Alternative Minimum Tax–2011

If AMTI minus the exemption is:		The Tax Is:	
Over—	But Not Over—		Of the Amount Over—
$0	$175,000*	26%	$0
175,000*		$45,500* – 28%	
175,000*			

*$87,500 and $22,750 for married taxpayers filing separately.

Social Security Tax–2011

Category	R	
OASDI	4.20% (6.20% for employer)	
Medicare	1.45%	None
Total	5.65%	

Self-Employment Tax–2011

Category	Rate	Dollar Limit
OASDI	10.40%	$106,800
Medicare	2.90%	None
Total	13.30%	

STANDARD DEDUCTION

Filing Status	2011 Amount
Married individuals filing joint returns and surviving spouses	$11,600
Heads of households	8,500
Unmarried individuals (other than surviving spouses and heads of households)	5,800
Married individuals filing separate return	5,800
Additional standard deductions for the aged and the blind	
Individual who is married and surviving spouses	1,150*
Individual who is unmarried and not a surviving spouse	1,450*
Taxpayer claimed as dependent on another taxpayer's return: Greater of (1) earned income plus $300, or (2) $950.	

*These amounts are $2,300 and $2,900, respectively, for a taxpayer who is both aged and blind.

Personal Exemption 2011: $3,700 Prior to 2010, personal exemptions were subject to a reduction for higher income tax-payers. This reduction has been eliminated for 2010 and future years although there has been some discussion about bringing this provision back into the law to raise additional revenue for the government.

Itemized Deductions

Prior to 2010, total itemized deductions were subject to a reduction for higher income taxpayers. This reduction has been eliminated for 2010 and future years. Whether the elimination is permanent is uncertain.

PRENTICE HALL'S
FEDERAL TAXATION
2012

Corporations, Partnerships, Estates & Trusts

EDITORS

KENNETH E. ANDERSON
University of Tennessee

THOMAS R. POPE
University of Kentucky

JOHN L. KRAMER
University of Florida

CONTRIBUTING AUTHORS

ANNA C. FOWLER
University of Texas at Austin (Emeritus)

RICHARD J. JOSEPH
Hult International Business School

DAVID S. HULSE
University of Kentucky

LEANN LUNA
University of Tennessee

MICHAEL S. SCHADEWALD
University of Wisconsin—Milwaukee

Prentice Hall
Boston   Columbus   Indianapolis   New York   San Francisco   Upper Saddle River
Amsterdam   Cape Town   Dubai   London   Madrid   Milan   Munich   Paris   Montreal   Toronto
Delhi   Mexico City   Sao Paulo   Sydney   Hong Kong   Seoul   Singapore   Taipei   Tokyo

VP, Editorial Director: Sally Yagan
AVP/Editor-in-Chief: Donna Battista
Product Development Manager: Ashley Santora
Editorial Project Manager: Melissa Pellerano
Editorial Assistant: Jane Avery
VP/Director of Marketing: Patrice Lumumba Jones
Marketing Assistant: Ian Gold
Senior Managing Editor: Cynthia Zonneveld
Senior Production Project Manager: Lynne Breitfeller
Operations Director: Nick Sklitis
Senior Operations Specialist: Diane Peirano
Cover Design: Gretchen Irmiger
Art Director: Jonathan Boylan
Cover Images: leungchopan/Shutterstock; javarman/Shutterstock;
  Yuri Arcurs/Shutterstock; shironosov/iStockphoto.com
Permissions Researcher: Marcy Lunetta
Production Media Project Manager: John Cassar
Editorial Media Project Manager: Allison Longley
Full-Service Project Management: Diane Kohnen/S4Carlisle Publishing Services
Composition: S4Carlisle Publishing Services
Printer/Binder: Courier/Kendallville
Cover Printer: Lehigh-Phoenix Color/Hagerstown
Text Font: 10/12 Sabon

Credits: chapter 1, pp. 1-5, 1-33, 1-34, and 1-35 Copyright 2010. American Institute of
Certified Public Accountants, Inc. All rights reserved. Used or adapted with permission.
Photo credits: chapter openers Mishella/Shutterstock; Jorg Hackerman/Shutterstock

Prentice Hall
is an imprint of

www.pearsonhighered.com

10 9 8 7 6 5 4 3 2 1
ISBN-10:   0-13-275414-2
ISBN-13: 978-0-13-275414-9

CONTENTS

CHAPTER 4
▶ CORPORATE NONLIQUIDATING DISTRIBUTIONS 4-1

CHAPTER 5
▶ OTHER CORPORATE TAX LEVIES 5-1

CHAPTER 6
▶ **CORPORATE LIQUIDATING DISTRIBUTIONS 6-1**

CHAPTER 7
▶ **CORPORATE ACQUISITIONS AND REORGANIZATIONS 7-1**

CHAPTER 8

▶ CONSOLIDATED TAX RETURNS 8-1

CHAPTER 9

▶ PARTNERSHIP FORMATION AND OPERATION 9-1

CHAPTER 13
▶ THE ESTATE TAX 13-1

CHAPTER 16
▶ U.S. TAXATION OF FOREIGN-RELATED TRANSACTIONS 16-1

APPENDICES

ABOUT THE EDITORS

KENNETH E. ANDERSON

Kenneth E. Anderson is the Pugh & Company Professor of Accounting at the University of Tennessee. He earned a B.B.A. from the University of Wisconsin–Milwaukee and subsequently attained the level of tax manager with Arthur Young (now part of Ernst & Young). He then earned a Ph.D. from Indiana University. He teaches corporate taxation, partnership taxation, and tax strategy, and has three times won the Beta Alpha Psi Outstanding Educator Award. Professor Anderson also is the Director of the Master of Accountancy Program. He has published articles in *The Accounting Review, The Journal of the American Taxation Association, Advances in Taxation,* the *Journal of Accountancy,* the *Journal of Financial Service Professionals,* and a number of other journals.

THOMAS R. POPE

Thomas R. Pope is the Ernst & Young Professor of Accounting at the University of Kentucky. He received a B.S. from the University of Louisville and an M.S. and D.B.A. in business administration from the University of Kentucky. He teaches international taxation, partnership and S corporation taxation, tax research and policy, and introductory taxation and has won outstanding teaching awards at the University, College, and School of Accountancy levels. He has published articles in *The Accounting Review,* the *Tax Adviser, Taxes, Tax Notes,* and a number of other journals. Professor Pope's extensive professional experience includes eight years with Big Four accounting firms. Five of those years were with Ernst & Whinney (now part of Ernst & Young), including two years with their National Tax Department in Washington, D.C. He subsequently held the position of Senior Manager in charge of the Tax Department in Lexington, Kentucky. Professor Pope also has been a leader and speaker at professional tax conferences all over the United States and is active as a tax consultant.

JOHN L. KRAMER

John L. Kramer is a former Professor of Accounting at the University of Florida. He was a recipient of a Teaching Improvement Program award given by the University of Florida in 1994. He holds a Ph.D. in Business Administration and an M.B.A. from the University of Michigan (Ann Arbor), and a B.B.A. from the University of Michigan (Dearborn). He is a past president of the American Taxation Association and the Florida Association of Accounting Educators, as well as a past editor of *The Journal of the American Taxation Association.* In 2001, Professor Kramer received the Ray M. Sommerfeld Outstanding Tax Education Award, co-sponsored by the American Taxation Association and Ernst & Young. Professor Kramer has taught for the American Institute of CPAs, American Tax Institute of Europe, and a number of national and regional accounting firms. He has been a frequent speaker at academic and professional conferences, as well as having served as an expert witness in a number of court cases. He has published over 50 articles in *The Accounting Review, The Journal of the American Taxation Association,* the *Tax Adviser,* the *Journal of Taxation,* and other academic and professional journals. Professor Kramer has been an editor on *The Prentice Hall Federal Tax* series since 1989.

Anna C. Fowler is the John Arch White Professor Emeritus in the Department of Accounting at the University of Texas at Austin. She received her B.S. in accounting from the University of Alabama and her M.B.A. and Ph.D. from the University of Texas at Austin. Active in the American Taxation Association throughout her academic career, she served on the editorial board of its journal and held many positions, including president. She is a former member of the American Institute of CPA's Tax Executive Committee and a former chair of the AICPA's Regulation/Tax Subcommittee for the CPA exam. She has published a number of articles, most of which have dealt with estate planning or real estate transaction issues. In 2002, she received the Ray M. Sommerfeld Outstanding Educator Award, co-sponsored by the American Taxation Association and Ernst & Young.

Richard J. Joseph is the Provost of Hult International Business School in Cambridge, Massachusetts. He is a current member of the Hult Accounting Faculty and a former member of the tax faculty of The University of Texas at Austin. A graduate *magna cum laude* of Harvard College (B.A.), Oxford University (M.Litt.), and The University of Texas at Austin School of Law (J.D.), he has taught individual, corporate, international, state and local taxation, tax research methods, and the fundamentals of financial and managerial accounting. Before embarking on his academic career, Provost Joseph worked as an investment banker and securities trader on Wall Street and as a mergers and acquisitions lawyer in Texas. He is co-editor of the *Oxford Handbook on Mergers and Acquisitions* and has written numerous commentaries in the *Financial Times, The Christian Science Monitor, Tax Notes,* and *Tax Notes International.* His book, *The Origins of the American Income Tax*, explores the original intent, rationale, and effect of the early American income tax.

David S. Hulse is the Deloitte & Touche Professor of Accountancy at the University of Kentucky. He received an undergraduate degree from Shippensburg University, an M.S. from Louisiana State University, and a Ph.D. from the Pennsylvania State University. He teaches introductory taxation and corporate taxation courses. Professor Hulse has published a number of articles on tax issues in academic and professional journals, including *The Journal of the American Taxation Association, Advances in Taxation,* the *Journal of Financial Service Professionals,* and *Tax Notes.*

LeAnn Luna is an Associate Professor of Accounting at the University of Tennessee. She is a C.P.A. and holds an undergraduate degree from Southern Methodist University, a M.T. from the University of Denver College of Law, and a Ph.D. from the University of Tennessee. She has taught introductory taxation, corporate and partnership taxation, tax research, and professional standards. Professor Luna also holds a joint appointment with the Center for Business and Economic Research at the University of Tennessee, where she interacts frequently with state policymakers on a variety of policy related issues. She has published articles in the *National Tax Journal, The Journal of the American Taxation Association, Tax Adviser, State Tax Notes,* and a number of other journals.

Michael S. Schadewald, Ph.D., CPA, is on the faculty of the University of Wisconsin-Milwaukee where he teaches graduate and undergraduate courses in business taxation. A graduate of the University of Minnesota, Professor Schadewald is a co-author of several books on multistate and international taxation and has published more than 40 articles in academic and professional journals, including *The Accounting Review, Journal of Accounting Research, Contemporary Accounting Research, The Journal of the American Taxation Association, CPA Journal, Journal of Taxation,* and *The Tax Adviser.* Professor Schadewald also has served on the editorial boards of *The Journal of the American Taxation Association, Journal of State Taxation, International Tax Journal, The International Journal of Accounting, Issues in Accounting Education,* and *Journal of Accounting Education.*

Why is the Pope/Anderson/Kramer series the best choice for you and your students?

The Pope/Anderson/Kramer 2012 Series in Federal Taxation is appropriate for use in any first course in federal taxation, and comes in a choice of three volumes:

Federal Taxation 2012: Individuals

Federal Taxation 2012: Corporations, Partnerships, Estates & Trusts (the companion book to *Individuals*)

Federal Taxation 2012: Comprehensive (includes 29 chapters; 14 chapters from *Individuals* and 15 chapters from *Corporations*)

** For a customized edition of any of the chapters for these texts, contact your Pearson representative and they can create a custom text for you.

- The *Corporations, Partnerships, Estates & Trusts* and *Comprehensive* volumes contain three comprehensive tax return problems whose data change with each edition, thereby keeping the problems fresh. Problem C:3-66 contains the comprehensive corporate tax return, Problem C:9-58 contains the comprehensive partnership tax return, and Problem C:11-64 contains the comprehensive S corporation tax return, which is based on the same facts as Problem C:9-58 so that students can compare the returns for these two entities.

- The *Corporations, Partnerships, Estates & Trusts* and *Comprehensive* volumes contain sections called Financial Statement Implications, which discuss the implications of Accounting Standards Codification (ASC) 740. The main discussion of accounting for income taxes appears in Chapter C:3. The financial statement implications of other transactions appear in Chapters C:5, C:7, C:8, and C:16 (*Corporations* volume only).

We want to stress that *all* entities are covered in the *Individuals* volume although the treatment is often briefer than in the *Corporations* and *Comprehensive* volumes. The *Individuals* volume, therefore, is appropriate for colleges and universities that require only one semester of taxation as well as those that require more than one semester of taxation. Further, this volume adapts the suggestions of the Model Tax Curriculum as promulgated by the American Institute of Certified Public Accountants.

What's New to this Edition?

Individuals

- Complete integration of the new laws contained in the Small Business Jobs Act of 2010 and the Tax Relief Act of 2010.
- Analysis of the new increased first year expense election of assets up to $500,000 under Sec. 179 for 2011 and 2012.
- Analysis of the new 100% bonus depreciation rules for part of 2010 and all of 2011.
- Increased discussion of Roth-type retirement plans.
- Discussion of the replacement of the Making Work Pay credit with the 2% decrease in Social Security taxes.
- Discussion of the extension of many itemized deductions through 2011 or 2012, including the deductibility of state and local sales taxes in lieu of state and local income taxes.
- Discussion of the 100% exclusion of gain on the sale of qualified small business stock.
- Coverage of the new exemption amounts for the alternative minimum tax for individual taxpayers.
- All tax rates schedules have been updated to reflect the rates and inflation adjustments for 2011.
- Whenever new updates become available, they will be accessible via MyAccountingLab.

Corporations

- The alternative minimum tax (AMT) portion of Chapter C:5 has been rewritten to make it clearer and better organized.
- The problems pertaining to Chapter C:5 have been modified to conform to the rewriting of the AMT portion of the text.
- New problems have been added to Chapter C:3 for the valuation allowance and uncertain tax positions.
- The comprehensive corporate tax return, Problem C:3-66 (previously Problem C:3-64), has all new numbers for the 2010 forms.
- The comprehensive partnership tax return, Problem C:9-58, has all new numbers for the 2010 forms.
- The comprehensive S corporation tax return, Problem C:11-64, has all new numbers for the 2010 forms.
- The changes enacted in the Small Business Jobs Act of 2010 and the Tax Relief Act of 2010 have been incorporated into the text where appropriate.
- Other changes affecting 2011 tax law, including inflation adjustments, have been incorporated into the text where appropriate
- All tax rate schedules have been updated to reflect the rates and inflation adjustments for 2011.
- Whenever new updates become available, they will be accessible via MyAccountingLab.

MyAccountingLab®

MyAccountingLab® is web-based, tutorial and assessment software for accounting that not only gives students more "I Get It" moments, but gives instructors the flexibility to make technology an integral part of their course. It also is an excellent supplementary resource for students.

For Instructors

MyAccountingLab provides instructors with a rich and flexible set of course materials, along with course-management tools that make it easy to deliver all or a portion of your course online.

- **Powerful Homework and Test Manager** Create, import, and manage online homework and media assignments, quizzes, and tests. Create assignments from online questions directly correlated to this and other textbooks. Homework questions include "Help Me Solve This" guided solutions to help students understand and master concepts. You can choose from a wide range of assignment options, including time limits, proctoring, and maximum number of attempts allowed. In addition, you can create your own questions—or copy and edit ours—to customize your students' learning path.
- **Comprehensive Gradebook Tracking** MyAccountingLab's online gradebook automatically tracks your students' results on tests, homework, and tutorials and gives you control over managing results and calculating grades. All MyAccountingLab grades can be exported to a spreadsheet program, such as Microsoft® Excel. The MyAccountingLab Gradebook provides a number of student data views and gives you the flexibility to weight assignments, select which attempts to include when calculating scores, and omit or delete results for individual assignments.
- **Department-Wide Solutions** Get help managing multiple sections and working with Teaching Assistants using MyAccountingLab Coordinator Courses. After your MyAccountingLab course is set up, it can be copied to create sections or "member courses." Changes to the Coordinator Course flow down to all members, so changes only need to be made once.

We will add the most current tax information to MyAccountingLab as it becomes available.

For Students

MyAccountingLab provides students with a personalized interactive learning environment, where they can learn at their own pace and measure their progress.

- **Interactive Tutorial Exercises** MyAccountingLab's homework and practice questions are correlated to the textbook, and "similar to" versions regenerate algorithmically to give students unlimited opportunity for practice and mastery. Questions offer helpful feedback when students enter incorrect answers, and they include "Help Me Solve This" guided solutions as well as other learning aids for extra help when students need it.
- **Study Plan for Self-Paced Learning** MyAccountingLab's study plan helps students monitor their own progress, letting them see at a glance exactly which topics they need to practice. MyAccountingLab generates a personalized study plan for each student based on his or her test results, and the study plan links directly to interactive, tutorial exercises for topics the student hasn't yet mastered. Students can regenerate these exercises with new values for unlimited practice, and the exercises include guided solutions and multimedia learning aids to give students the extra help they need.

View a guided tour of MyAccountingLab at http://www.myaccountinglab.com/support/tours.

Strong Pedagogical Aides

- Appropriate blend of technical content of the tax law with a high level of readability for students.
- Focused on enabling students to apply tax principles within the chapter to real-life situations.

What Would You Do in This Situation?

Unique to the Pope/Anderson/Kramer series, these boxes place students in a decision-making role. The boxes include many *current controversies* that are as yet unresolved or are currently being considered by the courts. These boxes make extensive use of **Ethical Material** as they represent choices that may put the practitioner at odds with the client.

Stop & Think

These "speed bumps" encourage students to pause and apply what they have just learned. Solutions for each issue are provided in the box.

Ethical Point

These comments provide the ethical implications of material discussed in the adjoining text. Apply what they have just learned.

Tax Strategy Tip

These comments suggest tax planning ideas related to material in the adjoining text.

Program Components

Materials for the instructor may be accessed at the Instructor's Resource Center (IRC) online, located at **www.pearsonhighered.com/phtax** or within the Instructor Resource section of MyAccountingLab. You may contact your Pearson representative for assistance with the registration process.

- *TaxACT 2010 Software:* Available on CD to be packaged with Individuals and Comprehensive Texts: This user-friendly tax preparation program includes more than 80 tax forms, schedules, and worksheets. TaxACT calculates returns and alerts the user to possible errors or entries.
- *Instructor's Resource Manual:* Contains sample syllabi, instructor outlines, and information regarding problem areas for students. It also contains solutions to the tax form/tax return preparation problems. In addition to being available electronically on the IRC online, it also is available in hardcopy.
- *Solutions Manual:* Contains solutions to discussion questions, problems, and comprehensive and tax strategy problems. It also contains all solutions to the case study problems, research problems, and "What Would You Do in This Situation?" boxes. In addition to being available electronically on the IRC online, it is also available in hardcopy.
- *Test Item File:* Offers a wealth of true/false, multiple-choice, and calculative problems. A computerized program is available to adopters.
- *PowerPoint Slides:* Include over 300 full-color electronic transparencies available for *Individuals and Corporations.*

Acknowledgments

Our policy is to provide annual editions and to prepare timely updated supplements when major tax revisions occur. We are most appreciative of the suggestions made by outside reviewers because these extensive review procedures have been valuable to the authors and editors during the revision process.

We also are grateful to the various graduate assistants, doctoral students, and colleagues who have reviewed the text and supplementary materials and checked solutions to maintain a high level of technical accuracy. In particular, we would like to acknowledge the following colleagues who assisted in the preparation of supplemental materials for this text:

Ann Burstein Cohen	SUNY at Buffalo
Caroline Strobel	University of South Carolina
Craig J. Langstraat	University of Memphis
Kate Demarest	Carroll Community College
Richard Newmark	University of Northern Colorado

In addition, we want to thank Myron S. Scholes, Mark A. Wolfson, Merle Erickson, Edward L. Maydew, and Terry Shevlin for allowing us to use the model discussed in their text, *Taxes and Business Strategy: A Planning Approach*, as the basis for material in Chapter I:18.

Please send any comments to Kenneth E. Anderson or Thomas R. Pope.

1

CHAPTER

TAX RESEARCH

LEARNING OBJECTIVES

After studying this chapter, you should be able to

1. Describe the steps in the tax research process

2. Explain how the facts influence the tax consequences

3. Identify the sources of tax law and understand the authoritative value of each

4. Consult tax services to research an issue

5. Grasp the basics of Internet-based tax research

6. Use a citator to assess tax authorities

7. Understand professional guidelines that CPAs in tax practice should follow

8. Prepare work papers and communicate to clients

This chapter introduces the reader to the tax research process. Its major focus is the sources of the tax law (i.e., the Internal Revenue Code and other tax authorities) and the relative weight given to each source. The chapter describes the steps in the tax research process and places particular emphasis on the importance of the facts to the tax consequences. It also describes the features of frequently used tax services and computer-based tax research resources. Finally, it explains how to use a citator.

The end product of the tax research process—the communication of results to the client—also is discussed. This text uses a hypothetical set of facts to provide a comprehensive illustration of the process. Sample work papers demonstrating how to document the results of research are included in Appendix A. The text also discusses two types of professional guidelines for CPAs in tax practice: the American Institute of Certified Public Accountants' (AICPA's) *Statements on Standards for Tax Services* (reproduced in Appendix E) and Treasury Department *Circular 230*.

OVERVIEW OF TAX RESEARCH

Tax research is the process of solving tax-related problems by applying tax law to specific sets of facts. Sometimes it involves researching several issues and often is conducted to formulate tax policy. For example, policy-oriented research would determine how far the level of charitable contributions might decline if such contributions were no longer deductible. Economists usually conduct this type of tax research to assess the effects of government policy.

Tax research also is conducted to determine the tax consequences of transactions to specific taxpayers. For example, client-oriented research would determine whether Smith Corporation could deduct a particular expenditure as a trade or business expense. Accounting and law firms generally engage in this type of research on behalf of their clients.

This chapter deals only with client-oriented tax research, which occurs in two contexts:

ADDITIONAL COMMENT

Closed-fact situations afford the tax advisor the least amount of flexibility. Because the facts are already established, the tax advisor must develop the best solution possible within certain predetermined constraints.

1. **Closed-fact or tax compliance situations:** The client contacts the tax advisor after completing a transaction or while preparing a tax return. In such situations, the tax consequences are fairly straightforward because the facts cannot be modified to obtain different results. Consequently, tax saving opportunities may be lost.

EXAMPLE C:1-1 ▶

Tom informs Carol, his tax advisor, that on November 4 of the current year, he sold land held as an investment for $500,000 cash. His basis in the land was $50,000. On November 9, Tom reinvested the sales proceeds in another plot of investment property costing $500,000. This is a closed fact situation. Tom wants to know the amount and the character of the gain (if any) he must recognize. Because Tom solicits the tax advisor's advice after the sale and reinvestment, the opportunity for tax planning is limited. For example, the possibility of deferring taxes by using a like-kind exchange or an installment sale is lost. ◀

ADDITIONAL COMMENT

Open-fact or tax-planning situations give a tax advisor flexibility to structure transactions to accomplish the client's objectives. In this type of situation, a creative tax advisor can save taxpayers dollars through effective tax planning.

2. **Open-fact or tax-planning situations:** Before structuring or concluding a transaction, the client contacts the tax advisor to discuss tax planning opportunities. Tax-planning situations generally are more difficult and challenging because the tax advisor must consider the client's tax and nontax objectives. Most clients will not engage in a transaction if it is inconsistent with their nontax objectives, even though it produces tax savings.

EXAMPLE C:1-2 ▶

Diane is a widow with three children and five grandchildren and at present owns property valued at $10 million. She seeks advice from Carol, her tax advisor, about how to minimize her estate taxes and convey the greatest value of property to her descendants. This is an open-fact situation. Carol could advise Diane to leave all but a few hundred thousand dollars of her property to a charitable organization so that her estate would owe no estate taxes. Although this recommendation would eliminate Diane's estate taxes, Diane is likely to reject it because she wants her children or grandchildren to be her primary beneficiaries. Thus, reducing estate taxes to zero is inconsistent with her objective of allowing her descendants to receive as much after-tax wealth as possible. ◀

When conducting research in a tax-planning context, the tax professional should keep a number of points in mind. First, the objective is not to minimize taxes per se but rather to maximize a taxpayer's after-tax return. For example, if the federal income tax rate is a constant 30%, an investor should not buy a tax-exempt bond yielding 5% when he or she could buy a corporate bond of equal risk that yields 9% before tax and 6.3% after tax. This is the case even though his or her explicit taxes (actual tax liability) would be minimized by investing in the tax-exempt bond.[1] Second, taxpayers typically do not engage in unilateral or self-dealing transactions; thus, the tax ramifications for all parties to the transaction should be considered. For example, in the executive compensation context, employees may prefer to receive incentive stock options (because they will not recognize income until they sell the stock), but the employer may prefer to grant a different type of option (because the employer cannot deduct the value of incentive stock options upon issuance). Thus, the employer might grant a different number of options if it uses one type of stock option versus another type as compensation. Third, taxes are but one cost of doing business. In deciding where to locate a manufacturing plant, for example, factors more important to some businesses than the amount of state and local taxes paid might be the proximity to raw materials, good transportation systems, the cost of labor, the quantity of available skilled labor, and the quality of life in the area. Fourth, the time for tax planning is not restricted to the beginning date of an investment, contract, or other arrangement. Instead, the time extends throughout the duration of the activity. As tax rules change or as business and economic environments change, the tax advisor must reevaluate whether the taxpayer should hold onto an investment and must consider the transaction costs of any alternatives.

One final note: the tax advisor should always bear in mind the financial accounting implications of proposed transactions. An answer that may be desirable from a tax perspective may not always be desirable from a financial accounting perspective. Though interrelated, the two fields of accounting have different orientations and different objectives. Tax accounting is oriented primarily to the Internal Revenue Service (IRS). Its objectives include calculating, reporting, and predicting one's tax liability according to legal principles. Financial accounting is oriented primarily to shareholders, creditors, managers, and employees. Its objectives include determining, reporting, and predicting a business's financial position and operating results according to Generally Accepted Accounting Principles. Because tax and financial accounting objectives may differ, planning conflicts could arise. For example, management might be reluctant to engage in tax reduction strategies that also reduce book income and reported earnings per share. Success in any tax practice, especially at the managerial level, requires consideration of both sets of objectives and orientations.

STEPS IN THE TAX RESEARCH PROCESS

In both open- and closed-fact situations, the tax research process involves six basic steps:

1. Determine the facts.
2. Identify the issues (questions).
3. Locate the applicable authorities.
4. Evaluate the authorities and choose those to follow where the authorities conflict.
5. Analyze the facts in terms of the applicable authorities.
6. Communicate conclusions and recommendations to the client.

---

[1] For an excellent discussion of explicit and implicit taxes and tax planning see M. S. Scholes, M. A. Wolfson, M. Erickson, L. Maydew, and T. Shevlin, *Taxes and Business Strategy: A Planning Approach,* fourth edition (Upper Saddle River, NJ: Pearson Prentice Hall, 2008). Also see Chapter I:18 of the *Individuals* volume. An example of an implicit tax is the excess of the before-tax earnings on a taxable bond over the risk-adjusted before-tax earnings on a tax-favored investment (e.g., a municipal bond).

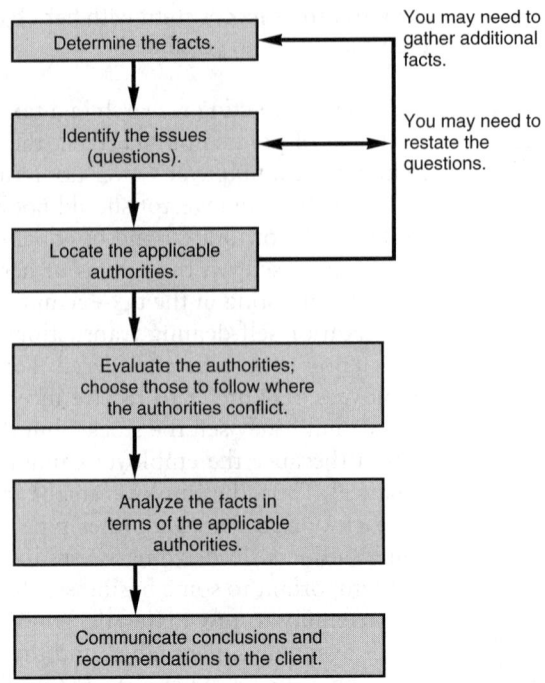

You may need to gather additional facts.

You may need to restate the questions.

FIGURE C:1-1 ▶ STEPS IN THE TAX RESEARCH PROCESS

ADDITIONAL COMMENT

The steps of tax research provide an excellent format for a written tax communication. For example, a good format for a client memo includes (1) statement of facts, (2) list of issues, (3) discussion of relevant authority, (4) analysis, and (5) recommendations to the client of appropriate actions based on the research results.

TYPICAL MISCONCEPTION

Many taxpayers think the tax law is all black and white. However, most tax research deals with gray areas. Ultimately, when confronted with tough issues, the ability to develop strategies that favor the taxpayer and then to find relevant authority to support those strategies will make a successful tax advisor. Thus, recognizing planning opportunities and avoiding potential traps is often the real value added by a tax advisor.

Although the above outline suggests a linear approach, the tax research process often is circular. That is, it does not always proceed step-by-step. Figure C:1-1 illustrates a more accurate process, and Appendix A provides a comprehensive example of this process.

In a closed-fact situation, the facts have already occurred, and the tax advisor's task is to analyze them to determine the appropriate tax treatment. In an open-fact situation, by contrast, the facts have not yet occurred, and the tax advisor's task is to plan for them or shape them so as to produce a favorable tax result. The tax advisor performs the latter task by reviewing the relevant legal authorities, particularly court cases and IRS rulings, all the while bearing in mind the facts of those cases or rulings that produced favorable results compared with those that produced unfavorable results. For example, if a client wants to realize an ordinary loss (as opposed to a capital loss) on the sale of several plots of land, the tax advisor might consult cases involving similar land sales. The advisor might attempt to distinguish the facts of those cases in which the taxpayer realized an ordinary loss from the facts of those cases in which the taxpayer realized a capital loss. The advisor then might recommend that the client structure the transaction based on the fact pattern in the ordinary loss cases.

Often, tax research involves a question to which no clearcut, unequivocally correct answer exists. In such situations, probing a related issue might lead to a solution pertinent to the central question. For example, in researching the issue described in the previous paragraph, i.e., whether the taxpayer may deduct a loss as ordinary instead of capital, the tax advisor might research the related issue of whether the presence of an investment motive precludes classifying a loss as ordinary. The solution to the latter issue might be relevant to the central question of whether the taxpayer may deduct the loss as ordinary.

Identifying the issue(s) to be researched often is the most difficult step in the tax research process. In some instances, the client defines the issue(s) for the tax advisor, such as where the client asks, "May I deduct the costs of a winter trip to Florida recommended by my physician?" In other instances, the tax advisor, after reviewing the documents submitted to him or her by the client, identifies and defines the issue(s) himself or herself. Doing so presupposes a firm grounding in tax law.[2]

---

[2] Often, in an employment context, supervisors define the questions to be researched and the authorities that might be relevant to the tax consequences.

Once the tax advisor locates the applicable legal authorities, he or she might have to obtain additional information from the client. Example C:1-3 illustrates the point. The example assumes that all relevant tax authorities are in agreement.

EXAMPLE C:1-3 ▶

Mark calls his tax advisor, Al, and states that he (1) incurred a loss on renting his beach cottage during the current year and (2) wonders whether he may deduct the loss. He also states that he, his wife, and their minor child occupied the cottage only eight days during the current year.

This is the first time Al has dealt with the Sec. 280A vacation home rules. On reading Sec. 280A(d), Al learns that a loss is *not* deductible if the taxpayer used the residence for personal purposes for longer than the greater of (1) 14 days or (2) 10% of the number of days the unit was rented at a fair rental value. He also learns that the property is *deemed* to be used by the taxpayer for personal purposes on any days on which it is used by any member of his or her family (as defined in Sec. 267(c)(4)). The Sec. 267(c)(4) definition of family members includes brothers, sisters, spouse, ancestors, or lineal descendants (i.e., children and grandchildren).

Mark's eight-day use is not long enough to make the rental loss nondeductible. However, Al must inquire about the number of days, if any, Mark's brothers, sisters, or parents used the property. (He already knows about use by Mark, his spouse, and his lineal descendants.) In addition, Al must find out how many days the cottage was rented to other persons at a fair rental value. Upon obtaining the additional information, Al proceeds to determine how to calculate the deductible expenses. Al then derives his conclusion concerning the deductible loss, if any, and communicates it to Mark. (This example assumes the passive activity and at-risk rules restricting a taxpayer's ability to deduct losses from real estate activities will not pose a problem for Mark. See Chapter I:8 of *Prentice Hall's Federal Taxation: Individuals* for a comprehensive discussion of these topics.) ◀

Many firms require that a researcher's conclusions be communicated to the client in writing. Members or employees of such firms may answer questions orally, but their oral conclusions should be followed by a written communication. According to the AICPA's *Statements on Standards for Tax Services* (reproduced in Appendix E),

> Although oral advice may serve a client's needs appropriately in routine matters or in well-defined areas, written communications are recommended in important, unusual, or complicated transactions. The member may use professional judgment about whether, subsequently, to document oral advice in writing.[3]

In addition, Treasury Department *Circular 230* covers all written advice communicated to clients. These requirements are more fully discussed at the end of this chapter and in Chapter C:15 (*Corporations, Partnerships, Estates, and Trusts* volume).

IMPORTANCE OF THE FACTS TO THE TAX CONSEQUENCES

OBJECTIVE 2

Explain how the facts influence the tax consequences

Many terms and phrases used in the Internal Revenue Code (IRC) and other tax authorities are vague or ambiguous. Some provisions conflict with others or are difficult to reconcile, creating for the researcher the dilemma of deciding which rules are applicable and which tax results are proper. For example, as a condition to claiming another person as a dependent, the taxpayer must provide a certain level of support for such person.[4] Neither the IRC nor the Treasury Regulations define "support." This lack of definition could be problematic. For example, if the taxpayer purchased a used automobile costing $8,000 for an elderly parent whose only source of income is $7,800 in Social Security benefits, the question of whether the expenditure constitutes support would arise. The tax advisor would have to consult court opinions, revenue rulings, and other IRS pronouncements to ascertain the legal meaning of the term "support." Only after thorough research would the meaning of the term become clear.

---

[3] AICPA, *Statement on Standards for Tax Services*, No. 7, "Form and Content of Advice to Taxpayers," 2010, Para. 6.

[4] Sec. 152(e)(1)(A) and Sec. 152(d)(1)(C).

In other instances, the legal language is quite clear, but a question arises as to whether the taxpayer's transaction conforms to a specific pattern of facts that gives rise to a particular tax result. Ultimately, the peculiar facts of a transaction or event determine its tax consequences. A change in the facts can significantly change the consequences. Consider the following illustrations:

Illustration One

Facts: A holds stock, a capital asset, that he purchased two years ago at a cost of $1,000. He sells the stock to B for $920. What are the tax consequences to A?

Result: Under Sec. 1001, A realizes an $80 capital loss. He recognizes this loss in the current year. A must offset the loss against any capital gains recognized during the year. Any excess loss is deductible from ordinary income up to a $3,000 annual limit.

Change of Facts: A is B's son.

New Result: Under Sec. 267, A and B are related parties. Therefore, A may not recognize the realized loss. However, B may use the loss if she subsequently sells the stock at a gain.

Illustration Two

Facts: C donates to State University ten acres of land that she purchased two years ago for $10,000. The fair market value (FMV) of the land on the date of the donation is $25,000. C's adjusted gross income is $100,000. What is C's charitable contribution deduction?

Result: Under Sec. 170, C is entitled to a $25,000 charitable contribution deduction (i.e., the FMV of the property unreduced by the unrealized long-term gain).

Change of Facts: C purchased the land 11 months ago.

New Result: Under the same IRC section, C is entitled to only a $10,000 charitable contribution deduction (i.e., the FMV of the property reduced by the unrealized short-term gain).

Illustration Three

Facts: Acquiring Corporation pays Target Corporation's shareholders one million shares of Acquiring voting stock. In return, Target's shareholders tender 98% of their Target voting stock. The acquisition is for a bona fide business purpose. Acquiring continues Target's business. What are the tax consequences of the exchange to Target's shareholders?

Result: Because the transaction qualifies as a reorganization under Sec. 368(a)(1)(B), Target's shareholders are not taxed on the exchange, which is solely for Acquiring voting stock.

Change of Facts: In the transaction, Acquiring purchases the remaining 2% of Target's shares with cash.

New Result: Under the same IRC provision, Target's shareholders are now taxed on the exchange, which is not solely for Acquiring voting stock.

CREATING A FACTUAL SITUATION FAVORABLE TO THE TAXPAYER

TYPICAL MISCONCEPTION

Many taxpayers believe tax practitioners spend most of their time preparing tax returns. In reality, providing tax advice that accomplishes the taxpayer's objectives is one of the most important responsibilities of a tax advisor. This latter activity is tax consulting as compared to tax compliance.

Based on his or her research, a tax advisor might recommend to a taxpayer how to structure a transaction or plan an event so as to increase the likelihood that related expenses will be deductible. For example, suppose a taxpayer is assigned a temporary task in a location (City Y) different from the location (City X) of his or her permanent employment. Suppose also that the taxpayer wants to deduct the meal and lodging expenses incurred in City Y as well as the cost of transportation thereto. To do so, the taxpayer must establish that City X is his or her tax home and that he or she temporarily works in City Y. (Section 162 provides that a taxpayer may deduct travel expenses while "away from home" on business. A taxpayer is deemed to be "away from home" if his or her employment at the new location does not exceed one year, i.e., it is "temporary.") Suppose the taxpayer wants to know the tax consequences of his or her working in City Y for ten months and then, within that ten-month period, finding permanent employment in City Y. What is tax research likely to reveal?

Tax research will lead to an IRS ruling stating that, in such circumstances, the employment will be deemed to be temporary until the date on which the realistic expectation about the temporary nature of the assignment changes.[5] After this date, the employment

---

[5] Rev. Rul. 93-86, 1993-2 C.B. 71.

will be deemed to be permanent, and travel expenses relating to it will be nondeductible. Based on this finding, the tax advisor might advise the taxpayer to postpone his or her permanent job search in City Y until the end of the ten-month period and simply treat his or her assignment as temporary. So doing would lengthen the time he or she is deemed to be "away from home" on business and thus increase the amount of meal, lodging, and transportation costs deductible as travel expenses. The taxpayer should compare the tax savings to any additional personal costs of maintaining two residences.

THE SOURCES OF TAX LAW

OBJECTIVE 3

Identify the sources of tax law and understand the authoritative value of each

The language of the IRC is general; that is, it prescribes the tax treatment of broad categories of transactions and events. The reason for the generality is that Congress can neither foresee nor provide for every conceivable transaction or event. Even if it could, doing so would render the statute narrow in scope and inflexible in application. Accordingly, interpretations of the IRC—both administrative and judicial—are necessary. Administrative interpretations are provided in Treasury Regulations, revenue rulings, revenue procedures, and several other pronouncements discussed later in this chapter. Judicial interpretations are presented in court opinions. The term *tax law* as used by most tax advisors encompasses administrative and judicial interpretations in addition to the IRC. It also includes the meaning conveyed in reports issued by Congressional committees involved in the legislative process.

THE LEGISLATIVE PROCESS

Tax legislation begins in the House of Representatives. Initially, a tax proposal is incorporated in a bill. The bill is referred to the House Ways and Means Committee, which is charged with reviewing all tax legislation. The Ways and Means Committee holds hearings in which interested parties, such as the Treasury Secretary and IRS Commissioner, testify. At the conclusion of the hearings, the Ways and Means Committee votes to approve or reject the measure. If approved, the bill goes to the House floor where it is debated by the full membership. If the House approves the measure, the bill moves to the Senate where it is taken up by the Senate Finance Committee. Like Ways and Means, the Finance Committee holds hearings in which Treasury officials, tax experts, and other interested parties testify. If the committee approves the measure, the bill goes to the Senate floor where it is debated by the full membership. Upon approval by the Senate, it is submitted to the President for his or her signature. If the President signs the measure, the bill becomes public law. If the President vetoes it, Congress can override the veto by at least a two-thirds majority vote in each chamber.

Generally, at each stage of the legislative process, the bill is subject to amendment. If amended, and if the House version differs from the Senate version, the bill is referred to a House-Senate conference committee.[6] This committee attempts to resolve the differences between the House and Senate versions. Ultimately, it submits a compromise version of the measure to each chamber for its approval. Such referrals are common. For example, in 1998 the House and Senate disagreed over what the taxpayer must do to shift the burden of proof to the IRS. The House proposed that the taxpayer assert a "reasonable dispute" regarding a taxable item. The Senate proposed that the taxpayer introduce "credible evidence" regarding the item. A conference committee was appointed to resolve the differences. This committee ultimately adopted the Senate proposal, which was later approved by both chambers.

After approving major legislation, the Ways and Means Committee and Senate Finance Committee usually issue official reports. These reports, published by the U.S. Government Printing Office (GPO) as part of the *Cumulative Bulletin* and as separate documents, explain the committees' reasoning for approving (and/or amending) the legislation.[7] In addition, the GPO publishes both records of the committee hearings and transcripts of the floor debates. The records are published as separate House or Senate documents. The transcripts are incorporated in the *Congressional Record* for the day of the

ADDITIONAL COMMENT

Committee reports can be helpful in interpreting new legislation because they indicate the intent of Congress. With the proliferation of tax legislation, committee reports have become especially important because the Treasury Department often is unable to draft the needed regulations in a timely manner.

---

[6] The size of a conference committee can vary. It is made up of an equal number of members from the House and the Senate.

[7] The *Cumulative Bulletin* is described in the discussion of revenue rulings on page C:1-12.

debate. In tax research, these records, reports, and transcripts are useful in deciphering the meaning of the statutory language. Where this language is ambiguous or vague, and the courts have not interpreted it, the documents can shed light on **Congressional intent**, i.e., what Congress *intended* by a particular term, phrase, or provision.

EXAMPLE C:1-4 ▶ In 1998, Congress passed legislation concerning shifting the burden of proof to the IRS. This legislation was codified in Sec. 7491. The question arises as to what constitutes "credible evidence" because the taxpayer must introduce such evidence to shift the burden of proof to the IRS. Section 7491 does not define the term. Because the provision was relatively new, few courts had an opportunity to interpret what "credible evidence" means. In the absence of relevant statutory or judicial authority, the researcher might have looked to the committee reports to ascertain what Congress intended by the term. Senate Report No. 105-174 states that "credible evidence" means evidence of a quality, which, "after critical analysis, the court would find sufficient upon which to base a decision on the issue if no contrary evidence were submitted."[8] This language suggests that Congress intended the term to mean evidence of a kind sufficient to withstand judicial scrutiny. Such a meaning should be regarded as conclusive in the absence of other authority. ◀

THE INTERNAL REVENUE CODE

The IRC, which comprises Title 26 of the United States Code, is the foundation of all tax law. First codified (i.e., organized into a single compilation of revenue statutes) in 1939, the tax law was recodified in 1954. The IRC was known as the Internal Revenue Code of 1954 until 1986, when its name was changed to the Internal Revenue Code of 1986. Whenever changes to the IRC are approved, the old language is deleted and new language added. Thus, the IRC is organized as an integrated document, and a researcher need not read through the relevant parts of all previous tax bills to find the current version of the law. Nevertheless, a researcher must be sure that he or she is working with the law in effect when a particular transaction occurred.

ADDITIONAL COMMENT

The various tax services, discussed later in this chapter, provide IRC histories for researchers who need to work with prior years' tax law.

The IRC contains provisions dealing with income taxes, estate and gift taxes, employment taxes, alcohol and tobacco taxes, and other excise taxes. Organizationally, the IRC is divided into subtitles, chapters, subchapters, parts, subparts, sections, subsections, paragraphs, subparagraphs, and clauses. Subtitle A contains rules relating to income taxes, and Subtitle B deals with estate and gift taxes. A set of provisions concerned with one general area constitutes a subchapter. For example, the topics of corporate distributions and adjustments appear in Subchapter C, and topics relating to partners and partnerships appear in Subchapter K. Figure C:1-2 presents the organizational scheme of the IRC.

An IRC section contains the operative provisions to which tax advisors most often refer. For example, they speak of "Sec. 351 transactions," "Sec. 306 stock," and "Sec. 1231 gains and losses." Although a tax advisor need not know all the IRC sections, paragraphs, and parts, he or she must be familiar with the IRC's organizational scheme to read and interpret it correctly. The language of the IRC is replete with cross-references to titles, paragraphs, subparagraphs, and so on.

EXAMPLE C:1-5 ▶ Section 7701, a definitional section, begins, "When used in this title . . ." and then provides a series of definitions. Because of this broad reference, a Sec. 7701 definition applies for all of Title 26; that is, it applies for purposes of the income tax, estate and gift tax, excise tax, and other taxes governed by Title 26. ◀

EXAMPLE C:1-6 ▶ Section 302(b)(3) allows taxpayers whose stock holdings are completely terminated in a redemption (a corporation's purchase of its stock from one or more of its shareholders) to receive capital gain treatment on the excess of the redemption proceeds over the stock's basis instead of ordinary income treatment on the entire proceeds. Section 302(c)(2)(A) states, "In the case of a distribution described in subsection (b)(3), section 318(a)(1) shall not apply if. . . ." Further, Sec. 302(c)(2)(C)(i) indicates "Subparagraph (A) shall not apply to a distribution to any entity unless. . . ." Thus, in determining whether a taxpayer will receive capital gain treatment in a stock redemption, a tax advisor must be able to locate and interpret various cross-referenced IRC sections, subsections, paragraphs, subparagraphs, and clauses. ◀

---

[8] S. Rept. No. 105-174, 105th Cong., 1st Sess. (unpaginated) (1998).

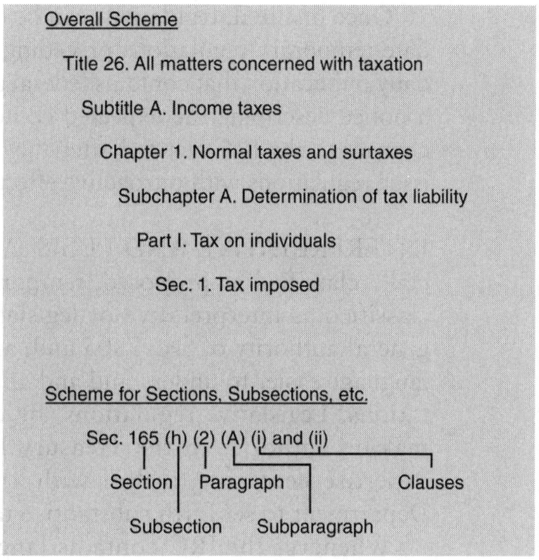

Overall Scheme

Title 26. All matters concerned with taxation

Subtitle A. Income taxes

Chapter 1. Normal taxes and surtaxes

Subchapter A. Determination of tax liability

Part I. Tax on individuals

Sec. 1. Tax imposed

Scheme for Sections, Subsections, etc.

Sec. 165 (h) (2) (A) (i) and (ii)

Section | Paragraph | Clauses

Subsection | Subparagraph

FIGURE C:1-2 ▶ ORGANIZATIONAL SCHEME OF THE INTERNAL REVENUE CODE

TREASURY REGULATIONS

The Treasury Department issues regulations that expound upon the IRC. Treasury Regulations often provide examples with computations that assist the reader in understanding how IRC provisions apply. Treasury Regulations are formulated on the basis of Treasury Decisions (T.D.s). The numbers of the Treasury Decisions that form the basis of a Treasury Regulation usually are found in the notes at the end of the regulation.

Because of frequent IRC changes, the Treasury Department does not always update the regulations in a timely manner. Consequently, when consulting a regulation, a tax advisor should check its introductory or end note to determine when the regulation was adopted. If the regulation was adopted before the most recent revision of the applicable IRC section, the regulation should be treated as authoritative to the extent consistent with the revision. Thus, for example, if a regulation issued before the passage of an IRC amendment specifies a dollar amount, and the amendment changed the dollar amount, the regulation should be regarded as authoritative in all respects except for the dollar amount.

PROPOSED, TEMPORARY, AND FINAL REGULATIONS. A Treasury Regulation is first issued in proposed form to the public, which is given an opportunity to comment on it. Parties most likely to comment are individual tax practitioners and representatives of organizations such as the American Bar Association, the Tax Division of the AICPA, and the American Taxation Association. The comments may suggest that the proposed rules could affect taxpayers more adversely than Congress had anticipated. In drafting a final regulation, the Treasury Department generally considers the comments and may modify the rules accordingly. If the comments are favorable, the Treasury Department usually finalizes the regulation with minor revisions. If the comments are unfavorable, it finalizes the regulation with major revisions or allows the proposed regulation to expire.

Proposed regulations are just that—proposed. Consequently, they carry no more authoritative weight than do the arguments of the IRS in a court brief. Nevertheless, they represent the Treasury Department's official interpretation of the IRC. By contrast, **temporary regulations** are binding on the taxpayer. Effective as of the date of their publication, they often are issued immediately after passage of a major tax act to guide taxpayers and their advisors on procedural or computational matters. Regulations issued as temporary are concurrently issued as proposed. Because their issuance is not preceded by a public comment period, they are regarded as somewhat less authoritative than final regulations.

Once finalized, regulations can be effective as of (1) the date they were proposed; (2) the date temporary regulations preceding them were first published in the *Federal Register*, a daily publication that contains federal government pronouncements; or (3) the date on which a notice describing the expected contents of the regulation was issued to the public.[9] For changes to the IRC enacted after July 29, 1996, the Treasury Department generally cannot issue regulations with retroactive effect.

INTERPRETATIVE AND LEGISLATIVE REGULATIONS. In addition to being officially classified as proposed, temporary, or final, Treasury Regulations are unofficially classified as interpretative or legislative. **Interpretative regulations** are issued under the general authority of Sec. 7805 and, as the name implies, merely make the IRC's statutory language easier to understand and apply. In addition, they often illustrate various computations. **Legislative regulations**, by contrast, arise where Congress delegates its rule-making authority to the Treasury Department. When Congress believes it lacks the expertise necessary to deal with a highly technical matter, it instructs the Treasury Department to set forth substantive tax rules relating to the matter.

Whenever the IRC contains language such as "The Secretary shall prescribe such regulations as he may deem necessary" or "under regulations prescribed by the Secretary," the regulations interpreting the IRC provision are legislative. The consolidated tax return regulations are an example of legislative regulations. In Sec. 1502, Congress delegated to the Treasury Department authority to issue regulations that determine the tax liability of a group of affiliated corporations filing a consolidated tax return. As a precondition to filing such a return, the corporations must consent to follow the consolidated return regulations.[10] Such consent generally precludes the corporations from later arguing in court that the regulatory provisions are invalid.

AUTHORITATIVE WEIGHT. Final regulations are presumed to be valid and have almost the same authoritative weight as the IRC. Despite this presumption, taxpayers occasionally argue that a regulation is invalid and, consequently, should not be followed. A court will not strike down an interpretative regulation unless, in its opinion, the regulation is "unreasonable and plainly inconsistent with the revenue statutes."[11] In other words, a court is unlikely to invalidate a legislative regulation because it recognizes that Congress has delegated to the Treasury Department authority to issue a specific set of rules. Nevertheless, courts have invalidated legislative regulations where, in their opinion, the regulations exceeded the scope of power delegated to the Treasury Department,[12] were contrary to the IRC,[13] or were unreasonable.[14]

In assessing the validity of Treasury Regulations, some courts apply the **legislative reenactment doctrine**. Under this doctrine, a regulation is deemed to receive Congressional approval whenever the IRC provision under which the regulation was issued is reenacted without amendment.[15] Underlying this doctrine is the rationale that, if Congress believed that the regulation offered an erroneous interpretation of the IRC, it would have amended the IRC to conform to its belief. Congress's failure to amend the IRC signifies approval of the regulation.[16] This doctrine is predicated on Congress's constitutional authority to levy taxes. This authority implies that, if Congress is dissatisfied with the manner in which either the executive or the judiciary have interpreted the IRC, it can invalidate these interpretations through new legislation.

STOP & THINK

Question: You are researching the manner in which a deduction is calculated. You consult Treasury Regulations for guidance because the IRC states that the calculation is to be done "in a manner prescribed by the Secretary." After reviewing these authorities, you

---

[9] Sec. 7805(b).

[10] Sec. 1501.

[11] *CIR v. South Texas Lumber Co.*, 36 AFTR 604, 48-1 USTC ¶5922 (USSC, 1948). In *U.S. v. Douglas B. Cartwright, Executor*, 31 AFTR 2d 73-1461, 73-1 USTC ¶12,926 (USSC, 1973), the Supreme Court concluded that a regulation dealing with the valuation of mutual fund shares for estate and gift tax purposes was invalid.

[12] *McDonald v. CIR*, 56 AFTR 2d 5318, 85-2 USTC ¶9494 (5th Cir., 1985).

[13] *Jeanese, Inc. v. U.S.*, 15 AFTR 2d 429, 65-1 USTC ¶9259 (9th Cir., 1965).

[14] *United States v. Vogel Fertilizer Co.*, 49 AFTR 2d 82-491, 82-1 USTC ¶9134 (USSC, 1982).

[15] *United States v. Homer O. Correll*, 20 AFTR 2d 5845, 68-1 USTC ¶9101 (USSC, 1967).

[16] One can rebut the presumption that Congress approved of the regulation by showing that Congress was unaware of the regulation when it reenacted the statute.

conclude that another way of doing the calculation arguably is correct under an intuitive approach. This approach would result in a lower tax liability for the client. Should you follow the Treasury Regulations or use the intuitive approach and argue that the regulations are invalid?

Solution: Because of the language "in a manner prescribed by the Secretary," the Treasury Regulations dealing with the calculation are legislative. Whenever Congress calls for legislative regulations, it explicitly authorizes the Treasury Department to write the "rules." As a consequence, such regulations are more difficult than interpretative regulations to be overturned by the courts. Thus, unless you intend to challenge the Treasury Regulations and believe you will prevail in court, you should follow them.

CITATIONS. Citations to Treasury Regulations are relatively easy to understand. One or more numbers appear before a decimal place, and several numbers follow the decimal place. The numbers immediately following the decimal place indicate the IRC section being interpreted. The numbers preceding the decimal place indicate the general subject of the regulation. Numbers that often appear before the decimal place and their general subjects are as follows:

Number	General Subject Matter
1	Income tax
20	Estate tax
25	Gift tax
301	Administrative and procedural matters
601	Procedural rules

The number following the IRC section number indicates the numerical sequence of the regulation, such as the fifth regulation. No relationship exists between this number and the subsection of the IRC being interpreted. An example of a citation to a final regulation is as follows:

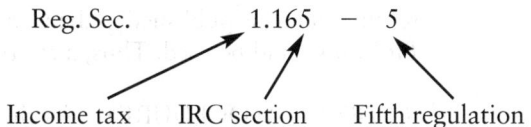

Citations to proposed or temporary regulations follow the same format. They are referenced as Prop. Reg. Sec. or Temp. Reg. Sec. For temporary regulations the numbering system following the IRC section number always begins with the number of the regulation and an upper case T (e.g., -1T).

Section 165 addresses the broad topic of losses and is interpreted by several regulations. According to its caption, the topic of Reg. Sec. 1.165-5 is worthless securities, which also is addressed in subsection (g) of IRC Sec. 165. Parenthetical information following the text of the Treasury Regulation indicates that the regulation was last revised on March 11, 2008, by Treasury Decision (T.D.) 9386. Section 165(g) was last amended in 2000. A researcher must always check when the regulations were last amended and be aware that an IRC change may have occurred after the most recent regulation amendment, potentially making the regulation inapplicable.

When referencing a regulation, the researcher should fine-tune the citation to indicate the precise passage that supports his or her conclusion. An example of such a detailed citation is Reg. Sec. 1.165-5(j), Ex. 2(i), which refers to paragraph (i) of Example 2, found in paragraph (j) of the fifth regulation interpreting Sec. 165.

ADMINISTRATIVE PRONOUNCEMENTS

The IRS interprets the IRC through **administrative pronouncements,** the most important of which are discussed below. After consulting the IRC and Treasury Regulations, tax advisors are likely next to consult these pronouncements.

REVENUE RULINGS.   In **revenue rulings**, the IRS indicates the tax consequences of specific transactions encountered in practice. For example, in a revenue ruling, the IRS might indicate whether the exchange of stock for stock derivatives in a corporate acquisition is tax-free.

The IRS issues more than 50 revenue rulings a year. These rulings do not rank as high in the hierarchy of authorities as do Treasury Regulations or federal court cases. They simply represent the IRS's view of the tax law. Taxpayers who do not follow a revenue ruling will not incur a substantial understatement penalty if they have substantial authority for different treatment.[17] Nonetheless, the IRS presumes that the tax treatment specified in a revenue ruling is correct. Consequently, if an examining agent discovers in an audit that a taxpayer did not adopt the position prescribed in a revenue ruling, the agent will contend that the taxpayer's tax liability should be adjusted to reflect that position.

Soon after it is issued, a revenue ruling appears in the weekly *Internal Revenue Bulletin* (cited as I.R.B.), published by the U.S. Government Printing Office (GPO). Revenue rulings later appear in the *Cumulative Bulletin* (cited as C.B.), a bound volume issued semiannually by the GPO. An example of a citation to a revenue ruling appearing in the *Cumulative Bulletin* is as follows:

Rev. Rul. 97-4, 1997-1 C.B. 5.

This is the fourth ruling issued in 1997, and it appears on page 5 of Volume 1 of the 1997 *Cumulative Bulletin*. Before the GPO publishes the pertinent volume of the *Cumulative Bulletin*, researchers should use citations to the *Internal Revenue Bulletin*. An example of such a citation follows:

Rev. Rul. 2009-3, 2009-5 I.R.B. 382.

For revenue rulings (and other IRS pronouncements) issued after 1999, the full four digits of the year of issuance are set forth in the title. For revenue rulings (and other IRS pronouncements) issued before 2000, only the last two digits of the year of issuance are set forth in the title. The above citation represents the third ruling for 2009. This ruling is located on page 382 of the *Internal Revenue Bulletin* for the fifth week of 2009. Once a revenue ruling is published in the *Cumulative Bulletin,* only the citation to the *Cumulative Bulletin* should be used. Thus, a citation to the I.R.B. is temporary.

REVENUE PROCEDURES.   As the name suggests, **revenue procedures** are IRS pronouncements that usually deal with the procedural aspects of tax practice. For example, one revenue procedure deals with the manner in which tip income should be reported. Another revenue procedure describes the requirements for reproducing paper substitutes for informational returns such as Form 1099.

As with revenue rulings, revenue procedures are published first in the *Internal Revenue Bulletin,* then in the *Cumulative Bulletin.* An example of a citation to a revenue procedure appearing in the *Cumulative Bulletin* is as follows:

Rev. Proc. 97-19, 1997-1 C.B. 644.

This pronouncement is found in Volume 1 of the 1997 *Cumulative Bulletin* on page 644. It is the nineteenth revenue procedure issued in 1997.

In addition to revenue rulings and revenue procedures, the *Cumulative Bulletin* contains IRS notices, as well as the texts of proposed regulations, tax treaties, committee reports, and U.S. Supreme Court decisions.

LETTER RULINGS.   **Letter rulings** are initiated by taxpayers who ask the IRS to explain the tax consequences of a particular transaction.[18] The IRS provides its explanation in the form of a letter ruling, a response personal to the taxpayer requesting an answer. Only the

---

[17] Chapter C:15 discusses the authoritative support taxpayers and tax advisors should have for positions they adopt on a tax return.

[18] Chapter C:15 further discusses letter rulings.

taxpayer to whom the ruling is addressed may rely on it as authority. Nevertheless, letter rulings are relevant for other taxpayers and tax advisors because they offer insight into the IRS's position on the tax treatment of particular transactions.

Originally the public did not have access to letter rulings issued to other taxpayers. As a result of Sec. 6110, enacted in 1976, letter rulings (with confidential information deleted) are accessible to the general public and have been reproduced by major tax services. An example of a citation to a letter ruling appears below:

Ltr. Rul. 200130006 (July 30, 2001).

The first four digits (two if issued before 2000) indicate the year in which the ruling was made public, in this case, 2001.[19] The next two digits denote the week in which the ruling was made public, here the thirtieth. The last three numbers indicate the numerical sequence of the ruling for the week, here the sixth. The date in parentheses denotes the date of the ruling.

OTHER INTERPRETATIONS

Technical Advice Memoranda. When the IRS audits a taxpayer's return, the IRS agent might ask the IRS national office for advice on a complicated, technical matter. The national office will provide its advice in a **technical advice memorandum**, released to the public in the form of a letter ruling.[20] Researchers can identify which letter rulings are technical advice memoranda by introductory language such as, "In response to a request for technical advice. . . ." An example of a citation to a technical advice memorandum is as follows:

ADDITIONAL COMMENT

A technical advice memorandum is published as a letter ruling. Whereas a taxpayer-requested letter ruling deals with prospective transactions, a technical advice memorandum deals with past or consummated transactions.

T.A.M. 9801001 (January 2, 1998).

This citation refers to the first technical advice memorandum issued in the first week of 1998. The memorandum is dated January 2, 1998.

Information Releases. If the IRS wants to disseminate information to the general public, it will issue an **information release**. Information releases are written in lay terms and are dispatched to thousands of newspapers throughout the country. The IRS, for example, may issue an information release to announce the standard mileage rate for business travel. An example of a citation to an information release is as follows:

I.R. 86-70 (June 12, 1986).

This citation is to the seventieth information release issued in 1986. The release is dated June 12, 1986.

Announcements and Notices. The IRS also disseminates information to tax practitioners in the form of **announcements** and **notices**. These pronouncements generally are more technical than information releases and frequently address current tax developments. After passage of a major tax act, and before the Treasury Department has had an opportunity to issue proposed or temporary regulations, the IRS may issue an announcement or notice to clarify the legislation. The IRS is bound to follow the announcement or notice just as it is bound to follow a revenue procedure or revenue ruling. Examples of citations to announcements and notices are as follows:

ADDITIONAL COMMENT

Announcements are used to summarize new tax legislation or publicize procedural matters. Announcements generally are aimed at tax practitioners and are considered to be "substantial authority" [Rev. Rul. 90-91, 1990-2 C.B. 262].

Announcement 2007-3, 2007-4 I.R.B. 376.
Notice 2007-9, 2007-5 I.R.B. 401.

The first citation is to the third announcement issued in 2007. It can be found on page 376 of the fourth *Internal Revenue Bulletin* for 2007. The second citation is to the ninth

---

[19] Sometimes a letter ruling is cited as PLR (private letter ruling) instead of Ltr. Rul.

[20] Technical advice memoranda are discussed further in Chapter C:15.

notice issued in 2007. It can be found on page 401 of the fifth *Internal Revenue Bulletin* for 2007. Notices and announcements appear in both the *Internal Revenue Bulletin* and the *Cumulative Bulletin.*

JUDICIAL DECISIONS

Judicial decisions are an important source of tax law. Judges are reputed to be unbiased individuals who decide questions of fact (the existence of a fact or the occurrence of an event) or questions of law (the applicability of a legal principle or the proper interpretation of a legal term or provision). Judges do not always agree on the tax consequences of a particular transaction or event. Therefore, tax advisors often must derive conclusions against a background of conflicting judicial authorities. For example, a U.S. district court might disagree with the Tax Court on the deductibility of an expense. Likewise, one circuit court might disagree with another circuit court on the same issue.

OVERVIEW OF THE COURT SYSTEM.   A taxpayer may begin tax litigation in any of three courts: the U.S. Tax Court, the U.S. Court of Federal Claims (formerly the U.S. Claims Court), or U.S. district courts. Court precedents are important in deciding where to begin such litigation (see page C:1-21 for a discussion of precedent). Also important is when the taxpayer must pay the deficiency the IRS contends is due. A taxpayer who wants to litigate either in a U.S. district court or in the U.S. Court of Federal Claims must first pay the deficiency. The taxpayer then files a claim for refund, which the IRS is likely to deny. Following this denial, the taxpayer must petition the court for a refund. If the court grants the taxpayer's petition, he or she receives a refund of the taxes in question plus accrued interest. If the taxpayer begins litigation in the Tax Court, on the other hand, he or she need not pay the deficiency unless and until the court decides the case against him or her. In that event, the taxpayer also must pay interest and penalties.[21] A taxpayer who believes that a jury would be sympathetic to his or her case should litigate in a U.S. district court, the only forum where a jury trial is possible.

If a party loses at the trial court level, it can appeal the decision to a higher court. Appeals of Tax Court and U.S. district court decisions are made to the court of appeals for the taxpayer's circuit. The appeals court system is comprised of 11 geographical circuits designated by numbers, the District of Columbia Circuit, and the Federal Circuit.[22] Table C:1-1 shows the states that lie in the various circuits. California, for example, lies in the Ninth Circuit. When referring to these appellate courts, instead of saying, for example, "the Court of Appeals for the Ninth Circuit," one generally says "the Ninth Circuit." All decisions of the U.S. Court of Federal Claims are appealable to one court—the Court of Appeals for the Federal Circuit—irrespective of where the taxpayer resides or does business.[23] The only cases the Federal Circuit hears are those that originate in the U.S. Court of Federal Claims.

The party losing at the appellate level can petition the U.S. Supreme Court to review the case under a **writ of certiorari**. If the Supreme Court agrees to hear the case, it grants certiorari.[24] If it refuses to hear the case, it denies certiorari. In recent years, the Court has granted certiorari in only about six to ten tax cases per year. Figure C:1-3 and Table C:1-2 provide an overview and summary of the court system with respect to tax matters.

THE U.S. TAX COURT.   The U.S. Tax Court was created in 1942 as a successor to the Board of Tax Appeals. It is a court of national jurisdiction that hears only tax-related cases. All taxpayers, regardless of their state of residence or place of business, may litigate in the Tax Court. It has 19 judges, including one chief judge.[25] The President, with the consent of the Senate, appoints the judges for a 15-year term and may reappoint them for an additional

SELF-STUDY
QUESTION
What are some of the factors that a taxpayer should consider when deciding in which court to file a tax-related claim?

ANSWER
(1) Each court's published precedent pertaining to the issue, (2) desirability of a jury trial, (3) tax expertise of each court, and (4) when the deficiency must be paid.

ADDITIONAL
COMMENT
Because the Tax Court deals only with tax cases, it presumably has a higher level of tax expertise than do other courts. Tax Court judges are appointed by the President, in part, due to their considerable tax experience. The Tax Court typically maintains a large backlog of tax cases, sometimes numbering in the tens of thousands.

---

[21] Revenue Procedure 2005-18, 2005-1 C.B. 798, provides procedures for taxpayers to make remittances or apply overpayments to stop the accrual of interest on deficiencies.

[22] The Federal Circuit has nationwide jurisdiction to hear appeals in specialized cases, such as those involving patent laws.

[23] The Court of Claims was reconstituted as the United States Court of Claims in 1982. In 1992, this court was renamed the U.S. Court of Federal Claims.

[24] The granting of certiorari signifies that the Supreme Court is granting an appellate review. The denial of certiorari does not necessarily mean that the Supreme Court endorses the lower court's decision. It simply means the court has decided not to hear the case.

[25] The Tax Court also periodically appoints, depending on budgetary constraints, a number of trial judges and senior judges who hear cases and render decisions with the same authority as the regular Tax Court judges.

▼ TABLE C:1-1
Federal Judicial Circuits

Circuit	States Included in Circuit
First	Maine, Massachusetts, New Hampshire, Rhode Island, Puerto Rico
Second	Connecticut, New York, Vermont
Third	Delaware, New Jersey, Pennsylvania, Virgin Islands
Fourth	Maryland, North Carolina, South Carolina, Virginia, West Virginia
Fifth	Louisiana, Mississippi, Texas
Sixth	Kentucky, Michigan, Ohio, Tennessee
Seventh	Illinois, Indiana, Wisconsin
Eighth	Arkansas, Iowa, Minnesota, Missouri, Nebraska, North Dakota, South Dakota
Ninth	Alaska, Arizona, California, Hawaii, Idaho, Montana, Nevada, Oregon, Washington, Guam, Northern Marina Islands
Tenth	Colorado, Kansas, New Mexico, Oklahoma, Utah, Wyoming
Eleventh	Alabama, Florida, Georgia
D.C.	District of Columbia
Federal	All jurisdictions (for taxpayers appealing from the U.S. Court of Federal Claims)

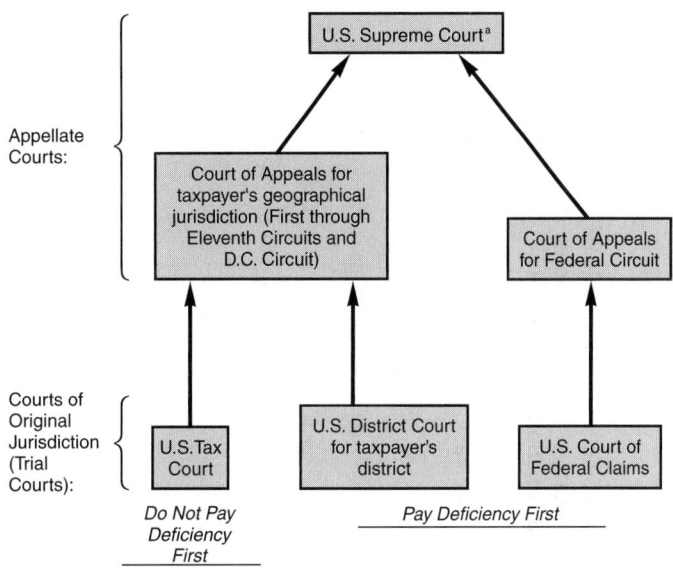

ª Cases are heard only if the Supreme Court grants certiorari.

FIGURE C:1-3 ▶ OVERVIEW OF COURT SYSTEM—TAX MATTERS

term. The judges, specialists in tax-related matters, periodically travel to roughly 100 cities throughout the country to hear cases. In most instances, only one judge hears a case.

The Tax Court issues both regular and memorandum (memo) decisions. Generally, the first time the Tax Court decides a legal issue, its decision appears as a **regular decision**. **Memo decisions,** on the other hand, usually deal with factual variations of previously decided cases. Nevertheless, regular and memo decisions carry the same authoritative weight.

At times, the chief judge determines that a particular case concerns an important issue that the entire Tax Court should consider. In such a situation, the words *reviewed by the court* appear at the end of the majority opinion. Any concurring or dissenting opinions follow the majority opinion. A judge who issues a concurring opinion agrees with the basic outcome of the majority's decision but not with its rationale. A judge who issues a dissenting opinion believes the majority reached an erroneous conclusion.

▼ TABLE C:1-2
Summary of Court System—Tax Matters

Court(s) (Number of)	Number of Judges on Each	Personal Jurisdiction	Subject Matter Jurisdiction	Determines Questions of Fact	Trial by Jury	Precedents Followed	Where Opinions Published
U.S. district courts (over 95)	1–28*	Local	General	Yes	Yes	Same court Court for circuit where situated U.S. Supreme Court	Federal Supplement American Federal Tax Reports United States Tax Cases
U.S. Tax Court (1)	19	National	Tax	Yes	No	Same court Court for taxpayer's circuit U.S. Supreme Court	Tax Court of the U.S. Reports CCH Tax Court Memorandum Decisions RIA Tax Court Memorandum Decisions
U.S. Court of Federal Claims (1)	16	National	Claims against U.S. Government	Yes	No	Same court Federal Circuit Court U.S. Supreme Court	Federal Reporter (pre-1982) U.S. Court of Federal Claims American Federal Tax Reports United States Tax Cases
U.S. Courts of Appeals (13)	About 20	Regional	General	No	No	Same court U.S. Supreme Court	Federal Reporter American Federal Tax Reports United States Tax Cases
U.S. Supreme Court (1)	9	National	General	No	No	Same court	U.S. Supreme Court Reports Supreme Court Reporter United States Reports, Lawyers' Edition American Federal Tax Reports United States Tax Cases

*Although the number of judges assigned to each court varies, only one judge hears a case.

Another phrase sometimes appearing at the end of a Tax Court opinion is *Entered under Rule 155.* This phrase signifies that the court has reached a decision concerning the tax treatment of an item but has left computation of the deficiency to the two litigating parties.

Small Cases Procedure. Taxpayers have the option of having their cases heard under the **small cases procedure** of the Tax Court if the amount in controversy on an annual basis does not exceed $50,000.[26] This procedure is less formal than the regular Tax Court procedure, and taxpayers can represent themselves without an attorney.[27] The cases are heard by special commissioners instead of by one of the 19 Tax Court judges. A disadvantage of the small cases procedure for the losing party is that the decision cannot be appealed. The opinions of the commissioners generally are not published and have no precedential value.

Acquiescence Policy. The IRS has adopted a policy of announcing whether, in future cases involving similar facts and similar issues, it will follow federal court decisions that are adverse to it. This policy is known as the IRS **acquiescence policy.** If the IRS wants taxpayers to know that it will follow an adverse decision in future cases involving similar facts and issues, it will announce its "acquiescence" in the decision. Conversely, if it wants taxpayers to know that it will not follow the decision in such future cases, it will announce its "nonacquiescence." The IRS does not announce its acquiescence or nonacquiescence in every decision it loses.

The IRS publishes its acquiescences and nonacquiescences as "Actions on Decision" first in the *Internal Revenue Bulletin,* then in the *Cumulative Bulletin.* Before 1991, the IRS acquiesced or nonacquiesced in regular Tax Court decisions only. In 1991, it broadened the scope of its policy to include adverse U.S. Claims Court, U.S. district court, and U.S. circuit court decisions.

In cases involving multiple issues, the IRS may acquiesce in some issues but not others. In decisions supported by extensive reasoning, it may acquiesce in the result but not the rationale (*acq. in result*). Furthermore, it may retroactively revoke an acquiescence or nonacquiescence. The footnotes to the relevant announcement in the *Internal Revenue Bulletin* and *Cumulative Bulletin* indicate the nature and extent of IRS acquiescences and nonacquiescences.

These acquiescences and nonacquiescences have important implications for taxpayers. If a taxpayer bases his or her position on a decision in which the IRS has nonacquiesced, he or she can expect an IRS challenge in the event of an audit. In such circumstances, the taxpayer's only recourse may be litigation. On the other hand, if the taxpayer bases his or her position on a decision in which the IRS has acquiesced, he or she can expect little or no challenge. In either case, the examining agent will be bound by the IRS position.

Published Opinions and Citations. Regular Tax Court decisions are published by the U.S. Government Printing Office in a bound volume known as the *Tax Court of the United States Reports.* Soon after a decision is made public, Research Institute of America (RIA) and CCH Incorporated (CCH) each publish the decision in its respective reporter of Tax Court decisions. An official citation to a Tax Court decision is as follows:[28]

MedChem Products, Inc., 116 T.C. 308 (2001).

The citation indicates that this case appears on page 308 in Volume 116 of *Tax Court of the United States Reports* and that the case was decided in 2001.

---

[26] Sec. 7463. The $50,000 amount includes penalties and additional taxes but excludes interest.

[27] Taxpayers also can represent themselves in regular Tax Court proceedings even though they are not attorneys. Where taxpayers represent themselves, the words *pro se* appear in the opinion after the taxpayer's name. The Tax Court is the only federal court before which non-attorneys, including CPAs, may practice.

[28] In a citation to a case decided by the Tax Court, only the name of the plaintiff (taxpayer) is listed. The defendant is understood to be the Commissioner of Internal Revenue whose name usually is not shown in the citation. In cases decided by other courts, the name of the plaintiff is listed first and the name of the defendant second. For non-Tax Court cases, the Commissioner of Internal Revenue is referred to as *CIR* in our footnotes and text.

From 1924 to 1942, regular decisions of the Board of Tax Appeals (predecessor of the Tax Court) were published by the U.S. Government Printing Office in the *United States Board of Tax Appeals Reports*. An example of a citation to a Board of Tax Appeals case is as follows:

J.W. Wells Lumber Co. Trust A., 44 B.T.A. 551 (1941).

This case is found in Volume 44 of the *United States Board of Tax Appeals Reports* on page 551. It is a 1941 decision.

If the IRS has acquiesced or nonacquiesced in a federal court decision, the IRS's action should be denoted in the citation. At times, the IRS will not announce its acquiescence or nonacquiescence until several years after the date of the decision. An example of a citation to a decision in which the IRS has acquiesced is as follows:

Security State Bank, 111 T.C. 210 (1998), *acq.* 2001-1 C.B. xix.

The case appears on page 210 of Volume 111 of the *Tax Court of the United States Reports* and the acquiescence is reported on page xix of Volume 1 of the 2001 *Cumulative Bulletin*. In 2001, the IRS acquiesced in this 1998 decision. A citation to a decision in which the IRS has nonacquiesced is as follows:

Estate of Algerine Allen Smith, 108 T.C. 412 (1997), *nonacq.* 2000-1 C.B. xvi.

The case appears on page 412 of Volume 108 of the *Tax Court of the United States Reports*. The nonacquiescence is reported on page xvi of Volume 1 of the 2000 *Cumulative Bulletin*. In 2000, the IRS nonacquiesced in this 1997 decision.

Tax Court memo decisions are not published by the U.S. Government Printing Office. They are, however, published by RIA in *RIA T.C. Memorandum Decisions* and by CCH in *CCH Tax Court Memorandum Decisions*. In addition, shortly after its issuance, an opinion is made available electronically and in loose-leaf form by RIA and CCH in their respective tax services. The following citation is to a Tax Court memo decision:

Edith G. McKinney, 1981 PH T.C. Memo ¶81,181, 41 TCM 1272.

McKinney is found at Paragraph 81,181 of Prentice Hall's (now RIA's)[29] 1981 *PH T.C. Memorandum Decisions* reporter, and in Volume 41, page 1272, of CCH's *Tax Court Memorandum Decisions*. The 181 in the PH citation indicates that the case is the Tax Court's 181st memo decision of the year. A more recent citation is formatted in the same way but refers to RIA memo decisions.

Paul F. Belloff, 1992 RIA T.C. Memo ¶92,346, 63 TCM 3150.

U.S. DISTRICT COURTS. Each state has at least one U.S. district court, and more populous states have more than one. Each district court is independent of the others and is thus free to issue its own decisions, subject to the precedential constraints discussed later in this chapter. Different types of cases—not just tax-related—are adjudicated in this forum. A district court is the only forum in which the taxpayer may have a jury decide questions of fact. Depending on the circumstances, a jury trial might be advantageous for the taxpayer.[30]

District court decisions are officially reported in the *Federal Supplement* (cited as F. Supp.) published by West Publishing Co. (West). Some decisions are not officially

ADDITIONAL COMMENT

Once the IRS has acquiesced in a federal court decision, other tax-payers generally will not need to litigate the same issue. However, the IRS can change its mind and revoke a previous acquiescence or nonacquiescence. References to acquiescences or nonacquiescences in federal court decisions can be found in the citators.

KEY POINT

To access all Tax Court cases, a tax advisor must refer to two different publications. The regular opinions appear in the *Tax Court of the United States Reports*, published by the U.S. Government Printing Office, and the memo decisions are published by both RIA (formerly PH) and CCH in their own court reporters.

---

[29] For several years the Prentice Hall Information Services division published its *Federal Taxes 2nd* tax service and a number of related publications, such as the *PH T.C. Memorandum Decisions*. Changes in ownership occurred, and in late 1991 Thomson Professional Publishing added the former Prentice Hall tax materials to the product line of its RIA tax publishing division. Some print products such as the *PH T.C. Memorandum Decisions* still have the Prentice Hall name on the spine of older editions.

[30] Taxpayers might prefer to have a jury trial if they believe a jury will be sympathetic to their case.

reported and are referred to as **unreported decisions**. Decisions by U.S. district courts on the topic of taxation also are published by RIA and CCH in secondary reporters that contain only tax-related opinions. RIA's reporter is *American Federal Tax Reports* (cited as AFTR).[31] CCH's reporter is *U.S. Tax Cases* (cited as USTC). A case not offically reported nevertheless might be published in the AFTR and USTC. An example of a complete citation to a U.S. district court decision is as follows:

Alfred Abdo, Jr. v. IRS, 234 F. Supp. 2d 553, 90 AFTR 2d 2002-7484, 2003-1 USTC ¶50,107 (DC North Carolina, 2002).

In the example above, the **primary citation** is to the *Federal Supplement*. The case appears on page 553 of Volume 234 of the second series of this reporter. **Secondary citations** are to *American Federal Tax Reports* and *U.S. Tax Cases*. The same case is found in Volume 90 of the second series of the AFTR, page 2002-7484 (meaning page 7484 in the volume containing 2002 cases) and in Volume 1 of the 2003 USTC at Paragraph 50,107. The parenthetical information indicates that the case was decided in 2002 by the U.S. District Court for North Carolina. Because some judicial decisions have greater precedential weight than others (e.g., a Supreme Court decision versus a district court decision), information relating to the identity of the adjudicating court is useful in evaluating the authoritative value of the decision.

U.S. COURT OF FEDERAL CLAIMS. The U.S. Court of Federal Claims, another court of first instance that addresses tax matters, has nationwide jurisdiction. Originally, this court was called the U.S. Court of Claims (cited as Ct. Cl.), and its decisions were appealable to the U.S. Supreme Court only. In a reorganization, effective October 1, 1982, the reconstituted court was named the U.S. Claims Court (cited as Cl. Ct.), and its decisions became appealable to the Circuit Court of Appeals for the Federal Circuit. In October 1992, the court's name was again changed to the U.S. Court of Federal Claims (cited as Fed. Cl.).

Beginning in 1982, U.S. Claims Court decisions were reported officially in the *Claims Court Reporter,* published by West from 1982 to 1992.[32] An example of a citation to a U.S. Claims Court decision appears below:

Benjamin Raphan v. U.S., 3 Cl. Ct. 457, 52 AFTR 2d 83-5987, 83-2 USTC ¶9613 (1983).

The *Raphan* case appears on page 457 of Volume 3 of the *Claims Court Reporter*. Secondary citations are to Volume 52, page 83-5987 of the AFTR, Second Series, and to Volume 2 of the 1983 USTC at Paragraph 9613.

Effective with the 1992 reorganization, decisions of the U.S. Court of Federal Claims are now reported in the *Federal Claims Reporter*. An example of a citation to an opinion published in this reporter is presented below:

Jeffrey G. Sharp v. U.S., 27 Fed. Cl. 52, 70 AFTR 2d 92-6040, 92-2 USTC ¶50,561 (1992).

The *Sharp* case appears on page 52 of Volume 27 of the *Federal Claims Reporter,* on page 6040 of the 70th volume of the AFTR, Second Series, and at Paragraph 50,561 of Volume 2 of the 1992 USTC reporter. Note that, even though the name of the reporter published by West has changed, the volume numbers continue in sequence as if no name change had occurred.

---

[31] The *American Federal Tax Reports* (AFTR) is published in two series. The first series, which includes opinions issued up to 1957, is cited as AFTR. The second series, which includes opinions issued after 1957, is cited as AFTR 2d. The *Alfred Abdo, Jr.* decision cited as an illustration of a U.S. district court decision appears in the second *American Federal Tax Reports* series.
[32] Before the creation in 1982 of the U.S. Claims Court (and the *Claims*

Court Reporter), the opinions of the U.S. Court of Claims were reported in either the *Federal Supplement* (F. Supp.) or the *Federal Reporter, Second Series* (F.2d). The *Federal Supplement* is the primary source of U.S. Court of Claims opinions from 1932 through January 19, 1960. Opinions issued from January 20, 1960, to October 1982 are reported in the *Federal Reporter, Second Series*.

CIRCUIT COURTS OF APPEALS. Lower court decisions are appealable by the losing party to the court of appeals for the circuit in which the litigation originated. Generally, if the case began in the Tax Court or a U.S. district court, the case is appealable to the circuit for the individual's residence as of the appeal date. For a corporation, the case is appealable to the circuit for the corporation's principal place of business. The Federal Circuit hears all appeals of cases originating in the U.S. Court of Federal Claims.

As mentioned earlier, there are 11 geographical circuits designated by numbers, the District of Columbia Circuit, and the Federal Circuit. In October 1981, the Eleventh Circuit was created by moving Alabama, Georgia, and Florida from the Fifth to a new geographical circuit. The Eleventh Circuit has adopted the policy of following as precedent all decisions of the Fifth Circuit during the time the states currently constituting the Eleventh Circuit were part of the Fifth Circuit.[33]

EXAMPLE C:1-7 ▶

In the current year, the Eleventh Circuit first considered an issue in a case involving a Florida taxpayer. In 1980, the Fifth Circuit had ruled on the same issue in a case involving a Louisiana taxpayer. Because Florida was part of the Fifth Circuit in 1980, under the policy adopted by the Eleventh Circuit, it will follow the Fifth Circuit's earlier decision. Had the Fifth Circuit's decision been rendered in 1982—after the creation of the Eleventh Circuit—the Eleventh Circuit would not have been bound by the Fifth Circuit's decision. ◀

As the later discussion of precedent points out, different circuits may reach different conclusions concerning similar facts and issues.

Circuit court decisions—regardless of topic (e.g., civil rights, securities law, and taxation)—are now reported officially in the *Federal Reporter, Third Series* (cited as F.3d), published by West. The third series was created in October 1993 after the volume number for the second series reached 999. The primary citation to a circuit court opinion should be to the *Federal Reporter*. Tax decisions of the circuit courts also appear in the *American Federal Tax Reports* and *U.S. Tax Cases*. Below is an example of a citation to a 1994 circuit court decision:

> *Leonard Greene v. U.S.,* 13 F.3d 577, 73 AFTR 2d 94-746, 94-1 USTC ¶50,022 (2nd Cir., 1994).

The *Greene* case appears on page 577 of Volume 13 of the *Federal Reporter, Third Series*. It also is published in Volume 73, page 94-746 of the AFTR, Second Series, and in Volume 1, Paragraph 50,022, of the 1994 USTC. The parenthetical information indicates that the Second Circuit decided the case in 1994. (A *Federal Reporter, Second Series* reference is found in footnote 33 of this chapter.)

ADDITIONAL COMMENT

A judge is not required to follow judicial precedent beyond his or her jurisdiction. Thus, the Tax Court, the U.S. district courts, and the U.S. Court of Federal Claims are not required to follow the others' decisions, nor is a circuit court required to follow the decision of a different circuit court.

U.S. SUPREME COURT. Whichever party loses at the appellate level can request that the U.S. Supreme Court hear the case. The Supreme Court, however, hears very few tax cases. Unless the circuits are divided on the tax treatment of an item, or the issue is deemed to be of great significance, the Supreme Court probably will not hear the case.[34] Supreme Court decisions are the law of the land and take precedence over all other court decisions, including the Supreme Court's earlier decisions. As a practical matter, a Supreme Court interpretation of the IRC is almost as authoritative as an act of Congress. If Congress does not agree with the Court's interpretation, it can amend the IRC to achieve a different result and has in fact done so on a number of occasions. If the Supreme Court declares a tax statute to be unconstitutional, the statute is invalid.

All Supreme Court decisions, regardless of subject, are published in the *United States Supreme Court Reports* (cited as U.S.) by the U.S. Government Printing Office, the *Supreme Court Reporter* (cited as S. Ct.) by West, and the *United States Reports, Lawyers' Edition* (cited as L. Ed.) by Lawyer's Co-operative Publishing Co. In addition,

---

[33] *Bonner v. City of Prichard,* 661 F.2d 1206 (11th Cir., 1981).
[34] *Vogel Fertilizer Co. v. U.S.,* 49 AFTR 2d 82-491, 82-1 USTC ¶9134 (USSC, 1982), is an example of a case the Supreme Court heard to settle a split in judicial authority. The Fifth Circuit, the Tax Court, and the Court of Claims had reached one conclusion on an issue, while the Second, Fourth, and Eighth Circuits had reached another.

the AFTR and USTC reporters published by RIA and CCH, respectively, contain Supreme Court decisions concerned with taxation. An example of a citation to a Supreme Court opinion appears below:

Boeing Company v. U.S., 537 U.S. 437, 91 AFTR 2d 2003-1088, 2003-1 USTC ¶50,273 (USSC, 2003).

According to the primary citation, this case appears in Volume 537, page 437, of the *United States Supreme Court Reports*. According to the secondary citation, it also appears in Volume 91, page 2003-1088, of the AFTR, Second Series, and in Volume 1, Paragraph 50,273, of the 2003 USTC.

Table C:1-3 provides a summary of how the IRC, court decisions, revenue rulings, revenue procedures, and other administrative pronouncements should be cited. Primary citations are to the reporters published by West or the U.S. Government Printing Office, and secondary citations are to the AFTR and USTC.

SELF-STUDY QUESTION

Is it possible for the Tax Court to intentionally issue conflicting decisions?

ANSWER

Yes. If the Tax Court issues two decisions that are appealable to different circuit courts and these courts have previously reached different conclusions on the issue, the Tax Court follows the respective precedent in each circuit and issues conflicting decisions. This is a result of the *Golsen* Rule.

PRECEDENTIAL VALUE OF VARIOUS DECISIONS.

Tax Court. The Tax Court is a court of national jurisdiction. Consequently, it generally rules uniformly for all taxpayers, regardless of their residence or place of business. It follows U.S. Supreme Court decisions and its own earlier decisions. It is not bound by cases decided by the U.S. Court of Federal Claims or a U.S. district court, even if the district court has jurisdiction over the taxpayer.

In 1970, the Tax Court adopted what is known as the *Golsen* Rule.[35] Under this rule, the Tax Court departs from its general policy of adjudicating uniformly for all taxpayers and instead follows the decisions of the court of appeals to which the case in question is appealable. Stated differently, the *Golsen* Rule mandates that the Tax Court rule consistently with decisions of the court for the circuit where the taxpayer resides or does business.

EXAMPLE C:1-8 ▶ In the year in which an issue was first litigated, the Tax Court decided that an expenditure was deductible. The government appealed the decision to the Tenth Circuit Court of Appeals and won a reversal. This is the only appellate decision regarding the issue. If and when the Tax Court addresses this issue again, it will hold, with one exception, that the expenditure is deductible. The exception applies to taxpayers in the Tenth Circuit. Under the *Golsen* Rule, these taxpayers will be denied the deduction. ◀

U.S. District Court. Because each U.S. district court is independent of the other district courts, the decisions of each have precedential value only within its own jurisdiction (i.e., only with respect to subsequent cases brought before that court). District courts must follow decisions of the U.S. Supreme Court, the circuit court to which the case is appealable, and the district court's own earlier decisions regarding similar facts and issues.

EXAMPLE C:1-9 ▶ The U.S. District Court for Rhode Island, the Tax Court, and the Eleventh Circuit have decided cases involving similar facts and issues. Any U.S. district court within the Eleventh Circuit must follow that circuit's decision in future cases involving similar facts and issues. Likewise, the U.S. District Court for Rhode Island must decide such cases consistently with its previous decision. Tax Court decisions are not binding on the district courts. Thus, all district courts other than the one for Rhode Island and those within the Eleventh Circuit are free to decide such cases independently. ◀

U.S. Court of Federal Claims. In adjudicating a case, the U.S. Court of Federal Claims must rule consistently with U.S. Supreme Court decisions, decisions of the Circuit Court of Appeals for the Federal Circuit, and its own earlier decisions, including those rendered when the court had a different name. It need not follow decisions of other circuit courts, the Tax Court, or U.S. district courts.

---

[35] The *Golsen* Rule is based on the decision in *Jack E. Golsen*, 54 T.C. 742 (1970).

▼ TABLE C:1-3
Summary of Tax-related Primary Sources—Statutory and Administrative

Source Name	Publisher	Materials Provided	Citation Example
U.S. Code, Title 26	Government Printing Office	Internal Revenue Code	Sec. 441(b)
Code of Federal Regulations, Title 26	Government Printing Office	Treasury Regulations (final)	Reg. Sec. 1.461-1(c)
		Treasury Regulations (temporary)	Temp. Reg. Sec. 1.62-1T(e)
Internal Revenue Bulletin	Government Printing Office	Treasury Regulations (proposed)	Prop. Reg. Sec. 1.671-1(h)
		Treasury decisions	T.D. 8756 (January 13, 1998)
		Revenue rulings	Rev. Rul. 2009-33, 2009-40 I.R.B. 447
		Revenue procedures	Rev. Proc. 2009-52, 2009-49 I.R.B. 744
		Committee reports	S.Rept. No. 105-33, 105th Cong., 1st Sess., p. 308 (1997)
		Public laws	P.L. 105-34, Sec. 224(a), enacted August 6, 1997
		Announcements	Announcement 2007-3, 2007-4 I.R.B. 376
		Notices	Notice 2009-21, 2009-13 I.R.B. 724
Cumulative Bulletin	Government Printing Office	Treasury Regulations (proposed)	Prop. Reg. Sec. 1.671-1(h)
		Treasury decisions	T.D. 8756 (January 12, 1998)
		Revenue rulings	Rev. Rul. 84-111, 1984-2 C.B. 88
		Revenue procedures	Rev. Proc. 77-28, 1977-2 C.B. 537
		Committee reports	S.Rept. No. 105-33, 105th Cong., 1st Sess., p. 308 (1997)
		Public laws	P.L. 105-34, Sec. 224(a), enacted August 6, 1997
		Announcements	Announcement 2006-8, 2006-1 C.B. 344
		Notices	Notice 88-74, 1988-2 C.B. 385

Summary of Tax-related Primary and Secondary Sources—Judicial

Reporter Name	Publisher	Decisions Published	Citation Example
U.S. Supreme Court Reports	Government Printing Office	U.S. Supreme Court	Boeing Company v. U.S., 537 U.S. 437 (2003)
Supreme Court Reports	West Publishing Company	U.S. Supreme Court	Boeing Company v. U.S., 123 S. Ct. 1099 (2003)
Federal Reporter (1st–3rd Series)	West Publishing Company	U.S. Court of Appeal Pre-1982 Court of Claims	Leonard Greene v. U.S., 13 F.3d 577 (2nd Cir., 1994)
Federal Supplement Series	West Publishing Company	U.S. District Court	Alfred Abdo, Jr. v. IRS, 234 F. Supp. 2d 553 (DC North Carolina, 2002)
U.S. Court of Federal Claims	West Publishing Company	Court of Federal Claims	Jeffery G. Sharp v. U.S., 27 Fed. Cl. 52 (1992)
Tax Court of the U.S. Reports	Government Printing Office	U.S. Tax Court regular	Security State Bank, 111 T.C. 210 (1998), acq. 2001-1 C.B. xix
Tax Court Memorandum Decisions	CCH Incorporated	U.S. Tax Court memo	Paul F. Belloff, 63 TCM 3150 (1992)
RIA Tax Court Memorandum Decisions	Research Institute of America	U.S. Tax Court memo	Paul F. Belloff, 1992 RIA T.C. Memo ¶92,346
American Federal Tax Reports	Research Institute of America	Tax: all federal courts except Tax Court	Boeing Company v. U.S., 91 AFTR 2d 2003-1 (USSC, 2003)
U.S. Tax Cases	CCH Incorporated	Tax: all federal courts except Tax Court	Ruddick Corp. v. U.S., 81-1 USTC ¶9343 (Ct. Cls., 1981)

EXAMPLE C:1-10 ▶   Assume the same facts as in Example C:1-9. In a later year, a case involving similar facts and issues is heard by the U.S. Court of Federal Claims. This court is not bound by precedents set by any of the other courts. Thus, it may reach a conclusion independently of the other courts. ◀

Circuit Courts of Appeals.   A circuit court is bound by U.S. Supreme Court decisions and its own earlier decisions. If neither the Supreme Court nor the circuit in question has already decided an issue, the circuit court has no precedent that it must follow, regardless of whether other circuits have ruled on the issue. In such circumstances, the circuit court is said to be writing on a clean slate. In rendering a decision, the judges of that court may adopt another circuit's view, which they are likely to regard as relevant.

EXAMPLE C:1-11 ▶   Assume the same facts as in Example C:1-9. Any circuit other than the Eleventh would be writing on a clean slate if it adjudicated a case involving similar facts and issues. After reviewing the Eleventh Circuit's decision, another circuit might find it relevant and rule in the same way. ◀

In such a case of "first impression," when the court has had no precedent on which to base a decision, a tax practitioner might look at past opinions of the court to see which other judicial authority the court has found to be "persuasive."

Forum Shopping.   Not surprisingly, courts often disagree on the tax treatment of the same item. This disagreement gives rise to differing precedents within the various jurisdictions (what is called a "split in judicial authority"). Because taxpayers have the flexibility of choosing where to file a lawsuit, these circumstances afford them the opportunity to **forum shop.** Forum shopping involves choosing where among the courts to file a lawsuit based on differing precedents.

An example of a split in judicial authority concerned the issue of when it became too late for the IRS to question the tax treatment of items that "flowed through" an S corporation's return to a shareholder's return. The key question was this: if the time for assessing a deficiency (limitations period) with respect to the corporation's, but not the shareholder's, return had expired, was the IRS precluded from collecting additional taxes from the shareholder? In *Kelley,*[36] the Ninth Circuit Court of Appeals ruled that the IRS would be barred from collecting additional taxes from the shareholder if the limitations period for the *S corporation's* return had expired. In *Bufferd,*[37] *Fehlhaber,*[38] and *Green,*[39] three other circuit courts ruled that the IRS would be barred from collecting additional taxes from the shareholder if the limitations period for the *shareholder's* return had expired. The Supreme Court affirmed the *Bufferd* decision,[40] establishing that the statute of limitations for the shareholder's return governed. This action brought about certainty and uniformity within the judicial system.

Dictum.   At times, a court may comment on an issue or a set of facts not central to the case under review. A court's remark not essential to the determination of a disputed issue, and therefore not binding authority, is called *dictum.* An example of dictum is found in *Central Illinois Public Service Co.*[41] In this case, the U.S. Supreme Court addressed whether lunch reimbursements received by employees constitute wages subject to withholding. Justice Blackman remarked in passing that earnings in the form of interest, rents, and dividends are not wages. This remark is dictum because it is not essential to the determination of whether lunch reimbursements are wages subject to withholding. Although not authoritative, dictum may be cited by taxpayers to bolster an argument in favor of a particular tax result.

---

[36] *Daniel M. Kelley v. CIR,* 64 AFTR 2d 89-5025, 89-1 USTC ¶9360 (9th Cir., 1989).

[37] *Sheldon B. Bufferd v. CIR,* 69 AFTR 2d 92-465, 92-1 USTC ¶50,031 (2nd Cir., 1992).

[38] *Robert Fehlhaber v. CIR,* 69 AFTR 2d 92-850, 92-1 USTC ¶50,131 (11th Cir., 1992).

[39] *Charles T. Green v. CIR,* 70 AFTR 2d 92-5077, 92-2 USTC ¶50,340 (5th Cir., 1992).

[40] *Sheldon B. Bufferd v. CIR,* 71 AFTR 2d 93-573, 93-1 USTC ¶50,038 (USSC, 1993).

[41] *Central Illinois Public Service Co. v. CIR,* 41 AFTR 2d 78-718, 78-1 USTC ¶9254 (USSC, 1978).

STOP & THINK

Question: You have been researching whether an amount received by your new client can be excluded from her gross income. The IRS is auditing the client's prior year tax return, which another firm prepared. In a similar case decided a few years ago, the Tax Court allowed an exclusion, but the IRS nonacquiesced in the decision. The case involved a taxpayer in the Fourth Circuit. Your client is a resident of Maine, which is in the First Circuit. Twelve years ago, in a case involving another taxpayer, the federal court for the client's district ruled that this type of receipt is not excludable. No other precedent exists. To sustain an exclusion, must your client litigate? Explain. If your client litigates, in which court of first instance should she begin her litigation?

Solution: Because of its nonacquiescence, the IRS is likely to challenge your client's tax treatment. Thus, she may be compelled to litigate. She would not want to litigate in her U.S. district court because it would be bound by its earlier decision, which is unfavorable to taxpayers generally. A good place to begin would be the Tax Court because it is bound by appellate court, but not district court, decisions and because of its earlier pro-taxpayer position. No one can predict how the U.S. Court of Federal Claims would rule because no precedent that it must follow exists.

ADDITIONAL COMMENT

A tax treaty carries the same authoritative weight as a federal statute (IRC). A tax advisor should be aware of provisions in tax treaties that will affect a taxpayer's worldwide tax liability.

TAX TREATIES

The United States has concluded **tax treaties** with numerous foreign countries. These treaties address the alleviation of double taxation and other matters. A tax advisor exploring the U.S. tax consequences of a U.S. corporation's operations in another country should determine whether a treaty between that country and the United States exists. If one does, the tax advisor should ascertain the applicable provisions of the treaty. (See Chapter C:16 of this text for a more extensive discussion of treaties.)

KEY POINT

Tax articles can be used to help *find* answers to tax questions. Where possible, the underlying statutory, administrative, or judicial sources referenced in the tax article should be cited as authority and not the author of the article. The courts and the IRS will place little, if any, reliance on mere editorial opinion.

TAX PERIODICALS

Tax periodicals assist the researcher in tracing the development of, and analyzing tax law. These periodicals are especially useful when they discuss the legislative history of a recently enacted IRC statute that has little or no administrative or judicial authority on point.

Tax experts write articles on landmark court decisions, proposed regulations, new tax legislation, and other matters. Frequently, those who write articles of a highly technical nature are attorneys, accountants, or professors. Among the periodicals that provide in-depth coverage of tax-related matters are the following:

> *The Journal of Taxation*
> *The Tax Adviser*
> *Practical Tax Strategies*
> *Taxes—The Tax Magazine*
> *Tax Law Review*
> *Tax Notes*
> *Corporate Taxation*
> *Business Entities*
> *Real Estate Taxation*
> *Estate Planning*

The first six journals are generalized; that is, they deal with a variety of topics. As their titles suggest, the next four are specialized; they deal with specific subjects. All these publications (other than *Tax Notes,* which is published weekly) are published either monthly or quarterly. Daily newsletters, such as the *Daily Tax Report,* published by the Bureau of National Affairs (BNA) in print and electronic formats, are used by tax professionals when they need updates more timely than can be provided by monthly or quarterly publications.

Tax periodicals and tax services are secondary authorities. The IRC, Treasury Regulations, IRS pronouncements, and court opinions are primary authorities. In presenting research results, the tax advisor should always cite primary authorities.

TAX SERVICES

OBJECTIVE 4

Consult tax services to research an issue

Various publishers provide multivolume commentaries on the tax law in what are familiarly referred to as **tax services**. Researchers often consult tax services at the beginning of the research process because a tax service helps identify the tax authorities pertaining to a particular tax issue. The actual tax authorities (e.g., IRC, Treasury Regulations, IRS pronouncements, and court cases), and not the tax services, are generally cited as support for a particular tax position. The services are available in print form via the publishers and electronic form via the Internet. (See further discussion at "The Internet as a Research Tool" later in this chapter). Although each major tax service is an outstanding resource, significant differences exist in the content and organizational scheme from one publisher to the next. For example, each service has its own special features and editorial approach to tax issues along with a great deal of proprietary content. The best way to acquaint oneself with the various tax services and the advantages and disadvantages of each is to use them in researching hypothetical or actual problems.

Organizationally, tax services fall into two types: annotated and topical (although this distinction has become somewhat blurred in the Internet version of these services). An **annotated tax service** is organized by IRC section. The IRC-arranged subdivisions of this service are likely to encompass several topics. The annotations accompany editorial commentaries and include digests or summaries of IRS pronouncements and court opinions that interpret a particular IRC section. They are classified by subtopic and cite pertinent primary authorities. A **topical tax service,** on the other hand, is organized by broad topic, including income taxes, estate and gift taxes, and excise taxes. The topically arranged subdivisions of this service are likely to encompass several IRC sections.

Annotated tax services include the *United States Tax Reporter* and the *Standard Federal Income Tax Reporter* services, both of which are organized by IRC section. Many tax advisors find these reporters easy to use because of their extensive indexing system. Topical tax services include RIA's *Federal Tax Coordinator 2d* and BNA's *Tax Management Portfolios*. *Tax Management Portfolios* are popular with many tax advisors because they are very readable yet still provide a comprehensive discussion of a broad range of tax issues. Each portfolio (e.g., Passive Loss Rules, Portfolio 549) covers a particular topic in great detail. However, because the published portfolios do not cover all areas of the tax law, another service may be necessary to supplement the gaps in a portfolio's coverage. Table C:1-4 summarizes the organization and key features of the major tax services.

▼ TABLE C:1-4
Summary of Key Features of Tax Services

Name	Publisher	Organization	Key Features
United States Tax Reporter	Thomson Reuters/RIA	IRC section number	• Editorial commentary • Index and findings list • Annotations
Standard Federal Income Tax Reporter	Wolters Kluwer/CCH	IRC section number	• Editorial commentary • Index and findings list • Annotations
Federal Tax Coordinator 2d	Thomson Reuters/RIA	Tax topic (income tax by topic, estate and gift taxes, excise taxes)	• Commentary organized by topic with references to primary authority and tabbed access to IRC and Treasury Regulations.
Tax Management Portfolios	Bureau of National Affairs (BNA)	U.S. income, foreign income, state tax, estate and gift tax	• Over 400 specialized booklets with extensive commentary by topic, heavily footnoted and referenced to primary authority.

THE INTERNET AS A RESEARCH TOOL

OBJECTIVE 5

Grasp the basics of Internet-based tax research

Internet databases are rapidly replacing print-based services as the principal source of tax related information. These databases encompass not only the IRC, Treasury Regulations, court cases, state laws, and other primary authorities, but also citators and secondary sources such as tax service reporters, treatises, journals, and newsletters. The principal advantages of using Internet-based tax services are ease and speed of access. These services eliminate the need for searching through several volumes of text, the need for consulting numerous cumulative supplements, and the time required to regularly update a print-based library. In addition, Internet based research tools put a vast amount of information in the hands of a tax practitioner without the cost and space requirements of a well equipped print-based tax library.

Because of these advantages, the Internet has become the principal medium for conveying tax related information to professionals. The most widely used Internet-based research services are RIA's Checkpoint™ (hereafter CHECKPOINT), accessible at *http://checkpoint.riag.com*, and CCH IntelliConnect™ (hereafter INTELLICONNECT), accessible at *http://intelliconnect.cch.com*.[42] Westlaw® and LexisNexus® are online legal research services that are predominately used by legal professionals.[43] This chapter limits its discussion to CHECKPOINT and INTELLICONNECT. Both subscription-based services are updated continuously and store information in databases, called libraries, principal among which are the following:[44]

CHECKPOINT	INTELLICONNECT
Newsstand	Tax News, Journals, and Newsletters
Federal	Federal Tax
State and Local	State Tax
International	International Tax
Estate Planning	Financial and Estate Planning
Pension and Benefits	Pension/Benefits
Payroll	Payroll

Newsstand on CHECKPOINT and *Tax News, Journals, and Newsletters* on INTELLICONNECT provide daily updates on recent tax developments. The *Federal* library on both series contains the text of the IRC, Treasury Regulations, IRS pronouncements, court opinions, and other primary sources. In addition to primary sources, the *Federal* library on CHECKPOINT contains the RIA citator, *Federal Tax Coordinator 2d*, and *United States Tax Reporter* annotations and explanations. The *Federal* library on INTELLICONNECT contains the *Standard Federal Income Tax Reporter* and the *Standard Federal Income Tax Reporter Explanations*. Tax reporters for all 50 states as well as multistate tax guides are found in the *State and Local* library on CHECKPOINT and the *State Tax* library on INTELLICONNECT. International tax treaties are found in the *International* library of both services. CHECKPOINT's *Estate Planning* offers the text of estate tax treaties, newsletters, journals, and Warren, Gorham & Lamont tax treatises. INTELLICONNECT's *Financial and Estate Planning* library supplies the *Federal Estate and Gift Tax Reporter*, as well as the text of estate and gift tax statutes, cases, and rulings. Finally, *Pension and Benefits* on CHECKPOINT and *Pension* on INTELLICONNECT contain the text of the Employee Retirement Income Security Act (ERISA), related Treasury Regulations, and Congressional committee reports, while *Payroll* provides the text of state and federal employment regulations and current withholding tables.

---

[42] Commerce Clearing House (CCH) is a member of the Wolters Kluwer Tax, Accounting and Legal Division. During 2009, CCH completed a major revision to its online research service, transitioning from the former Tax Research Network to IntelliConnect™ (hereafter INTELLICONNECT).

[43] The research products discussed in this section (e.g., CHECKPOINT, INTELLICONNECT, Westlaw, and LexisNexus) generally are available only to paid subscribers.

[44] INTELLICONNECT has numerous other databases, including Accounting and Audit, Banking, Corporate Government, Energy & Natural Resources, Health Care Compliance and Reimbursement. These specialty areas generally fall outside the tax arena and therefore are not described in this chapter.

CHECKPOINT and INTELLICONNECT libraries and databases can be searched in four basic ways:

▶ By keyword

▶ By index

▶ By citation

▶ By content

EXAMPLE C:1-12 ▶ Rhonda Researcher's client is a real estate developer and wants to exchange an office building for a residential condominium in the same town. The client wants to know if he can structure the transaction in a tax advantaged way. Rhonda immediately recognizes the situation as a potential like-kind exchange of real property. Therefore, she undertakes a keyword search of INTELLICONNECT using the term *like kind exchange* to quickly uncover potentially applicable documents. She also knows that Sec. 1031 is the relevant IRC section and can search the IRC or Treasury Regulations by citation. On the other hand, if she were unfamiliar with the topic, she could employ several other options. For example, INTELLICONNECT's Federal Tax editorial content has a heading for topic indexes. The "Exchange of property" term in the topical index directs Rhonda to "See Like-kind Exchanges; Sales and Exchanges; and Tax-free Exchanges." The index entries under these headings direct Rhonda to a number of entries potentially applicable to the transaction. Rhonda also conducts a similar research procedure on CHECKPOINT to see whether this alternative service provides any additional information. In particular, she searches in the *Federal Tax Coordinator 2d*, which is RIA's topical service. ◀

KEY WORD SEARCHES

Searching CHECKPOINT and INTELLICONNECT by keyword is relatively simple, particularly if the researcher is familiar with the Internet. The first step is to activate a database or multiple databases and refine the results after the initial query. The researcher can choose to search across any combination of the available databases. The CHECKPOINT Federal databases include primary sources such as the Internal Revenue Code, Treasury Regulations, and Federal Tax Cases along with editorial databases such as RIA's *Federal Tax Coordinator 2d*. Similar choices exist for INTELLICONNECT. Deciding which database to include in the search depends partly on the expected complexity of the research question and on the researcher's familiarity with the topic.

The search engines within the services look for the terms selected and many variations of the terms. For example, the search for *auto* will return documents with auto, car, automobile, motor vehicle, passenger vehicle, sedan, and others.[45] Searches will include both singular and plural variations. Any document with the term or terms is returned and ranked by best match according to the search. If two terms are used, the best matches generally are documents where the terms are close together. Picking key words and search terms is critical to success. The search must be broad enough to include relevant documents but not so broad to include hundreds or thousands of documents unlikely to be on point.

For example, if the researcher selects only the INTELLICONNECT Cases database, the term *property exchange* returns thousands of results that have both the words *property* and *exchange* somewhere in the document. Clearly this outcome is too broad for a researcher just beginning his or her research. Fortunately, several methods of narrowing the search exist. For example, the search for *property exchange* can be limited to all terms, any terms, near phrase, or exact phrase. Specifically, the keyword search "property exchange" that uses quotation marks around the search phrase will return documents only with that exact phrase. Thus, quotation marks should be used sparingly and only when the researcher knows the precise phrase. Using Boolean connectors is helpful as well. These connectors force the search engine to narrow the search based on the parameters set. Table C:1-5 provides a partial list of connectors available in CHECKPOINT and INTELLICONNECT.

Another way to narrow a search is to focus on terms unique to the research question at hand. The goal is to identify tax related terms likely to appear only in relevant tax

---

[45] Both CHECKPOINT and INTELLICONNECT provide a thesaurus tool, which can identify synonyms and suggest alternative terms related to search terms used by the researcher. The search engine automatically searches for synonyms unless the researcher restricts the search to specific terms using Boolean connectors or quotation marks. For example, a search for the specific phrase "automobile depreciation" will not return documents that refer to *auto*, *car*, or *vehicle*.

▼ TABLE C:1-5

Connectors Used in INTELLICONNECT and CHECKPOINT

INTELLICONNECT	CHECKPOINT	Description	Examples
and	&, and	Retrieves documents with both terms.	INTELLICONNECT: property and exchange CHECKPOINT: property & exchange
or	|, or	Retrieves documents with either term.	INTELLICONNECT: property or exchange CHECKPOINT: property | exchange
not	^	Retrieves documents with one term but not the other.	INTELLICONNECT: property not exchange CHECKPOINT: property ^ exchange
w/n	/n	Retrieves documents in which the first term is separated from the second term by no more than n number of words.	INTELLICONNECT: property w/5 exchange CHECKPOINT: property /5 exchange Locates property within 5 words of exchange
w/sen	/s	Retrieves documents that contain the first term within 20 words of the second term (or within the same sentence for RIA).	INTELLICONNECT: property w/sen exchange CHECKPOINT: property /s exchange
w/par	/p	Retrieves documents that contain the first term within 80 words of the second term (or within the same paragraph for RIA).	INTELLICONNECT: property w/par exchange CHECKPOINT: property /p exchange
" "	" "	Exact phrase.	INTELLICONNECT and CHECKPOINT: "property exchange"
*	*	Keyword variation.	Deprecia* returns depreciation, depreciate, depreciated, depreciating

authorities. For example, stamps are a type of collectible, but the term also will appear in documents discussing taxation of distilled spirits, food stamps, and store stamps and coupons. The researcher should begin the search with limiting terms such as *collectible* rather than the broader term *stamps*. Also, researchers with a good working knowledge of the IRC quickly learn that using IRC sections in search terms is a great way to obtain relevant documents.

Searching using key words is a skill that improves with practice. Researchers becoming familiar with using the databases will learn to craft search terms that include the most relevant elements of the question at hand. Once the researcher finds a document on point, the information within that document often can be used to narrow future searches. The search can be repeated by adding terms, or the documents returned originally can be searched using a new set of terms. Also, the "search within results" feature offered by both CHECKPOINT and INTELLICONNECT is helpful when the search returns too many documents. However, if searches by key word search do not return the desired results, other options exist.

SEARCH BY INDEX

Both CHECKPOINT and INTELLICONNECT offer traditional indexes. With INTELLI-CONNECT, the user can click on most databases to see an index of the contents. For example, clicking on the *Standard Federal Income Tax Reporter* Topical Index listed in the Federal Tax Editorial content database reveals a list from A to Z, and the researcher can easily click on a hyperlink for any letter and scroll through the alphabetized topics list. As an example, one can find the letter C, then scroll through the screens and find the topic "casualty losses" that directs the researcher to a variety of subheadings. CHECKPOINT has an Index option under the Search area of the Research tab. In CHECKPOINT, the researcher can choose the *Federal Tax Coordinator 2d* Topic Index database. Again, the researcher will find the letter C and scroll through the topics to find "casualty losses," which leads the researcher to subheadings with hyperlinks to CHECKPOINT's editorial materials.

In addition, both INTELLICONNECT and CHECKPOINT have topical indexes that use hyperlinks to the Internal Revenue Code. In INTELLICONNECT, the researcher begins with the Topical Index option located under Federal Tax Primary Sources, selects the Current Internal Revenue Code Topical Index, and begins his or her research with an A to Z list. In CHECKPOINT, the researcher selects the Current Code Topic Index located in the Indexes link on the Research tab.

SEARCH BY CITATION

Often the desired document is a specific IRC section, Treasury Regulation, court case, IRS pronouncement, or other document. If so, both services offer searches by specific citation. Researchers must be careful to use exact citations using this tool because close matches will not return the desired document.

Both CHECKPOINT and INTELLICONNECT citation search tools provide dedicated boxes in which to type the specific type of document requested. For example, to search for IRC Sec. 267, the researcher simply types 267 in the box labeled Current Code in CHECK-POINT under the "Find by Citation" link, or IRC Code & Hist. Sec. in INTELLICONNECT under the "Citation" link. Specific boxes also exist for various court decisions, revenue rulings, revenue procedures, and other IRS pronouncements.

SEARCH BY CONTENT

Each database also can be searched by content. Clicking on the hyperlink for each database will return a table of contents. Clicking through an entry will take the researcher further into the table of contents. For example, in INTELLICONNECT, several documents discussing adoption credits can be located by clicking on the following series of hyperlinks:

> Federal Tax
> > Federal Tax Editorial Content
> > > Standard Federal Income Tax Reporter
> > > > Credits
> > > > > Adoption expenses – Sec. 23

CHECKPOINT also has a Table of Contents, located in the upper right corner of the primary research screen. Documents discussing adoption credits may be found by clicking on the following series of hyperlinks:

> Federal Library
> > Federal Editorial Materials
> > > Federal Tax Coordinator 2d
> > > > Chapter A Individuals and Self-Employment Tax
> > > > > A-4400 Adoption Expense Credit

NONCOMMERCIAL INTERNET SERVICES

Many noncommercial institutions, such as governments and universities, allow access to their tax-related databases via the Internet. In "tax-surfing" the Internet, the researcher might first visit the IRS site located at *http://www.irs.gov*. Although oriented to the layman, this site contains a wealth of information useful to the tax professional. Such information includes guidelines for electronic filing, IRS forms and instructions, the full text of Treasury Regulations, and recent issues of the *Internal Revenue Bulletin*. Other useful sites include those maintained by the Library of Congress at *http://thomas.loc.gov* and the Government Printing Office at *http://www.gpoaccess.gov*. From these sites, the researcher can retrieve the text of recent court opinions, tax legislation, committee reports, state and federal tax laws, and much more.

An excellent gateway for starting tax related research is the Tax, Accounting, and Payroll Sites Directory at *http://www.taxsites.com*, maintained by AccountantsWorld,

LLC. This site provides hundreds of hyperlinks to federal, state, and international tax law and tax form databases. Instrumental in financial accounting searches is the Electronic Data Gathering, Analysis, and Retrieval (EDGAR) site at *http://www.sec.gov/edgar.shtml*. EDGAR is a document filing and retrieval service sponsored by the U.S. Securities and Exchange Commission (SEC). It provides access to the full text of documents filed with the SEC by publicly traded companies. These documents include annual financial statements on Form 10-K, quarterly financial statements on Form 10-Q, proxy statements, and prospectuses. The EDGAR database extends from January 1994 to the present and is accessible by company name, central index key, document file number, and keyword.

CITATORS

OBJECTIVE 6

Use a citator to assess tax authorities

Citators serve two functions. First, they trace the judicial history of a particular case (e.g., if the case under analysis is an appeals court decision, the citator indicates the lower court that heard the case and whether the Supreme Court reviewed the case). Second, they list other authorities (e.g., cases and IRS pronouncements) that cite the case or authority in question. These listed authorities are called *citing cases* or *citing rulings*. The judicial history also indicates whether the case is affirmed, reversed or remanded.[46]

Because tax law relies heavily on precedent, the citator provides an index of citing cases and rulings that help the researcher determine the strength of the case or ruling he or she is evaluating. The citator gives full citations for the citing case and lists where the citing cases can be found. It is important to note that the same case may have as many as three decisions (i.e., lower court, court of appeals, and Supreme Court) with each listing having its own list of citing cases. Therefore, if a citing case cites only the Supreme Court decision, the citator will list it only under the Supreme Court cite.

Two principal tax related commercial citators are those in INTELLICONNECT and CHECKPOINT. Both citators allow the researcher to enter case names or case citations. The discussion in this section focuses on the electronic version of the citators, although both CCH and RIA offer print versions as well.

The INTELLICONNECT citator analyzes every decision reported in the *Standard Federal Income Tax Reporter*, the *Excise Tax Reporter*, and the *Federal Estate and Gift Tax Reporter* and selectively lists cases that cite the decision under analysis. INTELLICONNECT lists only the citing cases that its editors believe will influence the precedential weight of the decision under analysis.

The CHECKPOINT citator also provides the history of each authority and lists the cases and pronouncements that have cited the authority. This citator, however, differs from the INTELLICONNECT citator in a couple of important ways. First, CHECKPOINT lists all citing cases, and not just those that the editors believe will serve as relevant precedent. Second, the CHECKPOINT citator provides additional information about the citing case, showing whether the citing authorities comment favorably or unfavorably on the cited case or whether they can be distinguished from the cited case.[47]

In addition to tax cases, the CHECKPOINT and INTELLICONNECT citators evaluate revenue rulings and other IRS pronouncements and lists any status changes. Before relying on a revenue ruling or pronouncement, a researcher must confirm that the pronouncement reflects the current position of the IRS. For example, a revoked ruling is

---

[46] If a case is *affirmed*, the decision of the lower court is upheld. *Reversed* means the higher court invalidated the decision of the lower court because it reached a conclusion different from that derived by the lower court. *Remanded* signifies that the higher court sent the case back to the lower court with instructions to address matters consistent with the higher court's ruling.

[47] When a court distinguishes the facts of one case from those of an earlier case, it suggests that its departure from the earlier decision is justified because the facts of the two cases are different.

▼ TABLE C:1-6
Terms to Describe Status Changes to IRS Rulings

Term	Description of Term
Amplified	No change in the prior published position has occurred, but the prior position is extended to cover a variation of the fact situation previously addressed.
Clarified	Language used in a prior published position is being made clear because the previous language has caused or could cause confusion.
Distinguished	The ruling mentions a prior ruling but points out an essential difference between the two rulings.
Modified	The substance of a previously published ruling is being changed, but the prior ruling remains in effect.
Obsoleted	A previously published ruling is no longer determinative with respect to future transactions, e.g., because laws or regulations have changed, or the substance of the ruling has been adopted into regulations.
Revoked	A previously published ruling has been determined to be incorrect, and the correct position is being stated in the new ruling.
Superseded	The new ruling merely restates the substance of a previously published ruling or series of rulings.
Supplemented	The ruling expands a previous ruling, e.g., by adding items to a list.
Suspended	The previously published ruling will not be applied pending some future action, such as the issuance of new or amended regulations.

Source: www.irs.gov.

one in which the ruling is no longer correct and the correct position is being stated in the new ruling. The IRS does not remove the old ruling from the *Internal Revenue Bulletin* or *Cumulative Bulletin*, but the old ruling does not have authority regarding a transaction occurring after the revocation. Thus, failure to confirm its status could result in an incorrect conclusion. Table C:1-6 provides a list of terms the IRS uses to describe changes in the status of a ruling.

USING THE CITATOR

Internet-based versions of the citators are easier to use than print-based citators. For example, assume the researcher is currently reading *Leonarda C. Diaz v. Commissioner of Internal Revenue*, 70 TC 1067 (1978). Using INTELLICONNECT, the researcher can click on the Citator button in the left column at the top left of the page, and the service opens up a new tab with a summary of activity of the case. The information in bold print with bullets to the left denotes that the *Diaz* case was first decided by the Tax Court (i.e., TC), and then by the Second Circuit Court of Appeals (i.e., CA-2). It shows that the Second Circuit affirmed (upheld) the Tax Court's decision. The three cases underneath the Second Circuit decision cite the *Diaz* decision and might be useful for the researcher to better understand the impact of the case. The seven cases listed beneath the Tax Court decision cite the Tax Court's opinion.

The CHECKPOINT citator is similarly easy to use. Once again, if the researcher is reading the *Diaz* case, he or she simply clicks on the Citator button at the top of the case window. The two main decisions (Tax Court and Second Circuit) appear in a list. Clicking on either case brings up the court decisions that have cited the *Diaz* decision. CHECKPOINT sometimes lists more cases than does INTELLICONNECT. In this example, CHECKPOINT lists ten cases that have cited the *Diaz* Second Circuit decision and 25 cases that have cited the Tax Court decision. CHECKPOINT also adds a brief description of the type of citation—cited favorably, cited unfavorable, case distinguished, or reasoning followed.

PROFESSIONAL GUIDELINES FOR TAX SERVICES

OBJECTIVE 7

Understand professional guidelines that CPAs in tax practice should follow

Professional guidelines for tax services are contained in both government-imposed and professional-imposed tax standards. The following sections briefly describe two types of guidelines—Treasury Department *Circular 230* (Rev. 4-2008) and the American Institute of Certified Public Accountants (AICPA) *Statements on Standards for Tax Services (SSTSs)*. A fuller discussion of these standards appears in Chapter C:15.

TREASURY DEPARTMENT *CIRCULAR 230*

Circular 230 sets forth rules to practice before the Internal Revenue Service and pertains to certified public accountants, attorneys, enrolled agents, and other persons representing taxpayers before the IRS. It presents the duties and restrictions relating to such practice and prescribes sanctions and disciplinary proceedings for violating these regulations.

Circular 230 rules, however, are not ethical standards. Instead, the document focuses on the right to represent clients before the IRS. These standards differ from the AICPA's SSTSs in the following ways:

▶ They apply only to federal tax issues and not state authorities.

▶ They generally apply only to federal income tax practice.

▶ They do not provide the depth of guidance found in the SSTSs.

▶ They give the government the authority to impose monetary penalties for violations of the rules.

Circular 230 also provides guidelines for written advice to taxpayers. These guidelines fall into two categories: (1) covered opinions[48] and (2) all other written advice.[49] The rules govern written advice in opinion letters, memoranda, presentations, studies, facsimiles, e-mail, and instant messaging, but they exclude oral advice, tax return preparation, certain post-filing advice, and internal written advice.

Tax advisors are often asked to give their opinion on the tax treatment of a transaction or proposed transaction. The advisor's written conclusions are called "reliance opinions" in *Circular 230* and include any written advice that concludes, at a confidence level of more likely than not, that a tax issue would be resolved in a taxpayer's favor. These opinions might include many routine tax issues encountered in a standard practice. Rather than comply with the detailed due diligence burdens imposed by *Circular 230*, many practitioners now include a standard disclaimer for routine written advice. See the sample client letter in Appendix A for the language of such disclaimers.

AICPA'S STATEMENTS ON TAX STANDARDS

Tax advisors confronted with ethical issues frequently turn to a professional organization for guidance. Although the guidelines set forth by such organizations are not *legally* enforceable, they carry significant moral weight, and may be cited in a negligence lawsuit as the proper "standard of care" for tax practitioners. They also may provide grounds for the termination or suspension of one's professional license. One such set of guidelines is the *Statements on Standards for Tax Services* (SSTSs),[50] issued by the American Institute of Certified Public Accountants (AICPA) and reproduced in Appendix E.

The SSTSs provide an ethical framework to govern the normative relationship between a tax advisor and his or her client, where, unlike an auditor, a tax advisor acts as the client's advocate. Thus, his or her primary duty is to the client, not the IRS. In

---

[48] Covered opinions include tax shelters, reportable transactions, marketed opinions as well as reliance opinions.
[49] *Circular 230* Section 10.35 applies to covered opinions and Section 10.37 applies to all other written advice.

[50] AICPA, *Statements on Standards for Tax Services*, 2009, effective January 1, 2010.

fulfilling this duty, the advisor is bound by the highest standards of care. The most recent version of the SSTSs includes seven standards that provide guidance for AICPA members in their professional tax practice.

SSTS No. 1—Tax Return Positions. Tax professionals often provide tax advice in situations where the authority is unclear or evolving. Frequently this advice involves recommending positions that could be reversed upon audit. This statement describes the minimum level of confidence a CPA must achieve to recommend a tax return position to a taxpayer. Members first must determine and comply with all standards imposed by the various taxing authorities. Regardless of those standards, a member should not recommend a position unless he or she has a good faith belief that the position has a "realistic possibility" of being sustained administratively or judicially on its merits if challenged. Members are not permitted to take the probability of audit into account.

If the position does not meet the realistic probability standard, a member still may recommend a tax return position if he or she concludes that the position has a "reasonable basis" and the position is properly disclosed. When recommending a tax return position and when preparing or signing a return on which a tax return position is taken, a member should, when relevant, advise the taxpayer regarding potential penalty consequences of such tax return position and the opportunity, if any, to avoid such penalties through disclosure.

The standard highlights the dual responsibility of the member. The U.S. tax system can function only when taxpayers file "true, correct, and complete" returns, but taxpayers also have no obligation to pay more in tax than they legally owe. The tax professional's duty is to meet his or her responsibilities to both the tax system and the taxpayer client.

SSTS No. 2—Answers to Questions on Returns. Return preparers often must sign a declaration that the return is "true, correct, and complete." A member should make a reasonable effort to obtain from the taxpayer the information necessary to provide appropriate answers to all questions on a tax return before signing as preparer. However, in certain circumstances, questions or information applicable to the taxpayer may be omitted. Reasonable grounds include the following situations:

▶ The omitted information is not readily available or is immaterial and has little effect on taxable income or loss or the tax liability.

▶ The meaning of the question as it relates to the taxpayer is uncertain.

▶ The requested information is voluminous, in which case the taxpayer can attach a statement indicating that the requested information will be supplied upon request.

SSTS No. 3—Certain Procedural Aspects of Preparing Returns. Tax returns are based on information provided by the client. This statement sets forth the applicable standards for members concerning this information. Specifically, in preparing or signing a return, members are not required to examine or verify a client's supporting data. A member may rely on information supplied by the taxpayer unless the information appears to be incorrect, incomplete, inconsistent, or unreasonable under the circumstances. However, if the applicable law or regulations impose a specific record keeping requirement to claim a deduction, the member should inquire and satisfy himself or herself that the required records do exist.

Members are specifically encouraged to make use of a taxpayer's returns for one or more prior years in preparing the current return, whenever feasible. The practice should help avoid the omission or duplication of items and provide a basis for the treatment of similar or related transactions.

SSTS No. 4—Use of Estimates. For various reasons, precise information about an amount required on a tax return might not be available at the time the tax return is prepared. For example, the taxpayer might not have a record of small transactions or might be missing certain records. In such cases, a member may advise on estimates used in the preparation of the tax return, but the taxpayer has the responsibility to provide the estimated data. Appraisals and valuations are not considered estimates.

If estimates are used, they generally need not be labeled as estimates, but they should not be presented in a manner that provides a misleading impression about the degree of factual accuracy. However, disclosure that estimates were used should be made in some unusual situations, including:

▶ A taxpayer has died or is ill at the time the return is prepared.

▶ A taxpayer has not received a schedule K-1 at the time the tax return is to be filed.

▶ Litigation is pending that affects the return.

▶ Fire, computer failure, or a natural disaster has destroyed the relevant records.

Notwithstanding this statement, the tax practitioner may not use estimates when such use is implicitly prohibited by the IRC. For example, Sec. 274(d) disallows deductions for certain expenses (e.g., meals and entertainment) unless the taxpayer can substantiate the expenses with adequate records or sufficient corroborating information. The documentation requirement effectively precludes the taxpayer from estimating such expenses and the practitioner from using such estimates.

SSTS No. 5—Departure from a Position Previously Concluded in an Administrative Proceeding or Court Decisions. Members can take positions that differ from a position determined in an administrative proceeding with respect to the taxpayer's prior return (such as an IRS audit, IRS appeals conference, or a court decision.) Departure might be warranted because of a change in the law or regulations, or favorable court decisions. In any event, if the member can otherwise meet the standards of SSTS No. 1, departure from previous positions is permissible.

SSTS No. 6—Knowledge of Error: Return Preparation and Administrative Proceedings. For purposes of this standard, the definition of an error has the common meaning, including a mathematical error, but the definition also encompasses any position that does not meet the standards of SSTS No. 1. A position also qualifies as an error if it met the standard when a return was originally filed but no longer does because of a retroactive legislative or legal proceeding. An error for this purpose does not include immaterial items.

A member should inform the taxpayer promptly upon becoming aware of (1) an error in a previously filed return, (2) an error in a return that is the subject of an administrative proceeding (e.g., an IRS audit or appeals conference), or (3) a taxpayer's failure to file a required return. A member should advise the taxpayer of the potential consequences of the error and recommend corrective measures to be taken. This advice can be given orally. The member is not obligated to inform the taxing authority of an error and, in fact, may not do so without the taxpayer's permission except when required by law.

However, if the taxpayer requests that a member prepare the current year's return and the taxpayer has not taken appropriate action to correct an error in a prior year's return, the member should consider whether to withdraw from preparing the return and whether to continue a professional or employment relationship with the taxpayer.

The standard recognizes that conflicts can arise between the member's interests and those of the client. For example, withdrawal from an engagement could have an adverse impact on the taxpayer. In some situations, the member should consult his or her own legal counsel before deciding on recommendations to the taxpayer and whether to continue the engagement. In situations involving potential fraud or criminal charges, the member should advise the client to consult with an attorney before taking any action.

SSTS No. 7—Form and Content of Advice to Taxpayers. A member should use professional judgment to ensure that tax advice provided to a taxpayer reflects competence and appropriately serves the taxpayer's needs. The advice can be communicated in writing or orally. When communicating tax advice to a taxpayer in writing, a member should comply with relevant taxing authorities' standards applicable to written tax advice. A member should use professional judgment about any need to document oral advice.

In deciding on the form of advice provided to a taxpayer, a member should consider factors such as:

▶ The importance of the transaction and the amounts involved

▶ The technical complexity involved

▶ The existence of authorities and precedents

▶ The tax sophistication of the taxpayer

▶ The need to seek other professional advice

▶ The potential penalty consequences of a tax return position and whether any penalties can be avoided through disclosure

This statement implies that practitioner-taxpayer dealings should not be casual, nonconsensual, or open ended. Rather, they should be professional, contractual, and definite. Oral advice may be appropriate in routine matters, but written communications are recommended in important, complicated, or significant dollar value transactions.

In addition to these obligations, the tax advisor has a strict duty of confidentiality to the client. Although not encompassed under the SSTSs, this duty is implied in the accountant client privilege. (For a discussion of this privilege, see Chapter C:15.)

STOP & THINK

Question: As described in the Stop & Think box on pages C:1-10 and C:1-11, you are researching the manner in which a deduction is calculated. The IRC states that the calculation is to be made "in a manner prescribed by the Secretary." After studying the IRC, Treasury Regulations, and committee reports, you conclude that another way of doing the calculation is arguably correct under an intuitive approach. This approach would result in a lower tax liability for the client. According to the *Statements on Standards for Tax Services*, may you take a position contrary to final Treasury Regulations based on the argument that the regulations are not valid?

Solution: You should not take a position contrary to the Treasury Regulations unless you have a "good-faith belief that the position has a realistic possibility of being sustained administratively or judicially on its merits." However, you can take a position that does not meet the above standard, provided you adequately disclose the position, and the position has a reasonable basis. Whether or not you have met the standard depends on all the facts and circumstances. Chapter C:15 discusses tax return preparer positions contrary to Treasury Regulations.

WHAT WOULD YOU DO IN THIS SITUATION?

Regal Enterprises and Macon Industries, unaffiliated corporations, have hired you to prepare their respective income tax returns. In preparing Regal's return, you notice that Regal has claimed a depreciation deduction for equipment purchased from Macon on February 22 at a cost of $2 million. In preparing Macon's return, you notice that Macon has reported sales proceeds of $1.5 million from the sale of equipment to Regal on February 22. One of the two figures must be incorrect. How do you proceed to correct it? Hint: See SSTS No. 3 in Appendix E.

SAMPLE WORK PAPERS AND CLIENT LETTER

OBJECTIVE 8

Prepare work papers and communicate to clients

Appendix A presents a set of sample work papers, including a draft of a client letter and a memo to the file. The work papers indicate the issues to be researched, the authorities addressing the issues, and the researcher's conclusions concerning the appropriate tax treatment, with rationale therefor.

The format and other details of work papers differ from firm to firm. The sample in this text offers general guidance concerning the content of work papers. In practice, work papers may include less detail.

PROBLEM MATERIALS

DISCUSSION QUESTIONS

C:1-1 Explain the difference between closed-fact and open-fact situations.

C:1-2 According to the AICPA's *Statements on Standards for Tax Services,* what duties does the tax practitioner owe the client?

C:1-3 Explain what is encompassed by the term *tax law* as used by tax advisors.

C:1-4 The U.S. Government Printing Office publishes both hearings on proposed legislation and committee reports. Distinguish between the two.

C:1-5 Explain how committee reports can be used in tax research. What do they indicate?

C:1-6 A friend notices that you are reading the Internal Revenue Code of 1986. Your friend inquires why you are consulting a 1986 publication, especially when tax laws change so frequently. What is your response?

C:1-7 Does Title 26 contain statutory provisions dealing only with income taxation? Explain.

C:1-8 Refer to IRC Sec. 301.
  a. Which subsection discusses the general rule for the tax treatment of a property distribution?
  b. Where should one look for exceptions to the general rule?
  c. What type of Treasury Regulations would relate to subsection (e)?

C:1-9 Why should tax researchers note the date on which a Treasury Regulation was adopted?

C:1-10 **a.** Distinguish between proposed, temporary, and final Treasury Regulations.
  b. Distinguish between interpretative and legislative Treasury Regulations.

C:1-11 Which type of regulation is more difficult for a taxpayer to successfully challenge, and why?

C:1-12 Explain the legislative reenactment doctrine.

C:1-13 **a.** Discuss the authoritative weight of revenue rulings.

b. As a practical matter, what consequences are likely to ensue if a taxpayer does not follow a revenue ruling and the IRS audits his or her return?

C:1-14 **a.** In which courts may litigation dealing with tax matters begin?
  b. Discuss the factors that might be considered in deciding where to litigate.
  c. Describe the appeals process in tax litigation.

C:1-15 May a taxpayer appeal a case litigated under the Small Cases Procedure of the Tax Court?

C:1-16 Explain whether the following decisions are of the same precedential value: (1) Tax Court regular decisions, (2) Tax Court memo decisions, (3) decisions under the Small Cases Procedures of the Tax Court.

C:1-17 Does the IRS acquiesce in decisions of U.S. district courts?

C:1-18 The decisions of which courts are reported in the AFTR? In the USTC?

C:1-19 Why do some revenue ruling citations refer to the *Internal Revenue Bulletin* (I.R.B.) and others to a *Cumulative Bulletin* (C.B.)?

C:1-20 Explain the *Golsen* Rule. Give an example of its application.

C:1-21 Assume that the only precedents relating to a particular issue are as follows:

Tax Court—decided for the taxpayer
Eighth Circuit Court of Appeals—decided for the taxpayer (affirming the Tax Court)
U.S. District Court for Eastern Louisiana—decided for the taxpayer
Fifth Circuit Court of Appeals—decided for the government (reversing the U.S. District Court of Eastern Louisiana)
  a. Discuss the precedential value of the foregoing decisions for your client, who is a California resident.

b. If your client, a Texas resident, litigates in the Tax Court, how will the court rule? Explain.

C:1-22 Which official publication(s) contain(s) the following:
   a. Transcripts of Senate floor debates
   b. IRS announcements
   c. Tax Court regular opinions
   d. Treasury decisions
   e. U.S. district court opinions
   f. Technical advice memoranda

C:1-23 Under what circumstances might a tax advisor find the provisions of a tax treaty useful?

C:1-24 What two functions does a citator serve?

C:1-25 Describe two ways that the information available from the CHECKPOINT citator differs from that available from the INTELLICONNECT citator.

C:1-26 List four methods of searching the CHECKPOINT and INTELLICONNECT databases.

C:1-27 Access INTELLICONNECT at *http://intelliconnect .cch.com* and RIA CHECKPOINT™ at *http://checkpoint.riag.com*. Then answer the following questions:
   a. What are the principal primary sources found in both Internet tax services?
   b. What are the principal secondary sources found in each Internet tax service?

C:1-28 Compare the features of the computerized tax services with those of Internet sites maintained by noncommercial institutions. What are the relative advantages and disadvantages of each? Could the latter sites serve as a substitute for a commercial tax service?

C:1-29 According to the *Statements on Standards for Tax Services*, what belief should a CPA have before taking a pro-taxpayer position on a tax return?

C:1-30 List an advisor's duties that are excluded under the AICPA's *Statements on Standards for Tax Services*.

C:1-31 List the two classifications of written advice under Treasury Department *Circular 230*.

C:1-32 Explain how Treasury Department *Circular 230* differs from the AICPA's *Statements on Standards for Tax Services*.

PROBLEMS

C:1-33 *Interpreting the IRC.* Under a divorce agreement executed in the current year, an ex-wife receives from her former husband cash of $25,000 per year for eight years. The agreement does not explicitly state that the payments are excludable from gross income.
   a. Does the ex-wife have gross income? If so, how much?
   b. Is the former husband entitled to a deduction? If so, is it for or from AGI?
   Refer only to the IRC in answering this question. Start with Sec. 71.

C:1-34 *Interpreting the IRC.* Refer to Sec. 385 and answer the questions below.
   a. Whenever Treasury Regulations are issued under this section, what type are they likely to be: legislative or interpretative? Explain.
   b. Assume Treasury Regulations under Sec. 385 have been finalized. Will they be relevant to estate tax matters? Explain.

C:1-35 *Using IRS Rulings.* Locate PLR 8733007 and Rev. Rul. 81-219.
   a. Briefly summarize the tax issue and conclusion of each ruling.
   b. Under what circumstances can a researcher rely on the private letter ruling?
   c. Under what circumstances can a researcher rely on the revenue ruling?

C:1-36 *Using Treasury pronouncements.* Which IRC section(s) does Rev. Rul. 2001-29 interpret? (Hint: consult the official pronouncement of the IRS.)

C:1-37 *Using CHECKPOINT for a Keyword Search.* The objective is to locate a general overview of available home office deductions. On the main research tab, select the *United States Tax Reporter—Explanations (RIA)* library. How many results does CHECKPOINT return for each search term?
   a. Search term: home office deduction.
   b. Search term: "home office" deduction.
   c. Search term: "home office" /5 deduction.
   d. Perform the search in Part a above. Select *Sort by Relevance*. How does this sort change the results? Does the sort make it easier to locate relevant documents?

C:1-38 *Using INTELLICONNECT for a Keyword Search.* The search objective is to determine the amount generally excludable on the sale of a married couple's home. Using Browse, locate the *Standard Federal Income Tax Reporter—Explanations* library. How many results does INTELLICONNECT return for each search term?
   a. Search term: home sale gain exclusion.
   b. Search term: "home sale" gain exclusion.

      c. Does limiting the results to only those documents containing the specific term "home sale" improve your results?

      d. How do most tax documents refer to a person's home?

C:1-39   *Determining Acquiescence.*

      a. What official action (acquiescence or nonacquiescence) did the IRS Commissioner take regarding the 1986 Tax Court decision in *John McIntosh*? (Hint: Consult Actions on Decisions.)

      b. Did this action concern *all* issues in the case? If not, explain. (Before answering this question, consult the headnote to the court opinion.)

C:1-40   *Determining Acquiescence.*

      a. What original action (acquiescence or nonacquiescence) did the IRS Commissioner take regarding the 1952 Tax Court decision in *Streckfus Steamers, Inc.*? (Hint: Consult Actions on Decisions.)

      b. Was the action complete or partial?

      c. Did the IRS Commissioner subsequently change his mind? If so, when?

C:1-41   *Determining Acquiescence.*

      a. What original action (acquiescence or nonacquiescence) did the IRS Commissioner take regarding the 1956 Tax Court decision in *Pittsburgh Milk Co.*? (Hint: Consult Actions on Decisions.)

      b. Did the IRS Commissioner subsequently change his mind? If so, when?

C:1-42   *Evaluating a Case.* Look up *James E. Threlkeld*, 87 T.C. 1294 (1988) and answer the questions below.

      a. Was the case reviewed by the court? If so, was the decision unanimous? Explain.

      b. Was the decision entered under Rule 155?

      c. Consult a citator. Was the case reviewed by an appellate court? If so, which one?

C:1-43   *Evaluating a Case.* Look up *Bush Brothers & Co.*, 73 T.C. 424 (1979) and answer the questions below.

      a. Was the case reviewed by the court? If so, was the decision unanimous? Explain.

      b. Was the decision entered under Rule 155?

      c. Consult a citator. Was the case reviewed by an appellate court? If so, which one?

C:1-44   *Writing Citations.* Provide the proper citations (including both primary and secondary citations where applicable) for the authorities listed below. (For secondary citations, reference both the AFTR and USTC.)

      a. *National Cash Register Co.*, a 6th Circuit Court decision

      b. *Thomas M. Dragoun v. CIR*, a Tax Court memo decision

      c. *John M. Grabinski v. U.S.*, a U.S. district court decision

      d. *John M. Grabinski v. U.S.*, an Eighth Circuit Court decision

      e. *Rebekah Harkness*, a 1972 Court of Claims decision

      f. *Hillsboro National Bank v. CIR*, a Supreme Court decision

      g. Rev. Rul. 78-129

C:1-45   *Writing Citations.* Provide the proper citations (including both primary and secondary citations where applicable) for the authorities listed below. (For secondary citations, reference both the AFTR and USTC.)

      a. Rev. Rul. 99-7

      b. *Frank H. Sullivan*, a Board of Tax Appeals decision

      c. *Tate & Lyle, Inc.*, a 1994 Tax Court decision

      d. *Ralph L. Rogers v. U.S.*, a U.S. district court decision

      e. *Norman Rodman v. CIR*, a Second Circuit Court decision

C:1-46   *Interpreting Citations.* Indicate which courts decided the cases cited below. Also indicate on which pages and in which publications the authority is reported.

      a. *Lloyd M. Shumaker v. CIR*, 648 F.2d 1198, 48 AFTR 2d 81-5353 (9th Cir., 1981)

      b. *Xerox Corp. v. U.S.*, 14 Cl. Ct. 455, 88-1 USTC ¶9231 (1988)

      c. *Real Estate Land Title & Trust Co. v. U.S.*, 309 U.S. 13, 23 AFTR 816 (USSC, 1940)

      d. *J. B. Morris v. U.S.*, 441 F. Supp. 76, 41 AFTR 2d 78-335 (DC TX, 1977)

      e. Rev. Rul. 83-3, 1983-1 C.B. 72

      f. *Malone & Hyde, Inc. v. U.S.*, 568 F.2d 474, 78-1 USTC ¶9199 (6th Cir., 1978)

C:1-47   *Using a Tax Service.* Use the topical index of the *United States Tax Reporter* to locate authorities dealing with the deductibility of the cost of a facelift.

      a. In which paragraph(s) does the *United States Tax Reporter* summarize and cite these authorities?

      b. List the authorities.

      c. May a taxpayer deduct the cost of a facelift paid in the current year? Explain.

C:1-48 *Using a Tax Service.* Locate Reg. Sec. 1.302-1 using either CHECKPOINT or INTELLI-CONNECT. Does this Treasury Regulation reflect recent amendments to the IRC? Explain.

C:1-49 *Using a Tax Service.* Using the topical index of the *Standard Federal Income Tax Reporter* in INTELLICONNECT, locate authorities addressing whether termite damage constitutes a casualty loss.
a. In which paragraph(s) does the *Standard Federal Income Tax Reporter* summarize and cite these authorities?
b. List the authorities.

C:1-50 *Using a Tax Service.*
a. Using the *Standard Federal Income Tax Reporter* in INTELLICONNECT, locate where Sec. 303(b)(2)(A) appears. This provision states that Sec. 303(a) applies only if the stock in question meets a certain percentage test. What is the applicable percentage?
b. Locate Reg. Sec. 1.303-2(a) in the same service. Does this Treasury Regulation reflect recent amendments to the IRC with respect to the percentage test addressed in Part a? Explain.

C:1-51 *Using a Tax Service.* Using the BNA tax service, identify the number of the BNA portfolio for the following subjects.
a. Innocent spouse relief.
b. Accounting methods.
c. Involuntary conversions.
d. IRAs.
e. Deductibility of legal and accounting fees, bribes, and illegal payments.

C:1-52 *Using a Tax Service.* This problem deals with CHECKPOINT's *Federal Tax Coordinator 2d.* Use the topical index CHECKPOINT to locate authorities dealing with the deductibility of the cost of work clothing by ministers (clergymen). List the authorities.

C:1-53 *Using a Citator.* Trace *Biltmore Homes, Inc.,* a 1960 Tax Court memo decision, in both the INTELLICONNECT and CHECKPOINT citators.
a. According to the CHECKPOINT citator, how many times has the Tax Court decision been cited by other courts on Headnote Number 5?
b. How many issues did the lower court address in its opinion? (Hint: Refer to the case headnote numbers.)
c. Did an appellate court review the case? If so, which one?
d. According to the INTELLICONNECT citator, how many times has the Tax Court decision been cited by other courts?
e. According to the INTELLICONNECT citator, how many times has the circuit court decision been cited by other courts on Headnote Number 5?

C:1-54 *Using a Citator.* Trace *Stephen Bolaris,* 776 F.2d 1428, in both the INTELLICONNECT and CHECKPOINT citators.
a. According to the CHECKPOINT citator, how many times has the Ninth Circuit's decision been cited?
b. Did the decision address more than one issue? Explain.
c. Was the decision ever cited unfavorably? Explain.
d. According to the INTELLICONNECT citator, how many times has the Ninth Circuit's decision been cited?
e. According to the INTELLICONNECT citator, how many times has the Tax Court's decision been cited on Headnote Number 1?

C:1-55 *Interpreting a Case.* Refer to the *Holden Fuel Oil Company* case (31 TCM 184).
a. In which year was the case decided?
b. What controversy was litigated?
c. Who won the case?
d. Was the decision reviewed at the lower court level?
e. Was the decision appealed?
f. Has the decision been cited in other cases?

C:1-56 *Internet Research.* Access the IRS Internet site at *http://www.irs.gov* and answer the following questions:
a. How does one file a tax return electronically?
b. How can the taxpayer transmit funds electronically?
c. What are the advantages of electronic filing?

C:1-57 *Internet Research.* Access the IRS Internet site at *http://www.irs.gov* and indicate the titles of the following IRS forms:
a. Form 4506
b. Form 973
c. Form 8725

C:1-58 *Internet Research.* Access the Federation of Tax Administrators Internet site at *http://www.taxadmin.org/fta/link/forms.html* and indicate the titles of the following state tax forms and publications:
a. Minnesota Form M-100
b. Illinois Individual Schedule CR
c. New York State Corporate Form CT-3-C

C:1-59 *Internet Research.* Access the Urban Institute and Brookings Institution Tax Policy Center at *http://taxpolicycenter.org.* On the home page, search for *state individual income tax rates* and locate the Tax Policy Center's latest summary of each state's rates. Researchers also can locate the file by looking under the *State* tab, *Main Features of State Tax Systems.*
a. How many states do not have a state individual income tax?
b. How many states tax only interest and dividends for individuals?
c. What is the top marginal individual income tax rate in Oregon?
d. Of those that do impose an income tax, which state's top marginal rate is lowest?

COMPREHENSIVE PROBLEM

C:1-60 Your client, a physician, recently purchased a yacht on which he flies a pennant with a medical emblem on it. He recently informed you that he purchased the yacht and flies the pennant to advertise his occupation and thus attract new patients. He has asked you if he may deduct as ordinary and necessary business expenses the costs of insuring and maintaining the yacht. In search of an answer, consult either INTELLICONNECT's *Standard Federal Income Tax Reporter* or CHECKPOINT's *United States Tax Reporter.* Explain the steps taken to find your answer.

TAX STRATEGY PROBLEM

C:1-61 Your client, Home Products Universal (HPU), distributes home improvement products to independent retailers throughout the country. Its management wants to explore the possibility of opening its own home improvement centers. Accordingly, it commissions a consulting firm to conduct a feasibility study, which ultimately persuades HPU to expand into retail sales. The consulting firm bills HPU $150,000, which HPU deducts on its current year tax return. The IRS disputes the deduction, contending that, because the cost relates to entering a new business, it should be capitalized. HPU's management, on the other hand, firmly believes that, because the cost relates to expanding HPU's existing business, it should be deducted. In contemplating legal action against the IRS, HPU's management considers the state of judicial precedent: The federal court for HPU's district has ruled that the cost of expanding from distribution into retail sales should be capitalized. The appellate court for HPU's circuit has stated in *dictum* that, although in some circumstances switching from product distribution to product sales entails entering a new trade or business, improving customer access to one's existing products generally does not. The Federal Circuit Court has ruled that wholesale distribution and retail sales, even of the same product, constitute distinct businesses. In a case involving a taxpayer from another circuit, the Tax Court has ruled that such costs invariably should be capitalized. HPU's Chief Financial Officer approaches you with the question, "In which judicial forum should HPU file a lawsuit against the IRS: (1) U.S. district court, (2) the Tax Court, or (3) the U.S. Court of Federal Claims?" What do you tell her?

CASE STUDY PROBLEM

C:1-62 A client, Mal Manley, fills out his client questionnaire for the previous year and on it provides information for the preparation of his individual income tax return. The IRS has never audited Mal's returns. Mal reports that he made over 100 relatively small cash contributions totaling $24,785 to charitable organizations. In the last few years, Mal's charitable contributions have averaged about $15,000 per year. For the previous year, Mal's adjusted gross income was roughly $350,000, about a 10% increase from the year before.

Required: Applying *Statements on Standards for Tax Services* No. 3, determine whether you can accept at face value Mal's information concerning his charitable contributions. Now assume that the IRS recently audited Mal's tax return for two years ago and denied 75% of that year's charitable contribution deduction because the deduction was not substantiated. Assume also that Mal indicates that, in the previous year, he contributed $25,000 (instead of $24,785). How do these changes of fact affect your earlier decision?

TAX RESEARCH PROBLEMS

C:1-63 The purpose of this problem is to enhance your skills in interpreting the authorities that you locate in your research. In answering the questions that follow, refer only to *Thomas A. Curtis, M.D., Inc.,* 1994 RIA TC Memo ¶94,015.
a. What was the principal controversy litigated in this case?
b. Which party—the taxpayer or the IRS—won?
c. Why is the corporation instead of Dr. and/or Ms. Curtis listed as the plaintiff?
d. What is the relationship between Ellen Barnert Curtis and Dr. Thomas A. Curtis?
e. Approximately how many hours a week did Ms. Curtis work, and what were her credentials?
f. For the fiscal year ending in 1989, what salary did the corporation pay Ms. Curtis? What amount did the court decide was reasonable?
g. What dividends did the corporation pay for its fiscal years ending in 1988 and 1989?
h. To which circuit would this decision be appealable?
i. According to *Curtis*, what five factors did the Ninth Circuit mention in *Elliotts, Inc.* as relevant in determining reasonable compensation?

C:1-64 Josh contributes $5,000 toward the support of his widowed mother, aged 69, a U.S. citizen and resident. She earns gross income of $2,000 and spends it all for her own support. In addition, Medicare pays $3,200 of her medical expenses. She does not receive financial support from sources other than those described above. Must the Medicare payments be included in the support that Josh's mother is deemed to provide for herself?

Prepare work papers and a client letter (to Josh) dealing with the issue.

C:1-65 Amy owns a vacation cottage in Maine. She predicts that the time during which the cottage will be used in the current year is as follows:

By Amy, solely for vacation	12 days
By Amy, making repairs ten hours per day and vacationing the rest of the day	2 days
By her sister, who paid fair rental value	8 days
By her cousin, who paid fair rental value	4 days
By her friend, who paid a token amount of rent	2 days
By three families from the Northeast, who paid fair rental value for 40 days each	120 days
Not used	217 days

Calculate the ratio for allocating the following expenses to the rental income expected to be received from the cottage: interest, taxes, repairs, insurance, and depreciation. The ratio will be used to determine the amount of expenses that are deductible and, thus, Amy's taxable income for the year.

For the tax manager to whom you report, prepare work papers in which you discuss the calculation method. Also, draft a memo to the file dealing with the results of your research.

C:1-66 Look up *Summit Publishing Company,* 1990 PH T.C. Memo ¶90,288, 59 TCM 833, and *J.B.S. Enterprises,* 1991 PH T.C. Memo ¶91,254, 61 TCM 2829, and answer the following questions:
a. What was the principal issue in these cases?
b. What factors did the Tax Court consider in resolving the central issue?
c. How are the facts of these cases similar? How are they dissimilar?

C:1-67 Your supervisor would like to set up a single Sec. 401(k) plan exclusively for the managers of your organization. Concerned that this arrangement might not meet the requirements for a qualified plan, he has asked you to request a determination letter from the IRS. In a brief memorandum, address the following issues:

a. What IRS pronouncements govern requests for determination letters?

b. What IRS forms must be filed with the request?

c. What information must be provided in the request?

d. What actions must accompany the filing?

e. Where must the request be filed?

2

C H A P T E R

CORPORATE FORMATIONS AND CAPITAL STRUCTURE

LEARNING OBJECTIVES

After studying this chapter, you should be able to

1. Explain the tax advantages and disadvantages of alternative business forms

2. Apply the check-the-box regulations to partnerships, corporations, and trusts

3. Determine the legal requirements for forming a corporation

4. Explain the requirements for deferring gain or loss upon incorporation

5. Understand the tax implications of alternative capital structures

6. Determine the tax consequences of worthless stock or debt obligations

When starting a business, entrepreneurs must decide whether to organize it as a sole proprietorship, partnership, corporation, limited liability company, or limited liability partnership. This chapter discusses the advantages and disadvantages of each form of business association. Because many entrepreneurs find organizing their business as a corporation advantageous, the chapter looks at the definition of a corporation for federal income tax purposes. It also discusses the tax consequences of incorporating a business. The chapter closes by examining the tax implications of capitalizing a corporation with equity and/or debt and describing the advantages and disadvantages of alternative capital structures.

This textbook takes a life-cycle approach to corporate taxation. The corporate life cycle starts with corporate formation, discussed in this chapter. Once formed and operating, the corporation generates taxable income (or loss), incurs federal income tax and other liabilities, and makes distributions to its shareholders. Finally, at some point, the corporation might outlive its usefulness and be liquidated and dissolved. The corporate life cycle is too complex to discuss in one chapter. Therefore, additional coverage follows in Chapters C:3 through C:8.

ORGANIZATION FORMS AVAILABLE

OBJECTIVE 1

Explain the tax advantages and disadvantages of alternative business forms

Businesses can be organized in several forms including

▶ Sole proprietorships

▶ Partnerships

▶ Corporations

▶ Limited liability companies

▶ Limited liability partnerships

A discussion of the tax implications of each form is presented below.

SOLE PROPRIETORSHIPS

ADDITIONAL COMMENT

The income/loss of a sole proprietorship reported on Schedule C carries to page 1 of Form 1040 and is included in the computation of the individual's taxable income. Net income, if any, also carries to Schedule SE of Form 1040 for computation of the sole proprietor's self-employment tax.

A **sole proprietorship** is an unincorporated business owned by one individual. It often is selected by entrepreneurs who are beginning a new business with a modest amount of capital. From a tax and legal perspective, a sole proprietorship is not a separate entity. Rather, it is a legal extension of its individual owner. Thus, the individual owns all the business assets and reports income or loss from the sole proprietorship directly on his or her individual tax return. Specifically, the individual owner (proprietor) reports all the business's income and expenses for the year on Schedule C (Profit or Loss from Business) or Schedule C-EZ (Net Profit from Business) of Form 1040. A completed Schedule C is included in Appendix B, where a common set of facts (with minor modifications) illustrates the similarities and differences in sole proprietorship, C corporation, partnership, and S corporation tax reporting.

If the business is profitable, the profit is added to the proprietor's other income.

EXAMPLE C:2-1 ▶ John, a single taxpayer, starts a new computer store, which he operates as a sole proprietorship. John reports a $15,000 profit from the store in its first year of operation. Assuming his marginal tax rate is 35%, John's tax on the $15,000 of profit from the store is $5,250 (0.35 × $15,000).[1] ◀

If the business is unprofitable, the loss reduces the proprietor's total taxable income, thereby generating tax savings.

EXAMPLE C:2-2 ▶ Assume the same facts as in Example C:2-1 except John reports a $15,000 loss instead of a $15,000 profit in the first year of operation. Assuming he still is taxed at a 35% marginal tax rate, the $15,000 loss produces tax savings of $5,250 (0.35 × $15,000). ◀

---

[1] The $15,000 Schedule C profit in Example C:2-1 will increase adjusted gross income (AGI). The AGI level affects certain deduction calculations (e.g., medical, charitable contributions, and miscellaneous itemized) and, because of limitations, may result in a taxable income increase different from the $15,000 AGI increase.

ADDITIONAL COMMENT

Although this chapter emphasizes the tax consequences of selecting the entity in which a business will be conducted, other issues also are important in making such a decision. For example, the amount of legal liability assumed by an owner is important and can vary substantially among the different business entities.

TAX ADVANTAGES. The tax advantages of conducting business as a sole proprietorship are as follows:

▶ The sole proprietorship is not subject to taxation as a separate entity. Rather, the sole proprietor, as an individual, is taxed at his or her marginal rate on income earned by the business.

▶ The proprietor's marginal tax rate may be lower than the marginal tax rate that would have applied had the business been organized as a corporation.

▶ The owner may contribute cash to, or withdraw profits from, the business without tax consequences.

▶ Although the owner usually maintains separate books, records, and bank accounts for the business, the money in these accounts belongs to the owner personally.

▶ The owner may contribute property to, or withdraw property from, the business without recognizing gain or loss.

▶ Business losses may offset nonbusiness income, such as interest, dividends, and any salary earned by the sole proprietor or his or her spouse, subject to the passive activity loss rules.

TAX DISADVANTAGES. The tax disadvantages of conducting business as a sole proprietorship are as follows:

▶ The profits of a sole proprietorship are currently taxed to the individual owner, whether or not the profits are retained in the business or withdrawn for personal use. By contrast, the profits of a corporation are taxed to its shareholders only if and when the corporation distributes the earnings as dividends.

▶ At times, corporate tax rates have been lower than individual tax rates. In such times, businesses conducted as sole proprietorships have been taxed more heavily than businesses organized as corporations.

▶ A sole proprietor must pay the full amount of Social Security taxes because he or she is not considered to be an employee of the business. By contrast, shareholder-employees must pay only half their Social Security taxes; the corporate employer pays the other half. (The employer, however, might pass this half onto employees in the form of lower wages.)

▶ Sole proprietorships may not deduct compensation paid to owner-employees. By contrast, corporations may deduct compensation paid to shareholder-employees.

▶ Certain tax-exempt benefits (e.g., premiums for group term life insurance) available to shareholder-employees are not available to owner-employees.[2]

▶ A sole proprietor must use the same accounting period for business and personal purposes. Thus, he or she cannot defer income by choosing a business fiscal year that differs from the individual's calendar year. By contrast, a corporation may choose a fiscal year that differs from the shareholders' calendar years.

PARTNERSHIPS

REAL-WORLD EXAMPLE

The IRS estimates the following business entity returns to be filed for 2010:

Entity	Number
Partnership	3.3 million
C corporation	2.0 million
S corporation	4.6 million

A **partnership** is an unincorporated business carried on by two or more individuals or entities for profit. The partnership form often is used by friends or relatives who engage in a business and by groups of investors who want to share the profits, losses, and expenses of an investment such as a real estate project.

A partnership is a tax reporting, but not taxpaying, entity. The partnership acts as a conduit for its owners. Its income, expenses, losses, credits, and other tax-related items pass through to the partners who report these items on their separate tax returns.

Each year a partnership must file a tax return (Form 1065—U.S. Partnership Return of Income) to report the results of its operations. When the partnership return is filed, the preparer must send each partner a statement (Schedule K-1, Form 1065) that reports the

---

[2] Section 162(l) permits self-employed individuals to deduct as a trade or business expense all of the health insurance costs incurred on behalf of themselves, their spouses, and their dependents.

partner's allocable share of partnership income, expenses, losses, credits, and other tax-related items. The partner then must report these items on his or her separate tax return. As with a sole proprietorship, the partner's allocable share of business profits is added to the partner's other income and taxed at that partner's marginal tax rate. A completed Form 1065 appears in Appendix B.

EXAMPLE C:2-3 ▶ Bob, a single taxpayer, owns a 50% interest in the BT Partnership, a calendar year entity. The BT Partnership reports a $30,000 profit in its first year of operation. Bob's $15,000 share flows through from the partnership to Bob's individual tax return. Assuming Bob is taxed at a 35% marginal rate, his tax on the $15,000 is $5,250 (0.35 × $15,000). Bob must pay the $5,250 tax whether or not the BT Partnership distributes any of its profits to him. ◀

If a partnership reports a loss, the partner's allocable share of the loss reduces that partner's other income and provides tax savings based on the partner's marginal tax rate. The passive activity loss rules, however, may limit the amount of any loss deduction available to the partner. (For a discussion of these rules, see Chapter C:9 of this textbook.)

EXAMPLE C:2-4 ▶ Assume the same facts as in Example C:2-3 except that, instead of a profit, the BT Partnership sustains a $30,000 loss in its first year of operation. Assuming Bob is taxed at a 35% marginal rate, his $15,000 share of the first year loss produces a $5,250 (0.35 × $15,000) tax savings. ◀

ADDITIONAL COMMENT

In some states, a limited partnership can operate as a limited liability limited partnership (LLLP) whereby the general partners obtain limited liability. See Chapter C:10 for additional discussion.

A partnership can be either general or limited. In a general partnership, the liability of each partner for partnership debts is unlimited. Thus, these partners are at risk for more than the amount of their capital investment in the partnership. In a limited partnership, at least one partner must be a general partner, and at least one partner must be a limited partner. As in a general partnership, the general partners are liable for all partnership debts, and the limited partners are liable only to the extent of their capital investment in the partnership, plus any amount they are obligated to contribute under their partnership agreement. Unless specified in that agreement, limited partners generally may not participate in the management of the partnership business.

TAX ADVANTAGES. The tax advantages of doing business as a partnership are as follows:

▶ The partnership as an entity pays no tax. Rather, the income of the partnership passes through to the separate returns of the partners and is taxed directly to them.

▶ A partner's tax rate may be lower than a corporation's tax rate for the same level of taxable income.

▶ Partnership income is not subject to double taxation. Although partnership profits are accounted for at the partnership level, they are taxed only at the partner level.

▶ Additional taxes generally are not imposed on distributions to the partners. With limited exceptions, partners can contribute money or property to, or withdraw money or property from, the partnership without recognizing gain or loss.

▶ Subject to limitations, partners can use losses to offset income from other sources.

▶ A partner's basis in a partnership interest is increased by his or her share of partnership income. This basis adjustment reduces the amount of gain recognized when the partner sells his or her partnership interest, thereby preventing double taxation.

TAX DISADVANTAGES. The tax disadvantages of doing business as a partnership are as follows:

▶ All the partnership's profits are taxed to the partners when earned, even if reinvested in the business.

▶ A partner's tax rate could be higher than a corporation's tax rate for the same level of taxable income.

▶ A partner is not considered to be an employee of the partnership. Therefore, he or she must pay the full amount of self-employment taxes on his or her share of partnership

ADDITIONAL COMMENT

If two or more owners exist, a business cannot be conducted as a sole proprietorship. From a tax compliance and recordkeeping perspective, conducting a business as a partnership is more complicated than conducting the business as a sole proprietorship.

income. Some tax-exempt fringe benefits (e.g., premiums for group term life insurance) are not available to partners.[3]

▶ Partners generally cannot defer income by choosing a fiscal year for the partnership that differs from the tax year of the principal partner(s). However, if the partnership demonstrates a business purpose, or if it makes a special election, it may use a fiscal year in general.

Chapters C:9 and C:10 of this volume discuss partnerships in greater detail.

CORPORATIONS

Corporations fall into two categories: C corporations and S corporations. A C corporation is subject to double taxation. Its earnings are taxed first at the corporate level when earned, then again at the shareholder level when distributed as dividends. An S corporation, by contrast, is subject to single-level taxation, much like a partnership. Its earnings are accounted for at the corporate level but are taxed only at the shareholder level.

C CORPORATIONS. A **C corporation** is a separate entity taxed on its income at rates ranging from 15% to 35%.[4] A C corporation must report all its income and expenses and compute its tax liability on Form 1120 (U.S. Corporation Income Tax Return). A completed Form 1120 appears in Appendix B. Shareholders are not taxed on the corporation's earnings unless these earnings are distributed as dividends. Through 2010, dividends received by a noncorporate shareholder are taxed at the same rate that applies to net capital gains. This dividend rate is 15% for taxpayers whose tax bracket exceeds 15%. (See Chapter I:5 of the *Individuals* volume for details of this provision.)

EXAMPLE C:2-5 ▶

Jane owns 100% of York Corporation stock. York reports taxable income of $50,000 for the current year. The first $50,000 of taxable income is taxed at a 15% rate, so York pays a corporate income tax of $7,500 (0.15 × $50,000). If the corporation distributes none of its earnings to Jane during the year, she pays no tax on York's earnings. However, if York distributes its current after-tax earnings to Jane, she must pay tax on $42,500 ($50,000 − $7,500) of dividend income. Assuming she is in the 35% marginal bracket, Jane's tax on the dividend income is $6,375 (0.15 × $42,500). The total tax on York's $50,000 of profits is $13,875 ($7,500 paid by York + $6,375 paid by Jane). ◀

Even when a corporation does not distribute its profits, double taxation may result. The profits are taxed to the corporation when they are earned. Then they may be taxed a second time (as capital gains) when the shareholder sells his or her stock or when the corporation liquidates.

EXAMPLE C:2-6 ▶

On January 2 of the current year, Carl purchases 100% of York Corporation stock for $60,000. In the same year, York reports taxable income of $50,000, on which it pays tax of $7,500. The corporation distributes none of the remaining $42,500 to Carl. On January 3 of the next year, Carl sells his stock to Mary for $102,500 (his initial investment plus the current year's accumulated earnings). Carl must report a capital gain of $42,500 ($102,500 − $60,000). Thus, York's profit is effectively taxed twice—first at the corporate level when earned and again at the shareholder level when Carl sells the appreciated stock at a gain. ◀

Tax Advantages. The tax advantages of doing business as a C corporation are as follows:

▶ A C corporation is an entity separate and distinct from its owners. Its marginal tax rate may be lower than its owners' marginal tax rates. So long as these earnings are not distributed and taxed to both the shareholders and the corporation, aggregate tax savings may result. If retained in the business, the earnings may be used for reinvestment and the retirement of debt. This advantage, however, may be limited by the accumulated earnings tax and the personal holding company tax. (See Chapter C:5 for a discussion of these two taxes.)

---

[3] Partners are eligible to deduct their health insurance costs in the same manner as a sole proprietor. See footnote 2 for details.

[4] As discussed in Chapter C:3, the corporate tax rate is 39% and 38% for certain levels of taxable income.

▶ Shareholders employed by the corporation are considered to be employees for tax purposes. Consequently, they are liable for only half their Social Security taxes, while their corporate employer is liable for the other half.

▶ Shareholder-employees are entitled to tax-free fringe benefits (e.g., premiums paid on group term life insurance and accident and health insurance). The corporation can provide these benefits with before-tax dollars (instead of after-tax dollars). By contrast, because sole proprietors and partners are not considered to be employees for tax purposes, they are ineligible for certain tax-free fringe benefits, although they are permitted to deduct their health insurance premiums.

▶ A corporation may deduct as an ordinary and necessary business expense compensation paid to shareholder-employees. Within reasonable limits, it may adjust this compensation upward to shelter corporate taxable income.

▶ A C corporation can use a fiscal instead of a calendar year as its reporting period. A fiscal year could permit a corporation to defer income to a later reporting period. (A personal service corporation, however, generally must use a calendar year as its tax year.[5])

▶ Special rules allow a shareholder to exclude 50% of the gain realized on the sale or exchange of stock held more than five years, provided the corporation meets certain requirements.

SELF-STUDY QUESTION

How are corporate earnings subject to double taxation?

ANSWER

Corporate earnings initially are taxed to the corporation. In addition, once these earnings are distributed to the shareholders (dividends), they are taxed again. Because the corporation does not receive a deduction for the distribution, these earnings have been taxed twice. Also, double taxation can occur when a shareholder sells his or her stock at a gain. Through 2012, qualified dividends and long-term capital gains both are subject to the 15% maximum tax rate.

Tax Disadvantages. The tax disadvantages of doing business as a C corporation are as follows:

▶ Double taxation of income results when the corporation distributes its earnings as dividends to shareholders or, effectively, when shareholders sell or exchange their stock.

▶ Shareholders generally cannot withdraw money or property from the corporation without recognizing income. A distribution of cash or property to a shareholder generally is taxable as a dividend if the corporation has sufficient earnings and profits (E&P). (See Chapter C:4 for a discussion of E&P.)

▶ Net operating losses confer no tax benefit to the owners in the year the corporation incurs them. They can be carried back or carried forward to offset the corporation's income in other years. For start-up corporations, these losses provide no tax benefit until the corporation earns a profit in a subsequent year. Shareholders cannot use these losses to offset income from other sources.

▶ Capital losses confer no tax benefit to the owners in the year the corporation incurs them. They cannot offset the ordinary income of either the corporation or its shareholders. These losses must be carried back or carried forward to offset corporate capital gains realized in other years.

S CORPORATIONS. An **S corporation** is so designated because special rules governing its tax treatment are found in Subchapter S of the IRC. Nevertheless, the general corporate tax rules apply unless overridden by the Subchapter S provisions. Like a partnership, an S corporation is a pass-through entity. Income, deductions, losses, and credits are accounted for by the S corporation, which generally is not subject to taxation. They pass through to the separate returns of its owners, who generally are subject to taxation. An S corporation offers its owners less flexibility than does a partnership. For example, the number and type of S corporation shareholders are limited, and the shareholders cannot allocate income, deductions, losses, and credits in a way that differs from their proportionate ownership. Like C corporation shareholders, S corporation shareholders enjoy limited liability.

To obtain S corporation status, a corporation must make a special election, and its shareholders must consent to that election. Each year, an S corporation files an information return, Form 1120S (U.S. Income Tax Return for an S Corporation), which reports the results of its operations and indicates the items of income, deduction, loss, and credit that pass through to the separate returns of its shareholders.

---

[5] Sec. 441. See Chapter C:3 for the special tax year restrictions applying to personal service corporations.

EXAMPLE C:2-7 ▶ Chuck owns 50% of the stock in Maine, an S corporation that uses the calendar year as its tax year. For its first year of operation, Maine reports $30,000 of taxable income, all ordinary in character. Maine pays no corporate income tax. Chuck, however, must pay tax on his $15,000 (0.50 × $30,000) share of Maine's income whether or not the corporation distributes this income to him. If his marginal rate is 35%, Chuck pays $5,250 (0.35 × $15,000) of tax on this share. If Maine instead reports a $30,000 loss, Chuck's $15,000 share of the loss reduces his tax liability by $5,250 (0.35 × $15,000). ◀

TAX STRATEGY TIP

If a corporation anticipates losses in its early years, it might consider operating as an S corporation so that the losses pass through to the shareholders. When the corporation becomes profitable, it can revoke the S election if it wishes to accumulate earnings for growth.

Tax Advantages.   The tax advantages of doing business as an S corporation are as follows:

▶ S corporations generally pay no tax. Corporate income passes through and is taxed to the shareholders.

▶ The shareholders' marginal tax rates may be lower than a C corporation's marginal tax rate, thereby producing overall tax savings.

▶ Corporate losses flow through to the separate returns of the shareholders and may be used to offset income earned from other sources. (Passive loss and basis rules, however, may limit loss deductions to shareholders. See Chapter C:11.) This treatment can be beneficial to owners of start-up corporations that generate losses in their early years of operation.

▶ Because capital gains, as well as other tax-related items, retain their character when they pass through to the separate returns of shareholders, the shareholders are taxed on these gains as though they directly realized them. Consequently, they can offset the gains against capital losses from other sources. Furthermore, they are taxed on these gains at their own capital gains rates.

▶ Shareholders generally can contribute money to or withdraw money from an S corporation without recognizing gain.

▶ Corporate profits are taxed only at the shareholder level in the year earned. Generally, the shareholders incur no additional tax liability when the corporation distributes the profits.

▶ A shareholder's basis in S corporation stock is increased by his or her share of corporate income. This basis adjustment reduces the shareholder's gain when he or she later sells the S corporation stock, thereby avoiding double taxation.

TAX STRATEGY TIP

Relatively low individual tax rates may increase the attractiveness of an S corporation relative to the C corporation form of doing business.

Tax Disadvantages.   The tax disadvantages of doing business as an S corporation are as follows:

▶ Shareholders are taxed on all of an S corporation's current year profits whether or not the corporation distributes these profits and whether or not the shareholders have the wherewithal to pay the tax on these profits.

▶ If the shareholders' marginal tax rates exceed those for a C corporation, the overall tax burden may be heavier, and the after-tax earnings available for reinvestment and debt retirement may be reduced.

▶ Nontaxable fringe benefits generally are not available to S corporation shareholder-employees.[6] Ordinarily, fringe benefits provided by an S corporation are deductible by the corporation and taxable to the shareholder. On the other hand, S corporation shareholder-employees pay half of Social Security taxes while the S corporation employer pays the other half.

▶ S corporations generally cannot defer income by choosing a fiscal year other than a calendar year unless the S corporation can establish a legitimate business purpose for a fiscal year or unless it makes a special election.

Chapter C:11 discusses S corporations in greater detail. In addition, Appendix F compares the tax treatment of C corporations, partnerships, and S corporations.

---

[6] S corporation shareholders may deduct their health insurance costs in the same manner as sole proprietors and partners. See footnote 2 for details.

ADDITIONAL COMMENT
All 50 states have adopted statutes allowing LLCs.

LIMITED LIABILITY COMPANIES

A **limited liability company** (LLC) combines the best features of a partnership with those of a corporation even though, from a legal perspective, it is neither. While offering its owners the limited liability of a corporation, an LLC with more than one owner generally is treated as a partnership for tax purposes. This limited liability extends to all the LLC's owners. In this respect, the LLC is similar to a limited partnership with no general partners. Unlike an S corporation, an LLC may have an unlimited number of owners who can be individuals, corporations, estates, and trusts. As discussed below, under the check-the-box regulations, the LLC may elect to be taxed as a corporation or be treated by default as a partnership. If treated as a partnership, the LLC files Form 1065 (U.S. Partnership Return of Income) with the IRS.

REAL-WORLD EXAMPLE
All the Big 4 accounting firms have converted general partnerships into LLPs.

LIMITED LIABILITY PARTNERSHIPS

Many states allow a business to operate as a **limited liability partnership** (LLP). This business form is attractive to professional service organizations, such as public accounting firms, that adopt LLP status primarily to limit their legal liability. Under state LLP laws, partners are liable for their own acts and omissions as well as the acts and omissions of individuals under their direction. On the other hand, LLP partners are not liable for the negligence or misconduct of the other partners. Thus, from a legal liability perspective, an LLP partner is like a limited partner with respect to other partners' acts but like a general partner with respect to his or her own acts, as well as the acts of his or her agents. Like a general partnership or LLC with more than one owner, an LLP can elect to be taxed as a corporation under the check-the-box regulations. If treated as a partnership by default, the LLP files Form 1065 (U.S. Partnership Return of Income) with the IRS.

CHECK-THE-BOX REGULATIONS

OBJECTIVE 2

Apply the check-the-box regulations to partnerships, corporations, and trusts

Most unincorporated businesses may choose to be taxed as a partnership or a corporation under rules commonly referred to as the **check-the-box regulations.** According to these regulations, an unincorporated business with two or more owners is treated by default as a partnership for tax purposes unless it elects to be taxed as a corporation. An unincorporated business with one owner is disregarded as a separate entity and thus treated as a sole proprietorship by default unless it elects to be taxed as a corporation.[7]

TAX STRATEGY TIP
When applying the federal check-the-box regulations, taxpayers also must check to see whether or not their state will treat the entity in a consistent manner.

An eligible entity (i.e., an unincorporated business) may elect its classification by filing Form 8832 (Entity Classification Election) with the IRS. The form must be signed by each owner of the entity, or any officer, manager, or owner of the entity authorized to make the election. The signatures must specify the date on which the election will be effective. The effective date cannot be more than 75 days before or 12 months after the date the entity files Form 8832. A copy of the form must be attached to the entity's tax return for the election year.

EXAMPLE C:2-8 ▶ On January 10 of the current year, a group of ten individuals organizes an LLC to conduct a bookbinding business in Texas. In the current year, the LLC is an eligible entity under the check-the-box regulations and thus may elect (with the owners' consent) to be taxed as a corporation. If the LLC does not make the election, it will be treated as a partnership for tax purposes by default. ◀

EXAMPLE C:2-9 ▶ Assume the same facts as in Example C:2-8 except only one individual organized the LLC. Unless the LLC elects to be taxed as a corporation, it will be disregarded for tax purposes by default. Consequently, its income will be taxed directly to the owner as if it were a sole proprietorship. ◀

---

[7] This rule does not apply to corporations, trusts, or certain special entities such as real estate investment trusts, real estate mortgage investment conduits, or publicly traded partnerships. Reg. Sec. 301.7701-2(b)(8). Publicly traded partnerships are discussed in Chapter C:10. Special check-the-box rules apply to foreign corporations. These rules are beyond the scope of this text.

If an entity elects to change its tax classification, it cannot make another election until 60 months after the effective date of the initial election. Following the election, certain tax consequences ensue. For example, following a partnership's election to be taxed as a corporation, the partnership is deemed to distribute its assets to the partners, who are then deemed to contribute the assets to a new corporation in a nontaxable exchange for stock. If an eligible entity that previously elected to be taxed as a corporation subsequently elects to be treated as a partnership or a disregarded entity, it is deemed to have distributed its assets and liabilities to its owners or owner in a liquidation as described in Chapter C:6. If a partnership, the deemed distribution is followed by a deemed contribution of assets and liabilities to a newly formed partnership.[8]

LEGAL REQUIREMENTS FOR FORMING A CORPORATION

OBJECTIVE 3

Determine the legal requirements for forming a corporation

The legal requirements for forming a corporation depend on state law. These requirements generally include

▶ Investing a minimum amount of capital

▶ Filing articles of incorporation

▶ Issuing stock

▶ Paying state incorporation fees

One of the first decisions an entrepreneur must make when organizing a corporation is the state of incorporation. Although most entrepreneurs incorporate in the state where they conduct business, many incorporate in other states with favorable corporation laws. Such laws might provide for little or no income, sales, or use taxes; low minimum capital requirements; and modest incorporation fees. Regardless of the state of incorporation, the entrepreneur must follow the incorporation procedure set forth in the relevant state statute. Typically, under this procedure, the entrepreneur must file articles of incorporation with the appropriate state agency. The articles must specify certain information, such as the formal name of the corporation; its purpose; the par value, number of shares, and classes of stock it is authorized to issue; and the names of the individuals who will initially serve on the corporation's board of directors. The state usually charges a fee for incorporation or filing. In addition, it periodically may assess a franchise tax for the privilege of doing business in the state.

ADDITIONAL COMMENT

States are not consistent in how they tax corporations. Certain states have no state income taxes. Other states do not recognize an S election, thereby taxing an S corporation as a C corporation.

TAX CONSIDERATIONS IN FORMING A CORPORATION

Once the entrepreneur decides on the corporate form, he or she must transfer money, property (e.g., equipment, furniture, inventory, and receivables), or services (e.g., accounting, legal, or architectural services) to the corporation in exchange for its debt or equity. These transfers may have tax consequences for both the transferor investor and the transferee corporation. For instance, the sale of property for stock usually is taxable to the transferor.[9] However, if Sec. 351(a) (which treats an investor's interest in certain transferred business assets to be "changed in form" rather than "disposed of") applies, any gain or loss realized on the exchange may be deferred. In determining the tax consequences of incorporation, one must answer the following questions:

▶ What property should be transferred to the corporation?

▶ What services should the transferors or third parties provide for the corporation?

[8] Reg. Sec. 301.7701-3(g). An alternative way for a corporation to be taxed as a pass-through entity is to make an election to be taxed as an S corporation. See Chapter C:11.

[9] Sec. 1001.

▶ What liabilities, in addition to property, should be transferred?

▶ How should the property be transferred (e.g., sale, contribution to capital, or loan)?

Example C:2-10 and Table C:2-1 compare the tax consequences of taxable and nontaxable property transfers.

EXAMPLE C:2-10 ▶ For several years Brad has operated a successful manufacturing business as a sole proprietorship. To limit his liability, he decides to incorporate his business as Block Corporation. Immediately preceding the incorporation, he reports the following balance sheet for his sole proprietorship, which uses the accrual method of accounting:

		Adjusted Basis	Fair Market Value
Assets:			
Cash		$ 10,000	$ 10,000
Accounts receivable		15,000	15,000
Inventory		20,000	25,000
Equipment	$120,000		
Minus: Depreciation	(35,000)	85,000	100,000
Total		$130,000	$150,000
Liabilities and owner's equity:			
Accounts payable		$ 30,000	$ 30,000
Note payable on equipment		50,000	50,000
Owner's equity		50,000	70,000
Total		$130,000	$150,000

When Brad transfers the assets to Block in exchange for its stock, he realizes a gain because the value of the stock received exceeds his basis in the assets. If the exchange is taxable, Brad recognizes $5,000 of ordinary income on the transfer of the inventory ($25,000 FMV − $20,000 basis) and, because of depreciation recapture, $15,000 of ordinary income on the transfer of the equipment ($100,000 FMV − $85,000 basis). However, if the exchange meets the requirements of Sec. 351(a), it is tax-free. In other words, Brad recognizes none of the income or gain realized on the transfer of assets and liabilities to Block. ◀

STOP & THINK

Question: Joyce has conducted a business as a sole proprietorship for several years. She needs additional capital and wants to incorporate her business. The assets of her business (building, land, inventory, etc.) have a $400,000 adjusted basis and a $1.5 million FMV. Joyce is willing to exchange the assets for 1,500 shares of Ace Corporation stock, each having a $1,000 fair market value. Bill and John each are willing to invest $500,000 in Joyce's business for 500 shares of stock. Why is Sec. 351 important to Joyce? Does it matter to Bill and John?

Solution: If not for Sec. 351, Joyce would recognize gain on the incorporation of her business. She realizes a gain of $1.1 million ($1,500,000 − $400,000) on her contribution of proprietorship assets to a new corporation in exchange for 60% of its outstanding shares (1,500 ÷ [1,500 + 500 + 500] = 0.60). However, she recognizes none of this gain because she meets the requirements of Sec. 351. Section 351 does not affect Bill or John because each is simply purchasing 20% of the new corporation's stock for $500,000 cash. They will not realize or recognize gain or loss unless they subsequently sell their stock at a price above or below the $500,000 cost.

If all exchanges of property for corporate stock were taxable, many entrepreneurs would find the tax cost of incorporating their business prohibitively high. In Example C:2-10, for example, Brad would recognize a $20,000 gain on the exchange of his assets for the corporate stock. Moreover, because losses also are realized in an exchange, without special rules, taxpayers could exchange loss property for stock and recognize the loss while maintaining an equity interest in the property transferred.

▼ TABLE C:2-1

Overview of Corporate Formation Rules

Tax Treatment for:	Taxable Property Transfer	Nontaxable Property Transfer
Transferors:		
1. Gain realized	FMV of stock received Money received FMV of noncash boot property (including securities) received Amount of liabilities assumed by transferee corporation Minus: Adjusted basis of property transferred Realized gain (Sec. 1001(a))	Same as taxable transaction
2. Gain recognized	Transferors recognize the entire amount of realized gain (Sec. 1001(c)) Losses may be disallowed under related party rules (Sec. 267(a)(1)) Installment sale rules may apply to the realized gain (Sec. 453)	Transferors recognize none of the realized gain unless one of the following exceptions applies (Sec. 351(a)): a. Boot property is received (Sec. 351(b)) b. Liabilities are transferred to the corporation for a nonbusiness or tax avoidance purpose (Sec. 357(b)) c. Liabilities exceeding basis are transferred to the corporation (Sec. 357(c)) d. Services, certain corporate indebtednesses, and interest claims are transferred to the corporation (Sec. 351(d)) The installment method may defer recognition of gain when a shareholder receives a corporate note as boot (Sec. 453)
3. Basis of property received	FMV (Cost) (Sec. 1012)	Basis of property transferred to the corporation Plus: Gain recognized Minus: Money received (including liabilities treated as money) 　　　FMV of noncash boot property Total basis of stock received (Sec. 358(a)) Allocation of total stock basis is based on relative FMVs Basis of noncash boot property is its FMV
4. Holding period of property received	Day after the exchange date	Holding period of stock received includes holding period of Sec. 1231 property or capital assets transferred; otherwise it begins the day after the exchange date
Transferee Corporation:		
1. Gain recognized	The corporation recognizes no gain or loss on the receipt of money or other property in exchange for its stock (including treasury stock) (Sec. 1032)	Same as taxable transaction except the corporation may recognize gain under Sec. 311 if it transfers appreciated noncash boot property (Sec. 351(f))
2. Basis	FMV (Cost) (Sec. 1012)	Generally, same as in transferor's hands plus any gain recognized by transferor (Sec. 362) If the total adjusted basis of all transferred property exceeds the total FMV of the property, the total basis to the transferor is limited to the property's total FMV
3. Holding period	Day after the exchange date	Transferor's carryover holding period for the property transferred regardless of the property's character (Sec. 1223(2)) Day after the exchange date if basis is reduced to FMV

To allow taxpayers to incorporate without incurring a high tax cost and to prevent taxpayers from recognizing losses while maintaining an equity claim to the loss assets, Congress enacted Sec. 351.

SECTION 351: DEFERRING GAIN OR LOSS UPON INCORPORATION

OBJECTIVE 4

Explain the requirements for deferring gain or loss upon incorporation

TAX STRATEGY TIP

A transferor who wishes to recognize gain or loss must take steps to avoid Sec. 351 by deliberately failing at least one of its requirements or by engaging in sales transactions. See Tax Planning Considerations later in this chapter for details.

Section 351(a) provides that transferors recognize no gain or loss when they transfer property to a corporation solely in exchange for the corporation's stock provided that, immediately after the exchange, the transferors are in control of the corporation. Section 351 does not apply to a transfer of property to an investment company, nor does it apply in certain bankruptcy cases.

This rule is based on the premise that, when property is transferred to a controlled corporation, the transferors merely exchange direct ownership for indirect ownership through stock ownership of the transferee corporation, which gives them an equity interest in the underlying assets. In other words, the transferors maintain a continuity of interest in the transferred property. Furthermore, if the only consideration the shareholders receive is stock, they have not generated cash with which to pay their taxes. If the transferors of property receive other consideration in addition to stock, such as cash or debt instruments, they will have the wherewithal to pay taxes and, under Sec. 351(b), may have to recognize some or all of their realized gain.

A transferor's realized gain or loss that is unrecognized for tax purposes, however, is not exempt from taxation. It is only *deferred* until the shareholder sells or exchanges the stock received in the Sec. 351 exchange. Shareholders who receive stock in such an exchange take a stock basis that reflects the deferred gain or loss. For example, if a shareholder receives stock in exchange for property and recognizes no gain or loss, the stock basis equals the basis of property transferred less liabilities assumed by the corporation (see Table C:2-1). This tax treatment is discussed later in this chapter. Under an alternative approach, the stock basis can be calculated as follows: FMV of qualified stock received, minus any deferred gain (or plus any deferred loss). This latter approach highlights the deferral aspect of this type of transaction. If the shareholder later sells the stock, he or she will recognize the deferred gain or loss inherent in the basis adjustment.

EXAMPLE C:2-11 ▶ Assume the same facts as in Example C:2-10. If Brad satisfies the conditions of Sec. 351, he will not recognize the $20,000 realized gain ($15,000 gain on equipment + $5,000 gain on inventory) when he transfers the assets and liabilities of his sole proprietorship to Block Corporation. Under the alternative approach, Brad's basis in the Block stock is decreased to reflect the deferred gain. Thus, Brad's basis in the Block stock is $50,000 ($70,000 FMV − $20,000 deferred gain). If Brad later sells his stock for its $70,000 FMV, he will recognize the $20,000 gain at that time. ◀

The specific requirements for deferral of gain and loss under Sec. 351(a) are

▶ The transferors must transfer property to the corporation.

▶ They must receive stock of the transferee corporation in exchange for their property.

▶ They must be in control of the corporation immediately after the exchange.

Each of these requirements is explained below.

THE PROPERTY REQUIREMENT

The rule of gain or loss nonrecognition applies only to transfers of property to a corporation in exchange for the corporation's stock. Section 351 does not define the term *property*. However, the courts and the IRS have defined *property* to include money and almost any other asset, including installment obligations, accounts receivable, inventory, equipment, patents and other intangibles representing know-how, trademarks, trade names, and computer software.[10]

Excluded from the statutory definition of property are[11]

▶ Services (such as legal or accounting services) rendered to the corporation in exchange for its stock

▶ Indebtedness of the transferee corporation not evidenced by a security

▶ Interest on transferee corporation debt that accrued on or after the beginning of the transferor's holding period for the debt

The first of these exclusions perhaps is the most important. A person receiving stock in compensation for services must recognize the stock's FMV as ordinary income for tax purposes. In other words, an exchange of services for stock is a taxable transaction even where concurrent transfers of property for stock are nontaxable under Sec. 351.[12] A shareholder's basis in the stock received in compensation for services is the stock's FMV.

EXAMPLE C:2-12 ▶ Amy and Bill form West Corporation. Amy exchanges property for 90 shares (90% of the outstanding shares) of West stock. Amy's exchange is nontaxable because Amy has exchanged property for stock and controls West immediately after the exchange. Bill performs accounting services in exchange for ten shares of West stock worth $10,000. Bill's exchange is taxable because he has provided services in exchange for stock. Thus, Bill recognizes $10,000 of ordinary income—the FMV of the stock—as compensation for his services. Bill's basis in the stock is its $10,000 FMV. ◀

THE CONTROL REQUIREMENT

Section 351 requires the transferors, as a group, to be in control of the transferee corporation immediately after the exchange. A transferor may be an individual or any type of tax entity (such as a partnership, another corporation, or a trust). Section 368(c) defines *control* as ownership of at least 80% of the total combined voting power of all classes of stock entitled to vote and at least 80% of the total number of shares of all other classes of stock (e.g., nonvoting preferred stock).[13] The minimum ownership levels for nonvoting stock apply to each class of stock rather than to the nonvoting stock in total.[14]

EXAMPLE C:2-13 ▶ Dan exchanges property having a $22,000 adjusted basis and a $30,000 FMV for 60% of newly created Sun Corporation's single class of stock. Ed exchanges $20,000 cash for the remaining 40% of Sun stock. The transaction qualifies as a nontaxable exchange under Sec. 351 because the transferors, Dan and Ed, together own at least 80% of the Sun stock immediately after the exchange. Therefore, Dan defers recognition of his $8,000 ($30,000 − $22,000) realized gain. (Ed realizes no gain because he contributes cash.) ◀

Because services do not qualify as property, stock received by a person who exclusively provides services does not count toward the 80% control threshold. Unless transferors of property own at least 80% of the corporation's stock immediately after the exchange, the control requirement will not be met, and the entire transaction will be taxable.

EXAMPLE C:2-14 ▶ Dana transfers property having an $18,000 adjusted basis and a $35,000 FMV to newly created York Corporation for 70 shares of York stock. Ellen provides legal services worth $15,000 for the remaining 30 shares of York stock. Because Ellen does not transfer property to York, her stock is not counted toward the 80% ownership threshold. On the other hand, because Dana transfers property to York, his stock is counted toward this threshold. However, Dana is not in control of York immediately after the exchange because he owns only 70% of York stock. Therefore, Dana recognizes all $17,000 ($35,000 − $18,000) of his gain realized on the exchange. Dana's basis in his York stock is its $35,000 FMV. Ellen recognizes $15,000 of ordinary income, the FMV of stock received for her services. Ellen's basis in her York stock is $15,000. The tax consequences to Ellen are the same whether or not Dana meets the control requirement. ◀

---

[10] For an excellent discussion of the definition of *property*, see footnote 6 of *D.N. Stafford v. U.S.*, 45 AFTR 2d 80-785, 80-1 USTC ¶9218 (5th Cir., 1980).
[11] Sec. 351(d).
[12] Secs. 61 and 83.
[13] In determining whether the 80% requirements are satisfied, the construc-

tive ownership rules of Sec. 318 do not apply (see Rev. Rul. 56-613, 1956-2 C.B. 212). See Chapter C:4 for an explanation of Sec. 318.
[14] Rev. Rul. 59-259, 1959-2 C.B. 115, as modified by Rev. Rul. 81-17, 1981-1 C.B. 75.

If the property transferors own at least 80% of the stock immediately after the exchange, they, but not the provider of services, will be in control of the transferee corporation.

EXAMPLE C:2-15 ▶ Assume the same facts as in Example C:2-14, except a third individual, Fred, contributes $35,000 in cash for 70 shares of York stock. Now Dana and Fred together own more than 80% of the York stock (140 ÷ 170 = 0.82) immediately after the exchange. Therefore, the Sec. 351 control requirement is met, and neither Dana nor Fred recognizes gain on the exchange. Ellen still must recognize $15,000 of ordinary income, the FMV of the stock she receives for her services. ◀

TRANSFERORS OF BOTH PROPERTY AND SERVICES. If a person transfers both services *and* property to a corporation in exchange for the corporation's stock, all the stock received by that person, including stock received in exchange for services, is counted toward the 80% control threshold.[15]

EXAMPLE C:2-16 ▶ Assume the same facts as in Example C:2-14 except that, in addition to providing legal services worth $15,000, Ellen contributes property worth at least $1,500. In this case, all of Ellen's stock counts toward the 80% ownership threshold. Because Dana and Ellen together own 100% of the York stock, the exchange meets the Sec. 351 control requirement. Therefore, Dana recognizes no gain on his property exchange. However, Ellen still must recognize $15,000 of ordinary income, the FMV of the stock received as compensation for services. ◀

When a person transfers both property and services in exchange for a corporation's stock, the property must have more than nominal value for that person's stock to count toward the 80% control threshold.[16] The IRS generally requires that the FMV of the stock received for transferred property be at least 10% of the value of the stock received for services provided. If the value of the stock received for the property is less than 10% of the value of the stock received for the services, the IRS will not issue an advance ruling to the effect that the transaction meets the requirements of Sec. 351.[17]

EXAMPLE C:2-17 ▶ Assume the same facts as in Example C:2-16 except that Ellen contributes only $1,000 worth of property in addition to $15,000 of legal services. In this case, the IRS will not issue an advance ruling that the transaction meets the Sec. 351 requirements because the FMV of stock received for the property ($1,000) is less than 10% of the value of the stock received for the services ($1,500 = 0.10 × $15,000). Consequently, if the IRS audits Ellen's tax return for the year of transfer, it probably will challenge Dana's and Ellen's position that the transfer is nontaxable under Sec. 351. ◀

TRANSFERS TO EXISTING CORPORATIONS. Section 351 applies to transfers to an existing corporation as well as transfers to a newly created corporation. The same requirements must be met in both cases. Property must be transferred in exchange for stock, and the property transferors must be in control of the corporation immediately after the exchange.

EXAMPLE C:2-18 ▶ Jack and Karen own 75 and 25 shares, respectively, of Texas Corporation stock. Jack transfers property with a $15,000 adjusted basis and a $25,000 FMV to the corporation in exchange for an additional 25 shares of Texas stock. The Sec. 351 control requirement is met because, immediately after the exchange, Jack owns 80% (100 ÷ 125 = 0.80) of Texas stock. Therefore, Jack recognizes no gain. ◀

If a shareholder transfers property to an existing corporation for additional stock but does not own at least 80% of the stock after the exchange, the control requirement is not met. Thus, Sec. 351 denies tax-free treatment for many transfers of property to an existing corporation by a new shareholder. A new shareholder's transfer of property to an existing corporation is nontaxable only if that shareholder acquires at least 80% of the corporation's stock, or if enough existing shareholders also transfer additional property so that the transferors as a group, including the new shareholder, control the corporation immediately after the exchange.

---

[15] Reg. Sec. 1.351-1(a)(2), Ex. (3).
[16] Reg. Sec. 1.351-1(a)(1)(ii).

[17] Rev. Proc. 77-37, 1977-2 C.B. 568, Sec. 3.07, as modified by T.D. 8761, 1998-1 C.B. 812.

EXAMPLE C:2-19 ▶ Alice owns all 100 shares of Local Corporation stock, valued at $100,000. Beth owns property with a $15,000 adjusted basis and a $100,000 FMV. Beth contributes the property to Local in exchange for 100 shares of newly issued Local stock. The Sec. 351 control requirement is not met because Beth owns only 50% of Local stock immediately after the exchange. Therefore, Beth recognizes an $85,000 ($100,000 − $15,000) gain. ◀

If an existing shareholder exchanges property for additional stock to enable another shareholder to qualify for tax-free treatment under Sec. 351, the stock received must be of more than nominal value.[18] For advance ruling purposes, the IRS requires that this value be at least 10% of the value of the stock already owned.[19]

EXAMPLE C:2-20 ▶ Assume the same facts as in Example C:2-19 except that Alice transfers additional property worth $10,000 for an additional ten shares of Local stock. Now both Alice and Beth are transferors, and the Sec. 351 control requirement is met. Consequently, neither Alice nor Beth recognizes gain on the exchange. If Alice receives fewer than ten shares, the IRS will not issue an advance ruling that the exchange is tax-free under Sec. 351. ◀

STOP & THINK

Question: Matthew and Michael each own 50 shares of Main Corporation stock having a $250,000 FMV. Matthew wants to transfer property with a $40,000 adjusted basis and a $100,000 FMV to Main in exchange for an additional 20 shares. Can Matthew avoid recognizing $60,000 ($100,000 − $40,000) of the gain realized on the transfer?

Solution: If Matthew simply exchanges the property for additional stock, he must recognize the gain. The Sec. 351 control requirement will not have been met because Matthew will own only 70 of the 120 outstanding shares (or 58.33%) immediately after the exchange.

Gain recognition can be avoided in two ways:

1. Matthew can transfer sufficient property (i.e., $750,000 worth) to Main to receive 150 additional shares so that, immediately after the exchange, he will own 80% (200 out of 250 shares) of Main stock.
2. Alternatively, Michael also can contribute additional property to qualify as a transferor. Specifically, he can contribute to the corporation at least $25,000, or 10% of the $250,000 value of the Main stock that he already owns so that together the two transferors will own 100% of Main stock immediately after the exchange.

DISPROPORTIONATE EXCHANGES OF PROPERTY AND STOCK. Section 351 does not require that the value of the stock received by the transferors be proportionate to the value of the property transferred. However, if the value of the stock received is *not* proportionate to the value of the property transferred, the exchange may be treated in accordance with its economic effect, that is, a proportional exchange followed by a constructive gift, compensation payment, or extinguishment of a liability owed by one shareholder to another.[20] If the deemed effect of the transaction is a gift from one transferor to another, for example, the "donor" will be treated as though he or she received stock equal in value to that of the property contributed and then gave some of the stock to the "donee."

EXAMPLE C:2-21 ▶ Don and his son John transfer property worth $75,000 (adjusted basis of $42,000 to Don) and $25,000 (adjusted basis of $20,000 to John), respectively, to newly formed Star Corporation in exchange for all 100 shares of Star stock. Don and John receive 25 and 75 shares of Star stock, respectively. Because Don and John are in control of Star immediately after the exchange, they recognize no gain or loss. However, because Don and John did not receive the stock in proportion to the FMV of their respective property contributions, Don might be deemed to have received 75 shares (worth $75,000), then to have given 50 shares (worth $50,000) to John. If the IRS deems such a gift, it might require Don to pay gift taxes. Don's basis in his remaining 25 shares is $14,000 [(25 ÷ 75) × $42,000 basis in the property transferred]. John's basis in the 75 shares is $48,000 [$20,000 basis in the property transferred by John + ($42,000 − $14,000) basis in the shares deemed to have been gifted by Don]. ◀

---

[18] Reg. Sec. 1.351-1(a)(1)(ii).
[19] Rev. Proc. 77-37, 1977-2 C.B. 568, Sec. 3.07, as modified by T.D. 8761, 1998-1 C.B. 812.

[20] Reg. Sec. 1.351-1(b)(1).

IMMEDIATELY AFTER THE EXCHANGE. Section 351 requires that the transferors be in control of the transferee corporation "immediately after the exchange." This requirement does not mean that all transferors must simultaneously exchange their property for stock. It does mean, however, that all the exchanges must be agreed to beforehand, and the agreement must be executed in an expeditious and orderly manner.[21]

EXAMPLE C:2-22 ▶

TAX STRATEGY TIP

If one shareholder has a prearranged plan to dispose of his or her stock, and the disposition drops the ownership of the transferor shareholders below the required 80% control, such disposition can disqualify the Sec. 351 transaction for all the shareholders. As a possible protection, all shareholders could provide a written representation that they do not currently have a plan to dispose of their stock.

Art, Beth, and Carlos form New Corporation. Art and Beth each transfer noncash property worth $25,000 in exchange for one-third of the New stock. Carlos contributes $25,000 cash for another one-third of the New stock. Art and Carlos transfer their property and cash, respectively, on January 10. Beth transfers her property on March 3. Because all three transfers are part of the same prearranged transaction, the transferors are deemed to be in control of the corporation immediately after the exchange. ◀

Section 351 does not require the transferors to retain control of the transferee corporation for any specific length of time after the exchange. Control is required only "immediately after the exchange." The IRS has interpreted this phrase to mean that the transferors must not have a prearranged plan to dispose of their stock outside the control group. If they do have such a plan, they are not considered to be in control immediately after the exchange.[22]

EXAMPLE C:2-23 ▶

Amir, Bill, and Carl form White Corporation. Each contributes to White appreciated property worth $25,000 in exchange for one-third of White stock. Before the exchange, Amir arranges to sell his stock to Dana as soon as he receives it. This prearranged plan implies that Amir, Bill, and Carl do *not* have control immediately after the exchange because Bill and Carl own only 66.7% of the stock while Amir has disposed of his interest. Therefore, each must recognize gain in the exchange. ◀

THE STOCK REQUIREMENT

Under Sec. 351, transferors who exchange property solely for transferee corporation stock recognize no gain or loss if they control the corporation immediately after the exchange. Stock for this purpose may be voting or nonvoting. On the other hand, nonqualified preferred stock is treated as boot. Preferred stock generally has a preferred claim to dividends and liquidating distributions. Such stock is nonqualified if

▶ The shareholder can require the corporation to redeem it,

▶ The corporation either is required to redeem the stock or is likely to exercise a right to redeem it, or

▶ The dividend rate on the stock varies with interest rates, commodity prices, or other similar indices.

These features render the preferred stock more like cash or debt than like equity. Thus, it is treated as boot subject to the rules discussed below. In addition, stock rights or stock warrants are not considered stock for purposes of Sec. 351.[23]

Topic Review C:2-1 summarizes the major requirements for a nontaxable exchange under Sec. 351.

EFFECT OF SEC. 351 ON THE TRANSFERORS

If all Sec. 351 requirements are met, the transferors recognize no gain or loss on the exchange of their property for stock in the transferee corporation. The receipt of property other than stock does not necessarily render the entire transaction taxable. Rather, it could result in the recognition of all or part of the transferors' realized gain.

RECEIPT OF BOOT. If a transferor receives any money or property other than stock in the transferee corporation, the additional money or property is considered to be **boot**. Boot may include cash, notes, securities, or stock in another corporation. Upon receiving boot, the transferor recognizes gain to the extent of the lesser of the transferor's realized

[21] Reg. Sec. 1.351-1(a)(1).
[22] Rev. Rul. 79-70, 1979-1 C.B. 144.

[23] Reg. Sec. 1.351-1(a)(1)(ii).

Topic Review C:2-1

Major Requirements of Sec. 351

1. The nonrecognition of gain or loss rule applies only to transfers of property in exchange for a corporation's stock. It does not apply to an exchange of services for stock.
2. The property transferors must be in control of the transferee corporation immediately after the exchange. Control means ownership of at least 80% of the voting power and at least 80% of the total number of shares of all other classes of stock. Stock disposed of after the exchange pursuant to a prearranged plan does not meet the "immediately after the exchange" requirement.
3. The nonrecognition rule applies only to the gain realized in an exchange of property for stock. If the transferor receives property other than stock, such property is considered to be boot. The transferor recognizes gain to the extent of the lesser of the FMV of any boot received or the realized gain.

gain or the FMV of the boot property received.[24] A transferor never recognizes a loss in an exchange qualifying under Sec. 351 whether or not he or she receives boot.

The character of the recognized gain depends on the type of property transferred. For example, if the shareholder transfers a capital asset such as stock in another corporation, the recognized gain is capital in character. If the shareholder transfers Sec. 1231 property, such as equipment or a building, the recognized gain is ordinary in character to the extent of any depreciation recaptured under Sec. 1245 or 1250.[25] Thus, depreciation is not recaptured unless the transferor receives boot and recognizes a gain on the depreciated property transferred.[26] If the shareholder transfers inventory, the recognized gain is entirely ordinary in character.

EXAMPLE C:2-24 ▶ Pam, Rob, and Sam form East Corporation and transfer the following property:

Transferor	Asset	Transferor's Adj. Basis	FMV	Consideration Received
Pam	Machinery	$10,000	$12,500	25 shares East stock
Rob	Land	18,000	25,000	40 shares East stock and $5,000 East note
Sam	Cash	17,500	17,500	35 shares East stock

The machinery and land are, respectively, Sec. 1231 property and a capital asset. The exchange meets the requirements of Sec. 351 except that, in addition to East stock, Rob receives boot of $5,000 (the FMV of the note). Rob realizes a $7,000 ($25,000 − $18,000) gain, of which he recognizes $5,000—the lesser of the $7,000 realized gain or the $5,000 boot received. The gain is capital in character because the property transferred was a capital asset in Rob's hands. Pam realizes a $2,500 gain on her exchange of machinery. However, even though Pam would have been required to recapture depreciation had she sold or exchanged the machinery, she recognizes no gain because she received no boot. Sam neither realizes nor recognizes gain on his cash purchase of East stock. ◀

ADDITIONAL COMMENT

If multiple assets were aggregated into one computation, any built-in losses would be netted against the gains. Such a result is inappropriate because losses cannot be recognized in a Sec. 351 transaction.

COMPUTING GAIN WHEN SEVERAL ASSETS ARE TRANSFERRED. Revenue Ruling 68-55 adopts a "separate properties approach" for computing gain or loss when a shareholder transfers more than one asset to a corporation.[27] Under this approach, the gain or loss realized and recognized is computed separately for each property transferred. The transferor is deemed to have received a proportionate share of stock, securities, and boot in exchange for each property transferred, based on the assets' relative FMVs.

EXAMPLE C:2-25 ▶ Joan transfers two assets to newly formed North Corporation in a transaction qualifying in part for tax-free treatment under Sec. 351. The total FMV of the assets is $100,000. The consideration

---

[24] Sec. 351(b).
[25] Section 1239 also may require some gain to be characterized as ordinary income. Section 1250 ordinary depreciation recapture will not apply to real property placed in service after 1986 because MACRS mandates straight-line depreciation.

[26] Secs. 1245(b)(3) and 1250(c)(3).
[27] 1968-1 C.B. 140, as amplified by Rev. Rul. 85-164, 1985-2 C.B. 117.

received by Joan consists of $90,000 of North stock and $10,000 of North notes. The following data illustrate how Joan determines her realized and recognized gain under the procedure set forth in Rev. Rul. 68-55.

	Asset 1	Asset 2	Total
Asset's FMV	$40,000	$60,000	$100,000
Percent of total FMV	40%	60%	100%
Consideration received in exchange for asset:			
Stock (Stock × percent of total FMV)	$36,000	$54,000	$ 90,000
Notes (Notes × percent of total FMV)	4,000	6,000	10,000
Total proceeds	$40,000	$60,000	$100,000
Minus: Adjusted basis	(65,000)	(25,000)	(90,000)
Realized gain (loss)	($25,000)	$35,000	$ 10,000
Boot received	$ 4,000	$ 6,000	$ 10,000
Recognized gain (loss)	None	$ 6,000	$ 6,000

Under the separate properties approach, the loss realized on the transfer of Asset 1 does not offset the gain realized on the transfer of Asset 2. Therefore, Joan recognizes $6,000 of the total $10,000 realized gain, even though she receives $10,000 of boot. Joan's selling Asset 1 to North so as to recognize the loss might be advisable. However, the Sec. 267 loss limitation rules may apply to Joan if she is a controlling shareholder (see pages C:2-34 and C:2-35). ◄

COMPUTING A SHAREHOLDER'S BASIS.

Boot Property. A transferor's basis in any boot property received is the property's FMV.[28]

Stock. A shareholder computes his or her adjusted basis in stock received in a Sec. 351 exchange as follows:[29]

	Adjusted basis of property transferred to the corporation
Plus:	Any gain recognized by the transferor
Minus:	FMV of boot received from the corporation
	Money received from the corporation
	Liabilities assumed by the corporation
	Adjusted basis of stock received

EXAMPLE C:2-26 ►

ADDITIONAL COMMENT

Because Sec. 351 is a deferral provision, any unrecognized gain must be reflected in the basis of the stock received by the transferor shareholder and is accomplished by substituting the transferor's basis in the property given up for the basis of the stock received. This substituted basis may be further adjusted by gain recognized and boot received.

Bob transfers a capital asset having a $50,000 adjusted basis and an $80,000 FMV to South Corporation. He acquired the property two years earlier. Bob receives all 100 shares of South stock, having a $70,000 FMV, plus a $10,000 90-day South note (boot property). Bob realizes a $30,000 gain on the exchange, computed as follows:

FMV of stock received	$70,000
Plus: FMV of 90-day note	10,000
Amount realized	$80,000
Minus: Adjusted basis of property transferred	(50,000)
Realized gain	$30,000

Bob's recognized gain is $10,000, i.e., the lesser of the $30,000 realized gain or the $10,000 FMV of the boot property. This gain is long-term and capital in character. The Sec. 351 rules effectively require Bob to defer $20,000 ($30,000 − $10,000) of his realized gain. Bob's basis in the South stock is $50,000, computed as follows:

SELF-STUDY QUESTION

What is an alternative method for determining the basis of the assets received by the transferor shareholder? How is this method applied to Bob in Example C:2-26?

Adjusted basis of property transferred	$50,000
Plus: Gain recognized by Bob	10,000
Minus: FMV of boot received	(10,000)
Adjusted basis of Bob's stock	$50,000 ◄

---

[28] Sec. 358(a)(2).

[29] Sec. 358(a)(1).

If a transferor receives more than one class of qualified stock, his or her basis must be allocated among the classes of stock according to their relative FMVs.[30]

EXAMPLE C:2-27 ▶

ANSWER

The basis of all boot property is its FMV, and the basis of stock received is the stock's FMV minus any deferred gain or plus any deferred loss. Bob's stock basis under the alternative method is $50,000 ($70,000 FMV of stock − $20,000 deferred gain).

Assume the same facts as in Example C:2-26 except Bob receives 100 shares of South common stock with a $45,000 FMV, 50 shares of South qualified preferred stock with a $25,000 FMV, and a 90-day South note with a $10,000 FMV. The total adjusted basis of the stock is $50,000 ($50,000 basis of property transferred + $10,000 gain recognized − $10,000 FMV of boot received). This basis must be allocated between the common and qualified preferred stock according to their relative FMVs, as follows:

$$\text{Basis of common stock} = \frac{\$45,000}{\$45,000 + \$25,000} \times \$50,000 = \$32,143$$

$$\text{Basis of preferred stock} = \frac{\$25,000}{\$45,000 + \$25,000} \times \$50,000 = \$17,857$$

Bob's basis in the note is its $10,000 FMV. ◀

TRANSFEROR'S HOLDING PERIOD. The transferor's holding period for any stock received in exchange for a capital asset or Sec. 1231 property includes the holding period of the property transferred.[31] If the transferor exchanged any other kind of property (e.g., inventory) for the stock, the transferor's holding period for the stock begins on the day after the exchange. Likewise, the holding period for boot property begins on the day after the exchange.

EXAMPLE C:2-28 ▶

Assume the same facts as in Example C:2-26. Bob's holding period for the stock includes the holding period of the capital asset transferred. His holding period for the note starts on the day after the exchange. ◀

STOP & THINK

Question: The holding period for stock received in exchange for a capital asset or Sec. 1231 property includes the holding period of the transferred item. The holding period for inventory or other assets begins on the day after the exchange. Why the difference?

Solution: Because stock received in a Sec. 351 exchange represents a "continuity of interest" in the property transferred, logically the stock should not only be valued and characterized in the same manner as the asset exchanged for the equity claim, but also accorded the same tax attributes. Because the holding period of a capital asset is relevant in determining the character of gain or loss realized (i.e., long-term or short-term) on the asset's subsequent sale, stock received in a tax-free exchange of the asset should be accorded the same holding period for the purpose of determining the character of gain or loss realized on the stock's subsequent sale. By the same token, because the holding period of a noncapital asset is less relevant in determining the character of gain or loss realized on the asset's subsequent sale, stock received in a tax-free exchange of the asset need not be accorded the same holding period for the purpose of determining the character of gain or loss realized on the stock's subsequent sale. Given the very nature of a noncapital asset, this gain or loss generally is ordinary in character, in any event. Moreover, if stock received in exchange for a noncapital asset were accorded a holding period that includes that of the transferred property, a transferor could sell the stock in a short time to realize a long-term capital gain, thereby converting ordinary income (potentially from the sale of the noncapital asset) into capital gain from the sale of stock.

Topic Review C:2-2 summarizes the tax consequences of a Sec. 351 exchange to the transferor(s) and the transferee corporation.

---

[30] Sec. 358(b)(1) and Reg. Sec. 1.358-2(b)(2).
[31] Sec. 1223(1). Revenue Ruling 85-164 (1985-2 C.B. 117) provides that a single share of stock may have two holding periods: a carryover holding period for the portion of such share received in exchange for a capital asset or Sec. 1231 property and a holding period that begins on the day after the exchange for the portion of such share received for inventory or other property. The split holding period is relevant only if the transferor sells the stock received within one year of the transfer date.

Topic Review C:2-2

Tax Consequences of a Sec. 351 Exchange

To Transferor(s):

1. Transferors recognize no gain or loss when they exchange property for stock. Exception: A transferor recognizes gain equal to the lesser of the realized gain or the sum of any money received plus the FMV of any non-cash property received. The character of the gain depends on the type of property transferred.
2. The basis of the stock received equals the adjusted basis of the property transferred plus any gain recognized by the transferor minus the FMV of any boot property received minus any money received (including liabilities assumed or acquired by the transferee corporation).
3. The holding period of stock received in exchange for capital assets or Sec. 1231 property includes the holding period of the transferred property. The holding period of stock received in exchange for any other property begins on the day after the exchange.

To Transferee Corporation:

1. A corporation recognizes no gain or loss when it exchanges its own stock for property or services.
2. The corporation's basis in property received is the transferor's basis plus any gain recognized by the transferor. However, if the total adjusted basis of all transferred property exceeds the total FMV of the property, the total basis to the transferee is limited to the property's total FMV.
3. The corporation's holding period for property received includes the transferor's holding period.

ADDITIONAL COMMENT

The nonrecognition rule for corporations that issue stock for property applies whether or not the transaction qualifies the transferor shareholder for Sec. 351 treatment.

TAX CONSEQUENCES TO TRANSFEREE CORPORATION

A corporation that issues stock or debt for property or services is subject to various IRC rules for determining the tax consequences of that exchange.

GAIN OR LOSS RECOGNIZED BY THE TRANSFEREE CORPORATION. Corporations recognize no gain or loss when they issue their own stock in exchange for property or services.[32] This result ensues whether or not Sec. 351 governs the exchange and whether or not the corporation issues new stock or treasury stock.

EXAMPLE C:2-29 ▶

West Corporation pays $10,000 to acquire 100 shares of its own stock from existing shareholders. The next year, West reissues these 100 treasury shares for land having a $15,000 FMV. West realizes a $5,000 ($15,000 − $10,000) gain on the exchange but recognizes none of this gain. ◀

Corporations also recognize no gain or loss when they exchange their own debt instruments for property or services. On the other hand, a corporation recognizes gain (but not loss) if it transfers appreciated property to a transferor as part of a Sec. 351 exchange. The amount and character of the gain are determined as though the property had been sold by the corporation immediately before the transfer.

EXAMPLE C:2-30 ▶

Alice, who owns 100% of Ace Corporation stock, transfers to Ace land having a $100,000 FMV and a $60,000 adjusted basis. In exchange, Alice receives 75 additional shares of Ace common stock having a $75,000 FMV, and Zero Corporation common stock having a $25,000 FMV. Ace's basis in the Zero stock, a capital asset, is $10,000. Alice realizes a $40,000 gain [($75,000 + $25,000) − $60,000] on the land transfer, of which she recognizes $25,000 (i.e., the FMV of the boot property received). In addition, Ace recognizes a $15,000 capital gain ($25,000 − $10,000) upon transferring the Zero stock to Alice. ◀

TRANSFEREE CORPORATION'S BASIS FOR PROPERTY RECEIVED. A corporation that acquires property in exhange for its stock in a transaction that is taxable to the transferor takes a current cost (i.e., its FMV) basis in the property. On the other hand, if

---

[32] Sec. 1032.

the exchange qualifies for nonrecognition treatment under Sec. 351 and is wholly or partially tax-free to the transferor, the corporation's basis in the property is computed as follows:[33]

Transferor's adjusted basis in property transferred to the corporation
Plus: Gain (if any) recognized by transferor
Minus: Reduction for loss property (if applicable)

Transferee corporation's basis in property

The transferee corporation's holding period for property acquired in a transaction satisfying the Sec. 351 requirements includes the period during which the property was held by the transferor.[34] This general rule applies to all types of property without regard to their character in the transferor's hands or the amount of gain recognized by the transferor. However, if the corporation reduces a property's basis to its FMV under the loss property limitation rule discussed below, the holding period will begin the day after the exchange date because no part of the new basis references the transferor's basis.

EXAMPLE C:2-31 ▶ Top Corporation issues 100 shares of its stock for land having a $15,000 FMV. Tina, who transferred the land, had a $12,000 basis in the property. If the exchange satisfies the Sec. 351 requirements, Tina recognizes no gain on the exchange. Top's basis in the land is $12,000, the same as Tina's. Top's holding period includes Tina's holding period. However, if the exchange does *not* satisfy the Sec. 351 requirements, Tina recognizes $3,000 of gain. Top's basis in the land is its $15,000 acquisition cost, and its holding period begins on the day after the exchange date. ◀

REDUCTION FOR LOSS PROPERTY. Section 362(e)(2) prevents shareholders from generating double losses by transferring loss property to a corporation. The double loss potential exists because the corporation would hold property with a built-in loss, and the shareholders would hold stock with a built-in loss. Accordingly, if a corporation's total adjusted basis (including any increase for gain recognized by the shareholder) for all properties transferred by the shareholder exceeds the properties' total FMV, the basis to the corporation of the properties must be reduced by this excess. The reduction in basis is allocated among the properties in proportion to their respective built-in losses. The limitation applies on a shareholder-by-shareholder basis. In other words, the property values and built-in losses of all shareholders are not aggregated.

EXAMPLE C:2-32 ▶ John transfers the following assets to Pecan Corporation in exchange for all of Pecan's stock worth $26,000.

Assets	Adjusted Basis to John	FMV
Inventory	$ 5,000	$ 8,000
Equipment	15,000	11,000
Furniture	9,000	7,000
Total	$29,000	$26,000

Although the transaction meets the requirements of Sec. 351, the total basis of the assets transferred ($29,000) exceeds their total FMV. Consequently, the total basis to Pecan is limited to the assets' FMV ($26,000). The $3,000 ($29,000 − $26,000) reduction in basis must be allocated among the assets in proportion to their respective built-in losses as follows:

Assets	Built-in Losses	Allocated Reduction
Equipment	$4,000	$2,000
Furniture	2,000	1,000
Total	$6,000	$3,000

---

[33] Sec. 362.   [34] Sec. 1223(2).

Thus, Pecan's bases for the assets transferred by John are:

Inventory	$ 5,000
Equipment ($15,000 − $2,000)	13,000
Furniture ($9,000 − $1,000)	8,000
Total	$26,000

Because each property's basis was not reduced to the property's FMV, the holding period of each property includes the transferor's holding period. ◄

A corporation subject to the basis reduction rules described above can avoid this result if the corporation and all its shareholders so elect. Under the election, the corporation need not reduce the bases of the assets received, but the affected shareholder's basis in stock received for the property is reduced by the amount by which the corporation would have reduced its basis absent the election.

EXAMPLE C:2-33 ▶ Assume the same facts as in Example C:2-32 except John and Pecan elect not to reduce the bases of the assets Pecan received. Under the election, John's basis in his Pecan stock is reduced to $26,000 ($29,000 − $3,000). ◄

A corporation and its shareholders can avoid the basis reduction rules altogether if each shareholder transfers enough appreciated property to offset any built-in losses of other property transferred. This avoidance opportunity exists because in making the comparison, each shareholder aggregates the adjusted bases and FMVs of his or her property transferred.

EXAMPLE C:2-34 ▶ Assume the same facts as in Example C:2-32 except the inventory's FMV is $12,000. In this case, total basis equals $29,000 and total FMV equals $30,000. Because total basis does not exceed total FMV, the limitation does not apply. Consequently, the corporation takes a carryover basis in each asset even though some assets have built-in losses. ◄

ASSUMPTION OF THE TRANSFEROR'S LIABILITIES

When a shareholder transfers property to a controlled corporation, the corporation often assumes the transferor's liabilities. The question arises as to whether the transferee corporation's assumption of liabilities is equivalent to a cash (boot) payment to the transferor. In certain types of transactions, the transferee's assumption of a transferor's liability is treated as a payment of cash to the transferor. For example, in a like-kind exchange, if a transferee assumes a transferor's liability, the transferor is treated as though he or she received a cash payment equal to the amount of the liability assumed. By contrast, if a transaction satisfies the Sec. 351 requirements, Sec. 357 provides relief from such treatment.

GENERAL RULE—SEC. 357(a). For the purpose of determining gain recognition, the transferee corporation's assumption of liabilities in a property transfer qualifying under Sec. 351 is *not* considered equivalent to the transferor's receipt of money. Consequently, the transferee corporation's assumption of liabilities does not result in the transferor's recognizing part or all of his or her realized gain. For the purpose of calculating the transferor's stock basis, however, the transferee corporation's assumption of liabilities *is* treated as money received and thus decreases the transferor's stock basis. Moreover, for the purpose of calculating the transferor's *realized* gain, the transferee corporation's assumption of liabilities is treated as part of the transferor's amount realized.[35]

EXAMPLE C:2-35 ▶ Roy and Eduardo transfer the following assets and liabilities to newly formed Palm Corporation:

---

[35] Sec. 358(d)(1).

Transferor	Asset/ Liability	Transferor's Adj. Basis	FMV	Consideration Received
Roy	Machinery	$15,000	$32,000	50 shares Palm stock
	Mortgage	8,000	—	Assumed by Palm
Eduardo	Cash	24,000	24,000	50 shares Palm stock

The transaction meets the requirements of Sec. 351. Roy's recognized gain is determined as follows:

FMV of stock received	$24,000
Plus: Palm's assumption of the mortgage liability	8,000
Amount realized	$32,000
Minus: Basis of machinery	(15,000)
Realized gain	$17,000
Boot received	$ –0–
Recognized gain	$ –0–

Although Palm's assumption of the mortgage liability increases Roy's amount realized, Roy recognizes none of his realized gain because the mortgage assumption is not considered to be boot (i.e., a cash equivalent). Eduardo recognizes no gain because he transferred only cash. Roy's stock basis is $7,000 ($15,000 basis of property transferred − $8,000 liability assumed by Palm). Eduardo's stock basis is $24,000. ◀

ADDITIONAL COMMENT

If any of the assumed liabilities are created for tax avoidance purposes, *all* the assumed liabilities are tainted.

ETHICAL POINT

Information about any transferor liabilities assumed by the transferee corporation must be reported with the transferee and transferor's tax returns for the year of transfer (see page C:2-36). Where a client asks a tax practitioner to ignore the fact that tax avoidance is the primary purpose for transferring a liability to a corporation, the tax practitioner must examine the ethical considerations of continuing to prepare returns and provide tax advice for the client.

The general rule of Sec. 357(a), however, has two exceptions. These exceptions, discussed below, relate to (1) transfers for the purpose of tax avoidance or without a bona fide business purpose and (2) transfers where the liabilities assumed by the corporation exceed the total basis of the property transferred.

TAX AVOIDANCE OR NO BONA FIDE BUSINESS PURPOSE—SEC. 357(b). All liabilities assumed by a controlled corporation *are* considered to be money received by the transferor, and therefore boot, if the principal purpose of the transfer of any portion of such liabilities is tax avoidance or if the liability transfer has no bona fide business purpose.

Liabilities the transfer of which might be considered to be motivated principally by tax avoidance are those the transferor incurred shortly before the transfer. Thus, the most important factor in determining whether a tax avoidance purpose exists may be the length of time between the incurrence of the liability and its transfer to, or assumption by, the corporation.

The assumption of liabilities normally is considered to have a business purpose if the transferor incurred the liabilities in the normal course of business or in the course of acquiring business property. Examples of liabilities without a bona fide business purpose and whose transfer would cause *all* liabilities transferred to be considered boot are personal obligations of the transferor, including a home mortgage or any other loans of a personal nature.

EXAMPLE C:2-36 ▶ David owns land having a $100,000 FMV and a $60,000 adjusted basis. The land is not encumbered by any liabilities. To obtain cash for his personal use, David transfers the land to his wholly owned corporation in exchange for additional stock and $25,000 cash. Because the cash is considered to be boot, David must recognize $25,000 of gain. Assume instead that David mortgages the land for $25,000 to obtain the needed cash. If shortly thereafter David transfers the land and the mortgage to his corporation for additional stock, the $25,000 mortgage assumed by the corporation will be considered to be boot because the transfer of the mortgage appears to have no bona fide business purpose. David's recognized gain will be $25,000, i.e., the lesser of the boot received ($25,000) or his realized gain ($40,000). This special liability rule prevents David from obtaining cash without boot recognition. ◀

LIABILITIES IN EXCESS OF BASIS—SEC. 357(c). Under Sec. 357(c), if the total amount of liabilities transferred to a controlled corporation exceeds the total adjusted basis of all property transferred, the excess liability is taxed as a gain to the transferor.

This rule applies regardless of whether the transferor realizes any gain or loss. The rationale for the rule is that the transferor has received a benefit (in the form of a release from liabilities) that exceeds his or her original investment in the transferred property. Therefore, the transferor should be taxed on this benefit. The character of the recognized gain depends on the type of property transferred to the corporation. The transferor's basis in any stock received is zero.

EXAMPLE C:2-37 ▶ Judy transfers $10,000 cash and land, a capital asset, to Duke Corporation in exchange for all its stock. At the time of the exchange, the land has a $70,000 adjusted basis and a $125,000 FMV. Duke assumes a $100,000 mortgage on the land for a bona fide business purpose. Although Judy receives no boot, Judy must recognize a $20,000 ($100,000 − $80,000) capital gain, the amount by which the liabilities assumed by Duke exceed the basis of the land and the cash. Judy's basis in the Duke stock is zero, computed as follows:

Judy's basis in the land transferred		$ 70,000
Plus:	Cash transferred	10,000
	Gain recognized	20,000
Minus:	Liabilities assumed by Duke	(100,000)
Judy's basis in the Duke stock		$ –0–

Note that, without the recogniton of the $20,000 gain, Judy's basis in the Duke stock would be a negative $20,000 ($80,000 − $100,000). ◀

STOP & THINK

Question: What are the fundamental differences between the liability exceptions of Sec. 357(b) and Sec. 357(c)?

Solution: Section 357(b) treats all "tainted" liabilities as boot so that gain recognition is the lesser of gain realized or the amount of boot. Excess liabilities under Sec. 357(c) are not treated as boot; they require gain recognition whether or not the transferor realizes any gain. Section 357(b) tends to be punitive in that the "tax avoidance" liabilities cause all the "offending" shareholder's transferred liabilities to be treated as boot even if the transfer of some liabilities do not have a tax avoidance purpose. Section 357(c) is not intended to be punitive. It recognizes that the shareholder has received an economic benefit to the extent of excess liabilities, and it prevents the occurrence of a negative stock basis. In short, Section 357(b) deters or punishes tax avoidance while Sec. 357(c) taxes an economic gain.

KEY POINT

Because of the "liabilities in excess of basis" exception, many cash basis transferor shareholders might inadvertently create recognized gain in a Sec. 351 transaction. However, a special exception exists that protects cash basis taxpayers. This exception provides that liabilities that would give rise to a deduction when paid are not treated as liabilities for purposes of Sec. 357(c).

LIABILITIES OF A CASH METHOD TAXPAYER—SEC. 357(c)(3). In a Sec. 351 tax-free exchange, special problems arise when a taxpayer using the cash or hybrid method of accounting transfers property and liabilities of an ongoing business to a corporation.[36] Often, the principal assets transferred are accounts receivable having a zero basis. Liabilities usually are transferred as well. Consequently, the amount of liabilities transferred may exceed the total basis (but not the FMV) of the property transferred.

Under the general rule of Sec. 357(c), the transferor recognizes gain equal to the amount by which the liabilities assumed exceed the total basis of the property transferred. Section 357(c)(3), however, provides that, in applying the general rule, the term *liabilities* does *not* include any amount that would give rise to a deduction when paid (e.g., accounts payable of a cash basis taxpayer). These amounts also are not considered liabilities for the purpose of determining the shareholder's basis in stock received.[37] Therefore, they generally do not reduce this basis. However, if after all other adjustments the stock's basis exceeds its FMV, these liabilities could reduce stock basis, but not below the stock's FMV.[38]

EXAMPLE C:2-38 ▶ Tracy operates a cash basis accounting practice as a sole proprietorship. She transfers the assets of her practice to Prime Corporation in exchange for all the Prime stock. The balance sheet for the transferred practice is as follows:

---

[36] Sec. 357(c)(3).
[37] Sec. 358(d)(2).

[38] Sec. 358(h)(1).

Assets and Liabilities	Adjusted Basis	FMV
Cash	$ 5,000	$ 5,000
Furniture	5,000	8,000
Accounts receivable	–0–	50,000
Total	$10,000	$63,000
Accounts payable (deductible expenses)	$ –0–	$25,000
Note payable (on office furniture)	2,000	2,000
Owner's equity	8,000	36,000
Total	$10,000	$63,000

If, for purposes of Sec. 357(c), the accounts payable were considered liabilities, the $27,000 of liabilities transferred (i.e., the $25,000 of accounts payable and the $2,000 note payable) would exceed the $10,000 total basis of assets transferred, and Troy would recognize a $17,000 gain. Because paying the $25,000 of accounts payable gives rise to a deduction, however, they are not considered liabilities for purposes of Sec. 357(c). On the other hand, the $2,000 note payable *is* considered a liability for this purpose because paying it would not give rise to a deduction. Thus, the total liabilities transferred to Prime amount to only $2,000. Because that amount does not exceed the $10,000 total basis of the assets transferred, Tracy recognizes no gain. Moreover, the accounts payable are not considered liabilities for purposes of computing Tracy's basis in her stock because the stock's basis ($8,000) does not exceed its FMV ($36,000). Thus, her basis in the Prime stock is $8,000 ($10,000 – $2,000). ◀

Topic Review C:2-3 summarizes the liability assumption and acquisition rules of Sec. 357.

OTHER CONSIDERATIONS IN A SEC. 351 EXCHANGE

RECAPTURE OF DEPRECIATION. If a Sec. 351 exchange is completely nontaxable (i.e., the transferor receives no boot), no depreciation is recaptured. Instead, the corporation inherits the entire amount of the transferor's recapture potential. Where the transferor recognizes some depreciation recapture as ordinary income (e.g., because of boot recognition), the transferee inherits the remaining recapture potential. If the transferee corporation subsequently disposes of the depreciated property, the corporation is subject to recapture rules on depreciation it claimed subsequent to the transfer, plus the recapture potential it inherited from the transferor.

EXAMPLE C:2-39 ▶ Azeem transfers machinery having a $25,000 original cost, an $18,000 adjusted basis, and a $35,000 FMV for all 100 shares of Wheel Corporation stock. Before the transfer, Azeem used the machinery in his business and claimed $7,000 of depreciation. In the transfer, Azeem recaptures no depreciation, and Wheel inherits the $7,000 recapture potential. After claiming an additional $2,000 of depreciation, Wheel has a $16,000 adjusted basis in the machinery. If

Topic Review C:2-3

Liability Assumption and Acquisition Rules of Sec. 357

1. *General Rule (Sec. 357(a)):* A transferee corporation's assumption of liabilities in a Sec. 351 exchange is not treated as boot by the shareholder for gain recognition purposes. On the other hand, the assumption of liabilities is treated as the receipt of money for purposes of determining the transferor's stock basis and amount realized.
2. *Exception 1 (Sec. 357(b)):* All liabilities assumed by a transferee corporation *are* considered to be money/boot received by the transferor if the principal purpose of the transfer of any of the liabilities is tax avoidance or if no bona fide business purpose exists for the transfer.
3. *Exception 2 (Sec. 357(c)):* If the total amount of liabilities assumed by a transferee corporation exceeds the total basis of property transferred, the transferor recognizes the excess as gain.
4. *Special Rule (Sec. 357(c)(3)):* For purposes of Exception 2, the term *liabilities* for a transferor using a cash or hybrid method of accounting does not include any amount that would give rise to a deduction when paid.

Wheel now sells the machinery for $33,000, it must recognize a $17,000 ($33,000 − $16,000) gain. Of this gain, $9,000 is ordinary income recaptured under Sec. 1245. The remaining $8,000 is a Sec. 1231 gain. ◄

COMPUTING DEPRECIATION. When a shareholder transfers depreciable property to a corporation in a nontaxable Sec. 351 exchange and the shareholder has not fully depreciated the property, the corporation must use the depreciation method and recovery period used by the transferor.[39] For the year of the transfer, the depreciation must be allocated between the transferor and the transferee corporation according to the number of months each party held the property. The transferee corporation is assumed to have held the property for the entire month in which the property was transferred.[40]

EXAMPLE C:2-40 ► On June 10 of Year 1, Carla paid $6,000 for a computer (five-year property for MACRS purposes), which she used in her sole proprietorship business. In Year 1, she claimed $1,200 (0.20 × $6,000) of depreciation. She did not elect Sec. 179 expensing and did not claim any bonus depreciation. On February 10 of Year 2, she transfers the computer and other sole proprietorship assets to King Corporation in exchange for King stock. Because Sec. 351 applies, she recognizes no gain or loss. King must use the same MACRS recovery period and method that Carla used. Depreciation for Year 2 is $1,920 (0.32 × $6,000). That amount must be allocated between Carla and King. The computer is considered to have been held by Carla for one month and by King for 11 months (including the month of transfer). The Year 2 depreciation amounts claimed by Carla and King are calculated as follows:

Carla	$6,000 × 0.32 × 1/12 = $ 160
King Corporation	$6,000 × 0.32 × 11/12 = $1,760

King's basis in the computer is calculated as follows:

Original cost		$6,000
Minus:	Year 1 depreciation claimed by Carla	(1,200)
	Year 2 depreciation claimed by Carla	(160)
Adjusted basis on transfer date		$4,640

King's depreciation for Year 2 and subsequent years is as follows:

Year 2 (as computed above)	$1,760
Year 3 ($6,000 × 0.1920)	1,152
Year 4 ($6,000 × 0.1152)	691
Year 5 ($6,000 × 0.1152)	691
Year 6 ($6,000 × 0.0576)	346
Total	$4,640 ◄

If the transferee corporation's basis in the depreciable property exceeds the transferor's basis (e.g., as a result of an upward adjustment to reflect gain recognized by the transferor), the corporation treats the excess amount as newly purchased MACRS property and uses the recovery period and method applicable to the class of property transferred.[41]

EXAMPLE C:2-41 ► Assume the same facts as in Example C:2-40 except that, in addition to King stock, Carla receives a King note. Consequently, she must recognize $1,000 of gain on the transfer of the computer. King's basis in the computer is calculated as follows:

Original cost	$6,000
Depreciation claimed by Carla	(1,360)
Adjusted basis on transfer date	$4,640
Plus: Gain recognized by Carla	1,000
Basis to King on transfer date	$5,640

The additional $1,000 of basis is depreciated as though it were separate, newly purchased five-year MACRS property. Thus, King claims depreciation of $200 (0.20 × $1,000) on this portion of

---

[39] Sec. 168(i)(7).
[40] Prop. Reg. Secs. 1.168-5(b)(2)(i)(B), 1.168-5(b)(4)(i), and 1.168-5(b)(8).
[41] Prop. Reg. Sec. 1.168-5(b)(7).

the basis in addition to the $1,760 of depreciation on the $4,640 carryover basis. Alternatively, King could elect to expense the $1,000 "new" basis under Sec. 179. ◄

ASSIGNMENT OF INCOME DOCTRINE. The **assignment of income doctrine** holds that income is taxable to the person who earned it and that it may not be assigned to another person for tax purposes.[42] The question arises as to whether the assignment of income doctrine applies where a cash method taxpayer transfers uncollected accounts receivable to a corporation in a Sec. 351 exchange. Specifically, who must recognize the income when it is collected—the taxpayer who transferred the receivable or the corporation that now owns and collects on the receivable? The IRS has ruled that the doctrine does *not* apply in a Sec. 351 exchange if the taxpayer transfers substantially all the business assets and liabilities, and a bona fide business purpose exists for the transfer. Instead, the accounts receivable take a zero basis in the corporation's hands, and the corporation includes their value in its income when it collects on the receivables.[43]

EXAMPLE C:2-42 ▶ For a bona fide business purpose, Ruth, a cash basis taxpayer, transfers all the assets and liabilities of her legal practice to Legal Services Corporation in exchange for all of Legal Services stock. The assets include $30,000 of accounts receivable that will generate earnings that Ruth has not included in her gross income. Because Ruth transfers substantially all the business assets and liabilities for a bona fide business purpose, the assignment of income doctrine does not apply to the receivables transferred, and Legal Services takes a zero basis in the receivables. Subsequently, Legal Services includes the value of the receivables in its income as it collects on them. ◄

The question of whether a transferee corporation can deduct the accounts payable transferred to it in a nontaxable transfer has frequently been litigated.[44] Most courts have held that ordinarily expenses are deductible only by the party that incurred those liabilities in the course of its trade or business. However, the IRS has ruled that in a nontaxable exchange the transferee corporation may deduct the payments it makes to satisfy the transferred accounts payable even though they arose in the transferor's business.[45]

CHOICE OF CAPITAL STRUCTURE

When a corporation is formed, the way it is financed will determine its capital structure. The corporation may obtain capital from shareholders, nonshareholders, and creditors. In exchange for their capital, shareholders may receive common or preferred stock; nonshareholders may receive benefits such as employment or special rates on products sold by the corporation; and creditors may receive long- or short-term debt. As explained below, each of these alternatives has tax advantages and disadvantages for the shareholders, creditors, and corporation.

CHARACTERIZATION OF OBLIGATIONS AS DEBT OR EQUITY

The deductibility of interest payments creates an incentive for corporations to incur as much debt as possible. Because debt financing often resembles equity financing (e.g., preferred stock), the IRS and the courts have refused to accept the form of the security as controlling.[46] In some cases, debt obligations that possess equity characteristics have been treated as common or preferred stock for tax purposes. In determining the appropriate tax treatment, the courts have relied on a number of factors.

[42] See, for example, *Lucas v. Guy C. Earl*, 8 AFTR 10287, 2 USTC ¶496 (USSC, 1930).
[43] Rev. Rul. 80-198, 1980-2 C.B. 113.
[44] See, for example, *Wilford E. Thatcher v. CIR*, 37 AFTR 2d 76-1068, 76-1 USTC ¶9324 (9th Cir., 1976), and *John P. Bongiovanni v. CIR*, 31 AFTR 2d 73-409, 73-1 USTC ¶9133 (2nd Cir., 1972).

[45] Rev. Rul. 80-198, 1980-2 C.B. 113.
[46] See, for example, *Aqualane Shores, Inc. v. CIR*, 4 AFTR 2d 5346, 59-2 USTC ¶9632 (5th Cir., 1959) and *Sun Properties, Inc. v. U.S.*, 47 AFTR 273, 55-1 USTC ¶9261 (5th Cir., 1955).

Congress enacted Sec. 385 to establish a workable standard for determining whether a security is debt or equity. Section 385 provides that the following factors be considered in the determination:

HISTORICAL NOTE

The Treasury Department at one time issued proposed and final regulations covering Sec. 385. These regulations were the subject of so much criticism that the Treasury Department eventually withdrew them. Section 385, however, makes it clear that Congress wants the Treasury Department to make further attempts at clarifying the debt-equity issue. So far, the Treasury Department has issued no "new" proposed or final regulations.

► Whether there is a written unconditional promise to pay on demand or on a specified date a certain sum of money in return for adequate consideration in the form of money or money's worth, in addition to an unconditional promise to pay a fixed rate of interest

► Whether the debt is subordinate to, or preferred over, other indebtedness of the corporation

► The ratio of corporate debt to equity

► Whether the debt is convertible into stock of the corporation

► The relationship between holdings of stock in the corporation and holdings of the interest in question[47]

DEBT CAPITAL

Various provisions govern the tax treatment of (1) the issuance of debt; (2) the payment of interest on debt; and (3) the extinguishment, retirement, or worthlessness of debt. The tax implications of each of these events are examined below.

SELF-STUDY QUESTION

From a tax perspective, why is the distinction between debt and equity important?

ANSWER

Interest paid with respect to a debt instrument is deductible by the payor corporation. Dividends paid with respect to an equity instrument are not deductible by the payor corporation. Thus, the determination of whether an instrument is debt or equity can provide different results to the payor corporation. Different results apply to the payee as well. Qualified dividends are subject to the 15% maximum tax rate (through 2012) while interest is ordinary income.

ISSUANCE OF DEBT. If a transferor transfers appreciated property in exchange for stock, the transfer will be nontaxable, provided the Sec. 351 requirements have been met. On the other hand, if the transferor transfers appreciated property in exchange for corporate debt as part of a Sec. 351 exchange, the FMV of the debt received will be treated as boot, possibly leading to gain recognition.

PAYMENT OF INTEREST. Interest paid on indebtedness is deductible by the corporation in deriving its taxable income.[48] Moreover, a corporation is not subject to the investment interest deduction limitation applicable to individual taxpayers. By contrast, the corporation cannot deduct dividends paid on equity securities.

If a corporation issues a debt instrument at a discount, Sec. 1272 requires the holder to amortize the original issue discount over the term of the obligation and treat the accrual as interest income. The debtor corporation amortizes the original issue discount over the term of the obligation and treats the accrual as an additional cost of borrowing.[49] If the corporation repurchases the debt instrument for more than the issue price (plus any original issue discount deducted as interest), the corporation deducts the excess of the purchase price over the issue price (adjusted for any amortization of original issue discount) as interest expense.[50]

Under Sec. 171, if a corporation issues a debt instrument at a premium, the holder may elect to amortize the premium over the term of the obligation and treat the accrual as a reduction in interest income earned on the obligation. For the debtor corporation, the premium reduces the amount of deductible interest.[51] If the corporation repurchases the debt instrument at a price greater than the issue price (minus any premium treated as income), the corporation deducts the excess of the purchase price over the issue price (adjusted for any amortization of premium) as interest expense.[52]

EXTINGUISHMENT OF DEBT. Generally, the retirement of debt is not a taxable event. Thus, a debtor corporation's extinguishing an obligation at face value does not result in the creditor's recognizing gain or loss. However, amounts received by the holder

---

[47] See also *O.H. Kruse Grain & Milling v. CIR,* 5 AFTR 2d 1544, 60-2 USTC ¶9490 (9th Cir., 1960), which lists additional factors that the courts might consider.

[48] Sec. 163(a).

[49] Sec. 163(e).

[50] Reg. Sec. 1.163-7(c).

[51] Reg. Sec. 1.163-12.

[52] Reg. Sec. 1.163-7(c).

of a debt instrument (e.g., note, bond, or debenture) at the time of its retirement are deemed to be "in exchange for" the obligation. Thus, if the obligation is a capital asset in the holder's hands, the holder must recognize a capital gain or loss if the amount received differs from its face value or adjusted basis, unless the difference is due to original issue or market discount.

EXAMPLE C:2-43 ▶

ADDITIONAL COMMENT

Even though debt often is thought of as a preferred instrument because of the deductibility of the interest paid, the debt must be repaid at its maturity, whereas stock has no specified maturity date. Also, interest usually must be paid at regular intervals, whereas dividends do not have to be declared if sufficient funds are not available to pay them or if the corporation needs to retain funds for operations or growth.

SELF-STUDY QUESTION

Does the transferee corporation recognize gain on the receipt of appreciated property from a shareholder?

ANSWER

No. A corporation does not recognize gain when it receives property from its shareholders, whether or not it exchanges its own stock. However, the transfer must qualify as a Sec. 351 exchange or the transaction will be taxable to the shareholders.

Titan Corporation issues a ten-year note at its $1,000 face amount. On the date of issuance, Rick purchases the note for $1,000. Because of a decline in interest rates, Titan calls the note at a price of $1,050 payable to each note holder. Rick reports the premium as a $50 capital gain, and Titan deducts as interest expense total premiums paid to all its note holders. ◀

Table C:2-2 presents a comparison of the tax advantages and disadvantages of a corporation's using debt in its capital structure.

EQUITY CAPITAL

Corporations can raise equity capital through the issuance of various types of stock. Some corporations issue only a single class of stock, whereas others issue numerous classes of stock. Reasons for the use of multiple classes of stock include

▶ Permitting nonfamily employees of family owned corporations to obtain an equity interest in the business while keeping voting control in the hands of family members

▶ Financing a **closely held corporation** through the issuance of preferred stock to an outside investor, while leaving voting control in the hands of existing common stockholders.

Table C:2-3 lists some of the major tax advantages and disadvantages of using common and preferred stock in a corporation's capital structure.

CAPITAL CONTRIBUTIONS BY SHAREHOLDERS

A corporation recognizes no income when it receives money or noncash property as a capital contribution from a shareholder.[53] If the shareholders make voluntary pro rata payments to a corporation but do not receive any additional stock, the payments are treated as additional consideration for the stock already owned.[54] The shareholders' respective bases in their stock are increased by the amount of money contributed, plus the basis of any noncash property contributed, plus any gain recognized by the shareholders. The

▼ TABLE C:2-2

Tax Advantages and Disadvantages of Using Debt in a Corporation's Capital Structure

Advantages:
1. A corporation can deduct interest paid on a debt obligation.
2. Shareholders do not recognize income in a debt retirement as they would in a stock redemption.

Disadvantages:
1. If at the time the corporation is formed or later when a shareholder makes a capital contribution, the shareholder receives a debt instrument in exchange for property, the debt is treated as boot, and the shareholder recognizes gain to the extent of the lesser of the boot's FMV or the realized gain.
2. If debt becomes worthless or is sold at less than its face value, the loss generally is a nonbusiness bad debt (treated as a short-term capital loss) or a capital loss. Section 1244 ordinary loss treatment applies only to stock (see pages C:2-32 and C:2-33).

---

[53] Sec. 118(a). [54] Reg. Sec. 1.118-1.

▼ TABLE C:2-3

Tax Advantages and Disadvantages of Using Equity in a Corporation's Capital Structure

Advantages:

1. A 70%, 80%, or 100% dividends-received deduction is available to a corporate shareholder who receives dividends. A similar deduction is not available for the receipt of interest (see Chapter C:3).
2. A shareholder can receive common and preferred stock in a tax-free corporate formation under Sec. 351 or a nontaxable reorganization under Sec. 368 without recognizing gain (see Chapters C:2 and C:7, respectively). Receipt of debt securities in each of these two types of transactions generally results in the shareholder's recognizing gain.
3. Common and preferred stock can be distributed tax-free to the corporation's shareholders as a stock dividend. Some common and preferred stock distributions, however, may be taxable as dividends under Sec. 305(b). Distributions of debt obligations generally are taxable as a dividend (see Chapter C:4).
4. Common or preferred stock that the shareholder sells or exchanges or that becomes worthless is eligible for ordinary loss treatment, subject to limitations, under Sec. 1244 (see pages C:2-32 and C:2-33). The loss recognized on similar transactions involving debt securities generally is treated as capital in character.
5. Section 1202 excludes 50% of capital gains realized on the sale or exchange of qualified small business (C) corporation stock that has been held for more than five years. For qualified stock acquired after February 17, 2009 and before September 28, 2010, the exclusion is 75%, and for qualified stock acquired after September 27, 2010 and before January 1, 2012, the exclusion is 100%.
6. Through 2012, qualified dividends are taxed at a maximum 15% tax rate.

Disadvantages:

1. Dividends are not deductible in determining a corporation's taxable income.
2. Redemption of common or preferred stock generally is taxable to the shareholders as a dividend. Under the general rule, none of the redemption distribution offsets the shareholder's basis for the stock investment. Redemption of common and preferred stock is eligible for exchange treatment only in situations specified in Secs. 302 and 303 (see Chapter C:4).
3. Preferred stock issued to a shareholder as a dividend may be treated as Sec. 306 stock. Sale, exchange, or redemption of such stock can result in the recognition of ordinary income instead of capital gain (see Chapter C:4). Through 2012, this ordinary income is taxed as a "deemed dividend" at 15%.

TYPICAL MISCONCEPTION

The characteristics of preferred stock can be similar to those of a debt security. Often, a regular dividend is required at a stated rate, much like what would be required with respect to a debt obligation. The holder of preferred stock, like a debt holder, may have preferred liquidation rights over holders of common stock. Also, preferred stock is not required to possess voting rights. However, differences remain. A corporation can deduct its interest expense but not dividends. Interest income is ordinary income to shareholders, but qualified dividends are subject to the 15% maximum tax rate (through 2012).

corporation's basis in any property received as a capital contribution from a shareholder equals the shareholder's basis, plus any gain recognized by the shareholder.[55] Normally, the shareholders recognize no gain when they transfer property to a controlled corporation as a capital contribution.

EXAMPLE C:2-44 ▶

Dot and Fred each own 50% of the stock in Trail Corporation, and each has a $50,000 basis in that stock. Later, as a voluntary contribution to Trail's capital, Dot contributes $40,000 in cash and Fred contributes property having a $25,000 basis and a $40,000 FMV. As a result of the contributions, Trail recognizes no income. Dot's basis in her stock is increased to $90,000 ($50,000 + $40,000), and Fred's basis in his stock is increased to $75,000 ($50,000 + $25,000). Trail's basis in the property contributed by Fred is $25,000—the same as Fred's basis in the property. ◀

If a shareholder-lender gratuitously forgives corporate debt, the debt forgiveness might be treated as a capital contribution equal to the principal amount of the forgiven debt. A determination of whether debt forgiveness is a capital contribution is based on the facts and circumstances surrounding the event.

---

[55] Sec. 362(a).

WHAT WOULD YOU DO IN THIS SITUATION?

Your corporate client wants to issue 100-year bonds. The corporation's CEO reads *The Wall Street Journal* regularly and has observed that similar bonds have been issued by several companies, including several Fortune 500 companies. He touts the fact that the interest rate on these bonds is slightly more than that for 30-year U.S. Treasury bonds. In addition, he expresses the belief that interest on the bonds would be deductible, whereas dividends on preferred or common stock would be nondeductible. You are concerned that the IRS might treat the bonds as equity because of their extraordinarily long term. If the IRS does treat the bonds as such, it might recharacterize the "interest" as dividends and deny your client an interest deduction.

What advice would you give the client now regarding the bond issue? What advice would you give it when it prepares its tax return after the new bonds have been issued?

CAPITAL CONTRIBUTIONS BY NONSHAREHOLDERS

BOOK-TO-TAX ACCOUNTING COMPARISON

The IRC requires capital contributions of property other than money made by a nonshareholder to be reported at a zero basis. Financial accounting rules, however, require donated capital to be reported at the FMV of the asset on the financial accounting books. Neither set of rules requires the property's value to be included in income.

Nonshareholders sometimes contribute capital to a corporation in the form of money or other property. For example, a city government might contribute land to a corporation to induce the corporation to locate within the city and provide jobs for citizens of the municipality. Such contributions are excluded from the corporation's gross income if the money or property contributed is neither a payment for goods or services nor a subsidy to induce the corporation to limit production.[56]

If a nonshareholder contributes noncash property to a corporation, the corporation's basis in such property is zero.[57] The zero basis precludes the corporation from claiming either a depreciation deduction or capital recovery offset with respect to the contributed property.

If a nonshareholder contributes money, the basis of any property acquired with the money during a 12-month period beginning on the day the corporation received the contribution is reduced by the amount of the money. This rule limits the corporation's deduction to the amount of funds it invested in the property. The amount of any money received from nonshareholders that the corporation did not spend to purchase property during the 12-month period reduces the basis of any noncash property held by the corporation on the last day of the 12-month period.[58]

The basis reduction applies to the corporation's property in the following order:

1. Depreciable property
2. Amortizable property
3. Depletable property
4. All other property

In the sequence of these downward adjustments, however, a property's basis may not be reduced below zero.

EXAMPLE C:2-45 ▶

To induce the company to locate in the municipality, the City of San Antonio contributes to Circle Corporation $100,000 in cash and a tract of land having a $500,000 FMV. Because of a downturn in Circle's business, the company spends only $70,000 of the contributed funds over a 12-month period. Circle recognizes no income as a result of the contribution. Circle's bases in the land and other property purchased with the contributed funds are zero. The basis of Circle's remaining assets, starting with its depreciable property, must be reduced by the $30,000 ($100,000 − $70,000) contributed but not spent. ◀

---

[56] Reg. Sec. 1.118-1.
[57] Sec. 362(c)(1).

[58] Sec. 362(c)(2).

WORTHLESSNESS OF STOCK OR DEBT OBLIGATIONS

Investors who purchase stock in, or lend money to, a corporation usually want to earn a profit and recover their investment. Some investments, however, do not offer an adequate return on capital, and an investor may lose part or all of the investment. In this event, the securities evidencing the investment become worthless. This section examines the tax consequences of stock or debt securities becoming worthless.

SECURITIES

A debt or equity **security** that becomes worthless results in a capital loss for the investor as of the last day of the tax year in which the security becomes worthless. For purposes of this rule, the term *security* includes (1) a share of stock in a corporation; (2) a right to subscribe for, or the right to receive, a share of stock in a corporation; or (3) a bond, debenture, note, or other evidence of indebtedness with interest coupons or in registered form issued by a corporation.[59]

In some situations, investors recognize an ordinary loss when a security becomes worthless. Investors who contribute capital, either in the form of equity or debt to a corporation that later fails, generally prefer ordinary losses because such losses are deductible against ordinary income. Ordinary losses that generate an NOL can be carried back two years or forward up to 20 years. In general, ordinary loss treatment is available in the following circumstances:

▶ *Securities that are noncapital assets.* An ordinary loss occurs when a security that is a noncapital asset in the hands of the taxpayer is sold or exchanged or becomes totally worthless. Securities in this category include those held as inventory by a securities dealer.

▶ *Affiliated corporations.* A domestic corporation can claim an ordinary loss for any affiliated corporation's security that becomes worthless during the tax year. The domestic corporation must own at least 80% of the total voting power of all classes of stock entitled to vote, and at least 80% of each class of nonvoting stock (other than stock limited and preferred as to dividends). At least 90% of the aggregate gross receipts of the loss corporation for all tax years must have been derived from nonpassive income sources.

▶ *Section 1244 stock.* Section 1244 permits a shareholder to claim an ordinary loss if qualifying stock issued by a small business corporation is sold or exchanged or becomes worthless. This treatment is available only to an individual who was issued the qualifying stock or who was a partner in a partnership at the time the partnership acquired the qualifying stock. In the latter case, the partner's distributive share of partnership losses includes the loss sustained by the partnership on such stock. Ordinary loss treatment is not available for stock inherited, received as a gift, or purchased from another shareholder. The ordinary loss is limited to $50,000 per year (or $100,000 if the taxpayer is married and files a joint return). Losses exceeding the dollar ceiling in any given year are considered capital in character.

EXAMPLE C:2-46 ▶ For $175,000, Tammy and her husband Cole purchased 25% of Minor Corporation's initial offering of a single class of stock. Minor is a small business corporation, and the Minor stock satisfies all Sec. 1244 requirements. On September 1 of the current year, Minor filed for bankruptcy. Two years later, the bankruptcy court notifies shareholders that the Minor stock is worthless. In that year, Tammy and Cole can deduct $100,000 of their initial investment as an ordinary loss. The remaining $75,000 loss is treated as capital in character. ◀

If a corporation issues Sec. 1244 stock for property whose adjusted basis exceeds its FMV immediately before the exchange, the stock's basis is reduced to the property's FMV for the purpose of determining the ordinary loss amount.

---

[59] Sec. 165(g).

EXAMPLE C:2-47 ▶ In a Sec. 351 nontaxable exchange, Penny transfers to Small Corporation property having a $40,000 adjusted basis and a $32,000 FMV for 100 shares of Sec. 1244 stock. Ordinarily, Penny's basis in the stock would be $40,000. However, for Sec. 1244 purposes, her stock basis is the property's FMV, or $32,000. If Penny sells the stock for $10,000, her recognized loss is $30,000 ($10,000 − $40,000). Her ordinary loss under Sec. 1244 is $22,000 ($10,000 − $32,000 Sec. 1244 basis). The remaining $8,000 loss is treated as capital in character. (Note also that, under Sec. 362(e)(2), Small would reduce its basis in the transferred property to its $32,000 FMV.) ◀

Section 1244 loss treatment requires no special election. Investors, however, should be aware that, if they fail to satisfy certain requirements, ordinary loss treatment will be unavailable, and their loss will be treated as capital in character. The requirements are as follows:

▶ The issuing corporation must be a small business corporation at the time it issues the stock. A small business corporation is a corporation that receives in the aggregate $1 million or less in money or noncash property (other than stock and securities) in exchange for its stock.[60]

▶ The issuing corporation must have derived more than 50% of its aggregate gross receipts from "active" sources (i.e., other than royalties, rents, dividends, interest, annuities, and gains on sales of stock and securities) during the five most recent tax years ending before the date on which the shareholder sells or exchanges the stock or the stock becomes worthless.

If a shareholder contributes additional money or property to a corporation after acquiring Sec. 1244 stock, the amount of ordinary loss recognized on the sale, exchange, or worthlessness of the Sec. 1244 stock is limited to the shareholder's capital contribution at the time the corporation issued the stock.

UNSECURED DEBT OBLIGATIONS

In addition to holding an equity interest, shareholders may lend funds to the corporation. The type of loss allowed if the corporation does not repay the borrowed funds depends on the nature of the loan or advance.

If the unpaid loan was not evidenced by a security (i.e., an unsecured debt obligation), it is considered to be either business or nonbusiness bad debt. Nonbusiness bad debts are treated less favorably than business bad debts. Under Sec. 166, nonbusiness bad debts are deductible as short-term capital losses (up to the $3,000 annual limit for net capital losses) when they become totally worthless. Business bad debts are deductible as ordinary losses without limitation when they become either partially or totally worthless. The IRS generally treats a loan made by a shareholder to a corporation in connection with his or her stock investment as nonbusiness in character.[61] It is understandable why a shareholder might attempt to rebut this presumption with the argument that a business purpose exists for the loan.

An advance in connection with the shareholder's trade or business, such as a loan to protect the shareholder's employment at the corporation, may be treated as an ordinary loss under the business bad debt rules. Regulation Sec. 1.166-5(b) states that whether a bad debt is business or nonbusiness related depends on the taxpayer's motive for making the advance. The debt is business related if the necessary relationship between the loss and the conduct of the taxpayer's trade or business exists at the time the debt was incurred, acquired, or became worthless.

In *U.S. v. Edna Generes,* the U.S. Supreme Court held that where multiple motives exist for advancing funds to a corporation, such as where a shareholder-employee advances funds to protect his or her employment, determining whether the advance is business or nonbusiness related must be based on the "dominant motivation" for the

TAX STRATEGY TIP

If a shareholder contributes additional money or property to an existing corporation, he or she should be sure to receive additional stock in the exchange so that it will qualify for Sec. 1244 treatment if all requirements are met. If the shareholder does not receive additional stock, the increased basis of existing stock resulting from the capital contribution will not qualify for Sec. 1244 treatment.

---

[60] Regulation Sec. 1.1244(c)-2 provides special rules for designating which shares of stock are eligible for Sec. 1244 treatment when the corporation has issued more than $1 million of stock.

[61] The assumption is made here that the loan is not considered to be an additional capital contribution. In such a case, the Sec. 165 worthless security rules apply instead of the Sec. 166 bad debt rules.

advance.[62] If the advance is only "significantly motivated" by considerations relating to the taxpayer's trade or business, such motivation will not establish a proximate relationship between the bad debt and the taxpayer's trade or business. Therefore, it may result in a nonbusiness bad debt characterization. On the other hand, if the advance is "dominantly motivated" by considerations relating to the taxpayer's trade or business, such motivation usually is sufficient to establish such a proximate relationship. Therefore, it may result in a business bad debt characterization.

Factors deemed important in determining the character of bad debt include the taxpayer's equity in the corporation relative to compensation paid by the corporation. For example, a modest salary paid by the corporation relative to substantial stockholdings in the corporation suggests an investment motive for the advance. Conversely, a substantial salary paid by the corporation relative to modest stockholdings suggests a business motive for the advance. The business motive at issue is the protection of the employee-lender's employment because the advance may help save the business from failing. Reasonable minds may differ on what is substantial and what is modest, and monetary stakes often are high in these cases. Consequently, the determination frequently involves litigation.

EXAMPLE C:2-48 ▶

Top Corporation employs Mary as its legal counsel. It pays Mary an annual salary of $100,000. In March of the current year, Mary advances the corporation $50,000 to assist it financially. In October of the current year, Top declares bankruptcy and liquidates. In the liquidation, Mary and other investors receive 10 cents on every dollar advanced. If Mary can show that her advance was dominantly motivated by her employment, her $45,000 ($50,000 × 0.90) loss will be treated as business bad debt, ordinary in character, and fully deductible in the current year. On the other hand, if Mary shows only that the advance was significantly motivated by her employment, her $45,000 loss will be treated as nonbusiness bad debt, capital in character, and deductible in this year and in subsequent years only to the extent of $3,000 in excess of any capital gains she recognizes. ◀

A loss sustained by a shareholder who guarantees a loan made by a third party to the corporation generally is treated as a nonbusiness bad debt. The loss can be claimed only to the extent the shareholder actually pays the third party and is unable to recover the payment from the debtor corporation.[63] Occasionally, the IRS treats the amount of a shareholder advance as additional paid-in capital. In such circumstances, any worthless security loss the shareholder claims for his or her equity investment may be increased by this amount.

TAX PLANNING CONSIDERATIONS

AVOIDING SEC. 351

Section 351 is not an elective provision. If its conditions are met, a corporate formation is tax-free, even if the taxpayer does not want it to be. Most often, taxpayers desire Sec. 351 treatment because it allows them to defer gains when transferring appreciated property to a corporation. In some cases, however, shareholders find such treatment disadvantageous because they would like to recognize gain or loss on the property transferred.

AVOIDING NONRECOGNITION OF LOSSES UNDER SEC. 351. If a shareholder transfers to a corporation property that has declined in value, the shareholder may want to recognize the loss so it can offset income from other sources. The shareholder can recognize the loss only if the Sec. 351 nonrecognition rules and the Sec. 267 related party rules do not apply to the exchange.

Avoiding Sec. 351 treatment requires that one or more of its requirements not be met. The simplest way to accomplish this objective is to ensure that the transferors of property do not receive 80% of the voting stock.

---

[62] 29 AFTR 2d 72-609, 72-1 USTC ¶9259 (USSC, 1972).   [63] Reg. Sec. 1.166-8(a).

Even if a shareholder avoids Sec. 351 treatment, he or she still may not be able to recognize the losses because of the Sec. 267 related party transaction rules. Under Sec. 267(a)(1), if the shareholder owns more than 50% of the corporation's stock, directly or indirectly, he or she is a related party and therefore cannot recognize loss on an exchange of property for the corporation's stock or other property. If the transferors of property receive less than 80% of the corporation's voting stock and if the transferor of loss property does not own more than 50% of the stock, the transferor of loss property may recognize the loss.

EXAMPLE C:2-49 ▶

Lynn owns property having a $100,000 basis and a $60,000 FMV. If Lynn transfers the property to White Corporation in a nontaxable exchange under Sec. 351, she will not recognize a loss, which will be deferred until she sells her White stock. If the Sec. 351 requirements are not met, she will recognize a $40,000 loss in the year she transfers the property. If Lynn receives 50% of the White stock in exchange for her property, Cathy, an unrelated individual, receives 25% of the stock in exchange for $30,000 cash, and John, another unrelated individual, receives the remaining 25% for services performed, the Sec. 351 control requirement will not be met because the transferors of property receive less than 80% of the White stock. Moreover, Lynn will not be a related party under Sec. 267 because she will not own more than 50% of the stock either directly or indirectly. Therefore, Lynn will recognize a $40,000 loss on the exchange. ◀

ADDITIONAL COMMENT

Any potential built-in gain on property transferred to the transferee corporation is duplicated because such gain may be recognized at the corporate level and at the shareholder level. This double taxation may be another reason for avoiding the nonrecognition of gain under Sec. 351.

AVOIDING NONRECOGNITION OF GAIN UNDER SEC. 351. Sometimes a transferor would like to recognize gain when he or she transfers appreciated property to a corporation so the transferee corporation can get a stepped-up basis in the transferred property. Some other reasons for recognizing gain are as follows:

▶ If the transferor's gain is capital in character, he or she can offset this gain with capital losses from other transactions.

▶ Individual long-term capital gains are taxed at a maximum 15% rate (through 2012). This rate is below the 35% top marginal tax rate applicable to corporate-level capital gains.

▶ The corporation's marginal tax rate may be higher than a noncorporate transferor's marginal tax rate. In such case, it might be beneficial for the transferor to recognize gain so the corporation can get a stepped-up basis in the property. A stepped-up basis would either reduce the corporation's gain when it later sells the property or allow the corporation to claim greater depreciation deductions when it uses the property.

A transferor who does not wish to recognize gain on the transfer of appreciated property to a corporation can avoid Sec. 351 treatment through one of the following planning techniques:

▶ The transferor can sell the property to the controlled corporation for cash.

▶ The transferor can sell the property to the controlled corporation for cash and debt. This transaction involves relatively less cash than the previous transaction. However, the sale may be treated as a nontaxable exchange if the IRS recharacterizes the debt as equity.[64]

▶ The transferor can sell the property to a third party for cash and have the third party contribute the property to the corporation for stock.

▶ The transferor can have the corporation distribute sufficient boot property so that, even if Sec. 351 applies to the transaction, he or she will recognize gain.

▶ The transferors can fail one or more of the Sec. 351 tests. For example, if the transferors do not own 80% of the voting stock immediately after the exchange, the Sec. 351 control requirement will not have been met, and they will recognize gain.

▶ To trigger gain recognition under Sec. 357(b) or (c), the transferors may transfer to the corporation either debt that exceeds the basis of all property transferred or debt that lacks a business purpose.

---

[64] See, for example, *Aqualane Shores, Inc. v. CIR*, 4 AFTR 2d 5346, 59-2 USTC ¶9632 (5th Cir., 1959) and *Sun Properties, Inc. v. U.S.*, 47 AFTR 273, 55-1 USTC ¶9261 (5th Cir., 1955).

EXAMPLE C:2-50 ▶ Ten years ago, Jaime purchased land as an investment for $100,000. The land is now worth $500,000. Jaime plans to transfer the land to Bell Corporation in exchange for all its stock. Bell will subdivide the land and sell individual tracts. Its gain on the land sales will be ordinary income. Jaime has realized a large capital loss in the current year and would like to recognize capital gain on the transfer of the land to Bell. One way for Jaime to accomplish this objective is to transfer the land to Bell in exchange for all the Bell stock plus a note for $400,000. Because the note is boot, Jaime will recognize $400,000 of gain even though Sec. 351 applies to the exchange. However, if the note is due in a subsequent year, Jaime's gain will be deferred until collection unless she elects out of the installment method. ◀

COMPLIANCE AND PROCEDURAL CONSIDERATIONS

REPORTING REQUIREMENTS UNDER SEC. 351

A taxpayer who receives stock or other property in a Sec. 351 exchange must attach a statement to his or her tax return for the period encompassing the date of the exchange.[65] The statement must include all facts pertinent to the exchange, including:

ADDITIONAL COMMENT

The required information provided to the IRS by both the transferor-shareholders and the transferee corporation should be consistent. For example, the FMVs assigned to the stock and other properties included in the exchange should be the same for both sides of the transaction.

▶ A description of the property transferred and its adjusted basis to the transferor

▶ A description of the stock received in the exchange, including its type, number of shares, and FMV

▶ A description of any other securities received in the exchange, including principal amount, terms, and FMV

▶ The amount of money received

▶ A description of any other property received, including its FMV

▶ A statement of the liabilities transferred to the corporation, including the nature of the liabilities, when and why they were incurred, and the business reason for their transfer

The transferee corporation must attach a statement to its tax return for the year in which the exchange took place. The statement must include

▶ A complete description of all property received from the transferors

▶ The transferors' adjusted bases in the property

▶ A description of the stock issued to the transferors

▶ A description of any other securities issued to the transferors

▶ The amount of money distributed to the transferors

▶ A description of any other property distributed to the transferors

▶ Information regarding the transferor's liabilities assumed by the corporation

---

[65] Reg. Sec. 1.351-3.

PROBLEM MATERIALS

DISCUSSION QUESTIONS

C:2-1   What entities or business forms are available for a new enterprise? Explain the advantages and disadvantages of each.

C:2-2   Alice and Bill plan to go into business together. They anticipate losses in the first two or three years, which they would like to use to offset income from other sources. They also are concerned about exposing their personal assets to business liabilities. Advise Alice and Bill as to what business form would best meet their needs.

C:2-3   Bruce and Bob organize Black LLC on May 10 of the current year. What is the entity's default tax classification? Are any alternative classification(s) available? If so, (1) how do Bruce and Bob elect the alternative classification(s) and (2) what are the tax consequences of doing so?

C:2-4   John and Wilbur form White Corporation on May 3 of the current year. What is the entity's default tax classification? Are any alternative classification(s) available? If so, (1) how do John and Wilbur elect the alternative classification(s) and (2) what are the tax consequences of doing so?

C:2-5   Barbara organizes Blue LLC on May 17 of the current year. What is the entity's default tax classification? Are any alternative classification(s) available? If so, (1) how does Barbara elect the alternative classification(s) and (2) what are the tax consequences of doing so?

C:2-6   Debate the following proposition: All corporate formation transactions should be taxable events.

C:2-7   What are the tax consequences for the transferor and transferee when property is transferred to a newly created corporation in an exchange qualifying under Sec. 351?

C:2-8   What items are considered to be property for purposes of Sec. 351(a)? What items are not considered to be property?

C:2-9   How is "control" defined for purposes of Sec. 351(a)?

C:2-10   Explain how the IRS has interpreted the phrase "in control immediately after the exchange" for purposes of a Sec. 351 exchange.

C:2-11   John and Mary each exchange property worth $50,000 for 100 shares of New Corporation stock. Peter exchanges services for 98 shares of New stock and $1,000 in cash for two shares of New stock. Are the Sec. 351 requirements met? Explain why or why not. What advice would you give the shareholders?

C:2-12   Does Sec. 351 require shareholders to receive stock equal in value to the property transferred? Suppose Fred and Susan each transfer property worth $50,000 to Spade Corporation. In exchange, Fred receives 25 shares of Spade stock and Susan receives 75 shares. Are the Sec. 351 requirements met? Explain the tax consequences of the exchange.

C:2-13   Does Sec. 351 apply to property transfers to an existing corporation? Suppose Carl and Lynn each own 50 shares of North Corporation stock. Karl transfers property worth $50,000 to North for an additional 25 shares. Does Sec. 351 apply? Explain why or why not. If not, what can be done to qualify the transaction for Sec. 351 treatment?

C:2-14   How are a transferor's basis and holding period determined for stock and other property (boot) received in a Sec. 351 exchange? How does the transferee corporation's assumption of liabilities affect the transferor's basis in the stock?

C:2-15   How are the transferee corporation's basis and holding period determined for property received in a Sec. 351 exchange?

C:2-16   Under what circumstances is a corporation's assumption of liabilities considered boot in a Sec. 351 exchange?

C:2-17   What factor(s) would the IRS likely consider to determine whether the transfer of a liability to a corporation in a Sec. 351 exchange was motivated by a business purpose?

C:2-18   Mark transfers all the property of his sole proprietorship to newly formed Utah Corporation in exchange for all the Utah stock. Mark has claimed depreciation on some of the property. Under what circumstances is Mark required to recapture previously claimed depreciation deductions? How is the depreciation deduction for the year of transfer calculated? What are the tax consequences if Utah sells the depreciable property?

C:2-19   How does the assignment of income doctrine apply to a Sec. 351 exchange?

C:2-20   What factors did Congress mandate to be considered in determining whether indebtedness is classified as debt or equity for tax purposes?

C:2-21   What are the advantages and disadvantages of using debt in a firm's capital structure?

C:2-22   How are capital contributions by shareholders and nonshareholders treated by the recipient corporation?

C:2-23 What are the advantages of Sec. 1244 loss treatment when a stock investment becomes worthless? What conditions must be met to qualify for this treatment?

C:2-24 What are the advantages of business bad debt treatment when a shareholder's loan or advance to a corporation cannot be repaid? What must the debtholder show to claim a business bad debt deduction?

C:2-25 Why might shareholders want to avoid Sec. 351 treatment? Explain three ways they can accomplish this end.

C:2-26 What are the Sec. 351 reporting requirements?

ISSUE IDENTIFICATION QUESTIONS

C:2-27 Peter Jones has owned all 100 shares of Trenton Corporation stock for the past five years. This year, Mary Smith contributes property with a $50,000 basis and an $80,000 FMV for 80 newly issued Trenton shares. At the same time, Peter contributes $15,000 in cash for 15 newly issued Trenton shares. What tax issues regarding the exchanges should Mary and Peter consider?

C:2-28 Carl contributes equipment with a $50,000 adjusted basis and an $80,000 FMV to Cook Corporation for 50 of its 100 shares of stock. His son, Carl Jr., contributes $20,000 cash for the remaining 50 Cook shares. What tax issues regarding the exchanges should Carl and his son consider?

C:2-29 Several years ago, Bill acquired 100 shares of Bold Corporation stock directly from the corporation for $100,000 in cash. This year, he sold the stock to Sam for $35,000. What tax issues regarding the stock sale should Bill consider?

PROBLEMS

C:2-30 *Transfer of Property and Services to a Controlled Corporation.* In 2011, Dick, Evan, and Fran form Triton Corporation. Dick contributes land (a capital asset) having a $50,000 FMV in exchange for 50 shares of Triton stock. He purchased the land in 2009 for $60,000. Evan contributes machinery (Sec. 1231 property purchased in 2008) having a $45,000 adjusted basis and a $30,000 FMV in exchange for 30 shares of Triton stock. Fran contributes services worth $20,000 in exchange for 20 shares of Triton stock.
a. What is the amount of Dick's recognized gain or loss?
b. What is Dick's basis in his Triton shares? When does his holding period begin?
c. What is the amount of Evan's recognized gain or loss?
d. What is Evan's basis in his Triton shares? When does his holding period begin?
e. How much income, if any, does Fran recognize?
f. What is Fran's basis in her Triton shares? When does her holding period begin?
g. What is Triton's basis in the land and the machinery? When does its holding period begin? How does Triton treat the amount paid to Fran for her services?

C:2-31 *Transfer of Property and Services to a Controlled Corporation.* In 2011, Ed, Fran, and George form Jet Corporation. Ed contributes land having a $35,000 FMV purchased as an investment in 2007 for $15,000 in exchange for 35 shares of Jet stock. Fran contributes machinery (Sec. 1231 property) purchased in 2007 and used in her business in exchange for 35 shares of Jet stock. Immediately before the exchange, the machinery had a $45,000 adjusted basis and a $35,000 FMV. George contributes services worth $30,000 in exchange for 30 shares of Jet stock.
a. What is the amount of Ed's recognized gain or loss?
b. What is Ed's basis in his Jet shares? When does his holding period begin?
c. What is the amount of Fran's recognized gain or loss?
d. What is Fran's basis in her Jet shares? When does her holding period begin?
e. How much income, if any, does George recognize?
f. What is George's basis in his Jet shares? When does his holding period begin?
g. What is Jet's basis in the land and the machinery? When does its holding period begin? How does Jet treat the amount paid to George for his services?
h. How would your answers to Parts a through g change if George instead contributed $5,000 in cash and services worth $25,000 for his 30 shares of Jet stock?

C:2-32 *Control Requirement.* In which of the following independent situations is the Sec. 351 control requirement met?

a. Olive transfers property to Quick Corporation for 75% of Quick stock, and Mary provides services to Quick for the remaining 25% of Quick stock.

b. Pete transfers property to Target Corporation for 60% of Target stock, and Robert transfers property worth $15,000 and performs services worth $25,000 for the remaining 40% of Target stock.

c. Herb and his wife, Wilma, each have owned 50 of the 100 outstanding shares of Vast Corporation stock since it was formed three years ago. In the current year, their son, Sam, transfers property to Vast for 50 newly issued shares of Vast stock.

d. Charles and Ruth develop a plan to form Tiny Corporation. On June 3 of this year, Charles transfers property worth $50,000 for 50 shares of Tiny stock. On August 1, Ruth transfers $50,000 cash for 50 shares of Tiny stock.

e. Assume the same facts as in Part d except that Charles has a prearranged plan to sell 30 of his shares to Sam on October 1.

C:2-33 *Control Requirement.* In which of the following unrelated exchanges is the Sec. 351 control requirement met? If the transaction does not meet the Sec. 351 requirements, suggest ways in which the transaction can be structured so as to meet these requirements.

a. Fred exchanges property worth $50,000 and services worth $50,000 for 100 shares of New Corporation stock. Greta exchanges $100,000 cash for the remaining 100 shares of New stock.

b. Maureen exchanges property worth $2,000 and services worth $48,000 for 100 shares of Gemini Corporation stock. Norman exchanges property worth $50,000 for the remaining 100 shares of Gemini stock.

C:2-34 *Sec. 351 Requirements.* Al, Bob, and Carl form West Corporation and transfer the following items to West:

| | | Item Transferred | | |
| | | Transferor's | | Shares Received |
Transferor	Item	Basis	FMV	by Transferor
Al	Patent	–0–	$25,000	1,000 common
Bob	Cash	$25,000	25,000	250 preferred
Carl	Services	–0–	7,500	300 common

The common stock has voting rights. The preferred stock does not.

a. Is the exchange nontaxable under Sec. 351? Explain the tax consequences of the exchange to Al, Bob, Carl, and West.

b. How would your answer to Part a change if Bob instead had received 200 shares of common stock and 200 shares of preferred stock?

c. How would your answer to Part a change if Carl instead had contributed $800 cash as well as services worth $6,700?

C:2-35 *Incorporating a Sole Proprietorship.* Tom incorporates his sole proprietorship as Total Corporation and transfers its assets to Total in exchange for all 100 shares of Total stock and four $10,000 interest-bearing notes. The stock has a $125,000 FMV. The notes mature consecutively on the first four anniversaries of the incorporation date. The assets transferred are as follows:

Assets		Adjusted Basis	FMV
Cash		$ 5,000	$ 5,000
Equipment	$130,000		
Minus: Accumulated depreciation	(70,000)	60,000	90,000
Building	$100,000		
Minus: Accumulated depreciation	(49,000)	51,000	40,000
Land		24,000	30,000
Total		$140,000	$165,000

a. What are the amounts and character of Tom's recognized gains or losses?

b. What is Tom's basis in the Total stock and notes?

c. What is Total's basis in the property received from Tom?

C:2-36 *Transfer to an Existing Corporation.* For the last five years, Ann and Fred each have owned 50 of the 100 outstanding shares of Zero Corporation stock. Ann transfers land having a $10,000 basis and a $25,000 FMV to Zero for an additional 25 shares of Zero stock. Fred transfers $1,000 cash to Zero for one additional share of Zero stock. What amount of the gain or loss must Ann recognize on the exchange? If the transaction does not meet the Sec. 351 requirements, suggest ways in which it can be structured so as to meet these requirements.

C:2-37 *Transfer to an Existing Corporation.* For the last three years, Lucy and Marvin each have owned 50 of the 100 outstanding shares of Lucky Corporation stock. Lucy transfers property having an $8,000 basis and a $12,000 FMV to Lucky for an additional ten shares of Lucky stock. How much gain or loss must Lucy recognize on the exchange? If the transaction does not meet the Sec. 351 requirements, suggest ways in which it can be structured so as to meet these requirements.

C:2-38 *Disproportionate Receipt of Stock.* Jerry transfers property with a $28,000 adjusted basis and a $50,000 FMV to Texas Corporation for 75 shares of Texas stock. Frank, Jerry's father, transfers property with a $32,000 adjusted basis and a $50,000 FMV to Texas for the remaining 25 shares of Texas stock.
a. What is the amount of each transferor's recognized gain or loss?
b. What is Jerry's basis in his Texas stock?
c. What is Frank's basis in his Texas stock?

C:2-39 *Sec. 351: Boot Property Received.* Sara transfers land (a capital asset) having a $30,000 adjusted basis to Temple Corporation in a Sec. 351 exchange. In return, Sara receives the following consideration:

Consideration	FMV
100 shares of Temple common stock	$100,000
50 shares of Temple qualified preferred stock	50,000
Temple note due in three years	20,000
Total	$170,000

a. What are the amount and character of Sara's recognized gain or loss?
b. What is Sara's basis in her common stock, preferred stock, and note?
c. What is Temple's basis in the land?

C:2-40 *Receipt of Bonds for Property.* Joe, Karen, and Larry form Gray Corporation. Joe contributes land (a capital asset) having an $8,000 adjusted basis and a $15,000 FMV to Gray in exchange for Gray ten-year bonds having a $15,000 face value. Karen contributes equipment (Sec. 1231 property) having an $18,000 adjusted basis and a $25,000 FMV for 50 shares of Gray stock. She previously claimed $10,000 of depreciation on the equipment. Larry contributes $25,000 cash for 50 shares of Gray stock.
a. What are the amount and character of Joe's, Karen's, and Larry's recognized gains or losses?
b. What basis do Joe, Karen, and Larry take in the stock or bonds they receive?
c. What basis does Gray take in the land and equipment? What happens to the $10,000 of depreciation recapture potential on the equipment?

C:2-41 *Transfer of Depreciable Property.* Nora transfers to Needle Corporation depreciable machinery originally costing $18,000 and now having a $15,000 adjusted basis. In exchange, Nora receives all 100 shares of Needle stock having an $18,000 FMV and a three-year Needle note having a $4,000 FMV.
a. What are the amount and character of Nora's recognized gain or loss?
b. What are Nora's bases in the Needle stock and note?
c. What is Needle's basis in the machinery?

C:2-42 *Transfer of Personal Liabilities.* Jim owns 80% of Gold Corporation stock. He transfers a business automobile to Gold in exchange for additional Gold stock worth $5,000 and Gold's assumption of both his $1,000 automobile debt and his $2,000 education loan. The automobile originally cost Jim $12,000 and, on the transfer date, has a $4,500 adjusted basis and an $8,000 FMV.
a. What are the amount and character of Jim's recognized gain or loss?
b. What is Jim's basis in his additional Gold shares?

c. When does Jim's holding period for the additional shares begin?

d. What basis does Gold take in the automobile?

C:2-43 *Liabilities in Excess of Basis.* Barbara transfers $10,000 cash and machinery having a $15,000 basis and a $35,000 FMV to Moore Corporation in exchange for 50 shares of Moore stock. The machinery was used in Barbara's business, originally cost Barbara $50,000, and is subject to a $28,000 liability, which Moore assumes. Sam exchanges $17,000 cash for the remaining 50 shares of Moore stock.

a. What are the amount and character of Barbara's recognized gain or loss?

b. What is Barbara's basis in the Moore stock?

c. What is Moore's basis in the machinery?

d. What are the amount and character of Sam's recognized gain or loss?

e. What is Sam's basis in the Moore stock?

f. When do Barbara and Sam's holding periods for their stock begin?

g. How would your answers to Parts a through f change if Sam received $17,000 of Moore stock for legal services (instead of cash)?

C:2-44 *Transfer of Business Properties.* Jerry transfers property having a $32,000 adjusted basis and a $50,000 FMV to Emerald Corporation in exchange for all of Emerald's stock worth $15,000 and Emerald's assumption of a $35,000 mortgage on the property.

a. What is the amount of Jerry's recognized gain or loss?

b. What is Jerry's basis in the Emerald stock?

c. What is Emerald's basis in the property?

d. How would your answers to Parts a through c change if the mortgage assumed by Emerald were $15,000 and the Emerald stock were worth $35,000?

C:2-45 *Incorporating a Cash Basis Proprietorship.* Ted decides to incorporate his medical practice. He uses the cash method of accounting. On the date of incorporation, the practice reports the following balance sheet:

	Basis	FMV
Assets:		
Cash	$ 5,000	$ 5,000
Accounts receivable	–0–	65,000
Equipment (net of $15,000 depreciation)	35,000	40,000
Total	$40,000	$110,000
Liabilities and Owner's Equity:		
Current liabilities	$ –0–	$ 35,000
Note payable on equipment	15,000	15,000
Owner's equity	25,000	60,000
Total	$40,000	$110,000

All the current liabilities would be deductible by Ted if he paid them. Ted transfers all the assets and liabilities to a professional corporation in exchange for all of its stock.

a. What are the amount and character of Ted's recognized gain or loss?

b. What is Ted's basis in the stock?

c. What is the corporation's basis in the property?

d. Who recognizes income on the receivables upon their collection? Can the corporation obtain a deduction for the liabilities when it pays them?

C:2-46 *Transfer of Depreciable Property.* On January 10, 2011, Mary transfers to Green Corporation a machine purchased on March 3, 2008, for $100,000. The machine has a $60,000 adjusted basis and a $110,000 FMV on the transfer date. Mary receives all 100 shares of Green stock, worth $100,000, and a two-year Green note worth $10,000.

a. What are the amount and character of Mary's recognized gain or loss?

b. What is Mary's basis in the stock and note? When does her holding period begin?

c. What are the amount and character of Green's gain or loss?

d. What is Green's basis in the machine? When does Green's holding period begin?

C:2-47   *Contribution to Capital by a Nonshareholder.* The City of Omaha donates land worth $500,000 to Ace Corporation to induce it to locate in Omaha and create an estimated 2,000 jobs for its citizens.

     a. How much income, if any, must Ace report on the land contribution?

     b. What basis does Ace take in the land?

     c. Assume the same facts except the City of Omaha also donated to Ace $100,000 cash, which the corporation used to pay a portion of the $250,000 cost of equipment that it purchased six months later. How much income, if any, must Ace report on the cash contribution? What basis does Ace take in the equipment?

C:2-48   *Choice of Capital Structure.* Kobe transfers $500,000 in cash to newly formed Bryant Corporation for 100% of Bryant's stock. In the first year of operations, Bryant's taxable income before any payments to Kobe is $120,000. What total amount of taxable income must Kobe and Bryant each report in the following two scenarios?

     a. Bryant pays a $70,000 dividend to Kobe.

     b. Assume that when Bryant was formed, Kobe transferred his $500,000 to the corporation for $250,000 of Bryant stock and $250,000 in Bryant notes. The notes are repayable in five annual installments of $50,000 plus 8% annual interest on the unpaid balance. During the current year, Bryant gives Kobe $50,000 in repayment of the first note plus $20,000 interest.

C:2-49   *Worthless Stock or Securities.* Tom and Vicki, husband and wife who file a joint return, each purchase for $75,000 one-half the stock in Guest Corporation from Al. Tom is employed full-time by Guest and earns $100,000 in annual salary. Because of Guest's financial difficulties, Tom and Vicki each lend Guest an additional $25,000. The $25,000 is secured by registered bonds and is repayable in five years, with interest accruing at the prevailing market rate. Guest's financial difficulties escalate, and it eventually declares bankruptcy. Tom and Vicki receive nothing for their Guest stock or Guest bonds.

     a. What are the amount and character of each shareholder's loss on the worthless stock and bonds?

     b. How would your answer to Part a change if the liability were not secured by bonds?

     c. How would your answer to Part a change if Tom and Vicki had purchased their stock for $75,000 each at the time Guest was formed?

C:2-50   *Worthless Stock.* Duck Corporation is owned equally by Harry, Susan, and Big Corporation. Harry and Susan are single. In 2003, Harry, Tom, and Big, the original investors in Duck, each paid $125,000 for their Duck stock. Susan purchased her stock from Tom in 2006 for $175,000. No adjustments to basis occur after the stock acquisition date. Duck encounters financial difficulties as a result of a lawsuit brought by a customer who suffered personal injuries from using a defective product. Duck files for bankruptcy, and uses all its assets to pay its creditors in 2011. What are the amount and character of each shareholder's loss?

C:2-51   *Sale of Sec. 1244 Stock.* Lois, who is single, transfers property with an $80,000 basis and a $120,000 FMV to Water Corporation in exchange for all 100 shares of Water stock. The shares qualify as Sec. 1244 stock. Two years later, Lois sells the stock for $28,000.

     a. What are the amount and character of Lois's recognized gain or loss?

     b. How would your answer to Part a change if the FMV of the property were $70,000?

C:2-52   *Transfer of Sec. 1244 Stock.* Assume the same facts as in Problem C:2-51 except that Lois gave the Water stock to her daughter, Sue, six months after she received it. The stock had a $120,000 FMV when Lois acquired it and when she made the gift. Sue sold the stock two years later for $28,000. How is the loss treated for tax purposes?

C:2-53   *Avoiding Sec. 351 Treatment.* Six years ago, Donna purchased land as an investment. The land cost $150,000 and is now worth $480,000. Donna plans to transfer the land to Development Corporation, which will subdivide it and sell individual tracts. Development's income on the land sales will be ordinary in character.

     a. What are the tax consequences of the asset transfer and land sales if Donna contributes the land to Development in exchange for all its stock?

     b. In what alternative ways can the transaction be structured to achieve more favorable tax results? Assume Donna's marginal tax rate is 35%, and Development's marginal tax rate is 34%.

COMPREHENSIVE PROBLEMS

C:2-54 On March 1 of the current year, Alice, Bob, Carla, and Dick form Bear Corporation and transfer the following items:

Property Transferred

Transferor	Asset	Basis to Transferor	FMV	Number of Common Shares Issued
Alice	Land	$12,000	$30,000	
	Building	38,000	70,000	400
	Mortgage on the land and building	60,000	60,000	
Bob	Equipment	25,000	40,000	300
Carla	Van	15,000	10,000	50
Dick	Accounting services	–0–	10,000	100

Alice purchased the land and building several years ago for $12,000 and $50,000, respectively. Alice has claimed straight-line depreciation on the building. Bob also receives a Bear note for $10,000 due in three years. The note bears interest at the prevailing market rate. Bob purchased the equipment three years ago for $50,000. Carla also receives $5,000 cash. Carla purchased the van two years ago for $20,000.
a. Does the transaction satisfy the requirements of Sec. 351?
b. What are the amount and character of the gains or losses recognized by Alice, Bob, Carla, Dick, and Bear?
c. What is each shareholder's basis in his or her Bear stock? When does the holding period for the stock begin?
d. What is Bear's basis in its property and services? When does the holding period for each property begin?

C:2-55 On June 3 of the current year, Eric, Florence, and George form Wildcat Corporation and transfer the following items:

Item Transferred

Transferor	Asset	Basis to Transferor	FMV	Number of Common Shares Issued
Eric	Land	$200,000	$50,000	500
Florence	Equipment	–0–	25,000	250
George	Legal services	–0–	25,000	250

Eric purchased the land (a capital asset) five years ago for $200,000. Florence purchased the equipment three years ago for $48,000. The equipment has been fully depreciated.
a. Does the transaction meet the requirements of Sec. 351?
b. What are the amount and character of the gains or losses recognized by Eric, Florence, George, and Wildcat?
c. What is each shareholder's basis in his or her Wildcat stock? When does the holding period for the stock begin?
d. What is Wildcat's basis in the land, equipment, and services? When does the holding period for each property begin?

TAX STRATEGY PROBLEMS

C:2-56 Assume the same facts as in Problem C:2-55.
a. Under what circumstances is the tax result in Problem C:2-55 beneficial, and for which shareholders? Are the shareholders likely to be pleased with the result?
b. If the shareholders decide that meeting the Sec. 351 requirements would generate a greater tax benefit, how might they proceed?

C:2-57 Paula Green owns and operates the Green Thumb Nursery as a sole proprietorship. The business has total assets with a $260,000 adjusted basis and a $500,000 FMV. Paula wants to expand into the landscaping business. She views this expansion as risky and therefore wants to incorporate so as not to put her personal assets at risk. Her friend, Mary Brown, is willing to invest $250,000 in the enterprise.

Although Green Thumb has earned approximately $55,000 per year, Paula and Mary expect that, when the landscaping business is launched, the new corporation will incur losses of $50,000 per year for the next two years. They expect profits of at least $80,000 annually, beginning in the third year. Paula and Mary earn approximately $50,000 from other sources. They are considering the following alternative capital structures and elections:

a. Green Thumb issues 50 shares of common stock to Paula and 25 shares of common stock to Mary.
b. Green Thumb issues 50 shares of common stock to Paula and a $250,000 ten-year bond bearing interest at 8% to Mary.
c. Green Thumb issues 40 shares of common stock to Paula plus a $100,000 ten-year bond bearing interest at 6% and 15 shares of common stock to Mary, plus a $100,000 ten-year bond bearing interest at 6%.
d. Green Thumb issues 50 shares of common stock to Paula and 25 shares of preferred stock to Mary. The preferred stock is nonparticipating but pays a cumulative preferred dividend at 8% of its $250,000 stated value.

What are the advantages and disadvantages of each of these alternatives? What considerations are relevant for determining the best alternative?

C:2-58 Assume the same facts as in Problem C:2-57.
a. Given the nursery's operating prospects, what business forms might Paula and Mary consider and why?
b. In light of their proposed use of debt and equity, how might Paula and Mary structure a partnership to achieve their various business and investment objectives?

CASE STUDY PROBLEMS

C:2-59 Bob Jones has a small repair shop that he has run for several years as a sole proprietorship. The proprietorship uses the cash method of accounting and the calendar year as its tax year. Bob needs additional capital for expansion and knows two people who might be interested in investing in the business. One would like to work for the business. The other would only invest.

Bob wants to know the tax consequences of incorporating the business. His business assets include a building, equipment, accounts receivable, and cash. Liabilities include a mortgage on the building and a few accounts payable, which are deductible when paid. Assume that Bob's ordinary tax rate is greater than 25%.

Required: Write a memorandum to Bob explaining the tax consequences of the incorporation. As part of your memorandum examine the possibility of having the corporation issue common and preferred stock and debt for the shareholders' property and money.

C:2-60 Eric Wright conducts a dry cleaning business as a sole proprietorship. The business operates in a building that Eric owns. Last year, Eric mortgaged for $150,000 the building and the land on which the building sits. He used the money for a down payment on his personal residence and college expenses for his two children. He now wants to incorporate his business and transfer the building and the mortgage to a new corporation, along with other assets and some accounts payable. The amount of the unpaid mortgage balance will not exceed Eric's adjusted basis in the land and building at the time he transfers them to the corporation. Eric is aware that Sec. 357(b) could impact the tax consequences of the transaction because no bona fide business purpose exists for the mortgage transfer, which the IRS might consider to have been for a tax avoidance purpose. However, Eric refuses to acknowledge this possibility when you confront him. He maintains that many taxpayers play the audit lottery and that, in the event of an audit, invoking this issue could be a bargaining ploy.

Required: What information about the transaction must be provided with the transferor and transferee's tax returns for the year in which the transfer takes place? Discuss the ethical issues raised by the AICPA's *Statements on Standards for Tax Services No. 1, Tax Return Positions* (which can be found in Appendix E) as it relates to this situation. Should the tax practitioner act as an advocate for the client? Should the practitioner sign the return?

TAX RESEARCH PROBLEMS

C:2-61 Anne and Michael own and operate a successful mattress business. They have decided to take the business public. They contribute all the assets of the business to newly formed Spring Corporation each in exchange for 20% of the stock. The remaining 60% is issued to an underwriting company that will sell the stock to the public and charge 10% of the sales proceeds as a commission. Prepare a memorandum for your tax manager explaining whether or not this transaction meets the tax-free requirements of Sec. 351.

C:2-62 Bob and Carl transfer property to Stone Corporation for 90% and 10% of Stone stock, respectively. Pursuant to a binding agreement concluded before the transfer, Bob sells half of his stock to Carl. Prepare a memorandum for your tax manager explaining why the exchange does or does not meet the Sec. 351 control requirement. Your manager has suggested that, at a minimum, you consult the following authorities:

- IRC Sec. 351
- Reg. Sec. 1.351-1

C:2-63 In an exchange qualifying for Sec. 351 tax-free treatment, Greta receives 100 shares of White Corporation stock plus a right to receive another 25 shares. The right is contingent on the valuation of a patent contributed by Greta. Because the patent license is pending, the patent cannot be valued for several months. Prepare a memorandum for your tax manager explaining whether the underlying 25 shares are considered "stock" for purposes of Sec. 351 and what tax consequences ensue from Greta's receipt of the 100 shares now and 25 shares later upon exercise of the right.

C:2-64 Your clients, Lisa and Matthew, are planning to form Lima Corporation. Lisa will contribute $50,000 cash to Lima for 50 shares of its stock. Matthew will contribute land having a $35,000 adjusted basis and a $50,000 FMV for 50 shares of Lima stock. Lima will borrow additional capital from a bank and then will subdivide and sell the land. Prepare a memorandum for your tax manager outlining the tax treatment of the corporate formation. In your memorandum, compare tax and financial accounting for this transaction. References:

- IRC Sec. 351
- Accounting Standards Codification (ASC) 845 (Nonmonetary Transactions), formerly APB No. 29

C:2-65 John plans to transfer the assets and liabilities of his business to Newco in exchange for all of Newco's stock. The assets have a $250,000 basis and an $800,000 FMV. John also plans to transfer $475,000 of business related liabilities to Newco. Under Sec. 357(c), can John avoid recognizing a $175,000 gain (the excess of liabilities over the basis of assets tranferred) by transferring a $175,000 personal promissory note along with the assets and liabilities?

C:2-66 Six years ago, Leticia, Monica, and Nathaniel organized Lemona Corporation to develop and sell computer software. Each individual contributed $10,000 to Lemona in exchange for 1,000 shares of Lemona stock (for a total of 3,000 shares issued and outstanding). The corporation also borrowed $250,000 from Venture Capital Associates to finance operating costs and capital expenditures.

Because of intense competition, Lemona struggled in its early years of operation and sustained chronic losses. This year, Leticia, who serves as Lemona's president, decided to seek additional funds to finance Lemona's working capital.

Venture Capital Associates declined Leticia's request for additional capital because of the firm's already high credit exposure to the software corporation. Hi-Tech Bank proposed to lend Limona $100,000, but at a 10% premium over the prime rate. (Other software manufacturers in the same market can borrow at a 3% premium.) Investment Managers LLC proposed to inject $50,000 of equity capital into Lemona, but on the condition that the investment firm be granted the right to elect five members to Lemona's board of directors. Discouraged by the "high cost" of external borrowing, Leticia turned to Monica and Nathaniel.

She proposed to Monica and Nathaniel that each of the three original investors contribute an additional $25,000 to Lemona, each in exchange for five 20-year debentures. The debentures would be unsecured and subordinated to Venture Capital Associates debt. Annual interest on the debentures would accrue at a floating 5% premium over the prime rate. The right to receive interest payments would be cumulative; that is, each debenture

TAX & FINANCIAL ACCOUNTING

holder would be entitled to past and current interest payents before Lemona's board could declare a common stock dividend. The debentures would be both nontransferable and noncallable.

Leticia, Monica, and Nathaniel have asked you, their tax accountant, to advise them on the tax implications of the proposed financing arrangement. After researching the issue, set forth your advice in a client letter. At a minimum, you should consult the following authorities:

- IRC Sec. 385
- *Rudolph A. Hardman*, 60 AFTR 2d 87-5651, 82-7 USTC ¶9523 (9th Cir., 1987)
- *Tomlinson v. The 1661 Corporation*, 19 AFTR 2d 1413, 67-1 USTC ¶9438 (5th Cir., 1967)

3

CHAPTER

THE CORPORATE INCOME TAX

LEARNING OBJECTIVES

After studying this chapter, you should be able to

1 Apply the requirements for selecting tax years and accounting methods to various types of C corporations

2 Compute a corporation's taxable income

3 Compute a corporation's income tax liability

4 Understand what a controlled group is and the tax consequences of being a controlled group

5 Understand how compensation planning can reduce taxes for corporations and their shareholders

6 Determine the requirements for paying corporate income taxes and filing a corporate tax return

7 Determine the financial statement implications of federal income taxes

A **corporation** is a separate taxpaying entity that must file an annual tax return even if it has no income or loss for the year. This chapter covers the tax rules for **domestic corporations** (i.e., corporations incorporated in one of the 50 states or under federal law) and other entities taxed as domestic corporations under the check-the-box regulations.[1] It explains the rules for determining a corporation's taxable income, loss, and tax liability and for filing corporate tax returns. See Table C:3-1 for the general formula for determining the corporate tax liability. It also discusses the financial implications of federal income taxes. Some of these implications appear briefly in the Book-to-Tax Accounting Comparisons, and a more detailed discussion appears at the end of this chapter.

The corporations discussed in this chapter are sometimes referred to as regular or C corporations because Subchapter C of the Internal Revenue Code (IRC) dictates much of their tax treatment. Corporations that have a special tax status include S corporations (see Chapter C:11) and affiliated groups of corporations that file consolidated returns (see Chapter C:8). A comparison of the tax treatments of C corporations, partnerships, and S corporations appears in Appendix F.

CORPORATE ELECTIONS

OBJECTIVE 1

Apply the requirements for selecting tax years and accounting methods to various types of C corporations

Once formed, a corporation must make certain elections, such as selecting its **tax year** and its accounting methods. The corporation makes these elections on its first tax return. They are important and should be considered carefully because, once made, they generally can be changed only with permission from the Internal Revenue Service (IRS).

CHOOSING A CALENDAR OR FISCAL YEAR

A new corporation may elect to use either a calendar year or a fiscal year as its accounting period. The corporation's tax year must be the same as the annual accounting period used for financial accounting purposes. The corporation makes the election by filing its first tax return for the selected period. A calendar year is a 12-month period ending on December 31. A fiscal year is a 12-month period ending on the last day of any month other than December. Examples of acceptable fiscal years are February 1, 2011, through January 31, 2012, and October 1, 2011, through September 30, 2012. A fiscal year that runs from September 16, 2011, through September 15, 2012, however, is not an acceptable tax year because it does not end on the last day of the month. The IRS requires that a corporation using an unacceptable tax year change to a calendar year.[2]

KEY POINT

Whereas partnerships and S corporations generally must adopt a calendar year, C corporations (other than personal service corporations) have the flexibility of adopting a fiscal year. The fiscal year must end on the last day of the month.

SHORT TAX PERIOD.   A corporation's first tax year might not cover a full 12-month period. If, for example, a corporation begins business on March 10, 2011, and elects a fiscal year ending on September 30, its first tax year covers the period from March 10, 2011, through September 30, 2011. Its second tax year covers the period from October 1, 2011, through September 30, 2012. The corporation must file a **short-period tax return** for its first tax year.[3] From then on, its tax returns will cover a full 12-month period. The last year of a corporation's life, however, also may be a short period covering the period from the beginning of the last tax year through the date the corporation ceases to exist.

RESTRICTIONS ON ADOPTING A TAX YEAR.   A corporation may be subject to restrictions in its choice of a tax year. For example, an S corporation generally must use a calendar year (see Chapter C:11), and members of an affiliated group filing a consolidated return must use the same tax year as the group's parent corporation (see Chapter C:8).

A **personal service corporation** (PSC) generally must use a calendar year as its tax year. This restriction prevents a personal service corporation with, for example, a January 31 year-end from distributing a large portion of its income earned during the February through December portion of 2011 to its calendar year shareholder-employees in January

---

[1] Sec. 7701(a)(4). Corporations that are not classified as domestic are **foreign corporations**. Foreign corporations are taxed like domestic corporations if they conduct a trade or business in the United States.

[2] Sec. 441. Section 441 also permits accounting periods of either 52 or 53 weeks that always end on the same day of the week (such as Friday).
[3] Sec. 443(a)(2).

▼ **TABLE C:3-1**

General Rules for Determining the Corporate Tax Liability

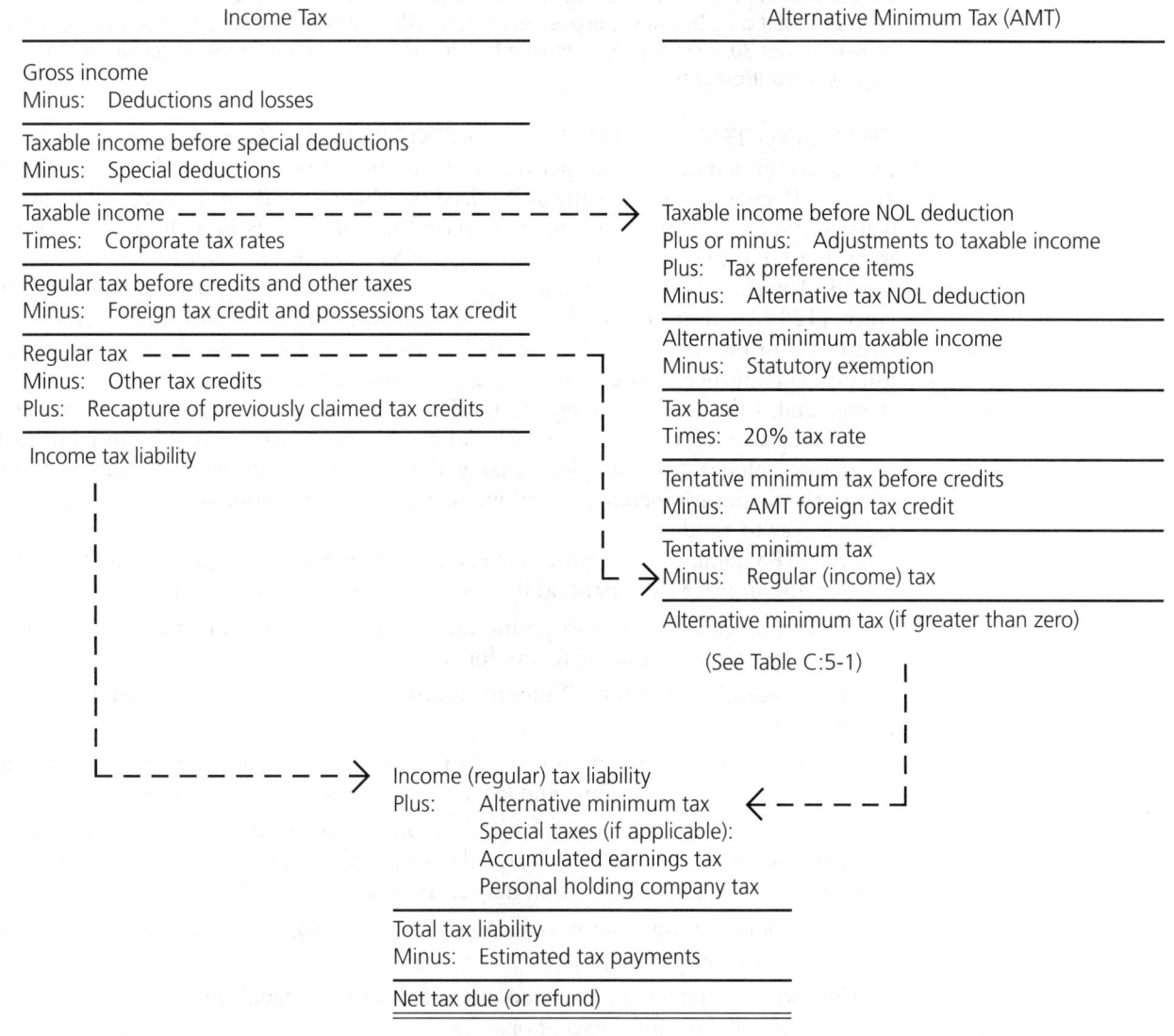

Income Tax	Alternative Minimum Tax (AMT)
Gross income Minus: Deductions and losses	
Taxable income before special deductions Minus: Special deductions	
Taxable income ‒ ‒ ‒ ‒ ‒ ‒ ‒ ‒ ‒ ‒ → Times: Corporate tax rates	Taxable income before NOL deduction Plus or minus: Adjustments to taxable income Plus: Tax preference items Minus: Alternative tax NOL deduction
Regular tax before credits and other taxes Minus: Foreign tax credit and possessions tax credit	Alternative minimum taxable income Minus: Statutory exemption
Regular tax ‒ ‒ ‒ ‒ ‒ ‒ ‒ ‒ ‒ ‒ Minus: Other tax credits Plus: Recapture of previously claimed tax credits	Tax base Times: 20% tax rate
Income tax liability	Tentative minimum tax before credits Minus: AMT foreign tax credit
	Tentative minimum tax Minus: Regular (income) tax
	Alternative minimum tax (if greater than zero)
	(See Table C:5-1)

Income (regular) tax liability
Plus: Alternative minimum tax ←
       Special taxes (if applicable):
       Accumulated earnings tax
       Personal holding company tax	

Total tax liability Minus: Estimated tax payments	
Net tax due (or refund)	

2012, thereby deferring income largely earned in 2011 to 2012. For this purpose, the IRC defines a PSC as a corporation whose principal activity is the performance of personal services by its employee-owners who own more than 10% of the stock (by value) on any day of the year.[4]

A PSC, however, may adopt a fiscal tax year if it can establish a business purpose for such a year. For example, it may be able to establish a natural business year and use that year as its tax year.[5] Deferral of income by shareholders is not an acceptable business purpose. Even when no business purpose exists, a new PSC may elect to use a September 30, October 31, or November 30 year-end if it meets minimum distribution requirements to employee-owners during the deferral period.[6] If it fails to meet these distribution requirements, the PSC may have to defer to its next fiscal year the deduction for amounts paid to employee-owners.[7]

[4] Sec. 441(i).

[5] The natural business year rule requires that the year-end used for tax purposes coincide with the end of the taxpayer's peak business period. (See the partnership and S corporation chapters and Rev. Proc. 2006-46, 2006-2 C.B. 859, for a further explanation of this exception.)

[6] Sec. 444.

[7] Sec. 280H.

EXAMPLE C:3-1 ▶ Alice and Bob form Cole Corporation with each shareholder owning 50% of its stock. Alice and Bob use the calendar year as their tax year. Alice and Bob are both active in the business and are the corporation's primary employees. The new corporation performs engineering services for the automotive industry. Cole must use a calendar year as its tax year unless it qualifies for a fiscal year based on a business purpose exception. Alternatively, it may adopt a fiscal year ending on September 30, October 31, or November 30, provided it complies with certain minimum distribution requirements. ◀

CHANGING THE ANNUAL ACCOUNTING PERIOD. A corporation that desires to change its annual accounting period must obtain the prior approval of the IRS unless Treasury Regulations specifically authorized the change or IRS procedures allow an automatic change. A change in accounting period usually results in a short period running from the end of the old annual accounting period to the beginning of the new accounting period. A corporation must request approval of an accounting period change by filing Form 1128 (Application for Change in Annual Accounting Period) on or before the fifteenth day of the third calendar month following the close of the short period. The IRS usually will approve a request for change if a substantial business purpose exists for the change and if the taxpayer agrees to the IRS's prescribed terms, conditions, and adjustments necessary to prevent any substantial distortion of income. A substantial distortion of income includes, for example, a change that causes the "deferral of a substantial portion of the taxpayer's income, or shifting of a substantial portion of deductions, from one taxable year to another."[8]

Under IRS administrative procedures, a corporation may change its annual accounting period without prior IRS approval if it meets the following conditions:

▶ The corporation files a short-period tax return for the year of change and annualizes its income when computing its tax for the short period.

▶ The corporation files full 12-month returns for subsequent years ending on the new year-end.

▶ The corporation closes its books as of the last day of the short-period and subsequently computes its income and keeps its books using the new tax year.

▶ If the corporation generates an NOL or capital loss in the short period, it may not carry back the losses but must carry them over to future years. However, if the loss is $50,000 or less, the corporation may carry it back.

▶ The corporation must not have changed its accounting period within the previous 48 months (with some exceptions).

▶ The corporation must not have an interest in a pass-through entity as of the end of the short period (with some exceptions).

▶ The corporation is not an S corporation, personal service corporation, tax-exempt organization, or other specialized corporation.[9]

ACCOUNTING METHODS

A new corporation must select the overall **accounting method** it will use for tax purposes. The method chosen must be indicated on the corporation's initial return. The three possible accounting methods are: accrual, cash, and hybrid.[10]

ACCRUAL METHOD. Under the accrual method, a corporation reports income in the year it earns the income and reports expenses in the year it incurs the expenses. A corporation must use the accrual method unless it qualifies under one of the following exceptions:

▶ It qualifies as a family farming corporation.[11]

BOOK-TO-TAX ACCOUNTING COMPARISON

Treasury Regulations literally require taxpayers to use the same overall accounting method for book and tax purposes. However, the courts have allowed different methods if the taxpayer maintains adequate reconciling workpapers. The IRS has adopted the courts' position on this issue.

---

[8] Reg. Sec. 1.442-1(b)(3). Also see Rev. Proc. 2002-39, 2002-1 C.B. 1046.
[9] Rev. Proc. 2006-45, 2006-2 C.B. 851. For automatic change procedures for S corporations and personal service corporations, see Rev. Proc. 2006-46, 2006-2 C.B. 859.
[10] Sec. 446.

[11] Sec. 448. Certain family farming corporations having gross receipts of less than $25 million may use the cash method of accounting. Section 447 requires farming corporations with gross receipts over $25 million to use the accrual method of accounting.

▶ It qualifies as a personal service corporation, which is a corporation substantially all of whose activities involve the performance of services in the fields of health, law, engineering, architecture, accounting, actuarial science, performing arts, or consulting; and substantially all of whose stock is held by current (or retired) employees performing the services listed above, their estates, or (for two years only) persons who inherited their stock from such employees.[12]

▶ It meets a $5 million gross receipts test for all prior tax years beginning after December 31, 1985. A corporation meets this test for any prior tax year if its average gross receipts for the three-year period ending with that prior tax year do not exceed $5 million. If the corporation was not in existence for the entire three-year period, the period during which the corporation *was* in existence may be used.

▶ It has elected S corporation status.

If a corporation meets one of the exceptions listed above, it may use either the accrual method or one of the following two methods.

CASH METHOD. Under the cash method, a corporation reports income when it actually or constructively receives the income and reports expenses when it pays them. Corporations in service industries such as engineering, medicine, law, and accounting generally use this method because they prefer to defer recognition until they actually receive the income. This method may not be used if inventories are a material income-producing factor. In such case, the corporation must use either the *accrual* method or the *hybrid* method of accounting.

HYBRID METHOD. Under the hybrid method, a corporation uses the accrual method of accounting for sales, cost of goods sold, inventories, accounts receivable, and accounts payable, and uses the cash method of accounting for all other income and expense items. Small businesses with inventories (e.g., retail stores) often use this method. Although they must use the accrual method of accounting for sales-related income and expense items, they often find the cash method less burdensome to use for other income and expense items, such as utilities, rents, salaries, and taxes.

ADDITIONAL COMMENT

Whereas partnerships and S corporations are generally allowed to be cash method taxpayers, most C corporations must use the accrual method of accounting. This restriction can prove inconvenient for many small corporations (with more than $5 million of gross receipts) that would rather use the less complicated cash method of accounting.

GENERAL FORMULA FOR DETERMINING THE CORPORATE TAX LIABILITY

Each year, C corporations must determine their corporate income (or regular) tax liability. In addition to the income tax, a C corporation may owe the corporate alternative minimum tax and possibly either the accumulated earnings tax or the personal holding company tax. A corporation's total tax liability equals the sum of its regular income tax liability plus any additional taxes that it owes.

This chapter explains how to compute a corporation's income (or regular) tax liability. Chapter C:5 explains the computation of the corporate alternative minimum tax, personal holding company tax, and accumulated earnings tax.

---

[12] The personal service corporation definition for the tax year election [Sec. 441(i)] is different from the personal service corporation definition for the cash accounting method election [Sec. 448].

COMPUTING A CORPORATION'S TAXABLE INCOME

OBJECTIVE 2

Compute a corporation's taxable income

Like an individual, a corporation is a taxpaying entity with gross income and deductions. However, a number of differences arise between individual and corporate taxation as summarized in Figure C:3-1. This section of the text expands on some of these items and discusses other tax aspects particular to corporations.

SALES AND EXCHANGES OF PROPERTY

Sales and exchanges of property generally are treated the same way for corporations as for an individual. However, special rules apply to capital gains and losses, and corporations are subject to an additional 20% depreciation recapture rule under Sec. 291 on sales of Sec. 1250 property.

1. **Gross income:** Generally, the same gross income definition applies to individuals and corporations. Certain exclusions are available to individuals but not to corporations (e.g, fringe benefits); other exclusions are available to corporations but not to individuals (e.g., capital contributions).
2. **Deductions:** Individuals have above-the-line deductions (*for* AGI), itemized deductions (*from* AGI), and personal exemptions. Corporations do not compute AGI, and their deductions are presumed to be ordinary and necessary business expenses.
3. **Charitable contributions:** Individuals are limited to 50% of AGI (30% for capital gain property). Corporations are limited to 10% of taxable income computed without regard to the dividends-received deductions, the U.S. production activities deduction, NOL and capital loss carrybacks, and the contribution deduction itself. Individuals deduct a contribution only in the year they pay it. Accrual basis corporations may deduct contributions in the year of accrual if the board of directors authorizes the contribution by year-end, and the corporation pays it by the fifteenth day of the third month of the next year.
4. **Depreciation on Sec. 1250 property:** Individuals generally do not recapture depreciation under the MACRS rules because straight-line depreciation applies to real property. Corporations must recapture 20% of the excess of the amount that would be recaptured under Sec. 1245. Individuals are subject to a 25% tax rate on Sec. 1250 gains. Corporations are not subject to this rate.
5. **Net capital gains:** Individuals usually are taxed at a maximum rate of 15% (however, through 2012, 0%, 25%, and 28% apply in special cases). Corporate capital gains are taxed at the regular corporate tax rates.
6. **Capital losses:** Individuals can deduct up to $3,000 of net capital losses to offset ordinary income. Individual capital losses carry over indefinitely. Corporations cannot offset any ordinary income with capital losses. However, capital losses carry back three years and forward five years and offset capital gains in those years.
7. **Dividends-received deduction:** Not available for individuals. Corporations receive a 70%, 80%, or 100% special deduction depending on the percentage of stock ownership.
8. **NOLs:** Individuals must make many adjustments to arrive at the NOL they are allowed to carry back or forward. A corporation's NOL is simply the excess of its deductions over its income for the year. The NOL carries back two years (or an extended period if applicable) and forward 20 years for individuals and corporations, or the taxpayer can elect to forgo the carryback and only carry the NOL forward.
9. For individuals, the U.S. production activities deduction is based on the lesser of qualified production activities income or AGI. For corporations, the deduction is based on the lesser of qualified production activities income or taxable income.
10. **Tax rates:** Individual's ordinary tax rates range from 10% to 35% (in 2011). Corporate tax rates range from 15% to 39%.
11. **AMT:** Individual AMT rates are 26% or 28%. The corporate AMT rate is 20%. Corporations are subject to a special AMTI adjustment, called adjusted current earnings (ACE), that does not apply to individuals.
12. **Passive Losses:** Passive loss rules apply to individuals, partners, S corporation shareholders, closely held C corporations, and PSCs. They do not apply to widely held C corporations.
13. **Casualty losses:** Casualty losses are deductible in full by a corporation because all corporate casualty losses are considered to be business related. Moreover, they are not reduced by a $100 offset, nor are they restricted to losses exceeding 10% of AGI, as are an individual's nonbusiness casualty losses.

FIGURE C:3-1 ▶ DIFFERENCES BETWEEN INDIVIDUAL AND CORPORATE TAXATION

CAPITAL GAINS AND LOSSES. A corporation has a capital gain or loss if it sells or exchanges a capital asset. As with individuals, a corporation must net all its capital gains and losses to obtain its net capital gain or loss position.

Net Capital Gain. A corporation includes all its net capital gains (net long-term capital gains in excess of net short-term capital losses) for the tax year in gross income. Unlike with individuals, a corporation's capital gains receive no special tax treatment and are taxed in the same manner as any other ordinary income item.

EXAMPLE C:3-2 ▶ Beta Corporation has a net capital gain of $40,000, gross profits on sales of $110,000, and deductible expenses of $28,000. Beta's gross income is $150,000 ($40,000 + $110,000). Its taxable income is $122,000 ($150,000 − $28,000). The $40,000 of net capital gain receives no special treatment and is taxed using the regular corporate tax rates described below. ◀

Net Capital Losses. If a corporation incurs a net capital loss, it cannot deduct the net loss in the current year. A corporation's capital losses can offset only capital gains. They never can offset the corporation's ordinary income.

A corporation must carry back a net capital loss as a short-term capital loss to the three previous tax years and offset capital gains in the earliest year possible (i.e., the losses carry back to the third previous year first). If the loss is not totally absorbed as a carryback, the remainder carries over as a short-term capital loss for five years. Any unused capital losses remaining at the end of the carryover period expire.

EXAMPLE C:3-3 ▶ In 2011, East Corporation reports gross profits of $150,000, deductible expenses of $28,000, and a net capital loss of $10,000. East reported the following capital gain net income (excess of gains from sales or exchanges of capital assets over losses from such sales or exchanges) during 2008 through 2010:

Year	Capital Gain Net Income
2008	$6,000
2009	–0–
2010	3,000

East has gross income of $150,000 and taxable income of $122,000 ($150,000 − $28,000) for 2011. East also has a $10,000 net capital loss that carries back to 2008 first and offsets the $6,000 capital gain net income reported in that year. East receives a refund for the taxes paid in 2008 on the $6,000 of capital gains. The $4,000 ($10,000 − $6,000) remainder of the loss carryback carries to 2010 and offsets East's $3,000 capital gain net income reported in that year. East still has a $1,000 net capital loss carry over to 2012. ◀

ADDITIONAL COMMENT

Under the modified accelerated cost recovery system (MACRS), Sec. 1250 depreciation recapture seldom, if ever, occurs for individuals because MACRS requires straight-line depreciation for Sec. 1250 property. Nevertheless, individuals would be subject to the 25% tax rate on Sec. 1250 gains.

SEC. 291: TAX BENEFIT RECAPTURE RULE. If a taxpayer sells Sec. 1250 property at a gain, Sec. 1250 requires that the taxpayer report the recognized gain as ordinary income to the extent the depreciation taken exceeds the depreciation that would have been allowed had the taxpayer used the straight-line method. This ordinary income is known as Sec. 1250 depreciation recapture. For individuals, any remaining gain is characterized as a combination of Sec. 1250 gain and Sec. 1231 gain. Corporations, however, must recapture as ordinary income an additional amount equal to 20% of the additional ordinary income that would have been recognized had the property been Sec. 1245 property instead of Sec. 1250 property.

EXAMPLE C:3-4 ▶ Texas Corporation purchased residential real estate several years ago for $125,000, of which $25,000 was allocated to the land and $100,000 to the building. Texas took straight-line MACRS depreciation deductions of $10,606 on the building during the period it held the building. In December of the current year, Texas sells the property for $155,000, of which $45,000 is allocated to the land and $110,000 to the building. Texas has a $20,000 ($45,000 − $25,000) gain on the land sale, all of which is Sec. 1231 gain. This gain is not affected by Sec. 291 because land is not Sec. 1250 property. Texas has a $20,606 [$110,000 sales price − ($100,000 original cost − $10,606 depreciation)] gain on the sale of the building. If Texas were an individual taxpayer, $10,606 would be a Sec. 1250 gain subject to a 25% tax rate, and the remaining $10,000 would

ADDITIONAL
COMMENT

Section 291 results in the recapture, as ordinary income, of an additional 20% of the gain on sales of Sec. 1250 property. This recapture requirement reduces the amount of net Sec.1231 gains that can be offset by corporate capital losses.

be a Sec. 1231 gain. However, a corporate taxpayer reports $2,121 of gain as ordinary income. These amounts are summarized below:

	Land	Building	Total
Amount of gain:			
Sales price	$45,000	$110,000	$155,000
Minus: adjusted basis	(25,000)	(89,394)	(114,394)
Recognized gain	$20,000	$ 20,606	$ 40,606
Character of gain:			
Ordinary income	$ –0–	$ 2,121[a]	$ 2,121
Sec. 1231 gain	20,000	18,485	38,485
Recognized gain	$20,000	$ 20,606	$ 40,606

[a]0.20 × lesser of $10,606 depreciation claimed or $20,606 recognized gain.

BUSINESS EXPENSES

Corporations are allowed deductions for ordinary and necessary business expenses, including salaries paid to officers and other employees of the corporation, rent, repairs, insurance premiums, advertising, interest, taxes, losses on sales of inventory or other property, bad debts, and depreciation. No deductions are allowed, however, for interest on amounts borrowed to purchase tax-exempt securities, illegal bribes or kickbacks, fines or penalties imposed by a government, or insurance premiums incurred to insure the lives of officers and employees when the corporation is the beneficiary.

ORGANIZATIONAL EXPENDITURES. When formed, a corporation may incur some organizational expenditures such as legal fees and accounting fees incident to the incorporation process. These expenditures normally must be capitalized. Nevertheless, under Sec. 248, a corporation may elect to deduct the first $5,000 of organizational expenditures. However, the corporation must reduce the $5,000 by the amount by which cumulative organizational expenditures exceed $50,000 although the $5,000 cannot be reduced below zero. The corporation can amortize the remaining organizational expenditures over a 180-month period beginning in the month it begins business.

EXAMPLE C:3-5 ▶ Sigma Corporation incorporates on January 10 of the current year, and begins business on March 3. Sigma elects a September 30 year-end. Thus, it conducts business for seven months during its first tax year. During the period January 10 through September 30, Sigma incurs $52,000 of organizational expenditures. Because these expenditures exceed $50,000, Sigma must reduce the first $5,000 by $2,000 ($52,000 − $50,000), leaving a $3,000 deduction. Sigma amortizes the remaining $49,000 ($52,000 − $3,000) over 180 months beginning in March of its first year. This portion of the deduction equals $1,906 ($49,000/180 × 7 months). Accordingly, its total first-year deduction is $4,906 ($3,000 + $1,906). ◀

WHAT WOULD YOU DO IN THIS SITUATION?

You are a CPA with a medium-size accounting firm. One of your corporate clients is an electrical contractor in New York City. The client is successful and had $10 million of sales last year. The contracts involve private and government electrical work. Among the corporation's expenses are $400,000 of kickbacks paid to people working for general contractors who award electrical subcontracts to the corporation, and $100,000 of payments to individuals in the electricians' union. Technically, these payments are illegal. However, your client says that everyone in this business needs to pay kickbacks to obtain contracts and to have enough electricians to finish the projects in a timely manner. He maintains that it is impossible to stay in business without making these payments. In preparing its tax return, your client wants you to deduct these expenses. What is your opinion concerning the client's request?

BOOK-TO-TAX ACCOUNTING COMPARISON

Most corporations amortize organizational expenditures for tax purposes over the specified period. For financial accounting purposes, they are expensed currently under ASC 720-15. Thus, the differential treatment creates a deferred tax asset.

For organizational expenditures paid or incurred after September 8, 2008, a corporation is deemed to have made the Sec. 248 election for the tax year the corporation begins business.[13] A corporation also can apply the amortization provisions for expenditures made after October 22, 2004, provided the statute of limitations is still open for the particular year. If the corporation chooses to forgo the deemed election, it can elect to capitalize the expenditures (without amortization) on a timely filed tax return for the tax year the corporation begins business. Either election, to amortize or capitalize, is irrevocable and applies to all organizational expenditures of the corporation.

A corporation begins business when it starts the business operations for which it was organized. Merely coming into existence is not sufficient. For example, obtaining a corporate charter does not in itself establish the beginning of business. However, acquiring assets necessary for operating the business may be sufficient.

Organizational expenditures include expenditures incident to the corporation's creation; chargeable to the corporation's capital account; and of a character that, if expended incident to the creation of a corporation having a limited life, would be amortizable over that life.

Specific organizational expenditures include

▶ Legal services incident to the corporation's organization (e.g., drafting the corporate charter and bylaws, minutes of organizational meetings, and terms of original stock certificates)

▶ Accounting services necessary to create the corporation

▶ Expenses of temporary directors and of organizational meetings of directors and stockholders

▶ Fees paid to the state of incorporation[14]

Organizational expenditures do not include expenditures connected with issuing or selling the corporation's stock or other securities (e.g., commissions, professional fees, and printing costs) and expenditures related to the transfer of assets to the corporation.

EXAMPLE C:3-6 ▶

Omega Corporation incorporates on July 12 of the current year, starts business operations on August 10, and elects a tax year ending on September 30. Omega incurs the following expenditures while organizing the corporation:

Date	Type of Expenditure	Amount
June 10	Legal expenses to draft charter	$ 2,000
July 17	Commission to stockbroker for issuing and selling stock	40,000
July 18	Accounting fees to set up corporate books	2,400
July 20	Temporary directors' fees	1,000
August 25	Directors' fees	1,500

Omega's first tax year begins July 12 and ends on September 30. Omega has organizational expenditures of $5,400 ($2,000 + $2,400 + $1,000). The commission for selling the Omega stock is treated as a reduction in the amount of Omega's paid-in capital. Omega deducts the directors' fees incurred in August as a trade or business expense under Sec. 162 because Omega had begun business operations by that date. Assuming a deemed election to amortize its organizational expenditures, Omega can deduct $5,000 in its first tax year and amortize the remaining $400 over 180 months. Thus, its first year deduction is $5,004 [$5,000 + ($400/180) × 2 months]. The following table summarizes the classification of expenditures:

Date	Expenditure	Amount	Organizational	Capital	Business
June 10	Legal	$ 2,000	$2,000		
July 17	Commission	40,000		$40,000	
July 18	Accounting	2,400	2,400		
July 20	Temporary directors' fees	1,000	1,000		
August 25	Directors' fees	1,500			$1,500
	Total	$46,900	$5,400	$40,000	$1,500	◀

---

[13] Temp. Reg. Sec. 1.148-1T. [14] Reg. Sec. 1.248-1(b)(2).

START-UP EXPENDITURES. A distinction must be made between a corporation's organizational expenditures and its start-up expenditures. Start-up expenditures are ordinary and necessary business expenses paid or incurred by an individual or corporate taxpayer

BOOK-TO-TAX ACCOUNTING COMPARISON

For tax purposes, a corporation amortizes start-up expenditures over 180 months (after the initial deduction). ASC 915 holds that the financial accounting practices and reporting standards used for development stage businesses should be no different for an established business. The two different sets of rules can lead to different reporting for tax and book purposes.

▶ To investigate the creation or acquisition of an active trade or business

▶ To create an active trade or business

▶ To conduct an activity engaged in for profit or the production of income before the time the activity becomes an active trade or business

Examples of start-up expenditures include the costs for a survey of potential markets; an analysis of available facilities; advertisements relating to opening the business; the training of employees; travel and other expenses for securing prospective distributors, suppliers, or customers; and the hiring of management personnel and outside consultants. The expenditures must be such that, if incurred in connection with the operation of an existing active trade or business, they would be allowable as a deduction in the year paid or incurred.

Under Sec. 195, a corporation may elect to deduct the first $5,000 of start-up expenditures. However, this amount is reduced (but not below zero) by the amount by which the cumulative start-up expenditures exceed $50,000. The corporation can amortize the remaining start-up expenditures over a 180-month period beginning in the month it begins business.

ADDITIONAL COMMENT

For 2010, a corporation could deduct up to $10,000 in the first year, with reduction beginning after $60,000.

For start-up expenditures paid or incurred after September 8, 2008, a corporation is deemed to have made the Sec. 195 election for the tax year the business to which the expenditures relate begins.[15] A corporation also can apply the amortization provisions for expenditures made after October 22, 2004, provided the statute of limitations is still open for the particular year. If the corporation chooses to forgo the deemed election, it can elect to capitalize the expenditures (without amortization) on a timely filed tax return for the tax year the business to which the expenditures relate begins. Either election, to amortize or capitalize, is irrevocable and applies to all start-up expenditures related to the business.

 STOP & THINK

Question: What is the difference between an organizational expenditure and a start-up expenditure?

Solution: Organizational expenditures are outlays made in forming a corporation, such as fees paid to the state of incorporation for the corporate chapter and fees paid to an attorney to draft the documents needed to form the corporation. Start-up expenditures are outlays that otherwise would be deductible as ordinary and necessary business expenses but that are capitalized because they were incurred prior to the start of the corporation's business activities.

A corporation may elect to deduct the first $5,000 of organizational expenditures and the first $5,000 of start-up expenditures. The corporation can amortize the remainder of each set of expenditures over 180 months. Like a corporation, a partnership can deduct and amortize its organizational and start-up expenditures. A sole proprietorship may incur start-up expenditures, but sole proprietorships do not incur organizational expenditures.

LIMITATION ON DEDUCTIONS FOR ACCRUED COMPENSATION. If a corporation accrues an obligation to pay compensation, the corporation must make the payment within 2½ months after the close of its tax year. Otherwise, the deduction cannot be taken until the year of payment.[16] The reason is that, if a payment is delayed beyond 2½ months, the IRS treats it as a deferred compensation plan. Deferred compensation cannot be deducted until the year the corporation pays it and the recipient includes the payment in income.[17]

EXAMPLE C:3-7 ▶ On December 10 of the current year, Bell Corporation, a calendar year taxpayer, accrues an obligation for a $100,000 bonus to Marge, a sales representative who has had an outstanding year. Marge owns no Bell stock. Bell must make the payment by March 15 of next year. Otherwise, Bell Corporation cannot deduct the $100,000 in its current year tax return but must wait until the year it pays the bonus. ◀

---

[15] Temp. Reg. Sec. 1.195-1T.
[16] Temp. Reg. Sec. 1.404(b)-1T.
[17] Sec. 404(b).

CHARITABLE CONTRIBUTIONS. The treatment of charitable contributions by individual and corporate taxpayers differs in three ways: the timing of the deduction, the amount of the deduction permitted for the contribution of certain noncash property, and the maximum deduction permitted in any given year.

Timing of the Deduction. Corporations may deduct contributions to qualified charitable organizations. Generally, the contribution must have been *paid* during the year (not just pledged) for a deduction to be allowed for a given year. A special rule, however, applies to corporations using the accrual method of accounting (corporations using the cash or hybrid methods of accounting are not eligible).[18] These corporations may elect to treat part or all of a charitable contribution as having been made in the year it accrued (instead of the year paid) if

▶ The board of directors authorizes the contribution in the year it accrued

▶ The corporation pays the contribution on or before the fifteenth day of the third month following the end of the accrual year.

The corporation makes the election by deducting the contribution in its tax return for the accrual year and by attaching a copy of the board of director's resolution to the return. Any portion of the contribution for which the corporation does not make the election is deducted in the year paid.

EXAMPLE C:3-8 ▶ Echo Corporation is a calendar year taxpayer using the accrual method of accounting. In the current year, its board of directors authorizes a $10,000 contribution to the Girl Scouts. Echo pays the contribution on March 10 of next year. Echo may elect to treat part or all of the contribution as having been paid in the current year. If the corporation pays the contribution after March 15 of next year, it may not deduct the contribution in the current year but may deduct it next year. ◀

TAX STRATEGY TIP

The tax laws do not require a corporation to recognize a gain when it contributes appreciated property to a charitable organization. Thus, except for inventory and limited other properties, a corporation can deduct the FMV of its donation without having to recognize any appreciation in its gross income. On the other hand, a decline in the value of donated property is not deductible. Thus, the corporation should sell the loss property to recognize the loss and then donate the sales proceeds to the chariable organization.

Deducting Contributions of Nonmonetary Property. If a taxpayer donates money to a qualified charitable organization, the amount of the charitable contribution deduction equals the amount of money donated. If the taxpayer donates property, the amount of the charitable contribution deduction generally equals the property's fair market value (FMV). However, special rules apply to donations of appreciated nonmonetary property known as ordinary income property and capital gain property.[19]

In this context, **ordinary income property** is property whose sale would have resulted in a gain other than a long-term capital gain (i.e., ordinary income or short-term capital gain). Examples of ordinary income property include investment property held for one year or less, inventory property, and property subject to depreciation recapture under Secs. 1245 and 1250. The deduction allowed for a donation of such property is limited to the property's FMV minus the amount of ordinary income or short-term capital gain the corporation would have recognized had it sold the property.

In three special cases, a corporation may deduct the donated property's adjusted basis plus one-half of the excess of the property's FMV over its adjusted basis (not to exceed twice the property's adjusted basis). This special rule applies to inventory if

1. The use of the property is related to the donee's exempt function, and it is used solely for the care of the ill, the needy, or infants;
2. The property is not transferred to the donee in exchange for money, other property, or services; and
3. The donor receives a statement from the charitable organization stating that conditions (1) and (2) will be complied with.

A similar rule applies to contributions of scientific research property if the corporation created the property and contributed it to a college, university, or tax-exempt scientific research organization for its use within two years of creating the property.

EXAMPLE C:3-9 ▶ King Corporation donates inventory having a $26,000 adjusted basis and a $40,000 FMV to a qualified public charity. A $33,000 [$26,000 + (0.50 × $14,000)] deduction is allowed for the

---

[18] Sec. 170(a).

[19] Sec. 170(e).

contribution of the inventory if the charitable organization will use the inventory for the care of the ill, needy, or infants, or if the donee is an educational institution or research organization that will use the scientific research property for research or experimentation. Otherwise, the deduction is limited to the property's $26,000 adjusted basis. If instead the inventory's FMV is $100,000 and the donation meets either of the two sets of requirements outlined above, the charitable contribution deduction is limited to $52,000, the lesser of the property's adjusted basis plus one-half of the appreciation [$63,000 = $26,000 + (0.50 × $74,000)] or twice the property's adjusted basis ($52,000 = $26,000 × 2). ◀

When a corporation donates appreciated property whose sale would result in long-term capital gain (also known as **capital gain property**) to a charitable organization, the amount of the contribution deduction generally equals the property's FMV. However, special restrictions apply if

▶ The corporation donates a patent, copyright, trademark, trade name, trade secret, know-how, certain software, or other similar property;

▶ A corporation donates tangible personal property to a charitable organization and the organization's use of the property is unrelated to its tax-exempt purpose; or

▶ A corporation donates appreciated property to certain private nonoperating foundations.[20]

In these cases, the amount of the corporation's contribution is limited to the property's FMV minus the long-term capital gain that would have resulted from the property's sale.

EXAMPLE C:3-10 ▶ Fox Corporation donates artwork to the MacNay Museum. The artwork, purchased two years earlier for $15,000, is worth $38,000 on the date Fox donates it. At the time of the donation, the museum's directors intend to sell the work to raise funds to conduct museum activities. Fox's deduction for the gift is limited to $15,000. If the museum plans to display the artwork to the public, the entire $38,000 deduction is permitted. Fox can avoid losing a portion of its charitable contribution deduction by, as a condition of the donation, placing restrictions on the sale or use of the property. ◀

Substantiation Requirements. Section 170(f)(11) imposes substantiation requirements for noncash charitable contributions. If the corporation does not comply, it will lose the charitable contribution deduction. The requirements are as follows:

▶ If the contribution deduction exceeds $500, the corporation must include with its tax return a description of the property and any other information required by Treasury Regulations.

▶ If the contribution deduction exceeds $5,000, the corporation must obtain a qualified appraisal and include with its tax return any information and appraisal required by Treasury Regulations. (Current regulations require an appraisal summary.)

▶ If the contribution deduction exceeds $500,000, the corporation must attach a qualified appraisal to the tax return.

The second and third requirements, however, do not apply to contributions of cash; publicly traded securities; inventory; or certain motor vehicles, boats, or aircraft the donee organization sells without any intervening use or material improvement. With regard to these vehicles, the donor corporation's deduction is limited to the amount of gross proceeds the donee organization receives on the sale.

Maximum Deduction Permitted. A limit applies to the amount of charitable contributions a corporation can deduct in a given year. The limit is calculated differently for corporations than for individuals. Contribution deductions by corporations are limited to 10% of adjusted taxable income. Adjusted taxable income is the corporation's taxable income computed without regard to any of the following amounts:

---

[20] Sec. 170(e)(5). The restriction on contributions of appreciated property to private nonoperating foundations does not apply to contributions of stock for which market quotations are readily available.

BOOK-TO-TAX ACCOUNTING COMPARISON

For financial accounting purposes, all charitable contributions can be claimed as an expense without regard to the amount of profits reported. For tax purposes, however, the charitable contribution deduction may be limited. Thus, the charitable contribution carryover for tax purposes creates a deferred tax asset, possibly subject to a valuation allowance.

▶ The charitable contribution deduction
▶ An NOL carryback
▶ A capital loss carryback
▶ The dividends-received deduction[21]
▶ The U.S. production activities deduction

Contributions that exceed the 10% limit are not deductible in the current year. Instead, they carry forward to the next five tax years. Any excess contributions not deducted within those five years expire. The corporation may deduct excess contributions in the carryover year only after it deducts any contributions made in that year. The total charitable contribution deduction (including any deduction for contribution carryovers) is limited to 10% of the corporation's adjusted taxable income in the carryover year.[22]

EXAMPLE C:3-11 ▶

Golf Corporation reports the following results in Year 1 and Year 2:

	Year 1	Year 2
Adjusted taxable income	$200,000	$300,000
Charitable contributions	35,000	25,000

Golf's Year 1 contribution deduction is limited to $20,000 (0.10 × $200,000). Golf has a $15,000 ($35,000 − $20,000) contribution carryover to Year 2. The Year 2 contribution deduction is limited to $30,000 (0.10 × $300,000). Golf's deduction for Year 2 is composed of the $25,000 donated in Year 2 and $5,000 of the Year 1 carryover. The remaining $10,000 carryover from Year 1 carries over to the next four years. ◀

Topic Review C:3-1 summarizes the basic corporate charitable contribution deduction rules.

Topic Review C:3-1

Corporate Charitable Contribution Rules

1. Timing of the contribution deduction
   a. General rule: A deduction is allowed for contributions paid during the year.
   b. Accrual method corporations can accrue contributions approved by their board of directors prior to the end of the accrual year and paid within 2½ months of that year-end.
2. Amount of the contribution deduction
   a. General rule: A deduction is allowed for the amount of money and the FMV of other property donated.
   b. Exceptions for ordinary income property:
      1. If donated property would result in ordinary income or short-term capital gain if sold, the deduction is limited to the property's FMV minus this potential ordinary income or short-term capital gain. Thus, for gain property the deduction equals the property's cost or adjusted basis.
      2. Special rule: For donations of (1) inventory used for the care of the ill, needy, or infants or (2) scientific research property or computer technology and equipment to certain educational institutions, a corporate donor may deduct the property's basis plus one-half of the excess of the property's FMV over its adjusted basis. The deduction may not exceed twice the property's adjusted basis.
   c. Exceptions for capital gain property: If the corporation donates tangible personal property to a charitable organization for a use unrelated to its tax-exempt purpose, or the corporation donates appreciated property to a private nonoperating foundation, the corporation's contribution is limited to the property's FMV minus the long-term capital gain that would result if the corporation sold the property.
3. Limitation on contribution deduction
   a. The contribution deduction is limited to 10% of the corporation's taxable income computed without regard to the charitable contribution deduction, any NOL or capital loss carryback, the dividends-received deduction, and the U.S production activities deduction.
   b. Excess contributions carry forward for a five-year period.

---

[21] Sec. 170(b)(2).

[22] Sec. 170(d)(2).

SPECIAL DEDUCTIONS

C corporations are allowed three special deductions: the U.S. production activities deduction, the dividends-received deduction, and the NOL deduction.

ADDITIONAL COMMENT

While discussed in this text under special deductions, the U.S. production activities deduction actually appears before Line 28 on Form 1120. This deduction also is referred to as the domestic production activities deduction or the manufacturing deduction.

BOOK-TO-TAX ACCOUNTING COMPARISON

The U.S. production activities deduction is not expensed for financial accounting purposes. Thus, it creates a permanent difference that affects the corporation's effective tax rate but not its deferred taxes.

U.S. PRODUCTION ACTIVITIES DEDUCTION. Section 199 allows a **U.S. production activities deduction** equal to 9% (in 2010 and thereafter) times the lesser of (1) qualified production activities income for the year or (2) taxable income before the U.S. production activities deduction. The deduction, however, cannot exceed 50% of the corporation's W-2 wages allocable to qualifying U.S. production activities for the year.

Qualified production activities income is the taxpayer's domestic production gross receipts less the following amounts:

▶ Cost of goods sold allocable to these receipts;

▶ Other deductions, expenses, and losses directly allocable to these receipts; and

▶ A ratable portion of other deductions, expenses, and losses not directly allocable to these receipts or to other classes of income.

Domestic production gross receipts include receipts from the following taxpayer activities:

▶ The lease, rental, license, sale, exchange, or other disposition of (1) qualified production property (tangible property, computer software, and sound recordings) manufactured, produced, grown, or extracted in whole or significant part within the United States; (2) qualified film production; or (3) electricity, natural gas, or potable water produced within the United States

▶ Construction performed in the United States

▶ Engineering or architectural services performed in the United States for construction projects in the United States

ADDITIONAL COMMENT

In addition to providing a benefit, the U.S. production activities deduction will increase a corporation's compliance costs because of the time necessary to determine what income and deductions pertain to U.S. production activities.

Domestic production gross receipts, however, do not include receipts from the sale of food and beverages the taxpayer prepares at a retail establishment and do not apply to the transmission of electricity, natural gas, or potable water.

The U.S. production activities deduction has the effect of reducing a corporation's marginal tax rate on qualifying taxable income. For example, a 9% deduction for a corporation in the 35% tax bracket decreases the corporation's marginal tax rate by about 3% ($0.09 \times 35\% = 3.15\%$).

EXAMPLE C:3-12 ▶ Gamma Corporation earns domestic production gross receipts of $1 million and incurs allocable expenses of $400,000. Thus, its qualified production activities income is $600,000. In addition, Gamma has $200,000 of income from other sources, resulting in taxable income of $800,000 before the U.S. production activities deduction. Its U.S. production activities deduction, therefore, is $54,000 ($600,000 × 0.09), and its taxable income is $746,000 ($800,000 − $54,000). ◀

EXAMPLE C:3-13 ▶ Assume the same facts as in Example C:3-12 except Gamma has $100,000 of losses from other sources rather than $200,000 of other income, resulting in taxable income of $500,000 before the U.S. production activities deduction. In this case, its U.S. production activities deduction is $45,000 ($500,000 × 0.09), and its taxable income is $455,000 ($500,000 − $45,000). ◀

DIVIDENDS-RECEIVED DEDUCTION. A corporation must include in its gross income any dividends received on stock it owns in another corporation. As described in Chapter C:2, the taxation of dividend payments to a shareholder generally results in double taxation. When a distributing corporation pays a dividend to a corporate shareholder and the recipient corporation subsequently distributes these earnings to its shareholders, potential triple taxation of the earnings can result.

EXAMPLE C:3-14 ▶ Adobe Corporation owns stock in Bell Corporation. Bell reports taxable income of $100,000 and pays federal income taxes on its income. Bell distributes its after-tax income to its shareholders. The dividend Adobe receives from Bell must be included in its gross income and, to the extent it reports a profit for the year, Adobe will pay taxes on the dividend. Adobe distributes its remaining after-tax income to its shareholders. The shareholders must include Adobe's dividends in their gross income and pay federal income taxes on the distribution. Thus, Bell's income in this example potentially is taxed three times. ◀

BOOK-TO-TAX ACCOUNTING COMPARISON

A corporation includes dividends in its financial accounting income but does not subtract a dividends-received deduction in determining its book net income. Thus, the dividends-received deduction creates a permanent difference that affects the corporation's effective tax rate but not its deferred taxes.

To partially mitigate the effects of multiple taxation, corporations are allowed a **dividends-received deduction** for dividends received from other domestic corporations and from certain foreign corporations.

General Rule for Dividends-Received Deduction. Corporations that own less than 20% of the distributing corporation's stock may deduct 70% of the dividends received. If the shareholder corporation owns 20% or more of the distributing corporation's stock (both voting power and value) but less than 80% of such stock, it may deduct 80% of the dividends received.[23]

EXAMPLE C:3-15 ▶ Hale Corporation reports the following results in the current year:

Gross income from operations	$300,000
Dividends from 15%-owned domestic corporation	100,000
Operating expenses	280,000

Gross income from operations and expenses both pertain to qualified production activities, so Hale's qualified production activities income is $20,000 ($300,000 − $280,000). Hale's dividends-received deduction is $70,000 (0.70 × $100,000). Thus, Hale's taxable income is computed as follows:

Gross income	$400,000
Minus: Operating expenses	(280,000)
Taxable income before special deductions	$120,000
Minus: Dividends-received deduction	(70,000)
Taxable income before the U.S. production activites deduction	$ 50,000
Minus: U.S. production activities deduction ($20,000 × 0.09)	(1,800)
Taxable income	$ 48,200 ◀

Limitation on Dividends-Received Deduction. In the case of dividends received from corporations that are less than 20% owned, the deduction is limited to the lesser of 70% of dividends received or 70% of taxable income computed without regard to any NOL deduction, any capital loss carryback, the dividends-received deduction itself, or the U.S. production activities deduction.[24] In the case of dividends received from a 20% or more owned corporation, the dividends-received deduction is limited to the lesser of 80% of dividends received or 80% of taxable income computed without regard to the same deductions.

EXAMPLE C:3-16 ▶ Assume the same facts as in Example C:3-15 except Hale Corporation's operating expenses for the year are $310,000 and that qualified production activities income is zero (or negative). Thus, the corporation cannot claim the U.S. production activities deduction. Hale's taxable income before the dividends-received deduction is $90,000 ($300,000 + $100,000 − $310,000). The dividends-received deduction is limited to the lesser of 70% of dividends received ($70,000 = $100,000 × 0.70) or 70% of taxable income before the dividends-received deduction ($63,000 = $90,000 × 0.70). Thus, the dividends-received deduction is $63,000. Hale's taxable income is $27,000 ($90,000 − $63,000). ◀

A corporation that receives dividends eligible for both the 80% dividends-received deduction and the 70% dividends-received deduction must compute the 80% dividends-received deduction first and then reduce taxable income by the aggregate amount of dividends eligible for the 80% deduction before computing the 70% deduction.

---

[23] Secs. 243(a) and (c).   [24] Sec. 246(b).

EXAMPLE C:3-17 ▶ Assume the same facts as in Example C:3-16 except Hale Corporation receives $75,000 of the dividends from a 25%-owned corporation and the remaining $25,000 from a 15%-owned corporation. The tentative dividends-received deduction from the 25%-owned corporation is $60,000 ($75,000 × 0.80), which is less than the $72,000 ($90,000 × 0.80) limitation. Thus, Hale can deduct the entire $60,000. The tentative dividends-received deduction from the 15%-owned corporation is $17,500 ($25,000 × .70). The limitation, however, is $10,500 [($90,000 − $75,000) × 0.70]. Note that, in computing this limitation, Hale reduces its taxable income by the entire $75,000 dividend received from the 25%-owned corporation. Thus, Hale can deduct only $10,500 of the $17,500 amount. Hale's taxable income is $19,500 ($90,000 − $60,000 − $10,500). ◀

Exception to the Limitation. The taxable income limitation on the dividends-received deduction does not apply if, after taking into account the full dividends-received deduction, the corporation has an NOL for the year.

EXAMPLE C:3-18 ▶ Assume the same facts as in Example C:3-16 except Hale Corporation's operating expenses for the year are $331,000. Hale's taxable income before the dividends-received deduction is $69,000 ($300,000 + $100,000 − $331,000). The tentative dividends-received deduction is $70,000 (0.70 × $100,000). Hale's dividends-received deduction is not restricted by the limitation of 70% of taxable income before the dividends-received deduction because, after taking into account the tentative $70,000 dividends-received deduction, the corporation has a $1,000 ($69,000 − $70,000) NOL for the year. ◀

The following table compares the results of Examples C:3-15, C:3-16, and C:3-18:

<table>
<tr><td></td><td>*Example C:3-15*</td><td>*Example C:3-16*</td><td>*Example C:3-18*</td></tr>
<tr><td>Gross income</td><td>$400,000</td><td>$400,000</td><td>$400,000</td></tr>
<tr><td>Minus: Operating expenses</td><td>(280,000)</td><td>(310,000)</td><td>(331,000)</td></tr>
<tr><td>Taxable income before special
  deductions</td><td>$120,000</td><td>$ 90,000</td><td>$ 69,000</td></tr>
<tr><td>Minus: Dividends-received
            deduction</td><td>(70,000)</td><td>(63,000)</td><td>(70,000)</td></tr>
<tr><td>   U.S. production
            activities deduction</td><td>(1,800)</td><td>–0–</td><td>–0–</td></tr>
<tr><td>Taxable income (NOL)</td><td>$ 48,200</td><td>$ 27,000</td><td>$ (1,000)</td></tr>
</table>

ADDITIONAL COMMENT

When the dividends-received deduction creates (or increases) an NOL, the corporation gets the full benefit of the deduction because it can carry back or carry forward the NOL.

TAX STRATEGY TIP

A corporation can avoid the dividends-received deduction limitation either by (1) increasing its taxable income before the dividends-received deduction so the limitation exceeds the tentative dividends-received deduction or (2) decreasing its taxable income before the dividends-received deduction so the tentative dividends-received deduction creates an NOL.

Of these three examples, the only case where the dividends-received deduction does not equal the full 70% of the $100,000 dividend is Example C:3-16. In that case, the deduction is limited to $63,000 because taxable income before special deductions is less than the $100,000 dividend *and* because the full $70,000 deduction would not create an NOL. The special exception to the dividends-received deduction can create interesting situations. For example, the additional $21,000 of deductions incurred in Example C:3-18 (as compared to Example C:3-16) resulted in a $28,000 reduction in taxable income. Corporate taxpayers should be aware of these rules and consider deferring income or recognizing expenses to ensure being able to deduct the full 70% or 80% dividends-received deduction. If the taxable income limitation applies, the corporation loses the unused dividends-received deduction.

ADDITIONAL COMMENT

If the affiliated group files a consolidated tax return, the recipient of the dividend does not claim the 100% dividends received deduction because the intercompany dividend gets eliminated in the consolidation (see Chapter C:8).

Members of an Affilliated Group. Members of an affiliated group of corporations can claim a 100% dividends-received deduction with respect to dividends received from other group members.[25] A group of corporations is affiliated if a parent corporation owns at least 80% of the stock (both voting power and value) of at least one subsidiary corporation, and at least 80% of the stock (both voting power and value) of each other corporation is owned by other group members. The 100% dividends-received deduction is not subject to a taxable income limitation and is taken before the 80% or 70% dividends-received deduction.[26]

---

[25] Sec. 243(a)(3).

[26] Secs. 243(b)(5) and 1504.

EXAMPLE C:3-19 ▶ Hardy Corporation reports the following results for the current year:

Gross income from operations	$520,000
Dividend received from an 80%-owned affiliated corporation	100,000
Dividend received from a 20%-owned corporation	250,000
Operating expenses	550,000

Hardy does not file a consolidated tax return with the 80%-owned affiliate. Because Hardy's qualified production activities income is negative, it cannot claim the U.S. production activities deduction. Hardy's taxable income before any dividends-received deduction is $320,000 ($520,000 + $100,000 + $250,000 − $550,000). Hardy can deduct the entire dividend received from the 80%-owned affiliate without limitation. The tentative dividends-received deduction from the 20%-owned corporation is $200,000 ($250,000 × 0.80). The limitation, however, is $176,000 [($320,000 − $100,000) × 0.80]. Note that, in computing this limitation, Hardy first reduces its taxable income by the $100,000 dividend received from the 80%-owned affiliate. Thus, Hardy can deduct only $176,000 of the $200,000 amount. Hardy's taxable income is $44,000 ($320,000 − $100,000 − $176,000). ◀

Dividends Received from Foreign Corporations. The dividends-received deduction applies primarily to dividends received from domestic corporations. The dividends-received deduction does not apply to dividends received from a foreign corporation because the U.S. Government does not tax its income. Thus, that income is not subject to the multiple taxation illustrated above.[27]

ADDITIONAL COMMENT

Stock purchased on which a dividend has been declared has an increased value. This value will drop when the corporation pays the dividend. If the dividend is eligible for a dividends-received deduction and the drop in value also creates a capital loss, corporate shareholders could use this event as a tax planning device. To avoid this result, no dividends-received deduction is available for stock held 45 days or less.

Stock Held 45 Days or Less. A corporation may not claim a dividends-received deduction if it holds the dividend paying stock for less than 46 days during the 91-day period that begins 45 days before the stock becomes ex-dividend with respect to the dividend.[28] This rule prevents a corporation from claiming a dividends-received deduction if it purchases stock shortly before an ex-dividend date and sells the stock shortly thereafter. (The ex-dividend date is the first day on which a purchaser of stock is not entitled to a previously declared dividend.) Absent this rule, such a purchase and sale would allow the corporation to receive dividends at a low tax rate—a maximum of a 10.5% [(100% − 70%) × 0.35] effective tax rate—and to recognize a capital loss on the sale of stock that could offset capital gains taxed at a 35% tax rate.

EXAMPLE C:3-20 ▶ Theta Corporation purchases 100 shares of Maine Corporation's stock for $100,000 one day before Maine's ex-dividend date. Theta receives a $5,000 dividend on the stock and then sells the stock for $95,000 shortly after the dividend payment date. Because the stock is worth $100,000 immediately before the $5,000 dividend payment, its value drops to $95,000 ($100,000 − $5,000) immediately after the dividend. The sale results in a $5,000 ($100,000 − $95,000) capital loss that may offset a $5,000 capital gain. Assuming a 35% corporate tax rate, the following table summarizes the profit (loss) to Theta with and without the 45-day rule.

	If Deduction Is Allowed	If Deduction Is Not Allowed
Dividends	$5,000	$5,000
Minus: 35% tax on dividend	(525)[a]	(1,750)
Dividend (after taxes)	$4,475	$3,250
Capital loss	$5,000	$5,000
Minus: 35% tax savings on loss	(1,750)	(1,750)
Net loss on stock	$3,250	$3,250
Dividend (after taxes)	$4,475	$3,250
Minus: Net loss on stock[b]	(3,250)	(3,250)
Net profit (loss)	$1,225	$ –0–

[a][$5,000 − (0.70 × $5,000)] × 0.35 = $525
[b]This example assumes the corporation has capital gains against which to deduct this capital loss.

---

[27] Sec. 245. A limited dividends-received deduction is allowed on dividends received from a foreign corporation that earns income by conducting a trade or business in the United States and, therefore, is subject to U.S. taxes.

[28] Sec. 246(c)(1).

ADDITIONAL COMMENT

Borrowing money with deductible interest to purchase a tax-advantaged asset, such as stock eligible for the dividends-received deduction, is an example of "tax arbitrage." Many provisions in the IRC, such as the limits on debt-financial stock, are aimed at curtailing tax arbitrage transactions.

The profit is not available if Theta sells the stock shortly after receiving the dividend because Theta must hold the Maine stock for at least 46 days to obtain the dividends-received deduction.   ◄

Debt-Financed Stock.   The dividends-received deduction is not allowed to the extent the corporation borrows money to acquire the dividend paying stock.[29] This rule prevents a corporation from deducting interest paid on money borrowed to purchase the stock, while paying little or no tax on the dividends received on the stock.

EXAMPLE C:3-21 ►

Palmer Corporation, whose marginal tax rate is 35%, borrows $100,000 at a 10% interest rate to purchase 30% of Sun Corporation's stock. The Sun stock pays an $8,000 annual dividend. If a dividends-received deduction were allowed for this investment, Palmer would have a net profit of $940 annually on owning the Sun stock even though the dividend received is less than the interest paid. The following table summarizes the profit (loss) to Palmer with and without the debt-financing rule.

REAL-WORLD EXAMPLE

Although sound in theory, the debt-financed stock limitation may be difficult to apply in practice. This difficulty became particularly apparent in a district court case, *OBH, Inc. v. U.S.,* 96 AFTR 2d, 2005-6801, 2005-2 USTC ¶50,627 (DC NB, 2005), where the IRS failed to establish that a corporation's debt proceeds were directly traceable to the acquisition of dividend paying stock.

	If Deduction Is Allowed	If Deduction Is Not Allowed
Dividends	$ 8,000	$ 8,000
Minus: 35% tax on dividend	(560)[a]	(2,800)
Dividend (after taxes)	$ 7,440	$5,200
Interest paid	$10,000	$10,000
Minus: 35% tax savings on deduction	(3,500)	(3,500)
Net cost of borrowing	$ 6,500	$6,500
Dividend (after taxes)	$ 7,440	$ 5,200
Minus: Net cost of borrowing	(6,500)	(6,500)
Net profit (loss)	$ 940	$(1,300)

[a][$8,000 − ($8,000 × 0.80)] × 0.35 = $560

This example illustrates how the rule disallowing the dividends-received deduction on debt-financed stock prevents corporations from making an after-tax profit by borrowing funds to purchase stocks paying dividends that are less than the cost of the borrowing.   ◄

NET OPERATING LOSSES (NOLs).   If a corporation's deductions exceed its gross income for the year, the corporation has a **net operating loss (NOL).** The NOL is the amount by which the corporation's deductions (including any dividends-received deduction) exceed its gross income.[30] In computing an NOL for a given year, no deduction is permitted for a carryover or carryback of an NOL from a preceding or succeeding year. However, unlike an individual's NOL, no other adjustments are required to compute a corporation's NOL. If the corporation has an NOL, it also would not be allowed a U.S. production activities deduction because it has no positive taxable income.

ADDITIONAL COMMENT

Recent tax acts allow eligible businesses having a calendar year to carry back applicable NOLs three, four, or five years instead of two years if the business so elects. An applicable NOL is one arising in a tax year ending after 2007 and before 2010. The business can make the election with respect to only one year, however.

A corporation's NOL carries back two years (or an extended period if applicable) and carries over 20 years. It carries to the earliest of the two preceding years first and offsets taxable income reported in that year. If the loss cannot be used in that year, it carries to the immediately preceding year, and then to the next 20 years in chronological order. The corporation may elect to forgo the carryback period entirely and instead carry over the entire loss to the next 20 years.[31]

EXAMPLE C:3-22 ►

In 2011, Gray Corporation, a calendar year taxpayer, has gross income of $150,000 (including $100,000 from operations and $50,000 in dividends from a 30%-owned domestic corporation) and $180,000 of expenses. Gray has a $70,000 [$150,000 − $180,000 − (0.80 × $50,000)] NOL. The NOL carries back to 2009 unless Gray elects to forego the carryback period. If Gray had

---

[29] Sec. 246A.
[30] Sec. 172(c).
[31] The two year carryback and 20-year carryforward applies to NOLs incurred in tax years beginning after August 5, 1997. The change does not

apply to NOLs carried forward from earlier years. These NOLs, in general, carried back three years and carried forward 15 years. NOLs incurred in 2001 and 2002 were allowed a five-year carryback period.

$20,000 of taxable income in 2009, $20,000 of Gray's 2011 NOL offsets that income. Gray receives a refund of all taxes paid in 2009. Gray carries the remaining $50,000 of the 2011 NOL to 2010. Any of the NOL not used in 2010 carries over to 2012 ◄

BOOK-TO-TAX ACCOUNTING COMPARISON

An NOL carryover for tax purposes creates a deferred tax asset, possibly subject to a valuation allowance.

A corporation might elect not to carry an NOL back because its income was taxed at a low marginal tax rate in the carryback period and the corporation anticipates income being taxed at a higher marginal tax rate in later years or because it used tax credit carryovers in the earlier year that were about to expire. The corporation must make this election for the entire carryback by the due date (including extensions) for filing the return for the year in which the corporation incurred the NOL. The corporation makes the election by checking a box on Form 1120 when it files the return. Once made for a tax year, the election is irrevocable.[32] However, if the corporation incurs an NOL in another year, the decision as to whether that NOL should be carried back is a separate decision. In other words, each year's NOL is treated separately and is subject to a separate election.

To obtain a refund due to carrying an NOL back to a preceding year, a corporation files Form 1139 (Corporation Application for a Tentative Refund) if one year or less has elapsed since the year in which the NOL occurred. If a longer period has elapsed, the corporation files Form 1120X (Amended U.S. Corporation Income Tax Return).

THE SEQUENCING OF THE DEDUCTION CALCULATIONS. The rules for charitable contributions, dividends-received, NOL, and U.S. production activities deductions require that these deductions be calculated in the following sequence:

1. All deductions other than the charitable contributions deduction, the dividends-received deduction, the NOL deduction, and the U.S. production activities deduction
2. The charitable contributions deduction
3. The dividends-received deduction
4. The NOL deduction
5. The U.S. production activities deduction

As stated previously, the charitable contributions deduction is limited to 10% of taxable income before the charitable contributions deduction, any NOL or capital loss carryback, the dividends-received deduction, or the U.S. production activities deduction, but *after* any NOL carryover deduction. Once the corporation determines its charitable contributions deduction, it adds back any NOL carryover deduction and subtracts the charitable contributions deduction before computing the dividends-received deduction. The corporation then subtracts the NOL deduction, if any, before determining its U.S. production activities deduction.

EXAMPLE C:3-23 ▶

East Corporation reports the following results for 2011:

Gross income from operations	$150,000
Dividends from 30%-owned domestic corporation	100,000
Operating expenses	100,000
Charitable contributions	35,000

In addition, East has $50,000 of qualified production activities income in the current year and a $40,000 NOL carryover from the previous year. East's charitable contributions deduction is computed as follows:

Gross income from operations	$150,000
Plus: Dividends	100,000
Gross income	$250,000
Minus: Operating expenses	(100,000)
NOL carryover	(40,000)
Base for calculation of the charitable contributions limitation	$110,000

East's charitable contributions deduction is limited to $11,000 (0.10 × $110,000). The $11,000 limitation means that East has a $24,000 ($35,000 − $11,000) excess contribution that carries over for five years. East Corporation computes its taxable income as follows:

[32] Sec. 172(b)(3)(C).

Gross income	$250,000
Minus: Operating expenses	(100,000)
Charitable contributions deduction	(11,000)
Taxable income before special deductions	$139,000
Minus: Dividends-received deduction ($100,000 × 0.80)	(80,000)
NOL carryover deduction	(40,000)
Taxable income before the U.S. production activities deduction	$ 19,000
Minus: U.S. production activities deduction ($19,000 × 0.09)	(1,710)
Taxable income	$ 17,290 ◄

Note that, if an NOL carries *back* from a later year, it is *not* taken into account in computing a corporation's charitable contributions limitation. In other words, the contribution deduction remains the same as in the year of the original return.

EXAMPLE C:3-24 ▶ Assume the same facts as in Example C:3-23, except the facts pertain to a prior year (e.g., 2009), and East carries back a $40,000 NOL to that year. East's base for calculation of the charitable contributions limitation was computed as follows when it filed the original return:

Gross income from operations	$150,000
Plus: Dividends	100,000
Gross income	$250,000
Minus: Operating expenses	(100,000)
Base for calculation of the charitable contributions limitation	$150,000

East's charitable contributions deduction was limited to $15,000 ($150,000 × 0.10). The $15,000 limitation means that East had a $20,000 ($35,000 − $15,000) contribution carryover from the prior year. East Corporation computes its taxable income after the NOL carryback as follows:

Gross income ($150,000 + $100,000)	$250,000
Minus: Operating expenses	(100,000)
Charitable contributions deduction	(15,000)
Taxable income before special deductions	$135,000
Minus: Dividends-received deduction ($100,000 × 0.80)	(80,000)
NOL carryback deduction	(40,000)
Taxable income before the U.S. production activities deduction	$ 15,000
Minus: U.S. production activities deduction ($15,000 × 0.06, the 2009 percentage)	(900)
Taxable income as recomputed	$ 14,100

Thus, East's prior-year charitable contributions deduction remains the same as originally claimed. ◄

STOP & THINK

Question: Why does a corporation's NOL or capital loss carryback not affect its charitable contributions deduction, but yet the corporation must take into account an NOL or capital loss carryover when calculating its charitable contribution limitation?

Solution: A carryback affects a tax return already filed in a prior year. If a carryback had to be taken into account when calculating the charitable contribution deduction limitation in the prior year, it might change the amount of the allowable charitable contribution. This change in turn might affect other items such as the carryback year's dividends-received deduction and some later years' deductions as well. For example, assume Alpha Corporation has a $10,000 NOL in 2011 that it carries back to 2009. If the NOL were permitted to reduce Alpha's allowable charitable contribution for 2009 by $1,000, Alpha's dividends-received deduction for 2009 and its charitable contribution deductions for 2010 as well might change.

To avoid these complications, which might force Alpha to amend its tax returns from the carryback year (2009) to the current year (2011), the law states that carrybacks are not taken into account in calculating the charitable contribution deduction limitation. Also, in the prior year, management made its charitable contribution decisions without knowledge of future NOLs. Altering the result of those prior decisions with future events might be unfair.

EXCEPTIONS FOR CLOSELY HELD CORPORATIONS

Congress has placed limits on certain transactions to prevent abuse in situations where a corporation is closely held. Some of these restrictions are explained below.

TRANSACTIONS BETWEEN A CORPORATION AND ITS SHAREHOLDERS. Special rules apply to transactions between a corporation and a controlling shareholder. Section 1239 may convert a capital gain realized on the sale of depreciable property between a corporation and a controlling shareholder into ordinary income. Section 267(a)(1) denies a deduction for losses realized on property sales between a corporation and a controlling shareholder. Section 267(a)(2) defers a deduction for accrued expenses and interest on certain transactions involving a corporation and a controlling shareholder.

In all three of the preceding situations, a controlling shareholder is one who owns more than 50% (in value) of the corporation's stock.[33] In determining whether a shareholder owns more than 50% of a corporation's stock, certain constructive stock ownership rules apply.[34] Under these rules, a shareholder is considered to own not only his or her own stock, but stock owned by family members (e.g., brothers, sisters, spouse, ancestors, and lineal descendants) and entities in which the shareholder has an ownership or beneficial interest (e.g., corporations, partnerships, trusts, and estates).

Gains on Sale or Exchange Transactions. If a controlling shareholder sells depreciable property to a controlled corporation (or vice versa) and the property is depreciable in the purchaser's hands, any gain on the sale is treated as ordinary income under Sec. 1239(a).

EXAMPLE C:3-25 ▶ Ann owns all of Cape Corporation's stock. Ann sells a building to Cape and recognizes a $25,000 gain, which usually would be Sec. 1231 gain or Sec. 1250 gain taxed (in 2011) at a maximum 15% or 25% capital gains tax rate, respectively. However, because Ann owns more than 50% of the Cape stock and the building is a depreciable property in Cape's hands, Sec. 1239 requires that Ann recognize the entire $25,000 gain as ordinary income. ◀

BOOK-TO-TAX ACCOUNTING COMPARISON

The denial of deductions for losses involving related party transactions is unique to the tax area. Financial accounting rules contain no such disallowance provision.

Losses on Sale or Exchange Transactions. Section 267(a)(1) denies a deduction for losses realized on a sale of property by a corporation to a controlling shareholder or on a sale of property by the controlling shareholder to the corporation. If the purchaser later sells the property to another party at a gain, that seller recognizes gain only to the extent it exceeds the previously disallowed loss.[35] Should the purchaser instead sell the property at a loss, the previously disallowed loss is never recognized.

EXAMPLE C:3-26 ▶ Quattros Corporation sells an automobile to Juan, its sole shareholder, for $6,500. The corporation's adjusted basis for the automobile is $8,000. Quattros realizes a $1,500 ($6,500 − $8,000) loss on the sale. Section 267(a)(1), however, disallows the loss to the corporation. If Juan later sells the auto for $8,500, he realizes a $2,000 ($8,500 − $6,500) gain. He recognizes only $500 of that gain, the amount by which his $2,000 gain exceeds the $1,500 loss previously disallowed to Quattros. If Juan instead sells the auto for $7,500, he realizes a $1,000 ($7,500 − $6,500) gain but recognizes no gain or loss. The previously disallowed loss reduces the gain to zero but may not create a loss. Finally, if Juan instead sells the auto for $4,000, he realizes and may be able to recognize a $2,500 ($4,000 − $6,500) loss. However, the $1,500 loss previously disallowed to Quattros is permanently lost. ◀

KEY POINT

Section 267(a)(2) is primarily aimed at the situation involving an accrual method corporation that accrues compensation to a cash method shareholder-employee. This provision forces a matching of the income and expense recognition by deferring the deduction to the year the shareholder recognizes the income.

Corporation and Controlling Shareholder Using Different Accounting Methods. Section 267(a)(2) defers a deduction for accrued expenses or interest owed by a corporation to a controlling shareholder or by a controlling shareholder to a corporation when the two parties use different accounting methods and the payee thereby includes the amount in gross income later than when the payer accrues the deduction. Under this rule, accrued expenses or interest owed by a corporation to a controlling shareholder may not be deducted until the shareholder includes the payment in gross income.

---

[33] Sec. 267(b)(2).
[34] Sec. 267(e)(3).

[35] Sec. 267(d).

EXAMPLE C:3-27 ▶ Hill Corporation uses the accrual method of accounting. Hill's sole shareholder, Ruth, uses the cash method of accounting. Both taxpayers use the calendar year as their tax year. The corporation accrues a $25,000 interest payment to Ruth on December 20 of the current year. Hill makes the payment on March 20 of next year. Hill, however, cannot deduct the interest in the current year but must wait until Ruth reports the income next year. Thus, the expense and income are matched. ◀

LOSS LIMITATION RULES

At-Risk Rules. If five or fewer shareholders own more than 50% (in value) of a C corporation's outstanding stock at any time during the last half of the corporation's tax year, the corporation is subject to the at-risk rules.[36] In such case, the corporation can deduct losses pertaining to an activity only to the extent the corporation is at risk for that activity at year-end. Any losses not deductible because of the at-risk rules must be carried over and deducted in a succeeding year when the corporation's risk with respect to the activity increases. (See Chapter C:9 for additional discussion of the at-risk rules.)

Passive Activity Limitation Rules. Personal service corporations (PSCs) and **closely held C corporations** (those subject to the at-risk rules described above) also may be subject to the **passive activity limitations**.[37] If a PSC does not meet the material participation requirements, its net **passive losses** and credits must be carried over to a year when it has **passive income**. In the case of closely held C corporations that do not meet material participation requirements, passive losses and credits are allowed to offset the corporation's net active income but not its portfolio income (i.e., interest, dividends, annuities, royalties, and capital gains on the sale of investment property).[38]

COMPUTING A CORPORATION'S INCOME TAX LIABILITY

OBJECTIVE 3

Compute a corporation's income tax liability

Once a corporation determines its taxable income, it then must compute its tax liability for the year. Table C:3-2 outlines the steps for computing a corporation's regular (income) tax liability. This section explains the steps involved in arriving at a corporation's income tax liability in detail.

▼ TABLE C:3-2

Computation of the Corporate Regular (Income) Tax Liability

Taxable income
Times: Income tax rates
Regular tax liability
Minus: Foreign tax credit (Sec. 27)
Regular tax
Minus: General business credit (Sec. 38)
Minimum tax credit (Sec. 53)
Other allowed credits
Plus: Recapture of previously claimed tax credits
Income tax liability

---

[36] Sec. 465(a).
[37] Secs. 469(a)(2)(B) and (C).

[38] Sec. 469(e)(2).

GENERAL RULES

REAL-WORLD EXAMPLE

In 2009, the IRS collected $225 billion from corporations, which was 9.8% of the $2.3 trillion collected by the IRS. This percentage is down from 13% in 2008.

All C corporations (other than members of controlled groups of corporations and personal service corporations) use the same tax rate schedule to compute their **regular tax** liability. The following table shows these rates, which also are reproduced on the inside back cover of this textbook.

Taxable Income Over	But Not Over	The Tax Is	Of the Amount Over
$ –0–	$ 50,000	15%	$ –0–
50,000	75,000	$ 7,500 + 25%	50,000
75,000	100,000	13,750 + 34%	75,000
100,000	335,000	22,250 + 39%	100,000
335,000	10,000,000	113,900 + 34%	335,000
10,000,000	15,000,000	3,400,000 + 35%	10,000,000
15,000,000	18,333,333	5,150,000 + 38%	15,000,000
18,333,333	—	6,416,667 + 35%	18,333,333

EXAMPLE C:3-28 ▶ Copper Corporation reports taxable income of $100,000. Copper's regular tax liability is computed as follows:

Tax on first $50,000:	0.15 × $50,000 =	$7,500
Tax on second $25,000:	0.25 × 25,000 =	6,250
Tax on remaining $25,000:	0.34 × 25,000 =	8,500
Regular tax liability		$22,250

This tax liability also can be determined from the above tax rate schedule. ◀

If taxable income exceeds $100,000, a 5% surcharge applies to the corporation's taxable income exceeding $100,000. The surcharge phases out the lower graduated tax rates that apply to the first $75,000 of taxable income for corporations earning between $100,000 and $335,000 of taxable income. The maximum surcharge is $11,750 [($335,000 − $100,000) × 0.05]. The above tax rate schedule incorporates the 5% surcharge by imposing a 39% (34% + 5%) rate on taxable income from $100,000 to $335,000.

EXAMPLE C:3-29 ▶ Delta Corporation reports taxable income of $200,000. Delta's regular tax liability is computed as follows:

Tax on first $50,000:	0.15 × $ 50,000 =	$ 7,500
Tax on next $25,000:	0.25 × 25,000 =	6,250
Tax on remaining $125,000:	0.34 × 125,000 =	42,500
Surcharge (income over $100,000):	0.05 × 100,000 =	5,000
Regular tax liability		$61,250

Alternatively, from the above tax rate schedule, the tax is $22,250 + [0.39 × ($200,000 − $100,000)] = $61,250. ◀

If taxable income is at least $335,000 but less than $10 million, the corporation pays a flat 34% tax rate on all of its taxable income. A corporation whose income is at least $10 million but less than $15 million pays $3.4 million plus 35% of the income above $10 million.

EXAMPLE C:3-30 ▶ Elgin Corporation reports taxable income of $350,000. Elgin's regular tax liability is $119,000 (0.34 × $350,000). If Elgin's taxable income is instead $12 million, its tax liability is $4.1 million [$3,400,000 + (0.35 × $2,000,000)]. ◀

If a corporation's taxable income exceeds $15 million, a 3% surcharge applies to the corporation's taxable income exceeding $15 million (but not exceeding $18,333,333). The surcharge phases out the one percentage point lower rate (34% vs. 35%) that applies to the first $10 million of taxable income. The maximum surcharge is $100,000 [($18,333,333 − $15,000,000) × 0.03]. The above tax rate schedule incorporates the 3%

surcharge by imposing a 38% (35% + 3%) rate on taxable income from $15 million to $18,333,333. A corporation whose taxable income exceeds $18,333,333 pays a flat 35% tax rate on all its taxable income.

STOP & THINK

Question: Planner Corporation has an opportunity to realize $50,000 of additional income in either the current year or next year. Planner has some discretion as to the timing of this additional income. Not counting the additional income, Planner's current year taxable income is $200,000, and it expects next year's taxable income to be $500,000. In what year should Planner recognize the additional $50,000?

Solution: Even though Planner's current year taxable income is lower than next year's expected taxable income, Planner will have a lower marginal tax rate next year. The current year's marginal tax rate is 39% because Planner's taxable income is in the 5% surtax range (or 39% "bubble"). Next year's taxable income is beyond the 39% bubble and is in the flat 34% range. Thus, Planner can save $2,500 (0.05 × $50,000) in taxes by deferring the $50,000 until next year.

PERSONAL SERVICE CORPORATIONS

Personal service corporations are denied the benefit of the graduated corporate tax rates. Thus, all the income of personal service corporations is taxed at a flat 35% rate.

Section 448(d) defines a personal service corporation as a corporation that meets the following two tests:

▶ Substantially all its activities involve the performance of services in the fields of health, law, engineering, architecture, accounting, actuarial science, performing arts, and consulting.

▶ Substantially all its stock (by value) is held directly or indirectly by employees performing the services or retired employees who performed the services in the past, their estates, or persons who hold stock in the corporation by reason of the death of an employee or retired employee within the past two years.

This rule encourages employee-owners of personal service corporations either to withdraw earnings from the corporation as deductible salary (rather than have the corporation retain them) or make an S election.

CONTROLLED GROUPS OF CORPORATIONS

OBJECTIVE 4

Understand what a controlled group is and the tax consequences of being a controlled group

Special tax rules apply to corporations under common control to prevent them from avoiding taxes that otherwise would be due. The rules apply to corporations that meet the definition of a controlled group. This section explains why special rules apply to controlled groups, how the IRC defines controlled groups, and what special rules apply to controlled groups.

WHY SPECIAL RULES ARE NEEDED

Special controlled group rules prevent shareholders from using multiple corporations to avoid having corporate income taxed at a 35% rate. If these rules were not in effect, the owners of a corporation could allocate the corporation's income among two or more corporations and take advantage of the lower 15%, 25%, and 34% rates on the first $10 million of corporate income for each corporation.

The following example demonstrates how a group of shareholders could obtain a significant tax advantage by dividing a business enterprise among several corporate entities. Each corporation then could take advantage of the graduated corporate tax rates. To prevent a group of shareholders from using multiple corporations to gain such tax advantages, Congress enacted laws that limit the tax benefits of multiple corporations.[39]

---

[39] Secs. 1561 and 1563.

EXAMPLE C:3-31 ▶ Axle Corporation reports taxable income of $450,000. Axle's regular tax liability on that income is $153,000 (0.34 × $450,000). If Axle could divide its taxable income equally among six corporations ($75,000 apiece), each corporation's federal income tax liability would be $13,750 [(0.15 × $50,000) + (0.25 × $25,000)], or an $82,500 total regular tax liability for all the corporations. Thus, Axle could save $70,500 ($153,000 − $82,500) in federal income taxes. ◀

The law governing controlled corporations requires special treatment for two or more corporations controlled by the same shareholder or group of shareholders. The most important restrictions on a controlled group of corporations are that the group must share the benefits of the progressive corporate tax rate schedule and pay a 5% surcharge on the group's taxable income exceeding $100,000, up to a maximum surcharge of $11,750, and also pay a 3% surcharge on the group's taxable income exceeding $15 million, up to a maximum surcharge of $100,000.

EXAMPLE C:3-32 ▶ White, Blue, Yellow, and Green Corporations belong to a controlled group. Each corporation reports $100,000 of taxable income (a total of $400,000). Only one $50,000 amount is taxed at 15% and only one $25,000 amount is taxed at 25%. Furthermore, the group is subject to the maximum $11,750 surcharge because its total taxable income exceeds $335,000. This surcharge is levied on the group member(s) that received the benefit of the 15 and 25% rates. Therefore, the group's total regular tax liability is $136,000 (0.34 × $400,000), as though one corporation earned the entire $400,000. Each corporation would be allocated $34,000 of this tax liability. ◀

WHAT IS A CONTROLLED GROUP?

A **controlled group** is comprised of two or more corporations owned directly or indirectly by the same shareholder or group of shareholders. Controlled groups fall into three categories: a parent-subsidiary controlled group, a brother-sister controlled group, and a combined controlled group. Each of these groups is subject to the limitations described above.

ADDITIONAL COMMENT

For purposes of the Sec. 179 expense dollar limitation, a more-than-50% threshold replaces the at-least-80% threshold in defining a parent-subsidiary controlled group.

PARENT-SUBSIDIARY CONTROLLED GROUPS. In a **parent-subsidiary controlled group**, one corporation (the parent corporation) must directly own at least 80% of the voting power of all classes of voting stock, or 80% of the total value of all classes of stock, of a second corporation (the subsidiary corporation).[40] The group can contain more than one subsidiary corporation. If the parent corporation, the subsidiary corporation, or any other members of the controlled group in total own at least 80% of the voting power of all classes of voting stock, or 80% of the total value of all classes of stock, of another corporation, that other corporation also is included in the parent-subsidiary controlled group.

EXAMPLE C:3-33 ▶ Parent Corporation owns 80% of Axle Corporation's single class of stock and 40% of Wheel Corporation's single class of stock. Axle also owns 40% of Wheel's stock. (See Figure C:3-2.) Parent, Axle, and Wheel are members of the same parent-subsidiary controlled group because Parent directly owns 80% of Axle's stock and therefore is its parent corporation, and Wheel's stock is 80% owned by Parent (40%) and Axle (40%).

If Parent and Axle together owned only 70% of Wheel's stock and an unrelated shareholder owned the remaining 30%, Wheel would not be included in the parent-subsidiary group. The controlled group then would consist only of Parent and Axle. ◀

EXAMPLE C:3-34 ▶ Beta Corporation owns 70% of Spectrum Corporation's single class of stock and 60% of Red Corporation's single class of stock. Blue Corporation owns the remaining stock of Spectrum (30%) and Red (40%). No combination of these corporations forms a parent-subsidiary group because no corporation has direct stock ownership of at least 80% of any other corporation's stock. ◀

---

[40] Sec. 1563(a)(1). Section 1563(d)(1) requires that certain attribution rules apply to determine stock ownership for parent-subsidiary controlled groups. If any person has an option to acquire stock, such stock is considered owned by the person having the option. Section 1563(c) excludes certain types of stock from the controlled group definition of stock.

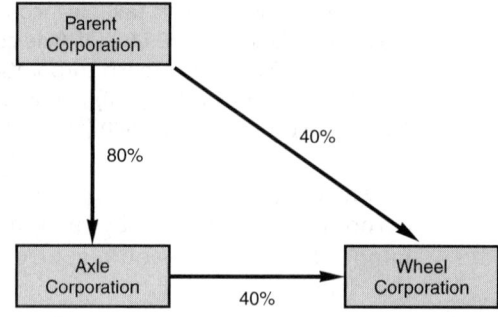

BROTHER-SISTER CONTROLLED GROUPS. The IRC contains two definitions of a **brother-sister controlled group.** This textbook will refer to them as the 50%-80% definition and the 50%-only definition. Under the 50%-80% definition, a group of two or more corporations is a brother-sister controlled group if five or fewer individuals, trusts, or estates own

▶ At least 80% of the voting power of all classes of voting stock (or at least 80% of the total value of the outstanding stock) of each corporation, and

▶ More than 50% of the voting power of all classes of stock (or more than 50% of the total value of the outstanding stock) of each corporation, taking into account only the stock ownership that is common with respect to each corporation.[41] A common ownership is the percentage of stock a shareholder owns that is common or identical in each of the corporations. For example, if a shareholder owns 30% of New Corporation and 70% of Old Corporation, his or her common ownership is 30%.

Thus, under the 50%-80% definition, the five or fewer shareholders not only must have more than 50% common ownership in the corporations, they also must own at least 80% of the stock of each corporation in the brother-sister group. This definition is narrow because the shareholders must meet two tests.

The 50%-only definition, on the other hand, is broader than the 50%-80% definition in that the five or fewer shareholders must satisfy only the 50% common ownership test described above. Consequently, in situations where the 50%-only definition applies, more corporations may be pulled into the controlled group than under the 50%-80% definition. Table C:3-3 on page C:3-29 indicates which definition applies to specific situations.

EXAMPLE C:3-35 ▶ North and South Corporations have only one class of stock outstanding, owned by the following individuals:

| | Stock Ownership Percentages | | |
Shareholder	North Corp.	South Corp.	Common Ownership
Walt	30%	70%	30%
Gail	70%	30%	30%
Total	100%	100%	60%

Five or fewer individuals (Walt and Gail) together own at least 80% (actually 100%) of each corporation's stock, and the same individuals own more than 50% (actually 60%) of the corporations' stock taking into account only their common ownership in each corporation. Because

---

[41] Sec. 1563(a)(2). Section 1563(d)(2) requires that certain attribution rules apply to determine stock ownership for brother-sister controlled groups. If any person has an option to acquire stock, such stock is considered to be owned by the person having the option. A proportionate amount of stock owned by a partnership, estate, or trust is attributed to partners having an interest of 5% or more in the capital or profits of the partnership or benefici-

aries having a 5% or more actuarial interest in the estate or trust. A proportionate amount of stock owned by a corporation is attributed to shareholders owning 5% or more in value of the corporate stock. Family attribution rules also can cause an individual to be considered to own the stock of a spouse, child, grandchild, parent, or grandparent.

their ownership satisfies both tests, North and South are a brother-sister controlled group under the 50%-80% definition and under the 50%-only definition. (See Figure C:3-3.) ◄

EXAMPLE C:3-36 ▶ East and West Corporations have only one class of stock outstanding, owned by the following individuals:

| | Stock Ownership Percentages | | Common Ownership |
Shareholder	East Corp.	West Corp.	
Javier	80%	25%	25%
Sara	20%	75%	20%
Total	100%	100%	45%

Five or fewer individuals (Javier and Sara) together own at least 80% (actually 100%) of each corporation's stock. However, those same individuals own only 45% of the corporations' stock taking into account only their common ownership. Because their ownership does not satisfy the more-than-50% test, East and West are not a brother-sister controlled group under either the 50%-80% or the 50%-only definition. Consequently, each corporation is taxed on its own income without regard to the earnings of the other. ◄

An individual's stock ownership can be counted for the 80% test only if that individual owns stock in each and every corporation in the controlled group.[42]

EXAMPLE C:3-37 ▶ Long and Short Corporations each have only a single class of stock outstanding, owned by the following individuals:

| | Stock Ownership Percentages | | Common Ownership |
Shareholder	Long Corp.	Short Corp.	
Al	50%	40%	40%
Beth	20%	60%	20%
Carol	30%	—	—
Total	100%	100%	60%

Carol's stock does not count for purposes of Long's 80% stock ownership requirement because she owns no stock in Short. Only Al's and Beth's stock holdings count, and together they own only 70% of Long's stock. Thus, the 80% test fails. Consequently, Long and Short are not a brother-sister controlled group under the 50%-80% defintion, but they are a brother-sister controlled group under the 50%-only definition. ◄

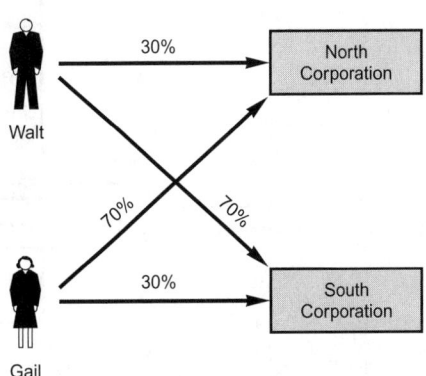

FIGURE C:3-3 ▶ BROTHER-SISTER CONTROLLED GROUP (EXAMPLE C:3-35)

---

[42] Reg. Sec. 1.1563-1(a)(3).

COMBINED CONTROLLED GROUPS. A **combined controlled group** is comprised of three or more corporations meeting the following criteria:

▶ Each corporation is a member of a parent-subsidiary controlled group or a brother-sister controlled group

▶ At least one of the corporations is both the parent corporation of a parent-subsidiary controlled group and a member of a brother-sister controlled group.[43]

EXAMPLE C:3-38 ▶

Able, Best, and Coast Corporations each have a single class of stock outstanding, owned by the following shareholders:

KEY POINT

The combined controlled group definition does just what its name implies: It combines a parent-subsidiary controlled group and a brother-sister controlled group. Thus, instead of trying to apply the controlled group rules to two different groups, the combined group definition eliminates the issue by combining the groups into one controlled group.

	Stock Ownership Percentages		
Shareholder	*Able Corp.*	*Coast Corp.*	*Best Corp.*
Art	50%	50%	—
Barbara	50%	50%	—
Able Corp.	—	—	100%

Able and Coast are a brother-sister controlled group under the 50%-80% *and* 50%-only definitions because Art's and Barbara's ownership satisfy both the 80% and 50% tests. Able and Best are a parent-subsidiary controlled group because Able owns all of Best's stock. Each of the three corporations is a member of either the parent-subsidiary controlled group (Able and Best) or the brother-sister controlled group (Able and Coast), and the parent corporation (Able) of the parent-subsidiary controlled group also is a member of the brother-sister controlled group. Therefore, Able, Best, and Coast Corporations are members of a combined controlled group. (See Figure C:3-4.) ◀

APPLICATION OF THE CONTROLLED GROUP TEST

Controlled group status generally is tested on December 31. A corporation is included in a controlled group if it is a group member on December 31 and has been a group member on at least one-half of the days in its tax year that precede December 31. A corporation that is not a group member on December 31, nevertheless, is considered a member for the tax year if it has been a group member on at least one-half the days in its tax year that precede December 31. Corporations are excluded from the controlled group if they were members for less than one-half the days in their tax year that precede December 31 or if they retain certain special tax statuses such as being a tax-exempt corporation.

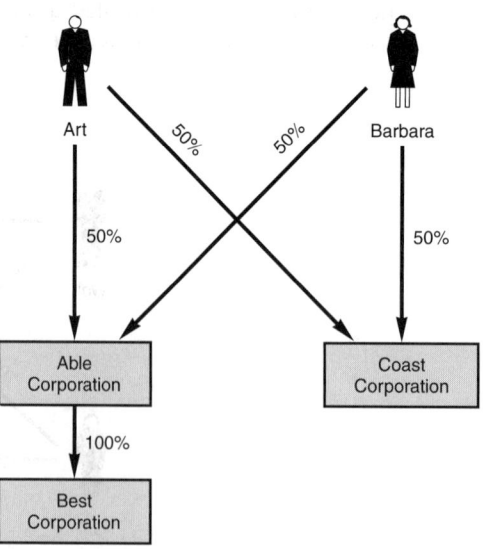

FIGURE C:3-4 ▶ COMBINED CONTROLLED GROUP (EXAMPLE C:3-38)

---

[43] Sec. 1563(a)(3).

▼ TABLE C:3-3

Items that Must be Apportioned if a Controlled Group Exists

Item	Brother-Sister 50%-Only	Brother-Sister 50%–80%	Parent-Subsidiary ≥ 80%	Parent-Subsidiary ≥ 50%
Low-bracket tax rates	X	X	X	
AMT exemption	X	X	X	
Minimum accumulated earnings tax credit	X	X	X	
Section 179 expense limitation		X	X	X
General business tax credit limitation		X	X	

EXAMPLE C:3-39 ▶ Ace and Copper Corporations are members of a parent-subsidiary controlled group of which Ace is the common parent. Both corporations are calendar year taxpayers and have been group members for the entire year. They do not file a consolidated return. Bell Corporation, which has a fiscal year ending on August 31, becomes a group member on December 1 of the current year. Although Bell is a group member on December 31 of the current year, it has been a group member for less than half the days in its tax year that precede December 31—only 30 of 121 days starting on September 1. Therefore, Bell is not a member of the Ace-Copper *controlled* group for its tax year beginning on September 1 of the current year. ◀

TAX STRATEGY TIP

A controlled group of corporations should elect to apportion the tax benefits in a manner that maximizes the tax savings from the tax benefits. See Tax Planning Considerations later in this chapter for details.

SPECIAL RULES APPLYING TO CONTROLLED GROUPS

As discussed earlier, if two or more corporations are members of a controlled group, the member corporations are limited to a total of $50,000 taxed at 15%, $25,000 being taxed at 25%, and $9,925,000 million being taxed at 34%. For brother-sister corporations, the broader 50%-only definition applies for limiting the reduced tax rates.

In addition, a controlled group must apportion certain other items among its group members, some of which are shown in Table C:3-3. For purposes of apportioning the Sec. 179 expense dollar limitation in a parent-subsidiary situation, the corporations are considered a controlled group if the ownership percentage is more than 50% rather than at least 80%.[44]

In addition to the above restrictions, Sec. 267(a)(1) allows no deduction for any loss on the sale or exchange of property between two members of the same controlled group. However, in contrast to losses between a corporation and controlling shareholder described earlier in this chapter, a loss realized on a transaction between members of a controlled group is deferred (instead of being disallowed). The original selling member recognizes the deferred loss when the property sold or exchanged in the intragroup transaction is sold outside the controlled group.

Section 267(a)(2) allows no deduction for certain accrued expenses or interest owed by one member of a controlled group to another member of the same controlled group when the two corporations use different accounting methods so that the payments would be reported in different tax years. (See page C:3-21 for a detailed discussion of Sec. 267.) The Sec. 1239 rules that convert capital gain into ordinary income on depreciable property sales between related parties also apply to sales or exchanges involving two members of the same controlled group. Sections 267 and 1239, however, provide special definitions of controlled groups that differ somewhat from those described above. These details are beyond the scope of this textbook.

TYPICAL MISCONCEPTION

The definitions of a parent-subsidiary controlled group and an affiliated group are similar, but not identical. For example, the 80% stock ownership test for controlled group purposes is satisfied if 80% of the voting power *or* 80% of the FMV of a corporation's stock is owned. For purposes of an affiliated group, 80% of both the voting power *and* the FMV of a corporation's stock must be owned.

CONSOLIDATED TAX RETURNS

WHO CAN FILE A CONSOLIDATED RETURN. Some groups of related corporations (i.e., affiliated groups) may elect to file a single income tax return called a **consolidated tax return**. An **affiliated group** is one or more chains of includible corporations connected through stock ownership with a common parent. In general, includible corporations are those other than foreign corporations, certain insurance companies, tax-exempt organiza-

[44] Secs. 179(d)(6) and (7).

tions, S corporations, and a few other specially defined corporations. The required ownership criteria are as follows:

▶ The common parent must directly own stock with at least 80% of the voting power *and* 80% of the value of at least one includible corporation.

▶ One or more group members must directly own stock with at least 80% of the voting power *and* 80% of the value of each other corporation included in the affiliated group.[45]

Many parent-subsidiary controlled groups also qualify as affiliated groups and thus are eligible to file a consolidated return in place of separate tax returns for each corporation. The parent-subsidiary portion of a combined group also can file a consolidated tax return if it also qualifies as an affiliated group. Brother-sister controlled groups, however, are not eligible to file consolidated returns because the requisite parent-subsidiary relationship does not exist.

An affiliated group elects to file a consolidated tax return by filing Form 1120, which includes all the income and expenses of each of its members. Each corporate member of the affiliated group must consent to the original election. Thereafter, any new member of the affiliated group must join in the consolidated return.

SELF-STUDY QUESTION

What is probably the most common reason for making a consolidated return election?

ANSWER

Filing consolidated returns allows the group to offset losses of one corporation against the profits of other members of the group.

ADVANTAGES OF FILING A CONSOLIDATED RETURN. A consolidated return, in effect, is one tax return for the entire affiliated group of corporations. The main advantages of filing a consolidated return are

▶ Losses of one member of the group can offset profits of another member of the group.

▶ Capital losses of one member of the group can offset capital gains of another member of the group.

▶ Profits or gains realized on intercompany transactions are deferred until a sale outside the group occurs (i.e., if one member sells property to another member, the gain is postponed until the member sells the property to someone outside the affiliated group).

In contrast, if the group members file separate returns, members with NOLs or capital losses must either carry back these losses to earlier years or carry them over to future years rather than offset another member's profits or gains.

Although the losses of one group member can offset the profits of another group member when the group files a consolidated return, some important limitations apply to the use of a member corporation's NOL. These limitations prevent one corporation from purchasing another corporation's NOL carryovers to offset its own taxable income or purchasing a profitable corporation to facilitate the use of its own NOL carryovers. (See Chapters C:7 and C:8.)

The following example illustrates the advantage of a consolidated return election.

EXAMPLE C:3-40 ▶

BOOK-TO-TAX ACCOUNTING COMPARISON

The corporations included in a consolidated tax return may differ from those included in consolidated financial statements. Page 1 of Schedule M-3 reconciles financial statement worldwide consolidated net income to financial statement net income (loss) of corporations included in the consolidated tax return.

Parent Corporation owns 100% of Subsidiary Corporation's stock. Parent reports $110,000 of taxable income, including a $10,000 capital gain. Subsidiary incurs a $100,000 NOL and a $10,000 capital loss. If Parent and Subsidiary file separate returns, Parent has a $26,150 [$22,250 + 0.39 × ($110,000 − $100,000)] tax liability. Subsidiary has no tax liability but may be able to use its $100,000 NOL and $10,000 capital loss to offset taxable income in other years. On the other hand, if Parent and Subsidiary file a consolidated return, the group's consolidated taxable income is zero and the group has no tax liability. By filing a consolidated return, the group saves $26,150 in taxes for the year. ◀

DISADVANTAGES OF FILING A CONSOLIDATED RETURN. The main disadvantages of a consolidated return election are

▶ The election is binding on all subsequent tax years unless the IRS grants permission to discontinue filing consolidated returns or the affiliated group terminates.

▶ Losses on intercompany transactions are deferred until a sale outside the group takes place.

▶ One member's Sec. 1231 losses offset another member's Sec. 1231 gains instead of being reported as an ordinary loss.

▶ Losses of an unprofitable member of the group may reduce the deduction or credit limitations of the group below what would be available had the members filed separate tax returns.

---

[45] Sec. 1504(a).

ADDITIONAL COMMENT

Under Sec. 267 discussed earlier, intercompany losses may be deferred even if the corporations file separate tax returns.

▶ The group may incur additional administrative costs in maintaining the records needed to file a consolidated return.

Determining whether to make a consolidated tax return election is a complex decision because of the various advantages and disadvantages and because the election is so difficult to revoke once made. Chapter C:8 provides detailed coverage of the consolidated return rules.

TAX PLANNING CONSIDERATIONS

OBJECTIVE 5

Understand how compensation planning can reduce taxes for corporations and their shareholders

COMPENSATION PLANNING FOR SHAREHOLDER-EMPLOYEES

Compensation paid to a shareholder-employee in the form of salary has the advantage of single taxation because, while taxable to the employee, salary is deductible by the corporation. Dividend payments, on the other hand, are taxed twice. The corporation is taxed on its income when earned, and the shareholder is taxed on profits distributed as dividends. Double taxation occurs because the corporation may not deduct dividend payments. The reduced tax rate on dividends available through 2012, however, makes the difference between salary and dividends much less substantial than when dividends are taxed at ordinary rates.

EXAMPLE C:3-41 ▶

Delta Corporation earns $500,000 and wishes to distribute $100,000 or as much of the $100,000 as possible to Mary, its sole shareholder and CEO. Mary's ordinary tax rate is 35%, and the corporation's marginal tax rate is 34%. Ignoring payroll taxes, the following table compares salary and dividend payments to Mary with respect to the $100,000 of partial earnings:

	Salary	Dividend at Ordinary Tax Rate	Dividend at Reduced Tax Rate
1. Corporate earnings (partial)	$100,000	$100,000	$100,000
2. Minus: Salary deduction	(100,000)	-0-	-0-
3. Corporate taxable income (partial)	$ -0-	$100,000	$100,000
4. Times: Corporate tax rate	0.34	0.34	0.34
5. Corporate income tax (on partial income)	$ -0-	$ 34,000	$ 34,000
6. Dividend to Mary (Line 1 − Line 5)	$100,000	$ 66,000	$ 66,000
7. Times: Mary's tax rate	0.35	0.35	0.15
8. Mary's tax	$ 35,000	$ 23,100	$ 9,900
9. Total tax (Line 5 + Line 8)	$ 35,000	$ 57,100	$ 43,900
10. Overall tax rate (Line 9 ÷ Line 1)	35%	57.1%	43.9%

Thus, the preferential dividend rate reduces the overall tax rate on the corporate earnings from 57.1% to 43.9% and lessens the difference between salary and dividends from 22.1% (57.1% − 35%) to 8.9% (43.9% − 35%). This example demonstrates Congress's intent of reducing the double taxation of corporate earnings when the corporation pays dividends. ◀

To avoid double taxation, some owners of closely held corporations prefer to be taxed under the rules of Subchapter S (see Chapter C:11). Other owners of closely held corporations retain C corporation status to use the 15% and 25% marginal corporate tax rates and to benefit from nontaxable fringe benefits such as health and accident insurance. These fringe benefits are nontaxable to the employee and deductible by the corporation. For both tax and nontax reasons, closely held corporations must determine the appropriate level of earnings to be withdrawn from the business in the form of salary and fringe benefits and the amount of earnings to be retained in the business.

ADVANTAGE OF SALARY PAYMENTS. If a corporation distributes all its profits as deductible salary and fringe benefit payments, it will eliminate double taxation. However, the following considerations limit such tax planning opportunities:

ADDITIONAL COMMENT

Reasonableness of a salary payment is a question of fact to be determined in each case. No formula can be used to determine a reasonable amount.

▶ Regulation Sec. 1.162-7(a) requires salary or fringe benefit payments to be reasonable in amount and to be paid for services rendered by the employee. If the IRS deems compensation to be unreasonable, it may disallow the portion of the salary it deems unreasonable while still requiring the employee to include all compensation in gross income (see Chapter C:4). This disallowance will result in double taxation. The reasonable compensation restriction primarily affects closely held corporations.

▶ A corporation may not deduct compensation paid to an executive of a publicly traded corporation that exceeds $1 million. However, this limitation does not apply to compensation paid to an executive other than the corporation's top five officers, or to performance-based compensation.[46]

▶ A corporation is a taxpaying entity independent of its owners. The first $75,000 of a corporation's earnings is taxed at 15% and 25% corporate tax rates. These rates are lower than the marginal tax rate that may apply to an individual taxpayer and provides an incentive to retain some earnings in the corporation instead of paying them out as salaries.

NEW LAW

In 2011 only, the employee portion is 4.2%, making the total 10.4% of the first $106,800 of wages in 2011. The overall total for 2011 is 13.3% (10.4% + 2.9%).

▶ A combined employee–employer social security tax rate of 15.3% applied in 2010 Employers and employees were each liable for 6.2% of old age security and disability insurance tax, or a total of 12.4% of the first $106,800 of wages in 2010. Employers and employees also are each liable for a 1.45% Medicare hospital insurance tax, for a total of 2.9% of all wages. In addition to these taxes, state and federal unemployment taxes may be imposed on a portion of wages paid.

TAX STRATEGY TIP

A fringe benefit probably is the most cost effective form of compensation because the amount of the benefit is deductible by the employer and never taxed to the employee. Thus, where possible, fringe benefits are an excellent compensation planning tool. For closely held corporations, however, the tax savings to shareholder-employees are reduced because the fringe benefit must be offered to all employees without discrimination.

ADVANTAGE OF FRINGE BENEFITS. Fringe benefits provide two types of tax advantages: a tax deferral or an exclusion. Qualified pension, profit-sharing, and stock bonus plans provide a tax deferral; that is, the corporation's contribution to such a plan is not taxable to the employees when the corporation makes the contribution. Instead, employees are taxed on the benefits when they receive them. Other common fringe benefits, such as group term life insurance, accident and health insurance, and disability insurance, are exempt from tax altogether; that is, the employee never is taxed on the value of these fringe benefits.

Because the employee excludes the value of fringe benefits from gross income, the marginal individual tax rate applicable to these benefits is zero. Thus, conversion of salary into a fringe benefit provides tax savings for the shareholder-employee equal to the amount of the converted salary times the employee's marginal tax rate, assuming the shareholder-employee could not purchase the same fringe benefit and deduct its cost on his or her individual tax return.

SPECIAL ELECTION TO ALLOCATE REDUCED TAX RATE BENEFITS

A controlled group may elect to apportion the tax benefits of the 15%, 25%, and 34% tax rates to the member corporations in any manner it chooses. If the corporations elect no special apportionment plan, the $50,000, $25,000, and $9,925,000 amounts allocated to the three reduced tax rate brackets are divided equally among all the corporations in the group.[47] If a controlled group has one or more group members that report little or no taxable income, the group should elect special apportionment of the reduced tax benefits to obtain the full tax savings resulting from the reduced rates. The following steps outline a set of procedures for apportioning tax rates for taxable income levels at or below $10 million.[48]

1. If aggregate positive taxable income is $100,000 or less, apportion the 15%, 25%, and 34% rates to members that have positive taxable income so as to maximize their benefit.

   a. To avoid "wasting" low tax rates on loss members, elect special apportionment of tax benefits.

---

[46] Sec. 162(m).
[47] Sec. 1561(a).

[48] For the sake of simplicity, we do not extend the procedures to taxable income exceeding $10 million but similar procedures apply.

b. Summing the members' taxes results in the same total tax as would occur by applying the corporate tax rate schedule to the group's aggregate positive taxable income.

2. If aggregate positive taxable income is between $100,000 and $335,000, apportion the 15%, 25%, and 34% brackets as in Step 1 above. Follow the next steps to apportion the 5% surtax.

   a. Calculate the surtax as 5% times (aggregate positive taxable income − $100,000).
   b. If the calculated surtax is $9,500 or less, apportion the calculated surtax in proportion to the way the corporations apportioned the 15% bracket.
   c. If the surtax is greater than $9,500 ($11,750 maximum), apportion the first $9,500 as in Step 2b, and apportion the excess in proportion to the way the corporations apportioned the 25% bracket in Step 1 above.
   d. Summing the members' taxes results in the same total tax as would occur by applying the corporate tax rate schedule to the group's aggregate positive taxable income.

3. If aggregate positive taxable income is from $335,000 to $10,000,000, the 15% and 25% tax brackets are fully phased out, so each member's tax equals a flat 34% of its taxable income, and the group's total tax equals 34% of aggregate positive taxable income.

EXAMPLE C:3-42 ▶ North and South Corporations are members of a controlled group. The corporations file separate tax returns for the current year and report the following results:

Corporation	Taxable Income (NOL)
North	$(25,000)
South	100,000

If they elect no special apportionment plan, North and South are limited to $25,000 each taxed at a 15% rate and to $12,500 each taxed at a 25% rate. The tax liability for each corporation is determined as follows:

Corporation	Calculation	Tax
North		$ –0–
South	15% tax bracket: 0.15 × $25,000	$ 3,750
	25% tax bracket: 0.25 × $12,500	3,125
	34% tax bracket: 0.34 × $62,500	21,250
	Subtotal for South Corporation	$28,125
Total for North-South controlled group		$28,125

If the corporations elect a special apportionment plan, the group may apportion the full $50,000 and $25,000 amounts for each of the reduced tax rate brackets to South. The tax liability for each corporation is determined as follows:

Corporation	Calculation	Tax
North		$ –0–
South	15% tax bracket: 0.15 × $50,000	$ 7,500
	25% tax bracket: 0.25 × $25,000	6,250
	34% tax bracket: 0.34 × $25,000	8,500
	Subtotal for South Corporation	$22,250
Total for North-South controlled group		$22,250

By shifting the benefit of low tax brackets away from a corporation that cannot use it (North) to a corporation that can (South), the special apportionment election reduces the total tax liability for the North-South controlled group by $5,875 ($28,125 − $22,250). ◀

If a controlled group's total taxable income exceeds $100,000 ($15 million), a 5% (3%) surcharge recaptures the benefits of the reduced tax rates. The component member (or members) that took advantage of the lower tax rates pays this additional tax.

EXAMPLE C:3-43 ▶ Alpha, Beta, and Gamma Corporations are members of a controlled group and report the following results:

Corporation	Taxable Income (Loss)
Alpha	$ 80,000
Beta	(25,000)
Gamma	230,000

The group, which has aggregate taxable income of $310,000 ($80,00 + $230,000), elects special apportionment. They apportion the 15% tax bracket to Alpha with the balance of Alpha's income taxed at 34% (before the surtax apportionment), and they apportion the 25% tax bracket to Gamma with the balance of Gamma's income taxed at 34% (before the surtax apportionment). The surtax in this case is $10,500 (0.05 × ($310,000 − $100,000)). Using the procedures outlined above, the members apportion $9,500 of the surtax to Alpha because that corporation received the entire 15% tax bracket, and they apportion the remaining $1,000 surtax to Gamma because that corporation received the entire 25% tax bracket. Accordingly, the tax liability for each corporation is as follows:

Alpha:		
Tax on $50,000 at 15%	$ 7,500	
Tax on $30,000 at 34%	10,200	
Surtax	9,500	
Total for Alpha		$27,200
Beta		–0–
Gamma:		
Tax on $25,000 at 25%	$ 6,250	
Tax on $205,000 at 34%	69,700	
Surtax	1,000	
Total for Alpha		76,950
Total for the group		$104,150

The total tax for the group is the same as if they applied the corporate tax rate schedule to the $310,000 aggregate positive taxable income as follows: $22,250 + ($210,000 × 0.39) = $104,150. ◀

EXAMPLE C:3-44 ▶ Hill, Jet, and King Corporations are members of a controlled group and report the following results:

Corporation	Taxable Income
Hill	$300,000
Jet	(50,000)
King	100,000

The group's aggregate positive taxable income is $400,000 ($300,000 + $100,000), which exceeds $335,000. Therefore, with special apportionment, Hill's and King's tax equals 34% of each corporation's taxable income as follows:

Hill ($300,000 × 0.34)	$102,000
Jet	–0–
King ($100,000 × 0.34)	34,000
Total for the group ($400,000 × 0.34)	$136,000 ◀

USING NOL CARRYOVERS AND CARRYBACKS

When a corporation incurs an NOL for the year, it has two choices:

▶ Carry the NOL back to the second and first preceding years in that order (assuming no extended carryback period), and then forward to the succeeding 20 years in chronological order until the NOL is exhausted.

▶ Forgo any carryback and just carry the NOL forward to the 20 succeeding years.

A corporation might elect to forgo an NOL carryback if it would offset income at a low tax rate, resulting in a small tax refund compared to a greater anticipated benefit if the NOL instead were carried over to a high tax rate year.

EXAMPLE C:3-45 ▶

Boyd Corporation, a calendar year taxpayer, incurs a $30,000 NOL in 2011. Boyd's 2009 taxable income was $50,000. If Boyd carries the NOL back to 2009, Boyd's tax refund is computed as follows:

Original tax on $50,000 (using 2009 rates)	$7,500
Minus: Recomputed tax on $20,000	
[($50,000 − $30,000) × 0.15]	(3,000)
Tax refund	$4,500

If Boyd anticipates taxable income (after reduction for any NOL carryovers) of $75,000 or more in 2012, carrying over the NOL will result in the entire loss offsetting taxable income that otherwise would be taxed at a 34% or higher marginal tax rate. The tax savings is computed as follows:

Tax on $105,000 of expected taxable income	$24,200
Minus: Tax on $75,000 ($105,000 − $30,000)	(13,750)
Tax savings in 2012	$10,450

Thus, if Boyd expects taxable income to be $105,000 in 2012, it might elect to forgo the NOL carryback and obtain the additional $5,950 ($10,450 − $4,500) tax benefit. Of course, by carrying the NOL over to 2012, Boyd loses the value of having the funds immediately available. However, Boyd may use the NOL to reduce its estimated tax payments for 2012. If the corporation expects the NOL carryover benefit to occur at an appreciably distant point in the future, the corporation would have to determine the benefit's present value to make it comparable to a refund from an NOL carryback. This example ignores the effect the NOL carryover has on the U.S. production activities deduction in the carryover year.   ◀

ETHICAL POINT

When tax practitioners take on a new client, they should review the client's prior year tax returns and tax elections for accuracy and completeness. Tax matters arising in the current year, such as an NOL, can affect prior year tax returns prepared by another tax practitioner. Positions taken or errors discovered in a prior year return may have ethical consequences for a practitioner who takes on a new client.

COMPLIANCE AND PROCEDURAL CONSIDERATIONS

ESTIMATED TAXES

Every corporation that expects to owe more than $500 in tax for the current year must pay four installments of estimated tax, each equal to 25% of its required annual payment.[49] For corporations that are not large corporations (defined below), the required annual payment is the lesser of 100% of the tax shown on the current year return or 100% of the tax shown on the preceding year return. A corporation may not base its required estimated tax amount on the tax shown on the preceding year return if the preceding year tax return showed a zero tax liability.[50] The estimated tax amount is the sum of the corporation's income tax and alternative minimum tax liabilities that exceeds its tax credits. The amount of estimated tax due may be computed on Schedule 1120-W (Estimated Tax for Corporations).

ESTIMATED TAX PAYMENT DATES.   A calendar year corporation must deposit estimated tax payments in a Federal Reserve bank or authorized commercial bank on or before April 15, June 15, September 15, and December 15.[51] This schedule differs from that of an individual taxpayer. The final estimated tax installment for a calendar year corporation is due in December of the tax year rather than in January of the following tax year, as is the case for individual taxpayers. For a fiscal year corporation, the due dates are the fifteenth day of the fourth, sixth, ninth, and twelfth months of the tax year.

---

[49] Sec. 6655.
[50] Rev. Rul. 92-54, 1992-2 C.B. 320.
[51] Sec. 6655(c)(2). Fiscal year corporations must deposit their taxes on or before the fifteenth day of the fourth, sixth, ninth, and twelfth month of their tax year. If the fifteenth falls on a weekend or holiday, the payment is due on the next business day.

EXAMPLE C:3-46 ▶ Garden Corporation, a calendar year taxpayer, expects to report the following results for the current year:

Regular tax	$119,000
Alternative minimum tax	25,000

Garden's current year estimated tax liability is $144,000 ($119,000 regular tax liability + $25,000 AMT liability). Garden's tax liability last year was $120,000. Assuming Garden is not a large corporation, its required annual payment for the current year is $120,000, the lesser of its prior year liability ($120,000) or its current year tax return liability ($144,000). Garden will not incur a penalty if it deposits four equal installments of $30,000 ($120,000 ÷ 4) on or before April 15, June 15, September 15, and December 15 of the current year. ◀

TYPICAL MISCONCEPTION

The easiest method of determining a corporation's estimated tax payments is to pay 100% of last year's tax liability. Unfortunately, for "large corporations," other than for its first quarterly payment, last year's tax liability is not an acceptable method of determining the required estimated tax payments. Also, last year's tax liability cannot be used if no tax liability existed in the prior year or if the corporation filed a short-year return for the prior year.

Different estimated tax payment rules apply to large corporations. A large corporation's required annual payment is 100% of the tax shown on the current year return. A large corporation's estimated tax payments cannot be based on the prior year's tax liability except the first installment. If a large corporation bases its first estimated tax installment on the prior year's liability, any shortfall between the required payment based on the current year's tax liability and the actual payment must be made up with the second installment.[52] A large corporation is one whose taxable income was $1 million or more in any of its three immediately preceding tax years. Controlled groups of corporations must allocate the $1 million amount among its group members.

EXAMPLE C:3-47 ▶ Assume the same facts as in Example C:3-46 except Garden is a large corporation (i.e., it had more than $1 million of taxable income in one of its prior three years). Garden can base its first estimated tax payment on either 25% of its current year tax liability or 25% of last year's tax liability. Garden should elect to use its prior year tax liability as the basis for its first installment because it can reduce the needed payment from $36,000 (0.25 × $144,000) to $30,000 (0.25 × $120,000). However, it must recapture the $6,000 ($36,000 − $30,000) shortfall when it pays its second installment. Therefore, the total second installment is $42,000 ($36,000 second installment + $6,000 recapture from first installment). The third and fourth installments are $36,000 each. ◀

KEY POINT

The amount of penalty depends on three factors: the applicable underpayment rate, the amount of the underpayment, and the amount of time that lapses until the corporation makes the payment.

PENALITES FOR UNDERPAYMENT OF ESTIMATED TAX. The IRS will assess a nondeductible penalty if a corporation does not deposit its required estimated tax installment on or before the due date for that installment. The penalty is the underpayment rate found in Sec. 6621 times the amount by which the installment due by a payment date exceeds the payment actually made.[53] The penalty accrues from the payment due date for the installment until the earlier of the actual date of the payment or the due date for the tax return (excluding extensions).

EXAMPLE C:3-48 ▶ Globe Corporation is a calendar year taxpayer that reported a $100,000 tax liability for 2010. Globe's tax liability for 2009 was $125,000. It should have made estimated tax payments of $25,000 ($100,000 ÷ 4) on or before April 15, June 15, September 15, and December 15, 2010. No penalty is assessed if Globe deposited the requisite amounts on or before each of the those dates. However, if Globe deposited only $16,000 ($9,000 less than the required $25,000) on April 15, 2010, and did not deposit the remaining $9,000 before the due date for the 2010 return, the corporation must pay a penalty on the $9,000 underpayment for the period of time from April 15, 2010, through March 15, 2011. If Globe deposits $34,000 on the second installment date (June 15, 2010), so that it has paid a total of $50,000 by the second installment due date, the penalty runs only from April 15, 2010, through June 15, 2010.

Now assume that Globe made the following estimated tax payments in 2010:

---

[52] Sec. 6655(d)(2)(B). A revision to the required estimated tax payment amount also may be needed if the corporation is basing its quarterly payments on the current year's tax liability. Installments paid after the estimate of the current year's liability has been revised must take into account any shortage or excess in previous installment payments resulting from the change in the original estimate.

[53] Sec. 6621. This interest rate is the short-term federal rate as determined by the Secretary of the Treasury plus three percentage points. It is subject to change every three months. The interest rate for large corporations is the short-term federal rate plus five percentage points. This higher interest rate begins 30 days after the issuance of either a 30-day or 90-day deficiency notice.

Date	Amount
April 15	$16,000
June 15	16,000
September 15	21,000
December 15	35,000

Form 2220 in Appendix B calculates the underpayments and resultant penalty given this pattern of payments. ◄

SPECIAL COMPUTATION METHODS.   In lieu of the current year and prior year methods, corporations can use either of two special methods for calculating estimated tax installments:

▶ The annualized income method

▶ The adjusted seasonal income method

The Annualized Income Method.   This method is useful if a corporation's income is likely to increase a great deal toward the end of the year. It allows a corporation to base its first and second quarterly estimated tax payments on its annualized taxable income for the first three months of the year. The corporation then bases its third payment on its annualized taxable income for the first six months of the year and its fourth payment on annualized taxable income for the first nine months of the year. (Two other options for the number of months used for each installment also are available.)

EXAMPLE C:3-49 ▶

Erratic Corporation, a calendar year taxpayer, reports taxable income of: $10,000 in each of January, February, and March; $20,000 in each of April, May, and June; and $50,000 in each of the last six months of the current year. Erratic's annualized taxable income and annualized tax are calculated as follows:

TAX STRATEGY TIP

Both the "annualized income exception" and the "adjusted seasonal income exception" are complicated computations. However, due to the large amounts of money involved in making corporate estimated tax payments along with the possible underpayment penalties, the time and effort spent in determining the least amount necessary for a required estimated tax payment are often worthwhile.

Through	Cumulative Taxable Income	Annualization Factor	Annualized Taxable Income	Tax on Annualized Taxable Income
Third month	$ 30,000	12/3	$120,000	$ 30,050
Sixth month	90,000	12/6	180,000	53,450
Ninth month	240,000	12/9	320,000	108,050

Assuming Erratic uses the annualized method for all four estimated tax payments, its installments will be as follows:

Installment Number	Annualized Tax	Applicable Percentage	Installment Amount	Cumulative Installment
One	$ 30,050	25%	$ 7,513[a]	$ 7,513
Two	30,050	50	7,512[b]	15,025
Three	53,450	75	25,063[c]	40,088
Four	108,050	100	67,962[d]	108,050

[a]$30,050 × 0.25
[b]($30,050 × 0.50) − $7,513
[c]($53,450 × 0.75) − $15,025
[d]($108,050 × 1.00) − $40,088

◄

A corporation may use the annualized income method for an installment payment only if it is less than the regular required installment. It must recapture any reduction in an earlier required installment resulting from use of the annualized income method by increasing the amount of the next installment that does not qualify for the annualized income method.

For small corporations, the sure way to avoid a penalty for the underpayment of estimated tax is to base the current year's estimated tax payments on 100% of last year's tax. This approach is not possible, however, for large corporations or for corporations that owed no tax in the prior year or that filed a short period tax return for the prior year. This approach also is not advisable if the corporation had a high tax liability in the prior year and expects a low tax liability in the current year.

Adjusted Seasonal Income Method. A corporation may base its installments on its adjusted seasonal income. This method permits corporations that earn seasonal income to annualize their income by assuming income earned in the current year is earned in the same pattern as in preceding years. As in the case of the annualized income exception, a corporation can use the seasonal income exception only if the resulting installment payment is less than the regular required installment. Once the exception no longer applies, any savings resulting from its use for prior installments must be recaptured.

REPORTING THE UNDERPAYMENT. A corporation reports its underpayment of estimated taxes and the amount of any penalty on Form 2220 (Underpayment of Estimated Tax by Corporations). A completed Form 2220 using the facts from Example C:3-47 appears in Appendix B.

PAYING THE REMAINING TAX LIABILITY. A corporation must pay its remaining tax liability for the year when it files its corporate tax return. An extension of time to file the tax return, however, does *not* extend the time to pay the tax liability. If any tax remains unpaid after the original due date for the tax return, the corporation must pay interest at the underpayment rate prescribed by Sec. 6621 from the due date until the corporation pays the tax. In addition to interest, the IRS assesses a penalty if the corporation does not pay the tax on time and cannot show reasonable cause for the failure to pay. The IRS presumes that reasonable cause exists if the corporation requests an extension of time to file its tax return and the amount of tax shown on the request for extension (Form 7004) or the amount of tax paid by the original due date of the return is at least 90% of the corporation's tax shown on its Form 1120.[54] A discussion of the failure-to-pay penalty and the interest calculation can be found in Chapter C:15.

STOP & THINK

Question: Why does the tax law permit a corporation to use special methods such as the annualized income method to calculate its required estimated tax installments?

Solution: A large corporation whose income varies widely may not be able to estimate its taxable income for the year until late in the year, and it is not allowed to base its estimates on last year's income. If, for example, a calendar year corporation earns income of $100,000 per month during the first six months of its year, it might estimate its first two installments on the assumption that it will earn a total taxable income of $1.2 million for the year. But if its income unexpectedly increases to $500,000 per month in the seventh month, it would need an annualized method to avoid an underpayment penalty for the first two installments. Were it not for the ability to use the annualized method, the corporation would have no way to avoid an underpayment penalty even though it could not predict its taxable income for the year when it made the first two installment payments.

OBJECTIVE 6

Determine the requirements for paying corporate income taxes and filing a corporate tax return

REQUIREMENTS FOR FILING AND PAYING TAXES

A corporation must file a tax return, Form 1120 (U.S. Corporation Income Tax Return), even if it has no taxable income for the year.[55] If the corporation did not exist for its entire annual accounting period (either calendar year or fiscal year), it must file a short period return for the part of the year it did exist. For tax purposes, a corporation's existence ends when it ceases business and dissolves, retaining no assets, even if state law treats the corporation as continuing for purposes of winding up its affairs.[56]

A completed Form 1120 corporate income tax return appears in Appendix B. A spreadsheet that converts book income into taxable income for the Johns and Lawrence business enterprise (introduced in Chapter C:2) is presented with the C corporation tax return.

---

[54] Reg. Sec. 301.6651-1(c)(4).
[55] Sec. 6012(a)(2).

[56] Reg. Sec. 1.6012-2(a)(2).

WHEN THE RETURN MUST BE FILED

Corporations must file their tax returns by the fifteenth day of the third month following the close of their tax year.[57] A corporation can obtain an automatic six-month extension to file its tax return by filing Form 7004 (Application for Automatic Extension of Time to File Certain Business Tax, Information, and Other Returns) by the original due date for the return. Corporations that fail to file a timely tax return are subject to the failure-to-file penalty. Chapter C:15 discusses this penalty in some detail.

EXAMPLE C:3-50 ▶

ADDITIONAL COMMENT

The IRS will not assess a late payment penalty if the corporation extends its due date and pays 90% of its total tax liability by the unextended due date and pays the balance by the extended due date.

Palmer Corporation's fiscal tax year ends on September 30. Its corporate tax return for the year ending September 30, 2011, is due on or before December 15, 2011. If Palmer files Form 7004 by December 15, 2011, it can obtain an automatic extension of time to file until June 15, 2012. Assuming Palmer expects its 2011 tax liability to be $72,000 and it has paid $68,000 in estimated tax during the year, it must pay the remaining $4,000 by December 15, 2011. A completed Form 7004 appears in Appendix B. ◀

Additional extensions beyond the automatic six-month period are not available. The IRS can rescind the extension period by mailing a ten-day notice to the corporation before the end of the six-month period.[58]

TAX RETURN SCHEDULES

BOOK-TO-TAX ACCOUNTING COMPARISON

Schedule L requires a financial accounting balance sheet rather than a tax balance sheet. However, for many small corporations, the tax balance sheet is the same as the financial accounting balance sheet.

SCHEDULE L (OF FORM 1120): THE BALANCE SHEET. Schedule L of Form 1120 requires a balance sheet showing the financial accounting results at the beginning and end of the tax year.

RECONCILIATION SCHEDULES. The IRS also requires the reconciliation of the corporation's financial accounting income (also known as book income) and its taxable income (before special deductions). Book income is calculated according to generally accepted accounting principles (GAAP) including rules promulgated by the Financial Accounting Standards Board (FASB). On the other hand, taxable income must be calculated using tax rules. Therefore, book income and taxable income usually differ.

Some small corporations that do not require audited statements keep their books on a tax basis. For example, they may calculate depreciation for book purposes the same way they do for tax purposes. Income tax expense for book purposes may simply reflect the federal income tax liability. Most corporations, however, must use GAAP to calculate net income per books. For such corporations, taxable income and book income may differ significantly. The reconciliation of book income and taxable income provides the IRS with information that helps it audit a corporation's tax return.

For many corporations, the reconciliation must be provided on Schedule M-1 of Form 1120. Corporations with total assets of $10 million or more on the last day of the tax year, however, must complete Schedule M-3 instead of Schedule M-1. This schedule provides the IRS with much more detailed information on differences between book income and taxable income than does Schedule M-1. This additional transparency of corporate transactions will increase the IRS's ability to audit corporate tax returns. Form 1120 also requires an analysis of unappropriated retained earnings on Schedule M-2.

BOOK-TO-TAX ACCOUNTING COMPARISON

The Internal Revenue Code and related authorities determine the treatment of items in the tax return while Accounting Standards Codification (ASC) 740 (Income Taxes) dictates the treatment of tax items in the financial statements.

BOOK-TAX DIFFERENCES. A corporation's book income usually differs from its taxable income for a large number of transactions. Some of these differences are permanent. **Permanent differences** arise because:

▶ Some book income is never taxed. Examples include:
   1. Tax-exempt interest received on state and municipal obligations
   2. Proceeds of life insurance carried by the corporation on the lives of key officers or employees
▶ Some book expenses are never deductible for tax purposes. Examples include:
   1. Expenses incurred in earning tax-exempt interest

---

[57] Sec. 6072(b).

[58] Reg. Sec. 1.6081-3.

2. Premiums paid for life insurance carried by the corporation on the lives of key officers or employees
3. Fines and expenses resulting from a violation of law
4. Disallowed travel and entertainment costs
5. Political contributions
6. Federal income taxes per books, which is based on GAAP (ASC 740)

▶ Some tax deductions are never taken for book purposes. Examples include:
1. The dividends-received deduction
2. The U.S. production activities deduction
3. Percentage depletion of natural resources in excess of their cost

Some of the differences are temporary. **Temporary differences** arise because:

▶ Some revenues or gains are recognized for book purposes in the current year but not reported for tax purposes until later years. Examples include:
1. Installment sales reported in full for book purposes in the year of sale but reported over a period of years using the installment method for tax purposes
2. Gains on involuntary conversions recognized currently for book purposes but deferred for tax purposes

▶ Some revenues or gains are taxable before they are reported for book purposes. These items are included in taxable income when received but are included in book income as they accrue. Examples include:
1. Prepaid rent or interest income
2. Advance subscription revenue

▶ Some expenses or losses are deductible for tax purposes after they are recognized for book purposes. Examples include:
1. Excess of capital losses over capital gains, which are expensed for book purposes but carry back or over for tax purposes
2. Book depreciation in excess of tax depreciation
3. Charitable contributions exceeding the 10% of taxable income limitation, which are currently expensed for book purposes but carry over for tax purposes
4. Bad debt accruals using the allowance method for book purposes and the direct write-off method for tax purposes
5. Organizational and start-up expenditures, which are expensed currently for book purposes but partially deducted and amortized for tax purposes
6. Product warranty liabilities expensed for book purposes when estimated but deducted for tax purposes when the liability becomes fixed
7. Net operating losses (NOLs) that, for tax purposes, carry back two years (or extended period if applicable) and carry over 20 years

▶ Some expenses or losses are deductible for tax purposes before they are recognized for book purposes. Examples include:
1. Tax depreciation in excess of book depreciation
2. Prepaid expenses deducted on the tax return in the period paid but accrued over a period of years for book purposes

For book purposes, temporary differences listed under the first and fourth bullets create deferred tax liabilities while those listed under the second and third bullets create deferred tax assets. The Financial Statement Implications section later in this chapter discusses the financial accounting treatment of book-tax differences.

SCHEDULE M-1. The Schedule M-1 reconciliation of book to taxable income begins with net income per books and ends with taxable income before special deductions, which corresponds with Line 28 of Form 1120. Thus, some book-tax differences enumerated above do not appear in the reconciliation, for example, the dividends-received deduction and the net operating loss deduction.

The left side of Schedule M-1 contains items the corporation adds back to book income. These items include the following categories:

▶ Federal income tax expense (per books)

▶ Excess of capital losses over capital gains

► Income subject to tax but not recorded on the books in the current year

► Expenses recorded on the books but not deductible for tax purposes in the current year

The right side of the schedule contains items the corporation deducts from book income. These items include the following categories:

► Income recorded on the books in the current year that is not taxable in the current year

► Deductions or losses claimed in the tax return that do not reduce book income in the current year

These categorizations, however, do not distinguish between permanent and temporary differences as does Schedule M-3 discussed below. The following example illustrates a Schedule M-1 reconciliation.

EXAMPLE C:3-51 ► Valley Corporation reports the following items for book and tax purposes in its first year of operations (2010):

	Book	Tax	Difference
Gross receipts	$1,500,000	$1,500,000	
MInus: Cost of goods sold	(550,000)	(550,000)	
Gross profit from operations	$ 950,000	$950,000	
Plus: Dividends from less than 20%-owned corporations	10,000	10,000	
Tax-exempt income	3,000	–0–	$ (3,000)
Prepaid rental income	–0–	8,000	8,000
Minus: Operating expenses	(300,000)	(300,000)	
Depreciation	(60,000)	(170,000)	(110,000)
Bad debt expense	(25,000)	(16,000)	9,000
Business interest expense	(75,000)	(75,000)	
Insurance premiums on life for key employee (Valley is the beneficiary)	(2,800)	–0–	2,800
Net capital loss disallowed for tax purposes	(12,000)	–0–	12,000
U.S. production activities deduction (rounded)	–0–	(35,000)	(35,000)
Net income before federal income taxes	$ 488,200		
Taxable income before special deductions		$372,000	
Minus: Federal income tax expense per books	(151,640)	–0–	155,604
Dividends-received deduction	–0–	(7,000)	(7,000)
Net income per books / Taxable income	$ 336,560	$365,000	
Federal tax liability ($365,000 × 0.34)		$124,100	
Effective tax rate ($151,640/$488,200)	31.06%		

Valley's Schedule M-1 reconciliation appears in Figure C:3-5.[59] ◄

BOOK-TO-TAX COMPARISON

Schedules M-1 and M-3 adjustments highlight the fact that financial accounting and tax accounting differ in many ways. A review of Schedule M-1 or M-3 is an excellent way to compare the financial accounting and tax accounting differences in a corporation.

SCHEDULE M-3. Schedule M-3 requires extensive detail in its reconciliation. Moreover, the schedule has the corporation distinguish between its permanent and temporary differences. The schedule contains three parts. Part I adjusts worldwide income per books to worldwide book income for only includible corporations. As described in Chapter C:8, some corporations may be included in the financial statement consolidation that might be excluded from the tax consolidated tax return. This resulting figure is then reconciled to taxable income before special deductions (again Line 28 of Form 1120). Part II enumerates the corporation's income and loss items, and Part III enumerates the expense and deduction items. The total items from Part III carry over to Part II for the final reconciliation. Both Parts II and III contain the following four columns: (a) book items, (b) temporary differences, (c) permanent differences, and (d) tax items.

---

[59] A worksheet for converting book income to taxable income for a sample Form 1120 return is provided in Appendix B with that return.

1	Net income (loss) per books	332,596	7	Income recorded on books this year not included on this return (itemize):		
2	Federal income tax per books	155,604				
3	Excess of capital losses over capital gains	12,000	a	Tax-exempt interest $ 3,000		
4	Income subject to tax not recorded on books this year (itemize):		b	Other (itemize):		
						3,000
	_____Prepaid rent_____	8,000	8	Deductions on this return not charged against book income this year (itemize):		
5	Expenses recorded on books this year not deducted on this return (itemize):		a	Depreciation . . $ 110,000		
a	Depreciation . . . . $		b	Charitable contributions $		
b	Charitable contributions $		c	Other (itemize):		
c	Travel and entertainment $			_U.S. prod. act. ded. 35,000_		
d	Other (itemize): Bad debt expense 9,000					145,000
	Premiums on life insurance 2,800	11,800	9	Add lines 7 and 8		148,000
6	Add lines 1 through 5	520,000	10	Income—line 6 less line 9		372,000

FIGURE C:3-5 ▶ VALLEY CORPORATION'S FORM 1120 SCHEDULE M-1 (EXAMPLE C:3-51)

Appendix B provides an example of Schedule M-3 using the data from Example C:3-50. Valley Corporation in that example is too small to be required to use Schedule M-3 although it may elect to do so. Nevertheless, that data is used to allow for comparison of Schedules M-1 and M-3. Note that Lines 1 and 2 of Schedule M-3, Part III, break the $151,640 federal income tax expense into its current and deferred components. The current expense ties to the current tax liability ($124,100), and the deferred expense ties to the change in net deferred tax liabilities and assets arising from temporary differences, specifically, depreciation, net capital loss, prepaid rent, and bad debt expense [$27,540 = 0.34 × ($110,000 − $12,000 − $8,000 − $9,000)]. These temporary differences appear in Column b of Schedule M-3, Parts II and III.

SCHEDULE M-2 (OF FORM 1120).   Schedule M-2 of Form 1120 requires an analysis of changes in unappropriated retained earnings from the beginning of the year to the end of the year. The schedule supplies the IRS with information regarding dividends paid during the year and any special transactions that caused a change in retained earnings for the year.

Schedule M-2 starts with the balance in the unappropriated retained earnings account at the beginning of the year. The following items, which must be added to the beginning balance amount, are listed on the left side of the schedule:

► Net income per books

► Other increases (e.g., refund of federal income taxes paid in a prior year taken directly to the retained earnings account instead of used to reduce federal income tax expense)

The following items, which must be deducted from the beginning balance amount, are listed on the right side of the schedule:

► Dividends (e.g., cash or property)

► Other decreases (e.g., appropriation of retained earnings made during the tax year)

The result is the amount of unappropriated retained earnings at the end of the year.

ADDITIONAL COMMENT

Schedule M-2 requires an analysis of a corporation's retained earnings. Retained earnings is a financial accounting number that has little relevance to tax accounting. It would seem much more worthwhile for the IRS to require an analysis of a corporation's earnings and profits, which is an extremely important number in determining the taxation of a corporation and its shareholders.

EXAMPLE C:3-52 ▶ In the current year, Beta Corporation reports net income and other capital account items as follows:

Unappropriated retained earnings, January 1, current year	$400,000
Net income	350,000
Federal income tax refund for capital loss carryback	15,000
Cash dividends paid in the current year	250,000
Unappropriated retained earnings, December 31, current year	515,000

Beta Corporation's Schedule M-2 appears in Figure C:3-6.   ◀

Topic Review C:3-2 summarizes the requirements for paying the taxes due and filing the corporate tax return.

Schedule M-2	**Analysis of Unappropriated Retained Earnings per Books**					
1	Balance at beginning of year	400,000	5	Distributions:	**a** Cash	250,000
2	Net income (loss) per books	350,000			**b** Stock	
3	Other increases (itemize):				**c** Property . . .	
			6	Other decreases (itemize):		
	Federal tax refund	15,000	7	Add lines 5 and 6	250,000
4	Add lines 1, 2, and 3	765,000	8	Balance at end of year (line 4 less line 7) .	515,000

FIGURE C:3-6 ▶ BETA CORPORATION'S FORM 1120 SCHEDULE M-2 (EXAMPLE C:3-52)

FINANCIAL STATEMENT IMPLICATIONS

OBJECTIVE 7

Determine the financial statement implications of federal income taxes

The book-tax differences discussed on pages C:3-39 and C:3-40 have implications not only for preparing the reconciliation Schedules M-1 and M-3 but also affect how a firm's financial statements present income taxes. Income taxes impact both the income statement and balance sheet. For example, the tax section of the income statement might appear as follows:

> Net income before federal income taxes
> Minus: Federal income tax expense
>
> Net income

Moreover, the **income tax expense** (also called the total tax provision) usually breaks down into a current component and a deferred component. The current component ties into the taxes payable for the current year, and the deferred component arises from book-tax temporary differences. The income tax expense also can contain a state tax component. For this textbook, however, we focus primarily on federal income taxes. Financial statements usually publish details concerning its tax provision in a footnote to the financial statements. Temporary differences also create **deferred tax liabilities** and **deferred tax assets,** which appear on the balance sheet.

The primary standard that dictates financial statement treatment is Accounting Standards Codification (ASC) 740, issued by the Financial Accounting Standards Board (FASB). This section first describes the basic principles of ASC 740 and then presents a comprehensive example to demonstrate its application.

Topic Review C:3-2

Requirements for Paying Taxes Due and Filing Tax Returns

1. Estimated Tax Requirement
   a. Corporations that expect to owe more than $500 in tax for the current year must pay four installments of estimated tax, each equal to 25% of its required annual payment.
   b. Taxes for which estimated payments are required of a C corporation include regular tax and alternative minimum tax, minus any tax credits.
   c. If a corporation is not a large corporation, its required annual payment is the lesser of 100% of the tax shown on the current year's return or 100% of the tax shown on the preceding year's return.
   d. If a corporation is a large corporation, its required annual payment is 100% of the tax shown on the current year's return. Its first estimated tax payment may be based on the preceding year's tax liability, but any shortfall must be made up when the second installment is due.
   e. Special rules apply if the corporation bases its estimated tax payments on the annualized income or adjusted seasonal income method.
2. Filing Requirements
   a. The corporate tax return is due by the fifteenth day of the third month after the end of the tax year.
   b. A corporate taxpayer may request an automatic six-month extension to file its tax return (but not to pay its tax due).

SCOPE, OBJECTIVES, AND PRINCIPLES OF ASC 740

ASC 740 establishes principles of accounting for current income taxes and for deferred taxes arising from temporary differences. Specifically, ASC 740 addresses the financial statement consequences of the following events:

▶ Revenues, expenses, gains, or losses recognized for tax purposes in an earlier or later year than recognized for financial statement purposes

▶ Other events that create differences between book and tax bases of assets and liabilities

▶ Operating loss and tax credit carrybacks or carryforwards

ASC 740 sets out two objectives: (1) to recognize current year taxes payable or refundable and (2) to recognize deferred tax liabilities and assets for the future tax consequences of events recognized in a firm's financial statements or tax return. To implement these objectives, ASC 740 applies the following principles:

▶ Recognize a current tax liability or asset for taxes payable or refundable on current year tax returns

▶ Recognize a deferred tax liability or asset for future tax effects attributable to temporary differences and carryforwards

▶ Measure current and deferred tax liabilities and assets using only enacted tax law, not anticipated future changes

▶ Reduce deferred tax assets by the amount of tax benefits the firm does not expect to realize, based on available evidence and adjusted via a valuation allowance

Interestingly, the only comment ASC 740 makes about permanent differences is that "[s]ome events do not have tax consequences. Certain revenues are exempt from taxation and certain expenses are not deductible." In this context, ASC 740 does not mention certain events that do have tax consequences but, nevertheless, create permanent differences, for example, the dividends-received deduction and the U.S. production activities deduction. As we show later, permanent differences do not affect deferred taxes, but they do impact the firm's effective tax rate.

TEMPORARY DIFFERENCES

Similarly to the discussion on pages C:3-39 and C:3-40, the following lists describe events that generate temporary differences and thus deferred tax liabilities and deferred tax assets. Deferred tax liabilities and assets appear on a firm's balance sheet.

Deferred tax liabilities occur when:

▶ Revenue or gains are recognized earlier for book purposes than for tax purposes

▶ Expenses or losses are deductible earlier for tax purposes than for book purposes

▶ Tax basis of an asset is less than its book basis

▶ Tax basis of a liability exceeds its book basis

Deferred tax assets occur when:

▶ Revenue or gains are recognized earlier for tax purposes than for book purposes

▶ Expenses or losses are deductible earlier for book purposes than for tax purposes

▶ Tax basis of an asset exceeds its book basis

▶ Tax basis of a liability is less than its book basis

▶ Operating loss or tax credit carryforwards exist

DEFERRED TAX ASSETS AND THE VALUATION ALLOWANCE

A deferred tax asset indicates that a firm will realize the tax benefit of an event some time in the future. For example, if the firm generates a net operating loss in the current year and, for tax purposes carries the loss forward, the firm will realize a tax benefit only if it earns sufficient future income to use the carryover before it expires. If the firm likely will not realize the entire tax benefit, it must record a **valuation allowance** to reflect the unrealizable portion. The valuation allowance is a contra-type account that reduces the deferred tax asset.

EXAMPLE C:3-53 ▶ Delta Corporation's NOL carryover is $200,000, and it expects to realize (deduct) the entire carryover at a 34% tax rate. Thus, Delta's deferred tax asset is $68,000 ($200,000 × 0.34), and it makes the following book journal entry:

Deferred tax asset	68,000	
Federal income tax expense (benefit)		68,000

Consequently, the deferred tax asset reduces the income tax expense or creates an income tax benefit.

If Delta determines that it likely will realize (deduct) only $150,000 of the NOL carryover, it must record a $17,000 ($50,000 × 0.34) valuation allowance. Accordingly, Delta makes the following book journal entry:

Deferred tax asset	68,000	
Valuation allowance		17,000
Federal income tax expense (benefit)		51,000	◀

ASC 740 specifically states that a deferred tax asset must be reduced by a valuation allowance if, based on the weight of evidence available, the firm *more likely than not* will fail to realize the benefit of the deferred tax asset. For this purpose, the term *more likely than not* means a greater than 50% likelihood. In assessing this likelihood, a firm must consider both negative and positive evidence, where negative evidence leads toward establishing a valuation allowance while positive evidence helps avoid a valuation allowance. ASC 740 lists several examples of each type of evidence. Examples of negative evidence include the following items:

▶ Cumulative losses in recent years

▶ A history of expiring loss or credit carryforwards

▶ Expected losses in the near future

▶ Unfavorable contingencies with future adverse effects

▶ Short carryback or carryover periods that might limit realization of the deferred tax asset

Examples of positive evidence include the following items:

▶ Existing contracts or sales backlogs that will produce sufficient income to realize the deferred tax asset

▶ Excess of appreciated asset value over tax basis (i.e., built-in gain) sufficient to realize the deferred tax asset

▶ A strong earnings history aside from the event causing the deferred tax asset along with evidence that the event is an aberration

In essence, a firm can realize (deduct) a deferred tax asset if it has sufficient taxable income to offset the deduction. ASC 740 suggests the following potential sources of such income:

▶ Future reversals of deferred tax liabilities

▶ Future taxable income other than reversing deferred tax liabilities

▶ Taxable income in carryback years assuming the tax law allows a carryback

▶ Taxable income from prudent and feasible tax planning strategies that a firm ordinarily would not take but nevertheless would pursue to realize an otherwise expiring deferred tax asset

ACCOUNTING FOR UNCERTAIN TAX POSITIONS

ASC 740 also prescribes acceptable accounting for uncertain tax positions. This standard addresses the following basic situation: For tax purposes, a firm may take a position in claiming a tax benefit that might not be sustained under IRS scrutiny. The FASB, however, believes that, for determining the financial statement tax provision, such uncertain tax positions either should not be recognized or should be recognized only partially.

REAL-WORLD EXAMPLE

The IRS has developed Schedule UTP for inclusion in Form 1120. This schedule requires certain taxpayers to provide information about their uncertain tax positions. The required information will provide the IRS a road map for auditing the tax return.

In applying the tax position standard, a firm takes a two-step approach. First, the firm determines whether the tax position has a *more likely than not* (greater than 50%) probability of being sustained upon an IRS examination. This determination requires substantial judgment and necessitates careful documentation for the financial statement audit and any IRS examination. If the tax position does not exceed this threshold, the firm cannot recognize the tax benefit for financial reporting purposes until one of the following three events occur:

▶ The position subsequently meets the *more likely than not* threshold.

▶ The firm favorably settles the tax issue with the IRS or in court.

▶ The statute of limitations on the transaction expires.

If the firm determines that a tax position meets the *more like than not* threshold, it then must measure the amount of benefit it can recognize for financial reporting purposes. This measure is the largest amount of tax benefit that exceeds a 50% probability of realization upon settlement with the taxing authorities. Further details of this measurement process and other procedures under the tax position standard become quite complex and are beyond the scope of this textbook.

EXAMPLE C:3-54 ▶ Lambda Corporation claims a $1 million deduction on its tax return, which provides a $350,000 tax savings, assuming a 35% tax rate. After some analysis and judgment, management determines the deduction has only a 45% chance of being allowed should the IRS audit Lambda's tax return. Assume for simplicity that Lambda has no deferred tax assets or liabilities. Assume further that Lambda's pretax book income and taxable income equal $20 million after taking the $1 million deduction. Thus, Lambda's tax liability is $7 million. Under the tax position standard, Lambda makes the following journal entry (ignoring potential penalties and interest):

Federal income tax expense	7,350,000	
Liability for unrecognized tax benefits		350,000
Federal income taxes payable		7,000,000

Suppose in a subsequent period Lambda negotiates a settlement with the IRS that allows $200,000 of the deduction, and Lambda pays $280,000 tax on the $800,000 disallowed portion. Ignoring penalties and interest, Lambda would make the following journal entry:

Liability for unrecognized tax benefits	350,000	
Cash		280,000
Federal income tax expense		70,000 ◀

EXAMPLE C:3-55 ▶ Assume the same facts as in Example C:3-54 except Lambda meets the *more likely than not* threshold. Lambda then measures the benefit more than 50% likely to be realized as $600,000 of the $1 million deduction taken. Thus, Lambda may not recognize $400,000 in determining its federal income tax expense for financial reporting purposes and, accordingly, makes the following journal entry:

Federal income tax expense	7,140,000	
Liability for unrecognized tax benefits		140,000
Federal income taxes payable		7,000,000 ◀

BALANCE SHEET CLASSIFICATION

Deferred tax liabilities and assets must be classified as either current or noncurrent. If related to another asset or liability, the classification is the same as the related asset. For example, a deferred tax asset pertaining to a difference between book and tax bad debt expense is current because it relates to accounts receivable. On the other hand, a deferred tax liability pertaining to a difference between book and tax depreciation is noncurrent because it relates to fixed assets. If a deferred tax liability or asset does not relate to a particular asset or liability, it is classified as current or noncurrent depending on its expected reversal date. Once classified as current and noncurrent, all current deferred tax liabilities and assets must be netted and presented as one amount. Similarly, all noncurrent deferred tax liabilities and assets must be netted and presented as another amount.

TAX PROVISION PROCESS

The following steps outline the approach used in this chapter to provide for income taxes in the financial statements. This process addresses only federal income taxes.

1. Identify temporary differences by comparing the book and tax bases of assets and liabilities, and identify tax carryforwards.
2. Prepare "roll forward" schedules of temporary differences that tabulate cumulative differences and current-year changes.
3. In the roll forward schedules, apply the appropriate statutory tax rates to determine the ending balances of deferred tax assets and liabilities.
4. Adjust deferred tax assets by a valuation allowance if necessary.
5. Adjust the income tax expense for uncertain tax positions if necessary.
6. Determine current federal income taxes payable, which, in many cases, also is the current federal income tax expense for book purposes.
7. Determining the total federal income tax expense (benefit).
8. Prepare and record tax related journal entries.
9. Prepare a tax provision reconciliation.
10. Prepare the tax rate reconciliation.
11. Prepare financial statements.

In practice, various firms may use slightly different approaches. For this chapter, however, the above steps provide a logical and systematic approach.

ADDITIONAL COMMENT

Determining the valuation allowance and uncertain tax position adjustments requires a great deal of professional judgment.

COMPREHENSIVE EXAMPLE – YEAR 1

To provide comprehensiveness, this example continues with the facts set forth in Example C:3-51. Thus, when completed, the two examples together provide the financial statement implications of federal income taxes as well as the tax return reporting in Schedules M-1 and M-3 for Year 1 (2010). We then continue the example with events occurring in Year 2 (2011).

In addition to the facts stated in Example C:3-51, Valley reports the following book and tax balance sheet items at the end of Year 1, prior to adjustment for tax related items. Step 11 below presents the completed book balance sheet after making tax related journal entries.

Assets:	Book	Tax	Difference
Cash	$ 230,200	$ 230,200	
Accounts receivable	300,000	300,000	
Minus: Allowance for bad debts	(9,000)	–0–	
Net accounts receivable	291,000	300,000	$ 9,000
Investment in corporate stock	90,000	90,000	
Investment in tax-exempt bonds	50,000	50,000	
Inventory	500,000	500,000	
Fixed assets	1,200,000	1,200,000	
Minus: Accumulated depreciation	(60,000)	(170,000)	
Net fixed assets	1,140,000	1,030,000	110,000
Liabilities and stock equity:			
Accounts payable	225,000	225,000	
Unearned rental income	8,000	–0–	8,000
Long-term liabilities	930,000	930,000	
Common stock	650,000	650,000	

Steps 1 through 3.

The book and tax balance sheets above indicate the items where the book and tax bases differ, thereby indicating temporary differences. In addition, the facts from Example C:3-51 indicates a nondeductible net capital loss, which creates a carryforward.

The following three roll forward schedules calculate the deferred tax assets and deferred tax liability associated with these temporary differences. The beginning and ending balances for the balance sheet items reflect the differences between the book and tax bases for these assets and liabilities. In the first schedule, the deferred tax asset for the net accounts receivable is current because it relates to a current asset. The deferred tax asset for the unearned rental income is current because Valley expects to earn that income in the next year. In the second schedule, the example assumes Valley does not expect to have sufficient capital gains to offset the capital loss carryover until three years from now. Therefore, this deferred tax asset will not reverse next year and is considered noncurrent. In the third schedule, the deferred tax liability pertaining to fixed assets is noncurrent because it relates to a noncurrent asset.

Current deferred tax asset:	Beg. of Year 1	End of Year 1	Change
Net accounts receivable	$ –0–	$ 9,000	$ 9,000
Unearned rental income	–0–	8,000	8,000
Total	$ –0–	$ 17,000	$ 17,000
Times: Tax rate	0.34	0.34	
Current deferred tax asset	$ –0–	$ 5,780	$ 5,780

Noncurrent deferred tax asset:	Beg. of Year 1	End of Year 1	Change
Net capital loss	$ –0–	$ 12,000	$ 12,000
Times: Tax rate	0.34	0.34	
Noncurrent deferred tax asset	$ –0–	$ 4,080	$ 4,080

Noncurrent deferred tax liability:	Beg. of Year 1	End of Year 1	Change
Net fixed assets	$ –0–	$110,000	$110,000
Times: Tax rate	0.34	0.34	
Noncurrent deferred tax liability	$ –0–	$ 37,400	$ 37,400

The amounts in the change column also appear as book-tax differences in the book and tax income schedules in Example C:3-51. In those schedules, the differences occur in the related income or expense accounts, specifically, bad debt expense, prepaid rental income, and depreciation.

One last aspect of these schedules needs mentioning. Specifically, the changes in the deferred tax assets and liabilities also represent the deferred federal tax expense or benefit for the current year. See Step 7 below.

Step 4.
Assuming evidence supports that Valley will realize the entire amount of its deferred tax assets, Valley need not establish a valuation allowance.

Step 5.
Assume that Valley requires no adjustments for uncertain tax positions.

Step 6.
As provided in Example C:3-51, current federal income taxes payable is $124,100. In this example, the current payable amount also is the current federal income tax expense for book purposes. (The equality of the current payable amount and the federal income tax expense may not occur, however, under some uncertain tax position situations and in other special circumstances.)

Step 7.

The net deferred federal tax expense from the roll forward schedules equals $27,540 ($37,400 − $5,780 − $4,080). Therefore, the total federal income tax expense for this year can be calculated as follows:

Current federal income tax expense	$124,100
Deferred income tax expense	27,540
Total federal income tax expense	$151,640

Step 8.

Given the amounts determined in previous steps, Valley makes the following book journal entry:

Current federal income tax expense	124,100	
Deferred federal income tax expense	27,540	
Current deferred tax asset	5,780	
Noncurrent deferred tax asset	4,080	
Noncurrent deferred tax liability		37,400
Federal income taxes payable		124,100

Alternatively, Valley could make the following combined book journal entry:

Total federal income tax expense	151,640	
Current deferred tax asset	5,780	
Net noncurrent deferred tax liability (37,400 − 4,080)		33,320
Federal income taxes payable		124,100

Step 9.

As a cross check on the previous steps, Valley can prepare the following tax provision reconciliation:

Net income before federal income taxes (FIT)	$488,200
Permanent differences:	
Nondeductible insurance premiums	2,800
Tax-exempt income	(3,000)
U.S. production activities deduction	(35,000)
Dividends-received deduction	(7,000)
Net income after permanent differences	$446,000
Temporary differences:	
Unearned rental income	8,000
Net capital loss disallowed for tax	12,000
Net accounts receivable (bad debt expense)	9,000
Net fixed assets (depreciation)	(110,000)
Taxable income	$365,000

Assuming no enacted change in future tax rates, net income after permanent differences times the tax rate results in the total federal income tax expense. Specifically, $446,000 \times 0.34 = \$151,640$. Similarly, taxable income times the tax rate results in current federal income taxes payable. Specifically, $365,000 \times 0.34 = \$124,100$.

Step 10.

A firm's effective tax rate is its income tax expense divided by its pretax book income. Because the income tax expense is based on net income after adjustment for permanent differences (see Step 9), these differences cause a firm's effective tax rate to differ from the statutory tax rate. In the footnotes to financial statements, firms reconcile the statutory tax rate to their effective tax rate. Accordingly, Valley's effective tax rate reconciliation is as follows:

ADDITIONAL COMMENT

This approach and the balance sheet approach may not always lead to the same result when enacted tax rates change, under some uncertain tax position situations, and in other special circumstances.

ADDITIONAL COMMENT

Remember that we are looking only at federal income taxes in these examples. Foreign, state, and local taxes also can affect a firm's effective tax rate.

Statutory tax rate	34.00%
Nondeductible insurance premiums ($2,800/$488,200 × 34%)	0.20%
Tax-exempt income [($3,000)/$488,200 × 34%]	(0.21)%
U.S. production activities deduction [($35,000)/$488,200 × 34%]	(2.44)%
Dividends-received deduction [($7,000)/$488,200 × 34%]	(0.49)%
Effective tax rate ($151,640/$488,200)	31.06%

In practice, a firm would not disclose the detail shown here but would aggregate small percentage amounts into an "other" category. Also, if the enacted future tax rate changes, that change also would be reflected in this schedule.

Step 11.

At this point, Valley can complete its financial statements. The income statement appears in Example C:3-51, but the tax portion is repeated here.

Partial income statement:

Net income before federal income taxes	$488,200
Minus: Federal income tax expense	(151,640)
Net income	$336,560
Effective tax rate ($151,640/$488,200)	31.06%

As shown in Step 7, the total federal income tax expense has two components as follows:

Current federal income tax expense	$124,100
Deferred income tax expense	27,540
Total federal income tax expense	$151,640

The book balance sheet for Year 1 is as follows:

Assets:		
Cash		$ 230,200
Accounts receivable	$ 300,000	
Minus: Allowance for bad debts	(9,000)	291,000
Investment in corporate stock		90,000
Investment in tax-exempt bond		50,000
Inventory		500,000
Current deferred tax asset		5,780
Fixed assets	$1,200,000	
Minus: Accumulated depreciation	(60,000)	1,140,000
Total assets		$2,306,980
Liabilities and equity:		
Accounts payable		$ 225,000
Unearned rental income		8,000
Federal income taxes payable		124,100
Noncurrent deferred liability ($37,400 − $4,080)		33,320
Long-term liabilities		930,000
Common stock		650,000
Retained earnings		336,560
Total liabilities and equity		$2,306,980

ADDITIONAL COMMENT

This example ignores estimated tax payments, so that the entire amount of federal income taxes payable appears on the balance sheet.

COMPREHENSIVE EXAMPLE – YEAR 2

Valley reports the following book and tax balance sheet items at the end of Year 2, prior to adjustment for tax related items. Pertinent to the temporary differences, in Year 2 Valley earned the rental income that was prepaid in Year 1 and did not collect additional amounts. It also adjusted its allowance for bad debts and claimed additional depreciation on fixed assets. It did not recognize any capital gains to offset the capital loss carryover. Step 11 below presents the completed book balance sheet after making tax related journal entries.

Assets:	Book	Tax	Difference
Cash	$ 318,800	$ 318,800	
Accounts receivable	400,000	400,000	
Allowance for bad debts	(37,000)	–0–	
Net accounts receivable	363,000	400,000	$ 37,000
Investment in corporate stock	90,000	90,000	
Investment in tax-exempt bonds	50,000	50,000	
Inventory	600,000	600,000	
Fixed assets	1,200,000	1,200,000	
Accumulated depreciation	(180,000)	(465,000)	
Net fixed assets	1,020,000	735,000	285,000
Liabilities and stock equity:			
Accounts payable	295,000	295,000	
Unearned rental income	–0–	–0–	
Long-term liabilities	530,000	530,000	
Common stock	650,000	650,000	

Valley also reports the following book income statement through net income before federal income taxes and tax return schedule through taxable income. The tax portion of the book income statement appears in Step 11.

	Book	Tax	Difference
Gross receipts	$2,000,000	$2,000,000	
Minus: Cost of goods sold	(700,000)	(700,000)	
Gross profit from operations	$1,300,000	$1,300,000	
Plus: Dividends from less than 20%-owned corporations	15,000	15,000	
Tax-exempt income	3,200	–0–	$ (3,200)
Prepaid rental income	8,000	–0–	(8,000)
Minus: Operating expenses	(500,000)	(500,000)	
Depreciation	(120,000)	(295,000)	(175,000)
Bad debt expense	(40,000)	(12,000)	28,000
Business interest expense	(60,000)	(60,000)	
Insurance premiums on life insurance for key employee (Valley is the beneficiary)	(3,500)	–0–	3,500
U.S. production activities deduction (rounded)	–0–	(39,000)	(39,000)
Dividends-received deduction	–0–	(10,500)	(10,500)
Net income before federal income taxes	$ 602,700		
Taxable income		$ 398,500	

Steps 1 through 3.

The book and tax balance sheets above indicate the items where the book and tax bases differ, thereby indicating temporary differences. In addition, the net capital loss carryforward remains unused.

The following three roll forward schedules calculate the deferred tax assets and deferred tax liability associated with these temporary differences. The beginning and ending balances for the balance sheet items reflect the differences between the book and tax bases for these assets and liabilities. In the first schedule, the net accounts receivable temporary difference increases, and the unearned rental income item reverses. In the second schedule, Valley has not realized the deferred tax asset because it recognized no capital gains in Year 2. Therefore, this deferred tax asset has not yet reversed. In the third schedule, the fixed asset temporary difference increases.

Current deferred tax asset:	Beg. of Year 2	End of Year 2	Change
Net accounts receivable	$ 9,000	$ 37,000	$ 28,000
Unearned rental income	8,000	–0–	(8,000)
Total	$ 17,000	$ 37,000	$ 20,000
Times: Tax rate	0.34	0.34	
Current deferred tax asset	$ 5,780	$ 12,580	$ 6,800

Noncurrent deferred tax asset:	Beg. of Year 2	End of Year 2	Change
Net capital loss	$ 12,000	$ 12,000	$ –0–
Times: Tax rate	0.34	0.34	
Noncurrent deferred tax asset	$ 4,080	$ 4,080	$ –0–

Noncurrent deferred tax liability:	Beg. of Year 2	End of Year 2	Change
Net fixed assets	$110,000	$285,000	$175,000
Times: Tax rate	0.34	0.34	
Noncurrent deferred tax liability	$ 37,400	$ 96,900	$ 59,500

The amounts in the change column also appear as book-tax differences in the above book and tax income schedules. In those schedules, the differences occur in the related income or expense accounts, specifically, bad debt expense, prepaid rental income, and depreciation.

As before, the changes in the deferred tax assets and liabilities also represent the deferred federal tax expense or benefit for the current year. See Step 7 below.

Step 4.
Assuming evidence supports that Valley still will realize the entire amount of its deferred tax assets, Valley need not establish a valuation allowance.

Step 5.
Assume again that Valley requires no adjustments for uncertain tax positions.

Step 6.
As provided in the schedule above, taxable income is $398,500. Therefore, current federal income taxes payable is $135,490 ($398,500 × 0.34). In this example, the current payable amount also is the current federal income tax expense for book purposes. (The equality of the current payable amount and the federal income tax expense may not occur, however, under some uncertain tax position situations and in other special circumstances.)

Step 7.
The net deferred federal tax expense from the roll forward schedules equals $52,700 ($59,500 − $6,800). Therefore, the total federal income tax expense for this year can be calculated as follows:

Current federal income tax expense	$135,490
Deferred income tax expense	52,700
Total federal income tax expense	$188,190

Step 8.
Given the amounts determined in previous steps, Valley makes the following book journal entry:

Current federal income tax expense	135,490	
Deferred federal income tax expense	52,700	
Current deferred tax asset	6,800	
Noncurrent deferred tax liability		59,500
Federal income taxes payable		135,490

Alternatively, Valley could make the following combined book journal entry:

Total federal income tax expense	188,190	
Current deferred tax asset	6,800	
Noncurrent deferred tax liability		59,500
Federal income taxes payable		135,490

Step 9.

As a cross check on the previous steps, Valley can prepare the following tax provision reconciliation:

Net income before federal income taxes (FIT)	$602,700
Permanent differences:	
Nondeductible insurance premiums	3,500
Tax-exempt income	(3,200)
U.S. production activities deduction	(39,000)
Dividends-received deduction	(10,500)
Net income after permanent differences	$553,500
Temporary differences:	
Unearned rental income	(8,000)
Net accounts receivable (bad debt expense)	28,000
Net fixed assets (depreciation)	(175,000)
Taxable income	$398,500

ADDITIONAL COMMENT

This approach and the balance sheet approach may not always lead to the same result when enacted tax rates change, under some uncertain tax position situations, and in other special circumstances.

Assuming no enacted change in future tax rates, net income after permanent differences times the tax rate results in the total federal income tax expense. Specifically, $553,500 \times 0.34 = $188,190$. Similarly, taxable income times the tax rate results in current federal income taxes payable. Specifically, $398,500 \times 0.34 = $135,490$.

Step 10.

Valley's Year 2 effective tax rate is its income tax expense divided by its pretax book income, or $188,190/$602,700 = 31.23%$ (rounded up). Accordingly, Valley's effective tax rate reconciliation is as follows:

Statutory tax rate	34.00%
Nondeductible insurance premiums ($3,500/$602,700 \times 34%)	0.20%
Tax-exempt income [($3,200)/$602,700 \times 34%]	(0.18)%
U.S. production activities deduction [($39,000)/$602,700 \times 34%]	(2.20)%
Dividends-received deduction [($10,500)/$602,700 \times 34%]	(0.59)%
Effective tax rate ($188,190/$602,700)	31.23%

Step 11.

At this point, Valley can complete its financial statements. The first part of the income statement appears in the schedule appearing before Steps 1 through 3, and the tax portion is as follows:

Partial income statement:	
Net income before federal income taxes	$602,700
Minus: Federal income tax expense	(188,190)
Net income	$414,510
Effective tax rate ($188,190/$602,700)	31.23%

As shown in Step 7, the federal income tax expense has two components as follows:

Current federal income tax expense	$135,490
Deferred income tax expense ($59,500 − $6,800)	52,700
Total federal income tax expense	$188,190

The book balance sheet for Year 2 is as follows:

Assets:

Cash		$ 318,800
Accounts receivable	$ 400,000	
Minus: Allowance for bad debts	(37,000)	363,000
Investment in corporate stock		90,000
Investment in tax-exempt bond		50,000
Inventory		600,000
Current deferred tax asset		12,580
Fixed assets	$1,200,000	
Minus: Accumulated depreciation	(180,000)	1,020,000
Total assets		$2,454,380

ADDITIONAL COMMENT

This example ignores estimated tax payments, so the entire amount of federal income taxes payable appears on the balance sheet.

Liabilities and equity:

Accounts payable	$ 295,000
Unearned rental income	–0–
Federal income taxes payable	135,490
Noncurrent deferred liability ($96,900 − $4,080)	92,820
Long-term liabilities	530,000
Common stock	650,000
Retained earnings	751,070
Total liabilities and equity	$2,454,380

OTHER TRANSACTIONS

Chapters C:5, C:7, C:8, and C:16 describe the financial statement implications of other transactions, for example, the alternative minimum tax (Chapter C:5), corporate acquisitions (Chapter C:7), intercompany transactions (Chapter C:8), and the foreign tax credit and deferred foreign earnings (Chapter C:16). Also, Problem C:3-64 provides a comprehensive tax return and financial accounting exercise.

PROBLEM MATERIALS

DISCUSSION QUESTIONS

C:3-1 High Corporation incorporates on May 1 and begins business on May 10 of the current year. What alternative tax years can High elect to report its initial year's income?

C:3-2 Port Corporation wants to change its tax year from a calendar year to a fiscal year ending June 30. Port is a C corporation owned by 100 shareholders, none of whom own more than 5% of the stock. Can Port change its tax year? If so, how can it accomplish the change?

C:3-3 Stan and Susan, two calendar year taxpayers, are starting a new business to manufacture and sell digital circuits. They intend to incorporate the business with $600,000 of their own capital and $2 million of equity capital obtained from other investors. The company expects to incur organizational and start-up expenditures of $100,000 in the first year. Inventories are a material income-producing factor. The company also expects to incur losses of $500,000 in the first two years of operations and substantial research and development expenses during the first three years. The company expects to break even in the third year and be profitable at the end of the fourth year, even though the nature of the digital circuit business will require continual research and development activities. What accounting methods and tax elections must Stan and Susan consider in their first year of operation? For each method and election, explain the possible alternatives and the advantages and disadvantages of each alternative.

C:3-4 Compare the tax treatment of capital gains and losses by a corporation and by an individual.

C:3-5 Explain the effect of the Sec. 291 recapture rule when a corporation sells depreciable real estate.

C:3-6 What are organizational expenditures? How are they treated for tax purposes?

C:3-7 What are start-up expenditures? How are they treated for tax purposes?

C:3-8 Describe three ways in which the treatment of charitable contributions by individual and corporate taxpayers differ.

C:3-9 Carver Corporation uses the accrual method of accounting and the calendar year as its tax year. Its board of directors authorizes a cash contribution on November 3, 2011, that the corporation pays on March 9, 2012. In what year(s) is it deductible? What happens if the corporation does not pay the contribution until April 20, 2012?

C:3-10 Zero Corporation contributes inventory (computers) to State University for use in its mathematics program. The computers have a $1,225 cost basis and an $2,800 FMV. How much is Zero's charitable contribution deduction for the computers? (Ignore the 10% limit.)

C:3-11 Why are corporations allowed a dividends-received deduction? What dividends qualify for this special deduction?

C:3-12 Why is a dividends-received deduction disallowed if the stock on which the corporation pays the dividend is debt-financed?

C:3-13 Crane Corporation incurs a $75,000 NOL in the current year. In which years can Crane use this NOL if it makes no special elections? When might a special election to forgo the carryback of the NOL be beneficial for Crane?

C:3-14 What special restrictions apply to the deduction of a loss realized on the sale of property between a corporation and a shareholder who owns 60% of the corporation's stock? What restrictions apply to the deduction of expenses accrued by a corporation at year-end and owed to a cash method shareholder who owns 60% of the corporation's stock?

C:3-15 Deer Corporation is a C corporation. Its taxable income for the current year is $200,000. What is Deer Corporation's income tax liability for the year?

C:3-16 Budget Corporation is a personal service corporation. Its taxable income for the current year is $75,000. What is Budget's income tax liability for the year?

C:3-17 Why do special restrictions on using the progressive corporate tax rates apply to controlled groups of corporations?

C:3-18 Describe the three types of controlled groups.

C:3-19 List five restrictions on claiming multiple tax benefits that apply to controlled groups of corporations.

C:3-20 What are the major advantages and disadvantages of filing a consolidated tax return?

C:3-21 What are the tax advantages of substituting fringe benefits for salary paid to a shareholder-employee?

C:3-22 Explain the tax consequences to both the corporation and a shareholder-employee if an IRS agent determines that a portion of the compensation paid in a prior tax year exceeds a reasonable compensation level.

C:3-23 What is the advantage of a special apportionment plan for the benefits of the 15%, 25%, and 34% tax rates to members of a controlled group?

C:3-24 What corporations must pay estimated taxes? When are the estimated tax payments due?

C:3-25 What is a "large" corporation for purposes of the estimated tax rules? What special rules apply to such large corporations?

C:3-26 What penalties apply to the underpayment of estimated taxes? The late payment of the remaining tax liability?

C:3-27 Describe the situations in which a corporation must file a tax return.

C:3-28 When is a corporate tax return due for a calendar-year taxpayer? What extension(s) of time in which to file the return are available?

C:3-29 List four types of differences that can cause a corporation's book income to differ from its taxable income.

ISSUE IDENTIFICATION QUESTIONS

C:3-30 X-Ray Corporation received a $100,000 dividend from Yancey Corporation this year. X-Ray owns 10% of the Yancey's single class of stock. What tax issues should X-Ray consider with respect to its dividend income?

C:3-31 Williams Corporation sold a truck with an adjusted basis of $100,000 to Barbara for $80,000. Barbara owns 25% of the Williams stock. What tax issues should Williams and Barbara consider with respect to the sale/purchase?

C:3-32 You are the CPA who prepares the tax returns for Don, his wife, Mary, and their two corporations. Don owns 100% of Pencil Corporation's stock. Pencil's current year taxable income is $100,000. Mary owns 100% of Eraser Corporation's stock. Eraser's current year taxable income is $150,000. Don and Mary file a joint federal income tax return. What issues should Don and Mary consider with respect to the calculation of the three tax return liabilities?

C:3-33 Rugby Corporation has a $50,000 NOL in the current year. Rugby's taxable income in each of the previous two years was $25,000. Rugby expects its taxable income for next year to exceed $400,000. What issues should Rugby consider with respect to the use of the NOL?

PROBLEMS

C:3-34 *Depreciation Recapture.* Young Corporation purchased residential real estate several year ago for $225,000, of which $25,000 was allocated to the land and $200,000 was allocated to the building. Young took straight-line MACRS deductions of $30,000 during the years it held the property. In the current year, Young sells the property for $285,000, of which $60,000 is allocated to the land and $225,000 is allocated to the building. What are the amount and character of Young's recognized gain or loss on the sale?

C:3-35 *Organizational and Start-up Expenditures.* Delta Corporation incorporates on January 7, begins business on July 10, and elects to have its initial tax year end on October 31. Delta incurs the following expenses between January and October related to its organization during the current year:

Date	Expenditure	Amount
January 30	Travel to investigate potential business site	$2,000
May 15	Legal expenses to draft corporate charter	2,500
May 30	Commissions to stockbroker for issuing and selling stock	4,000
May 30	Temporary directors' fees	2,500
June 1	Expense of transferring building to Delta	3,000
June 5	Accounting fees to set up corporate books	1,500
June 10	Training expenses for employees	5,000
June 15	Rent expense for June	1,000
July 15	Rent expense for July	1,000

a. What alternative treatments are available for Delta's expenditures?
b. What amount of organizational expenditures can Delta Corporation deduct on its first tax return for the fiscal year ending October 31?
c. What amount of start-up costs can Delta Corporation deduct on its first tax return?

C:3-36 *Charitable Contribution of Property.* Yellow Corporation donates the following property to the State University:

- ABC Corporation stock purchased two years ago for $18,000. The stock, which trades on a regional stock exchange, has a $25,000 FMV on the contribution date.

- Inventory with a $17,000 adjusted basis and a $22,000 FMV. State will use the inventory for scientific research that qualifies under the special Sec. 170(e)(4) rules.

- An antique vase purchased two years ago for $10,000 and having an $18,000 FMV. State University plans to sell the vase to obtain funds for educational purposes.

Yellow Corporation's taxable income before any charitable contributions deduction, NOL or capital loss carryback, or dividends-received deduction is $250,000.
a. What is Yellow Corporation's charitable contributions deduction for the current year?
b. What is the amount of its charitable contributions carryover (if any)?

C:3-37 *Charitable Contributions of Property.* Blue Corporation donates the following property to Johnson Elementary School:

- XYZ Corporation stock purchased two years ago for $25,000. The stock has a $19,000 FMV on the contribution date.

- ABC Corporation stock purchased three years ago for $2,000. The stock has a $16,000 FMV on the contribution date.

- PQR Corporation stock purchased six months ago for $12,000. The stock has an $18,000 FMV on the contribution date.

The school will sell the stock and use the proceeds to renovate a classroom to be used as a computer laboratory. Blue's taxable income before any charitable contribution deduction, dividends-received deduction, or NOL or capital loss carryback is $400,000.
a. What is Blue's charitable contributions deduction for the current year?
b. What is Blue's charitable contribution carryback or carryover (if any)? In what years can it be used?
c. What would have been a better tax plan concerning the XYZ stock donation?

C:3-38 *Charitable Contribution Deduction Limitation.* Zeta Corporation reports the following results for Year 1 and Year 2:

	Year 1	Year 2
Adjusted taxable income	$180,000	$125,000
Charitable contributions (cash)	20,000	12,000

The adjusted taxable income is before Zeta claims any charitable contributions deduction, NOL or capital loss carryback, dividends-received deduction, or U.S. production activities deduction.
a. How much is Zeta's charitable contributions deduction in Year 1? In Year 2?
b. What is Zeta's contribution carryover to Year 3, if any?

C:3-39 *Taxable Income Computation.* Omega Corporation reports the following results for the current year:

Gross profits on sales	$120,000
Dividends from less-than-20%-owned domestic corporations	40,000
Operating expenses	100,000
Charitable contributions (cash)	11,000

a. What is Omega's charitable contributions deduction for the current year and its charitable contributions carryover to next year, if any?
b. What is Omega's taxable income for the current year, assuming qualified production activities income is $20,000?

C:3-40 *Dividends-Received Deduction.* Theta Corporation reports the following results for the current year:

Gross profits on sales	$220,000
Dividends from less-than-20%-owned domestic corporations	100,000
Operating expenses	218,000

a. What is Theta's taxable income for the current year, assuming qualified production activities income is $2,000?
b. How would your answer to Part a change if Theta's operating expenses are instead $234,000, assuming qualified production activities income is zero or negative?
c. How would your answer to Part a change if Theta's operating expenses are instead $252,000, assuming qualified production activities income is zero or negative?
d. How would your answers to Parts a, b, and c change if Theta received $75,000 of the dividends from a 20%-owned corporation and the remaining $25,000 from a less-than-20%-owned corporation?

C:3-41 *Stock Held 45 Days or Less.* Beta Corporation purchased 100 shares of Gamma Corporation common stock (less than 5% of the outstanding stock) two days before the ex-dividend date for $200,000. Beta receives a $10,000 cash dividend from Gamma. Beta sells the Gamma stock one week after purchasing it for $190,000. What are the tax consequences of these three events?

C:3-42 *Debt-financed Stock.* Cheers Corporation purchased for $500,000 5,000 shares of Beer Corporation common stock (less than 5% of the outstanding Beer stock) at the beginning of the current year. It used $400,000 of borrowed money and $100,000 of its own cash to make this purchase. Cheers paid $50,000 of interest on the debt this year. Cheers received a $40,000 cash dividend on the Beer stock on September 1 of the current year.
a. What amount can Cheers deduct for the interest paid on the loan?
b. What dividends-received deduction can Cheers claim with respect to the dividend?

C:3-43 *Net Operating Loss Carrybacks and Carryovers.* In 2011, Ace Corporation reports gross income of $200,000 (including $150,000 of profit from its operations and $50,000 in dividends from less-than-20%-owned domestic corporations) and $220,000 of operating expenses. Ace's 2009 taxable income (all ordinary income) was $75,000, on which it paid taxes of $13,750.
a. What is Ace's NOL for 2011?
b. What is the amount of Ace's tax refund if Ace carries back the 2011 NOL to 2009?
c. Assume that Ace expects 2012's taxable income to be $400,000. Ignore the U.S. production activities deduction. What election could Ace make to increase the tax benefit from its NOL? What is the dollar amount of the expected benefit (if any)? Assume a 10% discount rate as a measure of the time value of money.

C:3-44 *Ordering of Deductions.* Beta Corporation reports the following results for the current year:

Gross income from operations	$180,000
Dividends from less-than-20%-owned domestic corporations	100,000
Operating expenses	150,000
Charitable contributions	20,000

In addition, Beta has a $50,000 NOL carryover from the preceding tax year, and its qualified production activities income is $30,000.
a. What is Beta's taxable income for the current year?
b. What carrybacks or carryovers are available to other tax years?

C:3-45 *Sale to a Related Party.* Union Corporation sells a truck for $18,000 to Jane, who owns 70% of its stock. The truck has a $24,000 adjusted basis on the sale date. Jane sells the truck to an unrelated party, Mike, for $28,000 two years later after claiming $5,000 in depreciation.
a. What is Union's realized and recognized gain or loss on selling the truck?
b. What is Jane's realized and recognized gain or loss on selling the truck to Mike?
c. How would your answers to Part b change if Jane instead sold the truck for $10,000?

C:3-46 *Payment to a Cash Basis Employee-Shareholder.* Value Corporation is a calendar year taxpayer that uses the accrual method of accounting. On December 10 of the current year, Value accrues a bonus payment of $100,000 to Brett, its president and sole shareholder. Brett is a calendar year taxpayer who uses the cash method of accounting.
a. When can Value deduct the bonus if it pays it to Brett on March 11 of next year? On March 18 of next year?
b. How would your answers to Part a change if Brett were an employee of Value who owns no stock in the corporation?

C:3-47 *Capital Gains and Losses.* Western Corporation reports the following results for the current year:

Gross profits on sales	$150,000
Long-term capital gain	8,000
Long-term capital loss	15,000
Short-term capital gain	10,000
Short-term capital loss	2,000
Operating expenses	61,000

a. What are Western's taxable income and income tax liability for the current year, assuming qualified production activities income is $89,000?
b. How would your answers to Part a change if Western's short-term capital loss is $5,000 instead of $2,000?

C:3-48 *Computing the Corporate Income Tax Liability.* What is Beta Corporation's income tax liability assuming its taxable income is (a) $94,000, (b) $300,000, and (c) $600,000. How would your answers change if Beta were a personal service corporation?

C:3-49 *Computing the Corporate Income Tax Liability.* Fawn Corporation, a C corporation, paid no dividends and recognized no capital gains or losses in the current year. What is its income tax liability assuming its taxable income for the year is
a. $50,000
b. $14,000,000
c. $18,000,000
d. $34,000,000

C:3-50 *Computing Taxable Income and Income Tax Liability.* Pace Corporation reports the following results for the current year:

Gross profit on sales	$120,000
Long-term capital loss	10,000
Short-term capital loss	5,000
Dividends from 40%-owned domestic corporation	30,000
Operating expenses	65,000
Charitable contributions	10,000

a. What are Pace's taxable income and income tax liability, assuming qualified production activities income is $55,000?
b. What carrybacks and carryovers (if any) are available and to what years must they be carried?

C:3-51 *Computing Taxable Income and Income Tax Liability.* Roper Corporation reports the following results for the current year:

Gross profits on sales	$80,000
Short-term capital gain	40,000
Long-term capital gain	25,000
Dividends from 25%-owned domestic corporation	15,000
NOL carryover from the preceding tax year	9,000
Operating expenses	45,000

What are Roper's taxable income and income tax liability, assuming qualified production activities income is $35,000?

C:3-52 *Controlled Groups.* Which of the following groups constitute controlled groups? (Any stock not listed below is held by unrelated individuals each owning less than 1% of the outstanding stock.) For brother-sister corporations, which definition applies?
a. Judy owns 90% of the single classes of stock of Hot and Ice Corporations.
b. Jones and Kane Corporations each have only a single class of stock outstanding. The two controlling individual shareholders own the stock as follows:

	Stock Ownership Percentages	
Shareholder	Jones Corp.	Kane Corp.
Tom	60%	80%
Mary	30%	0%

c. Link, Model, and Name Corporations each have a single class of stock outstanding. The stock is owned as follows:

	Stock Ownership Percentages	
Shareholder	Model Corp.	Name Corp.
Link Corp.	80%	50%
Model Corp.		40%

Link Corporation's stock is widely held by over 1,000 shareholders, none of whom owns directly or indirectly more than 1% of Link's stock.
d. Oat, Peach, Rye, and Seed Corporations each have a single class of stock outstanding. The stock is owned as follows:

	Stock Ownership Percentages			
Shareholder	Oat Corp.	Peach Corp.	Rye Corp.	Seed Corp.
Bob	100%	90%		
Oat Corp.			80%	30%
Rye Corp.				60%

C:3-53 *Controlled Groups of Corporations.* Sally owns 100% of the outstanding stock of Eta, Theta, Phi, and Gamma Corporations, each of which files a separate return for the current year. During the current year, the corporations report taxable income as follows:

Corporation	Taxable Income
Eta	$40,000
Theta	(25,000)
Phi	50,000
Gamma	10,000

a. What is each corporation's separate tax liability, assuming the corporations do not elect a special apportionment plan for allocating the corporate tax rates?
b. What is each corporation's separate tax liability, assuming the corporations make a special election to apportion the reduced corporate tax rates in such a way that minimizes the group's total tax liability? Note: More than one plan can satisfy this goal.
c. How does the result in Part b change if Gamma's income is $30,000 instead of $10,000?

C:3-54 *Compensation Planning.* Marilyn owns all of Bell Corporation's stock. Bell is a C corporation and employs 40 people. Marilyn is married, has two dependent children, and files a joint tax return with her husband. She projects that Bell will report $400,000 of pretax profits for the current year. Marilyn is considering five salary levels as shown below. Ignore the U.S. production activities deduction for this problem.

Total Income	Salary Paid to Marilyn	Earnings Retained by Bell Corporation	Marilyn	Bell Corporation	Total
				Tax Liability	
$400,000	$ –0–	$400,000			
400,000	$100,000	300,000			
400,000	200,000	200,000			
400,000	300,000	100,000			
400,000	400,000	–0–			

a. Determine the total tax liability for Marilyn and Bell for each of the five proposed salary levels. Assume no other income for Marilyn's family, and assume that Marilyn and her husband claim a combined itemized deduction and personal exemption of $30,000 regardless of AGI levels. Ignore employment taxes.
b. What recommendations can you make about a salary level for Marilyn that will minimize the total tax liability? Assume salaries paid up to $400,000 are considered reasonable compensation.
c. What is the possible disadvantage to Marilyn if Bell retains funds in the business and distributes some of the accumulated earnings as a dividend in a later tax year?

C:3-55 ***Fringe Benefits.*** Refer to the facts in Problem C:3-54. Marilyn has read an article explaining the advantages of paying nontaxable fringe benefits (premiums on group term life insurance, accident and health insurance, etc.) and having deferred compensation plans (e.g., qualified pension and profit-sharing plans). Provide Marilyn with information on the tax savings associated with converting $3,000 of her salary into nontaxable fringe benefits. What additional costs might Bell Corporation incur if it adopts a fringe benefit plan?

C:3-56 ***Estimated Tax Requirement.*** Zeta Corporation's taxable income for 2010 was $1.5 million, on which Zeta paid federal income taxes of $510,000. Zeta estimates calendar year 2011's taxable income to be $2 million, on which it will owe $680,000 in federal income taxes.
a. What are Zeta's minimum quarterly estimated tax payments for 2011 to avoid an underpayment penalty?
b. When is Zeta's 2011 tax return due?
c. When are any remaining taxes due? What amount of taxes are due when Zeta files its return assuming Zeta timely pays estimated tax payments equal to the amount determined in Part a?
d. If Zeta obtains an extension to file, when is its tax return due? Will the extension permit Zeta to delay making its final tax payments?

C:3-57 ***Filing the Tax Return and Paying the Tax Liability.*** Wright Corporation's taxable income for calendar years 2008, 2009, and 2010 was $120,000, $150,000, and $100,000, respectively. Its total tax liability for 2010 was $22,250. Wright estimates that its 2011 taxable income will be $500,000, on which it will owe federal income taxes of $170,000. Assume Wright earns its 2011 taxable income evenly throughout the year.
a. What are Wright's minimum quarterly estimated tax payments for 2011 to avoid an underpayment penalty?
b. When is Wright's 2011 tax return due?
c. When are any remaining taxes due? What amount of taxes are due when Wright files its return assuming it timely paid estimated tax payments equal to the amount determined in Part a?
d. How would your answer to Part a change if Wright's tax liability for 2010 had been $200,000?

C:3-58 ***Converting Book Income to Taxable Income.*** The following income and expense accounts appeared in the book accounting records of Rocket Corporation, an accrual basis taxpayer, for the current calendar year.

Account Title	Book Income Debit	Book Income Credit
Net sales		$3,230,000
Dividends		10,000 (1)
Interest		18,000 (2)
Gain on sale of stock		9,000 (3)
Key-person life insurance proceeds		100,000

Cost of goods sold	$2,000,000	
Salaries and wages	500,000	
Bad debts	13,000 (4)	
Payroll taxes	62,000	
Interest expense	12,000 (5)	
Charitable contributions	50,000 (6)	
Depreciation	70,000 (7)	
Other expenses	40,000 (8)	
Federal income taxes	166,000	
Net income	454,000	
Total	$3,367,000	$3,367,000

The following additional information applies.

1. Dividends were from Star Corporation, a 30%-owned domestic corporation.
2. Interest revenue consists of interest on corporate bonds, $15,000; and municipal bonds, $3,000.
3. The stock is a capital asset held for three years prior to sale.
4. Rocket uses the specific writeoff method of accounting for bad debts.
5. Interest expense consists of $11,000 interest incurred on funds borrowed for working capital and $1,000 interest on funds borrowed to purchase municipal bonds.
6. Rocket paid all contributions in cash during the current year to State University.
7. Rocket calculated depreciation per books using the straight-line method. For income tax purposes, depreciation amounted to $95,000.
8. Other expenses include premiums of $5,000 on the key-person life insurance policy covering Rocket's president, who died in December.
9. Qualified production activities income is $300,000, and the applicable percentage is 9%.
10. Rocket has a $90,000 NOL carryover from prior years.

Required:

a. Prepare a worksheet reconciling Rocket's book income with its taxable income (before special deductions). Six columns should be used—two (one debit and one credit) for each of the following three major headings: book income, Schedule M-1 adjustments, and taxable income. (See the sample worksheet with Form 1120 in Appendix B if you need assistance).

b. Prepare a tax provision reconciliation as in Step 9 of the Tax Provision Process. Assume a 34% corporate tax rate.

C:3-59 *Reconciling Book Income and Taxable Income.* Zero Corporation reports the following results for the current year:

Net income per books (after taxes)	$290,000
Federal income tax per books	150,000
Tax-exempt interest income	6,000
Interest on loan to purchase tax-exempt bonds	8,000
MACRS depreciation exceeding book depreciation	30,000
Net capital loss	5,000
Insurance premium on life of corporate officer where Zero is the beneficiary	4,000
Excess charitable contributions carried over to next year	3,000
U.S. production activities deduction	14,000

Prepare a reconciliation of Zero's taxable income before special deductions with its book income.

C:3-60 *Reconciling Unappropriated Retained Earnings.* White Corporation's financial accounting records disclose the following results for the period ending December 31 of the current year:

Retained earnings balance on January 1	$246,500
Net income for year	259,574
Contingency reserve established on December 31	60,000
Cash dividend paid on July 23	23,000

What is White's unappropriated retained earnings balance on December 31 of the current year?

C:3-61 *Tax Reconciliation Process.* Omega Corporation, a regular C corporation, presents you with the following partial *book* income statement for the current year:

Sales	$1,900,000	
Cost of goods sold	(1,100,000)	
Gross profit		$800,000
Operating expenses:		
Depreciation	$ 80,000	
Interest expense	18,000	
Warranty expense	12,000	
Fines and penalties	10,000	
Other business expenses	220,000	(340,000)
Net operating income		$460,000
Other income (losses):		
Interest received on municipal bonds	$ 1,000	
Income on installment sale	9,000	
Net losses on stock sales	(20,000)	(10,000)
Net income before federal income taxes		$450,000

Omega also provides the following partial balance sheet information:

	Book		Tax	
	Beg. of Year	End of Year	Beg. of Year	End of Year
Installment note receivable	$ –0–	$ 30,000	$ –0–	$ 30,000
Minus: Unrecognized income on note	–0–	–0–	–0–	(9,000)
Net basis of note receivable	–0–	30,000	–0–	21,000
Tax-exempt bonds	18,000	18,000	18,000	18,000
Current deferred asset	5,100	?	–0–	–0–
Investment stocks	100,000	40,000	100,000	40,000
Fixed assets	400,000	400,000	400,000	400,000
Minus: Accumulated depreciation	(40,000)	(120,000)	(80,000)	(208,000)
Net basis of fixed assets	360,000	280,000	320,000	192,000
Liability for warranties	–0–	12,000	–0–	–0–
Noncurrent deferred tax liability	13,600	?	–0–	–0–

You have gathered the following additional information:
1. Depreciation for tax purposes is $128,000.
2. Of the $18,000 interest expense, $2,000 is allocable to a loan used to purchase the municipal bonds.
3. The warranty expense is an estimated amount for book purposes. Omega expects actual claims on these warranties to be filed and paid next year.
4. Your research determines that the fines and penalties are not deductible for tax purposes.
5. In the current year, Omega sold property using the installment method as follows:

Selling price	$30,000
Adjusted basis	(21,000)
Gain	$9,000

Omega obtains a $30,000 installment note receivable this year and will receive the $30,000 sales proceeds next year. For book purposes, Omega recognizes the $9,000 gain in the current year. For tax purposes, Omega will recognize the $9,000 gain next year when it receives the $30,000 sales proceeds.
6. Omega sold a significant portion of its stock portfolio in the current year. The $20,000 net loss per books from these stock sales includes the following components:

Long-term capital gain	$15,000
Long-term capital loss	(38,000)
Short-term capital gain	3,000

Omega had no capital gains in prior years, so it cannot carry the net capital losses back.

7. Omega does not expect to realize capital gains next year, but it does expect sufficient capital gains within the next five years so that it can use the capital loss carryover before it expires. Thus, Omega determines that it needs no valuation allowance.
8. Omega has a $15,000 net operating loss carryover from last year, which it then expected to use in the next year (now the current year).
9. Qualified production activities income for the current year equals $300,000, which is less than taxable income before the U.S. production activities deduction. The applicable percentage is 9%.
10. Omega's tax rate is 34% and will remain so in future years.
11. The beginning deferred tax asset pertains to the NOL carryover, and the beginning deferred tax liability pertains to fixed assets. Other deferred tax assets and deferred tax liabilities may arise in the current year.
12. Omega determines that it needs no adjustment for uncertain tax positions.

Required: Perform the tax provision process steps as outlined in the text. For Step 11, just present partial income statement and balance sheet disclosures as allowed by the given facts.

C:3-62　*Valuation Allowance.* In the current year, Alpha Corporation generated $500,000 of ordinary operating income and incurred a $20,000 capital loss on the sale of marketable securities from its investment portfolio. Alpha expects to generate $500,000 of ordinary operating income in each of the next five years. Alpha incurred no capital gains in its previous three years, so it must carry over the $20,000 capital loss for up to five years. Alpha estimates that its remaining marketable securities would produce a $12,000 capital gain if sold. Thus, Alpha determines that, more likely than not, the corporation will not realize (deduct) $8,000 of the current year capital loss. Alpha has no other book-tax differences and is subject to a 34% tax rate.

Required:
a. Determine Alpha's deferred tax asset and valuation allowance for the current year.
b. Determine Alpha's current federal income tax expense, deferred federal income tax expense (benefit), total federal income tax expense, and federal income taxes payable.
c. Prepare the journal entry necessary to record the above amounts.
d. Prepare a tax provision reconciliation and effective tax rate reconciliation for the current year.

C:3-63　*Uncertain Tax Positions.* In the current year, Kappa Corporation earned $1 million of net income before federal income taxes. This amount of book income includes a $100,000 expense for what the company considers an ordinary and necessary business expense. Kappa also deducted the entire $100,000 for tax purposes. In assessing the expense for its tax provision, Kappa determines that it has a more-likely-than-not probability of sustaining some portion of the deduction upon an IRS examination. However, some uncertainty remains as to whether the entire amount is deductible. Any amount ultimately disallowed by the IRS would be a permanent disallowance and not merely a temporary item that could be amortized over time. Upon further analysis, Kappa measures the benefit that is more than 50% likely to be realized as $70,000. Thus, Kappa may not recognize $30,000 of the expense in determining its federal income tax provision. In addition, Kappa has a $25,000 temporary difference that decreases its taxable income to $975,000 and increases its deferred tax liability.

Required:
a. Determine Kappa's liability for unrecognized tax benefits, total federal income tax expense, deferred federal income tax expense, current federal income tax expense, increase in deferred tax liability, and federal income taxes payable.
b. Prepare the journal entry necessary to record the current year tax provision.

COMPREHENSIVE PROBLEM

C:3-64　Jackson Corporation prepared the following *book* income statement for its year ended December 31, 2011:

Sales	$950,000
Minus:　Cost of goods sold	(450,000)
Gross profit	$500,000

Plus:	Dividends received on Invest Corporation stock	$ 3,000	
	Gain on sale of Invest Corporation stock	30,000	
	Total dividends and gain		33,000
Minus:	Depreciation ($7,500 + $52,000)	$ 59,500	
	Bad debt expense	22,000	
	Other operating expenses	105,500	
	Loss on sale of Equipment 1	70,000	
	Total expenses and loss		(257,000)
	Net income per books before taxes		$276,000
Minus:	Federal income tax expense		(90,000)
	Net income per books		$186,000

Information on equipment depreciation and sale:

Equipment 1:

- Acquired March 3, 2009 for $180,000
- For books: 12-year life; straight-line depreciation
- Sold February 17, 2011 for $80,000

Sales price			$ 80,000
Cost		$180,000	
Minus:	Depreciation for 2009 (½ year)	$ 7,500	
	Depreciation for 2010 ($180,000/12)	15,000	
	Depreciation for 2011 (½ year)	7,500	
	Total book depreciation	(30,000)	
Book value at time of sale			(150,000)
Book loss on sale of Equipment 1			$(70,000)

- For tax: Seven-year MACRS property for which the corporation made no Sec. 179 election in the acquisition year and elected out of bonus depreciation.

Equipment 2:

- Acquired February 16, 2010 for $624,000
- For books: 12-year life; straight-line depreciation
- Book depreciation in 2011: $624,000/12 = $52,000
- For tax: Seven-year MACRS property for which the corporation made the Sec. 179 election in 2010 but elected out of bonus depreciation.

Other information:

- Under the direct writeoff method, Jackson deducts $15,000 of bad debts for tax purposes.
- Jackson has a $40,000 NOL carryover and a $6,000 capital loss carryover from last year.
- Jackson purchased the Invest Corporation stock (less than 20% owned) on June 21, 2009, for $25,000 and sold the stock on December 22, 2011, for $55,000.
- Jackson Corporation has qualified production activities income of $120,000, and the applicable percentage is 9%.

Required:
a. For 2011, calculate Jackson's tax depreciation deduction for Equipment 1 and Equipment 2, and determine the tax loss on the sale of Equipment 1.
b. For 2011, calculate Jackson's taxable income and tax liability.
c. Prepare a schedule reconciling net income per books to taxable income before special deductions (Form 1120, line 28).

TAX STRATEGY PROBLEM

C:3-65 Mike Barton owns Barton Products, Inc. The corporation has 30 employees. Barton Corporation expects $800,000 of net income before taxes in 2011. Mike is married and files a joint return with his wife, Elaine, who has no earnings of her own. They have one dependent son, Robert, who is 16 years old. Mike and Elaine have no other income and do not itemize. Mike's salary is $180,000 per year (already deducted in computing Barton Corporation's $500,000 net income). Assume that variations in salaries will not affect the U.S. production activities deduction already reflected in taxable income.

a. Should Mike increase his salary from Barton by $50,000 to reduce the overall tax burden to himself and Barton Products? Because of the Social Security cap, the corporation and Mike each would incur a 1.45% payroll tax with the corporate portion being deductible.

b. Should Barton employ Mike's wife Elaine for $50,000 rather than increase Mike's salary? Take into consideration employment taxes as well as federal income taxes. Note, that Elaine's salary would be well below the Social Security cap, so that she and the corporation each would incur the full amount of payroll taxes with the corporate portion being deductible. In 2011, Elaine's portion is 5.65%, and the corporation's is 7.65%. After 2011, Elaine's portion is 7.65%.

TAX FORM/RETURN PREPARATION PROBLEMS

C:3-66   Knoxville Musical Sales, Inc. is located at 5500 Kingston Pike, Knoxville, TN 37919. The corporation uses the calendar year and accrual basis for both book and tax purposes. It is engaged in the sale of musical instruments with an employer identification number (EIN) of 75-2012010. The company incorporated on December 31, 2006, and began business on January 2, 2007. Table C:3-4 contains balance sheet information at January 1, 2010, and December 31, 2010. Table C:3-5 presents an income statement for 2010. These schedules are presented on a book basis. Other information follows the tables.

▼ TABLE C:3-4

Knoxville Musical Sales, Inc.—Book Balance Sheet Information

Account	January 1, 2010 Debit	January 1, 2010 Credit	December 31, 2010 Debit	December 31, 2010 Credit
Cash	$ 108,439		$ 510,574	
Accounts receivable	429,570		499,500	
Allowance for doubtful accounts		$ 36,513		$ 42,458
Inventory	2,312,500		3,237,500	
Investment in corporate stock	150,000		46,000	
Investment in municipal bonds	30,000		30,000	
Cash surrender value of insurance policy	40,000		50,000	
Land	390,000		390,000	
Buildings	1,250,000		1,250,000	
Accumulated depreciation—Buildings		62,500		87,500
Equipment	928,000		2,840,000	
Accumulated depreciation—Equipment		154,667		259,333
Trucks	210,000		210,000	
Accumulated depreciation—Trucks		63,000		105,000
Deferred tax asset	15,815		14,436	
Accounts payable		300,000		270,000
Notes payable (short-term)		500,000		400,000
Accrued payroll taxes		13,875		17,344
Accrued state income taxes		8,325		13,875
Accrued federal income taxes				79,541
Bonds payable (long-term)		1,800,000		2,500,000
Deferred tax liability		150,444		560,020
Capital stock—Common		925,000		925,000
Retain earnings—Unappropriated		1,850,000		3,817,939
Totals	$5,864,324	$5,864,324	$9,078,010	$9,078,010

▼ TABLE C:3-5
Knoxville Musical Sales, Inc.—Book Income Statement 2010

Sales		$ 9,250,000
Returns		(231,250)
Net sales		$ 9,018,750
Beginning inventory	$2,312,500	
Purchases	5,087,500	
Ending inventory	(3,237,500)	
Cost of goods sold		(4,162,500)
Gross profit		$ 4,856,250
Expenses:		
Amortization	$ –0–	
Depreciation	229,267	
Repairs	19,240	
General ins.	50,875	
Net premium-Off. life ins.	41,625	
Officer's compensation	601,250	
Other salaries	370,000	
Utilities	66,600	
Advertising	44,400	
Legal and accounting fees	46,250	
Charitable contributions	27,750	
Payroll taxes	57,813	
Interest expense	194,250	
Bad debt expense	42,944	
Total expenses		(1,792,264)
Gain on sale of equipment		91,600
Interest on municipal bonds		4,625
Net gain on stock sales		35,000
Dividend income		11,100
Net income before income taxes		$ 3,206,311
Federal income tax expense		(1,076,497)
State income tax expense		(69,375)
Net income		$ 2,060,439

Estimated Tax Payments (Form 2220):
The corporation deposited estimated tax payments as follows:

April 15, 2010	$ 75,000
June 15, 2010	151,000
September 15, 2010	180,000
December 15, 2010	180,000
Total	$586,000

Taxable income in 2009 was $1,200,000, and the 2009 tax was $408,000. The corporation earned its 2010 taxable income evenly throughout the year. Therefore, it does not use the annualization or seasonal methods.

Inventory and Cost of Goods Sold (Schedule A):
The corporation uses the periodic inventory method and prices its inventory using the lower of FIFO cost or market. Only beginning inventory, ending inventory, and purchases should be reflected in Schedule A. No other costs or expenses are allocated to cost of goods sold. Note: the corporation is exempt from the uniform capitalization (UNICAP) rules because average gross income for the previous three years was less than $10 million.

Line 9 (a)	Check (ii)
(b), (c) & (d)	Not applicable
(e) & (f)	No

Compensation of Officers (Schedule E):

	(a)	(b)	(c)	(d)	(f)
Mary Travis	345-82-7091	100%	50%	$271,250
John Willis	783-97-9105	100%	25%	165,000
Chris Parker	465-34-2245	100%	25%	165,000
Total				$601,250

Bad Debts:

For tax purposes, the corporation uses the direct writeoff method of deducting bad debts. For book purposes, the corporation uses an allowance for doubtful accounts. During 2010, the corporation charged $37,000 to the allowance account, such amount representing actual writeoffs for 2010.

Additional Information (Schedule K):

1 b	Accrual	6-7	No
2 a	451140	8	Do not check box
b	Retail sales	9	Fill in the correct amount
c	Musical instruments	10	3
3	No	11	Do not check box
4 a	No	12	Not applicable
b	Yes; omit Schedule G	13	No
5 a	No		
b	No		

Organizational Expenditures:

The corporation incurred $9,500 of organizational expenditures on January 2, 2007. For book purposes, the corporation expensed the entire expenditure. For tax purposes, the corporation elected under Sec. 248 to deduct $5,000 in 2007 and amortize the remaining $4,500 amount over 180 months, with a full month's amortization taken for January 2007. The corporation reports this amortization in Part VI of Form 4562 and includes it in "Other Deductions" on Form 1120, Line 26.

Capital Gains and Losses:

The corporation sold 100 shares of PDQ Corp. common stock on October 7, 2010, for $89,000. The corporation acquired the stock on December 15, 2009, for $48,000. The corporation also sold 75 shares of JSB Corp. common stock on June 17, 2010, for $50,000. The corporation acquired this stock on September 18, 2008, for $56,000. The corporation has a $10,000 capital loss carryover from 2009.

Fixed Assets and Depreciation:

<u>For book purposes:</u> The corporation uses straight-line depreciation over the useful lives of assets as follows: Store building, 50 years; Equipment, 15 years (old) and ten years (new); and Trucks, five years. The corporation takes a half-year's depreciation in the year of acquisition and the year of disposition and assumes no salvage value. The book financial statements in Tables C:3-4 and C:3-5 reflect these calculations.

<u>For tax purposes:</u> All assets are MACRS property as follows: Store building, 39-year non-residential real property; Equipment, seven-year property; and Trucks, five-year property. The corporation acquired the store building for $1.25 million and placed it in service on January 2, 2007. The corporation acquired two pieces of equipment for $288,000 (Equipment 1) and $640,000 (Equipment 2) and placed them in service on January 2, 2007. The corporation acquired the trucks for $210,000 and placed them in service on July 18, 2008. The corporation did not make the expensing election under Sec. 179 on any property acquired before 2010. Accumulated tax depreciation through December 31, 2009, on these properties is as follows:

Store building	$ 94,863
Equipment 1	162,058
Equipment 2	360,128
Trucks	109,200

On September 1, 2010, the corporation sold for $322,000 Equipment 1 that originally cost $288,000 on January 2, 2007. The corporation had no Sec. 1231 losses from prior years. In a separate transaction on September 2, 2010, the corporation acquired and placed in service a piece of equipment costing $2.2 million. Assume these two transactions do *not* qualify as a like-kind exchange under Reg. Sec. 1.1031(k)-1(a). The new equipment is seven-year property. The corporation made the Sec. 179 expensing election with regard to the new equipment and claimed bonus depreciation. Where applicable, use published IRS depreciation tables to compute 2010 depreciation (reproduced in Appendix C of this text).

Other Information:

- The corporation's activities do not qualify for the U.S. production activities deduction.
- Ignore the AMT and accumulated earnings tax.
- The corporation received dividends (see Income Statement in Table C:3-5) from taxable, domestic corporations, the stock of which Knoxville Musical Sales, Inc. owns less than 20%.
- The corporation paid $92,500 in cash dividends to its shareholders during the year and charged the payment directly to retained earnings.
- The state income tax in Table C:3-5 is the exact amount of such taxes incurred during the year.
- The corporation is not entitled any credits.

Required: Prepare the 2010 corporate tax return for Knoxville Musical Sales, Inc. along with any necessary supporting schedules.

Optional: Prepare Schedule M-3 (and Schedule B) as well as Schedule M-1 even though the IRS does not require both Schedule M-1 and Schedule M-3.

Note to Instructor: See solution in the Instructor's Guide for other optional information to provide to students.

C:3-67 Permtemp Corporation formed in 2009 and, for that year, reported the following book income statement and balance sheet, excluding the federal income tax expense, deferred tax assets, and deferred tax liabilities:

Sales		$20,000,000
Cost of goods sold		(15,000,000)
Gross profit		$ 5,000,000
Dividend income		50,000
Tax-exempt interest income		15,000
Total income		$ 5,065,000
Expenses:		
Depreciation	$ 800,000	
Bad debts	400,000	
Charitable contributions	100,000	
Interest	475,000	
Meals and entertainment	45,000	
Other	3,855,000	
Total expenses		(5,675,000)
Net loss before federal income taxes		$ (610,000)
Cash		$ 500,000
Accounts receivable	$ 2,000,000	
Allowance for doubtful accounts	(250,000)	1,750,000
Inventory		4,000,000
Fixed assets	$10,000,000	
Accumulated depreciation	(800,000)	9,200,000
Investment in corporate stock		1,000,000
Investment in tax-exempt bonds		50,000
Total assets		$16,500,000
Accounts payable		$2,610,000
Long-term debt		8,500,000
Common stock		6,000,000
Retained earnings		(610,000)
Total liabilities and equity		$16,500,000

Additional information for 2009:

- The investment in corporate stock is comprised of less-than-20%-owned corporations.
- Depreciation for tax purposes is $1.4 million under MACRS.
- Bad debt expense for tax purposes is $150,000 under the direct writeoff method.
- Limitations to charitable contribution deductions and meals and entertainment expenses must be tested and applied if necessary.
- Qualified production activities income is zero.

Required for 2009:
a. Prepare page 1 of the 2009 Form 1120, computing the corporation's NOL.
b. Determine the corporation's deferred tax asset and deferred tax liability situation, and then complete the income statement and balance sheet to reflect proper GAAP accounting under ASC 740. Use the balance sheet information to prepare Schedule L of the 2009 Form 1120.
c. Prepare the 2009 Schedule M-3 for Form 1120.
d. Prepare a schedule that reconciles the corporation's effective tax rate to the statutory 34% tax rate.

Note: For 2009 forms, go to forms and publications, previous years, at the IRS website, *www.irs.gov.*

For 2010, Permtemp reported the following book income statement and balance sheet, excluding the federal income tax expense, deferred tax assets, and deferred tax liabilities:

Sales		$33,000,000
Cost of goods sold		(22,000,000)
Gross profit		$11,000,000
Dividend income		55,000
Tax-exempt interest income		15,000
Total income		$11,070,000
Expenses:		
Depreciation	$ 800,000	
Bad debts	625,000	
Charitable contributions	40,000	
Interest	455,000	
Meals and entertainment	60,000	
Other	4,675,000	
Total expenses		(6,655,000)
Net income before federal income taxes		$ 4,415,000
Cash		$ 2,125,000
Accounts receivable	$ 3,300,000	
Allowance for doubtful accounts	(450,000)	2,850,000
Inventory		6,000,000
Fixed assets	$10,000,000	
Accumulated depreciation	(1,600,000)	8,400,000
Investment in corporate stock		1,000,000
Investment in tax-exempt bonds		50,000
Total assets		$20,425,000
Accounts payable		$ 2,120,000
Long-term debt		8,500,000
Common stock		6,000,000
Retained earnings		3,805,000
		$20,425,000

Additional information for 2010:

- Depreciation for tax purposes is $2.45 million under MACRS.
- Bad debt expense for tax purposes is $425,000 under the direct writeoff method.
- Qualified production activities income is $3 million.

Required for 2010:

a. Prepare page 1 of the 2010 Form 1120, computing the corporation's taxable income and tax liability.

b. Determine the corporation's deferred tax asset and deferred tax liability situation, and then complete the income statement and balance sheet to reflect proper GAAP accounting ASC 740. Use the balance sheet information to prepare Schedule L of the 2010 Form 1120.

c. Prepare the 2010 Schedule M-3 for Form 1120.

d. Prepare a schedule that reconciles the corporation's effective tax rate to the statutory 34% tax rate.

CASE STUDY PROBLEMS

C:3-68 Marquette Corporation, a tax client since its creation three years ago, has requested that you prepare a memorandum explaining its estimated tax requirements for the current year. The corporation is in the fabricated steel business. Its earnings have been growing each year. Marquette's taxable income for the last three tax years has been $500,000, $1.5 million, and $2.5 million, respectively. The Chief Financial Officer expects its taxable income in the current year to be approximately $3 million.

Required: Prepare a one-page client memorandum explaining Marquette's estimated tax requirements for the current year, providing the necessary supporting authorities.

C:3-69 Susan Smith accepted a new corporate client, Winter Park Corporation. One of Susan's tax managers conducted a review of Winter Park's prior year tax returns. The review revealed that an NOL for a prior tax year was incorrectly computed, resulting in an overstatement of NOL carrybacks and carryovers to prior tax years. Apply the Statements on Standards for Tax Services (SSTSs) to the following situations. The SSTSs are in Appendix E of this text.

a. Assume the incorrect NOL calculation does not affect the current year's tax liability. What recommendations (if any) should Susan make to the new client? See SSTS No. 6.

b. Assume the IRS is currently auditing a prior year. What are Susan's responsibilities in this situation? See SSTS No. 6.

c. Assume the NOL carryover is being carried to the current year, and Winter Park does not want to file amended tax returns to correct the error. What should Susan do in this situation? See SSTS No. 1.

C:3-70 The Chief Executive Officer of a client of your public accounting firm saw the following advertisement in *The Wall Street Journal*:

> DONATIONS WANTED
> The Center for Restoration of Waters
> A Nonprofit Research and Educational Organization
> Needs Donations—Autos, Boats, Real Estate, Etc.
> ALL DONATIONS ARE TAX-DEDUCTIBLE

Prepare a memorandum to your client Phil Nickelson explaining how the federal income tax laws regarding donations of cash, automobiles, boats, and real estate apply to corporate taxpayers.

TAX RESEARCH PROBLEMS

C:3-71 Wicker Corporation made estimated tax payments of $6,000 in 2010. On March 11, 2011, it filed its 2010 tax return showing a $20,000 tax liability, and it paid the $14,000 balance at that time. On April 20, 2011, it discovers an error and files an amended return for 2010 showing a reduced tax liability of $8,000. Prepare a memorandum for your tax manager explaining whether Wicker can base its estimated tax payments for 2011 on the amended $8,000 tax liability for 2010, or must it use the $20,000 tax liability reported on its original return. Your manager has suggested that, at a minimum, you consult the following resources:

- IRC Sec. 6655(d)(1)
- Rev. Rul. 86-58, 1986-1 C.B. 365

C:3-72 Alice, Bill, and Charles each received an equal number of shares when they formed King Corporation a number of years ago. King has used the cash method of accounting since its inception. Alice, Bill, and Charles, the shareholder-employees, operate King as an environmental engineering firm with 57 additional employees. King had gross receipts of $4.3 million last year. Gross receipts have grown by about 15% in each of the last three years and were just under $5 million in the current year. The owners expect the 15% growth rate to continue for at least five more years. Outstanding accounts receivable average about $600,000 at the end of each month. Forty-four employees (including Alice, Bill, and Charles) actively engage in providing engineering services on a full-time basis. The remaining 16 employees serve in a clerical and support capacity (secretarial staff, accountants, etc.). Bill has read about special restrictions on the use of the cash method of accounting and requests information from you about the impact these rules might have on King's continued use of that method. Prepare a memorandum for your tax manager addressing the following issues: (1) If the corporation changes to the accrual method of accounting, what adjustments must it make? (2) Would an S election relieve King from having to make a change? (3) If the S election relieves King from having to make a change, what factors should enter into the decision about whether King should make an S election?

Your manager has suggested that, at a minimum, you should consult the following resources:

- IRC Secs. 446 and 448
- Temp. Reg. Secs. 1.448-1T and -2T
- H. Rept. No. 99-841, 99th Cong., 2d Sess., pp. 285–289 (1986)

C:3-73 James Bowen owns 100% of Bowen Corporation stock. Bowen is a calendar year, accrual method taxpayer. During the current year, Bowen made three charitable contributions:

Donee	Property Donated	FMV of Property
State University	Bates Corporation stock	$110,000
Red Cross	Cash	5,000
Girl Scouts	Pledge to pay cash	25,000

Bowen purchased the Bates stock three years ago for $30,000. Bowen holds a 28% interest, which it accounts for under GAAP using the equity method of accounting. The current carrying value for the Bates stock for book purposes is $47,300. Bowen will pay the pledge to the Girl Scouts by check on March 3 of next year. Bowen's taxable income for the current year before the charitable contributions deduction, dividends-received deduction, NOL deduction, and U.S. production activities deduction is $600,000. Your tax manager has asked you to prepare a memorandum explaining how these transactions are to be treated for tax purposes and for accounting purposes. Your manager has suggested that, at a minimum, you should consult the following resources:

- IRC Sec. 170
- Accounting Standards Codification (ASC) 720

C:3-74 Production Corporation owns 70% of Manufacturing Corporation's common stock and Rita Howard owns the remaining 30%. Each corporation operates and sells its product within the United States, and the corporations engaged in no intercompany transactions. Production's Chief Financial Officer (CFO) presents you with the following information pertaining to current year operations:

	Production Corporation	Manufacturing Corporation
Gross profit on sales	$500,000	$225,000
Minus: Operating expenses	(200,000)	(100,000)
Qualified production activities income	$300,000	$125,000
Plus: Dividends received from 20%-owned corporations	20,000	-0-
Minus: Dividends-received deduction	(16,000)	-0-
NOL carryover deduction	-0-	(15,000)
Taxable income before the U.S. production activities deduction	$304,000	$110,000

TAX & FINANCIAL ACCOUNTING

Operating expenses include W-2 wages allocable to U.S. production activities of $75,000 and $35,000 for Production and Manufacturing, respectively. Given this information, the CFO asks you to determine each corporation's qualified production activities deduction. The applicable deduction percentage is 9%. At a minimum, you should consult the following resources:

- IRC Sec. 199
- Reg. Sec. 1.199-7

4

CHAPTER

CORPORATE NONLIQUIDATING DISTRIBUTIONS

LEARNING OBJECTIVES

After studying this chapter, you should be able to

1. Calculate corporate current earnings and profits (E&P)

2. Distinguish between current and accumulated E&P

3. Determine the tax consequences of nonliquidating distributions

4. Determine the tax consequences of stock dividends and the issuance of stock rights

5. Discern when a stock redemption should be treated as a sale and when it should be treated as a dividend

6. Explain the tax treatment of preferred stock bailouts

7. Determine the applicability and tax consequences of Sec. 304 to stock sales

A corporation may distribute money, property, or stock to its shareholders. Shareholders who receive such distributions might have to recognize ordinary income, capital gain, or no taxable income at all. The distributing corporation might be required to recognize gain or loss when making the distribution. How the corporation and its shareholders treat distributions for tax purposes depends on not only what the corporation distributes but also the circumstances surrounding the distribution. Was the corporation in the process of liquidating? Was the distribution made in exchange for some of the shareholder's stock?

This chapter addresses distributions made when a corporation is not in the process of liquidating. It discusses the tax consequences of the following types of distributions:

▶ Distributions of cash or other property where the shareholder does not surrender any stock

▶ Distributions of stock or rights to acquire stock of the distributing corporation

▶ Distributions of property in exchange for the corporation's own stock (i.e., stock redemptions)

Chapter C:6 discusses **liquidating distributions**, and Chapter C:7 discusses distributions associated with corporate reorganizations.

NONLIQUIDATING DISTRIBUTIONS IN GENERAL

SELF-STUDY QUESTION

How does a shareholder classify a distribution for tax purposes?

ANSWER

Distributions are treated as follows: (1) dividends to the extent of corporate E&P, (2) return of capital to the extent of the shareholder's stock basis, and (3) gain from the sale of stock.

When a corporation makes a nonliquidating distribution to a shareholder, the shareholder must answer the following three questions:

▶ What is the amount of the distribution?

▶ To what extent is this amount treated as a dividend?

▶ What is the basis of the distributed property, and when does its holding period begin?

In addition, the distributing corporation must answer the following two questions:

▶ What are the amount and character of gain or loss the corporation must recognize?

▶ What effect does the distribution have on the distributing corporation's earnings and profits (E&P) account?

A brief summary of the rules for determining the taxability of a distribution follows, along with a simple example.

Section 301 requires a shareholder to include in gross income the amount of any corporate distribution to the extent it is treated as a dividend. Qualified dividends received by a noncorporate shareholder through 2010 are subject to a maximum 15% tax rate. Section 316(a) defines **dividend** as a distribution of property made by a corporation out of its earnings and profits (E&P), which are discussed in the next section of this chapter. Section 317(a) defines **property** broadly to include money, securities, and any other property except stock or stock rights of the distributing corporation. Distributed amounts that exceed a corporation's E&P are treated as a return of capital that reduces the shareholder's basis in his or her stock (but not below zero). Distributions exceeding the shareholder's basis are treated as gain from the sale of the stock. If the stock is a capital asset in the shareholder's hands, the gain is capital in character.

EXAMPLE C:4-1 ▶ On March 1, Gamma Corporation distributes $60,000 in cash to each of its two equal shareholders, Ellen and Bob. At the time of the distribution, Gamma's E&P is $80,000. Ellen's basis in her stock is $25,000, and Bob's basis in his stock is $10,000. Ellen and Bob each recognize $40,000 (0.50 × $80,000) of dividend income. This portion of the distribution reduces Gamma's E&P to zero. The additional $20,000 that each shareholder receives is treated first as a return of capital and then as a capital gain. The following table illustrates the relevant calculations:

	Ellen	Bob	Total
Distribution	$60,000	$60,000	$120,000
Dividend income[a]	(40,000)	(40,000)	(80,000)
Remaining distribution	$20,000	$20,000	$ 40,000
Return of capital[b]	(20,000)	(10,000)	(30,000)
Capital gain[c]	$ –0–	$10,000	$ 10,000

[a]Smaller of E&P allocable to the distribution or the distribution amount.
[b]Smaller of remaining distribution amount to shareholder or his or her stock basis.
[c]Any amount that exceeds the shareholder's basis in his or her stock.

◄

EARNINGS AND PROFITS (E&P)

TYPICAL MISCONCEPTION

Because E&P is such an important concept in many corporate transactions, one would assume that corporations know exactly what their E&P is. However, many corporations do not compute their E&P on a regular basis.

The term E&P is not defined in the IRC. Its meaning must be gleaned from judicial opinions, Treasury Regulations, and IRC rules regarding how certain transactions affect E&P.

To some extent, E&P measures a corporation's economic ability to pay dividends to its shareholders. Distributions are presumed to be made out of the corporation's E&P, unless the corporation reports no E&P.

CURRENT EARNINGS AND PROFITS

A corporation's E&P falls into two categories: current E&P and accumulated E&P. As explained below, **Current E&P** is calculated annually. **Accumulated E&P** is the sum of undistributed current E&P balances for all previous years reduced by the sum of all previous current E&P deficits and any distributions the corporation made out of accumulated E&P. Distributions are deemed to have been made first out of current E&P and then out of accumulated E&P to the extent that current E&P is insufficient.

EXAMPLE C:4-2 ▶

Zeta Corporation was formed in Year 1. Its current E&P balance (or deficit) and distributions for each year through Year 4 are as follows:

Year	Current E&P (Deficit)	Distributions
1	$(10,000)	–0–
2	15,000	–0–
3	18,000	$9,000
4	8,000	–0–

The corporation is deemed to have made the $9,000 distribution out of its Year 3 current E&P balance. At the beginning of Year 4, Zeta's accumulated E&P balance is $14,000 (− $10,000 + $15,000 + $18,000 − $9,000). At the beginning of Year 5, Zeta's accumulated E&P balance is $22,000 ($14,000 + $8,000). ◄

OBJECTIVE 1

Calculate corporate current earnings and profits (E&P)

COMPUTING CURRENT E&P. A corporation computes its current E&P on an annual basis at the end of each year. The starting point for computing current E&P is the corporation's taxable income or net operating loss (NOL) for the year. Taxable income or the NOL must be adjusted to derive the corporation's economic income or loss (current E&P) for the year. For example, federal income taxes must be deducted from taxable income to derive E&P. Because the corporation must pay these taxes to the U.S. government, they reduce the amount available to pay dividends to shareholders. On the other hand, tax-exempt income must be added to taxable income (or the NOL) because, even though not taxable, such income increases the corporation's ability to pay dividends.

Table C:4-1 lists some of the adjustments a corporation must make to taxable income (NOL) to derive current E&P. Some of these adjustments are explained below.[1]

---

[1] The adjustments are based on rules set forth in Sec. 312 and related Treasury Regulations.

▼ TABLE C:4-1
Computation of Current E&P

Taxable income

Plus: *Income excluded from taxable income but included in E&P*
  Tax-exempt interest
  Proceeds from a life insurance contract in which the corporation is named as the beneficiary
  Recoveries of bad debts and other deductions from which the corporation received no tax benefit
  Federal income tax refunds from prior years

Plus: *Income deferred to a later year when computing taxable income but included in E&P in the current year*
  Deferred gain on installment sales. Such gain is included in E&P in the year of sale.

Plus or
minus: *Income and deduction items that must be recomputed for E&P purposes*
  Income on long-term contracts must be based on the percentage of completion rather than the completed contract method
  Depreciation on personal and real property must be based on:
    The straight-line method for other than MACRS property
    The alternative depreciation system for MACRS property
  Excess of percentage depletion over cost depletion

Plus: *Deductions that are allowed for taxable income purposes but denied for E&P purposes*
  Dividends-received deduction
  NOL carryovers, charitable contribution carryovers, and capital loss carryovers applied in the current year
  U.S. production activities deduction

Minus: *Expenses and losses that are denied for taxable income purposes but allowed for E&P purposes*
  Federal income taxes
  Premiums on life insurance contracts in which the corporation is named as the beneficiary
  Excess capital losses that are not currently deductible
  Excess charitable contributions that are not currently deductible
  Expenses related to the production of tax-exempt income
  Nondeductible losses on sales to related parties
  Nondeductible penalties and fines
  Nondeductible political contributions and lobbying expenses

Current E&P balance (or deficit)

INCOME EXCLUDED FROM TAXABLE INCOME BUT INCLUDED IN E&P. Although certain items of income are excluded from taxable income, these items must be included in E&P if they increase the corporation's ability to pay dividends. For example, a corporation's current E&P includes both tax-exempt interest and life insurance proceeds. Current E&P also includes the recovery of an item deducted in a previous year if the deduction produced no tax benefit for the corporation and therefore was excluded from its taxable income.

EXAMPLE C:4-3 ▶ Ace Corporation deducted $10,000 of bad debts in Year 1. In the same year Ace generated an NOL that it could not carry back. Consequently, it derived no tax benefit from the deduction. In Year 2, Ace recovers $8,000 of the debt owed to it. Ace excludes the $8,000 from its gross income for Year 2 because it derived no tax benefit from the bad debt deduction in Year 1. However, Ace must add the $8,000 to its taxable income when computing current E&P for Year 2 because the NOL reduced current E&P in Year 1. (Ace also reduces its NOL carryover by $8,000 because of the recovery.) ◀

INCOME DEFERRED TO A LATER YEAR WHEN COMPUTING TAXABLE INCOME BUT INCLUDED IN E&P IN THE CURRENT YEAR. Gains and losses on property transactions generally are included in E&P in the same year they are recognized for taxable income purposes.

EXAMPLE C:4-4 ▶ Stone Corporation exchanges investment property with a $12,000 basis and an $18,000 fair market value (FMV) for $1,000 cash and investment property worth $17,000. Stone recognizes a $1,000 gain—the amount of boot received—in the like-kind exchange and defers the remaining $5,000 of realized gain. Stone includes the recognized gain in both taxable income and current E&P. It does not include the deferred gain in either taxable income or current E&P. ◀

In the case of an installment sale, the entire realized gain must be included in current E&P in the year of the sale. This rule applies to sales made by dealers and nondealers.

EXAMPLE C:4-5 ▶ In the current year, Tally Corporation sells land with a $12,000 basis and $20,000 FMV to Rick, an unrelated individual. Rick makes a $5,000 down payment this year and promises to pay Tally an additional $5,000 in each of the next three years, plus interest at the prevailing market rate on the unpaid balance. Tally's realized gain is $8,000 ($20,000 − $12,000). For taxable income purposes, Tally currently recognizes $2,000 of gain [($8,000 ÷ $20,000) × $5,000] under the installment method for nondealers. For E&P purposes, Tally includes all $8,000 of its realized gain in current E&P. Thus, in computing current E&P, Tally increases taxable income by $6,000. As it receives the installments, Tally will recognize the remaining $6,000 of gain ($2,000 per year) over the next three years for taxable income purposes. It will reduce E&P by $2,000 in each of those years because it included in E&P all $8,000 in the current year. ◀

INCOME AND DEDUCTION ITEMS THAT MUST BE RECOMPUTED FOR E&P PURPOSES. Some deductions are computed differently for E&P purposes than for taxable income purposes, thereby requiring adjustments.

▶ E&P must be computed under the percentage of completion method even where the corporation uses the completed contract method for taxable income purposes.

▶ Depreciation must be recomputed under the alternative depreciation system of Sec. 168(g). Also, the cost of property expensed under Sec. 179 must be recovered ratably over a five-year period starting with the month in which it was expensed. Other personal property must be depreciated over the property's class life under the half-year convention. Real property must be depreciated over a 40-year period under the straight-line method and mid-month convention.

EXAMPLE C:4-6 ▶ In January of Year 1, Radon Corporation paid $5,000 for equipment with a ten-year class life. In the same year, Radon expensed the cost of the equipment under Sec. 179. For E&P purposes, Radon's depreciation deduction is $1,000 ($5,000 ÷ 5) in each year from Year 1 through Year 5. ◀

▶ Cost depletion must be used for E&P purposes even where percentage depletion is used for taxable income purposes.

▶ Intangible drilling costs must be capitalized and amortized over 60 months.

DEDUCTIONS ALLOWED FOR TAXABLE INCOME PURPOSES BUT DENIED FOR E&P PURPOSES. Some deductions allowed for taxable income purposes are not allowed for E&P purposes.

▶ The dividends-received deduction is denied for E&P purposes because it does not reduce the corporation's ability to pay dividends. In the computation of E&P, this deduction must be added back to taxable income.

▶ NOL, charitable contribution, and capital loss carryovers that reduce current taxable income cannot be deducted to derive E&P. These excess losses or deductions reduce E&P in the year they are incurred or taken.

▶ The U.S. production activities deduction is disallowed for E&P purposes because it does not reduce the corporation's ability to pay dividends. It must be added back to taxable income to derive E&P.

▶ Deduction and amortization of organizational expenses is disallowed for E&P purposes.

EXAMPLE C:4-7 ▶ Thames Corporation's taxable income is $500,000 after deductions for the following items: a $10,000 NOL carryover from two years ago, $20,000 for dividends received, and $8,000 for U.S. production activities. To compute current E&P, Thames must add $38,000 to its taxable income. As a result, current E&P is $538,000. ◀

EXPENSES AND LOSSES DENIED FOR TAXABLE INCOME PURPOSES BUT ALLOWED FOR E&P PURPOSES. Some expenses and losses that are not deductible for taxable income purposes are deductible for E&P purposes.

▶ For taxable income purposes, federal income taxes are not deductible. For E&P purposes, however, federal income taxes are deductible in the year they accrue if the corporation uses the accrual method and in the year they are paid if the corporation uses the cash method.

EXAMPLE C:4-8 ▶ Perch Corporation, an accrual basis taxpayer, earns taxable income of $100,000 on which it owes $22,250 of federal income taxes. In computing current E&P, Perch reduces taxable income by $22,250. ◀

▶ For E&P purposes, charitable contributions are fully deductible. Thus, when current E&P is computed, taxable income must be reduced by any charitable contributions disallowed because of the 10% limitation.

EXAMPLE C:4-9 ▶ Dot Corporation computes $25,000 of taxable income before any charitable contribution deduction. Dot contributed $10,000 to the Red Cross. For taxable income purposes, Dot's charitable contribution deduction is limited to $2,500 because of the 10% limitation. However, Dot deducts the entire $10,000 in computing current E&P. To compute current E&P, it must subtract the remaining $7,500 from taxable income of $22,500 ($25,000 − $2,500). In a later year, when the corporation deducts the $7,500 carryover to compute taxable income, it must add that amount to taxable income to derive current E&P. ◀

▶ Premiums paid on insurance policies covering the lives of key corporate personnel (net of any increase in the cash surrender value) are not deductible when computing taxable income but are deductible when computing E&P.

▶ Capital losses exceeding capital gains cannot be deducted when computing taxable income but can be deducted when computing current E&P.

▶ Nondeductible expenses related to the production of tax-exempt income (e.g., interest charges to borrow money to purchase tax-exempt securities) are deductible when computing E&P.

▶ Losses on related party sales that are disallowed under Sec. 267 are allowed when computing E&P.

▶ Fines, penalties, and political contributions that are nondeductible for taxable income purposes are deductible for E&P purposes.

The foregoing items constitute only a partial list of adjustments that must be made to taxable income to compute current E&P. The basic rule is that an adjustment to taxable income must be made so that current E&P reflects the corporation's economic ability to pay dividends.

OBJECTIVE 2

Distinguish between current and accumulated E&P

DISTINCTION BETWEEN CURRENT AND ACCUMULATED E&P

A distinction must be made between current and accumulated E&P. A nonliquidating distribution is taxed as a dividend if made out of either current or accumulated E&P. Corporate distributions are deemed to be made first out of current E&P and then out of accumulated E&P to the extent that current E&P is insufficient.[2] If current E&P is sufficient to cover all distributions during the year, each distribution is treated as a taxable div-

---

[2] The distinction between current and accumulated E&P is explained in Reg. Sec. 1.316-2.

idend. This rule applies even where the corporation reports a deficit in its beginning accumulated E&P account. Current E&P is computed as of the last day of the tax year without reduction for distributions during the year.

EXAMPLE C:4-10 ▶

TAX STRATEGY TIP

A corporation with an accumulated deficit and current E&P may want to postpone distributions to a later year to avoid dividend treatment in the current year. See Example C:4-53 later in this chapter.

At the beginning of the current year, Water Corporation has a $30,000 accumulated E&P deficit. For the entire year, Water generates current E&P of $15,000. During the year, Water distributes $10,000 in cash to its shareholders. The $10,000 distribution is treated as a taxable dividend to the shareholders because it is deemed to be made out of current E&P. At the beginning of the next tax year, Water's accumulated E&P deficit is $25,000 (− $30,000 E&P deficit + $5,000 undistributed current E&P) computed as of the last day of the previous year. ◀

If distributions during the year exceed current E&P, current E&P is allocated on a pro rata basis regardless of when during the year the distributions occurred. Distributions exceeding current E&P are deemed to be made in chronological order out of accumulated E&P (if any). Distributions exceeding current and accumulated E&P are treated as a return of capital and reduce the shareholder's stock basis. However, such distributions cannot create an E&P deficit, which results only from losses. These rules are particularly relevant if stock changes hands during the year and total E&P is insufficient to cover all distributions.

EXAMPLE C:4-11 ▶

At the beginning of the current year, Cole Corporation has $20,000 of accumulated E&P. For the entire year, Cole's current E&P is $30,000. On April 10, Cole distributes $20,000 in cash to Bob, its sole shareholder. On July 15, Cole distributes an additional $24,000 in cash to Bob. On August 1, Bob sells all of his Cole stock to Lynn. On September 15, Cole distributes $36,000 in cash to Lynn. Cole's current and accumulated E&P must be allocated among the three distributions as follows:

Date	Distribution Amount	Current E&P	Accumulated E&P	Dividend Income	Return of Capital
April 10	$20,000	$ 7,500	$12,500	$20,000	$ –0–
July 15	24,000	9,000	7,500	16,500	7,500
September 15	36,000	13,500	–0–	13,500	22,500
Total	$80,000	$30,000	$20,000	$50,000	$30,000

The current E&P allocated to the April 10 distribution is calculated as follows:

$$\$30,000 \text{ (Current E\&P)} \times \frac{\$20,000 \text{ (April 10 distribution)}}{\$80,000 \text{ (Total distributions)}}$$

Note that the total amount of dividends paid by Cole equals $50,000, the sum of $30,000 of current E&P and $20,000 of accumulated E&P. Current E&P is allocated among all three distributions on a pro rata basis, whereas accumulated E&P is reduced first by the April 10 distribution ($12,500), then by the July 15 distribution, so that no accumulated E&P is available for the September 15 distribution. Thus, Bob's dividend income from Cole is $36,500 ($20,000 + $16,500). He also receives a $7,500 return of capital that reduces his stock basis accordingly. Lynn's dividend income from Cole is $13,500. She also receives a $22,500 return of capital that reduces her stock basis accordingly. Bob cannot determine his gain on the stock sale until after the end of the year. He must wait until he knows the extent to which the April 10 and July 15 distributions reduce his stock basis. ◀

If the corporation generates both a current E&P deficit and an accumulated E&P deficit, none of the distributions is treated as a dividend. Instead, all distributions are treated as a return of capital to the extent of the shareholder's stock basis. Distributions exceeding this basis are taxed as a capital gain.

EXAMPLE C:4-12 ▶

At the beginning of the current year, Rose Corporation has a $15,000 accumulated E&P deficit. Rose's current E&P deficit is $20,000. Rose distributes $10,000 on July 1. The distribution is treated not as a dividend but rather as a return of capital to the extent of the shareholder's stock basis. Any amount exceeding stock basis is taxed as a capital gain. Rose's accumulated E&P deficit on January 1 of next year is $35,000 because the distribution was not made out of E&P and because the negative balance in the current E&P account is transferred to the accumulated E&P account at the end of the current year. ◀

SELF-STUDY
QUESTION

When is E&P measured for purposes of determining whether a distribution is a dividend?

ANSWER

Usually at year-end. However, if a current deficit exists, the E&P available for measuring dividend income is determined at the distribution date.

If the corporation has a current E&P deficit and a positive accumulated E&P balance, it must net the two accounts at the time of the distribution to determine the dividend amount.[3] The deficit in current E&P that has accrued up through the day before the distribution reduces the accumulated E&P balance on that date. If the balance remaining after the reduction is positive, the distribution is treated as a dividend to the extent of the lesser of the distribution amount or the E&P balance. If the E&P balance is zero or negative, the distribution is treated as a return of capital. If the actual deficit in current E&P to the date of distribution cannot be determined, the current E&P deficit is prorated on a daily basis to the day before the distribution.

EXAMPLE C:4-13 ▶

Assume the same facts as in Example C:4-12 except that Rose Corporation has a $15,000 accumulated E&P balance. Unless information indicates otherwise, the current E&P deficit of $20,000 accrues on a daily basis. The amount of the July 1 distribution treated as a dividend is calculated as follows:

Date	Distribution Amount	Accumulated E&P	Dividend Income	Return of Capital
January 1	$ –0–	$15,000		
July 1	10,000	(9,918)[a]	$5,082	$4,918
Total	$10,000	$ 5,082[b]	$5,082	$4,918

[a]181/365 × $(20,000) = $(9,918)—the current E&P deficit accrued up to the distribution date. (The denominator in the 181/365 fraction assumes that the current year is not a leap year.)

[b]$15,000 − $9,918 = $5,082—accumulated E&P at beginning of year minus the current E&P deficit accrued up to the distribution date. ◀

? **STOP & THINK**

Question: Why is it necessary to keep separate balances for current and accumulated E&P, and why is it necessary to track E&P to individual distributions?

Solution: Separate balances are necessary because of the way dividends are accounted for. If total current and accumulated E&P is less than the total distributions to the shareholders, E&P must be allocated to all distributions during the year to determine the amount of each distribution that should be treated as a dividend. When no change in the shareholder's stock ownership occurs during the year and all distributions are proportional to stock ownership, an E&P allocation is needed only to track each shareholder's stock basis. Tracking E&P to individual distributions is necessary to determine the taxability of a particular distribution when a change in a shareholder's stock ownership occurs because current E&P is allocated on a pro rata basis and accumulated E&P is allocated chronologically. As a result of the chronological allocation, a greater portion of distributions early in a tax year may be taxed as a dividend relative to distributions later in the year. On the other hand, because accrued current E&P deficits offset accumulated E&P balances, a smaller portion of distributions later in a tax year may be taxed as a dividend relative to distributions earlier in the year.

NONLIQUIDATING PROPERTY DISTRIBUTIONS

OBJECTIVE 3

Determine the tax consequences of nonliquidating distributions

CONSEQUENCES OF NONLIQUIDATING PROPERTY DISTRIBUTIONS TO THE SHAREHOLDERS

Property includes money, securities, and any other property except stock in the corporation making the distribution (or rights to acquire such stock).[4] When a corporation distributes property to its shareholders, the following three questions must be answered:

---

[3] Reg. Sec. 1.316-2(b).   [4] Sec. 317(a).

▶ What is the amount of the distribution?

▶ To what extent is this amount treated as a dividend?

▶ What is the basis of the property to the shareholder, and when does its holding period begin?

For cash distributions, these questions are easy to answer. The distribution amount is the cash distributed, which is treated as a dividend to the extent of the corporation's current and accumulated E&P. The E&P account is reduced by the amount distributed, and the shareholder's basis in the cash received is its face value. The distributing corporation recognizes no gain or loss on cash distributions.

When the corporation distributes property, such as land or inventory, these questions are more difficult to answer. Neither the distribution amount nor the shareholder's basis in the property is immediately apparent. The corporation must recognize gain (but not loss) on the distribution, and the impact of the distribution on the corporation's E&P, as well as the taxability of the distribution, must be ascertained. The following sections set forth rules that address these issues.

When the corporation distributes property to a shareholder, the distribution amount is the property's FMV, determined as of the distribution date.[5] The amount of any liability assumed by the shareholder in the distribution, or to which the distributed property is subject, reduces the distribution amount, but never below zero. The distribution amount is treated as a dividend to the extent of the distributing corporation's E&P.

The shareholder takes a FMV basis in any property received. This basis is not reduced by any liabilities assumed by the shareholder or to which the property is subject.[6] The holding period for the property begins on the day after the distribution date and does not include the distributing corporation's holding period.

EXAMPLE C:4-14 ▶ Post Corporation has $100,000 of current and accumulated E&P. On March 1, Post distributes to Meg, its sole shareholder, land with a $60,000 FMV and a $35,000 adjusted basis. The land is subject to a $10,000 liability, which Meg assumes. The distribution amount is $50,000 ($60,000 − $10,000), all of which is treated as a dividend to Meg because it does not exceed Post's E&P balance. Meg's basis in the property is its $60,000 FMV, and her holding period for the property begins on March 2. ◀

 STOP & THINK

Question: When a corporation distributes property, why do liabilities reduce the amount of income realized by the shareholder but not the shareholder's adjusted basis in the property?

Solution: The liabilities reduce the amount of income realized, but not the shareholder's adjusted basis, because the distribution is analogous to the corporation's transferring an asset that it has financed with debt. Recall that financing the purchase of an asset has no bearing on the asset's cost basis. On the other hand, assuming a liability is tantamount to the transferee's settling the liability with the transferee's own funds, and thus receiving less value from the transferor.

Topic Review C:4-1 summarizes the tax consequences of a nonliquidating distribution to the shareholders.

CONSEQUENCES OF PROPERTY DISTRIBUTIONS TO THE DISTRIBUTING CORPORATION

Two questions must be answered with respect to a corporation that distributes property:

▶ What amount and character of gain or loss must the distributing corporation recognize?

▶ What effect does the distribution have on the corporation's E&P?

---

[5] Sec. 301(b).

[6] Sec. 301(d).

Topic Review C:4-1

Tax Consequences of a Nonliquidating Distribution to the Shareholders

1. The amount of a distribution equals money received plus the FMV of any noncash property received reduced by any liabilities assumed or acquired by the shareholder.
2. The distribution is treated as a dividend to the extent of the distributing corporation's current and accumulated E&P. Any distribution amount exceeding E&P is treated as a return of capital that reduces the shareholder's stock basis (but not below zero). Any additional excess is treated as a capital gain.
3. The shareholder's basis in the property received is its FMV.
4. The shareholder's holding period for the property begins on the day after the distribution date.

CORPORATE GAIN OR LOSS ON PROPERTY DISTRIBUTIONS. When a corporation distributes property that has appreciated in value, the corporation must recognize gain as though the corporation had sold the property for its FMV. On the other hand, a corporation does not recognize loss when it distributes property that has depreciated in value even though the corporation would have recognized a loss upon selling the property.[7]

EXAMPLE C:4-15 ▶

TAX STRATEGY TIP

Rather than distribute loss property, the corporation should consider selling it and distributing the proceeds. The sale will allow the corporation to deduct the loss.

Silver Corporation distributes to Mark, a shareholder, land (a capital asset) worth $60,000. Silver's adjusted basis in the land is $20,000. Upon distributing the land, Silver recognizes a $40,000 ($60,000 − $20,000) capital gain, as if Silver had sold the property. If the land instead had a $12,000 FMV, Silver would not have recognized a loss. ◀

If the distributed property is subject to a liability or the shareholder assumes a liability in the distribution, for the purpose of calculating gain, the property's FMV is deemed to be no less than the amount of the liability.[8]

EXAMPLE C:4-16 ▶

TAX STRATEGY TIP

If possible, a corporation should avoid distributing property subject to a liability exceeding the property's FMV because of the potential gain recognition caused by the excess liability.

Assume the same facts as in Example C:4-15 except the land's FMV instead is $25,000, and the land is subject to a $35,000 mortgage. For the purpose of calculating gain, the land's FMV is deemed to be $35,000 because this value cannot be less than the liability amount. Thus, Silver Corporation's gain is $15,000 ($35,000 − $20,000), the extent to which the land's deemed FMV exceeds its adjusted basis.[9] ◀

EFFECT OF PROPERTY DISTRIBUTIONS ON THE DISTRIBUTING CORPORATION'S E&P. Distributions have two effects on E&P:[10]

▶ When a corporation distributes appreciated property to its shareholders, it must increase E&P by the **E&P gain**, which is the excess of the property's FMV over its adjusted basis for E&P purposes. Because a property's **E&P adjusted basis** may differ from its tax basis (as discussed earlier in this chapter), this E&P gain may differ from the corporation's recognized gain for taxable income purposes.

▶ If the E&P adjusted basis of the noncash asset distributed equals or exceeds its FMV, E&P is reduced by the asset's E&P adjusted basis. If the FMV of the asset distributed exceeds its E&P adjusted basis, E&P is reduced by the asset's FMV. In either case, the E&P reduction is net of any liability to which the asset is subject or that the shareholder assumes in the distribution. E&P also is reduced by the income tax liability incurred on any gain recognized.[11]

---

[7] Sec. 311(a).
[8] Sec. 311(b)(2).
[9] The tax treatment of the shareholder is not entirely clear. Section 336(b), which Sec. 311(b)(2) makes applicable to nonliquidating distributions, specifically states that this liability rule applies only for determining the corporation's gain or loss. Thus, its applicability does not seem to extend to Sec. 301(d), which gives the shareholder a FMV basis in the distributed property. Some commentators have suggested that a strict interpretation of the statutory provision that gives the shareholder an actual FMV basis, rather than the greater

liability basis, produces an illogical result. (See B. C. Randall and D. N. Stewart, "Corporate Distributions: Handling Liabilities in Excess of the Fair Market Value of Property Remains Unresolved," *The Journal of Corporate Taxation*, 1992, pp. 55–64.) Also, in principle, given that the liability exceeds the distributed property's FMV, the shareholder's amount distributed should be zero, resulting in no dividend.
[10] Secs. 312(a) and (b).
[11] Secs. 312(a) and (c).

EXAMPLE C:4-17 ▶ Brass Corporation distributes to its shareholder, Joan, property with a $25,000 adjusted basis for taxable income purposes, a $22,000 adjusted basis for E&P purposes, and a $40,000 FMV. The property is subject to a $12,000 mortgage, which Joan assumes. In the distribution, Brass recognizes a $15,000 ($40,000 FMV − $25,000 tax adjusted basis) gain for taxable income purposes. For E&P purposes, Brass's E&P is increased by an $18,000 ($40,000 FMV − $22,000 E&P adjusted basis) gain and reduced by the amount of income taxes paid or accrued by Brass on the $15,000 tax gain. E&P is further reduced by the $28,000 ($40,000 FMV − $12,000 liability) net value of the distribution. ◀

A special rule applies when a corporation distributes its own obligations (e.g., its notes, bonds, or debentures) to a shareholder. In such case, the distributing corporation's E&P is reduced by the principal amount, not the fair market value, of the obligations.[12]

Topic Review C:4-2 summarizes the tax consequences of a nonliquidating distribution to the distributing corporation.

CONSTRUCTIVE DIVIDENDS

A **constructive dividend** (or deemed distribution) is the manner in which the IRS or the courts might recharacterize an excessive corporate payment to a shareholder to reflect the true economic benefit conferred upon the shareholder. As a result of the recharacterization, the IRS or courts usually recast a corporate-shareholder transaction as an E&P distribution, deny the corporation an offsetting deduction, and treat all or a portion of the income recognized by the shareholder as a dividend. Ordinarily, a corporate dividend involves a direct, pro rata distribution to all shareholders, which generally is declared by the board of directors. By contrast, a constructive dividend need not be direct or pro rata, nor be declared by the board of directors.

Constructive dividends generally are deemed to be paid in the context of a closely held corporation where the shareholders (or relatives of shareholders) and management groups overlap. In such situations, the dealings between the corporation and its shareholders are likely to be less formal and subject to closer review than dealings between a publicly held corporation and its shareholders. Constructive dividends also may occur in the context of a publicly held corporation.

INTENTIONAL EFFORTS TO AVOID DIVIDEND TREATMENT. The IRS's recharacterization of a payment as a constructive dividend often is in response to a shareholder's attempt either to bail out E&P without subjecting the corporation to taxation at the shareholder level or to obtain a deduction at the corporate level that otherwise would be disallowed. If a corporation generates sufficient E&P, dividend distributions are fully taxable to the shareholder but are not deductible by the distributing corporation. Therefore,

BOOK-TO-TAX ACCOUNTING COMPARISON

The distributing corporation reports dividends-in-kind at their FMV for financial accounting (book) purposes. For book purposes, the distributing corporation recognizes the difference between the property's FMV and its carrying value as a gain or loss. For tax purposes, however, the corporation recognizes gains but not losses.

ADDITIONAL COMMENT

The incentive to disguise dividends as salary, however, is somewhat diminished with the reduced tax rate on dividends.

Topic Review C:4-2

Tax Consequences of a Nonliquidating Property Distribution to the Distributing Corporation

1. When a corporation distributes appreciated property, it must recognize gain as if it sold the property for its FMV immediately before the distribution.
2. For gain recognition purposes, a property's FMV is deemed to be at least equal to any liability to which the property is subject or that the shareholder assumes in connection with the distribution.
3. A corporation recognizes no loss when it distributes to its shareholders property that has depreciated in value.
4. A corporation's E&P is increased by any E&P gain resulting from a distribution of appreciated property.
5. A corporation's E&P is reduced by (a) the amount of money distributed plus (b) the greater of the FMV or E&P adjusted basis of any noncash property distributed, minus (c) any liabilities to which the property is subject or that the shareholder assumes in connection with the distribution. E&P also is reduced by taxes paid or incurred on the corporation's recognized gain, if any.

---

[12] Sec. 312(a)(2).

shareholders may try to disguise a dividend as a salary payment. Without recharacterization, the payment would be taxable to the shareholder-employee and deductible by the distributing corporation as long as the payment is reasonable in amount. Shareholders also may try to disguise dividends as loans to themselves. Without recharacterization, a loan would be neither deductible by the corporation nor taxable to the shareholder. If the IRS recharacterizes either payment as a dividend, the payment is taxable to the shareholder and nondeductible by the corporation.

UNINTENTIONAL CONSTRUCTIVE DIVIDENDS. Some constructive dividends are inadvertent. Shareholders may not realize that the benefits they receive from the corporation are effectively taxable dividends until a tax advisor or the IRS examines the transactions. If a payment in the form of a salary, loan, lease, etc. is recast as a dividend, corresponding adjustments must be made at the corporate and shareholder levels. These adjustments may increase the shareholder's taxable income (e.g., because the distribution has been recharacterized as a dividend rather than a loan) or increase the distributing corporation's taxable income (i.e., because dividends are not deductible). Transactions most likely to be recast and treated as dividends are described below.

LOANS TO SHAREHOLDERS. Loans to shareholders may be viewed as disguised dividends unless the shareholders can prove that the loans are bona fide. Whether a loan is bona fide ordinarily depends on the shareholder's intent at the time he or she makes the loan. To prove that the loan is bona fide (and thus to avoid recharacterization of the loan as a dividend), the shareholder must show that he or she intends to repay the loan. Factors indicative of an intent to repay include

► Recording the loan on the corporate books

► Evidencing the loan by a written note

► Charging a reasonable rate of interest

► Scheduling regular payment of principal and interest

Factors that suggest the loan is *not* bona fide include

► Borrowing on "open account" (i.e., the shareholder borrows from the corporation with no fixed repayment schedule, whenever he or she needs cash)

► Failing to charge a market rate of interest

► Failing to enforce the regular payment of interest and principal

► Paying advances in proportion to stockholdings

► Paying advances to a controlling shareholder

If the corporation lends money to a shareholder and then, after a period of time, cancels the loan, the amount cancelled might be treated as a dividend to the extent of the corporation's E&P. If the corporation charges a below market interest rate, the IRS could impute interest on the loan. In such case, the corporation would be deemed to have earned interest income on the loan, and the shareholder would be allowed a deduction for interest deemed paid.

EXCESSIVE COMPENSATION PAID TO SHAREHOLDER-EMPLOYEES. Shareholders may be compensated for services in the form of salary, bonus, or fringe benefits. Ordinarily, the corporate employer may deduct such compensation as long as it represents an ordinary and necessary business expense and is reasonable in amount. However, if the IRS finds the compensation to be excessive, the excess amount will not be deductible by the corporation but still will be taxable to the shareholder. Depending upon the circumstances, this amount may be treated as a dividend or simply be included in the gross income of the recipient. No hard and fast rules offer guidance for determining when compensation is excessive. As a result, the issue frequently is litigated.

Before 2003, the IRS's main focus was the corporation's deducting the excess amount. The shareholder-employee recognized ordinary income regardless of whether the excess was characterized as compensation or a dividend. With the tax rate on dividends reduced to a 15% maximum through 2012, the corporation still will lose the deduction for excess compensation, but the IRS is unlikely to classify the excess as a dividend. Instead, the IRS probably will treat the excess as ordinary compensation to the shareholder-employee even though the corporation is not allowed to deduct it.[13]

EXCESSIVE COMPENSATION PAID TO SHAREHOLDERS FOR THE USE OF SHAREHOLDER PROPERTY. As with compensation, corporate payments to shareholders for the use of property (i.e., rents, interest, and royalties) are deductible under Sec. 162(a) if they are ordinary, necessary, and reasonable in amount. The corporation may not deduct any amount exceeding what it would have paid to an unrelated party in an arm's-length transaction.

CORPORATE PAYMENTS FOR THE SHAREHOLDER'S BENEFIT. If a corporation pays the personal obligation of a shareholder, the corporate payment may result in gross income to the shareholder. Such a payment may cover the shareholder's personal debt, expenses in connection with the shareholder's personal residence, expenses incurred for the improvement of the shareholder's real property, or an obligation personally guaranteed by the shareholder.

In addition, if the IRS denies a corporate deduction, the disallowed deduction may result in gross income to the shareholder if the expenditure associated with the deduction conferred an economic benefit upon the shareholder. Examples of such expenditures are unsubstantiated travel and entertainment expenses; club dues; and automobile, airplane, and yacht expenses related to the shareholder-employee's personal use.

BARGAIN PURCHASE OF CORPORATE PROPERTY. If a shareholder purchases corporate property at a discount relative to the property's FMV, the discount may be treated as a constructive dividend to the shareholder.

SHAREHOLDER USE OF CORPORATE PROPERTY. If a shareholder uses corporate property (such as a hunting lodge, yacht, or airplane) without paying adequate consideration to the corporation, the fair rental value of such property (minus any amounts paid) may be treated as a constructive dividend to the shareholder.

STOCK DIVIDENDS AND STOCK RIGHTS

OBJECTIVE 4

Determine the tax consequences of stock dividends and the issuance of stock rights

In 1919, the Supreme Court held in *Eisner v. Macomber* that a stock dividend is not income to the shareholder because it takes no property from the corporation and adds no property to the shareholder.[14] Subsequently, Congress enacted the Revenue Act of 1921, which provides that stock dividends are nontaxable. Although this general rule still applies today, Congress has carved out several exceptions to prevent abuses.

Section 305(a) states, "Except as otherwise provided in this section, gross income does not include the amount of any distribution of the stock of a corporation made by such corporation to its shareholders with respect to its stock." Thus, a distribution of additional common stock with respect to a shareholder's pre-existing common stock holdings represents a nontaxable stock dividend. However, whenever a stock dividend changes or has the potential to change the shareholders' proportionate interest in the distributing corporation, the distribution will be taxable. Taxable stock distributions include those where

► Any shareholder can elect to receive either stock of the distributing corporation or other property (e.g., money).

► Some shareholders receive property and other shareholders receive an increase in their proportionate interest in the distributing corporation's assets or E&P.

TYPICAL MISCONCEPTION

Stock dividends generally are nontaxable as long as a shareholder's proportionate interests in the corporation do not increase. If a shareholder's stock interest increases, Sec. 305(b) causes the dividend to be taxable.

---

[13] *Sterno Sales Corp. v. U.S.*, 15 AFTR 2d 979, 65-1 USTC ¶9419 (Ct. Cl., 1965).

[14] *Eisner v. Myrtle H. Macomber*, 3 AFTR 3020, 1 USTC ¶32 (USSC, 1919).

> ▶ Some holders of common stock receive preferred stock and others receive additional common stock.

> ▶ The underlying stock is preferred unless the distribution involves a change in the conversion ratio of convertible preferred stock to take into account a common stock dividend or a common stock split.

> ▶ The distributed stock is convertible preferred, unless it can be established that the distribution will have no disproportionate effect.

> The following example illustrates these exceptions.

EXAMPLE C:4-18 ▶ Two shareholders, Al and Beth, each own 100 of the 200 outstanding shares of Peach Corporation stock. Because Al's marginal tax rate is high, he does not want to recognize any additional income in the current year. Beth has a low marginal tax rate and needs additional cash. Peach, whose current E&P is $100,000, declares a dividend payable in stock or cash. Each taxpayer can receive one share of Peach stock (valued at $100) or $100 in cash for each share of Peach stock already owned. Al, who elects to receive stock, receives 100 additional Peach shares. Beth, who elects to receive cash, receives $10,000. Beth's distribution is taxable as a dividend. Absent any exceptions to Sec. 305, Al's dividend would be nontaxable because it was paid in Peach stock. After the distribution, however, Al owns two-thirds of the outstanding shares of Peach stock, whereas before the distribution he owned only one-half of Peach's outstanding shares. In this case, an exception to the general rule of Sec. 305(a) applies so that Al is deemed to have received a taxable dividend equal to the value of the additional shares he received. Even if both shareholders elected to receive a stock dividend, this dividend would be taxable because each shareholder had the option to receive cash. In this example, Al and Beth each recognize $10,000 of dividend income. Al's basis in his new shares is their $10,000 FMV. His basis in his original shares is unchanged. Peach reduces its E&P by $20,000, the amount of the taxable dividend to Al and Beth. ◀

NONTAXABLE STOCK DIVIDENDS

If a **stock dividend** is nontaxable, the basis of the stock with respect to which the distribution was made must be allocated between the old and new shares.[15] The holding period for the new shares includes the holding period for the old shares.[16]

If the old and new shares are identical, the basis of each share is determined by dividing the basis of the old shares by the total number of shares held by the shareholder after the distribution.

EXAMPLE C:4-19 ▶ Barbara owns 1,000 shares of Axle Corporation common stock having a $66,000 basis ($66 per share). Barbara receives a nontaxable 10% common stock dividend and now owns 1,100 Axle common shares. Her basis in each share becomes $60 ($66,000 ÷ 1,100). ◀

If the old and new shares are not identical, the basis of the old shares is allocated according to the relative FMVs of the old and new shares on the distribution date.

EXAMPLE C:4-20
REAL-WORLD EXAMPLE

Tracking the effects of nontaxable dividends, stock splits, stock dividends, and stock rights distributions on the basis of a stock investment can be difficult and time consuming. A number of publishers offer capital change reporters that provide a complete history of these four types of events for publicly traded companies. These reporters greatly simplify the making of stock basis calculations.

▶ Mark owns 1,000 shares of Axle Corporation common stock with a $60,000 basis. Mark receives 50 shares of Axle preferred stock in a nontaxable dividend. At the time of the distribution, the FMV of the common stock is $90,000 ($90 × 1,000 shares), and the FMV of the preferred stock is $10,000 ($200 × 50 shares). Subsequent to the distribution, $6,000 [($10,000 ÷ $100,000) × $60,000] of the common stock basis is allocated to the preferred stock, and the basis of the common stock is reduced from $60,000 to $54,000. ◀

NONTAXABLE STOCK RIGHTS

Under Sec. 305, a distribution of **stock rights** is nontaxable unless it changes, or has the potential to change, the shareholders' proportionate interest in the distributing corporation. The same Sec. 305(b) exceptions to the nontaxability of stock dividends also apply to distributions of stock rights.

If the value of the stock rights is less than 15% of the value of the stock with respect to which the rights were distributed (i.e., the underlying stock), the basis of the rights is zero unless the shareholder elects to allocate stock basis to the rights.[17] If the taxpayer intends to sell the

---

[15] Sec. 307(a) and Reg. Secs. 1.307-1 and -2.
[16] Sec. 1223(5).

[17] Sec. 307(b)(1).

rights, an allocation of his or her stock basis to the rights might be advisable so as to minimize the amount of gain recognized on the sale. The election to allocate stock basis to the rights must be made in a statement attached to the shareholder's return for the year in which the rights are received. The allocation must be based on the relative FMVs of the stock and the stock rights. The holding period for the rights includes the holding period for the underlying stock.[18]

EXAMPLE C:4-21 ▶ Linda owns 100 shares of Yale Corporation common stock with a $27,000 basis and a $50,000 FMV. Linda receives 100 nontaxable stock rights with a $4,000 FMV. Because the FMV of the stock rights is less than 15% of the FMV of the underlying stock (0.15 × $50,000 = $7,500), the basis of the stock rights is zero unless Linda elects to allocate the $27,000 stock basis between the stock and the stock rights. If Linda makes the election, the basis of the rights is $2,000 [($4,000 ÷ $54,000) × $27,000], and the basis of the stock is $25,000 ($27,000 − $2,000). ◀

If the value of the stock rights is 15% or more of the value of the underlying stock, the shareholder must allocate the basis of the underlying stock between the stock and the stock rights. This provision is mandatory, not elective.

EXAMPLE C:4-22 ▶ Kay owns 100 shares of Minor Corporation common stock with a $14,000 basis and a $30,000 FMV. Kay receives 100 stock rights with a total FMV of $5,000. Because the FMV of the stock rights is at least 15% of the stock's FMV (0.15 × $30,000 = $4,500), the $14,000 basis must be allocated between the stock rights and the underlying stock based on their relative FMVs. The basis of the stock rights is $2,000 [($5,000 ÷ $35,000) × $14,000], and the basis of the underlying stock is $12,000 [($30,000 ÷ $35,000) × $14,000]. ◀

TYPICAL MISCONCEPTION

Taxpayers often get confused about what happens to a stock right. A stock right may be sold or exercised, which means the actual stock is acquired. If the rights are not sold or exercised, they eventually will lapse.

If the taxpayer sells the stock rights, he or she calculates gain or loss by subtracting the allocated basis of the rights (if any) from the sale price. A shareholder cannot claim a loss if the stock rights expire. If the stock rights do expire, the allocated rights basis is added back to the basis of the underlying stock. If the taxpayer exercises the rights before they expire, the allocated rights basis is added to the basis of the stock purchased through the exercise of the rights.[19] The holding period for the stock acquired through exercise of the rights begins on the exercise date.[20]

EXAMPLE C:4-23 ▶ In a nontaxable distribution, Jeff receives ten stock rights to which no stock basis is allocated. Each stock right entitles Jeff to acquire one share of Jackson stock for $20. If Jeff exercises all ten rights, the Jackson stock acquired will have a $200 (10 rights × $20) basis. If instead Jeff sells the ten rights for $30 each, he will recognize a gain of $300 [($30 × 10 rights) − 0 basis]. If the rights expire, Jeff can claim no loss. ◀

EFFECT OF NONTAXABLE STOCK DIVIDENDS ON THE DISTRIBUTING CORPORATION

BOOK-TO-TAX ACCOUNTING COMPARISON

For financial accounting purposes, stock dividends reduce retained earnings. However, for tax purposes, nontaxable stock dividends have no effect on a corporation's E&P.

From a tax perspective, nontaxable distributions of stock and stock rights have no tax effect on the distributing corporation. The corporation recognizes no gain or loss and does not reduce its E&P balance.[21]

TAXABLE STOCK DIVIDENDS AND STOCK RIGHTS

If a distribution of stock or stock rights is taxable, the distribution amount equals the FMV of the stock or stock rights on the distribution date. The distribution is treated in the same way as any other property distribution. It is a dividend to the extent of the distributing corporation's E&P, and the recipient takes a FMV basis in the stock or stock rights received.[22] The holding period for the stock or stock rights begins on the day after the distribution date. No adjustment is made to the basis of the underlying stock. The distributing corporation recognizes no gain or loss on the distribution,[23] and the corporation reduces its E&P by the FMV of the stock or stock rights on the distribution date.

Topic Review C:4-3 summarizes the tax consequences of a stock dividend.

---

[18] Sec. 1223(5).
[19] Reg. Sec. 1.307-1(b).
[20] Sec. 1223(6).
[21] Secs. 311(a) and 312(d).

[22] Reg. Sec. 1.301-1(h)(2)(i).
[23] Sec. 311(a). Gain may be recognized when the shareholder can elect to receive either appreciated property or stock or stock rights of the distributing corporation.

Topic Review C:4-3

Tax Consequences of a Stock Dividend

Shareholders:
1. A stock dividend is nontaxable except where (1) a shareholder can elect to receive other property in lieu of the stock dividend; (2) some shareholders receive property and other shareholders increase their proportionate equity interest; (3) some common shareholders receive preferred and others receive common stock; (4) the underlying stock is preferred stock, unless the conversion ratio, if any, is adjusted to account for a common stock split or dividend; or (5) the distributed stock is convertible preferred, and the distribution has a disproportionate effect.
2. If the stock dividend meets one of the exceptions to nontaxable treatment, the stock dividend is treated as a property distribution under Sec. 301, where the FMV of the distribution is a taxable dividend to the extent of the distributing corporation's E&P.
3. If the stock dividend is nontaxable, (1) the basis of the underlying stock (old shares) is allocated among the old and new shares according to relative FMVs, and (2) the holding period for the new shares includes the holding period for the old shares.
4. If the stock dividend is taxable, (1) the distributed stock takes a basis equal to its FMV on the distribution date, and (2) the holding period begins the after the distribution.

Distributing Corporation:
1. The distributing corporation recognizes no gain or loss on the stock dividend, whether it is nontaxable or taxable.
2. If the stock dividend is nontaxable, the distributing corporation does not reduce its E&P.
3. If the stock dividend is taxable, the distributing corporation reduces its E&P to the extent the distribution is treated as a taxable dividend.

STOCK REDEMPTIONS

OBJECTIVE 5

Discern when a stock redemption should be treated as a sale and when it should be treated as a dividend

A **stock redemption** is a corporation's acquiring its own stock in exchange for corporate property. This property may be cash, securities of other corporations, or any other consideration the corporation uses to acquire its own stock.[24] The corporation may cancel the acquired stock, retire it, or hold it as treasury stock.

A stock redemption may be desirable for the following reasons:

▶ A shareholder may want to withdraw from the corporate business and sell his or her equity interest. In such a case, the shareholder may prefer that the corporation, rather than an outsider, purchase his or her stock so that the remaining shareholders (who may be family members) retain complete control and ownership of the corporation after his or her withdrawal from the business.

▶ A shareholder may be required to sell stock to the corporation under the terms of a stock purchase agreement with the issuing corporation.

▶ A shareholder may want to reduce his or her equity interest in a corporation but may be unwilling or unable to sell stock to outsiders. For example, no market may exist for the shares, or sales to outsiders may be restricted.

▶ A shareholder may want to withdraw assets from a corporation before a sale of the corporation's business. A potential purchaser may not be interested in acquiring all the assets or be able to pay full value for all outstanding shares. A withdrawal of some assets by the seller in exchange for some of his or her shares allows the purchaser to acquire the remaining shares and business assets at a lower total price.

▶ After the death of a major shareholder, a corporation may agree to purchase the decedent's stock from either the estate or a beneficiary to provide sufficient funds to pay estate and inheritance taxes and funeral and administrative expenses.

▶ Management may believe that the corporation's stock is selling at a low price and that, to increase share value, the corporation should acquire some of its stock in the open market.

---

[24] Sec. 317.

Whatever the reason for the redemption, the shareholder must answer the following questions:

▶ What are the amount and character of the income, gain, or loss recognized as a result of the redemption?

▶ What basis does the shareholder take in any property received in exchange for his or her stock?

▶ When does the holding period for the property begin?

▶ What basis does the shareholder take in any distributing corporation stock held after the redemption?

The distributing corporation must answer the following questions:

▶ What amount and character of gain or loss, if any, must the corporation recognize when it redeems stock with noncash property?

▶ What effect does the redemption have on the corporation's E&P?[25]

TAX CONSEQUENCES OF THE REDEMPTION TO THE SHAREHOLDER

KEY POINT

As far as a shareholder is concerned, the basic issue in a stock redemption is whether the redemption is treated as a dividend or a sale.

As a general rule, when a shareholder sells or exchanges corporate stock, any gain or loss in the transaction is capital in character. In some cases, a redemption is treated as a stock sale. In other cases, it is treated as a dividend. The reason for this difference is that some redemptions resemble a stock sale to a third party, whereas others are essentially equivalent to a dividend. The following two examples illustrate the difference between a redemption resembling a dividend and a redemption resembling a sale. (The IRC refers to a "sale or exchange," but for simplicity in this chapter, we will use only the term "sale.")

EXAMPLE C:4-24 ▶ John owns all 100 outstanding shares of Tango Corporation stock. John's basis in his shares is $50,000, and Tango's E&P is $100,000. If Tango redeems 25 of John's shares for $85,000, John still owns 100% of Tango stock. Because John's proportionate ownership of Tango has not changed as a result of the redemption, the redemption resembles a dividend (i.e., a distribution of corporate earnings). Accordingly, for tax purposes, John is deemed to have received an $85,000 dividend. ◀

EXAMPLE C:4-25 ▶ Carol has owned three of the 1,000 outstanding shares of Water Corporation stock for two years. Her basis in the shares is $1,000, and Water's E&P is $100,000. If Water redeems all three of Carol's shares for $5,000, Carol is essentially in the same position as a seller of stock to a third party. She has received $5,000 for her stock and has no further ownership interest in the corporation. Thus, the redemption resembles a sale and is not essentially equivalent to a dividend. Accordingly, Carol recognizes a $4,000 ($5,000 − $1,000) capital gain. ◀

Example C:4-24 is an extreme case involving a redemption that clearly should be treated as a dividend to the shareholder. Example C:4-25 also is an extreme case involving a redemption that clearly should be treated as a sale of stock by the shareholder. Many cases, however, fall between the two extremes, and the way the redemption should be treated is not immediately apparent. The problem for Congress and the courts has been how to distinguish redemptions that should be treated as sales from those that should be treated as dividends. Under current law, a redemption qualifies for sale treatment if it satisfies one of the following conditions:

▶ The redemption is substantially disproportionate.

▶ The redemption is a complete termination of the shareholder's interest.

▶ The redemption is not essentially equivalent to a dividend.

▶ The redemption involves a partial liquidation of the corporation in conjunction with its redeeming stock from a noncorporate shareholder.

▶ The redemption provides funds for an estate to pay death taxes.

If a redemption qualifies as a sale, the transaction is treated as though the shareholder sold stock to a third party. The shareholder recognizes gain or loss equal to the FMV of

---

[25] This discussion concerns the redemption of C corporation stock. Different rules apply to the redemption of S corporation stock.

the property received less the shareholder's adjusted basis in the stock surrendered. The gain or loss is capital in character if the stock is a capital asset in the hands of the shareholder. The shareholder's basis in any property received is its FMV. The holding period for the property begins on the day following the exchange date.

A redemption that does not satisfy any of the five conditions necessary for sale treatment is regarded as a property distribution under Sec. 301. Accordingly, the entire amount of the distribution is treated as a dividend to the extent of the distributing corporation's E&P.[26] The shareholder's stock basis is not taken into account in determining the dividend amount. Generally, this basis is added to the basis of any remaining shares owned by the shareholder. If all the shareholder's stock has been redeemed, the basis of the redeemed shares is added to the basis of shares owned by those individuals whose ownership is attributed to the shareholder under the rules described below.[27]

EXAMPLE C:4-26 ▶

Amy and Rose each own 50 of the 100 outstanding shares of stock in York Corporation, which reports $100,000 of E&P. On May 10, York redeems 20 of Amy's shares with property worth $25,000. Amy's adjusted basis in those shares is $20,000. If the redemption satisfies one of the conditions necessary for sale treatment, Amy recognizes a capital gain of $5,000 ($25,000 − $20,000). Her basis in the property received is its $25,000 FMV, and its holding period begins on May 11. If the redemption does not satisfy any of the conditions necessary for sale treatment, Amy recognizes $25,000 of dividend income. Her $20,000 basis in the surrendered shares is added to the basis of her remaining 30 shares. ◀

ADDITIONAL COMMENT

Prior to 2003, sale or exchange treatment provided a third advantage, specifically, the capital gain received preferential tax treatment as compared to ordinary income treatment for dividends. As a result of 2003 and 2010 Acts, however, dividends received by a noncorporate shareholder in 2003 through 2012 also obtain preferential treatment, thereby removing this advantage. Thus, because capital gains and qualified dividends are now taxed at the same rate, the difference in tax between exchange treatment and dividend treatment is solely a function of the taxpayer's basis in the redeemed stock.

Structuring a stock redemption as a sale offers two advantages. First, capital gains may be offset by capital losses. Second, in a sale, the basis of the shares redeemed reduces the amount of income recognized. By contrast, if a redemption is treated as a dividend, the basis of the shares redeemed does not reduce the dividend amount. Instead, the basis shifts to the shareholder's remaining stock, which reduces the gain (or increases the loss) recognized in a later sale of this stock.

Topic Review C:4-4 summarizes the tax consequences of stock redemptions to both the shareholder and the distributing corporation.

ATTRIBUTION RULES

Three of the five tests for determining how a redemption should be treated (i.e., as a sale or dividend) are based on stock ownership before and after the redemption. The tests measure the extent to which the shareholder's proportionate interest in the corporation has been reduced as a result of the exchange. In general, if the shareholder's proportionate interest has been substantially reduced, the redemption is treated as a sale. On the other hand, if this

Topic Review C:4-4

Tax Consequences of Stock Redemptions

Shareholders:

General Rule: The distribution amount received by a shareholder in exchange for his or her stock is treated as a dividend to the extent of the distributing corporation's E&P. The basis of the surrendered stock is added to the basis of the shareholder's remaining stock.

Sale Exception: If the redemption meets specific requirements, the distribution amount received by the shareholder is offset by the adjusted basis of the shares surrendered. The difference generally is treated as a capital gain or loss. No basis adjustment occurs.

Distributing Corporation:

Gain/Loss Recognition: Under either the general rule or sale exception, the corporation recognizes gain (but not loss) as though it had sold distributed noncash property for its FMV immediately before the redemption.

Earnings and Profits Adjustment: For a redemption treated as a dividend, E&P is reduced in the same manner as for a regular dividend (e.g., by the amount of any money or the FMV of any property distributed). For a redemption treated as a sale, E&P is reduced by the portion of current and accumulated E&P attributable to the redeemed stock. Any distribution amount exceeding this portion reduces the corporation's paid-in capital.

---

[26] Sec. 302(d).   [27] Reg. Sec. 1.302-2(c).

interest remains essentially the same or increases, the redemption is treated as a dividend (assuming sufficient E&P).

For the purpose of applying these tests, stock ownership is determined under the constructive ownership or attribution rules of Sec. 318.[28] According to these rules, a shareholder owns not only the shares he or she directly owns but also shares owned by his or her spouse, other immediate family members, and related entities. In addition, corporations, partnerships, trusts, and estates are considered to constructively own shares owned by their shareholders, partners, and beneficiaries.

The attribution rules prevent shareholders from taking advantage of favorable tax rules or avoiding unfavorable tax rules by transferring to family members or related entities stock that the shareholder previously owned. The proportionate stock ownership tests would be subject to abuse if only direct ownership were considered.

Section 318(a) sets forth four types of attribution rules: attribution among family members, attribution from entities, attribution to entities, and option attribution. These rules are discussed below.

FAMILY ATTRIBUTION. Under the first set of rules, an individual is considered to own constructively all stock owned by or for his or her spouse, children, grandchildren, and parents. An individual is not considered to own stock owned by his or her brothers, sisters, or grandparents.

Once attributed to an individual under one set of attribution rules, stock ownership may not be reattributed to another individual under the same set of rules. Thus, stock ownership attributed to one family member under the family attribution rules may not be reattributed to a second family member under the same set of rules. However, once attributed to an individual under one set of attribution rules, stock ownership may be reattributed to another individual under a different set of attribution rules. For example, stock ownership attributed from a corporation to its shareholder under the corporate attribution rules may be reattributed to the shareholder's spouse under the family attribution rules.

ADDITIONAL COMMENT

The family attribution rules of Sec. 318 are not as inclusive as the family attribution rules of Sec. 267 (covered in Chapter C:3). For example, siblings and grandparents are not considered family members by Sec. 318 but are included under Sec. 267.

EXAMPLE C:4-27 ▶ Harry; his wife, Wilma; their son, Steve; and Harry's father, Frank, each own 25 of the 100 outstanding shares of Strong Corporation stock. Under the family attribution rules, Harry is considered to own all 100 Strong shares (25 directly plus constructively the shares owned by Wilma, Steve, and Frank). Wilma is considered to own 75 shares (25 directly plus constructively the 50 shares owned by Harry and Steve). Ownership of Frank's shares is neither directly attributed to Wilma nor reattributed to Wilma through Harry. Steve is considered to own 75 shares (25 directly plus constructively the 50 shares owned by his parents Harry and Wilma). Ownership of Frank's shares is neither directly attributed to Steve nor reattributed to Steve through Harry. Frank is considered to own 75 shares (25 directly plus constructively the shares owned by Harry and Steve (his grandson)). Ownership of Wilma's shares is neither directly attributed to Frank nor reattributed to Frank through Harry.

The diagram below illustrates the constructive stock ownership of the four shareholders. The arrows indicate the direction(s) of ownership attribution.

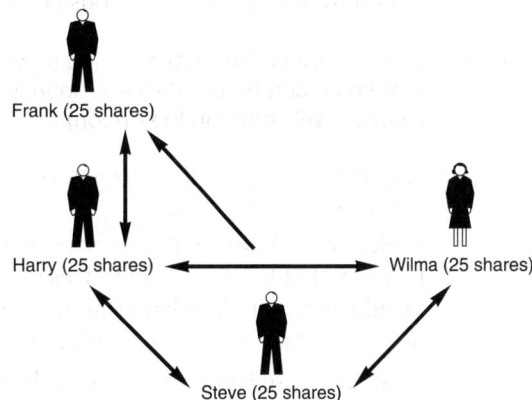

Frank (25 shares)

Harry (25 shares) — Wilma (25 shares)

Steve (25 shares)

The table below shows each shareholder's direct and constructive stock ownership. Note that the total number of shares owned directly and constructively by all shareholders may exceed the total number of actual shares issued and outstanding.

Shareholder	Direct Ownership	Spouse	Child	Grandchild	Parent(s)	Total
			Shares Constructively Owned From:			
Frank	25		25	25		75
Harry	25	25	25		25	100
Wilma	25	25	25			75
Steve	25				50	75
	100					

ATTRIBUTION FROM ENTITIES. Under the second set of attribution rules, stock owned by or for a partnership is considered to be owned proportionately by the partners. Stock owned by or for an estate is considered to be owned proportionately by the beneficiaries. Stock owned by or for a trust is considered to be owned by the beneficiaries in proportion to their actuarial interests. Stock owned by or for a C corporation is considered to be owned proportionately only by shareholders owning (directly or indirectly) 50% or more of the corporation's stock value.[29]

EXAMPLE C:4-28 ▶ Bill, who is married to Nancy, owns a 50% interest in Partnership A. Partnership A owns 40 of the 100 outstanding shares of Yellow Corporation stock, and Bill owns the remaining 60 shares. Under the entity attribution rules, Bill is considered to own 80 shares, 60 directly and 20 (0.50 × 40 shares) constructively. In addition, the stock ownership attributed to Bill under the entity attribution rules is reattributed to Nancy under the family attribution rules. ◀

ATTRIBUTION TO ENTITIES. Under the third set of attribution rules, all stock owned by or for a partner is considered to be constructively owned by the partnership. All stock owned by or for a beneficiary of an estate or a trust is considered to be constructively owned by the estate or trust. All stock owned by or for a shareholder who owns (directly or indirectly) 50% or more of a C corporation's stock value is considered to be constructively owned by the corporation.

Stock ownership attributed to a partnership, estate, trust, or corporation from a partner, beneficiary, or shareholder is not reattributed from the entity to another partner, beneficiary, or shareholder.

EXAMPLE C:4-29 ▶ Assume the same facts as in Example C:4-28. The partnership in which Bill is a partner is considered to own all 100 shares of Yellow stock (40 directly and 60 constructively through Bill). Bill's stock ownership attributed to the partnership cannot be reattributed from the partnership to Bill's partners. ◀

OPTION ATTRIBUTION. Under the last set of attribution rules, a person who holds an option to purchase stock is considered to own the underlying stock.

EXAMPLE C:4-30 ▶ John owns 25 of the 100 outstanding shares of Yard Corporation stock. He holds an option to acquire an additional 50 shares. John is considered to own 75 Yard shares (25 directly plus 50 constructively through the option). ◀

SUBSTANTIALLY DISPROPORTIONATE REDEMPTIONS

Under Sec. 302(b)(2), if a stock redemption is substantially disproportionate with respect to a shareholder, it is treated as a sale and thus qualifies for capital gain as opposed to dividend treatment. A redemption is substantially disproportionate with respect to a shareholder if all the following conditions are met:

▶ After the redemption, the shareholder owns less than 50% of the total combined voting power of all classes of voting stock.

---

[29] For purposes of the attribution rules, S corporations are treated as partnerships, not corporations. Thus, attribution occurs to and from shareholders owning less than 50% of the S corporation stock. Unless otherwise stated, all corporations in the examples are C corporations.

- ▶ After the redemption, the shareholder owns less than 80% of his or her percentage ownership of voting stock before the redemption.
- ▶ After the redemption, the shareholder owns less than 80% of his or her percentage ownership of common stock (whether voting or nonvoting) before the redemption.

These tests are applied mechanically to each shareholder's ownership interest. The 50% test precludes shareholders from qualifying for capital gains treatment if they own a controlling interest in the distributing corporation after the redemption. The 80% tests define a degree of change in the shareholder's proportionate interest that constitutes a substantial reduction in that interest. A redemption may be substantially disproportionate with respect to one shareholder but not another. If only one class of stock is outstanding, the second and third requirements are essentially the same.

TAX STRATEGY TIP

If possible, taxpayers should structure a redemption to meet the substantially disproportionate test rather than the subjective "not equivalent to a dividend" test (discussed on page C:4-23), thereby obtaining certainty of results.

EXAMPLE C:4-31 ▶

ADDITIONAL COMMENT

In calculating the percentage of stock owned *after* a redemption note that the denominator used is the number of shares outstanding *after* the redemption.

Long Corporation has issued 400 shares of common stock and plans to redeem 100 of these shares. Before the redemption, Ann, Bob, Carl, and Dana (all unrelated) own 100 shares each. Long redeems 55 shares from Ann, 25 shares from Bob, and 20 shares from Carl. The following table illustrates ownership before and after the redemption.

	Before Redemption			After Redemption	
Shareholder	No. of Shares Owned	Percentage of Ownership	Shares Redeemed	No. of Shares Owned	Percentage of Ownership
	(1)	(1) ÷ 400	(2)	(1) − (2)	[(1) − (2)] ÷ 300
Ann	100	25%	55	45	15.00%
Bob	100	25%	25	75	25.00%
Carl	100	25%	20	80	26.67%
Dana	100	25%	—	100	33.33%
Total	400	100%	100	300	100.00%

The redemption is substantially disproportionate with respect to Ann because, after the redemption, she owns less than 50% of Long's stock, and her stock ownership percentage (15%) is less than 80% of her stock ownership percentage before the redemption (0.80 × 25% = 20%). The redemption is not substantially disproportionate with respect to Bob because the percentage reduction in his stock ownership is not less than 80% of his pre-redemption ownership percentage. In fact, Bob owns the same percentage of stock (25%) after the redemption as he did before the redemption (25%). The redemption also is not substantially disproportionate with respect to Carl because his stock ownership percentage increases from 25% to 26.67%. Thus, only the redemption of Ann's shares is treated as a sale and qualifies for capital gains treatment. ◀

The constructive ownership rules of Sec. 318(a) apply in determining whether the shareholder has met the three conditions for a substantially disproportionate redemption.[30]

EXAMPLE C:4-32 ▶

Assume the same facts as in Example C:4-31 except that Ann is Bob's mother. In this case, the redemption is not substantially disproportionate with respect to either Ann or Bob because, before the redemption, each directly and constructively owns 200 shares, or 50% of the Long stock, and after the redemption each directly and constructively owns 120 shares, or 40% of the stock. Although the 50% test is met, neither Ann nor Bob satisfies the 80% test. After the redemption each directly and constructively owns *exactly* 80% of the percentage owned before the redemption (0.80 × 50% = 40%). ◀

COMPLETE TERMINATION OF THE SHAREHOLDER'S INTEREST

Under Sec. 302(b)(3), if a stock redemption completely terminates a shareholder's interest in the corporation, the redemption also is treated as a sale. At first glance, this rule does not offer a route to sale treatment that is not already provided by the other Sec. 302 rules. If a corporation redeems all of a shareholder's stock, in most cases the requirements for a substantially disproportionate redemption under Sec. 302(b)(2) would have been satisfied.

---

[30] Reg. Sec. 1.302-3(a).

However, the complete termination rule extends sale treatment to two redemptions not covered by the substantially disproportionate redemption rules:

▶ If a shareholder's interest in a corporation consists exclusively of nonvoting stock, a redemption of all the stock could not qualify as substantially disproportionate under Sec. 302(b)(2) because no reduction of voting power occurs. However, it could qualify as a complete termination of the shareholder's interest under Sec. 302(b)(3) because the interest need not consist of voting stock.

▶ If a shareholder owns some voting stock and the redemption terminates his or her entire interest in the corporation, the family attribution rules of Sec. 318(a)(1) may be waived. Consequently, the redemption could qualify for sale treatment even though other family members continue to own some or all of the corporation's stock.[31]

To have the family attribution rules waived, the shareholder must meet all of the following conditions:

▶ After the redemption, the shareholder must not retain any interest in the corporation except as a creditor. This restriction includes any interest as an officer, director, or employee.

▶ The shareholder must not acquire any such interest (other than by bequest or inheritance) for at least ten years from the date of the redemption.

▶ The shareholder must file a written agreement with the IRS that he or she will notify the IRS upon acquiring any prohibited interest.

The written agreement authorizes the IRS to assess additional taxes for the year of the redemption if the prohibited interest is acquired, even when the basic three-year limitations period has expired.

EXAMPLE C:4-33 ▶ Father and Son each own 50 of the 100 outstanding shares of Short Corporation stock. Short redeems all of Father's shares. Under the family attribution rules, Father is considered to own directly and constructively 100% of the Short stock both before and after the redemption. Thus, the redemption is not substantially disproportionate with respect to him. However, if Father agrees not to retain or acquire any interest in Short for ten years (except as a creditor, devisee, or heir), the family attribution rules may be waived. Consequently, the redemption could qualify as a complete termination of Father's interest and be treated as a stock sale. ◀

Waiver of the family attribution rules is not permitted in the following two situations involving related parties:

▶ Within the ten-year period ending on the distribution date, the distributee acquired, directly or indirectly, part or all of the redeemed stock from a person whose stock ownership would be attributable (at the time of the distribution) to the distributee under Sec. 318.

▶ Any person owns (at the time of the distribution) stock of the redeeming corporation the ownership of which is attributable to the distributee under Sec. 318, and such person acquired any stock in the redeeming corporation, directly or indirectly, from the distributee within the ten-year period ending on the distribution date.

The first restriction is aimed at an individual who transfers stock to a related party (e.g., family member or controlled entity) purportedly to enable the related party to invoke the complete termination provision to recognize a capital gain when the corporation redeems the transferred stock. The second restriction is aimed at an individual who transfers some of his or her stock to a related party purportedly to invoke the complete termination provision to recognize a capital gain when the corporation redeems his or her remaining stock. These prohibitions against waiving the family attribution rules do not apply if the shareholder transferred the stock more than ten years before the redemption or if the distributee can show that the acquisition or disposition of the stock did not have tax avoidance as one of its principal purposes. In the second situation above, the family attribution rules also can be waived if the corporation redeems as part of the same transaction stock previously transferred to the related party.

Note that only the family attribution rules can be waived. Entities may have the family attribution rules waived if both the entity and the individual whose stock is attributed to the entity agree not to acquire any prohibited interest in the corporation for at least ten years.

---

[31] Section 302(c)(2) provides for the waiver of family attribution rules.

EXAMPLE C:4-34 ▶ Andrew created the A Trust, which owns 30% of Willow Corporation stock. Andrew's wife, Wanda, is the sole beneficiary of the trust. Their son, Steve, owns the remaining 70% of Willow stock. Willow redeems all of its stock owned by the A Trust. At first glance, the redemption does not qualify for sale treatment because the trust is deemed to own all the stock owned by Wanda, and Wanda is deemed to own all the stock owned by Steve. However, if both A Trust and Wanda agree not to acquire any interest in the corporation for ten years, the family attribution rules may be waived. Consequently, the redemption will be treated as a complete termination of the trust's interest in Willow and will be eligible for sale treatment. ◀

REDEMPTIONS NOT ESSENTIALLY EQUIVALENT TO A DIVIDEND

KEY POINT

Section 302(b)(1) has generally been interpreted to require that a shareholder incur a "meaningful reduction" of its stock interest. What constitutes a "meaningful reduction" is the subject of controversy.

Section 302(b)(1) provides that a redemption will be treated as a sale if it is not essentially equivalent to a dividend. The tax law sets forth no mechanical test for determining when a redemption is not essentially equivalent to a dividend. Instead, it implies that a determination should be based on the facts and circumstances of each case.[32] Sec. 302(b)(1) does not provide a safe harbor similar to the rules for substantially disproportionate redemptions or redemptions that are a complete termination of a shareholder's interest. On the other hand, the provision prevents the redemption rules from being too restrictive, especially in the case of transactions involving preferred stock.

The Supreme Court's decision in *Maclin P. Davis* sets forth guidelines for determining when a redemption is not essentially equivalent to a dividend.[33] The Supreme Court held that (1) in this determination, a business purpose is irrelevant; (2) the Sec. 318 attribution rules must be applied to establish dividend equivalency; and (3) a redemption of part of a sole shareholder's stock is always essentially equivalent to a dividend. The Court further held that for Sec. 302(b)(1) purposes, there must be a "meaningful reduction" in the shareholder's proportionate interest in the corporation after taking into account the constructive ownership rules of Sec. 318(a). Despite this holding, the definition of "a meaningful reduction in interest" remains unclear.

Because of this lack of clarity, Sec. 302(b)(1) generally applies to a redemption of nonvoting preferred stock only where the shareholder does not own any common stock,[34] or to redemptions resulting in a substantial reduction in the shareholder's rights to vote and exercise control over the corporation, participate in earnings, and share in net assets upon liquidation. Generally, the IRS allows sale treatment if a controlling shareholder reduces his or her interest to a noncontrolling position,[35] or a noncontrolling shareholder further reduces his or her minority interest.[36] A shareholder does not qualify for sale treatment if he or she maintains control both before and after the redemption,[37] or if he or she assumes a controlling position.

EXAMPLE C:4-35 ▶ Four unrelated individuals own all of Thyme Corporation's single class of stock as follows: Alan, 27%; Betty, 24.33%; Clem, 24.33%; and David, 24.33%. Thyme redeems some of Alan's stock holdings, resulting in a reduction of Alan's interest to 22.27%. Betty, Clem, and David own equally the remaining 77.73% of Thyme stock. The redemption of Alan's stock does not qualify as substantially disproportionate because Alan's interest is not reduced below 21.6% (0.80 × 27% = 21.6%). Nor does the redemption qualify as a complete termination of Alan's interest because Alan still owns Thyme shares. However, the redemption might be treated as a sale under Sec. 302(b)(1) because the transaction results in a meaningful reduction of Alan's noncontrolling interest in Thyme. ◀

PARTIAL LIQUIDATIONS

Under Sec. 302(b)(4), a redemption of a noncorporate shareholder's stock qualifies for sale treatment if the redemption is in **partial liquidation** of the corporation. A partial liquidation occurs when a corporation discontinues one line of business, distributes assets used in that business to its shareholders, and continues at least one other line of business.[38] A distribution

---

[32] Reg. Sec. 1.302-2(b).
[33] *U.S. v. Maclin P. Davis*, 25 AFTR 2d 70-827, 70-1 USTC ¶9289 (USSC, 1970).
[34] Reg. Sec. 1.302-2(a).
[35] In Rev. Rul. 75-502, 1975-2 C.B. 111, a reduction in stock ownership from 57% to 50% where the shareholder no longer had control was considered a meaningful reduction in interest.
[36] In Rev. Rul. 76-364, 1976-2 C.B. 91, a reduction in stock ownership from 27% to 22% was considered a meaningful reduction in interest.

[37] See *Jack Paparo*, 71 T.C. 692 (1979), where reductions in stock ownership from 100% to 81.17% and from 100% to 74.15% were not considered meaningful reductions in interest.
[38] A partial liquidation also can occur when a corporation sells one line of business, distributes the sales proceeds (after paying taxes on any gain from the sale), and continues at least one other line of business. See Rev. Rul. 79-275, 1979-2 C.B. 137.

in partial liquidation qualifies for sale treatment if it is not essentially equivalent to a dividend. The distribution must be made within the tax year in which a plan of partial liquidation has been adopted or within the succeeding tax year.

DETERMINATION MADE AT THE CORPORATE LEVEL. For purposes of Sec. 302(b)(4), whether a distribution is not essentially equivalent to a dividend is determined at the corporate level.[39] The distribution must result from a bona fide contraction of the corporate business. In relevant Treasury Regulations and revenue rulings, the government provides guidance as to what constitutes a bona fide business contraction. Examples include

▶ The distribution of insurance proceeds received as a result of a fire that destroys part of a business.[40]

▶ Termination of a contract representing 95% of a domestic corporation's gross income.[41]

▶ Change in a corporation's business from a full-line department store to a discount apparel store, which results in the elimination of certain units; the elimination of most forms of credit; and a reduction in inventory, floor space, and employees.[42]

SAFE HARBOR RULE. Under Sec. 302(e)(2), a distribution satisfies the not-essentially-equivalent-to-a-dividend requirement and qualifies as a partial liquidation if

▶ The distribution is attributable to the distributing corporation's ceasing to conduct a qualified trade or business, or consists of the assets of a qualified trade or business; and

▶ Immediately after the distribution, the distributing corporation is engaged in the active conduct of at least one qualified trade or business.

A qualified trade or business is any trade or business that

▶ Has been actively conducted throughout the five-year period ending on the date of the redemption, and

▶ Was not acquired by the corporation within such five-year period in a partially or wholly taxable transaction.

The definition of an active trade or business is the same as that used for Sec. 355 (corporate division) purposes, as discussed in Chapter C:7.

EXAMPLE C:4-36 ▶ Sage Corporation has manufactured hats and gloves for the past five years. In the current year, Sage discontinues hat manufacturing, sells all of its hat manufacturing machinery, and distributes the proceeds to its shareholders in redemption of some of their Sage shares. The corporation continues glove manufacturing. The distribution is pursuant to a partial liquidation and thus qualifies for sale treatment. ◀

TAX CONSEQUENCES OF A PARTIAL LIQUIDATION TO THE SHAREHOLDERS. If a distribution is in partial liquidation of the corporation, a noncorporate shareholder treats the redemption of his or her stock as a sale, whether or not the distribution is pro rata. In contrast, a corporate shareholder treats the redemption distribution as a dividend unless the corporation meets one of the other tests for sale treatment (i.e., Sec. 302(b)(1)-(3) or Sec. 303). For a corporate shareholder, dividend treatment may be more advantageous than sale treatment because a corporation receives no preferential tax rate on capital gains, but may be eligible for a 70%, 80%, or 100% dividends-received deduction. In determining whether stock is owned by a corporate or noncorporate shareholder, stock held by a partnership, trust, or estate is considered to be held proportionately by its partners or beneficiaries.

EXAMPLE C:4-37 ▶ Assume the same facts as in Example C:4-36 except Sage Corporation is owned by Ted and Jolly Corporation. Each shareholder owns 50 shares of Sage stock with a $20,000 basis. Sage reports $100,000 of current and accumulated E&P. Sage distributes $18,000 to each shareholder in redemption of ten shares of stock worth $18,000. Because the redemption involves

---

[39] Sec. 302(e)(1)(A).
[40] Reg. Sec. 1.346-1.

[41] Rev. Rul. 75-3, 1975-1 C.B. 108.
[42] Rev. Rul. 74-296, 1974-1 C.B. 80.

a partial liquidation, Ted treats the transaction as a sale and recognizes a capital gain of $14,000 ($18,000 − $4,000). Jolly, however, cannot treat the transaction as a sale because Jolly is a corporate shareholder and thus must recognize $18,000 of dividend income. On the other hand, Jolly is eligible for a $14,400 (0.80 × $18,000) dividends-received deduction. Jolly's $4,000 basis in the ten redeemed shares is added to the basis of its 40 remaining shares, resulting in a $20,000 basis in those shares. (If Jolly owned the Sage stock since Sage's inception, Jolly would make no further basis adjustments. However, if Jolly did not own the Sage stock since inception, under Sec 1059(e), Jolly would reduce its basis in the Sage stock to $5,600 ($20,000 − $14,400) because the dividend would be considered extraordinary.) ◀

 STOP & THINK

Question: Why is a distribution in partial liquidation of a corporation treated as a sale by its noncorporate shareholders and as a dividend by its corporate shareholders?

Solution: The different tax treatment probably reflects different tax advantages. Noncorporate shareholders benefit most from sale treatment because they can offset their stock basis against any amount realized in the distribution. Corporate shareholders benefit most from dividend treatment because they can take the dividends-received deduction, thereby reducing the dividend tax burden. These disparate advantages stem from the different tax status of corporations, other entities, and individuals.

TAX STRATEGY TIP

An estate with liquidity problems owing to large holdings of a closely held business also may want to consider installment payment of the estate tax under Sec. 6166. See Chapter C:13 for further details.

REDEMPTIONS TO PAY DEATH TAXES

If corporate stock represents a substantial portion of a decedent's gross estate, a redemption of the stock from the estate or its beneficiaries may be eligible for sale treatment under Sec. 303. This IRC section helps shareholders who inherit stock in a closely held corporation pay estate and inheritance taxes and funeral and administrative expenses. If the stock is not readily marketable, a stock redemption may be the only way to provide the estate and its beneficiaries with sufficient liquidity to defray the costs of estate administration. Under the substantially disproportionate or complete termination rules, ownership attribution would disqualify the redemption from sale treatment. Consequently, the redemption would be treated as a dividend. Under Sec. 303, ownership attribution does not apply to the portion of a stock redemption that meets certain requirements.

Section 303 provides that a redemption of stock that was included in a decedent's gross estate is treated as a stock sale by the shareholder (i.e., either the estate or the beneficiary of the estate) if the following conditions are met:

1. The value of the redeeming corporation's stock included in the decedent's gross estate is more than 35% of the adjusted gross estate. The adjusted gross estate consists of the FMV of all property on the date of the decedent's death less allowable deductions for funeral and administrative expenses, claims against the estate, debts, and casualty and other losses.

EXAMPLE C:4-38 ▶

A decedent's gross estate, valued at $5.8 million, includes $3.4 million in cash and Pepper Corporation stock worth $2.4 million. Funeral and other deductible estate expenses amount to $1.8 million. Thus, the decedent's adjusted gross estate is $4 million ($5,800,000 − $1,800,000). Because the $2.4 million value of the Pepper stock included in the gross estate exceeds 35% of the adjusted gross estate ($1.4 million = 0.35 × $4,000,000), a redemption of this stock qualifies for sale treatment under Sec. 303. ◀

2. The maximum amount of the redemption distribution that can qualify for sale treatment is the sum of all federal and state estate and inheritance taxes, plus any interest due on those taxes, and all funeral and administrative expenses allowable as deductions in computing the federal estate tax. The redemption must be of stock held by the estate or by the decedent's heirs who are liable for estate taxes and other administrative expenses.

3. Section 303 applies to a redemption distribution only to the extent the shareholder's interest in the estate is reduced by the payment of death taxes and funeral and administration expenses. The maximum distribution eligible for sale treatment is the amount of estate taxes and expenses the shareholder is obligated to bear.

EXAMPLE C:4-39 ▶

Assume the same facts as in Example C:4-38 except that, before the decedent's death, all the stock was gifted to the decedent's son, Sam. The remaining assets were bequeathed to the decedent's wife, Wilma, who as beneficiary is indirectly liable for all estate taxes and administrative expenses. Section 303 sale treatment is not available to Sam because he is not liable for estate taxes or administrative expenses. If instead $1.6 million in nonstock assets had been gifted to Wilma before the decedent's death, and the remaining assets bequeathed to Sam, Sam as beneficiary would be indirectly liable for all estate taxes and administrative expenses. In such case, he could use Sec. 303 to obtain sale treatment for the redemption of enough of his stock to pay estate taxes and administrative expenses.   ◄

4. Section 303 applies only to distributions within certain time limits.

   a. In general, the redemption must occur not later than 90 days after the expiration of the period for assessing the federal estate tax. Because the limitations period for the federal estate tax expires three years after the estate tax return is due and because the return is due nine months after the date of death, the redemption generally must occur within four years after the date of death.

   b. If a petition for redetermination of an estate tax deficiency is filed with the Tax Court, the distribution period is extended to 60 days after the Tax Court's decision becomes final.

   c. If the taxpayer made a valid election under Sec. 6166 to defer paying of federal estate taxes under an installment plan, the distribution period is extended to the time the installment payments are due.

5. The stock of two or more corporations may be aggregated to meet the 35% threshold, provided that 20% or more of the value of each corporation's outstanding stock is included in the gross estate.

EXAMPLE C:4-40 ▶ A decedent's gross estate, valued at $5.8 million, includes 80% of the stock of Curry Corporation, valued at $800,000, and 90% of the stock of Brodie Corporation, valued at $900,000. Deductible funeral and administrative expenses amount to $1.8 million. Thus, the decedent's adjusted gross estate is $4 million. Although the value of neither the Curry stock nor the Brodie stock exceeds 35% of the $4 million adjusted gross estate, the total value of both corporations' stock ($1.7 million = $800,000 + $900,000) exceeds 35% of the adjusted gross estate ($1.4 million = 0.35 × $4,000,000). Therefore, a redemption of sufficient Curry stock and/or Brodie stock to pay estate taxes and funeral and administrative expenses qualifies for sale treatment under Sec. 303.   ◄

Although the legislative intent behind Sec. 303 is to provide liquidity for the payment of estate taxes and administrative expenses where a significant portion of the estate consists of stock in a closely held corporation, a redemption can qualify for Sec. 303 sale treatment even where the estate includes sufficient liquid assets to pay estate taxes and defray administrative costs. The redemption proceeds need not be used for these purposes.

The advantage of a Sec. 303 redemption is that the redeeming shareholder usually realizes little or no capital gain because his or her basis in the redeemed stock is the stock's FMV on date of the decedent's death (or an alternate valuation date, if applicable). If the redemption does *not* qualify as a sale, the redeeming shareholder recognizes dividend income equal to the distribution proceeds received in redemption of the stock.

EXAMPLE C:4-41 ▶

Chili Corporation pays $105,000 to redeem 100 shares of stock from Art, who inherited the stock from his father, Fred. The stock's FMV on Fred's date of death was $100,000. Chili reports an E&P balance of $500,000. If the redemption qualifies for sale treatment under Sec. 303, Art recognizes a $5,000 ($105,000 − $100,000) capital gain. On the other hand, if the redemption does not qualify for sale treatment under Sec. 303 or one of the other redemption provisions, Art recognizes $105,000 of dividend income. Although both the capital gain and the dividend income are subject to a maximum 15% tax rate (through 2012), the dividend amount significantly exceeds the capital gain amount.   ◄

EFFECT OF REDEMPTIONS ON THE DISTRIBUTING CORPORATION

As in the case of property distributions that are not in redemption of stock, two questions relating to property distributions in redemption of stock must be answered:

▶ What amount and character of gain or loss must the distributing corporation recognize?

▶ What effect does the distribution have on the corporation's E&P?

Each of these questions is addressed below.

CORPORATE GAIN OR LOSS ON PROPERTY DISTRIBUTIONS. The rules for gain or loss recognition for a corporation that distributes property in redemption of its stock are the same as the Sec. 311 rules pertaining to property distributions not in redemption of stock.

▶ The corporation recognizes gain when it redeems its stock by distributing property that has appreciated in value. The character of the gain depends on the character of the property distributed.

▶ The corporation recognizes no loss when it redeems its stock by distributing property that has declined in value.

EFFECT OF REDEMPTIONS ON E&P. A stock redemption affects a corporation's E&P in two ways. First, if the corporation distributes appreciated property, the excess of the property's FMV over its E&P adjusted basis increases the balance in the E&P account. Second, if the corporation distributes cash, or property, the corporation's E&P balance is reduced accordingly. The extent of the reduction depends on whether the shareholder treats the redemption as a sale or a dividend.

If the redemption is treated as a dividend, the corporation reduces its E&P by the amount of any cash, the principal amount of any obligations, and the greater of the adjusted basis or FMV of any other property distributed, in the same way as it does for a property distribution not in redemption of stock.

If the redemption is treated as a sale, the corporation reduces its E&P by the portion of its current and accumulated E&P attributable to the redeemed stock. In other words, E&P is reduced by the percentage of the total outstanding shares redeemed, not to exceed the actual distribution amount. Any distribution amount exceeding this percentage reduces the corporation's tax basis paid-in capital.[43] Ordinary dividend amounts are subtracted from current E&P before the subtraction of stock redemption amounts. No such sequencing exists for accumulated E&P. Both ordinary dividend distributions and redemption distributions reduce accumulated E&P in chronological order.

EXAMPLE C:4-42 ▶

Apex Corporation has 100 shares of stock outstanding, 30 of which are owned by Mona. On December 31, Apex pays $36,000 to redeem all 30 of Mona's shares in a redemption qualifying as a sale. At the time of the redemption, Apex has $60,000 in paid-in capital and $40,000 of E&P. Because Apex redeemed 30% of its outstanding stock, the distribution reduces Apex's E&P by $12,000 (0.30 × $40,000). The remaining $24,000 ($36,000 − $12,000) reduces Apex's tax basis paid-in capital to $36,000 ($60,000 − $24,000).[44] ◀

PREFERRED STOCK BAILOUTS

OBJECTIVE 6

Explain the tax treatment of preferred stock bailouts

The stock redemption rules permit sale treatment in certain situations and require dividend treatment in all others. Generally, taxpayers prefer sale treatment for two reasons. First, sale treatment allows taxpayers to offset their stock basis against the distribution proceeds. Second, gain on a stock sale generally is long-term and capital in character. Such gain may be entirely offset by the taxpayer's capital losses and thus not be taxed at all. With these results in mind, taxpayers have devised ways to obtain sale rather than dividend treatment.

---

[43] Sec. 312(n)(7). This adjustment to paid-in capital might be necessary for companies that maintain tax basis balance sheets, for example, to determine book-tax differences in complying with ASC 740, Income Taxes, which is the FASB Accounting Standards Codification for SFAS No. 109.

[44] Distributions during the year require a different calculation, which is beyond the scope of this text.

ADDITIONAL COMMENT

When the term *bailout* is used in the corporate context, it generally refers to a scheme that allows a corporation to make a dividend distribution that for tax purposes is treated as a sale of a capital asset.

One such method is a **preferred stock bailout**. Prior to Congress' enacting anti-tax avoidance measures, a preferred stock bailout typically proceeded as follows:

1. A corporation issued a nontaxable dividend of nonvoting preferred stock to its common shareholders. Under the rules relating to nontaxable stock dividends, a portion of the common stock basis was allocated to the preferred stock. Its holding period included the holding period for the common stock.

2. The recipient shareholder then sold the preferred stock at its FMV to an unrelated third party. As a result of the sale, the shareholder recognized a capital gain equal to the difference between the preferred stock's sale price and its allocated basis.

3. Next, the corporation redeemed the preferred stock from the third-party (usually at a small premium to reward the third party for his or her cooperation in the scheme).

4. As an alternative to steps 2 and 3, the corporation redeemed the preferred stock directly from the shareholder.

As a result of this preferred stock bailout, the shareholder extracted the corporation's E&P and converted what otherwise would have been a dividend into a long-term capital gain without changing his or her equity position. To deter such tax avoidance, Congress enacted Sec. 306, which "taints" certain stock (usually preferred stock) when distributed to a shareholder in a nontaxable stock dividend. Section 306 treats the distribution proceeds as a dividend if the corporation redeems the tainted stock directly from the shareholder and treats the amount realized as ordinary income if the shareholder sells the stock to a third party. Either way, Sec. 306 prevents shareholders from using a preferred stock bailout to convert ordinary income into capital gain.

The 2003 and 2010 Acts, however, took the "sting" out of Sec. 306 by reducing the tax rate on dividends to a maximum of 15%. Thus, through 2012, the dividend recognized on a direct redemption of Sec. 306 stock is taxed at 15%, and the amount realized on a third party sale of the stock is treated as a "deemed" dividend, also taxed at 15%. Nevertheless, the Sec. 306 taint is still disadvantageous because even though subject to the preferential capital gains tax rate, dividends cannot offset capital losses as can "real" capital gains. Also, if Sec. 306 recasts the redemption as a dividend, the shareholder is taxed on the entire amount of distribution proceeds rather than just the net gain.

SEC. 306 STOCK DEFINED

Section 306 stock is defined as follows:[45]

▶ Stock (other than common issued with respect to common) received in a nontaxable stock dividend

▶ Stock (other than common) received in a nontaxable corporate reorganization or corporate division if the effect of the transaction was substantially the same as the receipt of a stock dividend, or if the stock was received in exchange for Sec. 306 stock

▶ Stock that has a basis determined by reference to the basis of Sec. 306 stock (i.e., a substituted or transferred basis)

▶ Stock (other than common) acquired in an exchange to which Sec. 351 applies if the receipt of money (in lieu of the stock) would have been treated as a dividend

Preferred stock issued by a corporation with no current or accumulated E&P in the year the stock is issued is not Sec. 306 stock. Also, inherited stock is not Sec. 306 stock because the basis of such stock is its FMV on the date of the decedent's death (or alternate valuation date) and, therefore, is not determined by reference to the decedent's basis.[46]

DISPOSITIONS OF SEC. 306 STOCK

If a shareholder sells or otherwise disposes of Sec. 306 stock (except in a redemption), the amount realized is treated as a deemed dividend to the extent the shareholder would have recognized a dividend at the time of the distribution had money equal to the stock's FMV, instead of stock, been distributed. The shareholder's deemed dividend is measured by refer-

TYPICAL MISCONCEPTION

Although the amount of deemed dividend income recognized on a sale of Sec. 306 stock is measured by the E&P existing in the year the Sec. 306 stock was distributed, the E&P of the distributing corporation is not reduced by the amount of the deemed dividend.

[45] Sec. 306(c).

[46] Reg. Sec. 1.306-3(e).

ence to the corporation's E&P in the year the Sec. 306 stock was issued, although the corporation does not reduce its E&P upon the sale. Any additional amount received for the Sec. 306 stock generally is treated as a return of capital. If the additional amount exceeds the shareholder's basis in the Sec. 306 stock, the excess is treated as a capital gain. If the additional amount is less than the shareholder's basis, the unrecovered basis is not treated as a loss. Rather, it is added back to the shareholder's basis in his or her common shares.

EXAMPLE C:4-43 ▶

Carlos owns all 100 outstanding shares of Adobe Corporation common stock. His basis in the shares is $100,000. Adobe, which has $150,000 of E&P, distributes 50 shares of nonvoting preferred to Carlos in a nontaxable stock dividend. On the distribution date, the FMV of the preferred stock is $50,000, and the FMV of the common stock is $200,000. Carlos must allocate his $100,000 common stock basis between the common and preferred stock according to their relative FMVs as follows:

	FMV	Basis
Common stock	$200,000	$ 80,000[a]
Preferred stock	50,000	20,000[b]
Total	$250,000	$100,000

[a] $\dfrac{\$200,000}{\$250,000} \times \$100,000$ [b] $\dfrac{\$ 50,000}{\$250,000} \times \$100,000$

Carlos subsequently sells the preferred stock to Dillon for $50,000. The $50,000 sales proceeds are treated as a deemed dividend because Adobe's E&P in the year the corporation distributed the preferred stock exceeded the stock's FMV. Carlos's $20,000 basis in the preferred stock is added back to his basis in the common stock, thereby restoring his common stock basis to $100,000. If instead Carlos sells the preferred stock for $80,000, he recognizes a $50,000 deemed dividend, a $20,000 return of capital, and a $10,000 capital gain computed as follows:

Sales proceeds	$80,000
Minus: Deemed dividend income[a]	(50,000)
Remaining sales proceeds	$30,000
Minus: Return of capital[b]	(20,000)
Capital gain[c]	$10,000

[a]Smaller of E&P in year stock was issued or stock's FMV on the distribution date.
[b]Smaller of remaining sales proceeds or stock adjusted basis.
[c]Sales proceeds received in excess of stock adjusted basis.

◀

REDEMPTIONS OF SEC. 306 STOCK

KEY POINT

The amount realized in a redemption of Sec. 306 stock is a dividend to the extent of E&P existing in the year of redemption. Unlike a sale of Sec. 306 stock, E&P is reduced as a result of a redemption.

If the issuing corporation redeems Sec. 306 stock, the shareholder's total amount realized is treated as a distribution to which the Sec. 301 dividend rules apply. Specifically, it is treated as a dividend to the extent of the redeeming corporation's current and accumulated E&P measured *in the year of the redemption* and reduces corporate E&P accordingly. Amounts received in excess of the corporation's E&P are treated as a recovery of the shareholder's basis in his or her Sec. 306 stock, and then as a capital gain to the extent such amounts exceed basis. If all or a portion of the shareholder's basis in the redeemed stock is not recovered, the unrecovered amount increases the basis of the shareholder's common stock.

EXAMPLE C:4-44 ▶

Don owns all 100 shares of Brigham Corporation common stock with a total $300,000 adjusted basis. Four years ago, Brigham issued 50 shares of preferred stock to Don. On the distribution date, the FMVs of the preferred stock and common stock were $100,000 and $400,000, respectively. Brigham's E&P in the distribution year was $200,000. Don's allocated basis in the preferred stock was $60,000 {[$100,000 ÷ ($100,000 + $400,000)] × $300,000}. The basis of Don's common stock was reduced to $240,000 ($300,000 − $60,000) as a result of this allocation. On January 2 of the current year, Brigham redeems the preferred shares for $250,000. In the redemption year, Brigham's total E&P is $400,000. Thus, Don recognizes dividend income of $250,000. If Brigham's total E&P instead had been $200,000 in the redemption year, Don would have recognized $200,000 of dividend income and a $50,000 nontaxable return of capital.

Because Don's basis in his preferred stock is $60,000, the $10,000 unrecovered basis would have increased his basis in the common stock to $250,000 ($240,000 + $10,000). ◄

EXCEPTIONS TO SEC. 306 TREATMENT

Section 306 does not apply in the following situations.

► A shareholder sells all of his or her common and preferred stock, thereby completely terminating his or her interest in the issuing corporation.

► The corporation redeems all the shareholder's common and preferred stock, completely terminating the shareholder's interest in the corporation.

► The corporation redeems an individual shareholder's stock in a partial liquidation qualifying for sale treatment under Sec. 302(b)(4).

► A shareholder disposes of Sec. 306 stock in a way that triggers no gain or loss recognition (e.g., a gift). Although the donor recognizes no income when he or she disposes of Sec. 306 stock by gift, the stock retains its taint and remains Sec. 306 stock in the donee's hands. On the other hand, because heirs and devisees take a FMV basis in estate assets, the taint disappears when they inherit the stock.

► Section 306 does not apply if the taxpayer demonstrates to the IRS's satisfaction that the distribution and subsequent disposition of Sec. 306 stock did not have tax avoidance as a principal purpose.

STOCK REDEMPTIONS BY RELATED CORPORATIONS

OBJECTIVE 7

Determine the applicability and tax consequences of Sec. 304 to stock sales

If a shareholder sells stock in one corporation (the issuing corporation) to a second corporation (the acquiring corporation), the shareholder usually recognizes a capital gain or loss. However, if the shareholder controls both corporations, he or she may have to recognize dividend income because the net result may resemble a dividend more than a sale.

To prevent shareholders from using two corporations they commonly control to convert what is essentially a dividend into a capital gain, Sec. 304 requires that a sale of stock of one controlled corporation to a second controlled corporation be treated as a stock redemption. If the redemption meets the requirements for sale treatment (e.g., if the redemption is substantially disproportionate), the transaction will be treated as a sale. Otherwise, the redemption will be treated as a dividend to the extent of E&P. As in the case of Sec. 306 preferred stock bailouts, now that individuals pay a maximum tax rate of 15% on dividends and capital gains (through 2012), Sec. 304 no longer delivers the "sting" it had before 2003. Nevertheless, Sec. 304 still is in effect. When it does apply, shareholders may have to recognize dividend income rather than capital gain and cannot offset either stock basis or capital losses against this income.

Section 304 applies to two types of sales. The first is a sale of stock involving two brother-sister corporations. The second is a sale of a parent corporation's stock to one of its subsidiaries. The following sections define brother-sister and parent-subsidiary corporations and explain how Sec. 304 applies to each group.

BROTHER-SISTER CORPORATIONS

Two corporations are called brother-sister corporations when one or more shareholders control each of the corporations and a parent-subsidiary relationship does not exist. Control means ownership of at least 50% of the voting power or 50% of the total value of all the corporation's stock. The shareholder(s) who acquired such ownership are called controlling shareholders. If a controlling shareholder (or shareholders) transfers stock in one corporation to the other corporation in exchange for property, the exchange must be recast as a redemption.

To determine whether the redemption is treated as a sale or a dividend, reference is made to the shareholder's stock ownership in the issuing corporation. For purposes of this determination, the attribution rules of Sec. 318(a) apply.[47]

REDEMPTION TREATED AS A DISTRIBUTION. If the redemption does not qualify for sale treatment, it is treated as a dividend paid first by the acquiring corporation to the extent of its E&P, and then by the issuing corporation to the extent of its E&P. The shareholder's basis in the issuing corporation's stock sold is added to his or her basis in the acquiring corporation's stock. The acquiring corporation takes the same basis in the issuing corporation's stock as the shareholder's.

EXAMPLE C:4-45 ▶ Bert owns 60 of the 100 outstanding shares of First Corporation stock and 60 of the 100 outstanding shares of Second Corporation stock (see Fig. C:4-1). First and Second have $50,000 and $20,000 of E&P, respectively. Bert sells to Second for $20,000 20 shares of First stock with an adjusted basis of $10,000. Because Bert owns at least 50% of each corporation's stock, Bert is deemed to control both First and Second, and Sec. 304 governs the transaction. Accordingly, the sale is recast as a redemption. To determine whether the redemption qualifies for sale treatment, reference is made to Bert's percentage ownership of First stock. Before the redemption, Bert owned 60% of First stock. After the redemption, Bert owns 52% of First stock (40 shares directly and 12 [0.60 × 20] shares constructively through Second). Because the redemption satisfies none of the Sec. 302 tests for sale treatment, it is treated as a distribution subject to Sec. 301. Under this provision, the entire distribution is treated as a dividend because it does not exceed First's and Second's total E&P of $70,000. All $20,000 of the distribution is deemed to have been made out of Second's E&P because it is sufficient to cover the distribution amount. Second's basis in the First stock is $10,000, the same as Bert's. Bert increases his basis in Second stock by $10,000, his basis in the First stock he is deemed to have contributed to Second. ◀

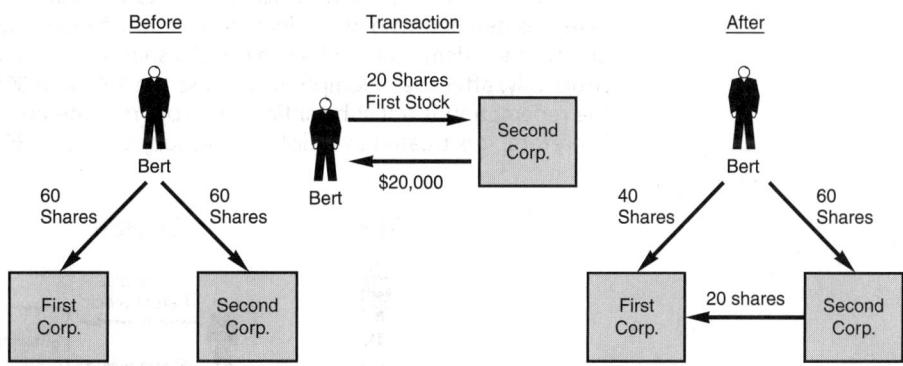

Bert's Ownership of First Corporation Stock:

Before: 60 shares (60%) directly
After: 52 shares [40 shares directly + 12 shares (60% × 20 shares) constructively]

FIGURE C:4-1 ▶ ILLUSTRATION OF A BROTHER-SISTER REDEMPTION (EXAMPLE C:4-45)

REDEMPTION TREATED AS A SALE. If the redemption qualifies for sale treatment, the shareholder's recognized gain or loss equals the difference between the amount received from the acquiring corporation and the shareholder's basis in the surrendered shares. The acquiring corporation is treated as having purchased the issuing corporation's shares and thus takes a cost basis in such shares.

EXAMPLE C:4-46 ▶ Assume the same facts as in Example C:4-45 except Bert sells 40 shares of First stock with an adjusted basis of $20,000 to Second Corporation for $40,000. After the redemption, Bert owns

---

[47] For Sec. 304 purposes, the attribution rules of Sec. 318(a) are modified so that a shareholder is considered to own an amount of stock proportionate to that owned by any corporation of which he or she owns 5% or more (instead of 50% or more) of the value of the stock.

44 shares of First stock (20 shares directly and 24 [0.60 × 40] shares constructively through Second). Therefore, he meets both the 50% and the 80% tests for substantially disproportionate redemptions, treats the redemption as a sale, and recognizes a capital gain of $20,000 ($40,000 received from Second − $20,000 adjusted basis in the First shares). Second's basis in the First shares acquired from Bert equals their $40,000 purchase price.   ◀

PARENT-SUBSIDIARY CORPORATIONS

If a shareholder sells stock in a parent corporation to a subsidiary of the parent, the sale is treated as a distribution in redemption of part or all of the shareholder's parent stock. A parent-subsidiary relationship exists if one corporation owns at least 50% of the voting power or 50% of the total value of all stock in another corporation.

To determine whether the redemption is treated as a sale or a dividend, reference is made to the shareholder's ownership of parent stock before and after the redemption. For this determination, the constructive ownership rules of Sec. 318 apply.

REDEMPTION TREATED AS A DIVIDEND. If the redemption does not qualify for sale treatment, the distribution is treated as a dividend, first from the subsidiary to the extent of its E&P and then from the parent to the extent of its E&P. This rule effectively sets the combined E&P of both corporations as the standard for measuring the amount of the distribution that constitutes a dividend. The shareholder's basis in his or her remaining parent shares is increased by his or her basis in the shares transferred to the subsidiary. The subsidiary's basis in the parent stock is the amount the subsidiary paid for the stock.[48]

EXAMPLE C:4-47 ▶

Of the 100 shares of Parent Corporation stock, Brian owns 60 with a $15,000 basis. Parent owns 60 of the 100 shares of Subsidiary stock. Parent and Subsidiary have $10,000 and $30,000 of E&P, respectively. Brian sells ten of his Parent shares to Subsidiary for $12,000. (See Figure C:4-2.) Parent is deemed to have redeemed its stock from Brian, who owned 60% of Parent stock before the redemption and 53 shares (50 shares directly and 3 [0.60 × 0.50 × 10] shares constructively) after the redemption. Because the 50% and 80% tests of Sec. 302(b)(2) are not met, the redemption is not substantially disproportionate and does not qualify for sale treatment. Therefore, it is treated as a distribution subject to Sec. 301. Under this provision, Brian recog-

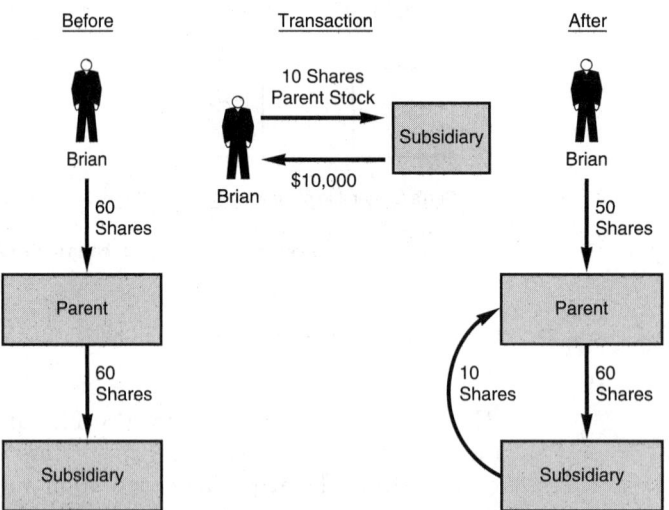

Brian's Ownership of Parent Corporation Stock:

Before: 60 shares (60%) directly
After: 53 shares [50 shares directly + 3 shares (50% × 60% × 10 shares) constructively]

FIGURE C:4-2   ▶   ILLUSTRATION OF A PARENT-SUBSIDIARY REDEMPTION (EXAMPLE C:4-47)

[48] Rev. Rul. 80-189, 1980-2 C.B. 106.

nizes a $12,000 dividend. This dividend is deemed to have been paid out of Subsidiary's E&P, which is sufficient to cover the entire distribution amount. Brian's $2,500 basis in the redeemed shares increases his $12,500 basis in his remaining Parent shares, so that his total basis in those shares remains $15,000. Subsidiary's basis in the ten Parent shares acquired from Brian is $12,000, the amount that Subsidiary paid for the shares. ◄

REDEMPTION TREATED AS A SALE.   If redemption of the parent's stock qualifies for sale treatment, the basis of the stock transferred to the subsidiary is subtracted from the amount realized in the distribution to derive the shareholder's recognized gain or loss.

EXAMPLE C:4-48 ▶   Assume the same facts as in Example C:4-47 except Brian sells 40 shares of Parent stock to Subsidiary for $48,000. Because Brian owns 60% of Parent stock before the redemption and 24.8% (20 shares directly and 4.8 [0.60 × 0.20 × 40] shares constructively) after the redemption, the redemption meets the Sec. 302(b)(2) 50% and 80% tests for a substantially disproportionate redemption. Consequently, Brian recognizes a capital gain of $38,000 ($48,000 − $10,000 adjusted basis in the 40 shares sold). Brian's adjusted basis in his remaining 20 shares of Parent stock is $5,000. Subsidiary's basis in the 40 Parent shares purchased from Brian is $48,000, the amount that Subsidiary paid for the shares. ◄

Topic Review C:4-5 summarizes the alternative treatments of stock redemptions.

Topic Review C:4-5

Alternative Treatments of Stock Redemptions

General Rule: A distribution in redemption of stock generally is treated as a dividend (Secs. 302(d) and 301).
Exception: The following transactions qualify for sale (i.e., capital gains) treatment:

1. Redemptions that are not essentially equivalent to a dividend (Sec. 302(b)(1))
2. Substantially disproportionate redemptions (Sec. 302(b)(2))
3. Complete terminations of a shareholder's interest (Sec. 302(b)(3))
4. Partial liquidations in redemption of a noncorporate shareholder's stock (Sec. 302(b)(4))
5. Redemptions to pay death taxes (Sec. 303)

Special Redemption Rules

1. Redemptions of Sec. 306 preferred stock generally are taxed as dividends to the shareholder (Sec. 306).
2. A sale of stock in one controlled corporation to another controlled corporation is treated as a redemption (Sec. 304).

TAX PLANNING CONSIDERATIONS

AVOIDING UNREASONABLE COMPENSATION

Chapter C:3 discussed the use of salary and fringe benefits to permit a shareholder of a closely held corporation to withdraw funds from the corporation and be subject to a single level of taxation. If a corporation pays too large a salary to a shareholder-employee, some of the salary may be disallowed as a corporate deduction while still taxed to the shareholder-employee. In such case, double taxation of the disallowed portion results.

Corporations can avoid this result by entering into a **hedge agreement** with a shareholder-employee. This agreement obligates the shareholder-employee to repay any portion of salary the IRS disallows as a corporate deduction. Under Sec. 162, the shareholder-employee may deduct this amount in the year he or she repays it, provided state law imposes a legal obligation to repay.[49] If a hedge agreement is not in effect, voluntary repayment of the salary is not deductible by the shareholder-employee.[50]

EXAMPLE C:4-49 ▶ Theresa owns one-half the stock in Marine Corporation and serves as its president. The remaining Marine stock is owned by eight investors, none of whom owns more than 10% of the outstanding shares. In 2006, Theresa and Marine conclude a hedge agreement requiring Theresa to repay all compensation the IRS declares unreasonable. In 2008, Marine pays Theresa a salary and bonus of $750,000. The IRS subsequently claims that $300,000 of the salary is unreasonable and thus nondeductible by Marine. After protracted negotiations, Marine and the IRS settle on $180,000 as unreasonable and nondeductible by Marine. Theresa repays the $180,000 in 2011. The entire $750,000 is taxable to Theresa in 2008. However, she can deduct the $180,000 as a trade or business expense in 2011. ◀

Hedge agreements also have been used in connection with other payments between a corporation and its shareholders (e.g., travel and entertainment expenses). Some employers are averse to hedge agreements because the IRS might consider the very existence of such an agreement as evidence of unreasonable compensation.

BOOTSTRAP ACQUISITIONS

A prospective purchaser who wants to acquire stock in a corporation may not have sufficient cash to do so. To facilitate the purchase, corporate funds could be used in the following way: a shareholder sells part of his or her stock to the purchaser and then causes the corporation to redeem the shareholder's remaining shares. Such an arrangement is called a **bootstrap acquisition**.

EXAMPLE C:4-50 ▶ Ted owns all 100 shares of Dragon Corporation stock having a $100,000 FMV. Vickie wants to purchase the stock from Ted but has only $60,000 in cash. Dragon has a large cash balance, which it does not need for its operations. Ted sells Vickie 60 shares of Dragon stock for $60,000 and then causes Dragon to redeem his remaining shares for $40,000. The redemption qualifies as a complete termination of Ted's interest under Sec. 302(b)(3) and, therefore, is eligible for sale treatment. ◀

Court cases have held that such redemptions qualify for sale treatment as long as the third-party sale and redemption are part of an integral plan to terminate the seller's entire corporate interest. Whether the redemption precedes the sale is immaterial.[51] The purchaser, however, must carefully avoid generating a dividend, actual or constructive. For example, a purchaser who contracts to acquire all the stock in a corporation on an installment basis and then causes the corporation to pay the installment obligations will recognize dividend income. The use of corporate funds constitutes a constructive dividend to the purchaser where the corporation discharges the purchaser's legal obligation. Even if the corporation uses its own funds to redeem the seller's shares, a purchaser who was legally obligated to purchase the shares is considered to have received a constructive dividend.[52]

EXAMPLE C:4-51 ▶ Assume the same facts as in Example C:4-50 except that, after Vickie purchases the 60 shares from Ted, she becomes legally obligated to purchase Ted's remaining 40 shares. After entering into the contract, Vickie causes Dragon Corporation to redeem the 40 shares. Because Dragon has extinguished Vickie's legal obligation, the corporation is deemed to have paid Vickie a $40,000 constructive dividend. No constructive dividend would have resulted had Vickie been legally obligated to purchase only 60 shares from Ted. ◀

Rev. Rul. 69-608 provides guidance to a bootstrap acquirer on how to avoid constructive dividend treatment.[53] According to this ruling, when the corporation redeems some of the seller's shares, the buyer will not be deemed to have received a constructive dividend as

---

[49] Rev. Rul. 69-115, 1969-1 C.B. 50, and *Vincent E. Oswald*, 49 T.C. 645 (1968), *acq.* 1968-2 C.B. 2.
[50] *Ernest H. Berger*, 37 T.C. 1026 (1962), and *John G. Pahl*, 67 T.C. 286 (1976).

[51] See, for example, *U.S. v. Gerald Carey*, 7 AFTR 2d 1301, 61-1 USTC ¶9428 (8th Cir., 1961).
[52] *H. F. Wall v. U.S.*, 36 AFTR 423, 47-2 USTC ¶9395 (4th Cir., 1947).
[53] Rev. Rul. 69-608, 1969-2 C.B. 42.

WHAT WOULD YOU DO IN THIS SITUATION?

One of the most cherished traditions observed by many professional firms involves the year-end bonus. Legal, medical, business, and accounting administrators often use bonus compensation to clear the books at the end of the year. In partnerships, bonuses are characterized as distributive shares or a form of compensation. As such, they are taxed only once as income paid to professionals for services rendered, net of appropriate accounting adjustments.

With the advent of the professional corporation, an entity designed to limit personal liability, many professionals have opted to do business as shareholders. The continued use of the year-end bonus in the professional corporation has come under close IRS scrutiny. The position taken by the IRS is clear. If the payments to the shareholder-professional are in exchange for his or her services rendered to the firm, the corporation may deduct them as salaries (assuming they are reasonable in amount). On the other hand, if they are a disguised payout of owners' profits, the corporation cannot deduct them. As a result, the corporation's taxable income will be increased by the amount of the disallowed deduction. The shareholder who receives the bonus must treat it as a dividend rather than salary. However, treating the bonus as a dividend generally results in less tax paid by the shareholder because dividends are taxed at a maximum rate of 15% (through 2012) as opposed to 35% for salary. The consequences are negative only to the corporation, which may not deduct the dividend payment.

This principle is illustrated in a case, *Rapco, Inc. v. CIR*, 77 AFTR 2d 2405, 96-1 USTC ¶50,297 (CA-2, 1996), decided by the Second Circuit. In *Rapco*, the court denied a deduction for bonus payments to the president of the company, even though he played a significant role in the company's rapid growth and had guaranteed third party loans to Rapco. Reasons cited by the court were that Rapco's compensation scheme was "bonus-heavy and salary light," suggesting dividend avoidance; Rapco had ignored its own bonus policy set forth in its preincorporation minutes; the corporation had a history of never paying dividends; the shareholder who determined the amount of his own salary owned 95% of the corporation's stock; and Rapco's own expert testified that $400,000 to $500,000 was fair compensation for the president's services. (The IRS allowed a salary deduction of $405,000).

Assuming your CPA firm is acting as a tax advisor to several similarly situated professional corporations, what advice that complies with the IRC, Treasury Regulations, and the AICPA's *Statements on Standards for Tax Services* would you give?

---

long as he or she does not have a primary and unconditional obligation to purchase the shares, and the corporation pays no more for the redeemed shares than their FMV. Furthermore, a purchaser who has an option—not a legal obligation—to purchase the seller's remaining shares, and who assigns the option to the redeeming corporation, is unlikely to generate a constructive dividend.[54]

TIMING OF DISTRIBUTIONS

Dividends can be paid only out of a corporation's E&P. Therefore, if a distribution can be made when the corporation has little or no E&P, it will be treated as a return of capital rather than as a dividend.

If a corporation generates a current E&P deficit, the deficit reduces accumulated E&P evenly throughout the year unless the corporation can demonstrate that it incurred the deficits on particular dates. Thus, if a corporation with a current E&P deficit, but a positive accumulated E&P balance, makes a distribution in the current year, the timing of the distribution will be critical in determining whether the distribution should be treated as a dividend or as a return of capital.

EXAMPLE C:4-52 ▶ Major Corporation has a $30,000 accumulated E&P balance at the beginning of the year and incurs a $50,000 deficit during the year. Because of its poor operating performance, Major pays to its sole shareholder only two of its four $5,000 quarterly dividends, the two being those ordinarily paid on March 31 and June 30. The tax treatment of the two distributions is determined as follows:

---

[54] *Joseph R. Holsey v. CIR*, 2 AFTR 2d 5660, 58-2 USTC ¶9816 (3rd Cir., 1958).

E&P balance, January 1	$30,000
Minus: Reduction for first quarter loss	(12,500)
Reduction for March 31 distribution	(5,000)
E&P balance, April 1	$12,500
Minus: Reduction for second quarter loss	(12,500)
E&P balance, June 30	$ –0–

The first and second quarter losses each are $12,500 [($50,000) × 0.25 = ($12,500)].

The operating loss reduces the accumulated E&P balance evenly throughout the year. All of the March 31 distribution is taxable because the corporation did not incur sufficient losses to offset the positive accumulated E&P balance at the beginning of the year. The second quarter loss results in a return of capital for the June 30 distribution and any other distributions before year-end (assuming that the shareholder's basis in his or her stock exceeds the distribution amount). Delaying all the distributions until late in the year could result in the tax-free return of capital. ◄

The timing of a distribution also can be critical if the distributing corporation has an accumulated E&P deficit and a positive current E&P balance.

EXAMPLE C:4-53 ▶ At the beginning of Year 1, Yankee Corporation has an accumulated E&P deficit of $250,000. During Year 1 and Year 2, Yankee reports the following current E&P balances and makes the following distributions to Joe, its sole shareholder:

Year	Current E&P	Distributions	Distribution Date
1	$100,000	$75,000	December 31
2	–0–	–0–	None

The $75,000 distribution in Year 1 is taxable as a dividend. The $25,000 of current E&P that is not distributed reduces Yankee's accumulated E&P deficit to $225,000. Had Yankee delayed distributing the $75,000 until sometime in Year 2, the distribution would have been treated as a nontaxable return of Joe's capital. ◄

COMPLIANCE AND PROCEDURAL CONSIDERATIONS

CORPORATE REPORTING OF NONDIVIDEND DISTRIBUTIONS

A corporation that makes a nondividend distribution to its shareholders must file with its income tax return Form 5452 (Corporate Report of Nondividend Distributions), along with supporting computations. Form 5452 reports the distributing corporation's E&P so as to enable the IRS to verify the tax treatment of the distribution. Form 5452 requires the following information: current and accumulated E&P, distribution amounts paid to shareholders during the tax year, the percentage of each payment that is taxable and non-taxable, and a detailed computation of E&P from the date of incorporation.

AGREEMENT TO TERMINATE INTEREST UNDER SEC. 302(b)(3)

As mentioned earlier, if a redemption completely terminates a shareholder's interest in a corporation, the family attribution rules of Sec. 318(a)(1) may be waived. To have the rules waived, the shareholder must agree in writing that he or she will notify the IRS upon acquiring any prohibited interest within the ten-year period following the redemption. A copy of this agreement (in the form of a signed statement in duplicate) must be attached to the first return filed by the shareholder for the tax year in which the redemption occurs. If the agreement cannot be filed on time, the IRS may grant an extension. Regulation Sec. 1.302-4(a) provides that an extension will be granted only if reasonable cause exists for failure to timely file the agreement and if the request for such an extension is filed within such time as the appropriate IRS official considers reasonable in the circumstances.

Treasury Regulations do not indicate what constitutes reasonable cause for failure to file or what constitutes a reasonable extension of time. In *Edward J. Fehrs* the U.S. Court of Claims held that late filing of a ten-year agreement was permissible where a taxpayer could not reasonably have expected that a filing would be necessary, where the taxpayer filed the agreement promptly after receiving notice that it was required, and where the agreement was filed before the issues in question were presented for trial.[55] However, in *Robin Haft Trust,* an agreement was filed *after* an adverse court ruling. In an appeal for a rehearing, the judge ruled that the filing of the agreement after the case was brought to trial was too late. Consequently, the judge denied the appeal for a rehearing.[56]

If the shareholder acquires a prohibited interest within the ten-year period following the redemption, the IRS may assess additional taxes. Such an acquisition ordinarily results in recasting the redemption as a dividend rather than a sale. The limitations period for assessing additional taxes extends to one year after the date the shareholder files with the IRS notice of acquiring the prohibited interest.[57]

PROBLEM MATERIALS

DISCUSSION QUESTIONS

C:4-1   Explain how a corporation computes its current and accumulated E&P balances.

C:4-2   Why is it necessary to distinguish between current and accumulated E&P?

C:4-3   Describe the effect of a $100,000 cash distribution paid on January 1 to the sole shareholder of a calendar year corporation whose stock basis is $25,000 when the corporation has
a. $100,000 of current E&P and $100,000 of accumulated E&P
b. A $50,000 accumulated E&P deficit and a $60,000 current E&P balance
c. A $60,000 accumulated E&P deficit and a $60,000 current E&P deficit
d. An $80,000 current E&P deficit and a $100,000 accumulated E&P balance
Answer Parts a through d again, assuming instead that the corporation makes the distribution on October 1 in a nonleap year.

C:4-4   Pecan Corporation distributes land to a noncorporate shareholder. Explain how the following items are determined:
a. The amount of the distribution
b. The amount of the dividend
c. The shareholder's basis in the land
d. When the holding period for the land begins. How would your answers change if the distribution were made to a corporate shareholder?

C:4-5   What effect do the following transactions have on the calculation of Young Corporation's current E&P? Assume that the starting point for the calculation is Young's taxable income for the current year.
a. The corporation earns tax-exempt interest income of $10,000.
b. Taxable income includes a $10,000 dividend and is reduced by a $7,000 dividends-received deduction.
c. A $5,000 capital loss carryover from the preceding tax year offsets $5,000 of capital gains.
d. The corporation accrued federal income taxes of $25,280.
e. The corporation took a U.S. production activities deduction of $3,000.

C:4-6   Badger Corporation was incorporated in the current year. It reports an $8,000 NOL on its initial tax return. Badger distributed $2,500 to its shareholders. Is it possible for this distribution to be taxed as a dividend to Badger's shareholders? Explain.

C:4-7   Does the timing of a distribution matter as to whether it is taxed as a dividend or treated as a return of capital? Explain.

C:4-8   Hickory Corporation owns a building with a $160,000 adjusted basis and a $120,000 FMV. Hickory's E&P is $200,000. Should the

[55] *Edward J. Fehrs v. U.S.,* 40 AFTR 2d 77-5040, 77-1 USTC ¶9423 (Ct. Cl., 1977).

[56] *Robin Haft Trust,* 62 T.C. 145 (1974).
[57] Sec. 302(c)(2)(A).

corporation sell the property and distribute the sale proceeds to its shareholders or distribute the property to its shareholders and let them sell the property? Why?

C:4-9 Walnut Corporation owns a building with a $120,000 adjusted basis and a $160,000 FMV. Walnut's E&P is $200,000. Should the corporation sell the property and distribute the sale proceeds to its shareholders or distribute the property to its shareholders and let them sell the property? Why?

C:4-10 What is a constructive dividend? Under what circumstances is the IRS likely to argue that a constructive dividend has been paid?

C:4-11 Why are stock dividends generally nontaxable? Under what circumstances are stock dividends taxable?

C:4-12 For tax purposes, how is a distribution of stock rights treated by a shareholder? By the distributing corporation?

C:4-13 What is a stock redemption? What are some reasons for redeeming stock? Why are some redemptions treated as sales and others as dividends?

C:4-14 Field Corporation redeems 100 shares of its stock from Andrew for $10,000. Andrew's basis in those shares is $8,000. Explain possible alternative tax treatments of Andrew's receiving the $10,000.

C:4-15 What conditions must be met for a redemption to be treated as a sale by the redeeming shareholder?

C:4-16 Explain the purpose of the attribution rules in determining stock ownership in a redemption. Describe the four types of attribution rules that apply to redemptions.

C:4-17 Abel, the sole shareholder of Ace Corporation, has an opporunity to purchase the assets of a sole proprietorship for $50,000 in cash. Ace has a substantial E&P balance. Abel does not have sufficient cash to personally make the purchase. If Abel obtains the needed $50,000 from Ace via a nonliquidating distribution, Abel will have to recognize dividend income. Alternatively, would Ace's purchase of the assets of the sole proprietorship followed by their distribution to Abel in redemption of part of his stock holdings constitute a partial liquidation? Explain.

C:4-18 Why does a redemption that qualifies for sale treatment under Sec. 303 usually result in the shareholder's recognizing little or no gain or loss?

C:4-19 Under what circumstances does a corporation recognize gain or loss when it distributes noncash property in redemption of its stock? What effect does a redemption distribution have on the distributing corporation's E&P?

C:4-20 What is a preferred stock bailout? How does Sec. 306 operate to prevent a shareholder from realizing the otherwise available tax benefits of a preferred stock bailout?

C:4-21 Bill owns all 100 of the outstanding shares of Plum Corporation stock and 80 of the 100 outstanding shares of Cherry Corporation stock. He sells 20 Plum shares to Cherry for $80,000. Explain why this transaction is treated as a stock redemption, and determine the tax consequences of the transaction.

C:4-22 Explain the tax consequences, to both the corporation and a shareholder-employee, of an IRS determination that a portion of the compensation paid in a prior tax year is unreasonable. What steps can the corporation and shareholder-employee take to avoid the double taxation usually associated with such a determination?

C:4-23 What is a bootstrap acquisition? What are the tax consequences of such a transaction?

ISSUE IDENTIFICATION QUESTIONS

C:4-24 Marsha receives a $10,000 cash distribution from Dye Corporation in April of the current year. Dye has $4,000 of accumulated E&P at the beginning of the year and $8,000 of current E&P. Dye also distributed $10,000 in cash to Barbara, who purchased all 200 shares of Dye stock from Marsha in June of the current year. What tax issues should be considered with respect to the distributions made to Marsha and Barbara?

C:4-25 Neil purchased land from Spring Harbor, his 100%-owned corporation, for $275,000. The corporation purchased the land three years ago for $300,000. Similar tracts of land located nearby have sold for $400,000 in recent months. What tax issues should be considered with respect to the corporation's sale of the land?

C:4-26 Price Corporation has 100 shares of common stock outstanding. Price repurchased all of Penny's 30 shares for $35,000 cash during the current year. Three years ago, Penny received the shares as a gift from her mother. Her basis in the shares is $16,000. Price has $100,000 of current and accumulated E&P. Penny's mother owns 40 of the remaining shares; unrelated individuals own the other 30 shares. What tax issues should be considered with respect to the corporation's purchase of Penny's shares?

C:4-27 George owns all 100 shares of Gumby's Pizza Corporation. The shares are worth $200,000, but George's basis is only $70,000. Mary and George have reached a tentative agreement under which George will sell all his shares to Mary. However, Mary is unwilling to pay more than $150,000 for the stock because the corporation currently has excess cash balances. They have agreed that George can withdraw $50,000 in cash from Gumby's before the stock sale. What tax issues should be considered with respect to George and Mary's agreement?

PROBLEMS

C:4-28   *Current E&P Calculation.* Beach Corporation, an accrual basis taxpayer, reports the following results for the current year:

Income:	
Gross profit from manufacturing operations	$250,000
Dividends received from 25%-owned domestic corporation	20,000
Interest income: Corporate bonds	10,000
Municipal bonds	12,000
Proceeds from life insurance policy on key employee	100,000
Section 1231 gain on sale of land	8,000
Expenses:	
Administrative expenses	110,000
Bad debts	5,000
Depreciation:	
Financial accounting	68,000
Taxable income	86,000
Alternative depreciation system (for E&P)	42,000
NOL carryover	40,000
Charitable contributions: Current year	8,000
Carryover from last year	3,500
Capital loss on sale of stock	1,200
U.S. production activities deduction	1,500
Penalty on late payment of federal taxes	450

a. What is Beach's taxable income?
b. What is Beach's current E&P?

C:4-29   *Current E&P Computation.* Water Corporation reports $500,000 of taxable income for the current year. The following additional information is available:

- For the current year, Water reports an $80,000 long-term capital loss and no capital gains.

- Taxable income includes $80,000 of dividends from a 10%-owned domestic corporation.

- Water paid fines and penalties of $6,000 that were not deducted in computing taxable income.

- In computing this year's taxable income, Water deducted a $20,000 NOL carryover from a prior tax year.

- Water claimed a $10,000 U.S. production activities deduction.

- Taxable income includes a deduction for $40,000 of depreciation that exceeds the depreciation allowed for E&P purposes.

Assume a 34% corporate tax rate. What is Water's current E&P for this year?

C:4-30   *Calculating Accumulated E&P.* Investors formed Peach Corporation in Year 1. Its current E&P (or current E&P deficit) and distributions for Years 1 through 4 are as follows:

Year	Current E&P (Deficit)	Distributions
1	$ (8,000)	$ 2,000
2	(12,000)	–0–
3	10,000	5,000
4	14,000	17,000

What is Peach's accumulated E&P at the beginning of Years 1 through 4?

C:4-31   *Consequences of a Single Cash Distribution.* Clover Corporation is a calendar year taxpayer. Connie owns all of its stock. Her basis for the stock is $10,000. On April 1 of the current (non-leap) year Clover distributes $52,000 to Connie. Determine the tax consequences of the cash distribution in each of the following independent situations:
a. Current E&P of $15,000; accumulated E&P of $25,000.

b. Current E&P of $30,000; accumulated E&P of ($20,000).

c. Current E&P of ($73,000); accumulated E&P of $50,000.

d. Current E&P of ($20,000); accumulated E&P of ($15,000).

C:4-32 ***Consequences of a Single Cash Distribution.*** Pink Corporation is a calendar year taxpayer. Pete owns one-third of Pink stock (100 shares). His basis in the stock is $25,000. Cheryl owns two-thirds of Pink stock (200 shares). Her basis in the stock is $40,000. On June 10 of the current year, Pink distributes $40,000 to Pete and $80,000 to Cheryl. Determine the tax consequences of the cash distributions to Pete and Cheryl in each of the following independent situations:

a. Current E&P of $60,000; accumulated E&P of $100,000.

b. Current E&P of $36,000; accumulated E&P of $30,000.

C:4-33 ***Consequences of Multiple Cash Distributions.*** At the beginning of the current (non-leap) year, Charles owns all of Pearl Corporation's outstanding stock. His basis in the stock is $80,000. On July 1, he sells all his stock to Donald for $125,000. During the year, Pearl, a calendar year taxpayer, makes two cash distributions: $60,000 on March 1 to Charles and $90,000 on September 1 to Donald. How are these distributions treated in the following independent situations? What are the amount and character of Charles' gain on his sale of stock to Donald? What is Donald's basis in his Pearl stock at the end of the year?

a. Current E&P of $40,000; accumulated E&P of $30,000.

b. Current E&P of $100,000; accumulated E&P (deficit) of ($50,000).

c. Current E&P (deficit) of ($36,500); accumulated E&P of $120,000.

C:4-34 ***Distribution of Appreciated Property.*** In the current year, Sedgwick Corporation has $100,000 of current and accumulated E&P. On March 3, Sedgwick distributes to its shareholder Dina a parcel of land (a capital asset) having a $56,000 FMV. The land has a $40,000 adjusted basis (for both taxable income and E&P purposes) to Sedgwick and is subject to an $8,000 mortgage, which Dina assumes. Assume a 34% marginal corporate tax rate.

a. What are the amount and character of the income Dina recognizes as a result of the distribution?

b. What is Dina's basis in the land?

c. What are the amount and character of Sedgwick's gain or loss as a result of the distribution?

d. What effect does the distribution have on Sedgwick's E&P?

C:4-35 ***Distribution of Property Subject to a Liability.*** On May 10 of the current year, Stowe Corporation distributes to its shareholder Arlene $20,000 in cash and land (a capital asset) having a $50,000 FMV. The land has a $15,000 adjusted basis (for both taxable income and E&P purposes) and is subject to a $60,000 mortgage, which Arlene assumes. Stowe has an E&P balance exceeding the amount distributed and is subject to a 34% marginal corporate tax rate.

a. What are the amount and character of the income Arlene recognizes as a result of the distribution?

b. What is Arlene's basis in the land?

c. What are the amount and character of Stowe's gain or loss as a result of the distribution?

C:4-36 ***Distribution of Depreciable Property.*** On May 15 of the current year, Quick Corporation distributes to its shareholder Calvin a building having a $250,000 FMV and used in Quick's business. The building originally cost $180,000. Quick claimed $30,000 of straight-line depreciation, so that the adjusted basis of the building on the date of distribution for taxable income purposes is $150,000. The adjusted basis of the building for E&P purposes is $160,000. The building is subject to an $80,000 mortgage, which Calvin assumes. Quick has an E&P balance exceeding the amount distributed and is subject to a 34% marginal tax rate.

a. What are the amount and character of the income Calvin recognizes as a result of the distribution?

b. What is Calvin's basis in the building?

c. What are the amount and character of Quick's gain or loss as a result of the distribution?

d. What effect does the distribution have on Quick's E&P?

C:4-37 ***Distribution of Various Types of Property.*** During the current year, Zeta Corporation distributes the assets listed below to its sole shareholder, Susan. For each asset listed, determine the gross income recognized by Susan, her basis in the asset, the amount of gain or loss recognized by Zeta, and the effect of the distribution on Zeta's E&P. Assume that Zeta has an E&P balance exceeding the amount distributed and is subject to a 34% marginal tax rate. Unless stated otherwise, adjusted bases for taxable income and E&P purposes are the same.

a. A parcel of land used in Zeta's business that has a $200,000 FMV and a $125,000 adjusted basis.

b. Assume the same facts as in Part a except that the land is subject to a $140,000 mortgage.

c. FIFO inventory having a $25,000 FMV and an $18,000 adjusted basis.

d. A building used in Zeta's business having an original cost of $225,000, a $450,000 FMV, and a $150,000 adjusted basis for taxable income purposes. Zeta has claimed $75,000 of depreciation for taxable income purposes under the straight-line method. Depreciation for E&P purposes is $60,000.

e. An automobile used in Zeta's business having an original cost of $12,000, an $8,000 FMV, and a $5,760 adjusted basis, on which Zeta has claimed $6,240 of MACRS depreciation for taxable income purposes. For E&P purposes, depreciation was $5,200.

f. Installment obligations having a $35,000 face amount (and FMV) and a $24,500 adjusted basis. The obligations were created when Zeta sold a Sec. 1231 asset.

C:4-38 *Disguised Dividends.* King Corporation is a profitable manufacturing concern with $800,000 of E&P. It is owned in equal shares by Harry and Wilma, husband and wife. Both individuals are actively involved in the business. Determine the tax consequences of the following independent events:

a. In reviewing a prior year tax return for King, the IRS determines that the $500,000 of salary and bonuses paid to Wilma is unreasonable and that reasonable compensation is $280,000.

b. King loaned Harry $400,000 over the past three years. None of the money has been repaid. Harry does not pay interest on the loans.

c. King sells a building to Wilma for $150,000 in cash. The property has an adjusted basis of $90,000 and is subject to a $60,000 mortgage, which Wilma assumes. The FMV of the building is $350,000.

d. Harry leases a warehouse to King for $50,000 per year. According to an IRS auditor, similar warehouses can be leased for $35,000 per year.

e. Wilma sells to King for $250,000 land on which King intends to build a factory. According to a recent appraisal, the FMV of the land is $185,000.

f. The corporation owns an airplane that it uses to fly executives to business meetings. When the airplane is not being used for business, Harry and Wilma use it to travel to their ranch in Idaho for short vacations. The approximate cost of their trips to the ranch in the current year is $8,000.

C:4-39 *Unreasonable Compensation.* Forward Corporation is owned by a group of 15 shareholders. During the current year, Forward pays $550,000 in salary and bonuses to Alvin, its president and controlling shareholder. The corporation's marginal tax rate is 34%, and Alvin's marginal tax rate is 35%. The IRS audits Forward's tax return and determines that reasonable compensation for Alvin is $350,000. Forward agrees to the adjustment. What effect does the disallowance of part of the salary and bonus deduction have on Forward's and Alvin's respective tax positions? Ignore payroll taxes, such as FICA.

C:4-40 *Stock Dividend Distribution.* Wilton Corporation has a single class of common stock outstanding. Robert owns 100 shares, which he purchased in 2005 for $100,000. In 2011, when the stock is worth $1,200 per share, Wilton declares a 10% dividend payable in common stock. On December 10, 2011, Robert receives ten additional shares. On January 30, 2012, he sells five of the ten shares for $7,000.

a. How much income must Robert recognize when he receives the stock dividend?

b. How much gain or loss must Robert recognize when he sells the common stock?

c. What is Robert's basis in his remaining common shares? When does his holding period in the new common shares begin?

C:4-41 *Stock Dividend Distribution.* Moss Corporation has a single class of common stock outstanding. Tillie owns 1,000 shares, which she purchased in 2007 for $100,000. Moss declares a stock dividend payable in 8% preferred stock having a $100 par value. Each shareholder receives one share of preferred stock for ten shares of common stock. On the distribution date—December 10, 2011—the common stock was worth $180 per share, and the preferred stock was worth $100 per share. On April 1, 2011, Tillie sells half of her preferred stock for $5,000.

a. How much income must Tillie recognize when she receives the stock dividend?

b. How much gain or loss must Tillie recognize when she sells the preferred stock? (Ignore the implications of Sec. 306.)

c. What is Tillie's basis in her remaining common and preferred shares after the sale? When does her holding period for the preferred shares begin?

C:4-42 *Stock Rights Distribution.* Trusty Corporation has a single class of common stock outstanding. Jim owns 200 shares, which he purchased for $50 per share two years ago. On April 10 of the current year, Trusty distributes to its common shareholders one right to purchase for $60 one common share for each common share owned. At the time of the distribution, each common share is worth $75, and each right is worth $15. On September 10, Jim sells 100 rights for $2,000 and exercises the remaining 100 rights. On November 10, he sells for $80 each 60 of the shares acquired through exercise of the rights.

a. What are the amount and character of income Jim recognizes upon receiving the rights?

b. What are the amount and character of gain or loss Jim recognizes upon selling the rights?

c. What are the amount and character of gain or loss Jim recognizes upon exercising the rights?

d. What are the amount and character of gain or loss Jim recognizes upon selling the newly acquired common shares?

e. What basis does Jim have in his remaining shares?

C:4-43 *Attribution Rules.* George owns 100 of the 1,000 outstanding shares of Polar Corporation common stock. Under the Sec. 318 family attribution rules, to which of the following individuals will ownership of George's stock be attributed? In other words, who is deemed to constructively own George's stock?

a. George's wife

b. George's father

c. George's brother

d. George's mother-in-law

e. George's daughter

f. George's son-in law

g. George's grandfather

h. George's grandson

i. George's mother's brother (his uncle)

C:4-44 *Attribution Rules.* Moose Corporation's 400 shares of outstanding stock are owned as follows:

Name	Shares
Lara (an individual)	60
LMN Partnership (Lara is a 20% partner)	50
LST Partnership (Lara is a 70% partner)	100
Lemon Corporation (Lara is a 30% shareholder)	100
Lime Corporation (Lara is a 60% shareholder)	90
Total	400

How many shares is Lara deemed to own under the Sec. 318 attribution rules?

C:4-45 *Redemption from a Sole Shareholder.* Paul owns all 100 shares of Presto Corporation stock. His basis in the stock is $10,000. Presto has $100,000 of E&P. Presto redeems 25 of Paul's shares for $30,000. What are the tax consequences of the redemption to Paul and to Presto?

C:4-46 *Multiple Redemptions.* Four unrelated shareholders own Benton Corporation's 400 shares of outstanding stock. Benton redeems 100 shares for $500 per share from the shareholders as shown below. Each shareholder has a $230 per share basis in his or her stock. Benton's current and accumulated E&P at the end of the tax year is $150,000.

Shareholder	Shares Held Before the Redemption	Shares Redeemed
Ethel	200	40
Fran	100	30
Georgia	50	30
Henry	50	–0–
Total	400	100

a. What are the tax consequences (e.g., basis of remaining shares and amount and character of recognized income, gain, or loss) of the redemptions to Ethel, Fran, and Georgia?

b. How would your answer to Part a change if Ethel is Georgia's mother?

C:4-47 *Partial Liquidation.* Unrelated individuals Amy, Beth, and Carla, and Delta Corporation each own 25 of the 100 outstanding shares of Axle Corporation stock. Axle distributes $20,000 cash to each shareholder in exchange for five Axle shares in a transaction that qualifies as a partial liquidation. Each share redeemed has a $1,000 basis to the shareholder and a $4,000 FMV. How does each shareholder treat the distribution for tax purposes?

C:4-48 *Redemption to Pay Death Taxes.* John died on March 3. His gross estate of $2.5 million includes First Corporation stock (400 of the 1,000 outstanding shares) worth $1.5 million. John's wife, Myra, owns the remaining 600 shares. Deductible funeral and administrative expenses amount to $250,000. John, Jr. is the sole beneficiary of John's estate. Estate taxes amount to $350,000.

a. Does a redemption of First stock from John's estate, John, Jr., or John's wife qualify for sale treatment under Sec. 303?

b. On September 10, First Corporation redeems 200 shares of its stock from John's estate for $800,000. How does the estate treat this redemption for tax purposes?

C:4-49 *Effect of Redemption on E&P.* White Corporation has 100 shares of stock outstanding. Ann owns 40 of these shares, and unrelated shareholders own the remaining 60 shares. White redeems 30 of Ann's shares for $30,000. In the year of the redemption, White has $30,000 of paid-in capital and $80,000 of E&P.

a. How does the redemption affect White's E&P balance if the redemption qualifies for sale treatment?

b. How does the redemption affect White's E&P balance if the redemption does *not* qualify for sale treatment?

C:4-50 *Various Redemption Issues.* Alan, Barbara, and Dave are unrelated. Each has owned 100 shares of Time Corporation stock for five years and each has a $60,000 basis in those shares. Time's E&P is $240,000. Time redeems all 100 of Alan's shares for their $100,000 FMV.

a. What are the amount and character of Alan's recognized gain or loss? What basis do Barbara and Dave take in their remaining shares? What effect does the redemption have on Time's E&P?

b. If Alan is Barbara's son, how would your answers to the questions in Part a change?

c. Assume the same facts as in Part b except Alan agrees with the IRS to waive the family attribution rules. Based on this assumption, how would your answers to the questions in Part a again change?

C:4-51 *Various Redemption Issues.* Andrew, Bea, Carl, and Carl, Jr. (Carl's son), and Tetra Corporation own all of the single class of Excel Corporation stock as follows:

Shareholder	Shares Held	Adjusted Basis
Andrew	20	$3,000
Bea	30	6,000
Carl	25	4,000
Carl, Jr.	15	3,000
Tetra Corporation	10	2,000
Total	100	

Andrew, Bea, and Carl are unrelated. Bea owns 75% of the Tetra stock, and Andrew owns the remaining 25%. Excel's E&P is $100,000. Determine the tax consequences of the following independent transactions to the shareholders and Excel:

a. Excel redeems 25 of Bea's shares for $30,000.

b. Excel redeems 10 of Bea's shares for $12,000.

c. Excel redeems all of Carl's shares for $30,000.

d. Assume the same facts as in Part c except the stock is redeemed from Carl's estate to pay death taxes, and the entire redemption qualifies for sale treatment under Sec. 303. The stock has a $28,000 FMV on the date of Carl's death. The alternative valuation date is not elected.

e. Excel redeems all of Andrew's shares for Excel land having a $6,000 basis for both taxable income and E&P purposes and a $24,000 FMV. Assume a 34% marginal corporate tax rate.

f. Assume that Carl owns 25 shares of Excel stock and that Carl, Jr. owns the remaining 75 shares. Determine the tax consequences to Carl and Excel if Excel redeems all 25 of Carl's shares for $30,000.

C:4-52 *Comparison of Dividends and Redemptions.* Bailey is one of four equal unrelated shareholders of Checker Corporation. Bailey has held Checker stock for four years and has a basis in her stock of $40,000. Checker has $280,000 of current and accumulated E&P and distributes $100,000 to Bailey.
a. What are the tax consequences to Checker and to Bailey if Bailey is an individual and the distribution is treated as a dividend?
b. In Part a, what would be the tax consequences if Bailey were a corporation?
c. What are the tax consequences to Checker and to Bailey (an individual) if Bailey surrenders all her stock in a redemption qualifying for sale treatment?
d. In Part c, what would be the tax consequences if Bailey were a corporation?
e. Which treatment would Bailey prefer if Bailey were an individual? Which treatment would Bailey Corporation prefer?

C:4-53 *Preferred Stock Bailout.* Does Sec. 306 apply in each of the following independent situations? If so, what is its effect?
a. Beth sells her Sec. 306 stock to Marvin in a year in which the issuing corporation has no E&P.
b. Zero Corporation redeems Sec. 306 stock from Jim in a year in which it has no E&P.
c. Zero Corporation redeems Sec. 306 stock from Ruth in a year in which it has a large E&P balance.
d. Joan gives 100 shares of her Sec. 306 stock to her nephew, Barry.
e. Ed completely terminates his interest in Zero Corporation by having Zero redeem all his common shares and Sec. 306 preferred stock.
f. Carl inherits 100 shares of Sec. 306 stock from his uncle Ted.

C:4-54 *Preferred Stock Bailout.* Fran owns all 100 shares of Star Corporation stock. Her stock basis is $60,000. On December 1 of the current year, Star distributes 50 shares of preferred stock to Fran in a nontaxable dividend. In the year of the distribution, Star's total E&P is $100,000, the preferred shares are worth $150,000, and the common shares are worth $300,000.
a. What are the tax consequences to Fran and to Star if Fran sells her preferred stock to Ken for $200,000 on January 10 of the following year? In that year, Star's current E&P is $75,000 (in addition to the $100,000 from the prior year)?
b. How would your answer to Part a change if Fran sells her preferred stock to Ken for $110,000 instead of $200,000?
c. How would your answer to Part a change if Star redeems Fran's preferred stock for $200,000 on January 10 of the following year?

C:4-55 *Brother-Sister Redemptions.* Bob owns 60 of the 100 outstanding shares of Dazzle Corporation stock and 80 of the 100 outstanding shares of Razzle Corporation stock. Bob's basis in his Dazzle shares is $12,000, and his basis in his Razzle shares is $8,000. Bob sells 30 of his Dazzle shares to Razzle for $50,000. At the end of the year of sale, Dazzle and Razzle have E&P of $25,000 and $40,000, respectively.
a. What are the amount and character of Bob's recognized gain or loss on the sale?
b. What is Bob's basis in his remaining shares of the Dazzle and Razzle stock?
c. How does the sale affect the E&P of Dazzle and Razzle?
d. What basis does Razzle take in the Dazzle shares it purchases?
e. How would your answer to Part a change if Bob owns only 50 of the 100 outstanding shares of Razzle stock?

C:4-56 *Parent-Subsidiary Redemptions.* Jane owns 150 of the 200 outstanding shares of Parent Corporation stock. Parent owns 160 of the 200 outstanding shares of Subsidiary Corporation stock. Jane sells 50 shares of her Parent stock to Subsidiary for $40,000. Jane's basis in her Parent shares is $15,000 ($100 per share). At the end of the year of sale, Subsidiary and Parent have E&P of $60,000 and $25,000, respectively.
a. What are the amount and character of Jane's recognized gain or loss on the sale?
b. What is Jane's basis in her remaining shares of Parent stock?
c. How does the sale affect the E&P of Parent and Subsidiary?
d. What basis does Subsidiary take in the Parent shares it purchases?
e. How would your answer to Part a change if Jane instead sells 100 of her Parent shares to Subsidiary for $80,000?

C:4-57   *Bootstrap Acquisition.* Jana owns all 100 shares of Stone Corporation stock having a $1 million FMV. Her basis in the stock is $400,000. Stone's E&P balance is $600,000. Michael would like to purchase the stock but wants only the corporation's non-cash assets valued at $750,000. Michael is willing to pay $750,000 for these assets.

a. What are the tax consequences to Jana, Michael, and Stone if Michael purchases 75 shares of Stone stock for $750,000 and Stone redeems Jana's remaining 25 shares for $250,000 cash?

b. How would your answer to Part a change (if at all) if Stone first redeems 25 shares of Jana's stock for $250,000 and then Michael purchases the remaining 75 shares from Jana for $750,000?

COMPREHENSIVE PROBLEM

C:4-58   Several years ago, Brian formed Sigma Corporation, a retail company ineligible for the U.S. production activities deduction. Sigma uses the accrual method of accounting. In 2011, the corporation reported the following items:

Gross profit	$290,000
Long-term capital gain	20,000
Tax-exempt interest received	7,000
Salary paid to Brian	80,000
Payroll tax on Brian's salary (Sigma's share)	6,000
Depreciation	25,000 ($21,000 for E&P purposes)
Other operating expenses	89,000
Dividend distribution to Brian	60,000

In addition to owning 100% of Sigma's stock, Brian manages Sigma's business and earns the $80,000 salary listed above. This salary is an ordinary and necessary business expense of the corporation and is reasonable in amount. The payroll tax on Brian's $80,000 salary is $12,000, $6,000 of which Sigma pays and deducts, and the other $6,000 of which Brian pays through Social Security (FICA) withholding. Brian is single with no dependents and claims the standard deduction.

a. Compute Sigma's and Brian's 2011 taxable income and total tax liability, as well as their combined tax liability. Also, calculate the corporation's current E&P after the dividend distribution.

b. Assume instead that Brian operates Sigma as a sole proprietorship. In the current year, the business reports the same operating results as above, and Brian withdraws $140,000 in lieu of the salary and dividend. Assume Brian's self-employment tax is $17,000. Compute Brian's total tax liability for 2011.

c. Assume a C corporation such as in Part a distributes all of its after-tax earnings. Compare the tax treatment of long-term capital gains, tax-exempt interest, and operating profits if earned by a C corporation with the tax treatment of these items if earned by a sole proprietorship.

TAX STRATEGY PROBLEM

C:4-59   John owns all 100 shares of stock in Jamaica Corporation, which has $100,000 of current E&P. John would like to receive a $50,000 distribution from the corporation. Jamaica owns the following assets that it could distribute to John. What are the tax consequences of Jamaica's distributing each of the following assets? Assume Jamaica has a 34% marginal tax rate and, unless stated otherwise, its bases for E&P and taxable income purposes are the same.

a. $50,000 cash.

b. 100 shares of XYZ stock purchased two years ago for $10,000 and now worth $50,000.

c. 100 shares of ABC stock purchased one year ago for $72,000 and now worth $50,000.

d. Equipment purchased four years ago for $120,000 that now has a tax adjusted basis of $22,000 and an E&P adjusted basis of $40,000. John would assume a liability of $31,000 on the equipment. The equipment is now worth $81,000.

e. An installment obligation with a face value of $50,000 and a basis of $32,000. Jamaica acquired this obligation three years ago when it sold land held as an investment.

f. Would your answers in Parts a–e change if Jamaica redeems 50 of John's shares for each of the properties listed?

g. Based on the foregoing results, which distribution would you recommend? Which distribution(s) should be avoided?

h. Would your answers in Parts a–e change if John's 100 shares represented one third of Jamaica's outstanding shares, unrelated parties owned the remaining 200 shares, and Jamaica exchanged all of John's shares for each of the properties listed?

i. If John were an investor, would treating the distribution as a sale be preferable to treating the distribution as a dividend? Why or why not?

CASE STUDY PROBLEMS

C:4-60 Amy, Beth, and Meg each own 100 of the 300 outstanding shares of Theta Corporation stock. Amy wants to sell her shares, which have a $40,000 basis and a $100,000 FMV. Either Beth and/or Meg can purchase Amy's shares (50 shares each) or Theta can redeem all of them. Theta has a $150,000 E&P balance.

Required: Write a memorandum comparing the tax consequences of the two options to the three sisters, who actively manage Theta.

C:4-61 Maria Garcia is a CPA whose firm has for many years prepared the tax returns of Stanley Corporation. A review of Stanley's last three tax returns by a new staff accountant, who has been assigned to the client for the first time, reveals that the corporation may be paying to one of its key officers excessive compensation that the IRS might deem to be a constructive dividend. The staff accountant feels that the firm should inform the IRS and/or report the excess amount as a nondeductible dividend. Although the facts are ambiguous, they tend to support the contention that the compensation paid in current and prior years is reasonable.

Required: In a client letter, discuss Maria's role as an advocate for Stanley, and discuss the possible tax consequences resulting from a subsequent audit.

TAX RESEARCH PROBLEMS

C:4-62 Fifteen years ago, husband and wife Stuart and Marsha Widell organized Widell Engineering Associates (WEA), a Delaware corporation that builds, repairs, and manages waste treatment plants throughout the Southwest. The Widells capitalized WEA with cash of $500,000 and industrial equipment having an adjusted basis of $4.5 million, each in exchange for 2,500 shares of WEA common stock. Three years later, Stuart and Marsha each gifted 500 shares of their WEA stock to their son Weymouth.

As a result of a sharp upswing in the economy, WEA's profits swelled under the joint management of Stuart and Weymouth. After ten years of joint control, however, and because of irreconcilable differences with his father, Weymouth decided to leave WEA and organize his own engineering firm, Fortunelle.

To keep WEA's business in the family and to give Stuart complete WEA management control, Stuart, Marsha, and Weymouth agreed that WEA would redeem all of Weymouth's 1,000 shares with waste treatment property worth $8.5 million. To ensure capital gains treatment, Weymouth obtained a waiver of the family attribution rules in return for an agreement with the IRS not to acquire an equity interest in WEA for ten years and to notify the IRS if he does so. Following the redemption, Weymouth transferred the property to Fortunelle in exchange for all 8,500 shares of Fortunelle common stock.

Last year, Stuart suffered a heart attack. He now has proceeded to reconcile his differences with Weymouth. To retain Widell family control of WEA's business, Stuart, Marsha, and Weymouth propose that WEA and Fortunelle conclude an "arms length" agreement under which Fortunelle would manage WEA's waste treatment plants in return annually for 20% of WEA's gross rental revenues, but no equity interest. The Widells are convinced that the proposed arrangement does not violate either the Sec. 302 waiver rules or Weymouth's agreement with the IRS. They have asked you to draft a letter that confirms this understanding. In researching the issue, consult at a minimum the following authorities:

- IRC Sec. 302(c)(2)
- Rev. Rul. 70-104, 1970 C.B. 66
- *Chertkof v. Commissioner*, 48 AFTR 2d 81-5194, 81-1 USTC ¶9462 (4th Cir, 1981)

C:4-63 When the IRS audited Winter Corporation's current year tax return, the IRS disallowed $10,000 of travel and entertainment expenses incurred by Charles, an officer-shareholder, because of inadequate documentation. The IRS asserted that the $10,000 expenditure was a constructive dividend to Charles, who maintained that the expense was business related. Charles argued that he derived no personal benefit from the expenditure and therefore received no constructive dividend. Prepare a memorandum for your tax manager explaining whether the IRS's assertion or Charles's assertion is correct. Your manager has suggested that, at a minimum, you consult the following resources:

- IRC Secs. 162 and 274
- Reg. Secs. 1.274-1 and -2

C:4-64 Scott and Lynn Brown each own 50% of Benson Corporation stock. During the current year, Benson made the following distributions to the shareholders:

Shareholder	Property Distributed	Adjusted Basis to Corporation	Property's FMV
Scott Brown	Land parcel A	$ 40,000	$75,000
Lynn Brown	Land parcel B	120,000	75,000

Benson had E&P of $250,000 immediately before the distributions. Prepare a memorandum for your tax manager explaining how Benson should treat these transactions for tax and financial accounting purposes. How will the two shareholders report the distributions? Assume Benson's marginal tax rate is 34%. Your manager has suggested that, at a minimum, you should consult the following resources:

- IRC Sec 301
- IRC Sec. 311
- IRC Sec. 312
- Accounting Standards Codification (ASC) 845, formerly APB No. 29

C:4-65 John and Jean own 80% and 20%, respectively, of Plum Corporation stock. Thanks to their hard work, Plum's software sales have sky rocketed. In its first year of operation Plum's earnings were minimal, but four years later, Plum grossed $10 million. Plum compensated John and Jean as follows: John received a bonus of 76% of net profits and Jean received a bonus of 19% of net profits at the end of each year. Plum never paid any dividends. Can Plum deduct any or all of the "salaries" paid to John and Jean?

C:4-66 Sara owns 60% of Mayfield Corporation's single class of stock. A group of five family members and three key employees own the remaining 40% of Mayfield stock. Mayfield is a calendar year taxpayer that uses the accrual method of accounting. Sara is a Mayfield officer and director and uses the cash method of accounting. During the period 2008–2010, Sara received the following amounts as salary and nontaxable fringe benefits from Mayfield: 2008, $160,000; 2009, $240,000; and 2010, $290,000. She earned these amounts evenly throughout the tax years in question. In 2011, upon auditing Mayfield's tax returns for 2008–2010, a revenue agent determined that reasonable compensation for Sara's services for the three years in question is $110,000, $165,000, and $175,000, respectively. The bylaws of Mayfield were amended on December 15, 2009, to provide that:

Any payments made to an officer of the corporation, including salary, commissions, bonuses, other forms of compensation, interest, rent, or travel and entertainment expenses incurred, and which shall be disallowed in whole or in part as a deductible expense by the Internal Revenue Service, shall be reimbursed by such officer to the corporation to the full extent of such disallowance.

Following the disallowance of $240,000 of the total salary expense, the board of directors met and requested that Sara reimburse Mayfield for the portion of her salary deemed to be excessive. Because of the large amount of money involved, the board of directors approved an installment plan whereby Sara would repay the $240,000 in five annual installments of $48,000 each over the period 2012–2016. The corporation would not charge Sara interest on the unpaid balance of $240,000. Prepare a memorandum for your tax manager explaining what salary and fringe benefits are taxable to Sara in the period 2008–2010 and what reimbursements Sara can deduct during the period 2012–2016.

5

CHAPTER

OTHER CORPORATE TAX LEVIES

LEARNING OBJECTIVES

After studying this chapter, you should be able to

▶ 1   Determine whether a corporation is liable for the alternative minimum tax

▶ 2   Calculate the corporation's alternative minimum tax liability (if any)

▶ 3   Determine whether a corporation is a personal holding company (PHC)

▶ 4   Calculate the corporation's PHC tax

▶ 5   Determine whether a corporation is liable for the accumulated earnings tax

▶ 6   Calculate the corporation's accumulated earnings tax

▶ 7   Explain how a corporation can avoid the personal holding company tax

▶ 8   Explain how a corporation can avoid the accumulated earnings tax

▶ 9   Understand the financial statement implications of the alternative minimum tax

Chapter C:3 examines a corporation's regular income tax and the procedures for calculating, reporting, and paying this tax. Chapter C:5 focuses on the following three additional taxes the tax law may impose on a C corporation: (1) the alternative minimum tax, (2) the personal holding company tax, and (3) the accumulated earnings tax. For a specific taxable year, a corporation could be liable for none, one, or two of these three taxes (as is discussed later in the chapter, a corporation cannot be liable for the personal holding company tax and accumulated earnings tax for the same taxable year). A corporation pays these additional taxes, if any, in addition to its regular tax liability. For each of these additional taxes, this chapter examines the requirements for the tax to be imposed, the calculation of the tax imposed, and the measures a corporation can take to avoid it.

THE ALTERNATIVE MINIMUM TAX

THE GENERAL FORMULA

OBJECTIVE 1

Determine whether a corporation is liable for the alternative minimum tax

The **alternative minimum tax (AMT)** is Congress' attempt to ensure that taxpayers with substantial economic income cannot use exclusions, deductions, and credits to avoid a significant part of their tax liability.[1] Chapter I:14 discusses the AMT as it applies to individuals. Some aspects of the AMT apply to corporations and individuals in the same way, but other aspects of the AMT apply to these two types of taxpayers in different ways.

Table C:5-1 summarizes the calculation of a corporation's AMT. Starting with its regular taxable income, the corporation adds AMT preference items and adds and/or subtracts AMT adjustment items, all of which results in **alternative minimum taxable income (AMTI)**. AMT preferences and adjustments are income and deduction items that are treated differently for regular tax and AMT purposes and are discussed more fully later in this chapter. The tax base for the AMT equals AMTI minus an AMT exemption amount. The corporation multiplies this tax base by a 20% tax rate and subtracts an AMT foreign tax credit to determine its **tentative minimum tax (TMT)**. AMT, then, is the amount by which the TMT exceeds the corporation's regular tax.[2]

The AMT exemption amount for corporations is $40,000 reduced by 25% of the amount by which AMTI exceeds $150,000. Thus, the AMT exemption amount is completely phased out if AMTI is $310,000 or more. If two or more corporations comprise a controlled group, they apportion among themselves one $40,000 AMT exemption amount (see Chapter C:3). In addition, the controlled group phases out its AMT exemption amount based on its members' combined AMTIs.

ADDITIONAL COMMENT

When AMTI exceeds $150,000 and is less than $310,000, the effective marginal AMT tax rate is 25% due to the AMT exemption amount phase-out [20% + (0.25 × 20%) = 25%].

EXAMPLE C:5-1 ▶

Yellow Corporation's AMTI is $200,000. Because its AMTI is more than $150,000 but less than $310,000, Yellow's AMT exemption amount equals $27,500 {$40,000 − [0.25 × ($200,000 − $150,000)]}.[3] ◀

EXAMPLE C:5-2 ▶

ADDITIONAL COMMENT

The AMT is a small part of corporate taxes. In 2007, the federal government collected $3.2 billion of AMT from corporations compared to $330 billion of regular income tax net of tax credits. Of the 1.9 million corporate tax returns (Form 1120) filed in 2007, only 11,266 reported any AMT.

Badger Corporation's regular taxable income is $400,000. It also has $350,000 of AMT preference items, $285,000 of positive AMT adjustment items, $35,000 of negative AMT adjustment items, and no tax credits. Badger's regular tax is $136,000 (0.34 × $400,000). Badger's AMTI is $1 million ($400,000 + $350,000 + $285,000 − $35,000). Its AMT exemption amount is zero because its AMTI exceeds $310,000. Thus, Badger's AMT tax base is $1 million ($1,000,000 AMTI − $0 AMT exemption amount), and its TMT is $200,000 (0.20 × $1,000,000 AMT tax base). Badger's AMT is $64,000 ($200,000 − $136,000). In total, Badger pays $200,000 ($136,000 + $64,000) of total federal income tax. ◀

A corporation is liable for any amount of positive AMT, no matter how small. Thus, a corporation needs to calculate its AMT every year (unless it is exempt from the AMT, at topic discussed later).

---

[1] S corporations are not subject to the AMT (Sec. 1363(a)). Instead, an S corporation's AMT preference and adjustment items pass through to their shareholders.

[2] The regular tax is the tax imposed on regular taxable income (see Chapter C:3), reduced by the regular foreign tax credit, the possessions tax credit, and the Puerto Rico economic activity credit. The regular tax does not include any accumulated earnings tax or personal holding company tax, which are discussed later in the chapter, and it does not include any AMT.

[3] In the examples, assume that all corporations are C corporations not exempt from the AMT.

▼ TABLE C:5-1

Calculation of a Corporation's Alternative Minimum Tax Liability

Regular taxable income or loss before the NOL deduction
Plus:　　Tax preference items
Plus or minus:　AMT adjustment items other than the ACE
　　　　　　　adjustment, the alternative tax NOL deduction, and the
　　　　　　　adjustment for the U.S. production activities deduction

Preadjustment AMTI
Plus or minus:　75% of the difference between pre-adjustment AMTI
　　　　　　　and adjusted current earnings (ACE)
Minus: Alternative tax NOL deduction
　　　　Adjustment for the U.S. production activities deduction

Alternative minimum taxable income (AMTI)
Minus: AMT exemption amount

Tax base for the AMT
Times: 0.20 tax rate

Tentative minimum tax before credits
Minus: AMT foreign tax credit

Tentative minimum tax (TMT)
Minus: Regular (income) tax

Alternative minimum tax (AMT, not less than zero)

STOP & THINK

Question: In Example C:5-2, Badger Corporation pays both the regular tax and the AMT because its TMT exceeds its regular tax. How is this result possible if the regular tax rate for corporations with $335,000 to $10 million of taxable income is 34% while the AMT rate is a flat 20%?

Solution: The result is possible because different tax bases are used to calculate the two taxes. The regular tax is based on regular taxable income while the TMT is based on AMTI minus the AMT exemption amount. The circumstances in which the TMT will exceed the regular tax can be expressed as follows (assuming the AMT exemption amount is completely phased out):

[Regular taxable Income (RTI) + Preferences (P) ± Adjustments (A)] × 0.20 > RTI × 0.34

The inequality can be simplified as follows:

$$0.20 \times (P \pm A) > 0.14 \times RTI$$
$$(P \pm A) > 0.70 \times RTI$$

For Example C:5-2, the inequality indicates that Badger will incur an AMT if its total AMT preference and adjustment items exceed $280,000 (0.70 × $400,000 regular taxable income). Badger's $600,000 ($350,000 + $285,000 − $35,000) of total AMT preference and adjustment items exceed $280,000, so the inequality correctly indicates that Badger incurs an AMT. If Badger's total AMT preference and adjustment items were $280,000, its AMTI would be $680,000 ($400,000 + $280,000), its TMT would be $136,000 (0.20 × $680,000), and its AMT would be zero because its TMT would not exceed its $136,000 regular tax.[a]

[a] The inequality will be different if the corporation's marginal regular tax rate is different than 34% as used above (i.e., it is 15%, 25%, 35%, 38%, or 39%) or if the AMT exemption amount is more than zero.

EXEMPTION FROM THE AMT FOR SMALL CORPORATIONS AND FIRST-YEAR CORPORATIONS

A qualifying small corporation is exempt from the AMT. To qualify, the corporation's average gross receipts generally must be $7.5 million or less for all three-taxable-year periods before the taxable year for which the corporation is determining qualification.[4] A corporation that did not exist for a full three-year period calculates its average gross receipts for the period it existed. For the corporation's first three-taxable-year (or shorter) period, average gross receipts must be $5 million or less to qualify for exemption from the AMT. A corporation generally is exempt from the AMT for its first year of existence, regardless of its gross receipts. If a corporation does not qualify for exemption from the AMT, it is subject to the AMT for the year it does not so qualify and all subsequent years.[5]

EXAMPLE C:5-3 ▶ Kiho Corporation forms on January 1 of Year 1 and has gross receipts as follows:

Year 1	$4,500,000
Year 2	6,000,000
Year 3	7,800,000
Year 4	8,400,000
Year 5	7,650,000
Year 6	6,300,000

Kiho is exempt from the AMT for Year 1 because it is the first year the corporation exists. For each subsequent year, Kiho calculates its average gross receipts and determines whether it is exempt from the AMT as follows:

Year 2: Before Year 2, Kiho exists for only one year, so it uses its Year 1 gross receipts as its average gross receipts. This $4.5 million amount is less than or equal to the $5 million maximum average gross receipts that applies for the first three-taxable-year (or shorter) period, so Kiho is exempt from the AMT for Year 2.

Year 3: Kiho exists for only two years before Year 3, so it averages its gross receipts for Years 1 and 2. This $5.25 million [($4,500,000 + $6,000,000) ÷ 2] average is less than or equal to the $7.5 million maximum average gross receipts that applies after the first three-taxable-year (or shorter) period, so Kiho is exempt from the AMT for Year 3.

Year 4: Kiho averages its gross receipts for Years 1 through 3. This $6.1 million [($4,500,000 + $6,000,000 + $7,800,000) ÷ 3] average is less than or equal to $7.5 million, so Kiho is exempt from the AMT for Year 4.

Year 5: Kiho averages its gross receipts for Years 2 through 4. This $7.4 million [($6,000,000 + $7,800,000 + $8,400,000) ÷ 3] average is less than or equal to $7.5 million, so Kiho is exempt from the AMT for Year 5.

Year 6: Kiho averages its gross receipts for Years 3 through 5. This $7.95 million [($7,800,000 + $8,400,000 + $7,650,000) ÷ 3] average is greater than $7.5 million, so Kiho is not exempt from the AMT for Year 6. However, Kiho's failure to qualify for exemption from the AMT does not necessarily mean it will pay any AMT for Year 6. Kiho would not pay any AMT if its TMT were less than its regular tax for Year 6.

Year 7: Kiho is not exempt from the AMT because it failed to so qualify in a prior year. It is irrelevant that Kiho's $7.45 million [($8,400,000 + $7,650,000 + $6,300,000) ÷ 3] average gross receipts for Years 4 through 6 is less than $7.5 million. ◀

Several additional rules apply to determine whether a corporation qualifies for exemption from the AMT:

▶ Gross receipts include total sales and amounts received for services. Gross receipts are not reduced for cost of goods sold and expenses. Gross receipts differ from gross income, gross profit, and taxable income. Thus, even though a corporation may have low gross profit or taxable income, it still may not qualify for exemption if it has high gross receipts.

▶ For any short taxable year (e.g., a corporation's initial year of existence), gross receipts are annualized.

▶ Gross receipts of a controlled group of corporations are aggregated. For example, if two corporations each have $4 million of average gross receipts and comprise a controlled group, the corporations will not be exempt from the AMT because their $8 million aggregate average gross receipts exceeds $7.5 million (or $5 million, if applicable).

ADDITIONAL COMMENT

Only a small fraction of corporations are subject to the AMT because most corporations' average gross receipts are less than $5 million.

---

[4] Sec. 55(e). To determine average gross receipts, the corporation takes into account only taxable years beginning after 1993.
[5] A corporation losing its exemption from the AMT applies the AMT on a prospective basis. For example, the AMT adjustment item for depreciation, discussed later, does not apply for property placed into service while the corporation is exempt from the AMT but whose recovery period includes years the corporation is subject to the AMT. This rule and similar rules for other AMT preference and adjustment items are beyond the scope of this chapter.

▶ A corporation that is a successor to another entity aggregates its gross receipts with those of its predecessor (e.g., a newly created subsidiary's gross receipts include those of its parent corporation).

OBJECTIVE 2

Calculate the corporation's alternative minimum tax (if any)

TAX PREFERENCE ITEMS

A corporation adds **tax preference items** to its regular taxable income when calculating preadjustment AMTI. Tax preference items always increase a corporation's AMTI. Tax preference items include:[6]

▶ The depletion deduction allowable for the tax year in excess of the depletable property's adjusted basis at the end of the tax year (before reducing the adjusted basis for the current year's depletion deduction).[7]

▶ The amount by which excess intangible drilling and development costs (IDCs) incurred in connection with oil, gas, and geothermal wells exceeds 65% of the net income from such property.[8]

▶ Tax-exempt interest on private activity bonds. A private activity bond is a bond issued by a state or local government whose proceeds are used wholly or partially for private business activities (e.g., the bond proceeds are used to construct a stadium used by professional sports teams).

ADDITIONAL COMMENT

Tax-exempt interest on private activity bonds issued before August 8, 1986 or in 2009 or 2010 is not treated as a tax preference item.

EXAMPLE C:5-4 ▶

Duffy Corporation mines iron ore. The adjusted basis for one of its properties is zero due to previous years' depletion deductions. Duffy earns $125,000 of gross income and $45,000 of taxable income from the sale of iron ore extracted from this property in the current year. The iron ore depletion percentage is 15%. Duffy's percentage deduction for regular taxable income before any reduction is $18,750 ($125,000 × 0.15), but Duffy reduces this deduction by $3,750 ($18,750 × 0.20) under Sec. 291(a)(2). Duffy's $15,000 ($18,750 − $3,750) deduction is less than the $22,500 ($45,000 × 0.50) maximum deduction. For AMT purposes, the $15,000 deduction for regular taxable income in excess of the property's zero adjusted basis is a tax preference item, which effectively disallows the $15,000 deduction for preadjustment AMTI. ◀

EXAMPLE C:5-5 ▶

Salek Corporation earns the following interest income in the current year:

Source	Amount
IBM Corporation bonds	$25,000
Wayne County School District bonds	30,000
City of Detroit bonds	15,000

The interest on the IBM bonds is taxable because the bonds are not issued by a state or local government, so Salek includes the $25,000 in its regular taxable income. The Wayne County School District issued its bonds to renovate school facilities. Thus, the bonds' proceeds were not used for private business activities and are not private activity bonds. Salek does not include the $30,000 in its regular taxable income, and it is not a tax preference item. The City of Detroit issued its bonds in 2006 to finance a parking garage, where 35% of the space is leased exclusively to a nonexempt corporation. Thus, the bonds are private activity bonds. Salek does not include the $15,000 in its regular taxable income but adds the $15,000 to its regular taxable income when calculating preadjustment AMTI. ◀

AMT ADJUSTMENT ITEMS

Although tax preference items always *increase* AMTI, **AMT adjustment items** can either *increase* or *decrease* AMTI. Common AMT adjustment items are discussed below.[9]

DEPRECIATION. Taxpayers calculate depreciation on some property differently for preadjustment AMTI than for regular taxable income (see Chapter I:10 for depreciation rules for

---

[6] Sec. 57(a).

[7] Independent producers and royalty owners are not required to treat the oil and gas depletion deduction in excess of the depletable property's adjusted basis as a tax preference item, so this tax preference item applies almost exclusively to integrated oil companies.

[8] Excess IDCs are the amount by which IDCs in the tax year exceed the deduction that would have been allowable if the IDCs had been capitalized

and amortized over a ten-year period. The oil and gas excess IDC preference applies to a more limited extent for independent oil companies than it does for integrated oil companies.

[9] Sec. 56(a).

regular tax purposes). These AMT depreciation rules apply to individual and corporate taxpayers. For simplicity, this chapter discusses rules for property placed in service after 1998.[10]

Personal Property Placed in Service After 1998. For AMT purposes, the taxpayer uses the same recovery period (e.g., MACRS recovery period) and same convention (i.e., half-year or mid-quarter) for AMT purposes as it uses for regular tax purposes. However, the taxpayer generally uses the 150% declining balance method to calculate AMT depreciation but uses the 200% declining balance method to calculate regular tax depreciation.[11] The AMT adjustment equals the difference between AMT and regular tax depreciation, and the adjustment could be positive or negative. For property depreciated under the half-year convention, see Table 1 in Appendix C for the regular tax depreciation rates and Table 10 for the AMT depreciation rates.

EXAMPLE C:5-6 ▶ In Year 1, Euclid Corporation places into service used office furniture costing $10,000. The property has a seven-year MACRS recovery period, and the half-year convention applies to it. Euclid does not elect Sec. 179 expensing for the property, and it does not qualify for bonus depreciation because it is not new property. In Year 1, regular tax depreciation is $1,429 ($10,000 × 0.1429), and AMT depreciation is $1,071 ($10,000 × 0.1071). Euclid adds the $358 ($1,429 − $1,071) difference in the depreciation amounts when calculating preadjustment AMTI. This AMT adjustment is positive because regular taxable income, which is the starting point for the preadjustment AMTI calculation, includes a larger depreciation deduction than is allowed for AMT purposes.

Toward the end of the recovery period, the depreciation adjustment becomes negative. For example, in Year 6, regular tax depreciation is $892 ($10,000 × 0.0892) while AMT depreciation is $1,225 ($10,000 × 0.1225). Thus, Euclid makes a negative $333 ($892 − $1,225) adjustment in Year 6. ◀

Any amount the taxpayer elects to expense under Sec. 179 for regular tax purposes also is allowed for AMT purposes.

EXAMPLE C:5-7 ▶ Assume the same facts as in Example C:5-6, except Euclid elects Sec. 179 expensing for $6,000 of the property's cost. In the current year, Euclid's regular tax depreciation is $6,572 [$6,000 + (0.1429 × ($10,000 − $6,000))], and its AMT tax depreciation is $6,428 [$6,000 + (0.1071 × ($10,000 − $6,000))]. Euclid makes a $144 ($6,572 − $6,428) positive AMT adjustment in the current year. ◀

Bonus Depreciation for Personal Property. For regular tax purposes, depreciation on *new* personal property acquired and placed in service in 2008 through 2012 generally is eligible for 50% bonus depreciation. However, 100% bonus depreciation applies for property acquired and place in service after September 8, 2010 and before January 1, 2012.[12] Bonus depreciation allows the taxpayer to deduct 50% (or 100%, if applicable) of the cost of qualified property in the year the taxpayer places the property in service. Qualified property is primarily computer software and personal property with a MACRS recovery period of 20 years or less. Any Sec. 179 expensing the taxpayer elects with respect to qualified property applies before applying bonus depreciation. Then, the taxpayer applies 50% (or 100%, if applicable) bonus depreciation to the property's cost minus the amount expensed under Sec. 179. Finally, the MACRS depreciation percentages apply to the remaining cost, if any. Property to which bonus depreciation applies is depreciated the same way for AMT purposes as it is for regular tax purposes. Thus, no AMT depreciation adjustment is required. However, a taxpayer can elect out of bonus

---

[10] AMT depreciation rules different than those discussed in the text apply to personal property and real property placed in service before 1999. For such property, the AMT adjustment usually differs from that which would apply to property placed in service after 1998.

[11] If a taxpayer elects to use the straight-line or 150% declining balance method of depreciation for personal property for regular tax purposes, AMT depreciation is the same as regular tax depreciation, so the taxpayer makes no AMT adjustment for depreciation.

[12] Sec. 168(k)(5). Fifty percent bonus depreciation also was allowed for new personal property acquired and placed in service after May 5, 2003 but before January 1, 2005, and 30% bonus depreciation was allowed for new personal property acquired and placed in service after September 11, 2001 but before May 6, 2003.

depreciation, in which case the taxpayer calculates AMT depreciation using the 150% declining balance method discussed above.[13]

EXAMPLE C:5-8 ▶ On August 25, 2010, Brighton Corporation purchased and placed in service $700,000 of new MACRS five-year property. For 2010, Brighton expenses $500,000 under Sec. 179. In addition, it claims $100,000 [0.50 × ($700,000 – $500,000)] of bonus depreciation on the cost that remains after Sec. 179 expensing. The corporation also claims $20,000 [0.20 × ($700,000 – $500,000 – $100,000)] of regular MACRS depreciation on the cost that remains after subtracting Sec. 179 expensing and bonus depreciation. Thus, for regular tax purposes, total 2010 depreciation is $620,000 ($500,000 + $100,000 + $20,000). This $620,000 also is 2010 AMT depreciation for the property, so Brighton has no AMT adjustment for depreciation on this property in 2010 or subsequent years. ◀

Real Property Placed in Service After 1998. Depreciation on real property is the same for preadjustment AMTI as it is for regular taxable income. Thus, the taxpayer makes no AMT adjustment for it.

BASIS CALCULATIONS. For regular tax purposes, a taxpayer reduces the adjusted basis of property for depreciation allowed for regular tax purposes. Similarly, a taxpayer reduces a property's AMT adjusted basis for allowable AMT depreciation. Thus, a property's adjusted basis for regular tax and AMT purposes will differ if these depreciation amounts differ. When selling such property, the taxpayer calculates separate amounts of gain or loss for regular tax and AMT purposes. Typically, a property's AMT adjusted basis will be more than its regular tax adjusted basis because regular tax depreciation is more accelerated than AMT depreciation, so the taxpayer has a smaller gain (or larger loss) for AMT purposes than it has for regular tax purposes. When calculating preadjustment AMTI, the taxpayer typically subtracts the regular tax gain in excess of the AMT gain (or subtracts the AMT loss in excess of the regular tax loss). These gain difference are a result of the differing regular tax and AMT bases.

EXAMPLE C:5-9 ▶ Assume the same facts as in Example C:5-6 except, on February 1 of Year 4, Euclid Corporation sells the property for $6,000. Euclid claims the following depreciation amounts each year for regular tax and AMT purposes.

Year	Regular Tax Depreciation (1)[a]		AMT Depreciation (2)[b]		AMT Adj. (1) – (2)
Year 1	$10,000 × 0.1429	$1,429	$10,000 × 0.1071	$1,071	$ 358
Year 2	$10,000 × 0.2449	2,449	$10,000 × 0.1913	1,913	536
Year 3	$10,000 × 0.1749	1,749	$10,000 × 0.1503	1,503	246
Year 4	$10,000 × 0.1249 × 0.5	625	$10,000 × 0.1225 × 0.5	613	12
Total		$6,252	Total	$5,100	$1,152

[a] See Table 1, Appendix C for depreciation percentages.
[b] See Table 10, Appendix C for depreciation percentages.

Because the mid-year convention applies to the property, Euclid claims a half-year of depreciation in Year 4, the year it sells the property. When Euclid sells the property, its adjusted basis for regular tax purposes is $3,748 ($10,000 – $6,252), and its adjusted basis for AMT purposes is $4,900 ($10,000 – $5,100). Thus, Euclid's gain when it sells the property is $2,252 ($6,000 – $3,748) for regular tax purposes and $1,100 ($6,000 – $4,900) for AMT purposes. Euclid makes a $1,152 ($2,252 – $1,100) negative AMT adjustment in Year 4 because the gain it includes in regular taxable income is $1,152 more than the gain it has for AMT purposes. This $1,152 difference is attributable to the regular tax depreciation in excess of the AMT depreciation for Years 1 through 4. For Year 4, Euclid's net AMT adjustment for the property is a negative $1,140 ($12 positive adjustment for depreciation minus $1,152 negative adjustment for the gain (basis) difference). ◀

ADDITIONAL COMMENT

In Example C:5-9, the $1,152 adjustment also can be calculated by subtracting the tax adjusted basis from the AMT adjusted basis ($4,900 – $3,748 = $1,152).

---

[13] Sec. 168(k)(2)(D)(iii) and Reg. Sec.1.168(k)-1(e)(6).

ADDITIONAL COMMENT

Because of the AMT small corporation exemption, many corporations that can use the completed contract method for regular tax purposes because their average gross receipts are $10 million or less do not have to make an AMT adjustment for long-term contracts.

LONG-TERM CONTRACTS. For regular tax purposes, taxpayers generally use the percentage of completion method to account for long-term contracts (e.g., a contract to construct a building). However, a taxpayer may use the completed contract method for construction contracts it expects to complete within two years if its average gross receipts for the three preceding tax years is $10 million or less. A taxpayer also may use the completed contract method for home construction contracts (see Chapter I:11). For AMT purposes, the completed contract method is allowed for home construction contracts, but the percentage of completion method must be used for other long-term contracts.

U.S. PRODUCTION ACTIVITES DEDUCTION. A special rule applies for the U.S. production activities deduction. For regular tax purposes in 2010 and later years, the deduction is 9% of qualified production activities income but is limited to 9% of taxable income before this deduction (see Chapter C:3). For AMT purposes, the deduction is limited to 9% of AMTI before the deduction, but the taxpayer does not have to recompute qualified production activities income based on the AMT rules.[14] Thus, the taxpayer usually will have an AMT adjustment for this deduction if its qualified production activities income is more than its regular taxable income and/or AMTI (both before the deduction). However, if qualified production activities income is less than regular taxable income and also is less than AMTI (both before the deduction), the taxpayer usually will not have to make an AMT adjustment for this deduction because the deduction will be 9% of qualified production activities income for both purposes.

ADDITIONAL COMMENT

Under the American Recovery and Reinvestment Act of 2009 and the Worker, Homeownership, and Business Assistance Act of 2009, a taxpayer generally can elect to carry back a 2008 or 2009 NOL three, four, or five years. In addition, the 90% limitation for the alternative tax NOL deduction is suspended for such NOLs that the taxpayer carries back for more than two years.

NOL DEDUCTION. For AMT purposes, a taxpayer claims the alternative tax NOL deduction instead of the regular tax NOL deduction. Similar to the regular tax NOL, the alternative tax NOL is the excess of deductions over gross income, but it is based on deductions and gross income determined under the AMT rules. The alternative tax NOL deduction is limited to 90% of AMTI before this deduction and the U.S. production activities deduction. A taxpayer generally carries its alternative tax NOL back two years and forward 20 years, but it foregoes the two-year carryback period for AMT purposes if it elects to do so for regular tax purposes.[15]

The following example illustrates the computation of **preadjustment AMTI** (see Table C:5-1). Preadjustment AMTI is a component of the ACE and AMTI calculations presented later.

EXAMPLE C:5-10 ▶

In the current year, Marion Corporation reports $300,000 of regular taxable income. The $300,000 includes a $70,000 deduction for percentage depletion (the $70,000 is after the 20% reduction under Sec. 291(a)(2)). The depletable property's adjusted basis at the beginning of the year is $40,000. Regular taxable income also includes an $80,000 deduction for MACRS depreciation. For AMT purposes, depreciation for the depreciable property is $55,000.

Regular taxable income	$300,000
Plus: Percentage depletion in excess	
of basis ($70,000 – $40,000)	30,000
AMT depreciation adjustment ($80,000 – $55,000)	25,000
Preadjustment AMTI	$355,000

◀

APPLICATION OF OTHER REGULAR TAX RULES. As discussed above, the IRC treats many income and deduction items differently for regular tax and AMT purposes. In addition, for AMT purposes, a corporation recomputes income and deduction items for which the regular tax and AMT rules do not differ, based on the regular tax rules and the AMT amounts.[16] For example, for regular tax purposes, the charitable contributions deduction is limited to 10% of taxable income before deducting certain items (see Chapter C:3). For AMT purposes, this limitation is 10% of AMTI before deducting those items. Similarly,

---

[14] Sec. 199(d)(6).
[15] Instructions for Form 4626, Alternative Minimum Tax—Corporations.

[16] Reg. Sec. 1.55-1(a). However, Reg. Sec. 1.56(g)-1(r) allows the taxpayer to elect to use a simplified inventory method for AMT purposes.

closely held corporations and personal service corporations recalculate their at-risk and passive activity losses, taking into account their AMT preference and adjustment items.

ADJUSTED CURRENT EARNINGS (ACE) ADJUSTMENT

ADDITIONAL COMMENT

In 2007, corporations' ACE adjustments totaled $7.4 billion while other AMT preference and adjustment items were a net positive $5.6 billion.

Congress added the ACE adjustment in an attempt to bring the AMT tax base closer to a corporation's economic income. The IRC requires C corporations, but not individuals and S corporations, to make the ACE adjustment when calculating the AMT.[17] The ACE adjustment generally equals 75% of ACE minus preadjustment AMTI. ACE is similar to the concept of earnings and profits (E&P) that determines whether a corporate distribution is a dividend (see Chapter C:4), but ACE is not exactly the same as E&P because the tax law treats some items differently for ACE purposes than for E&P purposes. ACE equals preadjustment AMTI plus and/or minus adjustments for items whose treatment differs for the two purposes. These differences are discussed below.

The ACE adjustment generally can be positive or negative. However, a corporation's negative ACE adjustment is limited to the cumulative net amount of its positive and negative ACE adjustment in all prior years. A corporation cannot carry over to another year any negative ACE adjustment that exceeds this limitation.

EXAMPLE C:5-11 ▶

Kantro Corporation's ACE adjustments prior to Year 1 net to a positive $10,000. Kantro reports the following ACE and preadjustment AMTI amounts for Years 1 through 3:

	Year 1	Year 2	Year 3
ACE	$600,000	$535,000	$570,000
Preadjustment AMTI	500,000	575,000	650,000

Kantro makes a positive $75,000 [0.75 × ($600,000 − $500,000)] ACE adjustment in Year 1 and a negative $30,000 [0.75 × ($535,000 − $575,000)] ACE adjustment in Year 2. Kantro's Year 2 negative ACE adjustment is limited to $85,000 ($10,000 + $75,000), so Kantro is allowed all $30,000 of the negative ACE adjustment. Kantro's Year 3 ACE adjustment is negative $60,000 [0.75 × ($570,000 − $650,000)] before considering the limitation on it. This negative adjustment is limited to $55,000 ($10,000 + $75,000 − $30,000), so Kantro's Year 3 ACE adjustment is negative $55,000. The total ACE adjustments over the three years is negative $10,000 ($75,000 − $30,000 − $55,000). ◀

ADDITIONAL COMMENT

Under the American Recovery and Reinvestment Act of 2009, interest on tax-exempt bonds issued in 2009 or 2010 is not treated as an adjustment for ACE purposes.

The following rules apply for determining ACE.[18]

▶ Any income or gains permanently excluded from gross income for preadjustment AMTI purposes but increase E&P are included in gross income for ACE purposes (e.g., interest on tax-exempt bonds that are not private activity bonds and life insurance proceeds).[19] A corporation adds these items to its preadjustment AMTI when calculating its ACE.

▶ Any expenses or losses deductible for preadjustment AMTI purposes but not deductible for E&P are not deductible for ACE purposes (e.g.,70% dividends-received deduction). A corporation adds these items to its preadjustment AMTI when calculating its ACE. The 80% and 100% dividends-received deductions and the U.S. production activities deduction are exceptions to this rule. These two deductions are allowed for ACE purposes even though they are not deductible for E&P.

▶ Any expenses or losses not deductible for preadjustment AMTI purposes but deductible for E&P are not deductible for ACE purposes (e.g., federal income taxes). A corporation does not adjust for these items when calculating ACE because they are not deductible for preadjustment AMTI or ACE.

---

[17] Sec. 56(c)(1) and (g)(6).

[18] Sec. 56(g)(4) and Reg. Sec. 1.56(g)-1. Depreciation on property placed in service before 1994 is calculated differently for ACE purposes than it is for preadjustment AMTI purposes. A corporation makes an adjustment for such property when calculating ACE. For property placed in service after 1993, depreciation for ACE purposes is that same as that for preadjustment AMTI purposes, so a corporation does not make any adjustment for such property when calculating ACE.

[19] The items are reduced by any deduction that would be allowable in computing preadjustment AMTI if the income were includible in preadjustment AMTI. No adjustment is made for timing differences (e.g., income or gains that are included in preadjustment AMTI and E&P but in different taxable years).

▶ The installment method generally is not allowed for ACE purposes. A corporation with a sale to which the installment method applies makes a positive adjustment to preadjustment AMTI to calculate ACE in the year of sale, and it makes a negative adjustment in the year(s) it receives the sales proceeds.

▶ Organizational expenditures are not deductible for ACE purposes. A corporation adds such a deduction to its preadjustment AMTI when calculating its ACE. Any organizational expenditures deducted for regular tax purposes are also deductible for preadjustment AMTI purposes, so a corporation makes no adjustment when calculating preadjustment AMTI.

▶ The increase or decrease in the annual LIFO recapture amount increases or decreases ACE. The LIFO recapture amount is the amount by which ending inventory under the first-in, first-out (FIFO) method exceeds ending inventory under the last-in, first-out (LIFO) method. This adjustment effectively converts the corporation's inventory method from LIFO to FIFO for ACE purposes.

▶ Depletion is determined under the cost method. For ACE purposes, a corporation amortizes intangible drilling costs over 60 months beginning with the month in which it pays or incurs them.

▶ For ACE purposes, a corporation recomputes income and deductions for which the preadjustment AMTI and ACE rules do not differ, based on the preadjustment AMTI rules and the ACE amounts.[20] For example, a corporation recalculates the charitable contribution and percentage depletion deduction limitations. For many corporations, recalculating the charitable contribution deduction limitation results in no adjustment to preadjustment AMTI because their charitable contributions are less than the limit for both preadjustment AMTI and ACE purposes.

Topic Review C:5-1 summarizes the ACE calculation.

COMPREHENSIVE EXAMPLE. Glidden Corporation does not qualify for the first year or small corporation exemption from the AMT. Glidden calculates its regular taxable income and regular tax as follows:

Gross profit from sales	$300,000
Dividends: From 30%-owned corporation	10,000
From 10%-owned corporation	20,000
Gain on sale of machine	12,778
Gain on installment sale of land	25,000
Gross income	$367,778
Operating expenses (other than depreciation)	(175,000)
Depreciation	(40,000)
Deduction for organizational expenditures	(500)
Dividends-received deduction	(22,000)
Total deductions	($237,500)
Taxable income	$130,278
Regular tax	$ 34,058

Assume the following additional facts:

▶ Glidden receives $15,000 of tax-exempt bond interest. The bonds are not private activity bonds and were issued in 2007.

▶ Glidden receives $100,000 of life insurance proceeds upon the death of one of its executives.

▶ Glidden sells land for a $77,000 gain, $25,000 of which it reports in the current year for regular tax purposes under the installment method.

▶ The gain on the machine sale for AMT purposes is $5,860.

---

[20] Reg. Sec. 1.56(g)-1(a)(5).

Topic Review C:5-1

Summary of Common Alternative Minimum Tax Preference and Adjustment Items

INCOME/EXPENSE ITEM	TYPICAL ADJUSTMENT TO:	
	REGULAR TAXABLE INCOME TO CALCULATE PREADJUSTMENT AMTI	PREADJUSTMENT AMTI TO CALCULATE ACE
Tax-exempt interest:		
Private activity bonds	Increase[a]	None
Other bonds	None	Increase[a]
Life insurance proceeds	None	Increase
Deferred gain on installment method sale:		
Year of sale	None	Increase
Subsequent years' proceeds received	None	Decrease
LIFO inventory adjustment	None	Increase or decrease
Depreciation	Increase or decrease	None[b]
"Basis adjustment" on asset sale	Decrease	None[c]
Excess charitable contributions:		
Year of contribution	Decrease	Decrease
Carryover year	Increase	Increase
Excess capital losses	None	None
Dividends-received deduction:		
80% and 100% DRD	None	None
70% DRD	None	Increase
U.S. production activities deduction	Decrease or None	None
Organizational expenditure deduction	None	Increase
Federal income taxes	None	None
Penalties and fines	None	None
Disallowed travel and entertainment expenses and club dues	None	None

[a] Except for bonds issued in 2009 or 2010.
[b] Increase or none for property placed into service before 1994.
[c] Decrease or none for property placed into service before 1994.

▶ Depreciation for AMT purposes is $32,500.

▶ Glidden incurred $12,500 of organizational expenditures three years ago. It expensed $5,000 of these expenditures in that year and is amortizing the remaining $7,500 over 180 months. The deduction for the current year is $500.

Glidden calculates its preadjustment AMTI as follows:

Taxable income	$130,278
Plus: Depreciation adjustment	7,500[a]
Minus: Basis adjustment on machine sale	(6,918)[b]
Preadjustment AMTI	$130,860

[a] $40,000 − $32,500 = $7,500.
[b] $5,860 − $12,778 = $(6,918).

Glidden makes the $7,500 depreciation adjustment because the depreciation method it uses for regular tax purposes differs from that for AMT purposes. Similarly, Glidden's gain on the machine sale differs for regular tax and AMT purposes because the different depreciation methods result in different adjusted bases for the property for these two purposes. Glidden makes no adjustment for preadjustment AMTI for the tax-exempt interest because it is not earned on private activity bonds, so Glidden treats the interest in the same manner for regular tax and preadjustment AMTI purposes. Likewise, Glidden makes no adjustment for the life insurance proceeds, the installment sale gain, or the organizational expenditures because it treats these items in the same manner to calculate regular taxable income and preadjustment AMTI.

Glidden calculates its ACE as follows:

Preadjustment AMTI	$130,860
Plus: Tax-exempt bond interest	15,000
Life insurance proceeds	100,000
Deferred gain on installment sale	52,000[a]
Deduction for organizational expenditures	500
Dividends-received deduction	14,000[b]
Adjusted current earnings	$312,360

[a] $77,000 − $25,000 = $52,000.
[b] $20,000 × 70% = $14,000.

The tax-exempt interest and life insurance proceeds are not included in regular taxable income and preadjustment AMTI but are included in ACE, so Glidden adds these items to preadjustment AMTI when calculating ACE. The portion of the installment sale gain whose taxation is deferred for regular tax and preadjustment AMTI purposes is not deferred for ACE purposes, so Glidden makes a positive adjustment for it. (Glidden will make negative adjustments in subsequent years as this deferred gain is recognized for regular tax and preadjustment AMTI purposes but not for ACE purposes.) Glidden adds the organizational expenditures and 70% dividends-received deductions because they are not allowed for ACE purposes.

Glidden calculates its AMT as follows:

Preadjustment AMTI		$130,860
Plus: ACE	$312,360	
Minus: Preadjustment AMTI	(130,860)	
Difference	$181,500	
Times: 75%	× 0.75	136,125
Alternative minimum taxable income (AMTI)		$266,985
Minus: AMT exemption amount		(10,754)[a]
AMT base		$256,231
Times: 20% tax rate		× 0.20
Tentative minimum tax (TMT)		$ 51,246
Minus: Regular tax		(34,058)[b]
Alternative minimum tax (AMT)		17,188

[a] $40,000 − [0.25 × ($266,985 − $150,000)] = $10,754.
[b] $22,250 + [0.39 × ($130,278 − $100,000)] = $34,058.

Glidden reduces its AMT exemption amount, but not to zero, because its AMTI is more than $150,000 and less than $310,000. Glidden's total federal income tax is $51,246 ($34,058 regular tax + $17,188 AMT), which equals its TMT. A completed Form 4626 for this comprehensive example appears in Appendix B.

MINIMUM TAX CREDIT

If applicable, a corporation incurs the AMT in addition to its regular tax. The AMT also creates a **minimum tax credit**, which the corporation may use to offset future regular taxes. The amount of unused minimum tax credits from prior years a corporation can use in a tax year is limited to the extent its regular tax (minus all credits other than refundable credits) exceeds its TMT. That is, a corporation's unused minimum tax credits can offset its regular tax but not its AMT. Also, the limitation prevents the minimum tax credit from reducing the regular tax below the TMT in a given year. A corporation's unused minimum tax credits carry forward indefinitely. Because of the minimum tax credit, the AMT generally accelerates a corporation's tax liability rather than permanently increasing it.[21] In effect, the AMT is a prepaid tax on corporate preferences and AMT adjustments.

---

[21] Sec. 53. Several of the differences between regular taxable income and AMTI are timing differences (e.g., depreciation). If no minimum tax credit were allowed, a corporation might incur AMT in one year when such a timing difference results in a positive AMT adjustment that causes its TMT to exceed its regular tax, but the corporation might not save AMT when the timing difference reverses and results in a negative AMT adjustment because its regular tax exceeds its TMT that year. Regular taxable income and AMTI can differ due to permanent differences that will never reverse (e.g., tax-exempt interest on private activity bonds or an ACE adjustment resulting from the 70% dividends-received deduction). A corporation generally is allowed a minimum tax credit for all of its AMT, whether it is due to timing or permanent differences. This treatment differs from that for individuals, who are allowed a minimum tax credit only for the AMT attributable to certain AMT preference and adjustment items (see Chapter I:14).

EXAMPLE C:5-12 ▶

ADDITIONAL COMMENT

In Example C:5-12, the $145,900 ($70,000 + $75,900) total tax that Woodford pays in the current year and next year equals the $145,900 ($59,300 + $86,600) total regular tax that Woodford pays in those years. This equality illustrates that the AMT generally accelerates a corporation's tax liability rather than permanently increasing it. With discounting, the total present value of the $70,000 and $75,900 amounts exceeds the total present value of the $59,300 and $86,600 amounts, demonstating the time value of money.

ADDITIONAL COMMENT

Because the general business credit limitation depends on the TMT, *every* corporation not exempt from the AMT needs to compute its TMT, even if it owes no AMT.

NEW TAX ACT

Under the Small Business Jobs Act of 2010, eligible small businesses carry back any general business credit exceeding the limitation for five years instead of one year. The 20-year carryforward still applies. An eligible small business also computes its general business credit limitation by taking into account only 25% of its net regular tax exceeding $25,000, disregarding its tentative minimum tax. These rules apply only for 2010.

EXAMPLE C:5-13 ▶

For the current year, Woodford Corporation's regular tax is $59,300, and its TMT is $70,000. Thus, Woodford's AMT is $10,700 ($70,000 − $59,300). This $10,700 of AMT generates a $10,700 minimum tax credit for Woodford. Woodford's total tax is $70,000 ($59,300 + $10,700).

In the next year, Woodford's regular tax is $86,600, and its TMT is $75,000. Thus, Woodford's AMT is zero. Woodford claims all $10,700 of its unused minimum tax credit because its use is limited to $11,600 ($86,600 − $75,000). Woodford's net tax for the next year is $75,900 ($86,600 − $10,700). If Woodford's regular tax in the next year had been $83,000 instead of $86,600, it could have taken only $8,000 ($83,000 − $75,000) of the minimum tax credit that year with $2,700 carrying forward to a subsequent year. ◀

TAX CREDITS AND THE AMT

AMT AND THE GENERAL BUSINESS CREDIT. The general business credit is the sum of many business credits, such as the credit for research activities (see Chapter I:14). The IRC limits the general business credit a taxpayer may claim for regular tax purposes, which the following points describe:[22]

▶ A taxpayer's general business credit limitation is:
 a. Net income tax in excess of
 b. Greater of:
  i. TMT, or
  ii. 25% of its net regular tax in excess of $25,000.

▶ The net income tax is the sum of the regular tax and AMT, reduced by the foreign tax credit, possessions tax credit, and Puerto Rico economic activity credit.

▶ The net regular tax is regular tax reduced by the same credits that reduce the net income tax.

▶ A small corporation exempt from the AMT is treated as having a zero TMT.

▶ The taxpayer can carry back one year and forward 20 years any general business credit that cannot be used in the current year because of the credit limitation.[23]

The effect of this limitation is that the general business credit can offset, at most, only the portion of the regular tax that exceeds the TMT, and it cannot offset any AMT.

In the current year (not 2010), Keene Corporation's regular tax before credits is $165,000, its TMT is $120,000, and the only available credit it has is a $55,000 general business credit. Keene's AMT is zero because its TMT does not exceed its regular tax. Keene calculates its general business credit limitation as follows:

Net income tax		$165,000
Minus: Greater of:		
(1) Tentative minimum tax, or	$120,000	
(2) 25% of regular tax (reduced by certain other credits) excess of $25,000 [0.25 × ($165,000 − $25,000)]	$ 35,000	(120,000)
General business credit limitation		$ 45,000

Keene may claim $45,000 of its general business credit in the current year, so its regular tax (net of credits) is $120,000 ($165,000 − $45,000). Keene's general business credit in excess of the limitation is $10,000 ($55,000 − $45,000), which it carries back one year and forward 20 years. ◀

AMT AND THE FOREIGN TAX CREDIT. A taxpayer may reduce its TMT by a modified version of the foreign tax credit. For regular tax purposes, the foreign tax credit is limited to the regular tax before credits multiplied by the ratio of foreign source regular taxable income to worldwide regular taxable income (see Chapter I:14). For AMT

---

[22] Sec. 38(c). Special rules apply for certain credits that comprise the general business credit, such as the empowerment zone employment credit.   [23] Sec. 39.

Topic Review C:5-2

Alternative Minimum Tax (AMT) for Corporations

1. Qualifying small corporations are exempt from the AMT. To qualify, a corporation's average gross receipts generally must be $7.5 million or less. Also, first-year corporations generally are exempt from the AMT. S corporations are exempt from the AMT and, instead, pass through their AMT preference and adjustment items to their shareholders.
2. The starting point for calculating preadjustment alternative minimum taxable income (AMTI) is regular taxable income. A taxpayer increases this amount for tax preference items and increases and/or decreases it for AMT adjustment items (other than the adjusted current earnings (ACE) adjustment and the alternative tax net operating loss (NOL) deduction). The resulting amount is preadjustment AMTI.
3. The ACE adjustment generally equals 75% of ACE minus preadjustment AMTI. ACE is a modified version of preadjustment AMTI.
4. AMTI equals preadjustment AMTI, plus or minus the ACE adjustment, and minus the alternative tax NOL deduction.
5. The AMT tax base is AMTI minus a $40,000 AMT exemption amount. The $40,000 amount phases out as AMTI increases from $150,000 to $310,000.
6. A corporation's tentative minimum tax (TMT) equals 20% of its AMT tax base. It is reduced by the AMT foreign tax credit allowed. The TMT can limit the amount of general business credit allowed for regular tax purposes.
7. The AMT is the excess of the TMT over the regular tax, which is levied in addition to the regular tax.
8. A corporation's AMT generates an equal amount of minimum tax credit, which the corporation can carry forward indefinitely to offset future regular taxes. Minimum tax credits can be used only to the extent the regular tax exceeds the TMT.
9. When determining its quarterly estimated tax payments, a taxpayer includes its regular tax and AMT.

purposes, a taxpayer calculates its credit limitation by substituting the TMT (before subtracting any AMT foreign tax credit) for the regular tax and by substituting AMTI for regular taxable income.[24]

Topic Review C:5-2 presents an overview of the AMT for corporations. Also see the financial statement implications of the AMT later in this chapter.

Personal holding company tax

A corporation that meets both a stock ownership test and a passive income test is classified as a **personal holding company (PHC)** for the tax year. Congress enacted the PHC tax to prevent taxpayers from using closely held corporations to shelter passive income from the higher individual tax rates. In tax years 2003 through 2012, this penalty tax applies at a 15% rate on the PHC's undistributed personal holding company income (UPHCI). After 2012, the PHC tax rate is scheduled to revert to the highest marginal tax rate for individuals. A corporation subject to the PHC tax pays this tax in addition to the regular tax and the alternative minimum tax. Corporations, however, can escape the PHC tax by intentionally failing either the stock ownership test or passive income test or through dividend distributions that reduce UPHCI to zero.

The significance of the PHC tax diminished after the 2003 Act. This act lowered the highest marginal rate for individuals to the same level as that for corporations (35%). In so doing, it reduced the attractiveness of using the C corporation as a vehicle for sheltering what are essentially individual earnings. Even with a narrowing or elimination of the individual-corporate tax rate gap, however, the PHC tax remains an important anti-tax avoidance tool, particularly where wealthy individuals in the 35% marginal tax bracket control corporations with effective tax rates less than 35%.

---

[24] Sec. 59(a). A taxpayer may elect to use a simplified AMT foreign tax credit limitation, which uses the ratio of foreign source regular taxable income to worldwide AMTI rather than the ratio of foreign source AMTI to worldwide AMTI.

ADDITIONAL
COMMENT

The Congressional intent behind
enacting the personal holding
company and accumulated earnings taxes was not to produce
large amounts of tax revenues.
However, the presence of these
taxes in the IRS's arsenal prevents
substantial revenue losses from
certain tax-motivated transactions
involving closely held
corporations.

PERSONAL HOLDING COMPANY DEFINED

A personal holding company is any corporation that (1) has five or fewer individual shareholders who own more than 50% of the corporation's outstanding stock at any time during the last half of its tax year and (2) has personal holding company income that is at least 60% of its adjusted ordinary gross income for the tax year.[25]

Corporations with special tax status generally are excluded from the PHC definition. Among these are S corporations and tax-exempt organizations.

STOCK OWNERSHIP REQUIREMENT

Section 542(a)(2) provides that a corporation satisfies the PHC stock ownership require-ment if more than 50% of the value of its outstanding stock is directly or indirectly owned by five or fewer individuals at any time during the last half of its tax year.[26] Any corpora-tion with fewer than ten individual shareholders at any time during the last half of its tax year, which is not an excluded corporation, will meet the stock ownership requirement.[27]

For purposes of determining whether the 50% requirement is satisfied, stock owned directly or indirectly by or for an individual is considered to be owned by that individual. The Sec. 544 stock attribution rules provide that

TYPICAL
MISCONCEPTION

The PHC tax applies to any corporation deemed to be a personal
holding company based on objective criteria. No improper intent is
necessary. Thus, the PHC tax truly
fits into the category of "a trap
for the unwary."

▶ Stock owned by a family member is considered to be owned by the other members of his or her family. Family members include a spouse, brothers and sisters, ancestors, and lineal descendants.

▶ Stock owned directly or indirectly by or for a corporation, partnership, estate, or trust is considered to be owned proportionately by its shareholders, partners, or beneficiaries.

▶ A person who holds an option to acquire stock is considered to own such stock whether or not the individual intends to exercise the option.

▶ Stock owned by a partnership's partner is considered to be owned by his or her part-ners.

▶ The family, partnership, and option rules can be used only to make a corporation a PHC. They cannot be used to prevent a corporation from acquiring PHC status.[28]

PASSIVE INCOME REQUIREMENT

A corporation whose shareholders satisfy the stock ownership requirement is not a PHC unless the corporation also earns predominantly passive income. The passive income requirement is met if at least 60% of the corporation's **adjusted ordinary gross income (AOGI)** for the tax year is personal holding company income (PHCI). The following text sections define AOGI and PHCI and outline ways in which a corporation can sidestep the passive income requirements.

KEY POINT

To be deemed a PHC, a corporation must satisfy two tests: a stock
ownership test and a passive
income test. Because most closely
held corporations satisfy the stock
ownership test, the passive
income test usually is decisive.

ADJUSTED ORDINARY GROSS INCOME DEFINED. The first step toward determin-ing AOGI is calculating the corporation's gross income (see Figure C:5-1). Gross income is determined under the same accounting method used to compute taxable income. Thus, an income item excluded from gross income also is excluded from AOGI. Gross receipts from sales are reduced by the corporation's cost of goods sold.

The next step toward determining AOGI is calculating the corporation's **ordinary gross income (OGI)**. To do this, the corporation's gross income is reduced by the amount of its capital gains and Sec. 1231 gains.[29] These items are neutral in determining whether a cor-poration is a PHC; that is, the realization and recognition of a large Sec. 1231 or capital gain cannot make a corporation a PHC.

---

[25] Sec. 542(a).
[26] The PHC stock ownership test also is used to determine whether a closely held C corporation is subject to the at-risk rules (Sec. 465) or the passive activity loss and credit limitation rules (Sec. 469). Thus, a closely held corpo-ration that is not a PHC may be subject to certain restrictions because of the PHC stock ownership rules.

[27] This statement may not be valid if entities own stock that might be attrib-uted to the individual owners.
[28] Sec. 544(a)(4)(A).
[29] Sec. 543(b)(1).

▼ FIGURE C:5-1
Determining Adjusted Ordinary Gross Income

Gross income (GI) reported for taxable income and PHC purposes
Minus: Gross gains on the sale of capital assets
Gross gains on the sale of Sec. 1231 property

Ordinary gross income (OGI)
Minus: Certain expenses relating to gross income from rents; mineral, oil,
and gas royalties; and working interests in oil or gas wells
Interest earned on certain U.S. obligations held for sale to customers by dealers
Interest on condemnation awards, judgments, or tax refunds
Certain expenses relating to rents from tangible personal property manufactured or
produced by the corporation, provided it has engaged in substantial manufacturing
or production of the same type of personal property in the current tax year

Adjusted ordinary gross income (AOGI)

Next, OGI is reduced by certain expenses. These expenses relate to the generation of rental income; mineral, oil, and gas (M, O, & G) royalties; and income from working interests in oil or gas wells.[30] The rental income adjustment is described below.

Reduction by Rental Income Expenses. Gross income from rents is reduced by deductions for depreciation or amortization, property taxes, interest, and rental payments. This net amount is known as **adjusted income from rents (AIR)**.[31] No other Sec. 162 expenses incurred in the generation of rental income reduce OGI. The expense adjustment cannot exceed total gross rental income.

EXAMPLE C:5-14 ▶

Ingrid owns all of Keno Corporation's single class of stock. Both Ingrid and Keno use the calendar year as their tax year. Keno reports the following results for the current year:

Rental income	$100,000
Depreciation	15,000
Interest expense	9,000
Real estate taxes	4,000
Maintenance expenses	8,000
Administrative expenses	12,000

Keno's AIR is $72,000 ($100,000 − $15,000 − $9,000 − $4,000). The maintenance and administrative expenses are deductible in determining taxable income and, consequently, UPHCI, but do not reduce the AIR amount. ◀

ADDITIONAL COMMENT

Income not included in AOGI cannot be PHCI. In calculating the 60% passive income test, PHCI is the numerator and AOGI is the denominator. Because the passive income test is purely objective, both the numerator and denominator can be manipulated. When the ratio is close to 60%, one planning opportunity is to accelerate the recognition of income that is AOGI but not PHCI.

PERSONAL HOLDING COMPANY INCOME DEFINED. **Personal holding company income** includes dividends, interest, annuities, adjusted income from rents, royalties, produced film rents, income from personal service contracts involving a 25% or more shareholder, rental income from corporate property used by a 25% or more shareholder, and distributions from estates or trusts.

PHCI is determined according to the following general rules:

▶ *Dividends:* Includes only distributions out of E&P. Any amounts that are tax exempt (e.g., return of capital distributions) or eligible for capital gain treatment (e.g., liquidating distributions) are excluded from PHCI.[32]

▶ *Interest income:* Includes interest included in gross income. Interest excluded from gross income also is excluded from PHCI.[33]

---

[30] Sec. 543(b)(2).
[31] Sec. 543(b)(3).

[32] Reg. Sec. 1.543-1(b)(1).
[33] Reg. Sec. 1.543-1(b)(2).

▶ *Annuity proceeds:* Includes only annuity amounts included in gross income. Annuity amounts excluded from gross income (for example, as a return of capital) also are excluded from PHCI.[34]

▶ *Royalty income:* Includes amounts received for the use of intangible property (e.g., patents, copyrights, and trademarks). Special rules apply to copyright royalties, mineral, oil, and gas royalties, active business computer software royalties, and produced film rents. Each of these four types of income constitutes a separate PHCI category that may be excluded under one of the exceptions discussed below and set forth in Table C:5-2.[35]

▶ *Distributions from an estate or trust:* Included in PHCI.[36]

In the calculation of PHCI, special rules apply that could result in the exclusion of rents; mineral, oil, and gas royalties; copyright royalties; produced film rents; rental income from the use of property by a 25% or more shareholder; and active business computer software royalties from PHCI. These rules, summarized in Table C:5-2, reduce the likelihood that a corporation will be deemed a PHC. The two most frequently encountered exclusions, for rental income and personal service contract income, are explained in the next two sections.

Exclusion for Rents. Adjusted income from rents (AIR) is included in PHCI unless a special exception applies for corporations earning predominantly rental income. PHCI does not include rents if (1) AIR is at least 50% of AOGI and (2) the dividends-paid deduction equals or exceeds the amount by which nonrental PHCI exceeds 10% of OGI.[37] The special exception permits corporations earning predominantly rental income and very little nonrental PHCI to avoid PHC status. The dividends-paid deduction is available for (1) dividends paid during the tax year, (2) dividends paid within 2½ months of the end of the tax year for which the PHC makes a special throwback election to treat the distribution as

▼ TABLE C:5-2

Tests to Determine Exclusions from Personal Holding Company Income

PHCI Category	A PHCI Category Is Excluded If:		
	Income in the Category Is:	Other PHCI Is:	Business Expenses Are:
Rents	≥50% of AOGI[a]	≤10% of OGI (unless reduced by distributions)	—
Mineral, oil, and gas royalties	≥50% of AOGI[a]	≤10% of OGI	≥15% of AOGI
Copyright royalties	≥50% of OGI	≤10% of OGI	≥25% of OGI
Produced film rents	≥50% of OGI	—	—
Compensation for use of property by a shareholder owning at least 25% of the outstanding stock	—	≤10% of OGI	—
Active business computer software royalties	≥50% of OGI	≤10% of OGI (unless reduced by distributions)	≥25% of OGI[b]
Personal services contract income	—[c]	—	—

[a] Measured in terms of adjusted income from rents or mineral, oil, and gas royalties, respectively.
[b] The deduction test can apply to either the single tax year in question or the five-year period ending with the tax year in question.
[c] Personal services income is excluded from PHCI if the corporation has the right to designate the person who is to perform the services or if the person performing the services owns less than 25% of the corporation's outstanding stock.

[34] Reg. Sec. 1.543-1(b)(4).
[35] Reg. Sec. 1.543-1(b)(3). Royalties include mineral, oil, and gas royalties, royalties on working interests in oil or gas wells, computer software royalties, copyright royalties, and all other royalties.

[36] Sec. 543(a)(8).
[37] Sec. 543(a)(2). AIR excludes rental income earned from leasing property to a shareholder owning 25% or more of the corporation's stock. Such income is included in PHCI as a separate category.

having been paid on the last day of the preceding tax year, and (3) consent dividends (see page C:5-21). Nonrental PHCI includes all PHCI (determined without regard to the exclusions for copyright royalties and mineral, oil, and gas royalties) *other than* adjusted income from rents and rental income earned from leasing property to a shareholder owning 25% or more of the corporation's stock.

EXAMPLE C:5-15 ▶ Karen owns all of Texas Corporation's single class of stock. Both Karen and Texas use the calendar year as their tax year. Texas reports the following results for the current year:

Rental income	$100,000
Operating profit from sales	40,000
Dividend income	15,000
Interest income on corporate bonds	10,000
Rental expenses:	
Depreciation	15,000
Interest	9,000
Real estate taxes	4,000
Other expenses	20,000

Texas pays no dividends during the current year or during the 2½-month throwback period following year-end. Because one shareholder owns all the Texas stock, Texas satisfies the stock ownership requirement. Texas's AOGI is calculated as follows:

Rental income		$100,000
Operating profit from sales		40,000
Dividends		15,000
Interest income		10,000
Gross income and OGI		$165,000
Minus: Depreciation	$15,000	
Interest expense	9,000	
Real estate taxes	4,000	(28,000)
AOGI		$137,000

The two AIR tests are illustrated as follows:

Test 1: Rental income	$100,000
Minus: Depreciation	(15,000)
Interest expense	(9,000)
Real estate taxes	(4,000)
AIR	$ 72,000
50% of AOGI (0.50 × $137,000 AOGI) [Test passed]	$ 68,500

Test 2: Dividends	$ 15,000
Interest income	10,000
Nonrental income	$ 25,000
Minus: 10% of OGI (0.10 × $165,000)	(16,500)
Minimum amount of distributions	$8,500
Actual dividends paid [Test failed]	$ –0–

AIR exceeds the 50% threshold, so Texas passes Test 1. Because Texas paid no dividends, its dividends-paid deduction is less than the nonrental income ceiling, and Texas fails Test 2. AIR is included in PHCI because Texas passed only one of the two tests. Application of the 60% PHC income test is illustrated below:

AIR	$ 72,000
Dividends	15,000
Interest income	10,000
PHCI	$ 97,000
AOGI	$137,000
Times: AOGI threshold	0.60
AOGI ceiling [Test passed]	$ 82,200

Texas is a PHC because PHCI exceeds 60% of AOGI and because it satisfies the stock ownership requirement.

Texas could have avoided PHC status by paying sufficient cash dividends during the current year or a consent dividend following year-end. The amount of dividends required to avoid PHC status is the excess of nonrental PHCI ($25,000) over 10% of OGI ($16,500), or $8,500. Thus, an $8,500 cash dividend paid during the current year or during the 2½-month throwback period in the next year or an $8,500 consent dividend would have permitted Texas to exclude the $72,000 of AIR from PHCI. PHCI then would have been $25,000 ($15,000 + $10,000), which is less than 60% of AOGI ($82,200). (Throwback dividends and consent dividends are discussed on page C:5-21.) ◄

ADDITIONAL COMMENT

Congress enacted the provision for personal service contracts to prevent entertainers, athletes, and other highly compensated professionals from incorporating their activities and, after paying themselves a below-normal salary, having the rest of the income taxed at the corporate rates. Even if it is apparent that a 25%-shareholder will perform the services, as long as no one other than the corporation has the right to designate who performs the services, the income is not PHCI. Thus, the careful drafting of contracts is important.

Exclusion for Personal Service Contracts. Income earned from contracts under which the corporation is obligated to perform personal services, as well as income earned on the sale of such contracts, is included in PHCI if the following two conditions are met:

▶ A person other than the corporation has the right to designate (by name or by description) the individual who is to perform the services, or the individual who is to perform the services is designated (by name or by description) in the contract.

▶ 25% or more of the value of the corporation's outstanding stock is directly or indirectly owned by the person who has performed, is to perform, or may be designated as the person to perform the services.[38]

The 25% or more requirement must be satisfied at some point during the tax year and is determined under the Sec. 544 constructive stock ownership rules. Congress enacted this provision to prevent professionals, entertainers, and sports figures from incorporating their activities, paying themselves a substandard salary, and sheltering at the lower corporate tax rates the difference between their actual earnings and their substandard salary.

EXAMPLE C:5-16 ▶

Dr. Kellner owns all the stock in a professional corporation that provides medical services. The professional corporation concludes with Dr. Kellner an exclusive employment contract that specifies the terms of his employment and that provides for the hiring of a qualified substitute when Dr. Kellner is off duty. The corporation provides office space for Dr. Kellner and employs office staff to enable Dr. Kellner to perform medical services. The income earned by Dr. Kellner does not constitute PHCI because (1) the normal patient–physician relationship generally does not involve a contract that designates a doctor who will perform the services, nor will the patient generally be permitted to designate a doctor who will perform the services, and (2) the professional corporation will be able to appoint a qualified substitute when Dr. Kellner is not on duty (for example, when he is on vacation or not on call).[39]

The income earned by the corporation in connection with Dr. Kellner's services would constitute PHCI if the contract with the patient specified that only Dr. Kellner would provide the services or if the services provided by Dr. Kellner were so unique that only he could provide them. Any portion of the corporation's income from the personal service contract attributable to "important and essential" services provided by persons other than Dr. Kellner is not included in PHCI.[40] ◄

OBJECTIVE 4

Calculate the corporation's PHC tax

CALCULATING THE PHC TAX

The PHC tax is calculated in two basic steps. First, the corporation determines the amount of its undistributed personal holding company income (UPHCI). It then applies the 15% PHC tax rate (in 2003–2012) to UPHCI. If the corporation owes the PHC tax, it can avoid paying the tax by making a timely consent or deficiency dividend distribution.

CALCULATING UPHCI. The starting point for calculating UPHCI is the corporation's taxable income. A series of adjustments are made to taxable income to derive UPHCI. The most important of these adjustments are outlined in Figure C:5-2 and discussed in the following paragraphs.

---

[38] Sec. 543(a)(7).
[39] Rev. Rul. 75-67, 1975-1 C.B. 169. See also Rev. Ruls. 75-249, 1975-1 C.B. 171 (relating to a composer), and 75-250, 1975-1 C.B. 172 (relating to an accountant).

[40] Reg. Sec. 1.543-1(b)(8)(ii).

▼ **FIGURE C:5-2**
Calculating the Personal Holding Company Tax

Regular taxable income
Plus: Positive adjustments
1. Dividends-received deduction
2. NOL deduction
3. Excess charitable contributions carried over from a preceding tax year and deducted in current year in determining regular taxable income
4. Net loss attributable to the operation or maintenance of certain property owned or operated by the corporation

Minus: Negative adjustments
1. Accrued U.S. and foreign income taxes
2. Current year charitable contributions that exceed the 10% corporate limitation
3. NOL (computed without regard to the dividends-received deduction) incurred in the immediately preceding tax year
4. Net capital gain minus the amount of any income taxes attributed to it

Minus: Dividends-paid deduction

Undistributed personal holding company income (UPHCI)
Times: 0.15 (in 2003–2012)

Personal holding company tax

KEY POINT

The PHC tax is assessed at a 15% rate in 2003–2012. This tax is in addition to the corporate income tax. Thus, the existence of both taxes reduces any advantage obtained by interposing a corporation between the taxpayer and his or her income-producing assets.

KEY POINT

The negative adjustments made to taxable income in deriving UPHCI (e.g., federal income taxes) represent items that do not reduce taxable income but reduce the earnings available for distribution to the shareholders. In contrast, positive adjustments made to taxable income (e.g., the dividends-received deduction) are not allowed in deriving UPHCI because they do not represent a reduction in earnings available for distribution to the shareholders.

TYPICAL MISCONCEPTION

A PHC does not adjust its taxable income for all items that affect taxable income differently than they affect the earnings available for distribution to its shareholders (e.g., no adjustment is required for tax-exempt interest and the U.S. production activities deduction).

Positive Adjustments to Taxable Income. The dividends-received deduction is not allowed for UPHCI. Thus, a PHC adds any dividends-received deduction to its regular taxable income when calculating its UPHCI.[41] Rental expenses that exceed rental income also are added back to taxable income to derive UPHCI.

Because PHCs may deduct only the NOL for the immediately preceding tax year, two NOL compensating adjustments must be made. First, the amount of the NOL deduction claimed in determining taxable income must be added back to taxable income. Second, the entire amount of the corporation's NOL (computed without regard to the dividends-received deduction) for the immediately preceding tax year must be subtracted from taxable income.[42] The U.S. production activities deduction, however, is not added back to taxable income.

Negative Adjustments to Taxable Income. Charitable contributions made by corporations are deductible for regular taxable income purposes up to 10% of taxable income without regard to the charitable contribution deduction, an NOL carryback, a capital loss carryback, the dividends-received deduction, and the U.S. production activities deduction. Charitable contributions made by individuals are deductible up to 20%, 30%, or 50% of adjusted gross income, depending on the type of contribution and type of donee. For purposes of a corporation's PHC tax, the deduction limitation is expanded from 10% to 20%, 30%, or 50% of taxable income (without regard to the same five items as for the 10% limitation), depending on the type of contribution and type of donee. Thus, a PHC has two adjustments for charitable contributions when calculating its UPHCI: (1) subtracting the amount of current year charitable contributions exceeding the 10% corporate limitation, but not exceeding the 20%, 30%, or 50% limitation, and (2) adding back charitable contribution carryovers deducted in the current year for regular tax purposes, but in an earlier year for PHC tax purposes.[43]

Income taxes (i.e., federal income taxes, the AMT, foreign income taxes, and U.S. possessions' income taxes) accrued by the corporation reduce UPHCI.[44]

[41] Sec. 545(b)(3).
[42] Sec. 545(b)(4) and Rev. Rul. 79-59, 1979-1 C.B. 209.
[43] Sec. 545(b)(2).
[44] Sec. 545(b)(1).

A PHC is allowed to deduct for UPHCI its net capital gain (i.e., net long-term capital gain over net short-term capital loss) minus income taxes attributable to the net capital gain.[45] The portion of federal income taxes attributable to the net capital gain equals the tax imposed on the corporation's taxable income minus the tax imposed on the corporation's taxable income excluding the net capital gain. The tax offset eliminates the possibility of a double benefit for federal income taxes, which are deductible in determining UPHCI.

The capital gains adjustment precludes a corporation from being classified as a PHC because of a large capital gain. Even where the corporation is classified as a PHC, the capital gains adjustment allows it to avoid the PHC tax on its long-term (but not short-term) capital gains.

AVOIDING THE PHC DESIGNATION AND TAX LIABILITY BY MAKING DIVIDEND DISTRIBUTIONS

The PHC can claim a **dividends-paid deduction** for distributions made during the current year if they are made out of the corporation's current or accumulated E&P.[46] A dividends-paid deduction is not available for **preferential dividends**. A dividend is preferential when (1) the amount distributed to a shareholder exceeds his or her ratable share of the distribution as determined by the number of shares of stock owned or (2) the amount received by a class of stock is greater or less than its rightful amount.[47] In either case, the entire distribution (and not just any excess distributions) is considered to be a preferential dividend.

Throwback dividends are distributions made in the first 2½ months after the close of the tax year. A dividend paid in the first 2½ months of the next tax year is treated as a throwback distribution in the preceding tax year only if the PHC makes the appropriate election.[48] Otherwise, the dividends-paid deduction is allowable only in the tax year in which the PHC actually makes the distribution. Throwback dividends paid by a PHC are limited to the lesser of the PHC's UPHCI or 20% of the amount of any dividends (other than consent dividends) paid during the tax year. Thus, a PHC that fails to make any dividend distributions during its tax year is precluded from paying a throwback dividend.

Consent dividends are hypothetical dividends deemed to have been paid to shareholders on the last day of the corporation's tax year. Consent dividends permit a corporation to reduce its PHC tax liability when it cannot make an actual dividend distribution because of a lack of cash, a restrictive loan covenant, or other financial or legal constraints. Any shareholder who owns stock on the last day of the corporation's tax year can elect to be treated as having received a consent dividend.[49] For PHC tax purposes, the election results in a hypothetical cash dividend on the last day of the PHC's tax year for which the dividends-paid deduction is claimed. The shareholder treats the consent dividend as received on the distribution date and then immediately contributed by the shareholder to the distributing corporation's capital account. The contribution increases the shareholder's stock basis. The shareholder can make the consent dividend election through the due date for the corporation's income tax return (including any permitted extensions).

Dividend Carryovers. Dividends paid in the preceding two tax years may be used as a dividend carryover to reduce the amount of the current year's PHC tax liability.[50] Section 564 permits a PHC to deduct the amount by which its dividend distributions eligible for a dividends-paid deduction in each of the two preceding tax years exceed the corporation's UPHCI for such year.

Liquidating Dividends. Section 562 allows a dividends-paid deduction for liquidating distributions made by a PHC within 24 months of adopting a plan of liquidation.[51]

Deficiency Dividends. Under Sec. 547, a corporation liable for the PHC tax can avoid paying the tax by electing to pay a **deficiency dividend**. The deficiency dividend provisions

ADDITIONAL COMMENT

The intent behind the PHC rules is not to collect taxes from a corporation. Instead, the rules are meant to compel the distribution of income by a closely held corporation so that such income will be taxed at the shareholders' individual tax rates. This purpose is evidenced by the flexibility of the dividends-paid deduction.

TYPICAL MISCONCEPTION

Do not confuse the dividends-paid deduction with the dividends-received deduction that is allowed for regular taxable income.

TAX STRATEGY TIP

If the corporation does not have the cash to pay a throwback dividend, it should consider a consent dividend. The consent dividend is not subject to the 20% limitation on throwback dividends and may be elected up to the extended due date for the corporation's tax return.

TAX STRATEGY TIP

A deficiency dividend can be beneficial if a corporation fails to eliminate its UPHCI, either under the erroneous assumption that it was not a PHC or due to a miscalculation of its UPHCI. If certain requirements are satisfied, a deficiency dividend can be retroactively paid and thus be deductible from UPHCI earned in a previous year.

---

[45] Sec. 545(b)(5).
[46] Secs. 561(a) and 562(a).
[47] Sec. 562(c).
[48] Sec. 563(b).
[49] Sec. 565.
[50] Sec. 561(a)(3).
[51] Sec. 562(b).

substitute a tax on the dividend at the shareholder level for the PHC tax at the corporate level. The distributing corporation's shareholders must include the deficiency dividend in their gross income in the tax year in which it is received, not the tax year for which the PHC claims a dividends-paid deduction. Payment of a deficiency dividend does not relieve the PHC from liability for interest and penalties relating to the PHC tax.

To claim a dividends-paid deduction for a deficiency dividend, a PHC must meet the following requirements:

▶ Obtain a determination (e.g., judicial decision or IRS agreement) that establishes the amount of the PHC tax liability.

▶ Pay a dividend within 90 days after this determination.

▶ File a claim for a dividends-paid deduction within 120 days of the determination date.[52]

EXAMPLE C:5-17 ▶ On its current year return, Boston Corporation characterizes a $200,000 distribution received pursuant to a stock redemption as a capital gain. Upon audit, the IRS and Boston agree that the distribution should be recharacterized as a dividend and that Boston is liable for the PHC tax. Boston can extinguish its PHC tax liability if it pays a deficiency dividend within 90 days after signing the agreement and if Boston files a timely claim. ◀

PHC TAX CALCULATION

The following example illustrates how UPHCI is calculated and how a corporation's regular tax and PHC tax liabilities are determined.

EXAMPLE C:5-18 ▶ Marlo Corporation is deemed to be a PHC for the current year, and reports $226,000 of taxable income on its federal income tax return as follows:

Operating profit	$100,000
Long-term capital gain	60,000
Short-term capital gain	30,000
Dividends (20%-owned corporation)	200,000
Interest	100,000
Gross income	$490,000
Salaries	(40,000)
General and administrative expenses	(20,000)
Charitable contributions	(43,000)[a]
Dividends-received deduction	(160,000)
U.S. production activities deduction	(1,000)
Taxable income	$226,000

a $43,000 limit = 0.10 × ($490,000 − $40,000 − $20,000).

Ignoring any AMT liability, Marlo determines its federal income tax liability to be $71,390 [$22,250 + (0.39 × $126,000)]. Marlo contributed $60,000 to charities in the current year and paid $50,000 in dividends in August.

Marlo's PHC tax liability is calculated as follows:

Taxable income			$226,000
Plus:	Dividends-received deduction		160,000
Minus:	Excess charitable contributions		(17,000)[b]
	Federal income taxes		(71,390)
	Dividends-paid deduction		(50,000)
	Long-term capital gain	$60,000	
	Minus: Federal income taxes	(23,400)[c]	
	LTCG adjustment		(36,600)
Undistributed personal holding company income			$211,010
Times: Tax rate			× 0.15
Personal holding company tax			$ 31,652

b $60,000 total contributions − $43,000 limitation = $17,000 excess contributions.
c Because Marlo is in the 39% tax bracket with and without the LTCG, it can calculate the applicable federal income tax as 0.39 × $60,000 = $23,400.

---

52 Secs. 547(c) through (e).

Marlo's total federal tax liability is $103,042 ($71,390 + $31,652). Marlo can avoid the $31,652 PHC tax by timely paying a deficiency dividend of $211,010, which equals the amount of UPHCI in the current year. ◀

Topic Review C:5-3 presents an overview of the personal holding company tax.

ACCUMULATED EARNINGS TAX

ADDITIONAL COMMENT

The accumulated earnings tax is a penalty tax imposed on corporations that accumulate unreasonable amounts of earnings for the purpose of avoiding shareholder-level taxes. When corporate tax rates are lower than individual rates, tax incentives exist for accumulating earnings inside a corporation. These opportunities should lead to the IRS imposing the accumulated earnings tax.

Corporations not subject to the personal holding company tax may be subject to the accumulated earnings tax. The **accumulated earnings tax** attempts "to compel the company to distribute any profits not needed for the conduct of its business so that, when so distributed, individual stockholders will become liable" for taxes on the dividends received.[53] Unlike its name, the tax is not levied on the corporation's total accumulated earnings balance but only on its current year addition to the balance. In other words, the tax is levied on current earnings that are not needed for a reasonable business purpose, such as excessive earnings invested by a corporation in speculative securities. Note, however, that the 15% maximum tax rate on qualified dividends through 2012 reduces the negative effect of double taxation.

CORPORATIONS SUBJECT TO THE PENALTY TAX

Section 532(a) states that the accumulated earnings tax applies "to every corporation . . . formed or availed of for the purpose of avoiding the income tax with respect to its shareholders . . . by permitting earnings and profits to accumulate instead of being divided or distributed." Certain corporate forms are excluded from the accumulated earnings tax, including the following:

▶ Personal holding companies
▶ Corporations exempt from tax under Secs. 501-530
▶ S corporations[54]

Topic Review C:5-3

Personal Holding Company (PHC) Tax

1. The PHC tax applies only to corporations deemed to be PHCs. A PHC has (1) five or fewer individual shareholders owning more than 50% in value of the corporation's stock at any time during the last half of the tax year and (2) PHCI that is at least 60% of its adjusted ordinary gross income for the tax year.
2. Two special exceptions to the PHC test may apply. First, certain types of corporations (e.g., S corporations) are excluded from the tax. Second, certain categories of income (e.g., rents and active business computer software royalties) are excluded if conditions relating to percentage of income, maximum level of other PHC income, and minimum level of business expenses are met. Table C:5-2 on page C:5-17 summarizes the excludable categories of income and related requirements.
3. The PHC tax equals 15% (in 2003–2012) times UPHCI. UPHCI equals taxable income plus certain positive adjustments (e.g., dividends-received deduction) and minus certain negative adjustments (e.g., federal income taxes, excess charitable contributions, and net capital gain reduced by federal income taxes attributable to the gain).
4. UPHCI can be reduced by a deduction for cash and property dividends paid during the tax year, as well as consent and throwback dividends distributed after year-end.
5. A PHC tax liability (but not liability for related interest and penalties) can be extinguished through payment of a deficiency dividend. Deficiency dividend provisions effectively substitute an income tax levy at the shareholder level for the corporate-level PHC tax.

---

[53] *Helvering v. Chicago Stock Yards Co.*, 30 AFTR 1091, 43-1 USTC ¶9379 (USSC, 1943).

[54] Secs. 532(b) and 1363(a).

WHAT WOULD YOU DO IN THIS SITUATION?

Shareholders formed Taylor Corporation on July 1 of the previous year, contributing $1 million of capital to the corporation. Because of delays in procuring manufacturing equipment, Taylor did not begin business until January of the current year. During the last six months of the previous year, the corporation earned $50,000 of taxable interest and incurred $20,000 of deductible expenses. A second-year accountant in a small accounting firm was assigned to prepare the Taylor corporate tax return. All of his previous assignments were for individual tax returns. The senior accountant responsible for the assignment told him that the return "would be simple and that all you need to do is input the interest and expense information into the Form 1120 software." Because of the rush to finish and deliver the return to the client by March 15, no one in the office noticed during the review process that Taylor might be deemed to be a personal holding company (PHC) in the previous year. The corporation filed its return on March 15 without paying any PHC tax. Another Taylor corporate issue arose in August of the current year and was assigned to you. When you considered the issue, you asked yourself, "Does Taylor have a PHC tax problem?" If so, what can Taylor and/or you do to resolve the problem?

In principle, the accumulated earnings tax applies to both large and small corporations.[55] In practice, however, it applies primarily to closely held corporations where management can implement a corporate dividend policy to reduce the tax liability of the shareholder group.

OBJECTIVE 5

Determine whether a corporation is liable for the accumulated earnings tax

PROVING A TAX-AVOIDANCE PURPOSE

Section 533(a) provides that the accumulation of E&P by a corporation beyond the reasonable needs of the business indicates a tax-avoidance purpose unless the corporation can prove that it is not accumulating the earnings merely to avoid taxes. In limited circumstances, this burden of proof may be shifted to the IRS under rules set forth in Sec. 534.

The existence of a tax-avoidance purpose may be inferred from all pertinent facts and circumstances. Regulation Sec. 1.533-1(a)(2) lists the following specific circumstances that suggest a tax-avoidance purpose:

▶ Dealings between the corporation and its shareholders (e.g., loans made by the corporation to its shareholders or funds expended by the corporation for the shareholders' personal benefit).

▶ Investments of undistributed earnings in assets having no reasonable connection to the corporation's business.

▶ The extent to which the corporation has distributed its E&P (e.g., a low dividend payout rate, low salaries, and substantial earnings accumulation may indicate a tax-avoidance purpose).

TAX STRATEGY TIP

When the IRS determines that the accumulation of earnings is unreasonable, it presumes that its determination is correct. To rebut this presumption, the taxpayer must show by a preponderance of the evidence that the IRS's determination is improper. Thus, periodic updating of the plans to use corporate earnings should be undertaken to reduce accumulated earnings tax problems.

Holding or investment companies are held to a standard different from that which applies to operating companies. Section 533(b) provides that holding or investment company status is prima facie evidence of a tax-avoidance purpose.[56] A holding company, like an operating company, can rebut this presumption by showing that it was neither formed nor availed of to avoid shareholder income taxes.

A tax-avoidance purpose may be only one of several reasons for the corporation's accumulation of earnings. In *U.S. v. The Donruss Company*, the Supreme Court held that tax avoidance does not have to be the dominant motive for the accumulation of earnings, which could lead to imposition of the accumulated earnings tax. According to the court,

---

[55] Sec. 532(c). See, however, *Technalysis Corporation v. CIR* [101 T.C. 397 (1993)] where the Tax Court held that the accumulated earnings tax can be imposed on a publicly held corporation regardless of the concentration of ownership or whether the shareholders are actively involved in corporate operations.

[56] Regulation Sec. 1.533-1(c) defines a holding or investment company for this purpose as "a corporation having practically no activities except holding property and collecting income therefrom or investing therein."

for a tax avoidance purpose to exist, the corporation must know about the tax consequences of accumulating earnings.[57] Such knowledge need not be the dominant motive or purpose for the accumulation of the earnings.

EVIDENCE CONCERNING THE REASONABLENESS OF AN EARNINGS ACCUMULATION

The courts have not specified any single factor that indicates an unreasonable level of accumulated earnings. Instead, they have alluded to several factors that suggest a tax-avoidance motive. The IRS and the courts have cited other factors that indicate reasonable business needs for the legitimate accumulation of earnings and profits.

EVIDENCE OF A TAX-AVOIDANCE MOTIVE. A corporation that wants to avoid liability for the accumulated earnings tax should act defensively. It can minimize this liability by avoiding or restricting the following transactions:

▶ Loans to shareholders

▶ Corporate expenditures for the personal benefit of shareholders

▶ Loans having no reasonable relation to the conduct of business (e.g., loans to relatives or friends of shareholders)

▶ Loans to a corporation controlled by the same shareholders that control the lending corporation

▶ Investments in property or securities unrelated to the activities of the corporation

▶ Insuring against unrealistic hazards[58]

Loans to shareholders or corporate expenditures for the personal benefit of shareholders are viewed as as substitutes for dividend payments to shareholders. Similarly, corporate loans made to relatives or friends of shareholders are viewed as substitutes for dividend payments to shareholders, who then make personal loans to their friends and relatives. All three measures suggest an unreasonable accumulation of corporate earnings, which should have been distributed as dividends.

Likewise, loans or corporate expenditures made for the benefit of a second corporation controlled by the shareholder (or the shareholder group) who also controls the first corporation may be considered to have a tax-avoidance purpose. Theoretically, the first corporation instead could have paid a dividend to the shareholder who in turn could have paid income taxes on the dividend and then contributed after-tax funds to the second corporation.

Another factor indicative of a tax-avoidance motive, but not mentioned in Treasury Regulations, is operating a corporation as a holding or investment company that pays little or no dividends.

 STOP & THINK

Question: In 2011, an IRS auditor examines Baylor Corporation's 2008 C corporation tax return. What items might the auditor scrutinize to assertain excess accumulated earnings?

Solution: The auditor might look first at the retained earnings accounts in the beginning and year-end balance sheets (Schedule L of Form 1120). Then, the auditor might review Schedule M-2 (Analysis of Unappropriated Retained Earnings per Books) for current year earnings, the amount of earnings distributed as dividends, and the manner in which the corporation used the undistributed earnings. Next, the auditor might examine the beginning and year-end balance sheets for evidence of transactions suggesting a tax-avoidance motive. Such transactions might include loans to stockholders (Schedule L, Line 7), loans to persons other than stockholders (Schedule L, Line 6), and portfolio investments

---

[57] *U.S. v. The Donruss Company,* 23 AFTR 2d 69-418, 69-1 USTC ¶9167 (USSC, 1969).   [58] Reg. Sec. 1.537-2(c).

(Schedule L, Lines 4, 5, 6, and 9). Information about expenditures of corporate funds made for the personal benefit of shareholders might be found in the noncurrent asset section of the balance sheets (e.g., corporate ownership of a boat, airplane, or second home of a major stockholder).

REASONABLE BUSINESS NEEDS.   Section 537 defines **reasonable business needs** as

▶ Reasonably anticipated needs of the business

▶ Section 303 (death tax) redemption needs of the business

▶ Excess business holdings redemption needs of the business

▶ Product liability loss reserves

Regulation Sec. 1.537-1(a) sets forth the following relevant standard of reasonableness:

An accumulation of the earnings and profits . . . is in excess of reasonable needs of the business if it exceeds the amount that a prudent businessman would consider appropriate for the present business purposes and for the reasonably anticipated future needs of the business. The need to retain earnings and profits must be directly connected with the needs of the corporation itself and must be for bona fide business purposes.

Specific, Definite, and Feasible Plans.   A corporation's accumulation of earnings is justified only if facts and circumstances indicate that the future needs of the business require such an accumulation. The corporation usually must have specific, definite, and feasible plans for the use of the accumulation.

No Specific Time Limitations.   The earnings accumulation need not be used within a short period of time after the close of the tax year. However, the plans must provide that, based on all the facts and circumstances associated with the future needs of the business, the corporation will use the accumulation within a reasonable period of time after the close of the tax year.

Impact of Subsequent Events.   A determination of the reasonably anticipated needs of the business is based on all relevant facts and circumstances that exist at the end of the tax year. Regulation Sec. 1.537-1(b)(2) provides that subsequent events may not be used to show that an earnings accumulation is unreasonable if all the elements of reasonable anticipation are present at the close of the tax year. However, subsequent events may be used to ascertain whether the taxpayer actually intended to consummate the plans for which the earnings were accumulated.

Treasury Regulations and the courts have cited as determinative or relevant a number of factors that represent reasonable needs for accumulating earnings. These factors include:

▶ Expansion of a business or replacement of plant

▶ Acquisition of a business enterprise

▶ Debt retirement

▶ Working capital build-up

▶ Loans to suppliers or customers

▶ Product liability losses

▶ Stock redemptions

▶ Business contingencies

Expansion of a Business or Replacement of Plant.   The IRS and the courts generally have viewed the expansion of a corporation's present business facilities or the replacement of existing plant and equipment as involving a reasonable need of a business. Taxpayers have encountered problems only when the plans are undocumented, indefinite, vague, or unfeasible.[59] Although the plans need not be reduced to writing, adequate documentation is advisable.

Acquisition of a Business Enterprise. The acquisition of a business enterprise might involve extension of the same business or expansion into a new business through the purchase of either the stock or the assets of a corporation conducting the new business. Taxpayers should be careful to acquire a sufficient interest in the new business so that it will not be considered a passive investment.

Working Capital: The Bardahl Formula. Working capital is defined generally as the excess of current assets over current liabilities. The *Bardahl* formula attempts to measure the amount of working capital necessary for an operating cycle. The operating cycle encompasses a period of time necessary for the corporation to acquire inventory, sell the inventory, generate accounts receivable, and collect on the receivables. Acquiring working capital for one operating cycle is considered a reasonable need of a business. Accordingly, accumulated earnings sufficient to finance such working capital is considered reasonable.

At one time, the courts used certain rules of thumb (e.g., a current ratio of 2 to 1 or 3 to 1 or the accumulation of funds to cover a single year's operating expenses) to establish adequate working capital. Later, in the first of two *Bardahl* cases, the Tax Court endorsed a mathematical formula for measuring an operating cycle. This formula is now used to estimate the amount of working capital required for the reasonable needs of the business.

The working capital needs of a manufacturing business differ from those of a service business. For a manufacturing business, an operating cycle is the "period of time required to convert cash into raw materials, raw materials into an inventory of marketable . . . products, the inventory into sales and accounts receivable, and the period of time to collect its outstanding accounts."[60]

In the second *Bardahl* case, the Tax Court ruled that amounts advanced to a corporation by its suppliers in the form of short-term credit (e.g., trade payables) reduce the required amount of working capital.[61] Based on this ruling, the ***Bardahl*** **formula** for determining average operating cycle has become

$$
\begin{array}{c} \text{Average} \\ \text{operating} \\ \text{cycle} \end{array} = \begin{array}{c} \text{Inventory} \\ \text{period} \end{array} + \begin{array}{c} \text{Accounts} \\ \text{receivable} \\ \text{period} \end{array} - \begin{array}{c} \text{Credit} \\ \text{period} \end{array}
$$

In this formula, the *inventory period* is the time (expressed as a percentage of a year) spanning the acquisition of raw materials inventory to the sale of finished goods inventory. The *accounts receivable period* is the time (expressed as a percentage of a year) spanning the sale date to the date on which accounts receivable are collected. The *credit period* is the time (expressed as a percentage of a year) from which the corporation incurs an expense or purchases inventory to the time at which it pays the liability.

The *Bardahl* formula can be expanded to include financial and operating data as follows:

$$
\begin{array}{c} \text{Average operating cycle} \\ \text{(as a percentage of a year)} \end{array} =
$$

$$
\left[\frac{\text{Inventory amount}}{\text{Annual cost of goods sold}} + \frac{\text{Accounts receivable amount}}{\text{Annual sales}} - \frac{\text{Accounts payable amount}}{\begin{array}{c}\text{Annual operating}\\\text{expenses and purchases}\\\text{(less noncash expenses)}\end{array}} \right] \times 100
$$

---

[59] See, for example, *Myron's Enterprises v. U.S.*, 39 AFTR 2d 77-693, 77-1 USTC ¶9253 (9th Cir., 1977) and *Atlas Tool Co., Inc. v. CIR*, 45 AFTR 2d 80-645, 80-1 USTC ¶9177 (3rd Cir., 1980).

[60] *Bardahl Manufacturing Corp.*, 1965 PH T.C. Memo ¶65,200, 24 TCM 1030, at 1044.

[61] *Bardahl International Corp.*, 1966 PH T.C. Memo ¶66,182, 25 TCM 935.

This formula is linked to the working capital requirements of the business through the following equation:

$$\text{Average operating cycle (as a percentage of a year)} \times \left[\text{Cost of goods sold} + \text{Operating expenses} \right] = \text{Working capital requirements}$$

Cost of goods sold is determined on a full-cost basis (i.e., including both direct and indirect expenses). Operating expenses exclude noncash expenses such as depreciation, amortization, and depletion, as well as capital expenditures and charitable contributions. The Tax Court has allowed federal income taxes (e.g., quarterly estimated tax payments) to be included as an operating expense.[62]

The working capital requirement for one operating cycle is compared with actual working capital employed at year-end. If the working capital requirement exceeds actual working capital, the excess, along with amounts required for specific needs of the business, is deemed to justify accumulating a portion of the corporation's earnings. If the working capital requirement is less than the corporation's actual working capital, the excess generally is deemed to reflect an unreasonable accumulation unless the corporation can somehow justify the excess (e.g., for plant replacement).

In establishing "adequate" working capital, the *Bardahl* formula may provide a false sense of mathematical precision because the IRS and the courts have interpreted it differently. Some courts have used peak month inventory, accounts receivable, and trade payables turnover (instead of an annual average) to measure an operating cycle.[63] Relative to the annual average method, the peak month method generally lengthens the corporation's operating cycle. Use of these two methods can lead to very different estimates of working capital requirements. As a result, significant disputes have arisen between the IRS and taxpayers over what constitutes "adequate" working capital.

TYPICAL MISCONCEPTION

No exact method exists for determining the working capital needs of a corporation. The *Bardahl* formula is merely a rule of thumb adopted by the Tax Court. The basic approaches (peak cycle approach versus the average cycle approach) sanctioned by the *Bardahl* formula are subject to dispute among the courts.

EXAMPLE C:5-19 ▶

Austin Corporation's managers believe that Austin may be liable for the accumulated earnings tax. They ask their tax advisor to determine the corporation's working capital requirement as of December 31 of the current year under the *Bardahl* formula. The following information from Austin's records for the current year is available:

Cost of goods sold	$2,700,000
Average inventory	675,000
Purchases	3,000,000
Sales (all on account)	6,000,000
Average accounts receivable	750,000
Operating expenses (including depreciation and other noncash charges)	875,000
Depreciation and other noncash charges	75,000
Average trade payables	350,000
Estimated federal income tax payments	100,000
Working capital on December 31	825,000

The operating cycle based on the annual average method is calculated as follows (assuming a nonleap year):

$$\text{Inventory turnover} = (\$675,000 \div \$2,700,000) \times 365 = 91.25 \text{ days}$$

$$\text{Receivables turnover} = (\$750,000 \div \$6,000,000) \times 365 = 45.625 \text{ days}$$

$$\text{Payables turnover} = \frac{\$350,000}{\$3,000,000 + \$800,000} \times 365 = 33.62 \text{ days}$$

$$\text{Operating cycle} = \frac{91.25 + 45.625 \ 2 \ 33.62}{365} \times 100 = 28.3\% \text{ of a year}$$

---

[62] *Doug-Long, Inc.*, 72 T.C. 158 (1979).
[63] *State Office Supply, Inc.*, 1982 PH T.C. Memo ¶82,292, 43 TCM 1481.

Based on this operating cycle, the tax advisor estimates Austin's working capital requirement as follows:

Annual operating expenses = \$2,700,000 + \$875,000 − \$75,000 + \$100,000 = \$3,600,000
Working capital requirement = \$3,600,000 × 0.283 = \$1,018,800

The estimated \$1,018,800 working capital requirement is \$193,800 more than the \$825,000 of actual working capital recorded on December 31. This excess justifies accumulating additional current earnings for working capital needs. ◀

The *Bardahl* formula also is used to estimate the working capital requirements of service companies. A different calculation is used because service companies generally hold little or no inventory. For service companies, one looks primarily at the financing of accounts receivables. Because their principal asset is key personnel, these companies must maintain adequate working capital to retain employees when a below-normal level of business is expected. Therefore, some amount may be added to actual working capital to cover the cost of retaining personnel for a period of time.[64]

Stock Redemptions. Section 537(a) permits corporations to accumulate earnings for two types of stock redemptions: Sec. 303 (death tax) redemptions and excess business holdings redemptions. In the first case, after the death of a shareholder, a corporation can accumulate earnings to redeem stock from the shareholder's estate or a beneficiary of the estate. These earnings cannot exceed the amount of stock redeemable under Sec. 303. In the second case, a corporation can accumulate earnings to redeem stock held by a private foundation to the extent the stock exceeds the business holdings limit imposed on such foundations.

Business Contingencies. The courts and IRS have sanctioned the accumulation of earnings for business contingencies not specifically mentioned in the Sec. 537 Treasury Regulations. Among these contingencies are actual or potential litigation, a likely decline in business activities following the loss of a major customer, insuring against a potential loss, providing for a threatened strike, and funding an employee retirement plan.

CALCULATING THE ACCUMULATED EARNINGS TAX

The accumulated earnings tax calculation is set forth in Figure C:5-3. The tax is levied at a 15% rate in 2003 through 2012. After 2012, the rate is scheduled to revert to the highest marginal tax rate for individuals. As with the PHC tax, a corporation can reduce its tax liability by paying dividends. However, corporations generally do not avail themselves of this tax planning device because they often pay only a nominal dividend or no dividend at all. Also, IRS auditors generally do not raise the accumulated earnings tax issue until one or more years after the corporation has filed its tax return. Unlike the PHC tax liability, the accumulated earnings tax liability cannot be extinguished through the payment of deficiency dividends.

ACCUMULATED TAXABLE INCOME. The starting point for calculating **accumulated taxable income** is the corporation's regular taxable income. A series of positive and negative adjustments to regular taxable income are made to derive accumulated taxable income.

Positive Adjustments to Regular Taxable Income. A corporation may not claim a dividends-received deduction. Thus, regular taxable income must be increased by the amount of this deduction in a manner similar to that under the PHC tax rules.[65] The U.S. production activities deduction, however, is not added back to regular taxable

---

[64] See, for example, *Simons-Eastern Co. v. U.S.*, 31 AFTR 2d 73-640, 73-1 USTC ¶9279 (D.C. GA, 1972).

[65] Sec. 535(b)(3).

▼ FIGURE C:5-3

Calculating the Accumulated Earnings Tax

Regular taxable income
Plus: Positive adjustments
                  1. Dividends-received deduction
                  2. NOL deduction
                  3. Excess charitable contributions carried over from a preceding tax year and
                      deducted in determining current year regular taxable income
                  4. Excess capital losses carried over from another tax year and deducted when calculating
                      current year regular taxable income
Minus: Negative adjustments
                  1. Accrued U.S. and foreign income taxes
                  2. Current year charitable contributions that exceed the 10% corporate limitation
                  3. Net capital losses (where capital losses for the year exceed capital gains)
                  4. Net capital gain minus the amount of any associated income taxes
Minus: Dividends-paid deduction
Minus: Accumulated earnings credit

Accumulated taxable income
Times: 0.15 (in 2003–2012)

Accumulated earnings tax

TYPICAL MISCONCEPTION

A corporation incurring the accumulated earnings tax does not adjust its taxable income for all items that affect its taxable income differently than they affect the earnings available for distribution to its shareholders (e.g., no adjustment is required for tax-exempt interest and the U.S. production activities deduction).

income to derive accumulated taxable income. Any NOL deduction claimed must be added back to regular taxable income. The IRC allows no special deduction for an NOL incurred in the immediately preceding year, as it does under the PHC tax rules.

Negative Adjustments to Taxable Income. Charitable contributions are deductible without regard to any percentage limitation. The same adjustments required for PHC tax purposes are required for accumulated earnings tax purposes.

U.S. and foreign income taxes accrued by the corporation reduce accumulated taxable income whether the corporation uses the accrual or cash method of accounting. A corporation may deduct the amount of its net capital gain, minus income taxes attributable to this gain. The capital gains adjustment prevents a corporation with substantial capital gains from paying the accumulated earnings tax on that portion of the gains retained in the business. Net capital losses (the excess of capital losses over capital gains for the year) represent a negative adjustment to regular taxable income.

WHAT WOULD YOU DO IN THIS SITUATION?

Magnum Corporation, your client, has manufactured handguns and rifles for years. Because of competition from foreign manufacturers, demand for U.S. manufactured guns has recently declined. The total historical cost of Magnum's operating assets at the end of its most recent fiscal year is $10 million. Total gross operating revenues are $18 million. Over the years, the company accumulated $2.5 million of earnings that Magnum's CEO Allen Blay invested in securities. The investment portfolio consists primarily of growth stocks, debt instruments, and Internet stocks. Along with his other duties as CEO, Allen manages this portfolio. With the recent surge in the stock market, the value of Magnum's investment securities have increased to more than $12 million. The portfolio took a small "hit" in the Fall of the previous year. The dividend and interest income earned on the portfolio represents only a small portion of Magnum's gross income. During a meeting with you, Allen brings to your attention this investment and its stellar performance. Is Magnum liable for the accumulated earnings tax? What action(s) do you recommend that the corporation take?

Dividends-Paid Deduction. A deduction is allowed for four types of dividends paid:

▶ Regular dividends

▶ Throwback dividends

▶ Consent dividends

▶ Liquidating distributions

With minor exceptions, the rules for the dividends-paid deduction are the same in the accumulated earnings tax calculation as in the PHC tax calculation. Nonliquidating distributions paid during the tax year are eligible for the dividends-paid deduction only if paid out of the corporation's E&P. A dividends-paid deduction is not available for preferential dividends.[66]

Throwback dividends are distributions made out of E&P in the first 2½ months following the close of the tax year. The accumulated earnings tax rules require that any distribution made in the first 2½ months following the close of the tax year be treated as if paid on the last day of the preceding tax year without regard to the amount of dividends actually paid during the preceding tax year.[67] Because the IRS generally does not raise the accumulated earnings tax issue until after it has audited a corporation's tax return, throwback and consent dividends are of limited use in avoiding the accumulated earnings tax. Liquidating distributions eligible for the dividends-paid deduction include those made in connection with a complete liquidation, a partial liquidation, or a stock redemption.[68]

Unlike the PHC tax, a corporation liable for the accumulated earnings tax cannot reduce the tax by electing to pay a deficiency dividend. Thus, if a determination (e.g., judicial decision or IRS agreement) establishes the amount of accumulated earnings tax, the corporation must pay the tax, as well as any related interest and penalties.

Accumulated Earnings Credit. The accumulated earnings credit permits a corporation to accumulate E&P up to either a minimum amount ($250,000 for most C corporations) or the level of its earnings accumulated for the reasonable needs of the business. Unlike other credits, the **accumulated earnings credit** does not offset the accumulated earnings tax liability on a dollar-for-dollar basis. Instead, it is like a deduction because it reduces accumulated taxable income. Different rules for the accumulated earnings credit exist for operating companies, service companies, and holding or investment companies.[69]

▶ Operating companies can claim a credit equal to the greater of (1) $250,000 minus accumulated E&P at the end of the preceding tax year[70] or (2) current E&P retained to meet the reasonable needs of the business.

▶ The accumulated E&P balance mentioned in the previous bullet point is reduced by the amount of any current year throwback distributions treated as having been made out of the preceding year's E&P.

▶ Current E&P is reduced by the dividends-paid deduction. Any net capital gains (reduced by federal taxes attributable to the gains) reduce the amount of current E&P retained for business needs.

▶ Special rules apply to personal service companies operating primary in the fields of health, law, engineering, architecture, accounting, actuarial science, performing arts, and consulting. For these companies, the basic calculation set forth above applies, but the $250,000 minimum credit is reduced to $150,000.

▶ Holding and investment companies may claim a credit equal to $250,000 minus accumulated E&P at the end of the preceding tax year. An increased credit based on the reasonable needs of the business is not available to a holding or investment company.

ADDITIONAL COMMENT

The minimum accumulated earnings credit is $250,000 ($150,000 for certain personal service corporations) reduced by accumulated E&P at the close of the preceding year. In many situations, corporations that have been in existence for some time have accumulated E&P exceeding $250,000. Thus, the minimum credit is of little practical significance for them.

TYPICAL MISCONCEPTION

The maximum accumulated earnings credit is the amount of current E&P retained to meet the reasonable needs of the business minus an adjustment for net capital gains. This amount does not include the entire accumulation for business needs but only the accumulation in the current tax year. Thus, to calculate the maximum credit, it is necessary to determine how much of prior accumulations are retained for reasonable business needs.

EXAMPLE C:5-20 ▶ Midway Corporation reports accumulated E&P, current E&P, and current E&P retained for business needs as shown in the table below. The corporation paid no dividends during the current year. Midway is a C corporation that is not a personal service or investment company. Its minimum credit is $250,000.

---

[66] Sec. 562(c). See page C:5-21 for a more detailed discussion.
[67] Sec. 563(a). Personal holding companies, on the other hand, may elect throwback treatment for dividends paid in the 2½ month period following the end of the tax year.
[68] Sec. 562(b)(1)(B).
[69] Sec. 535(c).
[70] Section 1561(a)(2) limits a controlled group of corporations to a single $250,000 amount for the accumulated earnings credit.

Tax Items	Scenario One	Scenario Two
1. Accumulated E&P	$ 75,000	$ 75,000
2. Lifetime minimum credit	250,000	250,000
2a. Current year minimum credit		
(2a = 2 − 1)	175,000	175,000
3. Current E&P	400,000	400,000
3a. Current E&P retained for business needs	300,000	50,000
3b. Current E&P exceeding business needs		
(3b = 3 − 3a)	100,000	350,000
4. Accumulated earnings credit	300,000	175,000
(Greater of 2a or 3a)		

In both scenarios, $175,000 of the minimum credit is available. In Scenario One, because the available $175,000 minimum credit is less than $300,000 of E&P retained for business needs, the accumulated earnings credit is $300,000. In Scenario Two, because the available $175,000 minimum credit is greater than the $50,000 of E&P retained for business needs, the accumulated earnings credit is $175,000. In both scenarios, no minimum credit is available in future years. All future accumulated earnings credits are based on E&P retained for business needs. ◀

COMPREHENSIVE EXAMPLE

The following example illustrates the calculation of accumulated taxable income and the accumulated earnings tax liability.

EXAMPLE C:5-21 ▶ Pasadena is a closely held C corporation that is not a personal holding company. Pasadena has conducted a successful manufacturing business for several years. On January 1 of the current year, Pasadena reports a $750,000 accumulated E&P balance. The following information pertains to current year operations:

Operating profit	$650,000
Long-term capital gain	30,000
Dividends received from a	
20%-owned corporation	150,000
Interest	70,000
Gross income	$900,000
Dividends-received deduction	(120,000)
Salaries	(100,000)
General and administrative expenses	(200,000)
Charitable contribution deduction	(60,000)[a]
U.S. production activities deduction	(10,000)
Regular taxable income	$410,000

[a] $60,000 = 0.10 × [$900,000 − ($100,000 + $200,000)].

Federal income taxes (based on current rates and assuming no alternative minimum tax liability) accrued by Pasadena are $139,400 ($410,000 × 0.34). Actual charitable contributions are $75,000. On June 30, the corporation pays cash dividends of $20,000. Pasadena's current E&P retained for the reasonable needs of the business (after the dividends-paid deduction) is $160,000.

If the IRS determines that Pasadena has accumulated earnings exceeding the reasonable needs of its business, Pasadena's accumulated earnings tax liability would be calculated as follows:

Regular taxable income			$410,000
Plus:	Dividends-received deduction		120,000
Minus:	Excess charitable contributions		(15,000)[a]
	Federal income taxes		(139,400)
	Long-term capital gain	$ 30,000	
	Minus: Federal income taxes	(10,200)[b]	(19,800)
	Dividends-paid deduction		(20,000)
	Accumulated earnings credit:		
	Increase in current year reasonable needs	$160,000	
	Minus: Long-term capital gain (net of taxes)	(19,800)	(140,200)

Accumulated taxable income	$195,600
Times: Tax rate	× 0.15
	$ 29,340
Accumulated earnings tax liability	

[a] $75,000 total contributions − $60,000 limitation = $15,000 excess contributions.
[b] $10,200 = $30,000 × 0.34

Pasadena's accumulated earnings credit is based on its current E&P retained for reasonable business needs (minus its net capital gain, net of taxes) because its $750,000 accumulated E&P exceeds the $250,000 minimum credit.

Assuming the corporation owes no AMT, Pasadena's total federal tax liability for the current year would be $168,740 ($139,400 + $29,340). ◀

Topic Review C:5-4 presents an overview of the accumulated earnings tax.

TAX PLANNING CONSIDERATIONS

This section examines five areas of tax planning: special accounting method elections for AMT purposes, eliminating the ACE adjustment, multiyear effects of the AMT, avoiding the PHC tax, and avoiding the accumulated earnings tax.

DEPRECIATION ELECTION

Personal property generally is depreciated using the 200% declining balance method for regular tax purposes but using the 150% declining balance method for AMT purposes. For regular tax purpose, a taxpayer can elect to use the same depreciation method used for AMT purposes.[71] Such an election can reduce a taxpayer's AMT compliance burden by eliminating the need to keep an additional set of depreciation records to determine the AMT depreciation adjustment, as well as the AMT adjustment that arises when the taxpayer sells depreciable property. This election usually will reduce a taxpayer's AMT but also increase its regular tax. The reduced AMT and increased regular tax often will exactly offset each other, as illustrated in the following example.

Topic Review C:5-4

Accumulated Earnings Tax

1. The accumulated earnings tax rules apply to all but certain types of corporations. As a practical matter, the tax is assessed primarily on closely held corporations (other than S corporations and personal holding companies).
2. Certain transactions generally lead IRS auditors to believe that an accumulated earnings tax problem exists. These transactions include loans made by the corporation to its shareholders, the expenditure of corporate funds for the personal benefit of shareholders, and investments in property or securities unrelated to the corporation's principal activities.
3. Earnings accumulated for the reasonable needs of the business are exempt from the accumulated earnings tax. Among such needs are a business acquisition, debt retirement, and the build up of working capital. A $250,000 minimum credit is available to reduce accumulated taxable income. The credit amount declines to $150,000 for certain personal service corporations.
4. The accumulated earnings tax is 15% (in 2003–2012) of accumulated taxable income. Accumulated taxable income is regular taxable income plus certain positive adjustments (e.g., dividends-received deduction) and minus certain negative adjustments (e.g., federal income taxes, excess charitable contributions, and a portion of net capital gains). An accumulated earnings credit equal to the greater of a fixed dollar amount or earnings accumulated during the year for the reasonable needs of the business also is available.
5. Accumulated taxable income can be reduced by cash and property dividends paid during the year as well as consent and throwback dividends paid after year-end. Deficiency dividends, available for PHC tax purposes, are not available for accumulated earnings tax purposes.

---

[71] Sec. 168(b)(2) and (5).

EXAMPLE C:5-22 ▶ Tremont Corporation places an asset into service in the current year. Current year depreciation for the asset based on the 200% and 150% declining balance methods is $20,000 and $15,000, respectively. Tremont's regular taxable income and AMT preference and adjustment items are $500,000 and $350,000, respectively, both before taking into account the depreciation deduction for the asset. The following shows the effect on Tremont's total income tax of the election to use AMT depreciation for regular tax purposes:

	Depreciation Used for Regular Tax Purposes	
	200% DB	150% DB
Regular taxable income before depreciation	$500,000	$500,000
Minus: Depreciation deduction	(20,000)	(15,000)
Regular taxable income	$480,000	$485,000
Times: Regular tax rate	0.34	0.34
Regular tax	$163,200	$164,900
Regular taxable income	$480,000	$485,000
Plus: AMT depreciation adjustment	5,000[a]	–0–[b]
Other AMT preference and adjustment items	350,000	350,000
AMTI	$835,000	$835,000
Times: AMT tax rate	0.20[c]	0.20[c]
Tentative minimum tax (TMT)	$167,000	$167,000
Minus: Regular tax	(163,200)	(164,900)
AMT	$ 3,800	$ 2,100
Regular tax	$163,200	$164,900
Plus: AMT	3,800	2,100
Total income tax	$167,000	$167,000

[a] $20,000 – $15,000 = $5,000
[b] No AMT depreciation adjustment because depreciation is the same for regular tax and AMT purposes.
[c] No AMT exemption amount is allowed because AMTI exceeds $310,000.

    Because Tremont incurs the AMT in the current year regardless of the depreciation method it uses, its total tax will equal its TMT. The TMT is based on AMTI, which is based on AMT depreciation. Thus, Tremont's total tax is $167,000 whether it chooses to use the 200% or 150% declining balance method for regular tax purposes. ◀

    For any tax year, a taxpayer may make this election with respect to one or more classes of property. The election applies to all property in such class(es) placed in service during the tax year. The taxpayer must make the election by the due date for that year's tax return (including permissible extensions). Depreciation for real property generally is the same for regular tax and AMT purposes, so the election is not relevant for such property.

ELIMINATING THE ACE ADJUSTMENT

C corporations make the ACE adjustment, which substantially increases AMTI for many C corporations. A C corporation can eliminate the ACE adjustment by electing to be taxed as an S corporation, assuming it qualifies to make the election (see Chapter C:11). S corporations are not subject to the AMT but pass through their tax preference and AMT adjustment items to their shareholders. On the other hand, a corporation that qualifies to make an S election also may have average gross receipts that qualify it to be exempt from the AMT. If such a corporation were taxed as a C corporation, it would incur no AMT and would not pass through any preference and adjustment items to its shareholders.

MULTIYEAR EFFECTS OF AMT

A corporation pays any AMT in addition to its regular tax, which increases its current tax liability. However, its AMT also generates the same amount of minimum tax credit, which can reduce its future regular tax liabilities. A corporation's tax planning with respect to the AMT should take into account the multiyear effects on its regular tax and AMT.

STOP & THINK

Question: Flair Corporation is considering investing in municipal bonds. Flair's Chief Financial Officer (CFO) thought that the interest earned on these bonds is tax-exempt, but she was surprised to learn that it could be taxed by the federal government at a rate of up to 20% if earned by a corporation. Can such tax-exempt interest be taxed at a rate of up to 20%?

Solution: If the bond is a private activity bond not issued in 2009 or 2010, the interest income is a tax preference item. Assuming its inclusion in AMTI does not affect the phase out of Flair's AMT exemption amount, each $1 of interest income on a private activity bond increases Flair's AMTI by $1 and its TMT by $0.20. The effect this $0.20 increase has on Flair's total income tax depends on its TMT versus its regular tax.

TMT < regular tax with and without the tax-exempt interest income: The tax-exempt interest income does not increase Flair's total income tax because it has zero AMT.

TMT > regular tax with and without the tax-exempt interest income: Each $1 of private activity bond interest income increases Flair's current year tax by $0.20 because it increases Flair's AMT by $0.20. However, this increased AMT also generates $0.20 of minimum tax credit that Flair can carry forward. Assuming Flair can use the credit in the subsequent year and it discounts cash flows at an 11% rate, the $0.20 of tax Flair saves has a $0.18 ($0.20 ÷ 1.11) present value. Thus, the net increase in the present value of Flair's taxes is $0.02 ($0.20 – $0.18). If Flair cannot use the $0.20 minimum tax credit until after the subsequent year, the net increase in the present value of Flair's taxes will be greater than $0.02 but less than $0.20, depending on the number of years until Flair can use the credit.

TMT < regular tax without tax-exempt interest income but TMT > regular tax with it: Each $1 of private activity bond interest income increases Flair's tax by less than $0.20 because part of the interest income merely increases its TMT up to its regular tax, but Flair's tax does increase because the rest of the interest income generates some AMT. This AMT creates an equal amount of minimum tax credit that Flair can carry forward. Thus, Flair should consider the present value of these future tax savings.

OBJECTIVE 7

Explain how a corporation can avoid the personal holding company tax

AVOIDING THE PERSONAL HOLDING COMPANY TAX

Five tax planning techniques can be used to avoid the PHC tax.

CHANGES IN THE CORPORATION'S STOCK OWNERSHIP. To circumvent the stock ownership rules, a potential PHC can issue additional stock to unrelated parties. The stock may be either common or preferred. The issuance of nonvoting preferred stock to unrelated parties permits the corporation to distribute stock ownership among a larger number of individuals without diluting the voting power of the current common shareholder group.

CHANGING THE AMOUNT AND TYPE OF INCOME EARNED BY THE CORPORATION. A corporation can change the amount and type of its income in the following ways:

▶ Adding "operating" activities to its business to decrease the proportion of passive or investment earnings in its total income.

▶ Converting taxable interest or dividends earned on an investment portfolio into nontaxable interest or long-term capital gains. Nontaxable interest and long-term capital gains are excluded from PHCI.

▶ Generating passive income of a type that is excludible from PHCI or in an amount that diminishes the proportion of other items includible in PHCI. For example, a corporation might attempt to increase the proportion of its rental income to more than 50% of AOGI so as to exclude from PHCI adjusted income from rents.

KEY POINT

One of the easiest ways to avoid the PHC penalty tax is a dividend distribution. If a corporation lacks the funds to pay a cash dividend, its shareholders can elect a consent dividend (which is a hypothetical dividend). In addition, throwback and consent dividends can be declared after year-end in after-the-fact tax planning.

DIVIDEND DISTRIBUTIONS. Dividend payments reduce the PHC tax base. A corporation can exclude certain categories of income (e.g., adjusted income from rents) from PHCI through the payment of dividends sufficient to reduce the amount of other PHCI to 10% or less of OGI. Some of these dividends (e.g., throwback and consent) can be declared after year-end, thereby allowing last-minute tax planning.

MAKING AN S CORPORATION ELECTION. As mentioned earlier, an S corporation election eliminates liability for the PHC tax because S corporations are exempt from this tax. The election also eliminates the double taxation of corporate earnings distributed as dividends (see Chapter C:11). Such an election is advantageous where corporate tax rates exceed individual tax rates. The LLC form offers many of the same tax and nontax benefits offered by the S corporation form.

LIQUIDATING THE CORPORATION. A PHC could liquidate and distribute its assets to the shareholders. Liquidating distributions made out of E&P are eligible for the dividends-paid deduction and thus can reduce UPHCI. This alternative, however, may be unattractive where top individual tax rates exceed corporate tax rates.

OBJECTIVE 8

Explain how a corporation can avoid the accumulated earnings tax

AVOIDING THE ACCUMULATED EARNINGS TAX

The primary defense against an IRS argument that the corporation has accumulated an unreasonable amount of earnings is that the earnings accumulations are necessary to meet the future needs of the business. Business plans in support of this defense should be documented and revised periodically. The plans should describe completed, but not abandoned, projects in sufficient detail. In the event of an IRS challenge, a tentative timetable for the completion of current projects should be set forth. Such plans might be incorporated into the minutes of one or more board meetings.

Transactions suggesting an unreasonable earnings accumulation (e.g., loans to shareholders or large investment portfolios) should be avoided. The business purpose for major transactions should be thoroughly documented.

Corporations potentially liable for the accumulated earnings tax should consider making an S corporation election. S corporations avoid accumulated earnings tax liability on a prospective basis. By implication, an S corporation election will not eliminate potential exposure to the accumulated earnings tax for tax years prior to the year in which the election becomes effective.

COMPLIANCE AND PROCEDURAL CONSIDERATIONS

ALTERNATIVE MINIMUM TAX

A corporation reports its AMT calculation on Form 4626 (Alternative Minimum Tax—Corporations). A completed Form 4626, based on the facts in the comprehensive example on pages C:5-10 through C:5-12, appears in Appendix B. The instructions for Form 4626 include a worksheet for calculating ACE. A corporation uses Form 8827 (Credit for Prior Year Minimum Tax—Corporations) to calculate the minimum tax credit it claims, as well as the minimum tax credit it carries forward to the subsequent year.

Section 6655(g) provides that a corporation's required quarterly estimated tax payments take into account its regular tax and AMT. A corporation whose estimated tax payments are not large enough incurs an underpayment penalty, which is discussed in Chapter C:3.

ETHICAL POINT

A tax practitioner has a responsibility to advise his or her client early in the year about potential PHC problems and steps that can be taken to avoid the penalty tax. Because the PHC tax is self-assessed, a Schedule PH must be filed with Form 1120 even if the corporation owes no PHC tax.

PERSONAL HOLDING COMPANY TAX

FILING REQUIREMENTS FOR TAX RETURNS. A PHC must file a corporate income tax return (Form 1120). Schedule PH must accompany the return. Schedule PH incorporates the tests for determining whether a corporation is a PHC and includes the UPHCI and PHC tax calculations. Section 6501(f) extends from three to six years the limitations period for the PHC tax if a PHC fails to file Schedule PH, even if the corporation owes no additional tax.

PAYMENT OF THE TAX, INTEREST, AND PENALTIES. Corporations ordinarily pay the PHC tax when they file Form 1120 and Schedule PH, or when the IRS or the courts determine that the corporation owes the tax. Unlike the AMT, the PHC tax is not

ETHICAL POINT

Notwithstanding the tax practitioner's responsibility to advise his or her client about potential accumulated earnings tax problems, because the tax is not self-assessed, the CPA or the client are under no duty to notify the IRS of the tax problem.

included in the corporation's required estimated tax payments. Corporations that pay the PHC tax after the due date for filing their return (without regard to extensions) generally will also owe interest and penalties on the unpaid PHC tax balance. Interest will accrue from the date the return is originally due (without regard to extensions) until the entire tax is paid.[72]

ACCUMULATED EARNINGS TAX

No schedule or return is required for reporting the accumulated earnings tax. Because of the ad hoc nature of this tax, a corporation generally will not pay it until some time after the IRS has audited its tax return. Sec. 6601(b) requires the charging of interest on the accumulated earnings tax balance from the original due date for the return (without regard to extensions) until the date the IRS receives full tax payment.[73] The IRS also may impose a penalty for negligent underpayment of an accumulated earnings tax.[74]

FINANCIAL STATEMENT IMPLICATIONS

OBJECTIVE 9

Understand the financial statement implications of the alternative minimum tax

ALTERNATIVE MINIMUM TAX

When a corporation pays AMT, it also obtains a minimum tax credit that it can carryforward indefinitely. Accounting Standards Codification (ASC) 740 prescribes the following rules for accounting for income taxes in financial statements when a firm pays AMT:

▶ For a firm's temporary differences and carryforwards, calculate its deferred tax assets and liabilities for regular tax temporary differences using the regular tax rate and the difference between the book basis and regular tax basis of its assets and liabilities.

▶ Include in a firm's deferred tax assets its minimum tax credit carryforwards, which may be comprised of minimum tax credits arising from AMT in the current year and unused minimum tax credits from prior years. As with other deferred tax assets, reduce the deferred tax asset for the minimum tax credit by a valuation allowance if, based on available evidence, it is more likely than not (i.e., greater than 50%) that all or some of the deferred asset will not be realized.

EXAMPLE C:5-23 ▶

In the current year, Alpha Corporation's regular tax is $40,000, and its AMT is $10,000. Alpha's current year AMT generates a $10,000 minimum tax credit. Alpha determines that it will realize (use) the entire credit in future years. Therefore, it need not establish a valuation allowance. Alpha has no book-tax differences, so the minimum tax credit carryover is the only deferred tax asset or liability item. Accordingly, Alpha makes the following book journal entry:

Federal income tax expense	40,000	
Deferred tax asset	10,000	
Taxes payable		50,000

Note that Alpha's $40,000 current year federal income tax expense for its financial statements equals its current year regular tax. This result occurs because Alpha pays $10,000 of AMT in the current year but expects to recover all $10,000 in subsequent years by using its minimum tax credit.

---

[72] *Hart Metal Products Corp. v. U.S.*, 38 AFTR 2d 76-6118, 76-2 USTC ¶9781 (Ct. Cls., 1976).

[73] Rev. Rul. 87-54, 1987-1 C.B. 349.
[74] Rev. Rul. 75-330, 1975-2 C.B. 496.

In the subsequent year, Alpha's regular tax is $90,000, and its tentative minimum tax is $70,000. Thus, its AMT is zero, and it can realize (use) the entire $10,000 minimum tax credit. Alpha's net tax liability is $80,000 ($90,000 − $10,000). Accordingly, it makes the following book journal entry:

Federal income tax expense	90,000	
Deferred tax asset		10,000
Taxes payable		80,000	◀

See Chapter C:3 for a general discussion of financial implications of federal income taxes.

PROBLEM MATERIALS

DISCUSSION QUESTIONS

C:5-1 Explain Congress' intent for enacting the AMT.

C:5-2 Define the following terms relating to the AMT:
a. Tax preference item
b. AMT adjustment item
c. Adjusted current earnings
d. Alternative minimum taxable income
e. AMT exemption amount
f. Tentative minimum tax
g. Minimum tax credit

C:5-3 Dunn Corporation is not a small corporation exempt from the AMT. Dunn's CPA does not calculate the AMT because he knows that Dunn's taxable income is less than the $40,000 AMT exemption amount allowed to corporations. Is the CPA correct in his belief? Explain.

C:5-4 What special rules (if any) apply to the AMT calculation for the following entities:
a. Corporations, particularly small ones
b. Controlled groups
c. S corporations

C:5-5 Agnew Corporation operates a small manufacturing business. During Year 1 (its first tax year, which is 12 months long), Agnew sells goods for $3.8 million for which the cost of goods sold is $2.8 million. Agnew's owner estimates that future sales and cost of goods sold will grow by 25% each year. Agnew is not related to any other corporations. Is Agnew exempt from the AMT in Year 1? In any of the next five years? Explain.

C:5-6 Menifee Corporation has conducted business for several years, and its annual gross receipts never have been more than $4 million. Jackie, who has owned all of Menifee's stock since she incorporated it, purchases all of Estill Corporation's stock in the current year. Estill's annual gross receipts have been approximately $6 million in recent years. Explain to Jackie how her acquisition of Estill's stock will affect the AMT that Menifee pays.

C:5-7 Determine whether the following statements relating to the AMT for a corporation are true or false. If false, explain why.

a. Tax preference items only increase AMTI.
b. A corporation uses the same NOL carryover amount for regular tax and AMT purposes.
c. A corporation is allowed a tax credit for the excess of its AMT over its regular tax.
d. The general business credit can reduce a corporation's regular tax and also its AMT.
e. The ACE adjustment only increases AMTI.
f. An S corporation is exempt from the AMT, regardless of its gross receipts.

C:5-8 Identify each of the following as a tax preference item (PREF), an AMT adjustment item to calculate preadjustment AMTI (ADJ), an item to adjust from preadjustment AMTI to ACE (ACE), or none of these (NONE):
a. Percentage depletion in excess of a property's adjusted basis at the beginning of the tax year
b. MACRS depreciation deducted on a machine placed in service in the current year
c. Sec. 179 expense deducted on delivery trucks placed in service in the current year
d. Gain or loss realized on the sale of a machine placed in service four years ago
e. Tax-exempt interest earned on State of Michigan private activity bonds
f. Tax-exempt interest earned on State of Michigan general revenue bonds
g. Long-term contract for which the taxpayer uses the completed contract method

C:5-9 What adjustment does a corporation make if ACE is more than preadjustment AMTI? If ACE is less than preadjustment AMTI?

C:5-10 Florida Corporation incurs AMT for the first time in the current year. The main reason for incurring the AMT is a $2 million gain on a current year installment sale that Florida is recognizing over ten years for regular tax purposes. Explain to Florida's president how the installment sale can cause Florida to incur the AMT, how its treatment for ACE is similar to and different from the E&P treatment with which she is familiar, and whether its ACE treatment will partially or completely reverse in future years.

C:5-11 Some tax scholars say tax-exempt interest on state or local bonds that are not private activity bonds can, because of the ACE adjustment, produce three different effective tax rates depending on the corporation's tax situation: (1) a 0% effective tax rate, (2) a 15% effective tax rate, or (3) between a 0% and 15% effective tax rate. Explain what the tax scholars mean.

C:5-12 Indicate whether the following items are includible in regular taxable income, preadjustment AMTI, and/or ACE. Also indicate whether a corporation must make a positive, negative, or zero adjustment when calculating preadjustment AMTI and when calculating ACE.
   a. Tax-exempt interest on private activity bonds (not issued in 2009 or 2010)
   b. Tax-exempt interest on a state's general revenue bonds (not issued in 2009 or 2010)
   c. Proceeds from a life insurance policy (with no cash surrender value) paid on account of a corporate officer's death
   d. Gain on a current year sale of property for which a corporation uses the installment method
   e. Gain on a previous year sale of property for which a corporation uses the installment method
   f. Deduction of organizational expenditures made in the previous year
   g. Deduction for a dividend received from a 25%-owned domestic corporation
   h. Deduction for a dividend received from a 5%-owned domestic corporation

C:5-13 Discuss the regular tax and AMT depreciation rules applicable to the following types of property acquired in the current year.
   a. Section 1250 property—a factory building
   b. Section 1245 property—a drill press

C:5-14 In the current year, Burbank Corporation incurs an AMT for the first time. Its AMT is due to an ACE adjustment resulting from Burbank's receiving $4 million of life insurance proceeds upon the death of the corporation's chief executive officer. The policy had no cash surrender value. Explain to Burbank's chief financial officer whether Burbank can reduce its future regular taxes by the AMT paid in the current year.

C:5-15 The personal holding company tax and the accumulated earnings tax reflect efforts to prevent use of the corporate entity to avoid taxation. Explain the congressional intent behind these two tax measures.

C:5-16 Which of the following corporate forms are exempt from the PHC tax? The accumulated earnings tax?
   a. Closely held corporations
   b. S corporations
   c. Professional corporations
   d. Tax-exempt organizations
   e. Publicly held corporations
   f. Corporations filing a consolidated tax return
   g. Limited liability companies

C:5-17 Because of its quality investments, Carolina Corporation has always generated 30% to 40% of its gross income from passive sources. In the current year, Carolina sold a block of stock in a company it acquired several years ago. As a result of the sale, the corporation realized a substantial long-term capital gain that will increase this year's investment income from 40% to 70% of gross income. Explain to Carolina's president why she should or should not be worried about the personal holding company tax.

C:5-18 Which of the following income items, when received by a corporation, are included in personal holding company income (PHCI)? Indicate whether any special circumstances would exclude an income item that is generally includible in PHCI.
   a. Dividends
   b. Interest on a corporate bond
   c. Interest on a general revenue bond issued by a state government
   d. Rental income from a warehouse leased to a third party
   e. Rental income from a warehouse leased to the corporation's sole shareholder
   f. Royalty income on a book whose copyright is owned by the corporation
   g. Royalty income on a computer software copyright developed by the corporation and leased to a software marketing firm
   h. Accounting fees earned by a professional corporation owned by three equal shareholders, which offers public accounting services to various clients
   i. Long-term capital gain on the sale of a stock investment

C:5-19 Which of the following dividends are eligible for the dividends-paid deduction in the calculation of the PHC tax? The accumulated earnings tax?
   a. Cash dividend paid on common stock during the tax year
   b. Annual cash dividend paid on preferred stock where no dividend is paid to the common shareholders
   c. Dividend payable in the stock of an unrelated corporation
   d. Stock dividend payable on the single class of stock of the distributing corporation
   e. Cash dividend paid two months after the close of the tax year

C:5-20 Define the term *consent dividend*. How can a consent dividend be used to avoid the PHC and accumulated earnings taxes? In each case, what requirements must be met by the distributing corporation and/or its shareholders to qualify a consent dividend for the dividends-paid deduction? What are the tax consequences of a consent dividend to the shareholders and the distributing corporation?

C:5-21 Explain the advantages of a deficiency dividend. What requirements must a PHC and its shareholders meet to use a deficiency dividend to reduce or eliminate the PHC tax liability? Can a deficiency dividend eliminate interest and penalties, in addition to the PHC tax liability?

C:5-22 Determine whether the following statements regarding the PHC tax are true or false:
   a. In a given tax year, a corporation might not owe the PHC tax even though it is deemed to be a PHC.
   b. A sale of a large tract of land held for investment can make a manufacturing corporation a PHC.
   c. Federal income taxes (including the alternative minimum tax) accrued by the PHC reduce UPHCI for the tax year.
   d. To reduce UPHCI, the corporation's shareholders can elect to be treated as having received consent dividends. They can make this election any time from the first day of the corporation's tax year through the due date for the corporation's tax return (including extensions).
   e. The payment of a deficiency dividend permits a PHC to eliminate its PHC tax liability, as well as related interest and penalties.
   f. A corporation deemed to be a PHC for a particular tax year also can be liable for the accumulated earnings tax for that year.
   g. A PHC can be subject to the alternative minimum tax.

C:5-23 Explain the implication of the following statement: "Like many dogs, the threat (bark) of the PHC tax is much worse than the actual penalties assessed in connection with its (bite)."

C:5-24 Explain the following statement: "Although the accumulated earnings tax can be imposed on both publicly held and closely held corporations, the tax is likely to be imposed primarily on closely held corporations."

C:5-25 The accumulated earnings tax is imposed only when the corporation is "formed or availed of for the purpose of avoiding the income tax." Does tax avoidance have to occur at the corporate or the shareholder level for the accumulated earnings tax to be imposed? Does tax avoidance have to be the sole motive for earnings accumulation before such imposition?

C:5-26 How, in its first year of operation, can a newly formed corporation be subject to the PHC tax but not the AMT and the accumulated earnings tax?

C:5-27 Gamma Corporation has generated substantial cash flows from its manufacturing activities. It has only a moderate need to reinvest its earnings in existing facilities or for expansion. In recent years, the corporation has amassed a large investment portfolio due to management's unwillingness to pay dividends. The corporation is unlikely to be deemed a PHC but is concerned about its exposure to the accumulated earnings tax. Explain to Gamma's president what steps he can take to avoid liability for the accumulated earnings tax in the current year? In future tax years? Do these steps require the payment of a cash dividend?

C:5-28 Explain the *Bardahl* formula. Why have some tax authorities said that this formula implies a greater degree of mathematical precision than is actually the case? Does the *Bardahl* formula apply to service companies?

C:5-29 Different rules for calculating the accumulated earnings credit apply to operating companies, holding and investment companies, and service companies. Explain the differences.

C:5-30 Determine whether the following statements about the accumulated earnings tax are true or false:
   a. Before the IRS can impose the accumulated earnings tax, it need only show that tax avoidance was one of the motives for the corporation's unreasonable accumulation of earnings.
   b. Long-term capital gains are included in the accumulated earnings tax base.
   c. Each corporate member of a controlled group can claim a separate $150,000 or $250,000 accumulated earnings credit.
   d. A dividends-paid deduction can be claimed for both cash and property distributions (other than nontaxable stock dividends) made by a corporation. This deduction reduces both regular taxable income and accumulated taxable income.
   e. The accumulated earnings tax liability cannot be eliminated by paying a deficiency dividend.
   f. Interest and penalties on the accumulated earnings tax deficiency accrue only from the date the IRS or the courts determine that the tax is owed.
   g. The accumulated earnings tax is self-reported on Form 1120-AET that is filed along with the corporate tax return.

C:5-31 For each of the following statements, indicate whether the statement is true for the PHC tax only (P), the accumulated earnings tax only (A), both taxes (B), or neither tax (N).
   a. The tax is imposed only if the corporation satisfies certain stock ownership and income requirements.
   b. The tax applies to both closely held and publicly traded corporations.
   c. The tax is ad hoc in nature (i.e., assessed in the course of an audit).
   d. Long-term capital gains are a neutral factor in determining the amount of the tax liability.
   e. Tax-exempt interest income is excluded from the tax base.
   f. A credit that reduces the tax liability on a dollar-for-dollar basis is available.
   g. Throwback dividends may be paid without limit.
   h. Consent dividends are eligible for a dividends-paid deduction.
   i. Throwback and consent dividends are effective in reducing or eliminating the tax liability.
   j. The tax can be avoided by paying a deficiency dividend.
   k. The tax applies to S corporations.

ISSUE IDENTIFICATION QUESTIONS

C:5-32 Bird Corporation purchases machinery for $3 million and places it in service in June 2012. Installation costs are $75,000. The machine replaces an old machine that Bird purchased several years ago, which Bird sells at a $125,000 financial accounting profit. What issues must you, as Bird's director of taxes, address because of the sale of the old machine and purchase of the new machine?

C:5-33 Parrish is a closely held C corporation. Robert and Kim Parrish own all its stock. The corporation, now in its second month of operation, expects to earn $200,000 of gross income in the current tax year. This income is expected to consist of approximately 40% dividends, 30% corporate bond interest, and 30% net real estate rentals (after interest expense, property taxes, and depreciation). Administrative expenses are estimated to be $40,000. What special problems does Parrish Corporation's earning substantial passive income present to you as its CPA?

C:5-34 McHale is a C corporation owned by eight individuals, three of whom own 51% of the stock and comprise the board of directors. The corporation operates a successful automobile repair parts manufacturing business. It has accumulated $2 million of E&P and expects to accumulate another $300,000 annually. Annual dividends are $30,000. Because Americans retain their vehicles longer than they did 20 years ago, demand for McHale's repair parts has been strong for the past five years. However, little expansion or replacement of the current plant is projected for three to five years. Management has invested $200,000 annually in growth stocks. Its current investment portfolio, which is held primarily as protection against a business downturn, is valued at $1.2 million. Loans to shareholder-employees currently amount to $400,000. As McHale's tax return preparer, what tax issues should you have your client consider?

PROBLEMS

C:5-35 *General Formula for AMT.* In the current year, Whitaker Corporation has taxable income of $700,000 and tax preference items of $100,000. It also has $250,000 of positive AMT adjustment items and $80,000 of negative AMT adjustment items (neither of which includes the ACE adjustment). Whitaker's ACE amount is $1.3 million. Whittaker is not a small corporation exempt from the AMT. Determine the following for Whitaker:
a. AMTI
b. Tentative minimum tax (TMT)
c. AMT
d. Minimum tax credit
e. How much smaller would Whitaker's tax preference and AMT adjustment items have to be for its AMT to be zero?

C:5-36 *General Formula for AMT.* Westwood Corporation has $100,000 of taxable income and $20,000 of tax preference items in the current year. Westwood's positive and negative AMT adjustment items (other than the ACE adjustment) are $38,000 and $45,000, respectively, and its ACE amount is $175,000. Westwood is not a small corporation exempt from the AMT. Determine Westwood's AMT for the current year.

C:5-37 *Small Corporation Exemption from AMT.* Willis Corporation is a calendar year corporation that forms on April 1 of Year 1. Willis Corporation reports the following gross receipts:

Year	Gross Receipts
1	$ 3,000,000
2	5,400,000
3	7,400,000
4	8,800,000
5	10,500,000
6	12,400,000

Willis is not a member of a controlled group and is not a successor to another corporation. In which year(s) is Willis exempt from the AMT?

C:5-38 *AMT Depreciation.* On June 1 of Year 1, Water Corporation places into service a machine costing $10,000. The machine is seven-year property under the MACRS rules and has a 12-year class life. Water does not elect Sec. 179 expensing and elects out of bonus depreciation. Based on the half-year convention, calculate each year's depreciation deductions for regular tax and AMT purposes, and determine the amount of Water's AMT depreciation adjustment each year.

C:5-39 *AMT Gain or Loss.* Assume the same facts as in Problem C:5-38 except Water Corporation sells the machine for $9,000 on August 31 of Year 3. Determine the following:
a. Water's gain or loss on the machine's sale for regular tax and AMT purposes.
b. The amount of Water's AMT adjustments for Year 3.

C:5-40 *ACE Adjustment.* Towne Corporation has the following amounts of ACE and preadjustment AMTI for Years 1 through 5:

	Year				
	1	2	3	4	5
ACE	$ 700	$ 700	$ 700	$700	$(700)
Preadjustment AMTI	(100)	1,300	1,000	–0–	(200)

Towne's net ACE adjustments prior to Year 1 are zero. Calculate Towne's ACE adjustment and AMTI for each year.

C:5-41 *Regular Tax and AMT Calculations.* Bronze Corporation reports the following data for the current year:

Net profit from recurring operations	$278,000
Other income and expenses not included in the $278,000 amount:	
Dividend from 10%-owned corporation	40,000
Life insurance proceeds received upon death of a Bronze officer	500,000
Tax-exempt interest on private activity bonds	25,000
Tax-exempt interest on general revenue bonds	30,000
Installment sale in current year:	
Total realized gain	400,000
Portion of gain on installment collections in current year	32,000
Depreciation:	
For regular tax purposes	120,000
For AMT purposes	85,000
Sec. 1245 property sold in current year:	
Gain for regular tax purposes	30,000
Basis for regular tax purposes	54,000
Basis for AMT purposes	60,000

Bronze is not a small corporation exempt from the AMT and has no AMT adjustment for the U.S. production activities deduction. The tax-exempt bonds were issued before 2009.
a. What is Bronze's regular taxable income and regular tax?
b. What is Bronze's preadjustment AMTI?
c. What is Bronze's ACE?
d. What is Bronze's AMTI?
e. What is Bronze's AMT?
f. What minimum tax credit does Bronze obtain in the current year? In what year(s) can Bronze use it?
g. Does Bronze have to include the AMT when determining its estimated tax payments and any tax underpayment penalty for the current year?

C:5-42 *Regular Tax and AMT Calculations.* Campbell Corporation reports regular taxable income of $210,000 in the current year. Campbell takes into account the following facts when calculating the $210,000 amount.

• Campbell deducts $100,000 of MACRS depreciation for regular tax purposes. Depreciation for AMT purposes is $75,000.

• Campbell recognizes a $12,000 Sec. 1245 gain on the sale of an asset. The asset's regular tax basis at the time of sale is $9,000 less than its AMT basis.

• Campbell's ACE is $290,000.

Campbell is not a small corporation exempt from the AMT and has no AMT adjustment for the U.S. production activities deduction.
a. What is Campbell's AMTI?
b. What is Campbell's AMT?

c. What minimum tax credit does Campbell obtain in the current year? In what year(s) can Campbell use it?

d. Does Campbell have to include the AMT when determining its estimated tax payments and any tax underpayment penalty for the current year?

C:5-43 *Regular Tax and AMT Calculations.* Sheldon Corporation reports regular taxable income of $150,000 in the current year. Its regular tax is $41,750. Sheldon takes into account the following facts when calculating the $150,000 amount.

- Sheldon deducts $90,000 of MACRS depreciation for regular tax purposes. Depreciation for AMT purposes is $60,000.
- Sheldon sells equipment for $28,000. The equipment's regular tax basis at the time of sale is $16,000, and its AMT basis is $25,000.
- Sheldon's ACE is $340,000.

Sheldon is not a small corporation exempt from the AMT and has no AMT adjustment for the U.S. production activities deduction.

a. What is Sheldon's AMT?

b. What minimum tax credit does Sheldon obtain in the current year? In what year(s) can Sheldon use it?

C:5-44 *Regular Tax and AMT Calculations.* Subach Corporation reports $600,000 of regular taxable income for the current year. Subach also reports the following information (reflected in regular taxable income, if applicable):

Depreciation:	
For regular tax purposes	$440,000
For AMT purposes	410,000
Tax-exempt interest:	
On general revenue bonds	100,000
On private activity bonds	75,000
Current year installment sale:	
Total realized gain	150,000
Portion of gain on current year installment collections	25,000
Prior year installment sale:	
Total realized gain	140,000
Portion of gain on current year installment collections	35,000
Life insurance proceeds received upon the death of a Subach executive	500,000
Organizational expenditures deducted in current year	5,000
Dividend received from 25%-owned corporation	90,000

Sheldon is not a small corporation exempt from the AMT and has no AMT adjustment for the U.S. production activities deduction. The general revenue bonds and private activity bonds were issued before 2009. What is Subach's total current year federal income tax?

C:5-45 *Regular Tax and AMT Calculations.* Alabama Corporation conducts a copper mining business. During the current year, it reports regular taxable income of $400,000, which includes a $100,000 deduction for percentage depletion. The depletable property's adjusted basis at year-end (before reduction for current year depletion) is $40,000. Cost depletion, had Alabama deducted it, would have been $30,000. Depreciation for other property is $140,000 for regular tax purposes and $90,000 for AMT purposes. Alabama sold an asset for which it included a $12,000 gain in regular taxable income. The asset's adjusted basis is $10,000 higher for AMT purposes than for regular tax purposes. Alabama's adjusted current earnings are $800,000. Alabama is not a small corporation exempt from the AMT and has no AMT adjustment for the U.S. production activities deduction.

a. What is Alabama's AMTI and AMT?

b. What minimum tax credit does Alabama obtain in the current year? In what year(s) can Alabama use it?

C:5-46 *Regular Tax and AMT Calculations.* What is Middle Corporation's regular tax, AMT, total federal income tax, and minimum tax credit generated in each of the following scenarios? Assume that Middle's ACE adjustments in prior years net to a positive $120,000 and that Middle is not a small corporation exempt from the AMT.

	Scenario 1	Scenario 2	Scenario 3
Regular taxable income	$200,000	$ 50,000	$300,000
AMT preference and adjustment items (other than the ACE adjustment)	100,000	25,000	160,000
Adjusted current earnings	500,000	150,000	400,000

C:5-47 *Regular tax and AMT Calculations.* For the current year, Delta Corporation reports taxable income of $2 million, tax preference items of $100,000, net positive AMT adjustment items (other than the ACE adjustment) of $600,000, and adjusted current earnings of $4 million. Delta is not a small corporation exempt from the AMT and has no AMT adjustment for the U.S. production activities deduction.
a. What is Delta's regular tax?
b. What is Delta's AMT?
c. What minimum tax credit does Delta obtain? In what year(s) can Delta use it?
d. Suppose Delta qualified as a small corporation exempt from the AMT. How would your answers to Parts a, b, and c change?

C:5-48 *Regular Tax and AMT Calculations.* Jones Corporation has $550,000 of regular taxable income, $120,000 of tax preference items, $240,000 of net positive AMT adjustment items (other than the ACE adjustment), and $970,000 of adjusted current earnings. Jones is not a small corporation exempt from the AMT and has no AMT adjustment for the U.S. production activities deduction.
a. What is Jones' total federal income tax?
b. What minimum tax credit does Jones obtain? In what year(s) can Jones use it?
c. Suppose Jones qualifies as a small corporation that is exempt from the AMT. How would your answers to Parts a and b change?

C:5-49 *Installment Sale and AMT.* Duncan Corporation sells land in the current year (Year 1) for $900,000. The land is Sec. 1231 property having a $360,000 adjusted basis. The purchaser of the land pays Duncan $300,000 in the current year and in each of the next two years. Duncan charges the purchaser a market interest rate on the unpaid balance. Duncan's CEO asks you to prepare a year-by-year analysis of the impact of this land sale on the firm's tax position. By how much will the land sale affect Duncan's regular tax and AMT each year? In your calculation, you can ignore the interest Duncan charges the purchaser. Assume that Duncan is not a small corporation exempt from the AMT, has no AMT adjustment for the U.S. production activities deduction, and has a 34% regular tax rate. Also assume that Duncan has AMT in each year whether or not it takes the land sale into consideration.

C:5-50 *Minimum Tax Credit.* Gulf Corporation reports the following amounts for Years 1 through 4:

Type of Tax	Year 1	Year 2	Year 3	Year 4
Regular tax	$75,000	$100,000	$120,000	$144,000
Tentative minimum tax	40,000	150,000	105,000	95,000

Gulf is not a small corporation exempt from the AMT. In what year(s) does Gulf obtain a minimum tax credit? In what year(s) can Gulf use the minimum tax credit?

C:5-51 *General Business Credit.* In the current year (not 2010), Edge Corporation's regular tax before credits is $165,000. Its tentative minimum tax is $100,000, and its only available tax credit is a $200,000 general business credit relating to research expenditures.
a. What amount of general business credit may Edge claim for the current year?
b. To what year(s) may Edge carry any unused general business credit from the current year?

C:5-52 *General Business Credit.* In the current year (not 2010), Harden Corporation has $700,000 of regular taxable income, $60,000 of tax preference items, $140,000 of net positive AMT adjustment items (other than the ACE adjustment), and $1 million of adjusted current earnings. Harden's only available tax credit is a $45,000 general business credit relating to research expenditures.
a. What is Harden's AMT for the current year?
b. What amount of general business credit may Harden claim for the current year?
c. To what year(s) may Harden carry any unused general business credit from the current year?

C:5-53 *Estimated Tax Payments and AMT.* Ajax Corporation expects to have a $100,000 regular tax and a $70,000 AMT for the current year. Last year, it had a $200,000 regular tax and no AMT. What minimum quarterly estimated tax payment must Ajax make for the current year?

C:5-54 *Estimated Tax Payments and AMT.* Dallas Corporation reports the following amounts for Years 1 and 2:

Type of Tax	Year 1	Year 2
Regular tax	$100,000	$150,000
AMT	–0–	25,000

Each tax year is a 12-month period. Dallas qualifies as a small corporation for purposes of estimated tax payments, but it does not qualify as a small corporation exempt from the AMT. Dallas makes $23,000 of estimated tax payments for each quarter of Year 2.
a. How much tax will Dallas owe when it files its Year 2 tax return?
b. Is Dallas liable for any estimated tax underpayment penalty? If so, how much did Dallas underpay in each quarter?

C:5-55 *PHC Definition.* In which of the following situations will Small Corporation be deemed to be a PHC? Assume that personal holding company income comprises more than 60% of Small's adjusted ordinary gross income.
a. Art owns 100% of Parent Corporation stock, and Parent owns 100% of Small's stock. Parent and Small file separate tax returns.
b. Art owns one-third of Small's stock. The PRS Partnership, of which Phil, Robert, and Sue each have a one-third capital and profits interest, also owns one-third of Small's stock. The remaining shares of Small's stock are owned by 50 individuals unrelated to Art, Phil, Robert, and Sue.
c. Art and his wife, Becky, each own 20% of Small's stock. The remaining shares of Small's stock are owned by the Whitaker Family Trust. Becky and her three sisters each have a one-fourth beneficial interest in the trust.

C:5-56 *Personal Holding Company Status.* In each of the following four scenarios, determine whether the corporation is a personal holding company. Assume the corporation's outstanding stock is owned equally by three individuals.

Item	Scenario 1	Scenario 2	Scenario 3	Scenario 4
Gross profit from sales	$40,000	$ 80,000	$40,000	$ 60,000
Capital gains	–0–	10,000	5,000	10,000
Taxable interest income	15,000	15,000	10,000	20,000
Dividends received	10,000	10,000	2,000	–0–
Rental income	80,000	150,000	–0–	–0–
Copyright royalties	–0–	5,000	80,000	–0–
Personal service income	–0–	–0–	–0–	100,000
Rent-related expenses	20,000	30,000	–0–	–0–
Copyright-related expenses	–0–	–0–	25,000	–0–
Dividends paid	8,000	10,000	5,000	10,000

C:5-57 *PHC Tax.* In the current year, Moore Corporation is deemed to be a PHC and reports the following results:

Taxable income	$200,000
Dividend received from an 18%-owned domestic corporation	50,000
Dividends paid	75,000

a. What is Moore's regular tax liability (ignoring any AMT implications)?
b. What is Moore's PHC tax liability?
c. What measures can Moore take to eliminate its PHC tax liability after year-end and before it files its tax return? After it files its tax return?

C:5-58 *PHC Tax.* In the current year, Kennedy Corporation is deemed to be a PHC and reports the following results:

Taxable income	$400,000
Federal income taxes	136,000
Dividends paid to Marlene, Kennedy's sole shareholder	75,000

The following information is available:
• The corporation received $100,000 of dividends from a 25%-owned domestic corporation.

- The corporation received $30,000 of tax-exempt interest income.
- The corporation recognized a $175,000 Sec. 1231 gain on the sale of land.

a. What is Kennedy's PHC tax liability?

b. What measures can Kennedy take to eliminate the PHC tax liability after year-end and before Kennedy files its tax return? After Kennedy files its tax return?

C:5-59 *PHC Tax.* Alice and Barry own all the shares of Alpha Corporation. For the current year, the corporation reports the following income and expenses:

Rental income	$ 750,000
Dividend income from less than 20%-owned corporations	200,000
Tax-exempt interest income	40,000
Gross profit on sale of merchandise	50,000
Long-term capital gain on the sale of stocks	200,000
Total income	$1,240,000

Minus: Rent related expenses:		
Interest expense	$140,000	
Depreciation expense	150,000	
Property taxes	175,000	
Other Sec. 162 expenses	165,000	(630,000)
Minus: Administrative expenses		(90,000)
Pre-tax profit		$ 520,000

During the current year, Alpha Corporation paid $50,000 in dividends to its shareholders. Assume Alpha is not eligible for the U.S. production activities deduction.

a. Is Alpha a personal holding company?

b. What is Alpha's regular tax liability?

c. What is Alpha's personal holding company tax liability (if any)?

C:5-60 *Unreasonable Accumulation of Earnings.* In each of the following scenarios, indicate why Adobe Corporation's accumulation of earnings might be unreasonable relative to its business needs. Provide one or more arguments the corporation might put forth to support its position that the accumulation is reasonable. Assume that Tess owns all the Adobe stock.

a. Ten years ago, Adobe established a sinking fund to retire its ten-year notes and has added cash to the fund annually. Six months ago, the corporation decided to refinance the notes at maturity at a lower interest rate through the issuance of a new series of bonds sold to an insurance company. The sinking fund balance is invested in stocks and commercial paper. A general plan exists to use the balance to purchase operating assets. No definite plans have been established by year-end.

b. Adobe regularly lends money to Tess at a rate slightly below the rate charged by a commercial bank. Tess has repaid about 20% of these loans. The current balance on the loans is $500,000, which approximates one year's net income for Adobe.

c. Adobe has heavily invested in stocks and bonds. The current market value of its investments is $2 million. The investment portfolio comprises approximately one-half of Adobe's assets.

d. Tess owns three other corporations, which, together with Adobe, form a brother-sister controlled group. Adobe regularly lends funds to Tess's three other corporations. Current loans amount to $500,000. The interest rate charged approximates the commercial rate for similar loans.

C:5-61 *Bardahl Formula.* Lion Corporation is concerned about a potential accumulated earnings tax liability. It accumulates E&P for working capital necessary to conduct its manufacturing business. The following data appear in its current year balance sheets.

Account	Beginning Balance	Ending Balance	Peak Balance for the Year
Accounts receivable	$300,000	$400,000	$400,000
Inventory	240,000	300,000	375,000
Accounts payable	150,000	200,000	220,000

Lion reports the following data in its current year income statement:

Sales	$3,200,000
Cost of goods sold	1,500,000
Purchases	1,200,000
Operating expenses (other than cost of goods sold)	1,000,000

Included in operating expenses are depreciation of $150,000 and federal income taxes of $100,000.

a. What is Lion's operating cycle in days? As a decimal?
b. What is Lion's reasonable working capital amount as determined under the *Bardahl* formula?
c. What steps must Lion take to justify accumulating earnings that exceed the amount prescribed under the *Bardahl* formula?

C:5-62 *Accumulated Earnings Credit.* In each of the following scenarios, calculate the accumulated earnings credit. Assume the corporation uses a calendar year as its tax year. Also assume that it realizes no current year capital gains.

a. Frank Corporation, a manufacturer of plastic toys, started business last year and reported E&P of $50,000. In the current year, the corporation reports E&P of $150,000 and pays no dividends. Of the $150,000 current E&P, the corporation retains $130,000 to meet its business needs.
b. How would your answer to Part a change if Frank were a service company that provides accounting services?
c. Hall Corporation's accumulated E&P balance at January 1 of the current year is $200,000. During the year, Hall, a glass container manufacturer, reports $100,000 of current E&P, all of which is retained to meet the reasonable needs of the business. Hall pays no dividends.

C:5-63 *Accumulated Earnings Tax.* Century Cleaning, Inc. provides cleaning services in Atlanta, Georgia. It is not a member of a controlled or an affiliated group. Century reports the following results for the current year:

Taxable income	$500,000
Federal income taxes (at 34%)	170,000
Dividends paid in August of the current year	75,000

Included in taxable income are the following items that may require special treatment:

Long-term capital gains	$ 30,000
Short-term capital gains	10,000
Dividends from 21%-owned domestic corporation	100,000
Excess charitable contributions from last year that are deductible in the current year	25,000

Century's accumulated E&P balance and its reasonable business needs on January 1 of the current year, were $125,000. The firm can justify the retention of $90,000 of current E&P to meet its reasonable business needs. Assume the corporation is not eligible for the U.S. production activities deduction.

a. What is Century's accumulated taxable income?
b. What is Century's accumulated earnings tax liability?

C:5-64 *Accumulated Earnings Tax.* Howard Corporation conducts a manufacturing business and has a compelling need to accumulate earnings. Its January 1, E&P balance is $600,000. It reports the following operating results for the current year:

Taxable income		$700,000
Federal income taxes		238,000
Dividends paid:	July 15 of the current year	50,000
	February 10 of the following year	100,000

Other information relating to Howard's current year operations is as follows:

NOL carryover from last year deducted in the current year	$100,000
Net capital gain	100,000
Dividends received from 10%-owned domestic corporation	75,000

Current year E&P before dividend payments is $400,000. Howard can justify the retention of $120,000 of current E&P to meet the reasonable needs of its business.

a. What is Howard's accumulated taxable income?

b. What is Howard's accumulated earnings tax liability?

C:5-65 *Financial Statement Implications.* Woodland Corporation reports the following financial accounting results and other depreciation information for the current year:

Sales revenue	$ 2,000,000
Plus: Interest income on municipal bonds	300,000
Minus: Depreciation for financial accounting purposes	(92,000)
Other operating expenses	(1,500,000)
Financial accounting net income before federal income taxes	$ 708,000
Depreciation for:	
For regular tax purposes	$ 152,000
For AMT purposes	114,000

Woodland's sales revenue and other operating expenses are the same for financial accounting, regular tax, and AMT purposes. The municipal bonds are not private activity bonds and were not issued in 2009 or 2010. The depreciation pertains to $900,000 of property Woodland acquired and placed in service during the current year. Assume that Woodland is not exempt from the AMT and has zero deferred tax assets and liabilities at the beginning of the current year. Also assume that Woodland does not have to establish a valuation allowance for any of its deferred tax assets and that the enacted tax rate for all future years is 34%.

a. Determine Woodland's regular taxable income, preadjustment AMTI, and ACE.

b. Determine Woodland's regular tax and AMT.

c. Prepare the journal entry to record Woodland's federal income tax expense, and determine Woodland's financial accounting net income.

COMPREHENSIVE PROBLEM

C:5-66 Stock in Random Corporation is owned equally by two individual shareholders. During the current year, Random reports the following results:

Income:	Rentals	$200,000
	Dividend (from a 25%-owned domestic corporation)	30,000
	Taxable interest	15,000
	Short-term capital gains	3,000
	Long-term capital gains	17,000
Expenses related to rental income:		
	Interest	30,000
	Depreciation	32,000
	Property taxes	11,000
	Other Sec. 162 expenses	50,000
General and administrative expenses		10,000
Dividend paid on June 30		15,000

a. What is Random's gross income?

b. What is Random's ordinary gross income?

c. What is Random's adjusted income from rents?

d. What is Random's adjusted ordinary gross income?

e. What is Random's personal holding company income?

f. Is Random a PHC?

g. What is Random's regular taxable income and regular tax liability?

h. What is Random's undistributed PHC income (UPHCI) and PHC tax liability?

i. What measures can Random take before year-end to avoid the PHC tax? Alternatively, what can Random do after year-end but before the corporation files its tax return? If the corporation takes no action before or after filing its return, what remedy does it have after filing?

j. Assume that Random's income and expense items will be similar in future years unless management changes Random's asset mix. What changes can management make to reduce the corporation's PHC exposure in future years?

k. If Random is a PHC, can it also be subject to the accumulated earnings tax?

TAX STRATEGY PROBLEMS

C:5-67 Galadriel and John, married with no children, own all the stock in Marietta Horse Supplies. The couple's C corporation has been in business for ten years. The business has been successful, permitting both owners to pay themselves a reasonable salary from its revenues. Although the salaries cover life's necessities, a review of industry statistics shows that the salary of each owner is about one-half or two-thirds of salaries paid by similar-sized horse supply businesses. The reason for the low salaries is that, for a number of years, the owners felt continual pressure to retain as much of the profits in the business as possible to have sufficient working capital to finance inventories and other business needs. In the past two years, the firm has established lines of credit with two local banks that have alleviated much of this pressure. However, the couple has never had time to review the level of their compensation. Recently, an IRS agent asked the couple about items reported in a previously filed tax return. The agent reviewed all three open years and proposed a settlement for the items in question. While in the office, the IRS agent indicated to you as the couple's CPA that, in her opinion, the company had unreasonably accumulated earnings and that she would be investigating the issue before closing the audit. What advice can you give the couple about their salaries and potential liability for the accumulated earnings tax?

C:5-68 Steve and Andrew write music and lyrics for popular songs. Two years ago, they organized S&A Music Corporation, each brother owning one-half of its stock. Through the end of the current year, they contributed a total of $250,000 in capital to the business. The songs that Steve and Andrew write and promote have been successful. Annually, the firm earns $300,000 of royalties from the copyrights that it owns. With the aid of their aunt who operates a local bookkeeping service, Steve and Andrew organized their business as a C corporation. The brothers decide that, with the success of their music business, perhaps they should move their accounting services to an accounting firm that specializes in providing tax advice for small- and medium-sized businesses. As a staff member of this accounting firm, what advice can you provide the brothers about possible tax problems and potential tax strategies?

TAX FORM/RETURN PREPARATION PROBLEM

C:5-69 King Corporation, I.D. No. 38-1534789, an accrual method taxpayer, reports the following results for 2010:

Regular taxable income before regular tax NOL deduction	$800,000
Minus: Regular tax NOL deduction	(200,000)
Regular taxable income	$600,000
Alternative tax NOL deduction	$175,000
AMT depreciation adjustment	148,000
Personal property acquired eight years ago and sold this year:	
Acquisition cost	50,000
Regular tax depreciation	38,845
AMT depreciation	26,845
Increase in LIFO recapture amount	75,000
Tax-exempt interest income:	
Private activity bonds (not issued in 2009 or 2010)	31,000
Other bonds (not issued in 2009 or 2010)	33,000
Dividends received (less than 1% ownership)	120,000
Dividends paid	110,000

King is not a small corporation exempt from the AMT, and it has no AMT adjustment for the U.S. production activities deduction. Regular taxable income includes $35,000 of Sec. 1231 gain from a prior year installment sale on which King's total realized gain was $350,000. Regular taxable income also includes $39,000 of Sec. 1231 gain from a 2010 installment sale on which King's total realized gain is $195,000. Prepare Form 4626 for King Corporation to report its 2010 AMT liability (if any).

CASE STUDY PROBLEMS

C:5-70 Eagle Corporation operates a family business established by Edward Eagle, Sr. ten years ago. Edward Eagle, Sr. died, and the Eagle stock passed to his children. The corporation operates rental property and also invests in dividend paying stock and corporate bonds. Eagle's tax advisor made the following profit projection for the current year:

Rentals	$260,000
Dividend income (from a 40%-owned domestic corporation)	90,000
Interest income	20,000
Gross income	$370,000
Rental expenses:	
Depreciation expense	$ 70,000
Interest expense	100,000
Property taxes	10,000
Other Sec. 162 expenses	20,000
General and administrative expenses	15,000
Total expenses	$215,000
Net profit	$155,000

Eagle paid dividends of $40,000 in each of the past three years. Eagle was not a PHC in prior years.

Required: Prepare a memorandum to Edward Eagle, Jr. regarding potential liability for the PHC tax. In your memorandum, discuss the following two questions:

a. Is Eagle likely to be deemed a PHC for the current year?

b. If Eagle is likely to be deemed a PHC for the current year, what measures (if any) should be taken before year-end to eliminate the PHC tax liability? After year-end?

C:5-71 Goss Corporation is a leading manufacturer of hangers for the laundry and dry cleaning industry. The family-owned business has prospered for many years and has generated approximately $100 million of sales and $8 million in after-tax profits. Your accounting firm has performed the audit and tax work for Goss and its executives since the company was created many years ago. The advent of plastic hangers and improved fabrics has kept the company's market share constant, and the corporation plans no major plant expansions or additions. Salaries paid to corporate executives, most of whom are family members, are above the national averages for similar officers. Dividend payments in recent years have not exceeded 10% of the after-tax profits. On December 1 of the current year, you were assigned to oversee the preparation of the current year Goss tax return. In undertaking the assignment, you review Goss tax returns for the past three years. You note from Schedule L (the balance sheet) that, during this period, the corporation made about $1.5 million in loans to three executives and regularly increased the size of its stock portfolio. This increase leads you to believe that Goss may be liable for the accumulated earnings tax in the current year and prior years.

Required:

a. What responsibility do you have to make Goss or the partner in charge of the Goss account aware of the potential accumulated earnings tax liability?

b. Should you advise the IRS of the potential liability for prior years? Should you disclose the potential liability on the current year return?

c. Prepare a list of measures that can be taken to reduce or eliminate Goss' liability for the accumulated earnings tax.

TAX RESEARCH PROBLEMS

C:5-72 Broadway Corporation is a C corporation not exempt from the AMT. During the current year, Broadway contributed significant amounts of cash to various charitable organizations. Should Broadway make any adjustment for its charitable contributions when calculating its alternative minimum taxable income and/or adjusted current earnings?

A partial list of sources is:

- IRC Sec. 170(b)(1) and (2)
- Reg. Sec. 1.55-1(a)
- Reg. Sec. 1.56(g)-1(a)(5)

- Ltr. Rul. 9320003 (February 1, 1993)
- Ltr. Rul. 9321063 (March 2, 1993)

C:5-73 Camp Corporation is owned by Hal and Ruthie, who have owned their stock since the corporation was formed fourteen years ago. The corporation uses the calendar year as its tax year and the accrual method of accounting. In 2010, Camp borrowed $4 million from a local bank. The loan is secured by a lien on its machinery. Camp loaned 90% of the borrowings to Vickers Corporation at the same annual rate as the rate on the bank loan. Vickers also is owned equally by Hal and Ruthie. Vickers sells to the automobile industry parts that are manufactured by Camp and unrelated companies. Camp's operating results suffered as a result of a slowdown in the automobile industry. The gross margin on its sales declined from $1 million in 2010 to $200,000 in 2011. Interest earned by Camp on the loan to Vickers is $432,000 in 2011. Other passive income earned by Camp is $40,000. Camp's accountant believes that the corporation is not a PHC because the interest income Camp earns can be netted against the $432,000 interest expense paid to the bank for the loan to Vickers. Is he correct in his belief?

A partial list of sources is

- IRC Secs. 542(a) and 543(a)(1)
- Reg. Sec. 1.543-1(b)(2)
- *Bell Realty Trust,* 65 T.C. 766 (1976)
- *Blair Holding Co., Inc.,* 1980 PH T.C. Memo ¶80,079, 39 TCM 1255

C:5-74 William Queen owns all the stock in Able and Baker Corporations. Able, a successful enterprise, has generated excess working capital of $3 million. Baker is still in its developmental stages and has had substantial capital needs. To meet some of these needs, William had Able lend Baker $2 million during 2009 and 2010. These loans are secured by Baker notes, but not other Baker property. Able has charged Baker interest at a rate ordinarily charged by a commercial lender. Upon reviewing Able's 2011 books in the audit of its 2009 tax return, an IRS agent indicates that Able is liable for the accumulated earnings tax because of its build up of excess working capital and its loans to Baker. Later this week, you will meet with the agent for a third time. Before this meeting, you must research whether loans to a related corporation to finance its working capital meet a reasonable need of the business. At a meeting to discuss this problem, William asks whether filing a consolidated tax return would eliminate this potential problem and, if so, how must the ownership structure change to accomplish this objective.

A partial list of research sources is

- IRC Secs. 532 and 537
- Reg. Secs. 1.537-2(c) and -3(b) and 1.1502-43
- *Latchis Theatres of Keene, Inc. v. CIR,* 45 AFTR 1836, 54-2 USTC ¶9544 (1st Cir., 1954)
- *Bremerton Sun Publishing Co.,* 44 T.C. 566 (1965)

6

C H A P T E R

CORPORATE
LIQUIDATING
DISTRIBUTIONS

LEARNING OBJECTIVES

After studying this chapter, you should be able to

1. Understand the difference between a complete liquidation and a dissolution

2. Apply the general shareholder gain and loss recognition rules for a corporate liquidation

3. Determine the tax consequences to the liquidating corporation when the general liquidation rules apply

4. Determine the tax consequences when the Sec. 332 and Sec. 337 nonrecognition rules apply to the liquidation of a subsidiary corporation

5. Determine the effect of a liquidation on the liquidating corporation's tax attributes

6. Understand the different tax treatments for open and closed liquidation transactions

7. Determine when a liquidating corporation recognizes gains and losses on the retirement of debt

**ADDITIONAL
COMMENT**

For noncorporate taxpayers,
capital gains recognized after
May 5, 2003, through 2012 are
taxed at a maximum 15% rate as
are qualified dividends received
in tax years 2003 through 2012.
Thus, dividends and capital gains
receive comparable tax rate treatment except that capital gain taxation is deferred until sale of
the stock or liquidation of the
corporation.

As part of the corporate life cycle, management may decide to discontinue the operations of a profitable or unprofitable corporation by liquidating it. As a result of this decision, the shareholders may receive liquidating distributions of the corporation's assets. Preceding the formal liquidation of the corporation, management may sell part or all the corporation's assets, which the shareholders may not want to receive in a liquidating distribution. An asset sale also generates cash to pay the corporation's liabilities (including federal income taxes incurred on the liquidation).

Ordinarily, the liquidation is motivated by a combination of tax and business reasons. However, sometimes it is undertaken principally for tax reasons.

▶ If the corporation liquidates and its shareholders hold the assets in an unincorporated form (e.g., sole proprietorship or partnership), the marginal tax rate may be reduced from the 35% top corporate rate to a lower 10%, 15%, 25%, 28%, or 33% individual rate (in 2011). For example, even low amounts of taxable income are taxed at 35% in a personal service corporation and thus could be taxed at a lower rate in noncorporate form.

▶ If the assets are producing losses, the shareholders may prefer to hold them in an unincorporated form and deduct the losses on their personal tax returns.

▶ Corporate earnings are taxed once under the corporate income tax rules and a second time when the corporation distributes the earnings as dividends or when the shareholder sells or exchanges the corporate stock at a gain. Liquidation of the corporation permits the assets to be held in an unincorporated form, thereby avoiding double taxation of subsequent earnings.

Liquidating a corporation carries a tax cost, however. The liquidating corporation is taxed as though it sold its assets, and the shareholders receiving liquidating distributions are taxed as though they sold their stock. A C corporation cannot simply elect to be treated as a pass-through entity under the check-the-box regulations (see Chapter C:2). Thus, the only route to converting a C corporation into a sole proprietorship, partnership, limited liability company, or limited liability partnership is via a taxable corporate liquidation followed by formation of the desired entity. Alternatively, a C corporation could obtain pass-through status without liquidating if it elects S corporation status. Even with this approach, the S corporation faces potential taxation on its built-in gains (see Chapter C:11).

This chapter explains the tax consequences of corporate liquidations to both the liquidating corporation and its shareholders. In so doing, the chapter presents two sets of liquidation rules. The general liquidation rules apply to liquidations of corporations not controlled by a parent corporation. Special rules apply to the liquidation of a controlled subsidiary.

OVERVIEW OF CORPORATE LIQUIDATIONS

This chapter initially presents an overview of the tax and nontax consequences of a corporate liquidation to both the shareholders and the distributing corporation.

THE SHAREHOLDER

Determining the tax consequences of the liquidation to each of the liquidating corporation's shareholders entails several questions:

▶ What are the amount, timing, and character of the shareholder's recognized gain or loss?

▶ What is the shareholder's adjusted basis of each property received?

▶ When does the holding period begin for each property received by the shareholder?

When a corporation liquidates under the general rules, a shareholder treats the liquidating distribution as an amount received in exchange for his or her stock. The shareholder recognizes a capital gain or loss equal to the excess of any money received plus the FMV of any noncash property received over the adjusted basis of his or her stock. The basis of each property received is stepped-up or stepped-down to the property's FMV on the liquidation date. The holding period for the asset begins the day after the liquidation date.

If a parent corporation liquidates a controlled subsidiary under special rules, however, the parent corporation (shareholder) recognizes no gain or loss. In addition, the bases and holding periods of the subsidiary's assets carry over to the parent.

THE CORPORATION

Two questions must be answered to determine the tax consequences of the liquidation transaction for the liquidating corporation:

▶ What are the amount and character of the corporation's recognized gain or loss?

▶ What happens to the corporation's tax attributes upon liquidation?

TAX STRATEGY TIP

Although the shareholders and corporation usually incur no tax cost upon forming a corporation, the tax costs of liquidating a corporation (other than a controlled subsidiary) may be substantial. The tax consequences of liquidating a corporation should be a consideration in the initial decision to use the corporate form. For example, assuming a 34% corporate tax rate and a 15% capital gains rate at the shareholder level, the effective tax cost of a complete liquidation is approximately 43.9% {34% + [(1 − 0.34) × 15%]}.

When a liquidation occurs under the general rules, the liquidating corporation recognizes gain or loss on the distribution of property to its shareholders. The recognized gain or loss is the same as what the corporation would recognize had it sold the distributed property to its shareholders. Some restrictions (discussed later in the chapter) limit loss recognition in certain potentially abusive situations. Also, tax attributions, such as net operating loss (NOL) carryovers and earnings and profits, disappear when the corporation liquidates under the general rules.

If the liquidating corporation is an 80%-controlled subsidiary of the parent corporation, the liquidating corporation recognizes no gain or loss under special rules. In this case, the subsidiary's tax attributes carry over to the parent corporation.

EXAMPLE C:6-1 ▶

Randy Jones owns Able Corporation, a C corporation. Randy's basis for his Able stock is $100,000. The corporation's assets are summarized below. In addition, Able Corporation owes $60,000 to its creditors.

Assets	Adjusted Basis	Fair Market Value
Cash	$ 50,000	$ 50,000
General stock	75,000	125,000
Machinery	115,000	200,000
Total	$240,000	$375,000

See Figure C:6-1 for an illustration of the corporate liquidation. In step 1, Able sells its machinery to an unrelated purchaser for $200,000 cash. The machinery originally cost $250,000, and Able has claimed $135,000 of depreciation on the machinery. Able recognizes a total gain on the machinery sale of $85,000 ($200,000 − $115,000). Because depreciation taken exceeds the amount of gain, the entire gain is Sec.1245 recapture (ordinary income). In step 2, Able uses $60,000 in cash to pay its creditors. In step 3, Able distributes remaining cash and the General stock, a capital asset, to Randy. Able recognizes a $50,000 ($125,000 − $75,000) capital gain on the General stock distribution. Assuming a 34% marginal tax rate, Able must pay $45,900 [($85,000 + $50,000) × 0.34] in federal income taxes on the distribution of the General stock and the sale of the machinery (step 4). The tax payment reduces Able's remaining cash to $144,100 ($50,000 + $200,000 sale proceeds − $60,000 paid to creditors − $45,900 paid in federal income taxes). Thus, Randy recognizes a $169,100 ($144,100 cash + $125,000 securities − $100,000 basis for stock) long-term capital gain on the liquidating distribution. The same federal income taxes would have occurred had Able sold both the General stock and machinery to unrelated purchasers, or had Able distributed both the stock and machinery to Randy because each of Able's noncash assets have FMVs exceeding their adjusted bases.[1] ◀

OBJECTIVE 1

Understand the difference between a complete liquidation and a dissolution

DEFINITION OF A COMPLETE LIQUIDATION

The term *complete liquidation* is not defined in the IRC, but Reg. Sec. 1.332-2(c) indicates that distributions made by a liquidating corporation must either completely cancel or redeem all its stock in accordance with a plan of liquidation or be one of a series of distributions that completely cancels or redeems all its stock in accordance with a plan of liquidation (see page C:6-21 for a discussion of plans of liquidation). When more than one distribution occurs, the corporation must be in a liquidation status when it makes the first

---

[1] The corporation's recognized gains and losses might be different if one or more of the properties had declined in value. The loss might be disallowed if the property were distributed to Randy Jones, where it would be recognized if the property had been sold to an unrelated purchaser.

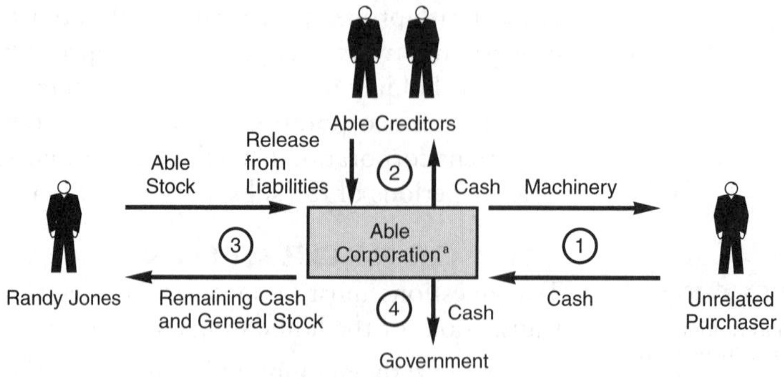

ᵃ Able Corporation liquidates and possibly dissolves.

FIGURE C:6-1 ▶ ILLUSTRATION OF CORPORATE LIQUIDATION (EXAMPLE C:6-1)

liquidating distribution under the plan, and such status must continue until the liquidation is completed. A distribution made before the corporation adopts a plan of liquidation is taxed to the shareholders as a dividend distribution or stock redemption (see Chapter C:4).

Liquidation status exists when the corporation ceases to be a going concern and its activities are for the purpose of winding up its affairs, paying its debts, and distributing any remaining property to its shareholders. A liquidation is completed when the liquidating corporation has divested itself of substantially all property. Retention of a nominal amount of assets (e.g., to retain the corporation's name) does not prevent a liquidation from occurring under the tax rules.

The liquidation of a corporation does not mean the corporation has undergone dissolution. **Dissolution** is a legal term that implies the corporation has surrendered the charter it received from the state. A corporation may complete its liquidation before surrendering its charter to the state and undergoing dissolution. Dissolution may never occur if the corporation retains its charter to protect the corporate name from being acquired by another party.

EXAMPLE C:6-2 ▶ Thompson Corporation adopts a plan of liquidation in December of the current year. The corporation distributes all but a nominal amount of assets to its shareholders in January of the next year. The nominal assets retained are the minimum amount needed to preserve the corporation's existence under state law and to prevent others from acquiring its name. Despite the retention of a nominal amount of assets, Thompson Corporation has liquidated for tax purposes even though it has not dissolved. ◀

STOP & THINK

Question: Peter Jenkins, age 58, is considering forming a new business entity to operate the rental real estate activities that he and his wife have owned personally for a number of years. He has heard about corporations and limited liability companies from reading various real estate journals. Because of their level of personal wealth and the liability protection afforded by the corporate form of doing business, Peter wants to use a corporation to own and operate their real estate. The assets Peter and his wife plan to transfer to the corporation have a $600,000 FMV and a $420,000 adjusted basis. As Peter's CPA, why should you consider the tax cost of liquidating the corporation as part of the overall analysis of the business entity selection decision?

Solution: A transfer of real estate by Peter and his wife to a corporation is nontaxable. A subsequent liquidation of the corporation is taxable, however, because both the corporation and the shareholder may recognize gain or loss. Peter and his wife have $180,000 ($600,000 − $420,000) of appreciation in their real estate. Even if no change in value occurs, liquidation of the real estate corporation at a later date will cause gain to be taxed twice, once at the corporate level and again at the shareholder level. On the other hand, creation and liquidation of a limited liability company are not taxable events to the entity or its owners. Thus, the difference in liquidation treatment at a future date is one of many differences the owners must consider when forming an entity. More information on liquidating a limited liability company can be found in Chapter C:10.

GENERAL LIQUIDATION RULES

This chapter section presents the general liquidation rules. These rules are considered in two parts: the effects of liquidating on the shareholders and the effects of liquidating on the corporation.

OBJECTIVE 2

Apply the general shareholder gain and loss recognition rules for a corporate liquidation

EFFECTS OF LIQUIDATING ON THE SHAREHOLDERS

Three aspects of the general liquidation rules are discussed below: amount and timing of gain or loss recognition, character of the recognized gain or loss, and basis and holding period of property received in the liquidation. Table C:6-1 summarizes the liquidation rules applying to shareholders under both the general liquidation rules and the controlled subsidiary corporation exception.

AMOUNT OF RECOGNIZED GAIN OR LOSS. Section 331(a) requires that liquidating distributions received by a shareholder be treated as full payment in exchange for his or her stock. The shareholder's recognized gain or loss equals the difference between the amount realized (the FMV of the assets received from the corporation plus any money) and his or her basis in the stock. If a shareholder assumes or acquires liabilities of the liquidating corporation, the amount of these liabilities reduces the shareholder's amount realized.

EXAMPLE C:6-3 ▶ Gamma Corporation liquidates, with Joseph receiving $10,000 in cash plus other property having a $12,000 FMV. Joseph's basis in his Gamma stock is $16,000. Joseph's amount realized is $22,000 ($12,000 + $10,000). Therefore, he recognizes a $6,000 ($22,000 − $16,000) gain on the liquidation. ◀

EXAMPLE C:6-4 ▶ Assume the same facts as in Example C:6-3 except Joseph also assumes a $2,000 mortgage attaching to the other property. The $2,000 liability assumed reduces Joseph's amount realized to $20,000 ($22,000 − $2,000). His recognized gain on the liquidation is $4,000 ($20,000 − $16,000). ◀

▼ TABLE C:6-1

Tax Consequences of a Liquidation to the Shareholders

	Amount of Gain or Loss Recognized	Character of Gain or Loss Recognized	Adjusted Basis of Property Received	Holding Period of Property Received
General rule	Shareholders recognize gain or loss (money + FMV of noncash property received − adjusted basis of stock) upon liquidation (Sec. 331).	Long-term or short-term capital gain or loss (Sec. 1222). Limited ordinary loss treatment available (Sec. 1244).	FMV of the property (Sec. 334(a)).	Begins on the day after the liquidation date (Sec. 1223(1)).
Controlled subsidiary corporation rule	Parent corporation recognizes no gain or loss when an 80% controlled subsidiary corporation liquidates into the parent corporation (Sec. 332).[a]	Not applicable.[a]	Carryover basis for property received from subsidiary corporation (Sec. 334(b)).[a]	Includes subsidiary corporation's holding period for the assets (Sec. 1223(2)).[a]

[a] Minority shareholders use the general rule.

Impact of Accounting Method. Shareholders who use the accrual method of accounting recognize gain or loss when all events have occurred that fix the amount of the liquidating distribution and the time the shareholders are entitled to receive the distribution upon surrender of their shares. Shareholders who use the cash method of accounting report the gain or loss when they have actual or constructive receipt of the liquidating distribution(s).[2]

When Stock Is Acquired. A shareholder may have acquired his or her stock at different times or for different per-share amounts. In this case, the shareholder must compute the gain or loss separately for each share or block of stock owned.[3]

CHARACTER OF THE RECOGNIZED GAIN OR LOSS. Generally, the liquidating corporation's stock is a capital asset in the shareholder's hands. The gain or loss recognized, therefore, is a capital gain or loss for most shareholders. Two exceptions to these rules are indicated below.

▶ Loss recognized by an individual shareholder on Sec. 1244 stock is an ordinary loss, within limits (see Chapter C:2).

▶ Loss recognized by a corporate shareholder on the worthlessness of the controlled subsidiary's stock is an ordinary loss under Sec. 165(g)(3) (see Chapter C:2).

BASIS AND HOLDING PERIOD OF PROPERTY RECEIVED IN THE LIQUIDATION. Section 334(a) provides that the shareholder's basis of property received under the general liquidation rules is its FMV on the distribution date. The holding period for the property starts on the day after the distribution date.

OBJECTIVE 3

Determine the tax consequences to the liquidating corporation when the general liquidation rules apply

EFFECTS OF LIQUIDATING ON THE LIQUIDATING CORPORATION

Two aspects of the general liquidation rules are discussed below: (1) the recognition of gain or loss by the liquidating corporation when it distributes property in redemption of its stock and (2) the special valuation rules used when the liabilities assumed or acquired by the shareholder exceed the property's adjusted basis in the liquidating corporation's hands. Table C:6-2 summarizes rules applying to the liquidating corporation.

RECOGNITION OF GAIN OR LOSS WHEN CORPORATION DISTRIBUTES PROPERTY IN REDEMPTION OF STOCK. Section 336(a) provides that the liquidating corporation must recognize gain or loss when it distributes property in a complete liquidation. The amount and character of the gain or loss are determined as if the corporation sold the property to the shareholder at its FMV.

EXAMPLE C:6-5 ▶

Under a plan of liquidation, West Corporation distributes land to one of its shareholders, Arnie. Arnie's basis in his stock is $70,000. The land, which is used in West's trade or business, has a $40,000 adjusted basis and a $120,000 FMV on the distribution date. West recognizes an $80,000 ($120,000 − $40,000) Sec. 1231 gain when it makes the liquidating distribution. Arnie recognizes a $50,000 ($120,000 − $70,000) capital gain on the distribution, and his basis for the land is its $120,000 FMV. A nonliquidating distribution would have produced similar results for the corporation. However, for the shareholder, the entire FMV would have been a dividend instead of a capital gain assuming sufficient E&P. Thus, both liquidating and nonliquidating distributions produce double taxation although the amount and character of the shareholder's gain or income differ. (Also, see Example C:6-1 for another illustration.) ◀

With limited exceptions, the liquidating corporation can recognize a loss when it distributes property that has declined in value to its shareholders. This rule eliminates the need for a liquidating corporation to sell property that has declined in value to recognize its losses.

EXAMPLE C:6-6 ▶

Assume the same facts as in Example C:6-5 except the land's FMV is instead $10,000. West recognizes a $30,000 ($10,000 − $40,000) Sec. 1231 loss when it distributes the land to Arnie. Arnie recognizes a $60,000 ($10,000 − $70,000) capital loss, and his basis for the land is $10,000. ◀

---

[2] Rev. Rul. 80-177, 1980-2 C.B. 109.   [3] Reg. Sec. 1.331-1(e).

▼ TABLE C:6-2

Tax Consequences of a Liquidation to the Liquidating Corporation

	Amount and Character of Gain, Loss, or Income Recognized	Treatment of the Liquidating Corporation's Tax Attributes
General rule	The liquidating corporation recognizes gain or loss when it distributes property as part of a complete liquidation (Sec. 336(a)).	Tax attributes disappear when the liquidation is completed.
Controlled subsidiary corporation rules	1. The liquidating subsidiary corporation recognizes no gain or loss upon a distribution of property to its parent corporation when the Sec. 332 nonrecognition rules apply to the parent corporation (Sec. 337(a)). 2. The liquidating subsidiary corporation recognizes no loss upon a distribution of property to minority shareholders when the Sec. 332 nonrecognition rules apply to the parent corporation (Sec. 336(d)(3)). It does recognize gains, however.	Tax attributes of a subsidiary corporation carry over to the parent corporation when the Sec. 332 rules apply (Sec. 381(a)).
Related party rule	The liquidating subsidiary corporation recognizes no loss upon a distribution of property to a related person unless the corporation distributes such property ratably to all shareholders *and* the liquidating corporation did not acquire the property in a Sec. 351 transaction or as a capital contribution during the five years preceding the distribution (Sec. 336(d)(1)).	
Tax avoidance rule	The liquidating subsidiary corporation recognizes no loss when a sale, exchange, or distribution of property occurs and the liquidating corporation acquired such property in a Sec. 351 transaction or as a capital contribution having as a principal purpose the recognition of loss (Sec. 336(d)(2)).	

TAX STRATEGY TIP

If possible, a corporation should avoid distributing property subject to a mortgage that exceeds the property's FMV. Such distributions cause excessive corporate gain recognition and uncertainty of results at the shareholder level.

LIABILITIES ASSUMED OR ACQUIRED BY THE SHAREHOLDERS. As described earlier, for purposes of determining the amount of gain or loss recognized under Sec. 336, property distributed by the liquidating corporation is treated as having been sold to the shareholder for its FMV on the distribution date. Section 336(b) contains a special restriction on valuing a liquidating property distribution when the shareholders assume or acquire liabilities. According to this rule, the FMV of the distributed property cannot be less than the amount of the liability assumed or acquired. Congress enacted Sec. 336(b) because the corporation realizes an economic gain or benefit equal to the amount of the liability the shareholder assumes or acquires (and not just the lower FMV of the property distributed) as part of the liquidation. Treatment at the shareholder level is not completely clear. Section 336(b) specifically states that this liability rule applies only for determining the corporation's gain or loss. Thus, it does not seem to extend to Sec. 334(a), which requires the shareholder to take a FMV basis in the distributed property. Some commentators have suggested that the strict statutory interpretation of giving the shareholders the actual FMV basis, rather than the greater liability basis, produces an illogical result.[4] Also, given that the liability exceeds the distributed property's FMV, the shareholder's amount realized should be zero, resulting in a capital loss equal to the shareholder's stock basis.

---

[4] For a detailed discussion, see B. C. Randall and D. N. Stewart, "Corporate Distributions: Handling Liabilities in Excess of the Fair Market Value of Property Remains Unresolved," *The Journal of Corporate Taxation*, Spring 1992, pp. 55–64.

EXAMPLE C:6-7 ▶ Jersey Corporation owns an apartment complex originally costing $3 million and, after depreciation, having a $2.4 million adjusted basis. The property is secured by a $2.7 million mortgage. Pursuant to a plan of liquidation, Jersey distributes the property and the mortgage to Rex, Jersey's sole shareholder, at a time when the property's FMV is $2.2 million. Rex's stock basis is $500,000. Jersey recognizes a $300,000 ($2,700,000 − $2,400,000) gain on distributing the property because its FMV cannot be less than the $2.7 million mortgage. The shareholder recognizes a $500,000 capital loss on the corporate stock and takes either a $2.2 million or $2.7 million basis in the property, depending on which interpretation applies. ◀

EXCEPTIONS TO THE GENERAL GAIN OR LOSS RECOGNITION RULE. The IRC provides four exceptions to the general recognition rule of Sec. 336(a). Two of these exceptions apply to liquidations of controlled subsidiary corporations and are covered later. The other two exceptions prevent certain abusive practices (e.g., the manufacturing of losses) from being accomplished and are examined below. Also, Sec 362(e)(2) may reduce a liquidating corporation's loss recognition. Specifically, for property contributed to a controlled corporation after October 22, 2004, the corporation must reduce the basis of loss property if the total adjusted basis of property contributed by a shareholder exceeds the total FMV of that property (see Chapter C:2 for details). Consequently, upon a later liquidating distribution, the corporation will realize a smaller loss or no loss at all.[5]

ADDITIONAL COMMENT

The disqualified property rule prohibits a shareholder from infusing loss property into the liquidating corporation and generating losses at both the corporate and shareholder levels by liquidating the corporation.

Distributions to Related Persons. Section 336(d)(1)(A) prevents loss recognition in connection with property distributions to a related person if (1) the distribution of loss property is other than pro rata to all shareholders based on their stock ownership or (2) the distributed property is disqualified property. Section 267(b) defines a related person as including, for example, an individual and a corporation whose stock is more than 50% owned (in terms of value) by such individual, as well as two corporations that are members of the same controlled group. Section 336(d)(1)(B) defines disqualified property as (1) any property acquired by the liquidating corporation in a transaction to which Sec. 351 applies, or as a contribution to capital, during the five-year period ending on the distribution date or (2) any property having an adjusted basis that carries over from disqualified property.

EXAMPLE C:6-8 ▶ Lei owns 60% and Betty owns 40% of Mesa Corporation's stock. Pursuant to a plan of liquidation, Mesa distributes Beta stock to Lei that Mesa purchased two years ago. The Beta stock, which is not disqualified property, has a $40,000 FMV and a $100,000 adjusted basis. Betty receives only cash in the liquidation. The non–pro rata distribution of the Beta stock (the loss property), however, prevents Mesa from claiming a $60,000 capital loss when it makes the distribution. If Mesa instead distributes the Beta stock 60% to Lei and 40% to Betty, Mesa deducts the entire capital loss, assuming Mesa has offsetting capital gains. ◀

EXAMPLE C:6-9 ▶ Assume the same facts as in Example C:6-8 except Mesa acquired the Beta stock two years ago as a capital contribution from Lei when the Beta stock basis was $100,000 and its FMV was $105,000. Thus, the stock was not subject to the Sec. 362(e)(2) basis reduction rule when contributed, and Mesa took a $100,000 carryover basis in the stock. The stock's FMV now is $40,000, and the corporation distributes it to Lei upon liquidation of the corporation. The Beta stock in this case is disqualified property. The $60,000 realized loss is disallowed because Lei is a related party under Sec. 267(b). If Mesa instead distributes the Beta stock 60% to Lei and 40% to Betty, Mesa still is prohibited from deducting the portion of the $60,000 capital loss attributable to the stock distributed to the related party even though Mesa distributed it ratably to Lei and Betty. Mesa can deduct only the $24,000 ($60,000 × 0.40) capital loss attributable to the Beta stock distributed to Betty because she is not a related party. Alternatively, a sale of the disqualified property to an unrelated purchaser permits Mesa to recognize the entire $60,000 loss, again assuming offsetting capital gains exist. ◀

EXAMPLE C:6-10 ▶ Assume the same facts as in Example C:6-9 except the Beta stock had an $85,000 FMV when contributed, and Mesa had to reduce its basis in the stock to $85,000 at that time. Upon liqui-

---

[5] For a detailed discussion, see B. C. Randall, B. C. Spilker, and J. M. Werlhof, "The Interaction of New Section 362(e)(2) With the Loss Disallowance Rules in Corporate Liquidations," *Corporate Taxation*, September/October 2005.

dation and distribution to Lei, Mesa realizes a $45,000 ($40,000 − $85,000) loss, which is disallowed under the related person, disqualified property rule. If instead Mesa distributes the Beta stock ratably to Lei and Betty, Mesa can deduct $18,000 ($45,000 × 0.40) of the loss attributable to the stock distributed to Betty, again assuming Mesa recognizes offsetting gains on other property. ◄

Sales Having a Tax-Avoidance Purpose. Section 336(d)(2) restricts loss recognition with respect to the sale, exchange, or distribution of property acquired in a Sec. 351 transaction, or as a contribution to capital, where the liquidating corporation acquired the property as part of a plan having the principal purpose of loss recognition by the corporation in connection with its liquidation. This loss limitation prevents a shareholder from transferring loss property into a corporation to reduce or eliminate the gain the liquidating corporation otherwise would have recognized from the distribution of other appreciated property.

Property acquired by the liquidating corporation in any Sec. 351 transaction or as a contribution to capital within two years of the date on which a plan of complete liquidation is adopted are treated as part of a plan having a tax-avoidance purpose unless exempted by forthcoming regulations. Treasury Regulations, when issued, should not prevent corporations from deducting losses associated with dispositions of assets that are contributed to the corporation and used in a trade or business (or a line of business), or dispositions occurring during the first two years of a corporation's existence.[6]

The basis of the contributed property for loss purposes equals its adjusted basis to the corporation at the time of liquidation reduced (but not below zero) by the excess (if any) of the property's adjusted basis over its FMV immediately after its contribution to the corporation. This adjusted basis already may include a reduction under Sec. 362(e)(2) for contributed loss property. No adjustment occurs to the contributed property's adjusted basis when determining the corporation's recognized gain.

TAX STRATEGY TIP

To avoid loss disallowance under Sec. 336(d)(2), a corporation should delay adopting a plan of liquidation until two years after receiving loss property in a Sec. 351 transaction.

TAX STRATEGY TIP

If the corporation made a basis reduction for contributed loss property under Sec. 362(e)(2), it might argue that no tax avoidance purpose existed, thereby making a Sec. 336(d) disallowance inapplicable. See article referenced in footnote 5.

EXAMPLE C:6-11 ►

Terry contributed a widget maker having a $1,000 adjusted basis and a $100 FMV to Pirate Corporation in exchange for additional stock on January 10, 2010. At the same time, Terry contributed a second property having a $2,000 FMV and a $900 adjusted basis. Because the total FMV of Terry's contributed property ($2,100) exceeded the total adjusted basis of that property ($1,900), the corporation did not reduce the loss property's basis under Sec. 362(e)(2) at that time. On April 1, 2011, Pirate adopts a plan of liquidation. Between January 10, 2010, and April 1, 2011, Pirate does not use the widget maker in its trade or business. Liquidation occurs on July 1, 2011, and Pirate distributes the widget maker and a second property that has a $2,500 FMV and a $900 adjusted basis. Because Terry contributed the widget maker to Pirate after April 1, 2009 (two years before Pirate adopted its plan of liquidation), and the widget maker is not used in Pirate's trade or business, its acquisition and distribution are presumed to be motivated by a desire to recognize the $900 loss. Unless Pirate can establish otherwise (e.g., by arguing that Sec. 362(e)(2) precludes a tax avoidance purpose), Sec. 336(d)(2) will apply to the distribution of the widget maker. Pirate's basis for determining its loss will be $100 [$1,000 − ($1,000 − $100)]. Thus, Pirate cannot claim a loss upon distributing the widget maker. This rule prevents Pirate from offsetting the $1,600 ($2,500 − $900) gain recognized on distributing the second property by the $900 loss realized on distributing the widget maker. ◄

The basis adjustment also affects sales, exchanges, or distributions of property made before the adoption of the plan of liquidation or in connection with the liquidation. Thus, losses claimed in a tax return filed before the adoption of the plan of liquidation may be restricted by Sec. 336(d)(2). The liquidating corporation may recapture these losses in the tax return for the tax year in which the plan of liquidation is adopted, or it can file an amended tax return for the tax year in which it originally claimed the loss.

EXAMPLE C:6-12 ►

Assume the same facts as in Example C:6-11 except Pirate sells the widget maker for $200 on July 10, 2010. Pirate reports an $800 loss ($200 − $1,000) on its 2010 tax return. The adoption of the plan of liquidation on April 1, 2011, causes the loss on the sale of the widget maker to be

---

[6] H. Rept. No. 99-841, 99th Cong., 2d Sess., p. II-201 (1986). The Conference Committee Report for the 1986 Tax Act indicates that property transactions occurring more than two years in advance of the adoption of the plan of liquidation will be disregarded unless no clear and substantial relationship exists between the contributed property and the conduct of the corporation's current or future business enterprises.

covered by the Sec. 336(d)(2) rules, again assuming a tax avoidance purpose exists. Pirate can file an amended 2010 tax return showing the $800 loss being disallowed, or it can file its 2011 tax return reporting $800 of income under the loss recapture rules.[7]   ◀

Topic Review C:6-1 summarizes the general corporate liquidation rules.

Topic Review C:6-1

Tax Consequences of a Corporate Liquidation

General Corporate Liquidation Rules

1. The shareholder's recognized gain or loss equals the amount of cash plus the FMV of the other property received minus the adjusted basis of stock surrendered. Corporate liabilities assumed or acquired by the shareholder reduce the amount realized.
2. The gain or loss is capital if the stock investment is a capital asset. If the shareholder recognizes a loss on the liquidation, Sec. 1244 permits ordinary loss treatment (within limits) for qualifying individual shareholders.
3. The adjusted basis of the property received is its FMV on the distribution date.
4. The shareholder's holding period for the property begins the day after the distribution date.
5. With certain limited exceptions, the distributing corporation recognizes gain or loss when making the distribution. The amount and character of the gain or loss are determined as if the corporation sold the property for its FMV immediately before the distribution. Special rules apply when the shareholders assume or acquire corporate liabilities and the amount of such liabilities exceeds the property's FMV.
6. The liquidated corporation's tax attributes disappear upon liquidation.

LIQUIDATION OF A CONTROLLED SUBSIDIARY CORPORATION

OBJECTIVE 4

Determine the tax consequences when the Sec. 332 and Sec. 337 nonrecognition rules apply to the liquidation of a subsidiary corporation

After a brief overview, the discussion of the controlled subsidiary exception is divided into three parts: the requirements for using the exception, the effects of liquidating on the parent corporation, and the effects of liquidating on the subsidiary corporation.

OVERVIEW

Section 332(a) provides that the parent corporation recognizes no gain or loss when a controlled subsidiary corporation liquidates into its parent corporation. This liquidation rule permits a corporation to modify its corporate structure without incurring any adverse tax consequences. Section 332 applies only to the parent corporation. Other shareholders owning a minority interest are taxed under the general liquidation rules of Sec. 331. When Sec. 332 applies to the parent corporation, Sec. 337 permits the liquidating corporation to recognize no gains or losses on the assets distributed to the parent corporation. The liquidating corporation, however, recognizes gains (but not losses) on distributions made to shareholders holding a minority interest. The nonrecognition of gain or loss rule is logical for the distribution to the parent corporation because the assets remain within the corporate group following the distribution. Thus, the subsidiary corporation can be liquidated and operated as a division of its parent corporation without gain or loss recognition.

EXAMPLE C:6-13 ▶ Parent Corporation owns all of Subsidiary Corporation's stock. Subsidiary's assets have a $1 million FMV and a $400,000 adjusted basis. Parent's basis for its Subsidiary stock is $250,000. The liquidation of Subsidiary results in a $600,000 ($1,000,000 − $400,000) realized gain for Subsidiary on the distribution of its assets, none of which is recognized. Parent

---

[7] The property has a $1,000 basis when determining Pirate's gain on the sale and a $100 ($1,000 − $900) basis when determining its loss on the sale.

Therefore, Pirate recognizes no gain or loss because the $200 sale price lies between the gain and loss basis amounts.

has a $750,000 ($1,000,000 − $250,000) realized gain on surrendering its Subsidiary stock, none of which is recognized. If Secs. 332 and 337 were not available, both Subsidiary and Parent would recognize their realized gains. In this case, Parent's gain would be reduced by the taxes paid by Subsidiary on its gain because Subsidiary's taxes reduce the amount available for distribution to Parent. ◄

REQUIREMENTS

All the following requirements must be met for a liquidation to qualify for the Sec. 332 nonrecognition rules:

▶ The parent corporation must own at least 80% of the total combined voting power of all classes of stock entitled to vote and 80% of the total value of all classes of stock (other than certain nonvoting preferred stock) from the date on which the plan of liquidation is adopted until receipt of the subsidiary corporation's property.[8]

▶ The property distribution must be in complete cancellation or redemption of all the subsidiary corporation's stock.

▶ Distribution of the property must occur within a single tax year or be one of a series of distributions completed within three years of the close of the tax year during which the subsidiary makes the first of the series of liquidating distributions.

If the corporations meet all these requirements, the Sec. 332 nonrecognition rules are mandatory. If one or more of the conditions listed above are not met, the parent corporation is taxed under the previously discussed general liquidation rules.

STOCK OWNERSHIP. For Sec. 332 to apply, the parent corporation must own the requisite amount of voting and nonvoting stock. In applying this requirement, the Sec. 318 attribution rules for stock ownership do not apply (see Chapter C:4).[9] The parent corporation must own the requisite 80% of voting and nonvoting stock from the date on which the plan of liquidation is adopted until the liquidation is completed. Failure to satisfy this requirement denies the transaction the benefits of Secs. 332 and 337.

CANCELLATION OF THE STOCK. The subsidiary corporation must distribute its property in complete cancellation or redemption of all its stock in accordance with a plan of liquidation. When more than one liquidating distribution occurs, the subsidiary corporation must have adopted a plan of liquidation and be in a status of liquidation when it makes the first distribution. This status must continue until the liquidation is completed. Regulation Sec. 1.332-2(c) indicates that a liquidation is completed when the liquidating corporation has divested itself of all its property. The liquidating corporation, however, may retain a nominal amount of property to permit retention or sale of the corporate name.

TIMING OF THE DISTRIBUTIONS. The distribution of all the subsidiary corporation's assets within one subsidiary tax year in complete cancellation or redemption of all its stock is considered a complete liquidation.[10] Although a formal plan of liquidation can be adopted, the shareholders' adoption of a resolution authorizing the distribution of the corporation's assets in complete cancellation or redemption of its stock is considered to be the adoption of a plan of liquidation when the distribution occurs within a single tax year. The tax year in which the liquidating distribution occurs does not have to be the same as the one in which the plan of liquidation is adopted.[11]

The subsidiary corporation can carry out the plan of liquidation by making a series of distributions that extend over a period of more than one tax year to cancel or redeem its stock. In this case, however, a formal plan of liquidation must be adopted, and the liquidation must be completed within three years of the close of the tax year in which the subsidiary makes the first distribution under the plan.[12]

TAX STRATEGY TIP

A parent corporation that does not own the requisite 80% should consider purchasing additional subsidiary stock from minority shareholders or consider having the subsidiary redeem shares from its minority shareholders. In either case, the strategy to attain 80% ownership must be applied before the corporations adopt a plan of liquidation. See Tax Planning Considerations for further details.

TYPICAL MISCONCEPTION

The 80% stock ownership requirement of Sec. 332 is not the same stock ownership requirement for corporate formations in Chapter C:2. Instead, the Sec. 332 ownership requirement is the same one used for affiliated groups filing consolidated tax returns (see Chapter C:8).

---

[8] The stock definition used for Sec. 332 purposes excludes any stock that is not entitled to vote, is limited and preferred as to dividends and does not participate in corporate growth to any significant extent, has redemption and liquidation rights that do not exceed its issue price (except for a reasonable redemption or liquidation premium), and is not convertible into another class of stock.

[9] Sec. 332(b)(1).
[10] Sec. 332(b)(2) and Reg. Sec. 1.332-3.
[11] Rev. Rul. 76-317, 1976-2 C.B. 98.
[12] Sec. 332(b)(3) and Reg. Sec. 1.332-4.

EFFECTS OF LIQUIDATING ON THE SHAREHOLDERS

RECOGNITION OF GAIN OR LOSS.

Parent Corporation. The Sec. 332(a) nonrecognition rules apply only to a parent corporation that receives a liquidating distribution from a solvent subsidiary. Section 332(a) does not apply to a parent corporation that receives a liquidating distribution from an insolvent subsidiary, to minority shareholders who receive liquidating distributions, or to a parent corporation that receives a payment to satisfy the subsidiary's indebtedness to the parent. All of these exceptions are discussed below.

Section 332 does not apply if the subsidiary corporation is insolvent at the time of the liquidation because the parent corporation does not receive the distributions in exchange for its stock investment. An insolvent subsidiary is one whose liabilities exceed the FMV of its assets. Regulation Sec. 1.332-2(b) requires that the parent corporation receive at least partial payment for the stock it owns in the subsidiary corporation to qualify for nonrecognition under Sec. 332. If the subsidiary is insolvent, however, the special worthless security rules of Sec. 165(g)(3) for affiliated corporations and the bad debt rules of Sec. 166 permit the parent corporation to recognize an ordinary loss with respect to its investment in the subsidiary's stock or debt obligations (see Chapter C:2).

EXAMPLE C:6-14 ▶

Parent Corporation owns all of Subsidiary Corporation's stock. Parent established Subsidiary to produce and market a product that proved unsuccessful. Parent has a $1.5 million basis in its Subsidiary stock. In addition, it made a $1 million advance to Subsidiary that is not secured by a note. Under a plan of liquidation, Subsidiary distributes all its assets, having a $750,000 FMV, to Parent in partial satisfaction of the advance after having paid all third-party creditors. No assets remain to pay the remainder of the advance or to redeem the outstanding stock. Because Subsidiary is insolvent immediately before the liquidating distribution, it distributes none of its assets in redemption of the Subsidiary stock. Therefore, the liquidation cannot qualify under the Sec. 332 rules. Parent, therefore, claims a $250,000 business bad debt with respect to the unpaid portion of the advance and a $1.5 million ordinary loss for its stock investment. ◀

STOP & THINK

Question: In Example C:6-14, assume Subsidiary Corporation had a $3 million net operating loss (NOL) carryover, which would disappear upon liquidation because Sec. 332 did not apply. To prevent this disappearance, Parent Corporation proposes to cancel the $1 million advance as a contribution to Subsidiary's capital. Thus, Parent would have a $2.5 million basis in its Subsidiary stock prior to the liquidation and no advances receivable. Now when Parent liquidates Subsidiary, all of Subsidiary's assets redeem Subsidiary's outstanding stock, and the transaction seems to qualify for Sec. 332 treatment. Under these circumstances, the $3 million NOL would carry over to Parent under Sec. 381, giving Parent $3 million worth of NOL deductions rather than $1.75 million worth of bad debt and worthless stock deductions under the original transaction. Do you think the IRS would condone this proposed transaction?

Solution: No. In Rev. Rul. 68-602, 1968-2 C.B. 135, the IRS held under similar circumstances that, because the cancellation "was an integral part of the liquidation and had no independent significance other than to secure the tax benefits of [Subsidiary's] net operating loss carryover, such step will be considered transitory and, therefore, disregarded." Thus, if Parent proceeded with the proposed transaction, the IRS would ignore it and treat the liquidation the same as originally done in Example C:6-14.

Minority Shareholders. Liquidating distributions made to minority shareholders are taxed under the Sec. 331 general liquidation rules. These rules require the minority shareholders to recognize gain or loss—which generally is capital—upon the redemption of their stock in the subsidiary corporation.

EXAMPLE C:6-15 ▶

Parent Corporation and Jane own 80% and 20%, respectively, of Subsidiary Corporation's single class of stock. Parent and Jane have adjusted bases of $100,000 and $15,000, respectively, for their stock interests. Subsidiary adopts a plan of liquidation on May 30 and makes liquidat-

SELF-STUDY
QUESTION

What bases do both the parent
and minority shareholders take in
the assets received in a Sec. 332
liquidation?

ANSWER

Because the parent corporation
recognizes no gain or loss in the
transaction, the parent corporation takes a carryover basis in its
assets. However, because the
minority shareholders are
involved in a taxable exchange,
they take a FMV basis in their
assets.

ing distributions of two parcels of land having $250,000 and $62,500 FMVs to Parent and Jane, respectively, on November 1 in exchange for their stock. Parent does not recognize its $150,000 ($250,000 − $100,000) gain because of Sec. 332. Jane recognizes a $47,500 ($62,500 − $15,000) capital gain under Sec. 331. (Subsidiary also faces gain recognition on the distribution of appreciated property to its minority shareholder as demonstrated in Example C:6-18.) ◄

BASIS OF PROPERTY RECEIVED.   Under Sec. 334(b)(1), the parent corporation's basis for property received in the liquidating distribution is the same as the subsidiary corporation's basis prior to the distribution. This carryover basis rule reflects the principle that the liquidating corporation recognizes no gain or loss when it distributes the property and that the property's tax attributes (e.g., the depreciation recapture potential) carry over from the subsidiary corporation to the parent corporation. The parent corporation's basis for its stock investment in the subsidiary corporation is ignored in determining the basis for the distributed property and disappears once the parent surrenders its stock in the subsidiary. Property received by minority shareholders takes a basis equal to its FMV.

EXAMPLE C:6-16 ▶ Assume the same facts as in Example C:6-15 and that the two parcels of land received by Parent Corporation and Jane have adjusted bases of $175,000 and $40,000, respectively, to Subsidiary. Parent takes a $175,000 carryover basis for its land, and Jane takes a $62,500 FMV basis for her land. ◄

A special rule prevents the importation of built-in losses upon the liquidation of a foreign subsidiary. Specifically, the parent takes a FMV basis in each transferred property if the following three conditions prevail: (1) the parent is a U.S. corporation, (2) the liquidating subsidiary is a foreign corporation, and (3) the aggregate adjusted basis of the transferred property exceeds the aggregate FMV.

STOP & THINK *Question:* Why should a corporation that is 100%-owned by another corporation be treated differently when it liquidates than a corporation that is 100%-owned by an individual?

Solution: A corporation that is 100%-owned by another corporation can file a consolidated tax return (see Chapters C:3 and C:8). As a result, the parent and its subsidiary corporations are treated as a single entity. This result is the same as if the subsidiary were one of a number of divisions of a single corporation. An extension of the single-entity concept is that a subsidiary corporation can be liquidated tax-free into its parent corporation. An individual and his or her corporation are treated as two separate tax entities when calculating their annual tax liabilities. As separate entities, nonliquidating distributions (e.g., ordinary distributions and stock redemptions) from the corporation to its shareholder(s) are taxable. The same principle applies to liquidating distributions.

EFFECTS OF LIQUIDATING ON THE SUBSIDIARY CORPORATION

RECOGNITION OF GAIN OR LOSS.   Section 337(a) provides that the liquidating corporation recognizes no gain or loss on the distribution of property to the 80% distributee in a complete liquidation to which Sec. 332 applies.[13] The term 80% distributee refers to a corporation that meets the 80% stock ownership requirement described on page C:6-11.

EXAMPLE C:6-17 ▶ Parent Corporation owns all the stock of Subsidiary Corporation. Pursuant to a plan of complete liquidation, Subsidiary distributes land having a $200,000 FMV and a $60,000 basis to Parent. Subsidiary recognizes no gain with respect to the distribution. Parent takes a $60,000 basis for the land. ◄

[13] Section 336(e) permits a corporation to sell, exchange, or distribute the stock of a subsidiary corporation and to elect to treat such a transaction as a disposition of all the subsidiary corporation's assets. The parent corporation recognizes no gain or loss on the sale, exchange, or distribution of the stock. The economic consequences of making this election for a stock sale are essentially the same as if the parent corporation instead liquidates the subsidiary in a transaction to which Sec. 332 applies and then immediately sells the properties to the purchaser.

The depreciation recapture provisions in Secs. 1245, 1250, and 291 do not override the Sec. 337(a) nonrecognition rule if a controlled subsidiary corporation liquidates into its parent corporation. Instead, the parent corporation assumes the depreciation recapture potential associated with the distributed property, and recapture occurs when the parent corporation sells or exchanges the property.[14]

The Sec. 337(a) nonrecognition rule applies only to distributions to the parent corporation. Liquidating distributions to minority shareholders are not eligible for nonrecognition under Sec. 337(a). Consequently, the liquidating corporation must recognize gain under Sec. 336(a) when it distributes appreciated property to the minority shareholders. Section 336(d)(3), however, prevents the subsidiary corporation from recognizing loss on distributions made to minority shareholders. Thus, for the subsidiary, liquidating distributions made to minority shareholders are treated the same way as nonliquidating distributions.

EXAMPLE C:6-18 ▶ Assume the same facts as in Example C:6-17 except Parent owns 80% of the Subsidiary stock, Chuck owns the remaining 20% of such stock, and Subsidiary distributes two parcels of land to Parent and Chuck. The parcels have FMVs of $160,000 and $40,000, and adjusted bases of $50,000 and $10,000, respectively. Subsidiary does not recognize the $110,000 ($160,000 − $50,000) gain realized on the distribution to Parent. However, Subsidiary does recognize the $30,000 ($40,000 − $10,000) gain realized on the distribution to Chuck because the Sec. 337(a) nonrecognition rule applies only to distributions to the 80% distributee. Assume that the land distributed to Chuck instead has a $40,000 FMV and a $50,000 adjusted basis. Subsidiary can deduct none of the $10,000 loss because it distributed the land to a minority shareholder. ◀

OBJECTIVE 5
Determine the effect of a liquidation on the liquidating corporation's tax attributes

TAX ATTRIBUTE CARRYOVERS. The **tax attributes** of the liquidating corporation disappear when the liquidation is completed under the general rules. They carry over, however, in the case of a controlled subsidiary corporation liquidated into its parent corporation under Sec. 332.[15] The following items are included among the carried-over attributes:

▶ NOL carryovers

▶ Earnings and profits

▶ Capital loss carryovers

▶ General business and other tax credit carryovers

The carryover amount is determined as of the close of the day on which the subsidiary corporation completes the distribution of all its property. Chapter C:7 contains further discussion of these rules.

Topic Review C:6-2 summarizes the special rules applicable to the liquidation of a controlled subsidiary corporation.

Topic Review C:6-2

Tax Consequences of a Corporate Liquidation

Tax Consequences of Liquidating a Controlled Subsidiary Corporation

1. Specific requirements must be met with respect to (a) stock ownership, (b) distribution of the property in complete cancellation or redemption of all the subsidiary's stock, and (c) distribution of all property within a single tax year or within a three-year period. To satisfy the stock ownership requirement, the parent corporation must own at least 80% of the total voting power of all voting stock and at least 80% of the total value of all stock.
2. The parent corporation recognizes no gain or loss when it receives distributed property from the liquidating subsidiary. Section 332 does not apply to liquidations of insolvent subsidiaries and distributions to minority shareholders.
3. The basis of the distributed property carries over from the subsidiary corporation to the parent corporation.
4. The parent corporation's holding period for the assets includes the subsidiary corporation's holding period.
5. The subsidiary corporation recognizes no gain or loss when making a distribution to an 80% distributee (parent). The liquidating subsidiary recognizes gain (but not loss) on distributions to minority shareholders. Also, the liquidating subsidiary recognizes no gain when it distributes appreciated property to satisfy certain subsidiary debts owed to the parent corporation.
6. The subsidiary corporation's tax attributes carry over to the parent corporation as part of the liquidation.

---

[14] Secs. 1245(b)(3) and 1250(d)(3).   [15] Sec. 381(a).

SPECIAL SHAREHOLDER REPORTING ISSUES

Four special shareholder reporting rules apply to liquidation transactions described below. These rules add different degrees of complexity to the general liquidation rules outlined above.

PARTIALLY LIQUIDATING DISTRIBUTIONS

Shareholders often receive a series of partially liquidating distributions that culminate in the redemption of all the corporation's stock. Section 346(a) treats this situation as a complete liquidation. Consequently, the distributions received are taxed under the Sec. 331 liquidation rules instead of under the Sec. 302 rules applying to redemptions in partial liquidation. The IRS permits the shareholder's basis to be recovered first and requires the recognition of gain once the shareholder fully recovers the basis of a particular share or block of stock. The shareholder cannot recognize a loss with respect to a share or block of stock until he or she receives the final liquidating distribution, or until it becomes clear that no more liquidating distributions will occur.[16]

EXAMPLE C:6-19 ▶ Diane owns 1,000 shares of Adobe Corporation stock purchased for $40,000 in 2005. Diane receives the following liquidating distributions: July 23, 2009, $25,000; March 12, 2010, $17,000; and April 5, 2011, $10,000. Diane recognizes no gain in 2009 because she has not fully recovered her $40,000 basis by year-end. The $15,000 ($40,000 − $25,000) unrecovered basis that exists after the first distribution is less than the $17,000 liquidating distribution received on March 12, 2010, so Diane recognizes a $2,000 gain at this time. She recognizes an additional $10,000 gain in 2011 when she receives the final liquidating distribution. ◀

EXAMPLE C:6-20 ▶ Assume the same facts as in Example C:6-19 except Diane paid $60,000 for her Adobe stock. The receipt of each of the liquidating distributions is nontaxable because Diane's $60,000 basis exceeds the $52,000 ($25,000 + $17,000 + $10,000) total of the distributions. Diane recognizes an $8,000 ($52,000 − $60,000) loss in 2011 when she receives the final liquidating distribution. ◀

SELF-STUDY QUESTION

If a cash method shareholder is subsequently obligated to pay a contingent liability of the liquidated corporation, what are the tax consequences of such a payment?

ANSWER

First, the prior tax year return is not amended. The additional payment results in a loss recognized in the year of payment. The character of the loss depends on the nature of the gain or loss recognized by the shareholder in the year of liquidation.

SUBSEQUENT ASSESSMENTS AGAINST THE SHAREHOLDERS

At some date after the liquidation, the shareholders may be required to pay a contingent liability of the corporation or a liability not anticipated at the time of the liquidating distribution (e.g., an income tax deficiency determined after the liquidation occurs or a judgment that is contingent when the corporation makes the final liquidating distribution). The additional payment does not affect the reporting of the initial liquidation. The tax treatment for the additional payment depends on the nature of the gain or loss originally reported by the shareholder and not on the type of loss or deduction the liquidating corporation would have reported had it paid the liability.[17] If the liquidation results in a recognized capital gain or loss, a cash method shareholder treats the additional payment as a capital loss in the year of payment (i.e., the shareholder does not file an amended tax return for the year in which he or she originally reported the gain or loss from the liquidation). An accrual method shareholder recognizes the capital loss when he or she incurs the liability.

EXAMPLE C:6-21 ▶ Coastal Corporation liquidated three years ago with Tammy, a cash method taxpayer, reporting a $30,000 long-term capital gain on the exchange of her Coastal stock. In the current year, Tammy pays $5,000 as her part of the settlement of a lawsuit against Coastal. All shareholders pay an additional amount because the settlement exceeds the amount of funds that Coastal placed into an escrow account as a result of the litigation. The amount placed into the escrow account was not included in the amount Tammy realized from the liquidating distribution

---

[16] Rev. Ruls. 68-348, 1968-2 C.B. 141, 79-10, 1979-1 C.B. 140, and 85-48, 1985-1 C.B. 126.

[17] *F. Donald Arrowsmith v. CIR*, 42 AFTR 649, 52-2 USTC ¶9527 (USSC, 1952).

three years ago. Because Tammy had not been taxed on the cash placed in the escrow account, she cannot deduct the amount of the payment made from the escrow account in the current year. Nevertheless, Tammy treats the $5,000 paid from her personal funds as a long-term capital loss in the current year. ◄

OBJECTIVE 6

Understand the different tax treatments for open and closed liquidation transactions

OPEN VERSUS CLOSED TRANSACTIONS

Sometimes the value of property received in a corporate liquidation cannot be determined by the usual valuation techniques. Property that can be valued only on the basis of uncertain future payments falls into this category. In such a case, the shareholders may attempt to rely on the **open transaction doctrine** of *Burnet v. Logan* and treat the liquidation as an open transaction.[18] Under this doctrine, the shareholder's gain or loss from the liquidation is not determined until the assets that cannot be valued are subsequently sold, collected, or able to be valued. Any assets that cannot be valued are assigned a zero value. The IRS's position is that the FMV of almost any asset should be ascertainable. Thus, the IRS assumes that the open transaction method should be used only in extraordinary circumstances. For example, an open transaction cannot be used merely because a market valuation for an investment in a closely held corporation is not readily available through market quotations for the stock.

ETHICAL POINT

A tax practitioner needs to ensure that the client obtains appropriate appraisals to support the values assigned to property distributed to shareholders in a corporate liquidation. A 20% substantial underpayment penalty may be imposed on corporations and shareholders that substantially understate their income tax liabilities.

INSTALLMENT OBLIGATIONS RECEIVED BY A SHAREHOLDER

Shareholders who receive an installment obligation as part of their liquidating distribution ordinarily report the FMV of their obligation as part of the consideration received to calculate the amount of the recognized gain or loss. Shareholders who receive an installment obligation that was acquired by the liquidating corporation in connection with the sale or exchange of its property are eligible for special treatment in reporting their gain on the liquidating transaction if the sale or exchange takes place during the 12-month period beginning on the date a plan of complete liquidation is adopted and the liquidation is completed during such 12-month period. These shareholders may report their gain as they receive the installment payments.[19]

SPECIAL CORPORATE REPORTING ISSUES

EXPENSES OF THE LIQUIDATION

The corporation can deduct the expenses incurred in connection with the liquidation. These expenses include attorneys' and accountants' fees, costs incurred in drafting the plan of liquidation and obtaining shareholder approval, and so on.[20] Such amounts ordinarily are deductible in the liquidating corporation's final tax return.

A liquidating corporation treats expenses associated with selling its property as an offset against the sales proceeds. When a corporation sells an asset pursuant to its liquidation, the selling expenses reduce the amount of gain or increase the amount of loss reported by the corporation.[21]

EXAMPLE C:6-22 ▶ Madison Corporation adopts a plan of liquidation on July 15 and shortly thereafter sells a parcel of land on which it realizes a $60,000 gain (excluding the effects of a $6,000 sales commission). Madison pays its legal counsel $1,500 to draft the plan of liquidation. Madison distributes all its remaining properties to its shareholders on December 15. The $1,500 paid to legal counsel is deductible as a liquidation expense in Madison's current year income tax return. The sales commission reduces the $60,000 gain realized on the land sale, so that Madison's recognized gain is $54,000 ($60,000 − $6,000). ◄

---

[18] *Burnet v. Edith A. Logan*, 9 AFTR 1453, 2 USTC ¶736 (USSC, 1931).
[19] Sec. 453(h)(1)(A). A tax deferral is available only with respect to the gain realized by the shareholder. The liquidating corporation must recognize the deferred gain when it distributes the installment obligation to the shareholder as if it had sold the obligation immediately before the distribution.

[20] *Pridemark, Inc. v. CIR*, 15 AFTR 2d 853, 65-1 USTC ¶9388 (4th Cir., 1965).
[21] See, for example, *J. T. Stewart III Trust*, 63 T.C. 682 (1975), *acq.* 1977-1 C.B. 1.

Any capitalized expenditures unamortized at the time of liquidation should be deducted if they have no further value to the corporation (e.g., unamortized organizational costs).[22] Capitalized expenditures that have value must be allocated to the shareholders receiving the benefit of such an outlay (e.g., prepaid insurance and prepaid rent).[23] Expenses related to issuing the corporation's stock are nondeductible, even at the time of liquidation, because they are treated as a reduction of paid-in capital. Unamortized bond premiums, however, are deductible at the time the corporation retires the bonds.

TREATMENT OF NET OPERATING LOSSES

TAX STRATEGY TIP

If a liquidating corporation creates an NOL in the year of liquidation or already has NOL carryovers, these losses may disappear with the liquidated corporation. If the liquidation qualifies under Sec. 332, however, the parent corporation acquires the NOL. If the liquidation falls under the general liquidation rules, the liquidating corporation may want to consider an S election for the liquidation year so any NOLs created in that year can pass through to the shareholders.

If the liquidating corporation reports little or no income in its final income tax return, the corporation may create an NOL when it deducts its liquidating expenses and any remaining capitalized expenditures. The NOL carries back to reduce corporate taxes paid in prior years. The resultant federal income tax refund increases (decreases) the gain (loss) previously reported by the shareholder. Alternatively, the shareholders might consider having the corporation make an S election for the liquidation year and have the flow-through loss reported on the shareholders' tax returns. (See Chapter C:11 for the tax treatment of S corporations.)

The need for a liquidating corporation to recognize gains when distributing appreciated property can be partially or fully offset by expenses incurred in carrying out the liquidation or by any available NOL carryovers. Losses recognized by the liquidating corporation when distributing property that has declined in value can offset operating profits or capital gains earned in the liquidation year. Should such losses produce an NOL or net capital loss, the losses may be carried back to provide a refund of taxes paid in a prior year, or they may be passed through to the corporation's shareholders if the corporation makes an S corporation election for the tax year.

RECOGNITION OF GAIN OR LOSS WHEN PROPERTY IS DISTRIBUTED IN RETIREMENT OF DEBT

OBJECTIVE 7

Determine when a liquidating corporation recognizes gains and losses on the retirement of debt

GENERAL RULE

A shareholder recognizes no gain or loss when the liquidating corporation pays off an unsecured debt obligation it owes to the shareholder. However, when the corporation retires a security at an amount different from the shareholder's adjusted basis for the obligation, the shareholder recognizes gain or loss for the difference. These rules apply whether the debtor corporation pays or retires the debt as part of its operations or as part of its liquidation. The debtor corporation recognizes no gain or loss when it uses cash to satisfy its debt obligations. However, the debtor corporation recognizes gain when it uses appreciated noncash property to satisfy its debt obligations. Similarly, a debtor corporation recognizes a loss when it uses noncash property that has declined in value to satisfy its debt obligations.

SATISFACTION OF THE SUBSIDIARY'S DEBT OBLIGATIONS

The Sec. 332(a) nonrecognition rules apply only to amounts received by the parent corporation in its role as a shareholder. The parent corporation, however, does recognize gain or loss upon receipt of property in payment of a subsidiary corporation indebtedness if the payment differs from the parent's basis in the debt.[24]

As mentioned above, the use of property to satisfy an indebtedness generally results in the debtor recognizing gain or loss at the time it transfers the property.[25] Section 337(b), however, prevents a liquidating subsidiary corporation from recognizing gain or loss

[22] Reg. Sec. 1.248-1(b)(3).
[23] *Koppers Co., Inc. v. U.S.*, 5 AFTR 2d 1597, 60-2 USTC ¶9505 (Ct. Cls., 1960).

[24] Sec. 1001(c). This general IRC section requires realized gains or losses to be recognized unless otherwise excluded or disallowed.
[25] Ibid.

WHAT WOULD YOU DO IN THIS SITUATION?

Andrea has operated her trendy, upscale clothing store as a C corporation for a number of years. Annually, the corporation earns $200,000 in pretax profits. Andrea's stock is worth about $800,000. Her stock basis is $125,000. One of her good friends, Jenna, has opened a clothing store as a limited liability company and has been telling Andrea about the advantage of not having to pay the corporate income tax. She also hears about the check-the-box regulations that permit corporations to elect to be taxed as partnerships and limited liability companies. She calls and tells you that she wants you to file the necessary paperwork with the IRS to make the change from being taxed as a C corporation to being taxed as a flow-through entity. What advice should you provide Andrea in this situation?

when it transfers noncash property to its parent corporation in satisfaction of an indebtedness. The IRC provides this exception because the property remains within the economic unit of the parent-subsidiary group.

Section 337(b) applies only to the subsidiary's indebtedness owed to the parent corporation on the date the plan of liquidation is adopted and that is satisfied by the transfer of property pursuant to a complete liquidation of the subsidiary corporation. It does not apply to liabilities owed to other shareholders or third-party creditors, or to liabilities incurred after the plan of liquidation is adopted. In addition, if the subsidiary corporation satisfies the indebtedness for less than its face amount, it may have to recognize income from the discharge of an indebtedness.

EXAMPLE C:6-23 ▶ Parent Corporation owns all of Subsidiary Corporation's single class of stock. When Parent acquired the Subsidiary stock, it also purchased $1 million of Subsidiary bonds at their face amount. Subsequently, Parent and Subsidiary adopt a plan of liquidation, and Subsidiary distributes to Parent property having a $1 million FMV and a $400,000 adjusted basis in cancellation of the bonds. Subsidiary also distributes its remaining property to Parent in exchange for all of its outstanding stock. Subsidiary recognizes no gain on the transfer of the property in cancellation of its bonds. Parent recognizes no gain on receipt of the property because the property's FMV equals Parent's adjusted basis of the bonds. Parent takes a $400,000 carryover basis for the noncash property it receives in cancellation of the bonds. ◀

TAX PLANNING CONSIDERATIONS

TIMING THE LIQUIDATION TRANSACTION

TAX STRATEGY TIP

Timing the distribution of loss property so that the losses may be used to offset high-bracket taxable income at the corporate level makes good tax sense if the general liquidation rules are applicable. However, this planning opportunity would not exist in a Sec. 332 parent-subsidiary liquidation because the liquidating subsidiary does not recognize losses.

Sometimes corporations adopt a plan of liquidation in one year but do not complete the liquidation until a subsequent year. Corporations planning to distribute properties that have both increased in value and decreased in value may find it advantageous to sell or distribute property that has declined in value in a tax year in which they also conducted business activities. As such, the loss recognized when selling or distributing the property can offset profits that are taxed at higher rates. Deferring the sale or distribution of property that has appreciated in value may delay the recognition of gain for one tax year and also place the gain in a year in which the marginal tax rate is lower.

EXAMPLE C:6-24 ▶ Miami Corporation adopts a plan of liquidation in November of the current year, a tax year in which it earns $150,000 in operating profits. Miami discontinues its operating activities before the end of the current year. Pursuant to the liquidation, it distributes assets, producing $40,000 of recognized ordinary losses. In January of next year, Miami distributes assets that have appreciated in value, producing $40,000 of recognized ordinary income. Distributing the loss property in the current year results in a $15,600 tax savings ($40,000 × 0.39). Only $6,000 ($40,000 × 0.15) in taxes result from distributing the appreciated property next year. The rate differential provides a $9,600 ($15,600 − $6,000) net savings to Miami. ◀

**ADDITIONAL
COMMENT**

In 2008 through 2012, the capital gains tax rate for taxpayers in the 15% or lower tax brackets is zero.

Timing the liquidating distributions should not proceed without the planner also considering the tax position of the various shareholders. Taxpayers should be careful about timing the liquidating distributions to avoid creating a short-term capital gain taxed at ordinary rates rather than long-term capital gains taxed at the maximum 15% rate. If the liquidation results in a recognized loss, shareholders should take advantage of the opportunity to offset the loss against capital gains plus $3,000 of ordinary income, as well as attempt to increase the portion of the loss eligible for ordinary loss treatment under Sec. 1244 (see next section).

RECOGNITION OF ORDINARY LOSSES WHEN A LIQUIDATION OCCURS

Shareholders sometimes recognize losses when a liquidation occurs. Individual shareholders should be aware that, because a complete liquidation is treated as an exchange transaction, Sec. 1244 ordinary loss treatment is available when a small business corporation liquidates. This treatment permits the shareholder to claim $50,000 of ordinary loss when he or she surrenders the stock ($100,000 if the taxpayer is married and files a joint return).

Ordinary loss treatment also is available for a domestic corporation that owns stock or debt securities in a subsidiary corporation. Because the rules in Sec. 332 regarding nonrecognition of gain or loss do not apply when a subsidiary corporation is insolvent (see page C:6-12), the parent corporation can recognize a loss when the subsidiary corporation's stocks and debt securities are determined to be worthless. This loss is an ordinary loss (instead of a capital loss) if the domestic corporation owns at least 80% of the voting stock and 80% of each class of nonvoting stock, and more than 90% of the liquidating corporation's gross income for all tax years has been other than passive income.[26]

OBTAINING 80% OWNERSHIP TO ACHIEVE SEC. 332 BENEFITS

The 80% stock ownership requirement provides tax planning opportunities when a subsidiary corporation liquidates. A parent corporation seeking nonrecognition under Sec. 332 may acquire additional shares of the subsidiary corporation's stock *before* the adoption of the plan of liquidation. This acquisition helps the parent corporation meet the 80% minimum and avoids gain recognition on the liquidation. If the parent corporation purchases these additional shares of stock from other shareholders to satisfy the 80% minimum *after* adopting the plan of liquidation, Sec. 332 will not apply.[27]

EXAMPLE C:6-25 ▶ Parent Corporation owns 75% of Subsidiary Corporation's single class of stock. On March 12, Parent purchases for cash the remaining 25% of the Subsidiary stock from three individual shareholders pursuant to a tender offer. Parent and Subsidiary adopt a plan of liquidation on October 1, and Subsidiary distributes its assets to Parent on December 1 in exchange for all of Subsidiary's outstanding stock. Parent recognizes no gain or loss on the liquidation of Subsidiary because all the Sec. 332 requirements had been satisfied prior to adoption of the plan of liquidation. ◀

Alternatively, the parent corporation might cause the subsidiary corporation to redeem some of its shares held by minority shareholders before the plan of liquidation is adopted. The IRS originally held that the intention to liquidate is present once the subsidiary corporation agrees to redeem the shares of the minority shareholders. Thus, redemption of a 25% minority interest did not permit Sec. 332 to be used even though the parent corporation owned 100% of the outstanding stock after the redemption.[28]

In *George L. Riggs, Inc.,* however, the Tax Court held that a parent corporation's tender offer to minority shareholders and the calling of the subsidiary's preferred stock do not invalidate the Sec. 332 liquidation because "the formation of a conditional intention to liquidate in the future is not the adoption of a plan of liquidation."[29] The IRS has acquiesced to the *Riggs* decision.

---

[26] Sec. 165(g)(3).
[27] Rev. Rul. 75-521, 1975-2 C.B. 120.

[28] Rev. Rul. 70-106, 1970-1 C.B. 70.
[29] *George L. Riggs, Inc.,* 64 T.C. 474 (1975), *acq.* 1976-2 C.B. 2.

Thus, careful planning can help both the parent corporation and subsidiary corporation avoid gain recognition under Secs. 332 and 337. Nonrecognition, however, does not extend to minority shareholders as discussed earlier.

EXAMPLE C:6-26 ▶

Parent Corporation owns 80% of Subsidiary Corporation's stock. Anthony owns the remaining 20% of Subsidiary stock. Parent and Anthony have adjusted bases of $200,000 and $60,000, respectively, for their Subsidiary stock. Subsidiary distributes land having a $250,000 adjusted basis and a $400,000 FMV to Parent and $100,000 in cash to Anthony. Subsidiary recognizes no gain or loss on the distribution of the land or the cash. Parent recognizes no gain on the liquidation and takes a $250,000 basis for the land. Anthony recognizes a $40,000 ($100,000 − $60,000) capital gain on the receipt of the money. Alternatively, distribution of the land and cash ratably to Parent and Anthony would require Subsidiary to recognize as gain the appreciation on the portion of land distributed to Anthony. ◀

AVOIDING SEC. 332 TO RECOGNIZE LOSSES

ADDITIONAL COMMENT

The parent corporation, however, would not acquire the subsidiary's tax attributes if a taxable liquidation occurs.

A parent corporation may want to avoid the Sec. 332 nonrecognition rules to recognize a loss when a solvent subsidiary corporation liquidates. Because the stock ownership requirement must be met during the entire liquidation process, the parent corporation apparently can sell some of its stock in the subsidiary corporation to reduce its stock ownership below the 80% level at any time during the liquidation process and be able to recognize the loss.[30] Such a sale permits the parent corporation to recognize a capital loss when it surrenders its stock interest in the subsidiary corporation. The parent corporation may desire this capital loss if it has offsetting capital gains.

The sale of a portion of the subsidiary's stock after the plan of liquidation is adopted prevents Sec. 332 from applying to the parent corporation. The Sec. 337 rules, which prevent the subsidiary corporation from recognizing gain or loss when making a liquidating distribution to an 80% distributee, also do not apply because nonrecognition is contingent on Sec. 332 applying to the distributee. Thus, the subsidiary corporation also can recognize a loss when it distributes property that has declined in value.

COMPLIANCE AND PROCEDURAL CONSIDERATIONS

GENERAL LIQUIDATION PROCEDURES

Section 6043(a) requires a liquidating corporation to file Form 966 (Corporate Dissolution or Liquidation) within 30 days after the adoption of any resolution or plan calling for the liquidation or dissolution of the corporation. The liquidating corporation files this form with the District Director of the IRS for the district in which it files its income tax return. Any amendment or supplement to the resolution or plan must be filed on an additional Form 966 within 30 days of making the amendment or supplement. The liquidating corporation must file Form 966 whether the shareholders' realized gain is recognized or not. The information included with Form 966 is described in Reg. Sec. 1.6043-1(b).

Regulation Sec. 1.6043-2(a) requires every corporation that makes a distribution of $600 or more during a calendar year to any shareholder in liquidation of part or all of its capital stock to file Form 1099-DIV (Dividends and Distributions). A separate Form 1099-DIV is required for each shareholder. The information that must be included with the Form 1099-DIV is described in Reg. Secs. 1.6043-2(a) and (b).

Regulation Sec. 1.6012-2(a)(2) requires a corporation that exists for part of a year to file a corporate tax return for the portion of the tax year that it existed. A corporation that ceases business and dissolves, while retaining no assets, is not considered to be in existence for federal tax purposes even though under state law it may be considered for certain purposes to be continuing its affairs (e.g., for purposes of suing or being sued).

---

[30] *CIR v. Day & Zimmerman, Inc.,* 34 AFTR 343, 45-2 USTC ¶9403 (3rd Cir., 1945).

ADDITIONAL COMMENT

As evidenced in this chapter, the compliance and procedural requirements of complete liquidations are formidable. Any taxpayer contemplating this type of corporate transactions should consult competent tax and legal advisors to ensure that the technical requirements of the proposed transaction are satisfied.

SECTION 332 LIQUIDATIONS

Regulation Sec. 1.332-6 requires every corporation receiving distributions in a Sec. 332 complete liquidation to maintain permanent records. A complete statement of all facts pertinent to the nonrecognition of gain or loss must be included in the corporate distributee's return for the tax year in which it receives a liquidating distribution. This statement includes the following: a certified copy of the plan of liquidation, a list of all property received upon the distribution, a statement of any indebtedness of the liquidating corporation to the recipient corporation, and a statement of stock ownership.

Treasury Regulations require a special waiver of the general three-year statute of limitations when the liquidation covers more than one tax year.[31] The distributee corporation must file a waiver of the limitations period on assessment for each of its tax years that falls partially or wholly within the liquidation period. The distributee corporation files this waiver at the time it files its income tax return. This waiver must extend the assessment period to a date at least one year after the last date of the period for assessment of such taxes for the last tax year in which the liquidation may be completed under Sec. 332.

PLAN OF LIQUIDATION

A **plan of liquidation** is a written document detailing the steps to be undertaken while carrying out the complete liquidation of the corporation. Although a formal plan of liquidation is not required, it may assist the corporation in determining when it enters a liquidation status and, therefore, when distributions to the shareholders qualify for exchange treatment under Sec. 331 (instead of possibly being treated as a dividend under Sec. 301). The adoption of a formal plan of liquidation can provide the liquidating corporation or its shareholders additional benefits under the tax laws. For example, the adoption of a plan of liquidation permits a parent corporation to have a three-year time period (instead of one tax year) to carry out the complete liquidation of a subsidiary corporation.

PROBLEM MATERIALS

DISCUSSION QUESTIONS

C:6-1   What is a complete liquidation? A partial liquidation? Explain the difference in the tax treatment accorded these two different events.

C:6-2   Summitt Corporation has manufactured and distributed basketball equipment for 20 years. Its owners would like to avoid the corporate income tax and are considering becoming a limited liability company (LLC). What tax savings may result from electing to be treated as an LLC? What federal tax costs will be incurred to make the change from a C corporation to an LLC? Would the same transaction costs be incurred if instead the corporation made an S election? Would the transaction costs be incurred had LLC status been adopted when the entity was initially organized?

C:6-3   Explain why tax advisors caution people who are starting a new business that the tax costs of incorporating a business may be low while the tax costs of liquidating a business may be high.

C:6-4   Explain the following statement: A corporation may be liquidated for tax purposes even though dissolution has not occurred under state corporation law.

C:6-5   Compare the tax consequences to the shareholder and the distributing corporation of the following three kinds of corporate distributions: ordinary dividends, stock redemptions, and complete liquidations.

C:6-6   What event or occurrence determines when a cash or accrual method of accounting taxpayer reports a liquidating distribution?

C:6-7   Explain why a shareholder receiving a liquidating distribution would prefer to receive either capital gain treatment or ordinary loss treatment.

C:6-8   A liquidating corporation could either (1) sell its assets and then distribute remaining cash to its shareholders or (2) distribute its assets directly to

---

[31] Reg. Sec. 1.332-4(a)(2).

the shareholders who then sell the distributed assets. Do the tax consequences of these alternatives differ?

C:6-9 Explain the circumstances in which a liquidating corporation does not recognize gain and/or loss when making a liquidating distribution.

C:6-10 Kelly Corporation makes a liquidating distribution. Among other property, it distributes land subject to a mortgage. The mortgage amount exceeds both the adjusted basis and FMV for the land. Explain to Kelly Corporation's president how the amount of its recognized gain or loss on the distribution and the shareholder's basis for the land are determined.

C:6-11 Explain the congressional intent behind the enactment of the Sec. 332 rules regarding the liquidation of a subsidiary corporation.

C:6-12 What requirements must be satisfied for the Sec. 332 rules to apply to a corporate shareholder?

C:6-13 Compare the general liquidation rules with the Sec. 332 rules for liquidation of a subsidiary corporation with respect to the following items:
a. Recognition of gain or loss by the distributee corporation
b. Recognition of gain or loss by the liquidating corporation
c. Basis of assets in the distributee corporation's hands
d. Treatment of the liquidating corporation's tax attributes

C:6-14 Parent Corporation owns 80% of the stock of Subsidiary Corporation, which is insolvent. Tracy owns the remaining 20% of the stock. The courts determine Subsidiary to be bankrupt. The shareholders receive nothing for their investment. How do they report their losses for tax purposes?

C:6-15 Parent Corporation owns all the stock of Subsidiary Corporation and a substantial amount of Subsidiary Corporation bonds. Subsidiary proposes to transfer appreciated property to Parent in redemption of its bonds pursuant to the liquidation of Subsidiary. Explain the tax consequences of the redemption of the stock and bonds to Parent and Subsidiary.

C:6-16 Explain the differences in the tax rules applying to distributions made to the parent corporation and a minority shareholder when a controlled subsidiary corporation liquidates.

C:6-17 Parent Corporation owns 80% of Subsidiary Corporation's stock. Sally owns the remaining 20% of the Subsidiary stock. Subsidiary plans to distribute cash and appreciated property pursuant to its liquidation. It has more than enough cash to redeem all of Sally's stock. What strategy for distributing the cash and appreciated property would minimize the gain recognized by Subsidiary on the distribution? Does the substitution of appreciated property for cash change the tax consequences of the liquidating distribution for Sally?

C:6-18 Parent Corporation owns 70% of Subsidiary Corporation's stock. The FMV of Subsidiary's assets is significantly greater than their basis to Subsidiary. The FMV of Parent's interest in the assets also substantially exceeds Parent's basis for the Subsidiary stock. Also, Parent's basis in its Subsidiary stock exceeds Subsidiary's basis in its assets. On January 30, Parent acquired an additional 15% of Subsidiary stock from one of Subsidiary's shareholders who owns none of the Parent stock. Subsidiary adopts a plan of liquidation on March 12. The liquidation is completed before year-end. What advantages accrue to Parent with respect to the liquidation by acquiring the additional Subsidiary stock?

C:6-19 Texas Corporation liquidates through a series of distributions to its shareholders after a plan of liquidation has been adopted. How are these distributions taxed?

C:6-20 Hill Corporation's shareholders are called on to pay an assessment that was levied against them as a result of a liability not anticipated at the time of liquidation. When will the shareholders claim the deduction for the additional payment, assuming they all use the cash method of accounting? What factors determine the character of the deduction claimed?

C:6-21 Able Corporation adopts a plan of liquidation. Under the plan, Robert, who owns 60% of the Able stock, is to receive 2,000 acres of land in an area where a number of producing oil wells have been drilled. No wells have been drilled on Able's land. Discussions with two appraisers have produced widely differing market values for the land, both of which are above Able's basis for the land and Robert's basis for the Able stock. Explain the alternatives available to Able and Robert for reporting the liquidating distribution.

C:6-22 Explain the IRS's position regarding whether a liquidation transaction will be considered open or closed.

C:6-23 For a corporation that intends to liquidate, explain the tax advantages to the shareholders of having the corporation (1) adopt a plan of liquidation, (2) sell its assets in an installment sale, and then (3) distribute the installment obligations to its shareholders.

C:6-24 Cable Corporation is 60% owned by Anna and 40% owned by Jim, who are unrelated. It has noncash assets, which it sells to an unrelated purchaser for $100,000 in cash and $900,000 in installment obligations due 50% in the current year and 50% in the following year. Cable will distribute its remaining cash, after payment of the federal income taxes on the sale and other corporate obligations, to Jim and Anna along with the installment obligations. Explain to the two shareholders the alternatives for reporting the gain realized on their receipt of the installment obligations.

C:6-25 Describe the tax treatment accorded the following expenses associated with a liquidation:
  a. Commissions paid on the sale of the liquidating corporation's assets
  b. Accounting fees paid to prepare the corporation's final income tax return
  c. Unamortized organizational expenditures
  d. Prepaid rent for office space occupied by one of the shareholders following the liquidation (Assume the prepaid rent was deducted in the preceding year's corporate tax return.)

C:6-26 Yancy owns 70% of Andover Corporation stock. At the beginning of the current year, the corporation has $400,000 of NOLs. Yancy plans to liquidate the corporation and have it distribute assets having a $600,000 FMV and a $350,000 adjusted basis to its shareholders. Explain to Yancy the tax consequences of the liquidation to Andover Corporation.

C:6-27 Nils Corporation, a calendar year taxpayer, adopts a plan of liquidation on April 1 of the current year. The final liquidating distribution occurs on January 5 of next year. Must Nils Corporation file a tax return for the current year? For next year?

C:6-28 What is a plan of liquidation? Why is it advisable for a corporation to adopt a formal plan of liquidation?

C:6-29 Indicate whether each of the following statements about a liquidation is true or false. If the statement is false, explain why.
  a. Liabilities assumed by a shareholder when a corporation liquidates reduce the amount realized by the shareholder on the surrender of his or her stock.
  b. The loss recognized by a shareholder on a liquidation generally is characterized as an ordinary loss.
  c. A shareholder's basis for property received in a liquidation is the same as the property's basis in the liquidating corporation's hands.
  d. The holding period for property received in a liquidation includes the period of time it is held by the liquidating corporation.
  e. The tax attributes of a liquidating corporation are assumed ratably by its shareholders.
  f. A parent corporation can elect to recognize gain or loss when it liquidates a controlled subsidiary corporation.
  g. A liquidating subsidiary recognizes no gain or loss when it distributes its property to its parent corporation.
  h. A parent corporation's basis for the assets received in a liquidation where gain is not recognized remains the same as it was to the liquidating subsidiary corporation.

ISSUE IDENTIFICATION QUESTIONS

C:6-30 Cable Corporation, which operates a fleet of motorized trolley cars in a resort city, is undergoing a complete liquidation. John, who owns 80% of the Cable stock, plans to continue the business in another city, and will receive the cable cars, two support vehicles, the repair parts inventory, and other tools and equipment. Peter, who owns the remaining 20% of the Cable stock, will receive a cash distribution. The corporation will incur $15,000 of liquidation expenses to break its lease on its office and garage space and cancel other contracts. What tax issues should Cable, John, and Peter consider with respect to the liquidation?

C:6-31 Parent Corporation, which operates an electric utility, created a 100%-owned corporation, Subsidiary, that built and managed an office building. Assume the two corporations have filed separate tax returns for a number of years. The utility occupied two floors of the office building, and Subsidiary offered the other ten floors for lease. Only 25% of the total rental space was leased because of the high crime rate in the area surrounding the building. Rental income was insufficient to cover the mortgage payments, and Subsidiary filed for bankruptcy because of the poor prospects. Subsidiary's assets were taken over by the mortgage lender. Parent lost its entire $500,000 investment. Another $100,000 of debts remained unpaid for the general creditors, which included a $35,000 account payable to Parent, at the time Subsidiary was liquidated. What tax issues should Parent and Subsidiary consider with respect to the bankruptcy and liquidation of Subsidiary?

C:6-32 Alpha Corporation is a holding company owned equally by Harry and Rita. They acquired the Alpha stock many years ago when the corporation was formed. Alpha has its money invested almost entirely in stocks, bonds, rental real estate, and land. Market quotations are available for all of its stock and bond investments except for 10,000 shares of Mayfair Manufacturing Corporation stock. Mayfair is privately held with 40 individuals owning all 100,000 outstanding shares. Last year, Mayfair reported slightly more than $3 million in net income. In a discussion with Harry and Rita, you find that they plan to liquidate Alpha Corporation in the next six months to avoid the personal holding company tax. What tax issues should Harry and Rita consider with respect to this pending liquidation?

PROBLEMS

C:6-33 *Shareholder Gain or Loss Calculation.* For seven years, Monaco Corporation has been owned entirely by Stacy and Monique, who are husband and wife. Stacy and Monique have a $165,000 basis in their jointly owned Monaco stock. The Monaco stock is Sec. 1244 stock. They receive the following assets in liquidation of their corporation: accounts receivable, $25,000 FMV; a car, $16,000 FMV; office furniture, $6,000 FMV; and $5,000 cash.

    a. What are the amount and character of their gain or loss?

    b. How would your answer change if the accounts receivable instead had a $140,000 FMV?

    c. What is the Monaco's basis for each property received in the liquidation in Parts a and b?

C:6-34 *Shareholder Gain or Loss Calculation.* For three years, Diamond Corporation has been owned equally by Arlene and Billy. Arlene and Billy have $40,000 and $20,000 adjusted bases, respectively, in their Diamond stock. Arlene receives a $30,000 cash liquidating distribution in exchange for her Diamond stock. Billy receives as a liquidating distribution a parcel of land having a $70,000 FMV and subject to a $45,000 mortgage, which he assumes, and $5,000 of cash in exchange for his Diamond stock.

    a. What are the amount and character of each shareholder's gain or loss?

    b. What is each shareholder's basis for the property received in the liquidation?

C:6-35 *Timing of Gain/Loss Recognition.* Peter owns 25% of Crosstown Corporation stock in which he has a $200,000 adjusted basis. In each of the following situations, what amount of gain/loss will Peter report in the current year? In the next year?

    a. Peter is a cash method of accounting taxpayer. Crosstown determines on December 24 of the current year that it will make a $260,000 liquidating distribution to Peter. Crosstown pays the liquidating distribution on January 3 of the next year.

    b. Assume the same facts as in Part a except that Peter is an accrual method of accounting taxpayer.

C:6-36 *Corporate Formation/Corporate Liquidation.* Len Wallace contributed assets with a $100,000 adjusted basis and a $400,000 FMV to Ace Corporation in exchange for all of its single class of stock. The corporation conducted operations for five years and was liquidated. Len received a liquidating distribution of $500,000 cash (less federal income taxes owed on the liquidation by the corporation) and the assets that he had contributed, which now have a $100,000 adjusted basis and a $500,000 FMV. Assume a 34% corporate tax rate.

    a. What are the tax consequences of the corporate formation transaction?

    b. What are the tax consequences of the corporate liquidation transaction?

    c. Would your answers to Parts a and b remain the same if instead the assets had been contributed by Wallace Corporation to Ace Corporation? If not, explain how your answer(s) would change?

C:6-37 *Gain or Loss on Making a Liquidating Distribution.* What are the amount and character of the gain or loss recognized by the distributing corporation when making liquidating distributions in the following situations? What is the shareholder's basis for the property received? In any situation where a loss is disallowed, indicate what changes would be necessary to improve the tax consequences of the transaction.

    a. Best Corporation distributes land having a $200,000 FMV and a $90,000 adjusted basis to Tanya, its sole shareholder. The land, a capital asset, is subject to a $40,000 mortgage, which Tanya assumes.

    b. Wilkins Corporation distributes depreciable property to its two equal shareholders. Robert receives a milling machine having a $50,000 adjusted basis and a $75,000 FMV. The corporation claimed $30,000 depreciation on the machine. The corporation purchased the milling machine from an unrelated seller four years ago. Sharon receives an automobile that originally cost $40,000 two years earlier and has a $26,000 FMV. The corporation claimed $25,000 depreciation on the automobile.

    c. Jordan Corporation distributes marketable securities having a $100,000 FMV and a $175,000 adjusted basis to Brad, a 66.67% shareholder. Jordan purchased the marketable securities three years ago. Jordan distributes $50,000 cash to Ann, a 33.33% shareholder.

    d. Assume the same facts as in Part c except the securities and cash are instead each distributed two-thirds to Brad and one-third to Ann.

C:6-38 *Gain or Loss Recognition by a Distributing Corporation.* Melon Corporation, which is owned equally by four individual shareholders, adopts a plan of liquidation for distributing the following property:

- Land (a capital asset) having a $30,000 FMV and a $12,000 adjusted basis.
- Depreciable personal property having a $15,000 FMV and a $9,000 adjusted basis. Melon has claimed depreciation of $10,000 on the property during the three years since its acquisition.
- Installment obligations having a $30,000 FMV and face amount and a $21,000 adjusted basis, acquired when Melon sold a Sec. 1231 property.
- Supplies that cost $6,000 and were expensed in the preceding tax year. The supplies have a $7,500 FMV.
- Marketable securities having a $15,000 FMV and an $18,000 adjusted basis. Melon purchased the marketable securities from a broker 12 months ago.

a. Which property, when distributed by Melon Corporation to one of its shareholders, will require the distributing corporation to recognize gain or loss?

b. How will your answer to Part a change if the distribution instead is made to Melon's parent corporation as part of a complete liquidation meeting the Sec. 332 requirements?

c. How will your answer to Part b change if the distribution instead is made to a minority shareholder?

C:6-39 *Distribution of Property Subject to a Mortgage.* Titan Corporation adopts a plan of liquidation. It distributes an apartment building having a $3 million FMV and a $1.8 million adjusted basis, and land having a $1 million FMV and a $600,000 adjusted basis, to MNO Partnership in exchange for all the outstanding Titan stock. MNO Partnership has an $800,000 basis in its Titan stock. Titan has claimed $600,000 of MACRS depreciation on the building. MNO Partnership agrees to assume the $3 million mortgage on the land and building. All of Titan's assets other than the building and land are used to pay its federal income tax liability.

a. What are the amount and character of Titan's recognized gain or loss on the distribution?

b. What are the amount and character of MNO Partnership's gain or loss on the liquidation? What is its basis for the land and building?

c. How would your answer to Parts a and b change if the mortgage instead was $4.5 million?

C:6-40 *Sale of Loss Property by a Liquidating Corporation.* In March 2010, Mike contributed the following two properties, which he acquired in February 2009, to Kansas Corporation in exchange for additional Kansas stock: (1) land having a $50,000 FMV and a $75,000 basis and (2) another property having an $85,000 FMV and a $70,000 adjusted basis. Kansas' employees uses the land as a parking lot until Kansas sells it in March 2011 for $45,000. One month after the sale, in April 2011, Kansas adopts a plan of liquidation.

a. What is Kansas' adjusted basis in the land immediately after the March 2010 contribution?

b. What is Kansas' recognized gain or loss on the subsequent land sale?

c. How would your answer to Part b change if the land were not used in Kansas' trade or business?

d. How would you answer to Part c change if Mike contributed the land and other property in March 2009 instead of March 2010?

e. How would your answer to Part c change if the corporation sold the land (contributed in March 2010) for $80,000 instead of $45,000?

C:6-41 *Tax Consequences of a Corporate Liquidation.* Marsha owns 100% of Gamma Corporation's common stock. Gamma is an accrual basis, calendar year corporation. Marsha formed the corporation six years ago by transferring $250,000 of cash in exchange for the Gamma stock. Thus, she has held the stock for six years and has a $250,000 adjusted basis in the stock. Gamma's balance sheet at January 1 of the current year is as follows:

Assets	Basis	FMV
Cash	$ 400,000	$ 400,000
Marketable securities	50,000	125,000
Inventory	300,000	350,000
Equipment	200,000	275,000
Building	500,000	750,000
Total	$1,450,000	$1,900,000

Liabilities and Equity

Accounts payable	$ 175,000	$ 175,000
Common stock	250,000	1,725,000
Retained earnings (and E&P)	1,025,000	
Total	$1,450,000	$1,900,000

Gamma has held the marketable securities for two years. In addition, Gamma has claimed $60,000 of MACRS depreciation on the machinery and $90,000 of straight-line depreciation on the building. On January 2 of the current year, Gamma liquidates and distributes all property to Marsha except that Gamma retains cash to pay the accounts payable and any tax liability resulting from Gamma's liquidation. Assume that Gamma has no other taxable income or loss. Determine the tax consequences to Gamma and Marsha.

C:6-42 *Sale of Assets Followed by a Corporation Liquidation.* Assume the same facts as in Problem C:6-41 except, on January 2 of the current year, Gamma Corporation sells all property other than cash to Acquiring Corporation for FMV. Gamma pays off the accounts payable and retains cash to pay any tax liability resulting from Gamma's liquidation. Gamma then liquidates and distributes all remaining cash to Marsha. Assume that Gamma has no other taxable income or loss. Determine the tax consequence to Gamma, Acquiring, and Marsha. How do these results compare to those in Problem C:6-41?

C:6-43 *Tax Consequences of a Corporate Liquidation.* Pamela owns 100% of Sigma Corporation's stock. She purchased her stock ten years ago, and her current basis for the stock is $300,000. On June 10, Pamela decided to liquidate Sigma. Sigma's balance sheet prior to the sale of the assets, payment of the liquidation expenses, and payment of federal income taxes is as follows:

Assets	Basis	FMV
Cash	$240,000	$ 240,000
Marketable securities	90,000	80,000
Equipment	150,000	200,000
Land	320,000	680,000
Total	$800,000	$1,200,000

Equity		
Common stock	$300,000	$1,200,000
Retained earnings (and E&P)	500,000	
Total	$800,000	$1,200,000

- The corporation has claimed depreciation of $150,000 on the equipment.
- The corporation received the marketable securities as a capital contribution from Pamela three years earlier at a time when their adjusted basis was $90,000 and their FMV was $70,000.
- Sigma incurred $20,000 in liquidation expenses in its final tax year.

a. What are the tax consequences of the liquidation to Pamela and Sigma Corporation? Assume a 34% corporate tax rate.

b. How would your answer change if Pamela contributed the marketable securities six years ago?

C:6-44 *Liquidation of a Subsidiary Corporation.* Parent Corporation owns 100% of Subsidiary Corporation's stock. The adjusted basis of its stock investment is $175,000. A plan of liquidation is adopted, and Subsidiary distributes to Parent assets having a $400,000 FMV and a $300,000 adjusted basis (to Subsidiary), and liabilities in the amount of $60,000. Subsidiary has a $150,000 E&P balance.

a. What are the amount and character of Subsidiary's recognized gain or loss on the distribution?

b. What are the amount and character of Parent's recognized gain or loss on the surrender of the Subsidiary stock?

c. What basis does Parent take in the assets?

d. What happens to Parent's basis in the Subsidiary stock and to Subsidiary's tax attributes?

C:6-45 *Liquidation of a Subsidiary Corporation.* Parent Corporation owns 100% of Subsidiary Corporation's single class of stock. Its adjusted basis for the stock is $175,000. After adopting a plan of liquidation, Subsidiary distributes the following property to Parent: money, $20,000; LIFO inventory, $200,000 FMV; and equipment, $150,000 FMV. The inventory has a $125,000 adjusted basis. The equipment originally cost $280,000. Subsidiary has claimed depreciation of $160,000 on the equipment. Subsidiary has a $150,000 E&P balance and a $40,000 NOL carryover on the liquidation date.

a. What are the amount and character of Subsidiary's recognized gain or loss when it makes the liquidating distributions?

b. What are the amount and character of Parent's recognized gain or loss on its surrender of the Subsidiary stock?

c. What is Parent's basis in each noncash property?

d. What happens to Subsidiary's E&P balance and NOL carryover following the liquidation?

e. What happens to Parent's $175,000 basis in the Subsidiary stock?

C:6-46 *Liquidation of a Subsidiary Corporation.* Parent Corporation owns 100% of Subsidiary Corporation's single class of stock and $2 million of Subsidiary debentures. Parent purchased the debentures in small blocks from various unrelated parties at a $100,000 discount from their face amount. Parent has a $1.3 million basis in the Subsidiary stock. Subsidiary adopts a plan of liquidation whereby it distributes property having a $4 million FMV and a $2.4 million adjusted basis in redemption of the Subsidiary stock. The debentures are redeemed for Subsidiary property having a $2 million FMV and a $2.2 million adjusted basis.

a. What income or gain does Subsidiary recognize as a result of making the liquidating distributions?

b. What gain or loss does Parent recognize on the surrender of the Subsidiary stock? The Subsidiary debentures?

c. What is Parent's basis for the property received from Subsidiary?

C:6-47 *Liquidation of an Insolvent Subsidiary.* Subsidiary Corporation is a wholly owned subsidiary of Parent Corporation. The two corporations have the following balance sheets:

Assets	Parent	Subsidiary
General assets	$1,500,000	$ 750,000
Investment in Subsidiary stock	200,000	
Note receivable from Subsidiary	1,000,000	
Total	$2,700,000	$ 750,000

Liabilities & Equity		
General liabilities	$1,500,000	$ 150,000
Note payable to Parent		1,000,000
Common Stock	300,000	200,000
Retained earnings (deficit)	900,000	(600,000)
Total	$2,700,000	$ 750,000

Other Facts:

• Parent's basis in its Subsidiary stock is $200,000, which corresponds to the $200,000 common stock on Subsidiary's balance sheet.

• The $1 million note payable on Subsidiary's balance sheet is payable to Parent and corresponds to the note receivable on Parent's balance sheet.

• The corporations do not file consolidated tax returns.

• Subsidiary has $600,000 of net operating loss (NOL) carryovers.

• The FMV and adjusted basis of Subsidiary's assets are the same amount.

• Just prior to the liquidation, Subsidiary uses $150,000 of its assets to pay off its general liabilities.

• Subsidiary transfers all its assets and liabilities to Parent upon a complete liquidation.

Determine the tax consequences to Parent and Subsidiary upon Subsidiary's liquidation.

C:6-48 *Liquidation of a Subsidiary Corporation.* Majority Corporation owns 90% of Subsidiary Corporation's stock and has a $45,000 basis in that stock. Mindy owns the other 10% and has a $5,000 basis in her stock. Subsidiary holds $20,000 cash and other assets having a $110,000 FMV and a $40,000 adjusted basis. Pursuant to a plan of liquidation, Subsidiary (1) distributes to Mindy assets having an $11,000 FMV and a $4,000 adjusted basis prior to the liquidation, (2) distributes to Majority assets having a $99,000 FMV and a $36,000 adjusted basis prior to the liquidation, and (3) distributes ratably to the two shareholders any cash remaining after taxes. Assume a 34% corporate tax rate and a 15% capital gains tax rate.

a. What are the tax consequences of the liquidation to Majority Corporation, Subsidiary Corporation, and Mindy?

b. Can you recommend a different distribution of assets that will produce better tax results than in Part a?

C:6-49 *Tax Consequences of a Corporate Liquidation.* Gabriel Corporation is owned 90% by Zeier Corporation and 10% by Ray Goff, a Gabriel employee. A preliquidation balance sheet for Gabriel is presented below:

Assets	Basis	FMV
Cash	$ 100,000	$ 100,000
Inventory	420,000	700,000
Equipment	80,000	100,000
Land	400,000	300,000
Total	$1,000,000	$1,200,000

Equity	Basis	FMV
Accounts payable	$ 100,000	$ 100,000
Bonds payable	500,000	500,000
Common stock	100,000	600,000
Retained earnings (and E&P)	300,000	
Total	$1,000,000	$1,200,000

Gabriel has claimed $150,000 of MACRS depreciation on the equipment. Gabriel purchased the land three years ago as a potential plant site. Plans to build the plant never were consummated, and Gabriel has held the land since then as an investment. Zeier and Ray Goff have $90,000 and $10,000 bases, respectively, in their Gabriel stock. Both shareholders have held their stock since the corporation's inception ten years ago. Zeier purchased the Gabriel bonds from an insurance company two years ago for $20,000 above their face amount. Gabriel adopts a plan of liquidation. Gabriel transfers $500,000 of inventory to Zeier to retire the bonds. The shareholders receive their share of Gabriel's remaining assets and assume their share of Gabriel's liabilities (other than federal income taxes). Gabriel pays federal income taxes owed on the liquidation. Assume a 34% corporate tax rate. What are the tax consequences of the liquidation to Ray Goff, Zeier Corporation, and Gabriel Corporation?

C:6-50 *Tax Consequences of a Corporate Liquidation.* Art owns 80% of Pueblo Corporation stock, and Peggy owns the remaining 20%. Art and Peggy have $320,000 and $80,000 adjusted bases, respectively, for their Pueblo stock. Pueblo owns the following assets: cash, $25,000; inventory, $150,000 FMV and $100,000 adjusted basis; marketable securities, $100,000 FMV and $125,000 adjusted basis; and equipment, $325,000 FMV and $185,000 adjusted basis. Pueblo purchased the equipment four years ago and subsequently claimed $215,000 of MACRS depreciation. The securities are not disqualified property. On July 1 of the current year, Pueblo adopts a plan of liquidation at a time when it has $250,000 of E&P and no liabilities. Pueblo distributes the equipment, $50,000 of inventory, the marketable securities, and $5,000 of money to Art before year-end as a liquidating distribution. Pueblo also distributes $20,000 of cash and $100,000 of inventory to Peggy before year-end as a liquidating distribution.

a. What are the gain and loss tax consequences of the liquidation to Pueblo Corporation and to Art and Peggy?

b. Can you offer any suggestions to Pueblo's management that could improve the tax consequences of the liquidation? Explain.

c. How would your answers to Parts a and b change if Art and Peggy instead were domestic corporations rather than individuals?

C:6-51 *Tax Attribute Carryovers.* Bell Corporation is 100% owned by George, who has a $400,000 basis in his Bell stock. Bell's operations have been unprofitable in recent years, and it has incurred small NOLs. Its operating assets currently have a $300,000 FMV and a $500,000 adjusted basis. George is approached by Time Corporation, which wants to purchase Bell's assets for $300,000. Bell expects to have approximately $200,000 in cash after the payment of its liabilities.

a. What are the tax consequences of the transaction if Bell adopts a plan of liquidation, sells the assets, and distributes the cash in redemption of the Bell stock within a 12-month period?

b. What advantages (if any) would accrue to Bell and George if the corporation remains in existence and uses the $200,000 of cash that remains after payment of the liabilities to conduct a new trade or business?

C:6-52 *Series of Liquidating Distributions.* Union Corporation is owned equally by Ron and Steve. Ron and Steve purchased their stock several years ago and have adjusted bases for their Union stock of $15,000 and $27,500, respectively. Each shareholder receives two liquidating distributions. The first liquidating distribution, made in the current year, results in each shareholder receiving a one-half interest in a parcel of land that has a $40,000 FMV and an $18,000 adjusted basis to Union Corporation. The second liquidating distribution, made in the next year, results in each shareholder receiving $20,000 in cash.

a. What are the amount and character of Ron and Steve's recognized gain or loss for the current year? For the next year?

b. What is the basis of the land in Ron and Steve's hands?

c. How would your answers to Parts a and b change if the land has a $12,000 FMV instead of a $40,000 FMV?

C:6-53 *Subsequent Assessment on the Shareholders.* Meridian Corporation originally was owned equally by five individual shareholders. Four years ago, Meridian adopted a plan of liquidation, and each shareholder received a liquidating distribution. Tina, a cash method taxpayer, reported a $30,000 long-term capital gain in the prior liquidation year on the redemption of her stock. Pending the outcome of a lawsuit in which Meridian is one of the defendants, $5,000 of Tina's liquidating distribution was held back and placed in escrow. Settlement of the lawsuit in the current year requires that the escrowed funds plus the interest earned on these funds be paid out to the plaintiff and that each shareholder pay an additional $2,500. Tina pays the amount due in the next year. How does Tina report the settlement of the lawsuit and the payment of the additional amount?

COMPREHENSIVE PROBLEM

C:6-54 The following facts pertain to Lifecycle Corporation:

- Able owns a parcel of land (Land A) having a $30,000 FMV and $16,000 adjusted basis. Baker owns an adjacent parcel of land (Land B) having a $20,000 FMV and $22,000 adjusted basis. On January 2, 2011, Able and Baker contribute their parcels of land to newly formed Lifecycle Corporation in exchange for 60% of the corporation's stock for Able and 40% of the corporation's stock for Baker. The corporation elects a calendar tax year and the accrual method of accounting.

- On January 2, 2011, the corporation borrows $2 million and uses the loan proceeds to build a factory ($1 million), purchase equipment ($500,000), produce inventory ($450,000), pay other operating expenses ($30,000), and retain working cash ($20,000). Assume the corporation sells all inventory produced and collects on all sales immediately so that, at the end of any year, the corporation has no accounts receivable or inventory balances.

- Operating results for 2011 are as follows:

Sales	$964,000	
Cost of goods sold	450,000	
Interest paid on loan	140,000	
Depreciation:		
Equipment	70,000	($25,000 for E&P)
Building	24,000	($24,000 for E&P)
Operating expenses	30,000	

Of these amounts, $250,000 is qualified production activities income. The deduction percentage is 9% in 2011.

- In 2012, Lifecycle Corporation invests $10,000 of excess cash in Macro Corporation stock (less than 20% owned) and $20,000 in tax-exempt bonds. In addition, the corporation pays Able a $12,000 salary and distributes an additional $42,000 to Able and $28,000 to Baker. The corporation also makes a $100,000 principal payment on the loan.
- Results for 2012 are as follows:

Sales	$990,000	
Cost of goods sold	500,000	
Interest paid on loan	130,000	
Depreciation:		
Equipment	125,000	($50,000 for E&P)
Building	25,000	($25,000 for E&P)
Operating expenses	40,000	
Salary paid to Able	12,000	
Dividend received on Macro Corporation stock	2,000	
Short-term capital gain on sale of portion of Macro Corporation stock holdings ($4,000 − $3,000)	1,000	
Tax-exempt interest received	1,500	
Charitable contributions	500	

Of these amounts, $158,000 is qualified production activities income. The deduction percentage is 9% in 2012.

- In 2013, the corporation did not pay a salary to Able and made no distributions to the shareholders. The corporation, however, made a $30,000 principal payment on the loan.
- Results for 2013 are as follows:

Sales	$500,000	
Cost of goods sold	280,000	
Interest paid on loan	125,000	
Depreciation:		
Equipment	90,000	($50,000 for E&P)
Building	25,000	($25,000 for E&P)
Operating expenses	60,000	
Long-term capital gain on sale of remaining Macro Corporation stock ($9,000 − $7,000)	2,000	
Long-term capital gain on sale of tax-exempt bond ($21,000 − $20,000)	1,000	

Of these amounts, qualified production activities income is zero (because it is negative).

- On January 2, 2014, the corporation receives a refund for the 2013 NOL carried back to 2011. When carrying back the NOL, remember to recalculate the U.S. production activities deduction in the carryback year because of the reduced taxable income resulting from carryback. In addition, the corporation sells its assets, pays taxes on the gain, and pays off the $1.87 million remaining debt.

	Sales Price	Tax Adj. Basis*	E&P Adj. Basis
Equipment	$ 250,000	$ 215,000	$ 375,000
Building	986,000	926,000	926,000
Land A	80,000	16,000	16,000
Land B	50,000	20,000	20,000
Total	$1,366,000	$1,177,000	$1,337,000

*Note: Technically, the equipment should be depreciated for ½ year in the year of disposition, and the building should be depreciated for ½ month (because of the January disposition). However, for simplicity, the above calculations ignore depreciation deductions in the disposition year, which creates an offsetting overstatement of adjusted basis. Section 362(e)(2) limits Land B basis to the FMV.

Immediately after these transactions, the corporation makes a liquidating distribution of the remaining cash to Able and Baker. The remaining cash is $348,639, which the corporation distributes in proportion to the shareholders' ownership (60% and 40%). Assume that long-term capital gains are taxed at 15% in 2014.

Required:
a. Determine the tax consequences of the corporate formation to Able, Baker, and Lifecycle Corporation.
b. For 2011–2013, prepare schedules showing corporate taxable income, taxes, and E&P activity. Assume that Lifecycle pays its taxes in the same year they accrue.
c. For 2014, prepare a schedule showing the results of this year's transactions on Lifecycle Corporation, Able, and Baker.
   Note: See Problem C:10-56 for a partnership variation of this problem.

TAX STRATEGY PROBLEMS

C:6-55 Sarah plans to invest $1 million in a business venture that will last five years. She is debating whether to operate the business as a C corporation or a sole proprietorship. If a C corporation, she will liquidate the corporation at the end of the five-year period. She expects the business to generate taxable income as follows:

Year	Taxable Income
1	$ 40,000
2	70,000
3	90,000
4	150,000
5	350,000

If incurred in corporate form, these taxable income amounts will be subject to the corporate tax rate schedule. If in proprietorship form, they will be subject to Sarah's 35% marginal tax rate. Assume that any capital gain upon corporate liquidation will be taxed at a 15% capital gains rate and that Sec. 1202 does not apply.

Required: Determine the after-tax amount Sarah will have at the end of five years under each alternative. Which alternative do you recommend?

C:6-56 One way to compare the accumulation of income by alternative business entity forms is to use mathematical models. The following models express the investment after-tax accumulation calculation for a particular entity form:

Flow-through entities and sole proprietorships: Contribution $\times [1 + R(1 - t_p)]^n$
C corporation: Contribution $\times \{[1 + R(1 - t_c)]^n(1 - t_g) + t_g\}$

Where: $\text{ATA} =$ after-tax accumulation in n years
$R =$ before-tax rate of return for the business entity
$t_p =$ owner's marginal tax rate on ordinary income
$t_c =$ corporation's marginal tax rate
$t_g =$ owner's tax rate on capital gains
$n =$ number of periods

In the C corporation model, the corporation operates for n years, paying taxes currently and distributing no dividends. At the end of its existence, the corporation liquidates, causing the shareholder to recognize a capital gain. In the flow-through model, the entity or sole proprietorship distributes just enough cash for the owner or owners to pay individual taxes, and the entity reinvests the remaining after-tax earnings in the business. (See Chapter I:18 of the *Individuals* volume for a detailed explanation of these models.)

Now consider the following facts. Twelve years ago, your client formed a C corporation with a $100,000 investment (contribution). The corporation's before-tax rate of return (R) has been and will continue to be 10%. The corporate tax rate (t_c) has been and will continue to be 35%. The corporation pays no dividends and reinvests all after-tax earnings in its business. Thus, the corporation's value grows at its after-tax rate of return. Your client's marginal ordinary tax rate (t_p) has been 33%, and her capital gains rate (t_g) has been 15%. Your client expects her ordinary tax rate to drop to 25% at the beginning of this year and stay at that level indefinitely. Her capital gains tax rate will remain at 15%. Assume the corporate stock does not qualify for the Sec. 1202 exclusion.

Your client wants you to consider two alternatives:
(1) Continue the business in C corporation form for the next 20 years and liquidate at that time (32 years in total).

(2) Liquidate the C corporation at the beginning of this year, invest the after-tax proceeds in a sole proprietorship, and operate as a sole proprietorship for the next 20 years.

The sole proprietorship's before-tax rate of return (R) also will be 10% for the next 20 years. Earnings from the sole proprietorship will be taxed currently at your client's ordinary tax rate, and your client will withdraw just enough earnings from the business to pay her taxes on the business's income. The remaining after-tax earnings will remain in the business until the end of the investment horizon (20 years from now).

Required: Show the results of each alternative along with supporting models and calculations. Ignore self employment taxes and the accumulated earnings tax. Which alternative should your client adopt?

Note: See Problem C:11-61 for a third alternative to consider.

CASE STUDY PROBLEMS

C:6-57 Paul, a long-time client of yours, has operated an automobile repair shop (as a C corporation) for most of his life. The shop has been fairly successful in recent years. His children are not interested in continuing the business. Paul is age 62 and has accumulated approximately $500,000 in assets outside of his business, most of which are in his personal residence and retirement plan. A recent balance sheet for the business shows the following amounts:

Assets	Adjusted Basis	FMV	Liabilities & Equity	Amount
Cash	$ 25,000	$ 25,000	Accounts payable	$ 30,000
Inventory	60,000	75,000	Mortgage payable	70,000
Equipment	200,000	350,000	Paid-in capital	120,000
Building	100,000	160,000	Retain earnings	205,000
Land	40,000	60,000		
Goodwill	–0–	100,000		
Total	$425,000	$770,000	Total	$425,000

The inventory is accounted for using the first-in, first-out inventory method. The corporation has claimed depreciation of $250,000 on the equipment. The corporation acquired the building 11 years ago and has claimed $25,000 of depreciation under the MACRS rules. The goodwill is an estimate that Paul feels reflects the value of his business over and above the other tangible assets.

Paul has received an offer of $775,000 from a competing automobile repair company for the noncash assets of his business, which will be used to establish a second location for the competing company. The corporation will sell the assets within 60 days and distribute remaining cash to Paul in liquidation of the corporation. The purchaser has obtained the necessary bank financing to make the acquisition. Paul's basis in his stock is $300,000.

Required: Prepare a memorandum for Paul outlining the tax consequences of the sale transaction and liquidation of the corporation.

C:6-58 Your accounting firm has done the audit and tax work for the Peerless family and their business entities for 20 years. Approximately 25% of your accounting and tax practice billings come from Peerless family work. Peerless Real Estate Corporation owns land and a building (MACRS property) having a $4.5 million FMV and a $1.0 million adjusted basis. The corporation owes a $1.3 million mortgage balance on the building. The corporation used substantial leverage to acquire the building so Myron Peerless and his brother Mark Peerless, who are equal shareholders in Peerless Real Estate, each have only $200,000 adjusted bases in their stock. Cash flows are good from the building, and only a small portion of the annual profits is needed for reinvestment in the building. Myron and Mark have decided to liquidate the corporation to avoid the federal and state corporate income taxes and continue to operate the business as a partnership. They want the MM Partnership, which has Mark and Myron equally sharing profits, losses, and liabilities, to purchase the building from the corporation for $400,000 cash plus their assumption of the $1.3 million mortgage. Mark knows a real estate appraiser who, for the right price, will provide a $1.7 million appraisal. Current corporate cash balances are sufficient to pay any federal and state income taxes owed on the sale of the building. Mark and Myron each would receive $200,000 from the corporation in cancellation of their stock.

Required: Prepare notes on the points you will want to cover with Myron and Mark Peerless about the corporate liquidation and the Peerless' desire to avoid federal and state corporate income taxes at your meeting tomorrow.

TAX RESEARCH PROBLEMS

C:6-59 Parent Corporation owns 85% of the common stock and 100% of the preferred stock of Subsidiary Corporation. The common stock and preferred stock have adjusted bases of $500,000 and $200,000, respectively, to Parent. Subsidiary adopts a plan of liquidation on July 3 of the current year, when its assets have a $1 million FMV. Liabilities on that date amount to $850,000. On November 9, Subsidiary pays off its creditors and distributes $150,000 to Parent with respect to its preferred stock. No cash remains to be paid to Parent with respect to the remaining $50,000 of its liquidation preference for the preferred stock, or with respect to any of the common stock. In each of Subsidiary's tax years, less than 10% of its gross income has been passive income. What are the amount and character of Parent's loss on the preferred stock? The common stock?

A partial list of research sources is

- IRC Secs. 165(g)(3) and 332(a)
- Reg. Sec. 1.332-2(b)
- *Spaulding Bakeries, Inc.*, 27 T.C. 684 (1957)
- *H. K. Porter Co., Inc.*, 87 T.C. 689 (1986)

C:6-60 Parent Corporation has owned 60% of Subsidiary Corporation's single class of stock for a number of years. Tyrone owns the remaining 40% of the Subsidiary stock. On August 10 of the current year, Parent purchases Tyrone's Subsidiary stock for cash. On September 15, Subsidiary adopts a plan of liquidation. Subsidiary then makes a single liquidating distribution on October 1. The activities of Subsidiary continue as a separate division of Parent. Does the liquidation of Subsidiary qualify for nonrecognition treatment under Secs. 332 and 337? Must Parent assume Subsidiary's E&P balance?

A partial list of research sources is

- IRC Secs. 332(b) and 381
- Reg. Sec. 1.332-2(a)

7

CHAPTER

CORPORATE ACQUISITIONS AND REORGANI- ZATIONS

LEARNING OBJECTIVES

After studying this chapter, you should be able to

1. Identify the types of taxable acquisitions

2. Distinguish between taxable and nontaxable acquisitions

3. Explain the types of nontaxable reorganizations and their requirements

4. Determine the tax consequences of a nontaxable reorganization to the target corporation

5. Determine the tax consequences of a nontaxable reorganization to the acquiring corporation

6. Determine the tax consequences of a nontaxable reorganization to target corporation shareholders and security holders

7. Understand judicial doctrines that govern the tax treatment of corporate reorganizations

8. Explain what happens to tax attributes in a reorganization

9. Explain restrictions on the use of NOL carryovers following an acquisition

10. Understand the financial statement implications of corporate acquisitions

A corporation's directors or shareholders may decide to acquire a second corporation (the target) either directly or indirectly. Alternatively, they may decide to divest the corporation of part or all of its assets, such as the assets of an operating division or stock in a subsidiary. These acquisitions or divestitures can be either taxable or nontaxable. In a taxable transaction, the entire realized gain or loss is recognized. To qualify as nontaxable, the transaction must meet certain statutory and judicial requirements. If the transaction meets these requirements, part or all of the realized gain or loss generally goes unrecognized. This unrecognized gain or loss is deferred until the assets or stock exchanged are sold or disposed of in a taxable transaction. The nontaxable reorganization rules embody the continuity of interest doctrine, which holds that no tax is imposed if the taxpayer retains a continuing equity interest. A tax is imposed, however, where the taxpayer receives money or property other than stock or securities.[1] On the other hand, taxpayers are likely to engage in a taxable transaction (instead of a nontaxable reorganization) where they prefer to recognize loss on an asset sale or stock disposition.

This chapter presents an overview of taxable and nontaxable acquisitions and divestitures. It also examines the statutory provisions and judicial doctrines that determine the tax consequences of these types of transactions.

TAXABLE ACQUISITION TRANSACTIONS

OBJECTIVE 1

Identify the types of taxable acquisitions

In taxable acquisitions, corporations acquire a **target corporation** in two principal ways.[2] First, they purchase the assets directly from the target corporation. Second, they acquire an equity claim to target corporation assets by purchasing a controlling interest in target corporation stock. Three options exist once the acquiring corporation has purchased the target stock.

▶ The acquiring corporation and its new subsidiary can exist as separate entities.

▶ The acquiring corporation can liquidate its new subsidiary in a nontaxable transaction. Following the liquidation, the parent corporation retains a direct interest in target corporation assets.

▶ The acquiring corporation can make a Sec. 338 election, which adjusts the basis of subsidiary assets to the price the acquiring corporation paid for the subsidiary stock, plus the amount of any subsidiary liabilities.

The principal asset and stock acquisitions are examined below. Table C:7-1 summarizes the tax consequences of these transactions.

ASSET ACQUISITIONS

From a tax perspective, accounting for an asset purchase is not difficult. The selling corporation calculates the gain or loss recognized on the sale of each asset. Sales of depreciable assets (e.g., Sec. 1245 and 1250 property) may result in the recapture of previously claimed depreciation.

The purchaser's bases in the acquired assets equal their acquisition cost.[3] The purchaser can claim depreciation based on the total acquisition cost of depreciable property.

A taxable asset acquisition provides the purchaser with two major advantages. First, a significant portion of the acquisition cost can be debt-financed. Interest accruing on the debt is deductible for federal income tax purposes. By contrast, in a nontaxable asset acquisition, the use of debt is either prohibited or restricted. Second, only assets and liabilities specified in the purchase-sale agreement are acquired. The purchaser need not acquire all or substantially all of target corporation's assets, as in the case of a taxable or

TAX STRATEGY TIP

Three types of state taxes may arise in an *asset* sale—transfer taxes, state income taxes, and sales taxes (some state sales tax laws allow certain bulk-sale exceptions). These taxes need to be taken into account by both the buyer and seller when drafting the sales agreement. When a *stock* sale occurs, these taxes can be avoided because the assets remain inside the same entity before and after the stock sale.

---

[1] The tax deferral can be permanent if the stock and securities are held until death. At death, the carryover or substituted basis is stepped up to its fair market value (FMV) without income tax consequences.

[2] The terms *target* and *acquired corporation* are used interchangeably here.
[3] Sec. 1012.

▼ TABLE C:7-1

Comparison of Taxable Acquisition Transactions

	Taxable Asset Acquisition	Taxable Stock Acquisition with:		
		No Liquidation of Target	Nontaxable Liquidation of Target	Sec. 338 Election for Target
Acquiring corporation's basis in stock	N/A	Cost basis	Cost basis initially; disappears upon liquidation of target corporation	Cost basis
Parent-subsidiary relationship created	No	Yes	Yes, until liquidation occurs	Yes
Consolidated tax return election available	No	Yes	Yes, until liquidation occurs	Yes
Gain/loss recognized by target corporation on asset sale	Yes	No	No	Yes, on deemed sale of assets from old target corporation to new target corporation
Gain/loss recognized by target corporation upon liquidating	Yes, if target elects to liquidate before or after the asset sale	N/A	No	No
Gain recognized by acquiring corporation in liquidating distribution	N/A	N/A	No	No
Acquiring corporation's basis in assets acquired	Cost basis to acquiring corporation	No change in basis of target corporation's assets	Carryover basis upon liquidation	Cost basis in target stock acquired plus amount of target corporation liabilities
Transfer of tax attributes to acquiring corporation	Remain with target corporation	Remain with target corporation	Carryover to acquiring corporation upon liquidation	Disappear upon deemed sale of assets by old target corporation

N/A = Not applicable.

nontaxable stock acquisition or a nontaxable asset acquisition. Similarly, the purchaser assumes only liabilities specified in the purchase-sale agreement. Contingent or unknown liabilities remain the responsibility of the seller.

The target (acquired) corporation recognizes gain or loss on the sale of assets and may subsequently liquidate. If it liquidates, any property retained by the target corporation is distributed to the shareholders as part of the liquidation. The liquidating corporation recognizes gain or loss on the distribution as if such property had been sold. Upon receiving the liquidating distribution, the target corporation's shareholders recognize capital gain or loss (see Chapter C:6).

EXAMPLE C:7-1 ▶ Six years ago, Ann, Bob, and Cathy each acquired one-third of Target Corporation stock. Each shareholder has a $20,000 basis in his or her stock. Acquiring Corporation purchases Target's noncash assets for $100,000 in cash and $300,000 in Acquiring debt obligations (three notes at $100,000 each). Target retains its $50,400 of cash. On the sale date, Target's noncash assets have a $280,000 adjusted basis and a $400,000 FMV. Its liabilities total $100,000 on the sale date. Target recognizes a $120,000 aggregate gain [($100,000 + $300,000) − $280,000]. The character of its separate asset gains and losses depends on the type of properties sold. Based on a 34% corporate tax rate, Target's tax liability on the sale is $40,800 ($120,000 × 0.34). Acquiring takes a

$400,000 basis in the noncash assets acquired. After Target pays its income tax and other liabilities, Target has remaining cash of $9,600 ($50,400 retained cash + $100,000 cash received − $100,000 liabilities paid − $40,800 tax paid) and holds the three $100,000 notes received. Ann, Bob, and Cathy then decide to liquidate Target with each receiving $3,200 cash ($9,600 ÷ 3) plus a $100,000 note. Thus, each shareholder recognizes a capital gain of $83,200 ($103,200 − $20,000 stock basis). ◄

Sometimes a target corporation liquidates before it sells its assets. In this case the target corporation distributes the assets to the shareholders who then sell them. The tax consequences of the liquidation are set forth in Chapter C:6. In general, the total tax liability of the corporation and its shareholders are the same whether the liquidation of the target corporation precedes or follows the asset sale.

STOCK ACQUISITIONS

STOCK ACQUISITION WITH NO LIQUIDATION. A stock purchase is the simplest of acquisition transactions. Gain recognized on the sale is capital in character if the stock is a capital asset in the seller's hands. If payment of part or all of the consideration is deferred to a later year, the seller can defer gain recognition under the installment method of accounting.[4] If part of the total amount received by the seller represents consideration for a promise not to compete with the purchaser, this portion is taxed as ordinary income.[5]

The purchaser's basis in the stock is its acquisition cost.[6] The target corporation's basis in its assets ordinarily does not change as a result of the stock sale. Any potential for depreciation recapture that exists on the transaction date remains with the target corporation's assets and, therefore, is assumed by the purchaser. If the target corporation has loss or credit carryovers, these carryovers can be subject to special limitations in the post-acquisition tax years (see pages C:7-43 through C:7-46).

Stock sales are popular with sellers because they often are less costly than asset sales due to a single level of taxation. No adjustment to the bases of the target corporation's assets is made after a stock sale even though the basis of the stock acquired may be substantially higher than the aggregate basis of these assets. Thus, one of the tax advantages of purchasing target corporation assets—a higher asset basis—is not available in a stock purchase unless the purchasing corporation makes a Sec. 338 deemed sale election (discussed later in this chapter).

EXAMPLE C:7-2 ►

Assume the same facts as in Example C:7-1 except Acquiring offers to purchase Target stock for $50 per share. Ann, Bob, and Cathy tender their 7,000 Target shares in response to Acquiring's offer. Acquiring's $350,000 (7,000 shares × $50/share) purchase price equals Target's net asset value ($450,000 − $100,000 liabilities). Ann, Bob, and Cathy each recognize a long-term capital gain on the sale of their stock. Target becomes a wholly-owned subsidiary of Acquiring and, without a Sec. 338 election, does not adjust the bases of its assets. ◄

If the purchasing corporation is a member of an affiliated group that files a consolidated tax return, the new subsidiary must join in the consolidated return election if the purchasing corporation owns at least 80% of the subsidiary's stock and if the subsidiary is an includible corporation (see Chapter C:8). Otherwise, the parent and subsidiary may make an initial consolidated return election.

STOCK ACQUISITION FOLLOWED BY A LIQUIDATION. The type of stock acquisition discussed in the preceding section can be followed by a liquidation of the acquired (subsidiary) corporation into its acquiring (parent) corporation. If the parent owns at least 80% of subsidiary stock, the liquidation is nontaxable under the Sec. 332 and 337 rules outlined in Chapter C:6.[7] The bases of the subsidiary's assets carry over to the parent. If the parent paid a premium for the assets (i.e., an amount exceeding the aggregate

4 Sec. 453(a).
5 The purchaser can amortize over a 15-year period any amounts paid to the seller with respect to the agreement not to compete (Sec. 197).

6 Sec. 1012.
7 The liquidation may be taxable to any minority shareholders and to the subsidiary corporation on distributions made to the minority shareholders.

asset adjusted basis), this premium is lost upon liquidation because the parent's basis in the stock disappears. The stock basis "loss" cannot be deducted and provides no tax benefit. If the parent paid less than the aggregate asset adjusted basis, the "excess" asset basis is included in the asset carryover basis, which can provide additional tax benefits.

EXAMPLE C:7-3 ▶ Assume the same facts as in Example C:7-2 except that, following the stock acquisition, Acquiring and Target Corporations continue to file separate tax returns, and Target liquidates into Acquiring shortly after the acquisition. Target's assets have the following adjusted bases and FMVs immediately before the sale:

Assets	Adjusted Basis	FMV
Cash	$ 50,000	$ 50,000
Marketable securities	49,000	55,000
Accounts receivable	60,000	60,000
Inventory	60,000	90,000
Building	27,000	44,000
Land	10,000	26,000
Machinery and equipment[a]	74,000	125,000
Total	$330,000	$450,000

[a]The machinery and equipment are Sec. 1245 property. Recapture potential of the machinery and equipment is $107,000.

Target and Acquiring recognize no gain or loss on the liquidation. Acquiring assumes Target's $100,000 in liabilities and takes a $330,000 total basis in Target assets, the basis of each asset carrying over. In addition, Acquiring inherits all of Target's tax attributes, including any NOL carryovers, E&P, and the $107,000 depreciation recapture potential of the machinery and equipment. ◀

ADDITIONAL COMMENT

A Sec. 338 election triggers immediate taxation to the target corporation. Therefore, in most situations it makes little sense to pay an immediate tax to obtain a step-up in basis when such additional basis can be recovered only in future years. The election can be beneficial, however, if the target corporation has enough NOLs to offset most or all of the gain recognized on the deemed asset sale. The election also can be beneficial if Sec. 338(h)(10) applies (see footnote 9).

SECTION 338 DEEMED SALE ELECTION. The Sec. 338 **deemed sale election** operates as follows: First target corporation's shareholders sell their stock to the acquiring corporation. Then the acquiring corporation makes a Sec. 338 deemed sale election with respect to the purchased stock. This election results in a hypothetical sale of the "old" target corporation's assets to a "new" target corporation for their **aggregate deemed sale price (ADSP)** in a transaction that requires the seller ("old" target) to recognize gains and losses on its final tax return. The "old" target corporation goes out of existence for tax purposes only.[8] The "new" target corporation is treated as a new entity for tax purposes (i.e., it makes new accounting method and tax year elections). The bases of old target corporation assets are stepped-up or stepped-down to the price paid by the acquiring corporation for target corporation stock plus the amount of target corporation liabilities (including any federal income taxes owed on the hypothetical sale). Corporate purchasers generally do not find the Sec. 338[9] election appealing because, in the year of the election, the target corporation usually incurs a significant tax liability.

PRACTICAL APPLICATION

The purchasing corporation most likely would not make a Sec. 338 election if it resulted in the target corporation's asset tax bases being stepped-down.

Eligible Stock Acquisitions. Section 338 requires the acquiring corporation to purchase 80% or more of target corporation voting stock and 80% or more of the total value of all classes of target stock except certain nonvoting preferred stock during a continuous 12-month (or shorter) qualified stock acquistion period.[10] The acquistion period begins on the date the acquiring corporation first purchases target stock and ends on the date the qualified stock purchase is completed. If the acquiring corporation does not acquire the necessary 80% minimum within the 12-month acquisition period, it cannot make a Sec. 338 election.

---

[8] The target corporation's legal existence does not change under the applicable corporation laws. For federal income tax purposes only, the target corporation (commonly referred to as "old" target) goes out of existence. A "new" target corporation is created. This new corporation acquires for tax purposes all the assets of the "old" corporation.

[9] An alternative Sec. 338 election is permitted under Sec. 338(h)(10) for members of an affiliated group. This election generally is used by affiliated groups that file consolidated tax returns. The Sec. 338(h)(10) election permits the target corporation (e.g., a subsidiary) to recognize gain or loss as if it had sold its assets in a single transaction. The corporation selling the stock (e.g., a parent corporation) does not recognize gain on the stock sale, thereby resulting in a single level of taxation. This special Sec. 338 election has become popular in recent years. The Treasury Department also has issued Prop. Reg. Secs. 1.336-2–1.336-5, which would allow a parent corporation to elect under Sec. 336(e) to treat certain dispositions of a subsidiary corporation's stock as a taxable sale of the subsidiary's underlying assets.

[10] The basic Sec. 332 liquidation of a controlled subsidiary stock definition outlined in Chapter C:6 also is used for Sec. 338 purposes.

EXAMPLE C:7-4 ▶ Missouri Corporation purchases a 25% block of Target Corporation's single class of stock on each of four dates: April 1, 2010; July 1, 2010; December 1, 2010; and February 1, 2011. Because Missouri acquires at least 80% of Target stock within a 12-month period (April 1, 2010, through February 1, 2011), it is eligible to make a Sec. 338 deemed sale election. ◀

EXAMPLE C:7-5 ▶ Assume the same facts as in Example C:7-4 except Missouri Corporation instead purchases the final 25% block on May 15, 2011. In this case, Missouri acquires only 75% of the Target stock during a 12-month period. Two possible 12-month periods may occur—April 1, 2010, through March 31, 2011, and May 16, 2010, through May 15, 2011. The 80% stock ownership minimum is not achieved in either period. Thus, Missouri is not eligible to make a Sec. 338 election. ◀

For the purpose of the 80% requirement, the following stock acquisitions are not treated as purchases:

▶ Stock whose adjusted basis is determined in whole or part by its basis in the hands of the person from whom it was acquired (e.g., stock acquired as a capital contribution)

▶ Stock whose basis is determined under Sec. 1014(a) (i.e., FMV on the date of decedent's death or alternative valuation date)

▶ Stock acquired in a nontaxable transaction under Sec. 351, 354, 355, or 356 (e.g., corporate formations, divisions, or reorganizations)

▶ Stock acquired from a related party where stock ownership may be attributed to the purchaser under Secs. 318(a)(1) through (3)

The Election. A Sec. 338 election must be made no later than the fifteenth day of the ninth month beginning after the month in which the acquisition date falls. The acquisition date is the first date during the 12-month acquisition period on which the 80% stock ownership requirement is met.[11]

EXAMPLE C:7-6 ▶ On April 1, 2011, Arizona Corporation purchased 40% of Target Corporation's single class of stock. On October 20, 2011, it purchases an additional 50% of Target stock. The acquisition date is October 20, 2011. Arizona must make a Sec. 338 election on or before July 15, 2012. ◀

Deemed Sale Transaction. When the acquiring corporation makes a Sec. 338 election, the target corporation is treated as having sold all its assets at their aggregate deemed sale price (ADSP) in a single transaction at the close of the acquisition date. The asset sale is a taxable transaction, with gain or loss recognized by the target corporation. ADSP is calculated as follows:[12]

$$\text{ADSP} = \frac{G + L - (T_R \times B)}{(1 - T_R)}$$

Where: G = Acquiring's grossed-up basis in recently purchased target corporation stock;

L = Target liabilities other than its tax liability for the deemed sale gain determined by reference to the ADSP;

T_R = the applicable federal income tax rate; and

B = the adjusted basis of the asset(s) deemed sold.

EXAMPLE C:7-7 ▶ Assume the same facts as in Examples C:7-2 and C:7-3 except Acquiring makes a timely Sec. 338 election. Also assume that Target's marginal tax rate is 34%. The aggregate deemed sale price is calculated as follows:

$$\text{ADSP} = \frac{G + L - (T_R \times B)}{(1 - T_R)}$$

---

[11] Secs. 338(g) and 338(h)(2).
[12] This equation is derived as follows:
$\text{ADSP} = G + L + [T_R \times (\text{ADSP} - B)]$
$\text{ADSP} = G + L + (T_R \times \text{ADSP}) - (T_R \times B)$

$\text{ADSP} - (T_R \times \text{ADSP}) = G + L - (T_R \times B)$
$\text{ADSP} \times (1 - T_R) = G + L - (T_R \times B)$
$\text{ADSP} = \dfrac{G + L - (T_R \times B)}{(1 - T_R)}$

$$ADSP = \frac{\$350{,}000 + \$100{,}000 - (0.34 \times \$330{,}000)}{(1 - 0.34)}$$

$$0.66\ ADSP = \$337{,}800$$

$$ADSP = \$511{,}818$$

Thus, Target recognizes a gain of $181,818 ($511,818 − $330,000) and pays taxes of $61,818 (0.34 × $181,818) on the gain. ◀

TAX STRATEGY TIP

Many taxpayers avoid Sec. 338 because it requires an advance payment of taxes to achieve a step-up in basis of target corporation's assets. A Sec. 338 election becomes more attractive, however, when the target corporation has NOLs that can offset its gain on the deemed sale of its assets, thereby reducing the cost of making the election.

The Sec. 338 election was intended for transactions in which the acquisition price of target stock exceeds the adjusted basis of target assets. In many of these transactions, the amount of gain recognized by the target corporation, as well as the associated tax liability, could be substantial. This potential tax cost might induce companies to forego the Sec. 338 election or lower the price they are willing to pay for target stock if they intend to make a Sec. 338 election.

Tax Basis of the Assets After the Deemed Sale. Similarly to the ADSP, the tax basis in the assets of the new target corporation is based on the amount paid by the acquiring corporation for target corporation stock. This amount is called the **adjusted grossed-up basis** in the target corporation stock. The adjusted grossed-up basis equals the sum of

▶ The purchasing corporation's grossed-up basis in recently purchased target corporation stock;

▶ The purchasing corporation's basis in nonrecently purchased target corporation stock;

▶ The liabilities of the new target corporation; and

▶ Other relevant items.[13]

The adjusted grossed-up basis is determined as of the beginning of the day following the acquisition date. Example C:7-10 illustrates the calculation of the adjusted grossed-up basis.

Target corporation stock owned by the acquiring corporation falls into two categories: recently purchased stock and nonrecently purchased stock. This categorization is necessary because only the recently purchased stock is treated as consideration used in a deemed purchase of target corporation assets. Recently purchased stock includes any target corporation stock held on the acquisition date that the acquiring corporation purchased during the 12-month (or shorter) acquisition period. Nonrecently purchased stock includes all other target corporation stock acquired before the acquisition period and held by the acquiring corporation on the acquisition date.[14] The basis of the purchasing corporation's ownership interest equals the grossed-up basis of the recently purchased stock plus the basis of the nonrecently purchased stock.

EXAMPLE C:7-8 ▶ On July 23 of the current year, Apple Corporation purchases all of Target Corporation's single class of stock. All the Target stock is considered to be recently purchased because it is purchased in a single transaction. The acquisition date is July 23 of the current year. ◀

EXAMPLE C:7-9 ▶ Assume the same facts as in Example C:7-8 except Apple already owns 10% of Target stock (purchased five years ago) and purchases the remaining 90% of Target stock. The original block of Target stock is not considered to be recently purchased because it was acquired more than 12 months before the acquisition date (July 23 of the current year). ◀

When the acquiring corporation does not own all of target corporation outstanding stock, the basis of the acquiring corporation's recently purchased stock must be increased or grossed-up to a hypothetical value that reflects ownership of all the stock.[15]

---

[13] Secs. 338(b)(1) and (2). The IRS has indicated that other relevant items include only items that arise from adjustment events that occur after the close of the new target's first tax year and items discovered as a result of an IRS examination of a tax return (e.g., the payment of contingent amounts for recently or nonrecently purchased stock).

[14] Sec. 338(b)(6). A special gain recognition election is available to adjust the basis of nonrecently purchased stock. This election, which is set forth in Sec. 338(b)(3), is beyond the scope of this text.

[15] Sec. 338(b)(4). The gross-up operation involves taking the purchasing corporation's basis for the recently purchased target stock and dividing it by the percentage (by value) of recently purchased target stock owned (expressed as a decimal).

Specifically, the basis of the recently purchased stock must be increased by the face amount of any target liabilities outstanding on the day following the acquisition date, plus the tax liability incurred on any gain realized in the deemed sale.[16] This liability adjustment embodies the notion that, if the acquisition had been structured as an asset purchase, the assumption of liabilities would have been reflected in the total purchase price.

Allocation of Basis to Individual Assets. The adjusted grossed-up basis of the stock is allocated among seven classes of assets under the residual method.[17] The residual method requires that the adjusted grossed-up basis be allocated to the corporation's tangible and intangible property (other than goodwill and going concern value) sequentially on a priority basis. Any amount exceeding the aggregate FMVs of this property is assigned to target corporation goodwill and going concern value.

The seven classes of assets to which the adjusted grossed-up basis is allocated are as follows:

▶ Class I: cash and general deposit accounts, including demand deposit and similar accounts in banks, savings and loan associations, and other financial institutions.

▶ Class II: actively traded personal property (as defined in Sec. 1092(d)(1)), such as U.S. government obligations and publicly traded securities.

▶ Class III: accounts receivable, mortgages, and credit card receivables that arise in the ordinary course of business.

▶ Class IV: inventory or other property held primarily for sale to customers in the ordinary course of business.

▶ Class V: all assets other than Class I, II, III, IV, VI, and VII assets. Included in this category are tangible and intangible property without regard to whether such property is depreciable, depletable, or amortizable.

▶ Class VI: all amortizable Sec. 197 intangible assets except goodwill and going concern value.

▶ Class VII: Sec. 197 intangible assets in the nature of goodwill and going concern value.[18]

Class VI and VII intangible assets are amortizable over a 15-year period if they are used in the active conduct of a trade or business. Among such assets are goodwill, going concern value, and covenants not to compete.

The adjusted grossed-up basis is first allocated to individual Class I assets based on their actual dollar amounts.[19] Any excess is allocated to Class II assets based on, and to the extent of, their relative gross FMVs. Similar allocations are made to Class III through VI assets based on, and to the extent of, the relative gross FMVs of individual assets within each class. The intra-class allocation is based on the asset's total gross FMV, not its net FMV (gross FMV minus liabilities secured by the property). Any remaining adjusted grossed-up basis is assigned to Class VII (goodwill).

PRACTICAL APPLICATION

Because goodwill now can be amortized, the fact that the residual purchase price is allocated to goodwill may be a desirable tax result. Goodwill was not amortized under pre-Sec. 197 law because it had an indefinite life. On the negative side, however, the required 15-year amortization period under Sec. 197 is longer than the time period used by many taxpayers under pre-Sec. 197 law to amortize intangible assets that had a shorter determinable life.

ADDITIONAL COMMENT

The residual method ensures that any premium paid for the target stock is reflected in goodwill. Because the residual method is the only acceptable allocation method, the only uncertainty that remains is to determine the FMVs of the assets listed in Classes II through VI.

EXAMPLE C:7-10 ▶ Assume the same facts as in Example C:7-7, with assets classified as follows:

Asset Class	Assets	FMV
I	Cash	$ 50,000
II	Marketable securities	55,000
III	Accounts receivable	60,000
IV	Inventory	90,000
V	Building	44,000
V	Land	26,000
V	Machinery and equipment	125,000
	Total	$450,000

---

[16] Sec. 338(b)(2) and Reg. Secs. 1.338(b)-1(f)(1) and (2).
[17] Reg. Sec. 1.338-6(a).

[18] Reg. Sec. 1.338-6(b).
[19] Ibid.

The adjusted grossed-up basis of Acquiring's interest in Target stock is calculated as follows:

Recently purchased stock	$350,000
Plus: Target corporation's nontax liabilities	100,000
Target corporation's tax liability [($511,818 − $330,000) × 0.34]	61,818
Adjusted grossed-up basis	$511,818

The adjusted grossed-up basis is allocated to Target's seven asset classes in the following steps:

Step 1: Allocate $50,000 to cash (Class I asset).

Step 2: Allocate $55,000 to marketable securities (Class II asset).

Step 3: Allocate $60,000 to accounts receivable (Class III asset).

Step 4: Allocate $90,000 to inventory (Class IV asset).

Step 5: Allocate $195,000 to the building, land, machinery, and equipment (Class V assets). Because the total basis that remains after the Step 4 allocation ($256,818) exceeds the aggregate FMV of the Class V assets ($195,000), each asset will take a basis exactly equal to its FMV.

Step 6: No allocation to Class VI assets.

Step 7: Allocate the residual $61,818 [$511,818 − ($50,000 + $55,000 + $60,000 + $90,000 + $195,000)] to goodwill (Class VII asset). The $61,818 is amortizable under Sec. 197. ◀

 STOP & THINK

Question: In Example C:7-10, Target Corporation is considering changing from the FIFO to the LIFO inventory method after all the Sec. 338 adjustments have been made. How and when will the $30,000 ($90,000 FMV − $60,000 cost) upward adjustment to the inventory's basis be recovered if Target makes the LIFO election?

Solution: The basis step-up will be recovered only if Target sells the LIFO inventory items in existence on the acquisition date. In general, such sales will not be made unless inventory levels are reduced below the amount held on the acquisition date. If Target retains the FIFO inventory method, the step-up in the inventory's basis will be included in cost of goods sold in the first post-election tax year. Some reasons for not making the Sec. 338 election include the lengthy capital recovery periods for the building and goodwill adjustments, and the inability to recover the adjustment made to the basis of the land through depreciation or amortization.

Tax Accounting Elections for the New Corporation. Because it is a separate legal entity, the "new" target corporation files a tax return separate from that of the acquiring corporation (unless the group files a consolidated return). For tax purposes, the "new" target corporation is a new entity.[20] Thus, without obtaining prior approval from the IRS, the target corporation may adopt any tax year that meets the requirements of Sec. 441 and any accounting method that meets the requirements of Sec. 446. In addition, the new target corporation can claim depreciation under the MACRS rules without regard to the elections made by the old target corporation and without regard to the anti-churning rules of Sec. 338.[21] The holding period for the new target corporation's assets begins on the day after the acquisition date.

For purposes of the tax attribute carryover rules, the new target corporation does not represent a continuation of the old target corporation.[22] As a result, when the purchasing corporation makes a Sec. 338 deemed sale election, tax attributes that exist on the acquisition date are permanently lost. Gain recognized on the deemed sale, however, may be offset by target corporation loss and credit carryovers that otherwise might be forfeited. Thus, if Target in Examples C:7-7 and C:7-10 had a $200,000 NOL on the acquisition

---

[20] The "old" target also files a separate tax return that includes the gains from the Sec. 338 deemed sale. The "old" target may not file a consolidated tax return with the acquiring corporation.

[21] Reg. Sec. 1.338-1(b)(1)(i).
[22] Sec. 381(a)(1).

date, the asset gain resulting from the Sec. 338 election would have been entirely offset by most of the NOL. Consequently, only a small portion of Target's $200,000 NOL would have been lost. The acquiring corporation must carefully consider the relative benefit of obtaining a stepped-up basis in target assets versus the economic value of target tax attributes (e.g., NOL carryovers).

Topic Review C:7-1 summarizes the requirements for, and tax consequences of, a Sec. 338 deemed sale election.

Topic Review C:7-1

Section 338 Deemed Sale Election

Election Requirements

1. The acquiring corporation must make a qualified stock purchase (i.e., within a 12-month period purchase 80% or more of target corporation voting stock and 80% or more of the total value of all target corporation stock).
2. Stock received in transactions that result in a substituted basis (e.g., nontaxable reorganizations, corporate formations, and gifts), transfers at death, and related party exchanges do not count toward the 80% minimum threshold.
3. The acquiring corporation must make the election not later than the fifteenth day of the ninth month beginning after the month in which the acquisition date falls. The acquisition date is the first date on which the 80% stock ownership requirement is met.

Tax Consequences of a Sec. 338 Election

1. The old target corporation is treated as having sold all its assets to the new target corporation at their aggregate deemed sales price in a single transaction at the close of the acquisition date. The old target corporation recognizes gain or loss on the deemed sale.
2. The new target corporation takes an aggregate asset basis equal to the acquiring corporation's adjusted grossed-up basis in the target stock, that is, the sum of the acquiring corporation's basis in the target corporation stock on the day following the acquisition date, the target corporation's liabilities on the day after the acquisition date, and other relevant items (e.g., contingent liabilities that become fixed).
3. The total adjusted grossed-up basis is allocated to individual assets under the residual method. This method requires allocation of basis first to cash and near-cash items, then to other tangible and intangible assets, and finally to goodwill and going concern value.
4. After the Sec. 338 deemed asset sale, the tax attributes of the old target corporation disappear.
5. The new target corporation makes new tax year and accounting method elections.

COMPARISON OF TAXABLE AND NONTAXABLE ACQUISITIONS

TAXABLE AND NONTAXABLE ASSET ACQUISITIONS

One way to illustrate the difference between taxable and nontaxable asset acquisitions is to identify the type of consideration used to acquire the assets and to compare the tax consequences of the transactions. For this discussion, we assume that the acquiring corporation acquires all the target corporation's assets and liabilities and that the target corporation liquidates immediately after the acquisition. If the acquiring corporation uses cash and/or other property to purchase the assets, the target corporation is taxed on the sale, and its shareholders are taxed on the liquidation. On the other hand, if the acquiring corporation uses its own stock, the asset acquisition may qualify as a reorganization that is nontaxable to the target corporation and its shareholders. If the acquiring corporation supplements its stock with a limited amount of cash and/or other property, the transaction still may qualify as a reorganization but may be partially taxable.

TAX CONSEQUENCES TO THE TARGET CORPORATION. Section 1001(c) requires that, with certain exceptions, the entire gain or loss realized on a sale or exchange of property be recognized. Thus, the target corporation recognizes all gains and losses realized on selling its assets.

A reorganization is one exception to the general rule. The target corporation generally recognizes no gain or loss when it exchanges its assets for acquiring corporation stock. It also recognizes no gain or loss when it distributes the acquiring corporation stock to its shareholders. The target corporation, however, could recognize gain if it receives boot and does not distribute the boot to its shareholders, or if it distributes boot or retained property whose FMV exceeds its adjusted basis. The term *retained property* refers to property not transferred to the acquiring corporation as part of the acquisition.

SELF-STUDY QUESTION

Why would an acquiring corporation want an acquisition to be nontaxable if it gets only a substituted basis rather than a FMV basis in the acquired assets?

ANSWER

Usually the motivation for an acquisition to be nontaxable comes from the target corporation and its shareholders. However, two reasons why the acquiring corporation may desire a nontaxable acquisition are (1) the acquiring corporation has no cash to acquire the assets, so it must use stock as the consideration for the purchase and (2) the target corporation may have favorable tax attributes (e.g., an NOL) that the acquiring corporation would like to use.

TAX CONSEQUENCES TO THE ACQUIRING CORPORATION. The acquiring corporation recognizes no gain or loss when it issues its stock in exchange for property in either a taxable or nontaxable acquisition. In a taxable acquisition, the acquiring corporation takes a cost (FMV) basis in the assets received, and the holding period for the acquired assets begins the day after the acquisition. In a reorganization, the acquiring corporation takes a carryover basis equal to target corporation's basis before the transfer. If the target corporation recognizes a gain because it does not distribute boot property to its shareholders, the carryover basis is adjusted upward to reflect this recognized gain. The acquiring corporation's holding period includes the target corporation's holding period.

In a taxable acquisition all the target corporation's tax attributes (e.g., an NOL carryover) disappear when it liquidates, while in a nontaxable reorganization, the acquiring corporation inherits the target corporation's tax attributes.

TAX CONSEQUENCES TO TARGET CORPORATION SHAREHOLDERS. If the target corporation liquidates as part of a taxable acquisition, its shareholders recognize gain or loss on the surrender of their stock. The target corporation assets they receive take a basis equal to their FMV. A reorganization requires the shareholders to recognize gain only to the extent they receive boot. The gain generally is capital in character. In some circumstances, however, target corporation shareholders could recognize dividend income. The stock and securities they receive take a substituted basis that references the basis of target corporation stock and securities surrendered. Their basis in any boot property received is its FMV.

ACCOUNTING FOR THE ACQUISITION. For financial reporting purposes, only the purchase method is available to account for acquisitions. Thus, the acquired assets must be recorded at their fair market values. Any goodwill created in the acquisition cannot be amortized, but rather must be periodically tested for impairment. Also, any impairment of an indefinite-life intangible asset must be reported in the acquiring corporation's financial statements as a loss from continuing operations. For other accounting issues, see Financial Statement Implications at the end of this chapter.

Topic Review C:7-2 compares various aspects of taxable and nontaxable asset acquisitions.

COMPARISON OF TAXABLE AND NONTAXABLE STOCK ACQUISITIONS

For purposes of this discussion, we assume that the acquiring corporation acquires all the stock of target corporation instead of its assets and that the target corporation becomes a controlled subsidiary of the acquiring corporation. If the acquiring corporation uses cash and/or other property alone or along with its own stock to acquire the target stock, the acquisition is taxable. If the acquiring corporation uses solely its voting stock or voting stock of its parent corporation to acquire the target corporation stock, the acquisition may qualify as a nontaxable reorganization.

TAX STRATEGY TIP

Taxes can be an important variable in determining the acquisition method used to acquire the target corporation's stock or assets. All parties also need to consider nontax variables associated with the transaction. For example, a stock-for-stock acquisition may minimize taxes but leave the target corporation's shareholders controlling the acquiring corporation. Facing loss of control, the acquiring corporation's owners may prefer financing the transaction with borrowed funds (and taxing the acquisition to the seller) while retaining control over the acquiring corporation.

TAX CONSEQUENCES TO THE TARGET CORPORATION. The target corporation's basis in its assets does not change as a result of either a taxable or nontaxable stock acquisition (unless the acquiring corporation makes a Sec. 338 election after a taxable

Topic Review C:7-2

Comparison of Taxable and Nontaxable Asset Acquisitions

TAX FEATURE	TAXABLE ACQUISITION	NONTAXABLE REORGANIZATION
1. Consideration used in acquisition	Primarily cash and debt instruments; may involve some stock of the acquiring corporation or its parent corporation.	Primarily stock and limited amount of cash or debt of the acquiring corporation or its parent corporation.
2. Target corporation		
a. Amount of gain or loss	All gains and losses are recognized. Installment method available if payments are deferred.	Generally, no gain or loss recognized. Gain recognized on an asset transfer when the target corporation receives boot property and does not distribute the boot property to its shareholders. Gain also recognized on the distribution of appreciated boot or retained property.
b. Character of gain or loss	Depends on nature of each asset transferred or distributed.	Depends on nature of each asset transferred or distributed.
c. Depreciation recapture	Sec. 1245 or 1250 depreciation is recaptured.	Sec. 1245 or 1250 depreciation is not recaptured unless boot triggers the recognition of gain.
3. Acquiring corporation		
a. Gain or loss when stock is exchanged for property	None recognized.	None recognized.
b. Gain or loss when boot is exchanged for property	Gain or loss recognized if noncash boot property is transferred to the target corporation.	Gain or loss recognized if noncash boot property is transferred to the target corporation.
c. Basis of acquired assets	Cost.	Same as the target corporation's basis, increased by gain recognized.
d. Holding period of acquired assets	Begins the day after the transaction date.	Includes holding period of the target corporation.
e. Acquisition of target corporation tax attributes	No.	Yes.
4. Target corporation shareholders		
a. Amount of gain or loss	Realized gain or loss is recognized. Installment method available if payments are deferred.	Realized gain is recognized to the extent of boot received; realized losses are not recognized.
b. Character of gain or loss	Capital gain or loss; may be Sec. 1244 loss.	Capital gain and/or dividend income in some circumstances.
c. Basis of stock and securities received	Cost; generally FMV of stock, securities, or other property received.	Substituted basis referenced to the stock and securities surrendered; FMV for boot property.
d. Holding period of stock and securities received	Begins the day after the transaction date.	Includes holding period for the stock and securities surrendered; day after the transaction date for boot property.

stock purchase). Any depreciation recapture potential on the transaction date stays with target corporation assets and, therefore, is inherited by the purchaser. Also, the target corporation retains any loss or credit carryovers, which may be subject to special limitations in the post-acquisition tax years.

If the acquiring corporation is a member of an affiliated group that files a consolidated tax return, the target corporation must join in the consolidated return election if the acquiring corporation owns at least 80% of the target corporation stock, and the target corporation is an includible corporation. Otherwise, the acquiring corporation and the target corporation can make an initial consolidated tax return election (see Chapter C:8).

TAX CONSEQUENCES TO THE ACQUIRING CORPORATION. In either a taxable or nontaxable stock acquisition, the acquiring corporation recognizes no gain or loss when it exchanges its own stock for target corporation stock. In a taxable acquisition, the acquiring corporation's basis in the target corporation stock is its acquisition cost. A taxable acquisition may qualify for the Sec. 338 deemed sale election. In a reorganization, the acquiring corporation's basis in the target corporation stock is the same as that in the hands of target corporation shareholders, and a Sec. 338 election is not available. The acquiring corporation recognizes gain or loss when it exchanges noncash boot property for target corporation stock.

TAX CONSEQUENCES TO TARGET CORPORATION SHAREHOLDERS. The gain recognized in a taxable stock sale is capital in character if the target corporation stock is a capital asset in the seller's hands. The seller can account for the gain under the installment method if payment of part or all of the consideration is deferred to a later tax year and if the stock is not traded on an established securities exchange. Consideration received by the seller that represents compensation for an agreement not to compete with the purchaser for a specified time period is taxable as ordinary income.

Because only voting stock may be used in a nontaxable stock acquisition, the target corporation's shareholders recognize no gain or loss. The shareholders take a substituted basis in the acquiring corporation stock, which is the same as their basis in the target corporation stock.

Topic Review C:7-3 compares various aspects of taxable and nontaxable stock acquisitions.

Topic Review C:7-3

Comparison of Taxable and Nontaxable Stock Acquisitions

TAX FEATURE	TAXABLE ACQUISITION	NONTAXABLE REORGANIZATION
1. Consideration used in acquisition	Primarily cash and debt instruments; may include some stock of the acquiring corporation or its parent corporation.	Solely voting stock of the acquiring corporation or its parent corporation.
2. Target corporation		
a. Parent-subsidiary relationship established	Yes.	Yes.
b. Consolidated tax return election available	Yes.	Yes.
c. Basis in assets	Unchanged by stock acquisition unless a Sec. 338 election is made.	Unchanged by stock acquisition. No Sec. 338 election available.
d. Tax attributes	Retained by the target corporation.	Retained by the target corporation.
3. Acquiring corporation		
a. Basis in stock acquired	Cost basis.	Carryover basis from the target corporation shareholders.
4. Target corporation shareholders		
a. Amount of gain or loss recognized	Realized gain or loss is recognized.	No boot is received; therefore, no gain is recognized.
b. Character of gain or loss	Capital gain or loss; may be Sec. 1244 loss.	Not applicable.
c. Basis of stock, securities, or other property received	Cost; generally FMV of stock, securities, or other property received.	Substituted basis from stock surrendered.
d. Holding period of stock, securities, or other property received	Begins the day after the transaction date.	Includes holding period of the stock surrendered.

TYPES OF REORGANIZATIONS

Section 368(a)(1) authorizes seven types of nontaxable reorganizations that correspond to the principal forms of business acquisitions, divestitures, and restructurings. Generally, tax practitioners refer to the reorganization type by the subparagraph of Sec. 368(a)(1) that defines it. For example, a merger is referred to as a *Type A* reorganization because it is defined in Sec. 368(a)(1)(A). The seven types of reorganizations also can be classified according to the transactional form, with the most common forms being acquisitive and divisive. In an **acquisitive reorganization**, the acquiring corporation obtains part or all of a target (or transferor) corporation's assets or stock. Types A, B, and C reorganizations generally are acquisitive. In a **divisive reorganization**, some of a transferor corporation's assets are transferred to a second corporation that is controlled by either the transferor or its shareholders. As part of the reorganization, the controlled (or transferee) corporation's stock or securities exchanged for the transferor's assets are distributed to the transferor's shareholders. Subsequent to the transfer, the transferor corporation can either remain in existence or be liquidated. If the transferor corporation remains in existence, its assets usually are divided between at least two corporations. Types D and G reorganizations may be either acquisitive or divisive.

Two types of reorganizations are neither acquisitive or divisive. A Type E reorganization—a recapitalization—involves a change in a corporation's capital structure. A Type F reorganization—a change in identity, legal form, or state of incorporation—involves the transfer of an existing corporation's assets to a new corporation, in which the shareholders of the transferor corporation generally retain the same equity interest.

Not all reorganizations fit neatly into one of the seven categories. Some reorganizations satisfy the requirements of two or more reorganization provisions. In this situation, the IRC or the IRS generally determines which reorganization rules prevail. In other situations, a reorganization may satisfy the requirements of a reorganization provision, but for various reasons the IRS and courts prescribe an entirely different tax treatment (e.g., if the transaction lacks a business purpose, it may be treated as taxable). These issues are discussed further in the next section.

TYPICAL MISCONCEPTION

For an acquisition to be treated as nontaxable, the transaction must qualify as a reorganization. The term *reorganization* includes only transactions enumerated in Sec. 368. Other transactions that may constitute reorganizations in a more general context are not considered nontaxable reorganizations.

KEY POINT

A summary of the acquisitive reorganizations is presented below:

Type	Description
A	Merger or consolidation
B	Stock-for-stock
C	Asset-for-stock
D	Asset-for-stock
G	Bankruptcy

TAX CONSEQUENCES OF REORGANIZATIONS

This section examines the tax consequences of a reorganization to the target (or transferor) corporation, the acquiring (or transferee) corporation, and the shareholders and other security holders.[23]

TARGET OR TRANSFEROR CORPORATION

RECOGNITION OF GAIN OR LOSS ON ASSET TRANSFER. Under Sec. 361(a), the target corporation recognizes no gain or loss on the exchange of property exclusively for stock in another corporation that is a party to the reorganization.[24] In addition, under Sec. 361(b), the target corporation recognizes no gain if it also receives money or noncash boot property as part of the reorganization and distributes such property to its shareholders or

---

[23] The corporation that transfers its assets as part of a reorganization is referred to as either a **target** or **transferor corporation**. The term *target corporation* generally is used in the context of an acquisitive reorganization where substantially all of a corporation's assets are acquired by the acquiring corporation. The term *transferor corporation* is used in the context of a divisive and other reorganizations where only part of a corporation's assets are transferred to a transferee corporation, and the transferor corporation may remain in existence. Tax law provisions generally are applied identically to

target or transferor corporations and acquiring or transferee corporations, so only a single reference to the target or acquiring corporation is provided in connection with an explanation.

[24] Section 361(a) permits securities (e.g., long-term debt obligations) to be received tax-free when the target corporation surrenders the same or a larger face amount of securities. Generally, a securities exchange does not occur in an acquisitive reorganization, so all debt obligations received by the target corporation are boot property.

TYPICAL MISCONCEPTION

One perplexing aspect of the reorganization provisions is the overlap between the different statutory reorganizations. One transaction often can qualify as more than one type of reorganization.

EXAMPLE C:7-11 ▶

TYPICAL MISCONCEPTION

Often, taxpayers do not realize that Sec. 361 applies to two exchanges. Section 361(a) applies to the exchange between the acquiring and target corporations (which already has been discussed). Section 361(c) deals with the exchange between the target corporation and its shareholders. Therefore, the target corporation is the only party to the reorganization that may recognize two separate gains.

SELF-STUDY QUESTION

How can the target corporation distribute appreciated boot property to its shareholders if it receives a FMV basis in all such property received from the acquiring corporation?

ANSWER

If the property appreciates in the hands of the target corporation before it is distributed, gain will result under Sec. 361(c). In addition, the target corporation may retain some of its own assets and distribute these assets to its shareholders, again causing the target corporation to recognize gain.

EXAMPLE C:7-12 ▶

OBJECTIVE 5

Determine the tax consequences of a nontaxable reorganization to the acquiring corporation

creditors. On the other hand, the target corporation recognizes gain equal to the lesser of the realized gain or the amount of money plus the FMV of any noncash boot property received unless it distributes the property to its shareholders. However, because most acquisitive and divisive reorganization provisions require the target corporation to be liquidated or distribute all its assets, the target corporation generally retains no boot and thus recognizes no gain on the exchange. (Note: the target corporation might recognize gain on the distribution of appreciated property to its shareholders, as discussed below.)

In a reorganization, Target Corporation transfers assets having a $175,000 adjusted basis to Acquiring Corporation in exchange for $400,000 of Acquiring common stock. In the exchange, Target realizes a $225,000 gain ($400,000 amount realized − $175,000 adjusted basis). Because Target received no boot, however, it recognizes none of the gain. If Target instead had received $350,000 of Acquiring common stock plus $50,000 of cash or other property, Target would have recognized no gain only if it had distributed the $50,000 of boot to its shareholders. ◀

DEPRECIATION RECAPTURE. The depreciation recapture rules of Secs. 1245 and 1250 do not override the gain or loss nonrecognition rules of Sec. 361.[25] The recapture potential that accumulates before the reorganization remains with the assets transferred to the acquiring corporation and is recognized when the acquiring corporation later sells or exchanges the assets in a taxable transaction.

ASSUMPTION OF LIABILITIES. Neither the acquiring corporation's assuming the target corporation's liabilities nor its acquiring the target corporation's property subject to a liability triggers gain recognition on the asset transfer. Section 357(c), however, requires the target corporation to recognize gain if the sum of the liabilities assumed or acquired exceeds the total adjusted bases of the property transferred *and* the transaction is a divisive Type D reorganization.

RECOGNITION OF GAIN OR LOSS ON DISTRIBUTION OF STOCK AND SECURITIES. The target corporation recognizes no gain or loss when, pursuant to a plan of reorganization, it distributes to its shareholders or creditors either (1) its stock, stock rights, or obligations or (2) any stock, stock rights, or obligations of a party to a reorganization that it received in the reorganization (see page C:7-47 for an explanation of a plan of reorganization).[26] Distributions of noncash boot property (including property retained by the target corporation) pursuant to the reorganization plan result in the recognition of gain (but not loss) in the same manner as if the target corporation had sold such property at its FMV.[27] Normally the gain recognized upon the distribution of boot property is inconsequential because of the brief period of time between the receipt of the boot from the acquiring corporation (with a basis equal to its FMV) and its distribution to the shareholders.

In a statutory merger (Type A reorganization), Target Corporation transfers all its assets and liabilities to Acquiring Corporation, which exchanges $300,000 of its common stock and $100,000 of cash to Target for Target assets. Target's basis in the assets is $250,000. In the exchange, Target realizes a $150,000 [($300,000 + $100,000) − $250,000] gain. Target recognizes none of this gain, even though it receives boot, because Target must liquidate as a reorganization requirement. Upon distributing the Acquiring stock to its shareholders, Target recognizes no gain. However, depending on their Target stock basis, Target shareholders who receive cash may have to recognize gain. ◀

ACQUIRING OR TRANSFEREE CORPORATION

AMOUNT OF GAIN OR LOSS RECOGNIZED. Under Sec. 1032, the acquiring corporation recognizes no gain or loss when it receives money or other property in exchange for its stock. Similarly, a target corporation recognizes no gain or loss when in a reorganization it

---

[25] Secs. 1245(b)(3) and 1250(d)(3). Similar provisions are found in the other recapture rules.

[26] Secs. 361(c)(1)–(c)(3).
[27] Sec. 361(c).

receives money or other property in exchange for its securities. Under Sec. 1001, however, the acquiring corporation recognizes gain or loss when it transfers noncash boot property to the target corporation or its shareholders.[28]

BASIS OF ACQUIRED PROPERTY. Under Sec. 362(b), property acquired from the target corporation in a reorganization takes a carryover basis, increased by the amount of gain recognized by the target corporation on the exchange. As a practical matter, however, because the target corporation generally recognizes no gain on the asset transfer, the carryover basis is not stepped up.

EXAMPLE C:7-13 ▶

Assume the same facts as in Example C:7-12. Acquiring's basis in the acquired property is the same as Target's basis, or $250,000. ◀

HOLDING PERIOD OF ACQUIRED PROPERTY. The acquiring corporation's holding period for acquired property includes the target corporation's holding period.[29]

SHAREHOLDERS AND SECURITY HOLDERS

AMOUNT OF GAIN OR LOSS RECOGNIZED. Under Sec. 354(a), shareholders recognize no gain or loss if, pursuant to a plan of reorganization, stock or securities in a corporate party to a reorganization are exchanged solely for stock or securities in the same corporation or another corporate party to the reorganization. The receipt of property other than stock or securities (nonqualifying property) does not necessarily disqualify the entire transaction from tax-free treatment. Section 356(a) requires that a shareholder or security holder recognize gain to the extent of the lesser of the realized gain or the amount of money received plus the FMV of any other property received. Thus, a shareholder recognizes gain to the extent he or she receives nonqualifying property that does not represent a continuation of the equity interest.

EXAMPLE C:7-14 ▶

Upon the liquidation of Target Corporation in a reorganization, Brian surrenders 1,000 Target shares having a $13,000 basis in exchange for Acquiring Corporation stock having a $28,000 FMV. Brian's realized gain is $15,000 ($28,000 − $13,000), none of which is recognized. If instead Brian had received $25,000 of Acquiring stock and $3,000 of cash, he would have recognized $3,000 of the $15,000 realized gain. ◀

With some limitations, the general rule of Sec. 354(a) permits a nontaxable exchange of stock for securities. The receipt of securities is completely nontaxable only if the principal amount of the securities surrendered equals or exceeds the principal amount of the securities received. If the principal amount of securities received exceeds the principal amount of securities surrendered, the FMV of the "excess" constitutes boot.[30] If no securities are surrendered, the FMV of the entire principal amount received constitutes boot. Certain types of preferred stock (e.g., preferred stock that the issuer must redeem) also may constitute boot.

EXAMPLE C:7-15 ▶

Assume the same facts as in Example C:7-14 except Brian instead receives $25,000 of Acquiring stock and Acquiring debt securities having a $3,000 principal amount and a $2,850 FMV. Brian's realized gain is $14,850 [($25,000 + $2,850) − $13,000], of which $2,850 is recognized. If Brian had received $3,000 in Acquiring securities and surrendered $2,000 of Target securities, the FMV of the $1,000 "excess" principal amount, or $950 [$1,000 × ($2,850/$3,000)], would have been treated as boot. ◀

CHARACTER OF THE RECOGNIZED GAIN. Section 356(a)(2) requires that the recognized gain be taxed as a dividend if the receipt of the boot property has the same effect as the payment of a dividend. The amount of this dividend equals the lesser of the shareholder's recognized gain or the shareholder's ratable share of the transferor or target cor-

---

[28] Rev. Rul. 72-327, 1972-2 C.B. 197.
[29] Sec. 1223(1).

[30] Secs. 354(a)(2) and 356(d)(2)(B). The FMV of the debt obligations surrendered is irrelevant when determining the amount of recognized gain.

poration's current and accumulated earnings and profits (E&P). Any additional recognized gain generally is capital in character.

The Sec. 302(b) stock redemption rules determine whether the exchange has the effect of a dividend.[31] (See Chapter C:4 for a review of the Sec. 302(b) rules.) Reorganizations generally do not involve the actual redemption of target corporation stock. For purposes of Sec. 356, however, they involve the hypothetical redemption of a portion of acquiring corporation stock. When the distribution of boot qualifies the hypothetical redemption for sale treatment under Sec. 302(b), the shareholder recognizes capital gain.

The following example applies the dividend equivalency test to the receipt of boot in a reorganization.

EXAMPLE C:7-16 ▶

Betty owns all 60 outstanding shares of Fisher Corporation stock. In a reorganization, Fisher merges with Gulf Corporation, with Betty receiving $250,000 in cash and 35 shares of Gulf stock worth $350,000. Four other individuals own the remaining 100 shares of Gulf stock. Betty's Fisher stock has a $200,000 basis. Fisher and Gulf have E&P balances of $300,000 and $500,000, respectively. Betty's realized gain is $400,000 [($350,000 stock + $250,000 cash) − $200,000 adjusted basis], of which $250,000 must be recognized because the cash is treated as boot property.

The Fisher stock initially is treated as having been exchanged for only Gulf stock. Because the Fisher stock is worth $600,000 and the Gulf stock is worth $10,000 per share ($350,000 ÷ 35), Betty is initially treated as owning 60 of the 160 (100 + 60) shares of Gulf stock immediately after the merger. The $250,000 in cash Betty receives is treated as having been exchanged for 25 ($250,000 ÷ $10,000 per share) of the 60 shares of Gulf stock that would have been received in an all-stock transaction. Because Betty owns 37.5% (60 shares ÷ 160 shares) of Gulf stock before the hypothetical redemption and 25.93% (35 shares ÷ 135 shares) after the hypothetical redemption, the $250,000 gain is capital in character under the Sec. 302(b)(2) substantially disproportionate redemption rules (i.e., 25.93% is less than 80% × 37.5% = 30%). ◀

The Sec. 302(b) test would apply in the same manner if securities were received in the reorganization. In such a case, the boot portion of the transaction would equal the FMV of the "excess" principal amount received by the shareholder or security holder.

Whether capital gain treatment is available for boot received in a reorganization depends on the relative sizes of the target and acquiring corporations. If the acquiring corporation is larger than the target corporation, the Sec. 302(b)(2) (substantially disproportionate redemption) or Sec. 302(b)(1) (not essentially equivalent to a dividend) rules generally will allow capital gain treatment. (See Chapter C:4 for an explanation of these rules.) If the acquiring corporation is smaller than the target corporation, the target corporation's shareholder could be considered as having received dividend income or a combination of dividend income and capital gain (e.g., if the boot received exceeds the shareholder's ratable share of E&P).

Prior to the 2003 Act, many noncorporate shareholders preferred capital gain treatment for their recognized gains because a 20% or lower capital gains tax rate was substantially less than the maximum tax rate applicable to ordinary dividend income. The 2003 Act reduced the maximum capital gains tax rate to 15% and extended the 15% rate to qualified dividends received by noncorporate shareholders. Thus, shareholders are taxed at 15% (though 2012) whether the gain is characterized as capital or a dividend, thereby diminishing the difference between the two types of treatments. Nevertheless, capital gains treatment can provide a benefit not available to dividend treatment in that the capital gains can be offset by (1) capital losses recognized in the current year or (2) capital loss carryovers from prior tax years. Dividend income, even though taxed at a 15% rate, cannot be offset by capital losses.

Corporate shareholders may prefer dividend treatment because they can claim a 70%, 80%, or 100% dividends-received deduction to reduce their tax liability. On the other hand, capital gains recognized in the reorganization can be offset by capital losses

---

[31] *CIR v. Donald E. Clark*, 63 AFTR 2d 89-1437, 89-1 USTC ¶9230 (USSC, 1989). The IRS has agreed to follow the *Clark* decision in Rev. Rul. 93-61, 1993-2 C.B. 118.

recognized by corporate and noncorporate shareholders in other transactions. Finally, Sec. 453(f)(6)(C) permits a corporate or noncorporate shareholder who is a party to a reorganization to use the installment method to defer recognizing part of the gain realized, provided such gain is not characterized as a dividend.[32]

STOP & THINK

Question: The character of the shareholder's recognized gain is determined under the Sec. 302(b) stock redemption rules. Why are the relative sizes of the acquiring and target corporations important in determining the character of the gain recognized in a reorganization?

Solution: If the target corporation is smaller than the acquiring corporation, the receipt of boot almost always will qualify for capital gains treatment under the redemption rules because generally no shareholder(s) will own more than 50% of the acquiring corporation's stock before and after the hypothetical redemption. If the boot is distributed proportionately to stock ownership, the pre-and post-redemption interests of the target corporation shareholder(s) are likely to be reduced. If the target corporation is larger than the acquiring corporation, a shareholder could own more than 50% of the acquiring corporation stock, resulting in the characterization of boot as a dividend.

KEY POINT

In a nontaxable reorganization, shareholders defer recognition of their realized gain or loss. Consequently, they take a substituted basis in the new nonrecognition property received (i.e., any deferred gain or loss is reflected in the basis of the nonrecognition property received).

BASIS OF STOCK AND SECURITIES RECEIVED. The basis of stock and securities (nonrecognition property) received by target corporation shareholders and security holders is determined according to the Sec. 358 rules, as discussed in Chapter C:2. Accordingly, the basis of nonrecognition property is calculated as follows:

Adjusted basis of stock and securities surrendered
Plus: Any gain recognized in the exchange
Minus: Money received in the exchange
            FMV of any noncash property received in the exchange

Basis of nonrecognition property received

If a shareholder or security holder receives no boot, the stock and securities take a substituted basis from the stock and securities surrendered. If the shareholder recognizes gain, the basis of stock and securities surrendered is increased by the amount of such gain and then reduced by the amount of money plus the FMV of any other boot property received in the reorganization. The basis of any other boot property is its FMV.

EXAMPLE C:7-17 ▶ Keith owns Target Corporation stock having a $10,000 adjusted basis. In a reorganization, Keith exchanges his Target stock for $12,000 of Acquiring stock and $4,000 of Acquiring securities. Keith realizes a $6,000 gain [($12,000 + $4,000) − $10,000], of which he must recognize $4,000 because he received securities worth $4,000 but surrendered no securities. The basis of the Acquiring securities that Keith received is $4,000. Keith's basis in the Acquiring stock is $10,000 ($10,000 basis of Target stock + $4,000 gain recognized − $4,000 FMV of Acquiring securities). ◀

When the target corporation shareholders initially own a single class of stock (or a single class of securities) and exchange that stock for two or more classes of stock or securities in a reorganization, the total basis in the nonrecognition property as calculated under the above formula must be allocated among the stock and/or securities in proportion to the relative FMVs of each class.[33]

HOLDING PERIOD. The holding period for the stock and securities that are nonrecognition property includes the holding period for the stock and securities surrendered. The holding period for boot property begins the day after the exchange date.[34]

---

[32] *King Enterprises, Inc. v. U.S.*, 24 AFTR 2d 69-5866, 69-2 USTC ¶9720 (Ct. Cls., 1969).

[33] Reg. Sec. 1.358-2(a)(2)-(4).
[34] Sec. 1223(1).

Topic Review C:7-4 summarizes the tax consequences of a reorganization to the target corporation, acquiring corporation, and target corporation shareholders and security holders.

Topic Review C:7-4

Tax Consequences of a Reorganization

TARGET CORPORATION

1. The target corporation recognizes no gain or loss on the asset transfer except to the extent that it receives and retains money or other boot property (Secs. 361(a)–(b)). Generally, boot is not retained because the reorganization provisions require the target corporation to liquidate or distribute all its assets.
2. The character of any recognized gain or loss depends on the nature of the assets transferred.
3. The acquiring corporation's assumption or acquisition of target corporation liabilities does not trigger recognition of gain on the asset transfer except where "excess" liabilities are assumed in divisive Type D reorganizations (Sec. 357(a)).
4. The target corporation recognizes no gain or loss when it distributes qualified property (i.e., stock and securities) to its shareholders and security holders. The target corporation recognizes gain (but not loss) when it distributes to its shareholders or security holders noncash boot property or retained assets (Sec. 361(c)).

ACQUIRING CORPORATION

1. The acquiring corporation recognizes no gain or loss when it receives money or other boot property in exchange for its stock or debt obligations (Sec. 1032).
2. On the other hand, the acquiring corporation recognizes gain or loss when it transfers noncash boot property to the target corporation or its shareholders (Sec. 1001).
3. The basis of noncash property received by the acquiring corporation equals its basis in the transferor's hands increased by any gain recognized by the transferor (Sec. 362(b)).
4. The acquiring corporation's holding period for such property includes the transferor's holding period (Sec. 1223(1)).

SHAREHOLDERS AND SECURITY HOLDERS

1. Shareholders and security holders recognize no gain or loss if they receive only stock (Sec. 354(a)). They recognize gain (but not loss) when they receive money, excess securities, or other boot property. The amount of recognized gain equals the lesser of the realized gain or the amount of money plus the FMV of any other boot property received (Sec. 356(b)).
2. The character of recognized gain is based on Sec. 302(b) as applied to receipt of acquiring corporation stock. Dividend income cannot exceed the shareholder's ratable share of the transferor or target corporation's E&P (Sec. 356(a)(2)).
3. The total basis of stock and securities received equals the adjusted basis of stock and securities surrendered plus any gain recognized by the shareholders and security holders on the exchange minus the sum of money and FMV of other boot property received. This basis is allocated among the stock and securities received according to their relative FMVs. The basis of boot property is its FMV (Sec. 358(a)).
4. The holding period for stock and securities received includes the holding period for stock and securities surrendered. The holding period for boot property received begins the day after the exchange date (Sec. 1223(1)).

ACQUISITIVE REORGANIZATIONS

This section is devoted to Types A, B, C, D, and G acquisitive reorganizations. Each of these types is explained below. Topic Review C:7-5 summarizes the tax aspects of acquisitive reorganizations.

TYPE A REORGANIZATION

Type A reorganizations encompass four transactional structures: mergers, consolidations, triangular mergers, and reverse triangular mergers. Each of these structures is discussed on the next page.

Topic Review C:7-5

Summary of Major Acquisitive Reorganizations

Type of Reorganization	Target (T) Corporation Property Acquired	Consideration That Can Be Used	What Happens to the Target (T) Corporation?	Shareholders' Recognized Gain	Other Requirements
A—Merger or consolidation	Assets and liabilities of T Corporation.[a]	Voting and nonvoting stock, securities, and other property of A Corporation.[b]	T Corporation liquidates as part of the merger.	Lesser of realized gain or boot received.	Transaction must have a business purpose and meet continuity of interest and business enterprise requirements.
B—Stock for stock	At least 80% of voting and 80% of nonvoting T Corporation stock.	Voting stock of A Corporation.	Becomes a subsidiary of A Corporation.	None	Boot paid by the transferor may render the entire transaction taxable.
C—Assets for stock	Substantially all T Corporation assets (and possibly some or all of its liabilities).	A Corporation stock, securities, and other property, provided at least 80% of the assets are acquired for voting stock.	Stock, securities, and boot received in the reorganization and all of T Corporation's remaining properties must be distributed to its shareholders and creditors; as a practical matter, T Corporation liquidates.	Lesser of realized gain or FMV of boot.	For advance ruling purposes, "substantially all" is 70% of the gross assets and 90% of the net assets of T Corporation.
D—Acquisitive	Substantially all T Corporation assets (and possibly some or all of its liabilities) are acquired by a "controlled" transferee corporation (A Corporation[b]).	A Corporation stock, securities, and other property.	Stocks, securities, and boot received in the reorganization and all of T Corporation's remaining property must be distributed to its shareholders and creditors; as a practical matter, T Corporation liquidates.	Lesser of realized gain or FMV of boot.	"Substantially all" definition is same as in a Type C reorganization; continuity of interest requirement applies; control is defined as 50% of the voting power or 50% of the value of A Corporation stock.

[a] T Corporation is the target or transferor corporation.
[b] A Corporation is the acquiring or controlled transferee corporation. In a Type D reorganization, A Corporation is 50% or more controlled by T Corporation shareholders.

MERGER OR CONSOLIDATION. In its broadest sense, a Type A reorganization is a **merger** or a **consolidation** that satisfies the corporation laws of the United States, a state, the District of Columbia, or a foreign country.[35] State law authorizes several different merger forms. Two common forms are discussed below. Other permitted forms, such as triangular mergers and reverse triangular mergers, are discussed later in this chapter. The first form involves the acquiring corporation's transferring its stock, securities, and other consideration (boot) to the target corporation in exchange for its assets and liabilities. The acquiring corporation stock, securities, and other consideration received by the target corporation are distributed to its shareholders and security holders in exchange for their target corporation stock and securities. The target corporation then goes out of existence. Figure C:7-1 illustrates this type of merger. The second form involves the acquiring corporation's exchanging its stock, securities, and other consideration directly for target corporation stock and securities held by target corporation shareholders and security holders. The acquiring corporation then liquidates the target corporation and acquires its assets and liabilities.

In a consolidation, a new corporation uses stock, securities, and other consideration to acquire the assets of two or more existing target corporations. Each target corporation distributes the stock, securities, and other consideration to its shareholders and security holders in exchange for its own stock and securities. It then liquidates. Figure C:7-2 illustrates this type of consolidation. In another type, the new acquiring corporation transfers its stock, securities, and other consideration directly to target corporation shareholders and security holders in exchange for their stock and securities. Each target corporation transfers its assets and liabilities to the acquiring corporation and then liquidates.

Requirements for Mergers and Consolidations. In terms of consideration, a Type A reorganization gives the acquiring corporation the greatest flexibility. Section 368 places no restrictions on the kind of consideration that can be used. Under the continuity of

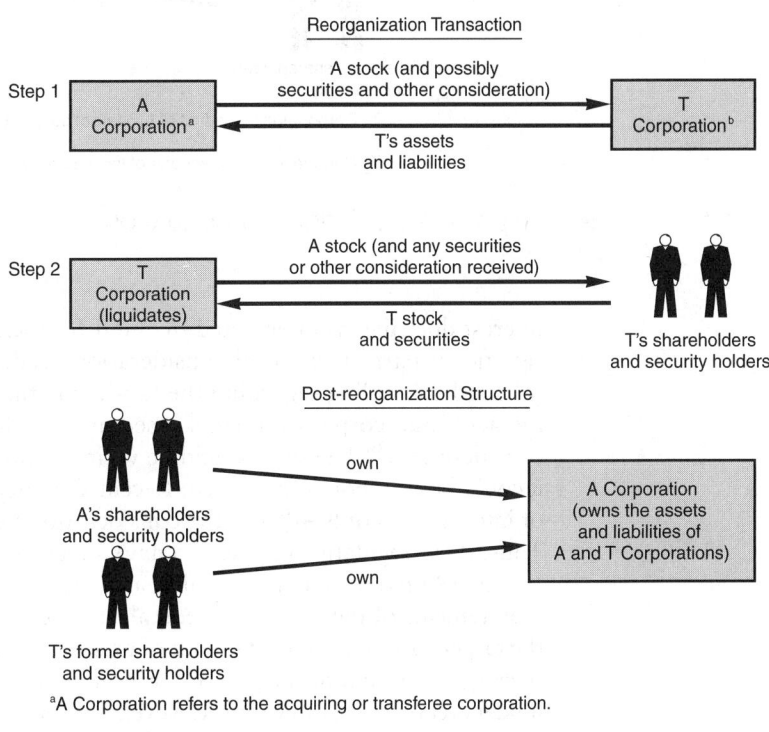

ᵃA Corporation refers to the acquiring or transferee corporation.

ᵇT Corporation refers to the target or transferor corporation.

FIGURE C:7-1 ▶ TYPE A REORGANIZATION—MERGER

---

[35] Sec. 368(a)(1)(A) and Reg. Sec. 1.368-2(b)(1).

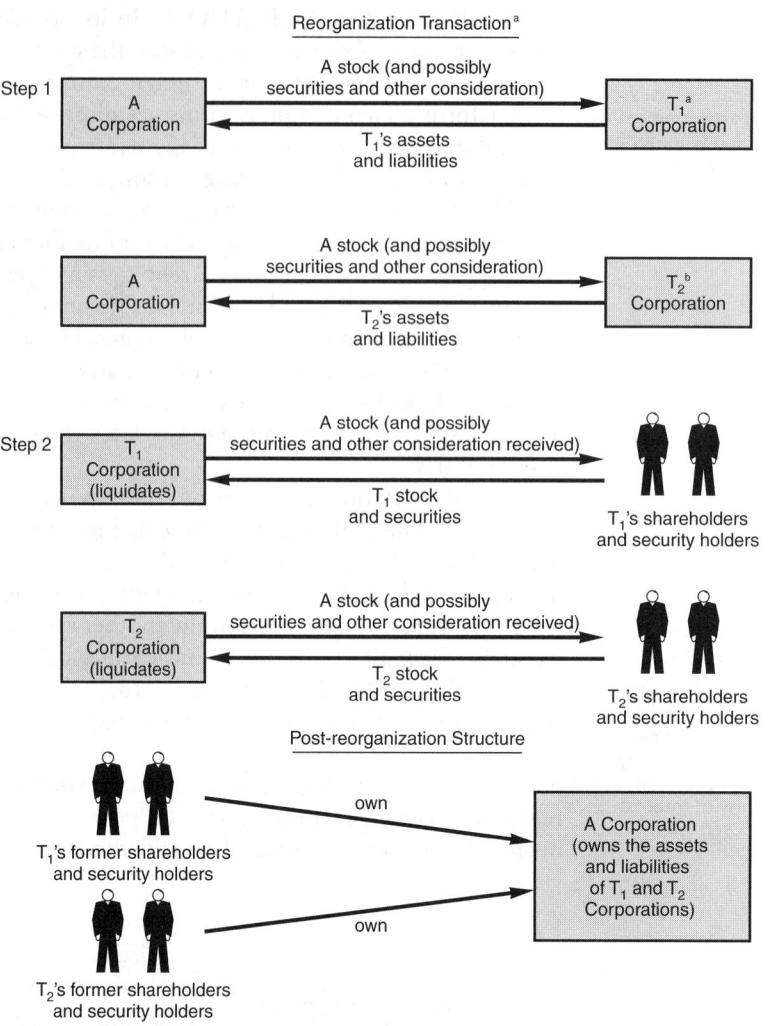

Reorganization Transaction[a]

Step 1 — A Corporation → A stock (and possibly securities and other consideration) → T_1[a] Corporation; T_1's assets and liabilities → A Corporation

A Corporation → A stock (and possibly securities and other consideration) → T_2[b] Corporation; T_2's assets and liabilities → A Corporation

Step 2 — T_1 Corporation (liquidates) → A stock (and possibly securities and other consideration received) → T_1's shareholders and security holders; T_1 stock and securities → T_1 Corporation

T_2 Corporation (liquidates) → A stock (and possibly securities and other consideration received) → T_2's shareholders and security holders; T_2 stock and securities → T_2 Corporation

Post-reorganization Structure

T_1's former shareholders and security holders — own → A Corporation (owns the assets and liabilities of T_1 and T_2 Corporations)

T_2's former shareholders and security holders — own → A Corporation (owns the assets and liabilities of T_1 and T_2 Corporations)

[a]T_1 Corporation is the first of two target corporations that are parties to the reorganization.

[b]T_2 Corporation is the second of two target corporations that are parties to the reorganization.

FIGURE C:7-2 ▶ TYPE A REORGANIZATION: CONSOLIDATION

interest doctrine, as interpreted by the IRS, stock of the acquiring corporation must be a significant part of the total consideration used. Traditionally, the IRS did not issued a private letter ruling regarding the tax-free nature of the transaction if the percentage of the acquiring corporation stock used as consideration was less than 50% of the total consideration.[36] The stock could be voting, nonvoting, or a combination of the two, and it could be common or preferred. Recent Treasury Regulations, however, allow continuity of interest with only 40% of the consideration being the acquiring corporation's stock.[37] Thus, these regulations appear to have superceded the IRS's previous ruling position.

The IRS requires that, to qualify as a Type A reorganization, the merger must meet the requirements of the applicable federal, state, or foreign corporate merger law. In addition, the target corporation must go out of existence.[38] An acquisition does not qualify as a Type A reorganization if the target corporation retains some assets and target corporation shareholders retain some target stock. Revenue Ruling 2000-5 holds that, if a target corporation merges under state law into two or more acquiring corporations and the target corporation does not go out of existence, the transaction does not qualify as a Type A reorganization.

---

[36] Rev. Proc. 77-37, 1977-2 C.B. 568, Sec. 3.02. In recent years, tax opinions from tax counsel have largely replaced private letter rulings for most acquisitive reorganizations.

[37] Temp. Reg. Sec. 1.368-1T(e)(2)(v), Example 1.
[38] Rev. Rul. 2000-5, 2000-1 C.B. 436.

ADDITIONAL COMMENT

Shareholder approval is time consuming, expensive, and not always possible to obtain.

Because a merger or consolidation must comply with state, federal, or foreign corporation laws, transactions that qualify as mergers or consolidations, and the procedures that must be followed to effect them, vary according to the laws of the jurisdictions in which the acquiring and target corporations are incorporated. Generally, these laws require approval by a majority of shareholders of the corporate parties to the merger. Where the stock in one or both of the companies is publicly traded, holding a shareholder's meeting, soliciting proxies, and obtaining the necessary corporate approvals may be costly and time consuming.

The rights of any dissenting shareholders are defined by the merger law. Among these rights are the right to dissent and have shares independently valued and purchased for cash. Liquidating the interests of a substantial number of dissenting shareholders may require a large cash outlay and could, in some circumstances, violate the continuity-of-interest doctrine.

A transaction that does not satisfy the requirements of the applicable corporation law does not qualify as a Type A reorganization.[39] Generally, this shortcoming renders the entire transaction taxable.

Advantages and Disadvantages of a Type A Reorganization. A Type A reorganization offers a number of advantages and disadvantages.

Advantages:

▶ A Type A reorganization is more flexible than other types of reorganizations because the consideration need not be solely voting stock, as in the case of some other types. Money, securities, other property, and the assumption of the target corporation's liabilities can be up to 60% of the total consideration used.[40]

▶ Substantially all the assets of the target corporation need not be acquired, as in the case of a Type C reorganization. Thus, dispositions of unwanted assets by the target corporation prior to, or as part of, the acquisition generally do not render the merger taxable.

Disadvantages:

▶ The parties to the merger must comply with applicable corporation laws. In most states, the shareholders of both the acquiring and target corporations must approve a plan of merger. Such approvals can take time and be costly if stock in one or both of the corporations is publicly traded.

▶ Dissenting shareholders of both corporations generally have the right to have their shares independently appraised and purchased for cash, which may require a substantial cash outlay.

▶ All liabilities of the target corporation, including unknown and contingent liabilities, must be assumed.

▶ A merger requires the transfer of real estate titles, leases, and contracts. The target corporation may have licenses, rights, or other privileges that are nontransferable. This limitation may necessitate a reverse triangular merger or other transactional structures discussed below.

Tax Consequences of a Merger. The following example illustrates the tax consequences of a merger.

EXAMPLE C:7-18 ▶ In a merger that qualifies as a Type A reorganization, Target Corporation transfers to Acquiring Corporation all its assets having a $2 million FMV and a $1.3 million adjusted basis, respectively, together with $400,000 in liabilities, in exchange for $1 million of Acquiring common stock and $600,000 of cash. At the time of the transfer, Acquiring's E&P balance is $1 million, and Target's is $750,000. Target distributes the Acquiring stock and cash to its sole shareholder, Millie, in exchange for all her Target stock, which has a $175,000 basis. If Millie had received only Acquiring stock, she would have held 6.25% of Acquiring stock (100,000 out of 1.6 million shares) immediately after the exchange.

---

[39] *Edward H. Russell v. CIR,* 15 AFTR 2d 1107, 65-2 USTC ¶9448 (5th Cir., 1965).
[40] Previous advance ruling requirements generally limited nonstock consider-ation to 50% of the total consideration. In certain circumstances, the courts have permitted the 50% ceiling to be exceeded. Treasury Regulations now allow up to 60% nonstock consideration. See footnote 37.

In the asset transfer, Target realizes a $700,000 gain [($1,000,000 stock + $600,000 cash + $400,000 liabilities) − $1,300,000 adjusted basis] but recognizes none of this gain. Acquiring takes a $1.3 million carryover basis in the assets it receives. Target recognizes no gain when it distributes the stock and cash to Millie. Upon Target's liquidation, Millie realizes a $1,425,000 gain [($1,000,000 stock + $600,000 cash) − $175,000 adjusted basis], of which $600,000 must be recognized because of the cash received. Each share of Acquiring stock is worth $16 ($1,600,000 total consideration ÷ 100,000 shares that would have been held if all stock had been received). The hypothetical redemption of Millie's Acquiring stock required under the *Clark* case and Rev. Rul. 93-61 (see pages C:7-16 and C:7-17) qualifies for Sec. 302(b)(2) sale treatment because the deemed redemption of 37,500 ($600,000 cash ÷ $16) shares of Acquiring stock reduces Millie's interest from 6.25% (100,000 shares ÷ 1,600,000 shares) to 4.00% (62,500 shares ÷ 1,562,500 shares). Millie's basis in her Acquiring stock is $175,000 ($175,000 basis of Target stock + $600,000 gain recognized − $600,000 cash received). Millie's holding period for the Acquiring stock includes her holding period for the Target stock. ◀

DROP-DOWN TYPE A REORGANIZATION. The reorganization rules permit the acquiring corporation to transfer (drop down) to a controlled subsidiary part or all the assets and liabilities acquired in the merger or consolidation.[41] The drop down does not affect the nontaxable nature of the transaction. Thus, neither the parent nor subsidiary recognize gain or loss. The subsidiary takes from its parent a carryover basis in the assets.

TRIANGULAR MERGERS. **Triangular mergers** are authorized by Sec. 368(a)(2)(D). They are similar to straight mergers (previously discussed) except the parent corporation uses a controlled subsidiary to acquire target corporation stock or assets. The target corporation then merges into the subsidiary under one of the two merger structures described earlier (see Figure C:7-3).

Triangular mergers must satisfy the same legal requirements as straight mergers. In addition, the stock used as consideration in the transaction is restricted to that of the parent corporation. On the other hand, a limited amount of subsidiary cash and securities can be used, and the subsidiary can assume the target corporation's liabilities.

The "Substantially All" Requirement. To be nontaxable, the subsidiary must acquire substantially all of target corporation's assets pursuant to a plan of reorganization. For advance ruling purposes, the IRS has defined *substantially all* to be at least 70% of the FMV of the target corporation's gross assets and 90% of the FMV of its net assets.[42]

EXAMPLE C:7-19 ▶

In a triangular merger, Acquiring Corporation's subsidiary, Acquiring-Sub Corporation, plans to acquire $2.5 million (FMV) in assets and $1 million in liabilities of Target Corporation. Under the IRS's advance ruling policy, Acquiring must acquire at least 70% of Target's gross assets ($1,750,000 = $2,500,000 FMV of assets × 0.70) and 90% of its net assets [$1,350,000 = ($2,500,000 FMV of assets − $1,000,000 liabilities) × 0.90], or $1.75 million in assets. Target can sell or otherwise dispose of the remaining assets. ◀

Advantages of a Triangular Merger. The tax treatment of a triangular merger is the same as for a straight merger. A triangular merger, however, offers three advantages over a straight merger:

▶ In a triangular merger, the target corporation's assets and liabilities become the responsibility of the subsidiary. Thus, the parent corporation generally cannot be held liable for any unknown or contingent liabilities. Potential claims against the parent corporation from the target corporation's creditors are thus minimized.

▶ Because the parent corporation is the principal shareholder in the acquiring subsidiary, shareholder approval for the transaction is readily available. If the parent corporation's stock is widely held, the cost of obtaining shareholder approval may be reduced.

[41] Sec. 368(a)(2)(C). As defined in Sec. 368(c), *control* requires the parent corporation to own at least 80% of the voting power and 80% of each class of nonvoting stock. The ability to "drop down" the assets acquired to a subsidiary corporation without recognizing any gain also applies to Type B, C, and G reorganizations.

[42] Rev. Proc. 77-37, 1977-2 C.B. 568, Sec. 3.01. Also see Rev. Rul. 2001-46, 2001-2 C.B. 321.

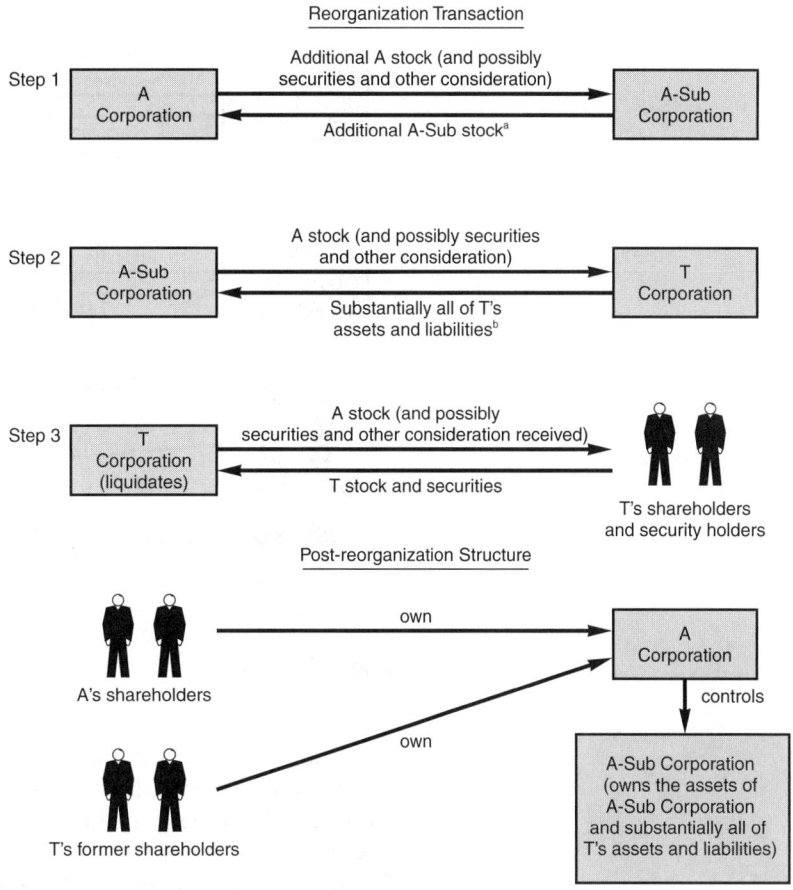

Reorganization Transaction

Step 1: A Corporation → Additional A stock (and possibly securities and other consideration) → A-Sub Corporation; A-Sub Corporation → Additional A-Sub stock[a] → A Corporation

Step 2: A-Sub Corporation → A stock (and possibly securities and other consideration) → T Corporation; T Corporation → Substantially all of T's assets and liabilities[b] → A-Sub Corporation

Step 3: T Corporation (liquidates) → A stock (and possibly securities and other consideration received) → T's shareholders and security holders; T's shareholders and security holders → T stock and securities → T Corporation (liquidates)

Post-reorganization Structure

A's shareholders own A Corporation; T's former shareholders own A Corporation; A Corporation controls A-Sub Corporation (owns the assets of A-Sub Corporation and substantially all of T's assets and liabilities)

[a]A Corporation must control A-Sub Corporation. If A already owns 100% of A-Sub, the A stock may be treated as additional paid-in capital for the shares that are already owned.

[b]T's shareholders may receive any remaining T Corporation assets that A Corporation did not acquire and that T Corporation did not sell to third parties.

FIGURE C:7-3 ▶ TRIANGULAR TYPE A REORGANIZATION

▶ Target corporation shareholders may prefer to receive parent corporation stock, especially if such stock is publicly traded, because of its increased marketability. By selling shares of this stock over an extended period of time, target shareholders can recognize the gain as if they were using the installment method of accounting.

ADDITIONAL COMMENT

In addition to the Type B reorganization, which will be discussed later, the reverse triangular merger is an acquisitive reorganization that keeps the target corporation in existence. It is a popular reorganization form because, unlike the Type B reorganization, the acquiring corporation can use a limited amount of boot.

REVERSE TRIANGULAR MERGERS. A **reverse triangular merger** is similar to the triangular merger illustrated in Figure C:7-3 except the subsidiary (A-Sub Corporation) merges into the target corporation (T Corporation), the target corporation remains in existence as a subsidiary of the parent corporation (A Corporation), and A-Sub Corporation goes out of existence. Continuing the target corporation as a going concern may be desirable from a business standpoint because of nontransferable rights, licenses, and contracts that it owns. Technical details of this type of acquisition are beyond the scope of this text.

TYPE C REORGANIZATION

A **Type C reorganization** is an asset-for-stock acquisition. This type of transaction, illustrated in Figure C:7-4, requires the acquiring corporation to obtain substantially all the target corporation's assets in exchange for acquiring corporation voting stock and possibly a limited amount of other consideration.[43]

---

[43] Sec. 368(a)(1)(C).

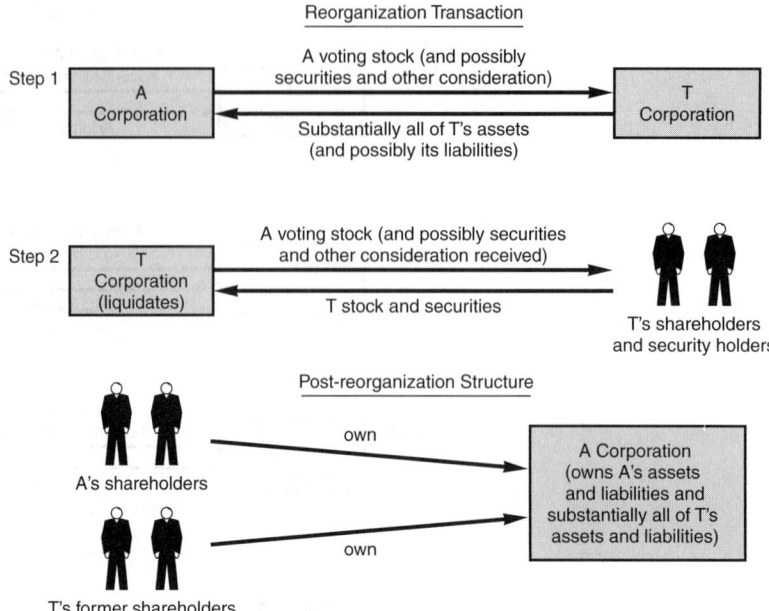

FIGURE C:7-4 ▶ TYPE C (ASSET-FOR-STOCK) REORGANIZATION

The term "substantially all" is not defined in the IRC or Treasury Regulations. For advance ruling purposes, however, the same minimum standard that applies to triangular Type A mergers (i.e., 70% of the FMV of gross assets and 90% of the FMV of net assets) applies to Type C reorganizations.[44]

In a Type C reorganization the target corporation must distribute the stock, securities, and other property it receives, plus any other property it retains, to its shareholders as part of the reorganization. Although the corporation need not formally dissolve, as a practical matter it usually liquidates.[45] If it does dissolve, any liabilities not assumed by the acquiring corporation usually become the responsibility of the target corporation's directors. Because the economic effect of a Type C reorganization is the same as that of a merger (i.e., the acquisition of target corporation assets) without dissolving the target corporation, many tax practitioners call it a practical merger.

In a Type C reorganization, the target corporation can retain its corporate charter to prevent others from using its corporate name or sell its corporate name to a third party. Assets other than the corporate charter can be retained to satisfy the minimum capital requirements of state law.[46]

ADDITIONAL COMMENT

Because of the solely-for-voting-stock requirement, a Type C reorganization is much less flexible than a Type A reorganization in terms of the consideration that can be used.

CONSIDERATION USED TO EFFECT THE REORGANIZATION. Section 368(a)(1)(C) requires that the consideration used to effect the reorganization be solely voting stock of the acquiring corporation (or its parent corporation). Both the acquiring corporation's assumption of part or all of target corporation liabilities and its acquiring property subject to a liability are disregarded for purposes of the solely-for-voting-stock requirement.

Section 368(a)(2)(B) permits the acquiring corporation to use other consideration in the reorganization, provided it obtains at least 80% of target property solely for its voting stock. Effectively, this provision allows the acquiring corporation to use money, securities, nonvoting stock, or other property to acquire up to 20% of target assets. Liabilities assumed or acquired reduce on a dollar-for-dollar basis the amount of money the acquiring corporation can use in the reorganization. If the liabilities assumed or acquired exceed 20% of the FMV of target assets, the transaction will qualify as a Type C reorganization only if the acquiring corporation uses no money, securities, nonvoting stock, or other property as consideration.

---

[44] Rev. Proc. 77-37, 1977-2 C.B. 568, Sec. 3.01.
[45] Sec. 368(a)(2)(G).
[46] Rev. Proc. 89-50, 1989-1 C.B. 631.

EXAMPLE C:7-20 ▶ Acquiring Corporation wants to acquire all of Target Corporation's assets and liabilities in a Type C reorganization. The following table illustrates how the solely-for-voting-stock test applies in four different situations:

	Situation 1	Situation 2	Situation 3	Situation 4
FMV of Target assets	$200,000	$200,000	$200,000	$200,000
Target liabilities assumed by Acquiring	–0–	30,000	100,000	100,000
Consideration given by Acquiring:				
FMV of Acquiring voting stock	160,000	160,000	100,000	99,900
Cash	40,000	10,000	–0–	100

In Situation 1, because the FMV of the Acquiring stock equals 80% of total assets, the transaction qualifies as a Type C reorganization. In Situation 2, although the liabilities assumed reduce the amount of cash Acquiring can pay, the transaction is still a Type C reorganization because the amount of cash and liabilities, in total, do not exceed 20% of the FMV of Target assets. In Situation 3, the high percentage of liabilities does not disqualify the transaction from Type C reorganization treatment because Acquiring paid no cash.[47] In Situation 4, the transaction fails as a Type C reorganization because Acquiring uses cash and stock, and the total amount of cash given plus liabilities assumed by Acquiring exceed 20% of the total FMV of Target assets. ◀

ADVANTAGES AND DISADVANTAGES OF A TYPE C REORGANIZATION. Relative to a merger, a Type C reorganization offers the following advantages and disadvantages.

▶ In a Type C reorganization, the acquiring corporation obtains only assets specified in the acquisition agreement. However, to be nontaxable, it must acquire substantially all the target corporation's assets. The target corporation might sell, dispose of, or retain assets the acquiring corporation does not want. These unwanted assets are not counted toward the "substantially all" test. Thus, disposition of a significant number of assets shortly before an asset-for-stock acquisition may disqualify the transaction as a Type C reorganization. By contrast, the "substantially all" test does not apply to a merger, and dispositions of unwanted assets generally will not disqualify a merger as a Type A reorganization.

▶ In a Type C reorganization, the acquiring corporation assumes only target corporation liabilities specified in the acquisition agreement. Unknown and contingent liabilities are not assumed, as they are in a merger.

▶ In a Type C reorganization, shareholders of the acquiring corporation generally need not approve the acquisition, thereby reducing the total transaction cost. In a merger, however, acquiring and target corporation shareholders must approve the transaction.

▶ In many cases, target liabilities assumed by the acquiring corporation are so substantial (i.e., exceeding 20% of total consideration) as to preclude the use of consideration other than voting stock. In a Type A reorganization, up to 60% of the consideration may be nonstock (see footnote 37).

▶ In both a Type A and Type C reorganization, dissenting shareholders of the target corporation may have the right under state law to have their shares independently appraised and purchased for cash.

TAX CONSEQUENCES OF A TYPE C REORGANIZATION. The following example illustrates the tax consequences of a Type C reorganization.

EXAMPLE C:7-21 ▶ Acquiring Corporation acquires all Target Corporation's assets and liabilities in exchange for $1.2 million of Acquiring voting stock. Target distributes the Acquiring stock to its sole shareholder, Andrew, in exchange for all his Target stock. Target's assets have a $1.4 million FMV and a $600,000 adjusted basis. Acquiring assumes liabilities of $200,000. Target has a $500,000 E&P

ADDITIONAL COMMENT

Target corporation liabilities assumed by the acquiring corporation are not a problem unless the target corporation receives boot as part of the consideration. In this case, when applying the 20% boot relaxation rule, liabilities are treated as money. Situation 4 in Example C:7-20 illustrates that, if the target corporation has liabilities exceeding 20% of the FMV of its assets, the boot relaxation rule is of no benefit.

SELF-STUDY QUESTION

Must the acquiring corporation assume all liabilities of the target corporation in a Type C reorganization?

ANSWER

No. The acquiring corporation may leave liabilities in the target corporation. These liabilities would then have to be satisfied with assets retained by the target corporation or with assets acquired by the target corporation in the reorganization.

---

[47] The IRS, however, may attempt to treat a transaction as a purchase under the continuity of proprietary interest doctrine (see page C:7-41) when the amount of liabilities assumed or acquired is high relative to the total FMV of the assets acquired.

balance. Andrew's basis in his Target stock is $400,000. Target realizes an $800,000 gain [($1,200,000 + $200,000) − $600,000], none of which is recognized. Acquiring recognizes no gain when it exchanges its stock for the assets, in which it takes a $600,000 basis. Upon surrendering his Target shares, Andrew realizes an $800,000 ($1,200,000 − $400,000) gain, none of which is recognized. Andrew's basis in the Acquiring stock is $400,000. Andrew's holding period for the Acquiring stock includes his holding period for the Target stock. Acquiring inherits all of Target's tax attributes, including the $500,000 E&P balance. ◄

TYPICAL MISCONCEPTION

As with a Type A reorganization, a Type C reorganization can be structured as a triangular (but not reverse triangular) acquisition. Although this feature provides greater flexibility in tax planning, it makes the tax consequences more confusing because of the substantial overlap between the different types of reorganizations.

DROP-DOWN AND TRIANGULAR TYPE C REORGANIZATIONS. Section 368(a)(2)(C) permits the acquiring corporation to transfer tax-free part or all of the assets and liabilities acquired in a Type C reorganization to a controlled subsidiary. Section 368(a)(1)(C) permits an acquiring subsidiary to use parent corporation voting stock to acquire substantially all the target corporation's assets. The triangular Type C reorganization requirements are the same as those for a basic Type C reorganization except the voting stock used by the acquiring subsidiary to acquire target corporation assets must consist solely of the parent's stock. The acquiring subsidiary, however, can provide additional consideration in the form of securities, money, or other property.

KEY POINT

When a Type D reorganization is used as an acquisitive reorganization, it generally involves commonly controlled corporations. However, its most common usage is as part of a divisive reorganization under Sec. 355 (discussed later in this chapter).

TYPE D REORGANIZATION

Type D reorganizations can be either acquisitive or divisive. (Divisive Type D reorganizations are discussed on pages C:7-33 through C:7-38.) In an acquisitive Type D reorganization, a target (transferor) corporation transfers substantially all its assets to an acquiring (transferee) corporation in exchange for the transferee's stock and securities (and possibly other consideration) pursuant to a plan of reorganization. The exchange must be followed by a distribution of the stock, securities, and other consideration received in the reorganization, plus any other property retained by the transferor corporation, to the transferor's shareholders and security holders pursuant to a complete liquidation.[48] (See Figure C:7-5 for an illustration of an acquisitive Type D reorganization.)

What constitutes "substantially all" is based on the facts and circumstances. For advance ruling purposes, however, the 70% of the FMV of gross assets and 90% of the FMV of net assets tests used in the triangular Type A and Type C reorganizations also apply here.[49]

ADDITIONAL COMMENT

The 50% control requirement makes the Type D reorganization a useful tool for the IRS to recast certain tax avoidance transactions.

CONTROL REQUIREMENTS. The transferor (target) corporation or one or more of its shareholders must control the transferee (acquiring) corporation immediately after the asset transfer. Section 368(a)(2)(H) defines control as either 50% or more of the total combined voting power of all classes of voting stock, or 50% or more of the total value of all classes of stock.

In one version of an acquisitive Type D reorganization, an acquiring corporation acquires all the assets of a larger corporation (target corporation), and target corporation shareholders control the acquiring corporation after the reorganization. Type C reorganizations (in which the target corporation does not control the acquiring corporation) and Type A reorganizations (which must comply with state, federal, or foreign merger law) are more common than acquisitive Type D reorganizations.

Section 368(a)(1)(D) does not explicitly limit the type of consideration that may be used in the transaction. The Treasury Department, IRS, and courts, however, require that the transferor corporation's shareholders maintain a continuing equity interest in the transferee corporation. For advance ruling purposes, the IRS traditionally required that transferor corporation shareholders receive transferee corporation stock equal to at least 50% of the value of the transferor corporation's outstanding stock, but recent Treasury Regulations now allow continuity of interest with 40% of the value.[50]

TAX CONSEQUENCES OF A TYPE D REORGANIZATION. Acquisitive Type D reorganization requirements are similar to those for a Type C reorganization. If the reorganization satisfies both the Type C and Type D reorganization requirements, Sec.

---

[48] Secs. 368(a)(1)(D) and 354(b)(1).
[49] Rev. Proc. 77-37, 1977-2 C.B. 568, Sec. 3.01.

[50] Rev. Proc. 77-37, 1977-2 C.B. 568, Sec. 3.02; Temp. Reg. Sec. 1.368-1T(e)(2)(v), Example 1.

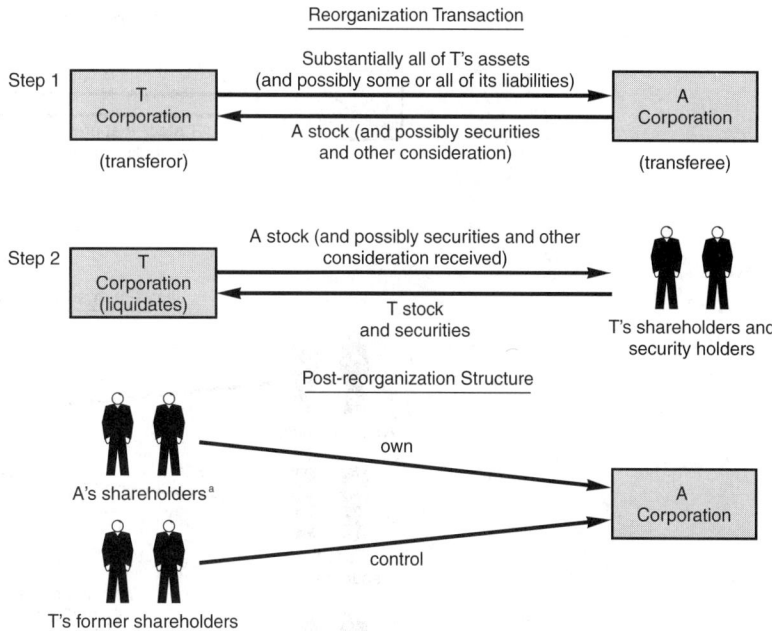

*Some or all of these shareholders also may have held T Corporation stock.

FIGURE C:7-5 ▶ ACQUISITIVE TYPE D REORGANIZATION

368(a)(2)(A) mandates that the reorganization be treated as Type D. The basic tax consequences of a Type D reorganization to the target corporation, the acquiring corporation, and target corporation shareholders are the same as those in a Type C reorganization.

TYPE B REORGANIZATION

ADDITIONAL COMMENT

If the acquiring corporation wants the target corporation to remain in existence, the two transactional alternatives in Sec. 368 that can accomplish this objective are a Type B reorganization or a reverse triangular merger.

A **Type B reorganization** is the simplest of acquisitive reorganizations. In this type of reorganization, target corporation shareholders exchange their stock for acquiring corporation voting stock, and the target corporation remains in existence as the acquiring corporation's subsidiary (see Figure C:7-6).

A Type B reorganization generally preserves the target corporation as a going concern. The basis of the target's assets (inside basis) and its tax attributes generally remain the same. After the reorganization, the target corporation and its parent may elect to file a consolidated tax return (see Chapter C:8). If the target corporation liquidates into its parent shortly after the stock-for-stock exchange, the IRS may attempt to collapse the two-step transaction into a single transaction and treat it as a Type C asset-for-stock reorganization.[51]

KEY POINT

The IRC allows no relaxation of the solely-for-voting-stock requirement for the Type B reorganization. Thus, the Type B reorganization has the least flexible consideration requirement of any of the reorganizations.

SOLELY-FOR-VOTING-STOCK REQUIREMENT. Under Sec. 368(a)(1)(B), the acquiring corporation must acquire target corporation stock in exchange solely for acquiring corporation voting stock. The acquiring corporation must own sufficient stock to be in control of the target corporation immediately after the exchange.

The solely-for-voting-stock requirement generally precludes the use of other property as consideration in the transaction. However, the voting stock used can be either common or preferred. If the acquiring corporation uses consideration other than voting stock (e.g., nonvoting preferred stock), the transaction will not qualify as a Type B reorganization and will be taxable to target corporation shareholders.

In a Type B reorganization, acquiring corporation debt obligations can be exchanged for target corporation debt obligations held by target shareholders, who will not recognize gain or loss if the face amounts of the two obligations are the same.[52]

---

[51] Rev. Rul. 67-274, 1967-2 C.B. 141. If the transaction is "collapsed" into a Type C reorganization, the Type C reorganization requirements (and not the Type B) must be satisfied.

[52] Rev. Rul. 98-10, 1998-1 C.B. 643.

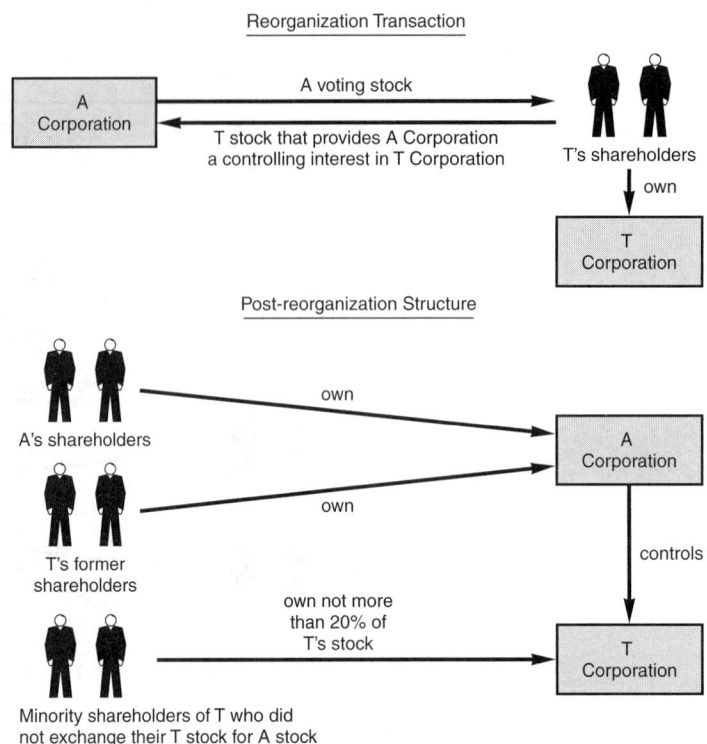

Reorganization Transaction

Post-reorganization Structure

FIGURE C:7-6 ▶ TYPE B (STOCK-FOR-STOCK) REORGANIZATION

Exceptions. The acquiring corporation can use cash in limited circumstances without violating the solely-for-voting-stock requirement. For example:

▶ Target corporation shareholders can receive cash in exchange for their right to receive a fractional share of acquiring corporation stock.[53]

▶ The acquiring corporation can pay reorganization expenses (such as legal expenses, accounting fees, and administrative costs) of the target corporation without violating the solely-for-voting-stock requirement.[54]

Control. For the purpose of a Type B reorganization, Section 368(c) defines control as 80% of the total combined voting power of all classes of voting stock and 80% of each class of nonvoting stock. Because the acquiring corporation need not acquire all the target corporation stock, a minority interest of up to 20% may remain. Under state law, minority shareholders can have their shares independently valued and acquired for cash without impairing the tax-free nature of the transaction. The target corporation can use its cash to redeem the minority shareholders' stock before or after the reorganization. The acquiring corporation, however, cannot use cash to purchase the dissenting minority shareholders' stock either before or as part of the reorganization. Doing so will render the entire transaction taxable.[55]

Timing of the Transaction. Some Type B reorganizations are conducted in a single transaction by exchanging stock of the acquiring corporation for 100% of target corporation shares. In other instances, the reorganization is accomplished through a series of transactions over an extended period of time. Regulation Sec. 1.368-2(c) provides that a cash purchase of stock may be disregarded for purposes of the solely-for-voting-stock requirement if it was independent of the stock-for-stock exchange. According to this regulation, stock acquisitions over a relatively short period of time—12 months or less—are to be aggregated for purposes of the solely-for-voting-stock requirement.

[53] Rev. Rul. 66-365, 1966-2 C.B. 116, as amplified by Rev. Rul. 81-81, 1981-1 C.B. 122.

[54] Rev. Rul. 73-54, 1973-1 C.B. 187.
[55] Rev. Rul. 68-285, 1968-1 C.B. 147.

EXAMPLE C:7-22 ▶ In July of last year, Acquiring Corporation purchased for cash 12% of Target Corporation's single class of stock. In January of the current year, Acquiring acquires the remaining 88% in a stock-for-stock exchange. The IRS probably will aggregate the cash and stock-for-stock acquisitions because they occurred within a 12-month period. Even though Acquiring achieves 80% control in a single stock-for-stock transaction, this transaction does not qualify as a Type B reorganization because, if the two stock purchases are aggregated, the solely-for-voting-stock requirement is not met. The transaction could qualify as a Type B reorganization if Acquiring unconditionally sold its 12% interest in Target and then acquired the requisite 80% interest in a single stock-for-stock exchange, or if Acquiring postponed the stock-for-stock exchange until after July of the current year, when the exchange might be considered independent of the cash purchase.[56] ◀

EXAMPLE C:7-23 ▶ Seven years ago, Acquiring Corporation acquired 85% of Target Corporation's single class of stock in a transaction that qualified as a Type B reorganization. In December of the current year, Acquiring acquires the remaining 15% of Target stock in a stock-for-stock exchange. Even though Acquiring already controls Target, the second transaction qualifies for Type B reorganization treatment because Acquiring owns at least 80% of Target after the exchange. ◀

TAX CONSEQUENCES OF A TYPE B REORGANIZATION. The tax consequences of a Type B reorganization are as follows:

▶ Target corporation shareholders recognize no gain or loss on the exchange unless their fractional shares are acquired for cash or the target corporation redeems some of their stock.

▶ Target corporation shareholders take a substituted basis in their acquiring corporation stock referenced to the basis of their target corporation stock surrendered. The holding period for the acquiring corporation stock includes the holding period for the target corporation stock.

▶ The acquiring corporation recognizes no gain or loss when it issues its voting stock for target corporation stock.

▶ The acquiring corporation's basis in the target corporation stock is the same as in the hands of target corporation shareholders.

EXAMPLE C:7-24 ▶ Mark owns all of Target Corporation's single class of stock, which has a $400,000 basis. Mark exchanges his Target stock for $700,000 of Acquiring Corporation voting stock. Mark realizes a $300,000 gain ($700,000 − $400,000), none of which is recognized. Mark's basis in the Acquiring stock is $400,000. Acquiring recognizes no gain or loss when it issues its stock to Mark, and it takes a $400,000 basis in the acquired Target stock. ◀

STOP & THINK

Question: Assume that stock in both Acquiring and Target Corporations is publicly traded and each corporation has several thousand shareholders. Acquiring Corporation acquires Target Corporation stock in a Type B reorganization. What problems might arise in determining Acquiring's basis in the Target stock?

Solution: Under Sec. 358(a), Acquiring's basis in the Target stock is the same as that in the hands of Target's shareholders. Many shareholders may not know their basis in stock purchased several years ago. The basis for these shares may have changed as a result of stock dividends, stock splits, or nonliquidating distributions. This lack of information may make it difficult to accurately determine Acquiring's basis in the Target stock acquired. To address the issue, the IRS allows sampling to extrapolate Acquiring's basis from the stock holdings of a small number of Target shareholders' aggregate stock basis.

ADDITIONAL COMMENT

The IRS has concluded that compliance with the sampling standards in Rev. Proc. 81-70, 1981-2 C.B. 729, may be "unduly burdensome or impossible." Thus, the IRS is seeking comments from those who perform basis studies and other interested parties in an effort to revise the revenue procedure (see Notice 2004-44, 2004-28 I.R.B. 32). So far, the IRS has not issued new guidance.

ADVANTAGES OF A TYPE B REORGANIZATION. A Type B reorganization has a number of advantages.

▶ The acquisition of target corporation stock usually can be accomplished in a single transaction without formal shareholder approval. Even if the target corporation's management does not approve the transaction, the acquiring corporation can acquire

---

[56] See, for example, *Eldon S. Chapman et al. v. CIR*, 45 AFTR 2d 80-1290, 80-1 USTC ¶9330 (1st Cir., 1980).

WHAT WOULD YOU DO IN THIS SITUATION?

You have just joined ProfessionalCPA, LLP as a new associate. ProfessionalCPA's principal audit client is Intergalactic Enterprises, a public company that accounts for roughly a quarter of ProfessionalCPA's revenues. Intergalactic wants to acquire the stock of Nebula Industries in a tender offer that qualifies as a Type B reorganization. In the proposed transaction, Intergalactic would offer three shares of Intergalactic stock for every two shares of Nebula stock. Currently, in the open market, Intergalactic stock trades at $15 a share while Nebula stock trades at $25 a share. Intergalactic would terminate the offer upon the tender of 55% of Nebula's outstanding shares.

Because Intergalactic's principal shareholder, Herman Islander, wants to retain control of the Intergalactic board of directors, he proposes to restrict the voting rights of Intergalactic stock issued to Nebula's share-holders. Under the proposed restriction, holders of the newly issued Intergalactic shares would have the right to vote for only two out of seven Intergalactic board members while holders of currently issued Intergalactic shares have the right to vote for all seven board members. Moreover, the voting rights inherent in all Nebula shares issued and outstanding are unrestricted.

Islander has requested from ProfessionalCPA a written opinion to the effect that the exchange of Nebula shares with unrestricted voting rights, for Intergalactic shares with restricted voting rights, meets the continuity of interest requirement. Although your supervisor questions whether the exchange in fact does meet the requirement, she recognizes that Intergalactic is a key audit client that contributes substantially to the firm's revenues.

Your supervisor approaches you with a request that you draft the opinion. What should be your response?

the necessary number of shares through a tender offer directly to target corporation shareholders.

▶ The target corporation remains in existence, and its assets, liabilities, and tax attributes need not be transferred to the acquiring corporation. However, the use of its NOLs may be limited under Sec. 382 (see pages C:7-43 through C:7-46).[57]

▶ The corporate name, goodwill, licenses, and rights of the target corporation may be preserved after the acquisition.

▶ The acquiring corporation does not directly assume the target corporation's liabilities, as is the case in some other reorganizations.

▶ The acquiring and target corporations can report their post-acquisition results on a consolidated basis (see Chapter C:8).

DISADVANTAGES OF A TYPE B REORGANIZATION.   Offsetting those advantages are a number of disadvantages.

▶ The acquiring corporation can use only voting stock as consideration in the transaction. Issuing this additional stock can dilute the voting power and control of acquiring corporation shareholders.

▶ The acquiring corporation must achieve at least 80% of target corporation stock even though effective control can be achieved through ownership of less than 80%.

▶ The acquisition of less than 100% of target corporation stock may give rise to dissenting minority shareholders. These shareholders have the right under state law to have their shares appraised and purchased for cash.

▶ The bases of target corporation stock (outside basis) and assets (inside basis) are not stepped-up (or stepped-down) to their FMVs upon the change in ownership, as would be the case in a taxable asset acquisition.

DROP-DOWN AND TRIANGULAR TYPE B REORGANIZATIONS.   As with Type A and C reorganizations, a triangular Type B reorganization, or a drop down of target corporation stock into a subsidiary before the stock-for-stock exchange, can be accomplished tax-free. In a triangular Type B reorganization, the acquiring subsidiary exchanges its parent stock for a controlling interest in the target corporation. As in a basic Type B reorganization,

---

[57] A Type B reorganization can result in an ownership change that, under Sec. 382, restricts the use of the target corporation's NOL carryovers but does not, in total, diminish the amount of its carryovers.

the target corporation remains in existence as a subsidiary of the acquiring subsidiary. Thus, it becomes a second-tier subsidiary of the parent corporation.

TYPE G REORGANIZATION

Section 368(a)(1)(G) defines a **Type G reorganization** as "a transfer by a corporation of part or all of its assets to another corporation in a Title 11 [bankruptcy] or similar case, but only if, in pursuance of the plan, stock or securities of the corporation to which the assets are transferred are distributed in a transaction that qualifies under sections 354, 355, or 356." Type G reorganizations are infrequent because the reorganization must occur pursuant to a court-approved plan in a bankruptcy, receivership, or similar situation.

In an acquisitive Type G reorganization, an insolvent corporation might transfer substantially all its assets to an acquiring corporation under a court-approved plan (e.g., a bankruptcy reorganization plan). It then might distribute all the stock, securities, and other property received in the exchange, plus any property retained, to its shareholders and creditors in exchange for their stock and debt obligations.

DIVISIVE REORGANIZATIONS

A divisive reorganization involves the transfer of some of a transferor corporation's assets to a controlled corporation in exchange for its stock and securities (and possibly boot property).[58] The transferor then distributes the stock and securities (and possibly boot property) to its shareholders. A divisive reorganization generally is governed by the Type D reorganization rules, although a divisive reorganization involving a financially troubled corporation could be governed by the Type G reorganization rules. Topic Review C:7-6 summarizes the requirements for divisive and other reorganizations.

DIVISIVE TYPE D REORGANIZATION

A divisive Type D reorganization must satisfy the requirements of Secs. 368(a)(1)(D) and 355, which are explained below.[59] Divisive Type D reorganizations can assume three forms: spin-offs, split-offs, and split-ups (see Figure C:7-7).

In the reorganization, a distribution of a controlled corporation's stock may be nontaxable under Sec. 355 even if the distributing corporation transfers no assets to the controlled corporation, in which case the division is not classified as a reorganization. To be a nontaxable Type D reorganization, however, both the asset transfer and the Sec. 355 distribution must be part of a single transaction governed by a plan of reorganization.

A divisive Type D reorganization can accomplish various business objectives, including

▶ Dividing an enterprise into two or more corporations to separate a high-risk business from a low-risk business

▶ Splitting up a single business among two or more disputing shareholders

▶ Dividing an enterprise according to functions, profit centers, or geographical areas

▶ Divesting operations because of antitrust laws

FORMS OF DIVISIVE TYPE D REORGANIZATIONS.   Three types of divisive transactions are nontaxable under Sec. 368(a)(1)(D):

▶ **Split-off**—the distributing corporation transfers some of its assets to a controlled corporation in exchange for stock and possibly securities, money, or other boot property. The distributing corporation then distributes stock in the controlled corporation to some or all of its shareholders in exchange for some of their stock. The context for such a transaction might be a management dispute between two distinct shareholder groups. To resolve the dispute, the parent corporation might redeem all the stock of one of the groups (see Figure C:7-7).

TYPICAL MISCONCEPTION

The existence of a corporate business purpose is necessary before the stock of a controlled subsidiary can be distributed to the shareholders of the distributing corporation. This requirement is much more difficult to satisfy in a Sec. 355 distribution than it is in an acquisitive reorganization.

---

[58] In a divisive Type D reorganization, Sec. 368(c) defines the term control because Sec. 355 (not Sec. 354) governs the distribution. In such a reorganization, control requires ownership of at least 80% of the voting and nonvoting stock. In an acquisitive Type D reorganization, on the other hand, control requires ownership of only 50% of the voting and nonvoting stock.

[59] The requirements of a divisive Type D reorganization are contrasted with the acquisitive Type D reorganization (previously discussed), where substantially all the transferor's assets must be transferred to a controlled corporation.

Topic Review C:7-6
Summary of Divisive and Other Reorganizations

Type of Reorganization	Distributing (D) or Transferor (T) Corporation Property Acquired	Consideration That Can Be Used	What Happens to the Distributing (D) or Transferor (T) Corporation?	Shareholders' Recognized Gain	Other Requirements
D—Divisive	D Corporation transfers part or all of its assets (and possibly some or all of its liabilities) to C Corporation.	Stock, securities, and other property of C Corporation.	D or T Corporation must distribute stock, securities, and boot received to its shareholders. D Corporation may liquidate or remain in existence.	Lesser of realized gain or FMV of boot received.	Transactions can assume three forms—spin-off, split-off, or split-up. Control is defined as 80% under Sec. 368(c).
E—Recapitalization	No increase or decrease in assets. The capital structure of T Corporation changes.	Stock, securities, and other property of T Corporation.	T Corporation remains in existence.	Lesser of realized gain or FMV of boot received.	May involve stock-for-stock, bond-for-bond, or bond-for-stock exchanges.
F—Change in form, identity, or place of organization	Old T Corporation transfers assets or stock to new T Corporation.	Stock, securities, and other property of new T Corporation.	Old T Corporation liquidates.	Lesser of realized gain or FMV of boot received.	Must involve only a single operating company.
G—Acquisitive or divisive	T Corporation transfers part or all of its assets (and possibly some or all of its liabilities) to A Corporation in bankruptcy.	Stock, securities, and other property of A Corporation.	T Corporation may liquidate, divide, or remain in existence.	Lesser of realized gain or FMV of boot received.	Stock and securities of A Corporation received by T Corporation must be distributed to its shareholders, security holders, or creditors.

Key:
D Corporation refers to the distributing corporation.
C Corporation refers to the controlled corporation.
T Corporation refers to the transferor corporation.
A Corporation refers to the transferee or acquiring corporation.

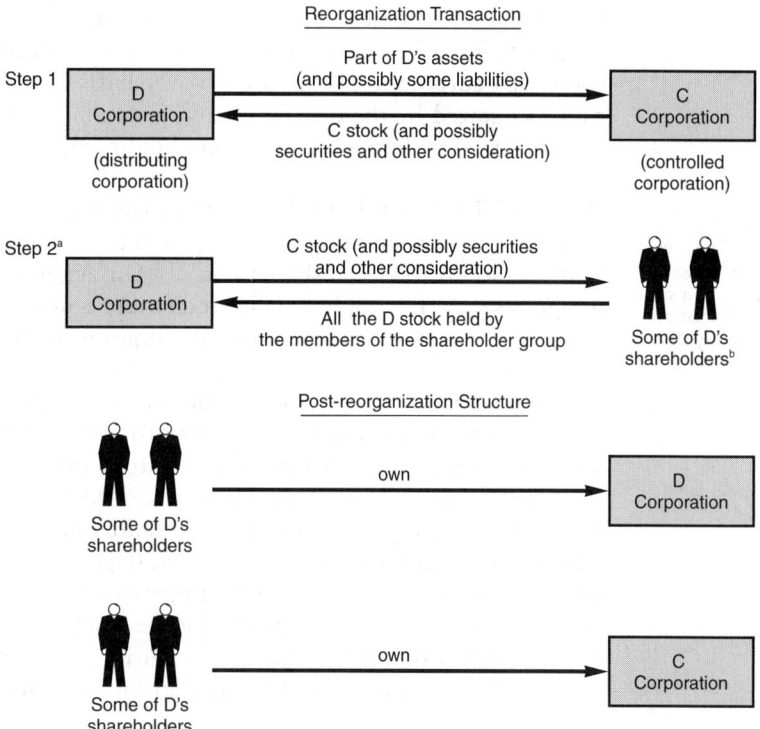

FIGURE C:7-7 ▶ DIVISIVE TYPE D REORGANIZATION (SPLIT-OFF FORM)

▶ **Spin-off**—the distributing corporation transfers some of its assets to a controlled corporation in exchange for stock and possibly securities, money, or other boot property. The distributing corporation then distributes stock in the controlled corporation ratably to all its shareholders who do not surrender their distributing corporation stock. Such a transaction might be motivated by a desire to minimize the risk associated with distinct operations (e.g., automobile manufacturing and financing) within a single corporation.

▶ **Split-up**—the distributing corporation transfers all its assets to two controlled corporations in exchange for stock and possibly securities, money, or other boot property. The distributing corporation then distributes stock in the two controlled corporations to all its shareholders, in exchange for all its outstanding stock. Such a transaction might be motivated by a desire to separate and continue distinct operations of an old corporation having a weak brand or little goodwill.

If the Sec. 355 requirements discussed below are *not* met, a spin-off is taxed as a dividend to the shareholders, a split-off is taxed as a stock redemption to the shareholders, and a split-up is taxed to its shareholders as a liquidation of the distributing corporation.

ASSET TRANSFER. The distributing corporation recognizes no gain or loss on the asset transfer except where it receives and retains boot property or where the controlled corporation acquires or assumes distributing corporation liabilities, and total liabilities exceed

ADDITIONAL COMMENT

If the IRS applies Sec. 351 to the asset transfer, and if the total adjusted basis for all property transferred exceeds the total FMV of that property, the subsidiary's total basis will be limited to the total FMV (see Chapter C:2 for details).

the total adjusted bases of the assets transferred.[60] The controlled corporation recognizes no gain or loss when it exchanges its stock for the distributing corporation's property. The controlled corporation takes a carryover basis in the acquired assets, increased by any gain recognized by the distributing corporation on the asset transfer. Its holding period includes the distributing corporation's holding period for the assets.

TYPICAL MISCONCEPTION

Section 355 can apply to a distribution of stock of an existing subsidiary as well as the distribution of stock of a new subsidiary that is created as part of the transaction.

DISTRIBUTION OF STOCK AND SECURITIES. In a Type D reorganization, the distributing corporation recognizes no gain or loss when it distributes controlled corporation stock (or securities) to its shareholders.[61] On the other hand, the distributing corporation recognizes gain (but not loss) when it distributes noncash boot property to its shareholders and when it makes a disqualified distribution of the controlled corporation's stock or securities.

The shareholders recognize no gain or loss on the receipt of the stock (and securities) except to the extent they receive boot property.[62] A shareholder's basis in the stock (or securities) equals his or her basis in the stock (or securities) held before the distribution, increased by any gain recognized and decreased by the sum of any money and the FMV of any other boot property received. If the shareholder holds more than one class of stock or securities before or after the distribution, the total basis in the nonrecognition property is allocated to each class based on their relative FMVs. The basis in any noncash boot property is its FMV. The holding period for the stock and nonboot securities received includes the holding period for the stock and securities surrendered. The holding period for boot property begins on the day after the distribution date.

EXAMPLE C:7-25 ▶

Distributing Corporation is owned equally by Ruth and Pat, who cannot agree on how Distributing should be managed. Ruth and Pat agree to divide the business by organizing Controlled Corporation and by exchanging Pat's Distributing shares for Controlled shares while leaving Ruth's equity interest intact (i.e., a split-up). Pat's basis in her Distributing shares is $400,000. Pursuant to this plan, Distributing transfers assets having a $600,000 FMV and a $350,000 adjusted basis to Controlled in exchange for all of Controlled's single class of stock. In the asset transfer, Distributing realizes a $250,000 gain ($600,000 − $350,000), none of which is recognized. Distributing recognizes no gain on the distribution of the Controlled shares to Pat. Upon surrendering her Distributing shares, Pat realizes a $200,000 ($600,000 − $400,000) gain, none of which is recognized. Her basis in the Controlled stock is $400,000. The holding period for the Controlled shares includes Pat's holding period for the Distributing shares. Upon issuing its stock for Distributing assets, Controlled recognizes no gain and takes a $350,000 basis in the acquired assets. ◀

SELF-STUDY QUESTION

Does the receipt of boot make the entire Sec. 355 transaction taxable to the shareholders?

ANSWER

No. The shareholders may have a partial recognition of gain. The amount and type of gain recognized depends on whether the shareholders surrender stock of the distributing corporation in the transaction.

Under Sec. 355, boot consists of money, short-term debt, property other than stock or securities of a controlled corporation, stock in the controlled corporation purchased within the previous five years in a taxable transaction, securities of the controlled corporation to the extent the principal amount of securities received exceeds the principal amount of securities surrendered, and stock or securities attributable to accrued interest.[63] When the shareholder receives boot, the amount and character of the recognized income or gain depend on whether he or she surrendered stock and securities in the distributing corporation (i.e., a split-off or split-up) or retained stock or securities (i.e., a spin-off).

When the shareholder receives boot in a spin-off, the FMV of the boot is treated as a dividend to the extent of the shareholder's ratable share of the distributing corporation's E&P. Any securities the shareholders receive in a spin-off are treated as boot because the

---

[60] Secs. 361(a) and 357(c)(1)(B).
[61] Sec. 361(c)(1). Two special rules may require the distributing corporation to recognize gain when it distributes stock and securities. A disqualifying distribution occurs if, immediately after the distribution, any person holds a 50% disqualified stock interest in either the distributing corporation or the controlled corporation. Disqualified stock generally is defined as any stock in the distributing or a controlled corporation purchased within the five-year period ending on the distribution date. The disqualifying distribution rules prevent a divisive transaction following a stock purchase to accomplish the disposition of a significant part of the historical shareholders' interests in one

or more of the divided corporations. A second set of rules, the anti-Morris Trust rules, also requires the distributing corporation to recognize gain when a distribution of stock or securities is made and is preceded or followed by a disposition of the stock or securities.
[62] Sec. 355(a). As with an acquisitive reorganization, Sec. 361(a) permits securities (e.g., long-term debt obligations) to be received tax-free in a divisive transaction when the shareholders surrender the same face amount of securities, or a larger amount. The excess amount of securities received constitutes boot property.
[63] Secs. 355(a)(3) and 356(b).

shareholders do not surrender any securities in this type of transaction. Thus, the FMV of the securities constitutes a dividend to the extent of the shareholder's ratable share of the distributing corporation's E&P.

In a split-off or split-up, in addition to the exchange of stock, a shareholder may receive boot property. If the shareholder realizes a loss on the exchange, the loss is not recognized, whether or not boot is received.[64] If the shareholder realizes a gain on the exchange, he or she recognizes the gain to the extent of the FMV of any boot received.

If the exchange is essentially equivalent to a dividend under the Sec. 302 stock redemption rules, the recognized gain is treated as a dividend to the extent of the shareholder's ratable share of the distributing corporation's E&P.[65] Otherwise it is treated as a capital gain. In either case, the income is taxed at a 15% rate. Under the Sec. 302 rules, the shareholder is treated as though he or she continued to own stock in the distributing corporation and surrendered only the portion of his or her shares equal in value to the amount of boot received. This hypothetical redemption is then tested under the Sec. 302(b) rules to determine whether the shareholder is entitled to sale or dividend treatment.[66]

EXAMPLE C:7-26 ▶

Distributing Corporation owns assets with a $60,000 FMV plus all the outstanding shares of Controlled Corporation stock valued at $40,000. Distributing formed Controlled by transferring some of its assets to Controlled as part of the reorganization. Distributing's E&P balance is $35,000. Carl and Diane each own 100 shares of Distributing stock. In a split-off, Distributing distributes all the Controlled stock to Carl in exchange for his 100 shares. Carl also receives $10,000 in cash. Carl's basis in the surrendered Distributing shares is $22,000. Carl has a $28,000 realized gain, calculated as follows:

FMV of Controlled stock	$40,000
Plus: Cash received	10,000
Amount realized	$50,000
Minus: Basis of Distributing stock	(22,000)
Realized gain	$28,000

Carl recognizes $10,000 of this gain (i.e., the lesser of the $28,000 realized gain or the $10,000 FMV of boot received). If Carl surrenders Distributing stock solely for the $10,000 cash, he would effectively be exchanging 20 Distributing shares ($10,000 boot ÷ $500 FMV for each share of Distributing stock) worth $10,000. Before this hypothetical redemption, he owns 50% of the outstanding Distributing shares (100 ÷ 200). Afterward, he owns 44% (80 ÷ 180). Thus, the hypothetical redemption is not substantially disproportionate under Sec. 302(b)(2) because the 44% post-redemption stock ownership exceeds 80% of the pre-redemption stock ownership (50% × 0.80 = 40%). If the exchange can meet one of the other tests for sale treatment (e.g., not essentially equivalent to a dividend), the $10,000 will be taxed as a capital gain. Otherwise it will be taxed as a dividend. ◀

In a split-off or split-up, a shareholder will receive securities of the controlled corporation tax-free only if the shareholder surrenders securities in the distributing corporation with an equal or larger principal amount. To the extent the principal amount of securities received exceeds the principal amount of securities surrendered, the excess will be taxable.

THE SEC. 355 REQUIREMENTS. Under Sec. 355, a distributing corporation's distribution of a controlled corporation's stock is nontaxable to the shareholders if all six of the following conditions are met:[67]

▶ The property distributed consists solely of stock or securities of a corporation controlled by the distributing corporation immediately before the distribution. The distributing corporation owns and distributes stock possessing at least 80% of the total

---

[64] Sec. 356(c).
[65] Sec. 356(a)(2).
[66] Rev. Rul. 93-62, 1993-2 C.B. 118.
[67] Sec. 355(a) and Reg. Secs. 1.355-2(b) and (c). Also, Rev. Proc. 2003-48, 2003-2 C.B. 86, provides a checklist questionnaire of the information that

must be included in a ruling request under Sec. 355. Appendix A of this revenue procedure contains guidelines regarding the business purpose of Sec. 355 transactions including information submission requirements for nine specific situations where rulings may or may not be granted.

ADDITIONAL COMMENT

The control requirement of Sec. 355 is the same control requirement relating to the formation of a corporation under Sec. 351 (see Chapter C:2).

TYPICAL MISCONCEPTION

The active trade or business requirement has two conditions: a pre-distribution five-year history must exist, and both the distributing and controlled corporations must be actively engaged in a trade or business immediately after the distribution.

combined voting power of all classes of stock entitled to vote and at least 80% of the total number of shares of all other classes of stock.[68]

▶ The distribution has not been used principally as a device to distribute the E&P of the distributing corporation, the controlled corporation, or both. Whether the distribution has been used as such a device will depend on the facts and circumstances of each case. A sale or exchange of distributing or controlled corporation stock after the distribution is evidence that the distribution was used as such a device, especially if the sale was prearranged.[69]

▶ Immediately after the distribution, the distributing and controlled corporations each engage in the active conduct of a trade or business that was actively conducted for at least five years before the distribution. This requirement prevents a corporation from spinning off a newly formed subsidiary whose only assets are unneeded cash and other liquid assets. The shareholders then could sell or liquidate the subsidiary and extract the liquid assets in a transaction characterized as a sale rather than a dividend.[70]

▶ The distributing corporation distributes either all controlled corporation stock and securities held by it immediately before the distribution or an amount of controlled corporation stock constituting control. The distributing corporation may retain some stock if it can establish to the IRS's satisfaction that the stock was not retained as part of a tax avoidance plan.

▶ The distribution has a substantial corporate business purpose. Qualifying distributions include those made to comply with antitrust laws and those made to separate businesses where the shareholders have major disagreements.[71]

▶ Shareholders who directly or indirectly owned the controlled corporation(s) and a substantial number of shareholders who owned the distributing corporation's stock before the distribution maintain a continuing equity interest in one or more of the corporations following the division.[72] The distribution of stock and securities need not be pro rata. Disproportionate distributions may be used to eliminate the stock ownership of dissenting shareholders. In a split-off, some shareholders may exchange all their distributing corporation stock for all the controlled corporation stock.

DIVISIVE TYPE G REORGANIZATION

A divisive Type G reorganization involves the transfer of some of a corporation's assets to a second corporation under a court-approved plan. The transferor corporation then distributes the transferee corporation's stock and securities to its shareholders, security holders, and creditors. The transferor corporation may continue as a separate going concern after restructuring its operations. Alternatively, the transferor corporation may liquidate under a court approved bankruptcy plan.

OTHER REORGANIZATIONS

Two types of transactions do not fit into the acquisitive or divisive reorganization categories: Type E reorganizations, which are recapitalizations, and Type F reorganizations, which are changes in identity, form, or state of incorporation. Topic Review C:7-6 presented earlier summarized the requirements for Type E and Type F reorganizations.

TYPE E REORGANIZATION

Section 368(a)(1)(E) refers to a **Type E reorganization** simply as a "recapitalization." A 1942 Supreme Court opinion defined **recapitalization** as "the reshuffling of the corporate

---

[68] Sec. 368(c).
[69] Reg. Sec. 1.355-2(d).
[70] Sec. 355(b)(2). A corporation is engaged in the active conduct of a trade or business if it actively conducts all activities necessary to generate a profit and these activities encompass all steps in the process of earning income.

Specifically excluded are passive investment activities such as merely holding stock, securities, and land.
[71] Reg. Sec. 1.355-2(b)(5), Exs. (1) and (2).
[72] Reg. Sec. 1.355-2(c).

KEY POINT

A Type E reorganization is neither acquisitive nor divisive in nature. Instead, it simply allows a single corporation to restructure its capital without creating a taxable exchange between the corporation and its shareholders or creditors.

structure within the framework of an existing corporation."[73] To qualify as a nontaxable reorganization, a recapitalization must have a bona fide business purpose. One reason for a recapitalization is to reduce a corporation's interest payments and debt-to-equity ratio by exchanging additional common or preferred stock for outstanding bonds. Alternatively, a family corporation might exchange newly issued preferred stock for part or all of the common stock held by a retiring, controlling shareholder so the shareholder can transfer management control to his or her children. This type of recapitalization also facilitates estate planning (see discussion after Example C:7-28).

Three types of corporate capital structure adjustments can qualify as a Type E reorganization: a stock-for-stock exchange, a bond-for-stock exchange, and a bond-for-bond exchange.[74] Normally, these exchanges do not result in an increase or decrease in the corporation's assets except to the extent shareholders or creditors receive a distribution of money or other property.

STOCK-FOR-STOCK EXCHANGE.   An exchange of common stock for common stock, or preferred stock for preferred stock, in the same corporation can qualify as a recapitalization if it is pursuant to a plan of reorganization. Section 1036 permits similar types of exchanges in a non-reorganization context. In either context, shareholders recognize no gain or loss on the exchange and take a substituted basis in the shares received that references the basis in the shares surrendered.

EXAMPLE C:7-27 ▶ The shareholders of Pilot Corporation exchange all their nonvoting Class B common stock for additional shares of Pilot voting Class A common stock. The exchange is nontaxable under Sec. 1036 even if not pursuant to a plan of reorganization. An exchange of some of Pilot Class A preferred stock for Class B preferred stock also would be nontaxable under Sec. 1036. ◀

Section 1036 does not apply to an exchange of common stock for preferred stock, or preferred stock for common stock, in the same corporation, or an exchange of stock of two corporations. On the other hand, the reorganization rules apply to an exchange of two different classes of stock (e.g., common for preferred) in the same corporation if the exchange is pursuant to a plan of reorganization. Under the Sec. 354(a) nonrecognition rules, the exchange is nontaxable to the shareholders except to the extent they receive boot property. If the FMV of stock received differs from that of stock surrendered, the difference may be recharacterized as a gift, a contribution to capital, compensation for services, a dividend, or a payment to satisfy a debt obligation, depending on the facts and circumstances.[75] The tax consequences of that portion of the exchange will not be governed by the reorganization rules.

EXAMPLE C:7-28 ▶ John owns 60% of Boise Corporation's common stock and all its preferred stock. The remainder of Boise common stock is held by 80 unrelated individuals. John's basis in his preferred stock is $300,000. The preferred stock is valued at $500,000. John exchanges his preferred stock for $400,000 of additional common stock and $100,000 in cash. In the exchange, John realizes a $200,000 [($400,000 + $100,000) − $300,000] gain, of which he recognizes $100,000 as dividend income (assuming Boise has sufficient E&P). None of the Sec. 302(b) exceptions that permit capital gain treatment applies. John's basis in the additional common stock is $300,000 ($300,000 + $100,000 gain recognized − $100,000 money received). ◀

A recapitalization often is used as an estate planning device whereby a parent's controlling common stock interest is exchanged for both common and preferred stock. The common stock often is gifted to a child who, following the recapitalization, owns a controlling common stock interest in the corporation and manages its business. The parent derives a steady stream of income from preferred stock dividends. The preferred stock's

---

[73] *Helvering v. Southwest Consolidated Corp.*, 28 AFTR 573, 42-1 USTC ¶9248 (USSC, 1942).
[74] An exchange of stock for bonds has been held in *J. Robert Bazely v. CIR* (35 AFTR 1190, 47-2 USTC ¶9288 [USSC, 1947]) not to be a recapitalization. Even if it were a recapitalization, it generally would be taxable because receipt of the entire principal amount of the bonds represents boot under

Sec. 356. Regulation Sec. 1.368-1(b) holds that continuity of interest and continuity of business enterprise are not necessary for a qualified Type E reorganization.
[75] Rev. Ruls. 74-269, 1974-2 C.B. 87, and 83-120, 1983-2 C.B. 170.

value is less likely to increase significantly over time, thereby limiting the value of that portion of the parent's estate and minimizing the estate tax liability. Relatively more capital appreciation will accrue to the child who owns the common stock.

Substantial income, estate, and gift tax planning opportunities previously existed in the recapitalization of a closely held corporation. To prevent abuses, Congress added Secs. 2701–2704, which, for transfer tax purposes, set forth procedures for more accurately valuing interests transferred to, and retained in, corporations and partnerships. Additional coverage of this topic is presented in Chapter C:12.

BOND-FOR-STOCK EXCHANGE. A bond-for-stock exchange is nontaxable to the shareholder except to the extent the shareholder receives a portion of the stock in satisfaction of the corporation's liability to him or her for accrued interest.[76] The latter portion is taxed as ordinary income.

BOND-FOR-BOND EXCHANGE. These exchanges are nontaxable only where the principal amount of the bonds received does not exceed the principal amount of the bonds surrendered. If the principal amount of the bonds received exceeds the principal amount of the bonds surrendered, the FMV of the "excess" is taxed to the bondholder as boot.

TYPE F REORGANIZATION

Section 368(a)(1)(F) defines a **Type F reorganization** as a "mere change in identity, form, or place of organization of one corporation, however effected." Typically, Type F reorganizations are used to change either the jurisdiction in which the business is incorporated or the name of a corporation, without requiring the old corporation or its shareholders to recognize gain or loss. In a Type F reorganization, the assets and liabilities of the old corporation are transferred to a new corporation in exchange for stock and possibly debt obligations. The shareholders and creditors of the old corporation then exchange their stock and debt interests for similar interests in the new corporation.

EXAMPLE C:7-29 ▶ Rider Corporation is incorporated in Illinois. Its management decides to change its state of incorporation to Delaware because of that state's favorable securities and corporation laws. To effect the change, Old Rider exchanges its assets for all the stock in New Rider, incorporated in Delaware. The shareholders of Old Rider then exchange their stock for New Rider stock. Old Rider goes out of existence. Neither the shareholders nor the "two" corporations recognize gain or loss. Each shareholder takes a substituted basis in the New Rider stock that references their basis in the Old Rider stock. Their holding period for the New Rider stock includes their holding period for the Old Rider stock. New Rider's asset bases are the same as Old Rider's asset bases, and New Rider acquires Old Rider's tax attributes. Although the two corporations are legally distinct, they represent the same enterprise that merely has changed its state of incorporation. ◀

The reorganization illustrated in Example C:7-29 also could be accomplished if Old Rider's shareholders exchanged their Old Rider stock for New Rider stock. Old Rider then would liquidate into New Rider. The tax consequences would be the same for both transactions.

JUDICIAL RESTRICTIONS ON THE USE OF CORPORATE REORGANIZATIONS

The U.S. Supreme Court has held that compliance with the letter of the law of reorganization provisions does not necessarily make a transaction nontaxable.[77] Through various judicial doctrines, the courts have placed four restrictions on reorganizations:

---

[76] Sec. 354(a)(2)(B).

[77] *Evelyn F. Gregory v. Helvering*, 14 AFTR 1191, 35-1 USTC ¶9043 (USSC, 1935).

OBJECTIVE 7

Understand judicial doctrines that govern the tax treatment of corporate reorganizations

▶ Continuity of proprietary interest

▶ Continuity of business enterprise

▶ A bona fide business purpose

▶ The step transaction doctrine

All four requirements elevate economic substance over legal form.

CONTINUITY OF PROPRIETARY INTEREST

The continuity of proprietary interest doctrine is based on the principle that the tax deferral associated with a reorganization is available because the shareholder merely has changed his or her investment from one form to another rather than liquidate it. According to Reg. Sec. 1.368-1(b), the requirements of this doctrine are met by a continuity of the business enterprise under a modified corporate form and a continuity of interest on the part of the shareholders who, directly or indirectly, own the enterprise before its reorganization. In a series of decisions, the courts have held that a continuing proprietary interest is ensured through ownership of common or preferred stock.[78] Thus, a transaction that involves the receipt of only cash or short-term debt obligations by the target corporation or its shareholders does not qualify as a nontaxable reorganization.

The IRC does not specify how much stock is necessary for continuity of proprietary interest. For advance ruling purposes, however, the IRS traditionally required that at least 50% of the total consideration received by target corporation shareholders consist of the acquiring corporation's stock. The courts, however, have accepted lower percentages, and Treasury Regulations now accept 40% as the continuity of interest threshold.[79]

TYPICAL MISCONCEPTION

The continuity of interest requirement has nothing to do with the relative sizes of the acquiring and target corporations. The target shareholders may end up with a minimal amount of the total outstanding stock of the acquiring corporation, and yet the merger will be a valid reorganization as long as 40% of the consideration received by the target shareholders is an equity interest in the acquiring corporation.

SELF-STUDY QUESTION

For which reorganizations is the continuity-of-interest requirement most important?

EXAMPLE C:7-30 ▶

In a Type C reorganization, Target Corporation transfers all its assets to Acquiring Corporation in exchange for $200,000 of Acquiring stock and the assumption of $800,000 of Target liabilities. Target distributes the Acquiring stock to its sole shareholder, Nancy, in exchange for all her Target stock. Even though the transaction meets the statutory requirements for a Type C reorganization, the IRS probably will claim that the transaction does not qualify for tax-free treatment because it lacks continuity of proprietary interest. Only 20% of the total consideration paid consists of an equity interest in Acquiring. ◀

ANSWER

The only limitation on consideration used for both regular and triangular mergers is the continuity-of-interest requirement. The other reorganizations, including reverse triangular mergers, have statutory requirements more restrictive than the continuity-of-interest doctrine.

Recently, the IRS amended Reg. Sec. 1.368-1(b) to clarify that neither the continuity of interest nor the continuity of business enterprise doctrine applies to Type E and Type F reorganizations.

CONTINUITY OF BUSINESS ENTERPRISE

Continuity of business enterprise implies that the acquiring corporation either continue the target corporation's business or use a significant portion of the target corporation's operating assets in a new business.[80] This doctrine limits nontaxable reorganizations to transactions involving *continuing interests* in the target's business or target property under a modified corporate form. The **continuity of business enterprise doctrine**, however, does not require that the target corporation's historic business be continued.

Whether the continuity of business enterprise requirement is met depends on the facts and circumstances of each case. The historical business requirement can be satisfied if the acquiring corporation continues one or more of the target corporation's significant lines of business.

SELF-STUDY QUESTION

Does the acquiring corporation have to continue its own historic business?

ANSWER

No. The IRS has specifically ruled that continuity of business enterprise requires only that the historic business of the target corporation be continued (Rev. Rul. 81-25, 1981-1 C.B. 132).

EXAMPLE C:7-31 ▶

Historically, Target Corporation has manufactured resins and chemicals and has distributed chemicals for the production of plastics. All three lines of business generate the same level of revenues. Target merges into Acquiring Corporation. Two months after the merger, Acquiring sells the resin manufacturing and chemicals distribution lines to an unrelated party for cash. The transaction satisfies the continuity of business enterprise requirement because Acquiring continues at least one of Target's three significant lines of business.[81] ◀

---

[78] See, for example, *V. L. LeTulle v. Scofield*, 23 AFTR 789, 40-1 USTC ¶9150 (USSC, 1940).

[79] Rev. Proc. 77-37, 1977-2 C.B. 568, Sec. 3.02. See also *John A. Nelson Co. v. Helvering*, 16 AFTR 1262, 36-1 USTC ¶9019 (USSC, 1935), in which the Supreme Court permitted a nontaxable reorganization where the stock exchanged constituted only 38% of the total consideration. Temp. Reg. Sec. 1.368-1T(e)(2)(v), Example 1.

[80] Reg. Sec. 1.368-1(d)(1).

[81] Reg. Secs. 1.368-1(d)(3) and -1(d)(5), Ex. (1).

The business (asset) continuity requirement is satisfied if the acquiring corporation uses in its business a significant portion of the assets used in the target corporation's business. Significance relates to the relative importance of the assets to target's historical business operations.

EXAMPLE C:7-32 ▶

ADDITIONAL COMMENT

Because the target corporation and its shareholders have the most to lose, they should protect themselves by stipulating that the acquiring corporation retain the historical assets. If not, the acquiring corporation can unilaterally dispose of the historical assets and invalidate the nontaxable reorganization.

Both Acquiring and Target Corporations manufacture computers. Target merges into Acquiring. Acquiring terminates Target's manufacturing activities and retains Target's equipment as a source of supply for its components. Acquiring satisfies the continuity of business enterprise requirement by continuing to use Target's business assets. Thus, Acquiring need not continue Target's historical business to satisfy the continuity of business enterprise requirement.[82] If instead Acquiring had sold Target's assets for cash and placed the proceeds in an investment vehicle, the continuity of business enterprise requirement would not have been met. ◀

Moreover, the acquiring corporation need not hold the target corporation's business assets for a prolonged period of time. The assets (business activities) may be held (conducted) by an 80%-or-more-owned subsidiary included in a chain of corporations that includes the acquiring corporation. In some cases, the acquired assets can be held by (or business conducted by) a partnership or LLC owned in full or in part by the acquiring corporation or one of its subsidiaries.

BUSINESS PURPOSE REQUIREMENT

A transaction must serve a bona fide **business purpose** to qualify for reorganization treatment.[83] Regulation Sec. 1.368-1(c) states that a transactional scheme that uses "the form of a corporate reorganization as a disguise for concealing its real character, and the object and accomplishment of which is the consummation of a preconceived plan having no business or corporate purpose, is not a plan of reorganization."

EXAMPLE C:7-33 ▶

KEY POINT

Business purpose is much more difficult to establish in divisive (Sec. 355) transactions than it is in acquisitive (Sec. 354) transactions.

Distributing Corporation transfers appreciated stock from its investment portfolio to newly created Controlled Corporation in exchange for all its stock. It then distributes the Controlled stock to its sole shareholder, Kathy, in exchange for some of her Distributing stock. Shortly after the stock transfer, Controlled liquidates, and Kathy receives the appreciated stock held by Controlled. If the liquidation were treated as a separate event, Kathy would recognize a capital gain, which she could use to offset capital loss carryovers from other tax years. In addition, she could step up the basis in the appreciated stock to its FMV without incurring a tax liability. Even though the stock transfer to Controlled complies with the letter of Sec. 368(a)(1)(D) for a divisive Type D reorganization, the IRS probably will claim that the Sec. 355 trade or business requirement has not been met. It also will rely on the Supreme Court's decision in *Gregory v. Helvering* to rule that the series of transactions serves no business purpose. As a result, Kathy's receipt of the appreciated stock from Controlled most likely will be treated as a dividend. ◀

STEP TRANSACTION DOCTRINE

The IRS can invoke the **step transaction doctrine** to collapse a multistep reorganization into a single taxable transaction. Alternatively, the IRS can invoke the doctrine to collapse a series of steps, which the taxpayer claims as independent taxable events, into an integral nontaxable reorganization. Both IRS actions prevent the taxpayer from elevating legal form over economic substance.

EXAMPLE C:7-34 ▶

Jody transfers business property from his sole proprietorship to wholly owned Target Corporation. Three days after this transaction, purportedly in a Type C reorganization, Target transfers all its assets to Acquiring Corporation in exchange for Acquiring stock. Subsequently, Target liquidates and distributes the Acquiring stock to Jody. After the liquidation, Jody owns 15% of the Acquiring stock. The IRS might collapse the two steps (the Sec. 351 asset transfer to Target and the Type C asset-for-stock reorganization) into a single transaction: an asset transfer by Jody to Acquiring. It might claim that the Sec. 351 requirements have not been met because Jody does not own at least 80% of the Acquiring stock immediately after the transfer. Furthermore, it might rule that, because Jody owns only 15% of Acquiring stock, Jody must recognize gain or loss on the asset transfer.[84] ◀

---

[82] Reg. Secs. 1.368-1(d)(4) and -1(d)(5), Ex. (2).
[83] *Evelyn F. Gregory v. Helvering*, 14 AFTR 1191, 35-1 USTC ¶9043 (USSC, 1935). Other Sec. 355 requirements, such as not constituting a device for distributing of E&P, probably were not met in this case.

[84] Rev. Rul. 70-140, 1970-1 C.B. 73.

TAX ATTRIBUTES

Under Sec. 381(a), the acquiring or transferee corporation inherits the target or transferor corporation's tax attributes (e.g., loss or tax credit carryovers) in certain types of reorganizations. Sections 269, 382, 383, and 384, however, restrict the taxpayer's ability to use certain corporate tax attributes (e.g., NOL carryovers) following the acquisition of a loss corporation's stock or assets.

ASSUMPTION OF TAX ATTRIBUTES

OBJECTIVE 8

Explain what happens to tax attributes in a reorganization

In Type A, C, acquisitive D, F, and acquisitive G reorganizations, the acquiring corporation obtains both the target corporation's tax attributes and assets. The tax attributes do not change hands in either a Type B or Type E reorganization because assets are not transferred from one corporation to another. Even though assets are transferred in divisive Type D and G reorganizations, the only tax attribute allocated to the transferee corporation is a pro rata portion of the transferor corporation's E&P.[85]

In acquisitive reorganizations, tax attributes carried over under Sec. 381(c) include

▶ Net operating losses

▶ Capital losses

▶ Earnings and profits (E&P)

▶ General business credits

▶ Inventory methods

KEY POINT

An often-cited advantage of a nontaxable asset reorganization over a taxable acquisition is that the tax attributes (e.g., NOLs and net capital losses) carry over to the acquiring corporation.

KEY POINT

The thrust of Sec. 381, as it relates to NOLs, is to allow Target's NOL carryovers to offset only the post-acquisition income of the acquiring corporation.

The target corporation's NOL carryover is determined as of the acquisition date and carries over to tax years ending after such date. Generally, the acquisition date for a reorganization is that on which the transferor or target corporation transfers the assets. When losses carryover from more than one tax year, the loss from the earliest tax year is used first. NOLs from the period following the acquisition date cannot be carried back by the acquiring corporation to offset target corporation profits earned in tax years preceding the acquisition date.[86]

EXAMPLE C:7-35 ▶

Target Corporation merges into Acquiring Corporation at the close of business on June 30 of the current year. Both corporations use the calendar year as their tax year. At the beginning of the year, Target reports a $200,000 NOL carryover from the preceding year. Target must file a final tax return for the period January 1 through June 30 of the current year. Target reports $60,000 of taxable income (before any NOL deductions) on its tax return for the short period. Target's taxable income for the January 1 through June 30 period reduces its NOL carryover to $140,000 ($200,000 − $60,000). Acquiring succeeds to this carryover. ◀

Section 381(c) restricts the acquiring corporation's use of the NOL carryover in its first tax year ending after the acquisition date. The NOL deduction is limited to the portion of the acquiring corporation's taxable income allocable on a daily basis to the post-acquisition period.

EXAMPLE C:7-36 ▶

Assume the same facts as in Example C:7-35 except Acquiring's accountants determine that its taxable income is $146,000, earned evenly throughout the current year. Acquiring can use Target's NOL carryover to offset $73,600 [(184 ÷ 365) × $146,000] of its taxable income attributable to the 184 days in the July 1 through December 31 current year post-acquisition period. The remaining NOL of $66,400 ($140,000 − $73,600) carries over to offset Acquiring's taxable income in the following year. Both the pre- and post-acquisition periods in the current year are treated as full tax years for loss carryover purposes. ◀

OBJECTIVE 9

Explain restrictions on the use of NOL carryovers following an acquisition

LIMITATION ON USE OF TAX ATTRIBUTES

Sections 382 and 269 are intended to discourage taxpayers from purchasing the assets or stock of a corporation having loss carryovers (known as the **loss corporation**) primarily to acquire the corporation's tax attributes. Similarly, Secs. 382 and 269 are intended to discourage

---

[85] Reg. Sec. 1.312-10.
[86] Special rules apply to Type F reorganizations. Because this type of reorganization involves only a change in form or identity of a single corporation,

NOLs generated after the acquisition date can be carried back to offset profits earned in pre-acquisition tax years.

a loss corporation from acquiring assets or stock of a profitable corporation primarily to use its carryovers. Section 383 imposes similar restrictions on acquisitions intended to facilitate the use of capital loss and tax credit carryovers. Additionally, Sec. 384 restricts use of pre-acquisition losses to offset built-in gains.

SECTION 382.   The Sec. 382 NOL restrictions are triggered when a substantial change in the stock ownership of the loss corporation occurs.

TYPICAL MISCONCEPTION

To effect an ownership change, the 5% shareholders must increase their stock ownership by more than 50 *percentage points.* For example, if shareholder A increases her stock ownership from 10% to 20%, this increase is not an ownership change even though it doubles A's ownership.

Stock Ownership Change.   A substantial change in stock ownership occurs where

▶ Stock ownership of any person(s) owning 5% or more of a corporation's stock has changed or a reorganization (other than a divisive Type D or G or a Type F reorganization) has occurred *and*

▶ The percentage of stock in the new loss corporation owned by one or more 5% shareholders has increased by more than 50 percentage points over the lowest percentage of stock in the old loss corporation owned by such shareholder(s) at any time during the preceding three-year (or shorter) "testing" period.[87]

The 5% shareholder test is based on the value of the loss corporation's stock. Nonvoting preferred stock is excluded from the calculation of ownership.

An **old loss corporation** is any corporation entitled to use an NOL carryover or that has an NOL for the tax year in which the ownership change occurs, and that undergoes the requisite stock ownership change. A **new loss corporation** is any corporation entitled to use an NOL carryover after the stock ownership change.[88] The old and new loss corporations are the same in most taxable acquisitions (e.g., the purchase of a loss corporation's stock by a new shareholder group). The old and new loss corporations differ, however, in many acquisitive reorganizations (e.g., a merger transaction where an unprofitable target [old loss] corporation merges into the acquiring [new loss] corporation).

KEY POINT

One of the burdensome aspects of Sec. 382 is that each time the stock ownership of a 5% shareholder changes, all 5% shareholders must be tested at that date to determine whether an ownership change has occurred.

Ownership changes are tested any time a transaction affects a person owning 5% or more of the stock either before or after the change. Such change may occur because a stock transaction involving a 5% shareholder or a person who does not own a 5% interest in the loss corporation affects the size of the stock interest owned by another 5% shareholder (i.e., a stock redemption). When applying the 5% rule, all shareholders owning less than 5% of the loss corporation's stock are considered to be a single shareholder.

EXAMPLE C:7-37 ▶

Stock in Spencer Corporation is publicly traded with no single individual owning more than 5% of its outstanding shares. In recent years, Spencer has incurred a series of NOLs. On July 3, Barry acquires for cash 80% of Spencer's single class of stock. Barry owned none of the Spencer stock before the acquisition. A substantial stock ownership change has occurred because, as a result of a stock purchase, a 5% shareholder (Barry) now owns 80 percentage points more stock than the 0% he owned at any time during the three-year testing period. Because Spencer incurred the losses prior to the ownership change and can use the NOLs after the change, it is considered to be both the old and new loss corporation. Consequently, Spencer's NOLs are subject to the Sec. 382 limitations.   ◀

In many acquisitive reorganizations, the Sec. 382 stock ownership test applies first with respect to the old loss (or target) corporation and then with respect to the new loss (or acquiring) corporation.

EXAMPLE C:7-38 ▶

Target Corporation has a single class of stock. None of its 300 shareholders owns more than 5% of the outstanding shares. Target has incurred substantial NOLs in recent years. Pursuant to a merger agreement, Target merges into Jackson Corporation. Jackson also has a single class of stock, and none of its 500 shareholders owns more than 5% of its outstanding shares, or any of the Jackson shares before the merger. After the merger, Target shareholders own 40% of the

[87] Sec. 382(g). For the purpose of determining the 50-percentage-point ownership change, special rules permit a testing period of less than three years. For example, where a recent previous change in stock ownership involving a 5% shareholder has occurred, the testing period begins on the date of the earlier ownership change.
[88] Secs. 382(k)(1)–(3).

Jackson stock. For purposes of applying the Sec. 382 stock ownership test, the stockholdings of all Jackson shareholders are aggregated. The Sec. 382 rules limit the use of Target NOL carryovers because Jackson shareholders owned none of the old loss corporation (Target) stock before the reorganization and own 60% of the new loss corporation (Jackson) stock immediately after the reorganization. ◄

Divisive Type D and G reorganizations or Type F reorganizations may be subject to the Sec. 382 limitations if the underlying transactions result in a more than 50 percentage point increase in the transferor corporation's stock ownership.

Loss Limitation. The Sec. 382 loss limitation for any tax year ending after the stock ownership change equals the value of the old loss corporation's stock (including nonvoting preferred) immediately before the ownership change multiplied by the long-term tax-exempt federal rate.[89] The IRS publishes the long-term tax-exempt federal rate, which is the highest of the adjusted federal long-term tax-exempt rates applicable in any month during the three-calendar-month period ending with the month in which the stock ownership change occurs.[90]

A new loss corporation first claims its current year deductions. It then deducts any NOLs from the old loss corporation (pre-change tax years) not limited by Sec. 382. If the NOL carryovers from the old loss corporation exceed the Sec. 382 loss limitation, the unused portion is deferred until the following year, provided the 20-year NOL carryforward period has not expired. If the Sec. 382 loss limitation exceeds the new loss corporation's taxable income for the current year, the unused loss portion carries forward and increases the Sec. 382 loss limitation in the following year.[91] Finally, any of its NOL and other carryovers from post-change taxable years are deducted. A new loss corporation that discontinues the business of the old loss corporation throughout the two-year period beginning on the stock ownership change date must use a zero Sec. 382 limitation for any post-change year. This zero limitation, in effect, disallows the use of the NOL carryovers.[92]

TYPICAL
MISCONCEPTION

Section 382 does not necessarily disallow NOLs. It merely limits the amount of NOL carryovers the new loss corporation can use on an annual basis.

ADDITIONAL
COMMENT

The new loss corporation's use of the old loss corporation's NOLs is limited annually to the FMV of the old loss corporation multiplied by the long-term tax-exempt federal rate because this limitation approximates the rate at which the old loss corporation could have used the NOLs.

EXAMPLE C:7-39 ►

KEY POINT

If the old loss corporation is a very large corporation relative to its NOL carryovers, Sec. 382 will not be a real obstacle in the use of the NOLs by the new loss corporation. Only when the old loss corporation has a small FMV relative to its NOL carryovers does Sec. 382 become a major obstacle.

Peter purchased all the stock in Taylor Corporation (the old and new loss corporation) from Karl at the close of business on December 31 of last year. Taylor manufactures brooms and has a $1 million NOL carryover from that year. Taylor continues to manufacture brooms after Peter's acquisition and in the current year earns $300,000 of taxable income. The value of the Taylor stock immediately before the acquisition is $3.5 million. Assume the applicable long-term tax-exempt federal rate is 5%. The requisite stock ownership change has occurred because Peter has increased his stock ownership from zero during the three-year testing period to 100% immediately after the acquisition. The Sec. 382 loss limitation for the current year is $175,000 ($3,500,000 × 0.05). Thus, Taylor can claim a $175,000 NOL deduction in the current year, thereby reducing its taxable income to $125,000. The remaining $825,000 ($1,000,000 − $175,000) NOL carries over to subsequent years, subject to the Sec. 382 limitation in those years. ◄

ADDITIONAL
COMMENT

Although the legislative intent of Sec. 382 has not been seriously questioned, the complexity of the statute with its accompanying Treasury Regulations is of concern to many tax practitioners.

Special rules apply to the loss corporation for the year in which the stock ownership change occurs. Taxable income earned before the change is not subject to the Sec. 382 limitation. Taxable income earned after the change, however, is subject to the limitation. Allocation of income earned during the tax year to the time periods before and after the stock ownership change is based on the number of days in each of the two time periods according to procedures similar to those for allocating tax attributes under Sec. 381.

Old loss corporation NOLs incurred before the date of the stock ownership change are limited by Sec. 382. These include NOLs incurred in tax years ending before the date of change plus the pre-change portion of the NOL for the tax year that includes the date of change. Allocation of an NOL for the tax year that includes the date of change is based on the number of days before and after the change.[93]

---

[89] Sec. 382(b)(1).
[90] Sec. 382(f).
[91] Sec. 382(b)(2).

[92] Sec. 382(c). Failure to continue the old loss corporation's business enterprise also may cause a corporate reorganization to lose its nontaxable status.
[93] Sec. 382(b)(3).

SECTION 383. Section 383 restricts the use of tax credit and capital loss carryovers when stock ownership changes under Sec. 382 occur. The same restrictions that apply to NOLs apply to the general business credit, the minimum tax credit, and the foreign tax credit.

SECTION 384. Section 384 restricts the use of pre-acquisition losses of either the acquiring or target corporation (the loss corporation) to offset built-in gains recognized by another corporation (the gain corporation) during the five-year post-acquisition recognition period. Such gains may be offset only by pre-acquisition losses of the gain corporation. This limitation applies if a corporation acquires either a controlling stock interest or the assets of another corporation and either corporation is a gain corporation.

SECTION 269. Section 269 applies where control of a corporation is obtained and the principal purpose of the transaction is "the evasion or avoidance of federal income tax by securing the benefit of a deduction" or credit that otherwise would not be available. The IRC defines control as 50% of the voting power or 50% of the value of the outstanding stock. The IRS can use this provision to disallow a loss or credit carryover in situations where Sec. 382 does not apply.

ADDITIONAL COMMENT

Section 269 represents the IRS's oldest and broadest weapon in dealing with trafficking in NOLs. However, because of the subjectivity of application, Secs. 382, 383, and 384 have turned out to be the IRS's main statutory weapons in this area.

Tax Planning Considerations

WHY USE A REORGANIZATION INSTEAD OF A TAXABLE TRANSACTION?

Choosing between a taxable and nontaxable transaction can be difficult. The advantages and disadvantages of a nontaxable reorganization are important for both the buyer and the seller. Depending on their relative importance, they may serve as points of negotiation and compromise in the effort to structure the transaction.

ETHICAL POINT

The choice between structuring an acquisition as taxable or nontaxable involves a large number of considerations for both the buyer and the seller. All parties must examine the tax, financial, and legal considerations with the assistance of their own experts.

From the target shareholders' perspective, several factors are relevant. First, a nontaxable reorganization affords shareholders a tax deferral except to the extent they receive boot. This tax deferral may permit a shareholder to preserve a higher percentage of his or her capital investment than otherwise would be possible in a taxable acquisition. Second, a taxable transaction permits target corporation shareholders to convert their former equity interests into liquid assets (e.g., when they receive cash or property other than stock or securities of the acquiring corporation). These liquid assets can be invested in whatever manner the shareholder chooses.

In a reorganization, the shareholder must obtain a proprietary interest in the acquiring corporation. The future success of the acquiring corporation is likely to enhance the value of this interest. Conversely, if the acquiring corporation encounters financial difficulties, the value of the shareholder's investment may diminish. Third, losses realized in a reorganization cannot be recognized. A taxable transaction permits the immediate recognition of realized losses. Fourth, gains recognized in a reorganization are taxed as dividends if the distribution of boot is substantially equivalent to a dividend. Taxable transactions generally result in the shareholder's recognizing capital gains. This difference is not as important now as in the past because both capital gains and dividend income are taxed at a maximum 15% rate. Finally, a taxable transaction permits the shareholder to step-up the basis of stock and securities received to their FMV. A nontaxable transaction, however, results in a substituted basis.

SELF-STUDY QUESTION

Is a nontaxable reorganization always preferable to a taxable acquisition?

ANSWER

No. What form an acquisition should take involves a myriad of issues relating to the parties involved in the transaction. A number of these issues are discussed in this section.

From the transferor corporation's point of view, a reorganization permits the exchange of assets without gain recognition. In addition, depreciation is not recaptured in a reorganization. Instead, the recapture potential shifts to the acquiring corporation.

From the acquiring corporation's point of view, a reorganization permits an acquisition without the expenditure of substantial amounts of cash or securities. Because the target corporation shareholders do not recognize gain unless they receive boot, they may be

TYPICAL MISCONCEPTION

When an acquisition structure is developed, the tax consequences are only one of many factors the parties must consider. Often, the final acquisition structure will not be optimal from a tax perspective because other factors may be deemed more important.

willing to accept a lower sales price than would otherwise be the case in a taxable acquisition. In a reorganization, the transferee takes the same property basis as the transferor's. The inability to step up basis to cost or FMV reduces the attractiveness of a reorganization and could lower the price the acquirer is willing to pay.

In a reorganization, the acquirer obtains the benefits of NOL, tax credit, and other carryovers from the target corporation (subject to limitations). In a taxable transaction, such tax attributes are not inherited by the buyer although they can be used to reduce the seller's tax cost in the sale.

AVOIDING THE REORGANIZATION PROVISIONS

TYPICAL MISCONCEPTION

The reorganization provisions are not elective. If a transaction qualifies as a Sec. 368 reorganization, it must be treated as such. It usually is not difficult to disqualify a nontaxable reorganization if the parties desire a taxable acquisition.

An acquisition can be converted from a nontaxable reorganization into a taxable transaction if the restrictions on the use of consideration incidental to a particular type of reorganization are violated. For example, the Type B reorganization rules can be skirted if the acquiring corporation obtains target corporation stock through a combination of acquiring corporation stock and cash. Because this structure does not meet the solely-for-voting-stock requirement, the transaction is taxable to the selling shareholders. It also is treated as a stock purchase, thereby permitting the acquiring corporation to make a Sec. 338 election and step-up the basis in target corporation assets.

EXAMPLE C:7-40 ▶

Acquiring Corporation offers to exchange one share of its common stock (valued at $40) plus $20 cash for each share of Target Corporation's single class of common stock. All of Target's shareholders accept the offer and exchange a total of 2,000 Target shares for 2,000 Acquiring shares and $40,000 cash. At the time of the exchange, Target's assets have a $35,000 adjusted basis and a $110,000 FMV. Target recognizes no gain or loss in the exchange. The basis of its assets remains $35,000 unless Acquiring makes a Sec. 338 election. Target's shareholders recognize gain or loss in the exchange whether or not Acquiring makes a Sec. 338 election. ◀

COMPLIANCE AND PROCEDURAL CONSIDERATIONS

SECTION 338 ELECTION

The acquiring corporation makes a Sec. 338 election by filing Form 8023 (Elections Under Section 338 for Corporations Making Qualified Stock Purchases) with the IRS. This election must be made by the fifteenth day of the ninth month beginning after the month of the acquisition date. The required information about the acquiring corporation, the target corporation, and the election is set forth in Reg. Sec. 1.338-1(d).

PLAN OF REORGANIZATION

Nonrecognition of gain by a transferor corporation in an asset acquisition (Sec. 361) or a shareholder in a stock acquisition (Sec. 354) requires that the acquisition be pursuant to a plan of reorganization. A **plan of reorganization** is a consummated transaction specifically defined as a reorganization. Nonrecognition of gain or loss is limited to exchanges or distributions that are a direct part of a reorganization undertaken to continue the business of a corporation that is a party to a reorganization.[94] Although a written plan is not required, it would be prudent for all parties to the reorganization to reduce the plan to writing, either as a communication to the shareholders, a document in the corporate records, or a written agreement between the parties. The transaction generally is taxable if a plan of reorganization does not exist or if a transfer or distribution is not pursuant to a plan.[95]

---

[94] Reg. Sec. 1.368-2(g).

[95] *A. T. Evans*, 30 B.T.A. 746 (1934), *acq.* XIII-2 C.B. 7; and *William Hewitt*, 19 B.T.A. 771 (1930).

PARTY TO A REORGANIZATION

For an asset or stock transfer to be nontaxable under Secs. 354 and 361, a shareholder or a transferor must be a party to a reorganization. Section 368(b) includes as a **party to a reorganization** "any corporation resulting from a reorganization, and both corporations involved in a reorganization where one corporation acquires the stock or assets of a second corporation." In a triangular reorganization, the corporation controlling the acquiring corporation, and whose stock is used to effect the reorganization, also is a party to the reorganization.

RULING REQUESTS

Before proceeding with an acquisition or disposition, some taxpayers request an advance ruling from the IRS on the tax consequences of the transaction. They generally do so because of the complexity of tax reorganization law and the substantial dollar amounts involved in the transaction. An after-the-fact determination by the IRS or the courts that a completed transaction is taxable could be costly to all parties. The IRS will issue an advance ruling only for reorganizations that conform to the guidelines of Rev. Proc. 77-37 and other IRS pronouncements. It will not issue an advance ruling for a reorganization if the consequences are adequately addressed in the IRC, Treasury Regulations, Supreme Court decisions, tax treaties, revenue rulings, revenue procedures, notices, or other IRS pronouncements.[96] Because of IRS policy not to issue these so-called "comfort rulings," many taxpayers instead seek opinion letters from tax counsel.

FINANCIAL STATEMENT IMPLICATIONS

OBJECTIVE 10

Understand the financial statement implications of corporate acquisitions

An acquiring corporation must use the acquisition method for financial statement purposes whether the business combination is a taxable purchase or a nontaxable reorganization.[97] However, differences occur in the recording of deferred tax accounts and the treatment of goodwill. Also, a stock acquisition has its own particularities because recording the transaction occurs in the process of consolidating the financial statements of the acquiring parent and the acquired subsidiary.

For subsequent illustrations, assume Theta Corporation (the target corporation) has the following balance sheet of identified assets and liabilities, where the tax basis and book basis are the same. Thus, prior to the acquisition, Theta has no temporary differences or deferred tax accounts.

	FMV	Basis	Difference
Accounts receivable	$ 12,000	$ 12,000	$ –0–
Inventory	30,000	25,000	5,000
Plant and equipment	100,000	75,000	25,000
Land	50,000	40,000	10,000
Total assets	$192,000	$152,000	$40,000
Liabilities	$ 20,000	$ 20,000	
Equity	172,000	132,000	
Total liabilities and equity	$192,000	$152,000	

TAXABLE ASSET ACQUISTION

In a taxable purchase, the acquiring corporation's tax basis in the purchased assets likely will be the same as the recorded book basis. If so, deferred tax liabilities and assets will not arise as a result of the business combination. Also, if tax goodwill and book goodwill

---

[96] Rev. Proc. 2011-1, 2011-1, I.R.B. 1, and Rev. Proc. 2011-3, 2011-1 I.R.B. 110.

[97] Accounting Standards Codification (ASC) 805, Business Combinations, which codifies SFAS No. 141R.

are equal, future amortization of tax goodwill under Sec. 197 will create temporary differences because book goodwill can be expensed only if impaired.[98] (If tax and book goodwill differ in a taxable business combination, the financial statement treatment gets complicated beyond the scope of this textbook.)

EXAMPLE C:7-41 ▶ At the beginning of the current year, Alpha Corporation purchases all of Theta Corporation's assets for $207,000 cash and does not assume Theta's liabilities. For both book and tax purposes, each asset gets a FMV allocation of this purchase price with the remainder allocated to goodwill. Because the book and tax bases are equal, Alpha records no deferred tax accounts. Accordingly, Alpha makes the following book journal entry to record the purchase:

Accounts receivable	12,000	
Inventory	30,000	
Plant and equipment	100,000	
Land	50,000	
Goodwill	15,000	
Cash		207,000

In the acquisition year, Alpha deducts $1,000 of goodwill amortization for tax purposes but takes no impairment loss for book purposes. Assuming no other book-tax differences, $150,000 of pretax book income, and a 35% tax rate, Alpha realizes the following results for this year.

Net income before FIT expense	$150,000
Goodwill amortization (temporary difference)	(1,000)
Taxable income	$149,000

Thus, Alpha's federal income tax expense is $52,500 ($150,000 × 0.35), and its federal tax liability is $52,150 ($149,000 × 0.35). Also, Alpha records a deferred tax liability of $350 ($1,000 × 0.35). Accordingly, Alpha makes the following book journal entry:

Federal income tax expense	52,500	
Deferred tax liability		350
Federal income taxes payable		51,150

The deferred tax liability will increase by the same amount each year of the 15-year tax amortization period and will reverse if and when Alpha takes an impairment loss on the book goodwill. ◀

NONTAXABLE ASSET ACQUISTION

In a nontaxable business combination, such as a Type A or Type C reorganization, the bases recorded for financial statement purposes differ from the carryover tax bases of acquired assets. For business combinations, the acquiring corporation recognizes a deferred tax asset or liability for differences between the assigned financial statement values and the tax bases of the transferred assets and liabilities.[99] Goodwill for which the corporation is not allowed an amortization deduction for tax purposes, the usual situation in a nontaxable acquisition, does not give rise to a temporary difference.

EXAMPLE C:7-42 ▶ At the beginning of the current year, Alpha Corporation acquires all of Theta's assets and assumes Theta's liabilities in a Type A merger. In addition to assuming the liabilities, Alpha issues $187,000 worth of its preferred stock as consideration, for a total consideration of $207,000. For tax purposes, Alpha takes a carryover basis in each asset, but for financial statement purposes, Alpha records each asset at its FMV. Assuming a 35% corporate tax rate, the $40,000 difference between the total book value and total tax basis creates a $14,000 ($40,000 × 0.35) deferred tax liability. Thus, aside from $15,000 of goodwill from the excess of consideration paid ($207,000) over the FMV of identified assets ($192,000), Alpha records $14,000 of additional goodwill. Accordingly, Alpha makes the following book journal entry to record the acquisition:

Accounts receivable	12,000	
Inventory	30,000	
Plant and equipment	100,000	

[98] Accounting Standards Codification (ASC) 350, Intangibles—Goodwill and Other, which codifies SFAS No. 142.

[99] Accounting Standards Codification (ASC) 740, Income Taxes, which codifies SFAS No. 109.

Land	50,000	
Goodwill	29,000	
Deferred tax liability		14,000
Liabilities		20,000
Preferred stock		187,000

In the acquisition year, Alpha's book net income before federal income tax (FIT) expense is $150,000, which includes $12,000 of book depreciation on the acquired plant and equipment and $2,800 of book goodwill impairment. For tax purposes, Alpha recognizes a $5,000 gain on the sale of the acquired inventory and takes $9,000 of depreciation on the acquired plant and equipment, but it amortizes no goodwill. The difference between the $2,800 book goodwill impairment and the zero tax goodwill amortization produces a permanent difference. The other book-tax differences are temporary, resulting in the following net income to taxable income reconciliation:

Net income before FIT expense	$150,000
Goodwill (permanent difference)	2,800
Net income after permanent differences	$152,800
Inventory sale (temporary difference)	5,000
Depreciation (temporary difference)	3,000
Taxable income	$160,800

Thus, assuming a 35% tax rate, Alpha's federal income tax expense is $53,480 ($152,800 × 0.35), and its federal tax liability is $56,280 ($160,800 × 0.35). Also, Alpha reduces its deferred tax liability by $2,800 ($8,000 × 0.35). Accordingly, Alpha makes the following book journal entry:

Federal income tax expense	53,480	
Deferred tax liability	2,800	
Federal income taxes payable		56,280	◄

STOCK ACQUISTION

In a stock acquisition, the target corporation remains intact as a subsidiary of the acquiring corporation. The adjustments necessary to implement acquisition accounting rules income tax accounting rules occur when the corporations prepare their consolidated financial statements.

EXAMPLE C:7-43 ▶ At the beginning of the current year, Alpha Corporation acquires 100% of Theta's stock for $187,000 cash. As a result, Theta's shareholders recognize gain or loss on their sale of the stock. Alpha makes the following book journal entry to record the purchase:

Investment in Theta Corporation	187,000	
Cash		187,000

If Alpha instead acquired the Theta stock in a Type B reorganization using $187,000 of common voting stock, Alpha would have made a similar journal entry with the credit being to common stock rather than cash. In the consolidating journal entry for either type acquisition, Alpha eliminates the investment account, adjusts Theta's tax bases to book value, and records the necessary deferred accounts as follows:

Inventory	5,000	
Plant and equipment	25,000	
Land	10,000	
Goodwill	29,000	
Theta's equity	132,000	
Deferred tax liability		14,000
Investment in Theta Corporation		187,000	◄

PRICING THE ACQUISITION

In the above examples, the numerical amount of consideration is the same for the taxable and nontaxable asset acquisitions ($207,000). Economically, however, they are not comparable because, in the taxable purchase, the seller bears the tax burden. In the nontaxable asset acquisition, however, the acquiring corporation assumes the tax burden because it pays the same amount of consideration for assets having a low tax basis and a built-in gain. Consequently, it incurs the tax liability when it sells or depreciates the low basis assets. To shift the tax burden back to the seller in a nontaxable acquisition, the acquiring corporation might want to negotiate a reduced price for the assets. Similarly, in either a taxable or nontaxable stock acquisition, the acquiring corporation obtains a subsidiary with low basis assets. Hence, it might want to negotiate a stock price that reflects that built-in tax liability.

NET OPERATING LOSSES

If the target corporation has net operation loss carryovers (NOLs), the acquiring corporation must establish a deferred tax asset along with a valuation allowance if necessary. See Chapter C:3 for a discussion of the valuation allowance as well as a general discussion of the financial implications of federal income taxes.

PROBLEM MATERIALS

DISCUSSION QUESTIONS

C:7-1 From the standpoint of Target Corporation shareholders, what is the advantage of a taxable stock acquisition by Purchaser Corporation compared to Purchaser acquiring all of Target's assets in a taxable transaction followed by a liquidating distribution from Target to its shareholders?

C:7-2 What tax advantages exist for a corporate buyer when it acquires the assets of another corporation in a taxable transaction? For a seller when he or she exchanges stock in a taxable transaction? In a nontaxable transaction?

C:7-3 What tax and nontax advantages and disadvantages accrue when an acquiring corporation purchases all of a target corporation's stock for cash and subsequently liquidates the target corporation?

C:7-4 Why might a parent corporation make a Sec. 338 election after acquiring a target corporation's stock? When would such an election not be advisable?

C:7-5 Explain the following items related to a Sec. 338 election:
   a. The rule used to determine the time period within which the Sec. 338 stock purchase(s) can be made.
   b. The types of stock acquisitions that are counted and not counted when determining whether a qualified stock purchase has occurred.
   c. The method for determining the sale price for target corporation assets.
   d. The method for determining the total basis for target corporation assets.
   e. The effect of the deemed sale on the target corporation's tax attributes.
   f. The date by which the Sec. 338 election must be made.
   g. Assuming goodwill results from a Sec. 338 election, can the goodwill be amortized? If so, over what period?

C:7-6 **a.** Holt Corporation acquires all the stock of Star Corporation and makes a timely Sec. 338 election. The adjusted grossed-up basis of the Star stock is $2.5 million. The FMV of tangible assets on Star's balance sheet is $1.8 million. How are the new bases in Star's individual assets determined?
   b. How would your answer change if instead the adjusted grossed-up basis were $1.4 million?

C:7-7 Compare the tax consequences of a taxable asset acquisition and an asset-for-stock reorganization, based on the following factors:
   a. Consideration used to effect the transaction.
   b. Recognition of gain or loss by the target corporation on the asset transfer.
   c. Basis of property to the acquiring corporation.
   d. Recognition of gain or loss when the target corporation liquidates.
   e. Use and/or carryover of the target corporation's tax attributes.

C:7-8 Which of the following events as part of an acquisitive reorganization require the target corporation to recognize gain? Assume in all cases that the target corporation liquidates in the reorganization.
   a. Transfer of appreciated target corporation assets in exchange for acquiring corporation stock and short-term notes.
   b. Transfer of appreciated target corporation assets in exchange for acquiring corporation stock and the assumption of the target corporation's liabilities.
   c. Assume the same facts as in Part b except the amount of liabilities assumed by the acquiring corporation exceeds the adjusted basis of the target corporation assets transferred.
   d. Transfer of appreciated target corporation assets in exchange for stock and money. Target distributes the money to its shareholders.

e. Transfer of appreciated target corporation assets in exchange for stock and money. Target uses the money to pay off its liabilities.

C:7-9 A shareholder receives stock and cash in an acquisitive reorganization. The shareholder recognizes a gain because of the boot (cash) received. What rules determine whether the character of the shareholder's recognized gain is dividend income or capital gain?

C:7-10 Evaluate the following statement: Individual shareholders who recognize gain as the result of receiving boot in a corporate reorganization generally prefer to report capital gain, whereas corporate shareholders generally prefer to report dividend income.

C:7-11 How is the basis in nonboot stock and securities received by a shareholder determined? How is the basis in boot property determined?

C:7-12 Which reorganization(s) are acquisitive? Divisive? Which reorganization(s) are neither acquisitive nor divisive? Which reorganization(s) can be either acquisitive or divisive?

C:7-13 Compare the types of consideration that can be used in Type A, B, and C reorganizations.

C:7-14 How does the IRS interpret the continuity of interest doctrine for a Type A reorganization?

C:7-15 How does the IRS interpret the continuity of business enterprise requirement for a Type A reorganization?

C:7-16 What are the advantages of a Type C asset-for-stock reorganization as opposed to a Type A merger reorganization? The disadvantages?

C:7-17 How does the IRS interpret the "substantially all" asset requirement for a Type C reorganization?

C:7-18 Explain why an acquiring corporation might be prohibited from using cash as part of the consideration paid in a Type C reorganization.

C:7-19 Some acquisitive transactions may be characterized as either a Type C or a Type D reorganization. Which reorganization provision controls if the two types overlap?

C:7-20 What is the difference between an acquisitive Type C reorganization and an acquisitive Type D reorganization?

C:7-21 Explain the circumstances in which money and other property can be used in a Type B reorganization.

C:7-22 Acquiring Corporation purchased for cash a 5% interest in Target Corporation stock. After buying the stock and examining Target's books, Acquiring's management wants to make a tender offer to acquire the remaining Target stock in exchange for Acquiring voting stock. Can this tender offer be accomplished as a Type B reorganization? What problems may be encountered in structuring the acquisition as a nontaxable reorganization?

C:7-23 Acquiring Corporation wants to exchange its voting common stock for all of Target Corporation's single class of stock in a tender offer. Only 85% of Target's shareholders agree to tender their shares. After the tender, what options exist for Acquiring to acquire the remaining shares as part of the reorganization? At a later date? How will a subsequent cash acquisition of the remaining outstanding shares affect the tax treatment of the tender offer?

C:7-24 Explain the structure of a triangular reorganization? What advantages would a triangular reorganization provide the acquiring corporation?

C:7-25 Compare and contrast the requirements for, and the tax treatment of, the spinoff, split-off, and split-up forms of divisive Type D reorganizations.

C:7-26 Stock in a controlled subsidiary corporation can be distributed tax-free to the distributing corporation's shareholders under Sec. 355. Explain the difference between such a distribution and a divisive Type D reorganization.

C:7-27 When is the distribution of a controlled corporation's stock or securities nontaxable to the distributing corporation's shareholders? What events trigger the recognition of gain or loss by the shareholders?

C:7-28 When does the distributing corporation recognize gain or loss on the distribution of stock or securities of a controlled corporation to its shareholders?

C:7-29 What is a recapitalization? What types of recapitalizations are nontaxable?

C:7-30 How can a recapitalization be used to transfer voting control tax-free within a family corporation from a senior generation that is in the process of retiring to a junior generation?

C:7-31 Explain why a transaction might satisfy the letter of Sec. 368 for a reorganization yet fail to be treated as a reorganization.

C:7-32 Which types of reorganizations (acquisitive, divisive, and other) permit the carryover of tax attributes from a target or transferor corporation to an acquiring or transferee corporation?

C:7-33 What restrictions are placed on the acquisition and use of a loss corporation's tax attributes?

C:7-34 Explain why Sec. 382 will not be an obstacle to the use of NOL carryovers following an acquisition if the value of the old loss corporation is large relative to its NOL carryovers.

C:7-35 What is a plan of reorganization? Does such a plan need to be reduced to writing?

C:7-36 Why do some taxpayers secure an advance ruling for a proposed reorganization transaction?

C:7-37 Does the receipt of a favorable advance ruling provide the taxpayer with a guarantee that the IRS will follow the ruling if it audits the completed transaction?

ISSUE IDENTIFICATION QUESTIONS

C:7-38   Rodger Powell owns all the stock in Fireside Bar and Grill Corporation in Pittsburgh. Now that he has turned 65, Rodger wants to sell his business and retire to sunny Florida. Karin Godfrey, a long-time bartender at Fireside, offers to purchase all the corporation's noncash assets in exchange for a 25% down payment, with the remaining 75% paid in five equal annual installments. Interest will accrue at a market rate on the unpaid installments. Rodger plans to liquidate the corporation that has operated the Bar and Grill. He also plans to have Fireside Bar and Grill distribute the installment notes and any remaining assets. What tax issues should Fireside Bar and Grill, Rodger, and Karin consider with respect to the proposed purchase?

C:7-39   Adolph Coors Co. transferred part of its assets to ACX Technologies Corporation in exchange for all of ACX's stock. The assets transferred included its aluminum unit, which makes aluminum sheet; its paper packaging unit, which makes consumer-products packaging; and its ceramic unit, which makes high-technology ceramics used in computer boards and automotive parts. The ACX Technologies stock received for the assets was distributed to the Coors shareholders. What tax issues should the parties to the divisive reorganization consider?

C:7-40   Johnson & Johnson announced that it had entered into a merger agreement with Alza Corporation, a research-based pharmaceutical company and a leader in drug delivery technologies. Alza shareholders were offered a fixed exchange ratio of 0.49 shares of Johnson & Johnson common stock for each share of Alza stock in a nontaxable reorganization. Alza had approximately 295 million shares outstanding at the time of the announcement. The boards of directors of both companies approved the merger. What tax issues might have been important to the two companies and to the two shareholder groups?

PROBLEMS

C:7-41   *Qualified Stock Purchase.* Acquiring Corporation purchased 20% of Target Corporation's stock on each of the following dates in the current year: January 2, April 1, June 1, October 1, and December 31.
   a. Has a qualified stock purchase occurred? If it so desires, when must Acquiring make the deemed sale election under Sec. 338?
   b. How would your answer to Part a change if instead the purchase dates were January 1, April 1, and September 2 of the current year, and January 3, and April 15 of the following year?
   c. If either Part a or b fails to be a qualified stock purchase, what is the latest date on which Acquiring can make the final stock purchase needed to qualify for a Sec. 338 election?

C:7-42   *Sec. 338 Election.* Acquiring Corporation purchases 20% of Target Corporation stock from Milt on August 10 of the current year. Acquiring purchases an additional 30% of the stock from Nick on November 15 of the current year. Acquiring purchases the remaining 50% of the Target stock from Phil on April 10 of the following year. The total price paid for the stock is $1.9 million. Target's balance sheet on April 10 of the following year shows assets with a $2.5 million FMV, a $1.6 million adjusted basis, and $500,000 in liabilities.
   a. What is the acquisition date for the Target stock for Sec. 338 purposes? By what date must Acquiring make the Sec. 338 election?
   b. If Acquiring makes a Sec. 338 election, what is the aggregate deemed sale price for the assets?
   c. What is the total basis of the assets following the deemed sale, assuming a 34% corporate tax rate?
   d. How does the tax liability attributable to the deemed sale affect the price Acquiring should be willing to pay for the Target stock?
   e. What happens to Target's tax attributes following the deemed sale?

C:7-43   *Sec. 338 Election.* Gator Corporation is considering the acquisition of Bulldog Corporation's stock in exchange for cash. Two options are under review: (1) Gator purchases the assets from Bulldog for $1.4 million or (2) Gator purchases the Bulldog stock for $1 million and makes a Sec. 338 election shortly after the stock purchase. Bulldog has no NOL or capital loss carryovers. Bulldog's balance sheet is presented below.

Assets	Adjusted Basis	FMV	Liabilities and Equity	Amount
Cash	$100,000	$ 100,000	Short-term debt	$ 200,000
Marketable securities	140,000	200,000	Long-term debt	200,000
Accounts receivable	100,000	100,000	Paid-in capital	300,000
Inventory (FIFO)	100,000	150,000	Retained earnings	700,000
Plant and equipment	200,000	500,000		
Intangibles	–0–	350,000		
Total	$640,000	$1,400,000	Total	$1,400,000

a. What advantages would accrue to Gator if it purchases the assets directly? What disadvantages would accrue to Bulldog if it sells the assets and then liquidates?

b. What advantages would accrue to Gator if it purchases the Bulldog stock for cash and subsequently makes a Sec. 338 election? What advantage would accrue to Bulldog if its shareholders sell the Bulldog stock?

c. How would your answers change if Bulldog had incurred $250,000 of NOLs in the current year that it cannot carry back in full due to insufficient taxable income in the preceding two years?

C:7-44 *Sec. 338 Basis Allocation.* Apache Corporation purchases all of Target Corporation's stock for $300,000 cash. Apache makes a timely Sec. 338 election. Target's balance sheet at the close of business on the acquisition date is as follows:

Assets	Adjusted Basis	FMV	Liabilities and Equity	Amount
Cash	$ 50,000	$ 50,000	Accounts payable	$ 40,000
Marketable securities	18,000	38,000	Note to bank	60,000
Accounts receivable	66,000	65,000	Owner's equity	300,000
Inventory (FIFO)	21,000	43,000		
Equipment[a]	95,000	144,000		
Land	6,000	12,000		
Building[b]	24,000	48,000		
Total	$280,000	$400,000	Total	$400,000

[a]The equipment cost $200,000.
[b]The building is MACRS property on which Target has claimed $10,000 of depreciation.

a. What is the aggregate deemed sale price for the Target assets (assume a 34% corporate tax rate)?

b. What amount and character of gain or loss must Target recognize on the deemed sale?

c. What is the adjusted grossed-up basis for the Target stock? What basis is allocated to each of the individual properties?

d. What happens to "old" Target's tax attributes? Do they carry over to "new" Target?

e. What amount (if any) of goodwill can Target amortize following the acquisition? Over what period and under what method does Target amortize the goodwill?

C:7-45 *Amount of Corporate Gain or Loss.* Thomas Corporation transfers all of its assets and $100,000 of its liabilities in exchange for Andrews Corporation voting common stock, having a $600,000 FMV, in a merger in which Thomas liquidates. Thomas's basis in its assets is $475,000.

a. What is the amount of Thomas's realized and recognized gain or loss on the asset transfer?

b. What is Andrews's basis in the assets received?

c. What is the amount of Thomas's realized and recognized gain or loss when it distributes the stock to its shareholders?

d. How would your answers to Parts a–c change if Thomas's basis in the assets instead had been $750,000?

e. How would your answers to Parts a–c change if Andrews instead had exchanged $600,000 cash for Thomas assets and Thomas subsequently liquidated. Assume a 34% corporate tax rate.

C:7-46 *Amount of Shareholder Gain or Loss.* Silvia exchanges all her Talbot Corporation stock (acquired August 1, 2008) for $300,000 of Alpha Corporation voting common stock pursuant to Talbot's merger into Alpha. Immediately after the stock-for-stock exchange Silvia owns 25% of Alpha's 2,000 outstanding shares of stock. Silvia's adjusted basis in the Talbot stock is $200,000 before the merger.

    a. What are the amount and character of Silvia's recognized gain or loss?

    b. What is Silvia's basis in the Alpha stock? When does her holding period begin?

    c. How would your answers to Parts a and b change if instead Silvia received Alpha common stock worth $240,000 and $60,000 cash?

C:7-47   *Amount and Character of Shareholder Gain or Loss.* Yong owns 100% of Target Corporation stock having a $600,000 adjusted basis. As part of the merger of Target into Allied Corporation, Yong exchanges his Target stock for Allied common stock having a $3 million FMV and $750,000 in cash. Yong retains a 60% interest in Allied's 100,000 shares of outstanding stock immediately after the merger.

    a. What are the amount and character of Yong's recognized gain?

    b. What is Yong's basis in the Allied stock?

    c. How would your answers to Parts a and b change if instead Yong's 60,000 Allied shares were one-third of Allied's outstanding shares?

C:7-48   *Amount and Character of Gain Recognized.* Springs Corporation has developed a nature park at the site of Blue Springs. The corporation has been extremely profitable. Because Newberry Corporation wants to develop several other springs in the area, Newberry wants to merge with Springs under Florida law. Newberry offers $650,000 of nonvoting preferred shares plus 1,000 shares of voting common (FMV of $50,000) to Springs in exchange for all of Springs' assets. As part of the merger, Springs' sole shareholder, Mr. High, exchanges all his shares in Springs for the shares in Newberry. Immediately before this transaction, Mr. High had a $240,000 basis in his Springs shares and owned no shares in Newberry. After the transaction he owns 20% of the value of the Newberry stock.

    a. Does this transaction qualify as a Type A reorganization?

    b. Does Springs recognize any gain or loss on the asset sale or the exchange of shares with Mr. High?

    c. Does Mr. High recognize any gain or loss? What is his basis and holding period in his Newberry shares?

C:7-49   *Characterization of the Shareholder's Gain or Loss.* Turbo Corporation has one million shares of common stock and 200,000 shares of nonvoting preferred stock outstanding. Pursuant to a merger under state law, Ace Corporation exchanges its common stock worth $15 million for the Turbo common stock and pays $10 million in cash for the Turbo preferred stock. Some shareholders of Turbo received only Ace common stock for their common stock. Some shareholders received only cash for their preferred stock. Some shareholders received both cash and Ace common stock for their Turbo preferred and common stock, respectively. Shareholders owning approximately 10% of the Turbo common stock also owned Turbo preferred stock. The total cash received by these shareholders amounted to $1.5 million. The Turbo common stockholders end up with 15% of the Ace stock. What is the tax treatment of the common stock and/or cash received by each of the three groups of Turbo shareholders? Assume that some Turbo shareholders realize a gain on the transaction while other shareholders realize a loss.

C:7-50   *Requirements for a Type A Reorganization.* Anchor Corporation plans to acquire all the assets of Tower Corporation in a merger under state law. Tower's assets have a $5 million FMV and a $2.2 million adjusted basis. Assuming Tower liquidates, which of the following transactions qualify as a Type A reorganization?

    a. The assets are exchanged for $5 million of Anchor common stock.

    b. The assets are exchanged for $5 million of Anchor nonvoting preferred stock.

    c. The assets are exchanged for $5 million of Anchor securities.

    d. The assets are exchanged for $3.5 million of Anchor nonvoting preferred stock and $1.5 million in cash.

    e. The assets are exchanged for $3 million of Anchor common stock and Anchor's assumption of $2 million of Tower liabilities.

    f. The assets are exchanged for $5 million in cash provided by Anchor. An "all cash" merger transaction is permitted under state law.

C:7-51   *Tax Consequences of a Merger.* Armor Corporation exchanges $1 million of its common stock and $300,000 of Armor bonds for all of Trail Corporation's outstanding stock. As part of the same transaction, Trail then merges into Armor, which receives assets having a $1.3 million FMV and an $875,000 adjusted basis. As part of the merger, Antonello exchanges his 20% interest (4,000 shares) in Trail's single class of stock, having an adjusted basis of $100,000, for $200,000 in Armor stock and $60,000 in Armor bonds. Following the reorganization, Antonello owns 5% (1,000 shares) of Armor's stock. Armor's E&P balance is $375,000.

a. What is the amount of Trail's recognized gain or loss on the asset transfer?

b. What is Armor's basis in the assets received in the exchange?

c. What are the amount and character of Antonello's recognized gain or loss?

d. What is Antonello's basis in the Armor stock? In the Armor bonds?

C:7-52 *Requirements for a Type C Reorganization.* Arnold Corporation plans to acquire all the assets of Turner Corporation in an asset-for-stock exchange. Turner's assets have a $600,000 adjusted basis and a $1 million FMV. Which of the following transactions qualify as a Type C reorganization (assuming Turner liquidates as part of the reorganization)?

a. The assets are exchanged for $800,000 of Arnold voting common stock and $200,000 of cash.

b. The assets are exchanged for $800,000 of Arnold voting common stock and $200,000 of Arnold bonds.

c. The assets are exchanged for $1 million of Arnold nonvoting preferred stock.

d. The assets are exchanged for $700,000 of Arnold voting common stock and Arnold's assumption of $300,000 of Turner's liabilities.

e. The assets are exchanged for $700,000 of Arnold voting common stock, Arnold's assumption of $200,000 of Turner's liabilities, and $100,000 in cash.

C:7-53 *Tax Consequences of a Type C Reorganization.* As part of a Type C reorganization, Ash Corporation exchanges $250,000 of its voting common stock and $50,000 of its bonds for all of Texas Corporation's assets. Texas liquidates, with each of its two shareholders receiving equal amounts of the Ash stock and bonds. Barbara has a $50,000 basis in her stock, and George has a $200,000 basis in his stock. George and Barbara, who are unrelated, each own 8% of Ash's stock (5,000 shares) immediately after the reorganization. At the time of the reorganization, Texas's E&P balance is $75,000, and its assets have an adjusted basis of $225,000.

a. What is the amount of Texas's recognized gain or loss on the asset transfer? On the distribution of the stock and bonds?

b. What is Ash's basis in the assets it acquired?

c. What are the amount and character of each shareholder's recognized gain or loss?

d. What is the basis of each shareholder's Ash stock? Ash bonds?

C:7-54 *Tax Consequences of a Type C Reorganization.* As part of a Type C reorganization, Tulsa Corporation exchanges assets having a $300,000 FMV and a $175,000 adjusted basis for $250,000 of Akron Corporation voting common stock and Akron's assumption of $50,000 of Tulsa's liabilities. Tulsa liquidates, with its sole shareholder, Michelle, receiving the Akron stock in exchange for her Tulsa stock having an adjusted basis of $100,000. Michelle owns 12% (2,500 shares) of Akron's stock immediately after the reorganization.

a. What is the amount of Tulsa's recognized gain or loss on the asset transfer? On the distribution of the stock?

b. What is Akron's basis in the assets it receives?

c. What effect would the transfer of Tulsa's assets to Subsidiary Corporation (controlled by Akron) have on the reorganization?

d. What are the amount and character of Michelle's recognized gain or loss?

e. What is Michelle's basis and holding period for her Akron stock?

f. What are the tax consequences of the transaction if Akron first transfers its stock to Akron-Sub Corporation, which then acquires Tulsa's assets?

C:7-55 *Requirements for a Type B Reorganization.* Allen Corporation plans to acquire all the stock in Taylor Corporation in a stock-for-stock exchange. Which of the following transactions will qualify as a Type B reorganization?

a. All of Taylor's common stock is exchanged for $1 million of Allen voting preferred stock.

b. All of Taylor's common stock is exchanged for $1 million of Allen voting common stock, and $500,000 face amount of Taylor bonds are exchanged for $500,000 face amount of Allen bonds. Both bonds are trading at their par values.

c. All of Taylor's stock is exchanged for $750,000 of Allen voting common stock and $250,000 of Allen bonds.

d. All of Taylor's stock is exchanged for $1 million of Allen voting common stock, and the shareholders of Taylor end up with less than 1% of Allen stock.

e. Ninety percent of Taylor's stock is exchanged for $900,000 of Allen voting common stock. One shareholder who owns 10% of the Taylor stock exercises his right under state law to have his shares independently appraised and redeemed for cash by Taylor. He receives $100,000.

f. Assume the same facts as in Part d except the Allen stock is contributed to Allen-Sub Corporation. The Allen stock is exchanged by Allen-Sub for all the Taylor stock.

C:7-56 *Tax Consequences of a Type B Reorganization.* Trent Corporation's single class of stock is owned equally by Juan and Miguel, who are unrelated. Juan has a $125,000 basis in his 1,000 shares of Trent stock, and Miguel has a $300,000 basis in his Trent stock. In a single transaction, Adams Corporation exchanges 2,500 shares of its voting common stock having a $100 per share FMV for each shareholder's Trent stock. Immediately after the reorganization, each shareholder owns 15% of the Adams stock.

a. What are the amount and character of each shareholder's recognized gain or loss?

b. What is each shareholder's basis in his Adams stock?

c. What is Adams's basis in the Trent stock?

d. How would your answers to Parts a–c change if Adams instead exchanged 2,000 shares of Adams common stock and $50,000 in cash for each shareholder's Trent stock?

C:7-57 *Tax Consequences of a Type B Reorganization.* Austin Corporation exchanges $1.5 million of its voting common stock for all of Travis Corporation's single class of stock. Ingrid, who owns all the Travis stock, has a $375,000 basis in her stock. Ingrid owns 25% of the 15,000 outstanding shares of Austin stock immediately after the reorganization.

a. What are the amount and character of Ingrid's recognized gain or loss?

b. What is Ingrid's basis in her Austin stock?

c. What is Austin's basis in the Travis stock?

d. What are the tax consequences for all parties to the acquisition if Austin subsequently liquidates Travis as part of the plan of reorganization?

e. As part of the reorganization, Austin exchanges $1 million of its 7% bonds for $1 million Travis 7% bonds held equally by ten private investors.

C:7-58 *Tax Consequences of a Type B Reorganization.* On January 30 of the current year, Ashton Corporation purchased 10% of Todd Corporation stock from Cathy for $250,000 in cash. On May 30 of the following year, Andrea and Bill each exchange one-half of the remaining 90% of the Todd stock for $1.2 million of Ashton voting common stock. Andrea and Bill each have a $150,000 basis in their Todd stock, and each owns 15% of the Ashton stock (12,000 shares) immediately after the reorganization.

a. What are the amount and character of each shareholder's recognized gain or loss?

b. What is each shareholder's basis in his or her Ashton stock?

c. What is Ashton's basis in the Todd stock?

d. How would your answers to Parts a–c change if instead Ashton had acquired the remaining Todd stock on May 30 of the current year?

e. What effect would the stock acquisition have on the adjusted bases of individual assets and the tax attributes of Todd?

f. Can the Ashton-Todd corporate group file a consolidated tax return?

g. Can a Sec. 338 election be made with respect to Todd's assets?

C:7-59 *Tax Consequences of a Divisive Type D Reorganization.* Road Corporation is owned equally by four shareholders. It conducts activities in two operating divisions: the road construction division and meat packing division. To segregate the two activities into distinct corporations, Road transferred the assets and liabilities of the meat packing division (60% of Road's total net assets) to Food Corporation in exchange for all of Food's single class of stock. The assets of the meat packing division have a $2.75 million FMV and a $1.1 million adjusted basis. A total of $500,000 of liabilities are transferred to Food. The $2.25 million of Food stock (90,000 shares) is distributed ratably to each of the four shareholders.

a. What is the amount of Road's recognized gain or loss on the asset transfer? On the distribution of the Food stock?

b. What are the amount and character of each shareholder's recognized gain or loss on the distribution? (Assume each shareholder's basis in Road stock is $200,000.)

c. What is the basis of each shareholder's Road and Food stock after the reorganization? (Assume the Road stock is worth $1.5 million immediately after the distribution.)

C:7-60 *Tax Consequences of a Divisive Type D Reorganization.* Light Corporation is owned equally by two individual shareholders, Bev and Tarek. The shareholders no longer agree on how to manage Light's operations. Tarek agrees to a plan whereby $500,000 of Light's assets (having an adjusted basis of $350,000) and $100,000 of Light's liabilities are transferred to Dark Corporation in exchange for all its single class of stock (5,000 shares). Tarek will exchange all his Light common stock, having a $150,000 adjusted basis, for the $400,000 of Dark stock. Bev will continue to operate Light.

a. What is the amount of Light's recognized gain or loss on the asset transfer? On the distribution of the Dark stock?

b. What are the amount and character of Tarek's recognized gain or loss?

c. What is Tarek's basis in his Dark stock?

d. What tax attributes of Light will be allocated to Dark?

C:7-61 *Distribution of Stock: Spin-Off.* Parent Corporation has been in the business of manufacturing and selling trucks for the past eight years. Its subsidiary, Diesel Corporation, has been in the business of manufacturing and selling diesel engines for the past seven years. Parent acquired control of Diesel six years ago when it purchased 100% of its single class of stock from Large Corporation. A federal court has ordered Parent to divest itself of Diesel pursuant to an antitrust judgment. Consequently, Parent distributes all its Diesel stock to its shareholders. Alan owns less than 1% of Parent's outstanding stock having a $40,000 basis. As a result of Parent's distribution, he receives 25 shares of Diesel stock having a $25,000 FMV. Parent distributes no cash or other assets. Parent's E&P at the end of the year in which the spinoff occurs is $2.5 million. The Parent stock held by Alan has a $75,000 FMV immediately after the distribution.

a. What are the amount and character of the gain, loss, or income Alan must recognize as a result of Parent's distributing the Diesel stock?

b. What basis does Alan take in the Diesel stock he receives?

c. When does Alan's holding period for the Diesel stock begin?

d. What amount and character of gain or loss does Parent recognize on the distribution?

e. How would your answer to Part a change if Parent had been in the truck business for only three years before the distribution, and it had acquired the Diesel stock in a taxable transaction only two years ago?

C:7-62 *Distribution of Stock: Split-Off.* Parent Corporation has owned all 100 shares of Subsidiary Corporation common stock since 2004. Parent has been in the business of manufacturing and selling light fixtures, and Subsidiary has been in the business of manufacturing and selling light bulbs. Amy and Bill are the two equal shareholders of the Parent stock and have owned their stock since 2004. Amy's basis in her 50 shares of Parent stock is $80,000, and Bill's basis in his 50 shares of Parent stock is $60,000. On April 10, 2011, Parent distributes all 100 shares of Subsidiary stock to Bill in exchange for all his Parent stock (which is cancelled). The distribution has a bona fide business purpose. The Subsidiary stock had a $30,000 basis to Parent on the distribution date. At the end of 2011, Parent has $150,000 of E&P. Immediately after the distribution, the FMVs of the Parent and Subsidiary stocks are $3,000 and $1,000 per share, respectively.

a. What are the amount and character of the gain, loss, or income Bill must recognize as a result of Parent's distributing the Subsidiary stock?

b. What basis does Bill take in the Subsidiary stock?

c. When does Bill's holding period for the Subsidiary stock begin?

d. Assume instead that Andrew formed Subsidiary in 2007 to manufacture and sell lightbulbs. Andrew sold the Subsidiary stock to Parent for cash in 2009. How would your answers to Parts a–c change?

C:7-63 *Distribution of Stock and Securities: Split-Off.* Ruby Corporation has 100 shares of common stock outstanding. Fred, a shareholder of Ruby, exchanges his 25% interest in the Ruby stock for Garnet Corporation stock and securities. Ruby purchased 80% of the Garnet stock ten years ago for $25,000. At the time of the exchange, Fred has a $50,000 basis in his Ruby stock, and the stock has an $80,000 FMV. Fred receives Garnet stock that has a $60,000 FMV and Garnet securities that have a $20,000 FMV. Ruby has $50,000 of E&P. Assume that all the requirements of Sec. 355 are met except for the receipt of boot.

a. What are the amount and character of Fred's recognized gain or loss on the exchange?

b. What is Fred's basis in the Garnet stock and the Garnet securities?

c. What are the amount and character of Ruby's recognized gain or loss on the distribution?

d. When does Fred's holding period begin for the Garnet stock and the Garnet securities?

e. How would your answers to Part a change if the exchange did not meet the requirements of Sec. 355 or Sec. 356?

C:7-64 *Distribution of Stock and Securities: Split-Up.* Jean Corporation has two divisions—home cookware and electric home appliances. Bill and Bob Jean own all of Jean Corporation's single class of stock. Bill, the older brother, owns 70% of the Jean stock, and Bob owns the remaining 30%. Bill and Bob's adjusted bases in their Jean stock are $700,000 and $300,000, respectively. They have owned the stock for eight years. The divisions have the following assets:

Division	FMV Assets	Adjusted Basis
Cookware	$980,000	$600,000
Home appliances	420,000	300,000

To divide the business, Jean transfers the cookware assets to Cookware Corporation in exchange for all of Cookware stock. Jean transfers the home appliance assets to Home Appliance Corporation in exchange for all of Home Appliance stock. Jean transfers the Cookware stock to Bill in exchange for all of his Jean stock. Jean transfers the Home Appliance stock to Bob in exchange for all of his Jean stock. Finally, Jean liquidates with its remaining cash used to pay its liabilities.

a. What gain or loss is recognized on the transfer of the Jean assets to Cookware and Home Appliance? What basis do the two corporations take in the assets transferred?

b. What gain or loss do Bill and Bob recognize when they transfer their Jean stock for the Cookware and Home Appliance stock? What basis does each shareholder take in his or her new stock?

C:7-65 *Requirements for a Type E Reorganization.* Master Corporation plans a recapitalization. Explain the tax consequences of each of the following unrelated transactions:

a. Holders of Class A nonvoting preferred stock exchange their stock for newly issued common stock. Master paid $300,000 of cash dividends in the current year and each prior year on the preferred stock.

b. Holders of Master bonds in the amount of $3 million exchange their bonds for a similar dollar amount of preferred stock. In addition, $180,000 of unpaid interest will be paid by issuing additional Master preferred stock to the former bondholders.

c. Because of a decline in the prevailing rate of interest, Master 9% bonds in the amount of $3 million are called and exchanged by their holders before their maturity date for a similar dollar amount of Master 6% bonds. In addition, Master will pay $180,000 of unpaid interest in cash.

C:7-66 *Tax Consequences of a Type E Reorganization.* Milan Corporation is owned by four shareholders. Andy and Bob each own 40% of the outstanding common and preferred stock. Chris and Doug each own 10% of the outstanding common and preferred stock. The shareholders want to retire the preferred stock that was issued five years ago when the corporation was in the midst of a major expansion. Retirement of the preferred stock will eliminate the need to pay annual preferred dividends. Explain the tax consequences of the following two alternatives to the shareholders:

- Milan redeems the $100 par preferred stock for its $120 call price. Each shareholder purchased his preferred stock at its par value five years ago.
- The shareholders exchange each share of the $100 par value preferred stock for $120 of additional common stock.

What nontax advantages might exist for selecting one alternative over the other?

C:7-67 *Types of Reorganizations.* Identify the type of each of the following reorganizations.

a. Briggs Corporation was originally incorporated in Georgia but now conducts most of its business activities in Florida. The firm transfers substantially all its Georgia assets to a new Florida corporation. The Georgia entity liquidates shortly after the transfer. All "Georgia" shareholders swap their "old" Briggs stock for "new" Briggs stock, thereby acquiring an ownership interest in the Florida entity.

b. Jones Corporation exchanges all $1 million of its $1,000 face amount, 6% bonds for a similar amount of new convertible bonds bearing a lower interest rate.

c. Bill Smith owns 100% of Smith Corporation and James Jones owns 100% of Jones Corporation. The two corporations are combined into a single entity called Smith & Jones Corporation. Each shareholder in the two original corporations receives stock in the new combined entity in proportion to the value of his original stock holdings.

d. Dupree Corporation is in bankruptcy. The corporation works out an agreement whereby bondholders and other creditors receive Dupree notes and stock in exchange for discharge of their original claims.

C:7-68 *Reorganization Requirements.* Discuss the tax consequences of the following corporate reorganizations to the parties to the reorganization:

a. Adobe Corporation and Tyler Corporation merge under Florida law. Tyler shareholders receive $300,000 of Adobe common stock and $700,000 of Adobe securities for their Tyler stock.

b. Alabama Corporation exchanges $1 million of its voting common stock for all the noncash assets of Texas Corporation. The transaction meets all requirements of a Type C reorganization. Alabama then splits the acquired business into two operating divisions: meat packing and meat distribution. Alabama retains the meat packing division's assets and continues to conduct its activities but sells for cash the assets of the meat distribution division. The meat distribution division's assets constitute 40% of Texas's noncash assets.

c. Parent Corporation transfers $500,000 of investment securities to Subsidiary Corporation in exchange for all its single class of stock. The Subsidiary stock is exchanged for one-third of the stock held by each of Parent's shareholders. Six months after the reorganization, Subsidiary distributes the investment securities to its shareholders pursuant to the liquidation of Subsidiary.

C:7-69 *Determining the Type of Reorganization Transaction.* For each of the following transactions, indicate its reorganization type (e.g., Type A, Type B, etc.). Assume all common stock is voting stock.

a. Anderson and Brown Corporations exchange their assets for all the single class of stock of newly created Computer Corporation. Following the exchange, Anderson and Brown liquidate. The transaction satisfies Michigan corporation law requirements.

b. Price Corporation (incorporated in Texas) exchanges all its assets for all the single class of stock of Price Corporation (incorporated in Delaware). Following the exchange, Price (Texas) liquidates.

c. All of Gates Corporation's noncumulative, 10% preferred stock is exchanged for Gates common stock.

d. Hobbs Corporation exchanges its common stock for 90% of the outstanding common stock and 80% of the outstanding nonvoting preferred stock of Calvin Corporation. The remaining Calvin stock is held by about 30 individual investors.

e. Scale Corporation transfers the assets of its two operating divisions to Major and Minor Corporations in exchange for all of each corporation's single class of stock. Scale then distributes the Major and Minor stock pursuant to the liquidation of Scale.

f. Tobias Corporation has $3 million of assets and $1 million of liabilities. Andrew Corporation exchanges $2 million of its voting common stock for all of Tobias' assets and liabilities. Tobias liquidates, and its shareholders end up owning 11% of the Andrew stock.

g. How would your answer to Part f change (if at all) should Tobias' balance sheet indicate that liabilities constituted 90% of the corporation's capital structure and common stock the remaining 10%?

C:7-70 *Tax Attribute Carryovers.* At the close of business on May 31, 2011, Alaska Corporation exchanges $2 million of its voting common stock for all the noncash assets of Tennessee Corporation. Tennessee uses its cash to pay off its liabilities and then liquidates. Tennessee and Alaska report the following taxable income:

Tax Year Ending	Alaska Corp.	Tennessee Corp.
December 31, 2008	($100,000)	($95,000)
December 31, 2009	60,000	20,000
December 31, 2010	70,000	(90,000)
May 31, 2011	XXX	(40,000)
December 31, 2011	73,000	XXX

a. What tax returns must Alaska and Tennessee file for 2011?

b. What amount of the NOL carryover does Alaska acquire?

c. Ignoring any implications of Sec. 382, what amount of Tennessee's NOL can Alaska use in 2011?

C:7-71 *Sec. 382 Limitation: Purchase Transaction.* Murray Corporation's stock is owned by about 1,000 shareholders, none of whom own more than 1% of the outstanding shares. Pursuant to a tender offer, Said purchases all the Murray stock for $7.5 million cash at the close of business on December 31, 2010. Before the acquisition, Said owned no Murray stock. Murray had incurred substantial NOLs, which at the end of 2010 totaled $1 million. Murray's taxable income is expected to be $200,000 and $600,000, respectively, for 2011 and 2012. Assuming the long-term tax-exempt federal rate is 5% and Murray continues in the same trade or business, what amount of NOLs can Murray use in 2011 and/or 2012? What amount of NOLs and Sec. 382 limitation carryover to 2013?

C:7-72 *Sec. 382 Limitation: Nontaxable Reorganization.* Albert Corporation is a profitable publicly traded corporation. None of its shareholders owns more than 1% of its outstanding shares. On December 31, 2010, Albert exchanges $8 million of its stock for all the stock of Turner Corporation as part of a merger. Turner is owned by Tara, who receives 15% of the Albert stock as part of the reorganization. Tara owned none of the Albert stock before the merger. Turner accumulated $2.5 million in NOL carryovers before merging into Albert. Albert expects to earn $1 million and $1.5 million in taxable income during 2011 and 2012, respectively. Assuming the long-term tax-exempt federal rate is 4.5%, what amount of NOLs can Albert use in 2011 and 2012?

COMPREHENSIVE PROBLEM

C:7-73 Sid Kess, a long-time tax client of yours, has decided to acquire the snow blower manufacturing firm owned by Richard Smith, one of his closest friends. Richard has a $200,000 adjusted basis in his Richard Smith Snow Blowers (RSSB) stock. Sid Kess Enterprises (SKE), a C corporation 100%-owned by Sid Kess, will make the acquisition. RSSB operates as a C corporation and reports the following assets and liabilities as of November 1 of the current year.

Assets	Adj. Basis	FMV
Cash	$ 200,000	$ 200,000
Inventory (LIFO)	470,000	600,000
Equipment	100,000	275,000
Building	200,000	295,000
Land	80,000	120,000
Goodwill	–0–	250,000
Total	$1,050,000	$1,740,000

Liabilities and Equity	Amount
Accounts payable	$ 60,000
Mortgage payable	120,000
Paid-in capital	220,000
Retained earnings	650,000
Total	$1,050,000

RSSB has claimed depreciation of $200,000 and $80,000 on the equipment and building, respectively, and has claimed no amortization on the goodwill. Retained earnings approximate RSSB's E&P. No NOL, capital loss, or credit carryovers exist at the time of the acquisition. What are the tax consequences of each alternative acquisition methods to SKE and RSSB? Assume a 34% corporate tax rate.

a. SKE acquires all the single class of RSSB stock for $1.56 million in cash. RSSB is not liquidated.

b. SKE acquires all the noncash assets of RSSB for $1.54 million in cash. RSSB is liquidated.

c. SKE acquires all the RSSB stock for $1.56 million in cash. RSSB is liquidated into SKE shortly after the acquisition.

d. SKE acquires all the RSSB stock for $1.56 million in cash. SKE makes a timely Sec. 338 election. RSSB's tax rate is 34%.

e. SKE exchanges $1.54 million of its common stock for all of RSSB's noncash assets ($1,540,000 = $1,740,000 total assets − $200,000 cash). SKE has 10,000 shares of stock outstanding with a $3 million FMV before the acquisition. RSSB liquidates as part of the transaction. RSSB uses part of the retained cash to pay off the corporation's liabilities. The remaining cash is distributed with the SKE stock in the liquidation of RSSB.

f. SKE exchanges $1.56 million of its common stock for all of Richard Smith's RSSB stock. Assume that RSSB does not liquidate. Each share of SKE stock has a $300 FMV.

g. Assume the same facts as in Part d except SKE transfers $1.56 million of its common stock to SKE-Sub. SKE-Sub serves as the acquiring corporation for the transaction and uses $1.56 million of the SKE stock to acquire RSSB's stock.

h. Assume the same facts as in Part e except SKE transfers $1.54 million of its common stock to SKE-Sub. SKE-Sub serves as the acquiring corporation for the transaction and uses $1.54 million of the SKE stock to acquire RSSB's noncash assets.

TAX STRATEGY PROBLEMS

C:7-74 Angel Macias is considering selling his business. The business (Target Corporation) has the following assets and liabilities:

Assets	Adjusted Basis	FMV
Cash	$ 400,000	$ 400,000
Securities	400,000	300,000
Inventory (LIFO)	100,000	200,000
Equipment	200,000	400,000
Building	50,000	300,000
Goodwill	–0–	200,000
Total	$1,150,000	$1,800,000

Target owes $200,000 of accounts payable and $400,000 in bank loans. No NOL carry-overs or carrybacks are available. Bill Jones and Sam Smith, each of whose net worth exceeds $1 million, are interested in acquiring the business by using their S&J Corporation as the vehicle for making the acquisition. Target's management and its owners are interested in selling the business. Assume that both entities are C corporations and their tax rate is a flat 34%. The individual owners are taxed at a 35% tax rate on their ordinary income and a 15% rate on their capital gains. What advice would you give Bill and Sam about acquiring the assets directly from Target, or indirectly by acquiring Target stock from its shareholders and then liquidating Target into S&J? Bill and Sam also have expressed a concern about possible differences in the financial reporting of a nontaxable versus a taxable acquisition.

C:7-75 Pedernales, a cash-rich Texas company that produces petrochemicals, would like to expand its operations in the Southwest. It considers acquiring Dorado, a Nevada corporation that disposes chemical wastes. Dorado owns key licenses, facilities, and technological processes. Over the years, it has accumulated substantial business and foreign tax credits. Because waste disposal sites are scarce in the United States, the value of Dorado's assets has increased threefold, while the value of Dorado stock has increased fivefold. The Rodriguez family, which owns a 52% equity stake in Pedernales, wants to retain control of the Texas company. How might Pedernales structure an acquisition? What tax and other issues should it consider?

C:7-76 Tom Smith owns 100% of Alpha Corporation's single class of stock, and Alpha owns 100% of Beta Corporation's single class of stock. Alpha and Beta have filed separate tax returns for a number of years. Neither corporation has any NOL carryovers. Although Alpha and Beta have been profitable in recent years, Beta needs an infusion of additional capital from outside investors. The corporations have received a proposal from an investor, Karla Boroff, to invest $2 million in Beta to enable Beta to expand its operations and to eliminate a current working capital shortage that cannot be rectified without additional funds. Karla has imposed one constraint on her capital contribution—that Alpha and Beta become two independent entities. Alpha would continue to be completely owned by Tom, but Beta would be owned by the two individuals, Tom and Karla, with each owning 50% of Beta's stock. What strategies can you offer for separating the two companies?

CASE STUDY PROBLEMS

C:7-77 *Comparative Acquisition Forms.* Bailey Corporation owns a number of automotive parts shops. Bill Smith owns an automotive parts shop that has been in existence for 40 years and has competed with one of Bailey's locations. Bill is considering retiring and would like to sell his business. He has his CPA prepare a balance sheet, which he presents to John Bailey, president, who has been a long-time friend.

Assets	Adjusted Basis	FMV
Cash	$ 250,000	$ 250,000
Accounts receivable	75,000	70,000
Inventories (LIFO)	600,000	1,750,000
Equipment	200,000	250,000
Building	30,000	285,000
Land	30,000	115,000
Total	$1,185,000	$2,720,000

If Bailey makes the acquisition, it will operate the automotive parts shop under its own tradename in the location Bill has used for 40 years. The president has asked you to prepare a summary of the tax consequences of the following three transactions: (1) a purchase of the noncash assets with cash, (2) a purchase of the stock of Bill's corporation with cash and Bailey notes, and (3) an asset-for-stock reorganization conducted exclusively with Bailey stock. Upon interviewing Bill, you obtain the following additional information: Bill's business is operated as a C corporation. Bill has a $160,000 adjusted basis in his stock. Accounts payable of $200,000 are outstanding. The corporation has depreciated the building under the straight-line method and has claimed $100,000 in depreciation. The equipment is Sec. 1245 property for which the corporation has claimed $150,000 in depreciation. The after-tax profits in each of the last three years have exceeded $300,000. Bill suspects that some goodwill value exists that is not shown on the balance sheet. No NOL carryovers are available from prior years.

Required: Prepare a memorandum that outlines the tax consequences of each of the three alternative acquisition transactions. Assume that the anticipated cash purchase price is $2.55 million for the noncash assets and $2.6 million for the stock and that the transaction takes place in the current year. How would the acquiring corporation report each of the three alternatives under GAAP?

C:7-78 The following advertisement appeared in *The Wall Street Journal*:

$17 MILLION CASH WITH
ADDITIONAL CASH AVAILABLE
$105 MM TAX LOSS GOOD THROUGH 2025
TIGERA GROUP, INC.
NASDAQ listed w/300 shareholders
WANTS TO ACQUIRE COMPANY
with Net Before Tax Audited Earnings of $7MM to $10MM
Exceptional Opportunity and Participation for Sellers and
Existing Management. Contact: Albert M. Zlotnick or Ross P.
Lederer, Tel: (000)-000-0000 and Fax: (000)-000-0000.

Required: Prepare a memorandum explaining the tax advantages that would accrue to the Tigera Group if it acquired the stock or assets of a profitable corporation in a nontaxable reorganization or a taxable transaction. Would the advantages be the same if a profitable corporation acquired Tigera? In addition, explain any tax law provisions that might restrict the use of these loss carryovers.

TAX RESEARCH PROBLEMS

C:7-79 On January 10 of the current year, Austin Corporation acquires 8% of Travis Corporation's single class of stock for cash. On August 25 of the current year, Austin makes a tender offer to exchange Austin common stock for the remaining Travis shares. Travis shareholders tender an additional 75% of the outstanding Travis stock. The exchange is completed on September 25 of the current year. Austin ends up with slightly more than 83% of the Travis shares. The remaining 17% of the Travis stock is held by about 100 former shareholders of Travis who own small blocks of stock. Your tax manager has asked you to draft a memorandum explaining whether one or both of the two acquisition transactions qualify as a nontaxable reorganization. If part or all of either transaction is taxable to Travis' shareholders, suggest ways to restructure the acquisitions so as to maximize tax benefits of the transaction. Assume that Austin does not want to make a Sec. 338 election.

Matt Bonner, CEO of Travis, asked a question that might be relevant to reporting the transaction: To simplify the corporate structure, can Austin liquidate Travis into Austin without recognizing any gain or loss?

At a minimum you should consult:

- IRC Sec. 368(a)(1)(B)
- Reg. Sec. 1.368-2(c)
- *Eldon S. Chapman, et al. v. CIR*, 45 AFTR 2d 80-1290, 80-1 USTC ¶9330 (1st Cir., 1980)
- *Arden S. Heverly, et al. v. CIR*, 45 AFTR 2d 80-1122, 80-1 USTC ¶9322 (3rd Cir., 1980)

C:7-80 ABC Corporation is the object of a hostile takeover bid by XYZ Corporation. ABC incurs a total of $400,000 in attorneys' fees, accounting fees, and printing costs for information mailed to ABC shareholders in an effort to defeat the XYZ takeover bid. XYZ finally concedes, and ABC remains a separate corporation. What is the appropriate tax treatment of the $400,000 in fees? Would that treatment be different if XYZ succeeds in acquiring ABC? Tax sources you should consult include the following:

- IRC Sec. 162
- IRC Sec. 165
- *INDOPCO, Inc. v. Comm.*, 69 AFTR 2d 92-694, 92-1 USTC ¶50,113 (USSC, 1992)
- *U.S. v. Federated Department Stores, Inc.*, 74 AFTR 2d 94-5519, 94-2 USTC ¶50,418 (S.D. Ohio, 1994)
- *A.E. Staley Manufacturing Co. v. Comm.*, 80 AFTR 2d 97-5060, 97-2 USTC ¶50,521 (7th Cir., 1997)
- Reg. Sec. 1.263(a)-5

C:7-81 Diversified Corporation is a successful bank with ten branches. Al, Bob, and Cathy created Diversified six years ago and own equally all the Diversified stock. Diversified has constructed a new building in downtown Metropolis that houses a banking facility on the first floor, offices for its employees on the second and third floors, and office space to be leased out to third party lessees on the fourth through twelfth floors. Since the building was completed six months ago, approximately 75% of the floor space on the upper floors has been occupied. Pursuant to a plan of reorganization, Diversified proposes to transfer the building to Metropolis Real Estate (MRE) Corporation in exchange for all the MRE common stock. A team of commercial real estate experts has been hired to manage MRE. Following the reorganization, the building will be the only property owned by MRE. Diversified owns no other real estate because it currently leases from third parties the facilities for its ten retail banking branches. Diversified will distribute the MRE common stock ratably to Al, Bob, and Cathy, who will end up with all the Diversified and MRE common stock. Your tax manager has asked you to draft a memorandum explaining whether or not the proposed transaction will satisfy the requirements of a nontaxable divisive reorganization. At a minimum you should consult:

- IRC Sec. 368(a)(1)(D)
- Reg. Sec. 1.355-3(b), (c)
- *Appleby v. Comm.*, 9 AFTR 2d 372, 62-1 USTC ¶9178 (3rd Cir., 1962)

8

CHAPTER

CONSOLIDATED TAX RETURNS

LEARNING OBJECTIVES

After studying this chapter, you should be able to

1. Determine whether a group of corporations is an affiliated group

2. Understand how an affiliated group makes a consolidated return election and how it discontinues the election

3. Calculate consolidated taxable income for a consolidated group

4. Determine whether a transaction is an intercompany transaction

5. Explain the reporting of an intercompany transaction

6. Calculate on a consolidated basis deductions and credits subject to limitations

7. Calculate the carryback or carryover of a consolidated NOL

8. Determine how the SRLY and Sec. 382 loss limitations restrict the use of NOL carrybacks and carryovers

9. Adjust the basis of stock of a subsidiary in a consolidated group

10. Explain the advantages and disadvantages of filing a consolidated tax return

11. Explain the procedures for making a consolidated return election

12. Understand the financial statement implications of various consolidated transactions

Many corporations have complex entity structures. For example, a corporation may have one or more subsidiaries, and some of these subsidiaries may have their own subsidiaries. A group of corporations form into complex entity structures for many reasons. For example, a parent corporation may want to insulate itself from liabilities related to its subsidiaries, or it may want to make it easier to implement a plan that links the compensation of the subsidiary's managers to the subsidiary's performance.

An **affiliated group** of corporations generally is a parent corporation and all its subsidiaries that are at least 80%-owned by the parent and other subsidiaries in the group (this topic will be discussed later in the chapter). The affiliated group has two options for filing its federal income tax returns:

▶ Each member of the group can file a separate tax return that reports its own income, deductions, credits, and other items.[1]

▶ The affiliated group can file a single, consolidated tax return that reports a combined result for all its group members.

If the affiliated group elects to file a **consolidated tax return**, it does not merely add up the members' incomes, deductions, and other items. Instead, the group must make adjustments so that it generally is treated as if it were a single corporation, as discussed in more detail later in the chapter. For example, the capital gains and losses for all group members are netted to determine the deductibility of capital losses against capital gains rather than netting these items separately for each group member. The group also must make adjustments for transactions among themselves, called *intercompany transactions*, so they do not affect the current year's consolidated taxable income.

Some consolidated tax returns include as few as two corporations. Other consolidated tax returns include hundreds of corporations. Most of the nation's largest corporate groups file consolidated tax returns. In 2007, only 43,348 consolidated tax returns were filed, which was less than 3% of all Form 1120s filed. However, these tax returns reported more than 99% of total taxable income and paid more than 99% of total income taxes of all corporations filing Form 1120.[2]

This chapter discusses the requirements for a group of corporations to qualify as an affiliated group that can elect to file a consolidated tax return. It also explains several rules that pertain to computing consolidated taxable income and the consolidated tax liability. The discussion then turns to some issues that arise when corporations enter or leave an affiliated group that is filing a consolidated tax return, such as when subsidiaries are bought and sold. The chapter also considers the advantages and disadvantages of filing a consolidated tax return instead of separate tax returns and discusses some financial statement implications.

DEFINITION OF AN AFFILIATED GROUP

REQUIREMENTS

STOCK OWNERSHIP REQUIREMENTS.   Only an affiliated group of corporations can elect to file a consolidated tax return. A group of corporations must satisfy the following stock ownership requirements to qualify as an affiliated group:

▶ The parent corporation must own directly at least 80% of the stock in one or more includible corporations (defined below).

▶ At least 80% of the stock of *each* corporation in the group (other than the parent corporation) must be owned directly by the parent corporation and other group members.

---

[1] If the affiliated group members file separate tax returns, some special tax rules apply because group members are related taxpayers under Sec. 267. These rules include, but are not limited to, matching of income and deductions (Sec. 267(a)(2)), deferral of loss on intragroup sales (Sec. 267(f)(2)), and

ordinary income recognition on intragroup sales of depreciable property (Sec. 1239). The members also may constitute a controlled group subject to the restrictions of Sec. 1563. See Chapter C:3 for details.
[2] Internal Revenue Service, Statistics of Income Division (*www.irs.gov*).

> ► Both 80% stock ownership requirements must be satisfied in two ways for each includible corporation (other than the parent): the stock owned directly must be at least 80% of the total voting power of all the includible corporation's outstanding stock entitled to vote, and it must be at least 80% of the total value of all the includible corporation's outstanding stock.[3]

EXAMPLE C:8-1 ► P Corporation owns 95% of S1 Corporation's stock, and S1 owns 100% of S2 Corporation's stock. Unrelated individuals own the remainder of S1's stock. P, S1, and S2 comprise an affiliated group because P owns at least 80% of S1's stock, and S1 owns at least 80% of S2's stock. The P-S1-S2 affiliated group can elect to file a consolidated tax return with P as the common parent.[4] ◄

EXAMPLE C:8-2 ► P Corporation owns 90% of S1 Corporation's stock and 35% of S2 Corporation's stock. S1 owns 50% of S2's stock. Unrelated individuals own the remainder of S1's and S2's stock. P, S1, and S2 comprise an affiliated group because P owns at least 80% of S1's stock, and P and S1 together own 85% (50% + 35%) of S2's stock. ◄

EXAMPLE C:8-3 ► Ted (an individual) owns all the stock of Alpha and Beta Corporations. Alpha and Beta are not an affiliated group because a parent-subsidiary relationship is not present even though the same individual owns 100% of each corporation. Alpha and Beta cannot elect to file a consolidated tax return. The Tax Strategy Tip on page C:8-4 suggests ways to restructure the corporations so they qualify as an affiliated group. ◄

EXAMPLE C:8-4 ► S Corporation has 1,000 shares of common stock and 600 shares of preferred stock outstanding. Each share of common stock has two votes and is worth $45. Each share of preferred stock has one vote and is worth $75. P Corporation owns all 1,000 shares of S's common stock and 150 shares of S's preferred stock. Unrelated individuals own the remaining preferred stock.

The total voting power of S's stock is 2,600 [(1,000 × 2) + (600 × 1)] votes, and the total value of S's stock is $90,000 [(1,000 × $45) + (600 × $75)]. P's ownership of S's stock possesses 2,150 [(1,000 × 2) + (150 × 1)] votes and is worth $56,250 [(1,000 × $45) + (150 × $75)]. This ownership is 82.69% (2,150 ÷ 2,600) of S's total voting power and 62.50% ($56,250 ÷ $90,000) of the value of S's stock. Because both 80% stock ownership requirements are not met, P and S are not an affiliated group. ◄

INCLUDIBLE CORPORATION REQUIREMENT. All corporations are includible except certain specified corporations having special tax statuses. Important types of corporations that are not includible are:

► Corporations exempt from tax under Sec. 501

► Life insurance companies subject to tax under Sec. 801[5]

► Foreign corporations[6]

► Regulated investment companies

► Real estate investment trusts

► S corporations

Most of the nation's largest corporations have a great number of subsidiaries, many of which are not part of an affiliated group because they are not includible corporations. Consequently, they cannot be included in a consolidated tax return, and they usually file their own separate corporate tax returns (if required to do so). Moreover, their stock ownership of other group members cannot be counted toward satisfying the 80% stock ownership requirement for an affiliated group.

---

[3] When determining whether these stock ownership requirements are met, nonvoting preferred stock is ignored if it is limited and preferred as to dividends (and does not participate in corporate growth to any significant extent), has redemption and liquidation rights limited to its issue price (plus a reasonable redemption or liquidation premium), and is not convertible into another class of stock (Sec. 1504(a)(4)).

[4] All corporations in this chapter are includible corporations and have a single class of stock unless otherwise indicated.

[5] Two or more Sec. 801 life insurance companies may elect to file a consoli-

dated tax return. If an affiliated group contains one or more Sec. 801 domestic life insurance companies, Sec. 1504(c)(2)(A) permits the parent corporation to elect to treat as includible corporations all such companies that have met the affiliated group stock ownership tests for the five immediately preceding tax years.

[6] Section 1504(d) allows a domestic corporation to elect to treat a 100%-owned Canadian or Mexican corporation as a domestic corporation if such foreign corporation is maintained solely for the purpose of complying with local law regarding title and operation of property.

EXAMPLE C:8-5 ►

ADDITIONAL COMMENT

In Example C:8-5, P, S1, S3, and S4 (but not S2, generally) comprise a parent-subsidiary controlled group. P constructively owns all of S4's stock for controlled group purposes but not for affiliated group purposes. Thus, S4 is in the same controlled group as P, S1, and S3 even though it is not in their affiliated group.

TYPICAL MISCONCEPTION

The terms *controlled group, affiliated group,* and *consolidated group* are easily confused. These terms have different definitions and applications.

TAX STRATEGY TIP

A brother-sister controlled group cannot file a consolidated tax return. One way to convert it into an affiliated group is for the owner(s) of one of the group's corporations to transfer 80% or more of the corporation's stock to one of its sibling corporations in a nontaxable transaction meeting the Sec. 351 requirements (see Chapter C:2). The two corporations, being in a parent-subsidiary relationship, then can make the consolidated return election and begin filing on a consolidated basis. Alternatively, the owner(s) could transfer the stock of all the sibling corporations to a new corporation, e.g., a holding company that would be the common parent.

EXAMPLE C:8-5 ►
P Corporation owns all the stock of S1 and S2 Corporations. S1 owns all of S3 Corporation's stock, and S2 (a foreign corporation) owns all of S4 Corporation's stock. S2 is not a member of the affiliated group because, as a foreign corporation, it is not an includible corporation. P, S1, S3, and S4 are includible corporations, but only P, S1, and S3 qualify as an affiliated group. Although S4 is an includible corporation, it is not a member of the affiliated group because the group's members (P, S1, and S3) do not own at least 80% of S4's stock. S2's ownership of S4's stock is disregarded because S2 is not an includible corporation even though S2 is wholly-owned by a group member. ◄

Under the check-the-box regulations discussed in Chapter C:2, noncorporate entities can elect to be treated as a corporation. A partnership or LLC that makes this election (and that does not elect to be treated as an S corporation) is an affiliated group member and is eligible to participate in a consolidated tax return provided it is an includible corporation and satisfies the stock ownership requirements. If a partnership or LLC does not elect to be treated as a corporation, it cannot be a member of the affiliated group and cannot participate in a consolidated tax return. Instead, the partnership's or LLC's income and losses pass through to each affiliated group member having an ownership interest in it.

COMPARISON WITH CONTROLLED GROUP DEFINITIONS

Chapter C:3 discusses the three types of controlled groups: parent-subsidiary, brother-sister, and combined controlled groups. Special tax rules apply to controlled groups of corporations to prevent them from avoiding taxes. For example, a controlled group's members are limited to a total of $50,000 of taxable income being taxed at 15%, $25,000 being taxed at 25%, and $9,925,000 being taxed at 34%. A brother-sister controlled group cannot elect to file a consolidated tax return because it does not qualify as an affiliated group, as illustrated in Example C:8-3. However, a parent-subsidiary controlled group and the parent-subsidiary portion of a combined controlled group often also qualify as an affiliated group and can elect to file a consolidated tax return if they so qualify.

The criteria for a parent-subsidiary controlled group and those for an affiliated group are similar but not identical. Differences in the criteria include:

▶ The stock ownership requirement for a parent-subsidiary controlled group is at least 80% of voting power *or* value. For an affiliated group, it is at least 80% of voting power *and* value.

▶ Through stock attribution rules, stock owned by certain related persons is taken into account in determining whether a controlled group exists. They are not used to determine whether an affiliated group exists.

▶ The types of corporations excluded from a controlled group differ from those excluded from an affiliated group.

▶ The controlled group definition is tested only on December 31, but the affiliated group definition is tested on each day of the year.

Because of these differences, a corporation could be a member of a controlled group but not be a member of an affiliated group.

CONSOLIDATED TAX RETURN ELECTION

OBJECTIVE 2

Understand how an affiliated group makes a consolidated return election and how it discontinues the election

CONSOLIDATED RETURN REGULATIONS

A consolidated group is an affiliated group of corporations that files a consolidated tax return. The IRC contains very few rules pertaining to consolidated tax returns, and these few rules primarily address the composition of affiliated groups. Instead of enacting voluminous IRC rules, Congress gave the Treasury Department the authority to issue regulations addressing the determination of the consolidated tax liability and the filing of consolidated tax returns. The IRC allows an affiliated group to elect to file a consolidated tax return, but it does so on the condition that all the group's members consent to the consolidated return regulations. The consolidated return regulations have essentially the same authority as the IRC because of the consent requirement and because they are legislative rather than interpretive in nature (see Chapter C:1). As a result, these regulations are seldom challenged in court and even more rarely found invalid.

ADDITIONAL COMMENT

Filing a consolidated tax return does not affect the reporting of other taxes, such as payroll, sales, or property taxes. Also, some states do not allow the filing of consolidated tax returns for state income tax purposes.

TERMINOLOGY. A **consolidated return year** is a corporation's tax year for which it files a consolidated tax return with the other members of its affiliated group. A **separate return year** is a corporation's tax year for which it files a separate tax return or files a consolidated tax return with another affiliated group. A corporation could have a separate return year because it was not a member of the affiliated group or because the group did not file a consolidated tax return.[7]

An affiliated group elects to file its tax return on a consolidated basis by filing a corporate tax return (Form 1120) that includes the income, expenses, etc. of all its members. The group must make the election no later than the due date for the common parent's tax return including any permitted extensions. Each corporation that is a member of the affiliated group during the initial consolidated return year must consent to the election. The Compliance and Procedural Considerations section later in this chapter provides further detail about election process.

TERMINATION OF CONSOLIDATED TAX RETURN FILING

TERMINATION OF THE AFFILIATED GROUP. Once an affiliated group has elected to file a consolidated tax return, it must continue to file on a consolidated basis as long as the affiliated group exists unless the IRS permits it to file separate tax returns. An affiliated group "remains in existence for a tax year if the common parent remains as the common parent and at least one subsidiary that was affiliated with it at the end of the prior year remains affiliated with it at the beginning of the year."[8] The parent corporation need not own the *same* subsidiary throughout the entire tax year nor own any subsidiary throughout the entire tax year as long as the parent owns a subsidiary at the beginning of the current tax year that it owned at the end of the prior tax year.

EXAMPLE C:8-6 ▶ P and S1 Corporations have filed a consolidated tax return for several calendar years. At the close of business on August 31 of the current year, P purchases all of S2 Corporation's stock. At the close of business on September 30, P sells all its S1 stock. The affiliated group, P-S1-S2, must file a consolidated tax return for the current year because P remained the common parent and at least one subsidiary that was affiliated with it at the end of the prior year remained affiliated with it at the beginning of the current year (i.e., S1).

Alternatively, assume the order of the purchase and sale transactions are reversed, i.e., P sells the S1 stock on August 31 and purchases the S2 stock on September 30. In this case, the affiliated group still must file a consolidated tax return for the current year. Even though P did not have a subsidiary from September 1 through September 30, it nevertheless remained as the common parent, and S1 was affiliated with it at the end of the prior year and at the beginning of the current year. In both cases, the consolidated tax return will include S1's and S2's income only for the portion of the year S1 and S2 were in the group. ◀

EXAMPLE C:8-7 ▶ P and S Corporations have filed a consolidated tax return for several calendar years. At the close of business on December 31 of the current year, P sells all its S stock to an unrelated individual. On January 1 of the next year, P purchases all of T Corporation's stock. P and S must file a consolidated tax return for the current year. However, the P-S affiliated group terminates at the end of the current year and a new affiliated group, P-T, forms in the next year. P and T may elect to file a consolidated tax return in the next year but are not required to do so. ◀

ADDITIONAL COMMENT

The IRS seldom grants permission to discontinue the filing of consolidated tax returns when the request relates to a change in the tax situation of the affiliated group that is not related to a tax law change.

GOOD CAUSE REQUEST TO DISCONTINUE CONSOLIDATION. The IRS may give an affiliated group permission to discontinue filing a consolidated tax return, even though the group remains in existence, if it makes a "good cause" request. The IRS ordinarily will grant the request if changes to the IRC or Treasury Regulations having effective dates in

---

[7] Reg. Sec. 1.1502-1.   [8] Reg. Sec. 1.1502-75(d)(1).

that tax year create a substantial adverse effect on the consolidated tax liability for the tax year (relative to what the aggregate tax liability would be if the group members filed separate tax returns).[9]

EFFECTS ON FORMER MEMBERS. The termination of a consolidated group affects its former members in several ways, two of which are examined later in this chapter.

▶ Any gains and losses that have been deferred on intercompany transactions (e.g., profits on inventory sales between group members) may have to be recognized under the acceleration rule.

▶ Consolidated tax attributes (e.g., NOLs, capital losses, tax credits, and charitable contribution carryovers) may have to be allocated among the former group members.

If a corporation departs an affiliated group and had been included in the group's consolidated tax return, it cannot be included again in the group's consolidated tax return (or that of another affiliated group with the same common parent corporation) until after the 60-month period beginning with the first tax year in which the corporation ceased to be a group member.[10] The IRS can waive this five-year rule.

CONSOLIDATED TAXABLE INCOME

ACCOUNTING PERIODS AND METHODS

OBJECTIVE 3

Calculate consolidated taxable income for a consolidated group

ACCOUNTING PERIODS. Beginning with the first year the affiliated group files a consolidated tax return, each subsidiary corporation in the group must adopt the parent corporation's tax year, and the group must file its return using the parent's tax year. The requirement for a common tax year also applies when a new member joins the affiliated group, such as when its stock is acquired.[11] Unless the IRS grants permission otherwise, a subsidiary that leaves a consolidated group must retain its former group's tax year (or adopt the tax year of the acquiring consolidated group, if applicable).

ACCOUNTING METHODS. Each group member determines the accounting methods it uses by applying the same rules as if it were filing a separate tax return unless the IRS grants it permission to change its accounting method.[12] This requirement applies when the group makes a consolidated tax return election and when a new corporation joins an existing consolidated group. Thus, one group member may use the cash method and another group member may use the accrual method with respect to the same consolidated tax return. The possibility of finding a mixture of cash and accrual basis corporations in an affiliated group is limited because of the Sec. 448 restrictions on the use of the cash method by C corporations (see Chapter C:3).

INCOME INCLUDED IN THE CONSOLIDATED TAX RETURN

KEY POINT

Even though members of a consolidated group must use the same tax year-end, members are not required to use the same tax accounting methods. For example, different inventory methods (e.g., LIFO and FIFO) can occur within the same consolidated group.

An affiliated group includes in its consolidated tax return the parent corporation's income for its entire tax year except for any part of the year it was a member of another affiliated group that filed a consolidated tax return. The group includes a subsidiary corporation's income in the consolidated tax return only for the part of the year that it was a group member. The subsidiary's income for any part of the year it was not a group member is included in its own separate tax return or the consolidated tax return of another affiliated group.[13]

EXAMPLE C:8-8 ▶ P and S Corporations were unaffiliated prior to 2011 and filed separate tax returns. P uses a fiscal year ending May 31 as its tax year, and S uses a calendar year. At the close of business on February 12, 2011, P acquires all of S's stock, and the P-S affiliated group elects to file a consol-

---

[9] Reg. Sec. 1.1502-75(c).
[10] Sec. 1504(a)(3).
[11] Reg. Sec. 1.1502-76(a).

[12] Reg. Sec. 1.1502-17(a).
[13] Reg. Sec. 1.1502-76(b)(1)(i).

idated tax return. S must change its tax year to a fiscal year ending May 31. The group's first consolidated tax return will include P's income for June 1, 2010 through May 31, 2011, and S's income for February 13, 2011, through May 31, 2011. S must file a separate, short period tax return for January 1, 2011, through February 12, 2011. ◄

EXAMPLE C:8-9 ▶ P1 Corporation owns all of S Corporation's stock, and the two corporations have filed consolidated tax returns for several years on a calendar year basis. At the close of business on August 8 of the current year, P1 sells all of S's stock to P2 Corporation, which has a September 30 tax year. P2 has filed consolidated tax returns for several years with its other subsidiaries. S must change its tax year from a calendar year to a fiscal year ending September 30 when it leaves the P1 consolidated group and enters the P2 consolidated group. ◄

EXAMPLE C:8-10 ▶ P and S1 Corporations have filed consolidated tax returns for several calendar years. At the close of business on August 31 of the current year, P sells all its S1 stock to an unrelated individual. At the close of business on September 30 of the current year, P purchases all of S2 Corporation's stock from an unrelated individual. S2 had been using a fiscal year ending March 31 as its tax year. As discussed in example C:8-6, the affiliated group, with P as the parent corporation, does not terminate. The current year's consolidated tax return includes P's income for the entire year, S1's income for January 1 through August 31 of the current year, and S2's income for October 1 through December 31 of the current year. S1 must file a short-period, separate tax return for September 1 through December 31 of the current year (unless the IRS grants it permission to change its tax year), and S2 must file a short-period, separate tax return for April 1 through September 30 of the current year. ◄

KEY POINT

Two basic rules determine what income must be included in a consolidated tax return: the common parent's income for the entire tax year and each subsidiary's income for the part of the tax year it is a member of the consolidated group.

A corporation that becomes or ceases to be a member of an affiliated group filing a consolidated tax return generally does so at the end of the day its status changes.[14] A corporation entering the consolidated group will have to file a separate tax return (or participate in the consolidated tax return of the affiliated group in which it previously was a member), and this tax return often will be a short-period return, which is a return for less than one year. However, the separate tax return does not require annualization of the corporation's taxable income.[15]

A corporation entering a consolidated group does not have to change its tax year if it already is using the same tax year as the group. In this case, the group can elect to ratably allocate the entering member's income, except for extraordinary items, between the separate return and consolidated return portions of the year. The group also can make this election for a departing group member that does not have to change its tax year.[16]

WHAT WOULD YOU DO IN THIS SITUATION?

The P-S-T affiliated group has filed consolidated tax returns for many years using the calendar year as its tax year. On October 1, P Corporation created a new subsidiary, X Corporation, with a $10,000 initial capital contribution, and X issued its stock to P. X opened a bank account and obtained a federal tax identification number. X did not conduct any business activities before year-end. Its only income was $125 in interest earned from the bank account. Due to a lack of communication or oversight, P's tax department did not include X's income in the current year's consolidated tax return.

Your CPA firm has provided tax advice to P for several years, but P's tax department has handled the federal tax return filings. Most of your work for P has been in the state and local tax area and on special federal tax assignments. You were aware of the affiliated group's future business plans for creating X. Will the oversight with respect to X disqualify the group from filing a consolidated tax return for the current year and future years? Can you avoid having to file a federal income tax return for X because of the small amount of its income? Does the failure to include X in this year's consolidated tax return prevent it from being included in future years? What advice can you give your client about needing to include X in the consolidated tax return?

---

[14] Reg. Sec. 1.1502-76(b)(1)(ii)(A).
[15] Reg. Sec. 1.1502-76(b)(2)(i).
[16] Reg. Sec. 1.1502-76(b)(2)(ii). The group can make this election only if the entering corporation does not have to change its accounting method

(e.g., entering the group allows the corporation to retain the cash method because the group's gross receipts do not exceed the $5 million limit under Sec. 448(c)).

EXAMPLE C:8-11 ▶ P Corporation acquires all the stock of S Corporation on February 26 of the current year (the 57th day of the year, which is not a leap year). P has been filing consolidated tax returns on a calendar year basis for several years with its other subsidiaries. S previously was unaffiliated and had been filing separate tax returns using a calendar year. S's income for the current year is $730,000 and includes no extraordinary items. The consolidated group can elect to ratably allocate the $730,000 because S does not have to change its tax year when entering the group. If it so elects, $114,000 ($730,000 × (57 days ÷ 365 days)) will be allocated to S's separate tax return for January 1 through February 26, and the other $616,000 ($730,000 × (308 days ÷ 365 days)) will be allocated to the consolidated tax return for the current year. ◀

If the consolidated group does not elect to ratably allocate an entering or departing group member's income, the group must allocate the member's income according to its accounting method, i.e., a closing of its books. This treatment also applies to extraordinary items, even if a ratable allocation is elected, and to an entering or departing member that must change its tax year. Extraordinary items include capital gains and losses, Sec. 1231 gains and losses, NOL carrybacks and carryovers, and several other items that are beyond the scope of this textbook.

CALCULATION OF CONSOLIDATED TAXABLE INCOME AND TAX

To arrive at its consolidated federal income tax liability, the group first must calculate **consolidated taxable income**. The process is more complicated than merely adding the consolidated group members' taxable incomes and losses. Instead, the group must make adjustments so that it generally is treated as if it were a single corporation. The calculation of consolidated taxable income involves the five steps presented in Table C:8-1. Later in the chapter, after discussing the various components of consolidated taxable income, we will discuss the consolidated tax calculation.

INTERCOMPANY TRANSACTIONS

OBJECTIVE 4

Determine whether a transaction is an intercompany transaction

Corporations in an affiliated group filing a consolidated tax return may engage in transactions with each other. The discussion here usually will designate the two consolidated group members involved in the intercompany transaction as S and B Corporations instead of the usual P and S Corporations. This designation makes it easier to remember which group member is the seller (S) or provider of services and which group member is the buyer (B) or recipient of services.

BASIC CONCEPTS

An **intercompany transaction** is a transaction between two corporations that are in the same consolidated group immediately after the transaction.[17] Intercompany transactions include:

▶ S's sale, exchange, contribution, or other transfer of property to B whether or not S recognizes gain or loss

▶ S's performance of services for B, and B's payment or accrual of its expense for the services

▶ S's licensing of technology, renting of property, or lending of money to B, and B's payment or accrual of its expense for these items

▶ A distribution by a subsidiary to its parent corporation in connection with the parent's investment in the subsidiary's stock, such as a dividend or a redemption

In general, S and B are treated as separate entities. S and B each report on their own books any income, gains, deductions, and losses related to intercompany transactions using the same basic rules that would apply if they were unaffiliated corporations. For

---

[17] Reg. Sec. 1.1502-13(b)(1)(i).

▼ **TABLE C:8-1**
Consolidated Taxable Income Calculation

Step 1: Compute each group member's taxable income (or loss) based on the member's own accounting methods as if it were filing its own separate tax return.

Step 2: Adjust each group member's taxable income as follows:
1. Income, gains, and losses on intercompany transactions occurring in the current year may be deferred until a later year.
2. Income, gains, and losses on intercompany transactions occurring in prior years may be taken into account in the current year.
3. Dividends received by one group member from another group member are excluded from the recipient's gross income.

Step 3: Remove certain items from each member's taxable income because they must be computed on a consolidated basis (see Step 5):
1. Section 1231 gains and losses
2. Capital gains and losses
3. Charitable contribution deduction
4. Dividends-received deduction
5. Net operating loss (NOL) deduction
6. U.S. production activities deduction

The result of making the adjustments to a member's taxable income in Steps 2 and 3 is the member's **separate taxable income** (**loss**).

Step 4: Combine the members' separate taxable incomes and losses. This amount is called the group's **combined taxable income**.

Step 5: Adjust the group's combined taxable income for the following items computed on a consolidated basis (see Step 3):
1. Determine and deduct the consolidated Sec. 1231 net loss.
2. Determine the consolidated net capital gain or loss (taking into account any capital loss carrybacks and carryovers and Sec. 1231 gains that are not treated as ordinary income). Add the consolidated net capital gain to combined taxable income.
3. Determine and deduct the consolidated charitable contribution deduction.
4. Determine and deduct the consolidated dividends-received deduction.
5. Determine and deduct the consolidated NOL deduction (taking into account any allowable NOL carryovers and carrybacks).
6. Determine and deduct the consolidated U.S. production activities deduction.

Consolidated taxable income (or consolidated NOL)[18]

ADDITIONAL COMMENT

These adjustments are listed in the same computational order as shown on page C:3-19, but they appear in a different order on an actual tax return.

example, if B purchases some property from S for cash, B's adjusted basis in the property would be B's cost to acquire it, and B's holding period for it would begin the day after B purchases the property.

To determine consolidated taxable income, S and B give special treatment to income, gains, deductions, and losses related to intercompany transactions. Specifically, the consolidated return regulations usually require that S's income, gains, deductions, or losses be deferred, and therefore excluded, in determining consolidated taxable income until a subsequent event occurs for B. These subsequent events include the following situations:

▶ B claims a depreciation, depletion, or amortization deduction on property it acquired in an intercompany transaction.

▶ B sells property it acquired in an intercompany transaction to a party outside the consolidated group.

▶ S or B leaves the consolidated group while B still owns property it acquired from S in an intercompany transaction.

---

[18] Reg. Sec. 1.1502-11.

▶ The corporations in an affiliated group discontinue filing a consolidated tax return and begin filing separate tax returns.

The intercompany transaction rules, in effect, have the members calculate consolidated taxable income as though S and B were a single entity. That is, if S and B were two divisions of a single corporation, any transactions between them would be ignored in computing the single corporation's taxable income. Likewise, consolidated taxable income should reflect only the consolidated group's income, gains, deductions, and losses from transactions with parties outside the group. The intercompany transaction rules adjust the consolidated group members' income, gains, deductions, and losses related to intercompany transactions, which the members reported on their separate books. Thus, the intercompany adjustments transform separate entity treatment into single entity treatment for calculating consolidated taxable income. This coexistence of separate entity treatment and single entity treatment is a challenging aspect of consolidated tax returns.

EXAMPLE C:8-12 ▶

S and B Corporations are members of a consolidated group. S owns marketable securities having a $120,000 basis. S sells the securities to B in the current year for $200,000 cash. S's $80,000 ($200,000 − $120,000) gain is determined and reported on its books on a separate entity basis in the current year. However, the $80,000 gain is not included in the current year's consolidated taxable income. On a single entity basis, the consolidated group did not sell the securities to an outside party, so it makes an adjustment to remove the gain from consolidated taxable income in the current year. B's basis in the securities is its $200,000 cost, and B's holding period begins the day after it purchases the securities from S. The group will take the $80,000 gain into account for consolidated taxable income at a later time, in accordance with the matching and acceleration rules discussed below. ◀

OBJECTIVE 5

Explain the reporting of an intercompany transaction

MATCHING AND ACCELERATION RULES

Treasury Regulations have two principal rules regarding intercompany transactions: the matching rule and the acceleration rule. Unlike many tax rules, the matching and acceleration rules are not detailed and mechanical. Instead, they are broad and conceptual, thereby allowing enough flexibility to apply to the wide variety of intercompany transactions that arise in practice.[19] The purpose of the intercompany transaction rules is to clearly reflect a consolidated group's taxable income by preventing intercompany transactions from creating, accelerating, avoiding, or deferring consolidated taxable income.[20] The following three terms will be used in the discussion of the intercompany transaction rules:[21]

▶ **Intercompany item:** S's income, gain, deduction, and loss from an intercompany transaction

▶ **Corresponding item:** B's income, gain, deduction, and loss from an intercompany transaction or from property acquired in an intercompany transaction

▶ **Recomputed corresponding item:** The corresponding item B would take into account if S and B were divisions of a single corporation and the transaction occurred between those divisions

EXAMPLE C:8-13 ▶

S and B Corporations are members of a consolidated group. S owns property having a $70 basis. S sells this property to B for $100. A few years later, B sells the property to a third party for $110. The sale from S to B is an intercompany transaction. The intercompany item is S's $30 ($100 − $70) gain on its sale of the property to B. The corresponding item is B's $10 ($110 − $100) gain on its sale of the property to the third party. The recomputed corresponding item is the $40 ($110 − $70) gain that B would realize on the sale to the third party had S and B been divisions of a single corporation. ◀

ADDITIONAL COMMENT

The intercompany transaction rules are an excellent example of the additional recordkeeping necessary to file consolidated tax returns.

MATCHING RULE. To determine consolidated taxable income, the matching rule requires a consolidated group to take into account an intercompany item in a manner that produces the same result as if the transaction were between two divisions of a single cor-

---

[19] Preamble to T.D. 8597.
[20] Reg. Sec. 1.1502-13(a)(1). Under Reg. Sec. 1.1502-13(e)(3), a consolidated group can request of the IRS that it take into account items from intercompany items on a separate entity basis. If the IRS grants this request, the group takes into account the items at the time of the intercompany transaction rather than deferring them.
[21] Reg. Secs. 1.1502-13(b)(2), (3), and (4).

poration.[22] That is, the amount of S's intercompany item taken into account for consolidated taxable income is such that, when combined (i.e., matched) with B's corresponding item, the result is the same as if the consolidated group were a single corporation. The amount of S's intercompany item taken into account for consolidated taxable income can be calculated as follows:

> Amount of recomputed corresponding item
> Minus: Amount of B's corresponding item
> _____
> Amount of S's intercompany item taken into account for consolidated taxable income

Working backwards from the desired outcome for consolidated taxable income, the starting point of the calculation is the amount of the recomputed corresponding item. The portion of the desired outcome comprised of B's corresponding item is subtracted out, leaving the amount of S's intercompany item that needs to be taken into account.[23]

EXAMPLE C:8-14 ▶

S and B Corporations are members of a consolidated group. S owns property having a $150 basis. S sells this property to B for $200 in Year 1. In Year 3, B sells the property to an unrelated corporation, X, for $215.

S's intercompany item is the $50 ($200 − $150) gain on its sale of the property to B. B's corresponding item is the $15 ($215 − $200) gain in Year 3 on its sale of the property to X. The recomputed corresponding item is the $65 ($215 − $150) gain in Year 3 that B would realize on the sale to X had S and B been divisions of a single corporation.

Year 1: If S and B were two divisions of a single corporation, the single corporation would realize no gain or loss, so the recomputed corresponding item for Year 1 is zero. B has no gain or loss in Year 1, so its corresponding item is zero. Thus, none of S's gain is taken into account for consolidated taxable income.

Year 3: If S and B were two divisions of a single corporation, it would realize a $65 gain. Subtracting B's $15 corresponding item from this $65 recomputed corresponding item yields the $50 amount of S's intercompany item taken into account for Year 3. Thus, recognition of S's $50 gain in Year 1 is deferred for consolidated taxable income until Year 3. In Year 3, S's $50 gain is matched with B's $15 gain to produce the $65 gain that accrued while the group held the property. ◀

EXAMPLE C:8-15 ▶

TAX STRATEGY TIP

A member of a consolidated group should consider selling property with a built-in loss to a party outside the group rather than to another group member. For example, S Corporation owns Sec. 1231 property with a $15,000 adjusted basis and a $9,000 FMV. If S sells the property to another group member, the $6,000 loss will not be deducted for consolidated taxable income until a later time. If S sells the property to an unrelated third party, the $6,000 loss will be deductible immediately for consolidated taxable income. Thus, the income tax savings from the $6,000 loss is accelerated.

Assume the same facts as in Example C8:14 except B sold the property to X for $180. The intercompany item again is S's $50 gain. However, B's corresponding item now is a $20 ($180 − $200) loss, and the recomputed corresponding item is a $30 ($180 − $150) gain.

Year 1: The property has not yet been sold outside the group, and B has not yet sold the property, so the recomputed corresponding item and B's corresponding item are both zero. None of S's gain is taken into account for consolidated taxable income.

Year 3: The property now has been sold to a person outside the consolidated group. Subtracting B's corresponding item ($20 loss) from the recomputed corresponding item ($30 gain) results in all of S's $50 intercompany item being taken into account for consolidated taxable income ($30 − (− $20) = $50). Note that a negative number is being subtracted because B's corresponding item is a loss. In summary, S's $50 gain is matched with B's $20 loss to produce the net $30 gain that accrued while the group held the property. ◀

ACCELERATION RULE. In some situations, it may not be possible to match S's intercompany item with B's corresponding item to produce the same outcome as if S and B were two divisions of a single corporation. For example, S may sell property to B while they are members of the same consolidated group, but B then departs the group before it has sold the property. In this situation, B's corresponding item will occur when B is outside the consolidated group, so it cannot be matched with S's intercompany item. The acceleration rule requires that the consolidated group take into account S's intercompany item immediately before the time it first becomes impossible to apply the matching rule.[24]

---

[22] Reg. Sec. 1.1502-13(c).
[23] In addition to the timing of income, gain, deduction, or loss, the matching rule requires that various other attributes be redetermined, such as the character and source of such amounts.

[24] Rec. Sec. 1.1502-13(d).

EXAMPLE C:8-16 ▶ Assume the same facts as in Example C8:14 except P, the common parent of S and B, sells all of its B stock to an unrelated corporation, Y, on June 4 of Year 2, which is before B sells the property to X. On that date, B departs the consolidated group, so it becomes impossible to match B's subsequent corresponding item with S's intercompany item. This situation triggers the acceleration rule, and the portion of S's intercompany item that has not yet been taken into account, which is all $50, now is taken into account in Year 2, immediately before the stock sale on June 4. ◀

APPLICATIONS OF MATCHING AND ACCELERATION RULES

The matching and acceleration rules are two principles used to implement the single entity approach to reporting intercompany transactions. The discussion below provides several examples to illustrate the two rules. Unless otherwise stated, S Corporation and B Corporation are in the same affiliated group, with P Corporation as their common parent. Also, the group has filed consolidated tax returns for several years on a calendar year basis.

EXAMPLE C:8-17 ▶ S purchased 1,000 shares of publicly traded stock as an investment several years ago for $175,000. In the current year (Year 1), S sells all the stock to B for $200,000. B sells 400 shares of the stock (40%) to a third party for $78,000 in Year 3, and B sells the other 600 shares (60%) to another third party for $134,000 in Year 5. S's intercompany item is its $25,000 ($200,000 − $175,000) gain on the sale to B. The timing of and extent to which S's intercompany item is taken into account for consolidated taxable income is as follows:

Year 1: No corresponding item or recomputed corresponding item occurs this year because B has not yet sold the stock. Therefore, none of S's $25,000 gain is taken into account.

Year 3: B's corresponding item is its $2,000 ($78,000 − (40% × $200,000)) loss on the sale of 400 shares to the third party. From the perspective of a single entity, the consolidated group acquired the 400 shares for $70,000 (40% × $175,000) and sold them for $78,000, producing an $8,000 gain (the recomputed corresponding item). To achieve this result in consolidated tax-able income, $10,000 of S's intercompany item is taken into account. The $10,000 gain, when matched with B's $2,000 loss, results in the $8,000 gain.

Year 5: B's corresponding item is its $14,000 ($134,000 − (60% × $200,000)) gain on the sale of the 600 shares. The recomputed corresponding item, from a single-entity perspective, is a $29,000 gain ($134,000 − (60% × $175,000)). The remaining $15,000 ($25,000 − $10,000) of S's gain is taken into account. The matching of this $15,000 with B's $14,000 corresponding item produces a $29,000 gain in consolidated taxable income, which is the outcome that would occur if S and B were two divisions of a single corporation. ◀

The timing and extent to which S's $25,000 gain in Example C8:17 is taken into account for consolidated taxable income can be determined by applying the following formula (with losses indicated as negative amounts):

	Year 1	Year 3	Year 5
Recomputed corresponding item	$ 0	$ 8,000	$29,000
Minus: B's corresponding item	0	(2,000)	14,000
S's intercompany item taken into account	$ 0	$10,000	$15,000

The consolidated group can report the three sales made by S and B in Example C8:17 by using a worksheet format such as that illustrated in the consolidated tax return exam-ple in Appendix B (see partial worksheet below). Each transaction initially is reported in the selling corporation's separate tax return column. The adjustments for the deferred gain on S's sale of the stock to B appear as negative and positive entries in the adjustments and eliminations column of the worksheet. The Year 1 negative adjustment removes the $25,000 gain realized on the intercompany transaction from Year 1 consolidated taxable income. The Year 3 and Year 5 positive adjustments restore the deferred gain when B sells the stock outside the consolidated group.

Transaction	Consolidated Taxable Income	Adjustments & Eliminations	S Corporation's Separate Reporting	B Corporation's Separate Reporting
S's sale to B in Year 1	$ –0–	$(25,000)	$25,000	
B's sale to third party in Year 3	8,000	10,000		$(2,000)
B's sale to third party in Year 5	29,000	15,000		14,000
Total	$37,000	$ –0–	25,000	$12,000

EXAMPLE C:8-18 ▶ Assume the same facts as in Example C:8-17 except S's and B's common parent corporation, P, sells all its B stock to a third party in Year 4. B's departure from the consolidated group triggers the acceleration rule in Year 4 because it is not possible to match B's subsequent corresponding item with the $15,000 portion of S's intercompany item that has not yet been taken into account. Thus, the $15,000 is included in Year 4 consolidated taxable income rather than Year 5 consolidated taxable income. The results would be the same if the common parent sold all of S's stock in Year 4 rather than all of B's stock. B still has a $14,000 gain in Year 5, but B includes the gain in its separate tax return (or the consolidated tax return of the affiliated group to which B belongs at that time). ◀

INSTALLMENT SALE OF PROPERTY FROM BUYER TO THIRD PARTY. Under the installment method, if some or all of the proceeds from the sale of property are to be received after the taxable year of sale, the seller spreads recognition of any gain on the sale over the years it collects the proceeds (see Chapter I:11). The installment method does not apply if the seller realizes a loss. Also, in a gain situation, the seller can elect to not use the installment method. Applying the matching rule to an installment sale requires an understanding of how the installment method operates on both a separate and single entity basis.

EXAMPLE C:8-19 ▶ S owns land having a $64,000 basis. In Year 1, S sells the land to B for $90,000. In Year 3, B sells the land to a third party for $100,000. The third party is to pay B $60,000 of the $100,000 in Year 4 and the remaining $40,000 in Year 5. B charges the third party an interest rate acceptable to the IRS on the unpaid balance.

Because S's sale of the land to B is an intercompany transaction, S's $26,000 ($90,000 − $64,000) gain on the sale will not be taken into account until a later time. When B sells the property in Year 3, it realizes a $10,000 ($100,000 − $90,000) gain. Under the installment method, B's gross profit percentage on the sale is 10% ($10,000 ÷ $100,000), so B has a $6,000 (10% × $60,000) corresponding item in Year 4 and a $4,000 (10% × $40,000) corresponding item in Year 5. From the perspective of a single entity, the consolidated group acquired the land for $64,000 and sold it for $100,000, which produces a $36,000 gain. The group's gross profit percentage is 36% ($36,000 ÷ $100,000), so the recomputed corresponding items are $21,600 (36% × $60,000) in Year 4 and $14,400 (36% × $40,000) in Year 5.

S's $26,000 gain on the intercompany transaction is taken into account for consolidated taxable income such that, when matched with B's corresponding items, they combine to be the same as the recomputed corresponding items as follows:

	Year 1	Year 3	Year 4	Year 5
Recomputed corresponding item	$–0–	$–0–	$21,600	$14,400
Minus: B's corresponding item	–0–	–0–	6,000	4,000
S's intercompany item taken into account	$–0–	$–0–	$15,600	$10,400 ◀

In Example C:8-19, all of S's $26,000 gain is removed in the calculation of Year 1 consolidated taxable income, $15,600 of it is restored in the calculation of Year 4 consolidated taxable income, and the other $10,400 of it is restored in Year 5.[25]

---

[25] Reg. Sec. 1.1502-13(c)(7) Example 5.

Transaction	Consolidated Taxable Income	Adjustments & Eliminations	S Corporation's Separate Reporting	B Corporation's Separate Reporting
S's sale to B in Year 1	$ –0–	$(26,000)	$26,000	
B's sale to third party in Year 3	–0–			
B's collection of first installment in Year 4	21,600	15,600		$ 6,000
B's collection of second installment in Year 5	14,400	10,400		4,000
Total	$36,000	$ –0–	$26,000	$10,000

EXAMPLE C:8-20 ▶ Assume the same facts as in Example C:8-19 except B sells the land to a third party for $80,000 in Year 3. The third party is to pay B $48,000 of the $80,000 in Year 4 and the remaining $32,000 in Year 5. B's corresponding item is now its $10,000 ($80,000 − $90,000) loss in Year 3. Unlike with a gain, the seller recognizes a loss under the installment method in the year of sale rather than spreading the loss over the years it receives the installment payments. From a single entity perspective, the consolidated group realizes a $16,000 ($80,000 − $64,000) gain, which produces a 20% ($16,000 ÷ $80,000) gross profit percentage. The group's recomputed corresponding items are $9,600 (20% × $48,000) in Year 4 and $6,400 (20% × $32,000) in Year 5. S's $26,000 gain on the intercompany transaction taken into account for consolidated taxable income is determined as follows:

	Year 1	Year 3	Year 4	Year 5
Recomputed corresponding item	$–0–	$ –0–	$9,600	$6,400
Minus: B's corresponding item	–0–	(10,000)	–0–	–0–
S's intercompany item taken into account	$–0–	$10,000	$9,600	$6,400 ◀

Example C:8-20 illustrates the process underlying the matching rule. It requires an understanding of how the transactions affect each of the group members on a separate entity basis and how the transactions would affect the corporations in the consolidated group if they were a single entity. Applying the same worksheet format used above, Example C:8-20 is presented as:

Transaction	Consolidated Taxable Income	Adjustments & Eliminations	S Corporation's Separate Reporting	B Corporation's Separate Reporting
S's sale to B in Year 1	$ –0–	$(26,000)	$26,000	
B's sale to third party in Year 3	–0–	10,000		$(10,000)
B's collection of first installment in Year 4	9,600	9,600		
B's collection of second installment in Year 5	6,400	6,400		
Total	$16,000	$ –0–	$26,000	$(10,000)

ADDITIONAL COMMENT

Section 168(i)(7) prevents B from obtaining a completely new depreciation schedule for property purchased from S, thereby preventing B from accelerating depreciation deductions.

INTERCOMPANY SALE OF DEPRECIABLE PROPERTY. When S sells depreciable property to B in an intercompany transaction, Sec. 168(i)(7) requires B to continue S's depreciation method and recovery period to the extent that B's basis equals or is less than S's adjusted basis. Any excess of B's basis over S's adjusted basis is treated as newly acquired property, so B uses the appropriate MACRS depreciation method and recovery period for this excess.[26] To the extent B's basis carries over from S, B's depreciation for the property is the same each year as S's depreciation would have been had S not sold the property.

S's intercompany item is its gain or loss on the sale of the depreciable property to B.[27] B's corresponding items are the depreciation deductions it takes for the property (and any gain or loss it recognizes on a subsequent sale of the property). The recomputed corresponding items are the depreciation deductions the consolidated group would have if S and B were two divisions of a single corporation.

EXAMPLE C:8-21 ▶

In Year 1, S purchases five-year MACRS property for $10,000. On January 3 of Year 3, S sells the property to B for $9,000. The mid-year convention applies, S does not elect Sec. 179 expensing, and S does not claim bonus depreciation. Accordingly, S claims the following depreciation deductions for the property (percentages are from Appendix C, Table 1):

Year 1: $10,000 × 20% = $2,000
Year 2: $10,000 × 32% = $3,200

In an intercompany sale of depreciable property, S and B prorate the depreciation deduction on a monthly basis, with B receiving the depreciation for the month of sale.[28] Because the intercompany sale occurred in January, S receives no Year 3 depreciation deduction for the property. S's adjusted basis in the property is $4,800 ($10,000 − $2,000 − $3,200), so it has a $4,200 ($9,000 − $4,800) gain on its sale to B.

B takes a $9,000 basis in the property, but it divides this basis into two portions to calculate its depreciation deductions. To the extent its basis equals or is less than S's adjusted basis ($4,800), B continues S's depreciation method and recovery period. B's $4,200 ($9,000 − $4,800) basis in excess of S's adjusted basis is treated as newly acquired five-year MACRS property. This $4,200 step-up in basis and S's $4,200 gain both result from B paying $4,200 more than S's adjusted basis for the property. B's depreciation deductions each year, which are its corresponding items, are calculated as follows:

ADDITIONAL COMMENT

Prop. Reg. Sec. 1.168-2(d)(3) provides a method for calculating B's depreciation when its basis for depreciable property purchased from S is less than S's adjusted basis.

		Depreciation on		
Year	Calculation	Carryover Basis	Step-Up in Basis	Total Depreciation
Year 3	$10,000 × 19.20% $4,200 × 20.00%	$1,920	$ 840	$2,760
Year 4	$10,000 × 11.52% $4,200 × 32.00%	1,152	1,344	2,496
Year 5	$10,000 × 11.52% $4,200 × 19.20%	1,152	806	1,958
Year 6	$10,000 × 5.76% $4,200 × 11.52%	576	484	1,060
Year 7	$4,200 × 11.52%		484	484
Year 8	$4,200 × 5.76%		242	242
Total		$4,800	$4,200	$9,000

The consolidated group's recomputed corresponding items are the depreciation deductions that would arise based on S's original $10,000 cost to purchase the property:

Year 3: $10,000 × 19.20% = $1,920
Year 4: $10,000 × 11.52% = $1,152
Year 5: $10,000 × 11.52% = $1,152
Year 6: $10,000 × 5.76% = $ 576

Subtracting B's corresponding items from the group's recomputed corresponding items, S's $4,200 gain on the sale to B will be taken into account for consolidated taxable income as follows (the amounts are negative because these are deduction items):

---

[26] Prop. Reg. Sec. 1.168-5(b)(7).
[27] Intercompany sales of property that will be depreciated in the purchasing group member's hands generally result in ordinary income under Sec. 1239 because the selling and purchasing consolidated group members usually are

members of a controlled group as well and, therefore, are related parties under Sec. 1239(b).
[28] Prop. Reg. Sec. 1.168-5(b)(4)(i).

	Year 3	Year 4	Year 5	Year 6	Year 7	Year 8
Recomputed corresponding item	$(1,920)	$(1,152)	$(1,152)	$ (576)	$ –0–	$ –0–
Minus: B's corresponding item	(2,760)	(2,496)	(1,958)	(1,060)	(484)	(242)
S's intercompany item taken into account	$ 840	$ 1,344	$ 806	$ 484	$ 484	$ 242

Applying the matching rule to this intercompany transaction causes S to report gain in consolidated taxable income to the same extent as the depreciation deductions attributable to B's step-up in basis. The two amounts offset, with only the depreciation deduction on the carryover portion of B's basis having an effect on consolidated taxable income. The following worksheet summarizes the consolidated group's reporting of these items:

Transaction	Consolidated Taxable Income	Adjustments & Eliminations	S Corporation's Separate Reporting	B Corporation's Separate Reporting
S's sale to B in Year 3	$ –0–	$(4,200)	$4,200	
B's depreciation of the property in:				
Year 3	(1,920)	840		$(2,760)
Year 4	(1,152)	1,344		(2,496)
Year 5	(1,152)	806		(1,958)
Year 6	(576)	484		(1,060)
Year 7	–0–	484		(484)
Year 8	–0–	242		(242)
Total	$(4,800)	$ –0–	$4,200	$(9,000)

EXAMPLE C:8-22 ▶ Assume the same facts as in Example C:8-21 except S's parent corporation, P, sells all its S stock on December 31 of Year 4. P continues to own all of B's stock. Because S no longer is a member of the consolidated group after that date, the remaining group can no longer match S's deferred gain on the intercompany transaction with B's post-Year 4 corresponding items. Consequently, the acceleration rule is triggered. Of S's $4,200 gain, the group has reported $2,184 ($840 in Year 3 + $1,344 in Year 4) in its consolidated taxable income. The consolidated group therefore must report the remaining $2,016 ($4,200 − $2,184) of deferred gain immediately before S departs the group. B continues to depreciate the property's total basis (carryover and step-up) as in the last column of the above schedules. ◀

PERFORMANCE OF SERVICES. Some intercompany transactions involve one consolidated group member performing services for another group member. For example, one group member may rent property or lend money to another group member. The matching rule generally applies in a manner similar to that for intercompany property transactions, matching S's intercompany item to B's corresponding item so their net effect results in the recomputed corresponding item.

EXAMPLE C:8-23 ▶ S rents land to B for $25,000 per year. S and B both use the accrual method of accounting. S's rental income is its intercompany item, and B's rental expense is its corresponding item. The recomputed corresponding item is zero because, from the perspective of a single corporation with divisions S and B, the single entity would have no rental income or expense. The group will take into account $25,000 ($0 − (−$25,000)) of S's annual rental income as B reports the $25,000 annual rental expense. Note that B's corresponding item is negative because it is an expense. S's rental income and B's rental expense are recognized simultaneously for consolidated taxable income and thus offset each other. ◀

EXAMPLE C:8-24 ▶ On March 1 of Year 1, S lends B $100,000 for one year. B pays the $100,000 debt, plus 12% annual interest, to S on March 1 of Year 2. S and B each use the accrual method of accounting. In determining their separate taxable incomes, S reports interest income of $10,000 ($100,000 × 12% × 10/12) in Year 1 and $2,000 ($100,000 × 12% × 2/12) in Year 2, and B reports interest expense of $10,000 in Year 1 and $2,000 in Year 2. The recomputed corresponding item is zero in Year 1 and in Year 2. Application of the matching rule results in S's intercompany items being reported in consolidated taxable income at the same time S reports them in its separate taxable income.

	Year 1	Year 2
Recomputed corresponding item	$ –0–	$ –0–
Minus: B's corresponding item	(10,000)	(2,000)
S's intercompany item taken into account	$ 10,000	$ 2,000	◄

Applying the worksheet format used for the earlier intercompany transactions, S and B report the interest income and expense as follows:

Year	Consolidated Taxable Income	Adjustments & Eliminations	S Corporation's Separate Reporting	B Corporation's Separate Reporting
Year 1	$–0–		$10,000	$(10,000)
Year 2	–0–		2,000	(2,000)
Total	$–0–		$12,000	$(12,000)

If S and B use different accounting methods, they might not report their respective sides of the intercompany transaction at the same time in determining their separate taxable incomes. The principle of the matching rule still applies, with S's intercompany item being matched with B's corresponding item.

EXAMPLE C:8-25 ► Assume the same facts as in Example C:8-24 except B uses the cash method of accounting. For separate taxable income, S reports interest income of $10,000 in Year 1 and $2,000 in Year 2, and B reports interest expense of $0 in Year 1 and $12,000 in Year 2. For consolidated taxable income, all $12,000 of S's interest income is reported in Year 2 under the matching rule.

	Year 1	Year 2
Recomputed corresponding item	$–0–	$ –0–
Minus: B's corresponding item	–0–	(12,000)
S's intercompany item taken into account	$–0–	$ 12,000	◄

ADDITIONAL COMMENT

Corporations filing a consolidated tax return are related parties under Sec. 267 because they also are members of the same controlled group. One consequence of their related status is that B cannot deduct its expense from an intercompany transaction with S before S reports its income from the transaction. This rule also can apply to transactions with corporations that are in the same controlled group but not the same consolidated group, such as brother-sister corporations.

Applying the worksheet format used previously, S and B report the interest income and expense as follows:

Year	Consolidated Taxable Income	Adjustments & Eliminations	S Corporation's Separate Reporting	B Corporation's Separate Reporting
Year 1	$–0–	$(10,000)	$10,000	$ –0–
Year 2	–0–	10,000	2,000	(12,000)
Total	$–0–	$ –0–	$12,000	$(12,000)

In some circumstances, B might capitalize its expenditure for the services S provides. B's corresponding item still would be its income, gain, deduction, and loss from an intercompany transaction or from property in an intercompany transaction. However, the corresponding item might occur at a time later than S's intercompany item, requiring that some or all of S's intercompany item be deferred under the matching rule.

EXAMPLE C:8-26 ► S operates a drilling business, and B operates a farming business. S and B both use the accrual method of accounting. In Year 1, S drills a water well and charges B $9,000 for the service. S incurs $8,000 of expenses in drilling the well, realizing a $1,000 profit. B capitalizes the $9,000 cost of its well and amortizes it over the four-year period Years 2 through 5.

From a single entity perspective, the group's cost of the well is $8,000, so its recomputed corresponding item is $2,000 ($8,000 ÷ 4 years) for each of Years 2 through 5. B's annual corresponding item is its $2,250 ($9,000 ÷ 4 years) amortization deduction. S's $1,000 intercompany item is reported for consolidated taxable income as follows:

	Year 1	Year 2	Year 3	Year 4	Year 5
Recomputed corresponding item	$–0–	$(2,000)	$(2,000)	$(2,000)	$(2,000)
Minus: B's corresponding item	–0–	(2,250)	(2,250)	(2,250)	(2,250)
S's intercompany item taken into account	$–0–	$ 250	$ 250	$ 250	$ 250

Transaction	Consolidated Taxable Income	Adjustments & Eliminations	S Corporation's Separate Reporting	B Corporation's Separate Reporting
Drilling of well in Year 1	$ –0–	$(1,000)	$1,000	
Amortization deductions:				
Year 2	(2,000)	250		$(2,250)
Year 3	(2,000)	250		(2,250)
Year 4	(2,000)	250		(2,250)
Year 5	(2,000)	250		(2,250)
Total	$(8,000)	$ –0–	$1,000	$(9,000) ◄

INTERCOMPANY SALE OF INVENTORY. Many consolidated groups have sales of inventory within the group. For example, one group member (S) may manufacture goods and sell them to another group member (B). B subsequently resells the goods to third-party customers. The matching rule applies in this situation and allows the consolidated group to defer taxation of profit from the intercompany transaction until B sells the inventory to a third party.[29]

EXAMPLE C:8-27 ► P, S, and B Corporations comprise a consolidated group with P being the common parent of subsidiaries S and B. S begins selling inventory items to B in Year 1, and both subsidiaries use the first-in, first-out (FIFO) inventory method. Information and treatment regarding S's inventory sales to B during Years 1 and 2 follow:

Year 1: S sells inventory to B for $400,000. The cost of this inventory to S was $300,000. Thus, S realizes a profit of $100,000 ($400,000 − $300,000) on the sale, which is S's intercompany item. During the year, B sells 88% of this inventory to third parties for $414,000. B's cost for this inventory is $352,000 ($400,000 × 0.88). Thus, B realizes a profit of $62,000 ($414,000 − $352,000) on the sale to third parties, which is B's corresponding item. S's cost for this same inventory had been $264,000 ($300,000 × 0.88). Thus, S realized a profit of $88,000 ($352,000 − $264,000) when it sold this portion of the inventory to B, which is S's intercompany item taken into account. From the perspective of a single entity, the consolidated group realizes a profit of $150,000 ($414,000 − $264,000) on the sale to third parties, which is the recomputed corresponding item. At year-end, B's inventory includes the remaining 12% of inventory it purchased from S in Year 1. B's cost in this remaining inventory is $48,000 ($400,000 × 0.12), and S's cost for this same inventory was $36,000 ($300,000 × 0.12). Thus, the remaining inventory contains a deferred profit of $12,000 ($48,000 − $36,000). Applying the matching rule, these transactions are summarized as follows:

Recomputed corresponding item	$150,000
Minus: B's corresponding item	(62,000)
S's intercompany item taken into account	$88,000

Year 2: B sells to third parties the remaining inventory it purchased from S in Year 1. The selling price is $55,000 and is deemed sold first in Year 2 under FIFO. Thus, B realizes a profit of $7,000 ($55,000 − $48,000) on this sale. From the perspective of a single entity, the consolidated group realizes a profit of $19,000 ($55,000 − $36,000) on this sale to third parties.

Also in Year 2, S sells additional inventory to B for $550,000. The cost of this inventory to S was $420,000. Thus, S realizes a profit of $130,000 ($550,000 − $420,000) on the sale. During the year, B sells 80% of this inventory to third parties for $515,000. B's cost for this inventory is $440,000 ($550,000 × 0.80). Thus, B realizes a profit of $75,000 ($515,000 − $440,000) on the sale to third parties. S's cost for this same inventory had been $336,000 ($420,000 × 0.80). Thus, S realized a profit of $104,000 ($440,000 − $336,000) when it sold this portion of the inventory to B. From the perspective of a single entity, the consolidated group realizes a profit of $179,000 ($515,000 − $336,000) on this sale to third parties. At year-end, B's inventory includes

---

[29] Reg. Sec. 1.1502-13(e)(1) provides simplifying rules for intercompany inventory sales when S or B uses a dollar-value LIFO method to account for intercompany transactions.

the remaining 20% of inventory it purchased from S in Year 2. B's cost in this remaining inventory is $110,000 ($550,000 × 0.20), and S's cost for this same inventory was $84,000 ($420,000 × 0.20). Thus, the remaining inventory contains a deferred profit of $26,000 ($110,000 − $84,000). Applying the matching rule, these transactions are summarized as follows:

Recomputed corresponding item ($19,000 + $179,000)	$198,000
Minus: B's corresponding item ($7,000 + $75,000)	(82,000)
S's intercompany item taken into account ($12,000 + $104,000)	$116,000

Applying the worksheet format for the intercompany transactions in Years 1 and 2, S and B report their inventory profits as follows:

Year	Consolidated Taxable Income	Adjustments & Eliminations	S Corporation's Separate Reporting	B Corporation's Separate Reporting
Year 1	$150,000	$(12,000)	$100,000	$ 62,000
Year 2	198,000	(14,000)*	130,000	82,000
Total	$348,000	$(26,000)	$230,000	$144,000

* Positive $12,000 adjustment for inventory S sold to B in Year 1 that B sells to third parties in Year 2, minus $26,000 adjustment for inventory S sells to B in Year 2 that B has not sold to third parties by the end of Year 2. ◄

EXAMPLE C:8-28 ▶ Assume the same facts as in Example C:8-27 except P sells all of B's stock on December 31 of Year 2. Because B no longer is a member of the consolidated group after that date, the remaining group cannot match S's intercompany items with B's corresponding items. Thus, the acceleration rule is triggered, and the $26,000 ($110,000 − $84,000) of S's intercompany inventory profits that otherwise would be included in Year 3 consolidated taxable income is now included in Year 2 consolidated taxable income. ◄

RELEVANCE OF MATCHING AND ACCELERATION RULES

The matching and acceleration rules are broad and conceptual, thereby allowing enough flexibility to apply to a wide variety of intercompany transactions that arise in practice. Applying the rules can seem tedious and irrelevant, possibly causing one to wonder why it is necessary to determine the intercompany items and corresponding items if the consolidated group's taxable income ultimately reflects the recomputed corresponding items. In response, we can cite the following reasons why the rules are important (some of which receive further discussion later in this chapter). The rules affect:

▶ The time for recognizing intercompany transactions, i.e., how much gain or loss to recognize currently or in the future.

▶ The amount by which a parent corporation adjusts the basis of stock it owns in its subsidiary corporations.

▶ The amount of consolidated net operating losses attributed to a particular consolidated group member.

▶ The amount of a member's separate return net operating losses that the group may use.

▶ The amount of each member's earning and profits (E&P).

Topic Review C:8-1 summarizes the intercompany transaction rules.

ITEMS COMPUTED ON A CONSOLIDATED BASIS

OBJECTIVE 6

Calculate on a consolidated basis deductions and credits subject to limitations

An affiliated group filing a consolidated tax return generally is treated as if it were a single corporation. To accomplish this treatment, the group calculates on a consolidated basis its deductions and credits that are subject to limitations. The computation of these items for a consolidated tax return is similar to their computation for an unaffiliated corporation. The group also must calculate its regular tax and its alternative minimum tax on a consolidated basis.

Topic Review C:8-1

Reporting Intercompany Transactions

INTERCOMPANY TRANSACTIONS

1. **Intercompany transaction:** A transaction between two corporations that are in the same consolidated group immediately after the transaction.
2. **Three concepts of reporting intercompany transactions:**
   a. **Intercompany item:** The selling corporation's income, gain, deduction, and loss from an intercompany transaction
   b. **Corresponding item:** The buying corporation's income, gain, deduction, and loss from an intercompany transaction or from property acquired in an intercompany transaction
   c. **Recomputed corresponding item:** The corresponding item the buying corporation would have if it and the selling corporation were two divisions of a single corporation and the transaction occurred between those divisions
3. **Separate entity concept:** The selling and buying corporations involved in the intercompany transaction generally are treated as separate entities in determining the amount of income, gain, deduction, and loss that each one incurs.
4. **Matching rule:** The selling corporation's intercompany item is taken into account for consolidated taxable income so that, when it is combined with the buying corporation's corresponding item, the result is the same as if the consolidated group were a single corporation (i.e., the recomputed corresponding item).
5. **Acceleration rule:** If it is not possible to apply the matching rule to match the selling corporation's intercompany item with the buying corporation's corresponding item, the consolidated group takes into account the selling corporation's intercompany item immediately before the time it first becomes impossible to apply the matching rule.
6. **Examples of events that can trigger recognition of an intercompany item:**
   a. The buying corporation sells to a third party property acquired in an intercompany transaction (matching rule).
   b. The buying corporation claims depreciation, amortization, or depletion deductions for property acquired in an intercompany transaction (matching rule).
   c. The selling corporation or buying corporation leaves the consolidated group (acceleration rule).
   d. The corporations in the affiliated group discontinue filing a consolidated tax return and begin filing separate tax returns (acceleration rule).

KEY POINT

The consolidated charitable contribution deduction could be greater than or less than the total of the charitable contribution deductions if the group filed separate tax returns. The outcome depends on each individual situation.

CHARITABLE CONTRIBUTION DEDUCTION

Chapter C:3 discusses the charitable contribution deduction for an unaffiliated C corporation. Recall that the deduction is limited to 10% of adjusted taxable income. Adjusted taxable income is the corporation's taxable income computed without regard to its charitable contribution deduction, NOL carryback, capital loss carryback, dividends-received deduction, and U.S. production activities deduction. The corporation can carry forward to the five succeeding tax years its charitable contributions that exceed the 10% limitation. Any unused contributions remaining at the end of the five-year carryover period expire.

The consolidated charitable contribution deduction is calculated by first aggregating the consolidated group members' charitable contributions. The deductibility of the aggregate charitable contributions is limited to 10% of consolidated adjusted taxable income, and any aggregate contributions exceeding the 10% limitation carry forward for five years.[30] Adjusted consolidated taxable income is determined similarly to an unaffiliated corporation's adjusted taxable income except the group uses consolidated amounts.[31]

EXAMPLE C:8-29 ▶ P, S1, and S2 Corporations comprise a consolidated group. The group members have the following charitable contributions and adjusted taxable incomes for the current year:

Group Member	Charitable Contributions	Adjusted Taxable Income
P	$12,500	$150,000
S1	5,000	(40,000)
S2	2,000	10,000
Total	$19,500	$120,000

---

[30] If a member leaves the consolidated group before the group fully uses its charitable contribution carryovers, the departing member takes with it its allocable share of the unused carryover. The allocation is based on the relative amount of the member's charitable contributions (when compared to the group's total charitable contributions) for the consolidated return year in which they were made. The allocation is similar to that for unused NOL carryovers discussed later in the chapter.

[31] Reg. Sec. 1.1502-24.

SELF-STUDY QUESTION

In Example C:8-29, what would be each corporation's current year charitable contribution deduction if the group filed separate tax returns?

ANSWER

$12,500 for P, $0 for S1, and $1,000 for S2. The total of these three deductions is $1,500 more than the $12,000 consolidated charitable contribution deduction. However, the total of the charitable contribution carryovers is $1,500 less than the consolidated charitable contribution carryover.

ADDITIONAL COMMENT

An affiliated group's ordinary gain or loss and capital gain or loss often will be different when it nets its various gains and losses on a consolidated basis rather than on a separate basis.

The consolidated group's charitable contribution deduction is limited to $12,000 (10% × $120,000). Because its aggregate charitable contributions exceed this limitation, it can deduct only $12,000 in the current year. The $7,500 ($19,500 − $12,000) excess charitable contribution carries over to the next five tax years in successive order until used. If not used, they expire at the end of the five-year carryover period.

NET SEC. 1231 GAIN OR LOSS

An unaffiliated corporation determines its net Sec. 1231 gain or loss by netting its recognized gains and losses from the sale or exchange of Sec. 1231 property (see Chapter I:13). The corporation treats any net Sec. 1231 loss as an ordinary loss. A net Sec. 1231 gain generally is treated as a long-term capital gain, although some or all of it may be converted to ordinary income if the corporation has any unrecaptured Sec. 1231 losses from the prior five years (the lookback rule). A consolidated group determines its net Sec. 1231 gain or loss by netting the members' Sec. 1231 gains and losses on a consolidated basis rather than for each member separately.[32]

CAPITAL GAINS AND LOSSES

Chapter C:3 discusses the treatment of capital gains and losses for an unaffiliated corporation. The corporation's capital gain net income or net capital loss is determined by netting its capital gains, capital losses, and net Sec. 1231 gains (to the extent they are not recaptured as ordinary income under the five-year lookback rule). Unlike with individuals, a corporation's net capital gain receives no preferential tax treatment. Also, a corporation cannot deduct a net capital loss. Instead, it must carry back the net capital loss to the three previous tax years and five following tax years, using the net capital loss in the earliest year(s) possible.

In a similar manner, the consolidated group determines its capital gain net income or net capital loss by netting the group members' capital gains and capital losses, as well as any consolidated net Sec. 1231 gain not recaptured under the lookback rule. If the group has a net capital loss for a tax year, it cannot deduct it in that year but must carry it back to the three preceding and forward to the five succeeding tax years. The consolidated net capital loss can offset any consolidated net capital gain in those eight carryback and carryover years.[33]

EXAMPLE C:8-30 ▶

KEY POINT

One member of the consolidated group may have a gain or loss from the sale of Sec. 1231 property or a capital asset to another group member. This sale is an example of an *intercompany transaction*, discussed earlier in the chapter. The consolidated group defers recognition of the gain or loss until a later time, and it does not include the gain or loss in the consolidated Sec. 1231 netting process or in the consolidated capital gain and loss netting process until that time.

P and S Corporations comprise a consolidated group. The group has no capital loss carryovers, and it has recognized no net Sec. 1231 losses in the previous five years. During the current year, the group reports $200,000 of ordinary income before taking into account the following gains and losses:

	Capital Gains and Losses				
Group Member	Short-Term		Long-Term		Net Sec. 1231 Gain (Loss)
	Gains	Losses	Gains	Losses	
P	$ –0–	$ –0–	$ 500	$1,500	$(3,100)
S	2,000	7,500	6,000	–0–	8,000
	$2,000	$7,500	$6,500	$1,500	$ 4,900

The P-S group's $4,900 consolidated net Sec. 1231 gain is treated as a long-term capital gain and is combined with the group's $5,000 ($6,500 − $1,500) net long-term capital gain and its $5,500 ($2,000 − $7,500) net short-term capital loss. Thus, the current year consolidated capital gain net income is $4,400 ($4,900 + $5,000 − $5,500). This amount is taxed at the regular corporate tax rates. ◀

DEPARTING GROUP MEMBERS' CAPITAL LOSSES. A particular issue arises with consolidated groups of corporations that does not arise with unconsolidated corporations. This issue pertains to the carryback and carryover of unused capital losses when the composition of the consolidated group changes. For example, suppose a consolidated group has capital loss carryovers when the parent corporation sells the stock in one of its

[32] Reg. Sec. 1.1502-23. [33] Reg. Sec. 1.1502-22.

ADDITIONAL COMMENT

In Example C:8-30, if P and S had filed separate tax returns, P's $3,100 net Sec. 1231 loss would have been treated as an ordinary loss, and P would have had a $1,000 ($500 − $1,500) net capital loss that would not have been deductible in the current year. S's $8,000 net Sec. 1231 gain would have been treated as a long-term capital gain, making S's capital gain net income $8,500 ($8,000 + $6,000 + $2,000 − $7,500).

ADDITIONAL COMMENT

The IRC does not allow corporations to forego the three-year carryback period for net capital losses. This restriction can complicate matters when some of the current year consolidated group members filed separate tax returns during any of the three prior years because they were not group members then.

subsidiaries. To what extent are the unused capital losses available to the departed group member on its separate tax return versus the remaining group members on their consolidated tax return? The group must determine the portion of the net capital loss attributable to the departing group member, and this portion is available to the departing group member and is not available to the remaining consolidated group members. The apportionment procedure is similar to that for NOLs for departing group members, which will be discussed later in the chapter.

SRLY LIMITATION. A consolidated group member may have net capital losses available from another tax year in which it was not member of the group. The consolidated group can use the net capital loss from this *separate return limitation year*, but the group's use of a member's SRLY net capital loss is limited to the member's cumulative contribution to consolidated capital gain net income. This restriction on the use of net capital losses is similar to the SRLY limitation on the use of NOLs, which will be discussed later in the chapter.

DIVIDENDS-RECEIVED DEDUCTION

Chapter C:3 discusses the dividends-received deduction for an unaffiliated corporation. Corporations that own less than 20% of the distributing corporation's stock may deduct 70% of the dividends received. If the shareholder (distributee) corporation owns 20% or more of the distributing corporation's stock but less than 80% of such stock, it may deduct 80% of the dividends received. The dividends-received deduction is limited to 70% of taxable income computed without regard to any NOL deduction, any capital loss carryback, the dividends-received deduction itself, or the U.S. production activities deduction. The limitation is 80% of such taxable income for dividends received qualifying for the 80% deduction. The limitation does not apply if, after taking into account the full dividends-received deduction, the corporation has an NOL for the year.

DIVIDENDS RECEIVED FROM NON-GROUP MEMBERS. The calculation of the consolidated dividends-received deduction for dividends received from corporations that are not members of the consolidated group is similar to the calculation for an unaffiliated corporation. The group members' dividends-received deductions, calculated without regard to the limitation on them, are added. The sum of these dividends-received deductions is limited to 70% (or 80%) of consolidated taxable income computed without regard to any NOL deduction, any capital loss carryback, the dividends-received deduction itself, or the U.S. production activities deduction. Similar to an unaffiliated corporation, the limitation does not apply if the consolidated group would have an NOL for the year after taking the full dividends-received deduction.

EXAMPLE C:8-31 ▶

ADDITIONAL COMMENT

In Example C:8-31, if P and S did not file a consolidated tax return, P would report an $11,200 dividends-received deduction on its separate tax return, which is the lesser of $14,000 (70% × $20,000) or $11,200 (70% × $16,000). S would report a $10,500 dividends-received deduction, which is the lesser of $10,500 (70% × $15,000) or $12,600 (70% × $18,000). The total dividends-received deductions of $21,700 ($11,200 + $10,500) would be less than the $23,800 dividends-received deduction allowed when P and S file a consolidated tax return.

P and S Corporations comprise a consolidated group. Taxable income (without considering any dividends-received deductions, NOLs, capital loss carrybacks, or U.S. production activities deductions) is $16,000 for P and $18,000 for S. P received $20,000 of dividends from unaffiliated corporations that are less than 20%-owned; S received $15,000 of such dividends. The consolidated dividends-received deduction is $23,800, computed as follows:

Dividends-received deduction before limitation (($20,000 × 70%) + ($15,000 × 70%))	$24,500
Limitation (($16,000 + $18,000) × 70%)	$23,800
Dividends-received deduction (lesser of $24,500 or $23,800)	$23,800 ◀

DIVIDENDS RECEIVED FROM GROUP MEMBERS. The deduction for dividends received by one affiliated group member from another member is determined differently than the deduction for dividends received from a non-group member. If the corporations in the affiliated group do not file a consolidated tax return, the distributee corporation may claim a 100% dividends-received deduction on its separate tax return. The 100% dividends-received deduction is not subject to the taxable income limitation and is taken before the 80% or 70% dividends received deduction.

If the affiliated group members file a consolidated tax return, the distribution of a dividend from one group member to another group member (e.g., from subsidiary to parent) qualifies as an intercompany transaction. An intercompany dividend distribution is not included in the distributee member's gross income if it produces a corresponding negative adjustment to that member's basis of its stock in the distributing member (this basis adjustment is discussed later in the chapter).[34] This exclusion eliminates the intercompany dividend from consolidated taxable income, but the consolidated group cannot also claim a 100% dividends-received deduction for the excluded dividend. If the intercompany distribution is in the form of property, the excess of the property's FMV over the distributing member's adjusted basis in it is reported by that member as a gain in its separate taxable income calculation under Sec. 311(b). However, the reporting of this gain for consolidated taxable income is deferred because it is an intercompany transaction. The consolidated group determines the timing of the gain's inclusion in consolidated taxable income by the matching and acceleration rules.[35]

EXAMPLE C:8-32 ▶

P, S1, and S2 Corporations comprise a consolidated group. Consolidated taxable income (without considering any dividends-received deduction, NOLs, capital loss carrybacks, or U.S. production activities deduction) is $200,000. The group members receive the following dividend income from unaffiliated corporations that are less than 20%-owned: P, $6,000; S1, $10,000; and S2, $34,000. In addition, P receives a $40,000 dividend from S1, and the distribution reduces P's basis in its S1 investment.

▶ P excludes from its gross income the $40,000 dividend received from S1 because the distribution reduces P's basis in its S1 investment.

▶ The 70% dividends-received deductions included in the separate taxable income calculations are P, $4,200 (70% × $6,000); S1, $7,000 (70% × $10,000); and S2, $23,800 (70% × $34,000). The total 70% dividends-received deduction of $35,000 ($4,200 + $7,000 + $23,800) is not restricted by the $140,000 dividends-received deduction limitation (70% × $200,000 consolidated taxable income given in the facts).

Thus, the consolidated dividends-received deduction is $35,000. ◀

 STOP & THINK

Question: Alpha Corporation has owned the stock of a 100%-owned subsidiary for many years. The CPA who has prepared both corporations' tax returns since their creation has been trying to persuade Alpha's Director of Federal Taxes to begin filing a consolidated tax return based on the tax exemption for intragroup dividends. Is the CPA right or wrong in this approach?

Solution: The CPA is wrong. If Alpha and its subsidiary file separate tax returns, Alpha can claim a 100% deduction for dividends received from its subsidiary, which will offset the dividend received. If the corporations file a consolidated tax return, Alpha can exclude the dividends from its gross income. Typically, these two alternatives result in the same outcome. The outcomes for these two alternatives may differ, however, when preparing state tax returns. The CPA should focus on other factors, such as deferring profits on intercompany transactions and offsetting profits and losses between the two corporations.

U.S. PRODUCTION ACTIVITIES DEDUCTION

The U.S. production activities deduction also is determined on a consolidated basis (see Chapter C:3 for a detailed discussion of this deduction). The deduction for an affiliated group must be calculated as if the corporations in the group were a single corporation, whether the group files a consolidated tax return or separate tax returns. Similar to an unaffiliated corporation, the deduction for an affiliated group is the least of (1) 9% of the group's aggregate qualified production activities income, (2) 9% of the group's aggregate taxable income before this deduction, or (3) 50% of the group's aggregate W-2 wages allocable to U.S. production activities. For purposes of the U.S. production activities deduction only, Congress expanded the definition of an affiliated group by reducing the

---

[34] Reg. Sec. 1.1502-13(f)(2)(ii).

[35] Reg. Sec. 1.1502-13(f)(2)(iii).

stock ownership threshold from at least 80% to more than 50% and by including insurance companies and corporations that use the possessions tax credit as eligible corporations. Accordingly, this deduction's calculation may involve entities that are not part of the group filing the consolidated tax return.

After calculating its U.S. production activities deduction, the expanded affiliated group must allocate the deduction among its members with positive qualified production activities income based on the relative amounts of such income. If the expanded affiliated group includes a consolidated group and one or more corporations that are not in the consolidated group, the corporations in the consolidated group are treated as one member of the expanded affiliated group. The consolidated group's share of the expanded affiliated group's U.S. production activities deduction is then allocated to the consolidated group members with positive qualified production activities income based on the relative amounts of such income.[36] Additional issues, such as aggregating the activities of the expanded affiliated group's members to determine whether their activities qualify for purposes of this deduction, are beyond the scope of this textbook.

REGULAR TAX LIABILITY

A consolidated group determines its consolidated regular income tax liability similarly to an unaffiliated corporation by applying the Sec. 11 corporate tax rates to its consolidated taxable income. These rates appear inside the back cover of this textbook.

The regular tax liability for a consolidated tax return resembles the total tax liability for a controlled group but is not exactly the same. As discussed in Chapter C:3, Sec. 1561 limits to an aggregate of $50,000 the taxable incomes of a controlled group's members to which the 15% tax rate applies, and it allows only an aggregate of $25,000 of the group's members' taxable incomes to be taxed at 25%. For a controlled group, however, each corporation computes its tax liability separately, with the benefits of the 15% and 25% tax brackets allocated among the group's members. In contrast, a consolidated group simply applies the normal corporate tax rate schedule to its consolidated taxable income.

ADDITIONAL COMMENT

An affiliated group filing a consolidated tax return is limited to a single $40,000 AMT exemption. As a controlled group, the corporations still would be limited to a single $40,000 AMT exemption even if they filed separate tax returns.

CORPORATE ALTERNATIVE MINIMUM TAX

A consolidated group determines its corporate alternative minimum tax (AMT) on a consolidated basis.[37] In so doing the group calculates its AMT using an approach similar in many ways to the AMT calculation for an unaffiliated corporation except the amounts involved are determined on a consolidated basis (see Chapter C:5 for a detailed discussion of the corporate AMT for an unaffiliated corporation). The group increases or decreases its regular taxable income for each of its AMT preference and adjustment items (e.g., the difference between MACRS and AMT depreciation and the adjusted current earnings (ACE) adjustment) to arrive at alternative minimum taxable income (AMTI). The consolidated group reduces its AMTI by a $40,000 AMT exemption, but this amount phases out from $150,000 to $310,000 of AMTI.

The group's tentative minimum tax (TMT) is 20% of its AMTI in excess of its AMT exemption, and this amount is reduced by the group's AMT foreign tax credit to arrive at its TMT. The AMT is the excess of the TMT over the regular tax liability for the tax year. The consolidated group must pay any consolidated AMT in addition to its regular tax liability, but this amount is available in future years as a consolidated minimum tax credit. The consolidated group is eligible for the small corporation exemption from the AMT, but the $5 million and $7.5 million tests are based on the entire group's gross receipts.

The consolidated group determines its preadjustment AMTI, ACE, and AMTI using an approach that generally parallels the determination of consolidated regular taxable income. For example, the group may defer recognition of income, gains, deductions, or losses from intercompany transactions, much like it would for consolidated regular taxable income. However, the intercompany items, corresponding items, and recomputed corresponding items may differ in amount for AMT and regular tax purposes, such as when the intercompany transaction involves depreciable property.

---

[36] Reg. Sec. 1.199-7.   [37] Prop. Reg. Sec. 1.1502-55.

KEY POINT

Determining the alternative minimum tax is complex for an unconsolidated corporation. Determining it on a consolidated basis adds greatly to the complexity of this computation.

Many complex issues arise for a consolidated group's AMT that do not arise for an unconsolidated corporation's AMT. For example, recall from Chapter C:5 that the negative ACE adjustment is limited to the cumulative net amount of positive and negative ACE adjustments. Applying this limitation on a consolidated basis requires the tracking of separate return and consolidated return positive and negative ACE adjustments in prior years if corporations enter or leave the consolidated group. Further discussion of these issues is beyond the scope of this textbook.

NEW TAX ACT

Under the Small Business Jobs Act of 2010, eligible small businesses carry back any general business credit exceeding the limitation for five years instead of one year. The 20-year carryforward still applies. An eligible small business also computes its general business credit limitation by taking into account only 25% of its net regular tax exceeding $25,000, disregarding its tentative minimum tax. These rules apply only for 2010.

TAX CREDITS

A consolidated group can claim all tax credits available to corporate taxpayers. The group calculates these credits in much the same way as would an unaffiliated corporation. The discussion that follows examines the two major credits claimed by most consolidated groups—the general business credit and the foreign tax credit.

GENERAL BUSINESS CREDIT.   A consolidated group determines its general business credit on a consolidated basis, combining its members' separate credit amounts into a single amount.[38] (See Chapter I:14 for more detailed coverage of the general business credit.) The extent to which this combined amount can be claimed as a credit is limited to the excess of the group's consolidated net income tax over the greater of (1) its consolidated tentative minimum tax or (2) 25% of its consolidated net regular tax liability exceeding $25,000. Any credit exceeding this limitation carries back one year and forward 20 years.[39]

The corporations in a consolidated group may find that the general business credit allowed in the current year is smaller on a consolidated basis than it would be on a separate return basis. For example, if the credit is attributable to a profitable group member and another group member has a loss, consolidation may result in that member's loss reducing the group's credit limitation. However, if the credit is attributable to an unprofitable group member, consolidation may allow the members to claim a greater amount of credit on a consolidated basis than on a separate return basis because the credit limitation is higher on a consolidated basis due to other group members' profits.

EXAMPLE C:8-33 ▶

P and S Corporations comprise a consolidated group. For the current year (after 2010), P and S have separate taxable income and losses of $300,000 and ($100,000), respectively. P has a $40,000 research credit, and S has a $10,000 employer provided child care credit. P and S have $125,000 of AMT preference and adjustment items.

The group has a $50,000 ($40,000 + $10,000) tentative general business credit. The group's consolidated regular taxable income is $200,000 ($300,000 − $100,000), assuming no intercompany transactions or other items that would cause consolidated taxable income to differ from the sum of the separate taxable income and loss. The group's regular tax is $61,250 [$22,250 + (0.39 x ($200,000 − $100,000))]. The group's tentative minimum tax is $65,000 (20% × ($200,000 + $125,000)); the AMT exemption is fully phased-out), so the consolidated AMT is $3,750 ($65,000 − $61,250). The group's general business credit limitation is calculated as follows:

BOOK-TO-TAX ACCOUNTING COMPARISON

A general business credit carryover creates a deferred tax asset on the group's consolidated financial statements. The group also establishes a valuation allowance for any part of the deferred tax asset that does not have a more likely than not probability of being realized, and it should record a liability for unrecognized tax benefit for the portion of it that is not more likely than not to be realized upon effective settlement with the IRS (see Chapter C:3 regarding uncertain tax positions under ASC 740).

Regular tax		$61,250
Plus: Alternative minimum tax		3,750
Minus: Credits allowed under Secs. 21-30C		–0–
Net income tax		$65,000
Minus: Greater of:		
(1) 25% of group's net regular tax liability exceeding $25,000 [0.25 × ($61,250 − $25,000)]	$ 9,062	
(2) Group's tentative minimum tax for the year	65,000	(65,000)
General business credit limitation		$ –0–

The $50,000 ($50,000 tentative credit − $0 credit limitation) of unused general business credits carries back one year and forward 20 years.   ◀

---

[38] Reg. Sec. 1.1502-3.   [39] Sec. 39(a).

FOREIGN TAX CREDIT. A consolidated group determines its foreign tax credit on a consolidated basis.[40] The parent corporation makes the election to claim either a deduction or a credit for the group's foreign income taxes. If the parent chooses to claim a credit, the consolidated group computes its foreign tax credit limitation by taking into account its consolidated foreign-source income, consolidated taxable income, and consolidated regular tax in the manner described in Chapter C:16.

ESTIMATED TAX PAYMENTS

For the first two years for which an affiliated group files consolidated tax returns, it may elect to make estimated tax payments on either a consolidated or separate basis. Once an affiliated group has filed consolidated tax returns for two consecutive years, it must pay estimated taxes on a consolidated basis and continue doing so until the group's members again file separate tax returns.[41] The group's estimated tax payments and any underpayment exceptions or penalties are based on its consolidated tax liability for the current and preceding tax years without regard to the number of corporations comprising the group. If new, profitable corporations join the group, this treatment can be advantageous due to the time value of money.

EXAMPLE C:8-34 ▶ The P-S1 affiliated group has filed consolidated tax returns for several years. In the preceding year, the group reported a $100,000 consolidated tax liability. The P-S1 group acquires all of S2 Corporation's stock during the current year. S2 is profitable and causes the P-S1-S2 group to report a $300,000 consolidated tax liability in the current year. Assuming the P-S1-S2 group does not fall under the large corporation rules discussed below, it can base its current year estimated tax payments on its $100,000 consolidated tax liability from the prior tax year. The group will not incur an underpayment penalty if it makes $25,000 ($100,000 ÷ 4) of estimated tax payments by the fifteenth day of the fourth, sixth, ninth, and twelfth months of its tax year. The group must pay the balance of its consolidated tax liability by the due date of its consolidated tax return (without regard to any extensions) to avoid a penalty. ◀

LARGE CORPORATION RULE. Chapter C:3 discusses the special underpayment rules for large corporations imposed by Sec. 6655(d)(2)(B). A large corporation's estimated tax payments cannot be based on its prior year's tax liability except for the first installment. A large corporation is one whose taxable income was $1 million or more in any of its three preceding tax years. A controlled group of corporations must allocate the $1 million amount among its group members. An affiliated group that files a consolidated tax return is treated as a single corporation for this purpose. An affiliated group that files separate tax returns generally must allocate this $1 million amount because it also qualifies as a parent-subsidiary controlled group.

CONSOLIDATED OR SEPARATE BASIS. During the first two tax years of filing consolidated tax returns, a consolidated group sometimes can reduce its quarterly tax payments by making estimated tax payments on a separate basis in the first year and on a consolidated basis in the second year or vice versa. These reduced quarterly estimated tax payments will cause the group to pay a larger balance of tax by the due date of its tax return (without extensions). The group can apply different exceptions for the underpayment penalty (e.g., prior year's liability or annualization of current year's income) on a consolidated or separate basis the first two years. Determination of the actual required estimated tax payments on a consolidated or separate basis, however, is beyond the scope of this textbook.

SHORT-PERIOD RETURN. If a corporation joins a consolidated group after the beginning of its tax year or leaves a consolidated group before its tax year ends, it generally must file a separate, short-period tax return covering the time period it was unaffiliated with the group (however, it would not file a separate tax return if it left one consolidated

---

[40] Reg. Sec. 1.1502-4.

[41] Reg. Sec. 1.1502-5.

group to enter another consolidated group). Treasury Regulations provide rules covering estimated tax payments for short tax years.[42] No estimated tax payment is required for a short tax year that is less than four months.

NET OPERATING LOSSES (NOLs)

ADDITIONAL COMMENT

Under the American Recovery and Reinvestment Act of 2009 and the Worker, Homeownership, and Business Assistance Act of 2009, a taxpayer generally can elect to carry back a 2008 or 2009 NOL three, four, or five years.

One advantage of filing a consolidated tax return is the ability of the consolidated group to offset one member's NOLs against the taxable income of other group members. However, the profitable group members' taxable income may not be sufficient to fully offset the other members' NOLs, resulting in a consolidated NOL. The consolidated NOL carries back two years and forward 20 years unless the parent elects out of the carryback. If corporations enter or depart the consolidated group between the year the NOL arose and the carryback or carryover year, the group must determine the portion of the NOL that carries to the entering or departing corporation's separate return year. In addition, if a corporation entering the consolidated group has unused NOLs from years prior to its entry into the group (or a departing corporation has unused NOLs from years after its departure), the group may be able to use the NOLs. Because of the potential for abuse, the tax law limits the group's ability to use a separate return NOL in a consolidated return year. In addition, NOL, capital loss, and tax credit carryovers can be subject to the consolidated limitations under Secs. 382-384. The rules that apply to carrybacks and carryovers are discussed below.

CURRENT YEAR NOL

KEY POINT

Generally, the most significant benefit of filing a consolidated tax return is the group's ability to offset one member's losses against the income of other members.

A consolidated group's NOL equals the excess of its deductions over its gross income (i.e., its negative taxable income).[43] The group combines each member's separate taxable income or loss to determine a combined taxable income before adjusting for NOL carryovers (see Table C:8-1). The combining process allows one group member's losses to offset the taxable income of other group members. The group determines its consolidated NOL after applying the intercompany transaction rules and after calculating on a consolidated basis the various items discussed earlier, such as Sec. 1231 and capital gains and losses. The group must use a member's current year loss to first offset other members' current-year profits. A group member cannot elect separately to carry back its own losses from a consolidated return year to one of its earlier or later profitable separate return years. Only the consolidated group's NOL (if any) may carry back or over.

EXAMPLE C:8-35 ▶

P and S Corporations comprise an affiliated group. During Year 1, their initial year of operation, P and S file calendar year separate tax returns. Beginning in Year 2, the group elects to file a consolidated tax return. P and S report the following results for Years 1 and 2:

Group Member	Taxable Income	
	Year 1	Year 2
P	($15,000)	$40,000
S	250,000	(27,000)
Consolidated taxable income	N/A	$13,000

N/A = Not applicable

P may not use its Year 1 NOL to offset S's Year 1 profits because they file separate returns. In its Year 2 consolidated tax return, the group must first offset S's $27,000 separate loss against P's separate taxable income. S cannot carry back the $27,000 to its Year 1 separate tax return. (Note that the tax savings from deducting the $27,000 would be greater if S could carry it back

---

[42] Reg. Sec. 1.6655-5.   [43] Reg. Sec. 1.1502-21(e).

to Year 1.) Because P did not exist before Year 1, P carries its Year 1 NOL forward to offset all $13,000 of Year 2 consolidated taxable income that the P-S group reports prior to deducting any of the NOL carryover. The group's Year 2 consolidated taxable income is zero. P carries over to Year 3 its remaining NOL of $2,000 ($15,000 NOL from Year 1 − $13,000 used in Year 2). ◀

<table>
<tr><td>**OBJECTIVE 7**</td><td></td></tr>
</table>

CARRYBACKS AND CARRYOVERS OF CONSOLIDATED NOLs

Calculate the carryback or carryover of a consolidated NOL

A consolidated NOL carries back to the two preceding tax years (or an extended period, if applicable) and carries over to the 20 succeeding tax years. The parent corporation may elect for the consolidated group to relinquish the carryback period for a consolidated NOL and use the NOL only as a carryforward to succeeding years.[44] (Chapter C:3 discusses reasons for making this election.)

If the same corporations comprise the consolidated group during the carryback and carryover periods as during the year in which the NOL occurs, the treatment of the consolidated NOL is much like the treatment of an unaffiliated corporation's NOL. However, if the group's composition changes, the treatment of a consolidated NOL becomes complicated.

GENERAL RULE. The consolidated group apportions a fraction of its consolidated NOL to each member that incurred a separate loss during the year the NOL arose as follows:[45]

$$\frac{\text{Separate NOL of the particular group member}}{\text{Sum of the separate NOLs of all group members having such losses}} \times \text{Consolidated NOL} = \begin{array}{c}\text{Portion of consolidated NOL attributable to the particular group member}\end{array}$$

EXAMPLE C:8-36 ▶

P, S1, and S2 Corporations comprise an affiliated group. The group filed separate tax returns in Years 1 and 2 but elected to file a consolidated tax return in Year 3. The members report the following amounts of income and loss (before any NOL deduction):

	Year 1	Year 2	Year 3
P	$80,000	$90,000	$ 75,000
S1	11,000	7,000	(60,000)
S2	4,400	3,300	(40,000)
Consolidated taxable income	N/A	N/A	$(25,000)

N/A = Not applicable

KEY POINT

In Example C:8-36, because the P-S1-S2 affiliated group did not file a consolidated tax return prior to Year 3, P must either forgo the NOL carryback or allow $22,700 of the consolidated NOL to be carried back to S1's and S2's Years 1 and 2 separate tax returns.

Of the $25,000 Year 3 consolidated NOL, the group apportions $15,000 [$25,000 × ($60,000 ÷ ($60,000 + $40,000))] to S1 and $10,000 [$25,000 × ($40,000 ÷ ($60,000 + $40,000))] to S2. Assuming P does not elect to forego the NOL carryback period, S1 carries back $11,000 of its apportioned NOL to offset all its Year 1 separate return taxable income and the remaining $4,000 ($15,000 − $11,000) to offset part of its Year 2 separate return taxable income. S2 carries back $7,700 of its $10,000 apportioned NOL to offset its Years 1 and 2 separate return taxable incomes. The remaining $2,300 ($10,000 − $4,400 − $3,300) of consolidated NOL attributable to S2 carries forward to Year 3. ◀

If a corporation ceases to be a member of a consolidated group, any consolidated NOL carryover apportioned to it first must be used to offset consolidated taxable income in the year of departure. This requirement applies even when the entire NOL carryover is attributable to the departing member. Any NOL carryover apportioned to the departing member not absorbed by departure year consolidated taxable income becomes the member's separate carryover and may be used in its subsequent separate return years.[46]

---

[44] Reg. Sec. 1.1502-21(b)(3)(i).
[45] Reg. Sec. 1.1502-21(b)(2)(iv). The member's separate NOL is determined in a manner similar to the calculation of separate taxable income except for a series of adjustments to take into account the member's charitable contributions, dividends-received deductions, and Sec. 1231 and capital gains and losses. The consolidated NOL apportioned to a member might be reduced under the unified loss rules of Reg. Sec. 1.1502-36, which are beyond the scope of this text.
[46] Reg. Sec. 1.1502-21(b)(2)(ii)(A).

EXAMPLE C:8-37 ▶ P, S1, and S2 Corporations comprise an affiliated group that has filed consolidated tax returns on a calendar year basis for several years. At the close of business on September 30 of Year 2, P sells all its S1 stock. Therefore, S1 must file a separate tax return for the period October 1 through December 31 of Year 2. The members report the following amounts of income and loss (before any NOL deduction):

	Year 1	Year 2
P	$ 48,000	$20,000
S1	(50,000)	43,000*
S2	(100,000)	10,000
Total	$(102,000)	$73,000

*S1 earns $30,000 from January 1 through September 30 and $13,000 from October 1 through December 31.

TAX STRATEGY TIP

In Example C:8-37, the group is entitled to use the consolidated NOL before S1 determines its NOL carryover. This privilege can have an impact on negotiating an equitable purchase price for S1.

Assuming P elects to forego the NOL carryback period, the consolidated NOL carryover of $102,000 from Year 1 offsets the $60,000 ($20,000 + $30,000 + $10,000) of taxable income reported by P, S1, and S2 in their Year 2 consolidated tax return. Of the remaining $42,000 ($102,000 − $60,000),the group apportions $14,000 [$42,000 × ($50,000 ÷ ($50,000 + $100,000))] to S1 and $28,000 [$42,000 × ($100,000 ÷ ($50,000 + $100,000))] to S2. Of S1's carryover, $13,000 can be used in its separate tax return for October 1 through December 31 of Year 2. The remaining $1,000 ($14,000 − $13,000) carries over to S1's Year 3 separate tax return. The consolidated group carries over S2's $28,000 apportioned share of the Year 1 NOL to Year 3 and subsequent years. ◀

OFFSPRING RULE.   The offspring rule pertains to the consolidated NOL apportioned to a loss corporation that was newly formed by one or more of the affiliated group's members. The rule permits the NOL apportioned to the loss corporation to be carried back to a consolidated return year before it was a group member or to a separate return year of the parent corporation. Normally, the NOL apportioned to a loss member cannot be carried back in this way. The offspring rule applies if:[47]

▶ The loss corporation did not exist in the carryback year, and

▶ The loss corporation has been a member of the affiliated group continually since its organization.

If these two requirements are met, the part of the consolidated NOL apportioned to the loss member carries back to the two preceding consolidated return years (or separate return year of the common parent). The offspring rule does not apply if the common parent was a member of a different consolidated group or affiliated group filing separate returns for the year to which the loss carries.

EXAMPLE C:8-38 ▶ P and S1 Corporations were affiliated during Years 1 and 2 and filed consolidated tax returns in those years. On January 1 of Year 3, P creates S2 Corporation and acquires all its stock. S2 becomes a member of the affiliated group on that date. P, S1, and S2 report the following results for Years 1 through 3 (before any NOL deduction):

	Year 1	Year 2	Year 3
P	$ 9,000	$11,000	$ 16,000
S1	8,000	7,000	4,000
S2	XXX	XXX	(30,000)
Consolidated taxable income	$17,000	$18,000	$(10,000)

SELF-STUDY QUESTION

In Example C:8-38, what is the reason for allowing S2's portion of the consolidated NOL to carry back to Years 1 and 2?

ANSWER

The assets that make up S2 really were P's assets in Years 1 and 2, so it makes sense to allow the NOL to carry back to whatever tax return P filed in Years 1 and 2.

The entire Year 3 consolidated NOL is apportioned to S2. As discussed earlier, S2's $30,000 separate NOL is first used to offset the Year 3 taxable income of P and S1, leaving only a $10,000 consolidated NOL. If P does not elect to forego the NOL carryback period, the offspring rule allows the $10,000 NOL to carry back and offset $10,000 of the $17,000 Year 1 consolidated taxable income. The requirements for the offspring rule are met because S2 did not exist in Year 1 (the carryback year) and has been a group member continually since its organization in Year 3.

---

[47] Reg. Sec. 1.1502-21(b)(2)(ii)(B).

If P elects to forego the NOL carryback period, the $10,000 consolidated NOL offsets consolidated taxable income in Year 4 and up to 19 subsequent years assuming S2 does not depart the consolidated group before the $10,000 NOL is used. ◀

EXAMPLE C:8-39 ▶ Assume the same facts as in Example C:8-38 except P and S1 Corporations did not begin filing consolidated tax returns until Year 2. The offspring rule's requirements are still met, so the $10,000 consolidated NOL apportioned to S2 can carry back to P's Year 1 separate tax return, offsetting its $9,000 of taxable income (assuming P does not elect to forego the NOL carryback period). The remaining $1,000 offsets $1,000 of the $18,000 Year 2 consolidated taxable income. ◀

If the loss corporation is not a member of the affiliated group immediately after its organization, that member's portion of the consolidated NOL carries back only to its prior separate return years.

EXAMPLE C:8-40 ▶ Assume the same facts as in Example C:8-39 except a third party created S2 in Year 2, and P acquired all of S2's stock from the third party on January 1 of Year 3. P, S1, and S2 report the following results for Years 1 through 3 (before any NOL deduction):

Group Member	Taxable Income		
	Year 1	Year 2	Year 3
P	$ 9,000	$11,000	$16,000
S1	8,000	7,000	4,000
S2	XXX	8,000	(30,000)
Consolidated taxable income	$17,000	$18,000[a]	($10,000)

[a] Includes only the results of P and S1.

The offspring rule does not apply because S2 was not affiliated with the P-S1 group in Year 2. Because the entire $10,000 consolidated NOL is attributable to S2, S2 can carry it back to Year 2 and offset all $8,000 of its taxable income on its Year 2 separate return. S2 cannot carry back the loss to Year 1 because S2 did not exist then. The remaining NOL of $2,000 ($10,000 − $8,000) carries over to offset the consolidated group's Year 4 and later taxable income. Alternatively, the P-S1-S2 affiliated group could elect to carry over the entire $10,000 loss to offset taxable income in Year 4 and later years. ◀

SPECIAL LOSS LIMITATIONS

The term NOL trafficking refers to attempts by one tax entity to acquire NOL deductions from another entity. For example, a profitable corporation might consider acquiring an unprofitable corporation merely to obtain a tax benefit from the acquired corporation's unused NOLs. To inhibit NOL trafficking, the tax law imposes special limitations on the use of NOLs. The **Sec. 382 loss limitation rules,** which were discussed in Chapter C:7 on a separate return basis, also could apply to affiliated groups filing consolidated tax returns. The **separate return limitation year (SRLY) rules** apply only to consolidated groups and limit the use in a consolidated return year of a member's NOL that arose in a separate return year. Specifically, the SRLY rules limit use of the NOL to the loss member's subsequent contribution to consolidated taxable income. The SRLY rules are explained in detail below, as well as special aspects of the Sec. 382 rules with respect to consolidated tax returns.

SEPARATE RETURN LIMITATION YEAR RULES. A SRLY generally is any separate return year (i.e., a year in which a corporation filed a separate tax return or joined in a consolidated tax return of another consolidated group). However, a SRLY does not include the following:[48]

▶ A separate return year of the group's parent corporation. The SRLY limitation thus does not apply to the parent corporation's NOLs, even if they arise in a separate return year.

---

[48] Reg. Sec. 1.1502-1(f).

KEY POINT

The SRLY rules limit a consolidated group's ability to acquire another corporation and use its already existing NOLs to offset the group's income.

ADDITIONAL COMMENT

These two exceptions to the SRLY rules exist because, in both cases, the group has not acquired already existing NOLs.

► A separate return year of a corporation that was a member of the affiliated group for every day of the loss year (e.g., the group did not elect to file a consolidated tax return in the loss year). The SRLY limitation does not apply in this circumstance because the loss year would not have been a SRLY had the group elected to file a consolidated tax return.

An NOL incurred in a SRLY carries back two years (or an extended period if applicable) and forward 20 years unless the corporation elects to carry forward the NOL only for 20 years. If the year to which the NOL carries is a consolidated return year, the NOL's deductibility is limited to the SRLY limitation for that group member:[49]

> Aggregate of consolidated taxable income for all consolidated return years of the group determined by taking into account only the loss member's items of income, gain, deduction, and loss
> Minus: Any of the loss member's NOLs previously absorbed by the consolidated group
>
> ---
> SRLY limitation (not less than zero)

The SRLY rules limit the consolidated group's use of the loss member's NOL to that member's aggregate contribution to consolidated taxable income in excess of zero. As a result, an NOL incurred in a SRLY that is deductible on a consolidated tax return equals the lesser of (1) the SRLY limitation, (2) consolidated taxable income, or (3) the amount of the NOL carryover or carryback. Any NOL carryover or carryback exceeding the lesser of these three amounts carries over to subsequent tax years.

EXAMPLE C:8-41 ►

SELF-STUDY QUESTION

What is the consequence of having NOLs subject to the SRLY limitations?

ANSWER

The effect of having a member's NOLs tainted as SRLY NOLs is that they can be used only to offset taxable income of the loss member. This restriction could delay deduction of the NOLs and increases the likelihood that they will expire unused.

P and S Corporations are calendar year corporations that formed in Year 1. P acquires 100% of S's stock at the close of business on December 31 of Year 1.[50] P and S file separate tax returns for Year 1 and begin filing a consolidated tax return for Year 2. Assume the U.S. production activities deduction does not apply. The corporations report the following taxable incomes (losses), before any NOL deductions, for Years 1 through 5:

| | Taxable Income | | | | |
Group Member	Year 1	Year 2	Year 3	Year 4	Year 5
P	$(9,000)	$17,000	$ 6,000	$(6,000)	$ 2,000
S	(20,000)	(2,000)	5,000	5,000	16,000
Consolidated taxable income	N/A	$15,000	$11,000	$(1,000)	$18,000

Under the SRLY rules, the P-S consolidated group uses the NOLs as follows:

► *Year 2:* P's Year 1 NOL offsets the group's consolidated taxable income (CTI). For P, Year 1 is not a SRLY because P is the group's parent corporation. S's only contribution to CTI by the end of Year 2 is its $2,000 loss in Year 2. Therefore, S's SRLY limitation for Year 2 is zero because S makes no positive aggregate contribution to CTI. The group's resulting CTI is $6,000 ($15,000 − $9,000).

► *Year 3:* S's SRLY limitation for Year 3 is $3,000 [($2,000) + $5,000]. S's $20,000 unused NOLs and the group's $11,000 CTI are both more than $3,000, so the group can deduct $3,000 of S's Year 1 NOL. The group's resulting CTI is $8,000 ($11,000 − $3,000), and $17,000 ($20,000 − $3,000) of S's NOL remains to carry forward.

► *Year 4:* S's SRLY limitation is $5,000 [($2,000) + $5,000 + $5,000 − $3,000]. However, none of S's Year 1 NOL can be used because the group has no positive CTI for the NOL to offset. Assuming the group carries back the Year 4 consolidated NOL to Year 2, CTI in Year 2 is reduced from $6,000 to $5,000 ($15,000 − $9,000 carryover from Year 1 − $1,000 carryback from Year 4).

---

[49] Reg. Sec. 1.1502-21(c). If multiple group members have unexpired NOLs or a loss member has unexpired NOLs from multiple SRLYs, the group uses the NOLs on a first-in, first-out (FIFO) basis. The group uses NOLs from tax years ending on the same date on a pro rata basis.

[50] P's acquisition of S stock might trigger both the SRLY rules and the Sec. 382 rules. To simplify the example, assume that the acquisition did not trigger the Sec. 382 rules. The SRLY-Sec. 382 overlap rules are discussed later in this chapter.

▶ *Year 5:* S's SRLY limitation is $21,000 [($2,000) + $5,000 + $5,000 − $3,000 + $16,000]. However, S has only $17,000 of NOLs remaining, so the group deducts this amount. The group's resulting CTI is $1,000 ($18,000 − $17,000), and no NOLs remain to carry forward to Year 6. ◀

The SRLY rules generally apply separately to each corporation that has a loss carryover from a SRLY.

EXAMPLE C:8-42 ▶ At the close of business on December 31 of Year 1, P Corporation purchases 100% of S Corporation's stock and 100% of T Corporation's stock. S and T were unaffiliated prior to these purchases. From Year 1, S has a $12,000 NOL carryover, and T has an $11,000 NOL carryover. Assume the Sec. 382 limitation does not apply to these stock purchases. The P-S-T affiliated group elects to file a consolidated tax return for Year 2, and the members report the following separate taxable income for that year:

P Corporation	$100,000
S Corporation	$ 14,000
T Corporation	$ 10,000

The Year 2 SRLY limitation for S's NOL is $14,000, and the limitation for T's NOL is $10,000. The P-S-T consolidated group can deduct all $12,000 of S's Year 1 NOL, but it can deduct only $10,000 of T's Year 1 NOL. As a result, the group's Year 2 consolidated taxable income is $102,000 ($100,000 + $14,000 + $10,000 − $12,000 − $10,000). The remaining $1,000 ($11,000 − $10,000) of T's Year 1 NOL carries forward to Year 3. ◀

The SRLY limitation applies to a SRLY subgroup on a joint basis rather than to each corporation separately. For NOL carryovers, a SRLY subgroup is the loss corporation and each other group member that (1) became a member of the current affiliated group at the same time as the loss corporation, (2) was affiliated with the loss corporation in another affiliated group before becoming a member of the current affiliated group, and (3) has been continuously affiliated with the loss corporation after ceasing to be a member of the former affiliated group.

EXAMPLE C:8-43 ▶ Assume the same facts as in Example C:8-42 except S owns 100% of T's stock, and P purchased 100% of S's stock at the close of business on December 31 of Year 1. S and T are a SRLY subgroup. The S-T subgroup SRLY limitation for Year 2 is $24,000 ($14,000 + $10,000), so the P-S-T consolidated group can deduct on its Year 2 tax return all $21,000 ($10,000 + $11,000) of S's and T's NOL carryovers from Year 1. ◀

KEY POINT

The SRLY rules apply to both carryovers and carrybacks. Remember that SRLYs stem from a year in which a member files a separate tax return or joins in the filing of a consolidated return with a different affiliated group.

In addition to NOL carryovers, the SRLY rules apply to NOL carrybacks. For example, suppose P Corporation owns 100% of S Corporation's stock, and they have filed consolidated tax returns for many years. P sells all its stock in S at the end of Year 2, and S incurs an NOL in Year 3. If S does not elect to forego the NOL carryback period, the Year 3 NOL first carries to the P-S Year 1 consolidated tax return, and any remaining NOL then carries to the P-S Year 2 consolidated tax return. In Years 1 and 2, the SRLY rules restrict the consolidated group's use of S's Year 3 NOL to S's contribution to consolidated taxable income for all consolidated return years.

The SRLY rules also limit the use of built-in losses. A built-in loss is a loss that accrues in a separate return year but is realized in a consolidated return year. For example, S Corporation purchases land in a separate return year for $100,000. The land's fair market value declines to $85,000 before P purchases all of S's stock, when they start filing tax returns on a consolidated basis. If S sells the land during the five-year period beginning on the date P purchases S's stock, the SRLY rules limit the extent to which the P-S consolidated group can use the realized loss. As with NOLs, the group must compute S's SRLY limitation in determining how much of the loss it can use.[51]

In a reverse acquisition, the acquired corporation's shareholders own more than 50% of the fair market value of the acquiring corporation's stock immediately after the

---

[51] Reg. Sec. 1.1502-15(a).

acquisition. In such an acquisition, the SRLY limitation applies to the acquiring corporation's NOLs and does not apply to the acquired corporation's NOLs.[52] For example, suppose P Corporation acquires all of S Corporation's stock in exchange for P stock. Because P is smaller than S, persons who were S shareholders immediately before the purchase own more than 50% of the fair market value of P's stock immediately after the purchase. The form of the transaction is that P acquires S, but its substance is that S acquires P. The transaction qualifies as a reverse acquisition, so the SRLY limitation applies to P's NOLs but not to S's NOLs. That is, S is treated as if it were the parent corporation for purposes of applying the SRLY limitation. The details of this rule and other aspects of the reverse acquisition rules are beyond the scope of this textbook.

A discussion of the financial statement implications of SRLY losses appears at the end of this chapter.

ADDITIONAL COMMENT

The Sec. 382 limitations do not apply to certain restructuring plans required by the Emergency Economic Stabilization Act of 2008.

CONSOLIDATED SEC. 382 RULES.   The Sec. 382 rules may apply when a consolidated group acquires a corporation with an unused NOL. Section 382 inhibits NOL trafficking by limiting the acquiring corporation's use of a loss corporation's NOL to the Sec. 382 limitation, which is the value of the old loss corporation's stock multiplied by the long-term tax-exempt federal interest rate.[53] The 50 percentage point stock ownership change needed to trigger the Sec. 382 rules can occur in acquisitive transactions involving a single corporation or a group of corporations that file separate or consolidated returns. (See Chapter C:7 for a discussion of Sec. 382.) The consolidated Sec. 382 rules generally provide that the ownership change and Sec. 382 limitation are determined with respect to the entire consolidated group (or a subgroup of a consolidated group) and not separately for each corporation.[54] The details of these rules are beyond the scope of this textbook.

SRLY-SEC. 382 OVERLAP.   A SRLY-Sec. 382 overlap occurs when an acquisition of a corporation falls under both the SRLY rules and the Sec. 382 rules (for example, a corporation in a consolidated group purchases 100% of the stock of a target corporation having an NOL carryover). Because both sets of rules inhibit NOL trafficking by restricting the use of NOLs, Treasury Regulations alleviate the burden of applying them by waiving the application of the SRLY rules in many SRLY-Sec. 382 overlap situations.[55]

To qualify for the overlap rule, a corporation must become a member of a consolidated group (the SRLY event) within six months of the date of an ownership change that triggers a Sec. 382 limitation (the Sec. 382 event). Often, the SRLY event and the Sec. 382 event are simultaneous.

EXAMPLE C:8-44 ▶

P Corporation purchases 60% of S Corporation's stock on February 28 of the current year. On June 30 of the current year, P purchases the other 40% of S's stock. P has filed consolidated tax returns with its other subsidiaries for several years. The Sec. 382 event occurs on February 28, when the 50 percentage-point ownership change takes place. The SRLY event occurs on June 30, when P's ownership of S reaches the 80% threshold needed to include S in the consolidated tax return. The overlap rule applies because the Sec. 382 event occurred within six months of the SRLY event, so the SRLY rules are waived beginning with the tax year that includes June 30. Instead, only the Sec. 382 rules apply. ◀

ADDITIONAL COMMENT

In some cases, the overlap rule will not apply. In Example C:8-44, if the 40% purchase had taken place on September 30, the SRLY event would have occurred more than six months after the Sec. 382 event. Consequently, the SRLY rules and the Sec. 382 rules both would apply.

If the SRLY event precedes the Sec. 382 event by six months or less, the overlap rule applies for the first tax year beginning after the Sec. 382 event (and the SRLY rules apply for the interim period). This situation could occur, for example, if the acquiring corporation had owned 45% of the target corporation's stock for many years, purchased 40% of the target's stock in the current year, and purchased the remaining 15% of the target's stock less than six months after the 40% purchase.

Topic Review C:8-2 summarizes the rules applying to carrybacks and carryovers of consolidated return and separate return NOLs.

---

[52] Reg. Sec. 1.1502-1(f)(3).
[53] The Sec. 382 limitation rules apply to the tax attributes limited by Secs. 382–384 (e.g., NOLs, capital losses, foreign tax credits, general business credits, minimum tax credit, built-in gains, and built-in losses).

[54] Reg. Sec. 1.1502-91(a)(1).
[55] Reg. Sec. 1.1502-21(g).

Topic Review C:8-2

Rules Addressing NOL Carrybacks and Carryovers To or From Consolidated Tax Return Years

LOSS YEAR	CARRYOVER/ CARRYBACK YEAR	RULE AND SPECIAL LIMITATIONS
CRY[a]	CRY	1. Consolidated NOLs carry back two years (or an extended period if applicable) and forward 20 years. The group's parent corporation can elect to forgo the carryback period. No special problems arise if the group members are the same in the loss year and the year to which the loss carries. 2. The Sec. 382 limitation applies to the loss carryover if a Sec. 382 ownership change occurs.
CRY	SRY[b]	1. Carryback to a member's prior separate return year is possible only if part or all of the NOL is apportioned to the member. Offspring rule permits carryback of an offspring member's allocable share of the consolidated NOL to a separate or consolidated return year of the group's parent corporation. 2. The departing member is allocated part of the consolidated NOL carryover. The consolidated NOL carryover is used first in the consolidated return year in which the member departs. The allocated share of the remaining consolidated NOL carryover is then available to be used in the departing member's first separate return year. The Sec. 382 loss limitation may apply to the loss carryover.
SRY	CRY	1. A separate return year NOL carries over to a consolidated return year, but the SRLY rules may limit the NOL's usage. The SRLY rules do not apply to the NOLs of the parent corporation or to a corporation that is a member of the affiliated group on each day of the loss year unless a reverse acquisition occurs. Section 382 loss limitation rules may apply to the loss carryover, but the SRLY rules may be waived under the overlap rule. 2. Carryback of a loss of a departed group member to a consolidated return year is a SRLY loss.

[a]Consolidated return year.
[b]Separate return year.

STOCK BASIS ADJUSTMENTS

OBJECTIVE 9

Adjust the basis of stock of a subsidiary in a consolidated group

A consolidated group member must annually adjust the basis of stock it owns in a subsidiary for the subsidiary's profits and losses, for distributions from the subsidiary, and for other items. These rules are similar to those that apply to partners of partnerships and shareholders of S corporations (see Chapters C:9 and C:11) and are intended to prevent the duplication of income or loss in consolidated taxable income.[56]

EXAMPLE C:8-45 ▶

KEY POINT

Positive stock basis adjustments reduce the amount of gain or increase the amount of loss reported when a sale of the stock of a consolidated group member (other than the parent) occurs.

P Corporation purchases all of S Corporation's stock on January 1 of the current year for $100,000. The corporations elect to file a consolidated tax return. S recognizes a $25,000 profit during the current year and pays no dividends to P. P sells all its S stock on December 31 of the current year for $125,000. P increases the basis of its S stock by $25,000. As a result, P realizes no gain or loss on the sale of its S stock [$125,000 amount realized − $125,000 basis ($100,000 + $25,000)].

Had P not adjusted its basis for S's profit, it would have realized a $25,000 gain on the stock sale ($125,000 − $100,000), and this gain would have been taxed on the current year's consolidated tax return. However, the increase in the S stock's value that led to this $25,000 gain is attributable to the $25,000 profit that S earned. Without the basis adjustment to the S stock, the consolidated group would have been taxed twice on the $25,000 gain. ◀

A consolidated group may be comprised of many tiers of corporations. For example, a parent corporation may have a subsidiary corporation (a first-tier subsidiary), and the subsidiary, in turn, may have its own subsidiary (a second-tier subsidiary). The stock basis

---

[56] Losses realized on the sale by one consolidated group member of another member's stock involve complicated rules and calculations that are beyond the scope of this text.

adjustments itemized below are discussed with respect to a parent corporation that owns stock of a subsidiary, but they also apply to a higher-tier subsidiary that owns stock of a lower-tier subsidiary.

The starting point for the calculation is the parent corporation's original basis in its subsidiary stock, which depends on the method used to acquire it (e.g., purchase, nontaxable corporate formation, or nontaxable reorganization). The parent makes the following adjustments to the original basis:[57]

▶ Increase basis for the subsidiary's income and gain items and decrease it for the subsidiary's deduction and loss items taken into account in determining consolidated taxable income. Items whose recognition is deferred under the intercompany transaction rules do not increase or decrease basis until they are taken into account for consolidated taxable income.

▶ Increase basis for the subsidiary's income permanently excluded from taxation (e.g., tax-exempt bond interest and federal income tax refunds).

▶ Increase basis for the subsidiary's deductions that do not represent a recovery of basis or an expenditure of money as if they were tax-exempt income (for example, the dividends-received and U.S. production activities deductions). However, the parent also decreases basis for the deductions themselves, so these two adjustments usually net to zero and thus have no net effect on the parent's basis in the subsidiary.[58]

▶ Decrease basis for the subsidiary's expenses that are not deductible and are not capital expenditures (e.g., federal income taxes, the nondeductible 50% of meals and entertainment expenses, expenses related to tax-exempt income, and losses disallowed under Sec. 267).

▶ Decrease basis for distributions received from the subsidiary (without regard to the subsidiary's E&P or whether the E&P accumulated before or after the subsidiary became a member of the consolidated group).

▶ Decrease basis for the subsidiary's NOLs that arise and are used in the current year against other group members' taxable income. NOLs that carry forward reduce basis in the year used. NOLs that carry back reduce basis in the year they arise. Expiring NOLs reduce basis in the year they expire. However, basis is not decreased when the subsidiary's pre-acquisition NOLs expire unused if the group waives the use of part or all of such losses. Similar rules apply to capital losses.

EXAMPLE C:8-46 ▶ On January 1 of the current year, P Corporation purchases all of S Corporation's stock for $1 million. P and S elect to file a consolidated tax return. During the current year, S reports taxable income of $300,000 and tax-exempt bond interest of $25,000, and S pays P a $40,000 dividend. On January 1 of the next year, P sells the S stock for $1.2 million. Assume that the portion of the consolidated tax liability allocable to S is $102,000 ($300,000 × 0.34) and that S pays it. P's basis in its S stock on the sale date is $1,183,000 ($1,000,000 + $300,000 + $25,000 − $102,000 − $40,000). Thus, P realizes a $17,000 gain on the stock sale ($1,200,000 − $1,183,000).[59] ◀

TIERING UP OF STOCK BASIS ADJUSTMENTS

In adjusting the basis of its first-tier subsidiary's stock, the parent corporation also takes into account the adjustments the first-tier subsidiary makes to its basis in second-tier subsidiary stock. The adjustments are applied in order of the tiers, from the lowest to the highest.

EXAMPLE C:8-47 ▶ P Corporation owns all of S Corporation's stock, and S owns all of T Corporation's stock. The three corporations have filed on a consolidated basis for several years. At the beginning of the current year, P's basis in its S stock was $800,000, and S's basis in its T stock was $500,000. During the current year, S reports $100,000 of taxable income, and T reports $50,000 of taxable

---

[57] Reg. Sec. 1.1502-32. If the parent owns less than 100% of the subsidiary's stock, it adjusts the stock basis by its ownership percentage multiplied by the various adjustment items.
[58] Reg. Sec. 1502-32(b)(3)(ii)(B).
[59] Separate basis calculations are required for regular tax and AMT purposes. The AMT basis calculations parallel those made for regular tax purposes but

use the appropriate numbers from the AMT calculation. Because the stock basis adjustments for regular tax and AMT purposes may differ (e.g., different amounts of expenses), the sale of subsidiary stock may result in different gain or loss amounts for the two purposes.

income. Assume that the portions of the consolidated tax liability allocable to S and T are $34,000 ($100,000 × 0.34) and $17,000 ($50,000 × 0.34), respectively, and that each pays its allocable portion. S increases the basis in its T stock to $533,000 ($500,000 + $50,000 − $17,000). P increases the basis in its S stock to $899,000 ($800,000 + $100,000 − $34,000 + $50,000 − $17,000), reflecting adjustments for both tiers below P. ◀

EXCESS LOSS ACCOUNT

If the negative basis adjustments (e.g., for losses and distributions) are sufficiently large, the parent reduces its basis in the subsidiary stock to zero. Additional negative basis adjustments create or increase an excess loss account. Creation of or change in the balance of an excess loss account does not trigger recognition of income or gain. Instead, it is treated as negative basis. Subsequent profits or other positive basis adjustments first reduce or eliminate the excess loss account before producing a positive basis in the subsidiary stock. A corporation disposing of a subsidiary's stock recognizes its excess loss account in the disposed shares as income or gain from the disposition.[60]

EXAMPLE C:8-48 ▶ P Corporation owns all of S Corporation's stock, and the two corporations have filed on a consolidated basis for several years. P's basis in its S stock was $900,000 at the beginning of the current year. During the current year, S incurs a $950,000 NOL, which offsets part of P's $2.5 million of taxable income. On January 1 of the next year, P sells its S stock for $80,000. P first reduces its basis in the S stock to zero, and the remaining $50,000 ($950,000 − $900,000) of the negative adjustment creates an excess loss account. When P sells the S stock, it recognizes a $130,000 gain ($80,000 amount realized − $0 basis + $50,000 excess loss account). ◀

TAX PLANNING CONSIDERATIONS

OBJECTIVE 10

Explain the advantages and disadvantages of filing a consolidated tax return

Filing a consolidated tax return has several advantages and disadvantages as discussed below. Thus, the decision whether or not to file a consolidated tax return is one of an affiliated group's tax planning considerations.

ADVANTAGES OF FILING A CONSOLIDATED TAX RETURN

▶ The consolidated group can offset one member's operating losses against another member's operating profits. This offset usually is beneficial because it allows the losses to immediately reduce taxes. If the group members filed separate returns, the losses carry back or forward as an NOL. However, discounting decreases the present value of the tax savings from an NOL that carries forward.

▶ The group can offset one member's net capital loss against another member's net capital gain. Again, this offset allows the net loss to immediately reduce taxes, and it reduces the chance that the losses will expire unused.

▶ The group computes various credit and deduction limitations on a consolidated basis (e.g., charitable contributions). If the group members filed separate tax returns, some members' credits or deductions might be only partially used due to the limitations, while other members' credits or deductions fall short of the limitations. By filing a consolidated tax return, group members with "excess" credits or deductions can take advantage of other members' "excess" limitations.

▶ In the consolidated tax return, the group eliminates dividends paid from one group member to another group member. However, the recipient member would be eligible for a 100% dividends-received deduction if they filed separate tax returns.

▶ The group defers gains and profits on intercompany transactions, which reduces the present value of the taxes on these items (assuming tax rates do not increase).

---

[60] Reg. Sec. 1.1502-19.

▶ The parent corporation (and upper tier corporations) increase their bases in subsidiary (and lower tier corporation) stock investments for the subsidiary's (and lower tier corporations') taxable income, much like pass-through entities, thereby eliminating double taxation.

▶ The group calculates its alternative minimum tax (AMT) on a consolidated basis. If the group members filed separate tax returns, some group members might incur an AMT because they have large amounts of AMT preference and adjustment items, while other group members have no AMT because they have relatively few preference and adjustment items. If the group files a consolidated tax return, members with "excess" tentative minimum taxes can use them to take advantage of other members' "excess" regular taxes.

DISADVANTAGES OF FILING A CONSOLIDATED TAX RETURN

▶ The group must continue to file consolidated tax returns for all subsequent tax years until the affiliated group terminates or the IRS grants permission for the group to discontinue filing on a consolidated basis. By filing a consolidated tax return, the group forfeits the flexibility to choose between filing on a separate or consolidated basis in future years.

▶ Offsetting one member's losses against other members' profits or gains reduces the limitations on various deductions and credits (e.g., charitable contributions), which may reduce the amounts of such items currrently allowed on a consolidated basis compared to those allowed on a separate return basis.

▶ All group members must use the same taxable year.

▶ The group defers losses and deductions on intercompany transactions, which reduces the present value of the tax savings on these items (assuming tax rates do not increase).

▶ The group may incur additional administrative costs to maintain the records necessary to account for intercompany transactions and the special loss limitations although it may realize some savings by filing a single tax return.

No general rule can be applied to determine whether an affiliated group should elect to file a consolidated tax return. Each group should examine the long- and short-term advantages and disadvantages of filing a consolidated tax return instead of separate tax returns before making this decision.

COMPLIANCE AND PROCEDURAL CONSIDERATIONS

THE BASIC ELECTION AND RETURN

OBJECTIVE 11

Explain the procedures for making a consolidated return election

As discussed earlier in this chapter, an affiliated group elects to file its tax return on a consolidated basis by filing a corporate tax return (Form 1120) that includes the income, expenses, etc. of all its members. The group must make the election no later than the due date for the common parent's tax return including any permitted extensions.[61] Each corporation that is a member of the affiliated group during the initial consolidated return year must consent to the election. The parent corporation consents by joining in the consolidated tax return. Each subsidiary corporation consents to the election by filing Form 1122 (Authorization and Consent of Subsidiary Corporation To Be Included in a Consolidated Income Tax Return) as part of the initial consolidated tax return. Only newly acquired subsidiary corporations file Form 1122 with subsequent consolidated tax returns.

Each year's consolidated tax return also must include Form 851 (Affiliations Schedule). This form includes names, addresses, and identification numbers of the

---

[61] Reg. Sec. 1.1502-75(a)(1).

corporations in the consolidated group; the corporations' tax prepayments; the ownership of their stock at the beginning of the tax year; and all stock ownership changes occurring during the tax year. Treasury Regulations require the group to file supporting statements with its consolidated tax return. These statements show in columnar form a reconciliation of the members' taxable incomes with consolidated taxable income, and they also show the details of each member's gross income and deductions so the IRS can readily audit them.[62] An example of such a reconciliation appears in the consolidated tax return included in Appendix B.

Similar to unaffiliated corporations, the due date for the consolidated tax return is the fifteenth day of the third month after the end of the consolidated group's tax year. A six-month extension for filing the tax return is allowed if the parent corporation files Form 7004 (Application for Automatic Extension of Time To File Certain Business Income Tax, Information, and Other Returns) and pays the estimated balance of the consolidated tax liability. If a subsidiary corporation enters or departs the consolidated group, the due date for its separate tax return for the part of the year it was not affiliated with the group depends on the date the group files its consolidated tax return.[63]

Appendix B presents a sample Form 1120 for reporting the current year's results for the Alpha affiliated group described in Example C:8-49. The Form 1120 involves the five intercompany transactions mentioned in the example, and a worksheet that summarizes the income and expense items for the five companies illustrates the reporting of the intercompany transactions and presents the details of the consolidated taxable income calculation.

EXAMPLE C:8-49 ▶

Alpha Manufacturing Corporation owns 100% of Beta, Charlie, Delta, and Echo Corporations' stock. The affiliated group has filed consolidated tax returns for several years using the calendar year as its tax year. The five corporations' separate taxable income components are reported on the supporting schedule of the group's consolidated tax return contained in Appendix B. This return illustrates the following five common transactions involving members of a consolidated group:

▶ The sale of inventory from Alpha to Beta, the profit from which is deferred for consolidated taxable income. Beta sells additional inventory to outsiders.

▶ Intragroup dividends paid from Beta and Echo to Alpha

▶ Payment of interest from Delta to Alpha

▶ The sale of a truck from Alpha to Beta

▶ Beta's depreciation of the truck acquired in the intercompany transaction ◀

Students should review this sample return to see how the group reports the transactions and how it transfers the numbers from the consolidated taxable income schedule to the consolidated group's Form 1120. Although not displayed in Appendix B, the consolidated return should include a Schedule M-3 if applicable (see Chapter C:3).

PARENT CORPORATION AS AGENT FOR THE CONSOLIDATED GROUP

A consolidated group's parent corporation generally acts as the sole agent for all matters relating to the group's consolidated tax liability.[64] This agency role means that a subsidiary corporation cannot act in its own behalf with respect to a consolidated return year except to the extent that Treasury Regulations prohibit the parent from acting in the subsidiary's behalf. For example, the parent, not the subsidiary, makes or changes any election used in computing the subsidiary's separate taxable income, corresponds with the IRS regarding a tax liability determination, files any requests for extensions of time in which to file a tax return, files a claim for a refund or credit relating to a consolidated return year, or elects to deduct or credit foreign tax payments.

---

[62] Reg. Sec. 1.1502-75(j).
[63] Reg. Sec. 1.1502-76(c). The details of these rules are beyond the scope of this text.

[64] Reg. Sec. 1.1502-77(a).

SEPARATE ENTITY TREATMENT OF INTERCOMPANY TRANSACTIONS

The consolidated group's common parent can request consent from the IRS to treat the group's intercompany transactions on a separate entity basis, where the transactions are treated as if the group members involved were not members of the same consolidated group. When deciding whether to grant such consent, the IRS considers whether such treatment reduces the group's tax compliance burden and whether it has more than a 5% effect on the group's consolidated taxable income or consolidated tax liability. The group can make the request for all its intercompany transactions (other than those involving group members' stock or obligations) or only one or more classes of intercompany transactions. The group applies such separate entity treatment for the consolidated return year for which the IRS grants consent and subsequent tax years. The group's common parent can revoke such separate entity treatment if the IRS consents to it, and the IRS can revoke the group's use of such treatment.[65]

LIABILITY FOR TAXES DUE

The parent corporation and every other corporation that was a group member for any part of the consolidated return year are severally liable for that year's consolidated tax liability.[66] Thus, the IRS may collect the entire consolidated tax liability from one group member if the other group members are unable to pay their allocable portion of the tax. The IRS can ignore any agreements among the group members to limit their share of the tax liability. A corporation that is a member of a consolidated group for even a few days during a tax year can be liable for the entire year's consolidated tax liability and related deficiencies.

An exception to this several liability rule occurs when a subsidiary corporation departs the consolidated group because its stock is sold or exchanged before the IRS assesses a deficiency against the group. The IRS can opt to assess a former subsidiary for only its allocable portion of the total deficiency if the IRS believes that the assessment and collection of the balance of the deficiency from the other group members will not be jeopardized.

FINANCIAL STATEMENT IMPLICATIONS

OBJECTIVE 12

Understand the financial statement implications of various consolidated transactions

INTERCOMPANY TRANSACTIONS

Intercompany transactions can raise deferred tax issues depending on the type of transaction and whether the affiliated group files consolidated tax returns or separate tax returns. The following discussion assumes a 100%-owned domestic subsidiary to avoid the complications of accounting for noncontrolling interests and for foreign subsidiaries. It also addresses just two types of intercompany transactions: (1) distributed and undistributed subsidiary profits and (2) intercompany sales of property.

For a parent with a 100%-owned domestic subsidiary, intercompany dividends and undistributed subsidiary earnings cause no temporary differences. If the group files a consolidated tax return, the intercompany dividend is eliminated for both tax and consolidated financial statement purposes. If the group files separate tax returns, the parent takes a 100% dividends-received deduction because it owns at least 80% of the subsidiary's stock. Therefore, in either case, no book-tax difference occurs that would create a temporary difference. Undistributed subsidiary earnings are included in consolidated financial statements, but a parent filing a separate tax return would not include these earnings in its income until the subsidiary distributes them as dividends. However, when ultimately distributed, the parent can take the 100% dividends-received deduction, thereby offsetting the dividend income. Consequently, undistributed subsidiary earnings also present no deferred tax issues (within the assumed parameters of this discussion).

---

[65] Reg. Sec. 1.1502-13(e)(3) and Rev. Proc. 2009-31, I.R.B. 2009-27.   [66] Reg. Sec. 1.1502-6(a).

Intercompany sales, however, do raise deferred tax issues in certain cases. If the group files a consolidated tax return, the group defers income or loss on intercompany sales of inventory and other property for both tax and consolidated financial statement purposes. Thus, temporary differences and deferred tax issues do not arise. On the other hand, if the group members each file a separate tax return, the selling member recognizes income or loss for tax purposes but not for consolidated financial statement purposes, thereby creating a temporary difference. Accounting Standards Codification (ASC) 810, (formerly ARB No. 51) requires the group to defer recognizing income taxes on intercompany profits on assets remaining within the group,[67] but ASC 740 (formerly SFAS No. 109) prohibits "recognition of a deferred tax asset for the intra-entity difference between the tax basis of the assets in the buyer's tax jurisdiction and their cost as reported in the consolidated financial statements."[68] Thus, even though the buyer's tax basis (the intercompany purchase price) may exceed the financial statement basis (e.g., the original cost), the group does not recognize a deferred tax asset. Instead, the group recognizes a prepaid asset for the seller's tax on the intercompany profit.

EXAMPLE C:8-50 ▶ Parent forms Subsidiary on January 2 of the current year as a 100%-owned subsidiary. The corporations have no temporary or permanent differences aside from those that might arise on intercompany transactions. For the current year, Parent and Subsidiary report the following transactions:

	Parent	Subsidiary
Net income before intercompany transactions	$300,000	$120,000
Profit on sale of inventory from Parent to Subsidiary	50,000	
Profit on partial sale of same inventory from Subsidiary to third parties		6,000
Dividend from Subsidiary to Parent	40,000	

The $50,000 profit to Parent is the difference between the inventory's $60,000 cost to Parent and its $110,000 selling price to Subsidiary. Subsidiary, in turn, sold 30% of this inventory to third parties for $39,000. This portion of the inventory had a $33,000 ($110,000 × 0.30) tax basis to Subsidiary, thereby generating the $6,000 profit.

If Parent and Subsidiary file a consolidated tax return for the current year, the $40,000 intercompany dividend and the $35,000 ($50,000 × 0.70) profit in the remaining inventory will be eliminated in both the consolidated financial statements and the consolidated tax return, leaving no temporary differences. Thus, consolidated taxable income (as well as net income before federal income taxes will equal $441,000 ($300,000 + $120,000 + $50,000 + $40,000 + $6,000 − $40,000 − $35,000)), and the federal income tax liability will be $149,940 ($441,000 × 0.34). Accordingly, the group makes the following book journal entry:

Federal income tax expense	149,940	
Federal income taxes payable		149,940

If instead Parent and Subsidiary file separate tax returns, Parent will claim a $40,000 dividends-received deduction. Parent, however, will eliminate the $35,000 inventory profit deferred for consolidated financial statement purposes but not for tax purposes. Thus, Parent's separate taxable income will be $350,000 ($300,000 + $50,000 + $40,000 − $40,000), and Subsidiary's taxable income will be $126,000 ($120,000 + $6,000). Even though Parent and Subsidiary do not file a consolidated tax return, they still comprise a parent-subsidiary controlled group. Consequently, Sec. 1563 limits the use of the 15% and 25% tax brackets. However, because the group's total taxable income ($350,000 + $126,000) exceeds $335,000, the benefit of the low brackets is completely phased out. Consequently, all taxable income for the group is taxed a flat 34% tax rate, giving Parent a $119,000 ($350,000 × 0.34) tax liability and Subsidiary a $42,840 ($126,000 × 0.34) tax liability, for a total of $161,840. At the same time, the group's consolidated net income before federal income taxes remains at $441,000, which is $35,000 ($350,000 + $126,000 − $441,000) less than the group's total taxable income. The group records as prepaid taxes the $11,900 ($35,000 × 0.34) tax that Parent pays on the eliminated intercompany inventory profit, so

---

[67] Accounting Standards Codification (ASC) 810-10-45-8.

[68] Accounting Standards Codification (ASC) 740-10-25-3.

the group's federal income tax expense is $149,940 ($161,840 − $11,900). This $149,940 also equals 34% of the group's $441,000 consolidated net income before federal income taxes. Accordingly, the group makes the following book journal entry:

Federal income tax expense	149,940	
Prepaid taxes	11,900	
Federal income taxes payable		161,840

Next year, Parent and Subsidiary earn the same income before intercompany transactions ($300,000 and $120,000, respectively) and file separate tax returns. However, they have no intercompany transactions next year, and Subsidiary sells the remaining inventory to third parties for a $14,000 profit. Thus, Parent's taxable income is $300,000, and Subsidiary's taxable income is $134,000 ($120,000 + $14,000). In addition, Parent's tax liability is $102,000 ($300,000 × 0.34), and Subsidiary's tax liability is $45,560 ($134,000 × 0.34), for a total of $147,560. At the same time, the group's consolidated net income after recognizing the $35,000 deferred profit but before federal income taxes is $469,000 ($300,000 + $134,000 + $35,000). The group now charges to federal income tax expense the $11,900 it previously recorded as prepaid taxes in the year the intercompany sale occurred, so the group's federal income tax expense is $159,460 ($147,560 + $11,900). This $159,460 also equals 34% of the group's $469,000 consolidated net income before federal income taxes. Accordingly, the group makes the following book journal entry:

Federal income tax expense	159,460	
Prepaid taxes		11,900
Federal income taxes payable		147,560

SRLY LOSSES

A net operating loss (NOL) from a separate return limitation year (SRLY) will create a deferred tax asset, possibly subject to a valuation allowance.

EXAMPLE C:8-51 ▶ Parent Corporation acquires 100% of Subsidiary Corporation at the beginning of the current year, when Subsidiary has a $200,000 NOL. Parent and Subsidiary elect to file a consolidated tax return for the current year. Assuming Parent's acquisition of Subsidiary is not a Sec. 382 ownership change, the SRLY limitation restricts the Parent-Subsidiary group's use of Subsidiary's NOL. Accordingly, management estimates that the group will be able to use only $150,000 of the NOL before it expires. The group's tax rate is 34%. The deferred tax asset is $68,000 ($200,000 × 0.34), and the valuation allowance is $17,000 ($50,000 × 0.34).

If Parent's acquisition of Subsidiary qualifies as a Sec. 382 ownership change, the SRLY limitation does not apply because of the overlap rule. However, the Sec. 382 limitation applies to restrict the group's use of Subsidiary's NOL. Assuming management estimates that the group will be able to use only $140,000 of the NOL before it expires, the deferred tax asset is $68,000 ($200,000 × 0.34), and the valuation allowance is $20,400 ($60,000 × 0.34).

If Parent and Subsidiary file separate tax returns, Subsidiary's use of its own NOL is restricted. If Parent's acquisition of Subsidiary does not qualify as a Sec. 382 ownership change, Subsidiary can use the $200,000 NOL only to offset the taxable income on its separate tax return, which restricts Subsidiary's use of its own NOL in much the same was as the SRLY limitation restricts it on a consolidated tax return. If the acquisition qualifies as a Sec. 382 ownership change, Subsidiary's use of its own NOL is limited to the same Sec. 382 limitation that applies had the corporations file a consolidated tax return. ◀

See Chapter C:3 for a general discussion of financial implications of federal income taxes.

PROBLEM MATERIALS

DISCUSSION QUESTIONS

C:8-1 What minimum level of stock ownership does the IRC require for a corporation to be included in an affiliated group?

C:8-2 Which of the following entities are includible in an affiliated group (if the 80% stock ownership requirements are met)?
a. Domestic C corporation.
b. Foreign corporation.
c. Life insurance company taxed under Sec. 801.
d. Limited liability company.

C:8-3 Pamela (an individual) owns 100% of P Corporation's stock and 100% of R Corporation's stock. P owns 100% of S Corporation's stock and 49% of T Corporation's stock. S owns the remaining 51% of T's stock. All the corporations are includible corporations and have only one class of stock.
a. Which entities comprise an affiliated group?
b. Which entities comprise a controlled group?
c. How would your answer to Part a change if S were instead a foreign corporation?

C:8-4 P Corporation purchases all of S Corporation's stock in the current year. Both corporations are includible corporations. S is P's only subsidiary. Explain their federal income tax return filing alternatives.

C:8-5 How do the stock ownership requirements for an affiliated group of corporations differ from those for a controlled group?

C:8-6 P Corporation owns 100% of the stock of S1 and S2 Corporations. S1 owns 51% of S3 Corporation's stock, and unrelated persons own the remaining 49%. S2 is a foreign corporation. Explain why the corporations included in a consolidated tax return can differ from the corporations included in a set of consolidated financial statements.

C:8-7 Explain why the consolidated return Treasury Regulations are legislative regulations.

C:8-8 P Corporation has owned all the stock of S and T Corporations for several years. P sells all of T's stock to Z Corporation during the current year.
a. Does P's sale of T's stock cause the affiliated group to cease to exist?
b. Is T required to file a consolidated tax return with Z?
c. If P purchases all of T's stock from Z three years after it sells T's stock to Z, is T required to file a consolidated tax return with P and S?
d. How would your answers change if P did not own any of S's stock?

C:8-9 P Corporation owns all the stock of S and T Corporations, and the three corporations elected to file a consolidated tax return for the prior year. What circumstances would allow the corporations to file separate tax returns for the current year?

C:8-10 Define the following terms:
a. Intercompany transaction.
b. Intercompany item.
c. Corresponding item.
d. Recomputed corresponding item.
e. Matching rule.
f. Acceleration rule.

C:8-11 P and S1 Corporations have filed consolidated tax returns for several years. S1 acquires all of S2 Corporation's stock at the close of business on June 15 of the current year. Which of the following current year transactions are intercompany transactions?
a. S1 sells machinery (Sec. 1245 property) to S2 on September 1.
b. P sells inventory to S1 throughout the year.
c. S2 performs services for S1 throughout the year.
d. P sells inventory to the S1-S2 Partnership on July 23. S1 and S2 are equal partners in the partnership.

C:8-12 P, S1, and S2 Corporations comprise a consolidated group. The group members use the accrual method of accounting. For each of the following intercompany transactions that occur during the current year, determine the intercompany item and corresponding item.
a. P lends S1 money, and P charges interest at a 10% annual rate. The money and interest remain unpaid at the end of the tax year.
b. S1 sells inventory to P. At year end, P holds the entire inventory purchased from S1.
c. P sells land (Sec. 1231 property) to S2. S2 holds the land (Sec. 1231 property) at year-end.
d. S1 provides engineering services that are capitalized as part of the cost of S2's new factory building.

C:8-13 One consolidated group member realizes a gain on the sale of seven-year MACRS property to another member of its consolidated group after owning the property for three years. Explain how the selling group member reports its gain and how the purchasing group member determines its basis and depreciation deductions for the property.

C:8-14 One consolidated group member lends money to another member of its group. Both corporations use the accrual method of accounting. Explain how the lending group member reports its interest income and how the borrowing group member reports its interest expense for consolidated tax return purposes. Discuss how this treatment compares to the consolidated financial accounting treatment of the transaction.

C:8-15 Brooklyn and Bronx Corporations become an affiliated group at the beginning of the current year. Will the corporations obtain a greater charitable contribution deduction for the current year by filing a consolidated tax return or separate tax returns?

C:8-16 An affiliated group elects to file a consolidated tax return. Explain why the group's consolidated capital gain net income or net capital loss is not merely the sum of the members' separate capital gain net incomes and net capital losses if they were to file separate tax returns.

C:8-17 Indicate the tax treatment for each of the following dividends received by a corporation that is a member of an affiliated group filing a consolidated tax return:
  a. Dividend received from a corporation that is 10%-owned by the group member.
  b. Dividend received from a corporation that is 100%-owned by the group member.
  c. Dividend received from a foreign corporation that is 80%-owned by the group's parent corporation.
  d. Dividend received from a life insurance company that is 100%-owned by the group's parent corporation.
  e. Dividend received from a corporation that is 50%-owned by the group member and 50%-owned by the group's parent corporation.

C:8-18 P, S, and T Corporations comprise a consolidated group. In the current year, P has a profit, while S and T both incur a loss. The net of P's profit with S's and T's losses result in a consolidated NOL. In what years can P, S, and/or T deduct the consolidated NOL?

C:8-19 An affiliated group has a consolidated NOL for the current year. What factors could determine whether it would be advantageous or disadvantageous for the group to elect to forgo the carryback of the consolidated NOL?

C:8-20 Define the term SRLY and explain its significance and application to a consolidated tax return.

C:8-21 What is the SRLY-Sec. 382 overlap rule? Explain its significance and application to a consolidated tax return.

C:8-22 P Corporation owns 100% of S Corporation's stock, and the corporations file a consolidated tax return.
  a. Explain why P must increase the basis in its S stock by S's taxable income and decrease the basis by the dividends S pays to P.
  b. Suppose S owns 100% of T Corporation's stock. Explain the basis adjustments that P and S must make.

C:8-23 P Corporation owns 100% of the stock of S1 and S2 Corporations. The corporations currently are filing separate tax returns. P and S1 are profitable. S2 is a start-up company that has reported losses for its first two years of operations. S1 eventually will be purchasing cosmetics from S2 and reselling them to retailers. What are the advantages and disadvantages of the three corporations filing a consolidated tax return?

C:8-24 The president of your CPA firm's largest client, a medium-size manufacturing company, advises you that the firm is about to acquire its largest supplier. Both companies have been profitable for the past ten years. The president wants to know what tax return filing options are available for the two companies and the advantages and disadvantages of the options. What factors are likely to be most important for this decision? What additional information do you need to give the president an informed answer?

C:8-25 During what time period can an affiliated group elect to file a consolidated tax return? How does it make the election? During what time period can it request to terminate its consolidation?

C:8-26 For which of the following tax-related matters can an affiliated group's parent corporation act as the group's agent?
  a. Making an initial consent for a subsidiary corporation to participate in a consolidated return election.
  b. Changing an accounting method election for a subsidiary corporation.
  c. Carrying on correspondence with the IRS during an audit regarding a transaction entered into by a subsidiary corporation that affects the group's determination of consolidated taxable income.
  d. Requesting an extension of time within which to file a consolidated tax return.

ISSUE IDENTIFICATION QUESTIONS

C:8-27 Mark owns all the stock of Red and Green Corporations. Red has been reporting $125,000 in taxable income for each of the past five years. Green has been reporting $30,000 NOLs annually, which have accumulated to $150,000. Approximately one-third of Red's profits come from sales to Green. Intercompany sales between Red and Green have increased during each of the last five years. What tax issues should Mark consider with respect to his investments in Red and Green Corporations?

C:8-28 Alpha and Baker Corporations, two accrual method of accounting corporations that use the calendar year as their tax year, have filed consolidated tax returns for several years. Baker, a 100%-owned subsidiary of Alpha, is transferring a patent, equipment, and working capital to newly created Charter Corporation in exchange for 100% of its stock. In the current year, Charter will begin to produce parts for the automotive industry. Charter expects to incur organizational expenditures of $12,000 and start-up expenditures of $60,000. What tax issues should Charter consider with respect to the selection of its over-all accounting method, inventory method, and tax year, the proper reporting of its organizational and start-up expenditures, and the type of income tax return to file?

C:8-29 Wildcat Corporation is the parent company of a three-member affiliated group. Wildcat and Badger Corporations have filed consolidated tax returns for several years. Early in the current year, Wildcat purchases Hawkeye Corporation, a start-up business that incurred net operating losses in each of its first three years prior to the purchase. Hawkeye's losses total $260,000. Can the Wildcat-Badger-Hawkeye group deduct the losses on its consolidated tax return? The group expects annual profits to be $300,000, with Hawkeye's contribution to the total being $50,000. What tax issues should the three corporations consider when determining how they can deduct the NOLs?

PROBLEMS

C:8-30 *Affiliated Group Definition.* In each of the following cases, determine the corporations that comprise an affiliated group. All corporations are includible corporations and have one class of stock.

a. B Corporation owns 100% of C Corporation's stock and 90% of D Corporation's stock. Unrelated persons own 10% of D's stock.

b. B Corporation owns 100% of C Corporation's stock and 90% of D Corporation's stock. C owns 80% of E Corporation's stock, and D owns 75% of F Corporation's stock. Unrelated persons own the remainder of D's, E's, and F's stock.

c. Luciano, an individual, owns all the stock of M and N Corporations.

d. Viviana, an individual, owns all the stock of W and X Corporations. W owns all of Y Corporation's stock, and X owns all of Z Corporation's stock.

C:8-31 *Affiliated Group Definition* In each of the following cases, determine the corporations that comprise an affiliated group. All corporations are includible corporations and have one class of stock unless otherwise indicated.

a. P Corporation owns all the stock of S and T Corporations. T owns all of U Corporation's stock. T and U are Belgian corporations.

b. Assume the same facts as in Part a except U is a domestic corporation.

c. Omar, an individual, owns 100% of P Corporation's stock and 30% of S Corporation's stock. P owns 70% of S's stock.

d. G is a German corporation. G owns all of P Corporation's stock. P owns all of S Corporation's stock.

e. P Corporation owns all of S Corporation's stock. P and S each own 50% of T, a domestic limited liability company.

C:8-32 *Stock Ownership Requirement.* Pierre Corporation's management is negotiating with Salem Corporation's management to purchase some of Salem's stock. Salem's outstanding shares are as follows:

Type of Stock	Votes per Share	Shares Outstanding	FMV per Share
Common stock	4	60,000	$40
Preferred stock	1	10,000	75

Pierre's management wants to acquire enough Salem stock to allow Pierre and Salem to file a consolidated tax return. Pierre and Salem are includible corporations.

a. If Pierre acquires all of Salem's common stock and none of Salem's preferred stock, will they be eligible to file a consolidated tax return?

b. What minimum amount of Salem's common stock and/or preferred stock must Pierre acquire for the two corporations to be eligible to file a consolidated tax return?

c. Suppose that Salem also has 10,000 shares of nonvoting preferred stock outstanding. Each share's FMV is $90. The stock is nonparticipating, has redemption and liquidation rights limited to its issue price, and is not convertible. If Pierre acquires all of Salem's common and voting preferred stock, what minimum amount of Salem nonvoting preferred stock must Pierre acquire for the two corporations to be eligible to file a consolidated tax return?

C:8-33 *Affiliated Group Termination.* P Corporation owns all of S Corporation's stock. P and S have filed consolidated tax returns for several years. Determine whether the affiliated group terminates in each of the following circumstances. Assume that all corporations use the calendar year as their tax year.

a. On February 1 of the current year, P purchases all of T Corporation's stock.

b. On March 1 of the current year, P purchases all of T Corporation's stock. On October 1 of the current year, P sells all of S's stock.

c. On April 1 of the current year, P sells all of S's stock. On September 1 of the current year, P purchases all of T Corporation's stock.

d. On May 1 of the current year, P sells all of S's stock. On January 1 of the next year, P purchases all of T Corporation's stock.

e. On June 1, R Corporation purchases all of P's stock. R had no subsidiaries prior to June 1.

f. On July 1, R Corporation purchases all of P's stock. On July 1, R has several wholly owned subsidiaries with which it has filed consolidated tax returns for several years.

C:8-34 *Consolidated Taxable Income.* Assume the same facts as in Problem C:8-33. What tax returns must the corporations file for the current year?

C:8-35 *Consolidated Taxable Income.* P Corporation owns all the stock of S1 and S2 Corporations. The corporations have filed calendar year, consolidated tax returns for several years. On September 15 of the current year, P sells all of S1's stock to Michelle, an unrelated individual. What effect does P's sale of S1's stock have on the P-S1-S2 group's current year consolidated taxable income?

C:8-36 *Consolidated Return Election.* P Corporation uses the calendar year as its tax year and the accrual method as its overall accounting method. S Corporation uses a fiscal year ending June 30 as its tax year and the cash method as its overall accounting method. On July 31, 2012, P acquires all of S's stock, and the P-S affiliated group elects to file a consolidated tax return for 2012.

a. What tax year must the group use in filing its consolidated tax return?

b. What overall accounting method(s) can P and S Corporations use?

c. What tax returns must the corporations file?

C:8-37 *Intercompany Transactions.* P, S1, and S2 Corporations have filed consolidated tax returns for several years. In the current year (Year 1), S1 sells land to S2 for $275,000. S1 purchased the land for $120,000 several years ago and has held it for possible expansion. S2 constructs a new plant facility on the land. In Year 3, S2 sells the land and the plant facility to a third party for cash, with $400,000 of the sales price attributable to the land.

a. What are the intercompany item, the corresponding item, and the recomputed corresponding item for this intercompany transaction?

b. In what year(s) are S1's gain or loss and S2's gain or loss included in consolidated taxable income?

C:8-38 *Intercompany Transactions.* P Corporation owns all the stock of S1 and S2 Corporations, and the three corporations have filed consolidated tax returns on a calendar year basis for several years. P owns 2,400 shares of publicly traded stock it purchased several years ago for $30 per share. P sells all the stock to S1 for $45 per share on January 25 of the current year (Year 1). S1 sells 1,400 shares of the stock to a third party for $48 per share on December 6 of Year 1, and S1 sells the other 1,000 shares to another third party for $52 per share on March 18 of Year 2.

a. What are the intercompany item, the corresponding items, and the recomputed corresponding items for this intercompany transaction?

b. In what year(s) are P's gain or loss and S1's gain or loss included in consolidated taxable income?

c. Suppose P sells all of S1's stock to a third party on December 30 of Year 1. How would your answer to Part b change?

d. Suppose S1 sells the 1,000 shares on March 18 of Year 2, for $44 per share instead of $52 per share. How would your answers to Parts a and b change?

C:8-39 *Intercompany Transactions.* P and S Corporations have filed consolidated tax returns for several years. In Year 1, P purchased land as an investment for $20,000. In Year 3, P sold the land to S for $60,000. S used the land for four years as additional parking space for its employees and made no improvements to the land. In Year 7, S sells the land to Z Corporation, an unrelated party, for $180,000. The sale's terms require Z to pay S $36,000 in each of Years 7 through 11. The terms also require Z to pay S interest at a rate acceptable to the IRS. Z pays all the required amounts.

a. What are the intercompany item, the corresponding items, and the recomputed corresponding items?

b. In what year(s) does the consolidated group include P's gain or loss and S's gain or loss in its taxable income?

c. How does the consolidated group report the interest income?

C:8-40 *Intercompany Transactions.* P owns all the stock of S1 and S2 Corporations. The corporations have filed consolidated tax returns for several years. In the current year (Year 1), S1 sells land to P for $100,000. S1 purchased the land several years earlier for $35,000. P sells the land to a unrelated third party in Year 3 for $115,000. The sale's terms require the third party to pay P $50,000 in Year 3, $40,000 in Year 4, and $25,000 in Year 5, plus interest at a rate acceptable to the IRS. The third party pays all the required amounts.
a. In what year(s) does the consolidated group include S1's gain or loss and P's gain or loss in its taxable income?
b. Suppose P sells all of S1's stock on December 31 of Year 4. How would this sale change your answer to Part a?
c. Suppose S1 sold the land to P in Year 1 for $120,000 instead of $100,000. How would this sale change your answer to Part a?

C:8-41 *Intercompany Transactions.* P and S Corporations have filed consolidated tax returns for several years. On June 10 of the current year (Year 1), P purchases a new machine (MACRS five-year property) for $20,000 cash. P makes no expensing election under Sec. 179 and elects out of bonus depreciation. On April 4 of Year 3, P sells the machine to S for $18,000 cash. S uses the property for two years before selling it to an unrelated party on March 10 of Year 5, for $15,000.
a. What are the amount and character of P's gain or loss?
b. What is S's basis for the machine? What depreciation method does S use for the machine? What are S's depreciation deductions for the machine?
c. What are the amount and character of S's gain or loss?
d. What are the intercompany item, the corresponding items, and the recomputed corresponding items?
e. In what year(s) does the consolidated group include P's gain or loss and S's gain or loss in its taxable income?

C:8-42 *Intercompany Transactions.* P and S Corporations have filed consolidated tax returns for several years. On January 1 of the current year (Year 1), P purchased a new machine (MACRS seven-year property) for $50,000. P did not make a Sec. 179 election for this acquisition and elected out of bonus depreciation. At the close of business on June 6 of Year 4, P sells the machine to S for $37,500. S sells the machine to an unrelated third party for $20,000 on March 15 of Year 7.
a. What are the amount and character of P's gain or loss? What is the amount of S's gain or loss?
b. In what years does the group include in its consolidated taxable income P's gain or loss and S's gain or loss?
c. Suppose P's and S's common parent corporation, R, sells all of P's stock to an unrelated third party on December 31 of Year 5. How does this sale affect your answers to Parts a and b?

C:8-43 *Intercompany Transactions.* P Corporation owns all of S Corporation's stock. Both corporations use the accrual method of accounting. P engages in two transactions with S: P sells to S for $30,000 an automobile having an $18,000 adjusted basis, and S provides to P $6,000 of cleaning services. Under the intercompany transaction rules, what are the similarities and differences in how the group reports the two transactions?

C:8-44 *Intercompany Transactions.* P and S Corporations have filed consolidated tax returns on a calendar year basis for several years. Both corporations use the accrual method of accounting. On August 1 of the current year (Year 1), P loans S $250,000 on a one-year note. P charges interest at a 12% simple rate. S repays the loan plus interest on July 31 of Year 2. How does this intercompany transaction affect the group's consolidated taxable income?

C:8-45 *Intercompany Transactions.* P and S Corporations have filed consolidated tax returns on a calendar year basis for several years. Both corporations use the accrual method of accounting. On January 1 of the current year, S begins renting a warehouse to P for $10,000 per month. P pays S $10,000 on the first day of each month of the current year. How does this transaction affect the group's consolidated taxable income?

C:8-46 *Intercompany Transactions.* P and S Corporations have filed consolidated tax returns for several years. In the current year (Year 1), P began selling inventory items to S. P and S use the first-in, first-out (FIFO) inventory method. P's profits on its Year 1 inventory sales to S are $75,000. S's sales to third parties during Year 1 include inventory items that P sells to S during Year 1 for a $40,000 profit; S sells these inventory items to third parties for a $25,000 profit. S's inventory at the end of Year 1 includes items that P sells to S for a $35,000 profit. S is deemed to sell these to third parties during Year 2 due to its use of the FIFO method and realizes a $22,000 profit on their sale. P's profits on its Year 2 inventory sales to S are $240,000.

S's sales to third parties during Year 2 include items that P sells to S during Year 2 for a $160,000 profit. S sells these inventory items to third parties for a $105,000 profit. S's inventory at the end of Year 2 includes items that P sells to S for an $80,000 profit. The group's consolidated taxable income (before taking into account any adjustments for profits on intercompany inventory sales) is $100,000 in Year 1 and $367,000 in Year 2. For simplicity, assume P and S have no other transactions in these two years. Also, ignore the U.S. production activities deduction. What is the group's consolidated taxable income for Years 1 and 2?

C:8-47 *Intercompany Transactions.* P and S Corporations have filed consolidated tax returns for several years. The group had no intercompany inventory sales before the current year (Year 1). P and S use the first-in, first-out (FIFO) inventory method. During Year 1, S sells 50,000 widgets to P, earning $8 per unit profit on the sale. Also during Year 1, P sells 37,500 of these widgets to third parties for an additional $6 per unit profit. Thus, P's inventory at the end of Year 1 includes 12,500 of unsold widgets. During Year 2, S sells 80,000 widgets to P, earning $9 per unit profit on the sale. Also during Year 2, P sells to third parties 65,000 of these widgets and also sells the 12,500 widgets from beginning inventory, all for an additional $6 per unit profit. Thus, P's inventory at the end of Year 2 includes 15,000 widgets P purchased from S in Year 2. No intercompany inventory sales occur in Year 3. However, during Year 3, P sells all widgets in beginning inventory. In addition to these intercompany transactions, P incurs a $40,000 loss and S earns $500,000 of profit in each year from other business activities. What is the group's consolidated taxable income for each of Years 1, 2, and 3? Ignore the U.S. production activities deduction.

C:8-48 *Charitable Contribution Deduction.* Topeka and Wichita Corporations have filed consolidated tax returns for several years. Topeka and Wichita report current year taxable incomes (without regard to any dividend income received, charitable contribution deduction, or dividends-received deduction) of $200,000 and $150,000, respectively. The $200,000 includes $30,000 profit on inventory that Topeka sold to Wichita on December 29 of the current year. Wichita sold none of the inventory before the end of the year. Topeka and Wichita received dividends of $10,000 and $4,000, respectively, during the current year that qualify for the 70% dividends-received deduction. Wichita's and Topeka's cash contributions to public charities during the current year are $45,000 and $5,000, respectively. Ignore the U.S. production activities deduction.
a. What is the Topeka-Wichita group's consolidated taxable income?
b. What is the amount of the charitable contribution carryover? How long can it be carried back and/or forward?
c. What is the Topeka-Wichita group's regular tax liability?

C:8-49 *Sec. 1231 Gains and Losses and Capital Gains and Losses.* Mobile, Newark, and Omaha Corporations comprise an affiliated group that has filed separate tax returns prior to the current year. The corporations report the following amounts for the current year:

Transaction	Mobile	Newark	Omaha	Total
Sec. 1231 gains	$ 18,000	$ 9,000	$ -0-	$ 27,000
Sec. 1231 losses	12,000	14,000	-0-	26,000
Short-term capital gains	3,500	-0-	-0-	3,500
Short-term capital losses	(2,000)	-0-	(6,200)	(8,200)
Long-term capital gains	-0-	8,100	5,500	13,600
Long-term capital losses	(2,400)	(7,300)	-0-	(9,700)
Other separate taxable income	300,000	200,000	100,000	600,000

The corporations have no intercompany transactions, no capital loss carryovers, and no nonrecaptured net Sec. 1231 losses. Ignore the U.S. production activities deduction.
a. Determine each corporation's current year taxable income if they file separate tax returns for the current year.
b. Determine the group's current year taxable income if the corporations elect to file a consolidated tax return.

C:8-50 *Capital Gains and Losses.* Alpha and Beta Corporations comprise an affiliated group that has filed separate tax returns prior to the current year. The corporations report the following amounts for the current year:

Transaction	Alpha	Beta	Total
Long-term capital gains	$ 20,000	$ 15,000	$ 35,000
Long-term capital losses	(11,900)	(17,000)	(28,900)
Other separate taxable income	80,000	70,000	150,000

Alpha's long-term capital gains include a $4,400 gain on land it sold to Beta during the current year. Beta had not sold the land by the end of the current year. The corporations have no other intercompany transactions and no capital loss carryovers. Ignore the U.S. production activities deduction.

a. Determine each corporation's current year taxable income if they file separate tax returns for the current year.

b. Determine the group's current year taxable income if the corporations elect to file a consolidated tax return.

C:8-51 *Dividends-Received Deduction.* P, S, and T Corporations have filed consolidated tax returns for several years. P, S, and T report taxable incomes or losses (without regard to any dividends received and dividends-received deductions) of $200,000, $(70,000), and $175,000, respectively, for the current year. P and S received cash dividends this year as follows:

Shareholder	Distributing Corporation	Amount
P Corporation	T Corporation	$125,000
P Corporation	100%-owned nonconsolidated U.S.-based life insurance company	15,000
S Corporation	25%-owned domestic corporation	40,000
P Corporation	51%-owned foreign corporation	10,000

a. What amount of dividend income does the group include in its consolidated taxable income?

b. What is the amount of the consolidated dividends-received deduction?

c. What is the amount of consolidated taxable income and consolidated regular tax liability? Ignore the U.S. production activities deduction.

C:8-52 *Regular Tax Liability.* Miami and Tampa Corporations comprise a parent-subsidiary controlled group. The corporations also comprise an affiliated group that has filed separate tax returns prior to the current year. In each case for the current year, determine each corporation's regular tax liability if they file separate tax returns, and determine the group's consolidated regular tax liability if they elect to file a consolidated tax return. Ignore the U.S. production activities deduction. Assume that, if they file separate tax returns, Miami and Tampa do not elect a special apportionment plan for allocating the corporate tax rates. Assume also that, if the group elects to file a consolidated tax return, its consolidated taxable income equals the sum of Miami's and Tampa's separate taxable incomes.

a. Miami's separate taxable income is $50,000, and Tampa's separate taxable income is $30,000.

b. Miami's separate taxable income is $70,000, and Tampa's separate taxable income is $(15,000), i.e., a loss.

c. Miami's separate taxable income is $45,000, and Tampa's separate taxable income is $40,000.

C:8-53 *Alternative Minimum Tax.* Dallas and Houston Corporations comprise an affiliated group that formed at the beginning of the current year. The following items pertain to Dallas and Houston for the current year:

Transaction	Dallas	Houston	Total
Taxable income	$500,000	$400,000	$ 900,000
AMT preference & adjustment items	175,000	210,000	385,000
Adjusted current earnings	740,000	720,000	1,460,000

Determine each corporation's AMT liability if they file separate tax returns, and determine the group's consolidated AMT liability if they elect to file a consolidated tax return. Assume that, if the group elects to file a consolidated tax return, its consolidated taxable income, consolidated AMT preference and adjustment items, and consolidated adjusted current earnings equal the sum of the corporations' separate amounts. Assume also that the corporations do not qualify for the small corporation exemption from the AMT. Ignore the U.S. production activities deduction.

C:8-54 *General Business Credit.* Peoria and Salem Corporations have filed consolidated tax returns for several years. For the current year (after 2010), consolidated adjusted current earnings are $750,000. Consolidated preadjustment alternative minimum taxable income is $400,000. Consolidated taxable income is $300,000. The consolidated general business credit amount (computed without regard to the overall limitation) is $15,000. Assume the Peoria-Salem group is not eligible for the small corporation exemption from the AMT. Ignore the U.S. production activities deduction.

a. What is the group's federal tax liability?

b. Are any credit carryovers created in the current year? How are they used?

C:8-55 *Consolidated NOL Carrybacks and Carryovers.* P and S Corporations form in Year 1 and immediately elect to file consolidated tax returns. The group reports the following results:

	Taxable Income				
Group Member	Year 1	Year 2	Year 3	Year 4	Year 5
P	$9,000	$10,000	$(6,000)	$ 20,000	$15,000
S	(7,800)	2,000	2,000	(30,000)	10,000
Consolidated taxable income (before NOL deduction)	$1,200	$12,000	$(4,000)	$(10,000)	$25,000

The group does not elect to forego any NOL carrybacks. Ignore the U.S. production activities deduction. In what years can the group deduct the Years 3 and 4 consolidated NOLs?

C:8-56 *Consolidated NOL Carryover.* P Corporation owns all the stock of S1 and S2 Corporations. The corporations have filed consolidated tax returns since their creation in Year 1. At the close of business on July 10 of Year 3, P sells all of its S2 stock. The group reports the following results:

	Taxable Income		
Group Member	Year 1	Year 2	Year 3
P	$ 8,000	$(18,000)	$16,000
S1	9,000	(24,000)	(4,000)
S2	10,000	(28,000)	7,000[a]
S2 (7/11-12/31)			8,000[b]
Consolidated taxable income (before NOL deduction)	$27,000	$(70,000)	$19,000[c]

[a] Taxable income from January 1 through July 10 of Year 3.
[b] Taxable income from July 11 through December 31 of Year 3, is included in S2's separate tax return.
[c] $16,000 − $4,000 + $7,000.

Ignore the U.S. production activities deduction.

a. In what year(s) can the corporations deduct the Year 2 consolidated NOL if the group does not elect to forego the carryback period?

b. In what year(s) can the corporations deduct the Year 2 consolidated NOL if the group elects to forego the carryback period?

C:8-57 *Separate Return and Consolidated NOL Carryovers and Carrybacks.* P Corporation acquires all of S Corporation's stock on January 1 of Year 2. In Year 1, the corporations were unrelated entities that filed separate returns. P and S report the following results:

	Taxable Income	
Group Member	Year 1	Year 2
P	$40,000	$(30,000)
S	(29,000)	20,000
Consolidated taxable income	N/A	$(10,000)

N/A = Not applicable

Ignore the Sec. 382 loss limitation that might apply to P's acquisition of S, and ignore the U.S. production activities deduction.

a. What are the Year 2 tax consequences if P and S file a consolidated tax return? What are the Year 2 tax consequences if P and S instead file separate tax returns?

b. P and S report the following taxable income in Year 3 before any NOL carryover: P, $21,000; S, $6,000. What is Year 3 consolidated taxable income if P and S file consolidated returns for Years 2 and 3?

C:8-58 *Consolidated NOL Carryovers and Intercompany Transactions.* P Corporation owns all the stock of S1 and S2 Corporations, and the group has filed consolidated tax returns on a calendar year basis for several years. In the current year (Year 1), S2 sells to S1 for $90,000 land S2 had purchased for $75,000. On December 31 of Year 2, S1 sells the land to a third party for $91,000. On January 18 of Year 3, P sells all of its S2 stock to a third party for a sales price equal to P's basis in the S2 stock. The consolidated group members report the following amounts of taxable income and loss (before deducting any NOLs or applying the matching and acceleration rules):

	Taxable Income (Loss)	
Group Member	*Year 2*	*Year 3*
P	$165,000	$(30,000)
S1	(120,000)	(20,000)
S2	(140,000)	7,000[a]
Consolidated taxable income or loss before deducting any NOLs or applying the matching and acceleration rules	$ (95,000)	$(43,000)

[a] Pertains to January 1 through January 18 of Year 3.

Assume that the group elects to forego the carryback period for the Year 2 consolidated NOL.
a. Determine the amount of NOL available for S2's Year 3 separate tax return.
b. Assume the same facts as in Part a except S1's land sale to a third party for $91,000 occurred on January 1 of Year 3. Determine the amount of NOL available for S2's Year 3 separate tax return.

C:8-59 *SRLY Limitation.* Bart, P's sole shareholder, creates P on January 1 of Year 1. P purchases all of S1's and S2's stock on September 1 of Year 1, after both corporations are in operation for about six months. P, S1, and S2 Corporations comprise the P-S1-S2 affiliated group and file separate tax returns for Year 1. The P-S1-S2 affiliated group then elects to file consolidated tax returns starting in Year 2. The group reports the following results:

	Taxable Income		
Group Member	*Year 1*	*Year 2*	*Year 3*
P	$(8,000)	$50,000	$10,000
S1	(24,000)	20,000	(18,000)
S2	(16,000)	(10,000)	15,000
Consolidated taxable income (before NOL deduction)	XXX	$60,000	$ 7,000

Ignore the Sec. 382 loss limitation that might apply to the acquisitions of S1 and S2, assume that P's purchase of S1 and S2 does not qualify as a reverse acquisition, and ignore the U.S. production activities deduction.
a. What is Year 2 consolidated taxable income?
b. What is Year 3 consolidated taxable income?
c. What NOL carryovers are available in Year 4?
d. How would your answer to Parts a through c change if Bart instead created P, S1, and S2 as an affiliated group on January 1 of Year 1?

C:8-60 *SRLY and Sec. 382 Loss Limitations.* P Corporation owns 100% of S Corporation's stock, and they have filed consolidated tax returns for several years. P also has owned 49% of T Corporation's stock for 10 years. On December 31 of the current year (Year 1), P purchases the other 51% of T's stock for $510,000 cash. T has $160,000 of NOLs it is carrying over on that date. In Year 2, the corporations report taxable profits as follows: P, $400,000; S, $250,000; and T, $90,000. Assume that the long-term tax-exempt federal interest rate is 5%.
a. Determine the amount of T's NOLs the group can deduct for its Year 2 consolidated taxable income.
b. Assume the same facts as in Part a except P purchases 45% of T's stock for $450,000 on December 31 of Year 1. Determine the amount of T's NOLs the group can deduct for its Year 2 consolidated taxable income.

C:8-61   *Stock Basis Adjustments.* P Corporation purchases 100% of S Corporation's stock for $2 million on January 1 of the current year. The corporations elect to file a consolidated tax return. During the current year, S reports $350,000 of taxable income and $30,000 of tax-exempt interest income, and it distributes a $100,000 dividend to P. Each corporation pays its portion of the consolidated tax liability. Assume a 34% corporate tax rate. What is P's basis for its S stock at the end of the current year?

C:8-62   *Stock Basis Adjustments.* P Corporation owns 100% of S Corporation's stock, and S owns 100% of T Corporation's stock. The three corporations have filed consolidated tax returns for several years. On January 1 of the current year, P's basis for its S stock is $5 million, and S's basis for its T stock is $3 million. The corporations' taxable incomes for the current year are $500,000 for P, $350,000 for S, and $250,000 for T. S and T pay no dividends during the year. Each corporation pays its portion of the consolidated tax liability. Assume a 34% corporate tax rate.

a. Determine P's basis for its S stock and S's basis for its T stock at the end of the current year.

b. Assume the same facts as in Part a except S pays an $80,000 dividend to P and T pays a $90,000 dividend to S. Determine P's basis for its S stock and S's basis for its T stock at the end of the current year.

C:8-63   *Financial Statement Implications.* P and S Corporations comprise an affiliated group that files separate tax returns. P and S had no intercompany inventory sales before the current year (Year 1). P and S use the first-in, first-out (FIFO) inventory method. During Year 1, S sells 40,000 widgets to P, earning $7 per unit profit on the sale. P's inventory at the end of Year 1 includes 10,000 of these widgets. During Year 2, S sells 75,000 widgets to P, earning $7.50 per unit profit on the sale. P's inventory at the end of Year 2 includes 12,000 of these widgets. During Year 3, no intercompany inventory sales occur, and P sells all widgets in beginning inventory. P's and S's taxable income each year (including any profits from intercompany inventory sales) is $380,000 and $300,000, respectively. Prepare the journal entries to record federal income tax expense for each of Years 1, 2, and 3. Assume a 34% corporate tax rate.

COMPREHENSIVE PROBLEM

C:8-64   P and S Corporations have filed consolidated tax returns for ten years. P and S use the accrual method of accounting, and they use the calendar year as their tax year. P and S report separate return taxable income (before any consolidation adjustments and eliminations, the NOL deduction, the charitable contributions deduction, and the dividends-received deduction) for the current year of $200,000 and $250,000, respectively. These amounts include the following current year transactions and events:

- P sells land to a third party for $80,000. P purchased the land from S two years ago for $70,000. S had purchased the land five years ago for $48,000.

- P's separate taxable income includes a $12,000 dividend S paid to P.

- P sold inventory to S in the previous year for which the deferred profit at the beginning of the current year is $5,000. S sells this inventory outside the consolidated group in the current year. P sells additional inventory to S in the current year, realizing a $100,000 profit. The intercompany profit on this unsold inventory is $8,000.

- The P-S group has a $20,000 consolidated NOL carryover available from the previous year. The NOL is wholly attributable to S.

- P receives $10,000 of dividends from corporations in which it owns less than 1% of the stock.

- P and S contribute cash to charities of $17,000 and $11,000, respectively.

- P lends S $150,000 early in the current year. S repays the loan later in the year. In addition, S pays P $6,000 interest at the time of repayment.

- S earns $1,600 of tax-exempt interest income, which is not included in S's $250,000 separate return taxable income.

- P and S have no qualified production activities income.

Determine the P-S group's consolidated taxable income and consolidated tax liability for the current year. What is P's basis for the S stock at the end of the current year? Assume that P's basis for the S stock was $1.4 million at the beginning of the current year.

C:8-65   Using the facts from Problem C:8-67 below, calculate the tax liabilities of Flying Gator and T Corporations for 2010. How much larger (or smaller) would be the total of the two separate return tax liabilities if they were to file separate tax returns than the affiliated group's consolidated return tax liability? What taxes are due (or refund available) if Flying Gator made $125,000 of estimated tax payments and T Corporation made $25,000 of estimated tax payments?

TAX STRATEGY PROBLEM

C:8-66   Sandra and John, who are unrelated, own all of Alpha and Beta Corporations. Sandra and John each own 50% of Alpha's stock and 50% of Beta's stock. For five years, Alpha has conducted manufacturing activities and sold machine parts primarily in the eastern United States. Alpha has reported $75,000 of operating profits in each of the last two years. Alpha's annual operating profits are expected to grow to $150,000 during the next five years. Alpha has $100,000 of NOLs it is carrying forward. Alpha sells 25% of its product to Beta. Beta has been working to establish a market niche for reselling Alpha products in the southwestern United States. In the start-up phase of establishing the market, Beta incurred $200,000 of NOLs. Under the sales arrangement with Alpha, probably the best that Beta can hope to achieve in the short-run is reach a break-even point.

Required: What suggestions can you offer Sandra and John about the short-term possibility of using Alpha's and Beta's NOLs against the profits that Alpha expects to earn and about minimizing their overall tax liabilities if both businesses become profitable? Sandra has specifically asked about merging the two companies into a single entity so the losses of one entity can offset the profits of the other and delay the need to pay income taxes to the federal government. Sandra indicates that the two companies were created for business reasons and not tax avoidance reasons. The operating situation has changed and, according to Sandra, now may be the time to combine the entities into one. However, John is not sure that bringing the two businesses together is a good idea.

TAX FORM/RETURN PREPARATION PROBLEM

C:8-67   The Flying Gator Corporation and its 100%-owned subsidiary, T Corporation, have filed consolidated tax returns for many years. Both corporations use the hybrid method of accounting and the calendar year as their tax year. During 2010 (which is the current year for this problem), they report the operating results as listed in Table C:8-2. Note the following additional information:

- Flying Gator and T Corporations are the only members of their controlled group.
- Flying Gator's address is 2101 W. University Ave., Gainesburg, FL 32611. Its employer identification number is 38-2345678. Flying Gator was incorporated on June 11, 1998. Its total assets are $430,000. Flying Gator made estimated tax payments of $150,000 for the consolidated group in the current year. Stephen Marks is Flying Gator's president.
- A $50,000 consolidated NOL carryover from the preceding year is available. The NOL is wholly attributable to Flying Gator.
- Flying Gator and T use the first-in, first-out (FIFO) inventory method. T began selling inventory to Flying Gator in the preceding year, which resulted in a $40,700 deferred intercompany profit at the end of the preceding year. Flying Gator is deemed to realize this profit in the current year because it uses the FIFO method. During the current year, T sells additional inventory to Flying Gator, realizing a $300,000 profit. At the end of the current year, Flying Gator holds inventory responsible for $45,100 of this profit.
- Flying Gator receives all its dividends from T. T receives all its dividends from a 60%-owned domestic corporation. All distributions are from E&P.
- Flying Gator receives all its interest income from T. T pays Flying Gator the interest on March 31 of the current year on a loan that was outstanding from October 1 of the preceding year through March 31 of the current year. Flying Gator and T did not accrue any interest at the end of the preceding year because they use the hybrid method of accounting. T pays $5,000 of its interest expense to a third party.
- Officer's salaries are $80,000 for Flying Gator and $65,000 for T. These amounts are included in salaries and wages in Table C:8-2.
- Flying Gator's capital losses include a $10,000 long-term loss on a sale of land to T in the current year. T holds the land at year-end.

▼ **TABLE C:8-2**

Current Year Operating Results for Flying Gator and T Corporations (Problem C:8-67)

Income or Deductions	Flying Gator	T	Total
Gross receipts	$2,500,000	$1,250,000	$3,750,000
Cost of goods sold	(1,500,000)	(700,000)	(2,200,000)
Gross profit	$1,000,000	$ 550,000	$1,550,000
Dividends	100,000	50,000	150,000
Interest	15,000		15,000
Sec. 1231 gain		20,000	20,000
Sec. 1245 gain		25,000	25,000
Long-term capital gain (loss)	(5,000)	6,000	1,000
Short-term capital gain (loss)		(3,000)	(3,000)
Total income	$1,110,000	$ 648,000	$1,758,000
Salaries and wages	175,000	200,000	375,000
Repairs	25,000	40,000	65,000
Bad debts	10,000	5,000	15,000
Taxes	18,000	24,000	42,000
Interest	30,000	20,000	50,000
Charitable contributions	22,000	48,000	70,000
Depreciation (other than that included in cost of goods sold)	85,000	40,000	125,000
Other expenses	160,000	260,000	420,000
Total deductions	$ 525,000	$ 637,000	$1,162,000
Separate return taxable income (before the USPAD, NOL ded., and DRD)	$ 585,000	$ 11,000	$ 596,000

- The corporations have no nonrecaptured net Sec. 1231 losses from prior tax years.
- T's Sec. 1245 gains include $20,000 realized on the sale of equipment to Flying Gator at the close of business on September 30 in the current year. The asset cost $100,000 and had been depreciated for two years by T as five-year property under the MACRS rules. T claims nine months of depreciation in the current (second) year. Flying Gator begins depreciating the property in the current year by using the MACRS rules and a five-year recovery period. Flying Gator claims the appropriate first-year MACRS depreciation on the property in the current year but does not elect Sec. 179 expensing and does not claim bonus depreciation.
- Qualified production activities income for Flying Gator is $340,000 and for T is $(35,000). The applicable percentage for 2010 is 9%.

Determine the consolidated group's 2010 tax liability. Prepare the front page of the consolidated group's current year corporate income tax return (Form 1120). Hint: Prepare a spreadsheet similar to the one included in Appendix B to arrive at consolidated taxable income.

CASE STUDY PROBLEMS

C:8-68　P Corporation operates six automotive service franchises in a metropolitan area. The service franchises have been a huge success in their first three years of operation, and P's annual taxable income exceeds $600,000. J Corporation owns the real estate associated with the six service franchises. P leases its automotive service franchise locations from J. J reports large interest and MACRS depreciation deductions because of a highly leveraged, capital intensive operation. As a result, J has reported NOLs in its first three years of operation. P and J file separate tax returns.

　　Carol owns 100% of both corporations. Carol sees the idea for the automotive service franchise chain starting to really develop and expects to add six more locations in each of the next two years. Because of the rapid expansion that is planned, she feels that she has outgrown her father's accountant and needs to have new ideas to help her save tax dollars so she can reinvest more money in the business.

Required: The tax partner that you are assigned to requests that you prepare a memorandum outlining your thoughts about Carol's tax problems and suggested solutions to those problems in preparation for his meeting next week with Carol.

TAX RESEARCH PROBLEMS

C:8-69 Angela owns all the stock of A, B, and P Corporations. P has owned all the stock of S1 Corporation for six years. The P-S1 affiliated group has filed a consolidated tax return in each of these six years using the calendar year as its tax year. On July 10 of the current year (a nonleap year), Angela sells her entire stock investment in A, which uses the calendar year as its tax year. No change takes place in Angela's ownership of B stock during the tax year. At the close of business on November 25 of this year, S1 purchases 90% of the common stock and 80% of the nonconvertible, nonvoting preferred stock (measured by value) of S2 Corporation. A, P, S1, and S2 are includible corporations. Which corporations are included in the affiliated group? In the controlled group? What income is included in the various tax returns? How is the allocation of the income between tax years made if the books are not closed on the sale or acquisition dates? If no special allocations are made, what portion of the reduced tax rate benefits of Sec. 11(b) can be claimed in the current year by the affiliated group? In future years?

A partial list of resources includes:

- IRC Sec. 1504
- IRC Sec. 1563
- Reg. Sec. 1.1502-76
- Reg. Sec. 1.1561-2

C:8-70 P, R, and T Corporations have filed a consolidated tax return for a number of years using the calendar year as its tax year. Current plans call for P to purchase all of X Corporation's stock at the close of business on June 30 of the current year from three individuals. X was created seven years ago and always has been an S corporation using the calendar year as its tax year. The chief financial officer of P comes to your office and makes a number of inquiries about the tax consequences of the acquisition including: Can X retain its S election? If so, does it file a federal income tax return separate from the consolidated group? Does X have to be included in the P-R-T group's consolidated tax return? Assuming the acquisition takes place as planned, what tax returns are required of the consolidated group and X? What income is included in the pre-affiliation tax return of X (if required) and the consolidated group's post-acquisition consolidated tax return? Prepare a brief memo for the chief financial officer outlining the answers to these questions and any other questions you feel are relevant.

A partial list of resources includes:

- IRC Sec. 1361(b)
- IRC Sec. 1362(d)(2)
- Reg. Sec. 1.1502-76

C:8-71 Mary owns all of Able Corporation's stock. Able owns all the shares of Baker and Cross Corporations. The three corporations have filed a consolidated calendar year tax return for several years. After consulting with her tax accountant, Mary decides that it will be more beneficial if the corporations are restructured as S corporations so their income is subject to a single layer of tax. The restructuring process is complex because Baker holds some valuable franchises that cannot be transferred. The restructuring occurred on October 23 of the current year. On October 23, Able transfers all of its assets and liabilities to Baker, and the two corporations merge with Baker as the survivor. As part of the restructuring, Mary receives all the stock of Baker. Six hours after the first transaction, Baker sells Mary all the stock in Cross for $2 million. Thus, the consolidated group survived for only six hours during the restructuring. Immediately after the restructuring, Baker incurs substantial losses. Can Baker file a consolidated return for the restructuring year and deduct the post-restructuring losses against prior year consolidated income?

A partial list of resources includes:

- Reg. Sec. 1.1502-75(a)(2)
- Reg. Sec. 1.1502-75(d)(2)
- Reg. Sec. 1.1502-76(b)(1)
- *The Falconwood Corporation v. U.S.* (96 AFTR 2d 2005-5977), 2005-2 USTC ¶50,597 (Fed. Cir., 2005)

CHAPTER

9

PARTNERSHIP FORMATION AND OPERATION

LEARNING OBJECTIVES

After studying this chapter, you should be able to

1. Differentiate between general and limited partnerships

2. Explain the tax results of a contribution of property or services in exchange for a partnership interest

3. Determine the permitted tax years for a partnership

4. Differentiate between items included in partnership ordinary income or loss and those that must be separately stated

5. Calculate a partner's distributive share of partnership income, gain, loss, deduction, or credit items

6. Explain the requirements for a special partnership allocation

7. Calculate a partner's basis in a partnership interest

8. Determine the limitations on a partner's deduction of partnership losses

9. Determine the tax consequences of a guaranteed payment

10. Explain the requirements for recognizing the holder of a partnership interest as a partner in a family partnership

11. Determine the allocation of partnership income between a donor and a donee of a partnership interest

12. Determine the requirements for filing a partnership tax return

9-1

CHAPTER OUTLINE

Partnerships have long been one of the major entities for conducting business activities. Partnerships vary in complexity from the corner gas station owned and operated by two brothers to syndicated tax partnerships with their partnership interests traded on major security markets. Two different sets of rules apply to partnerships depending on their size. The rules discussed in Chapter C:9 and most of Chapter C:10 apply to the majority of partnerships. A different set of rules, discussed at the end of Chapter C:10, apply to electing large partnerships. The partnership rules are found in Subchapter K of the IRC, which includes Secs. 701–777.

Chapters C:9 and C:10 discuss the income tax rules applying to partnership business operations. The first part of this chapter defines a partnership, describes the types of partnerships, and discusses the formation of a partnership. The remainder of the chapter deals with the ongoing operations of a partnership, such as the annual taxation of partnership earnings, transactions between partners and the partnership, and a partner's basis in a partnership interest. This chapter also considers procedural matters, such as reporting the annual partnership income and IRS audit procedures for partnerships and their partners. Chapter C:10 continues by discussing distributions to the partners and the tax implications of transactions used to terminate a partner's interest in a partnership. Chapter C:10 also discusses the unique problems of limited partnerships and the taxation of publicly traded partnerships and electing large partnerships.

DEFINITION OF A PARTNERSHIP

ADDITIONAL COMMENT

Even though the formation of a partnership requires no legal documentation, the partners should draft a formal written partnership agreement to prevent subsequent disagreements and arguments.

For tax purposes, the definition of a partnership includes "a syndicate, group, pool, joint venture, or other unincorporated organization" that carries on a business or financial operation or venture. However, a trust, estate, or corporation cannot be treated as a partnership. Unlike a corporation, which can exist only after incorporation documents are finalized, formation of a partnership requires no legal documentation. If two people (or business entities) work together to carry on any business or financial operation with the intention of making a profit and sharing that profit as co-owners, a partnership exists for federal income tax purposes.[1]

The IRC and Treasury Regulations define a **partner** simply as a member of a partnership. Years of case law and common business practice, however, have made clear that a partner can be an individual, trust, estate, or corporation. The only restriction on the number of partners is that a partnership must have at least two partners, but a large syndicated partnership may have hundreds or even thousands of partners.

GENERAL AND LIMITED PARTNERSHIPS

OBJECTIVE 1

Differentiate between general and limited partnerships

Each state has laws governing the rights and restrictions of partnerships. Almost all state statutes are modeled on the Uniform Partnership Act (UPA) or the Uniform Limited Partnership Act (ULPA) and thus have strong similarities to each other. A partnership can take two legal forms: a general partnership or a limited partnership. The differences between the two forms are substantial and extend to the partners' legal rights and liabilities as well as the tax consequences of operations to the partners. Because these differences are so important, we examine the two partnership forms before proceeding with further discussion of the partnership tax rules.

GENERAL PARTNERSHIPS. A **general partnership** exists any time two or more partners join together and do not specifically provide that one or more of the partners is a limited partner (as defined below). In a general partnership, each partner has the right to par-

---

[1] Section 761(a) allows an election to avoid the Subchapter K rules for a very limited group of business owners.

ticipate in the management of the partnership. However, a general partnership is flexible enough to allow its business affairs to be managed by a single partner chosen by the general partners.

Although only one (or a few) of the general partners may exercise management duties, each **general partner** has the ability to make commitments for the partnership.[2] In a general partnership, each partner has unlimited liability for all partnership debts. If the partnership fails to pay its debts, each partner may have to pay far more than the amount he or she has invested in the venture. Thus, each partner faces the risk of losing personal assets if the partnership incurs business losses. This exposure is the single biggest drawback to the general partnership form of doing business.

LIMITED PARTNERSHIPS. A **limited partnership** has two classes of partners. It must have at least one general partner, who essentially has the same rights and liabilities as any general partner in a general partnership,[3] and at least one **limited partner**. Even if a partnership becomes bankrupt, a limited partner can lose no more than his or her original investment plus any additional amount he or she has committed to contribute. However, a limited partner has no right to be active in the partnership's management.

The broad rights and obligations of general partners could make a general partnership an unwieldy form for operating a business with a large number of owners. On the other hand, a limited partnership having one (or a small number of) general partners can be useful for a business operation that needs to attract a large amount of capital. In fact, one common form for a tax shelter investment is a limited partnership having a corporation with a small amount of capital as its sole general partner. Such an arrangement allows the tax advantages of the partnership form while retaining the limited liability feature for virtually every investor.

Many of these limited partnerships are so large and widely held that in many ways they appear more like corporations than partnerships. As discussed in Chapter C:10, the tax laws provide that publicly traded partnerships may be reclassified for tax purposes as corporations.

LIMITED LIABILITY LIMITED PARTNERSHIPS (LLLPs). A recent variation on the limited partnership in some (but not all) states is the LLLP. As discussed above, a limited partnership, in addition to having limited partners, has one or more general partners whose personal liability exposure is unlimited. The LLLP is a partnership formed under a state's limited partnership laws but that can elect under the state's laws to provide the general partners with limited liability. Thus, the LLLP is similar to an LLC and becomes potentially useful in states that do not extend LLC status to personal service firms but allow such firms to operate as an LLLP.[4]

LIMITED LIABILITY COMPANIES (LLCs). With the advent of LLCs, businesses have the opportunity to be treated as a partnership for tax purposes while having limited liability protection for every owner. State law provides this limited liability. Unique tax rules for LLCs have not been developed. Instead, the check-the-box regulations (discussed in Chapter C:2) permit each LLC to choose whether to be treated as a partnership or taxed as a corporation. If an LLC is considered a partnership for tax purposes, the same tax rules apply to the LLC that apply to a traditional partnership. Chapter C:10 further discusses the tax treatment of LLCs.

LIMITED LIABILITY PARTNERSHIPS (LLPs). Initially, professional organizations in certain fields (e.g., public accounting and law) were not permitted to operate as LLCs and therefore remained general partnerships. Subsequently, many states have added LLPs to the list of permissible business forms. The primary difference between a general partnership and an LLP is that, in an LLP, a partner is not liable for damages resulting from failures in the

---

[2] Uniform Partnership Act.
[3] Uniform Limited Partnership Act.

[4] For a detailed discussion, see Shop Talk, "Service Firms Practicing as LLLPs: What Are the Tax Consequences?" *Journal of Taxation*, August 2005.

work of other partners or of people supervised by other partners. Under the check-the-box regulations, an LLP can be treated as a partnership or as a corporation. Like an LLC, the default tax classification of an LLP is a partnership. The same tax rules apply to an LLP that apply to a traditional partnership. Chapter C:10 further discusses the tax treatment of LLPs.

ELECTING LARGE PARTNERSHIPS.   Partnerships that qualify as "large partnerships" may elect to have a simplified set of reporting rules apply. To qualify as a large partnership, the partnership must not be a service partnership and must not be engaged in commodity trading. Further, to qualify to make this election, the partnership must have at least 100 partners throughout the tax year (excluding partners who provide substantial services in connection with the partnership's business activities). Once the partnership makes the election, it reports its income under a simplified reporting scheme, is subject to different rules about when the partnership terminates, and is subject to a different system of audits. The election is irrevocable without IRS permission. Chapter C:10 presents details about the tax treatment of electing large partnerships.

OVERVIEW OF TAXATION OF PARTNERSHIP INCOME

The following overview gives a broad perspective of the taxation of partnership income other than income earned by electing large partnerships. (Appendix F compares the tax characteristics of a partnership, a C corporation, and an S corporation.) More detailed descriptions follow this overview.

PARTNERSHIP PROFITS AND LOSSES

A partnership is not a taxpaying entity, and income earned by a partnership is not subject to two layers of federal income taxes. Instead, each partner reports a share of the partnership's income, gain, loss, deduction, and credit items in his or her income tax return. The partnership, however, must file Form 1065 (U.S. Partnership Return of Income), an information return that provides the IRS with information about partnership earnings as well as how the earnings are allocated among the partners. The partnership must elect a tax year and accounting methods to calculate its earnings. (Appendix B includes a completed partnership tax return that shows a Form 1065 and Schedule K-1 for a partner along with a set of supporting facts.)

Each partner receives a Schedule K-1 from the partnership, which informs the partner of the amount and character of his or her share of partnership items. The partner then combines his or her partnership earnings and losses with all other items of income or loss for the tax year, computes the amount of taxable income, and calculates the tax liability. Partnership income is taxed at the applicable tax rate for its partners, which can range from 10% to 35% (in 2011) for partners who are individuals, trusts, or estates. Corporate partners pay tax on partnership income at rates ranging from 15% to 39%.

One of the major advantages of the partnership form of doing business is that partnership losses are allocated among the partners. If the loss limitation rules (explained later in this chapter) do not apply, these losses offset the partners' other income, resulting in immediate tax savings for the partners. The immediate tax saving available to the partner contrasts sharply with the net operating loss (NOL) carrybacks or carryforwards that may result from a C corporation's operations.

THE PARTNER'S BASIS

A partner's basis in his or her partnership interest is a crucial element in partnership taxation. When a partner makes a contribution to a partnership or purchases a partnership interest, he or she establishes a beginning basis. Because partners can be personally liable for partnership debts, a partner's basis in his or her partnership interest is increased by his or her share of any partnership liabilities. Accordingly, the partner's basis fluctuates as the partnership borrows and repays loans or increases and decreases its accounts payable. In addition, a partner's basis in his or her partnership interest increases by the partner's share of partnership income and decreases by his or her share of partnership losses. Because a partner's basis in his or her partnership interest can never be negative, the basis serves as one limit on the amount of deductible partnership losses. (See the discussion on pages C:9-26 and C:9-27 about the various loss limitations.)

EXAMPLE C:9-1 ▶ Tom purchases a 20% interest in the XY Partnership for $8,000 on January 1 of Year 1 and begins to materially participate in the partnership's business. The XY Partnership uses the calendar year as its tax year. At the time of the purchase, the XY Partnership has $2,000 in liabilities, of which Tom's share is 20%. Tom's basis in his partnership interest on January 1 is $8,400 [$8,000 + (0.20 × $2,000)]. ◀

EXAMPLE C:9-2 ▶ Assume the same facts as in Example C:9-1 except, during Year 1, the XY Partnership incurs $10,000 in losses, and its liabilities increase by $4,000. Tom's basis on December 31 of Year 1 is calculated as follows:

January 1, Year 1, basis	$8,400
Plus: Share of liability increase ($4,000 × 0.20)	800
Minus: Share of partnership losses ($10,000 × 0.20)	(2,000)
December 31, Year 1, basis	$7,200 ◀

EXAMPLE C:9-3 ▶ Assume the same facts as in Example C:9-2, and further assume that, during Year 2, the XY Partnership incurs $60,000 in losses and its liabilities increase by $10,000. Tom's share of the losses is $12,000 ($60,000 × 0.20). The maximum amount Tom can deduct in Year 2 is calculated as follows:

January 1, Year 2, basis	$7,200
Plus: Share of liability increase	2,000
December 31, Year 2, basis before losses	$9,200
Minus: Maximum loss deduction allowed	(9,200)
December 31, Year 2, basis	$ –0–

Tom's remaining $2,800 in losses carry over to subsequent years, and he can deduct them when he regains sufficient basis in his partnership interest. ◀

PARTNERSHIP DISTRIBUTIONS

ADDITIONAL COMMENT

The increase in a partner's basis for earnings prevents double taxation of those earnings upon a subsequent distribution, sale of the partnership interest, or liquidation of the partnership.

When a partnership makes current (nonliquidating) distributions, the distributions generally are nontaxable to the partners because they represent the receipt of earnings that already have been taxed to the partners and that have increased the partners' bases in their partnership interests. Because they are a return of capital, these distributions reduce a partner's basis in his or her partnership interest. If a cash distribution is so large, however, that it exceeds a partner's basis in his or her partnership interest, the partner recognizes gain equal to the amount of the excess. When the partnership goes out of business or when a partner withdraws from the partnership, the partnership makes liquidating distributions to the partner. Like current distributions, these distributions cause the partner to recognize gain only if the cash received exceeds the partner's basis in his or her partnership interest. A partner may recognize a loss if he or she receives only cash, inventory, and unrealized receivables in complete liquidation of his or her partnership interest. Chapter C:10 presents detailed coverage of current and liquidating distributions.

TAX IMPLICATIONS OF FORMATION OF A PARTNERSHIP

When two or more individuals or entities decide to operate an unincorporated business together, they form a partnership. The following sections examine the tax implications of property contributions, service contributions, and organization and syndication expenditures.

OBJECTIVE 2

Explain the tax results of a contribution of property or services in exchange for a partnership interest

CONTRIBUTION OF PROPERTY

NONRECOGNITION OF GAIN OR LOSS. Section 721 governs the formation of a partnership. In most cases, a partner who contributes property in exchange for a partnership interest recognizes no gain or loss on the transaction. Likewise, the partnership recognizes no gain or loss on the contribution of property. The partner's basis for his or her partnership interest and the partnership's basis for the property are both the same as basis of the property transferred.[5]

Nonrecognition treatment is limited to transactions in which a partner receives a partnership interest in exchange for a contribution of property. As in the corporate formation area, the term *property* includes cash, tangible property (e.g., buildings and land), and intangible property (e.g., franchise rights, trademarks, and leases).[6] Services are specifically excluded from the definition of property, so a contribution of services for a partnership interest is a taxable transaction.

RECOGNITION OF GAIN OR LOSS. The general rule of Sec. 721(a) provides that neither the partnership nor any partner recognizes gain or loss when partners contribute property in exchange for a partnership interest. Three exceptions to this general rule may require a partner to recognize a gain upon the contribution of property to a partnership in exchange for a partnership interest:

▶ Contribution of property to a partnership that would be treated as an investment company if it were incorporated

▶ Contribution of property followed by a distribution in an arrangement that may be considered a sale rather than a contribution

▶ Contribution of property to a partnership along with the partnership's assumption of the partner's liabilities if, as a result, the partner's share of partnership liabilities exceeds his or her basis in the partnership.

The investment company exception of Sec. 721(b) requires recognition of gain only if the exchange results in diversification of the transferor's property interest.[7] If the contribution of property is to an investment partnership, the contributing partner must recognize any gain (but not loss) realized on the property transfer as if he or she sold the stock or securities.

Sections 707(a)(2)(A) and (B) set out the second exception, which holds that a property contribution followed by a distribution (or an allocation of income or gain) may be treated as a property sale by the partner to the partnership rather than as a contribution by the partner to the partnership. For example, Treasury Regulations may require sale treatment (and the recognition of gain or loss) if the distribution would not have occurred except for the contribution.

ADDITIONAL COMMENT

For contributions to a corporation to be nontaxable, the contributing shareholders must control (own at least 80%) the corporation immediately after the transaction. No such control requirement exists for contributions to a partnership to be nontaxable.

EXAMPLE C:9-4 ▶ In return for a 40% interest in the CD Partnership, Cara contributed land with a $100,000 fair market value (FMV). The partners agreed that the partnership would distribute $100,000 in cash to Cara immediately after the contribution. Because the cash distribution would not have occurred had Cara not first contributed the land and become a partner, the transaction is likely to be treated as a sale of the land by Cara to the partnership. ◀

If the distribution does not occur simultaneously with the contribution, the transaction is treated as a sale if the later distribution is not dependent on the normal business risk of the enterprise.

EXAMPLE C:9-5 ▶ Elena received a 30% interest in the DEF Partnership in return for her contribution of land having a $60,000 FMV. The partnership waits six months and then distributes $60,000 in cash to Elena. If the $60,000 distribution is not contingent on the partnership's earnings or ability to borrow funds or other normal risks of doing business, the distribution and contribution will be treated as a sale of land by Elena to the partnership. ◀

---

[5] Secs. 722 and 723.
[6] For an excellent discussion of the definition of the term *property*, see footnote 6 of *D.N. Stafford v. U.S.*, 45 AFTR 2d 80-785, 80-1 USTC ¶9218 (5th Cir., 1980).
[7] Reg. Sec. 1.351-1(c)(1). This investment is taxed only when immediately after the exchange more than 80% of the value of the partnership's assets (excluding cash and nonconvertible debt obligations) is held for investment or is readily marketable stocks, securities, or interests in regulated investment companies or real estate investment trusts.

EFFECTS OF LIABILITIES. The third condition that may cause a partner to recognize gain (but not loss) on the formation of a partnership is the contribution of property to a partnership along with the partnership's assumption of liabilities previously owed by the partner. Because each partner is liable for his or her share of partnership liabilities, increases and decreases in the partnership liabilities are reflected in each partner's basis. Specifically, Sec. 752 provides that two effects result from a partner's contribution of property to a partnership if the partnership also assumes the partner's liabilities.

▶ Each partner's basis is increased by his or her share of the partnership's liabilities as if he or she had contributed cash to the partnership in the amount of his or her share of partnership liabilities.

▶ The partner whose personal liabilities are assumed by the partnership has a reduction in the basis of his or her partnership interest as if the partnership distributed cash to him or her in the amount of the assumed liability. A cash distribution first reduces the partner's basis in the partnership interest. If the cash distribution exceeds the partner's predistribution basis in the partnership interest, the partner recognizes gain.

The net effect of these two basis adjustments, however, is seldom large enough to cause a transferor partner to recognize gain when he or she contributes property to the partnership. The transferor partner is deemed first to have made a contribution of property plus a contribution of cash equal to the partner's share of any partnership liabilities existing prior to his or her entrance into the partnership (or contributed by other partners concurrently with this transaction). The partner then is deemed to have received a cash distribution equal to the total amount of his or her own liability assumed by the *other* partners. (No basis adjustment is required for the portion of the liability transferred to the partnership by the transferor that he or she will retain as a partner.)

EXAMPLE C:9-6 ▶

In return for a 20% partnership interest, Mary contributes land having a $60,000 FMV and a $30,000 basis to the XY Partnership. The partnership assumes Mary's $15,000 liability arising from her purchase of the land, and Mary's share of partnership liabilities is 20%. The XY Partnership has $4,000 in liabilities immediately before her contribution. Mary's basis in her partnership interest is calculated as follows:

Basis of contributed property	$30,000
Plus: Mary's share of existing partnership liabilities ($4,000 × 0.20)	800
Minus: Mary's liabilities assumed by the other partners ($15,000 × 0.80)	(12,000)
Mary's basis in her partnership interest	$18,800

Mary recognizes no gain on the partnership's assumption of her liability because the deemed cash distribution from the assumption of her $12,000 in liabilities by the partnership does not exceed her $30,800 basis in the partnership interest immediately preceding the deemed distribution. ◀

EXAMPLE C:9-7 ▶

Assume the same facts as in Example C:9-6 except the amount of the liability assumed by the XY Partnership is $50,000. Mary's basis in her partnership interest is calculated as follows:

Basis of contributed property	$30,000
Plus: Mary's share of existing partnership liabilities ($4,000 × 0.20)	800
Predistribution basis	$30,800
Minus: Mary's liabilities assumed by the other partners ($50,000 × 0.80)	(40,000)
Basis in partnership interest (cannot be negative)	$ –0–

The cash deemed distributed in excess of Mary's predistribution basis causes her to recognize a $9,200 ($40,000 − $30,800) gain. Mary reduces her basis to zero by the distribution because a partner's basis in the partnership interest can never be less than zero. ◀

STOP & THINK

Question: Assume the land Mary contributed in Example C:9-6 has a $60,000 FMV and an $85,000 adjusted basis. Should Mary contribute it to the partnership?

Solution: If Mary contributes the land, she cannot recognize her $25,000 ($60,000 FMV − $85,000 adjusted basis) loss until the partnership disposes of the property. Accordingly, Mary might prefer to sell the property and recognize her loss now. If the partnership

ADDITIONAL COMMENT

If Mary's interest in the partnership exceeded 50%, she could not deduct the loss on the sale of property to the partnership. See page C:9-27.

can afford the $60,000 price and needs this property, Mary could sell the land to the partnership, recognize her loss on the sale, and then contribute the cash she receives from the partnership in exchange for her partnership interest. If the partnership does not need the property, Mary could sell the land to a third party, recognize her loss, and contribute the sales proceeds to the partnership in exchange for her partnership interest. However, a problem arises if the partnership needs this property and cannot afford to buy it from Mary. In that case, contributing the property to the partnership may be the only alternative despite the less-than-optimal tax results.

TYPICAL MISCONCEPTION

Example C:9-7 illustrates another difference between partnership and corporate formations. In the example, XY Partnership does not increase its basis in the property for the gain recognized by Mary, but if XY were a corporation, XY would increase its basis in the property by Mary's recognized gain.

Because the partnership's assumption of a partner's liabilities is treated as a cash distribution, the character of any gain recognized by the partner is controlled by the partnership distribution rules. Cash distributions exceeding predistribution basis always result in gain recognition, and that gain is deemed to be gain from the sale of the partnership interest.[8] Because a partnership interest is usually a capital asset, any gain arising from assumption of a partner's liabilities normally is a capital gain.

PARTNER'S BASIS IN THE PARTNERSHIP INTEREST (COMMONLY CALLED OUTSIDE BASIS). In general, the transferor partner's beginning basis in the partnership interest equals the sum of money contributed plus his or her basis in contributed property. If the partner recognizes any gain on the contribution because the partnership is an investment company, the amount of recognized gain increases his or her basis in the partnership interest.[9] Beginning basis also includes the partner's share of partnership liabilities at the time of contribution. Any gain recognized because of the effects of liabilities on the partner's basis does not increase the basis for the partnership interest because, in this situation, the basis is zero.

In some instances, a partner may contribute valuable property having little or no basis. For example, accounts receivable or notes receivable of a partner using the cash method of accounting can be a valued contribution to a partnership, but if the receivables' bases are zero, the beginning basis of the partnership interest also is zero.

TYPICAL MISCONCEPTION

If a partner contributes both ordinary income property and capital gain property to a partnership, the partner apparently has two different holding periods for his or her partnership interest.

HOLDING PERIOD FOR PARTNERSHIP INTEREST. The holding period for the partnership interest includes the transferor's holding period for the contributed property if that property is a capital asset or a Sec. 1231 asset in the transferor's hands.[10] If the contributed property is an ordinary income asset (e.g., inventory) to the partner, the holding period for the partnership interest begins the day after the contribution date.[11]

EXAMPLE C:9-8 ▶ On April 1, Sue contributes a building (a Sec. 1231 asset) to the ST Partnership in exchange for a 20% interest. Sue purchased the building three years ago. Her holding period for her partnership interest includes the three years she held the contributed building. ◀

EXAMPLE C:9-9 ▶ On April 1, Ted contributes inventory to the ST Partnership in exchange for a 20% interest. No matter when Ted acquired the inventory, his holding period for his partnership interest begins on April 2, the day after his contribution. ◀

BOOK-TO-TAX ACCOUNTING COMPARISON

Although the partnership takes a carryover tax basis in property, the partnership also records the property at FMV for book purposes. Thus, the partnership essentially maintains two sets of books.

PARTNERSHIP'S BASIS IN PROPERTY. Under Sec. 723, the partnership's basis for contributed property is the same as the property's basis in the hands of the contributing partner. If, however, the contributing partner recognizes gain because the partnership is an investment company, such gain increases the partnership's basis in the contributed property. Gain recognized by the contributing partner because of the assumption of a partner's liability does not increase the partnership's basis in the property.[12]

Not only does the property's basis carry over to the partnership from the contributing partner, but for some property the character of gain or loss on a subsequent disposition of the property by the partnership also references the character of the property in the contributing

8 Sec. 731(a).
9 Sec. 722.
10 Sec. 1223(1).

11 Reg. Sec. 1.1223-1(a).
12 Rev. Rul. 84-15, 1984-1 C.B. 158.

partner's hands. Section 724 prevents the transformation of ordinary income into capital gains (or capital losses into ordinary losses) when a partner contributes property to a partnership. Properties that were (1) unrealized receivables, inventory, or capital loss property in the hands of the contributing partner and (2) contributed to a partnership retain their character for some subsequent partnership dispositions.[13]

Unrealized Receivables. The concept of unrealized receivables plays a key role for tax purposes in many different partnership transactions. An **unrealized receivable** is any right to payment for goods or services the holder has not included in income because of the accounting method used.[14] The most common occurence of unrealized receivables is a cash basis taxpayer's accounts receivable.

If a partner contributes an unrealized receivable to his or her partnership, any gain or loss recognized on the partnership's later disposition or collection of the receivable is treated as ordinary income or loss. This rule mandates ordinary income or loss treatment regardless of how long the partnership holds the receivable or its character in the partnership's hands.

Inventory. If property was inventory to the contributing partner, its character remains ordinary for five years. Consequently, any gain or loss recognized by the partnership on the disposition of such property during the five-year period beginning on the date of contribution is ordinary gain or loss. Ordinary gain or loss treatment occurs even if the property is a capital asset or Sec. 1231 asset in the partnership's hands.

EXAMPLE C:9-10 ▶

On June 1, Jose, a real estate developer, contributes ten acres of land in an industrial park he developed to the Hi-Tech Partnership in exchange for a 30% interest in the partnership. Although Jose held the acreage in inventory, the land serves as the site for Hi-Tech's new research facility. Four years later Hi-Tech sells its research facility and the land. Although gain on the sale of the land usually would be taxed as Sec. 1231 gain, Hi-Tech must report it as ordinary income. ◀

ADDITIONAL COMMENT

Congress enacted Sec. 724 to eliminate the ability to transform the character of gain or loss on property by contributing the property to a partnership and having the partnership subsequently sell it.

Capital Loss Property. The final type of property whose character is fixed at the time of the contribution is property that would generate a capital loss if sold by the contributing partner rather than contributed to the partnership. A loss recognized by the partnership on the disposition of the property within five years of its contribution to the partnership is a capital loss. However, the amount of loss characterized as capital may not exceed the capital loss the contributing partner would have recognized had the partner sold the property on the contribution date. The character of any loss exceeding the difference between the property's FMV and its adjusted basis on the contribution date is determined by the property's character in the hands of the partnership.

EXAMPLE C:9-11 ▶

Pam holds investment land that she purchased six years ago for $50,000. The FMV of the land was only $40,000 two years ago when she contributed it to the PK Partnership, which is in the business of developing and selling lots. PK develops the contributed land and sells it in the current year for $28,000, or at a $22,000 loss. The $10,000 loss that accrued while Pam held the land as a capital asset retains its character as a capital loss. The remaining $12,000 of loss that accrues while the land is part of the partnership's inventory is an ordinary loss. ◀

PARTNERSHIP'S HOLDING PERIOD. Under Sec. 1223(2), the partnership's holding period for its contributed assets includes the holding period of the contributing partner. This rule applies without regard to the character the property has in the contributing partner's hands or the partnership's hands.

SECTION 1245 AND 1250 PROPERTY RULES. Although the Sec. 1245 and Sec. 1250 depreciation recapture rules override many gain nonrecognition provisions in the IRC, the partner incurs no depreciation recapture unless he or she recognizes gain upon contributing

---

[13] Sec. 724. The determination of whether property is an unrealized receivable, inventory, or a capital loss property in the contributing partner's hands occurs immediately before the contribution.
[14] Section 724(d)(1) references the unrealized receivables definition found in

Sec. 751(c). For distributions and sale transactions, the unrealized receivables definition is broadened to include certain recapture items. This difference is discussed more fully in Chapter C:10.

property in exchange for a partnership interest.[15] Instead, both the adjusted basis and depreciation recapture potential carry over to the partnership. If the partnership later sells the property at a gain, the Sec. 1245 and 1250 provisions affect the character of the gain. In addition, any Sec. 1250 gain potential carries over to the partnership to affect gain characterization upon a future sale. Section 1250 gain is taxed to individuals at a 25% capital gains tax rate under Sec. 1(h)(1)(D).

CONTRIBUTION OF PROPERTY AFTER FORMATION. Any time a partner contributes property in exchange for a partnership interest, the rules outlined above apply whether the contribution occurs during the formation of the partnership or at a later date. This treatment contrasts sharply with corporate contributions, where a nontaxable contribution after formation is rare because of the 80% control requirement. Most contributions of property in exchange for a partnership interest are nontaxable even if they occur years after forming the partnership.

CONTRIBUTION OF SERVICES

A partner who receives a partnership interest in exchange for services has been compensated as if he or she receives cash and thus must recognize ordinary income. The amount and timing of the income to be recognized are determined under Sec. 83. Consequently, receipt of an unrestricted interest in a partnership requires the service partner to immediately recognize income equal to the FMV of the partnership interest less any cash or property contributed by the partner. Generally, the service partner recognizes no income upon receiving a restricted interest in a partnership until the restriction lapses or the interest can be freely transferred.

ADDITIONAL COMMENT

The Treasury Department has issued proposed regulations, and the IRS will issue a new revenue procedure that will alter the landscape of taxing partnership interests transferred for services. The new rules also will make Rev. Proc. 93-27, discussed on the next page, obsolete. However, taxpayers may not rely on the proposed rules until they are finalized and may continue to rely on existing rules and procedures. See Notice 2005-43, 2005-24 I.R.B. 1221.

Although a partnership interest seems to be a unified interest, it really is made up of two components: a capital interest and a profits interest. A partner may receive both components or only a profits interest in exchange for his or her services. (A capital interest without a profits interest rarely occurs.) Treasury Regulations indicate that a **capital interest** can be valued by determining the amount the partner would receive if the partnership liquidated on the day the partner receives the partnership interest.[16] If the partner would receive proceeds from the sale of the partnership's assets or receive the assets themselves, he or she is considered to own a capital interest. Alternatively, if the partner's only interest is in the future earnings of the partnership (with no interest in the current partnership assets), the partner owns a **profits interest** (but not a capital interest).

Tax law has long been settled that receipt of a capital interest in a partnership in exchange for services is taxable under the rules outlined above. A profits interest, however, is no more than a right to future income taxable to the partners as the partnership earns it. To the extent the profits interest itself has a value, one might expect that value to be taxed when the partner receives the profits interest, as any other property received for services would be taxed.

EXAMPLE C:9-12 ▶ Carl arranges favorable financing for the purchase of an office building and receives a 30% profits interest in a partnership formed to own and operate the building. Less than three weeks later, Carl sells his profits interest to his partner for $40,000. Carl must recognize $40,000 as ordinary income from the receipt of a partnership profits interest in exchange for services. ◀

The facts in Example C:9-12 approximate those of *Sol Diamond,* a landmark partnership taxation case, which was the first case to tax the partner upon receipt of a profits interest.[17] The Tax Court pointed out that Sec. 61 included all compensation for services, and no other provision contained in the IRC or Treasury Regulations removed this transaction from taxation. The Seventh Circuit Court of Appeals seemed to limit the inclusion

---

[15] Secs. 1245(b)(3) and 1250(d)(3). Property acquired as a capital contribution where gain is not recognized under Sec. 721 is subject to the MACRS anti-churning rules of Sec. 168(i)(7)(A). In general, the anti-churning rules require the partnership to use the same depreciation method as the partner who contributed the property. See Chapter C:2 for a discussion of these rules in connection with a corporate formation transaction.

[16] Reg. Sec. 1.704-1(e)(1)(v). The capital interest definition in this regulation relates to family partnerships, but such definition should apply generally in the partnership area.

[17] 33 AFTR 2d 74-852, 74-1 USTC ¶9306 (7th Cir., 1974), *aff'g.* 56 T.C. 530 (1971).

of a profits interest to situations in which the market value of the profits interest could be determined. The IRS resolved much of the uncertainty in this area of tax law when it issued Rev. Proc. 93-27, which provides that the IRS generally will tax a profits interest received for services only in three specified instances in which a FMV is readily ascertainable.[18] In the general case, therefore, an income tax is not levied on the profits interest separately, but all partnership profits that pass through to the partner are taxed under the normal rules of partnership taxation.

CONSEQUENCES TO THE PARTNERSHIP. Payments by the partnership for services are either deductible as an expense or capitalized, including those paid for services with an interest in the partnership. If the payment constitutes a deductible expense, the partnership takes the deduction in the same year the partner includes the value of his or her partnership interest in income.[19] This rule matches the timing of the partnership's deduction to the partner's income recognition.

Allocating the Expense Deduction. The partnership allocates the expense deduction or the amortization of the capital expenditure among the partners other than the service partner. This allocation occurs because these partners make the outlay by relinquishing part of their interest in the partnership.

EXAMPLE C:9-13 ▶ In June of the current year Jay, a lawyer, receives a 1% capital and profits interest (valued at $4,000) in the JLK Partnership in return for providing legal services to JLK's employees during the first five months of the current year. The legal services were a fringe benefit for JLK's employees and were deductible by JLK. Jay must include $4,000 in his current year gross income, and JLK can deduct the expense in the current year. JLK allocates the $4,000 expense to all partners other than Jay. ◀

If the service performed is of a nature that should be capitalized, the partnership capitalizes the amount and amortizes it as appropriate. The related asset's basis is increased at the same time and in the same amount as the partner's gross income inclusion.[20]

EXAMPLE C:9-14 ▶ In June of the current year, Rob, an architect, receives a 10% capital and profits interest in the KLB Partnership for his services in designing a new building to house the partnership's operations. The June value of the partnership interest is $24,000. Rob must recognize $24,000 of ordinary income in the current year as a result of receiving the partnership interest. The KLB Partnership must capitalize the $24,000 as part of the building's cost and depreciate that amount (along with the building's other costs) over its recovery period. ◀

The timing of the partner's recognition of income is the same in the preceding two examples even though the partnership could deduct one payment but had to capitalize the other.

Partnership Gain or Loss. By exchanging an interest in the partnership for services, the partnership, in effect, pays for services by transferring an interest in the underlying partnership property. Generally, when a debtor uses property to pay a debt, the debtor must recognize gain or loss equal to the difference between the property's FMV and adjusted basis. Likewise, the partnership must recognize the gain or loss existing in the proportionate share of its assets deemed to be transferred to the service partner.[21] Furthermore, because the partnership recognizes gain or loss, it must adjust the bases of the assets.

EXAMPLE C:9-15 ▶ On January 1 of the current year, Maria is admitted as a 25% partner in the XYZ Partnership in exchange for services valued at $16,500. The partnership has no liabilities at the time but has assets with a basis of $50,000 and FMV of $66,000. The transaction is treated as if Maria received an undivided one-fourth interest in each asset. She is taxed on the $16,500 FMV of the

---

[18] 1993-2 C.B. 343. The three exceptions involve receipt of a profits interest having a substantially certain and predictable income stream, the partner disposes of the profits interest within two years of receipt, or the profits interest is a limited interest in a publicly traded partnership.

[19] Reg. Sec. 1.83-6(a)(1).
[20] Reg. Sec. 1.83-6(a)(4).
[21] Reg. Sec. 1.83-6(b).

assets and takes a $16,500 basis in her partnership interest. The partnership recognizes $4,000 of gain [0.25 × ($66,000 FMV − $50,000 adjusted basis)] on the assets deemed paid to Maria. The partnership calculates gain or loss for each asset XYZ holds, and the character of each asset determines the character of the gain or loss recognized. The recognized gain is allocated to the partners other than Maria. Also, the partnership's original basis in its assets ($50,000) is increased by the $4,000 recognized gain. ◄

ORGANIZATIONAL AND SYNDICATION EXPENDITURES

SELF-STUDY QUESTION

What is the importance of the distinction between organizational expenditures and syndication expenditures?

ANSWER

Organizational expenditures can be deducted up to $5,000 and then amortized over a period of 180 months, but syndication expenditures are *not* deductible or amortizable.

The costs of organizing a partnership are capital expenditures. However, under Sec. 709, the partnership can elect to deduct the first $5,000 of these expenditures in the tax year it begins business. As a limit, the partnership must reduce the $5,000 by the amount by which cumulative organizational expenditures exceed $50,000, although the $5,000 cannot not be reduced below zero. The partnership can amortize the remaining organizational expenditures over an 180-month period beginning in the month it begins business.

For organizational expenditures paid or incurred after September 8, 2008, a partnership is deemed to have made the Sec. 709 election for the tax year the partnership begins business.[22] A partnership also can apply the amortization provisions for expenditures made after October 22, 2004, provided the statute of limitations is still open for the particular year. If the partnership chooses to forgo the deemed election, it can elect to capitalize the expenditures (without amortization) on a timely filed tax return for the tax year the partnership begins business. Either election, to amortize or capitalize, is irrevocable and applies to all organizational expenditures of the partnership.

Organizational expenditures that can be capitalized and amortized must meet the same requirements as the costs incurred by a corporation making the Sec. 248 election to amortize organizational expenditures (see Chapter C:3). The organizational expenditures must be incident to the creation of the partnership, chargeable to a capital account, and of a character that would be amortizable over the life of the partnership if the partnership had a limited life. Eligible expenditures include legal fees for negotiating and preparing partnership agreements, accounting fees for establishing the initial accounting system, and filing fees. Syndication expenditures for the issuing and marketing of interests in the partnership are not organizational expenditures and cannot be included in this election.[23] The partnership deducts unamortized organizational expenditures (but not capitalized syndication expenditures) when it terminates or liquidates.

Topic Review C:9-1 summarizes the tax consequences of forming a partnership.

PARTNERSHIP ELECTIONS

OBJECTIVE 3

Determine the permitted tax years for a partnership

Once formed, the partnership must make a number of elections. For example, a partnership must select a tax year and elect accounting methods for all but a few items affecting the computation of partnership taxable income or loss.

PARTNERSHIP TAX YEAR

The partnership's selection of a tax year is critical because it determines when each partner reports his or her share of partnership income or loss. Under Sec. 706(a), each partner's tax return includes his or her share of partnership income, gain, loss, deduction, or credit items for any taxable year of the partnership ending within or with the partner's tax year.

EXAMPLE C:9-16 ▶ Vicki is a member of a partnership having a November 30 year-end. In her tax return for calendar year 2011, she must include her share of partnership items from the partnership tax year that ends November 30, 2011. Results of partnership operations in December 2011 are reported in Vicki's 2012 tax return along with her share of other partnership items from the partnership year that ends on November 30, 2012. She receives, in essence, a one-year deferral of the taxes due on December's partnership income. ◄

---

[22] Temp. Reg. Sec. 1.709-1T.

[23] Reg. Sec. 1.709-2(b).

Topic Review C:9-1

Formation of a Partnership

	CONTRIBUTION TO A PARTNERSHIP	
	PROPERTY	**SERVICES**
Recognition of gain, loss, or income by partner	Nontaxable unless (1) liabilities assumed by the partnership exceed partner's predistribution basis in partnership interest (gain recognized is amount by which liabilities assumed by partnership exceed predistribution basis), (2) the partnership formed is an investment partnership (gain recognized is excess of FMV of partnership interest over basis of assets contributed), or (3) a contribution is followed by a distribution that is treated as a sale (gain or loss recognized on sale transaction).	Taxable to partner equal to FMV of partnership interest received in exchange for the services.
Basis of partnership interest	Substituted basis from property contributed plus share of partnership liabilities assumed minus the partner's liabilities assumed by the partnership. Gain recognized because of the investment company rules increases the basis of the partnership interest.	Amount of income recognized plus share of partnership liabilities assumed by the partner minus partner's liabilities assumed by the partnership.
Gain or loss recognized by the partnership	No gain or loss recognized by the partnership.	1. Deduction or capitalized expense is created depending on the type of service rendered. 2. Gain or loss recognized equals difference between FMV of portion of assets used to pay service partner and the basis of such portion of the assets.
Basis of assets to the partnership	Carryover basis is increased by a partner's gain recognized only if gain results from the formation of an investment partnership. No basis adjustment occurs when assumption of partner's liabilities results in a partner's gain recognition. In a sale transaction, assets take a cost basis.	Increased or decreased to reflect the FMV of the assets paid to the service partner.

SECTION 706 RESTRICTIONS. Because of a substantial opportunity for tax deferral, Congress enacted Sec. 706 to restrict the available choices for a partnership's tax year. The partnership must use the same tax year as the one or more **majority partners** who have an aggregate interest in partnership profits and capital exceeding 50%. This rule must be used only if these majority partners have a common tax year and have had this tax year for the shorter of the three preceding years or the partnership's period of existence. If the tax year of the partner(s) owning a majority interest cannot be used, the partnership must use the tax year of all its principal partners (or the tax year to which all of its principal partners are concurrently changing). A **principal partner** is defined as one who owns a 5% or more interest in capital or profits.[24] If the principal partners do not have a common tax year, the partnership must use the tax year that allows the least aggregate deferral. The least aggregate deferral test provided in Treasury Regulations[25] requires that, for each possible tax year-end, each partner's ownership percentage be multiplied by the number of months the partner would defer income (number of months from partnership year-end to partner year-end). The number arrived at for each partner is totaled across all partners. The same procedure is followed for each alternative tax year, and the partnership must use the tax year that produces the smallest total.

EXAMPLE C:9-17 ▶ Jane, Kerry Corporation, and Lanier Corporation form the JKL Partnership. The three partners use tax years ending on December 31, June 30, and September 30, respectively. Jane, Kerry

---

[24] Sec. 706(b)(3).　　　　　　　　　　　　　[25] Reg. Sec. 1.706-1.

WHAT WOULD YOU DO IN THIS SITUATION?

Bob Krause and his large family corporation have been longtime clients of your accounting firm. During the current year, Bob and his adult son, Tom, formed the BT Partnership to develop and sell vacation homes on the Suwanee River. Bob contributed a 1,000-acre tract of land in exchange for a 50% interest in BT Partnership's profits and losses. The land had a $300,000 FMV and a $30,000 adjusted basis. Tom contributed $150,000 in cash for the remaining 50% interest in the partnership. Two months after being formed, BT

Partnership used the land as security for a $200,000 loan from a local bank. Of the $200,000 loan proceeds, the partnership used $50,000 to subdivide and plot the land. The partnership then distributed the other $150,000 of the loan proceeds to Bob. Bob plans not to report these transactions because property contributions in exchange for a partnership interest and distributions of money by a partnership that do not exceed the partner's basis are nontaxable transactions. What would you advise your client to do in this situation?

Corporation, and Lanier Corporation own 40%, 40%, and 20%, respectively, of the partnership. Neither the majority partner rule nor the principal partner rule can be applied to determine JKL's tax year because each partner has a different year-end. To determine the least aggregate deferral, all three possible year-ends must be analyzed as follows:

| | | | Possible Tax Year-Ends | | | | | |
| | | | 6/30 | | 9/30 | | 12/31 | |
Partnership Partner	Interest	Partner Tax Year	Months Deferred[a]	Total[b]	Months Deferred	Total	Months Deferred	Total
Jane	40%	12/31	6	2.4	3	1.2	0	0
Kerry	40%	6/30	0	0	9	3.6	6	2.4
Lanier	20%	9/30	3	0.6	0	0	9	1.8
				3.0		4.8		4.2

[a] Months from possible partnership tax year-end to partner tax year-end.
[b] Partnership interest × months deferred = Total.

The partnership must use a June 30 year-end because, with a total score of 3.0, that tax year-end produces the least aggregate deferral. ◀

If the partnership has a business purpose for using some tax year other than the year prescribed by these rules, the IRS may approve use of another tax year. Revenue Procedure 2002-39[26] states that an acceptable business purpose for using a different tax year is to end the partnership's tax year at the end of the partnership's natural business year. This revenue procedure explains that a business having a peak period and a nonpeak period completes its natural business year at the end of its peak season (or shortly thereafter). For example, a ski lodge has a natural business year that ends in early spring. Partnerships that do not have a peak period cannot use the natural business year exception.

EXAMPLE C:9-18 ▶

KEY POINT

Because of the Sec. 706 requirements, most partnerships are required to adopt a calendar year. As a compromise, a Sec. 444 election permits a fiscal tax year as long as no more than a three-month deferral exists and as long as the deferral is not increased from any deferral already approved.

Amy, Brad, and Chris are equal partners in the ABC Partnership. Each partner uses a December 31 tax year-end. ABC earns 30% of its gross receipts in July and August each year and has experienced this pattern of earnings for more than three years. This two-month period is the peak season for their business each year. The IRS probably would grant approval for the partnership to use an August 31 tax year-end. ◀

Section 444 provides an election that permits a partnership to use a year-end that results in a deferral of the lesser of the current deferral period or three months. The deferral period is the time from the beginning of the partnership's fiscal year to the close of the

---

[26] 2002-1 C.B. 1046. The IRS in Rev. Rul. 87-57, 1987-2 C.B. 117, has provided a series of situations illustrating the business purpose requirement. In addition, Rev. Proc. 2006-46, 2006-2 C.B. 859, provides expeditious IRS approval if the natural business year satisfies a 25% test. This test requires

that 25% of the partnership's gross receipts be earned in the last two months of the requested year and in the last two months of the two preceding similar 12-month periods.

first required tax year ending within such year (i.e., usually December 31). The **Sec. 444 election** is available to both new partnerships making an initial tax year election or existing partnerships that are changing tax years. A partnership that satisfies the Sec. 706 requirements described above or has established a business purpose for its choice of a year-end (i.e., natural business year) does not need a Sec. 444 election.

STOP & THINK

Question: Suppose the ABC Partnership has had a December 31 year-end for many years. All its partners are individuals with calendar tax year-ends. Using Sec. 444, what tax year-ends are available for ABC?

Solution: Only December 31 can be used for a tax year-end for ABC even with Sec. 444. Section 444 allows a minimum deferral of the shorter of three months or the existing deferral. Because the existing deferral is zero months (the required tax year-end and the existing tax year-end are both December 31), no deferral is allowed under Sec. 444. The section allows a deferral only for new partnerships or for partnerships that already have a deferral.

HISTORICAL NOTE
Congress enacted Sec. 444, in part, as a concession to tax return preparers who already have the majority of their clients with calendar year-ends.

A partnership that makes a Sec. 444 election must make a required payment under Sec. 7519. (See the Compliance and Procedural Considerations section of this chapter for a discussion of the Sec. 444 election and Sec. 7519 required payment.) The required payment has the effect of assessing a tax on the partnership's deferred income at the highest individual marginal tax rate plus one percentage point.

Topic Review C:9-2 summarizes the allowable partnership tax year elections.

OTHER PARTNERSHIP ELECTIONS

With the exception of three specific elections reserved to the partners, Sec. 703(b) requires that the partnership make all elections that can affect the computation of taxable income derived from the partnership.[27] The three elections reserved to the individual partners relate to income from the discharge of indebtedness, deduction and recapture of certain mining exploration expenditures, and the choice between deducting or crediting foreign income taxes. Other than these elections, the partnership makes all elections at the entity level. Accordingly, the partnership elects its overall accounting method, which can differ from the methods used by its partners. The partnership also elects its inventory and depreciation methods.

Topic Review C:9-2

Allowable Tax Year for a Partnership

Section 706 requires that a partnership select the highest ranked tax year-end from the ranking that follows:

1. The tax year-end used by the partners who own a majority interest in the partnership capital and profits.
2. The tax year-end used by all principal partners (i.e., partners who each owns an interest in at least 5% of the partnership capital or profits).
3. The tax year-end determined by the least aggregate deferral test.

The IRS may grant permission for the partnership to use a fiscal year-end if the partnership has a natural business year. If the partnership does not have a natural business year, it must either

▶ Use the tax year-end required by Sec. 706 or
▶ Elect a fiscal year-end under Sec. 444 and make a required payment that approximates the tax due on the deferred income.

---

[27] The partnership does not include depletion from oil or gas wells in its computation of income (Sec. 703(a)(2)(F)). Instead each partner elects cost or percentage depletion (Sec. 613A(c)(7)(D)).

PARTNERSHIP REPORTING OF INCOME

PARTNERSHIP TAXABLE INCOME

Although the partnership is not a taxable entity, the IRC requires that the partnership calculate **partnership taxable income** for various computational reasons, such as adjusting the partners' basis in their partnership interests. Partnership taxable income for partnerships that are not electing large partnerships is calculated in much the same way as the taxable income of individuals, with a few differences mandated by the IRC. First, taxable income is divided into separately stated items and ordinary income or loss. Section 703(a) specifies a list of deductions available to individuals but that cannot be claimed by a partnership. The forbidden deductions include income taxes paid or accrued to a foreign country or U.S. possession, charitable contributions, oil and gas depletion, and net operating loss (NOL) carrybacks or carryovers. The first three items must be separately stated and may or may not be deductible by the partner. Because all losses are allocated to the partners for deduction on their tax returns, the partnership itself never has an NOL carryover or carryback. Instead, a partner may have an NOL if his or her deductible share of partnership losses exceeds his or her other business income. These NOLs are used at the partner level without any further regard for the partnership entity.

SEPARATELY STATED ITEMS

Each partner must report his or her distributive share of partnership income. However, Sec. 702 establishes a list of items that must be separately stated at the partnership level so that their character can remain intact at the partner reporting level. Section 702(a) lists the following items that must be separately stated:

▶ Net short-term capital gains and losses

▶ Net long-term capital gains and losses

▶ Sec. 1231 gains and losses

▶ Charitable contributions

▶ Dividends eligible for the dividends-received deduction or the 15% maximum tax rate

▶ Taxes paid or accrued to a foreign country or to a U.S. possession

▶ Any other item provided by Treasury Regulations

Regulation Sec. 1.702-1(a)(8) adds several other items to this list, including:

▶ Tax-exempt or partially tax-exempt interest

▶ Any items subject to special allocations (discussed below)

As a general rule, an item must be separately stated if the income tax liability of any partner that would result from treating the item separately is different from the liability that would result if that item were included in partnership ordinary income.[28]

EXAMPLE C:9-19 ▶ Amy and Big Corporation are equal partners in the AB Partnership, which purchases new equipment during 2011 at a total cost of $650,000. In 2011, AB elects out of bonus depreciation, elects to expense $500,000 under Sec. 179, and allocates $250,000 to each partner. Big already has expensed $100,000 under Sec. 179 this year. The Sec. 179 expense must be separately stated because Big is subject to a separate $500,000 limit of its own. After the partnership allocation, Big has a remaining Sec. 179 expense limitation of $150,000 ($500,000 − $100,000 − $250,000). ◀

Once the partnership separately states each item and allocates a distributive share to each partner, the partners report the separately stated items on their tax returns as if the partnership entity did not exist. A partner's share of partnership net long-term capital

---

[28] Reg. Sec. 1.702-1(a)(8)(ii).

gains or losses is combined with the partner's personal long-term capital gains and losses to calculate the partner's net long-term capital gain or loss. Likewise, a partner's share of partnership charitable contributions is combined with the partner's own charitable contributions with the total subject to the partner's charitable contribution limitations. In summary, Sec. 702(b) requires that the character of each separately stated item be determined at the partnership level. The amount then passes through to the partners and is reported in each partner's return as if the partner directly realized the amount.

PARTNERSHIP ORDINARY INCOME

All taxable items of income, gain, loss, or deduction that do not have to be separately stated are combined into a total called **partnership ordinary income** or **loss**. This ordinary income amount sometimes is incorrectly referred to as partnership taxable income. Partnership taxable income is the sum of all taxable items among the separately stated items plus the partnership ordinary income or loss. Therefore, partnership taxable income often is substantially greater than partnership ordinary income.

Included in the partnership's ordinary income are items such as gross profit on sales, administrative expenses, and employee salaries. Such items are always ordinary income or expenses not subject to special limitations. Partnership ordinary income also includes Sec. 1245 depreciation recapture because such ordinary income is not eligible for preferential treatment.

The partnership allocates a share of partnership ordinary income or loss to each partner. Such an allocation is reported on Schedules K and K-1 of the partnership's Form 1065 (see the completed partnership tax return in Appendix B). An individual partner reports his or her distributive share of ordinary income, or the deductible portion of his or her distributive share of ordinary loss, on Schedule E of Form 1040. Schedule E includes rental and royalty income and income or losses from estates, trusts, S corporations, and partnerships. A corporate partner reports partnership ordinary income or loss in the Other Income category of Form 1120.

U.S. PRODUCTION ACTIVITIES DEDUCTION

Chapter C:3 describes the corporate version of the U.S. production activities deduction, whereby the deduction equals 9% times the lesser of (1) qualified production activities income for the year or (2) taxable income before the U.S. production activities deduction. Individuals use a modified form of AGI instead of taxable income for this computation. The deduction, however, cannot exceed 50% of the employer's W-2 wages allocable to production activities for the year. In the case of a partnership, the deduction applies at the partner level, so the partnership must report each partner's share of qualified production activities income on the partner's Schedule K-1. For the 50% salary limitation, each partner is allocated a share of the partnership's W-2 wages.

PARTNER REPORTING OF INCOME

PARTNER'S DISTRIBUTIVE SHARE

Once the partnership determines separately stated income, gain, loss, deduction, or credit items, and partnership ordinary income or loss, the partnership must allocate the totals among the partners. Each partner must report and pay taxes on his or her distributive share. Under Sec. 704(b), the partner's distributive share normally is determined by the terms of the partnership agreement or, if the partnership agreement is silent, by the partner's overall interest in the partnership as determined by taking into account all facts and circumstances.

Note that the term **distributive share** is misleading because it has nothing to do with the amount actually distributed to a partner. A partner's distributive share is the portion of partnership taxable and nontaxable income that the partner has agreed to report for tax purposes. Actual distributions in a given year may be more or less than the partner's distributive share.

PARTNERSHIP AGREEMENT.   The **partnership agreement** may describe a partner's distributive share by indicating the partner's profits and loss interest, or it may indicate separate profits and loss interests. For example, the partnership agreement may state that a partner has a 10% interest in both partnership profits and losses or a partner has only a 10% interest in partnership profits (i.e., profits interest) but has a 30% interest in partnership losses (i.e., loss interest).

If the partnership agreement states only one interest percentage, it is used to allocate both partnership profit and loss. If the partnership agreement states profit and loss percentages separately, the partnership's taxable income for the year is first totaled to determine whether a net profit or net loss has occurred. Then the appropriate percentage (either profit or loss) applies to each class of income for the year.[29]

EXAMPLE C:9-20 ▶ The ABC Partnership reports the following income and loss items for the current year:

Net long-term capital loss	$100,000
Net Sec. 1231 gain	90,000
Ordinary income	220,000

Carmelia has a 20% profits interest and a 30% loss interest in the ABC Partnership. Because the partnership earns a $210,000 ($90,000 + $220,000 − $100,000) net profit, Carmelia's distributive share is calculated using her 20% profits interest and is reported as follows:

Net long-term capital loss	$ 20,000
Net Sec. 1231 gain	18,000
Ordinary income	44,000

Her loss percentage is used only in years in which the partnership has a net loss.   ◀

VARYING INTEREST RULE. If a partner's ownership interest changes during the partnership tax year, the income or loss allocation takes into account the partner's varying interest.[30] This varying interest rule applies for changes occurring to a partner's interest as a result of buying an additional interest in the partnership, selling part (but not all) of a partnership interest, giving or being given a partnership interest, or admitting a new partner. The partner's ownership interest generally applies to the income earned on a pro rata basis.

EXAMPLE C:9-21 ▶ Maria owns 20% of the XYZ Partnership from January 1 through June 30 of the current year (not a leap year). On July 1 she buys an additional 10% interest in the partnership. During this year, XYZ Partnership has ordinary income of $120,000, which it earned evenly throughout the year. Maria's $30,049 ($11,901 + $18,148) distributive share of income is calculated as follows:

$$\text{Pre-July 1:} \qquad \$120,000 \times \frac{181 \text{ days}}{365 \text{ days}} \times 0.20 = \$11,901$$

$$\text{Post-June 30:} \qquad \$120,000 \times \frac{184 \text{ days}}{365 \text{ days}} \times 0.30 = \$18,148$$

Similar calculations would be made if the XYZ Partnership reported separately stated items such as capital gains and losses.   ◀

OBJECTIVE 6

Explain the requirements for a special partnership allocation

SPECIAL ALLOCATIONS

Special allocations are unique to partnerships (and LLCs treated as partnerships). They allow tremendous flexibility in sharing specific items of income and loss among the partners. Special allocations can provide a specified partner with more or less of an item of

---

[29] This rule is derived from the House and Senate reports on the original Sec. 704(b) provisions. The two reports are identical and read, "The income ratio shall be applicable if the partnership has taxable income . . . and the loss ratio shall be applicable [if] the partnership has a loss." H. Rept. No. 1337, 83d

Cong., 2d Sess., p. A223 (1954); S. Rept. No. 1622, 83d Cong., 2d Sess., p. 379 (1954).
[30] Sec. 706(d)(1).

income, gain, loss, or deduction than would be available using the partner's regular distributive share. Special allocations fall into two categories. First, Sec. 704 requires certain special allocations with respect to contributed property. Second, other special allocations are allowed as long as they meet the tests set forth in Treasury Regulations for having substantial economic effect. If the special allocation fails the substantial economic effect test, it is disregarded, and the income, gain, loss, or deduction is allocated according to the partner's interest in the partnership as expressed in the actual operations and activities.

ALLOCATIONS RELATED TO CONTRIBUTED PROPERTY. As previously discussed, when a partner contributes property to a partnership, the property takes a carryover basis that references the contributing partner's basis. With no special allocations, this carryover basis rule would require the partnership (and each partner) to accept the tax burden of any gain or loss that accrued to the property before its contribution.

> **BOOK-TO-TAX ACCOUNTING COMPARISON**
>
> For tax purposes, the partnership takes a carryover basis in contributed property. For book purposes, however, the partnership records the contributed property at its FMV.

EXAMPLE C:9-22 ▶ In the current year, Elizabeth contributes land having a $4,000 basis and a $10,000 FMV to the DEF Partnership. Assuming the property continues to increase in value, or at least does not decline in value, DEF's gain on the ultimate sale of this property is $6,000 greater than the gain that accrues while the partnership owns the property. Without a special allocation, this $6,000 precontribution gain would be allocated among all partners. ◀

Section 704(c), however, requires precontribution gains or losses to be allocated to the contributing partner. Thus, the precontribution gain of $6,000 in Example C:9-22 would be allocated to Elizabeth. In addition, income and deductions reported with respect to contributed property must be allocated to take into account the difference between the property's basis and FMV at the time of contribution.

EXAMPLE C:9-23 ▶ Kay and Sam form an equal partnership when Sam contributes cash of $10,000 and Kay contributes land having a $6,000 basis and a $10,000 FMV. If the partnership sells the land two years later for $12,000, the $4,000 precontribution gain ($10,000 FMV − $6,000 basis) is allocated only to Kay. The $2,000 gain that accrued while the partnership held the land ($12,000 sales price − $10,000 FMV at contribution) is allocated to Kay and Sam equally. Kay reports a total gain of $5,000 ($4,000 + $1,000), and Sam reports a $1,000 gain on the sale of the land. ◀

> **BOOK-TO-TAX ACCOUNTING COMPARISON**
>
> In Example C:9-23, the partnership records a $6,000 tax gain and a $2,000 book gain, which provides another example of the difference between partnership tax and book accounting.

The allocation of depreciation is another common example of the special deduction allocation related to contributed property that is necessary under these rules. Tax Research Problem C:9-61 addresses the depreciation allocation issue.

SUBSTANTIAL ECONOMIC EFFECT. Special allocations not related to contributed property must meet several specific criteria established by Treasury Regulations. These criteria ensure that the allocations affect the partner's economic consequences and not just their tax consequences.

> **BOOK-TO-TAX ACCOUNTING COMPARISON**
>
> The capital accounts for meeting the substantial economic effect requirements are maintained using book value accounting rather than tax accounting.

To distinguish transactions affecting only taxes from those affecting the partner's economic position, Treasury Regulations look at whether the allocation has an economic effect and whether the economic effect is substantial. Under the Sec. 704 regulations, the allocation has economic effect if it meets all three of the following conditions:

▶ The allocation results in the appropriate increase or decrease in the partner's capital account.

▶ The proceeds of any liquidation occurring at any time in the partnership's life cycle are distributed in accordance with positive capital account balances.

▶ Partners must make up negative balances in their capital accounts upon the liquidation of the partnership, and these contributions are used to pay partnership debts or are allocated to partners having positive capital account balances.[31]

EXAMPLE C:9-24 ▶ Arnie and Bonnie each contribute $100,000 to form the AB Partnership on January 1 of Year 1. The partnership uses these contributions plus a $1.8 million mortgage to purchase a $2 million

---

[31] Reg. Sec. 1.704-1(b)(2)(ii). Treasury Regulations provide other alternatives for meeting this portion of the requirements.

office building. To simplify the calculations, assume the partnership depreciates the building using the straight-line method over a 40-year life and that in each year income and expenses are equal before considering depreciation. AB makes a special allocation of depreciation to Arnie. The allocation reduces Arnie's capital account, and the partnership makes any liquidating distributions in accordance with the capital account balances. Allocations through Year 3 are as follows:

	Capital Account Balance	
	Arnie	Bonnie
January 1, Year 1, balance	$100,000	$100,000
Year 1 loss (from depreciation deduction)	(50,000)	–0–
Year 2 loss (from depreciation deduction)	(50,000)	–0–
Year 3 loss (from depreciation deduction)	(50,000)	–0–
December 31, Year 3, balance	$ (50,000)	$100,000

If we assume that the property has declined in value in an amount equal to the depreciation claimed and that the partnership now liquidates, the need for the requirement to restore negative capital account balances becomes apparent.

Sales price of property on December 31, Year 3	$1,850,000
Minus: Mortgage principal	(1,800,000)
Partnership cash to be distributed to partners	$ 50,000

If Arnie does not have to restore his negative capital account balance, Bonnie can receive only $50,000 in cash even though her capital account balance is $100,000. In effect, Bonnie has borne the economic burden of the Year 3 depreciation. Without a requirement to restore the negative capital account balance, the special allocation to Arnie would be ignored for Year 3, and Bonnie would receive the depreciation deduction. However, if Arnie must restore any negative capital account balance, he will contribute $50,000 when the partnership liquidates at the end of Year 3, and Bonnie will receive her full $100,000 capital account balance. The Year 3 special allocation to Arnie will then have economic effect. Note that Arnie's allocations for Years 1 and 2 are acceptable even without an agreement to restore negative capital account balances. This result occurs in each of these two years because Arnie has sufficient capital to absorb the economic loss if the property declines in value in an amount equal to the depreciation allocated to him.[32] ◀

ADDITIONAL COMMENT

The substantial economic effect rules ensure that cash flows ultimately conform to allocations and that allocations do not allow for abusive shifting of tax benefits among partners.

The second requirement for a special allocation to be accepted under Treasury Regulations is that the economic effect must be substantial, which requires that a reasonable possibility exists that the allocation will substantially affect the dollar amounts to be received by the partners independent of tax consequences.[33] Moreover, allocations that involve shifting will not pass the substantiality test. Shifting occurs when the following two conditions are present:

▶ The net change in the partner's capital accounts will be the same for a normal allocation and the special allocation.

▶ The total tax liability of the partners will be less with the special allocation than with a normal allocation.[34]

EXAMPLE C:9-25 ▶ The AB Partnership earns $10,000 in tax-exempt interest income and $10,000 in taxable interest income each year. Andy and Becky each have 50% capital and profit interests in the partnership. An allocation of the tax-exempt interest income to Andy, a 35% tax bracket partner, and the taxable interest income to Becky, a 15% tax bracket partner, does not have substantial economic effect. In particular, the allocation lacks substantiality because of shifting. The allocation increases each partner's capital account by $10,000 as would an equal allocation, and it reduces the partner's overall tax liability (see Problem C:9-36 at the end of this chapter). ◀

---

[32] Such allocations do not literally meet the three requirements outlined above for special allocations. However, allocations that meet the alternate standard—having sufficient capital to absorb the economic loss—are considered to have economic effect and will be allowed. See Reg. Sec. 1.704-1(b)(2)(ii)(d).

[33] Reg. Sec. 1.704-1(b)(2)(iii)(a). It should be noted that the substantial economic effect regulations go far beyond the rules covered in this text.

[34] Reg. Sec. 1.704-1(b)(2)(iii)(b). An allocation also can fail the substantiality test by being transitory, which is something like shifting except an allocation in one year is offset by another allocation in a future year (Reg. Sec. 1.704-1(b)(2)(iii)(c)).

STOP & THINK

Question: The special allocation rules require that a partner who receives a special allocation of loss or expense receive less cash or property when the partnership liquidates. As we will see later in this chapter, losses reduce the partner's basis in the partnership interest, so a sale or liquidation of the partnership interest will cause the partner to recognize a larger gain (or a smaller loss) than would have resulted without this loss allocation. Because the basis is reduced, the partner also is more likely to recognize taxable gain on a distribution from the partnership. With these negative consequences, why would anyone want to be given a special allocation of partnership loss or expense?

Solution: The answer is a matter of timing. The specially allocated loss reduces taxable income now and saves more taxes now for the partner than would a "normal" loss allocation. The negative consequences occur when the partner incurs a larger gain (or smaller loss) upon a future sale or liquidation of his or her partnership interest. The special allocation scenario may have a greater after-tax present value to the partner than would the after-tax present value of receiving a normal share of losses and an increased liquidating distribution.

BASIS FOR PARTNERSHIP INTEREST

OBJECTIVE 7

Calculate a partner's basis in a partnership interest

The calculation of a partner's beginning basis in a partnership interest depends on the method used to acquire the interest, with different valuation techniques for a purchased interest, a gifted interest, and an inherited interest. The results of the partnership's operations and liabilities both cause adjustments to the beginning amount. Additional contributions to the partnership and distributions from the partnership further alter the partner's basis.

BEGINNING BASIS

A partner's beginning basis for a partnership interest received for a contribution of property or services has been discussed. However, a partner also can acquire a partnership interest by methods other than contributing property or services to the partnership. If a person purchases the partnership interest from an existing partner, the new partner's basis is the price paid for the partnership interest, including assumption of partnership liabilities. If a person inherits the partnership interest, the heir's basis is the FMV of the partnership interest on the decedent's date of death or, if elected by the executor, the alternate valuation date but not less than liabilities assumed. If a person receives the partnership interest as a gift, the donee's basis generally equals the donor's basis (including the donor's ratable share of partnership liabilities) plus the portion of any gift tax paid by the donor that relates to appreciation attaching to the gift property. In summary, the usual rules for the method of acquisition dictate the beginning basis for a partnership interest.

EFFECTS OF LIABILITIES

The early part of this chapter briefly discussed the effect of partnership liabilities on the basis of a partnership interest in connection with the contribution of property subject to a liability. However, further explanation is necessary to fully convey the pervasive impact of liabilities on partnership taxation.

INCREASES AND DECREASES IN LIABILITIES. Two changes in a partner's liabilities are considered contributions of cash by the partner to the partnership.[35] The first is an increase in the partner's share of partnership liabilities. This increase can arise from either an increase in the partner's profit or loss interests or from an increase in total partnership liabilities. Accordingly, if a partnership incurs a large debt, the partners' bases in their partnership interests increase. The second way to increase a partner's basis is to have the partner assume partnership liabilities in his or her individual capacity.

ADDITIONAL COMMENT

A partner's basis in a partnership interest commonly is referred to as "outside basis" as opposed to "inside basis," which is the partnership's basis in its assets.

SELF-STUDY QUESTION

What are some of the common methods of acquiring a partnership interest, and what is the beginning basis?

ANSWER

1. Contribution—substituted basis from contributed property
2. Purchase—cost basis
3. Inheritance—FMV
4. Gift—usually donor's basis with a possible gift tax adjustment

---

[35] Sec. 752.

Conversely, two liability changes are treated as distributions of cash from the partnership to the partner. These changes are a decrease in a partner's share of partnership liabilities and a decrease in the partner's individual liabilities resulting from the partnership's assumption of the partner's liability. Often, both an increase and a decrease in a partner's basis for his or her interest can result from a single transaction. The framework below illustrates the steps used to calculate the partner's basis in his or her partnership interest.

	Partner's basis before changes in liabilities
Plus:	Increases in share of partnership liabilities
Minus:	Decreases in share of partnership liabilities
Plus:	Partnership liabilities assumed by this partner
Minus:	This partner's liabilities assumed by the partnership
	Partner's basis in the partnership interest

EXAMPLE C:9-26 ▶

Juan, a 40% partner in the ABC Partnership, has a $30,000 basis in his partnership interest before receiving a partnership distribution of land. As part of the transaction, Juan agrees to assume a $10,000 mortgage on the land. First, Juan's basis in his partnership interest will decrease by $4,000 for the decline in Juan's share of partnership liabilities resulting from the partnership no longer owing the $10,000 mortgage. Second, his basis in the partnership interest will increase by $10,000, which is the partnership liability he assumes in his individual capacity. The net change in basis in his partnership resulting from the liabilities is $6,000 (−$4,000 + $10,000). His basis in his partnership interest also must be decreased for the land distribution he receives. Distributions will be discussed further in Chapter C:10. ◀

A PARTNER'S SHARE OF LIABILITIES. Having explained the general impact of liabilities on a partner's basis for his or her partnership interest, we now turn to how the specific amount of the partner's share of a partnership's liabilities is determined. All examples so far have considered only general partners who have the same interest in profits and losses. Partnerships, however, commonly have one or more limited partners, and thus partners can have differing profit and loss ratios. Moreover, the type of liability affects how it is allocated. Treasury Regulations provide guidelines for allocating partnership liabilities to the individual partners.

Recourse and Nonrecourse Loans. A **recourse loan** is the usual kind of loan for which the borrower remains liable until the loan is paid. If the recourse loan is secured and the borrower fails to make payments as scheduled, the lender can sell the property used as security. If the sales proceeds are insufficient to repay a recourse loan, the borrower must make up the difference. Under Treasury Regulations, a recourse loan is one for which any partner or a related party will stand an economic loss if the partnership cannot pay the debt.[36] In contrast, a **nonrecourse loan** is one in which the lender may sell property used as security if the loan is not paid, but no partner is liable for any deficiency. In short, the lender has no recourse against the borrower for additional amounts. Nonrecourse debts most commonly occur in connection with the financing of real property that is expected to substantially increase in value over the life of the loan.

General and Limited Partners. A limited partner normally is not liable to pay partnership debts beyond the original contribution (which already is reflected in his or her basis in the partnership interest) and any additional amount the partner has pledged to contribute.[37] Therefore, recourse debt increases a limited partner's basis only to the extent the partner has a risk of economic loss. Nonrecourse debts increase a limited partner's basis based primarily on the profit ratio.[38]

ADDITIONAL COMMENT

That a partner gets basis for his or her share of recourse debt is not controversial. That a partner gets basis for debt on which the partner is not personally liable seems questionable, yet other rules, such as the at-risk provisions, limit the benefit of the basis created by the nonrecourse debt.

TYPICAL MISCONCEPTION

Nonrecourse debt is allocated among all partners primarily according to their profit ratios. Recourse debt, on the other hand, is allocated to the limited partners to the extent they bear an economic risk of loss, but generally a limited partner's economic risk of loss is not greater than any additional amounts that partner has pledged to contribute. The remaining recourse debt is allocated among the general partners according to their economic risk of loss.

---

[36] Reg. Sec. 1.752-1(a).

[37] This rule may be modified by the limited partner agreeing to assume some of the risk of economic loss despite his or her limited partner status. For example, a limited partner may guarantee the debt or may agree to reimburse the general partner some amount if the general partner has to pay the debt. These arrangements mean that the limited partner shares the risk of loss.

[38] Some nonrecourse debt allocations involve two steps before an allocation according to profits interests. These two steps of the allocation process are beyond the scope of this explanation.

A general partner's share of nonrecourse liabilities also is determined primarily by his or her profit ratio. On the other hand, because limited partners seldom receive an allocated share of the recourse liabilities, the general partners share all recourse liabilities beyond any amounts the limited partners can claim according to their economic loss potential.

The Sec. 752 Treasury Regulations require that recourse liabilities be allocated to the partner who will bear the economic loss if the partnership cannot pay the debt. The regulations provide a complex procedure using a hypothetical liquidation to determine who would bear the loss. In this text, we assume that the hypothetical liquidation analysis has been completed and that the appropriate shares of economic loss as determined by the hypothetical liquidation procedure are stated as part of the problem or example information.

EXAMPLE C:9-27 ▶ The ABC Partnership has one general partner (Anna) and a limited partner (Clay) with the following partnership interests:

	Anna (General)	Clay (Limited)
Loss interest	75%	25%
Profits interest	60%	40%
Basis before liabilities	$100,000	$100,000

Clay has an obligation to make an additional $5,000 contribution. He has made no other agreements or guarantees. The partnership has two liabilities at year-end: a $300,000 nonrecourse liability and a $400,000 recourse liability. Clay has an economic risk of loss only to the extent he has agreed to make additional contributions. The partners' year-end bases are calculated as follows:

	Anna (General)	Clay (Limited)
Year-end basis (excluding liabilities)	$100,000	$100,000
Share of:		
Recourse liability	395,000	5,000
Nonrecourse liability	180,000[a]	120,000[b]
Year-end basis	$675,000	$225,000

[a] 60% × $300,000 = $180,000
[b] 40% × $300,000 = $120,000 ◀

If the partnership has more than one general partner, the economic risk of loss computation entails computing a hypothetical loss and allocating that loss to the general partners. The hypothetical loss computation assumes the partnership sells all its assets (including cash) for the amount of nonrecourse liabilities. If the partnership does not have nonrecourse liabilities, the assets are deemed sold for zero dollars. The hypothetical loss then is subtracted from the partners' capital accounts to determine the economic risk of loss.

EXAMPLE C:9-28 ▶ Assume the same facts as in Example C:9-27 except that Clay is a general partner. In addition, the partnership has $900,000 of assets, and each partner's capital account is $100,000. If the partnership sold its assets for the amount of the nonrecourse liability, it would realize a $600,000 loss ($300,000 − $900,000). The economic risk of loss is calculated as follows:

	Anna (General)	Clay (General)
Capital accounts	$100,000	$100,000
Minus: Hypothetical loss (allocated according to loss percentages)	(450,000)	(150,000)
Economic risk of loss	($350,000)	($ 50,000)

The partners' year-end bases are calculated as follows:

	Anna (General)	Clay (General)
Year-end basis (excluding liabilities)	$100,000	$100,000
Share of:		
Recourse liability	350,000	50,000
Nonrecourse liability	180,000	120,000
Year-end basis	$630,000	$270,000 ◀

Determining the partners' share of recourse liabilities can be simplified if the partners have the same interest in losses as they do for profits and if their capital accounts are in accordance with those percentages. In this situation, the recourse liability allocation also will be in accordance with the profit/loss percentages.

EFFECTS OF OPERATIONS

A partner's basis is a summary of his or her contributions and the partner's share of partnership liabilities, earnings, losses, and distributions. Basis prevents a second tax levy on a distribution of income that was taxed previously as a partner's distributive share. Section 705 mandates a basis increase for additional contributions made by the partner to the partnership plus the partner's distributive share for the current and prior tax years of the following items:[39]

▶ Partnership taxable income (both separately stated items and partnership ordinary income)

▶ Tax-exempt income of the partnership

Basis is decreased (but not below zero) by distributions from the partnership to the partner plus the partner's distributive share for the current and prior tax years of the following items:

▶ Partnership losses (both separately stated items and partnership ordinary loss)

▶ Expenditures that are not deductible for tax purposes and that are not capital expenditures

The positive basis adjustment for tax-exempt income and the negative basis adjustment for nondeductible expenses preserve that tax treatment for the partner. If these adjustments were not made, tax-exempt income would be taxable to the partner upon a subsequent distribution or upon the sale or other disposition of the partnership interest.

BOOK-TO-TAX ACCOUNTING COMPARISON
Although a partner's basis in the partnership cannot go below zero, a partner's book capital account (equity) may be negative.

EXAMPLE C:9-29 ▶ LMN Partnership has only one asset—a $100,000 municipal bond. Marta has a $20,000 basis in her 20% partnership interest. In the current year, the partnership collects $4,000 tax-exempt interest from the bond. Marta's basis at year-end is calculated as follows:

Beginning basis	$20,000
Share of tax-exempt income	800
Basis at year end	$20,800

On the first day of the next year, the partnership sells the bond for $100,000 cash. At this point, the partnership has $104,000 in cash and no other assets. The partnership liquidates and distributes her 20% share of the cash ($20,800) to Marta. Marta has no gain or loss because her $20,800 basis exactly equals her distribution. If the tax-exempt income had not increased her basis, she would have recognized an $800 gain on the distribution ($20,800 cash distribution − $20,000 basis if no increase were made for the tax-exempt income). Thus, her basis must be increased by tax-exempt income to prevent a taxable gain upon its distribution. ◀

OBJECTIVE 8

Determine the limitations on a partner's deduction of partnership losses

LOSS LIMITATIONS. Each partner is allocated his or her distributive share of ordinary income or loss and separately stated income, gain, loss, or deduction items each year. The partner always reports income and gain items in his or her current tax year, and these items increase the partner's basis in the partnership interest. However, the partner may not be able to use his or her full distributive share of losses because Sec. 704(d) limits a partner's loss deduction to the amount of his or her basis in the partnership interest before the loss. All positive basis adjustments for the year and all reductions for actual or deemed distributions must be made before determining the amount of the deductible loss.[40]

EXAMPLE C:9-30 ▶ On January 1 of the current year, Miguel has a $32,000 basis for his general interest in the MT Partnership. He materially participates in the partnership's business activities. On December 1, Miguel receives a $1,000 cash distribution. His distributive share of MT's current items are a $4,000 net long-term capital gain and a $43,000 ordinary loss. Miguel's deductible loss is calculated as follows:

---

[39] Section 705 also contains adjustments pertaining to depletion.   [40] Reg. Sec. 1.704-1(d)(2).

January 1 basis	$32,000
Plus: Long-term capital gain	4,000
Minus: Distribution	(1,000)
Limit for loss deduction	$35,000

SELF-STUDY QUESTION

What happens to losses that are disallowed due to lack of basis in a partnership interest?

ANSWER

The losses are suspended until that partner obtains additional basis.

Miguel can deduct $35,000 of the ordinary loss in the current year, which reduces his basis to zero. He cannot deduct the remaining $8,000 of ordinary loss currently but can deduct it in the following year if he regains sufficient basis in his partnership interest. ◀

Any distributive share of loss that a partner cannot deduct because of the basis limit is simply noted in the partner's financial records. It is not reported on the partner's tax return, nor does it reduce the partner's basis. However, the losses carry forward until the partner again has positive basis from capital contributions, additional partnership borrowings, or partnership earnings.

EXAMPLE C:9-31 ▶

Assume the same facts as in Example C:9-30. Miguel makes no additional contributions in the following year, and the MT Partnership's liabilities remain unchanged. Miguel's distributive share of MT's partnership items in the following year is $2,500 of net short-term capital gain and $14,000 of ordinary income. These items restore his basis to $16,500 ($0 + $2,500 + $14,000), and he can deduct the $8,000 loss carryover. After taking these transactions into account, Miguel's basis is $8,500 ($16,500 − $8,000). ◀

Topic Review C:9-3 summarizes the rules for determining the initial basis for a partnership interest and the annual basis adjustments required to determine the adjusted basis of a partnership interest.

Topic Review C:9-3

Basis of a Partnership Interest

METHOD OF ACQUISITION	BEGINNING BASIS IS
Property contributed	Substituted basis from property contributed plus gain recognized for contributions to an investment partnership
Services contributed	Amount of income recognized for services rendered (plus any additional amount contributed)
Purchase	Cost
Gift	Donor's basis plus gift tax on appreciation
Inheritance	Fair market value at date of death or alternative valuation date

LIABILITY IMPACT ON BASIS	
Increase basis for	Increases in the partner's share of partnership liabilities Liabilities of the partnership assumed by the partner in his or her individual capacity
Decrease basis for	Decreases in the partner's share of partnership liabilities Liabilities of the partner assumed by the partnership

OPERATIONS IMPACT ON BASIS	
Increase basis for	Partner's share of ordinary income and separately stated income and gain items (including tax-exempt items) Additional contributions to the partnership Precontribution gain recognized
Decrease basis for	Distributions from the partnership to the partner Partner's share of ordinary loss and separately stated loss and deduction items (including items that are not deductible for tax purposes and are not capital expenditures) Precontribution loss recognized

SPECIAL LOSS LIMITATIONS

REAL-WORLD EXAMPLE

In 2008, 48% of all partnerships and LLCs reported net losses.

Three sets of rules limit the loss from a partnership interest that a partner may deduct. The Sec. 704(d) rules explained above limit losses to the partner's basis in the partnership interest. Two other rules establish more stringent limits. The at-risk rules limit losses to an amount called *at-risk basis*. The passive activity loss or credit limitation rules disallow most net passive activity losses.

AT-RISK LOSS LIMITATION

The Sec. 704(d) loss limitation rules were the only loss limits for many years. However, Congress became increasingly uncomfortable with allowing partners to increase their basis by a portion of the partnership's nonrecourse liabilities and then offset this basis with partnership losses. Accordingly, Congress established the **at-risk rules**, which limit loss deductions to the partner's at-risk basis. The **at-risk basis** is essentially the same amount as the regular partnership basis with the exception that liabilities increase the at-risk basis only if the partner is at risk for such an amount. The at-risk rules apply to individuals and closely held C corporations. Partners that are widely held C corporations are not subject to these rules.

Although much of the complexity of the *at-risk* term is beyond the scope of this text, a simplified working definition is possible. A partner is at risk for an amount if he or she would lose that amount should the partnership suddenly become worthless. Because a partner would not have to pay a partnership's nonrecourse liabilities even if the partnership became worthless, the usual nonrecourse liabilities cannot be included in any partner's at-risk basis. Under the at-risk rules, a partner's loss deduction may be substantially less than the amount deductible under the Sec. 704(d) rules.[41]

EXAMPLE C:9-32 ▶ Keesha is a limited partner in the KM Manufacturing Partnership. At the end of the partnership's tax year, her basis in the partnership interest is $30,000 ($10,000 investment plus a $20,000 share of nonrecourse financing). Keesha's distributive share of partnership losses for the tax year is $18,000. Although she has sufficient basis in the partnership interest, the at-risk rules limit her deduction to $10,000 because she is not at risk for the nonrecourse financing. ◀

The IRC allows one significant exception to the application of the at-risk rules. At-risk rules do not apply to nonrecourse debt if it is qualified real estate financing. The partner is considered at risk for his or her share of nonrecourse real estate financing if all of the following requirements are met:

TYPICAL MISCONCEPTION

The at-risk rules severely limit the use of nonrecourse debt to obtain loss deductions except for certain qualified real estate financing, yet this real estate exception is more apparent than real because of the final set of rules that must be satisfied: the passive activity limitations.

▶ The financing is secured by real estate used in the partnership's real estate activity.

▶ The debt is not convertible to any kind of equity interest in the partnership.

▶ The financing is from a qualified person or from any federal, state, or local government, or is guaranteed by any federal, state, or local government.[42] A qualified person is an unrelated party who is in the trade or business of lending money (e.g., bank, financial institution, or mortgage broker).

PASSIVE ACTIVITY LIMITATIONS

Subsequent to enacting the at-risk rules, Congress added still a third set of limitations to losses a partner may deduct: the passive activity loss and credit limitations of Sec. 469. Under these rules, income falls into one of three categories: (1) amounts derived from passive activities; (2) active income such as salary, bonuses, and income from businesses in which the taxpayer materially participates; and (3) portfolio income such as dividends, interest, and capital gains from investments other than passive activities. Generally, losses of an individual partner from a passive activity cannot be used to offset either active income or portfolio income. However, passive losses carry over to future years where they can offset passive income in those years. Moreover, passive losses are allowed in full when a taxpayer disposes of the entire interest in the passive activity. Passive losses generated by

---

[41] Sec. 465(a).　　　　　　[42] Sec. 465(b)(6).

a passive rental activity in which an individual partner is an active participant can be deducted up to a maximum of $25,000 per year. This deduction phases out by 50% of the amount of the partner's adjusted gross income (AGI) that exceeds $100,000, so that no deduction is allowed if the partner has AGI of $150,000 or more. (The phase-out begins at $200,000 for low-income housing or rehabilitation credits.) Losses disallowed under the phase-out are deductible to the extent of passive income.

A passive activity is any trade or business in which the taxpayer does not materially participate. A taxpayer who owns a limited partnership interest in any activity generally fails the material participation test. Accordingly, losses from most limited partnership interests can be used only to offset income from passive activities even if the limited partner has sufficient Sec. 704(d) and at-risk basis.[43]

Although passive activity limitations may greatly affect the taxable income or loss reported by a partner, they have no unusual effect on basis. Basis is reduced (but not below zero) by the partner's distributive share of losses whether or not the losses are limited under the passive loss rules.[44] When the suspended passive losses later become deductible, the partner's basis in the partnership interest is not affected.

TAX STRATEGY TIP

If a partner is unable to use all of his or her share of partnership losses due to a lack of basis, contributions to capital or increasing partnership liabilities may provide the additional needed tax basis. If the passive activity limitation rules are the reason the partnership losses cannot be used, the possibility of investing in passive activities that generate passive income may be the best planning alternative. See Tax Planning Considerations for further discussion.

EXAMPLE C:9-33 ▶

Chris purchases a 20% capital and profits interest in the CJ Partnership in the current year, but he does not participate in CJ's business. Chris owns no other passive investments. His Sec. 704(d) basis in CJ is $80,000, and his at-risk basis is $70,000. Chris's distributive share of the CJ Partnership's loss for the current year is $60,000. After the results of this year's operations are taken into account, Chris's Sec. 704(d) basis is $20,000 ($80,000 − $60,000), and his at-risk basis is $10,000 ($70,000 − $60,000). However, Chris cannot deduct any of the CJ loss in the current year because it is a passive activity loss. The $60,000 loss, however, can be used in a subsequent year if the partner generates passive income. Because the $60,000 loss already has reduced basis for purposes of both Sec. 704(d) and the at-risk rules, the disallowed loss need not be tested against those rules a second time. ◀

TRANSACTIONS BETWEEN A PARTNER AND THE PARTNERSHIP

The partner and the partnership are treated as separate entities for many transactions. Section 707(b) restricts sales of property between the partner and partnership by disallowing certain losses and converting certain capital gains into ordinary income. Section 707(c) permits a partnership to make guaranteed payments for capital and services to a partner that are separate from the partner's distributive share. Each of these rules is explored below.

SALES OF PROPERTY

LOSS SALES. Without restrictions, a controlling partner could sell property to the partnership to recognize a loss for tax purposes while retaining a substantial interest in the property through ownership of a partnership interest. Congress closed the door to such loss recognition with the Sec. 707(b) rules.

KEY POINT

The IRC disallows losses on sales between persons and certain related partnerships, similar to the related party rules of Sec. 267. The concern is that tax losses can be artificially recognized without the property being disposed of outside the economic group.

The rules for partnership loss transactions are quite similar to the Sec. 267 related party rules discussed in Chapter C:3. Under Sec. 707(b)(1), no loss can be deducted on the sale or exchange of property between a partnership and a person who directly or indirectly owns more than 50% of the partnership's capital or profits interests. (Indirect ownership includes ownership by related parties such as members of the partner's family.[45]) Similarly, losses are disallowed on sales or exchanges of property between two partnerships in which the same persons own, directly or indirectly, more than 50% of the capital

---

[43] Sec. 469(h)(2).
[44] S. Rept. No. 99-313, 99th Cong., 2d Sess., p. 723, footnote 4 (1986).
[45] For purposes of Sec. 707, related parties include an individual and mem-

bers of his or her family (spouse, brothers, sisters, lineal descendants, and ancestors), an individual and a more-than-50%-owned corporation, and two corporations that are members of the same controlled group.

or profits interests. If the seller is disallowed a loss under Sec. 707(b)(1), the purchaser can reduce any subsequent gain realized on a sale of the property by the previously disallowed loss.

EXAMPLE C:9-34 ▶ James, Karen, and Thelma own equal interests in the JKT Partnership. Karen and Thelma are siblings, but James is unrelated to the others. For purposes of Sec. 707, Karen owns two-thirds of the partnership (one-third directly and one-third indirectly from Thelma). Likewise, Thelma also owns two-thirds, but James has only a direct ownership interest of one-third. ◀

EXAMPLE C:9-35 ▶ Pat sold land having a $45,000 basis to the PTA Partnership for $35,000, its FMV. If Pat has a 60% capital and profits interest in the partnership, Pat realizes but cannot recognize a $10,000 loss on the sale. If Pat owns only a 49% interest, directly and indirectly, he can recognize the loss. ◀

EXAMPLE C:9-36 ▶ Assume the same facts as in Example C:9-35 except the partnership later sells the land for $47,000. The partnership's realized gain is $12,000 ($47,000 − $35,000 basis). If Pat has a 60% capital and profits interest, his previously disallowed loss of $10,000 reduces the partnership's recognized gain to $2,000. This $2,000 gain is then allocated to the partners according to the partnership agreement. ◀

GAIN SALES. When gain is recognized on the sale of a capital asset between a partnership and a related partner, Sec. 707(b)(2) requires that the gain be ordinary (and not capital gain) if the property will not be a capital asset to its new owner. Sales or exchanges resulting in the application of Sec. 707(b)(2) include transfers between (1) a partnership and a person who owns, directly or indirectly, more than 50% of the partnership's capital or profits interests, or (2) two partnerships in which the same persons own, directly or indirectly, more than 50% of the capital or profits interests.[46] This provision prevents related parties from increasing the depreciable basis of assets (and thereby reducing future ordinary income) at the cost of recognizing only a current capital gain.

EXAMPLE C:9-37 ▶ Sharon and Tony have the following capital and profits interests in two partnerships:

Partner	ST Partnership (%)	QRS Partnership (%)
Sharon	42	58
Tony	42	30
Other unrelated partners	16	12
Total	100	100

The ST Partnership sells land having a $150,000 basis to the QRS Partnership for $180,000. The land was a capital asset for the ST Partnership, but QRS intends to subdivide and sell the land. Because the land is ordinary income property to the QRS Partnership and because Sharon and Tony control both partnerships, the ST Partnership must recognize $30,000 of ordinary income on the land sale. ◀

GUARANTEED PAYMENTS

A corporate shareholder can be an employee of the corporation. However, a partner generally is not an employee of the partnership, and most fringe benefits are disallowed for a partner who is "employed" by his or her partnership.[47]

A partner who provides services to the partnership in an ongoing relationship might be compensated like any other employee. Section 707(c) provides for this kind of payment and labels it a **guaranteed payment**. The term *guaranteed payment* also includes certain payments made to a partner for the use of invested capital. These payments are similar to interest. Both types of guaranteed payments must be determined without regard to the partnership's income.[48] Conceptually, this requirement separates guaranteed payments from distributive shares. As indicated below, however, such a distinction may not be so clear in practice.

OBJECTIVE 9

Determine the tax consequences of a guaranteed payment

---

[46] Sec. 707(b)(2).
[47] Rev. Rul. 91-26, 1991-1 C.B. 184, holds that accident and health insurance premiums paid for a partner by the partnership are guaranteed payments.

[48] Sec. 707(c).

DETERMINING THE GUARANTEED PAYMENT. Sometimes the determination of the guaranteed payment is quite simple. For example, some guaranteed payments are expressed as specific amounts (e.g., $20,000 per year), with the partner also receiving his or her normal distributive share. Other times, the guaranteed payment is expressed as a **guaranteed minimum.** However, these guaranteed minimum arrangements make it difficult to distinguish the partner's distributive share and guaranteed payments because no guaranteed payment occurs under this arrangement unless the partner's distributive share is less than his or her guaranteed minimum. If the distributive share is less than the guaranteed minimum, the guaranteed payment is the difference between the distributive share and the guaranteed minimum.

EXAMPLE C:9-38 ▶ Tina manages the real estate owned by the TAV Partnership, in which she also is a partner. She receives 30% of all partnership income before guaranteed payments, but no less than $60,000 per year. In the current year, the TAV Partnership reports $300,000 in ordinary income. Tina's 30% distributive share is $90,000 (0.30 × $300,000), which exceeds her $60,000 guaranteed minimum. Therefore, she has no guaranteed payment. ◀

EXAMPLE C:9-39 ▶ Assume the same facts as in Example C:9-38 except the TAV Partnership reports $150,000 of ordinary income. Tina has a guaranteed payment of $15,000, which represents the difference between her $45,000 distributive share (0.30 × $150,000) and her $60,000 guaranteed minimum.[49] ◀

TAX IMPACT OF GUARANTEED PAYMENTS. Like salary or interest income, guaranteed payments are ordinary income to the recipient. The guaranteed payment must be included in income for the recipient partner's tax year during which the partnership year ends and the partnership deducts or capitalizes the payments.[50]

EXAMPLE C:9-40 ▶ In January 2011, a calendar year taxpayer, Will, receives a $10,000 guaranteed payment from the WRS Partnership, which uses the accrual method of accounting. WRS accrues and deducts the payment during its tax year ending November 30, 2010. Will must report the guaranteed payment in his 2010 tax return because that return includes the 2010 partnership income that reflects the impact of the guaranteed payment. ◀

The partnership treats the guaranteed payment as if it is made to an outsider. If the payment is for a service that is a capital expenditure (e.g., architectural services for designing a building for the partnership), the guaranteed payment must be capitalized and, if allowable, amortized. If the payment is for services deductible under Sec. 162, the partnership deducts the payment from ordinary income. Thus, deductible guaranteed payments offset the partnership's ordinary income but never its capital gains. If the guaranteed payment exceeds the partnership's ordinary income, the payment creates an ordinary loss that is allocated among the partners.[51]

EXAMPLE C:9-41 ▶ Theresa is a partner in the STU Partnership. She is to receive a guaranteed payment for deductible services of $60,000 and 30% of partnership income computed after the partnership deducts the guaranteed payment. The partnership reports $40,000 of ordinary income and a $120,000 long-term capital gain before deducting the guaranteed payment. Theresa's income from the partnership is determined as follows:

	STU Partnership	Theresa's Share Ratable Share	Theresa's Share Amount
Ordinary income (before guaranteed payment)	$ 40,000		
Minus: Guaranteed payment	(60,000)	100%	$60,000
Ordinary loss	($ 20,000)	30%	(6,000)
Long-term capital gain	$120,000	30%	36,000 ◀

---

[49] Reg. Sec. 1.707-1(c), Exs. (1) and (2).
[50] Reg. Secs. 1.707-1(c) and 1.706-1(a).
[51] Reg. Sec. 1.707-1(c), Ex. (4).

FAMILY PARTNERSHIPS

OBJECTIVE **10**

Explain the requirements for recognizing the holder of a partnership interest as a partner in a family partnership

CAPITAL OWNERSHIP

Because each partner reports and pays taxes on a distributive share of partnership income, a family partnership is an excellent way to spread income among family members and minimize the family's tax bill. However, to accomplish this tax minimization goal, the IRS must accept the family members as real partners. The question of whether someone is a partner in a family partnership is often litigated, but safe-harbor rules under Sec. 704(e) provide a clear answer if three tests are met: the partnership interest must be a capital interest, capital must be a material income-producing factor in the partnership's business activity, and the family member must be the true owner of the interest.

A capital interest gives the partner the right to receive assets if the partnership liquidates immediately upon the partner's acquisition of the interest. Capital is a material income-producing factor if the partnership derives substantial portions of gross income from the use of capital. For example, capital is a material income-producing factor if the business has substantial inventory or significant investment in plant or equipment. Capital is seldom considered a material income-producing factor in a service business.[52]

The remaining question is whether the family member is the true owner of the interest. Ownership is seldom questioned if one family member purchases the interest at a market price from another family member. However, when one family member gifts the interest to another, the major question is whether the donor retains so much control over the partnership interest that the donor is still the owner of the interest. If the donor still controls the interest, the donor is taxed on the distributive share.

TAX STRATEGY TIP

In certain situations, family partnerships provide an excellent tax-planning tool, but the family members must be real partners. The rules that determine who is a real partner in a family partnership are guided by the assignment-of-income principle.

DONOR RETAINED CONTROL. No mechanical test exists to determine whether the donor has retained too much control, but several factors may indicate a problem:[53]

▶ Retention of control over distributions of income can be a problem unless the retention occurs with the agreement of all partners or the retention is for the reasonable needs of the business.

▶ Retention of control over assets that are essential to the partnership's business can indicate too much control by the donor.

▶ Limitation of the donee partner's right to sell or liquidate his or her interest may indicate that the donor has not relinquished full control over the interest.

▶ Retention of management control that is inconsistent with normal partnership arrangements can be another sign that the donor retains control. This situation is not considered a fatal problem unless it occurs in conjunction with a significant limit on the donee's ability to sell or liquidate his or her interest.

If the donor has not directly or indirectly retained too much control, the donee is a full partner. As a partner, the donee must report his or her distributive share of income.

MINOR DONEES. When income splitting is the goal of a family, the appropriate donee for the partnership interest is often a minor. With the problem of donor-retained controls in mind, gifts to minors should be made with great attention to detail. Further, net unearned income of a child under age 18 is taxed to the child at the parents' marginal tax rate under the "kiddie tax" rules. This provision removes much of the incentive to transfer family partnership interests to young children, but gifting partnership interests to minors age 18 or older still can reap significant tax advantages, although in some situations the kiddie tax also applies to children ages 18 through 23.

OBJECTIVE **11**

Determine the allocation of partnership income between a donor and a donee of a partnership interest

DONOR-DONEE ALLOCATIONS OF INCOME

Partnership income must be properly allocated between a donor and a donee to be accepted by the IRS. Note that only the allocation between the donor and donee is questioned, with no impact on the distributive shares of any other partners.

---

[52] Reg. Sec. 1.704-1(e)(1)(iv).   [53] Reg. Sec. 1.704-1(e)(2)(ii).

Two requirements apply to donor-donee allocations. First, the donor must be allocated reasonable compensation for services rendered to the partnership. Then, after reasonable compensation is allocated to the donor, any remaining partnership income must be allocated based on relative capital interests.[54] This allocation scheme apparently overrides the partnership's ability to make special allocations of income.

EXAMPLE C:9-42 ▶

Andrew, a 40% partner in the ABC Partnership, gives one-half of his interest to his brother, John. During the current year, Andrew performs services for the partnership for which reasonable compensation is $65,000 but for which he accepts no pay. Andrew and John are each credited with a $100,000 distributive share, all of which is ordinary income. Reallocation between Andrew and John is necessary to reflect the value of Andrew's services.

Total distributive shares for the brothers	$200,000
Minus: Reasonable compensation for Andrew	(65,000)
Income to allocate	$135,000

John's distributive share: $\frac{20\%}{40\%} \times \$135,000 = \$67,500$

Andrew's distributive share: $\left(\frac{20\%}{40\%} \times \$135,000\right) + \$65,000 = \$132,500$ ◀

ETHICAL POINT

CPAs have a responsibility to review an entity's conduct of its activities to be sure it is operating as a partnership. If a donee receives a partnership interest as a gift and the donee is not the true owner of the interest (e.g., the donor retains too much control over the donee's interest), the partnership return must be filed without a distributive share of income or loss being allocated to the donee.

TAX PLANNING CONSIDERATIONS

TIMING OF LOSS RECOGNITION

The loss limitation rules provide a unique opportunity for tax planning. For example, if a partner knows that his or her distributive share of active losses from a partnership for a tax year will exceed the Sec. 704 basis limitation for deducting losses, he or she should carefully examine the tax situation for the current and upcoming tax years. Substantial current personal income may make immediate use of the loss desirable. Current income may be taxed at a higher marginal tax rate than will future income because of, for example, an extraordinarily good current year, an expected retirement, or a decrease in future years' tax rates. If the partner chooses to use the loss in the current year, he or she can make additional contributions just before year-end (perhaps even from funds the partner borrows, as long as the additional benefit exceeds the cost of the funds). Alternatively, one partner may convince the other partners to have the partnership incur additional liabilities so that each partner's basis increases. This last strategy should be exercised with caution unless a business reason (rather than solely a tax reason) exists for the borrowing.

EXAMPLE C:9-43 ▶

Ted, a 60% general partner in the ST Partnership, expects to be allocated partnership losses of $120,000 for the current year from a partnership in which he materially participates but where his partnership basis is only $90,000. Because he has a marginal tax rate of 35% for the current year (and anticipates only a 25% marginal tax rate for next year), Ted wants to use the ST Partnership losses to offset his current year income. He could make a capital contribution to raise his basis by $30,000. Alternatively, he could get the partnership to incur $50,000 in additional liabilities, which would increase his basis by his $30,000 ($50,000 × 0.60) share of the liability. The partnership's $50,000 borrowing must serve a business purpose for the ST Partnership. ◀

Alternatively, if a partner has little current year income and expects substantial income in the following year, the partner may prefer to delay the deduction of partnership losses that exceed the current year's loss limitation. Similarly, if a partner has loss, deduction, or credit carryovers that expire in the current year, deferral of the distributive share of

---

[54] Sec. 704(e)(2).

partnership losses to the following year again may be desirable. Should the partner opt to deduct the loss in a later year, he or she needs only to leave things alone so that the distributive share of losses exceeds the loss limitation for the current year.

COMPLIANCE AND PROCEDURAL CONSIDERATIONS

OBJECTIVE **12**

Determine the requirements for filing a partnership tax return

ADDITIONAL COMMENT

The partnership Schedule K in Appendix B of this text makes apparent that the large number of items now having to be separately stated has substantially complicated the preparation of Form 1065.

REPORTING TO THE IRS AND THE PARTNERS

FORMS. If the partnership is not an electing large partnership, the partnership must file a Form 1065 (U.S. Return of Partnership Income) with the IRS by the fifteenth day of the fourth month after the end of the partnership tax year. (See Appendix B for a completed Form 1065.) The IRS, however, allows an automatic five-month extension of time to file Form 1065. To obtain the extension, the partnership must file Form 7004 (Application for Automatic Extension of Time To File Certain Business Income Tax, Information, and Other Returns) on or before the partnership's normal filing date.[55] The IRS imposes penalties for failure to file a timely or complete partnership return. Because the partnership is only a conduit, Form 1065 is an information return and is not accompanied by any tax payment.[56] Included on the front page of Form 1065 are the ordinary items of income, gain, loss, and deduction that are not separately stated. Schedule K of Form 1065 reports both a summary of the ordinary income items and all the partnership's separately stated items. Schedule K-1, which the partnership must prepare for each partner, reflects a particular partner's distributive share of partnership ordinary income or loss, separately state items, and his or her special allocations. The partner's Schedule K-1 is notification of his or her share of partnership items for use in calculating income taxes and self-employment taxes.

SCHEDULE M-3. A partnership must file Schedule M-3 in lieu of Schedule M-1 if any one of the following conditions holds:

▶ The amount of total assets reported in Schedule L of Form 1065 (Balance Sheet per Books) equals or exceeds $10 million.

▶ The amount of adjusted total assets equals or exceeds $10 million, where adjusted total assets equal the Schedule L amount plus the following items that appear in Schedule M-2 of Form 1065: (1) capital distributions made during the year, (2) net book loss for the year, and (3) other adjustments.

▶ Total receipts equal or exceed $35 million.

▶ A reportable entity partner owns at least a 50% interest in the partnership on any day of the tax year, where a reportable entity partner is one that had to file its own Schedule M-3.

SECTION 444 ELECTION AND REQUIRED PAYMENTS. A partnership can elect to use a tax year other than a required year by filing an election under Sec. 444. This election is made by filing Form 8716 (Election to Have a Tax Year Other Than a Required Tax Year) by the earlier of the fifteenth day of the fifth month following the month that includes the first day of the tax year for which the election is effective or the due date (without regard to extension) of the income tax return resulting from the Sec. 444 election. In addition, a copy of Form 8716 must be attached to the partnership's Form 1065 for the first tax year for which the Sec. 444 election is made.

A partnership making a Sec. 444 election must make a required payment annually under Sec. 7519. The required payment has the effect of remitting a deposit equal to the

---

[55] Temp. Reg. 1.6081-2T.
[56] Reg. Sec. 301.6031-1(e)(2). Although the partnership pays no income tax, it still must pay the employer's share of social security taxes and any unemployment taxes as well as withhold income taxes from its employees' salaries.

Remember, however, that the partners are not considered to be employees. In addition, some publicly traded partnerships may pay a tax as explained in Chapter C:10.

tax (at the highest individual tax rate plus one percentage point) on the partnership's deferred income.

A partnership can obtain a refund if past payments exceed the tentative payment due on the deferred income for the current year. Similar refunds are available if the partnership terminates a Sec. 444 election or liquidates. The required payments are not deductible by the partnership and are not passed through to a partner. The required payments are in the nature of a refundable deposit.

The Sec. 7519 required payment is due on or before May 15 of the calendar year following the calendar year in which the election year begins. The partnership remits the required payment with Form 8752 (Required Payment or Refund Under Section 7519) along with a computational worksheet, which is illustrated in the instructions to Form 1065. Refunds of excess required payments also are obtained by filing Form 8752.

ESTIMATED TAXES. If the partnership is not an electing large partnership, it pays no income taxes and makes no estimated tax payments. However, the partners must make estimated tax payments based on their separate tax positions including their distributive shares of partnership income or loss for the current year. Thus, the partners are not making separate estimated tax payments for their partnership income but rather are including the effects of the partnership's results in the calculation of their normal estimated tax payments.

SELF-EMPLOYMENT INCOME. Every partnership must report the net earnings (or loss) for the partnership that constitute self-employment income to the partners. The instructions to Form 1065 contain a worksheet to make such a calculation. The partnership's self-employment income includes both guaranteed payments, partnership ordinary income and loss, and some separately stated items, but generally excludes capital gains and losses, Sec. 1231 gains and losses, interest, dividends, and rentals. The distributive share of self-employment income for each partner is shown on a Schedule K-1 and is included with the partner's other self-employment income in determining his or her self-employment tax liability (Schedule SE, Form 1040). The distributive share of partnership income allocable to a limited partner is not self-employment income.

EXAMPLE C:9-44 ▶ Adam is a general partner in the AB Partnership. His distributive share of partnership income and his guaranteed payment for the year are as follows:

Ordinary income	$15,000
Short-term capital gain	9,000
Guaranteed payment	18,000

Adam's self-employment income is $33,000 ($15,000 + $18,000). ◀

EXAMPLE C:9-45 ▶ Assume the same facts as in Example C:9-44 except that Adam is a limited partner. His self-employment income includes only the $18,000 guaranteed payment. ◀

IRS AUDIT PROCEDURES

Any questions arising during an IRS audit about a partnership item must be determined at the partnership level (instead of at the partner level).[57] Section 6231(a)(3) defines **partnership items** as virtually all items reported by the partnership for the tax year including tax preference items, credit recapture items, guaranteed payments, and the at-risk amount. In fact, almost every item that can appear on the partnership return is treated as a partnership item. Each partner must either report partnership items in a manner consistent with the Schedule K-1 received from the partnership or notify the IRS of the inconsistent treatment.[58]

The IRS can bring a single proceeding at the partnership level to determine the characterization or tax impact of any partnership item. All partners have the right to participate in the administrative proceedings, and the IRS must offer a consistent settlement to all partners.

---

[57] Sec. 6221. [58] Sec. 6222.

KEY POINT

To alleviate the administrative nightmare of having to audit each partner of a partnership, Congress has authorized the IRS to conduct audits of partnerships in a unified proceeding at the partnership level. This process is more efficient and should provide greater consistency in the treatment of the individual partners than did the previous system.

The partnership generally assigns a **tax matters partner** to facilitate communication between the IRS and the partners of a large partnership and to serve as the primary representative of the partnership.[59] If the partnership fails to assign the tax matters partner, the designation goes to the general partner having the largest profits interest at the close of the partnership's tax year.

These audit procedures, however, do not apply to small partnerships. For this purpose, a small partnership is defined as one having no more than ten partners who must be natural persons (but excluding nonresident aliens), C corporations, or estates. In counting partners, a husband and wife (or their estates) count as a single partner. Further, the IRS has announced that a partnership can be excluded from the audit procedures only if it can be established that all partners fully reported their shares of partnership items on timely filed tax returns.[60]

PROBLEM MATERIALS

DISCUSSION QUESTIONS

C:9-1 Yvonne and Larry plan to begin a business that will grow plants for sale to retail nurseries. They expect to have substantial losses for the first three years of operations while they develop their plants and their sales operations. Both Yvonne and Larry have substantial interest income, and both expect to work full-time in this new business. List three advantages for operating this business as a partnership instead of a C corporation.

C:9-2 Bob and Carol want to open a bed and breakfast inn as soon as they buy and renovate a turn-of-the-century home. What would be the major disadvantage of using a general partnership rather than a corporation for this business? Should they consider any other form for structuring their business?

C:9-3 Sam wants to help his brother, Lou, start a new business. Lou is a capable auto mechanic but has little business sense, so he needs Sam to help him make business decisions. Should this partnership be arranged as a general partnership or a limited partnership? Why? Should they consider any other form for structuring their business?

C:9-4 Doug contributes services but no property to the CD Partnership upon its formation. What are the tax implications of his receiving only a profits interest versus his receiving a capital and profits interest?

C:9-5 An existing partner wants to contribute property having a basis less than its FMV for an additional interest in a partnership.
  a. Should he contribute the property to the partnership?
  b. What are his other options?
  c. Explain the tax implications for the partner of these other options.

C:9-6 Jane contributes valuable property to a partnership in exchange for a general partnership interest. The partnership also assumes the recourse mortgage Jane incurred when she purchased the property two years ago.
  a. How will the liability affect the amount of gain that Jane must recognize?
  b. How will it affect her basis in the partnership interest?

C:9-7 Which of the following items can be deducted (up to $5,000) and amortized as part of a partnership's organizational expenditures?
  a. Legal fees for drawing up the partnership agreement
  b. Accounting fees for establishing an accounting system
  c. Fees for securing an initial working capital loan
  d. Filing fees required under state law in initial year to conduct business in the state
  e. Accounting fees for preparation of initial short-period tax return
  f. Transportation costs for acquiring machinery essential to the partnership's business
  g. Syndication expenses

C:9-8 The BW Partnership reported the following current year earnings: $30,000 interest from tax-exempt bonds, $50,000 long-term capital gain, and $100,000 net income from operations. Bob saw these numbers and told his partner, Wendy, that the partnership had $100,000 of taxable income. Is he correct? Explain your answer.

C:9-9 How will a partner's distributive share be determined if the partner sells one-half of his or her beginning-of-the-year partnership interest at the beginning of the tenth month of the partnership's tax year?

---

[59] Sec. 6231(a)(7).

[60] Rev. Proc. 84-35, 1984-1 C.B. 509.

C:9-10 Can a recourse debt of a partnership increase the basis of a limited partner's partnership interest? Explain.

C:9-11 The ABC Partnership has a nonrecourse liability that it incurred by borrowing from an unrelated bank. It is secured by an apartment building owned and managed by the partnership. The liability is not convertible into an equity interest. How does this liability affect the at-risk basis of general partner Anna and limited partner Bob?

C:9-12 Is the Sec. 704(d) loss limitation rule more or less restrictive than the at-risk rules? Explain.

C:9-13 Jeff, a 10% limited partner in the recently formed JRS Partnership, expects to have losses from the partnership for several more years. He is considering purchasing an interest in a profitable general partnership in which he will materially participate. Will the purchase allow him to use his losses from the JRS Partnership?

C:9-14 Helen, a 55% partner in the ABC Partnership, owns land (a capital asset) having a $20,000 basis and a $25,000 FMV. She plans to transfer the land to the ABC Partnership, which will subdivide the land and sell the lots. Discuss whether Helen should sell or contribute the land to the partnership.

C:9-15 What is the difference between a guaranteed payment that is a guaranteed amount and one that is a guaranteed minimum?

C:9-16 The TUV Partnership is considering two compensation schemes for Tracy, the partner who runs the business on a daily basis. Tracy can be given a $10,000 guaranteed payment, or she can be given a comparably larger distributive share (and distribution) so that she receives about $10,000 more each year. From the standpoint of when the income must be reported in Tracy's tax return, are these two compensation alternatives the same?

C:9-17 Roy's father gives him a capital interest in the Family Partnership. Discuss whether the Sec. 704(e) family partnership rules apply to this interest.

C:9-18 Andrew gives his brother Steve a 20% interest in the AS Partnership, and he retains a 30% interest. Andrew works for the partnership but is not paid. How will this arrangement affect the income from the AS Partnership that Andrew and Steve report?

ISSUE IDENTIFICATION QUESTIONS

C:9-19 Bob and Kate form the BK Partnership, a general partnership, as equal partners. Bob contributes an office building with a $130,000 FMV and a $95,000 adjusted basis to the partnership along with a $60,000 mortgage, which the partnership assumes. Kate contributes the land on which the building sits with a $50,000 FMV and a $75,000 adjusted basis. Kate will manage the partnership for the first five years of operations but will not receive a guaranteed payment for her work in the first year of partnership operations. Starting with the second year of partnership operations, Kate will receive a $10,000 guaranteed payment for each year she manages the partnership. What tax issues should Bob, Kate, and the BK Partnership consider with respect to the formation and operation of the partnership?

C:9-20 Suzanne and Laura form a partnership to market local crafts. In April, the two women spent $1,600 searching for a retail outlet, $1,200 to have a partnership agreement drawn up, and $2,000 to have an accounting system established. During April, they signed contracts with a number of local crafters to feature their products in the retail outlet. The outlet was fitted and merchandise organized during May. In June, the store opened and sold its first crafts. The partnership paid $500 to an accountant to prepare an income statement for the month of June. What tax issues should the partnership consider with regard to beginning this business?

C:9-21 Cara, a CPA, established an accounting system for the ABC Partnership and, in return for her services, received a 10% profits interest (but no capital interest) in the partnership. Her usual fee for the services would be approximately $20,000. No sales of profits interests in the ABC Partnership occurred during the current year. What tax issues should Cara and the ABC Partnership consider with respect to the payment made for the services?

C:9-22 George, a limited partner in the EFG Partnership, has a 20% interest in partnership capital, profits, and losses. His basis in the partnership interest is $15,000 before accounting for events of the current year. In December of the current year, the EFG Partnership repaid a $100,000 nonrecourse liability. The partnership earned $20,000 of ordinary income this year. What tax issues should George consider with respect to reporting the results of this year's activities for the EFG Partnership on his personal return?

C:9-23 Katie works 40 hours a week as a clerk in the mall and earns $20,000. In addition, she works five hours each week in the JKL Partnership's office. Katie, a 10% limited partner in the JKL Partnership, has been allocated a $2,100 loss from the partnership for the current year. The basis for her interest in JKL before accounting for current operations is $5,000. What tax issues should Katie consider with respect to her interest in, and employment by, the JKL Partnership?

C:9-24 Daniel has no family to inherit his 80% capital and profits interest in the CD Partnership. To ensure the continuation of the business, he gives a 20% capital and profits interest in the partnership to David, his best friend's son, on the condition that David work in the partnership for at least five years. David receives guaranteed payments for his work. Daniel takes no salary from the partnership, but he devotes all his time to the business operations of the partnership. What tax issues should Daniel and David consider with respect to the gift of the partnership interest and Daniel's employment arrangement with the partnership?

PROBLEMS

C:9-25 *Formation of a Partnership.* Suzanne and Bob form the SB General Partnership as equal partners. They make the following contributions:

Individual	Asset	Basis to Partner	FMV
Suzanne	Cash	$45,000	$ 45,000
	Inventory (securities)	14,000	15,000
Bob	Land	45,000	40,000
	Building	50,000	100,000

The SB Partnership assumes the $80,000 recourse mortgage on the building that Bob contributes, and the partners share the economic risk of loss on the mortgage equally. Bob has claimed $40,000 in straight-line depreciation under the MACRS rules on the building. Suzanne is a stockbroker and contributed securities from her inventory. The partnership will hold them as an investment.
  a. What amount and character of gain or loss must each partner recognize on the formation of the partnership?
  b. What is each partner's basis in his or her partnership interest?
  c. What is the partnership's basis in each asset?
  d. What is the partnership's initial book value of each asset?
  e. The partnership holds the securities for two years and then sells them for $20,000. What amount and character of gain must the partnership and each partner report?

C:9-26 *Formation of a Partnership.* On May 31, six brothers decided to form the Grimm Brothers Partnership to publish and print children's stories. The contributions of the brothers and their partnership interests are listed below. They share the economic risk of loss from liabilities according to their partnership interests.

Individual	Asset	Basis to Partner	FMV	Partnership Interest
Al	Cash	$15,000	$ 15,000	15%
Bob	Accounts receivable	–0–	20,000	20%
Clay	Office equipment	13,000	15,000	15%
Dave	Land	50,000	15,000	15%
Ed	Building	15,000	150,000	20%
Fred	Services	?	15,000	15%

The following other information about the contributions may be of interest:
 • Bob contributes accounts receivable from his proprietorship, which uses the cash method of accounting.
 • Clay uses the office equipment in a small business he owns. When he joins the partnership, he sells the remaining business assets to an outsider. He has claimed $8,000 of MACRS depreciation on the office equipment.
 • The partnership assumes a $130,000 mortgage on the building Ed contributes. Ed claimed $100,000 of straight-line MACRS depreciation on the commercial property.

- Fred, an attorney, drew up all the partnership agreements and filed the necessary paperwork. He receives a full 15% capital and profits interest for his services.
  a. How much gain, loss, or income must each partner recognize as a result of the formation?
  b. How much gain, loss, or income must the partnership recognize as a result of the formation?
  c. What is each partner's basis in his partnership interest?
  d. What is the partnership's basis in its assets?
  e. What is the partnership's initial book value of each asset?
  f. What effects do the depreciation recapture provisions have on the property contributions?
  g. How would your answer to Part a change if Fred received only a profits interest?
  h. What are the tax consequences to the partners and the partnership when the partnership sells for $9,000 the land contributed by Dave? Prior to the sale, the partnership held the land as an investment for two years.

C:9-27   *Formation of a Partnership.*   On January 1, Julie, Kay, and Susan form a partnership. The contributions of the three individuals are listed below. Julie received a 30% partnership interest, Kay received a 60% partnership interest, and Susan received a 10% partnership interest. They share the economic risk of loss from recourse liabilities according to their partnership interests.

Individual	Asset	Basis to Partner	FMV
Julie	Accounts receivable	$ –0–	$ 60,000
Kay	Land	30,000	58,000
	Building	45,000	116,000
Susan	Services	?	20,000

Kay has claimed $15,000 of straight-line MACRS depreciation on the building. The land and building are subject to a $54,000 mortgage, of which $18,000 is allocable to the land and $36,000 is allocable to the building. The partnership assumes the mortgage. Susan is an attorney, and the services she contributes are the drawing-up of all partnership agreements.
  a. What amount and character of gain, loss, or income must each partner recognize on the formation of the partnership?
  b. What is each partner's basis in her partnership interest?
  c. What is the partnership's basis in each of its assets?
  d. What is the partnership's initial book value of each asset?
  e. To raise some immediate cash after the formation, the partnership decides to sell the land and building to a third party and lease it back. The buyer pays $40,000 cash for the land and $80,000 cash for the building in addition to assuming the $54,000 mortgage. Assume the partnership claim no additional depreciation on the building before the sale. What is each partner's distributive share of the gains, and what is the character of the gains?

C:9-28   *Contribution of Services.*   Sean is admitted to the XYZ Partnership in December of the current year in return for his services managing the partnership's business during the year. The partnership reports ordinary income of $100,000 for the current year without considering this transaction.
  a. What are the tax consequences to Sean and the XYZ Partnership if Sean receives a 20% capital and profits interest in the partnership with a $75,000 FMV?
  b. What are the tax consequences to Sean and the XYZ Partnership if Sean receives only a 20% profits interest with no determinable FMV?

C:9-29   *Contribution of Services and Property.*   Marjorie works for a large firm whose business is to find suitable real estate, establish a limited partnership to purchase the property, and then sell the limited partnership interests. In the current year, Marjorie received a 5% limited partnership interest in the Eldorado Limited Partnership. Marjorie received this interest partially in payment for her services in selling partnership interests to others, but she also was required to contribute $5,000 in cash to the partnership. Similar limited partnership interests sold for $20,000 at approximately the same time that Marjorie received her interest. What are the tax consequences for Marjorie and the Eldorado Limited Partnership of Marjorie's receipt of the partnership interest?

C:9-30 *Partnership Tax Year.* The BCD Partnership is being formed by three equal partners, Beta Corporation, Chi Corporation, and Delta Corporation. The partners' tax year-ends are June 30 for Beta, September 30 for Chi, and October 31 for Delta. The BCD Partnership's natural business year ends on January 31.
a. What tax year(s) can the partnership elect without IRS permission?
b. What tax year(s) can the partnership elect with IRS permission?
c. How would your answers to Parts a and b change if Beta, Chi, and Delta own 4%, 4%, and 92%, respectively, of the partnership?

C:9-31 *Partnership Tax Year.* The BCD Partnership is formed in April of the current year. The three equal partners, Boris, Carlton Corporation, and Damien have had tax years ending on December 31, August 30, and December 31, respectively, for the last three years. The BCD Partnership has no natural business year.
a. What tax year is required for the BCD Partnership under Sec. 706?
b. Can the BCD Partnership make a Sec. 444 election? If so, what are the alternative tax years BCD could select?

C:9-32 *Partnership Income and Basis Adjustments.* Mark and Pamela are equal partners in MP Partnership. The partnership, Mark, and Pamela are calendar year taxpayers. The partnership incurred the following items in the current year:

Sales	$450,000
Cost of goods sold	210,000
Dividends on corporate investments	15,000
Tax-exempt interest income	4,000
Section 1245 gain (recapture) on equipment sale	33,000
Section 1231 gain on equipment sale	18,000
Long-term capital gain on stock sale	12,000
Long-term capital loss on stock sale	10,000
Short-term capital loss on stock sale	9,000
Depreciation (no Sec. 179 or bonus depreciation components)	27,000
Guaranteed payment to Pamela	30,000
Meals and entertainment expenses	11,600
Interest expense on loans allocable to:	
Business debt	42,000
Stock investments	9,200
Tax-exempt bonds	2,800
Principal payment on business loan	14,000
Charitable contributions	5,000
Distributions to partners ($40,000 each)	80,000

a. Compute the partnership's ordinary income and separately stated items.
b. Show Mark's and Pamela's shares of the items in Part a.
c. Compute Mark's and Pamela's ending basis in their partnership interests assuming their beginning balances are $150,000 each.

C:9-33 *Financial Accounting and Partnership Income.* Jim, Liz, and Keith are equal partners in the JLK Partnership, which uses the accrual method of accounting. All three materially participate in the business. JLK reports financial accounting income of $186,000 for the current year. The partnership used the following information to determine financial accounting income.

Operating profit (excluding the items listed below)	$94,000
Rental income	30,000
Interest income:	
Municipal bonds (tax-exempt)	15,000
Corporate bonds	3,000
Dividend income (all from less-than-20%-owned domestic corporations)	20,000
Gains and losses on property sales:	
Gain on sale of land held as an investment (contributed by Jim six	
years ago when its basis was $9,000 and its FMV was $15,000)	60,000
Long-term capital gains	10,000
Short-term capital losses	7,000
Sec. 1231 gain	9,000
Sec. 1250 gain	44,000

Depreciation:

Rental real estate	12,000
Machinery and equipment	27,000
Interest expense related to:	
Mortgages on rental property	18,000
Loans to acquire municipal bonds	5,000
Guaranteed payments to Jim	30,000
Low-income housing expenditures qualifying for credit	21,000

The following additional information is available about the current year's activities.

- The partnership received a $1,000 prepayment of rent for next year but has not recorded it as income for financial accounting purposes.
- The partnership recorded the land for financial accounting purposes at $15,000.
- MACRS depreciation on the rental real estate and machinery and equipment were $12,000 and $29,000, respectively, in the current year.
- MACRS depreciation for the rental real estate includes depreciation on the low-income housing expenditures.

a. What is JLK's financial accounting income?

b. What is JLK's partnership taxable income? (See Appendix B for an example of a financial accounting-to-tax reconciliation.)

c. What is JLK's ordinary income (loss)?

d. What are JLK's separately stated items?

C:9-34 *Partner's Distributive Shares.* On January of the current year, Becky (20%), Chuck (30%), and Dawn (50%) are partners in the BCD Partnership. During the current year, BCD reports the following results. All items occur evenly throughout the year unless otherwise indicated. Assume the current year is not a leap year.

Ordinary income	$120,000
Long-term capital gain (recognized September 1)	18,000
Short-term capital loss (recognized March 2)	6,000
Charitable contribution (made October 1)	20,000

a. What are the distributive shares for each partner, assuming they all continue to hold their interests at the end of the year?

b. Assume that Becky purchases a 5% partnership interest from Chuck on July 1 so that Becky and Chuck each own 25% from that date through the end of the year. What are Becky and Chuck's distributive shares for the current year?

C:9-35 *Allocation of Precontribution Gain.* Last year, Patty contributed land with a $4,000 basis and a $10,000 FMV in exchange for a 40% profits, loss, and capital interest in the PD Partnership. Dave contributed land with an $8,000 basis and a $15,000 FMV for the remaining 60% interest in the partnership. During the current year, PD Partnership reported $8,000 of ordinary income and sold the land that Patty contributed for $14,000, thereby producing a taxable long-term capital gain of $10,000 ($14,000 – $4,000). What income or gain must Patty and Dave report from the PD Partnership in the current year?

C:9-36 *Special Allocations.* Refer to Example C:9-25 in the text. Provide computations showing that the partners' total tax liability under the special allocation is less than their total liability under an equal allocation of the two types of interest income.

C:9-37 *Special Allocations.* Clark sold securities for a $50,000 short-term capital loss during the current year, but he has no personal capital gains to recognize. The C&L General Partnership, in which Clark has a 50% capital, profits, and loss interest, reported a $60,000 short-term capital gain this year. In addition, the partnership earned $140,000 of ordinary income. Clark's only partner, Lois, agrees to divide the year's income as follows:

Type of Income	Total	Clark	Lois
Short-term capital gain	$ 60,000	$50,000	$10,000
Ordinary income	140,000	50,000	90,000

Both partners and the partnership use a calendar year-end, and both partners have a 33% marginal tax rate.

a. Have the partners made a special allocation of income that has substantial economic effect?

b. What amount and character of income must each partner report on his or her tax return?

C:9-38 *Special Allocations.* Diane and Ed have equal capital and profits interests in the DE Partnership, and they share the economic risk of loss from recourse liabilities according to their partnership interests. In addition, Diane has a special allocation of all depreciation on buildings owned by the partnership. The buildings are financed with recourse liabilities. The depreciation reduces Diane's capital account, and liquidation is in accordance with the capital account balances. Depreciation for the DE Partnership is $50,000 annually. Diane and Ed each have $50,000 capital account balances on January 1 of Year 1. Will the special allocation be acceptable for Year 1, Year 2, and Year 3 in the following independent situations?

a. The partners have no obligation to repay negative capital account balances, and the partnership's operations (other than depreciation) each year have no net effect on the capital accounts.

b. The partners have an obligation to repay negative capital account balances.

c. The partners have no obligation to repay negative capital account balances. The partnership operates at its break-even point (excluding any depreciation claimed) and borrows $200,000 on a full recourse basis on December 31 of Year 2.

C:9-39 *Basis in Partnership Interest.* What is Kelly's basis for her partnership interest in each of the following independent situations? The partners share the economic risk of loss from recourse liabilities according to their partnership interests.

a. Kelly receives her 20% partnership interest for a contribution of property having a $14,000 basis and a $17,000 FMV. The partnership assumes her $10,000 recourse liability but has no other debts.

b. Kelly receives her 20% partnership interest as a gift from a friend. The friend's basis (without considering partnership liabilities) is $34,000. The FMV of the interest at the time of the gift is $36,000. The partnership has liabilities of $100,000 when Kelly receives her interest. No gift tax was paid with respect to the transfer.

c. Kelly inherits her 20% interest from her mother. Her mother's basis was $140,000. The FMV of the interest is $120,000 on the date of death and $160,000 on the alternate valuation date. The executor chooses the date of death for valuing the estate. The partnership has no liabilities.

C:9-40 *Basis in Partnership Interest.* Yong received a 40% general partnership interest in the XYZ Partnership in each of the independent situations below. In each situation, assume the general partners share the economic risk of loss related to recourse liabilities according to their partnership interests. What is Yong's basis in his partnership interest?

a. Yong designs the building the partnership will use for its offices. Yong normally would charge a $20,000 fee for a similar building design. Based on the other partner's contributions, the 40% interest has a FMV of $25,000. The partnership has no liabilities.

b. Yong contributes land with a $6,000 basis and an $18,000 FMV, a car (which he has used in his business since he purchased it) with a $15,000 adjusted basis and a $6,000 FMV, and $2,000 cash. The partnership has recourse liabilities of $100,000.

C:9-41 *Basis in Partnership Interest.* Tina purchases an interest in the TP Partnership on January 1 of the current year for $50,000. The partnership uses the calendar year as its tax year and has $200,000 in recourse liabilities when Tina acquires her interest. The partners share economic risk of loss associated with recourse debt according to their loss percentage. Her distributive share of partnership items for the year is as follows:

Ordinary income (excluding items listed below)	$30,000
Long-term capital gains	10,000
Municipal bond interest income	8,000
Charitable contributions	1,000
Interest expense related to municipal bond investment	2,000

TP reports the following liabilities on December 31:

Recourse debt	$100,000
Nonrecourse debt (not qualified real estate financing)	80,000

a. What is Tina's basis on December 31 if she has a 40% interest in profits and losses? TP is a general partnership. Tina has not guaranteed partnership debt, nor has she made any other special agreements about partnership debt.

b. How would your answer to Part a change if Tina instead had a 40% interest in profits and a 30% interest in losses? Assume TP is a general partnership, and all other agreements continue in place. Also assume the partners share recourse liabilities in accordance with their loss interest percentages.

c. How would your answer to Part a change if Tina were instead a limited partner having a 40% interest in profits and 30% interest in losses? The partnership agreement contains no guarantees or other special arrangements.

C:9-42 *At-Risk Loss Limitation.* The KC Partnership is a general partnership that manufactures widgets. The partnership uses a calendar year as its tax year and has two equal partners, Kerry and City Corporation, a widely held corporation. On January 1 of the current year, Kerry and City Corporation each has a $200,000 basis in the partnership interest. Operations during the year produce the following results:

Ordinary loss	$900,000
Long-term capital loss	100,000
Short-term capital gain	300,000

The only change in KC's liabilities during the year is KC's borrowing $100,000 as a nonrecourse loan (not qualified real estate financing) that remains outstanding at year-end.

a. What is each partner's deductible loss from the partnership's activities before any passive loss limitation?

b. What is each partner's basis in the partnership interest after the year's operations?

c. How would your answers to Parts a and b change if the KC Partnership's business were totally in real estate but not a rental activity? Assume the loan is qualified real estate financing.

C:9-43 *At-Risk Loss Limitation.* Mary and Gary are partners in the MG Partnership. Mary owns a 40% capital, profits, and loss interest. Gary owns the remaining interest. Both materially participate in partnership activities. At the beginning of the current year, MG's only liabilities are $30,000 in accounts payable, which remain outstanding at year-end. In November, MG borrows $100,000 on a nonrecourse basis from First Bank. The loan is secured by property with a $200,000 FMV. These are MG's only liabilities at year-end. Basis for the partnership interests at the beginning of the year is $40,000 for Mary and $60,000 for Gary before considering the impact of liabilities and operations. MG has a $200,000 ordinary loss during the current year. How much loss can Mary and Gary recognize?

C:9-44 *Passive Loss Limitation.* Eve and Tom own 40% and 60%, respectively, of the ET Partnership, which manufactures clocks. The partnership is a limited partnership, and Eve is the only general partner. She works full-time in the business. Tom essentially is an investor in the firm and works full-time at another job. Tom has no other income except his salary from his full-time employer. During the current year, the partnership reports the following gain and loss:

Ordinary loss	$140,000
Long-term capital gain	20,000

Before including the current year's gain and loss, Eve and Tom had $46,000 and $75,000 bases for their partnership interests, respectively. The partnership has no nonrecourse liabilities. Tom has no further obligation to make any additional investment in the partnership.

a. What gain or loss should each partner report on his or her individual tax return?

b. If the partnership borrowed an additional $100,000 of recourse liabilities, how would your answer to Part a change?

C:9-45 *Passive Loss Limitation.* Kate, Chad, and Stan are partners in the KCS Partnership, which operates a manufacturing business. The partners formed the partnership ten years ago with Kate and Chad each as general partners having a 40% capital and profits interest. Kate materially participates; Chad does not. Stan has a 20% interest as a limited partner. At the end of the current year, the following information was available:

	Kate	Chad	Stan
Basis in partnership (before gains and losses)	$100,000	$100,000	$50,000
Distributive share of:			
Nonrecourse liability (already included in basis and not qualified real estate financing)	50,000	50,000	25,000
Operating loss	(80,000)	(80,000)	(40,000)
Capital gain	20,000	20,000	10,000

a. How much operating loss can each partner deduct in the current year?

b. How much loss could each partner deduct if the KCS Partnership were engaged in rental activities? Assume Kate and Chad both actively participate, but Stan does not.

C:9-46 *At-Risk and Passive Loss Limitations.* At the beginning of year 1, Ed and Fran each contributed $1,000 cash to EF Partnership as equal partners. The partnership immediately borrowed $98,000 on a nonrecourse basis and used the contributed cash and loan proceeds to purchase equipment costing $100,000. The partnership leases out the equipment on a five-year lease for $10,000 per year. Over the five-year period, the partnership makes the following principal and interest payments on the loan:

Year	Principal	Interest
1	$3,000	$7,000
2	3,500	6,500
3	3,500	6,500
4	4,000	6,000
5	4,000	6,000

Assume the partnership depreciates the equipment according to the following hypothetical schedule:

Year	Depreciation
1	$40,000
2	25,000
3	15,000
4	8,000
5	8,000
6	4,000

At the beginning of Year 6, the partnership sells the equipment for $82,000. The partnership claims the last $4,000 of depreciation at the beginning of Year 6 as an expense, so the equipment has a zero basis when sold. At the beginning of Year 6, the partnership also pays off the $80,000 loan balance and distributes any remaining cash to Ed and Fran. Assume that each partner has a 35% ordinary tax rate and a 15% capital gains tax rate.

a. Determine the partnership's gain (loss) for each of the five years and the beginning of the sixth year.

b. Assume that depreciation recapture applies but that the at-risk and passive activity loss rules do not apply. Using the results from Part a and a 7% discount rate, determine the present value of tax savings for both partners combined over the five-year period including the beginning of the sixth year. Why do these tax savings occur?

c. Now assume the at-risk and passive activity loss rules do apply. Determine what the partners recognize over the five-year period including the beginning of the sixth year. Do the partners have any tax savings in this situation? Why or why not?

d. Provide a schedule analyzing each partner's outside basis over the five-year period including the sixth year.

C:9-47 *Related Party Transactions.* Susan, Steve, and Sandy own 15%, 35%, and 50%, respectively, in the SSS Partnership. Susan sells securities for their $40,000 FMV to the partnership. What are the tax implications of the following independent situations?

a. Susan's basis in the securities is $60,000. The three partners are siblings.

b. Susan's basis in the securities is $50,000. Susan is unrelated to the other partners.

c. Susan's basis in the securities is $30,000. Susan and Sandy are sisters. The partnership will hold the securities as an investment.

d. What are the tax consequences in Part a if the partnership subsequently sells the securities to an unrelated third party for $70,000? For $55,000? For $35,000?

C:9-48 *Related Party Transactions.* Kara owns 35% of the KLM Partnership and 45% of the KTV Partnership. Lynn owns 20% of KLM and 3% of KTV. Maura, Kara's daughter, owns 15% of KTV. No other partners own an interest in both partnerships or are related to other partners. The KTV Partnership sells to the KLM Partnership 1,000 shares of stock, which KTV has held for investment purposes, for its $50,000 FMV. What are the tax consequences of the sale in each of the following independent situations?

a. KTV's basis for the stock is $80,000.

    b. KTV's basis for the stock is $23,000 and KLM holds the stock as an investment.

    c. KTV's basis for the stock is $35,000 and KLM holds the stock as inventory.

    d. What are the tax consequences in Part a if the KLM Partnership subsequently sells the stock to an unrelated third party for $130,000? For $70,000? For $40,000?

C:9-49   *Guaranteed Payments.* Scott and Dave each invested $100,000 cash when they formed the SD Partnership and became equal partners. They agreed that the partnership would pay each partner a 5% guaranteed payment on his $100,000 capital account. Before the two guaranteed payments, current year results were $23,000 of ordinary income and $14,000 of long-term capital gain. What amount and character of income will Scott and Dave report for the current year from their partnership?

C:9-50   *Guaranteed Payments.* Allen and Bob are equal partners in the AB Partnership. Bob manages the business and receives a guaranteed payment. What amount and character of income will Allen and Bob report in each of the following independent situations?

    a. The AB Partnership earns $160,000 of ordinary income before considering Bob's guaranteed payment. Bob is guaranteed a $90,000 payment plus 50% of all income remaining after the guaranteed payment.

    b. Assume the same facts as Part a except Bob's distributive share is 50% with a guaranteed minimum of $90,000.

    c. The AB Partnership earns a $140,000 long-term capital gain and no ordinary income. Bob is guaranteed $80,000 plus 50% of all amounts remaining after the guaranteed payment.

C:9-51   *Guaranteed Payments.* Pam and Susan own the PS Partnership. Pam takes care of daily operations and receives a guaranteed payment for her efforts. What amount and character of income will each partner report in each of the following independent situations?

    a. The PS Partnership reports a $10,000 long-term capital gain and no ordinary income. Pam receives a $40,000 guaranteed payment plus a 30% distributive share of all partnership income after deducting the guaranteed payment.

    b. The PS Partnership reports $80,000 of ordinary income, before considering any guaranteed payment, and a $60,000 Sec. 1231 gain. Pam receives a $35,000 guaranteed payment plus a 20% distributive share of all partnership income after deducting the guaranteed payment.

    c. The PS Partnership reports $120,000 of ordinary income before considering any guaranteed payment. Pam receives 40% of partnership income but no less than $60,000.

C:9-52   *Family Partnership.* Dad gives Son a 20% capital and profits interest in the Family Partnership. Dad holds a 70% interest, and Fred, an unrelated individual, holds a 10% interest. Dad and Fred work in the partnership, but Son does not. Dad and Fred receive reasonable compensation for their work. The partnership earns $100,000 ordinary income, and the partners agree to divide this amount based on their relative ownership interests. What income must Father, Son, and Fred report if Family Partnership is a manufacturing firm with substantial inventories?

C:9-53   *Family Partnership.* Steve wishes to pass his business on to his children, Tracy and Vicki, and gives each daughter a 20% partnership interest to begin getting them involved. Steve retains the remaining 60% interest. Neither daughter is employed by the partnership, which buys and manages real estate. Steve draws only a $40,000 guaranteed payment for his work for the partnership. Reasonable compensation for his services would be $70,000. The partnership reports ordinary income of $120,000 after deducting the guaranteed payment. Distributive shares for the three partners are tentatively reported as: Steve, $72,000; Tracy, $24,000; and Vicki, $24,000. What is the proper distributive share of income for each partner?

COMPREHENSIVE PROBLEMS

C:9-54   Rick has a $50,000 basis in the RKS General Partnership on January 1 of the current year, and he owns no other investments. He has a 20% capital interest, a 30% profits interest, and a 40% loss interest in the partnership. Rick does not work in the partnership. The partnership's only liability is a $100,000 nonrecourse debt borrowed several years ago, which remains outstanding at year-end. Rick's share of the liability is based on his profits interest and is included in his $50,000 partnership basis. Rick and the partnership each report on a calendar year basis. Income for the entire partnership during the current year is:

Ordinary loss	$440,000
Long-term capital gain	100,000
Sec. 1231 gain	150,000

a. What is Rick's distributive share of income, gain, and loss for the current year?
b. What partnership income, gain, and loss should Rick report on his tax return for the current year?
c. What is Rick's basis in his partnership interest on the first day of next year?

C:9-55 Charles and Mary formed CM Partnership on January 1 of the current year. Charles contributed Inventory A with a $100,000 FMV and a $70,000 adjusted basis for a 40% interest, and Mary contributed $150,000 cash for a 60% interest. The partnership operates on a calendar year. The partnership used the cash to purchase equipment for $50,000, Inventory B for $80,000, and stock in ST Corporation for $5,000. The partnership used the remaining $15,000 for operating expenses and borrowed another $5,000 for operating expenses. During the year, the partnership sold one-half of Inventory A for $60,000 (tax basis, $35,000), one-half of Inventory B for $58,000 (tax basis, $40,000), and the ST stock for $6,000. The partnership claimed $7,000 of depreciation on the equipment for both tax and book purposes. Thus, for the year, the partnership incurred the following items:

Sales—Inventory A	$60,000
Sales—Inventory B	58,000
COGS—Inventory A	35,000
COGS—Inventory B	40,000
Operating expenses	20,000
Depreciation	7,000
Short-term capital gain	1,000
Interest on business loan	500

On December 31 of the current year, the partnership made a $1,000 principal payment on the loan and distributed $2,000 cash to Charles and $3,000 cash to Mary.
a. Determine partnership ordinary income for the year and each partner's distributive share.
b. Determine the separately stated items and each partner's distributive share.
c. Determine each partner's basis in the partnership at the end of the current year.
d. Determine each partner's book capital account at the end of the current year.
e. Provide an analysis of the ending cash balance.
f. Provide beginning and ending balance sheets using tax numbers.
g. Provide beginning and ending balance sheets using book values.

TAX STRATEGY PROBLEM

C:9-56 Sarah and Rex formed SR Entity on December 28 of last year. The entity operates on a calendar tax year. Each individual contributed $800,000 cash in exchange for a 50% ownership interest in the entity (common stock if a corporation; partnership interest if a partnership). In addition, the entity borrowed $400,000 from the bank. The entity operates on a calendar year. On December 28 of last year, the entity used the $2 million cash (contributions and loan) to purchase assets as indicated in the following balance sheet as of December 28 of last year:

Cash	$ 100,000
Inventory	1,770,000
Investment in tax-exempt bonds	50,000
Investment in corporate stock (less than 20%-owned)	80,000
Total	$2,000,000
Liability	$ 400,000
Equity*	1,600,000
Total	$2,000,000

*If a partnership, each partner's beginning capital account is $800,000.

The balance sheet did not change between December 28 of last year and the beginning of the current year. Thus, the above balance sheet also represents the balance sheet at January 1 of the current year.

The following data apply to the entity for the current year:

Sales	$3,000,000
Purchase of additional inventory	2,100,000
Ending inventory at December 31 of the current year	1,650,000
Gain on sale of corporate stock on December 31 of the current year	20,000
Dividends received on stock prior to its sale	4,000
Tax-exempt interest received	2,200
Operating expenses	500,000
Interest paid on loan (no principal paid)*	30,000
Distribution on December 31 of the current year:	
Sarah	50,000
Rex	50,000

*For simplicity, assume all the $30,000 interest expense pertains to business (and not to investments).

Sarah and Rex actively manage the entity's business, and the business does not qualify for the U.S. production activities deduction. At the individual level, Sarah and Rex are each single with no dependents. Each individual claims a standard deduction and one personal exemption (if applicable). Neither individual has income from sources other than listed above.

a. First, assume the entity is a regular C corporation and the distributions are dividends to Sarah and Rex. For the current year, determine the following:
   (1) The corporation's taxable income and tax liability.
   (2) Sarah's and Rex's individual AGI, taxable income, and tax liability.
   (3) The total tax liability for the corporation and its owners.
b. Next, assume the entity is a partnership. For the current year, determine the following:
   (1) Partnership ordinary income and each partner's share of partnership ordinary income.
   (2) Partnership separately stated items and each partner's share of each item.
   (3) Sarah's and Rex's AGI, taxable income, and total tax liability. Assume each partner will incur a $15,000 self-employment tax.
   (4) Each partner's basis in the partnership (outside basis) at the end of the current year.
c. Based on your analysis for the current year, which entity is better from an overall tax perspective? What are the shortcomings of examining only one year?
d. Given the corporate form, explain how the corporation can restructure the $50,000 distribution to each individual to reduce the overall tax liability.

TAX FORM/RETURN PREPARATION PROBLEM

C:9-57   The Dapper-Dons Partnership (employer identification no. 89-3456798) was formed ten years ago as a general partnership to custom tailor men's clothing. Dapper-Dons is located at 123 Flamingo Drive in Miami, Florida 33131. Bob Dapper (Social Security No. 654-32-1098) manages the business and has a 40% capital and profits interest. His address is 709 Brumby Way, Miami, Florida 33131. Jeremy Dons (Social Security No. 354-12-6531) owns the remaining 60% interest but is not active in the business. His address is 807 9th Avenue, North Miami, Florida 33134. The partnership values its inventory using the cost method and did not change the method used during the current year. The partnership uses the accrual method of accounting. Because of its simplicity, the partnership is not subject to the partnership audit procedures. The partnership has no foreign partners, no foreign transactions, no interests in foreign trusts, and no foreign financial accounts. This partnership is neither a tax shelter nor a publicly traded partnership. No changes in ownership of partnership interests occurred during the current year. The partnership made cash distributions of $155,050 and $232,576 to Dapper and Dons, respectively, on December 30 of the current year. It made no other property distributions. Financial statements for the current year are presented in Tables C:9-1 and C:9-2. Assume that Dapper-Dons' business qualifies as a U.S. production activity and that its qualified production activities income is $600,000. Dapper-Dons, being an eligible small pass-through partnership, uses the small business simplified overall method for reporting these activities (see discussion for Line 13d of Schedules K and K-1 in the Form 1065 instructions).
   Prepare a current year partnership tax return for Dapper-Dons Partnership.

▼ TABLE C:9-1

Dapper-Dons Partnership Income Statement for the 12 Months Ending December 31 of the Current Year (Problem C:9-57)

Sales		$2,350,000
Returns and allowances		(20,000)
		$2,330,000
Beginning inventory (FIFO method)	$ 200,050	
Purchases	624,000	
Labor	600,000	
Supplies	42,000	
Other costs[a]	12,000	
Goods available for sale	$1,478,050	
Ending inventory[b]	(146,000)	(1,332,050)
Gross profit		$ 997,950
Salaries for employees other than partners (W-2 wages)	$51,000	
Guaranteed payment for Dapper	85,000	
Utilities expense	46,428	
Depreciation (MACRS depreciation is $74,311)[c]	49,782	
Automobile expense	12,085	
Office supplies expense	4,420	
Advertising expense	85,000	
Bad debt expense	2,100	
Interest expense (all trade- or business-related)	45,000	
Rent expense	7,400	
Travel expense (meals cost $4,050 of this amount)	11,020	
Repairs and maintenance expense	68,300	
Accounting and legal expense	3,600	
Charitable contributions[d]	16,400	
Payroll taxes	5,180	
Other taxes (all trade- or business-related)	1,400	
Total expenses		494,115
Operating profit		$ 503,835
Other income and losses:		
Gain on sale of AB stock[e]	$ 18,000	
Loss on sale of CD stock[f]	(26,075)	
Sec. 1231 gain on sale of land[g]	5,050	
Interest on U.S. Treasury bills for entire year ($80,000 face amount)	9,000	
Dividends from 15%-owned domestic corporation	11,000	16,975
Net income		$ 520,810

[a] Additional Sec. 263A costs of $7,000 for the current year are included in other costs.
[b] Ending inventory includes the appropriate Sec. 263A costs, and no further adjustment is needed to properly state cost of sales and inventories for tax purposes.
[c] The partnership reports a $10,000 positive AMT adjustment for property placed in service after 1986. Dapper-Dons acquired and placed in service $40,000 of rehabilitation expenditures for a certified historical property this year. The appropriate MACRS depreciation on the rehabilitation expenditures already is included in the MACRS depreciation total.
[d] The partnership made all contributions in cash to qualifying charities.
[e] The partnership purchased the AB stock as an investment two years ago on December 1 for $40,000 and sold it on June 14 of the current year for $58,000.
[f] The partnership purchased the CD stock as an investment on February 15 of the current year for $100,000 and sold it on August 1 for $73,925.
[g] The partnership use the land as a parking lot for the business. The partnership purchased the land four years ago on March 17 for $30,000 and sold it on August 15 of the current year for $35,050.

▼ TABLE C:9-2

Dapper-Dons Partnership Balance Sheet for January 1 and December 31 of the Current Year (Problem C:9-57)

	Balance January 1	Balance December 31
Assets:		
Cash	$ 10,000	$ 40,000
Accounts receivable	72,600	150,100
Inventories	200,050	146,000
Marketable securities[a]	220,000	260,000
Building and equipment	374,600	465,000
Minus: Accumulated depreciation	(160,484)	(173,100)
Land	185,000	240,000
Total assets	$901,766	$1,128,000
Liabilities and equities:		
Accounts payable	$ 35,000	$ 46,000
Accrued salaries payable	14,000	18,000
Payroll taxes payable	3,416	7,106
Sales taxes payable	5,200	6,560
Mortgage and notes payable (current maturities)	44,000	52,000
Long-term debt	210,000	275,000
Capital:		
Dapper	236,060	289,334
Dons	354,090	434,000
Total liabilities and equities	$901,766	$1,128,000

[a] Short-term investment.

C:9-58 Knoxville Medical Supplies Company is located at 2400 20th Street, Knoxville, Tennessee 37919. The company is a general partnership that uses the calendar year and accrual basis for both book and tax purposes. It engages in the development and sale of specialized surgical tools to hospitals. The employer identification number (EIN) is 73-2012010. The company formed and began business on January 1, 2009. It has no foreign partners or other foreign dealings. The company is neither a tax shelter nor a publicly traded partnership. The company has made no distributions other than cash, and no changes in ownership have occurred during the current year. Dr. Bailey is the Tax Matters Partner. The partnership makes no special elections. Table C:9-3 contains book balance sheet information at the beginning and end of the current year, and Table C:9-4 presents a book income statement for the current year. Other information follows:

Information on Partnership Formation:
Two individuals formed the partnership on January 1, 2009: Dr. Leisa H. Bailey (1200 Kingston Pike, Knoxville, TN 37919; SSN 235-29-2820) and Dr. Thomas J. Firth (3600 Belmont Blvd., Nashville, TN 37215; SSN 279-27-9279). For a 30% interest, Dr. Bailey contributed $1.02 million cash. She is an active general partner who manages the company. For a 70% interest, Dr. Firth contributed $1,972,000 cash and 1,000 shares of Fastgrowth, Inc. stock having, at the time of contribution, a $408,000 fair market value (FMV) and an $81,600 adjusted basis. Dr. Firth is an active general partner who designs and develops new products. For book purposes, the company recorded the contribution of stock at fair market value.

Inventory and Cost of Goods Sold (Schedule A):
The company uses the periodic inventory method and prices its inventory using the lower of FIFO cost or market. Only beginning inventory, ending inventory, and purchases should be reflected in Schedule A. No other costs or expenses are allocated to cost of

▼ TABLE C:9-3

Knoxville Medical Supplies Company—Book Balance Sheet Information

Account	January 1, 2010 Debit	January 1, 2010 Credit	December 31, 2010 Debit	December 31, 2010 Credit
Cash	$ 336,360		$ 211,796	
Accounts receivable	734,400		816,000	
Inventory	1,360,000		1,632,000	
Investment in municipal bonds	22,000		22,000	
Investment in corporate stock	408,000		–0–	
Equipment	1,700,000		2,000,000	
Accumulated depreciation— Equipment		$ 242,930		$ 959,260
Accounts payable		136,000		176,800
Notes payable (short-term)		680,000		136,000
Accrued payroll expenses		4,760		7,140
Capital account balances:				
Dr. Leisa H. Bailey (30%)		1,049,121		1,020,779
Dr. Thomas J. Firth (70%)		2,447,949		2,381,817
Totals	$4,560,760	$4,560,760	$4,681,796	$4,681,796

goods sold. Note: the company is exempt from the uniform capitalization (UNICAP) rules because average gross income for the previous year was less than $10 million [Sec. 263A(b)(2)(B)].

Line 9 (a)	Check (ii)
(b) & (c)	Not applicable
(d) & (e)	No

Capital Gains and Losses (Schedule D):
The company sold all 1,000 shares of the Fastgrowth, Inc. common stock on July 1, 2010, for $1,224,000. Dr. Firth acquired the stock on January 2, 2007, for $81,600 and contributed the stock to the company on January 1, 2009, when its FMV was $408,000.

Fixed Assets and Depreciation (Form 4562):
The company acquired the equipment on January 2, 2009, and placed it in service on that date. The equipment, which originally cost $1.7 million, is MACRS seven-year property. The company did not elect Sec. 179 expensing in the acquisition year and elected out of bonus depreciation. The company claimed the following depreciation on this property:

Year	Book and Regular Tax Depreciation	AMT Depreciation
2009	$242,930	$182,070
2010	416,330	325,210

On March 1, 2010, the company acquired and placed in service additional equipment costing $300,000. The company made the Sec. 179 expensing election for the entire cost of this new equipment. No depreciation or expensing is reported on Schedule A.

Other Information

- The company paid Dr. Bailey a $170,000 guaranteed payment for her management services.

- The company made a $54,400 cash contribution to Fort Sanders Hospital System on December 1 of the current year.

- During the current year, the company made a $714,000 cash distribution to Dr. Bailey and a $1,666,000 million cash distribution to Dr. Firth.

▼ TABLE C:9-4
Knoxville Medical Supplies Company—Book Income Statement 2010

Sales		$6,800,000
Returns and allowances		(340,000)
Net sales		$6,460,000
Beginning inventory	$1,360,000	
Purchases	2,720,000	
Ending inventory	(1,632,000)	
Cost of goods sold		(2,448,000)
Gross profit		$4,012,000
Expenses:		
Depreciation (including Sec. 179)	$ 716,330	
Repairs	44,200	
General insurance	47,600	
Guaranteed payment (to Dr. Bailey)	170,000	
Other salaries	952,000	
Travel	27,200	
Utilities	81,600	
Rent expense	204,000	
Advertising expense	40,800	
Professional fees	68,000	
Employment taxes	95,200	
Business interest expense	32,640	
Investment expenses	4,896	
Investment interest expense	6,528	
Meals and entertainment	20,400	
Charitable contributions (cash)	54,400	
Total expenses		(2,565,794)
Other income:		
Interest on municipal bonds		880
Dividend income		22,440
Gain on stock sale:		
Selling price	$1,224,000	
Book value	(408,000)	
Book gain		816,000
Net income per books		$2,285,526

- The municipal bonds, acquired in 2009, are general revenue bonds, not private-activity bonds. Assume that no expenses of the company are allocable to the tax-exempt interest generated from the municipal bonds.
- Assume qualified production activities income (QPAI) equals $2.04 million. Employer's W-2 wages allocable to U.S. production activities equal $952,000. The company, being an eligible small pass-through partnership, uses the small business simplification overall method for reporting these activities (see discussion for Line 13d of Schedule K and Line 13 of Schedule K-1 in the Form 1065 instructions).
- Use book numbers for Schedule L, Schedule M-2, and Line 1 of Schedule M-1. Also use book numbers for Item L of Schedule K-1, and check the box for Sec. 704(b) book.
- The partners share liabilities, which are recourse, in the same proportion as their ownership percentages.

Required: Prepare the 2010 partnership tax return (Form 1065), including the following additional schedules and forms: Schedule D, Form 4562, and Schedule K-1.

Optional: Prepare a schedule for each partner's basis in his or her partnership interest.

CASE STUDY PROBLEMS

C:9-59 Abe and Brenda formed the AB Partnership ten years ago as a general partnership and have been very successful with the business. However, in the current year, economic conditions caused them to lose significant amounts, but they expect the economy and their business to return to profitable operations by next year or the year after. Abe manages the partnership business and works in it full-time. Brenda has a full-time job as an accountant for a $39,000 annual salary, but she also works in the partnership occasionally. She estimates that she spent about 120 hours working in the partnership this year. Abe has a 40% profits interest, a 50% loss interest, and a basis in his partnership interest on December 31 (before considering this year's operations) of $81,000. Brenda has a 60% profits interest, a 50% loss interest, and a basis of $104,000 on December 31 (before considering this year's operations). The partnership has no liabilities at December 31. Neither Abe nor Brenda currently has other investments. The AB Partnership incurs the following amounts during the year.

Ordinary loss	$100,000
Sec. 1231 gain	10,000
Tax-exempt municipal bond income	14,000
Long-term capital loss	14,000
Short-term capital loss	136,000

Early next year, the AB Partnership is considering borrowing $100,000 from a local bank to be secured by a mortgage on a building owned by the partnership with $150,000 FMV.

Required: Prepare a presentation to be made to Abe and Brenda discussing this matter. Points that should be discussed include: What amounts should Abe and Brenda report on their income tax return for the current year from the AB Partnership? What are their bases in their partnership interests after taking all transactions into effect? What happens to any losses they cannot deduct in the current year? What planning opportunities are presented by the need to borrow money early next year? What planning ideas would you suggest for Brenda?

C:9-60 On the advice of his attorney, Dr. Andres, a local pediatrician, contributed several office buildings, which he had previously owned as sole proprietor, to a new Andres Partnership in which he became a one-third general partner. He gave the remaining limited partnership interests to his two sons, Miguel and Esteban. Last year, when the partnership was formed, the boys were 14 and 16. The real estate is well managed and extremely profitable. Dr. Andres regularly consults with a full-time hired manager about the business, but neither of his sons has any dealings with the partnership. Under the terms of the partnership agreement, the boys can sell their partnership interest to no one but their father. Distributions from the partnership have been large, and Dr. Andres has insisted that the boys put all their distributions into savings accounts to pay for their college education.

Last year's return (the partnership's first) was filed by Mr. Jones, a partner in the local CPA firm of Wise and Johnson. Mr. Jones, who was Dr. Andres's accountant for a decade, retired last summer. Dr. Andres's business is extremely profitable and is an important part of the client base of this small-town CPA firm. Ms. Watson, the young partner who has taken over Dr. Andres's account, asked John, a second-year staff accountant, to prepare the current year's partnership return.

John has done considerable research and is positive that the Andres Partnership does not qualify as a partnership at all because the father has retained too much control over the sons' interests. John has briefly talked to Mr. Jones about his concerns. Mr. Jones said he was really rushed in the prior year when he filed the partnership return and admitted he never looked into the question of whether the arrangement met the requirements for being taxed as a partnership. After hearing more of the details, Mr. Jones stated that John was probably correct in his conclusion. Dr. Andres's tax bill will be significantly larger if he has to pay tax on all the partnership's income. When John approached Ms. Watson with his conclusions, her response was, "Oh, no! Dr. Andres already is unhappy because Mr. Jones is no longer preparing his returns. He'll really be unhappy if we give him a big tax increase, too." She paused thoughtfully, and then went on. "My first thought is just to leave well enough alone and file the partnership return. Are you positive, John, that this won't qualify as a partnership? Think about it and let me know tomorrow."

Required: Prepare a list of points you want to go over with the tax partner that would support finding that the business activity is a partnership. Prepare a second list of points that would support finding that the business activity is not a partnership.

TAX RESEARCH PROBLEMS

C:9-61 Caitlin and Wally formed the C & W Partnership on September 20, 2011. Caitlin contributed cash of $195,000, and Wally contributed office furniture with a FMV of $66,000. He bought the furniture for $60,000 on January 5, 2011, and placed it in service on that date. Wally will not claim Sec. 179 expensing on the furniture and elected out of bonus depreciation. He also contributed an office building and land with a combined FMV of $129,000. The land's FMV is $9,000. Wally bought the land in 2004 for $8,000 and had the building constructed for $100,000. The building was placed in service in June 2007.

Required: Your tax manager has asked you to prepare a schedule for the file indicating the basis of property at the time of contribution that Wally contributed, the depreciation for each piece of property that the partnership can claim, and the allocation of the depreciation to the two partners. Also indicate the amount and type of any recapture to which the contributed property may be subject at the time of the contribution and at a later time when the partnership sells the property. Your tax manager knows that, under Reg. Sec. 1.704-3, several alternatives exist for allocating depreciation relating to contributed property. He remembers that the Treasury Regulations describe a traditional method and a couple of others, but he's not sure what method applies in this situation. He wants you to check the alternatives and indicate which method should be used. Be certain to clearly label your schedule so that anyone who looks at the file later can determine where your numbers came from and the authority for your calculations. The manager has suggested that, at a minimum, you consult the following authorities:

- IRC Secs. 1(h), 168, 704, 1231, 1245
- Prop. Reg. Sec. 1.168-5(b)
- Reg. Sec. 1.704-1(b)(2)(iv)(g)(3)
- Reg. Sec. 1.704-3

C:9-62 Your clients, Lisa and Matthew, plan to form Lima General Partnership. Lisa will contribute $50,000 cash to Lima for a 50% interest in capital and profits. Matthew will contribute land having a $35,000 adjusted basis and a $50,000 FMV to Lima for the remaining 50% interest in capital and profits. Lima will borrow additional funds of $100,000 from a bank on a recourse basis and then will subdivide and sell the land. Prepare a draft memorandum for your tax manager's signature outlining the tax treatment for the partnership formation transaction. As part of your memorandum, compare the reporting of this transaction on the tax and financial accounting books. References:

- IRC Sec. 721
- Accounting Standards Codification (ASC) 845 (Nonmonetary Transactions)

C:9-63 Almost two years ago, the DEF Partnership was formed when Demetrius, Ebony, and Farouk each contributed $100,000 in cash. They are equal general partners in the real estate partnership, which has a December 31 year-end. The partnership uses the accrual method of accounting for financial accounting purposes but uses the cash method of accounting for tax purposes. The first year of operations resulted in a $50,000 loss. Because the real estate market plummeted, the second year of operations will result in an even larger ordinary loss. On November 30, calculations reveal that the year's loss is likely to be $100,000 for financial accounting purposes. Financial accounting results for the year are as follows:

	Quarter			
	First	*Second*	*Third*	*Fourth**
Revenue	$40,000	$60,000	$80,000	$100,000
Maintenance expense	(30,000)	(58,000)	(70,000)	(85,000)
Interest expense	(10,000)	(30,000)	(35,000)	(50,000)
Utilities expense	(3,000)	(3,000)	(3,000)	(3,000)
Projected loss	($ 3,000)	($31,000)	($28,000)	($38,000)

* Fourth quarter results are the sum of actual October and November results along with estimates for December results. December estimates are revenue, $33,000; maintenance, $60,000; interest, $20,000; and utilities, $1,000.

Cash has been short throughout the second year of operations, so more than $65,000 of expenses for second year operations have resulted in bills that are currently due or overdue. The unpaid bills are for July 1 through November 30 interest on a loan from the bank. In addition, all but essential maintenance has been postponed during the fourth quarter so that most of the fourth quarter maintenance is scheduled to be completed during December.

The DEF partners wants to attract a new partner to obtain additional capital. Raj is interested in investing $100,000 as a limited partner in the DEF Partnership if a good deal can be arranged. Raj would have a 25% profits and loss interest in the partnership but would expect something extra for the current year. In the current tax year, Raj has passive income of more than $200,000 from other sources, so he would like to have large passive losses allocated to him from DEF.

Required: Your tax partner has asked you to prepare a memorandum suggesting a plan to maximize the amount of current year loss that can be allocated to Raj. Assume none of the partners performs more than one-half of his or her personal service time in connection with real estate trades or businesses in which he or she materially participates. She reminded you to consider the varying interest rules for allocating losses to new partners found in Sec. 706 and to look into the possibilities of somehow capitalizing on the cash method of accounting or of using a special allocation. She wants you to be sure to check all the relevant case law for the plan you suggest.

C:9-64 Alice, Beth, and Carl formed the ABC partnership early in 2009. Alice and Beth each contributed $100,000 for their partnership interests, and Carl contributed land having a $100,000 FMV and $160,000 adjusted basis. The land remained a capital asset to the partnership. Late in 2010, Carl sold his interest in the partnership to Dan for $100,000. Shortly after that transaction, the partnership sold the land to an outside party for $100,000. The partnership has no Sec. 754 election in effect (discussed in Chapter C:10). The partners have asked that you explain the consequences these transactions have to the partnership and the partners, especially Carl and Dan. At a minimum, you should consult the following resources:

- IRC Sec. 704
- Reg. Sec. 1.704-3(a)

10

CHAPTER

SPECIAL PARTNERSHIP ISSUES

LEARNING OBJECTIVES

After studying this chapter, you should be able to

1. Determine the amount and character of gain or loss a partner recognizes in a nonliquidating partnership distribution

2. Determine the partner's basis of assets received in a nonliquidating partnership distribution

3. Identify the partnership's Sec. 751 assets

4. Determine the tax implications of a cash distribution when the partnership has Sec. 751 assets

5. Determine the amount and character of gain or loss a partner recognizes in a liquidating partnership distribution

6. Determine the partner's basis of assets received in a liquidating distribution

7. Determine the amount and character of the gain or loss recognized when a partner retires from the partnership or dies

8. Determine whether a partnership has terminated for tax purposes

9. Understand the effect of optional and mandatory basis adjustments

10. Determine the appropriate reporting for the income of an electing large partnership

Chapter C:10 continues the discussion of partnership taxation. The chapter first explains simple nonliquidating distributions and then discusses more complex nonliquidating and liquidating distributions. The chapter also explains methods of disposing of a partnership interest, including sales of the partnership interest and the retirement or death of a partner as well as transactions that terminate the entire partnership.

Finally, the chapter examines special partnership forms. These forms include publicly traded partnerships, limited liability companies, limited liability partnerships, and electing large partnerships.

NONLIQUIDATING DISTRIBUTIONS

Distributions from a partnership fall into two categories: liquidating distributions and nonliquidating (or current) distributions. A **liquidating distribution** is a single distribution, or one of a planned series of distributions, that terminates a partner's entire interest in the partnership. All other distributions, including those that substantially reduce a partner's interest in the partnership, are governed by the **nonliquidating (current) distribution** rules.

Although the tax consequences of the two types of distributions are similar in many respects, they are sufficiently different to require separate study. The chapter first discusses simple current distributions. It then covers complex current distributions involving Sec. 751 property and liquidating distributions.

OBJECTIVE 1

Determine the amount and character of gain or loss a partner recognizes in a nonliquidating partnership distribution

RECOGNITION OF GAIN

A current distribution that does not bring Sec. 751 into play cannot result in the recognition of a loss by either the partnership or the partner who receives the distribution. Moreover, the partnership usually recognizes no gain on a current distribution (except for Sec. 751 property, defined later in this chapter). Under Sec. 731, partners who receive distributions recognize a gain if they receive money distributions that exceed their basis in the partnership. For distribution purposes, money includes cash, deemed cash from reductions in a partner's share of liabilities, and the fair market value (FMV) of marketable securities.

EXAMPLE C:10-1 ▶

KEY POINT

Reductions in a partner's share of liabilities are treated as cash distributions.

Melissa is a 30% partner in the ABC Real Estate Partnership until Josh is admitted as a partner in exchange for a cash contribution. After Josh's admission, Melissa holds a 20% interest. Because of large loss deductions, Melissa's basis (before Josh's admission) is $20,000 including her 30% interest in the partnership liabilities of $250,000. She is deemed to receive a cash distribution equal to the $25,000 [(0.30 − 0.20) × $250,000] reduction in her share of partnership liabilities. Because the cash distribution exceeds her basis, Melissa recognizes a $5,000 ($25,000 distribution − $20,000 basis) gain. ◀

SELF-STUDY QUESTION

Can gain or loss be recognized in a current distribution?

ANSWER

Current distributions with no Sec. 751 implications do not create losses to either the partner or partnership. Ignoring Sec. 751, the partnership recognizes no gains. However, a partner recognizes a gain if the partner receives a money distribution exceeding his or her basis in his or her partnership interest. A distribution also may trigger recognition of precontribution gain or loss for a partner.

Precontribution Gain Recognition. Although a current distribution usually causes gain recognition only if money distributions exceed a partner's basis, a distribution also may trigger recognition of previously unrecognized precontribution gain or loss. A precontribution gain or loss is the difference between the FMV and adjusted basis of property when contributed to the partnership. Two different distribution events may trigger recognition of precontribution gain or loss.

First, if a partner contributes property with a precontribution gain or loss, the contributing partner must recognize the precontribution gain or loss when the partnership distributes the property to any other partner within seven years of the contribution. The amount of precontribution gain or loss recognized by the contributing partner equals the amount of precontribution gain or loss remaining that would have been allocated to the contributing partner had the property instead been sold for its FMV on the distribution date. The partnership's basis in the property immediately before the distribution and the contributing partner's basis in his or her partnership interest are both increased by any gain recognized or decreased by any loss recognized.[1]

EXAMPLE C:10-2 ▶ Several years ago, Michael contributed land with a $3,000 basis and a $7,000 FMV to the AB Partnership. In the current year, the partnership distributed the land to Stephen, another partner in the partnership. At the time of the distribution, the land had a $9,000 FMV. Stephen recognizes no gain on the distribution. Michael, however, recognizes his $4,000 precontribution gain when the partnership distributes the property to Stephen. Michael increases the basis in his partnership interest by $4,000, and the partnership's basis in the land immediately before the distribution increases by $4,000. This increase in the partnership's basis for the land also increases the land's basis to the distributee partner (Stephen). ◀

KEY POINT

Note the differences in the two distributions that cause a contributing partner to recognize remaining precontribution gains. In the first distribution, the *contributed property* is distributed to *another partner*. In the second distribution, *property other than the contributed property* is distributed to the *contributing partner*.

Second, under Sec. 737, property distributions to a partner may cause the partner to recognize his or her remaining precontribution gain if the FMV of the distributed property exceeds the partner's basis in his or her partnership interest before the distribution. The gain recognized under Sec. 737 is the lesser of the remaining precontribution net gain or the excess of the FMV of the distributed property over the adjusted basis of the partnership interest immediately before the property distribution (but after reduction for any money distributed at the same time).[2] The remaining precontribution gain is the net of all precontribution gains and losses for property contributed to the partnership in the seven years immediately preceding the distribution to the extent that such precontribution gains and losses have not already been recognized. The character of the recognized gain is determined by referencing the type of property that had precontribution gains or losses. The gain recognized under Sec. 737 is in addition to any gain recognized on the same distribution because of distributed cash exceeding the partner's basis in his or her partnership interest.

EXAMPLE C:10-3 ▶ Several years ago, Sergio contributed land, a capital asset, with a $20,000 FMV and a $15,000 basis to the STU Partnership in exchange for a 30% general interest in the partnership. The partnership still holds the land on January 31 of the current year, and none of the $5,000 precontribution gain has been recognized. On January 31 of the current year, Sergio has a $40,000 basis in his partnership interest when he receives an $8,000 cash distribution plus property purchased by the partnership with a $45,000 FMV and a $30,000 basis. Under the Sec. 731 distribution rules Sergio recognizes no gain because the cash distribution ($8,000) does not exceed Sergio's predistribution basis in his partnership interest ($40,000). However, under Sec. 737 he recognizes gain equal to the lesser of the $5,000 remaining precontribution gain or the $13,000 difference between the FMV of the property distributed ($45,000) and the basis of the partnership interest after the cash distribution but before any property distributions ($32,000 = $40,000 adjusted basis − $8,000 cash distributed). Thus, Sergio recognizes a $5,000 capital gain. ◀

EXAMPLE C:10-4 ▶ Assume the same facts as in Example C:10-3 except the distribution was $20,000 in cash and $23,000 (FMV) in marketable securities, which are treated like money, plus the property. Sergio recognizes a $3,000 gain under Sec. 731 because he received a money distribution exceeding his basis in the partnership interest ($43,000 money distribution − $40,000 adjusted basis before distributions). Under Sec. 737 he also recognizes gain equal to the lesser of the remaining precontribution gain ($5,000) or the $45,000 excess of the FMV of the property distributed ($45,000) over the zero basis of the partnership interest after money distributions but before property distributions ($0 = $40,000 adjusted basis − $43,000 money distributed). Sergio, therefore, recognizes both a $5,000 capital gain under Sec. 737 and a $3,000 capital gain under Sec. 731. ◀

If a partner recognizes gain under Sec. 737, that gain increases the partner's basis in his or her partnership interest (illustrated in the next section). Further, the recognized gain also increases the partnership's basis in the property that was the source of the precontribution gain.

---

[1] Sec. 704(c). See Chapter C:9 for a discussion of precontribution gains and losses.
[2] Section 737 does not apply if the property distributed was contributed by this same partner. Only the provisions of Sec. 731 would be considered in such a situation.

EXAMPLE C:10-5 ▶

OBJECTIVE 2

Determine the partner's basis of assets received in a nonliquidating partnership distribution

Assume the same facts as in Example C:10-3. At the time Sergio contributed the land, the partnership assumed Sergio's $15,000 basis in the land. Now, Sergio's $5,000 Sec. 737 gain increases the partnership's basis in the land to $20,000. ◀

BASIS EFFECTS OF DISTRIBUTIONS

In general, the partner's basis for property distributed by the partnership carries over from the partnership. The partner's basis in the partnership interest is reduced by the amount of money received and by the partner's basis in the distributed property.

EXAMPLE C:10-6 ▶

Jack has a $35,000 basis for his interest in the MLV Partnership before receiving a current distribution consisting of $7,000 in money, accounts receivable having a zero basis to the partnership, and land having an $18,000 basis to the partnership. Jack takes a carryover basis in the land and receivables. Following the distribution, his basis in the partnership interest is calculated as follows:

Predistribution basis in partnership interest		$35,000
Minus:	Money received	(7,000)
	Carryover basis in receivables	(–0–)
	Carryover basis in land	(18,000)
Postdistribution basis in partnership interest		$10,000

◀

The total bases of all distributed property in the partner's hands is limited to the partner's predistribution basis in his or her partnership interest plus any gain recognized on the distribution under Sec. 737.[3] If the partner's predistribution basis plus Sec. 737 gain is less than the sum of the money received plus the carryover basis of any noncash property received, the order in which the basis is allocated becomes crucial. First, cash and deemed cash distributions reduce the partner's basis in his or her partnership interest. Next, the remaining basis is allocated to provide a carryover of the partnership's basis for receivables and inventory. If the partner's predistribution basis is not large enough to allow a carryover of the partnership's basis for these two property categories, the partner's remaining basis is allocated among the receivables and inventory items based on both the partnership's basis in the assets and their FMV.[4] First, each asset is given its basis to the partnership. Then, the difference between the carryover basis from the partnership and the partner's basis in the partnership interest is cal-

WHAT WOULD YOU DO IN THIS SITUATION?

You have done the personal and business tax work for Betty and Thelma for a number of years. Betty and Thelma are partners in a retail shop. In addition, the two have decided they want to exchange some property that is not associated with their partnership. Betty wants to exchange undeveloped land she personally holds as an investment, having a $40,000 FMV and a $10,000 adjusted basis, for machinery and office equipment that Thelma owns but no longer uses. Thelma's machinery and office equipment in total have a $40,000 FMV and a $28,000 adjusted basis. Recently, a friend told Betty that several years ago he and an associate did a similar swap tax-free by contributing both pieces of property to be exchanged to a partnership, having the partnership hold the property for a few months, and then having the partnership distribute the property to the partner who wanted to receive it. The friend said the arrangement was nontaxable because the initial transfer qualified as a nontaxable contribution of property to the partnership in exchange for a partnership interest, and the distribution was nontaxable because it was simply a pro rata property distribution made by the partnership. Thelma and Betty have come to you asking that you structure their exchange using their retail shop partnership so that the transfer will be tax-free also. How should you respond to their request?

---

[3] Secs. 732(a)(2) and 737(c). Marketable securities have a basis equal to their Sec. 732 basis plus any gain recognized under Sec. 731(c).

[4] Sec. 732(c).

culated. A decrease must be allocated if the partner's basis in the partnership interest (after any money distribution) is less than the carryover basis from the partnership. The decrease is first allocated to any asset that has declined in value in an amount equal to the smaller of the decline in value for the asset or the asset's share of the decrease. If the decrease is not fully used at this point in the calculation, the remaining decrease is allocated to the assets based on their relative adjusted bases at this point in the calculation.

EXAMPLE C:10-7 ▶

KEY POINT

If different types of property are distributed, the partnership distribution rules assume that the property is distributed in the following order: (1) cash, (2) receivables and inventory, and (3) other property. This ordering can affect both the recognition of gain to the partner and the basis the partner takes in the distributed property.

Tracy has a $15,000 basis in her interest in the TP Partnership and no remaining precontribution gain immediately before receiving a current distribution that consists of $6,000 in money, power tools held as inventory with a $4,000 basis to the partnership and FMV of $3,500, and steel rod held as inventory with an $8,000 basis to the partnership and FMV of $9,200. The basis of the distributed property in Tracy's hands is determined as follows:

Predistribution basis in partnership interest	$15,000
Minus: Money received	(6,000)
Plus: Sec. 737 gain	–0–
Basis to be allocated	$ 9,000

The calculation of bases for the steel rod and power tools is as follows:

	Steel Rods	Power Tools	Total
FMV of asset	$9,200	$3,500	$12,700
Minus: Partnership's basis for asset	(8,000)	(4,000)	(12,000)
Difference	$1,200	($ 500)	$ 700
Step 1: Give each asset the partnership's basis for the asset	$8,000	$4,000	$12,000
Minus: Tracy's basis to be allocated			(9,000)
Decrease to allocate			$ 3,000
Step 2: Asset basis after Step 1	$8,000	$4,000	$12,000
Allocate the decrease first to assets that have declined in value	–0–	(500)	(500)
Adjusted bases at this point in the calculation	$8,000	$3,500	$11,500
Step 3: Allocate $2,500 remaining decrease based on relative adjusted bases at this point in the calculation	(1,739)[a]	(761)[b]	(2,500)
Tracy's bases in the assets	$6,261	$2,739	$ 9,000

[a][$8,000 ÷ ($8,000 + $3,500)] × $2,500 = $1,739
[b][$3,500 ÷ ($8,000 + $3,500)] × $2,500 = $ 761

This process results in Tracy's total basis in the two assets she receives being exactly equal to the $9,000 amount to be allocated. Moreover, Tracy's basis in her partnership interest is zero after the property distributions. ◀

EXAMPLE C:10-8 ▶

Assume the same facts as in Example C:10-7 except Tracy recognizes $1,000 of remaining precontribution gain under Sec. 737 as a result of the distribution. The basis of the distributed property in Tracy's hands is determined as follows:

Predistribution basis in partnership interest	$15,000
Minus: Money received	(6,000)
Plus: Sec. 737 gain	1,000
Amount to be allocated	$10,000

The calculation of the basis for the steel rods and power tools are as follows:

	Steel Rods	Power Tools	Total
FMV of asset	$9,200	$3,500	$12,700
Minus: Partnership's basis for asset	(8,000)	(4,000)	(12,000)
Difference	$1,200	($ 500)	$ 700

Step 1: Give each asset the partnership's basis for the asset	$8,000	$4,000	$12,000
Minus: Tracy's basis to be allocated			(10,000)
Decrease to allocate			$ 2,000

Step 2: Adjusted basis after Step 1	$8,000	$4,000	$12,000
Allocate the decrease first to assets that have declined in value	–0–	(500)	(500)
Adjusted basis at this point in the calculation	$8,000	$3,500	$11,500
Step 3: Allocate $1,500 remaining decrease based on relative adjusted bases at this point in the calculation	(1,043)[a]	(457)[b]	(1,500)
Tracy's bases in the assets	$6,957	$3,043	$10,000

[a][$8,000 ÷ ($8,000 + $3,500)] × $1,500 = $1,043
[b][$3,500 ÷ ($8,000 + $3,500)] × $1,500 = $ 457

Again, Tracy's basis in her partnership interest is zero after the distributions. ◀

If a partner's predistribution basis plus Sec. 737 gain recognized exceeds the sum of his or her money distribution plus the carryover basis for any receivables and inventory, a carryover basis is allocated to the other property received. If the partner has an insufficient basis in the partnership interest to provide a carryover basis for all the distributed property, the remaining basis for the partnership interest is allocated to the other property first to any decrease in FMV below basis and then based on the relative bases of such property in the partnership's hands just as was calculated above.

EXAMPLE C:10-9 ▶

SELF-STUDY QUESTION

Assume the same facts as in Example C:10-9 except the basis in the two parcels of land is only $4,000 in total. What are the tax consequences of the distribution?

ANSWER

If the basis in the two parcels of land were only $4,000 in total, the partner would take a $4,000 carryover basis in the land and retain a $2,000 basis in his partnership interest.

John has a $15,000 basis in his partnership interest and no remaining precontribution gain before receiving the following property as a current distribution:

Property	Basis to the Partnership	FMV
Money	$ 5,000	$5,000
Inventory	4,000	4,500
Land parcel 1	4,500	6,000
Land parcel 2	3,000	4,000

John's basis in his distributed property is calculated as follows:

Predistribution basis	$15,000
Minus: Money received	(5,000)
Plus: Sec. 737 gain	–0–
Basis for noncash property	$10,000
Minus: Carryover basis for inventory	(4,000)
Remaining basis to be allocated	$ 6,000

The calculation of the basis for the two parcels of land is as follows:

	Parcel One	Parcel Two	Total
FMV of asset	$6,000	$4,000	$10,000
Minus: Partnership's basis for asset	(4,500)	(3,000)	(7,500)
Difference	$1,500	$1,000	$ 2,500

Step 1: Give each asset the partnership's basis for the asset	$4,500	$3,000	$ 7,500
Minus: John's basis to be allocated			(6,000)
Decrease to allocate			$ 1,500

Step 2: Adjusted basis after Step 1	$4,500	$3,000	$ 7,500
Allocate the decrease first to assets that have declined in value	–0–	–0–	–0–
Adjusted basis at this point in the calculation	$4,500	$3,000	$ 7,500

Step 3: Allocate $1,500 remaining decrease
based on relative adjusted bases at
this point in the calculation

(900)ᵃ	(600)ᵇ	(1,500)

John's bases in the assets

$3,600	$2,400	$ 6,000

ᵃ[$4,500 ÷ ($4,500 + $3,000)] × $1,500 = $900
ᵇ[$3,000 ÷ ($4,500 + $3,000)] × $1,500 = $600

TYPICAL MISCONCEPTION

The partner's basis in his or her partnership interest cannot be less than zero. However, a partner's capital account can be less than zero. One must distinguish between references to a partner's basis in his or her partnership interest (his outside basis) and the balance in a partner's capital account.

John's basis in his partnership interest is zero after the distribution because all its basis is allocated to the money and other property received. ◄

Two other points should be noted. First, even when a partner's basis in the partnership interest is reduced to zero by a current distribution, he or she retains an interest in the partnership. If the partner has no remaining interest in the partnership (as opposed to a zero basis), the distribution would have been a liquidating distribution. Second, the distributee's basis in property distributed as a current distribution is always equal to or less than the carryover basis. Basis for distributed property cannot be increased above the carryover basis amount when received as a nonliquidating distribution.

HOLDING PERIOD AND CHARACTER OF DISTRIBUTED PROPERTY

The partner's holding period for property distributed as a current distribution includes the partnership's holding period for such property.[5] The length of time the partner owns the partnership interest is irrelevant when determining the holding period for the distributed property. Thus, if a new partner receives a distribution of property the partnership held for two years before he or she became a partner, the new partner's holding period for the distributed property is deemed to begin when the partnership purchased the property (i.e., two years ago) rather than on the more recent date when the partner purchases the partnership interest.

KEY POINT

Consistent with the discussion in Chapter C:9, certain rules ensure that neither contributions to nor distributions from a partnership can be used to alter the character of certain gains and losses on property held by the partnership or by the individual partners.

Special rules determine the character of gain or loss recognized when a partner subsequently sells or exchanges unrealized receivables or inventory distributed to the partner. These properties are defined in the next section of this chapter.

If the partnership distributes property that is an unrealized receivable in its hands, the distributee partner recognizes ordinary income or loss on a subsequent sale of that property. This ordinary income or loss treatment occurs without regard to the character of the property in the distributee partner's hands or the length of time the partner holds the property before its disposition.[6]

If the partnership distributes property that is inventory in its hands, the distributee partner recognizes ordinary income or loss on a subsequent sale that occurrs within five years of the distribution date.[7] The inventory rule mandates the ordinary income or loss result only for the five-year period beginning on the distribution date. After five years, the character of the gain or loss recognized on the sale of such property is determined by its character in the hands of the distributee partner.

NONLIQUIDATING DISTRIBUTIONS WITH SEC. 751

OBJECTIVE 3

Identify the partnership's Sec. 751 assets

So far, the discussion of current distributions has ignored the existence of the Sec. 751 property rules. Now, we must expand our discussion to include them.

SECTION 751 ASSETS DEFINED

Section 751 assets include unrealized receivables and inventory. These two categories encompass all property likely to produce ordinary income when sold or collected. Each of these categories must be carefully defined before further discussion of Sec. 751.

---

[5] Sec. 735(b).
[6] Sec. 735(a)(1).

[7] Sec. 735(a)(2).

UNREALIZED RECEIVABLES. **Unrealized receivables** includes a much broader spectrum of property than the name implies. Unrealized receivables are certain rights to payments to be received by a partnership to the extent they are not already included in income under the partnership's accounting methods. They include rights to payments for services performed or to be performed as well as rights to payment for goods delivered or to be delivered (other than capital assets). A common example of unrealized receivables is the accounts receivable of a cash method partnership.

In addition to rights to receive payments for goods and services, the term unrealized receivables includes most potential ordinary income recapture items. A primary example of this type of unrealized receivable is the potential Sec. 1245 or 1250 recapture on the partnership's depreciable property, which is the amount of depreciation that would be recaptured as ordinary income under Sec. 1245 or 1250 if the partnership sold property at its FMV.[8]

EXAMPLE C:10-10 ▶ The LK Partnership has two assets: $10,000 cash and a machine having a $14,000 basis and a $20,000 FMV. The partnership has claimed $8,000 of depreciation on the machine since its purchase. If the partnership sells the machine for its FMV, all $6,000 of the gain would be recaptured as ordinary income under Sec. 1245. Therefore, the LK Partnership has a $6,000 unrealized receivable. ◀

The definition of unrealized receivables is not limited to Sec. 1245 and 1250 depreciation recapture. Among the other recapture provisions creating unrealized receivables are Sec. 617(d) (mining property), Sec. 1252 (farmland), and Sec. 1254 (oil, gas, and geothermal property). Assets covered by Sec. 1278 (market discount bonds) and Sec. 1283 (short-term obligations) generate unrealized receivables to the extent the partnership would recognize ordinary income if it sold the asset. This type of unrealized receivable is deemed to have a zero basis.

INVENTORY. Inventory is equally surprising in its breadth. Inventory for purposes of Sec. 751 includes three major types of property:

▶ Items held for sale in the normal course of partnership business

▶ Any other property that, if sold by the partnership, would not be considered a capital asset or Sec. 1231 property

▶ Any other property held by the partnership that, if held by the selling or distributee partner, would be property of the two types listed above[9]

In short, cash, capital assets, and Sec. 1231 assets are the only properties that are not inventory.

For purposes of calculating the impact of Sec. 751 on distributions, inventory is considered a Sec. 751 asset only if the inventory is **substantially appreciated**. (This substantially appreciated rule does not apply to sales of partnership interests, discussed later in this chapter.) The test to determine whether inventory is substantially appreciated (and therefore falling under Sec. 751) is purely mechanical. Inventory is substantially appreciated if its FMV exceeds 120% of its adjusted basis to the partnership. For purposes of testing whether the inventory is substantially appreciated (but *only* for that purpose), inventory also includes unrealized receivables. The inclusion of unrealized receivables in the definition of inventory increases the likelihood that the inventory will be substantially appreciated.

EXAMPLE C:10-11 ▶ The ABC Partnership owns the following assets on December 31:

Assets	Basis	FMV
Cash	$10,000	$ 10,000
Unrealized receivables	–0–	40,000
Inventory	30,000	34,000
Land (Sec. 1231 property)	40,000	70,000
Total	$80,000	$154,000

[8] Sec. 751(c). Unrealized receivables may have basis if costs or expenses have been incurred but not taken into account under the partnership's method of accounting (e.g., the basis of property sold in a nondealer installment sale).

[9] Sec. 751(d)(2).

For purposes of the substantially appreciated inventory test, both ABC's unrealized receivables and inventory are included. The inventory's $74,000 FMV exceeds 120% of its adjusted basis [($30,000 + $0) × 1.20 = $36,000]. Therefore, the ABC Partnership has substantially appreciated inventory. ◀

EXCHANGE OF SEC. 751 ASSETS AND OTHER PROPERTY

A current distribution receives treatment under Sec. 751 only if the partnership has Sec. 751 assets and an exchange of Sec. 751 property for non-Sec. 751 property occurs. Accordingly, if a partnership does not have *both* Sec. 751 property and other property, the rules discussed above for simple current distributions control the taxation of the distribution. Similarly, a distribution that is proportionate to all partners or (1) consists of only the partner's share of either Sec. 751 property or non-Sec. 751 property and (2) does not reduce the partner's interest in other property is not affected by the Sec. 751 rules.

TYPICAL MISCONCEPTION

Even if a partnership has Sec. 751 property, Sec. 751 is not applicable as long as a partner's interest in the ordinary income type assets is not altered. However, if a distribution of the partnership assets is disproportionate, Sec. 751 treats that portion of the distribution as a deemed sale between the partnership and the distributee partner, with the corresponding income or loss being recognized.

However, any portion of the distribution that represents an exchange of Sec. 751 property for non-Sec. 751 property must be isolated and is not treated as a distribution at all. Instead, it is treated as a sale between the partnership and the partner, and any gain or loss realized on the sale transaction is fully recognized.[10] The character of the recognized gain or loss depends on the character of the property deemed sold. For the party deemed the seller of the Sec. 751 assets, the gain or loss is ordinary income or loss.

Analyzing the transaction to determine what property was involved in the Sec. 751 transaction is best accomplished by using an orderly, step-by-step approach.

STEP 1: DIVIDE THE ASSETS INTO SEC. 751 ASSETS AND NON-SEC. 751 ASSETS. Inventory must be tested at this time to see whether it is substantially appreciated to know whether it is a Sec. 751 asset for distribution purposes.

STEP 2: DEVELOP A SCHEDULE, SUCH AS THE ONE IN TABLE C:10-1, TO DETERMINE WHETHER THE PARTNER EXCHANGED SEC. 751 ASSETS FOR NON-SEC. 751 ASSETS OR VICE VERSA. This schedule must be based on the FMV of all the partnership's assets. To make the determination, compare the partner's interest in the partnership's assets before the distribution with his or her interest in the assets after the distribution. This part of the analysis assumes a hypothetical nontaxable pro rata distribution equal to the partner's decreased interest in the assets. We can see whether the partner exchanged Sec. 751 assets for non-Sec. 751 assets by comparing the hypothetical distribution with the actual distribution. Thus, in Table C:10-1,

KEY POINT

Steps 2 and 3 try to identify whether a disproportionate distribution of Sec. 751 assets has taken place. In Table C:10-1, if the column 5 total for Sec. 751 assets is zero, Sec. 751 is not applicable. But as the table illustrates, Anne received $10,000 more than her share of the partnership cash without receiving any of her $10,000 share of Sec. 751 assets.

▶ Column 1 represents the partner's interest (valued at FMV) in each asset before the distribution.

▶ Column 2 represents the partner's interest (valued at FMV) in each asset after the distribution.

▶ Column 3 shows a hypothetical proportionate distribution that would have occurred had the partner's ownership interest been reduced by the partner taking a pro rata share of each asset. (As such, the proportionate distribution would be nontaxable.)

▶ Column 4 shows the amounts actually distributed.

▶ Column 5 shows the difference between the hypothetical and actual distributions. This column indicates whether a Sec. 751 exchange has occurred (see Step 3).

STEP 3: ANALYZE COLUMN 5 TO DETERMINE WHETHER SEC. 751 ASSETS WERE EXCHANGED FOR NON-SEC. 751 ASSETS. If the column 5 total for the Sec. 751 assets section of Table C:10-1 is zero, no Sec. 751 exchange has occurred. The partner simply received an additional amount of one type of Sec. 751 asset in exchange for relinquishing an interest in some other type of Sec. 751 asset. For example, no Sec. 751 exchange occurs if a partner exchanges an interest in substantially appreciated inventory for an interest in unrealized receivables. However, if the column 5 total for the Sec. 751

---

[10] Sec. 751(b).

▼ TABLE C:10-1

Analysis of Sec. 751 Nonliquidating Distribution (Example C:10-12)

	Beginning Partnership Amount[a]	(1) Anne's Interest Before Distribution[a] (1/3)	(2) Anne's Interest After Distribution[a] (1/5)	(3) Hypothetical Proportionate Distribution (3) = (1) – (2)[a]	(4) Actual Distribution[a]	(5) Difference[b] (5) = (4) – (3)
Sec. 751 assets:						
Unrealized receivables	$15,000	$ 5,000	$ 3,000	$ 2,000	$ –0–	$ (2,000)
Inventory	60,000	20,000	12,000	8,000	–0–	(8,000)
Total Sec. 751 assets	$75,000	$25,000	$15,000	$10,000	$ –0–	$ (10,000)
Non-Sec. 751 assets:						
Cash	$75,000	$25,000	$10,000[c]	$15,000	$25,000	$ 10,000
Total non-Sec. 751 assets	$75,000	$25,000	$10,000	$15,000	$25,000	$ 10,000

[a]Valued at fair market value.
[b]A negative amount means that Anne gave up her interest in a particular property. A positive amount means that she received more than her proportionate interest.
[c]One-fifth interest in remaining cash of $50,000.

assets is an amount other than zero, a Sec. 751 exchange has occurred. One (or more) Sec. 751 properties has been exchanged for one (or more) non-Sec. 751 properties.

EXAMPLE C:10-12▶ On January 1, the ABC Partnership holds the assets listed below before making a $25,000 cash distribution to Anne that reduces her interest in the partnership from one-third to one-fifth.

Assets	Basis	FMV
Cash	$ 75,000	$ 75,000
Unrealized receivables	–0–	15,000
Inventory	30,000	60,000
Total	$105,000	$150,000

ABC owes no liabilities on January 1. Before the distribution, Anne has a $35,000 basis in her partnership interest. The following three steps indicate that a Sec. 751 exchange has occurred:

STEP 1. Determine ABC's Sec. 751 and non-Sec. 751 assets. ABC's Sec. 751 assets include the unrealized receivables and the substantially appreciated inventory. The cash is ABC's only non-Sec. 751 property.

STEP 2. Complete the table used to analyze the Sec. 751 distribution (see Table C:10-1).

STEP 3. Analyze column 5 of Table C:10-1 to see whether a Sec. 751 exchange has occurred. Because Anne's Sec. 751 asset total declined by $10,000, we know she gave up $10,000 of her proportionate interest in ABC's Sec. 751 assets in exchange for cash. ◀

ADDITIONAL COMMENT

Step 4 is crucial if a student is to understand the deemed sale that Sec. 751 creates. In Example C:10-13, Anne is treated as if she had exchanged her $10,000 interest in the unrealized receivables and inventory for $10,000 of cash. Thus, Anne has a taxable gain or loss on the deemed sale. To determine Anne's gain or loss on the deemed sale, the adjusted basis of the unrealized receivables and inventory equals whatever her basis would have been had the partnership actually distributed those assets to her.

STEP 4: DETERMINE THE GAIN OR LOSS ON THE SEC. 751 DEEMED SALE. We must assume that the exchange occurring in Step 3 above was a sale of the exchanged property between the partnership and the partner. This step follows logically from the premise that the partner "bargained" to receive the amounts actually distributed rather than a proportionate distribution. She sold her interest in some assets to receive more than her proportionate interest in other assets. As with any sale, the gain (or loss) equals the difference between the FMV of the property received and the adjusted basis of the property given up. Note that, up to this point, we have been dealing only in terms of the FMV, so the adjusted basis of property given up must be determined as if the hypothetical distribution actually had occurred.

EXAMPLE C:10-13▶

Assume the same facts as in Example C:10-12. The Sec. 751 sale portion of the distribution is analyzed as Anne receiving $10,000 more cash than her proportionate share and giving up a $2,000 (FMV) interest in the unrealized receivables and an $8,000 (FMV) interest in the inventory. By examining the balance sheet, we can see that the partnership's bases for the unrealized receivables and inventory are $0 and $4,000 [$8,000 × ($30,000 ÷ $60,000)]. If Anne received these properties in a current distribution, her basis would be the same as the property's basis in the partnership's hands, or $0 and $4,000, respectively. Therefore, Anne's deemed sale of the Sec. 751 assets is analyzed as follows:

Amount realized (cash)	$10,000
Minus: Adjusted basis of property deemed sold	(4,000)
Realized and recognized gain	$ 6,000

The character of the recognized gain depends on the character of the property deemed sold (in this case, the unrealized receivables and inventory). Therefore, Anne's $6,000 gain is ordinary income. ◀

STEP 5: DETERMINE THE IMPACT OF THE CURRENT DISTRIBUTION. The last step in analyzing the distribution's effect on the partner is to determine the impact of the portion of the distribution that is not a Sec. 751 exchange. This distribution is treated exactly like any other nonliquidating distribution.

EXAMPLE C:10-14▶

Assume the same facts as in Examples C:10-12 and C:10-13. Examining the distribution, we see in column 4 of Table C:10-1 that, as part of the Sec. 751 exchange, Anne received only $10,000 of the $25,000 cash actually distributed. The remaining $15,000 represents a current distribution. As described earlier in this chapter, a partner recognizes gain on a current distribution only if the money distributed exceeds his or her basis in the partnership interest. Thus, Anne recognizes no gain because she has a $16,000 basis in the partnership interest immediately after the current distribution. This basis is calculated as follows:

Predistribution basis for partnership interest	$35,000
Minus: Basis of property deemed distributed in Sec. 751 exchange	
($0 unrealized receivables + $4,000 inventory)	(4,000)
Basis before current distribution	$31,000
Minus: Money distributed	(15,000)
Postdistribution basis of partnership interest	$16,000

After the entire distribution is complete, Anne owns a one-fifth partnership interest with a basis of $16,000 and has $25,000 in cash. In addition, she has recognized $6,000 of ordinary income. ◀

STOP & THINK

Question: Do most current distributions made by a partnership require a Sec. 751 calculation?

Solution: No. A partnership makes many current distributions pro rata to all partners, so Sec. 751 is not involved. Even if the distribution is not pro rata, the distribution often does not create an exchange of an interest in Sec. 751 assets for an interest in other assets. This exchange happens only when (1) the partner is reducing his or her overall interest in the partnership, (e.g., from a 15% to a 5% general partner) or (2) an explicit agreement provides that the distribution results in a partner giving up all or part of his or her interest in some asset(s) maintained by the partnership. Most current distributions do not involve Sec. 751.

TERMINATING AN INTEREST IN A PARTNERSHIP

A partner can terminate or dispose of an interest in a partnership in a number of ways. The two most common are receiving a liquidating distribution and selling the interest. Other possibilities include giving the interest away, exchanging the interest for corporate stock, and transferring the interest at death. This part of the chapter considers each of these methods.

LIQUIDATING DISTRIBUTIONS

The IRC defines a liquidating distribution as a distribution, or one of a series of distributions, that terminates a partner's interest in the partnership.[11] If the partner's interest is drastically reduced but not terminated, the distribution is treated as a current distribution. A liquidating distribution can occur when only one member of a partnership terminates his or her interest, several partners terminate their interests but the partnership continues, or the entire partnership terminates and each partner receives a liquidating distribution. Rules for taxation of a liquidating distribution are the same whether one partner terminates his or her interest or the entire partnership liquidates.

GAIN OR LOSS RECOGNITION BY THE PARTNER. The rule for recognizing gain on a liquidating distribution is exactly the same rule used for a current distribution. A partner recognizes gain only if any money distributed exceeds the partner's predistribution basis in his or her partnership interest.[12] Distributed money includes money deemed distributed to the partner from a liability reduction or the FMV of marketable securities treated as money.

Although a partner can never recognize a loss from a current distribution, he or she can recognize a loss from a liquidating distribution. A partner recognizes a loss only if (1) the liquidating distribution consists of money (including money deemed distributed), unrealized receivables, and inventory, but no other property and (2) the partner's basis in the partnership interest exceeds the total basis of these distributed properties (including cash).[13] The amount of the loss is the difference between the partner's basis in the partnership interest before the distribution and the sum of money plus the bases of the receivables and inventory (to the partnership immediately before the distribution) that the partner receives.

Maria terminates her interest in the ABC Partnership when her basis in the partnership is $35,000. She receives a liquidating distribution of $10,000 cash and inventory with a $12,000 basis to the partnership. Her recognized loss is $13,000 [$35,000 − ($10,000 + $12,000)]. The inventory has a $12,000 basis to Maria. ◀

BASIS IN ASSETS RECEIVED. A partner's basis of an asset received in a liquidating distribution is determined using rules similar to those used to determine the basis of an asset received in a current distribution. For both kinds of distributions, the basis in unrealized receivables and inventory is generally the same as the property's basis in the partnership's hands. Under no condition is the basis of these two types of assets increased. Occasionally, however, the partner's basis in his or her partnership interest is so small that after making the necessary reduction for money (and deemed money) distributions, the basis in the partnership interest is smaller than the partnership's bases for the unrealized receivables and inventory distributed. In such cases, the remaining basis in the partnership interest must be allocated among the unrealized receivables and inventory items based first on their decline in value and then on their relative bases as adjusted to reflect the decline in value.[14] As a result, the bases for the unrealized receivables and inventory are reduced, and the amount of ordinary income a partner recognizes on their ultimate sale, exchange, or collection increases.

Remember that a liquidating distribution of money, unrealized receivables, and inventory having a total basis to the partnership less than the partner's basis in his or her partnership interest results in the recognition of a loss. However, the partner recognizes no loss if the distribution includes any property other than money, unrealized receivables, and inventory. Instead, all the remaining basis in the partnership interest must be allo-

---

[11] Sec. 761(d).
[12] Sec. 731(a)(1).

[13] Sec. 731(a)(2).
[14] Sec. 732(c).

cated to the other property received regardless of that property's basis to the partnership or its FMV. Application of this rule can create strange results.

EXAMPLE C:10-16▶

Assume the same facts as in Example C:10-15 except Maria's distribution also includes an office typewriter having a $50 basis to the partnership and a $100 FMV. The allocation of basis proceeds as follows:

Predistribution basis for partnership interest	$35,000
Minus: Money received	(10,000)
Basis after money distribution	$25,000
Minus: Basis of inventory to partnership	(12,000)
Remaining basis of partnership interest	$13,000

The entire $13,000 remaining basis of the partnership interest is allocated to the typewriter.

◀

TAX STRATEGY TIP

The partnership in Example C:10-16 should avoid distributing low basis property along with cash, unrealized receivables, and inventory so that the partner can obtain an immediate loss deduction.

The basis allocation procedure illustrated in Example C:10-16 delays loss recognition until Maria either depreciates or sells the typewriter. The allocation procedure also may change the character of the loss because Maria would recognize a capital loss when she receives the liquidating distribution in Example C:10-15. In Example C:10-16, however, the character of Maria's loss is determined by the character of the typewriter in her hands (or in some cases by a series of specific rules that are discussed below). Worst of all, if she converts the typewriter into personal-use property, the loss on its sale or exchange is nondeductible.

If the partnership distributes two or more assets other than unrealized receivables or inventory in the same distribution, the remaining basis in the partnership interest is allocated among them based on both their relative FMVs and bases in the partnership's hands. Such an allocation process can lead to either a decrease or increase in the total basis of these assets. This potential for increasing the assets' bases is unique to liquidating distributions.

The allocation that results in a decrease in the basis of a distributed asset is identical to the allocation process described for current distributions. However, if the amount to be allocated is greater than the carryover bases of the distributed assets, the basis is first allocated among the distributed assets in an amount equal to their carryover basis from the partnership. Then, allocations are made based on relative appreciation of the assets up to the amount of appreciation, and further allocations are made to the assets based on their relative FMVs.

EXAMPLE C:10-17▶

Before receiving a liquidating distribution, Craig's basis in his interest in the BCD Partnership is $62,000. The distribution consists of $10,000 in cash, inventory having a $2,000 basis to the partnership and a $4,000 FMV, and two parcels of undeveloped land (not held as inventory) having bases of $6,000 and $18,000 to the partnership and having FMVs of $10,000 and $24,000, respectively. Assume that Sec. 751 does not apply. His bases in the assets received are calculated as follows:

Predistribution basis for partnership interest	$62,000
Minus: Money received	(10,000)
Basis of inventory to the partnership	(2,000)
Basis allocated to two parcels of land	$50,000

The calculation of the basis for the two parcels of land are as follows:

	Parcel One	Parcel Two	Total
FMV of asset	$10,000	$24,000	$34,000
Minus: Partnership's basis for asset	(6,000)	(18,000)	(24,000)
Difference	$ 4,000	$ 6,000	$10,000
Step 1: Give each asset the partnership's basis for the asset	$ 6,000	$18,000	$24,000
Minus: Craig's basis to be allocated			(50,000)
Increase to allocate			$26,000

Step 2:	Adjusted basis after Step 1	$ 6,000	$18,000	$24,000
	Allocate the increase first to assets that have increased in value	4,000	6,000	10,000
	Adjusted basis at this point in the calculation	$10,000	$24,000	$34,000
Step 3:	Allocate $16,000 remaining increase based on relative FMVs	4,706[a]	11,294[b]	16,000
	Craig's bases in the assets	$14,706	$35,294	$50,000

[a]$10,000 ÷ ($10,000 + $24,000) × $16,000 = $ 4,706
[b]$24,000 ÷ ($10,000 + $24,000) × $16,000 = $11,294

◄

In a liquidating distribution, the amount of money received plus the distributee partner's total basis of the noncash property received normally equals the partner's predistribution basis in the partnership interest. The only two exceptions to this rule apply when the money received exceeds the partner's basis in his or her partnership interest, causing the partner to recognize a gain, or when money, unrealized receivables, and inventory are the only assets distributed and the partner recognizes a loss. In all other liquidating distributions, the distributee partner recognizes no gain or loss. Instead, that partner's predistribution basis in his or her partnership interest is transferred to the cash and other property received.

Holding Period in Distributed Assets. The distributee partner's holding period for any assets received in a liquidating distribution includes the partnership's holding period for such property.[15] If the partnership received the property as a contribution from a partner, the partnership's holding period also may include the period of time the contributing partner held the property prior to making the contribution (see Chapter C:9). The distributee partner's holding period for his or her partnership interest is irrelevant in determining the holding period of the assets received.

EXAMPLE C:10-18 ▶

George purchased an interest in the DEF Partnership on June 1, 2009, but he cannot get along with the other partners. Therefore, on July 1, 2011, he receives a liquidating distribution that terminates his interest in the partnership. George's distribution includes land that the partnership has owned since August 1, 2003. George's holding period for the land begins on August 1, 2003, even though his holding period for the partnership interest begins much later. ◄

The character of the gain or loss recognized on a subsequent sale of distributed property is determined using the same rules as for a current distribution.

EFFECTS OF SEC. 751. Section 751 has essentially the same impact on both liquidating and current distributions. To the extent the partner exchanges an interest in Sec. 751 assets for an interest in other assets (or vice versa), that portion of the transaction bypasses the distribution rules. Instead, this portion of the transaction is treated as a sale occurring between the partnership and the partner. One notable difference occurs between liquidating distributions and current distributions having Sec. 751 implications: the postdistribution interest in partnership assets is zero for the liquidating distribution because it terminates the partner's interest in the partnership.

EXAMPLE C:10-19 ▶

The ABC Partnership holds the assets listed below on December 31 before making a $50,000 cash distribution that reduces Al's one-third interest in the partnership to zero.

Assets	Basis	FMV
Cash	$75,000	$ 75,000
Unrealized receivables	–0–	15,000
Inventory	15,000	60,000
Total	$90,000	$150,000

---

[15] Sec. 735(b).

The partnership has no liabilities, and Al's predistribution basis in his partnership interest is $30,000. The following steps lead to the tax effects of the liquidating distribution:

STEP 1. Determine ABC's Sec. 751 and non-Sec. 751 assets. The Sec. 751 assets include the unrealized receivables and the substantially appreciated inventory. The cash is ABC's only non-Sec. 751 asset.

STEP 2. Complete the table used to analyze the Sec. 751 distributions (see Table C:10-2).

STEP 3. Analyze column 5 of Table C:10-2 to see whether a Sec. 751 exchange has occurred. Table C:10-2 shows that Al exchanges $5,000 of unrealized receivables and $20,000 of inventory for $25,000 cash.

SELF-STUDY QUESTION

What is the deemed Sec. 751 exchange shown in Table C:10-2?

ANSWER

Column 5 shows that Al received $25,000 of excess cash in lieu of $25,000 of Sec. 751 assets. Thus, the Sec. 751 exchange is a deemed sale by Al of $25,000 of unrealized receivables and inventory to the partnership in exchange for $25,000 of cash. With a table similar to Table C:10-2, the Sec. 751 computations are much easier to understand.

STEP 4. Determine the gain or loss on the Sec. 751 deemed sale. Al is deemed to have sold unrealized receivables and inventory for cash. Assume Al first got the receivables and inventory in a current distribution. He obtains the partnership's bases for the assets of $0 and $5,000, respectively. The subsequent deemed sale results in Al recognizing a $20,000 gain.

Amount realized (cash)	$25,000
Minus: Adjusted basis of property deemed sold	(5,000)
Realized and recognized gain	$20,000

Al's gain is ordinary income because it results from his deemed sale of receivables and inventory to the partnership.

STEP 5. Determine the impact of the non-Sec. 751 portion of the distribution. The liquidating distribution is only the $25,000 cash he receives that was *not* a part of the Sec. 751 transaction. To determine its impact, we first must find Al's basis in his partnership interest after the Sec. 751 transaction but before the $25,000 liquidating distribution.

Predistribution basis in the partnership interest	$30,000
Minus: Basis of receivables and inventory deemed distributed in Sec. 751 exchange	(5,000)
Basis before money distribution	$25,000
Minus: Money distribution	(25,000)
Gain recognized on liquidating distribution	$ –0–

Al recognizes no further gain or loss from the liquidating distribution portion of the transaction. ◄

▼ TABLE C:10-2

Analysis of Sec. 751 Liquidating Distribution (Example C:10-19)

	Beginning Partnership Amount[a]	(1) Al's Interest Before Distribution[a] (1/3)	(2) Al's Interest After Distribution[a] (–0–)	(3) Hypothetical Proportionate Distribution[a] (3) = (1) − (2)	(4) Actual Distribution[a]	(5) Difference[b] (5) = (4) − (3)
Sec. 751 assets:						
Unrealized receivables	$15,000	$ 5,000	$ –0–	$ 5,000	$ –0–	$ (5,000)
Inventory	60,000	20,000	–0–	20,000	–0–	(20,000)
Total Sec. 751 assets	$75,000	$25,000	$ –0–	$25,000	$ –0–	$ (25,000)
Non-Sec. 751 assets:						
Cash	$75,000	$25,000	$ –0–	$25,000	$50,000	$ 25,000
Total non-Sec. 751 assets	$75,000	$25,000	$ –0–	$25,000	$50,000	$ 25,000

[a]Valued at fair market value.
[b]A negative amount means that Al gave up his interest in a particular property. A positive amount means that Al received more than his proportionate interest.

SELF-STUDY QUESTION

What is the character of gain or loss on the sale of a partnership interest?

ANSWER

Because a partnership interest is generally a capital asset, the sale of a partnership interest results in the partner recognizing a capital gain or loss. However, if a partnership has Sec. 751 assets, the partner is deemed to sell his or her share of the underlying Sec. 751 assets, thereby causing a corresponding ordinary gain or loss to be recognized.

EFFECTS OF DISTRIBUTION ON THE PARTNERSHIP.   A partnership generally recognizes no gain or loss on liquidating distributions made to its partners.[16] If a Sec. 751 deemed sale occurs, however, the partnership may recognize gain or loss on assets deemed sold to its partner. Although a liquidating distribution normally does not itself terminate the partnership, the partnership terminates if none of the remaining partners continue to operate the business of the partnership in a partnership form. In this case, all partners will receive liquidating distributions. Finally, the partnership's assets may be subject to optional or mandatory basis adjustments (discussed later in this chapter).

Topic Review C:10-1 summarizes the tax consequences of current and liquidating distributions.

SALE OF A PARTNERSHIP INTEREST

Absence any contrary rules, a partner's sale or exchange of a partnership interest would generate a capital gain or loss under Sec. 741 because a partnership interest is usually a capital asset. Section 751, however, modifies this result by requiring the partner to recognize ordi-

Topic Review C:10-1

Current and Liquidating Distributions

TAX CONSEQUENCES	CURRENT DISTRIBUTIONS	LIQUIDATING DISTRIBUTIONS
Impact on Partner:		
Money (or deemed money from liability changes or marketable securities) distributed	Gain recognized only if money distributed exceeds basis in partnership interest before distribution.	Gain recognized only if money distributed exceeds basis in partnership interest before distribution.
Unrealized receivables and/or inventory distributed	Carryover basis (limited to basis in partnership interest before distribution reduced by money distributed).	Carryover basis (limited to basis in partnership interest before distribution reduced by money distributed).
	No gain or loss recognized.[a]	Loss recognized if partnership distributes money, inventory, and receivables with basis less than partner's basis in partnership interest before distribution and partnership distributes no other property.[a]
Other property distributed	Carryover basis (limited to basis in partnership interest before distribution reduced by money and carryover basis in inventory and receivables).	Basis equal to basis in partnership interest before distribution reduced by money and carryover basis in inventory and receivables.
	No gain or loss recognized.[a]	No gain or loss recognized.[a]
Impact on Partnership:		
General rule	No gain or loss recognized.	No gain or loss recognized.
Partnership assets	May be subject to optional basis adjustments.	May be subject to optional or mandatory basis adjustments.
Other Tax Consequences:	If a Sec. 751 deemed sale or exchange occurs, the partner and/or the partnership may recognize gain or loss on the deemed sale.	If a Sec. 751 deemed sale or exchange occurs, the partner and/or the partnership may recognize gain or loss on the deemed sale.

[a]A partner may recognize precontribution gain (but not loss) under Sec. 737 if a precontribution net gain remains and the FMV of the property distributed exceeds the adjusted basis of the partnership interest immediately before the property distribution (but after any money distribution). The contributing partner also may recognize precontribution gain or loss if the partnership distributes the contributed property to another partner within seven years of the contribution (Sec. 704(c)).

---

[16] Sec. 731(b).

nary income or loss (and possibly Sec. 1250 gain) on the sale or exchange of a partnership interest to the extent the consideration received is attributable to the partner's share of unrealized receivables and inventory items. The sale of a partnership interest also may have two other effects: the purchaser acquires the partner's share of the partnership's liabilities, and the partnership may be terminated. Each of these situations related to the sale of a partnership interest is examined below.

SECTION 751 PROPERTY.   The definition of Sec. 751 property is slightly different for sales or exchanges than for distributions because inventory does not have to be substantially appreciated to be included as Sec. 751 property. Thus, all inventory and all unrealized receivables are Sec. 751 assets in a sale or exchange situation.[17]

Treasury Regulations under Sec. 751 take a hypothetical asset sale approach to determine the amount of ordinary income or loss the partner recognizes on the sale or exchange of a partnership interest.[18] Under the regulations, the partnership is deemed to sell all its assets for their FMV immediately before the partner sells his or her interest in the partnership. The partner then is allocated his or her share of ordinary gain or loss (and possibly Sec. 1250 gain) attributable to the Sec. 751 assets. With this approach, the results of the sale or exchange can be determined using the following three steps:

STEP 1.   Determine the total gain or loss on the sale or exchange of the partnership interest.

STEP 2.   Determine the ordinary gain or loss component and the Sec. 1250 gain component, if applicable, using the hypothetical asset sale approach.[19]

STEP 3.   Determine the capital gain component by calculating the residual gain or loss after assigning the ordinary gain or loss and the Sec. 1250 gain components.

EXAMPLE C:10-20▶   Troy sells his one-fourth interest in the TV Partnership to Steve for $50,000 cash when the partnership's assets are as follows:

Assets	Basis	FMV
Cash	$ 20,000	$ 20,000
Unrealized receivables	–0–	24,000
Inventory	20,000	68,000
Building	40,000	56,000
Land	40,000	32,000
Total	$120,000	$200,000

The partnership has no liabilities on the sale date and has claimed $19,000 of straight-line depreciation on the building. Troy's basis in his partnership interest is $30,000 on such date. Both the receivables and inventory are Sec. 751 assets, and the building is Sec. 1250 property. Application of Step 1 yields the following gain on Troy's sale of his partnership interest:

Amount realized on sale	$50,000
Minus: Adjusted basis of partnership interest	(30,000)
Total gain realized	$20,000

Application of Step 2 yields the following allocation to Sec. 751 and Sec. 1250 property:

Deemed Sale of Assets	Partnership Gain (Loss)	Troy's Share (25%)
Unrealized receivables	$24,000	$ 6,000
Inventory	48,000	12,000
Building	16,000	4,000
Land	(8,000)	(2,000)

---

[17] Regulation Sec. 1.751-1(a)(1) is outdated to some extent and still speaks in terms of substantially appreciated inventory. However, Sec. 751(a) in the IRC, which deals with the sale or exchange of a partnership interest, includes all inventory items, not just those that are substantially appreciated.
[18] Reg. Sec. 1.751-1(a)(2). This hypothetical sale approach allows for easy incorporation of special allocations under Sec. 704 into the Sec. 751 calculation.

[19] The Sec. 1250 gain is the lesser of the hypothetical gain on Sec. 1250 property (e.g., buildings) or the amount of depreciation claimed on the Sec. 1250 property (assuming straight-line depreciation). This gain applies to noncorporate taxpayers and is subject to the 25% capital gains tax rate. A similar rule applies to a collectibles gain subject to the 28% capital gains tax rate. See Reg. Sec. 1.1(h)-1.

Thus, on the sale of his partnership interest, Troy recognizes ordinary income of $18,000 ($6,000 + $12,000). Because the $19,000 of depreciation exceeds the hypothetical gain on the building, the entire $16,000 gain is Sec. 1250 gain, $4,000 of which is Troy's share. Application of Step 3 yields the following residual allocation to capital gain or loss:

Total gain realized	$ 20,000
Minus: Allocation to ordinary income and Sec. 1250 gain	(22,000)
Capital loss recognized	$ (2,000)

In summary, on the sale of his partnership interest, Troy recognizes $18,000 of ordinary income, $4,000 of Sec. 1250 gain, and a $2,000 capital loss. Without Sec. 751, these three components would have been netted together as a $20,000 capital gain. ◀

STOP & THINK

Question: Bill owns 20% of Kraco and plans to sell his ownership interest for a $40,000 gain. Kraco has both unrealized receivables and inventory. If Kraco is a corporation, Bill will report a $40,000 capital gain. If Kraco is a partnership, part of the $40,000 gain (the gain on his 20% share of the Sec. 751 assets) will be ordinary income, and the remainder will be capital gain. Why did Congress decide to tax the gain on the sale of corporate stock differently from the gain on the sale of a partnership interest?

Solution: The corporation itself will pay tax on the ordinary income realized when it collects unrealized receivables or sells inventory, and the corporation's tax is unaffected by the identity of the shareholder. Under no conditions will the shareholder have to report any of the corporation's ordinary income. Accordingly, the sale of the corporate stock does not provide an opportunity to avoid ordinary income for the owner, nor can the owner convert ordinary income into capital gain by selling the corporate stock.[20]

Because the partners report and pay taxes on the ordinary income earned by the partnership, a sale of a partnership interest that produces only capital gains would represent an opportunity for a partner to avoid recognizing ordinary income and recognize capital gains instead. Imagine, for example, that Kraco is a cash basis service business whose only asset is a large account receivable where all work has been completed. If Bill stays in the partnership, he will recognize ordinary income when the partnership collects the receivable. If he were allowed to sell his partnership interest in this setting for a capital gain, he could convert his ordinary income into capital gain. However, Sec. 751 prevents this conversion from happening by requiring him to recognize ordinary income on the sale of the partnership interest to the extent the sales proceeds are attributable to Sec. 751 assets.

ADDITIONAL COMMENT

Section 751 treatment is another application of the aggregate theory of partnership taxation as opposed to the entity theory.

LIABILITIES. When a partnership has liabilities, each partner's distributive share of any liabilities is always part of the basis for the partnership interest. When a partner sells his or her partnership interest, the partner is relieved of the liabilities. Accordingly, the amount realized on the sale of a partnership interest is made up of money plus the FMV of noncash property received plus the seller's share of partnership liabilities assumed or acquired by the purchaser.

EXAMPLE C:10-21▶

Andrew is a 30% partner in the ABC Partnership when he sells his entire interest to Miguel for $40,000 cash. At the time of the sale, Andrew's basis is $27,000 (which includes his $7,000 share of partnership liabilities). The partnership has no Sec. 751 assets. Andrew's $20,000 gain on the sale is calculated as follows:

Amount realized:		
Cash	$40,000	
Liabilities assumed by purchaser	7,000	$47,000
Minus: Adjusted basis		(27,000)
Gain recognized on sale		$20,000

◀

---

[20] An exception used to exist for a so-called collapsible corporation. However, the 2003 Act and 2010 Tax Relief Act repealed these provisions for tax years beginning after 2003 and before 2013. A discussion of collapsible corporations is beyond the scope of this text.

IMPACT ON THE PARTNERSHIP. When one partner sells his or her partnership interest, the sale usually has no more impact on the partnership than the sale of corporate stock by one shareholder has on the corporation. Only the partner and the purchaser of the interest are affected. However, the partnership itself is affected if the partnership interest sold is sufficiently large that, under Sec. 708, its sale terminates the partnership for tax purposes. This effect is discussed later in this chapter. Also, the partnership may have to make optional or mandatory basis adjustments to its assets (discussed later in this chapter).

OBJECTIVE 7

Determine the amount and character of the gain or loss recognized when a partner retires from a partnership or dies

RETIREMENT OR DEATH OF A PARTNER

If a partner dies or retires from a partnership, that partner's interest can be sold either to an outsider or to one or more existing partners.[21] The results of such a sale are outlined above. Often, however, a partner or a deceased partner's successor-in-interest departs from the partnership in return for payments made by the partnership itself. When the partnership buys out the partner's interest, the analysis of the tax results focuses on two types of payments: payments made in exchange for the partner's interest in partnership property and other payments.

PAYMENTS FOR PARTNERSHIP PROPERTY. Generally, the IRS accepts the valuation placed on the retiring partner's interest in the partnership property by the partners in an arm's-length transaction. Payments made for the property interest are taxed under the liquidating distribution rules. Like any liquidating distribution made to a partner, payments made to a retiring partner or a deceased partner's successor-in-interest[22] in exchange for his or her property interest are not deductible by the partnership.[23]

If the retiring or deceased partner was a general partner and the partnership is a service partnership (i.e., capital is not a material income producing factor), payments made to a general partner for unrealized receivables and goodwill (when the partnership agreement does not provide for a goodwill payment on retirement or death) are not considered payments for property. Instead, any such payments are treated as other payments. The other payment treatment permits the partnership to deduct the amounts paid to the retiring or deceased partner or to reduce the distributive share allocable to the other partners.

OTHER PAYMENTS. Payments made to a retiring partner or to a deceased partner's successor-in-interest that exceed the value of that partner's share of partnership property have a different tax result for both the retiring partner and for the partnership. A few payments that do represent payments for property (e.g., payments to a general partner retiring from a service partnership for his or her interest in unrealized receivables and for his or her interest in partnership goodwill) also are taxed under these rules.

Under these rules, a payment is treated as either a distributive share or a guaranteed payment. If the excess payment is a function of partnership income (e.g., 10% of the partnership's net income), the income is considered a distributive share of partnership income.[24] Accordingly, the character of the income flows through to the partner, and each of the remaining partners is taxed on a smaller amount of partnership income. The income must be reported in the partner's tax year that includes the partnership year-end from which the distributive share arises, regardless of when the partner actually receives the distribution.

If the amount of the excess payment is determined without regard to the partnership income, the payment is treated as a guaranteed payment.[25] If the payment is a guaranteed payment, the retiring partner recognizes ordinary income, and the partnership generally has an ordinary deduction. Like all guaranteed payments, the income is includible in the

TYPICAL MISCONCEPTION

The significance of the two different kinds of payments is not readily apparent to some taxpayers. The payments for partnership property are not deductible by the partnership and often are not income to the retiring partner. However, payments considered in the second category are deductible by the partnership (or they reduce the distributive shares that other partners must recognize) and usually are income to the retiring partner.

TYPICAL MISCONCEPTION

The main difference between a payment being taxed as a distributive share or as a guaranteed payment is the character of the income recognized by the recipient partner. If the payment is taxed as a distributive share, the character of the income is determined by the type of income earned by the partnership. In contrast, the payment is always ordinary income if it is treated as a guaranteed payment.

---

[21] Retirement from the partnership in this context has nothing to do with reaching a specific age and leaving the employ of the partnership but instead refers to the partner's withdrawal at any age from a continuing partnership.

[22] A deceased partner's successor-in-interest is the party that succeeds to the rights of the deceased partner's partnership interest (e.g., the decedent's estate or an heir or legatee of the deceased partner). A deceased partner's successor-

in-interest is treated as a partner by the tax laws until his or her interest in the partnership has been completely liquidated.

[23] Sec. 736(b).

[24] Sec. 736(a)(1).

[25] Sec. 736(a)(2).

recipient's income for his or her tax year within which ends the partnership tax year in which the partnership claims its deduction (see Chapter C:9).

EXAMPLE C:10-22▶ When Sam retires from the STU Partnership, he receives a cash payment of $30,000. At the time of his retirement, his basis for his one-fourth limited partnership interest is $25,000. The partnership has no liabilities and the following assets:

Assets	Basis	FMV	Sam's 1/4 FMV
Cash	$ 40,000	$ 40,000	$10,000
Marketable securities	25,000	32,000	8,000
Land	35,000	48,000	12,000
Total	$100,000	$120,000	$30,000

In the absence of a valuation agreement, the partnership presumably pays Sam a ratable share of the FMV of each asset (and he receives no payment for any partnership goodwill). The $30,000 amount paid to Sam equals the FMV of his one-fourth interest in the partnership assets. The $30,000 Sam receives in exchange for his interest in partnership property is analyzed as a liquidating distribution in the following manner:

Cash distribution received	$30,000
Minus: Basis in partnership interest	(25,000)
Gain recognized on liquidating distribution	$ 5,000

Because the partnership holds no Sec. 751 assets, the entire gain is a capital gain. The partnership gets no deduction for the distribution. ◀

EXAMPLE C:10-23▶ Assume the same facts as in Example C:10-22 except Sam receives $34,000 instead of $30,000. This amount represents payment for Sam's one-fourth interest in partnership assets plus an excess payment of $4,000. Accordingly, this excess payment must be either a distributive share or a guaranteed payment. Because the $4,000 payment is not contingent on partnership earnings, it is taxed as a guaranteed payment. The partnership deducts the $4,000 payment, and Sam recognizes $4,000 of ordinary income.

In summary, Sam receives $34,000 as a payment on his retirement from the STU Partnership, $4,000 of which is considered a guaranteed payment taxed as ordinary income to Sam and deductible by the partnership. The remaining $30,000 Sam receives is in exchange for his interest in partnership property. Because the $30,000 cash payment exceeds his $25,000 basis in his partnership interest, he recognizes a $5,000 gain on the liquidating distribution. The partnership gets no deduction for the $30,000, which is considered a distribution. ◀

If the partnership has Sec. 751 assets, the calculations for a retiring partner are slightly more difficult. First, payments for substantially appreciated inventory and unrealized receivables are payments for property and must be analyzed using the liquidating distribution rules along with Sec. 751. The remainder of the transaction is analyzed as indicated above. (For partnership retirements only, unrealized receivables do not include recapture items.)

A retiring partner who receives payments from the partnership is considered to be a partner in that partnership for tax purposes until he or she receives the last payment. Likewise, a deceased partner's successor-in-interest is a member of the partnership until receiving the last payment.[26]

EXCHANGE OF A PARTNERSHIP INTEREST
EXCHANGE FOR ANOTHER PARTNERSHIP INTEREST. A partner also may terminate a partnership interest by exchanging it for either an interest in another partnership or a different interest in the same partnership. Exchanges involving interests in different partnerships do not qualify for like-kind exchange treatment.[27] Nevertheless, the IRS allows exchanges of interests within a single partnership.[28]

---

[26] Reg. Sec. 1.736-1(a)(1)(ii).
[27] Sec. 1031(a)(2)(D).

[28] Rev. Rul. 84-52, 1984-1 C.B. 157.

EXAMPLE C:10-24▶ Pam and Dean are equal partners in the PD General Partnership, which owns and operates a farm. The two partners agree to convert PD into a limited partnership, with Pam becoming a limited partner and Dean having both a general and a limited partnership interest in PD. Even though the partners exchange a general partnership interest for a limited partnership interest (plus an exchange of a general partnership interest for a general partnership interest for Dean), they recognize no gain or loss on the exchange. If, however, a partner's interest in the partnership's liabilities is changed, that partner's basis must be adjusted. If liabilities are reduced and a deemed distribution exceeding the basis for the partnership interest occurs, the partner must recognize gain on the excess. ◀

EXCHANGE FOR CORPORATE STOCK. A partnership interest may be exchanged for corporate stock in a transaction that qualifies under the Sec. 351 nonrecognition rules (see Chapter C:2). For Sec. 351 purposes, a partnership interest is property. If the other Sec. 351 requirements are met, a single partner's partnership interest can be transferred for stock in a new or an existing corporation in a nontaxable exchange. The partner treats this as if he or she had transferred any other property under the Sec. 351 rules. The basis in the corporate stock is determined by the partner's basis in the partnership interest. The holding period for the stock received in the exchange includes the holding period for the partnership interest. As a result of the exchange, one of the corporation's assets is an interest in a partnership, and the corporation (not the transferor) is now the partner of record. Thus, the corporation must report its distributive share of partnership income along with its other earnings.

INCORPORATION. When limited liability is important, the entire partnership may choose to incorporate. Normally such an incorporation can be structured to fall within the Sec. 351 provisions and can be partially or totally tax exempt. When a partnership chooses to incorporate, three possible alternatives are available:

▶ The partnership contributes its assets and liabilities to the corporation in exchange for the corporation's stock. The partnership then distributes the stock to the partners in a liquidating distribution of the partnership.

▶ The partnership liquidates by distributing its assets to the partners. The partners then contribute the property to the new corporation in exchange for its stock.

▶ The partners contribute their partnership interests directly to the new corporation in exchange for its stock. The partnership liquidates, with the corporation receiving all the partnership's assets and liabilities.

The tax implications of the incorporation and the impact of partnership liabilities, gain to be recognized, basis in the corporate assets, and the new shareholders' bases in their stock and securities may differ depending on the form chosen for the transaction.[29]

FORMATION OF AN LLC, LLP, OR LLLP. A second option for obtaining limited liability protection for all owners is for the partnership to become an LLC. Under Rev. Rul. 95-37,[30] the conversion is viewed as a partnership-to-partnership transfer. The property transfer does not cause the partners to recognize gain or loss nor does the transfer terminate the tax year for the partnership or any partner. The basis for the partners' interest in the partnership will be changed only if the liability shares for the partners change. Under the check-the-box regulations, an LLC with more than one member is treated as a partnership unless it elects to be taxed as a corporation (see Chapter C:2). If the LLC elects to be taxed as a C or an S corporation, the transfer of the property to the LLC falls under the incorporation rules discussed above.

If a partnership chooses LLP status to reduce some of the liability risks facing the partners, the change from partnership to LLP status also falls under the partnership-to-partnership transfer rules described above. The transfer does not cause the partners to recognize

---

[29] Rev. Rul. 84-111, 1984-2 C.B. 88. In addition, Reg. Secs. 301.7701-1, 2, and 3 describe the tax consequences of a partnership electing to be taxed as a corporation under the check-the-box regulations.

[30] 1995-1 C.B. 130.

gain or loss nor does the property transfer terminate the tax year for the partnership or any partner. Basis for the partners' interest in the partnership will be changed only if the liability shares for the partners change.[31] Finally, in some states, partners can achieve limited liability through a limited liability limited partnership (LLLP) (see page C:10-31).

Topic Review C:10-2 summarizes the tax consequences of a number of alternative methods for terminating an investment in a partnership.

INCOME RECOGNITION AND TRANSFERS OF A PARTNERSHIP INTEREST

The partnership tax year closes with respect to any partner who sells or exchanges his or her entire interest in a partnership or any partner whose interest in the partnership is liquidated. The partnership tax year closes on the sale or exchange date or the date of final payment on a liquidation. As a result, that partner's share of all items earned by the partnership must be reported in the partner's tax year that includes the transaction date.[32]

A partner's tax year also closes on the date of death. The partner's final return will include all partnership income up to the date of death.

OBJECTIVE 8

Determine whether a partnership has terminated for tax purposes

TERMINATION OF A PARTNERSHIP

EVENTS CAUSING A TERMINATION TO OCCUR. Because of the complex relationships among partners and their liability for partnership debts, state partnership laws provide for the termination of a partnership under a wide variety of conditions. Section 708(b), however, avoids the tax complexity created by the wide variety of state laws and the numerous termination conditions. This IRC section provides that a partnership terminates for tax purposes only if

Topic Review C:10-2

Terminating an Investment in a Partnership

METHOD	TAX CONSEQUENCES TO PARTNER
Death or retirement:	
Amounts paid for property[a]	Liquidating distribution tax consequences apply to the amount paid.
Amounts paid in excess of property values:	
Amounts not determined by reference to partnership income	Ordinary income.
Amounts determined by reference to partnership income	Distributive share of partnership income.
Sale of partnership interest to outsider	Capital gain (loss) except for ordinary income (loss) reported on Sec. 751 assets and Sec. 1250 gain on depreciable real property.
Exchange for partnership interest:	
In same partnership	No tax consequences
In different partnership	Capital gain (loss) except for ordinary income (loss) on Sec. 751 assets and Sec. 1250 gain on depreciable real property.
Exchange for corporate stock	No gain or loss generally recognized if it qualifies for Sec. 351 tax-free treatment.
	If the exchange does not qualify for Sec. 351 treatment, capital gain (loss) except for ordinary income (loss) on Sec. 751 assets and Sec. 1250 gain on depreciable real property.
Incorporation of partnership	Tax consequences depend on form of transaction used for incorporation.
Formation of LLC or LLP	No tax consequences except for distributions or contributions deemed to occur if liability shares change.

[a]Only for a general partner departing from a service partnership, property excludes unrealized receivables and goodwill if it is not mentioned in the partnership agreement.

---

[31] Ibid.   [32] Sec. 706(c)(2).

> ► No part of any business, financial operation, or venture of the partnership continues to be carried on by any of its partners in a partnership or
> ► Within a 12-month period a sale or exchange of at least 50% of the total interest in partnership capital and profits occurs.

NO BUSINESS OPERATED AS A PARTNERSHIP. If no partner continues to operate any business of the partnership through the same or another partnership, the original partnership terminates. To avoid termination, the partnership must maintain partners and business activity. For example, if one partner retires from a two-person partnership and the second partner continues the business alone, the partnership terminates. However, if one partner in a two-member partnership dies, the partnership does not terminate as long as the deceased's estate or successor-in-interest continues to share in the profits and losses of the partnership business.[33]

Likewise, a partnership terminates if it ceases to carry on any business or financial venture. The courts, however, have allowed a partnership to continue under this rule even though the partnership sold all its assets and retained only a few installment notes.[34] Despite the courts' flexibility in these circumstances, a partnership should maintain more than a nominal level of assets if continuation of the partnership is desired.

SALE OR EXCHANGE OF AT LEAST A 50% INTEREST. The second condition that terminates a partnership is the sale or exchange of at least a 50% interest in both partnership capital and profits within a 12-month period.[35] The relevant 12-month period is determined without reference to the tax year of either the partnership or any partner but rather is any 12 consecutive months. To cause termination, the partner must transfer the partnership interest by sale or exchange. Transactions or occurrences that do not constitute a sale or exchange (e.g., the gifting of a partnership interest or the transferring of a partnership interest at death) do not cause a partnership to terminate as long as partners continue the partnership business. Likewise, as long as at least two partners remain, the removal of a partner who owns more than 50% of the total partnership capital and profits interests can be accomplished without terminating the partnership by making a liquidating distribution.[36]

Measuring the portion of the total partnership capital and profits interest transferred often presents difficulties. Multiple exchanges of the same partnership interest are counted only once for purposes of determining whether the 50% maximum is exceeded. When several different small interests are transferred within a 12-month period, the partnership's termination occurs on the date of the transfer that first crosses the 50% threshold.[37]

EXAMPLE C:10-25 ►

On August 1, 2011, Miguel sells his 30% capital and profits interest in the LMN Partnership to Steve. On June 1, 2012, Steve sells the 30% interest acquired from Miguel to Andrew. For purposes of Sec. 708, the two sales are considered to be the transfer of a single partnership interest. Thus, the LMN Partnership does not terminate unless other sales of partnership interests occur totaling at least 20% of LMN's capital and profits interests during any 12-month period that includes either August 1, 2011, or June 1, 2012. ◄

EXAMPLE C:10-26 ►

On July 15, 2011, Kelly sells Carlos a 37% capital and profits interest in the KRS Partnership. On November 14, 2011, Rick sells Diana a 10% capital and profits interest in the KRS Partnership. On January 18, 2012, Sherrie sells Evan a 5% capital and profits interest in the KRS Partnership. The KRS Partnership terminates on January 18, 2012, because the cumulative interest sold within the 12-month period that includes January 18, 2012, first exceeds 50% on that date. ◄

EFFECTS OF TERMINATION.
Importance of Timing. When a partnership terminates, its tax year closes, requiring the partners to include their share of partnership earnings for the short-period partnership tax

---

[33] Reg. Sec. 1.708-1(b)(1)(i)(A).
[34] For example, see *Max R. Ginsburg v. U.S.*, 21 AFTR 2d 1489, 68-1 USTC ¶9429 (Ct. Cls., 1968).
[35] Under Sec. 774(c), an electing large partnership does *not* terminate solely because 50% or more of its interests are sold within a 12-month period.

[36] Reg. Sec. 1.708-1(b)(1)(ii).
[37] Ibid.

year in their tax returns. If the termination is not properly timed, partnership income for a regular 12-month tax year already may be included in the same return that must include the short tax year, resulting in more than 12 months of partnership income or loss being reported in some partners' tax returns. As partners and partnerships are increasingly forced to adopt the same tax year, this problem will lessen.

EXAMPLE C:10-27▶

Joy is a calendar year taxpayer who owns a 40% capital and profits interest in the ATV Partnership. ATV has a natural business year-end of March 31 and with IRS permission uses that date as its tax year-end. For the partnership tax year ending March 31, 2011, Joy has an $80,000 distributive share of ordinary income. Pat, who owns the remaining 60% capital and profits interests, sells his interest to Collin on November 30, 2011. Because more than 50% of the capital and profits interests have changed hands, the ATV Partnership terminates on November 30, 2011, and the partnership's tax year ends on that date.

Joy's tax return for the tax year ending December 31, 2011, must include the $80,000 distributive share from the partnership tax year for the period April 1, 2010, through March 31, 2011, and the distributive share of partnership income for the short tax year including the period April 1, 2011, through November 30, 2011. ◀

Liquidating Distributions and Contributions. When a termination occurs for tax purposes, the partnership is deemed to have made a pro rata liquidating distribution to all partners. Accordingly, the partners must recognize gain or loss under the liquidating distribution rules. An actual liquidating distribution may occur if the termination occurs because of the cessation of business. However, if the termination occurs because of a 50% or greater change in ownership of the capital and profits interests, an actual distribution usually does not occur. In this case, the new group of partners continue the business, and Treasury Regulations provide for the termination of the old partnership and the formation of a new partnership. Specifically, the old partnership is deemed to contribute all its property and liabilities to a new partnership in exchange for the interests in the new partnership. The old partnership then is deemed to liquidate by distributing its only remaining asset (the interests in the new partnership) to its partners.[38]

EXAMPLE C:10-28▶

The AB Partnership terminates for tax purposes on July 15 when Anna sells her 60% capital and profits interest to Diane for $123,000. The partnership has no liabilities, and its assets at the time of termination are as follows:

Assets	Basis	FMV
Cash	$ 20,000	$ 20,000
Receivables	30,000	32,000
Inventory	22,000	28,000
Building	90,000	95,000
Land	40,000	30,000
Total	$202,000	$205,000

Beth, a 40% partner in the AB Partnership, has an $80,800 basis in her partnership interest at the time of the termination. She has held her AB Partnership interest for three years at the time of the termination.

The old AB Partnership is deemed to transfer all its assets to a new partnership (NewAB) on July 15 in exchange for all the interests in NewAB. The old partnership then is deemed to transfer all the NewAB interests to the partners of the old partnership (Diane and Beth). At this point, the old AB Partnership ceases to exist because it no longer has partners, nor does it carry on any business.

The basis and holding period of the assets held by NewAB are identical to the basis and holding period of the old AB Partnership assets.[39] The basis of Beth's interest in NewAB is identical to her basis in her interest in the AB Partnership ($80,800).[40] Her holding period for the NewAB partnership interest begins when she acquired the old AB Partnership interest. Diane's basis in her partnership interest is its $123,000 cost, and her holding period begins when she purchases the interest. ◀

---

[38] Reg. Sec. 1.708-1(b)(1)(iv).
[39] Secs. 723 and 1223(2).
[40] Sec. 722.

Changes in Accounting Methods. The termination ends all partnership elections. Thus, the new partnership must make all elections concerning its tax year and accounting methods in its first new tax year.

MERGERS AND CONSOLIDATIONS

When two or more partnerships join together to form a new partnership, the parties to the transaction must determine which, if any, of the old partnerships are continued and which are terminated. An old partnership whose partner(s) own more than 50% of the profits and capital interests of the new partnership is considered to be continued as the new partnership.[41] Accordingly, the new partnership must continue with the tax year and accounting methods and elections of the old partnership that is considered to continue. All the other old partnerships are considered to have been terminated.

EXAMPLE C:10-29▶

The AB and CD Partnerships merge to form the ABCD Partnership. April and Ben each own 30% of ABCD, and Carole and David each own 20% of ABCD. The ABCD Partnership is considered a continuation of the AB Partnership because April and Ben, the former partners of AB, own 60% of ABCD. ABCD is bound by the tax year, accounting method, and other elections made by AB. CD, formerly owned by Carole and David, is considered to terminate on the merger date. ◀

In some combinations, the partners of two or more of the old partnerships might hold the requisite profits and capital interest in the new partnership. When two or more old partnerships satisfy this requirement, the old partnership credited with contributing the greatest dollar value of assets to the new partnership is considered the continuing partnership, and all other partnerships terminate. Sometimes, none of the old partnerships account for more than 50% of the capital and profits of the new partnership. In that case, all the old partnerships terminate, and the merged partnership is a new entity that can make its own tax year and accounting method elections.

EXAMPLE C:10-30▶

Three partnerships merge to form the ABCD Partnership. The AB Partnership (owned by Andy and Bill) contributes assets valued at $140,000 to ABCD. BC Partnership (owned by Bill and Cathy) and CD Partnership (owned by Cathy and Drew) contribute assets valued at $180,000 and $120,000, respectively. The capital and profits interests of the partners in the new partnership are Andy, 20%; Bill, 35%; Cathy, 19%; and Drew, 26%. Both the AB and BC Partnerships had partners who now own more than 50% of the new partnership (Andy and Bill own 55%, and Bill and Cathy own 54%). The BC Partnership contributed more assets ($180,000) to the new partnership than did the AB Partnership ($140,000). Therefore, the ABCD Partnership is a continuation of the BC Partnership. Both the AB and CD Partnerships terminate on the merger date. ◀

DIVISION OF A PARTNERSHIP

When a partnership divides into two or more new partnerships, all the new partnerships whose partners own collectively more than 50% of the profits and capital interests in the old partnerships are considered a continuation of the old partnership.[42] All partnerships that are continuations of the old partnership are bound by the old partnership's tax year and accounting method elections. Any other partnership created by the division is considered a new partnership eligible to make its own tax year and accounting method elections. If no new partnership meets the criteria for continuation of the divided partnership, the divided partnership terminates on the division date. The interest of any partner of the divided partnership who does not own an interest in a continuing partnership is considered to be liquidated on the division date.

EXAMPLE C:10-31▶

The RSTV Partnership is in the real estate and insurance business. Randy owns a 40% interest and Sam, Thomas, and Vicki each own 20% of RSTV. The partners agree to split the partnership, with the RS Partnership receiving the real estate operations and the TV Partnership receiving the insurance business. Because Randy and Sam own more than 50% of the RSTV Partnership (40% + 20% = 60%), the RS Partnership is a continuation of the RSTV Partnership and must report its results using the same tax year and accounting method elections that RSTV used.

---

[41] Sec. 708(b)(2)(A).

[42] Sec. 708(b)(2)(B).

Thomas and Vicki are considered to have terminated their interests in RSTV and to have received a liquidating distribution of the insurance business property. The TV Partnership makes its tax year and accounting method elections following the rules for a new partnership. ◀

OPTIONAL AND MANDATORY BASIS ADJUSTMENTS

OBJECTIVE 9

Understand the effect of optional and mandatory basis adjustments

In general, a partnership makes no adjustment to the basis of its property when a partner sells or exchanges his or her interest in the partnership, when a partner's interest transfers upon the partner's death, or when the partnership makes a property distribution to a partner. A partnership, however, may adjust basis of its assets if the partnership makes an **optional basis adjustment** election under Sec. 754. The following paragraphs compare the consequences of having no election to having such an election. The discussion focuses primarily on sale transactions but also briefly mentions distributions. Once made, the Sec. 754 election applies to all subsequent transfers of partnership interests (e.g., sales, exchanges, and transfers upon death) and all subsequent distributions. In addition, the partnership may have to make a **mandatory basis adjustment** in certain circumstances even if a Sec. 754 election is not in effect.

ADJUSTMENTS ON TRANSFERS

OPTIONAL ADJUSTMENT.   If a new incoming partner purchases his or her partnership interest from an existing partner, the new partner's basis in the partnership interest equals the purchase price plus the new partner's share of partnership liabilities. The new partner's basis in the partnership is likely to be different from his or her share of basis of the underlying assets in the partnership. This difference could lead to inequitable results as demonstrated by the following example.

EXAMPLE C:10-32 ▶

Amy, Bill, and Corey each own a one-third interest in ABC partnership, which has the following simple balance sheet:

	Basis	*FMV*
Assets:		
Cash	$30,000	$ 30,000
Inventory	60,000	90,000
Total	$90,000	$120,000
Liabilities and capital:		
Liabilities	$15,000	$ 15,000
Capital—Amy	25,000	35,000
—Bill	25,000	35,000
—Corey	25,000	35,000
Total	$90,000	$120,000

Eric purchases Amy's one-third interest for $35,000 cash and assumes her $5,000 share of partnerships liabilities. Eric pays this amount because one-third the FMV of the underlying partnership assets is $40,000 (1/3 × $120,000). In addition, the cash paid plus Eric's share of partnership liabilities gives him a $40,000 basis in his new partnership interest. Amy's basis at the time of sale is $30,000. Therefore, Amy recognizes a $10,000 gain ($40,000 amount realized − $30,000 basis). Amy's $10,000 gain also reflects her share of the difference between the inventory's FMV and basis at the partnership level. Thus, her gain will be ordinary income under Sec. 751.

Now suppose the partnership later sells the inventory for $90,000. The partnership recognizes $30,000 of ordinary income. Therefore, each partner, Bill, Corey, and Eric, recognizes a $10,000 distributive share of ordinary income from that sale, and each partner increases the basis of his partnership interest by the same amount. Accordingly, Eric increases his basis in the partnership from $40,000 to $50,000. In this situation, Eric appears to be taxed on the same gain as was Amy even though he paid a FMV price for his partnership interest (and the underlying partnership assets).

However, this result primarily is an issue of timing and possibly character of income and loss. For example, suppose further that, sometime after selling the inventory, the partnership distributes the $120,000 cash to the partners in liquidation. Eric would receive $40,000 and recognize a $10,000 ($40,000 distribution − $50,000 basis) capital loss.

In short, with no optional basis adjustment election in effect, Eric recognizes $10,000 of ordinary income when the partnership sells the inventory and a $10,000 capital loss when the partnership liquidates. This timing difference could be substantial if the partnership remains in existence for a long time. Also, the capital loss may offset only capital gains and up to $3,000 of ordinary income in the partner's personal tax return. ◀

ADDITIONAL COMMENT

The situation of a new partner purchasing an interest in a partnership is a good example of where a partner's outside basis can differ significantly from his or her share of the partnership's inside basis. The Sec. 754 election mitigates this difference.

AMOUNT OF THE ADJUSTMENT. An incoming partner might view the situation in Example C:10-32 as unacceptable and wish the partnership to make a Sec. 754 election. If the partnership makes such an election or has a Sec. 754 election already in effect, Sec. 743 mandates a special basis adjustment equal to the difference between the transferee (purchasing) partner's basis in the partnership interest and the transferee partner's share of basis of partnership assets. This basis adjustment, arising from a transfer, belongs only to the transferee partner (and not to the other partners), and it eliminates the inequities noted in Example C:10-32.

EXAMPLE C:10-33 ▶

Assume the same facts as in Example C:10-32 except the partnership makes a Sec. 754 election. Eric's optional basis adjustment is calculated as follows:

Cash purchase price	$35,000
Share of partnership liabilities	5,000
Initial basis in partnership	$40,000
Minus: Eric's share of partnership's basis in assets (1/3 × $90,000)[43]	(30,000)
Optional basis adjustment	$10,000

Now when the partnership sells the inventory, Eric has an additional $10,000 basis in his share of the inventory that offsets the $10,000 income he otherwise would recognize. The other partners, however, still recognize their $10,000 distributive shares of income. Because Eric recognizes no income, he does not increase his partnership basis. Suppose the partnership liquidates sometime after selling the inventory. Again, Eric receives a $40,000 distribution, but he recognizes no capital gain or loss ($40,000 distribution − $40,000 basis). Thus, the optional basis adjustment eliminated both the timing and character differences that occurred in Example C:10-32. ◀

MANDATORY ADJUSTMENT. The IRC imposes a mandatory basis adjustment for a sale or exchange of a partnership interest if the partnership has a substantial built-in loss and has no Sec. 754 optional basis adjustment election in effect. A substantial built-in loss exists if the partnership's adjusted basis in its property exceeds the FMV of the property by more than $250,000. This provision prevents the doubling of losses. Exceptions to the rule apply to certain specialized partnerships, discussion of which is beyond the scope of this textbook.

EXAMPLE C:10-34 ▶

David, Ellen, and Frank each own a one-third interest in DEF partnership, which has the following simple balance sheet:

	Basis	FMV
Assets:		
Cash	$ 100,000	$100,000
Land	1,100,000	800,000
Total	$1,200,000	$900,000

---

[43] In some cases, the calculation of the transferee's share of the partnership's basis in assets can be more complicated than shown in this example. See Reg. Sec. 1.743-1(d).

Capital:		
David	$ 400,000	$300,000
Ellen	400,000	300,000
Frank	400,000	300,000
Total	$1,200,000	$900,000

Gwen purchases David's one-third interest for $300,000 cash, which gives Gwen a $300,000 initial basis in her new partnership interest. David's partnership interest basis at the time of sale is $400,000. Therefore, he recognizes a $100,000 loss. David's $100,000 loss also reflects his share of the difference between the land's FMV and basis at the partnership level.

Now suppose the partnership has no optional basis adjustment election in effect and later sells the land for $800,000. The partnership recognizes a $300,000 loss. As a result, each partner, Ellen, Frank, and Gwen, recognizes a $100,000 distributive share of that loss, and each partner decreases the basis of his or her partnership interest by the same amount. As a result, both David and Gwen recognize a $100,000 loss. To prevent this doubling of losses, the partnership must make a $100,000 mandatory downward basis adjustment with respect to Gwen's share of the land, thereby nullifying her distributive share of loss on the land sale. The adjustment is mandatory because the partnership has a substantial built-in loss (i.e., its $300,00 built-in loss exceeds $250,000). Note that, without this mandatory adjustment, Gwen's $100,000 loss would be temporary because her partnership basis would be reduced to $200,000, causing her to recognize a $100,000 gain should the partnership liquidate and distribute $300,000 to her. Nevertheless, Congress chose to eliminate the initial doubling of losses by requiring the mandatory basis adjustment. ◄

OTHER ISSUES. Examples C:10-32 through C:10-34 assume inventory or land is the only asset other than cash. If the assets instead had been depreciable property, the basis adjustments would give the transferee partner additional depreciation deductions in Examples C:10-32 and C:10-33 or reduced depreciation deductions in example C:10-34. Also, if a partnership has more than one asset other than cash, the optional or mandatory basis adjustment must be allocated to the assets under special rules found in Sec. 755 and related Treasury Regulations. These allocation rules are beyond the scope of this text.

ADJUSTMENTS ON DISTRIBUTIONS

OPTIONAL ADJUSTMENT. As mentioned earlier, if a partnership distributes property to a partner, the partnership makes no adjustment to the basis of its remaining property unless an optional basis adjustment election is in place or unless the mandatory basis adjustment rule discussed later applies. If the partnership has made a Sec. 754 election, the partnership makes the following adjustments upon the distribution to a partner:

▶ Increases the basis of *partnership* property by:

1. Any gain recognized by the distributee partner on the distribution (e.g., cash distribution exceeding the partner's basis in his or her partnership interest)

2. The amount by which the distributee partner decreases the basis of property received in a property distribution from the basis of the property in the partnership's hands

▶ Decreases the basis of *partnership* property by:

1. Any loss recognized by the distributee partner on a liquidating distribution

2. The amount by which the distributee partner increases the basis of property received in a property distribution from the basis of the property in the partnership's hands

Unlike the optional basis adjustments arising from a transfer of partnership interest, the basis adjustments arising from a distribution belong to the partnership as a whole. These adjustments eliminate many (but not all) basis and timing disparities resulting from distributions.

A partnership should take care in making a Sec. 754 election because, once made, the election affects many transactions in complicated ways. Moreover, the election can cause downward as well as upward adjustments. Finally, the election has long-range implications because it can be revoked only with IRS approval. The IRS will not grant such approval if the primary purpose of the revocation is to avoid reducing the basis of partnership assets.

MANDATORY ADJUSTMENT.   The discussion of the optional basis adjustment for distributions included increases and decreases to partnership property. The IRC makes the decreasing basis adjustment for distributions mandatory if it exceeds $250,000. As with exchange transactions, this provision prevents the doubling of losses. In effect, the mandatory adjustment rule applies only to liquidating distributions because such decreasing adjustments cannot occur in nonliquidating distribution situations.

SPECIAL FORMS OF PARTNERSHIPS

Here, we examine a series of special partnership forms, including tax shelters organized as limited partnerships, publicly traded partnerships, limited liability companies, limited liability partnerships, and electing large partnerships.

TAX SHELTERS AND LIMITED PARTNERSHIPS

ADDITIONAL COMMENT

The passive activity loss limitations eliminate the deferral benefit of tax shelters.

Tax shelters at their best are good investments that reduce and/or defer the amount of an investor's tax bill. Traditionally, shelter benefits arise from leverage, income deferral, deduction acceleration, and tax credits.

Many years ago, limited partnerships were the primary vehicle for tax shelter investments. However, subsequent tax law greatly reduced the benefits of limited partnerships as tax shelters by invoking the passive activity loss limitations for activity conducted in a limited partnership form. The limited partnership, however, still allows an investor to limit liability while receiving the benefits of the shelter's tax attributes to save taxes on other passive income. Moreover, limited partnerships that generate passive income rather than losses have become popular investments for investors who already hold loss-generating limited partnership interests. (See Problem C:9-46 in the previous chapter for an example of tax deferred benefits and their elimination by the at-risk and passive activity loss limitations.)

PUBLICLY TRADED PARTNERSHIPS

The IRC restricts still further the benefits of tax shelter ownership by imposing special rules on **publicly traded partnerships** (PTPs). A PTP is a partnership whose interests are traded either on an established securities exchange or in a secondary market or the equivalent thereof. A partnership that meets the requirements is taxed as a C corporation under Sec. 7704.

Two exceptions apply to partnerships that otherwise would be classified as PTPs:

▶ Partnerships that have 90% or more of their gross income being "qualifying income" continue to be taxed under the partnership rules.

REAL-WORLD EXAMPLE

The Chicago Board of Partnerships acts as a secondary market for limited partnership interests. Trades can range from a few thousand dollars to millions of dollars. This market increases the liquidity of limited partnership investments. Some partnerships are publicly traded on the major stock exchanges.

▶ Partnerships that were in existence on December 17, 1987 and have not added a substantial new line of business since that date are grandfathered. In general, application of the PTP rules for these partnerships was delayed until tax years beginning after December 31, 1997.

The Taxpayer Relief Act of 1997 added an election that allows the grandfathered partnerships to continue to be treated as partnerships after the original ten-year window and until the election is revoked. To elect to continue to be treated as a partnership, the publicly traded partnership (which must have been taxed as a partnership under the grandfather provision) must agree to pay a 3.5% annual tax on gross income from the active conduct of any trade or business.[44] The election may be revoked by the partnership, but once revoked, it cannot be reinstated.

---

[44] Sec. 7704(g)(3).

For the 90% of gross income test, Sec. 7704(d) defines qualifying income to include certain interest, dividends, real property rents (but not personal property rents), income and gains from the sale or disposition of a capital asset or Sec. 1231(b) trade or business property held for the production of passive income, and gain from the sale or disposition of real property. It also includes gains from certain commodity trading and natural resource activities. Any PTP not taxed as a corporation because of this 90% exception is subject to separate and more restrictive Sec. 469 passive loss rules than are partnerships that are not publicly traded.

If a partnership is first classified as a PTP taxed as a corporation during a tax year, the PTP incurs a deemed contribution of all partnership assets and all partnership liabilities to a corporation in exchange for all the corporation's stock. The stock is then deemed distributed to the partners in complete liquidation of the partnership. This transaction is taxed exactly as if it had physically occurred.

LIMITED LIABILITY COMPANIES

In recent years, the limited liability company (LLC) has emerged as a popular form of business entity in the United States. The LLC combines the legal and tax benefits of partnerships and S corporations. Currently, all 50 states have adopted LLC laws. The LLC business form combines the advantage of limited liability for all its owners with the ability of achieving the conduit treatment and the flexibility of being taxed as a partnership.

In the past, whether an LLC was characterized as a corporation or a partnership for federal tax purposes depended on the number of corporate characteristics the entity possessed, such as limited liability, free transferability of interests, centralized management, and continuity of life. The process of determining tax treatment was complex and time consuming. To alleviate this complexity, the Treasury Department issued regulations that allow entities (other than corporations and trusts) to choose whether to be taxed as a partnership or as an association. (An association is an unincorporated entity taxed as a corporation.) According to these check-the-box regulations, an LLC with two or more members can choose either partnership or association tax treatment. With a written and properly filed election, any LLC can choose to be taxed as an association. If the LLC makes no such election, an LLC with two or more members is treated as a partnership for tax purposes, while a single member LLC is treated as a sole proprietorship.

As already mentioned, an LLC with two or more members that does not elect association status is a partnership for tax purposes and is subject to all the rules applicable to other partnerships. Thus, the formation of the LLC; income, gain, loss, and deductions that flow through to the LLC members; current and liquidating distributions; and sale, gift, or exchange of an interest in the LLC all fall under the partnership rules. An LLC treated as a partnership is subject to the Sec. 704 rules for special allocations and allocations of precontribution gain or loss, to the Sec. 736 rules for retirement distributions, and to the Sec. 751 rules pertaining to unrealized receivables and inventory.

Using the LLC form for a business with publicly traded ownership interests is likely to result in taxation as a corporation. Even if the LLC does not elect association status, the public trading of the ownership interest brings the LLC under the publicly traded partnership rules. As discussed above, these rules result in the business being taxed as a corporation unless 90% or more of the income is qualifying income or unless the LLC is covered under the grandfather rules. However, given the recency of LLCs as a form for conducting business, the grandfather provisions are unlikely to apply.

If an LLC is treated as a partnership, it offers greater flexibility than does an S corporation because it is not subject to the restrictions that apply to S corporations as to the number of shareholders, the number of classes of stock, or the types of investments in related entities that the entity can make. Moreover, unlike S corporations, LLCs can use the special allocation rules of Sec. 704 to allocate income, gain, loss or deductions to their members. Finally, each member's basis in the LLC interest includes that member's share of the organization's debts (and not just shareholder debt as with an S corporation).

TAX STRATEGY TIP

The list of advantages of an LLC over an S corporation is substantial and suggests that an LLC should always be seriously considered as an option for a pass-through entity. However, one current, important advantage of an S corporation is that the shareholders are not subject to self-employment taxes on their share of the entity's earnings.

LIMITED LIABILITY PARTNERSHIPS

Many states have added limited liability partnerships (LLPs) to the list of business forms that can be formed. Under the current state laws, the primary difference between a general partnership and an LLP is that in a limited liability partnership, a partner is not liable for damages resulting from failures in the work of other partners or of people supervised by other partners. For example, assume that a limited liability accounting partnership is assessed damages in a lawsuit that resulted from an audit partner in New York being negligent in an audit. The tax partner for the same firm, who is based in San Diego and who had no involvement with the audit or the auditor, should not be liable to pay damages resulting from the suit.

Like a general or limited partnership, this business form is a partnership for tax purposes. All the partnership tax rules and regulations apply to this business form just as they do to any other partnership.

 **STOP & THINK**

Question: What issues do you expect the check-the-box regulations to raise for new businesses making their initial choice of entity decision? What effect do you expect these regulations to have on existing corporations?

Solution: Consider the options facing a new business. The business can be formed as a C corporation, which provides limited liability protection to owners but subjects the corporate income to double taxation. A business formed as a C corporation can make an S election for tax purposes, which keeps the limited liability protection for the owners and eliminates the double taxation by taxing all income directly to the owners. However, as you will see in Chapter C:11, a number of restrictions prevent many corporations from electing S status. In addition, all income and loss of an S corporation must be allocated among the shareholders on a pro rata basis. A partnership offers the most flexible tax treatment with no double taxation of income, but the traditional partnership must have at least one general partner whose liability for partnership debts is not limited. An LLC, which is treated as a partnership, provides limited liability protection to its owners while avoiding both the double taxation of income found in a regular C corporation as well as the restrictions placed on S corporations. Because an LLC is treated as a partnership, the income and loss shares reported by each partner is flexible, and the partner's basis for his partnership interest includes his or her share of the LLC's liabilities. Thus, in some ways, the LLC has the best attributes of both the corporation and the partnership.

These are strong reasons why a new entity would choose to form as an LLC and be treated as a partnership. However, because the LLC is a relatively new business form, statutes, case law, and regulations are still being developed, and thus many areas of uncertainty remain to be resolved over time.

The check-the-box regulations are not helpful to existing C corporations and S corporations because an existing corporation cannot elect to be treated as a partnership. Instead, it must liquidate (with all the tax consequences of a liquidation, as described in Chapter C:6) before it can form as a partnership or an LLC. Potentially, the change in entity form has a high tax cost for an existing corporation.

LIMITED LIABILITY LIMITED PARTNERSHIP

Another recent innovation in some states (but not all) is the limited liability limited partnership (LLLP). Remember that a limited partnership, in addition to having limited partners, has one or more general partners whose personal liability exposure is unlimited. The LLLP is a partnership formed under a state's limited partnership laws but that can elect under the state's laws to provide the general partners with limited liability. Thus, the LLLP is similar to an LLC and becomes potentially useful in states that do not extend LLC status to personal service firms but allow such firms to operate as an LLLP.[45]

---

[45] For a detailed discussion, see Shop Talk, "Service Firms Practicing as LLLPs: What Are the Tax Consequences?" *Journal of Taxation*, August 2005.

OBJECTIVE **10**

Determine the appropriate reporting for the income of an electing large partnership

ELECTING LARGE PARTNERSHIPS

Partnerships that qualify as "large partnerships" may elect to be taxed under a simplified reporting arrangement.[46] The partnership must meet the following four qualifications to be treated as an electing large partnership:

▶ It must not be a service partnership.

▶ It must not be engaged in commodity trading.

▶ It must have at least 100 partners.

▶ It must file an election to be taxed as an electing large partnership.

Section 775 defines a service partnership as one in which substantially all the partners perform substantial services in connection with the partnership's activities or the partners are retired but in the past performed substantial services in connection with the partnership's activities. One example of a partnership that could not make this election is a partnership that provides accounting services. An electing large partnership also cannot be engaged in commodity trading. Further, to qualify to make this election, the partnership must have at least 100 partners (excluding those partners who do provide substantial services in connection with the partnership's business activities) throughout the tax year.

Once it makes the election, the partnership reports its income under a simplified reporting scheme, is subject to different rules about when the partnership terminates, and is subject to a different system of audits. The election is irrevocable without IRS permission.

REAL-WORLD EXAMPLE

In 2008, only 99 partnerships filed as electing large partnerships. Such partnerships file using Form 1065-B.

ELECTING LARGE PARTNERSHIP TAXABLE INCOME. Much like other partnerships, the calculation of electing large partnership taxable income includes separately stated income and other income. However, the items that must be separately stated are very different for the electing large partnership. Likewise, the items included in other income differ significantly. The main reason that Congress added electing large partnerships to the IRC was to provide a form of flow-through entity that does not require so much separate reporting to each partner of many different income, loss, and deduction items. Simpler reporting from the partnership to the partners was the goal, so fewer items are separately stated and many more items are combined at the partnership level.

Like a regular partnership, calculation of an electing large partnership's taxable income is similar to the calculation for an individual. For an electing large partnership (just like for other partnerships), the deductions for personal exemptions and net operating losses are disallowed as well as most additional itemized deductions, such as medical expenses and alimony. However, calculation of the items that would qualify as miscellaneous itemized deductions for an individual differs from the calculation for either individuals or other partnerships. For an electing large partnership, miscellaneous itemized deductions are combined at the partnership level and subject to a 70% deduction at the partnership level. After the 70% deduction, the remaining miscellaneous itemized deductions are combined with other income and passed through to the partners. Because they are combined with other income at the partnership level, they are not subject to the 2% nondeductible floor at the individual partner level.[47]

Instead of flowing through as a separately stated item as they do with a regular partnership, charitable contributions made by an electing large partnership are subject to the 10% of taxable income limit similar to the limit that normally applies to corporations. Once the limit is applied, the partnership deducts allowable charitable contribution from its ordinary income, and the partners do not report the charitable contributions as a separate item.[48]

For a regular partnership, the first-year expensing deduction allowed under Sec. 179 is both limited at the partnership level and is separately stated and limited at the partner level. For an electing large partnership, the only limit is at the partnership level. The

---

[46] Sec. 775.
[47] Sec. 773(b).

[48] Sec. 773(b)(2).

allowable deduction is calculated at the partnership level, and the deduction amount off-sets the partnership's ordinary income. For an electing large partnership, the Sec. 179 deduction is not separately stated and the impact of the Sec. 179 deduction is buried in the ordinary income amount reported by the partnership to the partners.

SEPARATELY STATED LARGE PARTNERSHIP ITEMS. An electing large partnership nevertheless is a pass-through entity, so some items still must be separately stated at the partnership level, and these items maintain their character when reported in the partners' tax returns. Section 772 lists the following items the electing large partnership must report separately:

▶ Taxable income or loss from passive loss limitation activities

▶ Taxable income or loss from other partnership activities

▶ Net capital gain or loss from passive loss limitation activities

▶ Net capital gain or loss from other partnership activities

▶ Tax-exempt interest

▶ Applicable net alternative minimum tax adjustment separately computed for passive loss limitation activities and other activities

▶ General credits

▶ Low income housing credit

▶ Rehabilitation credit

▶ Foreign income taxes

▶ Credit for producing fuel from a nonconventional source

▶ Any other item the IRS determines should be separately stated

The differences between the treatment of other partnerships versus electing large partnerships is significant. The most interesting aspect of this list is what items are combined for reporting by an electing large partnership. For example, Sec. 1231 gains and losses are netted at the partnership level, net 1231 losses are included in ordinary income or loss, and net 1231 gains are reported with capital gains and losses. The capital gains and losses also are combined at the partnership level with only a single, net number reported to the partners. The capital gain or loss is treated as long-term at the partner level. However, if the net is a short-term capital gain, that gain is treated as ordinary income and combined at the partnership level with other ordinary income items. All the partnership's credits are combined at the partnership level with the exceptions of the low income housing credit and the rehabilitation credit.

Both ordinary income and capital gains attributed to passive loss activities are reported separately from the results of other partnership activities. In addition, the taxable income or loss from activities other than passive activities generally are treated as items of income or expense with respect to property held for investment rather than as active trade or business income. Dividend income, for example, would fall into this category.

For the electing large partnership, all limits, such as the charitable contributions limit and the Sec. 179 expensing deduction limit, are applied at the partnership level rather than at the individual partner level with three exceptions. The three limits applied at the partner level are the Sec. 68 limit on itemized deductions, the limit on at risk losses, and the limit on passive activity losses.[49] For the limitation to be applied at the partner level, these items must be separately stated.

For separately stated items, the character of amounts flowing through the partnership retain their character when reported on the partners' tax returns. However, because many more items are combined at the partnership level and not separately stated, the character of many fewer kinds of income is retained to flow through with the electing large partnership form.

---

[49] Sec. 773(a)

EXAMPLE C:10-35 ▶

The ABC Partnership is an electing large partnership that reports the following transactions for the current year. ABC has no passive activities.

Net long-term capital loss	$100,000
Sec. 1231 gain	120,000
Ordinary income	40,000
Dividend income	10,000
Charitable contributions	30,000
Tax-exempt income	4,000

ABC will report these earnings to its partners as follows:

Long-term capital gain	$20,000
Ordinary income	33,000
Dividend income	10,000
Tax-exempt income	4,000

Because the partnership has a net Sec. 1231 gain, it is treated as a long-term capital gain ($120,000) and combined at the partnership level with the long-term capital loss ($100,000) to result in a net long-term capital gain of $20,000. At the partnership level, the charitable contribution deduction is limited to 10% of taxable income, or $7,000 [0.10 × ($20,000 capital gain + $10,000 dividend income + $40,000 ordinary income)] and is subtracted from ordinary income of $40,000 before ordinary income is reported to the partners. The character of the long-term capital gain, dividend income, tax-exempt income, and ordinary income pass through to the partner. ◀

REPORTING REQUIREMENT.   An electing large partnership files Form 1065-B and must provide a Schedule K-1 to each of its partners on or before March 15 following the close of the partnership tax year without regard to when the partnership tax return is due.[50] Partnerships that are not electing large partnerships are only required to provide the information return by the due date of the partnership tax return—which, for a calendar year partnership, is April 15. The March 15 provision will help reduce the number of partners who must file an extension of their individual tax returns because they do not receive the Schedule K-1 from a regular partnership early enough to file a timely individual return.

TERMINATION OF THE PARTNERSHIP.   Because electing large partnerships are quite large and often may be widely traded, Congress decided to change the conditions under which these partnership will be considered to terminate. An electing large partnership terminates only if its partners cease to conduct any business, financial operation, or venture in a partnership form. Unlike other partnerships, an electing large partnership will not terminate because of the sale or exchange of partnership interests involving at least a 50% interest in partnership capital or profits during a 12-month period.[51]

ELECTING LARGE PARTNERSHIP AUDITS.   An electing large partnership is not subject to the partnership audit rules but is subject to a much more restrictive set of partnership audit procedures.[52] First, all electing large partnership partners must report all items of partnership income, gain, loss, or deduction in the way the partnership reports the item. Deviations from that partnership reporting will be "corrected" by the IRS just as a math mistake is corrected.[53]

Because all partners are required to use identical reporting for partnership items, it becomes somewhat easier to audit partnership results only at the partnership level. Notice of audit proceedings, determination of errors, settlement offers, appeals proceedings, and court cases are all handled at the partnership level, and no individual partner can request separate treatment or refuse to participate in the partnership level result. In general, any adjustments determined at the partnership level by an audit agreement or court decision will be considered to be income or deduction that occurs in the year of the agreement or

[50] Sec. 6031.
[51] Sec. 774(c).
[52] Sec. 6240.
[53] Sec. 6241.

decision.[54] Accordingly, the effect of adjustments is borne by the partners who own interests in the year of the agreement or decision and not by the partners who originally reported the contested transaction results.

TAX PLANNING CONSIDERATIONS

LIQUIDATING DISTRIBUTION OR SALE TO PARTNERS

An unusual tax planning opportunity exists when one partner withdraws from a partnership and the remaining partners proportionately increase their ownership of the partnership. The partners can structure the ownership change as either a liquidating distribution made by the partnership or as a sale of the partnership interest to the remaining partners. In fact, the substance of the two transactions is the same, only the form is different. However, this difference in form can make a substantial difference in the tax consequences in a number of areas.

▶ If the transferor partner receives payment for his or her interest in the partnership's Sec. 751 assets, he or she must recognize ordinary income no matter how the transaction is structured. The partnership's basis in Sec. 751 assets is increased in the case of a liquidating distribution. When a sale transaction takes place, the partnership's basis in Sec. 751 assets is increased only if the partnership has an optional basis adjustment election in effect.

▶ If the partnership has an optional basis adjustment election in effect, the allocation of the adjustment to the individual partnership assets can be different depending on whether the transaction is structured as a sale or as a liquidating distribution.

▶ If the interest being transferred equals or exceeds 50% of the profits and capital interests, a sale to the remaining partners terminates the partnership. A liquidating distribution does not cause a termination to occur.

Because the tax implications of the sale transaction and liquidating distribution alternatives are both numerous and complex, the partners should make their choice only after careful consideration. (See the Tax Strategy Problem later in the Problem Material.)

PROBLEM MATERIALS

DISCUSSION QUESTIONS

C:10-1 Javier is retiring from the JKL Partnership. In January of the current year, he has a $100,000 basis in his partnership interest when he receives a $10,000 cash distribution. The partnership plans to distribute $10,000 each month this year, and Javier will cease to be a partner after the December payment. Is the January payment to Javier a current distribution or a liquidating distribution?

C:10-2 Lia has a $40,000 basis in her partnership interest just before receiving a parcel of land as a nonliquidating (current) distribution. The partnership purchased the land, and Lia has no precontribution gain. Under what conditions will Lia's basis in the land be $40,000? Under what conditions will Lia's basis in the land be a carryover basis from the partnership's basis in the land?

C:10-3 Mariel has a $60,000 basis in her partnership interest just before receiving a parcel of land as a liquidating distribution. She has no remaining precontribution gain and will receive no other distributions. Under what conditions will Mariel's basis in the land be $60,000?

[54] Sec. 6242.

C:10-4 Cindy has a $4,000 basis in her partnership interest before receiving a nonliquidating (current) distribution of property having a $4,500 basis and a $6,000 FMV from the CDE Partnership. Cindy has a choice of receiving either inventory or a capital asset. She will hold the distributed property as an investment for no more than two years before she sells it. What tax difference (if any) will occur as a result of Cindy's selection of one property or the other to be distributed by the partnership?

C:10-5 The AB Partnership purchases plastic components and assembles children's toys. The assembly operation requires a number of special machines that are housed in a building the partnership owns. The partnership has depreciated all its property under MACRS. The partnership sells the toys on account to a number of retail establishments and uses the accrual method of accounting. Identify any items you think might be classified as unrealized receivables.

C:10-6 Which of the following items are considered to be inventory for purposes of Sec. 751?
   a. Supplies
   b. Inventory
   c. Notes receivable
   d. Land held for investment purposes
   e. Lots held for resale

C:10-7 Explain the conditions under which Sec. 751 has an impact on nonliquidating (current) distributions.

C:10-8 What conditions are required for a partner to recognize a loss upon receipt of a distribution from a partnership?

C:10-9 Can the basis of unrealized receivables and inventory received in a liquidating distribution be greater to the partner than to the partnership? Can the basis of unrealized receivables and inventory received in a distribution be smaller to the partner than to the partnership? Explain.

C:10-10 Can a partner recognize both a gain and a loss on the sale of a partnership interest? If so, under what conditions?

C:10-11 Tyra has a zero basis in her partnership interest and a share in partnership liabilities, which are quite large. Explain how these facts will affect the taxation of her departure from the partnership using the following methods of terminating her interest in the partnership.
   a. A liquidating distribution of property
   b. A sale of the partnership interest to a current partner for cash

C:10-12 Tom is a 55% general partner in the RST Partnership. Tom wants to retire, and the other two partners, Stacy and Rich, want to continue the partnership business. They agree that the partnership will liquidate Tom's interest in the partnership by paying him 20% of partnership profits for each of the next ten years. Explain why Sec. 736 does (or does not) apply to the partnership's payments to Tom.

C:10-13 Lucia has a $20,000 basis in her limited partnership interest before her retirement from the partnership. Her share of partnership assets have a $23,000 FMV, and the partnership has no Sec. 751 assets. In addition to being paid cash for her full share of partnership assets, Lucia will receive a share of partnership income for the next three years. Explain Lucia's tax treatment for the payments she receives.

C:10-14 What are the advantages and disadvantages to the partnership and its partners when a partnership termination is caused by a sale of at least a 50% capital and profits interest?

C:10-15 What is a publicly traded partnership? Are all publicly traded partnerships taxed as corporations?

C:10-16 What are the advantages of a firm being formed as a limited liability company (LLC) instead of as a limited partnership?

C:10-17 What is an electing large partnership? What are the advantages to the partnership of electing to be taxed under the electing large partnership rules?

ISSUE IDENTIFICATION QUESTIONS

C:10-18 When Kayla's basis in her interest in the JKL Partnership is $30,000, she receives a current distribution of office equipment. The equipment has an FMV of $40,000 and basis of $35,000. Kayla will not use the office equipment in a business activity. What tax issues should Kayla consider with respect to the distribution?

C:10-19 Joel receives a $40,000 cash distribution from the JM Partnership, which reduces his partnership interest from one-third to one-fourth. The JM Partnership is a general partnership that uses the cash method of accounting and has substantial liabilities. JM's inventory has appreciated substantially since it was purchased. What issues should Joel consider with regard to the distribution?

C:10-20 Scott sells his one-third partnership interest to Sally for $43,000 when his basis in the partnership interest is $33,000. On the date of sale, the partnership has no liabilities and the following assets:

Assets	Basis	FMV
Cash	$30,000	$30,000
Inventory	12,000	21,000
Building	45,000	60,000
Land	12,000	18,000

The partnership has claimed $5,400 of straight-line depreciation on the building. What tax issues should Scott and Sally consider with respect to the sale transaction?

C:10-21 David owns a 60% interest in the DDD Partnership, a general partnership, which he sells to the two remaining partners—Drew and Dana. The three partners have agreed that David will receive $150,000 in cash from the sale. David's basis in the partnership interest before the sale is $120,000, which includes his $30,000 share of partnership recourse liabilities. The partnership has assets with a $300,000 FMV and a $200,000 adjusted basis. What issues should David, Drew, and Dana consider before this sale takes place?

C:10-22 Andrew and Beth are equal partners in the AB Partnership. On December 30 of the current year, the AB Partnership agrees to liquidate Andrew's partnership interest for a cash payment on December 30 of each of the next five years. What tax issues should Andrew and Beth consider with respect to the liquidation of Andrew's partnership interest?

C:10-23 Alex owns 60% of the Hot Wheels LLC, which is treated as a partnership. He plans to give 15% of the LLC (one-fourth of his interest) to his daughter Haley for her high school graduation. He plans to put her interest in a trust, and he will serve as the trustee until Haley is 21. The trust will receive any distributions from the LLC, but Haley is unlikely to be given any of the cash until she is age 21. Alex's 60% interest has a $120,000 FMV and an $80,000 adjusted basis including his $48,000 share of the LLC's liabilities. Alex works full time for the LLC for a small salary and his share of LLC income. Alex also has a special allocation of income from rental property he manages for the LLC. What issues should Alex consider before he completes the gift?

C:10-24 Three individuals recently formed Krypton Company as a limited liability company (LLC). The three individuals—Jeff, Susan, and Richard—own equal interests in the company, and they all have substantial income from other sources. Krypton is a manufacturing firm and expects to earn approximately $130,000 of ordinary income and $30,000 of long term capital gain each year for the next several years. Jeff will be a full time manager and will receive a salary of $60,000 each year. What tax issues should the owners consider regarding the LLC's initial year of operations?

C:10-25 XYZ Limited Partnership has more than 300 partners and is publicly traded. XYZ was grandfathered under the 1987 Tax Act and has consistently been treated as a partnership. In the current year, XYZ will continue to be very profitable and will continue to pay out about 30% of its income to its owners each year. The managing partners of XYZ want to consider the firm's options for taxation in the current and later years.

PROBLEMS

C:10-26 *Current Distributions.* Lisa has a $25,000 basis in her partnership interest before receiving a current distribution of $4,000 cash and land with a $30,000 FMV and a $14,000 basis to the partnership. Assume that any distribution involving Sec. 751 property is pro rata and that any precontribution gains have been recognized before the distribution.
   a. Determine Lisa's recognized gain or loss, Lisa's basis in distributed property, and Lisa's ending basis in her partnership interest.
   b. How does your answer to Part a change if the partnership's basis in the land is $24,000 instead of $14,000?
   c. How does your answer to Part a change if Lisa receives $28,000 cash instead of $4,000 (along with the land)?
   d. How does your answer to Part a change if, in addition to the cash and land, Lisa receives inventory with a $25,000 FMV and a $10,000 basis and receivables with a $3,000 FMV and a zero basis?

e. Suppose instead that Lisa receives the distribution in Part a from a C corporation instead of a partnership. The corporation has $100,000 of E&P before the distribution, and Lisa's stock basis before the distribution is $25,000. What are the tax consequences to Lisa and the C corporation?

f. Note: This part can be answered only after the student studies Chapter C:11 but is placed here to allow comparison with Parts a and e. Suppose instead that Lisa receives the distribution in Part a from an S corporation instead of a partnership. Lisa is a 50% owner in the corporation, and her stock basis before the distribution is $25,000. What are the tax consequences to Lisa and the S corporation?

C:10-27 *Current Distributions.* Complete the chart for each of the following independent distributions. Assume all distributions are nonliquidating and pro rata to the partners, and no contributed property was distributed. All precontribution gain has been recognized before these distributions.

	Partner's Basis and Gain/Loss	Property Distributed	Property's Basis to Partnership	Property's FMV	Property's Basis to Partner
a. Basis:					
Predistribution	$20,000	Cash	$ 6,000	$ 6,000	
Postdistribution	$_____	Land	4,000	15,000	$_____
Gain or loss	$_____	Machinery	3,000	2,000	$_____
b. Basis:					
Predistribution	$20,000	Cash	$ 3,000	$ 3,000	
Postdistribution	$_____	Land	6,000	4,000	$_____
Gain or loss	$_____	Inventory	7,000	7,500	$_____
c. Basis					
Predistribution	$26,000	Cash	$35,000	$35,000	
Postdistribution	$_____	Land—Parcel 1	6,000	10,000	$_____
Gain or loss	$_____	Land—Parcel 2	18,000	18,000	$_____
d. Basis:					
Predistribution	$28,000	Land—Parcel 1	$ 4,000	$ 6,000	$_____
Postdistribution	$_____	Land—Parcel 2	6,000	10,000	$_____
Gain or loss	$_____	Land—Parcel 3	4,000	10,000	$_____

C:10-28 *Current Distribution with Precontribution Gain.* Three years ago, Mario joined the MN Partnership by contributing land with a $10,000 basis and an $18,000 FMV. On January 15 of the current year, Mario has a basis in his partnership interest of $20,000, and none of his precontribution gain has been recognized. On January 15, Mario receives a current distribution of a property other than the contributed land with a $15,000 basis and a $23,000 FMV.

a. Does Mario recognize any gain or loss on the distribution?

b. What is Mario's basis in his partnership interest after the distribution?

c. What is the partnership's basis in the land Mario contributed after Mario receives this distribution?

C:10-29 *Current Distribution of Contributed Property.* Andrew contributed investment land having an $18,000 basis and a $22,000 FMV along with $4,000 in money to the ABC Partnership when it was formed. Two years later, the partnership distributed the investment land Andrew had contributed to Bob, another partner. At the time of the distribution, the land had a $21,000 FMV, and Andrew and Bob's bases in their partnership interests were $21,000 and $30,000, respectively.

a. What gain or loss must be recognized on the distribution, and who must recognize it?

b. What are the bases for Andrew and Bob's interests in the partnership after the distribution?

c. What is Bob's basis in the distributed land?

C:10-30 *Current Distribution of Contributed Property.* The ABC Partnership made the following current distributions in the current year. The dollar amounts listed are the amounts before considering any implications of the distribution.

Partner	Type of Property	Basis	FMV	Partner's Basis in Partnership Interest
		Property Received		
Alonzo	Land	$ 4,000	$10,000	$19,000
Beth	Inventory	1,000	10,000	15,000
Cathy	Cash	10,000	10,000	18,000

The land Alonzo received had been contributed by Beth two years ago when its basis was $4,000 and its FMV was $8,000. The inventory Beth received had been contributed by Cathy two years ago when its basis was $1,000 and its FMV was $4,000. For each independent situation, what gain or loss must be recognized? What is the basis of the distributed property after the distribution? What are the bases of the partnership interests after the distribution? Assume the distribution has no Sec. 751 implications.

C:10-31 *Current Distribution with Sec. 751.* The KLM Partnership owns the following assets on March 1 of the current year:

Assets	Partnership's Basis	FMV
Cash	$ 30,000	$ 30,000
Receivables	–0–	16,000
Inventory	50,000	52,000
Supplies	6,000	6,500
Equipment[a]	9,000	10,500
Land (investment)	40,000	65,000
Total	$135,000	$180,000

[a]The partnership has claimed depreciation of $4,000 on the equipment.

a. Which partnership items are unrealized receivables?
b. Is the partnership's inventory substantially appreciated?
c. Assume the KLM Partnership has no liabilities and that Kay's basis for her partnership interest is $33,750. On March 1 of the current year, Kay receives a $20,000 current distribution in cash, which reduces her partnership interest from one-third to one-fourth. What are the tax results of the distribution (i.e., the amount and character of any gain, loss, or income recognized and Kay's basis in her partnership interest)?

C:10-32 *Current Distribution with Sec. 751.* The JKLM Partnership owns the following assets on October 1 of the current year:

Assets	Partnership's Basis	FMV
Cash	$ 48,000	$ 48,000
Receivables	12,000	12,000
Inventory	21,000	24,000
Machinery[a]	190,000	240,000
Land	36,500	76,000
Total	$307,500	$400,000

[a]Sale of the machinery for its FMV would result in $50,000 of Sec. 1245 depreciation recapture. Thus, the machinery's FMV and original cost are the same numerical value, $240,000.

a. Which partnership items are unrealized receivables?
b. Is the partnership's inventory substantially appreciated?
c. Assume the JKLM Partnership has no liabilities and Jack's basis in his partnership interest is $76,875. On October 1 of the current year, Jack receives a $25,000 current distribution in cash, which reduces his partnership interest from one-fourth to one-fifth. What are the tax results of the distribution (i.e., the amount and character of any gain, loss, or income recognized and Jack's basis in his partnership interest)?

C:10-33 *Current Distribution with Sec. 751.* The PQRS Partnership owns the following assets on December 30 of the current year:

Assets	Partnership's Basis	FMV
Cash	$ 20,000	$ 20,000
Receivables	–0–	40,000
Inventory	80,000	100,000
Total	$100,000	$160,000

The partnership has no liabilities, and each partner's basis in his or her partnership interest is $25,000. On December 30 of the current year, Paula receives a current distribution of inventory having a $10,000 FMV, which reduces her partnership interest from one-fourth to one-fifth. What are the tax consequences of the distribution to the partnership, Paula, and the other partners?

C:10-34 *Liquidating Distributions.* Assume the same four independent distributions as in Problem C:10-27. Fill in the blanks in that problem assuming the only change in the facts is that the distributions are now liquidating distributions instead of nonliquidating distributions.

C:10-35 *Liquidating Distribution.* Marinda is a one-third partner in the MWH Partnership before she receives $100,000 cash as a liquidating distribution. Immediately before Marinda receives the distribution, the partnership has the following assets:

Assets	Partnership's Basis	FMV
Cash	$100,000	$100,000
Marketable securities	50,000	90,000
Investment land	90,000	140,000
Total	$240,000	$330,000

At the time of the distribution, the partnership has $30,000 of outstanding liabilities, which the three partners share equally. Marinda's basis in her partnership interest before the distribution was $80,000, which includes her share of liabilities. What are the amount and character of the gain or loss recognized by Marinda and the MWH Partnership on the liquidating distribution?

C:10-36 *Liquidating Distributions.* The AB Partnership pays its only liability (a $100,000 mortgage) on April 1 of the current year and terminates that same day. Alison and Bob were equal partners in the partnership but have partnership bases immediately preceding these transactions of $110,000 and $180,000, respectively, including his or her share of liabilities. The two partners receive identical distributions with each receiving the following assets:

Assets	Partnership's Basis	FMV
Cash	$ 20,000	$ 20,000
Inventory	33,000	35,000
Receivables	10,000	8,000
Building	40,000	60,000
Land	15,000	10,000
Total	$118,000	$133,000

The building has no depreciation recapture potential. What are the tax implications to Alison, Bob, and the AB Partnership of the April 1 transactions (i.e., basis of assets to Alison and Bob, amount and character of gain or loss recognized, etc.)?

C:10-37 *Liquidating Distribution.* The LQD Partnership distributes the following property to Larry in a distribution that liquidates Larry's interest in the partnership. Larry's basis in his partnership interest before the distribution is $40,000. The adjusted bases and FMVs of the distributed property to the partnership before the distribution are as follows:

Assets	Partnership's Basis	FMV
Cash	$ 2,500	$ 2,500
Inventory	8,000	9,000
Capital asset 1	10,000	15,000
Capital asset 2	15,000	17,500
Total	$35,500	$44,000

a. Determine Larry's basis in each distributed asset.
b. Same as Part a except Larry's partnership basis before the distribution is $46,500.
c. Same as Part b except the basis of capital asset 2 is $20,000 instead of $15,000.
d. Same as Part c except Larry's partnership basis before the distribution is $34,500.

C:10-38 *Sale of a Partnership Interest.* Pat, Kelly, and Yvette are equal partners in the PKY Partnership before Kelly sells her partnership interest. On January 1 of the current year, Kelly's basis in her partnership interest, including her share of liabilities, was $35,000. During January, the calendar year partnership earned $15,000 ordinary income and $6,000 of tax-exempt income. The partnership has a $60,000 recourse liability on January 1, and this amount remains constant throughout the tax year. Kelly's share of that liability is $20,000. The partnership has no other liabilities. Kelly sells her interest on February 1 to Margaret for a cash payment of $45,000. On the sale date the partnership had the following assets:

Assets	Partnership's Basis	FMV
Cash	$ 20,000	$ 20,000
Inventory	60,000	120,000
Building	36,000	40,000
Land	10,000	15,000
Total	$126,000	$195,000

The partnership has claimed $5,000 of depreciation on the building using the straight-line method.
a. What is Kelly's basis in her partnership interest on February 1 just before the sale?
b. What are the amount and character of Kelly's gain or loss on the sale?
c. What is Margaret's basis in her partnership interest?
d. What is the partnership's basis in its assets after the sale?

C:10-39 *Sale of Partnership Interest and Termination.* Clay owned 60% of the CAP Partnership and sold one-half of his interest (30%) to Steve for $75,000 cash. Before the sale, Clay's basis in his entire partnership interest was $168,000 including his $30,000 share of partnership liabilities and his share of income up to the sale date. Partnership assets on the sale date were

Assets	Partnership's Basis	FMV
Cash	$ 50,000	$ 50,000
Inventory	30,000	60,000
Land	200,000	190,000
Total	$280,000	$300,000

a. What are the amount and character of Clay's recognized gain or loss on the sale? What is his remaining basis in his partnership interest?
b. What is Steve's basis in his partnership interest?
c. How will the partnership's basis in its assets be affected?
d. How would your answers to Parts a and c change if Clay sold his entire interest to Steve for $150,000 cash?

C:10-40 *Sale of a Partnership Interest.* Alice, Bob, and Charles are one-third partners in the ABC Partnership. The partners originally formed the partnership with cash contributions, so no partner has precontribution gains or losses. Prior to Alice's sale of her partnership interest, the partnership has the following balance sheet:

	Partnership's Basis	FMV
Assets:		
Cash	$ 12,000	$ 12,000
Receivable	–0–	21,000
Inventory	57,000	72,000
Machinery[a]	90,000	132,000
Building[b]	120,000	165,000
Land	36,000	30,000
Investments[c]	15,000	48,000
Total	$330,000	$480,000

Liabilities and capital:		
Liabilities	$105,000	$105,000
Partners' capital:		
Alice	75,000	125,000
Bob	75,000	125,000
Charles	75,000	125,000
Total	$330,000	$480,000

[a]The machinery cost $126,000, and the partnership has claimed $36,000 of depreciation.
[b]The building cost $150,000, and the partnership has claimed $30,000 of straight-line depreciation.
[c]The partnership has held the investments for more than one year.

Alice has a $110,000 basis in her partnership interest including her share of partnership liabilities, and she sells her partnership interest to Darla for $125,000 cash.
a. What are the amount and character of Alice's recognized gain or loss on the sale?
b. What is Darla's basis in her partnership interest?

C:10-41 *Retirement of a Partner.* Suzanne retires from the BRS Partnership when the basis of her one-third interest is $105,000, which includes her share of liabilities. At the time of her retirement, the partnership had the following assets:

Assets	Partnership's Basis	FMV
Cash	$145,000	$145,000
Receivables	40,000	40,000
Land	130,000	220,000
Total	$315,000	$405,000

The partnership has $60,000 of liabilities when Suzanne retires. The partnership will pay Suzanne cash of $130,000 to retire her partnership interest.
a. What are the amount and character of the gain or loss Suzanne must recognize?
b. What is the impact of the retirement on the partnership and the remaining partners?

C:10-42 *Retirement of a Partner.* Brian owns 40% of the ABC Partnership before his retirement on April 15 of the current year. On that date, his basis in the partnership interest is $40,000 including his share of liabilities. The partnership's balance sheet on that date is as follows:

	Partnership's Basis	FMV
Assets:		
Cash	$ 60,000	$ 60,000
Receivables	24,000	24,000
Land	16,000	40,000
Total	$100,000	$124,000
Liabilities and capital:		
Liabilities	$ 20,000	$ 20,000
Capital—Abner	16,000	20,800
—Brian	32,000	41,600
—Charles	32,000	41,600
Total	$100,000	$124,000

What are the amount and character of gain or loss that Brian and the ABC Partnership recognize for the following independent retirement payments?
a. Brian receives $41,600 cash on April 15.
b. Brian receives $50,000 cash on April 15.

C:10-43 *Retirement of a Partner.* Kim retires from the KLM Partnership on January 1 of the current year. At that time, her basis in the partnership is $75,000, which includes her share of liabilities. The partnership reports the following balance sheet:

	Partnership's Basis	FMV
Assets:		
Cash	$100,000	$100,000
Receivables	30,000	30,000
Inventory	40,000	40,000
Land	55,000	100,000
Total	$225,000	$270,000
Liabilities and capital:		
Liabilities	$ 75,000	$ 75,000
Capital—Kim	50,000	65,000
—Larry	50,000	65,000
—Michael	50,000	65,000
Total	$225,000	$270,000

Explain the tax consequences (i.e., amount and character of gain or loss recognized and Kim's basis for any assets received) of the partnership making the retirement payments described in the following independent situations. Kim's share of liabilities is $25,000.

a. Kim receives $65,000 cash on January 1.

b. Kim receives $75,000 cash on January 1.

C:10-44 *Death of a Partner.* When Jerry died on April 16 of the current year, he owned a 40% interest in the JM Partnership, and Michael owns the remaining 60% interest. All his assets are held in his estate for a two-year period while the estate is being settled. Jerry's estate is his successor-in-interest for the partnership interest. Under a formula contained in the partnership agreement, the partnership must pay Jerry's successor-in-interest $40,000 cash shortly after his death plus $90,000 for each of the two years immediately following a partner's death. The partnership agreement provides that all payments to a retiring partner will first be payments for the partner's share of assets, and then any additional payments will be Sec. 736(a) payments. When Jerry died, the partnership had the following assets:

Assets	Partnership's Basis	FMV
Cash	$100,000	$100,000
Land	200,000	300,000
Total	$300,000	$400,000

Jerry's basis for the partnership interest on the date of his death was $120,000 including his $30,000 share of partnership liabilities.

a. How will the payments be taxed to Jerry's successor-in-interest?

b. What are the tax implications of the payments for the partnership?

C:10-45 *Death of a Partner.* Bruce died on June 1 of the current year. On the date of his death, he held a one-third interest in the ABC Partnership, which had a $100,000 basis including his share of liabilities. Under the partnership agreement, Bruce's successor-in-interest, his wife, is to receive the following amounts from the partnership: $130,000 cash, the partnership's assumption of Bruce's $20,000 share of partnership liabilities, plus 10% of partnership net income for the next three years. The partnership's assets immediately before Bruce's death are as follows:

Assets	Partnership's Basis	FMV
Cash	$100,000	$100,000
Receivables	90,000	90,000
Inventory	40,000	40,000
Land	70,000	220,000
Total	$300,000	$450,000

a. What are the amount and character of the gain or loss that Bruce's wife must recognize when she receives the first year's payment?

b. What is the character of the gain recognized from the partnership interest when she receives the payments in each of the following three years?

c. When does Bruce's successor-in-interest cease to be a member of the partnership?

C:10-46 *Liquidation or Sale of a Partnership Interest.* John has a 60% capital and profits interest in the JAS Partnership with a basis of $333,600, which includes his share of liabilities, when he decides to retire. Andrew and Stephen want to continue the partnership's business. On the date John retires, the partnership's balance sheet is as follows:

	Partnership's Basis	FMV
Assets:		
Cash	$160,000	$160,000
Receivables	100,000	100,000
Building[a]	200,000	300,000
Land	96,000	180,000
Total	$556,000	$740,000
Liabilities and capital:		
Liabilities	$120,000	$120,000
Capital—John	261,600	372,000
—Andrew	87,200	124,000
—Stephen	87,200	124,000
Total	$556,000	$740,000

[a]The partnership has claimed $60,000 of straight-line depreciation on the building.

a. What are the tax implications for John, Andrew, Stephen, and the JAS Partnership if Andrew and Stephen each purchase one-half of John's partnership interest for a cash price of $186,000 each? Include in your answer the amount and character of the recognized gain or loss, basis of the partnership assets, and any other relevant tax implications.

b. What are the tax implications for John, Andrew, Stephen, and the JAS Partnership if the partnership pays John a liquidating distribution equal to 60% of each partnership asset other than cash plus $24,000 of cash? Assume the assets are easily divisible.

C:10-47 *Liquidation or Sale of a Partnership Interest.* Amy, a one-third partner, retires from the AJS Partnership on January 1 of the current year. Her basis in her partnership interest is $120,000 including her share of liabilities. Amy receives $160,000 in cash from the partnership for her interest. On that date, the partnership balance sheet is as follows:

	Partnership's Basis	FMV
Assets:		
Cash	$180,000	$180,000
Receivables	60,000	60,000
Land	120,000	300,000
Total	$360,000	$540,000
Liabilities and capital:		
Liabilities	$ 60,000	$ 60,000
Capital—Amy	100,000	160,000
—Joan	100,000	160,000
—Stephanie	100,000	160,000
Total	$360,000	$540,000

a. What are the amount and character of Amy's recognized gain or loss?

b. How would your answers to Part a change if Joan and Stephanie each purchased one-half of Amy's partnership interest for $80,000 cash instead of having the partnership distribute the $160,000 in cash to Amy?

C:10-48 *Exchange of Partnership Interests.* Josh holds a general partnership interest in the JLK Partnership having a $40,000 basis and a $60,000 FMV. The JLK Partnership is a limited partnership that engages in real estate activities. Diana has an interest in the CDE Partnership having a $20,000 basis and a $60,000 FMV. The CDE Partnership is a general partnership that also engages in real estate activities. Neither partnership has any Sec. 751 assets or any liabilities.

a. What are the tax implications if Josh and Diana simply exchange their partnership interests?

b. What are the tax implications if instead Diana exchanges her general partnership interest in the CDE Partnership for a limited partnership interest in the same partnership (and Josh retains his general partnership interest in the JLK Partnership)?

C:10-49 *Termination of a Partnership.* Wendy, Xenia, and Yancy own 40%, 8%, and 52%, respectively, of the WXY Partnership. For each of the following independent situations occurring in the current year, determine whether the WXY Partnership terminates and, if so, the date on which the termination occurs.

a. Wendy sells her entire interest to Alan on June 1. Alan sells one-half of the interest to Beth on November 15.

b. Yancy receives a series of liquidating distributions totaling $100,000. He receives four equal annual payments on January 1 of the current year and the three subsequent years.

c. Wendy and Xenia each receive a liquidating distribution on September 14.

d. Yancy sells his interest to Karen on June 1 for $10,000 cash and a $90,000 installment note. The note will be paid in monthly installments of $10,000 principal plus interest (at a rate acceptable to the IRS) beginning on July 1.

e. The WXY and ABC Partnerships combine their businesses on December 30. Ownership of the new, combined partnership is as follows: Wendy, 20%; Xenia, 4%; Yancy, 26.5%; Albert, 20%; Beth, 19.5%; and Carl, 10%.

f. On January 1, the WXY Partnership divides its business into two new businesses. The WX Partnership is owned equally by Wendy and Xenia. Yancy continues his share of the business as a sole proprietorship.

C:10-50 *Termination of a Partnership.* For each of the following independent situations, determine which partnership(s) (if any) terminate and which partnership(s) (if any) continue.

a. The KLMN Partnership is created when the KL Partnership merges with the MN Partnership. The ownership of the new partnership is held 25% by Katie, 30% by Laura, 25% by Michael, and 20% by Neal.

b. The ABC Partnership, with $150,000 in assets, is owned equally by Amy, Beth, and Chuck. The CD Partnership, with $100,000 in assets, is owned equally by Chuck and Drew. The two partnerships merge, and the resulting ABCD Partnership is owned as follows: Amy, 20%; Beth, 20%; Chuck, 40%; and Drew, 20%.

c. The WXYZ Partnership results when the WX and YZ Partnerships merge. Ownership of WXYZ is held equally by the four partners. WX contributes $140,000 in assets, and YZ contributes $160,000 in assets to the new partnership.

d. The DEFG Partnership is owned 20% by Dawn, 40% by Eve, 30% by Frank, and 10% by Greg. Two new partnerships are formed by the division of DEFG. The two new partnerships, the DE and FG Partnerships, are owned in proportion to their relative interests in the DEFG Partnership by the individuals for whom they are named.

e. The HIJK Partnership is owned equally by its four partners, Hal, Isaac, Juan, and Katherine, before its division. Two new partnerships, the HI and JK Partnerships, are formed out of the division with the new partnerships owned equally by the partners for whom they are named.

C:10-51 *Disposal of a Tax Shelter.* Maria purchased an interest in a real estate tax shelter many years ago and deducted losses from its operation for several years. The real property owned by the tax shelter when Maria made her investment has been fully depreciated on a straight-line basis. Her basis in her limited partnership interest is zero, but her share of partnership liabilities is $100,000. Explain the tax results if Maria sells her partnership interest for $5 cash.

C:10-52 *Optional Basis Adjustment.* Patty pays $100,000 cash for Stan's one-third interest in the STU Partnership. The partnership has a Sec. 754 election in effect. Just before the sale of Stan's interest, STU's balance sheet appears as follows:

	Partnership's Basis	FMV
Assets:		
Cash	$ 80,000	$ 80,000
Land	160,000	220,000
Total	$240,000	$300,000
Partners' capital		
Stan	$ 80,000	$100,000
Traffic Corporation	80,000	100,000
Union Corporation	80,000	100,000
Total	$240,000	$300,000

a. What is Patty's total optional basis adjustment?
b. If STU Partnership sells the land for its $220,000 FMV immediately after Patty purchases her interest, how much gain or loss will the partnership recognize?
c. How much gain will Patty report as a result of the sale?

C:10-53 *Taxation of LLC Income.* ABC Company, a limited liability company (LLC) organized in the state of Florida, reports using a calendar tax year-end. The LLC chooses to be taxed as a partnership. Alex, Bob, and Carrie (all calendar year taxpayers) own ABC equally, and each has a basis of $40,000 in his or her ABC interest on the first day of the current tax year. ABC has the following results for the current year's operation:

Operating income	$30,000
Short-term capital gain	12,000
Long-term capital loss	6,000

Each owner received a $12,000 cash distribution during the current year.
a. What are the amount and character of the income, gain, and loss Alex must report on his tax return as a result of ABC's operations?
b. What is Alex's basis in his ownership interest in ABC after the current year's operations?

C:10-54 *Electing Large Partnership.* Austin & Becker is an electing large partnership. During the current year, the partnership has the following income, loss, and deduction items:

Ordinary income	$5,200,000
Rental loss	(2,000,000)
Long-term capital loss from investments	(437,100)
Short-term capital gain from investments	827,400
Charitable contributions	164,000

a. What ordinary income will Austin & Becker report?
b. What are the separately stated items for Austin & Becker?

C:10-55 *Electing Large Partnership.* Happy Times Film Distributions is an electing large partnership. During the current year, the partnership has the following income, loss, and deduction items:

Ordinary income	$ 700,000
Passive income	3,000,000
Sec. 1231 gains	27,000
Sec. 1231 losses	(134,800)
Long-term capital gains from investments	437,600
General business tax credits	43,000

a. What ordinary income will Happy Times report?
b. What are the separately stated items reported by Happy Times?

COMPREHENSIVE PROBLEMS

C:10-56 Refer to the facts in Comprehensive Problem C:6-54. Now assume the entity is a partnership named Lifecycle Partnership. Additional facts are as follows:

• Except for precontribution gains and losses, the partners agree to share profits and losses in a 60% (Able)—40% (Baker) ratio.

- The partners actively and materially participate in the partnership's business. Thus, the partnership is not a passive activity.
- Partnership debt is recourse debt.
- The salary to Able is a guaranteed payment.
- The refund for the NOL is not relevant to the partnership, nor are the E&P numbers.
- In addition to the numbers provided for the assets on January 2, 2014, the following partnership book values apply:

Equipment	$ 215,000
Building	926,000
Land A	30,000
Land B	20,000
Total	$1,191,000

- On January 2, 2014, the partnership sells its assets and pays off the $1.87 million debt. The partnership then makes liquidating distributions of the $490,000 remaining cash to Able and Baker in accordance with their book capital account balances.

   Required:
a. Determine the tax consequences of the partnership formation to Able, Baker, and Lifecycle Partnership.
b. For 2011–2013, prepare a schedule showing:
   (1) Partnership ordinary income and other separately stated items
   (2) Able's and Baker's book capital accounts at the end of 2011, 2012, and 2013
   (3) Able's and Baker's bases in their partnership interests at the end of 2011, 2012, and 2013
c. For 2014, determine:
   (1) The results of the asset sales
   (2) Able's and Baker's book capital accounts after the asset sales but before the final liquidating distribution
   (3) Able's and Baker's bases in their partnership interests after the asset sales but before the final liquidating distribution
   (4) The results of the liquidating distributions

C:10-57 Anne decides to leave the ABC Partnership after owning the interest for many years. She owns a 52% capital, profits, and loss interest in the general partnership (which is not a service partnership). Anne's basis in her partnership interest is $120,000 just before she leaves the partnership. The partnership agreement does not mention payments to partners who leave the partnership. The partnership has not made an optional basis adjustment election (Sec. 754). All partnership liabilities are recourse liabilities, and Anne's share is equal to her loss interest. When Anne leaves the partnership, the assets and liabilities for the partnership are as follows:

	Partnership's Basis	FMV
Assets:		
Cash	$240,000	$240,000
Receivables	–0–	64,000
Inventory	24,000	24,000
Land	60,000	100,000
Total	$324,000	$428,000
Liabilities	$ 60,000	$ 60,000

Analyze the following two alternatives, and answer the associated questions for each alternative.
a. Anne could receive a cash payment of $220,000 from the partnership to terminate her interest in the partnership. Does Anne or the partnership have any income, deduction, gain, or loss? Determine both the amount and character of any items.
b. Carrie already owns a 30% general interest in the ABC partnership prior to Anne's departure. Carrie is willing to buy Anne's partnership interest for a cash payment of $220,000. What income, gain, loss, or deduction will Anne recognize on the sale? What are the tax implications for the partnership if Carrie buys Anne's interest?

TAX STRATEGY PROBLEM

C:10-58   Consider the following balance sheet for DEF Partnership:

	Partnership's Basis	FMV
Assets:		
Cash	$60,000	$ 60,000
Receivables	–0–	60,000
Land A	10,000	20,000
Land B	10,000	20,000
Land C	10,000	20,000
Total	$90,000	$180,000
Partners' capital:		
Daniel	$30,000	$ 60,000
Edward	30,000	60,000
Frances	30,000	60,000
Total	$90,000	$180,000

Note: Land A, B, and C are Sec. 1231 property, and each partner's outside basis is $30,000.

Suppose Daniel wishes to exit the partnership completely. After discussions with Edward and Frances, the partners agree to let Daniel choose one of three options:
1. Daniel takes a liquidating distribution of $60,000 cash.
2. Daniel takes a pro rata liquidating distribution of $20,000 cash, $20,000 receivables, and Land A (FMV $20,000).
3. Daniel sells his entire partnership interest to Doris for $60,000 cash.
   Required:
a. Determine the tax consequences to Daniel of each option including gains (losses) realized, recognized, and deferred; character of gains (losses); and bases of assets.
b. Discuss the relative merits of each option to Daniel, that is, what are the advantages and disadvantages of each option? What factors could sway your recommendation one way or the other?
Note: See Case Study Problem C:10-59 for another situation involving various exit strategies.

CASE STUDY PROBLEM

C:10-59   Mark Green and his brother Michael purchased land in Orlando, Florida many years ago. At that time, they began their investing as Green Brothers Partnership with capital they obtained from placing second mortgages on their homes. Their investments have flourished both because of the prosperity and growth of the area and because they have shown an ability to select prime real estate for others to develop. Over the years, they have acquired a great amount of land and have sold some to developers.

   Their current tax year has just closed, and the partnership has the following balance sheet:

	Partnership's Basis	FMV
Assets:		
Cash	$200,000	$ 200,000
Accounts receivable	90,000	90,000
Land held for investment	310,000	1,010,000
Total	$600,000	$1,300,000
Liabilities and capital:		
Mortgages	$400,000	$ 400,000
Capital—Mark	100,000	450,000
—Michael	100,000	450,000
Total	$600,000	$1,300,000

Mark and Michael each have a basis in their partnership interest of $300,000 including their share of liabilities. They share the economic risk of loss from the liabilities equally. Last spring, Mark had a serious heart attack. On his doctor's advice, Mark wants to retire from all business activity and terminate his interest in the partnership. He is interested in receiving some cash now but is not averse to receiving part of his payment over time.

You have been asked to provide the brothers with information on how to terminate Mark's interest in the partnership. Several possibilities have occurred to Mark and Michael, and they want your advice as to which is best for Mark from a tax standpoint. Michael understands that the resulting choice may not be the best option for him. The possibilities they have considered include the following:

- Michael has substantial amounts of personal cash and could purchase Mark's interest directly. However, the brothers think that option probably would take almost all the cash Michael could raise, and they are concerned about any future cash needs Michael might have. They would prefer to have Mark receive $120,000 now plus $110,000 per year for each of the next three years. Mark also would receive interest at a market rate on the outstanding debt. This alternative would qualify for installment reporting. However, the installment sale rules for related parties would apply.

- The partnership could retire Mark's interest. They have considered the option of paying Mark $150,000 now plus 50% of partnership profits for the next three years. Alternatively, they could arrange for Mark to have a $150,000 payment now and a guaranteed payment of $100,000 per year for the next three years. They expect that the dollar amounts to be received by Mark would be approximately the same for the next three years under these two options. Mark also would receive interest at a market rate on any deferred payments.

- John Watson, a long-time friend of the family, has expressed an interest in buying Mark's interest for $450,000 cash immediately. Michael and John are comfortable that they could work well together.

Mark has substantial amounts of money in savings accounts and in stocks and bonds that have a ready market. He has invested in no other business directly. Assume that, for each year, Mark's ordinary tax rate is 35% and his capital gains tax rate is 15%.

Required: Prepare a memorandum summarizing the advice you would give the two brothers on the options that they have considered.

TAX RESEARCH PROBLEMS

C:10-60   Arnie, Becky, and Clay are equal partners in the ABC General Partnership. The three individuals each have a $120,000 tax basis in their partnership interest. For business reasons, the partnership needs to be changed into the ABC Corporation, and all three owners agree to the change. The partnership is expected to have the following assets on the date that the change is to occur:

Assets	Partnership's Tax Basis & Book Value	FMV
Cash	$ 50,000	$ 50,000
Accounts receivable	60,000	55,000
Inventory	150,000	200,000
Land	100,000	295,000
Total	$360,000	$600,000

Liabilities of $75,000 are currently outstanding. The liabilities are shared equally and are already included in the $120,000 bases of the partnership interests. The structure being considered for making the change is as follows:

- ABC Partnership transfers all its assets and liabilities to the new ABC Corporation in exchange for all the corporation's stock.

- ABC Partnership then liquidates by distributing the ABC stock to Arnie, Becky, and Clay.

Required: The tax manager you work for has asked you to determine the tax and financial accounting consequences. Describe the financial and tax treatments in a short memorandum to the partnership. Be sure to mention any relevant IRC sections, Treasury Regulations, revenue rulings, and accounting standards. Assume a 35% corporate tax rate.

C:10-61 Della retires from the BCD General Partnership when her basis in her partnership interest is $70,000 including her $10,000 share of liabilities. The partnership is in the business of providing house cleaning services for local residences. At the date of Della's retirement, the partnership's balance sheet is as follows:

	Partnership's Basis	FMV
Assets:		
Cash	$ 50,000	$ 50,000
Receivables	–0–	30,000
Equipment[a]	40,000	50,000
Building[b]	90,000	100,000
Land	30,000	40,000
Total	$210,000	$270,000
Liabilities and capital:		
Liabilities	$ 30,000	$ 30,000
Capital—Bruce	60,000	80,000
—Celia	60,000	80,000
—Della	60,000	80,000
Total	$210,000	$270,000

[a]If the equipment were sold for $50,000, the entire gain would be recaptured as Sec. 1245 ordinary income.
[b]The building has been depreciated using the straight-line method.

Della will receive payments of $20,000 cash plus 5% of partnership ordinary income for each of the next five years. The partnership agreement specifies that goodwill will be paid for when a partner retires. Bruce, Celia, and Della agree that the partnership has $21,000 in goodwill when Della retires and that she will be paid for her one-third share.

Required: A tax manager in your firm has asked you to determine the amount and character of the income Della must report for each of the next five years. In addition, he wants you to research the tax consequences of the retirement on the partnership for the next five years. (Assume the partnership earns $100,000 of ordinary income each year for the next five years.) Prepare an oral presentation to be made to Della explaining the tax consequences of the payments she will receive.

C:10-62 Pedro owns a 60% interest in the PD General Partnership having a $40,000 basis and $200,000 FMV. His share of partnership liabilities is $100,000. Because he is nearing retirement age, he has decided to give away his partnership interest on June 15 of the current year. The partnership's tax year ends on December 31. Pedro's tax year ends on June 30. He intends to give a 30% interest to his son, Juan, and the remaining 30% interest to the American Red Cross.

Required: A tax manager in your firm has asked you to prepare a letter to Pedro explaining fully the tax consequences of this gift to him, the partnership, and the donees. She reminds you to be sure to include information about the allocation of the current year's partnership income.

C:10-63 Frank, Greta, and Helen each have a one-third interest in the FGH Partnership. On December 31, 2010, the partnership reported the following balance sheet:

	Partnership's Basis	FMV
Assets:		
Cash	$120,000	$120,000
Asset 1	262,380	360,000
Asset 2	115,200	90,000
Total	$497,580	$570,000

Partners' Capital:

Frank	$165,860	$190,000
Greta	165,860	190,000
Helen	165,860	190,000
Total	$497,580	$570,000

The partnership placed Asset 1 (seven-year property) in service in 2008 and Asset 2 (five-year property) in service in 2009. The partnership did not elect Sec. 179 expensing and elected out of bonus depreciation in 2009. Accordingly, it computed the assets' adjusted bases at December 31, 2010 as follows:

		Asset 1		*Asset 2*
Cost		$600,000		$240,000
Depreciation:				
2008	$85,740			
2009	146,940		$48,000	
2010	104,940	(337,620)	76,800	(124,800)
Adjusted basis		$262,380		$115,200

On January 2, 2011, Helen sold her partnership interest to Hank for $190,000. At the time of sale, the partnership had a Sec. 754 optional basis election in effect but has not elected to use the remedial method for allocating partnership items.

Required: The partners have asked you to determine (1) the amount and character of Helen's gain or loss; (2) Hank's optional basis adjustment and its allocation to Asset 1 and Asset 2; and (3) the amount of depreciation allocated to Hank in 2011, including the effects of the optional basis adjustment. At a minimum, you should consult the following resources:

- IRC Secs. 743 and 751
- Reg. Sec. 1.743-1(j)
- Reg. Sec. 1.755-1

11

CHAPTER

S CORPORATIONS

LEARNING OBJECTIVES

After studying this chapter, you should be able to

1. ▶ Explain the requirements for being taxed under Subchapter S

2. ▶ Apply the procedures for electing to be taxed under Subchapter S

3. ▶ Identify the events that will terminate an S election

4. ▶ Determine the permitted tax years for an S corporation

5. ▶ Calculate ordinary income or loss

6. ▶ Calculate the amount of any special S corporation taxes

7. ▶ Calculate a shareholder's allocable share of ordinary income or loss and separately stated items

8. ▶ Determine the limitations on a shareholder's deduction of S corporation losses

9. ▶ Calculate a shareholder's basis in his or her S corporation's stock and debt

10. ▶ Determine the taxability of an S corporation's distributions to its shareholders

11. ▶ Apply the procedures for filing an S corporation tax return

12. ▶ Determine the estimated tax payments required of an S corporation and its shareholders

ADDITIONAL COMMENT

An LLC (or partnership) that wishes to be treated as an S corporation can file the S election (Form 2553) and automatically be classified as an association (corporation) under the check-the-box regulations without having to file the entity classification election (Form 8832).

This chapter discusses a special type of corporate entity known as an S corporation. The S corporation rules, located in Subchapter S of the Internal Revenue Code, permit small corporations to enjoy the nontax advantages of the corporate form of organization without being subject to the possible tax disadvantages of the corporate form (e.g., double taxation when the corporation pays a dividend to its shareholders). When enacting these rules, Congress stated three purposes:

▶ To permit businesses to select a particular form of business organization without being influenced by tax considerations

▶ To provide aid for small businesses by allowing the income of the business to be taxed to shareholders rather than being taxed at the corporate level

▶ To permit corporations realizing losses to obtain a tax benefit of offsetting the losses against income at the shareholder level[1]

As discussed in Chapter C:2, S corporations are treated as corporations for legal and business purposes. For federal income tax purposes, however, they are treated much like partnerships.[2] As in a partnership, the profits and losses of the S corporation pass through to the owners, and the S corporation can make nontaxable distributions of earnings previously taxed to its shareholders. Although generally taxed like a partnership, the S corporation still follows many of the basic Subchapter C tax provisions (e.g., S corporations use the corporate tax rules regarding formations, liquidations, and nontaxable reorganizations instead of the partnership rules). A tabular comparison of the S corporation, partnership, and C corporation rules appears in Appendix F.

Changes over the past several years have caused many businesses to reexamine the implications of an S election. First, the restrictive nature of the S corporation requirements has caused many new businesses that were potential S corporations to look at alternative business forms. All 50 states have adopted limited liability company (LLC) legislation. LLCs offer many of the same tax advantages of S corporations because they are treated as partnerships. LLCs, however, are not subject to the same requirements that an S corporation and its shareholders must satisfy to make and retain an S election. Partially because of the S corporation restrictions, some new businesses have organized as LLCs to take advantage of the greater operational flexibility the LLC form provides the entity and its owners, as well as its liability protection. A number of small businesses, however, elected to be S corporations because of the greater certainty available within the legal system for corporate entities.

Over the last several years, tax legislation has relaxed restrictions and increased the S corporation's popularity. For example, the shareholder limit was increased to 100, and the prohibitions against certain entities and trusts becoming S corporation shareholders were lessened. Moreover, current law now treats family members as one shareholder for the 100-shareholder limit. In effect, these changes have reduced some of the differences between S corporations and LLCs and have renewed interest in the S corporation form of doing business.

For many existing C corporations, the tax cost of liquidating the corporate entity and creating an LLC may be a prohibitively expensive way to avoid the corporate level income tax (see Chapter C:6). However, many of these C corporations have taken the next best alternative, that is, making an S election.

This chapter examines the requirements for making an S election and the tax rules that apply to S corporations and their shareholders.

---

[1] S. Rept. No. 1983, 85th Cong., 2d Sess., p. 87 (1958).

[2] Some states do not recognize an S corporation as a conduit for state income tax purposes. Instead, they are taxed under the state income tax laws in the same manner as a C corporation.

SHOULD AN S ELECTION BE MADE?

ADVANTAGES OF S CORPORATION TREATMENT

A number of advantages are available to a corporation that makes an S election.

REAL-WORLD EXAMPLE

The number of S corporations has grown from 725,000 in 1985 to four million in 2007. As a result of this rapid increase, the IRS has announced a major study of S corporation compliance to be conducted by the National Research Program (NRP).

▶ The corporation's income is exempt from the corporate income tax. An S corporation's income is taxed only to its shareholders, whose tax bracket may be lower than a C corporation's tax bracket.

▶ The corporation's losses pass through to its shareholders and can be used to reduce the taxes owed on other types of income. This feature can be especially important for new businesses. The corporation can make an S election, pass through the start-up losses to the owners, and terminate the election once a C corporation becomes advantageous.

▶ Undistributed income taxed to the shareholder is not taxed again when subsequently distributed unless the distribution exceeds the shareholder's basis for his or her stock.

▶ Capital gains, dividends, and tax-exempt income are separately stated and retain their character when passed through to the shareholders. Such amounts become commingled with other corporate earnings and are taxed as dividends when distributed by a C corporation. Through 2012, however, the 15% maximum tax rate on qualified dividends alleviates the detrimental tax effect of C corporation dividends.

▶ Deductions, losses, and tax credits are separately stated and retain their character when passed through to the shareholders. These amounts may be subject to the various limitations at the shareholder level. This treatment can permit the shareholder to claim a tax benefit when it otherwise would be denied to the corporation (e.g., a shareholder can claim the general business credit benefit even though the S corporation reports a substantial loss for the year).

▶ Splitting the S corporation's income among family members is possible. However, income splitting is restricted by the requirement that reasonable compensation be provided to family members who provide capital and services to the S corporation.

▶ An S corporation's earnings that pass through to the individual shareholders are not subject to the self-employment tax. In contrast, a partnership must determine what portion of each general partner's net earnings constitutes self-employment income.

▶ An S corporation is not subject to the personal holding company tax or the accumulated earnings tax (although, as discussed later, passive income can trigger a corporate-level tax in special circumstances).

DISADVANTAGES OF S CORPORATION TREATMENT

A number of tax disadvantages also exist for a corporation that makes an S election.

KEY POINT

The structure of an S corporation can create a real hardship for a shareholder if large amounts of income pass through without any compensation payments or distributions of cash to help pay the tax on the income.

▶ A C corporation is treated as a separate tax entity from its shareholders, thereby permitting its first $50,000 of income to be taxed at a 15% marginal rate instead of the shareholder's marginal rate.

▶ The S corporation's earnings are taxed to the shareholders even though they are not distributed. This treatment may require the corporation to make distributions or salary payments so the shareholder can pay taxes owed on the S corporation's earnings.

▶ S corporations are subject to an excess net passive income tax and a built-in gains tax. Partnerships are not subject to either of these taxes.

▶ Dividends received by the S corporation are not eligible for the dividends-received deduction, as is the case for a C corporation.

▶ Allocation of ordinary income or loss and the separately stated items is based on the stock owned on each day of the tax year. Special allocations of particular items are not permitted, as they are in a partnership.

▶ The loss limitation for an S corporation shareholder is smaller than for a partner in a partnership because of the treatment of liabilities. Shareholders can increase their loss limitations by the basis of any debt they loan to the S corporation. Partners, on the other hand, can increase their loss limitation by their ratable share of all partnership liabilities.

▶ S corporations and their shareholders are subject to the at-risk, passive activity limitation, and hobby loss rules. C corporations generally are not subject to these rules.

▶ An S corporation is somewhat restricted in the type and number of shareholders it can have and the capital structure it can use. Partnerships and C corporations are not so restricted.

▶ S corporations must use a calendar year as their tax year unless they can establish a business purpose for a fiscal year or unless they make a special election to use an otherwise nonpermitted tax year. Similar restrictions also apply to partnerships.

Once the owners decide to incorporate, no general rule determines whether the corporation should make an S election. Before making a decision, management and the shareholders should examine the long- and short-run tax and nontax advantages and disadvantages of filing as a C corporation versus filing as an S corporation. Unlike a consolidated return election, the S election can be revoked or terminated at any time with minimal effort.

S CORPORATION REQUIREMENTS

OBJECTIVE 1

Explain the requirements for being taxed under Subchapter S

The S corporation requirements are divided into two categories: shareholder-related and corporation-related requirements. A corporation that satisfies all the requirements is known as a small business corporation. Only small business corporations can make an S election. Each set of requirements is outlined below.

SHAREHOLDER-RELATED REQUIREMENTS

Three shareholder-related requirements must be satisfied on each day of the tax year.[3]

▶ The corporation must not have more than 100 shareholders.

▶ All shareholders must be individuals, estates, certain tax-exempt organizations, or certain kinds of trusts.

▶ None of the individual shareholders can be classified as a nonresident **alien**.

ADDITIONAL COMMENT

The Sec. 1244 stock rules (Chapter C:2) and the S corporation rules both use the term *small business corporations*. The definitions have different requirements, although most S corporation stock can qualify as Sec. 1244 stock.

100-SHAREHOLDER RULE. For purposes of applying the 100-shareholder limit, members of a family (and their estates) count as one shareholder. Members of a family include the common ancestor, lineal descendants of the common ancestor, spouses (or former spouses) of the common ancestor or lineal descendents, and estates of family members. An individual will not be considered a common ancestor if he or she is more than six generations removed from the youngest generation of family member shareholders. When two unmarried or nonfamily individuals own stock jointly (e.g., as tenants in common or as joint tenants), each owner is considered a separate shareholder.

REAL-WORLD EXAMPLE

In 2007, 60.4% of all S corporations had one owner. Only 0.094% of the four million S corporations that filed in 2007 had more than 30 owners.

ELIGIBLE SHAREHOLDERS. C corporations and partnerships cannot own S corporation stock. This restriction prevents a corporation or a partnership having a large number of owners from avoiding the 100-shareholder limitation by purchasing S corporation stock and being treated as a single shareholder. Organizations exempt from the federal

---

[3] Sec. 1361.

income tax under Sec. 501(a) (e.g., a tax-exempt public charity or private foundation) can hold S corporation stock, and each such organization counts as one shareholder when calculating the 100-shareholder limit.

Seven types of trusts can own S corporation stock: grantor trusts, voting trusts,[4] testamentary trusts, **qualified Subchapter S trusts (QSSTs)**,[5] qualified retirement plan trusts, small business trusts, and beneficiary-controlled trusts (i.e., trusts that distribute all their income to a single income beneficiary who is treated as the owner of the trust). Grantor trusts, QSSTs, and beneficiary-controlled trusts can own S corporation stock only if the grantor or the beneficiary is a qualified shareholder. Each beneficiary of a voting trust also must be an eligible shareholder. A qualified retirement plan trust is one formed as part of a qualified stock bonus, pension, or profit sharing plan or employee stock ownership plan (ESOP) that is exempt from the federal income tax under Sec. 501(a).

Small business trusts can own S corporation stock. These trusts can be complex trusts and primarily are used as estate planning devices. No interest in a small business trust can be acquired in a purchase transaction, that is, a transaction where the holder's interest takes a cost basis under Sec. 1012. Interests in small business trusts generally are acquired as a result of a gift or bequest. All current beneficiaries of a small business trust must be individuals, estates, or charitable organizations. Current beneficiaries are parties that can receive an income distribution for the period in question. Each beneficiary counts separately for purposes of the 100-shareholder limit. QSSTs and tax-exempt trusts are ineligible to elect to be a small business trust. The trustee must make an election to obtain small business trust status.

A testamentary trust (i.e., a trust created under the terms of a will) that receives S corporation stock can hold the stock and continue to be an eligible shareholder for a two-year period, beginning on the date the stock transfers to the trust. A grantor trust that held S corporation stock immediately before the death of the deemed owner, and which continues in existence after the death of the deemed owner, can continue to hold the stock and be an eligible shareholder for the two-year period beginning on the date of the deemed owner's death. Charitable remainder unitrusts and charitable remainder annuity trusts do not qualify as small business trusts.

ETHICAL POINT

Tax professionals must assist their clients in monitoring that the S corporation requirements are met on each day of the tax year. Failing to meet one of the requirements for even one day terminates the election. Ignoring a terminating event until the IRS discovers it upon an audit probably will cause the corporation to be taxed as a C corporation and prevent it from having the termination treated as being inadvertent.

EXAMPLE C:11-1 ▶

Joan, a U.S. citizen, owns 25% of Walden Corporation's stock. Walden is an S corporation. At the time of Joan's death in the current year, the Walden stock passes to her estate. The estate is a qualifying shareholder, and the transfer does not affect the S election. If the stock subsequently transfers to a trust provided for in Joan's will, the testamentary trust can hold the Walden stock for a two-year period before the S election terminates. ◀

The trust in Example C:11-1 can hold the S corporation stock for an indefinite period only if the trust's income beneficiary makes an election to have it treated as a QSST or small business trust. Otherwise, the S election terminates at the end of the two-year period.

ALIEN INDIVIDUALS.   Individuals who are not U.S. citizens (i.e., alien individuals) can own S corporation stock only if they are U.S. residents or are married to a U.S. citizen or resident alien and make an election to be taxed as a resident alien. The S election terminates if an alien individual purchases S corporation stock and does not reside in the United States or has not made the appropriate election.

CORPORATION-RELATED REQUIREMENTS

The corporation must satisfy the following three requirements on each day of the tax year:

---

[4] A **voting trust** is an arrangement whereby the stock owned by a number of shareholders is placed under the control of a trustee, who exercises the voting rights possessed by the stock. One reason for creating a voting trust is to increase the voting power of a group of minority shareholders in the selection of corporate directors or the establishment of corporate policies.

[5] A QSST is a domestic trust that owns stock in one or more S corporations

and distributes (or is required to distribute) all its income to its sole income beneficiary. The income beneficiary must make an irrevocable election to have the QSST rules of Sec. 1361(d) apply. The beneficiary is treated as the owner (and, therefore, the shareholder) of the portion of the trust consisting of the S corporation stock. A separate election is made for each S corporation's stock owned by the trust.

ADDITIONAL COMMENT

An unincorporated eligible entity that makes a valid S election is automatically treated as making an election to be treated as a corporation under the check-the-box regulations. Thus, the entity does not have to make two separate elections.

▶ The corporation must be a domestic corporation or an unincorporated entity that elects to be treated as a corporation under the check-the-box regulations.

▶ The corporation must not be an "ineligible" corporation.

▶ The corporation must have only one class of stock.[6]

The first requirement precludes a foreign corporation from making an S election.

A corporation may be an ineligible corporation and thereby violate the second requirement in one of two ways:

▶ Corporations that maintain a special federal income tax status are not eligible to make an S election. For example, financial institutions (e.g., banks) that use the reserve method to account for bad debts and insurance companies are not eligible.

▶ Corporations that have elected the special Puerto Rico and U.S. possessions tax credit (Sec. 936) or that had elected the special Domestic International Sales Corporation tax exemption are ineligible to make the S election.

ADDITIONAL COMMENT

Current S corporation stock ownership rules and the approval of the check-the-box regulations permit great flexibility in creating groups of entities that fit the business needs of their owners.

S corporations can own the stock of a C corporation without any limitation on the percentage of voting power or value held. However, as mentioned earlier, a C corporation cannot own the stock of an S corporation. An S corporation that owns the stock of a C corporation cannot participate in the filing of a consolidated tax return. An S corporation also can own the stock of a **Qualified Subchapter S Subsidiary (QSub)**. A QSub is a domestic corporation that qualifies as an S corporation, is 100% owned by an S corporation, and for which the parent S corporation elects to treat the subsidiary as a QSub. The assets, liabilities, income, deductions, losses, etc. of the QSub are treated as those of its S corporation parent and reported on the parent's tax return.[7]

A corporation that has two classes of stock issued and outstanding has violated the third requirement and cannot be an S corporation. The single class of stock determination is more difficult than it appears at first glance because of the many different financial arrangements that are possible between an S corporation and its shareholders. A corporation is treated as having only one class of stock if all of its outstanding shares of stock possess identical rights to distribution and liquidation proceeds and the corporation has not issued any instrument or obligation, or entered into any arrangement, that is treated as a second class of stock.[8] A second class of stock is not created if the only difference between the two classes of stock pertains to voting rights.[9]

EXAMPLE C:11-2 ▶

Kelly Corporation has two classes of common stock outstanding. The Class A and Class B common stock give the shareholders identical rights and interests in the profits and assets of the corporation. Class A stock has one vote per share. Class B stock is nonvoting. Kelly Corporation is treated as having only one class of stock outstanding and can make an S election. ◀

GENERAL RULES. The determination of whether all outstanding shares of stock confer identical rights to distribution and liquidation proceeds is based on the corporate charter, articles of incorporation, bylaws, applicable state law, and binding agreements relating to distribution and liquidation proceeds (i.e., the governing agreements).[10] Treasury Regulations permit certain types of state laws, agreements, distributions, etc., to be disregarded in determining whether all of a corporation's outstanding shares confer identical rights to distribution and liquidation proceeds. These include

▶ Agreements to purchase stock at the time of death, divorce, disability, or termination of employment

▶ Distributions made on the basis of the shareholder's varying stock interests during the year

▶ Distributions that differ in timing (e.g., one shareholder receives a distribution in the current year and a second shareholder receives a similar dollar amount distribution shortly after the beginning of the next tax year)

---

[6] Sec. 1361(b)(1).
[7] Sec. 1361(b)(3).
[8] Reg. Sec. 1.1361-1(l).

[9] Sec. 1361(c)(4).
[10] Reg. Sec. 1.1361-1(l)(2).

Agreements to increase cash or property distributions to shareholders who bear heavier state income tax burdens so as to provide equal after-tax distributions provide unequal distribution and liquidation rights. The unequal distributions probably will cause a second class of stock to be created. However, state laws that require a corporation to pay or withhold state income taxes on behalf of some or all of a corporation's shareholders are disregarded.

DEBT INSTRUMENTS.   Debt instruments, corporate obligations, and deferred compensation arrangements, in general, are not treated as a second class of stock. A number of safe harbors exist for characterizing corporate obligations as debt (and not as a second class of stock):[11]

▶ Unwritten advances from a shareholder that do not exceed $10,000 during the tax year, are treated as debt by the two parties, and are expected to be repaid within a reasonable time

▶ Obligations that are considered equity under the general tax laws but are owned solely by the shareholders in the same proportion as the corporations's outstanding stock

KEY POINT

If debt instruments satisfy the safe harbor rules, such instruments cannot be construed as equity. However, such debt must have been issued in an S corporation tax year.

In addition, Sec. 1361(c)(5) provides a safe harbor for straight debt instruments so that the debt is not treated as a second class of stock. For debt to qualify under the safe harbor, it must meet the following requirements if issued while an S election is in effect:

▶ The debt must represent an unconditional promise to pay a certain sum of money on a specified date or on demand.

▶ The interest rate and interest payment dates must not be contingent on profits, the borrower's discretion, or similar factors.[12]

▶ The debt must not be convertible directly or indirectly into stock.

▶ The creditor must be an individual, estate, or trust eligible to be an S corporation shareholder, or a nonindividual creditor actively and regularly engaged in the business of lending money.[13]

The safe harbor rules can apply to debt even if the debt otherwise would be considered a second class of stock under case law or other IRC provisions. An obligation that originally qualifies as straight debt may no longer qualify if it is materially modified so that it no longer satisfies the safe harbor or is transferred to a third party who is not an eligible shareholder.[14]

ELECTION OF S CORPORATION STATUS

OBJECTIVE 2

Apply the procedures for electing to be taxed under Subchapter S

The S election exempts a corporation from all taxes imposed by Chapter 1 of the Internal Revenue Code (Secs. 1-1399) except for the following:

▶ Sec. 1374 built-in gains tax

▶ Sec. 1375 excess net passive income tax

▶ Sec. 1363(d) LIFO recapture tax

This rule exempts the S corporation from the regular income tax, accumulated earnings tax, the personal holding company tax, and the corporate alternative minimum tax for all tax years the election remains in effect.

---

[11] Reg. Sec. 1.1361-1(l)(4). An exception applies to debt instruments, corporate obligations, and deferred compensation arrangements that are treated as stock under the general principles of the federal tax law where the principal purpose for the debt instrument, etc., is to circumvent the distribution or liquidation proceeds rights provided for by the outstanding stock or to circumvent the 100-shareholder limit.

[12] That the interest rate depends on the prime rate or a similar factor not related to the debtor corporation will not disqualify the instrument from coming under the safe harbor rules. If the interest being paid is unreasonably high, an appropriate portion may be treated as a payment of something other than interest.
[13] Sec. 1361(c)(5).
[14] Reg. Sec. 1.1361-1(l)(5)(ii) and (iii).

The S election affects the shareholders in three ways:

▶ Shareholders report their pro rata share of the S corporation's ordinary income or loss as well as any separately stated items.

▶ Shareholders treat most distributions as a nontaxable recovery of their stock investments.

▶ Shareholders' stock bases are adjusted for the shareholders' ratable share of ordinary income or loss and any separately stated items.

MAKING THE ELECTION

Only small business corporations can make the S election.[15] For a small business corporation to make a valid S election, the corporation must file a timely election (Form 2553), and all the corporation's shareholders must consent to the election. Existing corporations can make a timely S election at any time during the tax year preceding the year for which the election is to be effective or on or before the fifteenth day of the third month of the year for which the election is to be effective.

For a new corporation, the S election can be made at any time on or before the fifteenth day of the third month of its initial tax year. A new corporation's initial tax year begins with the first day the corporation has shareholders, acquires assets, or begins business.

If the corporation makes the S election during the first 2½ months of the tax year for which the election is first to be effective, the corporation also must meet all the small business corporation requirements on each day of the tax year preceding and including the election date. If the corporation fails to satisfy this requirement, the election becomes effective in the corporation's next tax year.

The tax law, however, provides some relief for improper elections. First, if the corporation misses the deadline for making the S corporation election, the IRS can treat the election as timely made if the IRS determines that the corporation had reasonable cause for making the late election. Second, if the election was ineffective because the corporation inadvertently failed to qualify as a small business corporation or because it inadvertently failed to obtain shareholder consents (see below), the IRS nevertheless can honor the election if the corporation and shareholders take steps to correct the deficiency within a reasonable period of time.[16]

EXAMPLE C:11-3 ▶

Wilco Corporation, a calendar year taxpayer, has been in existence for several years. Wilco wants to be treated as an S corporation for 2012 and subsequent years. The corporation can make the election any time during 2011 or from January 1 through March 15, 2012. If the corporation makes the election after March 15, 2012, it becomes effective in 2013. However, if Wilco can show reasonable cause for making the late election, the IRS may allow the election to be effective for 2012. ◀

CONSENT OF SHAREHOLDERS. Each person who is a shareholder on the election date must consent to the election. The consent is binding on the current tax year and all future tax years. No additional consents are required of shareholders who acquire the stock between the election date and its effective date or at any subsequent date.

Section 1362(b)(2) imposes a special rule on the shareholders when the corporation makes an election after the beginning of the tax year for which it is to be effective. Each shareholder who owned stock during any portion of the year preceding the election date, and who is not a shareholder on the election date, also must consent to the election.

EXAMPLE C:11-4 ▶

Sara and Harry own all of Kraft Corporation's stock. Sara sells all her Kraft stock to Lisa on February 10. The next day Kraft makes an S election. For the election to apply in the current year, Sara, Harry, and Lisa must consent to the election. If Sara refuses to consent, the election will not be effective until next year. ◀

---

[15] Election rules are in Sec. 1362.
[16] IRS spells out detailed procedures for relief in Rev. Proc. 97-48, 1997-2 C.B. 521, Rev. Proc. 2003-43, 2003-23 C.B. 998, Rev. Proc. 2004-48, 2004-2 C.B. 172, and Rev. Proc. 2007-62, 2007-41, I.R.B. 786.

Each tenant (whether or not husband and wife) must consent to the S election if the shareholders own the stock as tenants in common, joint tenants, or tenants in the entirety. If the shareholders own the S corporation stock as community property, each person having a community property interest must consent to the election. If the shareholder is a minor, either the minor or the minor's legal representative (e.g., a natural parent or legal guardian) can make the consent.

Topic Review C:11-1 summarizes the S corporation requirements and procedures for making the S election.

OBJECTIVE 3

Identify the events that will terminate an S election

TERMINATION OF THE ELECTION

Once made, the S election remains in effect until the corporation either revokes the election or terminates the election because it ceases to meet the small business corporation requirements. The following discussion examines each action and outlines the requirements for making a new S election following a termination.[17]

REVOCATION OF THE ELECTION. A corporation can revoke its S election in any tax year as long as it meets the requirements regarding shareholder consent and timeliness. Shareholders owning more than one-half the corporation's stock (including nonvoting stock) on the day the corporation makes the revocation must consent to the revocation. A revocation made on or before the fifteenth day of the third month of the tax year is effective on the first day of that tax year. A revocation made after the first 2½ months of the tax year takes effect on the first day of the next tax year. An exception permits the S corporation to select a prospective date for the revocation to be effective. The prospective date can be the date the corporation makes the revocation or any subsequent date.

Topic Review C:11-1

S Corporation Requirements and Election Procedures

Requirements

Shareholder-related:

1. The corporation may have no more than 100 shareholders. Family members and their estates count as one shareholder.
2. All shareholders must be individuals, estates, certain kinds of trusts, or certain kinds of tax-exempt organizations. Eligible trusts include grantor trusts, voting trusts, testamentary trusts, beneficiary-controlled trusts, qualified Subchapter S trusts, qualified retirement plan trusts, and small business trusts.
3. All the individual shareholders must be U.S. citizens or resident aliens.

Corporation-related:

1. The corporation must be a domestic corporation or an unincorporated entity. An unincorporated entity that makes an S election is automatically treated as having elected to be taxed as a domestic corporation under the check-the-box regulations.
2. The corporation must not be an ineligible corporation (e.g., an ineligible bank or other financial institution, an insurance company, or a foreign corporation).
3. The corporation must have only one class of stock issued and outstanding. Differences in voting rights are ignored.

Making the Election

1. The corporation can make the S election any time during the tax year preceding the year for which the election is effective or on or before the fifteenth day of the third month of the tax year for which the election is effective. Late elections are effective with the next tax year unless the corporation obtains IRS relief for reasonable cause.
2. Each shareholder who owns stock on the date the corporation makes the election must consent to the election. If the corporation makes the election after the beginning of the tax year, each person who was a shareholder during the portion of the tax year preceding the election also must consent to the election.

---

[17] Termination and revocation rules are in Sec. 1362.

EXAMPLE C:11-5 ▶ Adobe Corporation, a calendar year taxpayer, has been an S corporation for several years. However, the corporation has become quite profitable, and management feels that it would be advantageous to make a public stock offering to obtain additional capital during 2012. Adobe can revoke its S election any time on or before March 15, 2012, making the revocation effective on January 1, 2012. If the corporation revokes the election after March 15, 2012, it takes effect January 1, 2013. In either case, the corporation may specify a prospective 2012 effective date as long as the date occurs on or after the date it makes the revocation. ◀

TAX STRATEGY TIP

When it is difficult to obtain the majority shareholder vote necessary for revocation, consideration should be given to purposely triggering a termination event.

TERMINATION OF THE ELECTION. The S election terminates if the corporation fails one or more of the small business corporation requirements any time after the election's effective date. The termination generally occurs on the day of the terminating event. Events that can terminate the election include

▶ Exceeding the 100-shareholder limit

▶ Having an ineligible shareholder own some of the stock

▶ Creating a second class of stock

▶ Attaining a prohibited tax status

▶ Selecting an improper tax year

▶ Failing the passive investment income test for three consecutive years

The passive investment income test applies annually. It terminates the S election if more than 25% of the corporation's gross receipts are passive investment income for each of three consecutive tax years *and* the corporation has Subchapter C earnings and profits (E&P) at the end of each of the three consecutive tax years. If the corporation meets these conditions for three consecutive tax years, the election terminates on the first day of the next (fourth) tax year.

Passive investment income includes royalties, rents,[18] dividends, interest, annuities, and gains from the sale or exchange of stocks and securities. Treasury Regulations hold that passive investment income excludes income derived from the active conduct of a trade or business. Subchapter C E&P includes only earnings that accrued in tax years in which an S election was not in effect (i.e., the corporation was taxed under the C corporation rules).

EXAMPLE C:11-6 ▶ Shareholders formed Silver Corporation in the current year, and the corporation promptly made an S election. Silver can earn an unlimited amount of passive income during a tax year without any fear of losing its S corporation status or being subject to the Sec. 1375 tax on excess net passive income because it has never been a C corporation and thus has no Subchapter C E&P. However, if a C corporation containing E&P merged into Silver, Silver would then have potential exposure to the passive income rules. (See page C:11-16 for a discussion of the Sec. 1375 tax.) ◀

HISTORICAL NOTE

Previously, a termination was deemed effective on the first day of the tax year in which the terminating event occurred. To stop potential abuse, Congress changed the rule so that an S election terminates on the day of the terminating event.

ALLOCATION OF INCOME. A terminating event occurring at some time other than the first day of the tax year creates an S termination year. The **S termination year** is divided into an S short year and C short year. The **S short year** begins on the first day of the tax year and ends on the day preceding the termination date. The **C short year** begins on the termination date and continues through the last day of the corporation's tax year.

EXAMPLE C:11-7 ▶ Dixon Corporation has been an S corporation for several years. Paula and Frank each own one-half of Dixon's stock. Paula sells one-half of her Dixon stock to Eagle Corporation on July 1. The sale terminates the S election on July 1 because Eagle is an ineligible shareholder. Assuming Dixon is a calendar year taxpayer, the S short year runs from January 1 through June 30. The C short year runs from July 1 through December 31. ◀

---

[18] Regulation Sec. 1.1362-2(c)(5)(ii)(B)(2) excludes from rents payments received for the use or occupancy of property if the corporation provides significant services or incurs substantial costs in the rental business. See page C:11-37 for additional explanations of the significant services and substantial costs definitions.

TAX STRATEGY TIP

Income or loss can be allocated in the termination year under either of two methods. Careful consideration should be given to the possible tax advantages of a daily allocation versus an actual closing of the books. See Tax Planning Considerations for further details.

ADDITIONAL COMMENT

To use an actual closing of the books to allocate Dixon's income or loss in Example C:11-7, Eagle must consent. Due to the consequences of such an election, the method of allocation should be considered in negotiating the Dixon stock sale.

The S corporation's shareholders report the S short year income according to the normal reporting rules described below. The C corporation reports the income earned during the C short year and calculates its C short year income tax liability on an annualized basis (see Chapter C:3). The S short year and C short year returns are due on the due date for the corporation's tax return for the tax year had the termination not occurred (including any extensions).

An S corporation can use either of two rules to allocate the termination year's income between the S short year and the C short year. The general rule of Sec. 1362(e)(2) allocates the ordinary income or loss and the separately stated items between the S short year and C short year based on the number of days in each year. A special election under Sec. 1362(e)(3) permits an allocation that accords with the corporation's normal tax accounting rules if all persons who were shareholders at any time during the S short year and all persons who are shareholders on the first day of the C short year consent to the election. The corporation cannot use a daily allocation when an S termination year occurs and, during such year, sales or exchanges of 50% or more of the corporation's outstanding stock occur. In such a case, the corporation must use its normal accounting rules to make the allocation.

INADVERTENT TERMINATION. Special rules permit the corporation to continue its S election if an inadvertent termination occurs by its ceasing to be a small business corporation or by its failing the passive investment income test for three consecutive years. If such a termination occurs, the S corporation or its shareholders must take the necessary steps, within a reasonable time period after discovering the event creating the termination, to restore the corporation's small business status. If the IRS determines that the termination was inadvertent, the corporation and all persons owning stock during the termination period must agree to make the adjustments necessary to report the income for this period as if the S election had been in effect continuously.[19]

EXAMPLE C:11-8 ▶ Shareholders formed Frye Corporation in 2008 and operated it as a C corporation during that year. Frye made an S election in 2009. During 2008, the corporation incorrectly computed its E&P and believed that no Subchapter C E&P existed for its only pre–S corporation tax year. From 2009 through 2011, Frye earned large amounts of passive income but did not pay the Sec. 1375 excess net passive income tax or worry about terminating its election because it thought it had no accumulated E&P from 2008. Upon auditing Frye's tax returns, the IRS finds that Subchapter C E&P, in fact, did exist from 2008 and terminates the S election effective on January 1, 2012. If the corporation distributes the E&P and the shareholders report the dividend income, the IRS probably will treat the occurrence as an inadvertent termination and not revoke the election. ◀

The IRS also can grant relief for inadvertent terminations of the election to treat a subsidiary as a Qualified Subchapter S Subsidiary (QSub). For example, a parent S corporation might inadvertently transfer shares of a QSub to another person, thereby violating the 100% ownership requirement. If the S corporation takes the necessary steps to correct the inadvertent transfer, the IRS can grant relief, thereby allowing the election to remain in effect.

OTHER IRS WAIVERS. The IRS not only can waive a termination it deems to be inadvertent, it also can validate certain invalid elections. Validation of an invalid election can occur when the election failed to meet the basic S corporation requirements of Sec. 1361 or failed to provide the necessary shareholder consents. The IRS also can exercise this authority in situations where a corporation never filed an election. In addition, the IRS can treat a late S election as being timely filed if the IRS determines that reasonable cause

[19] Regulation Sec. 1.1362-4(b) holds that a termination will be inadvertent if the terminating event was not reasonably within the control of the corporation and was not part of a plan to terminate the election or if it took place without the corporation's knowledge and reasonable safeguards were in place to prevent the event from occurring.

existed for failing to make a timely election and the corporation meets certain other requirements.[20]

NEW ELECTION FOLLOWING A TERMINATION. A corporation that revokes or terminates its S election must wait five tax years before making a new election.[21] This delay applies unless the IRS consents to an earlier reelection. Regulation Sec. 1.1362-5(a) indicates that permission for an early reelection can occur (1) when more than 50% of the corporation's stock is owned by persons who did not own stock on the termination date or (2) when the event causing the termination was not reasonably within the control of the corporation or the shareholders having a substantial interest in the corporation *and* was not part of a plan to terminate the election involving the corporation or such shareholders.

EXAMPLE C:11-9 ▶ Terri owned Vector Corporation, a calendar year taxpayer that has been an S corporation for ten years. In January 2010, Terri sold all the Vector stock to Michelle with payments to be made over a five-year period. In March 2012, Michelle fails to make the necessary payments, and Terri repossesses the stock. During the time Michelle held the stock, Vector revoked its S election. Vector should immediately apply for reelection of S status because a more than 50% ownership change occurred since the revocation date. ◀

AVOIDING TERMINATION OF AN S ELECTION. Termination of an S election potentially can increase corporate or shareholder taxes. The S corporation's owners, management, and tax advisor need to understand the various events that can cause the termination of the S election. Some steps shareholders can take to prevent an untimely termination include the following:

▶ Monitor all transfers of S corporation stock. Make certain the purchaser or transferee of the stock is not an ineligible shareholder (e.g., corporation, partnership, or nonresident alien) or that the total number of shareholders does not exceed 100 (e.g., an excess shareholder resulting from creation of a joint interest).

▶ Establish procedures for the S corporation to purchase the stock of deceased shareholders to avoid the stock being acquired by a trust that is ineligible to be a shareholder.

▶ Establish restrictions on the transferability of the S corporation stock by having shareholders enter into a stock purchase agreement. Such an agreement could provide that the stock cannot be transferred without the prior consent of all other shareholders

---

WHAT WOULD YOU DO IN THIS SITUATION?

Harry Baker formed Xeno Corporation on January 4, 2009. The corporation filed a valid S corporation election on January 17, 2009, to be in effect for 2009. Harry, the corporation's sole shareholder, consented to the election. The corporation had business ties to Mexico, and to strengthen these ties, Harry sold 25% of his Xeno shares to Pedro Gonzales on February 12, 2010. Pedro is one of Harry's business associates and is a citizen and resident of Mexico. Harry continued to operate Xeno as an S corporation throughout 2010. Early in March 2011, Harry became aware that, by selling stock to an ineligible shareholder, he may have jeopardized the corporation's S election. Thus, Harry immediately contacted Pedro and persuaded Pedro to sell his Xeno shares back to him (Harry). Harry hires you as his tax advisor on December 17, 2011, at which time you learn about the sale and repurchase of the Xeno shares. However, Harry tells you not to worry because, by buying back the shares, he already has rectified the situation, and thus the IRS need not be told about the transfers. How do you advise Harry on this matter?

---

[20] See footnote 16.
[21] *Termination* includes both revocation of the S election and loss of the election because one or more of the small business corporation requirements were not met.

and, if the necessary consent cannot be obtained, the corporation will repurchase the stock at a specified price (e.g., at book value).

▶ Monitor the passive income earned by an S corporation that previously had been a C corporation for one or more years. Make certain the passive income requirement is not failed for three consecutive years by reducing the level of passive income or by distributing the Subchapter C E&P.

S CORPORATION OPERATIONS

S corporations make the same accounting period and accounting method elections that a C corporation makes. Each year, the S corporation must compute and report to the IRS and to its shareholders its ordinary income or loss and its separately stated items. The special S corporation rules are explained below.

OBJECTIVE 4

Determine the permitted tax years for an S corporation

TAXABLE YEAR

Section 1378(a) requires that the S corporation's taxable year be a permitted year, defined as

▶ A tax year ending on December 31 (including a 52–53 week year)

▶ Any fiscal year for which the corporation establishes a business purpose[22]

Section 1378(b) specifically notes that income deferral for the shareholders is not a necessary business purpose. An S corporation that adopts a fiscal year coinciding with its natural business year has satisfied the business purpose requirement. The natural business year for an S corporation depends on the type of business conducted. When a trade or business has nonpeak and peak periods of business, the natural business year is considered to end at, or soon after, the close of the peak business period. A business whose income is steady throughout the year, does not have a natural business year.[23]

EXAMPLE C:11-10 ▶

Sable Corporation, an S corporation, operates a ski resort and reports $1 million of gross receipts for each of its last three tax years. If at least $250,000 (25% of gross receipts) of the receipts occurred in February and March for each of the three consecutive years, Sable can adopt, or change to, or continue to use a natural business year ending March 31.[24] ◀

An S corporation's adoption of, or a change to, a fiscal year that is an ownership tax year also is permitted. An ownership tax year is the same tax year used by shareholders owning more than 50% of the corporation's outstanding stock. The 50% requirement must be met on the first day of the tax year to which the change relates. Failure to meet the 50% ownership requirement on the first day of any later tax year requires a change to a calendar year or other approved fiscal year. S corporations also can adopt or change to a fiscal year for which it obtains IRS approval, based on the facts and circumstances of the situation.[25]

Section 444 permits an S corporation to elect a fiscal year other than a permitted year. The fiscal year elected under Sec. 444 must have a deferral period of three months or less (e.g., a September 30 or later fiscal year-end for an S corporation otherwise required to use a calendar year). An S corporation that changes its tax year can elect to use a new fiscal year under Sec. 444 only if the deferral period is no longer than the shorter of three months or the deferral period of the tax year being changed.[26] A Sec. 444 election is not required of an S corporation that satisfies the business purpose exception.

ADDITIONAL COMMENT

The requirement that all S corporations adopt calendar years (with March 15 return due dates) caused a hardship for tax return preparers. Section 444 is a compromise provision that allows a fiscal year for filing purposes, but it mandates a special payment of the deferred taxes.

---

[22] Some S corporations use a "grandfathered" fiscal year, which is a fiscal year for which IRS approval was obtained after June 30, 1974. Excluded are fiscal years that result in an income deferral of three months or less.
[23] Rev. Procs. 2002-39, 2002-1 C.B. 1046, and 2006-46, 2006-2 C.B. 859.
[24] See Rev. Proc. 2006-46, 2006-2 C.B. 859, for an explanation of the 25% test.
[25] Regulation Sec. 1.1378-1 and Rev. Proc. 2006-46, 2006-2 C.B. 859, explain the procedures for an S corporation adopting a fiscal year or changing the tax

year of a new or existing S corporation. Rev. Rul. 87-57, 1987-2 C.B. 117, examines eight situations concerning whether the tax year is a permitted year.
[26] Special Sec. 444 transitional rules for 1986 permitted many S corporations to retain a previously adopted fiscal year (e.g., January 31) even though the deferral period is longer than three months.

S corporations that elect a fiscal year under Sec. 444 must make required payments under Sec. 7519, which approximate the deferral benefit of the fiscal year. Revocation or termination of the S election also terminates the Sec. 444 election unless the corporation becomes a personal service corporation. Termination of the Sec. 444 election permits the S corporation to obtain a refund of prior Sec. 7519 payments.

Topic Review C:11-2 summarizes the alternative tax years available to an S corporation.

ACCOUNTING METHOD ELECTIONS

As with a partnership, an S corporation makes accounting method elections independent of accounting method elections made by its shareholders. Three elections generally reserved for the S corporation's shareholders are as follows:

▶ Section 617 election relating to deduction and recapture of mining exploration expenditures

▶ Section 901 election to take a credit for foreign income taxes[27]

OBJECTIVE 5

Calculate ordinary income or loss

ORDINARY INCOME OR LOSS AND SEPARATELY STATED ITEMS

S corporations are treated much like partnerships and thus report both an ordinary income or loss amount and a series of separately stated items. Ordinary income or loss is the net of income and deductions other than the separately stated items described in the next paragraph.

KEY POINT

S corporations are much like partnerships in their method of reporting income and losses. Both are pass-through entities that provide K-1s to their owners with their respective shares of income and loss items.

The S corporation's separately stated items are the same ones that apply in partnership taxation under Sec. 702(a).[28] The items required to be separately stated by Sec. 702(a) include

▶ Net short-term capital gains and losses

▶ Net long-term capital gains and losses

▶ Sec. 1231 gains and losses

▶ Charitable contributions

Topic Review C:11-2

Alternative S Corporation Tax Years

Tax Year	Requirements
Calendar year (including certain 52–53 week years)	The permitted tax year unless an exception applies.
Permitted fiscal year:	IRS will grant approval if:
a. Ownership year	The tax year requested is the same as that used by shareholders owing more than 50% of the corporation's outstanding stock. This test must be met on the first day of the year for which approval is requested as well as for each succeeding year.
b. Natural business year	25% or more of the gross receipts for each of the three most recent 12-month periods are in the last two months of the requested tax year.
c. Facts and circumstances year	The corporation establishes a business purpose (other than an ownership year or natural business year) using the facts and circumstances of the situation.
Nonpermitted fiscal year	A Sec. 444 election permits the S corporation to use an otherwise nonpermitted tax year if the deferral period is three months or less and the corporation makes the necessary required payments.

---

[27] Secs. 1363(c).

[28] Sec. 1366(a).

▶ Dividends eligible for the 15% maximum tax rate or treated as investment income[29]

▶ Taxes paid to a foreign country or to a U.S. possession

▶ Any other item provided by Treasury Regulations

Regulation Sec. 1.702-1(a)(8) adds for partnerships several other items to the list. The same additions from the Treasury Regulations apply to S corporations and include the following:

▶ Tax-exempt or partially tax-exempt interest

▶ Soil and water conservation expenditures

▶ Intangible drilling and development costs

▶ Certain mining exploration expenditures

Additional separately stated items not mentioned in Sec. 702 or its regulations include

▶ Passive income and loss

▶ Portfolio income (e.g., dividends and interest)

For a more complete list of the separately stated items see Form 1120S, Schedule K included in Appendix B.

Section 1366(b) requires that the character of any separately stated item be determined as if the item were (1) realized directly by the shareholder from the same source from which it was realized by the corporation or (2) incurred by the shareholder in the same manner as it was incurred by the corporation. Thus, the character of an income, gain, deduction, loss, or credit item does not change merely because the item passes through to the shareholders.

DEDUCTIONS THAT CANNOT BE CLAIMED.   S corporations also have several deductions that it cannot claim, including

▶ The 70%, 80%, or 100% dividends-received deduction (because dividends pass through to the S corporation's shareholders)

▶ The U.S. production activities deduction (because that deduction passes through to the S corporation's shareholders)

▶ The same deductions disallowed to a partnership under Sec. 703(a)(2) (e.g., personal and dependency exemptions, additional itemized deductions for individuals, taxes paid or accrued to a foreign country or to a U.S. possession, charitable contributions, oil and gas depletion, and NOL carrybacks and carryforwards).[30]

SIMILARITY TO C CORPORATION TREATMENT.   S corporations are treated as corporations for certain tax matters. For example, an S corporation can elect to amortize its organizational expenditures under Sec. 248 (after deducting up to $5,000). Also, the 20% reduction in certain tax preference benefits under Sec. 291 applies to an S corporation if the corporation was a C corporation in any of its three preceding tax years.[31]

ADDITIONAL COMMENT

The 20-year carryover period continues to run on C corporation NOLS even during subsequent S corporation years.

CARRYOVERS AND CARRYBACKS WHEN STATUS CHANGES.   Some S corporations may operate as C corporations during a period of years that either precede the making of an S election or follow the termination of an S election. No carryovers or carrybacks that originate in a C corporation tax year can carry to an S corporation tax year other than carryovers that can be used to offset the built-in gains tax (see pages C:11-16 through C:11-18). Similarly, no carryovers or carrybacks created in an S corporation tax year can carry to a C corporation tax year.[32] Losses from an S corporation tax year pass through to the shareholder and, if greater than the shareholder's income for the year, can create an NOL carryover or carryback for the shareholder.

---

[29] Partnerships are permitted to have C corporations as owners of partnership interests. Thus, dividends eligible for the dividends-received deduction also are separately stated. Such is not the case with an S corporation, which cannot have a corporate shareholder.

[30] Sec. 1363(b)(2).
[31] Secs. 1363(b)(3) and (4).
[32] Sec. 1371(b).

U.S. PRODUCTION ACTIVITIES DEDUCTION

Chapter C:3 describes the C corporation version of the U.S. production activities deduction, whereby the deduction equals 9% times the lesser of (1) qualified production activities income for the year or (2) taxable income before the U.S. production activities deduction. Individuals use a modified form of AGI instead of taxable income for this computation. The deduction, however, cannot exceed 50% of the employer's W-2 wages allocable to U.S. production activities for the year. In the case of an S corporation, the deduction applies at the shareholder level, so the S corporation must report each shareholder's share of qualified production activities income on the shareholder's Schedule K-1. For the 50% salary limitation, each shareholder is allocated his or her share of the S corporation's W-2 wages.

OBJECTIVE 6
Calculate the amount of any special S corporation taxes

SPECIAL S CORPORATION TAXES

The S corporation is subject to three special taxes: the excess net passive income tax, the built-in gains tax, and the LIFO recapture tax. Each of these taxes is explained below.

EXCESS NET PASSIVE INCOME TAX. The **excess net passive income (or Sec. 1375) tax** applies when an S corporation has passive investment income for the tax year that exceeds 25% of its gross receipts and, at the close of the tax year, the S corporation has Subchapter C E&P. The excess net passive income tax equals the S corporation's excess net passive income times the highest corporate tax rate (35% in 2011).[33]

The **excess net passive income** is determined as follows:

$$\text{Excess net passive income} = \text{Net passive income} \times \frac{\text{Passive investment income} - 25\% \text{ of gross receipts}}{\text{Passive investment income}}$$

KEY POINT

The excess net passive income tax is of concern to a former C corporation that has accumulated E&P. A corporation that always has been an S corporation will not have a passive income problem.

The excess net passive income is limited to the corporation's taxable income, which is defined as a C corporation's taxable income except with no reduction for the NOL deduction or the dividends-received deduction. Net passive income equals passive investment income minus any deductions directly related to its production. Passive investment income excludes income derived from the active conduct of a trade or business.[34]

EXAMPLE C:11-11 ▶

Paoli Corporation, an S corporation, reports the following results for the current year:

Service (nonpassive) income	$35,000
Dividend income	37,000
Interest income	28,000
Passive income-related expenses	10,000
Other expenses	25,000

At the end of this year, Paoli's E&P from its prior C corporation tax years amounts to $60,000. Paoli's excess net passive income is determined as follows:

$$\$33,846 = (\$65,000 - \$10,000) \times \frac{\$65,000 - (0.25 \times \$100,000)}{\$65,000}$$

TAX STRATEGY TIP

A former C corporation can avoid the Sec. 1375 tax (and the possibility of having its S election terminated) by electing to distribute its Subchapter C E&P. See Tax Planning Considerations for further details.

The excess net passive income tax is $11,846 ($33,846 × 0.35). The special tax reduces (on a pro rata basis) the dividend income and interest income items that pass through to the shareholders. The S election is not terminated at the end of the current year unless Paoli also was subject to the tax in the prior two tax years. ◀

BUILT-IN GAINS TAX. A second corporate level tax may apply to gains recognized by an S corporation that formerly was a C corporation. This tax, called the **built-in gains (or Sec. 1374) tax**, applies to any income or gain the corporation would have included in

---

[33] Passive investment income and Subchapter C E&P for this purpose have the same definition here as given on page C:11-10.
[34] Reg. Sec. 1.1362-2(c)(5). Also, Reg. Sec. 1.1375-1(f), Ex. (2) indicates that

passive income subject to the Sec. 1375 tax includes municipal bond interest that otherwise is exempt from the federal income tax.

ADDITIONAL
COMMENT

A special rule provides a reduced recognition period for tax years beginning in 2009, 2010, and 2011. For example, a calendar year S corporation recognizes no built-in gains tax in 2009 or 2010 if the seventh year of the recognition period preceded 2009 or 2010. This rule will affect S corporations whose election was effective at the beginning of 2002 or 2003. For 2011, an S corporation recognizes no built-in gains tax if the fifth year of the recognition period precedes 2011, thereby affecting S corporations that elected in 2006.

gross income while a C corporation had the corporation used the accrual method of accounting (known as a **built-in gain**) and that the corporation reports during the ten-year period beginning on the date the S election took effect (known as the recognition period). **Built-in losses** are any deductions or losses the corporation would have deducted while a C corporation had the corporation used the accrual method of accounting and that the corporation reports during the ten-year period beginning on the date the S election took effect. Built-in gains and losses also include the differences between the FMVs and adjusted bases of assets held at the time the S election takes effect. Built-in losses reduce the amount of recognized built-in gains in determining the built-in gains tax liability.

Congress enacted this tax to prevent taxpayers from avoiding the corporate level tax by making an S election before distributing or selling its assets. The built-in gains tax applies to S corporation tax years beginning after December 31, 1986, where the S corporation was formerly a C corporation and made the current S election after December 31, 1986.

EXAMPLE C:11-12 ▶

Theta Corporation, a calendar year taxpayer, incorporated in 1998 and operated as a C corporation through the end of 2010. On February 5, 2011, Theta filed an S election that was effective for 2011 and later tax years. Theta is subject to the built-in gains tax for ten years starting with January 1, 2011. ◀

The Sec. 1374 tax is determined by using the following four-step calculation:

STEP 1: Determine the corporation's net recognized built-in gain for the tax year.

TAX STRATEGY TIP

An S corporation with NOL, capital loss, general business credit, and minimum tax credit carryovers from C corporation years can use these carryovers to reduce the effect of the built-in gains tax. Both NOL and capital loss carryforwards reduce the amount of recognized built-in gain taxed under Sec. 1374. The general business and minimum tax credit carryforwards reduce the actual built-in gains tax.

STEP 2: Reduce the net recognized built-in gain from Step 1 (but not below zero) by any NOL or capital loss carryovers from prior C corporation tax years.

STEP 3: Compute a tentative tax by multiplying the amount determined in Step 2 by the highest corporate tax rate (35% in 2011).

STEP 4: Reduce the tax determined in Step 3 (but not below zero) by the general business credit and minimum tax credit carryovers from any prior C corporation tax years and by the nonhighway use of gasoline and other fuels credit.

A recognized built-in gain or loss is any gain or loss recognized on an asset disposition during the ten-year recognition period unless the S corporation can establish that it did not hold the asset on the first day of the first tax year to which the S election applies. A recognized built-in gain cannot exceed the excess of a property's FMV over its adjusted basis on the first day of the ten-year recognition period. Dispositions include sales or exchanges and other events, including the collection of accounts receivable by a cash basis taxpayer, collection of an installment sale obligation, and the completion of a long-term contract by a taxpayer using the completed contract method.[35]

PRACTICAL
APPLICATION

The application of the Sec. 1374 tax requires detailed records, which enable the taxpayer to track the built-in gain assets and determine when the corporation recognizes these gains.

Built-in losses include not only losses originating from a disposition of property, but also any deductions claimed during the ten-year recognition period that are attributable to periods before the first S corporation tax year. A recognized built-in loss cannot exceed the excess of a property's adjusted basis over its FMV on the first day of the ten-year recognition period. Built-in losses, however, do not include any loss, deduction, or carryover originating from the disposition of an asset acquired before or during the recognition period where the principal purpose of such acquisition was avoiding the Sec. 1374 tax.

The net recognized built-in gain for a tax year is limited to the smaller of:

▶ The excess of (1) the net unrealized built-in gain (i.e., excess of the FMV of the S corporation's assets at the beginning of its first tax year for which the S election is in effect over their total adjusted basis on such date) over (2) the total net recognized built-in gain for prior tax years beginning in the ten-year recognition period.[36]

---

[35] Income and gains potentially can be taxed under both the excess net passive income (Sec. 1375) and built-in gains (Sec. 1374) taxes. Any such income or gain is fully taxed under the Sec. 1374 rules. The portion of the income or gain taxed under the Sec. 1374 tax is exempt from the Sec. 1375 tax.

[36] The recognition period can be extended beyond ten years if property having a carryover basis is acquired in a tax-free transaction (e.g., a tax-free reorganization) from a C corporation. For such property, the ten-year recognition period begins on the date the S corporation acquired the property.

▶ The S corporation's taxable income as if it were a C corporation but with no dividends-received deduction or NOL deduction allowed.

If the net of the recognized built-in gains and losses exceeds the corporation's taxable income and the corporation made the S election after March 30, 1988, the excess built-in gain carries over to the next tax year, where it may be subject to the Sec. 1374 built-in gains tax in the carryover year. The built-in gain carryover consists of a ratable share of each of the income categories (e.g., ordinary income or capital gains) making up the net recognized built-in gain for the tax year.

The built-in gains tax passes through to the shareholders as if it were a loss. The loss must be allocated proportionately among the net recognized built-in gains that resulted in the tax being imposed.

EXAMPLE C:11-13 ▶

Assume the same facts as in Example C:11-12 and that Theta Corporation uses the accrual method of accounting. Theta owns the following assets on January 1, 2011:

Assets	Adjusted Basis	FMV
Cash	$ 10,000	$ 10,000
Marketable securities	39,000	45,000
Accounts receivable	60,000	60,000
Inventory (FIFO)	60,000	75,000
Building	27,000	44,000
Land	10,000	26,000
Machinery and equipment[a]	74,000	140,000
Total	$280,000	$400,000

[a] $50,000 of the gain is subject to recapture under Sec. 1245.

During 2011, Theta collects $58,000 of accounts receivable and declares $2,000 uncollectible. It sells the FIFO inventory at a $25,000 profit in the first quarter of 2011, replacing the sold inventory with new inventory. It also sells two machines during 2011. One machine, having an $18,000 FMV and an $11,000 adjusted basis on January 1, produced a $7,000 gain (Sec. 1245 recapture income) on September 2. A second machine, having a $15,000 FMV and a $19,000 adjusted basis on January 1, produced a $4,000 loss on March 16.

▶ Theta recognizes no built-in gain or loss on collecting the receivables because it is an accrual method taxpayer. The $2,000 uncollectible debt is not a built-in loss because the loss arose after January 1. It is deductible as part of the ordinary income or loss calculation.

▶ Of the $25,000 inventory profit, $15,000 ($75,000 − $60,000) is a built-in gain taxed under Sec. 1374. Theta includes the entire $25,000 profit in ordinary income or loss.

▶ Theta recognizes a $7,000 built-in gain ($18,000 − $11,000) and a $4,000 ($15,000 − $19,000) built-in loss on the sale of the two machines. The $7,000 gain is ordinary income due to Sec. 1245 recapture and becomes part of Theta's S corporation ordinary income or loss. The $4,000 Sec. 1231 loss passes through separately to the shareholders.

In total, an $18,000 ($15,000 + $7,000 − $4,000) net recognized built-in gain is taxed under Sec. 1374, subject to the taxable income ceiling. Assuming C corporation taxable income (with no NOL deduction or dividends-received deduction) is at least $18,000, the built-in gains tax is $6,300 ($18,000 × 0.35). The entire tax amount reduces the shareholder's ordinary income from the inventory and machinery sales. ◀

ETHICAL POINT

A C corporation that has substantially appreciated assets and wants to make an S election should obtain an appraisal of its assets on or about the first day of the S election period. The S corporation's tax accountant must make sure the appraiser does not assign an artificially low value to these assets to minimize the potential built-in gains tax burden.

REAL-WORLD EXAMPLE

The special S corporation taxes account for only a small amount of federal revenues. In 2007, collections on the built-in gains and excess net passive income taxes were $843 and $70 million, respectively. In contrast, total C corporation tax revenues collected in 2007 were $395 billion.

LIFO RECAPTURE TAX. If a C corporation using the LIFO inventory method makes an S election, Sec. 1363(d)(3) requires the corporation to include its LIFO recapture amount in gross income for its last C corporation tax year. The LIFO recapture amount is the excess of the inventory's basis for tax purposes under the FIFO method over its basis under the LIFO method at the close of the final C corporation tax year. Any tax increase incurred in the final C corporation tax year is payable in four annual installments, on or before the due date for the final C corporation tax return and on or before the due date for the first three S corporation tax returns. The S corporation's inventory basis is increased by the LIFO recapture amount included in gross income.

EXAMPLE C:11-14▶ Taylor Corporation, a calendar year C corporation since its inception in 1994, made an S election on December 21, 2010, effective for its 2011 tax year. Taylor has used the LIFO inventory method for a number of years. Its LIFO inventory has a $400,000 adjusted basis, a $650,000 FIFO inventory value, and an $800,000 FMV. Taylor's LIFO recapture amount is $250,000 ($650,000 − $400,000). Taylor includes this amount in gross income reported on its 2010 corporate tax return. Assuming a 34% corporate tax, Taylor's increased tax liability is $85,000 (0.34 × $250,000), of which $21,250 (0.25 × $85,000) is due with Taylor's 2010 C corporation tax return. An additional $21,250 is due with the 2011 through 2013 S corporation tax returns. Taylor increases the basis of its inventory by the $250,000 LIFO recapture amount. ◀

? STOP & THINK

Question: Former C corporations that are now treated as S corporations are subject to three corporate level taxes—the **LIFO recapture tax**, the built-in gains tax, and the excess net passive income tax. Why did Congress enact these three taxes?

Solution: Prior to enacting the LIFO recapture tax, Congress debated making the conversion of a C corporation into an S corporation a taxable event subject to the corporate liquidation rules. The corporation would have recognized all gains and losses at the time of conversion. As a compromise, only LIFO users are subject to an "automatic" tax when conversion occurs, and this tax applies only to the LIFO recapture amount and not all inventory appreciation. The built-in gains tax applies only when the corporation sells or exchanges assets during its first ten years after the S election. Assets not sold or exchanged during this time period escape the tax. The excess net passive income tax encourages S corporations to distribute their accumulated E&P. No tax is imposed, however, if the corporation keeps its passive income below the 25% of gross receipts threshold. Thus, former C corporations and their shareholders generally are better off under the current system than had Congress mandated corporate liquidation treatment.

Taxation of the Shareholder

OBJECTIVE 7

Calculate a shareholder's allocable share of ordinary income or loss and separately stated items

INCOME ALLOCATION PROCEDURES

An S corporation's shareholders must report their pro rata share of the ordinary income or loss and separately stated items for the S corporation's tax year that ends with or within the shareholder's tax year.[37] Each shareholder's pro rata share of these items is determined by

1. Allocating an equal portion to each day in the tax year (by dividing the amount of the item by the number of days in the S corporation's tax year)
2. Allocating an equal portion of the daily amount to each share of stock outstanding on each day (by dividing the daily amount for the item by the number of shares of stock outstanding on a particular day)
3. Totaling the daily allocations for each share of stock
4. Totaling the amounts allocated for each share of stock held by the shareholder

TYPICAL MISCONCEPTION

An S corporation's income or loss is allocated basically the same as a partnership's except that a partnership may have the added flexibility of making certain special allocations under Sec. 704(b).

These allocation rules are known as the "per day/per share" method. Special allocations (such as those possible under the partnership tax rules) of the ordinary income or loss and separately stated items are not permitted.

If a sale of the S corporation stock occurs during the year, the transferor reports the earnings allocated to the transferred shares through the day of the transfer.[38] The transferee reports his or her share of the earnings from the day after the transfer date through the end of the tax year.

---

[37] Sec. 1366(a). If the shareholder dies during the S corporation's tax year, the income earned during the portion of the tax year preceding death is reported on the shareholder's tax return. Income for the period the estate holds the S corporation stock is reported on the estate's fiduciary tax return.

[38] Reg. Sec. 1.1377-1(a)(2)(ii). Also see examples under Reg. Sec. 1.1377-1(c).

EXAMPLE C:11-15▶ Fox Corporation is an S corporation owned equally by Arnie and Bonnie during all of the current year (not a leap year). During this year, Fox reports ordinary income of $146,000 and a long-term capital gain of $36,500. Arnie and Bonnie each report $73,000 (0.50 × $146,000) of ordinary income and $18,250 (0.50 × $36,500) of long-term capital gain. ◀

EXAMPLE C:11-16▶ Assume the same facts as in Example C:11-15, except Bonnie sells one-half of her shares to Clay on March 31 of the current year (the 90th day of Fox's tax year). Arnie reports the same ordinary income and long-term capital gain from his investment. Bonnie and Clay report ordinary income and long-term capital gain as follows:

Ordinary Income

$$\text{Bonnie:} \left(\$146,000 \times \frac{1}{2} \times \frac{90}{365} \right) + \left(\$146,000 \times \frac{1}{4} \times \frac{275}{365} \right) = \$45,500$$

$$\text{Clay:} \quad \$146,000 \times \frac{1}{4} \times \frac{275}{365} = \underline{27,500}$$

$$\text{Total} \qquad\qquad\qquad\qquad\qquad\qquad\qquad \underline{\underline{\$73,000}}$$

Long-Term Capital Gain

$$\text{Bonnie:} \left(\$36,500 \times \frac{1}{2} \times \frac{90}{365} \right) + \left(\$36,500 \times \frac{1}{4} \times \frac{275}{365} \right) = \$11,375$$

$$\text{Clay:} \quad \$36,500 \times \frac{1}{4} \times \frac{275}{365} = \underline{6,875}$$

$$\text{Total} \qquad\qquad\qquad\qquad\qquad\qquad\qquad \underline{\underline{\$18,250}}$$ ◀

KEY POINT

Shareholders of an S corporation need to be aware that when they dispose of their stock, they have the option of having income or loss determined by an actual closing of the books rather than an allocation on a daily basis.

A special election is available for allocating the ordinary income or loss and separately stated items when the shareholder's interest in the S corporation terminates or is substantially reduced during the tax year. Under this election, the income is allocated according to the accounting methods used by the S corporation (instead of on a daily basis). The election divides the S corporation's tax year into two parts ending on

▶ The day the shareholder's interest in the corporation terminates

▶ The last day of the S corporation's tax year

The corporation can make this election only if all affected shareholders agree to the election.[39] Affected shareholders include the shareholder whose interest terminated and all shareholders who received S corporation shares during the year. The Tax Planning Considerations section of this chapter explores this election in greater detail.

OBJECTIVE 8

Determine the limitations on a shareholder's deduction of S corporation losses

LOSS AND DEDUCTION PASS-THROUGH TO SHAREHOLDERS

The S corporation's ordinary loss and separately stated loss and deduction items pass through to the shareholders at the end of the corporation's tax year. The shareholders report these items in their tax year in which the S corporation's tax year ends.

ALLOCATION OF THE LOSS. Under the rules outlined above, allocation of the loss also occurs on a daily basis. Thus, shareholders receive an allocation of ordinary loss and separately stated items even if they own the stock for only a portion of the year. If ordinary loss and other separately stated loss and deduction pass-through items exceed the shareholder's income, the excess may create an NOL for the shareholder and result in a carryback or carryover at the shareholder level.

EXAMPLE C:11-17▶ Kauai Corporation, an S corporation, reports a $73,000 ordinary loss during the current year (not a leap year). At the beginning of the current year, Edward and Frank own equally all of Kauai's stock. On June 30 of the current year (the 181st day of Kauai's tax year), Frank gives

---

[39] Sec. 1377(a)(2).

one-fourth of his stock to his son George. Edward is allocated $36,500 ($73,000 × 0.50) of ordinary loss. Frank and George are allocated ordinary losses as follows:

Frank: $\left(\$73,000 \times \dfrac{1}{2} \times \dfrac{181}{365} \right) + \left(\$73,000 \times \dfrac{3}{8} \times \dfrac{184}{365} \right) = \$31,900$

George: $\$73,000 \times \dfrac{1}{8} \times \dfrac{184}{365} = \underline{4,600}$

Total $\underline{\underline{\$36,500}}$

All three shareholders can deduct these losses on their individual tax returns subject to the loss limitations described below. ◄

REAL-WORLD EXAMPLE

A U.S. Supreme Court case held that discharge of indebtedness income excluded from gross income under Sec. 108 nevertheless is a pass-through item that increases the shareholders' stock bases, thereby allowing loss pass-through items to be deducted by the shareholders. *Gitlitz et al. v. Comm.* 87 AFTR 2d 2001-417, 2001-1 USTC ¶50,147 (USSC, 2001). A subsequent tax act (2002), however, disallowed the pass-through and stock basis increase for debt cancellations after October 11, 2001. This situation is a good example of Congress "overruling" the Supreme Court with its legislative power.

SHAREHOLDER LOSS LIMITATIONS. Each shareholder's deduction for his or her share of the ordinary loss and the separately stated loss and deduction items is limited to the sum of the adjusted basis for his or her S corporation stock plus the adjusted basis of any indebtedness owed *directly* by the S corporation to the shareholder. Thus, a shareholder must account for stock basis and debt basis. Unlike the partnership taxation rules, however, a shareholder cannot increase his or her stock basis by a ratable share of the general S corporation liabilities.[40]

In determining the stock basis limitation for losses, the shareholder makes the following positive and negative adjustments:[41]

▶ Increase stock basis for any capital contributions during the year

▶ Increase stock basis for ordinary income and separately stated income or gain items

▶ Decrease stock basis for distributions not included in the shareholder's income

▶ Decrease stock basis for nondeductible, noncapital expenditures (unless the shareholder elects to determine the loss limitation without this decrease)

Sequencing the basis reduction for distributions ahead of losses means that distributions reduce the deductibility of S corporation loss and deduction pass-throughs, but losses do not affect the treatment of S corporation distributions.

TAX STRATEGY TIP

Rather than having the corporation borrow money, an S corporation shareholder might consider borrowing money directly from the bank and then lending the loan proceeds to the corporation with the corporation guaranteeing the bank loan. In this way, the shareholder obtains debt basis.

Many S corporations are nothing more than incorporated forms of sole proprietorships or partnerships. As a result, banks and other lending institutions often require one or more shareholders to personally guarantee loans the institutions make to the S corporation. The IRS and courts, however, have held that these guaranteed loans do not create corporate indebtedness to the shareholder. As a result, the shareholder's loss limitation does not increase until the shareholder pays part or all of the corporation's liability or the shareholder executes a note at the bank in full satisfaction of the corporation's liability. Such action by the shareholder converts the guarantee into an indebtedness of the corporation to the shareholder, which increases the shareholder's debt basis and loss limitation.[42]

The adjusted basis of S corporation stock and debt generally is determined as of the last day of the S corporation's tax year. If the shareholder disposes of the S corporation stock before that date, the stock and debt bases are instead determined immediately prior to the disposition.

Loss and deduction pass-through items are allocated to each share of stock and reduce each share's basis. Once the losses and deductions have reduced stock basis to zero, they then reduce the basis of any debt owed by the S corporation to the shareholder.

EXAMPLE C:11-18 ▶ Pat and Bill equally own Tillis Corporation, an S corporation. During the current year, Tillis reports an ordinary loss of $104,000. Tillis's liabilities at the end of the current year include $110,000 of accounts payable, $150,000 of mortgage payable, and a $20,000 note owed to Bill.

---

[40] Sec. 1366(d)(1). Amounts owed by an S corporation to a conduit entity that has the shareholder as an owner or beneficiary will not increase the shareholder's loss limitation.

[41] Sec. 1366(d) and Reg. Sec. 1.1366-2(a)(3). Special basis adjustment rules apply to oil and gas depletion.

[42] Rev. Ruls. 70-50, 1970-1 C.B. 178; 71-288, 1971-2 C.B. 319; and 75-144, 1975-1 C.B. 277. See also *Estate of Daniel Leavitt v. CIR*, 63 AFTR 2d 89-

1437, 89-1 USTC ¶9332 (4th Cir., 1989) among a series of decisions that uphold the IRS's position. However, see *Edward M. Selfe v. U.S.*, 57 AFTR 2d 86-464, 86-1 USTC ¶9115 (11th Cir., 1986) for a transaction where a guarantee was held to increase the shareholder's loss limitation because the transaction was structured so the bank looked primarily to the shareholder instead of the corporation for repayment.

Thus, Bill has a $20,000 debt basis for the amount he loaned to the corporation. Pat and Bill each had a $40,000 adjusted basis in their Tillis stock on January 1. The ordinary loss is allocated equally to Pat and Bill. Pat's $52,000 loss allocation is only partially deductible this year (i.e., up to $40,000) because the loss exceeds his $40,000 stock basis. Bill's $52,000 loss allocation is fully deductible this year because his loss limitation is $60,000 ($40,000 stock basis + $20,000 debt basis). After the loss pass-through, Pat and Bill each have a zero stock basis and Bill has an $8,000 debt basis.[43] ◄

Any loss or deduction pass-through not currently deductible is suspended until the shareholder regains basis in his stock or debt. The carryover period for the loss or deduction item is unlimited.[44] The additional adjusted basis amount can originate from a number of sources, including subsequent profits earned by the S corporation, additional capital contributions or loans made by the shareholder to the corporation, or purchases of additional stock from other shareholders.

EXAMPLE C:11-19 ► Assume the same facts as in Example C:11-18 and that Tillis Corporation reports ordinary income of $24,000 next year. Pat and Bill each are allocated $12,000 of ordinary income. This income provides Pat with the necessary $12,000 stock basis to deduct the $12,000 loss carryover. The $12,000 income allocated to Bill restores his debt basis to $20,000 (see pages C:11-25 through C:11-27). ◄

If a shareholder sells his or her S corporation stock still having unused losses due to lack of stock or debt basis, these losses do not transfer to the new shareholder. Instead, the unused losses lapse when the shareholder sells the stock. If the shareholder transfers the S corporation stock to a spouse or former spouse incident to a divorce, however, the suspended losses transfer to the spouse or former spouse. Thus, the spouse or former spouse can deduct the losses when he or she obtains sufficient basis.

SPECIAL SHAREHOLDER LOSS AND DEDUCTION LIMITATIONS. S corporation shareholders are subject to three special loss and deduction limitations. These limitations may prevent an S corporation's shareholder from using losses or deductions even though the general loss limitation described above does not otherwise apply. Application of the special loss limitations occurs as follows:

KEY POINT
An oft-quoted advantage of an S election is that losses pass through to the shareholders. This advantage is significantly limited by the at-risk and passive activity rules.

► *At-Risk Rules:* The Sec. 465 at-risk rules apply at the shareholder level. Thus, a shareholder can deduct a loss from a particular S corporation activity only to the extent the shareholder is at risk in the S corporation's activity at year-end.

► *Passive Activity Limitation Rules:* Losses and credits from a passive activity offset income earned from that passive activity or other passive activities in the same or subsequent tax year. An S corporation shareholder personally must meet the material participation standard for an activity to avoid the passive activity limitation. The S corporation's material participation in an activity does not allow a passive investor to deduct S corporation losses against his or her salary and other "active" income.

► *Hobby Loss Rules:* S corporation losses are subject to the Sec. 183 hobby loss rules, which limit deductions to the activity's gross income unless the S corporation can establish that it is engaged in the activity for profit.

In addition, various separately stated loss and deduction items are subject to shareholder limitations (e.g., charitable contributions, capital losses, and investment interest expenses), but they are not subject to corporate limitations. Conversely, some separately stated items are subject to corporate limitations but not shareholder limitations (e.g., the 50% nondeductible portion of meal and entertainment expenses).

POST-TERMINATION LOSS CARRYOVERS. Loss and deduction carryovers incurred in S corporation tax years can carry over at the shareholder level even though the S elec-

---

[43] See pages C:11-24 through C:11-27 for a detailed discussion of basis adjustments.

[44] Sec. 1366(d)(2). If more than one type of loss or deduction item passes through to the shareholder, the carryover amount is allocated to each of the pass-through items based on their relative amounts.

tion has terminated. Shareholders can deduct these carryovers only in the **post-termination transition period**.[45] The length of the post-termination transition period depends on the event causing the termination. In general, the period begins on the day after the last day of the corporation's final S corporation tax year and ends on the later of one year after the last day or the due date for the final S corporation tax return (including any extensions).

If the S election terminates for a prior tax year as a result of a determination, the period runs for 120 days beginning on the determination date. Section 1377(b)(2) defines a determination as a court decision that becomes final, a closing agreement entered into, a final disposition of a refund claim by the IRS, or an agreement between the corporation and the IRS that the corporation failed to qualify as an S corporation.

The shareholder can deduct the loss carryovers only up to his or her adjusted basis of the stock at the end of the post-termination transition period.[46] Losses that cannot be deducted because of the basis limitation are lost forever. Deducted losses reduce the shareholder's stock basis.

EXAMPLE C:11-20 ▶

Pearson Corporation has been a calendar year S corporation for several years. Helen's stock basis is $45,000. On July 1, 2011, its S election terminates when an ineligible shareholder acquires part of its stock. For the period ended June 30, 2011, Helen is allocated $60,000 of Pearson's ordinary loss. Helen can deduct only $45,000 of this loss because of her Pearson stock basis, which the loss reduces to zero. The $15,000 unused loss carries over to the post-termination transition period, which ends on June 30, 2012 (assuming Pearson does not extend the March 15, 2012, due date for the S short year tax return). Helen must have an adjusted basis for the Pearson stock of at least $15,000 at the close of business on June 30, 2012, to use the loss. Helen should consider making additional capital contributions of at least $15,000 between July 1, 2011, and June 30, 2012, to use the loss. ◀

Topic Review C:11-3 summarizes the rules governing deductibility of S corporation losses and deductions that pass through to the shareholders.

Topic Review C:11-3

Deductibility of S Corporation Losses and Deductions

Allocation Process
1. Losses and deductions are allocated based on the number of shares of stock owned by each shareholder on each day of the tax year. Special allocations of losses and deductions are not permitted.
2. Termination of the S election requires the tax year to be divided into two parts. The corporation can elect (with the shareholders' consent) to allocate the loss or deduction according to the corporation's accounting methods. This election also is available when a shareholder's interest in the S corporation terminates.

Loss Limitations
1. Losses and deductions pass through on a per-share basis and are limited to the shareholder's basis in stock and debt. Once the basis for all the shareholder's stock is reduced to zero, the losses reduce the basis of any S corporation indebtedness to the shareholder.
2. Losses and deductions that are not deducted carry over to a tax year in which the shareholder regains stock or debt basis. The time period for the carryover is unlimited. The unused losses lapse if the shareholder transfers the stock to anyone other than a spouse or former spouse incident to a divorce.
3. S corporation shareholders are subject to three special loss limitations:
   ▶ At-risk rules
   ▶ Passive activity limitations
   ▶ Hobby loss rules
   Some separately stated loss and deduction items also are subject to shareholder limitations (e.g., investment interest expense). Other separately stated items are subject to corporate limitations but not shareholder limitations (e.g., the 50% nondeductible portion of meal and entertainment expenses).

---

[45] Sec. 1366(d)(3). The loss carryovers that carry over include those disallowed by the at-risk rules.

[46] Sec. 1366(d)(3)(B).

FAMILY S CORPORATIONS

Family S corporations have been an important tax planning device. This type of tax planning often involves a high-tax-bracket taxpayer gifting stock to a minor child who generally has little other income. The transfer results in income splitting among family members. The IRS has enjoyed success in litigating cases dealing with intrafamily transfers of S corporation stock when the transferor (usually a parent) retains the economic benefits and control over the stock transferred to the transferee (usually a child).[47] The IRS has attained less success when one family member purchases the stock from another family member at its market value.

The IRS also has the statutory authority to adjust the income, loss, deduction, or credit items allocated to a family member to reflect the value of services rendered or capital provided to the corporation. Section 1366(e) defines family as including spouse, ancestors, lineal descendants, and trusts created for such individuals. This provision permits the reallocation of income to provide for full compensation of a shareholder or nonshareholder for services and capital provided to the corporation. It also reduces the residual income reported by the S corporation and allocated to the shareholders according to their stock ownership. Such a reallocation prevents not only the shifting of income from the family member providing the services or capital to other family members, but also the avoidance of employment taxes. Alternatively, the IRS can determine that the corporation paid too much compensation to a shareholder and reduce that shareholder's salary and increase the residual income allocated based on stock ownership.

ADDITIONAL COMMENT

The advantages of family S corporations have been somewhat curtailed. For example, income from stock of an S corporation gifted to a child under age 18 (and, in some cases, age 18 through 23) is subject to the "kiddie tax," where unearned income exceeding $1,900 (in 2011) is taxed at the parents' marginal tax rate.

EXAMPLE C:11-21 ▶

Harvest Corporation, an S corporation, reports ordinary income of $200,000 after it claims a $20,000 deduction for Sid's salary. Sid and his three children own the Harvest stock equally. Harvest employs none of Sid's three children. The IRS subsequently determines that reasonable compensation for Sid is $80,000. This adjustment increases Sid's salary income and Harvest's compensation deduction by $60,000 ($80,000 − $20,000) and reduces Harvest's ordinary income to $140,000 ($200,000 − $60,000). Each shareholder's ratable share of ordinary income is reduced from $50,000 ($200,000 ÷ 4) to $35,000 ($140,000 ÷ 4). These adjustments have a twofold effect. First, they increase the amount of income allocable to Sid ($80,000 + $35,000 vs. $20,000 + $50,000), where Sid may be in a higher tax bracket than his children. Second, the increased salary increases Sid's employment taxes. Alternatively, if the IRS can prove that the stock transfer to the three children is not a bona fide transfer, all $220,000 of Harvest's income is taxed to Sid—$80,000 as salary and $140,000 as an allocation of ordinary income. ◀

BASIS ADJUSTMENTS

OBJECTIVE 9

Calculate a shareholder's basis in his or her S corporation's stock and debt

Shareholder's must adjust their S corporation stock basis annually. In addition, if the S corporation is indebted to the shareholder, he or she may have to adjust the debt basis downward for loss or deduction pass-throughs and upward to reflect restoration of the debt basis when the corporation earns subsequent profits. Each of these adjustments is described below.

BASIS ADJUSTMENTS TO S CORPORATION STOCK

Basis adjustments to the shareholder's stock are made in the following order:[48]

Initial investment (or basis at beginning of tax year)
Plus: Additional capital contributions made during the year
Allocable share of ordinary income
Allocable share of separately stated income and gain items

---

[47] See, for example, *Gino A. Speca v. CIR*, 47 AFTR 2d 81-468, 80-2 USTC ¶9692 (7th Cir., 1980) and *Henry D. Duarte*, 44 T.C. 193 (1965), where the IRS's position prevailed. See also *Gavin S. Millar*, 1975 PH T.C. Memo

¶75,113, 34 TCM 554, and *Donald O. Kirkpatrick*, 1977 PH T.C. Memo ¶77,281, 36 TCM 1122, where the taxpayers prevailed.
[48] Sec. 1367(a) and Reg. Sec. 1.1367-1(f).

SELF-STUDY QUESTION

Why is the determination of stock basis in an S corporation important?

ANSWER

To determine gain or loss on the sale of the stock, to determine the amount of losses that can be deducted, and to determine the amount of distributions to shareholders that are nontaxable.

ADDITIONAL COMMENT

If Congress allows the repeal of the estate tax in 2010 to stand, special carryover basis rules apply that year.

Minus:	Distributions excluded from the shareholder's gross income
	Allocable share of any expense not deductible in determining ordinary income (loss) and not chargeable to the capital account (A shareholder, however, can elect to make this adjustment *after* the two following adjustments.)
	Allocable share of ordinary loss
	Allocable share of separately stated loss and deduction items

Adjusted basis for stock (but not less than zero)

A shareholder's initial basis for S corporation stock depends on how he or she acquires it. Stock purchased from the corporation or another shareholder takes a cost basis. Stock received as part of a corporate formation takes a substituted basis from the assets transferred. Stock acquired by gift takes the donor's basis (adjusted for gift taxes paid) or FMV (if lower). Stock acquired at death takes its FMV on the decedent's date of death or the alternate valuation date (if elected). The basis of S corporation stock inherited from a deceased shareholder is its FMV minus any corporate income that would have been income in respect of a decedent (see Chapter C:14) if the income had been acquired from the decedent. No basis adjustment occurs when the corporation makes the initial S election.

The basis adjustments to the S corporation stock parallel those made to a partnership interest. The ordinary income and separately stated income and gain items increase the shareholder's basis whether they are taxable, tax-exempt, or receive preferential tax treatment.

EXAMPLE C:11-22 ▶ Cathy owns Marlo Corporation, an S corporation. At the beginning of the current year, Cathy's adjusted basis in her Marlo stock is $105,000. Marlo reports the following operating results this year:

Ordinary income	$70,000
Municipal bond interest income	15,000
Dividends from domestic corporations	6,000
Long-term capital gain	8,000
Short-term capital loss	17,000

Cathy's adjusted basis in her Marlo stock at year-end is $187,000 ($105,000 + $70,000 + $15,000 + $6,000 + $8,000 − $17,000). ◀

Cathy makes the basis adjustment at the end of the S corporation's tax year, when the results for the entire period are known. Because profits and losses are allocated ratably on a daily basis to all shares held on each day of the tax year, a shareholder's gain or loss realized on the sale of S corporation stock during the tax year is not determinable until the ordinary income or loss and separately stated items allocable to the shares sold are known. Similarly, when S corporation stock becomes worthless during a tax year, the shareholder must make the necessary positive and negative basis adjustments before determining the amount of the worthless security loss.

EXAMPLE C:11-23 ▶ Mike, Carlos, and Juan equally own Diaz Corporation, an S corporation. Mike's 100 shares of Diaz stock have a $25,000 adjusted basis at the beginning of the current year (not a leap year). Diaz reports ordinary income of $36,500 and municipal bond interest income of $14,600 in the current year. On February 14 of the current year (the 45th day of Diaz's tax year), Mike sells all his Diaz stock for $30,000. Assuming the corporation uses the daily method to allocate the income items, Mike's basis for the Diaz stock is $27,100, determined as follows:

$$\$27,100 = \$25,000 + \left(\$36,500 \times \frac{45}{365} \times \frac{1}{3}\right) + \left(\$14,600 \times \frac{45}{365} \times \frac{1}{3}\right)$$

Mike reports a $2,900 ($30,000 − $27,100) gain on the sale. ◀

KEY POINT

Losses first reduce basis in stock and then any amount of debt owed to the shareholder by the S corporation. Subsequent *net* increases in basis are added first to debt and then to stock.

BASIS ADJUSTMENTS TO SHAREHOLDER DEBT

After the shareholder's basis in S corporation stock is reduced to zero, basis in any S corporation indebtedness to the shareholder is reduced (but not below zero) by the remainder of the available loss and deduction items.[49] If a shareholder has more than one loan outstanding at year-end, the basis reduction applies to all the indebtednesses based on the relative adjusted basis of each loan. Ordinary income and separately stated gain or income items allocated to the shareholder in subsequent tax years (net of distributions and losses to the shareholders) first restore debt basis. Once all previous decreases to debt basis are restored, any additional positive basis adjustments increase the shareholder's stock basis.[50]

Repayment of a shareholder indebtedness results in gain recognition to the shareholder if the payment amount exceeds the debt's adjusted basis. If the indebtedness is secured by a note, the difference is a capital gain. If the indebtedness is not secured by a note or other evidence of the indebtedness, the repayment is ordinary income.[51]

EXAMPLE C:11-24▶ At the beginning of 2011, Betty owns one-half the stock of Trailer Corporation, an S corporation. Betty's basis in the Trailer stock is $40,000. Trailer owes Betty $20,000 on January 1, 2011, evidenced by a note. Thus, Betty has a $20,000 debt basis. During 2011, Trailer reports an ordinary loss of $100,000 and during 2012 reports ordinary income of $10,000. Betty's $50,000 loss pass-through from 2011 first reduces her stock basis from $40,000 to zero. Next, the $10,000 remainder of the loss pass-through reduces Betty's debt basis from $20,000 to $10,000. Betty's $5,000 allocation of 2012's ordinary income increases her debt basis from $10,000 to $15,000. If the corporation repays the note before the end of 2012, Betty reports a $5,000 ($20,000 − $15,000) long-term capital gain resulting from the repayment plus $5,000 of ordinary income from Trailer's 2012 operations. If the debt instead were unsecured (i.e., an advance from the shareholder not secured by a note), the gain would be ordinary income. ◀

STOP & THINK

Question: The text preceding Example C:11-24 says that ordinary income and separately stated gain or income items (net of losses and distributions) restore debt basis before increasing stock basis; that is, debt is restored first by any net increase. The following rule also applies: total basis for the loss limitation equals (1) stock basis *after* all current year adjustments other than for losses plus (2) debt basis *before* any current year adjustments.

Consider the following situation: Omega Corporation is an S corporation with one shareholder. At the beginning of last year, the shareholder's stock basis was $15,000, and her debt basis was $20,000. Last year, Omega incurred a $45,000 ordinary loss, $35,000 of which the shareholder could deduct and $10,000 of which carries over. The loss affected basis as follows:

	Stock Basis	Debt Basis
Basis at beginning of last year	$15,000	$20,000
Ordinary loss last year ($45,000)	(15,000)	(20,000)
Basis at beginning of current year	$ –0–	$ –0–

In the current year, Omega earns $18,000 of ordinary income. What does the shareholder recognize in the current year, and what is the effect on her stock and debt bases? Why is the net increase rule for debt basis restoration beneficial to the shareholder?

Solution: The shareholder recognizes $18,000 of ordinary income and deducts the entire $10,000 loss carryover. Current year basis adjustments are as follows:

	Stock Basis	Debt Basis
Balance at beginning of current year	$ –0–	$ –0–
Ordinary income	10,000	8,000
Loss carryover allowed	(10,000)	–0–
Basis at end of current year	$ –0–	$8,000

The net increase approach benefits the shareholder because it allows her to deduct the $10,000 loss carryover in the current year rather than next year. The net increase for debt

---

[49] The shareholder makes no basis reductions to debt repaid before the end of the tax year. Regulation Sec. 1.1367-2(d)(1) holds that restoration occurs immediately before a shareholder repays or disposes of indebtedness during the tax year.

[50] Sec. 1367(b)(2)(B).

[51] Rev. Ruls. 64-162, 1964-1 (Part I) C.B. 304 and 68-537, 1968-2 C.B. 372.

restoration is $8,000 ($18,000 − $10,000), which leaves $10,000 of the $18,000 ordinary income to increase stock basis. This net increase approach to debt restoration allows a stock basis increase sufficient to use the loss carryover. Alternatively, if debt were restored by ordinary income without netting, the debt basis would increase by the entire $18,000, leaving no positive adjustment to the stock basis. This increase to debt basis would not help the shareholder in the current year because debt basis for the loss limitation is the balance before any current year adjustments. Under this hypothetical alternative approach, the shareholder could deduct the loss next year because next year's beginning debt basis would be $18,000. However, the net increase approach is better than the alternative because it allows the shareholder to deduct the loss in the current year.

S CORPORATION DISTRIBUTIONS

OBJECTIVE 10

Determine the taxability of an S corporation's distributions to its shareholders

Two sets of rules apply to S corporation distributions. One applies to S corporations having accumulated E&P. Accumulated E&P may exist if an S corporation was a C corporation in a pre–S election tax year. Another set of distribution rules applies to S corporations that do not have E&P (e.g., a corporation formed after 1982 that makes a timely S election in its initial tax year). These rules are explained below.

CORPORATIONS HAVING NO EARNINGS AND PROFITS

For S corporations with no accumulated E&P, a two-tier rule applies. Distributions are initially nontaxable and reduce the shareholder's stock basis (but not below zero). If the distribution exceeds the shareholder's stock basis, the shareholder treats the excess as a gain from the sale or exchange of the stock. Stock basis for determining excess distributions is that after positive adjustments for ordinary income and separately stated income and gain items but before negative adjustments.[52]

EXAMPLE C:11-25 ▶

Sandy owns 100% of Liberty Corporation, an S corporation. At the beginning of the current year, Sandy's adjusted basis in her Liberty stock (a capital asset) is $20,000, and she has no debt basis. In the current year, Liberty reports ordinary income of $30,000 and a long-term capital loss of $7,000. Liberty makes a $35,000 cash distribution to Sandy on June 15. Sandy's basis for the stock must be adjusted for the ordinary income before determining the taxability of the distribution. Because Sandy's $50,000 ($20,000 + $30,000) adjusted stock basis exceeds the $35,000 distribution, she excludes the entire distribution from her gross income. The distribution reduces her stock basis to $15,000 ($50,000 − $35,000). Because Sandy still has sufficient stock basis, she can deduct the $7,000 capital loss, which further reduces her stock basis to $8,000.

If Liberty instead reports only $5,000 of ordinary income and a $7,000 capital loss, $10,000 of the distribution is taxable. The ordinary income increases the stock's basis to $25,000 ($20,000 + $5,000). Because the distribution exceeds the stock's adjusted basis by $10,000 ($35,000 − $25,000), Sandy recognizes a capital gain on the excess distribution. The distribution not included in Sandy's income ($25,000) reduces her stock basis to zero at year-end. Because the stock basis after the distribution is zero, Sandy cannot deduct the $7,000 capital loss in the current year. She must wait until she regains a positive stock basis (or obtains debt basis by lending money to the corporation). ◀

SELF-STUDY QUESTION

Can distributions that exceed stock basis be tax-free to the extent of shareholder loans?

ANSWER

No. Although the amount of deductible losses can be increased by the amount of shareholder loans, nontaxable distributions are strictly limited to stock basis. Also, distributions never reduce debt basis.

If an S corporation distributes appreciated property to its shareholders, the S corporation recognizes gain as if it sold the property.[53] The corporation recognizes no loss, however, when it distributes property that has declined in value. The gain recognized on the distribution may be taxed at the corporate level as part of the S corporation's built-in gains or excess net passive income. The gain also becomes part of the S corporation's ordinary income or loss, or is passed through as a separately stated item, depending on the type of

[52] Secs. 1368(b) and (d).

[53] Sec. 311(b).

property distributed and the character of the gain recognized. After this recognition occurs, the distributed property causes no further taxation provided the sum of the money plus the FMV of the noncash property distributed does not exceed the shareholder's stock basis. The shareholder's stock basis is reduced by the FMV of the distribution, and the shareholder takes a FMV basis in the distributed property.

ADDITIONAL COMMENT

The distribution of appreciated stock in Example C:11-26 produced income to Echo, which passed through to Tad. A similar distribution by a C corporation would result in a double tax by causing income recognition to both Echo and Tad.

Tad owns 100% of Echo Corporation, which always has been an S corporation. Tad's stock basis at the beginning of the current year is $50,000. Echo reports $30,000 of ordinary income for this year (exclusive of the effects of a property distribution to Tad). On December 1, Echo distributes some Cable Corporation stock to Tad. The stock cost $40,000 and has a $100,000 FMV, and Echo has held it as an investment for three years. Echo reports $60,000 ($100,000 − $40,000) of capital gain from distributing the stock. Tad reports $30,000 of ordinary income and $60,000 of long-term capital gain from Echo's current year activities. Tad's stock basis increases to $140,000 ($50,000 + $30,000 + $60,000). The distribution is free of further taxation because the $140,000 stock basis exceeds the $100,000 distribution. The stock basis is $40,000 ($140,000 − $100,000) at year-end. Tad takes a $100,000 FMV basis in the Cable stock. ◀

CORPORATIONS HAVING ACCUMULATED EARNINGS AND PROFITS

PRIOR RULES. Under pre-1983 rules, a corporation's undistributed taxable income was taxed to its shareholders as a deemed distribution at year-end. This income accumulated in a **previously taxed income (PTI)** account, which can be a source of S corporation distributions. For simplicity in this text, however, the following discussion assumes that S corporation status occurs after 1982 and thus ignores the implications of PTI.

KEY POINT

The AAA represents the cumulative income and loss recognized in post-1982 S corporation years. To the extent the AAA is positive and sufficient basis exists in the stock, distributions from an S corporation are nontaxable and reduce stock basis.

CURRENT RULES. Under current (post-1982) rules, some S corporations have a post-1982 accumulated E&P balance earned while a C corporation. Part or all of a distribution may be treated as made from this balance. The current rules, however, also require S corporations that have accumulated E&P balances to maintain an **accumulated adjustments account (AAA)** from which they make most of their distributions. The existence of accumulated E&P and AAA balances makes the tax treatment of cash and property distributions somewhat more complicated than do the rules explained in the preceding section.

MONEY DISTRIBUTIONS. For corporations making a post-1982 S election and having an accumulated E&P balance, money distributions come from the two tiers of earnings illustrated in Table C:11-1. The corporation makes distributions from the first tier until it is exhausted. The corporation then makes distributions from the second tier until that tier is used up. Amounts distributed after the two tiers of earnings are exhausted reduce the shareholder's remaining basis in his or her S corporation stock. Any additional amounts distributed once stock basis has been reduced to zero are taxed to the shareholder as a capital gain. The corporation usually maintains these tiers as working paper accounts and not as general ledger accounts.

The AAA is the cumulative total of the ordinary income or loss and separately stated items accumulated for the S period but excluding tax-exempt income and expenses related to its production. The S period is the most recent continuous period during which the corporation has been an S corporation. No tax years beginning before 1983 are included in this period.[54]

The year-end AAA balance is determined as follows:

AAA balance at the beginning of the year
Plus: Ordinary income
             Separately stated income and gain items (except for tax-exempt income)

---

[54] Sec. 1368(e). An S corporation without accumulated E&P need not maintain the AAA to determine the tax effect of its distributions. If an S corporation having no E&P subsequently acquires E&P in a transaction where it assumes tax attributes under Sec. 381(a) (e.g., a merger), the corporation must calculate its AAA at the merger date to determine the tax effects of post-merger distributions. To accomplish this calculation, a firm may need to make calculations back to the original S election date. To reduce this hardship, the IRS, in the Form 1120S instructions, recommends that all S corporations maintain AAA information.

▼ TABLE C:11-1

**Source of Distributions Made by S Corporations Having
Accumulated Earnings and Profits**

		Types of Distributions Coming from Tier		
Tier	Classification	Money Distributions?	Property (Noncash) Distributions?	Taxable or Nontaxable Distributions?
1	Accumulated adjustments account	Yes	Yes	Nontaxable[a]
2	Accumulated E&P	Yes	Yes	Taxable
3	Basis of S corporation stock	Yes	Yes	Nontaxable[a]
4	Excess over stock basis	Yes	Yes	Taxable

[a] These distributions reduce the basis of the S corporation stock. Although generally nontaxable, gain can be recognized if the amount of money plus the FMV of the noncash property distributed exceeds the shareholder's adjusted basis in the S corporation stock as indicated in Tier 4.

Minus:	Distributions made from AAA (see first bullet item below)
	Ordinary loss
	Separately stated loss and deduction items (except for expenses or losses related to the production of tax-exempt income)
	Expenses not deductible in determining ordinary income (loss) and not chargeable to the capital account

AAA balance at the end of the year

Four differences exist between the positive and negative adjustments required for the AAA and the basis calculation for S corporation stock:

▶ Distributions not included in gross income reduce *stock* basis *before* other negative adjustments. Distributions reduce the AAA *after* other negative adjustments unless the other negative adjustments, when netted against positive adjustments, produce a "net negative adjustment." In this case, positive adjustments increase the AAA and negative adjustments other than distributions reduce the AAA to the extent of the positive adjustments. Then, distributions reduce the AAA before the net negative adjustment, and the net negative adjustment reduces the AAA after the distribution.[55]

▶ Tax-exempt income does not increase the AAA but increases the basis of S corporation stock.

▶ Nondeductible expenses that reduce stock basis also reduce the AAA except for expenses related to the production of tax-exempt income and federal income taxes related to a C corporation tax year.

TYPICAL MISCONCEPTION

Even though stock basis cannot be less than zero, the AAA can be negative if cumulative losses exceed cumulative profits.

▶ The AAA balance can be negative (e.g., when the cumulative losses exceed the cumulative profits), but a shareholder's stock basis cannot be less than zero.

Allocation of the AAA balance to individual distributions occurs at year-end after taking into account current year income and loss items. In general, the AAA balance is allocated ratably to individual distributions within a tax year (other than distributions coming from E&P) based on the amount of money or FMV of noncash property distributed.

---

[55] Reg. Secs. 1.1367-1(f) and 1.1368-2(a)(5). This ordering for AAA preserves tax-free treatment for S corporation earnings from prior years distributed in the loss year.

Corporations also maintain an Other Adjustments Account (OAA) if they have accumulated E&P at year-end. The corporation increases this account for tax-exempt income earned and decreases it by expenses incurred in earning the tax-exempt income, distributions out of the OAA, and federal taxes paid by the S corporation that are attributable to C corporation tax years. The effect of creating a separate account for tax-exempt income earned by companies having accumulated E&P is that the AAA is determined by taking into account only the taxable portion of the S corporation's income and any expenses and losses other than those related to the production of the tax-exempt income. Although the corporation reports the OAA balance on page 4 of the Form 1120S, it is not an accumulated earnings account. Municipal bond interest and other forms of tax-exempt income (net of related deductions) become part of the stock basis and thus appear after accumulated E&P in the distribution order. A corporation having an accumulated E&P balance might consider having the tax-exempt income-producing property owned at the shareholder level rather than at the corporate level.

EXAMPLE C:11-27▶ Omega Corporation is an S corporation with one shareholder, George. George's stock basis at the beginning of the current year is $22,000. Omega reports the following results for the current year:

Ordinary loss	$10,000
Dividend income	2,000

In addition, at the beginning of the current year, the corporation has a $12,000 AAA balance and a $4,000 accumulated E&P balance. In December of the current year, Omega distributes $7,500 cash to George. Because the ordinary loss and dividend income produce an $8,000 ($2,000 − $10,000) net negative adjustment, the predistribution AAA remains at $12,000 while the $2,000 dividend increases predistribution stock basis. Accordingly, the predistribution balances are as follows:

	Stock Basis	AAA	E&P
Beginning balances	$22,000	$12,000	$4,000
Dividend income	2,000	2,000	
Partial ordinary loss		(2,000)	
Predistribution balance	$24,000	$12,000	$4,000

Given these predistribution balances, the distribution has the following effects:

	Stock Basis	AAA	E&P
Predistribution balance	$24,000	$12,000	$4,000
AAA distribution	(7,500)	(7,500)	
Ordinary loss	(10,000)		
Net negative adjustment		(8,000)	
Ending balance	$ 6,500	($3,500)	$4,000

Because the net negative adjustment to the AAA occurs after the distribution, the entire distribution comes out of the AAA, and none comes out of accumulated E&P. Also, the distribution does not exceed the predistribution stock basis. Thus, the entire distribution is nontaxable. ◀

EXAMPLE C:11-28▶ Sigma Corporation, an S corporation, reports the following results during the current year:

Ordinary income	$30,000
Long-term capital gain	15,000
Municipal bond interest income	5,000
Dividend from domestic corporation	3,000
Charitable contribution	8,000

Sigma's sole shareholder, Silvia, has a $60,000 stock basis on January 1. On January 1, Sigma has a $40,000 AAA balance, a $27,000 accumulated E&P balance, and a zero OAA balance. Sigma makes $50,000 cash distributions to Silvia, its sole shareholder, on June 1 and December 1. The stock basis, AAA, OAA, and accumulated E&P activity for the year (before any distributions) is summarized as follows:

TYPICAL
MISCONCEPTION

If shareholders sell their S corporation stock, the AAA account
remains with the S corporation.
But if an S election terminates,
other than for the post-termination transition period, the AAA
disappears.

	Stock Basis	AAA	E&P	OAA
Beginning balance	$ 60,000	$40,000	$27,000	$ –0–
Ordinary income	30,000	30,000		
Long-term capital gain	15,000	15,000		
Municipal bond interest	5,000			5,000
Dividend income	3,000	3,000		
Charitable contribution		(8,000)		
Predistribution balance	$113,000	$80,000	$27,000	$5,000

The $80,000 AAA balance is allocated ratably to each of the distributions as follows:

$$\$40,000 = \$50,000 \times \frac{\$80,000}{\$50,000 + \$50,000}$$

The charitable contribution does not reduce the predistribution stock basis but does reduce the predistribution AAA because the reduction does not produce a net negative adjustment. Accordingly, $40,000 of each distribution comes out of AAA. This portion of the distribution is nontaxable because the AAA distributions in total are less than the stock's $113,000 predistribution basis. The remaining $10,000 ($50,000 − $40,000) of each distribution comes out of accumulated E&P and is taxable as dividend income. Accumulated E&P is reduced to $7,000 ($27,000 − $20,000) at year-end. The OAA balance reported on Form 1120S is not affected by the distribution because the accumulated E&P has not been exhausted. The stock's basis is $25,000 ($113,000 − $80,000 − $8,000) at year-end because a dividend distribution from accumulated E&P does not reduce its basis, but the charitable contribution does. After adjustment for the distribution, the AAA is zero. The effects of the distribution are summarized below:

	Stock Basis	AAA	E&P	OAA
Predistribution balance	$113,000	$80,000	$27,000	$5,000
AAA distribution	(80,000)	(80,000)		
E&P distribution			(20,000)	
Charitable contribution	(8,000)			
Ending balance	$ 25,000	$ –0–	$ 7,000	$5,000	◄

PROPERTY DISTRIBUTIONS. Property distributions (other than money) made by an S corporation having accumulated E&P trigger gain recognition according to the general rules described on page C:11-28. The FMV of the noncash property distributed reduces AAA.

TAX STRATEGY TIP

If a shareholder has NOL carryforwards that are about to expire,
the election to treat distributions
as dividend income to the extent
of E&P (as opposed to AAA distributions) may make sense. Also,
after 2012, the 15% maximum
tax rate on dividends is due to
expire. Thus, shareholders may
want to recognize dividend
income before ordinary tax rates
again apply to dividends.

DISTRIBUTION ORDERING ELECTIONS. An S corporation can elect to change the distribution order of E&P and the AAA. Specifically, the S corporation can elect to skip over the AAA in determining the source of a cash or property distribution, in which case distributions will come from accumulated E&P and then AAA. This election permits the S corporation to distribute Subchapter C E&P so as to avoid the excess net passive income tax and termination of the S election. The Tax Planning Considerations section of this chapter contains further discussion of this election.

POST-TERMINATION TRANSITION PERIOD. Nontaxable distributions of money made during the S corporation's post-termination transition period can be made to those shareholders who owned S corporation stock on the termination date. These distributions come first from the former S corporation's AAA balance and then from current and accumulated E&P. The amounts from the AAA are nontaxable and reduce the shareholder's stock basis.[56] The AAA balance disappears when the post-termination period ends. Even though the profits earned during the S election period no longer can be distributed tax-free from the AAA after the post-termination period ends, they still can be distributed tax-free to the extent of the shareholder's stock basis once the corporation

---

[56] Sec. 1371(e).

Topic Review C:11-4

Taxation of S Corporation Income and Distributions

Taxation of Income to the Corporation

1. Unlike with a partnership, special entity level taxes apply to an S corporation.
   a. Built-in gains tax: applicable to the net recognized built-in gain of an S corporation that formerly was a C corporation and that made its S election after December 31, 1986.
   b. Excess net passive income tax: applicable to S corporations that have Subchapter C E&P at year-end and that earn passive investment income exceeding 25% of gross receipts during the tax year.
   c. LIFO recapture tax: imposed when a C corporation that uses the LIFO inventory method in its final C corporation tax year makes an S election.

Allocation of Income to the Shareholders

1. Income and gains are allocated based on the number of shares of stock owned by each shareholder on each day of the tax year.
2. Termination of the S election or termination of the shareholder's interest in the S corporation during the tax year requires the tax year to be divided into two parts. The S corporation can elect to allocate the income or gain according to the general rule in (1) or the accounting methods used by the corporation.

Shareholder Distributions

1. Income and gain allocated to the shareholder increase the basis of the S corporation stock. For any S corporation that does not have an E&P balance, the amount of money plus the FMV of any noncash property distributed is nontaxable provided it does not exceed the shareholder's stock basis, determined before negative adjustments. The corporation recognizes gain (but not loss) when it distributes noncash property. The gain passes through to the shareholders.
2. If the S corporation made the S election after 1982 and has accumulated E&P, two earnings tiers must be maintained: the AAA and accumulated E&P. Distributions come from each tier in succeeding order until the tier is exhausted. Distributions out of accumulated E&P are taxable to the shareholder as dividends. Other distributions are nontaxable unless stock basis is reduced to zero, in which case the shareholder recognizes capital gain on the excess distribution.

distributes its current and accumulated E&P. Any distributions made from current or accumulated E&P and noncash distributions made during the post-termination transition period are taxable.

Topic Review C:11-4 summarizes the taxation of S corporation income and gains that pass through to the shareholders and the treatment of S corporation distributions.

STOP & THINK

Question: Special earnings tracking rules apply to S corporations that formerly were C corporations. Why do we need to have these special rules, which add complexity to the distribution topic?

Solution: Former C corporations that were profitable usually have an accumulated E&P balance when they become an S corporation. These earnings have never been taxed as a dividend to the corporation's shareholders. If separate tracking of the S corporation earnings (AAA) and C corporation earnings (accumulated E&P) did not occur, it would be impossible to determine which cash and property distributions came from S corporation earnings and which ones came from C corporation earnings, thereby frustrating the government's ability to collect taxes on distributed E&P.

OTHER RULES

In addition to the differences discussed above, S corporations differ from C corporations in a number of other ways. As discussed below, these differences include tax preference items and other alternative minimum tax (AMT) adjustments, expenses owed by the S corporation to a shareholder, related party sales and exchanges, and fringe benefits paid by the S corporation to a shareholder-employee.

TAX PREFERENCE ITEMS AND OTHER AMT ADJUSTMENTS

The S corporation is not subject to the corporate AMT. Instead, the S corporation computes and passes through tax preference items contained in Sec. 57(a) to its shareholders. The shareholders then include these tax preference items in their individual AMT calculations. Allocation of the tax preference items occurs on a daily basis unless the corporation makes one of the two special elections to allocate the items based on the corporation's tax accounting methods.

Section 56(a) prescribes a number of adjustments to the tax reporting of certain transactions and occurrences for AMT purposes from that used for income tax purposes. As with tax preference items, these special AMT adjustments pass through to the S corporation's shareholders to be included in their individual AMT calculations.

S corporations do not have to make an adjustment for the difference between adjusted current earnings and preadjustment alternative minimum taxable income that a C corporation makes in calculating its AMT liability. For certain corporations, this difference may make an S election attractive.[57]

TRANSACTIONS INVOLVING SHAREHOLDERS AND OTHER RELATED PARTIES

The Sec. 267(a)(2) related party transaction rules deny a payor a deduction for an expense paid to a related payee when a mismatching of the expense and income items occurs because of differences in accounting methods. A number of related party situations directly involve S corporations. Some of these transactions involve two S corporations or an S corporation and a C corporation where the same shareholders directly or indirectly own more than 50% of the value of each corporation's stock. Section 267(a)(2), for example, prevents an S corporation using the accrual method from currently deducting a year-end expense accrued for an item owed to a second S corporation that uses the cash method when the same shareholders own both corporations. The first S corporation can deduct the expense on the day the second S corporation includes the income in its gross income.

The S corporation, being a pass-through entity, is subject to Sec. 267(e), which extends the Sec. 267(a)(2) related party transaction rules described above to any payment made by the S corporation to *any* person who directly or indirectly owns S corporation stock. This rule prevents the S corporation from deducting a payment to be made to one of its shareholders or to someone who indirectly owns such stock until the payee reports the income. Payments made to the S corporation by a person who directly or indirectly owns S corporation stock are similarly restricted.

EXAMPLE C:11-29▶
Vassar Corporation, an S corporation, uses the accrual method of accounting and a calendar tax year. On September 1, 2011, Vassar borrows $50,000 from Joan, a cash basis taxpayer who owns 10% of the Vassar stock. Joan charges interest at an 8% annual rate. At year-end, Vassar accrues $1,000 of interest expense on the loan. The corporation pays six months of interest (including the $1,000 of accrued interest) to Joan on April 1, 2012. Vassar cannot deduct the 2011 accrued interest until it pays the interest in 2012. ◀

Section 267(a)(1) denies a deduction for losses incurred on the sale or exchange of property directly or indirectly between related parties. The same definition of a related party applies for this purpose as in applying Sec. 267(a)(2) to expense transactions involving an S corporation. Any loss disallowed to the seller on the related party sale or exchange can offset gains realized by the purchaser on a subsequent sale or exchange.

FRINGE BENEFITS PAID TO A SHAREHOLDER-EMPLOYEE

The S corporation is not treated as a corporate taxpayer with respect to many fringe benefits paid to 2% shareholders.[58] Instead, the S corporation is treated the same as a partnership,

---

[57] Sec. 56(g)(6).
[58] Section 1372(b) defines a 2% shareholder as any person who directly or indirectly owns on any day of the S corporation's tax year more than 2% of its outstanding stock or stock possessing more than 2% of its voting power. The Sec. 318 stock attribution rules apply to determine whether the 2% threshold has been exceeded.

TYPICAL MISCONCEPTION

Most fringe benefits provided by a C corporation are deductible to the corporation and nontaxable to the employee. However, fringe benefits paid to a more-than-2% shareholder-employee of an S corporation are in many cases nondeductible unless taxable to the shareholder-employee as compensation.

and a 2% shareholder is treated as a partner of such partnership.[59] Because of this restriction, many fringe benefits paid to a 2% shareholder-employee of an S corporation are taxable as compensation to the shareholder and deductible by the corporation if the benefit is not excludible from the shareholder's the gross income. Shareholders owning 2% or less of the S corporation stock are treated as ordinary employees.

The special fringe benefit rules apply only to statutory fringe benefits. They do not apply to stock options, qualified retirement plans, and nonqualified deferred compensation. The fringe benefits limited by the more-than-2%-shareholder rule include group term life insurance premiums (Sec. 79), accident and health benefit plan insurance premiums and payments (Secs. 105 and 106), meals and lodging furnished by the employer (Sec. 119), and cafeteria plan benefits (Sec. 125). Fringe benefits that may be excluded by more-than-2%-shareholders include compensation for injuries and sickness (Sec. 104), educational assistance program benefits (Sec. 127), dependent care assistance program benefits (Sec. 129), and certain other fringe benefits (Sec. 132). For purposes of the Sec. 162(l) above-the-line deduction for self-employed taxpayer's health insurance premiums, a more-than-2%-shareholder is deemed to be self-employed.

EXAMPLE C:11-30 ▶

Bill and his wife Cathy equally own Edison Corporation, an S corporation. Edison employs Bill and ten other individuals. All employees receive group term life insurance benefits based on their annual salaries. All employees except Bill can qualify for the Sec. 79 group term life insurance premium exclusion. Bill is treated as a partner and, therefore, does not qualify as an employee. Bill's premiums are treated as compensation and taxable to Bill. Edison can deduct the premiums paid to all its employees, including Bill. Because Bill is treated as self-employed under the 2% shareholder rules, he can deduct a portion of the premiums paid on the health insurance as a "for" AGI deduction under the Sec.162(l) rules applicable to health insurance payments made by all self-employed individuals. ◀

TAX PLANNING CONSIDERATIONS

ELECTION TO ALLOCATE INCOME BASED ON THE S CORPORATION'S ACCOUNTING METHODS

As a general rule, the S corporation's ordinary income or loss and separately stated items are allocated based on the amount of stock owned by each shareholder on each day of the S corporation's tax year. A special "closing of books" election allows the income to be allocated based on the S corporation's accounting methods when the S election terminates or when a shareholder terminates or substantially reduces his or her entire interest in the S corporation.[60] The use of the S corporation's tax accounting method to allocate the year's profit or loss can permit income shifting among shareholders.

EXAMPLE C:11-31 ▶

At the beginning of the current year (not a leap year), Rod and Dana equally own Apex Corporation, an S corporation. During the current year, Apex reports ordinary income of $146,000. On March 31 of the current year (the 90th day of Apex's tax year), Dana sells all his Apex stock to Randy. Apex earns $125,000 of its ordinary income after March 31 of the current year. Rod is allocated $73,000 ($146,000 × 0.50) of ordinary income. His income allocation is the same whether the corporation uses the daily allocation method or the special allocation election. In total, Dana and Randy are allocated $73,000 of ordinary income. Dana and Randy can allocate the ordinary income amount in the following ways:

---

[59] Sec. 1372(a).
[60] The shareholder, however, still can be a creditor, director, or employee of the corporation. Sections 1362(e) and 1377(a) prevent the daily allocation method from applying to any items resulting from a sale or exchange of 50% or more of the S corporation's stock during an S termination year.

	Daily Allocation	Closing of Books Election

$$\text{Dana: } \$146,000 \times \frac{1}{2} \times \frac{90}{365} = \$18,000 \qquad (\$146,000 - \$125,000) \times \frac{1}{2} = \$10,500$$

$$\text{Randy: } \$146,000 \times \frac{1}{2} \times \frac{275}{365} = \$55,000 \qquad \$125,000 \times \frac{1}{2} = \$62,500$$

The shifting of the $7,500 in income from Dana ($18,000 − $10,500) to Randy ($62,500 − $55,000) under the special election also reduces Dana's adjusted basis for his Apex stock when determining his gain or loss on the sale. The $7,500 difference between the income allocations under the two methods may be a point for negotiation between Dana and Randy, particularly if their marginal tax rates differ. ◀

By electing to use the S corporation's tax accounting method to allocate profits or losses between the C short year and S short year in the termination year, the corporation can shift losses into an S short year where the shareholders obtain an immediate benefit at a marginal tax rate of up to 35% (in 2011), or it can shift profits into a C short year to take advantage of the 15% and 25% marginal corporate tax rates. The C corporation, however, must annualize its short-year income in determining its tax liability.

EXAMPLE C:11-32▶ Delta Corporation has been an S corporation for several years using a calendar year as its tax year. The corporation has one shareholder whose marginal tax rate is 35%. Delta's S election terminates on July 1. The S short year includes January 1 through June 30, and the C short year includes July 1 through December 31. Total ordinary income this year is $10,000. If the corporation closes its books on June 30, $40,000 of ordinary loss is allocable to the S short year, and $50,000 of ordinary income is allocable to the C short year. Assuming each month has 30 days, the following income allocations are possible:

Period	Daily Allocation	Closing of Books Election
S short year	$ 5,000	($40,000)
C short year	5,000	50,000
Total	$10,000	$10,000

With the daily allocation, one-half the income is taxed to the shareholder, and the other half is taxed to the C corporation.[61] The daily allocation method causes the shareholder's tax to be $1,750 ($5,000 × 0.35) on the pass-through income and the C corporation's tax to be $750 ($5,000 × 2 × 0.15 × 0.5) on its annualized income, for a total tax of $2,500. By closing the books, the corporation passes the $40,000 S short year loss through to its shareholder and is taxed on the $50,000 C short year income as a C corporation. This method provides the shareholder with a $14,000 ($40,000 pass-through loss × 0.35) tax savings and causes the C corporation's tax to be $11,125 ($22,250 tax on $100,000 of annualized income × 0.5), for a net tax savings of $2,875 ($14,000 − $11,125). Thus, in this situation, the closing of books method provides the greater overall tax advantage ($2,875 vs. $2,500). ◀

INCREASING THE BENEFITS FROM S CORPORATION LOSSES

At the shareholder level, the deduction for S corporation pass-through losses is limited to the S corporation stock basis plus the basis of debt owed by the S corporation to the shareholder. Pass-through losses exceeding this limitation carry over to a subsequent tax year when the shareholder regains stock or debt basis. If the shareholder expects his or her marginal tax rate to be the same or lower in a carryover tax year, the shareholder should consider either increasing his or her stock basis or loaning additional funds to the corporation before the end of the current tax year. Conversely, if the shareholder never expects the loans to be repaid, he or she should not lend the S corporation additional amounts just to secure an additional tax deduction, which is worth at most 35 cents (at 2011 rates) for

---

[61] Section 1362(e)(5)(A) requires calculation of the tax liability for the C short year to be based on the annualized income of the former S corporation (see Chapter C:3 for a discussion of annualization).

each dollar loaned. If the shareholder expects his or her marginal tax rate to be higher in future tax years, the shareholder should consider deferring additional capital contributions or loans until after the end of the current tax year.

EXAMPLE C:11-33 ▶

KEY POINT

If an S corporation shareholder has losses that have been suspended due to lack of basis, either contributions to capital or bona fide loans to the corporation will create the necessary basis to use the losses.

Nancy owns 100% of Bailey Corporation, an S corporation. Bailey expects a $100,000 ordinary loss in the current year. Nancy's stock basis (before adjustment for the current loss) is $35,000. Bailey also owes Nancy $25,000. Nancy's current marginal tax rate is 35%, but she expects her marginal tax rate to decline to 15% next year. Nancy should consider making $40,000 [$100,000 loss − ($35,000 stock basis + $25,000 debt basis)] of additional capital contributions or loans before the end of the current year to obtain an additional $8,000 [(0.35 − 0.15) × $40,000] of tax benefits from deducting the loss in the current year rather than next year. If Nancy instead expects her marginal tax rates to be 15% in the current year and 35% next year, she can defer $8,000 [(0.35 − 0.15) × $40,000] of tax benefits (less the time value of money for one year) by postponing her capital contributions or loans until next year. Alternatively, Nancy could use the loss carryover to offset profits reported next year. These profits would restore part or all of her debt basis (and possibly increase her stock basis). The stock basis then would be partially or fully offset by the $40,000 loss carryover. ◀

The S corporation loss carryover is available only to the shareholder who held the stock when the loss occurred. A shareholder should consider increasing the stock basis to take advantage of the carryover before selling the stock. The purchasing shareholder does not acquire the carryover.

PASSIVE INCOME REQUIREMENTS

The S corporation can earn an unlimited amount of passive income each year without incurring any penalty provided it has no E&P accumulated in a C corporation tax year (known as Subchapter C E&P) at the end of its tax year. Thus, a corporation can make an S election to avoid the personal holding company tax that otherwise might apply to a C corporation's passive income.

S corporations that have operated as C corporations and have accumulated Subchapter C E&P are potentially liable for the excess net passive income tax. In addition, their S election may terminate if the passive investment income exceeds 25% of gross receipts for three consecutive tax years. The S corporation can avoid both of these possible problems by making a special election under Sec. 1368(e)(3) to distribute its entire Subchapter C E&P balance to its shareholders. A corporation that elects to distribute Subchapter C E&P before distributing from its accumulated adjustments account (AAA) can make a second special election to treat part or all of this "distribution" as a deemed dividend, which is deemed distributed to the shareholders and immediately contributed by the shareholders to the corporation on the last day of the corporation's tax year.[62] Such an election requires no cash outlay. The distribution, however, results in a tax cost for the shareholders who pay tax on the resulting deemed dividend income. To the shareholders, the cost of the election can be small if the accumulated E&P balance is insignificant or if the shareholder has a current year NOL (excluding the distribution) or an NOL carryover. The tax cost also is low given the current 15% maximum tax rate on dividends. The ultimate long-run benefit, however, may be great because it permits the S corporation to earn an unlimited amount of passive investment income free from corporate taxes in subsequent tax years.

EXAMPLE C:11-34 ▶

Hawaii Corporation incorporated 12 years ago and operated for a number of years as a C corporation, during which time it accumulated $30,000 of E&P. Most of Hawaii's gross income now comes from rentals and interest, constituting passive investment income. Hawaii makes an S election starting in the current year. The excess net passive income tax will apply in the current year if Hawaii's rentals and interest exceed 25% of its gross receipts for the year unless the corporation elects to distribute the accumulated E&P and then distributes the earnings by the end of the currrent year. ◀

---

[62] Reg. Sec. 1.1368-1(f)(3).

S corporations that earn rental income also can avoid the passive income tax and the possibility of having its election terminated if the corporation renders significant services to the occupant of the space or if the corporation incurs significant costs in the rental business.[63] Whether the corporation performs significant services or incurs substantial costs in the rental business depends on the facts and circumstances including, but not limited to, the number of persons employed to provide the services and the types and amounts of costs and expenses incurred (other than depreciation).

EXAMPLE C:11-35 ▶

Assume the same facts as in Example C:11-34 except Hawaii Corporation provides significant services to its tenants in connection with its rental activities. Because the services are significant, Hawaii has a passive income problem only if its interest income exceeds 25% of its gross receipts. If the 25% threshold is not exceeded, Hawaii can avoid having to distribute its Subchapter C E&P in the current year. ◀

S corporations that experience a passive income problem in two consecutive tax years should carefully monitor their passive income in the next year. If they see that their passive income for the third year will exceed the 25% threshold, they should elect to distribute their accumulated Subchapter C E&P before year-end. This strategy not only will prevent loss of the S election but also will avoid having to pay the Sec. 1375 tax.

COMPLIANCE AND PROCEDURAL CONSIDERATIONS

MAKING THE ELECTION

A corporation makes the S election by filing Form 2553 (Election by a Small Business Corporation). Any person authorized to sign the S corporation's tax return under Sec. 6037 can sign the election form. The corporation files Form 2553 with the IRS Service Center designated in the instructions. The IRS can treat a late election as timely made if the corporation can show reasonable cause.[64]

A shareholder can consent to the S election either on Form 2553 or on a separate consent statement signed by the shareholder and attached to the corporation's election form. Regulation Sec. 1.1362-6(b) outlines other information that must be provided with a separate consent. The IRS can grant extensions of time for filing shareholder consents to the S election.[65]

A corporation makes a Sec. 444 election to use a fiscal year on Form 8716, which the corporation must file by the earlier of (1) the fifteenth day of the fifth month following the month that includes the first day of the tax year for which the election will first be effective or (2) the due date for the income tax return resulting from the election.[66] The corporation must attach a copy of Form 8716 to Form 1120S for the first tax year for which the Sec. 444 election is effective. A corporation desiring to make a Sec. 444 election also must state its intention in a statement attached to its S election form (Form 2553).[67]

OBJECTIVE 11

Apply the procedures for filing an S corporation tax return

FILING THE CORPORATE TAX RETURN

All S corporations, whether or not they owe taxes under Secs. 1374 or 1375, must file a tax return if they exist for part or all of the tax year. An S corporation must file its corporate tax return not later than the fifteenth day of the third month following the end of the tax year.[68] The S corporation reports its results on Form 1120S (U.S. Income Tax Return for an S Corporation). A completed S corporation tax return and the facts supporting the return appear in Appendix B. An S corporation is allowed an automatic six-month extension of

---

[63] According to Reg. Sec. 1.1362-2(c)(5)(ii)(B)(2), however, significant services are not rendered and substantial costs are not incurred in connection with net leases.
[64] Sec. 1362(b)(5). Also see footnote 16.

[65] Reg. Sec. 1.1362-6(b)(3)(iii).
[66] Temp. Reg. Sec. 1.444-3T(b)(1).
[67] Temp. Reg. Sec. 1.444-3T(b)(3).
[68] Sec. 6072(b).

time for filing its tax return by filing Form 7004 (Application for Automatic Extension of Time to File Certain Business Income Tax, Information, and Other Returns), also illustrated in Appendix B.[69]

EXAMPLE C:11-36 ▶ Simpson Corporation, an S corporation, uses the calendar year as its tax year. Its tax return generally is due on March 15. Simpson can file Form 7004 and obtain an automatic six-month extension for the return, thereby extending its due date until September 15. ◀

All S corporations that file a tax return must furnish each person who is a shareholder at any time during the tax year with pertinent information from the tax return, usually via Form 1120S, Schedule K-1. The corporation must make the Schedule K-1 available to the shareholder not later than the day on which it files its tax return.[70] An individual shareholder reports the S corporation's pass-through ordinary income or loss and certain passive income or loss items on his or her Form 1040, Schedule E. The shareholder reports most separately stated items on other supporting schedules to Form 1040, as illustrated on the Form 1120S, Schedule K-1 presented in Appendix B.

An S corporation is subject to the same basic three-year statute of limitations that applies to other taxpayers. This three-year limitations period applies for purposes of determining the time period during which

▶ The corporation remains liable for assessments of the excess net passive income and built-in gains taxes

▶ The IRS can question the correctness of an S election made for a particular tax year

The limitation period for assessing the income tax liability of an S corporation shareholder (e.g., for an erroneous S corporation loss deduction claimed), however, runs from the date on which the shareholder files his or her return and not from the date the S corporation files its tax return.[71]

If the corporation elects a fiscal year under Sec. 444, it determines the Sec. 7519 required payment on a computation worksheet provided in the instructions for the Form 1120S. The corporation need not make a required payment if the total of such payments for the current year and all preceding years is $500 or less. Amounts equal to or less than the $500 threshold carry over to succeeding years. The required payment is due on or before May 15 regardless of the fiscal year used. The required payment and the computation worksheet must accompany a Form 8752, which also is used to secure a refund of prior Sec. 7519 payments.[72]

OBJECTIVE 12

Determine the estimated tax payments required of an S corporation and its shareholders

ESTIMATED TAX PAYMENTS

S corporations must make estimated tax payments if their estimated tax liability is reasonably expected to be $500 or more.[73] Estimated tax payments are required for the corporate liability attributable to the built-in gains tax (Sec. 1374) and the excess net passive income tax (Sec. 1375). In addition, the S corporation's shareholders must include their income, gain, loss, deduction, and credit pass-through items in their own estimated tax calculations.

The corporate estimated tax payment requirements described for a C corporation in Chapter C:3 also apply to an S corporation's tax liabilities. The required quarterly installment is 25% of the lesser of (1) 100% of the tax shown on the return for the tax year or (2) the sum of 100% of the built-in gains tax shown on the return for the tax year plus 100% of the excess net passive income tax shown on the return for the preceding tax year.

An S corporation cannot use the prior year tax liability exception when determining the required payment to be made with respect to the built-in gains tax. This exception, however, is available with respect to the excess net passive income tax portion of the

---

[69] Reg. Sec. 1.6081-3.
[70] Sec. 6037(b).
[71] *Sheldon B. Bufferd v. CIR*, 71 AFTR 2d 93-573, 93-1 USTC ¶50,038 (USSC, 1993).

[72] Temp. Reg. Sec. 1.7519-2T.
[73] Estimate tax rules appear in Sec. 6655.

required payment without regard to whether the corporation owed any tax in the prior year. All corporations can use the prior year tax liability exception for the excess net passive income tax whether or not they are "large" corporations under Sec. 6655(d)(2). The annualization election of Sec. 6655(e) also is available when determining the quarterly estimated tax payment amounts. An S corporation's failure to make timely estimated tax payments, or a timely final payment when it files the tax return, will trigger interest and penalties.

The S corporation's shareholders must include their ratable share of ordinary income or loss and separately stated items in determining their estimated tax liability. Such amounts are treated as having been received concurrently by the shareholders throughout the S corporation's tax year. Thus, ordinary income or loss and separately stated items for an S corporation tax year that ends with or within the shareholder's tax year are included in the estimated tax calculation to the extent they are attributable to months in the S corporation tax year that precede the month in which the installment is due.[74]

CONSISTENCY RULES

Section 6037(c) requires an S corporation shareholder to report on his or her return a Subchapter S item in a manner consistent with the treatment accorded the item on the S corporation's return. A Subchapter S item is any item (e.g., income, gain, deduction, loss, credit, accounting method, or tax year) of an S corporation where the reporting of the item is more appropriately determined at the corporation level than at the shareholder level. A shareholder must notify the IRS of any inconsistency when the corporation has filed a return but the shareholder's treatment on his return is (or may be) inconsistent with the treatment of the item on the corporation return. Failure to do so may result in the imposition of a negligence penalty under Sec. 6662. Any adjustment required to produce consistency with the corporate return is treated as a mathematical or clerical error for penalty calculation purposes. A similar notification also is required when the corporation has not filed a return. If a shareholder receives incorrect information from the S corporation regarding a Subchapter S item, the shareholder's consistent reporting of the item consistently with the information provided by the corporation generally will eliminate the imposition of any penalty.

SAMPLE S CORPORATION TAX RETURN

A sample S corporation Form 1120S and supporting Schedule K-1 appear in Appendix B, along with the facts supporting the return. Two differences should be noted between the S corporation tax return and a partnership tax return. First, the S corporation tax return provides for the determination of a corporate tax liability and the payment of the special taxes that can be levied on the S corporation. No such items appear in the partnership return. Second, the S corporation return does not require a reconciliation of the shareholders' basis adjustments as occurs on a partnership tax return. Schedule M-1, M-2, and M-3 reconciliations similar to those required of a C corporation are required of an S corporation. Schedule M-1 requires a reconciliation of book income with the income or loss reported on line 23 of Schedule K, which includes not only the ordinary income (loss) amount but also separately stated income and deduction items. For tax years ending on or after December 31, 2006, an S corporation must file Schedule M-3 in lieu of Schedule M-1 if the amount of total assets reported in Schedule L of Form 1120S (Balance Sheet per Books) equals or exceeds $10 million. The S corporation also may file Schedule M-3 voluntarily even if not required to do so. If the corporation files Schedule M-3, in either case, it checks the appropriate box on page 1 of Form 1120S and does not file Schedule M-1. (The sample tax return in Appendix B does not include Schedule M-3.) Schedule M-2 requires a reconciliation of the AAA, OAA, and PTI accounts. (The PTI account pertains to pre-1983 S corporations.) Only S corporations that have an accumulated E&P balance must provide the AAA reconciliation and OAA balance although the IRS recommends that all S corporations maintain AAA and OAA balances.

---

[74] For example, see Ltr. Rul. 8639008 (June 23, 1986).

PROBLEM MATERIALS

DISCUSSION QUESTIONS

C:11-1 List five advantages and five disadvantages of making an S election. Briefly explain each item.

C:11-2 Julio, age 50, is a U.S. citizen who has a 28% marginal tax rate. He has operated the A&B Automotive Parts Company for a number of years as a C corporation. Last year, A&B reported $200,000 of pre-tax profits, from which it paid $50,000 in salary and $25,000 in dividends to Julio. The corporation expects this year's pre-tax profits to be $300,000. To date, the corporation has created no fringe benefits or pension plans for Julio. Julio asks you to explain whether an S corporation election would reduce his taxes. How do you respond to Julio's inquiry?

C:11-3 Celia, age 30, is leaving a major systems development firm to establish her own firm. She will design computer-based systems for small- and medium-sized businesses. Celia will invest $100,000 in the business. She hopes to operate near her breakeven point during her first year, although a small loss is possible. Profits will build up slowly over the next four years until she is earning $150,000 a year in her fifth year. Celia has heard about S corporations and asks you whether the S corporation form would be advisable for her new business. How do you respond to Celia's inquiry?

C:11-4 Lance and Rodney are contemplating starting a new business to manufacture computer software games. They expect to encounter losses in the initial years. Lance's CPA has talked to them about using an S corporation. Rodney, while reading a business publication, encounters a discussion on limited liability companies (LLCs). The article talks about the advantages of using an LLC instead of an S corporation. How would you respond to their inquiry?

C:11-5 Which of the following classifications make a shareholder ineligible to own stock in an S corporation?
   a. U.S. citizen
   b. Domestic corporation
   c. Partnership where all the partners are U.S. citizens
   d. Estate of a deceased U.S. citizen
   e. Grantor trust created by a U.S. citizen
   f. Nonresident alien individual

C:11-6 Which of the following taxes do not apply to an S corporation?
   a. Regular (income) tax
   b. Accumulated earnings tax
   c. Corporate alternative minimum tax
   d. Built-in gains tax
   e. Personal holding company tax
   f. Excess net passive income tax
   g. LIFO recapture tax

C:11-7 Will the following events cause an S election to terminate?
   a. The S corporation earning 100% of its gross receipts in its first tax year from passive sources
   b. The S corporation issuing nonvoting stock that has a dividend preference
   c. The S corporation purchasing 100% of the single class of stock of a second domestic corporation that has conducted business activities for four years
   d. An individual shareholder donating 100 shares of S corporation stock to a charity that is exempt from tax under Sec. 501(c)(3)
   e. The S corporation earning tax-exempt interest income

C:11-8 What is an inadvertent termination? What actions must the S corporation and its shareholders take to correct an inadvertent termination?

C:11-9 After an S corporation revokes or terminates its S election, how long must the corporation wait to make a new election? What circumstances permit an early reelection?

C:11-10 What tax years can a newly created corporation that makes an S election adopt for its first tax year? If a fiscal year is permitted, does it require IRS approval?

C:11-11 At the time Cable Corporation makes its S election, it elects to use a fiscal year based on a Sec. 444 election. What other requirements must Cable satisfy to continue to use its fiscal year election for future tax years?

C:11-12 What are Subchapter C earnings and profits (E&P)? How does the existence of such E&P affect the S corporation's ability to earn passive income?

C:11-13 Explain the procedures for allocating an S corporation's ordinary income or loss to each of the shareholders. What special allocation elections are available?

C:11-14 What limitations apply to the amount of loss pass-through an S corporation shareholder can deduct? What happens to any losses exceeding this limitation? What happens to losses if the shareholder transfers his or her stock?

C:11-15 What actions can an S corporation shareholder take before year-end to increase the amount of the S corporation's losses he or she can deduct in the year they are incurred?

C:11-16 What is a post-termination transition period? What loss carryovers can an S corporation shareholder deduct during this period?

C:11-17 Explain the positive and negative adjustments to the basis of an S corporation shareholder's stock investment and the basis of an S corporation debt owed to the shareholder.

C:11-18 Explain the differences between the tax treatment accorded nonliquidating property distributions made by S corporations and partnerships.

C:11-19 What nonliquidating distributions made by an S corporation are taxable to its shareholders? Tax-free to its shareholders?

C:11-20 What is an accumulated adjustments account (AAA)? What income, gain, loss, and deduction items *do not* affect this account assuming the S corporation has an accumulated E&P balance?

C:11-21 Explain the differences between the way the following items are reported by a C corporation and an S corporation:

a. Ordinary income or loss
b. Dividend income
c. Capital gains and losses
d. Tax-exempt interest income
e. Charitable contributions
f. Nonliquidating property distributions
g. Fringe benefits paid to a shareholder-employee

C:11-22 When is the S corporation's tax return due? What extensions are available for filing the return?

C:11-23 What taxes must an S corporation prepay by making quarterly estimated tax payments? Can a shareholder owning S corporation stock use the corporation's estimated tax payments to reduce the amount of his or her individual estimated tax payments? Explain.

C:11-24 Review the completed C corporation, partnership, and S corporation tax returns presented in Appendix B. List three major tax reporting similarities and three major tax reporting differences in either content or format among the three tax returns.

ISSUE IDENTIFICATION QUESTIONS

C:11-25 Jennelle and Paula are equal partners in the J&P Manufacturing Partnership. The partnership will form J&P Corporation by exchanging the assets and liabilities of the J&P Manufacturing Partnership for all the corporation's stock on September 1 of the current year. The partnership then will liquidate by distributing the J&P Corporation stock equally to Jennelle and Paula. Both shareholders use the calendar year as their tax year and desire that the corporation make an S election. What tax issues should Jennelle and Paula consider with respect to the incorporation?

C:11-26 Williams Corporation has operated as a C corporation for the last seven years. The corporation has assets with a $450,000 adjusted basis and an $800,000 FMV. Liabilities amount to $100,000. Dan Williams, who uses a calendar year as his tax year, owns all the Williams Corporation stock. The corporation uses the accrual method of accounting and a June 30 year-end. Dan's CPA has suggested that he convert the corporation to S corporation status to reduce his total corporate/personal federal income tax liability. Dan would like to complete the conversion on the last day of the corporation's tax year. What tax issues should Dan and his CPA consider with respect to the S election?

C:11-27 Peter owns 50% of Air South Corporation, an air charter service. His S corporation stock basis at beginning of the year is $100,000. Air South has not done well this year and will report an ordinary loss of $375,000. Peter's marginal tax rate for the current year is 35%. What tax issues should Peter consider with respect to the loss?

C:11-28 Glacier Smokeries has been an S corporation since its inception six years ago. On January 1 of the current year, the corporation's two equal shareholders, Adam and Rodney, had adjusted bases of $175,000 and $225,000, respectively, for their S corporation's stock. The shareholders plan to have the corporation distribute land with a $75,000 adjusted basis and a $300,000 FMV in the current year. The shareholders also expect ordinary income to be $125,000 in the current year. What tax issues should Adam and Rodney consider with respect to the distribution?

PROBLEMS

C:11-29 *Comparison of Entity Forms.* Carl Carson, a single taxpayer, owns 100% of Delta Corporation. During 2011, Delta reports $150,000 of taxable income. Carl reports no income other than that earned from Delta, and Carl claims the standard deduction.

a. What is Delta's income tax liability assuming Carl withdraws none of the earnings from the C corporation? What is Carl's income tax liability? What is the total tax liability for the corporation and its shareholder?

b. Assume that Delta instead distributes $80,000 of its after-tax earnings to Carl as a dividend in the current year. What is the total income tax liability for the C corporation and its shareholder?

c. How would your answer to Part a change if Carl withdrew $80,000 from the business in salary? Assume the corporation pays $6,120 of Social Security taxes on the salary, which it can deduct from the $150,000 taxable income amount in Part a. Carl also pays $4,520 (in 2011) of Social Security taxes on the salary, which he cannot deduct.

d. How would your answers to Parts a–c change if Delta were instead an S corporation?

C:11-30 *Making the Election.* Voyles Corporation, a calendar year taxpayer formed five years ago, desires to make an S election beginning in 2011. Sue and Andrea each own one-half of the Voyles stock.

a. How does Voyles make the S election?

b. When can Voyles file its election form?

c. If in Part b the corporation does not file the election in a timely manner, when will the election take effect?

C:11-31 *Termination of the Election.* Orlando Corporation, a calendar year taxpayer, has been an S corporation for several years. On July 9, 2011, Orlando authorizes a second class of nonvoting preferred stock that pays a 10% annual dividend. The corporation issues the stock to Sid on September 13, 2011, to raise additional equity capital. Sid owns no other Orlando stock.

a. Does Orlando's S election terminate? If so, when is the termination effective?

b. What tax returns must Orlando file for 2011? When are they due?

c. How would your answer to Parts a and b change if instead the second class of stock were nonvoting Class B common stock?

C:11-32 *Revocation of the Election.* Tango Corporation, a calendar year taxpayer, has been an S corporation for several years. Tango's business activities have become very profitable in recent years. On June 16, 2011, its sole shareholder, who is in the 35% marginal tax bracket, desires to revoke the S election.

a. How does Tango revoke its S election? When does the revocation take effect?

b. Assume Tango files a prospective revocation effective July 1, 2011. What tax returns are required of Tango for 2011? For 2012? When are these returns due?

c. If the corporation makes a new S election after the revocation, when does it take effect?

C:11-33 *Sale of S Corporation Interest.* Peter and his wife, Alice, own all the stock of Galleon Corporation. Galleon made its S election 12 years ago. Peter and Alice sold one-half their Galleon stock to a partnership owned by Rob and Susan (not husband and wife) at the close of business on December 31, 2011, for a $75,000 profit. What are the tax consequences of the sale transaction for Peter and Alice? For the corporation? As Peter and Alice's CPA, do you have any advice for them if all parties would like the S election to continue?

C:11-34 *Selecting a Tax Year.* Indicate in each of the following independent situations whether the taxpayer can accomplish what is proposed. Provide adequate authority for your answer including any special elections that are needed or requirements that must be satisfied. Assume all individuals use the calendar year as their tax year unless otherwise indicated.

a. Will and Carol form Classic Corporation. They want the corporation to adopt a fiscal year ending January 31 as its tax year to provide a maximum deferral for their income. The corporation makes an S election for its initial tax year ending January 31, 2012.

b. Mark and Dennis have owned and operated the Plastic Corporation for several years. Plastic has used a fiscal year ending June 30 since its organization as a C corporation because it conforms to the corporation's natural business year. The corporation makes an S election for its tax year beginning July 1, 2011.

C:11-35 *Passive Income Tax.* Oliver organized North Corporation 15 years ago. The corporation made an S election last year after it accumulated $60,000 of E&P as a C corporation. As of December 31 of the current year, the corporation has distributed none of its accumulated E&P. In the current year, North reports the following results:

Dividends from domestic corporations	$ 60,000
Rental income	100,000
Services income	50,000
Expenses related to rental income	30,000
Expenses related to services income	15,000
Other expenses	5,000

The corporation has not provided significant services nor incurred substantial costs in connection with earning the rental income. The services income is derived from the active conduct of a trade or business.

a. Is North subject to the excess net passive income tax? If so, what is its tax liability?

b. What is the effect of the excess net passive income tax liability on North's pass-throughs of ordinary income and separately stated items?

c. What advice would you give North regarding its activities?

C:11-36 *Built-in Gains Tax.* Theta Corporation formed 15 years ago. In its first year, it elected to use the cash method of accounting and adopted a calendar year as its tax year. It made an S election on August 15 of last year, effective for Theta's current tax year. At the beginning of the current year, Theta had assets with a $600,000 FMV and a $180,000 adjusted basis. During the current year, Theta reports taxable income of $400,000.

- In the current year, Theta collects all $200,000 of accounts receivables outstanding on January 1 of the current year. The receivables had a zero adjusted basis.
- On February 1, Theta sells an automobile for $3,500. The automobile had a $2,000 adjusted basis and a $3,000 FMV on January 1 of the current year. Theta claimed $800 of MACRS depreciation on the automobile in the current year.
- On March 1, Theta sells land (a Sec. 1231 asset) that it held three years in anticipation of building its own office building for a $35,000 gain. The land had a $45,000 FMV and a $25,000 adjusted basis on January 1 of the current year.
- In the current year, Theta paid $125,000 of accounts payable outstanding on January 1 of the current year. All the payables are deductible expenses.

What is the amount of Theta's built-in gains tax liability?

C:11-37 *Determination of Pass-Throughs and Stock Basis Adjustments.* Mike and Nancy are equal shareholders in MN Corporation, an S corporation. The corporation, Mike, and Nancy are calendar year taxpayers. The corporation has been an S corporation during its entire existence and thus has no accumulated E&P. The shareholders have no loans to the corporation. The corporation incurred the following items in the current year:

Sales	$300,000
Cost of goods sold	140,000
Dividends on corporate investments	10,000
Tax-exempt interest income	3,000
Section 1245 gain (recapture) on equipment sale	22,000
Section 1231 gain on equipment sale	12,000
Long-term capital gain on stock sale	8,000
Long-term capital loss on stock sale	7,000
Short-term capital loss on stock sale	6,000
Depreciation	18,000
Salary to Nancy	20,000
Meals and entertainment expenses	7,800
Interest expense on loans allocable to:	
Business debt	32,000
Stock investments	6,400
Tax-exempt bonds	1,800
Principal payment on business loan	9,000
Charitable contributions	2,000
Distributions to shareholders ($15,000 each)	30,000

a. Compute the S corporation's ordinary income and separately stated items.

b. Show Mike's and Nancy's shares of the items in Part a.

c. Compute Mike's and Nancy's ending stock bases assuming their beginning balances are $100,000 each. When making basis adjustments, apply the adjustments in the order outlined on pages C:11-24 and C:11-25 of the text.

C:11-38 *Allocation of Income to Shareholders.* John owns all the stock of Lucas Corporation, an S corporation. John's basis for the 1,000 shares is $130,000. On June 11 of the current year (assume a non-leap year), John gifts 100 shares of stock to his younger brother Michael, who has been working in the business for one year. Lucas Corporation reports $125,000 of ordinary income for the current year. What amount of income is allocated to John? To Michael?

C:11-39 *Sale of S Corporation Interest.* Al and Ruth each own one-half the stock of Chemical Corporation, an S corporation. During the current year (assume a non-leap year), Chemical earns $15,000 per month of ordinary income. On April 5, Ruth sells her entire stock interest to Patty. The corporation sells a business asset on August 18 and realizes a $75,000 Sec. 1231 gain. What alternatives (if any) exist for allocating Chemical's current year income?

C:11-40 *Allocation of Income to Shareholders.* Toyland Corporation, an S corporation, uses the calendar year as its tax year. Bob, Alice, and Carter own 60, 30, and 10 shares, respectively, of the Toyland stock. Carter's basis for his stock is $26,000 on January 1 of the current year (assume a non-leap year). On June 30, Alice gifted one-half of her stock to Mike. On November 30, Carter sold his stock to Mike for $45,000. Toyland reports the following results for the current year:

Ordinary income	$120,000
Long-term capital loss	10,000
Charitable contributions	6,000

a. What amount of income, loss, or deduction do the four shareholders report (assuming the corporation makes no special allocation election)?

b. What gain or loss does Carter recognize when he sells the Toyland stock?

C:11-41 *Allocation of Income to Shareholders.* Redfern Corporation, a calendar year taxpayer, has been an S corporation for several years. Rod and Kurt each own 50% of Redfern's stock. On July 1 of the current year (assume a non-leap year), Redfern issues additional common stock to Blackfoot Corporation for cash. Rod, Kurt, and Blackfoot each end up owning one-third of Redfern's stock. Redfern reports ordinary income of $125,000 and a short-term capital loss of $15,000 in the current year. Eighty percent of the ordinary income and all the capital loss accrue after Blackfoot purchases its stock. Redfern makes no distributions to its shareholders in the current year. What income and losses do Redfern, Blackfoot, Rod, and Kurt report as a result of the current year's activities?

C:11-42 *Allocation of Income Between Family Members.* Bright Corporation, an S corporation, has been 100% owned by Betty since its creation 12 years ago. The corporation has been profitable in recent years and, in the current year (assume a non-leap year), reports ordinary income of $240,000 after paying Betty a $60,000 salary. On January 1, Betty gifts 15% of her Bright stock to each of her three sons, John, Andrew, and Stephen, hoping they will work in the family business. Betty pays gift taxes on the transfers. The sons are ages 24, 17, and 15 at present and are not currently active in the business. Bright distributes $7,500 in cash to each son and $27,500 in cash to Betty in the current year.

a. What income does Betty, John, Andrew, and Stephen report for the current year as a result of Bright's activities assuming the sons are considered bona fide owners of the stock? How will the income be taxed to the children?

b. Assuming the IRS determines a reasonable salary for Betty to be $120,000, how would your answer to Part a change?

c. How would your answer to Part a change if the sons were not considered bona fide owners of the stock?

C:11-43 *Use of Losses by Shareholders.* Monte and Allie each own 50% of Raider Corporation, an S corporation. Both individuals actively participate in Raider's business. On January 1, Monte and Allie have adjusted bases for their Raider stock of $80,000 and $90,000, respectively. During the current year, Raider reports the following results:

Ordinary loss	$175,000
Tax-exempt interest income	20,000
Long-term capital loss	32,000

Raider's balance sheet at year-end shows the following liabilities: accounts payable, $90,000; mortgage payable, $30,000; and note payable to Allie, $10,000.

a. What income and deductions will Monte and Allie report from Raider's current year activities?

b. What is Monte's stock basis on December 31?

c. What are Allie's stock basis and debt basis on December 31?

d. What loss carryovers are available for Monte and Allie?

e. Explain how the use of the losses in Part a would change if instead Raider were a partnership and Monte and Allie were partners who shared profits, losses, and liabilities equally.

C:11-44 *Use of Loss Carryovers.* Assume the same facts as in Problem C:11-43. Assume further that Raider Corporation reports $75,000 of ordinary income, $20,000 of tax-exempt income, and a $25,000 long-term capital gain in the next year.
   a. What income and deductions will Monte and Allie report from next year's activities?
   b. What is Monte's stock basis on December 31 of next year?
   c. What are Allie's stock basis and note basis on December 31 of next year?
   d. What loss carryovers (if any) are available to Monte and Allie?

C:11-45 *Use of Losses by Shareholders.* Tom owns 100% of Hammer Corporation, an S corporation. Tom has a $100,000 stock basis on January 1. Tom actively participates in Hammer's business. Hammer operating results were not good in the current year, with the corporation reporting an ordinary loss of $175,000. The size of the loss required Tom to lend Hammer $50,000 on August 10 of the current year to provide funds needed for operations. The loan is secured by a Hammer Corporation note. Hammer rebounds during the next year and reports ordinary income of $60,000. Hammer repays the $50,000 note on December 15.
   a. What amount of Hammer's current year loss can Tom deduct on his income tax return?
   b. What is Tom's basis for the Hammer stock and note at the end of the loss year?
   c. What income and deductions will Tom report next year from Hammer's activities and the loan repayment?

C:11-46 *Allocation of Losses to Shareholders.* Harry and Rita formed Alpha Corporation as an S corporation, with each shareholder contributing $10,000 in exchange for stock. In addition, Rita loaned the corporation $7,000, and the corporation borrowed another $8,000 from the bank. In the current year, the corporation incurred a $26,000 operating loss. In the next year, the corporation will earn $16,000 of operating income.
   a. For the current year and next year, determine the pass-through items for each shareholder and each shareholder's stock basis at the end of each year. Also, determine Rita's debt basis at the end of each year.
   b. Same as Part a except the corporation also distributes $6,000 cash to each shareholder at the end of next year.
   c. Assume the same facts as in Part b and that Alpha is a partnership instead of an S corporation. For the current year and next year, determine the pass-through items for each partner and each partner's basis in his or her partnership interest at the end of each year.

C:11-47 *Post-Termination Loss Use.* Stein Corporation, an S corporation, has 400 shares of stock outstanding. Chuck and Linda own an equal number of these shares, and both actively participate in Stein's business. Chuck and Linda each contributed $60,000 when they organized Stein on September 10, 2010. Start-up losses during 2010 resulted in Stein reporting a $210,000 ordinary loss. Stein's activities have since become profitable, and the corporation voluntarily revokes the S election on March 1, 2011, with no prospective revocation date being specified. In 2011, Stein reports $360,000 of taxable income ($30,000 per month). Stein makes no distributions to its shareholders in either year.
   a. What amount of loss can Chuck and Linda deduct in 2010?
   b. What amount of loss do Chuck and Linda carry over to 2011?
   c. If Chuck reported only $5,000 of other business income in 2010, what happens to the "excess" deductible S corporation losses?
   d. What portion of the loss carryover from Part b can Chuck and Linda deduct in 2011? What happens to any unused portion of the loss?
   e. What advice can you offer to Chuck and Linda to enhance their use of the Stein loss?

C:11-48 *Use of Losses by Shareholders.* Tina, a single taxpayer, owns 100% of Rocket Corporation, an S corporation. She has an $80,000 stock basis for her investment on January 1. During the first 11 months of 2011, Rocket reports an ordinary loss of $100,000. The corporation expects an additional $20,000 loss for December. Tina earns $295,000 of ordinary income from her other activities in 2011. She expects her other income to decline to $125,000 in 2012 and continue at that level in future years. The corporation expects 2012 losses to be only $20,000. Rocket projects a $35,000 profit for 2013 and each of the next four years. What advice can you offer Tina about using her Rocket losses and retaining S corporation status in future years? How would your answer change if Tina expected her income from other activities to be $75,000 in 2011 and $295,000 in 2012?

C:11-49 *Stock Basis Adjustment.* For each of the following items, indicate whether the item will increase, decrease, or cause no change in the S corporation's ordinary income (loss), AAA, and in the shareholder's stock basis. The corporation was formed four years ago and made its S election two years ago. During the time it was a C corporation, it accumulated $30,000 of E&P. The corporation has not distributed any of this accumulated E&P.

a. Operating profit
b. Dividend income received from domestic corporation
c. Interest income earned on corporate bond held as an investment
d. Life insurance proceeds paid on death of corporate officer
e. Long-term capital gain
f. Section 1231 loss
g. Section 1245 gain (recapture)
h. Charitable contributions
i. Fines paid for having overweight trucks
j. Depreciation
k. Pension plan contributions for employees
l. Salary paid to owner
m. Premiums paid on life insurance policy in Part d
n. Distribution of money (but not exceeding current year's earnings)

C:11-50 *Taxability of Distributions.* Tammy organized Sweets Corporation in January of the current year, and the corporation immediately elected to be an S corporation. Tammy, who contributed $40,000 in cash to start the business, owns 100% of the corporation's stock. Sweets' current year results are reported below:

Ordinary income	$36,000
Short-term capital loss	5,000

On July 10, Sweets makes a $10,000 cash distribution to Tammy.
a. What income (if any) do Sweets and Tammy recognize as a result of the distribution?
b. What is Tammy's basis for the Sweets stock on December 31?
c. How would your answers to Parts a and b change if Sweets' distribution were instead $80,000?

C:11-51 *Property Distributions.* George and Martha formed Washington Corporation as an S corporation several years ago. George and Martha each have a 50% interest in the corporation. At the beginning of the current year, their stock bases are $45,000 each. In the current year, the corporation earns $40,000 of ordinary income. In addition, the corporation distributes property to George having a $26,000 FMV and a $40,000 adjusted basis and distributes property to Martha having a $26,000 FMV and a $16,000 adjusted basis.
a. Determine what George and Martha recognize in the current year, and determine their ending stock bases. What bases do George and Martha have in the distributed property?
b. What tax planning disadvantages do you see with these property distributions?

C:11-52 *Taxability of Distributions.* Curt incorporates Vogel Corporation on January 15 of the current year. Curt makes a $70,000 capital contribution including land having a $12,000 FMV, and Vogel makes a timely S election for this year. Vogel reports $60,000 of ordinary income, $40,000 of Sec. 1231 gain, $5,000 of tax-exempt interest income, and $3,000 of charitable contributions this year. On December 1, Vogel distributes $5,000 cash plus the land contributed by Curt because the corporation no longer needs it in the business. The land, which had a $10,000 basis and a $12,000 FMV when contributed to the corporation in January, has an $18,000 FMV when distributed.
a. What income do Vogel Corporation and Curt report as a result of the distribution?
b. What is Curt's basis in the Vogel stock on December 31?
c. What is Vogel's accumulated adjustments account (AAA) balance on December 31?

C:11-53 *Taxability of Distributions.* Hal organized Stable Corporation five years ago and has continued to own all its stock. The corporation made an S election one year after its incorporation. At the beginning of the current year, Stable reports the following earnings accumulations:

Accumulated adjustments account (AAA)	$85,000
Accumulated E&P	22,000

Hal's basis in his Stable stock on January 1 of the current year is $120,000. During the current year, Stable reports the following results from its operations:

Ordinary income	$30,000
Tax-exempt interest income	15,000
Long-term capital loss	20,000

Stable makes a $65,000 cash distribution to Hal on August 8.

a. What income, gain, or loss (if any) do Stable and Hal recognize as a result of the distribution?

b. What is Hal's basis in the Stable stock on December 31?

c. What are Stable's AAA, E&P, and OAA balances on December 31?

d. How would your answers to Parts a-c change if Stable instead distributed $120,000?

C:11-54 *Taxability of Distributions.* Sigma Corporation, an S corporation with one shareholder, incurred the following items Year 1 and Year 2:

Year 1

| Tax-exempt income | $ 5,000 |
| Ordinary income | 30,000 |

Year 2

| Ordinary loss | ($40,000) |
| Cash distribution | 15,000 |

At the beginning of Year 1, the corporation had AAA and OAA balances of zero and accumulated E&P of $6,000. At the beginning of Year 1, the shareholder had a $10,000 basis in stock and a $12,000 basis in debt he loaned to the corporation.

a. Determine items reported by the shareholder in Year 1 and Year 2.

b. Determine the balances in each corporate account and the shareholder's stock and debt bases at the end of each year.

c. Determine the results if the distribution in Year 2 is $35,000 instead of $15,000.

d. How does the answer to Part c change if, in Year 2, the corporation has an $18,000 long-term capital gain in addition to the $40,000 ordinary loss?

C:11-55 *Taxability of Distributions.* Beta Corporation, an S corporation with one shareholder, incurred the following items:

Year 1

| Ordinary loss | ($40,000) |

Year 2

| Ordinary income | $27,000 |
| Cash distribution | 10,000 |

Year 3

| Ordinary income | $22,000 |
| Cash distribution | 17,000 |

At the beginning of Year 1, the shareholder's stock basis was $20,000, and her debt basis was $16,000.

a. Assuming the corporation has no accumulated E&P, show items reported by the shareholder in each year, show all basis adjustments to stock and debt, and show the stock and debt bases at the end of each year.

b. Redo Part a for Year 2 and Year 3 assuming ordinary income in Year 2 is $8,000 instead of $27,000.

c. Go back to the original facts and again redo Part a for all years assuming that, at the beginning of Year 1, the corporation had a AAA balance of zero and accumulated E&P of $12,000.

COMPREHENSIVE PROBLEMS

C:11-56 *Comparison of Entity Formations.* Cara, Bob, and Steve want to begin a business on January 1, 2011. The individuals are considering three business forms—C corporation, partnership, and S corporation.

• Cara has investment land with a $36,000 adjusted basis and a $50,000 FMV that she is willing to contribute. The land has a rundown building on it having a $27,000 basis and a $15,000 FMV. Cara has never used the building nor rented it. She would like to get rid of the building. Because she needs cash, Cara will take out a $25,000 mortgage on the property before the formation of the new business and have the new business assume the debt. Cara obtains a 40% interest in the entity.

- Bob will contribute machinery and equipment, which he purchased for his sole proprietorship in January 2006. He paid $100,000 for the equipment and has used the MACRS rules with a half-year convention on this seven-year recovery period property. He did not make a Sec. 179 expensing election for this property, and bonus depreciation did not apply in 2006. The FMV of the machinery and equipment is $39,000. Bob obtains a 39% interest in the entity.

- Steve will contribute cash of $600 and services worth $20,400 for his interest in the business. The services he will contribute include drawing up the necessary legal documentation for the new business and setting up the initial books. Steve obtains a 21% interest in the entity.

To begin operations, the new business plans to borrow $50,000 on a recourse basis from a local bank. Each owner will guarantee his or her ownership share of the debt.

What are the tax and nontax consequences for the new business and its owners under each alternative? Assume that any corporation will have 200 shares of common stock authorized and issued. For the partnership alternative, each partner receives a capital, profits, and loss interest. How would your answer to the basic facts change if instead Steve contributes $2,600 in cash and $18,400 in services?

C:11-57 *Comparison of Operating Activities.* RST business entity reported the following items during the current year:

Dividends from 25%-owned domestic corporation	$ 19,000
State of Florida bond interest	18,000
General Electric Corporation bond interest	29,000
Gain on land contributed by Karen[a]	40,000
Operating profit (excluding depreciation)[b]	120,000
MACRS depreciation	36,000
Section 1245 gain (recapture)	5,000
Section 1231 loss	28,000
Long-term capital losses	4,000
Short-term capital losses	5,000
Charitable contributions	23,000
Investment interest expense (related to General Electric bonds)	16,000
Salary (guaranteed payment)	37,000

[a] Karen held the land as an investment prior to contributing it to RST business entity three years ago in exchange for her ownership interest. When Karen contributed the land, it had a basis of $15,000 and a FMV of $40,000. RST sold the land in the current year for $55,000. RST business entity held the land as an investment. Assume that Sec. 351 applied to any corporate formation transaction.

[b] Assume that qualified production activities income is $47,000 and that operating profit includes sufficient W-2 wages so as not to be a limiting factor. The deduction percentage is 9%.

a. What is the corporate taxable income and income tax liability for the current year if RST is taxed as a C corporation?
b. What is the ordinary income and separately stated items for the current year if RST elects to be an S corporation? Assume that RST has never operated as a C corporation.
c. What are the ordinary income and separately stated items if RST is treated as a general partnership?

C:11-58 *Comparison of Nonliquidating Distributions.* Jeff and John organized Tampa Corporation 18 years ago and have each owned 50% of the corporation since its inception. In the current year, Tampa reports ordinary income/taxable income of $40,000. Assume the business does not qualify for the U.S. production activities deduction. On April 5, Tampa distributes $100,000 cash to Jeff and distributes land with a $100,000 FMV and a $70,000 adjusted basis to John. Tampa had purchased the land as an investment two years ago. What are the tax implications to Tampa, Jeff, and John of the land distribution in each of the four situations that follow?

a. Tampa has been a C corporation since its formation. On January 1 of the current year, Jeff's basis in his stock is $50,000, and John's stock basis is $45,000. Tampa has accumulated E&P of $155,000 on January 1 of the current year.

b. Tampa was formed as a C corporation but made an S election three years after its formation. On January 1 of the current year, Jeff's basis in his stock is $100,000, and John's stock basis is $80,000. Tampa had the following earnings balances on January 1 of the current year:

Accumulated Adjustments Account $125,000
Accumulated E&P 30,000

c. Tampa was formed as a partnership and continues to operate in that form. On January 1 of the current year, Jeff's basis in his partnership interest is $100,000, and John's partnership basis is $80,000. The partnership has no liabilities and no unrecognized precontribution gains.

d. How would your answers to Parts a–c change if the land held as an investment and then distributed to John had been contributed to Tampa by Jeff two years ago? At the time of Jeff's contribution, the land had a FMV of $95,000 and a $70,000 basis.

TAX STRATEGY PROBLEMS

C:11-59 Alice, a single taxpayer, will form Morning Corporation in the current year. Alice plans to acquire all of Morning's common stock for a $100,000 contribution to the corporation. Morning will obtain additional capital by borrowing $75,000 from a local bank. Morning will conduct a variety of service activities with little need to retain its capital in the business. Alice expects start-up losses of $90,000 during Morning's first year of operation. She expects the corporation to earn pre-tax operating profits of $250,000 (before reduction for Alice's salary) starting next year. Alice plans to withdraw $100,000 of Morning's profits as salary. Her other income consists primarily of ordinary income (no dividends) from other sources, and she expects these amounts to total $120,000 annually. What advice can you provide Alice about the advisability of making an S election in the initial tax year? In the next tax year? In answering these questions, compare the following alternatives: (1) S corporation in both the current year and the next year, (2) S corporation in the current year and C corporation in the next year (i.e., by revoking the S election next year), (3) C corporation in both the current year and the next year, and (4) C corporation in the current year and S corporation in the next year. When analyzing these alternatives, consider the total taxes associated with each alternative, specifically, at the corporate and shareholder levels and across both years. Ignore payroll taxes, however. Also, assume the following facts: (1) for both years, Alice's combined standard deduction and exemption is $9,500; (2) 2011 tax rate schedules remain the same for both years; and (3) a 7% discount rate applies for present value calculations. Although this problem asks for only a two-year analysis, discuss some shortcomings of such a short time frame. Ignore the U.S. production activities deduction for this problem.

C:11-60 One way to compare the accumulation of income by alterative business entity forms is to use mathematical models. The following models express the investment after-tax accumulation calculation for a particular entity form:

Flow-through entities (S corporations, partnerships, and LLCs): $ATA = [1 + R(1 - t_p)]^n$
C corporation: $ATA = [1 + R(1 - t_c)]^n(1 - t_g) + t_g$
where: ATA = after-tax accumulation in n years
R = before-tax rate of return;
t_p = owner's marginal tax rate on ordinary income
t_c = corporation's marginal tax rate
t_g = owner's tax rate on capital gains
n = number of periods

For each alternative business form, the owner makes an initial investment of $1. The following operating assumptions apply:

Before-tax rate of return $(R) = 0.18$
Marginal tax rate for owner $(t_p) = 0.35$
Corporate tax rate $(t_c) = 0.34$
Capital gains rate $(t_g) = 0.15$ for regular capital gains (assume the Sec. 1202 50% exclusion for small business corporations does not apply)
Investment horizon $(n) = 2, 4, 20, 50,$ or 101 years

A flow-through entity distributes only enough cash each year for the owners to pay their taxes. The corporation pays no dividends. The shareholders sell their stock at the end of the investment horizon, and their gains are taxed at capital gains rates. (See Chapter I:18 of the *Individuals* volume for a detailed explanation of these models.)

Required: What is the after-tax accumulation if each business form is operated for the investment horizon and then sold for the amount of the accumulation? Which entity form is best for each investment horizon? How would your calculations and conclusions change if the C corporation's tax rate is 25%?

C:11-61 Problem C:6-56 considered two alternative forms for doing business. Now consider a third alternative. The C corporation could make an S election effective at the beginning of the current year, operate as an S corporation for the next 20 years, and liquidate the S corporation at that time (32 years in total). Compare this alternative to the other two alternatives in Problem C:6-56.

C:11-62 Assume the corporation in Problem C:11-61 (and C:6-56) had been an S corporation for its first 12 years, during which it distributed just enough cash for the shareholder to pay taxes on the pass-through income. Thus, the S corporation reinvested after-tax income. Now the corporation is considering revoking its S election and operating as a C corporation for the remaining 20 years with no dividend distributions. Show the results of remaining an S corporation versus revoking the election. Also show supporting models and calculations. Which alternative should the corporation adopt? Ignore the accumulated earnings tax for C corporations. How does your answer change if the C corporation's tax rate is 15% instead of 35%?

TAX FORM/RETURN PREPARATION PROBLEM

C:11-63 Bottle-Up, Inc., was organized on January 8, 2001, and made its S election on January 24, 2000. The necessary consents to the election were filed in a timely manner. Its federal tax identification number is 38-1507869. Its address is 1234 Hill Street, Gainesville, FL 32607. Bottle-Up uses the calendar year as its tax year, the accrual method of accounting, and the first-in, first-out (FIFO) inventory method. Bottle-Up manufactures ornamental glass bottles. It made no changes to its inventory costing methods this year. It uses the specific identification method for bad debts for book and tax purposes. Herman Hiebert (S.S. No. 123-45-6789) and Melvin Jones (S.S. No. 100-67-2000) own 500 shares each. Both individuals materially participate in Bottle-Up's single activity. Herman Hiebert is the tax matters person. Financial statements for Bottle-Up for the current year are shown in Tables C:11-2 through C:11-4. Assume that Bottle-Up's business qualifies as a U.S. production activity and that its qualified production activities income is $90,000. The S corporation uses the small business simplified overall method for reporting these activities (see discussion for Line 12d of Schedules K and K-1 in the Form 1120S instructions). Prepare a current year S corporation tax return for Bottle-Up, showing yourself as the paid preparer.

C:11-64 Refer to the facts in Tax Form/Return Preparation Problem C:9-58. Now assume the company is an S corporation rather than a partnership. Additional facts are as follows:

- Drs. Bailey and Firth formed the corporation on January 1, 2009, and the corporation immediately elected S corporation status effective at the beginning of 2009.

- Upon formation of the corporation, Dr. Bailey received common stock worth $1.02 million, and Dr. Firth received common stock worth $2.38 million.

- The balance sheet information is the same as in Table C:9-3 except the equity section is as follows:

	January 1, 2010	December 31, 2010
Common stock	$3,400,000	$3,400,000
Retained earnings	97,070	2,596

- The $170,000 paid to Dr. Bailey is salary constituting W-2 wages (instead of a guaranteed payment). Ignore employment taxes (Social Security, etc.) on Dr. Bailey's salary.

- Qualified production activities income (QPAI) still equals $2.04 million, but employer's W-2 wages allocable to U.S. production activities equal $1,122,000 million (because of Dr. Bailey's salary). The company, being an eligible small pass-through S corporation, uses the small business simplification overall method for reporting these activities (see discussion for Line 12d of Schedule K and Line 12 of Schedule K-1 in the Form 1120S instructions).

- Use book numbers for Schedule L and Schedule M-1 in Form 1120S.

▼ TABLE C:11-2

Bottle-Up, Inc. Income Statement for the Year Ended December 31 of the Current Year (Problem C:11-63)

Sales		$2,500,000
Returns and allowances		(15,000)
Net sales		$2,485,000
Beginning inventory	$ 102,000	
Purchases	900,000	
Labor	200,000	
Supplies	80,000	
Utilities	100,000	
Other manufacturing costs	188,000[a]	
Goods available for sale	$1,570,000	
Ending inventory	(96,000)	1,474,000[b]
Gross profit		$1,011,000
Salaries[c]	$ 451,020	
Utilities expense	54,000	
Depreciation (MACRS depreciation is $36,311)	11,782	
Automobile and truck expense	26,000	
Office supplies expense	9,602	
Advertising expense	105,000	
Bad debts expense	620	
Rent expense	30,000	
Interest expense[d]	1,500	
Meals and entertainment expense	21,000	
Selling expenses	100,000	
Repairs and maintenance expense	38,000	
Accounting and legal expense	4,500	
Charitable contributions[e]	9,000	
Insurance expense[f]	24,500	
Hourly employees' fringe benefits	11,000	
Payroll taxes	36,980	
Other taxes	2,500	
Penalties (fines for overweight trucks)	1,000	(938,004)
Operating profit		$ 72,996
Other income and losses:		
Long-term gain on sale of capital assets	$ 48,666[g]	
Sec. 1231 loss	(1,100)[h]	
Interest on U.S. Treasury bills	1,200	
Interest on State of Florida bonds	600	
Dividends from domestic corporations	11,600	
Investment expenses	(600)	60,366
Net income		$ 133,362

[a] Total MACRS depreciation is $74,311. Assume that $38,000 of depreciation has been allocated to cost of sales for both book and tax purposes so that the book and tax inventory and cost of sales amounts are the same. The AMT depreciation adjustment on personal property is $9,000.

[b] The cost of goods sold amount reflects the Uniform Capitalization Rules of Sec. 263A. The appropriate restatements have been made in prior years.

[c] Officer salaries of $120,000 are included in the total. All are employer's W-2 wages.

[d] Investment interest expense is $500. All other interest expense is trade- or business-related. None of the interest expense relates to the production of tax-exempt income.

[e] The corporation made all contributions in cash to qualifying charities.

[f] Includes $3,000 of premiums paid for policies on lives of corporate officers. Bottle-Up is the beneficiary for both policies.

[g] The corporation acquired the capital assets on March 3, 2008 for $100,000 and sold them on September 15, 2010, for $148,666.

[h] The corporation acquired the Sec. 1231 property on June 5, 2009 for $10,000 and sold it on December 21, 2010, for $8,900.

▼ TABLE C:11-3

Bottle-Up, Inc. Balance Sheet for January 1 and December 31 of the Current Year (Problem C:11-63)

	January 1	December 31
Assets:		
Cash	$ 15,000	$116,948
Accounts receivable	41,500	45,180
Inventories	102,000	96,000
Stocks	103,000	74,000
Treasury bills	15,000	16,000
State of Florida bonds	10,000	10,000
Building and equipment	374,600	375,000
Minus: Accumulated depreciation	(160,484)	(173,100)
Land	160,000	190,000
Total	$660,616	$750,028
Liabilities and equities:		
Accounts payable	$ 36,000	$ 10,000
Accrued salaries payable	12,000	6,000
Payroll taxes payable	3,416	7,106
Sales taxes payable	5,200	6,560
Due to Mr. Hiebert	10,000	5,000
Mortgage and notes payable (current maturities)	44,000	52,000
Long-term debt	210,000	260,000
Capital stock	10,000	10,000
Retained earnings	330,000	393,362
Total	$660,616	$750,028

▼ TABLE C:11-4

Bottle-Up, Inc. Statement of Change in Retained Earnings, for the Current Year Ended December 31 (Problem C:11-63)

Balance, January 1		$330,000[a]
Plus: Net income	$133,362	
Minus: Dividends	(70,000)	63,362
Balance, December 31		$393,362

[a] The January 1 accumulated adjustments account balance is $274,300.

Required: Prepare the 2010 S corporation tax return (Form 1120S), including the following additional schedules and forms: Schedule D, Form 4562, and Schedule K-1.

Optional: (1) Complete Schedule M-2 in Form 1120S even though the company has never been a C corporation. For this purpose, the accumulated adjustments account at the beginning of 2010 is $97,070. (2) Prepare a schedule for each shareholder's basis in his or her S corporation stock. For this purpose, Bailey's stock basis at the beginning of 2010 is $1,049,121, and Firth's is $2,121,549.

CASE STUDY PROBLEM

C:11-65 Debra has operated a family counseling practice for a number of years as a sole proprietor. She owns the condominium office space that she occupies in addition to her professional library and office furniture. She has a limited amount of working capital and little need to accumulate additional business assets. Her total business assets are about

$150,000, with an $80,000 mortgage on the office space being her only liability. Typically, she has withdrawn any unneeded assets at the end of the year. Debra has used her personal car for business travel and charged the business for the mileage at the appropriate mileage rate provided by the IRS. Over the last three years, Debra's practice has grown so that she now forecasts $80,000 of income being earned this year. Debra has contributed small amounts to an Individual Retirement Account (IRA) each year, but her contributions have never reached the annual limits. Although she has never been sued, Debra recently has become concerned about legal liability. An attorney friend of hers has suggested that she incorporate her business to protect herself against being sued and to save taxes.

Required: You are a good friend of Debra's and a CPA; she asks your opinion on incorporating her business. You are to meet with Debra tomorrow for lunch. Prepare a draft of the points you feel should be discussed over lunch about incorporating the family counseling practice.

TAX RESEARCH PROBLEMS

C:11-66 Cato Corporation incorporated on July 1, 2006, in California, with Tim and Elesa, husband and wife, owning all the Cato stock. On August 15, 2006, Cato made an S election effective for 2006. Tim and Elesa filed the necessary consents to the election. On March 10, 2010, Tim and Elesa transferred 15% of the Cato stock to the Reid and Susan Trust, an irrevocable trust created three years earlier for the benefit of their two minor children. In early 2011, Tim and Elesa's tax accountant learns about the transfer and advises the couple that the transfer of the stock to the trust may have terminated Cato's S election. Prepare a memorandum for your tax manager indicating any action Tim and Elesa can take that will permit Cato to retain its S election. Research sources suggested by the tax manager include Secs. 1361(c)(2), 1362(d)(2), and 1362(f).

C:11-67 One of your wealthy clients, Cecile, invests $100,000 for sole ownership of an electing S corporation's stock. The corporation is in the process of developing a new food product. Cecile anticipates that the new business will need approximately $200,000 in capital (other than trade payables) during the first two years of its operations before it starts to earn sufficient profits to pay a return on the shareholder's investment. The first $100,000 of this total is to come from Cecile's contributed capital. The remaining $100,000 of funds will come from one of the following three sources:

- Have the corporation borrow the $100,000 from a local bank. Cecile is required to act as a guarantor for the loan.
- Have the corporation borrow $100,000 from the estate of Cecile's late husband. Cecile is the sole beneficiary of the estate.
- Have Cecile lend $100,000 to the corporation from her personal funds.

The S corporation will pay interest at a rate acceptable to the IRS. During the first two years of operations, the corporation anticipates losing $125,000 before it begins to earn a profit. Your tax manager has asked you to evaluate the tax ramifications of each of the three financing alternatives. Prepare a memorandum to the tax manager outlining the information you found in your research.

C:11-68 Joe Stephens formed Sigma Corporation on January 4, 2009, and the corporation immediately made an S election effective for 2009. In forming the corporation, Joe contributed $50,000 cash in exchange for 100% of Sigma's stock. Shortly thereafter, the corporation obtained a $75,000 bank loan to assist with operations. Sigma's first two years did not go as well as expected, with Sigma incurring a $60,000 ordinary loss in 2009 and a $12,000 ordinary loss in 2010. Moreover, in 2010, Joe and his wife Marsha divorced. As part of the divorce settlement, on March 31, 2010, Joe gave Marsha 50% of the Sigma stock. In 2011, Sigma's performance improved, with the corporation earning $40,000 of ordinary income. Joe asks your help in determining the tax consequences of these events, particularly the usage of the S corporation losses. At a minimum, you should consider the following resources:

- IRC Sec. 1366
- Reg. Sec. 1.1366-2

12

CHAPTER

THE GIFT TAX

LEARNING OBJECTIVES

After studying this chapter, you should be able to

1. Understand the concept of the unified transfer tax system

2. Describe the gift tax formula

3. Identify a number of transactions subject to the gift tax

4. Determine whether an annual gift tax exclusion is available

5. Identify deductions available for gift tax purposes

6. Apply the gift-splitting rules

7. Calculate the gift tax liability

8. Understand how basis affects the overall tax consequences

9. Recognize the filing requirements for gift tax returns

The **gift tax** is a **wealth transfer tax** that applies if a person transfers property while alive. It is similar to the estate tax, which applies to transfers associated with death. Both the gift tax and the estate tax are part of the unified transfer tax system that subjects gratuitous transfers of property between persons to taxation. The vast majority of all property transfers are exempt from these transfer taxes because of the annual exclusion and the various deductions and credits.[1] However, planning for reducing these transfer taxes is a significant matter for wealthy or moderately wealthy individuals. The Economic Growth and Tax Relief Reconciliation Act of 2001 (the 2001 Act) provided for phased in increases to the unified credit and phased in reductions in the unified tax rate schedule beginning in 2002. In addition, it repealed the estate and generation skipping transfer taxes, *but not the gift tax*, effective January 1, 2010. The 2001 Act also provided that, if no further legislation passed, the rules for gift, estate, and generation skipping taxes would revert on January 1, 2011, to the rules in effect before the 2001 Act. Congress adopted this "sunsetting" provision to comply with the Congressional Budget Act of 1974.

The Tax Relief, Unemployment Insurance Reauthorization, and Job Creation Act of 2010 (hereinafter referred to as the Tax Relief Act) enacted in December 2010 provides that, for 2011 and 2012, the top rate for both estate and gift taxes is 35%, and the amount that can be transferred tax free in either context is $5 million. This amount will be indexed for 2012. In the absence of further legislation, in 2013 the rules will return to those in effect before the 2001 Act. In addition, for decedents who died in 2010, the Tax Relief Act allows the executor to choose between (1) no estate tax with a modified carryover basis or (2) the estate tax with a $5 million applicable exclusion amount, a top rate of 35%, and FMV bases for the estate's assets. Thus, estates below the $5 million threshold can step up the assets' bases to FMV without incurring any estate tax liability. A step-up occurs when the estate's assets have a FMV exceeding their bases. A step-down could occur for assets whose bases exceed their FMV.

This chapter discusses both the structure of the gift tax (including the exclusion, deduction, and credit provisions) and exactly which property transfers fall within its purview. It reviews the income tax basis rules in the context of their implications for selecting properties to transfer by gift instead of at death.

CONCEPT OF TRANSFER TAXES

OBJECTIVE 1

Understand the concept of the unified transfer tax system

ADDITIONAL COMMENT

The continuity of the estate tax was broken for 2010 for estates whose executors elect to have the estate tax not apply for that year, with a modified carryover basis rule to apply instead.

The recipient of a gift incurs no income tax liability because Sec. 102 explicitly excludes gifts and inheritances from the recipient's gross income.[2] The gift tax, a type of excise tax, is levied on the donor, the person who transferred the property. The gift tax applies to the act of transferring property to a recipient who pays either no consideration or consideration smaller than the value of the property received.

HISTORY AND PURPOSE OF TRANSFER TAXES

The United States has had an estate tax since 1916 and a gift tax continuously since 1932. The structure of the gift and estate taxes has remained fairly constant, but details such as the amount of the exclusion and the rate schedules have changed numerous times. The Tax Reform Act of 1976 (the 1976 Act) made a very significant change by enacting a unified rate schedule for gift and estate tax purposes.

The gift tax has had several purposes, one of the most important of which was to raise revenue. However, because of the fairly generous annual exclusion and unified credit legislated by Congress, the gift tax yields only a small fraction of the federal government's total revenues. Only donors making relatively large gifts owe any gift taxes. Another purpose of the gift tax is to serve as a backstop to the estate tax and to prevent individuals from avoiding a significant amount of—or all—estate taxes by disposing of property before death. For example, without the gift tax, persons who know they are terminally ill could dispose of property "on their deathbed" and escape the transfer tax. In addition, the gift tax

---

[1] In 1998, for example, only 47,500 estates owed any tax, and most of the tax was paid by estates above $5 million. See "House Republicans Shift Their Strategy in Effort to Push Two Popular Tax Cuts," *The Wall Street Journal* (August 22, 2000), p. A20.

[2] The income earned from property received as a gift or an inheritance, however, is not exempt from the income tax.

ADDITIONAL
COMMENT

The lower tax rate on dividend income will reduce or eliminate the income tax savings formerly available from having dividends taxed to donees in low tax brackets.

provides revenue to offset some of the reduction in income tax revenue resulting from the fact that income from gifted property sometimes is shifted to persons in lower income tax brackets. Another purpose for levying gift and estate taxes is to redistribute wealth.

No one knows what the distribution of wealth would have been had Congress not enacted transfer taxes. However, one study estimated that the top 1% of the population held 22.5% of this nation's personal wealth in 1995, about the same percentage as in 1992.[3]

THE UNIFIED TRANSFER TAX SYSTEM

In 1976, Congress greatly revamped the transfer tax system by combining the separate estate and gift tax systems into one unified transfer tax system. Although Chapters C:12 and C:13 use the terms *gift tax* and *estate tax,* these taxes actually are components of the same unified transfer tax system. The system also includes the generation-skipping transfer tax, a topic discussed in Chapter C:13. The unification of the transfer tax system removed the previous law's bias favoring the tax treatment of lifetime gifts in comparison with transfers at death. The three most significant elements of the unified system—the unified rate schedule, the inclusion of taxable gifts in the death tax base, and the unified credit—are discussed below.

UNIFIED RATE SCHEDULE

SELF-STUDY
QUESTION

Use the rate schedule inside the back cover of this text to determine the amount of gift tax (before credits) on 2011 taxable gifts of $6 million.

ANSWER

The tax is $2,080,800 [$155,800 + 0.35 × ($6,000,000 − $500,000)].

Before the 1976 Act mandated a **unified rate schedule,** effective for gifts made after 1976 and deaths occurring after 1976 and applicable to both lifetime transfers and transfers at death, the gift tax rates were only 75% of the estate tax rates on a transfer of the same size. The rates are progressive and have varied over the years. The 2001 Act reduced the unified transfer tax rates beginning in 2002 by replacing the former top two brackets (on amounts exceeding $2.5 million) with a 50% maximum tax rate in 2002. The top rate declined to 49% in 2003, 48% in 2004, 47% in 2005, and 46% in 2006. In those years, the top rate applies to tax bases above $2 million. In 2007 through 2009, for both estate and gift tax purposes, a maximum tax rate of 45% applied to tax bases exceeding $1.5 million.

For 2010 through 2012, the top estate and gift tax rate is 35%, applicable to tax bases exceeding $500,000. If, however, an estate's executor so elects for 2010, the estate tax will not apply that year, but the 35% tax rate nevertheless will apply to 2010 gifts. Unless Congress acts otherwise, the estate and gift tax rules will revert to their pre-2001 Act levels after 2012. The estate and gift tax unified transfer tax rates appear inside the back cover of this textbook.

IMPACT OF TAXABLE GIFTS ON DEATH TAX BASE

Before 1977, a separate system applied to lifetime gifts compared with dispositions at death. By making gifts, an individual could shift the taxation of property from the top of the estate tax rate schedule to the bottom of the gift tax rate schedule. Few taxpayers could take advantage of this shifting, however, because only people with a relatively large amount of property could afford to part with sizable amounts of their assets while alive.

ADDITIONAL
COMMENT

At the taxpayer's death, the unified tax is computed on the sum of the taxable estate plus the adjusted taxable gifts. The tax on this sum is reduced by the tax that would have been payable (at current rates) on the taxable gifts made after December 31, 1976.

Under today's unified system, taxable gifts affect the size of the tax base at death. Any post-1976 taxable gifts (other than gifts included in the gross estate) are called **adjusted taxable gifts,** and such gifts are included in the donor's death tax base. Although they are valued at their fair market value (FMV) on the date of the gift, the addition of such taxable gifts to the tax base at death can cause the donor-decedent's estate to be taxed at a higher marginal tax rate. However, such gifts are not taxed for a second time upon the donor's death because gift taxes (computed at current rates) on these gifts are subtracted in determining the estate tax liability.

EXAMPLE C:12-1 ▶ In 1994, Dan made taxable gifts totaling $500,000. When Dan died the value of the gifted property had tripled. Dan's death tax base includes the $500,000 of post-1976 taxable gifts.

---

[3] "Tax Report," *The Wall Street Journal* (April 19, 2000), p. A1.

They are valued for estate tax purposes at their FMV on the date of the gift; the post-gift appreciation escapes the transfer tax system. Thus, the transfer tax value is fixed or frozen at the date-of-gift value. ◄

Note that unification (including taxable gifts that become part of the tax base at death) extends only to gifts made after 1976. Congress exempted gifts made before 1977 from unification because it did not want to retroactively change the two separate transfer tax systems of the prior tax regime.

UNIFIED CREDIT

The **unified credit** reduces dollar for dollar a certain amount of the tax computed on the taxable gifts or the taxable estate. The amount of the credit has varied depending on the year of the transfer (see discussion on page C:12-6). In the gift and estate tax formulas, the full credit is available for lifetime transfers and again in determining the tax payable at death. In concept, however, an individual's estate does not receive the benefit of this unified credit amount at death to the extent the decedent had used the credit against lifetime transfers (as explained in Chapter C:13). The gift tax formula, including the unified credit, is discussed below.

GIFT TAX FORMULA

OBJECTIVE 2

Describe the gift tax formula

The formula described in this section is used to calculate a donor's gift tax liability for the year of the transfer. Gift tax reporting is done on an annual basis, always on a calendar year. Figure C:12-1 illustrates the formula for determining the donor's annual gift tax liability. This formula is discussed in detail later in the chapter.

ADDITIONAL COMMENT

The gift tax applies to cumulative lifetime gifts made since the enactment of the gift tax in 1932. The unified gift and estate tax, enacted in 1976, applies only to cumulative lifetime taxable gifts made after 1976. Thus, a taxable gift of $75,000 made in 1970 would not be included in a decedent's unified tax base for calculating the estate tax but would affect the gift tax payable by that person.

DETERMINATION OF GIFTS

The starting point in the process is to determine which, if any, of the taxpayer's transfers constitute gifts. The next section discusses the various types of transfers that the statute views as gifts. All gifts are valued at their FMVs on the date of the gift. Next, the aggregate amount of gifts for the period is determined. The aggregate gifts are then reduced by any exclusions and deductions. Finally, the tax is computed according to the formula illustrated in Figure C:12-1.

EXCLUSIONS AND DEDUCTIONS

For many years the maximum amount excludible annually was a fixed amount of $10,000 per donee, but Congress amended the IRC to allow indexation beginning with gifts made after 1998. Inflation adjustments are rounded to the next *lowest* multiple of $1,000.[4] Accordingly, the annual exclusion rose to $11,000 for 2002 through 2005, to $12,000 for 2006 through 2008, and to $13,000 beginning in 2009. If the gifts made to a donee are less than the annual exclusion amount, the amount excludible is limited to the amount of the gift made to that donee. A donor may claim exclusions for transfers to an unlimited number of donees.

Two types of deductions (marital and charitable) reduce the amount of the taxable gifts. Most transfers to one's spouse generate a marital deduction; there is no ceiling on the amount of this deduction. Similarly, most transfers to charitable organizations are cancelled out by the charitable contribution deduction, which also is unlimited.

KEY POINT

The annual exclusion applies to each *donee* per year; therefore, the total amount of tax-free gifts in a given year can be much greater than the annual exclusion amount. Also, gift-splitting can double the tax-free amount per donee.

GIFT-SPLITTING ELECTION

Congress authorized gift-splitting provisions to achieve more comparable tax consequences between taxpayers of community property and noncommunity property (common law) states.[5] Under **community property law**, assets acquired after marriage are community property unless they are acquired by gift or inheritance. Typically, in a **community property state**, a large portion of the spouses' assets is community property, property in which each spouse has a one-half interest. One-half of a community property gift is automatically

---

[4] Sec. 2503(b).
[5] The eight traditional community property states are Louisiana, Texas, New Mexico, Arizona, California, Washington, Idaho, and Nevada. Wisconsin's marital property law, though not providing for community property, is basically the same as community property.

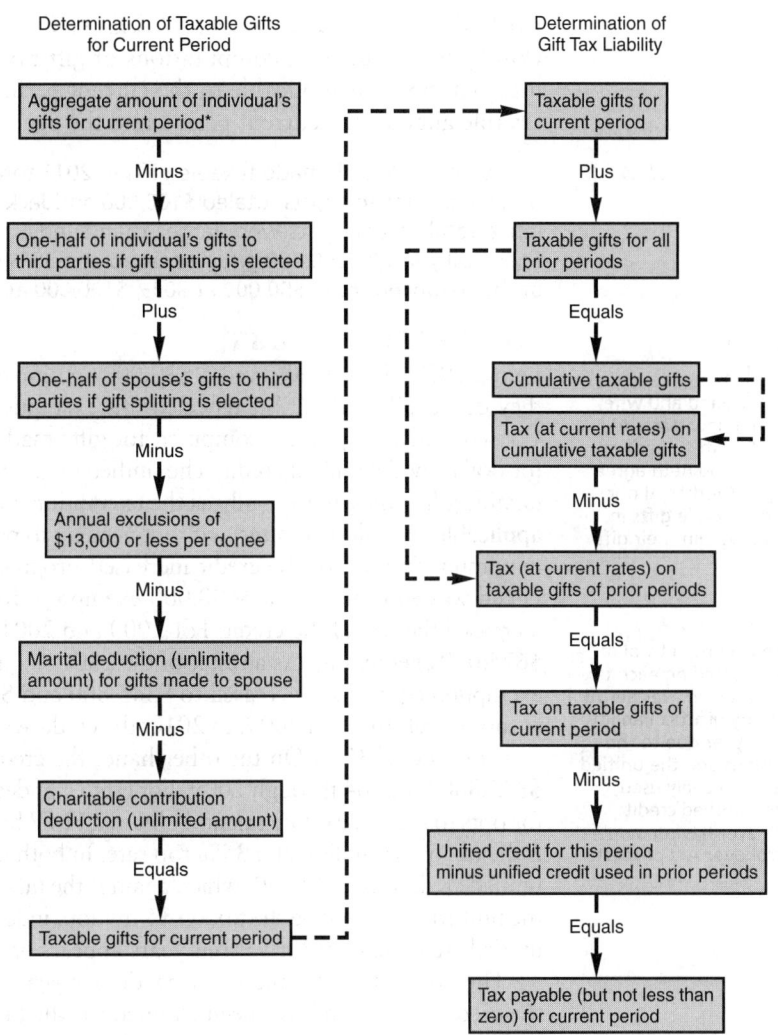

Determination of Taxable Gifts
for Current Period

Aggregate amount of individual's
gifts for current period*

Minus

One-half of individual's gifts to
third parties if gift splitting is elected

Plus

One-half of spouse's gifts to third
parties if gift splitting is elected

Minus

Annual exclusions of
$13,000 or less per donee

Minus

Marital deduction (unlimited
amount) for gifts made to spouse

Minus

Charitable contribution
deduction (unlimited amount)

Equals

Taxable gifts for current period

Determination of
Gift Tax Liability

Taxable gifts for
current period

Plus

Taxable gifts for all
prior periods

Equals

Cumulative taxable gifts

Tax (at current rates) on
cumulative taxable gifts

Minus

Tax (at current rates) on
taxable gifts of prior periods

Equals

Tax on taxable gifts of
current period

Minus

Unified credit for this period
minus unified credit used in prior periods

Equals

Tax payable (but not less than
zero) for current period

* Valued at FMV on date of gift.

FIGURE C:12-1 ▶ THE GIFT TAX FORMULA

considered to be given by each spouse. By contrast, in a **common law state**, all assets acquired during the marriage are the property of the acquiring spouse. The other spouse does not automatically acquire an interest in the property. Thus, sometimes only one spouse owns enough assets to consider making large gifts.

Section 2513 authorizes spouses to elect gift splitting, which treats gifts made by each spouse to third parties as if each spouse made one-half of the gift. As a result, spouses in common law states can achieve the same benefits that apply automatically for gifts of community property. Thus, both spouses can claim a $13,000 per donee exclusion although only one spouse actually makes the gift, and the spouses can give each donee a total of $26,000 before either spouse's gift becomes taxable.

EXAMPLE C:12-2 ▶

ADDITIONAL COMMENT

Because the gift tax is a tax on *cumulative* lifetime gifts, taxpayers must keep track of all taxable gifts. All previous taxable gifts are part of the calculation for current gift tax due, and post-1976 taxable gifts affect the estate tax liability.

Andy and Bonnie, residents of a common law state, are married throughout 2011. In that year, Andy gives his brother $100,000 cash. Andy and Bonnie may elect gift splitting and thereby treat the $100,000 gift as if each spouse gave $50,000. As a result, the excludible portion of the gift totals $26,000 ($13,000 per donee for each of the two deemed donors). If they elect gift splitting, each donor's $37,000 taxable gift may be taxed at a lower marginal tax rate. In addition, Bonnie can use a unified credit amount that she might not otherwise be able to use. As a result of gift splitting, the tax consequences are the same as if Andy and Bonnie were residents of a community property state and each gave $50,000 of community property to Andy's brother. ◀

CUMULATIVE NATURE OF GIFT TAX

Unlike the income tax, computations of gift tax liabilities are cumulative in nature. The marginal tax rate applicable to the current period's taxable gifts is a function of both the taxable gifts for the current period and the aggregate taxable gifts for all earlier periods.

EXAMPLE C:12-3 ▶ Sandy and Jack each made taxable gifts in 2011 totaling $200,000. However, for previous periods, Sandy's taxable gifts totaled $100,000 and Jack's totaled $1.5 million. Because Jack's cumulative total taxable gifts were larger than Sandy's, Jack's marginal tax rate exceeded Sandy's. Specifically Jack's $200,000 gift was taxed at a 35% rate, while Sandy's $200,000 gift was taxed at the following rates: $50,000 at 30%, $100,000 at 32%, and $50,000 at 34%. ◀

SELF-STUDY QUESTION

Al and Beth, husband and wife, live in a common law state. Al gives a $620,000 gift to each of two children. Al and Beth agree to split the gift. Neither Al nor Beth has made taxable gifts in any prior year. Explain their gift tax liability.

ANSWER

One-half of each gift, a total of $620,000, is reported on each taxpayer's gift tax return. Neither Al nor Beth has any gift tax liability for the current year due to the annual exclusions and the unified credit. Al has effectively used some of Beth's unified credit without Beth ever having ownership or control over Al's property.

UNIFIED CREDIT

Before 1977, the IRC allowed a $30,000 specific exemption deductible by donors whenever they desired. The 1976 Act repealed this exemption and replaced it with the unified credit.[6] Consequently, the gift tax computed for gifts made in 1977 and later years is reduced dollar for dollar by the unified credit. The unified credit allows donors to make a certain amount of taxable gifts (known originally as the **exemption equivalent** and now referred to in the IRC as **applicable exclusion amount**) without needing to pay the gift tax. For 1977 through 1987, the maximum amount of the credit increased progressively until in 1987 it reached $192,800, which was equivalent to a $600,000 exemption from the gift tax. Legislation in 1997 again increased the size of the credit. For 2000 and 2001, the credit was $220,550 (equivalent to a $675,000 exemption). As a result of the 2001 Act, the credit against gift taxes and the gift tax exemption equivalent increased to $345,800 and $1 million, respectively, in 2002 and stayed at those levels through 2009. In 2010, the credit was $330,800, which is the tax on $1 million at a top rate of 35%. On the other hand, the credit for estate tax purposes increased above $345,800 for 2004 through 2009. For estates of decedents dying in 2010 for which the executor opts to incur the estate tax and obtain a FMV basis, the unified credit is $1,730,800, which is the tax on $5 million at a 35% top rate. In both the estate and gift tax context for 2011, the unified credit is $1,730,800, which again is the tax on $5 million at a 35% top rate. For 2012, the unified credit will be the tax on $5 million, indexed for inflation, at a top rate of 35%. The unified credit amount for various years appears on the inside back cover of this textbook.

The amount creditable for a particular year is the credit amount for that year minus the credit that could have been claimed for the taxable gifts made by the individual in earlier years. However, because of the lowering of the top rate to 35% in 2010 through 2012, the credit is reduced not by the credit actually claimed in earlier years but by what the unified credit would have been, if lower, had the credit been calculated using the rates for the current year. Recall that no credit was allowed for gifts made before 1977.[7]

EXAMPLE C:12-4 ▶ Zheng made her first taxable gift ($325,000) in 1984. She used the $96,300 unified credit available for 1984 (as shown on the inside back cover) to reduce her $96,300 gift tax liability to zero. Zheng made her next taxable gift ($100,000) in 1985. Zheng's 1985 gift tax is computed as follows:

Tax on cumulative gifts [$70,800 + 0.34 × ($425,000 − $250,000)]	$130,300
Minus: Unified credit taken in 1984	(96,300)
Tax before 1985 credit	$ 34,000
Minus: Unified credit in 1985 ($121,800 − $96,300)	(25,500)
Tax in 1985	$ 8,500

Thus, by 1985, Zheng has claimed credits totaling $121,800. If she makes taxable gifts in 2011, the maximum credit she can claim against her 2011 tax is $1,609,000 ($1,730,800 − $121,800 already used). In this situation, the credit actually claimed and the amount of the credit calculated using the 2011 rate are the same because the earlier gifts were not taxed at rates above 35%. ◀

ADDITIONAL COMMENT

Taxpayers must keep a record of how much of the specific exemption they used between September 9 and December 31, 1976, to determine how much of the unified credit is available to them.

After passage of the 1976 Act, prospective donors quickly realized they could make gifts before the end of 1976 and avoid the unification provisions, but Congress adopted a special rule that affects donors who used any portion of their specific exemption between September 9, 1976, and December 31, 1976.[8] The rule reduced the amount of unified

---

[6] Sec. 2505.
[7] Also, no credit is used for a gift that is completely nontaxable.

[8] Sec. 2505(b). Congress repealed this exemption for post-1976 years.

credit otherwise available to such donors by 20% of the amount of the specific exemption they claimed against gifts made between September 9 and December 31, 1976. The maximum reduction in the unified credit as a result of this provision is $6,000 (0.20 × $30,000 maximum specific exemption).

EXAMPLE C:12-5 ▶ In November 1976, Maria made a large taxable gift, her first gift, and used her $30,000 specific exemption. As a result, the unified credit that Maria could otherwise claim after 1976 is reduced by $6,000 (0.20 × $30,000). Her 1976 taxable gifts are not includible in her death tax base. ◀

TRANSFERS SUBJECT TO THE GIFT TAX

OBJECTIVE 3

Identify a number of transactions subject to the gift tax

In general, property transferred for less than adequate consideration in money or money's worth is deemed to be a gift in the gift tax context. The gift occurs when the donor gives up control over the transferred property. Congress has legislated several provisions that exempt various property transfers that otherwise might be viewed as gifts from the scope of the gift tax. These exemptions include direct payments of medical expenses and tuition, transfers to political organizations, property settlements in conjunction with a divorce, and qualified disclaimers.

TRANSFERS FOR INADEQUATE CONSIDERATION

As mentioned earlier, the initial step in determining the donor's gift tax liability is deciding which transactions constitute gifts for gift tax purposes. Section 2501(a) states that a gift tax is imposed on "the transfer of property by gift." Thus, if *property* is transferred *by gift*, the transferor potentially incurs a gift tax liability. Perhaps surprisingly, the IRC does not define the term *gift*. Section 2511(a), however, elaborates on the gift concept by indicating that the tax is applicable "whether the transfer is in trust or otherwise, whether the gift is direct or indirect, and whether the property is real or personal, tangible or intangible."

A transaction is subject to the gift tax even though not entirely gratuitous if "the value of the property transferred by the donor exceeds the value in money or money's worth of the consideration given therefor."[9] In such circumstances, the amount of the gift is the difference between the value of the property the donor gives up and the value of the consideration in money or money's worth received. The following discussion examines in more depth the scope of the rule regarding transfers for less than adequate consideration.

ADDITIONAL COMMENT

At times, a transferor can inadvertently make a gift by selling property to a family member for an amount determined in an IRS audit to be less than its fair market value.

BARGAIN SALES. Often, an individual wants to sell an asset to a family member, but the prospective buyer cannot afford to pay the full FMV of the property. If the buyer pays consideration of less than the FMV of the transferred property, the seller makes a gift to the buyer equal to the bargain element of the transaction, which is the excess of the property's FMV over its sales price.

EXAMPLE C:12-6 ▶ Martha sells her ranch, having a $1 million FMV, to her son Stan, who can afford to pay only $300,000 of consideration. In the year of the sale, Martha makes a gift to Stan of $700,000, the excess of the ranch's FMV over the consideration received. ◀

TRANSFERS IN NORMAL COURSE OF BUSINESS. Treasury Regulations provide an exception to the general rule that a transfer for inadequate consideration triggers a gift. Specifically, a transaction arising "in the ordinary course of business (a transaction which is bona fide, at arm's length, and free from any donative intent)" is considered to have been made for adequate consideration.[10] Thus, no gift arises when a buyer acquires property for less than its FMV *if* the acquisition is in the ordinary course of business.

EXAMPLE C:12-7 ▶ John, a merchant, has a clearance sale and sells a diamond bracelet valued at $30,000 to Bess who pays $14,000, the clearance sale price. Because the clearance sale arose in the ordinary course of John's business, the bargain element ($16,000) does not constitute a gift to Bess. ◀

[9] Reg. Sec. 25.2512-8.   [10] Ibid.

STATUTORY EXEMPTIONS FROM THE GIFT TAX

For various reasons, including simplifying the administration of the gift tax, Congress enacted several provisions that exempt certain transactions from the purview of the gift tax. In the absence of these statutory rules, some of these transactions could constitute gifts.

PAYMENT OF MEDICAL EXPENSES OR TUITION. Section 2503(e) states that a qualified transfer is not treated as a transfer of property by gift. The IRC defines *qualified transfer* as an amount paid on behalf of an individual to an educational organization for tuition or to any person who provides medical care as payment for such medical care. Such payments are exempt from gift treatment only if made *directly* to the educational organization or to the person or entity providing the medical care. *Educational organization* has the same definition as for charitable contribution purposes,[11] and *medical care* has the same definition as for medical expense deduction purposes.[12] Note that the rule addresses only tuition, not room, board, and books. Moreover, the identity of the person whose expenses are paid is not important. The special exemption applies even if an individual makes payments on behalf of a non-relative.

If one taxpayer pays amounts benefitting someone else and the expenditures constitute support that the payor must furnish under state law, such payments are support, not gifts. State law determines the definition of support. Generally, payments of medical expenses for one's minor child would be categorized as support and not a gift, even in the absence of Sec. 2503(e). On the other hand, state law generally does not require parents to pay medical expenses or tuition for an adult child. Thus, the enactment of Sec. 2503(e) removed such payments from the gift tax.

According to the Staff of the Joint Committee on Taxation, special rules concerning tuition and medical expense payments were enacted because

> Congress was concerned that certain payments of tuition made on behalf of children who have attained their majority, and of special medical expenses on behalf of elderly relatives, technically could be considered gifts under prior law. The Congress believed such payments should be exempt from gift taxes.[13]

SELF-STUDY QUESTION

Ben's adult son Clarence, who is not Ben's dependent, needs a liver transplant. Because Clarence cannot afford the surgical procedure, Ben pays the medical fee directly to the hospital. Is the payment for Clarence's benefit a taxable gift?

ANSWER

The payment is not a taxable gift because of Sec. 2503(e).

EXAMPLE C:12-8 ▶ Sergio (a widower) pays $20,000 for his adult grandson's tuition at medical school and $15,000 for the grandson's room and board in the medical school's dormitory. Sergio makes all payments directly to the educational organization. Section 2503(e) exempts the direct payment of the tuition to the medical school (but not the room and board) from being treated as a gift. Because Sergio is not required under state law to pay room and board for an adult grandson, such payments are not support. Sergio has made a $15,000 gift to the grandson. ◀

EXAMPLE C:12-9 ▶ Assume the same facts as in Example C:12-8 except that Sergio writes a $35,000 check to his grandson, who in turn pays the medical school. Sergio has made a $35,000 gift. Because Sergio does not pay the tuition directly to the school, Sergio does not meet all the conditions for exempting the tuition payments from gift tax treatment. Here, and in Example C:12-8, Sergio receives a $13,000 annual exclusion. ◀

TRANSFERS TO POLITICAL ORGANIZATIONS. Congress adopted a provision specifically exempting transfers to political organizations from being deemed to be a transfer of property by gift.[14] Without this special rule, these transfers generally would be subjected to gift tax treatment.

EXAMPLE C:12-10 ▶ Ann transfers $2,000 to a political organization founded to promote Thomas's campaign for governor. Ann's $2,000 transfer does not fall within the statutory definition of a gift. ◀

PROPERTY SETTLEMENTS IN CONJUNCTION WITH DIVORCE. To reduce litigation, Congress enacted special rules addressing property transfers in the context of a divorce. Section 2516 and underlying Treasury Regulations specify the circumstances in which it automatically exempts property settlements in connection with a divorce from being treated as gifts.

For Sec. 2516 to be applicable, the spouses must adopt a written agreement concerning their marital and property rights and the divorce must occur during a three-year

---

[11] Section 170(b)(1)(A)(ii) defines *educational organization* in the context of the charitable contribution deduction.
[12] Section 213(d) defines *medical care* in the context of the medical expense deduction.

[13] U.S. Congress, Staff of the Joint Committee on Taxation, *General Explanation of the Economic Recovery Tax Act of 1981* (Washington, DC: U.S. Government Printing Office, 1981), p. 273.
[14] Sec. 2501(a)(4).

WHAT WOULD YOU DO IN THIS SITUATION?

You are a CPA with a very wealthy elderly client, Ms. Atsushi Trong. She is a model of the U.S. success story. Having struggled in her native country, she immigrated to the United States as a teenager and studied clothing trends among her peers in both high school and college. She started her own clothing company and over the years has led the way by promoting such trends as miniskirts, bell-bottom pants, the so-called "Mature Elvis" look, and the hip-hop-rap grunge fashion. She has a net worth of over $100 million and no immediate family.

She has decided to plow some of her good fortune back into the educational system, which provided the intellectual foundation for her success. She selected the current class of her old high school, P.S. 101, and in 2011 gave each of 100 graduating students $100,000 to be used to pay tuition costs for four years at her college alma mater. Each of the 100 student donees used the $100,000 to prepay the four-year tuition costs. All these transactions took place during the current tax year.

You have been asked to determine the tax consequences of these transactions. What position would you take after considering the requirements of the IRC and *Statements on Standards for Tax Services* (reproduced in Appendix E)?

period beginning one year before they make the agreement. No gift arises from any transfer made in accordance with such agreement if a spouse transfers property to settle the other spouse's marital or property rights or to provide reasonable support for the children while they are minors.

EXAMPLE C:12-11▶ In June 2010, Hal and Wanda signed a property agreement whereby Hal is to transfer $750,000 to Wanda in settlement of her property rights. Hal makes the transfer in May 2011. Hal and Wanda receive a divorce decree in July 2011. Hal is not deemed to have made a gift to Wanda when he transferred property to her. ◀

QUALIFIED DISCLAIMERS. Sometimes a person named to receive property under a decedent's will prefers not to receive such property and would like to disclaim (not accept) it. Typically, the person is quite ill and/or elderly or very wealthy. State disclaimer statutes allow individuals to say "no thank you" to the property willed to them. State law or another provision in the will addresses how to determine who will receive the property after the original beneficiary (the disclaimant) declines to accept it.

ADDITIONAL COMMENT

Individuals who execute disclaimers, in a sense, participate in shifting wealth to another.

Section 2518(a) states that people making a qualified disclaimer are treated as if the disclaimed property were never transferred to them. Thus, the person making the disclaimer is not deemed to have made a gift to the person who receives the property because of the disclaimer.

A **qualified disclaimer** must meet the following four tests:

▶ It must be an irrevocable, unqualified, written refusal to accept property.

▶ The transferor or his or her legal representative must receive the refusal no later than nine months after the later of the day the transfer is made or the day the person named to receive the property becomes age 21.

▶ The disclaiming person must not have accepted the property interest or any of its benefits.

▶ As a result of the disclaimer, the property must pass to the decedent's spouse or a person other than the one disclaiming it. In addition, the person disclaiming the property cannot direct who is to receive the property.[15]

EXAMPLE C:12-12▶ Doug dies on February 1, 2011, and wills 500 acres of land to Joan. If Joan disclaims the property in a manner that meets all four of the tests for a qualified disclaimer, Joan will not be treated as making a gift to the person who receives the property as a result of her disclaimer. ◀

---

[15] Sec. 2518(b).

EXAMPLE C:12-13 ▶ Assume the same facts as in Example C:12-12 except Joan instead disclaims the property on January 2, 2012. Joan's action arose too late to meet the second qualified disclaimer test above. Thus, Joan makes a gift to the person who receives the property she disclaims. ◀

CESSATION OF DONOR'S DOMINION AND CONTROL

A gift occurs when a transfer becomes complete and is valued as of the date the transfer becomes complete. Thus, the concept of a completed transfer is important in two contexts: determination of whether a gift has arisen and, if so, the value of the gift. According to Treasury Regulations, a gift becomes complete—and is thus deemed made and valued—when the donor "has so parted with dominion and control as to leave in him no power to change its disposition, whether for his own benefit or for the benefit of another."[16] A gift is not necessarily complete just because the transferor cannot receive any further personal benefits, such as income, from the property. If the transferor still can influence the benefits others may receive from the transferred property, the transfer is incomplete with respect to the portion of the property over which the transferor retained control.

REVOCABLE TRUSTS. A transferor who conveys property to a revocable trust has made an incomplete transfer because the creator of a revocable trust can change the trust provisions, including the identity of the beneficiaries. Moreover, the creator may demand the return of the trust property. Because the transferor does not give up any control over property conveyed to a revocable trust, the individual does not make a gift upon funding the trust. Once the trustee distributes trust income to a beneficiary, however, the creator of the trust loses control over the distributed funds and then makes a completed gift of the income the trustee pays out.

EXAMPLE C:12-14 ▶ On May 1, Ted transfers $500,000 to a revocable trust with First National Bank as trustee. The trustee must pay out all the income to Ed during Ed's lifetime and at Ed's death distribute the property to Ed, Jr. On December 31, the trustee distributes $35,000 of income to Ed. The May 1 transfer is incomplete because Ted may revoke the trust; thus, no gift arises upon the funding of the trust. A $35,000 gift to Ed occurs on December 31 because Ted no longer has control over the income distributed to Ed. The gift is eligible for the annual exclusion. ◀

EXAMPLE C:12-15 ▶ Assume the same facts as in Example C:12-14 and that Ted amends the trust instrument on July 7 of the next year to make the trust irrevocable. By this date, the trust property has appreciated to $612,000. Ted makes a completed gift of $612,000 on July 7 of the next year because he gives up his powers over the trust. The gift is eligible for the annual exclusion. ◀

KEY POINT

If the donor retains control over any portion of the property, no gift is considered to have been made with respect to the portion of the property the donor still controls.

OTHER RETAINED POWERS. Transfers to an irrevocable trust can be deemed incomplete for the portion of the trust over which the creator kept control. Treasury Regulations state that if "the donor reserves any power over its [the property's] disposition, the gift may be wholly incomplete, or may be partially complete and partially incomplete, depending upon all the facts in the particular case."[17] One must examine the trust agreement language to determine the scope of the donor's retention of control. The regulations elaborate by indicating that "[a] gift is . . . incomplete if and to the extent that a reserved power gives the donor the power to name new beneficiaries or to change the interests of the beneficiaries."[18]

EXAMPLE C:12-16 ▶ On May 3, Art transfers $300,000 of property in trust with a bank as trustee. Art names his friends Bob and/or Sue to receive the trust income for 15 years and Karl to receive the trust property at the end of 15 years. Art reserves the power to determine how that income is to be divided between Bob and Sue each year, but the trustee must distribute all of the income each year. Because Art reserves the power over payment of the income for the 15-year period, this portion of the transfer is incomplete on May 3. Actuarial tables discussed in the next section of the chapter address the valuation of the completed gift to Karl. As discussed in Chapter C:14, under the grantor trust rules, Art is taxed on the trust income. ◀

---

[16] Reg. Sec. 25.2511-2(b).
[17] Ibid.

[18] Reg. Sec. 25.2511-2(c).

EXAMPLE C:12-17▶ Assume the same facts as in Example C:12-16 and that on December 31 Art instructs the trustee to distribute the trust's $34,000 of income as follows: $18,000 to Bob and $16,000 to Sue. Once the trustee pays out income, Art loses control over it. Thus, Art makes an $18,000 gift to Bob and a $16,000 gift to Sue on December 31. Each gift qualifies for the annual exclusion. ◀

EXAMPLE C:12-18▶ Assume the same facts as in Example C:12-16 and that on May 3 of the next year, when the trust assets are valued at $360,000, Art relinquishes his powers over payment of income and gives this power to the trustee. Art's transfer of the income interest (with a remaining term of 14 years) becomes complete on May 3 of the next year. The valuation of the gift of a 14-year income interest is determined from actuarial tables in Appendix H. ◀

Topic Review C:12-1 provides examples of various complete, incomplete, and partially complete transfers.

VALUATION OF GIFTS

GENERAL RULES. All gifts are valued at their FMV as of the date of the gift (i.e., the date the transfer becomes complete). Treasury Regulations state that a property's value is "the price at which such property would change hands between a willing buyer and a willing seller, neither being under any compulsion to buy or to sell, and both having reasonable knowledge of relevant facts."[19] According to the regulations, stocks and bonds traded on a stock exchange or over the counter are valued at the mean of the highest and lowest selling price on the date of the gift.[20] In general, the guidelines for valuing properties are the same, regardless of whether the property is conveyed during life or at death. An exception is life insurance policies, which are less valuable while the insured is alive. Valuation of life insurance policies is discussed in a later section of this chapter, as well as in Chapter C:13's coverage of the estate tax.

LIFE ESTATES AND REMAINDER INTERESTS. Often a donor transfers less than his or her entire interest in an asset. For example, an individual may transfer property in trust and reserve the right to the trust's income for life and name another individual to receive the property upon the transferor's death. In such a situation, the transferor retains a **life estate** and gives a **remainder interest**. In general, only the remainder interest is subject to the gift tax. An exception applies if the gift is to a family member, as discussed in the estate freeze section below. If the transferor keeps an annuity (a fixed amount) for life and names another person to receive the remainder at the transferor's death, in all situations the gift is of just the remainder interest.

A grantor also may transfer property in trust with the promise that another person will receive the income for a certain number of years and at the end of that time period the

ADDITIONAL COMMENT

Because the determination of value is such a subjective issue, a large number of gift tax controversies are nothing more than valuation disagreements.

KEY POINT

The value of the life estate plus the value of the remainder interest equals the total FMV of the property.

Topic Review C:12-1

Examples of Complete and Incomplete Transfers

1. Complete Transfers, Subject to Gift Tax:
   a. Property transferred outright to donee
   b. Property transferred to an irrevocable trust over which the donor retains no powers
2. Incomplete Transfers, Not Subject to Gift Tax:
   a. Property transferred to a revocable trust
   b. Property transferred to an irrevocable trust for which the donor retains discretionary powers over both income and the remainder interest
3. Partially Complete Transfers, Only a Portion Subject to Gift Tax:
   a. Property transferred to an irrevocable trust for which the donor retains discretionary powers over who receives the income but not the remainder interest[a]

[a]The gift of the remainder interest constitutes a completed transfer.

---

[19] Reg. Sec. 25.2512-1.   [20] Reg. Sec. 25.2512-2.

property will revert to the grantor. In this case, the donor retains a reversionary interest, whereas the other party receives a **term certain interest**.[21] As explained later in the discussion of estate freezes, unless the donee is a family member, only the term certain interest is subject to the gift tax. Trusts in which the grantor retains a reversionary interest have disadvantageous income tax consequences to the grantor if they were created after March 1, 1986. Chapter C:14 discusses the income tax treatment of such trusts.

Life estates, annuity interests, remainders, and term certain interests are valued from actuarial tables that incorporate the Sec. 7520 interest rate. In general, these tables must be used regardless of the actual earnings rate of the transferred assets. Excerpts from the tables appear in Appendix H. Table S is used for valuing life estates and remainders and Table B for term certain interests. The factor for a life estate or term certain interest is 1.0 minus the remainder factor. The remainder factor simply represents the present value of the right to receive a property at the end of someone's life (in the case of Table S) or at the end of a specified time (in the case of Table B). The value of the income interest plus the remainder interest is 1.0, the entire value of the property. The factor for an annuity is the life estate or the term factor divided by the Sec. 7520 interest rate. Section 7520 calls for the interest rate to be revised every month to the rate, rounded to the nearest 0.2%, that is 120% of the federal midterm rate applicable for the month of the transfer.[22] Congress mandated that at least once every ten years the tables be revised to reflect mortality experience. The most recent revised life tables are effective for transfers beginning on May 1, 2009.

EXAMPLE C:12-19 ▶ Refer to Example C:12-16, in which on May 3 Art transfers $300,000 of property in trust with a bank as trustee. Art names his friends Bob and Sue to receive the trust income for 15 years but reserves the power to determine how the income is to be divided between them each year. However, the trustee must distribute all the income. Art specifies that Karl is to receive the trust property at the end of the fifteenth year. Only the gift of the remainder interest is a completed transfer on May 3. The gift is valued from Table B. If the interest rate is 4%, the amount of the gift is $166,580 (0.555265 × $300,000), the present value of the property to be received by Karl at the end of 15 years. ◀

EXAMPLE C:12-20 ▶ Assume the same facts as in Example C:12-19 and that three years later, when the trust assets are valued at $360,000, Art relinquishes to the trustee his power over the payment of trust income. The income interest has a remaining term of 12 years. The gift is the present value of the 12-year income interest, which is valued from Table B by subtracting the factor for a remainder interest (0.624597 if the interest rate is 4%) from 1.0. Thus, the amount of the gift is $135,145 [(1.0 − 0.624597) × $360,000]. ◀

EXAMPLE C:12-21 ▶ On July 5 of the current year, Don transfers $100,000 of property in trust and names his friends Larry (age 60) to receive all of the income for the rest of Larry's life and Ruth (age 25) to receive the trust assets upon Larry's death. Don names a bank as the trustee. The amount of each donee's gift is reported on the gift tax return and is determined from Table S. If the interest rate is 4% and Larry is age 60, the value of the remainder interest gift to Ruth, as calculated from the single life remainder factors column of Table S, is $46,310 (0.46310 × $100,000). This amount represents the present value of the property Ruth will receive after the death of Larry, age 60. The remaining portion of the $100,000 of property, $53,690 ($100,000 − $46,310), is the value of the life estate transferred to Larry. The total value of the income plus remainder interests is 1.0. ◀

EXAMPLE C:12-22 ▶ In July of the current year, Amy (age 62) transferred $1 million of stock to a trust from which she retained the right to receive $120,000 per year for five years. She provided that the remainder will pass to her son, Arthur, at the end of the fifth year. Assume that 4% was the Sec. 7520 rate at the time of her transfer. She anticipated that the stock would continue to appreciate at its recent appreciation rate of 6% a year. The factor for a five-year annuity, assuming a 4%

---

[21] *Term certain interest* means that a particular person has an interest in the property held in trust for a specified time period. The person having such interest does not own or hold title to the property but has a right to receive the income from such property for a specified time period. At the end of the time period, the property reverts to the grantor (or passes to another person, the remainderman).

[22] The IRS regularly issues revenue rulings with applicable rate information.

rate, is 4.451825 [(1.0 − 0.821927, the factor for a remainder interest)/(0.04, the Sec. 7520 rate)]. Thus, Amy is deemed to have retained $534,219 (4.451825 × $120,000) and is deemed to have gifted the difference of $465,781 ($1,000,000 − $534,219) to Arthur. ◀

 STOP & THINK

Question: In which scenario would the amount of the gift be larger: (1) a gift of a remainder interest to a friend if a 68-year-old donor retained the income for life or (2) a gift of a remainder interest to a friend if an 86-year-old donor retained the income for life? Assume that each donor makes the gift on the same day so that the applicable interest rates are the same for each scenario.

Solution: The gift of the remainder interest would be larger if the donor is 86, instead of 68, because the actuarial value of the income interest the donor retains would be smaller if the donor is older. Under actuarial assumptions, older donors have shorter life expectancies.

ADDITIONAL COMMENT

In estate freeze transfers, Congress provided rules that generally increase the amount classified as a gift at the time of the actual transfer.

SPECIAL VALUATION RULES: ESTATE FREEZES. A number of years ago, Congress became concerned that individuals were able to shift wealth to other individuals, usually in a younger generation, without paying their "fair share" of the transfer taxes. An approach donors commonly used was to recapitalize a corporation (by exchanging common stock for both common and preferred shares) and then to give the common stock to individuals in the younger generation. This technique was one of a variety of transactions known as estate freezes.

In 1990, Congress decided to address the perceived problem of estate freezes by writing new valuation rules that apply for certain gifts. The thrust of these rules—current IRC Chapter 14 (Secs. 2701 through 2704)—is to ensure that gifts are not undervalued. A couple of the more common situations governed by the new rules are described below, but the rules are too complicated to warrant a complete discussion. If a parent owns 100% of a corporation's stock and then gives the common stock to his or her children and retains the preferred stock, the value of the right to the preferred dividends is treated as zero unless the stock is cumulative preferred. Consequently, unless the donor retains *cumulative* preferred stock, the value assigned to the common stock given away is relatively high. If the donor creates a trust in which he or she retains an interest and in which he or she gives an interest to a family member, the value of the transferor's retained interest is treated as zero unless the interest is an annuity interest (fixed payments) or a unitrust interest (calling for distributions equal to a specified percentage of the current FMV of the trust). Thus, the donor who retains an income interest is treated as having kept nothing. The effect of these rules increases the gift amount, compared with the result under prior law, unless the transferor structures the transaction to avoid having a zero value assigned to his or her retained interest.[23]

GIFT TAX CONSEQUENCES OF CERTAIN TRANSFERS

Some transactions that cause the transferor to make a gift are straightforward. It is easy to see that the disposition is within the scope of the gift tax if, for example, an individual places the title to stock or real estate solely in another person's name and receives less than adequate consideration in return. Treasury Regulations include the following examples of transactions that may be subject to the gift tax: forgiving of a debt; assignment of the benefits of a life insurance policy; transfer of cash; and transfer of federal, state, or municipal bonds.[24] The gratuitous transfer of state and local bonds falls within the scope of the gift tax, even though interest on such bonds is exempt from federal income taxation. The following discussion concerns the gift tax rules for several transfers that are more complicated than, for example, transferring the title to real property or stock to another person.

---

[23] See Reg. Secs. 25.2701-1 through -6 and 25.2702-1 through -6 for guidance concerning the estate freeze provisions.

[24] Reg. Sec. 25.2511-1(a).

CREATION OF JOINT BANK ACCOUNTS. Parties depositing money to a jointly owned bank account potentially face gift tax consequences. Funding a joint bank account is an incomplete transfer because the depositor is free to withdraw the amount deposited into the account. A gift occurs when one party withdraws an amount exceeding the amount he or she deposited.[25] The transfer is complete at that time because only the person who withdrew funds can control those funds.

EXAMPLE C:12-23 ▶ On May 1, Connie deposits $100,000 into a joint bank account in the names of Connie and Ben. Her friend Ben makes no deposits. On December 1, Ben withdraws $30,000 from the joint account and purchases an automobile. No gift arises upon the creation of the bank account. However, on December 1, Connie makes a gift to Ben of $30,000, the excess of Ben's withdrawal over Ben's deposit. ◀

CREATION OF OTHER JOINT TENANCIES. **Joint tenancy** is a popular form of property ownership from a convenience standpoint because, when one joint owner dies, the property is automatically owned by the survivor(s). Each joint tenant is deemed to have an equal interest in the property. A completed gift arises when the transferor titles real estate or other property in the names of himself or herself and another (e.g., a spouse, a sibling, or a child) as joint tenants. The person furnishing the consideration to acquire the property is deemed to have made a gift to the other joint tenant in an amount equal to the value of the donee's pro rata interest in the property.[26]

EXAMPLE C:12-24 ▶ Kwame purchases land for $250,000 and immediately has it titled in the names of Kwame and Kesha, as joint tenants with right of survivorship. Kwame and Kesha are not husband and wife. Kwame makes a gift to Kesha of $125,000, or one-half the value of the property. ◀

TAX STRATEGY TIP

An owner of a life insurance policy who wishes to gift the ownership to someone else, such as the beneficiary, can use the following strategies to avoid the gift tax:
(1) Before making the gift, borrow enough against the policy to reduce its net value to the amount of the annual exclusion ($13,000 in 2011). The former owner (borrower) then can pay premiums and make loan repayments, not to exceed the annual exclusion in any given year.
(2) Have the insurance company rewrite the policy into separate policies, each having a value that does not exceed the annual exclusion. Then, gift one policy each year for several years.

TRANSFER OF LIFE INSURANCE POLICIES. The mere naming of another as the beneficiary of a life insurance policy is an incomplete transfer because the owner of the policy can change the beneficiary designation at any time. However, if an individual irrevocably assigns all ownership rights in an insurance policy to another party, this event constitutes a gift of the policy to the new owner.[27] Ownership rights include the ability to change the beneficiary, borrow against the policy, and cash the policy in for its cash surrender value.

The payment of a premium on an insurance policy owned by another person is considered a gift to the policy's owner. The amount of the gift is the amount of the premium paid. The tax result is the same as if the donor transferred cash to the policy owner and the owner used the cash to pay the premium.

According to Reg. Sec. 25.2512-6, the value of the gift of a life insurance policy is the amount it would cost to purchase a comparable policy on the date of the gift. The regulations point out, however, that if the policy is several years old, the cost of a comparable policy is not readily ascertainable. In such a situation, the policy is valued at its interpolated terminal reserve (i.e., an amount similar to the policy's cash surrender value) plus the amount of any unexpired premiums. The insurance company will furnish information concerning the interpolated terminal reserve.

EXAMPLE C:12-25 ▶ On September 1, Bill transfers his entire ownership rights in a $300,000 life insurance policy on his own life to his sister Susan. The policy's interpolated terminal reserve is $24,000 as of September 1. On July 1, Bill had paid the policy's $4,800 annual premium. Bill makes a gift to Susan on September 1 of $28,000 [$24,000 + (10/12 × $4,800)] because he transferred ownership to Susan. If, however, the policy had been a term insurance policy, which has no interpolated terminal reserve, the gift would have been $4,000 (10/12 × $4,800), the amount of the unexpired premium.

On July 1 of the next year, Bill pays the $4,800 annual premium on the policy now owned by Susan. As a result of the premium payment, Bill makes a $4,800 gift to Susan that year, the same result as if he had given her $4,800 of cash to pay the premium. ◀

---

[25] Reg. Sec. 25.2511-1(h)(4).
[26] Reg. Sec. 25.2511-1(h)(5). If the two joint tenants are husband and wife, no taxable gift will arise because of the unlimited marital deduction.

[27] Reg. Sec. 25.2511-1(h)(8).

EXAMPLE C:12-26▶ Assume the same facts as in Example C:12-25 except that Susan, who now owns the policy, changes the beneficiary of the policy from Frank to John. Susan does not make a gift because she has not given up control; she can change the beneficiary again in the future. ◀

EXERCISE OF A GENERAL POWER OF APPOINTMENT.   Section 2514 provides the rules concerning powers of appointment. A **power of appointment** exists when a person transfers property (perhaps in trust) and grants someone else the power to specify who eventually will receive the property. Thus, possession of a power of appointment has some of the same benefits as ownership of the property. Powers can be general or special. *Potential* gift tax consequences are associated with the powerholder's exercise of a **general power of appointment**. A person possesses a general power of appointment if he or she has the power to appoint the property (have the property distributed) to him- or herself, his or her creditors or estate, or the creditors of his or her estate. The words *his or her estate* mean that there are no restrictions concerning to whom the individual may bequeath the property.

A gift occurs when a person exercises a general power of appointment and names some other person to receive the property.[28] The donee is the person the powerholder names to receive the property. A person who exercises a general power of appointment in favor of himself or herself does not make a gift (i.e., one cannot make a gift to him- or herself).

EXAMPLE C:12-27▶ In 2011, Tina funds an irrevocable trust with $600,000 and names Van to receive the income for life. In addition, Tina grants Van a general power of appointment exercisable during his life as well as at his death. Tina made a gift to Van of $600,000 at the time she transferred the property to the trust in 2011. In 2012, Van instructs the bank trustee to distribute $50,000 of trust property to Kay. Through the exercise of his general power of appointment in favor of Kay, Van makes a $50,000 gift to Kay in 2012 because he diverted property to her. ◀

NET GIFTS.   A **net gift** occurs when an individual makes a gift to a donee who agrees to pay the gift tax as a condition of receiving the gift. The donee's payment of the gift tax is treated as consideration paid to the donor. The amount of the gift is the excess of the FMV of the transferred property over the amount of the gift tax paid by the donee. Because the amount of the gift depends on the amount of gift tax payable, which in turn depends on the amount of the gift, the calculations require the use of simultaneous equations.[29]

The net gift strategy is especially attractive for people who would like to remove a rapidly appreciating asset from their estate but are unable to pay the gift tax because of liquidity problems. However, a net gift has one potential disadvantage: the Supreme Court has ruled that the donor must recognize as a gain the excess of the gift tax payable over his or her adjusted basis in the property.[30] The Court's rationale is that the donee's payment of the donor's gift tax liability constitutes an "amount realized" for purposes of determining the gain or loss realized on a sale, exchange, or other disposition. From a practical standpoint, this decision affects only donors who transfer property so highly appreciated that the property's adjusted basis is less than the gift tax liability.

EXAMPLE C:12-28▶ Mary transferred land with a $3 million FMV to her son, Sam, who agreed to pay the gift tax liability. Mary's adjusted basis in the land was $15,000. Earlier in 2011, she gave him $13,000, which was covered by the annual exclusion. The taxable gift was $3 million, less the gift tax paid by Sam. Simultaneous equations are necessary to calculate the amount of the gift and the gift tax liability. Mary had to recognize gain equal to the excess of the gift tax liability paid by Sam minus Mary's $15,000 basis in the property.

---

[28] In general, the exercise of a special power of appointment is free of gift tax consequences. In the case of special powers of appointment, the holder of the power does not have an unrestricted ability to name the persons to receive the property. For example, he or she may be able to appoint to only his or her descendants.
[29] In Rev. Rul. 75-72 (1975-1 C.B. 310), the IRS explained how to calculate

the amount of the net gift and the gift tax. In Ltr. Rul. 7842068 (July 20, 1978), the IRS stated that the donor's available unified credit, not the donee's, is used to calculate the gift tax payable.
[30] *Victor P. Diedrich v. CIR*, 50 AFTR 2d 82-5054, 82-1 USTC ¶9419 (USSC, 1982).

TAX STRATEGY TIP

As a general rule, substantially appreciated property should not be transferred by gift. It should be transferred at death to take advantage of the step-up in basis to the estate tax value (usually FMV at date of death). If Mary in Example C:12-28 were elderly, it might be better to transfer an asset other than the land to get a step-up in basis for the land.

Assume that, because of sizable previous taxable gifts, any additional gifts Mary made were subject to the 35% maximum gift tax rate for 2011, Assume Mary had used all of her unified credit. If G represents the amount of the gift and T is the amount of the tax, then

$$G = \$3,000,000 - T$$
$$T = 0.35G$$

Substituting 0.35G for T in the first equation and solving for G yields G = $3,000,000 ÷ 1.35 = $2,222,222, the amount of the gift. The tax is 35% of this amount, or $777,778. The calculation increases in difficulty when, because of splitting brackets, more than one gift tax rate applies. Mary's gain equals the $777,778 gift tax paid by Sam minus her $15,000 basis in the property, or $762,778. ◀

EXCLUSIONS

OBJECTIVE 4

Determine whether an annual gift tax exclusion is available

In many instances, a portion or all of a transfer by gift is tax-free because of the annual exclusion authorized by Sec. 2503(b). In 1932, the Senate Finance Committee explained the purpose of the **annual exclusion** as follows:

> Such exemption . . . is to obviate the necessity of keeping an account of and reporting numerous small gifts, and . . . to fix the amount sufficiently large to cover in most cases wedding and Christmas gifts and occasional gifts of relatively small amount.[31]

In most gift transactions, the donor makes no taxable gift because of the annual exclusion. Consequently, administration of the gift tax provisions is a much simpler task than it otherwise would be.

AMOUNT OF THE EXCLUSION

The amount of this exclusion, which is analogous to an exclusion from gross income for income tax purposes, is $13,000.[32] It is available each year for an unlimited number of donees. For transfers made in trust, each beneficiary is deemed to be a separate donee. Any number of donors may make a gift to the same donee, and each is eligible to claim the exclusion. The only limitations on the annual exclusion are the donor's wealth, generosity, and imagination in identifying donees.

EXAMPLE C:12-29 ▶

In 2011, Ann and Bob each give $13,000 cash to each of Tad and Liz. Ann and Bob again make $13,000 cash gifts to Tad and Liz in 2012. For both 2011 and 2012, Ann receives $26,000 of exclusions ($13,000 for the gift to Tad and $13,000 for the gift to Liz). The same result applies to Bob. (This example assumes the $13,000 exclusion amount will remain at this level in 2012.) ◀

TAX STRATEGY TIP

Gifts up to the amount of the annual exclusion not only remove the gifted amounts from the donor's estate with no gift tax cost but also remove the property's future income from the donor's estate. In addition, the property's income can be shifted to someone whose tax bracket might be lower than the donor's, thereby reducing income taxes.

The annual exclusion is a significant tax planning device that has no estate tax counterpart. So long as a donor's gifts to a particular donee do not exceed the excludable amount, the donor will never make any taxable gifts or incur any gift tax liability. Because taxable gifts will be zero, the donor's estate tax base will not include any adjusted taxable gifts. A donor, who each year for ten years prior to 2002 gave $10,000 per donee to each of ten donees, removed $1 million (10 × $10,000 × 10) from being taxed in his or her estate. The donor accomplished these transfers without making any taxable gifts or paying any gift tax. If retained, the $1 million would have been taxed in the donor's estate, at perhaps the top estate tax rate, unless the property was willed to the donor's surviving spouse.

PRESENT INTEREST REQUIREMENT

Although we generally speak of the annual exclusion as if it were available automatically for all gifts, in actuality it is not. A donor receives an exclusion only for gifts that constitute a present interest.

---

[31] S. Rept. No. 665, 72nd Cong., 1st Sess. (1932), reprinted in 1939-1 C.B. (Part 2), pp. 525–526.
[32] On January 1, 1982, Congress increased the annual exclusion from $3,000 to $10,000. Later, Congress provided that the exclusion would be indexed after 1998, with inflation adjustments rounded to the next lowest multiple of $1,000. In 2002, the exclusion rose to $11,000 and remained there through 2005. It rose to $12,000 in 2006 and to $13,000 in 2009.

DEFINITION OF PRESENT INTEREST. A **present interest** is "an unrestricted right to the immediate use, possession, or enjoyment of property or the income from property (such as a life estate or term certain)."[33] Only present interests qualify for the annual exclusion. If only a portion of a transfer constitutes a present interest, the excluded portion of the gift may not exceed the value of the present interest.

DEFINITION OF FUTURE INTEREST. A future interest is the opposite of a present interest. A **future interest** "is a legal term, and includes reversions, remainders, and other interests . . . which are limited to commence in use, possession, or enjoyment at some future date or time."[34] Gifts of future interests are ineligible for the annual exclusion. The following examples help demonstrate the attributes of present and future interests.

EXAMPLE C:12-30 ▶

Nancy transfers $500,000 of property to an irrevocable trust with a bank serving as trustee. Nancy names Norm (age 55) to receive all the trust income quarterly for the rest of Norm's life. At Norm's death, the property is to pass to Ellen (age 25) or Ellen's estate. Norm receives an unrestricted right to immediate enjoyment of the income. Thus, Norm has a present interest. Ellen, however, has a future interest because Ellen cannot enjoy the property or any of the income until Norm dies. The taxable gift is $487,000 ($500,000 − $13,000). ◀

EXAMPLE C:12-31 ▶

Greg transfers $800,000 of property to an irrevocable trust with a bank serving as trustee and instructs the trustee to distribute all the trust income semiannually to Greg's three adult children, Jill, Katy, and/or Laura. The trustee is to use its discretion in deciding how much to distribute to each beneficiary. Moreover, the trustee is authorized to distribute nothing to a particular beneficiary if it deems such action to be in the beneficiary's best interest. Although all the income must be paid out, the trustee has complete discretion to determine how much to pay to a particular beneficiary. None of the beneficiaries has the assurance that he or she will receive a trust distribution. Thus, Greg created no present interests, and the annual exclusion does not apply. The taxable gift, therefore, is $800,000. ◀

SPECIAL RULE FOR TRUSTS FOR MINORS. Congress realized that many donors would not want to require trusts for minor children to distribute all their income to the young children. Accordingly, Congress enacted Sec. 2503(c), which authorizes special trusts for minors, to address donors' concerns about the distribution of trust income to minors. Section 2503(c) authorizes an annual exclusion for gifts to trusts for beneficiaries under age 21 even though the trusts need not distribute all their income annually. Such trusts, known as **Sec. 2503(c) trusts**, allow donors to claim the annual exclusion if the following two conditions are met:

▶ Until the beneficiary becomes age 21, the trustee may pay the income and/or the underlying assets to the beneficiary.

▶ Any income and underlying assets not paid to the beneficiary will pass to that beneficiary when he or she reaches age 21. If the beneficiary should die before becoming age 21, the income and underlying assets are payable to either the beneficiary's estate or to any person the minor may appoint if the minor possesses a general power of appointment over the property.

If the trust instrument contains both the provisions listed above, no part of the trust is considered to be a gift of a future interest. Therefore, the entire transfer is treated as a present interest and is eligible for the annual exclusion.

As a result of Sec. 2503(c), donors creating trusts for donees under age 21 receive an exclusion even though the trustee has discretion over paying out the trust income. However, the IRC requires the trustee to distribute the assets and accumulated income at age 21.

CRUMMEY TRUST. The **Crummey trust** is yet another technique that allows the donor to obtain an annual exclusion upon funding a discretionary trust. The trust can terminate at whatever age the donor specifies and can be created for a beneficiary of any age. Thus, the *Crummey* trust is a much more flexible arrangement than the Sec. 2503(c) trust.

ADDITIONAL COMMENT

The donor may serve as trustee of a Sec. 2503(c) trust, but this approach generally is not advisable. If the donor's powers are not sufficiently limited, the trust property will be included in the donor's estate if the donor's death occurs before the trust terminates.

ADDITIONAL COMMENT

The holder of a *Crummey* power must be given notice of a contribution to the trust to which the power relates and must be given a reasonable time period within which to exercise the power. The donor receives the annual exclusion regardless of whether the donee exercises the power.

---

[33] Reg. Sec. 25.2503-3(b).

[34] Reg. Sec. 25.2503-3(a).

The *Crummey* trust is named for a Ninth Circuit Court of Appeals decision holding that the trust beneficiaries received a present interest as a result of certain language in the trust instrument.[35] That language, which is referred to interchangeably as a *Crummey* power, *Crummey* demand power, or *Crummey* withdrawal power, entitled each beneficiary to demand a distribution of the lesser of $4,000 (the amount in the case) or the amount transferred to the trust that year. If the beneficiary did not exercise the power by a specified date, it expired. The trust instrument included the "lesser of" language for the demand power because the donor does not have to create a present interest larger than the annual exclusion amount. In years in which the gift is smaller than the annual exclusion amount, the donor simply needs to be able to exclude the amount of that year's gift. In addition, the donor wants to restrict the amount to which the beneficiary can have access. Because of potential changes in the annual exclusion amount, the trust instrument often states that the maximum amount the beneficiary can withdraw is "an amount equal to the annual exclusion for federal gift tax purposes" or twice that amount if gift splitting is anticipated.

The court held that the demand power provided each beneficiary with a present interest equal to the maximum amount the beneficiary could require the trustee to pay over to him or her that year. Use of the *Crummey* trust technique entitles the donor to receive the annual exclusion while creating a discretionary trust that terminates at whatever age the donor deems appropriate. The donor thereby avoids the restrictive rules of Sec. 2503(c). Generally, the donor hopes the beneficiary will not exercise the demand right.

EXAMPLE C:12-32 ▶

Al funds two $100,000 irrevocable trusts and names First Bank the trustee. The first trust is for the benefit of Kay, his 15-year-old daughter. The trustee has discretion to distribute income and/or principal to Kay until she reaches age 21. If she dies before age 21, the trust assets are payable to whomever she appoints in her will or to her estate if she dies without a will. The second trust is for the benefit of Bob, Al's 25-year-old son. Income and/or principal are payable to Bob in the trustee's discretion until Bob reaches age 35, whereupon Bob will receive the trust assets. Bob may demand by December 31 of each year that the trustee pay him the lesser of the amount of the gift tax annual exclusion or the amount transferred to the trust that calendar year. The trust for Kay is a Sec. 2503(c) trust, and the one for Bob is a *Crummey* trust. An annual exclusion is available for each trust. ◀

 STOP & THINK

Question: For which of the following gifts would the donor receive an annual exclusion:

▶ A gift of a remainder interest in land if the donor retains the income interest for life

▶ A gift outright of a life insurance policy that has a cash surrender value

▶ A gift to a discretionary trust that is classified as a Sec. 2503(c) trust

▶ A gift to a Crummey trust?

Solution: All the transfers except the gift of the remainder interest (a future interest) are eligible for the annual exclusion. Even though the gift to the Sec. 2503(c) trust does not literally involve a gift of a present interest (the right to current income or enjoyment), the IRC explicitly allows this kind of transfer to qualify for the annual exclusion.

GIFT TAX DEDUCTIONS

OBJECTIVE 5

Identify deductions available for gift tax purposes

The formula for determining taxable gifts allows both an unlimited marital deduction and an unlimited charitable contribution deduction. The **marital deduction** is for transfers to one's spouse. The **charitable contribution deduction** is for gifts to charitable organizations. Section 2524 states that the deductible amount in either case may not exceed the amount of the "includible gift"—that is, the amount of the gift exceeding the annual exclusion. Thus, the lowest possible taxable gift is zero, not a negative number, as could be the case if the deduction equaled the total amount of the gift.

---

[35] *D. Clifford Crummey v. CIR*, 22 AFTR 2d 6023, 68-2 USTC ¶12,541 (9th Cir., 1968).

MARITAL DEDUCTION

ADDITIONAL
COMMENT
Congress allowed a marital
deduction because a taxpayer
who transfers property to his or
her spouse has not made a transfer outside the economic (hus-
band/wife) unit. For similar reasons, the interspousal gift has no
income tax consequences. The
donor spouse recognizes no gain
or loss, and the donee spouse
takes a carryover basis.

Generally, the marital deduction results in tax-free interspousal transfers, but an exception discussed below applies to gifts of certain terminable interests. Congress enacted the marital deduction in 1948 to provide more uniform treatment of community property and noncommunity property donors. To recap, in community property states, most property acquired after marriage is owned equally by each spouse. In noncommunity property states, however, the spouses' wealth often is divided unequally, and such spouses can equalize each individual's share of the wealth only by engaging in a gift-giving program. As a result of the marital deduction, spouses can shift wealth between themselves completely free of any gift tax consequences.

UNLIMITED AMOUNT. Over the years, the maximum marital deduction has varied, but since 1981 a spouse has been able to deduct up to 100% of the amount of gifts made to the other spouse. The amount of the marital deduction, however, is limited to the portion of the gift that exceeds the annual exclusion.[36] After 1981, transfers of community property became eligible for the marital deduction.

EXAMPLE C:12-33 ▶   A wife gives her husband stock valued at $450,000. She excludes $13,000 because of the annual exclusion and claims a $437,000 marital deduction. Thus, no taxable gift arises.   ◀

GIFTS OF TERMINABLE INTERESTS: GENERAL RULE.
Nondeductible Terminable Interests.   A **terminable interest** is an interest that ends or is terminated when some event occurs (or fails to occur) or a specified amount of time passes. Some, but not all, terminable interests are ineligible for the marital deduction.[37] A marital deduction is denied only when the transfer is of a *nondeductible* terminable interest. A nondeductible terminable interest has one of the following characteristics:

▶ The donee-spouse's interest ceases at a set time (such as at death) and the property then either passes back to the donor or passes to a third party who does not pay adequate consideration.

▶ Immediately after making the gift, the donor has the power to name someone else to receive an interest in the property, and the person named may possess the property upon the termination of the donee-spouse's interest.[38]

The next three examples illustrate some of the subtleties of the definition of nondeductible terminable interests. In Example C:12-34, a marital deduction is available because the transfer involves neither characteristic of a nondeductible terminable interest.

EXAMPLE C:12-34 ▶   A donor gives a patent to a spouse. A patent is a terminable interest because the property interest terminates at the end of the patent's legal life. Nevertheless, the patent does not constitute a nondeductible terminable interest. When the patent's legal life expires, a third party will not possess an interest in the patent. Thus, a donor will receive a marital deduction.   ◀

In Example C:12-35, a marital deduction is denied because the first of the two alternative characteristics of a nondeductible terminable interest exists.

EXAMPLE C:12-35 ▶   A donor transfers property in trust and (1) names his wife to receive trust income, at the trustee's discretion, annually for the next 15 years and (2) states that at the end of the 15-year period the trust's assets are to be distributed to their child. The donor has given his wife a nondeductible terminable interest. When the spouse's interest ceases, the property passes to their child, a recipient who did not pay adequate consideration. Thus, the donor receives no marital deduction.   ◀

In Example C:12-36, a marital deduction is available. In addition to having a lifetime income interest, the donee-spouse has a general power of appointment over the trust's assets and can specify who eventually receives the property.

---

[36] Sec. 2524.
[37] Sec. 2523(b).

[38] Ibid.

EXAMPLE C:12-36▶ The donor gives his wife the right to all the income from a trust annually for life plus a general power of appointment over the trust's assets. He has transferred an interest eligible for the marital deduction. The general power of appointment may be exercisable during life, at death, or at both times. In addition, the donee-spouse is entitled to receive the income annually. ◀

TAX STRATEGY TIP

A general power of appointment can qualify a transfer for the marital deduction. For example, assume that last year Brad transferred property to a trust, income to be distributed annually to his wife Sonia until her death, with a general power of appointment in Sonia over the remainder. Sonia's general power of appointment allowed the transfer to be eligible for the gift tax marital deduction.

TAX STRATEGY TIP

By using a QTIP, a donor can achieve a marital deduction while exercising some control over the property. For example, assume the same facts as in the previous annotation except that Brad has been married twice. He had two children by his first wife and three children with Sonia. Brad could not be sure his first two children would receive any assets from the trust because Sonia could exercise her general power of appointment in favor of just their three children (or someone else). If Brad funded a QTIP, the trust instrument could specify that the remainder, on Sonia's death, would go equally to all five children. Brad could thus control the ultimate disposition of the remainder and still receive a marital deduction.

The rationale behind the nondeductible terminable interest rule is that a donor should obtain a marital deduction only if he or she conveys an interest that will have transfer tax significance to the donee-spouse. In other words, when a donee spouse later gives away property received as a result of an interspousal transfer, a transfer subject to the gift tax occurs. If the donee-spouse retains such property until death, the asset is included in the donee-spouse's gross estate.

QTIP PROVISIONS. Beginning in 1982, Congress made a major change to the nondeductible terminable interest rule and allowed transfers of qualified terminable interest property to be eligible for the marital deduction.[39] Such transfers are commonly referred to as *QTIP transfers*. **Qualified terminable interest property** is property

▶ That is transferred by the donor-spouse,

▶ In which the donee has a "qualifying income interest for life," and

▶ For which a special election has been made.

A spouse has the necessary "qualifying income interest for life" if

▶ The spouse is entitled to all the income from the property annually or more often, and

▶ No person has a power to appoint any part of the property to any person other than the donee-spouse unless the power cannot be exercised while the spouse is alive.

The QTIP rule enhances the attractiveness of making transfers to one's spouse because a donor can receive a marital deduction—and thereby make a nontaxable transfer—without having to grant the spouse full control over the gifted property. The QTIP rule is especially attractive for a donor who wants to ensure that the children by a previous marriage will receive the property upon the donee-spouse's death.

The donor does not have to claim a marital deduction even though the transfer otherwise qualifies as a QTIP transfer. Claiming the deduction on such transfers is elective.[40] If the donor elects to claim a marital deduction, the donee-spouse must include the QTIP trust property in his or her estate at its value as of the donee-spouse's date of death. Thus, as with other transfers qualifying for the marital deduction, the interspousal transfer is tax-free, and the taxable event is postponed until the donee-spouse transfers the property.

EXAMPLE C:12-37▶ Jo transfers $1 million of property in trust with a bank acting as trustee. All the trust income is payable to Jo's husband, Ed (age 64), quarterly for the rest of his life. Upon Ed's death, the property will pass to Jo's nieces. This gift is eligible for a marital deduction. If Jo elects to claim the marital deduction, she will receive a $987,000 ($1,000,000 − $13,000) marital deduction. The deduction is limited to the amount of the includible gift, i.e., the gift exceeding the annual exclusion. Jo's taxable gift will be zero. ◀

Note that Jo's marital deduction in the preceding example is for $987,000 and not for the value of Ed's life estate. If Jo elects to claim the marital deduction, Ed's gross estate will include the value of the entire trust, valued as of the date of Ed's death. The QTIP provision permits Jo to receive a marital deduction while still being able to specify who will receive the property upon her husband's death.

Topic Review C:12-2 summarizes the eligibility of a transfer for the marital deduction and the amount of the marital deduction that can be claimed.

---

[39] Sec. 2523(f).
[40] The donor might decide not to claim the marital deduction if the donee-spouse has substantial assets already or a short life expectancy, especially if the gifted property's value is expected to appreciate at a high annual rate.

Topic Review C:12-2

Eligibility for and Amount of the Marital Deduction

Examples of Transfers Eligible for the Marital Deduction
Property transferred to spouse as sole owner
Property transferred in trust with all the income payable to the spouse for life and over which the donee-spouse has a general power of appointment
Property transferred in trust with all the income payable annually or more often to the spouse for life and for which the donor-spouse designated the remainderman—marital deduction available if elected under QTIP rule

Examples of Transfers Ineligible for the Marital Deduction
Property transferred in trust with the income payable in the trustee's discretion to the spouse for life, and for which the donor-spouse designated the remainderman
Property transferred in trust with all the income payable to the spouse for a specified number of years and for which the donor-spouse designated the remainderman

Amount of the Marital Deduction, if Available
The amount of the transfer minus the portion eligible for the annual exclusion

CHARITABLE CONTRIBUTION DEDUCTION

If a donor is not required to file a gift tax return to report noncharitable gifts, the donor does not have to report gifts to charitable organizations on a gift tax return, provided a charitable contribution deduction is available and the charitable organization receives the donor's entire interest in the property. Claiming an income tax deduction for a charitable contribution does not preclude the donor from also obtaining a gift tax deduction. In contrast with the income tax provisions, the gift tax charitable contribution deduction has no percentage limitation. The only ceiling on the deduction is imposed by Sec. 2524, which limits the deduction to the amount of the gift that exceeds the excluded portion.

EXAMPLE C:12-38 ▶ Julio gives stock valued at $76,000 to State University. Julio receives a $13,000 annual exclusion and a $63,000 charitable contribution deduction for *gift* tax purposes. However, he need not report the gift on a gift tax return if he does not have to file a return to report gifts to noncharitable donees. On his *income* tax return, he receives a $76,000 charitable contribution deduction, subject to AGI limitations. ◀

TAX STRATEGY TIP

A charitably minded taxpayer could avoid the gift (and the estate) tax entirely by giving all his or her property to a qualified charitable organization. Actually, in 2011 the taxpayer could give $5 million plus the amount shielded by the annual exclusion to noncharitable donees and still pay no gift tax, assuming the taxpayer had not earlier made any taxable gifts.

TRANSFERS ELIGIBLE FOR THE DEDUCTION. To be deductible, the gift must be made to a charitable organization. The rules defining charitable organizations are quite similar for income, gift, and estate tax purposes.[41] According to Sec. 2522, a gift tax deduction is available for contributions to the following:

▶ The United States or any subordinate level of government within the United States as long as the transfer is solely for public purposes

▶ A corporation, trust fund, etc., organized exclusively for religious, charitable, scientific, literary, or educational purposes, or to foster amateur sports competition, including the encouragement of art and the prevention of cruelty to children or animals

▶ A fraternal society or similar organization operating under the lodge system if the gifts are to be used in the United States only for religious, charitable, scientific, literary, or educational purposes

▶ A war veterans' post or organization organized in the United States or one of its possessions if no part of its net earnings accrues to the benefit of private shareholders or individuals

---

[41] In contrast to the income tax rules, a charitable contribution deduction is available under the gift tax rules for transfers made to foreign charitable organizations. No deduction is available, however, for gifts made to foreign governments.

SPLIT-INTEREST TRANSFERS.   Specialized rules apply when a donor makes a transfer for both private (i.e., an individual) and public (i.e., a charitable organization) purposes. Such arrangements are known as **split-interest transfers**. An example of a split-interest transfer is the gift of a residence to one's sister for life with the remainder interest to a university. If a donor gives a charitable organization a remainder interest, the donor forfeits the charitable contribution deduction unless the remainder interest is in either a personal residence (not necessarily the donor's principal residence), a farm, a charitable remainder annuity trust or unitrust, or a pooled income fund.[42] A split-interest gift of a present interest to a charity qualifies for a charitable contribution deduction only if the charity receives a guaranteed annuity interest or a unitrust interest. Actuarial tables are used to value split-interest transfers (see Appendix H).

EXAMPLE C:12-39▶

Al transfers $800,000 of property to a charitable remainder annuity trust. He reserves an annuity of $56,000 per year for his remaining life and specifies that upon his death the trust property will pass to the American Red Cross. Al must report this transaction on a gift tax return because the Red Cross did not receive his entire interest in the property. In the same year, Al gives a museum a remainder interest in his antique furniture collection and reserves a life estate for himself.

Each of these is a split-interest transfer. Unfortunately for the donor, only the remainder interest in the charitable remainder annuity trust is eligible for a charitable contribution deduction. Consequently, Al makes a taxable gift equal to the value of the remainder interest in the antique furniture. (If Al had given a remainder interest in a personal residence or farm, he would have received a charitable contribution deduction for this gift.) Even though the furniture is not an income-producing property, the value of the remainder interest is determined from the actuarial tables found in Appendix H.

Assume that Al was age 60 at the time of the gifts and that the Sec. 7520 interest rate was 4%. What is the amount of Al's charitable contribution deduction?

Answer: The portion of the annuity trust retained by Al is $751,660 {[(1.0 − 0.46310)/0.04] × $56,000}. The charitable deduction on the gift tax return is $48,340 ($800,000 − $751,660), the value of the remainder interest, a future interest. The same amount also is allowable—subject to the ceiling rules—as a charitable contribution deduction on Al's income tax return for that year. ◀

THE GIFT-SPLITTING ELECTION

OBJECTIVE 6

Apply the gift-splitting rules

The gift-splitting provisions of Sec. 2513 allow spouses to treat a gift actually made by just one of them as if each spouse made one-half of the gift. This election offers several advantages, as follows:

▶ If only one spouse makes a gift to a particular donee, the election enables a spouse to give $26,000 (instead of $13,000) to the donee before a taxable gift arises.

▶ If per-donee annual transfers exceed $26,000 and taxable gifts occur, the election may reduce the applicable marginal gift tax rate.

▶ Each spouse may use a unified credit to reduce the gift tax payable.

TAX STRATEGY TIP

Donors can magnify the benefits of the annual exclusion by using gift splitting techniques.

To take advantage of the gift-splitting election, the spouses must meet the following requirements at the time of the transfer:

▶ They must be U.S. citizens or residents.

▶ At the time of the gift(s) for which the spouses make an election, the donor-spouse must be married to the person who consents to gift splitting. In addition, the donor-spouse must not remarry before the end of the year.

---

[42] In a **charitable remainder annuity trust**, an individual receives trust distributions for a certain time period or for life. The annual distributions are a uniform percentage (5% or higher) of the value of the trust property, valued on the date of the transfer. For a **charitable remainder unitrust**, the distributions are similar, except that they are a uniform percentage (5% or higher) of the value of the trust property, revalued at least annually. Thus, the annual distributions from a unitrust, but not an annuity trust, vary from one year to the next. Both unitrusts and annuity trusts must meet the requirements that the payout rate does not exceed 50% of the value of the property and the value of the remainder interest is at least 10% of the initial FMV. A **pooled income fund** is similar in concept to a mutual fund. The various individual beneficiaries receive annual distributions of their proportionate shares of the pooled income fund's total income.

ADDITIONAL COMMENT

A wife makes a gift of $40,000 to a child in March and a gift of $60,000 to another child in November of the same year. The gift-splitting election, if made, will apply to both gifts because the election to gift split applies to all gifts made during the year. With gift splitting, her husband will be treated as making one-half of each gift.

The gift-splitting election is effective for all transfers to third parties made during the portion of the year that the spouses were married to each other.

A spouse living in a community property state who makes a gift of separate property (e.g., an asset received by inheritance) may desire to use gift splitting. In this case, the election automatically extends to gifts of community property even though splitting each spouse's gifts of community property has no impact on the "bottom-line" amount of taxable gifts.

Note that gift splitting is an all-or-nothing proposition. Spouses wanting to elect it for one gift must elect it for all gifts to third parties for that year. Each year's election stands alone, however, and is not binding on future years.[43] The procedural aspects of the gift-splitting election are discussed in the Compliance and Procedural Considerations section of this chapter.

EXAMPLE C:12-40▶

Eli marries Joy on April 1 of the current year. They are still married to each other at the end of the year. In March, Eli gave Amy $60,000. In July, Eli gave Barb $52,000, and Joy gave Claire $28,000. If the couple elects gift splitting, the election is effective only for the July gifts. Each spouse is treated as giving $26,000 and $14,000 to Barb and Claire, respectively. Because they may not elect gift splitting for the gift Eli makes before their marriage, Eli is treated as giving $60,000—the amount he actually transfers—to Amy. Under gift splitting, both Eli and Joy exclude $13,000 of gifts to both Barb and Claire, or a total of $52,000. Eli also excludes $13,000 of his gift to Amy. ◀

ADDITIONAL COMMENT

The gift-splitting election is a year-by-year election. For example, a husband and wife could elect to gift split in 2006, 2008, and 2010, but not elect to gift split in 2007, 2009, and 2011.

Upon the death of the actual donor or the spouse who consented to gift splitting, such decedent's estate tax base includes that decedent's post-1976 taxable gifts, known as adjusted taxable gifts. By electing gift splitting, a couple can reduce the amount of the taxable gifts the donor-decedent is deemed to have made. Under gift splitting, the adjusted taxable gifts include only the portions of the gifts that are taxable on the gift tax returns filed by the donor-decedent. Of course, the nondonor-spouse's estate reports his or her post-1976 taxable gifts.

? STOP & THINK

Question: Bob made taxable gifts of $4 million in 2001, and Betty, his spouse, has not made any taxable gifts. Betty inherited a large fortune last year and is contemplating gifting $500,000 in 2011 to each of her two children. Bob does not anticipate making any taxable gifts in 2011. Should they elect gift splitting for Betty's gifts?

Solution: They should not necessarily elect gift splitting because the main advantage of the election will be that the aggregate annual exclusions will be $52,000 instead of $26,000. An adverse effect will be that Bob, who has exhausted his unified credit (except for the increase from $220,550 in 2001 to the current year amount) and is in a higher marginal tax bracket, will be the deemed donor of $474,000 [(0.50 × $1,000,000) − $26,000] of taxable gifts.

COMPUTATION OF THE GIFT TAX LIABILITY

OBJECTIVE 7

Calculate the gift tax liability

EFFECT OF PREVIOUS TAXABLE GIFTS

The gift tax computation involves a cumulative process. All the donor's previous taxable gifts (i.e., those made in 1932 or later years) plus the donor's taxable gifts for the current year affect the marginal tax rate for current taxable gifts. Thus, two donors making the same taxable gifts in the current period may incur different gift tax liabilities because one donor may have made substantially larger taxable gifts in earlier periods than did the other donor. The process outlined below must be used to compute the gross tax levied on the current period's taxable gifts.

1. Determine the gift tax liability (at current rates) on the donor's cumulative taxable gifts (taxable gifts of current period plus aggregate taxable gifts of previous periods).

---

[43] If the nondonor-spouse has made substantial taxable gifts relative to those made by the donor-spouse, the gift tax liability for the period in question may be lower if the spouses do not elect gift splitting because the nondonor-spouse may have little or no unified credit left and may have reached the highest marginal transfer tax rate.

2. Determine the gift tax liability (at current rates) on the donor's cumulative taxable gifts made through the end of the preceding period.
3. Subtract the gift tax determined in Step 2 from that in Step 1. The difference equals the gross gift tax on the current period's taxable gifts.

This calculation process results in taxing the gifts on a progressive basis over the donor's lifetime.

Note that, although the gift tax rates have varied over the years, the current rate schedule is used in the calculation even when the donor made some or all the gifts when different rates were in effect. This process ensures that current taxable gifts are taxed at the appropriate rate, given the donor's earlier gift history.

EXAMPLE C:12-41 ▶ In 1975, Tony made $2 million in taxable gifts. These gifts were the first Tony ever made. The tax imposed under the 1975 rate schedule was $564,900. Tony's next taxable gifts were made in 2011. The taxable amount of these gifts was $400,000. The tax on Tony's 2011 taxable gifts before applying the unified credit is calculated as follows:

Tax at current rates on $2.4 million of cumulative taxable gifts	$820,800
Minus: Tax at current rates on $2 million of prior period taxable gifts	(680,800)
Tax on $400,000 of taxable gifts made in the current period	$140,000 ◀

This cumulative process results in the $400,000 gift in Example C:12-41 being taxed at the maximum 35% gift tax rate for 2011, which applied to taxable transfers exceeding $500,000. If the gift tax computations were not cumulative, the tax on the $400,000 of gifts would be determined by using the lowest marginal rates and would have been only $121,800. Because the tax on taxable transfers made in previous periods is determined by reference to the current rate schedule, Tony's actual 1975 gift tax liability, incurred when the gift tax rates were lower, is not relevant to the determination of his current gift tax. As discussed below, the unified credit will reduce the tax liability.

UNIFIED CREDIT AVAILABLE

Congress enacted a unified credit for both gift and estate tax purposes beginning in 1977. The unified credit reduces the amount of the gross gift tax owed on current period gifts. The size of the tax base for which the unified credit exactly offsets the tax liability is referred to as the exemption equivalent (or applicable exclusion amount). The amount of the credit has increased over the years (see inside back cover). As a result of the 2001 Act, the credit for gift tax purposes rose to $345,800 in 2002 and remained at that amount through 2009 even though the credit against estate taxes increased further through 2009. In 2010, the unified credit for gift taxes was $330,800. In 2011, the credit is $1,730,800, which is the tax at a maximum 35% tax rate on the $5 million exemption equivalent. Donors who have made taxable gifts in the post-1976 period have used some of their credit. The amount of the credit available to those donors for the current year is reduced by the aggregate amount allowable as a credit in all preceding years. Because of the reduction of the top rate to 35%, beginning in 2010, the credit for the current year is reduced by what the credit would have been, if lower, calculated using the rates for the current year.

EXAMPLE C:12-42 ▶ Hu made her first taxable gift in 1985. The taxable amount of the 1985 gift was $100,000, which resulted in a gross gift tax of $23,800. Hu claimed $23,800 (of the $121,800 credit then available) on her 1985 return to reduce her net gift tax liability to zero. Hu made her next taxable gift in 1994. The taxable amount of the gift was $400,000. The tax on the $400,000 gift equaled (1) the tax on $500,000 of total gifts (at 1994 gift tax rates) of $155,800 minus (2) the tax on $100,000 of previous gifts (at 1994 gift tax rates) of $23,800, or $132,000. The credit amount for 1994 was $192,800. Hu's gift tax was reduced to zero by a credit of $132,000 because for 1994 she had a credit of $169,000 ($192,800 − $23,800) left. If in 2011 Hu made additional taxable gifts, $1,575,000 [$1,730,800 − ($23,800 + $132,000)] of unified credit was available to reduce Hu's gift tax liability in 2011. Note that none of Hu's gifts were taxed at rates above 35%. Thus, the credit available for the current year is reduced by the total amount of the credits claimed earlier. ◀

? STOP & THINK

Question: In the process of preparing a current year gift tax return, you reviewed a 2009 gift tax return a different CPA prepared for your new client, George Winston. The tax return reported 2009 taxable gifts of $1 million and $500,000 of taxable gifts made in 1992. You note that the return showed tax of $345,800, claimed a unified credit of $345,800, and thus reported zero gift tax payable. What should you discuss with your new client?

Solution: You should explain that the 2009 unified credit of $345,800 (which equaled the tax on the first $1 million of taxable gifts) was not an annual credit maximum but rather the credit available during a donor's lifetime. Because in 1992 the client made $500,000 of taxable gifts, he exhausted $155,800 of his $192,800 unified credit then available. In addition, you should explain the cumulative nature of the gift tax calculations. The tax calculated on the first $1 million of taxable gifts was $345,800. If the other CPA claimed a $345,800 unified credit and showed zero tax payable, he or she did not calculate the tax on the $1 million 2009 taxable gift by performing the cumulative calculations that take into effect the $500,000 of earlier taxable gifts. The tax *before* the credit was calculated incorrectly. The credit available was $190,000 ($345,800 − $155,800), the 2009 credit less the credit already used. Therefore, you should advise the client to file an amended return and pay the correct gift tax.

COMPREHENSIVE ILLUSTRATION

The following comprehensive illustration demonstrates the computation of one donor's gift tax liability for the situation where the spouses elect gift splitting. It demonstrates the computation of the wife's gift tax liability.

ADDITIONAL COMMENT

This illustration pertains to 2009 because, at the time the textbook went to press, the IRS had not published the 2010 gift tax forms. They were delayed because of the late passage of the Tax Relief Act of 2010.

BACKGROUND DATA

Hugh and Wilma Brown are married to each other throughout 2009. Hugh made no taxable gifts in earlier periods. Wilma's previous taxable gifts were $300,000 in 1975 and $200,000 in 1988. In August 2009, Wilma makes the following gratuitous transfers:

► $80,000 in cash to son Billy

► $28,000 in jewelry to daughter Betsy

► $30,000 in medical expense payments to Downtown Infirmary for medical care of grandson Tim

► Remainder interest in vacation cabin to friend Ruth Cain. Wilma (age 60) retains a life estate. The vacation cabin is valued at $100,000.

► $600,000 of stocks to a bank in trust with all of the income payable semiannually to husband Hugh (age 72) for life and remainder payable at Hugh's death to Jeff Bass, Wilma's son by an earlier marriage, or Jeff's estate. Wilma wants to elect the marital deduction.

In 2009, Hugh's only gifts were

► $80,000 of stock to State University

► $600,000 of land to daughter Betsy

Assume the applicable interest rate for valuing life estates and remainders is 4%.

CALCULATION OF TAX LIABILITY

Section 2503(e) exempts the medical expense payments from the gift tax. The Browns need to report the gift made to State University even though the university received Hugh's entire interest in the property, and even though the transfer is nontaxable, because they must file a gift tax return to report gifts to noncharitable donees. The vacation cabin is valued at $100,000, and the remainder interest therein at $46,310 (0.46310 × $100,000) (see Table S, age 60, 4%, in Appendix H). The stock is transferred to a QTIP trust, and the marital deduction election treats the entire interest (not just the life estate) as having been given to Hugh Brown.

Table C:12-1 shows the computation of Wilma's gift tax liability for 2009. Recall that the annual exclusion for 2009 was $13,000. These same facts are used for the sample United States Gift Tax Return, Form 709, in Appendix B. The form's format for reporting the gift-splitting aspects differs slightly from the format in the table. On the form, Part 1 of Schedule A splits the gifts earlier than Table C:12-1 does.

▼ TABLE C:12-1

Comprehensive Gift Tax Illustration

Wilma's actual 2009 gifts:		
Billy, cash		$ 80,000
Betsy, jewelry		28,000
Ruth, remainder interest in vacation cabin (future interest)		46,310
Husband Hugh and son Jeff, transfer to QTIP trust		600,000
Total gifts made by Wilma		$754,310
Minus:	One-half of Wilma's gifts made to third parties that are deemed made by Hugh [0.50 × ($80,000 + $28,000 + $46,310)]	(77,155)
Plus:	One-half of Hugh's gifts made to third parties (Betsy and State University) that are deemed made by Wilma [0.50 × ($80,000 + $600,000)]	340,000
Minus:	Annual exclusions for gifts of present interests ($13,000 each for gifts made to Billy, Betsy, Hugh, and State University)	(52,000)
Minus:	Marital deduction ($600,000 − $13,000 exclusion)	(587,000)
Minus:	Charitable contribution deduction ($40,000 deemed gift by Wilma − $13,000 exclusion)	(27,000)
Taxable gifts for current period		$351,155
Tax on cumulative taxable gifts of $851,155[a]		$287,750
Minus:	Tax on previous taxable gifts of $500,000 (current rate schedule)	(155,800)
Tax on taxable gifts of $351,155 for the current period		$131,950
Minus:	Unified credit:	
Credit for 2009	$345,800	
Minus: Credit allowable for prior periods	(68,000)[b]	(277,800)[c]
Tax payable for 2009		$ –0–

[a]$300,000 (in 1975) + $200,000 (in 1988) + $351,155 (in 2009).
[b]$0 (for 1975) + $68,000 (for 1988). The $68,000, which is smaller than the maximum credit of $192,800 for 1988, is the excess of the $155,800 tax on cumulative taxable gifts less the $87,800 tax on the $300,000 previous taxable gifts.
[c]Actually, for 2009 Wilma uses only $131,950 of her remaining credit.

BASIS CONSIDERATIONS FOR A LIFETIME GIVING PLAN

OBJECTIVE 8

Understand how basis affects the overall tax consequences

Prospective donors should consider the tax-saving features of making a series of lifetime gifts (discussed in the Tax Planning Considerations section of this chapter). Lifetime giving plans can remove income from the donor's income tax return and transfer it to the donee's income tax return, where it may be taxed at a lower marginal tax rate. A series of gifts may permit property to be transferred to a donee without incurring a gift tax liability and thus enable the donor to eliminate part or all of his or her estate tax liability. These two advantages must be weighed against the unattractive basis rules (discussed below) applicable for such transfers.

PROPERTY RECEIVED BY GIFT

The carryover basis rules apply to property received by gift. Provided the property's FMV on the date of the gift exceeds its adjusted basis, the donor's basis in the property carries over as the donee's basis. In addition, the donee's basis may be increased by some or all of the gift tax paid by the donor. For pre-1977 gifts, all the gift taxes paid by the donor may be added to the donor's adjusted basis. For post-1976 transfers, however, the donee may add only the portion of the gift taxes represented by the following fraction:

SELF-STUDY
QUESTION

Barkley purchased land in 1965 for $90,000. In 1974, when the FMV of the land was $300,000, he gave the land to his son Tracy, claimed a $3,000 annual exclusion, and paid gift taxes of $23,000. What is Tracy's basis in the land? What if the gift had been made in 2010? For simplicity, assume the 2010 tax was $23,000.

ANSWER

If the gift were made in 1974, Tracy's basis is $90,000 plus the $23,000 gift tax, or $113,000. Had Barkley made the gift in 2010, Tracy's basis would be $90,000 plus [($210,000/$287,000) × $23,000], or $106,829.

ADDITIONAL
COMMENT

Phil owns investment property worth $350,000 in which his adjusted basis is $500,000. Unless there are reasons why the property should be kept in the family, Phil should sell the property and recognize an income tax loss. If he gifts the property to his child, the loss basis in the child's hands is $350,000 (and the gain basis is $500,000). Thus, if the value does not increase, a loss deduction for the $150,000 decline in market value can never be taken. If Phil dies holding the loss property, his heirs will take the estate tax return value (FMV) as their basis, and the potential income tax loss will not be recognized.

$$\frac{\text{Amount of property's appreciation}}{\text{from acquisition date}}{\text{through date of gift}}$$

$$\text{FMV of property on the date of the gift}$$
$$\text{minus exclusions and deductions}$$

In no event, however, can the gift tax adjustment increase the donee's basis above the property's FMV on the date of the gift.[44]

If the gifted property's FMV on the date of the gift is less than the donor's adjusted basis, the basis rules are more complicated. For purposes of determining gain, the donee's basis is the same as the donor's adjusted basis. For purposes of determining loss, the donee's basis is the property's FMV on the date of the gift. If the donee sells the property for an amount between its FMV as of the date of the gift and the donor's adjusted basis, the donee recognizes no gain or loss. The property's basis cannot be increased by any gift taxes paid if the donor's adjusted basis exceeds the property's FMV as of the date of the gift. In general, prospective donors should dispose of property that has declined in value by selling it instead of gifting it.

PROPERTY RECEIVED AT DEATH

In general, the basis rules that apply to property received as a result of another's death call for a step up or step down to the property's FMV as of the decedent's date of death. The recipient's basis is the same as the amount at which the property is valued on the estate tax return, which is its FMV on either the decedent's date of death or the alternate valuation date. Generally, the alternate valuation date is six months after the date of death. Although these rules are usually thought of as providing for a step-up in basis, if the property has declined in value as of the transferor's death, the basis is stepped-down to its FMV at the date of death or alternate valuation date.

In certain circumstances, no step up in basis occurs for appreciated property transferred at death.[45] This exception applies if both of the following conditions are present:

▶ The decedent receives the appreciated property as a gift during the one-year period preceding his or her death, and

▶ The property passes to the donor or to the donor's spouse as a result of the donee-decedent's death.

Before the enactment of this rule, a widely publicized planning technique involved transferring appreciated property to an ill spouse who, in turn, could will the property back to the donor-spouse, who would receive the property at a stepped-up basis. Interspousal transfers by gift and at death are tax-free because of the unlimited marital deduction for both gift tax and estate tax purposes. Consequently, before the rule change, the property received a step-up in basis at no transfer tax cost.

EXAMPLE C:12-43 ▶ In June 2008, Sarah gave property valued at $700,000 to Tom, her husband. Sarah's adjusted basis in the property was $120,000. Tom died in March 2011. At this time, the property was worth $740,000. If the property passed back to Sarah under Tom's will upon Tom's death, Sarah's basis would be $120,000. However, if the property passed to someone other than Sarah at Tom's death, its basis would be stepped-up to $740,000. If Tom lived for more than one year after receiving the gift, the basis was stepped-up to its FMV as of Tom's date of death regardless of whether the property passed at Tom's death to Sarah or someone else. If Tom (the donee) sold the property a few months before his death in March 2011, Tom's basis would be the same as Sarah's was, or $120,000. ◀

For estates of decedents dying in 2010, the executor can elect to be exempt from the estate tax and forego the basis step-up and use instead a modified carryover basis rule. Under this rule, a person receiving property from a decedent will have a basis equal to the lesser of (1) the decedent's adjusted basis in the property or (2) the property's fair market value at the date of the decedent's death. A special rule, however, will allow a total basis increase of

---

[44] See Reg. Sec. 1.1015-5(c) for examples of how to calculate the gift tax that can increase the property's basis.

[45] Sec. 1014(e).

$1.3 million to all assets (and an additional $3 million basis increase for property transferred to a surviving spouse) not to exceed the property's fair market value. For example, assume the decedent's estate consists of $10 million cash and land the decedent purchased for $2 million. He dies in 2010, when the land is worth $12 million and leaves the land to his surviving spouse and the cash to his children. The executor elects to be exempt from the estate tax. The spouse's basis will be $6.3 million ($2,000,000 + $1,300,000 + $3,000,000), compared with $12 million under the fair market value basis rule. Some additional special rules will apply to the basis of property received from a decedent but are not detailed in this text.

BELOW-MARKET LOANS: GIFT AND INCOME TAX CONSEQUENCES

GENERAL RULES

Section 7872 provides rules concerning the gift and income tax consequences of below-market loans. In general, it treats the lender as both making a gift to the borrower and receiving interest income. The borrower is treated as receiving a gift and paying interest expense.

In the case of a demand loan, the lender is treated as having made a gift in each year in which the loan is outstanding. The amount of the gift equals the forgone interest income for the portion of the year the loan is outstanding. The forgone interest income is calculated by referring to the excess of the federal short-term rate of Sec. 1274(d), for the period in question, over the interest rate the lender charged.

For income tax purposes, the forgone interest is treated as being retransferred from the borrower to the lender on the last day of each calendar year in which the loan is outstanding. The amount of the forgone interest is the same as for gift tax purposes and is reported by the lender as income for the year in question. The borrower gets an interest expense deduction for the same amount unless one of the rules limiting the interest deduction applies (e.g., personal interest or investment interest limitations).

EXAMPLE C:12-44 ▶ On July 1, Frank lends $500,000 to Susan, who signs an interest-free demand note. The loan is still outstanding on December 31. Assume that 10% is the applicable annual interest rate. Frank is deemed to have made a gift to Susan on December 31 of $25,000 (0.10 × $500,000 × 6/12). Frank must report $25,000 of interest income. Susan deducts $25,000 of interest expense provided the interest expense deduction rules do not otherwise limit or disallow her deduction. ◀

DE MINIMIS RULES

Under one of the *de minimis* rules, neither the income nor the gift tax rules apply to any gift loan made directly between individuals for any day on which the aggregate loans outstanding between the borrower and the lender are $10,000 or less. The *de minimis* exception does not apply to any loan directly attributable to the purchase or carrying of income-producing assets.

A second *de minimis* exception potentially permits loans of $100,000 or less to receive more favorable income tax (but not gift tax) treatment by limiting the lender's imputed income to the borrower's net investment income (as defined in Sec. 163(d)(3)) for the year. Moreover, if the borrower's net investment income for the year is $1,000 or less, such amount is treated as being zero.

The *de minimis* provisions do not apply to transactions having tax avoidance as a principal purpose and do not apply to any day on which the total outstanding loans between the borrower and the lender exceed $100,000. For purposes of the $100,000 or $10,000 loan limitations, a husband and wife are treated as one person.

EXAMPLE C:12-45 ▶ On August 1, Mike lends $100,000 to Don. No other loans are outstanding between the parties. Avoidance of federal taxes is not a principal purpose of the loan. Don signs an interest-free demand note when 10% is the applicable interest rate. The loan is still outstanding on December 31. Mike is treated as having made a present interest gift to Don on December 31 of $4,167 [$100,000 × 0.10 × 5/12]. Mike need not report this gift on a gift tax return unless his aggregate gifts to Don this year exceed the $13,000 gift tax annual exclusion.

The income tax consequences depend on Don's (the borrower's) net investment income. If Don's net investment income for the year exceeds $4,167, Mike reports $4,167 of imputed interest income under Sec. 7872. Subject to rules that may disallow some or all of the interest expense deduction, Don deducts the $4,167 interest expense imputed under Sec. 7872 . If Don's net investment income is between $1,001 and $4,167, each party reports imputed interest income or expense equal to Don's net investment income. Mike and Don report no interest income or expense under Sec. 7872 if Don's net investment income is $1,000 or less. ◄

TAX PLANNING CONSIDERATIONS

The 1976 Act, which introduced the unification concept, reduced the tax law's bias in favor of lifetime transfers. The 2001 Act, on the other hand, was more favorable toward transfers at death because the unified credit for gift tax purposes peaked at $345,800 beginning in 2004 whereas the credit against the estate tax continued to increase. Beginning in 2011, the unified credit again becomes the same amount for gift and estate tax purposes. Nevertheless, lifetime gifts provide more advantages than disadvantages. Many factors, including the expected appreciation rate and the donor's expectations about whether permanant repeal of the estate tax will occur, affect the decision of whether to make gifts. Thus, the optimal result is not always clear. The pros and cons of lifetime gifts from an estate planning perspective are discussed below.

TAX-SAVING FEATURES OF INTER VIVOS GIFTS

USE OF ANNUAL EXCLUSION. The annual exclusion offers donors the opportunity to start making gifts to several donees per year relatively early in their lifetime and keep substantial amounts of property off the transfer tax rolls. The tax-free amount doubles if a husband and wife use the gift-splitting election.

The law provides no estate tax counterpart to the annual gift tax exclusion. Consequently, a terminally ill person whose will includes bequests of approximately $13,000 to each of several individuals would realize substantial transfer tax savings if gifts—instead of bequests—were made to these individuals.

REMOVAL OF POST-GIFT APPRECIATION FROM TAX BASE. Another important advantage of lifetime gifts is that their value is frozen at their date-of-gift value. That is, any post-gift appreciation escapes the transfer tax rolls. Consequently, transfer tax savings are maximized if the donor gives away the assets that appreciate the most.

REMOVAL OF GIFT TAX AMOUNT FROM TRANSFER TAX BASE. With one exception, gift taxes paid by the donor are removed from the transfer tax base. The lone exception applies to gift taxes paid on gifts the donor makes within three years of dying. Under the gross-up rule (discussed in Chapter C:13), the donor's gross estate includes only gift taxes paid on gifts made within three years of the donor's death.

INCOME SHIFTING. Originally, one of the most favorable consequences of lifetime gifts was income shifting, but the compression of the income tax rate schedules beginning in 1987 has lessened these benefits. In addition, the 2003 Act, which lowered the tax rate on dividends, further reduced income shifting benefits from giving stock. The income produced by the gifted property is taxed to the donee, whose marginal income tax rate may be lower than the donor's. If income tax savings do arise, they accrue each year during the post-gift period. Thus, the income tax savings can be quite sizable over a span of several years. This tax saving aspect of gifts is a major reason Congress retained the gift tax in the 2001 Act.

GIFT IN CONTEMPLATION OF DONEE-SPOUSE'S DEATH. At times, a terminally ill spouse may have very few assets. If such a spouse died, a sizable portion of his or her unified credit would be wasted because the decedent's estate would be well below the amount of the exemption equivalent provided by the unified credit. If the healthier spouse is relatively wealthy, he or she could make a gift to the ill spouse to create an estate in an amount equal to the estate tax exemption equivalent. Because of the unlimited marital deduction, the gift would be tax-free. Upon the death of the donee-spouse, no estate tax would be payable because the estate tax liability would not exceed the unified credit. The donee-spouse should not transfer his or her property back to the donor-spouse at death. Otherwise, the donee-spouse's unified credit would be wasted, and the original tax planning would be negated. Moreover, the retransferred property would be included in the surviving spouse's estate.

A gift of appreciated property in contemplation of the donee-spouse's death provides an additional advantage. If the property does not pass back to the donor-spouse, its basis is increased to its value on the donee's date of death. In the event the property is willed to the donor-spouse, a step-up in basis still occurs if the date of the gift precedes the donee-spouse's date of death by more than one year.

LESSENING STATE TRANSFER TAX COSTS.   Currently about 20 states levy an estate or inheritance tax, but only two states impose a gift tax.[46] State death taxes are deductible in calculating the taxable estate, but they still add to death-associated costs. Therefore, in some states, the tax cost of lifetime transfers is lower than that for transfers at death.

INCOME TAX SAVINGS FROM CHARITABLE GIFTS.   Some individuals desire to donate a portion of their property to charitable organizations. Assuming the donation is eligible for a charitable contribution deduction, the transfer tax implications are the same—no taxable transfer—irrespective of whether the transfer occurs *inter vivos* or at death. From an income tax standpoint, however, a lifetime transfer is preferable because only lifetime transfers produce an income tax deduction for charitable contributions.

NEGATIVE ASPECTS OF GIFTS

LOSS OF STEP-UP IN BASIS.   Taxpayers deliberating about whether to make gifts or which property to give should keep in mind that the donee receives no step-up in basis for property acquired by gift. From a practical standpoint, sacrifice of the step-up in basis is insignificant if the donee does not plan to sell the property or if the property is not subject to an allowance for depreciation. Also, keep in mind that gain on the sale is likely to be taxed at the preferential long-term capital gain rate (e.g., 15%), and property in the estate may be taxed at rate close to 50%.

PREPAYMENT OF ESTATE TAX.   A donor who makes taxable gifts that exceed the exemption equivalent (applicable exclusion amount) must pay a gift tax. Upon the donor's death, the taxable gift is included in his or her estate tax base as an adjusted taxable gift. Because the gift tax paid during the donor's lifetime reduces the donor's estate tax liability, in a sense, the donor's payment of the gift tax results in prepayment of a portion of the estate tax.

COMPLIANCE AND PROCEDURAL CONSIDERATIONS

OBJECTIVE 9

Recognize the filing requirements for gift tax returns

FILING REQUIREMENTS

Section 6019 specifies the circumstances in which a donor should file a gift tax return. In general, the donor will file Form 709 (United States Gift Tax Return). A completed Form 709 appears in Appendix B. The facts used in the preparation of the completed Form 709 are the same as the facts in the comprehensive illustration, which uses a format for the gift-splitting aspects that differs slightly from that used in the form.

---

[46] The two states that impose a gift tax are Connecticut and Tennessee. Beginning with 2010, the Connecticut gift tax applies only if cumulative gifts exceed $3.5 million. Louisiana repealed its gift tax effective July 1, 2008, and North Carolina its gift tax effective January 2009.

As is the case for income tax returns, a return can be necessary even though the taxable amount and the tax payable are both zero. A donor must file a gift tax return for any calendar year in which the donor makes gifts other than

▶ Gifts to the spouse that qualify for the marital deduction

▶ Gifts that are fully shielded from taxation because they fall within the annual exclusion amount or are exempted from classification as a gift under the exception for educational or medical expenses

▶ Gifts to charitable organizations if the gift is deductible and the organization receives the donor's entire interest in the property

In addition, if the gift to the spouse is of qualified terminable interest property (QTIP), the donor must report the gift on the gift tax return. The marital deduction is not available for these transfers unless the donor makes the election, which is done by claiming a marital deduction on the gift tax return.

United States persons who receive aggregate gifts from foreign corporations or foreign partnerships exceeding $14,375 (in 2011) or aggregate gifts or bequests from nonresident aliens or foreign estates exceeding $100,000 (in 2011) must report such amounts as prescribed in Treasury Regulations.[47]

DUE DATE

All gift tax returns must be filed on a calendar-year basis. Under the general rule, gift tax returns are due no later than April 15 following the close of the year of the gift.[48] An extension of time granted for filing an individual income tax return is deemed to automatically extend the filing date for the individual's gift tax return for that year. The automatic extension period is until October 15.

If the donor dies early in the year in which a gift is made, the due date for the donor's final gift tax return may be earlier than April 15. Because information concerning the decedent's taxable gifts is necessary to complete the estate tax return, the gift tax return for the year of death is due no later than the due date (including extensions) for the donor's estate tax return.[49] Estate tax returns are due nine months after the date of death.

Receipt of an extension for filing a gift tax return does not postpone the due date for payment of the tax. Interest is imposed on any gift tax not paid by April 15. Donors should submit Form 8892 if they anticipate owing gift tax and/or if they need an extension for only their gift tax return. Unlike with the income tax, a donor does not have to make estimated payments of gift taxes.

GIFT-SPLITTING ELECTION

For taxable gifts to be computed under the gift-splitting technique, both spouses must indicate their consent to gift splitting in one of the following ways:[50]

▶ Each spouse signifies his or her consent on the other spouse's gift tax return.

▶ Each spouse signifies his or her consent on his or her own gift tax return.

▶ Both spouses signify their consent on one of the gift tax returns.

Treasury Regulations state that the first approach listed above is the preferred manner for designating consent.

KEY POINT

Similarly to a husband and wife filing a joint income tax return, if gift splitting is elected, the husband and wife have joint and several liability for the entire gift tax liability regardless of who actually made the gifts.

LIABILITY FOR TAX

The donor is responsible for paying the gift tax,[51] and if the spouses consent to gift splitting, the entire gift tax liability is a joint and several liability of the spouses.[52] Thus, if spouses do not pay the tax voluntarily, the IRS may attempt to collect whatever amount it deems appropriate from either spouse, irrespective of the size of the gift that spouse actually made.

In the rare event that the donor does not pay the gift tax, the donee becomes personally liable for the gift tax.[53] However, a donee's liability is limited to the value of the gift.

---

[47] Sec. 6039F.
[48] Sec. 6075(b).
[49] The decedent's post-1976 taxable gifts affect the size of his or her estate tax base, as discussed in the next chapter.

[50] Reg. Sec. 25.2513-2(a)(1).
[51] Sec. 2502(c).
[52] Sec. 2513(d).
[53] Reg. Sec. 301.6324-1.

DETERMINATION OF VALUE

One of the most difficult problems encountered by donors and their tax advisors is determining the gifted property's FMV. This task is especially difficult if the gifted property is stock in a closely held business, an oil and gas property, or land in an area where few sales occur.

If a transaction involves a sale, the IRS can argue that the asset's value exceeds its sales price and, thus, there is a gift to the extent of the bargain element. This problem is especially common with sales to family members. If the donor gives or sells to a family member property whose value is not readily determinable, the donor should obtain an appraisal of the property before filing the gift tax return.

PENALTY FOR UNDERVALUATION. Section 6662 imposes a penalty, at one of two rates, on underpayments of gift or estate taxes resulting from too low a valuation of property. The amount on which the penalty is imposed is the underpayment of the transfer tax attributable to the valuation understatement.

No penalty applies if the valuation shown on the return exceeds 65% of the amount determined during an audit or court trial to be the correct value. If the value reported on the return is 65% or less of the correct value, the penalty rate is as shown below.

Ratio of Value per Return to Correct Value	Penalty Rate
More than 40% but 65% or less	20%
40% or less	40%

Section 6662(g)(2) exempts a taxpayer from the penalty if the underpayment is less than $5,000.

EXAMPLE C:12-46 ▶ Assume Donna already had used her available unified credit. She gave land to her son and reported its value at $400,000 on her 2009 gift tax return. The IRS audited Donna's return in 2011, and she agreed that $900,000 was the correct value of the property. Because the value stated on the return was 44.44% [($400,000 ÷ $900,000) × 100] of the correct value, the IRS levied a 20% penalty on the underpayment attributable to the valuation understatement. If Donna was in the 45% marginal gift tax bracket, the gift tax underpayment was $225,000 [0.45 × ($900,000 − $400,000)]. Thus, the penalty is $45,000 (0.20 × $225,000) unless Donna can demonstrate reasonable cause and good faith for the valuation. ◀

STATUTE OF LIMITATIONS

In general, the statute of limitations for gift tax purposes is three years after the later of the date the return was filed or the return's due date.[54] The statute of limitations increases from three to six years if the donor omits from the gift tax return gifts whose total value exceeds 25% of the gifts reported on the return. If the donor files no return because, for example, he or she is unaware that he or she made any gifts, the IRS may assess the tax at any time.

The cumulative nature of the gift tax causes the taxable gifts of earlier years to affect the gift tax owed in subsequent periods. After the statute of limitations had expired for pre-1997 gifts, the IRS could not argue that taxable gifts of prior periods were undervalued (and thus that the current period's gifts should be taxed at a higher rate than that used by the donor) as long as the donor had paid gift tax on the earlier gifts. However, for gifts reported after August 5, 1997, this rule applies even if the donor has paid no gift tax.[55]

For gifts made in 1997 and later, it is important to adequately disclose potential gift transactions for which the gift status is unclear. The statute of limitations will not expire on a transaction unless the donor makes adequate disclosure.[56]

EXAMPLE C:12-47 ▶ Andy filed a gift tax return for 2011, reporting taxable gifts of $1.85 million made in October 2011. Andy paid gift tax. If Andy adequately disclosed all potential gifts, once the statute of limitations expires for 2011, the IRS cannot contend that, for purposes of calculating the tax on later taxable gifts, the 2011 taxable gifts exceeded $1.85 million. ◀

---

[54] Sec. 6501.
[55] Sec. 2504(c).

[56] Sec. 6501(c)(9).

PROBLEM MATERIALS

DISCUSSION QUESTIONS

C:12-1 Describe two ways in which the transfer tax (estate and gift tax) system is a unified system.

C:12-2 What was the Congressional purpose for enacting the gift-splitting provisions?

C:12-3 Determine whether the following statement is true or false: Every donor who makes a taxable gift incurs a gift tax liability. Explain your answer.

C:12-4 Under what circumstances must the amount of the unified credit usually available be reduced (by a maximum amount of $6,000) even though the donor has never claimed any unified credit?

C:12-5 Does the exemption from the gift tax for direct payment of tuition encompass payments of non-relatives' tuition? Explain.

C:12-6 Steve is considering the following actions. Explain to him which actions will constitute gifts for gift tax purposes.
  a. Transferring all his ownership rights in a life insurance policy to another person
  b. Depositing funds into a joint bank account in the names of himself and another party (who deposits nothing)
  c. Paying half the consideration for land and having it titled in the names of Steve and his son as joint tenants with right of survivorship if the son furnishes the other half of the consideration
  d. Paying a hospital for the medical expenses of a neighbor
  e. Making a $1 million demand loan to an adult child and charging no interest

C:12-7 Dick wants to transfer property with a $600,000 FMV to an irrevocable trust with a bank as the trustee. Dick will name his distant cousin Earl to receive all of the trust income annually for the next eight years. Then the property will revert to Dick. In the last few years, the income return (yield) on the property has been 6%. Assume this yield is not likely to decline and that the applicable rate from the actuarial tables is 4%.
  a. What will be the amount of Dick's gift to Earl?
  b. Would you recommend that Dick transfer the property yielding 6% to this type of a trust? Explain. If not, what type of property would you recommend that Dick transfer to the trust?

C:12-8 Antonio would like to make a gift of a life insurance policy. Explain to him what action he must take to make a completed gift.

C:12-9 In what circumstances might a potential donor be interested in making a net gift? Explain the potential income tax problem with making a net gift.

C:12-10 What is the purpose of the gift tax annual exclusion?

C:12-11 In what circumstances do gifts fail to qualify for the annual exclusion?

C:12-12 Compare and contrast a Sec. 2503(c) trust and a *Crummey* trust.

C:12-13 From a nontax standpoint, would a parent probably prefer to make a transfer to a minor child by using a Sec. 2503(c) trust or a *Crummey* trust?

C:12-14 Explain the requirements for classifying a transaction as a transfer of a qualified terminable interest property (QTIP).

C:12-15 Why do some donors consider the qualified terminable interest property (QTIP) transfer an especially attractive arrangement for making gifts to their spouses?

C:12-16 A client is under the impression that a donor cannot incur a gift tax liability if he or she makes gifts to only U.S. charitable organizations. What should you say to the client?

C:12-17 Describe to a married couple three advantages of making the gift-splitting election.

C:12-18 Both Damien and Latoya make taxable gifts of $250,000 in the current year. Will their current year gift tax liabilities necessarily be identical? Explain.

C:12-19 A donor made his first taxable gift in 1979 and his second taxable gift in the current year. In the intervening years, the highest gift tax rates declined. In calculating the tax on taxable gifts of previous periods, which rate schedule is applicable: the one for the year in which the donor made the earlier gift or the one for the current period?

C:12-20 A mother is trying to decide which of the two assets listed below to give to her adult daughter.

Asset	FMV	Adjusted Basis	Annual Net Income from the Asset
Apartment	$600,000	$400,000	$(10,000)
Bonds	600,000	530,000	80,000

The mother's marginal income tax rate exceeds her daughter's. Describe the pros and cons of giving each of the two properties.

C:12-21 Phil and Marcy have been married for a number of years. Marcy is very wealthy, but Phil is not. In fact, Phil, who has only $10,000 of property, is very ill, and his doctor believes that he probably will die within the next few months. Make one (or more) tax planning suggestions for the couple. Assume that Phil might die in 2012.

C:12-22 Assume the same facts as in Problem C:12-21 and that Marcy has decided to give Phil property valued at $4.99 million. Phil probably will leave the gifted property to their children under his will.

a. What are the gift tax consequences to Marcy and the estate tax consequences to Phil of the transfer (assuming the property does not appreciate before his death)?

b. Assume Marcy is trying to decide whether to give Phil stock with an adjusted basis of $1,285,000 or land with an adjusted basis of $2.8 million. Each asset is valued at $4.99 million. Which asset would you recommend she give and why?

C:12-23 Carlos has heard about the unified transfer tax system and does not understand how making gifts can be beneficial. Explain to Carlos how a lifetime gift fixes (freezes) the gifted property's value for transfer tax purposes.

C:12-24 Describe for a client five advantages and two disadvantages of disposing of property by gift instead of at death, assuming an estate tax is in effect.

C:12-25 In general, what is the due date for the gift tax return? What are two exceptions?

C:12-26 In 2003, Frank made an installment sale of real property to Stu, his son, for $1 million. Frank did not file a gift tax return. In 2012, the IRS audits Frank's 2010 income tax return and discovers the sale. The IRS then contends that the property Frank sold was worth $2.5 million in 2003 and that Frank made a $1.5 million gift to Stu in 2003.

a. Can the IRS collect the gift tax on the 2003 gift? If not, will the 2003 gift affect the tax due on later gifts that Frank makes?

b. Will Frank potentially incur any penalty? Explain.

ISSUE IDENTIFICATION QUESTIONS

C:12-27 Kwambe is thinking of making a substantial gift of stock to his fiancée, Maya. The wedding is scheduled for October 1 of the current year. Kwambe already has exhausted his unified credit. He also is considering giving $26,000 cash this year to each of his three children by a previous marriage. What tax issues should Kwambe consider with respect to the gifts he plans to make to Maya and his three children?

C:12-28 Janet is considering transferring assets valued at $4 million to an irrevocable trust (yet to be created) for the benefit of her son, Gordon, age 15, with Farmers Bank as trustee. Her attorney has drafted a trust agreement that provides that Gordon is to receive income in the trustee's discretion for the next 20 years and that at age 35 the trust assets will be distributed equally between Gordon and his sister Joanna. Janet anticipates that her husband will consent to gift splitting. What tax issues should Janet and her husband consider with respect to the trust?

C:12-29 Melvin funds an irrevocable trust with Holcomb Bank as trustee and reserves the right to receive the income for seven years. He provides that at the end of the seventh year the trust assets will pass outright to his adult daughter, Pamela, or to Pamela's estate should Pamela not be alive. Melvin transfers assets valued at $1 million to the trust; the assets at present are producing income of about 4.5% per year. Assume that the Sec. 7520 rate per the actuarial tables for the month of the transfer is 6%. What tax issues should Melvin consider regarding the trust?

PROBLEMS

C:12-30 *Calculation of Gift Tax.* In 2011, Sondra makes taxable gifts aggregating $300,000. Her only other taxable gifts amount to $200,000, all of which she made in 1997.

a. What is Sondra's 2011 gift tax liability?

b. What is her 2011 gift tax liability under the assumption that she made the $200,000 of taxable gifts in 1974 instead of 1997?

C:12-31 *Calculation of Gift Tax.* Amir made taxable gifts as follows: $800,000 in 1975, $1.2 million in 1999, and $600,000 in 2011. What is Amir's gift tax liability for 2011?

C:12-32 *Determination of Taxable Gifts.* In the current year, Beth, who is single, sells stock valued at $40,000 to Linda for $18,000. Later that year, Beth gives Linda $12,000 in cash.

a. What is the amount of Beth's taxable gifts?

b. How would your answer to Part a change if Beth instead gave the cash to Patrick?

C:12-33 *Determination of Taxable Gifts.* In the current year, Clay gives $32,000 cash to each of his eight grandchildren. His wife makes no gifts during the current year.

a. What are Clay's taxable gifts, assuming Clay and his wife do *not* elect gift splitting?

b. How would your answer to Part a change if the couple elects gift splitting?

C:12-34 *Determination of Taxable Gifts.* In the current year, David gives $180,000 of land to David, Jr. In the current year, David's wife gives $200,000 of land to George and $44,000 cash to David, Jr. Assume the couple elects gift splitting for the current year.
a. What are the couple's taxable gifts?
b. How would your answer to Part a change if David's wife gave the $44,000 of cash to Ollie (instead of to David, Jr.)?

C:12-35 *Recognition of Transactions Treated as Gifts.* In the current year, Emily, a widow, engages in the following transactions. Determine the amount of the completed gift, if any, arising from each of the following occurrences.
a. Emily names Lauren the beneficiary of a $100,000 life insurance policy on Emily's life. The beneficiary designation is not irrevocable.
b. Emily deposits $50,000 cash into a checking account in the joint names of herself and Matt, who deposits nothing to the account. Later that year, Matt withdraws $15,000 from the account.
c. Emily pays $22,000 of nephew Noah's medical expenses directly to County Hospital.
d. Emily transfers the title to land valued at $60,000 to Olive.

C:12-36 *Calculation of Gift Tax.* Refer to the facts of Problem C:12-35 and assume the current year is 2011. Emily's prior gifts are as follows:

Year	Amount of Taxable Gifts
1974	$ 500,000
1998	1,000,000

What is the gift tax liability with respect to Emily's 2011 gifts?

C:12-37 *Recognition of Transactions Treated as Gifts.* In the current year, Marge (age 67) engages in the following transactions. Determine the amount of the completed gift, if any, arising from each of the following events. Assume 4% is the applicable interest rate.
a. Marge transfers $100,000 of property in trust and irrevocably names herself to receive $8,000 per year for life and daughter Joy (age 37) to receive the remainder.
b. Marge pays her grandson's $15,000 tuition to State University.
c. Marge gives the same grandson stock valued at $72,000.
d. Marge deposits $150,000 into a revocable trust. Later in the year, the bank trustee distributes $18,000 of income to the named beneficiary, Gail.

C:12-38 *Recognition of Transactions Treated as Gifts.* Determine the amount of the completed gift, if any, arising from each of the following occurrences.
a. A parent sells real estate valued at $1.8 million to an adult child, who pays $1 million in consideration.
b. A furniture store holds a clearance sale and sells a customer a $5,000 living room suite for $1,500.
c. During the year, a father purchases food and clothing costing $8,500 for his minor child.
d. A citizen contributes $1,500 cash to a political organization.
e. Zeke lends $600,000 interest free to Henry, who signs a demand note on August 1. Assume 6% is the applicable interest rate and the note remains unpaid at year-end.

C:12-39 *Determination of Unified Credit.* In March 1976, Sue made a taxable gift of $200,000. In arriving at the amount of her taxable gift, Sue elected to deduct the $30,000 specific exemption formerly available. In 2011, Sue makes her next gift; the taxable amount is $1.5 million.
a. What unified credit can Sue claim on her 2011 return?
b. What unified credit can Sue claim on her 2011 return if she made the 1976 gift in December instead of March?

C:12-40 *Valuation of Gifts.* On September 1 of the current year, Mario irrevocably transfers a $100,000 whole life insurance policy on his life to Mario, Jr. as owner. On September 1, the policy's interpolated terminal reserve is $30,000. Mario paid the most recent annual premium ($1,800) on June 1. What is the amount of the gift Mario made in the current year?

C:12-41 *Determination of Gift Tax Deductions.* In June, Tina makes cash gifts of $700,000 to her husband and $100,000 to the City Art Museum. What are the amounts of the deductions available for these gifts when calculating Tina's income tax and gift tax liabilities if she does not elect gift splitting?

C:12-42 *Determination of Annual Exclusion.* For each of the following transactions that occur in the current year, indicate the amount of the annual exclusion available. Explain your answer.

a. Tracy creates a trust in the amount of $300,000 for the benefit of her eight-year-old daughter, May. She names a bank as trustee. Before May reaches age 21, the trustee in its discretion is to pay income or corpus (trust assets) to May or for her benefit. When May reaches age 21, she will receive the unexpended portion of the trust income and corpus. If May dies before reaching age 21, the unexpended income and corpus will be paid to her estate or a party (or parties) she appoints under a general power of appointment.

b. Assume the same facts as in Part a except May is age 28 when Tracy creates the trust and the trust agreement contains age 41 wherever age 21 appears in Part a.

c. Assume the same facts as in Part b except the trust instrument allows May to demand a distribution by December 31 of each year equal to the lesser of the amount of the annual exclusion for federal gift tax purposes or the amount transferred to the trust that year.

C:12-43 *Determination of Annual Exclusion.* During 2011, Will gives $40,000 cash to Will, Jr. and a remainder interest in a few acres of land to his friend Suzy. The remainder interest is valued at $32,000. Will and his wife, Helen, elect gift splitting, and during the current year Helen gives Joyce $8,000 of stock. What is the total amount of the annual gift tax exclusions available to Will and Helen?

C:12-44 *Availability of Annual Exclusion.* Bonnie, a widow, irrevocably transfers $1 million of property to a trust and names a bank as trustee. For as long as Bonnie's daughter Carol is alive, Carol is to receive all the trust income annually. Upon Carol's death, the property is to be distributed to Carol's children. Carol is age 32 and currently has three children. How many gift tax exclusions does Bonnie receive for the transfer?

C:12-45 *Calculation of Gift Tax.* Before last year, neither Hugo nor Wanda, his wife, made any taxable gifts. In 2010, Hugo gave $13,000 cash to each of his 30 nieces, nephews, and grandchildren. This year (2011), Wanda gives $34,000 of stock to each of the same people. What is the *minimum* legal gift tax liability (*before* reduction for the unified credit) for each spouse for each year?

C:12-46 *Calculation of Marital Deduction.* Hugh makes the gifts listed below to Winnie, his wife, age 37. What is the amount of the marital deduction, if any, attributable to each?

a. Hugh transfers $500,000 to a trust with a bank named as trustee. All the income must be paid to Winnie monthly for life. At Winnie's death, the property passes to Hugh's sisters or their estates.

b. Hugh transfers $300,000 to a trust with a bank named as trustee. Income is payable at the trustee's discretion to Winnie annually until the earlier of her death or her remarriage. When payments to Winnie cease, the trustee must distribute the property to Hugh's children by a previous marriage or to their estates.

C:12-47 *Calculation of the Marital Deduction.* In the current year, Louise makes the transfers described below to Lance, her husband, age 47. Assume 4% is the applicable interest rate. What is the amount of her marital deduction, if any, attributable to each transfer?

a. In June, she gives him land valued at $45,000.

b. In October, she gives him a 12-year income interest in a trust with a bank named as trustee. She names their daughter to receive the remainder interest. She funds the irrevocable trust with $400,000 in assets.

C:12-48 *Charitable Contribution Deduction.* Tien (age 70) transfers a remainder interest in a vacation cabin (with a total value of $100,000) to a charitable organization and retains a life estate in the cabin for herself.

a. What is the amount of the gift tax charitable contribution deduction, if any, attributable to this transfer? Assume that 4% is the applicable interest rate.

b. How will your answer to Part a change if Tien instead gives a remainder interest in a valuable oil painting (worth $100,000) to the organization?

C:12-49 *Calculation of Gift Tax.* In 2011, Homer and his wife, Wilma (residents of a non–community property state) make the gifts listed below. Homer's previous taxable gifts consist of $100,000 made in 1975 and $1.4 million made in 1996. Wilma has made no previous taxable gifts.

Wilma's current year gifts were	
to Art	$400,000
to Bart	6,000
Homer's current year gifts were	
to Linda	$600,000
to a charitable organization	100,000
to Norma (future interest)	200,000

a. What are the gift tax liabilities of Homer and Wilma for 2011 if they elect gift splitting and everyone except Norma receives a present interest?

b. How would the gift tax liabilities for each spouse in Part a change if they do not elect gift splitting?

C:12-50 *Calculation of Gift Tax.* In 2011, Henry and his wife, Wendy, made the gifts shown below. All gifts are of present interests. What is Wendy's gift tax payable for 2011 if the couple elects gift splitting and Wendy's previous taxable gifts (made in 1995) total $1 million?

Wendy's current gifts were	
to Janet	$80,000
to Cindy	70,000
to Henry	50,000
Henry's current gifts were	
to Janet	30,000

C:12-51 *Basis Rules.* In June 2010, Karen transfers property with a $75,000 FMV and a $20,000 adjusted basis to Hal, her husband. Hal dies in March 2011; the property has appreciated to $85,000 in value by then. His gross estate is $1 million.

a. What is the amount of Karen's taxable gift in 2010?

b. What gain would Hal recognize if he sells the property for $95,000 in July 2010?

c. If Hal wills the property to Dot, his daughter, what basis would Dot have?

d. How would your answer to Part c change if Hal instead willed the property to Karen?

e. How would your answer to Part d change if Hal did not die until August 2011?

C:12-52 *Basis Rules.* Siu is considering giving away stock in Ace Corporation or Gold Corporation. Each has a current FMV of $500,000, and each has the same estimated future appreciation rate. Siu's basis in the Ace stock is $100,000, and her basis in the Gold stock is $450,000. Assume Siu has total assets of $1 million. Which stock would you suggest that she give away and why, or does it make any difference?

C:12-53 *Below-Market Loans.* On October 1, Sam lends Tom $10 million. Tom signs an interest-free demand note. The loan is still outstanding on December 31. Explain the income tax and gift tax consequences of the loan to both Sam and Tom. Assume that the federal short-term rate is 5%.

COMPREHENSIVE PROBLEM

C:12-54 In 2011, Ginger Graham, age 46 and wife of Greg Graham, engaged in the transactions described below. Determine Ginger's gift tax liability for 2011 if she and Greg elect gift splitting and Greg gave their son Stevie stock valued at $80,000 during 2011. Ginger's grandmother Mamie died November 12, 2010, and Mamie's will bequeathed $250,000 to Ginger. On March 4, 2011, Ginger irrevocably disclaimed the $250,000 in writing, and, as a result, the property passed instead to Ginger's sister Gertie. In 2011, Ginger gave $100,000 cash to her alma mater, State University. In 1996, Ginger had given ownership of a life insurance policy on her own life to her daughter, Denise, and in 2011 Ginger paid the $22,000 annual premium on the policy. In 2010, Ginger deposited $45,000 into a bank account in the name of herself and son Stevie, joint tenants with rights of survivorship. Stevie deposited nothing. Neither party made a withdrawal until 2011, when Stevie withdrew $30,000. In 2011, Ginger created a trust with County Bank as trustee and transferred $300,000 of stock to the irrevocable trust. She named her husband Greg (age 47) to receive all the trust income semi-annually for life and daughter Drucilla to receive the remainder. In 2011, she gave a remainder interest in her beach cottage to the American Red Cross and kept the right to use the cottage rent free for the rest of her life. The fair market value of the cottage was $70,000.

Other information: Ginger's earlier *taxable* gifts are $175,000, all made in 1996. Ginger will make whatever elections are necessary to minimize her current gift tax liability. Assume the Sec. 7520 interest rate is 4%.

TAX STRATEGY PROBLEM

C:12-55 Ilene Ishi is planning to fund an irrevocable charitable remainder annuity trust with $100,000 of cash. She will designate her sister, age 60, to receive an annuity of $5,000 per year for 15 years and State University to receive the remainder at the end of the fifteenth year. The valuation of the charitable portion of the transfer, according to Reg. Sec. 25.2522(c)-3(d)(2)(i), is to be determined under Reg. Sec. 1.664-2(c), an income tax regulation. Regulation Sec. 1.664-2(c) provides that, in valuing the remainder interest, the donor may elect to use the Sec. 7520 interest rate for either of the two months preceding the month of the transfer as an alternative to using the rate for the actual month of transfer. Otherwise, the value will be determined by using the Sec. 7520 rate for the month of the transfer. Assume that in the month of the transfer the interest rate was 4% but that in the two preceding months the rate was 4.2%. Should the donor elect to calculate the value of the remainder interest by using the interest rate for one of the two preceding months? Explain your answer. Note: The 4.2% rate does not appear in the excerpts from the actuarial tables, but the absence of such rate from the tables will not preclude you from answering this question.

TAX FORM/RETURN PREPARATION PROBLEMS

NOTE

These problems pertain to 2009 because, when this textbook went to press, the IRS had not published estate or gift tax returns for 2010.

C:12-56 Use the information presented below to prepare a gift tax return (Form 709) for 2009 for Theresa Stone (343-52-6678). Theresa and her husband, Adolf Stone (653-99-0734), reside at 1325 Apple Lane, Brandon, FL 33511 and want to elect gift splitting. Both are U.S. residents. For simplicity, assume that the Sec. 7520 rate is 4%. Theresa's transactions (all in August) are as shown below.

	Amount
1. Stock given to grandson, Stanley Stone	$ 52,000
2. Land given to granddaughter, Eliza Stone	84,000
3. Medical expenses paid to City Hospital for Adolf's unemployed nephew, Dudley Stone	38,000
4. Cash paid to First Methodist Church for building fund	28,000
5. Stock given to charitable remainder trust with remainder to American Cancer Society and an annual annuity of $8,000 for life to Theresa's mother, Audrey Alsup (age 82); Bank Three is trustee	120,000
6. Stock given to Bank of Florida as trustee with all the income payable annually to Adolf Stone (age 58) for life and remainder to daughter, Betsey Stone-Marbelle (age 30)	200,000

During 2009, Adolf gave Stanley Stone cash of $30,000 and did the same for Eliza Stone. Theresa's previous taxable gifts consisted of a $120,000 taxable gift made in 1998 and a $60,000 taxable gift made in 2003. Adolf made a $210,000 taxable gift in 2001.

C:12-57 Alice Arnold, Social Security number 572-13-4409, a widow, engages in the transactions listed below in 2009. Use this information to prepare a gift tax return (Form 709) for Alice.

	Amount
1. Stock given to daughter, Brenda Bell.	$700,000
2. Cash transferred to son, Al Arnold.	600,000
3. $500,000 interest-free demand loan made to Brenda Bell on July 1. The loan is still outstanding on December 31.	
4. Land given to niece, Lou Lane	100,000

Assume 6% is the applicable interest rate. Alice has made only one previous taxable gift: $300,000 (taxable amount) in 2000. Alice, a U.S. citizen, resides at 105 Peak Rd., Denver, Colorado 80309.

CASE STUDY PROBLEMS

C:12-58 Your client, Karen Kross, recently married Larry Kross. Karen is age 72, quite wealthy, and in reasonably good health. To date, she has not made any taxable gifts, but Larry made taxable gifts totaling $900,000 in 1998. Karen is considering giving each of her five college-age grandchildren approximately $34,000 of cash for them to use to pay their college expenses of tuition and room and board for the year. In addition, she is considering giving her three younger grandchildren $3,000 each to use for orthodontic bills. Karen wants to give her daughter property valued at $400,000. She is trying to choose between giving her daughter cash or stock with a basis of $125,000. She would like to give her son $400,000 of property also, but prefers to tie the property up in a discretionary trust with a bank as trustee for the son for at least 15 years. An agricultural museum approached Karen about making a contribution to it and, as a result, she is contemplating deeding her family farm to the museum but retaining a life estate in the farm.

Required: Prepare a memorandum to the tax partner of your firm that discusses the transfer tax and income tax consequences of the proposed transactions described above. Also, make any recommendations that you deem appropriate.

C:12-59 Morris Jory, a long-time tax client of the firm you work for, has made substantial gifts during his lifetime. Mr. Jory transferred Jory Corporation stock to 14 donees in December 2010. Each donee received shares valued at $13,000. Two of the donees were Mr. Jory's adult children, Amanda and Peter. The remaining 12 donees were employees of Jory Corporation who are not related to Mr. Jory. Mr. Jory, a widower, advised the employees that within two weeks of receiving the stock certificates they must endorse such certificates over to Amanda and Peter. Six of the donees were instructed to endorse their certificates to Amanda and six to Peter. During 2010, Mr. Jory also gave $35,000 cash to his favorite grandchild, Robin. Your firm has been engaged to prepare Mr. Jory's 2010 gift tax return. In January 2011, you meet with Mr. Jory, who insists that his 2010 taxable gifts will be only $23,000 ($36,000 to Robin − $13,000 annual exclusion). After your meeting with Mr. Jory, you are uncertain about his position regarding the amount of his 2010 gifts and have scheduled a meeting with your firm's senior tax partner, who has advised Mr. Jory for more than 20 years. In preparation for the meeting, prepare a summary of the tax and ethical considerations (with supporting authority where possible) regarding whether you should prepare a gift tax return that reports the taxable gifts in accordance with Mr. Jory's wishes.

TAX RESEARCH PROBLEMS

C:12-60 Karl Kremble funded an irrevocable trust in March 2011 with oil and gas property valued at $400,000. Assume the Sec. 7520 interest rate for the actuarial tables was 6% on the date of funding. Karl named a bank trustee and provided that his distant cousin, Louise Lane, will receive all the trust income annually for the next 50 years. Then the assets will revert (pass back) to Karl or his estate. The trust instrument specifically states that the trust is not to maintain a reserve for depletion (that is, no portion of the royalties received from the oil and gas properties is to be transferred to the trust's principal account to account for the wasting nature of the trust assets, and depletion will not reduce the trust's accounting income). Your manager has requested that you research whether the amount of Karl's gift to Louise may be determined by using the actuarial tables and that you write a memo summarizing your conclusions. Your manager indicated further that your memo should address the amount of the gift Karl is deemed to have made.

C:12-61 In July of the current year, Horace Hiatt, a widower, transferred $13,000 worth of publicly traded stock to an irrevocable trust with Benton National Bank as trustee. He named his granddaughter, Heather, then age 15, the beneficiary. The trust instrument provides that, until Heather reaches age 21, the trustee is to distribute amounts of income and/or principal to her as it "shall deem to be in the best interest of Heather." In addition, the trust instrument states that, if Heather dies before reaching age 21, the trust assets are to be distributed in accordance with Heather's appointment under a general power of appointment. The trust instrument provides further that the trust assets, including undistributed income, will be paid over to Heather upon her attaining age 21. However, if Heather does not ask for such property within 60 days of being notified of her right to ask for it, the trust is to continue until Heather reaches age 45, and the trustee is to continue to have the distribution powers it received at inception. Your manager asks you to research the effect, if any, on the availability of the gift tax annual exclusion of the language stating that the trust will continue until age 45 if Heather does not ask for the trust assets within a certain time frame. Your manager suggests that she seems to recall reading a 2006 letter ruling on this issue and asks that you try to locate it and that you also try to locate applicable higher authority, if any. Draft a memo to your manager addressing the availability of the annual exclusion.

C:12-62 Janet Mason filed a 2008 gift tax return to report the gift on June 3, 2008, of closely held stock in Mason Meat Co., Inc. The tax return, which your firm prepared, reflected a value of $1,500 per share (determined by an appraiser) and a taxable gift of $1.1 million. This was Janet's first taxable gift, and she exhausted her full unified credit of $345,800. On October 22, 2009, Janet's father, Mason Meat's CEO and founder, died unexpectedly at age 59. In addition, two months prior to her father's death the firm had recalled much of its meat from distributors and supermarkets because of contamination in the meat plant. The meat plant closed for six weeks while the contamination problem was corrected. An appraiser valued the stock for her father's estate at $1,000 per share. Janet, a new client, would like for your firm to prepare an amended gift tax return and value her gift at $1,000 per share because of the decline in value resulting from the two events described. She would like to receive a refund of the gift tax she paid and have some of her unified credit restored. Prepare a memo that addresses whether Janet should be entitled to a refund of the gift tax paid and restoration of some of her unified credit.

C:12-63 *Internet Research Problem.* In 2011, Robert Rath, a widower who has two adult sons and who lives in Memphis, Tennessee, made a $75,000 gift of cash to his niece, Ruby Rath Rubin. Use the Internet to determine the amount of Tennessee state gift tax he will owe on this gift if it is his first taxable gift.

C:12-64 *Internet Research Problem.* Your manager wants you to participate in delivering a staff training course on the basics of gift taxation. Your assignment is to discuss *Crummey* trusts. You want to improve your understanding of some of the advantages and disadvantages of such trusts. Conduct research on the Internet and summarize the advantages and disadvantages. Also indicate which site(s) is (are) the source(s) of your information.

C:12-65 *Internet Research Problem.* What was the Sec. 7520 rate for May, June, and July 2010?

13

C H A P T E R

THE ESTATE TAX

LEARNING OBJECTIVES

After studying this chapter, you should be able to

1. Describe the formula for the estate tax

2. Describe the methods for valuing interests in the gross estate

3. Determine which interests are includible in the gross estate

4. Identify deductions available for estate tax purposes

5. Calculate the estate tax liability

6. Identify tax provisions that alleviate liquidity problems

7. Recognize the filing requirements for estate tax returns

REAL-WORLD EXAMPLE

In 2004, the top 2.73 million wealth holders held total assets worth $11.1 trillion in the following proportions:

Personal residences	9.2%
Other real property	12.6
Closely held stock	10.2
Other stock	20.3
Tax exempt bonds	6.3
Various taxable bonds	2.9
Cash accounts	8.9
Retirement assets	9.5
Various other assets	20.1

Gift taxes and estate taxes are part of a unified system that taxes the transfer of wealth. Thus, they are fundamentally different than income or property taxes. Chapter C:12 discussed their history and purposes.

As previously noted, the term *gift taxes* applies to lifetime transfers and the term *estate taxes* applies to dispositions of property resulting from the transferor's death. This chapter discusses the structure of the federal estate tax and examines the types of interests and transactions that cause inclusions in the decedent's gross estate. It also discusses the various deductions and credits affecting the federal estate tax liability and the rules concerning the taxable gifts that affect the estate tax base, an important issue because of the unified nature of the tax levied at death.

As described in Chapter C:12, the Economic Growth and Tax Relief Reconciliation Act of 2001 (the 2001 Act) provided phased-in increases to the unified credit and phased-in reductions to the unified tax rate schedule beginning with 2002. In addition, it provided that the estate and generation skipping transfer taxes would not apply, effective January 1, 2010. However, the 2001 Act further provided that, in the absence of additional legistation, the rules for gift, estate, and generation skipping taxes would revert on January 1, 2011, to what they were before the 2001 Act.

Thus, as of January 1, 2010, the estate tax was automatically repealed and was scheduled to return in 2011 at pre-2001 Act levels. Several very high-wealth individuals died in 2010, and their estates were not subject to any estate tax under the rules in effect at their dates of death. However, with the repeal of the estate tax, a decedent's assets, except for a limited amount, were not permitted to be stepped-up to fair market value. Rather, the basis of the assets transferred to beneficiaries was determined using a modified carryover basis system discussed at C:12-27 and 12-28. In December 2010, Congress finally enacted the Tax Relief, Unemployment Insurance Reauthorization, and Job Creation Act of 2010 (hereinafter referred to as the Tax Relief Act), which reinstated the estate tax retroactive to January 1, 2010 along with assets being stepped up or down to fair market value at date of death. However, for decedents who died in 2010, the Tax Relief Act allows the executor to choose between (1) no estate tax with a modified carryover basis or (2) the estate tax with a $5 million applicable exclusion amount, a top rate of 35%, and FMV bases for the estate's assets. Thus, estates below the $5 million threshold can step up the assets' bases to FMV without incurring any estate tax liability. A step-up occurs when the estate's assets have a FMV exceeding their bases. A step-down could occur for assets whose bases exceed their FMV.

The Tax Relief Act provides that for 2011 and 2012 the maximum rate for both estate and gift taxes is 35% and the amount that can be transferred tax free in either context is $5 million; this amount is indexed for 2012. In the absence of further legislation, in 2013 the rules will return to those in effect before the 2001 Act.

ESTATE TAX FORMULA

OBJECTIVE 1

Describe the formula for the estate tax

The tax base for the federal estate tax is the *total* of the decedent's taxable estate (i.e., the gross estate less the deductions discussed below) and adjusted taxable gifts (post-1976 taxable gifts). After the gross tax liability on the tax base is determined, various credits—including the unified credit—are subtracted to arrive at the net estate tax payable. The estate tax formula appears in Figure C:13-1.

GROSS ESTATE

As illustrated in Figure C:13-1, calculation of the decedent's estate tax liability begins with determining which items are included in the gross estate. Such items are valued at either the decedent's date of death or the alternate valuation date.[1] As a transfer tax, the estate tax is levied on dispositions that are essentially testamentary in nature. Transactions are viewed as being essentially **testamentary transfers** if the transferor's control or enjoyment of the property in question ceases at death, not before death.[2]

---

[1] Under Sec. 2032, the alternate valuation date is the earlier of six months after the date of death or the date the property is disposed of.

[2] An example of a transaction that is essentially **testamentary** in nature is a situation where the donor transfers property in trust but reserves a lifetime right to receive the trust income and, thus, continues to enjoy the economic benefits.

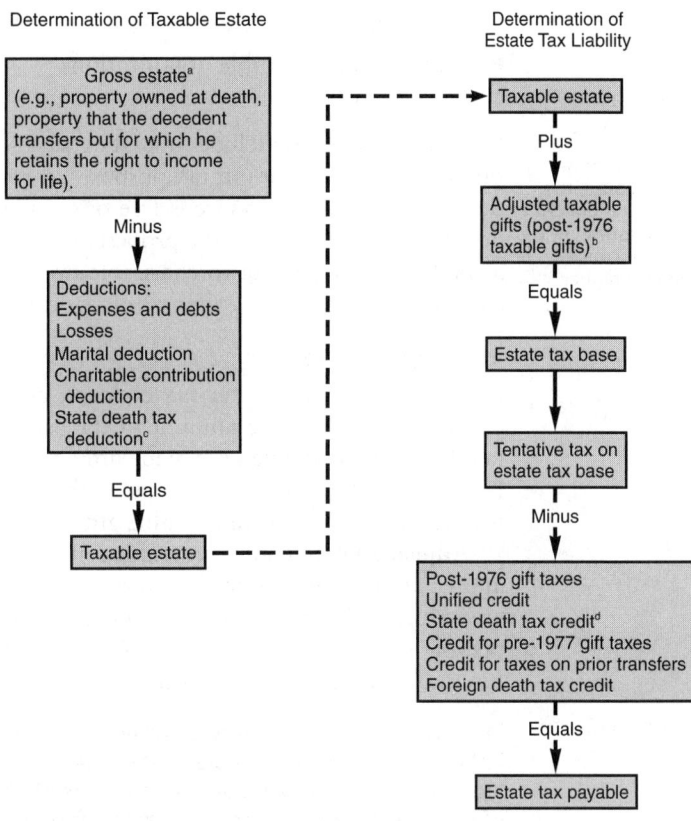

Determination of Taxable Estate

Determination of Estate Tax Liability

[a]Valued at decedent's date of death or alternate valuation date.
[b]Valued at date of gift.
[c]For decedents dying after 2004.
[d]For decedents dying before 2005.

FIGURE C:13-1 ▶ ESTATE TAX FORMULA

Inclusions in the gross estate extend to a much broader set of properties than merely assets to which the decedent holds title at the time of death. Making a lifetime transfer that generates a taxable gift does not guarantee that the donor removes the transferred property from his or her gross estate. Although an individual usually removes property from his or her gross estate by giving it to another before death, the donor's gross estate must include the gifted property if the donor retains either the right to receive the income generated by the transferred property or control over the property for the donor's lifetime.

EXAMPLE C:13-1 ▶ In the current year, Ted transfers stocks to an irrevocable trust with a bank named as trustee. Under the terms of the trust agreement, Ted is to receive the trust income annually for the rest of his life and Ted's cousin Ed (or Ed's estate) is to receive the remainder. In the current year, Ted made a taxable gift of the remainder interest (but not the income interest) in the trust. If, for example, Ted already has used his entire unified credit, he incurs a gift tax liability. When Ted dies, the entire value of the trust is included in Ted's gross estate, even though Ted has made a taxable gift and does not have legal title to the property. Because the shift in the right to the income does not occur until Ted's death, the transfer is testamentary in nature. ◀

The categories of items included in the gross estate and their valuation are examined in detail later in this chapter. Once the components of the gross estate have been determined and valued, the deductions from the gross estate are calculated.

SELF-STUDY QUESTION

In 2007, Barb transferred $500,000 in trust, income for life to herself, remainder to her daughter. What part, if any, of the value of the trust's assets will be included in Barb's estate?

ANSWER

The value of the entire trust will be included in Barb's estate, because she retained the income from the trust until her death.

DEDUCTIONS

The IRC authorizes five categories of items that may be deducted in arriving at the amount of the taxable estate:

▶ Expenses and debts

▶ Casualty and theft losses

► Transfers to the decedent's spouse

► Transfers to charitable organizations

► State death taxes

ADDITIONAL COMMENT

If a decedent leaves all his or her property to his or her spouse, the decedent wastes his or her unified credit. In addition, the estate of the surviving spouse is increased and may be pushed into higher tax brackets.

Deductible expenses include funeral expenses and expenses of administering the decedent's property. As is true for gift tax purposes, there is no ceiling on the marital deduction. Thus, the death of the first spouse is free of estate taxes if the decedent's spouse receives all the decedent's property, or all the property except for an amount equal to the exemption equivalent.[3] Property passing to charitable organizations qualifies, in general, for a charitable contribution deduction, with no ceiling on the amount of such deductions.

ADJUSTED TAXABLE GIFTS AND TAX BASE

Under the unified transfer tax concept, adjusted taxable gifts are added to the taxable estate to determine the amount of the estate tax base. Section 2001(b) defines adjusted taxable gifts as taxable gifts made after 1976 *other than* gifts included in the gross estate. Because very few gifts are included in the gross estate, almost every post-1976 taxable gift is classified as an adjusted taxable gift.

Adjusted taxable gifts are valued at their date-of-gift values. Therefore, any post-gift appreciation escapes both the gift tax and estate tax. Allowable deductions and exclusions are subtracted from the gift's value in determining taxable gifts and, thus, the adjusted taxable gifts amount. Increasing the taxable estate by adjusted taxable gifts potentially forces the estate into a higher marginal tax rate.

EXAMPLE C:13-2 ►

In 1992, Amy made $5 million of taxable gifts, none of which were included in her gross estate. In 2011, Amy died with a taxable estate of $4 million. The property Amy gave away in 1992 appreciated to $7 million in value by her date of death. In 1998, Amy gave stock valued at $10,000 to one of her children. Amy made no taxable gift and incurred no transfer tax on the 1998 transaction. The stock had appreciated to $70,000 when Amy died. Amy's estate tax base is calculated as follows:

ADDITIONAL COMMENT

Income earned on gifted property is the donee's and is not included in the donor's estate.

Taxable estate	$4,000,000
Plus: Adjusted taxable gifts (valued at date-of-gift values)	5,000,000
Estate tax base	$9,000,000

The $2 million of post-gift appreciation on the property gifted in 1992 escapes transfer taxation. Amy's $9 million tax base includes the gifted property, whose value was "frozen" at its date-of-gift value. The 1998 gift did not affect Amy's estate tax base because the 1998 *taxable gift* was zero. ◄

TENTATIVE TAX ON ESTATE TAX BASE

Once the amount of the tax base has been determined, the next step is to calculate the tax on this base using the unified tax rates, which are reproduced on the inside back cover of this textbook. In 2007 through 2009, a maximum tax rate of 45% applied to tax bases exceeding $1.5 million for both estate and gift tax purposes. For 2010 through 2012, the top estate and gift tax rate is 35%, applicable to tax bases exceeding $500,000. If, however, an estate's executor so elects for 2010, the estate tax will not apply that year, but the 35% tax rate nevertheless will apply to 2010 gifts.

EXAMPLE C:13-3 ►

Assume the same facts as in Example C:13-2. The gross tax on Amy's $9 million tax base was $3,130,800. The estate was taxed at a 35% marginal tax rate, the highest rate applicable in the year Amy died. ◄

REDUCTION FOR POST-1976 GIFT TAXES

Adjusted taxable gifts, in effect, are not taxed twice because Sec. 2001(b)(2) allows a reduction to the estate tax for gift taxes imposed on post-1976 taxable gifts. If the rate schedule for the year of death differs from the schedule applicable for the year of the gift, the tax on post-1976 taxable gifts is determined by using the rate schedule in effect for the year of

---

[3] The estate tax exemption equivalent ($5 million for 2011), as explained in Chapter C:12, is the size of the tax base for which the estate tax liability is exactly cancelled by the unified credit, $1,730,800 in 2011.

death. The unified credit subtracted from the gift tax is recalculated to arrive at what the credit would have been if the tax rates in effect at the date of death had been in effect at the time of the gift. The rule regarding rates works to the disadvantage of decedents who made taxable gifts and paid taxes at a higher rate than the rate in effect on the date of death. This recalculation approach ensures that the estate pays tax at the current marginal tax rate applicable for the decedent's amount of taxable estate and adjusted taxable gifts.

EXAMPLE C:13-4 ▶

Assume the same facts as in Examples C:13-2 and C:13-3. Recall that in 1992 Amy made $5 million of taxable gifts. The tax on $5 million of 1992 taxable gifts was $2,390,800. Amy was entitled to a $192,800 unified credit and paid $2,198,000 of gift taxes. Amy's 1992 gifts were taxed at a 55% marginal rate. For the year of Amy's death (2011), the marginal rate for $5 million of transfers is 35%. Consequently, the reduction for gift taxes on post-1976 taxable gifts is limited to the amount of gift taxes that would be payable if the 2011 rate schedule were in effect in the year of the gift. This amount is calculated as follows:

Tax on $5 million at 2011 rates	$1,730,800
Minus: Unified credit for 1992 (the year of the gift) if 35% had been the top rate	(190,800)
Tax that would have been payable on $5 million if 2011 rates were in effect	$1,540,000

Note that the only changes to the gift tax computation are that the 2011 transfer tax rates are used. The credit applicable for the year of the gift (and not the credit for the year of death) is subtracted. However, this amount is recalculated to take into consideration the tax rates in effect for the year of the donor's death. Thus, the credit used in the above calculation is $190,800 [$155,800 + 0.35 × ($600,000 − $500,000)], where $600,000 is the exemption equivalent for 1992. ◀

EXAMPLE C:13-5 ▶

From Examples C:13-3 and C:13-4, Amy's estate tax, before reduction for any credits, is calculated as follows:

Tax on $9 million tax base (Example C:13-3)	$3,130,800
Minus: Tax that would have been payable on $5 million of post-1976 taxable gifts, at 2011 rates (Example C:13-4)	(1,540,000)
Estate tax, before reduction for credits (discussed below)	$1,590,800 ◀

UNIFIED CREDIT

As shown in the inside back cover, the unified credit has varied over the years since its inception in 1977. The credit enables a certain size tax base, referred to as the exemption equivalent or applicable exclusion amount, to be completely free of transfer taxes. For 2009, the unified credit was the equivalent of the tax on $3.5 million for estates and $1 million for gifts. The Tax Relief Act did not revise the amount in effect for 2010 for gift tax purposes. It, however, increased the exempt amount to $5 million for estate tax purposes for the years 2010, 2011, and 2012 and for gift tax purposes for 2011 and 2012. As a result, the unified credit is $1,730,800. In addition, this amount will be indexed in 2012. After 2012, absent further Congressional action, the amount will decrease to $1 million. This exempt amount often is referred to as the exemption equivalent and/or the applicable exclusion amount, and in 2011 and 2012 it is called the basic exclusion amount.

The estate tax computation permits an estate to subtract the entire unified credit applicable for the year of death (reduced by any phaseout for certain pre-1977 gifts) regardless of how much unified credit the decedent claimed for gift tax purposes. As a conceptual matter, however, only one unified credit is available. Under the unification concept, the estate tax is computed on a tax base consisting of the taxable estate plus the adjusted taxable gifts. The tentative tax on the tax base is reduced not by the amount of the "gross" tax on the adjusted taxable gifts, but by the "gross" tax on such gifts reduced by the unified credit. Ignoring changes in the amount of the unified credit, this computation achieves the same result as allowing the unified credit amount to be subtracted only once against all of a person's transfers but allowing a reduction to the estate tax for the gift tax liability *before* reduction for the unified credit.

OTHER CREDITS

In addition to the unified credit—the only credit available for gift tax purposes—the IRC authorizes three credits for estate tax purposes. (Prior to 2005, estates also were allowed a credit for state death taxes.) These additional credits (shown in Figure C:13-1) are discussed in more detail on pages C:13-24 and C:13-25.

SELF-STUDY QUESTION

Taxpayer made $3 million of taxable gifts in 1992 and paid gift taxes of $1,098,000 (gross tax of $1,290,800 minus the unified credit of $192,800). Taxpayer died in 2011 with a taxable estate of $100,000. At 2011 rates and a credit recalculated at 2011 rates, the gift taxes payable on $3 million would be $840,000 ($1,030,800 − $190,800). Determine the amount of her estate tax liability.

ANSWER

The unified transfer tax base was $3.1 million, the sum of the $3 million of 1992 taxable gifts and the $100,000 estate. The 2011 tax on $3.1 million is $1,065,800. The unified credit of $1,730,800 and the subtraction for gift taxes of $840,000 reduce the tax liability to zero.

THE GROSS ESTATE: VALUATION

OBJECTIVE 2

Describe the methods for valuing interests in the gross estate

DATE-OF-DEATH VALUATION

All property included in the gross estate is valued at either its fair market value (FMV) on the date of death or the alternate valuation date. The valuation date election is an all-or-nothing proposition. Each item included in the gross estate must be valued as of the same date. In other words, the executor (called the personal representative in some states) may not value some items as of the date of death and others as of the alternate valuation date.

TYPICAL MISCONCEPTION

The basis of inherited property is the FMV of the property on the decedent's date of death, which could be higher or lower than the decedent's basis. This change is referred to as a step-up or a step-down in basis. Many taxpayers hear so much about step-up that they forget that a step-down can occur. However, see pages C:12-27 and C:12-28 for carryover basis rules applicable to deaths in 2010.

Fair market value is defined as "the price at which the property would change hands between a willing buyer and a willing seller, neither being under any compulsion to buy or to sell and both having reasonable knowledge of relevant facts."[4] In general, the FMV of a particular asset on a certain date is the same regardless of whether the property is being valued for gift or estate tax purposes. Life insurance on the life of the transferor is an exception to this rule. Upon the death of the insured, the policy is valued at its face value, whereas it is valued at a lesser amount while the insured is alive. Generally, this lesser amount is either the cost of a comparable contract or the policy's interpolated terminal reserve plus the unexpired portion of the premium.

For certain types of property, Treasury Regulations contain detailed descriptions of the valuation approach. However, the valuation of interests in closely held businesses is described in only very general terms. Judicial decisions and revenue rulings provide additional guidance for valuation of assets. Valuation rules for several interests are discussed below. For purposes of this discussion, it is assumed that date-of-death valuation is elected.

ETHICAL POINT

Valuation of interests in closely held corporations and real estate is an area where the executor may need to engage a qualified appraiser. Because appraisals are subjective, two appraisers may arrive at different values. Using the highest appraisal may mean additional estate taxes, but it will provide a greater step-up in basis. Using too low an appraisal may subject the estate to undervaluation penalties (see page C:13-35).

LISTED STOCKS. Stocks traded on a stock exchange are valued at the average of their highest and lowest selling prices on the date of death.[5] If no sales occur on the date of death, but sales do take place within a few days of such date, the estate tax value is a weighted average of the high and low sales prices on the nearest trade dates before and after the date of death. The average is weighted inversely in relation to the number of days separating the sales dates and the date of death.

EXAMPLE C:13-6 ▶

Juan, who died on November 15, 2011, owned 100 shares of Jet Corporation stock. Jet stock, traded on the New York Stock Exchange, traded at a high of $120 and a low of $114 on November 15. On Juan's estate tax return, the stock was valued at $117 per share, the average of $120 and $114. The total value of the block of Jet stock was $11,700 (100 × $117). ◀

EXAMPLE C:13-7 ▶

Susan, who died on May 7, 2011 owned 100 shares of Top Corporation stock, traded on the New York Stock Exchange. No sales of Top stock occurred on May 7. The sales occurring closest to May 7 took place two business days before May 7 and three business days after May 7. On the earlier date, the stock traded at a high of $500 and a low of $490, with an average of $495. On the later date, the high was $492 and the low was $490, for an average of $491. The date-of-death per-share valuation of the stock is computed under the inverse weighted average approach, as follows:

$$\frac{[3 \times \$495] + [2 \times \$491]}{5} = \$493.40$$

The total value of the block of Top stock is $49,340 (100 × $493.40). ◀

In certain circumstances, the decedent may own such a large block of stock that the price at which the stock trades in the market may not represent the FMV per share for the decedent's number of shares. In such circumstances, Treasury Regulations allow a departure from the traditional valuation rule for stocks. These regulations, referred to as the blockage regulations, state that

---

[4] Reg. Sec. 20.2031-1(b).   [5] Reg. Sec. 20.2031-2(b).

In certain exceptional cases, the size of the block of stock to be valued in relation to the number of shares changing hands in sales may be relevant in determining whether selling prices reflect the fair market value of the block of stock to be valued. If the executor can show that the block of stock to be valued is so large in relation to the actual sales on the existing market that it could not be liquidated in a reasonable time without depressing the market, the price at which the block could be sold as such outside the usual market, as through an underwriter, may be a more accurate indication of value than market quotations.[6]

INTERESTS IN FIRMS WHOSE STOCK IS NOT PUBLICLY TRADED. Often, the decedent owns stock in a firm whose shares are not publicly traded. Treasury Regulations do not specifically address the valuation rules for this type of an interest. However, detailed guidelines about relevant factors, including book value and earning capacity, are found in Rev. Rul. 59-60.[7] If the stock is a minority interest in a closely held firm, the courts often grant a discount for the minority interest.

REAL ESTATE. Perhaps surprisingly, Treasury Regulations do not specifically address the valuation approach for real estate. Thus, the general valuation principles concerning a price that would be acceptable to a willing buyer and a willing seller must be implemented without the benefit of more specific guidance. Appraisal literature discusses three techniques for valuing real property: comparable sales, reproduction cost, and capitalization of earnings.[8] Unfortunately, for some properties, it may be difficult to locate a comparable real estate sale. The reproduction cost, of course, is not applicable to valuing land. Capitalization of earnings often is used in valuing commercial real property. At times, an appraiser may use all three approaches.

ANNUITIES, INTERESTS FOR LIFE OR A TERM OF YEARS, REVERSIONS, REMAINDERS. Actuarial tables are used to value annuities, interests for life or a term of years, reversions, and remainders included in the gross estate.[9] The same tables apply for both estate and gift tax purposes. (See Chapter C:12 for a discussion of the use of these tables.) The following example illustrates a situation when the actuarial tables must be used to value an inclusion in the decedent's estate.

EXAMPLE C:13-8 ▶ Tony gives property to a trust with a bank named as trustee and his cousin named to receive all of the trust income for the next 15 years (i.e., a term certain interest). At the end of the fifteenth year, the property reverts to Tony or his estate. Tony dies exactly four years after creating the trust, and the trust property is valued at $100,000 at Tony's death. At Tony's death, the trust has 11 years to continue until the property reverts to Tony's estate. The inclusion in Tony's estate is the value of a reversionary interest following a term certain interest with 11 remaining years. If 4% is the applicable rate, the reversionary interest is valued at $64,958 (0.649581 × $100,000) from Table B of the actuarial tables included in Appendix H. ◀

ALTERNATE VALUATION DATE

Section 2032 authorizes the executor to elect to value all property included in the gross estate at its FMV on the alternate valuation date. Congress enacted this provision in response to the stock market crash of 1929 to make sure that an entire estate could not be confiscated for taxes because of a sudden, substantial drop in values.

In general, the **alternate valuation date** is six months after the date of death. However, if the property is distributed, sold, exchanged, or otherwise disposed of within six months of the date of death, the alternate valuation date is the date of sale or other disposition.

EXAMPLE C:13-9 ▶ Ron died on March 3, 2011. Ron's estate included two items: stock and land. The estate still owned the stock on September 3, but the executor sold the land on August 20. If Ron's executor elected the alternate valuation date, the stock was valued as of September 3. The land, however, was valued as of August 20 because it was disposed of before the end of the six-month period. Of course, the value of land generally would change very little, if any, between August 20 and September 3. ◀

---

[6] Reg. Sec. 20.2031-2(e). As examples of cases dealing with the blockage discount, see *Horace Havemeyer v. U.S.*, 33 AFTR 1069, 45-1 USTC ¶10,194 (Ct. Cls., 1945); *Estate of Charles M. Prell*, 48 T.C. 67 (1967); and *Estate of David Smith*, 57 T.C. 650 (1972). The *Smith* case extended the blockage concept to large holdings of works of art.
[7] 1959-1 C.B. 237.

[8] For a discussion of techniques for appraising real estate, see The Appraisal Institute, *The Appraisal of Real Estate*, 11th ed. (Arlington Heights, IL: The Appraisal Institute, 1996).
[9] Section 7520 provides that the interest rate potentially changes every month. Regulation Sec. 20.7520-1(a)(2) provides these tables. An excerpt from these tables is included in Appendix H.

REAL-WORLD EXAMPLE

Proposed Treasury Regulations, if adopted, would allow the alternative valuation only for reductions due to "market conditions."

If the executor elects the alternate valuation date, generally any changes in value that occur *solely* because of a "mere lapse of time" must be ignored in determining the property's value.[10] In a limited number of situations, one must concentrate on the meaning of the phrase "the mere passage of time." For example, if the executor elects the alternate valuation date to value a patent, he or she must ignore any change in value attributable to the fact that the patent's remaining life is six months shorter on the alternate valuation date than it was on the date of death. Changes in value resulting from the invention of a competing patented product are relevant.

The alternate valuation date election can be made only if it decreases the value of the gross estate *and* the estate tax liability (after reduction for credits).[11] As a result of this provision, electing the alternate valuation date cannot produce a higher step-up in basis. Congress enacted this strict rule because the alternate valuation date formerly offered a substantial tax planning advantage in situations where, because of the unlimited marital deduction, no estate tax was owed. If the property appreciated between the date of death and the alternate valuation date, the recipient could receive an increased basis if the executor elected the alternate valuation date.[12] Because of the unlimited marital deduction, the estate formerly could achieve an additional step-up in basis without increasing the estate tax liability.

STOP & THINK

Question: Joan died on December 1, 2011. Her estate consisted of three assets: an apartment building valued at $3.2 million on December 1, 2011, stock valued at $3.7 million on December 1, and $400,000 of cash. On June 1 of the next year, 1, the values were as follows: apartment building—$3.5 million, stock—$3.1 million, and cash of $400,000. Joan willed all her property to her son, who anticipates owning the property for a long time. The deductions for Joan's estate were negligible. Is there an estate tax benefit in electing the alternate valuation date? Is there an income tax benefit in electing the alternate valuation date?

Solution: An estate tax benefit results from using the alternate valuation date. The estate tax liability would be lower because the taxable estate would be $300,000 smaller if the alternate valuation date value ($7 million minus deductions) were used instead of the date of death value ($7.3 million minus deductions). Some income tax benefit also results from using the alternate valuation date. By using the alternate valuation date value, the tax basis for calculating cost recovery on the apartment building is $300,000 higher, ignoring any allocation of value to the land. However, a related detriment occurs because the basis of the stock is $600,000 lower with the alternate valuation date. If the son sells the stock in the near future, the $600,000 capital loss that would arise by using the date of death value might permit Joan's son to sell a number of highly-appreciated assets and offset a very large capital gain with the $600,000 capital loss.

THE GROSS ESTATE: INCLUSIONS

OBJECTIVE 3

Determine which interests are includible in the gross estate

As Figure C:13-1 illustrates, the process of calculating the decedent's estate tax liability begins with determining the components of the gross estate. The **gross estate** is analogous to gross income. Once the components of the gross estate have been identified, they must be valued. As previously mentioned, the gross estate encompasses a much wider array of items than merely those to which the decedent held legal title at death. For example, under certain statutory provisions, referred to as the *transferor sections*, the gross estate includes items previously transferred by the decedent. For decedents other than nonresident aliens, the fact that property is located in a foreign country does not preclude it from being included in the gross estate. Table C:13-1 provides an overview of the inclusions in the gross estate.

---

[10] Reg. Sec. 20.2032-1(f).
[11] Sec. 2032(c).

[12] Sec. 1014(a).

▼ TABLE C:13-1
Inclusions in the Gross Estate

IRC Section	Type of Property or Transaction Included
2033	Property in which the decedent had an interest
2035	Gift taxes on property given away within three years of death *plus* certain property (primarily life insurance) given away within three years of death
2036	Property that the decedent transferred during life but in which the decedent retained economic benefits or the power to control enjoyment
2037	Property that the decedent transferred during life but for which the decedent has too large a reversionary interest
2038	Property that the decedent transferred during life but over which the decedent held the power to alter, amend, revoke, or terminate an interest
2039	Annuities
2040	Jointly owned property
2041	Property over which the decedent possessed a general power of appointment
2042	Life insurance on the decedent's life
2044	QTIP trust for which a marital deduction was claimed by the decedent's spouse

COMPARISON OF GROSS ESTATE WITH PROBATE ESTATE

The gross estate is a federal tax law concept, and the probate estate is a state law concept. To oversimplify, the **probate estate** can be defined as encompassing property that passes subject to the will (or under an intestacy statute) and is subject to court administration. Often, a decedent's gross estate is substantially larger than his or her probate estate. For example, suppose that at the time of death, a decedent owned a life insurance policy on his own life with his daughter as the beneficiary. The policy is not a part of the decedent's probate estate because the policy proceeds are payable directly to the named beneficiary (the daughter), but it is included in the gross estate.

STOP & THINK

Question: Karl died in 2011, and Karl's executor included the following properties in Karl's gross estate: life insurance payable to the beneficiary, Karl's wife; savings account solely in Karl's name; land titled in the names of Karl and his son as joint tenants with right of survivorship; and a trust created under the will of Karl's mother. Karl had an income interest in the trust for his lifetime and complete power to designate the owners of the property on his death. With the exception of the trust assets (willed to his children), Karl's will left all his property to his beloved cousin, Karla. Which assets passed under the terms of Karl's will? Which assets did Karla receive?

Solution: This scenario illustrates the difference between the property included in a decedent's gross estate and in the probate estate. Karl's gross estate was larger than his probate estate. Only two assets included in his gross estate—the savings account and the trust property—passed under the terms of Karl's will. Karla received only the savings account because Karl willed the trust property to his children. The life insurance passed outside the will to the named beneficiary, the spouse, and the land passed outside the will to the surviving joint tenant, the son.

PROPERTY IN WHICH THE DECEDENT HAD AN INTEREST

Section 2033, sometimes called the *generic section*, provides that the gross estate includes the value of all property the decedent beneficially owned at the time of death. Its broad language taxes such items as a personal residence, an automobile, stocks, and any other asset titled in the decedent's name. Because the rule refers to beneficial ownership,

SELF-STUDY QUESTION

Which of the following properties will be included in (1) the probate estate, (2) the gross estate, (3) both the probate and gross estate, or (4) neither estate?
1. Real property held in joint tenancy with the decedent's spouse. (The answer is 2.)
2. Real property held as a tenant in common with the decedent's spouse. (The answer is 3.)
3. A life insurance policy owned by the decedent in which the decedent's spouse is named the beneficiary. (The answer is 2.)
4. A life insurance policy always owned by the decedent's spouse in which the decedent's children are named the beneficiaries. (The answer is 4.)

however, its scope extends beyond assets to which the decedent held legal title. For example, such items as remainder interests also are included in the gross estate.

At the time of his death in 2011, Raj held the following assets in his name: personal residence, mountain cabin, Zero Corporation stock, checking account, and savings account. Raj beneficially owned each of these items when he died. Under Sec. 2033, each item was included in Raj's gross estate. ◀

Ken's will named Ann to receive trust income for life and Raj or Raj's estate to receive the trust remainder upon Ann's death. Raj's gross estate, therefore, included the value of the remainder interest if Raj predeceased Ann because Raj's will controlled the passage of the remainder interest Raj beneficially owned. The transfer was associated with Raj's death, and, hence, was subject to the estate tax. ◀

DOWER OR CURTESY RIGHTS

Certain state laws provide wealth protection to surviving spouses through **dower** or **curtesy** rights.

▶ Dower is a widow's interest in her deceased husband's property.

▶ Curtesy is a widower's interest in his deceased wife's property.

ADDITIONAL COMMENT

Any property that passes outright to the decedent's spouse, due to dower or curtesy rights under state law, is eligible for the marital deduction and will not increase the unified tax base.

Dower or curtesy rights entitle the surviving spouse to a certain portion of the decedent spouse's estate, even though the decedent may have willed a smaller portion to the spouse. Because the decedent spouse does not have complete control over the portion of his or her estate that is subject to dower or curtesy rights, some might think that the portion of the estate that the surviving spouse is entitled to receive is excluded from the gross estate. Thus, Congress made it crystal clear that the decedent's gross estate is not reduced for the value of the property in which the surviving spouse has a dower or curtesy interest or some other statutory interest.[13]

SELF-STUDY QUESTION

When Dorothy died on April 10, 2011, she owned Z Corporation bonds, which paid interest on April 1 and October 1, and stock in X and Y Corporations. X Corporation had declared a dividend on March 15 payable to stockholders of record on April 1. Y Corporation had declared a dividend on March 31 payable to stockholders of record on April 15. Dorothy's estate received the interest and dividends on the payment dates. Are any of the interest or dividends includible in Dorothy's gross estate?

ANSWER

The X Corporation dividend is included because the date of record preceded Dorothy's death. The Y Corporation dividend is not included because the date of record was after her death. The Z Corporation bond interest included is the interest that accrued between the April 1 payment date and the April 10 date of death.

The laws of a certain state provide that widows are entitled to receive one-third of their deceased husband's property. The husband's gross estate does not exclude his widow's dower rights (one-third interest) in his property. ◀

TRANSFEROR PROVISIONS

Sections 2035 through 2038 are called the *transferor provisions*. They apply if the decedent made a transfer while alive of a type specified in the IRC section in question, *and* the decedent did not receive adequate consideration in money or money's worth for the transferred interest. If one of the transferor provisions applies, the gross estate includes the transferred property at its date-of-death or alternate valuation date value.

GIFTS MADE WITHIN THREE YEARS OF DEATH. Section 2035(a) specifies the circumstances in which a gift that a decedent makes within three years of death triggers an inclusion in the gross estate. The scope of this provision, which is relatively narrow, encompasses the following two types of transfers made by the donor-decedent within three years before death:

▶ A life insurance policy on the decedent's life that would have been taxed under Sec. 2042 (life insurance proceeds received by the executor or for the benefit of the estate) had the policy not been given away, or

▶ An interest in property that would have been taxed under Sec. 2036 (transfers with a retained life estate), Sec. 2037 (transfers taking effect at death), or Sec. 2038 (revocable transfers) had it not been transferred.

Of these situations, the most common involves the insured's gifting a life insurance policy on his or her own life and dying within three years of the transfer. With new insurance policies, the potential for an inclusion can be avoided if the decedent never owns the new policy. In other words, instead of the insured purchasing a new policy and then giving it to a transferee as owner, the other party should buy the new policy. A common planning

---

[13] Sec. 2034.

technique involves a transfer of cash by an individual to a trust, and the trust (a life insurance trust) using the cash to purchase an insurance policy on the transferor's life.

EXAMPLE C:13-13▶

On April 1, 2008, Roy transferred to Sally ownership of a $400,000 life insurance policy on his own life purchased in 1996. Sally is the policy's beneficiary. Roy died on February 3, 2011. Because Roy died within three years of giving away the policy, the policy was included in Roy's gross estate. The estate tax value of the policy is its $400,000 face value. If Roy had died on April 2, 2011, the policy transfer would have fallen outside the three-year rule, and the policy would not have been included in Roy's gross estate. ◀

EXAMPLE C:13-14▶

Roy made a gift of stock to Troy on May 1, 2010. Roy died on February 3, 2011. The stock was worth $80,000 on the gift date and was worth $125,000 at the time of Roy's death. The gifted property was not included in Roy's gross estate because it is not life insurance on Roy's life, nor is it property that would have been taxed in Roy's estate under Secs. 2036 through 2038 had he kept such property. ◀

GROSS-UP RULE. The donor-decedent's gross estate is increased by any gift tax that he or she, or his or her estate pays on any gift the decedent or his or her spouse makes during the three-year period ending with the decedent's death.[14] This provision, known as the gross-up rule, applies to the gift tax triggered by a gift of any type of property during the three-year look-back period.

The purpose of the gross-up rule is to foreclose the opportunity that existed under pre-1977 law to reduce one's gross estate (and thereby one's taxable estate) by removing the gift tax on "deathbed" gifts from the gross estate. Because the donor's estate received a credit for some or all of the gift tax paid, under the pre-1977 rules, a person on his or her deathbed in effect could prepay a portion of his or her estate tax and at the same time reduce his or her gross estate by the amount of the gift tax.

The gross-up rule, as illustrated in the two examples below, reinstates the estate to the position it would have been in had no gift tax liability been incurred.

EXAMPLE C:13-15▶

In late 2008, Cheron made her first gift, a $2.5 million taxable gift of stock, and paid a gift tax of $660,000 ($1,005,800 gross tax − $345,800 unified credit). Cheron died in early 2011. Cheron's gross estate did not include the stock, but it did include the $660,000 gift tax paid because she made the gift within three years of her death. ◀

EXAMPLE C:13-16▶

SELF-STUDY QUESTION

Refer to Example C:13-16. Assume that Hal, the spouse who actually made the gift, paid Wanda's $660,000 gift tax as well as his own $660,000 gift tax. Would Wanda's $660,000 gift tax be included in her gross estate?

ANSWER

No. It would not be included because payment of the tax from Hal's account did not reduce Wanda's cash balance.

In late 2008, Hal gave Jody stock having a $5,024,000 FMV, and he and Wanda, his wife, elected gift splitting. Each was deemed to have made a $2.5 million [($5,024,000 ÷ 2) − $12,000 annual exclusion] taxable gift, and each paid $660,000 ($1,005,800 gross tax − $345,800 unified credit) of gift tax. Wanda died in early 2011. Wanda's gross estate included the $660,000 in gift tax she paid on the portion of her husband's gift that she was deemed to have made within three years of her death. Her cash balance declined because of paying the gift tax, and the gross-up for the tax reinstated her estate to the position it would have been in had she paid no gift tax. ◀

TRANSFERS WITH RETAINED LIFE ESTATE. Section 2036, although titled "Transfers with Retained Life Estate," extends beyond taxing solely lifetime transfers made by the decedent in which he or she retained a life estate (the right to income or use for life). The two primary types of transfers taxed under Sec. 2036 are those for which the decedent

▶ Kept possession or enjoyment of the property or the right to its income

▶ Retained the power to designate the person who is to possess or enjoy the property or to receive its income

Thus, Sec. 2036 applies when the transferor kept the income or enjoyment *or* the right to control other individuals' income or enjoyment.

The direct or indirect retention of voting rights in stock of a controlled corporation that the decedent transferred also can cause the gifted stock to be included in the

---

[14] Sec. 2035(b).

transferor's gross estate.[15] A controlled corporation is one in which the decedent owned (directly, indirectly, or constructively), or had the right to vote, stock that possessed at least 20% of the voting power.[16]

The retention of income, control, or voting rights for one of the three retention periods listed below causes the transferred property to be included in the transferor's gross estate. The three periods are

▶ The transferor's lifetime

▶ A period that cannot be determined without referring to the transferor's death (e.g., the transferor retained the right to quarterly payments of income, but payments ceased with the last quarterly payment before the transferor's death)

▶ A period that does not end, in fact, before the transferor's death

An implied agreement or understanding is sufficient to trigger inclusion. For example, if a mother gives a residence to her daughter and continues to occupy the residence alone and rent-free, the residence probably will be included in the mother's gross estate under the argument that the parties had an implied understanding allowing the mother to reside in the residence for life without paying rent.

If Sec. 2036 applies to a transfer and if the decedent's retention of enjoyment or control extends to all the transferred property, 100% of the transferred property's value is included in the transferor's gross estate.[17] However, if the transferor keeps the right to only one-third of the income for life and retains no control over the remaining two-thirds, his estate includes just one-third of the property's date-of-death value. The following three examples illustrate some of the transactions that cause Sec. 2036 to apply.

EXAMPLE C:13-17▶

In 2005, David (age 30) transferred an office building to Ellen but retained the right to collect all the income from the building for life. David died in 2011. Because David retained the income right for life, the Sec. 2036 inclusion applied. The amount included was 100% of the building's date-of-death value. ◀

EXAMPLE C:13-18▶

Assume the same facts as in Example C:13-17 except that David retained the right to income for only 15 years. David died six years after the transfer; therefore, David had the right to receive the income for the remaining nine-year period. Because the retention period did not *in fact* end before David's death, his gross estate included 100% of the property's date-of-death value. ◀

EXAMPLE C:13-19▶

Tracy created a trust with a bank as trustee and named Alice, Brad, and Carol to receive the trust income for their joint lives and Dick to receive the remainder upon the death of the first among Alice, Brad, or Carol to die. Tracy reserved the right to designate the portion of the income to be paid to each income beneficiary each year. Only the transfer to Dick was a completed transfer and subject to gift taxes. Tracy predeceased the other parties. Because her control over the flow of income did not end before Tracy's death, the date-of-death value of the trust assets was included in Tracy's gross estate even though a portion of the transfer was subject to gift taxes. If Tracy had instead "cut the string" and not kept control over the income flow, she could have removed the trust property from her estate. ◀

SELF-STUDY QUESTION

Refer to Example C:13-19. Assume the same facts except that the trustee was directed to distribute its annual income equally to Alice, Brad, and Carol for their joint lives. Also assume that Tracy named Dick the remainderman. Was the value of the trust included in Tracy's gross estate?

ANSWER

No, because Tracy retained no power to control the enjoyment of the property.

REVERSIONARY INTERESTS. If the chance exists that the property will pass back to the transferor under the terms of the transfer, the transferor has a **reversionary interest.** Under Sec. 2037, the transferor's gross estate includes earlier transferred property if the decedent stipulates that another person must survive him or her to own the property and the value of the decedent's reversionary interest exceeds 5% of the value of the transferred property. Actuarial techniques are used to value the reversionary interest.[18] Section 2037 does not apply if the value of the reversionary interest does not exceed the 5% *de minimis* amount.

EXAMPLE C:13-20▶

Beth transferred an asset to Tammy for life and then to Doug for life. The asset is to revert to Beth, if Beth is still alive, upon the death of either Tammy or Doug, whoever dies second. If Beth is not alive upon the death of the survivor of Tammy and Doug, the asset is to pass to Don or to

---

[15] Sec. 2036(b)(1).

[16] Sec. 2036(b)(2).

[17] Reg. Sec. 20.2036-1(a).

[18] The **reversionary interest** is the interest that will return to the transferor. Often, it will return only if certain contingencies occur. The value of Beth's

reversionary interest in Example C:13-20 is a function of the present value of the interest Beth would receive after the deaths of Tammy and Doug, valued as from actuarial tables (see Appendix H), and coupled with the probability that Tammy and Doug would die before Beth.

a charitable organization if Don is not alive. Thus, Don must live longer than Beth to receive the property. The property is included in Beth's estate if the value of Beth's reversionary interest exceeds 5% of the property's value. The amount included is not the value of Beth's reversionary interest, but rather the date-of-death value of the asset less the value of Tammy's and Doug's intervening life estates. ◄

ADDITIONAL COMMENT

Sections 2036 through 2038 draw back into the gross estate certain previously transferred property and include it at its FMV on the date of the decedent's death. For income tax purposes, if the property has appreciated in value, donees will obtain a stepped-up basis rather than a carryover gift tax basis for property included in the gross estate.

REVOCABLE TRANSFERS. Section 2038 covers the rules for revocable transfers (i.e., revocable trusts). However, this provision also taxes all transfers over which the decedent has, at the time of his or her death, the power to change the enjoyment of property by altering, amending, revoking, or terminating an interest. Revocable trusts, sometimes called living trusts, are popular arrangements from a non-tax standpoint because assets held by a revocable trust pass outside of probate. Advantages of avoiding probate include lower probate costs and easier administration for real property located in a state that is not the decedent's state of domicile. In addition, unlike a will, a revocable trust is not a matter of public record.

Section 2038 can apply even though the decedent does not originally retain powers over the property. The crucial factor is that the transferor possesses the powers at the time of death regardless of whether the transferor retained such powers originally. The estate includes only the value of the interest that is subject to the decedent's power to change. Sections 2038 and 2036 overlap greatly, and if one amount is taxable under one section and a different amount is taxable under the other section, the gross estate includes the larger amount. Two types of transfers taxed by Sec. 2038 are illustrated in the following examples.

EXAMPLE C:13-21 ► Joe funded a revocable trust and named his son to receive the income for life and his grandson to receive the property upon the son's death. Because the trust was revocable, Joe could change the terms of the trust or take back the trust property during his lifetime. Joe's power to revoke the transfer extended to the entire trust. Thus, Joe's gross estate included the date-of-death value of the entire trust. ◄

EXAMPLE C:13-22 ► Vicki created a trust and irrevocably named Gina to receive the income for life and Matt to receive the remainder. Vicki, however, retained the right to substitute Liz (for Matt) as remainderman. When Vicki died, she had the authority to change the enjoyment of the remainder. Thus, the value of the trust's remainder interest was includible in Vicki's estate. ◄

ANNUITIES AND OTHER RETIREMENT BENEFITS

SELF-STUDY QUESTION

Reggie purchased an annuity and elected to collect benefits for 15 years. If Reggie dies before the end of the 15-year term of the annuity, his estate will be entitled to the remaining payments. Assume Reggie died after receiving nine payments. Will the value of the remaining six payments be included in Reggie's estate?

ANSWER

Yes. Section 2039 requires that the cost of a comparable contract of six payments be included in his gross estate.

Section 2039 explicitly addresses the estate tax treatment of annuities. Even if this section had not been enacted, some annuities probably would have been taxable under the general language of Sec. 2033 because the decedent would have been viewed as having an interest in the property. For an annuity to be included in the gross estate, it must involve payments made under a contract or an agreement. In addition, the decedent must be receiving such payments at the time of his or her death or must have the right to collect such payments alone or with another person. If the annuity simply ceases with the death of the decedent in question, nothing is to be received by another party and nothing is included in the gross estate. For the payments to be included in the decedent's estate, they must be payable for the decedent's life, a period that may not be determined without referring to the decedent's date of death or for a period that does not actually end before the decedent's death.

ANNUITIES NOT RELATED TO EMPLOYMENT. The purchase of an annuity designed to pay benefits to the purchaser and then to a named survivor upon the purchaser's death, or to both parties simultaneously and then to the survivor, is a form of wealth shifting. The survivor receives wealth that originates with the purchaser. This type of transfer is different from most other wealth transfers because it involves a series of annuity payments instead of a transfer of a tangible property.

The amount included in the gross estate with respect to annuities or other retirement benefits is a fraction (described below) of the value of the annuity or lump-sum payment to be received by the surviving beneficiary. Annuities are valued at the cost of a comparable contract.[19] To determine the inclusion in the gross estate, this cost is multiplied by a fraction that represents the portion of the purchase price the decedent contributed.

EXAMPLE C:13-23▶

Twelve years ago, Jim purchased a joint and survivor annuity and selected benefits to be paid to himself and his son concurrently and then to the survivor for life. Jim and his son started collecting payments four years before Jim died, survived by his son. At the time of Jim's death, the cost of a comparable contract providing the same benefits was $180,000. Because Jim provided all the consideration to purchase the annuity, his gross estate included 100% of the $180,000 cost of a comparable contract. This annuity arrangement represents a shifting of wealth from Jim to his son upon Jim's death. ◀

SELF-STUDY QUESTION

On his retirement at age 65, Winslow elected to take a joint and survivor annuity from his qualified pension plan. The plan provided Winslow and his wife with a monthly pension of $2,500 until the death of the survivor. Winslow died seven years later. What amount (if any) was included in Winslow's gross estate if his wife survived?

EMPLOYMENT-RELATED RETIREMENT BENEFITS. Recall that, to determine the amount of an annuity includible in the decedent's gross estate, the cost of a comparable contract is multiplied by a fraction representing the portion of the purchase price contributed by the decedent. Section 2039(b) states that contributions from the decedent's employer (or former employer) are treated as contributions made by the decedent, provided such payments are made as a result of the employment relationship. Thus, 100% of the benefits from an employment-related annuity are included in the gross estate.

EXAMPLE C:13-24▶

ANSWER

The gross estate included the cost of a comparable contract providing $2,500 a month for the rest of the spouse's life. The younger the spouse, the higher the cost.

Pat was employed by Wheel Corporation at the time of his death. Wheel Corporation maintains a qualified retirement plan to which it makes 60% of the contributions and its employees contribute 40%. Pat's spouse is to receive an annuity valued at $350,000 from the retirement plan. Because the employer's contributions are considered to have been made by the employee, Pat is deemed to have provided all the consideration for the retirement benefits. Consequently, Pat's gross estate includes 100% of the annuity's $350,000 date-of-death value. ◀

JOINTLY OWNED PROPERTY

Section 2040 addresses the estate tax treatment of jointly owned property (i.e., property owned in a joint tenancy with right of survivorship or tenancy by the entirety arrangement).[20] An important characteristic of this form of ownership is that, upon the death of one joint owner, the decedent's interest passes automatically (by right of survivorship) to the surviving joint owner(s). Thus, the property is not part of the probate estate and does not pass under the will. Section 2040 contains two sets of rules, one for property jointly owned by spouses and one for all other jointly owned properties.

OWNERSHIP INVOLVING PERSONS OTHER THAN SPOUSES. When persons other than spouses or persons in addition to spouses own property as joint owners, the amount includible is determined by the consideration-furnished test.[21] Under this test, property is included in a joint owner's gross estate in accordance with the portion of the consideration he or she furnished to acquire the property. Obviously, this portion can range between 0% and 100%.

---

[19] Reg. Sec. 20.2031-8(a).

[20] Both joint tenancies with right of survivorship and tenancies by the entirety have the feature of survivorship. When one joint owner dies, his or her interest passes by right of survivorship to the remaining joint owner(s). Only spouses may use the tenancy by the entirety arrangement, whereas any persons may own as joint tenants with right of survivorship. A joint tenancy with right of survivorship may be severed by the action of any joint owner, whereas a tenancy by the entirety arrangement continues unless severed by the joint action of both joint owners.

The following definitions are from Henry Campbell Black, *Black's Law Dictionary*, Rev. 6th ed., Ed. by Joseph R. Nolan and Jacqueline M. Nolan-Haley (St. Paul, MN: West Publishing Co., 1990), p. 1465.

Joint tenancy with right of survivorship: The primary incident of joint tenancy is survivorship, by which the entire tenancy on the decease of any joint tenant remains to the survivors, and at length to the last survivor.

Tenancy by the entirety: A tenancy which is created between husband and wife and by which together they hold title to the whole with right of survivorship so that upon death of either, other takes whole to exclusion of deceased heirs. It is essentially a "joint tenancy" modified by the common-law theory that husband and wife are one person, and survivorship is the predominant and distinguishing feature of each. Neither party can alienate or encumber the property without the consent of the other.

[21] Sec. 2040(a).

EXAMPLE C:13-25▶

ADDITIONAL COMMENT
The tracing rule is easy to understand but difficult to implement. Suppose a joint tenancy between a parent and a child was created in a parcel of real estate 30 years ago when the parent paid for the property. The child died of a heart attack, and the parent is senile. Nothing should be included in the child's gross estate. Unfortunately the burden of proof to keep a portion of the property out of the estate is on the estate, not the IRS.

EXAMPLE C:13-26▶

SELF-STUDY QUESTION

Fred and Myrtle, husband and wife, held title to their home in joint tenancy with right of survivorship. Fred died in an airplane crash. What part of the value of the residence was included in Fred's gross estate? Who will own the residence if Fred willed all his property to their children?

EXAMPLE C:13-27▶

ANSWER

One-half the value of the residence was included in Fred's gross estate. Myrtle will own the residence after Fred's death because it passed to her by right of survivorship.

EXAMPLE C:13-28▶

Seven years ago, Fred and Jack provided $10,000 and $30,000 of consideration, respectively, to purchase real property titled in the names of Fred and Jack as joint tenants with right of survivorship. Fred died and was survived by Jack. The real property was valued at $60,000. Fred's gross estate included $15,000 (0.25 × $60,000) because Fred furnished 25% of the consideration to acquire the property. If Jack instead predeceased Fred when the property was worth $60,000, his estate would have included $45,000 (0.75 × $60,000). ◀

If part of the consideration furnished by one joint tenant is originally received gratuitously from another joint tenant, the consideration is attributable to the joint tenant who made the gift. If all joint owners acquire their interests by gift, devise, bequest, or inheritance, the decedent joint owner's estate includes his or her proportionate share of the date-of-death value of the jointly owned property.

Ray gave stock valued at $50,000 to Sam. Three years later Sam transferred this stock (now valued at $60,000) as partial consideration to acquire real property costing $120,000. Ray furnished the remaining $60,000 of consideration. The real property was titled in the names of Ray and Sam as joint tenants with right of survivorship. Because Sam received the asset that he used for consideration as a gift from Ray (the other joint tenant), Sam is treated as having furnished no consideration. If Sam dies before Ray, Sam's estate will include none of the real property's value. If Ray predeceases Sam, however, Ray's estate will include the entire date-of-death value. ◀

OWNERSHIP INVOLVING ONLY SPOUSES. If spouses are the only joint owners, the property is classified as a **qualified joint interest**. Section 2040(b)(1) provides that, in the case of qualified joint interests, the decedent's gross estate includes one-half the value of the qualified joint interest. The 50% inclusion rule applies automatically regardless of the relative amount of consideration provided by either spouse.

Wilma provided all the consideration to purchase stock costing $80,000. She registered the stock in her name and her husband's name as joint tenants with right of survivorship. The estate of the first spouse to die, regardless of which spouse it is, will include 50% of the value of the jointly owned stock. Upon the second spouse's death, all the property will be included in that spouse's gross estate because the property no longer is jointly owned property. ◀

GENERAL POWERS OF APPOINTMENT

Section 2041 requires inclusion in the gross estate of certain property interests that the decedent never owns in a legal sense. Inclusion occurs because the decedent had the power to designate who eventually would own the property. The authority to designate the owner—a significant power—is called a power of appointment. Powers of appointment can be general or special (i.e., more restricted).

Only a general power of appointment results in an addition to the gross estate. If a general power was created before October 22, 1942, however, no inclusion occurs unless the decedent exercised the power. For a post-1942 general power of appointment, inclusion occurs regardless of whether the power is exercised. A general power of appointment exists if the holder can exercise the power in favor of him- or herself, his or her estate or creditors, *or* the creditors of his or her estate. Being exercisable in favor of the decedent's estate means there is no restriction on the powerholder's ability to specify the person(s) to receive the property. The power may be exercisable during the decedent's life, by his or her will, or both.

When Kathy died in 1999, her will created a trust from which Doris is to receive the income for life. In addition, Doris was granted the power to designate by will the person or persons to receive the trust's assets. Doris has a testamentary general power of appointment. The trust's assets are included in Doris's gross estate regardless of whether Doris exercises the power. If Kathy had instead died in 1940, Doris would have had a pre-1942 power of appointment. Such powers are taxed only if exercised. ◀

Sometimes a powerholder can exercise a power for only specified purposes and/or in favor of only certain persons. Appointment powers that are governed by a so-called "ascertainable standard" are free of estate tax consequences because they may be exercised solely for purposes of the decedent's health, support, maintenance, or education.

EXAMPLE C:13-29▶

Assume the same facts as in Example C:13-28 except that Kathy's will merely empowered Doris to name which of her descendants shall receive the trust assets. Doris now has only a special power of appointment because she does not have the power to leave the property to whomever she desires (e.g., the power to appoint the property to her estate). Because Doris's power of appointment is only a special power, the value of the trust is not included in Doris's gross estate. ◀

LIFE INSURANCE

Section 2042 addresses the estate tax treatment of life insurance policies on the decedent's life. Life insurance policies owned by the decedent on the lives of others are taxed under the general language of Sec. 2033. According to Sec. 2042, a decedent's gross estate includes the value of policies on his or her own life if the proceeds are receivable by the executor or for the benefit of the estate, or if the decedent had any "incidents of ownership" in the policy at the time of death. Treasury Regulations list the following powers as a partial inventory of the incidents of ownership:

▶ To change the beneficiary

▶ To surrender or cancel the policy

▶ To borrow against the policy

▶ To pledge the policy for a loan

▶ To revoke an assignment of the policy[22]

Examples in the regulations pertaining to incidents of ownership involve economic rights over the insurance policies. Judicial decisions also have been important in defining what constitutes incidents of ownership. In some jurisdictions, the phrase has been interpreted to be broader than simply relating to economic powers.[23]

If the decedent could have exercised the incidents of ownership only in conjunction with another party, the policy nevertheless is included in the gross estate. Moreover, it is the legal power to exercise ownership rights, not the practical ability to do so, that leads to an inclusion. The Supreme Court in the *Estate of Marshal L. Noel* emphasized the importance of the decedent-insured's legal versus practical powers in a situation where the insured was killed in a plane crash and the policies he owned on his life were on the ground in the possession of his spouse. The Court held that the decedent possessed incidents of ownership and thus the policies were includible in his gross estate.[24]

EXAMPLE C:13-30▶

Tracy purchased an insurance policy on her life, and several years later she transferred all her incidents of ownership in the policy to her daughter. Seven years after the transfer, Tracy died. Tracy's niece has always been the policy's beneficiary. The policy was not included in Tracy's gross estate because Tracy did not have any incidents of ownership in the policy at the time of her death, nor was her estate the beneficiary. (Also, she did not give the policy away within three years of death.) ◀

EXAMPLE C:13-31▶

Assume the same facts as in Example C:13-30 except that Tracy's estate instead was the policy's beneficiary. Because Tracy's estate was designated as the beneficiary, the policy was included in her gross estate and valued at its face value. ◀

It is not sufficient to consider only Sec. 2042 in determining whether a life insurance policy on the decedent's life is includible in the gross estate. Recall from the discussion earlier in this chapter that a life insurance policy is includible in a decedent's gross estate if the individual makes a gift of a life insurance policy on his or her own life within three years of dying.[25]

EXAMPLE C:13-32▶

Two years prior to his death, Peng gave all his incidents of ownership in a life insurance policy on his own life to his son, Phong. The face value of the policy is $400,000. Phong was

---

[22] Reg. Sec. 20.2042-1(c)(2).

[23] See, for example, *Estate of James H. Lumpkin, Jr. v. CIR*, 31 AFTR 2d 73-1381, 73-1 USTC ¶12,909 (5th Cir., 1973), wherein the court held that the right to choose how the proceeds were to be paid—in a lump sum or in installments—was an incident of ownership.

[24] *CIR v. Estate of Marshal L. Noel*, 15 AFTR 2d 1397, 65-1 USTC ¶12,311 (USSC, 1965).

[25] The gifted insurance policy is included under Sec. 2035(a)(2).

always the beneficiary. Because Peng died within three years of giving Phong the policy, Peng's gross estate included the policy, valued at its $400,000 date-of-death value. The potential problem of making a transfer of a life insurance policy within three years of death could have been avoided had Phong been the original owner of the policy. In that case, Peng would not have made a transfer and need not have been concerned with the three-year rule. ◄

CONSIDERATION OFFSET

Property is included in the gross estate at its FMV on the date of death or alternate valuation date. Section 2043 allows an offset against the amount included in the gross estate for consideration received in certain transactions.[26] This offset is allowed only if the decedent received some, but less than adequate, consideration in connection with an earlier transaction. The gross estate is reduced by an offset for the partial consideration received. The offset is for the actual dollars received, not for the pro rata portion of the cost paid by the decedent. This offset, called the consideration offset, serves the same function as a deduction in that it reduces the taxable estate. If the decedent receives consideration equal to the value of the property transferred, the property in question is not included in the gross estate. No offset is permitted if the property is excluded from the decedent's gross estate.

The consideration offset prevents a double counting of property in the decedent's estate. For example, if an individual makes a transfer that is includible in the gross estate and receives partial consideration in return, the consideration received is part of the gross estate unless it has been consumed. Sections 2035 through 2038 also require the transferred property to be included in the gross estate, even though the transferor does not own it at the date of death.

TAX STRATEGY TIP

An individual may be concerned that his or her estate will not have sufficient cash to pay its estate taxes. The individual could buy life insurance so his or her estate will have sufficient cash. However, if the individual owns the policy or names his or her estate the beneficiary of the policy, the proceeds of the policy will be taxed in the gross estate. In this case, the individual should have his or her children (or an irrevocable life insurance trust) buy the life insurance and name themselves the beneficiaries, even if the individual has to provide the funds for the premiums (by making gifts). If the children are the beneficiaries, they can use the policy proceeds to buy an asset from the estate so the estate can raise cash needed to pay the estate taxes.

EXAMPLE C:13-33 ►

Two years ago, Steve transferred a $300,000 life insurance policy on his life to Earl. The policy was worth $75,000 at the time of transfer, but Earl paid only $48,000 consideration for the policy. Steve dies in the current year with the $48,000 still in his savings account. Steve's gross estate includes both the amount in the savings account and the $300,000 face value of the insurance policy. Under Sec. 2043, Steve's gross estate is reduced by the $48,000 consideration received on the transfer of the insurance policy. The insurance policy on Steve's life would be excluded from Steve's estate if Steve survived the transfer by more than three years, and no consideration offset would be permitted because the insurance is not included in the gross estate. ◄

RECIPIENT SPOUSE'S INTEREST IN QTIP TRUST

Recall from Chapter C:12 that a gift tax marital deduction is available for transferring qualified terminable interest property (QTIP) to one's spouse. A QTIP interest involves a transfer entitling the recipient spouse to all the income for life. The estate tax rules for QTIP interests are explained on page C:13-22. Claiming a marital deduction with respect to QTIP interests is voluntary. If the donor or the executor elects to claim a marital deduction for QTIP interests transferred to the spouse during life or at death, the transferred property generally is included in the recipient spouse's gross estate.[27] A QTIP interest included in the gross estate, like other property included in the gross estate, is valued at its date-of-death or alternate valuation date value.

The gross estate of the surviving spouse excludes the QTIP interest if the transferor spouse does not elect to claim a marital deduction. If the recipient spouse has a life estate, has no general power of appointment, and was not the transferor, no IRC sections other than Sec. 2044 (dealing with QTIPs) include the property in the gross estate.

No inclusion in the gross estate is required for QTIP interests for which a marital deduction is elected if the recipient spouse disposes of all or a portion of his or her income interest during his or her lifetime. However, dispositions of all or a portion of a spouse's income interest in a QTIP are treated under Sec. 2519 as a transfer of all interests in the QTIP other than the qualifying income interest. Thus, such dispositions are subject to the gift tax.

---

[26] Section 2043 provides a consideration offset for items included in the gross estate under Secs. 2035 through 2038 and Sec. 2041.

[27] Sec. 2044.

EXAMPLE C:13-34 ▶ Henry died, and his will created a $3 million QTIP trust for his widow, Wendy, age 75. Henry's executor elected to claim a marital deduction for the QTIP trust. Wendy died five years later. By then, the assets in the QTIP trust had appreciated to $3.8 million. Wendy's gross estate included the QTIP trust, valued at $3.8 million. If Henry's executor had not claimed a marital deduction for the QTIP trust, the value of the trust would have been excluded from Wendy's estate. If Henry's executor had made a partial QTIP election for 70% of the trust, only 70% of the $3.8 million value would have been in Wendy's gross estate. ◀

DEDUCTIONS

OBJECTIVE 4

Identify deductions available for estate tax purposes

As mentioned earlier in this chapter, deductions from the gross estate currently fall into five categories. Three of these categories (debts and funeral and administration expenses, casualty and theft losses, and state death taxes) allow the tax base to reflect the net wealth passed to the decedent's heirs, legatees, or devisees. Two other deduction categories reduce the estate tax base for transfers to the surviving spouse (the marital deduction) or to charitable organizations (the charitable contribution deduction). No deduction is available, however, for the amount of wealth diverted to the federal government in the form of estate taxes. The aggregate amount of the deductions is subtracted from the gross estate amount to determine the taxable estate. Each deduction category is examined below. Table C:13-2 provides an overview of the estate tax deductions.

DEBTS AND FUNERAL AND ADMINISTRATION EXPENSES

Section 2053 authorizes deductions for mortgages and other debts owed by the decedent, as well as for the decedent's funeral and administration expenses. Mortgages and all other debts of the decedent are deductible provided they represent bona fide contracts for an adequate and full consideration in money or money's worth. Even personal debts relating to an expenditure for which no income tax deduction would be allowable are deductible. Interest, state and local taxes, and trade or business expenses accrued at the date of death are deductible on both the estate tax return (as a debt of the decedent) and on the estate's income tax return (as an expense known as a deduction in respect of a decedent) when they are paid. (See Chapter C:14 for a discussion of the income tax implications.)

Examples of administration expenses include executor's commissions, attorneys' fees, court costs, accountants' fees, appraisers' fees, and expenses of preserving and distributing the estate. The executor must decide whether to deduct administration expenses on the estate tax return (Form 706) or the estate's income tax return (Form 1041). Such expenses cannot be deducted twice, although some may be deducted on the estate tax return and others on the estate's income tax return.

▼ TABLE C:13-2
Estate Tax Deductions

IRC Section	Type of Deduction
2053	Funeral and administration expenses[a] and debts
2054	Casualty and theft losses[a]
2055	Charitable contributions[b]
2056	Marital deduction[b]
2058	State death taxes[c]

[a]Deductible on the estate tax return or on the estate's income tax return.
[b]No limit on deductible amount.
[c]Available (instead of a credit) after 2004.

An estate that owes no estate tax (e.g., because of the unlimited marital deduction or the unified credit) should deduct administration expenses on its income tax return because no tax savings will result from a deduction on the estate tax return. If an estate owes estate taxes, its marginal estate tax rate will be 35% because this rate applies to tax bases exceeding $500,000. Similarly, the highest income tax rate for an estate is 35%. Thus, at times, the tax savings will be identical regardless of where the administration expenses are deducted.

Funeral expenses are deductible only on the estate tax return. The estate may deduct any funeral expenses allowable under local law including "[a] reasonable expenditure for a tombstone, monument, or mausoleum, or for a burial lot, either for the decedent or his family, including a reasonable expenditure for its future care." The transportation costs of the person bringing the body to the burial place also are deductible as funeral expenses.[28]

EXAMPLE C:13-35 ▶

At Ed's date of death in 2011, Ed owed a $75,000 mortgage on his residence, plus $280 of interest accrued thereon, and $320 of personal expenditures charged to a department store charge card. The estate's administration expenses were $32,000. His funeral expenses totaled $12,000. Under Sec. 2053, Ed's estate could deduct $75,600 ($75,000 + $280 + $320) for debts and $12,000 for funeral expenses. The $32,000 of administration expenses were deductible on the estate tax return, on the estate's income tax return for the year in which they were paid, or some on each return. As Chapter C:14 points out, Ed's estate receives an income tax deduction for the accrued mortgage interest whenever it is paid. ◀

TAX STRATEGY TIP

The executor should elect to deduct any casualty or theft loss, when such loss is allowable, from the estate tax return if the marginal estate tax rate exceeds the marginal income tax rate.

LOSSES

Section 2054 authorizes a deduction for losses incurred from theft or casualty while the estate is being settled. Just as in the context of the income tax, examples of casualties include fires, storms, and earthquakes. Any insurance compensation received affects the amount of the loss. If the alternate valuation date is elected, the loss may not be used to reduce the alternate value and then used again as a loss deduction. As with administration expenses, the executor must decide whether to deduct the loss on the estate tax return or the estate's income tax return. No double deduction is allowed for these losses, and the nondeductible floor applicable for income tax purposes does not exist for estate tax purposes.

EXAMPLE C:13-36 ▶

Sam dies on May 3, 2011. One of the items included in Sam's gross estate is a mountain cabin valued at $125,000. The uninsured cabin is totally destroyed in a landslide on August 18. If the date-of-death valuation is chosen, the cabin is included in the gross estate at $125,000. The executor must choose between claiming a Sec. 2054 loss deduction on the estate tax return or a Sec. 165 casualty loss deduction on the estate's income tax return. ◀

EXAMPLE C:13-37 ▶

Assume the same facts as in Example C:13-36 except that Sam's executor elects the alternate valuation date. The cabin is valued at zero when determining the value of the gross estate. No loss deduction is available for the casualty on the estate tax return. The estate cannot claim an income tax deduction for the casualty loss either because the property's adjusted basis in its hands is zero. ◀

CHARITABLE CONTRIBUTION DEDUCTION

Section 2055 authorizes a deduction for transfers to charitable organizations. The rules concerning eligible donee organizations are the same as for gift tax purposes.

Because the estate tax charitable contribution deduction is unlimited, a decedent could eliminate his or her estate tax liability by willing all his or her property (or all property except for an amount equal to the exemption equivalent) to a charitable organization. Similarly, a decedent could eliminate an estate tax liability by willing an amount equal to the exemption equivalent to the children and the rest of the estate to the surviving spouse and a charitable organization (e.g., in equal shares).[29] People who desire to leave some property to a charity at their death should be encouraged to consider giving the property before death, so they can obtain an income tax deduction for the gift and also reduce their gross estate by the amount of the gift.

---

[28] Reg. Sec. 20.2053-2.
[29] Another way the estate could owe no taxes is if all of the property, or all of the property except for the exemption equivalent, is shielded from taxation by the marital deduction.

COMPUTING THE DEDUCTION. In certain circumstances, computation of the estate tax charitable contribution deduction can be somewhat complicated. Suppose the decedent (a widow) has an $11 million gross estate and no Sec. 2053 or 2054 deductions. The decedent's will specifies that her son is to receive $8 million and a charitable organization is to receive the residue (the rest not explicitly disposed of). Assume that state law specifies that death taxes are payable from the residue. Because $8 million of property passes to the decedent's child, the estate will definitely owe some estate taxes. The charitable organization will receive $3 million, less the estate taxes payable therefrom. The estate tax liability depends on the amount of the charitable contribution deduction, which in turn depends on the amount of the estate tax liability. Simultaneous equations are required to calculate the amount of the charitable contribution deduction.[30]

EXAMPLE C:13-38 ▶ Ahmed, a widower, died with a gross estate of $9 million. Ahmed willed State University $1 million and the residue of his estate to his children. Under state law, death taxes are payable from the residue. In this scenario, Ahmed's estate receives a charitable contribution deduction for $1 million because the estate taxes were charged against the children's share (the residue). ◀

SPLIT-INTEREST TRANSFERS. If the decedent's will provides for a split-interest transfer (i.e., a transfer of interests to both an individual and a charitable organization), the rules concerning whether a charitable contribution deduction is available are very technical. Basically, the rules are the same as for gift tax purposes (discussed in Chapter C:12).

EXAMPLE C:13-39 ▶ Jane dies in a year with an estate tax having a gross estate of $8 million. In 2000, she gave City Art Museum a remainder interest in her personal residence but retained the right to live there rent-free for the rest of her life. Upon Jane's death, no other individuals have an interest in the residence. Jane received an income tax deduction in 2000 for the value of the remainder interest and incurred no gift tax liability. Under Sec. 2036, Jane's gross estate includes her residence, valued at $350,000. Her estate receives a $350,000 charitable contribution deduction.

Her lifetime transfer triggers no added estate tax cost. The residence is included in her gross estate, but the inclusion is a wash because of the estate tax charitable contribution deduction claimed for the value of the residence. ◀

MARITAL DEDUCTION

The fourth category of deductions is the marital deduction for certain property passing to the decedent's surviving spouse.[31] Because the marital deduction is unlimited, the decedent's estate does not owe any federal estate taxes if all the items includible in the gross estate (or all items except an amount equal to the exemption equivalent) pass to the surviving spouse.[32] If the surviving spouse is not a U.S. citizen, however, a marital deduction is not available unless the decedent's property passes to a special trust called a qualified domestic trust.

TAX STRATEGY TIP

The marital deduction defers the estate tax until the death of the surviving spouse and protects against liquidity problems when the first spouse dies. Moreover, the surviving spouse can reduce the overall estate tax through personal consumption and a lifetime gifting program.

The marital deduction provides equal treatment for decedents of common law and community property states. As mentioned in Chapter C:12, marital property is treated differently under each type of state law. In community property states, for example, a large portion of the assets acquired after a couple marries constitutes community property (i.e., property owned equally by each spouse). On the other hand, in common law states, one spouse may own the majority of the assets acquired after marriage. Thus, with no marital deduction, the progressive estate tax rates could cause the combined estate tax liability to be higher for a couple living in a noncommunity property state. Nevertheless, a marital deduction is available to decedents who own nothing but community property.

Only certain transfers to the surviving spouse are eligible for the marital deduction. The estate does not receive a marital deduction unless the interest conveyed to the surviving spouse will be subject to either the estate tax in the recipient spouse's estate or to the

---

[30] The simultaneous equation problem generally does not occur if a charity receives a bequest of a specific dollar amount. See Reg. Sec. 20.2055-3 for a discussion of death taxes payable from charitable transfers.
[31] Sec. 2056.
[32] Some states have not adopted an unlimited marital deduction; therefore,

some estates may owe state death taxes even though no federal liability would otherwise exist. Payment of substantial sums to a state as taxes will reduce the amount passing to the spouse as a marital deduction and can cause federal taxes to be owed.

gift tax if transferred while the surviving spouse is alive. In other words, the surviving spouse generally can escape transfer taxation on the transferred property only by consuming it.

The following three tests must be met before an interest qualifies for the marital deduction:

▶ The property must be included in the decedent's gross estate.

▶ The property must pass to the recipient spouse in a qualifying manner.

▶ The interest conveyed must not be a nondeductible terminable interest.

TEST 1: INCLUSION IN THE GROSS ESTATE. No property passing to the surviving spouse is eligible for the marital deduction unless the property is included in the decedent's gross estate. The reason for this rule is obvious: Assets excluded from the gross estate cannot generate a deduction.

EXAMPLE C:13-40 ▶ Gail is insured under a life insurance policy for which her husband, Al, is the beneficiary. Gail's sister always had the incidents of ownership in the policy. Gail held the title to the personal residence in which she and Al lived. She willed the residence to Al, and the residence qualifies for the marital deduction. Even though the insurance proceeds are payable to Al, Gail's estate receives no marital deduction for the insurance. The policy is excluded from Gail's gross estate because she had no incidents of ownership, her estate was not the beneficiary, and the policy was not transferred within three years of her death. ◀

TEST 2: THE PASSING REQUIREMENT. Property is not eligible for the marital deduction unless it passes to the decedent's spouse in a qualifying manner. According to Sec. 2056(c), property is deemed to pass from one spouse to the other if the surviving spouse receives the property because of

▶ A bequest or devise under the decedent's will

▶ An inheritance resulting from the decedent dying intestate

▶ Dower or curtesy rights

▶ An earlier transfer from the decedent

▶ Right of survivorship

▶ An appointment by the decedent under a general power of appointment or in default of appointment

▶ A designation as the beneficiary of a life insurance policy on the decedent's life

In addition, a surviving spouse's interest in a retirement benefit plan is considered to have passed from the decedent to the survivor to the extent the retirement benefits are included in the gross estate.[33]

TEST 3: THE TERMINABLE INTEREST RULE. The last statutory test (also applicable for gift tax purposes) requires that the recipient-spouse's interest *not* be classified as a nondeductible terminable interest.[34] A terminable interest is one that ceases with the passage of time or the occurrence of some event. Some terminable interests qualify for the marital deduction, however, because only *nondeductible* terminable interests fail to generate a marital deduction. Nondeductible terminable interests have the following features:

▶ An interest in the property must pass or have passed from the decedent to a person other than the surviving spouse, and such person must have paid less than adequate consideration in money or money's worth.

▶ The other person may possess or enjoy any part of the property after the termination of the surviving spouse's interest.

Thus, if the decedent makes a transfer granting the surviving spouse the right to receive all the income annually for life and a general power of appointment over the

---

[33] Reg. Sec. 20.2056(e)-1(a)(6).

[34] Nondeductible terminable interests also are precluded from eligibility for the marital deduction for gift tax purposes.

property, the property is eligible for the marital deduction. As discussed below, as a result of the QTIP provisions a marital deduction is available for certain transfers that otherwise would be disqualified under the nondeductible terminable interest rule.

EXAMPLE C:13-41 ▶

SELF-STUDY QUESTION

A decedent, by will, creates a trust with income to the surviving spouse for 25 years, the remainder to their children. The surviving spouse's life expectancy is 16 years. Does the property qualify for the marital deduction?

ANSWER

The property does not qualify because the surviving spouse's interest terminates at the end of a specified number of years. The spouse's shorter life expectancy is irrelevant.

SELF-STUDY QUESTION

How does the donor spouse or decedent spouse who establishes a QTIP trust control the disposition of the trust corpus?

ANSWER

The donor or decedent spouse states in the trust instrument or in his or her will who will receive the remainder interest on the death of the recipient spouse.

Louis wills a copyright with a ten-year remaining legal life to his wife, Tina, age 42. His will also sets up a trust for the benefit of Tina, whom he entitles to receive all of the income semiannually until the earlier of her remarriage or her death. Upon Tina's remarriage or death, the trust property is to be distributed to the couple's children or their estates. Both the copyright and the trust are terminable interests. The copyright is eligible for the marital deduction because it is not a nondeductible terminable interest; the copyright simply ends at the expiration of its legal life. No person other than Tina receives an interest in the copyright. No marital deduction is available for the trust because it is a nondeductible terminable interest. Upon the termination of Tina's interest, the children will possess the property, and they receive their interests from Louis without paying adequate consideration. ◀

QTIP TRANSFERS. Section 2056(b)(7) authorizes a marital deduction for transfers of qualified terminable interest property (called QTIP transfers). The QTIP provisions are somewhat revolutionary compared with earlier law because they allow a marital deduction in situations where the recipient spouse holds no power to designate which parties eventually receive the property.

Qualified terminable interest property is defined as property that passes from the decedent, in which the surviving spouse has a qualifying income interest for life, and to which an election applies. A spouse has a qualifying income interest for life if the following are true:

▶ He or she is entitled to all the income from the property, payable at least annually.

▶ No person has a power to appoint any portion of the property to anyone other than the surviving spouse unless the power cannot be exercised during the spouse's lifetime (e.g., it is exercisable only at or after the death of the surviving spouse).

Claiming the marital deduction with respect to QTIP transfers is not mandatory, and partial elections also are allowed. In the event the executor elects to claim a marital deduction for 100% of the QTIP transfer, the marital deduction is for the entire amount of the QTIP transfer. In other words, the deduction is not limited to the value of the surviving spouse's life estate.

If the marital deduction is elected in the first spouse's estate, the property is taxed in the surviving spouse's estate under Sec. 2044 or is subject to the gift tax in such spouse's hands if disposed of during the spouse's lifetime.[35] Thus, as with other interspousal transfers, the QTIP provisions allow a postponement of the taxable event until the second spouse dies or disposes of the interest by gift. If the taxable event is postponed, the property is valued at its FMV as of the date the second spouse transfers the property by gift or at death. See the Tax Planning Considerations section of this chapter for a discussion of planning opportunities (including partial QTIP elections) with the marital deduction.

EXAMPLE C:13-42 ▶

ADDITIONAL COMMENT

Refer to Example C:13-42. The executor may elect QTIP status for less than the entire property in the trust. For example, the executor might elect QTIP treatment for only 60% of the $1 million placed in the trust. On Mary's death, 60% of $2.2 million, or $1.32 million, is included in Mary's gross estate.

Tom died in 2004, survived by his wife, Mary. Tom's will called for setting up a $1 million trust from which Mary would receive all the income quarterly for the rest of her life. Upon Mary's death, the property is to be distributed to Tom's children by a previous marriage. If Tom's executor elects to claim a marital deduction, Tom's estate receives a $1 million marital deduction. At Mary's death, the trust assets are valued at $2.2 million. Section 2044 includes $2.2 million in Mary's gross estate. If Tom's executor forgoes electing the marital deduction, Mary's gross estate excludes the value of the trust. In either event, the trust assets will be taxed in the estate of one of the spouses, but not both. ◀

STATE DEATH TAXES. For estates of decedents dying after 2004, Sec. 2058 allows a deduction for state death taxes. Eligible taxes include estate, inheritance, legacy, and succession taxes paid to a state or the District of Columbia. The taxes must be paid no later than four years after the filing of the estate tax return. The amount of the deduction is the amount paid and, unlike the state death tax credit formerly available, is not restricted to a maximum amount.

---

[35] Section 2519 states that, if a recipient spouse disposes of a qualifying income interest for life for which the donor or the executor elected a marital deduction under the QTIP rules, the recipient spouse is treated as having made a gift of everything except the qualifying income interest. Under the generic gift rules of Sec. 2511, the gift of the income interest is treated as a gift.

COMPUTATION OF TAX LIABILITY

OBJECTIVE 5

Calculate the estate tax liability

As mentioned earlier, the estate tax base is the aggregate of the decedent's taxable estate and his or her adjusted taxable gifts. Figure C:13-1 earlier in this chapter illustrates how the estate tax formula combines these two concepts.

TAXABLE ESTATE AND TAX BASE

The gross estate's value is reduced by the deductions to arrive at the amount of the taxable estate. Under the unification provisions effective after 1976, the estate tax base consists of the taxable estate plus the adjusted taxable gifts, defined as *all* taxable gifts made *after 1976 other than* gifts included in the gross estate. The addition of the adjusted taxable gifts to the estate tax base may cause an estate to be taxed at a higher marginal tax rate. If the decedent elects gift splitting (discussed in Chapter 12), the decedent's adjusted taxable gifts equal the amount of the taxable gifts the individual is deemed to have made after applying the gift-splitting provisions. Adjusted taxable gifts can arise from consenting to gift splitting, even though the decedent never actually gives away any property.

Adjusted taxable gifts are valued at date-of-gift values; therefore, any post-gift appreciation is exempt from the transfer taxes. The estate tax computations for decedents who never made gifts exceeding the excludable amount reflect no adjusted taxable gifts.

TENTATIVE TAX AND REDUCTION FOR POST-1976 GIFT TAXES

The tentative tax is computed on the estate tax base, which is the sum of the taxable estate and the adjusted taxable gifts, if any.[36] The unified transfer tax rates are found in Sec. 2001(c) and are reproduced on the inside back cover. The tentative tax is reduced by the decedent's post-1976 gift taxes. In determining the tax on post-1976 taxable gifts, the effect of gift splitting is taken into consideration. That is, the amount of the post-1976 gift taxes is usually the levy imposed on the taxable gifts the decedent is deemed to have made after applying any gift-splitting election.

If the tax rates change between the time of the gift and the time of death, the subtraction for gift taxes equals the amount of gift taxes that would have been payable on post-1976 gifts had the rate schedule applicable in the year of death been in effect in the year of the gift. The only "as if" computation is for the gross tax amount; the unified credit actually used on the gift tax return is subtracted to determine the amount of gift tax that would have been payable at current rates.

UNIFIED CREDIT

The excess of the tentative tax over the post-1976 gift taxes is reduced by the unified credit. The amount of this credit has changed over the years and it increased through 2009; in 2009 it was $1,455,800 (see inside back cover). For estates of decedents dying in 2010 for which the executor opts to incur the estate tax and obtain a FMV basis, the unified credit is $1,730,800, which is the tax on $5 million at a 35% top rate. In both the estate and gift tax context for 2011, the unified credit is $1,730,800, which again is the tax on $5 million at a 35% top rate. For 2012, the unified credit will be the tax on $5 million, indexed for inflation, at a top rate of 35%. With a credit of $1,730,800, the tax on a $5 million tax base is completely eliminated. The unified credit never generates a refund; the most relief it can provide is to eliminate an estate's federal estate tax liability.

Section 2010(c) provides that the unified credit otherwise available for estate tax purposes must be reduced because of certain pre-1977 gifts. Before 1977, a $30,000 lifetime exemption was available for the gift tax. Donors could claim some or all of this exemption whenever they so desired. For post-1976 years, Congress repealed the exemption and replaced it with the unified credit. If the decedent claimed any portion of the $30,000 exemption against gifts made after September 8, 1976, and before January 1, 1977, the unified credit was reduced by 20% of the exemption claimed.

SELF-STUDY QUESTION

Verda died penniless in 2011. Because of consenting to gift splitting, her taxable gifts made in 1999 were $1.75 million. She paid $457,000 of gift taxes on these gifts. What was her unified tax base?

ANSWER

Her unified tax base was $1.75 million, the amount of her lifetime taxable gifts. Note that the gifts are valued at what they were worth on the date of the gift.

SELF-STUDY QUESTION

Refer to the previous self-study question. What was the amount of the unified tax before credits? After credits?

ANSWER

The unified tax before credits was $593,300. This tax was reduced by the unified credit of $1,730,800 and post-1976 gift taxes, which leaves zero tax due. Verda's unified tax base of $1.75 million was below the $5 million exemption equivalent for 2011.

---

[36] Sec. 2001(b).

EXAMPLE C:13-43 ▶ Carl died in 2011 with a tax base of $6 million. In October 1976, Carl made his first taxable gift. Carl claimed the $30,000 exemption to reduce the amount of his taxable gifts. Thus, Carl's $1,730,800 unified credit is reduced by $6,000 (0.20 × $30,000). If Carl claimed the exemption by making a gift on or before September 8, 1976, his estate would have been entitled to the full $1,730,800 credit. ◀

PORTABILITY BETWEEN SPOUSES OF EXEMPTION AMOUNT

Prior to 2011, both a husband and wife had estate tax exemption amounts that could be used only by that individual. For example, in 2009, when the exempt amount was $3.5 million, the husband could use $3.5 million at his death, and the wife could use $3.5 million at her death. This situation was the case even if one spouse's estate was much smaller than $3.5 million and the other spouse's estate was considerably larger than $3.5 million. For many years, a number of estates used a technique called "credit shelter trusts" to make sure the $3.5 million (the 2009 amount) or the relevant amount for the year of death passed in such a way as to take advantage of the unified credit. Under the Tax Relief Act, the so-called basic exclusion amount of $5 million is portable between spouses for 2011 and 2012, which means that any basic exclusion amount that remains unused at the first spouse's death can be used by the second spouse. However, this benefit applies only if the executor elects portability. Further, unless Congress takes further action, this provision is in effect for only 2011 and 2012. If a spouse has been predeceased by more than one spouse who died after 2010, the surviving spouse can use only the unused exemption amount of the last deceased spouse.

EXAMPLE C:13-44 ▶ Joe died early in 2011 with a taxable estate of $2 million. He is survived by his spouse, Joanne. If Joe's executor elects, Joe's remaining $3 million basic exclusion amount is added to Joanne's $5 million, so she now would have an exempt amount of $8 million. Under current law, this benefit applies only if Joanne dies before 2013. ◀

EXAMPLE C:13-45 ▶ Joanne from the previous example married Karl late in 2011. Karl died in July 2012 with a taxable estate of $11 million. Thus, Karl has no unused exemption. If Joanne dies in December 2012, her exempt amount will be $5 million as she cannot use Joe's remaining basic exclusion. ◀

OTHER CREDITS

The IRC authorizes three additional credits: a gift tax credit on pre-1977 gifts, a credit for another decedent's estate taxes paid on prior transfers, and a credit for foreign death taxes. (Prior to 2005, the IRC also allowed a state death tax credit.) These credits apply less often than the unified credit. Like the unified credit, these credits cannot exceed the amount of the estate tax actually owed.

PRE-2005 STATE DEATH TAX CREDIT. For many years, all states levied some form of death tax: an inheritance tax, an estate tax, or both. Many states enacted a simple system whereby the state death tax liability equaled the credit for state death taxes allowed on the federal estate tax return.

Prior to 2005, Sec. 2011 allowed a credit calculated in accordance with the table contained in Sec. 2011(b). As mentioned earlier, beginning in 2005, a deduction replaced the credit. Consequently, if a jurisdiction had earlier imposed a state death tax equal to the credit allowed on the federal return for state death taxes, no state death tax will be owed after 2004 *unless* that jurisdiction changes its tax rules.

EXAMPLE C:13-46 ▶ John died in 2011 with a taxable estate of $6 million. If he resided in a state whose statute imposes an estate tax equal to the credit available on the federal return for state death taxes, his estate owed nothing to the state. In effect, his state no longer has an estate tax. On the other hand, if he resided in a state that levies an inheritance tax based on the value of the property the various heirs receive, his estate received a deduction (not a credit) for the inheritance tax paid. ◀

CREDIT FOR PRE-1977 GIFT TAXES. Section 2012(a) authorizes a credit for gift taxes paid by the decedent on pre-1977 gifts that must be included in the gross estate. Remember that Sec. 2001(b)(2) allows a reduction for gift taxes paid on post-1976 gifts, but the IRC does not refer to this item as a credit.

In general, the credit for pre-1977 gift taxes equals the amount of gift taxes paid with respect to transfers included in the gross estate. Because of a ceiling rule, however, the amount of the credit sometimes is lower than the amount of gift taxes paid. A discussion of the credit ceiling computation is beyond the scope of this text.

CREDIT FOR TAX ON PRIOR TRANSFERS. The credit available under Sec. 2013 for the estate taxes paid on prior transfers reduces the cost of having property taxed in more than one estate in quick succession. Without this credit, the overall tax cost could be quite severe if the legatee dies soon after the original decedent. The credit applies if the person who transfers the property (i.e., the transferor-decedent) to the decedent in question (i.e., the transferee-decedent) dies no more than ten years before, or within two years after, the date of the transferee-decedent's death. The potential credit is the smaller of the federal estate tax of the transferor-decedent attributable to the transferred interest or the federal estate tax of the transferee-decedent attributable to the transferred interest.

To determine the final credit, the potential credit is multiplied by a percentage that varies inversely with the period of time separating the two dates of death. If the transferor dies no more than two years before or after the transferee, the credit percentage is 100%. As specified in Sec. 2013(a), the other percentages are as follows:

Number of Years by Which Transferor's Death Precedes the Transferee's Death	Credit Percentage
More than 2, but not more than 4	80
More than 4, but not more than 6	60
More than 6, but not more than 8	40
More than 8, but not more than 10	20

EXAMPLE C:13-47▶ Mary died on March 1, 2006. All of Mary's property passed to Debra, her daughter. Debra died on June 1, 2011. All of Debra's property passed to her son. Both Mary's and Debra's estates paid federal estate taxes. Debra's estate was entitled to a credit for a percentage of some, or all, of the taxes paid by Mary's estate. Because Mary's death preceded Debra's death by five years and three months, the credit for the tax paid on prior transfers was 60% of the potential credit. ◀

EXAMPLE C:13-48▶ Ed died on August 7, 2009. One of the items included in Ed's estate was a life insurance policy on Sam's life. Sam gave Ed all his incidents of ownership in this policy on December 13, 2008. Sam died on June 15, 2011, within three years of making a gift of the insurance policy on his own life. The policy was included in Sam's gross estate under Sec. 2035. Because Sam died within two years of Ed's death, Ed's estate was entitled to a credit for 100% of the potential credit and an amended return had to be filed to claim this credit. ◀

FOREIGN DEATH TAX CREDIT. Under Sec. 2014, the estate is entitled to a credit for some or all of the death taxes paid to a foreign country for property located in that foreign country and included in the gross estate. The maximum credit is the smaller of the foreign death tax attributable to the property located in the foreign country that imposed the tax or the federal estate tax attributable to the property located in the foreign country and taxed by such country.

COMPREHENSIVE ILLUSTRATION

The following comprehensive illustration demonstrates the computation of the estate tax liability.

BACKGROUND DATA

Herman Estes died on October 13, 2009. Herman, a Florida resident, was survived by his widow, Ann, and three adult children. During his lifetime, Herman made three gifts, as follows:

▶ In 1974, he gave his son Billy $103,000 cash. Herman claimed the $30,000 exemption (then available) and a $3,000 annual exclusion available then. The taxable gift was $70,000.

▶ In 1978, he gave his daughter, Dotty, $203,000 cash. He claimed a $3,000 annual exclusion available then and thus made a $200,000 taxable gift on which he paid a $28,000 gift tax, after claiming the $34,000 unified credit.

▶ In December 2006, he gave his son, Johnny, stock then worth $1,512,000. Herman claimed a $12,000 annual exclusion and thus made a $1.5 million taxable gift. He claimed the available unified credit of $311,800 ($345,800 − $34,000) and paid a $287,900 ($599,700 − $311,800) gift tax. On October 13, 2009, the stock was worth $1.75 million.

Property discovered after Herman's death appears below. All amounts represent date-of-death values.

▶ Checking account containing $19,250.

▶ Savings account containing $75,000.

▶ Land worth $400,000 held in the names of Herman and Ann, joint tenants with right of survivorship (JTWROS). Herman provided all the consideration to buy the land in January 1993.

▶ Life insurance policy 123-A with a face value of $200,000. Herman had incidents of ownership; Johnny is the beneficiary.

▶ A personal residence titled in Herman's name worth $325,000.

▶ Stock in Ajax Corporation worth $3.2 million.

▶ Qualified pension plan to which Herman's employer made 60% of the contributions and Herman made 40%. Ann is to receive a lump-sum distribution of $240,000.

▶ A trust created under the will of Herman's mother, Amelia, who died in 1992. Herman was entitled to receive all the income quarterly for life. In his will, Herman could appoint the trust assets to such of his descendants as he desired. The trust assets are valued at $375,000.

At his death, Herman owes a $25,200 bank loan, including $200 accrued interest. Balances due on his various charge cards total $6,500. Herman's funeral expenses are $15,000, and his administration expenses are $70,000. The maximum tax savings will occur by deducting the administration expenses on the estate tax return instead of on the income tax return.

Herman's will contains the following provisions:

▶ "To my wife, Ann, I leave my residence, my savings account, and $10,000 from my checking account."

▶ "I leave $200,000 of property in trust with First Bank as trustee. My wife, Ann, is to receive all the income from this trust fund quarterly for the rest of her life. Upon Ann's death, the trust property is to be divided equally among our three children."

▶ "To the American Cancer Society I leave $10,000."

▶ "I appoint the property in the trust created by my mother, Amelia Estes, to my daughter, Dotty."

▶ "The residue of my estate is to be divided equally between my sons, Johnny and Billy."

CALCULATION OF TAX LIABILITY

Table C:13-3 illustrates the computation of Herman's estate tax liability. These same facts are used for the sample Estate Tax Return (Form 706) included in Appendix B. For illustration purposes, it is assumed that the executor elects to claim the marital deduction on the QTIP trust and that the laws for Florida levy death taxes equal to the maximum federal credit for state death taxes. As mentioned earlier, after 2004 an estate receives a deduction instead of a credit for state death taxes. Thus, because the federal government allows no credit for state death taxes, Herman's estate owes nothing to the state.

▼ TABLE C:13-3
Comprehensive Estate Tax Illustration

Gross estate:	
Checking account (Sec. 2033)	$ 19,250
Savings account (Sec. 2033)	75,000
Land held in joint tenancy with wife (0.50 × $400,000) (Sec. 2040)	200,000
Life insurance (Sec. 2042)	200,000
Personal residence (Sec. 2033)	325,000
Ajax stock (Sec. 2033)	3,200,000
Qualified pension plan (Sec. 2039)	240,000
Gross-up for gift tax paid on 2006 gift (Sec. 2035)	287,900
Total gross estate	$4,547,150
Minus:	
Debts (Sec. 2053):	
Bank loan, including $200 accrued interest	(25,200)
Charge cards	(6,500)
Funeral expenses (Sec. 2053)	(15,000)
Administration expenses (Sec. 2053)	(70,000)
Marital deduction (Sec. 2056):	
Residence (under will)	(325,000)
Cash from checking account (under will)	(10,000)
Savings account (under will)	(75,000)
QTIP trust (under will)	(200,000)
Land (JTWROS)	(200,000)
Qualified pension plan (beneficiary)	(240,000)
Charitable contribution deduction (Sec. 2055)	(10,000)
Total reductions to gross estate	($1,176,700)
Taxable estate	$3,370,450
Plus adjusted taxable gifts (Sec. 2001(b)):	
1978 taxable gifts	200,000[a]
2006 taxable gifts	1,500,000[a]
Estate tax base	$5,070,450
Tentative tax on tax base (2009 tax rates) (Sec. 2001)	$2,162,503
Minus:	
Reduction for post-1976 gift taxes (Sec. 2001(b))	(315,900)[b]
Unified credit (Sec. 2010)	(1,455,800)
Estate tax payable	$ 390,803

[a]Valued at date-of-gift fair market values.
[b]$28,000 (for 1978) + $287,900 (for 2006) = $315,900.

ADDITIONAL COMMENT

Note that, in 2011 and 2012, 35% will be the top rate for estate and income tax purposes. Also, if Herman dies in 2011 or 2012, the portability of the estate tax exemption would not apply because his tax base would exceed $5 million.

Note that several factors affect the computation set out in Table C:13-3:

▶ Herman had only a special power of appointment over the assets in the trust created by his mother because he could will the property only to his descendants. Therefore, the trust property is not included in his estate.

▶ Assets that pass to the surviving spouse outside the will, such as by survivorship and by beneficiary designation, can qualify for the marital deduction.

▶ Adjusted taxable gifts (added to the taxable estate) include only post-1976 taxable gifts.

▶ The estate tax payable is not reduced by pre-1977 gift taxes unless the gifted property is included in the gross estate.

▶ Because the highest marginal income tax rate for the estate is less than its 45% marginal estate tax rate and because the estate owes a tax liability (even with the available credits), administration expenses should be deducted on the estate tax return.

LIQUIDITY CONCERNS

OBJECTIVE 6

Identify tax provisions that alleviate liquidity problems

Liquidity is one of the major problems facing individuals planning their estates and executors eventually managing the estates. Individuals often use life insurance to help address this problem. In general, the entire amount of the estate tax liability is due nine months after the decedent's death. Certain provisions, however, allow the executor to pay some or all of the estate tax liability at a later date. Deferral of part or all of the estate tax payments and two other provisions aimed at alleviating a liquidity problem are discussed below.

DEFERRAL OF PAYMENT OF ESTATE TAXES

REASONABLE CAUSE. Section 6161(a)(1) authorizes the Secretary of the Treasury to extend the payment date for the estate taxes for a *reasonable period*, defined as a period of not longer than 12 months. Moreover, the Secretary of the Treasury may extend the payment date for a maximum period of ten years if the executor shows reasonable cause for not being able to pay some, or all, of the estate tax liability on the regular date.[37]

Whenever the executor pays a portion of the estate tax after the regular due date, the estate owes interest on the portion of the tax for which it postpones payment. In general, the interest rate, which is governed by Sec. 6621, is the same as that applicable to underpayments. The interest rate on underpayments potentially fluctuates quarterly with changes in the rate paid on short-term U.S. Treasury obligations.[38]

REMAINDER OR REVERSIONARY INTERESTS. If the gross estate includes a relatively large remainder or reversionary interest, liquidity problems could result if the estate has to pay the entire estate tax liability soon after the decedent's death. For example, the estate might include a remainder interest in an asset in which a healthy, 30-year-old person has a life estate. The estate might not gain possession of the assets until many years after the decedent's death. Section 6163 permits the executor to elect to postpone payment of the tax attributable to a remainder or reversionary interest until six months after the other interests terminate, which in the example would be after the person currently age 30 died. In addition, upon being convinced of reasonable cause, the Secretary of the Treasury may grant an additional extension of not more than three years.

INTERESTS IN CLOSELY HELD BUSINESSES. Section 6166 authorizes the executor to pay a portion of the estate tax in as many as ten annual installments in certain situations. Executors may elect to apply Sec. 6166 if

▶ The gross estate includes an interest in a closely held business, and

▶ The value of the closely held business exceeds 35% of the value of the adjusted gross estate.

TAX STRATEGY TIP

A person who owns a substantial interest in a small business might choose to gift property other than the business interest. He or she may want to retain the business interest so that his or her estate will qualify for the five-year deferral, ten-installment option of Sec. 6166. See Tax Planning Considerations for further details.

Closely held businesses are defined as proprietorships and partnerships or corporations having no more than 45 owners.[39] If a corporation or partnership has more than 45 owners, it nevertheless can be classified as closely held if the decedent's gross estate includes 20% or more of the capital interest (in the partnership) or 20% or more of the value of the voting stock (in the corporation).[40]

The adjusted gross estate is defined as the gross estate less *allowable* Sec. 2053 and 2054 deductions. Consequently, in determining whether the estate meets the 35% requirement, all administration expenses and casualty and theft losses are subtracted, regardless of whether the executor elects to deduct them on the estate tax return or the estate's income tax return.

Once the election is chosen, the following provisions apply:

▶ The portion of the estate tax that can be paid in installments is the ratio of the value of the closely held business interest to the value of the adjusted gross estate.

---

[37] Sec. 6161(a)(2).
[38] Sec. 6621. The interest rate is discussed in Chapter C:15.

[39] Sec. 6166(b)(1).
[40] Ibid.

▶ The first of the ten allowable installments generally is not due until five years after the due date for the return. (This provision defers the last payment for as many as 15 years.)

▶ Interest on the tax due is payable annually, even during the first five years.

Some or all of the installment payments may accrue interest at a rate of only 2%. The maximum amount of deferred tax to which the 2% rate applies is (1) the tax on the total of $1 million of value (as indexed) and the exemption equivalent amount less (2) the unified credit. In no event, however, may the amount exceed the tax postponed under Sec. 6166.[41] The $1 million amount is indexed for inflation with inflation adjustments rounded to the next lowest $10,000; for 2011, this amount is $1.36 million. The interest rate on any additional deferred tax is 45% of the rate applicable to underpayments. The downside is the interest paid is not deductible as interest expense on the estate's income tax return or as an administrative expense on the estate tax return.

STOCK REDEMPTIONS TO PAY DEATH TAXES

Sometimes an estate's major asset is stock in a closely held corporation. In this situation, the corporation may have to redeem some of the corporate stock to provide the estate sufficient liquidity to pay death taxes. As discussed in Chapter C:4, stock redemptions generally receive sale or exchange treatment only if they meet certain requirements under Sec. 302, such as being substantially disproportionate or involving a complete termination of the shareholder's interest. Without exchange treatment and assuming sufficient earnings and profits, the redeemed shareholder (e.g., the estate) would recognize a dividend equal to the redemption proceeds rather than a capital gain equal to the difference between the redemption proceeds and the stock's adjusted basis. Because of the 15% maximum tax rate on dividends (through 2010), the primary benefit of sale or exchange treatment is being able to apply basis against proceeds. To reduce the income tax cost upon a shareholder's death, Sec. 303 allows the estate to treat a redemption as an exchange even if it does not satisfy the stringent Sec. 302 requirements. This treatment minimizes any gain recognized because the stock's adjusted basis, which is subtracted from the redemption proceeds, is stepped up to its FMV upon the decedent's death.

To qualify for Sec. 303 treatment, the stock in the corporation redeeming the shares must make up more than 35% of the value of the decedent's gross estate, less any *allowable* Sec. 2053 and 2054 deductions. The maximum amount of redemption proceeds eligible for exchange treatment is the total of the estate's death taxes and funeral and administration expenses, regardless of whether they are deducted on the estate tax return or the estate's income tax return.

SPECIAL USE VALUATION OF FARM REAL PROPERTY

In 1976, Congress became concerned that farms sometimes had to be sold to generate funds to pay estate taxes. This situation was attributable, in part, to the FMV of farm land in many areas being relatively high, perhaps because of suburban housing being built nearby. Congress enacted Sec. 2032A, which allows real property used for farming or in a trade or business other than farming to be valued using a formula approach that attempts to value the property at what it is worth for farming purposes. The lowest valuation permitted is $750,000 less than the property's FMV, but the $750,000 became indexed after 1998 with adjustments rounded to the next lowest $10,000. For 2011 the indexed amount is $1.02 million.

The estate must meet a number of requirements before the executor can elect the special valuation rules.[42] Moreover, if during the ten-year period after the decedent's death the new owner of the property disposes of it or no longer uses it as a farm, in general, an additional tax equal to the estate tax savings that arose from the lower Sec. 2032A valuation is levied.

SELF-STUDY QUESTION

Why might an heir to farmland want an estate to forego the special valuation method of Sec. 2032A?

ANSWER

The heir may contemplate selling the land and prefer the higher basis he or she would get if FMV is used rather than the special farmland value, especially if the estate taxes are payable out of the residual estate and the heir does not share in that residual.

---

[41] Sec. 6601(j).

[42] For example, the farm real and personal property must make up at least 50% of the adjusted value of the gross estate, and the farm real property must make up 25% or more of the adjusted value of the gross estate.

GENERATION-SKIPPING TRANSFER TAX

The Tax Reform Act of 1976 enacted a third transfer tax—the generation-skipping transfer tax (GSTT)—to fill a void in the gift and estate tax structure. In 1986, Congress repealed the original GSTT retroactive to its original effective date and replaced it with a revised GSTT. The revised GSTT generally applies to *inter vivos* transfers made after September 25, 1985, and transfers at death made after October 22, 1986.

For years, a popular estate planning technique, especially among the very wealthy, involved giving individuals in several generations an interest in the same property. For example, a decedent might set up a testamentary trust creating successive life estates for a child and a grandchild and a remainder interest for a great grandchild. Under this arrangement, an estate tax would be imposed at the death of the person establishing the trust but not again until the great grandchild's death. The GSTT's purpose is to ensure that some form of transfer taxation is imposed one time a generation. It accomplishes its purpose by subjecting transfers that escape gift or estate taxation for one or more generations to the GSTT.

Originally, every grantor was entitled to a $1 million exemption from the GSTT, but the exemption became indexed for inflation (with adjustments rounded to the next lowest $10,000) for estates of decedents dying after 1998.[43] Beginning in 2004, Congress changed the exemption to the same amount as the "applicable exclusion amount" for estate tax purposes, which was $3.5 million in 2009. With the increase in the unified credit under the Tax Relief Act, the exemption is $5 million in 2011. The grantor elects when, and against which transfers, to apply this exemption. Appreciation on the property for which the exemption is elected is also exempt from the GSTT.

The GSTT is levied at a flat rate, the highest estate tax rate.[44] The tax applies to direct skip gifts and bequests and to taxable terminations of and taxable distributions from generation-skipping transfers. A **generation-skipping transfer** involves a disposition that

▶ Provides interests for more than one generation of beneficiaries who are in a younger generation than the transferor, or

▶ Provides an interest solely for a person two or more generations younger than the transferor.[45]

The recipient must be a skip person, a person two or more generations younger than the decedent (or the donor). For family members, generation assignments are made according to the family tree. Transfers to skip persons outside of a trust are known as direct skips because they skip one or more generations.

EXAMPLE C:13-49▶ Tom transfers an asset directly to Tom III his grandson. This is a direct skip type of generation-skipping transfer because the transferee (Tom III) is two generations younger than the transferor (Tom). ◀

The termination of an interest in a generation-skipping arrangement is known as a taxable termination.[46] This event triggers imposition of the GSTT. The tax is levied on the before-tax amount transferred, and the trustee pays the tax.

EXAMPLE C:13-50▶ Tom created a trust with income payable to his son, Tom, Jr., for life and a remainder interest distributable to Tom III upon the death of Tom, Jr. (his father). This is a generation-skipping transfer because Tom, Jr., and Tom III are one and two generations younger, respectively, than the transferor (Tom). A taxable termination occurs when Tom, Jr., dies. ◀

---

[43] Sec. 2631(a).
[44] Sec. 2641.

[45] Sec. 2611.
[46] Sec. 2612(a).

EXAMPLE C:13-51▶ The trust in Example C:13-50 was worth $2 million when Tom, Jr., died in 2011. Tom, Jr., had used his GSTT exemption against other transfers. The amount of the taxable termination was $2 million. The tax was $700,000 (0.35 × $2,000,000). The trustee paid the tax and distributed the $1.3 million of remaining assets to the beneficiary. ◀

In the case of a direct skip, the amount subject to the GSTT is the value of the property received by the transferee.[47] The transferor is liable for the tax. If the direct skip occurs *inter vivos*, the GSTT paid by the transferor is treated as an additional transfer subject to the gift tax.[48] As a result, the total transfer tax liability (GSTT plus gift tax) can exceed the value of the property the donee received.

EXAMPLE C:13-52▶ In 2012, Susan gave $1 million to her granddaughter. Susan had used her entire unified credit and was in the 35% marginal gift tax bracket; ignore the annual exclusion and the exemption. The GSTT was $350,000 (0.35 × $1,000,000). The amount subject to the gift tax was the value of the property transferred ($1 million) plus the GSTT paid ($350,000). Thus, the gift tax is $472,500 (0.35 × $1,350,000). It cost $822,500 ($350,000 + $472,500) to shift $1 million of property to the granddaughter. ◀

TAX PLANNING CONSIDERATIONS

The effectiveness of many of the pre-1977 transfer tax-saving strategies was diluted by the unification of the transfer tax system in general and by the adoption of a unified rate schedule and the concept of adjusted taxable gifts in particular. To some extent, provisions that allow a larger tax base to be free of estate taxes and permit most interspousal transfers to be devoid of transfer tax consequences counterbalance unification. This section discusses various tax planning considerations that tax advisors should explore to reduce the transfer taxes applicable to a family unit.

WHAT WOULD YOU DO IN THIS SITUATION?

You are a CPA specializing in wealth transfer taxation. One of your clients is an unmarried resident of Aspen, Colorado and his health has recently taken a downhill turn. His doctor told him to consider putting his affairs in order.

This client is a merchant who owns a number of assets with FMVs totaling approximately $5.4 million. His largest asset is his Victorian era store building. Based on comparable sales in the area, your client's building appears to be worth approximately $760,000. Because your client is in poor health, he does not use all the store space and occasionally rents out some space to other vendors. During the ski season, the full price fair market rental value of the space would be over $1,000 per week.

Your client's only son has indicated that he is not interested in moving to Aspen but plans to continue the rental practices initiated by his father.

The estate probably will have no deductions. Would you propose to the client that this asset be listed in the estate as Special Use Value property pursuant to Sec. 2032A? Would it be ethical to propose a valuation method based on the historical income generated by this property for the client's estate tax return? Using the historical income stream, the capitalized value would be $350,000. With this value, his estate would be lower by $410,000 and no tax would be owed because of an overall valuation of slightly under $5 million for the entire estate.

---

[47] Sec. 2623.

[48] Sec. 2515.

USE OF *INTER VIVOS* GIFTS

SELF-STUDY QUESTION

What types of property should one consider gifting?

ANSWER

Give property that is expected to appreciate substantially in future years, produces substantial amounts of income, or is a family heirloom that probably will be passed from the donee to the donee's heirs and not be sold.

One of the most significant strategies for reducing transfer taxes is a well-designed, long-term gift program. As long as the gifts to each donee do not exceed the per donee annual exclusion, there will be no additions to the gross estate and no adjusted taxable gifts. A donor may pass thousands of dollars of property to others free of any transfer tax consequences if he or she selects enough donees and makes gifts over a substantial number of years. If taxable gifts do occur, the donor removes the post-gift appreciation from the estate tax base. Moreover, if the donor lives more than three years after the date of the gift, the gift tax paid is removed from the gross estate.

Prospective donors should weigh the opportunities for reducing transfer taxes through the use of lifetime gifts against the income tax disadvantage of foregoing the step up in basis that occurs if the donor retains the property until death. However, unless the donee is the donor's spouse, income taxes on the income produced by the gifted property can be reduced if shifted to a donee in a lower tax bracket.

USE OF EXEMPTION EQUIVALENT

ADDITIONAL COMMENT

As mentioned earlier, the so-called basic exclusion amount of $5 million is portable between spouses for 2011 and 2012. Thus, any basic exclusion amount that remains unused at the first spouse's death can be used by the second spouse. However, this benefit applies only if the executor elects portability and only for the years 2011 and 2012 unless Congress takes further action.

The exemption equivalent allows a certain amount of property—$5 million in 2011—to pass to people other than the decedent's spouse without any estate taxes being extracted therefrom. The exemption equivalent also is called the applicable exclusion amount or, in 2011 and 2012, the basic exclusion amount. In addition, a donor can transfer property to a spouse tax-free without limit. Thus, because the spouse presumably will die before any children or grandchildren (i.e., individuals to whom people often will property), a wealthy person should contemplate leaving at least an amount equal to the exemption equivalent to people other than his or her spouse. (If one leaves this amount of property in trust, the trust is often called a credit shelter or bypass trust.) Otherwise, in general, he or she will waste some or all of the exemption equivalent, and the property will be taxed when the surviving spouse dies.

Making full use of the exemption equivalent enables a husband and wife to transfer to third parties an aggregate of $10 million (using 2011 amounts) without incurring any estate taxes. The strategy of making gifts to an ill spouse, who is not wealthy, to keep the donee-spouse's exemption equivalent from being wasted was discussed earlier (see Chapter C:12). Under this technique, the wealthier spouse makes gifts to the other spouse free of gift taxes because of the marital deduction. The recipient spouse then has an estate that can be passed tax-free to children, grandchildren, or other individuals because of the exemption equivalent.

 STOP & THINK

Question: Sol made $600,000 in taxable gifts six years before his death but did not have to pay any gift tax. Sol died in 2011, when the gifted property was worth $825,000. Sol's taxable estate (gross estate minus estate tax deductions) was $5 million. Did the exemption equivalent enable Sol's estate to owe zero tax?

Solution: No. In concept, the unified credit of $1,730,800, which cancels out the tax on the 2011 $5 million exemption equivalent, is available only once. Sol's total tranfers—by gift and at death—exceeded $5 million. Calculation of Sol's estate tax payable would be as follows:

Taxable estate	$5,000,000
Plus: Adjusted taxable gifts	600,000
Estate tax base	$5,600,000
Tentative tax on estate tax base	$1,940,800
Minus:	
Post-1976 gift tax (on $600,000 gift)	–0–
Unified credit	(1,730,800)
Estate tax payable	$ 210,000

The $210,000 represents the tax on the incremental $600,000, the amount over and above the $5 million *aggregate* taxable amount that could be passed free of transfer taxes (both gift and estate).

WHAT SIZE MARITAL DEDUCTION IS BEST?

To reiterate, the tax law imposes no ceiling on the amount of property eligible for the marital deduction. Even so, the availability of an unlimited marital deduction does not necessarily mean that a person should use it. From a tax perspective, wealthier people should leave an amount equal to the exemption equivalent to someone other than the spouse. Alternatively, they could leave the spouse an income interest in property equal to the exemption equivalent along with the power to invade such property for reasons of health, support, maintenance, or education. These powers do not cause an inclusion in the gross estate.

In certain circumstances, it may be preferable for an amount exceeding the exemption equivalent to pass directly to third parties. It might be beneficial for the first spouse's estate to pay some estate taxes if the surviving spouse already has substantial property and has a relatively short life expectancy, especially if the decedent spouse's assets are expected to rapidly increase in value.

ADDITIONAL COMMENT

This discussion ignores exemption amount portability, which currently applies only for deaths in 2011 and 2012.

 STOP & THINK

Question: Tarik died recently at age 78. He was survived by his wife, Saliah, and several children and grandchildren. Saliah is 54 and in excellent health. Tarik's adjusted gross estate was $8 million, and his will left $5 million outright to his children and the rest to a trust for Saliah. The trust is eligible for the QTIP election. An investment advisor believes that the trust assets will likely appreciate annually at the rate of at least 10%. Name two advantages and one disadvantage of electing the marital deduction on the entire trust.

Solution: One advantage is that the tax on the trust will be deferred, perhaps for a long time, given the wife's age and health. Another advantage is that, because no tax is owed at Tarik's death, the trust assets remain intact to appreciate and produce more income for Saliah. That is, there is no current capital drain to pay transfer taxes. A disadvantage is that, because of the anticipated appreciation and the long time before Saliah's estimated death, the amount taxed in Saliah's estate will likely be much greater than the residue (here, $3 million) Tarik willed to Saliah. Note that Tarik took full advantage of his unified credit.

USE OF DISCLAIMERS

Because the IRC does not treat a **qualified disclaimer** as a gift, disclaimers can be valuable estate planning tools (see Chapter C:12). For example, if a decedent wills all his or her property to the surviving spouse, such spouse could disclaim an amount at least equal in size to the exemption equivalent and thereby enable the decedent's estate to take full advantage of the unified credit. Alternatively, a decedent's children might disclaim some bequests if, as a result of their disclaimer, the property would pass instead to the surviving spouse. This approach might be desirable if the estate otherwise would receive a relatively small marital deduction. Another scenario where a disclaimer could be appropriate is where the disclaimant is elderly and in poor health and wishes to preclude the property from being taxed again relatively soon. (Of course, the credit for tax on prior transfers would provide some relief from double taxation.) Bear in mind, however, that the person making the qualified disclaimer has no input concerning which people receive the disclaimed property.

ROLE OF LIFE INSURANCE

Life insurance is an important asset with respect to estate planning for the following reasons:

► It can help provide the liquidity for paying estate taxes and other costs associated with death.

► It has the potential for large appreciation. If the insured gives away his or her incidents of ownership in the policy and survives the gift by more than three years, his or her estate benefits by keeping the policy's increased value out of the estate.

Assume an individual is contemplating purchasing a new insurance policy on his or her life and transferring it to another individual as a gift. The insured must live for more than three years after making the gift to exclude the face amount of the policy from his or her gross estate. Should the insured die within three years of gifting the policy, the donor's gross estate includes the policy's face amount. If the donee instead purchases the policy, the insured will not make a gift of the policy, and the three-year rule will not be of concern.

QUALIFYING THE ESTATE FOR INSTALLMENT PAYMENTS

It can be quite beneficial for an estate owning an interest in a closely held business to qualify for installment payment of estate taxes under Sec. 6166. In a sense, the estate can borrow a certain amount of dollars from the government at 2% and the rest at a higher, but still favorable, rate. The closely held business interest must comprise more than 35% of the adjusted gross estate, defined as the gross estate less Sec. 2053 and Sec. 2054 deductions.

Retaining closely held business interests and gifting other assets will increase the likelihood of the estate's being able to elect the installment payments. However, closely held business interests often have a potential for great appreciation. Consequently, from the standpoint of reducing the size of the estate by freezing values, they are good candidates for gifts.

People cannot make gifts to restructure their estates and thereby qualify for Sec. 6166 if they postpone restructuring until soon before their death. If the decedent makes gifts within three years of dying, the closely held business interest must make up more than 35% of the adjusted gross estate in both of the following calculations:

1. Calculate the ratio of the closely held business to the actual adjusted gross estate.
2. Redo the calculations after revising the ratio to include (at date-of-death values) any property given away within three years of death.

EXAMPLE C:13-53 ▶ Joe died in 2011. Joe's gross estate included a closely held business interest valued at $2 million and other property valued at $3.6 million. Joe's allowable Sec. 2053 and 2054 deductions totaled $100,000. In 2009, partly in hopes of qualifying his estate for Sec. 6166 treatment, Joe made gifts of listed securities of $300,000 (at 2011 valuations) and paid no gift tax on the gifts. The two tests for determining whether Joe's estate qualified for Sec. 6166 are as follows:

Excluding gifts: $2,000,000 ÷ $5,500,000 = 36.36%
Including gifts: $2,000,000 ÷ $5,800,000 = 34.48%

The estate could not elect Sec. 6166 treatment because it met the greater than 35% test in only one of the two computations. ◀

WHERE TO DEDUCT ADMINISTRATION EXPENSES

Another tax planning opportunity concerns the choice of where to deduct administration expenses: on the estate tax return, on the estate's income tax return, or some in each place. The executor should claim the deduction where it will yield the greatest tax savings. For 2011 and 2012, the top tax rate for both estate and income tax purposes is 35%. Thus, for many estates, the tax savings will be the same regardless of where the expenses are deducted. However, some decedents may have made bequests to certain persons or charitable organizations based on the size of the adjusted gross or taxable estate. In such circumstances, the tax return on which the administration expenses are deducted will affect the amount of the adjusted gross and taxable estates and the amount that some beneficiaries of the estate receive. If no estate taxes are owed because of the exemption equivalent or the marital and/or charitable contribution deduction, administration expenses should be deducted on the estate's income tax return.

COMPLIANCE AND PROCEDURAL CONSIDERATIONS

OBJECTIVE 7

Recognize the filing requirements for estate tax returns

FILING REQUIREMENTS

Section 6018 indicates the circumstances in which estate tax returns are necessary. In general, no return is necessary unless the value of the gross estate plus adjusted taxable gifts exceeds the exemption equivalent (also known as the applicable exclusion amount). An exception applies, however, if the decedent made any post-1976 taxable gifts or claimed any portion of the $30,000 specific exemption after September 8, 1976, and before January 1, 1977. In such circumstances, a return must be filed if the value of the gross estate exceeds the amount of the exemption equivalent reduced by the total of the decedent's adjusted taxable gifts and the amount of the specific exemption claimed against gifts made after September 8, 1976, and before January 1, 1977.

A completed sample Estate Tax Return (Form 706) appears in Appendix B. The facts on which the preparation of the return is premised are the same as for the comprehensive illustration appearing on pages C:13-25 through C:13-27.

REAL-WORLD EXAMPLE

The IRS expects 43,500 estate tax returns to be filed for 2009. However, the Treasury Inspector General for Tax Administration reports that only 2% of decedents are required to file an estate tax return and even fewer pay any tax because of deductions and credits.

DUE DATE

Estate tax returns generally must be filed within nine months after the decedent's death.[49] The Secretary of the Treasury is authorized to grant a reasonable extension of time for filing.[50] The maximum extension period is six months. Obtaining an extension does not extend the time for paying the estate tax. Section 6601 imposes interest on any portion of the tax not paid by the due date of the return, determined without regard to the extension period. Thus, to avoid interest, the estate must pay the tax by the original due date.

VALUATION

One of the most difficult tasks of preparing estate tax returns is valuing the items included in the gross estate. Some items (e.g., one-of-a-kind art objects) may truly be unique. For many properties the executor should arrange for appraisals by experts.

If the value of any property reported on the return is 65% or less of the amount determined to be the proper value during an audit or court case, a 20% undervaluation penalty is imposed.[51] The penalty is higher if a gross valuation misstatement occurs; that is, the estate tax valuation is 40% or less than the amount determined to be the proper value.[52] Chapter C:12 discusses these penalties in more detail.

ELECTION OF ALTERNATE VALUATION DATE

The executor may value the gross estate on the alternate valuation date instead of on the date of death by making an irrevocable election on the estate tax return. The election does not necessarily have to be made on a timely return, but no election is possible if the return is filed more than a year after the due date (including extensions).

PROBLEM MATERIALS

DISCUSSION QUESTIONS

C:13-1 In general, at what amount are items includible in the gross estate valued? (Answer in words.) Indicate one exception to the general valuation rules and the reason for this exception.

C:13-2 A client requests that you explain the valuation rules used for gift tax and estate tax purposes. Explain the similarities and differences of the two sets of rules.

---

[49] Sec. 6075(a).
[50] Sec. 6081(a).

[51] Sec. 6662(g).
[52] Sec. 6662(h).

C:13-3 Compare the valuation for gift and estate tax purposes of a $150,000 group term life insurance policy on the transferor's life.

C:13-4 Explain how shares of stock traded on a stock exchange are valued. What is the blockage rule?

C:13-5 Assume that the properties included in Alex's gross estate have appreciated during the six-month period immediately after his death. May Alex's executor elect the alternate valuation date and thereby achieve a larger step-up in basis? Explain.

C:13-6 Explain to an executor an advantage and a disadvantage of electing the alternate valuation date.

C:13-7 A decedent transferred land to an adult child by gift two years before death. Is the land included in the decedent's gross estate? In the estate tax base?

C:13-8 From a tax standpoint, which of the following alternatives is more favorable for a client's estate?
  a. Buying a new insurance policy on his life and soon thereafter giving it to another person
  b. Encouraging the other person to buy the policy with funds previously received from the client
  Explain your answer.

C:13-9 Explain the difference between the estate tax treatment for gift taxes paid on gifts made two years before death and on gifts made ten years before death.

C:13-10 A client is considering making a very large gift. She wants to know whether the gross-up rule will apply to the entire amount of gift taxes paid by both her and her spouse if the spouses elect gift splitting and she dies within three years of the gift. Explain.

C:13-11 A widow owns a valuable eighteenth-century residence that she would like the state historical society to own someday. Explain to her the estate tax consequences of the following two alternatives:
  a. Deeding the state historical society a remainder interest in the residence and reserving the right to live there rent free for the rest of her life.
  b. Giving her entire interest in the house to the society and moving to another home for the rest of her life.

C:13-12 Which three retention periods can cause Sec. 2036 (transfers with retained life estate) to apply to a transferor's estate?

C:13-13 What characteristics do Secs. 2035 through 2038 have in common?

C:13-14 When does the consideration furnished test apply to property that the decedent held as a joint tenant with right of survivorship?

C:13-15 In which two circumstances is life insurance on the decedent's life includible in the gross estate under Sec. 2042? If insurance policies on the decedent's life escape being included under Sec. 2042, are they definitely excluded from the gross estate? Explain.

C:13-16 Indicate two situations in which property that has previously been subject, at least in part, to gift taxation is nevertheless included in the donor-decedent's gross estate.

C:13-17 Joe's will required property to be put in trust with a bank as trustee. His will named his sister Tess to receive the trust income annually for life and empowered Tess to will the property to whomever she so desires. In addition, Tess may require that the trustee make distributions of principal to her for her health or support needs. Tess plans to leave the property by will to two of her three children in equal shares. Tess seeks your advice about whether the trust will be included in her gross estate. Respond to Tess.

C:13-18 Determine the accuracy of the following statement: The gross estate includes a general power of appointment possessed by the decedent only if the decedent exercised the power.

C:13-19 Carlos died six years before his wife. His will called for the creation of a trust to be funded with $1 million of property. The bank trustee was required to distribute all the trust income semiannually to Carlos's widow for the rest of her life. Upon her death, the trust assets were to be distributed to the couple's children. When the widow died, the trust assets had appreciated to $1.7 million. Are the trust assets included in the widow's gross estate? Explain.

C:13-20 List the various categories of estate tax deductions, and compare them with the categories of gift tax deductions. What differences exist?

C:13-21 Compare the tax treatment of administration expenses with that of the decedent's debts.

C:13-22 Judy died and was survived by her husband, Jason, who received the following interests as a result of his wife's death. Does Judy's estate receive a marital deduction for them? Explain.
  a. $400,000 of life insurance proceeds; Jason is the beneficiary; Judy held the incidents of ownership.
  b. Outright ownership of $700,000 of land held by Judy and Jason as joint tenants. Jason provided all the consideration to purchase the land.

C:13-23 Compare the credits available for estate tax purposes with the credits available for gift tax purposes. What differences exist?

C:13-24 Explain to a client the tax policy reason Congress allowed an estate to make installment payments of the portion of the estate taxes attributable to closely held business interests.

C:13-25 Assume that Larry is wealthier than Jane, his wife, and that he is likely to die before her. From an overall tax standpoint (considering transfer taxes and income taxes), is it preferable for Larry to transfer property to Jane *inter vivos* or at death, or does it matter? Explain.

C:**13-26** Bala desires to freeze the value of his estate. Explain which of the following assets you would recommend that Bala transfer during his lifetime (more than one asset may be suggested):
  a. Life insurance on his life
  b. Cash
  c. Corporate bonds (assume interest rates are expected to rise)
  d. Stock in a firm with a bright future
  e. Land in a boom town

C:**13-27** Refer to Problem C:13-26. Explain the negative tax considerations (if any) with respect to Bala's making gifts of the assets that you recommended.

C:**13-28** From a tax standpoint, why is it advisable for a wealthy married person to dispose of an amount equal to the exemption equivalent (applicable exclusion amount or basic exclusion amount) to individuals other than his or her spouse?

C:**13-29** In general, when is the estate tax due? What are some exceptions?

ISSUE IDENTIFICATION QUESTIONS

C:**13-30** Henry Arkin (a widower) is quite elderly and is beginning to engage in some estate planning. His goal is to reduce his transfer taxes. He is considering purchasing land with a high potential for appreciation and having it titled in his name and the name of his grandson as joint tenants with rights of survivorship. Henry would provide all of the consideration, estimated to be about $8 million. What tax issues should Henry Arkin consider with respect to the purchase of the land?

C:**13-31** Annie James died early in 2011. All her property passed subject to her will, which provides that her surviving husband, Dave James, is to receive all the property outright. Her will further states that any property Dave disclaims will pass instead to their children in equal shares. Annie's gross estate is about $5.6 million, and her Sec. 2053 deductions are very small. Dave, who is in poor health, already owns about $3 million of property. What tax issues should Dave James consider with respect to the property bequested to him by his wife?

C:**13-32** Assume the same facts as in Problem C:13-31 except that Annie's will leaves all her property to a QTIP trust for Dave for life with the remainder to their children. What tax issues should Dave James and the estate's executor consider with respect to the property that passes to the QTIP trust?

C:**13-33** Jeung Hong, a widower, died in March 2011. His gross estate was $6.5 million and, at the time of his death, he owed debts of $60,000. His will made a bequest of $200,000 to his undergraduate alma mater and left the rest of his property to his children. His administrative expenses were $75,000. Jeung made no taxable gifts. What tax issues should the estate's CPA consider when preparing Jeung's estate tax return and his estate's income tax return?

PROBLEMS

C:**13-34** *Valuation.* Beth died on May 5, 2011. Her executor elected date-of-death valuation. Beth's gross estate included, among other properties, the items listed below. What is the estate tax value of each item?
  a. 4,000 shares of Highline Corporation stock, traded on a stock exchange on May 5, 2011 at a high of 30, a low of 25, and a close of 26.
  b. Life insurance policy on the life of Beth having a face value of $600,000. The cost of a comparable policy immediately before Beth's death was $187,430.
  c. Life insurance policy on the life of Beth's son having a face value of $100,000. The interpolated terminal reserve immediately before Beth's death was $14,000. Unexpired premiums were $920.
  d. Beach cottage appraised at a FMV of $175,000 and valued for property tax purposes at $152,000.

C:**13-35** *Valuation.* Mary died on April 3, 2011. As of this date, Mary's gross estate was valued at $6.5 million. On October 3, Mary's gross estate was valued at $5.8 million. The estate neither distributed nor sold any assets before October 3, 2011. Mary's estate had no deductions or adjusted taxable gifts. What was Mary's *lowest* possible estate tax liability?

C:13-36 *Estate Tax Formula.* Sue died on May 3, 2011. On October 1, 2008, Sue gave Tom land valued at $2,012,000. Sue applied a unified credit of $345,800 against the gift tax due on this transfer. On Sue's date of death the land was valued at $2.4 million.

a. With respect to this transaction, what amount was included in Sue's gross estate?

b. What is the amount of Sue's adjusted taxable gifts attributable to the 2008 gift?

C:13-37 *Transferor Provisions.* Val died on May 13, 2011. On July 3, 2008, she gave a $400,000 life insurance policy on her own life to son Ray. Because the value of the policy was relatively low, the transfer did not cause any gift tax to be payable.

a. What amount was included in Val's gross estate as a result of the 2008 gift?

b. What amount was included in Val's gross estate if the property given was land instead of a life insurance policy?

c. Refer to Part a. What amount would have been included in Val's gross estate if she instead gave Ray the policy on April 30, 2007?

C:13-38 *Transferor Provisions.* In December 2008, Jody transferred stock having a $1,112,000 FMV to her daughter Joan. Jody paid $41,000 of gift taxes on this transfer. When Jody died in January 2011, the stock was valued at $920,000. Jody made no other gifts during her lifetime. With respect to this gift transaction, what amount was includible in Jody's gross estate, and what amount was reportable as adjusted taxable gifts?

C:13-39 *Transferor Provisions.* In December 2008, Curt and Kate elected gift splitting to report $2,224,000 million of gifts of stocks Curt made. Each paid gift taxes of $41,000 by spending his or her own funds. Kate died in January 2011 and was survived by Curt. Her only taxable gift was the one reported for 2008. When Kate died in 2011, the stock had appreciated to $2.8 million. With respect to the 2008 gift, what amount was included in Kate's gross estate, and what amount was reportable as adjusted taxable gifts?

C:13-40 *Transferor Provisions.* John died in 2011. What amount, if any, was included in his gross estate in each of the following situations:

a. In 1994, John created a revocable trust, funded it with $400,000 of assets, and named a bank as trustee. The trust instrument provided that the income is payable to John annually for life. Upon John's death, the assets were to be divided equally among John's descendants. When John died at the age of 72, the trust was still revocable. The trust assets were then worth $480,000.

b. In 1995, John transferred title to his personal residence to a charitable organization but retained the right to live there rent free for 20 years. The residence was worth $150,000 on the transfer date. At John's death, the residence was worth $230,000.

c. In 1995, John created an irrevocable trust, funded it with $200,000 of assets, and named a bank as trustee. According to the trust agreement, all the trust income was to be paid out annually for 25 years. The trustee, however, is to decide how much income to pay each year to each of the three beneficiaries (John's children). Upon termination of the trust, the assets are to be distributed equally among John's three children (now adults) or their estates. The trust's assets were worth $500,000 when John died.

d. In 1996, John created an irrevocable trust with a bank named as trustee. He designated his grandson Al as the beneficiary of all the income for life. Upon Al's death, the property is to be distributed equally among Al's descendants. The trust assets were worth $400,000 when John died.

C:13-41 *Transferor Provisions.* Latoya transferred property to an irrevocable trust in 2002 with a bank trustee. Latoya named Al to receive the trust income annually for life and Pat or Pat's estate to receive the remainder upon Al's death. Latoya reserved the power to designate Mike or Mike's estate (instead of Pat or Pat's estate) to receive the remainder. Upon Latoya's death in August 2011, the trust assets were valued at $200,000; Al was age 50; Mike, age 27; and Pat, age 32. Assume a 4% rate for the actuarial tables.

a. How much, if any, is included in Latoya's gross estate?

b. How much would have been included in Latoya's gross estate if she had *not* retained any powers over the trust?

C:13-42 *Annuities.* Maria died two years after her retirement. At the time of her death at age 67, she was covered by the two annuities listed below.

• An annuity purchased by Maria's father providing benefits to Maria upon her attaining age 65. Upon Maria's death, survivor benefits are payable to her sister. The sister's total benefits are valued at $45,000.

- An annuity purchased by Maria's former employer under a qualified plan to which only the employer contributed. Benefits became payable to Maria upon her retirement. Upon Maria's death a survivor annuity valued at $110,000 is payable to her son.
  a. What is the amount of the inclusion in Maria's gross estate with respect to each annuity?
  b. How would your answer for the first annuity change if Maria had instead purchased the annuity?
  c. How would your answer for the second annuity change if the employer had instead made 70% of the contributions to the qualified plan and Maria had made the remaining 30%?

C:13-43 *Jointly Owned Property.* In 2004, Art purchased land for $60,000 and immediately titled it in the names of Art and Bart, joint tenants with right of survivorship. Bart paid no consideration. In 2011, Art died and was survived by Bart, his brother. The land's value had appreciated to $300,000.
  a. What was the amount of the inclusion in Art's gross estate?
  b. Assume Bart died (instead of Art). What amount would have been included in Bart's gross estate?
  c. Assume that Art died in January 2011 and Bart died in November 2011, when the land was worth $320,000. What amount was included in Bart's gross estate?

C:13-44 *Jointly Owned Property.* Five years ago, Andy and Sandy, siblings, pooled their resources and purchased a warehouse. Andy provided $50,000 of consideration, and Sandy furnished $100,000. Andy died and was survived by Sandy. The property, which they had titled in the names of Andy and Sandy, joint tenants with right of survivorship, was valued at $450,000 when Andy died. What amount was includible in Andy's gross estate?

C:13-45 *Jointly Owned Property.* Mrs. Cobb purchased land costing $80,000 in 2000. She had the land titled in the names of Mr. and Mrs. Cobb, joint tenants with right of survivorship. Mrs. Cobb died and was survived by Mr. Cobb. At Mrs. Cobb's death, the land's value was $200,000.
  a. What amount was included in Mrs. Cobb's gross estate?
  b. What amount, if any, of the marital deduction could Mrs. Cobb's estate claim for the land?
  c. Assume Mr. Cobb died after Mrs. Cobb and the land was worth $240,000 at his death. What amount was included in his gross estate?

C:13-46 *Powers of Appointment.* Tai was the sole income beneficiary for life of each of the trusts described below. For each trust, indicate whether and why it was includible in Tai's gross estate.
  a. A trust created under the will of Tai's mother, who died in 1996. Upon Tai's death, the trust assets are to pass to those of Tai's descendants whom Tai directs by his will. Should Tai fail to appoint the trust property, the trust assets are to be distributed to the Smithsonian Institution. Tai willed the property to his twin daughters in equal shares.
  b. An irrevocable *inter vivos* trust created in 2001 by Tai's father. The trust agreement authorizes Tai to appoint the property to whomever he so desires. The appointment could be made only by his will. In his will, Tai appointed the property to an elderly neighbor.
  c. An irrevocable trust funded by Tai in 2002. The trust instrument specifies that, upon Tai's death, the property is to pass to his children.
  d. A trust created under the will of Tai's great-grandmother, who died in 1941. Her will authorizes Tai to appoint the property by his will to whomever he so desires. In default of appointment, the property is to pass to Tai's descendants in equal shares. Tai's will did not mention this trust.
  e. Assume the same facts as in Part b except Tai's will did not mention the trust property.

C:13-47 *Life Insurance.* Joy died on November 5, 2011. Soon after Joy's death, the executor discovered the following insurance policies on Joy's life. Indicate the amount includible in Joy's gross estate for each policy.

Policy Number	Owner	Beneficiary	Face Value
123	Joy	Joy's husband	$400,000
757	Joy's son	Joy's estate	225,000
848	Joy's son	Joy's son	300,000
414	Joy's daughter	Joy's husband	175,000

Joy transferred ownership of policies 757 and 848 to her son in 1997. She gave ownership of policy 414 to her daughter in 2009.

C:13-48 *Life Insurance.* Refer to Problem C:13-47. What is the net addition to Joy's *taxable estate* with respect to the insurance policies listed above if all the property passing under Joy's will was left to Joy's son?

C:13-49 *Deductions.* When Yuji died in March 2011, his gross estate was valued at $8 million. He owed debts totaling $300,000. Funeral and administration expenses were $12,000 and $120,000, respectively. The marginal estate tax rate exceeded his estate's marginal income tax rate because the estate collected only about $8,000 of income. Yuji willed his church $300,000 and his spouse $1.1 million. Calculate Yuji's taxable estate.

C:13-50 *Marital Deduction.* Assume the same facts as in Problem C:13-49 except that Yuji's will also provided for setting up a trust to be funded with $400,000 of property with a bank named as trustee. His wife is to receive all the trust income semiannually for life, and upon her death the trust assets are to be distributed equally among Yuji's children and grandchildren.
a. What was the amount of Yuji's taxable estate? Provide two possible answers.
b. Assume Yuji's widow died in December 2011. With respect to Yuji's former assets, which items will be included in the widow's gross estate? Provide two possible answers, but you need not indicate amounts.

C:13-51 *Marital Deduction.* Assume the same facts as in Problem C:13-50 and that before Yuji's death his wife already owned property valued at $300,000. Assume that each asset owned by each spouse increased 8% in value by the surviving spouse's date of death and that Yuji's executor elected to claim the maximum marital deduction possible. Assume there were no state death taxes. From a tax standpoint, was the executor's strategy of electing the marital deduction on the QTIP trust a wise decision? Support your answer with computations.

C:13-52 *Portability of Exclusion.* Sam Snider died February 14, 2011, survived by his spouse Janet and several children. Sam had not made any taxable gifts. Sam's gross estate was $7 million. In each of the following independent situations, indicate the amount of Sam's basic exclusion that is portable to Janet and that can be used by Janet's estate if Sam's executor makes the appropriate election.
a. Sam's deductions, including the marital deduction, total $3.7 million; Janet dies in 2012.
b. Sam's deductions, including the marital deduction, total $1.1 million; Janet dies in 2012.
c. Sam's deductions, including the marital deduction, total $6 million; Janet dies in 2016.
d. Sam's deductions, including the marital deduction, total $5.5 million. Janet remarries late in 2011. Her new spouse dies early in 2012 with a $9 million taxable estate, and Janet dies late in 2012.

C:13-53 *Adjusted Taxable Gifts.* Will, a bachelor, died in 2011. At that time, his sole asset was cash of $6 million. Assume no debts or funeral and administration expenses. His gift history was as follows:

Date	Amount of Taxable Gifts	FMV of Gift Property at Date of Death
October 1987	$270,000	$290,000
October 1991	90,000	65,000

a. What was Will's estate tax base?
b. How would your answer to Part a change if Will made the first gift in 1974 (instead of 1987)?

C:13-54 *Estate Tax Base.* Bess died in 2011. Her gross estate, which totaled $7 million, included a $100,000 life insurance policy on her life that she gave away in 2009. The taxable gift that arose from giving away the policy was $15,000. In 2008, Bess made a $740,000 taxable gift of stock whose value increased to $790,000 by the time Bess died. Assume her estate tax deductions totaled $80,000.
a. What was her estate tax base?
b. What unified credit could her estate claim?

C:13-55 *Installment Payments.* Elaine died on May 1, 2011. Her gross estate consisted of the following items:

Cash	$ 40,000
Stocks traded on a stock exchange	4,200,000
Personal residence	550,000
25% capital interest in a 60-person partnership	3,100,000

Elaine's Sec. 2053 deductions totaled $200,000. She had no other deductions.

a. What percentage of Elaine's federal estate taxes could be paid in installments under Sec. 6166? When was the first installment payment due?

b. Could Elaine's estate elect Sec. 6166 treatment if the stocks were valued at $6.2 million instead of $4.2 million?

C:13-56 *State Death Taxes.* Giovanni died in 2011 with a gross estate of $6.9 million and debts of $30,000. He made post-1976 taxable gifts of $100,000, valued at $80,000 when Giovanni died. His estate paid state death taxes of $110,200. Calculate his estate tax base.

COMPREHENSIVE PROBLEMS

C:13-57 Bonnie died on June 1, 2011, survived by her husband, Abner, and two sons, Carl and Doug. Bonnie's only lifetime taxable gift was made in October 2008 in the taxable amount of $1.25 million. She did not elect gift splitting. By the time of her death, the value of the gifted property (stock) had declined to $1.1 million.

Bonnie's executor discovered the items shown below. Amounts shown are the FMVs of the items as of June 1, 2011.

Cash in checking account in her name	$ 127,750
Cash in savings account in her name	430,000
Stock in names of Bonnie and Doug, joint tenants with right of survivorship. Bonnie provided all the consideration ($3,000) to purchase the stock.	25,000
Land in names of Bonnie and Abner, joint tenants with right of survivorship. Abner provided all the consideration to purchase the land.	360,000
Personal residence in only Bonnie's name	450,000
Life insurance on Bonnie's life. Bonnie was owner, and Bonnie's estate was beneficiary (face value)	5,000,000
Trust created under the will of Bonnie's mother (who died in 2000). Bonnie was entitled to all the trust income for life, and she could will the trust property to whomever she desired. She willed it to her sons in equal amounts.	700,000

Bonnie's debts, as of her date of death, were $60,000. Her funeral and administration expenses were $9,000 and $71,000, respectively. Her estate paid state death taxes of $65,000. The executor elected to deduct the administration expenses on the estate tax return.

Bonnie's will included the following:

I leave my residence to my husband Abner.

$250,000 of property is to be transferred to a trust with First Bank named as trustee. All of the income is to be paid to my husband, Abner, semiannually for the rest of his life. Upon his death the property is to be divided equally between my two sons or their estates.

I leave $47,000 to the American Cancer Society.

Assume the executor elected to claim the maximum marital deduction possible. Compute the following with respect to Bonnie's estate:

a. Gross estate

b. Taxable estate

c. Adjusted taxable gifts

d. Estate tax base and basic exclusion amount portable to Abner

e. Tentative tax on estate tax base

f. Federal estate tax payable

C:13-58 Assume the same facts as in Problem C:13-57 except the joint tenancy land was held in the names of Bonnie and her son Doug, joint tenants with right of survivorship. Also assume that Bonnie provided 55% of the consideration to buy the land and that Bonnie's executor did not elect to claim the marital deduction on the QTIP trust. Assume further that no taxable gift arose on the purchase of the joint tenancy land.

TAX STRATEGY PROBLEMS

C:13-59 Gaylord Gunnison (GG) died January 13, 2011, and his gross estate consisted of three properties—cash, land, and stock in a public company. The amount of cash on the date of his death was $2.9 million, which went into the estate. On January 13, 2011, the land had a fair market value of $1 million, and the stock had a fair market value of $2 million. On July 13, 2011, the fair market values of the land and stock were $1.1 million and $1.6 million, respectively, and the cash remained at $2.9 million. Assume, for simplicity, that the estate has no deductions and GG made no taxable gifts. GG willed all of his property to his daughter, Gilda, who anticipated that, beginning in July 2011, the stock would appreciate at the rate of 9% per year before taxes. She anticipates selling the stock on or about July 13, 2017. Assume that the land's fair market value will remain at $1.1 million through 2017 and that she anticipates retaining the land for the rest of her life.

Considering both income tax and estate tax effects, compare after-tax wealth using the alternate valuation date or the date of death to value the estate. Which date should the executor have elected? For simplicity, assume that the cash is not invested. (Incidentally, the factor for the future value, six years hence, at 9% is 1.677.) Prepare a worksheet on which you calculate the amount of after-tax wealth using the two possible valuation dates. Assume that the gain will be taxed at a 20% rate in 2017.

C:13-60 Steve Silver, a new client, owns stock in HyTeche, Inc., which recently had an initial public offering. In early 2011, his stock is valued at $8 million. His only other asset is $9 million of cash. Unfortunately, he has a terminal illness and has a life expectancy of less than a year. He believes that the stock's value will escalate to about $10 million by the time of his death. Steve is a widower and wants his daughter Sylvia to end up with the stock. He wants you to do a projection of his total transfer tax cost (gift and estate) if he gives the stock to Sylvia immediately compared with his total transfer tax cost if he leaves the stock to Sylvia under his will. He explains that Sylvia is not likely to sell the stock. Thus, the stock's basis is a moot issue. Prepare projections for the total transfer tax cost of the gift now versus pass on at death scenarios under the assumption that he will die in late 2011 when the stock will be worth $11 million.

C:13-61 Matt Patterson died in early 2011 with a $4.5 million gross estate and no deductions other than a potential marital deduction. He bequeathed all his property to his spouse, Nancy, with the provision that, if Nancy predeceases him, the couple's two adult children will receive the entire property in equal amounts. Nancy survived Matt, but she has a recently diagnosed terminal illness. Nancy's own assets have an estimated $5.3 million fair market value as of Matt's date of death. Her estate will likely have only a minimal amount of deductions. Her current will leaves her property 50% each to the two children. Your manager will soon meet with Nancy, who wants to discuss the implications of disclaiming Matt's bequest to her. Your manager requests that you prepare projections of the combined estate tax liability of Matt and Nancy if Nancy disclaims and does not disclaim. Assume the assets do not appreciate by Nancy's date of death. Nancy requested the projections be based on the assumption that her death will occur near the end of 2012, at the latest.

TAX FORM/RETURN PREPARATION PROBLEMS

NOTE
These problems pertain to 2009 because, when this textbook went to press, the IRS had not published estate or gift tax returns for 2010.

C:13-62 Prepare an Estate Tax Return (Form 706) for Judy Griffin (464-55-3434), who died on June 30, 2009. Judy is survived by her husband, Greg, and her daughter, Candy. Judy was a resident of 17 Fiddlers Way, Nashville, Tennessee 37205. She was employed as a corporate executive with Sounds of Country, Inc., a recording company, at the time of her death. The assets discovered at Judy's death are listed below at their date-of-death values.

Certificates of deposit in Judy's name	$2,190,000
Checking account in Judy's name	10,000
Personal residence (having a $200,000 mortgage)	500,000

Household furnishings	75,000
400 shares of stock in Omega Corporation (quotes on June 30, 2008 are high of 70, low of 60, close of 67)	?
Real estate in New York (inherited from her mother in 1991)	640,000
Porsche purchased by Greg in 2007, as an anniversary gift to Judy	45,000

Other items include the following:
1. Life insurance policy 1: Judy purchased a $200,000 life insurance policy on her life on November 1, 2006 and paid the first annual premium of $2,500. The next day, she transferred the policy to her brother, Todd Williams, who also is the beneficiary. Judy paid the premium on August 1, 2007, and August 1, 2008.
2. Life insurance policy 2: A $150,000 whole life policy on Greg's life. Judy purchased the policy in 1995 and has always paid the $1,200 semiannual premium due on March 30 and September 30. Interpolated terminal reserve is $25,000. The beneficiary is Judy or her estate. Judy is the owner of the policy.
3. Employer annuity: Judy's employer established a qualified pension plan in 1982. The employer contributes 60% and the employee pays 40% of the required annual contributions. Judy chose a settlement option that provides for annual payments to Greg until his death. The annuity receivable by Greg is valued at $600,000.

Other information includes the following:
1. In October 2006, Judy transferred to her brother, Todd, $1,524,000 of stock that she received as a gift. Judy and Greg elected gift splitting. This was the first taxable gift for each spouse, and they paid their own portion of the gift tax (if any) from their own funds. When Judy dies, the stocks have appreciated to $1.6 million.
2. Unpaid bills at death include $2,500 owed on a bank credit card.
3. The cost of Judy's funeral and tombstone totals $25,000.
4. Judy's administration expenses are $55,000. Her estate's marginal transfer tax rate will be higher than the estate's marginal income tax rate.
5. Judy's will includes the following dispositions of property:

> I leave $60,000 of property in trust with Fourth Bank named as trustee. All income is to be paid semiannually to my husband, Greg, for life or until he remarries, whichever occurs first. At the termination of Greg's interest, the property will pass to my daughter, Candy, or her estate.

> To my beloved husband, Greg, I leave my Omega stock. The rest of my property I leave to my daughter, Candy, except that I leave $10,000 to the University of Tennessee.

6. Assume that Judy's state does not impose an estate tax.
7. Make the QTIP election if possible.

C:13-63 Prepare an Estate Tax Return (Form 706) for Adam Zugg (331-22-4589) of 45 Cornfield Place, Palatine, IL 60094. Adam died October 31, 2009. He was survived by his wife, Callie, and their son, Zebulon. At the time of his death, Adam was employed by a farm equipment distributor as its office manager. The executor reports that he has discovered the property listed below.

Checking account, Adam and Callie, joint tenants with right of survivorship	$ 10,200
Stocks in public companies in the name of Adam	1,300,000
Undeveloped land (not leased or farmed) in the name of Adam	2,400,000
Qualified retirement plan funded by Adam's employer	800,000
Face value of term life insurance policy on Adam's life	2,000,000
Automobile in Adam's name	22,000

Other information includes the following:
1. Adam owned the life insurance policy, and his estate is the beneficiary.
2. Callie is the beneficiary of the retirement plan.
3. Adam willed his stocks to Callie and the rest of his property to Zebulon.
4. Adam owed $13,200 on a car loan.
5. The estate's administrative expenses were $32,000, and his funeral expenses were $8,000.
6. Assume that the estate paid state estate taxes of $45,000.
7. Adam made his only taxable gift, $2 million in amount, in 2007 and paid all the gift taxes from an account solely in his name.

CASE STUDY PROBLEMS

C:13-64 Your long-time client, Harold (Hal) Holland will meet with your supervising partner next week for an estate planning appointment. Hal has been married to Winona Holland since 1990. Hal is age 68 and retired. Winona, age 60, retired early to spend more time with Hal. They are residents of Topeka, Kansas. Hal is a U.S. citizen, and Winona is a citizen of Australia. Winona has indicated she plans to return to Australia if Hal predeceases her. Your supervising partner has requested that you identify any potential pitfalls in Hal's current estate plan so she can bring them to his attention.

Hal has stated that, in addition to providing some wealth transfers to his wife Winona, he wants to treat his three children by his prior marriage (Gina, Halbert, and Julianna) approximately equally in terms of total wealth received from him by gift and as a result of his death.

Hal and Winona prepared and submitted via e-mail the list of assets shown below.

- Principal residence in Topeka titled in the names of Hal and Winona, joint tenants with right of survivorship; purchased with $280,000 of consideration furnished solely by Winona; fair market value of $400,000.

- Household furnishings in the Topeka house; fair market value of $34,000. Winona owned almost all of these furnishings before she married Hal.

- Portfolio of publicly traded stocks in Hal's name; fair market value of $7.12 million.

- Mountain cabin and land in Vail, Colorado. Hal purchased the property in 1998 for $60,000; fair market value is $460,000. Hal never visits the cabin, but Halbert spends every summer and several weeks during the winter at the cabin.

- Stock (12 shares) in Harold's Hammocks, Inc. (a closely held C corporation) transferred to the Oz State Bank Revocable Trust in 1992; fair market value of $226,000, and basis of $15,000. Hal acquired the 12 shares in 1988 in a Sec. 351 transaction. Julianna and Gina own the remaining stock, 44 shares each, which Hal gifted to them in 2009.

- Individual retirement account at ToKan State Bank. The account consists of the funds rolled directly into the IRA from the non-contributory qualified retirement plan of Hal's former employer when Hal retired. Fair market value of the IRA is $540,000. Hal has not yet received any distributions. He is the IRA beneficiary, and Winona is the contingent beneficiary if Hal predeceases her.

- Cash of $825,000 in checking and savings accounts in Hal's name.

- Mutual fund shares in the names of Hal and Julianna, joint tenants with right of survivorship. Hal provided all the consideration ($9,000); fair market value of $64,000. He intended to use the money to finance Julianna's education, but she received a full scholarship.

- Stock in Dolrah, Inc. (a firm that elected S corporation status in 1990 upon its formation). The stock is in Hal's name, and he is one of six stockholders; fair market value of $79,000.

Hal's current will reads as follows:

> To my wife, Winona, I leave outright any household furnishings that I own, $500,000 of stock from my portfolio of publicly traded stocks, and all of my stock in Dolrah, Inc.
>
> To my grandchild, Halbert, Jr., I leave $5,750,000 of stock from my portfolio.
>
> I leave the rest of my estate outright in equal shares to my children, Gina, Halbert, and Julianna.

Required:
Prepare a memo to your supervising partner to help her prepare for the appointment with Hal. In the memo, advise the partner of any pitfalls (problems) you have identified that she should discuss with Hal. You need not make any calculations of estate tax liabilities.

C:13-65 Your client is Jon Jake, the executor of the Estate of Beth Adams, a widow. Mrs. Adams died 11 years after the death of her husband, Sam. Mr. Jake seeks assistance in the preparation of the estate tax return for Mrs. Adams, whose estate consists primarily of real estate. Mrs. Adams's estate will be divided among her three adult children except for $50,000 willed to charity. The real estate has been appraised at $6.8 million by her son-in-law (who is married to one of Mrs. Adams's three children), an experienced real estate appraiser. You have a number of real estate clients and have considerable familiarity with property values for real estate located in the same general area as the estate's property. Your "gut feeling" is that the appraised values may be somewhat understated. As a tax advisor, what responsibilities do you have to make additional inquiries? What information should you provide Mr. Jake concerning possible penalties?

TAX RESEARCH PROBLEMS

C:13-66   Arthur Zolnick died at age 84 on June 7, 2011. In March 2005, he transferred $4 million of stock to a charitable remainder annuity trust (CRAT) from which he named himself to receive $280,000 per year for life. He designated a charitable organization to receive the remainder interest after his death and appointed his nephew Luther as trustee. Luther never distributed cash to Arthur because Arthur indicated he had no need for additional funds that "would just add to my gross estate." At Arthur's date of death, the value of the assets in the CRAT had risen to $4.3 million. Another firm prepared the estate tax return, on which it claimed a charitable contribution deduction for the CRAT. The IRS proposed disallowing the deduction. Should a charitable contribution deduction be available?

C:13-67   In May 2005, Jasper Mason died, survived by his spouse Amber Mason and four adult children. His gross estate was valued at $3 million, and he had Sec. 2053 deductions of $120,000. His will left the personal residence on which the mortgage had been paid off to Amber. Its value was $450,000. The will stated that the rest of Jasper's property was to pass to a trust at Seaman's Bank with Amber to receive all the trust income semi-annually for life and the four children to receive the remainder in equal shares. Amber was the beneficiary of a $1 million life insurance policy included in Jasper's gross estate. The insurance policy was the only non-probate asset. Jasper made no post-1976 taxable gifts. A CPA with a small firm that does not specialize in taxation prepared the estate tax return for Jasper's estate and elected to claim the marital deduction for the trust. The firm with whom you are employed has been engaged to prepare the estate tax return for Amber, who died in May 2011. The Seaman's Bank trust has increased in value to $3 million as of Amber's date of death. Amber owned assets valued at $4 million in her own name. Your manager asks you to research whether the Seaman's Bank trust has to be included in Amber's gross estate. He is hoping that it does not because, even if the marital deduction had not been claimed for the trust, Jasper's estate still would not have owed any tax. Draft a memo to your manager reporting the results of your research. Confine your research to IRS pronouncements.

C:13-68   Gladys Green died March 4, 2009. Her will named Scott Spencer, a neighbor and a criminal court judge, as her executor. Spencer had no experience with being an executor and no expertise regarding taxation. He consulted with a partner (Omar Oake) in a prominent law firm for a recommendation about an attorney who could answer questions for him regarding Green's estate. Oake suggested Carl Cable, one of his partners. Relying on Oake's recommendation, Spencer engaged Cable to prepare Green's estate tax return. Spencer first reviewed Cable's resume and information about Cable posted on the law firm's web site. Spencer provided records to Cable and regularly "checked in" with Cable with respect to his progress on the return preparation. Cable assured Spencer that preparation was going smoothly and "on target." However, on December 3, 2009 Cable advised Spencer that he had encountered a problem in his research and could not complete the return by December 4, 2009. He volunteered that he, Cable, would request an additional extension of six months and that, even if the IRS denied the extension, he would have ten days after receipt of information of the denial to file a timely return. On February 27, 2009, Spencer submitted the return, which Cable had given him on the preceding day. In 2011, the IRS audited Green's estate tax return and assessed failure to file and failure to pay penalties against the estate on the grounds that the return was not filed timely and the tax not timely paid. Your manager has requested that you research whether Spencer should argue against imposition of the penalty on the grounds that he reasonably relied on the advice of a professional, Cable. Draft a memo with your conclusions.

C:13-69   Zan Zwang, a widower, died September 4, 2011, and was survived by his three adult children. On September 4, 2008, he gave each child stock valued at $2 million and paid gift tax with the return he filed in 2009. Exclusive of any gross-up, Zwang's gross estate is valued at $6.2 million. You are preparing Zwang's estate tax return, and your manager advises you that she seems to recollect reading a technical advice memo addressing when the three-year period begins in this context. Prepare a memo to your manager in which you address when the three-year period begins and, thus, whether Zwang's gross estate must include a gross-up for the taxes on the 2008 gift.

Internet Research Problem. You have been asked to make a presentation to a group of laypersons and explain which types of property do not pass under the decedent's will (that is, they pass outside probate). Consult the Internet address *http://wills.about.com* and enter the phrase non-probate property in the "search" box. Then select "What Are Non Probate Assets and Are They Included in Your Estate?" Prepare a presentation explaining several types of property that do not pass under the terms of the will; that is, they pass outside probate.

Internet Research Problem. Soon you will be meeting with a client who is considering moving to one of several other states and who does not currently have a will. You want to do some research regarding how property typically passes if the decedent dies intestate (without a will). The client plans to execute a will soon but makes the inquiry because of his busy schedule and tendency to procrastinate. The client is interested in just the typical rules until he decides to which state he will relocate. Consult the Internet address *http://www.suffolklaw.com.* On the left side, select "Legal News," then select "What Happens If You Die Without a Will?" Prepare a brief memo about what you learn.

14

C H A P T E R

INCOME TAXATION OF TRUSTS AND ESTATES

LEARNING OBJECTIVES

After studying this chapter, you should be able to

1. ▶ Understand the basic concepts concerning trusts and estates

2. ▶ Distinguish between the accounting concepts of principal and income

3. ▶ Calculate the tax liability of a trust or an estate

4. ▶ Understand the significance of distributable net income

5. ▶ Determine the taxable income of a simple trust

6. ▶ Determine the taxable income of a complex trust and an estate

7. ▶ Recognize the significance of income in respect of a decedent

8. ▶ Explain the effect of the grantor trust provisions

9. ▶ Recognize the filing requirements for fiduciary returns

Chapters C:12 and C:13 examined two components of the transfer tax system: the gift tax and the estate tax. This chapter returns to income taxation by exploring the basic rules for taxing trusts and estates, two special tax entities often called **fiduciaries**. Income generated by property owned by an estate or a **trust** is reported on an income tax return for that entity. In general, the tax rules governing estates and trusts are identical. Unless the text states that a rule applies to only one of these entities, the discussion concerns both estates and trusts. Subchapter J (Secs. 641-692) of the IRC contains the special tax rules applicable to estates and trusts, and this chapter describes its basic provisions.

This chapter also discusses principles of fiduciary accounting, a concept that influences the tax consequences. The chapter focuses on determining the fiduciary's taxable income and the amount taxable to the beneficiaries. It includes comprehensive examples concerning the computations of taxable income, and Appendix B displays completed tax returns (Form 1041) for both a simple and a complex trust. The chapter also explores the circumstances that cause the grantor (transferor) to be taxed on the trust's income.

BASIC CONCEPTS

INCEPTION OF TRUSTS

Often a relatively wealthy person (one concerned with gift and/or estate taxes) will create trusts for tax and/or other reasons (e.g., conserving assets). A person may create a trust at any point in time by transferring property to the trust. A **trustee** (named by the transferor) administers the trust property for the benefit of the beneficiary. The trustee may be either an individual or an institution, such as a bank, and there can be more than one trustee.

OBJECTIVE **1**

Understand the basic concepts concerning trusts and estates

If the transfer occurs during the transferor's lifetime, the trust is called an **inter vivos trust,** meaning among the living. The transferor is known as the **grantor** or the **trustor**. A trust created under the direction of a decedent's will is called a **testamentary trust** and contains assets formerly held by the decedent's estate. A trust may continue to exist for whatever time the trust instrument or the will specifies subject to the constraints of the **Rule Against Perpetuities.**[1]

INCEPTION OF ESTATES

ADDITIONAL COMMENT

The IRS projects that 4.1 million fiduciary income tax returns will be filed in 2011.

Estates originate only upon the death of the person whose assets are being administered. The estate continues in existence until the executor[2] (i.e., the person(s) named in the will to manage the property and distribute the assets) or administrator (where the decedent died without a will) completes his or her duties. An executor's or administrator's duties include collecting the assets, paying the debts and taxes, and distributing the property. The time needed to perform the duties may vary from a year or two to over a decade, depending on many factors (e.g., whether anyone contests the will).

Because the estate is a separate tax entity, continuing the estate's existence results in an additional personal exemption and achieves having some income taxed to yet another taxpayer, but the estate's income tax rates are very compressed. Nevertheless, the decedent's survivors sometimes can reduce their personal income taxes by preserving the estate's existence as a separate taxpayer. Treasury Regulations provide, however, that if the IRS considers that the administration of an estate has been unreasonably prolonged, it will view the estate as having been terminated for federal tax purposes after a reasonable period for performance of the administrative duties has expired.[3] In such a situation, the income is taxed directly to the individuals entitled to receive the estate's assets, and sometimes these individuals have a higher marginal tax rate than does the estate.

---

[1] The Rule Against Perpetuities addresses how long property may be tied up in trust and is the "principle that no interest in property is good unless it must vest, if at all, not later than 21 years, plus period of gestation, after some life or lives in being at time of creation of interest." Henry Campbell Black, *Black's Law Dictionary,* Rev. 6th ed., Ed. by Joseph R. Nolan and Jacqueline

M. Nolan-Haley (St. Paul, MN: West Publishing Co., 1990), p. 1331. Some states have abolished the Rule Against Perpetuities.
[2] In some states, this individual is called a personal representative.
[3] Reg. Sec. 1.641(b)-3(a).

REASONS FOR CREATING TRUSTS

A myriad of reasons—both tax and nontax—exist for creating trusts. A discussion of some of these reasons follows.

KEY POINT

A trust is a contract between two parties: the grantor and the trustee. The grantor gives the trustee legal title to property, which the trustee holds for the benefit of a third party(ies), the beneficiary(ies). The trustee, acting in a fiduciary capacity, manages the property for the duration of the trust. Beneficiaries of a trust may have an income interest, which means that they receive part or all of the trust's income, or they may have a remainder interest, which means that they will receive the property held by the trust on some specified future date. A beneficiary may hold both an income interest and a remainder interest. The grantor may be a beneficiary and/or the trustee.

TAX SAVING ASPECTS OF TRUSTS. If the trust is irrevocable, meaning the grantor cannot require the trustee to return the assets, one of the primary tax purposes for establishing the trust traditionally was to achieve income splitting. Historically, with income splitting, the income from the trust assets was taxed to at least one taxpayer (i.e., the trust or the beneficiary) at a lower marginal tax rate than that of the grantor. Today's compressed fiduciary tax rate schedules, under which the top rate of 35% (in 2011) occurs at an income level above $11,350, often make achieving income tax reduction difficult. Sometimes the trust instrument authorizes the trustee to use his or her discretion in "sprinkling" the income among several beneficiaries or accumulating it within the trust. In such circumstances, the trustee may consider the tax effects of making a distribution of income to one beneficiary rather than to another or retaining income in the trust.

Individuals also have created trusts to minimize their estate taxes. As discussed in Chapter C:13, for the transferor to exclude the property conveyed to the trust from the gross estate, the transferor must not retain the right to receive the trust income or the power to control which other people receive the income or have, at the time of death, the power to alter the identity of anyone named earlier to receive such assets.[4]

NONTAX ASPECTS OF TRUSTS. Reduction of taxes is not always the foremost reason for establishing trusts. Individuals often use trusts, including Sec. 2503(c) trusts and *Crummey* trusts, when minors are the donees so that a trustee can manage the assets. (See Chapter C:12 for a discussion of such trusts.) Even when the donee is an adult, donors sometimes may prefer that the assets be managed by a trustee deemed to have better management skills than the donee. Other donors may want to avoid conveying property directly to a donee if they fear the donee would soon consume most of the assets. In addition, donors sometimes use trusts to protect assets from creditors.

The creation of a **revocable trust** (i.e., one in which the grantor may demand that the assets be returned) does not yield any income or estate tax savings for the grantor. Nevertheless, donors often establish revocable trusts, including ones in which the grantor is also the beneficiary, for nontax purposes such as having the property managed by another person or an institution with superior management skills. Use of a revocable trust reduces probate costs because assets in a revocable trust avoid probate. Such a strategy is especially important in states where probate costs are high. In this text, a trust is deemed to be an **irrevocable trust** unless explicitly denoted as being revocable.

BASIC PRINCIPLES OF FIDUCIARY TAXATION

Throughout the rest of this chapter, you should keep several basic principles of **fiduciary taxation** in mind. These features (discussed below) apply to all trusts other than grantor trusts, a type of trust where generally the grantor instead of the trust or the beneficiary pays tax on the income. (See pages C:14-30 through C:14-33 for a description of the tax treatment of grantor trusts.)

TRUSTS AND ESTATES AS SEPARATE TAXPAYERS. An estate or a trust is a separate taxpaying entity that files a Form 1041, and if it has any taxable income, it pays an income tax. The 2011 tax rates applicable to estates and trusts appear on the inside back cover. These rates, which are indexed annually for inflation, are very compressed in comparison with the rates for individuals. As is true for individuals, an estate's or trust's long-term capital gains and qualified dividends are taxed at a top tax rate of 15% (through 2012).

---

[4] Sec. 2036, relating to retention of income or control, and Sec. 2038, relating to the power to alter the identity of beneficiaries.

EXAMPLE C:14-1 ▶ For calendar year 2011, a trust reports taxable income of $15,000, none from dividends or long-term capital gains. Its tax liability is $4,215. In contrast, an unmarried individual not qualifying as a head of household would owe taxes of $1,825 on $15,000 of taxable income. ◀

NO DOUBLE TAXATION. Unlike the situation for corporations, no double taxation of income earned by an estate or trust (a fiduciary taxpayer) occurs because an estate or trust receives a deduction for the income it distributes to its beneficiaries. The beneficiaries, in turn, report the taxable portion of their receipts as income on their individual returns. Thus, the current income is taxed once, to the fiduciary or to the beneficiary or some to each, depending on how much is distributed. In total, all the estate or trust's current income is taxed, sometimes some to the fiduciary and the remaining amount to the beneficiary. One of the primary purposes of the Subchapter J rules is to address exactly where the estate or trust's current income is taxed.

EXAMPLE C:14-2 ▶ In the current year, the Lopez Trust receives corporate bond interest of $25,000, $15,000 of which the trustee in its discretion distributes to Lupe. Lupe is taxed on $15,000, the amount of the distribution. The trust is taxed on the income it retains or accumulates, $10,000 in this case, less a $100 personal exemption (discussed on pages C:14-9 and C:14-10). ◀

CONDUIT APPROACH. A conduit approach governs fiduciary income taxation. Under this approach, the distributed income has the same character in the hands of the beneficiary as it has to the trust. Thus, if the trust distributes nontaxable interest income on state and local bonds, such income retains its tax-free character at the beneficiary level.

EXAMPLE C:14-3 ▶ In the current year, the Lopez Trust receives $15,000 of dividends and $10,000 of nontaxable interest. It distributes all of its receipts to its beneficiary, who is deemed to receive $15,000 of dividend income and $10,000 of nontaxable interest. The 15% tax rate applies to the dividends assuming the beneficiary's tax bracket equals or exceeds 15%. ◀

SELF-STUDY QUESTION

King Trust receives interest on a savings account and distributes it to Anne. Because the trust is treated as a conduit, the interest is reported by Anne as taxable interest. Why might this be important?

ANSWER

For purposes of the limitation on the investment interest deduction, the interest from the trust is part of Anne's investment income. For purposes of the passive loss limitations, it is classified as portfolio income.

SIMILARITY TO RULES FOR INDIVIDUALS. Section 641(b) states "[T]he taxable income of an estate or trust shall be computed in the same manner as in the case of an individual, except as otherwise provided in this part." Sections 641-683 appear in this part (Part I) of Subchapter J. Thus, the tax effect for fiduciaries is the same as for individuals if the provisions of Secs. 641-683 do not specify rules that differ from those applicable for individual taxpayers. Sections 641-683 do not provide any special treatment for interest income from state and local bonds or for state and local tax payments. Consequently, an estate or trust receives an exclusion for state and local bond interest and the same deductions as individuals for state and local taxes. On the other hand, Sec. 642(b) specifies the amount of the personal exemption for fiduciaries. Thus, this subsection preempts the Sec. 151 rule concerning the amount of the personal exemption for individuals.

PRINCIPLES OF FIDUCIARY ACCOUNTING

OBJECTIVE 2

Distinguish between the accounting concepts of principal and income

To better understand the special tax treatment of fiduciary income, especially the determination of to whom the estate or trust's current income is taxed, one needs a general knowledge of the principles of fiduciary accounting. In a sense, fiduciary accounting is similar to fund accounting for government entities. Instead of having separate funds, however, receipts and disbursements are classified in either the income or principal (corpus) account.

THE IMPORTANCE OF IDENTIFYING INCOME AND PRINCIPAL

When computing taxable income, we generally are concerned with whether a particular item is included in or deducted from gross income. When answering fiduciary tax questions, however, we also need to consider whether an item is classified as principal (corpus) or income for fiduciary accounting purposes. For example, certain items (e.g., interest on state bonds) may constitute fiduciary accounting gross income but are not included in calculating gross income for tax purposes. Other items (e.g., capital gains) may be included in gross income but classified as principal for fiduciary accounting purposes. If the trust instrument stipulates that the trustee can distribute only income prior to the termination of the trust, the amount of fiduciary accounting income sets the ceiling on the current distribution that the trustee can make to a beneficiary.

One of the most difficult aspects of feeling comfortable with the fiduciary taxation rules is appreciating the difference between fiduciary accounting income and income in the general tax sense. To understand and apply the IRC, one has to know in which context the word *income* is used. Section 643(b) provides guidance for this matter by providing that the word *income* refers to income in the fiduciary accounting context unless other words, such as "distributable net," "undistributable net," "taxable," or "gross," modify the word *income*. In this text, the term **net accounting income** is used to refer to the excess of accounting gross income over expenses charged to accounting income.

Under state law, the definitions in the trust instrument that classify items as principal or income preempt any definitions contained in state statutes. In the absence of definitions in the trust instrument, the applicable state statute controls. For purposes of defining principal and income, many states follow the Revised Uniform Principal and Income Act (enacted in 1962 and hereafter referred to as the Uniform Act of 1962) in its entirety or with minor modifications.[5] However, a number of states have adopted the Uniform Principal and Income Act (1997), which is more flexible.

The 1997 Act allows the trustee to make adjustments between the principal and income accounts to the extent the trustee deems them necessary (such as to increase the amount distributable), provided certain additional requirements are met. A trustee, however, will not always deem adjustments necessary. The rationale behind allowing adjustments is grounded in modern portfolio theory. By allowing trustees to transfer cash from principal to income, the 1997 Act enables a trustee to apply prudent investor standards when making investment decisions. If dividends are low because of growth stock investments, the trustee can transfer some cash to the income account, thereby increasing the amount distributable to a beneficiary entitled to receive only income.

The categorization of a receipt or disbursement as principal or income generally affects the amount that can be distributed and the amount taxed to the fiduciary or the beneficiary. For example, if a gain is classified as principal and the trustee can distribute only income, the trust is taxed on the gain. A trustee cannot distribute a receipt that constitutes gross income for tax purposes if it constitutes principal under the fiduciary accounting rules unless the trust instrument authorizes the trustee to distribute principal or unless, under the 1997 Act, the trustee makes adjustments by transferring some cash from principal to income.

SELF-STUDY QUESTION

A trust agreement provides that all trust income is to be distributed to Janet until her thirty-fifth birthday, at which time the trust is to terminate and distribute all of its corpus to Joe. Stock is the only property owned by the trust. If the trust sells the stock, is Janet entitled to a distribution equal to the gain?

ANSWER

This question stresses the importance of differentiating between income and principal. The trustee must follow the definitions of income and corpus stated in the trust agreement, or if not there, under state law. Janet receives no distribution if the proceeds are classified as corpus unless the trustee under the 1997 Act makes an adjustment and moves money from corpus to income.

EXAMPLE C:14-4 ▶

In the current year, the Bell Trust collects $18,000 of dividends, classified as accounting income. In addition, it sells stock for a $40,000 capital gain. Under state law, which is based on the Uniform Act of 1962 (discussed below), the gain is allocated to principal. The trust instrument (which does not define principal or income) requires the trustee to distribute all the trust's income to Beth annually until she reaches age 45. The trust assets are to be held and paid to Beth on her forty-fifth birthday (five years from now). The trustee must distribute $18,000 to Beth in the current year. The capital gain cannot be distributed currently because it is allocated to principal, and the trustee is not empowered to make distributions of principal. The trust will pay tax on the gain. ◀

PRINCIPAL AND INCOME: THE UNIFORM ACT

INCOME RECEIPTS. The Uniform Act of 1962 defines *income* as "the return in money or property derived from the use of principal." It lists income as including the following: rent, interest, corporate distributions of dividends, distributions by a regulated investment company from ordinary income, and the net profits of a business. The rules are more

---

[5] The *Revised Uniform Principal and Income Act* (1962) is a model set of rules proposed by the National Conference of Commissioners on Uniform State Laws. States can voluntarily adopt such provisions verbatim or in amended form.

detailed for receipts from the disposition of natural resources. A portion (27.5%) of the receipts from royalties is added to principal as a depletion allowance. The remainder of the royalties constitutes income. The 1997 Act provides different rules for allocating of royalty receipts.

ADDITIONAL COMMENT

The Commissioners approved and recommended for enactment the *Uniform Principal and Income Act* (1997). A number of states have adopted the 1997 Act, which differs in many ways from the 1962 Act.

PRINCIPAL RECEIPTS. *Principal* is defined in the Uniform Act of 1962 as "the property which has been set aside by the owner or the person legally empowered so that it is held in trust eventually to be delivered to the **remainderman** while the return or use of the principal is in the meantime taken or received by or held for accumulation for an **income beneficiary**." Among the categories of receipts included in principal are the following: consideration received on the sale or other transfer of principal or on repayment of a loan, stock dividends, receipts from disposition of corporate securities, and 27.5% of royalties received from natural resources.

EXPENDITURES. The Uniform Act of 1962 provides guidance for expenditures also. Among the important charges that reduce income are the following:

► Ordinary expenses, including regularly recurring property taxes, insurance premiums, interest, and ordinary repairs

► A reasonable allowance for depreciation

► Tax payable by the trustee if it is levied on receipts classified as income

Some of the significant expenditures chargeable to principal are

► Principal payments on debts

► Extraordinary repairs or expenses incurred in making a capital improvement

► Any tax levied on gain or other receipts allocated to principal even if the tax is described as an income tax

Frequently, the agreement between the grantor and the trustee specifies the respective portions of the trustee's fee that are chargeable to income and corpus.

EXAMPLE C:14-5 ►

SELF-STUDY QUESTION

Wilson Trust, which owns a commercial building, is required to distribute all of its income each year. The building is leased to a tenant on a net lease, so the trust's only expense is depreciation. The rental income is $25,000, and the depreciation is $11,000. If depreciation is chargeable to income, the distribution to the income beneficiary will be $14,000, and the trustee will set aside $11,000 of the income for the remainderman. What is the impact if depreciation is chargeable to principal?

ANSWER

The income distribution will be $25,000. If the trust holds the building to the end of its useful life, the building will theoretically "turn to dust" overnight, and the remainderman would receive nothing (as far as the building is concerned) because the trust had no depreciation reserve.

The governing instrument for the Wang Trust does not define income and principal. The state in question has adopted the Uniform Act of 1962. In the current year, the trust reports the following receipts and disbursements:

Dividends	$12,000
Proceeds from sale of stock, including $20,000 of gain	70,000
Trustee's fee, all charged to income	1,000
CPA's fee for preparation of tax return	500

The trust's net accounting income is $10,500 ($12,000 − $1,000 − $500). The gain on the sale of stock and the remaining sales proceeds constitute corpus. Consequently, if the trustee can distribute nothing but income, the maximum distribution is $10,500. ◄

CATEGORIZATION OF DEPRECIATION

As mentioned above, the Uniform Act of 1962 charges depreciation to income. Depreciation thereby reduces net accounting income and the maximum amount that can be distributed to a beneficiary if the trust instrument does not authorize the distribution of corpus. Many states have departed from the Uniform Act's treatment of depreciation by providing that depreciation is a charge against principal (instead of against income). If depreciation is charged against principal, the maximum amount that can be distributed to the income beneficiaries is not reduced by the depreciation deduction. This result is advantageous to the income beneficiary. (See page C:14-9 for a discussion of the tax treatment of depreciation.)

Some trust instruments require the trustee to set aside (and not distribute) a certain amount of income as a depreciation reserve. A statement in the trust instrument concerning the accounting treatment for depreciation overrides a provision of state law.

EXAMPLE C:14-6 ►

Park Trust, whose trust instrument is silent with respect to depreciation, collects rental income of $17,000 and pays property taxes of $1,000. Its depreciation expense is $4,000. Under state law, all depreciation is charged to principal. Therefore, the trust's net accounting income is $16,000 ($17,000 − $1,000). If the trust instrument mandates current distribution of all the income, the beneficiary receives $16,000. If the trust instrument states that depreciation is charged against income, the income distribution is limited to $12,000. ◄

Topic Review C:14-1 summarizes the treatment under the Uniform Act of 1962 of the major receipts and expenditures of fiduciaries. The discussion in the rest of the chapter assumes the Uniform Act of 1962 governs the trust or that, if the 1997 Act applies, the trustee makes no adjustments from principal to income.

FORMULA FOR TAXABLE INCOME AND TAX LIABILITY

OBJECTIVE 3

Calculate the tax liability of a trust or an estate

With three major exceptions, the formula for determining a fiduciary's taxable income and income tax liability is very similar to the formula applicable to individuals. A fiduciary's deductions are not divided between deductions *for* and *from* adjusted gross income (AGI). Instead, a fiduciary's deductions are simply deductible in arriving at taxable income. A fiduciary receives no standard deduction. A type of deduction unique to fiduciaries—the distribution deduction—is available in computing a fiduciary's taxable income. Figure C:14-1 illustrates the formula for computing a fiduciary's taxable income and tax liability.

GROSS INCOME

The items included in a trust or estate's gross income are the same as those included in an individual's gross income. However, the categorization of a fiduciary's income is not identical for tax and accounting purposes. For example, a gain usually constitutes principal for accounting purposes, but it is part of gross income for tax purposes.

EXAMPLE C:14-7 ▶ In the current year, Duke Trust receives $8,000 interest on corporate bonds, $20,000 interest on state bonds, and a $50,000 capital gain. The trust reports gross income of $58,000 ($8,000 + $50,000). Its accounting income is $28,000 ($8,000 + $20,000) because tax-exempt interest is accounting income, and the gain is part of principal. ◀

DEDUCTIONS FOR EXPENSES

Fiduciaries incur numerous deductible expenses that parallel those of individuals and include interest, taxes (e.g., state and local income taxes and property taxes), fees for tax return preparation, expenses associated with producing rental income, and trade or business expenses. In addition, fiduciaries may deduct some or all of the trustee's fee under Sec. 212 as an expense incurred for the management of property held for the production of income.

Topic Review C:14-1

Classification of Receipts and Expenditures as Principal or Income Under the Uniform Act of 1962

INCOME ACCOUNT	PRINCIPAL ACCOUNT

Income:
  Rent
  Interest
  Dividends
  Net profits of a business
  72.5% of royalties[a]
	Receipts:
	  Consideration (including gains) received upon
	    disposition of property
	  Stock dividends
	  27.5% of royalties[a]

Expenses:
  Ordinary expenses (e.g., property taxes,
    insurance, interest, and ordinary repairs)
  Taxes levied on accounting income
  Depreciation[b]
	Expenditures:
	  Principal payments on debt
	  Extraordinary repairs and capital improvements
	  Taxes levied on gains and other items of principal

[a]The Uniform Principal and Income Act (1997) provides a different allocation.
[b]Many state laws depart from the Uniform Act and characterize depreciation as a charge to principal.

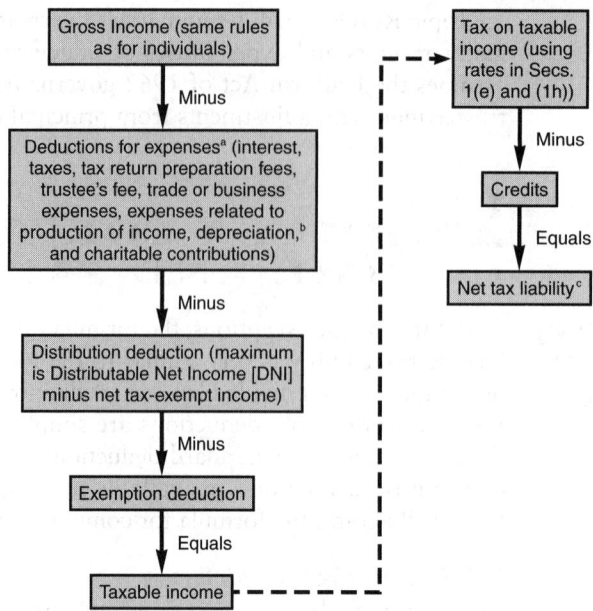

ᵃ No deduction is available for expenses allocable to tax-exempt income.

ᵇ When the trust instrument is silent, depreciation is allocated for tax purposes between the fiduciary and the beneficiary according to the portion of income attributable to each.

ᶜ Trusts and estates are subject to the alternative minimum tax (AMT). The AMT may be owed by a trust or estate in addition to the income tax levy described in this figure. The AMT is calculated in the same way as for individual taxpayers. Trusts and estates, however, are allowed only a $22,500 statutory exemption. This exemption is phased-out from $75,000 to $165,000 of alternative minimum taxable income.

FIGURE C:14-1 ▶ FORMULA FOR DETERMINING THE TAXABLE INCOME AND TAX LIABILITY OF A FIDUCIARY

For individuals, miscellaneous itemized deductions are deductible only to the extent the aggregate amount of such deductions exceeds 2% of the taxpayer's AGI. Estates and trusts do not literally have AGI, but Sec. 67(e) provides that a hypothetical AGI amount for an estate or trust is determined in the same fashion as for an individual *except* that (1) expenses paid or incurred in connection with the administration of the estate or trust *that would not have been incurred if the property were not held in such trust or estate,* (2) the personal exemption, and (3) the distribution deduction are treated as deductible for hypothetical AGI. Thus, these deductions are not subject to the 2% floor, and by being subtracted to arrive at hypothetical AGI, they reduce the amount of disallowed miscellaneous deductions. The cost of preparing of a fiduciary return, for example, would have been avoided if the trust or estate had not existed and therefore is excepted from the 2% floor.[6] In recent years, controversy arose about whether investment counsel fees paid by trusts were subject to the 2% of AGI floor. In 2008, the Supreme Court resolved the issue in *Knight*[7] and concluded that, to escape the 2% rule, the costs must be "uncommon, unusual, or unlikely" for a hypothetical individual to incur. It emphasized that individuals commonly engage the services of investment advisers and concluded that the fees in question were subject to the 2% floor. The IRS issued guidance for tax years beginning before 2010 by stating that it would allow bundled trustee's fees (fees where the billing does not provide detailed amounts of specific fees for each of several services performed) to be fully deductible even if some of the fee was for services normally subject to the 2% floor if paid to an investment advisory firm.[8] The IRS has not provided additional guidance for later years. In this chapter, we assume that all trustee fees are exempt from classification as a miscellaneous itemized deduction.

[6] 71 AFTR 2d 93-2052, 93-1 USTC ¶50,332 (6th Cir., 1993), reversing 98 T.C. 227 (1992), nonacq., I.R.B. 1994-38, 4.

[7] *Knight vs. Comm.*, 101 AFTR 2d 2008-544, 2008-1 USTC ¶50,332 (USSC, 2008). Prior to the Supreme Court's decision, the Treasury Department issued Prop. Reg. 1.67-4, which adopted a harsher position than that of the Supreme Court. It provided that miscellaneous expenses incurred by estates and trusts need to be expenses *unique* to estates and trusts to avoid the 2% floor rule. To date, the Treasury Department has not issued revised proposed regulations as a result of the *Knight* case.

[8] Notice 2010-32, 2010-16 I.R.B. 594.

An executor can deduct administration expenses on the estate's income tax return if he or she does not deduct such items on the estate tax return. Unlike the situation for individuals, a fiduciary's charitable contribution deduction is not limited. The IRC does not allow a deduction, however, unless the trust instrument authorizes a charitable contribution.[9]

A depreciation or depletion deduction is available to an estate or trust only to the extent it is not allowable to beneficiaries under Secs. 167(d) or 611(b).[10] According to Sec. 167(d), the depreciation deduction for trusts is apportioned between the income beneficiaries and the trust pursuant to the terms of the trust instrument. If the instrument is silent, the depreciation is divided between the parties on the basis of the trust income allocable to each. For estates, however, the depreciation always must be apportioned according to the share of the income allocable to each party. The Sec. 611(b) rules for depletion parallel those described above for the allocation of depreciation.

EXAMPLE C:14-8 ▶ In the current year, Nunn Trust distributes 20% of its income to Bob and 50% to Clay. It accumulates the remaining 30%. The trust's current year depreciation is $10,000. The trust instrument is silent concerning the depreciation deduction, and state law, which charges depreciation to principal, controls. Even though net accounting income and the maximum distributable amount are not reduced by the depreciation deduction, Bob receives a $2,000 (0.20 × $10,000) depreciation deduction, and Clay receives a $5,000 (0.50 × $10,000) depreciation deduction. The remaining $3,000 (0.30 × $10,000) of depreciation is deducted in calculating the trust's taxable income. ◀

DISTRIBUTION DEDUCTION

SIMPLE TRUSTS. Some trusts must distribute all their income currently and are not empowered to make charitable contributions. Treasury Regulations refer to such trusts as **simple trusts**.[11] According to Sec. 651(a), these trusts receive a distribution deduction for the income required to be distributed currently, that is, 100% of the trust income. No words modify the word *income*; therefore, *income* means accounting income. If the accounting income that must be distributed exceeds the trust's distributable net income, the distribution deduction may not exceed the distributable net income (see discussion beginning on page C:14-10). As used in this context, distributable net income does not include any tax-free income (net of related deductions) that the trust earned.[12] Whatever amount is deductible at the trust level is taxed to the beneficiaries, and they are taxed on all the income, irrespective of the amount they receive.

KEY POINT

If a trust *must* distribute all of its income currently, has no charitable beneficiary, *and* does *not* distribute corpus during the year, it is a simple trust for that year. *Income,* as used here, is accounting net income.

COMPLEX TRUSTS. Trusts that are not required to distribute all their income currently are referred to as **complex trusts**.[13] The distribution deduction for complex trusts and all estates is the sum of the income required to be distributed currently and any other amounts (such as discretionary payments) properly paid, credited, or required to be distributed for the year. As is the case for simple trusts, the distribution deduction may not exceed the trust or estate's distributable net income (reduced by its tax-exempt income net of any related deductions).[14] The complex trust or estate's beneficiaries report, in the aggregate, gross income equal to the amount of the distribution deduction.[15]

EXAMPLE C:14-9 ▶ Green Trust must distribute 25% of its income annually to Amy. In addition, the trustee in its discretion may distribute additional income to Amy or Brad. In the current year, the trust has net accounting income and distributable net income of $100,000, none from tax-exempt sources. The trust makes a $25,000 mandatory distribution to Amy and discretionary distributions of $10,000 each to Amy and Brad. The trust's distribution deduction is $45,000 ($25,000 + $10,000 + $10,000). Amy and Brad report trust income of $35,000 and $10,000, respectively, on their individual returns. ◀

PERSONAL EXEMPTION

One of the differences between the rules for individuals and for fiduciaries is the amount of the personal exemption. Under Sec. 151, individuals are allowed personal exemptions. Section 642(b) authorizes an exemption for fiduciaries that applies in lieu of the amount for individuals. A trust or estate, however, receives no exemption in the year of its termination.

[9] Sec. 642(c)(1).
[10] Sec. 642(e).
[11] Reg. Sec. 1.651(a)-1.
[12] Sec. 651(b).
[13] Reg. Sec. 1.661(a)-1.
[14] Secs. 661(a) and (c).
[15] Sec. 662(a).

Estates are entitled to a $600 exemption. The exemption amount for trusts differs, depending on the terms of the trust. If the trust instrument requires that the trustee distribute all the income annually, the trust receives a $300 exemption. Otherwise, $100 is the exemption amount. Some trusts may be required to make current distributions of all their income in certain years, whereas in other years they may be directed to accumulate the income or to make distributions at the trustee's discretion. For such trusts the exemption amount is $300 in some years and $100 in other years.

EXAMPLE C:14-10 ▶

Marion Gold establishes a trust in 2011 with Jack Silver as the beneficiary. The trust instrument instructs the trustee to make discretionary distributions of income to Jack during the years 2011 through 2015. Beginning in 2016, the trustee is to pay all the trust income to Jack currently. For 2011 through 2015, the trust's exemption is $100. Beginning in 2016, it rises to $300. ◀

Recall that a trust receives a distribution deduction for income currently distributed to its beneficiaries. At first blush, it appears that the distribution deduction balances out the income of trusts that must distribute all their income currently, and such trusts receive no tax benefits from their exemption deduction. True, the exemption produces no tax savings for such trusts if they have no gains credited to principal. Tax savings do result from the personal exemption, however, if the trust has undistributed gains. The exemption reduces the amount of gain otherwise taxed at the trust level.

EXAMPLE C:14-11 ▶

Rizzo Trust must distribute all of its income currently. Capital gains are characterized as principal. In the current year, Rizzo Trust has $25,000 of interest income from corporate bonds and a $10,000 capital gain. It has no expenses. It receives a distribution deduction of $25,000 and a $300 personal exemption. Its taxable income is $9,700 ($25,000 + $10,000 − $25,000 − $300), which represents the capital gain less the personal exemption. ◀

SELF-STUDY QUESTION

A trust, although not required to do so, distributes all of its income for the year. In the same year, it has a long-term capital gain. The trust agreement allocates the gain to principal. The trust does not distribute corpus, and none of its beneficiaries are charities. Is the trust a simple trust? What is its personal exemption?

ANSWER

It is a complex trust because it is not required to distribute all of its income. The exemption is $100 because distributions are discretionary.

The personal exemption amount for individuals is adjusted annually for changes in the consumer price index, but no comparable provision exists for the personal exemption for fiduciaries. On the other hand, the tax rate schedules for both fiduciaries and individuals are indexed for inflation.

CREDITS

In general, the rules for tax credits for fiduciaries are the same as those for individuals, but a fiduciary generally does not incur expenditures of the type that trigger some of the personal credits, such as the credit for household and dependent care expenses. Trusts and estates are allowed a foreign tax credit determined in the same manner as for individual taxpayers except that the credit is limited to the amount of foreign taxes not allocable to the beneficiaries.[16]

U.S. PRODUCTION ACTIVITIES DEDUCTION

The 2004 Jobs Act added a new deduction for businesses engaged in U.S. production activities for tax years beginning after 2004. Chapter C:3 describes the corporate version of this deduction, but the deduction also applies to individuals. Upon the death of a sole proprietor, his or her business passes to an estate or trust. To the extent income is distributed from the estate or trust, the U.S. production activities deduction applies at the beneficiary level. Thus, the estate or trust will need to determine each beneficiary's share of the business's qualified production activities income and report these amounts to the beneficiaries. Further discussion of this topic with respect to estates and trusts is beyond the scope of this text.

DISTRIBUTABLE NET INCOME

OBJECTIVE 4

Understand the significance of distributable net income

As stated earlier in this chapter, the primary function of Subchapter J is to determine to whom—the fiduciary, the beneficiary, or some to each—the estate or the trust's current income is to be taxed. **Distributable net income (DNI)** plays a key role in determining the amount taxed to each party. In fact, DNI has been called the pie to be cut for tax purposes.[17]

---

[16] Sec. 642(a)(1).
[17] M. Carr Ferguson, James L. Freeland, and Richard B. Stephens, *Federal Income Taxation of Estates and Beneficiaries* (Boston, MA: Little, Brown, 1970), p. 1x.

SIGNIFICANCE OF DNI

DNI sets the ceiling on the amount of distributions taxed to the beneficiaries. As mentioned earlier, beneficiaries are taxed on the lesser of the amount of the distributions they receive or their share of DNI (reduced by net tax-exempt income).

Just as the total amount taxed to the beneficiaries equals the fiduciary's distribution deduction, DNI represents not only the maximum that can be taxed to the beneficiaries but also the maximum that can be deducted at the fiduciary level. Recall from the preceding section that the distribution deduction is the smaller of the amount distributed or the fiduciary's DNI. The distribution deduction, however, may not include any portion of tax-exempt income (net of any related deductions) deemed to have been distributed.

DNI also determines the character of the beneficiaries' income. Under the conduit approach, each beneficiary's distribution is deemed to consist of various categories of income (net of deductions) in the same proportion as the total of each class of income bears to the total DNI. For example, if 40% of the trust's income consists of dividends, 40% of each beneficiary's distribution is deemed to consist of dividends.

EXAMPLE C:14-12▶

Southern Trust has $30,000 of DNI for the current year. Its DNI includes $10,000 of rental income and $20,000 of corporate bond interest. The trust instrument requires that each year the trustee distribute 30% of the trust's income to Jose and 70% to Petra. Because the trust has no tax-exempt income and must distribute all of its income, it receives a $30,000 distribution deduction.

Jose reports $9,000 (0.30 × $30,000) of trust income, and Petra reports $21,000 (0.70 × $30,000) of trust income. Because rents make up one-third ($10,000 ÷ $30,000) of DNI, the composition of the income reported by Jose and Petra is one-third rental income and two-thirds corporate bond interest. ◀

SELF-STUDY QUESTION

What functions does distributable net income (DNI) serve?

ANSWER

1. It establishes the maximum amount on which the beneficiaries may be taxed.
2. It establishes the maximum amount the trust or estate may deduct as a distribution deduction.
3. It establishes the character of the income or expense in DNI that flows to the beneficiaries (income or expense flows to the beneficiaries in proportion to the part each different type of income or expense bears to DNI).

DEFINITION OF DNI

Section 643(a) defines *DNI* as the fiduciary's taxable income, adjusted as follows:

▶ No distribution deduction is subtracted.

▶ No personal exemption is subtracted.

▶ Capital gains are not included and capital losses are not subtracted unless such gains and losses are allocated to accounting income instead of to principal.

▶ Extraordinary dividends and taxable stock dividends are not included if they are allocable to principal.

▶ An addition is made for tax-exempt interest (minus the expenses allocable thereto).

Because one purpose of DNI is to set a ceiling on the distribution deduction, the distribution deduction is not subtracted from taxable income in determining DNI. If capital gains and extraordinary dividends are allocated to corpus, they are excluded from DNI because they cannot be distributed. Tax-exempt interest is part of accounting income and can be distributed even though it is excluded from gross income. Consequently, DNI includes tax-exempt income (net of the nondeductible expenses allocable to such income). Even though net tax-exempt income is included in DNI, no distribution deduction is available for the portion of the distribution deemed to consist of tax-exempt income.

Aside from complicated scenarios, net accounting income and DNI are the same, with one other exception. Any expenses (e.g., trustee's fees) charged to principal reduce DNI even though they do not lessen net accounting income. The trustee's fees (whether charged to income or to principal) are deductible in arriving at taxable income, and no adjustment is made to taxable income for such expenses when calculating DNI. Reducing DNI by the expenses charged to principal provides a tax advantage for the income beneficiary because these fees lessen the amount taxable to the beneficiary. However, such fees do not decrease the money that can be distributed to the beneficiary.

KEY POINT

A significant difference between net accounting income and DNI is that DNI is reduced by certain expenses charged to principal. These expenses do not decrease net accounting income, nor do they decrease the amount of money that can be distributed.

MANNER OF COMPUTING DNI

The amount of taxable income is in large measure a function of the distribution deduction, and the distribution deduction depends on the amount of DNI. The distribution deduction cannot exceed DNI. Thus, the Sec. 643(a) definition of DNI, which involves making adjustments to a fiduciary's taxable income, is not a workable definition from a practical standpoint because the computation is circular. The distribution deduction must be computed to arrive at the amount of income taxable to the fiduciary, and the distribution deduction depends, in part, on the amount of DNI.

However, there are two practical means of determining DNI. The first approach, as illustrated below, begins with taxable income exclusive of the distribution deduction and makes the adjustments (other than the distribution deduction) to taxable income that the IRC specifies.

EXAMPLE C:14-13▶ In the current year, Darby Trust reports the following results. The trust must distribute all of its income annually.

	Amounts Allocable to	
	Income	*Principal*
Corporate bond interest	$20,000	
Rental income	30,000	
Gain on sale of investment land		$40,000
Property taxes	5,000	
Trustee's fee charged to corpus		2,000
Distribution to beneficiary	45,000	

The trust's taxable income exclusive of the distribution deduction is computed as follows:

Corporate bond interest	$20,000
Rental income	30,000
Capital gain	40,000
Minus: Property taxes	(5,000)
Trustee's fee	(2,000)
Personal exemption	(300)
Taxable income exclusive of distribution deduction	$82,700

Now that taxable income exclusive of the distribution deduction has been determined, DNI can be computed in the following manner:

Taxable income exclusive of distribution deduction	$82,700
Plus: Personal exemption	300
Minus: Capital gain	(40,000)
DNI	$43,000 ◀

A second method that often can be used to determine DNI is to calculate net accounting income and reduce such amount by expenses charged to corpus (e.g., the trustee's fee). In some complicated situations, however, DNI would not be correctly arrived at under this approach, but the discussion of such situations is beyond the scope of this book.

EXAMPLE C:14-14▶ Assume the same facts as in Example C:14-13. The following steps illustrate the second approach to calculating the DNI amount.

Corporate bond interest	$20,000
Rental income	30,000
Minus: Property taxes	(5,000)
Net accounting income	$45,000
Minus: Trustee's fee charged to corpus	(2,000)
DNI	$43,000 ◀

Although the beneficiary receives a cash distribution of $45,000 (net accounting income), he or she reports only $43,000 (DNI) as income. The beneficiary receives $2,000 tax-free. Thus, an income beneficiary benefits from trustee's fees charged to principal by getting to report a smaller amount of gross income than the amount of cash he or she receives. The trust's distribution deduction cannot exceed $43,000 (DNI) even though the amount paid to the beneficiary exceeds this amount.

Topic Review C:14-2 summarizes the DNI concept.

STOP & THINK

Question: Wei is the beneficiary of a two unrelated simple trusts. From which simple trust would Wei's after-tax cash flow be larger?

▶ Trust A collects corporate bond interest of $40,000 and pays a trustee's fee of $1,000. The trustee's fee is charged to corpus.

▶ Trust B collects corporate bond interest of $40,000 and pays a trustee's fee of $800. The trustee's fee is charged to income.

Solution: Wei would receive $40,000 in cash from Trust A but pay federal income taxes on only $39,000, which is the trust's DNI. The trust's distribution is based on net accounting income, which is not reduced by the trustee's fee charged to corpus. Wei's gross income is based on the trust's DNI, which is reduced by the trustee's fee. Wei would receive $39,200 in cash from Trust B. He would pay federal income taxes on the same $39,200 amount, which is the trust's DNI. The trustee's fee paid by Trust B reduces both net accounting income and DNI. Even though the trust's economic income is larger with Trust B, Wei would have a larger amount of after-tax cash flow from Trust A.

DETERMINING A SIMPLE TRUST'S TAXABLE INCOME

OBJECTIVE 5

Determine the taxable income of a simple trust

The term *simple trust* does not appear in the IRC. Treasury Regulations interpreting Secs. 651 and 652—the statutory rules for trusts that distribute current income only—introduce the term *simple trust*. The provisions of Secs. 651 and 652 govern only trusts whose trust agreements require that all income be distributed currently and do not authorize charitable contributions. Moreover, such provisions are inapplicable if the trust makes distributions of principal.

Some trust instuments may require trusts to pay out all their income currently in certain years but permit them to retain a portion of their income in other years. In some of the years in which the instument mandates distribution of all the income, it also permits distributions of principal. These trusts are simple trusts in some years and complex trusts in others. The amount of the personal exemption, however, turns not on whether the trust is simple or complex but on whether it must pay out all its income currently. Suppose, for

Topic Review C:14-2

The Distributable Net Income (DNI) Concept

Significance of DNI

DNI, exclusive of net tax-exempt interest included therein, sets the ceiling on:

1. The distribution deduction, and
2. The aggregate amount of gross income reportable by the beneficiaries.

Calculation of DNI

Taxable income, exclusive of distribution deduction[a]	
Plus:	Personal exemption
Minus:	Capital gains (or plus deductible capital losses)
Plus:	Tax-exempt interest (net of allocable expenses)
Distributable net income (DNI)[b]	

[a]Gross income (dividends, taxable interest, rents, and capital gains) minus deductible expenses and the personal exemption.
[b]Frequently, DNI is the same amount as net accounting income minus trustee's fees charged to corpus.

▼ TABLE C:14-1
Trust Classification Rules and the Size of the Exemption

Situation	Classification	Exemption Amount
Required to pay out all of its income, makes no charitable contributions, distributes no principal	Simple	$300
Required to pay out all of its income, makes no charitable contributions, distributes principal	Complex	$300
Required to pay out all of its income, authorized to make charitable contributions, distributes no principal	Complex	$300
Authorized to make discretionary distributions of income, makes no charitable contributions, distributes no principal	Complex	$100
Authorized to make discretionary distributions of income and principal, makes no charitable contributions	Complex	$100

example, a trust must pay out all of its current income and one-fourth of its principal. Because the trust distributes principal, it is a complex trust. It claims a $300 personal exemption because of the mandate to distribute all of its income. Table C:14-1 highlights the trust classification rules and the $300 or $100 exemption dichotomy.

ALLOCATION OF EXPENSES TO TAX-EXEMPT INCOME

Recall that expenses related to producing tax-exempt income are not deductible.[18] Thus, if a trust with income from both taxable and tax-exempt sources incurs expenses that are not directly attributable to the production of taxable income, a portion of such expenses may not be deducted. Regulation Secs. 1.652(b)-3 and 1.652(c)-4(e) address the issue of the allocation of deductions. An expense directly attributable to one type of income, such as a repair expense for rental property, is allocated thereto. Expenses not directly related to a particular item of income, such as a trustee's fee for administering the trust's assets, may be allocated to any type of income included in computing DNI, provided a portion of the expense is allocated to nontaxable income. Regulation Sec. 1.652(b)-3 sets forth the following formula for determining the amount of indirect expenses allocable to nontaxable income:

$$\frac{\text{Tax-exempt income (net of expenses directly attributable thereto)}}{\text{Accounting income (net of all direct expenses)}^{19}} \times \frac{\text{Expenses not directly attributable to any item of income}}{} = \frac{\text{Indirect expenses allocable to nontaxable income}}{}$$

EXAMPLE C:14-15 ▶ In the current year, the Mason Trust reports the following results:

Dividends	$16,000
Interest from corporate bonds	6,000
Tax-exempt interest from state bonds	18,000
Capital gain (allocated to corpus)	20,000
Trustee's fee, all allocated to corpus	4,000

---

[18] Sec. 265(a)(1).

[19] A discrepancy exists in the Treasury Regulations with respect to how to allocate expenses to tax-exempt income. According to Reg. Sec. 1.652(b)-3(b), the denominator is accounting income net of direct expenses. Regula-

tion Sec. 1.652(c)-4(e), however, shows computations where the denominator is accounting income unreduced by direct expenses. The text uses the latter approach.

SELF-STUDY QUESTION

A trust can allocate indirect expenses arbitrarily (after the appropriate allocation is made to tax-exempt income). Hill Trust has rental income, taxable interest income, and dividend income. Its sole beneficiary has unused passive rental losses of her own. To which income would you suggest allocating the trustee's fee?

ANSWER

If possible, the trust should take into consideration the tax status of its beneficiaries. The trust should not allocate the fee to its rental income so that passive rental income is maximized. Moreover, because of the low tax rate on dividends, the trust should allocate the fee against interest income.

Accounting gross income is $40,000 ($16,000 + $6,000 + $18,000). The trustee's fee is an indirect expense that must be allocated to the tax-exempt income as follows:

$$\frac{\$18,000}{\$40,000} \times \$4,000 = \$1,800$$

Thus, the Mason Trust cannot deduct $1,800 of its $4,000 trustee's fee. The remaining $2,200 may be allocated to dividends or corporate bond interest in whatever amounts the return preparer selects. Because of the low tax rate on dividends, allocating the fee to the higher taxed interest income would reduce taxes. ◄

DETERMINATION OF DNI AND THE DISTRIBUTION DEDUCTION

As mentioned above, DNI is defined as taxable income with several adjustments, including a subtraction for capital gains credited to principal. As described earlier, a practical technique for determining DNI involves beginning with taxable income exclusive of the distribution deduction. Once DNI has been determined, both the distribution deduction and the trust's taxable income can be calculated.

A simple trust must distribute all of its net accounting income currently. Thus, a simple trust generally receives a distribution deduction equal to the amount of its net accounting income.[20] The following two exceptions modify this general rule:

▶ The distribution deduction may not exceed DNI. Therefore, if a trust has expenses that are charged to corpus (as in Example C:14-13), the distribution deduction is limited to the DNI amount because DNI is smaller than net accounting income.

▶ Because tax-exempt income is not included in the trust's gross income, no distribution deduction is available for tax-exempt income (net of the expenses allocable thereto) included in DNI.[21]

TAX TREATMENT FOR BENEFICIARY

The aggregate gross income reported by the beneficiaries equals the trust's net accounting income, subject to the constraint that the aggregate of their gross income amount does not exceed the trust's DNI. If DNI is lower than net accounting income and the trust has more than one beneficiary, each beneficiary's share of gross income is the following fraction of total DNI:[22]

$$\frac{\text{Income required to be distributed to such beneficiary}}{\text{Income required to be distributed to } \textit{all} \text{ beneficiaries}}$$

The income received by the beneficiaries retains the character it had at the trust level. Thus, if the trust receives tax-exempt interest, the beneficiaries are deemed to have received tax-exempt interest. Unless the trust instrument specifically allocates particular types of income to certain beneficiaries, each beneficiary is viewed as receiving income consisting of the same fraction of each category of income as the total of such category bears to total DNI.

EXAMPLE C:14-16 ▶

In the current year, Crane Trust collects $22,000 of tax-exempt interest and $66,000 of dividends and pays $8,000 of trustee's fees from corpus. Its net accounting income is $88,000, and its DNI is $80,000: $20,000 of net tax-exempt interest and $60,000 of net dividends. The trust instrument requires distribution of one-eighth of the income annually to Matt and the remaining seven-eighths of the income to Pat. The cash distributions to Matt and Pat are $11,000 and $77,000, respectively. The distribution deduction and the aggregate gross income of the beneficiaries are limited to $60,000 ($80,000 DNI − $20,000 net tax-exempt interest). Matt and Pat will report gross income of $7,500 (0.125 × $60,000) and $52,500 (0.875 × $60,000), respectively. Dividends make up 75% ($60,000 ÷ $80,000) of DNI and 100% ($60,000 ÷ $60,000) of taxable DNI. Therefore, all of Matt's and Pat's *gross* income is deemed to consist of dividends. Matt and Pat also are deemed to receive $2,500 (0.125 × $20,000) and $17,500 (0.875 × $20,000), respectively, of tax-exempt interest. ◄

---

[20] Sec. 651(a).
[21] Sec. 651(b).

[22] Sec. 652(a).

Because a simple trust must distribute all of its income currently, trustees cannot defer the taxation of trust income to the beneficiaries by postponing distributions until the next year. Beneficiaries of simple trusts are taxed currently on their pro rata share of taxable DNI regardless of the amount distributed to them during the year.[23]

SHORTCUT APPROACH TO PROVING CORRECTNESS OF TAXABLE INCOME

A shortcut approach may be used to verify the correctness of the amount calculated as a simple trust's taxable income. Because a simple trust must distribute all of its income currently, the only item taxable at the trust level should be the amount of gains (net of losses) credited to principal, reduced by the personal exemption. The taxable income calculated under the shortcut approach should equal the taxable income determined under the formula illustrated in Figure C:14-1. The steps of the shortcut approach are as follows:

1. Start with the excess of gains over losses credited to principal.
2. Subtract the $300 personal exemption.

EXAMPLE C:14-17▶ In the current year, West Trust, which must distribute all of its income currently, reports $25,000 of corporate bond interest, a $44,000 long-term capital gain, and a $4,000 long-term capital loss. Under the shortcut approach, the test-check calculation of its taxable income is $39,700 [($44,000 − $4,000) − $300 personal exemption]. On its tax return, the trust reports $25,000 of gross income from interest, $40,000 from net long-term capital gains, a $25,000 distribution deduction, and a $300 exemption. ◀

EFFECT OF A NET OPERATING LOSS

If a trust incurs a net operating loss (NOL), the loss does not pass through currently to the beneficiaries unless the loss arises in the year the trust terminates, but the trust can carry the NOL back and forward. In determining the amount of the NOL, deductions are not allowed for charitable contributions or the distribution deduction.[24] In the year a trust terminates, any loss that would otherwise qualify for a loss carryover at the trust level passes through to the individual return(s) of the beneficiary(ies) succeeding to the trust's property.[25]

EXAMPLE C:14-18▶ In 2011, the year it terminates, New Trust incurs a $10,000 NOL. It also has a $40,000 NOL carryover from 2009 and 2010. At termination, New Trust distributes 30% of its assets to Kay and 70% to Liz. Because 2011 is the termination year, Kay may report a $15,000 (0.30 × $50,000) NOL on her 2011 return, and Liz may report a $35,000 (0.70 × $50,000) NOL on her 2011 return. Before 2011, the beneficiaries cannot report any of the trust's NOLs on their returns. ◀

EFFECT OF A NET CAPITAL LOSS

The maximum capital loss that a trust can deduct is the lesser of $3,000 or the excess of its capital losses over capital gains.[26] Because simple trusts must distribute all of their accounting income currently and the distribution deduction reduces their taxable income to zero, they receive no current tax benefit from capital losses that exceed capital gains. Nevertheless, the trust's taxable income for the year of the loss is reduced by its net capital loss, up to $3,000. In determining the capital loss carryover, capital losses that produced no tax benefit are available as a carryover to offset capital gains realized by the trust in subsequent years. In addition, if all of the capital loss carryovers have not been absorbed by capital gains before the trust's termination date, the remaining capital loss is passed through in the termination year to the beneficiaries succeeding to the trust's property.[27]

---

[23] Reg. Sec. 1.652(a)-1.
[24] Reg. Sec. 1.642(d)-1(b).
[25] Reg. Sec. 1.642(h)-1. A trust is never categorized as a simple trust in the year it terminates because in its final year it always makes distributions of principal.

[26] Sec. 1211(b).
[27] Reg. Sec. 1.642(h)-1.

EXAMPLE C:14-19▶

SELF-STUDY QUESTION

Why do Treasury Regulations (see footnotes 26 and 27) allow unused NOLs and capital losses to be used by the remainderman on the termination of a trust?

ANSWER

Losses have depleted the corpus of the trust. Because the remainderman's interest has been depleted by these losses, it is reasonable to allow the trust to pass these losses through to the remainderman at the end of its life.

Old Trust, which must distribute all of its income currently, sells two capital assets before it terminates. In 2009, it sold an asset at a $20,000 loss. In 2010, it sold an asset for a $6,000 gain. In 2011, it terminates and distributes its assets equally between its two beneficiaries, Joy and Tim. The trust is not a simple trust in 2011 because it distributes principal that year. Because the $20,000 loss provided no benefit on the 2009 return, the carryover to 2010 was $20,000, and $6,000 of it offset 2010's $6,000 capital gain. The remaining $14,000 carries over to 2011. Because 2011 is the termination year, a $7,000 (0.50 × $14,000) capital loss passes through to both Joy's and Tim's individual returns for 2011. Joy realizes a $12,000 capital gain by selling assets in 2011. Joy offsets the $7,000 trust loss against her own gain. Tim sells no assets in 2011. Therefore, Tim deducts $3,000 of the loss from the trust against his other income. His remaining $4,000 loss carries over to 2012. ◀

Topic Review C:14-3 describes how to calculate a trust's taxable income.

COMPREHENSIVE ILLUSTRATION: DETERMINING A SIMPLE TRUST'S TAXABLE INCOME

The following comprehensive illustration reviews a number of the points discussed previously. The facts for this illustration are used to complete the Form 1041 for a simple trust that appears in Appendix B.

BACKGROUND DATA

Zeb Brown established the Bob Adams Trust by a gift in 1993. The trust instrument requires that the trustee (First Bank) distribute all of the trust income at least annually to Bob Adams for life. Capital gains are credited to principal. The 2010 results of the trust are as follows:

	Amounts Allocable to	
	Income	Principal
Dividends	$30,000	
Rental income from land	5,000	
Tax-exempt interest	15,000	
Rental expenses (realtor's commission on rental income)	1,000	
Trustee's fee		$ 1,200
Fee for preparation of tax return	500	
Capital gain on sale of stock[a]		12,000
Distribution of net accounting income to Bob	48,500	
Payments of estimated tax		2,600

[a]The trust sold the stock in October, having acquired it four years earlier.

Topic Review C:14-3

Calculation of Trust Taxable Income

Gross income[a]
Minus: Deductions for expenses[a]
            Distribution deduction[b]
            Personal exemption ($300 or $100)
Taxable income

[a]Rules for calculating these amounts are generally the same as for individual taxpayers.
[b]Deduction cannot exceed the amount of DNI from taxable sources.

TRUSTEE'S FEE

As mentioned earlier, a portion of the trustee's fee is nondeductible because it must be allocated to tax-exempt income. The trust receives $50,000 ($30,000 + $5,000 + $15,000) of gross accounting income, of which $15,000 is tax-exempt. Therefore, $360 [($15,000 ÷ $50,000) × $1,200] of the trustee's fee is allocated to tax-exempt income and is nondeductible. The entire return preparation fee is deductible because no such fee would have been incurred had the trust's income been entirely from tax-exempt sources.

DISTRIBUTION DEDUCTION AND DNI

One of the key amounts affecting taxable income is the distribution deduction. Taxable income exclusive of the distribution deduction can be the starting point for determining the amount of DNI, a number crucial in quantifying the distribution deduction. The trust's taxable income, exclusive of the distribution deduction, is calculated as follows:

Dividends		$30,000
Rental income		5,000
Capital gain on sale of stock		12,000
Minus:	Rental expenses	(1,000)
	Deductible portion of trustee's fee	(840)
	Fee for tax return preparation	(500)
	Personal exemption	(300)
Taxable income, exclusive of distribution deduction		$44,360

DNI now can be calculated by making the adjustments shown below to taxable income, exclusive of the distribution deduction.[28]

Taxable income, exclusive of distribution deduction		$44,360
Plus:	Personal exemption	300
Minus:	Capital gain on sale of stock	(12,000)
Plus:	Tax-exempt interest ($15,000), net of $360 of allocable expenses	14,640
DNI		$47,300

Recall that the distribution deduction cannot exceed the DNI, as reduced by tax-exempt income (net of any allocable expenses). Nor can it exceed net accounting income of $48,500 ($30,000 + $5,000 + $15,000 − $1,000 − $500). The distribution deduction may be computed as follows:

Smaller of:	Net accounting income ($48,500) or DNI ($47,300)		$47,300
Minus:	Tax-exempt interest	$15,000	
	Minus: Allocable expenses	(360)	(14,640)
Distribution deduction			$32,660

TRUST'S TAXABLE INCOME

Once the amount of the distribution deduction is determined, the trust's taxable income can be calculated as illustrated in Table C:14-2.

CATEGORIZING A BENEFICIARY'S INCOME

Because income reported by the beneficiary retains the character it had at the trust level, the amount of each category of income received by the beneficiary must be determined. Bob is deemed to have received dividends, rents, and tax-exempt interest. Rental expenses are charged entirely against rental income. The deductible portion of the trustee's fee and the tax return preparation fee can be allocated in full to rents or dividends, or some to each. However, because of the low tax rate on dividends, the fees should be allocated

---

[28] Another way of determining the amount of DNI in this scenario is to reduce the net accounting income of $48,500 by the $1,200 of expenses charged to principal. The resulting amount is $47,300.

against the higher taxed rents. Consequently, the character of Bob's income is determined as follows:

	Dividends	Rents	Tax-Exempt Interest	Total
Accounting income	$30,000	$5,000	$15,000	$50,000
Minus: Expenses:				
Rental expenses		(1,000)		(1,000)
Trustee's fee		(840)	(360)	(1,200)
Tax return preparation fee		(500)		(500)
DNI	$30,000	$2,660	$14,640	$47,300

Bob reports $30,000 of dividend income and $2,660 of rental income on his individual return. His dividend income is taxed at the low rate applicable to dividends.

DETERMINING TAXABLE INCOME FOR COMPLEX TRUSTS AND ESTATES

OBJECTIVE 6

Determine the taxable income of a complex trust and an estate

The caption to Subpart C of Part I of Subchapter J (Secs. 661-664) reads "Distribution for Estates and Trusts Accumulating or Distributing Corpus." In general, the rules applicable to estates and these trusts (complex trusts) are the same. The IRC does not contain the term *complex trust*, but according to Treasury Regulations, "A trust to which subpart C is applicable is referred to as a 'complex' trust."[29] Recall from the discussion about simple trusts that a trust that must distribute all of its income currently can be classified as a

▼ TABLE C:14-2

Comprehensive Illustration: Determining a Simple Trust's Taxable Income and Tax Liability

Gross income:	
Dividends	$30,000
Rental income	5,000
Capital gain on sale of stock	12,000[a]
Minus: Expense deductions:	
Rental expenses	(1,000)
Deductible portion of trustee's fee	(840)
Tax return preparation fee	(500)
Minus: Distribution deduction	(32,660)
Minus: Personal exemption	(300)
Taxable income	$11,700[b]
Tax liability (2010 rates)	$1,410[c]
Minus: Estimated tax payments	(2,600)
Tax owed (refunded)	$(1,190)

[a]The stock sale took place in October and involved stock purchased four years earlier.
[b]The short-cut approach to verifying taxable income is as follows:

Long-term capital gain	$12,000
Minus: Personal exemption	(300)
Taxable income	$11,700

[c]The taxable income consists of a long-term capital gain, which, in 2010, is taxed at a maximum rate of 0% on the first $2,300 and 15% on the rest.

ADDITIONAL COMMENT

The short-cut approach to computing taxable income used in Table C:14-2 consists of reducing the income allocated to corpus by the personal exemption.

[29] Reg. Sec. 1.661(a)-1.

complex trust for a particular year if it also pays out some principal during the year. Trusts that can accumulate income are categorized as complex trusts, even in years in which they make discretionary distributions of all their income. A trust is a complex trust also if the trust instrument provides for amounts to be paid to, or set aside for, charitable organizations (see Table C:14-1).

Many of the rules are the same for simple and complex trusts, but some differences exist. Different rules are used to determine the distribution deduction for the two types of trusts. The rules for determining an estate's distribution deduction are the same as those applicable to complex trusts. The personal exemption, however, is $600 for an estate and $300 or $100 for a complex trust. The $300 amount applies for years in which a trust must pay out all of its income; otherwise, the exemption is $100.

TAX STRATEGY TIP

Trust managers can reduce overall taxes by carefully planning the amount and timing of distributions. See Tax Planning Considerations later in text for details.

DETERMINATION OF DNI AND THE DISTRIBUTION DEDUCTION

Section 661(a) defines the distribution deduction for complex trusts and estates as the sum of the total current income *required* to be paid out currently plus any other amounts "properly paid or credited or required to be distributed" (i.e., discretionary distributions) to the beneficiary during the year. If the fiduciary can make mandatory distributions from either the income or the principal account, distributions are treated as "current income required to be paid" if paid out of the trust's income account; thus, some of the income is taxed to the beneficiary. Like simple trusts, the amount of the trust's DNI limits the amount of the distribution deduction.

EXAMPLE C:14-20▶

In the current year, Able Trust has net accounting income and DNI of $30,000, all from taxable sources. It makes a $15,000 mandatory distribution of income to Kwame and a $4,000 discretionary distribution to Kesha. Its distribution deduction is computed as follows:

Income required to be distributed currently	$15,000
Plus: Other amounts properly paid, etc.	4,000
Tentative distribution deduction	$19,000
DNI	$30,000
Distribution deduction (lesser of tentative distribution deduction or DNI)	$19,000 ◀

As is the case for simple trusts, an additional constraint applies to the amount of the distribution deduction. No distribution deduction is allowed with respect to tax-exempt income (net of allocable expenses).

EXAMPLE C:14-21▶

Assume the same facts as in Example C:14-20 except that net accounting income and DNI consist of $20,000 of corporate bond interest and $10,000 of tax-exempt interest. Because one-third ($10,000 ÷ $30,000) of the DNI is from tax-exempt sources, tax-exempt income is deemed to make up one-third of the distributions. Thus, the distribution deduction is only $12,667 (0.667 × $19,000). ◀

If a trust makes charitable contributions, DNI is not reduced by the charitable contribution deduction when determining the maximum distribution deduction available for mandatory distributions. However, DNI is reduced by the charitable contribution deduction when calculating the deduction for discretionary distributions.

EXAMPLE C:14-22▶

Assume instead that the trust in Example C:14-20 has net accounting income and DNI (exclusive of the charitable contribution deduction) of $16,000. The trust makes a $15,000 mandatory distribution to Kwame and a $4,000 mandatory distribution to Kesha. In accordance with its trust instrument, the trust pays $3,000 to a charitable organization.

Tentative distribution deduction (required distributions)	$19,000
DNI (excluding charitable contribution deduction)	16,000
Distribution deduction (lesser of tentative distribution deduction or DNI)	16,000

If the distributions to both Kwame and Kesha were discretionary, the $3,000 charitable contribution would be deductible by the trust and would first reduce DNI to $13,000, thereby limiting the distribution deduction to $13,000. Thus, in total, the beneficiaries would report $3,000 ($19,000 − $16,000) less gross income. ◀

TAX TREATMENT FOR BENEFICIARY

GENERAL RULES. In general, the amount of distributions from estates or complex trusts includible in a beneficiary's gross income equals the sum of income required to be distributed currently to the beneficiary plus any other amounts properly paid or credited, or required to be distributed (i.e., discretionary distributions) to the beneficiary during the year.[30] This general rule has three exceptions, all discussed later in this section.

Because income retains the character it has at the fiduciary level, beneficiaries do not include distributions of tax-exempt income in their gross income. Each beneficiary's distribution is deemed to consist of tax-exempt income in the proportion that total tax-exempt income bears to total DNI.[31] Thus, if 30% of DNI is from tax-exempt income, 30% of each beneficiary's distribution is deemed to consist of tax-free income.

Even in the absence of distributions of principal, mandatory payments to beneficiaries can exceed DNI because at times accounting income exceeds DNI. When the total income required to be distributed currently exceeds DNI (before reduction for the charitable contribution deduction), each beneficiary reports as gross income the following ratio of DNI attributable to taxable sources:

$$\frac{\text{Income required to be distributed currently to this beneficiary}}{\text{Aggregate income required to be distributed to all beneficiaries currently}}[32]$$

In calculating the portion of DNI includible in the gross income of each beneficiary who receives mandatory distributions, DNI is not reduced for the charitable contribution deduction.

EXAMPLE C:14-23 ▶

In the current year, Yui Trust reports net accounting income of $125,000 but DNI of only $95,000 because of certain expenses charged to principal. The trust must distribute $100,000 of income to Tai and $10,000 to Tien. It makes no discretionary distributions or charitable contributions. Because the trust's mandatory distributions of $110,000 exceed its DNI of $95,000, the amount each beneficiary reports as gross income is as follows:

Beneficiary	Gross Income
Tai	$86,364 = ($100,000 ÷ $110,000) × $95,000
Tien	$8,636 = ($10,000 ÷ $110,000) × $95,000

◀

EXCEPTION—THE TIER SYSTEM. Some trust instruments require mandatory distributions to some beneficiaries and discretionary distributions to those or other beneficiaries. If the sum of current income required to be distributed currently and all other amounts distributed (e.g., discretionary payments of income or any payments of corpus) exceed DNI, the amount taxable to each beneficiary is calculated under a tier system. Beneficiaries to whom income distributions must be made are commonly called **tier-1 beneficiaries**.[33] All other beneficiaries are known as **tier-2 beneficiaries**. An individual who receives both mandatory and discretionary payments in the same year can be both a tier-1 and a tier-2 beneficiary.

Under the tier system, tier-1 beneficiaries are the first to absorb income. The total income taxed to this group is the lesser of the aggregate mandatory distributions or DNI, which is determined without reduction for charitable contributions. If required income distributions plus all other payments exceed DNI, each tier-2 beneficiary includes in income a fraction of the remaining DNI, the DNI minus the income required to be distributed currently. Section 662(a)(2) states that the fraction is as follows:

$$\frac{\text{Other amounts properly paid or required to be distributed to the beneficiary}}{\text{Aggregate of amounts properly paid or required to be distributed to \textit{all} beneficiaries}}$$

[30] Sec. 662(a).
[31] Sec. 662(b).
[32] Sec. 662(a)(1).

[33] The terms *tier-1* and *tier-2* do not appear in the IRC or Treasury Regulations.

EXAMPLE C:14-24▶

In the current year, Eagle Trust reports net accounting income and DNI of $80,000, all from taxable sources. The trust instrument requires the trustee to distribute $30,000 of income to Holly currently. In addition, the trustee makes $60,000 of discretionary distributions, $15,000 to Holly and $45,000 to Irene. The trust distributes $90,000 total and pays $10,000 of the $60,000 discretionary distributions from corpus. The gross income reported by each beneficiary is determined as follows.

1. Gross income from mandatory distributions:	
Lesser of:	
a. Amount required to be distributed, or	$30,000
b. DNI	80,000
Amount reportable by Holly	30,000
2. Gross income from other amounts paid:	
Lesser of:	
a. All other amounts paid, or	60,000
b. DNI minus amount required to be distributed ($80,000 − $30,000)	50,000
Amount reportable by Holly and Irene	50,000
3. Total amount reportable (1) + (2) = (3)	80,000

The portions of the $50,000 from Step 2 to be reported by each beneficiary are calculated under a pro rata approach as follows:

Holly: $50,000 × ($15,000 ÷ $60,000) = $12,500
Irene: $50,000 × ($45,000 ÷ $60,000) = $37,500

A recapitulation of the beneficiaries' gross income is as follows:

	Amount Reported by	
Type of Distribution	Holly	Irene
Mandatory distributions	$30,000	$ –0–
Discretionary distributions	12,500	37,500
Total	$42,500	$37,500 ◀

Tier-1 beneficiaries generally have gross income equal to their total distributions if they receive no tax-exempt interest, whereas tier-2 beneficiaries are more likely to receive a portion of their distributions tax-free. Thus, tier-2 beneficiaries potentially receive more favorable tax treatment than tier-1 beneficiaries.

SELF-STUDY QUESTION

What is the ultimate effect of the separate share rule?

ANSWER

It has the effect of treating a trust or estate as two or more separate entities, each with its own DNI. This "separate" DNI is allocated to the specific beneficiary of each share of the trust or estate.

EXCEPTION—SEPARATE SHARE RULE. Some trusts and estates with more than one beneficiary can be treated as consisting of more than one entity in determining the amount of the distribution deduction and the beneficiaries' gross income.[34] In calculating the fiduciary's income tax liability, however, these trusts or estates are treated as one entity with the result that taxable income is taxed under one rate schedule. Entities eligible for this treatment, known as the **separate share rule,** have governing instruments requiring that distributions be made in substantially the same manner as if separate entities had been created.[35] If the separate share rule applies, the amount of the income taxable to a beneficiary can differ from the amount taxable under the general rules. Because of this rule, beneficiaries often report gross income that is less than the distributions they receive.

EXAMPLE C:14-25▶

Bart Berry created the Berry Trust for the benefit of Dale and John. According to the trust instrument, no income is to be distributed until a beneficiary reaches age 21. Moreover, income is to be divided into two equal shares. Once a beneficiary reaches age 21, the trustee may make discretionary distributions of income and principal to such beneficiary, but distributions may not exceed a beneficiary's share of the trust. Each beneficiary is to receive his remaining share of the trust assets on his thirtieth birthday. Earlier distributions of income and principal must be taken into account in determining each beneficiary's final distribution.

On January 1 of the current year, Dale reaches age 21; John is age 16. In the current year, the trust has DNI and net accounting income of $50,000, all from taxable sources. During the cur-

---

[34] Sec. 663(c).

[35] Reg. Sec. 1.663(c)-3(a).

rent year, the trustee distributes $25,000 of income (Dale's 50% share) and $80,000 of principal to Dale. The trustee makes no distribution of income or corpus to John. Under the separate share rule, the trust's distribution deduction and Dale's gross income inclusion cannot exceed his share of DNI, or $25,000. Dale receives the remaining $80,000 distribution tax-free. Berry Trust pays tax on John's separate share of the income (all accumulated), or $25,000, less the personal exemption. In the absence of the separate share rule, Dale would be taxed on $50,000 (the lesser of DNI or his total distributions). ◄

EXCEPTION—SPECIFIC BEQUESTS. Recall that a beneficiary is taxed on other amounts properly paid, credited, or required to be distributed,[36] subject to the constraint that the maximum amount taxed to all beneficiaries is the fiduciary's DNI. Thus, a beneficiary can be required to report gross income even though he or she receives a distribution paid from the principal account.

EXAMPLE C:14-26► Doug died in 2010, leaving a will that bequeathed all his property to his sister Tina. During 2011, Doug's estate reports $50,000 of DNI, all from taxable sources. During 2011, the executor distributes Doug's coin collection, valued at $22,000, to Tina. The adjusted basis of the coin collection also is $22,000, its value at the date of death. The distribution of the coin collection is classified as an "other amount properly paid" and, even though the executor distributes nothing from the income account, Tina must report $22,000 of gross income. If the coin collection's adjusted basis and FMV exceed $50,000 (DNI), Tina's gross income would be only $50,000, the DNI amount. ◄

ADDITIONAL COMMENT

The executor of an estate should carefully consider the timing of property distributions where the property being distributed is not the subject of a specific bequest. If possible, property (other than specific bequests) should be distributed in a year when the trust has little or no DNI.

On the other hand, a distribution of property does not trigger a distribution deduction at the estate level or the recognition of gross income at the beneficiary level if such property constitutes a bequest of a specific sum of money or of specific property to be paid at one time or in not more than three installments.[37] If Doug's will in Example C:14-26 instead includes specific bequest language (e.g., "I bequeath my coin collection to Tina"), Tina would not report any gross income upon receiving the coin collection.

More income is generally taxed at the estate level (and less at the beneficiary level) if the decedent's will includes numerous specific bequests. If the estate has a lower marginal income tax rate than its beneficiaries' marginal tax rates, the optimal tax result is to have the income taxed to the estate because the tax liability is lower.

EXAMPLE C:14-27► Dick died in 2010 and bequeathed $100,000 cash to Fred and devised his residence, valued at $300,000, to Gary. The executor distributes the cash and the residence in 2011, when the estate has $80,000 of DNI, all from taxable sources. Because the cash and residence constitute specific bequests, the estate receives no distribution deduction and the beneficiaries report no gross income. ◄

STOP & THINK

Question: Sally is the sole beneficiary of her uncle Harry's estate. In the current year, the estate had DNI of $36,000, all from dividends and corporate interest. During the current year, the estate's executor distributed to Sally $12,200 of cash and her uncle Harry's rare book collection, valued at $5,400 on both date of death and date of distribution. Uncle Harry's will made a specific bequest of the rare book collection to Sally. Another part of his will left Sally the rest of his estate. How much gross income should Sally report from the estate during the current year? What is the amount of the estate's distribution deduction?

Solution: Sally does not have to report gross income as a result of receiving the specific bequest of the book collection. Because Sally's $12,200 cash distribution does not exceed the estate's $36,000 DNI, Sally should report gross income equal to the cash distributed to her ($12,200). The estate's distribution deduction equals the amount included in Sally's gross income ($12,200). If Harry had not specifically willed the books to Sally, the distribution of the books would be taxable to Sally because the $17,600 ($12,200 + $5,400) distributed by the estate is less than the estate's DNI.

---

[36] Sec. 662(a)(2).　　　　[37] Sec. 663(a)(1).

KEY POINT

Generally, the tax consequences of both NOLs and net capital losses are the same for estates, complex trusts, and simple trusts.

EFFECT OF A NET OPERATING LOSS

As with simple trusts, an NOL of an estate or complex trust can be carried back and carried forward. In the year the trust or estate terminates, any remaining NOL passes through to the beneficiaries who succeed to the assets. In addition, in its year of termination the estate passes through to its beneficiaries any excess of current nonoperating expenses (e.g., executor's fees) over current income. If the estate incurs NOLs over a series of years, a tax incentive exists for terminating the estate as early as possible so the loss can pass through to the beneficiaries.

EFFECT OF A NET CAPITAL LOSS

The tax effect of having capital losses that exceed capital gains generally is the same for estates and complex trusts as for simple trusts. As for an individual taxpayer, the maximum capital loss deduction is the lesser of $3,000 or the excess of its capital losses over capital gains.[38] Simple trusts, however, receive no immediate tax benefit when capital losses exceed capital gains because no income is retained against which to offset the capital loss. Estates and complex trusts often do not distribute all their income and, thus, have taxable income against which they can offset a capital loss.

EXAMPLE C:14-28 ▶

For 2010, Green Trust reported $30,000 of net accounting income and DNI, all from taxable sources. It made discretionary distributions totaling $7,000 to Amy. It sold one capital asset at an $8,000 long-term capital loss. The trust deducted $3,000 of capital losses in arriving at its 2010 taxable income. The trust carries over the remaining $5,000 of capital loss to 2011. If in 2011, Green Trust sells a capital asset for a $7,000 long-term capital gain, it will offset the $5,000 loss carryover against the $7,000 capital gain. ◀

COMPREHENSIVE ILLUSTRATION: DETERMINING A COMPLEX TRUST'S TAXABLE INCOME

The comprehensive illustration below reviews a number of points discussed earlier. A sample Form 1041 for a complex trust appears in Appendix B; it is prepared on the basis of the facts in this illustration.

BACKGROUND DATA

Ted Tims established the Cathy and Karen Stephens Trust on March 12, 1994. Its trust instrument empowers the trustee (Merchants Bank) to distribute income in its discretion to Cathy and Karen for the next 20 years. The trust will then be terminated, and the trust assets will be divided equally between Cathy and Karen, irrespective of the amount of distributions each has previously received. In other words, no separate shares are to be maintained. Under state law, capital gains are part of principal.

The 2010 income and expenses of the trust appear below. With the exception of the information concerning distributions and payments of estimated tax, the amounts are the same as in the comprehensive illustration for a simple trust discussed previously in the chapter. As before, the holding period for the stock sold in October was four years.

	Amounts Allocable to	
	Income	Principal
Dividends	$30,000	
Rental income from land	5,000	
Tax-exempt interest	15,000	
Rental expenses (realtor's commissions on rental income)	1,000	

---

[38] Sec. 1211(b).

Trustee's fee		$ 1,200
Fee for preparation of tax return	500	
Capital gain on sale of stock		12,000
Distribution of net accounting income to:		
Cathy	14,000	
Karen	7,000	
Payments of estimated tax	5,240	3,360

TRUSTEE'S FEE

Recall that some of the trustee's fee must be allocated to tax-exempt income, with the result that this portion is nondeductible. Of the trust's gross accounting income of $50,000 ($30,000 + $5,000 + $15,000), $15,000 is from tax-exempt sources. Consequently, the nondeductible trustee's fee is $360 [($15,000 ÷ $50,000) × $1,200]. The remaining $840 of the fee is deductible, as is the $500 tax return preparation fee.

DISTRIBUTION DEDUCTION AND DNI

Recall that the primary function of the Subchapter J rules is to provide guidance for calculating the amounts taxable to the beneficiaries and to the fiduciary. One of the crucial numbers in the process is the distribution deduction, which requires knowledge of the DNI amount. Taxable income, exclusive of the distribution deduction, is the starting point for calculating DNI and is computed as follows:

Dividends		$30,000
Rental income		5,000
Capital gain on sale of stock		12,000
Minus:	Rental expenses	(1,000)
	Deductible portion of trustee's fee	(840)
	Fee for tax return preparation	(500)
	Personal exemption	(100)
Taxable income, exclusive of distribution deduction		$44,560

DNI is calculated by adjusting taxable income, exclusive of the distribution deduction, as follows:

Taxable income, exclusive of distribution deduction		$44,560
Plus:	Personal exemption	100
Minus:	Capital gain on sale of stock	(12,000)
Plus:	Tax-exempt interest (net of $360 of allocable expenses)	14,640
DNI		$47,300

The distribution deduction is the lesser of (1) amounts required to be distributed, plus all other amounts properly paid or credited, or required to be distributed, or (2) DNI. This lesser-of amount must be reduced by tax-exempt income (net of allocable expenses). DNI, exclusive of net tax-exempt income, is calculated as follows:

DNI		$47,300
Minus:	Tax-exempt income (net of $360 of allocable expenses)	(14,640)
DNI, exclusive of net tax-exempt income		$32,660

In no event may the distribution deduction exceed $32,660, the DNI, exclusive of net tax-exempt income. The DNI ceiling is of no practical significance in this example, however, because the trust distributed only $21,000.

Because a portion of the payments to each beneficiary is deemed to consist of tax-exempt income, the distribution deduction is less than the $21,000 distributed. Each beneficiary's share of tax-exempt income is determined by dividing DNI into categories of income. In this categorization process, the rental expenses are direct expenses that must be charged against rental income, and $360 of the trustee's fees must be charged against tax-exempt income. In this example, the deductible trustee's fee and the tax

ADDITIONAL COMMENT

This example dealing with a complex trust clearly illustrates the computational complexity that exists in situations with multiple categories of income and multiple beneficiaries.

return preparation fee are charged against rental income. Alternatively, they could be charged against dividend income or pro rata against each income category, but an allocation to dividend income would be disadvantageous because dividends are taxed at a preferential rate. As with the simple trust illustrated earlier, total DNI of $47,300 consists of the following categories:

	Dividends	Rents	Tax-Exempt Interest	Total
Accounting income	$30,000	$5,000	$15,000	$50,000
Minus: Expenses:				
Trustee's fee		(840)	(360)	(1,200)
Rental expenses		(1,000)		(1,000)
Tax return preparation fee		(500)		(500)
DNI	$30,000	$2,660	$14,640	$47,300

Because the complex trust illustration involves two beneficiaries and three categories of income, we must calculate the amount of each beneficiary's distribution attributable to each income category. These steps were not needed in the simple trust illustration because the simple trust had only one beneficiary.

Category of Income	Proportion of DNI
Dividends	63.4249% = $30,000 ÷ $47,300
Rental income	5.6237% = $ 2,660 ÷ $47,300
Tax-exempt income	30.9514% = $14,640 ÷ $47,300
Total	100.0000%

As shown above, 30.9514% of each beneficiary's distribution represents tax-exempt interest and is ineligible for a distribution deduction. The amount of the distribution deduction (which cannot exceed the $32,660 DNI, exclusive of net tax-exempt income) is determined as follows:

Total amount distributed	$21,000
Minus: Net tax-exempt income deemed distributed (0.309514 × $21,000)	(6,500)
Distribution deduction	$14,500

The distributions received by the beneficiaries are deemed to consist of three categories of income in the amounts shown below.

Components of Distributions	Cathy	Karen	Total
Dividends (63.4249%)	$ 8,879	$4,440	$13,319
Plus: Rental income (5.6237%)	788	393	1,181
Gross income (69.0486%)	$ 9,667	$4,833	$14,500
Plus: Tax-exempt interest (30.9514%)	4,333	2,167	6,500
Total income (100%)	$14,000	$7,000	$21,000

TRUST'S TAXABLE INCOME

Once the taxable and tax-exempt distributions have been quantified, the trust's taxable income can be calculated. Table C:14-3 illustrates this calculation. Unlike the simple trust situation, no short-cut approach exists for verifying taxable income for complex trusts and estates except in the years when they distribute all their income.

ADDITIONAL OBSERVATIONS

A few additional observations are in order concerning the Stephens Trust:

▶ If the entity is an estate instead of a trust, all amounts except the personal exemption are the same. The estate's personal exemption would be $600 instead of $100.

▼ TABLE C:14-3

Comprehensive Illustration: Determining a Complex Trust's Taxable Income and Tax Liability

Gross income:	
Dividends	$30,000
Rental income	5,000
Capital gain on sale of stock	12,000
Minus: Expense deductions:	
Rental expenses	(1,000)
Deductible portion of trustee's fee	(840)
Tax return preparation fee	(500)
Minus: Distribution deduction	(14,500)
Minus: Personal exemption	(100)
Taxable income	$30,060
Tax liability (2010 rates)[a]	$ 4,371
Minus: Estimated taxes	(8,600)
Tax owed (refunded)	$ (4,229)

[a]The $12,000 long-term capital gain and the $16,681 of dividends retained by the trust ($28,681 in total) are taxed at the lower rates. The $16,681 amount is $30,000 minus the $13,319 dividends distributed, as calculated on p. C:14-26. The tax liability is calculated as follows:

Tax on ordinary, non-dividend income [0.15 × $1,379 (where $1,379 = $30,060 − $12,000 − $16,631)]	$ 207
Plus: Tax on capital gains and dividends at 0% [0.0 × $921 (where $921 = $2,300 − $1,379)]	–0–
Tax on capital gains and dividends at 15% [0.15 × ($28,681 − $921)]	4,164
Total tax	$4,371

▶ Assume that (1) the trust owns a building instead of land and incurs $2,000 of depreciation expense, chargeable against principal under state law, and (2) the trust instrument does not require a reserve for depreciation. Because approximately 56% of the trust's income is accumulated (i.e., $26,300 of its $47,300 DNI), $1,120 (0.56 × $2,000) of the depreciation is deductible by the trust and its taxable income is $1,120 lower. The remaining $880 (0.44 × $2,000) is deductible on the beneficiaries' returns and is divided between them according to their pro rata share of the total distributions. Cathy deducts $587 [$880 × ($14,000 ÷ $21,000)], and Karen deducts $293 [$880 × ($7,000 ÷ $21,000)]. In summary, the depreciation is deductible as follows $1,120 to the trust, $587 to Cathy, and $293 to Karen.

▶ If the trust instrument had mandated a reserve for depreciation equal to the depreciation expense for tax purposes, accounting income would have been reduced by the depreciation. In addition, the entire $2,000 of depreciation would have been deducted by the trust, and DNI would have been $45,300 instead of $47,300.

INCOME IN RESPECT OF A DECEDENT

OBJECTIVE 7

Recognize the significance of income in respect of a decedent

DEFINITION AND COMMON EXAMPLES

Section 691 specifies the tax treatment for specific types of income known as income in respect of a decedent. **Income in respect of a decedent (IRD)** is gross income that the decedent earned before death but was not includible on the decedent's income tax return for the tax year ending with the date of death or for an earlier tax year because the decedent (a cash basis taxpayer) had not collected the income. Because most individuals use the cash method of accounting, IRD generally consists of income earned, but not actually or constructively received, prior to death. Common examples of IRD include the following:

▶ Interest earned, but not received, before death

▶ Salary, commission, or bonus earned, but not received, before death

▶ Dividends collected after the date of death, for which the record date precedes the date of death

▶ The gain portion of principal collected on a pre-death installment sale

SIGNIFICANCE OF IRD

DOUBLE TAXATION. Recall from Chapter C:13 that a decedent's gross estate includes property to the extent of his or her interest therein. The decedent has an interest in any income earned but not actually or constructively received before death. Thus, the decedent's gross estate includes income accrued as of the date of death. If the decedent used the cash method of accounting, the decedent did not include this accrued income in gross income because he or she had not yet collected it. The income is taxed to the party (i.e., the estate or a named individual) entitled to receive it. Thus, IRD is taxed under both the transfer tax system and the income tax system. The income also is taxed twice if the decedent collects a dividend check, deposits it into his or her bank account, and dies before consuming the cash. In the latter case, the dividend is included in the decedent's individual income tax return, and the cash (from the dividend check) is included in the decedent's gross estate. The income taxes owed on the dividend income are deductible as a debt on the estate tax return.

EXAMPLE C:14-29 ▶ Doug dies on July 1. Included in Doug's gross estate is an 8%, $1,000 corporate bond that pays interest each September 1 and March 1. Doug's gross estate also includes accrued interest for the period March 2 through July 1 of $27 ($1,000 × 0.08 × 4/12). On September 1, Doug's estate collects $40 of interest, of which $27 constitutes IRD. The calendar year income tax return for Doug's estate includes $40 of interest income, consisting of $27 of IRD and $13 earned after death. ◀

DEDUCTIONS IN RESPECT OF A DECEDENT. Section 691(b) authorizes **deductions in respect of a decedent (DRD)**. Such deductions include trade or business expenses, expenses for the production of income, interest, taxes, depletion, etc. that are accrued before death but are not deductible on the decedent's final income tax return because the decedent used the cash method of accounting. Because these accrued expenses have not been paid before death, they also may be deductible as debts on the estate tax return. In addition, the accrued expenses are deductible on the estate's income tax return when paid by the estate (if they are for deductible expenses). Thus, a double benefit can be obtained for DRD.

EXAMPLE C:14-30 ▶

Dan dies on September 20. At the time of his death, Dan owes $18,000 of salaries to the employees of his proprietorship. The executor pays the total September payroll of $29,000 on September 30. The $18,000 of accrued salaries is deductible as a debt on the estate tax return. As a trade or business (Sec. 162) expense, the salaries also constitute DRD. The $18,000 of DRD, plus any other salaries paid, is deductible on the estate's income tax return for the period of payment. ◀

SECTION 691(c) DEDUCTION. The Sec. 691(c) deduction provides some relief for the double taxation of IRD. This deduction equals the federal estate taxes attributable to the net IRD included in the gross estate. The total Sec. 691(c) deduction is the excess of the decedent's actual federal estate tax over the federal estate tax that would be payable if the net IRD were excluded from the decedent's gross estate. Net IRD means IRD minus deductions in respect of a decedent (DRD). If the IRD is collected in more than one tax year, the Sec. 691(c) deduction for a particular tax year is determined by the following formula:[39]

$$\begin{array}{c}\text{Sec. 691(c)}\\\text{deduction}\\\text{for the year}\end{array} = \begin{array}{c}\text{Total}\\\text{Sec. 691(c)}\\\text{deduction}\end{array} \times \dfrac{\text{Net IRD included in gross income for the year}}{\text{Total Net IRD}}$$

---

[39] Sec. 691(c)(1).

EXAMPLE C:14-31▶

Latoya died in 2009 with a taxable estate and estate tax base of $4.5 million. Latoya's gross estate included $300,000 of IRD, primarily from gains on installment sales, none of which was received by her surviving spouse. Her estate had no DRD. The estate collects $250,000 of the IRD during its 2011 tax year. The Sec. 691(c) deduction for Latoya's estate for 2011 is calculated as shown below.

Actual 2009 federal estate tax on base of $4.5 million		$450,000
Minus: 2009 federal estate tax on base of $4.2 million determined		
by excluding net IRD from gross estate		(315,000)
Total Sec. 691(c) deduction		$135,000
Sec. 691(c) deduction available in 2011: ($250,000 ÷ $300,000) × $135,000 =		$112,500 ◀

NEW TAX LAW

For decedents dying in 2010, Congress retroactively reinstated the estate tax along with the FMV basis rule. However, for 2010, estate executors can elect out of the estate tax and use the modified carryover basis rules that were in effect for 2010 before the reinstatement.

NO STEP-UP IN BASIS. Most property received as the result of a decedent's death acquires a basis equal to its FMV on the date of death or the alternate valuation date. Property classified as IRD retains the basis it had in the decedent's hands.[40]

This carryover basis rule for IRD items is especially unfavorable when the decedent sells a highly appreciated asset soon before death, collects a relatively small portion of the sales price before death, and reports the sale under the installment method of accounting. For example, if the gain is 80% of the sales price, 80% of each principal payment in the post-death period will continue to be characterized as gain. If the sale instead had been postponed until after the date of death, the gain would be restricted to the post-death appreciation (if any) because the step-up in basis rules apply to the asset.

EXAMPLE C:14-32▶
SELF-STUDY
QUESTION

Roger (a cash basis taxpayer) died leaving $150,000 of accounts receivable. What basis does his estate have in these accounts receivable?

ANSWER

Zero. The accounts receivable constitute IRD. If they were stepped-up in basis, they would never be subject to an income tax.

On June 3, 2011, Joel sells a parcel of investment land for $40,000. The land has a $10,000 adjusted basis in Joel's hands. The buyer pays $8,000 down and signs a $32,000 note at an interest rate acceptable to the IRS. The note is payable June 3, 2012. Joel, a cash basis taxpayer, uses the installment method for reporting the $30,000 ($40,000 − $10,000) gain. The gross profit ratio is 75% ($30,000 gain ÷ $40,000 contract price). Joel dies accidentally on June 13, 2011 with a gross estate of $1 million. Joel's final individual income tax return reports a gain of $6,000 (0.75 × $8,000). The estate reports a gain of $24,000 (0.75 × $32,000) on its 2012 income tax return because it collects the $32,000 balance on June 3, 2012. Had the sale contract been entered into immediately after Joel's death, the gain would have been zero because the land's basis would have been its $40,000 FMV at the date of death. ◀

? STOP & THINK

Question: Isaac, a cash basis, calendar year taxpayer, died on May 12 of the current year. On which income tax return—Isaac's or his estate's—should the following income and expenses be reported? Assume the estate's tax year is the calendar year.

▶ Dividends declared in January and paid in February

▶ Interest income on a corporate bond that pays interest each June 30 and December 31

▶ Rent collected in June for a vacation home rented to tenants for the month of March, but the tenants were allowed to pay after occupying the property

▶ Balance due on Isaac's state income taxes for the previous year, paid in July because the return was extended

▶ Federal estimated income tax for the previous year that Isaac paid in January

Solution: Income received before death and deductible expenses paid before death (in this case the dividends and nothing more) should be reported on Isaac's individual return. Income received after his death, even though earned before his death, is to be reported on the estate's income tax return. The same is true for deductible expenses paid by the estate. Items to be reported on the estate's income tax return include the interest income, the rental income, and the state income taxes. The federal income taxes paid are not deductible on the federal income tax return of either taxpayer. The tax payment, however, reduced the cash Isaac owned at his date of death and thereby his gross estate.

---

[40] Sec. 1014(c).

GRANTOR TRUST PROVISIONS

This portion of the chapter examines the provisions affecting a special type of trust known as a **grantor trust,** which is governed by Secs. 671-679. As discussed previously, income of a regular (or nongrantor) trust or an estate is taxed to the beneficiary to the extent distributed and to the fiduciary to the extent accumulated. In the case of a grantor trust, however, the trust's grantor (creator) is taxed on some or all of the trust's income even if such income is distributed to the beneficiary. In certain circumstances, a person other than the grantor or the beneficiary (e.g., a person with powers over the trust) must pay taxes on the trust's income.

PURPOSE AND EFFECT

The grantor trust rules require grantors who do not give up enough control or economic benefits when they create a trust to pay a price by being taxed on part or all of the trust's income. A grantor must report some or all of a trust's income on his or her individual tax return if he or she does not part with enough control over the trust assets or give up the right to income produced by the assets for a sufficiently long time period. For transfers after March 1, 1986, the grantor generally is taxed on the trust's income if the trust property will eventually return to the grantor or the grantor's spouse.[41] According to the Tax Court, the grantor trust rules have the following purpose and result:

> This subpart [Secs. 671–679] enunciates the rules to be applied where, in described circumstances, a grantor has transferred property to a trust but has not parted with complete dominion and control over the property or the income which it produces. . . . [42]

Sections 671–679 use the term *treated as owner* instead of taxed. Section 671 specifies that when a grantor is treated as owner, the income, deductions, and credits attributable to the portion of the trust with respect to which the grantor is treated as owner are reported directly on the grantor's tax return and not on the trust's return. The fiduciary return contains only the items attributable to the portion of the trust for which the grantor is not treated as the owner.

ADDITIONAL COMMENT

Many trust provisions can cause the grantor trust rules to apply. A trust need *not* be a revocable trust to be a grantor trust.

Unfortunately, the rules governing when the grantor has given up enough to avoid being taxed on the trust's income do not agree completely with the rules concerning whether the transfer is complete for gift tax purposes or the transferred property is removed from the donor's gross estate. In certain circumstances, a donor can make a taxable gift and still be taxed on the income from the transferred property. For example, if a donor transfers property to a trust with the income payable annually to the donor's cousin for six years and a reversion of the property to the donor at the end of the sixth year, the donor makes a gift, subject to the gift tax, of the value of a six-year income interest. Under the grantor trust rules, however, the donor is taxed on the trust's income because the property reverts to the donor within too short a time period.

Retention of certain powers over property conveyed in trust can cause the trust assets to be included in the donor's gross estate even though these powers do not result in the donor being taxed on the trust income. Assume a donor to a trust reserves the discretionary power to pay out or accumulate trust income until the beneficiary (a grandchild) reaches age 21. The trust assets, including any accumulated income, are to be distributed to the beneficiary on his or her twenty-first birthday. The donor is not taxed on the trust income because he can exercise his powers only until the beneficiary reaches age 21. If the donor dies before the beneficiary attains age 21, however, the donor's gross estate will include the trust property because the donor retained control over the beneficiary's economic benefits (see discussion of Sec. 2036 in Chapter C:13).

---

[41] For trusts created before March 2, 1986, the grantor was treated as the owner with respect to the trust's capital gains but not its ordinary income if the property returned to the grantor after a period of more than ten years. In such a situation, the grantor is taxed on the capital gains and the trust and/or the beneficiary on the ordinary income. The trusts usually terminated slightly more than ten years after their funding. Thus, few (if any) of these trusts exist today.

[42] *William Scheft,* 59 T.C. 428, at 430-431 (1972).

REVOCABLE TRUSTS

The grantor of a revocable trust can control assets conveyed to the trust by altering the terms of the trust (including changing the identity of the beneficiaries) and/or withdrawing assets from the trust. Not surprisingly, Sec. 676 provides that the grantor is treated as the owner of the trust and therefore is taxed on the income generated by the trust. As Chapter C:12 points out, a transfer of assets to a revocable trust is an incomplete transfer and not subject to the gift tax.

EXAMPLE C:14-33 ▶

ADDITIONAL COMMENT

A common use of the revocable trust is to avoid probate for the property held by the trust. On the death of the grantor, the trustee of the revocable trust distributes the trust property in accordance with the trust agreement. Because the trustee holds legal title to the property, he or she can distribute the property without the trust assets going through the probate process. The trust assets are included in the gross estate.

In the current year, Tom transfers property to a revocable trust and names Ann to receive the income for life and Beth to receive the remainder. The trust's income for the current year consists of $15,000 of dividends and an $8,000 long-term capital gain. The trustee distributes the dividends to Ann but retains the gain and credits it to principal. Because the trust is revocable, the dividend and capital gain income are taxed directly to Tom on his current year individual tax return. Nothing is taxed to the trust or its beneficiaries. ◀

POST-1986 REVERSIONARY INTEREST TRUSTS

The 1986 Tax Reform Act amended Sec. 673(a) for transfers made after March 1, 1986, to provide that, generally, the grantor is treated as the owner of the trust and is taxed on the accounting income of the trust if he or she has a reversionary interest in either income or principal. Under Sec. 672(e), a grantor is treated as holding any interest held by his or her spouse. These rules have two exceptions.

The first exception makes the grantor trust rules inapplicable if, as of the inception of the trust, the value of the reversionary interest, as valued under the actuarial tables, does not exceed 5% of the value of the trust. The second exception applies if the reversion will occur only if the beneficiary dies before reaching age 21 and the beneficiary is a lineal descendant of the grantor.

EXAMPLE C:14-34 ▶

In the current year, Paul establishes a trust with income payable to his elderly parents for 15 years. The assets of the trust will then revert to Paul. The value of Paul's reversionary interest exceeds 5%. Because Paul has a reversionary interest valued at above 5% and the transfer arose after March 1, 1986, Paul is taxed currently on the trust's accounting income and capital gains. ◀

EXAMPLE C:14-35 ▶

In the current year, Paul transfers property to a trust with income payable to his daughter Ruth until Ruth reaches age 21. On Ruth's twenty-first birthday, she is to receive the trust property outright. In the event Ruth dies before reaching age 21, the trust assets will revert to Paul. Paul is not taxed on the accounting income because his reversion is contingent on the death of the beneficiary (a lineal descendant) before age 21. ◀

RETENTION OF ADMINISTRATIVE POWERS

Under Sec. 675, the grantor is taxed on the accounting income and gains if he or she or his or her spouse holds certain administrative powers. Such powers include, but are not limited to, the following:

▶ The power to purchase or exchange trust property for less than adequate consideration in money or money's worth

▶ The power to borrow from the trust without adequate interest or security except where the trustee (who is someone other than the grantor) has a general lending power to make loans irrespective of interest or security

▶ The power exercisable in a role other than as trustee to (1) vote stock of a corporation in which the holdings of the grantor and the trust are significant from the standpoint of voting control and (2) reacquire the trust property by substituting other property of equal value.

RETENTION OF ECONOMIC BENEFITS

Section 677 taxes the grantor on the portion of the trust with respect to which the income may be

▶ Distributed to the grantor or his or her spouse,

▶ Held or accumulated for future distribution to the grantor or his or her spouse, or

▶ Used to pay premiums on life insurance policies on the life of the grantor or his or her spouse

Use of trust income to provide support for a child whom the grantor is legally obligated to support yields obvious economic benefits to the grantor. A grantor is taxed on any trust income distributed by the trustee to support individuals whom the grantor is legally obligated to support (e.g., children). However, the mere existence of the discretionary power to use trust income for support purposes does not cause the grantor to be taxed on the trust income. Taxation turns on whether the trust income is actually used to meet the support obligation.

The next example concerns use of trust income to support the grantor's minor child.

EXAMPLE C:14-36 ▶

Hal creates a trust and empowers the bank trustee to distribute income to his minor son, Louis, until the son reaches age 21. When Louis reaches age 21, the trust assets including accumulated income are to be paid over to the child. In the current year, when Louis is age 15, the trustee distributes $5,000 that is used to support Louis and $8,000 that is deposited into Louis's savings account. The remaining $12,000 of income is accumulated. Hal (the grantor) is taxed on the $5,000 used to support his son. Louis includes $8,000 in his gross income, and the trust pays tax on $12,000 less its $100 exemption. Note, however, that the kiddie tax rules apply to Louis's income of $8,000. ◀

The following example deals with the payment of premiums on an insurance policy on the grantor's life.

EXAMPLE C:14-37 ▶

ADDITIONAL COMMENT

If the trust were created by a person other than the insured, say a parent, the income required to be used for paying life insurance premiums would not be taxed to the grantor because the insured is not the grantor or the grantor's spouse.

Maria is the grantor of the Martinez Trust, one of whose assets is a life insurance policy on Maria's life. The trust instrument requires that $1,000 of trust income be used to pay the annual insurance premiums and that the rest be distributed to Maria's adult son Juan. Section 677 requires Maria (the grantor and insured) to be taxed on $1,000 of accounting income. The remaining income is taxed to Juan under the general trust rules. ◀

CONTROL OF OTHERS' ENJOYMENT

Section 674 taxes the grantor on trust income if he or she, his or her spouse, or someone without an interest in the trust (e.g., a trustee) has the power to control others' beneficial enjoyment such as by deciding how much income to distribute. Many exceptions, including one for independent trustees, exist for the general rule.

EXAMPLE C:14-38 ▶

Otto is grantor and trustee of a trust over which the trustee has complete discretion to pay out the income or corpus in any amount he deems appropriate to some or all of its three adult beneficiaries, Kay, Fay, and May (none related to Otto). In the current year, the trustee distributes all the income to Kay. Otto, the grantor, is taxed on the income. If instead the trustee were independent, Kay would be taxed on the amount she received. ◀

Under Sec. 678, an individual other than the trust's grantor or beneficiary can be required to report the trust income. This individual is taxed on the trust income if he or she has the power under the trust instrument to vest the trust principal or the income in him- or herself, provided such power is exercisable solely by such individual.

Topic Review C:14-4 summarizes the grantor trust rules.

WHAT WOULD YOU DO IN THIS SITUATION?

You, a CPA, have prepared the income tax returns for the Candy Cain Trust, an irrevocable trust, since the inception of the trust five years ago. The grantor is Able Cain, another client and the father of Candy Cain, the income beneficiary. First Bank, the trustee, is authorized to distribute income at its discretion to Candy, who reached age 18 August of last year. Last year, the trust's DNI of $4,000, all from interest on corporate bonds, was distributed to Candy in June to pay her medical bills incurred in an accident. You advised Mr. Cain that he must include the $4,000 trust distribution on his individual tax return because the distribution was used to satisfy his obligation to support Candy until age 18. Candy began working after her high school graduation and, last year, used her earned income to provide over half of her own support. Mr. Cain reminds you of how many clients he has referred to you and demands that you instead show the distribution as taxable to Candy so the income will be taxed at his daughter's low rates instead of at his rate, the highest marginal rate. How will you react to Mr. Cain's request?

Topic Review C:14-4

Grantor Trust Rules

FACTUAL SITUATION	TAX TREATMENT
1. Trust is revocable.	Ordinary income (including dividends) and capital gains are taxed to grantor.
2. Irrevocable trust is funded on or after March 2, 1986, with income payable to third-party beneficiary for 25 years after which property reverts to grantor; the value of the reversionary interest exceeds 5% of the value of the trust.	Ordinary income (including dividends) and capital gains are taxed to grantor.
3. The grantor of an irrevocable trust retains administrative powers described in the IRC.	Ordinary income (including dividends) and capital gains are taxed to grantor.
4. The income of an irrevocable trust is disbursed to meet the grantor's obligation to support his or her children.	Ordinary income (including dividends) used for support are taxed to grantor.
5. The income of an irrevocable trust is disbursed to pay the premium on a life insurance policy on the life of the grantor or the grantor's spouse.	Ordinary income (including dividends) and capital gains are taxed to grantor to the extent they may be used to pay the premiums.

TAX PLANNING CONSIDERATIONS

Many tax planning opportunities exist with respect to estates and trusts, including the ability to shift income to the fiduciary and/or the beneficiaries and the opportunity for executors or trustees of discretionary trusts to consider the tax consequences of the timing of distributions. These and other tax planning considerations are discussed below.

ABILITY TO SHIFT INCOME

Before 1987, one of the primary tax advantages of using trusts was the ability to shift income from the grantor to the trust or the beneficiary. Three changes have reduced the tax advantages of shifting income. First, the tax rate schedules for all taxpayers—but especially for fiduciaries—are very compressed. In fact, an estate or trust has only $2,300 (in 2011) of income subject to the 15% tax rate. Second, unearned income exceeding $1,900 (in 2011) of children under age 18 (and in some cases age 18 through 23) is taxed at the higher of the parents' or the child's tax rate, even if distributed from a trust or estate. Third, dividend income is eligible for a low or zero tax rate regardless of whether it is taxed to the grantor, the beneficiary, or the trust. Depending on whether the trust income is distributed or retained, it is taxed to the trust or the beneficiary or a portion to each. Because the trust is a separate taxpayer, income taxed to the trust is taxed under the trust's rate schedule. If the beneficiary has income from other sources, the income shifted to the beneficiary is not necessarily taxed in the lowest tax bracket. An income tax savings nevertheless can occur whenever a portion of the shifted income is taxed at a rate lower than the rate the grantor would pay on such income.

TIMING OF DISTRIBUTIONS

Individuals managing estates and discretionary trusts can reduce taxes by carefully planning the timing of distributions. From a tax standpoint, the executor or trustee should consider the beneficiary's income from other sources and make distributions in amounts that equalize the marginal tax rates of the beneficiary and the fiduciary. If the trust is a **sprinkling trust** (a discretionary trust with several beneficiaries), the trustee can accomplish tax savings for the beneficiaries by making distributions to the beneficiaries who have the lowest marginal tax rate that year. Of course, nontax reasons might require a trustee to distribute income to other beneficiaries as well. A special 65-day

ADDITIONAL COMMENT

In 2011, the first $2,350 of trust income is taxed at 15%. A complex trust pays no tax on $100 of income (because of its personal exemption) and only 15% on the next $2,350 of income. If the trust distributes income to a child subject to the kiddie tax rules who is a dependent and has no other unearned income, the child pays no tax on the first $950 of that income and pays taxes at his or her own rate on the next $950. The rest is taxed at the parents' rates. If the parents are always in the top income tax bracket, nontrivial income tax savings still can be achieved by using a trust to spread non-dividend income over different taxpayers. For the situation described here, a Sec. 2503(c) trust (trust for minors) is commonly used.

KEY POINT

Given that one often cannot determine the exact amount of income a trust (or any other entity) has earned until after the end of the tax year, the importance of the 65-day rule for distribution planning becomes readily apparent.

rule allows trustees of complex trusts and estates to treat distributions made during the first 65 days of the new tax year as if they had been made on the last day of the preceding tax year. If the trustee or executor does not make the election, the distributed income is deducted by the fiduciary and taxed to the beneficiary in the year of the actual distribution.

PROPERTY DISTRIBUTIONS

Under the general rule affecting property distributions, the trust receives a distribution deduction equal to the lesser of the fiduciary's adjusted basis in the property or the property's FMV.[43] If the trust distributes appreciated property, however, the trustee can elect to recognize a gain on the distribution equal to the excess of the property's FMV over its adjusted basis on the distribution date. If the trustee does not make the election, the trust recognizes no gain when it distributes the property.

If the trustee elects to recognize the gain, the distribution deduction equals the property's FMV. The beneficiary, in turn, takes a basis equal to the property's adjusted basis to the trust plus the gain the trust recognized on the distribution. If the beneficiary likely will sell the property soon after distribution, the election provision allows the trustee to choose where the appreciation will be taxed, at the trust level or the beneficiary level. If the distribution involves appreciated capital gain property, the capital gain the trust recognizes can offset the trust's current capital loss and carryovers from prior tax years.

EXAMPLE C:14-39▶ Todd Trust owns a number of assets, including an asset with a FMV of $35,000 and an adjusted basis of $12,000. In the current year, the trust distributes the asset to its sole beneficiary, Susan. The trust does not make any other distributions to Susan. If the trustee elects to recognize gain of $23,000, the trust receives a distribution deduction of $35,000, the FMV of the asset. Susan includes $35,000 of income in her tax return and obtains a $35,000 basis in the asset. Thus, if she sells the asset for $35,000, she will report no gain. If the trustee had not elected to recognize gain on the in-kind distribution, the distribution deduction would have been $12,000, the asset's adjusted basis to the trust. Susan's basis in the asset also would have been $12,000, and she would have reported $12,000 income from the trust. ◀

CHOICE OF YEAR-END FOR ESTATES

Distributions from an estate or trust are taxed to the beneficiaries in the beneficiaries' tax year in which the fiduciary's year ends.[44] Congress in 1986 required all trusts (even existing fiscal-year trusts) other than tax-exempt and wholly charitable trusts to use a calendar year as their tax year to eliminate their ability to defer the taxation of trust distributions to beneficiaries by choosing a noncalendar year.[45] Estates, however, are completely free to choose a year-end as long as the tax year does not exceed 12 months.

EXAMPLE C:14-40▶ Molly Madison died on February 7, 2010. Madison Estate adopted a fiscal year ending January 31. During the period February 7, 2010, through January 31, 2011, Madison Estate distributes $30,000 to Bob, a calendar year beneficiary. The estate's DNI exceeds $30,000. Bob reports $30,000 of estate income on his individual return for 2011, Bob's tax year during which the estate's tax year ended. By choosing the January 31 year-end (instead of a calendar year-end), the executor postpones the taxation of income to Bob from 2010 to 2011. ◀

ADDITIONAL COMMENT

For 2011 and 2012, 35% is the top tax rate for both income and estate tax purposes, so the deduction may produce the same tax savings on either tax return.

DEDUCTION OF ADMINISTRATION EXPENSES

Chapter C:13 points out that the executor elects where to deduct administration expenses, i.e., on the estate tax return, the estate's income tax return, or some on each return. Unlike the situation for deductions in respect of a decedent, Sec. 642(g) denies a double deduction for administration expenses. Such expenses should be deducted where they will yield the greatest tax savings. Of course, if the surviving spouse receives all the

---

[43] Sec. 643(e)(2).
[44] Secs. 652(c) and 662(c).

[45] Sec. 644.

decedent's property or all except for an amount equal to the exemption equivalent, deducting administration expenses on the estate tax return will produce no tax savings because the estate will owe no estate taxes.

COMPLIANCE AND PROCEDURAL CONSIDERATIONS

OBJECTIVE 9

Recognize the filing requirements for fiduciary returns

FILING REQUIREMENTS

GENERAL RULE. Every estate that has gross income of at least $600 for the tax year must file an income tax return (Form 1041-U.S. Income Tax Return for Estates and Trusts). A trust income tax return (generally Form 1041) is required for every trust that has taxable income or has gross income of $600 or more.[46] In addition, every estate or trust that has a nonresident alien as a beneficiary must file a return.[47]

DUE DATE FOR RETURN AND TAX

The due date for fiduciary returns (Form 1041) is the same as for individuals, the fifteenth day of the fourth month following the end of the tax year.[48] If an extension is desired, Form 7004 must be filed. The automatic extension period is five months.

Both trusts and estates generally must make estimated tax payments using the general rules applicable to individual taxpayers.[49] The IRC, however, exempts estates from making estimated tax payments for their first two tax years. If the fiduciary's tax liability exceeds the estimated tax payments, the balance of the tax is due on or before the due date for the return.[50] Estimated tax payments for a trust or an estate should be accompanied by Form 1041-ES (Estimated Income Tax for Fiduciaries).

DOCUMENTS TO BE FURNISHED TO IRS

Although the executor or the trustee need not file a copy of the will or the trust instrument with the return, at times the IRS may request a copy of such documents. If the IRS makes such a request, the executor or the trustee also should transmit the following:

▶ A statement signed under penalty of perjury that the copy is true and complete

▶ A statement naming the provisions of the will or trust agreement that the executor or the trustee believes control how the income is to be divided among the fiduciary, the beneficiaries, and the grantor (if applicable)

SAMPLE SIMPLE AND COMPLEX TRUST RETURNS

Appendix B contains samples of simple and complex trust returns (Form 1041). The Appendix also illustrates completed Schedules K-1 for the reporting of distributed income, etc. to the beneficiaries. One copy of Schedule K-1 for each beneficiary is filed with Form 1041. In addition, each beneficiary receives a copy of his or her Schedule K-1, so that he or she knows the amount and type of gross income to report for the distributions received as well as other pertinent information.

In the two sets of facts illustrated in the sample returns, the trusts do not owe the alternative minimum tax (AMT). Trusts that owe the AMT report it on Schedule I of Form 1041.

ETHICAL POINT

Individual beneficiaries report their share of income from trusts and estates on their Form 1040. CPAs have a responsibility to monitor clients' beneficial interests in trusts and estates to prevent underreporting. Some clients may unintentionally forget to disclose income from a simple trust because they received no cash distributions from the fiduciary during the year.

---

[46] Secs. 6012(a)(3) and (4). A special grantor trust rule, however, permits a revocable trust's income to be reported on the grantor's tax return. See Reg. Sec. 1.671-4(b).

[47] Sec. 6012(a)(5).

[48] Sec. 6072(a).

[49] Sec. 6654(l).

[50] Sec. 6151(a).

PROBLEM MATERIALS

DISCUSSION QUESTIONS

C:14-1 Explain to a client in laymen's language what portion of the income of an estate or trust is subject to taxation at the fiduciary level.

C:14-2 Given the tax rate schedule for trusts, what reasons (tax and/or nontax) exist today for creating a trust?

C:14-3 List some major differences between the taxation of individuals and trusts.

C:14-4 Explain to a client the significance of the income and principal categorization scheme used for fiduciary accounting purposes.

C:14-5 List some common examples of principal and income items under the 1962 Act.

C:14-6 A client asks about the relevance of state law in classifying items as principal or income. Explain the relevance.

C:14-7 A trust whose instrument provides that Irene is entitled to receive for life distributions of income only and Beth is to receive the remainder interest sells property at a gain. Income and corpus are classified in accordance with the 1962 Uniform Act. Will Irene receive a distribution equal to the amount of the gain? Explain.

C:14-8 Refer to Question C:14-7. Which taxpayer (the trust, Irene, or Beth) pays the tax on the gain?

C:14-9 A trust owns an asset on which depreciation is claimed. The trust distributes all of its income to its sole income beneficiary. Whose taxable income is reduced by the depreciation?

C:14-10 What is the amount of the personal exemption for trusts and estates?

C:14-11 A client inquires about the significance of distributable net income (DNI). Explain.

C:14-12 a. Are net accounting income and DNI always the same amount?
b. If not, explain a common reason for a difference.
c. Are capital gains usually included in DNI?

C:14-13 Explain how to determine the deductible portion of a trustee's fee.

C:14-14 Assume that a trust collects rental income and interest income on tax-exempt bonds. Will a portion of the rental expenses, such as repairs, have to be allocated to tax-exempt income and thereby become nondeductible? Explain.

C:14-15 a. Describe the shortcut approach for verifying that the amount calculated as a simple trust's taxable income is correct.
b. Can a shortcut verification process be applied for trusts and estates that accumulate some of their income? Explain.

C:14-16 When does the NOL of a trust or estate produce tax deductions for the beneficiaries?

C:14-17 The Mary Morgan Trust, a simple trust, sells one capital asset in the current year. The sale results in a loss.
a. When will the capital loss produce a tax benefit for the trust or its beneficiary? Explain.
b. Would the result necessarily be the same for a complex trust? Explain.

C:14-18 A colleague states that simple trusts receive no tax benefit from a personal exemption. Is your colleague correct?

C:14-19 Describe the tier system for taxing trust beneficiaries.

C:14-20 Determine the accuracy of the following statement: Under the tier system, beneficiaries who receive mandatory distributions of income are more likely to be taxed on the entire distributions they receive than are beneficiaries who receive discretionary distributions.

C:14-21 a. Describe to a client what income in respect of a decedent (IRD) is.
b. Describe to the client one tax disadvantage and one tax advantage that occur because of the classification of a receipt as IRD.

C:14-22 Describe three situations that cause trusts to be subject to the grantor trust rules.

C:14-23 Can a client escape the grantor trust rules by providing in a trust instrument that income is payable to a nephew for 20 years and that the trust assets pass at the end of 20 years to the client's spouse?

C:14-24 A client is under the impression that, if the grantor trust rules apply to a trust, the grantor is always taxed on the trust's ordinary income (including dividends) and capital gains. Is the client correct? Explain.

C:14-25 What is the benefit of the 65-day rule?

C:14-26 a. When are fiduciary income tax returns due?
b. Must estates and trusts pay estimated income taxes?

ISSUE IDENTIFICATION QUESTIONS

C:14-27 Art Rutter sold an apartment building in May 2011 for a small amount of cash and a note payable with payments beginning in 2012. Principal and interest payments are due annually on the note in April of 2012 through 2016. Art died in August 2011. He willed all his assets to his daughter Amelia. Art's gross estate is about $6 million, and his estate tax deductions are very small. What tax issues should the executor of his estate consider with respect to reporting the sale of the building and the collection of the installments?

C:14-28 For the first five months of its existence (August through December 2011), the Estate of Amy Ennis had gross income (net of expenses) of $7,000 per month. For January through July 2012, the executor estimates that the estate will have gross income (net of expenses) totaling $5,000. The estate's sole beneficiary is Amy's uncle, Joe, who is a calendar year taxpayer. Joe incurred a large NOL from his sole proprietorship years ago, and $34,000 of the NOL carryover remains but expires at the end of 2011. During 2011, Joe received only $9,000 of income from part-time employment. What tax issues should the executor of Amy's estate consider with respect to distributions of the estate's income?

C:14-29 Raj Kothare funded an irrevocable simple trust in May of last year. The trust benefits Raj's son for life and grandson upon the son's death. One of the assets he transferred to the trust was Webbco stock, which had a $35,000 FMV on the transfer date. Raj's basis in the stock was $39,000, and he paid no gift tax on the transfer. The stock's value has dropped to $27,000, and the trustee thinks that now (October of the current year) might be the time to sell the stock and recognize the loss. For the current year, the trust will have $20,000 of income exclusive of any gain or loss. Raj's taxable income is approximately $15,000. What tax and non-tax issues should the trustee consider concerning the possible sale of the stock?

PROBLEMS

C:14-30 *Calculation of the Tax Liability.* A trust has taxable income of $30,000 in 2011. The $30,000 includes $5,000 of long-term capital gains and $25,000 of interest. What is its income tax liability? Compare this tax to the amount of tax a married individual filing a joint return would pay on the same amount of taxable income.

C:14-31 *Determination of Taxable Income.* A simple trust has the following receipts and expenditures for the current year. The long-term capital gain and trustee's fees are part of principal.

Dividends	$20,000
Long-term capital gain	15,000
Trustee's fees	1,500
Distribution to beneficiary	20,000

a. What is the trust's taxable income under the formula approach of Figure C:14-1?
b. What is the trust's taxable income under the short-cut approach?

C:14-32 *Determination of Taxable Income.* Refer to Problem C:14-31. How would your answer to Part a change if the trust in addition received $8,000 interest from tax-exempt bonds, and it distributed $28,000 instead of $20,000?

C:14-33 *Determination of Taxable Income and Tax Liability.* A simple trust has the following receipts and expenditures for 2011. The trust instrument is silent with respect to capital gains, and state law concerning trust accounting income follows the Uniform Act. Assume the trustee's fee is charged to income.

Corporate bond interest	$40,000
Tax-exempt interest	9,000
Long-term capital gain	5,000
Trustee's fee	2,000
Distribution to beneficiary	47,000

a. What is the trust's taxable income under the formula approach of Figure C:14-1?
b. What is the trust's tax liability?

C:14-34 *Determination of Taxable Income.* During the current year, a simple trust has the following receipts and expenditures. Assume that trustee's fees are charged to income and that the 1962 Uniform Act governs the accounting classification.

Corporate bond interest	$60,000
Long-term capital gain	20,000
Trustee's fees	3,000

a. How much must be distributed to the beneficiary?
b. What is the trust's taxable income under the shortcut approach?

C:14-35 *Determination of Distribution Deduction.* A trust has net accounting income of $24,000 and incurs a trustee's fee of $1,000 in its principal account. What is its distribution deduction under the following situations:
a. It distributes $24,000, and all of its income is from taxable sources.
b. It distributes $24,000, and it has tax-exempt income (net of allocable expenses) of $2,000.
c. It distributes $10,000, and all of its income is from taxable sources.

C:14-36 *Determination of Beneficiary's Income.* A trust is authorized to make discretionary distributions of income and principal to its two beneficiaries, Roy and Sandy. Separate shares are not required. For the current year, it has DNI and net accounting income of $80,000, all from taxable sources. It distributes $60,000 to Roy and $40,000 to Sandy. How much gross income should each beneficiary report?

C:14-37 *Determination of Beneficiary's Income.* Refer to Problem C:14-36. How would your answer change if the trust instrument required that $10,000 per year be distributed to Sandy, and the trustee also made discretionary distributions of $60,000 to Roy and $30,000 to Sandy with separate shares not required?

C:14-38 *Determination of Accounting Income and Distribution.* The Trotter Trust has the receipts and expenditures listed below for the current year. Assume the Uniform Act (1962) governs an item's classification as principal or income. The trustee's fee is charged one-half to principal and one-half to income. What is the trust's net accounting income and the maximum amount it can distribute? Assume the trust cannot pay out principal.

Dividends	$15,000
Interest on tax-exempt bonds	7,000
Loss on sale of capital asset	(9,000)
Rental income from land	6,000
Property taxes on rental property	1,000
Trustee's fee	1,800

C:14-39 *Determination of Taxable Income.* Refer to Problem C:14-38. Assume the trustee must pay out all of its income currently to its beneficiary, Julio.
a. What is the deductible portion of the trustee's fee?
b. What is the trust's taxable income exclusive of the distribution deduction?
c. What is the trust's DNI?
d. What is the trust's taxable income using the formula approach of Figure C:14-1?

C:14-40 *Determination of Taxable Income.* Refer to Problem C:14-39. How would your answers change if the trust were a discretionary trust that distributes $12,000 to its beneficiary, Julio?

C:14-41 *Calculation of Deductible Expenses.* The George Grant Trust reports the receipts and expenditures listed below. What are the trust's *deductible* expenses?

U.S. Treasury interest	$25,000
Rental income	9,000
Interest from tax-exempt bonds	6,000
Property taxes on rental property	2,000
CPA's fee for tax return preparation	800
Trustee's fee	1,900

C:14-42 *Tax Treatment of Capital Losses.* A simple trust had a long-term capital loss of $10,000 for 2010 and a long-term capital gain of $15,000 for 2011. Its net accounting income and DNI are equal. Explain the tax treatment for the 2010 capital loss assuming the trust is in existence at the end of 2012.

C:14-43   *Tax Treatment of Capital Losses.* Refer to Problem C:14-42. How would your answer change if instead the trust were a complex trust that makes no distributions in 2010 and 2011? Assume the trust earns $8,000 of corporate bond interest income each year.

C:14-44   *Revocable Trusts.* A revocable trust created by Amir realizes $30,000 of rental income and a $5,000 capital loss. It distributes $25,000 to Ali, its beneficiary. How much income is taxed to the trust, the grantor, and the beneficiary?

C:14-45   *Reversionary Interest Trusts.* Holly funded the Holly Marx Trust in January 2011. The entire trust income is payable to her adult son, Jack for 20 years. At the end of the twentieth year, the trust assets are to pass to Holly's husband. In the current year, the trust realizes $30,000 of dividend income and a $15,000 long-term capital gain. How much income is taxed to the trust, the grantor, and the beneficiary in the current year?

C:14-46   *Reversionary Interest Trusts.* Refer to Problem C:14-45. Explain how your answers would change for each independent situation indicated below:
a. At the end of the trust term, the property passes instead to Holly's nephew.
b. Holly creates the trust in October 2011 for a term of 25 years, after which the property reverts to her.

C:14-47   *Income in Respect of Decedent.* The following items are reported on the first income tax return for the Ken Kimble Estate. Mr. Kimble, a cash method of accounting taxpayer, died on July 1, 2011.

Dividends	$10,000
Interest on corporate bonds	18,000
Collection on installment note from sale of investment land	24,000

The record date was June 14 for $6,000 of the dividends and October 31 for the remaining $4,000 of dividends. The bond interest is payable annually on October 1. Mr. Kimble's basis in the land was $8,000. He sold it in 2010 for a total sales and contract price of $48,000 and reported his gain under the installment method. Ignore interest on the installment note. What amount of IRD is reported on the estate's calendar year income tax return?

C:14-48   *Income in Respect of Decedent.* Julie Brown died on May 29 of the current year. She was employed before her death at a gross salary of $4,000 per month. Her pay day was the last day of each month, and her employer did not pro rate her last monthly salary payment. She owned preferred stock that paid quarterly dividends of $800 per quarter each March 31, June 30, September 30, and December 31. The record date for the June dividend was June 10. Assume her estate chooses a calendar year as its tax year. What amount of gross income should be reported on the estate's first income tax return? Identify the IRD included in gross income.

C:14-49   *Property Distributions.* In the current year, Maddox Trust, a complex trust, distributed an asset with a $42,000 adjusted basis and a $75,000 FMV to its sole beneficiary, Marilyn Maddox-Mason. The trustee elected to recognize gain on the distribution. Marilyn received no other distributions from the trust during the year. The distributable net income for the year was $87,000, and none of it was from tax-exempt sources.
a. What is the trust's distribution deduction?
b. On her individual income tax return, how much gross income should Marilyn report from the trust?
c. What is Marilyn's basis in the asset distributed in kind from the trust?

C:14-50   *Income Recognition by Beneficiary.* Joan died April 17, 2010. Joan's executor chose March 31 as the tax year end for the estate. The estate's only beneficiary, Kathy, reports on a calendar year. The executor of Joan's estate makes the following distributions to Kathy:

June 2010	$ 5,000
August 2010	10,000
March 2011	12,000
August 2011	14,000

The 2010 and 2011 distributions do not exceed DNI. How much income should Kathy report on her 2010 return as a result of the distributions from the estate? On her 2011 return?

COMPREHENSIVE PROBLEM

C:14-51 Dana Dodson died October 31, 2009, with a gross estate of $6.7 million, debts of $200,000, and a taxable estate of $6.5 million. Dana made no adjusted taxable gifts. All of her property passed under her will to her son, Daniel Dodson. The estate chose a June 30 year-end. Its receipts, disbursements, and gains for the period ended June 30, 2011, were as follows:

Dividend income	$27,000
Interest income from corporate bonds	18,000
Interest income from tax-exempt bonds	9,000
Gain on sale of land	10,000
Executor's fee (charged to principal)	4,000
Distribution to Daniel Dodson	–0–

Of the $27,000 dividends received in the estate's first tax year, $7,000 were declared October 4, 2009, with a record date of October 25 and a payment date of November 4, 2009. The corporate bonds pay interest each August 31 and February 28. The estate collected $18,000 corporate bond interest in February 2010 and February 2011. The tax-exempt bonds pay interest each June 30 and December 31. The estate collected $4,500 in December 2009 and 2010 and $4,500 in June 2010 and 2011 from the tax-exempt bonds. Dana, a cash basis taxpayer, sold land in 2008 for a total gain of $60,000 and used installment reporting. She collected principal in 2008 and 2009 and reported gain of $30,000 on her 2008 return and $10,000 on her 2009 return. The estate collected additional principal in March 2010 and the remaining principal payment in March 2011. The gain attributable to the March 2010 and March 2011 principal collections is $10,000 per tax year. Ignore interest on the sale.
   Calculate the following:
a. Deductible executor's fee.
b. Total IRD and the IRD reported on the return for the period ended June 30, 2011.
c. Total Sec. 691(c) deduction if none of the debts are DRD.
d. Section 691(c) deduction deductible on the estate's income tax return for the period ended June 30, 2011.
e. Taxable income of the estate for its tax year ended June 30, 2011.
f. Marginal income tax rate for the estate for its tax year ended June 30, 2011.

TAX STRATEGY PROBLEM

C:14-52 Glorietta Trust is an irrevocable discretionary trust that Grant Glorietta funded in 1999. The discretionary income beneficiary for life is Grant's son, Gordon Glorietta (single). Gordon is a partner in a partnership in which he materially participates, and he has a large basis in his partnership interest. For 2011, the trust had $50,000 of corporate bond interest, net of expenses, and no other income. It made no distributions to Gordon in 2011. Assume that it is now February 22, 2012, and Gordon has just learned that his share of loss from the partnership will be $72,000. Gordon has other income for 2011 of approximately $52,000. The trustee anticipates distributing $40,000 cash to Gordon before the end of February. For the last few years, Gordon's marginal tax rate was 15%. He claims the standard deduction, has only one exemption, and files as a single individual. Discuss a tax-saving opportunity presented by this scenario. Also show a comparative analysis of the alternatives.

C:14-53 Carla plans to transfer to a new trust oil and gas properties producing royalty income. She will transfer no other properties. The sole income beneficiary of the trust will be Carla's son, Marshall, who is in the top marginal income tax bracket and is expected to remain there. Carla estimates that the trust, a simple trust, will receive about $30,000 of royalty income each year and have $2,000 of cash expenses each year. The situs of the trust will be in Virginia, which has enacted the Uniform Principal and Income Act (1997). Carla seeks your advice about the total combined income tax cost to the trust and Marshall if the Uniform Principal and Income Act governs compared with the combined tax cost to the two taxpayers if the trust instrument states that 27.5% of the royalty income is to be allocated to principal (corpus) and the rest to income. For simplicity, use 2011 tax rates and ignore the depletion deduction that would actually be available with respect to the royalty income. You will need to follow the instructions for Problem C:14-63 to learn about the Virginia rules under the Uniform Principal and Income Act.

C:14-54 Cate Cole died in 2009, and her will left her entire estate in equal shares to her two adult children, Calvin and Corrine. Both children have been in the top income tax bracket for at least ten years and anticipate remaining there unless the rate structure changes substantially. The Cate Cole Estate is a calendar year taxpayer. The year 2011 is almost over, and to date the estate has received $18,000 of interest income from a certificate of deposit (CD). The executor does not expect to collect any more income before the end of the year. However, in January 2012, the estate will collect $1,500 of interest income from the CD. The executor has distributed all the estate's assets except for the CD, which matures in early January 2012. The executor anticipates distributing the funds from the CD when it matures, after which he will close the estate. Because the taxable estate did not exceed the "exemption equivalent," the executor did *not* deduct administration expenses on the estate tax return. The estate now owes administration expenses totaling $25,000. Propose an income tax minimization strategy for timing, between 2011 and 2012, the payment of the administration expenses, and prepare a schedule to support your recommendation.

TAX FORM/RETURN PREPARATION PROBLEMS

C:14-55 Marion Mosley created the Jenny Justice Trust in 1995 with First Bank named as trustee. For 20 years, the trust is to pay out all its income semiannually to the beneficiary, Jenny Justice. At the end of the twentieth year, the trust assets are to be distributed to Jenny's descendants. Capital gains are credited to principal, and depreciation is charged to principal. For the current year, the irrevocable trust reports the following results:

	Amounts Allocable to	
	Income	Principal
Rental income	$15,000	
Corporate bond interest	27,000	
Interest on tax-exempt (non-private activity) bonds	8,000	
Long-term capital gain on sale of land		30,000[a]
Maintenance and repairs of rental property	1,500	
Property taxes on rental property	700	
Fee for tax return preparation	500	
Trustee's fee		2,000
Depreciation		2,400
Estimated federal income taxes paid		9,000

[a]The sales price and adjusted basis are $110,000 and $80,000, respectively. The trustee acquired the land in 2002 and the trustee sold it in November of the current year.

Prepare a Form 1041, including any needed Schedule K-1s, for the Jenny Justice Trust. Ignore the alternative minimum tax (AMT). The trustee's address is P.O. Box 100, Dallas, TX 75202. The identification number of the trust is 74-6224343. Jenny, whose Social Security number is 252-37-1492, resides at 2 Mountain View, Birmingham, AL 35205.

C:14-56 In 2001, Belinda Barclay established the Barclay Trust, an irrevocable trust, and named as trustee Local Bank, 1234 Tide Freeway, Tuscaloosa, AL 35487. She funded the trust with corporate and municipal bonds. The trustee is directed to distribute income and/or principal at its discretion to Belinda's adult sons, Anthony Barclay (421-78-0443) and Patrick Barclay (421-78-0445), for 15 years and then to pay out the remaining trust assets, including any accumulated income, equally between the two sons. The tax ID number for the trust is 74-5434127. Half of the trustee's fee is charged to principal and half to income. During the current year, the trustee distributed $12,400 to Anthony, who resides at 37 Crimson Cove, Tuscaloosa, AL 35487, and nothing to Patrick. Other current year information for the trust is as follows:

Corporate bond interest	$17,000
Municipal bond interest	19,000
Long-term capital gain on sale of corporate bonds	2,200
CPA's fee for prior year's tax return	800
Trustee's fee	1,500
Estimated federal income taxes paid	3,700

The trust has a $700 short-term capital loss carryover from the prior year.

Prepare a Form 1041, and any needed Schedule K-1s, for the Barclay Trust. Ignore the alternative minimum tax (AMT). The bonds are not private activity bonds.

C:14-57 Mark Meadows funded a trust in 2004 with Merchants Bank named as trustee. He paid no gift tax on the transfer. The trustee in its discretion is to pay out income to Mark's children, Angela and Barry, for 15 years. Then the trust will terminate, and its assets, including accumulated income, will be paid to Angela and Barry in equal amounts. (Separate shares are *not* to be maintained.) In the current year, the trustee distributes $3,000 to Angela and $9,000 to Barry. The trust paid estimated federal income taxes of $15,000 and reported the following additional results for the current year.

	Amounts Allocable to	
	Income	Principal
Dividends	$50,000	
Interest on corporate bonds	4,000	
Interest on City of Cleveland (non-private activity) bonds	9,000	
Long-term capital loss on sale of stock		$12,000ª
Trustee's fee		2,400
CPA's fee for tax return preparation	400	

ªMr. Meadows purchased the stock for $30,000 in 1990. It was valued at $44,000 when he transferred it to the trust in 2004. The trust sold the stock for $18,000 in December of the current year.

Prepare a Form 1041, including any needed Schedule K-1s, for the trust established by Mr. Meadows. Ignore the alternative minimum tax (AMT). The trustee's address is 201 Fifth Ave., New York, NY 10017. The trust's identification number is 74-5271322. Angela (127-14-1732) and Barry (127-14-1733) reside at 3 East 246th St., Huntington, NY 11743.

CASE STUDY PROBLEMS

C:14-58 Arthur Rich, a widower, is considering setting up a trust (or trusts) with a bank as trustee for his three minor children. He will fund the trust at $900,000 (or $300,000 each in the case of three trusts). A friend suggested that he might want to consider a January 31 year-end for the trusts. The friend also suggested that Arthur might want to make each trust a complex discretionary trust. Arthur is a little apprehensive about the idea of a trust that would be complex. The friend warned that trust income should not be spent on support of the children.

Required: Prepare a memorandum to the tax partner of your firm concerning the above client matter. As part of your analysis, consider the following:

a. What tax reasons, if any, can you think of for having three trusts instead of one?
b. Why do you think the friend suggested a January 31 year-end?
c. What is your reaction to the friend's suggestion about the year-end?
d. Which taxpayer, the beneficiary or the trust, is taxed on the income from a discretionary trust?
e. To what extent do trusts serve as income-shifting arrangements?
f. What can you advise Arthur concerning his apprehension about a complex trust?
g. Why did the friend warn against spending trust income for the children's support?

C:14-59 You are preparing a 2010 individual tax return for Robert Lucca, a real estate developer and long-time client. While preparing Robert's individual tax return you learn that he has interest income from a trust his 75-year-old father created in 2009. His 2010 income from the trust is properly reflected on a Schedule K-1 prepared by the accounting firm that prepared the trust's 2010 return. Robert prepared the trust's return for 2009, and decided that he should not be taxed on any of the trust's income because the trust distributed nothing to him. Upon reviewing Robert's copy of the trust instrument, you learn that the instrument calls for mandatory distributions of all the income to Robert every year. Assume that the trust reported $8,000 of taxable income for 2009 and claimed no distribution deduction and that Robert was in the highest marginal tax bracket for 2009.

a. What responsibility do you have in 2011 to correct the error made for the tax year 2009? Refer to the *Statements on Standards for Tax Services* in Appendix E.
b. Assume instead that an IRS agent has just begun to audit Robert's 2009 individual tax return. What is your responsibility if you have discovered the error on the 2009 trust return, and you are representing Robert in the audit?

TAX RESEARCH PROBLEMS

C:14-60 The Latimer Trust instrument directs that all income be paid annually to Laura Lee Latimer for life with remainder to Laura Lee's son Lance Latimer or his estate. The trust instrument does not authorize the trustee to make charitable contributions. The Latimer Trust owns a 15% interest in LLL Partnership, which operates a retail store. A Schedule K-1 the Latimer Trust received from the partnership reported, among other information, that the trust's share of charitable contributions made by the partnership for 2011 was $350. The trust had DNI of $25,000. What charitable contribution deduction, if any, may the trust deduct? Is the trust a simple or complex trust in 2011?

C:14-61 Roy Ritter died two years ago. Among the assets he owned were Ritter Ranch, a cattle ranch consisting of 12,220 acres in Texas. In accordance with Roy's will, the ranch passed to a testamentary trust (the Ritter Trust) with grandson Gene Ritter as trustee. The sole asset of the trust is the ranch, and unfortunately the ranch is operating at a loss. Gene is an accountant and devotes some hours to day-to-day ranching issues but does not meet the material participation test in the context of the passive activity loss (PAL) rules. Gene employs a well-trained, full-time ranch manager and 20 "ranch hands." Ritter Trust is a new client of your firm. Write a memo in which you discuss the applicability of the PAL rules to the Ritter Trust. In particular, you should discuss whether "material participation" is measured by just the trustee's hours and activities or whether the hours and efforts of the trustee, the ranch manager, and all of the other employees should be considered. Recall that Sec. 469 is the primary IRC section for the PAL rules.

C:14-62 Joyce Ingalls is the daughter of the late Fred Ingalls, who died August 15, 2011. One of the items included in his gross estate was a traditional (regular/non-Roth) IRA valued at several million dollars. Mr. Ingalls's estate will owe taxes, but no estate taxes had been paid by March 1, 2012, the date Joyce filed her 2011 individual income tax return, which she prepared. Included in her gross income for 2011 was a $50,000 distribution from her father's IRA. After talking with a friend, she wonders whether a Sec. 691(c) deduction was available on her 2011 return, and she has contacted you to resolve this issue. Write a memo in which you address whether Joyce is entitled to claim a Sec. 691(c) deduction for income in respect of a decedent (IRD) she collected, given that no estate tax has yet been paid on the IRD or any other inclusion in her father's gross estate. Also address in a conceptual manner how the deduction, assuming it is available, is calculated. At a minimum you should consult the following sources:

- IRC Sec. 691(c)
- FSA 200011023

C:14-63 *Internet Research Problem.* Your client is considering funding a trust with some oil and gas properties. The trust will be governed by the laws of Virginia, which has adopted the 1997 version of the Uniform Principal and Income Act (the 1997 Act). Your client wants to know how oil and gas royalty income will be allocated between the principal and income accounts under the 1997 Act, compared with the 1962 version of the Act. Start your research by going to *www.nccusl.org*, the Web site for the National Conference of Commissioners of Uniform State Laws. Go to "Final Acts & Legislation." Select "Principal and Income Act," and "Virginia." Under "Final Act," consult Section 411 of the Act. Prepare a memo that addresses the client's question.

C:14-64 *Internet Research Problem.* You are preparing for a client meeting at which the client has indicated he wants to discuss revocable trusts. Use the search engine Google and locate a discussion about revocable trusts (also known as living trusts). Summarize the points from a site's discussion about revocable (living) trusts, and indicate which Web site you visited.

15

CHAPTER

ADMINISTRATIVE PROCEDURES

LEARNING OBJECTIVES

After studying this chapter, you should be able to

1. ▶ Understand the role of the IRS in our tax system

2. ▶ Discuss how returns are selected for audit and the alternatives available to taxpayers whose returns are audited

3. ▶ Describe the IRS's ruling process

4. ▶ Identify due dates for tax returns

5. ▶ Understand tax-related penalties generally

6. ▶ Calculate the penalty for not paying estimated taxes

7. ▶ Describe more severe penalties, including the fraud penalty

8. ▶ Understand the statute of limitations

9. ▶ Explain from whom the government may collect unpaid taxes

10. ▶ Understand professional and government standards for tax practitioners

This chapter provides an overview of the administrative and procedural aspects of tax practice, an area with which all tax advisors should be familiar. The specific matters discussed include the role of the Internal Revenue Service (IRS) in tax enforcement and collection, the manner in which the IRS chooses tax returns for audit, taxpayers' alternatives to immediately agreeing to pay a proposed deficiency, due dates for returns, taxpayer penalties, and the statute of limitations. Chapter C:1 briefly discussed the AICPA's *Statements on Standards for Tax Services* and Treasury Department *Circular 230* guidelines for tax practioners. Chapter C:15 expands the discussion on professional standards and examines additional tax practice topics, including Internal Revenue Code (IRC) penalty provisions that affect tax advisors and tax return preparers.

ROLE OF THE INTERNAL REVENUE SERVICE

OBJECTIVE 1

Understand the role of the IRS in our tax system

The IRS is part of the Treasury Department. Its chief administrative officer is the IRS Commissioner. Overseeing the activities of the IRS is a nine-member board consisting of the Secretary of the Treasury, the IRS Commissioner, a public sector representative, and six private sector representatives. All board members are appointed by the President of the United States.

ENFORCEMENT AND COLLECTION

One of the IRS's most significant functions is enforcing tax laws.[1] The IRS is responsible for ensuring that taxpayers file returns, correctly report their tax liabilities, and pay any tax due.

Voluntary compliance with U.S. tax laws is relatively high. However, because some persons do not voluntarily comply, the IRS must audit selected taxpayers' returns and investigate the activities of nonfilers. In addition, because numerous ambiguities (gray areas) in the tax law exist, taxpayers and the IRS do not always agree on the proper tax treatment of transactions and events. As part of its enforcement duties, the IRS attempts to discover whether the reporting of these transactions and events differs from the way the IRS thinks they should be reported. As we point out later, taxpayers who disagree with the IRS in an audit may litigate.

The IRS must ensure that taxpayers not only report the correct tax liability, but also pay their taxes on time. For various reasons, some taxpayers file returns without paying any or all of the tax owed. The IRS's collection agents are responsible for collecting as much of the tax as possible from such persons.

INTERPRETATION OF THE STATUTE

As noted in Chapter C:1, the statutory language of the Internal Revenue Code (IRC) often is so vague that the courts and IRS must interpret it so that it can be readily applied. The IRS publishes its interpretations in revenue rulings, revenue procedures, notices, and information releases, which are available to the general public. In addition, the IRS offers guidance to specific taxpayers in the form of letter rulings, which have no precedential value for third-party taxpayers. Each of these authorities is discussed in detail in Chapter C:1.

KEY POINT

The U.S. tax structure is based on a self-assessment system. The level of voluntary compliance actually is quite high, but one of the principal purposes of the IRS is to enforce the federal tax laws and identify taxpayers who willfully or inadvertently fail to pay their fair share of the tax burden.

---

[1] The IRS, however, does not have enforcement duties with respect to the taxes on guns and alcohol.

AUDITS OF TAX RETURNS

OBJECTIVE 2

Discuss how returns are selected for audit and the alternatives available to taxpayers whose returns are audited

The IRS operates service centers across the country, which receive and process tax returns.[2] One of the IRS's principal enforcement functions is auditing these returns. All returns are subject to some verification. One task the IRS service centers perform is checking whether amounts are properly calculated and faithfully carried from one line of a return to another. Another task is determining whether any items, such as signatures and Social Security numbers, are missing. Computers compare (or "match") by Social Security number the amounts reported on a taxpayer's return with employer- or payer-prepared documents (Forms W-2 and 1099) filed with the IRS service center.[3] To date, however, a 100% matching of these documents with tax return information has been difficult to achieve.

If the service center detects a calculation error in the tax reported on the return, it will send to the taxpayer a notice proposing an additional tax or granting a refund. If the information reported on a return is inconsistent with the information on Forms W-2 or 1099 reported by an employer or payer, the IRS asks the taxpayer to account for the discrepancy in writing or pay some additional tax.

PERCENTAGE OF RETURNS EXAMINED

REAL-WORLD EXAMPLE

Percentage examined of all returns filed in 2008:

Individuals	1.0%
C corporations	1.3%
S corporations	0.4%
Partnerships	0.4%

The IRS exams only a small fraction of all returns filed. For example, see the Real World Example in the margin. However, for individuals with total positive income (i.e., gross income before losses and other deductions) of $1 million or more, the audit rate was 6.4%, and corporations with assets of at least $250 million faced a 25.7% audit rate. As a result of its audit activities, the IRS recommended additional taxes and penalties totaling $49.3 billion in that year.[4]

The examination percentages described above may be misleading because over half the returns filed are subject to a computerized matching in which the IRS compares the tax return information with documents (Forms 1099 and W-2) submitted by taxpayers and employers. Because wages, interest, alimony, pensions, unemployment compensation, Social Security benefits, and other items of income are reported to the IRS by the payers, and because state income taxes, local real estate taxes, home mortgage interest, and other items of deduction are reported to the IRS by the payees, taxpayers who report only these items on their returns effectively face a 100% audit rate. According to a former IRS commissioner, "[M]ore than half of the individual returns filed are simple enough so that a matching with forms filed by employers and interest payors is sufficient to insure compliance."[5] In fact, 52% of individual assessments were by correspondence.

SELECTION OF RETURNS FOR AUDIT

Returns are chosen for audit in various ways, with many being selected under the *discriminant function (DIF)* process described below. The IRS's objective in using the DIF process is to make the audit process as productive as possible by maximizing the number of audits that result in the collection of additional taxes.[6] The DIF process has improved the IRS's ability to select returns for audit. In recent years, the IRS failed to collect additional taxes on only 10% to 15% of the individual returns audited by its revenue agents and examiners. By comparison, in the late 1960s, before the advent of the DIF program, the IRS failed to collect additional taxes in 45% to 50% of its audits.[7] The IRS conducts an audit initiative known as the Market Segment Specialization Program (MSSP). Examples of market segments include manufacturing, wholesale trade, retail trade (auto

---

[2] For returns filed during calendar year 2011, individuals will send their returns to Atlanta, Georgia; Austin, Texas; Fresno, California; or Kansas City, Missouri.

[3] Form W-2 reports employees' salaries and withholding tax, and Form 1099 reports income such as interest and dividends.

[4] "Examination Coverage: Recommended and Average Recommended Additional Tax Examination, by Type and Size of Return, Fiscal Year 2009," *Internal Revenue Service 2009 Data Book*, available for download at *http://www.irs.gov*, Tax Stats link. Examinations are performed by revenue agents, tax auditors, and service center personnel.

[5] Bureau of National Affairs, *BNA Daily Tax Reports*, June 20, 1984, p. G-1.

[6] J. L. Wedick, Jr., "Looking for a Needle in a Haystack—How the IRS Selects Returns for Audit," *The Tax Adviser*, November 1983, pp. 673–674.

[7] Letter from Sheldon S. Cohen, former IRS Commissioner, to Representative Nancy L. Johnson, Chairman of House Ways and Means Subcommittee on Oversight Regarding the TCMP, dated July 20, 1995, reprinted in *Tax Notes Today*, August 10, 1995, Document 95 TNT 156-63.

and boat dealers and service stations), and services (medical and health).[8] Under the MSSP, IRS personnel develop industry expertise, and the IRS prepares MSSP audit guidelines. As IRS personnel become more familiar with specific industries, their ability to spot industry-specific items that taxpayers incorrectly report likely will improve.

HISTORICAL NOTE

Taxpayers have made several attempts to make the DIF variables public information. However, so far the courts have refused to require the IRS to provide such information. The basic thrust of the DIF program is that a return will be flagged if enough items on the return are out of the norm for a taxpayer in that particular income bracket.

DISCRIMINANT FUNCTION (DIF) PROGRAM.   Of the individual returns audited in 1982, the IRS selected two-thirds under the **DIF** program. In fiscal year 2006, the IRS selected only 27% under the DIF program, with the rest being selected under 12 different audit initiatives, some of which involve nonfilers, tax-shelter related write-offs, computer matching of third-party information, claims for refund, return preparers, and unallowable items.[9]

Returns with a relatively high DIF score have characteristics in common with returns for which the IRS earlier assessed a deficiency upon audit (e.g., the return may have reported a relatively high casualty loss or charitable contribution deduction). Because the IRS does not have the resources to audit all returns with a relatively high DIF score, IRS agents choose which of the higher scored returns should receive top priority for an audit.[10]

The IRS developed its DIF formulas based on data gathered in its **Taxpayer Compliance Measurement Program (TCMP)**. Under the TCMP, the IRS conducted special audits of taxpayers selected at random. In these audits, the IRS examined every line item of taxpayers' returns to develop a statistical norm for the taxpayers' industry or profession as a whole. The IRS "indefinitely postponed" the TCMP in 1995, but in 2002, the IRS launched the **National Research Program (NRP)**. The NRP updates data compiled in TCMP audits and develops new statistical models for identifying returns most likely to contain errors. The NRP differs from the TCMP in two significant respects. First, it relies on pre-existing audit data as well as data compiled in ordinary, as opposed to special, audits. Second, it focuses on specific portions of a tax return, not all line-by-line items, some of which can be verified without face-to-face meetings. Like the TCMP, the NCR is based on data gathered primarily in audits of randomly selected individual tax returns.[11] Starting in 2007, the IRS began selecting 13,000 returns per year and will combine the audit results over rolling three year periods.

The IRS also conducts what are called "financial status" or "lifestyle" audits. These audits seek to identify inconsistencies between the income that a taxpayer reports and income suggested by his or her lifestyle. In the course of the audit, IRS agents review the taxpayer's overall economic situation. They may ask questions concerning where the taxpayer vacations, where his or her children go to school, and the cost and model of his or her vehicles. Although the courts generally have sanctioned the use of financial status audits, Congress has limited their use to situations in which the IRS has a reasonable indication of unreported income.

OTHER METHODS.   The IRS widely uses other methods for selecting returns for audit. Some returns are chosen because the taxpayer filed a claim for a refund of taxes paid previously, and the IRS decides to audit the tax return before refunding the requested amount. A few returns are audited because the IRS receives a tip from one taxpayer (perhaps a disgruntled former employee or ex-spouse) that another taxpayer did not file a correct return. If the IRS does collect additional taxes as a result of the audit, it is authorized to pay a reward to the individual who provided the tip. The reward is completely discretionary although, in most cases, it cannot exceed 15% of the additional tax and penalties due.[12] If the tax, penalties, and interest exceed $2 million, the reward ranges from 15% to 30% of the amount collected. Sometimes, examining the return of an entity (e.g., a corporation) leads to an audit of a related party's return (e.g., a major stockholder).

Occasionally, the IRS investigates particular types of transactions or entities to ascertain taxpayer compliance with the tax law. As a result of these investigations, the IRS may select a number of returns for audit. For example, in 1989 the IRS examined 3,000 to

---

[8] K. D. Bakhai and G. E. Bowers, "A New Era in IRS Auditing," *Florida CPA Today*, November 1994, pp. 26–30.
[9] J. L. Wedick, Jr., "Looking for a Needle in a Haystack—How the IRS Selects Returns for Audit," *The Tax Adviser*, November 1983, pp. 673–674.
[10] Ibid.

[11] The NRP also targets taxes other than individual taxes. For example, the IRS is in the final stages of a project involving S corporations. It also announced a multi-year employment tax project beginning in 2010.
[12] Sec. 7623 and Reg. Sec. 301.7623-1(c).

4,000 individual returns to determine whether taxpayers avoided classifying expenses as miscellaneous itemized deductions to escape the 2% floor. In 1997, the IRS investigated the returns of about 200,000 trusts (representing approximately 7% of total trust returns) to determine whether taxpayers had established them to avoid taxes.[13] In 2003, through a combination of audits, summons, and targeted litigation, the IRS launched an initiative to identify and deter promoters of abusive tax shelters.[14] In November 2009, the IRS announced its first major employment tax research study in 25 years.

The IRS has implemented a tier system to rank issues that might arise during audit. Tier I issues are the most pressing, affect the most industries, and receive the most attention from the IRS. Taxpayers identified as having an existing Tier I issue will almost certainly be audited. Tier II issues are those with substantial non-compliance risk for an industry. Tier III issues generally are industry specific.

DISCLOSURE OF UNCERTAIN TAX POSITIONS

Beginning in 2010, the IRS began phasing in a new reporting requirement on Form 1120, Schedule UTP (Uncertain Tax Position Statement). An uncertain tax position is a tax position taken on a tax return that would result in an adjustment to a line on the tax return if the position is not sustained. Schedule UTP requires a description of each uncertain tax position for which the taxpayer recorded a reserve in its audited financial statements or for which no reserve has been recorded because of expected litigation. Taxpayers also must rank the uncertain positions and disclose whether any tax position exceeds 10% of the aggregate amount of the reserves for all tax positions. For 2010 and 2011 tax years, corporations with assets exceeding $100 million that issue audited financial statements must report uncertain tax positions on Schedule UTP. By 2014, business taxpayers with assets of $10 million or greater will be required to file the schedule.

The schedule will help the IRS identify and prioritize issues for audit. The IRS hopes that Schedule UTP will make their auditors more efficient and increase taxpayer compliance. Taxpayers' primary objection is that the schedule provides a detailed roadmap of vulnerable tax positions, which would affect who was audited and what issues should be addressed. In response to this concern (in Announcement 2010-76), the IRS expanded its policy of restraint and will refrain from requesting particular documents related to uncertain tax positions and the workpapers used to complete Schedule UTP. As part of the restraint policy, the IRS will not assert that the attorney-client privilege, tax advice privilege under Sec. 7525, or the work product doctrine has been waived by providing otherwise privileged documents to financial auditors for their use in preparing financial statements. However, privilege is not created for any other document of the taxpayer or third party. Refer to "Accountant-Client Privilege" on page C:15-36.

ALTERNATIVES FOR A TAXPAYER WHOSE RETURN IS AUDITED

When the IRS notifies a taxpayer of an impending audit, the notice indicates whether the audit is a correspondence, office, or field audit. In a correspondence audit, communication, such as documenting a deduction or explaining why the taxpayer did not report certain income, is handled through the mail. In an office audit, the taxpayer and/or his or her tax advisor meet with an IRS employee at a nearby IRS office. The audit notice indicates which items the IRS will examine and what information the taxpayer should bring to the audit. Field audits are common for business returns and complex individual returns. IRS officials conduct these audits either at the taxpayer's place of business or residence or at his or her tax advisor's office.

SPECIAL RELIEF RULE. A special relief rule exists for repetitive audit examinations of the same item. A taxpayer who receives an audit notice can request that the IRS suspend the examination and review whether the audit should proceed if (1) the IRS audited the taxpayer's return for the same item in at least one of the two previous years and (2) the earlier audit did

ADDITIONAL COMMENT

This special relief rule was designed to reduce the likelihood that the IRS could harass a taxpayer by repeatedly auditing a taxpayer on the same issue.

[13] Jacob M. Schlesinger, "IRS Cracks Down on Trusts It Believes Were Set up as Tax-Avoidance Schemes," *The Wall Street Journal,* April 4, 1997, p. A2.

[14] I.R. 2003-51, April 15, 2003.

not result in a change to his or her tax liability. To request the suspension, the taxpayer should call the IRS official whose name and telephone number appear on the audit notice.

EXAMPLE C:15-1 ▶ In October 2011, the IRS notifies Tony that it will audit his 2009 medical expense deduction. Two years ago, the IRS audited Tony's 2007 medical expense deduction but did not assess an additional tax. Consequently, Tony may request that the IRS suspend the audit of his 2009 return regarding this issue. ◀

EXAMPLE C:15-2 ▶ Assume the same facts as in Example C:15-1 except the IRS audited Tony's 2007 employee business expenses. Because that audit dealt with a different item, Tony may not request a suspension. ◀

ADDITIONAL COMMENT

Taxpayers should encourage the tax practitioner to handle an IRS audit. Because taxpayers usually have a limited understanding of the complexities of the tax law and its administration, having the taxpayer present at the audit generally is not a good idea.

TYPICAL MISCONCEPTION

Taxpayers should be cautious in signing a Form 870. Once this form is executed, the taxpayer no longer is permitted to administratively pursue the items under audit.

MEETING WITH A REVENUE AGENT.   Generally, the first step in the audit process is a meeting between the IRS agent and the taxpayer or the taxpayer's advisor. If the taxpayer is fortunate, the agent will agree that the return was correct as filed or, even better, that the taxpayer is entitled to a refund. In most instances, however, the agent will contend that the taxpayer owes additional taxes. Taxpayers who do not agree with the outcome of their meeting may ask to confer with the agent's supervisor. A meeting with the supervisor could lead to an agreement concerning the additional tax due.

Should the taxpayer agree and the agent's supervisor concur in the amount owed, the taxpayer must sign Form 870 (Waiver of Statutory Notice). This form indicates that the taxpayer waives any restrictions on the IRS's authority to assess the tax and consents to the IRS's collecting it. However, signing Form 870 does not preclude the taxpayer from filing a refund claim later.

If the taxpayer agrees that he or she owes additional tax and pays the tax upon signing the Form 870 waiver, interest accrues on the tax deficiency from the due date of the return through the payment date. Interest also ceases to accrue 30 days after the taxpayer signs the Form 870 waiver but begins to accrue again when the IRS issues a notice and demand for payment. However, the IRS charges no additional interest if the taxpayer pays the tax due within 21 days of the notice and demand (ten days for $100,000 or more).

TECHNICAL ADVICE MEMORANDA.   Occasionally, a highly technical issue with which an IRS agent or appeals officer has had little or no experience arises in the course of the audit. Regardless of the type of audit, the official may request advice from the IRS's national office. Sometimes, the taxpayer urges the official to seek such advice. The advice is given in a Technical Advice Memorandum, which the IRS makes public in the form of a letter ruling. If the advice is favorable to the taxpayer, the agent or appeals officer must follow it. Even if the advice is pro-IRS, the official may consider the hazards of litigation in deciding whether to compromise.

APPEAL TO APPEALS DIVISION.   If the taxpayer does not sign the Form 870 waiver, the IRS will send the taxpayer a **30-day letter**, detailing the proposed changes in the taxpayer's liability and advising the taxpayer of his or her right to pursue the matter with the IRS appeals office. The taxpayer has 30 days from the date of the letter to request a conference with an IRS appeals officer.

If the audit was a field audit and the amount of additional tax plus penalties and interest in question exceeds $10,000, the taxpayer must submit a **protest letter** within the 30-day period. Only a brief written statement is necessary if the amount is between $2,501 and $10,000. An oral request is acceptable in the case of office audits, regardless of the amount of the additional tax, penalties, and interest. If the taxpayer does not respond to the 30-day letter, the IRS will follow up with a 90-day letter, discussed below.

Protest letters are submitted to an official in the appropriate IRS functional division and should include the following information:

▶ The taxpayer's name, address, and telephone number

▶ A statement that the taxpayer wishes to appeal the IRS findings to the appeals office

▶ A copy of the letter showing the proposed adjustments

▶ The tax years involved

> ▶ A list of the proposed changes with which the taxpayer disagrees
> ▶ A statement of facts supporting the taxpayer's position on any issue with which he or she disagrees
> ▶ The law or other authority on which the taxpayer relied[15]

The taxpayer must declare, under penalties of perjury, that the statement of facts is true. If the taxpayer's representative prepares the protest letter, the representative must indicate whether he or she knows personally that the statement of facts is true.

Unlike IRS agents, appeals officers generally have the authority to settle (compromise) cases after considering the hazards of litigation. For example, if the appeals officer believes that the IRS has approximately a 40% chance of winning in court, the appeals officer may agree to close the case if the taxpayer will pay an amount equal to 40% of the originally proposed deficiency. The settlement authority of appeals officers extends to questions of fact and law.

In some matters, however, an appeals officer has no settlement authority. For example, if the matter involves an appeals coordinated issue, the appeals officer must obtain concurrence or guidance from a director of appeals to reach a settlement. An **appeals coordinated issue** usually has wide impact or importance, frequently involving an entire industry or occupation group, for which the IRS desires consistent treatment. An example of an appeals coordinated issue is the income tax treatment of a sale in/lease out (SILO) transaction.[16]

If, after the appeals conference, the taxpayer completely agrees with the IRS's position, he or she signs a Form 870 waiver. However, if the appeals officer makes some concessions and the parties agree that the additional tax is less than that originally proposed, the taxpayer signs Form 870-AD (Waiver of Restrictions on Assessment and Collection). Unlike the case of a Form 870 waiver, a Form 870-AD waiver generally does not permit the taxpayer later to file a refund claim for the tax year in question. A Form 870-AD waiver is effective only if accepted by the IRS.

90-DAY LETTER

If the taxpayer and appeals officer fail to reach an agreement, or if the taxpayer does not file a written protest within 30 days of the date of the initial letter, the IRS issues a **90-day letter** (officially, a "Statutory Notice of Deficiency").[17] The 90-day letter specifies the amount of the deficiency; explains how the amount was calculated; and states that the IRS will assess it unless, within 90 days of the date of mailing, the taxpayer files a petition with the Tax Court.[18] During the 90-day period (and whether or not the taxpayer files the petition), the IRS may not assess the deficiency or attempt to collect it. After the 90-day period (and only if the taxpayer timely files the petition), the IRS still may not assess or collect the deficiency until the Court's decision becomes final.

LITIGATION

As mentioned earlier, taxpayer litigation can begin in one of three courts of first instance: the Tax Court, a U.S. district court, and the U.S. Court of Federal Claims. Before deciding where to litigate, a taxpayer should consider the precedents, if any, of the various courts. Chapter C:1 discusses the issues of precedent and "forum shopping." After considering the time and expense of litigation, some taxpayers decide to pay the deficiency even though they believe their position is correct.

U.S. TAX COURT. Taxpayers seeking to litigate in the Tax Court must file their petition with the Tax Court within 90 days of the date on which the IRS mails the Statutory Notice of Deficiency. The Tax Court strictly enforces this time limit. Before the scheduled hearing date, taxpayers still may reach an agreement with the IRS. Going the Tax Court route has some advantages, including not having to pay the deficiency as a precondition to filing suit.

---

[15] IRS, *Publication No. 5* [Your Appeal Rights and How to Prepare a Protest If You Don't Agree], January 1999, p. 1. A sample protest letter is published in Robert E. Meldman and Richard J. Sideman, *Federal Taxation Practice and Procedure,* Ninth Edition (Chicago: CCH Incorporated, 2006).
[16] IRS Appeals Coordinated Issue Program Settlement Guidelines, UIL No. 9300.38-00.

[17] Upon request, the IRS may grant an extension of time for filing a protest letter.
[18] Sec. 6213(a). If the notice is addressed to a person outside the United States, the time period is 150 days instead of 90.

If the amount in question does not exceed $50,000 for a given year, the taxpayer may use the informal small cases procedure, an alternative not available in other courts. A potential disadvantage of this procedure is that the taxpayer may not appeal the Court's decision.

Taxpayers must pay the additional tax, plus any interest and penalties, if they lose in Tax Court and choose not to appeal their case. In some situations, the Tax Court leaves the computation of the additional tax up to the litigating parties. When this happens, the phrase "Entered under Rule 155" appears at the end of the Tax Court's opinion.

U.S. DISTRICT COURT OR U.S. COURT OF FEDERAL CLAIMS.   To litigate in either a U.S. district court or the U.S. Court of Federal Claims, the taxpayer must first pay the deficiency and then file a claim for a refund with the IRS. In all likelihood, the IRS will deny this claim on the ground that the IRS correctly calculated the deficiency amount and properly assessed it. Upon notice of denial or six months after filing the claim, whichever is earlier, the taxpayer may sue the IRS for a refund. In no event, however, may the taxpayer file this lawsuit two years after the IRS denies the claim.

APPEAL OF A LOWER COURT'S DECISION.   Whichever party loses—the taxpayer or the IRS—may appeal the lower court's decision to an appellate court. If the lawsuit was filed in the Tax Court or a federal district court, the case is appealable to the circuit court of appeals with jurisdiction over the taxpayer. For individuals, the taxpayer's place of residence generally determines which court of appeals has jurisdiction. In the case of corporations, the firm's principal place of business or state of incorporation generally controls. Cases originating in the U.S. Court of Federal Claims are appealable to the Circuit Court of Appeals for the Federal Circuit; that is, all the latter cases are heard by the same circuit, irrespective of the taxpayer's residence, principal place of business, or state of incorporation.

Either the taxpayer or the government can request that the U.S. Supreme Court review an appellate court's decision. If the Supreme Court decides to hear a case, it grants **certiorari**. If the Court decides not to hear a case, it denies certiorari. In any given year, the Supreme Court hears only a few cases dealing with tax matters.

STOP & THINK

Question: Two years ago, Pete deducted an expenditure in the year he paid it. Recently, the IRS audited Pete's return for that year and contended that the expenditure is not deductible. Pete is a resident of California, which is in the Ninth Circuit. In a similar case a few years ago, the Tax Court held that the expenditure is deductible, and the IRS did not appeal the decision. In yet another similar case litigated in a U.S. district court in California, the government lost at the trial level but won on appeal to the Ninth Circuit. If Pete decides to litigate, in which forum (lower court) should he file suit, and why?

Solution: If he litigates in the Tax Court, he need not pay the proposed deficiency tax in advance. However, under the *Golsen* Rule (see Chapter C:1), the Tax Court would depart from its earlier pro-taxpayer decision and rule for the IRS. (Pete's case would be appealable to the Ninth Circuit, and the Ninth Circuit has adopted a pro-government position.) Because the court for his California district would be bound by Ninth Circuit precedent, he should not litigate in that court. This likely outcome would disappoint Pete if he believed that a jury would rule in his favor because only U.S. district courts allow for jury trials. The only forum in which he could win is the U.S. Court of Federal Claims. No precedent that this court must follow exists because neither the U.S. Supreme Court, the Court of Appeals for the Federal Circuit, nor the U.S. Court of Federal Claims has previously adjudicated the issue. (For a discussion of "forum-shopping," see Chapter C:1.)

BURDEN OF PROOF.   In civil cases, the IRS has the burden of proving any factual issue relevant to a determination of the taxpayer's liability, provided the taxpayer meets four conditions.[19] First, the taxpayer introduces "credible evidence" regarding the issue. Credible evidence means evidence of a quality sufficient to serve as the basis of a court decision.[20]

---

[19] See Sec. 7491.   [20] See S. Rept. No. 105-174, (PL. 105-206), pp. 45-46.

Second, the taxpayer complies with the recordkeeping and substantiation requirements of the IRC. These requirements include the proper documentation of meal and entertainment expenses (Sec. 274), charitable contributions (Sec. 170), and foreign controlled businesses (Sec. 6038). Third, the taxpayer "cooperates" with the reasonable requests of the IRS for witnesses, information, documents, meetings, and interviews. Cooperation includes providing access to, and inspection of, persons and items within the taxpayer's control. It also includes exhausting all administrative remedies available to the taxpayer.[21] Fourth, the taxpayer is either a legal person with net worth not exceeding $7 million, or a natural person.

REQUESTS FOR RULINGS

OBJECTIVE 3

Describe the IRS's ruling process

As discussed in Chapter C:1, a taxpayer can seek to clarify the tax treatment of a transaction by requesting that the IRS rule on the transaction. The IRS will respond to certain requests by issuing a letter ruling (sometimes referred to as a private letter ruling) directly to the taxpayer. A letter ruling is a written determination that interprets and applies the tax laws to the taxpayer's specific set of facts.[22] The IRS releases letter rulings to the public but eliminates all confidential information before doing so. The IRS charges a user fee for issuing a ruling, with the 2011 fees ranging from $150 for identical accounting method changes to $50,000 for pre-filing agreements. The fee Also for ruling on a proposed transaction is $14,000.[23]

ADDITIONAL COMMENT

The information requirements for requesting a letter ruling are very precise (see Rev. Proc. 2009-1). In general, a tax professional experienced in dealing with the national office of the IRS should be consulted. Also, a good blueprint of what should be included in a ruling request often can be found by locating an already-published letter ruling and examining its format.

INFORMATION TO BE INCLUDED IN TAXPAYER'S REQUEST

Early each calendar year, the IRS issues a revenue procedure that details how to request a letter ruling and the information that the request must contain. Taxpayers or tax advisors should consult this procedure before requesting a ruling. Appendix B of the procedure contains a checklist the taxpayer may use to ensure that the request is in order. The IRS has issued additional guidelines concerning the data to be included in the ruling request. For example, the IRS has specified what information the taxpayer must provide in a request for a ruling on the tax effects of transfers to a controlled corporation under Sec. 351. All ruling requests must contain a statement of all the relevant facts, including the following:

► Names, addresses, telephone numbers, and taxpayer identification numbers of all interested parties

► The taxpayer's annual accounting period and method

► A description of the taxpayer's business operations

► A complete statement of the business reasons for the transaction

► A detailed description of the transaction[24]

The taxpayer also should submit copies of the contracts, agreements, deeds, wills, instruments, and other documents that pertain to the transaction. The taxpayer must provide an explicit statement of all the relevant facts and not merely incorporate by reference language from the documents. The taxpayer also should indicate what confidential data should be deleted from the ruling before its release to the public.

If the taxpayer takes a position, he or she must disclose the basis for this position and the authorities relied on. Even if the taxpayer does not argue for a particular position, he or she must furnish an opinion of the expected tax effects, along with a statement of authorities supporting this opinion. In addition, the taxpayer should disclose and discuss any authorities to the contrary. The IRS suggests that, if no authorities to the contrary exist, the taxpayer should state so.

---

[21] Ibid.
[22] Rev. Proc. 2011-1, 2011-1 I.R.B. 1, Sec. 2.01.
[23] Rev. Proc. 2011-1, 2011-1 I.R.B. 1, Appendix A.
[24] Rev. Proc. 2011-1, 2011-1 I.R.B. 1, Sec. 7.01. Certain revenue procedures provide a checklist of information to be included for frequently occurring

transactions. See, for example, Rev. Proc. 83-59, 1983-2 C.B. 575, which includes guidelines for requesting rulings regarding a corporate formation under Sec. 351.

The person on whose behalf a ruling is requested should sign the following declaration: "Under penalties of perjury, I declare that I have examined this request, including accompanying documents, and, to the best of my knowledge and belief, the request contains all the relevant facts relating to the request, and such facts are true, correct, and complete."[25]

WILL THE IRS RULE?

In income and gift tax matters, the IRS will rule only on proposed transactions and on completed transactions for which the taxpayer has not yet filed a return.[26] In estate tax matters, the IRS generally will not rule if the estate has filed a tax return. On the other hand, the IRS will rule on the estate tax consequences of a living person.[27] If no temporary or final Treasury Regulations relating to a particular statutory provision have been issued, the following policies govern a ruling unless another IRS pronouncement holds otherwise:

▶ If the answer seems clear by applying the statute to the facts, the IRS will rule under the usual procedures.

▶ If the answer seems reasonably certain by applying the statute to the facts, but not entirely free from doubt, the IRS will likewise rule.

▶ If the answer does not seem reasonably certain, the IRS will rule if so doing is in the best interests of tax administration.[28]

The IRS will not rule on a set of alternative ways of structuring a proposed transaction or on the tax consequences of hypothetical transactions. Generally, the IRS will not rule on certain issues because of the factual nature of the problem involved or for other reasons.[29]

From time to time, the IRS discloses, by means of a revenue procedure, the topics with respect to which it will not rule. The list of topics, however, is not all-inclusive. The IRS may refuse to rule on other topics whenever, in its opinion, the facts and circumstances so warrant.

According to Rev. Proc. 2011-3, the matters on which the IRS will not rule include the following:

▶ Whether property qualifies as the taxpayer's principal residence

▶ Whether compensation is reasonable in amount

▶ Whether a capital expenditure for an item ordinarily used for personal purposes (e.g., a swimming pool) has medical care as its primary purpose

▶ The determination of the amount of a corporation's earnings and profits.[30]

In addition, the IRS will not rule privately on issues that it proposes to address in revenue rulings, revenue procedures, or otherwise, or that the Treasury Department proposes to address in Treasury Regulations.

WHEN RULINGS ARE DESIRABLE

Private letter rulings serve to "insure" the taxpayer against adverse, after-the-fact tax consequences. They are desirable where (1) the transaction is proposed, (2) the potential tax liability is high, and (3) the law is unsettled or unclear. They also are desirable where the IRS has issued to another taxpayer a favorable ruling regarding similar facts and issues. Because only the other taxpayer may rely on the latter ruling, *this* taxpayer may seek a ruling on which he or she may confidently rely. On the other hand, private letter rulings are undesirable where the IRS has issued to another taxpayer an unfavorable ruling regarding similar facts and issues. They also are undesirable where the IRS might publicly rule on a related matter, and the taxpayer has an interest in this matter. Private letter rulings offer insight into the IRS's thinking on the tax treatment of proposed transactions. Although third parties may not cite them as authority for the tax consequences of their transactions, they may cite them as authority for avoiding a substantial understatement penalty (discussed later in this chapter).

TYPICAL MISCONCEPTION

It is easy to be confused about the difference between letter rulings, which pertain to either prospective transactions or completed transactions for which a return has not yet been filed, and Technical Advice Memoranda, which pertain to completed transactions for which the return has been filed and is under audit.

SELF-STUDY QUESTION

How are letter rulings different from other IRS administrative pronouncements (i.e., revenue rulings, revenue procedures, notices, and information releases)?

ANSWER

Letter rulings are written for specific taxpayers (not the general public) and have no precedential value.

ADDITIONAL COMMENT

Requesting a letter ruling makes most sense for transactions that the taxpayer would not undertake without being assured of certain tax consequences. For example, certain divisive reorganizations are tax-free under Sec. 355. Taxpayers often request a ruling that a proposed transaction satisfies the intricate requirements of Sec. 355.

---

[25] Rev. Proc. 2011-1, 2011-1 I.R.B. 1, Sec. 7.01.
[26] Ibid., Sec. 5.01.
[27] Ibid., Sec. 5.06.

[28] Ibid., Sec. 5.14.
[29] Ibid., Sec. 6.
[30] Rev. Proc. 2011-3, 2011-1 I.R.B. 110, Sec. 3.

DUE DATES

OBJECTIVE 4

Identify the due dates for tax returns

DUE DATES FOR RETURNS

Returns for individuals, fiduciaries, and partnerships are due on or before the fifteenth day of the fourth month following the year-end of the individual or entity.[31] C corporation and S corporation tax returns are due no later than the fifteenth day of the third month after the corporation's year-end. To be subject to reporting requirements, individuals and fiduciaries, but not corporations and partnerships, must have earned a minimum level of gross income during the year.[32]

EXTENSIONS

Congress realized that, in some instances, gathering the requisite information and completing the return by the designated due date is difficult. Consequently, it authorized extensions of time for filing returns. Unless the taxpayer is abroad, the extension period cannot exceed six months.[33]

INDIVIDUALS. By filing Form 4868 (Application for Automatic Extension of Time to File U.S. Individual Income Tax Return), an individual taxpayer may request an automatic six-month extension of time to file the tax return.[34] The extension is automatic in the sense that the taxpayer need not convince the IRS that an extension is necessary.

EXAMPLE C:15-3 ▶ Bob and Alice, his wife, are calendar year taxpayers. By filing Form 4868, they may get an automatic extension until October 15 of the following year for filing their current year's return. However, if the fifteenth falls on Saturday, Sunday, or a holiday, the due date is the next business day. ◀

CORPORATIONS. Corporations request an automatic extension by filing Form 7004 (Application for Automatic Extension of Time to File Corporation Income Tax Return) by the original due date for the return. Although the IRC specifies an automatic extension period of three months, Treasury Regulations and the Form 7004 instructions specify six months.[35] No additional extensions are available.

EXAMPLE C:15-4 ▶ Lopez Corporation reports on a fiscal year ending March 31. The regular due date for its return is June 15. It may file Form 7004 and request an automatic six-month extension that postpones the due date until December 15. ◀

DUE DATES FOR PAYMENT OF THE TAX

TYPICAL MISCONCEPTION

Obtaining an extension defers the date by which the return must be filed, but it does *not* defer the payment date of the tax liability. Therefore, an extension for filing must be accompanied by a payment of an estimate of the taxpayer's tax liability. Computing this estimated tax liability can be difficult because much of the information necessary to complete the return may be incomplete or not yet available.

The granting of an extension merely postpones the due date for filing the return. It does not extend the due date for paying the tax. In general, the due date for the tax payment is the same as the unextended due date for filing the return.[36] In addition, the first estimated tax installment for extinguishing an individual's annual income tax liability must be paid by the due date for the preceding year's return, and the remaining payments must be made, respectively, two, five, and nine months later. Taxpayers who elect to let the IRS compute their tax must pay it within 30 days of the date the IRS mails a notice of the amount payable.[37]

When individuals request an automatic extension, they should project the amount of their tax liability to the extent possible. Any tax owed, net of tax withholding and estimated tax payments, should be remitted with the extension request. In addition, if an extension for filing a gift tax return is requested (on the same form), the estimated amount of gift tax liability should be remitted. Similarly, corporations should remit with their automatic extension request the amount of tax they estimate to be due, reduced by any estimated tax already paid.

---

[31] Sec. 6072(a). Section 6072(c) extends the due date for returns of nonresident alien individuals and foreign corporations to the fifteenth day of the sixth month after the end of their tax year.
[32] Secs. 6012(a) and 6031(a).
[33] Sec. 6081(a).
[34] Reg. Sec. 1.6081-4.

[35] Sec. 6081(b) and Reg. Sec. 1.6081-3(a).
[36] Sec. 6151(a).
[37] Sec. 6151(b)(1). The estimated tax payment rules for C corporations, S corporations, and trusts and estates are described in Chapters C:3, C:11, and C:14, respectively, of this volume.

INTEREST ON TAX NOT TIMELY PAID

Interest accrues on any tax not paid by the original due date for the return even if the tax-payer extends the filing date.[38] Taxpayers incur interest charges in four situations.

▶ They file late, without having requested an extension, and pay late.

▶ They request an extension for filing but underestimate their tax liability and, thus, must pay additional tax when they file their return.

▶ They file in a timely manner but are not financially able to pay some, or all, of the tax.

▶ The IRS audits their return and determines that they owe additional taxes.

RATE DETERMINATION. The IRS fixes the interest rate that it charges taxpayers under rules provided in Sec. 6621 and announces changes in Revenue Rulings. The rate varies with fluctuations in the quarterly federal short-term rate. Thus, the interest rate could change at the beginning of each calendar quarter. For noncorporate taxpayers, the interest rate on both underpayments and overpayments is three percentage points higher than the federal rate. For corporate tax overpayments exceeding $10,000, the interest rate is reduced to the federal short-term rate plus one-half percentage point. For corporate underpayments exceeding $100,000, the rate is five percentage points above the federal short-term rate if the deficiency is not paid before a certain date. Rates are rounded to the nearest full percent. Recent applicable interest rates are as follows:

Period	General Rate for Underpayments and Overpayments
January 1, 2011, through March 31, 2011	3%
April 1, 2009, through Decemer 31, 2010	4%
January 1, 2009, through March 31, 2009	5%
October 1, 2008, through December 31, 2008	6%
July 1, 2008, through September 30, 2008	5%
April 1, 2008, through June 30, 2008	6%
January 1, 2008, through March 31, 2008	7%

EXAMPLE C:15-5 ▶ Ann filed her 2008 individual return in a timely manner on April 15, 2009 and the IRS audits it in March 2011. Ann is a calendar year taxpayer. The IRS contends that Ann owes $2,700 of additional taxes. Ann pays the additional taxes on March 31, 2011. Ann also must pay interest on the $2,700 deficiency for the period April 16, 2009, through March 31, 2011. The applicable interest rates for the various segments of time during this period appear in the schedule just before this example. ◀

HISTORICAL NOTE

Probably two of the most significant changes in tax administration have been the daily compounding of interest and tying the interest rate charged to the federal short-term rate, which has resulted in a higher rate used to calculate the interest charge than in years past. Before these two changes, taxpayers who played the "audit lottery" and took aggressive positions incurred little risk.

DAILY COMPOUNDING. Daily compounding applies to both the interest taxpayers owe to the government and the interest the government owes to taxpayers who have over-paid their taxes. The IRS has issued Rev. Proc. 95-17 containing tables to be used for calculating interest.[39] The major tax services have published these tables. In addition, software packages are available for interest calculations.

ACCRUAL PERIOD. Interest usually accrues from the original due date for the return until the payment date. However, two important exceptions apply. First, if the IRS fails to send an individual taxpayer a notice within 36 months after the original due date or the date on which a return is timely filed (including extensions), whichever is later, the accrual of interest (and penalties) is suspended.[40] The suspension period begins on the

---

[38] Secs. 6601(a) and (b)(1).
[39] Rev. Proc. 95-17, 1995-1 C.B. 556.

[40] Sec. 6404(g).

day after the 36-month period and ends 21 days after the IRS sends the requisite notice. Second, if the IRS does not issue a notice and demand for payment within 30 days after the taxpayer signs a Form 870 waiver, no interest is charged for the period between the end of the 30-day period and the date the IRS issues its notice and demand.[41] Taxpayers litigating in the Tax Court may make a deposit to reduce interest potentially owed. If the court decides that the taxpayer owes a deficiency, interest will not accrue on the deposit.

EXAMPLE C:15-6 ▶ Cindy receives an automatic extension for filing this year's return. On June 24 of the following year, she submits her return, along with the $700 balance she owes on this year's tax liability. She owes interest on $700 for the period April 16 of this year through June 24 of the following year. Interest is compounded daily based on the interest rate for underpayments determined under Sec. 6621. ◀

EXAMPLE C:15-7 ▶ After filing for an automatic extension, Hans files his 2011 return on August 15, 2012. On August 28, 2015, the IRS sends Hans a notice of deficiency in which it assesses interest. Because the IRS failed to send Hans the notice by August 15, 2015 (36 months after the date on which the return was timely filed), the accrual of interest is suspended. The suspension period begins on August 16, 2015 (the day after the 36-month period) and ends on September 18, 2015 (21 days after the IRS sends the requisite notice). ◀

EXAMPLE C:15-8 ▶ Raj filed his 2008 individual return on March 16, 2009 (March 15 fell on a Sunday). The IRS audits the return in 2011, and on January 25, 2011, Raj signs a Form 870 waiver, in which he agrees that he owes a $780 deficiency. The IRS does not issue a notice and demand for payment until March 22, 2011. Raj pays the deficiency two days later. Raj owes interest, compounded daily at the Sec. 6621 underpayment rate, for the period April 16, 2009, through February 24, 2011. No interest can be assessed for the period February 24 through March 22, 2011, because the IRS did not issue its notice and demand for payment until more than 30 days after Raj signed the Form 870 waiver. ◀

ABATEMENT. The IRS does not abate interest except for unreasonable errors or delays resulting from its managerial or ministerial acts.[42] A "managerial act" involves the temporary or permanent loss of records or the exercise of judgment or discretion relating to the management of personnel.[43] A "ministerial act" involves routine procedure without the exercise of judgment or discretion.[44] A decision concerning the proper application of federal law is neither a managerial nor a ministerial act.

EXAMPLE C:15-9 ▶ Omar provides documentation to an audit agent, who assures him that he will receive a copy of an audit report shortly. Before the agent has had an opportunity to act, however, the divisional manager transfers him to another office. An extended period of time elapses before the manager assigns another audit agent to Omar's case. The decision to reassign is a managerial act. The IRS may abate interest attributable to any unreasonable delay in payment resulting from this act. ◀

EXAMPLE C:15-10 ▶ Chanelle requests information from an IRS employee concerning the balance due on her current year tax liability. The employee fails to access the most current computerized database and provides Chanelle with incorrect information. Based on this information, Chanelle pays less than the full balance due. The employee's failing to access the most current database is a ministerial act. The IRS may abate interest attributable to any unreasonable delay in payment resulting from this act. ◀

FAILURE-TO-FILE AND FAILURE-TO-PAY PENALTIES

OBJECTIVE 5

Understand tax-related penalties generally

Penalties add teeth to the accounting and reporting provisions of the Internal Revenue Code. Without them, these provisions would be mere letters on the books of the legislature—words without effect. Tax-related penalties fall into two broad categories: taxpayer and preparer. As the name suggests, taxpayer penalties apply only to taxpayers, be they individuals, corporations, estates, or trusts. Preparer penalties apply only to tax return

---

[41] Sec. 6601(c).
[42] Sec. 6404(e).

[43] Reg. Sec. 301.6404-2(b)(1).
[44] Reg. Sec. 301.6404-2(b)(2).

REAL-WORLD EXAMPLE

In 2009, as a result of the audit process, the IRS assessed a total of $29.8 billion in civil penalties and abated about $15.9 billion for reasonable cause.

preparers, be they firms that employ tax professionals or the professionals themselves. Within these broad categories are two distinct subcategories: civil and criminal. Civil penalties are imposed on taxpayers for negligently, recklessly, or intentionally failing to fulfill their accounting or reporting obligations. Criminal penalties are imposed for maliciously or willfully failing to do so. Taxpayers may raise as a defense to some penalties "reasonable cause" and a good faith belief in the correctness of their position. Sometimes, for the defense to be valid, they also must disclose this position on their tax return. This section of the text discusses two commonly encountered penalties in income, estate, and gift taxation: failure to file and failure to pay. The IRS may assess these penalties, in addition to interest, on overdue tax liabilities. Subsequent sections of the text discuss other taxpayer and preparer penalties. Topic Review C:15-1 presents a summary of IRC penalty provisions. The Topic Review is provided here rather than later in the chapter to give readers a framework for following the discussion of the various penalties.

Topic Review C:15-1

Overview of Penalties

PENALTY	IRC SECTION	APPLICABILITY	RULES/CALCULATION	DEFENSES/WAIVER
A. TAXPAYER—CIVIL				
Failure to file	6651(a)	All persons	*General rule:* 5% per month or fraction thereof; 25% maximum *Minimum penalty if late more than 60 days:* lesser of $135 or 100% of tax due *Fraudulent reason for not filing:* 15% per month or fraction thereof; 75% maximum	Reasonable cause, not willful neglect
Failure to pay tax	6651(a)	All persons	*General rule:* 0.5% per month or fraction thereof; 25% maximum*	Reasonable cause, not willful neglect
Failure by individual to pay estimated tax	6654	Individuals, certain estates, trusts	*General rule:* penalty at same rate as interest rate for deficiency; imposed for period between due date for estimated tax payments and earlier of payment date or due date for return	Waiver in unusual circumstances
Failure by corporation to pay estimated tax	6655	Corporations	*General rule:* penalty at same rate as interest rate for deficiency; imposed for period between due date for estimated tax payments and earlier of payment date or due date for return	—
Negligence	6662(c)	All persons	*General rule:* 20% of underpayment attributable to negligence	Reasonable cause, good faith
Substantial understatement	6662(d)	All persons	*General rule:* 20% of underpayment attributable to substantial understatement (portion for which no substantial authority and no disclosure exists)	Reasonable cause, good faith; also, substantial authority, disclosure
Civil fraud	6663	All persons	*General rule:* 75% of portion of understatement attributable to fraud.	Reasonable cause, good faith
B. TAXPAYER—CRIMINAL				
Willful attempt to evade tax	7201	All persons	*General rule:* $100,000 ($500,000 for corporations) and/or up to five years in prison	—
Willful failure to collect or pay over tax	7202	All persons	*General rule:* $10,000 and/or up to five years in prison	—
Willful failure to pay or file	7203	All persons	*General rule:* $25,000 ($100,000 for corporations) and/or up to one year in prison	—
Willfully making false or fraudulent statements	7206	All persons	*General rule:* $100,000 ($500,000 for corporations) and/or up to three years in prison	—

Topic Review C:15-1 (cont.)

C. PREPARER—CIVIL

Understatement of tax by preparer	6694(a)	Tax return preparers	*General rule:* greater of $1,000 or half of preparer's income from return	Reasonable cause, good faith; also, disclosure
Willful attempt to understate taxes	6694(b)	Tax return preparers	*General rule:* greater of $5,000 or half of preparer's income from return	—
Failure to furnish copy to taxpayer	6695(a)	Tax return preparers	*General rule:* $50; $25,000 maximum	Reasonable cause, not willful neglect
Failure to sign return	6695(b)	Tax return preparers	*General rule:* $50; $25,000 maximum	Reasonable cause, not willful neglect
Failure to furnish identifying number	6695(c)	Tax return preparers	*General rule:* $50; $25,000 maximum	Reasonable cause, not willful neglect
Failure to retain copy or list	6695(d)	Tax return preparers	*General rule:* $50; $25,000 maximum	Reasonable cause, not willful neglect
Failure to file correct information returns	6695(e)	Tax return preparers	*General rule:* $50 for each failure to file a return or each failure to set forth an item in a return; $25,000 maximum	Reasonable cause, not willful neglect
Improper negotiation of checks	6695(f)	Tax return preparers	*General rule:* $500 per check	—
Aiding and abetting in understatement	6701(b)	All persons	*General rule:* $1,000 ($10,000 for corporations)	—

* If the taxpayer owes both the failure-to-file and the failure-to-pay penalties for a given month, the total penalty for such month is limited to 5% of the net tax due.

FAILURE TO FILE

Taxpayers who do not file a return by the due date generally are liable for a penalty of 5% per month (or fraction thereof) of the net tax due.[45] A fraction of a month, even just a day, counts as a full month. The maximum penalty for failing to file is 25%. If the taxpayer receives an extension, the extended due date is treated as the original due date. In determining the net tax due (i.e., the amount subject to the penalty), the IRS reduces the taxpayer's gross tax by any taxes paid by the return's due date (e.g., withholding and estimated tax payments) and tax credits claimed on the return.[46] If any failure to file is fraudulent, the penalty rate is 15% per month up to a maximum penalty of 75%.[47] For purposes of this provision, "fraud" is actual, intentional wrongdoing or the commission of an act for the specific purpose of evading a tax known or believed to be due.[48]

Penalties are not levied if a taxpayer can prove that he or she failed to file a timely return because of reasonable cause (as opposed to willful neglect). According to Treasury Regulations, reasonable cause exists if "the taxpayer exercised ordinary business care and prudence and was nevertheless unable to file the return within the prescribed time."[49] Not surprisingly, much litigation deals with the issue of reasonable cause.

ADDITIONAL COMMENT

The most common reason given by taxpayers to support reasonable cause for failing to file a timely tax return is reliance on one's tax advisor. Other reasons include severe illness or serious accident. Reliance on a tax advisor is not always sufficient cause to obtain a waiver of the penalties.

Note that the penalty imposed for not filing on time generally is a function of the net tax due. However, a minimum penalty applies in some cases.[50] Congress enacted the minimum penalty provision because of the cost to the IRS of identifying nonfilers. If a taxpayer does not file an income tax return within 60 days of the due date (including any extensions), the penalty will be no less than the smaller of $135 or 100% of the tax due on the return. Taxpayers who owe no tax are not subject to the **failure-to-file penalty**. Also, the IRS may waive the penalty if the taxpayer shows reasonable cause for not filing.

---

[45] Sec. 6651(a).
[46] Sec. 6651(b)(1).
[47] Sec. 6651(f).
[48] *Robert W. Bradford v. CIR,* 58 AFTR 2d 86-5532, 86-2 USTC ¶9602 (9th Cir., 1996: *Chris D. Stoltzfus v. U.S.,* 22 AFTR 2d 5251, 68-2 USTC ¶9499

(3rd Cir., 1968): and *William E. Mitchell v. CIR,* 26 AFTR 684, 41-1 USTC ¶9317 (5th Cir., 1941).
[49] Reg. Sec. 301.6651-1(c)(1).
[50] Sec. 6651(a).

EXAMPLE C:15-11 ▶ Earl files his current year individual income tax return on July 5 of the following year. Earl requested no extension and did not have reasonable cause for his late filing, but he committed no fraud. Earl's current year return shows a balance due of $400. Under the regular rules, the late filing penalty would be $60 (0.05 × 3 months × $400). Earl's penalty is $135 because of the minimum penalty provision applicable to his failure to file the return within 60 days of the due date. ◀

In general under Sec. 6601(e)(2), interest does not accrue on any penalty paid within 21 days of the date that the IRS notifies the taxpayer of the penalty (ten days if the amount exceeds $100,000). However, interest accrues on the failure-to-file penalty, from the due date of the return (including any extensions) until the payment date.

FAILURE TO PAY

The **failure-to-pay penalty** is imposed at 0.5% per month (or fraction thereof).[51] The maximum penalty is 25%. The penalty is based on the gross tax shown on the return less any tax payments made and credits earned before the beginning of the month for which the penalty is calculated.[52] As with the failure-to-file penalty, the IRS may waive the failure-to-pay penalty if the taxpayer shows reasonable cause.

Because the tax is due on the original due date for the return, taxpayers who request an extension without paying 100% of their tax liability potentially owe a failure-to-pay penalty. Treasury Regulations provide some relief by exempting a taxpayer from the penalty if the additional tax due with the filing of the extended return does not exceed 10% of the tax owed for the year.[53]

EXAMPLE C:15-12 ▶ Gary requests an extension for filing his current year individual income tax return. His current year tax payments include withholding of $4,500, estimated tax payments of $2,000, and $1,000 submitted with his request for an automatic extension. He files his return on June 6 of the following year, showing a total tax of $8,000 and a balance due of $500. Gary is exempt from the failure-to-pay penalty because the $500 balance due does not exceed 10% of his current year liability (0.10 × $8,000 = $800). Had Gary's current year tax instead been $9,000, he would have owed an additional tax of $1,500 and a failure-to-pay penalty of $15 (0.005 × 2 months × $1,500). ◀

The 0.5% penalty increases to 1% a month, or fraction thereof, in certain circumstances. The rate is 1% for any month beginning after the earlier of

▶ Ten days after the date the IRS notifies the taxpayer that it plans to levy on his or her salary or property and

▶ The day the IRS notifies and demands immediate payment from the taxpayer because it believes that collection is in jeopardy

EXAMPLE C:15-13 ▶ Ginny filed her 2008 individual income tax return on April 13, 2009. However, Ginny did not pay her tax liability. On October 4, 2011, the IRS notifies Ginny of its plans to levy on her property. The failure-to-pay penalty is 0.5% per month for the period April 15, 2009 through October 14, 2011. Beginning on October 15, 2011, the penalty rises to 1% per month, or fraction thereof. ◀

SELF-STUDY QUESTION

If a taxpayer does not have sufficient funds to pay his or her tax liability by the due date, should the taxpayer wait until the funds are available before filing the tax return?

ANSWER

No. He or she should file the return on a timely basis. This filing avoids the 5% per month failure-to-file penalty. The taxpayer still will owe the failure-to-pay penalty, but at least this penalty is only 0.5% per month.

Some taxpayers file on time to avoid the failure-to-file penalty even though they cannot pay the balance of the tax due. Barring a showing of reasonable cause, these taxpayers still will incur the failure-to-pay penalty. Because taxpayers who do not timely file a return are likely to owe additional taxes, they often owe both the failure-to-file and the failure-to-pay penalties.

The IRC provides a special rule for calculating the 5% per month failure-to-file penalty for periods in which the taxpayer owes both penalties. The 5% per month failure-to-file penalty is reduced by the failure-to-pay penalty.[54] Thus, the total penalties for a given month will not exceed 5%. For months when the taxpayer incurs both penalties, the failure-to-file penalty is effectively 4.5% (5% − 0.5%). Note, however, that no reduction occurs if the minimum penalty for failure to file applies.

---

[51] Sec. 6651(a)(2).
[52] Sec. 6651(b).

[53] Reg. Sec. 301.6651-1(c)(3) and (4).
[54] Sec. 6651(c)(1).

EXAMPLE C:15-14▶ Tien files her current year individual income tax return on August 5 of the following year, without having requested an extension. Her total tax is $20,000. Tien pays $15,000 in a timely manner and the $5,000 balance when she files the return. Although Tien committed no fraud, she can show no reasonable cause for the late filing and late payment. Tien's penalties are as follows:

Failure-to-pay penalty:		
$5,000 × 0.005 × 4 months		$ 100
Failure-to-file penalty:		
$5,000 × 0.05 × 4 months	$1,000	
Minus: Reduction for failure-to-pay penalty imposed for same period	(100)	900
Total penalties		$1,000 ◀

EXAMPLE C:15-15▶ Assume the same facts as in Example C:15-14 except that Tien instead pays the $5,000 balance on November 17 of the following year. The penalties are as follows:

Failure-to-pay penalty:		
$5,000 × 0.005 × 8 months (April 16 through November 17)		$ 200
Failure-to-file penalty:		
$5,000 × 0.05 × 4 months (April 16 through August 5)	$1,000	
Minus: Reduction for failure-to-pay penalty levied for April 16 through August 5 ($5,000 ×0.005 × 4 months)	(100)	900
Total penalties		$1,100 ◀

ESTIMATED TAXES

OBJECTIVE 6

Calculate the penalty for not paying estimated taxes

Individuals earning only salaries and wages generally pay their annual income tax liability through payroll withholding. The employer is responsible for remitting these withheld amounts, along with Social Security taxes, to a designated federal depository. By contrast, individuals earning other types of income, as well as C corporations, S corporations, and trusts, must estimate their annual income tax liability and prepay their taxes on a quarterly basis.[55] Estates must do the same with respect to income earned during any tax year ending two years after the decedent's death.[56] Although partnerships do not pay estimated income taxes, their separate partners do if they are individuals or taxable entities. Chapters C:3, C:11, and C:14 discuss the estimated income tax requirements for C corporations, S corporations, and fiduciaries, respectively.

PAYMENT REQUIREMENTS

Individuals should pay quarterly estimated income taxes if they have a significant amount of income from sources other than salaries and wages. The amount of each payment should be the same if this outside income accrues uniformly throughout the year. To avoid an estimated income tax penalty for the current year, individuals with AGI of $150,000 or less in the previous year should calculate each payment as follows:

Step 1: Determine the lesser of
    a. 90% of the taxpayer's regular tax, alternative minimum tax (if any), and self-employment tax for the current year, or
    b. 100% of the taxpayer's prior year regular tax, alternative minimum tax (if any), and self-employment tax if the taxpayer filed a return for the prior year and the year was not a short tax year.

Step 2: Calculate the total of
    a. Tax credits for the current year
    b. Taxes withheld on the current year's wages
    c. Overpayments of the prior year's tax liability the taxpayer requests be credited against the current year's tax

---

[55] S corporations must pay quarterly estimated taxes on their net recognized built-in gains, passive investment income, and credit recapture amounts.
[56] For example, if the decedent's death were June 15 of the current year, and the assets of the decedent's estate are not distributed by June 14 of the following year, the estate must pay estimated taxes on income earned on estate assets for the following tax year.

Step 3: Multiply the excess of the amount from Step 1 over the amount from Step 2 by 25%.[57]

Calendar year individual taxpayers should pay their quarterly installments on April 15, June 15, September 15, and January 15.

Individuals with AGI exceeding $150,000 ($75,000 for married filing separately) in the prior year can avoid the estimated tax penalty for the current year if they pay at least 90% of the current year's tax, or at least 110% of the prior year's tax.[58]

EXAMPLE C:15-16 ▶

Mike's regular tax on his current year taxable income is $35,000. Mike also owes $2,000 of self-employment tax but no alternative minimum tax. Mike's total liability last year for both income and self-employment taxes was $24,000. His AGI last year did not exceed $150,000. Taxes withheld from Mike's current year wages were $8,000. Mike did not overpay his tax last year or earn any credits this year. For the current year, Mike should have made quarterly estimated tax payments of $4,000, as calculated below.

Lesser of:	90% of current year's tax (0.90 × $37,000 = $33,300) or	
	100% of prior year's $24,000 tax liability	$24,000
Minus:	Taxes withheld from current year's wages	(8,000)
Minimum estimated tax payment to avoid penalty under general rule		$16,000
Quarterly estimated tax payments (0.25 × $16,000)		$ 4,000 ◀

ADDITIONAL COMMENT

Although it is simpler to use the amount of tax paid (or, if necessary, the applicable percentage of the amount of tax paid) in the preceding year as a safe harbor, the estimate of the current year's tax liability is preferable if the current year's tax liability is expected to be significantly less than the preceding year's tax liability.

The authority to make estimated tax payments based on the preceding year's income is especially significant for taxpayers with rising levels of income. To avoid an estimated income tax penalty, these taxpayers need to pay only an amount equal to the prior year's tax liability. Using this safe harbor eliminates the need for estimating the current year's tax liability with a high degree of accuracy.

EXAMPLE C:15-17 ▶

Peter, a single calendar year taxpayer, incurs a regular tax liability of $76,000 in the current year. Peter owes no alternative minimum tax liability nor can he claim any tax credits. No overpayments of last year's taxes are available to offset this year's tax liability. Taxes withheld evenly from Peter's wages throughout the current year are $68,000. Peter's AGI last year exceeded $150,000, and his regular tax liability was $60,000. Because Peter's $17,000 of withholding for each quarter exceeds the $15,000 minimum required quarterly payments, as calculated below, he incurs no underpayment penalty.

Lesser of:	90% of current year's (0.90 × $76,000 = $68,400) or	
	110% of prior year's $60,000 tax liability	$66,000
Minus:	Taxes withheld from current year's wages	(68,000)
Minimum estimated tax payment to avoid penalty under general rule		$ –0–

The $8,000 ($76,000 − $68,000) balance of the current's year taxes is due on or before April 15 of next year with the filing of the return or the request for extension of time to file. ◀

ADDITIONAL COMMENT

If a taxpayer is having taxes withheld and making estimated tax payments, a certain amount of tax planning is possible. Withholdings are deemed to have occurred equally throughout the year. Thus, disproportionately large amounts could be withheld in the last quarter to allow the taxpayer to avoid the underpayment penalty.

PENALTY FOR UNDERPAYING ESTIMATED TAXES

With the exceptions discussed in the next section, taxpayers who do not remit the requisite amount of estimated tax by the appropriate date are subject to a penalty for underpayment of estimated taxes. The penalty is calculated at the same rate as the interest rate applicable under Sec. 6621 to late payments of tax.[59] The penalty for each quarter is calculated separately on Form 2210.

The amount subject to the penalty is the excess of the total tax that should have been paid during the quarter (e.g., $6,000 [$24,000 prior year's tax liability ÷ 4] in Example C:15-16) over the sum of the estimated tax actually paid during that quarter on or before

---

[57] Secs. 6654(d), (f), and (g).
[58] Sec. 6654(d)(1)(C). Included in the definition of *individuals* are estates and trusts. Section 67(e) defines AGI for estates and trusts. (See Chapter C:14.)

[59] Daily compounding is not applicable in calculating the penalty.

the installment date plus the withholding attributable to that quarter. Unless the taxpayer proves otherwise, the withholding is deemed to take place equally during each quarter. This rule creates a planning opportunity. Taxpayers who have not paid sufficient amounts of estimated tax in the first three quarters can avoid a penalty by having large amounts of tax withheld during the last quarter.

The penalty is assessed for the time period beginning on the due date for the quarterly installment and ending on the earlier of the date the underpayment actually is paid or the due date for the return (April 15 assuming a calendar year taxpayer). The next example illustrates the computation of the underpayment penalty.

EXAMPLE C:15-18▶

Assume the same facts as in Example C:15-16 except Mike pays only $3,000 of estimated tax payments on April 15, June 15, and September 15 of the current year and January 15 of next year and, for simplicity, that 6% is the Sec. 6621 underpayment rate for the entire time period. Mike files his current year return on March 30 of next year and pays the $17,000 ($37,000 − $8,000 withholding − $12,000 estimated taxes) balance due at that time. Mike's underpayment penalty is determined as follows:

	Quarter			
	First	Second	Third	Fourth
Amount that should have been paid ($24,000 ÷ 4)	$6,000	$6,000	$6,000	$6,000
Minus: Wage withholding	(2,000)	(2,000)	(2,000)	(2,000)
Estimated tax payment	(3,000)	(3,000)	(3,000)	(3,000)
Underpayment	$1,000	$1,000	$1,000	$1,000
Number of days of underpayment (ends March 30 of next year because earlier than April 15 of next year);	349	288	196	74
Penalty at 6% assumed annual rate for number of days of underpayment	$ 57	$ 47	$ 32	$ 12

The total penalty equals $148 ($57 + $47 + $32 + $12). The $148 penalty is not deductible. ◀

TYPICAL MISCONCEPTION

Many self-employed taxpayers assume they are not liable for estimated taxes if they have sufficient itemized deductions and exemptions to create zero taxable income or a taxable loss. However, a self-employment tax liability may exist even if the individual has no taxable income. Thus, taxpayers in this situation can end up with an overall tax liability and an accompanying estimated tax penalty.

Interest does not accrue on underpayments of estimated tax.[60] However, if the entire tax is not paid by the due date for the return, interest and perhaps also a failure-to-pay penalty will be levied on the unpaid amount.

EXCEPTIONS TO THE PENALTY

In certain circumstances, individuals who have not remitted the required estimated tax payments nevertheless will be exempt from the underpayment penalty. The IRS imposes no penalty if the taxpayer's tax liability exceeds by less than $1,000 taxes actually withheld from wages during the year. Similarly, the taxpayer will not owe a penalty, regardless of the underpayment amount, if the taxpayer owed no taxes for the prior tax year, the prior tax year consisted of the full 12 months, and the taxpayer was a U.S. citizen or resident alien throughout that year. The Secretary of the Treasury can waive the penalty otherwise due in the case of "casualty, disaster, or other unusual circumstances" or for newly retired or disabled individuals.[61]

EXAMPLE C:15-19▶

Paul's current year tax liability is $2,200, the same as last year's. His wage withholding amounts to $1,730, and Paul does not pay any estimated taxes. Paul pays the $470 balance due on March 15 of next year. Under the general rules, Paul is subject to the underpayment penalty because he does not reach either the 90% of the current year tax threshold or 100% of the prior year

---

[60] Sec. 6601(h).　　　　　　[61] Sec. 6654(e).

tax threshold. However, because Paul's tax exceeds wage withholding by less than $1,000, he owes no penalty for underpaying his estimated tax liability. ◄

Taxpayers are exempt from the underpayment penalty in certain other circumstances, a discussion of which is beyond the scope of this text. Chapter I:14 of *Prentice Hall's Federal Taxation: Principles* and *Comprehensive* texts, however, discusses one such circumstance where the taxpayer annualizes his or her income and bases the estimated tax payment on the annualized amount.[62] Annualizing income often is beneficial for taxpayers who realize a high percentage of their income later in the year (e.g., large year-end bonus).

OTHER MORE SEVERE PENALTIES

OBJECTIVE 7

Describe more severe penalties, including the fraud penalty

In addition to the penalties for failure to file, failure to pay, and underpayment of estimated tax, taxpayers may be subject to other more severe penalties. These include the accuracy-related penalty (applicable in several contexts) and the fraud penalty, each of which is discussed below. A 20% accuracy-related penalty applies to any underpayment attributable to negligence, any substantial understatement of income tax, transactions without economic substance, and various types of errors, a discussion of which is beyond the scope of this text.[63] An accuracy-related penalty is not levied, however, if the government imposed the fraud penalty or if the taxpayer filed no return.

ADDITIONAL COMMENT

To shift the burden of proof to the IRS, the taxpayer must introduce credible evidence regarding a factual issue relating to his or her tax liability.

NEGLIGENCE

The accuracy-related **negligence penalty** applies whenever the IRS determines that a taxpayer has underpaid any part of his or her taxes as a result of negligence or disregard of the rules or regulations (but without intending to defraud).[64] The penalty is 20% of the underpayment attributable to negligence. Interest accrues on the negligence penalty at the rate applicable to underpayments.[65]

EXAMPLE C:15-20 ▶

The IRS audits Ted's individual return and assesses a $7,500 deficiency, of which $2,500 is attributable to negligence. Ted agrees to the assessment and pays the additional tax of $7,500 the following year. Ted incurs a negligence penalty of $500 (0.20 × $2,500). ◄

The IRC defines *negligence* as "any failure to make a reasonable attempt to comply with the provisions" of the IRC. It defines disregard of the rules or regulations as "any careless, reckless, or intentional disregard."[66] According to Treasury Regulations, a presumption of negligence exists if the taxpayer does not include in gross income an amount of income reported on an information return or does not reasonably attempt to ascertain the correctness of a deduction, credit, or exclusion that a reasonable and prudent person would think was "too good to be true."[67]

A taxpayer is careless if he or she does not diligently try to determine the correctness of his or her position. A taxpayer is reckless if he or she exerts little or no effort to determine whether a rule or regulation exists. A taxpayer's disregard is intentional if he or she knows about the rule or regulation he or she disregards.[68]

The penalty will not be imposed for any portion of an underpayment if the taxpayer had reasonable cause for his or her position and acted in good faith.[69] Failure to follow a regulation must be disclosed on Form 8275-R (Regulation Disclosure Statement), but disclosure alone is not sufficient as a defense against negligence.

---

[62] Section 6654(d)(2) allows for computation of the underpayments, if any, by annualizing income. Relief from the underpayment penalty may result from applying the annualization rules. Corporations, but not individuals, are permitted a seasonal adjustment to the annualization rules.
[63] Secs. 6662(a) and (b).
[64] Secs. 6662(b) and (c).

[65] Sec. 6601(e)(2)(B).
[66] Sec. 6662(c).
[67] Reg. Sec. 1.6662-3(b)(1).
[68] Reg. Sec. 1.6662-3(b)(2).
[69] Sec. 6664(c)(1).

EXAMPLE C:15-21▶ The IRS audits Mario's current year individual return, and Mario agrees to a $4,000 deficiency. Mario had reasonable cause for adopting his tax return positions (which were not contrary to the applicable rules or regulations) and acted in good faith. Mario will not be liable for a negligence penalty. ◀

SUBSTANTIAL UNDERSTATEMENT

ADDITIONAL COMMENT

Theoretically, penalties are designed to deter taxpayers from willfully disregarding federal tax laws. Some taxpayers have been concerned that the IRS has used the multitude of tax penalties primarily as a source of revenue. The IRS achieved this result by "stacking" penalties (i.e., applying several penalties to a single underpayment). Recent legislation has alleviated some of this concern.

Taxpayers who substantially understate their income tax are liable for an accuracy-related penalty for their substantial understatements. The IRC defines a substantial understatement as an understatement of tax exceeding the greater of 10% of the tax required to be shown on the return or $5,000 (or $10,000 in the case of a C corporation). For a C corporation, an additional rule applies. Specifically, if 10% of the required tax exceeds $10 million, a substantial understatement exists if the understatement exceeds $10 million.[70] The penalty equals 20% of the underpayment of tax attributable to the substantial understatement. It does not apply to understatements for which the taxpayer shows reasonable cause and good faith for his or her position.

UNDERSTATEMENT VERSUS UNDERPAYMENT. The amount of tax attributable to the substantial understatement may be less than the amount of the underpayment. In general, the amount of the understatement is calculated as the amount by which the tax required to be shown (i.e., the correct tax) exceeds the tax shown on the return. Because the amount of tax attributable to certain items is not treated as an understatement, the additional tax attributed to such items is not subject to the penalty. An underpayment for an item other than a tax shelter is *not* an understatement if either of the following is true:

SELF-STUDY QUESTION

How is an understatement different from an underpayment?

ANSWER

An underpayment can be larger than an understatement. Understatements do not include underpayments for which there was either substantial authority or adequate disclosure.

▶ The taxpayer has substantial authority (discussed below) for the tax treatment of the item.

▶ The taxpayer discloses, either on the return or in a statement attached to the return, the relevant facts affecting the tax treatment of the item, and the taxpayer has a reasonable basis for such treatment.

Although neither the IRC nor Treasury Regulations define "reasonable basis," Reg. Sec. 1.6662-3(b)(3) states that a "reasonable basis" standard is significantly higher than the "not frivolous" standard that usually applies to tax preparers. The latter standard involves a tax position that is not patently improper. The taxpayer meets the adequate disclosure requirement if he or she properly completes either Form 8275 or Form 8275-R and attaches it to the return, or discloses information on the return in a manner prescribed by an annual revenue procedure.[71] Large corporations required to disclose uncertain tax positions will meet the disclosure requirement by filing Schedule UTP.

EXAMPLE C:15-22▶ The IRS examines Val's current year individual income tax return, and Val agrees to a $9,000 deficiency, which increases her tax liability from $25,000 to $34,000. Val neither made adequate disclosure concerning the items for which the IRS assessed the deficiency nor had substantial authority for her tax treatment. Thus, Val's understatement also is $9,000. This understatement is substantial because it exceeds both 10% of her correct tax liability ($3,400 = 0.10 × $34,000) and the $5,000 minimum. Val incurs a substantial understatement penalty of $1,800 (0.20 × $9,000). ◀

EXAMPLE C:15-23▶ Assume the same facts as in Example C:15-22 except Val has substantial authority for the tax treatment of an item that results in a $1,000 additional assessment. In addition, she makes adequate disclosure for a second item with respect to which the IRS assesses additional taxes of $1,500. Although Val's underpayment is $9,000, her understatement is only $6,500 [$9,000 − ($1,000 + $1,500)]. The $6,500 understatement is substantial because it is more than the greater of 10% of Val's tax or $5,000. Thus, the penalty in this case is $1,300 (0.20 × $6,500). ◀

Like the negligence penalty, the substantial understatement penalty bears interest at the rate applicable for underpayments. The interest accrues from the due date of the return.

---

[70] Sec. 6662(d)(1).
[71] Reg. Secs. 1.6662-4(f)(1) and (2). See Rev. Proc. 99-41, 1999-2 C.B. 566, Rev. Proc. 2001-11, 2001-1 C.B. 275, and Rev. Proc. 2002-66, 2002-2 C.B.

724, where the Treasury Department identifies circumstances where disclosure of a position on a taxpayer's return is adequate to reduce the understatement penalty of Sec. 6662(d) and tax preparer penalties of Sec. 6694(a).

ADDITIONAL COMMENT

Even though the substantial understatement penalty is a taxpayer penalty, tax preparers have a duty to make their clients aware of the potential risk of substantial understatement. In some situations, failure to do so has resulted in the client's attempting to collect the amount of the substantial understatement penalty from the preparer.

CONCEPT OF SUBSTANTIAL AUTHORITY.   Treasury Regulations indicate that substantial authority

▶ Exists only if the weight of authorities supporting the tax treatment of an item is substantial relative to the weight of those supporting the contrary treatment, and

▶ Is based on an objective standard involving an analysis of law and its application to the relevant facts. This standard is more stringent than the "reasonable basis" standard that the taxpayer must meet to avoid the negligence penalty but less stringent than the "more likely than not" standard that applies to tax shelters.[72] (See discussion below.)

According to these regulations, the following are considered to be "authority": statutory provisions; proposed, temporary, and final regulations; court cases; revenue rulings; revenue procedures; tax treaties; Congressional intent as reflected in committee reports and joint statements of a bill's managers; private letter rulings; technical advice memoranda; information or press releases; notices; and any other similar documents published by the IRS in the *Internal Revenue Bulletin* and the *General Explanation of the Joint Committee on Taxation* (also known as the "Blue Book"). Conclusions reached in treatises, periodicals, and the opinions of tax professionals are not considered to be authority. The applicability of court cases in the taxpayer's district is not taken into account in determining the existence of substantial authority. On the other hand, the applicability of court cases in the taxpayer's circuit *is* taken into account in determining the existence of substantial authority.

EXAMPLE C:15-24▶

Authorities addressing a particular issue are as follows:

▶ For the government: Tax Court and Fourth Circuit Court of Appeals

▶ For taxpayers: U.S. District Court for Rhode Island and First Circuit Court of Appeals

The taxpayer (Tina) is a resident of Rhode Island, which is in the First Circuit. Tina would have substantial authority for a pro-taxpayer position because such a position is supported by the circuit court of appeals for Tina's geographical jurisdiction. ◀

Taxpayers should be aware that, while sparing them a substantial understatement penalty, disclosure (even with a reasonable basis for the tax treatment of the item) might raise a "red flag" that could prompt an IRS audit.

TAX SHELTERS AND REPORTABLE TRANSACTIONS.   A different set of rules applies to a tax shelter, which is any arrangement for which a significant purpose is the avoidance or evasion of federal income tax.[73] See page C:15-30 and C:15-31 for a discussion of this topic.

TRANSACTIONS WITHOUT ECONOMIC SUBSTANCE

As part of its 2010 health care legislation, Congress added Sec. 6662(b)(6) and created a 20% accuracy-related penalty for underpayments that result from transactions lacking economic substance.[74] Further, if the understatement results from a nondisclosed noneconomic substance transaction, the penalty is increased to 40%.

Prior to 2010, the law existed in the form of a judicial doctrine (i.e., the economic substance doctrine), but the courts did not agree on what constituted economic substance. Section 7701(o)(1) states that a transaction will have economic substance if (1) the transaction changes in a meaningful way the taxpayer's economic position (apart from federal income tax effects) and (2) the taxpayer has a substantial business purpose (apart from federal income tax effects) for entering into the transaction.

CIVIL FRAUD

Fraud differs from simple, honest mistakes and negligence in that it involves a deliberate attempt to deceive. Because the IRS cannot establish intent per se, it attempts to prove

---

[72] Reg. Sec. 1.6662-4(d). Substantial authority usually is considered to require a 40% chance that the position would be sustained if challenged.

[73] Sec. 6662(d)(2)(C).

[74] Health Care and Education Reconciliation Act of 2010, P.L. 111–152.

intent indirectly by emphasizing the taxpayer's actions and the circumstances surrounding these actions. One leading authority refers to fraud cases in this manner:

> Fraud cases ordinarily involve systematic or substantial omissions from gross income or fictitious deductions or dependency claims, accompanied by the falsification or destruction of records or false or inconsistent statements to the investigating agents, especially where records are not kept by the taxpayer. The taxpayer's education and business experience are relevant.[75]

The penalty equals 75% of the portion of the underpayment attributable to fraud. If the IRS establishes that any portion of an underpayment is due to fraud, the entire underpayment is treated as having resulted from fraud unless the taxpayer establishes otherwise by a preponderance of the evidence. Like the negligence penalty, the fraud penalty bears interest.[76]

EXAMPLE C:15-25 ▶ The IRS audits Ned's individual return and claims that Ned's underpayment is due to fraud. Ned agrees to the $40,000 deficiency but establishes that only $32,000 of the deficiency is attributable to fraud. The remainder results from mistakes that the IRS did not believe were due to fraud. Ned's civil fraud penalty is $24,000 (0.75 × $32,000).　◀

The fraud penalty can be imposed on taxpayers filing income, gift, or estate tax returns. If it is imposed, the negligence and substantial understatement penalties are not assessed on the portion of the underpayment attributable to fraud.[77] With respect to a joint return, no fraud penalty can be imposed on a spouse who has not committed fraud.[78] In other words, one spouse is not liable for the other spouse's fraudulent acts.

STOP & THINK

Question: A few years ago, Joyce filed her individual income tax return in which she reported $250,000 of taxable income. She paid all the tax shown on the return on the day she filed. She, however, fraudulently omitted an additional $100,000 of gross income and, of course, does not have substantial authority for this omission. If the IRS proves that Joyce committed fraud, will she be liable for both the civil fraud penalty and the substantial understatement penalty? What are the rates for the two penalties?

Solution: Because the penalties cannot be stacked, Joyce will not owe both penalties. If the IRS successfully proves fraud, she will owe a penalty of 75% of the tax due on the omitted income. She will not owe the 20% penalty for substantial understatements.

CRIMINAL FRAUD

Civil and criminal fraud are similar in that both involve a taxpayer's intent to misrepresent facts. They differ primarily in terms of the weight of evidence required for conviction. Civil fraud requires proof by a preponderance of the evidence. Criminal fraud requires proof beyond a reasonable doubt. Because the latter standard is more stringent than the former, the government charges relatively few taxpayers with criminal fraud. To do so, the IRS and Justice Department must agree on the charges.

CRIMINAL FRAUD INVESTIGATIONS. The Criminal Investigation Division of the IRS conducts criminal fraud investigations. The agents responsible for the investigation are called **special agents**. Under IRS policy, at the first meeting of the special agent and the taxpayer, the special agent must

▶ Identify himself or herself as such

▶ Advise the taxpayer that he or she is the subject of a criminal investigation

▶ Advise the taxpayer of his or her rights to remain silent and consult legal counsel

REAL WORLD EXAMPLE

In fiscal 2009, the IRS initiated 4,121 criminal investigations (up from 3,749 in 2008), and it referred 2,570 for prosecution. During fiscal 2009, the IRS filed 2,335 indictments, and sentences were handed down in 2,229 of those cases.

---

[75] Boris I. Bittker and Lawrence Lokken, *Federal Taxation of Income, Estates, and Gifts* (Boston, MA: Warren, Gorham & Lamont, 1999), vol. 4, ¶ 114–6.

[76] Sec. 6601(e)(2)(B).
[77] Sec. 6662(b).
[78] Sec. 6663(c).

ADDITIONAL COMMENT

Any time a tax professional learns a client has engaged in activities that may constitute criminal fraud, he or she immediately should refer the client to qualified legal counsel. Counsel should then hire the accountant as a consultant. Taxpayer's communications will be confidential under the attorney–client relationship. This relationship encompasses agents of the attorney.

PENALTY PROVISIONS. Sections 7201-7216 provide for criminal penalties. Three of these penalties are discussed below.

Section 7201. Section 7201 provides for an assessment of a penalty against any person who "willfully attempts . . . to evade or defeat any tax." The maximum penalty is $100,000 ($500,000 for corporations), a prison sentence of up to five years, or both.

Section 7203. Section 7203 imposes a penalty on any person who willfully fails to pay any tax or file a return. The maximum penalty is $25,000 ($100,000 for corporations), a prison sentence of no more than one year, or both. If the government charges the taxpayer with willfully failing to prepare a return, it need not prove that the taxpayer owes additional tax.

Section 7206. Persons other than the taxpayer can be charged under Sec. 7206. This section applies to any person who

> [W]illfully aids or assists in, or procures, counsels, or advises the preparation or presentation under, or in connection with any matter arising under the internal revenue laws, of a return, affidavit, claim, or other document, which is fraudulent or is false as to any material matter, whether or not such falsity or fraud is with the knowledge or consent of the person authorized or required to present such return, affidavit, claim, or document.[79]

What constitutes a material matter has been litigated extensively.[80] The maximum penalty under Sec. 7206 is $100,000 ($500,000 for corporations), a prison sentence of up to three years, or both. The government need not prove that the taxpayer owes additional tax.

STATUTE OF LIMITATIONS

OBJECTIVE 8

Understand the statute of limitations

The **statute of limitations** has the same practical implications in a tax context as in other contexts. It specifies a timeframe (called the "limitations period") during which the government must assess the tax or initiate a court proceeding to collect the tax. The statute of limitations also defines the limitations period during which a taxpayer may file a lawsuit against the government or a claim for a refund.

GENERAL THREE-YEAR RULE

Under the general rule of Sec. 6501(a), the limitations period is three years after the date on which the return is filed, regardless of whether the return is timely filed. A return filed before its due date is treated as filed on the due date.[81]

EXAMPLE C:15-26 ▶ Ali files his 2011 individual return on March 5, 2012. The government may not assess additional taxes for 2011 after April 15, 2015. If instead, Ali files his 2011 individual return on October 6, 2012, the limitations period for his return expires on October 6, 2015. ◀

SIX-YEAR RULE FOR SUBSTANTIAL OMISSIONS

INCOME TAX RETURNS. In the case of substantial omissions, the limitations period is six years after the later of the date the return is filed or the return's due date. For income tax purposes, the six-year period is applicable if the taxpayer omits from gross income an amount exceeding 25% of the gross income shown on the return. If an item is disclosed either on the return or in a statement attached to the return, it is not treated as an omission if the disclosure is "adequate to apprise the [Treasury] Secretary of the nature and amount of such item."[82] In the case of taxpayers conducting a trade or business, gross income for purposes of the 25% omission test means the taxpayer's sales revenues (not the taxpayer's gross profit).[83] Taxpayers benefit from this special definition because it renders the 25% test applicable to a gross amount (implying a higher threshold).

---

[79] Sec. 7206(2).
[80] See, for example, *U.S. v. Joseph DiVarco*, 32 AFTR 2d 73-5605, 73-2 USTC ¶9607 (7th Cir., 1973), wherein the court held that the source of the taxpayer's income as stated on the tax return is a material matter.

[81] Sec. 6501(b)(1).
[82] Sec. 6501(e).
[83] Regulation Sec. 1.61-3(a) defines *gross income* as sales less cost of goods sold.

WHAT WOULD YOU DO IN THIS SITUATION?

After working eight years for a large CPA firm, you begin your practice as a sole practitioner CPA. Your practice is not as profitable as you had expected, and you consider how you might attract additional clients. One idea is to obtain for your clients larger refunds than they anticipate. Your reputation for knowing tax-saving tips might grow, and your profits might increase. You think further and decide that maybe you could claim itemized deductions for charitable contributions that actually were not made and for business expenses that actually were not paid. You are aware of Sec. 7206, regarding false and fraudulent statements but think that you can avoid the "as to any material matter" stipulation by keeping the deduction overstatements relatively insubstantial. Would you try this scheme for increasing your profits? If so, would you escape the scope of Sec. 7206? What ramifications might these deeds have on your standing as a CPA under the AICPA's *Statements on Standards for Tax Services* and *Code of Professional Conduct*?

EXAMPLE C:15-27 ▶ Peg files her 2011 return on March 31, 2012. Her return shows $6,000 of interest from corporate bonds and $30,000 of salary. Peg attaches a statement to her return that indicates why she thinks a $2,000 receipt is nontaxable. However, because of an oversight, she does not report an $8,000 capital gain. Peg is deemed to have omitted only $8,000 rather than $10,000 (the $8,000 capital gain plus the $2,000 receipt) because she disclosed the $2,000 receipt. The $8,000 amount is 22.22% ($8,000/$36,000) of her reported gross income. Because the omission does not exceed 25% of Peg's reported gross income, the limitations period expires on April 15, 2015. ◀

EXAMPLE C:15-28 ▶ Assume the same facts as in Example C:15-27 except Peg does not make adequate disclosure of the $2,000 receipt. Thus, she is considered to have omitted $10,000 from gross income. The $10,000 amount is 27.77% ($10,000/$36,000) of her reported gross income. Therefore, the limitations period expires on April 16, 2018 (April 15 falls on a Sunday). ◀

EXAMPLE C:15-29 ▶ Rita conducts a business as a sole proprietorship. Rita's 2011 return, filed on March 16, 2012, indicates sales of $100,000 and cost of goods sold of $70,000. Rita inadvertently fails to report $9,000 of interest earned on a loan to a relative. For purposes of the 25% omission test, her gross income is $100,000, not $30,000. The omitted interest is 9% ($9,000/$100,000) of her reported gross income. Because the $9,000 does not exceed 25% of the gross amount, the limitations period expires on April 15, 2015. ◀

KEY POINT

A 25% omission of gross income extends the basic limitations period to six years, whereas a 25% overstatement of deductions is still subject to the basic three-year limitations period. However, if fraud can be shown, there is no limitations period.

Note that the six-year rule applies only to omitted income. Thus, claiming excessive deductions will not result in a six-year limitations period. Moreover, if the omission involves fraud, no limitations period applies.

GIFT AND ESTATE TAX RETURNS. A similar six-year limitations period applies for gift and estate tax purposes. If the taxpayer omits items that exceed 25% of the gross estate value or the total amount of gifts reported on the return, the limitations period expires six years after the later of the date the return is filed or the due date. Items disclosed on the return or in a statement attached to the return "in a manner adequate to apprise the [Treasury] Secretary of the nature and amount of such item" do not constitute omissions.[84] Understatements of the value of assets disclosed on the return also are not considered omissions.

EXAMPLE C:15-30 ▶ On April 3, 2012, John files a gift tax return for 2011. The return reports a cash gift of $600,000. In 2011, John sold land to his son for $700,000. At the time of the sale, John thought the land's FMV was $700,000 and did not disclose any additional amount on the gift tax return. Upon audit, the IRS determines that the FMV of the land on the sale date was $900,000. Thus, John effectively gave an additional $200,000 to his son. The $200,000 amount is 33⅓% ($200,000/$600,000) of all gifts reported. The limitations period expires on April 16, 2018 (April 15 falls on a Sunday). ◀

---

[84] Sec. 6501(e)(2).

WHEN NO RETURN IS FILED

No limitations period exists if the taxpayer does not file a return.[85] Thus, the government may assess the tax or initiate a court proceeding for collection at any time.

EXAMPLE C:15-31 ▶

Jill does not file a tax return for 2011. No limitations period applies. Consequently, if the government discovers 20 years later that Jill did not file a return, it may assess the 2011 tax, along with penalties and interest. ◀

OTHER EXCEPTIONS TO THREE-YEAR RULE

EXTENSION OF THE THREE-YEAR LIMITATIONS PERIOD. The IRC provides other exceptions to the three-year statute of limitations rule, some of which are discussed here. The taxpayer and the IRS can mutually agree in writing to extend the limitations period for taxes other than the estate tax.[86] In such situations, the limitations period is extended until the date agreed on by the two parties. Such agreements usually are concluded when the IRS is auditing a return near the end of the statutory period. Taxpayers often agree to extending the limitations period because they think that, if they do not do so, the IRS will assess a higher deficiency than otherwise would have been the case. Before concluding such an agreement, the IRS must notify the taxpayer that he or she may refuse to extend the limitations period or may limit the extension to particular issues.

NOL CARRYBACKS. For a year to which a net operating loss (NOL) carries back, the applicable limitations period is for the year in which the NOL arose.[87]

WHEN FRAUD IS PROVEN.
Deficiency and Civil Fraud Penalty. If the government successfully proves that a taxpayer filed a false or fraudulent return "with the intent to evade tax" or engaged in a "willful attempt . . . to defeat or evade tax," there is no limitations period.[88] In other words, the government may at any time assess the tax or begin a court proceeding to collect the tax and the interest thereon. In addition, if the government proves fraud, it may impose a civil penalty. If it fails to prove fraud and the normal three-year limitations period and special six-year period for 25% omissions have expired, it may not assess additional taxes. The fraud issue is significant in tax litigation because the burden of proving fraud is unconditionally on the government.

EXAMPLE C:15-32 ▶

The IRS audits Trey's 2015 return late in 2018. It also examines Trey's prior years' returns and contends that Trey has willfully attempted to evade tax on his timely filed 2011 return. Trey litigates in the Tax Court, and the Court decides the fraud issue in his favor. Because the IRS did not prove fraud, it may not assess additional taxes for 2011. Had the IRS proven fraud, the limitations period for the 2011 return would have remained open, and the IRS could have assessed the additional taxes. ◀

Criminal Provisions. If taxpayers are not indicted for criminal violations of the tax law within a certain period of time, they are home free. For most criminal offenses, the maximum period is six years after the commission of the offense.[89] Taxpayers cannot be prosecuted, tried, or punished unless an indictment is made within that timeframe. The six-year period begins on the date the taxpayer committed the offense, not the date he or she files the return. Taxpayers who file fraudulent returns might commit offenses related to the returns at a subsequent date. An example of an offense that some taxpayers commit after filing a return is depositing money into a new bank account under a fictitious name.

EXAMPLE C:15-33 ▶

In March 2012, Tony files a fraudulent 2011 return through which he attempts to evade tax. Before filing, Tony keeps a double set of books. In 2011, Tony deposits some funds into a bank account under a fictitious name. In 2013, he moves to another state, and on May 4, 2013, he transfers these funds to a new bank account under a different fictitious name. Depositing

---

SELF-STUDY QUESTION

Should a taxpayer ever agree to extend the limitations period?

ANSWER

Yes. When an audit is in progress, if a taxpayer refuses to extend the limitations period, the agent may assert a deficiency for each item in question. Had the taxpayer granted an extension, perhaps many of the items in question never would have been included in the examining agent's report.

ADDITIONAL COMMENT

Even though a taxpayer is home free from criminal prosecution after six years of an act or omission, he or she still is subject to civil fraud penalties if fraud is proven at any time after the six-year period.

---

[85] Sec. 6501(c)(3).
[86] Sec. 6501(c)(4).
[87] Sec. 6501(h).

[88] Secs. 6501(c)(1) and (2).
[89] Sec. 6531.

money into the new account is an offense relating to the fraudulent return. Provided Tony commits no additional offenses, the limitations period for indictment expires on May 4, 2019. ◄

REFUND CLAIMS

Taxpayers generally are not entitled to a refund for overpayments of tax unless they file a claim for refund by the later of three years from the date they file the return or two years from the date they pay the tax.[90] The limitations period for individuals is suspended when the individual is financially disabled. A return filed before the due date is deemed to have been filed on the due date. The due date is determined without regard to extensions. In most cases, taxpayers pay the tax concurrently with filing the return. Typically, the taxpayer files a claim for a refund in the following circumstance: the IRS has audited the taxpayer's return, has proposed a deficiency, and has assessed additional taxes. The taxpayer may have paid the additional taxes two years after the due date for the return. In such a situation, the taxpayer may file a claim for a refund at any time within two years after making the additional payment (or a total of four years after the filing date). If the taxpayer does not file a claim until more than three years after the date of filing the return, the maximum refund is the amount of tax paid during the two-year period immediately preceding the date on which he or she files the claim.[91]

EXAMPLE C:15-34 ▶ Pat files his 2011 return on March 12, 2012. The return reports a tax liability of $5,000, and Pat pays this entire amount when he files his return. He pays no additional tax. Pat must file a claim for refund by April 15, 2015. The maximum refundable amount is $5,000. ◄

EXAMPLE C:15-35 ▶ Assume the same facts as in Example C:15-34 except the IRS audits Pat's 2011 return, and Pat pays a $1,200 deficiency on October 3, 2014. Pat may file a claim for refund as late as October 3, 2016. However, if Pat files the claim later than April 15, 2015, the refund may not exceed $1,200 (the amount of tax paid during the two-year period immediately preceding the filing of the claim). ◄

LIABILITY FOR TAX

Taxpayers are primarily liable for paying their tax. Spouses and transferees may be secondarily liable, as discussed below.

OBJECTIVE 9

Explain from whom the government may collect unpaid taxes

JOINT RETURNS

Ordinarily, if spouses file a joint return, their liability to pay the tax is joint and several.[92] **Joint and several liability** means that each spouse is potentially liable for the full amount due. If one spouse fails to pay any or all of the tax, the other spouse is responsible for paying the deficiency. Joint and several liability has facilitated IRS collection efforts where one spouse absconds from the country, and the other spouse remains behind.

VALIDITY OF JOINT RETURN. To be valid, a joint return generally must include the signatures of both spouses. However, if one spouse cannot sign because of a disability, the return still is valid if that spouse orally consents to the other spouse's signing for him or her.[93] A joint return is invalid if one spouse forces the other to file jointly.

INNOCENT SPOUSE PROVISION. Congress has provided for **innocent spouse relief** where holding one spouse liable for the taxes due from both spouses would be inequitable. Relief is available if all five of the following conditions are met:[94]

▶ The spouses file a joint return.

▶ The return contains an understatement of tax attributable to the erroneous item(s) of an individual filing it.

---

[90] Sec. 6511(a).
[91] Under Sec. 6512, special rules apply if the IRS has mailed a notice of deficiency and if the taxpayer files a petition with the Tax Court.

[92] Sec. 6013(d)(3).
[93] Reg. Sec. 1.6012-1(a)(5).
[94] Sec. 6015(b).

▶ The other individual establishes that he or she neither knew nor had reason to know of any or all of the understatement.

▶ Based on all the facts and circumstances, holding the other individual liable for the deficiency would be inequitable.

▶ The other individual elects innocent spouse relief no later than two years after the IRS begins its collection efforts.

The degree of relief available depends on the extent of the electing spouse's knowledge. If the spouse neither knew nor had reason to know of *an understatement*, full relief will be granted. Full relief encompasses liability for taxes, interest, and penalties attributable to the full amount of the understatement. On the other hand, if the spouse either knew or had reason to know of an understatement, but not *the extent of the understatement*, only partial relief will be granted.[95] Partial relief encompasses liability for taxes, interest, and penalties attributable to that portion of the understatement of which the spouse was unaware.

EXAMPLE C:15-36 ▶ Jim and Joy jointly filed a tax return for 2010. Joy fraudulently reported on Schedule C two expenses: one amounting to $4,000 and the other amounting to $3,000. The IRS audits the return, assesses a $2,170 deficiency, and begins its collection efforts on June 2, 2012. If (1) Jim elects innocent spouse relief no later than June 2, 2014, (2) Jim establishes that he neither knew nor had reason to know of the understatement, and (3) if holding Jim liable for the deficiency would be inequitable under the circumstances, Jim will be relieved of liability for the full $2,170. ◀

EXAMPLE C:15-37 ▶ Same facts as in Example C:15-36 except Jim had reason to know the $3,000 expense was fraudulent. If (1) Jim elects innocent spouse relief no later than June 2, 2014, (2) Jim establishes that he neither knew nor had reason to know the *extent* of the understatement (i.e., $7,000 as opposed to $3,000), and (3) if holding Jim liable for the full amount of the deficiency would be inequitable under the circumstances, Jim will be relieved of liability for that portion of the deficiency attributable to the $4,000 expense. ◀

Proportional liability is liability for only that portion of a deficiency attributable to the taxpayer's separate taxable items. A joint filer incurs proportional liability if all the following conditions are met:[96]

▶ The joint filer elects proportional liability within two years after the IRS begins its collection efforts.

▶ The electing filer is either divorced or separated at the time of the election.

▶ The electing filer did not reside in the same household as the other filer at any time during the 12-month period preceding the election.

▶ The electing filer does not have actual knowledge of any item giving rise to the deficiency.

The electing filer bears the burden of proving the amount of his or her proportional liability. The fraudulent transfer of property between joint filers immediately before the election will invalidate it.

EXAMPLE C:15-38 ▶ Sam and Sue jointly filed a 2009 tax return. Sam intentionally omitted to report $8,000 in gambling winnings. Sue fraudulently deducted $1,600 in business expenses. The IRS audits the return, assesses a $3,600 deficiency, and begins its collection efforts on August 17, 2012. Sam and Sue are subsequently divorced. If Sue (1) elects innocent spouse relief no later than August 17, 2014, (2) did not reside in the same household as Sam at any time during the 12-month period preceding the election, and (3) did not actually know of Sam's omission, she will be liable for only that portion of the deficiency attributable to her fraudulent deduction. ◀

The Effect of Community Property Laws. Community property laws are ignored in determining to whom income (other than income from property) is attributable. For example, if one spouse living in a community property state wins money by gambling, the gambling income is not treated as community property for purposes of the innocent spouse provisions. If the gambling winnings are omitted from a joint return, they are deemed to be solely the income of the spouse who gambled.

---

[95] Sec. 6015(b)(2).   [96] Sec. 6015(c).

TRANSFEREE LIABILITY

TYPICAL MISCONCEPTION

A taxpayer cannot escape paying taxes by transferring assets to a transferee (donee, heir, legatee, etc.) or a fiduciary (executor, trustee, etc.).

Section 6901 authorizes the IRS to collect taxes from persons other than the taxpayer. The two categories of persons from whom the IRS may collect taxes are transferees and fiduciaries. Transferees include donees, heirs, legatees, devisees, shareholders of dissolved corporations, parties to a reorganization, and other distributees.[97] Fiduciaries include executors and administrators of estates. In general, the limitations period for transferees expires one year after the limitations period for transferors. The transferors may be income earners in the case of income taxes, executors in the case of estate taxes, and donors in the case of gift taxes.

EXAMPLE C:15-39 ▶

Lake Corporation is liquidated in the current year, and it distributes all its assets to its sole share-holder, Leo. If the IRS audits Lake's return and assesses a deficiency, Leo (the distributee) is responsible for paying the deficiency. ◀

TAX PRACTICE ISSUES

OBJECTIVE 10

Understand professional and governmental standards for tax practitioners

A number of statutes and guidelines address what constitutes proper behavior of CPAs and others engaged in tax practice, including the AICPA's *Statements on Standards for Tax Services* (see Appendix E).

STATUTORY PROVISIONS CONCERNING TAX RETURN PREPARERS

Sections 6694–6696 impose penalties on tax return preparers for misconduct. Section 7701(a)(36) defines a tax return preparer as a "person who prepares for compensation, or who employs one or more persons to prepare for compensation, any return of tax imposed by this title or any claim for refund of tax imposed by this title."[98] Tax return preparers are divided into two categories: signing preparers and non-signing preparers. A signing preparer has primary responsibility for the overall substantive accuracy of the preparation of the return or refund claim. A non-signing preparer gives advice to a taxpayer or another preparer, and the advice leads to a position or entry that is a substantial portion of the return or refund claim. As a result, more than one preparer can be subject to the preparer penalties. The 2007 Small Business Act expanded the definition of a preparer from "one preparer per firm" to "one preparer per position per firm." The preparer responsible for the position giving rise to the understatement is subject to preparer penalties related to that position.[99]

KEY POINT

As evidenced by the formidable list of possible penalties, an individual considering becoming a tax return preparer needs to be aware of certain procedures set forth in the IRC.

Section 6695 imposes penalties for

▶ Failure to furnish the taxpayer with a copy of the return or claim ($50 per failure)

▶ Failure to sign a return or claim ($50 per failure)

▶ Failure to furnish one's identification number ($50 per failure)

▶ Failure to keep a copy of a return or claim or, in lieu thereof, to maintain a list of taxpayers for whom returns or claims were prepared ($50 per failure)

▶ Failure to file a correct information return ($50 per failure)

▶ Endorsement or other negotiation of an income tax refund check made payable to anyone other than the preparer ($500 per check)

▶ Failure to be diligent in determining eligibility for the earned income credit ($100 per case)

The first five penalties are not assessable if the preparer shows that the failure is due to reasonable cause and not willful neglect, and the maximum penalty cannot exceed $25,000 for a return period.[100]

Under Sec. 6694, a preparer will owe a maximum penalty equal to $1,000 or 50% of the income derived from the return if he or she lacked substantial authority for a non-disclosed position.[101] Substantial authority is an objective standard that involves the analysis of the law

---

[97] Reg. Sec. 301.6901-1(b).
[98] The 2007 Small Business Act broadened the definition of tax return preparer to include a person preparing non-income tax returns, such as estate, gift, excise, or employment tax returns.
[99] Reg. Sec. 1.6694-1(b).

[100] Regulation Sec. 1.6695-1(b)(3) states that, for the purpose of avoiding the failure-to-sign penalty, reasonable cause is "a cause which arises despite ordinary care and prudence exercised by the individual preparer."
[101] Sec. 6694(a).

REAL-WORLD EXAMPLE

In addition to these penalties, the IRS may suspend or bar a tax practitioner from practicing before the IRS. Each week the IRS publishes a list of suspended practitioners.

and application of the law to the relevant facts.[102] The standard is less stringent than the "more likely than not" (greater than 50%) test but more stringent than the reasonable basis standard. Reasonable basis refers to a position that is arguable and reasonably based on an acceptable authority such as the Internal Revenue Code, Treasury Regulations, court cases, and other pronouncements listed in Reg. Sec. 1.6662-4(d)(3).[103] Consequently, pertinent Treasury Regulations imply that a tax position meets the substantial authority test if the authorities supporting the position are more substantial than authorities that take a contrary position. The preparer may avoid the penalty if the preparer has reasonable basis for the position and the position is properly disclosed.[104] The IRS will impose no penalty if the preparer shows that he or she has reasonable cause for the understatement, and he or she acted in good faith.[105]

If any portion of the understatement results from the preparer's willful attempt to understate taxes or from reckless or intentional disregard of rules or regulations, the penalty will be the greater of $5,000 or 50% of the income derived from the return. Proposed Reg. Sec. 1.6694-3 states that preparers are considered to have willfully understated taxes if they have attempted to wrongfully reduce taxes by disregarding pertinent information. A preparer generally is deemed to have recklessly or intentionally disregarded a rule or regulation if he or she adopts a position contrary to a rule or regulation about which he or she knows, or is reckless in not knowing about such rule or regulation. A preparer may adopt a position contrary to a revenue ruling if the position has reasonable basis. In addition, a preparer may depart from following a Treasury Regulation without penalty if he or she has a good faith basis for challenging its validity and adequately discloses his or her position on Form 8275-R (Regulation Disclosure Statement).

STOP & THINK

Question: While preparing a client's tax return two days before the due date, Tevin reviews an item that arguably is deductible. He weighs the cost of researching whether he has substantial authority for the position. In so doing, he calculates that researching the issue will cost him $300 in forgone revenues and that not researching the issue will cost him $250 in preparer penalties. What should Tevin do?

Solution: Undoubtedly, Tevin should research the issue and determine whether the deduction either has substantial authority or has a reasonable basis. If he has a reasonable basis, he should disclose his position on the tax return. At stake here is not merely $300 in foregone revenues but also Tevin's professional reputation. His taking a position that does not meet the applicable standards subjects not only him as tax preparer, but also his client as taxpayer, to penalties. If the IRS imposes a penalty on the client, the client might terminate the professional relationship with Tevin or sue Tevin for negligence. Besides, Tevin may have miscalculated his own professional liability. If the IRS determines that Tevin recklessly or intentionally disregarded tax rules and regulations, it may impose a penalty of $5,000, not $250.

Tax preparers who offer advice relating to the preparation of a document, knowing that such advice will result in a tax understatement, will be liable for aiding and abetting in the understatement.[106] The penalty for aiding and abetting is $1,000 for advice given to noncorporate taxpayers and $10,000 for advice given to corporate taxpayers. If a preparer is assessed an aiding-and-abetting penalty, the preparer will not be assessed a Sec. 6694 preparer penalty for the same infraction.

REPORTABLE TRANSACTION DISCLOSURES

The IRS has continued its focus on tax shelters, including reportable and listed transactions, and has issued extensive and detailed reporting requirements on individuals who advise clients on certain aggressive tax schemes. Section 6111 sets forth the required disclosures by material advisors for reportable transactions, and Section 6112 requires material advisors to maintain a list of tax shelter clients and file information returns with the IRS.

---

[102] Reg. Sec. 1.6662-4(d).
[103] Reg. Sec. 1.6662-3(b)(3).
[104] Sec. 6694(a)(2)(B).

[105] Sec. 6694(b)(3).
[106] Sec. 6701.

A reportable transaction is any transaction required to be disclosed because the IRS has determined it to have the potential for tax evasion or avoidance.[107] Reportable transactions include the following: (1) listed transactions as defined by the IRS, (2) confidential transactions, (3) transactions with contractual protection, (4) loss transactions where the losses claimed exceed certain thresholds ranging from $50,000 in a single year for individuals to $20 million for corporations over a number of years, (5) transactions of interest as designated by the IRS, and (6) patented transactions.[108]

A material advisor is any person who provides material aid, assistance, or advice with respect to any reportable transaction, and who receives gross income from the activity in excess of $50,000 if the tax benefits flow primarily to individuals or $250,000 for corporations and other entities.[109] The income thresholds are sharply reduced for listed transactions and transactions of interest ($10,000 for individuals and $25,000 for corporations).[110]

In general, a material advisor complies with the disclosure requirements by filing Form 8918 which details the transaction, the expected tax treatment, and the potential tax benefits in sufficient detail for the IRS to fully understand the transaction. Failure to make the required disclosures subjects taxpayers and material advisors to severe penalties as follows:

▶ *Imposed on the taxpayer:* Failure to disclose a reportable or listed transaction (ranging from $10,000 to $200,000, depending on the nature of the transaction and the status of the taxpayer)[111]

▶ *Imposed on the taxpayer:* Accuracy-related penalty for listed and reportable transactions (20% of the understatement for disclosed transactions; 30% for undisclosed transactions)[112]

▶ *Imposed on the organizer or advisor:* Failure to furnish information on reportable transactions ($50,000 in the case of tax benefits provided to individuals; $250,000 in any other case).[113]

▶ *Imposed on the organizer or advisor:* Failure to maintain an investor list ($10,000 per day after the twentieth business day following notice)[114]

▶ *Imposed on the organizer or advisor:* Tax shelter fraud (50% of gross income derivable from the tax shelter)[115]

In addition, if a taxpayer fails to report information regarding a listed transaction on a required return or statement, the limitations period is extended to one year after the earlier of the date on which the information is furnished to the IRS or the date on which a material advisor meets the list maintenance requirements.[116]

RULES OF *CIRCULAR 230*

Treasury Department *Circular 230* regulates the practice of attorneys, CPAs, enrolled agents, and enrolled actuaries before the IRS. Practice before the IRS includes representing taxpayers in meetings with IRS audit agents and appeals officers. Tax professionals who do not comply with the rules and regulations of *Circular 230* can be barred from practicing before the IRS and may be subject to censure and/or monetary penalties. Such professionals are entitled to an administrative hearing before being penalized.

The IRS plans to extend *Circular 230* rules to all paid preparers (signing and non-signing) and create a new practice designation called the "registered tax return preparer" (RTRP). The proposed changes require all paid preparers to register with the IRS, pay an annual fee, and obtain a preparer tax identification number (PTIN). Additional initiatives scheduled to take place in 2011 include mandatory testing and continuing education for those who are not CPAs, attorneys, or enrolled agents. These changes attempt to ensure that all tax preparers adhere to professional standards. Accordingly, all RTRPs will be governed by *Circular 230*. An RTRP is limited to preparing and signing tax returns, claims for refund, and other documents to be filed with the IRS and may represent a taxpayer before revenue agents, Taxpayer

ETHICAL POINT

In deciding whether to adopt a pro-taxpayer position on a tax return or in rendering tax advice, a tax advisor should keep in mind his or her responsibilities under the tax return preparer rules of the IRC, *Treasury Department Circular 230*, and the *Statements on Standards for Tax Services*, especially Statement No. 1. Statement No. 1 (reproduced in Appendix E) requires that a CPA have a good faith belief that the position adopted on the tax return is supported by existing law or by a good faith argument for extending, modifying, or reversing existing law.

---

[107] Sec. 6707A(c).
[108] Reg. Sec. 1.6011-4 and Prop. Reg. Sec. 1.6011-4.
[109] Sec 6111(b).
[110] Reg. Sec. 301.6111-3.
[111] Sec. 6707A.

[112] Sec. 6662A.
[113] Sec. 6111.
[114] Sec. 6708.
[115] Sec. 6700(a).
[116] Sec. 6501(c)(10).

Advocate Service representatives, or similar employees of the IRS. However, RTRPs may not provide tax advice beyond the advice necessary to prepare the tax return and may not represent taxpayers before appeals officers, counsel, or similar IRS employees.

Among the rules governing the conduct of practitioners before the IRS are the following:[117]

▶ If the practitioner knows that a client has not complied with federal tax laws or has made an error in or an omission from any return, the practitioner should promptly advise the client of the error or omission. The practitioner also must advise the client of possible corrective action and the consequences of not taking such action.

▶ Each person practicing before the IRS must exercise due diligence in preparing returns, determining the correctness of representations made to the Treasury Department, and determining the correctness of representations made to clients about tax matters.

Circular 230 provides that a practitioner may not advise a client to take a position on or submit to the IRS a document, affidavit, or other paper unless the position is not frivolous.[118] The current (2008) revisions for *Circular 230* omit the sections dealing with tax return preparation because the corresponding penalty sections in the IRC were simultaneously changed. The Treasury Department and the IRS have determined that the professional standards of *Circular 230* should conform with the civil penalty standards for return preparers in Sec. 6694, which now require substantial authority for a tax return position. See previous discussion on preparer penalties.

Circular 230 also lists best practices standards for tax advisors.[119] Such standards include the following:

▶ Communicate clearly with the client regarding the terms of the engagement.

▶ Establish the relevant facts, evaluate the reasonableness of assumptions or representations, relate the applicable law to the relevant facts, and arrive at a conclusion supported by the law and relevant facts.

▶ Advise the client of the implications of conclusions reached, including the applicability of accuracy-related penalties.

▶ Act fairly and with integrity in practice before the IRS.

Circular 230 also provides detailed substantive and format requirements for practitioners who provide written advice. Written advice fall into two categories: (1) covered opinions and (2) all other written advice.[120] A covered opinion is written advice concerning at least one federal issue arising from any one of the following items:

▶ A listed transaction

▶ Any plan or arrangement, the *principal* purpose of which is tax avoidance, or

▶ Any plan or arrangement, a significant purpose of which is tax avoidance if the written advice also is a marketed opinion, a contractual protection opinion, a confidential transaction opinion, or a reliance opinion.

A reliance opinion or other written advice could include written advice on a routine matter, such as whether certain entertainment expenses are deductible. As a practical matter, many practitioners include a standard disclaimer with such written correspondence not explicitly intended to comply with the *Circular 230* substantive and format requirements. See the client letter in Appendix A for an example of the disclaimer language.

STATEMENTS ON STANDARDS FOR TAX SERVICES

Tax advisors confronted with ethical issues frequently turn to a professional organization for guidance. Although the guidelines set forth by such organizations are not *legally* enforceable, they carry significant moral weight, and may be cited in a negligence lawsuit

---

[117] *Treasury Department Circular 230* (2008), Secs. 10.21 and 10.22.
[118] Ibid., Sec. 10.34.
[119] Ibid., Sec. 10.33.

[120] Covered opinions are discussed in Sec. 10.35 and all other written advice is discussed in Sec. 10.37.

as the proper "standard of care" for tax practitioners. They also may provide grounds for the termination or suspension of one's professional license. One such set of guidelines is the *Statements on Standards for Tax Services* (SSTSs), issued by the American Institute of Certified Public Accountants (AICPA) and reproduced in Appendix E.[121] Inspired by the principles of honesty and integrity, these guidelines define standards of ethical conduct for CPAs engaged in tax practice. In the words of the AICPA:

> In our view, practice standards are the hallmark of calling one's self a professional. Members should fulfill their responsibilities as professionals by instituting and maintaining standards against which their professional performance can be measured. The promulgation of practice standards also reinforces one of the core values of the AICPA Vision—that CPAs conduct themselves with honesty and integrity.[122]

The SSTSs are professionally enforceable; that is, they may be enforced through a disciplinary proceeding conducted by the AICPA, which may terminate or suspend a practitioner from AICPA membership.

Statement No. 1 defines the circumstances under which a CPA should (or should not) recommend a tax return position to a taxpayer. It also prescribes a course of conduct that the CPA should follow when making such a recommendation. Specifically,

▶ A member should not recommend that a tax return position be taken with respect to any item unless the member has a good-faith belief that the position has a realistic possibility of being sustained administratively or judicially on its merits if challenged.

▶ [A] member may recommend a tax return position that the member concludes that the position has a reasonable basis and the member recommends that the taxpayer appropriately disclose the position.

▶ When recommending tax return positions and when preparing or signing a return on which a tax return position is taken, a member should, when relevant, advise the taxpayer regarding potential penalty consequences of such tax return position and the opportunity, if any, to avoid such penalties through disclosure.

The *realistic possibility standard* set forth in Statement No. 1 parallels that of Sec. 6694. Regulation Sec. 1.6694-2(b)(2) states that the relevant authorities for the realistic-possibility-of-being-sustained test are the same as those that apply in the substantial authority context. The IRS will treat a position as having met the realistic possibility of being sustained on "its merits" if a reasonable and well informed analysis by a person knowledgeable in the tax law would lead such a person to conclude that the position has approximately a one in three, or greater, likelihood of being sustained on its merits.

However, the *realistic possibility standard* set forth in Statement No. 1 differs from the IRC standard in that it allows as support for a tax return position well reasoned articles or treatises, in addition to primary tax authorities. The IRC standard allows as support for a tax return position only primary tax authorities.

Statement No. 2 sets forth the standards when signing the preparer's declaration that the return is true, correct, and complete. Specifically,

▶ A member should make a reasonable effort to obtain all necessary information from the taxpayer to provide answers to all questions on the tax return.

▶ A request for information may necessitate a disclosure for the return to be considered complete or to avoid penalties.

Statement No. 3 addresses (1) whether tax practitioners can reasonably rely on information supplied to them by the taxpayer, (2) when they have a duty to examine or verify such information, (3) when they have a duty to make inquiries of the taxpayer, and (4) what information they should consider in preparing a tax return. Specifically,

---

[121] The AICPA's Tax Executive Committee issued revised standards in November 2009, which were effective January 1, 2010.

[122] Letter to AICPA members by David A. Lifson, Chair, AICPA Tax Executive Committee, and Gerald W. Padwe, Vice President, AICPA Taxation Section (April 18, 2000).

▶ In preparing or signing a return, a member may in good faith rely, without verification, on information furnished by the taxpayer or by third parties. However, a member should make reasonable inquiries if the information furnished appears to be incorrect, incomplete, or inconsistent either on its face or on the basis of other facts known to a member.

▶ If the tax law or regulations impose a condition with respect to the deductibility or other tax treatment of an item . . . a member should make appropriate inquiries to determine to the member's satisfaction whether such condition has been met.

▶ When preparing a tax return, a member should consider information actually known to that member from the tax return of another taxpayer if the information is relevant to that tax return and its consideration is necessary to properly prepare that tax return.

Note that the duty to verify arises only when taxpayer provided information appears "strange" on its face. Otherwise, the tax practitioner has no duty to investigate taxpayer facts and circumstances. The taxpayer has the ultimate responsibility for the contents of the return.

Statement No. 4 defines the circumstances in which a tax practitioner may use estimates in preparing a tax return. In addition, it cautions practitioners as to the manner in which they may use estimates. Specifically,

▶ A member may advise on estimates used in the preparation of a tax return, but the taxpayer has the responsibility to provide the estimated data. Appraisals or valuations are not considered estimates.

▶ [A] member may use the taxpayer's estimates in the preparation of a tax return if it is not practical to obtain exact data and if the member determines that the estimates are reasonable. If the taxpayer's estimates are used, they should be presented in a manner that does not imply greater accuracy than exists.

Notwithstanding this statement, the tax practitioner may not use estimates when such use is implicitly prohibited by the IRC. For example, Sec. 274(d) disallows deductions for certain expenses (e.g., meals and entertainment) unless the taxpayer can substantiate the expenses with adequate records or sufficient corroborating information. The documentation requirement effectively precludes the taxpayer from estimating such expenses and the practitioner from using such estimates.

Statement No. 5 sets forth the standards for members in recommending a tax return position that departs from the position determined in an administrative proceeding or in a court decision with respect to the taxpayer's prior return.

Statement No. 6 defines a tax practitioner's duty when he or she becomes aware of an error in the taxpayer's return or a return that is the subject of an administrative proceeding. Specifically,

▶ A member should inform the taxpayer promptly upon becoming aware of (1) an error in a previously filed return, (2) an error in a return that is the subject of an administrative proceeding (e.g., an IRS audit or appeals conference), or (3) a taxpayer's failure to file a required return. A member should advise the taxpayer of the potential consequences of the error and recommend the corrective measures to be taken. The member is not obligated to inform the taxing authority, and a member may not do so without the taxpayer's permission, except when required by law.

▶ If a member is requested to prepare the current year's return and the taxpayer has not taken appropriate action to correct an error in a prior year's return, the member should consider whether to withdraw from preparing the return and whether to continue a professional or employment relationship with the taxpayer.

▶ If a member is representing a taxpayer in an administrative proceeding with respect to a return that contains an error of which the member is aware, the member should request the taxpayer's agreement to disclose the error to the taxing authority.

This statement implies that the tax practitioner's primary duty is to the taxpayer, not the taxing authority. Furthermore, upon the taxpayer's failure to correct a tax related error, the practitioner may exercise discretion in deciding whether or not to terminate the professional relationship. The standard also permits the member to provide oral recommendations, but the member should document any oral advice.

Finally, Statement No. 7 addresses the quality of advice provided by the tax practitioner, what consequences presumably ensue from such advice, and whether the practitioner has a duty to update advice to reflect subsequent developments. Specifically,

▶ A member should use professional judgment to ensure that tax advice provided to a taxpayer reflect competence and appropriately serves the taxpayer's needs. When communicating tax advice to a taxpayer in writing, a member should comply with relevant taxing authorities' standards applicable to written tax advice. A member should use professional judgment about any need to document oral advice.

▶ A member should assume that tax advice provided to a taxpayer will affect the manner in which the matters or transactions considered would be reported on the taxpayer's tax returns.

▶ A member has no obligation to communicate with a taxpayer when subsequent developments affect advice previously provided with respect to significant matters except while assisting a taxpayer in implementing procedures or plans associated with the advice provided or when a member undertakes an obligation by specific agreement.

The statement implies that practitioner-taxpayer dealings should not be casual, nonconsensual, open ended. Rather, they should be professional, contractual, and definite. Oral advice may be appropriate in routine matters, but written communications are recommended in important, complicated, or significant dollar value transactions. When giving tax advice, a member should consider the standards in SSTS No. 1.

TAX ACCOUNTING AND TAX LAW

Accountants and lawyers frequently deal with the same issues. These issues pertain to incorporation and merger, bankruptcy and liquidation, purchases and sales, gains and losses, compensation and benefits, and estate planning. Both types of professionals are competent to practice in many of the same areas. In some areas, however, accountants are more competent than lawyers, and in other areas, lawyers are more competent than accountants. What are these areas, and where does one draw the line?

In the realm of federal taxation, achieving a clear delineation always has been difficult. When an accountant prepares a tax return, he or she invariably delves into the intricacies of tax law. When a lawyer gives tax advice, he or she frequently applies principles of accounting. Toward clarifying the responsibilities of each, the AICPA and American Bar Association have issued the *Statement on Practice in the Field of Federal Income Taxation*.[123] This statement indicates five areas in which CPAs and attorneys are equally competent to practice and several areas in which each is exclusively competent to practice. The areas of mutual competence are as follows:

▶ Preparing federal income tax returns
▶ Determining the tax effects of proposed transactions
▶ Representing taxpayers before the Treasury Department
▶ Practicing before the U.S. Tax Court
▶ Preparing claims for refunds

Areas in which an accountant is exclusively competent to practice include:

▶ Resolving accounting issues
▶ Preparing financial statements included in financial reports or submitted with tax returns
▶ Advising clients as to accounting methods and procedures
▶ Classifying transactions and summarizing them in monetary terms
▶ Interpreting financial results

---

[123] National Conference of Lawyers and Certified Public Accountants, *Statement on Practice in the Field of Federal Income Taxation*, November 1981.

Areas in which an attorney is exclusively competent to practice include:

► Resolving issues of law

► Preparing legal documents such as agreements, conveyances, trust instruments, and wills

► Advising clients as to the sufficiency or effect of legal documents

► Taking the necessary steps to create, amend, or dissolve a partnership, corporation, or trust

► Representing clients in criminal investigations

State bar and CPA associations have issued similar guidelines for their constituencies, and the courts generally have followed these and the national guidelines.[124]

What happens if an accountant oversteps his or her professional bounds? The transgression may constitute the **unauthorized practice of law.** The unauthorized practice of law involves the engagement, by nonlawyers, in professional activities traditionally reserved for the bar. In most states, it is actionable by injunction, damages, or both. Allegations of the unauthorized practice of law typically arise in the context of a billing dispute.[125] The CPA bills a client for professional services, and the client disputes the bill on the ground that the accountant engaged in the unauthorized practice of law. Occasionally, the court sustains the client's allegation and thus denies the accountant the amount in dispute. With this and the public interest in mind, accountants should always confine their practice to areas in which they are most competent.

ACCOUNTANT-CLIENT PRIVILEGE

According to judicial doctrine, certain communications between an attorney and a client are "privileged," i.e., nondiscoverable in the course of litigation. In 1998, Congress extended this privilege to similar communications between a federally authorized tax advisor and a client. A federally authorized tax advisor includes a certified public accountant.

The accountant-client privilege is similar to the attorney-client privilege in two respects. First, it encompasses communications for the purpose of obtaining or giving professional advice. Second, it excludes communications for the sole purpose of preparing a tax return. The accountant-client privilege is dissimilar in three respects. First, it is limited only to *tax* advice. Second, it may be asserted only in a noncriminal tax proceeding before a federal court or the IRS. Third, it excludes written communications between an accountant and a corporation regarding a tax shelter. A tax shelter is any plan or arrangement, a significant purpose of which is tax avoidance or evasion.

EXAMPLE C:15-40 ► Alec, Chief Financial Officer of MultiCorp, has solicited the advice of his tax accountant, Louise, concerning a civil dispute with the IRS. Louise has advised Alec in a series of letters spanning the course of five months. An IRS appeals officer asks Louise if he can review the letters. Louise may refuse the officer's request because her professional advice was offered in anticipation of civil litigation and therefore is "privileged." ◄

EXAMPLE C:15-41 ► Assume the same facts as in Example C:15-40 except Louise sends Alec a letter concerning a foreign sales scheme. Because Louise communicates tax advice to a corporation concerning a "tax shelter" and because this communication is written, it is *not* privileged. ◄

The creation of an accountant-client privilege reflects Congress' belief that the selection of a tax advisor should not hinge on the question of privilege. It ensures that all tax advice is accorded the same protection regardless of the tax advisor's professional status.

[124] See for example *Lathrop v. Donahue,* 367 U.S. 820, 81 S. Ct. 1826 (1961), *U.S. v. Gordon Buttorff,* 56 AFTR 2d 85-5247, 85-1 USTC ¶9435 (5th Cir., 1985), *Morton L. Simons v. Edgar T. Bellinger,* 643 F.2d 774, 207 U.S. App. D.C. 24 (1980), *Emilio L. Ippolito v. The State of Florida,* 824 F. Supp. 1562, 1993 U.S. Dist. LEXIS 13091 (M.D. Fla., 1993), *In re*

Application of New Jersey Society of Certified Public Accountants, 102 N.J. 231, 507 A.2d 711 (1986).
[125] See for example, *In re Bercu,* 299 N.Y. 728, 87 N.E.2d 451 (1949), and *Agran v. Shapiro,* 46 AFTR 896, 127 Cal. App.2d 807 (App. Dept. Super. Ct., 1954).

PROBLEM MATERIALS

DISCUSSION QUESTIONS

C:15-1 Describe how the IRS verifies tax returns at its service centers.

C:15-2 Name some of the IRS administrative pronouncements.

C:15-3
a. Through what programs has the IRS gathered data to develop its DIF statistical models?
b. How do these programs differ?
c. How has the IRS used these programs to select returns for audit?

C:15-4 On his individual return, Al reports salary and exemptions for himself and seven dependents. His itemized deductions consist of mortgage interest, real estate taxes, and a large loss from breeding dogs. On his individual return, Ben reports self-employment income, a substantial loss from partnership operations, a casualty loss deduction equal to 25% of his AGI, charitable contribution deductions equal to 30% of his AGI, and an exemption for himself. Al's return reports higher taxable income than does Ben's. Which return is more likely to be selected for audit under the DIF program? Explain.

C:15-5 The IRS notifies Tom that it will audit his current year return for an interest deduction. The IRS audited Tom's return two years ago for a charitable contribution deduction. The IRS, however, did not assess a deficiency for the prior year return. Is any potential relief available to Tom with respect to the audit of his current year return?

C:15-6 The IRS informs Brad that it will audit his current year employee business expenses. Brad just met with a revenue agent who contends that Brad owes $775 of additional taxes. Discuss briefly the procedural alternatives available to Brad.

C:15-7 What course(s) of action is (are) available to a taxpayer upon receipt of the following notices:
a. The 30-day letter?
b. The 90-day letter?
c. IRS rejection of a claim for a refund?

C:15-8 List the courts in which a taxpayer can begin tax-related litigation.

C:15-9 Why do taxpayers frequently litigate in the Tax Court?

C:15-10 In what situations is a protest letter necessary?

C:15-11 What information should be included in a request for a ruling?

C:15-12 What conditions must the taxpayer meet to shift the burden of proof to the IRS?

C:15-13 In what circumstances will the IRS rule on estate tax issues?

C:15-14 On which of the following issues will the IRS likely issue a private letter ruling and why? In your answer, assume that no other IRS pronouncement addresses the issue and that pertinent Treasury Regulations are not forthcoming.
a. Whether the taxpayer correctly calculated a capital gain reported on last year's tax return.
b. The tax consequences of using stock derivatives in a corporate reorganization.
c. Whether a mathematical formula correctly calculates the fair market value of a stock derivative.
d. Whether the cost of an Internet course that purports to improve existing employment skills may be deducted this year as a business expense.

C:15-15 Tracy wants to take advantage of a "terrific business opportunity" by engaging in a transaction with Homer. Homer, domineering and impatient, wants Tracy to conclude the transaction within two weeks and under the terms proposed by Homer. Otherwise, Homer will offer the opportunity to another party. Tracy is unsure about the tax consequences of the proposed transaction. Would you advise Tracy to request a ruling? Explain.

C:15-16 Provide the following information relating to both individual and corporate taxpayers:
a. Due date for an income tax return assuming the taxpayer requests no extension.
b. Due date for the return assuming the taxpayer files an automatic extension request.
c. Latest possible due date for the return

C:15-17 Your client wants to know whether she must file any documents for an automatic extension to file her tax return. What do you tell her?

C:15-18 A client believes that obtaining an extension for filing an income tax return would give him additional time to pay the tax at no additional cost. Is the client correct?

C:15-19 Briefly explain the rules for determining the interest rate charged on tax underpayments. Is this rate the same as that for overpayments? In which months might the rate(s) change?

C:15-20 In April of the current year, Stan does not have sufficient assets to pay his tax liability for the previous year. However, he expects to pay the tax by August of the current year. He wonders if he should request an extension for filing his return instead of simply filing his return and paying the tax in August. What is your advice?

C:15-21 At what rate is the penalty for underpaying estimated taxes imposed? How is the penalty amount calculated?

C:15-22 The IRS audited Tony's return, and Tony agreed to pay additional taxes plus the negligence penalty. Is this penalty necessarily imposed on the total additional taxes that Tony owes? Explain.

C:**15-23** Assume that a taxpayer owes additional taxes as a result of an audit. Give two reasons why the IRS might not impose a substantial understatement penalty on the additional amount owed.

C:**15-24** Upon audit, the IRS determines Maria's tax liability to be $40,000. Maria agrees to pay a $7,000 deficiency. Will she necessarily have to pay a substantial understatement penalty? Explain.

C:**15-25** Distinguish between the circumstances that give rise to the civil fraud penalty and those that give rise to the negligence penalty.

C:**15-26** Distinguish between the burdens of proof the government must meet to prove civil and criminal fraud.

C:**15-27** Explain why the government might bring criminal fraud charges against a taxpayer under Sec. 7206 instead of Sec. 7201. Compare the maximum penalties imposed under Secs. 7201, 7203, and 7206.

C:**15-28** In general, when does the limitations period for tax returns expire? List four exceptions to the general rule.

C:**15-29** What is the principal purpose of the innocent spouse provisions?

C:**15-30** Is the tax return preparer limited to the person who signs the return? Explain.

C:**15-31** List five IRC penalties that can be imposed on tax return preparers. Does the IRC require a CPA to verify the information a client furnishes?

C:**15-32** According to *Treasury Department Circular 230*, what standard should a CPA meet to properly take a position on a tax return?

C:**15-33** Under the AICPA's *Statements on Standards for Tax Services*, what is the tax practitioner's professional duty in each of the following situations?
   a. Client erroneously deducts $5,000 (instead of $500) on a previous year's tax return.
   b. Client refuses to file an amended return to correct the deduction error.
   c. Client informs tax practitioner that client incurred $200 in out-of-pocket office supplies expenses.
   d. Client informs tax practitioner that client incurred $700 in business related entertainment expenses.
   e. Tax practitioner learns that the exemption amount for single taxpayers has been increased by $1,000. Client is a single taxpayer.

ISSUE IDENTIFICATION QUESTIONS

C:**15-34** You are preparing the tax return of Bold Corporation, which had sales of $60 million. Bold made a $1 million expenditure for which the appropriate tax treatment—deductible or capitalizable—is a gray area. Bold's director of federal taxes and chief financial officer urgently wants to deduct the expenditure. What tax compliance issues should you consider in advising her?

C:**15-35** Your client, Hank Goedert, earned $100,000 of salary and received $40,000 of dividends in the current year. His itemized deductions total $37,000. In addition, Hank received $47,000 from a relative who was his former employer. You have researched whether the $47,000 should be classified as a gift or compensation and are confident that substantial authority exists for classifying the receipt as a gift. What tax compliance issues should you consider in deciding whether to include or exclude the amount in Hank's gross income?

C:**15-36** The IRS audited the tax returns of Darryl Strawberry, a former major league outfielder. It contended that, between 1986 and 1990, Strawberry earned $422,250 for autograph signings, appearances, and product endorsements, but he reported only $59,685 of income. Strawberry attributed the shortfall to his receipt of cash for autograph sessions and promotional events. He allegedly concealed the cash payments in separate bank accounts of which his CPA was unaware. What tax compliance issues regarding the alleged underreporting are pertinent?

PROBLEMS

C:**15-37** *Calculation of Penalties.* Amy files her current year tax return on August 13 of the following year. She pays the amount due without requesting an extension. The tax shown on her return is $24,000. Her current year wage withholding amounts to $15,000. Amy pays no estimated taxes and claims no tax credits on her current year return.
   a. What penalties will the IRS likely impose on Amy (ignoring the penalty for underpayment of estimated taxes)? Assume Amy committed no fraud.
   b. On what dollar amount, and for how many days, will Amy owe interest?

C:**15-38** *Calculation of Penalties.* In the preceding problem, how would your answers change if Amy instead files her return on June 18 and, on September 8 pays the amount due? Assume her wage withholding tax amounts to
   a. $19,000
   b. $24,500
   c. How would your answer to Part a change if Amy requests an automatic extension?

C:15-39 *Calculation of Penalties.* The taxes shown on Hu's tax returns for 2010 and 2011 are $5,000 and $8,000, respectively. Hu's wage withholding for 2011 was $5,200, and she paid no estimated taxes. Hu filed her 2011 return on March 17, 2012, but she did not have sufficient funds to pay any taxes on that date. She paid the $2,800 balance due on June 22, 2013. Hu's AGI for 2010 did not exceed $150,000. Calculate the penalties Hu owes with respect to her 2011 tax return.

C:15-40 *Calculation of Penalties.* Ted's 2011 return reported a tax liability of $1,800. Ted's wage withholding for 2011 was $2,200. Because of his poor memory, Ted did not file his 2011 return until May 28, 2012. What penalties (if any) does Ted owe?

C:15-41 *Calculation of Penalties.* Bob, a calendar year taxpayer, files his current year individual return on July 17 of the following year without having requested an extension. His return indicates an amount due of $5,100. Bob pays this amount on November 3 of the following year. What are Bob's penalties for failing to file and failing to pay his tax on time? Assume Bob committed no fraud.

C:15-42 *Calculation of Penalties.* Carl, a calendar year taxpayer, requests an automatic extension for filing his 2011 return. By April 16, 2012 (April 15 falls on a Sunday), he has paid $20,000 of taxes in the form of wage withholding and estimated taxes. He does not pay any additional tax with his extension request. Carl files his return and pays the balance of the taxes due on June 18, 2012. For 2010, his tax liability was $19,000, and his AGI did not exceed $150,000. What penalties will Carl owe if his 2011 tax is $23,000? $20,800?

C:15-43 *Determination of Interest.* Refer to the preceding problem.
a. Will Carl owe interest? If so, on what amount and for how many days?
b. Assume the applicable interest rate is 6%. Compute Carl's interest payable if his 2011 tax is $23,000. (See a major tax service for the compounding tables.)

C:15-44 *Penalty for Underpayment of Estimated Taxes.* Ed's tax liability for last year was $24,000. Ed projects that his tax for this year will be $34,000. Ed is self-employed and, thus, will have no withholding. His AGI for last year did not exceed $150,000. How much estimated tax should Ed pay for this year to avoid the penalty for underpaying estimated taxes?

C:15-45 *Penalty for Underpayment of Estimated Taxes.* Refer to the preceding problem. Assume that Ed expects his income for this year to decline and his tax liability for this year to be only $15,000. What minimum amount of estimated taxes should Ed pay this year? What problem will Ed encounter if he pays this minimum amount and his income exceeds last year's because of a large capital gain realized in December of this year?

C:15-46 *Penalty for Underpayment of Estimated Taxes.* Pam's 2010 income tax liability was $23,000. Her 2010 AGI did not exceed $150,000. On April 2, 2012, Pam, a calendar year taxpayer, files her 2011 individual return, which indicates a $30,000 income tax liability (before reduction for withholding). In addition, the return indicates self-employment taxes of $2,600. Taxes withheld from Pam's salary total $20,000; she has paid no estimated taxes.
a. Will Pam owe a penalty for not paying estimated taxes? Explain.
b. What amount (if any) per quarter is subject to the penalty? For what period will the penalty be imposed for each quarter's underpayment?
c. How would your answers to Parts a and b change if Pam's 2011 tax liability (including self-employment taxes) instead were $17,000?

C:15-47 *Penalty for Underpayment of Estimated Taxes.* Amir's projected tax liability for the current year is $23,000. Although Amir has substantial dividend and interest income, he does not pay any estimated taxes. Amir's withholding for January through November of the current year is $1,300 per month. He wants to increase his withholding for December to avoid the penalty for underpaying estimated taxes. Amir's previous year's liability (excluding withholding) is $21,000. His previous year's AGI did not exceed $150,000. What amount should Amir have withheld from his December paycheck? Explain.

C:15-48 *Negligence Penalty.* The IRS audits Tan's individual return for the current year and assesses a $9,000 deficiency, $2,800 of which results from Tan's negligence. What is the amount of Tan's negligence penalty? Does the penalty bear interest?

C:15-49 *Negligence Penalty.* The IRS audits Pearl's current year individual return and determines that, among other errors, she negligently failed to report dividend income of $8,000. The deficiency relating to the dividends is $2,240. The IRS proposes an additional $12,000 deficiency for the other errors that do not involve negligence. What is the amount of Pearl's negligence penalty for the $14,240 in deficiencies?

C:15-50 *Substantial Understatement Penalty.* Carmen's current year individual return reports a $6,000 deduction for a questionable item not relating to a tax-shelter. Carmen does not make a disclosure regarding this item. The IRS audits Carmen's return, and she consents to a deficiency. As a result, her tax liability increases from $20,000 to $21,860. Assume Carmen lacks substantial authority for the deduction.
  a. What substantial understatement penalty (if any) will be imposed?
  b. Will the penalty bear interest?
  c. How would your answer to Parts a and b change if Carmen reported a $20,000 deduction instead of $6,000, and her tax liability increased by $6,200 to $26,200?

C:15-51 *Substantial Understatement Penalty.* Refer to Part c of the previous problem. Assume that Carmen discloses her position, which is not frivolous. How would your original answer change assuming the item does not involve a tax shelter?

C:15-52 *Fraud Penalty.* Luis, a bachelor, owes $56,000 of additional taxes, all due to fraud.
  a. What is the amount of Luis' civil fraud penalty?
  b. What criminal fraud penalty might the government impose on Luis under Sec. 7201?

C:15-53 *Fraud Penalty.* Hal and Wanda, his wife, are in the 35% marginal tax bracket in the current year. Wanda fraudulently omits from their joint return $50,000 of gross income. Hal does not participate in or know of her fraudulent act. Hal, however, overstates his deductions by $10,000 because of an oversight.
  a. If the government successfully proves fraud in a civil suit against Wanda, what fines and/or penalties might she owe? If Hal and Wanda establish that the overstatement is not attributable to fraud, can the government impose a civil fraud penalty on Hal?
  b. If the government successfully proves fraud in a criminal suit against Wanda, what fines or penalties might she owe? Could she or Hal be sentenced to prison?

C:15-54 *Statute of Limitations.* Frank, a calendar year taxpayer, reports $100,000 of gross income and $60,000 of taxable income on his 2011 return, which he files on March 12, 2012. He fails to report on the return a $52,000 long-term capital gain and a $10,000 short-term capital loss. When does the limitations period for the government's collecting the tax deficiency expire if
  a. Frank's omission results from an oversight?
  b. His omission results from a willful attempt to evade the tax?

C:15-55 *Statute of Limitations.* Refer to the previous problem. Assume Frank commits fraud with respect to his 2011 return as late as October 8, 2013. When does the limitations period for charging Frank with criminal tax fraud expire?

C:15-56 *Claim for Refund.* On March 12, 2012, Maria, a calendar year taxpayer, files her 2011 individual return and pays the amount of tax due. She later discovers that she overlooked some deductions that she should have reported on the return. By what date must she file a claim for refund?

C:15-57 *Innocent Spouse Provisions.* Wilma earns no income in 2011 but files a joint return with her husband, Hank. Their 2011 return reports $40,000 of gross income and AGI, and $24,000 of taxable income. Hank realizes $12,000 of gambling winnings (no losses) in 2011 but fails to report the winnings on the return. Wilma does not know about Hank's gambling activities, much less his winnings. The IRS audits the 2011 return and assesses additional taxes. Is Wilma entitled to innocent spouse relief? Explain.

C:15-58 *Innocent Spouse Provisions.* Joe and Joan file a joint return for the current year. They are in the 35% marginal tax bracket. Unbeknownst to Joe, Joan fails to report on the return the $8,000 value of a prize she won. She, however, used the prize to buy Joe a new boat. Is Joe entitled to innocent spouse relief? Explain.

C:15-59 *Unauthorized Practice of Law.* Your client, Meade Technical Solutions, proposes to merge with Dealy Cyberlabs. In advance of the merger, you (a) issue an opinion concerning the FMV of Dealy, (b) prepare pro forma financials for the merged entity to be, (c) draft Meade shareholder resolutions approving the proposed merger, (d) file a shareholder proxy statement with the U.S. Securities and Exchange Commission, and (e) advise Meade's board of directors concerning the advantages of a Type A versus a Type B reorganization. Which of these activities, if any, constitutes the unauthorized practice of law?

C:15-60 *Unauthorized Practice of Law.* Your client, Envirocosmetics, recently has filed for bankruptcy. In the course of bankruptcy proceedings, you (a) prepare a plan of reorganization that alters the rights of preferred stockholders, (b) notify the Envirocosmetics' creditors of an impending bulk transfer of the company's assets, (c) review IRS secured claims against these assets, (d) restructure the company's debt by reducing its principal amount and extending its maturity, (e) advise the bankruptcy court as to how this restructuring will impact the company's NOLs. Which of these activities, if any, constitutes the unauthorized practice of law?

C:15-61 *Accountant-Client Privilege* Which of the following communications between an accountant and client are privileged?

    a. For tax preparation purposes only, client informs the accountant that she contributed $10,000 to a homeless shelter.

    b. Client informs the accountant that he forgot to report on his tax return the $5,000 value of a prize and asks how he should correct the error.

    c. Client informs the accountant that she no longer will pay alimony to her ex-husband.

C:15-62 *Accountant-Client Privilege.* Which of the following communications between an accountant and client are *not* privileged?

    a. In a closed-door meeting, the accountant orally advises the client to set up a foreign subsidiary to shift taxable income to a low-tax jurisdiction.

    b. In a closed-door meeting, the accountant submits to the client a plan for shifting taxable income to a low-tax jurisdiction.

    c. In soliciting professional advice relating to criminal fraud, the client informs the accountant that he (the client) lied to the IRS.

COMPREHENSIVE PROBLEM

C:15-63 This year, Ark Corporation acquired substantially all the voting stock of BioTech Consultants, Inc. for cash. Subsequent to the acquisition, Ark's chief financial officer, Jonathan Cohen, approached Edith Murphy, Ark's tax advisor, with a question: Could Ark amortize the "general educational skills" of BioTech's employees? Edith researched the issue but found no primary authorities on point. She did, however, find a tax journal article, co-authored by two prominent academics, that endorsed amortizing "general educational skills" for tax purposes. The article referred to numerous primary authorities that support the amortization of "technical skills," but not "general educational skills." Edith consulted these authorities directly. Based on her research, Edith in good faith advised Jonathan that Ark could amortize the "general educational skills" over a 15-year period. In so doing, has Edith met the "realistic possibility standard" of

    a. The IRC?

    b. The AICPAs *Statements on Standards for Tax Services* (see Appendix E)?

TAX STRATEGY PROBLEM

C:15-64 The IRS is disputing a deduction reported on your 2010 tax return, which you filed on April 14, 2011. On April 4, 2014, the IRS audit agent asks you to waive the statute of limitations for the entire return so as to give her additional time to obtain a Technical Advice Memorandum. The agent proposes in return for the waiver a "carrot"—the prospect of an offer in compromise—and a "stick"—the possibility of a higher penalty. Although you have substantial authority for the deduction, you consider the following alternatives: (1) waive the statute of limitations for the entire return, (2) waive the statute of limitations for the deduction only, or (3) do not waive the statute of limitations in any way, shape, or form. Which alternative should you choose, and why?

CASE STUDY PROBLEM

C:15-65 A long-time client, Horace Haney, wishes to avoid currently recognizing revenue in a particular transaction. A recently finalized Treasury Regulation provides that, in such a transaction, revenue should be currently recognized. Horace insists that you report no revenue from the transaction and, furthermore, that you make no disclosure about contravening the regulation. The IRC is unclear about whether the income should be recognized currently. No relevant cases, revenue rulings, or letter rulings deal specifically with the transaction in question.

    Required: Discuss whether you, a CPA, should prepare Horace's tax return and comply with his wishes. Assume that recognizing the income in question would increase Horace's tax liability by about 25%.

TAX RESEARCH PROBLEMS

C:15-66 Art is named executor of the Estate of Stu Stone, his father, who died on February 3 of the current year. Art hires Larry to be the estate's attorney. Larry advises Art that the estate must file an estate tax return but does not mention the due date. Art, a pharmacist, has no experience in tax matters other than preparing his own tax returns. Art provides Larry with all the necessary information by June 15 of the current year. On six occasions, Art contacts Larry to check on the progress of the estate tax return. Each time, Larry assures

Art that "everything is under control." On November 15, Art contacts Larry for the seventh time. He learns that because of a clerical oversight, the return—due on November 2 of the current year—has not been filed. Larry apologizes and says he will make sure that an associate promptly files the return. The return, which reports an estate tax liability of $75,200, is filed on December 7 of the current year. Your manager requests that you prepare a memorandum addressing whether the estate will owe a failure-to-file penalty. Your manager suggests that, at a minimum, you consult

- IRC Sec. 6151(a)
- *U.S. v. Robert W. Boyle*, 55 AFTR 2d 85-1535, 85-1 USTC ¶13,602 (USSC, 1985)

C:15-67 Harold and Betty, factory workers who until this year prepared their own individual tax returns, purchased an investment from a broker last year. Although they reviewed the prospectus for the investment, the broker explained the more complicated features of the investment. Early this year, they struggled to prepare their individual return for last year but, because of the investment, found it too complicated to complete. Consequently, they hired a CPA to prepare the return. The CPA deducted losses generated from the investment against income that Harold and Betty generated from other sources. The IRS audited the return for last year and contended that the loss is not deductible. After consulting their CPA, who further considered the tax consequences of the investment, Harold and Betty agreed that the loss is not deductible and consented to paying the deficiency. The IRS also contended that the couple owes the substantial understatement penalty because they did not disclose the value of the investment on their return and did not have substantial authority for their position. Assume you are representing the taxpayers before the IRS and intend to argue that they should be exempted from the substantial understatement penalty. Your tax manager reminds you to consult Secs. 6662 and 6664 when conducting your research.

C:15-68 Gene employed his attorney to draft identical trust instruments for each of his three minor children: Judy (age 5), Terry (age 7), and Grady (age 11). Each trust instrument names the Fourth City Bank as trustee and states that the trust is irrevocable. It provides that, until the beneficiary reaches age 21, the trustee at its discretion is to pay income and/or principal (corpus) to the beneficiary. Upon reaching age 21, the beneficiary will have 60 days in which to request that the trust assets be paid over to him or her. Otherwise, the assets will stay in the trust until the beneficiary reaches age 35. The beneficiary also is granted a general testamentary power of appointment over the trust assets. If the beneficiary dies before the trust terminates and does not exercise his or her power of appointment (because, for example, he or she dies without a will), trust assets will be distributed to family members in accordance with state intestacy laws. Each trust will be funded with property valued at $100,000. Before he signs the instruments, Gene wants to obtain a ruling from the IRS concerning whether the trusts qualify for the annual gift tax exclusion. Your task is to prepare a request for a letter ruling.

A partial list of research sources is

- IRC Secs. 2503(b) and (c)
- Reg. Sec. 25.2503-4
- Rev. Rul. 67-270, 1967-2 C.B. 349
- Rev. Rul. 74-43, 1974-1 C.B. 285
- Rev. Rul. 81-7, 1981-1 C.B. 474

C:15-69 On April 15, 2010, Adam and Renee Tyler jointly filed a 2009 return that reported AGI of $68,240 ($20,500 attributable to Renee) and a tax liability of $3,050. They paid this amount in a timely fashion. On their return, the Tylers claimed a $18,405 deduction for Adam's distributive share of a partnership loss. If not for the loss, the Tylers' tax liability would have been $8,358. In the previous year, Adam had withdrawn $20,000 cash from the partnership, which he used to buy Renee a new car. Although Renee, a marketing consultant, is not active in the partnership business, she has worked for the partnership as a part-time receptionist. Adam and his partner (who incidentally is Renee's brother) failed to file a partnership return for 2009. Upon audit, the IRS discovered that the 2009 partnership records were missing. In June 2011, Adam had a heart attack. He remains in serious condition. Unable to reach Adam, the IRS sends Renee a 30-day letter proposing a $5,308 deficiency. She intends to protest. Your supervisor has asked you to write a memorandum discussing Renee's potential liabilities and defenses. In your memorandum, you should consult the following authorities:

- IRC Secs. 6013 and 6662
- *Rebecca Jo Reser v. CIR*, 79 AFTR 2d 97-2743, 97-1 USTC ¶50,416 (5th Cir., 1997)

C:15-70 A colleague comes to you with the following investment proposal that he would like to market for Client:

- Client obtains cash of $60,000 from Bank.
- Bank loan agreement specifies that $40,000 of this amount represents principal; the remaining $20,000 represents interest.
- Client contributes the $60,000 cash to Partnership, which agrees to assume Client's $40,000 debt.
- Under Sec. 752, Partnership's debt assumption is treated as a distribution of money that reduces Client's basis in partnership interest from $60,000 to $20,000.
- Partnership invests the $60,000 in a resort hotel project.
- Before the project comes onstream, Client sells partnership interest for $15,000.

Net result: Partnership, not Client, is responsible for repayment of Bank loan. Client realizes a $5,000 capital loss without having spent any of its own funds.

Prepare a memorandum that sets forth the tax and reporting implications of this investment proposal. At a minimum, consult the following authorities:

- IRC Secs. 6707A and 6111
- Reg. Secs. 1.6111-4 and 301.6112-1
- Notice 2000-44, 2000-2 C.B. 255

C:15-71 Five years ago, Spyros Dietrich wanted to sell IMPEXT, Inc., his wholly owned import-export business. He also wanted to avoid recognizing the substantial gain that would result from his selling his IMPEXT shares on the open market. Spyros' basis in the shares ($100,000) was well below their market value ($600,000).

To avoid gain recognition, Spyros formed the SH Partnership with his brother Hussein. To capitalize the partnership, Spyros transferred all his IMPEXT shares to SH in exchange for 99 SH Partnership units. Hussein transferred $100 cash in exchange for one SH Partnership unit. Subsequently, Spyros formed Fu Yung, Inc., an S corporation, and transferred his 99 SH Partnership units to Fu Yung in exchange for 99 Fu Yung shares.

Under Sec. 708, the transfer to Fu Yung technically caused a dissolution of SH. However, Spyros and Hussein agreed to continue the SH "business" in reconstituted form as the FYH Partnership. Thereupon, FYH elected under Sec. 754 to step up its basis in the IMPEXT shares from $100,000 to $600,000. Then FYH sold the IMPEXT shares to disinterested investor Gonzalez for $615,000, thereby realizing only a $15,000 gain. Ninety-nine percent of this gain passed through to Spyros' separate return via Fu Yung and FYH.

The series of transactions went unnoticed by the IRS until the current year, when it audited Spyros' return. On that return, Spyros reported $525,000 of ordinary income and $14,850 (i.e., 99% of $15,000) of capital gain. When the IRS alleged that Spyros had substantially understated his income, Spyros raised the "statute of limitations" as a defense. Is the IRS correct in its allegation? If so, is it precluded by the statute of limitations from collecting additional taxes from Spyro?

Before answering these questions, please consult the following sources:

- IRC Secs. 708, 704, 6501
- *Brandon Ridge Partners v. U.S.*, 100 AFTR 2d 2007-5347, 2007-2 USTC ¶50,573 (DC FL, July 30, 2007)

16

CHAPTER

U.S. TAXATION OF FOREIGN-RELATED TRANSACTIONS

LEARNING OBJECTIVES

After studying this chapter, you should be able to

1. Understand the principles underlying U.S. authority to tax foreign-related transactions

2. Determine the foreign tax credit available to U.S. taxpayers

3. Calculate the earned income exclusion available to U.S. individuals working abroad

4. Determine whether a foreign citizen is a U.S. resident or nonresident alien

5. Calculate the U.S. tax liability of a nonresident alien

6. Calculate the deemed paid credit available to a U.S. stockholder in a foreign corporation

7. Understand tax provisions applicable to controlled foreign corporations (CFCs)

8. Be aware of special international tax incentives formerly available to U.S. taxpayers

9. Explain the transactional structure and taxation of inversions

10. Understand the financial statement implications of various international transactions

When making their business decisions, taxpayers must consider the potential U.S. tax consequences of international transactions. These consequences impact whether a foreign business should be conducted directly by a U.S. corporation or indirectly through a foreign subsidiary. They also impact the placement and compensation of U.S. employees abroad. In many cases, these employees can exempt part or all of their foreign salaries and housing allowances from U.S. taxation. Such an exemption reduces the cost of employing American citizens abroad.

This chapter presents a general overview of the U.S. taxation of cross-border and foreign-related transactions. Coverage also includes the U.S. taxation of income derived from domestic and foreign activities conducted by U.S. citizens, resident and nonresident aliens, and domestic and foreign entities.

JURISDICTION TO TAX

OBJECTIVE 1

Understand the principles underlying U.S. authority to tax foreign-related transactions

U.S. authority to tax foreign-related transactions is based on three factors:

▶ The taxpayer's country of citizenship

▶ The taxpayer's country of residence

▶ Where income is earned

The U.S. tax laws prescribe different tax treatments of income items according to the taxpayer's country of citizenship or country of organization. The United States taxes U.S. citizens and corporations[1] on their worldwide income and taxes foreign citizens and corporations primarily on income earned within U.S. territorial limits.

Individuals who are not U.S. citizens are called "aliens." The U.S. income tax laws divide aliens into two classes: resident and nonresident. A **resident alien** is an individual who resides in the United States *but* is not a U.S. citizen. A **nonresident alien** is an individual who resides outside the United States *and* is not a U.S. citizen.

Like U.S. citizens and domestic corporations, resident aliens are taxed on their worldwide income. In general, the same rules apply to the various classes of income they earn, whether the income is earned in the United States, a foreign country, or a U.S. possession. However, certain items of income earned in foreign countries or U.S. possessions are subject to special treatment.

TYPICAL MISCONCEPTION

Many people believe that income earned outside the United States is not subject to taxation by the United States. This belief is incorrect. U.S. citizens, resident aliens, and domestic corporations are taxed by the United States on their worldwide income.

▶ Compensation received by a U.S. citizen or resident alien who works in a foreign country for an extended period of time is eligible for a special inflation adjusted annual exclusion of up to $91,500 in 2010 and $92,900 in 2011.

▶ The income taxes paid by a U.S. taxpayer to a foreign country or a U.S. possession may be credited against the U.S. tax liability.

To some extent, the tax treatment accorded nonresident aliens and foreign corporations depends on whether they conducted a trade or business in the United States at some time during the year. If they did not conduct a U.S. trade or business, the nonresident aliens and foreign corporations are taxed only on their U.S.-source investment income. If they did conduct a U.S. trade or business, the nonresident aliens and foreign corporations are taxed on both their U.S.-source investment income and their U.S.-source (and certain foreign-source) income that is connected with the conduct of the U.S. trade or business. Trade or business and investment income earned outside the United States by nonresident aliens and foreign corporations generally escape U.S. taxation.

An overview of international tax issues relating to the various types of tax entities that operate in the United States is presented in Table C:16-1. This table adds structure to the following discussion of the U.S. tax rules that apply to foreign-related transactions.

---

[1] Secs. 7701(a)(3) and (4). A domestic corporation is a corporation created or organized under federal law or the laws of one of the 50 states or the District of Columbia. All other corporations are **foreign corporations**. A domestic corporation includes a noncorporate entity that elects under the check-the-box regulations to be taxed as a corporation. See Chapter C:2.

▼ TABLE C:16-1

Overview of International Tax Issues

Entity Form	U.S. Tax Base	U.S. Tax Issues
Individuals:		
U.S. citizen	Worldwide income	1, 2
U.S. resident alien	Worldwide income	1, 2
U.S. nonresident alien	U.S. territorial	3, 4
Corporations:		
U.S. parent with foreign branch	Worldwide income	1, 3
U.S. parent with foreign subsidiary	Worldwide income	1, 5, 6
Foreign parent with U.S. branch	U.S. territorial	3, 4, 6, 7
Foreign parent with U.S. subsidiary	Worldwide	1, 3, 4, 6

U.S. Tax Issues Listing

1. Foreign tax credit
2. Foreign earned income exclusion
3. U.S. income tax liability
4. Withholding of U.S. taxes on payments by U.S. persons to non-U.S. persons
5. Deferral of U.S. taxation of foreign profits
6. Transfer pricing
7. Branch profits tax

TAXATION OF U.S. CITIZENS AND RESIDENT ALIENS

This section examines two foreign tax provisions applicable to U.S. citizens and resident aliens: the foreign tax credit and the foreign-earned income exclusion. Both provisions alleviate the double taxation of income earned by these individuals in a foreign country.

OBJECTIVE 2

Determine the foreign tax credit available to U.S. taxpayers

FOREIGN TAX CREDIT

The **foreign tax credit** alleviates double taxation by allowing U.S. taxpayers to credit income taxes paid or accrued to a foreign country (including its political subdivisions such as provinces and cities) or a U.S. possession[2] against their U.S. income tax liability. The foreign tax credit reduces a U.S. taxpayer's total effective tax rate on income earned in foreign countries or U.S. possessions to the higher of the U.S. or the foreign tax rate.

STOP & THINK

Question: The United States uses the foreign tax credit as its principal mechanism for alleviating double taxation. What are the advantages and disadvantages of the foreign tax credit?

Solution: The foreign tax credit is based on the premise that all taxable income should be subject to the same effective tax rate no matter where it is earned. The U.S. Government taxes foreign source income but allows a credit for foreign income taxes paid or accrued up to the amount of U.S. taxes owed on all foreign-source income. The credit system requires that a taxpayer report the income, file a tax return, and apply the credit to reduce

---

[2] For Sec. 901 purposes, U.S. possessions include Puerto Rico, the Virgin Islands, Guam, the Northern Mariana Islands, and American Samoa. See Reg. Sec. 1.901-1(g)(4).

his or her U.S. tax liability. This requirement ensures that taxpayers report to the U.S. tax authorities their non-U.S. income taxed in a foreign jurisdiction. It also provides additional U.S. tax revenues to the extent that U.S. tax rates are higher than foreign tax rates. The reporting requirement, however, increases compliance costs for U.S. taxpayers. The credit provides an incentive for foreign governments to raise their tax rates to the level of U.S. tax rates (in the form of "soak up taxes"). Such increases will not alter a taxpayer's worldwide tax costs but will increase tax revenues accruing to a foreign treasury at the expense of the U.S. Treasury.

KEY POINT

This double taxation results when two different jurisdictions tax the same stream of income rather than one jurisdiction taxing the same stream of income twice (such as dividends a shareholder receives from a C corporation).

CREDITABLE TAXES. Income taxes paid or accrued to a foreign country or a U.S. possession may be credited against the U.S. tax liability. Other foreign taxes are deductible under the rules of Sec. 164, which are explained in Chapter I:7 of the companion volume, *Prentice Hall's Federal Taxation: Individuals*. The IRS regularly issues pronouncements relating to the creditability of certain foreign taxes.[3] These pronouncements save taxpayers time and effort in determining whether a specific tax is creditable. Major tax services summarize these pronouncements, as well as judicial decisions concerning creditable taxes.

REAL-WORLD EXAMPLE

The foreign tax credit is the largest U.S. tax credit. In 2007, U.S. corporations claimed $86.2 billion in foreign tax credits, which is 5.5 times larger than their general business credits. These two credits reduced corporations' U.S. tax liability by 23.4%.

ELIGIBILITY FOR THE CREDIT. Section 901(a) permits U.S. citizens and resident aliens to elect to claim a foreign tax credit for income taxes paid or accrued to a foreign country or a U.S. possession. This type of tax credit is known as a *direct credit*. Most taxpayers annually elect to credit their foreign income taxes against their U.S. tax liability. As discussed in the Tax Planning Consideration section of this chapter, however, taxpayers sometimes prefer to deduct their foreign income taxes from gross income.

A taxpayer who uses the accrual method of accounting claims the foreign tax credit in the year in which the tax accrues. A taxpayer who uses the cash method of accounting claims the foreign tax credit in the year in which the tax is paid unless the taxpayer makes a special election to accrue the tax (the advantages of this election are discussed in the Tax Planning Considerations section of this chapter).

ADDITIONAL COMMENT

Foreign income taxes also are deductible under Sec. 164. However, taxpayers may not both deduct and credit the same foreign income taxes. Whether a taxpayer credits or deducts the foreign income taxes requires an annual election.

TRANSLATION OF THE FOREIGN TAX PAYMENTS. Determining the credit amount necessitates translating the tax paid or accrued in a foreign currency into U.S. dollars. To do the translation, cash method taxpayers use the exchange rate as of the payment date. Accrual method taxpayers use the average exchange rate for the tax year over which the tax accrues. They may elect to translate the tax amount into U.S. dollars based on the exchange rate prevailing on the payment date, provided the tax is denominated in a currency other than that used in the taxpayer's regular course of business. (The latter currency is referred to as the taxpayer's "functional currency.") If accrual method taxpayers pay their taxes two years after the close of the tax year to which the taxes relate, they must use the exchange rate prevailing on the payment date to account for any potential currency fluctuation.[4]

EXAMPLE C:16-1 ▶

U.S. citizen Bill is a resident of Country A during the current year. Country A permits its residents to make a single tax payment on the first day of the third month following the close of the tax year. Bill's tax year for both U.S. and Country A tax reporting is the calendar year. Bill remits a 60,000 pirog payment for current year Country A taxes on March 1 of the following year. The average pirog-U.S. dollar exchange rate for the current calendar year is 1 pirog = $0.50 (U.S.). The exchange rate on the March 1 payment date is 1 pirog = $0.60 (U.S.). If Bill uses the cash method of accounting (and does not elect to accrue his foreign taxes), he can claim a $36,000 (60,000 pirogs × $0.60) foreign tax credit. If Bill uses the accrual method of accounting, he can claim a $30,000 (60,000 pirogs × $0.50) foreign tax credit based on the average dollar/pirog exchange rate for the accrual period. ◀

---

[3] Reg. Sec. 1.901-2. See, for example, Rev. Rul. 91-45, 1991-2 C.B. 336, relating to the creditability of the Mexican asset tax and the Mexican income tax.
[4] Temp. Reg. Sec. 1.905-3T. An amended U.S. tax return must be filed to report the increase or decrease in the credit amount if the taxpayer has filed his or her U.S. tax return by the date the foreign tax is paid. The average exchange rate translation method applies to 1998 and later tax years.

ADDITIONAL COMMENT

The numerator of the limitation fraction is U.S. taxable income from foreign sources. The foreign taxes actually paid or accrued are computed under the tax laws of the foreign jurisdiction. Because these tax laws may differ significantly from the U.S. tax laws, determining whether the fraction is a limiting factor cannot necessarily be determined by simply comparing the statutory tax rates of the two countries.

FOREIGN TAX CREDIT LIMITATION.

Calculating the General Limitation. Congress enacted the foreign tax credit limitation to prevent taxpayers from crediting foreign taxes owed on income earned outside the United States against U.S. taxes owed on income earned in the United States. This limit, which corresponds to the amount of U.S. tax payable on income earned outside the United States, is calculated as follows:

$$\text{Foreign tax credit limitation} = \text{Total U.S. tax liability} \times \frac{\text{Foreign source taxable income}}{\text{Total worldwide taxable income}}$$

The foreign tax credit equals the lesser of (1) creditable taxes paid or accrued to all foreign countries and U.S. possessions or (2) the foreign tax credit limitation. The limitation permits taxpayers to offset during the same tax year excess foreign taxes paid in one country against excess limitation amounts relative to taxes paid in other countries (known as cross-crediting). However, the total foreign taxes paid or accrued on foreign source taxable income may not exceed the total U.S. tax due on such income.[5] Also, only foreign taxes allocable to the same income baskets (discussed later) may be cross-credited. Before claiming the foreign tax credit, individuals must reduce taxable income by nonrefundable credits allowed under Secs. 21–26.[6]

EXAMPLE C:16-2 ▶

SELF-STUDY QUESTION

Kathy Richards, a U.S. citizen, earns active business income of $100,000 in Country X, $200,000 in Country Z, and $200,000 in the United States. She pays $10,000 in taxes to X and $90,000 in taxes to Z. Assume a 35% U.S. tax rate. What is Richards's post-credit U.S. tax liability?

ANSWER

Pre-credit U.S. tax = $175,000 ($500,000 × 0.35). The credit is the lesser of the $100,000 ($10,000 + $90,000) of foreign taxes paid or the $105,000 ($175,000 × 300/500) foreign tax credit limitation. Although Richards pays taxes to Country Z at a much higher rate (45%) than the U.S. rate, all the foreign taxes are creditable because the limitation is computed on an overall basis and because the Country X tax rate is so low (5%).

U.S. citizen Theresa earns $10,000 of taxable income (wages) from U.S. sources and $20,000 of taxable income (wages) from Country B in the current year. Theresa pays $6,000 of taxes to Country B in the current year. Assuming a 25% U.S. tax rate, Theresa's gross U.S. tax liability is calculated as follows:

Source of Income	Taxable Income	U.S. Tax Liability before FTC
United States	$10,000	$2,500
Country B	20,000	5,000
Total	$30,000	$7,500

Theresa's foreign tax credit limitation is determined as follows:

$$\$5,000 = \$7,500 \times \frac{\$20,000}{\$30,000}$$

Without a foreign tax credit limitation, Theresa could credit $1,000 of Country B taxes against the $2,500 of U.S. taxes assessed on her U.S. income. Accordingly, an unlimited credit would decrease her U.S. tax liability to $1,500 ($7,500 − $6,000). The foreign tax credit limitation, however, reduces the amount of foreign tax that Theresa can credit to the extent of U.S. taxes owed on the Country B income, or $5,000. This limitation ensures that Theresa pays the full $2,500 of U.S. taxes assessed on her U.S. income. The $1,000 ($6,000 − $5,000) excess credit carries back and over to other tax years as discussed below. ◀

Section 904(k) exempts an individual with less than $300 of creditable foreign taxes ($600 for joint filers) from the foreign tax credit limitation, provided his or her foreign source income is exclusively passive.

Determining the Income Amounts. The taxable income amount in the numerator of the credit limitation formula is determined according to the source of income ("sourcing") rules found in Secs. 861–865. These rules are summarized as follows:

▶ *Personal service income:* Compensation for personal services is considered to be earned in the place where the taxpayer performs the services.

---

[5] Sec. 904(a). An "excess" foreign tax amount is the excess of the foreign taxes paid or accrued over the foreign tax credit limitation. An "excess" limitation amount is the excess of the foreign tax credit limitation over foreign taxes paid or accrued.

[6] Sec. 904(i).

▶ *Sales of personal property (other than inventory):* Income derived from a U.S. resident's sale of noninventory personal property (e.g., investment securities) is considered to be earned in the United States. Income derived from a nonresident's sale of such property is considered to be earned outside the United States.[7]

▶ *Sales of inventory:* Income derived from the sale of merchandise inventory (i.e., final goods purchased for resale) is considered to be earned in the country where the sale occurs. Income derived from the sale of manufactured inventory (i.e., goods manufactured and sold) is considered to be earned partly in the country of manufacture and partly in the country of sale.[8]

▶ *Sales of real property:* Income derived from the sale of real property is considered to be earned in the country where the property is located.

▶ *Rents and royalties:* Rents are considered to be earned in the place where the tangible property is located, and royalties in the place where the intangible property (e.g., patent, copyright, or trademark) is used. The latter rule applies to the sale of intangible property if the sale is contingent on the productivity, use, or disposition of the property.

▶ *Interest income:* Interest generally is considered to be earned in the debtor's country of residence. For purpose of this rule, a U.S. resident includes a foreign partnership or foreign corporation that has derived most of its income from a U.S. trade or business over the past three years.

▶ *Dividends:* Dividends generally are considered to be earned in the distributing corporation's country of incorporation.

In deriving foreign-source taxable income, a taxpayer allocates deductions and losses to foreign-source gross income according to the rules outlined in Reg. Sec. 1.861-8.

▶ For individual taxpayers, taxable income is computed without any reduction for personal exemptions.

▶ In general, deductions are matched with the income with which they are associated.

▶ Deductions not associated with a specific class of income (such as itemized deductions and the standard deduction) are allocated ratably among all classes of income.

Foreign Tax Credit Carrybacks and Carryovers. Excess foreign tax credits can be carried back one year and carried over ten years to a tax year in which the taxpayer has an excess foreign tax credit limitation (i.e., an unused limitation amount). The total of the foreign taxes paid or accrued in a tax year, plus any carryback or carryover to that year, cannot exceed the taxpayer's foreign tax credit limitation. When a taxpayer reports excess credits in more than one year, the excess credits are used on a first-in, first-out (FIFO) basis.[9]

EXAMPLE C:16-3 ▶ U.S. citizen Kathy accrues $95,000 of creditable foreign taxes in 2011. Kathy's 2011 foreign tax credit limitation is $80,000. The $15,000 of 2011 excess credits carry back to 2010, then over to 2012 through 2021, until used up. The credit carryback and carryover procedure is illustrated below:

	2010	*2011*	*2012*
Foreign tax accrual	$ 90,000	$95,000	$100,000
Foreign tax credit limitation	100,000	80,000	95,000
Excess credits		15,000	5,000
Excess limitation	10,000		

---

[7] Sec. 865(a). Income derived by a nonresident alien from the sale of personal property (including inventory) attributable to an office or place of business located in the United States is considered to be earned in the United States. Section 865(g) defines the terms *resident* and *nonresident* for the purpose of personal property sales. The definition generally is based on the individual's domicile.

[8] Sec. 865(b) and Reg. Secs. 1.863-3(b) and (c). For tax purposes, an inventory sale generally occurs at the location where title passes from the buyer to the seller. The IRS may depart from this general rule where the primary purpose of the sale is tax-avoidance .

[9] Sec. 904(c). For foreign tax credits arising before October 23, 2004, the carryback period is two years, and the carryover period is five years.

The excess credits first carry back to 2010, and Kathy must file an amended return for 2010 to claim the $10,000 carryback. The remaining $5,000 ($15,000 − $10,000) of excess credits carry over to 2012 and are added to the $5,000 of credits generated in that year. The resulting $10,000 of credits carry forward. Any portion of the carryover not fully used by 2021 will expire. ◀

ADDITIONAL COMMENT

U.S. corporate tax rates tend to be higher than the tax rates of many foreign jurisdictions. This fact, coupled with the imposition of separate limitation baskets, has caused U.S. multinational corporations to remain in an excess foreign tax limitation position.

Special Foreign Tax Credit Limitations. For some taxpayers, more than one foreign tax credit calculation is required. Before 2007, the Sec. 904 foreign tax credit limitation rules created nine baskets of income, for which separate foreign tax credit limitation calculations had to be made.

Beginning in 2007, the number of foreign tax credit limitation baskets was reduced to two, one for passive income and the other for general limitation income.[10] The separate baskets prevent taxpayers from cross-crediting excess foreign taxes levied on one type of income against excess limitations associated with another type of income. Without the separate baskets, taxpayers could "load up" on income items traditionally taxed at low rates to inflate the numerator in the foreign tax credit limitation formula without increasing the total amount of taxes to be credited.

Dividends received by a U.S. shareholder from a foreign corporation in which the shareholder owns at least a 10% equity stake, as well as interest, rents, and royalties received by a U.S. shareholder from a controlled foreign corporation (i.e., a majority-U.S.-owned foreign corporation) are treated as income earned in the separate baskets on a look-through basis (i.e., as if the foreign corporation were a conduit entity).

Compensation and manufacturing income fall into the general limitation basket. Taxpayers who earn only such income must make one foreign tax credit calculation. Other taxpayers must make two calculations.

Excess foreign taxes in one basket cannot offset excess limitation amounts in another basket. Because items in each basket must be accounted for separately, taxpayers generally cannot use excess credits arising from foreign taxes paid or accrued at a high rate (e.g., taxes on salary or business profits in one basket) to offset U.S. taxes owed on income taxed by a foreign country at a low rate or not taxed at all (e.g., taxes on interest or dividends).

EXAMPLE C:16-4 ▶ Assume the same facts as in Example C:16-2 except, in Country C, Theresa also earns $15,000 of interest income that is not subject to local taxation. The additional U.S. tax liability resulting from this interest income is $3,750 ($15,000 × 0.25). Theresa's total U.S. tax liability is $11,250 ($7,500 [from Example C:16-2] + $3,750). Two foreign tax credit limitations must be calculated for Theresa:

$$\text{Interest income } \$3,750 = \$11,250 \times \frac{\$15,000}{\$45,000}$$

$$\text{Wages } \$5,000 = \$11,250 \times \frac{\$20,000}{\$45,000}$$

SELF-STUDY QUESTION

Do any limitations restrict the carryback or carryforward of excess foreign taxes?

ANSWER

Yes. The carryback and carryover provision can occur only within the separate baskets. In Example C:16-4, the $1,000 of excess foreign taxes can be offset only against an excess limitation in the general limitation basket for a carryback or carryover year.

Theresa's foreign tax credit position is summarized in the following table:

Type of Income Earned	U.S. Tax Liability before FTC	Foreign Taxes Paid or Accrued	Foreign Tax Credit Limitation	U.S. Tax Liability after FTC	Excess Foreign Tax Payments
Interest	$ 3,750	$ –0–	$3,750	$3,750	$ –0–
Wages	7,500	6,000	5,000	2,500	1,000
Total	$11,250	$6,000	$8,750	$6,250	$1,000

Theresa can claim a $5,000 foreign tax credit—the lesser of the $5,000 foreign tax credit limitation or the $6,000 foreign tax paid—for the Country B wages. She can claim no foreign

---

[10] Sec. 904(d)(1).

tax credit for the Country C interest income because she paid no foreign tax on this income. The interest income is foreign-source, and U.S. taxpayers calculate the foreign tax credit limitation based on worldwide income. Nevertheless, the $1,000 of excess taxes paid on the Country B wages cannot be used to offset the U.S. taxes owed on the Country C interest income because the interest income is included in the passive income basket and the salary income is included in the general limitation basket. Theresa can carry the excess foreign taxes allocable to the general limitation basket back to the preceding tax year then forward up to ten years. ◀

Topic Review C:16-1 summarizes the foreign tax credit provisions. A discussion of the financial statement implications of the foreign tax credit appears at the end of this chapter.

FOREIGN-EARNED INCOME EXCLUSION

Special income exclusions are available to individuals working in foreign countries, Puerto Rico, and certain U.S. possessions. One such exclusion—the foreign earned income exclusion under Sec. 911—is important to employers because it provides tax relief to their U.S. employees stationed in foreign countries. Many such employers reimburse their overseas employees for their incremental worldwide tax costs relative to the costs they would have incurred had they stayed in the United States. By reducing the U.S. tax liability of these employees, the Sec. 911 exclusion decreases the amount of this reimbursement and thus reduces employers' costs.

U.S. CITIZENS AND RESIDENT ALIENS WORKING ABROAD. The United States taxes U.S. citizens and resident aliens, including those working abroad, on their worldwide income. While working outside the country, these taxpayers may incur additional costs to maintain the same standard of living they enjoyed in the United States. In addition, they may endure inconveniences, substandard living conditions, hardships, or political hazards that warrant additional compensation in the form of special allowances. The allowances may be taxed in both the United States and the country of residence. The U.S. employer generally reimburses U.S. employees for these tax costs to relieve them of any incremental tax burden. The total compensation package can make hiring a U.S. citizen or resident alien more expensive than hiring a foreign resident or citizen with the same set of skills.

Topic Review C:16-1

Foreign Tax Credit

▶ Foreign income taxes paid or accrued to a foreign country or a U.S. possession are deductible or creditable by U.S. taxpayers.

▶ The election to deduct or credit foreign taxes is made annually. Generally, a taxpayer will elect to credit foreign taxes because of the dollar-for-dollar tax benefit derived from a credit as opposed to a deduction.

▶ Cash method taxpayers can elect to accrue their foreign taxes. This election can accelerate by one year the time for claiming the credit and may reduce the need to carry back or carry over excess credits.

▶ A direct credit is available for foreign taxes paid or accrued by the taxpayer, as well as for foreign taxes withheld by a foreign payer.

▶ Foreign taxes generally are translated into U.S. dollars at the exchange rate for the date on which they are paid or the period over which they accrue, depending on the taxpayer's accounting method.

▶ The foreign tax credit limitation prevents crediting foreign taxes against the U.S. tax liability on U.S. source income. The amount of credit that can be claimed is the lesser of (a) the creditable taxes paid or accrued to all foreign countries and U.S. possessions, or (b) the overall foreign tax credit limitation. Excess credits may be carried back one year and then forward up to ten years. Taxpayers must account for the credit by income type, or foreign tax credit basket. An excess credit in one basket cannot offset an excess credit limitation in another basket.

ADDITIONAL
COMMENT

The foreign income exclusion is elective and is made by filing Form 2555 with the income tax return (or amended return) for the first tax year for which the election is to be effective. A completed Form 2555 is reproduced in Appendix B.

To enable U.S. firms to compete abroad, the U.S. government established a policy of reducing the U.S. tax burden on U.S. citizens and resident aliens living abroad for an extended period of time. Taxpayers who are bona fide residents of a foreign country (or countries) for an entire tax year, or who are physically present in a foreign country (or countries) for 330 full days[11] out of a 12-month period, can exclude up to $91,500 in 2010 and $92,900 in 2011 of foreign-earned income from their gross income.[12] This benefit, which is known as the *foreign-earned income exclusion*, is indexed for inflation and is available to taxpayers who meet one of two tests: the bona fide residence test or the physical presence test.

KEY POINT

Whether a U.S. citizen has established foreign residency is based on all the pertinent facts and circumstances. This rule is different from the determination of whether a foreign citizen has established U.S. residency. The latter is based on either a green card or the substantial physical presence test (discussed later in this chapter).

BONA FIDE RESIDENCE TEST. A U.S. citizen (but not a resident alien) satisfies the bona fide residence test of Sec. 911(d)(1)(A) if he or she has resided in a foreign country (or countries) for an uninterrupted period that includes an entire tax year and has maintained a tax home in a foreign country (or countries) during the period of residence.

For Sec. 911 purposes, an individual's tax home is defined in the same way as it is for determining the deductibility of travel expenses incurred while away from home on business.[13] In other words, an individual's tax home is his or her regular or principal place of business. Temporary absences from the foreign country for trips back to the United States or to other foreign countries normally do not disqualify foreign residency.

An individual is not a bona fide resident of a foreign country if he or she submits to the taxing authorities of that country a statement claiming to be a nonresident and obtains from that country's taxing authorities an earned income exemption based on nonresident status.[14] An individual does not qualify for the foreign earned income exclusion until he or she has been a foreign resident for an *entire tax year*. At the end of that period, the individual can retroactively claim Sec. 911 benefits from the date he or she became a foreign resident.

EXAMPLE C:16-5 ▶

TYPICAL MISCONCEPTION

A day is not just any 24-hour period. To count a day, the taxpayer must be in a foreign country for a period of 24 hours beginning and ending at midnight.

U.S. citizen Mark, who uses the calendar year as his tax year, is transferred by his employer to Country P. Mark becomes a Country P resident upon his arrival at noon on July 15, 2008. At that time, Mark establishes his tax home in P's capital. Mark's residency in P is maintained until his return to the United States at 2 p.m. on January 10, 2012. Mark first qualifies as a bona fide resident of a foreign country on December 31, 2009 after a full tax year. This qualification permits Mark to claim the foreign earned income exclusion as of July 15, 2008. Mark can continue to claim the exclusion through January 10, 2012. ◀

SELF-STUDY QUESTION

During a 12-month period, U.S. citizen Robert's work requires him to be physically present in a foreign country for 317 days. If Robert delays his return to the U.S. by vacationing overseas for 13 more days, will he qualify for the foreign-earned income exclusion?

ANSWER

Yes. The foreign physical presence can be for any reason.

PHYSICAL PRESENCE TEST. A taxpayer who cannot satisfy the bona fide residence test still can qualify for Sec. 911 benefits by satisfying the physical presence test of Sec. 911(d)(1)(B). To do so, the taxpayer must meet two requirements:

▶ Be physically present in a foreign country (or countries) for at least 330 *full* days during a 12-month period.

▶ Maintain a tax home in a foreign country (or countries) during the period of physical presence.

The 330 days need not be consecutive, nor must the taxpayer be in the same country at all times. The 12-month period may begin on any day of the calendar year. The period ends on the day before the corresponding calendar day in the twelfth succeeding month.

---

[11] A full day is a continuous 24-hour period beginning with midnight and ending with the following midnight.
[12] The IRS adjusts the exclusion each year for inflation.
[13] Sec. 911(d)(3).

[14] Sec. 911(d)(5). The Sec. 911 bona fide residence test is different from the Sec. 7701(b) test used to determine whether an alien individual is a resident or nonresident of the United States. The latter test is discussed on page C:16-14.

EXAMPLE C:16-6 ▶ Assume the same facts as in Example C:16-5. The 330 days of physical presence begin with the first full day Mark is present in Country P (July 16, 2008) and include a total of 169 days through the end of 2008. The 161 additional days needed to complete the 330-day period include January 1, 2009, through June 10, 2009. One possible 12-month period for Mark thus begins on July 16, 2008, and runs through July 15, 2009. An alternative 12-month period might be June 9, 2008, through June 10, 2009, where the 330 days of physical presence fall at the end of the period. ◀

ADDITIONAL COMMENT

Note that in Example C:16-6, Mark would prefer to use the 12-month period of June 9, 2008, through June 10, 2009, when computing the exclusion for 2009 to have more days of the year in the qualifying period and, hence, a larger exclusion. This 12-month period places the 330 days of qualifying time at the end of the 12-month period.

FOREIGN EARNED INCOME DEFINED. For purposes of the exclusion, earned income means wages, salaries, professional fees, and other compensation for personal services actually rendered.[15] Earned income is excludible only if it is foreign source. The sourcing rules previously discussed are used to determine whether income is earned in the United States or a foreign country. In general, income is sourced according to where the services are performed. If the taxpayer performs services in more than one location during the tax year, he or she must allocate the income between the two or more locations based on the number of days worked at each location.[16]

Fringe benefits excluded from gross income under an IRC provision other than Sec. 911 (e.g., meals and lodging furnished for the convenience of the employer, excludible under Sec. 119) do not diminish the excludible amount. Items that generally are taxable to the recipient, but which do not comprise earned income for Sec. 911 purposes, include pensions and annuities, compensation paid by the United States or one of its agencies to an employee,[17] and amounts received more than one tax year after the tax year in which services are performed.

AMOUNT OF THE EXCLUSION. The foreign earned income exclusion is available only for the number of days in the tax year during which the taxpayer meets either the bona fide residence test or the physical presence test. Section 911(b)(2)(A) limits the foreign earned income exclusion to the lesser of the following:

▶ The individual's foreign-earned income

▶ The amount of the daily exclusion times the number of days during the tax year that the individual qualifies for the exclusion

The 2011 annual and daily limits are $92,900 and $254.52, respectively. The 2010 annual and daily limits were $91,500 and $250.68, respectively. For 2008 and 2009, the annual limits were $87,600 and $91,400, respectively, and the daily limits were $239.34 and $250.41, respectively.

EXAMPLE C:16-7 ▶ U.S. citizen Lee, who uses the calendar year as his tax year, establishes a tax home and residency in Country A on November 1, 2008 (the 306th day of the year). Lee maintains his tax home and residency until March 31, 2010 (the 90th day), when Lee returns to the United States. While employed abroad, Lee earns salary and allowances at $15,000 monthly. Lee's exclusion is calculated as follows:

Tax Year	Foreign-Earned Income	Qualifying Days (1)	Daily Exclusion Amount (2)	Total Amount Excluded (3) = (1) × (2)
2008	$ 30,000	61	239.34	$14,600
2009	180,000	365	250.41	91,400
2010	45,000	90	250.68	22,561 ◀

Individuals satisfying the bona fide residence test can claim the exclusion for each day they "reside" in a foreign country whether or not they are physically present in that country on each day. Individuals satisfying the physical presence test can claim the exclusion for each day of a 12-month period that falls within the tax year, whether or not they are

---

[15] Sec. 911(d)(2).
[16] Sec. 911(b)(1)(A).
[17] Under Sec. 912, civilian officers and employees of the U.S. government

who are employed abroad can exclude from gross income certain foreign area and cost-of-living allowances.

physically present in a foreign country on all 365 days. Because an individual need only be physically present in a foreign country for 330 days out of the 12-month period (365 days in a non-leap year, 366 days in a leap year) and because the exclusion applies to income earned during the full 12-month period, an individual might qualify for the exclusion for as many as 35 days before arrival in the foreign country or as many as 35 days after departure from the foreign country. Such an extension of the qualifying period in the year of arrival or departure may favor calculating the exclusion for these years based on the physical presence test.[18]

EXAMPLE C:16-8 ▶ Assume the same facts as in Example C:16-7 except Lee was physically present in Country A at all times from his arrival in 2008 to his departure in 2010. Lee's first 330 full days in Country A extend from November 2, 2008, through September 27, 2009. Lee's last 330 full days in Country A extend from May 5, 2009, through March 30, 2010. Lee's two corresponding 12-month periods extend from September 26, 2008 (the 270th day of 2008) through September 27, 2009, and from May 5, 2009, through May 4, 2010 (the 124th day of 2010). The amount of Lee's exclusion is calculated below:

Taxable Year	Foreign- Earned Income	Qualifying Days (1)[19]	Daily Exclusion Amount (2)	Amount Excluded (3) = (1) × (2)
2008	$ 30,000	97	$239.34	$23,216
2009	180,000	365	250.41	91,400
2010	45,000	124	250.68	31,084

Lee obtains a larger exclusion in 2008 and 2010 under the physical presence test because he effectively gets credit for the additional days (97–61 and 124–90) extending beyond the 330-day period, but included in the corresponding 12-month period. ◀

KEY POINT

A taxpayer may elect to use the foreign-earned income exclusion and the housing cost exclusion. Once made, the exclusion election is effective for that year and all subsequent years. See pages C:16-34 and C:16-35 for a discussion of why a taxpayer might elect out of the Sec. 911 exclusion.

HOUSING COST EXCLUSION OR DEDUCTION. Section 911 permits a taxpayer who is eligible for the foreign earned income exclusion also to exclude or deduct a **housing cost amount,** which is determined as follows:

$$\text{Housing cost amount} = \text{Housing expenses} - \text{Base housing amount}$$

$$\text{Base housing amount} = 0.16 \times \begin{array}{c}\text{Maximum foreign}\\\text{earned income}\\\text{exclusion}\end{array} \times \begin{array}{c}\underline{\text{Number of qualifying}}\\\underline{\text{days in the tax year}}\\\text{Number of days in}\\\text{the tax year}\end{array}$$

For 2011, the maximum foreign earned income exclusion is $92,900.[20] Thus, for taxpayers qualifying for Sec. 911 benefits for the entire tax year, the base housing amount for 2011 is $14,864, and the daily base housing amount is $40.72. The 2010 annual and daily base housing amounts were $14,640 and $40.11, respectively.

Housing costs include any reasonable expense paid or incurred for foreign housing for the taxpayer, his or her spouse, and any dependents during the part of the year the taxpayer qualifies for Sec. 911 benefits. Housing costs also include expenses incurred for a second home outside the United States if, because of adverse living conditions, the taxpayer must maintain a home for his or her spouse and dependents at a location other than the tax home.[21]

ADDITIONAL COMMENT

Employer-provided amounts include all compensation provided by the employer (salary, bonus, allowances, etc.), not just the amount identified as the housing allowance.

The exclusion is limited to 30% of the maximum foreign earned income exclusion (computed on a daily basis). Employer-provided amounts encompass any income that is foreign earned and included in the employee's gross income (without regard to Sec. 911 benefits) for

---

[18] Reg. Sec. 1.911-3(d).
[19] September 26, 2008, through December 31, 2008, encompasses 97 days, and January 1, 2010, through May 4, 2010, encompasses 124 days.
[20] The corresponding figure for 2010 was $91,500.
[21] Sec. 911(c)(3)(B). The IRS provides a list of countries with adverse living

conditions. Individuals residing in these countries were required to leave them because of war, civil unrest, or other similar conditions that precluded the normal conduct of business. The most recent list appeared in Rev. Proc. 2004-17, 2004-1 C.B. 562, that covered tax year 2003.

the tax year. Such amounts include, but are not limited to, salary or allowances paid by the employer (including allowances other than for housing), reimbursements to the employee for housing expenses, in-kind housing (other than that excluded under Sec. 119), and reimbursements to third parties on behalf of the employee.

EXAMPLE C:16-9 ▶ U.S. citizen John is a bona fide resident of Country M for all of 2011. John, who uses the calendar year as his tax year, receives $120,000 in salary and allowances from his employer. Included in this total is a $15,000 housing allowance. In 2011, John incurred eligible housing expenses of $18,000. Thus, John's housing cost amount is $3,316 ($18,000 − $14,864). Because this amount is less than the foreign housing cost limit of $27,870 (0.30 × $92,900), John can exclude the full housing cost amount. In addition, he can exclude $92,900 of his foreign earned income because he qualified for all of 2011. Therefore, his total exclusion is $96,216 ($3,316 + $92,900), so only $23,784 ($120,000 − $96,216) of his total compensation is subject to U.S. taxation. ◀

ADDITIONAL COMMENT

If an individual has only W-2 income (no self-employment income), he or she is eligible for only the housing cost exclusion because the entire housing cost amount is attributable to employer-provided amounts. The housing cost exclusion and deduction can both be taken only in situations where an individual has both W-2 income and self-employment income. Proration of the housing cost amount between a deduction and an exclusion is based on the relative amounts of the taxpayer's W-2 income and self-employment income.

Any portion of the housing cost amount that is not provided by an employer is a *for-*AGI deduction.[22] Thus, if an individual has only self-employment income, the entire housing cost amount is deductible. Such would be the case in Example C:16-9 if John were self-employed and the $120,000 were commission income. His $3,360 housing cost amount could be claimed only as a *for-*AGI deduction.

The housing cost deduction is limited to the taxpayer's foreign earned income minus the sum of the foreign earned income and housing cost exclusions. If the deduction for housing costs exceeds its limitation, the excess amount carries forward as a deduction in the next year (subject to that year's limitation).

DISALLOWANCE OF DEDUCTIONS AND CREDITS. Section 911(d)(6) prohibits taxpayers from claiming deductions or credits relating to their excluded income. The rules used to determine the nondeductible portion of an individual's employment-related expenses and the noncreditable portion of an individual's foreign taxes are discussed below.

Employment-related Expenses. Any employment-related expense associated with a taxpayer's excluded foreign earned income is nondeductible. By contrast, expenses relating to the employee's taxable income are deductible in full.[23] However, although foreign housing expenses may be related to excludible foreign earned income, no restriction is placed on deducting the housing cost amount.

EXAMPLE C:16-10 ▶ In 2011, Don reports $150,000 of foreign-earned income and $15,000 of foreign employment-related expenses that are subject to the 2% of AGI floor. Don takes $12,000 of other itemized deductions not directly related to foreign earned income and not subject to the 2% of AGI floor. Don may exclude $92,900 (or 61%) of his foreign earned income. Based on the calculation below, the exclusion precludes Don from deducting 62% or $9,290 ($15,000 total expenses − $5,710 deductible expenses) of foreign employment-related expenses. Don can deduct the full $12,000 of the other itemized deductions.

$$\$5,710 \text{ (Deductible expenses)}^a = \$15,000 \begin{pmatrix} \text{Expenses directly attributable to foreign earned income} \end{pmatrix} \times \left[1 - \frac{\$92,900 \text{ (Excluded foreign earned income)}}{\$150,000 \text{ (Total foreign earned income)}} \right]$$

ᵃ Subject to the 2% AGI floor.

The employment-related expenses are deductible only to the extent they exceed 2% of Don's $57,100 AGI ($150,000 − $92,900). Thus, Don can deduct $4,568 [$5,710 − ($57,100 × 0.02)] of employment-related expenses plus the $12,000 of other itemized deductions not subject to the 2% floor. ◀

---

[22] Sec. 911(c)(4)(A).
[23] Sec. 911(d)(6) and Reg. Sec. 1.911-6(a). Miscellaneous itemized expenses are subject to the 2% AGI floor whether the taxpayer is eligible for the Sec. 911 exclusion or not.

REAL-WORLD EXAMPLE

A number of websites provide the costs of sending an employee on an overseas assignment or the cost of maintaining an employee who already is on an overseas assignment. Some sites also provide information on foreign, U.S., and state taxation. In addition, many of the sites provide cultural information and financial advice.

Foreign Income Taxes. Foreign income taxes paid or accrued on excludible foreign earned income cannot be credited or deducted for U.S. income tax purposes. Creditable foreign taxes are determined under the following formula.[24]

$$\text{Creditable taxes} = \begin{array}{c} \text{Foreign} \\ \text{income} \\ \text{taxes} \\ \text{paid or} \\ \text{accrued} \end{array} \times \left[1 - \frac{\begin{array}{c}\text{Excludible foreign earned income (minus non-} \\ \text{deductible foreign employment-related expenses)}\end{array}}{\begin{array}{c}\text{Total foreign earned income (minus} \\ \text{expenses relating to foreign earned} \\ \text{income) subject to foreign tax}\end{array}} \right]$$

If foreign income taxes are paid or accrued on earned and other types of income, and the taxes cannot be allocated between the two amounts, the denominator of the fraction must include the total of all income subject to foreign tax (minus all related expenses).

EXAMPLE C:16-11 ▶ Assume the same facts as in Example C:16-10 except Don also incurs $33,750 of Country F income taxes on his foreign earned income. Don's $13,163 of creditable foreign taxes are 39% of the total foreign taxes. The creditable taxes are computed as follows:

$$\$12,848 = \$33,750 \times \left[1 - \frac{\$92,900 - \$9,290}{\$150,000 - \$15,000} \right]$$ ◀

Topic Review C:16-2 summarizes the foreign earned income and housing cost exclusions.

Topic Review C:16-2

Foreign Earned Income and Housing Cost Exclusions

1. Only U.S. citizens can qualify under the bona fide residence test. According to this test, they must have (a) resided in a foreign country(ies) for an uninterrupted period that includes an entire tax year and (b) maintained a tax home in a foreign country(ies) during the residence period.
2. U.S. citizens and resident aliens can qualify under the physical presence test. According to this test, they must have (a) been physically present in a foreign country(ies) for at least 330 full days during a 12-month period and (b) maintained a tax home in a foreign country(ies) during the period of physical presence.
3. The exclusion equals the lesser of the taxpayer's foreign earned income or the daily exclusion ($250.68 in 2010 and $254.52 in 2011) times the number of days in the tax year that the taxpayer qualifies for the exclusion.
4. Under the bona fide residence test, qualifying days include the number of days in the tax year during which the taxpayer "resided" in a foreign country. Under the physical presence test, qualifying days encompass the full 12-month period within which at least 330 days of physical presence fall.
5. Subject to limitations, employees can exclude a housing cost amount in addition to foreign earned income. Self-employed individuals can deduct the housing cost amount. The housing cost amount equals housing expenses incurred minus the base housing amount (16% × maximum foreign earned income exclusion) for the part of the tax year during which the taxpayer qualifies for the foreign earned income exclusion.
6. Taxpayers who exclude foreign earned income may not claim deductions or credits associated with their excluded income.

---

[24] Reg. Sec. 1.911-6(c).

TAXATION OF NONRESIDENT ALIENS

Whether a foreign national is a U.S. resident or a nonresident determines the U.S. tax treatment of that person's income. Under Sec. 871, U.S. taxing authority over nonresident aliens is limited to their U.S.-source investment income and any U.S. (and certain foreign) income effectively connected with the conduct of a U.S. trade or business.

The taxation of nonresident aliens is important for both U.S. and foreign companies that employ foreign nationals in the United States. Just like companies that employ U.S. citizens or residents abroad, companies that employ foreign citizens in the United States often assist them in complying with the U.S. tax laws and reimburse them for additional tax costs. In addition, U.S. businesses that pay U.S.-source income to nonresident aliens, foreign corporations, or foreign conduit entities (e.g., foreign partnerships) must withhold U.S. taxes on this income to avoid certain penalties.

OBJECTIVE 4

Determine whether a foreign citizen is a U.S. resident or nonresident alien

DEFINITION OF NONRESIDENT ALIEN

With certain exceptions,[25] foreign nationals who do not satisfy the Sec. 7701(b) tests set forth below are nonresident aliens. Foreign nationals who satisfy the tests are resident aliens.

▶ *Lawful permanent residency test:* The foreign national must have been a lawful permanent resident of the United States at any time during the tax year. A foreign national with a "green card" is considered to be a lawful permanent resident.

▶ *Substantial presence test:* The foreign national must have been present in the United States for 31 or more days during the current calendar year *and* a total of 183 or more days during the current and the two preceding tax years. The 183-day prong of the test is based on a weighted average calculation, according to which the more recent the period, the greater the weight. Specifically, each day in the current year is weighted one, each day in the first preceding year is weighted one-third, and each day in the second preceding year is weighted one-sixth.

EXAMPLE C:16-12 ▶

Marco, a citizen of Country X, is present in the United States for 122 days in each of 2009, 2010, and 2011. Marco satisfies the 31-day requirement because he is present in the United States for at least 31 days in 2011. The following table illustrates the weighting of days for purposes of the 183-day requirement:

Year	Days Present In the United States	Portion of Day Counted	Total Days Counted
2011	122	Full day	122.00
2010	122	1/3 of full day	40.67
2009	122	1/6 of full day	20.33
Total			183.00

Marco is a resident alien because he satisfies both the 31-day and 183-day requirements. ◀

Even though foreign nationals satisfy the physical presence test, they are nonresident aliens if they are nominally present in the United States (i.e., physically present in the United States for less than 30 days in the current year, notwithstanding a three-year total of 183 or more days) or if they have a closer connection with a foreign country than with the United States. Under the "closer connection" rule, the individual must be present in the United States for less than 183 days in the current year, maintain a tax home in a for-

---

[25] A nonresident alien also can become a resident alien by marrying a U.S. citizen or resident alien and electing to be treated as a resident alien under Sec. 6013(g). (See the Tax Planning Considerations section of this chapter.)

eign country for the entire year, and have maintained more significant contacts with the foreign country than with the United States.

Foreign nationals typically have dual status in their first and last years of U.S. residency. Dual status implies that the foreign national resides in the United States for part of the year and in a foreign country for the other part. Therefore, his or her tax computation is based on nonresident alien status for part of the tax year and resident alien status for the other part. An individual who satisfies the lawful permanent residency test (but not the substantial presence test) begins his or her residency period on the first day of the first year in which he or she is physically present as a lawful permanent resident in the United States. An individual who satisfies the substantial presence test in his or her first year becomes a resident on the first day of the first year in which he or she is physically present in the United States.

Foreign nationals terminate their residency on the last day of the last year in which they are lawful permanent residents. Foreign nationals who satisfy the physical presence test for a particular year maintain residency through the last day of such year (ignoring periods of nominal U.S. presence).

The United States amended its tax laws to reduce the incentive for U.S. citizens and residents to forfeit their U.S. citizenship or residency. The U.S. government can impose an expatriation tax when an individual terminates his or her U.S. citizenship or long-term residency status. The IRC sets forth a tax avoidance presumption that references the individual's average taxes for the five-year period preceding the termination, as well as the individual's net worth. The expatriation tax is based on an expanded U.S. source of income definition that applies to nonresident aliens who are liable for the additional income tax.[26] Modified estate and gift tax rules subject certain property to U.S. taxation if transferred within ten years of the event triggering the loss of citizenship or residency.[27]

INVESTMENT INCOME

OBJECTIVE 5

Calculate the U.S. tax liability of a nonresident alien

Passive investment income is taxed to a nonresident alien only if it is U.S.-source. Section 871(a)(1)(A) places the following types of income in this category: interest, dividends, rents, salaries,[28] premiums; annuities; compensation; and other fixed or determinable annual or periodical gains and profits (sometimes referred to as "FDAP income"). Capital gains realized by a nonresident alien in the United States (other than in the conduct of a U.S. trade or business) are taxed to that individual only if he or she is physically present in the United States for at least 183 days during the tax year.[29] Two important exceptions to this general rule are as follows:

▶ Interest income earned by a nonresident alien on deposits in a U.S. bank, the foreign office of a U.S. bank, or other financial institution is exempt from U.S. taxation, provided the interest is not effectively connected with the foreign national's conduct of a U.S. trade or business.

▶ Portfolio interest (i.e., interest on obligations issued by U.S. persons and held by a nonresident alien as a portfolio investment) is exempt from U.S. taxation.[30]

The sale of personal property in the United States is not considered to generate fixed or determinable annual or periodic income. As a result, casual sales of inventory that are not regular, continuous, and substantial are not subject to U.S. taxation. To the extent the sales proceeds are contingent on the productivity, use, or disposition of an intangible asset (e.g., patent, copyright, trademark), gain from the sale of the asset is taxed as ordinary income. It is U.S.-source if the asset is used in the United States and foreign-source if the asset is used in a foreign country. To the extent the sales proceeds are noncontingent, the

TYPICAL MISCONCEPTION

Foreign nationals who are U.S. residents are taxed on their worldwide income, just as U.S. citizens are. They file Form 1040. Nonresident aliens who are subject to U.S. taxation file Form 1040NR.

---

[26] Sec. 877.
[27] Secs. 2107 and 2501.
[28] Compensation for personal services ordinarily is trade or business income. Salaries are trade or business income even if the foreign national does not conduct a U.S. trade or business in the tax year in which the income is reported (e.g., no services are performed in the United States in the year in which a final paycheck is collected by a cash method taxpayer) if it is attrib-utable to an earlier tax year and would have been treated as effectively connected with the conduct of a U.S. trade or business in that year.
[29] Sec. 871(a)(2). The capital gains are reduced by U.S. capital losses, and only the net gain is taxed.
[30] Portfolio obligations include, for example, bonds issued by a U.S. corporation in the Eurobond market.

gain is capital in character. It is U.S.-source if a U.S. resident sells the asset and foreign-source if a nonresident sells the asset.

EXAMPLE C:16-13 ▶ Paula, a citizen and resident of Country A, sells a patent to a U.S. corporation in consideration for a $2 fee for each unit produced under the patent in the United States. In the current year, Paula receives $18,000 for 9,000 units produced. The $18,000 is a contingent payment. It is U.S.-source because the patent is used in the United States and thus is subject to U.S. taxing authority. If Paula instead received a single $18,000 payment in exchange for all rights to the patent, the $18,000 less Paula's adjusted basis in the patent would have been a capital gain. It would have been foreign-source, and thus would have escaped U.S. taxation, because Paula is a foreign resident. ◀

ADDITIONAL COMMENT

Many tax treaties reduce this flat 30% rate for specific types of income.

Investment income and capital gains earned by a nonresident alien are taxed at a flat 30% rate, applicable to the gross amount.[31] Often, this rate is reduced by tax treaty (see discussion under Tax Planning Considerations later in this chapter). The 30% rate applies to capital gains of a nonresident alien only if he or she is present in the United States for at least 183 days during a tax year. In many cases, an individual who is present in the United States for 183 or more days has already acquired resident alien status. In general, U.S. payers must withhold the tax from the gross amount and remit the tax to the IRS.[32] If the U.S. payer fails to do so, and the nonresident alien fails to pay the tax voluntarily, the U.S. payer may be liable for the tax, as well as penalties for failing to withhold.[33]

EXAMPLE C:16-14 ▶ First State Bank issues dividend checks for a domestic corporation. One of the corporation's shareholders is Kelly, a nonresident alien entitled to a $30,000 dividend. Because the dividend represents U.S.-source investment income paid to a nonresident alien, First State Bank must withhold $9,000 ($30,000 × 0.30) of U.S. tax from Kelly's payment and remit the tax to the IRS. Kelly need not report or voluntarily pay the tax to the IRS. ◀

TRADE OR BUSINESS INCOME

A nonresident alien is engaged in a U.S. trade or business if he or she, with the intent to make a profit, conducts an activity in the United States that is regular, continuous, and substantial. A partner in a partnership or a beneficiary of a trust or estate is considered to indirectly conduct a U.S. trade or business if the partnership, trust, or estate directly conducts the U.S. trade or business.

Nonresident aliens who (1) are in the United States for less than 90 days during the year; (2) are employed by a nonresident alien, foreign partnership, or foreign corporation that does not conduct a U.S. trade or business, or by a foreign office maintained by a U.S. person; and (3) do not earn more than $3,000 for their services are considered not to have conducted a U.S. trade or business. In addition, their wages are exempt from U.S. taxation because such wages are foreign source.

Nonresident aliens who invest in securities through a broker also are considered not to have conducted a U.S. trade or business. Their capital gains are exempt from U.S. taxation unless they are present in the United States for more than 183 days during the year.

SPECIAL ELECTION FOR REAL ESTATE INVESTORS. Nonresident aliens may elect to have their U.S. real estate activities be treated as a U.S. trade or business even though the activities are passive. This election permits the nonresident aliens to claim all deductions and losses associated with the activities and thus be taxed on a net basis. If the election is not made and the activity does not constitute a trade or business, the real estate income is subject to the flat 30% withholding tax levied on a gross basis (i.e., without any reduction for deductions and losses).[34] Gains from the sale of U.S. real property interests (whether capital or ordinary) are treated as effectively connected with the conduct of a U.S. trade or business. Ownership of a U.S. real estate interest may be direct or indirect

---

[31] Sec. 871(a).
[32] If a nonresident alien voluntarily files a tax return, he or she can deduct casualty and theft losses related to (1) personal use property that exceed the $100/10% of AGI floor, (2) transactions entered into for a profit even if not

connected with a trade or business, and (3) charitable contributions otherwise deductible under Sec. 170.
[33] Secs. 1441(a) and 1461.
[34] Sec. 871(d).

(e.g., an investment in a corporation or a partnership that owns substantial U.S. real estate).[35]

EFFECTIVELY CONNECTED TESTS. Income is effectively connected with the conduct of a U.S. trade or business if one of two tests is met: an "asset use" test or a "business activities" test. Under the asset use test, income is effectively connected with the conduct of a U.S. trade or business if the income is derived from assets used in the business. For example, interest earned on a certificate of deposit (CD) may be either investment or business related, depending on how the CD is used. If a nonresident alien holds the CD to support the operating cycle of his or her U.S. business, the interest is derived from an asset used in the business and thus is effectively connected with the conduct of the business. Under the business activities test, income is effectively connected with the conduct of a U.S. trade or business if the activities of the business are a material factor in generating the income. For example, short-term gains realized by the U.S. branch of a foreign securities firm are effectively connected with the conduct of a U.S. business because the activities of the business (i.e., securities trading) are a material factor in generating the income. Capital gain income that is effectively connected with the conduct of a U.S. trade or business under either test is taxable without regard to the number of days the individual is physically present in the United States.

Income from the sale of inventory or other personal property by a nonresident alien is U.S.-source and, therefore, taxable in the United States if the alien has a U.S. office and the sale is attributable to that office. On the other hand, the income is foreign-source and therefore exempt from U.S. taxation if the property is for foreign use or disposition and if a non-U.S. office materially participated in the sale. When a foreign national manufactures or creates personal property in the United States and then sells it abroad, a portion of the sales income is allocated to U.S. production and thus is subject to U.S. taxation. The remainder is allocated to the location where the sale occurred.

CALCULATING THE TAX. A foreign national who conducts a U.S. trade or business may have to make two separate tax calculations. Investment income that is unrelated to the conduct of a U.S. trade or business is taxed on a gross basis at a flat 30% rate (unless reduced by a tax treaty). This tax is collected through withholding. Trade or business income is taxed at graduated rates on a net basis (i.e., reduced by all associated expenses and losses). Nonresident aliens

▶ Cannot use the standard deduction otherwise available to individual taxpayers

▶ Must itemize their deductions

▶ Are generally limited to a single personal exemption[36]

Individual tax rates apply to taxable income derived from an unincorporated U.S. trade or business. The trade or business income of unmarried nonresident aliens is taxed at the marginal rates for single taxpayers. Married nonresident aliens use the tax rate schedule for married individuals filing separately unless they elect to file a joint return under Sec. 6013(g) (see the Tax Planning Considerations section of this chapter). The U.S. trade or business income of nonresident aliens may be subject to the alternative minimum tax for individuals. The taxes owed on trade or business income can be reduced by any available tax credits. The taxpayer then pays the net U.S. tax liability through estimated tax installments and, if a balance remains, through a final remittance when he or she files an annual return.

EXAMPLE C:16-15 ▶ Maria, a single taxpayer, is a citizen and resident of Country D. In the current year, Maria reports $40,000 of U.S. dividends that are unrelated to Maria's U.S. trade or business and $1,000 of itemized deductions. Maria's U.S. trade or business generates $300,000 of gross income from sales activities, $20,000 of interest income, $225,000 of expenses, and $500 of tax credits.

---

[35] Secs. 897(a) and (c).
[36] Section 873(b) permits certain personal deductions (for example, casualty losses, charitable contributions, and personal exemptions) not directly related to trade or business activities.

SELF-STUDY QUESTION

In Example C:16-15, assume Maria also earned $10,000 of capital gain income on the sale of investment property she had owned in the United States. How would this change Maria's total U.S. tax liability?

ANSWER

Maria's U.S. tax liability would not increase unless the capital gain was connected with a U.S. trade or business, or it was investment gain and Maria was present in the United States for 183 days or more, and the gain was U.S. source income.

Maria's tax liability on her dividend income is $12,000 ($40,000 × 0.30), on the assumption that no U.S. tax treaty with Country D reduces the statutory 30% rate. The taxes owed on Maria's trade or business income are calculated as follows:

Gross income:	
Sales	$300,000
Interest	20,000
Total gross income	$320,000
Minus: Trade or business expenses	(225,000)
Adjusted gross income	$ 95,000
Minus: Personal exemption (2011)	(3,700)
Itemized deductions	(1,000)
Taxable income	$ 90,300
Gross tax liability (single rate schedule)	$ 18,901
Minus: Tax credits	(500)
Net tax liability	$ 18,401

Maria's total U.S. tax liability is $30,401 ($12,000 + $18,401). ◀

Topic Review C:16-3 summarizes the tax rules applicable to nonresident aliens.

TAXATION OF U.S. BUSINESSES OPERATING ABROAD

The IRC offers numerous tax breaks to U.S. enterprises that conduct business abroad. For example, it generally exempts from U.S. taxation income earned by foreign subsidiaries of U.S. corporations unless the income is derived from a U.S. trade or business or from a U.S. investment. This exemption extends to the foreign subsidiary's U.S. owners, who generally are not taxed on their share of the subsidiary's earnings until they receive the earnings in the form of a dividend (but see discussion of controlled foreign corporations below). The remainder of this chapter examines the conduct of overseas businesses and the special tax treatment of their owners.

DOMESTIC SUBSIDIARY CORPORATIONS

The use of domestic subsidiaries to sell goods or provide services to foreign consumers offers two nontax advantages to U.S. multinationals. First, the foreign activities of the multinationals can be conducted separately from their domestic activities. Second, a subsidiary's liabilities can be separated from those of its parent corporation, thereby shielding the parent's assets from the subsidiary's foreign creditors.

Profits from overseas business activities are taxed in the United States when earned. Losses are deductible when incurred. Because the foreign activities are conducted by a domestic corporation, they can be reported as part of a consolidated tax return that includes both the parent's and its domestic subsidiaries' operating results (see Chapter C:8 of this text). Thus, foreign losses can offset domestic profits and vice versa with respect to domestic losses.

FOREIGN BRANCHES

A domestic corporation may choose to conduct its overseas business through a foreign branch. A **foreign branch** is an unincorporated office or other fixed place of business (e.g., a manufacturing plant) maintained by a domestic entity in a foreign country. For tax purposes, a branch is treated as a legal extension of the domestic corporation. The domestic corporation reports profits attributable to the branch's foreign activities in the year in which the profits are earned, whether or not the branch remits the profits to the United States. Foreign income taxes paid or accrued on these profits are creditable against the domestic corporation's U.S. tax liability.

ADDITIONAL COMMENT

The use of limited liability companies (LLCs) is popular with overseas activities. The profits and losses of an LLC pass through to its U.S. owners. In many cases, the U.S. owner of a foreign LLC is a U.S. corporation. Once the LLC becomes profitable, the U.S. owner can elect to be taxed as a C corporation under the check-the-box regulations and receive the benefits of the deferral privilege (see page C:16-20) or can continue to be treated as an LLC under its default classification.

Topic Review C:16-3

Taxation of Nonresident Aliens

1. Nonresident aliens are foreign nationals who do not reside in the United States. A foreign citizen can acquire U.S. resident alien status by satisfying either the lawful permanent residency test or the substantial presence test as set forth in U.S. law.
2. Foreign nationals generally have dual status in their first and last years of U.S. residency. The foreign national may be taxed as a resident alien for part of the year and as a nonresident alien for the remainder of the year. Two different tax computations for the year may be required.
3. Passive investment income (e.g., dividends, interest, rents) is taxed to a nonresident alien only if such income is U.S. source. The income is taxed at a flat 30% rate, unless reduced by tax treaty, with no allowance for deductions or exemptions.
4. Capital gains earned in the United States (other than those related to the conduct of a U.S. trade or business) are taxed at the 30% rate only if the foreign national is physically present in the United States for 183 or more days during the tax year.
5. The U.S. tax on investment income or capital gains is collected through withholding by the U.S. person who pays the income or gains to the nonresident alien.
6. The United States taxes a nonresident alien's ordinary income and capital gains that are effectively connected with the conduct of a U.S. trade or business. Related business expenses and losses are deductible from effectively connected income. In computing their U.S. tax liability, nonresident aliens can claim a single personal exemption but not a standard deduction. Graduated individual tax rates apply to the nonresident alien's U.S. taxable income. The foreign national voluntarily pays the tax owed on the effectively connected income through estimated tax payments and an annual remittance.
7. A special election to file a joint return with their U.S.-citizen or resident-alien spouse is available to nonresident aliens. If the nonresident alien makes the election, he or she is subject to U.S. taxation on his or her worldwide income.

Similarly, the domestic corporation reports losses attributable to the branch's foreign activities in the year in which the losses are incurred. Because deducting the losses reduces taxes on domestic profits, such deductibility is a major advantage of conducting initial overseas activities through a branch. By using a branch, a domestic corporation can deduct start-up losses when incurred. Subject to branch loss recapture provisions, once the overseas activities become profitable, the domestic corporation can incorporate the branch in a foreign country and defer U.S. taxes on overseas profits until the profits are remitted to the United States.

FOREIGN CORPORATIONS

Conducting an overseas business through a foreign corporation offers the following four advantages:

▶ The foreign corporation's liabilities are separate from the assets of the parent corporation, thereby limiting the parent's losses to the extent of its capital investment in the foreign corporation.

▶ Unless the foreign corporation is "controlled" (see discussion of controlled foreign corporations below), the U.S. income tax on a U.S. stockholder's ratable share of the foreign corporation's earnings is deferred until the earnings are remitted to the United States.

▶ A domestic corporation that receives a dividend from a foreign corporation in which it owns at least 10% of the stock can claim a deemed paid tax credit for a ratable share of foreign income taxes paid or accrued by the foreign corporation.

▶ A domestic corporation that receives a dividend from a foreign corporation in which it owns at least 10% of the stock can claim a dividends-received deduction for the portion of any dividend paid out of the foreign corporation's undistributed profits that are effectively connected with the conduct of a U.S. trade or business. A dividends-received deduction is not available for dividends paid out of the foreign corporation's non-U.S. trade or business earnings.

The last three of these advantages, as well as the tax treatment of a foreign corporation's U.S. trade or business income, are discussed below.

ADDITIONAL COMMENT

This deferral privilege is eliminated for certain types of income of controlled foreign corporations. This topic is discussed later in the chapter.

DEFERRAL PRIVILEGE. For U.S. tax purposes, foreign corporations are entities separate and distinct from their shareholders. The IRC effectively grants a **deferral privilege** to U.S. shareholders with respect to the foreign corporation's earnings. Under this privilege, the U.S. shareholders are not taxed on the foreign corporation's earnings until the earnings are remitted to them as dividends.

EXAMPLE C:16-16 ▶

Adobe, a U.S. corporation, owns all the stock in Delta, a foreign corporation. In 2007, Delta reported $300,000 in after-tax profits from foreign manufacturing activities. Delta reinvested these profits outside the United States and remitted them to Adobe as a dividend in 2011. No U.S. income taxes are due on Delta's profits until 2011. This result contrasts with that for a foreign branch, whose earnings would have been taxable in the United States to Adobe in 2007. In principle, the value of the tax deferral (known as the "deferral privilege") equals the amount of U.S. taxes deferred times the time value of money for four years. ◀

TAX STRATEGY TIP

To enjoy the deferral privilege consider using a corporation rather than a branch for foreign operations.

Losses incurred by a foreign corporation cannot be deducted by any of its U.S. shareholders. Instead, the losses reduce profits earned in other years.

EXAMPLE C:16-17 ▶

Boston, a U.S. corporation, owns all the stock in Gulf, a foreign corporation. In the current year, Gulf reports $125,000 in losses. None of Gulf's current losses can be used to reduce Boston's current profits. Instead, in other years the losses can reduce Gulf's profits that might be distributed to Boston as dividends. Had the $125,000 of losses instead been incurred by a foreign branch, Boston could have used the current losses to offset its current profits. ◀

ADDITIONAL COMMENT

The deemed paid foreign tax credit is not available to individual U.S. shareholders.

FOREIGN TAX CREDIT. If a U.S. corporation conducts a foreign business through a foreign branch, it is directly liable for foreign taxes owed on the branch's earnings and can claim a direct U.S. credit for all such taxes paid or accrued. On the other hand, if a U.S. corporation conducts a foreign business through a foreign subsidiary, the foreign subsidiary is directly liable for foreign taxes owed on the subsidiary's earnings, and the U.S. corporation can claim a direct U.S. credit only for foreign taxes withheld from the subsidiary's dividend payments. Because most foreign countries impose taxes on foreign profits that are higher than taxes withheld on dividends, the foreign tax credit rules could discourage the use of foreign subsidiaries to conduct foreign businesses. To remedy this situation, Congress enacted the Sec. 902 **deemed paid credit** provisions relating to foreign income taxes paid or accrued by a foreign corporation.

OBJECTIVE 6

Calculate the deemed paid credit available to a U.S. stockholder in a foreign corporation

For a U.S. corporation to claim a deemed paid credit, two conditions must be met:

▶ The foreign corporation must pay a dividend to the U.S. corporation out of the foreign corporation's earnings and profits (E&P).

▶ The U.S. corporation must own at least 10% of the foreign corporation's voting stock on the distribution date.[37]

TYPICAL MISCONCEPTION

The deemed paid credit is available from first- through sixth-tier foreign corporations (but not for seventh- and lower-tier corporations). The credit becomes available only as an *actual* dividend is paid from each subsidiary to its parent. The U.S. corporation claims the credit when the first-tier foreign corporation pays a dividend to the U.S. corporation.

Calculating the Deemed Paid Credit. The deemed paid credit for the post-1986 tax years of a domestic corporate shareholder is calculated as follows:[38]

$$\text{Deemed paid credit} = \frac{\text{Dividend paid to domestic corporation out of undistributed earnings}}{\text{Accumulated undistributed earnings}} \times \text{Creditable taxes paid or accrued by the foreign corporation}$$

ADDITIONAL COMMENT

The foreign corporation's earnings and profits must be calculated under U.S. tax principles.

The undistributed earnings amount is not reduced by current dividends and is determined at the end of the current year. Dividends paid to all shareholders (U.S. and foreign) during the year reduce undistributed earnings at year-end. Creditable taxes also are determined at the end of the current year and include taxes paid, accrued, or deemed

---

[37] Secs. 902(a) and 902(b)(1)–(3). Foreign taxes paid by foreign subsidiaries of foreign corporations also qualify for the deemed paid credit.

[38] Sec. 902(a). Deemed paid foreign taxes are not deductible under Sec. 164. The calculation below pertains to post-1986 earnings and credits. Different rules apply to pre-1987 deemed paid credit calculations.

paid by the foreign corporation. Taxes attributable to all dividends paid during the current year reduce total taxes at year-end. The definition of "dividend" in the numerator of the fraction is the same as that for domestic corporate distributions out of E&P (see Chapter C:4).

Both the dividend received by the domestic corporation and the income equivalent of the pro rata share of foreign taxes associated with it are included in the domestic corporation's gross income.[39] This "gross up" for a pro rata share of foreign income taxes paid or accrued by the foreign corporation (equal to the amount of the deemed paid credit) precludes the domestic corporation's benefiting from both a deduction and a credit for such taxes (i.e., a deduction at the foreign corporate level and a credit at the domestic shareholder level).

EXAMPLE C:16-18▶ Coastal, a U.S. corporation, owns 40% of the stock in Bay, a foreign corporation. During the current year, Bay reports $200,000 of E&P, pays $50,000 in foreign income taxes, and remits $60,000 in dividends to Coastal. Bay withholds $6,000 in foreign taxes from the dividend payment. In prior tax years, Bay reported $100,000 of E&P, paid $40,000 in foreign income taxes, and paid no dividends. Based on a 34% corporate tax rate, Coastal's calculation of the deemed paid credit for the current year dividend is as follows:

$$\$18,000 = \frac{\$60,000}{\$200,000 + \$100,000} \times (\$50,000 + \$40,000)$$

The $18,000 credit amount is included in Coastal's income as a "gross up" and enters into the calculation of its U.S. tax liability:

Dividend	$60,000
Plus: Deemed paid credit gross up	18,000
Gross income	$78,000
Times: Corporate tax rate	× 0.34
Gross U.S. tax liability	$26,520
Minus: Deemed paid credit	(18,000)
Direct credit	(6,000)
Net U.S. tax liability	$ 2,520

◀

Translating the Dividend and Foreign Taxes into U.S. Dollars. Normally, a foreign corporation's books and records are maintained in the currency of the country in which the corporation operates. For U.S. tax reporting purposes, the dividend must be translated into U.S. dollars. If the distributee is a domestic corporation eligible for the deemed paid credit, the foreign corporation's E&P and foreign taxes also must be translated into U.S. dollars. The exchange rate for the date on which the dividend is included in gross income is used to translate the dividend paid by a noncontrolled foreign corporation, as well as the underlying E&P.[40] Translation of foreign taxes withheld from the dividend is based on the exchange rate in effect on the dividend payment date. For purposes of calculating the deemed paid credit, translation of foreign taxes is based on the exchange rate in effect on the date the foreign corporation pays the taxes.[41]

EXAMPLE C:16-19▶ Houston, a U.S. corporation, owns 40% of the stock in Far East, a foreign corporation that began operations in Year 1. In Year 2, Far East pays Houston a 70,000 pira dividend. In Year 1 and Year 2, Far East earns 400,000 pira in pretax profits. It pays 30,000 and 20,000 pira in home country taxes respectively in Year 1 and Year 2. On the dividend payment date, the pira-U.S. dollar exchange rate is 1 pira = $0.22 (U.S.). Far East paid the Year 1 and Year 2 foreign taxes when the exchange rates were 1 pira = $0.20 (U.S.) and 1 pira = $0.25 (U.S.), respectively. Far East's E&P is 350,000 (400,000 pretax profits − 50,000 taxes) pira. The translated dividend amount is 70,000 pira × $0.22 = $15,400. The translated foreign tax amount is $11,000 [(30,000 pira × $0.20) + (20,000 pira × $0.25)]. The translated foreign taxes attributable to the dividend are $2,200 [$11,000 × (70,000 pira ÷ 350,000 pira)]. ◀

---

[39] Sec. 78.
[40] Reg. Secs. 1.301-1(b) and 1.902-1(g) and *The Bon Ami Co.*, 39 B.T.A. 825 (1939).

[41] Sec. 986(b).

A discussion of the financial statement implications of deferred foreign earnings appears at the end of this chapter.

FOREIGN TAX CREDIT BASKETS.   Before 2003, dividends received by a corporate shareholder owning at least 10% but no more than 50% of a foreign corporation's stock were accounted for in a separate limitation basket. These dividends are called Sec. 902 dividends because that IRC section governs their tax treatment. They also are called 10/50 dividends because of the range of required taxpayer ownership in the stock of the dividend paying corporation. Until 2003, separate foreign tax credit limitations were calculated for this basket. The existence of a separate 10/50 dividend basket permitted the cross-crediting of foreign taxes paid on dividends received from noncontrolled (10/50) foreign corporations. Cross-crediting was allowed only with respect to distributions made out of the foreign corporation's earnings and profits accumulated before January 1, 2003. As an illustration, in Example C:16-18, before 2003, the dividends received by Coastal Corporation from Bay Corporation (as well as from all other 10/50 corporations) would have been placed in Coastal's 10/50 dividend basket. Coastal then would have calculated separate limitations for the purpose of determining the amount of foreign taxes attributable to the dividends that were creditable.

Now, U.S. corporate taxpayers that receive dividends from a 10/50 corporation must "look through" the foreign corporation to ascertain the source and character of the foreign corporation's earnings and profits out of which the dividends were paid. They then must apportion the dividends according to this source and character and assign them to one of two baskets (i.e., passive income and general limitation) into which the underlying earnings and profits would have been placed. (See the previous discussion of Special Foreign Tax Credit Limitations on p. C:16-7.) To apply the Sec. 902 dividend "look through" rules, minority U.S. shareholders must rely on foreign corporations to supply them with information on the source and character of the corporation's earnings and profits.

TAXATION OF A FOREIGN CORPORATION'S U.S. TRADE OR BUSINESS INCOME
Regular and Alternative Minimum Taxes.   A foreign corporation that invests in the United States or that conducts a U.S. trade or business is taxed by the U.S. government in the same way as a nonresident alien. Section 881(a) taxes the U.S.-source investment income of a foreign corporation on a gross basis at a flat 30% rate (or lower rate specified by tax treaty). Capital gains that are not effectively connected with the conduct of a U.S. trade or business are exempt from U.S. taxation. The U.S. taxes on the investment income are collected through withholding.[42] Section 882(a) taxes that portion of the foreign corporation's income that is effectively connected with the conduct of a U.S. trade or business on a net basis at graduated rates. These earnings are not taxed to the foreign corporation's U.S. shareholders until they are distributed.

Section 245(a) allows a domestic corporation to deduct dividends (or a portion thereof) received from a foreign corporation in which it has at least a 10% stock interest. To be deductible, the dividends (or a portion thereof) must have been paid out of the foreign corporation's undistributed profits that are effectively connected with the conduct of a U.S. trade or business. The percentage (i.e., 70%, 80%, or 100%) of the effectively connected dividend amount that is deductible depends on the extent of the domestic corporation's stock ownership in the foreign corporation. The deductibility of the effectively connected dividend amount alleviates the double taxation of the foreign corporation's earnings that were previously taxed by the United States.

Branch Profits Tax.   Income earned by a U.S. subsidiary of a foreign corporation is taxed twice: first, at the U.S. corporate level when earned; second, at the foreign shareholder level when distributed. The corporate level tax is assessed on a net basis at graduate rates. The U.S. subsidiary pays it voluntarily. The shareholder level tax is assessed on a gross dividend basis at a flat 30% rate, which may be reduced by treaty. The U.S. subsidiary withholds the tax and remits it to the IRS.

ADDITIONAL COMMENT

Dividends paid by a foreign corporation out of its U.S. trade or business E&P are eligible for a dividends-received deduction.

---

[42] Sec. 1442.

In a similar manner, income earned by an unincorporated U.S. branch of a foreign corporation also is taxed twice: first, at the branch level when earned; second, at the foreign corporate level when "remitted." The branch level tax is imposed on branch income effectively connected with the conduct of a U.S. trade or business. It is assessed on a net basis at graduated rates. The corporate level tax is imposed on a "dividend equivalent amount" deemed to have been paid by the U.S. branch to the foreign corporation. This tax is assessed on a gross basis at a flat 30% rate, which may be reduced by treaty. The foreign corporation pays both of these taxes voluntarily.

The latter tax on deemed-distributed branch earnings is called the **branch profits tax.**[43] It is analogous to the 30% withholding tax on U.S. corporate dividends paid to foreign shareholders. The branch profits tax effectively places foreign corporations that conduct their U.S. business through an unincorporated U.S. branch on par with foreign corporations that conduct their U.S. business through a U.S. subsidiary. It ensures that both sets of foreign corporations are treated in the same way.

The branch profits tax equals 30% (or a lower rate specified in a tax treaty) times the dividend equivalent amount. The dividend equivalent amount equals the foreign corporation's E&P that is effectively connected with the conduct of its U.S. trade or business increased by the decrease (or decreased by the increase) in the foreign corporation's net equity investment in its branch assets during the year. Thus, the branch profits tax base is (1) increased by earnings remitted to the foreign corporation during the year as reflected by a decrease in the branch's U.S. trade or business assets and (2) decreased by earnings reinvested in branch operations during the year as reflected by an increase in the branch's U.S. trade or business assets. Under allocable interest rules, certain interest paid by a U.S. branch is taxed as if it were paid by a U.S. corporation. The interest income accruing to foreign creditors is considered to be U.S. source and hence subject to a 30% U.S. withholding tax (or a lower rate specified in a tax treaty).

CONTROLLED FOREIGN CORPORATIONS

OBJECTIVE 7

Understand tax provisions applicable to controlled foreign corporations (CFCs)

UNDER PRE-SUBPART F RULES. Before the 1962 enactment of the **controlled foreign corporation (CFC)** provisions (known as the Subpart F rules, discussed later), U.S. corporations set up majority owned foreign subsidiaries in "tax-haven" countries to minimize their U.S. tax liability on income earned from overseas operations. The typical scenario proceeded as follows:

► A U.S. manufacturer formed a sales subsidiary in a foreign country that imposed little or no corporate income tax.

► The U.S. manufacturer sold goods to foreign purchasers.

► The U.S. manufacturer shipped the goods directly to the foreign purchasers.

► The U.S. manufacturer billed the sales subsidiary for the goods at an artificially low price.

► The sales subsidiary, in turn, billed the foreign purchasers for the goods at an artificially high price.

► Through this scheme, the U.S. manufacturer effectively shifted its sale profits from the United States to the foreign country in which the sales subsidiary operated.

A U.S. firm that performed services for foreign clients could devise a similar scheme. The following example illustrates how, absent Subpart F rules, a U.S. corporation could defer recognition of U.S. taxable income by conducting its foreign business through a foreign subsidiary as opposed to a foreign branch.

EXAMPLE C:16-20 ► Under pre-CFC rules, Chicago, a U.S. corporation, forms a foreign branch to conduct its overseas widget sales. The foreign country in which the branch operates imposes no income taxes. Chicago's overseas widget sales generate $1 million of profits annually. Chicago pays $340,000 ($1,000,000 × 0.34) in U.S. taxes and no foreign taxes in the year the income is earned. Had the same profit been divided equally between Chicago and Island Corporation, a newly formed foreign sales subsidiary, the worldwide tax cost would have been reduced substantially. Figure C:16-1 illustrates this result.

---

[43] Sec. 884(a).

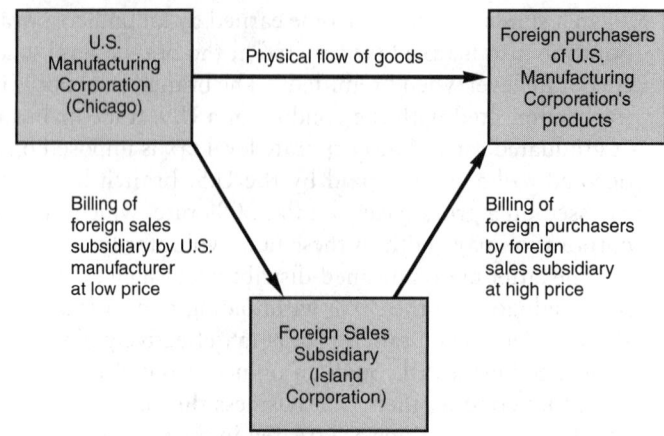

Sales made by Chicago's foreign branch:
$1,000,000 profit x 0.34 = $340,000 U.S. tax liability for Chicago. No foreign tax liability.

Sales made by Chicago. Profit divided equally between Chicago and Island Corporation in the absence of Subpart F rules:
  Chicago: $500,000 profit x 0.34 = $170,000 U.S. tax liability.
  Island: $500,000 profit x 0 = $0 Foreign Country tax liability (and no U.S. tax
          liability for Chicago until part or all of the profit is remitted to the United States.)

Sales made by Chicago. Profit divided equally between Chicago and Island Corporation in the absence of Subpart F rules:
Chicago: $500,000 profit on sales to Island x 0.34 = $170,000 U.S. tax liability.
         $500,000 Subpart F income x 0.34 = $170,000 U.S. tax liability.
         No U.S. tax liability when Island remits its profits to the United States.
Island: $500,000 profit x 0 = $0 Foreign Country tax liability and no U.S. tax liability.

FIGURE C:16-1 ▶ ILLUSTRATION OF USE OF FOREIGN SALES SUBSIDIARY (EXAMPLE C:16-20)

KEY POINT

The tainted income is taxable to Chicago (the CFC's U.S. parent) as a deemed paid dividend, rather than taxable directly to the CFC.

Chicago's $500,000 share of the profit results in a $170,000 ($500,000 × 0.34) U.S. tax liability. Island owes no U.S. or foreign tax on its $500,000 share of the profit. Chicago owes no U.S. tax on Island's share of the profits because the earnings have not been remitted as a dividend to its parent corporation in the United States. An attempt by Chicago to maximize its tax deferral by selling its widgets to Island at an artificially low price probably would be challenged by the IRS under the Sec. 482 transfer pricing rules (see page C:16-30). Section 482 would limit Island's profit to the portion of the $1 million total profit that it had earned, based on the value it had added to the goods. This amount may be less than the amount allocated under a 50–50 profit split method. ◀

UNDER SUBPART F RULES. In the foregoing scenario, the Subpart F rules eliminate tax deferral by accelerating U.S. recognition of certain types of "tainted" income (see Figure C:16-2 for a summary of the Subpart F income categories).

EXAMPLE C:16-21 ▶ Assume the same facts as in Example C:16-20 except that Island is a CFC. Under current U.S. tax law, Island's profit on widgets manufactured by a related party outside Island's country of incorporation and resold to third parties outside Island's country of incorporation is considered tainted or Subpart F income. This profit is deemed to be distributed to Chicago on the last day of Island's tax year. Only the portion, if any, of Island's profits attributable to widget sales in Island's country of incorporation is untainted and thus deferred. If Island sells all the widgets outside its country of incorporation, its $500,000 of profits would be taxed directly to Chicago under the Subpart F rules. This result is basically the same as if Chicago had conducted its foreign sales through a foreign branch. ◀

Because of the increased tax cost associated with the Subpart F rules, U.S. businesses often arrange their overseas activities in such a way as to avoid CFC status or structure their transactions to avoid generating Subpart F income.

CFC DEFINED. A CFC is a foreign corporation in which more than 50% of the voting stock or more than 50% of the value of all outstanding stock is owned by U.S. share-

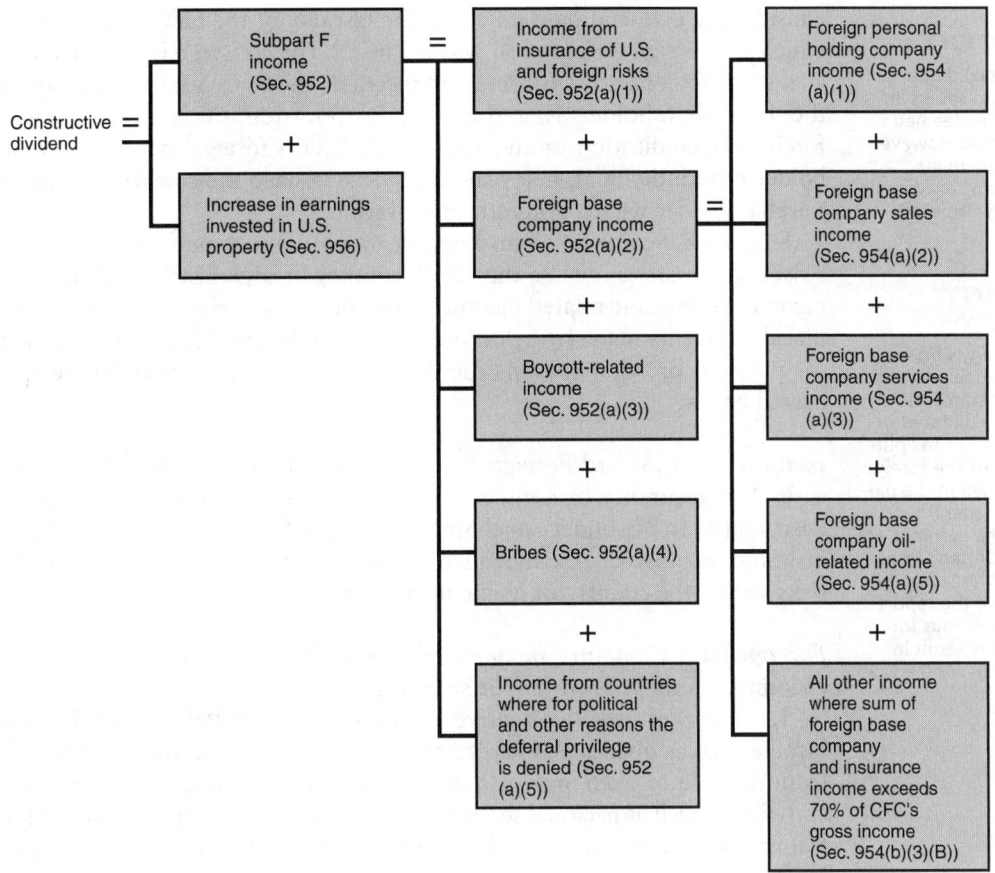

▶ TYPES OF INCOME EARNED BY A CONTROLLED FOREIGN CORPORATION (CFC) INCLUDIBLE IN THE GROSS INCOME OF ITS U.S. SHAREHOLDER(S)

holders on any day of the corporation's tax year.[44] A **U.S. shareholder** is a U.S. person who owns at least 10% of the foreign corporation's voting stock.[45] Ownership may be direct, indirect, or constructive. Constructive ownership is determined under the attribution rules of Sec. 318 (see Chapter C:4) with modifications specified in Sec. 958(b).

EXAMPLE C:16-22 ▶ Europa, a foreign corporation, is owned by five unrelated individuals. Al, Bill, and Connie are U.S. citizens who own 24%, 20%, and 9%, respectively, of Europa's voting and nonvoting stock. Duane and Elaine are nonresident aliens who own 40% and 7%, respectively, of Europa's voting and nonvoting stock. Only Al and Bill are considered U.S. shareholders because they are U.S. persons who own at least 10% of Europa's voting stock. Europa is not a CFC because Al and Bill together own only 44% of its voting and nonvoting stock. If Al instead were Connie's father, Connie would be a U.S. shareholder because, under the Sec. 318 family attribution rules, she would own 33% (9% directly + 24% constructively from Al) of Europa's voting stock. Europa then would be a CFC because its three U.S. shareholders together would own 53% (24% + 20% + 9%) of its voting and nonvoting stock. Double-counting Al's 24% interest to take into consideration both Al's and Connie's stockholdings is not permitted. ◀

CONSTRUCTIVE DISTRIBUTIONS OF SUBPART F INCOME. A U.S. shareholder is taxed on its ratable share of Subpart F income if the foreign corporation has been a CFC for at least 30 days during the tax year. Each U.S. shareholder reports its share as a

---

[44] Sec. 957(a). A CFC must adopt the same tax year as its majority U.S. shareholder if on the first day of the CFC's tax year (or other days as prescribed by the IRS) 50% or more of the voting power or value of all classes of the CFC's stock is directly, indirectly, or constructively owned by a single U.S. shareholder.

[45] Sec. 951(b). A U.S. person includes a U.S. citizen or resident alien, a domestic corporation, a domestic partnership, and a domestic trust or estate.

constructive dividend paid on either the last day of the CFC's tax year or the last day on which the foreign corporation was a CFC.[46] The constructive dividend is included in the U.S. shareholder's gross income and increases the shareholder's basis in the CFC stock. If the U.S. shareholder is a domestic corporation, it is entitled to a deemed paid foreign tax credit for a ratable share of the CFC's foreign income taxes. If the U.S. shareholder is an individual, he or she may elect to have the constructive dividend taxed as if the shareholder were a domestic corporation.

Subpart F income falls into five categories: (1) income from insuring U.S. and foreign risks that originate outside the CFC's country of organization, (2) foreign base company income, (3) boycott-related income, (4) income equal to the amount of any bribes or other illegal payments made by or on behalf of the CFC, and (5) income from countries where for political or other reasons the deferral privilege is denied. These categories are discussed below.

Insurance of U.S. and Foreign Risks. Income derived by the CFC from issuing (or reinsuring) an insurance or annuity contract is Subpart F income if the income would have been subject to tax under Subchapter L of the IRC had it been earned by a domestic (U.S.) insurance company.[47] Excluded from this rule is income earned by the CFC from insuring risks within the country of its incorporation.

Foreign Base Company Income. The broadest of all, this Subpart F income category encompasses the following four subcategories.

1. *Foreign personal holding company income* (FPHCI) includes passive investment income such as dividends, interest, royalties, annuities, and rents. FPHCI also includes gain from the sale or exchange of non-income-producing property, commodities, or foreign currency, as well as personal services contract income. It excludes rents and royalties received from a related corporation for the use of property within the CFC's country of incorporation. It also excludes income derived from the CFC's active conduct of a trade or business with an unrelated person. For years beginning before January 1, 2012, a special exception from the Subpart F rules applies to (1) active banking and finance income earned by a CFC predominantly or substantially engaged in a banking, financing, or similar business and (2) income from services related to the production of banking and finance income. An exception also applies to gains from property sales by security dealers. Dividends and interest are not FPHCI if received from a related corporation organized in the CFC's country of incorporation and whose principal assets are used in a trade or business in that country.[48]

Time is a CFC incorporated in Country X. Time receives interest and dividends from its two foreign subsidiaries, East Corporation and West Corporation. East is incorporated in Country V and conducts all its business in that country. West is incorporated in Country X and conducts all its business in that country. Only the interest and dividends received from East are FPHCI because East is not incorporated in the same country as Time. West's interest and dividends are not FPHCI because West is incorporated in Country X. ◀

2. *Foreign base company sales income* includes fees and profits earned from the sale, or purchase and sale, of personal property outside the CFC's country of incorporation to or from a related party. The related party transactions that result in foreign base company sales income are[49]

▶ The purchase of personal property from a related person and its sale to any person

▶ The sale of personal property to any person on behalf of a related person (e.g., commission income)

▶ The purchase of personal property from any person and its sale to a related person

▶ The purchase of personal property from any person on behalf of a related person

---

[46] Sec. 951(a).
[47] Sec. 953(a)(1).
[48] Sec. 954(c). Section 954(d)(3) defines "related person" for Subpart F purposes as (a) any individual, corporation, partnership, trust, or estate that controls, or is controlled by, the CFC, or (b) any corporation, partnership, trust,

or estate controlled by the same persons who control the CFC. "Control" means direct, indirect, or constructive ownership of 50% or more of the total voting power or total value of the CFC's stock.
[49] Sec. 954(d)(1).

Foreign base company sales income excludes profits derived from the sale of products either manufactured in the CFC's country of incorporation, sold for use in the CFC's country of incorporation, or produced by the CFC.[50]

EXAMPLE C:16-24▶

ADDITIONAL COMMENT

Goods are deemed to have been manufactured by the CFC if it substantially transforms the product (such as making screws and bolts from steel rods) or if its direct labor and factory overhead account for 20% or more of the total cost of goods sold.

Dublin Corporation is a CFC organized in Country F. Dublin purchases machine tools from its U.S. parent for sale to unrelated parties. Dublin sells 70% of the tools in Country E and 30% in Country F. Only the profit earned from the sale of tools in Country E constitutes foreign base company sales income. If Dublin manufactured the machine tools, none of its profit from the Country E or Country F sales would be foreign base company sales income. ◀

3. *Foreign base company services income* includes compensation for services provided for or on behalf of a related person outside the CFC's country of incorporation. In general, compensation for personal services is considered to be earned at the location where the services are performed.[51]

EXAMPLE C:16-25▶

Andes Corporation, organized in Country A, is 100% owned by Hi-Tech, a U.S. corporation. Hi-Tech sells industrial machines to unrelated Amazon Corporation for use in Country B. Hi-Tech assigns the portion of the sales contract covering the installation and maintenance of the machines to Andes, and Hi-Tech pays Andes for these services. Earnings derived from the installation and maintenance is foreign base company services income because Andes performs these services for a related party (Hi-Tech) outside its country of incorporation (Country A). ◀

4. *Foreign base company oil-related income* includes earnings derived from oil and gas related activities (other than the extraction of oil and gas) conducted in a foreign country. Such activities include the transport, shipping, processing, and distribution of oil and gas and any related service. Foreign base company oil-related income is not taxed under Subpart F if it is earned in the foreign country in which the oil and gas was extracted.[52]

WHAT WOULD YOU DO IN THIS SITUATION?

You are a tax manager assigned to the U.S. Manufacturing and Export Corporation (USM&E) account. USM&E manufactures machine tools for distribution throughout North and South America. USM&E sells its products to six 100%-owned foreign subsidiaries that resell the products in various North and South American markets. In reviewing USM&Es operating results, you notice that sales to the U.S. and Canadian subsidiaries account for the largest profit margin. USM&E revenues from sales to the four Central and South American subsidiaries are barely above related manufacturing costs. Upon examining prior year information, you discover that Canadian income tax rates are nearly the same as U.S. rates while the rates in the other countries are substantially lower. The sales manager at USM&E tells you that this organizational structure has been in place for years and the operations of the six sales subsidiaries are substantially identical. He also informs you that none of the other tax professionals who have worked on the account has ever questioned USM&E's sales and pricing. In reviewing USM&E's data, you discover that additional costs were incurred to ship the goods from the United States to Central and South America, but these costs do not justify the price differences between the sales made in these regions and the sales made in the United States and Canada. You suspect that a transfer pricing problem exists. What benefit can USM&E derive from its current pricing scheme? Can you advise your client about possible negative tax consequences of inappropriate pricing? Under U.S. tax laws, are any alternatives available to USM&E that might permit it to use different pricing methods or non-arm's-length transfer prices? Can USM&E obtain advice from the IRS concerning the soundness of its pricing methods?

---

[50] Sec. 954(d) and Reg. Sec. 1.954-3(a)(4)(i).
[51] Sec. 954(e).
[52] Sec. 954(g).

Subpart F income specifically excludes

▶ Income earned by the CFC in the conduct of a U.S. trade or business. Such income is taxed directly to the CFC.[53]

▶ Foreign base company income or insurance income that is subject to an effective foreign tax rate greater than 90% of the maximum U.S. corporate rate.[54]

▶ Foreign base company income and insurance income that in total are less than the smaller of 5% of the CFC's gross income or $1 million.[55]

▶ Income earned by the CFC that cannot be repatriated to the United States because of currency or other restrictions.[56]

When foreign base company income and insurance income exceed 70% of the CFC's total gross income, all the CFC's gross income is deemed to be foreign base company income or insurance income.[57]

REAL-WORLD EXAMPLE

Countries that participate in, or cooperate with, international boycotts include Kuwait, Lebanon, Libya, Qatar, Saudi Arabia, Syria, the United Arab Emirates, and the Republic of Yemen. In 2006, 2,270 boycott reports were filed. The tax effects were a $733,077 reduction in foreign tax credits, and a $11.7 million increase in Subpart F income.

Boycott-related Income. This category includes any income derived by the CFC from the participation in, or cooperation with, an international boycott against a particular nation (or group of nations). The portion of the CFC's profits that are boycott-related is determined under the rules of Sec. 999.

Bribes, Kickbacks, and Other Illegal Payments. The CFC loses its deferral privilege for the earnings equivalent of all bribes, kickbacks, and other illegal payments that it makes.

Earnings Derived in Certain Foreign Countries. U.S. shareholders of a CFC cannot defer income derived from activities in certain countries. These countries include those the U.S. government does not recognize, those with whom the U.S. Government has frozen or severed diplomatic relations, and those the U.S. Government believes support international terrorism.

Related Deductions. Subpart F income is reduced by any related deductions, the allocation of which are based on rules set forth in Reg. Sec. 1.861-8.[58]

ADDITIONAL COMMENT

Income derived from the following countries is not eligible for the deferral privilege: Cuba, Iran, North Korea, Sudan, and Syria.

INCREASE IN EARNINGS INVESTED IN U.S. PROPERTY. Dividends paid by a CFC to its U.S. shareholders may be both taxed to the shareholders in the United States and subject to tax withholding in the foreign country. In the absence of special rules, the CFC could avoid the U.S. tax by either investing its earnings in U.S. property or lending funds to its U.S. shareholders, thereby affording them the beneficial use of CFC earnings without an actual earnings distribution. To close this loophole, Congress enacted a special IRC provision that taxes the U.S. shareholders on their respective pro rata shares of any increase in CFC earnings invested in U.S. property. Under this provision, each U.S. shareholder is deemed to receive a constructive distribution equal to the lesser of the shareholder's ratable share of U.S. property held by the CFC minus the CFC's E&P previously taxed as a constructive distribution, or the shareholder's ratable share of CFC earnings for the year.[59] CFC earnings previously taxed as Subpart F income may be invested in U.S. property without the shareholder's incurring additional tax liability. Such amounts, if distributed, would not constitute a dividend.

ADDITIONAL COMMENT

If the CFC guarantees an obligation of a U.S. person, it is deemed to hold that obligation. Thus, if a CFC guarantees a loan of its U.S. parent, the guarantee constitutes the acquisition of U.S. property. This result can be a tax trap for the unwary.

The U.S. property value is based on the average adjusted basis (minus any liability to which the property is subject) as of the last day of each quarter of the CFC's tax year. U.S. property includes tangible property located in the United States, stock in domestic corporations, obligations of U.S. persons, and intangibles developed by the CFC for use in the United States.[60] U.S. property excludes U.S. government obligations, U.S. bank deposits, stock in domestic corporations that are not U.S. shareholders of the CFC or more than 25% owned by a U.S. shareholder, U.S. securities acquired by CFC security dealers, obligations issued by non-corporate U.S. persons unrelated to the CFC, and U.S. property acquired before the first and after the last day on which the foreign corporation was "controlled."

---

[53] Sec. 952(b).
[54] Sec. 954(b)(4).
[55] Sec. 954(b)(3)(A).
[56] Sec. 964(b).

[57] Sec. 954(b)(3)(B).
[58] Sec. 954(b)(5).
[59] Sec. 951(a)(2).
[60] Sec. 956(c)(1).

EXAMPLE C:16-26▶

SELF-STUDY
QUESTION

If $500,000 of the $1 million in
Example C:16-26 had been Subpart
F income (and thus currently taxed
to the CFC's U.S. shareholders),
would the acquisition of the U.S.
property also be taxed currently?

ANSWER

The E&P invested in U.S. property
is deemed to come first out of the
E&P that has been previously
taxed. Therefore, the U.S. shareholders would incur no additional
tax liability as a result of the U.S.
investment.

Forco is a CFC in its initial year of operation. During the current year, Forco reports $1 million of earnings, none of which is taxed as Subpart F income. On December 31, Forco invests in U.S. property worth $400,000. Because of this additional investment, $400,000 of Forco's earnings are no longer deferred and are taxed ratably to Forco's U.S. shareholders. ◀

DISTRIBUTIONS FROM A CFC. Distributions from a CFC are deemed to be made first out of any increase in earnings invested in U.S. property and the CFC's most recently accumulated Subpart F income, then out of its U.S. tax-deferred earnings, if any. Distributions of previously taxed income (i.e., the increase in earnings invested in U.S. property and Subpart F income) are tax-free to the U.S. shareholder and reduce his or her basis in CFC stock.[61]

EXAMPLE C:16-27▶

Bulldog, a domestic corporation, owns all the stock in Marine, a CFC. Bulldog's cost basis in the Marine stock is $600,000. Since the time Bulldog acquired the stock, Marine generated $400,000 of E&P, of which $175,000 was taxed to Bulldog as Subpart F income. Marine distributes $200,000 cash to Bulldog. Of this amount, $175,000 is deemed to be a nontaxable distribution of previously taxed Subpart F income. The remaining $25,000 is deemed to be a taxable distribution of earnings that were not previously taxed under Subpart F. After the distribution, Bulldog's basis in the Marine stock is $600,000 ($600,000 + $175,000 − $175,000). ◀

KEY POINT

Section 1248 is a backstop to the
Subpart F rules in that it subjects
gain from disposition of CFC stock
to taxation as ordinary income to
the extent that it previously has
not been taxed.

DISPOSITION OF CFC STOCK. Section 1248 applies to U.S. persons who own at least 10% of a foreign corporation's voting stock and who sell or exchange the stock within five years after any time the foreign corporation was a CFC. The gain recognized on the sale or exchange is taxed as a dividend to the extent of the U.S shareholder's pro rata share of the CFC's untaxed E&P. This amount is further prorated to reflect the time the U.S. person held the stock and the period during which the foreign corporation was a CFC.[62] The remaining portion of the gain is treated as capital in character. Foreign taxes associated with the dividend portion of the gain qualify for the deemed paid foreign tax credit.

EXAMPLE C:16-28▶

On November 1, 2009, Texas, a domestic corporation, purchased 200 of the 500 outstanding shares of Le Chien Corporation's stock. Texas holds the shares until March 31, 2011, when it sells the stock for a $60,000 gain. Le Chien is a CFC at all times while the stock is owned. Le Chien's E&P amounts not previously taxed to Texas under the Subpart F rules are as follows: 2009, $60,000; 2010, $30,000; and 2011, $70,000. The untaxed E&P attributable to the stock sold or exchanged is determined under the following formula:

$$\text{CFC's untaxed E\&P for tax year} \times \frac{\text{Number of shares sold or exchanged}}{\text{Number of shares outstanding}} \times \frac{\text{Number of days shares are owned while corporation is a CFC}}{\text{Number of days in CFC's tax year}} = \text{CFC's untaxed E\&P attributable to shares sold or exchanged}$$

$$2009: \$60,000 \times \frac{200}{500} \times \frac{61}{365} = \$ 4,011$$

$$2010: \$30,000 \times \frac{200}{500} \times \frac{365}{365} = 12,000$$

$$2011: \$70,000 \times \frac{200}{500} \times \frac{90}{365} = \underline{6,904}$$

$$\text{Total} \qquad \underline{\$22,915}$$

ADDITIONAL
COMMENT

For U.S. taxpayers operating in a
foreign country with a high tax
rate, Sec. 1248 is a tax benefit and
not a tax detriment. The combination of Sec. 1248's dividend treatment and the availability of the
Sec. 902 deemed paid credit
reduces the U.S. tax liability to
below the U.S. tax liability if the
gain were instead taxed as a
capital gain.

Thus, $22,915 of the gain is treated as a dividend, and $37,085 ($60,000 − $22,915) is treated as capital in character. Texas can claim a deemed paid credit for a pro rata share of foreign taxes actually paid by Le Chien on the earnings out of which the CFC paid the dividend. ◀

---

[61] Secs. 959(c) and 961(b).

[62] Sec. 1248(a).

**TYPICAL
MISCONCEPTION**

Section 482 applies to transactions involving two U.S. entities as well as to transactions involving a U.S. entity and a foreign entity.

SECTION 482 RULES AND TAX AVOIDANCE. Transactions between a domestic corporation and its foreign subsidiary, or between a foreign corporation and its U.S. subsidiary, present an opportunity for tax avoidance. For example, the domestic corporation could sell goods to, or provide services for, the subsidiary at a price less than the price that would be obtained in an arm's-length dealing (see Figure C:16-1 and related text). Alternatively, the foreign subsidiary could pay a less-than-arm's-length price for the use of intangibles (such as patents or trademarks). Both transactions increase the foreign subsidiary's profits that may be deferred for U.S. tax purposes.

EXAMPLE C:16-29 ▶ Taylor, a U.S. corporation, sells widgets to its wholly owned foreign subsidiary, Wheeler Corporation. Wheeler is incorporated in, pays taxes to, and sells the widgets in Country Z. Taylor normally sells widgets at a price of $10 per unit to a U.S. wholesaler that provides services similar to those provided by Wheeler. Both the U.S. wholesaler and Wheeler incur similar costs. If Taylor sells the widgets to Wheeler at $8 per unit, Wheeler's profits increase by $2 per unit, and Taylor's profits decrease by $2 per unit. The additional profit is not Subpart F income because it is derived from sales by the CFC within its country of incorporation. Thus, the additional profit is isolated in Country Z. It is not taxed by the United States until Wheeler remits it to Taylor as a dividend. ◀

EXAMPLE C:16-30 ▶ Assume the same facts as in Example C:16-29 except Taylor instead issues a license to Wheeler to manufacture the widgets and charges a $1 per-unit royalty for each unit produced and sold. A licensing agreement between Taylor and an unrelated foreign widget producer specifies a $3 per-unit royalty payment. The reduced royalty rate increases Wheeler's profits by an additional $2 per unit. Because the profit is derived from manufacturing performed by a CFC, the additional profit is not taxed to Taylor as Subpart F income. Such profit is U.S. tax deferred until Wheeler remits it to Taylor as a dividend. ◀

Section 482 authorizes the IRS to distribute, apportion, or allocate gross income, deductions, credits or allowances between or among controlled entities to prevent tax evasion and to clearly reflect income. The IRS may use this authority under the following circumstances:

▶ Two or more organizations, trades, or businesses exist.

▶ They are owned or controlled by the same persons.

▶ A transaction between or among the entities does not reflect the income that would have been earned in an arm's-length transaction.

The **Sec. 482 rules** can apply to transactions between two unincorporated entities, two incorporated entities, or one incorporated entity and one unincorporated entity. The related persons can be domestic or foreign and need not be members of an affiliated group that files a consolidated return. In the two preceding examples, Sec. 482 would authorize the IRS to adjust the prices and/or profits reported by Taylor and Wheeler to reflect an arm's-length transaction.

Treasury Regulations under Sec. 482 provide guidance for determining an arm's-length standard in various types of transactions, including

▶ Loans or advances

▶ Performance of services

▶ Sales, transfers, or use of intangible property

▶ Sales, transfers, or use of tangible property

▶ Cost sharing arrangements[63]

These rules create safe harbors for taxpayers engaged in related party transactions. If the transaction price meets the standard set forth in the Sec. 482 Treasury Regulations, the IRS generally will not challenge it.

Treasury Regulations finalized in 1994 offer additional guidance. For example, Reg. Sec. 1.482-3(b)(2) states that a transaction involving the transfer of tangible property (as in Example C:16-29) between controlled taxpayers meets the arm's-length standard if the

---

[63] Reg. Sec. 1.482-1 through -6 and -8.

REAL-WORLD EXAMPLE

The IRS entered into 904 advance pricing agreements (APAs) with taxpayers as of December 31, 2009. APAs provide advance Sec. 482 approval for the transfer pricing procedures used by the taxpayer on transfers of tangible personal property or financial instruments. Most APAs cover a five-year period, at which time they must be renewed.

results are consistent with the outcome that would have been obtained had uncontrolled taxpayers engaged in a *comparable* transaction under *comparable* circumstances. The transaction and circumstances are comparable only if minor differences between the transactions have no effect on the amount charged, or if these differences can be reconciled through a reasonable number of adjustments to the uncontrolled transaction. If no uncontrolled transaction is comparable, the resale price, cost-plus, comparable profits, profit-split, or any other appropriate method approved by the IRS can be used.

For intangibles (as in Example C:16-30), the arm's-length price in a controlled transfer of an intangible is the same as that in a comparable uncontrolled transfer. An uncontrolled transfer is comparable to a controlled transfer if it involves comparable intangible property and occurs under similar circumstances, as explained in Reg. Sec. 1.482-4(c)(2). If significant differences exist between the controlled and uncontrolled transfers that make them substantially dissimilar, the comparable profits method may not be used. The comparable profits method derives the arm's-length price paid in a controlled transfer of property from objective measures of profitability (e.g., profit level indicators such as rates of return) specific to uncontrolled persons engaged in similar business activities with other uncontrolled persons under similar circumstances. If the comparable profits method cannot be used, the taxpayer can petition the IRS to use another method.

Section 482 permits the IRS periodically to adjust the level of payments for the use of an intangible to reflect its current revenue yield. Thus, in setting the initial royalty rate, related parties should consider projected operating results, including changes in the income stream attributed to the intangible.

A net Sec. 482 transfer pricing adjustment for the provision of services, or the sale or use of property, could constitute a substantial valuation misstatement under Sec. 6662(e)(1)(B) if it exceeds the lesser of $5 million or 10% of the taxpayer's gross receipts. If so, an accuracy-related penalty equal to 20% of the tax underpayment attributable to the valuation misstatement may be imposed.

ADDITIONAL COMMENT

Many federal government documents are available to the general public under the Freedom of Information Act (FOIA). Advance pricing arrangements (APAs), however, receive special treatment under the FOIA. APAs, both past and present, and their related background files are treated as confidential tax return information.

OBJECTIVE 8

Be aware of special international tax incentives formerly available to U.S. taxpayers

FOREIGN SALES CORPORATIONS REGIME AND EXTRATERRITORIAL INCOME EXCLUSION

Before 2005, two special tax incentives to encourage the export of U.S. goods abroad were available to U.S. taxpayers: the foreign sales corporation (FSC) regime and the extraterritorial income (ETI) exclusion. The FSC regime exempted from U.S. taxation a portion of foreign trade income earned by an FSC organized by a U.S. taxpayer in a treaty country. The ETI exclusion exempted from U.S. taxation foreign trading gross receipts accruing to a U.S. corporation as a result of activities conducted abroad. In response to World Trade Organization rulings that the FSC regime and the ETI exclusion constitute prohibited export subsidies, Congress repealed both measures. The ETI repeal, however, does not apply to transactions conducted in the ordinary course of business under a binding contract, between unrelated persons, in effect since September 2003. As a phase-out of the ETI exclusion, 80% of the otherwise available ETI benefits were available to U.S. taxpayers in 2005, and 60% of the benefits were available in 2006.

OBJECTIVE 9

Explain the transactional structure and taxation of inversions

INVERSIONS

In our federal system of taxation, the tax treatment of U.S. corporations differs significantly from the tax treatment of foreign corporations. Specifically, U.S. corporations are taxed on their worldwide income, both U.S.- and foreign-source. By contrast, foreign corporations are taxed almost exclusively on their U.S.-source business and investment income. Unless effectively connected with the conduct of a U.S. trade or business (or attributable to a U.S. "permanent establishment" under the terms of a treaty), the foreign-source income of foreign corporations largely escapes U.S. taxation.

This difference in tax treatment creates an incentive for U.S. corporations with substantial foreign-source income to reorganize as a foreign corporation in transactions known as **inversions**. Typically, in an inversion, a U.S. corporation (1) merges into a foreign entity or transfers substantially all of its assets to the foreign entity; (2) the owners of the U.S. business exchange stock in the U.S. corporation for equity in the foreign entity; and (3) the same owners continue to conduct their U.S. business, as well as their foreign operations, through the foreign entity. Following the merger or asset transfer, income from the U.S. business continues to be subject to U.S. taxation, but income from the foreign business largely escapes U.S. taxation.

Because inversions erode the U.S. corporate tax base, Congress added two anti-inversion provisions to Secs. 367 and 7874. Under the first provision, a foreign corporation will be deemed to be a U.S. corporation for U.S. tax purposes if (1) the foreign corporation acquired substantially all the assets of a U.S. corporation, (2) former shareholders of the U.S. corporation own 80% or more (by vote or value) of stock in the foreign corporation by reason of their U.S. stock ownership, and (3) the foreign corporation and its affiliates do not conduct substantial business in the foreign country of incorporation.

Under the second anti-inversion provision, income recognized in an inversion transaction, as well as related taxes, cannot be offset by the U.S. corporation's otherwise available tax attributes (e.g., net operating losses or foreign tax credits) for a ten-year period if conditions (1) through (3) in the previous paragraph are met, with the substitution of 60% ownership for 80% ownership. Thus, if in the inversion, (1) the foreign corporation acquires substantially all the assets of a U.S. corporation, (2) former shareholders of the U.S. corporation own between 60% and 80% of the foreign corporation's stock by reason of their U.S. stock ownership, and (3) the foreign corporation and its affiliates do not conduct substantial business in the foreign country of incorporation, income recognized on the asset transfer cannot be reduced by the U.S. corporation's otherwise available net operating losses, and taxes owed on this income cannot be offset with the U.S. corporation's otherwise available foreign tax credits. Excepted from the rule are sales of inventory and similar property to a foreign related person.

EXAMPLE C:16-31 ▶ Gomez, Nguyen, Jones, and Ahmed own equal shares of Wilmington-Domestic, a U.S. corporation. The corporation generates $20 million of income from its U.S. business and $60 million of income from a business conducted in Country X. In an attempt to remove its foreign business income from U.S. taxing jurisdiction, Wilmington-Domestic reorganizes as Wilmington-Foreign in Country Z. In the reorganization, Gomez, Nguyen, Jones, and Ahmed exchange their stock in Wilmington-Domestic for an equal number of shares in Wilmington-Foreign, and Wilmington-Domestic merges into Wilmington-Foreign. Following the reorganization, Wilmington-Foreign conducts the U.S. and Country X businesses but conducts no business in Country Z. Under the first anti-inversion rule, Wilmington-Foreign will be treated as a U.S. corporation, and thus taxed on its worldwide income, because (1) Wilmington-Foreign acquired substantially all the assets of Wilmington-Domestic; (2) Gomez, Nguyen, Jones, and Ahmed own more than 80% of Wilmington-Foreign stock by reason of their Wilmington-Domestic stock ownership; and (3) Wilmington-Foreign conducts no business in Country Z. ◀

EXAMPLE C:16-32 ▶ Assume the same facts as in the preceding example except that only Gomez, Nguyen, and Jones exchange their stock in Wilmington-Domestic for an equal number of shares in Wilmington-Foreign (75% of the total). Under the second anti-inversion rule, any income recognized on the merger of Wilmington-Domestic into Wilmington-Foreign cannot be reduced by Wilmington-Domestic's otherwise available net operating losses, if any. Moreover, taxes owed on this income cannot be offset by Wilmington-Domestic's otherwise available foreign tax credits, if any. ◀

TAX PLANNING CONSIDERATIONS

DEDUCTION VERSUS CREDIT FOR FOREIGN TAXES

Taxpayers may elect annually to deduct or credit any paid or accrued foreign income taxes.[64] Nearly all taxpayers elect to credit them. The advantage of doing so is illustrated in the following example.

---

[64] Sec. 901(a).

EXAMPLE C:16-33 ▶

Phil, a U.S. citizen, earns $100 of foreign income. Phil pays $25 in foreign income taxes and is subject to a 28% marginal tax rate. He makes the following calculations to compare the advantages of crediting the taxes versus deducting them.

	Deduction	Credit
Gross income	$100	$100
Minus: Foreign tax deduction	(25)	–0–
Taxable income	$ 75	$100
Times: Marginal tax rate	× 0.28	× 0.28
Gross U.S. tax liability	$ 21	$ 28
Minus: Foreign tax credit	–0–	(25)
Net U.S. tax liability	$ 21	$ 3

If Phil deducts the foreign income taxes, his total U.S. and foreign tax liability is $46 ($25 + $21). By claiming the credit, Phil reduces his total U.S. and foreign tax liability to $28 ($25 + $3). ◀

Some taxpayers deduct their foreign income taxes when they incur foreign losses or when they cannot credit the taxes either in the current year or in any of the one carryback or ten carryover years. The deduction provides current tax benefits where U.S. profits exceed foreign losses. If no U.S. profits are earned, the foreign taxes increase the taxpayer's NOL.

ELECTION TO ACCRUE FOREIGN TAXES

Cash method taxpayers may elect to accrue foreign taxes for credit purposes. The election permits them to credit foreign income taxes that have accrued but have not yet been paid. It does not affect the application of the cash method of accounting to other taxable items. The election is not available for the purpose of deducting foreign taxes. It is binding on all tax years and can be revoked only with IRS consent.[65]

Topic Review C:16-4

Taxation of U.S. Persons Doing Business Abroad

TYPE OF ENTITY USED	TAX TREATMENT
Domestic subsidiary	Profits are taxed to the subsidiary (or the consolidated group) in the year earned. A direct foreign tax credit is available for foreign taxes paid or accrued. Losses are deducted in the year incurred.
Foreign branch	Foreign branches are unincorporated extensions of domestic entities. Branch profits are taxed to the entity in the year earned. A direct foreign tax credit is available for foreign taxes paid or accrued on branch profits. Branch losses are deducted in the year incurred.
Foreign corporation (less than 50% U.S.-owned)	A foreign corporation's earnings are tax deferred until repatriated to the United States. A domestic corporation can claim a deemed paid foreign tax credit with respect to dividends received from a foreign corporation in which it owns at least a 10% interest.
Controlled foreign corporation (CFC, more than 50% U.S.-owned)	Same rules as for previous entry. Subpart F income of the CFC is taxed to its U.S. shareholders in the year in which earned. The increase in CFC earnings invested in U.S. property is subject to U.S. taxation. Previously taxed income is distributed tax-free. Special rules apply to the sale or exchange of CFC stock.

---

[65] Sec. 905(a).

Two advantages ensue from this election.

▶ It accelerates use of the foreign tax credit by one or more tax years.

▶ It eliminates the problem of matching foreign income with foreign taxes for credit limitation purposes. In many cases, it obviates the need for a carryback or carryover of excess credits.

EXAMPLE C:16-34 ▶ In 2008, Tulsa, a U.S. corporation and cash method taxpayer, began a business in Country Z. Z's tax laws require the use of a calendar year for tax reporting purposes. Taxes owed on income earned during the year must be paid by the first day of the third month following year-end. Tulsa conducts its foreign operations for three years before ceasing business on December 31, 2011. Its results are as follows:

	2008	2009	2010	2011
Foreign source taxable income	$1,000	$1,000	$1,000	$–0–
Foreign taxes accrued (30% rate)	300	300	300	–0–
Foreign taxes paid	–0–	300	300	300
Foreign tax credit limitation (34% U.S. corporate rate)	340	340	340	–0–
Foreign tax credit:				
Cash method	–0–	300	300	300
Accrual method	300	300	300	–0–

Under the cash method, Tulsa pays its 2008 U.S. taxes without the benefit of a foreign tax credit. In 2011, Tulsa generates $300 of excess credits because of the annual mismatching of income and tax payments. Of the 2011 foreign tax payment, $40 can be carried back to 2010, but $220 [$300 − ($40 + $40)] in foreign tax credits are lost because Tulsa discontinued its foreign activities in 2010. If such activities had not been discontinued, the excess foreign taxes could have been carried over and used in later years when the credit limitation exceeds foreign taxes paid. No mismatching occurs, however, where Tulsa uses the accrual method to report the foreign tax credit. ◀

SPECIAL EARNED INCOME ELECTIONS

Taxpayers may revoke a previous election to exclude foreign-earned income or not make the initial election if they find themselves in one of two situations:

▶ They are employed in a foreign country where the foreign tax rate exceeds the U.S. tax rate (e.g., Canada or Germany).

▶ They incur a substantial loss from overseas employment or in a trade or business.

In the first situation, the available foreign tax credits exceed the taxpayer's gross U.S. tax liability. The foreign-earned income exclusion diminishes the utility of the excess credits. By including foreign earned income in gross income, the taxpayer can use the entire amount of excess credits as a carryback or carryover (subject to separate basket limitations). These excess credits might be beneficial if, for example, the taxpayer earned self-employment income in another year in a foreign country where the tax rate is lower than the U.S. rate.

In the second situation, the foreign deductions of taxpayers who incur substantial losses may exceed their foreign gross income. If these taxpayers exclude part or all of their foreign-earned income from their total gross income, a pro rata portion of the related foreign expenses will be disallowed. This disallowance reduces the amount of any available NOL carryback or carryover. Including foreign earnings in the taxpayer's gross income allows the excess foreign expense portion to be deducted.

Taxpayers may not elect to exclude or deduct the housing cost amount. A qualifying taxpayer who receives only this amount (reported as W-2 income) from his or her employer must exclude it from gross income. If the taxpayer earns only self-employment income, he or she must deduct the housing cost amount. If the taxpayer earns both salary (or wages) and self-employment income, he or she must apportion the housing cost amount between an exclusion and a deduction based on the relative amounts of income earned.

A taxpayer can forego the foreign earned income benefits by so electing on his or her current return or on an amended return. If the taxpayer revokes the initial election, he or she may not make a new election for five years or until the IRS consents.[66] Thus, a taxpayer who revokes an election while residing in a country with a tax rate higher than the U.S. rate may not elect to exclude foreign earned income if shortly thereafter he or she moves to a country with a tax rate lower than that in the United States.

TAX TREATIES

ADDITIONAL COMMENT

With certain exceptions, whenever a treaty and the IRC are in conflict, the treaty takes precedence.

A treaty is an agreement between two or more sovereign nations. The United States has concluded tax treaties with over 60 countries. Income **tax treaties** have numerous objectives, including

▶ To reduce or eliminate double taxation

▶ To facilitate the exchange of information among taxing authorities

▶ To provide a mechanism for resolving disputes between residents or citizens of one country and residents or citizens of another country

In addition to income tax treaties, the United States has concluded estate and gift tax treaties, as well as Social Security tax totalization agreements.

A tax treaty to which the United States is a party cannot be used by U.S. citizens or U.S. corporations to reduce the scope of their income subject to U.S. taxation. Notwithstanding the provisions of any treaty, U.S. citizens and U.S. corporations are still taxed on their worldwide income at regular U.S. rates. On the other hand, a tax treaty can reduce the foreign taxes that U.S. citizens or U.S. corporations pay on their foreign-source investment income, and it allows them to credit against their U.S. tax liability foreign taxes paid on their foreign-source business income. Conversely, a tax treaty can reduce the U.S. taxes that foreign citizens or foreign corporations pay on their U.S.-source investment income, and it allows them to credit against their foreign tax liability U.S. taxes paid on their U.S.-source business income.

ADDITIONAL COMMENT

Tax treaties designate a competent authority to represent each country when an international tax dispute arises between the treaty partners. The U.S. competent authority is the Assistant Commissioner (International) of the IRS.

The second objective is intended to prevent or eliminate tax evasion. The third objective is achieved through a "competent authority" procedure under which taxpayers of one treaty partner can settle tax disputes with taxpayers of the other treaty partner through the latter country's tax authorities.

Section 6114 requires a taxpayer who takes a position based on a treaty provision that preempts an IRC provision to disclose such position on his or her tax return or on a statement attached to the return.

SPECIAL RESIDENT ALIEN ELECTIONS

Two special elections permit nonresident aliens to be treated as resident aliens for U.S. tax purposes. The first election is usually made when a foreign national moves to the United States too late in the year to qualify as a resident (see page C:16-14). This election is available if the foreign national

▶ Does not qualify as a resident under the lawful residency test or substantial presence test for the calendar year for which the election is made (i.e., election year)

▶ Does not qualify as a resident for the calendar year preceding the election year

▶ Qualifies as a resident under the substantial presence test in the calendar year immediately following the election year, and was present in the United States

  a. For at least 31 consecutive days in the election year and

  b. For at least 75% of the days during the period beginning with the first day of the 31-consecutive-day or longer period and ending with the last day of the election year.

The election is made on the nonresident alien's tax return for the election year and may not be revoked without the IRS's consent. The election cannot be made before the foreign national has met the substantial presence test for the calendar year following the election year.[67]

---

[66] Sec. 911(e)(2).

[67] Sec. 7701(b)(4).

ADDITIONAL
COMMENT

The special resident alien election is made by attaching to a joint return a statement that the Sec. 6013(g) election is being made. This election must be made within the time period designated for filing a claim for credit or refund.

Section 6013(g) permits nonresident aliens who are married to U.S. citizens or resident aliens to elect to be taxed as resident aliens. Such an election requires both spouses to agree to be taxed on their worldwide income and to provide all books, records, and information necessary to determine either spouse's tax liability. The election permits nonresident aliens to file a joint tax return with their spouses. By filing a joint return, the spouses can take advantage of the lower tax rates available to married persons filing jointly.

Another election permits nonresident aliens to be treated as resident aliens for income tax and wage withholding purposes. To qualify for the election, the foreign national must be a nonresident alien at the beginning of the tax year and a resident alien at the end of the year and must be married to a U.S. citizen or resident alien at the end of the tax year. Both spouses must make the election, which provides the same tax benefits as a Sec. 6013(g) election and eliminates nonresident alien tax treatment for part of the year and resident alien tax treatment for the remainder of the year.

COMPLIANCE AND PROCEDURAL CONSIDERATIONS

FOREIGN OPERATIONS OF U.S. CORPORATIONS

U.S. corporations must provide a summary of their overseas business activities on Form 1120, Schedule N (Foreign Operations of U.S. Corporations). This form reports information relating to interests in foreign partnerships, stock in controlled foreign corporations, and foreign bank and securities accounts.

REPORTING THE FOREIGN TAX CREDIT

Individual taxpayers claim the foreign tax credit on Form 1116. Corporate taxpayers claim the credit on Form 1118. Separate forms must be filed for each of the foreign tax credit limitation baskets. A completed Form 1116 is illustrated in Appendix B. This form is based on the following situation:

EXAMPLE C:16-35▶ Andrew Roberts is a U.S. citizen and resident who files jointly with his wife. They have no children. His Social Security number is 123-45-6789. In 2010, he reports $18,000 (Canadian) of dividend income on which $2,700 (Canadian) in income taxes are withheld on December 31, 2010. Assume that on December 31, 2010, 1.01 Canadian dollars equal $1 (U.S.). The Canadian dollars translate into $17,822 (U.S.) of dividend income and $2,673 ($17,822 × 0.15) (U.S.) of income taxes. Roberts owns 3% of the distributing foreign corporation's outstanding stock. The Canadian taxes are translated at the exchange rate for the date on which they were withheld (December 31, 2010). The $17,822 (U.S.) of gross income is reduced by an allocable portion of Andrew's deductions. As indicated on Form 1116, Andrew can claim $2,495 of the $2,673 (U.S.) foreign tax withheld from the dividend, as a foreign tax credit subject to Andrew's credit limitation for the passive income basket. The Roberts' taxable income before exemptions (Form 1040, Line 41) is $86,000, and their tax before credits (Form 1040, Line 44) is $12,038. ◀

REPORTING THE EARNED INCOME EXCLUSION

The elections for the foreign earned income and housing cost exclusions are made separately on Form 2555 or Form 2555-EZ. The latter form can be used by a taxpayer who meets the bona fide residence or physical presence test and maintains a tax home in a foreign country during the requisite period. In addition, the taxpayer must (1) be a U.S. citizen or resident alien, (2) have earned wages/salaries in a foreign country, (3) report total foreign earned income of no more than $92,900 (in 2011) or $91,500 (in 2010), (4) file a tax return for a 12-month period, (5) have earned no self-employment income, and (6) have incurred no business and/or moving expenses. Each election must be made

KEY POINT

Taxpayers who regularly reside in a foreign country generally qualify under both the physical presence and bona fide residence tests. Tax practitioners must indicate on Form 2555 which one of the two tests has been met when claiming the foreign earned exclusion. Determining whether one is a foreign resident is more difficult than merely calculating one's physical presence during the tax year. If a taxpayer fails the physical presence test, he or she should retain documentation (e.g., rent receipts, employment contract, and visas) to support bona fide residence.

on an income tax return that is timely filed (including any extensions), a later amended return filed within the appropriate limitations period, or an original income tax return filed within one year after the return's due date. Once made, the election remains in effect for that year and all subsequent years unless the IRS consents to revocation. Thus, a new election is not required when an individual either moves from one foreign country to another or moves to the United States and then returns to a foreign country years later.[68]

At the end of their first year in a foreign country, U.S. expatriates often face a dilemma. They would like to claim the foreign earned income and/or housing cost exclusion (deduction) for the current year but have not yet met either the bona fide residence or physical presence test. As a result, despite their intention to remain in the foreign country until such time as they have met one these tests, they might have to include their foreign earnings in gross income and pay U.S. taxes on an otherwise excludible amount. If in a subsequent year they eventually meet either test because of their extended stay in the foreign country, they might have to file an amended return or a refund claim to retroactively recover the foregone Sec. 911 benefits for the previous year. To avoid this result, Treasury Regulations grant these taxpayers an extension for filing their first year return until such time as they will have met either the residence or physical presence test.[69] Regulations also grant these taxpayers a general filing extension to the fifteenth day of the sixth month following the close of the tax year.[70]

Appendix B contains a completed Form 2555 based on the following situation:

EXAMPLE C:16-36▶

Lawrence Smith, a U.S. citizen, Social Security number 234-56-7890, is employed by the Very Public Corporation in Paris, France. In 2010, he earned $60,000 in salary and received the following benefits:

Cost of living allowance	$27,000
Education allowance	8,000
Home leave stipend	6,400
Housing allowance	21,300
Total	$62,700

Smith is eligible for the Sec. 911 earned income exclusion for all of 2010 even though he spent five business days in the United States. While in the United States, he earned $1,200. For 2010, Smith can exclude up to $91,500 under the foreign earned income exclusion and an additional $6,660 ($21,300 qualifying expenses − $14,640 base housing amount) under the housing cost exclusion. This $98,160 ($91,500 + $6,660) is not reduced by any disallowed-for-AGI deductions because Smith deducts all his employment-related expenses as miscellaneous itemized deductions. ◀

FILING REQUIREMENTS FOR ALIENS AND FOREIGN CORPORATIONS

A nonresident alien reports income on Form 1040-NR on or before the fifteenth day of the sixth month following the close of the tax year. If the nonresident alien's wages are subject to tax withholding, Form 1040-NR must be filed on or before the fifteenth day of the fourth month following the close of the tax year.[71]

A foreign corporation reports income on Form 1120-F, U.S. Income Tax Return of a Foreign Corporation. If the foreign corporation maintains no U.S. office or place of business, the due date for its income tax return is the fifteenth day of the sixth month following the close of its tax year. If the corporation maintains a U.S. office or place of business, the due date is the fifteenth day of the third month following the close of its tax year.

---

[68] Reg. Sec. 1.911-7(a).
[69] Reg. Sec. 1.911-7(c).

[70] Reg. Sec. 1.6081-5(a).
[71] Reg. Sec. 1.6072-1(c).

FINANCIAL STATEMENT IMPLICATIONS

OBJECTIVE 10

Understand the financial statement implications of various international transactions

FOREIGN TAX CREDIT

A corporation having excess foreign taxes because of the foreign tax credit (FTC) limitation will record a deferred tax asset, possibly subject to a valuation allowance. The valuation allowance, in turn, will increase the corporation's effective tax rate. On the other hand, full use of the foreign tax credit without limitation will not affect the corporation's effective tax rate.

EXAMPLE C:16-37▶

Upsilon Corporation operates in the United States and in Country Low using a foreign branch. Country Low's tax rate is 20%. In the current year, Upsilon earns $1 million from its U.S. operations and $400,000 from its Country Low operations. Thus, Upsilon pays $80,000 ($400,000 × 0.20) of foreign taxes to Country Low, producing the following tax results:

U.S.-source income	$1,000,000
Foreign-source income	400,000
Taxable income	$1,400,000
Times: U.S. tax rate	0.34
U.S. tax before FTC	$ 476,000
Minus: Foreign tax credit	(80,000)
U.S. taxes payable	$ 396,000

For book purposes, Upsilon's total income tax expense is $476,000 ($396,000 U.S. + $80,000 foreign). Accordingly, Upsilon makes the following book journal entry:

Total income tax expense	476,000	
Total income taxes payable		476,000

In this case, Upsilon reports the following book results:

Net income before income tax expense	$1,400,000
Minus: Total income tax expense	(476,000)
Net income	$ 924,000
U.S. taxes ($396,000/$1,400,000)	28.29%
Foreign taxes ($80,000/$1,400,000)	5.71%
Total effective tax rate	34.00% ◀

EXAMPLE C:16-38▶

Assume the same facts as in Example C:16-37 except Upsilon's foreign branch is in Country High instead of Country Low. Country High imposes a 45% tax rate. In this case, Upsilon's foreign taxes are $180,000 ($400,000 × 0.45), with the FTC limited to $136,000 ($476,000 × $400,000/$1,400,000). Assuming no carryback opportunity, the $44,000 ($180,000 − $136,000) excess carries over for ten years. Upsilon's net U.S. tax is $340,000 ($476,000 − $136,000), and its total tax liability is $520,000 ($340,000 U.S. + $180,000 foreign).

For book purposes, Upsilon records a $44,000 deferred tax asset for the FTC carryover. However, if Upsilon continues to operate only in Country High, it likely will not realize the deferred tax asset because of the FTC limitation. Therefore, Upsilon also must record a $44,000 valuation allowance. Accordingly, Upsilon makes the following book journal entry:

Total income tax expense	520,000	
Deferred tax asset	44,000	
Valuation allowance		44,000
Total income taxes payable		520,000

In this case, Upsilon reports the following book results:

Net income before income tax expense	$1,400,000
Minus: Total income tax expense	(520,000)
Net income	$ 880,000

U.S. taxes ($340,000/$1,400,000)	24.28%
Foreign taxes ($180,000/$1,400,000)	12.86%
Total effective tax rate	37.14%

This effective tax rate reconciles to the 34% statutory tax rate as follows:

Statutory tax rate	34.00%
Valuation allowance ($44,000/$1,400,000)	3.14%
Total effective tax rate	37.14%

EXAMPLE C:16-39▶

Assume the same facts as in Example C:16-38 except Upsilon plans to open second branch in Country Low. Because all income falls into the general limitation basket, Upsilon can offset the excess foreign taxes from Country High against the excess FTC limitation from Country Low and thereby use the FTC carryover within the next ten years. With these alternative facts, Upsilon need not record the valuation allowance, so its U.S. income tax expense per books reflects the entire foreign tax credit. Thus, Upsilon's U.S. tax expense is $296,000 ($476,000 − $180,000), and its foreign tax expense is $180,000, for a total of $476,000. Accordingly, Upsilon makes the following book journal entry:

Total income tax expense	476,000	
Deferred tax asset	44,000	
Total income taxes payable		520,000

In this case, Upsilon reports the following book results:

Net income before income tax expense	$1,400,000
Minus: Total income tax expense	(476,000)
Net income	$ 924,000
U.S. taxes ($296,000/$1,400,000)	21.14%
Foreign taxes ($180,000/$1,400,000)	12.86%
Total effective tax rate	34.00%

DEFERRED FOREIGN EARNINGS

As discussed earlier in this chapter, a U.S. parent does not include a foreign subsidiary's earnings in its (the parent's) gross income until the subsidiary repatriates (remits) the earnings as a dividend. (An exception to this deferral privilege was discussed earlier in the text under Controlled Foreign Subsidiaries.) Under normal income tax accounting principles, this deferred income would create a deferred tax liability.[72] However, in this situation, an exception for indefinite reinvestment applies.[73] Specifically, a reporting entity does not recognize a deferred tax asset for the excess of financial reporting basis over tax basis of an investment in a foreign subsidiary unless that temporary difference will reverse in the foreseeable future. Such a basis difference will occur if the consolidated financial statements recognize the foreign earnings but the U.S. parent's tax return does not. If the group does not invoke the indefinite reinvestment exception because it expects to repatriate the earnings in the future, the deferral and subsequent repatriation will not affect the effective tax rate. One the other hand, if the group does invoke the exception, the deferral is treated as a permanent difference that reduces the effective tax rate. However, if the subsidiary nevertheless remits the earnings in a future year, the repatriation will increase the effective tax rate. Thus, using the exception could cause wide swings in effective tax rates. These potential swings might induce management to forgo the exception or, if using the exception, inhibit management from repatriating the foreign earnings.

EXAMPLE C:16-40▶

Parent Corporation operates in the United States and in Country Low using Foreign Subsidiary in which Parent holds a 100% interest. Country Low's tax rate is 20%. In the current year, Parent earns $1 million from its U.S. operations, and Foreign earns $400,000 from its Country Low operations. Thus, Foreign pays $80,000 ($400,000 × 0.20) of foreign taxes to Country Low, and Parent incurs a $340,000 ($1,000,000 × 0.34) tax liability on its U.S.-source income. Thus, the

---

[72] Accounting Standards Codification (ASC) 740, which codifies SFAS No. 109.

[73] Accounting Standards Codification (ASC) 740-30-25-17, which incorporates the pre-codification APB No. 23 exception for indefinite reinvestment.

total tax liability is $420,000 ($340,000 + $80,000), and Parent defers $56,000 of U.S. taxes on the foreign earnings, computed as follows:

Gross foreign earnings	$400,000
Times: U.S. tax rate	0.34
Tax liability before FTC	$136,000
Minus: Potential deemed paid FTC	(80,000)
Deferred tax liability	$ 56,000

For book purposes, the consolidated financial statements include the foreign earnings, so the group's U.S. income tax expense is $396,000, computed as follows:

U.S.-source income	$1,000,000
Foreign-source income	400,000
Net income before income tax expense	$1,400,000
Times: U.S. tax rate	0.34
U.S. income tax expense before FTC	$ 476,000
Minus: Deemed paid FTC	(80,000)
U.S. income tax expense	$ 396,000

Consequently, the group's total income tax expense is $476,000 ($396,000 U.S. + $80,000 foreign). Assuming the group does not invoke the indefinite reinvestment exception, the group recognizes a deferred tax liability and makes the following book journal entry:

Total income tax expense	476,000	
Deferred tax liability		56,000
Total income taxes payable		420,000

In this case, the group reports the following book results:

Net income before income tax expense	$1,400,000
Minus: Total income tax expense	(476,000)
Net income	$ 924,000
U.S. taxes ($396,000/$1,400,000)	28.29%
Foreign taxes ($80,000/$1,400,000)	5.71%
Total effective tax rate	34.00%

In a subsequent year, Parent again earns $1 million from its U.S. operations, but Foreign has no earnings that year. Nevertheless, Foreign remits a $320,000 dividend to Parent out of prior year earnings from which it paid the $80,000 of foreign taxes. For tax purposes, Parent grosses up the dividend by the deemed paid FTC to $400,000 ($320,000 + $80,000) and claims the deemed paid FTC. Consequently, Parent's U.S. tax on the foreign earnings is $56,000 ($136,000 − $80,000), and its total liability is $396,000 ($340,000 + $56,000).

For book purposes, the group recognizes only the $1 million of U.S.-source earnings, so its total income tax expense is $340,000. Accordingly, the group makes the following book journal entry:

Total income tax expense	340,000	
Deferred tax liability	56,000	
Total income taxes payable		396,000

In this case, the group reports the following book results:

Net income before income tax expense	$1,000,000
Minus: Total income tax expense	(340,000)
Net income	$ 660,000
U.S. taxes ($340,000/$1,000,000)	34.00%
Foreign taxes ($0/$1,000,000)	–0–%
Total effective tax rate	34.00%

Thus, the effective tax rate is the same in each year. ◀

EXAMPLE C:16-41 ▶ Now assume the group in Example C:16-40 invokes the indefinite reinvestment exception in the first year thinking it will leave the foreign earnings invested in Foreign indefinitely. Nevertheless, subsequent events lead the group to repatriate the earnings in the later year. In the first year, the group treats the $56,000 deferral as permanent. For book purposes, the consolidated financial statements include the foreign earnings, but the income tax expense does not reflect the permanent difference, so the group's U.S. income tax expense is $340,000, computed as follows:

U.S.-source income	$1,000,000
Foreign-source income	400,000
Net income before income tax expense	$1,400,000
Minus: Foreign source income treated as a permanent difference	(400,000)
Net income after permanent differences	$1,000,000
Times: U.S. tax rate	0.34
U.S. income tax expense	$ 340,000

Consequently, the group's total tax income tax expense is $420,000 ($340,000 U.S. + $80,000 foreign), and the group makes the following book journal entry:

Total income tax expense	420,000	
Total income taxes payable		420,000

In this case, the group reports the following book results:

Net income before income tax expense	$1,400,000
Minus: Total income tax expense	(420,000)
Net income	$ 980,000
U.S. taxes ($396,000/$1,400,000)	24.29%
Foreign taxes ($80,000/$1,400,000)	5.71%
Total effective tax rate	30.00%

This effective tax rate reconciles to the 34% statutory tax rate as follows:

Statutory tax rate	34.00%
Foreign tax treated as a permanent difference ($56,000/$1,400,000)	(4.00%)
Total effective tax rate	30.00%

In the subsequent year when Foreign remits the dividend, the group reverses the "permanent" difference, so the group's U.S. income tax expense is $476,000, computed as follows:

U.S.-source income	$1,000,000
Foreign-source income	–0–
Net income before income tax expense	$1,000,000
Plus: Reversed permanent difference	400,000
Net income after permanent differences	$1,400,000
Times: U.S. tax rate	0.34
U.S. income tax expense before FTC	$ 476,000
Minus: Deemed paid FTC	(80,000)
U.S. income tax expense	$ 396,000

The group's total tax income tax expense also is $396,000 because it incurred no foreign taxes in this year. Accordingly, the group makes the following book journal entry:

Total income tax expense	396,000	
Total income taxes payable		396,000

In this case, the group reports the following book results:

Net income before income tax expense	$1,000,000
Minus: Total income tax expense	(396,000)
Net income	$ 604,000

U.S. taxes ($396,000/$1,000,000)	39.60%
Foreign taxes ($0/$1,000,000)	–0–%
Total effective tax rate	39.60%

This effective tax rate reconciles to the 34% statutory tax rate as follows:

Statutory tax rate	34.00%
Reversal of foreign tax treated as a permanent difference ($56,000/$1,000,000)	5.60%
Total effective tax rate	39.60%

Thus, the effective tax rate varied from 30% in the first year to 39.6% in the subsequent year.

◄

One other point deserves mention. The foreign operations may occur in a high tax foreign country such that the deemed paid FTC completely eliminates the U.S. tax on the repatriated earnings. Consequently, the group would not reduce its effective tax rate by invoking the indefinite reinvestment exception. Therefore, corporations in this situation typically do not treat foreign earnings as indefinitely reinvested.

See Chapter C:3 for a general discussion of financial implications of federal income taxes.

PROBLEM MATERIALS

DISCUSSION QUESTIONS

C:16-1 What three factors have the drafters of U.S. tax laws considered in determining the scope of U.S. tax jurisdiction? Explain the importance of each factor.

C:16-2 Why is it important for a foreign national to ascertain whether he or she is a resident of the United States?

C:16-3 Explain the alternatives available to individual taxpayers in accounting for foreign taxes paid or accrued on their taxable income.

C:16-4 What types of foreign taxes are eligible to be credited?

C:16-5 In what circumstances might a taxpayer prefer to deduct, rather than credit, foreign taxes?

C:16-6 Why did Congress enact the foreign tax credit limitation rules?

C:16-7 Explain how the separate basket approach to calculating the foreign tax credit has created excess foreign tax credit issues for some U.S. taxpayers.

C:16-8 What advantages does a cash method taxpayer gain by electing to accrue foreign taxes for foreign tax credit purposes?

C:16-9 What requirements must be satisfied for a U.S. citizen or resident living abroad to qualify for the foreign-earned income exclusion?

C:16-10 Tony, a U.S. citizen, uses the calendar year as his tax year. Tony is transferred to Foreign Country C on June 15, 2009, and he immediately becomes a resident of that country. His employer transfers him back to the United States on March 10, 2011. Does Tony qualify for the foreign-earned income exclusion as a bona fide resident? If not, can he qualify in any other way?

C:16-11 Explain why a taxpayer might prefer to claim his or her foreign-earned income exclusion under the physical presence test instead of the bona fide residence test.

C:16-12 Why might a taxpayer choose to forego the foreign-earned income exclusion? If the taxpayer does so in the current tax year, what negative tax consequences might this choice have in future tax years?

C:16-13 Compare the U.S. tax treatment of a nonresident alien and a resident alien, both of whom earn U.S. trade or business and U.S. investment income.

C:16-14 Explain how a nonresident alien is taxed in the year of arrival and departure if he or she arrives in the United States on July 1, 2009, and immediately establishes U.S. residency, and departs from the United States on October 1, 2011, thereby terminating his or her U.S. residency.

C:16-15 How is a nonresident alien's U.S. source investment income taxed? What planning tool(s) is (are) available to reduce the tax rate below 30%? What mechanism is used to collect the tax?

C:16-16 Why is the effectively connected income concept important in taxing a nonresident alien's trade or business?

C:16-17 During the current year, Manuel, a nonresident alien, conducts a U.S. business. He earns $100,000 in sales commissions and $25,000 of interest income. What factor(s) do U.S. taxing authorities consider to determine whether the interest is investment income not subject to U.S. taxation or business income subject to U.S. taxation?

C:16-18 What are the advantages of a U.S. corporation's conducting a foreign business through a foreign branch? Through a foreign subsidiary?

C:16-19 What is the deferral privilege? What tax provisions result in the current U.S. taxation of part or all of a foreign corporation's earnings?

C:16-20 Why did Congress enact the deemed paid foreign tax credit provisions?

C:16-21 What are the "look through" rules? To whom do they apply and for what purposes? What taxable items are subject to these rules?

C:16-22 Kilarney, a foreign corporation, is incorporated in Country J and is 100%-owned by Maine, a domestic corporation. During the current year, Kilarney earns $500,000 from its Country J operations and $100,000 from its U.S. trade or business activities. None of the Country J income is Subpart F. None of Kilarney's after-tax profits are distributed as a dividend to Maine.
  a. Explain how Kilarney is taxed in the U.S. and whether any of Kilarney's income is taxed to Maine.
  b. How would your answer change if Kilarney earned none of its income from U.S. operations and if Kilarney paid a $50,000 dividend to Maine?

C:16-23 What is the branch profits tax? Explain Congressional intent behind its enactment.

C:16-24 What is a controlled foreign corporation (CFC)? How does the tax treatment of a U.S. stockholder's share of distributed and undistributed CFC profits differ from that of U.S. stockholders in a noncontrolled foreign corporation?

C:16-25 Explain the concept of Subpart F income. What major income categories are taxed under the Subpart F rules?

C:16-26 A primary purpose of Subpart F is to prevent the use of related entities in tax-haven countries to shelter foreign profits from U.S. taxation. Explain how application of the following income concepts accomplish this purpose:
  a. Foreign personal holding company income
  b. Foreign base company sales income
  c. Foreign base company services income

C:16-27 A U.S. manufacturer wants to conduct business through a foreign subsidiary organized in a low tax jurisdiction. How might it do so without being currently taxed on the subsidiary's foreign earnings?

C:16-28 How is the increase in CFC earnings invested in U.S. property measured? Explain why Congress decided to tax this amount to U.S. shareholders.

C:16-29 Explain the tax consequences to a U.S. shareholder of a CFC distribution of previously taxed Subpart F income.

C:16-30 How does the taxation of a gain recognized when a U.S. shareholder sells stock in a CFC differ from that of a gain recognized when a U.S. shareholder sells stock in a non-CFC?

C:16-31 Explain how the Sec. 482 transfer pricing and CFC rules work together to discourage a domestic corporation's use of a foreign sales subsidiary to avoid U.S. taxation.

C:16-32 What are the tax consequences of an inversion where former shareholders of the merged U.S. corporation own 85% of the voting stock in the new foreign corporation by reason of their U.S. stock ownership? Where they own 75% of this stock by reason of their U.S. stock ownership?

C:16-33 Adam, Britt, and Casey own equal shares of Yankee, Inc., a U.S. corporation. Yankee generates $10 million of taxable income from its U.S. business and $40 million of taxable income from a business conducted in the Republic of Boleckia. Yankee reincorporates as AlienCorp in Boleckia. In the reincorporation, Adam and Britt exchange their shares of Yankee voting stock for an equal number of shares of AlienCorp voting stock, and Yankee merges into AlienCorp. Subsequently, Adam and Britt conduct the U.S. and Boleckia businesses from an office in New York under the AlienCorp logo. Analyze the transaction under the anti-inversion rules, and indicate how it will be taxed.

C:16-34 King, a U.S. corporation, owns 25% of each of two foreign corporations. King's foreign business activities are taxed at foreign tax rates that are higher than those prevailing in the United States. Consequently, King finds itself in an excess foreign tax credit position. Corporation A is located in a country that has concluded a tax treaty with the United States. The treaty reduces from 15% to 5% the withholding on dividends paid to a U.S. corporation. Corporation B is located in a non-treaty country where the withholding rate is 15%. A and B both pay local income taxes at a 20% effective tax rate. If King wants to repatriate profits, which corporation(s) should pay the dividend to minimize the repatriation cost? Can King use such a payment to reduce its excess foreign tax credits associated with its other foreign income?

ISSUE IDENTIFICATION QUESTIONS

C:16-35 Plato Toys has created a new line of plastic toys that it wants to market in Canada. The corporation's headquarters are located in Detroit, Michigan. The company currently exports about $500,000 worth of toys to Canada each year. Most of the toys are sold in the province of Ontario through a Canadian distributor. Profits on current sales average 30% of the selling price to the Canadian distributor. Plato has never had a Canadian office or plant. Because of the corporation's desire to expand its operations, Plato is planning to open branch offices in other Canadian provinces that have large population centers. If a high volume of Canadian sales materializes, the company would like to open a manufacturing facility in Canada at a future date. Your accounting firm has performed audit and tax services for Plato for a number of years. One October morning, Plato's director of taxes, Kelly Hunt, comes to your office and asks that you prepare a presentation to corporate management about the U.S. tax consequences of the company's opening additional sales offices (or a Canadian sales subsidiary). If Canadian activities sufficiently expand, the firm might send U.S. personnel to work in Canada. Plato's CFO has had reservations about transferring employees to Canada and opening branch offices. She wants you to identify possible tax and business problems, in addition to explaining whether it is necessary to operate in Canada to obtain U.S. tax breaks. Prepare a list of tax and non-tax issues faced by Plato that you want to cover in your presentation.

C:16-36 In January of the current year, George Kratzer's U.S. firm assigned him to its Brussels office. During the year, George earned salary, a cost-of-living allowance, a housing allowance, a home leave allowance that permitted him to return home once each year, and an education allowance to pay for his daughter's U.S. schooling. George and his wife, Geneva, have rented an apartment in Brussels and paid Belgian income taxes. What U.S. tax issues should George consider when preparing his tax return?

C:16-37 During the current year, Bailey, a U.S. corporation, began operating overseas. It manufactures machine tools in the United States and sells them to Canadian customers through a branch office located in Toronto. Bailey purchased a 40% investment in a Brazilian corporation from which it later received a dividend. The company received royalties from an English firm that licences machine tool patents owned by Bailey. The English firm uses the patents to manufacture machine tools that the firm sells in England. What international tax issues regarding these activities should Bailey's director of taxes consider?

C:16-38 During the current year, Sanders, a U.S. corporation, organized a foreign subsidiary in Country Z. The subsidiary purchases components from Sanders, assembles them into finished products using Country Z labor, and sells the products to unrelated wholesalers in Countries X, Y, and Z through its own sales force. Assembly costs are 25% of the wholesale price. The foreign subsidiary has paid Sanders (its parent) no dividends this year. What tax issues regarding these activities should Sanders' director of taxes consider?

PROBLEMS

C:16-39 *Translation of Foreign Tax Payments.* Arnie, a U.S. citizen who uses the calendar year as his tax year and the cash method of accounting, operates a sole proprietorship in Country Z. In Year 1, he reports 500,000 dubles of pretax profits. On June 1 of Year 2, he pays Country Z income taxes of 150,000 dubles for calendar Year 1. Duble-U.S. dollar exchange rates on various dates in Year 1 and Year 2 are as follows:

December 31, Year 1	4.00 dubles = $1 (U.S.)
Year 1 average	3.75 dubles = $1 (U.S.)
June 1, Year 2	4.25 dubles = $1 (U.S.)

a. What is the U.S. dollar amount of Arnie's foreign tax credit? In what year can Arnie claim the credit?

b. How would your answer to Part a change if Arnie elected to accrue his foreign income taxes on December 31 of Year 1, and filed his Year 1 U.S. income tax return on April 15 of Year 2?

c. What adjustment to the credit claimed in Part b would Arnie have to make when he pays his Country Z taxes on June 1 of Year 2?

C:16-40 *Foreign Tax Credit Limitation.* During the current year, Jackson, a U.S. corporation and accrual method taxpayer, engages in both U.S. and foreign business activities. All its overseas activities are conducted by a branch in Country S. The results of Jackson's current year operations are as follows:

U.S. source taxable income	$2,000,000
Foreign source taxable income	1,500,000
Accrued Country S income taxes	600,000

a. What is the amount of Jackson's foreign tax credit (assuming the corporate tax rate is 34% and income from all foreign activities fall into a single basket)?

b. Are any foreign tax credit carrybacks or carryovers available? If so, in what years can they be used?

C:16-41 *Foreign Tax Credit Limitation.* Tucson, a U.S. corporation organized in Year 1, reports the following items for a three-year period.

	Year 1	Year 2	Year 3
Foreign tax accrual	$ 100,000	$ 120,000	$ 180,000
Foreign source taxable income	400,000	300,000	500,000
Worldwide taxable income	1,000,000	1,000,000	1,000,000

The foreign source and worldwide taxable income items are determined under U.S. law.

a. What is Tucson's foreign tax credit limitation for each of the three years (assume a 34% U.S. corporate tax rate and that income from all foreign activities fall into a single basket)?

b. How are Tucson's excess foreign tax credits (if any) treated? Do any carryovers remain after Year 3?

c. How would your answers to Parts a and b change if the IRS determines that $100,000 of expenses allocable to U.S.-source income should have been allocable to foreign-source income?

d. What measures should Tucson consider if it expects its current excess foreign tax credit position to persist in the long-run?

C:16-42 *Foreign-Earned Income Exclusion.* Julia, a U.S. citizen, leaves the United States at noon on August 1, 2009 and arrives in Country P at 8:00 a.m. the next day. She immediately establishes in Country P a permanent residence, which she maintains until her return to the United States at 3:00 p.m. on April 5, 2011. Her only trips outside Country P are related to temporary employment in Country B from November 1, 2009, through December 10, 2009, and a U.S. vacation beginning at 5:00 p.m. on June 1, 2010, and ending at 10:00 p.m. on June 30, 2010. Does Julia qualify for the Sec. 911 benefits? If so, what is the amount of her foreign earned income exclusion for the years 2009–2011?

C:16-43 *Foreign-Earned Income Exclusion.* Fred, a U.S. citizen, arrives in Country K on July 15, 2009 and proceeds to a construction site in its oil fields. Once there, he moves into employer-provided housing where he is required to reside. Except for brief periods of local travel and the months of July and August 2010 when he is on vacation in the United States, he remains at the site until his departure on December 1, 2011. He provides no services while in the United States. Fred earns $10,000 per month in salary and allowances while employed overseas. In addition, while in Country K, he receives meals and lodging valued at $1,750 per month. What is the amount of Fred's Sec. 911 exclusions for the years 2009–2011?

C:16-44 *Foreign-Earned Income Exclusion.* Dillon, a U.S. citizen, resides in Country K for all of 2011. Dillon is married, files a joint return and claims two personal exemptions. The following items pertain to his 2011 activities:

Salary and allowances (other than for housing)[a]	$175,000
Housing allowance	28,000
Employment-related expenses[b]	7,500
Housing costs	30,000
Other itemized deductions	4,000
Country K income taxes	12,000

[a]All of Dillon's salary and allowances are attributable to services performed in Country K.

[b]Dillon claims the employment-related expenses as itemized deductions.

What is Dillon's net U.S. tax liability for 2011 (assume that Dillon excludes his earned income and housing cost amount)?

C:16-45 *Tax Calculation for a Nonresident Alien.* Tien is a citizen of Country C, which does not have an income tax treaty with the United States. During the current year (2011), she is a nonresident alien for U.S. tax purposes and earns the following amounts:

Dividend received from a U.S. corporation	$ 2,500
Rentals from leasing a U.S. building	13,000
Interest received from a foreign corporation	5,000

Tien does not conduct a U.S. trade or business. Her interest and depreciation expenses from leasing the building under a net lease arrangement total $7,000.
a. Assuming the real estate income is investment related, what is Tien's U.S. tax liability? How is the tax collected?
b. How does your answer to Part a change if Tien makes an election to treat the real estate activity as a U.S. trade or business?

C:16-46 *Taxation of a Nonresident Alien.* Pierre, a single nonresident alien, conducts a U.S. trade or business for 80 days during the current year. Pierre reports the following income items from his U.S. activities. Indicate how each of these items will be taxed and how the tax will be collected.
a. $25,000 of dividends earned on a U.S. portfolio stock investment unrelated to Pierre's trade or business.
b. $75,000 of sales commissions Pierre earned as an employee of a foreign corporation. Pierre generated $50,000 from sales in the United States and $25,000 from sales outside the United States.
c. A $10,000 capital gain on the sale of stock in a U.S. corporation realized by Pierre while in the United States.
d. $3,000 of interest earned on a bank account in Pierre's home country and $1,800 of interest earned on a bank account located in Jacksonville, Florida.

C:16-47 *Deemed Paid Foreign Tax Credit.* Paper, a U.S. corporation, owns 40% of the stock in Sud, a foreign corporation. Sud reports post-1986 earnings and profits of $200,000 (before the payment of any current dividends) and post-1986 foreign income taxes of $50,000. In the current year, Sud pays a total of $90,000 in dividends to all its shareholders. It withholds from the gross dividends paid to nonresident shareholders a 15% Country T income tax.
a. What gross income amount does Paper report upon receiving the dividend?
b. To what extent is Paper's U.S. tax liability increased as a result of the dividend (assume a 34% U.S. corporate tax rate)?
c. How would your answers to Parts a and b change if the post-1986 foreign income taxes instead had been $80,000?

C:16-48 *Deemed Paid Foreign Tax Credit.* Duke, a U.S. corporation, owns all the stock in Taiwan, a foreign corporation. In the current year, Taiwan pays to Duke a $125,000 dividend from which $12,500 in foreign taxes are withheld. Taiwan's post-1986 operating results indicate $1 million of earnings and profits (before payment of the dividend) and $300,000 of foreign income taxes. Assume Duke has no other foreign source income and its U.S. taxable income (excluding the dividend) is $1 million.
a. What is the amount of Duke's deemed paid foreign tax credit?
b. To what extent is Duke's U.S. tax liability increased as a result of the dividend (assume a 34% U.S. corporate tax rate)?
c. How would your answers to Parts a and b change if the $125,000 dividend were instead paid to U.S. citizen Donna (instead of to Duke), whose marginal tax rate is 35%? Assume the foreign-source dividend does not qualify for the 15% reduced tax rate.

C:16-49 *Translation of a Dividend.* Dayton, a U.S. corporation, owns all the stock in Fiero, a foreign corporation organized in the current year. During the year, Fiero earns 400,000 pirogs of pretax profits and accrues 100,000 pirogs of Country Z income taxes. On August 25 of the current year, Fiero pays to Dayton a 150,000 pirog dividend on which 7,500 pirogs in Country Z taxes are withheld. On March 1 of the following year, Fiero pays 100% of its Country Z income taxes for the current year. Assume Dayton has no other foreign source income, and its U.S. taxable income (excluding the dividend) is $1 million. The pirog-U.S. dollar exchange rate on various dates are as follows:

January 1 of the current year	9.0 pirogs = $1 (U.S.)
August 25 of the current year	10.0 pirogs = $1 (U.S.)
Current year average	9.5 pirogs = $1 (U.S.)
March 1 of the following year	11.0 pirogs = $1 (U.S.)

a. For U.S. tax reporting purposes, what are Dayton's dividend and deemed paid foreign tax credit amounts in U.S. dollars?

b. What is Dayton's net U.S. tax liability as a result of the dividend?

C:16-50 *Worldwide Tax Rates.* Young Corporation conducts a business in both the United States and a foreign country. In each of the following scenarios, what is Young's worldwide (combined U.S. and foreign) tax rate relative to the branch income it earns in the foreign country? Assume that Young wants to claim the maximum foreign tax credit possible.

Scenario	U.S. Tax Rate	Foreign Tax Rate
1	34%	0%
2	34%	15%
3	34%	34%
4	34%	40%

What incentive exists for the foreign country to increase its tax rates if the United States taxes foreign income when earned? What incentive exists for a foreign country to lower its tax rates if a foreign subsidiary earns income in one year but is taxed in a later year when the income is repatriated to the United States?

C:16-51 *Section 902 Dividend Look Through Rules.* Hamilton, a U.S. corporation, reports the following results from its current year activities:

U.S.-source taxable income	$1,000,000
Foreign-source taxable income from manufacturing branch in Country M	1,000,000
Foreign taxes paid on branch income	390,000
Gross U.S. income tax liability	799,000

Hamilton owns 20% of the stock in Beauvais, a foreign corporation. Beauvais pays a $350,000 dividend to Hamilton on April 20 of the current year. Beauvais' pretax profits from post-1986 tax years are $6 million, and its Country X taxes from post-1986 tax years are $1.2 million. Beauvais' E&P under U.S. rules is $4 million, $3.6 million of which was derived from foreign manufacturing and $400,000 of which was earned on foreign securities. All of the foregoing figures were recorded before payment of the dividend.

a. For foreign tax credit purposes, into which of Hamilton's limitation baskets should the dividend from Beauvais be placed and in what amounts?

b. Calculate Hamilton's current year foreign tax credit.

c. How should any excess credits be treated?

C:16-52 *Definition of a CFC.* In each of the following scenarios, determine whether a foreign corporation with a single class of stock outstanding, is a controlled foreign corporation.

a. The foreign corporation's stock is owned equally by Alpha, a U.S. corporation, and Bart, a U.S. citizen, who owns no Alpha stock.

b. Assume the same facts as in Part a except Bart is a nonresident alien.

c. The foreign corporation's stock is owned 7% by Art, 49% by Phong, 29% by Colleen, and 15% by Danielle. Art, Colleen, and Danielle are U.S. citizens, and Phong is a nonresident alien. All four individuals are unrelated.

d. Assume the same facts as in Part c except Danielle is Art's daughter.

C:16-53 *Definition of Foreign Base Company Income.* Manila Corporation is organized in Country J. All of Manila's stock is owned by Simpson, a U.S. corporation. Indicate which of the following transactions generate Subpart F income.

a. Manila purchases a product from Simpson and sells it to unrelated parties in Countries J and X.

b. Manila receives a dividend from Manila-Sub, a foreign corporation organized and operating exclusively in Country J. All of Manila-Sub's stock has been owned by Manila since its incorporation.

c. Manila purchases raw materials locally, manufactures products in Country J, and sells the products to an unrelated purchaser for use in Country Z.

d. Manila services machinery manufactured by an unrelated Country J corporation. Revenues from servicing this machinery outside of Country J constitute 80% of Manila's gross income.

e. Manila purchases a product from a related U.S. corporation and sells the product to unrelated persons in Country Z.

C:16-54 *Definition of Foreign Base Company Income.* Apache, a U.S. corporation, owns 80% of the stock in Burrito, incorporated in Country Y. Burrito reports the following results for the current year:

	Gross Income	Deductions
Foreign base company sales income	$300,000	$120,000
Foreign base company services income	150,000	90,000
Dividend from Kane, a 70%-owned Country Y corporation	70,000	–0–
Rental income earned in Country Y	280,000	220,000

Kane conducts substantially all its business in Country Y.
a. What amount of income must Apache recognize as a result of Burrito's activities?
b. How would your answer to Part a change if Kane were instead a 70%-owned Country M corporation?
c. How would your answer to Part b change if foreign base company sales income before deductions were instead $500,000?

C:16-55 *Transfer Pricing Rules.* Arrow, a U.S. corporation, annually sells one million starter motors to Bentley, a wholly owned foreign subsidiary organized in Country K. Bentley sells the starters as replacement parts through auto dealers in Country K. The statutory Country K tax rate is 20%.
a. What is the value of Arrow's annual U.S. tax deferral if the starters cost Arrow $30 to produce, are sold to Bentley for $50, and are re-sold to the auto dealers for $70? Assume Bentley's operating expenses are $4 million.
b. What additional benefit would accrue to Arrow annually if it reduced the sale price of each starter from $50 to $30? What mechanisms are likely to be used by U.S. tax authorities to address this situation?
c. How would your answer to Part a change if Bentley sold one-half of the starters to auto dealers in Country M under the same terms as it sold them to auto dealers in Country K?

C:16-56 *Sale of CFC Stock.* On April 1, 2009, Irvan, a U.S. corporation, acquired for $300,000 all the stock in DeLeon, a foreign corporation. At the close of business on September 30, 2011, Irvan sells the DeLeon stock for $825,000. Irvan reports $25,000 of Subpart F income as a result of DeLeon's 2009–2011 activities. DeLeon reports E&P balances for the period as follows:

Year	E&P
2009	$120,000
2010	110,000
2011	144,000

a. What are the amount and character of Irvan's gain on the sale of the DeLeon stock?
b. Can Irvan use any of DeLeon foreign taxes to reduce its U.S. tax liability on the stock gain?

COMPREHENSIVE PROBLEM

C:16-57 Allen Blay owns 100% of the stock in AB Corporation, organized ten years ago under the laws of California. AB operates a foreign branch in Country A. In the current year, AB reports $500,000 of taxable income from U.S. activities. The branch reports a 400,000 pirog loss, which translates into a $60,000 (U.S.) loss. Neither the branch nor the U.S. corporation paid Country A income taxes in the current year.

AB owns 50% of FC1, incorporated in Country B. Bob Haynes, a resident of Country B, owns the remaining FC1 stock. In the current year, FC1 generated 200,000 kira of Country B taxable income. The Country B corporate income tax rate is 25%. On December 31, FC1 remitted 50,000 kira of current year profits to AB. The kira-U.S. dollar exchange rate on December 31 was 1.25 kira = $1.00 (U.S.). Amounts repatriated to the United States are subject to a 15% Country B withholding tax. The United States-Country B tax treaty reduces this rate to 10%.

AB owns 100% of the stock in FC2, incorporated in Country C. FC2 purchases electronic testing equipment from AB and employs a local sales force to distribute the equipment throughout the region. Forty percent of the FC2 sales are made to customers in

Country C. The remaining sales are made to customers in Country D. Total pre-tax profits from FC2's sales were 275,000 tesos in the current year. FC2 remitted none of its profits to AB. FC2 earned an additional 200,000 tesos of pre-tax profits from manufacturing electronic testing equipment from parts produced by Country C companies and from selling this equipment in Countries C and D. FC2 paid 60,000 tesos of Country C income taxes on its current year activities. The teso-U.S. dollar exchange rate on December 31 was 1.5 tesos = $1.00 (U.S.). FC2 remitted no profits to the United States. The profit margins on sales of electronic testing equipment in the Country C and D markets are substantially higher than those in the United States.

In June of the current year, AB assigned Brad Gould to work for FC2. Brad relocated from Sunnyvale, California, to Country C under a three-year employment contract.

Required: Explain the U.S. tax consequences of each of AB's overseas activities.

TAX STRATEGY PROBLEM

C:16-58 Miami-based Florida Corporation manufactures electronic games that it has sold overseas for the past two years. Its foreign operations are conducted primarily through two distributors in South America who divide up the South American market and handle sales activities within their assigned areas. Florida has been shipping Spanish and Portuguese versions of its U.S. video games directly from Miami to its two South American distributors and billing the distributors for the shipments. All South American advertising, distribution, and billing activities are the responsibility of the two distributors.

In talking with Florida's chief financial officer (CFO), you learn that the company has been paying U.S. corporate income taxes at a 34% rate on its $2 million of profits generated from sales to the two distributors. The company has paid no foreign taxes on this profit because the sales to the two South American distributors have occurred in the United States. The CFO believes that the company can avoid foreign taxation because it has not set up a permanent establishment in any foreign country. The CFO indicates that she would like to reduce or defer the U.S. tax burden on part or all of these profits by setting up a South American subsidiary to distribute the games throughout South America. The subsidiary would be located in a South American country where the income tax rate is substantially less than the 34% U.S. corporate tax rate. She has found two countries that offer favorable business climates in which to establish an overseas presence. The maximum income tax rate in each country is 15%.

The CFO believes she can shift all or a large portion of the foreign sales profits to the country in which the subsidiary is established. By shifting part or all of the profits on the overseas sales to this country, the CFO hopes to defer the 34% U.S. corporate income tax until the profits are repatriated to the United States. Florida also hopes to obtain a tax holiday that would permit deferral or exemption of foreign income taxes as an incentive for investing in the foreign country. Ideally, the effective foreign tax rate would be 15% or lower.

Required: Florida's CFO would like you to advise her on alternative ways to conduct the foreign sales so as to reduce and/or defer the the company's worldwide tax liability. Compare the after-tax earnings that accrue to a foreign branch and a foreign subsidiary over a five-year period. What alternative business forms can Florida use to conduct its overseas activities? For each alternative, identify the U.S. tax treatment, determine the available tax savings, and indicate whether such savings reflect a tax deferral or a permanent exclusion from U.S. income taxation. In addition, identify whether Florida must establish a foreign office or manufacturing facility in a foreign country to obtain tax reductions or deferrals.

TAX FORM/RETURN PREPARATION PROBLEMS

C:16-59 Stephen R. and Rachel K. Bates, both U.S. citizens, resided in Country K for the entire current year except when Stephen was temporarily assigned to his employer's home office in the United States. They file a joint return and use the calendar year as their tax year. Their taxpayer identification number is 123-45-6789. The Bateses report the following current-year income and expense items:

Salary and allowances:	United States	$ 20,000
	Country K	150,000
Dividends:	From U.S. corporation	2,000
	From Country K corporation	15,000

Unreimbursed foreign business expenses (directly allocable to Country K earned income and deductible as a miscellaneous itemized deduction)	5,000
Charitable contributions paid to U.S. charities (not directly allocable to any income item)	8,000
Country K income taxes paid on April 1 of current year (in dollars)	12,500
Personal and dependency exemptions	2

Last year, the Bateses elected to accrue their foreign income taxes for foreign tax credit purposes. No foreign tax credit carryovers to the current year are available. Stephen Bates estimates the family will owe 75,000 tesos in Country K income taxes for this year on the Country K salary and dividends. The average annual exchange rate for the current year is 4 tesos to $1 (U.S.). The teso-U.S. dollar exchange rate did not change between year-end and the date the Bates paid their Country K taxes. No Country K taxes were withheld on the foreign corporation dividend.

Complete the two Form 1116s the Bateses must file with their income tax return to claim a credit for the foreign taxes paid on the salary and dividends. Use 2010 tax forms and ignore the implications of the Sec. 911 earned income exclusion, itemized deduction and personal exemption phase-outs, and alternative minimum tax provisions.

C:16-60 John Lawrence Bailey (Social Security number 234-56-7890) is employed in Country T by American Conglomerate Corporation. Bailey has resided with his wife and three children in Country T for seven years. He made one five-day business trip back to the United States in the current year, and $2,000 of his salary (but none of the allowances) is allocable to the U.S. business trip. Bailey reports the following tax-related information for the current year:

Income:	
Base salary	$100,000
Overseas premium in addition to base salary	15,000
Cost-of-living allowance	37,500
Housing allowance	30,000
Education allowance	16,000
Home leave travel allowance	11,000
Income tax reimbursement from employer for preceding tax year	25,000
Expenditures:	
Tuition at U.S. school	12,000
Housing expenses (rental of home and related expenses)	32,500
Itemized deductions (including $4,000 of unreimbursed employee expenses)	10,000
Foreign income taxes	12,000

Complete a 2010 Form 2555 for the Baileys' current tax year. Assume Mr. Bailey established foreign residency in 2006, and all prior tax returns were filed with a Form 2555 claiming that Mr. Bailey was a bona fide foreign resident.

CASE STUDY PROBLEMS

C:16-61 You have performed tax services for Mark Pruett, a U.S. citizen who is being transferred abroad by his employer. Mark's 2011 salary and allowances in Country M will be $210,000, which is substantially above his salary for last year. The salary differential is due to the higher cost of living in Country M and Mark's added responsibilities. Of the allowances, $30,000 is for housing although Mark's 2011 housing costs are expected to be $40,000. The Country M income tax rate is 40%. Mark's employer conducts business at a second location in Country T, where Mark probably will be transferred in three or four years. The Country T income tax rate is 20%.

The transfer date is February 1. Mark's wife and three-year-old daughter will accompany him. Mark expects to return to the United States for one week of training each year starting in September 2011. Mark takes four weeks of vacation each year. Because Mark still has family in the United States, he may spend substantial vacation time in the United States.

Required: Your tax manager has asked you to draft for her review a memorandum explaining the tax consequences of the relocation, whether Mark is entitled to the foreign earned income exclusion, and what records Mark must maintain to file his tax return for the year of transfer.

C:16-62 Ralph Sampson was hired last year by a small international trading company. You have prepared Ralph's tax returns for a number of years while he worked in the U.S. offices of a large international bank. You continue to perform tax services for Ralph while he is overseas to manage the trading company's office in Country T (a nontreaty country). Ralph has been assigned abroad since November 1 of Year 1, and has continuously resided in a company-provided apartment located in Country T's capital. His wife and child have maintained their old residence in the United States to enable Mrs. Sampson to continue her career as a university professor and their son to finish high school. During Year 1, Ralph was in Country T and other foreign countries for all of November and December. During Year 2, Ralph was in the United States for 93 days (spread out evenly throughout the four quarters of that year) and in Country T and other foreign countries for the remainder of the year. Ralph wants you to file an amended Year 1 tax return and an initial Year 2 tax return claiming on each return the maximum possible foreign earned income exclusion. (The Year 1 return originally was filed without claiming the foreign earned income exclusion because Ralph had not yet qualified for the exclusion when the return was due.) Ralph knows that he does not meet the physical presence test, but he has assured you that he meets the bona fide residence test. However, because of his heavy Year 2 travel schedule, he has not yet been able to document that he is a Country T resident.

In June of Year 3, the Sampsons' son will graduate from high school. Mrs. Sampson plans to join her son overseas and obtain a teaching position in an American school for U.S. expatriates. The Sampsons' son will spend 2½ months of summer with his parents overseas but will return to the United States to attend the University of Tennessee. He will join his parents for an additional four weeks in December and January during the university's holiday break.

Required: Should you file the Sampson's amended Year 1 tax return and new Year 2 income tax return claiming the maximum foreign-earned income exclusion for which Ralph has asked? What information should you ask Ralph to provide before you prepare his return? What ethical issues are raised by your filing the return based on Ralph's promise to obtain the requisite information? When will Mrs. Sampson first be eligible for the foreign earned income exclusion? Under which of the two tests will she likely qualify after she begins her Country T teaching job in June of Year 3?

TAX RESEARCH PROBLEMS

C:16-63 Spike "Spitball" Weaver, a hard-throwing pitcher, was approaching the end of his major league baseball career. After becoming a free agent at the end of the Year 1 baseball season, he signed a lucrative three-year contract (which specified a substantial signing bonus) to play for the Tokyo Bombers in the fledgling World Baseball League starting in Year 2. The team's management paid 50% of the bonus in Year 1 and will pay the remaining 50% during Years 2 through 4. This league includes 12 teams, only four of which are located in the United States. Although Spike's salary is paid over a 12-month period, he resides in Japan only for the seven-month regular season, the preseason training period, and the post-season playoffs (if his team makes the playoffs). He spends the remainder of his time at his home in Fitzgerald, Georgia. The tax manager for whom you regularly work has asked you to prepare a memorandum to the file indicating what factors should be considered in allocating Spike's bonus and salary according to work performed at the U.S. and non-U.S. locations.

She suggests that at a minimum you consider

- Reg. Sec. 1.861-4
- Rev. Rul. 76-66, 1976-1 C.B. 189
- Rev. Rul. 87-38, 1987-1 C.B. 176
- *Peter Stemkowski v. CIR*, 50 AFTR 2d 82-5739, 82-2 USTC ¶9589 (2nd Cir., 1982)

C:16-64 Determine whether each of the taxes listed below may be credited against a U.S. income tax liability.
a. Saudi Arabian tax on companies producing petroleum
b. French Company Income Tax
c. Ontario (Canada) Corporations Tax
d. Japan Corporation Tax
  A partial list of research sources includes:
- Research Institute of America (RIA), *United States Tax Reporter*, ¶9015.03

- Commerce Clearing House (CCH), *Standard Federal Tax Reporter,* ¶27,826.318
- Bureau of National Affairs (BNA), *Tax Management Portfolios,* individual country portfolios on Saudi Arabia, France, Canada, and Japan

For additional authority, the researcher might consult the tax treaties that the United States has concluded with each of the four countries.

TAX & FINANCIAL ACCOUNTING

C:16-65 MedTec was incorporated five years ago under the laws of Georgia. It manufactures products for doctors and hospitals in the United States. Because of lower labor costs outside the United States, MedTec establishes in Country X a foreign subsidiary that will manufacture some of its products for shipment back to the United States as well as to other foreign countries. Country X tax rates are lower than U.S. tax rates. In addition, Country X has provided special tax incentives that lead you to believe the subsidiary will pay local income taxes at a 10% rate for the first five years, and at a 25% rate for subsequent years. Only a small portion, if any, of the foreign earnings will be taxed to MedTec under Subpart F. According to financial projections, the foreign subsidiary will generate $500,000 of pre-tax profits each year. Because of MedTec's need for capital to expand its foreign operations, none of the foreign profits will be repatriated to the United States in the first ten years of operations.

Prepare a memorandum for your boss that outlines the proper financial accounting treatment of MedTec's U.S. income taxes with respect to its investment in the Country X subsidiary.

A partial list of research sources is:

- Accounting Standards Codification (ASC) 740 (Income Taxes) formerly SFAS No. 109
- IRC Sec. 951

C:16-66 AmeriCorp, a U.S. corporation based in Houston, manufactures telecommunications equipment. It sells the equipment to retailers throughout the world. To promote its Latin American sales, AmeriCorp conducts its business through three entities: TelMexico, a *sociedad anonima* organized under Mexican law and 100% owned by AmeriCorp; TelBrazilco, a *sociedade limitada*, organized under Brazilian law and 51% owned by AmeriCorp; and TelCaymanco, an ordinary nonresident company organized under Cayman Islands law and 100% owned by TelBrazilco. Foreign investors own the remaining 49% of TelBrazilco voting stock.

TelMexico routinely purchases telecommunications equipment from AmeriCorp and sells the equipment to independent retailers throughout Central America. This entity derives 20% of its revenues from equipment sales outside of Mexico. TelBrazilco manufactures telecommunications equipment in Brazil and sells the equipment to independent retailers throughout South America. This entity derives 65% of its income from equipment sales outside of Brazil. TelCaymanco purchases telecommunications equipment exclusively from TelBrazilco and sells the equipment to independent retailers throughout Europe. This entity derives 99% of its revenues from equipment sales outside the Cayman Islands. Periodically, TelMexico pays dividends to AmeriCorp, and TelCaymanco pays dividends to TelBrazilco.

AmeriCorp's chief financial officer has approached you with the following questions:

1. What are the tax implications of this organizational structure? Specifically, are the entities controlled foreign corporations, and do their activities generate Subpart F income?
2. Can AmeriCorp use the check-the-box regulations to change the tax treatment of any foreign entity?
3. What tax consequences would ensue if AmeriCorp elected to have,
   a. TelCaymanco and TelBrazilco taxed as corporations (i.e., associations)?
   b. TelBrazilco taxed as a corporation (TelCaymanco would be disregarded as a taxable entity)?

Write a memorandum that addresses these questions. At a minimum, consult the following authorities:

- Reg. Secs. 301.7701-2 and 301.7701-3

A P P E N D I X A

TAX RESEARCH WORKING PAPER FILE

INDEX TO TAX RESEARCH FILE*

*Most accounting firms maintain a **client file** for each of their clients. Typically, this file contains copies of client letters, memoranda-to-the-file, relevant primary and secondary authorities, and billing information. In our case, the client file for Mercy Hospital would include copies of the following: (1) the December 12 letter to Elizabeth Feghali, (2) the December 9 memorandum-to-the-file, (3) Sec. 119, (4) Reg. Sec. 1.119-1, (5) the *Kowalski* opinion, (6) the *Standard Federal Tax Reporter* annotation, and (7) pertinent billing information.

TAX RESEARCH FILE

As mentioned in Chapter C:1 the tax research process entails six steps.

1. Determine the facts
2. Identify the issues
3. Locate applicable authorities
4. Evaluate these authorities
5. Analyze the facts in terms of applicable authorities
6. Communicate conclusions and recommendations to others.

Let us walk through each of these steps.

Determine the Facts Assume that we have determined the facts to be as follows:

> *Mercy Hospital maintains a cafeteria on its premises. In addition, it rents space to MacDougal's, a privately owned sandwich shop. The cafeteria closes at 8:00 p.m. MacDougal's is open 24 hours. Mercy provides meal vouchers to each of its 240 medical employees to enable them to remain on call in case of emergency. The vouchers are redeemable either at the cafeteria or at MacDougal's. Although the employees are not required to remain on or near the premises during meal hours, they generally do. Elizabeth Fegali, Mercy's Chief Administrator, has approached you with the following question: Is the value of a meal voucher includible in the employees' gross income?*

At this juncture, be sure you understand the facts before proceeding further. Remember, researching the wrong facts could produce the wrong results.

Identify the Issues Identifying the issues presupposes a minimum level of proficiency in tax accounting. This proficiency will come with time, effort, and perseverance. The central issue raised by the facts is the taxability of the meal vouchers. A resolution of this issue will hinge on the resolution of other issues raised in the course of the research.

Locate Applicable Authorities For some students, this step is the most difficult in the research process. It raises the perplexing question, "Where do I begin to look?" The answer depends on the tax resources at one's disposal, as well as one's research preferences. Four rules of thumb apply:

1. *Adopt an approach with which you are comfortable, and that you are confident will produce reliable results.*
2. *Always consult the IRC and other primary authorities.*
3. *Be as thorough as possible, taking into consideration time and billing constraints.*
4. *Make sure that the authorities you consult are current.*

One approach is to conduct a topical search. Begin by consulting the index to the Internal Revenue Code (IRC). Then read the relevant IRC section(s). If the language of the IRC is vague or ambiguous, turn to the Treasury Regulations. Read the relevant regulation section that elaborates or expounds on the IRC provision. If the language of the regulation is confusing or unclear, go to a commercial tax service. Read the relevant tax service paragraphs that explain or analyze the statutory and regulatory provisions. For references to other authorities, browse through the footnotes and annotations of the service. Then, consult these authorities directly. Finally, check the currency of the authorities consulted, with the aid of a citator or status (finding) list.

If a pertinent court decision or IRS ruling has been called to your attention, consult this authority directly. Alternatively, browse through the status (finding) list of a tax service for references to tax service paragraphs that discuss this authority. Better still, consult a citator or status list for references to court opinions or rulings that cite the authority. If you subscribe to a computerized tax service, conduct a keyword, citation, contents, or topical search. (For a discussion of these types of searches, see the computerized research supplement available for download at *www.prenhall.com/phtax*.) Then, hyperlink to the authorities cited within the text of the documents retrieved. So numerous are the approaches to tax research that one is virtually free to pick and choose. All that is required of the researcher is a basic level of skill and some imagination.

Let us adopt a topical approach to the issue of the meal vouchers. If we consult an index to the IRC, we are likely to find the heading "Meals and Lodging." Below this heading are likely to be several subheadings, some pertaining to deductions, others to exclusions. Because the voucher issue pertains to an exclusion, let us browse through these subheadings. In so doing, we will notice that most of these subheadings refer to Sec. 119. If we look up this IRC section, we will see the following passage:

Sec. 119. Meals or lodging furnished for the convenience of the employer.

(a) **Meals and lodging furnished to employee, his spouse, and his dependents, pursuant to employment.**
There shall be excluded from gross income of an employee the value of any meals or lodging furnished to him . . . by, or on behalf of his employer for the convenience of the employer, but only if—

   (1) in the case of meals, the meals are furnished on the business premises of the employer . . .

(b) **Special rules.** For purposes of subsection (a)—
   (4) **Meals furnished to employees on business premises where meals of most employees are otherwise excludable.** All meals furnished on the business premises of an employer to such employer's employees shall be treated as furnished for the convenience of the employer if . . . more than half of the employees to whom such meals are furnished on such premises are furnished such meals for the convenience of the employer.

Section 119 appears to be applicable. It deals with meals furnished to an employee on the business premises of the employer. Our case deals with meal vouchers furnished to employees for redemption at employer-maintained and employer-rented-out facilities. But here, additional issues arise. For purposes of Sec. 119, are meal vouchers the same as "meals"? (Do not assume they are.) Are employer-maintained and employer-rented-out facilities the same as "the business premises of the employer"? (Again, do not assume they are.) And what does the IRC mean by "for the convenience of the employer"? Because the IRC offers no guidance in this respect, let us turn to the Treasury Regulations.

The applicable regulation is Reg. Sec. 1.119-1. How do we know this? Because Treasury Regulation section numbers track the IRC section numbers. Regulation Sec. 1.119-1 is the only regulation under Sec. 119. If we browse through this regulation, we will find the following provision:

(a) **Meals . . .**
   (2) **Meals furnished without a charge**
      (i) Meals furnished by an employer without charge to the employee will be regarded as furnished for the convenience of the employer if such meals are furnished for a substantial noncompensatory business reason of the employer . . .
      (ii) (a) Meals will be regarded as furnished for a substantial noncompensatory business reason of the employer when the meals are furnished to the employee during his working hours to have the employee available for emergency call during his meal period . . .
(c) **Business premises of the employer.**
   (1) **In general.** For purposes of this section, the term "business premises of the employer" generally means the place of employment of the employee . . .

Based on a reading of this provision, we might conclude that the hospital meals are furnished "for the convenience of the employer." Why? Because they are furnished for a "substantial noncompensatory business reason of the employer," namely, to have the employees available for emergency call during their meal periods. They also are furnished during the employees' working hours. Moreover, under Sec. 119(b)(4), if more than half the employees satisfy the "for the convenience of the employer" test, all employees will be regarded as satisfying the test. But are the meals furnished on "the business premises of the employer"? Under the regulation, the answer would depend. If the meals are furnished in the hospital cafeteria, they probably are furnished on "the business premises of the employer." The hospital is the place of employment of the medical employees. The cafeteria is part of the hospital. On the other hand, if the meals are furnished at MacDougal's, they probably are not furnished on "the business premises of the employer." MacDougal's is not the place of employment of the medical employees. Nor is it a part of the hospital. Thus, Reg. Sec. 1.119-1 is enlightening with respect to two statutory terms: "for the convenience of the employer" and "the business premises of the employer." However, it is obscure with respect to the third term, "meals." Because of this obscurity, let us turn to a tax service.

Although the index to CCH's *Standard Federal Tax Reporter* does not list "meal vouchers," it does list "cash allowances in lieu of meals" as a subtopic under Meals and Lodging. Are meal vouchers the same as cash meal allowances?—perhaps so; let us see. Next to the heading "cash allowances in lieu of meals" is a reference to CCH ¶7222.59. If we look up this reference, we will find the following annotation:

¶7222.59 **Meal allowances.**—Cash meal allowances received by an employee (state trooper) from his employer were not excludible from income. *R.J. Kowalski*, SCt, 77-2 USTC ¶9748, 434 US 77.[1]

Here we discover that, in the *Kowalski* case, the U.S. Supreme Court decided that cash meal allowances received by an employee were not excludible from the employee's income. Is the *Kowalski* case similar to our case? It might be. Let us find out. If we turn to paragraph 9748 of the second 1977 volume of *United States Tax Cases*, we will find the text of the *Kowalski* opinion. A synopsis of this opinion is present below.

In the mid-1970s, the State of New Jersey provided cash meal allowances to its state troopers. The state did not require the troopers to use the allowances exclusively for meals. Nor did it require them to consume their meals on its business premises. One trooper, Robert J. Kowalski, failed to report a portion of his allowance on his tax return. The IRS assessed a deficiency, and Kowalski took the IRS to court. In court, Kowalski argued that the meal allowances were excludible, because they were furnished "for the convenience of the employer." The IRS contended that the allowances were taxable because they amounted to compensation. The Supreme Court took up the case and sided with the IRS. The Court held that the Sec. 119 income exclusion does not apply to cash payments; it applies only to meals in kind.[2]

For the sake of illustration, let us assume that Sec. 119, Reg. Sec. 1.119-1, and the *Kowalski* case are the *only* authorities "on point." How should we evaluate them?

Evaluate Authorities Section 119 is the key authority applicable to our case. It supplies the operative rule for resolving the issue of the meal vouchers. It is vague, however, with respect to three terms: "meals," "business premises of the employer," and "for the convenience of the employer." The principal judicial authority is the *Kowalski* case. It provides an official interpretation of the term "meals." Because the U.S. Supreme Court decided *Kowalski*, the case should be assigned considerable weight. The relevant administrative authority is Reg. Sec. 1.119-1. It expounds on the terms "business premises of the employer" and "for the convenience of the employer." Because neither the IRC nor *Kowalski* explain these terms, Reg. Sec. 1.119-1 should be accorded great weight. But what if *Kowalski* had conflicted with Reg. Sec. 1.119-1? Which should be considered more authoritative? As a general rule, high court decisions "trump" the Treasury Regulations (and all IRS pronouncements for that matter). The more recent the decision, the greater its precedential weight. Had there been no Supreme Court decision and a division of appellate authority, equal weight should have been assigned to each of the appellate court decisions.

Analyze the Facts in Terms of Applicable Authorities Analyzing the facts in terms of applicable authorities involves applying the abstraction of the law to the concreteness of the facts. It entails expressing the generalities of the law in terms of the specifics of the facts. In this process, every legal condition must be satisfied for the result implied by the

---

[1] The researcher also might read the main *Standard Federal Tax Reporter* paragraph that discusses meals and lodging furnished by the employer (CCH ¶7222.01). Within this paragraph are likely to be references to other primary authorities.

[2] At this juncture, the researcher should consult a citator to determine whether *Kowalski* is still "good law," and to locate other authorities that cite *Kowalski*.

general rule to ensue. Thus, in our case, the conditions of furnishing "meals," "on the business premises of the employer," and "for the convenience of the employer" must be satisfied for the value of the "meals" to be excluded from the employee's income.

When analyzing the facts in terms of case law, the researcher should always draw an *analogy* between case facts and client facts. Likewise, he or she should always draw a *distinction* between case facts and client facts. Remember, under the rule of precedent, a court deciding the client's case will be bound by the precedent of cases involving *similar* facts and issues. By the same token, it will *not* be bound by the precedent of cases involving *dissimilar* facts and issues.

The most useful vehicle for analyzing client facts is the memorandum-to-the-file (see page A-6). The purpose of this document is threefold: first, it assists the researcher in recollecting transactions long transpired; second, it apprises colleagues and supervisors of the nature of one's research; third, it provides "substantial authority" for the tax treatment of a particular item. Let us analyze the facts of our case by way of a memorandum-to-the-file. Notice the format of this document; it generally tracks the steps in the research process itself.

Communicate Conclusions and Recommendations to Others For three practical reasons, research results always should be communicated to the client *in writing*. First, a written communication can be made after extensive revisions. An oral communication cannot. Second, in a written communication, the researcher can delve into the intricacies of tax law. Often, in an oral communication, he or she cannot. Third, a written communication reinforces an oral understanding. Alternatively, it brings to light an oral misunderstanding.

The written communication usually takes the form of a client letter (see page A-7). The purpose of this letter is two-fold: first, it apprises the client of the results of one's research and, second, it recommends to the client a course of action based on these results. A sample client letter is presented below. Notice the organization of this document; it is similar to that of the memorandum-to-the-file.

Memorandum-to-the-File

Date: December 9, 20X1
From: Rosina Havacek
Re: The taxability of meal vouchers furnished by Mercy Hospital to its medical staff.

Facts
[*State only the facts that are relevant to the Issue(s) and necessary for the Analysis.*] Our client, Mercy Hospital ("Mercy"), provides meal vouchers to its medical employees to enable them to remain on emergency call. The vouchers are redeemable at Mercy's onsite cafeteria and at MacDougal's, a privately owned sandwich shop. MacDougal's rents business space from the hospital. Although Mercy does not require its employees to remain on or near its premises during their meal hours, the employees generally do. Elizabeth Fegali, Mercy's Chief Administrator, has asked us to research whether the value of the meal vouchers is taxable to the employees.

Issues
[*Identify the issue(s) raised by the facts. Be specific.*] The taxability of the meal vouchers depends on three issues: first, whether the meals are furnished "for the convenience of the employer"; second, whether they are furnished "on the business premises of the employer"; and third, whether the vouchers are equivalent to cash.

Applicable Law
[*Discuss those legal principles that both strengthen and weaken the client's case. Because the primary authority for tax law is the IRC, begin with the IRC.*] Section 119 provides that the value of meals is excludible from an employee's income if the meals are furnished for the convenience of, and on the business premises of the employer. [*Discuss how administrative and/or judicial authorities expound on statutory terms.*] Under Reg. Sec. 1.119-1, a meal is furnished "for the convenience of the employer" if it is furnished for a "substantial noncompensatory business reason." A "substantial noncompensatory business reason" includes the need to have the employee available for emergency calls during his or her meal period. Under Sec. 119(b)(4), if more than half the employees satisfy the "for the convenience of the employer" test, all employees will be regarded as satisfying the test. Regulation Sec. 1.119-1 defines "business premises of the employer" as the place of employment of the employee.

[*When discussing court cases, present case facts in such a way as to enable the reader to draw an analogy with client facts.*] A Supreme Court case, *Kowalski v. CIR*, 434 U.S. 77, 77-2 USTC ¶9748, discusses what constitutes "meals" for purposes of Sec. 119. In *Kowalski*, the State of New Jersey furnished cash meal allowances to its state troopers to enable them to eat while on duty. It did not require the troopers to use the allowances exclusively for meals. Nor did it require them to consume their meals on its business premises. One trooper, R.J. Kowalski, excluded the value of his allowances from his income. The IRS disputed this treatment, and Kowalski took the IRS to Court. In Court, Kowalski argued that the allowances were excludible because they were furnished "for the convenience of the employer." The IRS contended that the allowances were taxable because they amounted to compensation. The U.S. Supreme Court took up the case and decided for the IRS. The Court held that the Sec. 119 income exlusion does not apply to payments in cash.

Analysis
[*The analysis should (a) apply applicable law to the facts and (b) address the issue(s). In this section, every proposition should be supported by either authority, logic, or plausible assumptions.*]

Issue 1: The meals provided by Mercy seem to be furnished "for the convenience of the employer." They are furnished to have employees available for emergency call during their meal breaks. This is a "substantial noncompensatory reason" within the meaning of Reg. Sec. 1.119-1.

Issue 2: Although the hospital cafeteria appears to be the "business premises of the employer," MacDougal's does not appear to be. The hospital is the place of employment of the medical employees. MacDougal's is not.

Issue 3: [*In applying case law to the facts, indicate how case facts are similar to/dissimilar from client facts. If the analysis does not support a "yes-no" answer, do not give one.*] Based on the foregoing authorities, it is unclear whether the vouchers are equivalent to cash. On the one hand, they are redeemable only in meals. Thus, they resemble meals-in-kind. On the other hand, they are redeemable at more than one institution. Thus, they resemble cash. Nor is it clear whether a court deciding this case would reach the same conclusion as the Supreme Court did in *Kowalski*. In the latter case, the State of New Jersey provided its meal allowances in the form of cash. It did not require its employees to use the allowances exclusively for meals. Nor did it require them to consume their meals on its business premises. In our case, Mercy provides its meal allowances in the form of vouchers. Thus, it indirectly requires its employees to use the allowances exclusively for meals. On the other hand, it does not require them to consume their meals on its business premises.

Conclusion
[*The conclusion should (a) logically flow from the analysis, and (b) address the issue(s).*] Although it appears that the meals acquired by voucher in the hospital cafeteria are furnished "for the convenience of the employer" and "on the business premises of the employer," it is unclear whether the vouchers are equivalent to cash. If they *are* equivalent to cash, *or* if they are redeemed at MacDougal's, their value is likely to be taxable to the employees. On the other hand, if they are not equivalent to cash, *and* they are redeemed only in the hospital cafeteria, their value is likely to be excludible.

Professional Accounting Associates
2701 First City Plaza
Suite 905
Dallas, Texas 75019

December 12, 20X1

Elizabeth Feghali, Chief Administrator
Mercy Hospital
22650 West Haven Drive
Arlington, Texas 75527

Dear Ms. Feghali:

[*Introduction. Set a cordial tone.*] It was great to see you at last Thursday's football game. If not for that last minute fumble, the Longhorns might have taken the Big 12 Conference championship!

[*Issue/Purpose.*] In our meeting of December 6, you asked us to research whether the value of the meal vouchers that Mercy provides to its medical employees is taxable to the employees. [*Short Answer.*] I regret to inform you that if the vouchers are redeemed at MacDougal's, their value is likely to be taxable to the employees. On the other hand, if the vouchers are redeemed in the hospital cafeteria, their value is likely to be excludible from the employee's income. [*The remainder of the letter should elaborate, support, and qualify this answer.*]

[*Steps taken in deriving conclusion.*] In reaching this conclusion, we consulted relevant provisions of the Internal Revenue Code ("IRC"), applicable Treasury Regulations under the IRC, and a pertinent Supreme Court case. In addition, we reviewed the documents on employee benefits that you submitted to us at our earlier meeting.

[*Facts. State only the facts that are relevant to the issue and necessary for the analysis.*] The facts as we understand them are as follows: Mercy provides meal vouchers to its medical employees to enable them to eat while on emergency call. The vouchers are redeemable either in the hospital cafeteria or at MacDougal's. MacDougal's is a privately owned institution that rents business space from the hospital. Although Mercy's employees are not required to remain on or near the premises during their meal hours, they generally do.

[*Applicable law. State, do not interpret.*] Under the IRC, the value of meals is excludible from an employee's income if two conditions are met: first, the meals are furnished "for the convenience of the employer" and second, they are provided "on the business premises of the employer." Although the IRC does not explain what is meant by "for the convenience of the employer," "business premises of the employer," and "meals," other authorities do. Specifically, the Treasury Regulations define "business premises of the employer" to be the place of employment of the employees. The regulations state that providing meals during work hours to have an employee available for emergency calls is "for the convenience of the employer." Moreover, under the IRC, if more than half the employees satisfy the "for the convenience of the employer" test, all the employees will be regarded as satisfying the test. The Supreme Court has interpreted "meals" to mean food-in-kind. The Court has held that cash allowances do not qualify as "meals."

[*Analysis. Express the generalities of applicable law in terms of the specifics of the facts.*] Clearly, the meals furnished by Mercy are "for the convenience of the employer." They are furnished during the employees' work hours to have the employees available for emergency call. Although the meals provided in the hospital cafeteria appear to be furnished "on the business premises of the employer," the meals provided at MacDougal's do not appear to be. The hospital is the place of employment of the medical employees. MacDougal's is not. What is unclear is whether the meal vouchers are equivalent to food-in-kind. On the one hand, they are redeemable at more than one institution and thus resemble cash allowances. On the other hand, they are redeemable only in meals and thus resemble food-in-kind.

[*Conclusion/Recommendation.*] Because of this lack of clarity, we suggest that you modify your employee benefits plan to allow for the provision of meals-in-kind exclusively in the hospital cafeteria. In this way, you will dispel any doubt that Mercy is furnishing "meals," "for the convenience of the employer," "on the premises of the employer."

[*Closing/Follow Up.*] Please call me at 475-2020 if you have any questions concerning this conclusion. May I suggest that we meet next week to discuss the possibility of revising your employee benefits plan.

[*Circular 230 Disclaimer.*] U.S. Treasury Regulations require us to advise you that, unless otherwise specifically noted, any federal tax advice in this communication (including any attachments, enclosures, or other accompanying materials) was not intended or written to be used, and it cannot be used, by any taxpayer for the purpose of avoiding penalties; furthermore, this communication was not intended or written to support the promotion or marketing of any of the transactions or matters it addresses.

Very truly yours,
Professional Accounting Associates

By: Rosina Havacek, Junior Associate

A P P E N D I X B

COMPLETED TAX FORMS

*At the time this textbook went to press, the IRS had not published these 2010 forms, so 2009 forms are illustrated here.

SCHEDULE C
(Form 1040)

Department of the Treasury
Internal Revenue Service (99)

Profit or Loss From Business

(Sole Proprietorship)

▶ **Partnerships, joint ventures, etc., generally must file Form 1065 or 1065-B.**
▶ **Attach to Form 1040, 1040NR, or 1041.**   ▶ **See Instructions for Schedule C (Form 1040).**

OMB No. 1545-0074

20**10**

Attachment
Sequence No. **09**

Name of proprietor	Social security number (SSN)
Andrew Lawrence	297-63-2110

A	Principal business or profession, including product or service (see instructions)	B Enter code from pages C-9, 10, & 11
	Manufacturing Furniture	▶ 3 3 7 0 0 0

C	Business name. If no separate business name, leave blank.	D Employer ID number (EIN), if any
		5 9 2 0 2 9 7 6 3

E   Business address (including suite or room no.) ▶ 1234 University Avenue
City, town or post office, state, and ZIP code   Gainesville, FL 32611

F   Accounting method: **(1)** ☐ Cash   **(2)** ☒ Accrual   **(3)** ☐ Other (specify) ▶

G   Did you "materially participate" in the operation of this business during 2010? If "No," see instructions for limit on losses   ☒ Yes   ☐ No

H   If you started or acquired this business during 2010, check here . . . . ▶ ☐

Part I   Income

1	Gross receipts or sales. **Caution.** See instructions and check the box if:		
	• This income was reported to you on Form W-2 and the "Statutory employee" box on that form was checked, or	▶ ☐	
	• You are a member of a qualified joint venture reporting only rental real estate income not subject to self-employment tax. Also see instructions for limit on losses.	1	869,658
2	Returns and allowances	2	29,242
3	Subtract line 2 from line 1	3	840,416
4	Cost of goods sold (from line 42 on page 2)	4	540,204
5	**Gross profit.** Subtract line 4 from line 3	5	300,212
6	Other income, including federal and state gasoline or fuel tax credit or refund (see instructions)	6	
7	**Gross income.** Add lines 5 and 6 . . . . ▶	7	300,212

Part II   Expenses. Enter expenses for business use of your home **only** on line 30.

8	Advertising	8	13,000	18	Office expense	18	16,000
9	Car and truck expenses (see instructions).	9	4,000	19	Pension and profit-sharing plans .	19	2,000
				20	Rent or lease (see instructions):		
10	Commissions and fees .	10	10,400	a	Vehicles, machinery, and equipment	20a	36,000
11	Contract labor (see instructions)	11		b	Other business property . . .	20b	
12	Depletion	12		21	Repairs and maintenance . . .	21	
13	Depreciation and section 179 expense deduction (not included in Part III) (see instructions).	13	12,476	22	Supplies (not included in Part III) .	22	
				23	Taxes and licenses	23	9,840
				24	Travel, meals, and entertainment:		
				a	Travel	24a	4,000
14	Employee benefit programs (other than on line 19). .	14	4,000	b	Deductible meals and entertainment (see instructions) .	24b	4,000
15	Insurance (other than health)	15		25	Utilities	25	
16	Interest:			26	Wages (less employment credits) .	26	52,000
a	Mortgage (paid to banks, etc.)	16a		27	Other expenses (from line 48 on page 2)	27	8,650
b	Other	16b	8,000				
17	Legal and professional services.	17					

28	**Total expenses** before expenses for business use of home. Add lines 8 through 27 . . . . . . ▶	28	184,366
29	Tentative profit or (loss). Subtract line 28 from line 7	29	
30	Expenses for business use of your home. Attach **Form 8829**	30	115,846
31	**Net profit or (loss).** Subtract line 30 from line 29.		
	• If a profit, enter on both **Form 1040, line 12,** and **Schedule SE, line 2,** or on **Form 1040NR, line 13** (if you checked the box on line 1, see instructions). Estates and trusts, enter on **Form 1041, line 3.**	31	115,846
	• If a loss, you **must** go to line 32.		

32	If you have a loss, check the box that describes your investment in this activity (see instructions).		
	• If you checked 32a, enter the loss on both **Form 1040, line 12,** and **Schedule SE, line 2,** or on **Form 1040NR, line 13** (if you checked the box on line 1, see the line 31 instructions). Estates and trusts, enter on **Form 1041, line 3.**	32a ☒ All investment is at risk. 32b ☐ Some investment is not at risk.	
	• If you checked 32b, you **must** attach **Form 6198.** Your loss may be limited.		

For Paperwork Reduction Act Notice, see your tax return instructions.   Cat. No. 11334P   Schedule C (Form 1040) 2010

| Part III | **Cost of Goods Sold** (see instructions) |

33 Method(s) used to
value closing inventory: **a** [X] Cost **b** [ ] Lower of cost or market **c** [ ] Other (attach explanation)

34 Was there any change in determining quantities, costs, or valuations between opening and closing inventory?
If "Yes," attach explanation . . . . [ ] **Yes** [ ] **No**

35	Inventory at beginning of year. If different from last year's closing inventory, attach explanation . . .	35	64,000
36	Purchases less cost of items withdrawn for personal use	36	340,800
37	Cost of labor. Do not include any amounts paid to yourself	37	143,204
38	Materials and supplies	38	
39	Other costs	39	97,000
40	Add lines 35 through 39	40	645,004
41	Inventory at end of year	41	104,800
42	**Cost of goods sold.** Subtract line 41 from line 40. Enter the result here and on page 1, line 4 . . .	42	540,204

| Part IV | **Information on Your Vehicle.** Complete this part **only** if you are claiming car or truck expenses on line 9 and are not required to file Form 4562 for this business. See the instructions for line 13 to find out if you must file Form 4562. |

43 When did you place your vehicle in service for business purposes? (month, day, year) ▶ 3 / 12 / 09

44 Of the total number of miles you drove your vehicle during 2010, enter the number of miles you used your vehicle for:

a Business 17,000   **b** Commuting (see instructions) 4,500   **c** Other 12,000

45 Was your vehicle available for personal use during off-duty hours? . . . . [X] Yes [ ] No

46 Do you (or your spouse) have another vehicle available for personal use? . . . . [X] Yes [ ] No

47a Do you have evidence to support your deduction? . . . . [X] Yes [ ] No

b If "Yes," is the evidence written? . . . . [X] Yes [ ] No

| Part V | **Other Expenses.** List below business expenses not included on lines 8–26 or line 30. |

Repairs	4,800
General and administrative	3,000
Miscellaneous	850

48	**Total other expenses.** Enter here and on page 1, line 27	48	8,650

Schedule C (Form 1040) 2010

FACTS FOR SOLE PROPRIETORSHIP (SCHEDULE C)

Andrew Lawrence is the sole proprietor of a business that operates under the name Andrew Lawrence Furniture (Business Code 337000). The proprietorship is located at 1234 University Ave., Gainesville, FL 32611. Its employer identification number is 59-2029763. Andrew started the business with a $200,000 capital investment on June 1, 2004. The proprietorship uses the calendar year as its tax year (the same as its proprietor) and the accrual method of accounting. The following information pertains to its 2010 activities:

A trial balance is included as part of the accompanying worksheet. Notes accompanying the account balances are presented below.

1. Cost of goods sold is determined as follows:

Inventory at beginning of year	$ 64,000
Plus: Purchases	340,800
Cost of labor	143,204
Additional Sec. 263A adjustment	7,000
Other costs	90,000
Goods available for sale	$645,004
Minus: Inventory at end of year	(104,800)
Cost of goods sold	$540,204

The proprietorship values its inventory using the first-in, first-out method and historical costs. The Sec. 263A rules apply to the proprietorship. No change in valuing inventories occurred between the beginning and end of the tax year.

2. The proprietorship uses MACRS depreciation for tax purposes. The current year tax depreciation is $27,476. Of this amount, $15,000 is included in cost of goods sold and inventory. The AMT depreciation adjustment on post-1986 personal property is $1,514. This amount is reported on Andrew Lawrence's Form 6251 (Alternative Minimum Tax—Individuals), which is not reproduced here.

3. Using its excess funds, the proprietorship has purchased various temporary investments, including a 2% investment in Plaza Corporation stock, 50 shares of Service Corporation stock, and some tax-exempt municipal bonds. The proprietorship has held the Plaza stock for two years and sold it in July for $4,500 more than its $7,000 adjusted basis. Prior to the sale, Plaza paid a $1,000 dividend. The 50 shares of Service stock, which had been purchased during the year, was declared worthless during the year. The proprietorship recovered none of its $2,100 adjusted basis.

4. Employees other than Andrew Lawrence receive limited fringe benefits. One employee also receives a $2,000 contribution to an Individual Retirement Account paid by the proprietorship.

5. Miscellaneous expenses include $150 of expenses related to the production of the dividend income.

6. The proprietorship paid no estimated taxes.

7. Balance sheet information is not provided for the sole proprietorship because it is not reported on the Schedule C. Balance sheet information, however, can be found on page 4 of the C corporation tax return.

Andrew Lawrence, Sole Proprietorship Reconciliation of Book and Taxable Income For Year Ending December 31, 2010

Account Name	Book Income Debit	Book Income Credit	Adjustments Debit	Adjustments Credit	Taxable Income Debit	Taxable Income Credit	Schedule C	Other Tax Forms
Sales		$869,658				$869,658	$869,658	
Sales returns & allowances	$ 29,242				$ 29,242		(29,242)	
Cost of sales	540,204				540,204		(540,204)	
Dividends		1,000			1,000	1,000		$ 1,000 (Sch. B)
Tax-exempt interest		18,000	$18,000			0		
Gain on July stock sale		4,500				4,500		4,500 (Sch. D)
Worthless stock loss	2,100				2,100			(2,100) (Sch. D)
Proprietor's salary(a)	36,000			$36,000	0		0	
Other salaries	52,000				52,000		(52,000)	
Rentals	36,000				36,000		(36,000)	
Bad debts	4,000				4,000		(4,000)	
Interest:								
Working capital loans	8,000				8,000		(8,000)	
Purchase tax-exempt bonds	2,000			2,000	0			
Employment taxes	8,320				8,320		(8,320)	
Taxes	1,520				1,520		(1,520)	
Repairs	4,800				4,800		(4,800)	
Depreciation(b)	12,000		476		12,476		(12,476)	
Charitable contributions	12,000				12,000			(12,000) (Sch. A)
Travel	4,000				4,000		(4,000)	
Meals and entertainment(c)	8,000			4,000	4,000		(4,000)	
Office expenses	16,000				16,000		(16,000)	
Advertising	13,000				13,000		(13,000)	
Transportation expense	10,400				10,400		(10,400)	
General and administrative	3,000				3,000		(3,000)	
Pension plans(d)	2,000				2,000		(2,000)	
Employee benefit programs(e)	4,000				4,000		(4,000)	
Miscellaneous	1,000				1,000		(850)	(150) (Form 4952)
Net profit/Taxable income	83,572		23,524		107,096		115,846	
Total	$893,158	$893,158	$42,000	$42,000	$875,158	$875,158	$115,846	

(a) The $3,000 monthly salary for Andrew Lawrence is treated as a withdrawal from the proprietorship and is not deducted on Schedule C. The salary does not reduce Schedule C income and therefore is taxed as self-employment income.

(b) MACRS depreciation is $27,476 − $15,000 = $12,476

(c) 50% of the meals and entertainment expense is not deductible for tax purposes.

(d) The pension plan expense is the same for book and tax purposes for this business. No pension expenses relate to pensions for the proprietor.

(e) The employee benefit expense is the same for book and tax purposes for this business. None relates to proprietor benefits.

Form **1120**	**U.S. Corporation Income Tax Return**	OMB No. 1545-0123
Department of the Treasury Internal Revenue Service	For calendar year 2010 or tax year beginning _____, 2010, ending _____, 20 _____ ▶ See separate instructions.	2010

A Check if:

1a Consolidated return (attach Form 851) ☐
b Life/nonlife consolidated return . . ☐
2 Personal holding co. (attach Sch. PH) . ☐
3 Personal service corp. (see instructions) . ☐
4 Schedule M-3 attached ☐

Print or type

Name: **Johns and Lawrence, Inc.**
Number, street, and room or suite no. If a P.O. box, see instructions.
1234 University Avenue
City or town, state, and ZIP code
Gainesville, FL 32611

B Employer identification number 76-3456789
C Date incorporated 6/1/2004
D Total assets (see instructions) $ 479,324

E Check if: (1) ☐ Initial return (2) ☐ Final return (3) ☐ Name change (4) ☐ Address change

Income

1a	Gross receipts or sales 869,658 b Less returns and allowances 29,242 c Bal ▶	1c	840,416
2	Cost of goods sold (Schedule A, line 8)	2	540,204
3	Gross profit. Subtract line 2 from line 1c	3	300,212
4	Dividends (Schedule C, line 19)	4	1,000
5	Interest	5	
6	Gross rents	6	
7	Gross royalties	7	
8	Capital gain net income (attach Schedule D (Form 1120)) *Not Reproduced*	8	2,400
9	Net gain or (loss) from Form 4797, Part II, line 17 (attach Form 4797)	9	
10	Other income (see instructions—attach schedule)	10	
11	**Total income.** Add lines 3 through 10 ▶	11	303,612

Deductions (See instructions for limitations on deductions.)

12	Compensation of officers (Schedule E, line 4) ▶	12	36,000
13	Salaries and wages (less employment credits)	13	52,000
14	Repairs and maintenance	14	4,800
15	Bad debts	15	4,000
16	Rents	16	36,000
17	Taxes and licenses	17	16,000
18	Interest	18	8,000
19	Charitable contributions	19	7,694
20	Depreciation from Form 4562 not claimed on Schedule A or elsewhere on return (attach Form 4562)	20	12,476
21	Depletion	21	
22	Advertising	22	13,000
23	Pension, profit-sharing, etc., plans	23	2,000
24	Employee benefit programs	24	4,000
25	Domestic production activities deduction (attach Form 8903) *Not Reproduced*	25	6,169
26	Other deductions (attach schedule)	26	38,400
27	**Total deductions.** Add lines 12 through 26 ▶	27	240,539
28	Taxable income before net operating loss deduction and special deductions. Subtract line 27 from line 11	28	63,073
29	**Less: a** Net operating loss deduction (see instructions) . . . 29a		
	b Special deductions (Schedule C, line 20) . . . 29b 700	29c	700

Tax, Refundable Credits, and Payments

30	**Taxable income.** Subtract line 29c from line 28 (see instructions)	30	62,373
31	**Total tax** (Schedule J, line 10)	31	10,593
32a	2009 overpayment credited to 2010 . . 32a		
b	2010 estimated tax payments . . . 32b 14,000		
c	2010 refund applied for on Form 4466 32c ( ) d Bal ▶ 32d 14,000		
e	Tax deposited with Form 7004 . . . . 32e		
f	Credits: (1) Form 2439 _____ (2) Form 4136 _____ 32f		
g	Refundable credits from Form 3800, line 19c, and Form 8827, line 8c 32g	32h	14,000
33	Estimated tax penalty (see instructions). Check if Form 2220 is attached . . . ▶ ☐	33	
34	**Amount owed.** If line 32h is smaller than the total of lines 31 and 33, enter amount owed	34	
35	**Overpayment.** If line 32h is larger than the total of lines 31 and 33, enter amount overpaid	35	3,407
36	Enter amount from line 35 you want: **Credited to 2011 estimated tax** ▶ 3,407 **Refunded** ▶	36	

Sign Here

Under penalties of perjury, I declare that I have examined this return, including accompanying schedules and statements, and to the best of my knowledge and belief, it is true, correct, and complete. Declaration of preparer (other than taxpayer) is based on all information of which preparer has any knowledge.

▶ *Andrew Lawrence* Signature of officer   3-15-11 Date   ▶ **Vice-President** Title

May the IRS discuss this return with the preparer shown below (see instructions)? ☒ Yes ☐ No

Paid Preparer Use Only

Print/Type preparer's name **Michael Kramer**	Preparer's signature *Michael Kramer*	Date 3-14-11	Check ☒ if self-employed	PTIN 104121
Firm's name ▶ Michael S. Kramer			Firm's EIN ▶ 59-2029763	
Firm's address ▶ 1110 McMillian Gainesville, FL 32611			Phone no. 352 555-2000	

For Paperwork Reduction Act Notice, see separate instructions.   Cat. No. 11450Q   Form **1120** (2010)

Form 1120 (2010)   Page **2**

Schedule A   Cost of Goods Sold (see instructions)

1	Inventory at beginning of year	1	64,000
2	Purchases	2	340,800
3	Cost of labor	3	143,204
4	Additional section 263A costs (attach schedule)	4	7,000
5	Other costs (attach schedule)	5	90,000
6	**Total.** Add lines 1 through 5	6	645,004
7	Inventory at end of year	7	104,800
8	**Cost of goods sold.** Subtract line 7 from line 6. Enter here and on page 1, line 2	8	540,204

9a Check all methods used for valuing closing inventory:

  (i) ☒ Cost

  (ii) ☐ Lower of cost or market

  (iii) ☐ Other (Specify method used and attach explanation.) ▶ ------------------------------

  b Check if there was a writedown of subnormal goods . . . . ▶ ☐

  c Check if the LIFO inventory method was adopted this tax year for any goods (if checked, attach Form 970) . . . . . ▶ ☐

  d If the LIFO inventory method was used for this tax year, enter percentage (or amounts) of closing
     inventory computed under LIFO . . . . | 9d | |

  e If property is produced or acquired for resale, do the rules of section 263A apply to the corporation? . . . . ☒ Yes ☐ No

  f Was there any change in determining quantities, cost, or valuations between opening and closing inventory? If "Yes,"
     attach explanation . . . . ☐ Yes ☒ No

Schedule C   Dividends and Special Deductions (see instructions)

		(a) Dividends received	(b) %	(c) Special deductions (a) × (b)
1	Dividends from less-than-20%-owned domestic corporations (other than debt-financed stock)	1,000	70	700
2	Dividends from 20%-or-more-owned domestic corporations (other than debt-financed stock)		80	
3	Dividends on debt-financed stock of domestic and foreign corporations		see instructions	
4	Dividends on certain preferred stock of less-than-20%-owned public utilities		42	
5	Dividends on certain preferred stock of 20%-or-more-owned public utilities		48	
6	Dividends from less-than-20%-owned foreign corporations and certain FSCs		70	
7	Dividends from 20%-or-more-owned foreign corporations and certain FSCs		80	
8	Dividends from wholly owned foreign subsidiaries		100	
9	**Total.** Add lines 1 through 8. See instructions for limitation			700
10	Dividends from domestic corporations received by a small business investment company operating under the Small Business Investment Act of 1958		100	
11	Dividends from affiliated group members		100	
12	Dividends from certain FSCs		100	
13	Dividends from foreign corporations not included on lines 3, 6, 7, 8, 11, or 12			
14	Income from controlled foreign corporations under subpart F (attach Form(s) 5471)			
15	Foreign dividend gross-up			
16	IC-DISC and former DISC dividends not included on lines 1, 2, or 3			
17	Other dividends			
18	Deduction for dividends paid on certain preferred stock of public utilities			
19	**Total dividends.** Add lines 1 through 17. Enter here and on page 1, line 4 ▶	1,000		
20	**Total special deductions.** Add lines 9, 10, 11, 12, and 18. Enter here and on page 1, line 29b . . . . . ▶			700

Schedule E   Compensation of Officers (see instructions for page 1, line 12)

Note: *Complete Schedule E only if total receipts (line 1a plus lines 4 through 10 on page 1) are $500,000 or more.*

	(a) Name of officer	(b) Social security number	(c) Percent of time devoted to business	Percent of corporation stock owned		(f) Amount of compensation
				(d) Common	(e) Preferred	
1	Stephen Johns	386-05-9174	100 %	50 %	%	18,000
	Andrew Lawrence	297-63-2110	100 %	50 %	%	18,000
			%	%	%	
			%	%	%	
			%	%	%	
2	Total compensation of officers					36,000
3	Compensation of officers claimed on Schedule A and elsewhere on return					
4	Subtract line 3 from line 2. Enter the result here and on page 1, line 12					36,000

Form **1120** (2010)

Form 1120 (2010)   Page **3**

Schedule J	**Tax Computation** (see instructions)		
1	Check if the corporation is a member of a controlled group (attach Schedule O (Form 1120)) . . . . . ▶ ☐		
2	Income tax. Check if a qualified personal service corporation (see instructions) . . . . ▶ ☐	**2**	10,593
3	Alternative minimum tax (attach Form 4626)	**3**	
4	Add lines 2 and 3	**4**	10,593
5a	Foreign tax credit (attach Form 1118)	5a		
b	Credit from Form 8834, line 29	5b		
c	General business credit (attach Form 3800)	5c		
d	Credit for prior year minimum tax (attach Form 8827)	5d		
e	Bond credits from Form 8912	5e		
6	**Total credits.** Add lines 5a through 5e	**6**	-0-
7	Subtract line 6 from line 4	**7**	10,593
8	Personal holding company tax (attach Schedule PH (Form 1120))	**8**	
9	Other taxes. Check if from: ☐ Form 4255 ☐ Form 8611 ☐ Form 8697		
	☐ Form 8866 ☐ Form 8902 ☐ Other (attach schedule) . . .	**9**	
10	**Total tax.** Add lines 7 through 9. Enter here and on page 1, line 31	**10**	10,593

Schedule K	**Other Information** (see instructions)		Yes	No
1	Check accounting method: **a** ☐ Cash **b** ☒ Accrual **c** ☐ Other (specify) ▶ _____			
2	See the instructions and enter the:			
a	Business activity code no. ▶ **337,000**			
b	Business activity ▶ **Manufacturing**			
c	Product or service ▶ **Furniture**			
3	Is the corporation a subsidiary in an affiliated group or a parent-subsidiary controlled group?			X
	If "Yes," enter name and EIN of the parent corporation ▶ _____			
4	At the end of the tax year:			
a	Did any foreign or domestic corporation, partnership (including any entity treated as a partnership), trust, or tax-exempt organization own directly 20% or more, or own, directly or indirectly, 50% or more of the total voting power of all classes of the corporation's stock entitled to vote? If "Yes," complete Part I of Schedule G (Form 1120) (attach Schedule G)			X
b	Did any individual or estate own directly 20% or more, or own, directly or indirectly, 50% or more of the total voting power of all classes of the corporation's stock entitled to vote? If "Yes," complete Part II of Schedule G (Form 1120) (attach Schedule G) ＊.		X	
5	At the end of the tax year, did the corporation:			
a	Own directly 20% or more, or own, directly or indirectly, 50% or more of the total voting power of all classes of stock entitled to vote of any foreign or domestic corporation not included on **Form 851,** Affiliations Schedule? For rules of constructive ownership, see instructions. If "Yes," complete (i) through (iv).			X

(i) Name of Corporation	(ii) Employer Identification Number (if any)	(iii) Country of Incorporation	(iv) Percentage Owned in Voting Stock

Form **1120** (2010)

＊**Schedule G is not attached. If attached, it would list the same individuals listed in Schedule E.**

Form 1120 (2010)   Page **4**

Schedule K	Continued			Yes	No

b Own directly an interest of 20% or more, or own, directly or indirectly, an interest of 50% or more in any foreign or domestic partnership (including an entity treated as a partnership) or in the beneficial interest of a trust? For rules of constructive ownership, see instructions | | | | | X |

If "Yes," complete (i) through (iv).

(i) Name of Entity	(ii) Employer Identification Number (if any)	(iii) Country of Organization	(iv) Maximum Percentage Owned in Profit, Loss, or Capital

6 During this tax year, did the corporation pay dividends (other than stock dividends and distributions in exchange for stock) in excess of the corporation's current and accumulated earnings and profits? (See sections 301 and 316.) . . . . | | X |

If "Yes," file **Form 5452,** Corporate Report of Nondividend Distributions.

If this is a consolidated return, answer here for the parent corporation and on Form 851 for each subsidiary.

7 At any time during the tax year, did one foreign person own, directly or indirectly, at least 25% of **(a)** the total voting power of all classes of the corporation's stock entitled to vote or **(b)** the total value of all classes of the corporation's stock? . . . . | | X |

For rules of attribution, see section 318. If "Yes," enter:

(i) Percentage owned ▶ _____ and **(ii)** Owner's country ▶ _____

(c) The corporation may have to file **Form 5472,** Information Return of a 25% Foreign-Owned U.S. Corporation or a Foreign Corporation Engaged in a U.S. Trade or Business. Enter the number of Forms 5472 attached ▶ _____

8 Check this box if the corporation issued publicly offered debt instruments with original issue discount . . . . . ▶ ☐

If checked, the corporation may have to file **Form 8281,** Information Return for Publicly Offered Original Issue Discount Instruments.

9 Enter the amount of tax-exempt interest received or accrued during the tax year ▶ $ _18,000_____

10 Enter the number of shareholders at the end of the tax year (if 100 or fewer) ▶ _____2_____

11 If the corporation has an NOL for the tax year and is electing to forego the carryback period, check here . . . . . ▶ ☐

If the corporation is filing a consolidated return, the statement required by Regulations section 1.1502-21(b)(3) must be attached or the election will not be valid.

12 Enter the available NOL carryover from prior tax years (do not reduce it by any deduction on line 29a.) ▶ $ _-0-_____

13 Are the corporation's total receipts (line 1a plus lines 4 through 10 on page 1) for the tax year **and** its total assets at the end of the tax year less than $250,000? . . . . | | X |

If "Yes," the corporation is not required to complete Schedules L, M-1, and M-2 on page 5. Instead, enter the total amount of cash distributions and the book value of property distributions (other than cash) made during the tax year. ▶ $ _____

14 Is the corporation required to file Schedule UTP (Form 1120), Uncertain Tax Position Statement (see instructions)? . . . .

If "Yes," complete and attach Schedule UTP.

Form **1120** (2010)

Form 1120 (2010)

Page **5**

Schedule L	**Balance Sheets per Books**	Beginning of tax year		End of tax year	
	Assets	**(a)**	**(b)**	**(c)**	**(d)**
1	Cash		60,000		72,600
2a	Trade notes and accounts receivable	25,000		24,000	
b	Less allowance for bad debts	(1,000)	24,000	(1,000)	23,000
3	Inventories		64,000		104,800
4	U.S. government obligations				
5	Tax-exempt securities (see instructions)		200,000		200,000
6	Other current assets (attach schedule)		7,000		
7	Loans to shareholders				
8	Mortgage and real estate loans				
9	Other investments (attach schedule)				
10a	Buildings and other depreciable assets	151,600		151,600	
b	Less accumulated depreciation	(45,200)	106,400	(72,676)	78,924
11a	Depletable assets				
b	Less accumulated depletion	( )		( )	
12	Land (net of any amortization)				
13a	Intangible assets (amortizable only)				
b	Less accumulated amortization	( )		( )	
14	Other assets (attach schedule)				
15	Total assets		461,400		479,324
	Liabilities and Shareholders' Equity				
16	Accounts payable		26,000		19,000
17	Mortgages, notes, bonds payable in less than 1 year		4,000		4,000
18	Other current liabilities (attach schedule)		3,600		3,600
19	Loans from shareholders				
20	Mortgages, notes, bonds payable in 1 year or more		130,000		119,724
21	Other liabilities (attach schedule)				
22	Capital stock: **a** Preferred stock				
	b Common stock	200,000	200,000	200,000	200,000
23	Additional paid-in capital				
24	Retained earnings—Appropriated (attach schedule)				
25	Retained earnings—Unappropriated		97,800		133,000
26	Adjustments to shareholders' equity (attach schedule)				
27	Less cost of treasury stock		( )		( )
28	Total liabilities and shareholders' equity		461,400		479,324

Schedule M-1	**Reconciliation of Income (Loss) per Books With Income per Return**		
	Note: Schedule M-3 required instead of Schedule M-1 if total assets are $10 million or more—see instructions		

1	Net income (loss) per books	63,412	7	Income recorded on books this year	
2	Federal income tax per books	14,000		not included on this return (itemize):	
3	Excess of capital losses over capital gains			Tax-exempt interest $ 18,000	
4	Income subject to tax not recorded on books this year (itemize):				18,000
			8	Deductions on this return not charged against book income this year (itemize):	
5	Expenses recorded on books this year not deducted on this return (itemize):		a	Depreciation . . $ 476	
a	Depreciation . . . $ 4,306		b	Charitable contributions $	
b	Charitable contributions . $ 4,000			U.S. prod. act. ded. $6,169	
c	Travel and entertainment . $				6,645
	Nondeductable interest* $2,000	10,306	9	Add lines 7 and 8	24,645
6	Add lines 1 through 5	87,718	10	Income (page 1, line 28)—line 6 less line 9	63,073

Schedule M-2	**Analysis of Unappropriated Retained Earnings per Books (Line 25, Schedule L)**		
1	Balance at beginning of year	97,800	5	Distributions: **a** Cash	28,212
2	Net income (loss) per books	63,412		**b** Stock	
3	Other increases (itemize):			**c** Property	
			6	Other decreases (itemize):	
			7	Add lines 5 and 6	28,212
4	Add lines 1, 2, and 3	161,212	8	Balance at end of year (line 4 less line 7)	133,000

*On loans to acquire municipal bonds.

Form **1120** (2010)

FACTS FOR C CORPORATION (FORM 1120)

The same basic facts presented for the Andrew Lawrence proprietorship are used for the C corporation except for the following:

1. Andrew Lawrence and Stephen Johns are the two 50% shareholders of Johns and Lawrence, Inc., a furniture manufacturer (Business Code 337000). Johns and Lawrence is located at 1234 University Ave., Gainesville, FL 32611. Its employer identification number is 76-3456789. The following information pertains to the 2010 corporate tax return:

Compensation of Officers

Name	S.S. No.	Share	Title	Compensation
Stephen Johns	386-05-9174	1,000	President	$18,000
Andrew Lawrence	297-63-2110	1,000	V.P.	18,000
Total		2,000		$36,000

The corporation paid all salaries owed to the shareholders in 2010. The corporation paid none of the interest or rentals to the shareholders.

2. The book income for the corporation appears in the attached worksheet, which reconciles the corporation's book income and its taxable income before special deductions.

3. The company was incorporated on June 1, 2004. Each of the two officers hold one-half the stock, which they acquired on that date for a total cash and property contribution of $200,000. No change in the stockholdings has occurred since incorporation. Johns and Lawrence each devote 100% of their time to the business. The corporation provides no expense allowances. The corporation, however, reimburses properly substantiated expenses. Both officers are U.S. citizens. Johns and Lawrence is not a member of a controlled group.

4. Addresses for the officers are: Andrew Lawrence, 436 N.W. 24th Ave., Gainesville, FL 32607; Stephen Johns, 1250 N.E. 12th Ave., Gainesville, FL 32601.

5. The corporation paid estimated taxes of $14,000 for tax year 2010.

6. Other deductions include:

Travel	$ 4,000
Meals and entertainment	8,000
Minus: 50% disallowance	(4,000)
Office expenses	16,000
Transportation	10,400
General and administrative	3,000
Miscellaneous	1,000
Total	$38,400

7. The charitable contributions deduction limitation is $7,694 (see footnote b in Reconciliation worksheet on next page). The remaining $4,306 ($12,000 − $7,694) carries over to 2011 and the four succeeding tax years.

8. Qualified production activities income (QPAI) equals $80,000. Employer's W-2 wages allocable to U.S. production activities equal $88,000.

9. The $28,212 of withdrawals made by the two owners are dividends out of the corporation's earnings and profits. They are reported as gross income on the shareholders' individual tax returns.

10. The beginning-of-the-year balance sheets for all entity forms are the same, which permits a direct comparison of the 2010 tax differences. Actually, the corporation would have reported tax differences in all prior years (2004 through 2009), which would have been included in the January 1, 2010 balance sheet. If these differences were so included, the direct comparisons would be much more difficult.

Johns and Lawrence, Inc. (C Corporation) Reconciliation of Book Income to Taxable Income before Special Deductions for Year Ending December 31, 2010

Account Name	Book Income Debit	Book Income Credit	Adjustments Debit	Adjustments Credit	Taxable Income Debit	Taxable Income Credit
Sales		$869,658				$869,658
Sales returns & allowances	$ 29,242				$ 29,242	
Cost of sales	540,204				540,204	
Dividends		1,000				1,000
Tax-exempt interest		18,000	$18,000			0
Gain on stock sale		4,500				4,500
Worthless stock loss	2,100				2,100	
Officers' salaries	36,000				36,000	
Other salaries	52,000				52,000	
Rentals	36,000				36,000	
Bad debts	4,000				4,000	
Interest:						
Working capital loans	8,000				8,000	
Purchase tax-exempt bonds	2,000			$ 2,000	0	
Employment taxes	14,480				14,480	
Taxes	1,520				1,520	
Repairs	4,800				4,800	
Depreciation(a)	12,000		476		12,476	
Charitable contributions(b)	12,000			4,306	7,694	
Travel	4,000				4,000	
Meals and entertainment(c)	8,000			4,000	4,000	
Office expenses	16,000				16,000	
Advertising	13,000				13,000	
Transportation expense	10,400				10,400	
General and administrative	3,000				3,000	
Pension plans	2,000				2,000	
Employee benefit programs	4,000				4,000	
Miscellaneous	1,000				1,000	
U.S. prod. act. ded.	0		6,169		6,169	
Federal income taxes	14,000			14,000	0	
Net income/Taxable income before spec. deds.	63,412			339	63,073(e)	
Total	$893,158	$893,158	$24,645	$24,645	$875,158	$875,158

(a) MACRS depreciation = $27,476 total − $15,000 included in COGS = $12,476

(b) Charitable contribution deduction limitation:

Total income (Form 1120, page 1, line 11)	$303,612
Minus: Deductions other than char. cont., DRD, & U.S. prod. act. ded.	(226,676)
Charitable contribution base	$ 76,936
Times: 10%	0.10
Charitable contribution deduction	$ 7,694

(c) $8,000 × 0.50 disallowance rate = $4,000 disallowed expenses

(d)

Total income (Form 1120, page 1, line 11)	$303,612
Minus: Deductions other than the U.S. prod. act. ded.	(235,070)
Taxable income before the U.S. prod. act. ded.	$ 68,542
Times: 9%	0.09
U.S. prod. act. ded.	$ 6,169

(e) Taxable income:

Taxable income before spec. deds.	$ 63,073
Minus: Div. rec. ded. ($1,000 × 0.70)	(700)
Taxable income	$ 62,373

Form **7004**	**Application for Automatic Extension of Time To File Certain Business Income Tax, Information, and Other Returns**	OMB No. 1545-0233

Form **7004**
(Rev. December 2009)
Department of the Treasury
Internal Revenue Service

▶ File a separate application for each return.
▶ See separate instructions.

Type or Print

File by the due date for the return for which an extension is requested. See instructions.

Name	Identifying number
Palmer Corporation	38-1505286

Number, street, and room or suite no. (If P.O. box, see instructions.)

1631 W. University Avenue

City, town, state, and ZIP code (If a foreign address, enter city, province or state, and country (follow the country's practice for entering postal code)).

Gainesville, FL 32601

Note. See instructions before completing this form.

Part I	Automatic 5-Month Extension Complete if Filing Form 1065, 1041, or 8804

1a Enter the form code for the return that this application is for (see below) . . . .

Application Is For:	Form Code	Application Is For:	Form Code
Form 1065	09	Form 1041 (estate)	04
Form 8804	31	Form 1041 (trust)	05

Part II	Automatic 6-Month Extension Complete if Filing Other Forms

b Enter the form code for the return that this application is for (see below) . . . .

Application Is For:	Form Code	Application Is For:	Form Code
Form 706-GS(D)	01	Form 1120-PC	21
Form 706-GS(T)	02	Form 1120-POL	22
Form 1041-N	06	Form 1120-REIT	23
Form 1041-QFT	07	Form 1120-RIC	24
Form 1042	08	Form 1120S	25
Form 1065-B	10	Form 1120-SF	26
Form 1066	11	Form 3520-A	27
Form 1120	12	Form 8612	28
Form 1120-C	34	Form 8613	29
Form 1120-F	15	Form 8725	30
Form 1120-FSC	16	Form 8831	32
Form 1120-H	17	Form 8876	33
Form 1120-L	18	Form 8924	35
Form 1120-ND	19	Form 8928	36
Form 1120-ND (section 4951 taxes)	20		

2 If the organization is a foreign corporation that does not have an office or place of business in the United States, check here . . . . ▶ ☐

3 If the organization is a corporation and is the common parent of a group that intends to file a consolidated return, check here . . . . ▶ ☐

If checked, attach a schedule, listing the name, address, and Employer Identification Number (EIN) for each member covered by this application.

Part III	All Filers Must Complete This Part

4 If the organization is a corporation or partnership that qualifies under Regulations section 1.6081-5, check here . ▶ ☐

5a The application is for calendar year 20 ____, or tax year beginning __Oct. 1__ 20 _10_, and ending __Sept. 30__, 20 _11_

b Short tax year. If this tax year is less than 12 months, check the reason:
☐ Initial return   ☐ Final return   ☐ Change in accounting period   ☐ Consolidated return to be filed

6	Tentative total tax	6	72,000
7	**Total** payments and credits (see instructions)	7	68,000
8	**Balance due.** Subtract line 7 from line 6. **Generally, you must deposit this amount using the Electronic Federal Tax Payment System (EFTPS), a Federal Tax Deposit (FTD) Coupon, or Electronic Funds Withdrawal (EFW)** (see instructions for exceptions)	8	4,000

For Privacy Act and Paperwork Reduction Act Notice, see separate Instructions.   Cat. No. 13804A   Form **7004** (Rev. 12-2009)

Form **2220**

Department of the Treasury
Internal Revenue Service

Underpayment of Estimated Tax by Corporations

▶ See separate instructions.
▶ Attach to the corporation's tax return.

OMB No. 1545-0142

20**10**

Name	Employer identification number
Globe Corporation	38-1505087

Note: *Generally, the corporation is not required to file Form 2220 (see Part II below for exceptions) because the IRS will figure any penalty owed and bill the corporation. However, the corporation may still use Form 2220 to figure the penalty. If so, enter the amount from page 2, line 38 on the estimated tax penalty line of the corporation's income tax return, but* **do not** *attach Form 2220.*

Part I   Required Annual Payment

1	Total tax (see instructions)	**1**	100,000
2a	Personal holding company tax (Schedule PH (Form 1120), line 26) included on line 1	**2a**	
b	Look-back interest included on line 1 under section 460(b)(2) for completed long-term contracts or section 167(g) for depreciation under the income forecast method	**2b**	
c	Credit for federal tax paid on fuels (see instructions)	**2c**	
d	**Total.** Add lines 2a through 2c	**2d**	
3	Subtract line 2d from line 1. If the result is less than $500, **do not** complete or file this form. The corporation does not owe the penalty	**3**	100,000
4	Enter the tax shown on the corporation's 2009 income tax return (see instructions). **Caution:** *If the tax is zero or the tax year was for less than 12 months, skip this line and enter the amount from line 3 on line 5*	**4**	125,000
5	**Required annual payment.** Enter the **smaller** of line 3 or line 4. If the corporation is required to skip line 4, enter the amount from line 3	**5**	100,000

Part II   Reasons for Filing—Check the boxes below that apply. If any boxes are checked, the corporation **must** file Form 2220 even if it does not owe a penalty (see instructions).

6	☐	The corporation is using the adjusted seasonal installment method.
7	☐	The corporation is using the annualized income installment method.
8	☐	The corporation is a "large corporation" figuring its first required installment based on the prior year's tax.

Part III   Figuring the Underpayment

			(a)	(b)	(c)	(d)
9	Installment due dates. Enter in columns (a) through (d) the 15th day of the 4th (**Form 990-PF filers:** Use 5th month), 6th, 9th, and 12th months of the corporation's tax year	**9**	4-15-10	6-15-10	9-15-10	12-15-10
10	Required installments. If the box on line 6 and/or line 7 above is checked, enter the amounts from Schedule A, line 38. If the box on line 8 (but not 6 or 7) is checked, see instructions for the amounts to enter. If none of these boxes are checked, enter 25% of line 5 above in each column	**10**	25,000	25,000	25,000	25,000
11	Estimated tax paid or credited for each period (see instructions). For column (a) only, enter the amount from line 11 on line 15	**11**	16,000	16,000	21,000	35,000
	Complete lines 12 through 18 of one column before going to the next column.					
12	Enter amount, if any, from line 18 of the preceding column	**12**		-0-	-0-	-0-
13	Add lines 11 and 12	**13**		16,000	21,000	35,000
14	Add amounts on lines 16 and 17 of the preceding column	**14**		9,000	18,000	22,000
15	Subtract line 14 from line 13. If zero or less, enter -0-	**15**	16,000	7,000	3,000	13,000
16	If the amount on line 15 is zero, subtract line 13 from line 14. Otherwise, enter -0-	**16**		-0-	-0-	
17	**Underpayment.** If line 15 is less than or equal to line 10, subtract line 15 from line 10. Then go to line 12 of the next column. Otherwise, go to line 18	**17**	9,000	18,000	22,000	12,000
18	**Overpayment.** If line 10 is less than line 15, subtract line 10 from line 15. Then go to line 12 of the next column	**18**				

Go to Part IV on page 2 to figure the penalty. Do not go to Part IV if there are no entries on line 17—no penalty is owed.

For Paperwork Reduction Act Notice, see separate instructions.   Cat. No. 11746L   Form **2220** (2010)

Form 2220 (2010)   Page **2**

Part IV   Figuring the Penalty

		(a)	(b)	(c)	(d)
19	Enter the date of payment or the 15th day of the 3rd month after the close of the tax year, whichever is earlier (see instructions). *(Form 990-PF and Form 990-T filers:* Use 5th month instead of 3rd month.) **19**	6-15-10	9-15-10	12-15-10	3-15-11
20	Number of days from due date of installment on line 9 to the date shown on line 19 **20**	61	92	91	90
21	Number of days on line 20 after 4/15/2010 and before 7/1/2010 **21**	61	15		
22	Underpayment on line 17 × $\frac{\text{Number of days on line 21}}{365}$ × 4% **22**	$ 60	$ 30	$	$
23	Number of days on line 20 after 6/30/2010 and before 10/1/2010 **23**		77	15	
24	Underpayment on line 17 × $\frac{\text{Number of days on line 23}}{365}$ × 4% **24**	$	$ 152	$ 36	$
25	Number of days on line 20 after 9/30/2010 and before 1/1/2011 **25**			76	16
26	Underpayment on line 17 × $\frac{\text{Number of days on line 25}}{365}$ × 4% **26**	$	$	$ 183	$ 21
27	Number of days on line 20 after 12/31/2010 and before 4/1/2011 **27**				74
28	Underpayment on line 17 × $\frac{\text{Number of days on line 27}}{365}$ × 3% **28**	$	$	$	$ 73
29	Number of days on line 20 after 3/31/2011 and before 7/1/2011 **29**				
30	Underpayment on line 17 × $\frac{\text{Number of days on line 29}}{365}$ × *% **30**	$	$	$	$
31	Number of days on line 20 after 6/30/2011 and before 10/1/2011 **31**				
32	Underpayment on line 17 × $\frac{\text{Number of days on line 31}}{365}$ × *% **32**	$	$	$	$
33	Number of days on line 20 after 9/30/2011 and before 1/1/2012 **33**				
34	Underpayment on line 17 × $\frac{\text{Number of days on line 33}}{365}$ × *% **34**	$	$	$	$
35	Number of days on line 20 after 12/31/2011 and before 2/16/2012 **35**				
36	Underpayment on line 17 × $\frac{\text{Number of days on line 35}}{366}$ × *% **36**	$	$	$	$
37	Add lines 22, 24, 26, 28, 30, 32, 34, and 36 **37**	$ 60	$ 182	$ 219	$ 94

38   **Penalty.** Add columns (a) through (d) of line 37. Enter the total here and on Form 1120, line 33; or the comparable line for other income tax returns .   **38** $ 555

*Use the penalty interest rate for each calendar quarter, which the IRS will determine during the first month in the preceding quarter. These rates are published quarterly in an IRS News Release and in a revenue ruling in the Internal Revenue Bulletin. To obtain this information on the Internet, access the IRS website at **www.irs.gov.** You can also call 1-800-829-4933 to get interest rate information.

Form **2220** (2010)

SCHEDULE M-3 (Form 1120)	Net Income (Loss) Reconciliation for Corporations With Total Assets of $10 Million or More	OMB No. 1545-0123
Department of the Treasury Internal Revenue Service	▶ Attach to Form 1120 or 1120-C. ▶ See separate instructions.	20**10**

Name of corporation (common parent, if consolidated return)	Employer identification number
Valley Corporation	

Check applicable box(es):   (1) ☒ Non-consolidated return   (2) ☐ Consolidated return (Form 1120 only)

(3) ☐ Mixed 1120/L/PC group   (4) ☐ Dormant subsidiaries schedule attached

Part I   **Financial Information and Net Income (Loss) Reconciliation** (see instructions)

1a Did the corporation file SEC Form 10-K for its income statement period ending with or within this tax year?
    ☐ **Yes.** Skip lines 1b and 1c and complete lines 2a through 11 with respect to that SEC Form 10-K.
    ☒ **No.** Go to line 1b. See instructions if multiple non-tax-basis income statements are prepared.
   b Did the corporation prepare a certified audited non-tax-basis income statement for that period?
    ☐ **Yes.** Skip line 1c and complete lines 2a through 11 with respect to that income statement.
    ☒ **No.** Go to line 1c.
   c Did the corporation prepare a non-tax-basis income statement for that period?
    ☒ **Yes.** Complete lines 2a through 11 with respect to that income statement.
    ☐ **No.** Skip lines 2a through 3c and enter the corporation's net income (loss) per its books and records on line 4a.
2a Enter the income statement period: Beginning   1/1/10 DD/YYYY   Ending   12/31/10 DD/YYYY
   b Has the corporation's income statement been restated for the income statement period on line 2a?
    ☐ **Yes.** (If "Yes," attach an explanation and the amount of each item restated.)
    ☒ **No.**
   c Has the corporation's income statement been restated for any of the five income statement periods preceding the period on line 2a?
    ☐ **Yes.** (If "Yes," attach an explanation and the amount of each item restated.)
    ☒ **No.**
3a Is any of the corporation's voting common stock publicly traded?
    ☐ **Yes.**
    ☒ **No.** If "No," go to line 4a.
   b Enter the symbol of the corporation's primary U.S. publicly traded voting common stock . . . .
   c Enter the nine-digit CUSIP number of the corporation's primary publicly traded voting common stock . . . .

4a Worldwide consolidated net income (loss) from income statement source identified in Part I, line 1 . .	**4a**	372,000
b Indicate accounting standard used for line 4a (see instructions): (1) ☒ GAAP (2) ☐ IFRS (3) ☐ Statutory (4) ☐ Tax-basis (5) ☐ Other (specify) _____		
5a Net income from nonincludible foreign entities (attach schedule)	**5a**	( )
b Net loss from nonincludible foreign entities (attach schedule and enter as a positive amount)	**5b**	
6a Net income from nonincludible U.S. entities (attach schedule)	**6a**	( )
b Net loss from nonincludible U.S. entities (attach schedule and enter as a positive amount)	**6b**	
7a Net income (loss) of other includible foreign disregarded entities (attach schedule)	**7a**	
b Net income (loss) of other includible U.S. disregarded entities (attach schedule)	**7b**	
c Net income (loss) of other includible entities (attach schedule)	**7c**	
8 Adjustment to eliminations of transactions between includible entities and nonincludible entities (attach schedule)	**8**	
9 Adjustment to reconcile income statement period to tax year (attach schedule)	**9**	
10a Intercompany dividend adjustments to reconcile to line 11 (attach schedule)	**10a**	
b Other statutory accounting adjustments to reconcile to line 11 (attach schedule)	**10b**	
c Other adjustments to reconcile to amount on line 11 (attach schedule)	**10c**	
11 **Net income (loss) per income statement of includible corporations.** Combine lines 4 through 10 . . .	**11**	372,000
Note. Part I, line 11, must equal the amount on Part II, line 30, column (a), and Schedule M-2, line 2.		

12 Enter the total amount (not just the corporation's share) of the assets and liabilities of all entities included or removed on the following lines.

	Total Assets	Total Liabilities
a Included on Part I, line 4* . . . . ▶	2,306,980	1,320,420
b Removed on Part I, line 5 . . . . ▶		
c Removed on Part I, line 6 . . . . ▶		
d Included on Part I, line 7 . . . . ▶		

For Paperwork Reduction Act Notice, see the Instructions for Form 1120.	Cat. No. 37961C	Schedule M-3 (Form 1120) 2010

*For this information, see Comprehensive Example, Year 1, Step 11 on text Page C:3-50.

Schedule M-3 (Form 1120) 2010

Page **2**

Name of corporation (common parent, if consolidated return)	Employer identification number
Valley Corporation	

Check applicable box(es): **(1)** ☐ Consolidated group   **(2)** ☐ Parent corp   **(3)** ☐ Consolidated eliminations   **(4)** ☐ Subsidiary corp   **(5)** ☐ Mixed 1120/L/PC group

Check if a sub-consolidated: **(6)** ☐ 1120 group   **(7)** ☐ 1120 eliminations

Name of subsidiary (if consolidated return)	Employer identification number

Part II   **Reconciliation of Net Income (Loss) per Income Statement of Includible Corporations With Taxable Income per Return** (see instructions)

Income (Loss) Items (Attach schedules for lines 1 through 11)	(a) Income (Loss) per Income Statement	(b) Temporary Difference	(c) Permanent Difference	(d) Income (Loss) per Tax Return
1 Income (loss) from equity method foreign corporations				
2 Gross foreign dividends not previously taxed				
3 Subpart F, QEF, and similar income inclusions				
4 Section 78 gross-up				
5 Gross foreign distributions previously taxed				
6 Income (loss) from equity method U.S. corporations				
7 U.S. dividends not eliminated in tax consolidation	10,000			10,000
8 Minority interest for includible corporations				
9 Income (loss) from U.S. partnerships				
10 Income (loss) from foreign partnerships				
11 Income (loss) from other pass-through entities				
12 Items relating to reportable transactions (attach details)				
13 Interest income (attach Form 8916-A) ***	3,000		(3,000)	-0-
14 Total accrual to cash adjustment				
15 Hedging transactions				
16 Mark-to-market income (loss)				
17 Cost of goods sold (attach Form 8916-A)	(550,000)			(550,000)
18 Sale versus lease (for sellers and/or lessors)				
19 Section 481(a) adjustments				
20 Unearned/deferred revenue *Prepaid rent*	-0-	8,000		8,000
21 Income recognition from long-term contracts				
22 Original issue discount and other imputed interest				
23a Income statement gain/loss on sale, exchange, abandonment, worthlessness, or other disposition of assets other than inventory and pass-through entities	(12,000)	12,000		
b Gross capital gains from Schedule D, excluding amounts from pass-through entities				
c Gross capital losses from Schedule D, excluding amounts from pass-through entities, abandonment losses, and worthless stock losses				
d Net gain/loss reported on Form 4797, line 17, excluding amounts from pass-through entities, abandonment losses, and worthless stock losses				
e Abandonment losses				
f Worthless stock losses (attach details)				
g Other gain/loss on disposition of assets other than inventory				
24 Capital loss limitation and carryforward used				
25 Other income (loss) items with differences (attach schedule)				
26 **Total income (loss) items.** Combine lines 1 through 25	(549,000)	20,000	(3,000)	(532,000)
27 **Total expense/deduction items** (from Part III, line 38)	(314,440)	(110,000)	128,440	(296,000)
28 Other items with no differences **	1,200,000			1,200,000
29a Mixed groups, see instructions. All others, combine lines 26 through 28	336,560	(90,000)	125,440	372,000
b PC insurance subgroup reconciliation totals				
c Life insurance subgroup reconciliation totals				
30 **Reconciliation totals.** Combine lines 29a through 29c	336,560	(90,000)	125,440	372,000

Note. Line 30, column (a), must equal the amount on Part I, line 11, and column (d) must equal Form 1120, page 1, line 28.

Schedule M-3 (Form 1120) 2010

*Tax-exempt interest $3,000

**Sales $1,500,000 minus operating expenses $300,000

Schedule M-3 (Form 1120) 2010 | Page **3**

Name of corporation (common parent, if consolidated return)	Employer identification number
Valley Corporation	

Check applicable box(es): **(1)** ☐ Consolidated group **(2)** ☐ Parent corp **(3)** ☐ Consolidated eliminations **(4)** ☐ Subsidiary corp **(5)** ☐ Mixed 1120/L/PC group

Check if a sub-consolidated: **(6)** ☐ 1120 group **(7)** ☐ 1120 eliminations

Name of subsidiary (if consolidated return)	Employer identification number

Part III Reconciliation of Net Income (Loss) per Income Statement of Includible Corporations With Taxable Income per Return—Expense/Deduction Items (see instructions)

Expense/Deduction Items	(a) Expense per Income Statement	(b) Temporary Difference	(c) Permanent Difference	(d) Deduction per Tax Return
1 U.S. current income tax expense .*	124,100		(124,100)	
2 U.S. deferred income tax expense * . . .	27,540		(27,540)	
3 State and local current income tax expense . .				
4 State and local deferred income tax expense . .				
5 Foreign current income tax expense (other than foreign withholding taxes)				
6 Foreign deferred income tax expense				
7 Foreign withholding taxes				
8 Interest expense (attach Form 8916-A) ** . . .	75,000			75,000
9 Stock option expense				
10 Other equity-based compensation				
11 Meals and entertainment				
12 Fines and penalties				
13 Judgments, damages, awards, and similar costs				
14 Parachute payments				
15 Compensation with section 162(m) limitation . .				
16 Pension and profit-sharing				
17 Other post-retirement benefits				
18 Deferred compensation				
19 Charitable contribution of cash and tangible property				
20 Charitable contribution of intangible property .				
21 Charitable contribution limitation/carryforward .				
22 Domestic production activities deduction . . .			35,000	35,000
23 Current year acquisition or reorganization investment banking fees				
24 Current year acquisition or reorganization legal and accounting fees				
25 Current year acquisition/reorganization other costs				
26 Amortization/impairment of goodwill				
27 Amortization of acquisition, reorganization, and start-up costs				
28 Other amortization or impairment write-offs . .				
29 Section 198 environmental remediation costs .				
30 Depletion				
31 Depreciation	60,000	110,000		170,000
32 Bad debt expense	25,000		(9,000)	16,000
33 Corporate owned life insurance premiums . .	2,800		(2,800)	-0-
34 Purchase versus lease (for purchasers and/or lessees)				
35 Research and development costs (attach schedule)				
36 Section 118 exclusion (attach schedule) . . .				
37 Other expense/deduction items with differences (attach schedule)				
38 **Total expense/deduction items.** Combine lines 1 through 37. Enter here and on Part II, line 27, reporting positive amounts as negative and negative amounts as positive	314,440	110,000	(128,440)	296,000

Schedule M-3 (Form 1120) 2010

*$151,640 FIT per books – $124,100 FIT liability (current income tax expense) = $27,540 deferred income tax expense. Also see Comprehensive Problem, Year 1, Step 7 on text Page C:3-49.

**Business interest

Form **4626**	**Alternative Minimum Tax—Corporations**	OMB No. 1545-0175
Department of the Treasury Internal Revenue Service	► See separate instructions. ► Attach to the corporation's tax return.	20**10**

Name	Employer identification number
Glidden Corporation	38-1505786

Note: *See the instructions to find out if the corporation is a small corporation exempt from the alternative minimum tax (AMT) under section 55(e).*

1	Taxable income or (loss) before net operating loss deduction	**1**	130,278
2	**Adjustments and preferences:**		
a	Depreciation of post-1986 property	**2a**	7,500
b	Amortization of certified pollution control facilities.	**2b**	
c	Amortization of mining exploration and development costs	**2c**	
d	Amortization of circulation expenditures (personal holding companies only)	**2d**	
e	Adjusted gain or loss	**2e**	(6,918)
f	Long-term contracts	**2f**	
g	Merchant marine capital construction funds.	**2g**	
h	Section 833(b) deduction (Blue Cross, Blue Shield, and similar type organizations only)	**2h**	
i	Tax shelter farm activities (personal service corporations only)	**2i**	
j	Passive activities (closely held corporations and personal service corporations only)	**2j**	
k	Loss limitations	**2k**	
l	Depletion	**2l**	
m	Tax-exempt interest income from specified private activity bonds	**2m**	
n	Intangible drilling costs	**2n**	
o	Other adjustments and preferences	**2o**	
3	Pre-adjustment alternative minimum taxable income (AMTI). Combine lines 1 through 2o.	**3**	130,860

4	**Adjusted current earnings (ACE) adjustment:**				
a	ACE from line 10 of the ACE worksheet in the instructions	**4a**	312,360		
b	Subtract line 3 from line 4a. If line 3 exceeds line 4a, enter the difference as a negative amount (see instructions).	**4b**	181,500		
c	Multiply line 4b by 75% (.75). Enter the result as a positive amount	**4c**	136,125		
d	Enter the excess, if any, of the corporation's total increases in AMTI from prior year ACE adjustments over its total reductions in AMTI from prior year ACE adjustments (see instructions). **Note:** *You **must** enter an amount on line 4d (even if line 4b is positive)*	**4d**	311,296		
e	ACE adjustment. • If line 4b is zero or more, enter the amount from line 4c • If line 4b is less than zero, enter the **smaller** of line 4c or line 4d as a negative amount			**4e**	136,125
5	Combine lines 3 and 4e. If zero or less, stop here; the corporation does not owe any AMT			**5**	266,985
6	Alternative tax net operating loss deduction (see instructions)			**6**	-0-
7	**Alternative minimum taxable income.** Subtract line 6 from line 5. If the corporation held a residual interest in a REMIC, see instructions			**7**	266,985

8	**Exemption phase-out** (if line 7 is $310,000 or more, skip lines 8a and 8b and enter -0- on line 8c):				
a	Subtract $150,000 from line 7 (if completing this line for a member of a controlled group, see instructions). If zero or less, enter -0-	**8a**	116,985		
b	Multiply line 8a by 25% (.25).	**8b**	29,246		
c	Exemption. Subtract line 8b from $40,000 (if completing this line for a member of a controlled group, see instructions). If zero or less, enter -0-			**8c**	10,754
9	Subtract line 8c from line 7. If zero or less, enter -0-			**9**	256,231
10	Multiply line 9 by 20% (.20)			**10**	51,246
11	Alternative minimum tax foreign tax credit (AMTFTC) (see instructions)			**11**	-0-
12	Tentative minimum tax. Subtract line 11 from line 10			**12**	51,246
13	Regular tax liability before applying all credits except the foreign tax credit			**13**	34,058
14	**Alternative minimum tax.** Subtract line 13 from line 12. If zero or less, enter -0-. Enter here and on Form 1120, Schedule J, line 3, or the appropriate line of the corporation's income tax return			**14**	17,188

For Paperwork Reduction Act Notice, see the instructions.	Cat. No. 12955I	Form **4626** (2010)

Adjusted Current Earnings (ACE) Worksheet

▶ See ACE Worksheet Instructions (which begin on page 8).

1	Pre-adjustment AMTI . Enter the amount from line 3 of Form 4626	**1**		**130,860**
2	ACE depreciation adjustment:			
a	AMT depreciation	**2a**	**32,500**	
b	ACE depreciation:			
	(1) Post-1993 property	**2b(1)** **32,500**		
	(2) Post-1989, pre-1994 property	**2b(2)**		
	(3) Pre-1990 MACRS property	**2b(3)**		
	(4) Pre-1990 original ACRS property	**2b(4)**		
	(5) Property described in sections 168(f)(1) through (4)	**2b(5)**		
	(6) Other property	**2(b6)**		
	(7) Total ACE depreciation. Add lines 2b(1) through 2b(6)	**2b(7)** **32,500**		
c	ACE depreciation adjustment. Subtract line 2b(7) from line 2a	**2c**		**-0-**
3	Inclusion in ACE of items included in earnings and profits (E&P):			
a	Tax-exempt interest income	**3a**	**15,000**	
b	Death benefits from life insurance contracts	**3b**	**100,000**	
c	All other distributions from life insurance contracts (including surrenders)	**3c**		
d	Inside buildup of undistributed income in life insurance contracts	**3d**		
e	Other items (see Regulations sections 1.56(g)-1(c)(6)(iii) through (ix) for a partial list)	**3e**		
f	Total increase to ACE from inclusion in ACE of items included in E&P. Add lines 3a through 3e	**3f**		**115,000**
4	Disallowance of items not deductible from E&P:			
a	Certain dividends received	**4a**	**14,000**	
b	Dividends paid on certain preferred stock of public utilities that are deductible under section 247	**4b**		
c	Dividends paid to an ESOP that are deductible under section 404(k)	**4c**		
d	Nonpatronage dividends that are paid and deductible under section 1382(c) . . .	**4d**		
e	Other items (see Regulations sections 1.56(g)-1(d)(3)(i) and (ii) for a partial list)	**4e**		
f	Total increase to ACE because of disallowance of items not deductible from E&P. Add lines 4a through 4e	**4f**		**14,000**
5	Other adjustments based on rules for figuring E&P:			
a	Intangible drilling costs	**5a**		
b	Circulation expenditures	**5b**		
c	Organizational expenditures	**5c**	**500**	
d	LIFO inventory adjustments	**5d**		
e	Installment sales	**5e**	**52,000**	
f	Total other E&P adjustments. Combine lines 5a through 5e	**5f**		**52,500**
6	Disallowance of loss on exchange of debt pools	**6**		
7	Acquisition expenses of life insurance companies for qualified foreign contracts	**7**		
8	Depletion	**8**		
9	Basis adjustments in determining gain or loss from sale or exchange of pre-1994 property	**9**		
10	**Adjusted current earnings.** Combine lines 1, 2c, 3f, 4f, and 5f through 9. Enter the result here and on line 4a of Form 4626	**10**		**312,360**

Form **1120**		**U.S. Corporation Income Tax Return**				OMB No. 1545-0123	

Department of the Treasury
Internal Revenue Service

For calendar year 2010 or tax year beginning _____, 2010, ending _____, 20 _____

► **See separate instructions.**

2010

A Check if:

1a Consolidated return (attach Form 851) **[X]**

b Life/nonlife consolidated return . . **[ ]**

2 Personal holding co. (attach Sch. PH) . **[ ]**

3 Personal service corp. (see instructions) . **[ ]**

4 Schedule M-3 attached **[ ]**

Print or type

Name Alpha Manufacturing Corp. and Subsidaries

Number, street, and room or suite no. If a P.O. box, see instructions. 820 N.W. 1st Place

City or town, state, and ZIP code Gainesville, FL 32601

B Employer identification number 38-0000001

C Date incorporated 9/15/2000

D Total assets (see instructions) $ 3,976,492

E Check if: **(1)** [ ] Initial return **(2)** [ ] Final return **(3)** [ ] Name change **(4)** [ ] Address change

Income

1a	Gross receipts or sales	6,256,000	**b** Less returns and allowances	-0-	**c** Bal ► **1c**	6,256,000
2	Cost of goods sold (Schedule A, line 8)				**2**	2,410,000
3	Gross profit. Subtract line 2 from line 1c				**3**	3,846,000
4	Dividends (Schedule C, line 19)				**4**	40,000
5	Interest				**5**	156,000
6	Gross rents				**6**	195,000
7	Gross royalties				**7**	
8	Capital gain net income (attach Schedule D (Form 1120)) .				**8**	67,939
9	Net gain or (loss) from Form 4797, Part II, line 17 (attach Form 4797)				**9**	37,080
10	Other income (see instructions—attach schedule) . . .				**10**	10,000
11	**Total income.** Add lines 3 through 10 . . . . . ►				**11**	4,352,019

Deductions (See instructions for limitations on deductions.)

12	Compensation of officers (Schedule E, line 4) . . . . . . ►		**12**	165,000
13	Salaries and wages (less employment credits)		**13**	1,356,000
14	Repairs and maintenance		**14**	83,000
15	Bad debts		**15**	48,500
16	Rents		**16**	179,000
17	Taxes and licenses		**17**	138,000
18	Interest		**18**	58,000
19	Charitable contributions		**19**	15,000
20	Depreciation from Form 4562 not claimed on Schedule A or elsewhere on return (attach Form 4562) . .		**20**	168,693
21	Depletion		**21**	
22	Advertising		**22**	269,140
23	Pension, profit-sharing, etc., plans		**23**	140,000
24	Employee benefit programs		**24**	105,000
25	Domestic production activities deduction (attach Form 8903) . .		**25**	27,962
26	Other deductions (attach schedule)		**26**	1,284,000
27	**Total deductions.** Add lines 12 through 26 . . . . . ►		**27**	4,037,295
28	Taxable income before net operating loss deduction and special deductions. Subtract line 27 from line 11 .		**28**	314,724
29	**Less: a** Net operating loss deduction (see instructions)	**29a**		
	b Special deductions (Schedule C, line 20)	**29b**	32,000	**29c**	32,000

Tax, Refundable Credits, and Payments

30	**Taxable income.** Subtract line 29c from line 28 (see instructions)		**30**	282,724
31	**Total tax** (Schedule J, line 10)		**31**	93,512
32a	2009 overpayment credited to 2010	**32a**		
b	2010 estimated tax payments	**32b**	100,000	
c	2010 refund applied for on Form 4466	**32c** ( ) **d** Bal ►	**32d**	100,000
e	Tax deposited with Form 7004		**32e**	
f	Credits: **(1)** Form 2439	**(2)** Form 4136	**32f**	
g	Refundable credits from Form 3800, line 19c, and Form 8827, line 8c . . .	**32g**	**32h**	100,000
33	Estimated tax penalty (see instructions). Check if Form 2220 is attached . . . . ► [ ]		**33**	
34	**Amount owed.** If line 32h is smaller than the total of lines 31 and 33, enter amount owed . . .		**34**	
35	**Overpayment.** If line 32h is larger than the total of lines 31 and 33, enter amount overpaid		**35**	6,488
36	Enter amount from line 35 you want: **Credited to 2011 estimated tax** ► 6,488	**Refunded** ►	**36**	

Sign Here

Under penalties of perjury, I declare that I have examined this return, including accompanying schedules and statements, and to the best of my knowledge and belief, it is true, correct, and complete. Declaration of preparer (other than taxpayer) is based on all information of which preparer has any knowledge.

► *U. R. Stuck* | 3-15-11 | ► President
Signature of officer | Date | Title

May the IRS discuss this return with the preparer shown below (see instructions)? [ ] **Yes** [ ] **No**

Paid Preparer Use Only

Print/Type preparer's name	Preparer's signature	Date	Check [X] if self-employed	PTIN
John A. Kramer	*John A. Kramer*	3-14-11		104122

Firm's name ► Kramer and Associates | Firm's EIN ► 01-0000001

Firm's address ► 4710 N.W. 68th Terrace Gainesville, FL | Phone no. 352 555-5555

For Paperwork Reduction Act Notice, see separate instructions. | Cat. No. 11450Q | Form **1120** (2010)

Form 1120—Consolidated Taxable Income Computation

Line	Title	Consolidated	Adjustments and Eliminations	Alpha Mfg. Corp. 1	Beta Corp. 2	Charlie Corp. 3	Delta Corp. 4	Echo Corp. 5
1	Net gross receipts	$6,256,000	$85,000[1] (109,000)[2]	$1,566,000	$2,680,000	$676,000		$1,249,000
2	Cost goods/Operations	(2,410,000)		(783,000)	(1,390,000)	(128,000)		-0-
3	Gross profit	$3,846,000	($24,000)	$ 783,000	$1,290,000	$548,000	$ -0-	$1,249,000
4	Dividends (Sch. C)	40,000	(170,000)[3]	210,000				
5	Interest	156,000[5]		46,000	89,000			21,000
6	Gross rents	195,000					$195,000	
7	Gross royalties							
8	Capital gain net income (Sch. D)	67,939		67,939				
9	Net gain or loss from Form 4797	37,080	(14,600)[6]	52,760	(4,000)			
10	Other income	10,000[4]	2,920[6]	10,000				
11	Total income	$4,352,019	($205,680)	$1,169,699	$1,375,000	$548,000	$195,000	$1,270,000
12	Compensation of officers	$ 165,000		$ 165,000	$ 240,000	$377,000	$ 36,000	$ 565,000
13	Salaries and wages	1,356,000		138,000	18,000	7,000	18,000	21,000
14	Repairs	83,000		19,000	36,500	4,000		8,000
15	Bad debts	48,500			39,000	11,000		36,000
16	Rents	179,000		93,000	27,000	10,000	16,000	49,000
17	Taxes	138,000[4]		36,000			29,000[5]	2,000
18	Interest	58,000		27,000				2,000
19	Contributions	15,000[4]		9,000	4,000			
20	Depreciation	168,693		24,500	62,930	24,370	24,043	32,850
21	Depletion	-0-						
22	Advertising	269,140			223,140	27,000		19,000
23	Pension, profit sharing, etc. plans	140,000		39,000	21,000	35,000		45,000
24	Employee benefit programs	105,000		26,000	16,000	29,000		34,000
25	U.S. prod. act. ded.	27,962[7]			19,052			8,910
26	Other deductions	1,284,000[4]		409,000	401,000	72,000	49,000	353,000
27	Total deductions	$4,037,295	$ -0-	$ 985,500	$1,107,622	$596,370	$172,043	$1,175,760

Line	Title	Consolidated	Adjustments and Eliminations	1 Alpha Mfg. Corp.	2 Beta Corp.	3 Charlie Corp.	4 Delta Corp.	5 Echo Corp.
28	Taxable income before NOL ded. and special deductions	$314,724	($205,680)	$184,199	$267,378	($48,370)	$22,957	$94,240
29a	NOL deduction							
29b	Special deductions	(32,000)	(32,000)³					
30	Taxable income	$282,724	($237,680)					

Explanatory Notes

¹ Beta's inventory at the beginning of the current year includes items Alpha sold to Beta in the preceding year for an $85,000 profit. Beta sells the items to third parties in the current year. Under the matching rule, the group defers inclusion of the $85,000 in consolidated taxable income from the preceding year to the current year, so a positive $85,000 adjustment is needed for the current year.

² Beta's inventory at the end of the current year includes items Alpha sold to Beta in the current year for a $109,000 profit. Under the matching rule, the group defers inclusion of the $109,000 in consolidated taxable income from the current year to a subsequent year, so a negative $109,000 elimination entry is needed for the current year.

³ Dividends of $100,000 and $70,000 paid by Beta and Echo, respectively, to Alpha are an adjustment to consolidated taxable income because they were included in Alpha's separate tax return. The remaining $40,000 of dividends are from unaffiliated domestic corporations that are more than 20%-owned and eligible for an 80% dividends-received deduction (see Line 29b). The group claims a $32,000 dividends-received deduction.

⁴ The supporting schedule of component items is not reproduced here.

⁵ Alpha Manufacturing loaned money to Delta Corporation. Delta accrued and paid $12,000 in interest during the year. Under the matching rule, Delta's $12,000 of interest expense (the corresponding item) is matched with Alpha's $12,000 of interest income (the intercompany item). The two amounts offset, resulting in a zero net effect on consolidated taxable income (the recomputed corresponding item). The individual firms reported these amounts in their separate expense and income items, so no adjustment or elimination is needed.

⁶ Alpha sells a truck to Beta on June 1 of the current year for $25,000. The truck (a five-year MACRS property) cost $26,000 when purchased new on June 1 two years ago. Alpha did not elect Sec. 179 expensing or bonus depreciation on the truck and thus claimed depreciation of $13,520 [$26,000 × (0.20 + 0.32)] on the truck in the prior two years. Alpha claims depreciation of $2,080 ($26,000 × 0.192 × 5/12) in the current year. Alpha claims a total of $15,600 ($13,520 + $2,080) in depreciation prior to the sale. Alpha's deferred gain (intercompany item) on the sale is $14,600 [$25,000 − ($26,000 − $15,600)]. (See Line 9, Adjustments and Eliminations.) The truck is recorded as two separate MACRS properties on Beta's tax books. Beta depreciates the original $26,000 basis for the truck using the remainder of Alpha's five-year recovery period. Depreciation on this portion of the basis is $2,912 ($26,000 × 0.1920 × 7/12) in the current year. Beta also can depreciate the second MACRS property; that is, the step-up in basis that results from the intercompany sale. Beta elects to depreciate this portion of the basis as a five-year MACRS property and claims an additional $2,920 ($14,600 × 0.2000) of depreciation in the current year. Under the matching rule, the $2,920 is the portion of the deferred gain (Sec. 1245 income) Alpha reported in the current year.

⁷ The consolidated U.S. production activities deduction is computed as $310,686 × 0.09, where $310,686 is consolidated taxable income before that deduction and is less than consolidated qualified production activities income. The deduction is then allocated to the group members based on Reg. Sec. 1.199-7. The calculations assume that only Beta and Echo have positive qualified production activities income, 68.135% allocable to Beta and 31.865% allocable to Echo.

U.S. Return of Partnership Income

Form **1065**

Department of the Treasury
Internal Revenue Service

For calendar year 2010, or tax year beginning _____, 2010, ending _____, 20 ____ .

▶ See separate instructions.

OMB No. 1545-0099

20**10**

A Principal business activity		Name of partnership	D Employer identification number
Manufacturing		**Johns and Lawrence**	**76-3456789**
B Principal product or service	Print or type.	Number, street, and room or suite no. If a P.O. box, see the instructions.	E Date business started
Furniture		**1234 University Avenue**	**6-1-2004**
C Business code number		City or town, state, and ZIP code	F Total assets (see the instructions)
337000		**Gainesville, FL 32611**	$ **499,484**

G Check applicable boxes: **(1)** ☐ Initial return **(2)** ☐ Final return **(3)** ☐ Name change **(4)** ☐ Address change **(5)** ☐ Amended return
   (6) ☐ Technical termination - also check (1) or (2)

H Check accounting method: **(1)** ☐ Cash **(2)** ☒ Accrual **(3)** ☐ Other (specify) ▶ _____

I Number of Schedules K-1. Attach one for each person who was a partner at any time during the tax year ▶ _____

J Check if Schedules C and M-3 are attached . . . . ☐

Caution. *Include **only** trade or business income and expenses on lines 1a through 22 below. See the instructions for more information.*

Income	1a	Gross receipts or sales	1a	869,658			
	b	Less returns and allowances	1b	29,242	1c	840,416	
	2	Cost of goods sold (Schedule A, line 8)			2	540,204	
	3	Gross profit. Subtract line 2 from line 1c			3	300,212	
	4	Ordinary income (loss) from other partnerships, estates, and trusts *(attach statement)* . .			4		
	5	Net farm profit (loss) *(attach Schedule F (Form 1040))*			5		
	6	Net gain (loss) from Form 4797, Part II, line 17 *(attach Form 4797)*			6		
	7	Other income (loss) *(attach statement)*			7		
	8	**Total income (loss).** Combine lines 3 through 7			8	300,212	
Deductions (see the instructions for limitations)	9	Salaries and wages (other than to partners) (less employment credits)			9	52,000	
	10	Guaranteed payments to partners			10	36,000	
	11	Repairs and maintenance			11	4,800	
	12	Bad debts			12	4,000	
	13	Rent			13	36,000	
	14	Taxes and licenses . **(8,320 + 1,520)**			14	9,840	
	15	Interest			15	8,000	
	16a	Depreciation (*if required, attach Form 4562*)	16a	27,476			
	b	Less depreciation reported on Schedule A and elsewhere on return	16b	15,000	16c	12,476	
	17	Depletion **(Do not deduct oil and gas depletion.)**			17		
	18	Retirement plans, etc.			18	2,000	
	19	Employee benefit programs			19	4,000	
	20	Other deductions *(attach statement)*			20	51,250	
	21	**Total deductions.** Add the amounts shown in the far right column for lines 9 through 20 .			21	220,366	
	22	**Ordinary business income (loss).** Subtract line 21 from line 8			22	79,846	

Sign Here

Under penalties of perjury, I declare that I have examined this return, including accompanying schedules and statements, and to the best of my knowledge and belief, it is true, correct, and complete. Declaration of preparer (other than general partner or limited liability company member manager) is based on all information of which preparer has any knowledge.

▶ *Andrew Lawrence*
Signature of general partner or limited liability company member manager

▶ **4-10-11**
Date

May the IRS discuss this return with the preparer shown below (see instructions)? ☐ Yes ☐ No

Paid Preparer Use Only	Print/Type preparer's name	Preparer's signature	Date	Check ☒ if self-employed	PTIN
	Michael S. Kramer	*Michael S. Kramer*	**4-7-11**		**104121**
	Firm's name ▶ **Michael S. Kramer**			Firm's EIN ▶ **59-2029763**	
	Firm's address ▶ **1110 McMillon Gainesville, FL 37611**			Phone no. **(352) 555-2000**	

For Paperwork Reduction Act Notice, see separate instructions. Cat. No. 11390Z Form **1065** (2010)

Form 1065 (2010) Page **2**

Schedule A	**Cost of Goods Sold** (see the instructions)		
1	Inventory at beginning of year	1	64,000
2	Purchases less cost of items withdrawn for personal use	2	340,800
3	Cost of labor	3	143,204
4	Additional section 263A costs (attach statement)	4	7,000
5	Other costs (attach statement)	5	90,000
6	**Total.** Add lines 1 through 5	6	645,004
7	Inventory at end of year	7	104,800
8	**Cost of goods sold.** Subtract line 7 from line 6. Enter here and on page 1, line 2	8	540,204

9a Check all methods used for valuing closing inventory:

(i) ☐ Cost as described in Regulations section 1.471-3

(ii) ☒ Lower of cost or market as described in Regulations section 1.471-4

(iii) ☐ Other (specify method used and attach explanation) ▶ _____

b Check this box if there was a writedown of "subnormal" goods as described in Regulations section 1.471-2(c) . . . ▶ ☐

c Check this box if the LIFO inventory method was adopted this tax year for any goods (if checked, attach Form 970) . . ▶ ☐

d Do the rules of section 263A (for property produced or acquired for resale) apply to the partnership? . . . . ☒ Yes ☐ No

e Was there any change in determining quantities, cost, or valuations between opening and closing inventory? . . ☐ Yes ☒ No
If "Yes," attach explanation.

Schedule B	**Other Information**		Yes	No

1 What type of entity is filing this return? Check the applicable box:

a ☒ Domestic general partnership   **b** ☐ Domestic limited partnership

c ☐ Domestic limited liability company   **d** ☐ Domestic limited liability partnership

e ☐ Foreign partnership   **f** ☐ Other ▶ _____

2 At any time during the tax year, was any partner in the partnership a disregarded entity, a partnership (including an entity treated as a partnership), a trust, an S corporation, an estate (other than an estate of a deceased partner), or a nominee or similar person? . . . . | | X

3 At the end of the tax year:

a Did any foreign or domestic corporation, partnership (including any entity treated as a partnership), trust, or tax-exempt organization own, directly or indirectly, an interest of 50% or more in the profit, loss, or capital of the partnership? For rules of constructive ownership, see instructions. If "Yes," attach Schedule B-1, Information on Partners Owning 50% or More of the Partnership . . . . | | X

b Did any individual or estate own, directly or indirectly, an interest of 50% or more in the profit, loss, or capital of the partnership? For rules of constructive ownership, see instructions. If "Yes," attach Schedule B-1, Information on Partners Owning 50% or More of the Partnership* . . . .   X | |

4 At the end of the tax year, did the partnership:

a Own directly 20% or more, or own, directly or indirectly, 50% or more of the total voting power of all classes of stock entitled to vote of any foreign or domestic corporation? For rules of constructive ownership, see instructions. If "Yes," complete (i) through (iv) below . . . . | | X

(i) Name of Corporation	(ii) Employer Identification Number (if any)	(iii) Country of Incorporation	(iv) Percentage Owned in Voting Stock

b Own directly an interest of 20% or more, or own, directly or indirectly, an interest of 50% or more in the profit, loss, or capital in any foreign or domestic partnership (including an entity treated as a partnership) or in the beneficial interest of a trust? For rules of constructive ownership, see instructions. If "Yes," complete (i) through (v) below . . | | X

(i) Name of Entity	(ii) Employer Identification Number (if any)	(iii) Type of Entity	(iv) Country of Organization	(v) Maximum Percentage Owned in Profit, Loss, or Capital

*Schedule B-1 is not attached. If attached, it would list Stephen Johns and Andrew Lawrence, each of whom own a 50% interest in the partnership.

Form **1065** (2010)

Form 1065 (2010)   Page **3**

		Yes	No
5	Did the partnership file Form 8893, Election of Partnership Level Tax Treatment, or an election statement under section 6231(a)(1)(B)(ii) for partnership-level tax treatment, that is in effect for this tax year? See Form 8893 for more details		X
6	Does the partnership satisfy **all four** of the following conditions?		
a	The partnership's total receipts for the tax year were less than $250,000.		
b	The partnership's total assets at the end of the tax year were less than $1 million.		
c	Schedules K-1 are filed with the return and furnished to the partners on or before the due date (including extensions) for the partnership return.		
d	The partnership is not filing and is not required to file Schedule M-3		X
	If "Yes," the partnership is not required to complete Schedules L, M-1, and M-2; Item F on page 1 of Form 1065; or Item L on Schedule K-1.		
7	Is this partnership a publicly traded partnership as defined in section 469(k)(2)?		X
8	During the tax year, did the partnership have any debt that was cancelled, was forgiven, or had the terms modified so as to reduce the principal amount of the debt?		X
9	Has this partnership filed, or is it required to file, Form 8918, Material Advisor Disclosure Statement, to provide information on any reportable transaction?		X
10	At any time during calendar year 2010, did the partnership have an interest in or a signature or other authority over a financial account in a foreign country (such as a bank account, securities account, or other financial account)? See the instructions for exceptions and filing requirements for Form TD F 90-22.1, Report of Foreign Bank and Financial Accounts. If "Yes," enter the name of the foreign country. ▶		X
11	At any time during the tax year, did the partnership receive a distribution from, or was it the grantor of, or transferor to, a foreign trust? If "Yes," the partnership may have to file Form 3520, Annual Return To Report Transactions With Foreign Trusts and Receipt of Certain Foreign Gifts. See instructions		X
12a	Is the partnership making, or had it previously made (and not revoked), a section 754 election?		X
	See instructions for details regarding a section 754 election.		
b	Did the partnership make for this tax year an optional basis adjustment under section 743(b) or 734(b)? If "Yes," attach a statement showing the computation and allocation of the basis adjustment. See instructions		X
c	Is the partnership required to adjust the basis of partnership assets under section 743(b) or 734(b) because of a substantial built-in loss (as defined under section 743(d)) or substantial basis reduction (as defined under section 734(d))? If "Yes," attach a statement showing the computation and allocation of the basis adjustment. See instructions.		X
13	Check this box if, during the current or prior tax year, the partnership distributed any property received in a like-kind exchange or contributed such property to another entity (other than entities wholly-owned by the partnership throughout the tax year) . . . . ▶ ☐		
14	At any time during the tax year, did the partnership distribute to any partner a tenancy-in-common or other undivided interest in partnership property?		X
15	If the partnership is required to file Form 8858, Information Return of U.S. Persons With Respect To Foreign Disregarded Entities, enter the number of Forms 8858 attached. See instructions ▶		
16	Does the partnership have any foreign partners? If "Yes," enter the number of Forms 8805, Foreign Partner's Information Statement of Section 1446 Withholding Tax, filed for this partnership. ▶		X
17	Enter the number of Forms 8865, Return of U.S. Persons With Respect to Certain Foreign Partnerships, attached to this return. ▶ ------------------------------------		

Designation of Tax Matters Partner (see instructions)

Enter below the general partner designated as the tax matters partner (TMP) for the tax year of this return:

Name of designated TMP ▶	Andrew Lawrence	Identifying number of TMP ▶	297-63-2110
If the TMP is an entity, name of TMP representative ▶		Phone number of TMP ▶	
Address of designated TMP ▶	436 N.W. 24th Ave. Gainesville, FL 32607		

Form **1065** (2010)

Form 1065 (2010)   Page **4**

Schedule K		Partners' Distributive Share Items			Total amount	
Income (Loss)	1	Ordinary business income (loss) (page 1, line 22)		1	79,846	
	2	Net rental real estate income (loss) (attach Form 8825)		2		
	3a	Other gross rental income (loss)	3a			
	b	Expenses from other rental activities (attach statement) .	3b			
	c	Other net rental income (loss). Subtract line 3b from line 3a		3c		
	4	Guaranteed payments		4	36,000	
	5	Interest income		5		
	6	Dividends: a Ordinary dividends		6a	1,000	
		b Qualified dividends	6b	1,000		
	7	Royalties		7		
	8	Net short-term capital gain (loss) (attach Schedule D (Form 1065))		8	(2,100)	
	9a	Net long-term capital gain (loss) (attach Schedule D (Form 1065))		9a	4,500	
	b	Collectibles (28%) gain (loss)	9b			
	c	Unrecaptured section 1250 gain (attach statement) . .	9c			
	10	Net section 1231 gain (loss) (attach Form 4797)		10		
	11	Other income (loss) (see instructions) Type ▶		11		
Deductions	12	Section 179 deduction (attach Form 4562)		12		
	13a	Contributions		13a	12,000	
	b	Investment interest expense		13b	150	
	c	Section 59(e)(2) expenditures: **(1)** Type ▶ _____ **(2)** Amount ▶		13c(2)		
	d	Other deductions (see instructions) Type ▶		13d	*	
Self-Employment	14a	Net earnings (loss) from self-employment		14a	115,846	
	b	Gross farming or fishing income		14b		
	c	Gross nonfarm income		14c	300,212	
Credits	15a	Low-income housing credit (section 42(j)(5))		15a		
	b	Low-income housing credit (other)		15b		
	c	Qualified rehabilitation expenditures (rental real estate) (attach Form 3468)		15c		
	d	Other rental real estate credits (see instructions) Type ▶		15d		
	e	Other rental credits (see instructions) Type ▶		15e		
	f	Other credits (see instructions) Type ▶		15f		
Foreign Transactions	16a	Name of country or U.S. possession ▶				
	b	Gross income from all sources		16b		
	c	Gross income sourced at partner level		16c		
		Foreign gross income sourced at partnership level				
	d	Passive category ▶ _____ **e** General category ▶ _____ **f** Other ▶		16f		
		Deductions allocated and apportioned at partner level				
	g	Interest expense ▶ _____ **h** Other . . . . ▶		16h		
		Deductions allocated and apportioned at partnership level to foreign source income				
	i	Passive category ▶ _____ **j** General category ▶ _____ **k** Other ▶		16k		
	l	Total foreign taxes (check one): ▶ Paid ☐ Accrued ☐		16l		
	m	Reduction in taxes available for credit (attach statement)		16m		
	n	Other foreign tax information (attach statement)				
Alternative Minimum Tax (AMT) Items	17a	Post-1986 depreciation adjustment		17a	1,514	
	b	Adjusted gain or loss		17b		
	c	Depletion (other than oil and gas)		17c		
	d	Oil, gas, and geothermal properties—gross income		17d		
	e	Oil, gas, and geothermal properties—deductions		17e		
	f	Other AMT items (attach statement)		17f		
Other Information	18a	Tax-exempt interest income		18a	18,000	
	b	Other tax-exempt income		18b		
	c	Nondeductible expenses		18c	6,000	**
	19a	Distributions of cash and marketable securities		19a	28,212	
	b	Distributions of other property		19b		
	20a	Investment income		20a	1,000	***
	b	Investment expenses		20b		
	c	Other items and amounts (attach statement)				

Form **1065** (2010)

*Qualified production activities income (QPAI) equals $80,000. Employer's W-2 wages allocable to U.S. production activities equal $52,000.

**Disallowed meals and entertainment expenses ($4,000) and interest on loan used to purchase tax-exempt bonds ($2,000).

***If partners elect to tax dividends at ordinary rates under Sec. 163(d)(4)(B).

Form 1065 (2010)   Page **5**

Analysis of Net Income (Loss)

1	Net income (loss). Combine Schedule K, lines 1 through 11. From the result, subtract the sum of Schedule K, lines 12 through 13d, and 16l					**1**	**107,096**

2	Analysis by partner type:	**(i)** Corporate	**(ii)** Individual (active)	**(iii)** Individual (passive)	**(iv)** Partnership	**(v)** Exempt organization	**(vi)** Nominee/Other
a	General partners		107,096				
b	Limited partners						

Schedule L — Balance Sheets per Books

	Assets	Beginning of tax year (a)	(b)	End of tax year (c)	(d)
1	Cash		60,000		92,760
2a	Trade notes and accounts receivable . . .	25,100		24,000	
b	Less allowance for bad debts	1,000	24,000	1,000	23,000
3	Inventories		64,000		104,800
4	U.S. government obligations				
5	Tax-exempt securities		200,000		200,000
6	Other current assets (*attach statement*) . .		7,000		-0-
7	Mortgage and real estate loans . . .				
8	Other investments (*attach statement*) . . .				
9a	Buildings and other depreciable assets . .	151,600		151,600	
b	Less accumulated depreciation	45,200	106,400	72,760	78,924
10a	Depletable assets				
b	Less accumulated depletion				
11	Land (net of any amortization)				
12a	Intangible assets (amortizable only) . . .				
b	Less accumulated amortization				
13	Other assets (*attach statement*) . . .				
14	Total assets		461,400		499,484
	Liabilities and Capital				
15	Accounts payable		26,000		19,000
16	Mortgages, notes, bonds payable in less than 1 year		4,000		4,000
17	Other current liabilities (*attach statement*) .		3,600		3,600
18	All nonrecourse loans				
19	Mortgages, notes, bonds payable in 1 year or more		130,000		119,724
20	Other liabilities (*attach statement*)				
21	Partners' capital accounts		297,800		353,160
22	Total liabilities and capital		461,400		499,484

Schedule M-1 — Reconciliation of Income (Loss) per Books With Income (Loss) per Return

Note. Schedule M-3 may be required instead of Schedule M-1 (see instructions).

1	Net income (loss) per books	83,572	6	Income recorded on books this year not included on Schedule K, lines 1 through 11 (itemize):		
2	Income included on Schedule K, lines 1, 2, 3c, 5, 6a, 7, 8, 9a, 10, and 11, not recorded on books this year (itemize): _____		a	Tax-exempt interest $ __18,000__		18,000
3	Guaranteed payments (other than health insurance)	36,000	7	Deductions included on Schedule K, lines 1 through 13d, and 16l, not charged against book income this year (itemize):		
4	Expenses recorded on books this year not included on Schedule K, lines 1 through 13d, and 16l (itemize):		a	Depreciation $ __476__		
a	Depreciation $					476
b	Travel and entertainment $ __4,000__		8	Add lines 6 and 7		18,476
	__Interest on loans*__ __2,000__	6,000	9	Income (loss) (Analysis of Net Income (Loss), line 1). Subtract line 8 from line 5 .		107,096
5	Add lines 1 through 4	125,572				

Schedule M-2 — Analysis of Partners' Capital Accounts

1	Balance at beginning of year . . .	297,800	6	Distributions: **a** Cash		28,212
2	Capital contributed: **a** Cash . . .			**b** Property		
	b Property . .		7	Other decreases (itemize): _____		
3	Net income (loss) per books	83,572		_____		
4	Other increases (itemize): _____					
	_____		8	Add lines 6 and 7		28,212
5	Add lines 1 through 4	381,372	9	Balance at end of year. Subtract line 8 from line 5		353,160

*To buy tax-exempt bonds.

Form **1065** (2010)

651110

☐ Final K-1   ☐ Amended K-1   OMB No. 1545-0099

Schedule K-1 (Form 1065)

20**10**

Department of the Treasury
Internal Revenue Service

For calendar year 2010, or tax

year beginning _____, 2010

ending _____, 20 _____

Partner's Share of Income, Deductions, Credits, etc.

► See back of form and separate instructions.

Part III	**Partner's Share of Current Year Income, Deductions, Credits, and Other Items**		
1	Ordinary business income (loss) **39,923**	15	Credits
2	Net rental real estate income (loss)		
3	Other net rental income (loss)	16	Foreign transactions
4	Guaranteed payments **18,000**		
5	Interest income		
6a	Ordinary dividends **500**		
6b	Qualified dividends **500**		
7	Royalties		
8	Net short-term capital gain (loss) **(1,050)**		
9a	Net long-term capital gain (loss) **2,250**	17	Alternative minimum tax (AMT) items **A 757**
9b	Collectibles (28%) gain (loss)		
9c	Unrecaptured section 1250 gain		
10	Net section 1231 gain (loss)	18	Tax-exempt income and nondeductible expenses
11	Other income (loss)	**A**	**9,000**
		C	**3,000**
		19	Distributions **A 14,106**
12	Section 179 deduction		
13	Other deductions **A 6,000**	20	Other information **A 500****
	G 75 **U 40,000** **V 26,000**		
14	Self-employment earnings (loss) **A 57,923**		
	A 150,106		

Part I Information About the Partnership

A Partnership's employer identification number

76-3456789

B Partnership's name, address, city, state, and ZIP code

Johns and Lawrence
1234 University Ave.
Gainesville, FL 32611

C IRS Center where partnership filed return

Ogden, UT

D ☐ Check if this is a publicly traded partnership (PTP)

Part II Information About the Partner

E Partner's identifying number

297-63-2110

F Partner's name, address, city, state, and ZIP code

Andrew Lawrence*
436 N.W. 24th Ave.
Gainesville, FL 32607

G ☒ General partner or LLC member-manager   ☐ Limited partner or other LLC member

H ☐ Domestic partner   ☐ Foreign partner

I What type of entity is this partner? **Individual**

J Partner's share of profit, loss, and capital (see instructions):

	Beginning	Ending
Profit	50 %	50 %
Loss	50 %	50 %
Capital	50 %	50 %

K Partner's share of liabilities at year end:

Nonrecourse	$
Qualified nonrecourse financing	$
Recourse	$ 73,162

L Partner's capital account analysis:

Beginning capital account	$ 148,900
Capital contributed during the year	$ -0-
Current year increase (decrease)	$ 41,786
Withdrawals & distributions	$ (14,106)
Ending capital account	$ 176,580

☐ Tax basis   ☒ GAAP   ☐ Section 704(b) book
☐ Other (explain)

M Did the partner contribute property with a built-in gain or loss?
☐ Yes   ☒ No
If "Yes", attach statement (see instructions)

*See attached statement for additional information.

For IRS Use Only

*Schedule K-1 for Stephen Johns is similar to this one and is not reproduced here.

**If partner elects to tax dividends at ordinary rates under Sec. 163(d)(4)(B).

This list identifies the codes used on Schedule K-1 for all partners and provides summarized reporting information for partners who file Form 1040. For detailed reporting and filing information, see the separate Partner's Instructions for Schedule K-1 and the instructions for your income tax return.

1. **Ordinary business income (loss).** Determine whether the income (loss) is passive or nonpassive and enter on your return as follows.

	Report on
Passive loss	See the Partner's Instructions
Passive income	Schedule E, line 28, column (g)
Nonpassive loss	Schedule E, line 28, column (h)
Nonpassive income	Schedule E, line 28, column (j)

2. **Net rental real estate income (loss)** — See the Partner's Instructions
3. **Other net rental income (loss)**

Net income	Schedule E, line 28, column (g)
Net loss	See the Partner's Instructions

4. **Guaranteed payments** — Schedule E, line 28, column (j)
5. **Interest income** — Form 1040, line 8a
6a. **Ordinary dividends** — Form 1040, line 9a
6b. **Qualified dividends** — Form 1040, line 9b
7. **Royalties** — Schedule E, line 4
8. **Net short-term capital gain (loss)** — Schedule D, line 5, column (f)
9a. **Net long-term capital gain (loss)** — Schedule D, line 12, column (f)
9b. **Collectibles (28%) gain (loss)** — 28% Rate Gain Worksheet, line 4 (Schedule D instructions)
9c. **Unrecaptured section 1250 gain** — See the Partner's Instructions
10. **Net section 1231 gain (loss)** — See the Partner's Instructions
11. **Other income (loss)**

Code

A	Other portfolio income (loss)	See the Partner's Instructions
B	Involuntary conversions	See the Partner's Instructions
C	Sec. 1256 contracts & straddles	Form 6781, line 1
D	Mining exploration costs recapture	See Pub. 535
E	Cancellation of debt	Form 1040, line 21 or Form 982
F	Other income (loss)	See the Partner's Instructions

12. **Section 179 deduction** — See the Partner's Instructions
13. **Other deductions**

A	Cash contributions (50%)	
B	Cash contributions (30%)	
C	Noncash contributions (50%)	
D	Noncash contributions (30%)	See the Partner's Instructions
E	Capital gain property to a 50% organization (30%)	
F	Capital gain property (20%)	
G	Contributions (100%)	
H	Investment interest expense	Form 4952, line 1
I	Deductions—royalty income	Schedule E, line 18
J	Section 59(e)(2) expenditures	See the Partner's Instructions
K	Deductions—portfolio (2% floor)	Schedule A, line 23
L	Deductions—portfolio (other)	Schedule A, line 28
M	Amounts paid for medical insurance	Schedule A, line 1 or Form 1040, line 29
N	Educational assistance benefits	See the Partner's Instructions
O	Dependent care benefits	Form 2441, line 12
P	Preproductive period expenses	See the Partner's Instructions
Q	Commercial revitalization deduction from rental real estate activities	See Form 8582 instructions
R	Pensions and IRAs	See the Partner's Instructions
S	Reforestation expense deduction	See the Partner's Instructions
T	Domestic production activities information	See Form 8903 instructions
U	Qualified production activities income	Form 8903, line 7b
V	Employer's Form W-2 wages	Form 8903, line 17
W	Other deductions	See the Partner's Instructions

14. **Self-employment earnings (loss)**

Note. *If you have a section 179 deduction or any partner-level deductions, see the Partner's Instructions before completing Schedule SE.*

A	Net earnings (loss) from self-employment	Schedule SE, Section A or B
B	Gross farming or fishing income	See the Partner's Instructions
C	Gross non-farm income	See the Partner's Instructions

15. **Credits**

A	Low-income housing credit (section 42(j)(5)) from pre-2008 buildings	See the Partner's Instructions
B	Low-income housing credit (other) from pre-2008 buildings	See the Partner's Instructions
C	Low-income housing credit (section 42(j)(5)) from post-2007 buildings	Form 8586, line 11
D	Low-income housing credit (other) from post-2007 buildings	Form 8586, line 11
E	Qualified rehabilitation expenditures (rental real estate)	
F	Other rental real estate credits	See the Partner's Instructions
G	Other rental credits	
H	Undistributed capital gains credit	Form 1040, line 71; check box a
I	Alcohol and cellulosic biofuel fuels credit	Form 6478, line 8
J	Work opportunity credit	Form 5884, line 3

Code		*Report on*
K	Disabled access credit	See the Partner's Instructions
L	Empowerment zone and renewal community employment credit	Form 8844, line 3
M	Credit for increasing research activities	See the Partner's Instructions
N	Credit for employer social security and Medicare taxes	Form 8846, line 5
O	Backup withholding	Form 1040, line 61
P	Other credits	See the Partner's Instructions

16. **Foreign transactions**

A	Name of country or U.S. possession	
B	Gross income from all sources	Form 1116, Part I
C	Gross income sourced at partner level	

Foreign gross income sourced at partnership level

D	Passive category	
E	General category	Form 1116, Part I
F	Other	

Deductions allocated and apportioned at partner level

G	Interest expense	Form 1116, Part I
H	Other	Form 1116, Part I

Deductions allocated and apportioned at partnership level to foreign source income

I	Passive category	
J	General category	Form 1116, Part I
K	Other	

Other information

L	Total foreign taxes paid	Form 1116, Part II
M	Total foreign taxes accrued	Form 1116, Part II
N	Reduction in taxes available for credit	Form 1116, line 12
O	Foreign trading gross receipts	Form 8873
P	Extraterritorial income exclusion	Form 8873
Q	Other foreign transactions	See the Partner's Instructions

17. **Alternative minimum tax (AMT) items**

A	Post-1986 depreciation adjustment	
B	Adjusted gain or loss	See the Partner's
C	Depletion (other than oil & gas)	Instructions and
D	Oil, gas, & geothermal—gross income	the Instructions for
E	Oil, gas, & geothermal—deductions	Form 6251
F	Other AMT items	

18. **Tax-exempt income and nondeductible expenses**

A	Tax-exempt interest income	Form 1040, line 8b
B	Other tax-exempt income	See the Partner's Instructions
C	Nondeductible expenses	See the Partner's Instructions

19. **Distributions**

A	Cash and marketable securities	
B	Distribution subject to section 737	See the Partner's Instructions
C	Other property	

20. **Other information**

A	Investment income	Form 4952, line 4a
B	Investment expenses	Form 4952, line 5
C	Fuel tax credit information	Form 4136
D	Qualified rehabilitation expenditures (other than rental real estate)	See the Partner's Instructions
E	Basis of energy property	See the Partner's Instructions
F	Recapture of low-income housing credit (section 42(j)(5))	Form 8611, line 8
G	Recapture of low-income housing credit (other)	Form 8611, line 8
H	Recapture of investment credit	See Form 4255
I	Recapture of other credits	See the Partner's Instructions
J	Look-back interest—completed long-term contracts	See Form 8697
K	Look-back interest—income forecast method	See Form 8866
L	Dispositions of property with section 179 deductions	
M	Recapture of section 179 deduction	
N	Interest expense for corporate partners	
O	Section 453(l)(3) information	
P	Section 453A(c) information	
Q	Section 1260(b) information	
R	Interest allocable to production expenditures	See the Partner's Instructions
S	CCF nonqualified withdrawals	
T	Depletion information—oil and gas	
U	Amortization of reforestation costs	
V	Unrelated business taxable income	
W	Precontribution gain (loss)	
X	Section 108(i) information	
Y	Other information	

FACTS FOR GENERAL PARTNERSHIP (FORM 1065)

The same basic facts presented for the Andrew Lawrence proprietorship are used for the partnership except for the following:

1. Johns and Lawrence is instead a general partnership. Andrew Lawrence and Stephen Johns are both general partners and have equal capital and profits interests. The partners formed the partnership on June 1, 2004. Johns and Lawrence each exchanged their $100,000 of property for a 50% interest in capital and profits.

2. The book income for Johns and Lawrence is presented in the attached worksheet, which reconciles book income and partnership taxable income.

3. The $18,000 salaries paid to each partner are stipulated in the partnership agreement and are treated as guaranteed payments.

4. The partnership pays federal and state employment taxes on the wages paid to employees other than the partners Johns and Lawrence. The employment tax expense is $52,000 × 0.16 = $8,320. The guaranteed payments made to Johns and Lawrence are treated as self-employment income by the two partners.

5. The partnership paid no estimated federal income taxes.

6. The partnership distributed $14,106 to each of the two partners.

7. Other deductions include:

Travel	$ 4,000
Meals and entertainment	8,000
Minus: 50% disallowance	(4,000)
Office expenses	16,000
Transportation	10,400
General and administrative	3,000
Advertising	13,000
Miscellaneous*	850
Total	$51,250

*$150 of the miscellaneous expenses are related to the production of the dividend income and are separately stated.

8. The following schedule reconciles net income for the C corporation and the partnership:

Net income per books for C corporation	$63,412
Plus: Federal income taxes	14,000
Employment tax adjustment ($14,480 − $8,320)	6,160
Net income per books for partnership	$83,572

9. Total paid-in capital and accumulated profits were divided equally between the two partners in accordance with the actual contributions and allocation of partnership profits in the partnership agreement. Actual business operations may provide for an unequal allocation.

10. Qualified production activities income (QPAI) equals $80,000. Employer's W-2 wages allocable to U.S. production activities equal $52,000.

11. The balance sheet for Johns and Lawrence appears on page 4 of Form 1065.

Johns and Lawrence General Partnership Reconciliation of Book and Taxable Income For Year Ending December 31, 2010

Account Name	Book Income Debit	Book Income Credit	Adjustments Debit	Adjustments Credit	Taxable Income Debit	Taxable Income Credit	Form 1065 Schedule K Ordinary Income	Form 1065 Schedule K Separately Stated Items
Sales		$869,658				$869,658	$869,658	
Sales returns & allowances	$ 29,242				$ 29,242		(29,242)	
Cost of sales	540,204				540,204		(540,204)	
Dividends		1,000				1,000		$ 1,000
Tax-exempt interest		18,000	$18,000			0		18,000
Gain on stock sale		4,500				4,500		4,500
Worthless stock loss	2,100				2,100			(2,100)
Guaranteed payments[a]	36,000			$36,000	0		(36,000)	
Other salaries	52,000				52,000		(52,000)	
Rentals	36,000				36,000		(36,000)	
Bad debts	4,000				4,000		(4,000)	
Interest:								
Working capital loans	8,000				8,000		(8,000)	
Purchase tax-exempt bonds	2,000			2,000	0			(2,000)
Employment taxes	8,320				8,320		(8,320)	
Taxes	1,520				1,520		(1,520)	
Repairs	4,800				4,800		(4,800)	
Depreciation[b]	12,000		476		12,476		(12,476)	
Charitable contributions	12,000				12,000			(12,000)
Travel	4,000				4,000		(4,000)	
Meals and entertainment[c]	8,000			4,000	4,000		(4,000)	
Meals and ent. nondeductible								(4,000)
Office expenses	16,000				16,000		(16,000)	
Advertising	13,000				13,000		(13,000)	
Transportation expense	10,400				10,400		(10,400)	
General and administrative	3,000				3,000		(3,000)	
Pension plans[d]	2,000				2,000		(2,000)	
Employee benefit programs[e]	4,000				4,000		(4,000)	
Miscellaneous	1,000				1,000		(850)	(150)
Net profit/Taxable income	83,572		$23,524		107,096			
Total	$893,158	$893,158	$42,000	$42,000	$875,158	$875,158	$ 79,846	

[a] Guaranteed payments have no net effect on taxable income. The guaranteed payments both reduce ordinary income and increase separately stated income items that are taxable.

[b] MACRS depreciation = $27,476 total − $15,000 allocated to COGS= $12,476

[c] 50% of the meals and entertainment expense is not deductible for tax purposes but must be separately stated on Schedules K and K-1.

[d] The pension plan expense is the same for book and tax purposes for this partnership. No pension expenses relate to pensions for the partners.

[e] The employee benefit expense is the same for book and tax purposes for this partnership. None relates to partner benefits.

Form **1120S**		**U.S. Income Tax Return for an S Corporation**		OMB No. 1545-0130

▶ Do not file this form unless the corporation has filed or is attaching Form 2553 to elect to be an S corporation.
▶ See separate instructions.

Department of the Treasury
Internal Revenue Service

2010

For calendar year 2010 or tax year beginning _____ , 2010, ending _____ , 20___

A S election effective date		Name	**D** Employer identification number
6-13-2004	**TYPE OR PRINT**	**Johns and Lawrence, Inc.**	**76-3456789**
B Business activity code number *(see instructions)*		Number, street, and room or suite no. If a P.O. box, see instructions.	**E** Date incorporated
337000		**1234 University Avenue**	**6-1-2004**
C Check if Sch. M-3 attached ☐		City or town, state, and ZIP code **Gainsville, FL 32611**	**F** Total assets *(see instructions)* $ **498,324**

G Is the corporation electing to be an S corporation beginning with this tax year? ☐ Yes ☐ No   If "Yes," attach Form 2553 if not already filed

H Check if: **(1)** ☐ Final return   **(2)** ☐ Name change   **(3)** ☐ Address change
(4) ☐ Amended return   **(5)** ☐ S election termination or revocation

I Enter the number of shareholders who were shareholders during any part of the tax year . . . . ▶ **2**

Caution. Include **only** trade or business income and expenses on lines 1a through 21. See the instructions for more information.

Income

1a	Gross receipts or sales	**869,658**	**b** Less returns and allowances **29,242**	**c** Bal ▶	**1c**	**840,416**
2	Cost of goods sold (Schedule A, line 8)				**2**	**540,204**
3	Gross profit. Subtract line 2 from line 1c				**3**	**300,212**
4	Net gain (loss) from Form 4797, Part II, line 17 *(attach Form 4797)*				**4**	
5	Other income (loss) *(see instructions—attach statement)*				**5**	
6	**Total income (loss).** Add lines 3 through 5			▶	**6**	**300,212**

Deductions (see instructions for limitations)

7	Compensation of officers	**7**	**36,000**
8	Salaries and wages (less employment credits)	**8**	**52,000**
9	Repairs and maintenance	**9**	**4,800**
10	Bad debts	**10**	**4,000**
11	Rents	**11**	**36,000**
12	Taxes and licenses	**12**	**16,000**
13	Interest	**13**	**8,000**
14	Depreciation not claimed on Schedule A or elsewhere on return *(attach Form 4562)*	**14**	**12,476**
15	Depletion **(Do not deduct oil and gas depletion.)**	**15**	
16	Advertising	**16**	**13,000**
17	Pension, profit-sharing, etc., plans	**17**	**2,000**
18	Employee benefit programs	**18**	**4,000**
19	Other deductions *(attach statement)*	**19**	**38,250**
20	**Total deductions.** Add lines 7 through 19 ▶	**20**	**226,526**
21	**Ordinary business income (loss).** Subtract line 20 from line 6	**21**	**73,686**

Tax and Payments

22a	Excess net passive income or LIFO recapture tax *(see instructions)*	**22a**		
b	Tax from Schedule D (Form 1120S)	**22b**		
c	Add lines 22a and 22b *(see instructions for additional taxes)*		**22c**	**NONE**
23a	2010 estimated tax payments and 2009 overpayment credited to 2010	**23a**		
b	Tax deposited with Form 7004	**23b**		
c	Credit for federal tax paid on fuels *(attach Form 4136)*	**23c**		
d	Add lines 23a through 23c		**23d**	**NONE**
24	Estimated tax penalty *(see instructions)*. Check if Form 2220 is attached ▶ ☐		**24**	
25	**Amount owed.** If line 23d is smaller than the total of lines 22c and 24, enter amount owed		**25**	**NONE**
26	**Overpayment.** If line 23d is larger than the total of lines 22c and 24, enter amount overpaid		**26**	
27	Enter amount from line 26 **Credited to 2011 estimated tax** ▶ _____ Refunded ▶		**27**	

Under penalties of perjury, I declare that I have examined this return, including accompanying schedules and statements, and to the best of my knowledge and belief, it is true, correct, and complete. Declaration of preparer (other than taxpayer) is based on all information of which preparer has any knowledge.

Sign Here

▶ *Andrew Lawrence* Signature of officer | 3-15-11 Date   ▶ **Vice-President** Title

May the IRS discuss this return with the preparer shown below (see instructions)? ☒ Yes ☐ No

Paid Preparer Use Only	Print/Type preparer's name **Michael Kramer**	Preparer's signature *Michael Kramer*	Date **3-14-11**	Check ☒ if self-employed	PTIN **104121**
	Firm's name ▶ **Michael S. Kramer**			Firm's EIN ▶ **59-2029763**	
	Firm's address ▶ **1110 McMillon Gainesville, FL 32611**			Phone no. **(352) 555-2000**	

For Paperwork Reduction Act Notice, see separate instructions.   Cat. No. 11510H   Form **1120S** (2010)

Schedule A	**Cost of Goods Sold** (see instructions)		
1	Inventory at beginning of year	1	64,000
2	Purchases	2	340,800
3	Cost of labor	3	143,204
4	Additional section 263A costs (attach statement)	4	7,000
5	Other costs (attach statement)	5	90,000
6	**Total.** Add lines 1 through 5	6	645,004
7	Inventory at end of year	7	104,800
8	**Cost of goods sold.** Subtract line 7 from line 6. Enter here and on page 1, line 2	8	540,204

9a Check all methods used for valuing closing inventory: (i) ☒ Cost as described in Regulations section 1.471-3

 (ii) ☐ Lower of cost or market as described in Regulations section 1.471-4

 (iii) ☐ Other (Specify method used and attach explanation.) ▶ ---------------------------------

 b Check if there was a writedown of subnormal goods as described in Regulations section 1.471-2(c) . . . . ▶ ☐

 c Check if the LIFO inventory method was adopted this tax year for any goods (if checked, attach Form 970) . . . . . . ▶ ☐

 d If the LIFO inventory method was used for this tax year, enter percentage (or amounts) of closing inventory computed under LIFO . . . . | 9d |

 e If property is produced or acquired for resale, do the rules of section 263A apply to the corporation? . . . . ☒ Yes ☐ No

 f Was there any change in determining quantities, cost, or valuations between opening and closing inventory? . . ☐ Yes ☒ No
 If "Yes," attach explanation.

Schedule B	**Other Information** (see instructions)		Yes	No

1 Check accounting method: **a** ☐ Cash **b** ☒ Accrual **c** ☐ Other (specify) ▶ ---------------------

2 See the instructions and enter the:
 a Business activity ▶ *Manufacturing*   **b** Product or service ▶ *Furniture*

3 At the end of the tax year, did the corporation own, directly or indirectly, 50% or more of the voting stock of a domestic corporation? (For rules of attribution, see section 267(c).) If "Yes," attach a statement showing: **(a)** name and employer identification number (EIN), **(b)** percentage owned, and **(c)** if 100% owned, was a qualified subchapter S subsidiary election made?   X

4 Has this corporation filed, or is it required to file, **Form 8918,** Material Advisor Disclosure Statement, to provide information on any reportable transaction? . . . .

5 Check this box if the corporation issued publicly offered debt instruments with original issue discount . . . . ▶ ☐

 If checked, the corporation may have to file **Form 8281,** Information Return for Publicly Offered Original Issue Discount Instruments.

6 If the corporation: **(a)** was a C corporation before it elected to be an S corporation **or** the corporation acquired an asset with a basis determined by reference to the basis of the asset (or the basis of any other property) in the hands of a C corporation **and (b)** has net unrealized built-in gain in excess of the net recognized built-in gain from prior years, enter the net unrealized built-in gain reduced by net recognized built-in gain from prior years (see instructions) . . . . ▶ $ -----------------

7 Enter the accumulated earnings and profits of the corporation at the end of the tax year. $ --------------

8 Are the corporation's total receipts (see instructions) for the tax year **and** its total assets at the end of the tax year less than $250,000? If "Yes," the corporation is not required to complete Schedules L and M-1   X

9 During the tax year, was a qualified subchapter S subsidiary election terminated or revoked? If "Yes," see instructions .

Schedule K	**Shareholders' Pro Rata Share Items**			Total amount
	1	Ordinary business income (loss) (page 1, line 21)	1	73,686
	2	Net rental real estate income (loss) (attach Form 8825)	2	
	3a	Other gross rental income (loss)	3a	
	b	Expenses from other rental activities (attach statement) . . .	3b	
	c	Other net rental income (loss). Subtract line 3b from line 3a	3c	
I	4	Interest income	4	
n	5	Dividends: **a** Ordinary dividends	5a	1,000
c		**b** Qualified dividends	5b	1,000
o	6	Royalties	6	
m	7	Net short-term capital gain (loss) (attach Schedule D (Form 1120S))	7	(2,100)
e	8a	Net long-term capital gain (loss) (attach Schedule D (Form 1120S))	8a	4,500
(Loss)	b	Collectibles (28%) gain (loss)	8b	
	c	Unrecaptured section 1250 gain (attach statement)	8c	
	9	Net section 1231 gain (loss) (attach Form 4797)	9	
	10	Other income (loss) (see instructions) . . . Type ▶	10	

Form 1120S (2010) Page **3**

		Shareholders' Pro Rata Share Items (continued)		Total amount
Deductions	**11**	Section 179 deduction (*attach Form 4562*)	**11**	12,000
	12a	Contributions	**12a**	150
	b	Investment interest expense	**12b**	
	c	Section 59(e)(2) expenditures **(1)** Type ▶ _____ **(2)** Amount ▶	**12c(2)**	*
	d	Other deductions (*see instructions*) . . . Type ▶	**12d**	
Credits	**13a**	Low-income housing credit (section 42(j)(5))	**13a**	
	b	Low-income housing credit (other)	**13b**	
	c	Qualified rehabilitation expenditures (rental real estate) (*attach Form 3468*)	**13c**	
	d	Other rental real estate credits (*see instructions*) Type ▶ _____	**13d**	
	e	Other rental credits (*see instructions*) . . . Type ▶ _____	**13e**	
	f	Alcohol and cellulosic biofuel fuels credit (*attach Form 6478*)	**13f**	
	g	Other credits (*see instructions*) . . . . . Type ▶	**13g**	
Foreign Transactions	**14a**	Name of country or U.S. possession ▶ _____		
	b	Gross income from all sources	**14b**	
	c	Gross income sourced at shareholder level	**14c**	
		Foreign gross income sourced at corporate level		
	d	Passive category	**14d**	
	e	General category	**14e**	
	f	Other (*attach statement*)	**14f**	
		Deductions allocated and apportioned at shareholder level		
	g	Interest expense	**14g**	
	h	Other	**14h**	
		Deductions allocated and apportioned at corporate level to foreign source income		
	i	Passive category	**14i**	
	j	General category	**14j**	
	k	Other (*attach statement*)	**14k**	
		Other information		
	l	Total foreign taxes (check one): ▶ ☐ Paid ☐ Accrued . .	**14l**	
	m	Reduction in taxes available for credit (*attach statement*) . . .	**14m**	
	n	Other foreign tax information (*attach statement*)		
Alternative Minimum Tax (AMT) Items	**15a**	Post-1986 depreciation adjustment	**15a**	1,514
	b	Adjusted gain or loss	**15b**	
	c	Depletion (other than oil and gas)	**15c**	
	d	Oil, gas, and geothermal properties—gross income	**15d**	
	e	Oil, gas, and geothermal properties—deductions	**15e**	
	f	Other AMT items (*attach statement*)	**15f**	
Items Affecting Shareholder Basis	**16a**	Tax-exempt interest income	**16a**	18,000
	b	Other tax-exempt income	**16b**	
	c	Nondeductible expenses	**16c**	6,000 **
	d	Distributions (*attach statement if required*) (*see instructions*) . .	**16d**	28,212
	e	Repayment of loans from shareholders	**16e**	
Other Information	**17a**	Investment income	**17a**	1,000 ***
	b	Investment expenses	**17b**	
	c	Dividend distributions paid from accumulated earnings and profits	**17c**	
	d	Other items and amounts (*attach statement*)		
Reconciliation	**18**	**Income/loss reconciliation.** Combine the amounts on lines 1 through 10 in the far right column. From the result, subtract the sum of the amounts on lines 11 through 12d and 14l	**18**	64,936

Form **1120S** (2010)

*Qualified production activities income (QPAI) equals $80,000.
Employer's W-2 wages allocable to U.S. production activities equal $88,000.

**Disallowed meals and entertainment expenses ($4,000) and interest on loan used to purchase tax-exempt bonds ($2,000).

***If shareholders elect to tax dividends at ordinary rates under Sec. 163(d)(4)(B).

Form 1120S (2010) Page **4**

Schedule L	Balance Sheets per Books	Beginning of tax year		End of tax year	
	Assets	(a)	(b)	(c)	(d)
1	Cash		60,000		86,600
2a	Trade notes and accounts receivable	25,000		24,000	
b	Less allowance for bad debts	(1,000)	24,000	(1,000)	23,000
3	Inventories		64,000		104,800
4	U.S. government obligations				
5	Tax-exempt securities (see instructions)		200,000		200,000
6	Other current assets (attach statement)		7,000		
7	Loans to shareholders				
8	Mortgage and real estate loans				
9	Other investments (attach statement)				
10a	Buildings and other depreciable assets	151,600		151,600	
b	Less accumulated depreciation	(45,200)	106,400	(72,676)	78,924
11a	Depletable assets				
b	Less accumulated depletion	( )		( )	
12	Land (net of any amortization)				
13a	Intangible assets (amortizable only)				
b	Less accumulated amortization	( )		( )	
14	Other assets (attach statement)				
15	Total assets		461,400		493,324
	Liabilities and Shareholders' Equity				
16	Accounts payable		26,000		19,000
17	Mortgages, notes, bonds payable in less than 1 year		4,000		4,000
18	Other current liabilities (attach statement)		3,600		3,600
19	Loans from shareholders				
20	Mortgages, notes, bonds payable in 1 year or more		130,000		119,724
21	Other liabilities (attach statement)				
22	Capital stock		200,000		200,000
23	Additional paid-in capital				
24	Retained earnings		97,800		147,000
25	Adjustments to shareholders' equity (attach statement)				
26	Less cost of treasury stock		( )		( )
27	Total liabilities and shareholders' equity		461,400		493,324

Schedule M-1	Reconciliation of Income (Loss) per Books With Income (Loss) per Return

Note: Schedule M-3 required instead of Schedule M-1 if total assets are $10 million or more—see instructions

1	Net income (loss) per books	77,412	5	Income recorded on books this year not included on Schedule K, lines 1 through 10 (itemize):	
2	Income included on Schedule K, lines 1, 2, 3c, 4, 5a, 6, 7, 8a, 9, and 10, not recorded on books this year (itemize):		a	Tax-exempt interest $ 18,000	18,000
3	Expenses recorded on books this year not included on Schedule K, lines 1 through 12 and 14l (itemize):		6	Deductions included on Schedule K, lines 1 through 12 and 14l, not charged against book income this year (itemize):	
a	Depreciation $		a	Depreciation $ 476	
b	Travel and entertainment $ 4,000				476
	Interest on loans* $2,000	6,000	7	Add lines 5 and 6	18,476
4	Add lines 1 through 3	83,412	8	Income (loss) (Schedule K, line 18). Line 4 less line 7	64,936

Schedule M-2	Analysis of Accumulated Adjustments Account, Other Adjustments Account, and Shareholders' Undistributed Taxable Income Previously Taxed (see instructions)

		(a) Accumulated adjustments account	(b) Other adjustments account	(c) Shareholders' undistributed taxable income previously taxed
1	Balance at beginning of tax year	86,100	11,700	
2	Ordinary income from page 1, line 21	73,686		
3	Other additions	5,500**	18,000	
4	Loss from page 1, line 21	( )		
5	Other reductions	(18,250***)	(2,000)	
6	Combine lines 1 through 5	147,036	27,700	
7	Distributions other than dividend distributions	28,212		
8	Balance at end of tax year. Subtract line 7 from line 6	118,824	27,700	

Form **1120S** (2010)

*For municipal bonds
**$1,000 + $4,500 = $5,500
***$12,000 + $4,000 + $150 +$2,100 = $18,250

671110

☐ Final K-1	☐ Amended K-1		OMB No. 1545-0130

Schedule K-1
(Form 1120S)
Department of the Treasury
Internal Revenue Service

20**10**

For calendar year 2010, or tax
year beginning _____, 2010
ending _____ , 20 _____

Shareholder's Share of Income, Deductions,
Credits, etc.   ▶ See back of form and separate instructions.

Part I	**Information About the Corporation**

A Corporation's employer identification number
76-3456789

B Corporation's name, address, city, state, and ZIP code

Johns and Lawrence, Inc.
1234 University Ave.
Gainesville, FL 32611

C IRS Center where corporation filed return
Ogden, UT

Part II	**Information About the Shareholder**

D Shareholder's identifying number
297-63-2110

E Shareholder's name, address, city, state, and ZIP code

Andrew Lawrence
436 N.W. 24th Ave.
Gainesville, FL 32607

F Shareholder's percentage of stock
ownership for tax year . . . . _____50%____ %

For IRS Use Only

Part III	**Shareholder's Share of Current Year Income, Deductions, Credits, and Other Items**		
1 Ordinary business income (loss)	36,843	**13** Credits	
2 Net rental real estate income (loss)			
3 Other net rental income (loss)			
4 Interest income			
5a Ordinary dividends	500		
5b Qualified dividends	500	**14** Foreign transactions	
6 Royalties			
7 Net short-term capital gain (loss)	(1,050)		
8a Net long-term capital gain (loss)	2,250		
8b Collectibles (28%) gain (loss)			
8c Unrecaptured section 1250 gain			
9 Net section 1231 gain (loss)			
10 Other income (loss)		**15** Alternative minimum tax (AMT) items	
		A	757
11 Section 179 deduction		**16** Items affecting shareholder basis	
		A	9,000
12 Other deductions		C	3,000
A	6,000	D	14,106
G	75		
Q	40,000		
R	44,000		
		17 Other information	
		A	500 **

* See attached statement for additional information.

For Paperwork Reduction Act Notice, see Instructions for Form 1120S.   Cat. No. 11520D   Schedule K-1 (Form 1120S) 2010

*Schedule K-1 for Stephen Johns is similar to this
  one and is not reproduced here.

**If shareholder elects to tax dividends at ordinary rates under Sec. 163(d)(4)(B).

This list identifies the codes used on Schedule K-1 for all shareholders and provides summarized reporting information for shareholders who file Form 1040. For detailed reporting and filing information, see the separate Shareholder's Instructions for Schedule K-1 and the instructions for your income tax return.

1. **Ordinary business income (loss).** Determine whether the income (loss) is passive or nonpassive and enter on your return as follows:

	Report on
Passive loss	See the Shareholder's Instructions
Passive income	Schedule E, line 28, column (g)
Nonpassive loss	Schedule E, line 28, column (h)
Nonpassive income	Schedule E, line 28, column (j)

2. **Net rental real estate income (loss)**   See the Shareholder's Instructions

3. **Other net rental income (loss)**

Net income	Schedule E, line 28, column (g)
Net loss	See the Shareholder's Instructions

4. **Interest income**   Form 1040, line 8a

5a. **Ordinary dividends**   Form 1040, line 9a

5b. **Qualified dividends**   Form 1040, line 9b

6. **Royalties**   Schedule E, line 4

7. **Net short-term capital gain (loss)**   Schedule D, line 5, column (f)

8a. **Net long-term capital gain (loss)**   Schedule D, line 12, column (f)

8b. **Collectibles (28%) gain (loss)**   28% Rate Gain Worksheet, line 4 (Schedule D instructions)

8c. **Unrecaptured section 1250 gain**   See the Shareholder's Instructions

9. **Net section 1231 gain (loss)**   See the Shareholder's Instructions

10. **Other income (loss)**

Code		
A	Other portfolio income (loss)	See the Shareholder's Instructions
B	Involuntary conversions	See the Shareholder's Instructions
C	Sec. 1256 contracts & straddles	Form 6781, line 1
D	Mining exploration costs recapture	See Pub. 535
E	Other income (loss)	See the Shareholder's Instructions

11. **Section 179 deduction**   See the Shareholder's Instructions

12. **Other deductions**

A	Cash contributions (50%)	
B	Cash contributions (30%)	
C	Noncash contributions (50%)	
D	Noncash contributions (30%)	See the Shareholder's Instructions
E	Capital gain property to a 50% organization (30%)	
F	Capital gain property (20%)	
G	Contributions (100%)	
H	Investment interest expense	Form 4952, line 1
I	Deductions—royalty income	Schedule E, line 18
J	Section 59(e)(2) expenditures	See the Shareholder's Instructions
K	Deductions—portfolio (2% floor)	Schedule A, line 23
L	Deductions—portfolio (other)	Schedule A, line 28
M	Preproductive period expenses	See the Shareholder's Instructions
N	Commercial revitalization deduction from rental real estate activities	See Form 8582 instructions
O	Reforestation expense deduction	See the Shareholder's Instructions
P	Domestic production activities information	See Form 8903 instructions
Q	Qualified production activities income	Form 8903, line 7b
R	Employer's Form W-2 wages	Form 8903, line 17
S	Other deductions	See the Shareholder's Instructions

13. **Credits**

A	Low-income housing credit (section 42(j)(5)) from pre-2008 buildings	
B	Low-income housing credit (other) from pre-2008 buildings	See the Shareholder's Instructions
C	Low-income housing credit (section 42(j)(5)) from post-2007 buildings	Form 8586, line 11
D	Low-income housing credit (other) from post-2007 buildings	Form 8586, line 11
E	Qualified rehabilitation expenditures (rental real estate)	See the Shareholder's Instructions
F	Other rental real estate credits	
G	Other rental credits	
H	Undistributed capital gains credit	Form 1040, line 71, box a
I	Alcohol and cellulosic biofuel fuels credit	Form 6478, line 8
J	Work opportunity credit	Form 5884, line 3
K	Disabled access credit	See the Shareholder's Instructions
L	Empowerment zone and renewal communtiy employment credit	Form 8844, line 3

Code		*Report on*
M	Credit for increasing research activities	See the Shareholder's Instructions
N	Credit for employer social security and Medicare taxes	Form 8846, line 5
O	Backup withholding	Form 1040, line 61
P	Other credits	See the Shareholder's Instructions

14. **Foreign transactions**

A	Name of country or U.S. possession	
B	Gross income from all sources	Form 1116, Part I
C	Gross income sourced at shareholder level	

Foreign gross income sourced at corporate level

D	Passive category	
E	General category	Form 1116, Part I
F	Other	

Deductions allocated and apportioned at shareholder level

G	Interest expense	Form 1116, Part I
H	Other	Form 1116, Part I

Deductions allocated and apportioned at corporate level to foreign source income

I	Passive category	
J	General category	Form 1116, Part I
K	Other	

Other information

L	Total foreign taxes paid	Form 1116, Part II
M	Total foreign taxes accrued	Form 1116, Part II
N	Reduction in taxes available for credit	Form 1116, line 12
O	Foreign trading gross receipts	Form 8873
P	Extraterritorial income exclusion	Form 8873
Q	Other foreign transactions	See the Shareholder's Instructions

15. **Alternative minimum tax (AMT) items**

A	Post-1986 depreciation adjustment	
B	Adjusted gain or loss	See the Shareholder's Instructions and the Instructions for Form 6251
C	Depletion (other than oil & gas)	
D	Oil, gas, & geothermal—gross income	
E	Oil, gas, & geothermal—deductions	
F	Other AMT items	

16. **Items affecting shareholder basis**

A	Tax-exempt interest income	Form 1040, line 8b
B	Other tax-exempt income	
C	Nondeductible expenses	See the Shareholder's Instructions
D	Distributions	
E	Repayment of loans from shareholders	

17. **Other information**

A	Investment income	Form 4952, line 4a
B	Investment expenses	Form 4952, line 5
C	Qualified rehabilitation expenditures (other than rental real estate)	See the Shareholder's Instructions
D	Basis of energy property	See the Shareholder's Instructions
E	Recapture of low-income housing credit (section 42(j)(5))	Form 8611, line 8
F	Recapture of low-income housing credit (other)	Form 8611, line 8
G	Recapture of investment credit	See Form 4255
H	Recapture of other credits	See the Shareholder's Instructions
I	Look-back interest—completed long-term contracts	See Form 8697
J	Look-back interest—income forecast method	See Form 8866
K	Dispositions of property with section 179 deductions	
L	Recapture of section 179 deduction	
M	Section 453(l)(3) information	
N	Section 453A(c) information	
O	Section 1260(b) information	
P	Interest allocable to production expenditures	See the Shareholder's Instructions
Q	CCF nonqualified withdrawals	
R	Depletion information—oil and gas	
S	Amortization of reforestation costs	
T	Section 108(i) information	
U	Other information	

FACTS FOR S CORPORATION (FORM 1120S)

The same basic facts presented for the Andrew Lawrence proprietorship are used for the S corporation except for the following:

1. Johns and Lawrence, Inc. made an S corporation election on June 13, 2004. The election was effective for its initial tax year.

2. The book income for Johns and Lawrence is presented in the attached worksheet, which reconciles book income and S corporation taxable income.

3. The $18,000 salaries paid to each employee are subject to the same employment tax requirements as when paid by the C corporation. The total employment taxes ($14,480) are the same as for the C corporation.

4. The S corporation paid no estimated federal income taxes.

5. The corporation distributed $14,106 to each of the two shareholders.

6. Other deductions include:

Travel	$ 4,000
Meals and entertainment	8,000
Minus: 50% disallowance	(4,000)
Office expenses	16,000
Transportation	10,400
General and administrative	3,000
Miscellaneous*	850
Total	$38,250

*$150 of the miscellaneous expenses are related to the production of the dividend income and are separately stated.

7. The following schedule reconciles net income for the C corporation and the S corporation:

Net income per books for C corporation	$63,412
Plus: Federal income taxes	14,000
Net income per books for S corporation	$77,412

The S corporation return can be tied back to the partnership return. The only difference between the two returns is that the S corporation pays an additional $6,160 in employment taxes with respect to the shareholder-employee salaries, as compared to the partnership's guaranteed payments. This dollar difference is reflected in the net income numbers, the ordinary income numbers, capital account balances, and total asset amounts.

8. Qualifed production activities income (QPAI) equals $80,000. Employer's W-2 wages allocable to U.S. production activities equal $88,000.

9. The balance sheet for Johns and Lawrence appears on page 4 of Form 1120S.

Johns and Lawrence, Inc. (S Corporation) Reconciliation of Book and Taxable Income For Year Ending December 31, 2010

| | Book Income | | Adjustments | | Taxable Income | | Form 1120S Schedule K | |
| | | | | | | | Ordinary | Separately |
Account Name	Debit	Credit	Debit	Credit	Debit	Credit	Income	Stated Items
Sales		$869,658				$869,658	$869,658	
Sales returns & allowances	$ 29,242				$ 29,242		(29,242)	
Cost of sales	540,204				540,204		(540,204)	
Dividends		1,000				1,000		1,000
Tax-exempt interest		18,000	$18,000			0		$18,000
Gain on stock sale		4,500				4,500		4,500
Worthless stock loss	2,100				2,100			(2,100)
Officers salaries[a]	36,000				36,000		(36,000)	
Other salaries	52,000				52,000		(52,000)	
Rentals	36,000				36,000		(36,000)	
Bad debts	4,000				4,000		(4,000)	
Interest:								
Working capital loans	8,000				8,000		(8,000)	
Purchase tax-exempt bonds	2,000			$ 2,000	0			(2,000)
Employment taxes	14,480				14,480		(14,480)	
Taxes	1,520				1,520		(1,520)	
Repairs	4,800				4,800		(4,800)	
Depreciation[b]	12,000		476		12,476		(12,476)	
Charitable contributions	12,000				12,000			(12,000)
Travel	4,000				4,000		(4,000)	
Meals and entertainment[c]	8,000			4,000	4,000		(4,000)	
Meals and ent. nondeductible								(4,000)
Office expenses	16,000				16,000		(16,000)	
Advertising	13,000				13,000		(13,000)	
Transportation expense	10,400				10,400		(10,400)	
General and administrative	3,000				3,000		(3,000)	
Pension plans[d]	2,000				2,000		(2,000)	
Employee benefit programs[e]	4,000				4,000		(4,000)	
Miscellaneous	1,000				1,000		(850)	(150)
Net profit/Taxable income	77,412			12,476	64,936			
Total	$893,158	$893,158	$18,476	$18,476	$875,158	$875,158	$ 73,686	

[a] Salaries for the S corporation's shareholder-employees are deductible by the S corporation and are subject to the same employee taxes imposed on nonshareholder-employees.

[b] MACRS depreciation = $27,476 total − $15,000 allocated to COGS = $12,476

[c] 50% of the meals and entertainment expense is not deductible for tax purposes but must be separately stated on the Schedules K and K-1.

[d] The pension plan expense is the same for book and tax purposes for this corporation. No pension expenses relate to pensions for the shareholder-employees.

[e] The employee benefit expense is the same for book and tax purposes for this corporation. None relates to shareholder-employee benefits.

Form **709**	United States Gift (and Generation-Skipping Transfer) Tax Return	OMB No. 1545-0020

Department of the Treasury
Internal Revenue Service

(For gifts made during calendar year 2009)

▶ **See separate instructions.**

2009

Part 1 — General Information

1 Donor's first name and middle initial	2 Donor's last name	3 Donor's social security number
Wilma	Brown	123-45-6789

4 Address (number, street, and apartment number)	5 Legal residence (domicile)
2 Main Street	Georgia

6 City, state, and ZIP code	7 Citizenship (see instructions)
Dalton, GA 35901	U.S.A.

		Yes	No
8	If the donor died during the year, check here ▶ ☐ and enter date of death _____ , _____		
9	If you extended the time to file this Form 709, check here ▶ ☐		
10	Enter the total number of donees listed on Schedule A. Count each person only once. ▶ 6		
11a	Have you (the donor) previously filed a Form 709 (or 709-A) for any other year? If "No," skip line 11b	X	
b	If the answer to line 11a is "Yes," has your address changed since you last filed Form 709 (or 709-A)?		X
12	**Gifts by husband or wife to third parties.** Do you consent to have the gifts (including generation-skipping transfers) made by you and by your spouse to third parties during the calendar year considered as made one-half by each of you? (See instructions.) (If the answer is "Yes," the following information must be furnished and your spouse must sign the consent shown below. **If the answer is "No," skip lines 13–18 and go to Schedule A.**)	X	
13	Name of consenting spouse Hugh Brown 14 SSN 987-65-4321		
15	Were you married to one another during the entire calendar year? (see instructions)	X	
16	If 15 is "No," check whether ☐ married ☐ divorced or ☐ widowed/deceased, and give date (see instructions) ▶		
17	Will a gift tax return for this year be filed by your spouse? (If "Yes," mail both returns in the same envelope.)		X
18	**Consent of Spouse.** I consent to have the gifts (and generation-skipping transfers) made by me and by my spouse to third parties during the calendar year considered as made one-half by each of us. We are both aware of the joint and several liability for tax created by the execution of this consent.		

Consenting spouse's signature ▶ *Hugh Brown*   Date ▶ 3-2-2010

Part 2 — Tax Computation

1	Enter the amount from Schedule A, Part 4, line 11	1	351,155
2	Enter the amount from Schedule B, line 3	2	500,000
3	Total taxable gifts. Add lines 1 and 2	3	851,155
4	Tax computed on amount on line 3 (see *Table for Computing Gift Tax* in separate instructions)	4	287,750
5	Tax computed on amount on line 2 (see *Table for Computing Gift Tax* in separate instructions)	5	155,800
6	Balance. Subtract line 5 from line 4	6	131,950
7	Maximum unified credit (nonresident aliens, see instructions)	7	345,800 | 00
8	Enter the unified credit against tax allowable for all prior periods (from Sch. B, line 1, col. C)	8	68,000
9	Balance. Subtract line 8 from line 7	9	277,800
10	Enter 20% (.20) of the amount allowed as a specific exemption for gifts made after September 8, 1976, and before January 1, 1977 (see instructions)	10	-0-
11	Balance. Subtract line 10 from line 9	11	277,800
12	Unified credit. Enter the smaller of line 6 or line 11	12	131,950
13	Credit for foreign gift taxes (see instructions)	13	-0-
14	Total credits. Add lines 12 and 13	14	131,950
15	Balance. Subtract line 14 from line 6. Do not enter less than zero	15	-0-
16	Generation-skipping transfer taxes (from Schedule C, Part 3, col. H, Total)	16	-0-
17	Total tax. Add lines 15 and 16	17	-0-
18	Gift and generation-skipping transfer taxes prepaid with extension of time to file	18	-0-
19	If line 18 is less than line 17, enter **balance due** (see instructions)	19	-0-
20	If line 18 is greater than line 17, enter **amount to be refunded**	20	

Under penalties of perjury, I declare that I have examined this return, including any accompanying schedules and statements, and to the best of my knowledge and belief, it is true, correct, and complete. Declaration of preparer (other than donor) is based on all information of which preparer has any knowledge.

Sign Here

▶ *Wilma Brown*   3-2-2010
  Signature of donor   Date

May the IRS discuss this return with the preparer shown below (see instructions)? ☒ Yes ☐ No

Attach check or money order here.

Paid Preparer's Use Only

Preparer's signature ▶ *Sally Preparer*	Date 3-1-2010	Check if self-employed ☒	Preparer's SSN or PTIN 123-45-6789
Firm's name (or yours if self-employed), address, and ZIP code ▶ Sally Preparer, 110 Last Bank Tower Dalton, GA 35901		EIN	
			Phone no. 706-934-5000

For Disclosure, Privacy Act, and Paperwork Reduction Act Notice, see page 12 of the separate instructions for this form.   Cat. No. 16783M   Form **709** (2009)

Note: Page 4, which is not pertinent to the tax consequences, is omitted because the donor made no generation skipping transfers.

Form 709 (2009)   Page **2**

SCHEDULE A	Computation of Taxable Gifts (Including transfers in trust) (see instructions)

A   Does the value of any item listed on Schedule A reflect any valuation discount? If "Yes," attach explanation   . . . . . .   Yes ☐   No ☒

B   ☐ ◄ Check here if you elect under section 529(c)(2)(B) to treat any transfers made this year to a qualified tuition program as made ratably over a 5-year period beginning this year. See instructions. Attach explanation.

Part 1—Gifts Subject Only to Gift Tax. Gifts less political organization, medical, and educational exclusions. (see instructions)

A Item number	B • Donee's name and address • Relationship to donor (if any) • Description of gift • If the gift was of securities, give CUSIP no. • If closely held entity, give EIN	C	D Donor's adjusted basis of gift	E Date of gift	F Value at date of gift	G For split gifts, enter ½ of column F	H Net transfer (subtract col. G from col. F)
1 1-4	} Schedule attached		593,000	2009	754,310	77,155	677,155

Gifts made by spouse —*complete **only** if you are splitting gifts with your spouse and he/she also made gifts.*

5	State University, stock		32,000*	2009	80,000	40,000	40,000
6	Betsy Brown, land		112,000*	2009	600,000	300,000	300,000

Total of Part 1. Add amounts from Part 1, column H . . . . ►   **1,017,155**

Part 2—Direct Skips. Gifts that are direct skips and are subject to both gift tax and generation-skipping transfer tax. You must list the gifts in chronological order.

A Item number	B • Donee's name and address • Relationship to donor (if any) • Description of gift • If the gift was of securities, give CUSIP no. • If closely held entity, give EIN	C 2632(b) election out	D Donor's adjusted basis of gift	E Date of gift	F Value at date of gift	G For split gifts, enter ½ of column F	H Net transfer (subtract col. G from col. F)
1							

Gifts made by spouse —*complete **only** if you are splitting gifts with your spouse and he/she also made gifts.*

Total of Part 2. Add amounts from Part 2, column H . . . . ►

Part 3—Indirect Skips. Gifts to trusts that are currently subject to gift tax and may later be subject to generation-skipping transfer tax. You must list these gifts in chronological order.

A Item number	B • Donee's name and address • Relationship to donor (if any) • Description of gift • If the gift was of securities, give CUSIP no. • If closely held entity, give EIN	C 2632(c) election	D Donor's adjusted basis of gift	E Date of gift	F Value at date of gift	G For split gifts, enter ½ of column F	H Net transfer (subtract col. G from col. F)
1							

Gifts made by spouse —*complete **only** if you are splitting gifts with your spouse and he/she also made gifts.*

Total of Part 3. Add amounts from Part 3, column H . . . . ►

(If more space is needed, attach additional sheets of same size.)   Form **709** (2009)

*Assumed amounts not listed in the facts.

Form 709 (2009)   Page **3**

Part 4—Taxable Gift Reconciliation

1	Total value of gifts of donor. Add totals from column H of Parts 1, 2, and 3	**1**	1,017,155
2	Total annual exclusions for gifts listed on line 1 (see instructions)	**2**	52,000 **
3	Total included amount of gifts. Subtract line 2 from line 1	**3**	965,155

Deductions (see instructions)

4	Gifts of interests to spouse for which a marital deduction will be claimed, based on item numbers ____4____ of Schedule A . . .	**4**	600,000		
5	Exclusions attributable to gifts on line 4	**5**	13,000		
6	Marital deduction. Subtract line 5 from line 4	**6**	587,000		
7	Charitable deduction, based on item nos. ____5____ less exclusions .	**7**	27,000		
8	Total deductions. Add lines 6 and 7			**8**	614,000
9	Subtract line 8 from line 3			**9**	351,155
10	Generation-skipping transfer taxes payable with this Form 709 (from Schedule C, Part 3, col. H, Total) . .			**10**	
11	**Taxable gifts.** Add lines 9 and 10. Enter here and on page 1, Part 2—Tax Computation, line 1			**11**	351,155

Terminable Interest (QTIP) Marital Deduction. (See instructions for Schedule A, Part 4, line 4.)

If a trust (or other property) meets the requirements of qualified terminable interest property under section 2523(f), and:

a. The trust (or other property) is listed on Schedule A, and

b. The value of the trust (or other property) is entered in whole or in part as a deduction on Schedule A, Part 4, line 4,

then the donor shall be deemed to have made an election to have such trust (or other property) treated as qualified terminable interest property under section 2523(f).

If less than the entire value of the trust (or other property) that the donor has included in Parts 1 and 3 of Schedule A is entered as a deduction on line 4, the donor shall be considered to have made an election only as to a fraction of the trust (or other property). The numerator of this fraction is equal to the amount of the trust (or other property) deducted on Schedule A, Part 4, line 6. The denominator is equal to the total value of the trust (or other property) listed in Parts 1 and 3 of Schedule A.

If you make the QTIP election, the terminable interest property involved will be included in your spouse's gross estate upon his or her death (section 2044). See instructions for line 4 of Schedule A. If your spouse disposes (by gift or otherwise) of all or part of the qualifying life income interest, he or she will be considered to have made a transfer of the entire property that is subject to the gift tax. See *Transfer of Certain Life Estates Received From Spouse* on page 4 of the instructions.

12 Election Out of QTIP Treatment of Annuities

☐ ◄ Check here if you elect under section 2523(f)(6) **not** to treat as qualified terminable interest property any joint and survivor annuities that are reported on Schedule A and would otherwise be treated as qualified terminable interest property under section 2523(f). See instructions. Enter the item numbers from Schedule A for the annuities for which you are making this election ► _____

SCHEDULE B   **Gifts From Prior Periods**

If you answered "Yes" on line 11a of page 1, Part 1, see the instructions for completing Schedule B. If you answered "No," skip to the Tax Computation on page 1 (or Schedule C, if applicable).

A Calendar year or calendar quarter (see instructions)	B Internal Revenue office where prior return was filed	C Amount of unified credit against gift tax for periods after December 31, 1976	D Amount of specific exemption for prior periods ending before January 1, 1977	E Amount of taxable gifts
1975	Atlanta, GA	-0-		300,000
1988	Atlanta, GA	68,000		200,000

1	Totals for prior periods	**1**	68,000		500,000
2	Amount, if any, by which total specific exemption, line 1, column D is more than $30,000			**2**	
3	Total amount of taxable gifts for prior periods. Add amount on line 1, column E and amount, if any, on line 2. Enter here and on page 1, Part 2—Tax Computation, line 2			**3**	500,000

(If more space is needed, attach additional sheets of same size.)   Form **709** (2009)

**$13,000 each for Billy, Betsy, State University, and Hugh.

Form 709 (2009), Schedule A, Part 1

A	B	C	D	E	F	G	H
1	Billy Brown, cash		$ 80,000	2009	$ 80,000	$40,000	$ 40,000
2	Betsy Brown, jewelry		18,000*	2009	28,000	14,000	14,000
3	Ruth Cain, remainder interest in vacation cabin (0.46310 x 100,000)		15,000*	2009	46,310	23,155	23,155
4	Trust at First Bank, income to Hugh Brown for life. Remainder to Jeff Bass (QTIP trust)		480,000*	2009	600,000	-0-	600,000
			$593,000		$754,310	$77,155	$677,155

*Assumed amounts not listed in the facts.

Form **706**
(Rev. September 2009)

Department of the Treasury
Internal Revenue Service

United States Estate (and Generation-Skipping Transfer) Tax Return

Estate of a citizen or resident of the United States (see separate instructions).
To be filed for decedents dying after December 31, 2008, and before January 1, 2010.

OMB No. 1545-0015

1a Decedent's first name and middle initial (and maiden name, if any) **Herman**	**1b** Decedent's last name **Estes**	**2** Decedent's Social Security No. **999-11-4444**

Part 1—Decedent and Executor

3a County, state, and ZIP code, or foreign country, of legal residence (domicile) at time of death

Montgomery, OH 45347

3b Year domicile established **1939**   **4** Date of birth **1923**   **5** Date of death **10-13-2009**

6b Executor's address (number and street including apartment or suite no.; city, town, or post office; state; and ZIP code) and phone no.

**10 Main Place
Dayton, OH 45347**

6a Name of executor (see page 5 of the instructions)

John Johnson

6c Executor's social security number (see page 5 of the instructions)

998-12-5732

Phone no. (   )

7a Name and location of court where will was probated or estate administered

7b Case number

8 If decedent died testate, check here ▶ ☒ and attach a certified copy of the will.   **9** If you extended the time to file this Form 706, check here ▶ ☐

10 If Schedule R-1 is attached, check here ▶ ☐

Part 2—Tax Computation

1	Total gross estate less exclusion (from Part 5—Recapitulation, page 3, item 12)	**1**	4,547,150
2	Tentative total allowable deductions (from Part 5—Recapitulation, page 3, item 22)	**2**	1,176,700
3a	Tentative taxable estate (before state death tax deduction) (subtract line 2 from line 1) . .	**3a**	3,370,450
b	State death tax deduction	**3b**	
c	Taxable estate (subtract line 3b from line 3a)	**3c**	3,370,450
4	Adjusted taxable gifts (total taxable gifts (within the meaning of section 2503) made by the decedent after December 31, 1976, other than gifts that are includible in decedent's gross estate (section 2001(b)))	**4**	1,700,000
5	Add lines 3c and 4	**5**	5,070,450
6	Tentative tax on the amount on line 5 from Table A on page 4 of the instructions	**6**	2,162,503
7	Total gift tax paid or payable with respect to gifts made by the decedent after December 31, 1976. Include gift taxes by the decedent's spouse for such spouse's share of split gifts (section 2513) only if the decedent was the donor of these gifts and they are includible in the decedent's gross estate (see instructions)	**7**	315,900
8	Gross estate tax (subtract line 7 from line 6)	**8**	1,846,603
9	Maximum unified credit (applicable credit amount) against estate tax . **9** 1,455,800		
10	Adjustment to unified credit (applicable credit amount). (This adjustment may not exceed $6,000. See page 6 of the instructions.) . . . **10**		
11	Allowable unified credit (applicable credit amount) (subtract line 10 from line 9)	**11**	1,455,800
12	Subtract line 11 from line 8 (but do not enter less than zero)	**12**	390,803
13	Credit for foreign death taxes (from Schedule(s) P). (Attach Form(s) 706-CE.) **13**		
14	Credit for tax on prior transfers (from Schedule Q) **14**		
15	Total credits (add lines 13 and 14)	**15**	
16	Net estate tax (subtract line 15 from line 12)	**16**	390,803
17	Generation-skipping transfer (GST) taxes payable (from Schedule R, Part 2, line 10) . . .	**17**	
18	Total transfer taxes (add lines 16 and 17)	**18**	390,803
19	Prior payments. Explain in an attached statement	**19**	
20	Balance due (or overpayment) (subtract line 19 from line 18)	**20**	390,803

Under penalties of perjury, I declare that I have examined this return, including accompanying schedules and statements, and to the best of my knowledge and belief, it is true, correct, and complete. Declaration of preparer other than the executor is based on all information of which preparer has any knowledge.

Sign Here

▶ *John Johnson*
Signature of executor

▶ **5-14-10**
Date

▶
Signature of executor

▶
Date

Paid Preparer's Use Only

Preparer's signature	*Mary Wilson, CPA*	Date **5-12-10**	Check if self-employed ▶ ☒	Preparer's SSN or PTIN **631-17-8487**
Firm's name (or yours if self-employed), address, and ZIP code	**Mary Wilson, CPA** **15 Main Place, Dayton, OH 45347**		EIN ▶	
			Phone no. ( )	

For Privacy Act and Paperwork Reduction Act Notice, see page 30 of the separate instructions for this form.   Cat. No. 20548R   Form **706** (Rev. 9-2009)

Note: Pages not pertinent to the tax consequences are omitted.

Form 706 (Rev. 9-2009)

Estate of: Herman Estes

	Decedent's Social Security Number
	999-11-4444

Part 3—Elections by the Executor

Please check the "Yes" or "No" box for each question (see instructions beginning on page 7).

Note. Some of these elections may require the posting of bonds or liens.

			Yes	No
1	Do you elect alternate valuation?	1		X
2	Do you elect special-use valuation? If "Yes," you must complete and attach Schedule A-1.	2		X
3	Do you elect to pay the taxes in installments as described in section 6166? If "Yes," you must attach the additional information described on pages 10 through 12 of the instructions. **Note.** By electing section 6166, you may be required to provide security for estate tax deferred under section 6166 and interest in the form of a surety bond or a section 6324A lien.	3		X
4	Do you elect to postpone the part of the taxes attributable to a reversionary or remainder interest as described in section 6163?	4		X

Part 4—General Information

(**Note.** Please attach the necessary supplemental documents. **You must attach the death certificate.**) (see instructions on page 12)

Authorization to receive confidential tax information under Regs. sec. 601.504(b)(2)(i); to act as the estate's representative before the IRS; and to make written or oral presentations on behalf of the estate if return prepared by an attorney, accountant, or enrolled agent for the executor:

Name of representative (print or type)	State	Address (number, street, and room or suite no., city, state, and ZIP code)
Mary Wilson	OH	15 Main Place, Dayton, OH 45347

I declare that I am the ☐ attorney/ ☒ certified public accountant/ ☐ enrolled agent (you must check the applicable box) for the executor and prepared this return for the executor. I am not under suspension or disbarment from practice before the Internal Revenue Service and am qualified to practice in the state shown above.

Signature	CAF number	Date	Telephone number
Mary Wilson, CPA		5-12-10	

1 Death certificate number and issuing authority (attach a copy of the death certificate to this return).

1246, County Coroner

2 Decedent's business or occupation. If retired, check here ▶ ☒ and state decedent's former business or occupation.

Executive

3 Marital status of the decedent at time of death:

☒ Married

☐ Widow or widower—Name, SSN, and date of death of deceased spouse ▶ _____

☐ Single
☐ Legally separated
☐ Divorced—Date divorce decree became final ▶

4a Surviving spouse's name	4b Social security number	4c Amount received (see page 12 of the instructions)
Ann Estes	555-77-9999	1,050,000

5 Individuals (other than the surviving spouse), trusts, or other estates who receive benefits from the estate (do not include charitable beneficiaries shown in Schedule O) (see instructions).

Name of individual, trust, or estate receiving $5,000 or more	Identifying number	Relationship to decedent	Amount (see instructions)
Johnny Estes	555-61-4107	Son	1,445,874
Billy Estes	556-63-4437	Son	1,245,874
Daughter, Dorothy Estes, received the corpus in the special power of appointment trust created by Amelia Estes.			

All unascertainable beneficiaries and those who receive less than $5,000   ▶

Total		2,691,748

Please check the "Yes" or "No" box for each question.

		Yes	No
6	Does the gross estate contain any section 2044 property (qualified terminable interest property (QTIP) from a prior gift or estate) (see page 12 of the instructions)?		X
7a	Have federal gift tax returns ever been filed? If "Yes," please attach copies of the returns, if available, and furnish the following information:	X	

7b Period(s) covered	7c Internal Revenue office(s) where filed
1974, 1978, 2006	Cincinnati, OH

8a	Was there any insurance on the decedent's life that is not included on the return as part of the gross estate?		X
b	Did the decedent own any insurance on the life of another that is not included in the gross estate?		X

(continued on next page)

Form 706 (Rev. 9-2009)

Part 4—General Information (continued)

		Yes	No
If you answer "Yes" to any of questions 9–16, you must attach additional information as described in the instructions.			
9	Did the decedent at the time of death own any property as a joint tenant with right of survivorship in which **(a)** one or more of the other joint tenants was someone other than the decedent's spouse, and **(b)** less than the full value of the property is included on the return as part of the gross estate? If "Yes," you must complete and attach Schedule E		X
10a	Did the decedent, at the time of death, own any interest in a partnership (for example, a family limited partnership), an unincorporated business, or a limited liability company; or own any stock in an inactive or closely held corporation?		X
b	If "Yes," was the value of **any** interest owned (from above) discounted on this estate tax return? If "Yes," see the instructions for Schedule F on page 20 for reporting the total accumulated or effective discounts taken on Schedule F or G	N/A	
11	Did the decedent make any transfer described in section 2035, 2036, 2037, or 2038 (see the instructions for Schedule G beginning on page 15 of the separate instructions)? If "Yes," you must complete and attach Schedule G	X	
12a	Were there in existence at the time of the decedent's death any trusts created by the decedent during his or her lifetime? .	X	X
b	Were there in existence at the time of the decedent's death any trusts not created by the decedent under which the decedent possessed any power, beneficial interest, or trusteeship?	X	
c	Was the decedent receiving income from a trust created after October 22, 1986, by a parent or grandparent?	X	
	If "Yes," was there a GST taxable termination (under section 2612) upon the death of the decedent?		X
d	If there was a GST taxable termination (under section 2612), attach a statement to explain. Provide a copy of the trust or will creating the trust, and give the name, address, and phone number of the current trustee(s).		
e	Did the decedent at any time during his or her lifetime transfer or sell an interest in a partnership, limited liability company, or closely held corporation to a trust described in question 12a or 12b? . . . . If "Yes," provide the EIN number to this transferred/sold item. ▶		X
13	Did the decedent ever possess, exercise, or release any general power of appointment? If "Yes," you must complete and attach Schedule H		X
14	Did the decedent have an interest in or a signature or other authority over a financial account in a foreign country, such as a bank account, securities account, or other financial account?		X
15	Was the decedent, immediately before death, receiving an annuity described in the "General" paragraph of the instructions for Schedule I or a private annuity? If "Yes," you must complete and attach Schedule I	X	
16	Was the decedent ever the beneficiary of a trust for which a deduction was claimed by the estate of a pre-deceased spouse under section 2056(b)(7) and which is not reported on this return? If "Yes," attach an explanation		X

Part 5—Recapitulation

Item number	Gross estate		Alternate value	Value at date of death
1	Schedule A—Real Estate	1		325,000
2	Schedule B—Stocks and Bonds	2		3,200,000
3	Schedule C—Mortgages, Notes, and Cash	3		94,250
4	Schedule D—Insurance on the Decedent's Life (attach Form(s) 712) . .	4		200,000
5	Schedule E—Jointly Owned Property (attach Form(s) 712 for life insurance) .	5		200,000
6	Schedule F—Other Miscellaneous Property (attach Form(s) 712 for life insurance) .	6		
7	Schedule G—Transfers During Decedent's Life (att. Form(s) 712 for life insurance)	7		287,900
8	Schedule H—Powers of Appointment	8		
9	Schedule I—Annuities	9		240,000
10	Total gross estate (add items 1 through 9)	10		4,547,150
11	Schedule U—Qualified Conservation Easement Exclusion	11		
12	Total gross estate less exclusion (subtract item 11 from item 10). Enter here and on line 1 of Part 2—Tax Computation	12		4,547,150

Item number	Deductions		Amount
13	Schedule J—Funeral Expenses and Expenses Incurred in Administering Property Subject to Claims . . .	13	85,000
14	Schedule K—Debts of the Decedent	14	31,700
15	Schedule K—Mortgages and Liens	15	
16	Total of items 13 through 15	16	116,700
17	Allowable amount of deductions from item 16 (see the instructions for item 17 of the Recapitulation) .	17	116,700
18	Schedule L—Net Losses During Administration	18	
19	Schedule L—Expenses Incurred in Administering Property Not Subject to Claims	19	
20	Schedule M—Bequests, etc., to Surviving Spouse	20	1,050,000
21	Schedule O—Charitable, Public, and Similar Gifts and Bequests	21	10,000
22	Tentative total allowable deductions (add items 17 through 21). Enter here and on line 2 of the Tax Computation	22	1,176,700

Page 3

Form 706 (Rev. 9-2009)

Estate of: Herman Estes

Decedent's Social Security Number
999-11-4444

SCHEDULE A—Real Estate

- For jointly owned property that must be disclosed on Schedule E, see the instructions on the reverse side of Schedule E.
- Real estate that is part of a sole proprietorship should be shown on Schedule F.
- Real estate that is included in the gross estate under section 2035, 2036, 2037, or 2038 should be shown on Schedule G.
- Real estate that is included in the gross estate under section 2041 should be shown on Schedule H.
- If you elect section 2032A valuation, you must complete Schedule A and Schedule A-1.

Item number	Description	Alternate valuation date	Alternate value	Value at date of death
1	Personal residence, house and lot, located at 105 Elm Court, Dayton, OH			325,000
	Total from continuation schedules or additional sheets attached to this schedule . .			
	TOTAL. (Also enter on Part 5—Recapitulation, page 3, at item 1.)			325,000

(If more space is needed, attach the continuation schedule from the end of this package or additional sheets of the same size.)

(See the instructions on the reverse side.)

Form 706 (Rev. 9-2009)

Estate of: Herman Estes

Decedent's Social Security Number
999-11-4444

SCHEDULE B—Stocks and Bonds

(For jointly owned property that must be disclosed on Schedule E, see the instructions for Schedule E.)

Item number	Description, including face amount of bonds or number of shares and par value for identification. Give CUSIP number. If trust, partnership, or closely held entity, give EIN	CUSIP number or EIN, where applicable	Unit value	Alternate valuation date	Alternate value	Value at date of death
1	Stock in Ajax Corporation 1,000 shares, $10 per share		3,200			3,200,000
	Total from continuation schedules (or additional sheets) attached to this schedule . .					
	TOTAL. (Also enter on Part 5—Recapitulation, page 3, at item 2.)					3,200,000

(If more space is needed, attach the continuation schedule from the end of this package or additional sheets of the same size.)

(The instructions to Schedule B are in the separate instructions.)

Schedule B—Page 12

Form 706 (Rev. 9-2009)

Estate of: Herman Estes	Decedent's Social Security Number 999-11-4444

SCHEDULE C—Mortgages, Notes, and Cash

(For jointly owned property that must be disclosed on Schedule E, see the instructions for Schedule E.)

Item number	Description	Alternate valuation date	Alternate value	Value at date of death
1	Checking account			19,250
2	Savings account (includes accrued interest through date of death)			75,000
	Total from continuation schedules (or additional sheets) attached to this schedule .			
	TOTAL. (Also enter on Part 5—Recapitulation, page 3, at item 3.)			94,250

(If more space is needed, attach the continuation schedule from the end of this package or additional sheets of the same size.)
(See the instructions on the reverse side.)

Form 706 (Rev. 9-2009)

Estate of: Herman Estes

Decedent's Social Security Number
999-11-4444

SCHEDULE D—Insurance on the Decedent's Life

You must list all policies on the life of the decedent and attach a Form 712 for each policy.

Item number	Description	Alternate valuation date	Alternate value	Value at date of death
1	Life insurance policy No. 123-A issued by the Life Insurance Company of Ohio. Beneficiary — Johnny Estes			200,000
	Total from continuation schedules (or additional sheets) attached to this schedule .			
	TOTAL. (Also enter on Part 5—Recapitulation, page 3, at item 4.)			200,000

(If more space is needed, attach the continuation schedule from the end of this package or additional sheets of the same size.)

(See the instructions on the reverse side.)

Schedule D—Page 15

Form 706 (Rev. 8-2009)

Estate of: **Herman Estes**	**Decedent's Social Security Number** **999-11-4444**

SCHEDULE E—Jointly Owned Property
(If you elect section 2032A valuation, you must complete Schedule E and Schedule A-1.)

PART 1. Qualified Joint Interests—Interests Held by the Decedent and His or Her Spouse as the Only Joint Tenants (Section 2040(b)(2))

Item number	Description. For securities, give CUSIP number. If trust, partnership, or closely held entity, give EIN	CUSIP number or EIN, where applicable	Alternate valuation date	Alternate value	Value at date of death
1	Land				400,000
	Total from continuation schedules (or additional sheets) attached to this schedule				
1a	Totals	**1a**			400,000
1b	Amounts included in gross estate (one-half of line **1a**)	**1b**			200,000

PART 2. All Other Joint Interests

2a State the name and address of each surviving co-tenant. If there are more than three surviving co-tenants, list the additional co-tenants on an attached sheet.

	Name	Address (number and street, city, state, and ZIP code)
A.		
B.		
C.		

Item number	Enter letter for co-tenant	Description (including alternate valuation date if any). For securities, give CUSIP number. If trust, partnership, or closely held entity, give EIN	CUSIP number or EIN, where applicable	Percentage includible	Includible alternate value	Includible value at date of death
1						
		Total from continuation schedules (or additional sheets) attached to this schedule				
2b	Total other joint interests			**2b**		
3	**Total includible joint interests** (add lines 1b and 2b). Also enter on Part 5—Recapitulation, page 3, at item 5			**3**		200,000

(If more space is needed, attach the continuation schedule from the end of this package or additional sheets of the same size.)
(See the instructions on the reverse side.)

Schedule E—Page 17

Form 706 (Rev. 8-2009)

Estate of: Herman Estes

Decedent's Social Security Number
999-11-4444

SCHEDULE G—Transfers During Decedent's Life

(If you elect section 2032A valuation, you must complete Schedule G and Schedule A-1.)

Item number	Description. For securities, give CUSIP number. If trust, partnership, or closely held entity, give EIN	Alternate valuation date	Alternate value	Value at date of death
A.	Gift tax paid or payable by the decedent or the estate for all gifts made by the decedent or his or her spouse within 3 years before the decedent's death (section 2035(b))	X X X X X		287,900
B. 1	Transfers includible under section 2035(a), 2036, 2037, or 2038:			
	Total from continuation schedules (or additional sheets) attached to this schedule .			
	TOTAL. (Also enter on Part 5—Recapitulation, page 3, at item 7.)			287,900

SCHEDULE H—Powers of Appointment

(Include "5 and 5 lapsing" powers (section 2041(b)(2)) held by the decedent.)

(If you elect section 2032A valuation, you must complete Schedule H and Schedule A-1.)

Item number	Description	Alternate valuation date	Alternate value	Value at date of death
1				
	Total from continuation schedules (or additional sheets) attached to this schedule .			
	TOTAL. (Also enter on Part 5—Recapitulation, page 3, at item 8.)			

(If more space is needed, attach the continuation schedule from the end of this package or additional sheets of the same size.)

(The instructions to Schedules G and H are in the separate instructions.)

Schedules G and H—Page 21

Form 706 (Rev. 8-2009)

Estate of: Herman Estes	**Decedent's Social Security Number** 999-11-4444

SCHEDULE I—Annuities

Note. Generally, no exclusion is allowed for the estates of decedents dying after December 31, 1984 (see page 17 of the instructions).

	Yes	No
A Are you excluding from the decedent's gross estate the value of a lump-sum distribution described in section 2039(f)(2) (as in effect before its repeal by the Deficit Reduction Act of 1984)? . . . . If "Yes," you must attach the information required by the instructions.		X

Item number	Description. Show the entire value of the annuity before any exclusions	Alternate valuation date	Includible alternate value	Includible value at date of death
1	Qualified pension plan issued by Buckeye Corporation. Beneficiary — Ann Estes, spouse			240,000
	Total from continuation schedules (or additional sheets) attached to this schedule .			
	TOTAL. (Also enter on Part 5—Recapitulation, page 3, at item 9.)			240,000

(If more space is needed, attach the continuation schedule from the end of this package or additional sheets of the same size.)

Schedule I—Page 22

(The instructions to Schedule I are in the separate instructions.)

Form 706 (Rev. 9-2009)

Estate of:	Herman Estes	**Decedent's Social Security Number**
		999-11-4444

SCHEDULE J—Funeral Expenses and Expenses Incurred in Administering Property Subject to Claims

Note. Do not list on this schedule expenses of administering property not subject to claims. For those expenses, see the instructions for Schedule L.

If executors' commissions, attorney fees, etc., are claimed and allowed as a deduction for estate tax purposes, they are not allowable as a deduction in computing the taxable income of the estate for federal income tax purposes. They are allowable as an income tax deduction on Form 1041 if a waiver is filed to waive the deduction on Form 706 (see the Form 1041 instructions).

Item number	Description	Expense amount	Total amount
1	**A. Funeral expenses:**	15,000	
	Total funeral expenses . . . . ▶		15,000
	B. Administration expenses:		
	1 Executors' commissions—amount estimated/agreed upon/paid. (Strike out the words that do not apply.)		70,000
	2 Attorney fees—amount estimated/agreed upon/paid. (Strike out the words that do not apply.)		
	3 Accountant fees—amount estimated/agreed upon/paid. (Strike out the words that do not apply.)		

		Expense amount
	4 Miscellaneous expenses:	
	Total miscellaneous expenses from continuation schedules (or additional sheets) attached to this schedule	
	Total miscellaneous expenses . . . . ▶	

TOTAL. (Also enter on Part 5—Recapitulation, page 3, at item 13.) . . . . ▶	85,000

(If more space is needed, attach the continuation schedule from the end of this package or additional sheets of the same size.)
(See the instructions on the reverse side.) **Schedule J—Page 23**

Form 706 (Rev. 8-2009)

Estate of: Herman Estes

Decedent's Social Security Number
999-11-4444

SCHEDULE K—Debts of the Decedent, and Mortgages and Liens

Item number	Debts of the Decedent—Creditor and nature of claim, and allowable death taxes	Amount unpaid to date	Amount in contest	Amount claimed as a deduction
1	Bank loan (including $200 interest accrued through date of death)	25,200		25,200
2	American Express, Visa, and Master Card credit card debts	6,500		6,500
	Total from continuation schedules (or additional sheets) attached to this schedule			
	TOTAL. (Also enter on Part 5—Recapitulation, page 3, at item 14.)			31,700

Item number	Mortgages and Liens—Description	Amount
1		
	Total from continuation schedules (or additional sheets) attached to this schedule	
	TOTAL. (Also enter on Part 5—Recapitulation, page 3, at item 15.)	

(If more space is needed, attach the continuation schedule from the end of this package or additional sheets of the same size.)
(The instructions to Schedule K are in the separate instructions.)

Form 706 (Rev. 8-2009)

Estate of: Herman Estes

Decedent's Social Security Number
999-11-4444

SCHEDULE M—Bequests, etc., to Surviving Spouse

Election To Deduct Qualified Terminable Interest Property Under Section 2056(b)(7). If a trust (or other property) meets the requirements of qualified terminable interest property under section 2056(b)(7), and

a. The trust or other property is listed on Schedule M and

b. The value of the trust (or other property) is entered in whole or in part as a deduction on Schedule M,

then unless the executor specifically identifies the trust (all or a fractional portion or percentage) or other property to be excluded from the election, the executor shall be deemed to have made an election to have such trust (or other property) treated as qualified terminable interest property under section 2056(b)(7).

If less than the entire value of the trust (or other property) that the executor has included in the gross estate is entered as a deduction on Schedule M, the executor shall be considered to have made an election only as to a fraction of the trust (or other property). The numerator of this fraction is equal to the amount of the trust (or other property) deducted on Schedule M. The denominator is equal to the total value of the trust (or other property).

Election To Deduct Qualified Domestic Trust Property Under Section 2056A. If a trust meets the requirements of a qualified domestic trust under section 2056A(a) and this return is filed no later than 1 year after the time prescribed by law (including extensions) for filing the return, and

a. The entire value of a trust or trust property is listed on Schedule M and

b. The entire value of the trust or trust property is entered as a deduction on Schedule M, then unless the executor specifically identifies the trust to be excluded from the election, the executor shall be deemed to have made an election to have the entire trust treated as qualified domestic trust property.

		Yes	No
1	Did any property pass to the surviving spouse as a result of a qualified disclaimer? **1**		X
	If "Yes," attach a copy of the written disclaimer required by section 2518(b).		
2a	In what country was the surviving spouse born? **United States**		
b	What is the surviving spouse's date of birth? **3-12-1946**		
c	Is the surviving spouse a U.S. citizen? **2c**	X	
d	If the surviving spouse is a naturalized citizen, when did the surviving spouse acquire citizenship? **N/A**		
e	If the surviving spouse is not a U.S. citizen, of what country is the surviving spouse a citizen? **N/A**		
3	**Election Out of QTIP Treatment of Annuities.** Do you elect under section 2056(b)(7)(C)(ii) not to treat as qualified terminable interest property any joint and survivor annuities that are included in the gross estate and would otherwise be treated as qualified terminable interest property under section 2056(b)(7)(C)? (see instructions) **3**		X

Item number	Description of property interests passing to surviving spouse. For securities, give CUSIP number. If trust, partnership, or closely held entity, give EIN	Amount
A1	QTIP property: Trust with First Bank as trustee	200,000
B1	All other property: Residence Savings account Checking account Land held in joint tenancy Qualified pension plan	325,000 75,000 10,000 200,000 240,000

	Total from continuation schedules (or additional sheets) attached to this schedule			
4	**Total** amount of property interests listed on Schedule M	**4**	1,050,000	
5a	Federal estate taxes payable out of property interests listed on Schedule M . .	**5a**		
b	Other death taxes payable out of property interests listed on Schedule M . .	**5b**		
c	Federal and state GST taxes payable out of property interests listed on Schedule M	**5c**		
d	Add items 5a, 5b, and 5c	**5d**		
6	Net amount of property interests listed on Schedule M (subtract 5d from 4). Also enter on Part 5—Recapitulation, page 3, at item 20	**6**	1,050,000	

(If more space is needed, attach the continuation schedule from the end of this package or additional sheets of the same size.)
(See the instructions on the reverse side.)

Schedule M—Page 27

Form 706 (Rev. 8-2009)

Estate of: Herman Estes

Decedent's Social Security Number
999-11-4444

SCHEDULE O—Charitable, Public, and Similar Gifts and Bequests

	Yes	No
1a If the transfer was made by will, has any action been instituted to have interpreted or to contest the will or any of its provisions affecting the charitable deductions claimed in this schedule? . . . . If "Yes," full details must be submitted with this schedule.		X
b According to the information and belief of the person or persons filing this return, is any such action planned? If "Yes," full details must be submitted with this schedule.		X
2 Did any property pass to charity as the result of a qualified disclaimer? . . . . If "Yes," attach a copy of the written disclaimer required by section 2518(b).		X

Item number	Name and address of beneficiary	Character of institution	Amount
1	American Cancer Society	Charity	10,000

Total from continuation schedules (or additional sheets) attached to this schedule 10,000

3 Total	**3**	
4a Federal estate tax payable out of property interests listed above . . .	**4a**	
b Other death taxes payable out of property interests listed above . . .	**4b**	
c Federal and state GST taxes payable out of property interests listed above	**4c**	
d Add items 4a, 4b, and 4c	**4d**	
5 Net value of property interests listed above (subtract 4d from 3). Also enter on Part 5—Recapitulation, page 3, at item 21	**5**	10,000

(If more space is needed, attach the continuation schedule from the end of this package or additional sheets of the same size.)
(The instructions to Schedule O are in the separate instructions.)

Form **1041**
Department of the Treasury—Internal Revenue Service
U.S. Income Tax Return for Estates and Trusts 20**10**

OMB No. 1545-0092

For calendar year 2010 or fiscal year beginning _____ , 2010, and ending _____ , 20 ____

A Type of entity (see instr.):
☐ Decedent's estate
☒ Simple trust
☐ Complex trust
☐ Qualified disability trust
☐ ESBT (S portion only)
☐ Grantor type trust
☐ Bankruptcy estate-Ch. 7
☐ Bankruptcy estate-Ch. 11
☐ Pooled income fund

Name of estate or trust (If a grantor type trust, see page 15 of the instructions.)
Bob Adams Trust (Simple Trust)

Name and title of fiduciary
First Bank

Number, street, and room or suite no. (If a P.O. box, see page 15 of the instructions.)
Post Office Box 100

City or town, state, and ZIP code
Nashville, TN 37203

C Employer identification number
74-1237211

D Date entity created
1993

E Nonexempt charitable and split-interest trusts, check applicable boxes (see page 16 of the instr.):
☐ Described in section 4947(a)(1)
☐ Not a private foundation
☐ Described in section 4947(a)(2)

B Number of Schedules K-1 attached (see instructions) ▶ **1**

F Check applicable boxes:
☐ Initial return ☐ Final return ☐ Amended return
☐ Change in fiduciary ☐ Change in fiduciary's name
☐ Change in trust's name ☐ Change in fiduciary's address

G Check here if the estate or filing trust made a section 645 election . . . . ▶ ☐

Income

1	Interest income	1	
2a	Total ordinary dividends	2a	30,000
b	Qualified dividends allocable to: (1) Beneficiaries **30,000** (2) Estate or trust **-0-**		
3	Business income or (loss). Attach Schedule C or C-EZ (Form 1040) . .	3	
4	Capital gain or (loss). Attach Schedule D (Form 1041)	4	12,000
5	Rents, royalties, partnerships, other estates and trusts, etc. Attach Schedule E (Form 1040) (see below.)	5	4,000
6	Farm income or (loss). Attach Schedule F (Form 1040) . . .	6	
7	Ordinary gain or (loss). Attach Form 4797	7	
8	Other income. List type and amount _____	8	
9	**Total income.** Combine lines 1, 2a, and 3 through 8 . . . . ▶	9	46,000

Deductions

10	Interest. Check if Form 4952 is attached ▶ ☐	10	
11	Taxes	11	
12	Fiduciary fees . . **($1,200 – $360)**	12	840
13	Charitable deduction (from Schedule A, line 7)	13	
14	Attorney, accountant, and return preparer fees	14	500
15a	Other deductions **not** subject to the 2% floor (attach schedule) . . .	15a	
b	Allowable miscellaneous itemized deductions subject to the 2% floor . .	15b	
16	Add lines 10 through 15b . . . . ▶	16	1,340
17	Adjusted total income or (loss). Subtract line 16 from line 9 . . .	17	44,660
18	Income distribution deduction (from Schedule B, line 15). Attach Schedules K-1 (Form 1041)	18	32,660
19	Estate tax deduction including certain generation-skipping taxes (attach computation) . . .	19	
20	Exemption	20	300
21	Add lines 18 through 20 . . . . ▶	21	32,960

Tax and Payments

22	Taxable income. Subtract line 21 from line 17. If a loss, see page 23 of the instructions . . .	22	11,700
23	**Total tax** (from Schedule G, line 7)	23	1,410
24	Payments: a 2010 estimated tax payments and amount applied from 2009 return . . .	24a	2,600
b	Estimated tax payments allocated to beneficiaries (from Form 1041-T) . . .	24b	
c	Subtract line 24b from line 24a	24c	2,600
d	Tax paid with Form 7004 (see page 24 of the instructions)	24d	
e	Federal income tax withheld. If any is from Form(s) 1099, check ▶ ☐ . .	24e	
	Other payments: f Form 2439 _____; g Form 4136 _____; Total ▶	24h	
25	**Total payments.** Add lines 24c through 24e, and 24h . . . . . ▶	25	2,600
26	Estimated tax penalty (see page 24 of the instructions)	26	
27	**Tax due.** If line 25 is smaller than the total of lines 23 and 26, enter amount owed	27	
28	**Overpayment.** If line 25 is larger than the total of lines 23 and 26, enter amount overpaid . .	28	1,190
29	Amount of line 28 to be: **a** Credited to 2011 estimated tax ▶ **1,190** ; **b** Refunded ▶	29	-0-

Sign Here

Under penalties of perjury, I declare that I have examined this return, including accompanying schedules and statements, and to the best of my knowledge and belief, it is true, correct, and complete. Declaration of preparer (other than taxpayer) is based on all information of which preparer has any knowledge.

▶ *Tom Trusty* 3-15-11 ▶ 35-1505087
Signature of fiduciary or officer representing fiduciary | Date | EIN of fiduciary if a financial institution

May the IRS discuss this return with the preparer shown below (see instr.)? ☒ Yes ☐ No

Paid Preparer Use Only

Print/Type preparer's name	Preparer's signature	Date	Check ☒ if self-employed	PTIN
Karen Certified	*Karen Certified*	3-14-11		104123

Firm's name ▶ Karen Certified Firm's EIN ▶ 74-1234567
Firm's address ▶ One Opryland Place, Nashville TN 37204 Phone no. (615) 372-1800

For Paperwork Reduction Act Notice, see the separate instructions. Cat. No. 11370H Form **1041** (2010)

Line 5: Net rental income = Rental income $5,000 – Realtor's commissions $1,000 = $4,000

Note: Pages concerning the AMT are omitted because the trust does not owe the AMT.

Form 1041 (2010)   Page **2**

Schedule A	**Charitable Deduction.** Do not complete for a simple trust or a pooled income fund.		
1	Amounts paid or permanently set aside for charitable purposes from gross income (see page 25)	1	
2	Tax-exempt income allocable to charitable contributions (see page 25 of the instructions) . . .	2	
3	Subtract line 2 from line 1	3	
4	Capital gains for the tax year allocated to corpus and paid or permanently set aside for charitable purposes	4	
5	Add lines 3 and 4	5	
6	Section 1202 exclusion allocable to capital gains paid or permanently set aside for charitable purposes (see page 25 of the instructions)	6	
7	**Charitable deduction.** Subtract line 6 from line 5. Enter here and on page 1, line 13	7	

Schedule B	**Income Distribution Deduction**		
1	Adjusted total income (see page 25 of the instructions)	1	44,660
2	Adjusted tax-exempt interest . ($15,000 – $360)	2	14,640
3	Total net gain from Schedule D (Form 1041), line 15, column (1) (see page 26 of the instructions) .	3	
4	Enter amount from Schedule A, line 4 (minus any allocable section 1202 exclusion)	4	
5	Capital gains for the tax year included on Schedule A, line 1 (see page 26 of the instructions) . .	5	
6	Enter any gain from page 1, line 4, as a negative number. If page 1, line 4, is a loss, enter the loss as a positive number	6	(12,000)
7	**Distributable net income.** Combine lines 1 through 6. If zero or less, enter -0-	7	47,300
8	If a complex trust, enter accounting income for the tax year as determined under the governing instrument and applicable local law . | 8 |		
9	Income required to be distributed currently	9	48,500
10	Other amounts paid, credited, or otherwise required to be distributed	10	-0-
11	Total distributions. Add lines 9 and 10. If greater than line 8, see page 26 of the instructions . .	11	48,500
12	Enter the amount of tax-exempt income included on line 11	12	14,640
13	Tentative income distribution deduction. Subtract line 12 from line 11	13	33,860
14	Tentative income distribution deduction. Subtract line 2 from line 7. If zero or less, enter -0- . .	14	32,660
15	**Income distribution deduction.** Enter the smaller of line 13 or line 14 here and on page 1, line 18	15	32,660

Schedule G	**Tax Computation** (see page 27 of the instructions)			
1	**Tax: a** Tax on taxable income (see page 27 of the instructions) . .	1a	1,410	
	b Tax on lump-sum distributions. Attach Form 4972	1b		
	c Alternative minimum tax (from Schedule I (Form 1041), line 56)	1c		
	d Total. Add lines 1a through 1c . . . . ▶	1d		1,410
2a	Foreign tax credit. Attach Form 1116	2a		
b	General business credit. Attach Form 3800	2b		
c	Credit for prior year minimum tax. Attach Form 8801	2c		
d	Bond credits. Attach Form 8912	2d		
3	**Total credits.** Add lines 2a through 2d . . . . ▶	3		
4	Subtract line 3 from line 1d. If zero or less, enter -0-	4		1,410
5	Recapture taxes. Check if from: ☐ Form 4255 ☐ Form 8611	5		
6	Household employment taxes. Attach Schedule H (Form 1040)	6		
7	**Total tax.** Add lines 4 through 6. Enter here and on page 1, line 23 . . . . ▶	7		1,410

	Other Information	Yes	No
1	Did the estate or trust receive tax-exempt income? If "Yes," attach a computation of the allocation of expenses	X	
	Enter the amount of tax-exempt interest income and exempt-interest dividends ▶ $ _15,000 (see below)_		
2	Did the estate or trust receive all or any part of the earnings (salary, wages, and other compensation) of any individual by reason of a contract assignment or similar arrangement?		X
3	At any time during calendar year 2010, did the estate or trust have an interest in or a signature or other authority over a bank, securities, or other financial account in a foreign country?		X
	See page 29 of the instructions for exceptions and filing requirements for Form TD F 90-22.1. If "Yes," enter the name of the foreign country ▶		
4	During the tax year, did the estate or trust receive a distribution from, or was it the grantor of, or transferor to, a foreign trust? If "Yes," the estate or trust may have to file Form 3520. See page 29 of the instructions		X
5	Did the estate or trust receive, or pay, any qualified residence interest on seller-provided financing? If "Yes," see page 29 for required attachment		X
6	If this is an estate or a complex trust making the section 663(b) election, check here (see page 29) . . ▶ ☐		
7	To make a section 643(e)(3) election, attach Schedule D (Form 1041), and check here (see page 29) . . ▶ ☐		
8	If the decedent's estate has been open for more than 2 years, attach an explanation for the delay in closing the estate, and check here ▶ ☐		
9	Are any present or future trust beneficiaries skip persons? See page 29 of the instructions		X

Form **1041** (2010)

Line 2: Allocation of expenses: $\frac{\$15,000}{\$50,000}$ x $1,200 = $360 of trustees fee allocated to tax-exempt income

SCHEDULE D
(Form 1041)

Department of the Treasury
Internal Revenue Service

Capital Gains and Losses

▶ **Attach to Form 1041, Form 5227, or Form 990-T. See the Instructions for Schedule D (Form 1041) (also for Form 5227 or Form 990-T, if applicable).**

OMB No. 1545-0092

20**10**

Name of estate or trust	Employer identification number
Bob Adams Trust	74-1237211

Note: *Form 5227 filers need to complete **only** Parts I and II.*

Part I — Short-Term Capital Gains and Losses—Assets Held One Year or Less

(a) Description of property (Example: 100 shares 7% preferred of "Z" Co.)	(b) Date acquired (mo., day, yr.)	(c) Date sold (mo., day, yr.)	(d) Sales price	(e) Cost or other basis (see instructions)	(f) Gain or (loss) for the entire year Subtract (e) from (d)
1a					

b Enter the short-term gain or (loss), if any, from Schedule D-1, line 1b . . . . | **1b** | |

2 Short-term capital gain or (loss) from Forms 4684, 6252, 6781, and 8824 . . . . | **2** | |

3 Net short-term gain or (loss) from partnerships, S corporations, and other estates or trusts . . . | **3** | |

4 Short-term capital loss carryover. Enter the amount, if any, from line 9 of the 2009 Capital Loss Carryover Worksheet . . . . | **4** (|) |

5 **Net short-term gain or (loss).** Combine lines 1a through 4 in column (f). Enter here and on line 13, column (3) on the back . . . . ▶ | **5** | |

Part II — Long-Term Capital Gains and Losses—Assets Held More Than One Year

(a) Description of property (Example: 100 shares 7% preferred of "Z" Co.)	(b) Date acquired (mo., day, yr.)	(c) Date sold (mo., day, yr.)	(d) Sales price	(e) Cost or other basis (see instructions)	(f) Gain or (loss) for the entire year Subtract (e) from (d)
6a 1,000 shares of ABC Corp.	2006	Oct. 2010	15,000	3,000	12,000

b Enter the long-term gain or (loss), if any, from Schedule D-1, line 6b . . . . | **6b** | |

7 Long-term capital gain or (loss) from Forms 2439, 4684, 6252, 6781, and 8824 . . . . | **7** | |

8 Net long-term gain or (loss) from partnerships, S corporations, and other estates or trusts . . . | **8** | |

9 Capital gain distributions . . . . | **9** | |

10 Gain from Form 4797, Part I . . . . | **10** | |

11 Long-term capital loss carryover. Enter the amount, if any, from line 14 of the 2009 Capital Loss Carryover Worksheet . . . . | **11** (|) |

12 **Net long-term gain or (loss).** Combine lines 6a through 11 in column (f). Enter here and on line 14a, column (3) on the back . . . . ▶ | **12** | 12,000 |

For Paperwork Reduction Act Notice, see the Instructions for Form 1041.   Cat. No. 11376V   Schedule D (Form 1041) 2010

Schedule D (Form 1041) 2010   Page **2**

Part III	Summary of Parts I and II Caution: *Read the instructions **before** completing this part.*		(1) Beneficiaries' (see instr.)	(2) Estate's or trust's	(3) Total
13	Net short-term gain or (loss)	13			
14	Net long-term gain or (loss):				
a	Total for year	14a		12,000	12,000
b	Unrecaptured section 1250 gain (see line 18 of the wrksht.) .	14b			
c	28% rate gain	14c			
15	Total net gain or (loss). Combine lines 13 and 14a . . ▶	15		12,000	12,000

Note: *If line 15, column (3), is a net gain, enter the gain on Form 1041, line 4 (or Form 990-T, Part I, line 4a). If lines 14a and 15, column (2), are net gains, go to Part V, and **do not** complete Part IV. If line 15, column (3), is a net loss, complete Part IV and the **Capital Loss Carryover Worksheet,** as necessary.*

Part IV	Capital Loss Limitation

16   Enter here and enter as a (loss) on Form 1041, line 4 (or Form 990-T, Part I, line 4c, if a trust), the **smaller** of:

a   The loss on line 15, column (3)   **or b** $3,000   . . . .   16 (   )

Note: *If the loss on line 15, column (3), is more than $3,000, **or** if Form 1041, page 1, line 22 (or Form 990-T, line 34), is a loss, complete the **Capital Loss Carryover Worksheet** on page 7 of the instructions to figure your capital loss carryover.*

Part V	Tax Computation Using Maximum Capital Gains Rates

Form 1041 filers. Complete this part **only** if both lines 14a and 15 in column (2) are gains, or an amount is entered in Part I or Part II and there is an entry on Form 1041, line 2b(2), **and** Form 1041, line 22, is more than zero.

Caution: *Skip this part and complete the worksheet on page 8 of the instructions if:*

- Either line 14b, col. (2) or line 14c, col. (2) is more than zero, or
- Both Form 1041, line 2b(1), and Form 4952, line 4g are more than zero.

Form 990-T trusts. Complete this part **only** if both lines 14a and 15 are gains, or qualified dividends are included in income in Part I of Form 990-T, **and** Form 990-T, line 34, is more than zero. Skip this part and complete the worksheet on page 8 of the instructions if either line 14b, col. (2) or line 14c, col. (2) is more than zero.

17	Enter taxable income from Form 1041, line 22 (or Form 990-T, line 34) . .			17	11,700	✓	
18	Enter the **smaller** of line 14a or 15 in column (2) but not less than zero	18	12,000 ✓				
19	Enter the estate's or trust's qualified dividends from Form 1041, line 2b(2) (or enter the qualified dividends included in income in Part I of Form 990-T) . . .	19	-0- ✓				
20	Add lines 18 and 19	20	12,000 ✓				
21	If the estate or trust is filing Form 4952, enter the amount from line 4g; otherwise, enter -0- . . ▶	21	-0-				
22	Subtract line 21 from line 20. If zero or less, enter -0-			22	12,000	✓	
23	Subtract line 22 from line 17. If zero or less, enter -0-			23	-0-	✓	
24	Enter the **smaller** of the amount on line 17 or $2,300			24	2,300	✓	
25	Is the amount on line 23 equal to or more than the amount on line 24?						
	☐ **Yes.** Skip lines 25 and 26; go to line 27 and check the "No" box.						
	☒ **No.** Enter the amount from line 23			25	-0-	✓	
26	Subtract line 25 from line 24			26	2,300	✓	
27	Are the amounts on lines 22 and 26 the same?						
	☐ **Yes.** Skip lines 27 thru 30; go to line 31. ☒ **No.** Enter the **smaller** of line 17 or line 22			27	11,700	✓	
28	Enter the amount from line 26 (If line 26 is blank, enter -0-)			28	2,300	✓	
29	Subtract line 28 from line 27			29	9,400	✓	
30	Multiply line 29 by 15% (.15)			30	1,410		✓
31	Figure the tax on the amount on line 23. Use the 2010 Tax Rate Schedule for Estates and Trusts (see the Schedule G instructions in the instructions for Form 1041)			31	-0-		✓
32	Add lines 30 and 31			32	1,410		✓
33	Figure the tax on the amount on line 17. Use the 2010 Tax Rate Schedule for Estates and Trusts (see the Schedule G instructions in the instructions for Form 1041)			33	3,071		
34	**Tax on all taxable income.** Enter the **smaller** of line 32 or line 33 here and on Form 1041, Schedule G, line 1a (or Form 990-T, line 36)			34	1,410		

Schedule D (Form 1041) 2010

661110

□ Final K-1   □ Amended K-1   OMB No. 1545-0092

Schedule K-1
(Form 1041)

20**10**

Department of the Treasury
Internal Revenue Service

For calendar year 2010,
or tax year beginning _____ , 2010,
and ending _____ , 20 _____

Beneficiary's Share of Income, Deductions, Credits, etc.

▶ See back of form and instructions.

Part I	Information About the Estate or Trust

A Estate's or trust's employer identification number

74-1237211

B Estate's or trust's name

Bob Adams Trust

C Fiduciary's name, address, city, state, and ZIP code

First Bank
Post OfficeBox 100
Nashville, TN 37203

D □ Check if Form 1041-T was filed and enter the date it was filed

_____ / _____ / _____

E □ Check if this is the final Form 1041 for the estate or trust

Part II	Information About the Beneficiary

F Beneficiary's identifying number

389-16-4001

G Beneficiary's name, address, city, state, and ZIP code

Bob Adams
3 Andrew Jackson Highway
Nashville, TN 37211

H [X] Domestic beneficiary   □ Foreign beneficiary

Part III	Beneficiary's Share of Current Year Income, Deductions, Credits, and Other Items

1	Interest income	**11**	Final year deductions
2a	Ordinary dividends **30,000**		
2b	Qualified dividends **30,000**		
3	Net short-term capital gain		
4a	Net long-term capital gain		
4b	28% rate gain	**12**	Alternative minimum tax adjustment
4c	Unrecaptured section 1250 gain		
5	Other portfolio and nonbusiness income		
6	Ordinary business income		
7	Net rental real estate income **2,660***	**13**	Credits and credit recapture
8	Other rental income		
9	Directly apportioned deductions		
		14	Other information
10	Estate tax deduction		**A 14,640**

*See attached statement for additional information.

Note. A statement must be attached showing the beneficiary's share of income and directly apportioned deductions from each business, rental real estate, and other rental activity.

For IRS Use Only

For Paperwork Reduction Act Notice, see the Instructions for Form 1041.   Cat. No. 11380D   **Schedule K-1 (Form 1041) 2010**

*5,000 − ($1,000 + $840 + $500) = $2,660

This list identifies the codes used on Schedule K-1 for beneficiaries and provides summarized reporting information for beneficiaries who file Form 1040. For detailed reporting and filing information, see the Instructions for Beneficiary Filing Form 1040 and the instructions for your income tax return.

	Report on
1. Interest income	Form 1040, line 8a
2a. Ordinary dividends	Form 1040, line 9a
2b. Qualified dividends	Form 1040, line 9b
3. Net short-term capital gain	Schedule D, line 5
4a. Net long-term capital gain	Schedule D, line 12
4b. 28% rate gain	Line 4 of the worksheet for Schedule D, line 18
4c. Unrecaptured section 1250 gain	Line 11 of the worksheet for Schedule D, line 19
5. Other portfolio and nonbusiness income	Schedule E, line 33, column (f)
6. Ordinary business income	Schedule E, line 33, column (d) or (f)
7. Net rental real estate income	Schedule E, line 33, column (d) or (f)
8. Other rental income	Schedule E, line 33, column (d) or (f)

9. Directly apportioned deductions

Code	
A Depreciation	Form 8582 or Schedule E, line 33, column (c) or (e)
B Depletion	Form 8582 or Schedule E, line 33, column (c) or (e)
C Amortization	Form 8582 or Schedule E, line 33, column (c) or (e)
10. Estate tax deduction	Schedule A, line 28

11. Final year deductions

A Excess deductions	Schedule A, line 23
B Short-term capital loss carryover	Schedule D, line 5
C Long-term capital loss carryover	Schedule D, line 12; line 5 of the wksht. for Sch. D, line 18; and line 16 of the wksht. for Sch. D, line 19
D Net operating loss carryover — regular tax	Form 1040, line 21
E Net operating loss carryover — minimum tax	Form 6251, line 11

12. Alternative minimum tax (AMT) items

Code	Report on
A Adjustment for minimum tax purposes	Form 6251, line 15
B AMT adjustment attributable to qualified dividends	
C AMT adjustment attributable to net short-term capital gain	
D AMT adjustment attributable to net long-term capital gain	See the beneficiary's instructions and the Instructions for Form 6251
E AMT adjustment attributable to unrecaptured section 1250 gain	
F AMT adjustment attributable to 28% rate gain	
G Accelerated depreciation	
H Depletion	
I Amortization	
J Exclusion items	2011 Form 8801

13. Credits and credit recapture

A Credit for estimated taxes	Form 1040, line 62
B Credit for backup withholding	Form 1040, line 61
C Low-income housing credit	Form 8586 (also see the beneficiary's instructions)
D Rehabilitation credit and energy credit	See the beneficiary's instructions
E Other qualifying investment credit	See the beneficiary's instructions
F Work opportunity credit	Form 5884, line 3
G Credit for small employer health insurance premiums	Form 8941, line 15
H Alcohol and cellulosic biofuel fuels credit	Form 6478, line 8 (also see the beneficiary's instructions)
I Credit for increasing research activities	Form 3800, line 1c
J Renewable electricity, refined coal, and Indian coal production credit	See the beneficiary's instructions
K Empowerment zone and renewal community employment credit	Form 8844, line 3
L Indian employment credit	Form 3800, line 1g
M Orphan drug credit	Form 3800, line 1h
N Credit for employer-provided child care and facilities	Form 3800, line 1k
O Biodiesel and renewable diesel fuels credit	Form 8864, line 9 (also see the beneficiary's instructions)
P Nonconventional source fuel credit	Form 3800, line 1o
Q Credit to holders of tax credit bonds	Form 8912, line 8
R Agricultural chemicals security credit	Form 3800, line 1v
S Energy efficient appliance credit	Form 3800, line 1q
T Credit for employer differential wage payments	Form 3800, line 1w
U Recapture of credits	See the beneficiary's instructions

14. Other information

A Tax-exempt interest	Form 1040, line 8b
B Foreign taxes	Form 1040, line 47 or Sch. A, line 8
C Qualified production activities income	Form 8903, line 7, col. (b) (also see the beneficiary's instructions)
D Form W-2 wages	Form 8903, line 17
E Net investment income	Form 4952, line 4a
F Gross farm and fishing income	Schedule E, line 42
G Foreign trading gross receipts (IRC 942(a))	See the Instructions for Form 8873
H Other information	See the beneficiary's instructions

Note. If you are a beneficiary who does not file a Form 1040, see instructions for the type of income tax return you are filing.

Form **1041**
Department of the Treasury—Internal Revenue Service
U.S. Income Tax Return for Estates and Trusts 2010
OMB No. 1545-0092

A Type of entity (see instr.):

☐ Decedent's estate
☐ Simple trust
☒ Complex trust
☐ Qualified disability trust
☐ ESBT (S portion only)
☐ Grantor type trust
☐ Bankruptcy estate-Ch. 7
☐ Bankruptcy estate-Ch. 11
☐ Pooled income fund

For calendar year 2010 or fiscal year beginning _____ , 2010, and ending _____ , 20 _____

Name of estate or trust (If a grantor type trust, see page 15 of the instructions.)
Cathy and Karen Stephens Trust (Complex Trust)

Name and title of fiduciary
Merchants Bank

Number, street, and room or suite no. (If a P.O. box, see page 15 of the instructions.)
3000 Sun Plaza I

City or town, state, and ZIP code
Tampa, FL 32843

C Employer identification number
74-5727422

D Date entity created
3-12-94

E Nonexempt charitable and split-interest trusts, check applicable boxes (see page 16 of the instr.):
☐ Described in section 4947(a)(1)
☐ Not a private foundation
☐ Described in section 4947(a)(2)

B Number of Schedules K-1 attached (see instructions) ▶ **2**

F Check applicable boxes:
☐ Initial return ☐ Final return ☐ Amended return
☐ Change in fiduciary ☐ Change in fiduciary's name

☐ Change in trust's name
☐ Change in fiduciary's address

G Check here if the estate or filing trust made a section 645 election . . . . . . ▶ ☐

Income

1	Interest income	**1**	
2a	Total ordinary dividends	**2a**	30,000
b	Qualified dividends allocable to: **(1)** Beneficiaries 13,319 **(2)** Estate or trust 16,681		
3	Business income or (loss). Attach Schedule C or C-EZ (Form 1040) . .	**3**	
4	Capital gain or (loss). Attach Schedule D (Form 1041)	**4**	12,000
5	Rents, royalties, partnerships, other estates and trusts, etc. Attach Schedule E (Form 1040) .	**5**	4,000
6	Farm income or (loss). Attach Schedule F (Form 1040) . . . ⤶ see below	**6**	
7	Ordinary gain or (loss). Attach Form 4797	**7**	
8	Other income. List type and amount _____	**8**	
9	**Total income.** Combine lines 1, 2a, and 3 through 8 . . . . . . ▶	**9**	46,000

Deductions

10	Interest. Check if Form 4952 is attached ▶ ☐	**10**	
11	Taxes	**11**	
12	Fiduciary fees ($1,200. — $360)	**12**	840
13	Charitable deduction (from Schedule A, line 7)	**13**	
14	Attorney, accountant, and return preparer fees	**14**	500
15a	Other deductions **not** subject to the 2% floor (attach schedule) . .	**15a**	
b	Allowable miscellaneous itemized deductions subject to the 2% floor . .	**15b**	
16	Add lines 10 through 15b . . . . ▶	**16**	1,340
17	Adjusted total income or (loss). Subtract line 16 from line 9 . . **17** 44,660		
18	Income distribution deduction (from Schedule B, line 15). Attach Schedules K-1 (Form 1041)	**18**	14,500
19	Estate tax deduction including certain generation-skipping taxes (attach computation) . .	**19**	
20	Exemption	**20**	100
21	Add lines 18 through 20 . . . . ▶	**21**	14,600

Tax and Payments

22	Taxable income. Subtract line 21 from line 17. If a loss, see page 23 of the instructions . . .	**22**	30,060
23	**Total tax** (from Schedule G, line 7)	**23**	4,371
24	**Payments: a** 2010 estimated tax payments and amount applied from 2009 return	**24a**	8,600
b	Estimated tax payments allocated to beneficiaries (from Form 1041-T) . . .	**24b**	
c	Subtract line 24b from line 24a	**24c**	8,600
d	Tax paid with Form 7004 (see page 24 of the instructions)	**24d**	
e	Federal income tax withheld. If any is from Form(s) 1099, check ▶ ☐ . . .	**24e**	
	Other payments: **f** Form 2439 _____ ; **g** Form 4136 _____ ; Total ▶	**24h**	
25	**Total payments.** Add lines 24c through 24e, and 24h . . . . . ▶	**25**	8,600
26	Estimated tax penalty (see page 24 of the instructions)	**26**	
27	**Tax due.** If line 25 is smaller than the total of lines 23 and 26, enter amount owed . .	**27**	
28	**Overpayment.** If line 25 is larger than the total of lines 23 and 26, enter amount overpaid . .	**28**	4,229
29	Amount of line 28 to be: **a Credited to 2011 estimated tax** ▶ 4,229 ; **b Refunded** ▶	**29**	-0-

Sign Here

Under penalties of perjury, I declare that I have examined this return, including accompanying schedules and statements, and to the best of my knowledge and belief, it is true, correct, and complete. Declaration of preparer (other than taxpayer) is based on all information of which preparer has any knowledge.

▶ *Fred Fidus* | 3-14-11 | ▶ 38-4371419
Signature of fiduciary or officer representing fiduciary | Date | EIN of fiduciary if a financial institution

May the IRS discuss this return with the preparer shown below (see instr.)? ☒ Yes ☐ No

Paid Preparer Use Only

Print/Type preparer's name	Preparer's signature	Date	Check ☒ if self-employed	PTIN
Sarah Public	*Sarah Public*	3-13-11		104124

Firm's name ▶ Sarah Public
Firm's address ▶ 200 Sun Plaza Tampa, FL 32843

Firm's EIN ▶ 38-9876543
Phone no. (863) 437-1000

For Paperwork Reduction Act Notice, see the separate instructions. Cat. No. 11370H Form **1041** (2010)

Line 4: Net Rental income = Rental income $5,000 — Rental expenses $1,000 = $4,000

Note: Pages concerning the AMT are omitted because the trust does not owe the AMT.

Form 1041 (2010)

Page **2**

Schedule A	**Charitable Deduction.** Do not complete for a simple trust or a pooled income fund.		
1	Amounts paid or permanently set aside for charitable purposes from gross income (see page 25)	1	
2	Tax-exempt income allocable to charitable contributions (see page 25 of the instructions) . . .	2	
3	Subtract line 2 from line 1	3	
4	Capital gains for the tax year allocated to corpus and paid or permanently set aside for charitable purposes	4	
5	Add lines 3 and 4	5	
6	Section 1202 exclusion allocable to capital gains paid or permanently set aside for charitable purposes (see page 25 of the instructions)	6	
7	**Charitable deduction.** Subtract line 6 from line 5. Enter here and on page 1, line 13	7	

Schedule B	**Income Distribution Deduction**		
1	Adjusted total income (see page 25 of the instructions)	1	44,660
2	Adjusted tax-exempt interest ($15,000. − $360.)	2	14,640
3	Total net gain from Schedule D (Form 1041), line 15, column (1) (see page 26 of the instructions) .	3	
4	Enter amount from Schedule A, line 4 (minus any allocable section 1202 exclusion)	4	
5	Capital gains for the tax year included on Schedule A, line 1 (see page 26 of the instructions) . .	5	
6	Enter any gain from page 1, line 4, as a negative number. If page 1, line 4, is a loss, enter the loss as a positive number	6	(12,000)
7	**Distributable net income.** Combine lines 1 through 6. If zero or less, enter -0-	7	47,300
8	If a complex trust, enter accounting income for the tax year as determined under the governing instrument and applicable local law . **8** 48,500		
9	Income required to be distributed currently	9	-0-
10	Other amounts paid, credited, or otherwise required to be distributed	10	21,000
11	Total distributions. Add lines 9 and 10. If greater than line 8, see page 26 of the instructions . .	11	21,000
12	Enter the amount of tax-exempt income included on line 11	12	6,500
13	Tentative income distribution deduction. Subtract line 12 from line 11	13	14,500
14	Tentative income distribution deduction. Subtract line 2 from line 7. If zero or less, enter -0- . .	14	32,660
15	**Income distribution deduction.** Enter the smaller of line 13 or line 14 here and on page 1, line 18	15	14,500

Schedule G	**Tax Computation** (see page 27 of the instructions)				
1	**Tax: a** Tax on taxable income (see page 27 of the instructions) . .	1a	4,371	✓	
	b Tax on lump-sum distributions. Attach Form 4972	1b			
	c Alternative minimum tax (from Schedule I (Form 1041), line 56)	1c			
	d **Total.** Add lines 1a through 1c . . . . ▶	1d		4,371	
2a	Foreign tax credit. Attach Form 1116	2a			
b	General business credit. Attach Form 3800	2b			
c	Credit for prior year minimum tax. Attach Form 8801	2c			
d	Bond credits. Attach Form 8912	2d			
3	**Total credits.** Add lines 2a through 2d . . . . ▶	3			
4	Subtract line 3 from line 1d. If zero or less, enter -0-	4		4,371	
5	Recapture taxes. Check if from: ☐ Form 4255 ☐ Form 8611 . . .	5			
6	Household employment taxes. Attach Schedule H (Form 1040)	6			
7	**Total tax.** Add lines 4 through 6. Enter here and on page 1, line 23 . . . . . . ▶	7		4,371	

	Other Information	Yes	No
1	Did the estate or trust receive tax-exempt income? If "Yes," attach a computation of the allocation of expenses Enter the amount of tax-exempt interest income and exempt-interest dividends ▶ $ _15,000; (see below)_	X	
2	Did the estate or trust receive all or any part of the earnings (salary, wages, and other compensation) of any individual by reason of a contract assignment or similar arrangement?		X
3	At any time during calendar year 2010, did the estate or trust have an interest in or a signature or other authority over a bank, securities, or other financial account in a foreign country?		X
	See page 29 of the instructions for exceptions and filing requirements for Form TD F 90-22.1. If "Yes," enter the name of the foreign country ▶		
4	During the tax year, did the estate or trust receive a distribution from, or was it the grantor of, or transferor to, a foreign trust? If "Yes," the estate or trust may have to file Form 3520. See page 29 of the instructions		X
5	Did the estate or trust receive, or pay, any qualified residence interest on seller-provided financing? If "Yes," see page 29 for required attachment		X
6	If this is an estate or a complex trust making the section 663(b) election, check here (see page 29) . . ▶ ☐		
7	To make a section 643(e)(3) election, attach Schedule D (Form 1041), and check here (see page 29) . . ▶ ☐		
8	If the decedent's estate has been open for more than 2 years, attach an explanation for the delay in closing the estate, and check here ▶ ☐		
9	Are any present or future trust beneficiaries skip persons? See page 29 of the instructions		X

Form **1041** (2010)

Line 2: Allocation of expenses: $\dfrac{\$15,000}{\$50,000}$ x $1,200 = $360 of trustee's fee allocated to tax-exempt income

SCHEDULE D (Form 1041)	**Capital Gains and Losses**	OMB No. 1545-0092
Department of the Treasury Internal Revenue Service	▶ Attach to Form 1041, Form 5227, or Form 990-T. See the Instructions for Schedule D (Form 1041) (also for Form 5227 or Form 990-T, if applicable).	20**10**

Name of estate or trust	Employer identification number
Cathy and Karen Stephens Trust	74-5724722

Note: *Form 5227 filers need to complete **only** Parts I and II.*

Part I Short-Term Capital Gains and Losses—Assets Held One Year or Less

(a) Description of property (Example: 100 shares 7% preferred of "Z" Co.)	(b) Date acquired (mo., day, yr.)	(c) Date sold (mo., day, yr.)	(d) Sales price	(e) Cost or other basis (see instructions)	(f) Gain or (loss) for the entire year Subtract (e) from (d)
1a					

b Enter the short-term gain or (loss), if any, from Schedule D-1, line 1b	**1b**		
2 Short-term capital gain or (loss) from Forms 4684, 6252, 6781, and 8824	**2**		
3 Net short-term gain or (loss) from partnerships, S corporations, and other estates or trusts . . .	**3**		
4 Short-term capital loss carryover. Enter the amount, if any, from line 9 of the 2009 Capital Loss Carryover Worksheet	**4** (	)
5 **Net short-term gain or (loss).** Combine lines 1a through 4 in column (f). Enter here and on line 13, column (3) on the back . . . . ▶	**5**		

Part II Long-Term Capital Gains and Losses—Assets Held More Than One Year

(a) Description of property (Example: 100 shares 7% preferred of "Z" Co.)	(b) Date acquired (mo., day, yr.)	(c) Date sold (mo., day, yr.)	(d) Sales price	(e) Cost or other basis (see instructions)	(f) Gain or (loss) for the entire year Subtract (e) from (d)
6a 1,000 shares of ABC Corporation stock	2006	Oct. 2010	15,000	3,000	12,000

b Enter the long-term gain or (loss), if any, from Schedule D-1, line 6b	**6b**		
7 Long-term capital gain or (loss) from Forms 2439, 4684, 6252, 6781, and 8824	**7**		
8 Net long-term gain or (loss) from partnerships, S corporations, and other estates or trusts . . .	**8**		
9 Capital gain distributions	**9**		
10 Gain from Form 4797, Part I	**10**		
11 Long-term capital loss carryover. Enter the amount, if any, from line 14 of the 2009 Capital Loss Carryover Worksheet	**11** (	)
12 **Net long-term gain or (loss).** Combine lines 6a through 11 in column (f). Enter here and on line 14a, column (3) on the back . . . . ▶	**12**	12,000	

For Paperwork Reduction Act Notice, see the Instructions for Form 1041.　　Cat. No. 11376V　　Schedule D (Form 1041) 2010

Schedule D (Form 1041) 2010   Page **2**

Part III Summary of Parts I and II	**(1)** Beneficiaries' (see instr.)	**(2)** Estate's or trust's	**(3)** Total
Caution: *Read the instructions **before** completing this part.*			
13 **Net short-term gain or (loss)** 13			
14 **Net long-term gain or (loss):**			
a Total for year 14a		12,000	12,000
b Unrecaptured section 1250 gain (see line 18 of the wrksht.) . 14b			
c 28% rate gain 14c			
15 **Total net gain or (loss).** Combine lines 13 and 14a . . ▶ 15		12,000	12,000

Note: *If line 15, column (3), is a net gain, enter the gain on Form 1041, line 4 (or Form 990-T, Part I, line 4a). If lines 14a and 15, column (2), are net gains, go to Part V, and **do not** complete Part IV. If line 15, column (3), is a net loss, complete Part IV and the **Capital Loss Carryover Worksheet,** as necessary.*

Part IV Capital Loss Limitation

16   Enter here and enter as a (loss) on Form 1041, line 4 (or Form 990-T, Part I, line 4c, if a trust), the **smaller** of:

    a   The loss on line 15, column (3) **or** b $3,000 . . . . 16 (   )

Note: *If the loss on line 15, column (3), is more than $3,000, **or** if Form 1041, page 1, line 22 (or Form 990-T, line 34), is a loss, complete the **Capital Loss Carryover Worksheet** on page 7 of the instructions to figure your capital loss carryover.*

Part V Tax Computation Using Maximum Capital Gains Rates

Form 1041 filers. Complete this part **only** if both lines 14a and 15 in column (2) are gains, or an amount is entered in Part I or Part II and there is an entry on Form 1041, line 2b(2), **and** Form 1041, line 22, is more than zero.

Caution: *Skip this part and complete the worksheet on page 8 of the instructions if:*

- *Either line 14b, col. (2) or line 14c, col. (2) is more than zero, or*
- *Both Form 1041, line 2b(1), and Form 4952, line 4g are more than zero.*

Form 990-T trusts. Complete this part **only** if both lines 14a and 15 are gains, or qualified dividends are included in income in Part I of Form 990-T, **and** Form 990-T, line 34, is more than zero. Skip this part and complete the worksheet on page 8 of the instructions if either line 14b, col. (2) or line 14c, col. (2) is more than zero.

17	Enter taxable income from Form 1041, line 22 (or Form 990-T, line 34) . .	**17**	30,060
18	Enter the **smaller** of line 14a or 15 in column (2) but not less than zero **18** 12,000		
19	Enter the estate's or trust's qualified dividends from Form 1041, line 2b(2) (or enter the qualified dividends included in income in Part I of Form 990-T) **19** 16,681		
20	Add lines 18 and 19 . . . . **20** 12,000		
21	If the estate or trust is filing Form 4952, enter the amount from line 4g; otherwise, enter -0- . . ▶ **21** -0-		
22	Subtract line 21 from line 20. If zero or less, enter -0-	**22**	28,681
23	Subtract line 22 from line 17. If zero or less, enter -0-	**23**	1,379
24	Enter the **smaller** of the amount on line 17 or $2,300	**24**	2,300
25	Is the amount on line 23 equal to or more than the amount on line 24?		
	☐ **Yes.** Skip lines 25 and 26; go to line 27 and check the "No" box.		
	☒ **No.** Enter the amount from line 23	**25**	1,379
26	Subtract line 25 from line 24	**26**	921
27	Are the amounts on lines 22 and 26 the same?		
	☐ **Yes.** Skip lines 27 thru 30; go to line 31. ☒ **No.** Enter the **smaller** of line 17 or line 22	**27**	28,681
28	Enter the amount from line 26 (If line 26 is blank, enter -0-)	**28**	921
29	Subtract line 28 from line 27	**29**	27,760
30	Multiply line 29 by 15% (.15)	**30**	4,164
31	Figure the tax on the amount on line 23. Use the 2010 Tax Rate Schedule for Estates and Trusts (see the Schedule G instructions in the instructions for Form 1041)	**31**	207
32	Add lines 30 and 31	**32**	4,371
33	Figure the tax on the amount on line 17. Use the 2010 Tax Rate Schedule for Estates and Trusts (see the Schedule G instructions in the instructions for Form 1041)	**33**	9,497
34	**Tax on all taxable income.** Enter the **smaller** of line 32 or line 33 here and on Form 1041, Schedule G, line 1a (or Form 990-T, line 36)	**34**	4,371

Schedule D (Form 1041) 2010

661110

☐ Final K-1   ☐ Amended K-1   OMB No. 1545-0092

Schedule K-1
(Form 1041)
Department of the Treasury
Internal Revenue Service

2010

For calendar year 2010,
or tax year beginning _____, 2010,
and ending _____, 20 _____

Beneficiary's Share of Income, Deductions, Credits, etc.

▶ See back of form and instructions.

Part I	Information About the Estate or Trust

A Estate's or trust's employer identification number

74-5727422

B Estate's or trust's name

Cathy and Karen Stephens Trust

C Fiduciary's name, address, city, state, and ZIP code

Merchants Bank
3000 Sun Plaza 1
Tampa, FL 32843

D ☐ Check if Form 1041-T was filed and enter the date it was filed

_____ / _____ / _____

E ☐ Check if this is the final Form 1041 for the estate or trust

Part II	Information About the Beneficiary

F Beneficiary's identifying number

411-36-4761

G Beneficiary's name, address, city, state, and ZIP code

Cathy Stephens
13 Sunny Shores
Miami Beach, FL 33131

H ☒ Domestic beneficiary   ☐ Foreign beneficiary

Part III	Beneficiary's Share of Current Year Income, Deductions, Credits, and Other Items

1 Interest income		**11** Final year deductions	
2a Ordinary dividends	8,879		
2b Qualified dividends	8,879		
3 Net short-term capital gain			
4a Net long-term capital gain			
4b 28% rate gain		**12** Alternative minimum tax adjustment	
4c Unrecaptured section 1250 gain			
5 Other portfolio and nonbusiness income			
6 Ordinary business income			
7 Net rental real estate income	788	**13** Credits and credit recapture	
8 Other rental income			
9 Directly apportioned deductions			
		14 Other information	
10 Estate tax deduction		A	4,833

*See attached statement for additional information.

Note. A statement must be attached showing the beneficiary's share of income and directly apportioned deductions from each business, rental real estate, and other rental activity.

For IRS Use Only

For Paperwork Reduction Act Notice, see the Instructions for Form 1041.   Cat. No. 11380D   **Schedule K-1 (Form 1041) 2010**

661110

☐ Final K-1   ☐ Amended K-1   OMB No. 1545-0092

Schedule K-1
(Form 1041)

20**10**

Department of the Treasury
Internal Revenue Service

For calendar year 2010,
or tax year beginning _____ , 2010,
and ending _____ , 20 _____

Beneficiary's Share of Income, Deductions, Credits, etc.

▶ See back of form and instructions.

Part I	Information About the Estate or Trust

A Estate's or trust's employer identification number

74-5727422

B Estate's or trust's name

Cathy and Karen Stephens Trust

C Fiduciary's name, address, city, state, and ZIP code

Merchants Bank
3000 Sun Plaza I
Tampa, FL 32843

D ☐ Check if Form 1041-T was filed and enter the date it was filed

_____ / _____ / _____

E ☐ Check if this is the final Form 1041 for the estate or trust

Part II	Information About the Beneficiary

F Beneficiary's identifying number

456-78-1230

G Beneficiary's name, address, city, state, and ZIP code

Karen Stephens
1472 Ski Run
Vail, CO 74820

H ☒ Domestic beneficiary   ☐ Foreign beneficiary

Part III	Beneficiary's Share of Current Year Income, Deductions, Credits, and Other Items

1	Interest income	11	Final year deductions
2a	Ordinary dividends 4,440		
2b	Qualified dividends 4,440		
3	Net short-term capital gain		
4a	Net long-term capital gain		
4b	28% rate gain	12	Alternative minimum tax adjustment
4c	Unrecaptured section 1250 gain		
5	Other portfolio and nonbusiness income		
6	Ordinary business income		
7	Net rental real estate income 393	13	Credits and credit recapture
8	Other rental income		
9	Directly apportioned deductions		
		14	Other information
10	Estate tax deduction	A 2,167	

*See attached statement for additional information.

Note. A statement must be attached showing the beneficiary's share of income and directly apportioned deductions from each business, rental real estate, and other rental activity.

For IRS Use Only

For Paperwork Reduction Act Notice, see the Instructions for Form 1041.   Cat. No. 11380D   **Schedule K-1 (Form 1041) 2010**

This list identifies the codes used on Schedule K-1 for beneficiaries and provides summarized reporting information for beneficiaries who file Form 1040. For detailed reporting and filing information, see the Instructions for Beneficiary Filing Form 1040 and the instructions for your income tax return.

	Report on
1. **Interest income**	Form 1040, line 8a
2a. **Ordinary dividends**	Form 1040, line 9a
2b. **Qualified dividends**	Form 1040, line 9b
3. **Net short-term capital gain**	Schedule D, line 5
4a. **Net long-term capital gain**	Schedule D, line 12
4b. **28% rate gain**	Line 4 of the worksheet for Schedule D, line 18
4c. **Unrecaptured section 1250 gain**	Line 11 of the worksheet for Schedule D, line 19
5. **Other portfolio and nonbusiness income**	Schedule E, line 33, column (f)
6. **Ordinary business income**	Schedule E, line 33, column (d) or (f)
7. **Net rental real estate income**	Schedule E, line 33, column (d) or (f)
8. **Other rental income**	Schedule E, line 33, column (d) or (f)

9. **Directly apportioned deductions**

    Code

A Depreciation	Form 8582 or Schedule E, line 33, column (c) or (e)
B Depletion	Form 8582 or Schedule E, line 33, column (c) or (e)
C Amortization	Form 8582 or Schedule E, line 33, column (c) or (e)
10. **Estate tax deduction**	Schedule A, line 28

11. **Final year deductions**

A Excess deductions	Schedule A, line 23
B Short-term capital loss carryover	Schedule D, line 5
C Long-term capital loss carryover	Schedule D, line 12; line 5 of the wksht. for Sch. D, line 18; and line 16 of the wksht. for Sch. D, line 19
D Net operating loss carryover — regular tax	Form 1040, line 21
E Net operating loss carryover — minimum tax	Form 6251, line 11

12. **Alternative minimum tax (AMT) items**

    Code   *Report on*

A Adjustment for minimum tax purposes	Form 6251, line 15
B AMT adjustment attributable to qualified dividends	
C AMT adjustment attributable to net short-term capital gain	
D AMT adjustment attributable to net long-term capital gain	See the beneficiary's instructions and the Instructions for Form 6251
E AMT adjustment attributable to unrecaptured section 1250 gain	
F AMT adjustment attributable to 28% rate gain	
G Accelerated depreciation	
H Depletion	
I Amortization	
J Exclusion items	2011 Form 8801

13. **Credits and credit recapture**

A Credit for estimated taxes	Form 1040, line 62
B Credit for backup withholding	Form 1040, line 61
C Low-income housing credit	Form 8586 (also see the beneficiary's instructions)
D Rehabilitation credit and energy credit	See the beneficiary's instructions
E Other qualifying investment credit	See the beneficiary's instructions
F Work opportunity credit	Form 5884, line 3
G Credit for small employer health insurance premiums	Form 8941, line 15
H Alcohol and cellulosic biofuel fuels credit	Form 6478, line 8 (also see the beneficiary's instructions)
I Credit for increasing research activities	Form 3800, line 1c
J Renewable electricity, refined coal, and Indian coal production credit	See the beneficiary's instructions
K Empowerment zone and renewal community employment credit	Form 8844, line 3
L Indian employment credit	Form 3800, line 1g
M Orphan drug credit	Form 3800, line 1h
N Credit for employer-provided child care and facilities	Form 3800, line 1k
O Biodiesel and renewable diesel fuels credit	Form 8864, line 9 (also see the beneficiary's instructions)
P Nonconventional source fuel credit	Form 3800, line 1o
Q Credit to holders of tax credit bonds	Form 8912, line 8
R Agricultural chemicals security credit	Form 3800, line 1v
S Energy efficient appliance credit	Form 3800, line 1q
T Credit for employer differential wage payments	Form 3800, line 1w
U Recapture of credits	See the beneficiary's instructions

14. **Other information**

A Tax-exempt interest	Form 1040, line 8b
B Foreign taxes	Form 1040, line 47 or Sch. A, line 8
C Qualified production activities income	Form 8903, line 7, col. (b) (also see the beneficiary's instructions)
D Form W-2 wages	Form 8903, line 17
E Net investment income	Form 4952, line 4a
F Gross farm and fishing income	Schedule E, line 42
G Foreign trading gross receipts (IRC 942(a))	See the Instructions for Form 8873
H Other information	See the beneficiary's instructions

Note. If you are a beneficiary who does not file a Form 1040, see instructions for the type of income tax return you are filing.

Form **1116** Department of the Treasury Internal Revenue Service (99)	**Foreign Tax Credit** (Individual, Estate, or Trust) ▶ Attach to Form 1040, 1040NR, 1041, or 990-T. ▶ See separate instructions.	OMB No. 1545-0121 20**10** Attachment Sequence No. **19**

Name **Andrew Roberts**	**Identifying number** as shown on page 1 of your tax return **123-45-6789**

Use a separate Form 1116 for each category of income listed below. See **Categories of Income** in the instructions. Check only one box on each Form 1116. Report all amounts in U.S. dollars except where specified in Part II below.

a ☒ Passive category income **c** ☐ Section 901(j) income **e** ☐ Lump-sum distributions

b ☐ General category income **d** ☐ Certain income re-sourced by treaty

f Resident of (name of country) ▶ **United States**

Note: *If you paid taxes to only one foreign country or U.S. possession, use column A in Part I and line A in Part II. If you paid taxes to* ***more than one*** *foreign country or U.S. possession, use a separate column and line for each country or possession.*

Part I Taxable Income or Loss From Sources Outside the United States (for Category Checked Above)

		Foreign Country or U.S. Possession			Total (Add cols. A, B, and C.)
		A	**B**	**C**	
g	Enter the name of the foreign country or U.S. possession . . . . ▶	**Canada**			
1a	Gross income from sources within country shown above and of the type checked above (see instructions):				
	Dividends	**17,822**			1a **17,822**
b	Check if line 1a is compensation for personal services as an employee, your total compensation from all sources is $250,000 or more, and you used an alternative basis to determine its source (see instructions) . . ▶ ☐				
	Deductions and losses (*Caution: See instructions*):				
2	Expenses **definitely related** to the income on line 1a (attach statement)				
3	Pro rata share of other deductions **not definitely related:**				
a	Certain itemized deductions or standard deduction (see instructions)				
b	Other deductions (attach statement)				
c	Add lines 3a and 3b				
d	Gross foreign source income (see instructions) .				
e	Gross income from all sources (see instructions) .				
f	Divide line 3d by line 3e (see instructions) . .				
g	Multiply line 3c by line 3f				
4	Pro rata share of interest expense (see instructions):				
a	Home mortgage interest (use worksheet on page 14 of the instructions)				
b	Other interest expense				
5	Losses from foreign sources				
6	Add lines 2, 3g, 4a, 4b, and 5	**-0-**			6 **-0-**
7	Subtract line 6 from line 1a. Enter the result here and on line 14, page 2 . . . . ▶			7	**17,822**

Part II Foreign Taxes Paid or Accrued (see instructions)

Country	Credit is claimed for taxes (you must check one)	Foreign taxes paid or accrued								
		In foreign currency				In U.S. dollars				
	(h) ☒ Paid (i) ☐ Accrued	Taxes withheld at source on:			**(n)** Other foreign taxes paid or accrued	Taxes withheld at source on:			**(r)** Other foreign taxes paid or accrued	**(s)** Total foreign taxes paid or accrued (add cols. (o) through (r))
	(j) Date paid or accrued	**(k)** Dividends	**(l)** Rents and royalties	**(m)** Interest		**(o)** Dividends	**(p)** Rents and royalties	**(q)** Interest		
A	**12-31-10**	**2,700***				**2,673**				**2,673**
B										
C										
8	Add lines A through C, column (s). Enter the total here and on line 9, page 2 . . . . ▶								8	**2,673**

For Paperwork Reduction Act Notice, see instructions. Cat. No. 11440U Form **1116** (2010)

*Canadian dollars

Form 1116 (2010)   Page **2**

Part III **Figuring the Credit**

9	Enter the amount from line 8. These are your total foreign taxes paid or accrued for the category of income checked above Part I . .	9	**2,673**
10	Carryback or carryover (attach detailed computation)	10	
11	Add lines 9 and 10	11	**2,673**
12	Reduction in foreign taxes (see instructions)	12	

13	Subtract line 12 from line 11. This is the total amount of foreign taxes available for credit (see instructions)	13	**2,673**

14	Enter the amount from line 7. This is your taxable income or (loss) from sources outside the United States (before adjustments) for the category of income checked above Part I (see instructions)	14	**17,822**
15	Adjustments to line 14 (see instructions)	15	
16	Combine the amounts on lines 14 and 15. This is your net foreign source taxable income. (If the result is zero or less, you have no foreign tax credit for the category of income you checked above Part I. Skip lines 17 through 21. However, if you are filing more than one Form 1116, you must complete line 19.)	16	**17,822**
17	**Individuals:** Enter the amount from Form 1040, line 41, or Form 1040NR, line 39. **Estates and trusts:** Enter your taxable income without the deduction for your exemption	17	**86,000**

Caution: *If you figured your tax using the lower rates on qualified dividends or capital gains, see instructions.*

18	Divide line 16 by line 17. If line 16 is more than line 17, enter "1"	18	**0.207233**
19	**Individuals:** Enter the amount from Form 1040, line 44. If you are a nonresident alien, enter the amount from Form 1040NR, line 42. **Estates and trusts:** Enter the amount from Form 1041, Schedule G, line 1a, or the total of Form 990-T, lines 36 and 37	19	**12,038**[*]

Caution: *If you are completing line 19 for separate category **e** (lump-sum distributions), see instructions.*

20	Multiply line 19 by line 18 (maximum amount of credit)	20	**2,495**
21	Enter the **smaller** of line 13 or line 20. If this is the only Form 1116 you are filing, skip lines 22 through 26 and enter this amount on line 27. Otherwise, complete the appropriate line in Part IV (see instructions) . . . . ▶	21	**2,495**

Part IV **Summary of Credits From Separate Parts III** (see instructions)

22	Credit for taxes on passive category income	22	**2,495**		
23	Credit for taxes on general category income	23			
24	Credit for taxes on certain income re-sourced by treaty	24			
25	Credit for taxes on lump-sum distributions	25			
26	Add lines 22 through 25			26	**2,495**
27	Enter the **smaller** of line 19 or line 26			27	**2,495**
28	Reduction of credit for international boycott operations. See instructions for line 12			28	
29	Subtract line 28 from line 27. This is your **foreign tax credit.** Enter here and on Form 1040, line 47; Form 1040NR, line 45; Form 1041, Schedule G, line 2a; or Form 990-T, line 40a . . . . . . ▶			29	**2,495**

Form **1116** (2010)

[*]Tax on $86,000 − (2 x $3,650) = $78,700 taxable income. The figure reported on Line 41 of Form 1040 is net of the standard deduction or itemized deductions.

Form **2555**	**Foreign Earned Income**	OMB No. 1545-0074
Department of the Treasury Internal Revenue Service	▶ See separate instructions. ▶ Attach to Form 1040.	20**10** Attachment Sequence No. **34**

For Use by U.S. Citizens and Resident Aliens Only

Name shown on Form 1040	Your social security number
Lawrence E. Smith	234-56-7890

Part I **General Information**

1 Your foreign address (including country)
123 Rue de Harve 75011 Paris France

2 Your occupation
Financial Vice-President

3 Employer's name ▶ Very Public Corporation

4a Employer's U.S. address ▶ 90 Fifty Avenue, New York, NY 10011

b Employer's foreign address ▶ 11 Rue de Nanettes/5 e'Etage, 75011 Paris France

5 Employer is (check any that apply): ▶
- **a** ☐ A foreign entity
- **b** ☒ A U.S. company
- **c** ☐ Self
- **d** ☐ A foreign affiliate of a U.S. company
- **e** ☐ Other (specify) ▶

6a If, after 1981, you filed Form 2555 or Form 2555-EZ, enter the last year you filed the form. ▶ 2009

b If you did not file Form 2555 or 2555-EZ after 1981 to claim either of the exclusions, check here ▶ ☐ and go to line 7.

c Have you ever revoked either of the exclusions? . . . . ☐ Yes ☒ No

d If you answered "Yes," enter the type of exclusion and the tax year for which the revocation was effective. ▶

7 Of what country are you a citizen/national? ▶ United States

8a Did you maintain a separate foreign residence for your family because of adverse living conditions at your tax home? See **Second foreign household** on page 3 of the instructions . . . . ☐ Yes ☒ No

b If "Yes," enter city and country of the separate foreign residence. Also, enter the number of days during your tax year that you maintained a second household at that address. ▶ N/A

9 List your tax home(s) during your tax year and date(s) established. ▶ 123 Rue de Harve, 75011 Paris France
July 10, 2009

Next, complete either Part II or Part III. If an item does not apply, enter "NA." If you do not give the information asked for, any exclusion or deduction you claim may be disallowed.

Part II **Taxpayers Qualifying Under Bona Fide Residence Test** (see page 2 of the instructions)

10 Date bona fide residence began ▶ July 10, 2009 , and ended ▶ Presently a resident

11 Kind of living quarters in foreign country ▶
- **a** ☐ Purchased house
- **b** ☒ Rented house or apartment
- **c** ☐ Rented room
- **d** ☐ Quarters furnished by employer

12a Did any of your family live with you abroad during any part of the tax year? . . . . ☒ Yes ☐ No

b If "Yes," who and for what period? ▶ Wife and two children for entire year

13a Have you submitted a statement to the authorities of the foreign country where you claim bona fide residence that you are not a resident of that country? See instructions . . . . ☐ Yes ☒ No

b Are you required to pay income tax to the country where you claim bona fide residence? See instructions . ☒ Yes ☐ No

If you answered "Yes" to 13a and "No" to 13b, you do not qualify as a bona fide resident. Do not complete the rest of this part.

14 If you were present in the United States or its possessions during the tax year, complete columns (a)–(d) below. **Do not** include the income from column (d) in Part IV, but report it on Form 1040.

(a) Date arrived in U.S.	(b) Date left U.S.	(c) Number of days in U.S. on business	(d) Income earned in U.S. on business (attach computation)	(a) Date arrived in U.S.	(b) Date left U.S.	(c) Number of days in U.S. on business	(d) Income earned in U.S. on business (attach computation)
2-19-10	2-23-10	5	1,200				

15a List any contractual terms or other conditions relating to the length of your employment abroad. ▶ Indefinite

b Enter the type of visa under which you entered the foreign country. ▶ Resident

c Did your visa limit the length of your stay or employment in a foreign country? If "Yes," attach explanation . ☐ Yes ☒ No

d Did you maintain a home in the United States while living abroad? . . . . ☒ Yes ☐ No

e If "Yes," enter address of your home, whether it was rented, the names of the occupants, and their relationship to you. ▶ 4710 N.W. 68th Terrace, Gainesville, FL 32601 (rented to unrelated party)

For Paperwork Reduction Act Notice, see the Form 1040 instructions.   Cat. No. 11900P   Form **2555** (2010)

Form 2555 (2010)

Page **2**

Part III — Taxpayers Qualifying Under Physical Presence Test (see page 2 of the instructions)

16 The physical presence test is based on the 12-month period from ▶ ___N/A___ through ▶ _____

17 Enter your principal country of employment during your tax year. ▶ _____

18 If you traveled abroad during the 12-month period entered on line 16, complete columns **(a)–(f)** below. Exclude travel between foreign countries that did not involve travel on or over international waters, or in or over the United States, for 24 hours or more. If you have no travel to report during the period, enter "Physically present in a foreign country or countries for the entire 12-month period." **Do not** include the income from column **(f)** below in Part IV, but report it on Form 1040.

(a) Name of country (including U.S.)	**(b)** Date arrived	**(c)** Date left	**(d)** Full days present in country	**(e)** Number of days in U.S. on business	**(f)** Income earned in U.S. on business (attach computation)

Part IV — All Taxpayers

Note: *Enter on lines 19 through 23 all income, including noncash income, you earned and actually or constructively received during your 2010 tax year for services you performed in a foreign country. If any of the foreign earned income received this tax year was earned in a prior tax year, or will be earned in a later tax year (such as a bonus), see the instructions. **Do not** include income from line 14, column **(d)**, or line 18, column **(f)**. Report amounts in U.S. dollars, using the exchange rates in effect when you actually or constructively received the income.*

If you are a cash basis taxpayer, report on Form 1040 all income you received in 2010, no matter when you performed the service.

2010 Foreign Earned Income		Amount (in U.S. dollars)
19 Total wages, salaries, bonuses, commissions, etc.	**19**	58,800*
20 Allowable share of income for personal services performed (see instructions):		
a In a business (including farming) or profession	**20a**	
b In a partnership. List partnership's name and address and type of income. ▶ _____		
_____	**20b**	
21 Noncash income (market value of property or facilities furnished by employer—attach statement showing how it was determined):		
a Home (lodging)	**21a**	
b Meals	**21b**	
c Car	**21c**	
d Other property or facilities. List type and amount. ▶ _____		
_____	**21d**	
22 Allowances, reimbursements, or expenses paid on your behalf for services you performed:		
a Cost of living and overseas differential	**22a** 27,000	
b Family	**22b**	
c Education	**22c** 8,000	
d Home leave	**22d** 6,400	
e Quarters	**22e** 21,300	
f For any other purpose. List type and amount. ▶ _____		
_____	**22f**	
g Add lines 22a through 22f	**22g**	62,700
23 Other foreign earned income. List type and amount. ▶ _____		
_____	**23**	
24 Add lines 19 through 21d, line 22g, and line 23	**24**	121,500
25 Total amount of meals and lodging included on line 24 that is excludable (see instructions)	**25**	
26 Subtract line 25 from line 24. Enter the result here and on line 27 on page 3. This is your **2010 foreign earned income** . . . . ▶	**26**	121,500

*$60,000 salary — $1,200 U.S. source income from Part II, Line 14(d).

Form **2555** (2010)

Form 2555 (2010)																				Page **3**

Part V   All Taxpayers

27	Enter the amount from line 26	**27**	**121,500**	

Are you claiming the housing exclusion or housing deduction?
☒ **Yes.** Complete Part VI.
☐ **No.**   Go to Part VII.

Part VI   Taxpayers Claiming the Housing Exclusion and/or Deduction

28	Qualified housing expenses for the tax year (see instructions)	**28**	**21,300**
29a	Enter location where housing expenses incurred (see instructions) ▶ **France**		
b	Enter limit on housing expenses (see instructions)	**29b**	**27,450**
30	Enter the **smaller** of line 28 or line 29b	**30**	**21,300**
31	Number of days in your qualifying period that fall within your 2010 tax year (see instructions) . . . . **31** **365** days		
32	Multiply $40.11 by the number of days on line 31. If 365 is entered on line 31, enter $14,640.00 here	**32**	**14,640**
33	Subtract line 32 from line 30. If the result is zero or less, do not complete the rest of this part or any of Part IX	**33**	**6,660**
34	Enter employer-provided amounts (see instructions) **34** **121,500**		
35	Divide line 34 by line 27. Enter the result as a decimal (rounded to at least three places), but do not enter more than "1.000"	**35**	**×1 . 00**
36	**Housing exclusion.** Multiply line 33 by line 35. Enter the result but do not enter more than the amount on line 34. Also, complete Part VIII . . . . ▶	**36**	**6,660**

Note: *The housing deduction is figured in Part IX. If you choose to claim the foreign earned income exclusion, complete Parts VII and VIII before Part IX.*

Part VII   Taxpayers Claiming the Foreign Earned Income Exclusion

37	Maximum foreign earned income exclusion	**37**	$91,500	00
38	• If you completed Part VI, enter the number from line 31. • All others, enter the number of days in your qualifying period that fall within your 2010 tax year (see the instructions for line 31). **38** **365** days			
39	• If line 38 and the number of days in your 2010 tax year (usually 365) are the same, enter "1.000." • Otherwise, divide line 38 by the number of days in your 2010 tax year and enter the result as a decimal (rounded to at least three places).	**39**	**×1 . 00**	
40	Multiply line 37 by line 39	**40**	**91,500**	
41	Subtract line 36 from line 27	**41**	**114,840**	
42	**Foreign earned income exclusion.** Enter the **smaller** of line 40 or line 41. Also, complete Part VIII ▶	**42**	**91,500**	

Part VIII   Taxpayers Claiming the Housing Exclusion, Foreign Earned Income Exclusion, or Both

43	Add lines 36 and 42	**43**	**98,160**
44	Deductions allowed in figuring your adjusted gross income (Form 1040, line 37) that are allocable to the excluded income. See instructions and attach computation	**44**	
45	Subtract line 44 from line 43. Enter the result here and in parentheses on **Form 1040, line 21.** Next to the amount enter "Form 2555." On Form 1040, subtract this amount from your income to arrive at total income on Form 1040, line 22	**45**	**98,160**

Part IX   Taxpayers Claiming the Housing Deduction— Complete this part only if **(a)** line 33 is more than line 36 and **(b)** line 27 is more than line 43.

46	Subtract line 36 from line 33	**46**	
47	Subtract line 43 from line 27	**47**	
48	Enter the **smaller** of line 46 or line 47	**48**	

Note: *If line 47 is **more than** line 48 and you could not deduct all of your 2009 housing deduction because of the 2009 limit, use the worksheet on page 4 of the instructions to figure the amount to enter on line 49. Otherwise, go to line 50.*

49	Housing deduction carryover from 2009 (from worksheet on page 4 of the instructions) . . .	**49**	
50	**Housing deduction.** Add lines 48 and 49. Enter the total here and on Form 1040 to the left of line 36. Next to the amount on Form 1040, enter "Form 2555." Add it to the total adjustments reported on that line . . . . ▶	**50**	**N/A**

Form **2555** (2010)

MACRS TABLES

MACRS, ADS and ACRS Depreciation Methods Summary

System	Characteristics	Depreciation Method		Table No.[a]	
		MACRS	ADS	MACRS	ADS
MACRS & ADS	Personal Property:				
	1. Accounting convention	Half-year or mid-quarter	Half-year or mid-quarter[b]		
	2. Life and method				
	a. 3-year, 5-year, 7-year, 10-year	200% DB or elect straight-line	150% DB or elect straight-line	1, 2, 3, 4, 5	10, 11[c]
	b. 15-year, 20-year	150% DB or elect straight-line	150% DB or elect straight-line[d]	1, 2, 3, 4, 5	
	3. Luxury Automobile Limitations			6	
	Real property:				
	1. Accounting convention	Mid-month	Mid-month		
	2. Life and method				
	a. Residential rental property	27.5 years, straight-line	40 years straight-line	7	12
	b. Nonresidential real property	39 years, straight-line[e]	40 years straight-line	9	12

System	Characteristics	ACRS
ACRS[f]	Personal Property	
	1. Accounting convention	Half-year
	2. Life and method	
	a. 3-year, 5-year, 10-year, 15-year	150% DB or elect straight-line
	Real Property	
	1. Accounting convention	First of month or mid-month
	2. Life	
	a. 15-year property	Placed in service after 12/31/80 and before 3/16/84
	b. 18-year property	Placed in service after 3/15/84 and before 5/9/85
	c. 19-year property	Placed in service after 5/8/85 and before 1/1/87
	3. Method	
	a. All but low-income housing	175% DB or elect straight-line
	b. Low-income housing property	200% DB or elect straight-line

[a]All depreciation tables in this appendix are based upon tables contained in Rev. Proc. 87-57, as amended.
[b]General and ADS tables are available for property lives from 2.5–50.0 years using the straight-line method. These tables are contained in Rev. Proc. 87-57 and are only partially reproduced here.
[c]The mid-quarter tables are available in Rev. Proc. 87-57, but are not reproduced here.
[d]Special recovery periods are assigned certain MACRS properties under the alternative depreciation system.
[e]A 31.5-year recovery period applied to nonresidential real property placed in service under the MACRS rules prior to May 13, 1993 (see Table 8).
[f]ACRS was effective for years 1981–1986. ACRS tables are no longer reproduced in this textbook.

▼ TABLE 1

General Depreciation System—MACRS
Personal Property Placed in Service after 12/31/86
Applicable Convention: Half-year
Applicable Depreciation Method: 200 or 150 Percent Declining Balance Switching to Straight Line

If the Recovery Year Is:	And the Recovery Period Is:					
	3-Year	5-Year	7-Year	10-Year	15-Year	20-Year
	The Depreciation Rate Is:					
1	33.33	20.00	14.29	10.00	5.00	3.750
2	44.45	32.00	24.49	18.00	9.50	7.219
3	14.81	19.20	17.49	14.40	8.55	6.677
4	7.41	11.52	12.49	11.52	7.70	6.177
5		11.52	8.93	9.22	6.93	5.713
6		5.76	8.92	7.37	6.23	5.285
7			8.93	6.55	5.90	4.888
8			4.46	6.55	5.90	4.522
9				6.56	5.91	4.462
10				6.55	5.90	4.461
11				3.28	5.91	4.462
12					5.90	4.461
13					5.91	4.462
14					5.90	4.461
15					5.91	4.462
16					2.95	4.461
17						4.462
18						4.461
19						4.462
20						4.461
21						2.231

▼ TABLE 2

General Depreciation System—MACRS
Personal Property Placed in Service after 12/31/86
Applicable Convention: Mid-quarter (Property Placed in Service in First Quarter)
Applicable Depreciation Method: 200 or 150 Percent Declining Balance Switching to Straight Line

If the Recovery Year Is:	And the Recovery Period Is:					
	3-Year	5-Year	7-Year	10-Year	15-Year	20-Year
	The Depreciation Rate Is:					
1	58.33	35.00	25.00	17.50	8.75	6.563
2	27.78	26.00	21.43	16.50	9.13	7.000
3	12.35	15.60	15.31	13.20	8.21	6.482
4	1.54	11.01	10.93	10.56	7.39	5.996
5		11.01	8.75	8.45	6.65	5.546
6		1.38	8.74	6.76	5.99	5.130
7			8.75	6.55	5.90	4.746
8			1.09	6.55	5.91	4.459
9				6.56	5.90	4.459
10				6.55	5.91	4.459
11				0.82	5.90	4.459
12					5.91	4.460
13					5.90	4.459
14					5.91	4.460
15					5.90	4.459
16					0.74	4.460
17						4.459
18						4.460
19						4.459
20						4.460
21						0.557

▼ TABLE 3

General Depreciation System—MACRS
Personal Property Placed in Service after 12/31/86
Applicable Convention: Mid-quarter (Property Placed in Service in Second Quarter)
Applicable Depreciation Method: 200 or 150 Percent Declining Balance Switching to Straight Line

If the Recovery Year Is:	And the Recovery Period Is: 3-Year	5-Year	7-Year	10-Year	15-Year	20-Year
	The Depreciation Rate Is:					
1	41.67	25.00	17.85	12.50	6.25	4.688
2	38.89	30.00	23.47	17.50	9.38	7.148
3	14.14	18.00	16.76	14.00	8.44	6.612
4	5.30	11.37	11.97	11.20	7.59	6.116
5		11.37	8.87	8.96	6.83	5.658
6		4.26	8.87	7.17	6.15	5.233
7			8.87	6.55	5.91	4.841
8			3.33	6.55	5.90	4.478
9				6.56	5.91	4.463
10				6.55	5.90	4.463
11				2.46	5.91	4.463
12					5.90	4.463
13					5.91	4.463
14					5.90	4.463
15					5.91	4.462
16					2.21	4.463
17						4.462
18						4.463
19						4.462
20						4.463
21						1.673

▼ TABLE 4

General Depreciation System—MACRS
Personal Property Placed in Service after 12/31/86
Applicable Convention: Mid-quarter (Property Placed in Service in Third Quarter)
Applicable Depreciation Method: 200 or 150 Percent Declining Balance Switching to Straight Line

If the Recovery Year Is:	And the Recovery Period Is:					
	3-Year	5-Year	7-Year	10-Year	15-Year	20-Year
	The Depreciation Rate Is:					
1	25.00	15.00	10.71	7.50	3.75	2.813
2	50.00	34.00	25.51	18.50	9.63	7.289
3	16.67	20.40	18.22	14.80	8.66	6.742
4	8.33	12.24	13.02	11.84	7.80	6.237
5		11.30	9.30	9.47	7.02	5.769
6		7.06	8.85	7.58	6.31	5.336
7			8.86	6.55	5.90	4.936
8			5.53	6.55	5.90	4.566
9				6.56	5.91	4.460
10				6.55	5.90	4.460
11				4.10	5.91	4.460
12					5.90	4.460
13					5.91	4.461
14					5.90	4.460
15					5.91	4.461
16					3.69	4.460
17						4.461
18						4.460
19						4.461
20						4.460
21						2.788

▼ TABLE 5

General Depreciation System—MACRS
Personal Property Placed in Service after 12/31/86
Applicable Convention: Mid-quarter (Property Placed in Service in Fourth Quarter)
Applicable Depreciation Method: 200 or 150 Percent Declining Balance Switching to Straight Line

If the Recovery Year Is:	And the Recovery Period Is:					
	3-Year	5-Year	7-Year	10-Year	15-Year	20-Year
	The Depreciation Rate Is:					
1	8.33	5.00	3.57	2.50	1.25	0.938
2	61.11	38.00	27.55	19.50	9.88	7.430
3	20.37	22.80	19.68	15.60	8.89	6.872
4	10.19	13.68	14.06	12.48	8.00	6.357
5		10.94	10.04	9.98	7.20	5.880
6		9.58	8.73	7.99	6.48	5.439
7			8.73	6.55	5.90	5.031
8			7.64	6.55	5.90	4.654
9				6.56	5.90	4.458
10				6.55	5.91	4.458
11				5.74	5.90	4.458
12					5.91	4.458
13					5.90	4.458
14					5.91	4.458
15					5.90	4.458
16					5.17	4.458
17						4.458
18						4.459
19						4.458
20						4.459
21						3.901

▼ TABLE 6

Luxury Automobile Depreciation Limits

	Year Automobile is Placed in Service[a]				
	2011 and 2010	2009	2008	2007	2006
Maximum Allowable Depreciation (100% Business Use):					
Year 1	$3,060[b]	$2,960[c]	$2,960[d]	$3,060	$2,960
Year 2	4,900	4,800	4,800	4,900	4,800
Year 3	2,950	2,850	2,850	2,850	2,850
Year 4 and Each Succeeding Year	1,775	1,775	1,775	1,775	1,775

[a]For years prior to 2006, see the Revenue Procedure for the appropriate year.
[b]$11,060 in Year 1 (2011 or 2010) if taxpayer claims bonus depreciation.
[c]$10,960 in Year 1 (2009) if taxpayer claims bonus depreciation.
[d]$10,960 in Year 1 (2008) if taxpayer claimed bonus depreciation.

▼ TABLE 6 (continued)
Truck and Van Depreciation Limits

	Year Truck or Van is Placed in Service[a]					
	2011	2010	2009	2008	2007	2006
Maximum Allowable Depreciation (100% Business Use):						
Year 1	$3,260[b]	$3,160[d]	$3,060[c]	$3,160[d]	$3,260	$3,260
Year 2	5,200	5,100	4,900	5,100	5,200	5,200
Year 3	3,150	3,050	2,950	3,050	3,050	3,150
Year 4 and Each Succeeding Year	1,875	1,875	1,775	1,875	1,875	1,875

[a]For years prior to 2006, see the Revenue Procedure for the appropriate year.
[b]$11,260 in Year 1 (2011) if taxpayer claims bonus depreciation.
[c]$11,060 in Year 1 (2009) if taxpayer claims bonus depreciation.
[d]$11,160 in Year 1 (2010 and 2008) if taxpayer claimed bonus depreciation.

▼ TABLE 7

General Depreciation System—MACRS
Residential Rental Real Property Placed in Service after 12/31/86
Applicable Recovery Period: 27.5 Years
Applicable Convention: Mid-month
Applicable Depreciation Method: Straight Line

If the Recovery Year Is:	And the Month in the First Recovery Year the Property Is Placed in Service Is:											
	1	2	3	4	5	6	7	8	9	10	11	12
	The Depreciation Rate Is:											
1	3.485	3.182	2.879	2.576	2.273	1.970	1.667	1.364	1.061	0.758	0.455	0.152
2	3.636	3.636	3.636	3.636	3.636	3.636	3.636	3.636	3.636	3.636	3.636	3.636
3	3.636	3.636	3.636	3.636	3.636	3.636	3.636	3.636	3.636	3.636	3.636	3.636
4	3.636	3.636	3.636	3.636	3.636	3.636	3.636	3.636	3.636	3.636	3.636	3.636
5	3.636	3.636	3.636	3.636	3.636	3.636	3.636	3.636	3.636	3.636	3.636	3.636
6	3.636	3.636	3.636	3.636	3.636	3.636	3.636	3.636	3.636	3.636	3.636	3.636
7	3.636	3.636	3.636	3.636	3.636	3.636	3.636	3.636	3.636	3.636	3.636	3.636
8	3.636	3.636	3.636	3.636	3.636	3.636	3.636	3.636	3.636	3.636	3.636	3.636
9	3.636	3.636	3.636	3.636	3.636	3.636	3.636	3.636	3.636	3.636	3.636	3.636
10	3.637	3.637	3.637	3.637	3.637	3.637	3.636	3.636	3.636	3.636	3.636	3.636
11	3.636	3.636	3.636	3.636	3.636	3.636	3.637	3.637	3.637	3.637	3.637	3.637
12	3.637	3.637	3.637	3.637	3.637	3.637	3.636	3.636	3.636	3.636	3.636	3.636
13	3.636	3.636	3.636	3.636	3.636	3.636	3.637	3.637	3.637	3.637	3.637	3.637
14	3.637	3.637	3.637	3.637	3.637	3.637	3.636	3.636	3.636	3.636	3.636	3.636
15	3.636	3.636	3.636	3.636	3.636	3.636	3.637	3.637	3.637	3.637	3.637	3.637
16	3.637	3.637	3.637	3.637	3.637	3.637	3.636	3.636	3.636	3.636	3.636	3.636
17	3.636	3.636	3.636	3.636	3.636	3.636	3.637	3.637	3.637	3.637	3.637	3.637
18	3.637	3.637	3.637	3.637	3.637	3.637	3.636	3.636	3.636	3.636	3.636	3.636
19	3.636	3.636	3.636	3.636	3.636	3.636	3.637	3.637	3.637	3.637	3.637	3.637
20	3.637	3.637	3.637	3.637	3.637	3.637	3.636	3.636	3.636	3.636	3.636	3.636
21	3.636	3.636	3.636	3.636	3.636	3.636	3.637	3.637	3.637	3.637	3.637	3.637
22	3.637	3.637	3.637	3.637	3.637	3.637	3.636	3.636	3.636	3.636	3.636	3.636
23	3.636	3.636	3.636	3.636	3.636	3.636	3.637	3.637	3.637	3.637	3.637	3.637
24	3.637	3.637	3.637	3.637	3.637	3.637	3.636	3.636	3.636	3.636	3.636	3.636
25	3.636	3.636	3.636	3.636	3.636	3.636	3.637	3.637	3.637	3.637	3.637	3.637
26	3.637	3.637	3.637	3.637	3.637	3.637	3.636	3.636	3.636	3.636	3.636	3.636
27	3.636	3.636	3.636	3.636	3.636	3.636	3.637	3.637	3.637	3.637	3.637	3.637
28	1.970	2.273	2.576	2.879	3.182	3.485	3.636	3.636	3.636	3.636	3.636	3.636
29	0.000	0.000	0.000	0.000	0.000	0.000	0.152	0.455	0.758	1.061	1.364	1.667

▼ TABLE 8

General Depreciation System—MACRS
Nonresidential Real Property Placed in Service after 12/31/86 and before 5/13/93
Applicable Recovery Period: 31.5 Years
Applicable Convention: Mid-month
Applicable Depreciation Method: Straight Line

If the Recovery Year Is:	And the Month in the First Recovery Year the Property Is Placed in Service Is:											
	1	2	3	4	5	6	7	8	9	10	11	12
	The Depreciation Rate Is:											
1	3.042	2.778	2.513	2.249	1.984	1.720	1.455	1.190	0.926	0.661	0.397	0.132
2	3.175	3.175	3.175	3.175	3.175	3.175	3.175	3.175	3.175	3.175	3.175	3.175
3	3.175	3.175	3.175	3.175	3.175	3.175	3.175	3.175	3.175	3.175	3.175	3.175
4	3.175	3.175	3.175	3.175	3.175	3.175	3.175	3.175	3.175	3.175	3.175	3.175
5	3.175	3.175	3.175	3.175	3.175	3.175	3.175	3.175	3.175	3.175	3.175	3.175
6	3.175	3.175	3.175	3.175	3.175	3.175	3.175	3.175	3.175	3.175	3.175	3.175
7	3.175	3.175	3.175	3.175	3.175	3.175	3.175	3.175	3.175	3.175	3.175	3.175
8	3.175	3.174	3.175	3.174	3.175	3.174	3.175	3.175	3.175	3.175	3.175	3.175
9	3.174	3.175	3.174	3.175	3.174	3.175	3.174	3.175	3.174	3.175	3.174	3.175
10	3.175	3.174	3.175	3.174	3.175	3.174	3.175	3.174	3.175	3.174	3.175	3.174
11	3.174	3.175	3.174	3.175	3.174	3.175	3.174	3.175	3.174	3.175	3.174	3.175
12	3.175	3.174	3.175	3.174	3.175	3.174	3.175	3.174	3.175	3.174	3.175	3.174
13	3.174	3.175	3.174	3.175	3.174	3.175	3.174	3.175	3.174	3.175	3.174	3.175
14	3.175	3.174	3.175	3.174	3.175	3.174	3.175	3.174	3.175	3.174	3.175	3.174
15	3.174	3.175	3.174	3.175	3.174	3.175	3.174	3.175	3.174	3.175	3.174	3.175
16	3.175	3.174	3.175	3.174	3.175	3.174	3.175	3.174	3.175	3.174	3.175	3.174
17	3.174	3.175	3.174	3.175	3.174	3.175	3.174	3.175	3.174	3.175	3.174	3.175
18	3.175	3.174	3.175	3.174	3.175	3.174	3.175	3.174	3.175	3.174	3.175	3.174
19	3.174	3.175	3.174	3.175	3.174	3.175	3.174	3.175	3.174	3.175	3.174	3.175
20	3.175	3.174	3.175	3.174	3.175	3.174	3.175	3.174	3.175	3.174	3.175	3.174
21	3.174	3.175	3.174	3.175	3.174	3.175	3.174	3.175	3.174	3.175	3.174	3.175
22	3.175	3.174	3.175	3.174	3.175	3.174	3.175	3.174	3.175	3.174	3.175	3.174
23	3.174	3.175	3.174	3.175	3.174	3.175	3.174	3.175	3.174	3.175	3.174	3.175
24	3.175	3.174	3.175	3.174	3.175	3.174	3.175	3.174	3.175	3.174	3.175	3.174
25	3.174	3.175	3.174	3.175	3.174	3.175	3.174	3.175	3.174	3.175	3.174	3.175
26	3.175	3.174	3.175	3.174	3.175	3.174	3.175	3.174	3.175	3.174	3.175	3.174
27	3.174	3.175	3.174	3.175	3.174	3.175	3.174	3.175	3.174	3.175	3.174	3.175
28	3.175	3.174	3.175	3.174	3.175	3.174	3.175	3.174	3.175	3.174	3.175	3.174
29	3.174	3.175	3.174	3.175	3.174	3.175	3.174	3.175	3.174	3.175	3.174	3.175
30	3.175	3.174	3.175	3.174	3.175	3.174	3.175	3.174	3.175	3.174	3.175	3.174
31	3.174	3.175	3.174	3.175	3.174	3.175	3.174	3.175	3.174	3.175	3.174	3.175
32	1.720	1.984	2.249	2.513	2.778	3.042	3.175	3.174	3.175	3.174	3.175	3.174
33	0.000	0.000	0.000	0.000	0.000	0.000	0.132	0.397	0.661	0.926	1.190	1.455

▼ TABLE 9

General Depreciation System—MACRS
Nonresidential Real Property Placed in Service after 5/12/93
Applicable Recovery Period: 39 years
Applicable Depreciation Method: Straight Line

If the Recovery Year Is:	And the Month in the First Recovery Year the Property Is Placed in Service Is:											
	1	2	3	4	5	6	7	8	9	10	11	12
	The Depreciation Rate Is:											
1	2.461	2.247	2.033	1.819	1.605	1.391	1.177	0.963	0.749	0.535	0.321	0.107
2-39	2.564	2.564	2.564	2.564	2.564	2.564	2.564	2.564	2.564	2.564	2.564	2.564
40	0.107	0.321	0.535	0.749	0.963	1.177	1.391	1.605	1.819	2.033	2.247	2.461

▼ TABLE 10

Alternative Depreciation System—MACRS (Partial Table)
Property Placed in Service after 12/31/86
Applicable Convention: Half-year
Applicable Depreciation Method: 150 Percent Declining Balance
Switching to Straight Line

If the Recovery Year Is:	And the Recovery Period Is:					
	3	4	5	7	10	12
	The Depreciation Rate Is:					
1	25.00	18.75	15.00	10.71	7.50	6.25
2	37.50	30.47	25.50	19.13	13.88	11.72
3	25.00	20.31	17.85	15.03	11.79	10.25
4	12.50	20.31	16.66	12.25	10.02	8.97
5		10.16	16.66	12.25	8.74	7.85
6			8.33	12.25	8.74	7.33
7				12.25	8.74	7.33
8				6.13	8.74	7.33
9					8.74	7.33
10					8.74	7.33
11					4.37	7.32
12						7.33
13						3.66

▼ TABLE 11

Alternative Depreciation System—MACRS (Partial Table)
Property Placed in Service after 12/31/86
Applicable Convention: Half-year
Applicable Depreciation Method: Straight Line

If the Recovery Year Is:	And the Recovery Period Is:					
	3	4	5	7	10	12
	The Depreciation Rate Is:					
1	16.67	12.50	10.00	7.14	5.00	4.17
2	33.33	25.00	20.00	14.29	10.00	8.33
3	33.33	25.00	20.00	14.29	10.00	8.33
4	16.67	25.00	20.00	14.28	10.00	8.33
5		12.50	20.00	14.29	10.00	8.33
6			10.00	14.28	10.00	8.33
7				14.29	10.00	8.34
8				7.14	10.00	8.33
9					10.00	8.34
10					10.00	8.33
11					5.00	8.34
12						8.33
13						4.17

▼ TABLE 12

Alternative Depreciation System—MACRS
Real Property Placed into Service after 12/31/86
Applicable Recovery Period: 40 years
Applicable Convention: Mid-month
Applicable Depreciation Method: Straight Line

If the Recovery Year Is:	And the Month in the First Recovery Year the Property Is Placed in Service Is:											
	1	2	3	4	5	6	7	8	9	10	11	12
	The Depreciation Rate Is:											
1	2.396	2.188	1.979	1.771	1.563	1.354	1.146	0.938	0.729	0.521	0.313	0.104
2 to 40	2.500	2.500	2.500	2.500	2.500	2.500	2.500	2.500	2.500	2.500	2.500	2.500
41	0.104	0.312	0.521	0.729	0.937	1.146	1.354	1.562	1.771	1.979	2.187	2.396

▼ TABLE 13

Lease Inclusion Dollar Amounts for Automobiles (Other Than for Trucks, Vans, or Electronic Automobiles) With a Lease Term Beginning in Calendar Year 2010[a]

Fair Market Value of Passenger Automobile		Tax Year During Lease				
Over	Not Over	1st	2nd	3rd	4th	5th and Later
$18,500	$19,000	7	15	22	26	31
19,000	19,500	8	17	25	30	35
19,500	20,000	9	19	29	34	39
20,000	20,500	10	21	32	38	44
20,500	21,000	11	23	35	42	48
21,000	21,500	12	26	38	45	53
21,500	22,000	13	28	41	50	57
22,000	23,000	14	31	46	56	63
23,000	24,000	16	36	52	63	73
24,000	25,000	18	40	59	71	81
25,000	26,000	20	44	66	78	90
26,000	27,000	22	49	71	86	100
27,000	28,000	24	53	78	94	108
28,000	29,000	26	57	85	101	118
29,000	30,000	28	61	92	109	126
30,000	31,000	30	66	97	117	135
31,000	32,000	32	70	104	125	144
32,000	33,000	34	74	111	132	153
33,000	34,000	36	79	117	140	161
34,000	35,000	38	83	123	148	171
35,000	36,000	40	87	130	156	179
36,000	37,000	42	92	136	163	188
37,000	38,000	44	96	143	170	198
38,000	39,000	46	100	149	179	206
39,000	40,000	48	105	155	186	215
40,000	41,000	50	109	162	194	224
41,000	42,000	52	113	169	201	233
42,000	43,000	54	118	174	210	241
43,000	44,000	56	122	181	217	251
44,000	45,000	58	126	188	225	259
45,000	46,000	60	131	194	232	269
46,000	47,000	61	135	201	240	277
47,000	48,000	63	140	207	248	286
48,000	49,000	65	144	213	256	295
49,000	50,000	67	148	220	263	304
50,000	51,000	69	153	226	271	313
51,000	52,000	71	157	232	279	322
52,000	53,000	73	161	239	287	331
53,000	54,000	75	166	245	294	340
54,000	55,000	77	170	252	302	348
55,000	56,000	79	174	258	310	358
56,000	57,000	81	178	265	318	366
57,000	58,000	83	183	271	325	375
58,000	59,000	85	187	278	333	384

[a]*Per Rev. Proc.* 2010-18. The table for 2011 had not been released at the date of the printing.

▼ TABLE 13ᵃ (continued)

Fair Market Value of Passenger Automobile		Tax Year During Lease				
Over	Not Over	1st	2nd	3rd	4th	5th and Later
$ 59,000	$ 60,000	87	191	284	341	393
60,000	62,000	90	198	294	352	406
62,000	64,000	94	207	306	368	424
64,000	66,000	98	215	320	382	443
66,000	68,000	102	224	332	398	460
68,000	70,000	106	232	346	413	478
70,000	72,000	110	241	358	429	496
72,000	74,000	114	250	371	444	513
74,000	76,000	118	258	384	460	531
76,000	78,000	122	267	396	476	549
78,000	80,000	126	276	409	491	566
80,000	85,000	132	291	432	518	598
85,000	90,000	142	313	464	556	643
90,000	95,000	152	334	497	594	687
95,000	100,000	162	356	528	634	731
100,000	110,000	177	388	577	691	798
110,000	120,000	196	432	641	768	887
120,000	130,000	216	475	705	846	976
130,000	140,000	236	518	770	922	1,065
140,000	150,000	256	561	834	1,000	1,154
150,000	160,000	275	605	898	1,077	1,243
160,000	170,000	295	648	963	1,153	1,333
170,000	180,000	315	691	1,027	1,231	1,421
180,000	190,000	334	735	1,091	1,308	1,510
190,000	200,000	354	778	1,155	1,386	1,599
200,000	210,000	374	821	1,220	1,462	1,688
210,000	220,000	393	865	1,284	1,539	1,777
220,000	230,000	413	908	1,348	1,617	1,866
230,000	240,000	433	951	1,413	1,693	1,956
240,000	and up	453	995	1,476	1,771	2,044

ᵃ*Per Rev. Proc.* 2010-18. The table for 2011 had not been released at the date of the printing.

▼ TABLE 14

Lease Inclusion Dollar Amounts for Trucks and Vans
With a Lease Term Beginning in Calendar Year 2010[a]

REV. PROC. 2010-18 TABLE 4 DOLLAR AMOUNTS FOR TRUCKS AND VANS
WITH A LEASE TERM BEGINNING IN CALENDAR YEAR 2010

Fair Market Value of Truck or Van		Tax Year During Lease				
Over	Not Over	1st	2nd	3rd	4th	5th Later
$18,500	$19,000	6	12	19	22	24
19,000	19,500	7	15	21	26	29
19,500	20,000	8	17	25	29	34
20,000	20,500	9	19	28	33	38
20,500	21,000	10	21	31	37	43
21,000	21,500	11	23	35	41	47
21,500	22,000	12	25	38	45	51
22,000	23,000	13	29	42	51	58
23,000	24,000	15	33	49	58	67
24,000	25,000	17	37	56	66	76
25,000	26,000	19	42	62	73	85
26,000	27,000	21	46	68	82	93
27,000	28,000	23	50	75	89	103
28,000	29,000	25	55	81	97	111
29,000	30,000	27	59	88	104	121
30,000	31,000	29	63	94	113	129
31,000	32,000	31	68	100	120	138
32,000	33,000	33	72	107	127	148
33,000	34,000	35	76	114	135	156
34,000	35,000	37	81	119	143	165
35,000	36,000	39	85	126	151	174
36,000	37,000	41	89	133	158	183
37,000	38,000	43	94	139	166	191
38,000	39,000	45	98	145	174	201
39,000	40,000	47	102	152	182	209
40,000	41,000	49	106	159	189	218
41,000	42,000	51	111	164	198	227
42,000	43,000	53	115	171	205	236
43,000	44,000	55	119	178	213	245
44,000	45,000	57	124	184	220	254
45,000	46,000	59	128	190	228	263
46,000	47,000	60	133	197	235	272
47,000	48,000	62	137	203	244	280
48,000	49,000	64	142	209	251	290
49,000	50,000	66	146	216	259	298
50,000	51,000	68	150	223	266	308
51,000	52,000	70	154	229	275	316
52,000	53,000	72	159	235	282	325
53,000	54,000	74	163	242	290	334
54,000	55,000	76	167	249	297	343
55,000	56,000	78	172	254	305	352
56,000	57,000	80	176	261	313	361
57,000	58,000	82	180	268	320	370
58,000	59,000	84	185	274	328	378
59,000	60,000	86	189	280	336	388
60,000	62,000	89	195	291	347	401
62,000	64,000	93	204	303	363	418

[a]Per *Rev. Proc.* 2010-18. The table for 2011 had not been released at the date of the printing.

▼ TABLE 14ª (continued)

REV. PROC. 2010-18 TABLE 4 DOLLAR AMOUNTS FOR TRUCKS AND VANS WITH A LEASE TERM BEGINNING IN CALENDAR YEAR 2010

Fair Market Value of Automobiles		Tax Year During Lease				
Over	Not Over	1st	2nd	3rd	4th	5th and Later
$ 64,000	$ 66,000	97	213	315	379	436
66,000	68,000	101	221	329	394	454
68,000	70,000	105	230	341	410	472
70,000	72,000	109	239	354	424	490
72,000	74,000	113	247	367	440	508
74,000	76,000	117	256	380	455	526
76,000	78,000	121	264	393	471	543
78,000	80,000	125	273	406	486	561
80,000	85,000	131	289	428	513	592
85,000	90,000	141	310	461	552	636
90,000	95,000	151	332	492	591	681
95,000	100,000	161	353	525	629	726
100,000	110,000	176	386	573	686	793
110,000	120,000	195	430	637	763	882
120,000	130,000	215	473	701	841	971
130,000	140,000	235	516	766	918	1,059
140,000	150,000	255	559	830	995	1,149
150,000	160,000	274	603	894	1,072	1,238
160,000	170,000	294	646	958	1,150	1,326
170,000	180,000	314	689	1,023	1,226	1,416
180,000	190,000	333	733	1,087	1,303	1,505
190,000	200,000	353	776	1,151	1,381	1,594
200,000	210,000	373	819	1,216	1,457	1,683
210,000	220,000	392	863	1,280	1,534	1,772
220,000	230,000	412	906	1,344	1,612	1,861
230,000	240,000	432	949	1,409	1,689	1,949
240,000	250,000	452	992	1,473	1,766	2,039

[a]Per *Rev. Proc.* 2010-18. The table for 2011 had not been released at the date of the printing.

GLOSSARY

Accounting method The rules used to determine the tax year in which income and expenses are reported for tax purposes. Generally, the same accounting method must be used for tax purposes as is used for keeping books and records. The accounting treatment used for any item of income or expense and for specific items (e.g., installment sales and contracts) is included in this term.

Accounting period See Tax year.

Accumulated adjustments account (AAA) Account that must be kept by S corporations. The cumulative total of the ordinary income or loss and separately stated items for the most recent S corporation election period.

Accumulated earnings and profits The sum of the undistributed current earnings and profits balances (and deficits) from previous years reduced by any distributions that have been made out of accumulated earnings and profits.

Accumulated earnings credit Deduction that reduces the accumulated taxable income amount. It does not offset the accumulated earnings tax on a dollar-for-dollar basis. Different rules apply for operating companies, service companies, and holding or investment companies.

Accumulated earnings tax Penalty tax on corporations other than those subject to the personal holding company tax among others. It is levied on a corporation's current year addition to its accumulated earnings balance exceeding the amount needed for reasonable business purposes and not distributed to the shareholders. This tax is intended to discourage companies from retaining excessive amounts of earnings if the funds are invested in activities unrelated to business needs. The tax is 15% (in 2011) of accumulated taxable income.

Accumulated taxable income The tax base for the accumulated earnings tax, which is determined by taking the corporation's taxable income and increasing (decreasing) it by positive (negative) adjustments and decreasing it by the accumulated earnings credit and available dividends-paid deductions.

Accumulation distribution rules (throwback rules) Exception to the general rule that distributable net income (DNI) serves as a ceiling on the amount taxable to a beneficiary. Under the general rule, the beneficiary excludes the portion of any distribution exceeding DNI from his gross income. Accumulation distributions made by a trust are taxable to the beneficiaries in the year received.

ACE See Adjusted current earnings.

Acquiescence policy IRS policy of announcing whether it agrees or disagrees with a court decision decided in favor of the taxpayer. Such statements are not issued for every case.

Acquisitive reorganization A transaction in which the acquiring corporation obtains all or part of the stock or assets of a target corporation.

Adjusted current earnings (ACE) Alternative minimum taxable income for the tax year plus or minus a series of special adjusted current earnings adjustments specified in Sec. 56(g)(4) (special depreciation calculation, special E&P rules, etc.).

Adjusted current earnings adjustment 75% of the excess (if any) of the adjusted current earnings of the corporation over the preadjustment AMTI. A downward adjustment is provided for 75% of the excess (if any) of preadjustment AMTI over the adjusted current earnings of the corporation.

Adjusted grossed-up basis For Sec. 338 purposes, the sum of (1) the basis of a purchasing corporation's stock interest in a target corporation plus (2) an adjustment for the target corporation's liabilities on the day following the acquisition date plus or minus (3) other relevant items.

Adjusted income from rents (AIR) This amount equals the corporation's gross income from rents reduced by the deductions claimed for amortization or depreciation, property taxes, interest, and rent.

Adjusted ordinary gross income (AOGI) A corporation's adjusted ordinary gross income is its ordinary gross income reduced by (1) certain expenses incurred in connection with gross income from rents, mineral, oil and gas royalties, and working interests in oil or gas wells, (2) interest received by dealers on certain U.S. obligations, (3) interest received from condemnation awards, judgments, or tax refunds, and (4) rents from certain tangible personal property manufactured or produced by the corporation.

Adjusted taxable gift Taxable gifts made after 1976 that are valued at their date-of-gift value. These gifts affect the size of the transfer tax base at death.

Administrative pronouncement Treasury Department or IRS statement that interprets provisions of the IRC. Such pronouncements may be in the form of Treasury regulations, revenue rulings, or revenue procedures.

Advance ruling See Letter ruling.

Affiliated group A group consisting of a parent corporation and at least one subsidiary corporation.

Aggregate Deemed Sale Price (ADSP) Price at which old target is deemed to have sold all of its assets pursuant to a Sec. 338 deemed sale election.

AIR See Adjusted income from rents.

Alien An individual who is not a U.S. citizen.

Alternate valuation date The alternate valuation date is the earlier of six months after the date of death or the date the property is sold, exchanged, distributed, etc. by the estate. Unless this option is elected, the gross estate is valued at its FMV on the date of the decedent's death.

Alternative minimum tax (AMT) Tax that applies to individuals, corporations, and estates and trusts if it exceeds the taxpayer's regular tax. Most taxpayers are not subject to this tax, including corporations meeting the small corporation exception. This tax equals the amount by which the tentative minimum tax exceeds the regular tax.

Alternative minimum taxable income (AMTI) The taxpayer's taxable income (1) increased by tax preference items and (2) adjusted for income, gain, deduction, and loss items that have to be recomputed under the AMT system.

AMT See Alternative minimum tax.

AMTI See Alternative minimum taxable income.

Annotated tax service A multivolume tax commentary organized by IRC section number. The IRC-arranged subdivisions contain the IRC provision, related Treasury Regulations, publisher-provided commentary and explanations, and annotations that summarize related cases and IRS pronouncements. The service has a topical index to assist research.

Announcement Information release issued by the IRS to provide a technical explanation of a current tax issue. Announcements are aimed at tax practitioners rather than the general public.

Annual exclusion An exemption intended to relieve a donor from keeping an account of and reporting the numerous small gifts (e.g., wedding and Christmas gifts) made throughout the year. This exclusion currently is $13,000 per donee (in 2011).

AOGI See Adjusted ordinary gross income.

Appeals coordinated issue Issue over which the appeals officer must obtain a concurrence of guidance from the regional director of appeals to render a decision.

Applicable exclusion amount Portion of the estate and gift tax base that is completely free of transfer taxes because of the unified credit (previously called the exemption equivalent).

Assignment of income doctrine A judicial requirement that income be taxed to the person that earns it.

At-risk basis Essentially the same amount as the regular partnership basis with the exception that liabilities increase the at-risk basis only if the partner is at-risk for such an amount.

At-risk rules These rules limit the partner's loss deductions to his or her at-risk basis.

Bardahl formula Mathematical formula for determining the amount of working capital that a business reasonably needs for accumulated earnings tax purposes. For a manufacturing company, the formula is based on the business's operating cycle.

Boot Property that may not be received tax-free in certain nontaxable transactions (i.e., any money, debt obligations, and so on).

Bootstrap acquisition An acquisition where an investor purchases part of a corporation's stock and then has the corporation redeem the remainder of the seller's stock.

Branch profits tax Special tax levied by the U.S. government on the branch activities of a foreign corporation doing business in the United States.

Brother-sister controlled group Under the narrow 50%-80% definition, this type of controlled group exists if (1) five or fewer individuals, estates, or trusts own at least 80% of the voting stock or 80% of the value of each corporation and (2) the shareholders have common ownership of more than 50% of the voting power or 50% of the value of all classes of stock. Under the broad 50%-only definition, the five or fewer shareholders need only meet the 50% test.

Built-in deduction A deduction that accrues in a separate return limitation year but which is recognized for tax purposes in a consolidated return year.

Built-in gain A gain that accrued prior to the conversion of a C corporation to an S corporation.

Built-in gains (Sec. 1374) tax Tax on built-in gains recognized by the S corporation during the ten-year period beginning on the date the S corporation election took effect.

Built-in loss A loss that accrued prior to the conversion of a C corporation to an S corporation.

Business purpose A judicial doctrine established by the U.S. Supreme Court that a transaction cannot be solely motivated by a tax avoidance purpose. Transactions that serve no business purpose usually are ignored by the IRS and the courts.

Capital gain property For charitable contribution deduction purposes, property upon which a long-term capital gain would be recognized if that property were sold at its FMV.

Capital interest An interest in the assets owned by a partnership.

C corporation Form of business entity taxed as a separate taxpaying entity. Its income is subject to an initial tax at the corporate level. Its shareholders are subject to a second tax if the corporation pays dividends from its earnings and profits. This type of corporation is sometimes referred to as a regular corporation.

Certiorari An appeal from a lower court (i.e., a federal court of appeals) that the U.S. Supreme Court agrees to hear. Such appeals, which are made as a writ of certiorari, generally are not granted unless (1) a constitutional issue needs to be decided or (2) a conflict among the lower court decisions must be clarified.

CFC See Controlled foreign corporation.

Charitable contribution deduction Contributions of money or property made to qualified organizations (i.e., public charities and private nonoperating foundations). For income tax purposes, the amount of the deduction depends on (1) the type of charity receiving the contribution, (2) the type of property contributed, and (3) other limitations mandated by the tax law. Charitable contributions also are deductible under the unified transfer tax (i.e., gift tax and estate tax rules).

Charitable remainder annuity trust This type of trust makes distributions to individuals for a certain time period or for life. The annual distributions are a uniform percentage (5% or higher) of the value of the trust property as valued on the date of transfer.

Charitable remainder unitrust This type of trust makes annual distributions for either a specified time period or for life. The distributions are a uniform percentage (5% or higher) of the value of the property as revalued annually.

Check-the-box regulations Treasury Regulations that permit certain entities (e.g., partnerships and limited liability companies) to select an income tax status different from their basic classification.

Circular 230 Rules and standards issued by the Treasury Department regarding practice before the IRS.

Clifford trust A trust that normally is held for a ten-year period after which the principal reverts to the grantor. The trust accounting income generally is not taxed to the grantor.

Closed-fact or tax compliance situation Situation or transaction in which the facts have already occurred. In such situations, the tax advisor's task is to analyze the facts to determine the appropriate tax treatment.

Closed transaction Situation where the property in question (e.g., property distributed in a corporate liquidation) can be valued with reasonable certainty. The gain or loss reported on the transaction is determinable at the time the transaction occurs. See Open transaction doctrine.

Closely held corporation A corporation owned by either a single individual or a small group of individuals who may or may not be family members.

Closely held C corporation For purposes of the at-risk rules, a C corporation in which more than 50% of the stock is owned by five or fewer individuals at any time during the last half of the corporation's tax year.

Combined controlled group A group of three or more corporations that are members of a parent-subsidiary or brother-sister controlled group. In addition, at least one of the corporations must be the parent corporation of the parent-subsidiary controlled group and a member of a brother-sister controlled group.

Combined taxable income The total amount of the separate taxable incomes of the individual group members of an affiliated group that is filing a consolidated tax return.

Common law state All states other than the community property states are common law states. In such states, all assets acquired during the marriage are the property of the acquiring spouse.

Community property law Law in community property states mandating that all property acquired after marriage generally is community property unless acquired by gift or inheritance. Each spouse owns a one-half interest in community property.

Community property state The eight traditional community property states (Louisiana, Texas, New Mexico, Arizona, California, Washington, Idaho, and Nevada) and Wisconsin (which adopted a similar law). These states do not follow the common law concept of property ownership.

Complex trust Trust that is not required to distribute all of its income currently.

Congressional intent What Congress *intended* by a particular statutory term, phrase, or provision as gleaned from House and Senate committee reports, records of committee hearings, and transcripts of floor debates.

Consent dividend Hypothetical dividend generally deemed paid to a personal holding company's shareholders on the last day of the corporation's tax year. Also may be paid to avoid the personal holding company tax or accumulated earnings tax.

Consolidated return year A tax year for which a consolidated return is filed or is required to be filed by an affiliated group.

Consolidated taxable income The taxable income reported on a consolidated return filed by a group of affiliated corporations. The calculation of this amount is determined by establishing each member's separate taxable income and then following a series of steps that result in a consolidated amount.

Consolidated tax return A single tax return filed by an affiliated group of includible corporations.

Consolidation A nontaxable reorganization involving two or more corporations whose assets are acquired by a new corporation. The stock, securities, and other consideration transferred by the acquiring corporation is then distributed by each target corporation to its shareholders and security holders in exchange for their stock and securities.

Constructive dividend The manner in which the IRS or the courts might recharacterize an excessive corporate payment to a shareholder to reflect the true economic benefit conferred upon the shareholder. As a result of the recharcterization, the IRS or the courts usually recast a corporate-shareholder transaction as an E&P distribution, deny the corporation an offsetting deduction, and treat all or a portion of the income recognized by the shareholder as a dividend.

Continuity of interest doctrine The judicial requirement that shareholders who transfer property to a transferee corporation continue their ownership in the property through holding the transferee corporation's stock to defer recognition of their gains.

Controlled foreign corporation (CFC) Foreign corporation that is directly or indirectly controlled by U.S. shareholders at any time during the taxable year, provided that such U.S. shareholders control more than 50% of its voting power or more than 50% of the value of the outstanding stock.

Controlled group Two or more separately incorporated businesses owned by a related group of individuals or entities. Such groups include parent-subsidiary groups, brother-sister groups, or combined groups.

Corporation A separate taxpaying entity (such as an association, joint stock company, or insurance company) that must file a tax return every year, even when it had no income or loss for the year.

Corresponding item The buyer's income, gain, deduction, or loss from an intercompany transaction, or from property acquired in an intercompany transaction.

Crummey trust Technique that allows a donor to set up a discretionary trust and obtain an annual exclusion. Such a trust arrangement allows the beneficiary to demand an annual distribution of the lesser of the annual exclusion ($13,000 in 2011) or the amount transferred to the trust that year.

C short year That portion of an S termination year that begins on the day on which the termination is effective and continues through to the last day of the corporation's tax year.

Current distribution See Nonliquidating distribution.

Current earnings and profits Earnings and profits calculated annually by (1) adjusting the corporation's taxable income (or net operating loss) for items that must be recomputed, (2) adding back any excluded income items, income deferrals, and deductions not allowed in computing earnings and profits, and (3) subtracting any expenses and losses not deductible in computing the corporation's taxable income.

Curtesy A widower's interest in his deceased wife's property.

Deductions in respect of a decedent (DRD) Deduction accrued prior to death but not includible on decedent's final tax return because of the decedent's method of accounting.

Deemed paid credit An indirect foreign tax credit available to a domestic corporation owning at least 10% of the voting stock of a foreign corporation when the foreign corporation pays or accrues creditable foreign taxes.

Deemed sale election Election under Sec. 338 permitting an acquiring corporation that acquires a controlling interest in a target corporation's stock to step-up or step-down the basis of the target corporation's assets to their adjusted grossed-up basis via a deemed sale and purchase of its assets.

Deferral privilege A tax exemption provided U.S. taxpayers who own stock of a foreign corporation. The foreign corporation's earnings generally are not taxed in the United States until repatriated unless an exception such as the Subpart F rules applies.

Deferred tax asset A book balance sheet item that results from temporary differences that produce tax deductions in the future when the differences reverse. The amount is the applicable tax rate times the temporary difference.

Deferred tax liability A book balance sheet item that results from temporary differences that produce taxable income in the future when the differences reverse. The amount is the applicable tax rate times the temporary difference.

Deficiency dividend This type of dividend substitutes an income tax levy on the dividend payment at the shareholder level for the payment of the personal holding company tax.

DIF See Discriminant Function Program.

Discriminant Function Program (DIF) Program used by the IRS to select individual returns for audit. This system is intended to identify those tax returns that are most likely to contain errors.

Dissolution A legal term implying that a corporation has surrendered the charter it originally received from the state.

Distributable net income (DNI) Maximum amount of distributions taxed to the beneficiaries and deducted by a trust or estate.

Distributive share The portion of partnership taxable and nontaxable income, losses, credits, and so on that the partner must report for tax purposes.

Dividend A distribution of property made by a corporation out of its earnings and profits.

Dividends-paid deduction Distributions made out of a corporation's earnings and profits are eligible for this deduction for personal holding company tax and accumulated earnings tax purposes. The deduction is equal to the amount of money plus the adjusted basis of the noncash property distributed.

Dividends-received deduction This deduction attempts to mitigate the triple taxation that would occur if one corporation paid dividends to a corporate shareholder who, in turn, distributed such amounts to its individual shareholders. Certain restrictions and limitations apply to this deduction.

Divisive reorganization Transaction in which part of a transferor corporation's assets are transferred to a second, newly created corporation controlled by either the transferee or its shareholders.

DNI See Distributable net income.

Domestic corporation Corporation incorporated in one of the 50 states or under federal law.

Dower A widow's interest in her deceased husband's property.

DRD See Deductions in respect of a decedent.

E&P See Earnings and profits.

E&P adjusted basis Adjusted basis obtained by using special calculations required under the E&P rules (e.g., calculation using straight-line depreciation under the alternative depreciation system).

E&P gain The difference between an asset's FMV an its E&P adjusted basis, which may differ from an asset's tax gain.

Earnings and profits (E&P) A measure of the corporation's ability to pay a dividend from its current and accumulated earnings without an impairment of capital.

Effective tax rate Total book income tax expense divided by pretax book income. In footnotes to the financial statements, firms reconcile the effective tax rate to the statutory tax rate.

Electing large partnership A partnership having at least 100 partners for the preceding tax year (excluding service partners). Electing large partnerships have a simplified reporting procedure that reduces the number of income, gain, loss, deductions, and credit items passing through to the partners.

Estate A legal entity that comes into being only upon the death of the person whose assets are being administered. The estate continues in existence until the duties of the executor have been completed.

Excess loss account A negative investment account of a member of an affiliated group that files a consolidated tax return which attaches to an investment in a lower-tier subsidiary corporation.

Excess net passive income An amount equal to the S corporation's net passive income multiplied by the fraction consisting of its passive investment income less 25% of its gross receipts divided by its passive investment income. It is limited to the corporation's taxable income.

Excess net passive income (Sec. 1375) tax Tax levied when (1) an S corporation has passive investment income for the taxable year that exceeds 25% of its gross receipts and (2) at the close of the tax year the S corporation has earnings and profits from C corporation tax years.

Exemption equivalent That portion of the tax base that is completely free of transfer taxes because of the unified credit. (Now called the applicable exclusion amount.)

Failure-to-file penalty Penalty imposed for the failure to file a timely return. The penalty is assessed at 5% per month (or fraction thereof) on the amount of the net tax due. The maximum penalty for failing to file is 25%. The minimum penalty is the lesser of $135 or 100% of the tax due.

Failure-to-pay penalty Penalty imposed at 0.5% per month (or fraction thereof) on the amount of tax shown on the return less any tax payments made before the beginning of the month for which the penalty is being calculated. The maximum penalty is 25%.

Fair market value (FMV) The amount that would be realized from the sale of a property at a price that is agreeable to both the buyer and the seller when neither party is obligated to participate in the transaction.

Fiduciary A person or other entity (e.g., a guardian, executor, trustee, or administrator) who holds and manages property for someone else.

Fiduciary taxation The special tax rules that apply to fiduciaries (e.g., trusts and estates).

FMV See Fair market value.

Foreign branch An office or other establishment of a domestic entity that operates in a foreign country.

Foreign corporation A corporation that is incorporated under the laws of a country other than the United States.

Foreign tax credit Tax credit given to mitigate the possibility of double taxation faced by U.S. citizens, residents, and corporations earning foreign income.

Forum shopping The ability to consider differing precedents in choosing the forum for litigation.

Future interest Such interests include reversions, remainders, and other interests that may not be used, owned, or enjoyed until some future date.

General partner Partner or partners with (1) the authority to make management decisions and commitments for the partnership and (2) unlimited liability for all partnership debts.

General partnership A partnership with two or more partners where no partner is a limited partner.

General power of appointment Power of appointment under which the holder can appoint the property to himself, his estate, his creditors, or the creditors of his estate. Such power may be exercisable during the decedent's life, by his will, or both.

Generation-skipping transfer A disposition that (1) provides interests for more than one generation of beneficiaries who are in a younger generation than the transferor or (2) provides an interest solely for a person two or more generations younger than the transferor.

Gift tax A wealth transfer tax that applies if the property transfer occurs during a person's lifetime.

Grantor The transferor who creates a trust.

Grantor trust Trust governed by Secs. 671 through 679. The income from such trusts is taxed to the grantor even if some or all of the income has been distributed.

Gross estate The gross estate includes items to which the decedent held title at death as well as certain incomplete transfers made by the decedent prior to death.

Guaranteed minimum Minimum amount of payment guaranteed to a partner. This amount is important if the partner's distributive share is less than his guaranteed minimum. See also Guaranteed payment.

Guaranteed payment Minimum amount of payment guaranteed to a partner in the form of a salary-like payment made for services provided to the partnership and interest-like payments for the use of invested capital. Guaranteed payments, which may be in the form of a guaranteed minimum amount or a set amount, are taxed as ordinary income. See also Guaranteed minimum.

Headnote An editorial summary of a particular point of case law that appears immediately before the text of a judicial opinion.

Hedge agreement An obligation on the part of a shareholder-employee to repay to the corporation any portion of salary disallowed by the IRS as a deduction. It also is used in connection with other corporate payments to shareholder-employees (e.g., travel and entertainment expenses).

Housing cost amount A special deduction or exclusion equal to the housing expenses incurred by a taxpayer eligible for the Sec. 911 earned income exclusion minus the base housing amount.

Income beneficiary Entity or individual that receives the income from a trust.

Income in respect of a decedent (IRD) Amount to which the decedent was entitled as gross income but which was not properly includible in computing his or her taxable income for the tax year ending with his or her date of death or for a previous tax year under the method of accounting employed by the decedent.

Income tax expense A subtraction item in the book income statement that represents a firm's current and deferred tax expense for the year. It is the total tax expense and sometimes is called the total tax provision.

Information release An administrative pronouncement concerning an issue that the IRS thinks the general public will be interested in. Such releases are issued in lay terms and widely published.

Innocent spouse relief This provision exempts a spouse from penalty and liability for tax if such spouse meets certain requirements.

Intercompany item The seller's income, gain, deduction, or loss from an intercompany transaction.

Intercompany transaction Transaction that takes place during a consolidated return year between corporations that are members of the same group immediately after the transaction.

Interpretative regulations Treasury Regulations that serve to interpret the provisions of the Internal Revenue Code. Interpretative regulations are less authoritative than legislative regulations.

Inter vivos trust Transfer to a trust that is made during the grantor's lifetime.

Inversion A transaction in which a U.S. corporation reorganizes as a foreign entity for the purpose of removing foreign-source income not associated with a U.S. business from U.S. taxing jurisdiction.

IRD See Income in respect of a decedent.

Irrevocable trust Trust under which the grantor cannot require the trustee to return the trust's assets.

Joint and several liability The potential liability for the full amount of tax due. If one joint filer is unable to pay any or all of the tax, the other joint filer is liable for the deficiency. Also see Proportional liability.

Joint tenancy A popular form of property ownership that serves as a substitute for a will. Each joint tenant is deemed to have an equal interest in the property.

Judicial decisions Decision rendered by a court deciding the case that is presented to it by a plaintiff and defendant. These decisions are important sources of the tax law and can come from trial courts and appellate courts.

Legislative reenactment doctrine Rule holding that Congress's failure to change the wording in the IRC over an extended period signifies that Congress has approved the treatment provided in Treasury Regulations.

Legislative regulations Treasury Regulations that are treated as law because Congress has delegated its rulemaking authority to the Treasury Department. Such regulations may be overturned by the courts on the grounds that they exceed the scope of the delegated authority or are unreasonable.

Letter ruling A letter ruling originates from the IRS at the taxpayer's request. It describes how the IRS will treat a proposed transaction. It is binding only on the person requesting the ruling provided the transaction is completed as proposed in the ruling. Letter rulings that are of general interest are published as revenue rulings.

Life estate A property transfer in trust that results in the transferor reserving the right to income for life. Another individual is named to receive the property upon the transferor's death.

LIFO recapture tax A tax imposed on a C corporation that uses the LIFO inventory method and which elects S corporation treatment. The tax is imposed in the final C corporation tax year and is paid over a four-year period.

Limited liability company (LLC) A business entity that combines the legal and tax benefits of partnerships and S corporations. These entities are taxed as partnerships for federal tax purposes unless they elect to be taxed as corporations under the check-the-box regulations.

Limited liability partnership (LLP) Similar to a limited liability company, but formed under a separate state statute that generally applies to service companies.

Limited partner Partner who has no right to be active in the management of the partnership and whose liability is limited to his original investment plus any additional amounts he or she is obligated to contribute.

Limited partnership A partnership where one or more of the partners is designated as a limited partner and at least one partner is a general partner.

Liquidating distribution A distribution that (1) liquidates a partner's entire partnership interest due to retirement, death, or other business reason or (2) partially or totally liquidates a shareholder's stock interest in a corporation following the adoption of a plan at liquidation.

Loss corporation A corporation entitled to use a net operating loss carryover or having a net operating loss for the taxable year in which an ownership change occurs.

Majority partners The one or more partners in a partnership who have an aggregate interest in partnership profits and capital exceeding 50%.

Mandatory basis adjustment Required basis adjustment if the partnership has a substantial built-in loss at the time a partner sells his or her partnership interest or if the partnership has a decreasing basis adjustment at the time of a liquidating distribution.

Marital deduction Deduction allowed for tax-free inter-spousal transfers other than those for gifts of certain terminable interests.

Memorandum (memo) decision Decision issued by the Tax Court dealing with a factual variation on a matter where the law already has been decided in an earlier case.

Merger A nontaxable reorganization one form of which has the acquiring corporation transfer its stock, securities, and other consideration to the target corporation in exchange for its assets and liabilities. The target corporation then distributes the consideration it receives to its shareholders and security holders in exchange for their stock and securities.

Minimum tax credit (MTC) A tax credit allowed for the amount of alternative minimum tax that arose because of deferral and permanent adjustments and preference items. This credit carries over to offset regular tax liabilities in subsequent years.

MTC See Minimum tax credit.

National Research Program (NRP) An IRS program designed to develop new statistical models for identifying returns most likely to contain errors. The models are based on pre-existing audit data as well as data compiled in ordinary audits.

Negligence The IRC defines negligence as (1) any failure to reasonably attempt to comply with the IRC and (2) "careless, reckless, or intentional disregard" of the rules and regulations.

Negligence penalty Penalty assessed if the IRS finds that the taxpayer has filed an incorrect return because of negligence. Generally, this penalty is 20% of the underpayment attributable to negligence.

Net accounting income The excess of accounting income over expenses for a fiduciary (i.e., an estate or trust). Excluded are any items credited to or charged against capital.

Net gift A gift upon which the donee pays the gift tax as a condition of receiving the gift.

Net operating loss (NOL) A net operating loss occurs when business expenses exceed business income for any taxable year. Such losses may be carried back two years (unless an extended carryback period applies) or carried forward 20 years to a year in which the taxpayer has taxable income. The loss is carried back first and must be deducted from years in chronological order unless the taxpayer makes a special election to forgo the carryback.

New loss corporation Any corporation permitted to use a net operating loss carryover after an ownership change occurs.

Ninety (90)-day letter Officially called a Statutory Notice of Deficiency, this letter is sent when (1) the taxpayer does not file a protest letter within 30 days of receipt of the 30-day letter or (2) the taxpayer has met with an appeals officer but no agreement was reached. The letter notifies the taxpayer of the amount of the deficiency, how that amount was determined, and that a deficiency will be assessed if a petition is not filed with the Tax Court within 90 days. The taxpayer also is advised of the alternatives available to him.

NOL See Net operating loss.

Nonliquidating (current) distribution Distribution that (1) reduces, but does not eliminate, a partner's partnership interest or (2) is made with respect to a shareholder's stock interest in a corporation at a time when no plan of liquidation has been adopted and may or may not reduce the shareholder's interest in the corporation.

Nonrecourse loan Loan for which the borrower has no personal liability. Usually, the lender can look only to the secured property for satisfaction.

Nonresident alien Individual whose residence is not the United States and who is not a U.S. citizen.

Notice An interpretation by the IRS that provides quidance concerning how to interpret a statute, perhaps one recently enacted.

OGI See Ordinary gross income.

Old loss corporation Any corporation allowed to use a net operating loss carryover, or that has a net operating loss for the tax year in which an ownership change occurs, and that undergoes the requisite stock ownership change.

Open-fact or tax-planning situation Situation or transaction in which the facts have not yet occurred. In such situations, the tax advisor's task is to plan for the facts or shape them so as to produce a favorable tax result.

Open transaction doctrine Valuation technique for property that can be valued only on the basis of uncertain future payments. This doctrine determines the shareholder's gain or loss when the asset is sold, collected, or able to be valued. Assets that cannot be valued are assigned a value of zero.

Optional basis adjustment An elective technique that adjusts the basis for the underlying partnership assets up or down as a result of (1) distributions from the partnership to its partners, (2) sales of partnership interests by existing partners, or (3) transfers of the interest following the death of a partner.

Ordinary gross income (OGI) A corporation's ordinary gross income is its gross income reduced by capital gains and Sec. 1231 gains.

Ordinary income property For charitable contribution deduction purposes, any property that would result in the recognition of ordinary income if it were sold. Such property includes inventory, works of art or manuscripts created by the taxpayer, capital assets that have been held for one year or less, and Sec. 1231 property that results in ordinary income due to depreciation recapture.

Other intercompany transactions An intercompany transaction that is not a deferred intercompany transaction. See Intercompany transaction.

Parent-subsidiary controlled group To qualify as such, a common parent must own at least 80% of the voting stock or at least 80% of the value of at least one subsidiary corporation and at least 80% of each other component member of the controlled group must be owned by other members of the controlled group.

Partial liquidation Occurs when a corporation discontinues one line of business, distributes the assets related to that business to its shareholders, and continues at least one other line of business.

Partner A member of a partnership. The member may be an individual, trust, estate, or corporation. Also see General partner and Limited partner.

Partnership Syndicate, group, pool, joint venture, or other unincorporated organization that carries on a business or financial operation or venture and that has at least two partners.

Partnership agreement Agreement that governs the relationship between the partners and the partnership.

Partnership item Virtually all items reported by the partnership for the tax year, including tax preference items, credit recapture items, guaranteed payments, and at-risk amounts.

Partnership ordinary income The positive sum of all partnership items of income, gain, loss, or deduction that do not have to be separately stated.

Partnership ordinary loss The negative sum of all partnership items of income, gain, loss, or deduction that do not have to be separately stated.

Partnership taxable income The sum of all taxable items among the separately stated items plus the partnership ordinary income or ordinary loss.

Party to a reorganization Such parties include corporations that result from a reorganization and the corporations involved in a reorganization where one corporation acquires the stock or assets of the other corporation.

Passive activity limitation Separate limitation on the amount of losses and credits that can be claimed with respect to a passive activity.

Passive foreign investment company (PFIC) A foreign corporation having passive income as 75% or more of its gross income for the tax year, or at least 50% of the average value of its assets during the tax year producing or held for producing passive income.

Passive income Income from an activity that does not require the taxpayer's material involvement or participation. Thus, income from tax shelters and rental activities generally fall into this category.

Passive loss Loss generated from a passive activity. Such losses are computed separately. They may be used to offset income from other passive activities but may not be used to offset either active income or portfolio income.

Permanent difference Items reported in taxable income but not book income or vice versa. Such differences include book income items that are nontaxable in the current year and will never be taxable and book expense items that are nondeductible in computing taxable income for the current year and will never be deductible.

Personal holding company (PHC) A closely held corporation (1) that is owned by five or fewer shareholders who own more than 50% of the corporation's outstanding stock at any time during the last half of its tax year and (2) whose PHC income equals at least 60% of the corporation's adjusted ordinary gross income for the tax year. Certain corporations (e.g., S corporations) are exempt from this definition.

Personal holding company income (PHCI) Categories of income including the following: dividends; interest; annuities; royalties (other than minerals, oil and gas, computer software, and copyright royalties); adjusted income from rents; adjusted income from mineral, oil and gas royalties, or working interests in oil and gas wells; computer software royalties; copyright royalties; produced film rents; income from personal service contracts involving a 25% or more shareholder; rental income from corporate property used by a 25% or more shareholder; and distributions from estates and trusts.

Personal holding company (PHC) tax This tax equals 15% (in 2011) of the undistributed personal holding company income and, if applicable, is assessed in addition to the regular corporate income tax and the AMT.

Personal service corporation Corporation whose principal activity is the performance of personal services.

PHC See Personal holding company.

PHCI See Personal holding company income.

Plan of liquidation A written document detailing the steps to be undertaken while carrying out the complete liquidation of a corporation.

Plan of reorganization A consummated transaction that is specifically defined as a reorganization.

Pooled income fund A fund in which individuals receive an income interest for life and a charitable contribution deduction equal to the remainder interest for amounts contributed to the fund. The various individual beneficiaries receive annual distributions of income based upon their proportionate share of the fund's earnings.

Post-termination transition period The period of time following the termination of the S corporation election during which (1) loss and deduction carryovers can be deducted or (2) distributions of S corporation previously taxed earnings can be made tax-free.

Power of appointment The power to designate the eventual owner of a property. Such appointments may be general or specific. Also see General power of appointment.

Preadjustment AMTI Alternative minimum taxable income determined without the adjusted current earnings adjustment and the alternative tax NOL deduction.

Preferential dividend Dividends are preferential if (1) the amount distributed to a shareholder exceeds his ratable share of the distribution as determined by the number of shares owned or (2) the distribution amount for a class of stock is more or less than its rightful amount.

Preferred stock bailout A tax treatment mandated by Sec. 306 that prevents shareholders who receive nontaxable preferred stock dividends from receiving capital gain treatment upon the sale or redemption of the preferred stock.

Present interest An unrestricted right to the immediate use, possession, or enjoyment of property or the income from property (e.g., a life estate or term certain).

Previously taxed income (PTI) Income earned in a pre-1983 S corporation tax year and that was taxed to the shareholder. A money distribution of PTI can be distributed tax-free once all of a corporation's AAA balance has been distributed. See Accumulated adjustments account.

Primary citation The highest level official reporter that reports a particular case.

Principal partner Partner who owns at least a 5% interest in the partnership's capital or profits.

Private Letter Ruling See Letter ruling.

Probate estate Properties that (1) pass subject to the will or under an intestacy statute and (2) are subject to court administration are part of the probate estate.

Profits interest Interest in the partnership's future earnings.

Property Cash, tangible property (e.g., buildings and land), and intangible property (e.g., franchise rights, trademarks, and leases).

Proportional liability The liability for one's pro rata share of the amount of tax due. If one joint filer is unable to pay any or all the tax, the other joint filer is liable only for the portion of the tax attributable to his or her separate taxable items. Also see Joint and several liability.

Protest letter If the additional tax in question is more than $10,000 and the IRS audit was a field audit, the taxpayer must file a protest letter within 30 days. If no such letter is sent, the IRS will follow-up with a 90-day letter. Also see Ninety (90)-day letter.

Publicly traded partnership A partnership that is actively traded on an established securities exchange or is traded in a secondary market or the equivalent thereof. Such partnerships formed after December 17, 1987, are taxed as corporations unless they earn predominantly passive income; publicly traded partnerships that existed before that date will be treated as partnerships if they agree to pay a special excise tax on their gross income.

QTIP See Qualified terminable interest property.

Qualified disclaimer Disclaimer made by a person named to receive property under a decedent's will who wishes to renounce the property and any of its benefits. Such a disclaimer must be in written form and be irrevocable. In addition, it must be made no later than nine months after the later of the day the transfer is made or the day the recipient becomes 21 years old. The property must pass to either the decedent's spouse or another person not named by the person making the disclaimer.

Qualified joint interest If spouses are the only joint owners of a property, that property is classified as a qualified joint interest.

Qualified Subchapter S Subsidiary (QSub) An S corporation that is 100%-owned by another S corporation. The income earned by a QSub is treated and reported as if earned by its parent corporation.

Qualified Subchapter S trusts (QSSTs) A domestic trust that owns stock in one or more S corporations and distributes (or is required to distribute) all of its income to its sole income beneficiary. The beneficiary must make an irrevocable election to be treated as the owner of the trust consisting of the S corporation stock. A separate QSST election must be made for each corporation's stock owned by the trust.

Qualified terminable interest property (QTIP) QTIP property is property for which a special election has been made that makes it eligible for the marital deduction. Such property must be transferred by the donor-spouse to a donee-spouse who has a qualifying interest for life. In other words, the donor

does not have to grant full control over the property to his spouse.

Reasonable business needs For accumulated earnings tax purposes, the amount that a prudent business person would consider appropriate for the business's bona fide present and future needs, Sec. 303 (death tax) redemption needs, and excess business holding redemption needs.

Recapitalization A nontaxable change in the capital structure of an existing corporation for a bona fide business purpose.

Recomputed corresponding item The corresponding item that would occur if the selling and buying group members were divisions of a single corporation.

Recourse loan Loan for which the borrower remains liable until repayment is complete. If the loan is secured, the lender can be repaid by selling the security. Any difference in the sale amount and the loan amount must be paid by the borrower.

Regular corporation See C corporation.

Regular decision Tax Court decision issued on a particular issue for the first time.

Regular tax A corporation's tax liability for income tax purposes reduced by foreign tax credits allowable for income tax purposes.

Remainder interest The portion of an interest in property retained by a transferor who is not transferring his entire interest in the property.

Remainderman The person entitled to the remainder interest.

Reorganization A corporate acquistion or division that meets specific requirements to qualify as nontaxable transaction. Reorganizations are classified as Type A, B, C, D, E, F, or G.

Resident alien An individual whose residence is the United States but who is not a U.S. citizen.

Revenue procedure Issued by the national office of the IRS and reflects the IRS's position on procedural aspects of tax practice issues. Revenue procedures are published in the Cumulative Bulletin.

Revenue ruling Issued by the national office of the IRS and reflects the IRS's interpretation of a narrow tax issue. Revenue rulings, which are published in the Cumulative Bulletin, have less weight than Treasury Regulations.

Reverse triangular merger Type of nontaxable transaction in which a subsidiary corporation is merged into a target corporation, and the target corporation stays alive as a subsidiary of the parent corporation.

Reversionary interest An interest in property that might revert back to the transferor under the terms of the transfer. If the amount of reversionary interest is 5% or less, it is not included in the gross estate.

Revocable trust Trust under which the grantor may demand that the assets be returned.

Rule against perpetuities The requirement that no property interest vest more than 21 years, plus the gestation period, after some life or lives in being at the time the interest is created.

S corporation Election that can be made by small business corporations that allows them to be taxed like partnerships rather than like C corporations. Small business corporations are those that meet the 100-shareholder limitation, the type of shareholder restrictions, and the one class of stock restriction.

Secondary citation Citation to a secondary source (i.e., an unofficial reporter) for a particular case.

Section 306 stock Preferred stock received as a stock dividend or a part of a nontaxable reorganization. Sec. 306 stock is subject to the special preferred stock bailout rules when sold or redeemed. See Preferred stock bailouts.

Section 382 loss limitation rules Limitation that principally prevents trafficking in NOLs. Applies to corporate acquisitions, stock redemptions, and reorganizations when a more than 50 percentage point change in ownership occurs. The NOL that can be used in a tax year is limited to the value of the loss corporation's stock times a federal long-term tax exempt rate.

Section 444 election Personal service corporations, partnerships, and S corporations that are unable to otherwise elect a fiscal year instead of their required tax year, under Sec. 444 can elect a fiscal year as their taxable year.

Section 482 rules The IRS has the power under Sec. 482 to distribute, apportion, or allocate income, deductions, credits, or allowances between or among controlled entities to prevent tax evasion and to clearly reflect the income of the entities.

Section 2503(c) trust Trust created for children under age 21 that need not distribute all of its income annually. The undistributed interest passes to the beneficiary when he or she attains age 21 or to his or her estate should he or she die before age 21.

Security A security includes (1) shares of stock in a corporation; (2) a right to subscribe for, or the right to receive, a share of stock in a corporation; and (3) a bond, debenture, note, or other evidence of indebtedness issued by a corporation with interest coupons or in registered form.

Separate return limitation year Any separate return year except (1) a separate return year of the group member designated as the parent corporation for the consolidated return year to which the tax attribute is carried or (2) a separate return year of any corporation that was a group member for every day of the loss year.

Separate return limitation year (SRLY) rules Limitation on the amount of net operating loss and other deduction and loss amounts from a separate return year that can be used by an affiliated group in a consolidated return year to the member's contribution to consolidated taxable income.

Separate return year A tax year for which a corporation files a separate return or joins in the filing of a consolidated return with a different affiliated group.

Separate share rule Rule permitting a trust with several beneficiaries to treat each beneficiary as having a separate trust interest for purposes of determining the amount of the distribution deduction and the beneficiary's gross income.

Separate taxable income (loss) The taxable income (loss) of an individual corporate member of an affiliated group filing a consolidated tax return. This amount is used to calculate the group's combined taxable income.

Short-period tax return A tax return covering a period of less than 12 months. Short period returns are commonly filed in the first or final tax year or when a change in tax year is made.

Short-term trust Trust whose period is long enough for the grantor to escape being taxed on the trust's accounting income. A *Clifford* trust is a short-term trust.

Simple trust Trust that must distribute all of its income currently and is not empowered to make a charitable contribution.

Small business trust A type of trust that can own stock in a small business corporation that has made an S election to be taxed as an S corporation.

Small cases procedure A Tax Court procedure for adjudicating tax-related claims of $50,000 or less. Small cases procedure decisions are not appealable and have no precedential value.

Sole proprietorship Form of business owned by an individual who reports all items of income and expense on Schedule C (or Schedule C-EZ) of his individual return.

Special agents The IRS agents responsible for criminal fraud investigations.

Spin-off A nontaxable distribution in which a parent corporation distributes the stock and securities of a subsidiary to its shareholders without receiving anything in exchange.

Split-interest transfer A transfer made for both private (i.e., an individual) and public (i.e., a charitable organization) purposes.

Split-off A nontaxable distribution in which a parent corporation distributes a subsidiary's stock and securities to some or all of its shareholders in exchange for part or all of their stock and securities in the parent corporation.

Split-up A nontaxable distribution in which a parent corporation distributes the stock or securities of two or more subsidiaries to its shareholders in exchange for all of their

stock and securities in the parent corporation. The parent corporation then goes out of existence.

Sprinkling trust A discretionary trust with several beneficiaries.

S short year That portion of an S termination year that begins on the first day of the tax year and ends on the day preceding the day on which the termination is effective.

SSTS See Statements on Standards for Tax Services.

Statements on Standards for Tax Services (SSTS) Ethical standards of practice and compliance set by the Tax Division of the American Institute of Certified Public Accountants. The AICPA enforces these standards, and thus they have a great deal of influence on ethics in tax practice.

Statute of limitations A period of time as provided by law after which a taxpayer's return may not be changed either by the IRS or the taxpayer. The limitations period is generally three years from the later of the date the tax return is filed or its due date. A fraudulent return has no statute of limitations.

Step transaction doctrine A judicial doctrine that the IRS can use to collapse a multistep transaction into a single transaction (either taxable or nontaxable) to prevent the taxpayers from arranging a series of business transactions to obtain a tax result that is not available if only a single transaction is used.

S termination year A tax year in which a termination event occurs on any day other than the first day of the tax year. It is divided into an S short year and a C short year.

Stock dividend A dividend paid in the form of stock in the corporation issuing the dividend.

Stock redemption The acquisition by a corporation of its own stock in exchange for property. Such stock may be cancelled, retired, or held as treasury stock.

Stock rights Rights issued by a corporation to its shareholders or creditors that permit the purchase of an additional share(s) of stock at a designated exercise price with the surrender of one or more of the stock rights.

Subpart F income A series of income categories deemed distributed to the U.S. shareholders of a controlled foreign corporation on the last day of its tax year. Subpart F income includes income from insurance of U.S. and foreign risks, foreign base company income, boycott-related income, bribes, and income from countries where for political reasons, etc. the deferral privilege is denied.

Substantially appreciated inventory This type of inventory includes (1) items held for sale in the normal course of partnership business, (2) other property that would not be considered a capital asset or Sec. 1231 property if it were sold by the partnership, and (3) any other property held by the partnership that would fall into the above classification if it were held by the selling or distributee partner.

Target corporation The corporation that transfers its assets as part of a taxable or nontaxable acquisition. Also may be known as the acquired or transferor company.

Tax attributes Corporations have various tax items, such as earnings and profits, deduction and credit carryovers, and depreciation recapture potential, that are called tax attributes. The tax attributes of a target or liquidating corporation are assumed by the acquiring or parent corporation, respectively, in acquisitive reorganizations and tax-free liquidations.

Tax matters partner Partner who is designated by the partnership or who is the general partner having the largest profits interests at the close of the partnership's tax year.

Taxpayer Compliance Measurement Program (TCMP) A stratified random sample used to select tax returns for audit. The program is intended to test the extent to which taxpayers are in compliance with the law.

Tax preference items Designated items that increase taxable income to arrive at AMTI. Unlike AMT adjustments, tax preference items do not reverse in later years and reduce AMTI.

Tax research The process of solving a specific tax-related question on the basis of both tax law sources and the specific circumstances surrounding the particular situation.

Tax services Multivolume commentaries on the tax law. Generally, these commentaries contain copies of the Internal Revenue Code and the Treasury Regulations. Also included are editorial comments prepared by the publisher of the tax service, current matters, and a cross-reference to various government promulgations and judicial decisions. Most tax services now are available on the Internet.

Tax treaties Bilateral agreements entered into between two nations that address tax and other matters. Treaties provide for modifications to the basic tax laws involving residents of the two countries (e.g., reductions in the withholding rates).

Tax year The period of time (usually 12 months) selected by taxpayers to compute their taxable income. The tax year may be a calendar year or a fiscal year. The election is made on the taxpayer's first return and cannot be changed without IRS approval. The tax year may be less than 12 months if it is the taxpayer's first or final return or if the taxpayer is changing accounting periods.

TCMP See Taxpayer Compliance Measurement Program.

Technical advice memorandum Such memoranda are administrative interpretations issued by the national office of the IRS in the form of a letter ruling. Taxpayers may request them if they need guidance about the tax treatment of complicated technical matters being audited.

Temporary differences Items that are included in book income in the current year but that were included in taxable income in the past or will be included in the future. Book income items that are nontaxable in the current year even though they were taxed in the past or will be taxed in the future and book expenses that are not currently deductible even though that status was different in the past or will be different in the future are categorized as temporary differences.

Temporary regulations Regulations issued by the Treasury Department relating to an IRC provision. Such regulations are effective for a limited period of time, usually three years. Issuance of temporary regulations is not preceded by a public hearing on their substance. Temporary regulations have the same precedential value as final regulations.

Tentative minimum tax (TMT) Tax calculated by (1) multiplying 20% times the corporation's alternative minimum taxable income less a statutory exemption amount and (2) deducting allowable foreign tax credits.

Term certain interest A person holding such an interest has a right to receive income from property for a specified term but does not own or hold title to such property. The property reverts to the grantor at the end of the term.

Terminable interest A property interest that ends when some event occurs (or fails to occur) or when a specified amount of time passes.

Testamentary Of, pertaining to, or of the nature of a testament or will.

Testamentary transfers A transferor's control or enjoyment of a property ceases at death.

Testamentary trust Trust created under the direction of a decedent's will and funded by the decedent's estate.

Thirty (30)-day letter A report sent to the taxpayer if the taxpayer does not sign Form 870 (Waiver of Statutory Notice) concerning any additional taxes assessed. The letter details the proposed changes and advises the taxpayer of his or her right to pursue the matter with the Appeals Office. The taxpayer then has 30 days in which to request a conference.

Throwback dividends For accumulated earnings tax and personal holding company tax purposes, these are distributions made out of current or accumulated earnings and profits in the first two and one-half months after the close of the tax year.

Tier-1 beneficiary Beneficiary to whom a distribution must be made.

Tier-2 beneficiary Beneficiary who receives a discretionary distribution.

TMT See Tentative minimum tax.

Topical tax service A multivolume tax commentary organized by topic. Topics might include, for example, deferred compensation, Type A reorganizations, or S corporations. These volumes are an excellent place to begin research in an unfamiliar area.

Transferor corporation The corporation that transfers its assets as part of a reorganization. Also may be known as acquired or target corporation.

Triangular merger A type of merger transaction where the parent corporation uses a subsidiary corporation to serve as the acquiring corporation.

Triangular reorganization A type of reorganization (i.e., Type A, B, or C) where the parent corporation uses a subsidiary corporation to serve as the acquiring corporation. Also see Triangular merger.

Trust An arrangement created either by will or by an inter vivos declaration whereby trustees take title to property for the purpose of protecting it or conserving it for the beneficiaries.

Trustee An individual or institution that administers a trust for the benefit of a beneficiary.

Trustor The grantor or transferor of a trust.

Type A reorganization Type of corporate reorganization that meets the requirements of state or federal law. It may take the form of a consolidation, merger, triangular merger, or reverse triangular merger.

Type B reorganization Reorganization characterized by a stock-for-stock exchange. The target corporation remains in existence as a subsidiary of the acquiring corporation.

Type C reorganization A transaction that requires the acquiring corporation to obtain substantially all the target corporation's assets in exchange for its voting stock and a limited amount of other consideration. The target corporation generally is liquidated.

Type D reorganization This type of reorganization may be either acquisitive or divisive. In the former, substantially all the transferor corporation's assets (and possibly some or all of its liabilities) are acquired by a controlled corporation. The target corporation is liquidated. The latter involves the acquisition of the part or all of the transferor corporation's assets (and liabilities) by a controlled subsidiary corporation(s). The transferor corporation may either remain in existence or be liquidated.

Type E reorganization This type of reorganization changes the capital structure of a corporation. The corporation remains in existence.

Type F reorganization The old corporation's assets or stock are transferred to a single newly formed corporation in this type of transaction. The "old" corporation is liquidated.

Type G reorganization This type of reorganization may be either acquisitive or divisive. In either case, part or all the target or transferor corporation's assets (and possibly some or all of its liabilities) are transferred to another corporation as part of a bankruptcy

proceeding. The target or transferor corporation may either remain in existence or be liquidated.

Unauthorized practice of law The engagement of nonlawyers in professional activities traditionally relegated to the legal profession. Such activities include preparing legal documents, formalizing business entities, and representing clients in criminal investigations.

Unified credit The unified credit enables a tax base of a certain size (i.e., the exemption equivalent or applicable exclusion amount) to be completely free of transfer taxes. It may be subtracted only once against all of a person's transfers—throughout one's lifetime and at death. See Exemption equivalent and Applicable exclusion amount.

Unified rate schedule Progressive rate schedule for estate and gift taxes. These rates are effective for gifts made after 1976 and deaths occurring after 1976.

Unrealized receivable Right to payment for goods and services that has not been included in the owner's income because of its method of accounting.

Unreported decisions District court decisions that are not reported in official reporters. Such decisions may be reported in secondary reporters that report only tax-related cases.

U.S. production activities deduction A deduction equal to a percentage times the lesser of (1) qualified production activities income for the year or (2) taxable income before the U.S. production activities deduction. The phased-in percentages were 3% for 2005 and 2006, 6% for 2007–2009, and 9% for 2010 and thereafter. The deduction, however, cannot exceed 50% of the corporation's W-2 wages allocable to U.S. production activities for the year.

U.S. shareholder For controlled foreign corporation purposes, a U.S. person who owns at least 10% of the foreign corporation's voting stock.

Valuation allowance A contra-type account that represents the portion of a deferred tax asset that likely will not be realized.

Voting trust An arrangement whereby the stock owned by a number of shareholders is placed under the control of a trustee for purposes of exercising the voting rights possessed by the stock. This practice increases the voting power of the minority shareholders.

Wealth transfer taxes Estate taxes (i.e., the tax on dispositions of property that occur as a result of the transferor's death) and gift taxes (i.e., the tax on lifetime transfers) are wealth transfer taxes.

Writ of certiorari See Certiorari.

Note: The AICPA released revised Statements on Standards for Tax Services (SSTS) effective on January 1, 2010. These statements are enforceable standards of tax practice for AICPA members. Changes to Statements No. 1 and 7 (formerly No. 8) were substantive in nature. As a result, Interpretations No. 1-1 and 1-2 relating to former Statement No. 1 are currently under revision. The new statements as well as the old statements can be found on the AICPA website at www.aicpa.org.

• AICPA STATEMENTS ON STANDARDS FOR TAX SERVICES NOS. 1–7 (NOVEMBER 2009)

PREFACE

1. Standards are the foundation of a profession. The AICPA aids its members in fulfilling their ethical responsibilities by instituting and maintaining standards against which their professional performance can be measured. Compliance with professional standards of tax practice also reaffirms the public's awareness of the professionalism that is associated with CPAs as well as the AICPA.

2. This publication sets forth enforceable tax practice standards for members of the AICPA, Statements on Standards for Tax Services (SSTSs or statements). These statements apply to all members providing tax services regardless of the jurisdictions in which they practice. Interpretations of these statements may be issued as guidance to assist in understanding and applying the statements. The SSTSs and their interpretations are intended to complement other standards of tax practice, such as Treasury Department Circular No. 230, *Regulations Governing the Practice of Attorneys, Certified Public Accountants, Enrolled Agents, Enrolled Actuaries, Enrolled Retirement Plan Agents, and Appraisers before the Internal Revenue Service*; penalty provisions of the Internal Revenue Code; and state boards of accountancy rules.

3. The SSTSs are written in as simple and objective a manner as possible. However, by their nature, practice standards provide for an appropriate range of behavior and need to be interpreted to address a broad range of personal and professional situations. The SSTSs recognize this need by, in some sections, providing relatively subjective rules and by leaving certain terms undefined. These terms are generally rooted in tax concepts and, therefore, should be readily understood by tax practitioners. Accordingly, enforcement of these rules, as part of the AICPA's Code of Professional Conduct Rule 201, *General Standards*, and Rule 202, *Compliance With Standards* (AICPA, *Professional Standards*, vol. 2, ET sec. 201 par. .01 and ET sec. 202 par. .01),

will be undertaken on a case-by-case basis. Members are expected to comply with them.

HISTORY

4. The SSTSs have their origin in the Statements on Responsibilities in Tax Practice (SRTPs), which provided a body of advisory opinions on good tax practice. The guidelines as originally set forth in the SRTPs became more important than many members had anticipated when the guidelines were issued. The courts, the IRS, state accountancy boards, and other professional organizations recognized and relied on the SRTPs as the appropriate articulation of professional conduct in a CPA's tax practice. The SRTPs became *de facto* enforceable standards of professional practice, because state disciplinary organizations and courts regularly held CPAs accountable for failure to follow the guidelines set forth in the SRTPs.

5. The AICPA's Tax Executive Committee concluded it was appropriate to issue tax practice standards that would become a part of the AICPA's *Professional Standards*. At its July 1999 meeting, the AICPA Board of Directors approved support of the executive committee's initiative and placed the matter on the agenda of the October 1999 meeting of the AICPA's governing Council. On October 19, 1999, Council approved designating the Tax Executive Committee as a standardsetting body, thus authorizing that committee to promulgate standards of tax practice. As a result, the original SSTSs, largely mirroring the SRTPs, were issued in August 2000.

6. The SRTPs were originally issued between 1964 and 1977. The first nine SRTPs and the introduction were promulgated in 1976; the tenth SRTP was issued in 1977. The original SRTPs concerning the CPA's responsibility to sign the tax return (SRTP No. 1, *Signature of Preparers*, and No. 2, *Signature of Reviewer: Assumption of Preparer's Responsibility*) were withdrawn in 1982 after Treasury Department regulations were issued adopting

substantially the same standards for all tax return preparers. The sixth and seventh SRTPs, concerning the responsibility of a CPA who becomes aware of an error, were revised in 1991. The first interpretation of the SRTPs, Interpretation No. 1-1, "Realistic Possibility Standard," was approved in December 1990. The SSTSs and Interpretation No. 1-1, "Realistic Possibility Standard," of SSTS No. 1, *Tax Return Positions*, superseded and replaced the SRTPs and their Interpretation No. 1-1, effective October 31, 2000. Although the number and names of the SSTSs, and the substance of the rules contained in each of them, remained the same as in the SRTPs, the language was revised to both clarify and reflect the enforceable nature of the SSTSs. In addition, because the applicability of these standards is not limited to federal income tax practice (as was the case with the SRTPs), the language was changed to indicate the broader scope. In 2003, in connection with the tax shelter debate, SSTS Interpretation No. 1-2, "Tax Planning," of SSTS No. 1 was issued to clarify a member's responsibilities in connection with tax planning; that interpretation became effective December 31, 2003.

7. When the original SSTSs were issued, an effort was made to keep to a minimum any changes in the language of the SSTSs from that of the predecessor SRTPs. This was done to alleviate concerns regarding the enforceability of standards that differed from the SRTPs under which members had been practicing. Since the issuance of the original SSTSs, members have asked for clarification on certain matters, such as the duplication of the language in SSTS No. 6, *Knowledge of Error: Return Preparation*, and No. 7, *Knowledge of Error: Administrative Proceedings*. Also, certain changes in federal and state tax laws have raised concerns regarding the need to revise SSTS No. 1. As a result, in 2008, the original SSTS Nos. 1–8 were updated, effective January 1, 2010. The original SSTS Nos. 6–7 were combined into the revised SSTS No. 6, *Knowledge of Error: Return Preparation and Administrative Proceedings*. The original SSTS No. 8, *Form and Content of Advice to Taxpayers*, was renumbered SSTS No. 7. In addition, various revisions were made to the language of the original SSTSs.

ONGOING PROCESS

8. The following SSTSs and any interpretations issued thereunder reflect the AICPA's standards of tax practice and delineate members' responsibilities to taxpayers, the public, the government, and the profession. The statements are intended to be part of an ongoing process of articulating standards of tax practice for members. These standards are subject to change as necessary or appropriate to address changes in the tax law or other developments in the tax practice environment.

9. Members are encouraged to assess the adequacy of their practices and procedures for providing tax services in conformity with these standards. This process will vary according to the size of the practice and the nature of tax services performed.

10. The Tax Executive Committee promulgates the SSTSs and their interpretations. Acknowledgment is also due to the

many members who have devoted their time and efforts over the years to developing and revising the AICPA's standards.

STATEMENT ON STANDARDS FOR TAX SERVICES NO. 1, *TAX RETURN POSITIONS*

INTRODUCTION

1. This statement sets forth the applicable standards for members when recommending tax return positions, or preparing or signing tax returns (including amended returns, claims for refund, and information returns) filed with any taxing authority. For purposes of these standards

 a. a *tax return position* is (i) a position reflected on a tax return on which a member has specifically advised a taxpayer or (ii) a position about which a member has knowledge of all material facts and, on the basis of those facts, has concluded whether the position is appropriate.

 b. a *taxpayer* is a client, a member's employer, or any other third-party recipient of tax services.

2. This statement also addresses a member's obligation to advise a taxpayer of relevant tax return disclosure responsibilities and potential penalties.

3. In addition to the AICPA, various taxing authorities, at the federal, state, and local levels, may impose specific reporting and disclosure standards with regard to recommending tax return positions or preparing or signing tax returns.[1] These standards can vary between taxing authorities and by type of tax.

STATEMENT

4. A member should determine and comply with the standards, if any, that are imposed by the applicable taxing authority with respect to recommending a tax return position, or preparing or signing a tax return.

5. If the applicable taxing authority has no written standards with respect to recommending a tax return position or preparing or signing a tax return, or if its standards are lower than the standards set forth in this paragraph, the following standards will apply:

 a. A member should not recommend a tax return position or prepare or sign a tax return taking a position unless the member has a good-faith belief that the position has at least a realistic possibility of being sustained administratively or judicially on its merits if challenged.

 b. Notwithstanding paragraph 5(a), a member may *recommend a tax return position* if the member (i) concludes that there is a reasonable basis for the position and

---

[1] A member should refer to the current version of Internal Revenue Code Section 6694, Understatement of taxpayer's liability by tax return preparer, and other relevant federal, state, and jurisdictional authorities to determine

the reporting and disclosure standards that are applicable to preparers of tax returns.

(ii) advises the taxpayer to appropriately disclose that position. Notwithstanding paragraph 5(a), a member may *prepare or sign a tax return* that reflects a position if (i) the member concludes there is a reasonable basis for the position and (ii) the position is appropriately disclosed.

6. When recommending a tax return position or when preparing or signing a tax return on which a position is taken, a member should, when relevant, advise the taxpayer regarding potential penalty consequences of such tax return position and the opportunity, if any, to avoid such penalties through disclosure.

7. A member should not recommend a tax return position or prepare or sign a tax return reflecting a position that the member knows

a. exploits the audit selection process of a taxing authority, or

b. serves as a mere arguing position advanced solely to obtain leverage in a negotiation with a taxing authority.

8. When recommending a tax return position, a member has both the right and the responsibility to be an advocate for the taxpayer with respect to any position satisfying the aforementioned standards.

EXPLANATION

9. The AICPA and various taxing authorities impose specific reporting and disclosure standards with respect to tax return positions and preparing or signing tax returns. In a given situation, the standards, if any, imposed by the applicable taxing authority may be higher or lower than the standards set forth in paragraph 5. A member is to comply with the standards, if any, of the applicable taxing authority; if the applicable taxing authority has no standards or if its standards are lower than the standards set forth in paragraph 5, the standards set forth in paragraph 5 will apply.

10. Our self-assessment tax system can function effectively only if taxpayers file tax returns that are true, correct, and complete. A tax return is prepared based on a taxpayer's representation of facts, and the taxpayer has the final responsibility for positions taken on the return. The standards that apply to a taxpayer may differ from those that apply to a member.

11. In addition to a duty to the taxpayer, a member has a duty to the tax system. However, it is well established that the taxpayer has no obligation to pay more taxes than are legally owed, and a member has a duty to the taxpayer to assist in achieving that result. The standards contained in paragraphs 4–8 recognize a member's responsibilities to both the taxpayer and the tax system.

12. In reaching a conclusion concerning whether a given standard in paragraph 4 or 5 has been satisfied, a member may consider a well-reasoned construction of the applicable statute, well-reasoned articles or treatises, or pronouncements issued by the applicable taxing authority, regardless of whether such sources would be treated as *authority* under Internal Revenue Code Section 6662, *Imposition of accuracy-related penalty on underpayments*, and the regulations thereunder. A position would not fail to meet these standards merely because it is later abandoned for practical or procedural considerations during an administrative hearing or in the litigation process.

13. If a member has a good-faith belief that more than one tax return position meets the standards set forth in paragraphs 4–5, a member's advice concerning alternative acceptable positions may include a discussion of the likelihood that each such position might or might not cause the taxpayer's tax return to be examined and whether the position would be challenged in an examination. In such circumstances, such advice is not a violation of paragraph 7.

14. A member's determination of whether information is appropriately disclosed by the taxpayer should be based on the facts and circumstances of the particular case and the disclosure requirements of the applicable taxing authority. If a member recommending a position, but not engaged to prepare or sign the related tax return, advises the taxpayer concerning appropriate disclosure of the position, then the member shall be deemed to meet the disclosure requirements of these standards.

15. If particular facts and circumstances lead a member to believe that a taxpayer penalty might be asserted, the member should so advise the taxpayer and should discuss with the taxpayer the opportunity, if any, to avoid such penalty by disclosing the position on the tax return. Although a member should advise the taxpayer with respect to disclosure, it is the taxpayer's responsibility to decide whether and how to disclose.

16. For purposes of this statement, preparation of a tax return includes giving advice on events that have occurred at the time the advice is given if the advice is directly relevant to determining the existence, character, or amount of a schedule, entry, or other portion of a tax return.

STATEMENT ON STANDARDS FOR TAX SERVICES NO. 2, *ANSWERS TO QUESTIONS ON RETURNS*

INTRODUCTION

1. This statement sets forth the applicable standards for members when signing the preparer's declaration on a tax return if one or more questions on the return have not been answered. The term *questions* includes requests for information on the return, in the instructions, or in the regulations, whether or not stated in the form of a question.

STATEMENT

2. A member should make a reasonable effort to obtain from the taxpayer the information necessary to provide appropriate answers to all questions on a tax return before signing as preparer.

EXPLANATION

3. It is recognized that the questions on tax returns are not of uniform importance, and often they are not applicable to the particular taxpayer. Nevertheless, there are at least three reasons why

a member should be satisfied that a reasonable effort has been made to obtain information to provide appropriate answers to the questions on the return that are applicable to a taxpayer:

    a. A question may be of importance in determining taxable income or loss, or the tax liability shown on the return, in which circumstance an omission may detract from the quality of the return.

    b. A request for information may require a disclosure necessary for a complete return or to avoid penalties.

    c. A member often must sign a preparer's declaration stating that the return is true, correct, and complete.

4. Reasonable grounds may exist for omitting an answer to a question applicable to a taxpayer. For example, reasonable grounds may include the following:

    a. The information is not readily available and the answer is not significant in terms of taxable income or loss, or the tax liability shown on the return.

    b. Genuine uncertainty exists regarding the meaning of the question in relation to the particular return.

    c. The answer to the question is voluminous; in such cases, a statement should be made on the return that the data will be supplied upon examination.

5. A member should not omit an answer merely because it might prove disadvantageous to a taxpayer.

6. A member should consider whether the omission of an answer to a question may cause the return to be deemed incomplete or result in penalties.

7. If reasonable grounds exist for omission of an answer to an applicable question, a taxpayer is not required to provide on the return an explanation of the reason for the omission.

STATEMENT ON STANDARDS FOR TAX SERVICES NO. 3, *CERTAIN PROCEDURAL ASPECTS OF PREPARING RETURNS*

INTRODUCTION

1. This statement sets forth the applicable standards for members concerning the obligation to examine or verify certain supporting data or to consider information related to another taxpayer when preparing a taxpayer's tax return.

STATEMENT

2. In preparing or signing a return, a member may in good faith rely, without verification, on information furnished by the taxpayer or by third parties. However, a member should not ignore the implications of information furnished and should make reasonable inquiries if the information furnished appears to be incorrect, incomplete, or inconsistent either on its face or on the basis of other facts known to the member. Further, a member should refer to the taxpayer's returns for one or more prior years whenever feasible.

3. If the tax law or regulations impose a condition with respect to deductibility or other tax treatment of an item, such as taxpayer maintenance of books and records or substantiating documentation to support the reported deduction or tax treatment, a member should make appropriate inquiries to determine to the member's satisfaction whether such condition has been met.

4. When preparing a tax return, a member should consider information actually known to that member from the tax return of another taxpayer if the information is relevant to that tax return and its consideration is necessary to properly prepare that tax return. In using such information, a member should consider any limitations imposed by any law or rule relating to confidentiality.

EXPLANATION

5. The preparer's declaration on a tax return often states that the information contained therein is true, correct, and complete to the best of the preparer's knowledge and belief based on all information known by the preparer. This type of reference should be understood to include information furnished by the taxpayer or by third parties to a member in connection with the preparation of the return.

6. The preparer's declaration does not require a member to examine or verify supporting data; a member may rely on information furnished by the taxpayer unless it appears to be incorrect, incomplete, or inconsistent. However, there is a need to determine by inquiry that a specifically required condition, such as maintaining books and records or substantiating documentation, has been satisfied and to obtain information when the material furnished appears to be incorrect, incomplete, or inconsistent. Although a member has certain responsibilities in exercising due diligence in preparing a return, the taxpayer has the ultimate responsibility for the contents of the return. Thus, if the taxpayer presents unsupported data in the form of lists of tax information, such as dividends and interest received, charitable contributions, and medical expenses, such information may be used in the preparation of a tax return without verification unless it appears to be incorrect, incomplete, or inconsistent either on its face or on the basis of other facts known to a member.

7. Even though there is no requirement to examine underlying documentation, a member should encourage the taxpayer to provide supporting data where appropriate. For example, a member should encourage the taxpayer to submit underlying documents for use in tax return preparation to permit full consideration of income and deductions arising from security transactions and from pass-through entities, such as estates, trusts, partnerships, and S corporations.

8. The source of information provided to a member by a taxpayer for use in preparing the return is often a pass-through entity, such as a limited partnership, in which the taxpayer has an interest but is not involved in management. A member may accept the information provided by the pass-through entity without further inquiry, unless there is reason to believe it is incorrect,

incomplete, or inconsistent, either on its face or on the basis of other facts known to the member. In some instances, it may be appropriate for a member to advise the taxpayer to ascertain the nature and amount of possible exposure to tax deficiencies, interest, and penalties by taxpayer contact with management of the pass-through entity.

9. A member should make use of a taxpayer's returns for one or more prior years in preparing the current return whenever feasible. Reference to prior returns and discussion of prior-year tax determinations with the taxpayer should provide information to determine the taxpayer's general tax status, avoid the omission or duplication of items, and afford a basis for the treatment of similar or related transactions. As with the examination of information supplied for the current year's return, the extent of comparison of the details of income and deduction between years depends on the particular circumstances.

STATEMENT ON STANDARDS FOR TAX SERVICES NO. 4, *USE OF ESTIMATES*

INTRODUCTION

1. This statement sets forth the applicable standards for members when using the taxpayer's estimates in the preparation of a tax return. A member may advise on estimates used in the preparation of a tax return, but the taxpayer has the responsibility to provide the estimated data. Appraisals or valuations are not considered estimates for purposes of this statement.

STATEMENT

2. Unless prohibited by statute or by rule, a member may use the taxpayer's estimates in the preparation of a tax return if it is not practical to obtain exact data and if the member determines that the estimates are reasonable based on the facts and circumstances known to the member. The taxpayer's estimates should be presented in a manner that does not imply greater accuracy than exists.

EXPLANATION

3. Accounting requires the exercise of professional judgment and, in many instances, the use of approximations based on judgment. The application of such accounting judgments, as long as not in conflict with methods set forth by a taxing authority, is acceptable. These judgments are not estimates within the purview of this statement. For example, a federal income tax regulation provides that if all other conditions for accrual are met, the exact amount of income or expense need not be known or ascertained at year end if the amount can be determined with reasonable accuracy.

4. When the taxpayer's records do not accurately reflect information related to small expenditures, accuracy in recording some

data may be difficult to achieve. Therefore, the use of estimates by a taxpayer in determining the amount to be deducted for such items may be appropriate.

5. When records are missing or precise information about a transaction is not available at the time the return must be filed, a member may prepare a tax return using a taxpayer's estimates of the missing data.

6. Estimated amounts should not be presented in a manner that provides a misleading impression about the degree of factual accuracy.

7. Specific disclosure that an estimate is used for an item in the return is not generally required; however, such disclosure should be made in unusual circumstances where nondisclosure might mislead the taxing authority regarding the degree of accuracy of the return as a whole. Some examples of unusual circumstances include the following:

a. A taxpayer has died or is ill at the time the return must be filed.
b. A taxpayer has not received a Schedule K-1 for a pass-through entity at the time the tax return is to be filed.
c. There is litigation pending (for example, a bankruptcy proceeding) that bears on the return.
d. Fire, computer failure, or natural disaster has destroyed the relevant records.

STATEMENT ON STANDARDS FOR TAX SERVICES NO. 5, *DEPARTURE FROM A POSITION PREVIOUSLY CONCLUDED IN AN ADMINISTRATIVE PROCEEDING OR COURT DECISION*

INTRODUCTION

1. This statement sets forth the applicable standards for members in recommending a tax return position that departs from the position determined in an administrative proceeding or in a court decision with respect to the taxpayer's prior return.

2. For purposes of this statement, *administrative proceeding* includes an examination by a taxing authority or an appeals conference relating to a return or a claim for refund.

3. For purposes of this statement, *court decision* means a decision by any court having jurisdiction over tax matters.

STATEMENT

4. The tax return position with respect to an item as determined in an administrative proceeding or court decision does not restrict a member from recommending a different tax position in a later year's return, unless the taxpayer is bound to a specified treatment

in the later year, such as by a formal closing agreement. Therefore, the member may recommend a tax return position or prepare or sign a tax return that departs from the treatment of an item as concluded in an administrative proceeding or court decision with respect to a prior return of the taxpayer provided the requirements of Statement on Standards for Tax Services (SSTS) No. 1, *Tax Return Positions*, are satisfied.

EXPLANATION

5. If an administrative proceeding or court decision has resulted in a determination concerning a specific tax treatment of an item in a prior year's return, a member will usually recommend this same tax treatment in subsequent years. However, departures from consistent treatment may be justified under such circumstances as the following:

a. Taxing authorities tend to act consistently in the disposition of an item that was the subject of a prior administrative proceeding but generally are not bound to do so. Similarly, a taxpayer is not bound to follow the tax treatment of an item as consented to in an earlier administrative proceeding.

b. The determination in the administrative proceeding or the court's decision may have been caused by a lack of documentation. Supporting data for the later year may be appropriate.

c. A taxpayer may have yielded in the administrative proceeding for settlement purposes or not appealed the court decision, even though the position met the standards in SSTS No. 1.

d. Court decisions, rulings, or other authorities that are more favorable to a taxpayer's current position may have developed since the prior administrative proceeding was concluded or the prior court decision was rendered.

6. The consent in an earlier administrative proceeding and the existence of an unfavorable court decision are factors that the member should consider in evaluating whether the standards in SSTS No. 1 are met.

STATEMENT ON STANDARDS FOR TAX SERVICES NO. 6, *KNOWLEDGE OF ERROR: RETURN PREPARATION AND ADMINISTRATIVE PROCEEDINGS*

INTRODUCTION

1. This statement sets forth the applicable standards for a member who becomes aware of (a) an error in a taxpayer's previously filed tax return; (b) an error in a return that is the subject of an administrative proceeding, such as an examination by a taxing authority or an appeals conference; or (c) a taxpayer's failure to file a required tax return. As used herein, the term *error* includes any position, omission, or method of accounting that, at the time the return is filed, fails to meet the standards set out in Statement on Standards for Tax Services (SSTS) No. 1, *Tax Return Positions*. The term *error* also includes a position taken on a prior year's return that no longer meets these standards due to legislation, judicial decisions, or administrative pronouncements having retroactive effect. However, an error does not include an item that has an insignificant effect on the taxpayer's tax liability. The term *administrative proceeding* does not include a criminal proceeding.

2. This statement applies whether or not the member prepared or signed the return that contains the error.

3. Special considerations may apply when a member has been engaged by legal counsel to provide assistance in a matter relating to the counsel's client.

STATEMENT

4. A member should inform the taxpayer promptly upon becoming aware of an error in a previously filed return, an error in a return that is the subject of an administrative proceeding, or a taxpayer's failure to file a required return. A member also should advise the taxpayer of the potential consequences of the error and recommend the corrective measures to be taken. Such advice and recommendation may be given orally. The member is not allowed to inform the taxing authority without the taxpayer's permission, except when required by law.

5. If a member is requested to prepare the current year's return and the taxpayer has not taken appropriate action to correct an error in a prior year's return, the member should consider whether to withdraw from preparing the return and whether to continue a professional or employment relationship with the taxpayer. If the member does prepare such current year's return, the member should take reasonable steps to ensure that the error is not repeated.

6. If a member is representing a taxpayer in an administrative proceeding with respect to a return that contains an error of which the member is aware, the member should request the taxpayer's agreement to disclose the error to the taxing authority. Lacking such agreement, the member should consider whether to withdraw from representing the taxpayer in the administrative proceeding and whether to continue a professional or employment relationship with the taxpayer.

EXPLANATION

7. While performing services for a taxpayer, a member may become aware of an error in a previously filed return or may become aware that the taxpayer failed to file a required return. The member should advise the taxpayer of the error and the potential consequences, and recommend the measures to be taken. Similarly, when representing the taxpayer before a taxing authority in an administrative proceeding with respect to a return containing an error of which the member is aware, the member should advise the taxpayer to disclose the error to the taxing authority and of the potential consequences of not disclosing the error. Such advice and recommendation may be given orally.

8. It is the taxpayer's responsibility to decide whether to correct the error. If the taxpayer does not correct an error, a member should consider whether to withdraw from the engagement and whether to continue a professional or employment relationship with the taxpayer. Although recognizing that the taxpayer may not be required by statute to correct an error by filing an amended return, a member should consider whether a taxpayer's decision not to file an amended return or otherwise correct an error may predict future behavior that might require termination of the relationship.

9. Once the member has obtained the taxpayer's consent to disclose an error in an administrative proceeding, the disclosure should not be delayed to such a degree that the taxpayer or member might be considered to have failed to act in good faith or to have, in effect, provided misleading information. In any event, disclosure should be made before the conclusion of the administrative proceeding.

10. A conflict between the member's interests and those of the taxpayer may be created by, for example, the potential for violating Code of Professional Conduct Rule 301, *Confidential Client Information* (AICPA, *Professional Standards*, vol. 2, ET sec. 301 par. .01) (relating to the member's confidential client relationship); the tax law and regulations; or laws on privileged communications, as well as by the potential adverse impact on a taxpayer of a member's withdrawal. Therefore, a member should consider consulting with his or her own legal counsel before deciding upon recommendations to the taxpayer and whether to continue a professional or employment relationship with the taxpayer.

11. If a member believes that a taxpayer may face possible exposure to allegations of fraud or other criminal misconduct, the member should advise the taxpayer to consult with an attorney before the taxpayer takes any action.

12. If a member decides to continue a professional or employment relationship with the taxpayer and is requested to prepare a tax return for a year subsequent to that in which the error occurred, the member should take reasonable steps to ensure that the error is not repeated. If the subsequent year's tax return cannot be prepared without perpetuating the error, the member should consider withdrawal from the return preparation. If a member learns that the taxpayer is using an erroneous method of accounting and it is past the due date to request permission to change to a method meeting the standards of SSTS No. 1, the member may sign a tax return for the current year, providing the tax return includes appropriate disclosure of the use of the erroneous method.

13. Whether an error has no more than an insignificant effect on the taxpayer's tax liability is left to the professional judgment of the member based on all the facts and circumstances known to the member. In judging whether an erroneous method of accounting has more than an insignificant effect, a member should consider the method's cumulative effect, as well as its effect on the current year's tax return or the tax return that is the subject of the administrative proceeding.

14. If a member becomes aware of the error while performing services for a taxpayer that do not involve tax return preparation or representation in an administrative proceeding, the member's responsibility is to advise the taxpayer of the existence of the error and to recommend that the error be discussed with the taxpayer's tax return preparer. Such recommendation may be given orally.

STATEMENT ON STANDARDS FOR TAX SERVICES NO. 7, *FORM AND CONTENT OF ADVICE TO TAXPAYERS*

INTRODUCTION

1. This statement sets forth the applicable standards for members concerning certain aspects of providing advice to a taxpayer and considers the circumstances in which a member has a responsibility to communicate with a taxpayer when subsequent developments affect advice previously provided. The statement does not, however, cover a member's responsibilities when the expectation is that the advice rendered is likely to be relied on by parties other than the taxpayer.

STATEMENT

2. A member should use professional judgment to ensure that tax advice provided to a taxpayer reflects competence and appropriately serves the taxpayer's needs. When communicating tax advice to a taxpayer in writing, a member should comply with relevant taxing authorities' standards, if any, applicable to written tax advice. A member should use professional judgment about any need to document oral advice. A member is not required to follow a standard format when communicating or documenting oral advice.

3. A member should assume that tax advice provided to a taxpayer will affect the manner in which the matters or transactions considered would be reported or disclosed on the taxpayer's tax returns. Therefore, for tax advice given to a taxpayer, a member should consider, when relevant (*a*) return reporting and disclosure standards applicable to the related tax return position and (*b*) the potential penalty consequences of the return position. In ascertaining applicable return reporting and disclosure standards, a member should follow the standards in Statement on Standards for Tax Services No. 1, *Tax Return Positions*.

4. A member has no obligation to communicate with a taxpayer when subsequent developments affect advice previously provided with respect to significant matters, except while assisting a taxpayer in implementing procedures or plans associated with the advice provided or when a member undertakes this obligation by specific agreement.

EXPLANATION

5. Tax advice is recognized as a valuable service provided by members. The form of advice may be oral or written and the subject matter may range from routine to complex. Because the range of advice is so extensive and because advice should meet the specific needs of a taxpayer, neither a standard format nor guidelines for communicating or documenting advice to the taxpayer can be established to cover all situations.

6. Although oral advice may serve a taxpayer's needs appropriately in routine matters or in welldefined areas, written

communications are recommended in important, unusual, substantial dollar value, or complicated transactions. The member may use professional judgment about whether, subsequently, to document oral advice.

7. In deciding on the form of advice provided to a taxpayer, a member should exercise professional judgment and should consider such factors as the following:

  a. The importance of the transaction and amounts involved
  b. The specific or general nature of the taxpayer's inquiry
  c. The time available for development and submission of the advice
  d. The technical complexity involved
  e. The existence of authorities and precedents
  f. The tax sophistication of the taxpayer
  g. The need to seek other professional advice
  h. The type of transaction and whether it is subject to heightened reporting or disclosure requirements
  i. The potential penalty consequences of the tax return position for which the advice is rendered
  j. Whether any potential applicable penalties can be avoided through disclosure
  k. Whether the member intends for the taxpayer to rely upon the advice to avoid potential penalties

8. A member may assist a taxpayer in implementing procedures or plans associated with the advice offered. When providing such assistance, the member should review and revise such advice as warranted by new developments and factors affecting the transaction.

9. Sometimes a member is requested to provide tax advice but does not assist in implementing the plans adopted. Although such developments as legislative or administrative changes or future judicial interpretations may affect the advice previously provided, a member cannot be expected to communicate subsequent developments that affect such advice unless the member undertakes this obligation by specific agreement with the taxpayer.

10. Taxpayers should be informed that (a) the advice reflects professional judgment based upon the member's understanding of the facts, and the law existing as of the date the advice is rendered and (b) subsequent developments could affect previously rendered professional advice. Members may use precautionary language to the effect that their advice is based on facts as stated and authorities that are subject to change.

11. In providing tax advice, a member should be cognizant of applicable confidentiality privileges.

These Statements on Standards for Tax Services were unanimously adopted by the assenting votes of the 17 members of the 18-member Tax Executive Committee who participated in the August 6, 2009, Tax Executive Committee meeting.

Note: *Statements on Standards for Tax Services are issued by the Tax Executive Committee, the senior technical body of the AICPA designated to promulgate standards of tax practice. Rule 201, General Standards, and Rule 202, Compliance With Standards, of the Code of Professional Conduct (AICPA, Professional Standards, vol. 2, ET sec. 201 par. .01 and ET sec. 202 par. .01), require compliance with these standards.*

APPENDIX F

COMPARISON OF TAX ATTRIBUTES FOR C CORPORATIONS, PARTNERSHIPS, AND S CORPORATIONS

APPENDIX F: COMPARISON OF TAX ATTRIBUTES FOR C CORPORATIONS, PARTNERSHIPS, AND S CORPORATIONS

Tax Attribute	C Corporation	Partnership	S Corporation
I. General Characteristics			
1. Application of the separate entity versus conduit (flow through) concept.	*Entity:* The corporation is treated as a separate taxpaying entity. If the corporation distributes income to shareholders in the form of dividends, the shareholders are subject to a second tax on such amounts. Shareholders also are subject to a second tax if they sell their stock.	*Conduit:* The partners report their distributive share of partnership ordinary income and separately stated items on their tax returns. Most elections, such as depreciation methods, accounting period and methods, are made at the partnership level. Special tax rules apply to electing large partnerships.	*Conduit:* Similar to the partnership form of organization. However, the S corporation may be subject to tax at the corporate level on excess net passive income, or built-in gains under special circumstances.
2. Period of existence.	Continues until dissolution; not affected by stock sales by shareholders.	Termination can occur by agreement, or by death, retirement, or disaffiliation of a partner.	Same as for C corporation.
3. Transferability of interest.	Stock can be transferred easily; corporation may retain right to buy back shares.	Addition of new partner or transfer of partner's interest generally requires approval of other partners.	Same as for C corporation.
4. Liability exposure.	Shareholders generally liable only for capital contributions.	General partners are personally, jointly, and severally liable for partnership obligations. Limited partners usually are liable only for capital contributions.	Same as for C corporation.
5. Management responsibility.	Shareholders may be part of management or may hire outside management.	All general partners participate in management. Limited partners generally do not participate.	Because of limited number of shareholders, shareholders usually are part of management.
II. Election and Restrictions			
1. Restrictions on: a. Type of owners.	No restriction.	No restriction.	Limited to individuals, estates, charitable organizations, and certain kinds of trusts.
b. Number of owners.	No restriction.	No restriction.	Limited to 100 shareholders, where a family counts as one shareholder.
c. Type of entity.	Includes domestic or foreign corporations, unincorporated entities known as associations, and certain kinds of trusts. A publicly traded partnership is taxed as a corporation unless more than 90% of its income is qualifying passive income. Grandfathered publicly traded partnerships can avoid corporate taxation by paying an excise tax. Partnerships, LLCs, and proprietorships can elect to be taxed as a corporation under the check-the-box regulations.	Includes a variety of unincorporated entities including limited liability company and limited liability partnership forms. Certain joint undertakings are excluded from partnership status.	Domestic corporations and unincorporated entities (e.g., associations) are eligible. A partnership, LLC, or proprietorship that elects to be treated as an S corporation automatically is considered to have elected to be treated as a corporation under the check-the-box regulations.

APPENDIX F: COMPARISON OF TAX ATTRIBUTES FOR C CORPORATIONS, PARTNERSHIPS, AND S CORPORATIONS

Tax Attribute	C Corporation	Partnership	S Corporation
d. Special tax classifications.	No restriction.	No restriction.	S corporation cannot be a former Domestic International Sales Corporation, or have elected the special Puerto Rico and U.S. Possessions tax credit. Certain financial institutions and insurance companies also are ineligible.
e. Investments made by entity.	No restriction.	No restriction.	S corporation can own 80% or more of a C corporation but cannot file a consolidated tax return with the C corporation.
f. Capital structure.	No restriction.	No restriction.	Limited to a single class of stock that is outstanding. Differences in voting rights are disregarded. Special "safe harbor" rules are available for debt issues.
g. Passive interest income.	No restriction.	No restriction.	Passive investment income cannot exceed 25% of gross receipts for three consecutive tax years when the corporation also has Subchapter C E&P at the end of the year.
2. Election and shareholder consent.	No election required.	No election required.	Election can be made during the preceding tax year or first 2½ months of the tax year. Shareholders must consent to the election.
3. Termination of election.	Not applicable.	The partnership can terminate if it does not carry on any business, financial operation, or venture or if a sale or exchange of at least 50% of the profits and capital interests occurs within a 12-month period.	Occurs if one of the requirements is failed after the election is first effective or if the passive investment income test is failed for three consecutive tax years. IRS can waive invalid elections and permit inadvertent terminations not to break the S election.
4. Revocation of election.	Not applicable.	Not applicable.	Election may be revoked only by shareholders owning more than one-half of the stock. Must be made in first 2½ months of tax year or on a prospective basis.
5. New election.	Not applicable.	Not applicable.	Not permitted for five-year period without IRS consent to early reelection.

APPENDIX F: COMPARISON OF TAX ATTRIBUTES FOR C CORPORATIONS, PARTNERSHIPS, AND S CORPORATIONS

Tax Attribute	C Corporation	Partnership	S Corporation
III. Accounting Periods and Elections			
1. Taxable year.	Calendar year or fiscal year is permitted. Personal service corporations are restricted to using a calendar year unless IRS grants approval to use a fiscal year. A special election is available to use a fiscal year resulting in a three-month or less income deferral if the corporation meets a series of minimum distribution requirements.	Generally use tax year of majority or principal partners. Otherwise use of the least aggregate deferral year is required. Can use a fiscal year that has a business purpose for which IRS approval is obtained. An electing partnership may use a fiscal year resulting in a three-month or less income deferral if an additional required payment is made.	Can use a fiscal year that has a business purpose for which IRS approval is obtained. An S corporation may use a fiscal year resulting in a three-month or less income deferral if an additional required payment is made. If neither of the above applies, a calendar year must be used.
2. Accounting methods.	Elected by the corporation. Use of cash method of accounting is restricted for certain personal service corporations and C corporations having $5 million or more annual gross receipts.	Elected by the partnership. Restrictions on the use of the cash method of accounting apply to partnerships having a C corporation as a partner or that are tax shelters.	Elected by the S corporation. Restrictions on the use of the cash method of accounting apply to S corporations that are tax shelters.
IV. Taxability of Profits			
1. Taxability of profits.	Ordinary income and capital gains are taxed to the corporation. Profits are taxed a second time when distributed.	Ordinary income and separately stated income and gain items pass through to the partners at the end of the partnership's tax year whether or not distributed.	Same as partnership.
2. Allocation of profits.	Not applicable.	Based on partnership agreement. Special allocations are permitted.	Based on stock ownership on each day of the tax year. Special allocations are not permitted.
3. Character of income.	Distributed profits (including tax-exempt income) are dividends to extent of earnings and profits (E&P).	Items receiving special treatment (e.g., capital gains or tax-exempt income) pass through separately to the partner and retain same character as when earned by the partnership.	Same as partnership.
4. Maximum tax rate for earnings.	15% on the first $50,000; 25% from $50,000 to $75,000; 34% from $75,000 to $10 million. The rate is 35% for taxable income above $10 million. A 5% surcharge applies to taxable income between $100,000 and $335,000, and a 3% surcharge applies to taxable income between $15 million and $18,333,333. Special rules apply to controlled groups. Personal service corporations are taxed at a flat 35% rate.	Rates of tax applicable to noncorporate partners from 10% through 35% (in 2011) are levied on pass-through income from the partnership. C corporation rates apply to corporate partners.	Same as partnership except for certain special situations where a special corporate tax applies to the S corporation.

Tax Attribute	C Corporation	Partnership	S Corporation
5. Special tax levies.	Can be subject to accumulated earnings tax, personal holding company tax, and corporate alternative minimum tax.	Not applicable.	Can be subject to built-in gains tax, excess net passive income tax, and LIFO recapture tax.
6. Income splitting between family members.	Only possible when earnings are distributed to shareholder. Dividends received by shareholder under age 18 (or, in some cases, ages 18 through 23) are taxed at parents' marginal tax rate.	Transfer of partnership interest by gift will permit income splitting. Subject to special rules for transactions involving family members requiring payment of reasonable compensation for capital and services. Income received by partner under age 18 is taxed at parents' marginal tax rate.	Transfer of S corporation interest by gift will permit income splitting. Special rules apply to transactions involving family members requiring payment of reasonable compensation for capital and services. Income received by shareholder under age 18 is taxed at parents' marginal tax rate.
7. Sale of ownership interest.	Gain is taxed as capital gain; 50% of gain may be excluded under Sec. 1202 qualified small business stock rules. Loss is eligible for Sec. 1244 treatment.	Gain may be either ordinary income or capital gain depending on the nature of underlying partnership assets. Losses usually are capital.	Gain is capital in nature but is not eligible for special Sec. 1202 small business stock rules. Loss is eligible for Sec. 1244 treatment.

V. Treatment of Special Income, Gain, Loss, Deduction and Credit Items

Tax Attribute	C Corporation	Partnership	S Corporation
1. Capital gains and losses.	Long-term capital gains are taxed at regular tax rates. Capital losses offset capital gains; excess losses carried back three years and forward five years.	Passed through to partners (according to partnership agreement).	Passed through to shareholders (on a daily basis according to stock ownership).
2. Section 1231 gains and losses.	Eligible for long-term capital gain or ordinary loss treatment. Loss recapture occurs at the corporate level.	Passed through to partners. Loss recapture occurs at the partner level.	Same as partnership.
3. Dividends received from domestic corporation.	Eligible for 70%, 80%, or 100% dividends-received deduction.	Passed through to noncorporate partners, subject to the maximum 15% tax rate if qualified. Corporate partners may be eligible for the dividends-received deduction.	Same as partnership except S corporation cannot have corporate shareholders.
4. U.S. production activities deduction.	Deduction equals a 9% (in 2011) times the lesser of (1) qualified production activities income for the year or (2) taxable income before the U.S. production activities deduction. The deduction, however, cannot exceed 50% of the corporation's W-2 wages allocable to U.S. production activities for the year.	Passed through to partners. Limitations apply at partner level.	Same as partnership.
5. Organizational expenditures.	Deduct up to $5,000 and amortize balance over 180 months.	Same as C corporation.	Same as partnership.
6. Charitable contributions.	Limited to 10% of taxable income.	Passed through to partners. Limitations apply at partner level.	Same as partnership.
7. Expensing of asset acquisition costs.	Limited to $500,000 (in 2011).	Limited to $500,000 (in 2011) for the partnership and for each partner.	Same as partnership.

APPENDIX F: COMPARISON OF TAX ATTRIBUTES FOR C CORPORATIONS, PARTNERSHIPS, AND S CORPORATIONS

Tax Attribute	C Corporation	Partnership	S Corporation
8. Expenses owed to related parties.	Regular Sec. 267 rules apply to payments and sales or exchanges made to or by the corporation and certain other related parties (e.g., controlling shareholder and corporation or members of a controlled group).	Regular Sec. 267 rules can apply. Special Sec. 267 rules for passthrough entities apply to payments made by the partnership to a partner.	Same as partnership.
9. Employment-related tax considerations.	An owner-employee may be treated as an employee for Social Security tax and corporate fringe benefit purposes. The corporate qualified pension and profit-sharing benefits available to owner-employees are comparable to the plan benefits for self-employed individuals (partners and sole proprietors).	A partner is not considered an employee of the business. Therefore, the partner must pay self-employment tax on the net self-employment income from the business. Corporate fringe benefit exclusions such as group term life insurance are not available (i.e., the premiums are not deductible by the business and are not excludable from the partner's income). Fringe benefits may be provided as nontaxable distribution or as taxable compensation.	Corporate fringe benefit exclusions generally are not available to S corporation shareholders. Fringe benefits usually are provided as nontaxable distribution or taxable compensation. S corporation shareholders may be treated as employees, however, for Social Security tax payments and qualified pension and profit sharing plan rules.
10. Tax preference items and AMT adjustments.	Subject to the corporate alternative minimum tax at the corporate level.	Passed through to partners and taxed under the alternative minimum tax rules applicable to the partner.	Same as partnership.

VI. Deductibility of Losses and Special Items

Tax Attribute	C Corporation	Partnership	S Corporation
1. Deductibility of losses.	Losses create net operating loss (NOL) that carry back two years (unless an extended carryback period applies) or forward 20 years or capital loss that carry back three years or forward five years.	Ordinary losses and separately stated loss and deduction items pass through to the partners at the end of the partnership tax year. May create a personal NOL.	Same as partnership.
2. Allocation of losses.	Not applicable.	Based on partnership agreement. Special allocations are permitted.	Based on stock ownership on each day of the tax year. Special allocations are not permitted.
3. Shareholder and entity loss limitations.	Passive losses may be restricted under the passive activity limitation if the C corporation is closely held.	Limited to partner's basis for the partnership interest. Ratable share of all partnership liabilities is included in basis of partnership interest. Excess losses carry over indefinitely until partnership interest again has a basis. Subject to at-risk, passive activity, and hobby loss restrictions.	Limited to shareholder's basis for the stock interest plus basis of S corporation debts to the shareholder. Excess losses carry over indefinitely until shareholder again has basis for stock or debt. Subject to the at-risk, passive activity, and hobby loss restrictions.
4. Basis adjustments for debt and equity interests.	Not applicable.	Basis in partnership interest reduced by loss and deduction passthrough. Subsequent profits increase basis of partnership interest.	Basis in S corporation stock reduced by loss and deduction passthrough. Once basis of stock has been reduced to zero, any other losses and deductions reduce basis of debt (but not below zero). Subsequent net increases restore basis reductions to debt before increasing basis of stock.

APPENDIX F: COMPARISON OF TAX ATTRIBUTES FOR C CORPORATIONS, PARTNERSHIPS, AND S CORPORATIONS

Tax Attribute	C Corporation	Partnership	S Corporation
5. Investment interest deduction limitation.	Not applicable.	Investment interest expenses and income pass through to the partners. Limitation applies at partner level.	Same as partnership.
VII. Distributions			
1. Taxability of nonliquidating distributions to shareholder.	Taxable as dividends if made from current or accumulated E&P. Additional distributions first reduce shareholder's basis for stock, and distributions exceeding stock basis trigger capital gain recognition.	Nontaxable unless money, money equivalents, or marketable securities received by the partner exceeds his or her basis for the partnership interest.	Nontaxable if made from the accumulated adjustment account or shareholder's basis for his or her stock. Taxable if made out of accumulated E&P or after stock basis has been reduced to zero.
2. Taxability of nonliquidating distributions to distributing entity.	Gain (but not loss) recognized as if the corporation had sold the property for its FMV immediately before the distribution.	No gain or loss recognized by the partnership except when a disproportionate distribution of Sec. 751 property occurs.	Gain (but not loss) recognized and passed through to the shareholders as if the corporation had sold the property for its FMV immediately before the distribution. Gain may be taxed to the S corporation under one of the special tax levies.
3. Basis adjustment to owner's investment for distribution.	None unless the distribution exceeds E&P.	Amount of money or adjusted basis of distributed property reduces basis in partnership interest.	Amount of money or FMV of distributed property reduces basis of stock except when distribution is made out of accumulated E&P.
VIII. Other Items			
1. Tax return.	Form 1120. Schedule M-3 may be required.	Form 1065 (Information Return). Schedule M-3 may be required.	Form 1120S (Information Return). Schedule M-3 may be required.
2. Due date.	March 15 for calendar year C corporations.	April 15 for calendar year partnerships.	March 15 for calendar year S corporations.
3. Extensions of time permitted.	Six months.	Five months.	Six months.
4. Estimated tax payments required.	Yes—April 15, June 15, September 15, and December 15 for calendar year C corporations.	No—Estimated taxes are required of the partners for passed through income, etc.	Yes—Applies to built-in gains tax and excess net passive income tax.
5. Audit rules.	IRS audits corporation independently of its shareholders.	Special audit rules apply requiring audit of partnership and requiring partners to take a position consistent with the partnership tax return.	Special rules require consistent tax treatment for Subchapter S items on the corporation and shareholder returns.

APPENDIX G

RESERVED

APPENDIX H

ACTUARIAL TABLES

TRANSFERS MADE AFTER APRIL 30, 2009
EXCERPT FROM TABLE S
SINGLE LIFE REMAINDER FACTORS

| | INTEREST RATE | | | | | | | |
AGE	2%	4%	6%	8%	AGE	2%	4%	6%	8%
25	.36464	.14924	.06960	.03724	58	.64573	.43790	.31103	.23053
26	.37134	.15440	.07288	.03929	59	.65553	.45041	.32348	.24197
27	.37819	.15980	.07639	.04153	60	.66534	.46310	.33625	.25380
28	.38520	.16542	.08012	.04396	61	.67515	.47595	.34933	.26603
29	.39233	.17126	.08406	.04656	62	.68494	.48892	.36267	.27862
30	.39959	.17730	.08820	.04933	63	.69470	.50200	.37625	.29155
31	.40698	.18355	.09255	.05229	64	.70443	.51519	.39010	.30484
32	.41449	.19002	.09712	.05543	65	.71411	.52849	.40420	.31850
33	.42213	.19671	.10192	.05878	66	.72385	.54203	.41872	.33273
34	.42988	.20360	.10693	.06231	67	.73359	.55575	.43363	.34749
35	.43774	.21070	.11217	.06605	68	.74331	.56963	.44887	.36272
36	.44572	.21803	.11764	.06999	69	.75299	.58360	.46438	.37837
37	.45381	.22557	.12335	.07416	70	.76260	.59764	.48013	.39443
38	.46201	.23334	.12932	.07856	71	.77215	.61176	.49614	.41090
39	.47032	.24133	.13554	.08320	72	.78162	.62593	.51237	.42776
40	.47873	.24954	.14201	.08807	73	.79098	.64009	.52876	.44494
41	.48724	.25797	.14873	.09319	74	.80019	.65417	.54523	.46235
42	.49585	.26662	.15572	.09856	75	.80923	.66813	.56169	.47991
43	.50457	.27552	.16301	.10422	76	.81807	.68192	.57810	.49754
44	.51338	.28465	.17057	.11016	77	.82671	.69553	.59444	.51525
45	.52228	.29400	.17843	.11640	78	.83515	.70894	.61068	.53298
46	.53129	.30360	.18659	.12294	79	.84337	.72213	.62680	.55071
47	.54037	.31343	.19505	.12980	80	.85135	.73507	.64272	.56836
48	.54955	.32351	.20383	.13699	81	.85910	.74773	.65844	.58590
49	.55882	.33383	.21294	.14453	82	.86660	.76009	.67391	.60330
50	.56819	.34442	.22242	.15247	83	.87385	.77214	.68909	.62050
51	.57766	.35528	.23226	.16080	84	.88084	.78385	.70396	.63745
52	.58722	.36641	.24249	.16957	85	.88757	.79521	.71849	.65412
53	.59687	.37781	.25309	.17876	86	.89402	.80619	.73264	.67046
54	.60658	.38945	.26406	.18837	87	.90021	.81679	.74638	.68642
55	.61635	.40131	.27537	.19838	88	.90612	.82700	.75971	.70200
56	.62613	.41335	.28697	.20875	89	.91176	.83681	.77259	.71714
57	.63593	.42555	.29887	.21947	90	.91713	.84620	.78500	.73181

Source: Reg. Sec. 20.2031-7T(d)(7).

EXCERPT FROM TABLE B
TERM CERTAIN REMAINDER FACTORS

YEARS	INTEREST RATE			
	2%	4%	6%	8%
1	.980392	.961538	.943396	.925926
2	.961169	.924556	.889996	.857339
3	.942322	.888996	.839619	.793832
4	.923845	.854804	.792094	.735030
5	.905731	.821927	.747258	.680583
6	.887971	.790315	.704961	.630170
7	.870560	.759918	.665057	.583490
8	.853490	.730690	.627412	.540269
9	.836755	.702587	.591898	.500249
10	.820348	.675564	.558395	.463193
11	.804263	.649581	.526788	.428883
12	.788493	.624597	.496969	.397114
13	.773033	.600574	.468839	.367698
14	.757875	.577475	.442301	.340461
15	.743015	.555265	.417265	.315242
16	.728446	.533908	.393646	.291890
17	.714163	.513373	.371364	.270269
18	.700159	.493628	.350344	.250249
19	.686431	.474642	.330513	.231712
20	.672971	.456387	.311805	.214548
21	.659776	.438834	.294155	.198656
22	.646839	.421955	.277505	.183941
23	.634156	.405726	.261797	.170315
24	.621721	.390121	.246979	.157699
25	.609531	.375117	.232999	.146018

Source: Reg. Secs. 20.7520-1(a)(1) and 20.2031-7(d)(6).

APPENDIX K

INDEX OF GOVERNMENT PROMULGATIONS

INDEX OF COURT CASES

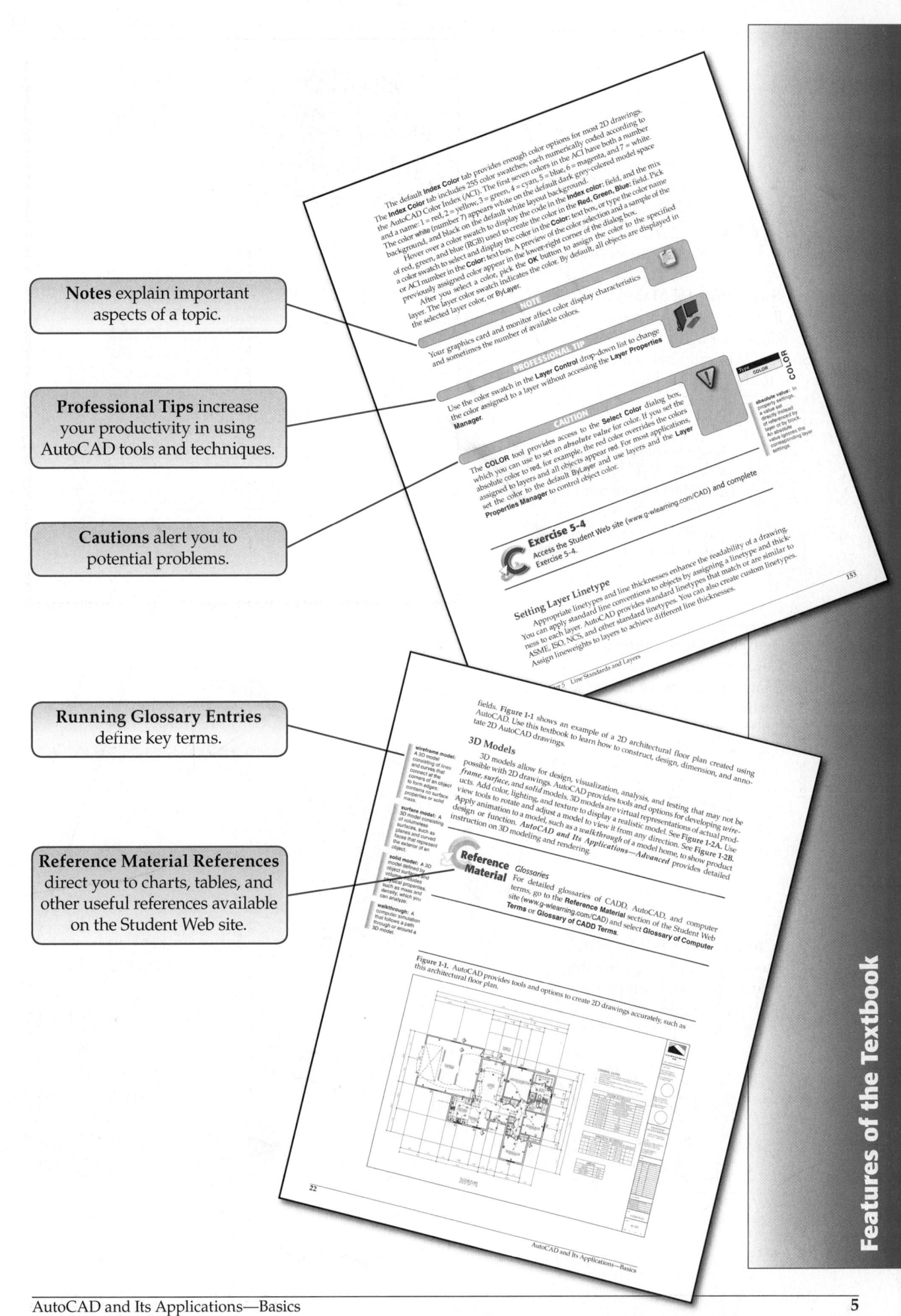

Notes explain important aspects of a topic.

Professional Tips increase your productivity in using AutoCAD tools and techniques.

Cautions alert you to potential problems.

Running Glossary Entries define key terms.

Reference Material References direct you to charts, tables, and other useful references available on the Student Web site.

Features of the Textbook

Exercise References direct you to exercises on the Student Web site.

Supplemental Material References direct you to additional material on the Student Web site that is relevant to the current chapter.

Express Tool References direct you to information on the Student Web site about AutoCAD Express Tools.

Template Development References direct you to Template Development material on the Student Web site.

Chapter Tests reinforce the knowledge gained by reading the chapter and completing the exercises.

---

the plot, pick **Click to view plot and publish details...** to display the **Plot and Publish Details** dialog box. You can also access the **Plot and Publish Details** dialog box using the **VIEWPLOTDETAILS** tool.

NOTE

AutoCAD provides additional tools for exporting drawings, automating the process of transmitting drawings electronically (**eTransmit**), and *publishing*. Publishing a set of sheets is described later in this textbook.

publishing: Preparing a sequential set of multiple drawings for hard copy or electronic plotting of the set.

Exercise 29-9

Access the Student Web site (www.g-wlearning.com/CAD) and complete Exercise 29-9.

Plotting to a PLT File

If a plot device is not available, but you are ready to plot, an alternative is to plot to a file. A plot file saves with a PLT extension. The file stores all the drawing geometry, plot styles, and plot settings assigned to the drawing. Some offices or schools with only one printer or plotter attach a *plot spooler* to the printer or plotter to plot a PLT file. The plot spooler device usually allows you to take a PLT file from a storage disk and copy it to the plot spooler, which in turn plots the drawing.

plot spooler: A disk drive with memory that allows you to plot files.

To plot to a file, open the **Plot** dialog box, select the plot device from the **Name:** drop-down list, and check the **Plot to file** check box. The setting in the **Plot and Publish** tab of the **Options** dialog box determines the location in which the plot file is saved. To specify the path, pick the ellipsis (...) button for the **Select default location for all plot-to-file operations** dialog box.

Supplemental Material — *Additional Plotting Options*
For information about several additional plot settings in the **Plot and Publish** tab of the **Options** dialog box, go to the Student Web site (www.g-wlearning.com/CAD), select this chapter, and select **Additional Plotting Options**.

Express Tools Chapter 29 — The **Layout** panel of the **Express Tools** ribbon tab includes additional layout tools. For information about the most useful layout express tools, go to the Student Web site (www.g-wlearning.com/CAD), select this chapter, and select **Layout Express Tools**.

Template Development Chapter 8 — For detailed instructions on choosing a more appropriate point style to use for construction purposes, go to the Student Web site (www.g-wlearning.com/CAD), select this chapter, and select **Template Development**.

Chapter Test

Answer the following questions. Write your answers on a separate sheet of paper or go to the Student Web site (www.g-wlearning.com/CAD) and complete the electronic chapter test.

1. List two ways to establish an offset distance using the **OFFSET** tool.
2. Which option of the **OFFSET** tool allows you to remove the source offset object?
3. How do you draw a single point, and how do you draw multiple points?
4. How do you access the **Point Style** dialog box?
5. If you use the **DIVIDE** tool and nothing seems to happen, what should you do to make the points more visible?
6. How do you change the point size in the **Point Style** dialog box?
7. What tool can you use to place point objects that mark 24 equal segments on a line?
8. What is the difference between the **DIVIDE** and **MEASURE** tools?
9. Why is it a good idea to put construction lines on their own layer?
10. Name the option that allows you to draw infinite construction lines.
11. What is the difference between the construction lines drawn with a construction line and rays drawn with the **RAY** tool?
12. What in Question 10 and rays drawn with the **RAY** tool?
13. What ASME drafting standard applies to multiview drawings?
14. Provide at least four guidelines for selecting the front view of an orthographic multiview drawing.
15. How do you determine how many views of an object are necessary in a multiview drawing?
16. When can you describe a part with only one view?
17. When does a drawing require an auxiliary view, and what does an auxiliary view show?
18. List two methods of aligning the views in a multiview drawing.
19. What is the angle of projection from the slanted surface into the auxiliary view?
20. Describe an effective method of constructing an auxiliary view even if you do not know the angle of the inclined surface.

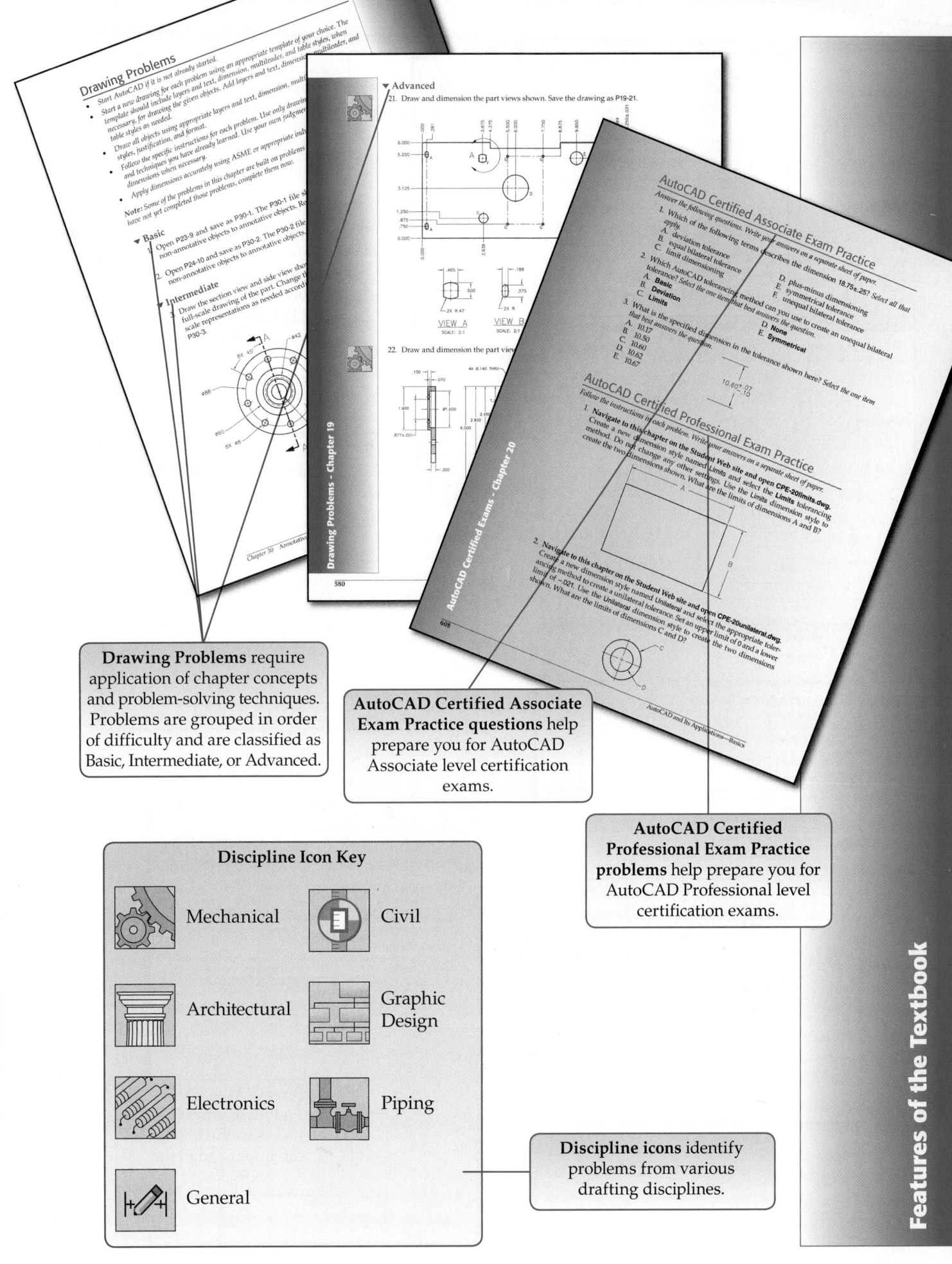

Drawing Problems require application of chapter concepts and problem-solving techniques. Problems are grouped in order of difficulty and are classified as Basic, Intermediate, or Advanced.

AutoCAD Certified Associate Exam Practice questions help prepare you for AutoCAD Associate level certification exams.

AutoCAD Certified Professional Exam Practice problems help prepare you for AutoCAD Professional level certification exams.

Discipline Icon Key

Mechanical

Civil

Architectural

Graphic Design

Electronics

Piping

General

Discipline icons identify problems from various drafting disciplines.

Features of the Textbook

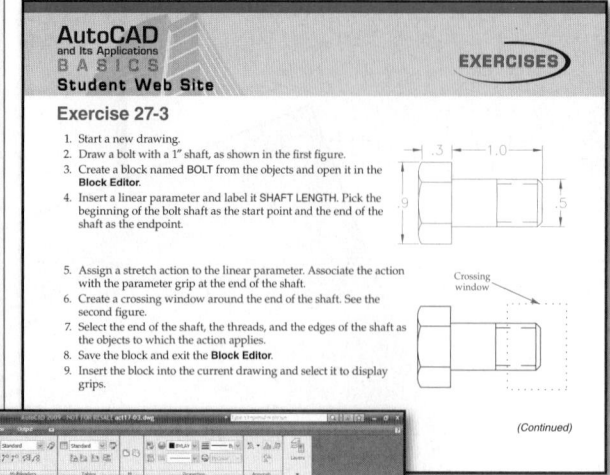

(Continued)

Exercises. Chapter exercises are provided on the Student Web site, allowing you to switch between the exercise directions and AutoCAD on-screen.

AutoCAD Software. Pick this button to access a Web site from which you can download the AutoCAD software at no cost for use with this book.

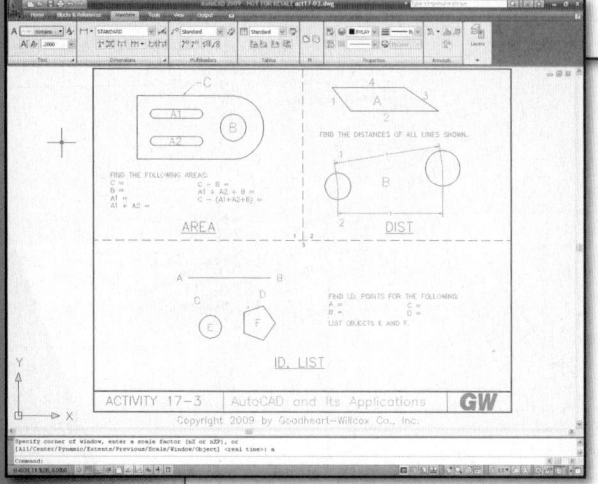

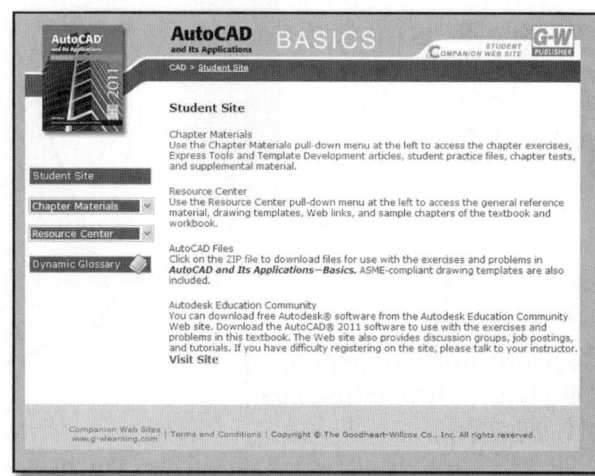

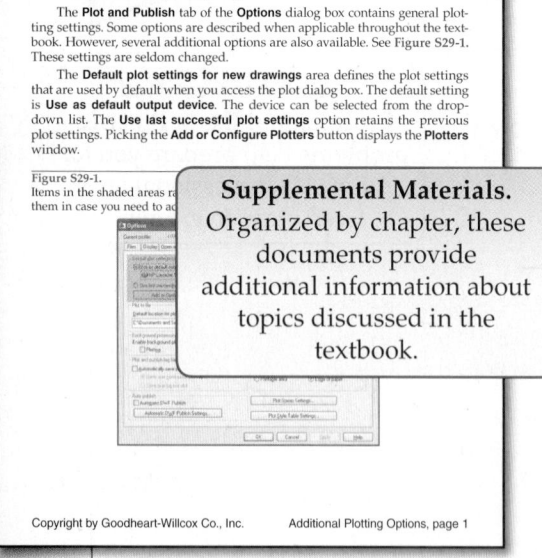

Supplemental Materials. Organized by chapter, these documents provide additional information about topics discussed in the textbook.

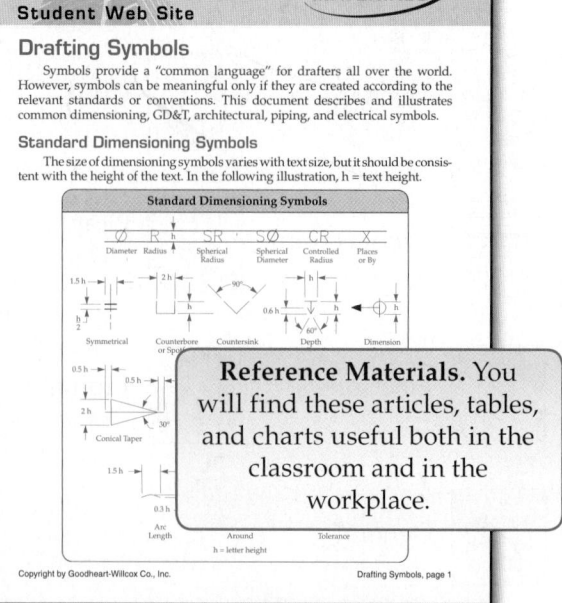

Reference Materials. You will find these articles, tables, and charts useful both in the classroom and in the workplace.

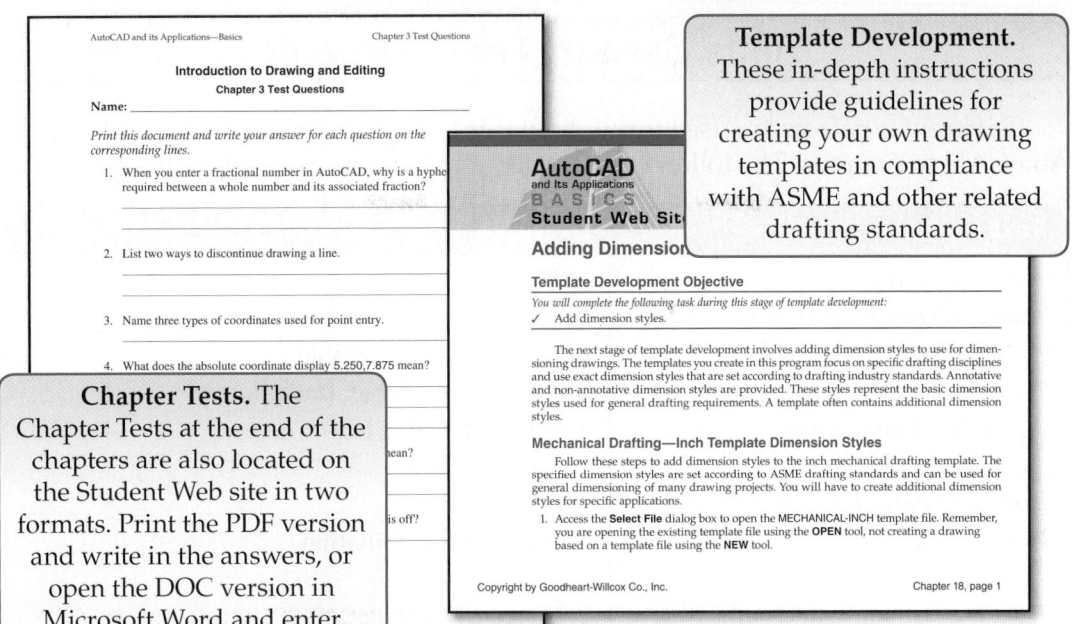

Chapter Tests. The Chapter Tests at the end of the chapters are also located on the Student Web site in two formats. Print the PDF version and write in the answers, or open the DOC version in Microsoft Word and enter your answers electronically.

Template Development. These in-depth instructions provide guidelines for creating your own drawing templates in compliance with ASME and other related drafting standards.

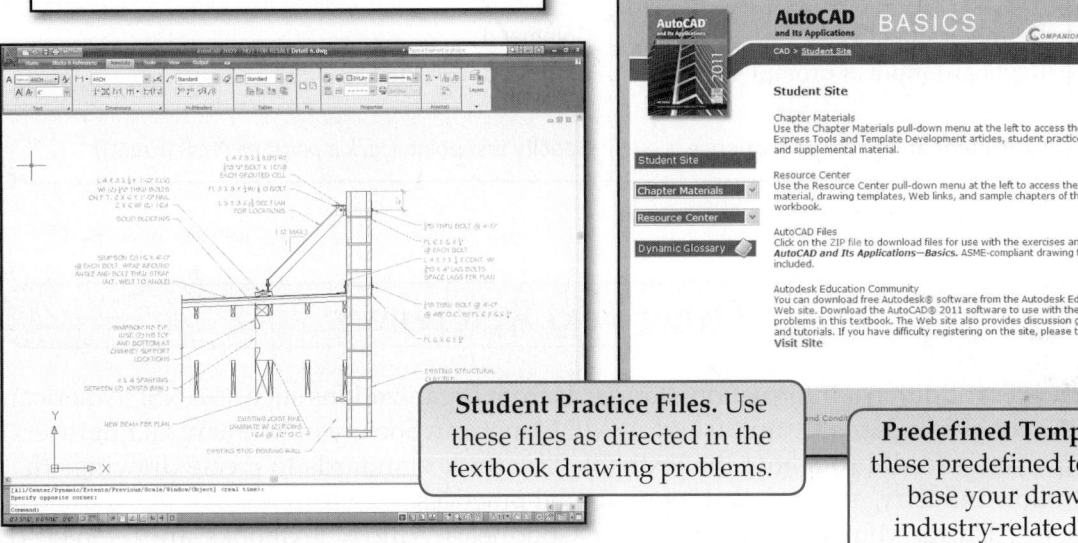

Student Practice Files. Use these files as directed in the textbook drawing problems.

Predefined Templates. Use these predefined templates to base your drawings on industry-related drawing standards and conventions.

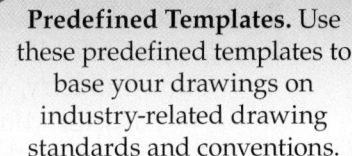

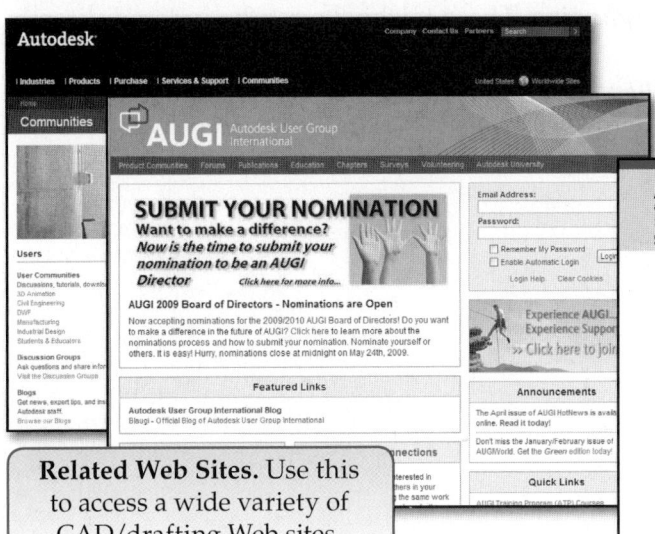

Related Web Sites. Use this to access a wide variety of CAD/drafting Web sites.

Express Tools Material. Express Tools are supplemental AutoCAD functions. Notes in the textbook refer to these components.

Features of the Student Web Site

Fonts Used in This Textbook

Different typefaces are used throughout this textbook to define terms and identify AutoCAD commands. The following typeface conventions are used in this textbook:

Text Element	Example
AutoCAD tools	**LINE** tool
AutoCAD menu browser menus	**Draw > Arc > 3 Points**
AutoCAD system variables	**LTSCALE** system variable
AutoCAD toolbars and buttons	**Quick Access** toolbar, **Undo** button
AutoCAD dialog boxes	**Insert Table** dialog box
Keyboard entry (in text)	Type LINE
Keyboard keys	[Ctrl]+[1] key combination
File names, folders, and paths	C:\Program Files\AutoCAD 2011\mydrawing.dwg
Microsoft Windows features	Start menu, Programs folder
Prompt sequence	Command:
Keyboard input at prompt sequence	Command: **L** *or* **LINE**↵
Comment at a prompt sequence	Specify first point: (*pick a point or press* [Enter])

Other Text References

For additional information, standards from organizations such as ANSI (American National Standards Institute) and ASME (American Society of Mechanical Engineers) are referenced throughout the textbook. Use these standards to create drawings that follow industry, national, and international practices.

Also for your convenience, other Goodheart-Willcox textbooks are referenced. Referenced textbooks include *AutoCAD and Its Applications—Advanced* and *Geometric Dimensioning and Tolerancing*. These textbooks can be ordered directly from Goodheart-Willcox.

AutoCAD and Its Applications—Basics covers basic AutoCAD applications. For a textbook covering the advanced AutoCAD applications, please refer to *AutoCAD and Its Applications—Advanced*.

Contents in Brief

About the Authors

Terence M. Shumaker is Faculty Emeritus, the former Chairperson of the Drafting Technology Department, and former Director of the Autodesk Premier Training Center at Clackamas Community College. Terence taught at the community college level for over 25 years. He has professional experience in surveying, civil drafting, industrial piping, and technical illustration. He is the author of Goodheart-Willcox's *Process Pipe Drafting* and coauthor of the *AutoCAD and Its Applications* series.

David A. Madsen is the president of Madsen Designs Inc. (www.madsendesigns.com). David is Faculty Emeritus and the former Chairperson of Drafting Technology and the Autodesk Premier Training Center at Clackamas Community College in Oregon City, Oregon. David was an instructor and a department chairperson at Clackamas Community College for nearly 30 years. In addition to teaching at the community college level, David was a Drafting Technology instructor at Centennial High School in Gresham, Oregon. David is a former member of the American Design Drafting Association (ADDA) Board of Directors. He was honored with Director Emeritus status by the ADDA in 2005. David has extensive experience in mechanical drafting, architectural design and drafting, and building construction. He holds a Master of Education degree in Vocational Administration and a Bachelor of Science degree in Industrial Education. David is coauthor of the *AutoCAD and Its Applications* series, *Architectural Drafting Using AutoCAD*, *Geometric Dimensioning and Tolerancing*, and other drafting and design textbooks.

David P. Madsen is the vice president of Madsen Designs Inc. (www.madsendesigns.com) and operates the Madsen Designs Inc. consulting service. Dave has been a professional drafter since 1996 and has extensive experience in a variety of drafting, design, and engineering disciplines. Dave has provided drafting and computer-aided design and drafting instruction to secondary and postsecondary learners since 1999. He has extensive curriculum experience, in addition to considerable program coordination and development experience. Dave holds a Master of Science degree in Educational Policy, Foundations, and Administrative Studies with a specialization in Postsecondary, Adult, and Continuing Education; a Bachelor of Science degree in Technology Education; and an Associate of Science degree in General Studies and Drafting Technology. Dave is the author of the Goodheart-Willcox textbook *Inventor and Its Applications* and coauthor of *AutoCAD and Its Applications—Basics*, *AutoCAD and Its Applications—Comprehensive*, *Architectural Drafting Using AutoCAD*, and *Geometric Dimensioning and Tolerancing*.

Acknowledgments

Technical Assistance and Contribution of Materials

Margo Bilson of Willamette Industries, Inc.
Fitzgerald, Hagan, & Hackathorn
Bruce L. Wilcox, Johnson and Wales University School of Technology

Contribution of Technical Information

Arthur Baker	International Source for Ergonomics
Autodesk	Jim Webster
CADalyst magazine	Kunz Associates
CADENCE magazine	Myonetics, Inc.
Chris Lindner	Norwest Engineering
EPCM Services, Ltd.	Schuchart & Associates, Inc.
Harris Group, Inc.	Willamette Industries, Inc.

Trademarks

Autodesk, the Autodesk logo, AutoCAD, DesignCenter, AutoCAD Learning Assistance, AutoSnap, and AutoTrack are either registered trademarks or trademarks of Autodesk, Inc. in the U.S.A. and/or other countries.

Microsoft, Windows, and Windows Vista are registered trademarks of Microsoft Corporation in the United States and/or other countries.

Contents

Basic Drawing and Printing

Dimensioning and Tolerancing

Using Layouts

Student Web Site Content

Using the Web Site

Express Tools

Exercises

Template Development

Chapter Tests

Reference Materials

Supplemental Materials

Student Practice Files

Predefined Templates

Download Student AutoCAD

Related Web Links

Introduction to AutoCAD

Learning Objectives

After completing this chapter, you will be able to do the following:

✓ Define computer-aided design and drafting.
✓ Describe typical AutoCAD applications.
✓ Explain the value of planning your work and system management.
✓ Describe the purpose and importance of drawing standards.
✓ Demonstrate how to start and exit AutoCAD.
✓ Recognize the AutoCAD interface and access AutoCAD tools.
✓ Use help resources.

Computer-aided design and drafting (CADD) is the process of using a computer with CADD software to design and produce drawings and models according to specific industry and company standards. The terms *computer-aided design (CAD)* and *computer-aided drafting (CAD)* refer to specific aspects of the CADD process. This chapter introduces the AutoCAD CADD system. You will begin working with AutoCAD and learn to control the AutoCAD environment.

> **computer-aided design and drafting (CADD):** The process of using a computer with CADD software to design and produce drawings and models.

AutoCAD Applications

AutoCAD *tools* and *options* allow you to draw objects of any size or shape. Use AutoCAD to prepare two-dimensional (2D) drawings, three-dimensional (3D) models, and animations. AutoCAD is a universal CADD program that applies to any drafting, design, or engineering discipline. For example, you can use AutoCAD to design and document mechanical parts and assemblies, architectural buildings, civil and structural engineering projects, and electronics.

> **tool (command):** An instruction issued to the computer to complete a specific task. For example, use the **LINE** tool to draw lines.

> **option:** A choice associated with a tool, or an alternative function of a tool.

2D Drawings

2D drawings display object length and width, or width and height, in a flat (2D) form. 2D drawings are useful for documenting engineering and design requirements. A 2D drawing typically includes dimensions and annotations that fully describe features on the drawing. This practice results in a document used to manufacture or construct a product. 2D drawings are common in all drafting, design, and engineering fields. **Figure 1-1** shows an example of a 2D architectural floor plan created using AutoCAD. Use this textbook to learn how to construct, design, dimension, and annotate 2D AutoCAD drawings.

3D Models

3D models allow for design, visualization, analysis, and testing that may not be possible with 2D drawings. AutoCAD provides tools and options for developing *wireframe*, *surface*, and *solid* models. 3D models are virtual representations of actual products. Add color, lighting, and texture to display a realistic model. See **Figure 1-2A**. Use view tools to rotate and adjust a model to view it from any direction. See **Figure 1-2B**. Apply animation to a model, such as a *walkthrough* of a model home, to show product design or function. *AutoCAD and Its Applications—Advanced* provides detailed instruction on 3D modeling and rendering.

Reference Material

Glossaries

For detailed glossaries of CADD, AutoCAD, and computer terms, go to the **Reference Material** section of the Student Web site (www.g-wlearning.com/CAD) and select **Glossary of Computer Terms** or **Glossary of CADD Terms**.

Figure 1-1. AutoCAD provides tools and options to create 2D drawings accurately, such as this architectural floor plan.

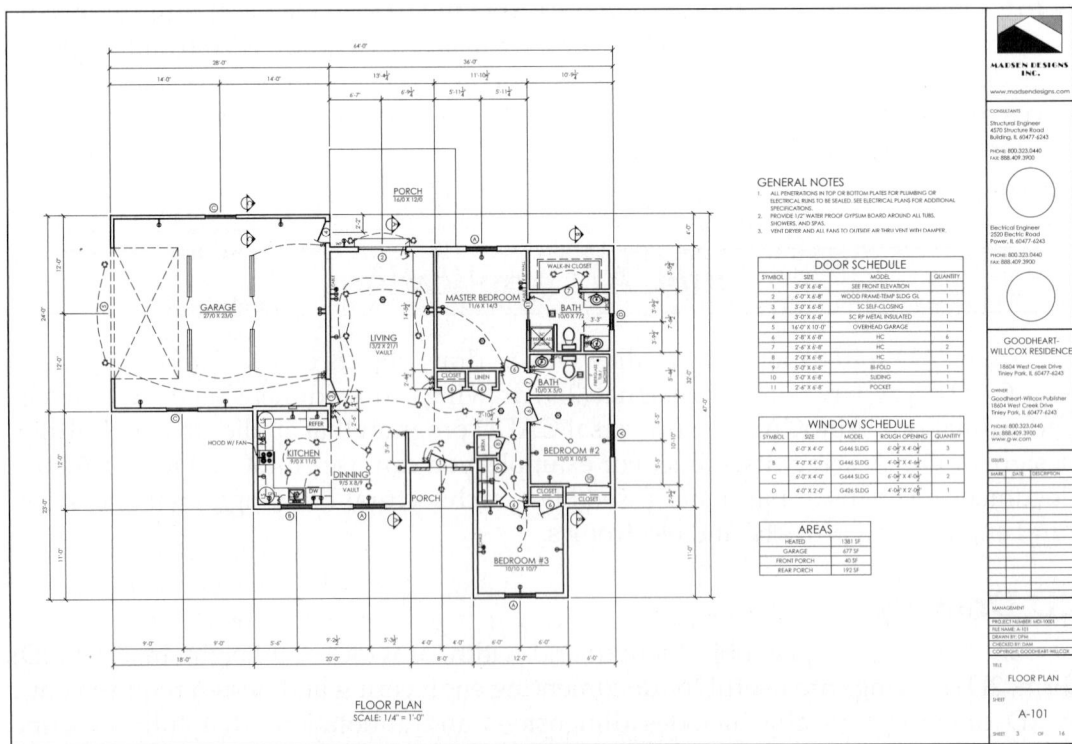

Figure 1-2. A 3D AutoCAD model of a mechanical assembly. A—A wireframe model (left) with realistic colors and textures added (right). B—You can rotate, zoom in and out, and view a model from any location in 3D space.

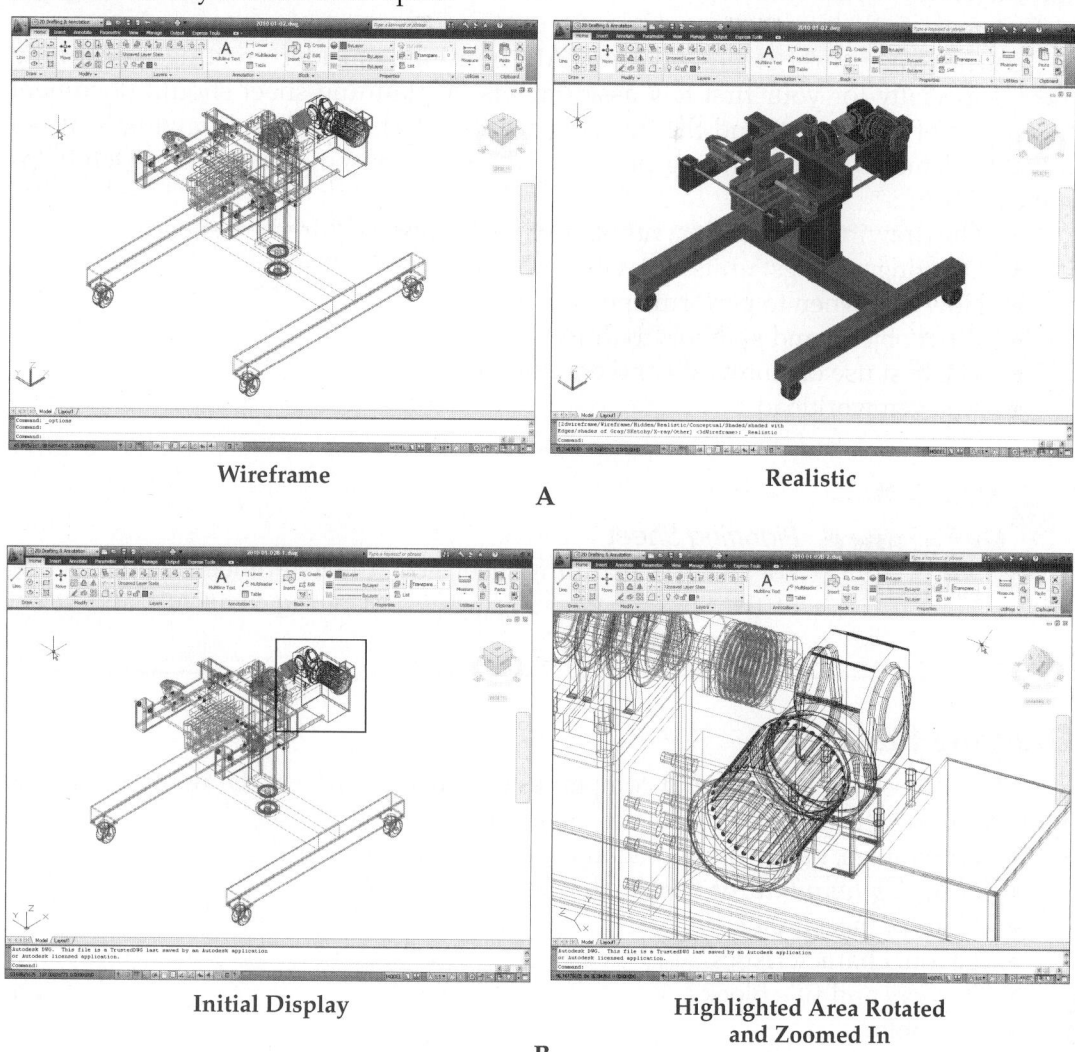

Wireframe   Realistic

A

Initial Display   Highlighted Area Rotated
                              and Zoomed In

B

Before You Begin

Designing and drafting effectively with a computer requires a skilled CADD operator. To be a proficient AutoCAD user, you must have detailed knowledge of AutoCAD tools and processes, and know when each tool and process is best suited for a specific task. You must also understand and be able to apply design and drafting systems and conventions when using AutoCAD.

As you begin your CADD training, develop effective methods for managing your work. First, plan your *drawing sessions* thoroughly to organize your thoughts. Second, learn and use industry, classroom, or office standards. Third, save your work often. If you follow these procedures, you will find it easier to use AutoCAD tools and methods, and your drawing experience will be more productive and enjoyable.

drawing sessions: Time spent working on a drawing project, including analyzing design parameters and using AutoCAD.

Planning Your Work

A drawing plan involves thinking about the entire process or project in which you are involved and determining how to approach a project. Your drawing plan focuses on the content you want to present, the objects and symbols you intend to create, and the appropriate use of standards. You may want processes to happen immediately or to be automatic, but if you hurry and do little or no planning, you may become frustrated and waste time while drawing. Take as much time as needed to develop drawing and project goals so that you can proceed with confidence.

During your early stages of AutoCAD training, consider creating a planning sheet, especially for your first few assignments. A planning sheet should document all aspects of a drawing, and the drawing session. A sketch of the drawing is also a valuable element of the planning process. Creating a drawing plan and sketch helps you establish:

- The drawing layout: area, number of views, and required free space
- Drawing settings: units, drawing aids, layers, and styles
- How and when to perform specific tasks
- What objects and symbols to draw
- The best use of AutoCAD and equipment
- An even workload

Reference Material

Planning Sheet
For a sample planning sheet, go to the **Reference Material** section of the Student Web site (www.g-wlearning.com/CAD) and select **Planning Sheet**.

Drawing Standards

standards: Guidelines that specify drawing requirements, appearance, and techniques, operating procedures, and record keeping methods.

Most industries, schools, and companies establish *standards*. Drawing standards apply to most settings and procedures, including:

- File storage, naming, and backup
- *Drawing template*, or *template*, files
- Units of measurement
- Layout characteristics
- Borders and title blocks
- Symbols
- Layers
- Text, table, dimension, and multileader styles
- Plot styles and plotting

drawing template (template): A file that contains standard drawing settings and objects for use in new drawings.

Company or school drawing standards should follow appropriate national industry standards whenever possible. Although standards vary in content, the most important aspect is that standards exist and are understood and used by all CADD personnel. When you follow drawing standards, drawings are consistent, you become more productive, and the classroom or office functions more efficiently.

This textbook presents mechanical drafting standards developed by the American Society of Mechanical Engineers (ASME) and accredited by the American National Standards Institute (ANSI). This textbook also references International Standards Organization (ISO) mechanical drafting standards, and discipline-specific standards when appropriate, including the United States National CAD Standard® (NCS) and American Welding Society (AWS) standards.

Reference Material

Drawing Standards
For more information about drawing standards, go to the **Reference Material** section of the Student Web site (www.g-wlearning.com/CAD) and select **Drawing Standards**.

You may consider other drafting standards when preparing drawings, such as the *BSI*, *DIN*, *GB*, *GOST*, and *JIS* standards.

BSI: The British Standards Institution.

DIN: Deutsches Institut Für Normung, established by the German Institute for Standardization.

GB: Chinese Guóbiāo standard.

GOST: Gosudarstvennyy standart, maintained by the Euro-Asian Council for Standardization.

JIS: Japanese Industrial Standards.

Saving Your Work

Drawings are lost due to software error, hardware malfunction, power failure, or accident. Prepare for such an event by saving your work frequently. Develop a habit of saving your work at least every 10 to 15 minutes. You can set the automatic save option, described in Chapter 2, to save drawings automatically at set intervals. However, you should also frequently save your work manually.

Working Procedures Checklist

Proficient use of AutoCAD requires several skills. Use the following checklist to become comfortable with AutoCAD, and to help you work quickly and efficiently:

✓ Carefully plan your work
✓ Frequently check object and drawing settings, such as layers, styles, and properties, to see which object characteristics and drawing options are in effect
✓ Follow the prompts, tooltips, notifications, and *alerts* that appear as you work
✓ Constantly check for the correct options, instructions, or keyboard entry
✓ *Right-click* to access shortcut menus and review available options
✓ Think ahead to prepare for each stage of the drawing session
✓ Learn tools and options that increase your speed and efficiency
✓ Save your work at least every 10 to 15 minutes
✓ Learn to use available resources, such as this textbook, to help solve problems and answer questions

alert: A pop-up that indicates a required action or potential problem.

right-click: Use the right mouse button to select.

Workplace Comfort
For information about maintaining comfort and productivity while operating a CADD workstation, go to the Student Web site (www.g-wlearning.com/CAD), select this chapter, and select **Workplace Comfort**.

Exercise 1-1

Access the Student Web site (www.g-wlearning.com/CAD) and complete Exercise 1-1.

double-click: Quickly press the left mouse button twice to select.

icon: Small graphic representing an application, file, or tool.

Starting AutoCAD

pick (click): Press the left mouse button to select.

button: A "hot spot" on the screen that you pick to access an application, tool, or option.

One of the quickest methods to start AutoCAD is to *double-click* on the AutoCAD 2011 Windows desktop *icon*. The desktop icon is set to appear during AutoCAD installation. A second option is to *pick* the Start *button* in the lower-left corner of the Windows desktop, then *hover* over or pick Programs, then select Autodesk, followed by AutoCAD 2011, and finally AutoCAD 2011.

NOTE

AutoCAD 2011 operates with Windows 7 and specific versions of Windows Vista and Windows XP. Do not be concerned if you see illustrations in this textbook that appear slightly different from those on your screen.

Initial Setup

The **Initial Setup** wizard appears when you first launch AutoCAD. See **Figure 1-3.** The **Initial Setup** wizard guides you through the initial process of building a custom work environment according to the type of drawings you create, tools you commonly use, and the drawing template you use most often.

If you are a new AutoCAD user, you may not recognize most of the choices in the **Initial Setup** wizard. Additionally, this textbook explains 2D drawing applications related to a variety of drafting, design, and engineering disciplines. Therefore, pick the **Skip** button on the first page of the **Initial Setup** wizard to exit setup. Select the **Start AutoCAD 2011** button to launch AutoCAD. When you skip the initial setup, AutoCAD loads the *default* **2D Drafting & Annotation** workspace, which is appropriate for use with this textbook.

NOTE

To access the **Initial Setup** wizard at any time, pick the **Initial Setup...** button on the **User Preferences** tab of the **Options** dialog box. To display the **Options** dialog box, pick the **Options** button at the bottom of the **Application Menu**.

Exiting AutoCAD

Access the **EXIT** tool to end an AutoCAD session. Pick the program **Close** button, located in the upper-right corner of the AutoCAD window; double-click the **Application Menu** button in the upper-left corner of the AutoCAD window; select the **Exit AutoCAD** button in the **Application Menu**; or with a file open, type EXIT or QUIT and press [Enter]. See **Figure 1-4.**

NOTE

If you attempt to exit before saving your work, AutoCAD prompts you to save or discard changes.

Figure 1-3. Use the **Initial Setup** wizard to customize AutoCAD initially according to discipline, interface, and template preferences.

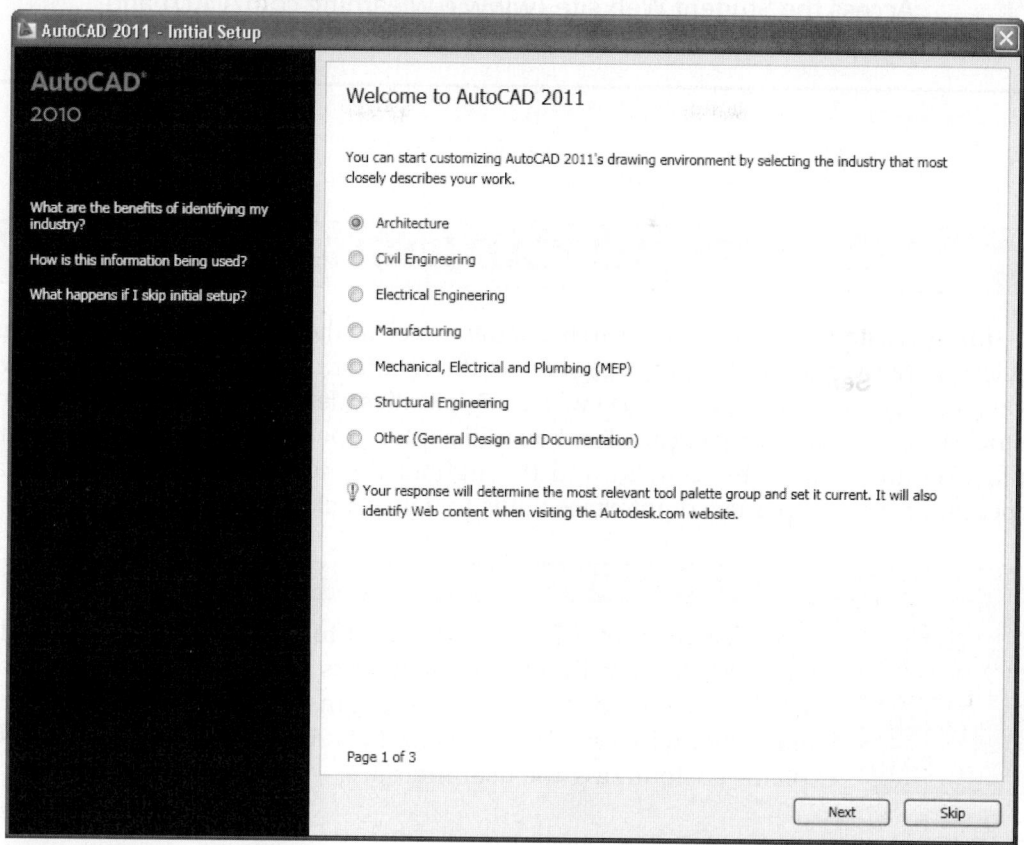

Figure 1-4. Use any of several techniques to exit AutoCAD when you finish a drawing session.

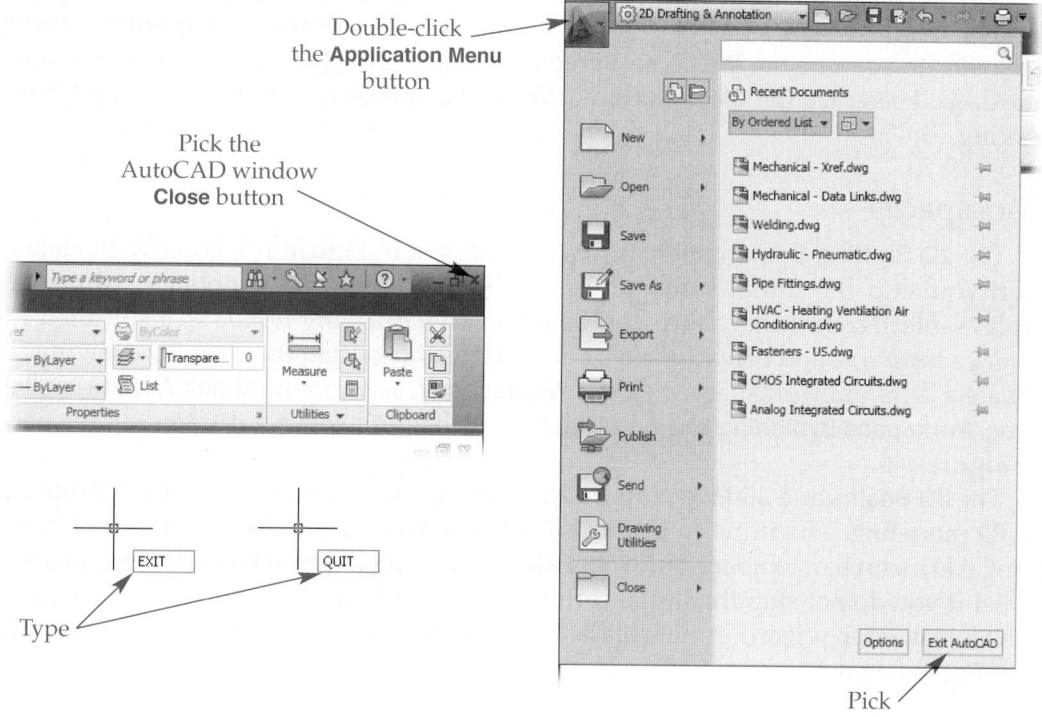

Exercise 1-2

Access the Student Web site (www.g-wlearning.com/CAD) and complete Exercise 1-2.

The AutoCAD Interface

interface: Items that allow you to input data to and receive outputs from a computer system.

graphical user interface (GUI): On-screen features that allow you to interact with a software program.

Interface items include devices to input data, such as the keyboard and mouse, and devices to receive computer outputs, such as the monitor. AutoCAD uses a Windows-style *graphical user interface (GUI)* with an **Application Menu**, ribbon, dialog boxes, and AutoCAD-specific items. See **Figure 1-5.** You will explore specific elements of the unique AutoCAD interface in this chapter and throughout this textbook. Learn the format, appearance, and proper use of interface items to help quickly master AutoCAD.

> **NOTE**
>
> As you learn AutoCAD, you may want to customize the graphical user interface according to common tasks and specific applications. Customize AutoCAD manually or begin customization using the **Initial Setup** window. *AutoCAD and Its Applications—Advanced* explains customizing the user interface.

AutoCAD
NEW

Welcome Screen

The **Welcome Screen** is an element of the AutoCAD help system and appears by default when you launch AutoCAD. Refer again to **Figure 1-5.** Pick an option from the menu to view a video of the selected topic. You can also access additional help system features, described later in this chapter. Deselect the **Show this dialog box at startup** *check box* to prevent the **Welcome Screen** from appearing the next time you launch AutoCAD. Then pick the **Close** button of **Welcome Screen** to exit the screen and begin working.

check box: A selectable box that turns an item on (when checked) or off (when unchecked).

Workspaces

workspace: Preset work environment containing specific interface items.

drawing window (graphics window): The largest area in the AutoCAD window, where drawing and modeling occurs.

flyout: Set of related buttons that appear when you pick the arrow next to certain tool buttons.

The **2D Drafting & Annotation** *workspace,* shown in **Figure 1-5,** is active by default when you skip the initial setup process. The **2D Drafting & Annotation** workspace displays interface features above and below a large *drawing window,* also called the *graphics window,* and contains tools and options most often used for 2D drawing. To activate a different workspace, pick the **Workspace** *flyout* on the **Quick Access** toolbar or the **Workspace Switching** button on the status bar and select a different workspace. See **Figure 1-6.**

The **3D Basics** and **3D Modeling** workspaces provide tools and options appropriate for 3D modeling. The universal **AutoCAD Classic** workspace displays the traditional AutoCAD menu bar, toolbars, and **Tool Palettes.** The **Initial Setup Workspace** appears in the list if you do not skip the initial setup process, and includes the settings specified in the **Initial Setup** wizard. A new **Initial Setup Workspace** forms each time you use the **Initial Setup** wizard.

Figure 1-5. The default AutoCAD window with the **2D Drafting & Annotation** workspace active.

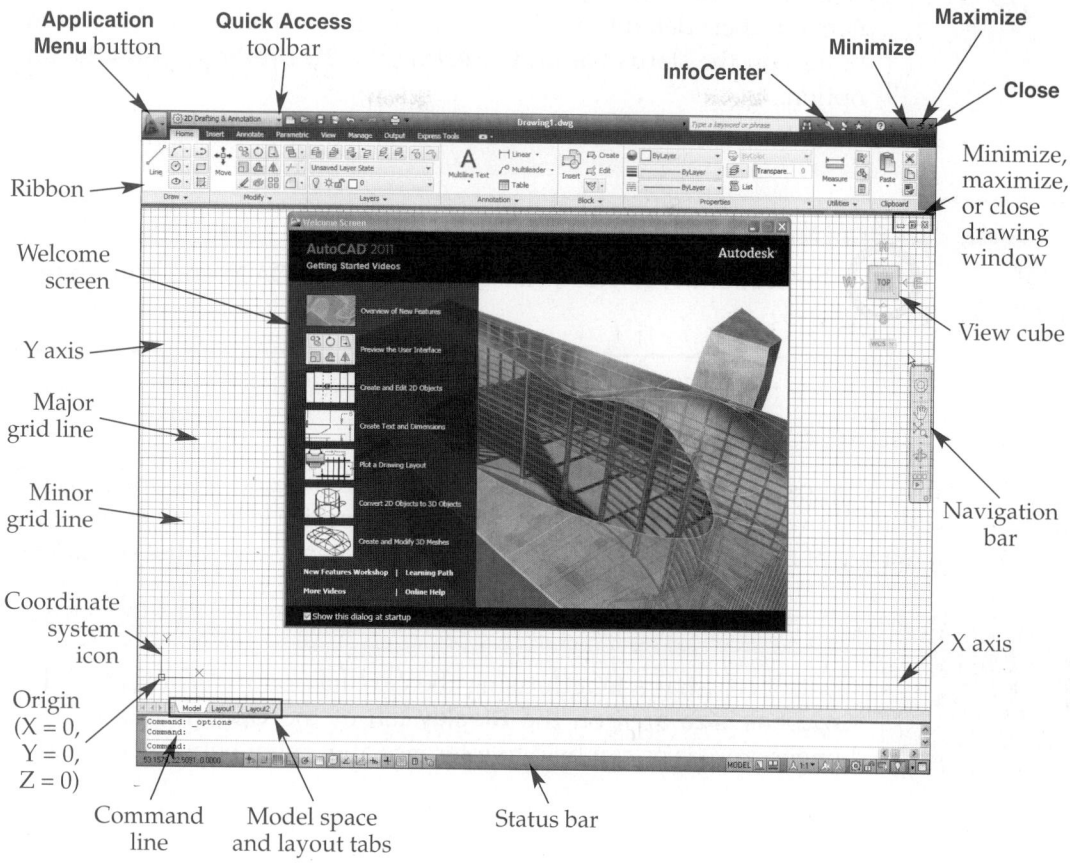

Figure 1-6. Use the **Workspace Switching** flyout on the **Quick Access** toolbar or the **Workspace Switching** button on the status bar to change to a different workspace, create a new workspace, or customize the user interface.

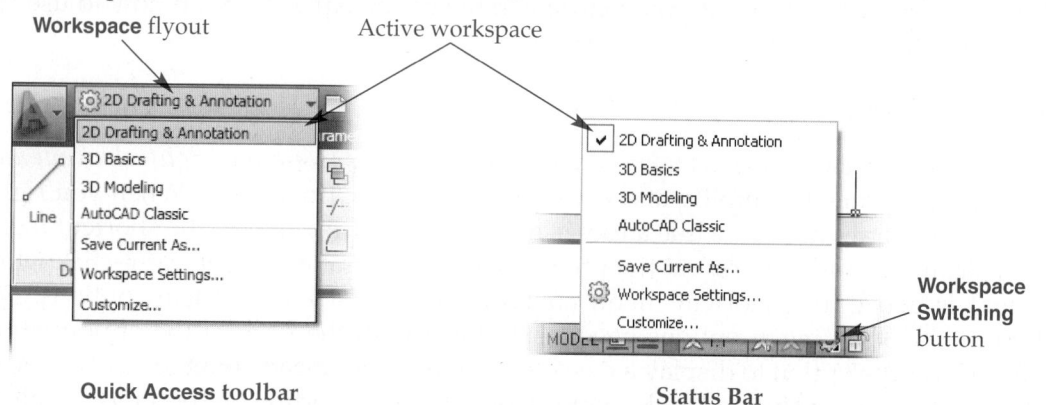

Quick Access toolbar

Status Bar

NOTE

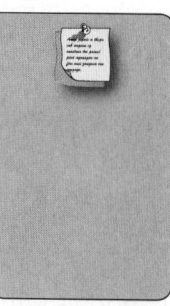

This textbook focuses on the default **2D Drafting & Annotation** workspace, except in specific situations that require additional interface items. The default model space drawing window background color is dark gray (33,40,48), but this textbook shows a white background for clarity. Add items and AutoCAD tools to the interface as needed. *AutoCAD and Its Applications—Advanced* details the **3D Modeling** workspace and explains how to customize a workspace.

Reload the **2D Drafting & Annotation** workspace to return interface items to their default locations by picking the **Workspace Switching** button on the status bar and selecting the **2D Drafting & Annotation** option.

Exercise 1-3

Access the Student Web site (www.g-wlearning.com/CAD) and complete Exercise 1-3.

Crosshairs and Cursor

The AutoCAD crosshairs is the primary means of pointing to and selecting objects or locations within a drawing. The crosshairs changes to the familiar Windows cursor when you move it outside of the drawing area or over an interface item, such as the status bar.

Control crosshairs length using the *text box* or *slider* found in the **Crosshair size** area on the **Display** tab of the **Options** dialog box. Longer crosshairs can help to reference alignment between objects.

text box: A box in which you type a name, number, or single line of information.

slider: A movable bar that increases or decreases a value when you slide the bar.

tooltip: A pop-up that provides information about the item over which you hover.

Tooltips

A *tooltip* displays when you hover over most interface items. See **Figure 1-7**. Tooltip content varies depending on the item. Many tooltips expand as you continue to hover. The initial tooltip might display the tool name, a brief description of the tool, and the command name. As you continue to hover, an explanation on how to use the tool and other information may appear.

Shortcut Menus

AutoCAD uses *shortcut menus*, also known as *cursor menus*, *right-click menus*, or *pop-up menus*, to simplify and accelerate tool and option access. When you right-click in the drawing area while a tool is not active, the first item in the shortcut menu is typically an option to repeat the previous tool or operation. If you right-click while a tool is active, the shortcut menu contains *context-sensitive* menu options. See **Figure 1-8**. Some menu options have a small arrow to the right of the option name. Hover over the option to display a *cascading menu*. The **Recent Input** cascading menu shows a list of recently used tools, options, or values, depending on the shortcut menu. Pick from the list to reuse a function or value.

shortcut menu (cursor menu, right-click menu, pop-up menu): Context-sensitive menu available by right-clicking on interface items or objects.

context-sensitive: Specific to the active tool or option.

cascading menu: A menu of options related to the chosen menu item.

Controlling Windows

Control the AutoCAD and drawing windows using the same methods you use to control other windows within the Windows operating system. To minimize, maximize, restore, or close the AutoCAD window or individual drawing windows, pick the appropriate button in the upper-right corner of the window. You can also adjust the AutoCAD window by right-clicking on the title bar and choosing from the standard window control menu. Window sizing operations are also the same as those for other windows within the Windows operating system.

Figure 1-7. Examples of tooltips that appear when you hover over an item.

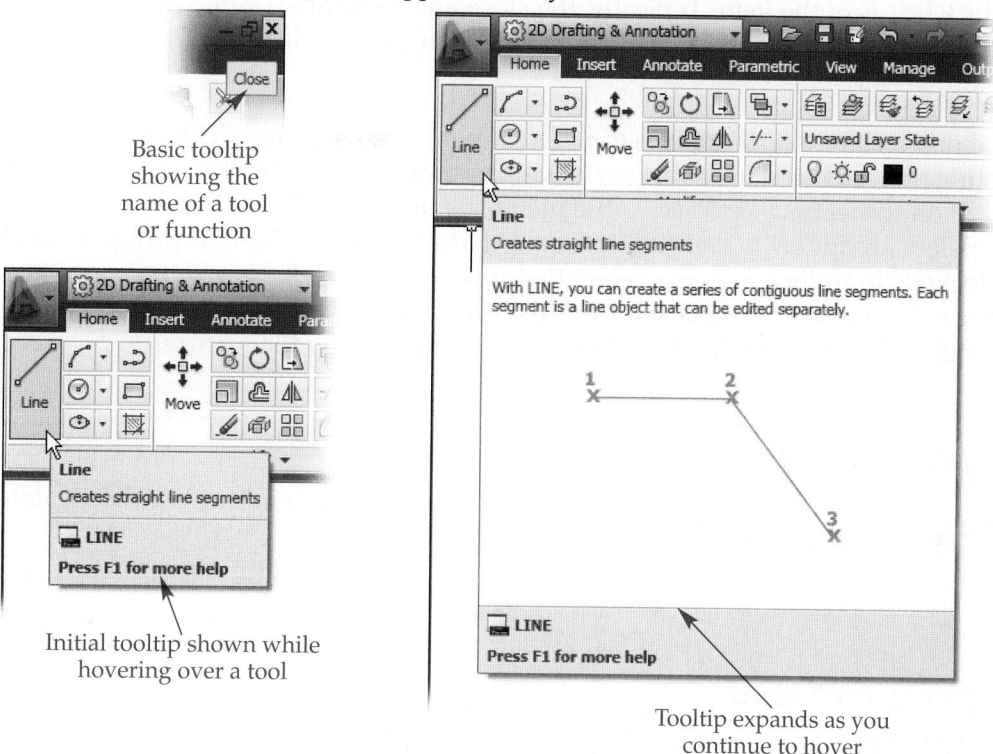

Basic tooltip showing the name of a tool or function

Initial tooltip shown while hovering over a tool

Tooltip expands as you continue to hover

Figure 1-8. Shortcut menus provide instant access to tools and options related to the current drawing or editing operation.

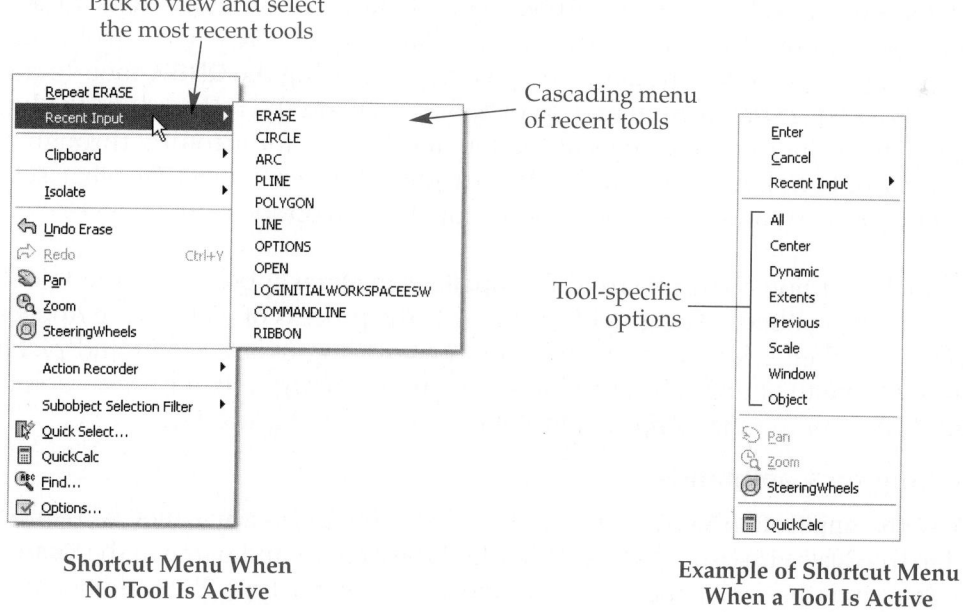

Pick to view and select the most recent tools

Cascading menu of recent tools

Tool-specific options

Shortcut Menu When No Tool Is Active

Example of Shortcut Menu When a Tool Is Active

float: Describes interface items that appear within a border and can be resized or moved.

dock: Describes interface items locked into position on an edge of the AutoCAD window (top, bottom, left, or right).

Floating and Docking

Several interface items, including the AutoCAD and drawing windows, can *float* or *dock*. Some items, such as the drawing window, have a title bar at the top or side. You can move and resize floating windows in the same manner as other windows. However, drawing windows will only move and resize within the AutoCAD window.

Different options are available depending on the particular interface item and the float or dock status of the item. Typically, the close and minimize or maximize options are available. Some floating items, such as sticky panels, include *grab bars*.

Locking

Lock certain interface items to prevent them from moving accidentally in either a floating or a docked state. To access locking options, pick the **Toolbar/Window Positions** button on the status bar to access the menu shown in **Figure 1-9**.

Select an option to lock the interface items that reside in that group as floating or docked. To unlock a group, select the option again. To lock or unlock all interface items, select **Locked** or **Unlocked** from the **All** cascading menu. Move a locked feature without unlocking it by holding down [Ctrl] while moving the feature.

Exercise 1-4

Access the Student Web site (www.g-wlearning.com/CAD) and complete Exercise 1-4.

Application Menu

The **Application Menu** provides access to application- and file-related tools and settings through a menu system. The **Application Menu** displays when you pick the **Application Menu** button, located in the upper-left corner of the AutoCAD window. See **Figure 1-10**.

Using the Buttons and Menus

Items on the left side of the **Application Menu** function as buttons to activate common application tools, and except for the **Save** button, they also display menus. For example, press the **New** button to begin a new file using the **QNEW** tool. To display a menu, hover over the menu name, or pick the arrow on the right side of the button. Long menus include small arrows at the top and bottom for scrolling through selections. Some options have a small arrow to the right of the item name that, when selected or hovered over, expands to provide a submenu. Pick an option from the list to activate the tool.

A tool or option accessible from the **Application Menu** appears as a graphic in the margin of this textbook. The graphic represents the process of picking the **Application Menu** button, then selecting a menu button or hovering over a menu and picking a menu or submenu option. The example shown in this margin illustrates accessing the **PAGESETUP** tool from the **Application Menu**, as shown in **Figure 1-10**.

Searching for Commands

Use the **Application Menu** search tool to locate and access any AutoCAD command listed in the Customize User Interface (CUI) file. Type a command name in the **Search** text box. Commands that match the letters you enter appear as you type. Type additional letters

---

Figure 1-9.
You can lock some or all interface items in position.

Lock specific types of interface items

Lock all interface items

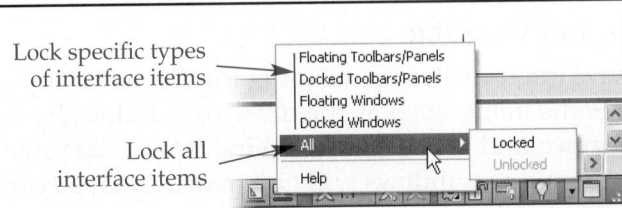

to narrow the search, with the best-matched command listed first. **Figure 1-11** shows using the **Search** text box to locate the **SAVE** tool for saving a file. Pick a command from the list to activate the command.

Figure 1-10.
Use the **Application Menu** to access common application and file management tools and settings, search for commands, and view open and recently used documents.

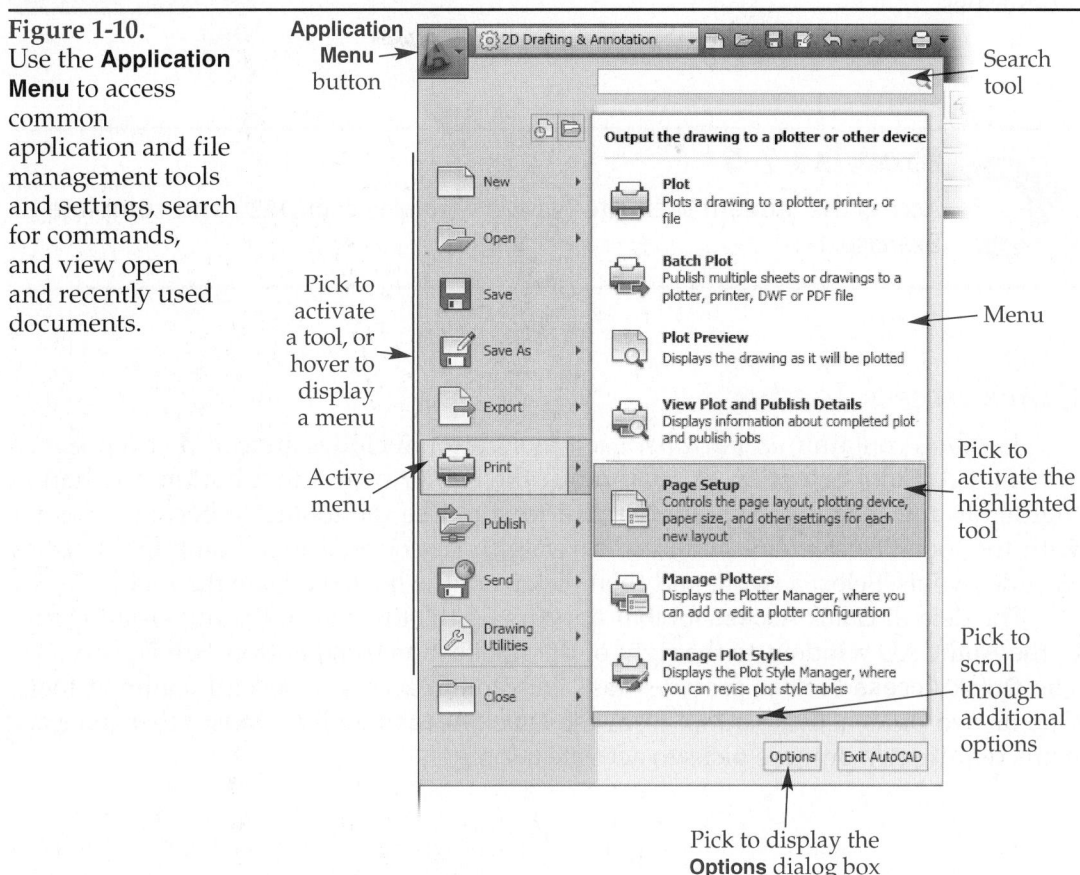

Figure 1-11.
Use the **Application Menu** to search for a command. Pick the command from the list to activate the command.

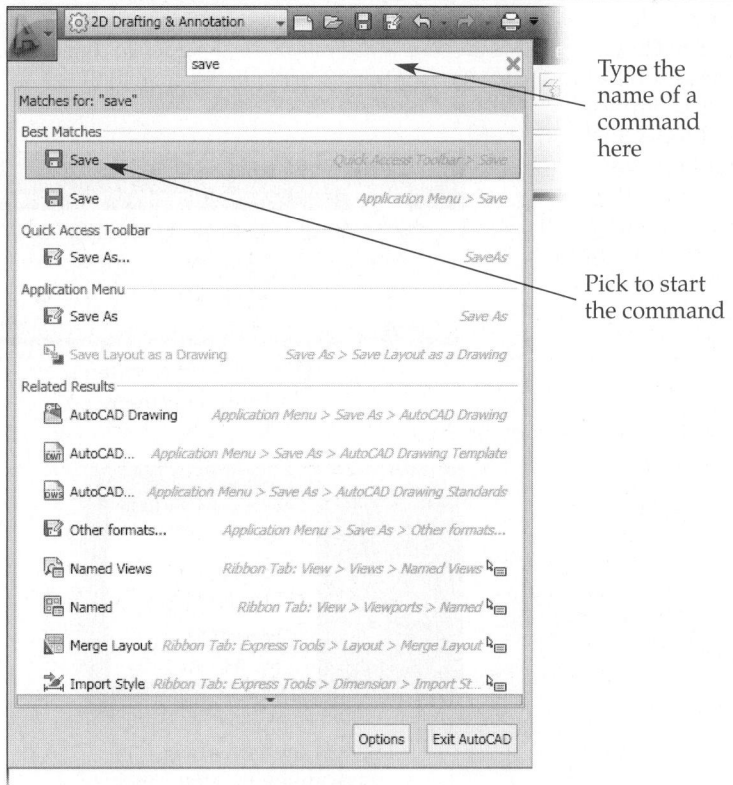

The **Recent Documents** and **Open Documents** features of the **Application Menu** provide access to recent and active files, as Chapter 2 describes.

Exercise 1-5

Access the Student Web site (www.g-wlearning.com/CAD) and complete Exercise 1-5.

Quick Access Toolbar

toolbars: Interface items that contain tool buttons or drop-down lists.

tool buttons: Interface items used to start tools.

Toolbars contain *tool buttons*. Each tool button includes an icon that represents an AutoCAD tool or option. As you move the cursor over a tool button, the button highlights and may display a border and tooltip. Use the tooltip to become familiar with the tool. Select a tool button to activate the associated tool. Some tool buttons include flyouts. Select a flyout and then pick from the list to activate the tool.

The default **Quick Access** toolbar appears on the title bar in the upper-left corner of the AutoCAD window, to the right of the **Application Menu** button. See **Figure 1-12**. The **Quick Access** toolbar provides fast, convenient access to several common tools. One or two picks activate a tool from the **Quick Access** toolbar. Most other interface items require two or more picks to activate a tool.

Figure 1-12.
Use the **Quick Access** toolbar to access commonly used tools. Pick a tool button to activate the corresponding tool or pick a flyout to access related or alternative tools.

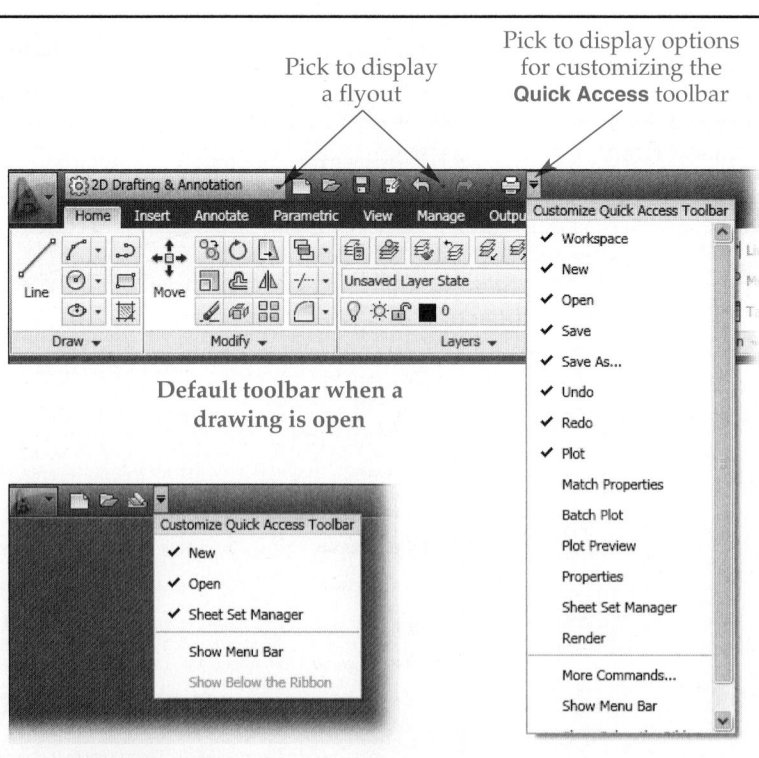

Default toolbar when a drawing is open

Default toolbar when no drawing is open

When a drawing is open and the default **2D Drafting & Annotation** workspace is active, the **Quick Access** toolbar contains **New**, **Open**, **Save**, **Save As**, **Undo**, **Redo**, and **Plot** buttons. When no drawings are open, the **New**, **Open**, and **Sheet Set Manager** buttons display. The **Quick Access** toolbar is fully customizable by adding, removing, and relocating tool buttons. To make basic adjustments, pick the **Customize Quick Access Toolbar** flyout on the right side of the toolbar. *AutoCAD and Its Applications—Advanced* further explains customizing the user interface.

A tool or option accessible from the **Quick Access** toolbar appears as a graphic in the margin of this textbook. The graphic represents the process of picking a **Quick Access** toolbar button from the toolbar or flyout. The example shown in this margin illustrates accessing the **REDO** tool from the **Quick Access** toolbar to redo a previously undone operation.

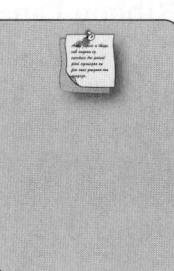

REDO

NOTE

Several toolbars appear in the **AutoCAD Classic** workspace. These toolbars are usually application- or task-specific. The **Application Menu**, **Quick Access** toolbar, and ribbon replace classic toolbars in all other workspaces. Refer to *AutoCAD and Its Applications—Advanced* for information about displaying toolbars and interface customization.

Exercise 1-6

Access the Student Web site (www.g-wlearning.com/CAD) and complete Exercise 1-6.

Ribbon

The ribbon docks horizontally below the AutoCAD window title bar by default and is the primary means of accessing tools and options. See **Figure 1-13**. The ribbon provides a convenient location from which to select tools and options that traditionally would require access by extensive typing, multiple toolbars, or several menus. The ribbon allows you to spend less time looking for tools and options and reduces clutter in the AutoCAD window.

Figure 1-13. The ribbon docked at the top of the drawing window is the most often used palette. Palettes provide access to tools, options, properties, and settings.

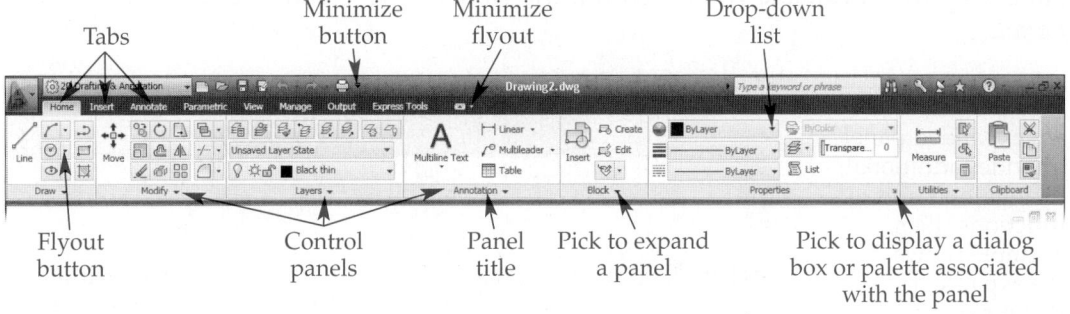

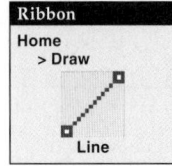

The ribbon appears by default in all workspaces except the **AutoCAD Classic** workspace. Use the *tabs* along the top of the ribbon to access collections of related *ribbon panels*, or *panels*. Each panel houses groups of similar tools. For example, the **Annotate** tab includes several panels, each with specific tools for creating, modifying, and formatting annotations, such as text. The tabs and panels shown when the **2D Drafting & Annotation** workspace is active provide access to 2D drawing tools. Highlighted, context-sensitive tabs appear when some tools, such as the **HATCH** tool, are active or you are when working in a unique environment, such as the **Block Editor**.

A tool or option accessible from the ribbon appears in a graphic located in the margin of this textbook. The graphic identifies the tab and panel where the tool is located. You may need to expand the panel or pick a flyout to locate the tool. The example shown in this margin illustrates using the ribbon to access the **LINE** tool.

Ribbon Panels

The large tool button in a panel typically signifies the most often used panel tool. In addition to tool buttons, panels can contain flyouts, *drop-down lists*, and other items. Some panels have a triangle, or arrow, next to the panel name. If you see this arrow, pick the bottom, or title, of the panel to display additional related tools and functions. See **Figure 1-14.** To show the expanded list on-screen at all times, select the pushpin button in the lower-left corner of the expanded panel.

> **NOTE**
>
> When you pick an option from a ribbon flyout, the option becomes the new default and appears in the ribbon. This makes it easier to select the same option the next time you use the tool.

Some panels include a small arrow in the lower-right corner of the panel. Pick this arrow to access a dialog box or palette closely associated with the panel. For example, pick the arrow in the lower-right corner of the **Annotate** tab, **Dimensions** panel, as shown in **Figure 1-14,** to display the **Dimension Style Manager** dialog box.

Basic Adjustment

The ribbon appears maximized by default. You can minimize the display to show only tabs, panel titles, or panel buttons by repeatedly pressing the **Minimize** button to the right of the tabs, or by selecting the appropriate option from the **Minimize** flyout. Picking the **Minimize** button corresponds to the **Cycle though All** flyout selection. When **Minimize to Tabs** is active, pick a tab to show all panels in the tab. When **Minimize to Panel Titles** is active, pick a panel title to display the panel. When **Minimized to Panel Buttons** is active, pick a panel button to display the panel.

Right-click on a portion of the ribbon unoccupied by a panel to access the options briefly described in **Figure 1-15.** *AutoCAD and Its Applications—Advanced* provides additional information on customizing the ribbon, including repositioning tabs and panels, options available when floating the ribbon, and creating and using a *sticky panel*.

Figure 1-14.
An expanded panel provides additional, related tools and functions. This example shows the expanded **Dimensions** panel.

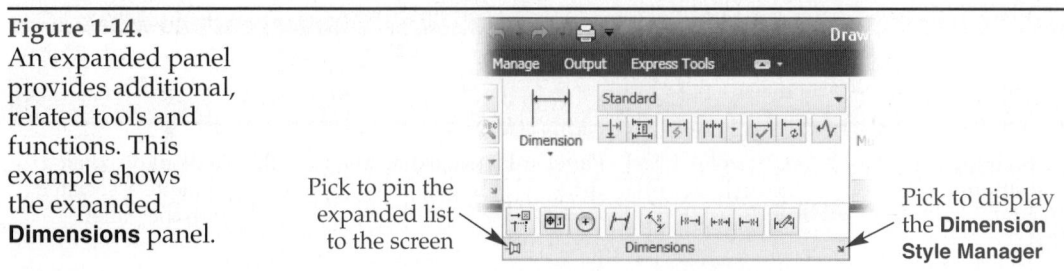

Pick to pin the expanded list to the screen

Pick to display the **Dimension Style Manager**

Figure 1-15. Right-click options for displaying and organizing ribbon elements.

Selection	Result
Show Related Tool Palette Group	Displays tool palette groups customized to associate with a ribbon tab.
Tool Palette Group	Allows you to select which related tool palette groups to show.
Show Tabs	Allows you to choose which tabs to display; also available by right-clicking on a panel.
Show Panels	Allows you to select which panels to display; also available by right-clicking on a panel.
Show Panel Titles	Uncheck to hide panel titles.
Undock	Changes the ribbon to a floating state. Double-click the ribbon title bar or drag and drop to dock the floating ribbon.
Close	Closes the ribbon. Use the **RIBBON** tool to redisplay the ribbon.

NOTE

The **Application Menu**, **Quick Access** toolbar, and ribbon replace the traditional menu bar in workspaces other than the **AutoCAD Classic** workspace. To display the menu bar, pick the **Customize Quick Access Toolbar** flyout on the right side of the **Quick Access** toolbar and choose **Show Menu Bar**.

Palettes

Palettes, also known as *modeless dialog boxes*, control many AutoCAD functions. Palettes can look like extensive toolbars or more like dialog boxes, depending on the function and floating or docked state. You can consider the ribbon a palette used to access tools and options. Palettes can contain tool buttons, flyouts, drop-down lists, and many other features, such as *list boxes* and *scroll bars*. Unlike a dialog box, palettes need not be closed to use other tools and work on the drawing. Like the ribbon, panels divide some palettes into groups of tools. Large palettes are divided into separate pages or windows, which you commonly access using tabs.

To display a palette, pick a palette button from the **Palettes** panel in the **View** ribbon tab. You can also display most palettes using palette-specific access techniques. For example, to access the **Properties** palette, pick the arrow in the lower-left corner of the **Properties** panel in the **Home** ribbon tab; double-click on most objects in the drawing window; select an object, right-click and select **Properties**; or type **PROPERTIES**.

When you display a palette for the first time, it is often in a floating state, although you can dock some palettes. Right-click on the palette title bar or pick the **Properties** button to select from a list of undocked palette control options. The **Auto-hide** option allows the palette to minimize when the cursor is away from the palette, conserving drawing space. Deselect the **Allow Docking** palette property or menu option to disable the ability to dock palettes. The **Properties** button or shortcut menu on some palettes includes other functions, such as the **Transparency...** option. This option makes the palette transparent, allowing you to view drawing geometry behind the palette. See **Figure 1-16**.

palette (modeless dialog box): Special type of window containing tool buttons and features common to dialog boxes. Palettes can remain open while other tools are active.

list box: A boxed area that contains a list of items or options from which to select.

scroll bar: A bar tipped with arrow buttons used to scroll through a list of options or information.

Figure 1-16. Pick the **Properties** button or right-click in the title bar and select **Transparency…** to access the **Transparency** dialog box. This example shows the transparent **Layer Properties Manager** palette positioned over a mechanical model.

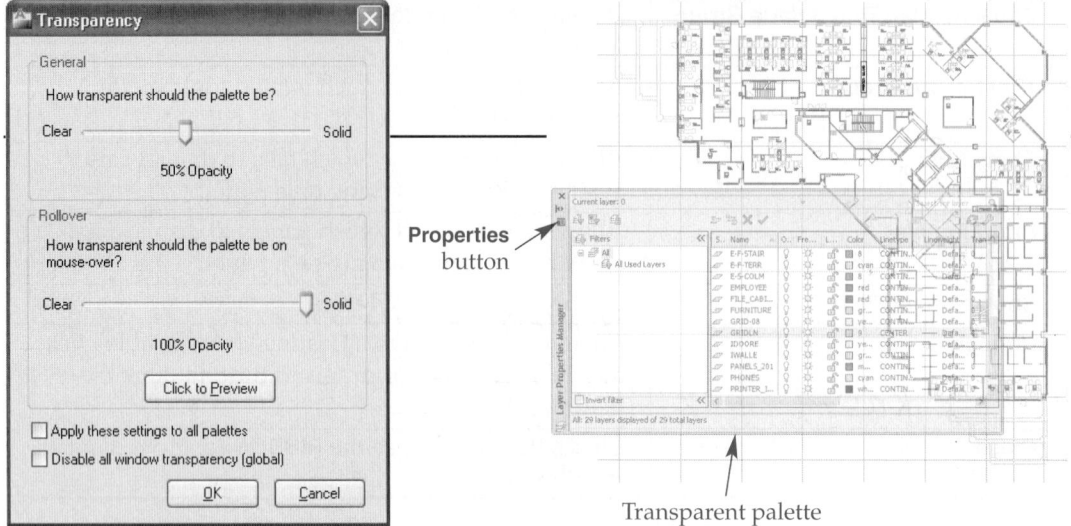

Properties button

Transparent palette

PROFESSIONAL TIP

Resize a floating palette using the resizing arrows that appear when you move the cursor over the edge. Then pick the **Auto-hide** button to have quick access to the palette while displaying the largest possible drawing area.

Exercise 1-7

Access the Student Web site (www.g-wlearning.com/CAD) and complete Exercise 1-7.

Status Bars

AutoCAD provides two types of status bars. The application status bar applies to all open drawing or drawing template files. A drawing status bar, when activated, appears above the *command line* and is specific to each drawing or drawing template. Status bars are the quickest and most effective way to manage certain drawing settings.

command line: Area where you can type commands (tool names) and options.

Application Status Bar

The application status bar appears along the bottom of the AutoCAD window. See **Figure 1-17.** The application status bar includes areas that display and control a variety of drawing aids and tools. The coordinate display field, located on the left side of the application status bar, shows the location, or coordinates, of the crosshairs in drawing space. *Status toggle buttons* appear next to the coordinate display field. Status toggle buttons show icons by default. To change the display from icons to names, right-click on any status toggle button and deselect **Use Icons**.

status toggle buttons: Buttons that toggle drawing aids and tools on and off.

The items on the right side of the application status bar control windows and the drawing environment, activate tools, and adjust annotation scaling. This area also includes a notification tray that identifies the status of and provides notifications for some AutoCAD tools and applications.

AutoCAD and Its Applications—Basics

Figure 1-17. Picking buttons on the application status bar is the quickest and most effective way to manage certain drawing settings.

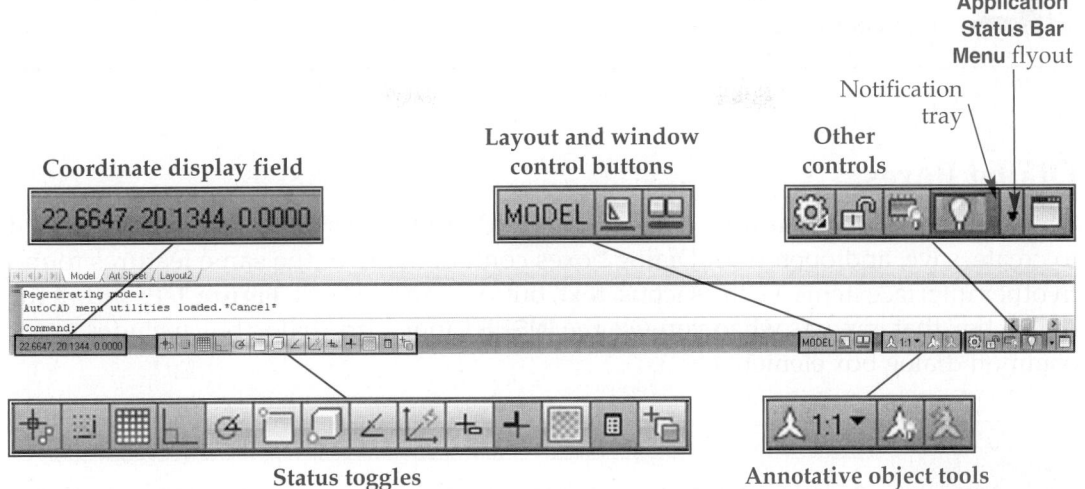

NOTE

Right-click on the application status bar, away from the coordinate display field or a button, or pick the **Application Status Bar Menu** flyout to access options for modifying the display of the application status bar. Uncheck an item on the list to hide the item from the status bar. *AutoCAD and Its Applications—Advanced* further describes how to customize the status bar.

Drawing Status Bar

Select the **Drawing Status Bar** option from the application status bar shortcut menu or the **Display** tab of the **Options** dialog box to display a separate drawing status bar in the drawing window. The **Annotation Scale**, **Annotation Visibility**, and **AutoScale** tools and the notification tray move from the application status bar to the drawing status bar. A **Drawing Status Bar Menu** flyout also appears. See **Figure 1-18**. The settings are unique to each open file.

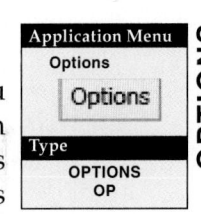

PROFESSIONAL TIP

Right-click on the coordinate display field or a button in the application or drawing status bar to view a shortcut menu specific to the item. Picking options from a status bar shortcut menu is often the most efficient method of controlling drawing settings.

Figure 1-18. The drawing status bar, when displayed, is specific to the current drawing. Each open drawing has its own drawing status bar.

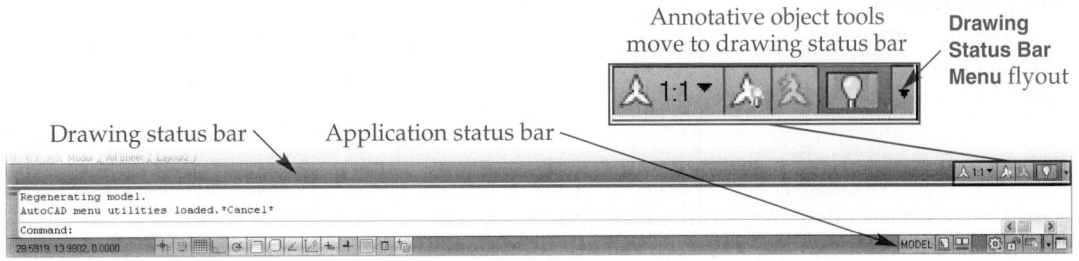

Exercise 1-8

Access the Student Web site (www.g-wlearning.com/CAD) and complete Exercise 1-8.

Dialog Boxes

dialog box: A window-like item that contains various settings and information.

You will see many *dialog boxes* during a drawing session, including those used to create, save, and open files. Dialog boxes contain many of the same features found in other interface items, such as icons, text, buttons, and flyouts. **Figure 1-19** shows the dialog box that appears when you use the **INSERT** tool. This dialog box includes many common dialog box elements.

> **NOTE**
>
> A dialog box appears when you pick any menu selection or button displaying an ellipsis (…).

preview box: An area in a dialog box that shows the results of the options and settings you select.

Use the cursor to set variables and select items in a dialog box. Many dialog boxes include images, *preview boxes*, or other cues to help you to select appropriate options. When you pick a button in a dialog box that includes an ellipsis (…), another dialog box appears. You must make a selection from the second dialog box before returning to the original dialog box. A button with an arrow icon requires you to select in the drawing area.

> **CAUTION**
>
> The AutoCAD interface includes several other unique items, such as the **Model** and **Layout** tabs, ViewCube, and navigation bar. Refer back to **Figure 1-5** to recognize these features. You will explore these features and their specific control operations throughout this textbook. Do not use or adjust these tools until you learn about their function, because doing so can unexpectedly change the interface display and operation. Ensure that the **Model** tab is active.

Figure 1-19.
A dialog box appears when you pick a menu item with a name followed by an ellipsis (...) or a button displaying an ellipsis. The dialog box shown here displays when you select the **INSERT** tool.

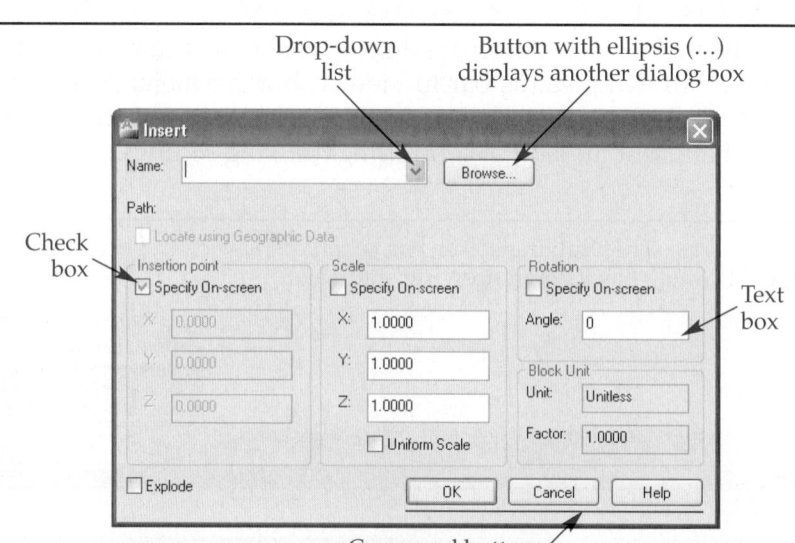

Exercise 1-9

Access the Student Web site (www.g-wlearning.com/CAD) and complete
Exercise 1-9.

System Options

The **Options** dialog box contains AutoCAD system options. System options apply
to the entire program and are not specific to a file. Many system options help configure
the work environment, such as the background color of the drawing window. This
textbook focuses on the default system options and references the **Options** dialog box
when applicable.

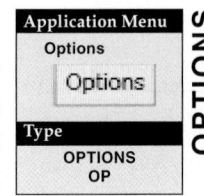

Accessing Tools

Tools are available by direct access from the ribbon, shortcut menus, **Application
Menu**, **Quick Access** toolbar, palettes, status bar, ViewCube, and navigation bar. An
alternative is to type the command that activates a tool using *dynamic input* or the
command line. To activate a tool by typing, type the single-word command name
or the *command alias* and press [Enter] or the space bar, or right-click. You can use
uppercase, lowercase, or a combination of uppercase and lowercase letters. You can
only issue one command at a time.

You can activate all tools and options by typing. All command names and aliases,
along with other access techniques available in the **2D Drafting & Annotation** workspace, appear in a graphic in the margin of this textbook. The example displayed in
this margin shows the command name (**LINE**) and alias (**L**) you can use to access the
LINE tool.

A major benefit of accessing a tool using a method other than typing is that you
do not need to memorize command names or aliases. Another advantage is that tools,
options, and your drawing activities appear on-screen as you work, using visual icons,
tooltips, and prompts. As you work with AutoCAD, you will become familiar with the
display and location of tools. Decide which tool selection technique works best for you.
A combination of tool selection methods often proves most effective.

**dynamic
input:** Area near
the crosshairs
where you can type
commands and
options and view
context-oriented
information.

command aliases:
Abbreviated
command names
entered at the
keyboard.

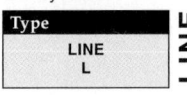

Reference Material

Command Aliases

For a detailed list of command aliases, go to the **Reference Material** section of the Student Web site (www.g-wlearning.com/CAD) and select **Command Aliases**.

Dynamic Input

Dynamic input allows you to keep your focus at the crosshairs while you draw. When dynamic input is on, a temporary input area appears in the drawing window, below and to the right of the crosshairs by default. See **Figure 1-20**.

Depending on the tool in progress, different information and options appear in the dynamic input area. For example, **Figure 1-21** shows the display after starting the **RECTANGLE** tool. The first portion of the dynamic input area is the prompt, which reads Specify first corner point or. In this case, to draw a rectangle, you need to pick in the drawing window or enter *coordinates* to specify the first corner of the rectangle, or access other options as suggested by the "or" portion of the prompt.

coordinates:
Numerical values used to locate a point in the drawing area.

Figure 1-20. Use dynamic input to type or select tools and values from a temporary input area next to the crosshairs.

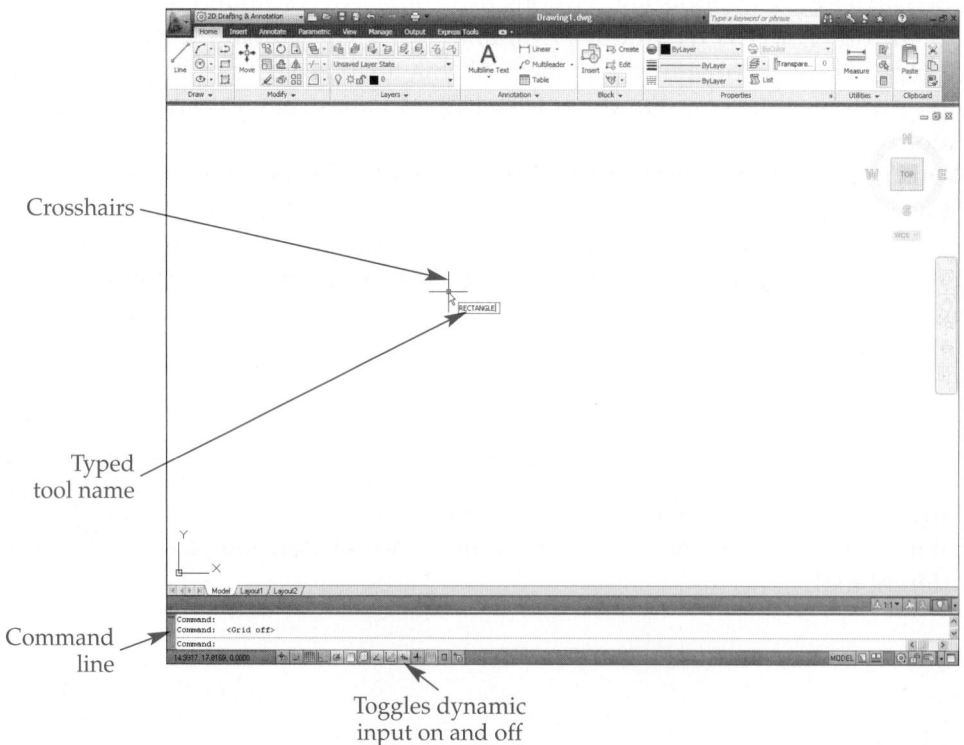

Crosshairs

Typed tool name

Command line

Toggles dynamic input on and off

Figure 1-21.
The dynamic input fields that appear after you enter the **RECTANGLE** tool.

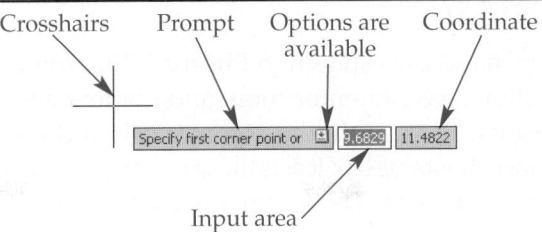

Crosshairs   Prompt   Options are available   Coordinate

Specify first corner point or   9.6829   11.4822

Input area

Press the down arrow key to display available tool options. See **Figure 1-22.** Select an option using the cursor, or press the down arrow again to cycle through the options, as indicated by a bullet next to the option. Press [Enter] to select the highlighted option. You can also choose an option by right-clicking and picking an option from the shortcut menu. The information displayed in the dynamic input area changes while you work with a tool, depending on the actions you choose. **Figure 1-23** shows the dynamic input display when the **LINE** tool is active.

> **NOTE**
>
> Toggle dynamic input on and off by picking the **Dynamic Input** button on the status bar or pressing [F12]. You can issue commands without dynamic input on.

Figure 1-22.
Press the down arrow key to display tool options. Pick an option with the cursor, or use the up and down arrow keys to highlight the desired option and press [Enter] to select.

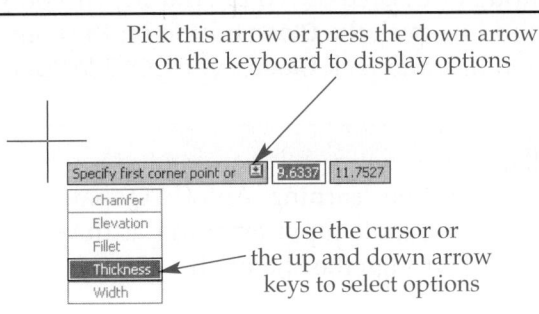

Pick this arrow or press the down arrow on the keyboard to display options

Specify first corner point or   9.6337   11.7527

Chamfer
Elevation
Fillet
Thickness
Width

Use the cursor or the up and down arrow keys to select options

Figure 1-23.
Dynamic input fields change while a tool is in use. In this example, the crosshairs coordinates appear first. Once you select the first endpoint, the distance and angle of the crosshairs relative to the first endpoint are displayed.

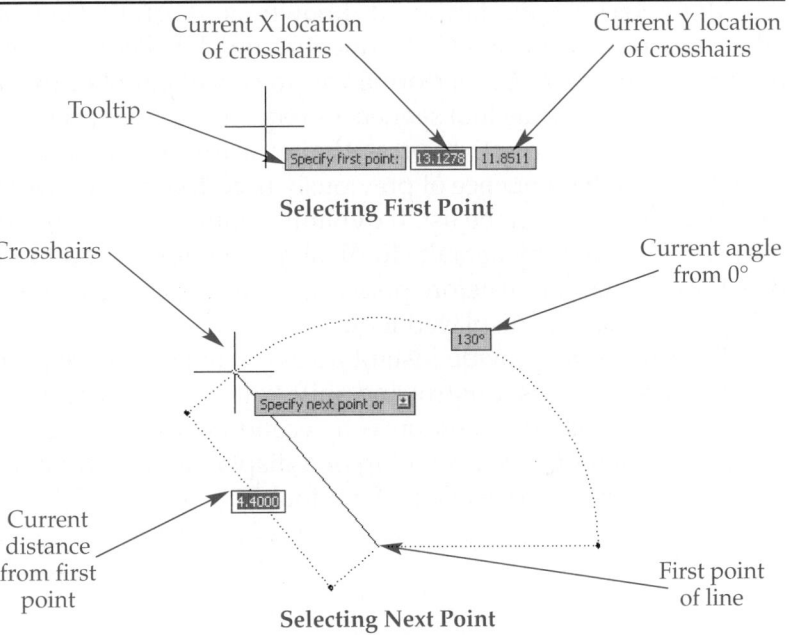

Current X location of crosshairs   Current Y location of crosshairs

Tooltip

Specify first point: 13.1278   11.8511

Selecting First Point

Crosshairs

Current angle from 0°

130°

Specify next point or

4.4000

Current distance from first point

First point of line

Selecting Next Point

Command Line

The command line, shown in **Figure 1-20**, provides the same function as dynamic input, but allows you to enter tools and context-specific information in a traditional window format. By default, the command line docks at the bottom of the AutoCAD window, above the status bar. It acts like a palette, displays the Command: prompt, and reflects any commands you issue. The command line also displays prompts that supply information or request input.

When you issue a command, AutoCAD either performs the specified operation or prompts for additional information. The commands that activate AutoCAD tools have the following standard format:

> Command: **COMMANDNAME.**↵
> Current settings: Setting1 Setting2 Setting3
> Prompt [Option1/oPtion2/opTion3/...] <default option or value>:

Settings or options associated with a command display as shown. The prompt indicates what you should do to continue the operation. The square brackets contain available options. Each option has an alias, or unique combination of uppercase characters, that you can enter at the prompt rather than typing the entire option name. Angle brackets (<>) surround the default option; press [Enter] to accept this option instead of typing the value again.

Each default AutoCAD workspace includes the command line. The command line can float or dock, resize, and lock. The floating command line contains the **Autohide** and **Properties** buttons found on palettes. You can use the command line with dynamic input, or disable the command line if you use only dynamic input. To hide the command line, pick the **Close** button on the command line title bar, right-click on the command line and pick **Close**, type COMMANDLINEHIDE, or press [Ctrl]+[9].

PROFESSIONAL TIP

While learning AutoCAD, pay close attention to prompts in the dynamic input area and at the command line. Prompts guide you through the operation.

Keyboard Shortcuts

shortcut key (keyboard shortcut): Single key or key combination used to issue a command or select an option.

escape key: Keyboard key used to cancel a tool or exit a dialog box.

function keys: The keys labeled [F1] through [F12] along the top of the keyboard.

Many keys on the keyboard, known as *shortcut keys* or *keyboard shortcuts*, allow you to perform AutoCAD functions quickly. Become familiar with these keys to improve your AutoCAD performance. To cancel a tool or exit a dialog box, press the *escape key* [Esc]. Some tool sequences require that you press [Esc] twice to cancel.

When no tool is active, press the up arrow key as many times as necessary to cycle through the sequence of previously used tool names. Use the down arrow key to return to a later tool in the list. If dynamic input is active, previously used tools appear near the crosshairs by default. To display previously used tools at the command line, pick the command line before pressing the up arrow, or turn off dynamic input. Press [Enter] to activate the displayed tool.

Function keys provide instant access to tools and are programmable to perform a series of commands. Control and shift key combinations require that you press and hold [Ctrl] or [Shift] and then press a second character. You can activate several tools using [Ctrl] combinations. A tooltip or a display in a shortcut menu typically indicates if a key combination is available for a tool.

Reference Material

Shortcut Keys

For a complete list of keyboard shortcuts, go to the **Reference Material** section of the Student Web site (www.g-wlearning.com/CAD) and select **Shortcut Keys**.

Exercise 1-10

Access the Student Web site (www.g-wlearning.com/CAD) and complete Exercise 1-10.

Getting Help

If you need help with a specific tool, option, or AutoCAD feature, use this textbook as a guide. AutoCAD also includes a help system. The **Welcome Screen** you see when you launch AutoCAD for the first time is an element of the help system and provides access to the **AutoCAD 2011 Help** Web site, as shown in **Figure 1-24**. The graphic shown in this margin identifies several other ways to access the **AutoCAD 2011 Help** Web site. You can also open the **AutoCAD 2011 Help** Web site from the **InfoCenter**, described later in this chapter, or by selecting **Help** from a shortcut menu.

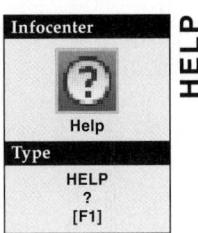

Figure 1-24. The **AutoCAD 2011 Help** Web site and the **InfoCenter** found in the AutoCAD window.

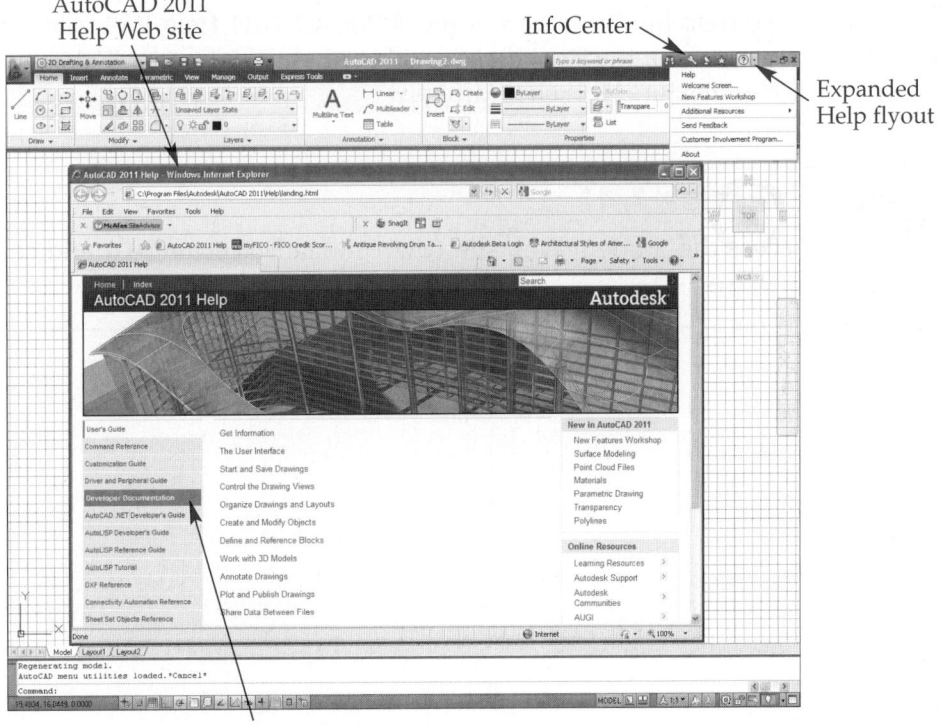

AutoCAD 2011 Help Web site

InfoCenter

Expanded Help flyout

Select an option to display related help content

Help system files install with AutoCAD, allowing you to view the **AutoCAD 2011 Help** site offline. If you cannot view the Web version, force AutoCAD to display the installed help system by deselecting the **Use online help from Autodesk website when available** check box in the **Help** area on the **System** tab of the **Options** dialog box. The **Help** area also includes *radio buttons* to specify the appropriate browser to display help.

The **AutoCAD 2011 Help** Web site uses a typical Web site format with menus of links, navigation options, and a search function. Select a topic from the main menu on the left side of the Web site to access links to AutoCAD help data. Smaller menus are also available and provide direct access to content such as features new to AutoCAD 2011 and Autodesk support. To search the help system index for a specific topic, such as a tool or option, type in the **Search** box, located in the upper-right corner of the **AutoCAD 2011 Help** Web site.

PROFESSIONAL TIP

Press [F1] while using a tool to display *context-oriented help*. This saves time when you are looking for help with the current tool and drawing task.

InfoCenter

The **InfoCenter**, located on the right side of the title bar as shown in **Figure 1-24,** allows you to search for help topics without first displaying the **AutoCAD 2011 Help** Web site. Type in the text box to search for related topics. Then select the appropriate topic from the list to display it in the **AutoCAD 2011 Help** Web site, or choose a specific location to search using the **Search** flyout. Pick the star icon next to a topic to add the topic to the **Favorites** list for future reference.

Pick the **Subscription Center** button to access information associated with your license and subscription eligibility, options, and services. Pick the **Communication Center** button to access content on a variety of help topics. Pick the **Favorites** button to access stored help topics. Select the **Help** button to access the **AutoCAD 2011 Help** Web site, or choose a help system option from the **Help** flyout, such as redisplaying the **Welcome Screen** or accessing the **New Feature Workshop** directly.

Exercise 1-11

Access the Student Web site (www.g-wlearning.com/CAD) and complete Exercise 1-11.

Chapter Test

Answer the following questions. Write your answers on a separate sheet of paper or go to the Student Web site (www.g-wlearning.com/CAD) and complete the electronic chapter test.

1. Describe at least one application for AutoCAD software.
2. Briefly explain what is involved in planning a drawing.
3. What are drawing standards?
4. Why should you save your work every 10 to 15 minutes?
5. What is the quickest method of starting AutoCAD?
6. Name one method of exiting AutoCAD.
7. What is the name for an interface that includes on-screen features?
8. Define or explain the following terms:
   A. Default
   B. Pick (or click)
   C. Hover
   D. Button
   E. Function key
   F. Option
   G. Tool
9. What is a workspace?
10. What is a flyout?
11. How do you change from one workspace to another?
12. How do you access a shortcut menu?
13. What does it mean when a shortcut menu is described as context-sensitive?
14. What is the difference between a docked interface item and a floating interface item?
15. How do you select the locking options to lock the interface items in either their floating or docked state?
16. Explain the basic function of the **Application Menu**.
17. Describe the **Application Menu** search tool and briefly explain how to use it.
18. Briefly describe an advantage of using the ribbon.
19. What is the function of tabs in the ribbon?
20. What is another name for a palette?
21. Describe the function of the application status bar.
22. What is the meaning of the … (ellipsis) in a menu option or button?
23. What are the two primary methods for accessing AutoCAD tools? List interface items associated with each.
24. Briefly describe the function of dynamic input.
25. Briefly explain the function of the [Esc] key.
26. How do you access previously used tools when dynamic input is on?
27. Name the function keys that execute the following tasks. (Refer to the Shortcut Keys document in the **Reference Material** section on the Student Web Site.)
   A. Snap mode (toggle)
   B. Grid mode (toggle)
   C. Ortho mode (toggle)
28. Describe two ways to access the **AutoCAD 2011 Help** Web site.
29. What is context-oriented help, and how is it accessed?
30. Describe the purpose of the **InfoCenter**, and explain how to use the **InfoCenter** text box.

Problems

Start AutoCAD if it is not already started. Follow the specific instructions for each problem.

▼ Basic

1. Perform the following tasks:
   A. Open the **AutoCAD 2011 Help** Web site.
   B. At the main menu, pick the **User's Guide** link if it is not already selected.
   C. Pick the **Find the Information You Need** link.
   D. Pick the **Find Information Using InfoCenter** link.
   E. Read each topic.
   F. Close the **AutoCAD 2011 Help** Web site, and then close AutoCAD.

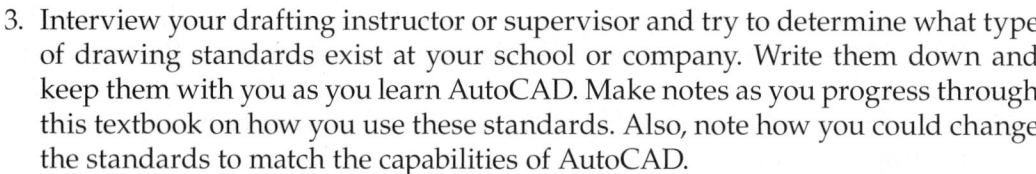

2. Perform the following tasks:
   A. Move the cursor over the buttons in the status bar and read the tooltip for each.
   B. Slowly move the cursor over each of the ribbon panels and read the tooltips.
   C. Pick the **Application Menu** to display it. Hover over the **File** menu, and then use the right arrow key to move to the **File** options. Then use the down arrow key to move through all the menu options.
   D. Press [Esc] to dismiss the menu.
   E. Close AutoCAD.

▼ Intermediate

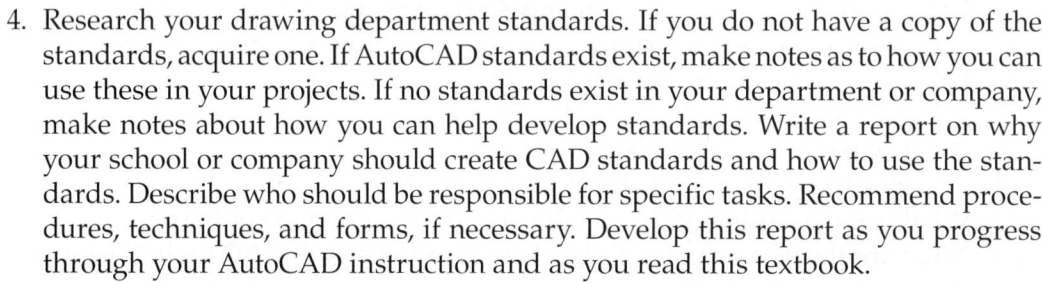

3. Interview your drafting instructor or supervisor and try to determine what type of drawing standards exist at your school or company. Write them down and keep them with you as you learn AutoCAD. Make notes as you progress through this textbook on how you use these standards. Also, note how you could change the standards to match the capabilities of AutoCAD.

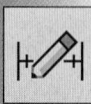

4. Research your drawing department standards. If you do not have a copy of the standards, acquire one. If AutoCAD standards exist, make notes as to how you can use these in your projects. If no standards exist in your department or company, make notes about how you can help develop standards. Write a report on why your school or company should create CAD standards and how to use the standards. Describe who should be responsible for specific tasks. Recommend procedures, techniques, and forms, if necessary. Develop this report as you progress through your AutoCAD instruction and as you read this textbook.

5. Develop a drawing planning sheet for use in your school or company. List items you think are important for planning a CAD drawing. Make changes to this sheet as you learn more about AutoCAD.

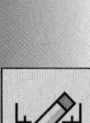

6. Create a freehand sketch of the default AutoCAD window with the **2D Drafting & Annotation** workspace active. Label each of the screen areas. To the side of the sketch, write a short description of the function of each screen area.

7. Create a freehand sketch showing three examples of tooltips displayed as you hover over an item. To the side of the sketch, write a short description of each example's function.

8. Using the **Application Menu** search tool, type the letter C and review the information provided in the **Application Menu**. Then add the letter L. How does the information change? Continue typing O, S, and E to complete the **CLOSE** command. Write a short paragraph explaining how you might use this search tool to find a command if you are unsure how the command is spelled or where it is located.

▼ Advanced

9. Research and write a report of approximately 250 words covering the American Society of Mechanical Engineers (ASME) and American National Standards Institute (ANSI) drafting standards.

10. Research and write a report of approximately 250 words covering the International Standards Organization (ISO) drafting standards.

11. Research and write a report of approximately 250 words covering the United States National CAD Standard (NCS).

12. Research and write a report of approximately 250 words covering workplace ethics, especially as related to CADD applications and CADD-related software.

13. Research and write a report of approximately 150 words covering an ergonomically designed CADD workstation. Include a sketch of what you consider a high-quality design for a workstation and label its characteristics.

14. Go to the Autodesk Education Community Web site at http://students.autodesk.com/, and register to join the Autodesk Education Community. After you register, download a student version of AutoCAD to your home or laptop computer. Use your copy of AutoCAD to complete assignments and study AutoCAD when you are unable to access a CADD lab. The Autodesk Education Community Web site provides complete information on the registration and download process. If you do not have a school-supplied e-mail account, your instructor can register and invite you to participate.

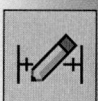

Drawing Problems - Chapter 1

AutoCAD Certified Associate Exam Practice

Answer the following questions. Write your answers on a separate sheet of paper.

1. Which workspaces are present by default in the AutoCAD 2011 software? *Select all that apply.*
   A. **3D Basics**
   B. **3D Animation**
   C. **3D Modeling**
   D. **AutoCAD Classic**
   E. **2D Modeling**
   F. **2D Drafting & Annotation**

2. Which of the following is a method of starting the AutoCAD software? *Select the one item that best answers the question.*
   A. Access the Windows Start menu, select Run..., and enter autocad.exe
   B. Right-click on the Windows desktop and select AutoCAD 2011 from the shortcut menu
   C. Double-click the AutoCAD 2011 icon on the Windows desktop
   D. Navigate to http://autodesk.com and double-click AutoCAD 2011

3. If you cannot view the Web version, you can force AutoCAD to display the installed help system by deselecting the **Use online help from Autodesk website when available** check box in which of the following locations? *Select the one item that best answers the question.*
   A. **InfoCenter**
   B. **Options** dialog box, **System** tab
   C. **Application Menu**, **Drawing Utilities** menu
   D. Application status bar

AutoCAD Certified Professional Exam Practice

Follow the instructions in each problem. Write your answers on a separate sheet of paper.

1. **Start AutoCAD using one of the methods described in the chapter.**
   Turn off dynamic input. At the Command: prompt, type the letters LA and press [Enter]. What command does AutoCAD execute? (The command appears at the command line in capital letters after the LA you typed.)

2. **Start AutoCAD using one of the methods described in the chapter.**
   Access the **Application Menu** search tool and type the letters C, L, and O. Review the results of the search. What entry appears in the Ribbon Tab: Home category?

Drawings and Templates

Learning Objectives

After completing this chapter, you will be able to do the following:

✓ Begin a new drawing.
✓ Save your work.
✓ Close files.
✓ Open saved files.
✓ Work with multiple open documents.
✓ View and adjust drawing properties.
✓ Determine and specify drawing units and limits.
✓ Create drawing template files.

In this chapter, you will learn how to start new drawings, save drawings, open existing drawings, and begin the process of preparing drawing templates. This chapter also explains tools and options that assist in organizing and setting up a drawing session, including basic drawing settings. You will find the drawing settings described in this chapter very useful as you begin working with drawing and drawing template files.

Beginning a New Drawing

AutoCAD uses or recognizes several different types of files for specific functions. The primary file types are *drawing files*, which have a .dwg extension, and *drawing template files*, also known as *templates*, which have a .dwt extension. You typically begin a new drawing by referencing a template that includes standard drawing settings and objects. A new drawing based on a template includes all of the template settings and content. To help avoid confusion as you learn AutoCAD, remember that a new drawing file references a drawing template file, but the drawing file is where you draw.

A new drawing file appears by default when you launch AutoCAD. The drawing references a default template. If you skip the initial setup process as advised in this textbook, the drawing you initially see references the acad.dwt template installed with AutoCAD. The drawing is appropriate for initial drawing applications and uses basic

drawing files: Files you use to create and store drawings.

drawing template files (templates): Files you reference to develop new drawings; contain standard drawing settings and objects.

decimal unit settings, with a U.S. Customary (inch) unit preference. You are ready to draw, then save and close the file. To start another new drawing, use a template or start from scratch.

Starting from a Template

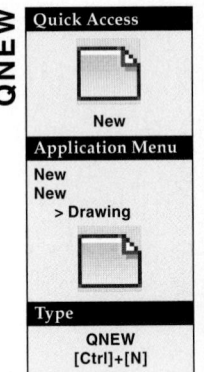

The **QNEW** tool is the primary means of starting a new drawing. By default, the **Select template** dialog box appears when you access the **QNEW** tool. See **Figure 2-1**. The **Select template** dialog box lists the templates found in the specified drawing template folder. The default template folder shown in **Figure 2-1** includes a variety of templates supplied with AutoCAD.

> **NOTE**
>
> All file navigation dialog boxes, including the **Select template** dialog box and those used to save, close, and open files, support auto-complete. Type in the **File Name** text box to view a list of files matching the characters you enter.

The tutorial templates for manufacturing and architecture include a border and title block. All of the other supplied templates are blank, but include drawing settings specific to the requirements of a certain industry or drawing. For general 2D drawing applications, use the default acad.dwt template, or select the acadiso.dwt template, which uses basic decimal unit settings according to metric ISO standards. To use a template to begin a new drawing, double-click on the file name, right-click on the file and pick **Select**, or select the file and pick the **Open** button.

Figure 2-1. Use the **Select template** dialog box to begin a new drawing. Choose a template to reference, or pick the arrow next to the **Open** button and select an **Open with no Template** option to start a drawing from scratch.

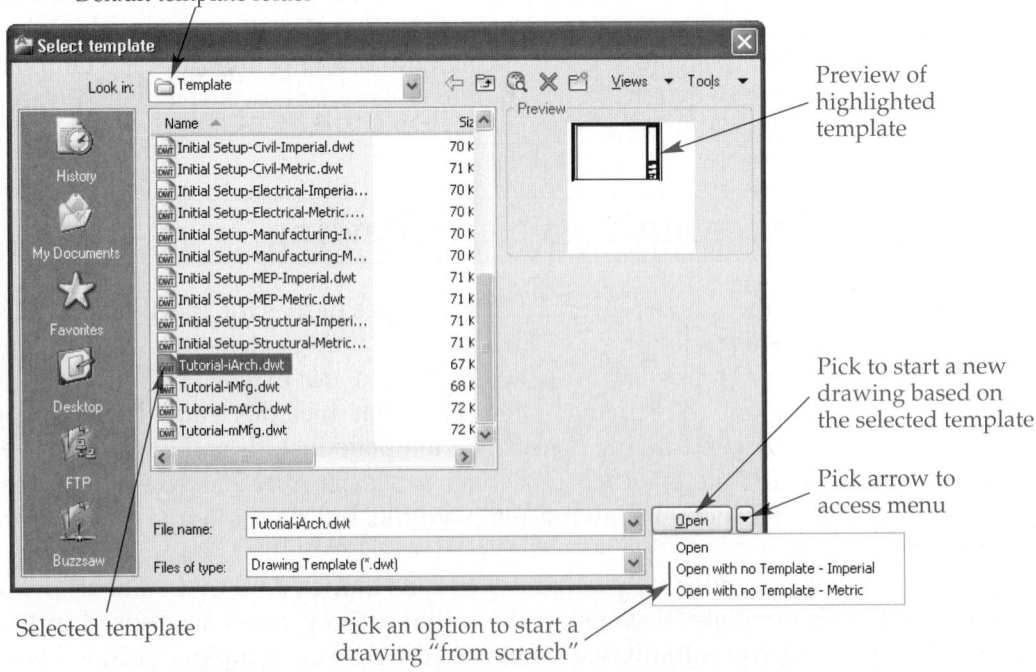

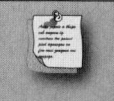

Starting from Scratch

For a new AutoCAD user, an effective way to begin a new drawing is to start "from scratch" using a blank drawing file without a border, title block, modified layouts, or customized drawing settings. Start from scratch when you just begin to learn AutoCAD, when units and drawing settings are unknown, and when creating your own template. To start from scratch, pick the flyout next to the **Open** button in the **Select template** dialog box. See **Figure 2-1**. Then, to begin a drawing using basic inch unit settings, pick **Open with no Template-Imperial**, or to begin a drawing using basic metric unit settings, pick **Open with no Template-Metric**.

Setting the Quick Start Template

The **Options** dialog box provides a quick start feature to begin a drawing using the **QNEW** tool and a specific template, skipping the **Select template** dialog box. Pick the **Files** tab, expand the Template Settings option, and then expand the Default Template File Name for QNEW function. See **Figure 2-2**. None displays by default and causes the **Select template** dialog box to appear. Pick the **Browse...** button to select a specific template to launch each time you use the **QNEW** tool.

Figure 2-2. Specifying a template for the **QNEW** tool.

Files tab

No template specified

Pick to specify template

Saving Your Work

You should save your drawing or template immediately after you begin work. Then save at least every 10 to 15 minutes while working to avoid the possibility of losing work. Several AutoCAD tools allow you to save your work. In addition, when you close a file or exit AutoCAD, an alert appears asking if you want to save changes. This gives you a final opportunity to save or discard changes.

File Storage and Naming

Store drawings on your computer or a network drive according to school or company practice. Back up files to a removable storage device or other system to help ensure that information is not permanently lost during a system failure.

Develop an organized structure of file folders, and use subfolders as needed to help organize each project. Using a standard naming system allows you to find drawings quickly and easily by content, category, or other criteria. For example, you might save all of your textbook exercises to an Exercises folder, or create chapter-specific folders to store exercises, tests, and problems. An example of a mechanical drafting project is a main folder titled ACME.4001 based on the company name ACME, Inc. and project and assembly number 4001. An example of an architectural drafting project is a main folder titled JAMES0110 to identify the first James Residence project of 2010.

file properties:
Values used to define a variety of file and design characteristics.

The name you assign to a file is one of several *file properties*. File naming is typically based on a specific system associated with the product and approved drawing standards. A file name should be concise and allow you to determine the content of the file. A basic example is the file naming scheme applied to exercises in this textbook. You save Exercise 2-1, for example, as EX2-1. **Figure 2-3** provides other examples of drawing file names. File name characteristics vary greatly depending on the product, specific drawing requirements, and drawing standard interpretation and options.

Rules and restrictions apply to naming folders and files. When naming files, you can use most alphabetic and numeric characters and spaces, as well as most punctuation symbols. You can use 255 characters. You cannot use the quotation mark ("), asterisk (*), question mark (?), forward slash (/), and backward slash (\).You do not have to include the file extension, such as .dwg or .dwt, with the file name. File names are not case sensitive. For example, you can name a drawing PROBLEM 2-1, but Windows interprets Problem 2-1 as the same file name.

NOTE

The U.S. National CAD Standard (NCS) includes a comprehensive file naming structure for architectural and construction-related drawings. You can adapt the system for other disciplines.

Figure 2-3.
Examples of mechanical, architectural, and structural drawing file naming schemes. The architectural and structural examples follow the U.S. National CAD Standard (NCS) file naming format.

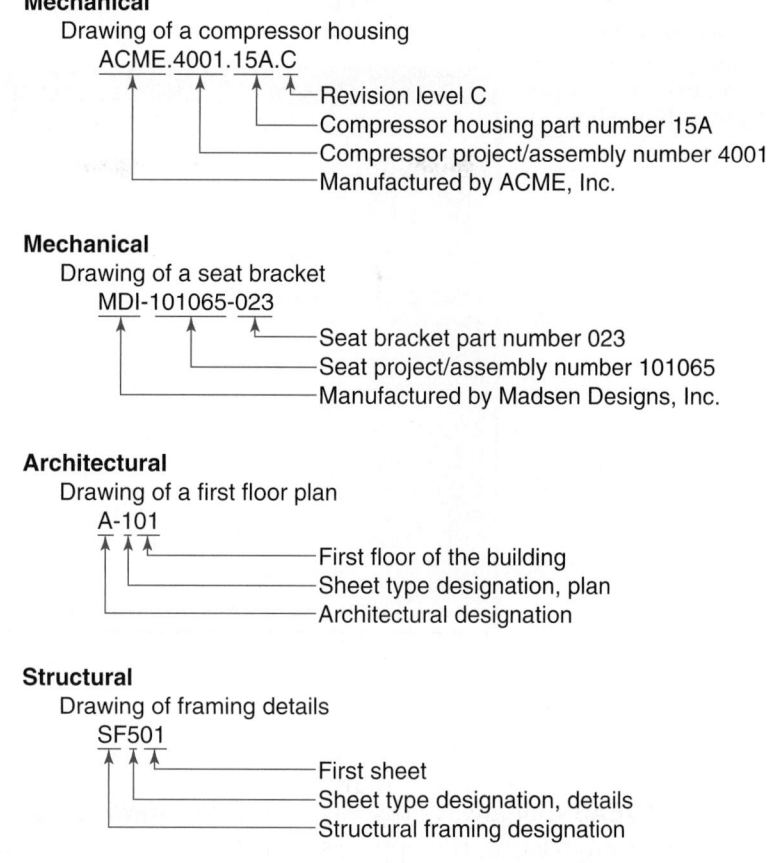

Mechanical
Drawing of a compressor housing
ACME.4001.15A.C
— Revision level C
— Compressor housing part number 15A
— Compressor project/assembly number 4001
— Manufactured by ACME, Inc.

Mechanical
Drawing of a seat bracket
MDI-101065-023
— Seat bracket part number 023
— Seat project/assembly number 101065
— Manufactured by Madsen Designs, Inc.

Architectural
Drawing of a first floor plan
A-101
— First floor of the building
— Sheet type designation, plan
— Architectural designation

Structural
Drawing of framing details
SF501
— First sheet
— Sheet type designation, details
— Structural framing designation

Using the QSAVE Tool

If you have not yet saved a file, the **QSAVE** tool displays the **Save Drawing As** dialog box. See **Figure 2-4.** To save a file, first choose the type of file to save from the **Files of type:** drop-down list. Select AutoCAD 2011 Drawing (*.dwg) for most applications. Use AutoCAD Drawing Template (*.dwt) to save a template file. To share a file with someone using an older version of AutoCAD, choose the appropriate older AutoCAD version from the list. You also have the option of saving a *drawing exchange file (DXF)* or *drawing standards file (DWS)*.

Next, select the folder in which to store the file from the **Save in:** drop-down list. To move upward from the current folder, pick the **Up one level** button. To create a new folder in the current location, pick the **Create New Folder** button and type a new folder name.

The name Drawing1 appears in the **File name:** text box if the file is the first file since the launch of AutoCAD. Change the name to the desired file name. After you specify the correct location and file name, pick the **Save** button to save the file. You can also press [Enter] to activate the **Save** button.

If you saved the file previously, the **QSAVE** tool updates, or resaves, the file based on the current file state. In this situation, **QSAVE** issues no prompts and displays no dialog box.

Using the SAVEAS Tool

Use the **SAVEAS** tool to save a copy of a file using a different name or file type. You can also use the **SAVEAS** tool when you *open* a drawing template file to use as a basis for another drawing. This leaves the template unchanged and ready to use for starting other drawings.

QSAVE

Quick Access
Save
Application Menu
Save
Type
QSAVE
[Ctrl]+[S]

drawing exchange file (DXF): A common file format recognized by other CADD systems.

drawing standards file (DWS): A file used to check the standards of another file using AutoCAD standards-checking tools.

Figure 2-4.
The **Save Drawing As** dialog box is a standard file selection dialog box.

Select folder where drawing will be saved

Move up one level from current folder

Create a new folder

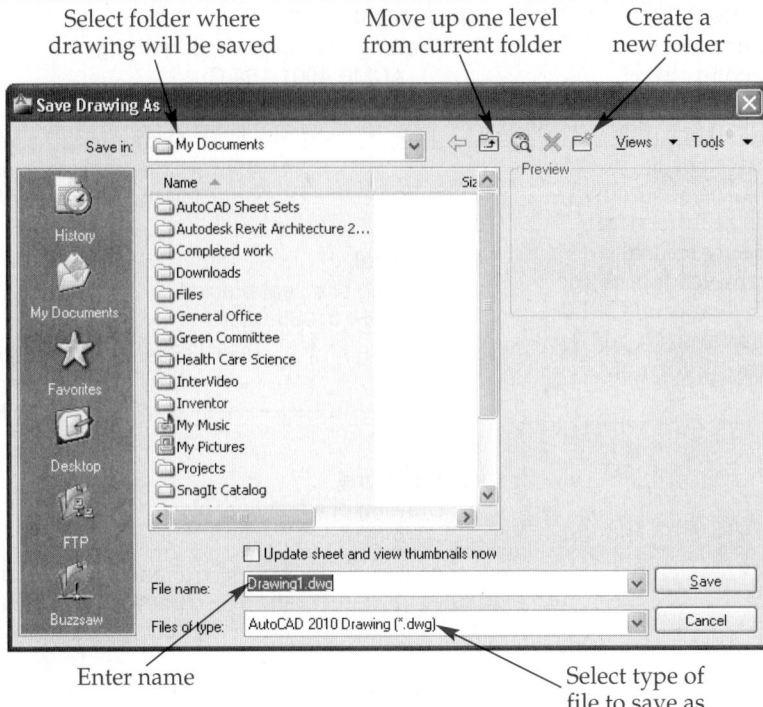

Enter name

Select type of file to save as

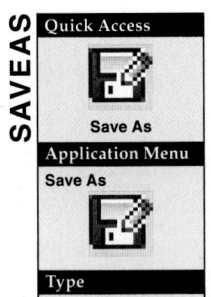

SAVEAS

The **SAVEAS** tool always displays the **Save Drawing As** dialog box. The location and name of an existing file appears. Confirm that the **Files of type:** drop-down list displays the desired file type and that the **Save in:** drop-down list displays the correct drive and folder. Type the new file name in the **File name:** text box and pick the **Save** button.

> **NOTE**
>
> Pick an option from the **Save As** menu in the **Application Menu** to preset the file type in the **Save Drawing As** dialog box.

> **PROFESSIONAL TIP**
>
> When you save a version of a drawing in an earlier format, give the file a name that is different from the AutoCAD 2011 version to prevent accidentally overwriting your working drawing with the older format.

Automatic Saves

automatic save: A save procedure that occurs at specified intervals without your input.

AutoCAD provides an *automatic save* tool that automatically creates a temporary backup file while you work. Settings in the **File Safety Precautions** area of the **Open and Save** tab in the **Options** dialog box control automatic saves. See **Figure 2-5.** Automatic save is on by default and saves every 10 minutes. Type the number of minutes between saves in the **Minutes between saves** text box. By default, AutoCAD names automatically saved files *FileName_n_n_nnnn*.sv$ in the C:\Documents and Settings*user*\Local Settings\Temp folder.

Figure 2-5. Use the **Open and Save** tab in the **Options** dialog box to set up the automatic save feature and backup files.

Activates autosave

Autosave timer setting

Creates backup copies

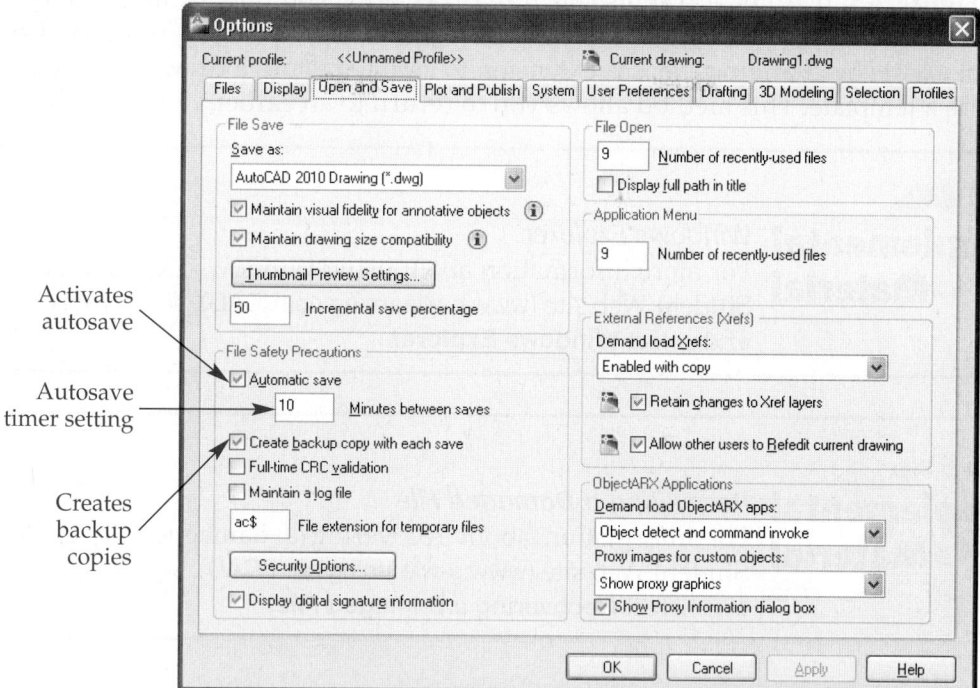

The automatic save timer starts as soon as you make a change to the file and resets when you save the file. The file saves automatically when you start the first tool after reaching the automatic save time. Keep this in mind if you let the computer remain idle; an automatic save does not execute until you return and use a tool. Be sure to save your file manually if you plan to be away from your computer for an extended period.

The automatic save file is available for use if AutoCAD shuts down unexpectedly. Therefore, when you close a file normally, the automatic save file is deleted. However, after a system failure, the **Drawing Recovery Manager** displays the next time you open AutoCAD. It contains a node for every file to display all of the available versions of the file: the original file, the recovered file saved at the time of the system failure, the automatic save file, and the .bak file. Pick a version in the **Drawing Recovery Manager** to view, determine which version you want to save, and then save that file. You can save the recovered file over the original file name.

Application Menu

Drawing
> Open the
 Drawing
 Recovery
 Manager

Type

DRAWING
RECOVERY

> **NOTE**
>
>
>
> The **Automatic Save File Location** item in the **Files** tab of the **Options** dialog box determines the folder where automatic save files are stored.

Backup Files

By default, an AutoCAD backup file is saved in the same folder as the drawing or template file. Backup files have a .bak extension. When you save a drawing or template, the file updates, and the old file overwrites the backup file. Therefore, the backup file is always one save behind the drawing or template file.

The backup feature is on by default and is controlled using the **Create backup copy with each save** check box in the **Open and Save** tab of the **Options** dialog box. See **Figure 2-5.** If AutoCAD shuts down unexpectedly, you may be able to recover a file from the backup version using the **Drawing Recovery Manager.** You can also use a backup file by changing the .bak extension to .dwg to restore a drawing, or to .dwt to restore a template. This method allows you to return to an earlier version of the file.

Supplemental Material

Windows Explorer

For more information about using Windows Explorer, go to the Student Web site (www.g-wlearning.com/CAD), select this chapter, and select **Windows Explorer.**

Supplemental Material

Recovering a Damaged File

For information about recovering a damaged file, go to the Student Web site (www.g-wlearning.com/CAD), select this chapter, and select **Recovering a Damaged File.**

Closing Files

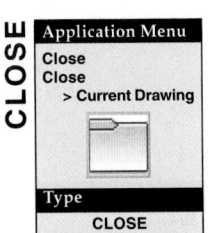

CLOSE

Application Menu
Close
Close
> Current Drawing

Type
CLOSE

Use the **CLOSE** tool to close the current file without exiting AutoCAD. One of the quickest methods of closing a file is to pick the **Close** button from the title bar of a drawing window. If you close a file before saving, AutoCAD prompts you to save or discard changes. Pick the **Yes** button to save the file, or pick the **No** button to discard any changes made to the file since the previous save. Pick the **Cancel** button if you decide not to close the drawing.

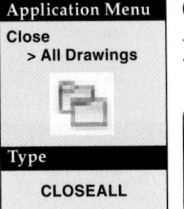

CLOSEALL

Application Menu
Close
> All Drawings

Type
CLOSEALL

AutoCAD allows you to have multiple files open at the same time. Use the **CLOSEALL** tool to close all open files. AutoCAD prompts you to save each file to which you made changes.

NOTE

You can also close files using the **Quick View Drawings** tool, described later in this chapter.

Exercise 2-1

Access the Student Web site (www.g-wlearning.com/CAD) and complete Exercise 2-1.

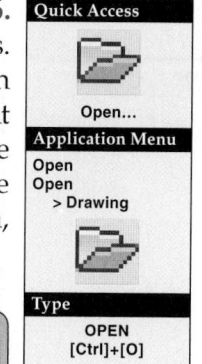

Opening a Saved File

Use the **OPEN** tool to open a saved file. You can also conveniently open a recent document from the **Application Menu** or open a file from Windows Explorer.

Using the OPEN Tool

Access the **OPEN** tool to display the **Select File** dialog box shown in **Figure 2-6**. The buttons on the left side of the dialog box provide instant access to certain folders. See **Figure 2-7**. Double-click on a folder to display the contents. Pick a file to view an image of the file in the **Preview** area. This provides an easy way for you to view the content of a file without loading it into AutoCAD. You can quickly preview other files using the up and down arrow keys to move vertically, and the left and right arrow keys to move horizontally. To open the highlighted file, double-click on a file, pick the **Open** button, or press [Enter].

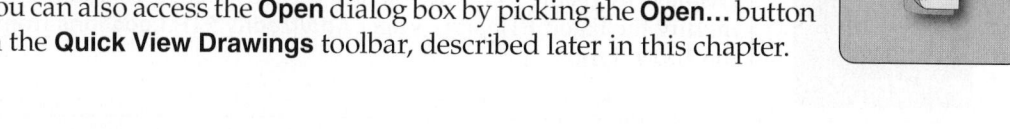

> **NOTE**
>
> You can also access the **Open** dialog box by picking the **Open...** button in the **Quick View Drawings** toolbar, described later in this chapter.

Exercise 2-2

Access the Student Web site (www.g-wlearning.com/CAD) and complete Exercise 2-2.

Figure 2-6. The **Select File** dialog box is a standard file selection dialog box that allows you to open an AutoCAD file. The AutoCAD 2011\Sample folder is open in this illustration. The Architectural – Annotation Scaling and Multileaders drawing is selected and appears in the File name: text box and in the preview area.

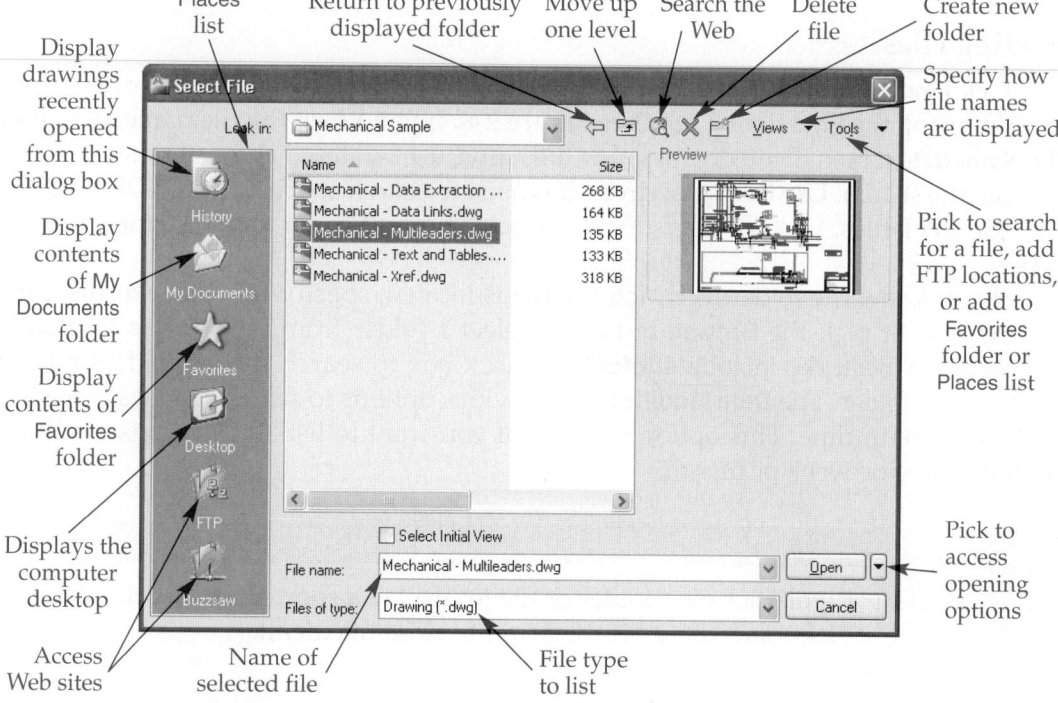

Figure 2-7. Additional features in the **Select File** dialog box. Right-click on the list to access options for adding, removing, and adjusting folders, and for restoring the original folders.

Button	Description
History	Lists drawing files recently opened from the **Select File** dialog box.
My Documents	Displays the files and folders contained in the My Documents folder for the current user.
Favorites	Displays files and folders located in the Favorites folder for the current user. To add the folder displayed in the **Look in:** box to the favorites list, select **Add to Favorites** from the **Tools** flyout.
FTP	Displays available FTP (file transfer protocol) sites. To add or modify the listed FTP sites, select **Add/Modify FTP Locations** from the **Tools** flyout.
Desktop	Lists the files, folders, and drives located on the computer desktop.
Buzzsaw	Displays projects on the Buzzsaw Web site. Buzzsaw.com is designed for the building industry. After setting up a project hosting account, users can access drawings from a given construction project on the Web site. This allows the various companies involved in the project to have instant access to the drawing files.

Finding Files

Pick **Find…** from the **Tools** flyout at the top of the **Select File** dialog box to search for files using the **Find** dialog box. See **Figure 2-8.** If you know the file name, type it in the **Named:** text box. If you do not know the name, use wildcard characters, such as *, to narrow the search. Use the **Type:** drop-down list to search specifically for DWG, DWS, DXF, or DWT files. Use Windows Explorer or Windows Search to search for other file types.

If you know the folder in which the file is located, specify the folder in the **Look in:** text box, or pick the **Browse** button to select a folder from the **Browse for Folder** dialog box. Check the **Include subfolders** check box to search the subfolders within the selected folder. The **Date Modified** tab provides options to search for files modified within a certain time. This option is useful if you want to list all drawings modified within a specific week or month.

NOTE

Right-click on a folder or file to display a shortcut menu of options. Pick somewhere off the menu to close the menu.

Figure 2-8.
Use the **Find** dialog box to locate AutoCAD files.

Enter file name or wildcards

Select type of file to search for

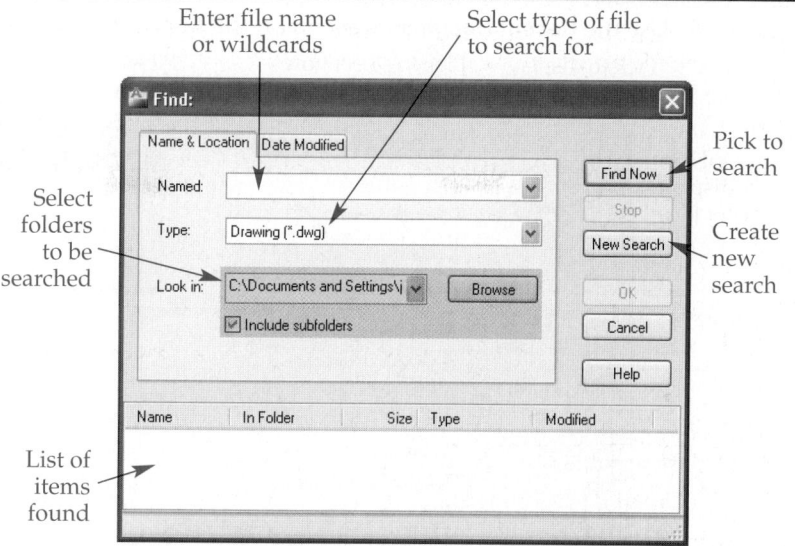

Select folders to be searched

Pick to search

Create new search

List of items found

PROFESSIONAL TIP

Certain file management capabilities are available in file dialog boxes, similar to those in Windows Explorer. For example, to rename an existing file or folder, slowly double-click on the name. This places the name in a text box for editing. Type the new name and press [Enter].

CAUTION

Use caution when deleting or renaming files and folders. Never delete or rename anything if you are not certain you should. If you are unsure, ask your instructor or system administrator for assistance.

Exercise 2-3

Access the Student Web site (www.g-wlearning.com/CAD) and complete Exercise 2-3.

Using the Recent Documents Menu

Pick the **Recent Documents** button in the **Application Menu** to display a list of recently opened documents. See **Figure 2-9**. This provides convenient access to files that may be related to the current project. Nine of the most recent AutoCAD files appear by default.

Use the **Ordered List** drop-down list to organize the files. Select **By Ordered List**, **By Access Date**, **By Size**, or **By Type** according to how you want files arranged. Select from the display options flyout to specify how recent files appear. Choose the appropriate option to display files as icons, small images, medium images, or large images.

Figure 2-9. Use the **Recent Documents** menu on the **Application Menu** to open a recent file.

Pick to display open files · Pick to select how to list recent files · Pick to select a display option

Pick to display recent files

Recently opened files

Pick to pin the file to the list

Tooltip displays when you hover over a file name

Hover over a file in the list to display a tooltip with file information and a preview of the file. Pick a file from the list to open. Pick the pushpin icon to the right of the file to keep the file in the recent documents list. Unpinned files eventually are removed from the recent documents list as you open other files.

PROFESSIONAL TIP

Specify the number of files displayed in the **Recent Documents** list by accessing the **Open and Save** tab of the **Options** dialog box. The **Number of recently-used files** text box in the **Application Menu** area controls this function.

NOTE

If you try to open a deleted or moved file, AutoCAD displays the message Cannot find the specified drawing file. Please verify that the file exists. AutoCAD then opens the **Select File** dialog box.

Using Windows Explorer

Double-click on an AutoCAD file from Windows Explorer to open the file. If AutoCAD is not already running, it starts and the file opens. You can also drag and drop a file onto the AutoCAD **Command** line. If AutoCAD is not running, you can drag and drop the file onto the AutoCAD 2011 icon on your desktop. AutoCAD starts and opens the drawing file.

Opening Old Files

When using AutoCAD 2011, you can open AutoCAD files created in AutoCAD Release 12 or later. When you save a file from a previous release in AutoCAD 2011, AutoCAD automatically updates the file to the current file format. A file saved in AutoCAD 2011 displays in the **Preview** image tile in the **Select File** dialog box.

> **NOTE**
>
> In order to view the original format of an older release file opened in AutoCAD 2011, you must use the **SAVEAS** tool to save it back to the appropriate file format.

Opening as Read-Only or Partial Open

You can open files in various modes by selecting the appropriate option from the **Open** flyout in the **Select File** dialog box. When you open a file as *read-only*, you cannot save changes to the original file. However, you can make changes to the file and then use the **SAVEAS** tool to save changes using a different file name. This ensures that the original file remains unchanged.

read-only: Describes a drawing file intended for viewing only. To keep any changes made to the drawing, use the **SAVEAS** tool to the save the file using a different name.

When opening a large drawing, you may choose to issue a *partial open*. This allows you to open a portion of a drawing by selecting specific views and layers to open. Views and layers are described in later chapters. You can also partially open a drawing in the read-only mode.

partial open: Describes opening a portion of a file by specifying only the views and layers you need to see.

Managing Multiple Documents

Most drafting projects include several closely related files. Each file presents or organizes a different aspect of the project. Examples of drawings for a mechanical drafting project include an assembly drawing, subassembly drawings, and detail drawings of each part. Examples of drawings for a basic architectural drafting project include a site plan, a floor plan, electrical and plumbing plans, and details. You can open multiple AutoCAD files at the same time to work with different portions of a project. Drag-and-drop and similar operations allow you to easily share content between documents.

Controlling Windows

Each file you start or open in AutoCAD appears in its own drawing window. The name of the active file appears on the AutoCAD window title bar, and on a title bar of a floating drawing window. Control drawing windows using the minimize, maximize, restore, and close buttons located in the upper-right corner of each window. See **Figure 2-10**. Resize windows using standard window sizing operations.

The **Windows** panel of the **View** ribbon tab provides one method to access additional window management tools. Pick the **Switch Windows** flyout to display a list of all open files. Select a file from the flyout to activate. The **Tile Horizontally**, **Tile Vertically**, and **Cascade** buttons allow you to control the arrangement of floating drawing windows. Select the **Tile Vertically** button to tile drawings in a vertical arrangement, with the

Figure 2-10. A—Float drawing windows when more than one file is open to work efficiently between drawings. B—Minimize drawing windows to display title bars only. Pick the title bar to display a window control menu.

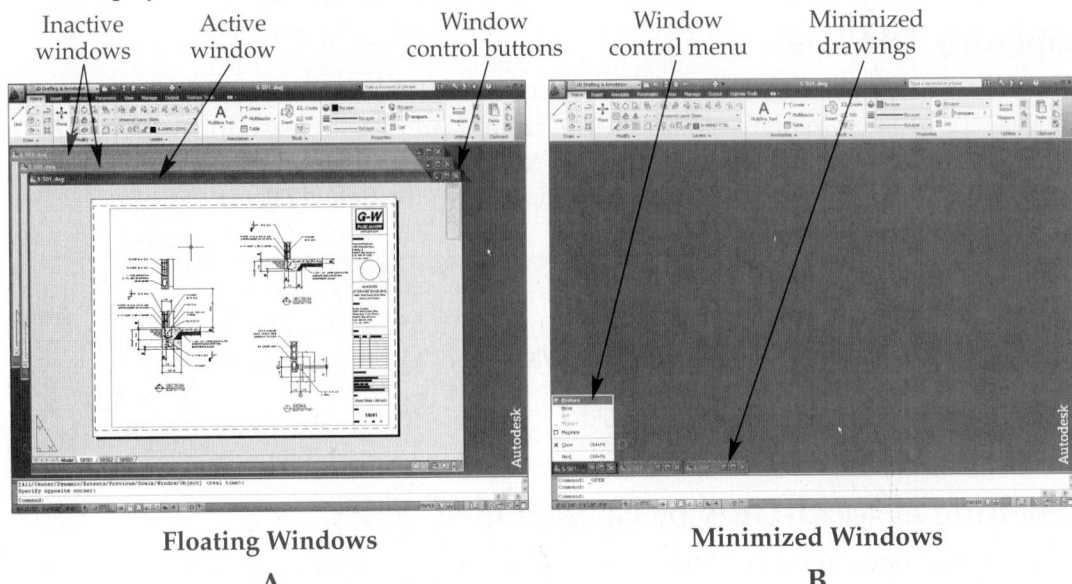

Inactive windows Active window Window control buttons Window control menu Minimized drawings

Floating Windows
A

Minimized Windows
B

active window placed on the left. Pick the **Tile Horizontally** option to tile drawings in a horizontal arrangement, with the active window placed on top. Pick the **Cascade** option to arrange drawing windows in a cascading style. See **Figure 2-11.**

You can also switch drawing windows from the **Application Menu** by picking the **Open Documents** button. Files are listed alphanumerically in the order opened. You can display open files as icons, small images, medium images, or large images by picking the appropriate option from the display options flyout. Pick a file from the list to activate the corresponding drawing window.

Using the Quick View Drawings Tool

The **Quick View Drawings** tool allows you to see and control open AutoCAD files without changing drawing windows. The quickest way to access the **Quick View Drawings** tool is to pick the **Quick View Drawings** button on the status bar. The **Quick View Drawings** tool appears in the lower center of the AutoCAD window. See **Figure 2-12.**

A thumbnail image and file name identify each open file. Files are arranged in the order opened, with the file opened first on the left side of the row. The current file is highlighted when you initially access the **Quick View Drawings** tool. Pick the thumbnail of a different file to make the drawing window current, or move the cursor over a thumbnail to show additional options for controlling the drawing window.

The **Quick View Drawings** tool includes a small toolbar below the file thumbnail images. See **Figure 2-13.** By default, the **Quick View Drawings** tool disappears when you pick a thumbnail to switch files. To keep the tool on-screen after you select a thumbnail, pick the **Pin Quick View Drawings** button on the left side of the toolbar. The **New...** button activates the **QNEW** tool, and the **Open...** button activates the **OPEN** tool. The **New...** and **Open...** buttons are especially useful for starting a new drawing or opening an existing drawing that relates to the current project. Select the **Close Quick View Drawings** button to close the **Quick View Drawings** tool.

Figure 2-11. Examples of tiled and cascading floating drawing windows. The effect of tiling drawing windows varies depending on the number of windows and the tile option you choose.

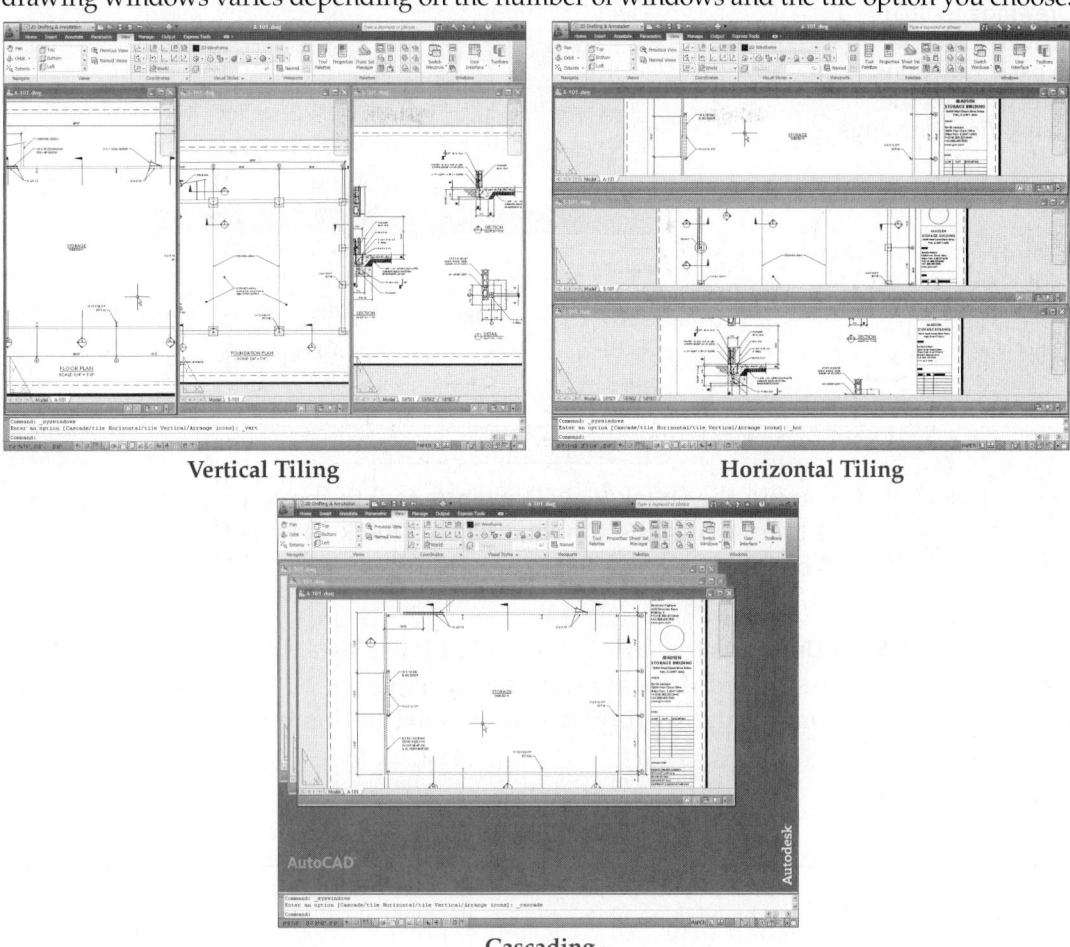

Vertical Tiling   Horizontal Tiling

Cascading

Figure 2-12. The **Quick View Drawings** tool offers an effective visual method for switching and controlling open drawings.

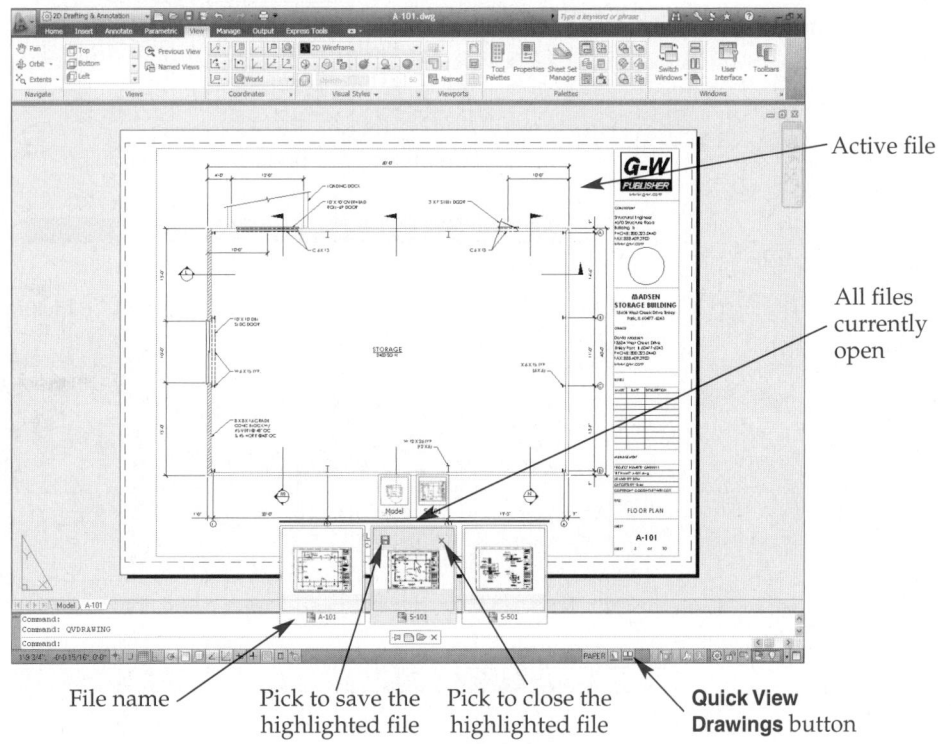

Active file

All files currently open

Quick View Drawings button

File name

Pick to save the highlighted file

Pick to close the highlighted file

Figure 2-13.
The **Quick View Drawings** toolbar provides access to basic functions directly from the **Quick View Drawings** tool.

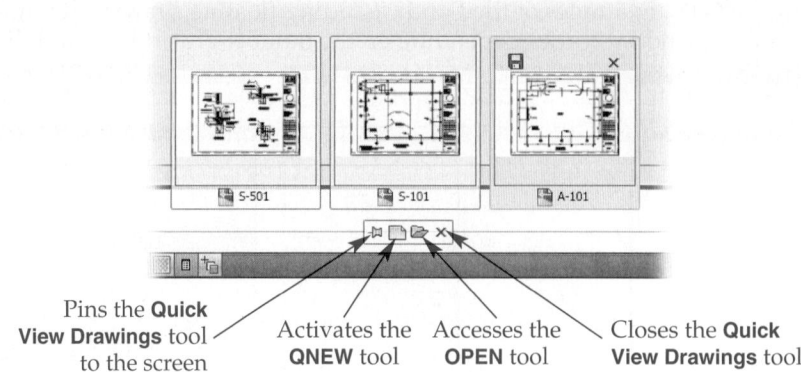

Pins the **Quick View Drawings** tool to the screen

Activates the **QNEW** tool

Accesses the **OPEN** tool

Closes the **Quick View Drawings** tool

NOTE

If you pin the **Quick View Drawings** tool to the screen, close the tool and then access the tool again, the **Quick View Drawings** tool will still be in the pinned state.

The **Quick View Drawings** tool also allows you to display a drawing layout without first activating the associated drawing window. See **Figure 2-14.** Layouts are used to prepare a drawing for plotting, as fully described later in this textbook.

Figure 2-14.
A—The initial display when you hover over a file thumbnail. B—Hover over the model space and layout thumbnails to enlarge.

Model space in the highlighted file

Layouts defined in the highlighted file

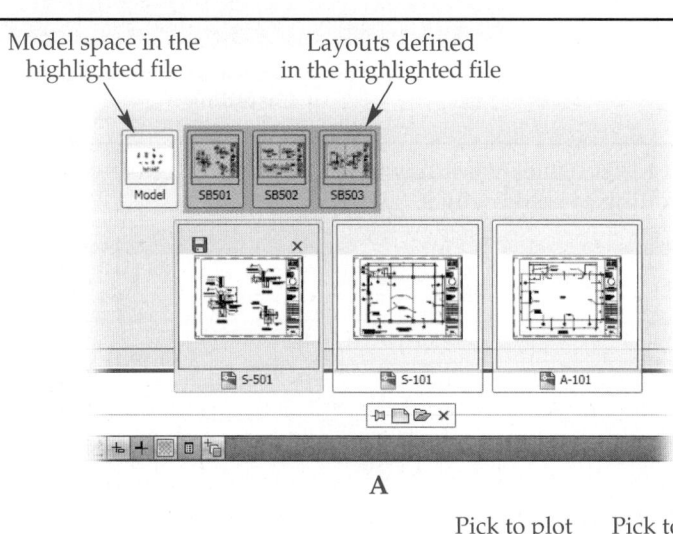

A

Pick to plot   Pick to publish

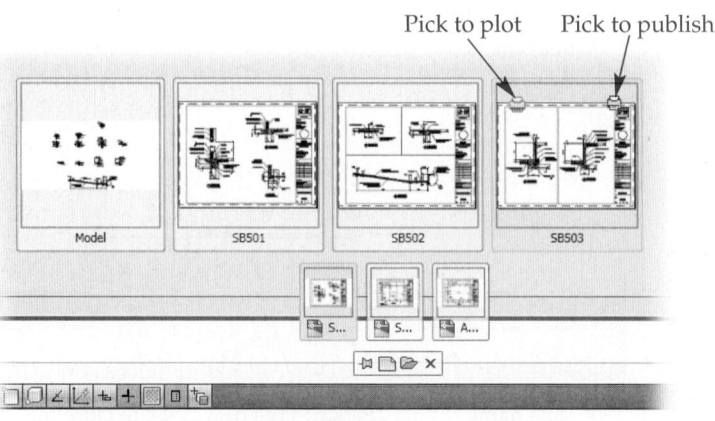

B

Right-click on a thumbnail image to access a shortcut menu of options for controlling open files. The **Windows** cascading menu provides the same features found in the **Windows** panel of the **View** ribbon tab, and the additional **Arrange Icons** option to arrange minimized drawings neatly along the bottom of the drawing window area. Pick **Copy File as a Link** to copy the entire file to the Clipboard for pasting into a drawing or document. Select **Close All** to close all open documents. Pick **Close other files** to close all files except the active file. Choose **Save All** to save all open documents. Select **Close** to close the active file.

PROFESSIONAL TIP

Another technique for switching between open drawings is to press [Ctrl]+[F6]. This is a very effective way to cycle through open drawings quickly.

NOTE

Typically, you can change the active drawing window as desired. However, you cannot activate a different window during certain operations, such as while a dialog box is open. You must complete or cancel the operation before switching.

Exercise 2-4

Access the Student Web site (www.g-wlearning.com/CAD) and complete Exercise 2-4.

Drawing Properties

An AutoCAD file stores drawing properties that identify the file. The file type and name are fundamental examples of file properties. Add values to drawing properties to record common drawing information, such as the title of the product represented by the drawing. You can then reference drawing properties for a variety of purposes, such as adding text to a title block, or creating a bill of materials or report. Additionally, content in the drawing linked to drawing properties updates when you make changes to values in the **Properties** dialog box.

NOTE

The **Properties** dialog box is different from the **Properties** palette, which will be explained in later chapters. The **Properties** dialog box contains properties of the drawing file. The **Properties** palette provides access to the properties of objects created in the drawing file.

Application Menu

Drawing Utilities
> Drawing
    Properties

Type

DWGPROPS

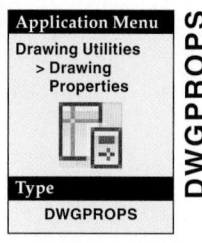

DWGPROPS

Access the **Properties** dialog box to view and make changes to drawing properties. See **Figure 2-15.** Values form in the **General** and **Statistics** tabs when you save the file. You cannot edit general and statistic properties using the **Properties** dialog box. The

Summary tab includes basic file properties, such as the title and author, that you can modify using the text boxes. Use the **Custom** tab to add properties to the file, such as the name of your school or company or the design revision level. Pick the **Add** button to create a custom property name and default value using the **Add Custom Property** dialog box. Remove a custom property using the **Delete** button.

Figure 2-15. Use the **Properties** dialog box to add information about the file. You can then link drawing content, such as text, to the drawing properties.

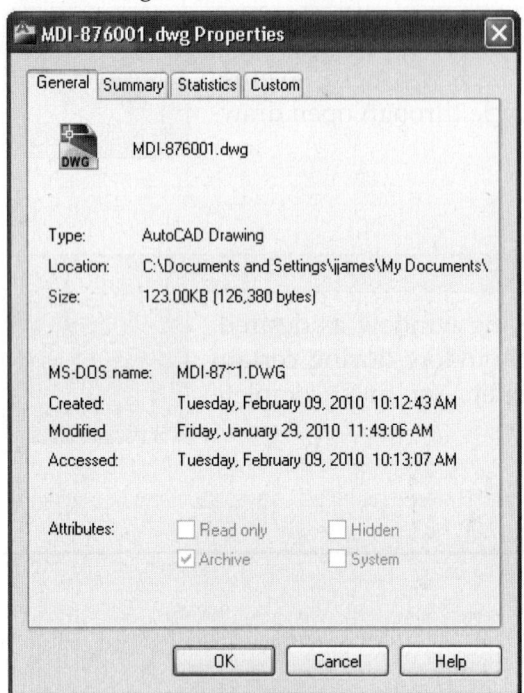

General Tab

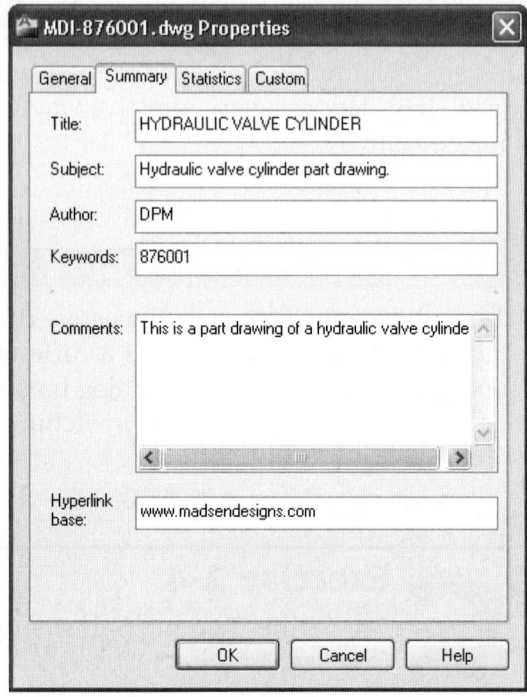

Summary Tab

Pick to remove a custom property

Pick to create a custom property

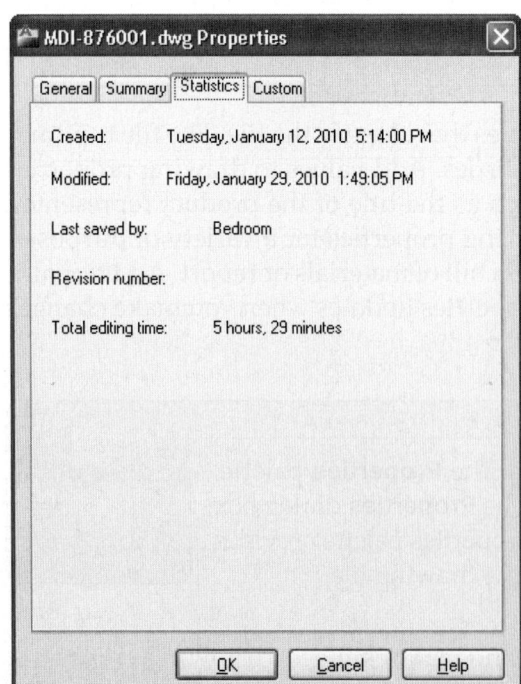

Statistics Tab

Custom Tab

You can view some drawing properties in Windows Explorer by right-clicking on a file and picking **Properties**.

Specify properties that will be used throughout a project and those that are common to multiple projects in template files. These properties will then be predefined every time you begin a new file. You will create template files later in this chapter.

Exercise 2-5

Access the Student Web site (www.g-wlearning.com/CAD) and complete Exercise 2-5.

Basic Drawing Settings

Drawing settings determine the general characteristics of a drawing, such as the units of measurement. You can change drawing settings as needed throughout the drawing process. However, you can specify appropriate drawing settings in template files to preset common drawing properties every time you begin a new file. You will create templates later in this chapter.

AutoCAD includes many drawing settings. The most basic drawing settings control the units of measurement and limits.

Introduction to Model Space

Before you adjust drawing settings and begin drawing, you should understand the two environments in which you can work. *Model space* is where you design and draft the *model* of a product. In mechanical drafting, for example, use model space to draw part and assembly views. In architectural drafting, use model space to draw building plans, elevations, sections, and details.

Once you complete the drawing or model in model space, you switch to *paper (layout) space*, where you prepare a *layout*. A layout represents the sheet of paper used to organize and scale, or lay out, and plot or export a drawing or model. Layouts typically include a border, title block, and general notes. A single drawing can have multiple layouts.

You know you are in model space when you see the model space coordinate system icon, the active **Model** tab, the **MODEL** button on the status bar, and no representation of a sheet in the drawing area. See **Figure 2-16.** You know you are working with a layout when you see the paper space coordinate system icon, an active layout tab, the **PAPER** button on the status bar, and a representation of a sheet in the drawing area. See **Figure 2-17.** If you find that you are not in model space, pick the **Model** tab or the **PAPER** button on the status bar, or use **Quick View Drawings** or **Quick View Layouts**. You will explore **Quick View Layouts** later in this textbook.

model space: The environment in AutoCAD in which the majority of drawing usually occurs, including the design and drafting of drawing views.

model: A term that usually describes a 3D model, but in AutoCAD also refers to 2D drawing geometry, typically created at full size.

paper (layout) space: The environment in AutoCAD in which you create layouts for plotting and display purposes.

layout: An arrangement in paper space of sheet elements, typically including a border, title block, general notes, and a display of items drawn in model space.

Figure 2-16. Model space is the environment in which you design and draft product geometry, such as the views of this hydraulic valve cylinder.

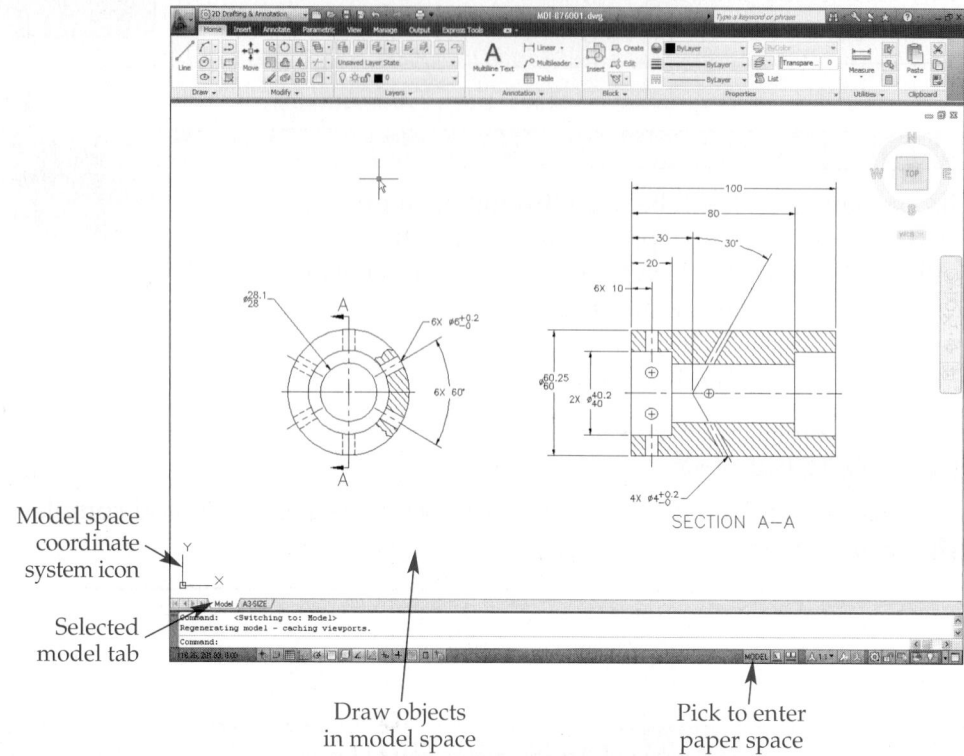

Model space coordinate system icon

Selected model tab

Draw objects in model space

Pick to enter paper space

Figure 2-17. Paper space is the environment in which you lay out model space geometry to complete the drawing and prepare for plotting or export. This example shows common items added to a layout sheet, including an ASME border, title block, revision block, and general notes.

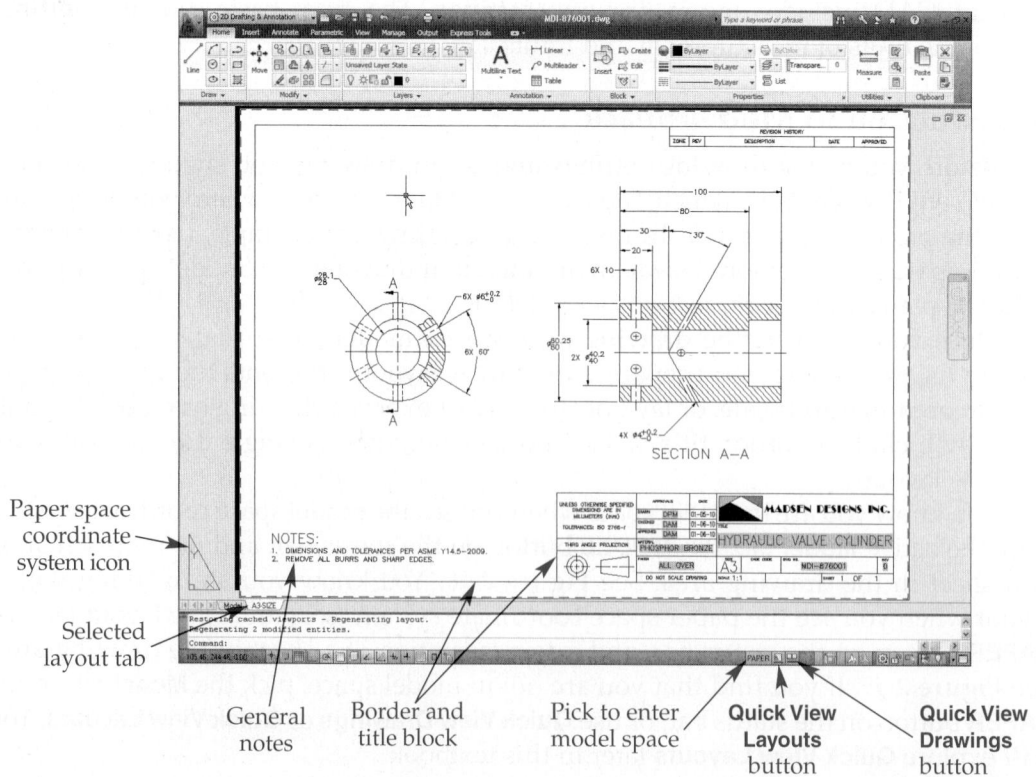

Paper space coordinate system icon

Selected layout tab

General notes

Border and title block

Pick to enter model space

Quick View Layouts button

Quick View Drawings button

Drawing Units

Drawing units define the linear and angular units of measurement used while drawing and the precision to which these measurements display. *You* determine what "1 unit" means in AutoCAD. For example, 1 unit can mean 1 inch, 1 millimeter, 1 meter, or 1 mile. Most AutoCAD users generally think of 1 unit to be 1 inch or 1 millimeter. Access the **Drawing Units** dialog box to set linear and angular units. See **Figure 2-18**. Specify linear unit characteristics in the **Length** area. Use the **Type:** drop-down list to set the linear units format, and use the **Precision:** drop-down list to specify the precision of linear units. **Figure 2-19** describes linear unit formats.

> **drawing units:** The standard linear and angular units and precision of measurement.

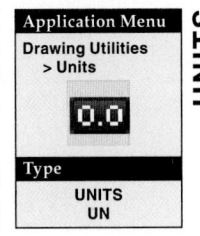

Set the angular unit format and precision in the **Type:** and **Precision:** drop-down lists in the **Angle** area of the **Drawing Units** dialog box. Select the **Clockwise** check box to change the direction for angular measurements to clockwise from the default setting of counterclockwise.

Pick the **Direction...** button to access the **Direction Control** dialog box. See **Figure 2-20**. Pick the **East**, **North**, **West**, or **South** radio button to set the compass orientation. The **Other** radio button activates the **Angle:** text box and the **Pick an angle** button. Enter an angle for zero direction in the **Angle:** text box. The **Pick an angle** button allows you to pick two points on-screen to establish the angle zero direction.

Figure 2-18.
Use the **Drawing Units** dialog box to set linear and angular unit values.

Select linear units

Select linear precision

Specifies the units used to insert objects, but does not preset the drawing to use a specific unit of measurement

Select angular units

Select angular precision

Pick to change direction of angular measurement

Access the **Direction Control** dialog box

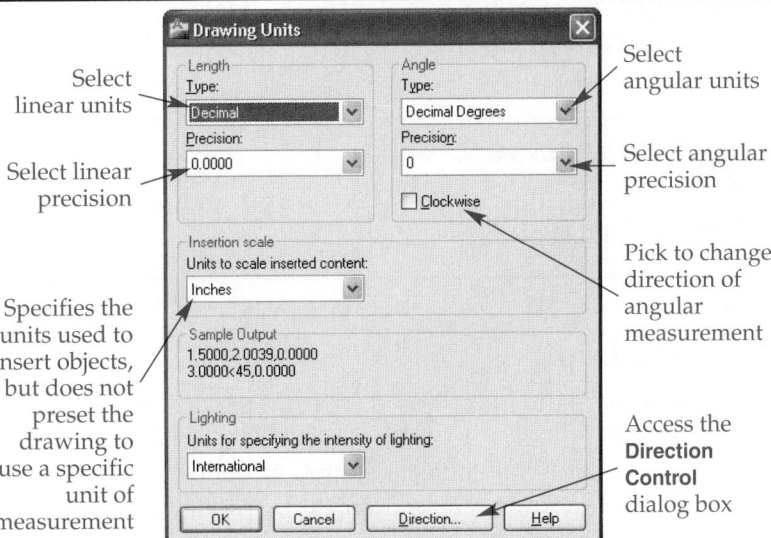

Figure 2-19. Linear unit formats available in the **Drawing Units** dialog box. Select the appropriate type and precision for the specific drawing application.

Type	Typical Applications	Characteristics	Example
Decimal	Mechanical—inch or metric, architectural, structural, civil—metric	• Decimal inches or millimeters. • Conforms to the ASME Y14.5 dimensioning and tolerancing standard. • Four decimal place default precision.	14.1655
Engineering	Civil—feet and inch	• Feet and decimal inches. • Four decimal place default precision.	1'-2.1655"
Architectural	Architectural, structural—feet and inch	• Feet, inches, and fractional inches. • 1/16" default precision.	1'-2 3/16"
Fractional	Mechanical—fractional	• Fractional parts of any common unit of measure. • 1/16" default precision.	14 3/16
Scientific	Chemical engineering, astronomy	• E+01 means the base number is multiplied by 10 to the first power. • Used when very large or small values are required. • Four decimal place default precision.	1.4166E+01

Figure 2-20.
The **Direction Control** dialog box.

Set direction of 0°

Specify another angle

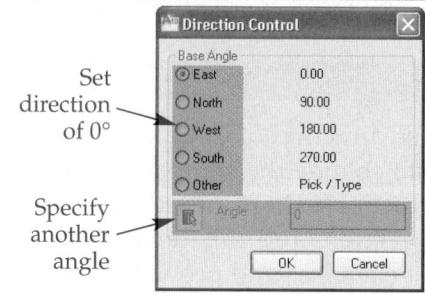

Figure 2-21 describes angular unit formats. After selecting the linear and angular units and precision, pick the **OK** button to exit the **Drawing Units** dialog box.

Exercise 2-6

Access the Student Web site (www.g-wlearning.com/CAD) and complete Exercise 2-6.

Drawing Limits

You prepare an AutoCAD drawing at actual size, or full scale, regardless of the type of drawing, the units used, or the size of the final layout on paper. Use model space to draw full-scale objects. AutoCAD allows you to specify the size of a virtual model space drawing area, known as the model space drawing limits, or *limits*. You typically set limits in a template, but you can change limits as necessary.

limits: The size of the virtual drawing area in model space.

Figure 2-21. Angular unit formats available in the **Drawing Units** dialog box. Select the appropriate type and precision for the specific drawing application.

Type	Applications and Characteristics	Example
Decimal Degrees	• Mechanical, architectural, and structural drafting applications. • Degrees and decimal parts of a degree. • Initial default setting.	45°
Deg/Min/Sec	• Civil and sometimes mechanical, architectural, and structural drafting applications. • Degrees, minutes, and seconds. • 1 degree = 60 minutes; 1 minute = 60 seconds.	45°0′0″
Grads	• Grad is the abbreviation for *gradient*. • One-quarter of a circle has 100 grads; a full circle has 400 grads.	50.000g
Radians	• A radian is an angular unit of measurement in which 2π radians = 360° and π radians = 180°. Pi (π) is approximately equal to 3.1416. • A 90° angle has $\pi/2$ radians and an arc length of $\pi/2$. • Changing the precision displays the radian value rounded to the specified decimal place.	0.785r
Surveyor	• Civil drafting applications. • Degrees, minutes, and seconds. • Uses bearings. A bearing is the direction of a line with respect to one of the quadrants of a compass. Bearings are measured clockwise or counterclockwise (depending on the quadrant), beginning from either north or south. • An angle measuring 55°45′22″ from north toward west is expressed as N55°45′22″W. • Set precision to degrees, degrees/minutes, degrees/minutes/seconds, or decimal display accuracy of the seconds part of the measurement.	N45°E

The concept of limits is somewhat misleading, because the AutoCAD drawing area is infinite in size. For example, if you set limits to 17″ × 11″, you can still create objects that extend past the 17″ × 11″ area, such as a line that is 1200′ long. Therefore, you can choose not to consider limits while developing a template or creating a drawing. Conversely, as you learn AutoCAD, you may decide that setting appropriate drawing limits is helpful, especially when you are drawing large objects. Regardless of whether you choose to acknowledge limits, you should be familiar with the concept and recognize that some AutoCAD tools, such as **ZOOM** and **PLOT**, provide options for using limits. The **ZOOM** and **PLOT** tools are explained in later chapters.

Access the **LIMITS** tool to set model space drawing limits. The first prompt asks you to specify the coordinates for the lower-left corner of the drawing limits. Press [Enter] to accept the default 0,0 value or enter a new value and press [Enter]. The next prompt asks you to specify the coordinates for the upper-right corner of the virtual drawing area. For example, type 17,11 and then press [Enter] to set limits of 17 units × 11 units. The first value is the horizontal measurement of the limits, and the second value is the vertical measurement. A comma separates the values.

In general, you should set limits larger than the objects you plan to draw. You can determine limits accurately by identifying the drawing scale, converting the scale to a scale factor, and then multiplying the scale factor by the size of sheet on which

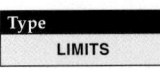

LIMITS

you plan to plot the drawing. For now, calculate the approximate total length and width of all objects you plan to draw, and add extra space for dimensions and notes. For example, when drawing a 48′ × 24′ building floor plan, allow 10′ on each side for dimensions and notes to make a total virtual drawing area of 68′ × 44′.

NOTE

The **LIMITS** tool provides a limits-checking feature that, when turned on, restricts your ability to draw outside of the drawing limits. Turn on limits checking by entering or selecting the **ON** option of the **LIMITS** tool. Turn off limits checking using the **OFF** option.

Introduction to Templates

Drawing templates allow you to use an existing drawing as a starting point for a new drawing. A template includes drawing settings for specific applications that are preset each time you begin a new drawing. Templates are incredible productivity boosters. They help ensure that everyone at your school or company uses the same drawing standards. Templates usually include the following, set according to the drawing requirements:

- ✓ Units and limits
- ✓ Drawing aids, such as dynamic input, grid display, and snaps
- ✓ Layers with specific line standards
- ✓ Text, dimension, multileader, table, and plot styles
- ✓ Common symbols and blocks
- ✓ Layouts with a border, title block, and general notes

sheet: The paper used to lay out and plot drawings.

sheet size: Size of the paper used to lay out and plot drawings.

Drawing Sheets

For tables describing *sheet* characteristics, including *sheet size*, drawing scale, and drawing limits, go to the **Reference Material** section of the Student Web site (www.g-wlearning.com/CAD) and select **Drawing Sheets**. Additional information regarding sheet parameters and selection is described later in this textbook.

Template Development

Starting from scratch or using a template supplied with AutoCAD is an appropriate way to begin drawing as you first learn AutoCAD. However, you may soon discover it necessary to create your own templates. Creating your own templates helps you reduce setup time significantly, increase productivity, and consistently adhere to drafting standards. Begin the basic process of template development now, and continue to add content to your templates while you learn AutoCAD.

You can save *any* drawing or template file as a template using the **SAVEAS** tool and **Save Drawing As** dialog box. Pick AutoCAD Drawing Template (*.dwt) from the **Files of type:** drop-down list, and then specify a template name and storage location. Template names typically relate to the drawing application, such as Mechanical Template for mechanical part and assembly drawings, or Architectural floor plans for architectural floor plan drawings.

By default, the file list box in the **Save Drawing As** dialog box shows the drawing templates currently found in the Template folder. See **Figure 2-22A**. You can store templates in any appropriate location, but if you place them in the Template folder, they automatically appear in the **Select template** dialog box. Pick the **Save** button to save the template and display the **Template Options** dialog box. See **Figure 2-22B**. Type a brief description of the template file in the **Description** area. Specify English or Metric units in the **Measurement** drop-down list and pick the **OK** button.

NOTE

Pick **AutoCAD Drawing Template** from the **Save As** menu of the **Application Menu** to preset the template file type in the **Save Drawing As** dialog box.

Figure 2-22.
A—Save a template using the .dwt file extension. If desired, save it in the AutoCAD Template folder. B—Type a description of the new template in the **Template Options** dialog box.

Select the folder in which to save the template

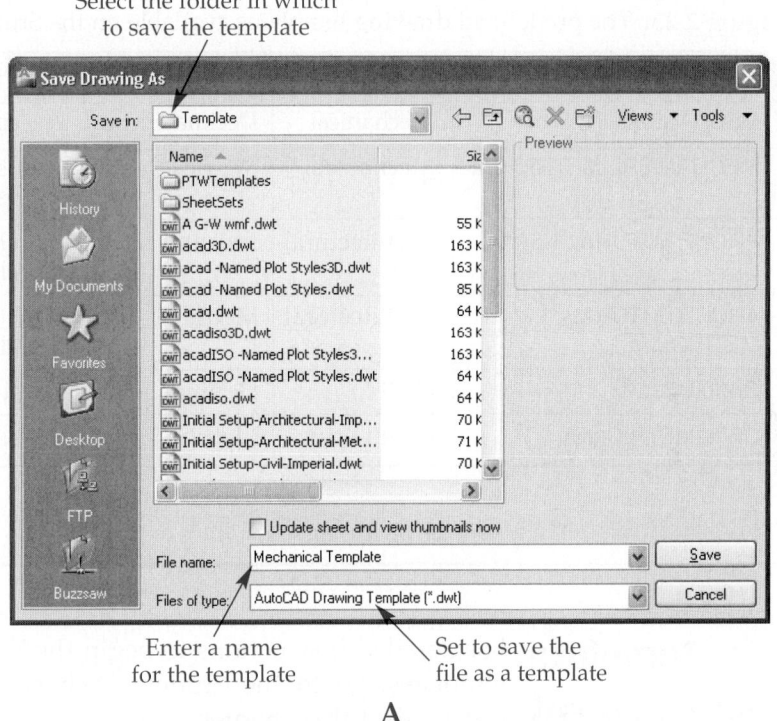

Enter a name for the template

Set to save the file as a template

A

Enter a description for the template

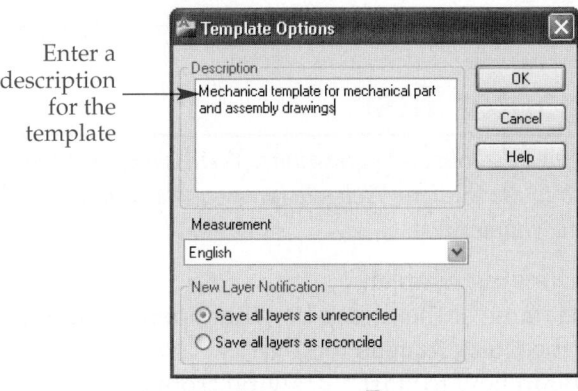

B

The Student Web site contains several predefined templates that you can use to create drawings in accordance with correct mechanical, architectural, and civil drafting standards. **Figure 2-23** describes each available template. The mechanical drafting templates follow American Society of Mechanical Engineers ASME/ANSI and ISO drafting standards. The architectural and civil drafting templates follow appropriate architectural and civil drafting standards, including standards specified in the NCS.

In addition to the complete, ready-to-use templates on the Student Web site, the Template Development sections at the end of several chapters refer you to the Student Web site for important template creation topics and procedures. Use the Template Development feature of this textbook to learn gradually how to prepare templates in accordance with correct mechanical, architectural, and civil drafting standards.

Figure 2-23. The predefined drawing templates available on the Student Web site.

Template File	Discipline	Units	Layout Sheet Sizes
MECHANICAL-INCH.dwt	Mechanical	Decimal inches	A-size, B-size, C-size, D-size
MECHANICAL-METRIC.dwt	Mechanical	Metric	A4-size, A3-size, A2-size, A1-size
ARCHITECTURAL-US.dwt	Architectural	Feet and inches	Architectural C-size, Architectural D-size
ARCHITECTURAL-METRIC.dwt	Architectural	Metric	Architectural A2-size, Architectural A1-size
CIVIL-US.dwt	Civil	Decimal inches	C-size, D-size
CIVIL-METRIC.dwt	Civil	Metric	A2-size, A1-size

Template Development
Chapter 2

For detailed instructions to begin the development of drawing templates, go to the Student Web site (www.g-wlearning.com/CAD), select this chapter, and select the **Template Development** link.

Chapter Test

Answer the following questions. Write your answers on a separate sheet of paper or go to the Student Web site (www.g-wlearning.com/CAD) and complete the electronic chapter test.

1. What is a drawing template?
2. What is the name of the dialog box that opens by default when you pick the **New** button on the **Quick Access** toolbar?
3. Briefly explain how to start a drawing from scratch.

4. How often should you save your work?
5. Explain the benefits of using a standard system for naming drawing files.
6. Name the tool that allows you to save your work quickly without displaying a dialog box.
7. What tool allows you to save a drawing file in an older AutoCAD format?
8. How do you set AutoCAD to save your work automatically at designated intervals?
9. Identify the tool you would use if you want to exit a drawing file, but remain in the AutoCAD session.
10. How can you close all open drawing windows at the same time?
11. How can you set the number of recently opened files listed in the **Application Menu**?
12. What does the term *read-only* mean?
13. Describe the advantages of using the **Quick View Drawings** tool to work with multiple open drawings.
14. How do you keep the **Quick View Drawings** tool on-screen after you pick a thumbnail image?
15. What is the function of drawing properties?
16. What is the advantage of adding values to drawing properties?
17. Name three settings you can specify in the **Drawing Units** dialog box.
18. What is sheet size?
19. Explain the benefit of using a drawing template file to create a new drawing.
20. How can you convert a drawing file into a drawing template?

Drawing Problems

Start AutoCAD if it is not already started. Follow the specific instructions for each problem.

▼ Basic

1. Start a new drawing using the **acad-Named Plot Styles** template supplied by AutoCAD. Save the new drawing as a file named P2-1.dwg.

2. Start a new drawing using the **Tutorial-iArch** template supplied by AutoCAD. Save the new drawing as a file named P2-3.dwg.

▼ Intermediate

Problems 3 and 4 refer to drawings available at www.autodesk.com/autocad-samples.

3. Locate and click on the Lineweights drawing to open it. Enter Z and A to view the entire drawing. Describe the drawing.

4. Locate and click on the TrueType drawing to open it. Enter Z and A to view the entire drawing. Describe the drawing.

▼ Advanced

For Problems 5–7, create the specified template for possible future use.

5. Create a template with decimal units with 0.0 precision, decimal degrees with 0.0 precision, default angle measure and orientation, and limits of 0,0 × 17,11. Save the template as P2-8.dwt. Enter an appropriate description for the template.

Drawing Problems - Chapter 2

6. Create a template with metric units with 0.0 precision, decimal degrees with 0.0 precision, default angle measure and orientation, and limits of 0,0 × 22,17. Save the template as P2-9.dwt. Enter an appropriate description for the template.

7. Create a template with architectural units with 0'-0" precision, decimal degrees with 0 precision, and limits of 0,0 × 1632,1056. Save the template as P2-10.dwt. Enter an appropriate description for the template.

8. Research the requirements for a set of working drawings of a mechanical assembly. Identify a mechanical assembly consisting of several parts, and possibly subassemblies. Describe the product and provide a detailed list of each drawing required in the set of working drawings. Create, in writing only, a complete directory for storing and organizing the drawing files. Use an appropriate system to name each folder and file.

9. Research the requirements for a set of working drawings for a single-family home according to national and local codes. Provide a detailed list of each drawing required in the set of working drawings. Create, in writing only, a complete directory for storing and organizing the drawing files. Use an appropriate system to name each folder and file. Refer to the U.S. National CAD Standard if available.

AutoCAD Certified Associate Exam Practice

Answer the following questions. Write your answers on a separate sheet of paper.

1. Which of the following methods can you use to close an AutoCAD drawing file? *Select all that apply.*
   A. Enter **CLOSEFILE** at the keyboard
   B. Pick the **Close** button on the drawing window title bar
   C. Pick **Close** in the **Application Menu**
   D. Right-click in the drawing area and pick **Close...**
   E. Select **Close** and then select **Current Drawing** in the **Application Menu**

2. Which of the following tasks can you accomplish using the **Application Menu**? *Select all that apply.*
   A. Access the **Options** dialog box
   B. Open a new drawing
   C. Specify the limits for a drawing
   D. Specify the units and precision for a drawing
   E. Access **Quick View Drawings**

AutoCAD Certified Professional Exam Practice

Follow the instructions in each problem. Write your answers on a separate sheet of paper.

1. **Open the db_samp.dwg file in the Database Connectivity subfolder of the AutoCAD Sample folder.**
   Access the **LIMITS** tool and press [Enter] repeatedly to cycle through the prompts. Do not change any of the values. What are the coordinates for the upper-right corner of the drawing limits for this drawing?

2. **Open the Mechanical - Multileaders.dwg file in the Mechanical Sample subfolder of the AutoCAD Sample folder.**
   Access the **Drawing Units** dialog box. Do not change any of the values. What type of linear drawing units are specified for this drawing, and at what precision?

Introduction to Drawing and Editing

Learning Objectives

After completing this chapter, you will be able to do the following:
- ✓ Use appropriate values when responding to prompts.
- ✓ Apply basic viewing methods.
- ✓ Draw given objects using the **LINE** tool.
- ✓ Describe and use several point entry tools and methods.
- ✓ Describe and use basic drawing aids.
- ✓ Use the **ERASE**, **UNDO**, **U**, **REDO**, and **OOPS** tools appropriately.
- ✓ Create selection sets using various selection options.

This chapter introduces a variety of fundamental drawing and editing concepts and processes. You will learn to pick points, draw lines, select objects, and erase objects. You will also use basic drawing aids and explore several other primary AutoCAD tools and operations.

Responding to Prompts

AutoCAD tools prompt, or ask, you to perform a specific task. For example, when you draw a line, prompts ask you to specify line endpoints. When you erase an object, a prompt asks you to select objects to erase. You must understand how to respond to prompts before you begin drawing. Many prompts provide options that you can select instead of responding to the immediate request. For example, after you pick the first point of a line, a prompt asks you to select the next point, or you can choose the **Undo** option to remove the previous selection.

Responding with Numbers

Many tools require you to enter specific numerical data, such as the location of a point, or the radius of a circle. Acceptable values vary depending on the tool and prompt. AutoCAD understands that a number is positive without the plus sign (+) in front of the value. However, you must add a hyphen (-) in front of a negative number, such as -6.375. Do not include a space when responding to a prompt, because the space bar functions like [Enter] to end the input.

The drawing units have some effect on values that you can enter when responding to prompts. All drawing length units accept decimal or fractional values. For example, you can type 2.5 or 2-1/2 to specify two and one half units. (Remember, you are responsible for applying the appropriate units.) Architectural units recognize this example value as 2 1/2″, decimal units as 2.5 units, engineering units as 2.5″, fractional units as 2 1/2 units, and scientific units as 2.5E+0 units, depending on the precision.

AutoCAD only accepts the inch (″) and foot (′) symbols when a drawing is set up with architectural or engineering units, and does not recognize other suffixes, such as mm. The numerator and denominator of fractions must be whole numbers greater than zero, such as 1/2 or 2/3. You must include a hyphen between a whole number and a fraction for values greater than one, such as 2-3/4, because of the function of the space bar. The numerator can be larger than the denominator, as in 3/2, but only if you do not include a whole number with the fraction. For example, 1-3/2 is not a valid input.

AutoCAD assumes inches when a drawing is set up with architectural and engineering length units. Do not add inch marks (″) when specifying an inch value; they are unnecessary and time-consuming. Values can be whole numbers, decimals, or fractions. For measurements in feet, place the foot symbol (′) after the number, as in 24′. Do not include a space or hyphen when specifying a value in feet and whole inches. For example, 24′6 is the proper input for the value 24′-6″. Separate fractional inches with a hyphen, such as 24′6-1/2. Never mix feet with inch values greater than one foot. For example, 24′18 is invalid; type 25′6 instead.

Ending and Canceling Tools

Some AutoCAD tools remain active until stopped. For example, you can continue to pick points to create new line segments until you end the **LINE** tool. You can usually end a tool by pressing [Enter] or the space bar, or by right-clicking and selecting **Enter**. Press [Esc] to cancel an active tool or abort data entry. It may be necessary to press [Esc] twice to cancel certain tools completely.

TEXTSCR

Ribbon
View
> Windows
> User
Interface
> Text
Window
Type
TEXTSCR
[F2]

If you press the wrong key or misspell a word when answering a prompt, use [Backspace] to correct the error. This works only if you notice your mistake *before* you accept the value. If you enter an invalid value or option, AutoCAD usually responds with an error message. Access the **AutoCAD Text Window** to view lengthy error messages, or to review entries. Return to the graphics screen using the same method you used to access the text window, or pick any visible portion of the graphics screen.

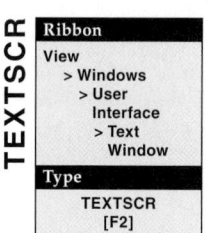

PROFESSIONAL TIP

You can cancel the active tool and access a new tool at the same time by picking a ribbon button or an **Application Menu** option.

point entry:
Locating a point, such as the endpoint of a line, on the AutoCAD coordinate system.

Cartesian (rectangular) coordinate system: A system that locates points in space according to distances from three intersecting axes.

rectangular coordinates: A set of numerical values that identify the location of a point on the X, Y, and Z axes of the Cartesian coordinate system.

Introduction to Drawing

Most object drawing tools use *point entry* to locate and size geometry. Examples of point entry include specifying the two endpoints of a line, locating the center and a point on the edge of a circle, and specifying the points at opposite corners of a rectangle. The most basic point entry technique is to pick a random location in space using the left mouse button. Specific coordinate entry methods and drawing aids allow for accurate point entry, as explained later in this textbook.

AutoCAD uses the *Cartesian (rectangular) coordinate system* of X, Y, and Z coordinate values. These values, called *rectangular coordinates*, locate any point in

3D space. In 2D drafting, the *origin* divides the coordinate system into four quadrants on the XY plane. See **Figure 3-1.** The origin is usually at the lower-left corner of the drawing. This setup places all points in the upper-right quadrant of the XY plane, where both X and Y coordinate values are positive. See **Figure 3-2.** To locate a point in 3D space, a third dimension rises up from the surface of the XY plane along the Z axis.

Describe a coordinate location with the X value first, followed by the Y value, and finally the Z value. A comma separates each value. For example, the coordinate location of 3,1,6 represents a point that is three units from the origin in the X direction, one unit from the origin in the Y direction, and six units from the origin in the Z direction. *AutoCAD and Its Applications—Advanced* describes how to use the Z axis to construct 3D models.

origin: The intersection point of the X, Y, and Z axes. The position of the default 2D origin is 0,0, where X = 0 and Y = 0.

Figure 3-1.
The 2D Cartesian coordinate system consists of X and Y axes. The origin is located at the intersection of the axes.

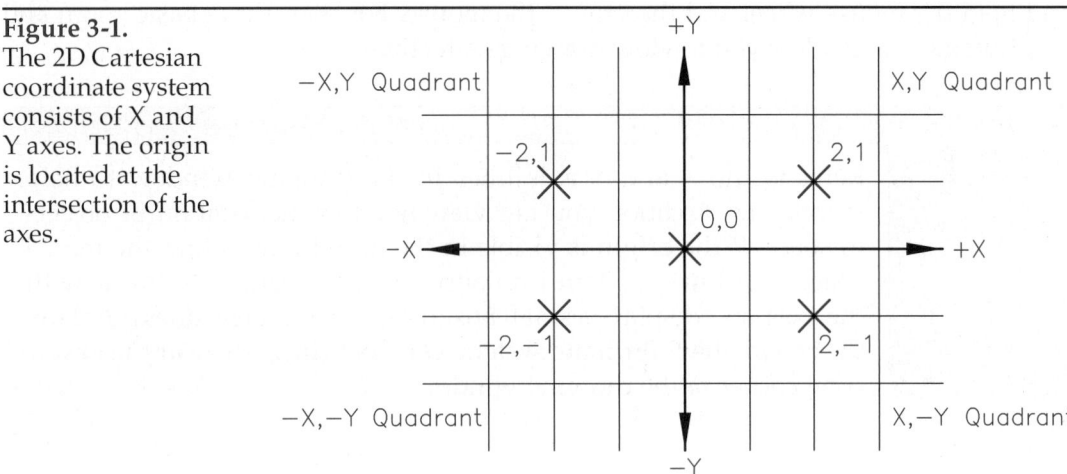

Figure 3-2. By default, the upper-right quadrant of the Cartesian coordinate system fills the screen. The model space coordinate system, or UCS, icon identifies the coordinate system orientation.

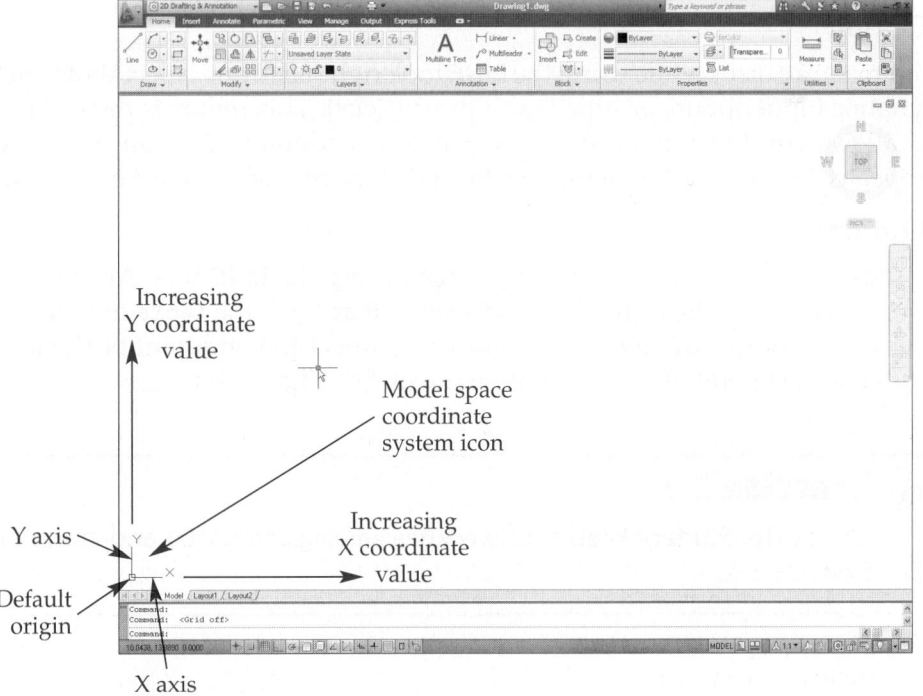

Exercise 3-1

Access the Student Web site (www.g-wlearning.com/CAD) and complete Exercise 3-1.

Basic Viewing Methods

zoom: Make objects appear bigger (zoom in) or smaller (zoom out) on the screen without affecting their actual size.

pan: Change the drawing display so that different portions of the drawing are visible on-screen.

zoom out: Change the display area to show a larger part of the drawing at a lower magnification.

zoom in: Change the display area to show a smaller part of the drawing at a higher magnification.

View tools allow you to navigate the infinite AutoCAD drawing area and observe and work more efficiently with a specific portion of a drawing. Chapter 6 explains the many view tools available to adjust the display of a 2D drawing. However, as you begin drawing, you should be able to apply basic *zoom* and *pan* operations. To *zoom out*, roll the mouse wheel forward. To *zoom in*, roll the mouse wheel back. Double-click the wheel to zoom to the furthest extents of objects in the drawing. To pan, press and hold the mouse wheel and then move the mouse. For now, these basic zoom and pan functions will allow you to view drawings effectively.

> **NOTE**
>
> Refer to the X and Y axis lines in the drawing window to help identify the location you are viewing, and the location of objects in space. If the origin is visible in the drawing window, the model space coordinate system icon appears at the origin, collinear with the axes, and displays a small box. If the current view does not show the origin, the coordinate system icon floats in space near the lower-right corner of the drawing window.

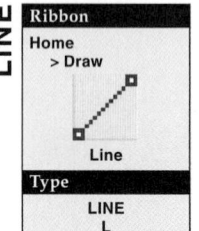

LINE

Ribbon
Home
> Draw

Line

Type
LINE
L

rubberband line: A reference line that extends from the crosshairs with certain drawing tools after you make the first selection.

polygon: Closed plane figure with at least three sides, such as a triangle or rectangle.

Drawing Lines

To draw a line, access the **LINE** tool and specify a start point, which is the first line endpoint. As you move the crosshairs, a *rubberband line* appears connecting the first point and the crosshairs. Continue locating points to connect a series of line segments. Then press [Enter] or the space bar, or right-click and select **Enter** to end the **LINE** tool.

Undo Option

If you make an error while using the **LINE** tool, right-click and select **Undo**, pick the **Undo** dynamic input option, or type U and press [Enter]. This removes the most recent line and allows you to continue from the previous endpoint. You can use the **Undo** option repeatedly to delete line segments until the entire line is gone. See **Figure 3-3.**

Close Option

The **Close** option aids in drawing a *polygon* using the **LINE** tool. After you draw two or more line segments, right-click and select **Close**, pick the **Close** dynamic input option, or type C or CLOSE and press [Enter] to connect the endpoint of the last line segment to the start point of the first line segment. See **Figure 3-4.**

Exercise 3-2

Access the Student Web site (www.g-wlearning.com/CAD) and complete Exercise 3-2.

Figure 3-3.
Using the **Undo** option of the active **LINE** tool. The dashed lines represent the undone lines, and do not appear when you use the **Undo** option.

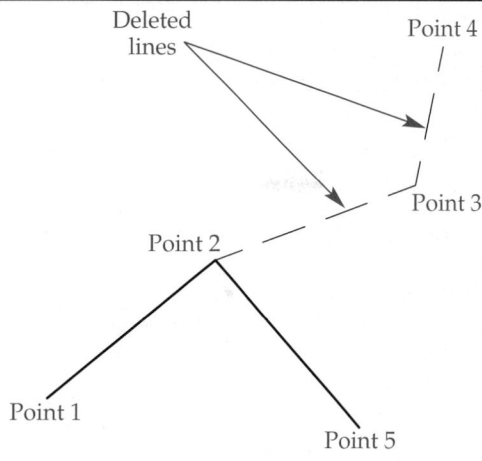

Figure 3-4.
Constructing the final segment of a rectangle using the **Close** option of the **LINE** tool.

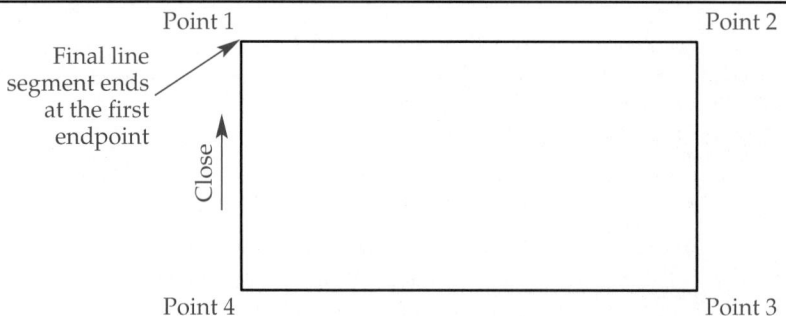

Coordinate Entry Methods

Creating an object by picking random points in space with the left mouse button is typically not accurate. Specific coordinate input is one way to locate points precisely to create accurate geometry. Another option is to use drawing aids, as explained later in this chapter.

Absolute Coordinates

Points located using *absolute coordinates* measured from the origin (0,0). For example, a point located two units horizontally (X = 2) and two units vertically (Y = 2) from the origin is at the absolute coordinate 2,2. **Figure 3-5A** shows using absolute coordinates to draw a line starting at 2,2 and ending at 4,4. The first point of a line is often positioned using absolute coordinates. Remember, when using the absolute coordinate system, you locate each point from 0,0. If you enter negative X and Y values, the selection occurs outside of the upper-right XY plane quadrant.

absolute coordinates: Coordinate distances measured from the origin.

Relative Coordinates

When using *relative coordinates*, think of the previous point as the "temporary origin." The @ symbol specifies coordinates as relative. For example, input @2,2 to locate the second point shown in **Figure 3-5B** at the absolute coordinate 4,4.

relative coordinates: Coordinates specified from, or relative to, the previous position, rather than from the origin.

Polar Coordinates

To apply *polar coordinates*, specify the length of the line, followed by the less than (<) symbol, and then the angle at which the line is drawn. **Figure 3-6** shows the default angular values used for polar coordinate entry. Precede a polar coordinate with the @ symbol to locate the point relative to the previous point. Otherwise the

polar coordinates: Coordinates based on the distance from a fixed point at a given angle.

coordinate is located relative to the origin. For example, to draw a line 2 units long at a 45° angle, starting 2 units from 0,0 at a 45° angle, type 2<45 for the first point, and @2<45 for the second point. See **Figure 3-7.**

Figure 3-5.
A—Drawing a line segment using absolute coordinates. B—Drawing the same line segment, but locating points using relative coordinates.

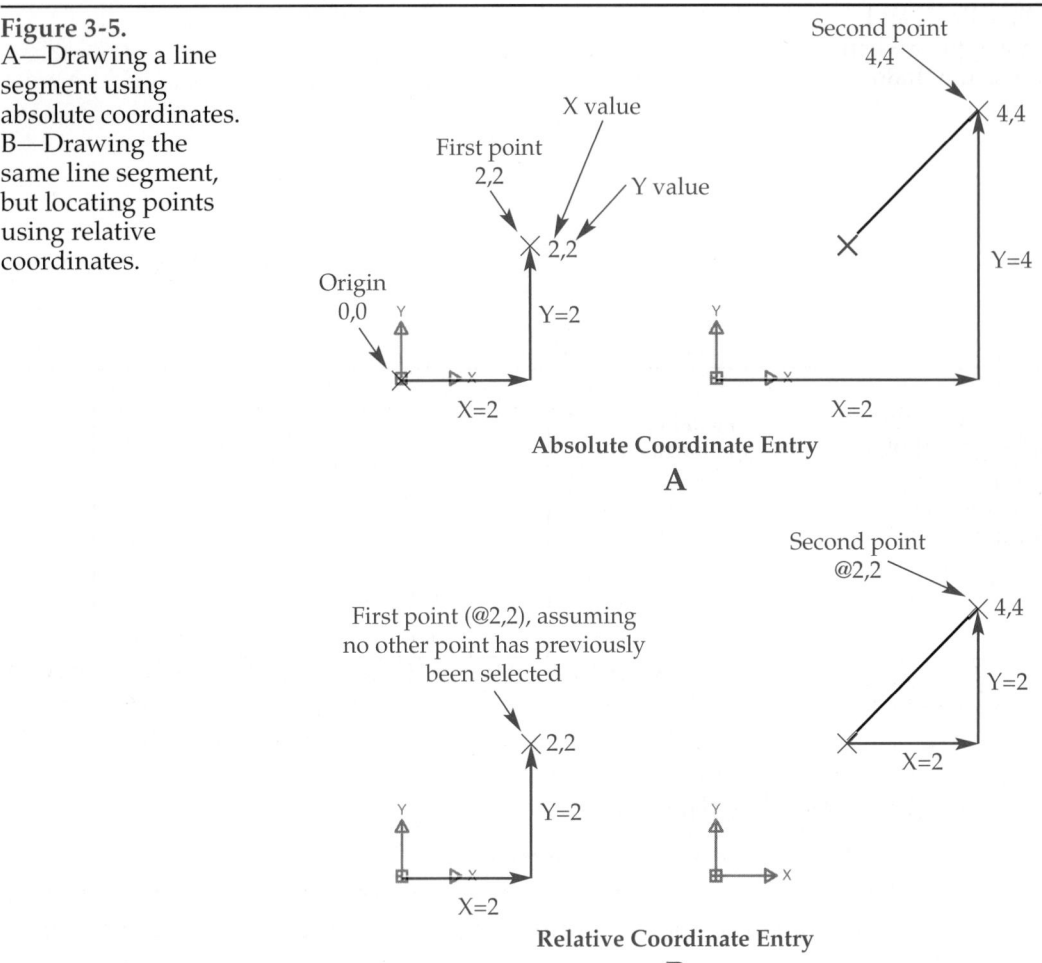

Absolute Coordinate Entry
A

Relative Coordinate Entry
B

Figure 3-6.
The default angles used when entering polar coordinates. 0° is to the right, or east, and angles are measured counterclockwise. For specific applications, such as when measuring azimuths, you can adjust the direction and rotation using options in the **Drawing Units** dialog box.

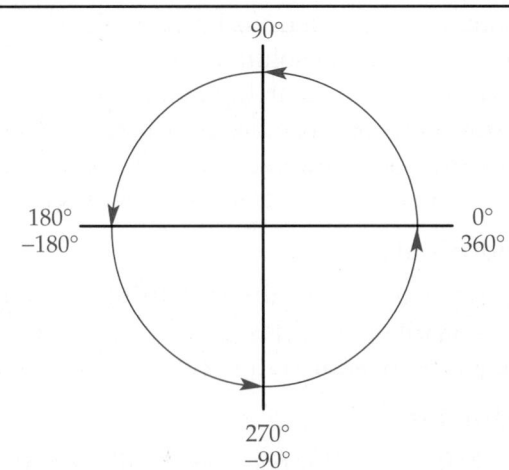

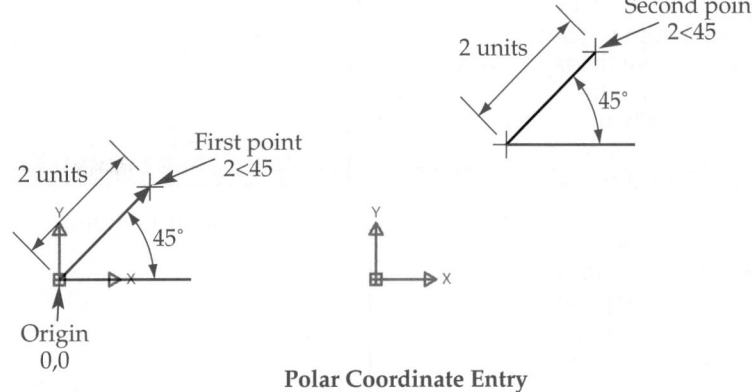

Figure 3-7.
Locating points using polar coordinates.

Polar Coordinate Entry

Crosshairs Coordinates

The area on the left side of the status bar shows the coordinate display field. The drawing units determine the format and precision shown. To toggle the display on or off, pick the display field or right-click and select **On** or **Off**. When coordinate display is on, the coordinates constantly change as the crosshairs moves. When coordinate display is off, the coordinates are "grayed out," but update to identify the location of the last point you select.

You can choose the coordinate display mode when a tool such as **LINE** is active and you have selected a point. Right-click on the display field and choose **Relative** to view the coordinates of the crosshairs as polar coordinates relative to the previously picked point. The coordinates update each time you pick a new point. Select **Absolute** to view the coordinates of the crosshairs relative to the origin. The **Geographic** mode is available if you specify the geographic drawing location, as explained in *AutoCAD and Its Applications—Advanced.*

Dynamic Input

Dynamic input is on by default and is a very effective way to enter coordinates. A quick way to toggle dynamic input on and off is to pick the **Dynamic Input** button on the status bar. Dynamic input provides the same function as the command line, but allows you to keep your focus at the crosshairs while you draw. Dynamic input also offers additional coordinate entry techniques. When dynamic input is active, point entry functions differently, according to dynamic input settings.

When you start the **LINE** tool, dynamic input prompts you to specify the first point. The X coordinate input field is active, and the Y coordinate input field appears. See **Figure 3-8.** Use *pointer input* to specify the absolute, relative, or polar coordinates of the first point. Absolute coordinates are the default when you select the first point. Type the X value, and then press [Tab] or type a comma to lock in the X value and move to the Y coordinate input field. Type the Y value and right-click or press [Enter] to select the point.

pointer input: The process of entering points using dynamic input.

Polar coordinates are the other likely option for specifying the first point. To specify polar coordinates, type the distance from origin in the distance input field, followed by the less than symbol (<) to move to the angle input field. Type the angle from the origin and right-click or press [Enter] to select the point. Dynamic input fields automatically change to anticipate the next entry.

Dynamic input also provides a *dimensional input* feature that allows you to enter the length of a line and the angle at which the line is drawn. To use dimensional input, access the **LINE** tool and specify a start point. Distance and angle input fields appear by default. See **Figure 3-9A.** Move the crosshairs toward where you want to locate the endpoint, type the length of the line in the distance input field, and press [Tab]. This

dimensional input: An instinctive dynamic input point entry technique, similar to polar coordinate entry.

Figure 3-8.
Dynamic input displays these fields after you start the **LINE** tool. When you type @ to use relative coordinates, the symbol appears in a field to the right of the prompt. When you use polar coordinates, the less than symbol (<) appears before the angle input field.

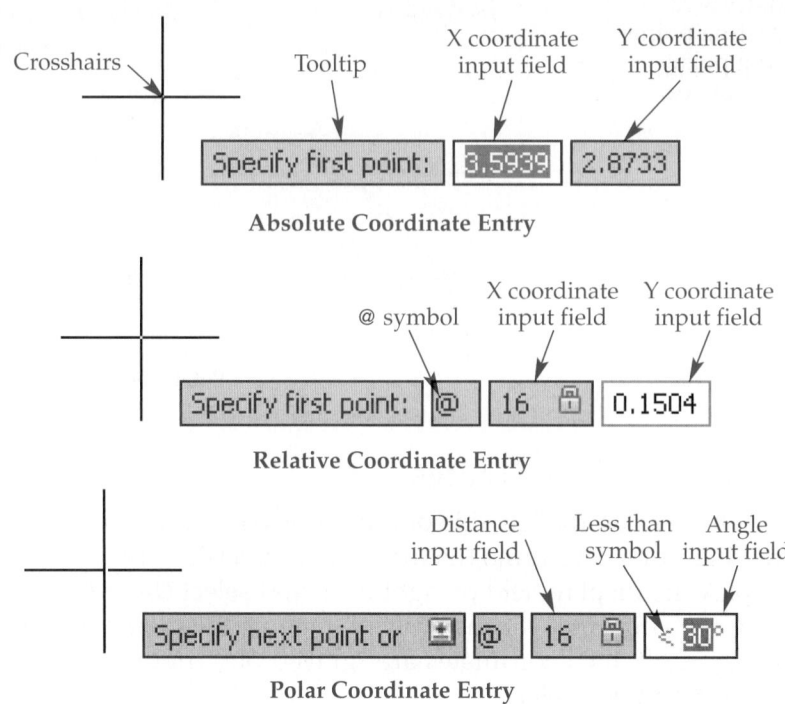

Absolute Coordinate Entry

Relative Coordinate Entry

Polar Coordinate Entry

locks in the distance and moves the cursor to the angle input field. Type the angle of the line and right-click or press [Enter] to select the point. Dimensional input does not follow the same rules as polar coordinates, and drawing units do not control direction and rotation. All angles relate to the location of the crosshairs from 0° east. **Figure 3-9B** shows additional examples of specifying dimensional input angles.

You can also use pointer input to pick additional points once you select the start point of the line. Relative coordinates are active by default, which means you do not need to type @ before entering the X and Y values. To select the second point using a relative coordinate entry, type the X value in the distance input field, then type a comma to lock in the X value and move to the Y coordinate input field. Type the Y value and right-click or press [Enter] to select the point.

Dimensional input is on by default, but you can turn it off temporarily by typing # before entering values. When dimensional input is off, dynamic input defaults to polar format. Type the length of the line in the distance input field, and press [Tab] to lock in the length and move to the angle input field. Enter the angle of the line and right-click or press [Enter] to select the point. In order to use an absolute coordinate entry with the default settings, type #, enter the X coordinate in the active field, type a comma, type the Y value, and right-click or [Enter] to select the point.

PROFESSIONAL TIP

Use [Tab] to cycle through dynamic input fields. You can make changes to values before accepting the coordinates.

Supplemental Material

Dynamic Input Settings
For more information about adjusting dynamic input options, go to the Student Web site (www.g-wlearning.com/CAD), select this chapter, and select **Dynamic Input Settings**.

Figure 3-9. A—Steps for using dimensional input to define the length and angle of a line. B—Pay close attention to the location of the crosshairs and the reading in the angle input field. All angles relate to the location of the crosshairs from 0° east.

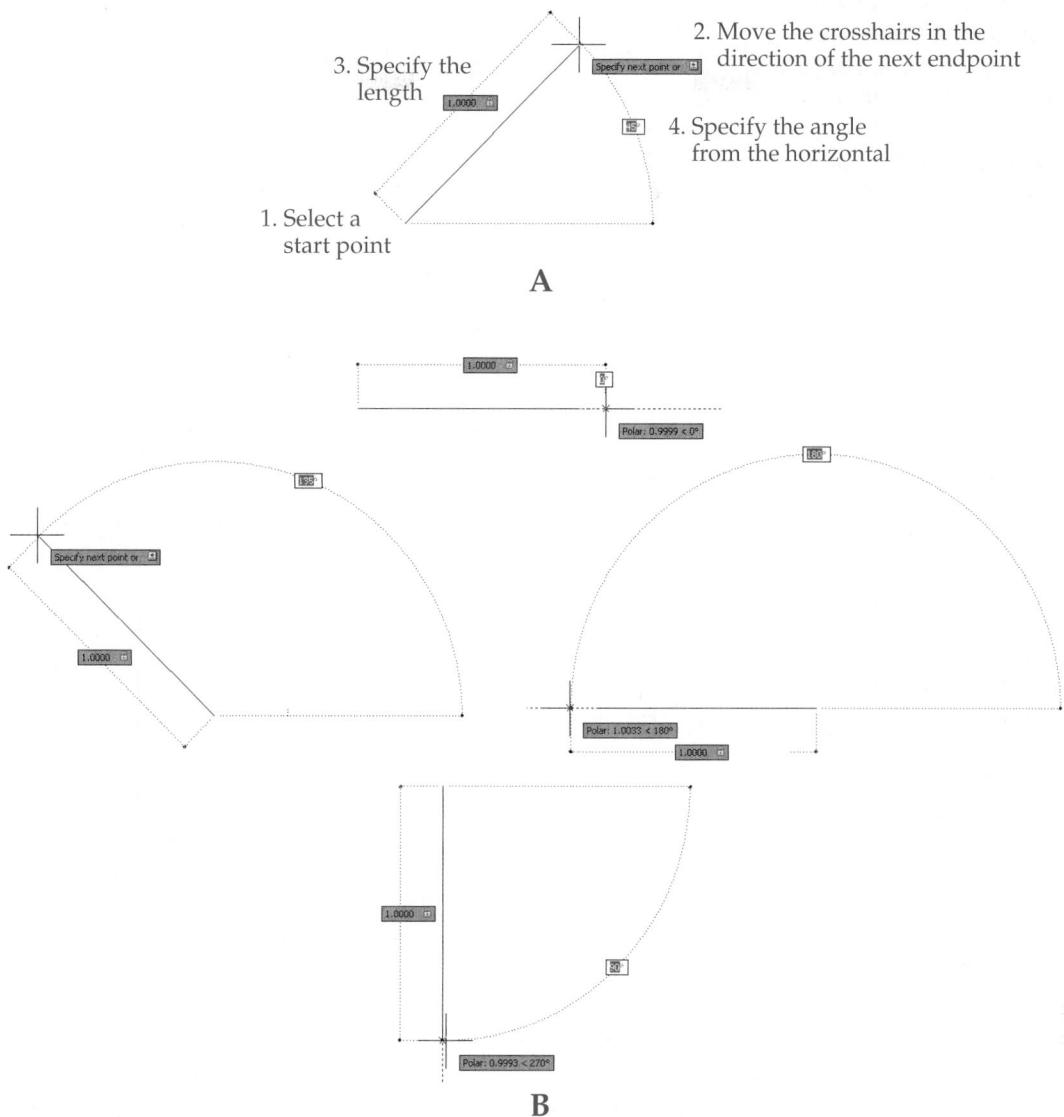

Command Line

You can use the command line at the same time as dynamic input, or you can disable dynamic input to use only the command line. Another option is to hide the command line to free additional drawing space and focus on using dynamic input. Absolute, relative, and polar point entry methods accomplish the same tasks whether you enter them using dynamic input or the command line. However, dimensional input and quick input settings are unavailable with the command line, and coordinate entry is slightly different when using the command line.

The next three figures provide examples of point entry using the command line. **Figure 3-10** applies to absolute coordinate entry, **Figure 3-11** applies to relative coordinate entry, and **Figure 3-12** applies to polar coordinate entry. You can apply the same examples to dynamic input. Even if you choose not to use the command line, review these examples to help better understand point entry techniques. You must disable dynamic input in order for these exact command sequences to work properly.

Figure 3-10. Drawing a shape using the **LINE** tool and absolute coordinates.

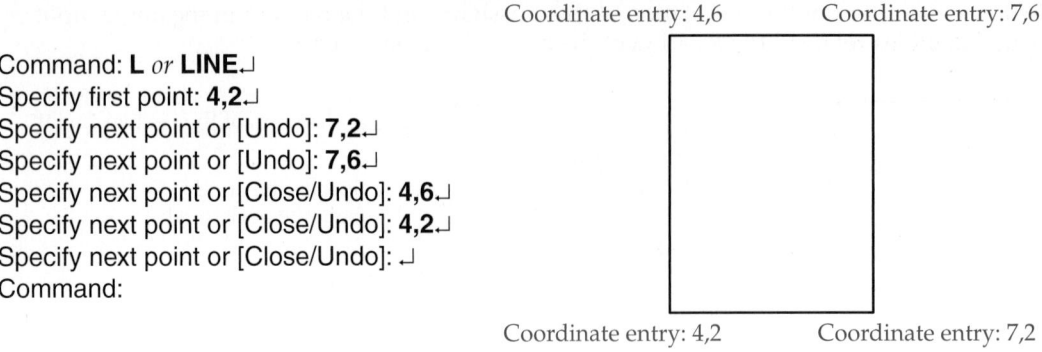

Coordinate entry: 4,6   Coordinate entry: 7,6

Command: **L** *or* **LINE**⏎
Specify first point: **4,2**⏎
Specify next point or [Undo]: **7,2**⏎
Specify next point or [Undo]: **7,6**⏎
Specify next point or [Close/Undo]: **4,6**⏎
Specify next point or [Close/Undo]: **4,2**⏎
Specify next point or [Close/Undo]: ⏎
Command:

Coordinate entry: 4,2   Coordinate entry: 7,2

Absolute Coordinate Entry

Figure 3-11. Drawing a shape using the **LINE** tool and a combination of absolute and relative coordinates. Notice that negative (–) values are used and the coordinates are entered counterclockwise from the first point, in this case 2,2.

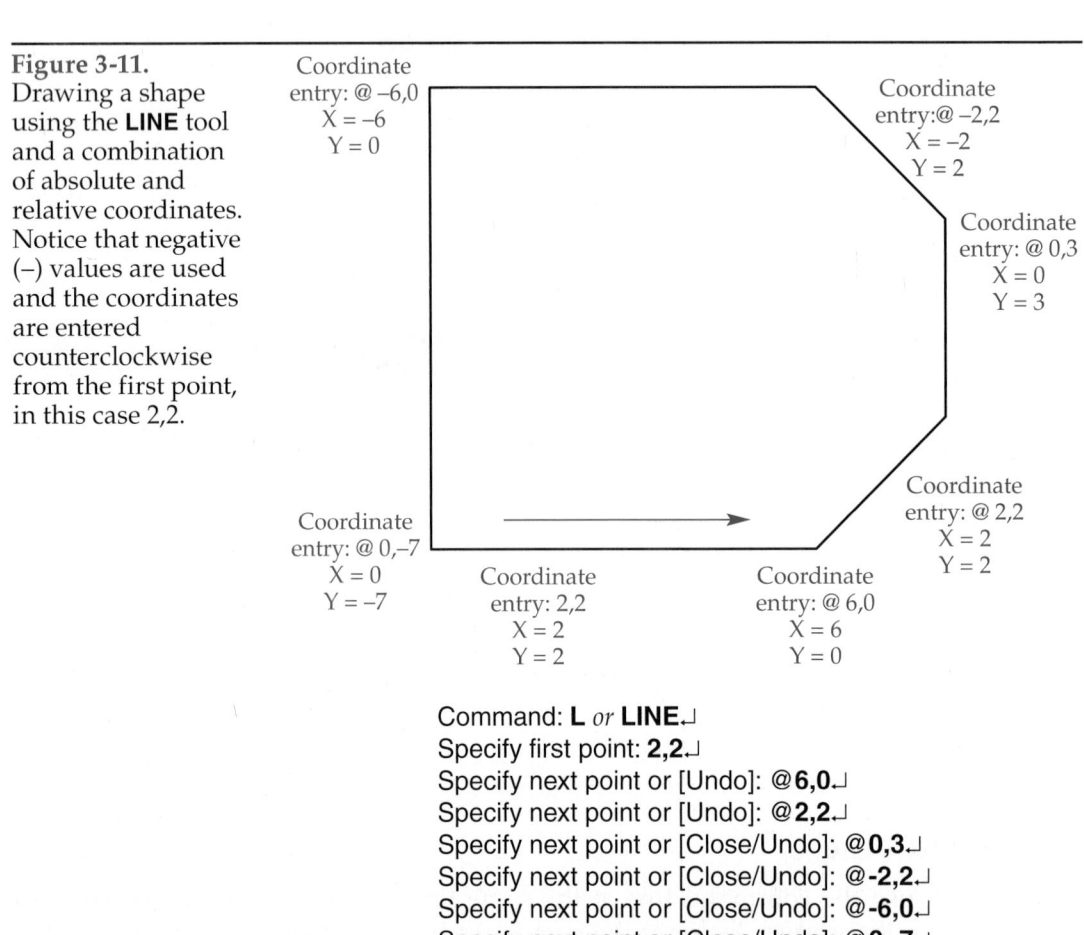

Coordinate entry: @ –6,0
X = –6
Y = 0

Coordinate entry:@ –2,2
X = –2
Y = 2

Coordinate entry: @ 0,3
X = 0
Y = 3

Coordinate entry: @ 2,2
X = 2
Y = 2

Coordinate entry: @ 0,–7
X = 0
Y = –7

Coordinate entry: 2,2
X = 2
Y = 2

Coordinate entry: @ 6,0
X = 6
Y = 0

Command: **L** *or* **LINE**⏎
Specify first point: **2,2**⏎
Specify next point or [Undo]: **@6,0**⏎
Specify next point or [Undo]: **@2,2**⏎
Specify next point or [Close/Undo]: **@0,3**⏎
Specify next point or [Close/Undo]: **@-2,2**⏎
Specify next point or [Close/Undo]: **@-6,0**⏎
Specify next point or [Close/Undo]: **@0,-7**⏎
Specify next point or [Close/Undo]: ⏎
Command:

Relative Coordinate Entry

Figure 3-12.
Drawing shapes using the **LINE** tool and a combination of absolute and polar coordinates.

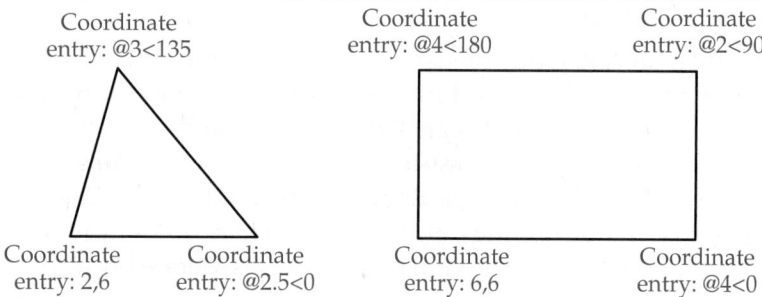

Coordinate entry: @3<135
Coordinate entry: @4<180
Coordinate entry: @2<90
Coordinate entry: 2,6
Coordinate entry: @2.5<0
Coordinate entry: 6,6
Coordinate entry: @4<0

Command: **L** *or* **LINE**↵
Specify first point: **2,6**↵
Specify next point or [Undo]: **@2.5<0**↵
Specify next point or [Undo]: **@3<135**↵
Specify next point or [Close/Undo]: **2,6**↵
Specify next point or [Close/Undo]: ↵
Command: ↵
LINE Specify first point: **6,6**↵
Specify next point or [Undo]: **@4<0**↵
Specify next point or [Undo]: **@2<90**↵
Specify next point or [Close/Undo]: **@4<180**↵
Specify next point or [Close/Undo]: **@2<270**↵
Specify next point or [Close/Undo]: ↵
Command:

Polar Coordinate Entry

Exercises 3-3, 3-4, and 3-5

Access the Student Web site (www.g-wlearning.com/CAD) and complete Exercise 3-3, Exercise 3-4, and Exercise 3-5.

PROFESSIONAL TIP

To position the start point of a line at the last point entered, right-click or press [Enter] or the space bar when you see the Specify first point: prompt. To select the last point entered at any point selection prompt, type @ and press [Enter]. You can reference the coordinates of other previously selected points by pressing the up arrow key when you receive a point selection prompt. Dynamic input or the command line lists the coordinates, and a symbol appears at each point on-screen. Press [Enter] or right-click and choose **Enter** to select the desired coordinates.

Introduction to Drawing Aids

AutoCAD includes many drawing aids that increase accuracy and productivity. The crosshairs coordinates on the status bar and dynamic input are examples of drawing aids. This chapter describes basic drawing aids, and provides an overview of several important drawing aids that are explained in detail later in this textbook.

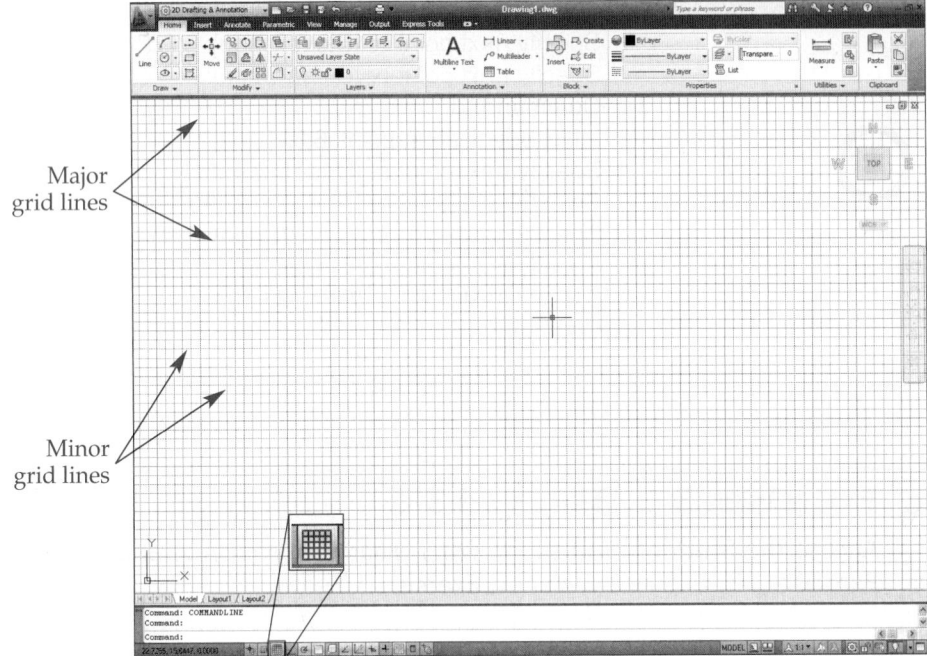

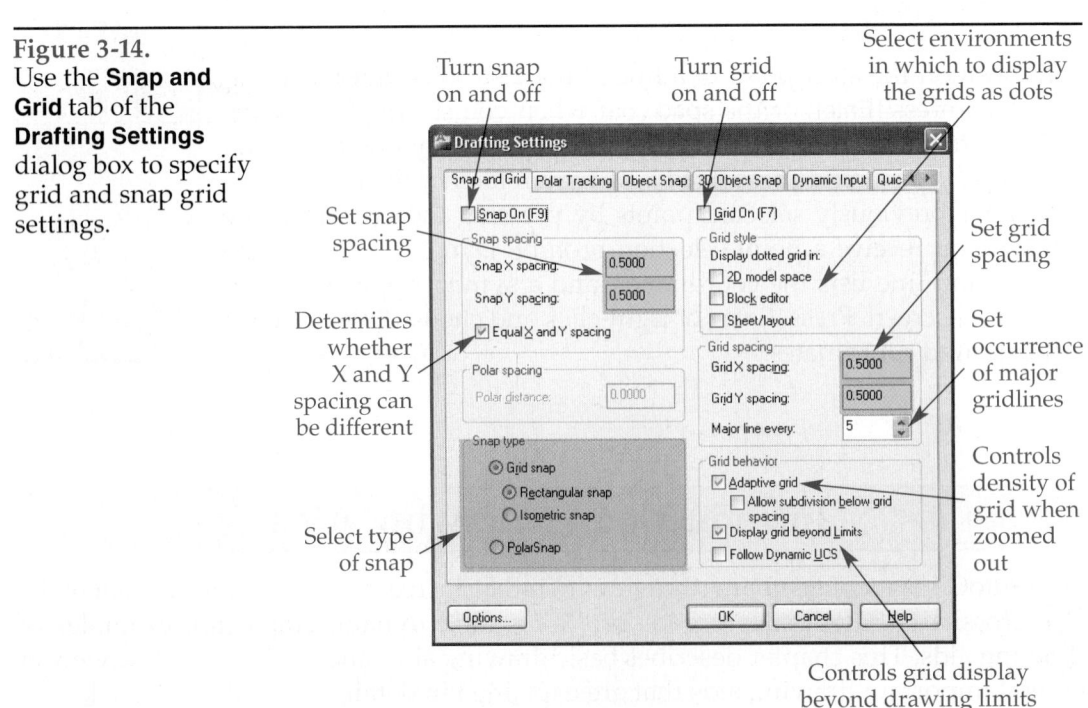

grid: A pattern of lines that appears on-screen for reference; analogous to graph paper.

DSETTINGS GRID

Type
GRID
[CTRL]+[G]
F7

Type
DSETTINGS
DS
SE

Grid Mode

Turn on **Grid** mode to display a *grid* on-screen. See **Figure 3-13**. The grid functions like virtual graph paper, but appears for reference only, as a visual aid to drawing layout. A quick way to toggle **Grid** mode on and off is to pick the **Grid Display** button on the status bar.

Use the options on the **Snap and Grid** tab of the **Drafting Settings** dialog box to adjust grid mode settings. See **Figure 3-14**. A quick way to access the **Snap and Grid** tab is to right-click on the **Grid Display** or **Snap Mode** button on the status bar and select

Figure 3-13. By default, lines represent grid spacing when **Grid** mode is active.

Major grid lines

Minor grid lines

Figure 3-14.
Use the **Snap and Grid** tab of the **Drafting Settings** dialog box to specify grid and snap grid settings.

Turn snap on and off

Set snap spacing

Determines whether X and Y spacing can be different

Select type of snap

Turn grid on and off

Select environments in which to display the grids as dots

Set grid spacing

Set occurrence of major gridlines

Controls density of grid when zoomed out

Controls grid display beyond drawing limits

Settings... Turn the grid on and off using the **Grid On** check box. The grid appears as lines by default. Use the check boxes in the **Grid style** area to replace the grid lines with dots in selected environments.

Set the grid spacing in the **Grid spacing** area by typing values in the **Grid X spacing:** and **Grid Y spacing:** text boxes. For decimal units, set the grid spacing to standard decimal increments such as .125, .25, .5, or 1 for an inch drawing or 1, 10, 20, or 50 for a metric drawing, depending on the size of objects. For architectural units, use standard increments such as 1, 6, and 12 (for inches) or 1, 2, 4, 5, and 10 (for feet). A very large drawing might have a grid spacing of 12 (one foot), or 120 (ten feet), while a small drawing may use a spacing of .125 or less. Type the number of grid rows to display between the bold, major grid lines in the **Major line every** text box.

The options in the **Grid behavior** area determine how the grid appears on-screen. When **Adaptive Grid** is checked and you zoom out to a display where the grid spacing becomes too dense, AutoCAD adjusts the grid display to show the grid at a larger scale. The **Display grid beyond Limits** option determines whether the grid appears only within the drawing limits. The **Allow subdivision below grid spacing** and **Follow Dynamic UCS** options apply to 3D applications.

Snap Mode

Turn on **Snap** mode to activate the *snap grid*, also known as *snap resolution* or *snap*. A quick way to toggle snap on and off is to pick the **Snap Mode** button on the status bar. By default, snap is off, allowing the crosshairs to move freely on-screen. Turn snap on to move the crosshairs in specific increments. Snap is different from the grid, because snap controls the movement of the crosshairs, while the grid is only a visual guide. However, grid and snap settings typically complement each other.

The **Snap and Grid** tab of the **Drafting Settings** dialog box includes options for setting snaps. Refer again to **Figure 3-14.** Turn snap on or off using the **Snap On** check box. Set the snap increment in the **Snap spacing** area by typing values in the **Snap X spacing:** and **Snap Y spacing:** text boxes. For example, if you set the X and Y grid spacing to .5, an appropriate X and Y snap spacing is .125 or .25. With these settings, each mode plays a separate role in assisting drawing layout. Often the most effective use of grid and snap is to set equal X and Y spacing. However, if many horizontal features conform to one increment and most vertical features correspond to another, you may choose to set different X and Y values.

Use the **Snap type** area to control how snaps function. The default, previously described snap type is **Grid snap** with the **Rectangular snap** style. Select the **Grid snap** type and **Isometric snap** style to aid in creating isometric drawings. The **PolarSnap** type allows you to snap to precise distances along alignment paths when you use polar tracking, as explained in Chapter 7.

Type

SNAP
[CTRL]+[B]
[F9]

SNAP

snap grid (snap resolution, snap): An invisible grid that allows the crosshairs to move in, or snap to, specified increments.

NOTE

Adjust the grid and snap settings as needed, such as when larger or smaller values would assist you with a certain drawing task. Changing grid and snap settings does not affect the location of existing points or objects.

Exercise 3-6

Access the Student Web site (www.g-wlearning.com/CAD) and complete Exercise 3-6.

Supplemental Material

Introduction to Isometric Drawings

For an introduction to pictorial drawings and information about isometric snaps, go to the Student Web site (www.g-wlearning.com/CAD), select this chapter, and select **Introduction to Isometric Drawings**.

Polar Tracking

polar tracking: A drawing aid that causes the drawing crosshairs to "snap" to predefined angle increments.

direct distance entry: Entering points by dragging the crosshairs for direction and typing a number for distance.

Polar tracking causes the drawing crosshairs to "snap" to predefined angle increments. Chapter 7 fully explains polar tracking, but because polar tracking is on by default, you should have a basic understanding of the tool. Turn polar tracking on or off by picking the **Polar Tracking** button on the status bar or by pressing [F10]. You can use polar tracking to draw lines at accurate lengths and angles using *direct distance entry*. As you move the crosshairs toward a polar tracking angle, AutoCAD displays an alignment path and tooltip. The default polar angle increments are 0°, 90°, 180°, or 270°.

To apply direct distance entry using polar tracking, access the **LINE** tool and specify a start point. Then move the crosshairs in alignment with a polar tracking angle. Type the length of the line and press [Enter] or right-click and select **Enter**. See **Figure 3-15**.

Exercise 3-7

Access the Student Web site (www.g-wlearning.com/CAD) and complete Exercise 3-7.

Ortho Mode

ORTHO

Type
ORTHO
[CTRL]+[L]
[F8]

ortho: From *orthogonal*, which means "at right angles."

Ortho mode forces a horizontal or vertical line. **Ortho** mode is off by default. Pick the **Ortho Mode** button on the status bar to toggle **Ortho** mode on and off. If **Ortho** mode is off, you can temporarily turn it on while drawing by holding down [Shift]. You can use **Ortho** mode to draw accurate lengths of horizontal and vertical lines using direct distance entry.

Figure 3-15. Using polar tracking and direct distance entry to draw connected and perpendicular lines at specific lengths. 0° and 90° tracking are the defaults. This example shows dynamic input active, but the same technique applies when you use the command line.

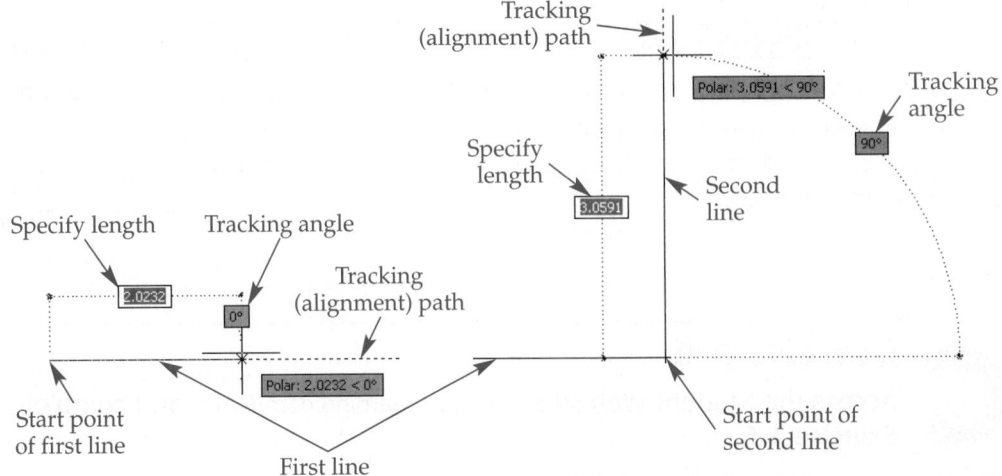

To apply direct distance entry using **Ortho** mode, access the **LINE** tool and specify a start point. Move the crosshairs to display a horizontal or vertical rubberband line in the direction you want to draw. Then type the length of the line and press [Enter] or right-click and select **Enter**. See **Figure 3-16**.

> **NOTE**
>
> You can use direct distance entry to specify the length of a line at any angle. However, direct distance entry itself is not very useful unless you incorporate drawing aids such as polar tracking or **Ortho** mode.

Exercise 3-8

Access the Student Web site (www.g-wlearning.com/CAD) **and complete Exercise 3-8.**

Figure 3-16. Using **Ortho** mode and direct distance entry to construct a rectangle. Notice that the crosshairs specifies the general direction of the line endpoint and do not attach to the rubberband line. This example shows dynamic input active. The same technique applies when you use the command line.

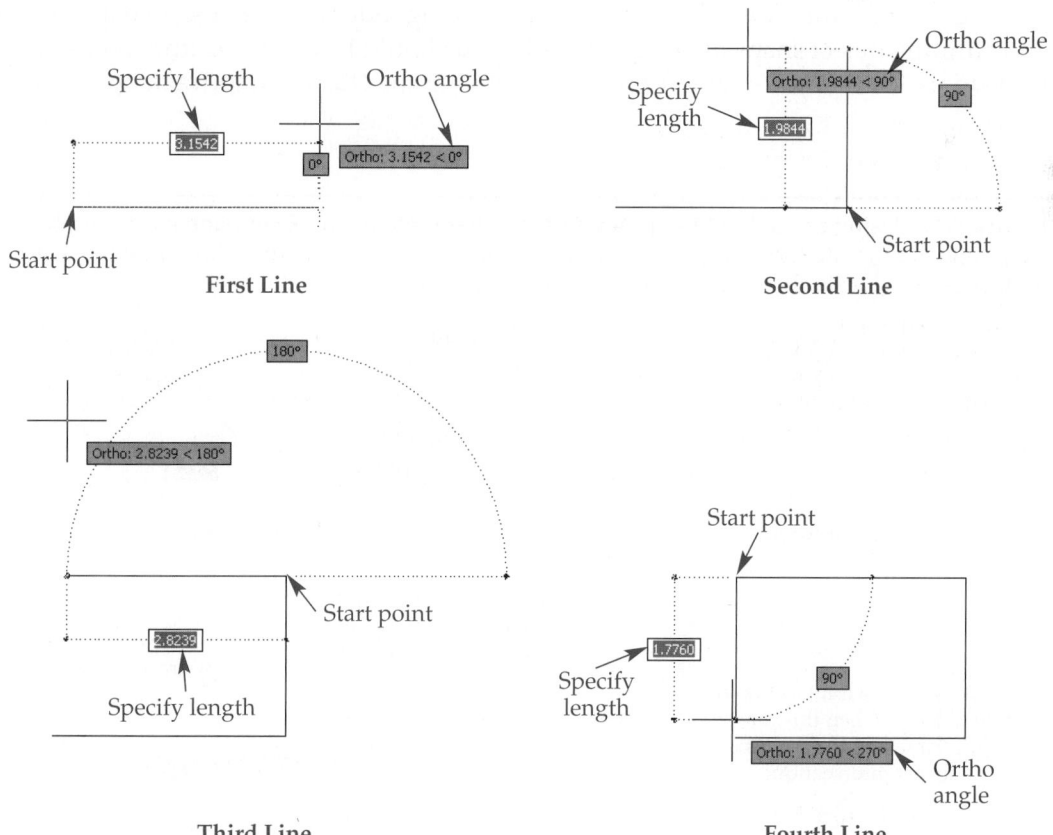

Object Snap

Object snap increases drafting performance and accuracy through the concept of *snapping.* Chapter 7 fully explains object snap, but because *running object snaps* are on by default, you should have a basic understanding of how to use them. Turn running object snaps on or off by picking the **Object Snap** button on the status bar or pressing [F3]. Object snap modes identify the points on objects to which the crosshairs snap. The **Endpoint**, **Center**, **Intersection**, and **Extension** running object snap modes are active by default. The AutoSnap feature is also on by default, and displays *markers* at each active snap point. After a brief pause, a tooltip appears to indicate the object snap mode. See **Figure 3-17.**

You can snap to a point whenever you receive a point selection prompt, such as picking the start point or endpoint of a line segment. **Figure 13-17** shows a basic example of locating the start point of a line using each default running object snap mode. Follow the instructions shown to snap to the corresponding point.

Exercise 3-9

Access the Student Web site (www.g-wlearning.com/CAD) and complete Exercise 3-9.

Object Snap Tracking

Object snap tracking has two requirements: running object snaps must be active, and the crosshairs must hover over the intended selection long enough to acquire the point. Chapter 7 fully explains object snap tracking, but because object snap tracking and running object snaps are on by default, you should have a basic understanding of these tools. Turn object snap on and off by picking the **Object Snap Tracking** button on

Figure 3-17. Using the default **Endpoint**, **Center**, **Intersection**, and **Extension** running object snap modes to locate the start point of a line. When you see the correct AutoSnap marker and tooltip, pick to locate the point at the exact snap location.

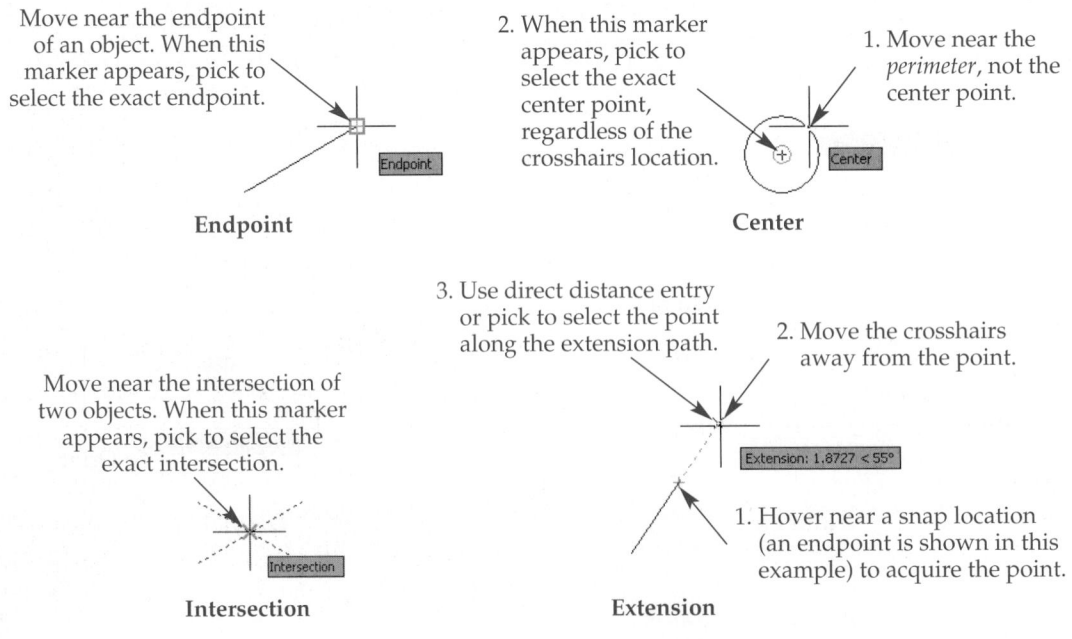

Move near the endpoint of an object. When this marker appears, pick to select the exact endpoint.

Endpoint

2. When this marker appears, pick to select the exact center point, regardless of the crosshairs location.

1. Move near the *perimeter,* not the center point.

Center

Move near the intersection of two objects. When this marker appears, pick to select the exact intersection.

Intersection

3. Use direct distance entry or pick to select the point along the extension path.

2. Move the crosshairs away from the point.

Extension: 1.8727 < 55°

1. Hover near a snap location (an endpoint is shown in this example) to acquire the point.

Extension

the status bar or pressing [F11]. **Figure 3-18** shows an example of using the **Endpoint** running object snap with object snap tracking to locate the endpoint of a line exactly vertical to another endpoint.

PROFESSIONAL TIP

Practice using different point entry techniques and drawing aids, and decide which method works best for specific situations.

Exercise 3-10

Access the Student Web site (www.g-wlearning.com/CAD) and complete Exercise 3-10.

Inferring Geometric Constraints

Chapter 22 describes the process of constraining, or applying relationships between, objects. However, before continuing you should be aware of a tool that automatically forms, or *infers*, constraints. A constrained drawing functions differently than an unconstrained drawing. Until you have read Chapter 22 and are ready to constrain objects, confirm that the **Infer Constraints** tool is off before drawing. The **Infer Constrains** button on the status bar toggles the **Infer Constraints** tool on and off.

Introduction to Editing

AutoCAD includes many *editing* tools for making changes to a drawing and increasing productivity. One of the most basic ways to edit a drawing is to remove objects using the **ERASE** tool. You will also learn to use the **OOPS**, **UNDO**, **U**, and **REDO** tools, common while drawing and editing.

editing: A procedure used to modify an existing object.

The standard approach to editing is to access a tool, such as **ERASE**, select the objects to modify, and then complete the operation by right-clicking, or pressing [Enter] or the space bar. Another approach is to select options first using the crosshairs, then access the editing tool, and finally complete the operation. The process of selecting

Figure 3-18.
Using the **Endpoint** running object snap and object snap tracking to construct the top side of a rectangle using the **LINE** tool. Polar tracking is active to create a horizontal line.

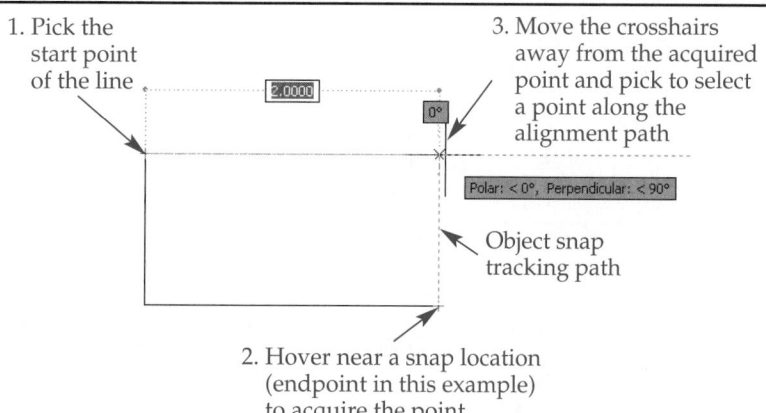

1. Pick the start point of the line

2. Hover near a snap location (endpoint in this example) to acquire the point

3. Move the crosshairs away from the acquired point and pick to select a point along the alignment path

Object snap tracking path

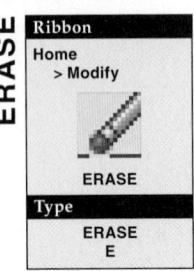

objects is the same for both methods. Choose the technique you prefer, but selecting objects first is most appropriate when you are editing using *grips*. Chapter 14 explains grip editing.

ERASE Tool

Access the **ERASE** tool to remove objects from the drawing. The Select objects: prompt appears and an object selection target, or *pick box*, replaces the screen crosshairs. Move the pick box over the item to erase and pick. The object becomes highlighted and the Select objects: prompt remains active, allowing you to select additional objects to erase. When you finish selecting objects, erase the selection set by right-clicking, or pressing [Enter] or the space bar. See **Figure 3-19.** If you choose to select objects before accessing the **ERASE** tool, you have the option to erase the selected objects by pressing [Delete].

> **NOTE**
>
> By default, when you hover over an object, the object changes to a thicker lineweight, appears dashed, and basic object properties appear. When you move the crosshairs or pick box off the object, the object display returns to normal. This allows you to preview the object before you select. When a small area contains many objects, this feature helps you select the correct object the first time and often eliminates the need to cycle through stacked objects.

Exercise 3-11

Access the Student Web site (www.g-wlearning.com/CAD) and complete Exercise 3-11.

Figure 3-19. Using the **ERASE** tool to erase a single object. A—The initial display before you access the **ERASE** tool. B—The pick box that appears when you access the **ERASE** tool. C—Selecting a single object. D—The completed erase operation.

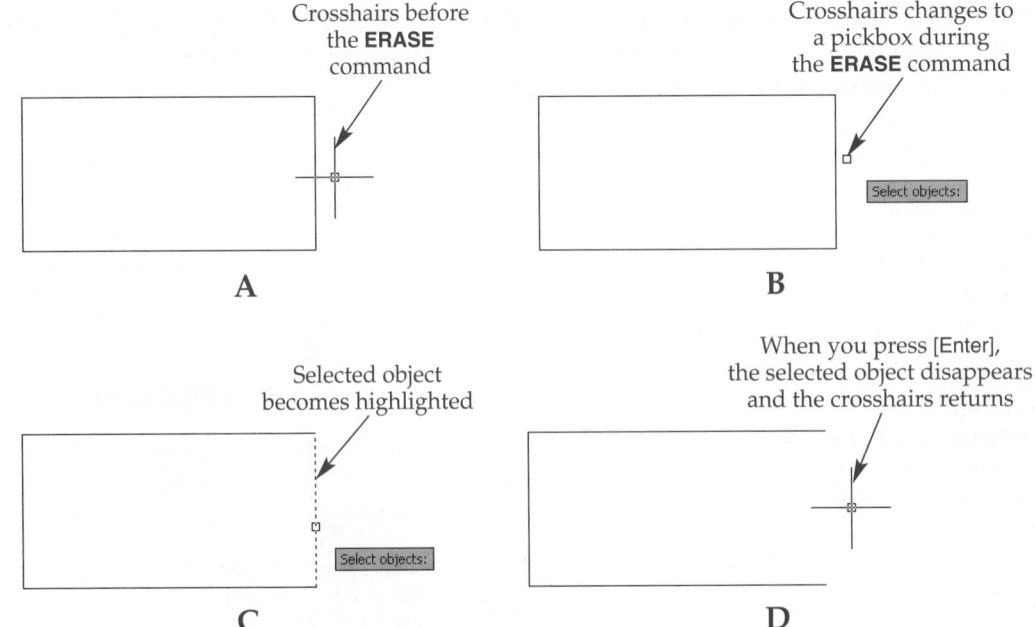

U Tool

The **U** tool undoes the effect of the last tool you entered. You can reissue the **U** tool to continue undoing tool actions, but you can only undo one tool at a time. Actions are undone in the order you used them.

> **NOTE**
>
> You can also activate the **U** tool by right-clicking in the drawing window and selecting **Undo** *current*.

UNDO Tool

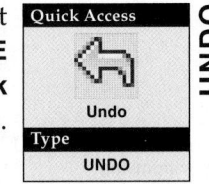

The **UNDO** tool allows you to undo a single operation or a number of operations at once. The **UNDO** tool is different from the **Undo** option of certain tools, such as the **LINE** tool. The quickest way to use the **UNDO** tool is to pick the **Undo** button on the **Quick Access** toolbar. Select the button as many times as needed to undo multiple operations. An alternative is to pick the flyout and select all of the tools to undo from the list.

Supplemental Material

UNDO Options

For detailed information about the options available when you access the **UNDO** tool from a source other than the **Quick Access** toolbar, go to the Student Web site (www.g-wlearning.com/CAD), select this chapter, and select **UNDO Options**.

REDO Tool

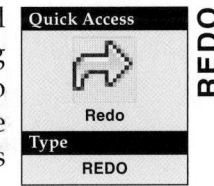

Use the **REDO** tool to reverse the action of the **UNDO** and **U** tools. The **REDO** tool works only *immediately* after you have undone something. The **REDO** tool does not bring back line segments removed using the **Undo** option of the **LINE** tool. The quickest way to use the **REDO** tool is to pick the **Redo** button on the **Quick Access** toolbar. Select the button as many times as needed to redo multiple undone operations. An alternative is to pick the flyout and select one or more undone operations from the list to redo.

Exercise 3-12

Access the Student Web site (www.g-wlearning.com/CAD) and complete Exercise 3-12.

OOPS Tool

The **OOPS** tool brings back the last object you *erased*. Unlike the **UNDO** and **U** tools, **OOPS** only returns objects erased in the most recent procedure. It has no effect on other modifications. If you erase several objects in the same tool sequence, all of the objects return to the screen.

Editing tools and similar operations prompt you to select the objects to modify. So far, you have selected objects individually. However, when you need to select more than one object, a more efficient method is to create a *selection set*. This chapter describes several options for creating selection sets.

selection set: A group of one or more selected objects, typically created to perform an editing operation on the selection.

Window and Crossing Selection

Window selection allows you to select objects by creating a box, or "window," around the objects. Only objects entirely within the window are selected. Crossing selection also requires you to create a box, but all objects within *and crossing* the box are selected. The window selection box has a solid outline and light blue background to distinguish it from the crossing selection box, which has a dotted outline and light green background.

automatic windowing (implied windowing): Selection method that allows you to select multiple objects at one time without entering a selection option.

The quickest and most effective way to use window or crossing selection is through a feature known as *automatic windowing*, or *implied windowing*, which is on by default. To apply automatic window selection, pick a point clearly above or below and to the *left* of the objects to be selected. Then move the opposite corner of the selection box to the right and up or down to cover the objects you want to select. Pick to locate the second corner and select the objects. Right-click or press [Enter] or the space bar to complete the operation. See **Figure 3-20.**

To apply automatic crossing selection, pick a point clearly above or below and to the *right* of the objects to be selected. Then move the corner of the selection box to the left and up or down, across the objects you want to select. Right-click or press [Enter] or the space bar to complete the operation. See **Figure 3-21.**

NOTE

You can type W or WINDOW at the Select objects: prompt to use manual window selection, or C or CROSSING to use manual crossing selection. When you use manual window or crossing selection, the selection box uses the window or crossing format regardless of where you pick to create the box.

Figure 3-20. Using window selection on a mechanical part drawing view to select and erase all objects that lie completely inside the window selection box. Notice that the selection set does not include the circles that are only partially inside the window.

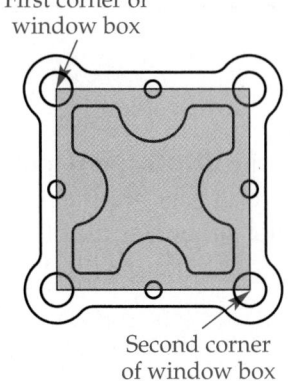
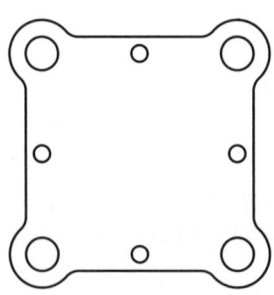

First corner of window box

Second corner of window box

Window Selection   **Objects Selected**   **Objects Erased**

Figure 3-21. Using crossing selection on an architectural floor plan to select all objects inside the selection box as well as all those that touch the sides of the box.

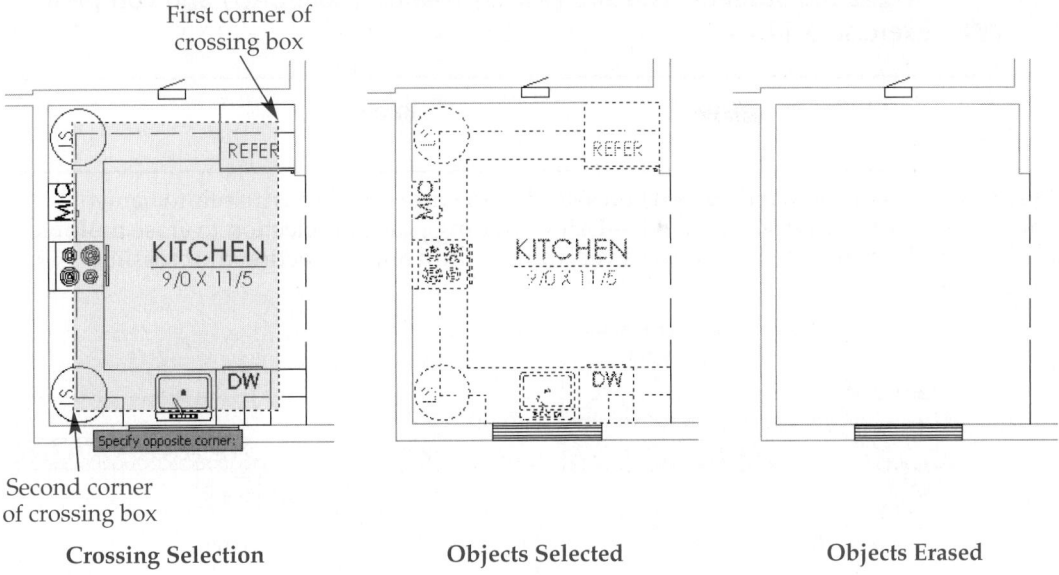

First corner of
crossing box

Second corner
of crossing box

Crossing Selection   Objects Selected   Objects Erased

Exercise 3-13

Access the Student Web site (www.g-wlearning.com/CAD) and complete Exercise 3-13.

Window and Crossing Polygon Selection

The window and crossing polygon selection methods are useful for creating a selection set when it is difficult to use a standard rectangular window or crossing selection box. To use window polygon selection, type WPOLYGON or WP at the Select objects: prompt. Then pick points to draw a polygon enclosing the objects you want to select. See **Figure 3-22A.** To use crossing polygon selection, type CPOLYGON or CP at the Select objects: prompt. Then pick points to draw a polygon around and through the objects to select. See **Figure 3-22B.**

> **PROFESSIONAL TIP**
>
> In window or crossing polygon selection, AutoCAD does not allow you to select a point that causes the lines of the selection polygon to intersect each other. Pick locations that do not result in an intersection. Use the **Undo** option if you need to go back and relocate a previous pick point.

Fence Selection

Fence selection allows you to select all objects that contact a "fence" of connected segments you draw while using an edit tool. To use fence selection, type FENCE or F at the Select objects: prompt. Then pick points to draw a fence through objects to select them. See **Figure 3-23.** Often you only need to draw a single segment to create a useful selection set.

Exercise 3-14

Access the Student Web site (www.g-wlearning.com/CAD) and complete Exercise 3-14.

Figure 3-22. A—Using window polygon selection to erase only the wire reinforcement symbol from a structural slab detail. B—Using crossing polygon selection to erase multiple objects from the structural slab detail. Everything within and contacting the crossing polygon selects.

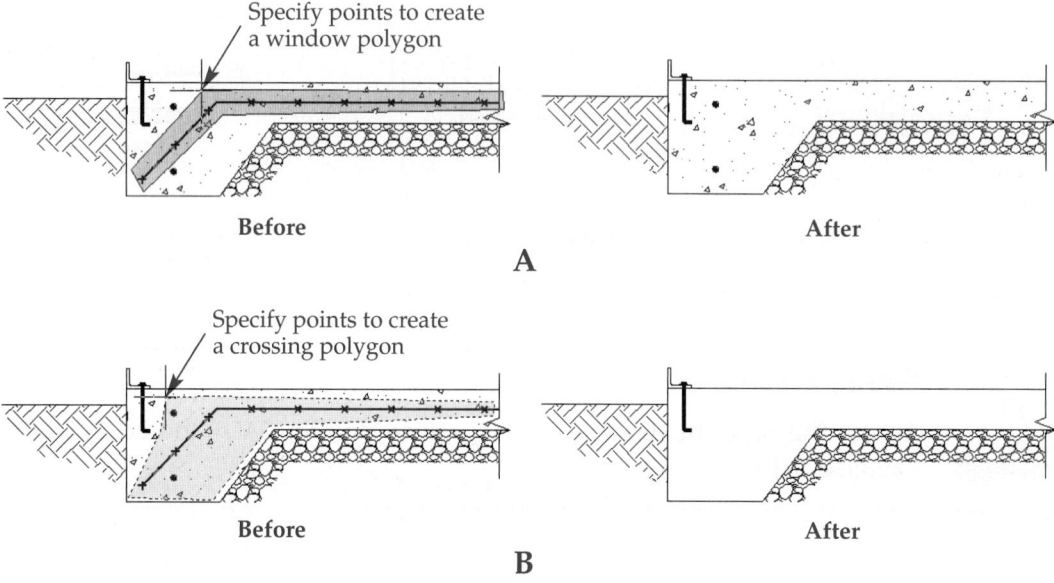

Figure 3-23. Using fence selection to erase specific objects from a mechanical part drawing view. The fence can be staggered, as shown, or a single straight segment.

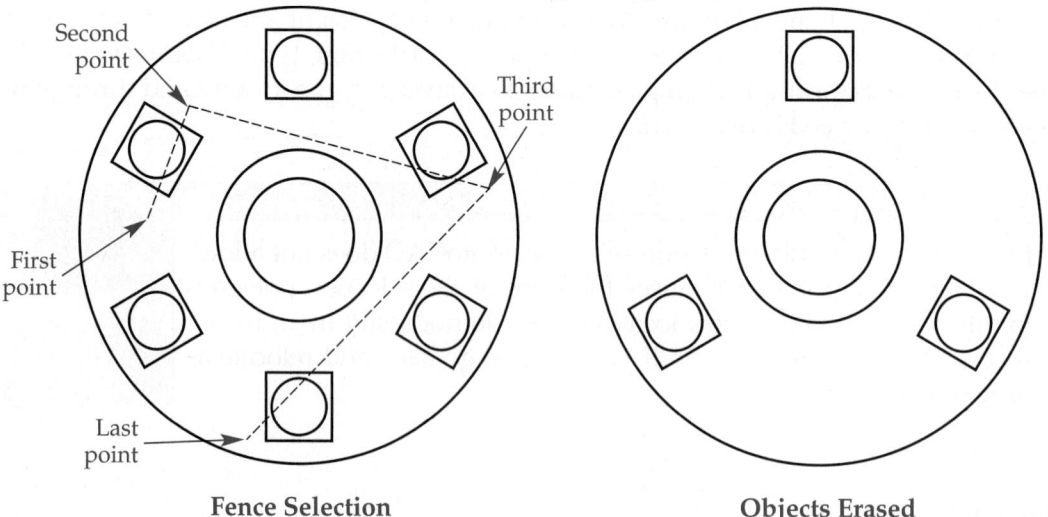

Last Selection

Type LAST or L at the Select objects: prompt to select the last object drawn. You must access a single tool, such as **ERASE**, repeatedly and use LAST selection each time to select individual items in reverse order. Other selection options are usually much faster than LAST selection.

Previous Selection

Type Previous or P at the Select objects: prompt to reselect all the objects selected in the previous selection set. Previous selection is especially useful when you need to carry out more than one editing operation on a specific group of objects. Use Previous selection to reselect the objects you just edited.

NOTE

Previous selection does not reselect erased objects.

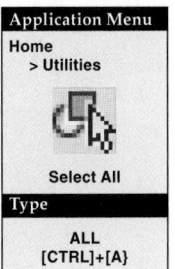

Selecting All Objects

Use the **Select All** tool to select every object in the drawing that is not on a frozen layer, including objects that are outside of the current drawing window display. Chapter 5 describes layers.

Application Menu
Home
> Utilities
Select All
Type
ALL
[CTRL]+[A]

Changing the Selection Set

The quickest way to remove one or more objects from a selection set is to hold down [Shift] and reselect the objects. This is possible only for individual picks and automatic windowing. To change the selection set while using automatic windowing, hold down [Shift], pick the first corner, then release [Shift] and pick the second corner. Select objects as usual to add them back to the selection set.

Another option for removing objects from a selection set is to type REMOVE or R at the Select objects: prompt. This enters the **Remove** option, and changes the Select objects: prompt to Remove objects:, allowing you to pick objects to remove from the selection set. To switch back to selection mode, type ADD or A at the Remove objects: prompt. This enters the **Add** option and restores the Select objects: prompt, allowing you to select additional objects.

PROFESSIONAL TIP

Removing items from a selection set is especially effective if you first use the **Select All** selection option. This allows you to keep a few specific objects while erasing everything else.

Exercise 3-15

Access the Student Web site (www.g-wlearning.com/CAD) and complete Exercise 3-15.

Cycling through Stacked Objects

stacked objects: Objects that overlap in a drawing. When you pick with the mouse, the topmost object is selected by default.

cycle: Repeatedly select a series of stacked objects until the desired object highlights.

While drawing, you will sometimes create *stacked objects*, intersecting objects, or objects that become very close together. To *cycle* through overlapping objects to find the object to select, first access an editing tool, such as **ERASE**. When the Select objects: prompt appears, move the pick box over the intersecting objects, then hold down [Shift] and press the space bar repeatedly to cycle through the stacked objects. When the object you want to select is highlighted, release [Shift] and pick (left-click) to select. See **Figure 3-24**.

AutoCAD also includes a **Selection Cycling** tool for cycling through stacked objects before you access a tool, which is common for grip editing. Pick the **Selection Cycling** button on the status bar to toggle **Selection Cycling** on and off. Move the crosshairs over stacked objects. When you see the **Selection Cycling** icon, pick using the left mouse button to display a list of stacked objects. Move the cursor over an object in the list to highlight the corresponding object in the drawing. Select an object from the list box or choose **None** to exit. See **Figure 3-25A**. Use the options on the **Selection Cycling** tab of the **Drafting Settings** dialog box to adjust **Selection Cycling** settings. See **Figure 3-25B**. A quick way to access the **Selection Cycling** tab is to right-click on the **Selection Cycling** button on the status bar and select **Settings...**.

NOTE

You can only cycle through objects if the objects are close enough together that a portion of each object fits inside the pick box.

Supplemental Material

Selection Display Options

For detailed information about adjusting selection display options, go to the Student Web site (www.g-wlearning.com/CAD), select this chapter, and select **Selection Display Options**.

Figure 3-24. Access the **ERASE** tool and then cycle through a series of stacked bushes on a site plan to locate a specific bush to erase.

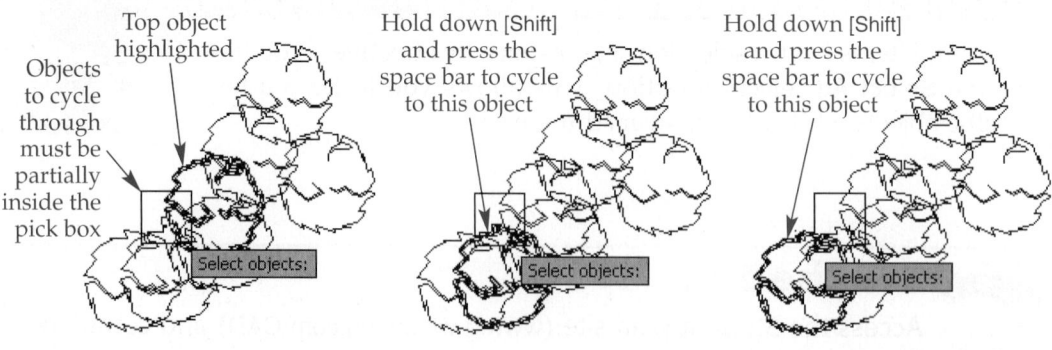

Figure 3-25. A—Turn on **Selection Cycling** to cycle though stacked objects before you access a tool. B—Use the **Selection Cycling** tab of the **Drafting Settings** dialog box to specify **Selection Cycling** preferences.

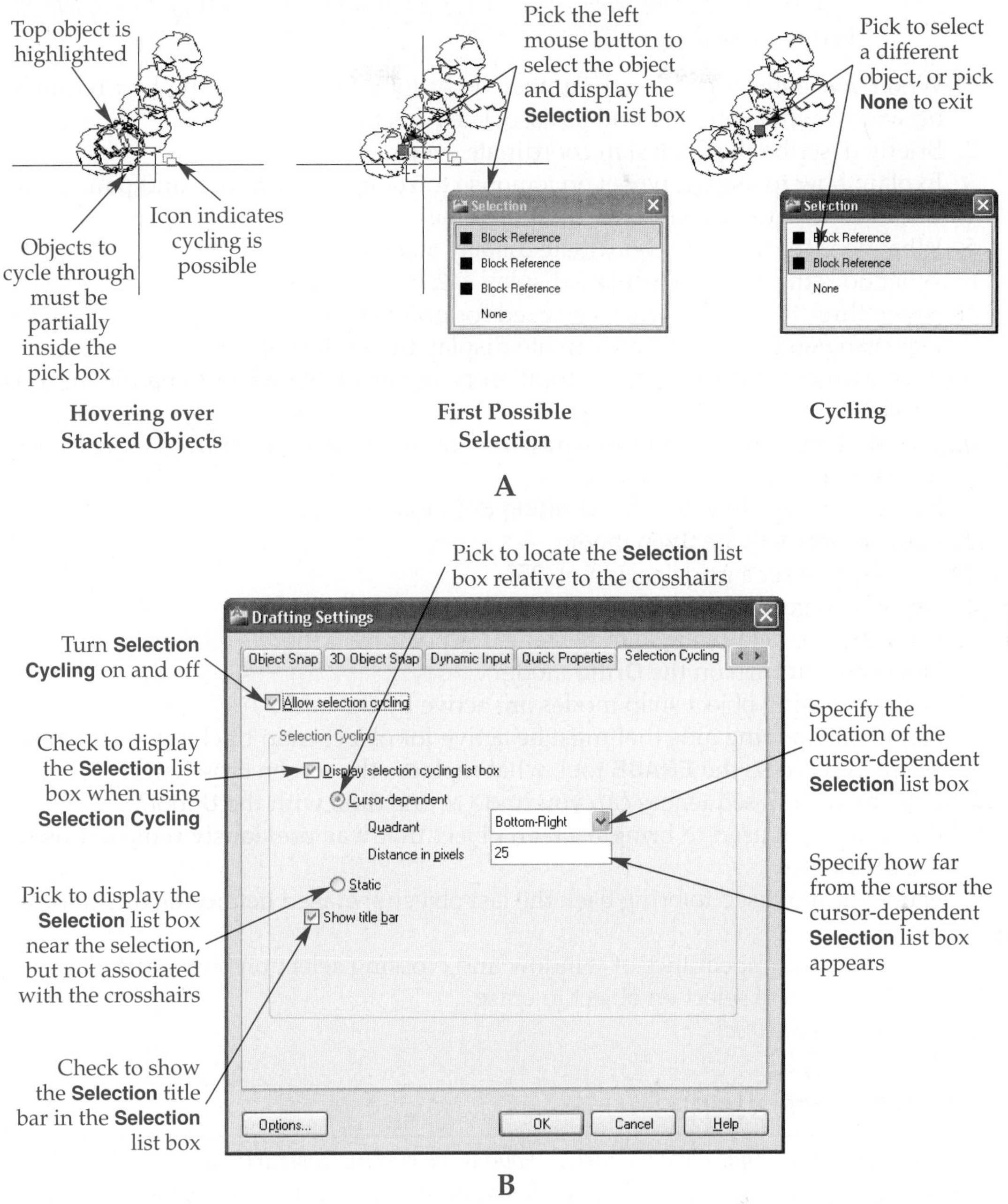

Top object is highlighted

Objects to cycle through must be partially inside the pick box

Icon indicates cycling is possible

Hovering over Stacked Objects

Pick the left mouse button to select the object and display the **Selection** list box

Selection
■ Block Reference
■ Block Reference
■ Block Reference
None

First Possible Selection

Pick to select a different object, or pick **None** to exit

Selection
■ Block Reference
■ Block Reference
None

Cycling

A

Pick to locate the **Selection** list box relative to the crosshairs

Turn **Selection Cycling** on and off

Check to display the **Selection** list box when using **Selection Cycling**

Pick to display the **Selection** list box near the selection, but not associated with the crosshairs

Check to show the **Selection** title bar in the **Selection** list box

Drafting Settings

Object Snap | 3D Object Snap | Dynamic Input | Quick Properties | Selection Cycling

☑ Allow selection cycling

Selection Cycling
☑ Display selection cycling list box
◉ Cursor-dependent
Quadrant   Bottom-Right
Distance in pixels   25
○ Static
☑ Show title bar

Options...   OK   Cancel   Help

Specify the location of the cursor-dependent **Selection** list box

Specify how far from the cursor the cursor-dependent **Selection** list box appears

B

Template Development Chapter 3

For detailed instructions on setting grid and snap values for specific drawing templates, go to the Student Web site (www. g-wlearning.com/CAD), select this chapter, and select **Template Development**.

Chapter Test

Answer the following questions. Write your answers on a separate sheet of paper or go to the Student Web site (www.g-wlearning.com/CAD) and complete the electronic chapter test.

1. When you enter a fractional number in AutoCAD, why is a hyphen required between a whole number and its associated fraction?
2. Briefly describe the Cartesian coordinate system.
3. Explain how to use the wheel on a mouse to zoom in, zoom out, and pan.
4. List two ways to discontinue drawing a line.
5. What does the absolute coordinate display 5.250,7.875 mean?
6. What does the polar coordinate display @2.750<90 mean?
7. Name three types of coordinates used for point entry.
8. How can you turn on the coordinate display field if it is off?
9. What two general methods of point entry are available when dynamic input is active?
10. Explain how you can continue drawing another line segment from a previously drawn line.
11. Name two ways to access the **Drafting Settings** dialog box.
12. How do you activate **Snap** mode?
13. How do you set a grid spacing of .25?
14. Explain, in general terms, how direct distance entry works.
15. What are the default angle increments for polar tracking?
16. How can you turn on the **Ortho** mode?
17. Which running object snap modes are active by default?
18. Name the drawing aids that must be active for object snap tracking to function.
19. When you access the **ERASE** tool, what replaces the screen crosshairs?
20. How many tool sequences can you undo at one time with the **U** tool?
21. Name the tool used to bring back an object that was previously removed using the **UNDO** tool.
22. Name the tool used to bring back the last object(s) erased before starting another tool.
23. How does the appearance of window and crossing selection boxes differ?
24. List five ways to select an object to erase.
25. Define *stacked objects*.

Drawing Problems

Start AutoCAD if it is not already started. Follow the specific instructions for each problem. Use only drawing tools and techniques you have already learned. Do not draw dimensions or text. Use your own judgment and approximate dimensions when necessary.

▼ Basic

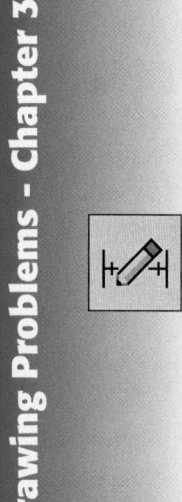

1. Start a new drawing from scratch or use a template of your choice. Use the status bar to turn off all drawing aids, including grid, snap, polar tracking, object snap tracking, ortho, and inferred constraints. Use the **LINE** tool to draw the following objects as accurately as possible.
   - Right triangle
   - Isosceles triangle
   - Rectangle
   - Square
   Save the drawing as P3-1.

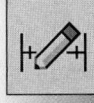

2. Start a new drawing from scratch or use a template of your choice. Draw the same objects specified in Problem 1, but this time, turn the snap grid on. Observe the difference between having snap mode on for this problem and off for the previous problem. Save the drawing as P3-2.

3. Start a new drawing from scratch or use a decimal-unit template of your choice. Draw an object by connecting the following point coordinates. Use dynamic input to enter the coordinates. Save your drawing as P3-3.

Point	Coordinates	Point	Coordinates
1	2,2	8	@-1.5,0
2	@1.5,0	9	@0,1.25
3	@.75<90	10	@-1.25,1.25
4	@1.5<0	11	@2<180
5	@0,-.75	12	@-1.25,-1.25
6	@3,0	13	@2.25<270
7	@1<90		

4. Start a new drawing from scratch or use an architectural-unit template of your choice. Draw the front and side views of a wide flange, similar to the wide flange shown. Use grid and snap modes, default running object snaps, and object snap tracking when possible. Save the drawing as P3-4.

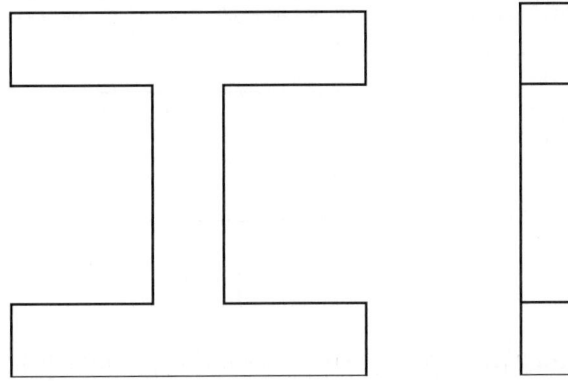

5. Start a new drawing from scratch or use a template of your choice. Draw the bar graph shown using direct distance entry and polar tracking. Each grid square represents one unit. Do not draw the grid lines. Save the drawing as P3-5.

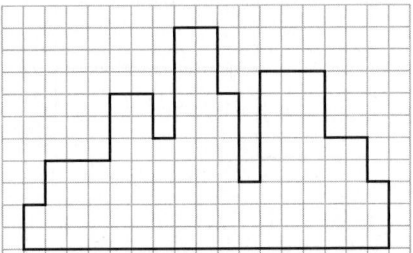

Drawing Problems - Chapter 3

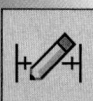

6. Start a new drawing from scratch or use a template of your choice. Draw the hexagon shown using the dimensional input feature of dynamic input. Each side of the hexagon is 2 units. Begin at the start point, and draw the lines in the direction indicated by the arrows. Save the drawing as P3-6.

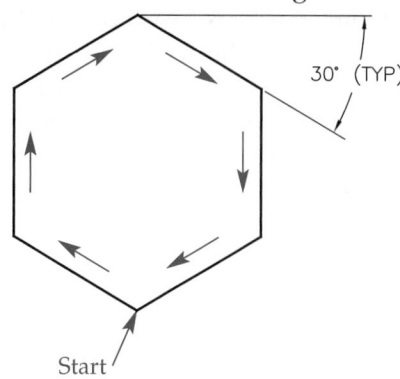

▼ Intermediate

7. Start a new drawing from scratch or use a fractional-unit template of your choice. Draw the part views shown using absolute, relative, and polar coordinate entry methods. Set the units to decimal and the precision to 0.0 when drawing Object A. Draw Object A three times, using a different point entry system each time. Set the units to fractional and the precision to 1/16 when drawing Object B. Draw Object B once, using at least two methods of coordinate entry. Save the drawing as P3-7.

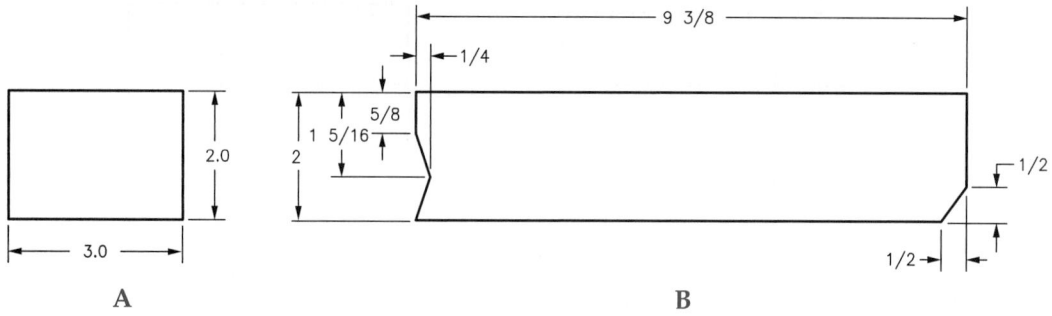

For Problems 8–9, start a new drawing from scratch or use a decimal-unit template of your choice. Draw the part view shown. Save the drawings as P3-8 and P3-9.

8.

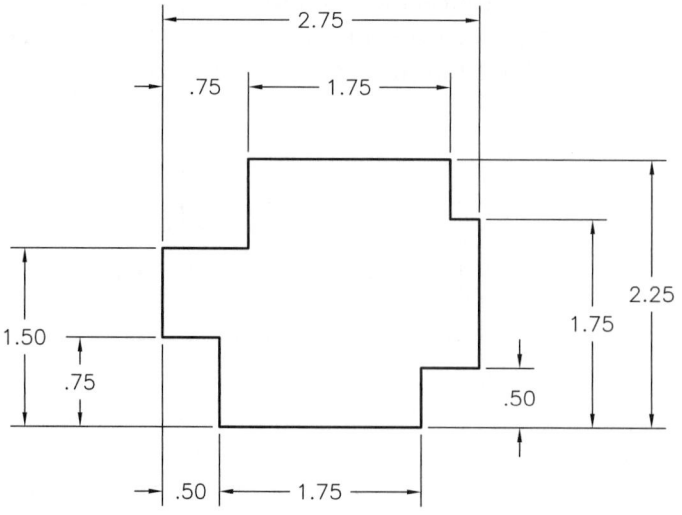

9.

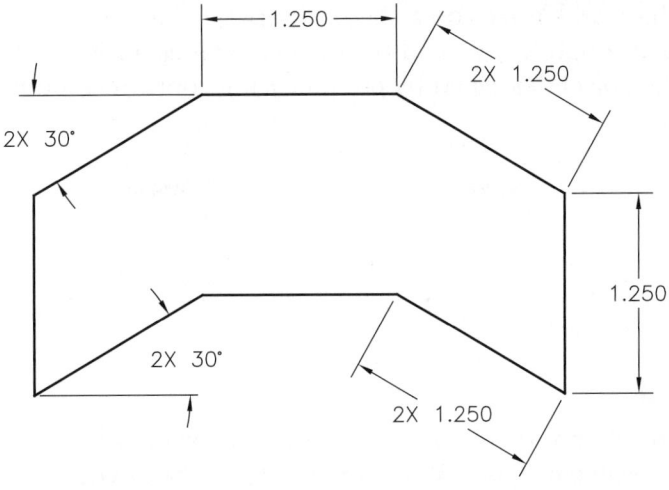

10. Start a new drawing from scratch or use a decimal-unit template of your choice. Draw the part views shown in A and B. Begin at the start point and then discontinue the **LINE** tool at the point shown. Complete each view by continuing from the previous endpoint. Save the drawing as P3-10.

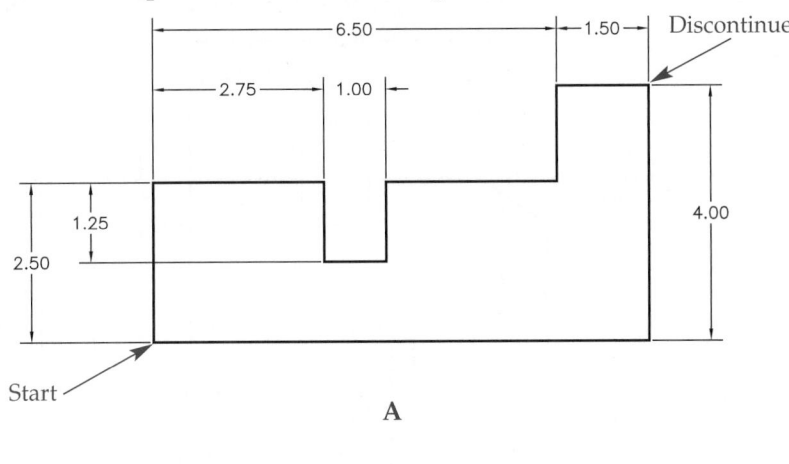

A

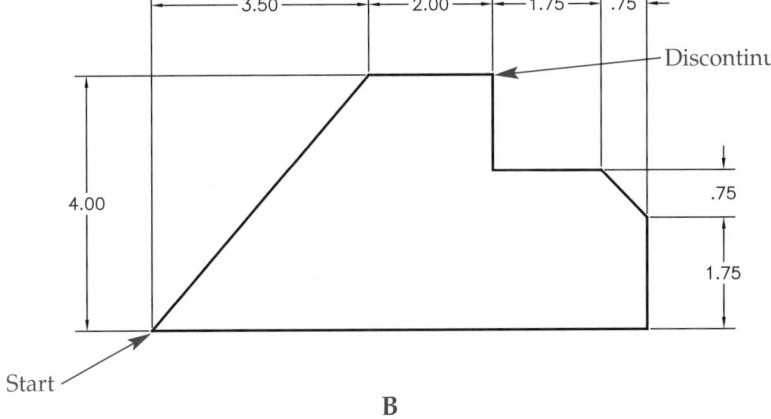

B

11. Sketch the X and Y axes on a sheet of paper. Label the origin, the positive values for X = 1 through X = 10, and the positive values for Y = 1 through Y = 10. Then sketch the object described by the following coordinate points:

2,2	4,6
8,2	4,3
8,7	3,3
7,7	3,7
7,3	2,7
6,3	2,2
6,6	

▼ Advanced

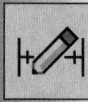

12. Sketch the X and Y axes of the Cartesian coordinate system as you did for the previous problem. Then sketch an object outline of your choice within the axes. List, in order, the rectangular coordinates of the points a drafter would need to specify in AutoCAD to recreate the object in your sketch.

For Problems 13–15, start a new drawing from scratch or use a decimal-unit template of your choice. Draw the part view shown. Save the drawings as P3-13, P3-14, *and* P3-15.

13.

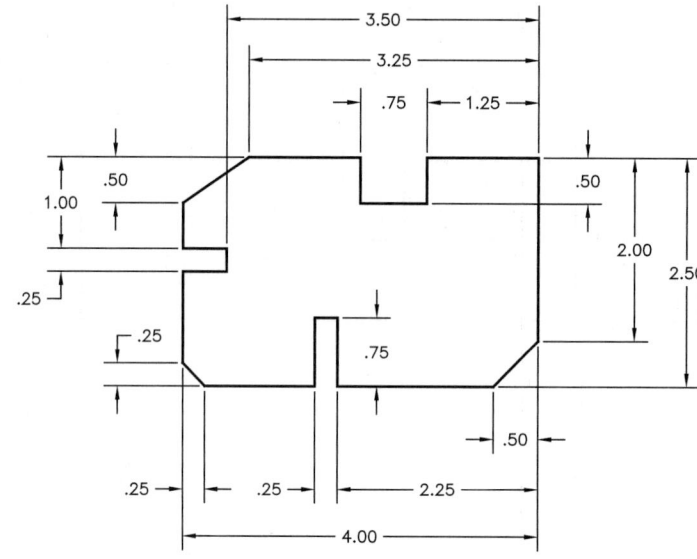

14.

15.

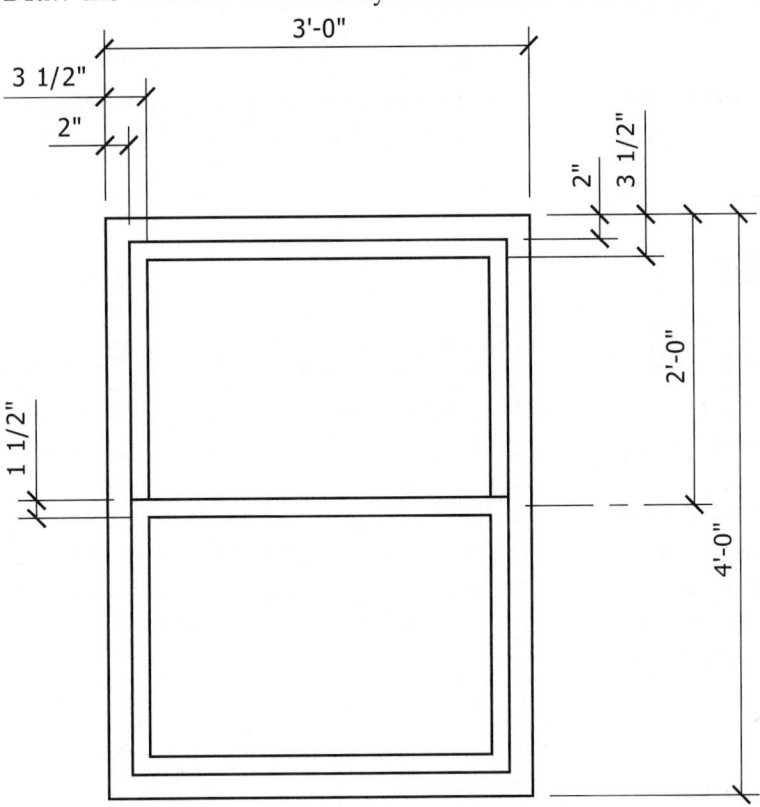

16. Start a new drawing from scratch or use an architectural-unit template of your choice. Draw the window elevation symbol shown. Save the drawing as P3-16.

17. Create a 2D hand-drawn sketch of the view of your computer monitor you see when looking at the screen. Use available measuring devices, such as a tape measure and caliper to dimension the size and location of each feature accurately. Convert any round objects to rectangular shapes that you can draw using the **LINE** tool. Start a new drawing from scratch or use a decimal-unit template of your choice. Draw the monitor from your sketch. Save the drawing as P3-17.

18. Create a dimensioned 2D sketch of the floor plan of a room in your school or company, complete with furniture. Use a tape measure to dimension the size and location of walls, doors, windows, and furniture accurately. Convert any round objects to rectangular shapes that you can draw using the **LINE** tool. Start a new drawing from scratch or use an architectural-unit template of your choice. Draw the room from your sketch. Save the drawing as P3-18.

AutoCAD Certified Associate Exam Practice

Answer the following questions. Write your answers on a separate sheet of paper.

1. If a drawing is set to architectural units, which of the following can you enter to specify a line length of 11 3/4"? *Select all that apply.*
   A. 11.75"
   B. 11.75
   C. 11 3/4
   D. 11-3/4
   E. 11 3/4"

2. Which of the following can you enter at the Select objects: prompt to select objects that lie partially within the selection boundary? *Select all that apply.*
   A. C
   B. W
   C. CP
   D. WP

3. Which tool or tools allow you to undo more than one operation at one time? *Select all that apply.*
   A. **OOPS**
   B. **REDO**
   C. **U**
   D. **UNDO**

AutoCAD Certified Professional Exam Practice

Follow the instructions in each problem. Write your answers on a separate sheet of paper.

1. **Navigate to this chapter on the Student Web site and open the CPE-03line.dwg file.**
   With dynamic input off, use the coordinates below to create the object shown. Do not change any settings in the drawing file. When you finish, use the **Endpoint** object snap mode to select point A. According to the coordinate display field in the lower-left corner of the screen, what are the coordinates of this point?
   Coordinate Values:
   2,3
   @6.25<0
   @4<50
   @3.5<90
   @4<130
   @6.25<180
   CLOSE

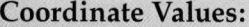

2. **Navigate to this chapter on the Student Web site and open the CPE-03intersect.dwg file.**
   With dynamic input off, use the coordinates below to create the object shown. Do not change any settings in the drawing file. Use the **Intersection** object snap mode to select point B. According to the coordinate display field in the lower-left corner of the screen, what are the coordinates of this point?
   Coordinate Values:
   5,2
   @3.45<60
   @4.75<180
   @8<−15

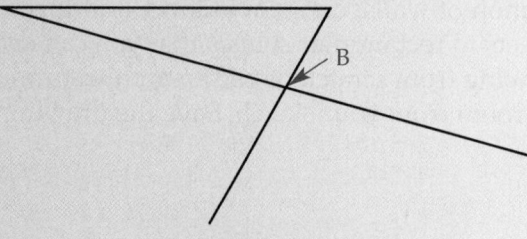

Basic Object Tools

Learning Objectives

After completing this chapter, you will be able to do the following:

✓ Draw circles using **CIRCLE** tool options.
✓ Draw arcs using **ARC** tool options.
✓ Use the **ELLIPSE** tool to draw ellipses and elliptical arcs.
✓ Use the **PLINE** tool to draw polylines.
✓ Draw regular polygons using the **POLYGON** tool.
✓ Draw rectangles using **RECTANGLE** tool options.
✓ Draw donuts and filled circles using the **DONUT** tool.
✓ Draw true spline curves using the **SPLINE** tool.

This chapter describes several basic object tools and their options. This chapter presents the ribbon as the primary way to access object tools, because the ribbon often provides a direct link to a specific tool option. Prompts associated with the option appear when you draw to automate the process. In contrast, when you issue a tool using dynamic input or the command line, you must choose specific options while you draw to receive appropriate prompts for constructing the object. You can draw objects using point entry or drawing aids, similar to locating endpoints while using the **LINE** tool. Several object tools also offer the option to input a direct value, such as the radius of a circle.

Drawing Circles

The **CIRCLE** tool provides several options to draw *circles*. Choose the appropriate option based on the information you know about locating and constructing the circle. The ribbon is an effective way to access circle tool options. See **Figure 4-1.**

Center, Radius Option

Access the **Center, Radius** option to specify the center of the circle, followed by the radius. Use point entry or drawing aids to locate the center point. If you know the radius, type a value and press [Enter] or the space bar, or right-click and pick **Enter**. You can also define the radius using point entry or drawing aids. See **Figure 4-2.**

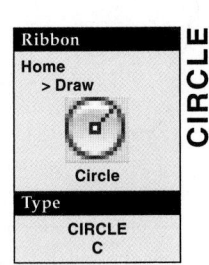

Ribbon

Home
> Draw

Circle

Type
CIRCLE
C

CIRCLE

circle: A closed curve with a constant radius around a center point; usually dimensioned according to the diameter.

Figure 4-1.
Select a **Circle** tool option from the **Draw** panel of the **Home** ribbon tab to preset the **Circle** tool to display appropriate prompts.

Pick the **Circle** flyout to display the **Circle** options

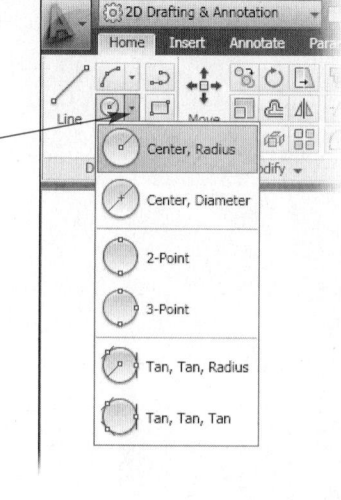

Figure 4-2.
Drawing a circle by specifying the center point and radius. Notice the rubberband line that appears when you move the crosshairs away from the center point.

1. Define the center point

2. Enter the radius or specify a point

Radius, rubberband line

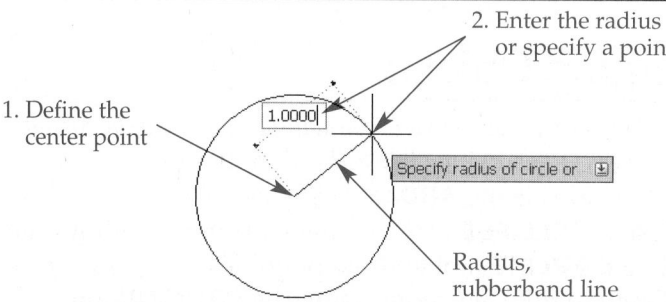

 **NOTE**

AutoCAD stores the radius of the circle you draw as the new default radius setting, allowing you to draw another circle with the same radius.

Center, Diameter Option

Access the **Center, Diameter** option to specify the center of the circle, followed by the diameter. The **Center, Diameter** option is convenient because on most designs, circular holes, shafts, and features are sized according to diameter. Use point entry or drawing aids to locate the center point. If you know the diameter, type a value and press [Enter] or the space bar, or right-click and pick **Enter**. You can also define the diameter using point entry or drawing aids. See **Figure 4-3**.

Figure 4-3.
Drawing a circle by specifying the center point and diameter. Notice that the crosshairs measures the diameter, but the rubberband line passes midway between the center and the crosshairs.

2. Enter the diameter or specify a point

Crosshairs position

Rubberband line

Diameter

1. Define a center point

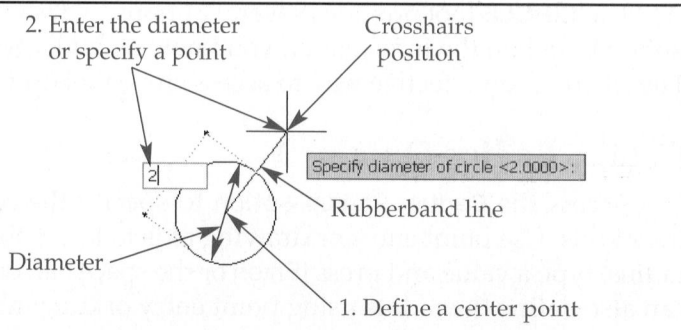

If you use the **Center, Radius** option to draw a circle after using the **Diameter** option, AutoCAD changes the default to a radius measurement based on the previous diameter.

2-Point Option

Access the **2-Point** option to specify diameter using two points on opposite sides of the circle. The **2-Point** option is useful when you know the diameter of the circle, but the center is difficult to locate. A common example is drawing a circle between two existing objects. Use point entry or drawing aids to locate the endpoints. See **Figure 4-4.**

3-Point Option

Select the **3-Point** option to draw a circle according to three known points on the circumference of the circle. The **3-Point** option is most commonly used when the location of the center point, the radius, and the diameter are unknown. Specify the three points in any order using point entry or drawing aids. See **Figure 4-5.**

Tan, Tan, Radius Option

Access the **Tan, Tan, Radius** option to pick two objects *tangent* to a circle and the circle radius. Hover the crosshairs over the first line, arc, or circle to which the new circle will be tangent. When you see the **Deferred Tangent** object snap marker, pick to select the first *point of tangency*. Repeat the process to select the second object to which the new circle will be tangent. The order in which you pick is not critical.

tangent: A line, circle, or arc that meets another circle or arc at only one point.

point of tangency: The point shared by tangent objects.

Figure 4-4.
Using the **2-Point** option of the **CIRCLE** tool. A common application is drawing a circle between two existing objects, such as these lines.

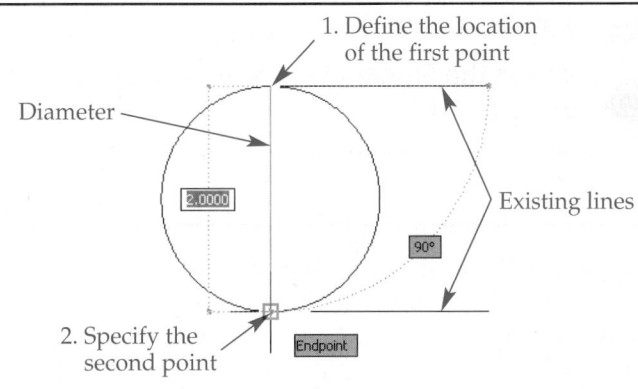

Figure 4-5.
Using the **3-Point** option of the **CIRCLE** tool. A common application is drawing a circle by referencing three known points, such as the endpoints of these lines.

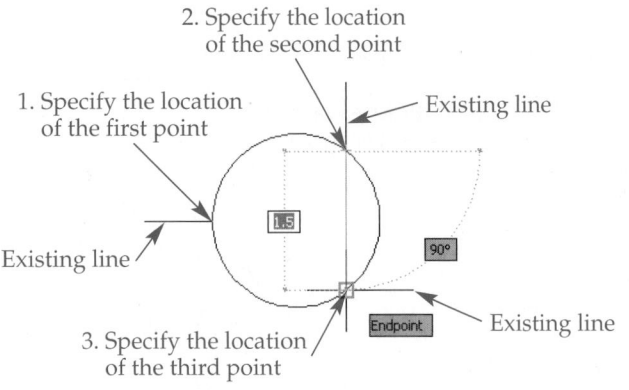

If you know the radius, type a value and press [Enter] or the space bar, or right-click and pick **Enter**. You can also define the radius using point entry or drawing aids. See Figure 4-6.

NOTE

If the radius you enter while using the **Tan, Tan, Radius** option is too small, AutoCAD displays the message Circle does not exist.

Tan, Tan, Tan Option

Select the **Tan, Tan, Tan** option to draw a circle tangent to three existing objects. Hover the crosshairs over the first line, arc, or circle to which the new circle will be tangent. When you see the **Deferred Tangent** object snap marker, pick to select the first point of tangency. Repeat the process to select the second and third objects to which the new circle will be tangent. You must make selections when you see the **Deferred Tangent** object snap marker, but the order in which you pick is not critical. See Figure 4-7.

NOTE

Unlike the **Tan, Tan, Radius** option, the **Tan, Tan, Tan** option does not automatically recover when you pick a point where no tangent exists. In such a case, you must manually reactivate the **Tangent** object snap to make additional picks. Chapter 7 describes the **Tangent** object snap. For now, type TAN and press [Enter] at the point selection prompt to pick again.

Exercise 4-1

Access the Student Web site (www.g-wlearning.com/CAD) and complete Exercise 4-1.

Figure 4-6.
Two examples of drawing circles tangent to two given objects using the **Tan, Tan, Radius** option.

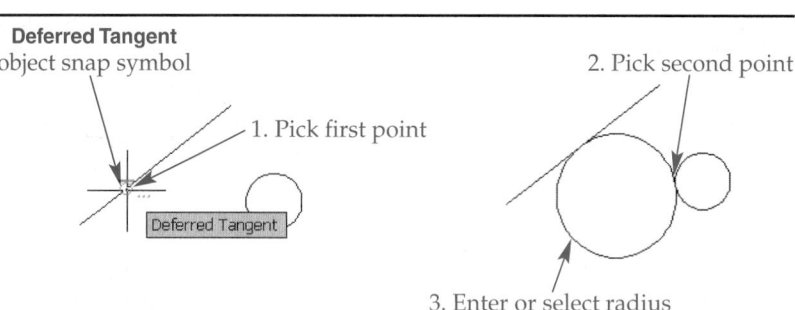

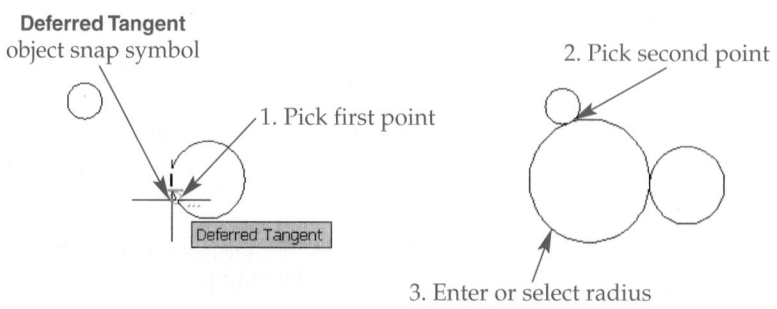

Figure 4-7.
Two examples of drawing circles tangent to three given objects using the **Tan, Tan, Tan** option.

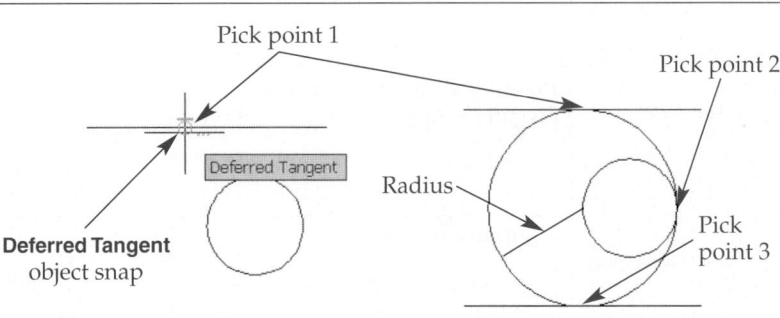

Drawing Arcs

The **ARC** tool offers multiple options to draw *arcs*. Select the appropriate option based on the information you know about locating and constructing the arc. The ribbon is an effective way to access arc tool options. See **Figure 4-8.**

Figure 4-9 provides a step-by-step example of using each **ARC** tool option. The selections and values you enter determine arc placement. Some options prompt for the

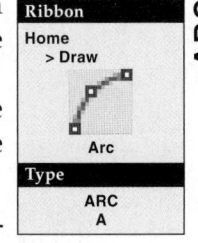

ARC

Ribbon
Home
> Draw
Arc

Type
ARC
A

arc: Any portion of a circle; usually dimensioned according to the radius.

Figure 4-8.
Selecting an **Arc** tool option from the **Draw** panel of the **Home** ribbon tab to preset the **Arc** tool to display appropriate prompts.

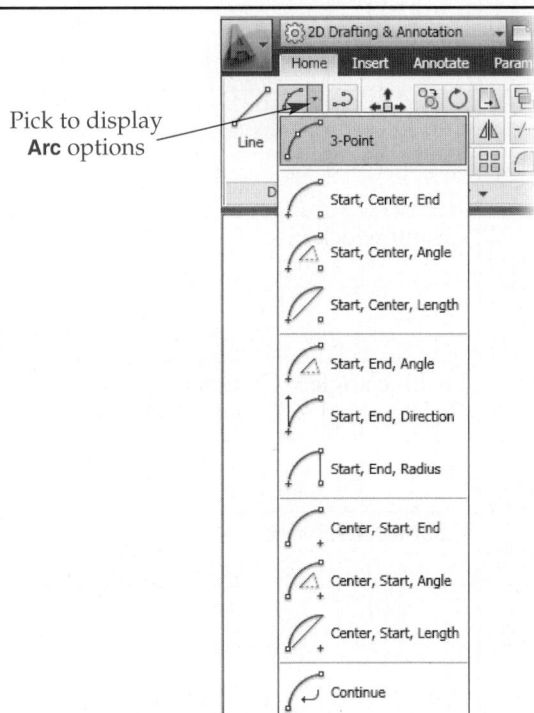

Pick to display **Arc** options

Figure 4-9. Select the appropriate **Arc** tool option based on the information you know about locating and constructing the arc.

Option	Direction	Steps
3-Point	Clockwise or counterclockwise	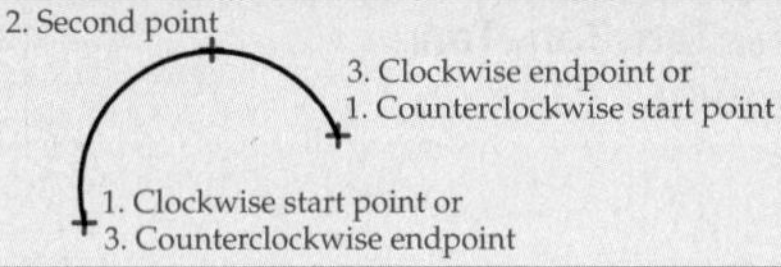 2. Second point; 3. Clockwise endpoint or 1. Counterclockwise start point; 1. Clockwise start point or 3. Counterclockwise endpoint
Start, Center, End	Counterclockwise	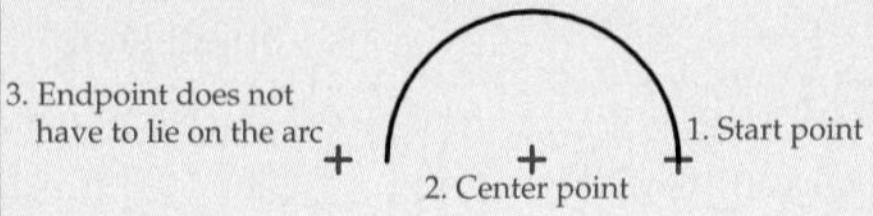 3. Endpoint does not have to lie on the arc; 2. Center point; 1. Start point
Start, Center, Angle	Positive angle = Clockwise Negative angle = Counterclockwise	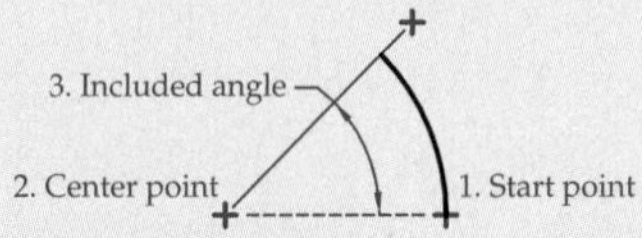 3. Included angle; 2. Center point; 1. Start point
Start, Center, Length	Counterclockwise	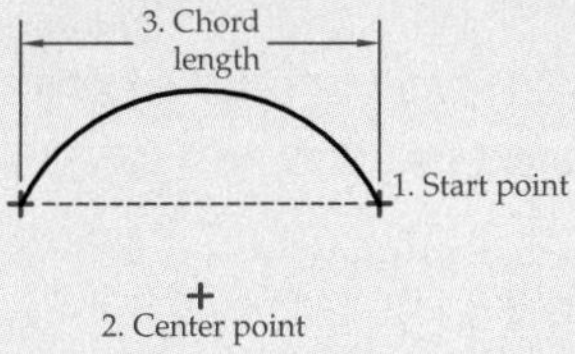 3. Chord length; 1. Start point; 2. Center point
Start, End, Angle	Positive angle = Clockwise Negative angle = Counterclockwise	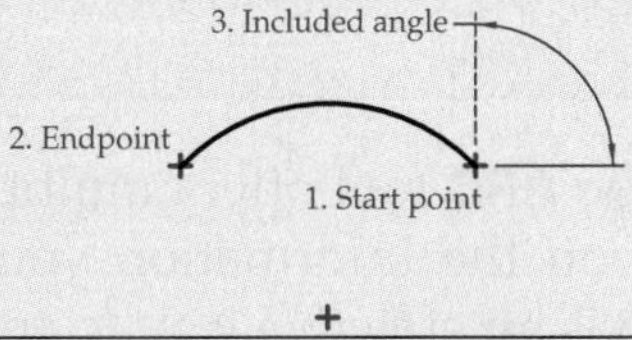 3. Included angle; 2. Endpoint; 1. Start point
Start, End, Direction	Tangent to specified direction	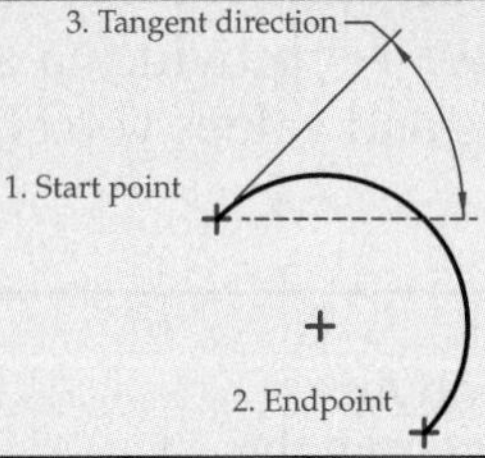 3. Tangent direction; 1. Start point; 2. Endpoint
Start, End, Radius	Counterclockwise	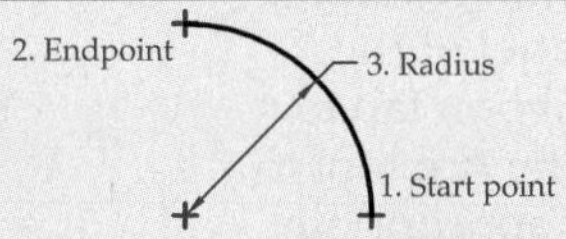 2. Endpoint; 3. Radius; 1. Start point
Center, Start, End	Counterclockwise	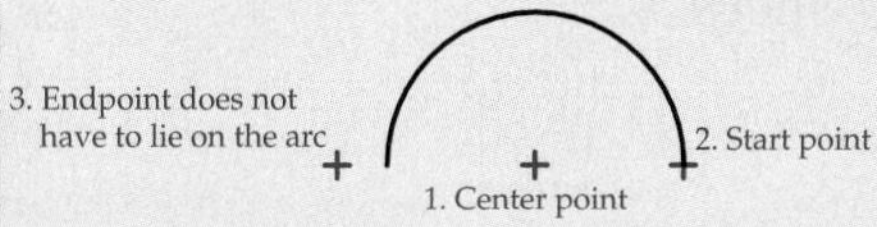 3. Endpoint does not have to lie on the arc; 2. Start point; 1. Center point
Center, Start, Angle	Positive angle = Clockwise Negative angle = Counterclockwise	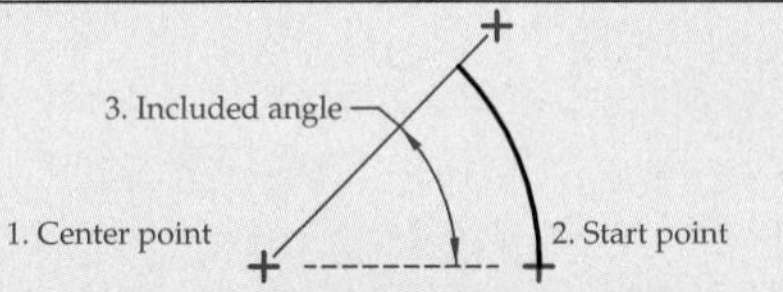 3. Included angle; 1. Center point; 2. Start point
Center, Start, Length	Counterclockwise	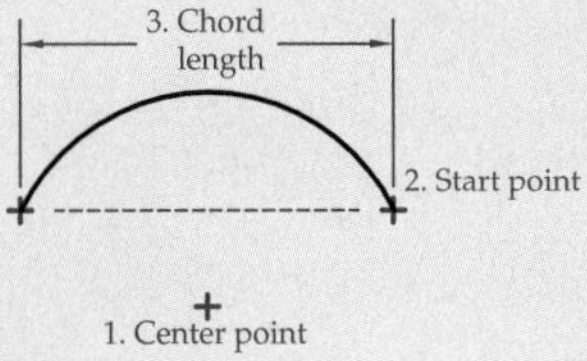 3. Chord length; 2. Start point; 1. Center point

included angle, and others prompt for the *chord length*. Locating points in a clockwise or counterclockwise pattern affects the result in most arc options. The values you specify, including the use of positive or negative numbers, also affects the result.

included angle:
The angle formed between the center, start point, and endpoint of an arc.

chord length: The linear distance between two points on a circle or arc.

NOTE

The **3-Point** option is default when you enter the **ARC** tool at the keyboard.

Reference Material

Chord Length Table
For a chord length table and other reference tables, go to the **Reference Material** section of the Student Web site (www.g-wlearning.com/CAD) and select **Standard Tables**.

Exercises 4-2 and 4-3

Access the Student Web site (www.g-wlearning.com/CAD) and complete Exercise 4-2 and Exercise 4-3.

Continue Option

Use the **Continue** option to continue an arc from the endpoint of a previously drawn line or arc. The arc automatically attaches to the endpoint of the previously drawn line or arc, and the Specify endpoint of arc: prompt appears. Pick the endpoint of the new arc to create the arc.

The **Continue** option is a quick way to draw an arc beginning at the endpoint of a previously drawn line, tangent to the line. See **Figure 4-10**. Use this technique for applications such as drawing slots. When you draw a series of arcs using the **Continue** option, each arc is tangent to the previous arc. The start point and direction occur from the endpoint and direction of the previous arc. See **Figure 4-11**.

Figure 4-10.
Continuing an arc from the previous line. Point 2 is the start of the arc, and Point 3 is the end of the arc. The arc and line are tangent at Point 2.

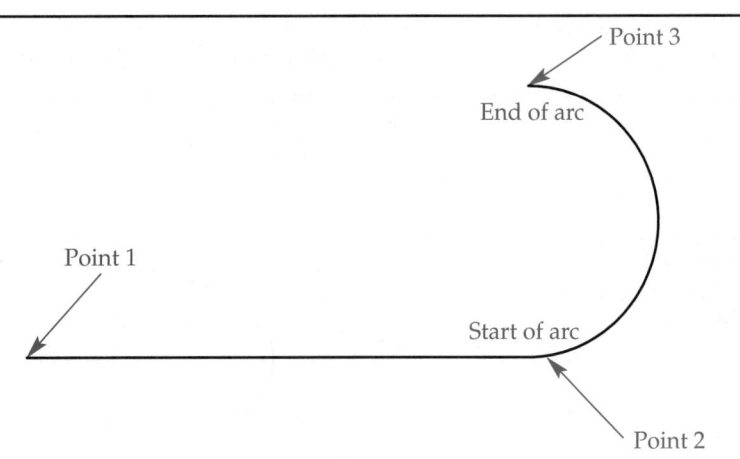

Figure 4-11.
Using the **Continue** option to draw three tangent arcs.

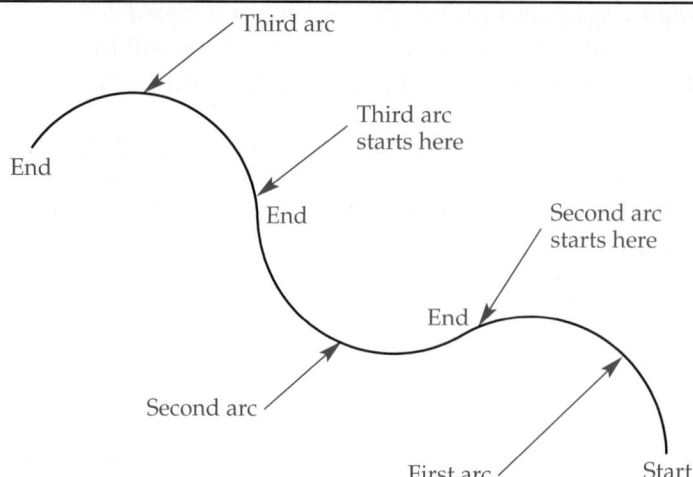

Third arc

Third arc starts here

End

End

Second arc starts here

End

Second arc

First arc

Start

NOTE

You can also access the **Continue** option by beginning the **ARC** tool and pressing [Enter] or the space bar, or by right-clicking and selecting **Enter** when prompted to specify the start point of the arc.

Exercise 4-4

Access the Student Web site (www.g-wlearning.com/CAD) and complete Exercise 4-4.

Drawing Ellipses

ELLIPSE

Ribbon
Home
> Draw

Ellipse

Type
ELLIPSE
EL

An *ellipse* has a *major axis* and a *minor axis*. See **Figure 4-12.** A circle appears as an ellipse when you view the circle at an angle. For example, a 30° ellipse is a circle rotated 30° from the line of sight.

The **ELLIPSE** tool offers several options to draw elliptical shapes. Choose the appropriate option based on the information you know about locating and constructing the ellipse, and whether the ellipse is whole or an elliptical arc.

ellipse: An oval shape that contains two centers of equal radius.

major axis: The longer of the two axes in an ellipse.

minor axis: The shorter of the two axes in an ellipse.

Figure 4-12.
The parts of an ellipse.

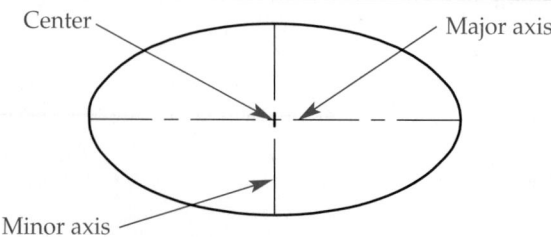

Center

Major axis

Minor axis

Center Option

Select the **Center** option to specify the center of the ellipse, then an endpoint of the first axis, and finally an endpoint of the second axis. Axes endpoints originate from the center of the ellipse, forming half of the major and minor axes. See **Figure 4-13.**

Axis, End Option

Choose the **Axis, End** option to specify the first endpoint of an axis, then the second endpoint of the same axis, and finally one endpoint of the second axis. The first axis can be the major or minor axis. See **Figure 4-14.**

Rotation Option

Use the **Rotation** option to create an ellipse by specifying the angle at which a circle rotates from the line of sight. For example, a 30° ellipse is a circle rotated 30° from the line of sight. Begin by constructing an ellipse as usual, but be sure to create the major axis when you specify the first axis endpoint. Then, when the Specify distance to other axis or: prompt appears, select the **Rotation** option instead of picking the second axis endpoint. Finally, enter the angle at which the circle rotates from the line of sight, such as 30 for a 30° rotation. **Figure 4-15** shows examples of rotation angles.

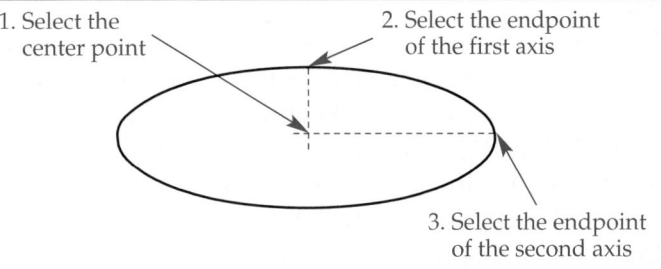

Figure 4-13. Drawing an ellipse by picking the center and an endpoint for each axis. The order in which you specify axis endpoints is not critical. The distance from each endpoint to the center point determines the major and minor axes.

1. Select the center point
2. Select the endpoint of the first axis
3. Select the endpoint of the second axis

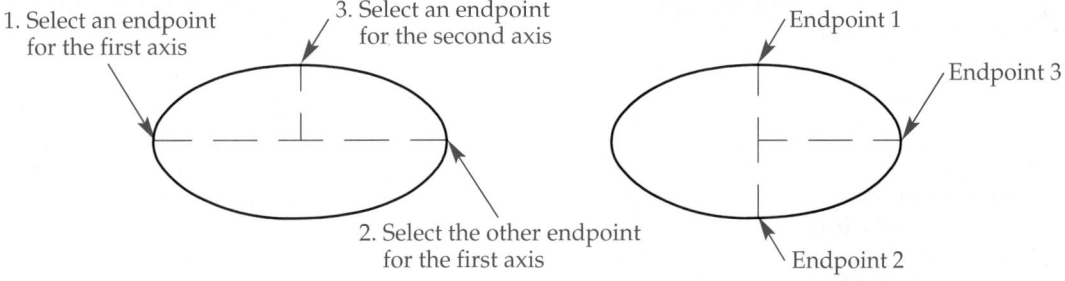

Figure 4-14. Constructing the same ellipse by choosing different axis endpoints. Select points based on known information or the location of existing objects.

1. Select an endpoint for the first axis
3. Select an endpoint for the second axis
2. Select the other endpoint for the first axis

Endpoint 1
Endpoint 3
Endpoint 2

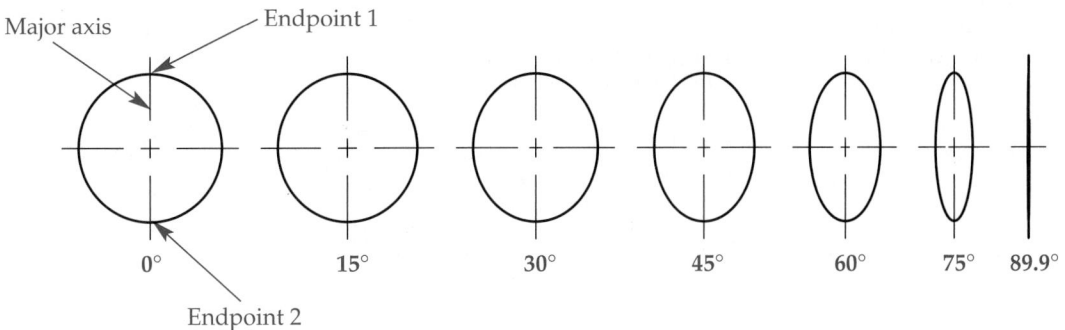

Figure 4-15. The relationship among several ellipses having the same major axis length, but different rotation angles.

Major axis
Endpoint 1
Endpoint 2

0°   15°   30°   45°   60°   75°   89.9°

Exercise 4-5

Access the Student Web site (www.g-wlearning.com/CAD) and complete Exercise 4-5.

Drawing Elliptical Arcs

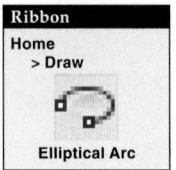

Ribbon
Home
> Draw

Elliptical Arc

Use the **Arc** option to draw elliptical arcs. Drawing an elliptical arc is just like drawing an ellipse, but with two additional steps that define the start and end of the elliptical arc. Several options are available for defining the size and shape of an elliptical arc.

The default elliptical arc option is similar to the **Axis, End** ellipse option. Specify the first endpoint of an axis, then the second endpoint of the same axis, and then one endpoint of the second axis. Finally, select the start and end angles for the elliptical arc. See **Figure 4-16.** The start and end angles are the angular relationships between the center of the ellipse and the arc endpoints. The angle of the first axis establishes the angle of the elliptical arc. For example, a 0° start angle begins the arc at the first endpoint of the first axis. A 45° start angle begins the arc 45° counterclockwise from the first endpoint of the first axis. End angles are also counterclockwise from the start point.

Figure 4-17 briefly describes additional elliptical arc options. Use the **Center** option when appropriate instead of the default axis endpoint method. The **Parameter, Included angle,** and **Rotation** options are available when you create axis endpoint or center elliptical arcs.

Figure 4-16.
The steps required to draw an elliptical arc using a 0° start angle and a 90° end angle. The three examples at the bottom were created using the same steps, but different start and end angles.

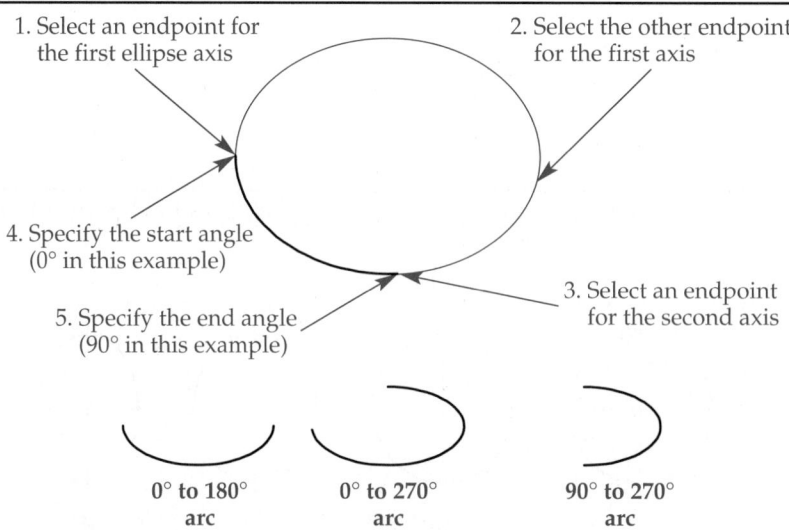

1. Select an endpoint for the first ellipse axis

2. Select the other endpoint for the first axis

4. Specify the start angle (0° in this example)

3. Select an endpoint for the second axis

5. Specify the end angle (90° in this example)

0° to 180° arc   0° to 270° arc   90° to 270° arc

Figure 4-17. Additional options for drawing elliptical arcs.

Option	Application	Process
Center	Lets you establish the center of the elliptical arc. **Rotation, Parameter,** and **Included angle** options are available.	1. Select the ellipse center point. 2. Select the endpoint of one of the ellipse axes. 3. Pick the endpoint of the other axis to form the ellipse. 4. Enter the start angle for the elliptical arc. 5. Select the end angle.
Parameter	Use instead of picking the start angle of the elliptical arc. AutoCAD uses a different means of vector calculation to create the elliptical arc.	1. Specify the start parameter point. 2. Specify the end parameter point.
Included angle	Establishes an included angle beginning at the start angle.	1. Specify the included angle.
Rotation	Allows you to rotate the elliptical arc about the first axis by specifying a rotation angle. **Parameter** and **Included angle** options are available.	1. Specify the rotation around the major axis. 2. Specify the start angle for the elliptical arc. 3. Specify the end angle.

Exercise 4-6

Access the Student Web site (www.g-wlearning.com/CAD) and complete Exercise 4-6.

Isometric Circles and Arcs

For information about using the **Isocircle** option of the **ELLIPSE** tool to draw isometric circles and arcs, go to the Student Web site (www.g-wlearning.com/CAD), select this chapter, and select **Isometric Circles and Arcs**.

Drawing Polylines

Use the **PLINE** tool to draw *polylines*. When you use the default polyline settings, drawing polyline segments is identical to drawing line segments using the **LINE** tool. Access the **PLINE** tool and use point entry or drawing aids to locate polyline endpoints. Press [Enter], the space bar, or [Esc], or right-click and select **Enter** to exit. The difference between a polyline and a line is that all of the segments of a polyline act as a single object. The **PLINE** tool also provides more flexibility than the **LINE** tool, allowing you to draw a single object composed of straight lines and arcs of varying thickness.

The **PLINE** tool includes the same **Undo** and **Close** options available with the **LINE** tool. Use the **Undo** option to remove the last segment of a polyline without leaving the **PLINE** tool and continue from the previous endpoint. You can use the **Undo** option

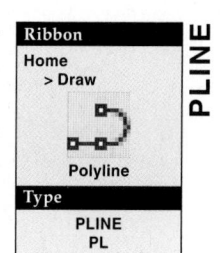

Ribbon
Home
> Draw

Polyline

Type
PLINE
PL

PLINE

polyline: A series of lines and arcs that constitute a single object.

repeatedly to delete polyline segments until the entire object is gone. Use the **Close** option to connect the endpoint of the last polyline segment to the start point of the first polyline segment.

Setting Polyline Width

The default polyline settings create a polyline with a constant width of 0. A polyline with a constant width of 0 is similar to a standard line and accepts the lineweight applied to the layer on which the polyline is drawn. Chapter 5 explains layers. Adjust the polyline width to create thick and tapered polyline objects.

To change the width of a polyline segment, access the **PLINE** tool, select the first point, and choose the **Width** option. AutoCAD prompts you to specify the starting width of the line, followed by the ending width of the line. Enter the same starting and ending width value to draw a polyline with constant width. See **Figure 4-18A.** The rubberband line from the first point reflects the width settings. The location of the start point and endpoint is at the center of the segment width.

To create a tapered line segment for applications such as an arrowhead, enter different values for the starting and ending widths. See **Figure 4-18B.** To draw an arrowhead with a sharp point, use the **Width** option and specify 0 as the starting or ending width, and then use an appropriate value greater than 0 for the other width.

NOTE

A starting or ending width value other than 0 overrides the lineweight applied to the layer on which you draw the polyline.

Setting Polyline Halfwidth

Choose the **Halfwidth** option to specify the width of the polyline from the center to one side, as opposed to the total width of the polyline defined using the **Width** option. Access the **PLINE** tool, pick the first polyline endpoint, and then choose the **Halfwidth** option. Specify starting and ending values at the appropriate prompts. **Figure 4-19** shows a polyline drawn using the **Halfwidth** option and the same width values applied in **Figure 4-18B**, resulting in a polyline that is twice as wide.

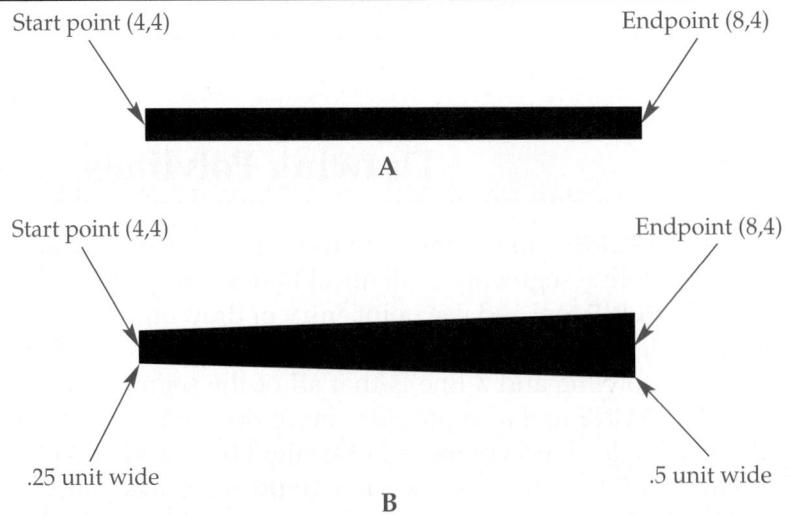

Figure 4-18.
A—A thick polyline drawn using the **Width** option of the **PLINE** tool.
B—Using the **Width** option of the **PLINE** tool to draw a tapered polyline.

Start point (4,4)   Endpoint (8,4)

A

Start point (4,4)   Endpoint (8,4)

.25 unit wide   .5 unit wide

B

Figure 4-19.
Specifying the width
of a polyline using
the **Halfwidth** option.
A starting value
of .25 produces a
polyline width of .5
unit, and an ending
value of .5 produces
a polyline width of
1 unit.

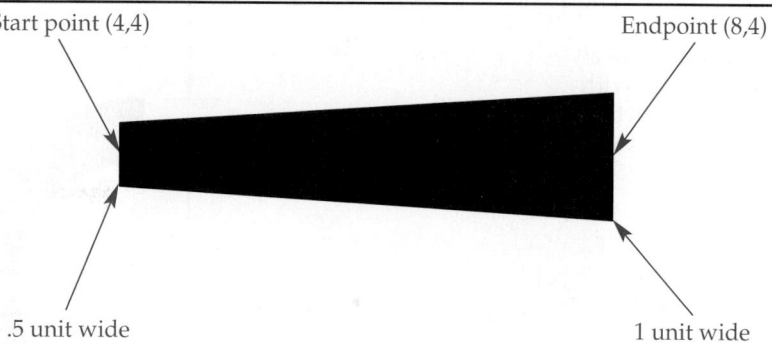

Start point (4,4) Endpoint (8,4)

.5 unit wide 1 unit wide

NOTE

All polyline objects with width—including polylines, polygons drawn using the **POLYGON** tool, rectangles drawn using the **RECTANGLE** tool, and donuts—can appear filled or empty. The **Apply solid fill** setting in the **Display performance** area of the **Display** tab in the **Options** dialog box controls the appearance. You can also type FILL or FILLMODE and use the **On** or **Off** option. Polyline objects are filled by default. The fill display for previously drawn polyline objects updates when the drawing regenerates. You can regenerate the drawing manually by typing REGEN.

Length Option

The **Length** option allows you to draw a polyline parallel to a previously drawn line or polyline. After you draw a line or polyline, access the **PLINE** tool and pick a start point. Choose the **Length** option and specify the length. The resulting polyline is automatically drawn parallel to the previous line or polyline using specified length.

Exercises 4-7 and 4-8

Access the Student Web site (www.g-wlearning.com/CAD) and complete Exercise 4-7 and Exercise 4-8.

Drawing Polyline Arcs

Use the **Arc** option to draw polyline arcs. Polyline arcs can continue from or to polyline segments drawn during the same operation to form a single object. You can use the **Width** or **Halfwidth** option to add width to a polyline arc, ranging from 0 to the radius of the arc. You can also set different starting and ending arc widths. See **Figure 4-20.** Enter the **Width** or **Halfwidth** and **Arc** options in either order. Use the **Line** option to return the **PLINE** tool back to straight-line segment mode.

In addition to the **Close**, **Undo**, **Width**, and **Halfwidth** options, the polyline **Arc** option includes functions for controlling the size and location of polyline arcs. Many of the polyline **Arc** options allow you to create polyline arcs using the same methods available for drawing arcs using the **ARC** tool. Select the appropriate option and follow the prompts to create the polyline arc. Review the **ARC** tool options described in **Figure 4-21** to help recognize the function of similar polyline **Arc** options.

Figure 4-20.
An example of a
polyline arc with
different starting
and ending widths.

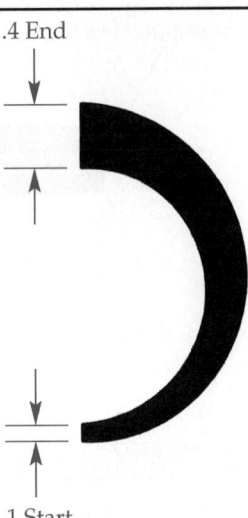

.4 End

.1 Start

Figure 4-21. Additional options available for drawing polyline arcs.

Option	Application	Options for Completion
Angle	Specify the polyline arc size according to an included angle.	1. Specify an endpoint. 2. Use the **Center** option to select the center point. 3. Use the **Radius** option to enter the radius.
Center	Specify the location of the polyline arc center point, instead of allowing AutoCAD to calculate the location automatically.	1. Specify an endpoint. 2. Use the **Angle** option to specify the included angle. 3. Use the **Length** option to specify the chord length.
Direction	Alter the polyline arc bearing, or tangent direction, instead of allowing the polyline arc to form tangent to the last object drawn.	1. Specify an endpoint.
Radius	Specify the polyline arc radius.	1. Specify an endpoint. 2. Use the **Angle** option to specify the included angle.
Second point	Draw a three-point polyline arc.	1. Pick the second point, followed by the endpoint.

Exercise 4-9

Access the Student Web site (www.g-wlearning.com/CAD) and complete Exercise 4-9.

Multilines

For information about drawing and editing multiline objects, go to the Student Web site (www.g-wlearning.com/CAD), select this chapter, and select **Multilines**.

Drawing Regular Polygons

Access the **POLYGON** tool to draw any *regular polygon* with up to 1024 sides. Polygons drawn using the **POLYGON** tool are single polyline objects. The first prompt asks for the number of sides. For example, to draw an octagon, which is a regular polygon with eight sides, enter 8. Next, decide how to describe the size and location of the polygon. The default setting involves choosing the center and radius of an imaginary circle. To use this method, specify a location for the polygon center point. A prompt then asks if you want to form an *inscribed polygon* or a *circumscribed polygon*. Select the appropriate option and specify the radius to create the polygon. See **Figure 4-22**.

regular polygon: A closed geometric figure with three or more equal sides and equal angles.

inscribed polygon: A polygon drawn inside an imaginary circle so that its corners touch the circle.

circumscribed polygon: A polygon drawn outside an imaginary circle so that the sides of the polygon are tangent to the circle.

NOTE

The number of polygon sides you enter, the **Inscribed in circle** or **Circumscribed about circle** option you select, and the radius you specify are stored as the new default settings, allowing you to draw another polygon with the same characteristics.

PROFESSIONAL TIP

Regular polygons, such as the *hexagons* commonly drawn to represent bolt heads and nuts on mechanical drawings, are normally dimensioned across the flats. Use the **Circumscribed about circle** option to draw a polygon dimensioned across the flats. The radius you enter is equal to one-half the distance across the flats. Use the **Inscribed in circle** option to dimension a polygon across the corners or to confine the polygon within a circular area.

hexagon: Six-sided regular polygon.

Edge Option

Use the **Edge** option to construct a polygon if you do not know the center point location or radius of the imaginary circle, but you do know the size and location of a polygon edge. After you access the **POLYGON** tool and enter the number of sides, choose the **Edge** option at the Specify center of polygon or [Edge]: prompt. Specify a point for the first endpoint of one side, followed by the second endpoint of the side. See Figure 4-23.

Figure 4-22.
Regular polygons can be inscribed in a circle or circumscribed around a circle.

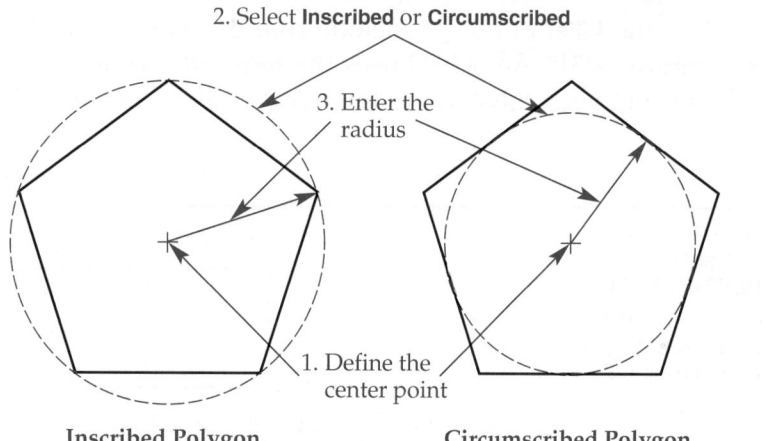

2. Select **Inscribed** or **Circumscribed**

3. Enter the radius

1. Define the center point

Inscribed Polygon   Circumscribed Polygon

Figure 4-23.
Use the **Edge** option of the **POLYGON** tool to construct a regular polygon according to the location and size of an edge.

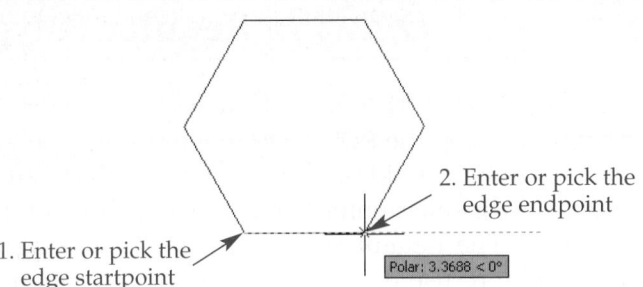

1. Enter or pick the edge startpoint

2. Enter or pick the edge endpoint

Polar: 3.3688 < 0°

Exercise 4-10

Access the Student Web site (www.g-wlearning.com/CAD) and complete Exercise 4-10.

Drawing Rectangles

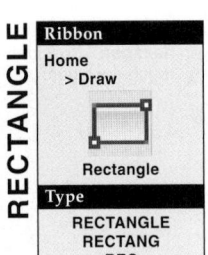
Use the **RECTANGLE** tool to draw rectangles easily. Rectangles drawn using the **RECTANGLE** tool are single polyline objects. To draw a rectangle using default settings, specify the point of one corner, followed by point of the diagonally opposite corner. See **Figure 4-24.** By default, the **RECTANGLE** tool draws a rectangle at a 0° angle with sharp corners.

Adding Chamfered Corners

chamfer: In mechanical drafting, a small angled surface used to relieve a sharp corner.

Use the **Chamfer** option to include *chamfered* corners during rectangle construction. See **Figure 4-25A.** When prompted, enter the first chamfer distance, followed by the second chamfer distance. Entering 0 at the first or second chamfer distance prompt creates a rectangle with sharp corners. After setting the distances, you can either draw the rectangle or set additional options. However, using the **Fillet** option overrides the **Chamfer** option. The rectangle you draw must be large enough to accommodate the specified chamfer distances. Otherwise, the rectangle will have sharp corners. New rectangles are drawn with the specified chamfer until you reset the chamfer distances to 0 or use the **Fillet** option to create rounded corners.

Adding Rounded Corners

fillet: A rounded interior corner.

round: A rounded exterior corner.

Use the **Fillet** option to include rounded corners during rectangle construction. See **Figure 4-25B.** AutoCAD uses the term *fillet* to describe both *fillets* and *rounds*. When prompted, enter the radius for all fillets and rounds. Entering a radius of 0

Figure 4-24.
Using the **RECTANGLE** tool and point entry or drawing aids to construct a rectangle.

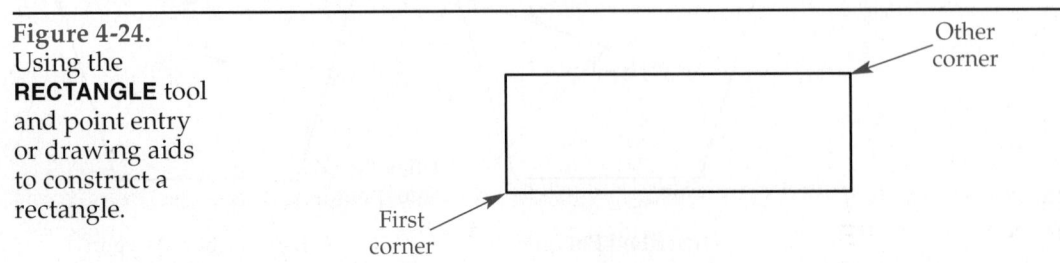

Other corner

First corner

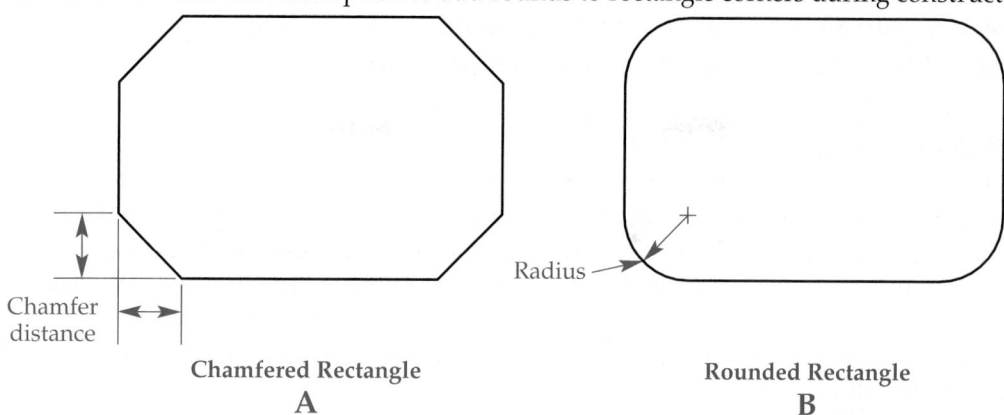

Figure 4-25. A—Use the **Chamfer** option to add chamfers to rectangle corners during construction. B—Use the **Fillet** option to add rounds to rectangle corners during construction.

Chamfer distance

Chamfered Rectangle
A

Radius

Rounded Rectangle
B

creates a rectangle with sharp corners. After setting the radius, you can either draw the rectangle or set additional options. However, using the **Chamfer** option overrides the **Fillet** option. The rectangle you draw must be large enough to accommodate the specified round radii. Otherwise, the rectangle will have sharp corners. New rectangles are drawn with the specified fillets until you reset the fillet radius to 0 or use the **Chamfer** option to create chamfered corners.

> **NOTE**
>
> This chapter introduces adding chamfers and rounds while creating rectangles. Chapter 12 covers adding chamfers using the **CHAMFER** tool and rounds using the **FILLET** tool.

Setting the Width

Select the **Width** option to adjust rectangle line width, or "boldness." Do not confuse width with lineweight, described in Chapter 5. A prompt asks you to enter the line width. For example, to create a rectangle with lines that are .5 wide, enter .5. After setting the rectangle width, you can either draw the rectangle or set additional options. All new rectangles are drawn using the specified width. Reset the **Width** option to 0 to create new rectangles using a standard "0-width" line.

Specifying the Area

The **Area** option is available after you pick the first corner point. This option is useful for drawing a rectangle when you know the area of the rectangle and the length of one side. Choose the **Area** option, and then specify the total area for the rectangle using a value that corresponds to the current units. For example, enter 45 to draw a rectangle with an area of 45 units^2. Next, choose the **Length** option if you know the length of a side (the X value), or choose the **Width** option if you know the width of a side (the Y value). When prompted, enter the length or width to complete the rectangle. AutoCAD calculates the unspecified dimension and draws the rectangle.

Specifying Rectangle Dimensions

The **Dimensions** option is available after you pick the first corner of the rectangle and allows you to specify the length and width of the rectangle. Choose the **Dimensions** option and specify the length of a side to indicate the X value. Next, enter the width of a side to indicate the Y value. AutoCAD now prompts for the other corner point. To change the dimensions, select the **Dimensions** option again. If the dimensions are correct, specify another point to complete the rectangle. The second point determines which of four possible rectangles you draw. See **Figure 4-26.**

Drawing a Rotated Rectangle

Use the **Rotation** option, available after you pick the first corner of the rectangle, to draw a rectangle at an angle other than 0°. When prompted, specify the angle to rotate the rectangle from the default of 0°. Then locate the opposite corner of the rectangle. An alternative is to use the **Pick points** option when you see the Specify rotation angle or [Pick points]: prompt. If you select the **Pick points** option, the prompt asks you to select two points to define the angle. The rotation value becomes the new default angle for using the **Rotation** option.

NOTE

The **Elevation** and **Thickness** options of the **RECTANGLE** tool are appropriate for 3D applications, as explained in *AutoCAD and Its Applications—Advanced.*

PROFESSIONAL TIP

You can use a combination of rectangle settings to draw a single rectangle. For example, you can enter a width value, chamfer distances, and length and width dimensions to create a rectangle.

Exercise 4-11

Access the Student Web site (www.g-wlearning.com/CAD) and complete Exercise 4-11.

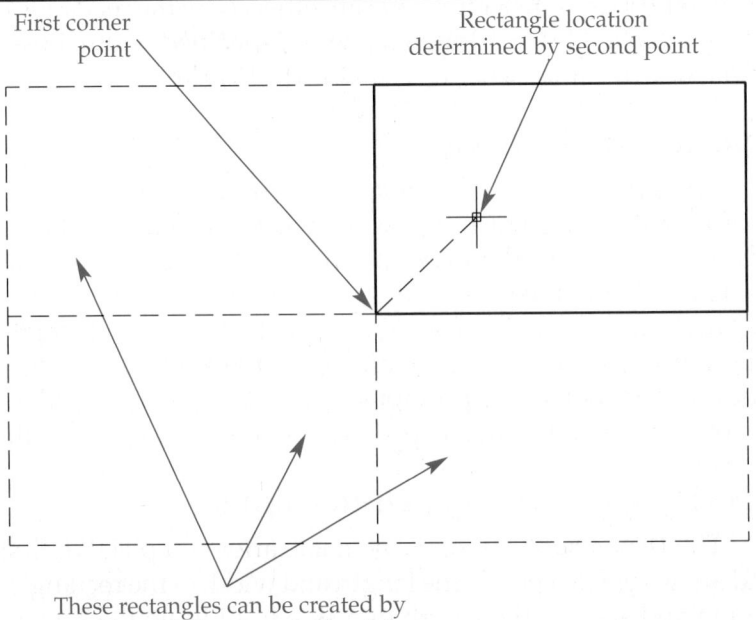

Figure 4-26.
The second corner point, or quadrant, determines the orientation of the rectangle relative to the first corner point.

First corner point

Rectangle location determined by second point

These rectangles can be created by picking a different second point

Drawing Donuts and Filled Circles

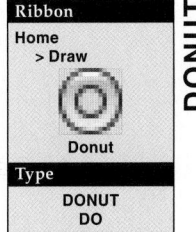

The **DONUT** tool allows you to draw a thick or filled circle. See **Figure 4-27**. A donut is a single polyline object. After activating the **DONUT** tool, enter the inside diameter and then the outside diameter of the donut. Enter a value of 0 for the inside diameter to create a completely filled donut, or solid circle.

The center point of the donut attaches to the crosshairs, and the Specify center of donut or <exit>: prompt appears. Pick a location to place the donut. The **DONUT** tool remains active until you right-click or press [Enter], the space bar, or [Esc]. This allows you to place multiple donuts of the same size using a single instance of the **DONUT** tool.

Exercise 4-12

Access the Student Web site (www.g-wlearning.com/CAD) and complete Exercise 4-12.

Drawing True Splines

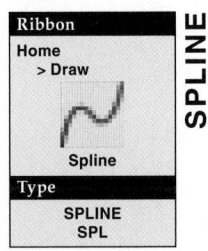

Access the **SPLINE** tool to create a special type of curve called a ***non-uniform rational B-spline (NURBS) curve***, or ***spline***. Examples of splines on a 2D drawing include curved edges on the drawing of an ergonomic consumer product and contour lines on a site plan. To draw a default spline, specify fit points using point entry or drawing aids. By default, the spline forms, or fits, though the points. When you are finished locating points, press [Enter] or the space bar, or right-click and select **Enter** to create the spline and exit the tool. **Figure 4-28** shows a spline drawn using absolute coordinates. Use the **Undo** option to remove the last segment of a spline without leaving the **SPLINE** tool.

non-uniform rational B-spline (NURBS) curve: A true (mathematically correct) spline.

Figure 4-27.
The appearance of a donut depends on its inside and outside diameters and the current **FILL** mode.

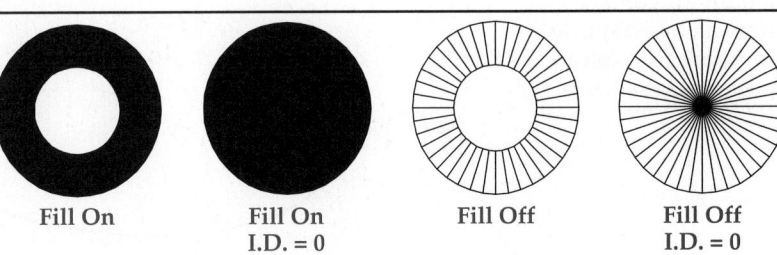

Fill On   Fill On I.D. = 0   Fill Off   Fill Off I.D. = 0

Figure 4-28.
A spline drawn using the default settings of the **SPLINE** tool and three fit points.

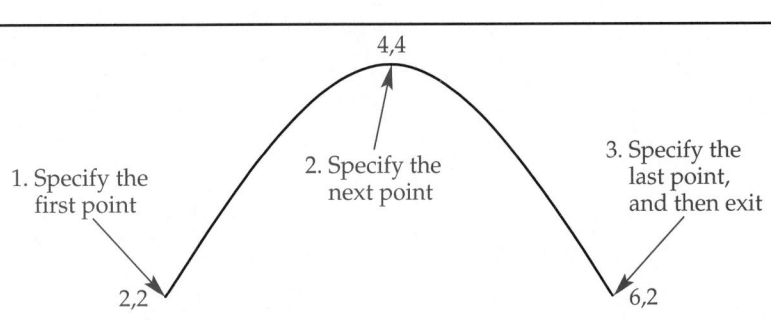

1. Specify the first point

2. Specify the next point

3. Specify the last point, and then exit

Drawing Closed Splines

Use the **Close** option after locating at least two control points to connect the last point to the first point. When you issue the **Close** option with the default **Fit** spline creation method, AutoCAD prompts you specify the tangent direction. Press [Enter] or the space bar or right-click and select **Enter** to accept the default tangent direction calculated by AutoCAD. See **Figure 4-29.** Specify a tangent direction to adjust the spline shape.

Exercise 4-13

Access the Student Web site (www.g-wlearning.com/CAD) and complete Exercise 4-13.

Spline Options
For information about options available while drawing splines, go to the Student Web site (www.g-wlearning.com/CAD), select this chapter, and select **Spline Options**.

Figure 4-29.
Using the **Close** option of the **SPLINE** tool with AutoCAD default tangents to draw a closed spline. Compare this spline to the spline shown in Figure 4-28.

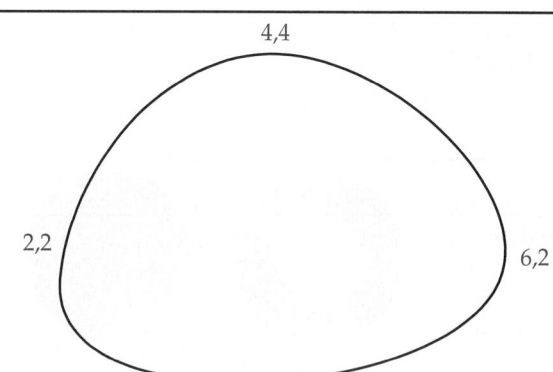

Chapter Test

Answer the following questions. Write your answers on a separate sheet of paper or go to the Student Web site (www.g-wlearning.com/CAD) and complete the electronic chapter test.

1. When you use the **CIRCLE** tool, what are the options for responding to the prompt Specify radius of circle?
2. Explain how to create a circle with a diameter of 2.5 units.
3. What option of the **CIRCLE** tool creates a circle of a specific radius that is tangent to two existing objects?
4. Define the term *point of tangency*.
5. Explain how to draw a circle tangent to three objects.
6. Explain the procedure to draw an arc beginning with the center point and having a 60° included angle.
7. Define the term *included angle* as it applies to an arc.
8. What is the default option if you enter the **ARC** tool at the keyboard?
9. List three input options that you can use to draw an arc tangent to the endpoint of a previously drawn arc.
10. Name the two axes found on an ellipse.
11. Briefly describe the procedure to draw an ellipse using the **Axis, End** option.
12. What **ELLIPSE** rotation angle results in a circle?
13. How do you draw a filled arrow using the **PLINE** tool?
14. Which **PLINE** tool option allows you to specify the width from the center to one side?
15. Explain how to turn off **FILL** mode.
16. Briefly describe how to create a polyline parallel to a previously drawn line or polyline.
17. Explain how to draw a hexagon measuring 4″ (102 mm) across the flats.
18. Name at least three tools you could use to create a rectangle.
19. Name the tool option used to draw rectangles with rounded corners.
20. Name the tool option designed for drawing rectangles with a specific line thickness.
21. Explain how to draw a rectangle at an angle other than 0°.
22. Describe a method for drawing a solid circle.
23. Explain how to draw two donuts with an inside diameter of 6.25 and an outside diameter of 9.50.
24. Name the tool you can use to create a true spline.
25. How do you accept the AutoCAD defaults for the start and end tangents of a spline?

Drawing Problems

Start AutoCAD if it is not already started. Start a new drawing from scratch or use an appropriate template of your choice. Follow the specific instructions for each problem. Use only drawing tools and techniques you have already learned. Do not draw dimensions or text. Use your own judgment and approximate dimensions when necessary.

▼ Basic

1. Use **LINE**, **CIRCLE**, and **RECTANGLE** tool options to draw the objects shown. Save the drawing as P4-1.

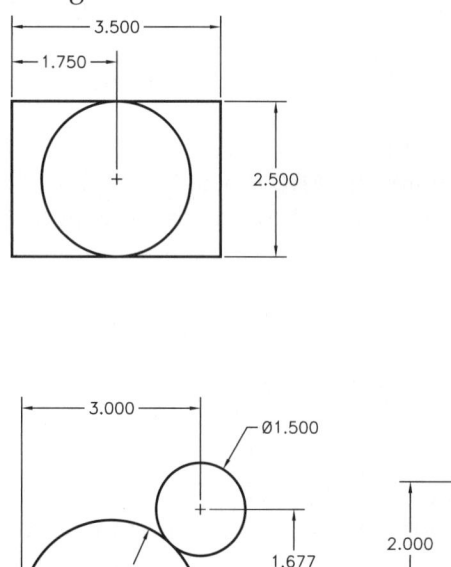

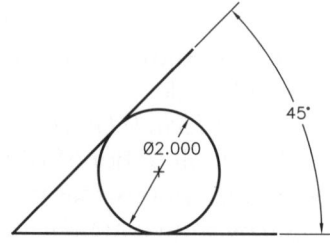

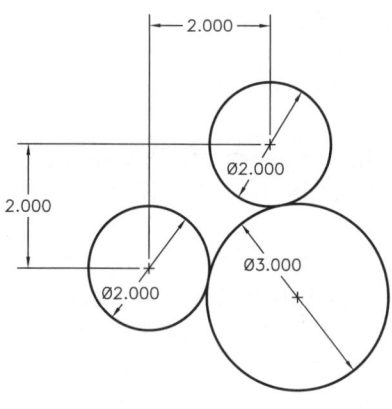

2. Use **CIRCLE** and **ARC** tool options to draw the object shown. Save the drawing as P4-2.

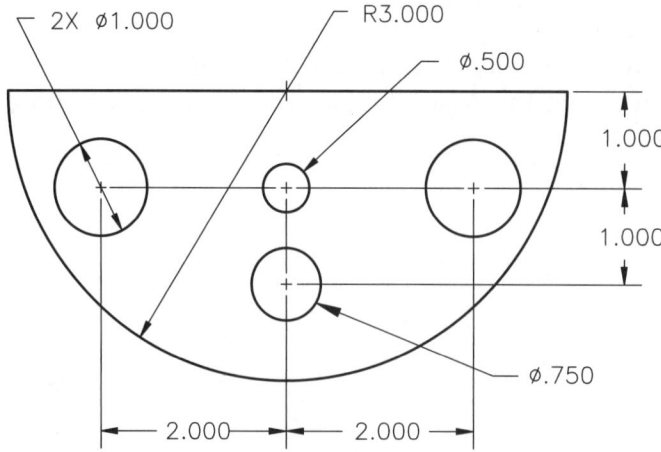

AutoCAD and Its Applications—Basics

3. Draw the spacer shown. Save the drawing as P4-3.

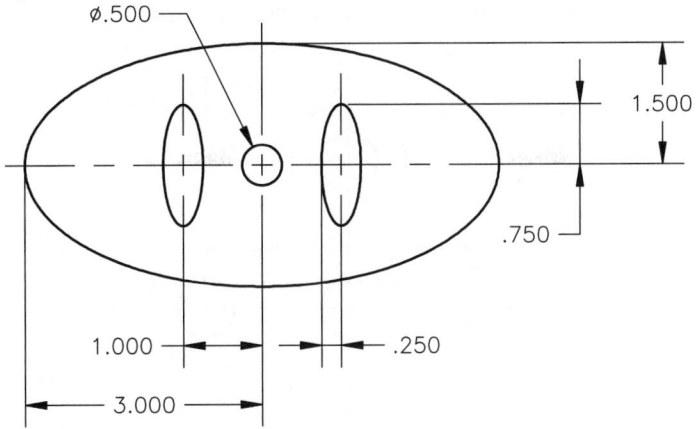

4. Draw the part view shown. Save the drawing as P4-4.

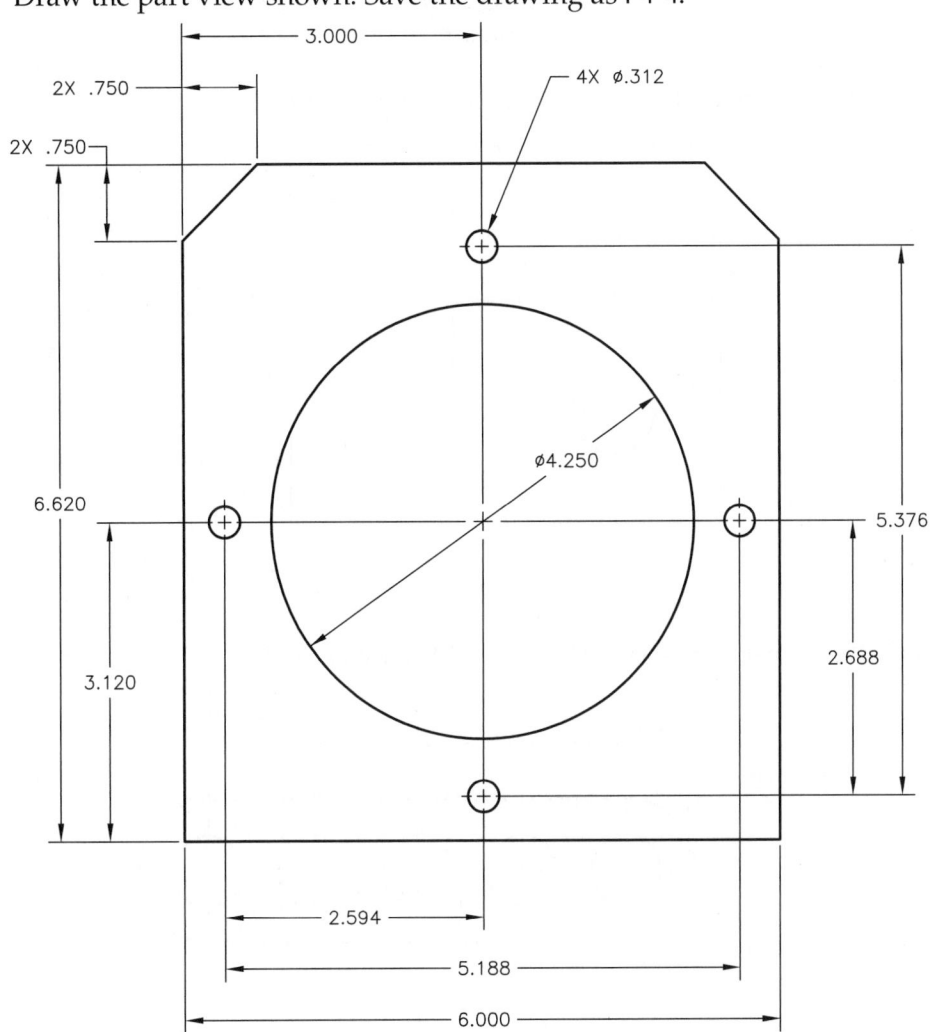

5. Draw the part view shown. Save the drawing as P4-5.

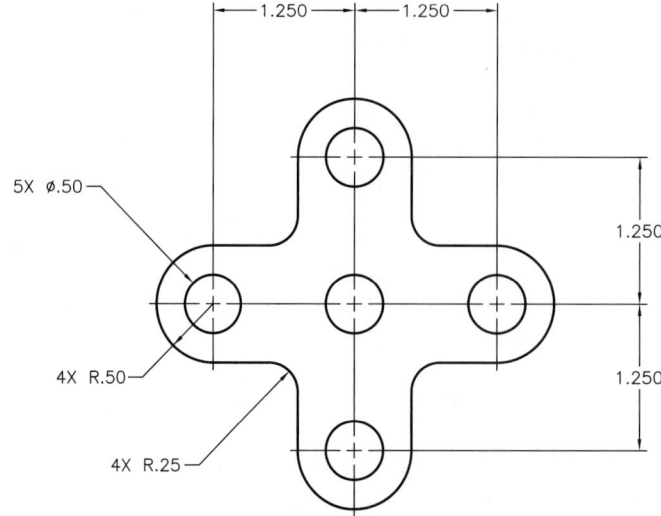

6. Draw the part view shown. Save the drawing as P4-6.

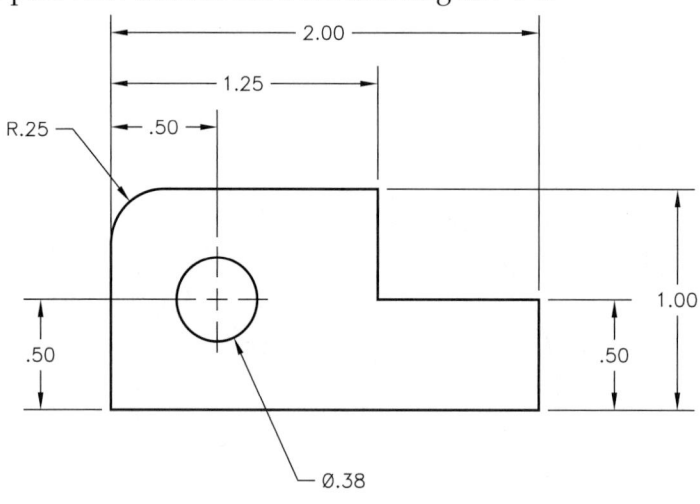

7. Draw the pipe spacer shown. Save the drawing as P4-7.

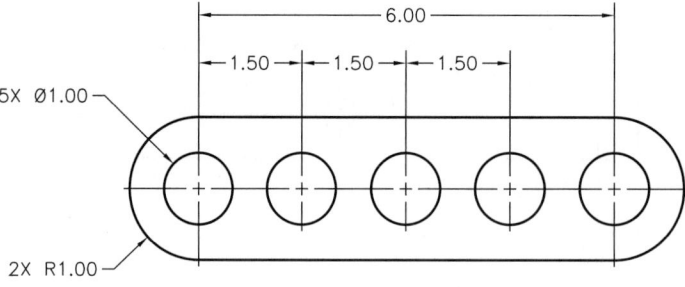

8. Use the **PLINE** tool and a .032 width to draw the object shown. Save the drawing as P4-8.

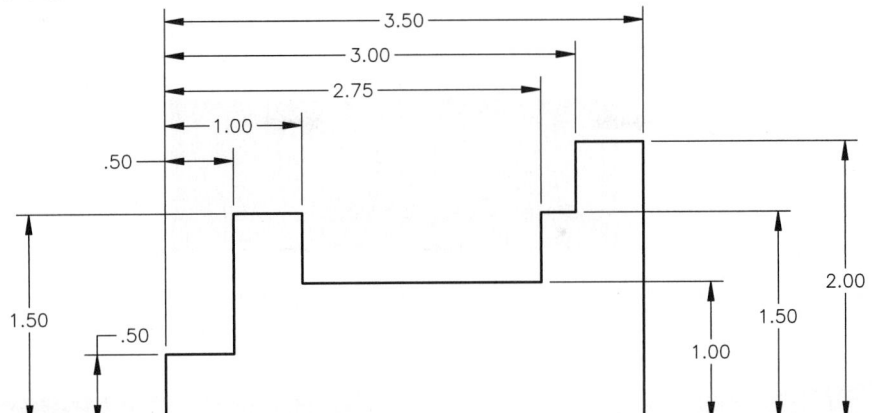
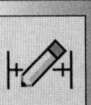

9. Use the **PLINE** tool and a .032 width to draw the object shown. Save the drawing as P4-9.

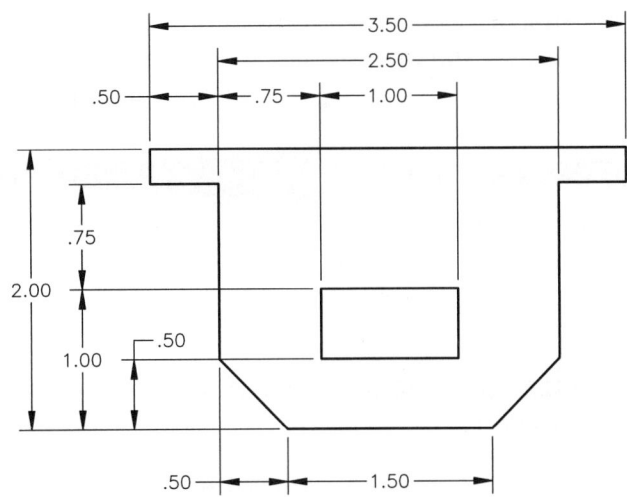

10. Use the **PLINE** tool and a .032 width to draw the object shown.
    A. Deactivate solid fills and use the **REGEN** tool, and reactivate solid fills and reissue the **REGEN** tool.
    B. Observe the difference with solid fills enabled.
    C. Save the drawing as P4-10.

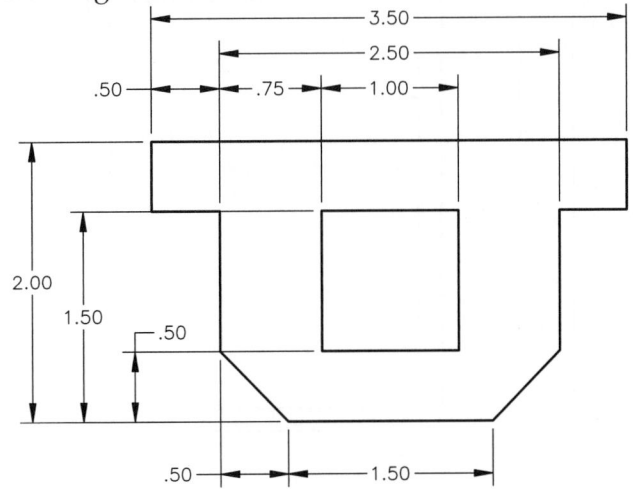

Drawing Problems - Chapter 4

11. Use the **PLINE** tool to draw the filled rectangle shown. Save the drawing as P4-11.

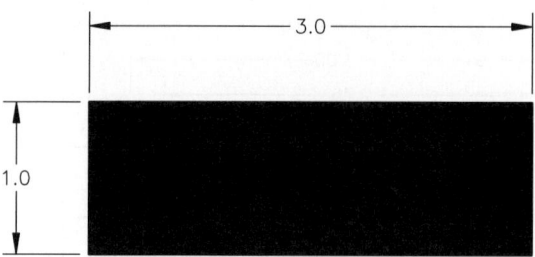

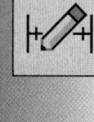

12. Draw the arrowheads shown. Save the drawing as P4-12.

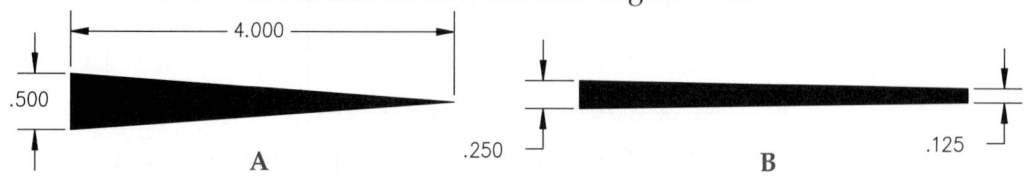

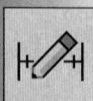

13. Draw the arrow shown. Set decimal units, .25 grid spacing, .0625 snap spacing, and limits of 11,8.5. Save the drawing as P4-13.

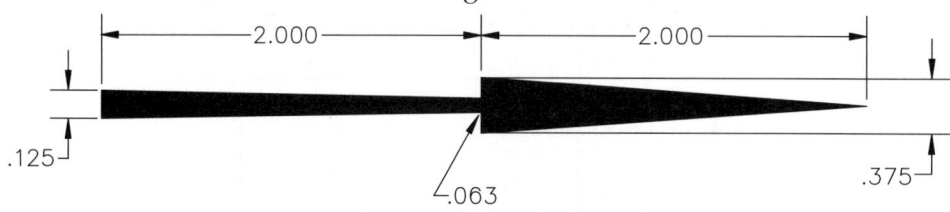

▼ Intermediate

14. Use the **RECTANGLE** and **CIRCLE** tools to draw the single kitchen sink shown. Save the drawing as P4-14.

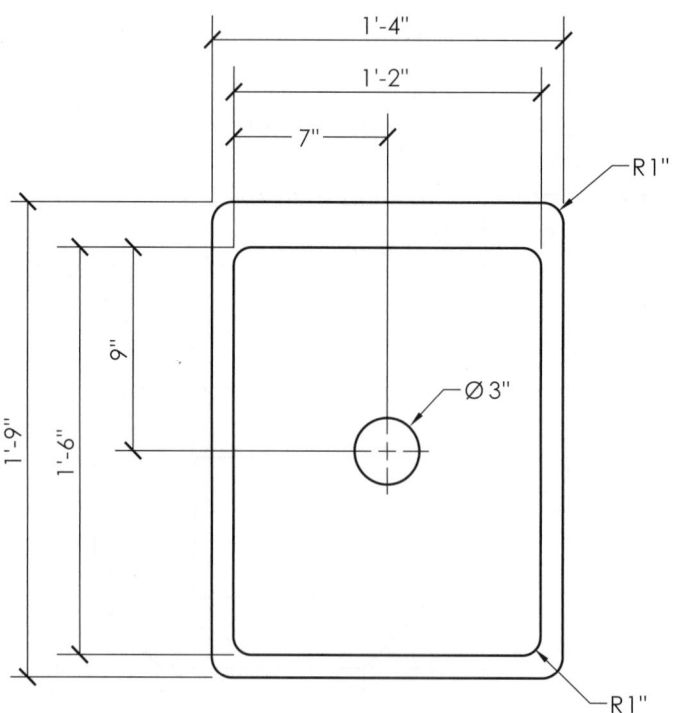

15. Draw the single polyline shown. Use the **Arc**, **Width**, and **Close** options of the **PLINE** tool to complete the shape. Set the polyline width to 0, except at the points indicated. Save the drawing as P4-15.

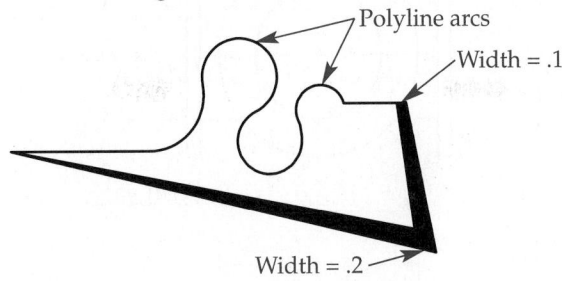

Polyline arcs

Width = .1

Width = .2

16. Draw the two curved arrows shown using the **Arc** and **Width** options of the **PLINE** tool. The arrowheads should have a starting width of 1.4 and an ending width of 0. The body of each arrow should have a beginning width of .8 and an ending width of .4. Save the drawing as P4-16.

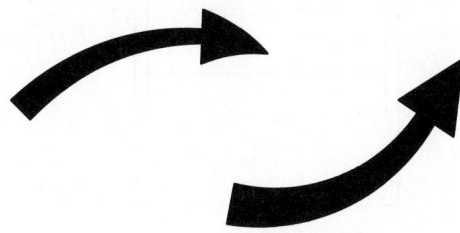

17. Draw the wrench shown. Save the drawing as P4-17.

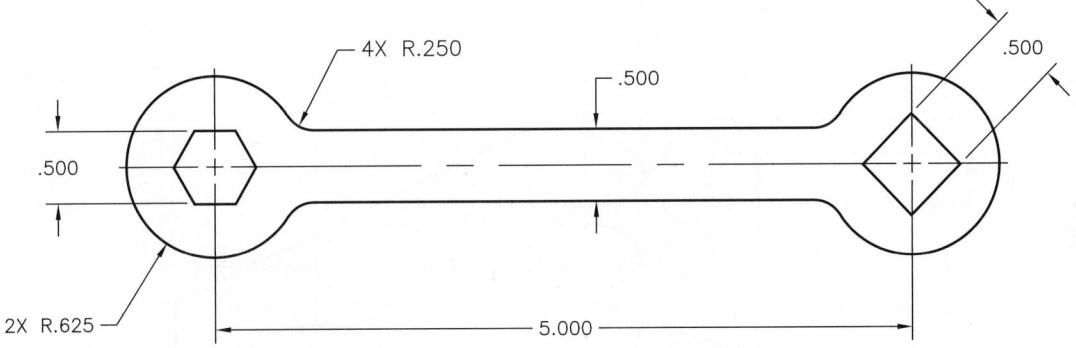

4X R.250

.500

.500

.500

2X R.625

5.000

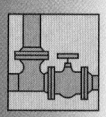

18. Draw the pipe fitting shown. Save the drawing as P4-18.

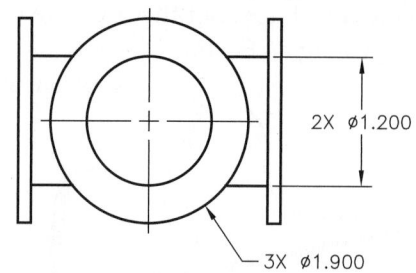

2X ⌀1.200

3X ⌀1.900

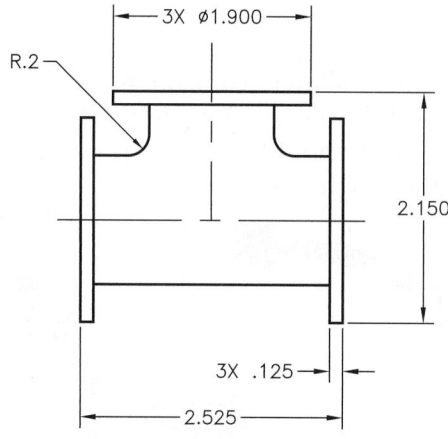

3X ⌀1.900

R.2

2.150

3X .125

2.525

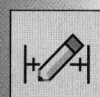

19. Draw the ellipse template shown. Save the drawing as P4-19.

ELLIPSE TABLE		
KEY	MAJOR DIA	MINOR DIA
A	.9951	.5745
B	1.0717	.6187
C	1.1482	.6629
D	1.2247	.7071
E	1.3013	.7513
F	1.3778	.7955
G	1.4544	.8397
H	1.5309	.8839
I	1.6075	.9281
J	1.6840	.9723
K	1.7606	1.0165
L	1.8371	1.0607
M	1.9902	1.1490
N	2.1433	1.2374
O	2.2964	1.3258
P	2.4495	1.4142

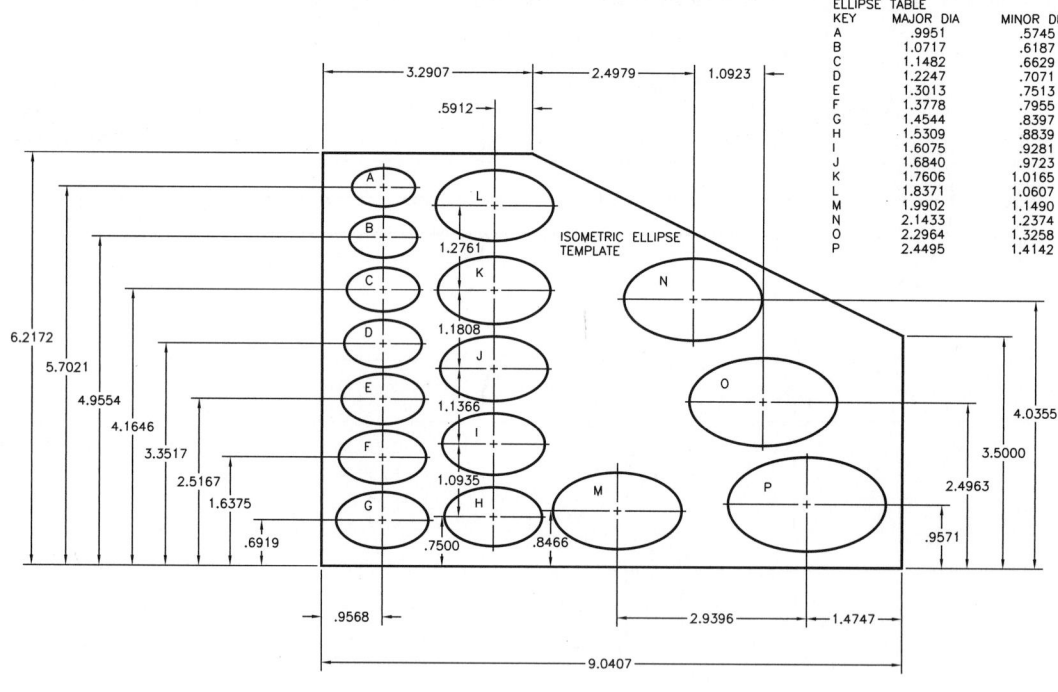

20. Draw the gasket shown. Save the drawing as P4-20.

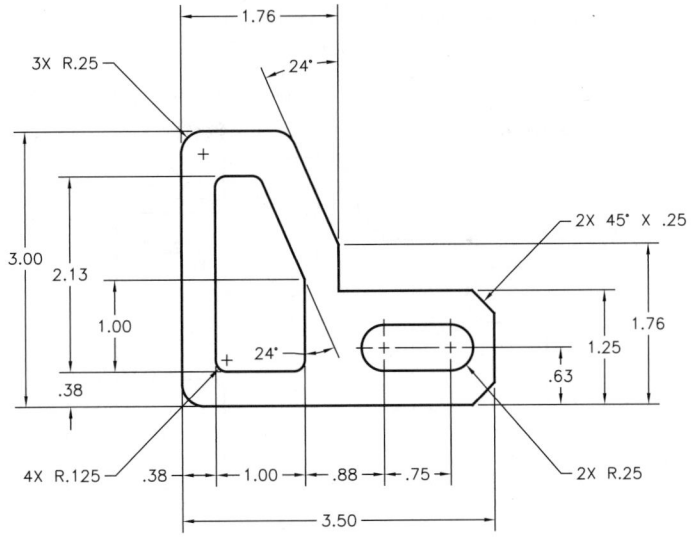

21. Use the **SPLINE** tool to draw the curve for the cam displacement diagram. Use the following guidelines and the drawing shown to complete this problem:
   A. The total rise equals 2.000.
   B. The total displacement can be any length.
   C. Divide the total displacement into 30° increments.
   D. Draw a half circle divided into 6 equal parts on one end.
   E. Draw a horizontal line from each division of the half circle to the other end of the diagram.
   F. Draw the displacement curve with the **SPLINE** tool by picking points where the horizontal and vertical lines cross.
   G. Label the displacement increments along the horizontal scale as shown. Save the drawing as P2-21.

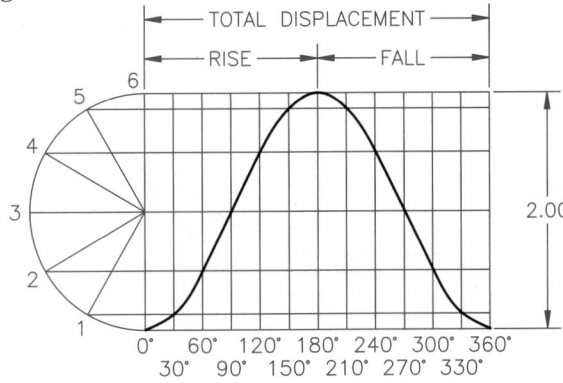

22. Draw the part view shown. Save the drawing as P4-22.

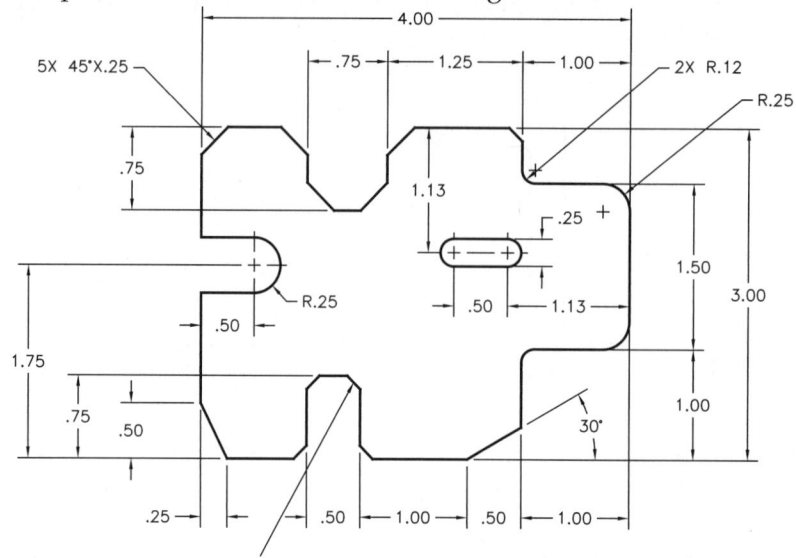

23. Draw the part view shown. Save the drawing as P4-23.

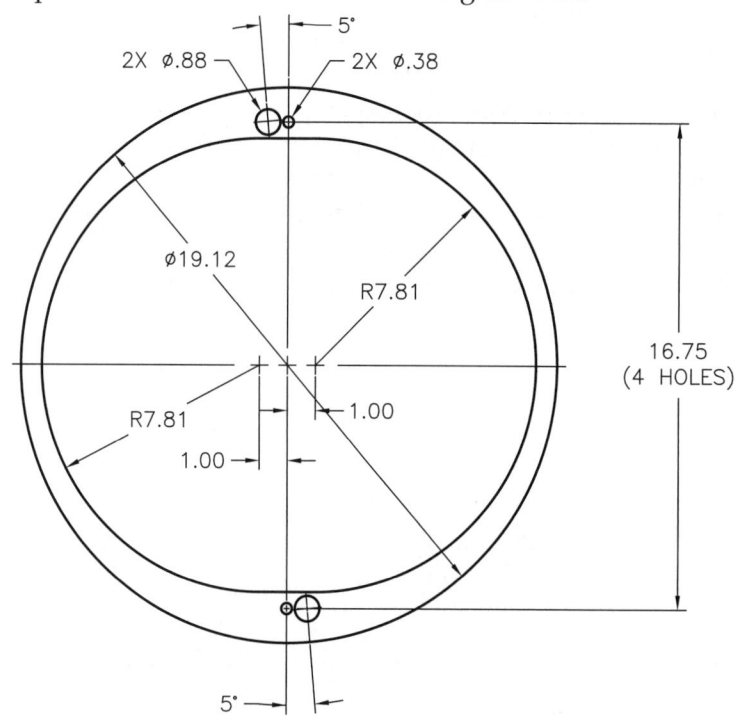

24. Create a drawing from the sketch of a car design shown. Use the **LINE** tool and selected shape tools to draw the car using appropriate size and scale features. Use a tape measure to measure an actual car for reference if necessary. Consider the tools and techniques used to draw the car, and try to minimize the number of objects. Save your drawing as P4-24.

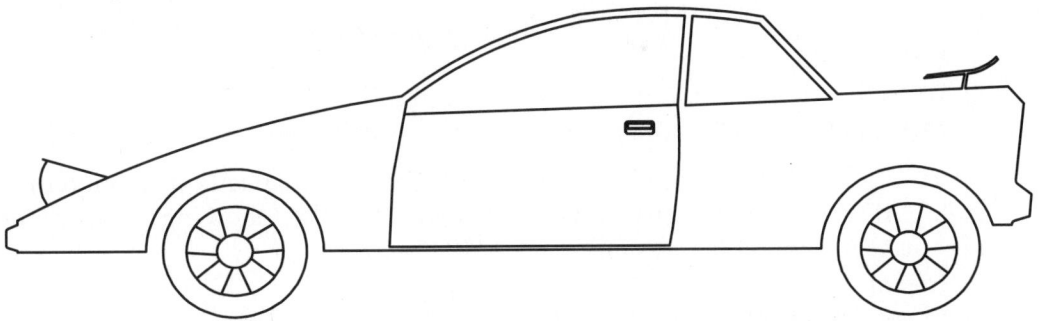

25. Draw the elevation shown using the **ARC**, **ELLIPSE**, **RECTANGLE**, and **DONUT** tools. Draw objects proportionate to the drawing shown. Use dimensions based on your experience, research, and measurements. Save the drawing as P4-25.

26. Research the design of an existing squeeze bottle with the following specifications: 8 ounce capacity, contaminant-resistant style, integral spout, nozzle and draw tube are externally molded to the bottle, clear polyethylene material. Hand-draw a dimensioned 2D sketch of the existing design from the manufacturer's specifications, or take measurements from an actual squeeze bottle. Start a new drawing from scratch or use a decimal-unit template of your choice. Draw the squeeze bottle from your sketch. Save the drawing as P4-26.

27. Find a door at your school, company, or home that includes features with several different shapes. Hand-draw a 2D sketch of the door elevation complete with casework and hardware. Use measuring devices such as a tape measure and caliper to dimension the size and location of door features accurately. Start a new drawing from scratch or use an architectural-unit template of your choice. Draw the door from your sketch. Save the drawing as P4-27.

AutoCAD Certified Associate Exam Practice

Answer the following questions. Write your answers on a separate sheet of paper.

1. Which tool allows you to draw a rectangle? *Select all that apply.*
   A. **LINE**
   B. **PLINE**
   C. **RECTANGLE**
   D. **DONUT**
   E. **POLYGON**

2. If you use the **Rotation** option of the **ELLIPSE** tool and specify a rotation of 45, AutoCAD creates a circle rotated 45° from which of the following? *Select the one item that best answers the question.*
   A. line of sight
   B. major axis of the ellipse
   C. minor axis of the ellipse
   D. X axis
   E. Z axis

3. When you use the **2-Point** option of the **CIRCLE** tool to create a circle, which of the following is defined by the points you specify? *Select the one item that best answers the question.*
   A. radius of the circle
   B. circumference of the circle
   C. diameter of the circle
   D. area of the circle

AutoCAD Certified Professional Exam Practice

Follow the instructions in each problem. Write your answers on a separate sheet of paper.

1. **Navigate to this chapter on the Student Web site and open the CPE-04circle. dwg file.**
   Use the **CIRCLE** tool to create a circle that is tangent to both of the lines in the drawing and has a radius of 7.3. Do not change any settings in the drawing file. When you finish, type LIST, select the circle, and press [Enter] to display a list of information about the circle in a text window. (The **LIST** tool is explained in more detail in Chapter 16.) According to the listed information, what are the coordinates of the center point of the circle?

2. **Navigate to this chapter on the Student Web site and open the CPE-04arc.dwg file.**
   Use the ARC tool to create the arc shown below. Specify the center point and start point of the arc using the **Endpoint** object snap, and specify an angle of 37°. Do not change any settings in the drawing file. Then use the **Endpoint** object snap mode to select the upper endpoint of the arc (Point A). According to the coordinate display field in the lower-left corner of the screen, what are the coordinates of this point?

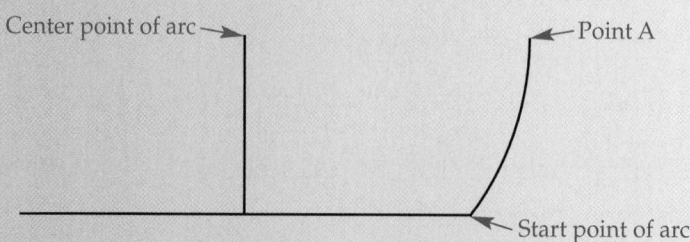

Center point of arc — Point A
Start point of arc

Line Standards and Layers

Learning Objectives

After completing this chapter, you will be able to do the following:

✓ Describe basic line conventions.
✓ Explain how drawing layers are used in various drafting fields.
✓ Create and manage layers.
✓ Draw objects on separate layers.
✓ Use **DesignCenter** to copy layers and linetypes between drawings.

AutoCAD has a layer system that allows you to organize and assign several properties to objects. *Layers* help you conform to drawing standards and conventions and help create unique displays, views, and sheets. This chapter introduces line conventions and the AutoCAD layer system. You will also use **DesignCenter** to reuse drawing content.

layers:
Components of the AutoCAD overlay system that allow you to separate objects into logical groups for formatting and display purposes.

Line Standards

Drafting is a graphic language that uses lines, symbols, and text to describe how to manufacture or construct a product. *Line conventions* provide a way to classify the content of a drawing to enhance readability. Layers provide a way to apply line conventions while drawing with AutoCAD. Use line conventions as a guide to develop layers.

The ASME Y14.2 standard, *Line Conventions and Lettering,* recommends two line thicknesses to establish contrasting lines. See **Figure 5-1.** Lines are thick or thin. Thick lines are twice as thick as thin lines. The recommended thicknesses are 0.6 mm for thick lines and 0.3 mm for thin lines. **Figure 5-2** describes the most common linetypes. **Figure 5-3** shows an example of a drawing with several common linetypes.

The U.S. National CAD Standard (NCS) recommends a specific line thickness and characteristics for architectural and similar drawings. Thicknesses range from *extra fine* at 0.13 mm to *4X* at 2 mm. Use the range of NCS-recommended line thicknesses to provide accents to drawings as needed. A common practice is to select a few of the line thicknesses that correlate best to specific applications. See **Figure 5-4.**

line conventions:
Standards related to line thickness, type, and purpose.

Figure 5-1. Line conventions adapted from ASME Y14.2. Thick lines have a 0.6 mm width. Thin lines have a 0.3 mm line width.

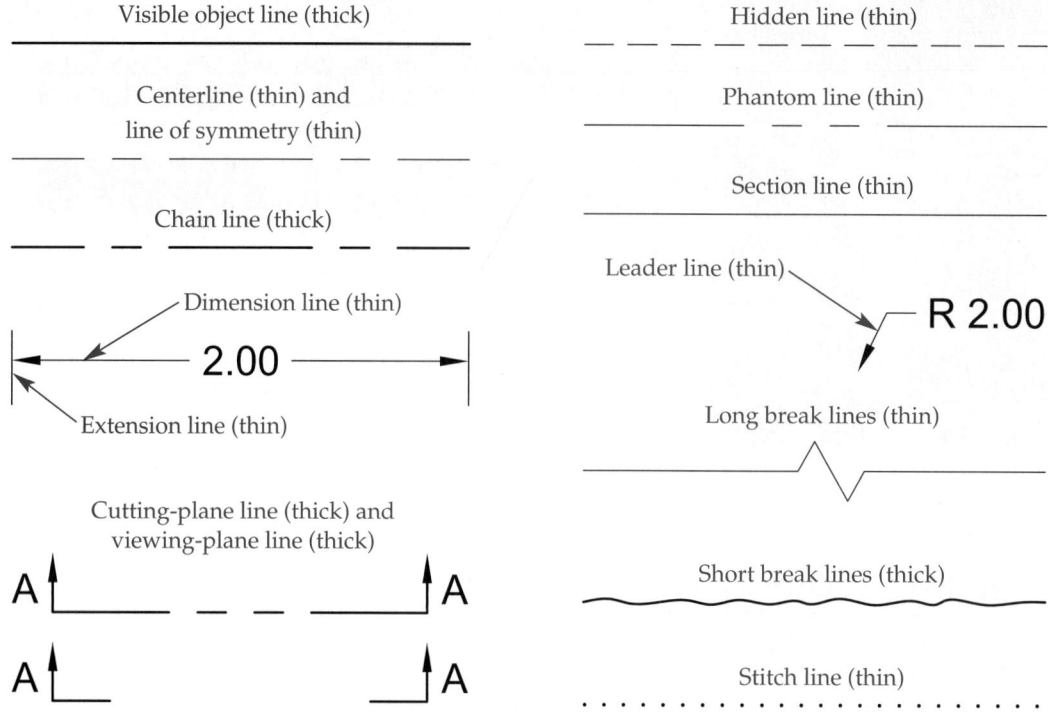

Figure 5-2. Descriptions of common lines and line standards. Line characteristics and spacing are measured at full scale. Specifications vary according to drawing size.

Type	Purpose	Linetype	Standards
Object lines (visible, outline)	Show the contour or outline of objects.	Continuous	Thick, solid.
Hidden lines	Represent features that are hidden in the current view.	HIDDEN or DASHED	Thin, dashed. Dashes are .125″ (3 mm) long and are spaced .06″ (1.5 mm) apart.
Centerlines	Locate the centers of circles and arcs, and show the axis of cylindrical or symmetrical shapes.	CENTER	Thin. Extend .125″ to .25″ (3 mm to 6 mm) past objects. Centerlines consist of one .125″ dash alternating with one .75″ to 1.5″ (19 mm to 38 mm) dash. A .06″ (1.5 mm) space separates the dashes. Small centerline dashes should cross only at the center of a circle.
Extension lines	Show the extent of a dimension.	Continuous	Thin, solid. Begin .06″ (1.5 mm) from an object and extend .125″ (3 mm) beyond the last dimension line. Can cross object lines, hidden lines, and centerlines, but should not cross dimension lines. Centerlines become extension lines when used to show the extent of a dimension.

(Continued)

AutoCAD and Its Applications—Basics

Figure 5-2. *(Continued)*

Type	Purpose	Linetype	Standards
Dimension lines	Show the distance being measured.	Continuous	Thin, solid. Broken near the center for placement of the dimension numeral in mechanical drafting. Unbroken in architectural and structural drawings, with dimension placed on top of the dimension line. Arrows terminate the ends of dimension lines, except in architectural drafting, where slashes (ticks) or dots are often used.
Leader lines	Connect a specific note to a feature on a drawing.	Continuous	Thin, solid. Often terminate with an arrowhead at the feature. May be curved on architectural drawings. Straight leader lines often have a small shoulder at the note.
Cutting-plane lines	Identify the location and viewing direction of a section view.	PHANTOM or DASHED	Thick. Can be drawn in one of two ways.
Viewing-plane lines	Identify the location of a view.	PHANTOM or DASHED	Thick. Can be drawn in one of two ways.
Section lines	In a section view, show where material has been cut away.	(Varies)	Thin, usually drawn in a pattern. Different linetypes can be used to indicate specific or different material.
Break lines	Show where a portion of an object has been removed for clarity or convenience.	Continuous	Thin or thick depending on the symbol, solid. Break representation is based on the object or material being broken.
Phantom lines	Identify repetitive details, show alternate positions of moving parts, and locate adjacent positions of related parts.	PHANTOM	Thin. Two .125″ (3 mm) dashes, alternating with one .75″ to 1.5″ (19 mm to 38 mm) dash. Spaces between dashes are .06″ (1.5 mm).
Chain lines	Indicate special features or unique treatment for a surface.	CENTER	Thick.

Figure 5-3. An example of a mechanical assembly drawing with several common types of lines.

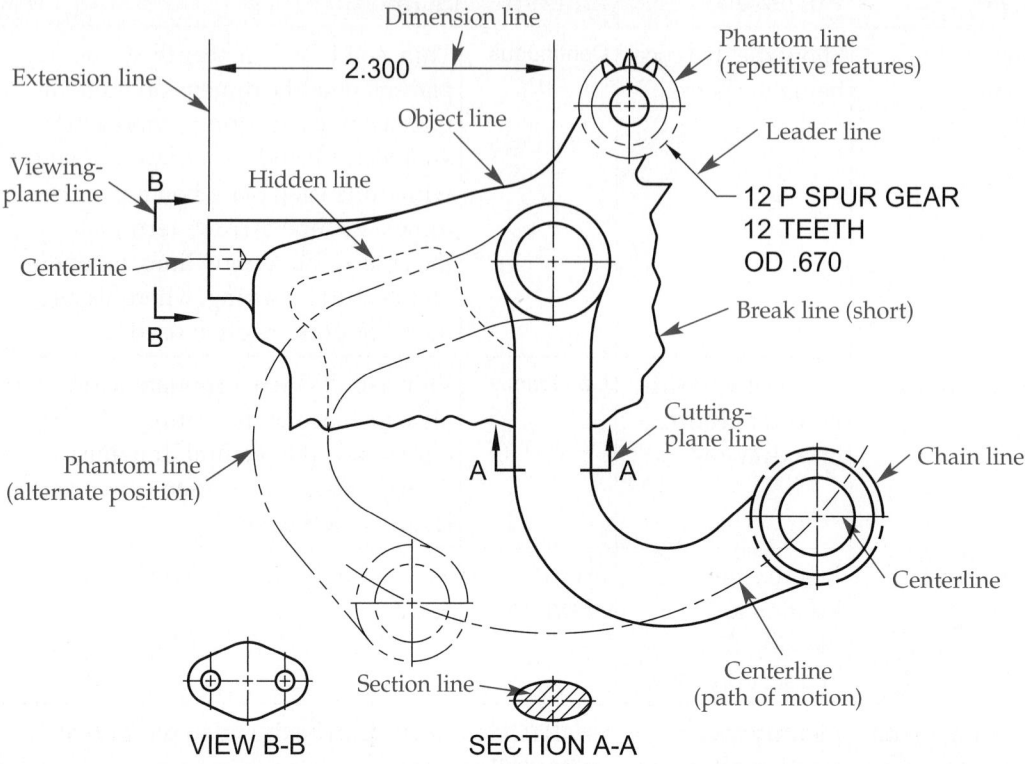

Figure 5-4. A few of the most common U.S. National CAD Standard line thicknesses.

Thickness	Application
Thin, 0.25 mm	Dimension elements, phantom lines, hidden lines, centerlines, long break lines, schedule grid lines, adn background objects.
Medium, 0.35 mm	Object lines, text for dimension values, notes and schedules, terminator marks, door and window elevations, and schedule grid accent lines.
Wide, 0.5 mm	Major object lines at elevation edges, cutting-plane lines, short break lines, title text, minor title underlines, and border lines.
Extra wide, 0.7 mm	Major title underlines, schedule outlines, large titles, special emphasis object lines, elevation and section grade lines, property lines, sheet borders, adn schedule borders.

NOTE

Many AutoCAD tools simplify and automate the process of applying correct line standards. You will learn applications and techniques for drawing specific types of lines in this textbook.

Introduction to Layers

In AutoCAD, you can use an *overlay system* of layers to separate different objects and elements of a drawing. For example, draw all object lines on an Object layer and all dimensions on a Dimension layer. You can display both layers to show the complete drawing with dimensions, or hide the Dimension layer to show only the objects. The following is a list of ways you can use layers to increase productivity and add value to a drawing:

overlay system:
A system of separating drawing components by layer.

✓ Assign each layer a unique color, linetype, and lineweight to correspond to line conventions and to help improve clarity.

✓ Make changes to layer properties that immediately update all objects drawn on the layer.

✓ Turn off or freeze selected layers to decrease the amount of information displayed on-screen or to speed screen regeneration.

✓ Plot each layer in a different color, linetype, or lineweight, or set a layer not to plot at all.

✓ Use separate layers to group specific information. For example, draw a floor plan using floor plan layers, an electrical plan using electrical layers, and a plumbing plan using plumbing layers.

✓ Create several sheets from the same drawing file by controlling layer visibility to separate or combine drawing information. For example, use layers to display a floor plan and electrical plan together to send to an electrical contractor, or display a floor plan and plumbing plan together to send to a plumbing contractor.

Layers Used in Drafting Fields

The drawing typically determines the function of each layer. In mechanical drafting, you usually assign a specific layer to each different type of line or object. For example, draw object lines on an Object layer that is black in color, has a solid (Continuous) linetype, and is 0.6 mm wide. Draw hidden lines on a green Hidden layer that uses a 0.3 mm hidden (HIDDEN or DASHED) linetype.

Architectural and civil drawings can require hundreds of layers, each used to produce a specific item. For example, draw full-height floor plan walls on a black A-WALL-FULL layer that has a 0.5 mm solid (Continuous) linetype. Add plumbing fixtures to a floor plan on a blue P-FLOR-FIXT layer that has a 0.35 mm solid (Continuous) linetype.

You can create layers for any type of drawing: detail parts, assemblies, floor plans, foundation plans, partition layouts, plumbing systems, electrical systems, structural systems, roof drainage systems, reflected ceiling systems, HVAC systems, site plans, profiles, topographic maps, and details. Interior designers may use floor plan, interior partition, and furniture layers. Electronics drafters may draw each level of a circuit on its own layer.

Creating and Using Layers

Use the **LAYER** tool to open the **Layer Properties Manager**, where you can create and control layers. See **Figure 5-5**. The columns in the list view pane on the right side of the **Layer Properties Manager** list layers and provide layer property controls.

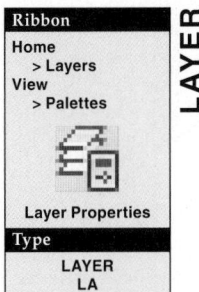

Ribbon
Home
> Layers
View
> Palettes

LAYER

Layer Properties
Type
LAYER
LA

Properties in each column appear as an icon or as an icon and a name. See **Figure 5-6**. Pick a property to change the corresponding layer settings. The tree view pane on the left side of the **Layer Properties Manager** displays filters for limiting the number of layers displayed in the list view pane.

The default 0 layer is the only required layer in an AutoCAD drawing. The 0 layer is primarily reserved for drawing blocks, as described later in this textbook. You cannot delete, rename, or purge the 0 layer. Draw each object on a layer specific to the object. For example, draw object lines on an Object layer, draw floor plan walls on an A-WALL layer, and draw construction lines on a Construction or A-ANNO-NPLT layer.

Figure 5-5. The **Layer Properties Manager**. Layer 0 is the AutoCAD default layer.

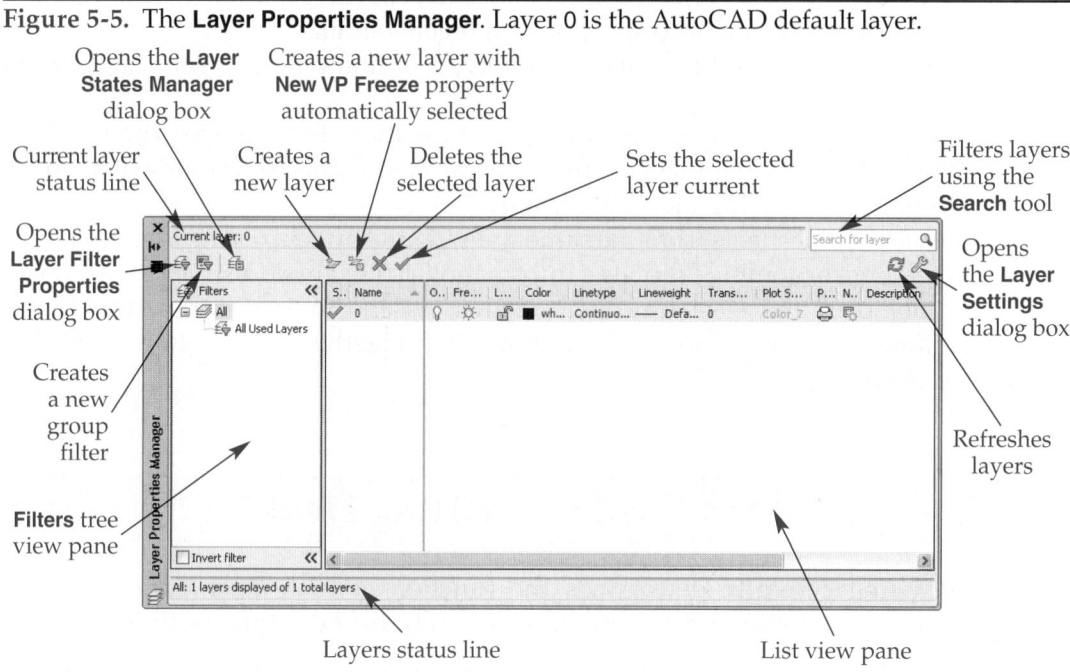

Figure 5-6. Pick an icon in the **Layer Properties Manager** to change layer settings.

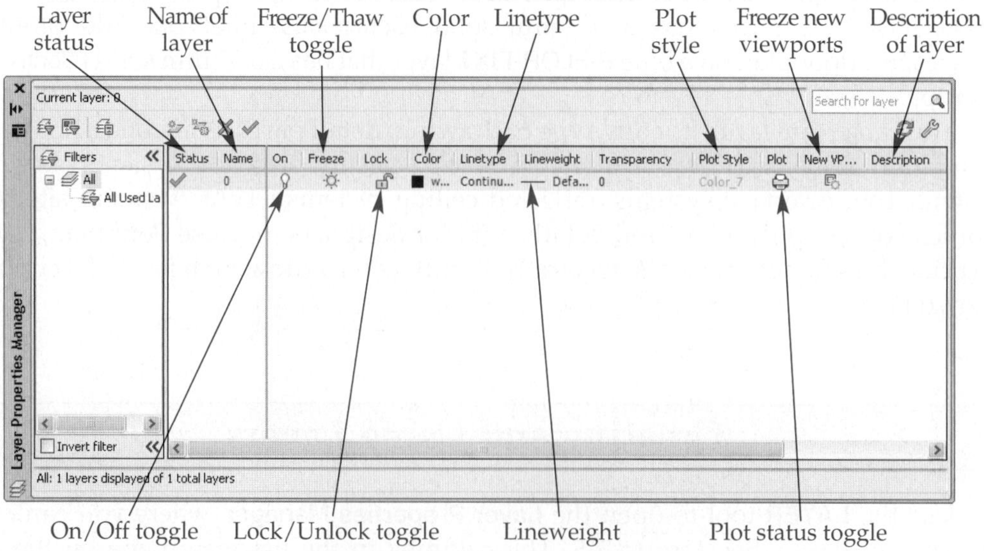

Adding Layers

Add layers to a drawing to meet the needs of the current drawing project. To add a new layer, select an existing layer with properties similar to those you want to assign to the new layer. Reference the 0 layer to create the first new layer using a default template. Then pick the **New Layer** button, right-click in the list view, and select **New Layer** or press [Enter] or [Alt]+[N]. A new layer appears, using a default name. The layer name is highlighted, allowing you to type a new name. See **Figure 5-7.** Pick away from the layer in the list or press [Enter] to accept the layer.

Layer Names

Name layers to reflect drawing content. Layer names can include letters, numbers, and certain other characters, including spaces. Layer names are usually set according to specific industry or company standards. Some examples of typical mechanical, architectural, civil, and electronic drafting layer names are shown in **Figure 5-8.**

However, simple or generic drawings may use a more basic naming system. For example, the name Continuous-White indicates a layer assigned a continuous linetype and white color. The name Object-7 identifies a layer for drawing object lines, assigned color 7. Another option is to assign the linetype a numerical value. For example, name object lines 1, hidden lines 2, and centerlines 3. If you use this method, keep a written record of the numbering system for reference.

More complex layer names are appropriate for some applications, and may include items such as drawing number, color code, and layer content. For example, the name Dwg100-2-Dimen refers to drawing DWG100, color 2, for use when adding dimensions. The American Institute of Architects (AIA) *CAD Layer Guidelines*, associated with the NCS, specifies a layer naming system for architectural and related drawings. The system uses a highly detailed layer naming process that assigns each layer a discipline designator and major group, and if necessary, one or two minor groups and a status field. The AIA system allows complete identification of drawing content.

Figure 5-7. AutoCAD names a new layer Layer*n* by default and provides the opportunity for you to change the name immediately.

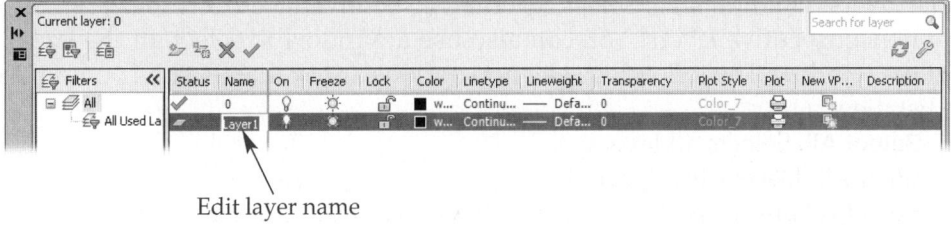

Edit layer name

Figure 5-8. Examples of typical layer names in common drafting fields.

Mechanical	Architectural	Civil	Electronic
Object	A-WALL-FULL	G-BLDG	Capacitor
Hidden	A-GLAZ	C-WATR	Coil
Center	A-DOOR	C-TOPO	Resistor
Dimension	E-LITE	C-PROP	Diode
Construction	P-FLOR-FIXT	C-NGAS	Transistor
Section	S-FNDN	C-SSWR	Notation
Border	M-HVAC	C-ELEV	Coupling

Layer names are listed alphanumerically as you create new layers. See **Figure 5-9**. Pick any column heading in the list view to sort layer names in ascending or descending order according to that column. The **Layer Properties Manager** is a palette, so new layers and changes made to existing layers automatically save and apply to the drawing. There is no need to "apply" changes or close the palette to see the effects of the layer changes in the drawing.

PROFESSIONAL TIP

If you need to create multiple layers, accelerate the process by pressing the comma key [,] after typing each layer name to create another new layer.

Renaming Layers

To change a layer name using the **Layer Properties Manager**, slowly double-click on the existing name in the **Name** column to highlight it. Type the new name and press [Enter] or pick outside of the text box. You can also rename a layer by picking the name once to highlight it and then pressing [F2], or by right-clicking and selecting **Rename Layer**. You cannot rename layer 0 or layers associated with an external reference.

Exercise 5-1

Access the Student Web site (www.g-wlearning.com/CAD) and complete Exercise 5-1.

Selecting Multiple Layers

Select multiple layers to speed the process of deleting or applying the same properties to several layers. Use standard selection practices or the shortcut menu to select multiple layers. Hold [Shift] to select several consecutive layers, or hold [Ctrl] to select several nonconsecutive layers. You can also use a window to select all the layers that contact the window. The following selection options are available when you right-click in the list view:

- **Select All.** Selects all layers.
- **Clear All.** Deselects all layers.
- **Select All but Current.** Selects all layers except the current layer.
- **Invert Selection.** Deselects all selected layers and selects all deselected layers.

Figure 5-9. Layer names are automatically listed in alphanumeric order when you create new layers or change layer names.

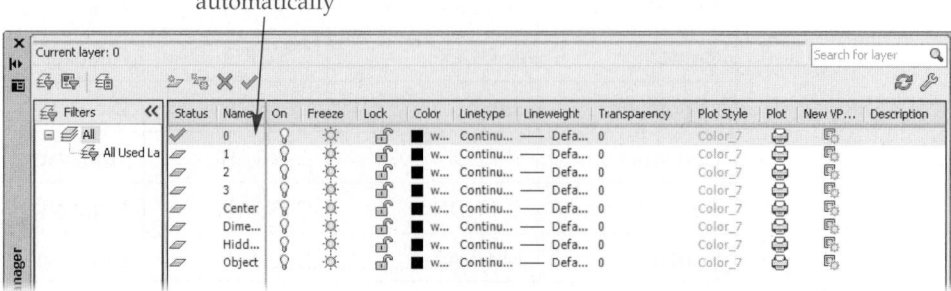

Exercise 5-2

Access the Student Web site (www.g-wlearning.com/CAD) and complete Exercise 5-2.

Layer Status

The icon in the **Status** column describes the status, or use of a layer. A green check mark indicates the *current layer*. The status line at the top of the **Layer Properties Manager** also identifies the current layer.

A white sheet of paper, or **Not In Use** icon, in the **Status** column indicates a non-current layer that is not used by the drawing. A blue sheet of paper, or **In Use** icon, in the **Status** column means the layer is assigned to objects, but the layer is not current. The **In Use** icon can also mean that you cannot delete or purge the layer, even if no objects are assigned to the layer.

current layer: The active layer. Whatever you draw is placed on the current layer.

Current

Not in Use

In Use

> **NOTE**
>
> If the **Layer Properties Manager** does not indicate layers in use, pick the **Settings** button in the upper-right corner to display the **Layer Settings** dialog box and select the **Indicate layers in use** check box.

Setting the Current Layer

To set a layer current using the **Layer Properties Manager**, double-click the layer name, pick the layer name and select the **Set Current** button, or right-click on the layer and choose **Set Current**. You can also make a layer current without using the **Layer Properties Manager** by picking the layer name from the **Layer Control** drop-down list of the **Home** ribbon tab. See **Figure 5-10.** Use the vertical scroll bar to move up and down through a long list. The **Layer Control** drop-down list is the most effective way to activate and manage layers while drawing.

Figure 5-10.
The **Layer Control** drop-down list allows you to change the current layer and adjust specific layer properties.

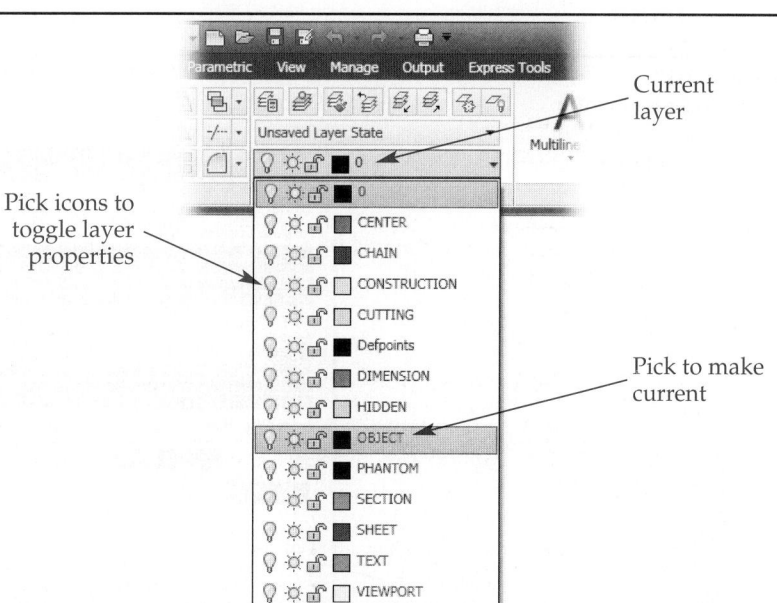

Current layer

Pick icons to toggle layer properties

Pick to make current

You can use the **Layer Properties Manager** or the **Layer Control** drop-down list to change the current layer or layer properties while a tool is active. For example, draw a line segment using the current layer, and then without exiting the **LINE** tool, make a different layer current to draw the next line segment on a different layer.

To assign a different layer to existing objects, select the objects and then choose the layer using the **Layer Properties Manager** or the **Layer Control** drop-down list.

Exercise 5-3

Access the Student Web site (www.g-wlearning.com/CAD) and complete Exercise 5-3.

Setting Layer Color

You can assign a unique color to each layer to help distinguish objects on-screen. You also have the options of using layer colors to plot a drawing in color or to control object properties. Although plotting in color and controlling object properties using color are not common, assigning colors to layers is very important for drawing clarity, organization, workability, and format. Layer colors should highlight important features and symbols and not cause eyestrain.

Use the **Color** column of the **Layer Properties Manager** to assign a color to each layer. Pick the existing color swatch to change the color using the **Select Color** dialog box. See **Figure 5-11.** The **Select Color** dialog box includes an **Index Color** tab, a **True Color** tab, and a **Color Books** tab. Each tab provides a different method for color selection.

Figure 5-11.
Use the **Select Color** dialog box to assign a color to a layer.

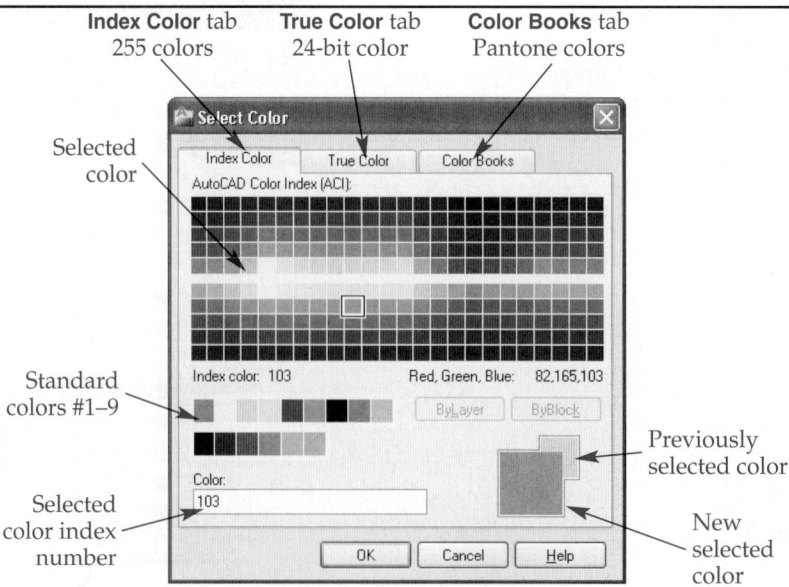

The default **Index Color** tab provides enough color options for most 2D drawings. The **Index Color** tab includes 255 color swatches, each numerically coded according to the AutoCAD Color Index (ACI). The first seven colors in the ACI have both a number and a name: 1 = red, 2 = yellow, 3 = green, 4 = cyan, 5 = blue, 6 = magenta, and 7 = white. The color white (number 7) appears white on the default dark grey-colored model space background, and black on the default white layout background.

Hover over a color swatch to display the code in the **Index color:** field, and the mix of red, green, and blue (RGB) used to create the color in the **Red, Green, Blue:** field. Pick a color swatch to select and display the color in the **Color:** text box, or type the color name or ACI number in the **Color:** text box. A preview of the color selection and a sample of the previously assigned color appear in the lower-right corner of the dialog box.

After you select a color, pick the **OK** button to assign the color to the specified layer. The layer color swatch indicates the color. By default, all objects are displayed in the selected layer color, or ByLayer.

NOTE

Your graphics card and monitor affect color display characteristics and sometimes the number of available colors.

PROFESSIONAL TIP

Use the color swatch in the **Layer Control** drop-down list to change the color assigned to a layer without accessing the **Layer Properties Manager**.

CAUTION

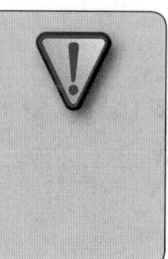

The **COLOR** tool provides access to the **Select Color** dialog box, which you can use to set an *absolute value* for color. If you set the absolute color to red, for example, the red color overrides the colors assigned to layers and all objects appear red. For most applications, set the color to the default ByLayer and use layers and the **Layer Properties Manager** to control object color.

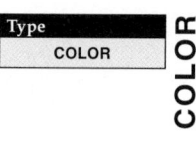

COLOR

absolute value: In property settings, a value set directly instead of referenced by layer or by block. An absolute value ignores the corresponding layer settings.

Exercise 5-4

Access the Student Web site (www.g-wlearning.com/CAD) and complete Exercise 5-4.

Setting Layer Linetype

Appropriate linetypes and line thicknesses enhance the readability of a drawing. You can apply standard line conventions to objects by assigning a linetype and thickness to each layer. AutoCAD provides standard linetypes that match or are similar to ASME, ISO, NCS, and other standard linetypes. You can also create custom linetypes. Assign lineweights to layers to achieve different line thicknesses.

Use the **Linetype** column of the **Layer Properties Manager** to assign a linetype to each layer. Pick the existing linetype to change the linetype using the **Select Linetype** dialog box. See **Figure 5-12.** By default, the Continuous linetype is the only linetype in the **Loaded linetypes** list box. Use the Continuous linetype to draw solid lines with no breaks.

Loading Linetypes

AutoCAD maintains linetypes in external linetype definition files. Before you can apply a linetype other than Continuous to a layer, you must load the linetype into the **Select Linetype** dialog box. Pick the **Load...** button to display the **Load or Reload Linetypes** dialog box. See **Figure 5-13.** The acad.lin or acadiso.lin file is active, depending on the template you use to begin the drawing. The acad.lin and acadiso.lin files are identical except that the acadiso.lin file applies a 25.4 scale factor to non-ISO linetypes to convert inches to millimeters for metric drawings. Pick the **File...** button and use the **Select Linetype File** dialog box to select a different linetype definition file.

The **Available Linetypes** list displays the name and a description, which includes an image, of each linetype available from the active linetype definition file. Use the scroll bars to view all available linetypes, and use the image in the **Description** column to aid in selecting the appropriate linetypes to load. Choose a single linetype, or select multiple linetypes using standard selection practices or the shortcut menu. Pick the **OK** button to return to the **Select Linetype** dialog box, where the linetypes you selected now appear. See **Figure 5-14.** In the **Select Linetype** dialog box, pick the linetype to assign to the layer, and then pick the **OK** button. **Figure 5-15** shows the HIDDEN linetype selected in **Figure 5-14** assigned to the layer named Hidden.

Figure 5-12.
The **Select Linetype** dialog box allows you to load linetypes for use in the current drawing.

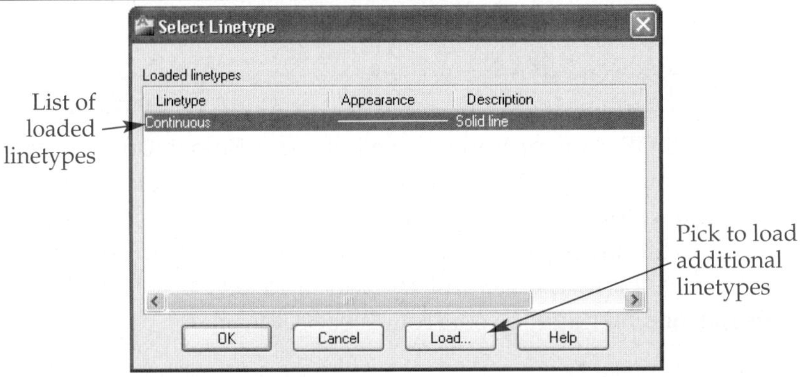

List of loaded linetypes

Pick to load additional linetypes

Figure 5-13.
The **Load or Reload Linetypes** dialog box displays linetypes available for loading.

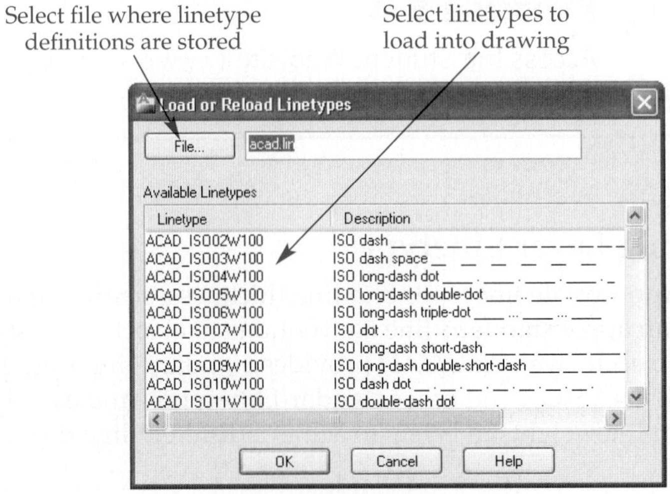

Select file where linetype definitions are stored

Select linetypes to load into drawing

Figure 5-14.
Linetypes loaded
into the drawing
using the **Load or
Reload Linetypes**
dialog box appear in
the **Loaded linetypes**
list box.

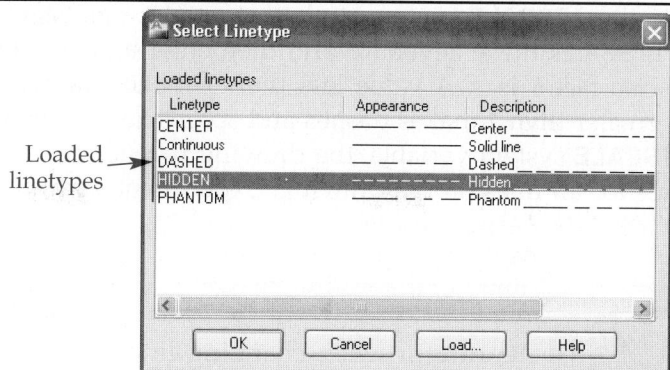

Figure 5-15. Objects drawn on the Hidden layer will have the HIDDEN linetype.

Linetype changed
to HIDDEN

CAUTION

The **LINETYPE** tool provides access to the **Linetype Manager,** which
you can use to set an absolute value for linetype. If you set the absolute linetype to HIDDEN, for example, the HIDDEN linetype overrides
the linetype assigned to layers and all objects appear in the hidden
linetype. For most applications, set linetype to ByLayer and use
layers and the **Layer Properties Manager** to control object linetype.

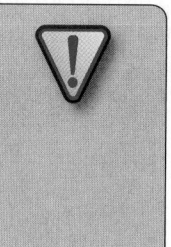

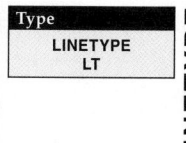

Type

LINETYPE
LT

LINETYPE

Exercise 5-5

Access the Student Web site (www.g-wlearning.com/CAD) and complete
Exercise 5-5.

Setting Linetype Scale

You can change the *linetype scale* to adjust the lengths of dashes and spaces in
linetypes to make a drawing more closely match standard drafting practices. Changing
the *global linetype scale* is the preferred method for adjusting linetype scale, though
it is possible to change the linetype scale of specific objects.

linetype scale: The
lengths of dashes
and spaces in
linetypes.

**global linetype
scale:** A linetype
scale applied to
every linetype in the
current drawing.

system variable:
A command that configures AutoCAD to accomplish a specific task or exhibit a certain behavior. The value of each variable is saved with the drawing, so the next time the drawing is opened, the value remains the same.

Use the **LTSCALE** *system variable* to make a global change to the linetype scale. Enter LTSCALE at the keyboard and then enter a new value. The default global linetype scale factor is 1. A value less than 1 makes dashes and spaces smaller, and a value greater than 1 makes dashes and spaces larger. See **Figure 5-16.** When you exit the **LTSCALE** system variable, the drawing regenerates and the global linetype scale changes for all lines on the drawing. Experiment with different linetype scales until you achieve the desired results.

CAUTION

Be careful when changing linetype scales to avoid making your drawing look odd and not in accordance with drafting standards.

Reference Material

System Variables
For a detailed listing and description of AutoCAD system variables, go to the **Reference Material** section of the Student Web site (www.g-wlearning.com/CAD) and select **System Variables**.

Setting Layer Lineweight

lineweight: The assigned width of lines for display and plotting.

Assign a *lineweight* to a layer to manage the weight, or thickness, of objects. You can adjust the lineweight to match ASME, ISO, NCS, or other standards. Use the **Lineweight** column of the **Layer Properties Manager** to assign lineweight to each layer. Pick the existing lineweight to change the lineweight using the **Lineweight** dialog box. See **Figure 5-17.** The **Lineweight** dialog box displays fixed AutoCAD lineweights. Scroll through the **Lineweights:** list and select the lineweight to assign to the layer. Pick the **OK** button to apply the lineweight and return to the **Layer Properties Manager**.

The **LINEWEIGHT** tool provides access to the **Lineweight Settings** dialog box, shown in **Figure 5-18.** Use the **Units for Listing** area to set the lineweight thickness to **Millimeters (mm)** or **Inches (in)**. The units apply only to values in the **Lineweight** and **Lineweight Settings** dialog boxes, helping you to select lineweights based on a known unit of measurement.

LINEWEIGHT

Type
LINEWEIGHT
LWEIGHT
LW

NOTE

You can also access the **Lineweight Settings** dialog box by right-clicking on the **Show/Hide Lineweight** button on the status bar and selecting **Settings...**.

Figure 5-16.
The CENTER linetype at different linetype scales.

Scale Factor	Line
0.5	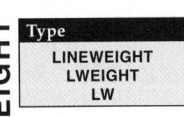
1.0	
1.5	

Figure 5-17.
Use the **Lineweight**
dialog box to assign
a lineweight to a
layer.

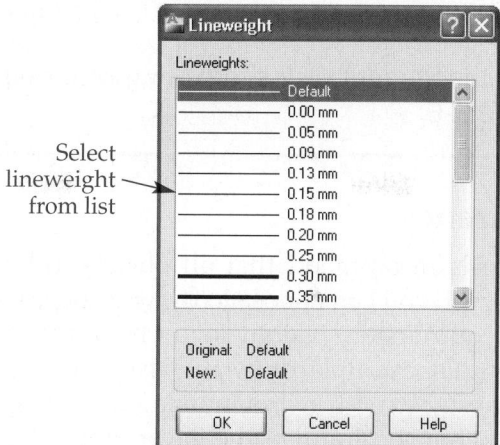

Select
lineweight
from list

Figure 5-18.
The **Lineweight**
Settings dialog box.

Select
lineweight

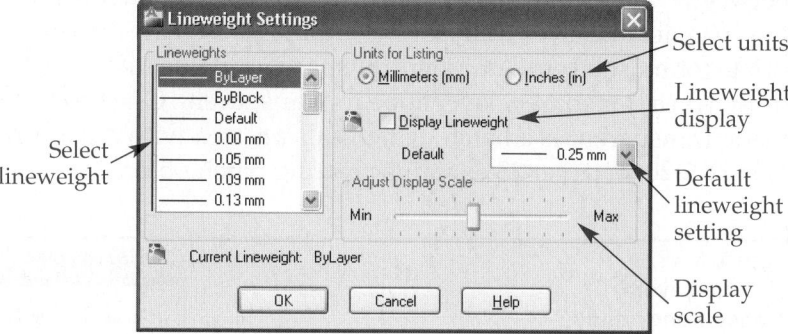

Select units

Lineweight
display

Default
lineweight
setting

Display
scale

Check the **Display Lineweight** box to display object lineweight on-screen. Use the **Adjust Display Scale** slider to adjust the lineweight display scale to improve the appearance of lineweights when lineweight display is on. When lineweight display is off, all objects display a 0, or one-pixel, thickness regardless of the lineweight assigned to the layer. You can also toggle screen lineweight on and off using the **Show/Hide Lineweight** button on the status bar.

The **Default** drop-down list sets the value used when you assign the Default lineweight to a layer. The Default lineweight is an application setting and applies to any drawing you open. The Default lineweight is not template-specific and remains set until you change the value. Do not assign the Default lineweight to layers if you anticipate using a different *default* lineweight for different drawing applications. Assign a specific lineweight, other than Default, to each layer to maintain flexibility and consistency between drawings.

CAUTION

You can use the **Lineweights** area of the **Lineweight Settings** dialog box to set an absolute value for lineweight. If you set the absolute lineweight to 0.30 mm, for example, the 0.30 mm lineweight overrides the lineweight assigned to layers and all objects appear 0.30 mm thick. For most applications, set lineweight to ByLayer and use layers and the **Layer Properties Manager** to control object lineweight.

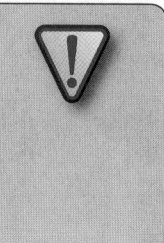

Exercise 5-6

Access the Student Web site (www.g-wlearning.com/CAD) **and complete** Exercise 5-6.

2011

AutoCAD
NEW

Layer Transparency

ASME standards recommend that all objects to be opaque and dark for most applications. However, you can choose to draw transparent, or see-though, objects for specific drawing requirements, usually for architectural, civil, technical illustration, or related applications. For example, draw an existing building using transparent objects to highlight a proposed structure drawn using nontransparent objects.

Use the **Transparency** column of the **Layer Properties Manager** to assign a level of transparency to each layer. Pick the existing transparency value to change the level of transparency using the **Layer Transparency** dialog box. See **Figure 5-19**. Type a value between 0 and 90 or select a value from the drop-down list.

The default layer transparency value of 0 creates nontransparent objects, appropriate for most layers. A higher transparency value increases transparency. Any object drawn on a transparent layer appears transparent. One type of object that is commonly made transparent is a hatch, which fills an area with a pattern, solid, or gradient. See **Figure 5-20**. Chapter 23 explains creating hatch objects.

Figure 5-19.
Use the **Layer Transparency** dialog box to assign a level of transparency to a layer.

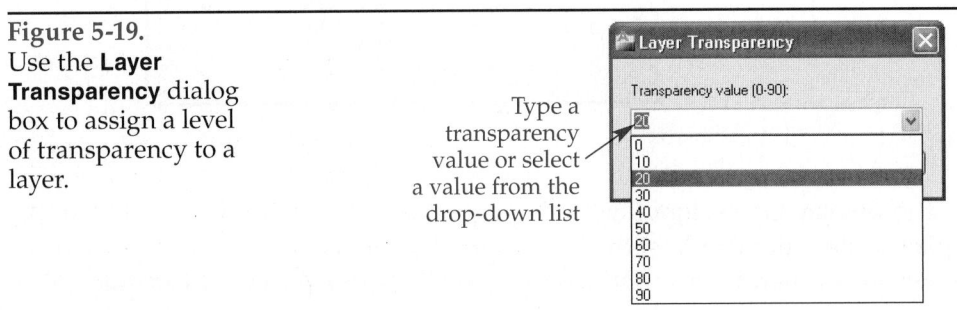

Type a transparency value or select a value from the drop-down list

Figure 5-20. An example of a portion of a storm water pollution control plan with transparent solid hatch objects that represent different impervious and non-impervious surfaces.

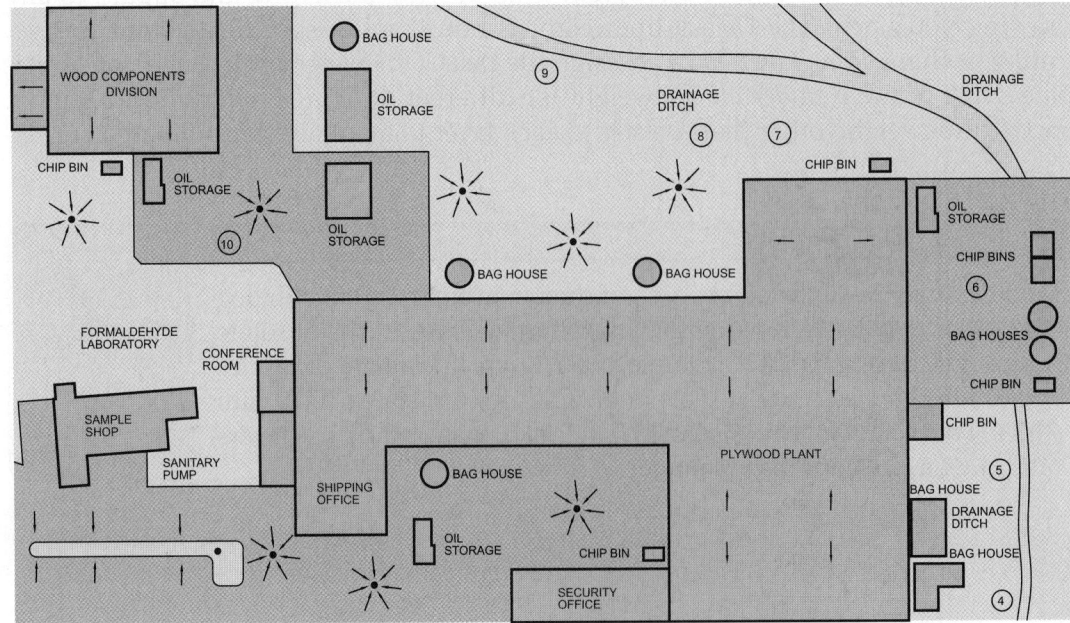

Showing and Hiding Transparency

Show or hide transparency using the **Show/Hide Transparency** button on the status bar. Transparency is on by default, and all objects drawn using a transparent layer appear at their transparent level. Disabling transparency using the **Show/Hide Transparency** button makes all transparent objects appear nontransparent, but does not change the layer transparency property.

CAUTION

You can override layer transparency for specific objects, but for most applications, set transparency to ByLayer and use layers and the **Layer Properties Manager** to control object transparency.

PROFESSIONAL TIP

Layers should simplify and support drafting. Set color, linetype, lineweight, and transparency using layers, and do not override these properties for individual objects. Also, once you establish layers, avoid resetting and mixing color, linetype, lineweight, and transparency, which can lead to confusion and disorder.

Layer Plotting Properties

Use the **Plot Style** column of the **Layer Properties Manager** to assign a named plot style to each layer. AutoCAD uses color-dependent plot styles by default, so the plot style property is disabled. This textbook explains plot styles when appropriate.

Use the **Plot** column of the **Layer Properties Manager** to disable a layer from printing or plotting. Pick the printer, or **Plot**, icon to change it to the **No Plot** icon if the layer should not plot. The layer displays on-screen and is selectable, but does not plot.

Plot   No Plot

Adding a Layer Description

Use the **Description** column of the **Layer Properties Manager** to describe each layer. To add or change a description, slowly double-click on the blank area or existing description, type a description, and press [Enter] or pick outside of the **Description** text box. Another method is to right-click and select **Change Description**.

Turning Layers On and Off

Use the **On** column of the **Layer Properties Manager** to turn a layer on or off. The lit light bulb, or **On** icon, indicates that the layer is turned on. Objects assigned to an "on" layer display on-screen, are selectable, regenerate, and can plot. Pick the lit light bulb to turn the layer off, indicated by the gray light bulb, or **Off** icon. Objects assigned to an "off" layer do not display on-screen and do not plot. You can still select and edit objects that are on these layers using advanced selection techniques. Objects that are off also regenerate.

On   Off

NOTE

Turn a layer on or off using the **Layer Control** drop-down list in the **Layers** panel on the **Home** ribbon tab.

Freeze Thaw

Freezing and Thawing Layers

Use the **Freeze** column of the **Layer Properties Manager** to thaw or freeze a layer. The sun, or **Thaw** icon, indicates a thawed layer. Objects assigned to a thawed layer display on-screen, are selectable, regenerate, and can plot. Pick the sun to freeze the layer, indicated by the snowflake, or **Freeze** icon. Objects assigned to a frozen layer do not display on-screen, plot, or regenerate. You cannot select or edit objects that are frozen. Freeze layers to hide objects and ensure that you do not accidentally modify the objects.

Use the **New VP Freeze** column to control thawing or freezing of layers when you create a new viewport. Additional layer functions also apply to layouts and viewports. This textbook explains layouts and viewports when appropriate.

VP Freeze

VP Thaw

> **NOTE**
>
> You can also freeze or thaw a layer using the **Layer Control** drop-down list in the **Layers** panel of the **Home** ribbon tab. You cannot freeze the current layer or make a frozen layer current.

> **CAUTION**
>
> You cannot modify frozen objects, but you can modify objects that are off. For example, if you turn off layers and use the **All** selection option with the **Erase** tool, even the objects assigned to the off layers are erased. However, if you freeze the layers, the objects are not selected or erased.

Locking and Unlocking Layers

Lock Unlock

Use the **Lock** column of the **Layer Properties Manager** to unlock or lock a layer. The unlocked padlock, or **Unlock** icon, indicates an unlocked layer. Pick the unlocked padlock to lock the layer, indicated by the locked padlock, or **Lock** icon. A **Lock** icon also appears next to the cursor when you hover over an object on a locked layer. Objects assigned to a locked layer display on-screen, and you can use a locked layer to draw new objects. However, you cannot select or edit locked objects. Lock layers to display objects, but eliminate the possibility of selecting the objects.

> **NOTE**
>
> You can also lock or unlock a layer using the **Layer Control** drop-down list in the **Layers** panel on the **Home** ribbon tab.

Locked Layer Fading

By default, all locked layers fade, allowing unlocked layers to stand out on-screen. The quickest way to control locked layer fading is to use the options available in the expanded **Layers** panel of the **Home** ribbon tab. See **Figure 5-21**. Pick the **Locked layer fading** button to allow or disable locked layer fading. Use the **Locked Layer Fading** slider to increase or decrease fading, or type a fading percentage between 0 and 90. The default fade value is 50%. A higher fade value increases fading. **Figure 5-22** shows an example of using locked layer fading on an architectural drawing.

Figure 5-21.
Locked layers fade by default. Increase or decrease fading and enable or disable locked layer fading as needed.

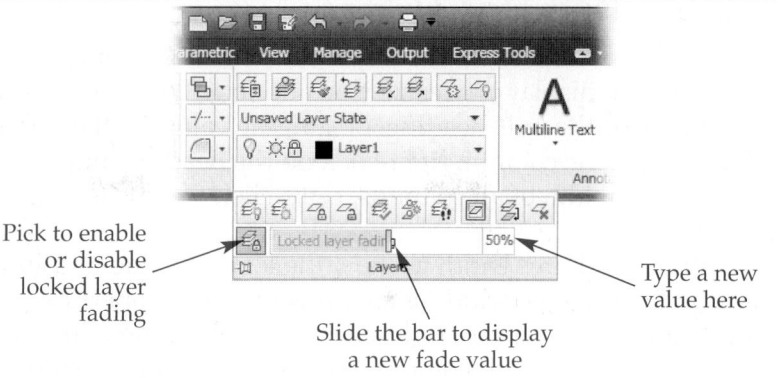

Pick to enable or disable locked layer fading

Slide the bar to display a new fade value

Type a new value here

Figure 5-22. An example of a floor plan with all layers locked except the A-WALL-FULL layer, which contains the walls. A—Locked layer fading disabled. B—Locked layer fading enabled and set to a fade value of 75.

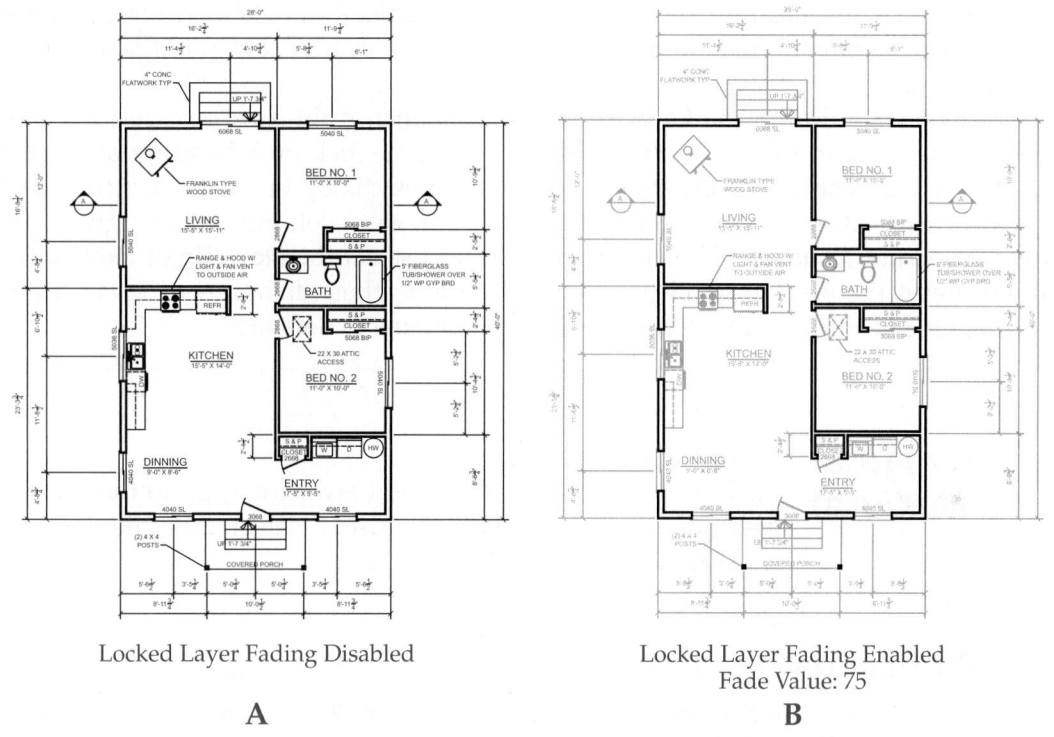

Locked Layer Fading Disabled

A

Locked Layer Fading Enabled
Fade Value: 75

B

> **NOTE**
>
> Transparency is a layer property that makes objects transparent. Locked layer fading is a function of the lock state, intended for on-screen drawing purposes only. For example, you can plot transparent objects, but you cannot plot locked faded layers.

Deleting Layers

To delete a layer using the **Layer Properties Manager**, select the layer and pick the **Delete Layer** button, or right-click on the layer and choose **Delete Layer**. You cannot delete or purge the 0 layer, the current layer, layers containing objects, or layers associated with an external references.

Adjusting Property Columns

To resize a column in the **Layer Properties Manager**, move the cursor over the column edge to display the resize icon and drag the column width. Maximize column width to show the full heading or longest value in the column. To maximize the width of a specific column, right-click on the heading and select **Maximize column**. To maximize the width of all columns, right-click on any heading and select **Maximize all columns**.

Optimize column width to show the longest value in columns that list properties as text and reduce the width of columns that list properties as icons. To optimize the width of a specific column, right-click on the heading and select **Optimize column**. To optimize the width of all columns, right-click on any heading and select **Optimize all columns**.

By default, a vertical bar appears on the right side of the **Name** column. Any column to the left of the bar is "frozen" to remain in position when you move the scroll bar near the bottom of the **Layer Properties Manager**. Scroll columns to the right of the vertical bar using the horizontal scroll bar. To disable the column freeze function, right-click on a heading and select **Unfreeze column**. Right-click on a heading and select **Freeze column** to turn on the freeze function for every column to the left of the selected column.

To hide a column in the **Layer Properties Manager**, right-click on a heading and deselect the column name. Another option is to right-click on a heading and select **Customize...** to display the **Customize Layer Columns** dialog box. Deselect the check boxes corresponding to the columns to hide. To move a column left or right in the **Layer Properties Manager**, pick a column name and select the **Move Up** or **Move Down** button. Reset the display of all property columns to their default settings by right-clicking on a heading and selecting **Restore all columns to defaults**.

Supplemental Material

Additional Layer Tools
For information about additional layer tools, go to the Student Web site (www.g-wlearning.com/CAD), select this chapter, and select **Additional Layer Tools**.

Introduction to Layer Filters

layer filters: Settings that screen out, or filter, layers you do not want to display in the list view pane of the Layer Properties Manager.

The filter tree view pane on the left side of the **Layer Properties Manager** controls *layer filters*. See **Figure 5-23**. Layer filters are typically appropriate when it becomes difficult to manage a very large number of layers. Filter a large list of layers to make it easier to work with layers needed for a specific drawing task.

Layer filters are listed in alphabetical order inside the **All** node. Select the **All** node to display all layers in the drawing. Pick the **All Used Layers** filter to display only layers used to create objects in the drawing. When you insert external references and save the drawing, an Xref filter node appears, allowing you to filter the display of layers associated with external references. This textbook explains external references when appropriate. You can create custom filters as needed.

> **NOTE**
>
> Collapse the filter tree view of the **Layer Properties Manager** by picking the **Collapse Layer filter tree** button. To display all filters and layers in the list view, right-click in the layer list area and select **Show Filters in Layer List**.

Figure 5-23.
Create and restore layer filters using the filter tree view of the **Layer Properties Manager**.

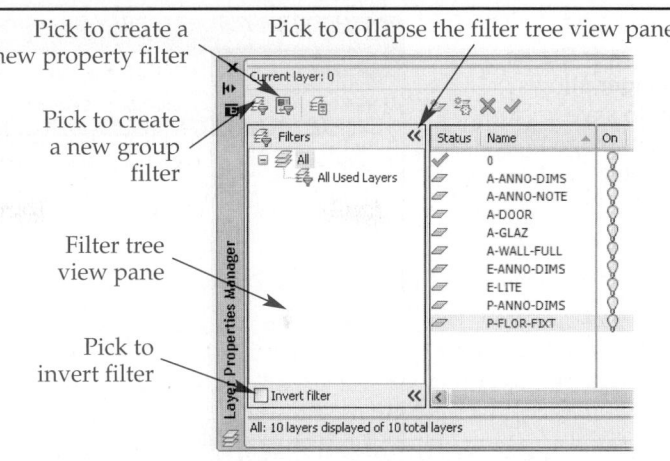

Pick to create a new property filter

Pick to collapse the filter tree view pane

Pick to create a new group filter

Filter tree view pane

Pick to invert filter

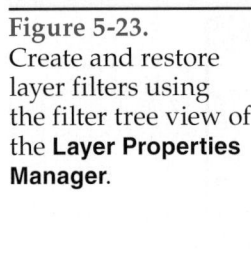

Supplemental Material

Creating Layer Filters
For information about creating and managing layer filters, go to the Student Web site (www.g-wlearning.com/CAD), select this chapter, and select **Creating Layer Filters**.

Layer States

Once you save a *layer state*, you can readjust layer settings to meet drawing tasks, with the option to restore a saved layer state when needed. For example, a basic architectural drawing might use the layers shown in **Figure 5-23**. You can use the drawing file to prepare a floor plan, a plumbing plan, and an electrical plan. **Figure 5-24** shows the layer settings for each of the three drawings.

Save each of the three groups of settings as an individual layer state. Then restore a layer state to return the layer settings for a specific drawing. This method is easier than changing the settings for each layer individually.

Use the **Layer States Manager**, shown in **Figure 5-25**, to create a new layer state. Pick the **New...** button to display the **New Layer State to Save** dialog box. See **Figure 5-26**. Type a name in the **New layer state name:** text box and a description in the **Description:** text box. Pick the **OK** button to save the new layer state. Once you create a layer state, you can adjust layer properties as needed. **Figure 5-27** describes the areas, options, and buttons available in the **Layer States Manager**.

layer state: A saved setting, or state, of layer properties for all layers in the drawing.

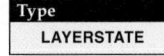

LAYERSTATE

Figure 5-24. Use layer states to manage the layers needed for several different plans.

Layer	Description	Floor Plan	Plumbing Plan	Electrical Plan
0		Off	Off	Off
A-NNO-DIM	Floor Plan Dimensions	On	Frozen	Frozen
A-ANNO-NOTE	Floor Plan Notes	On	Frozen	Frozen
A-DOOR	Doors	On	Frozen	Locked
A-GLAZ	Windows	On	Frozen	Locked
A-WALL-FULL	Full Height Walls	On	Locked	Locked
E-ANNO-DIMS	Electrical Panel Dimensions	Frozen	Frozen	On
E-LITE	Electrical Plan Lights	Frozen	Frozen	On
P-ANNO-DIMS	Plumbing Plan Dimensions	Frozen	On	Frozen
P-FLOR-FIXT	Plumbing Plan Fixtures	Locked	On	Locked

Figure 5-25.
The **Layer States Manager** allows you to save, restore, and manage layer settings.

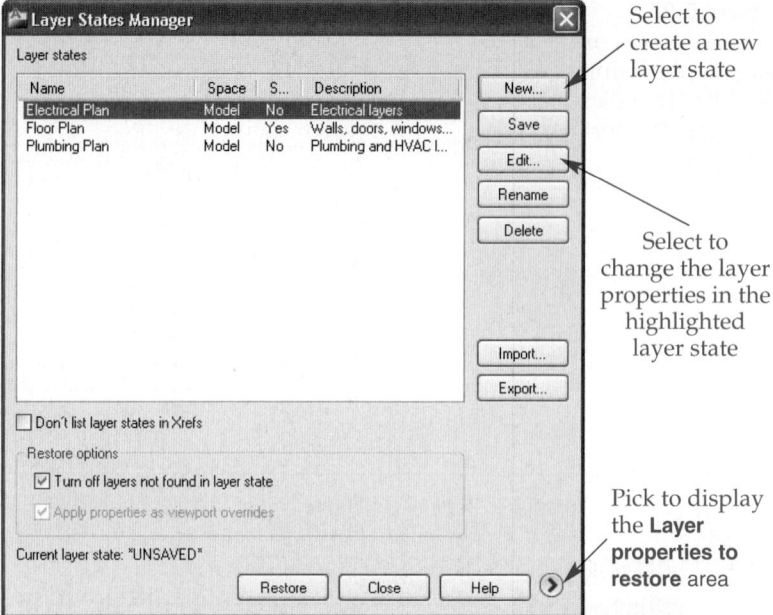

Select to create a new layer state

Select to change the layer properties in the highlighted layer state

Pick to display the **Layer properties to restore** area

Figure 5-26.
Creating a new layer state.

Enter the layer state name

Enter a description for the layer state

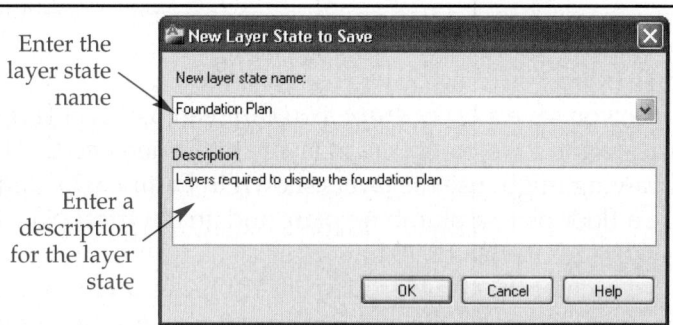

NOTE

You can also access the **Layer States Manager** by picking the **Layer States Manager** button from the **Layer Properties Manager** or right-clicking in the layer list view of the **Layer Properties Manager** and selecting **Restore Layer State**. To save a layer state outside the **Layer States Manager**, pick the **New Layer State…** option from the **Layer States** drop-down list in the **Layers** panel on the **Home** ribbon tab.

PROFESSIONAL TIP

Importing a layer state file (.las) to a drawing that does not contain any layers other than 0 adds the layers from the layer state file to the drawing.

After you create a layer state, you can restore layer properties to the settings saved in the layer state at any time. To activate a layer state using the ribbon, select it from the **Layer States** drop-down list in the **Layers** panel on the **Home** ribbon tab. You can also restore a layer state using the **Layer States Manager** by selecting the layer state from the list and picking the **Restore** button.

AutoCAD and Its Applications—Basics

Figure 5-27. Layer state options available in the **Layer States Manager**.

Item	Feature
Layer states	Displays saved layer states. The **Name** column provides the name of the layer state. The **Space** column indicates whether the layer state was saved in model space or paper space. The **Same as DWG** column indicates whether the layer state is the same as the current layer properties. The **Description** column lists the layer state description added when the layer state was saved.
Save	Pick to resave and override the selected layer state with the current layer properties.
Edit	Opens the **Edit Layer State** dialog box, where you can adjust the properties of each layer state without exiting the **Layer States Manager**.
Rename	Activates a text box that allows you to rename the current layer state.
Delete	Deletes the selected layer state.
Import	Opens the **Import layer state** dialog box, used to import an LAS file containing an existing layer state into the **Layer States Manager**.
Export	Opens the **Export layer state** dialog box, used to save a layer state as an LAS file. The file can be imported into other drawings, allowing you to share layer states between drawings containing identical layers.
Don't list layer states in Xrefs	Hides layer states associated with external reference drawings. External references are described in Chapter 30.
Restore options	Check the **Turn off layers not found in layer state** check box to turn off new layers or layers removed from a layer state when the layer state is restored. Check **Apply properties as viewport overrides** to apply layer viewport overrides when you are adjusting layer states within a layout.
Layer properties to restore	Check the layer properties that you want to restore when the layer state is restored. Pick the **Select All** button to pick all properties. Pick the **Clear All** button to deselect all properties.

Supplemental Material

Layer Settings

For information about options available in the **Layer Settings** dialog box, go to the Student Web site (www.g-wlearning.com/CAD), select this chapter, and select **Layer Settings**.

Reusing Drawing Content

In nearly every drafting discipline, many of the drawings created for a given project may share a number of common elements. All the drawings within a specific drafting project generally have the same set of standards. You often duplicate *drawing content*, such as layers, text and dimension characteristics, symbols, layouts, and details, in many different drawings. One of the most fundamental advantages of CADD is the ease with which you can share content between drawings. Once you create a common drawing element, you can reuse the item as needed in any number of drawing applications.

Drawing templates are one way to reuse drawing content. Customized templates provide an effective way to start each new drawing using standard settings. Another

drawing content: All of the objects, settings, and other components that make up a drawing.

way to reuse drawing content is to seek out data from existing files. This is a common requirement when developing related drawings for a specific project, or working on similar projects. Sharing drawing content is also common when revising drawings and when duplicating standards used by a consultant, vendor, or client. AutoCAD provides several ways to share drawing content, as described throughout this textbook. One of the most useful tools is **DesignCenter**.

Introduction to DesignCenter

ADCENTER

Ribbon
View
> Palettes
Insert
> Content

DesignCenter

Type
ADCENTER
ADC

DesignCenter is a palette for managing drawing content between files. See **Figure 5-28.** You can use **DesignCenter** to locate and reuse layers, linetypes, blocks, dimension styles, multileader styles, table styles, text styles, external references, and raster image files. **DesignCenter** allows you to load content from a file without actually opening a file and copying and pasting the content. **DesignCenter** floats by default. You can resize, move, Auto-hide, or dock the floating **DesignCenter**.

Copying Layers and Linetypes

To copy content using **DesignCenter**, first pick a tab below the **DesignCenter** toolbar to locate a file with drawing content. Pick the **Folders** tab to explore the folders and files found on the hard drive and network, similar to using Windows Explorer. Pick the **Open Drawings** tab to list only drawings that are currently open. The **History** tab lists recently opened drawings and templates. Double-click on a recent file or right-click on the file and choose **Explore** to navigate to the file in the **Folders** tab.

The **Tree View** pane is displayed directly below the tabs by default. If the **Tree View** pane is not visible, toggle it on by picking the **Tree View Toggle** button from the **DesignCenter** toolbar. Use the **Tree View** pane with the **Folders** or **Open Drawings** tab to select a file with the content to reuse. Double-click the file or pick the plus sign (+) to view content categories. Pick Layers to load the **Content** pane with layers found in the selected drawing. See **Figure 5-29.**

Figure 5-28. Use the **DesignCenter** to copy content from one drawing to another.

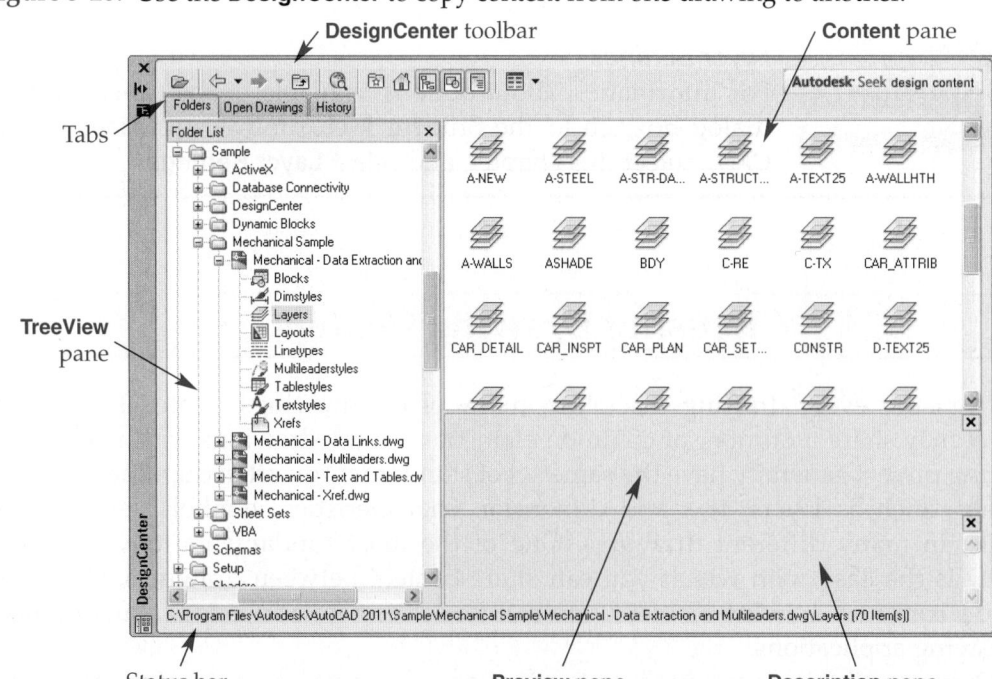

Figure 5-29. Using **DesignCenter** to display the layers found in a drawing.

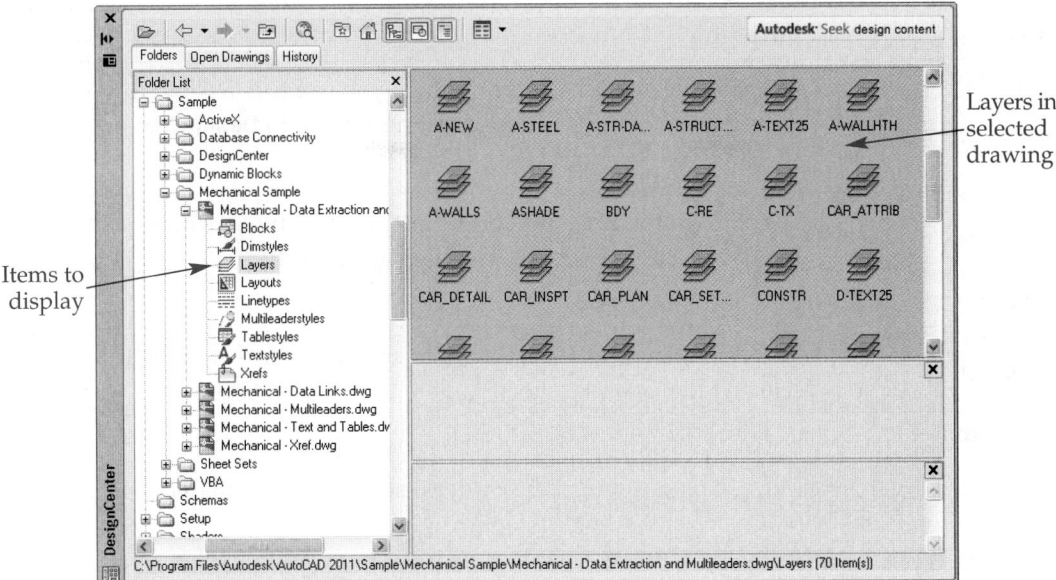

Items to display

Layers in selected drawing

Use a drag-and-drop operation to import content into the current drawing. Use standard selection practices to select multiple layers. Press and hold down the pick button on the layers to import, and then drag the cursor to the drawing window. See **Figure 5-30**. Release the pick button to add the layers to the current file. An alternative is to right-click on the layers in the **Content** pane and pick **Add Layer(s)**.

Use **DesignCenter** to copy linetypes from one file to another using the same procedure as copying layers. In the **Tree View** pane, select and expand the file containing the linetypes to copy. Pick the Linetypes category to display the linetypes in the **Content** pane. Use drag-and-drop or the shortcut menu to add the linetypes to the current drawing. **Figure 5-31** briefly describes several additional **DesignCenter** features.

Figure 5-30. To copy layers shown in **DesignCenter** into the current drawing, drag and drop the layers into the drawing area.

Select layer(s) to copy

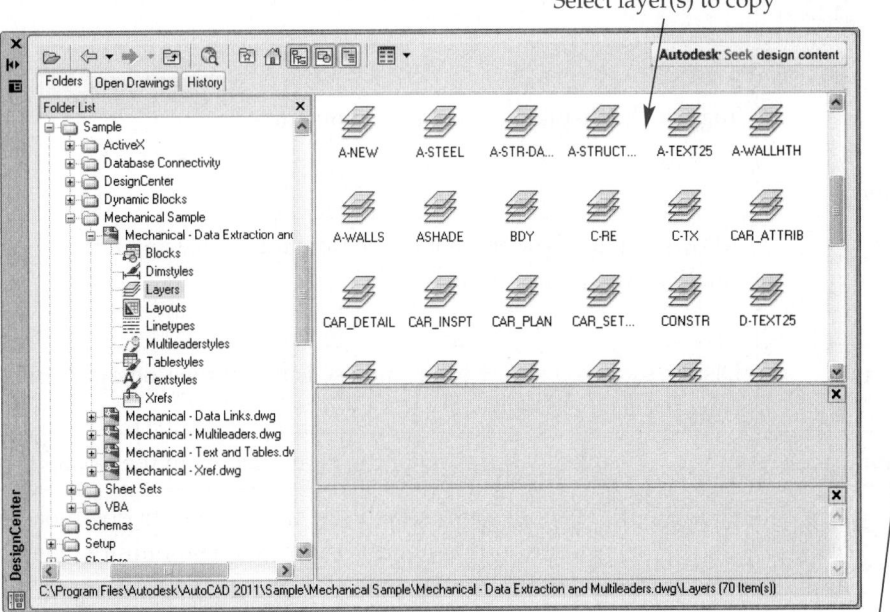

Cursor appearance during drag-and-drop operation

Figure 5-31. Additional items available in **DesignCenter**.

Item	Function
Load	Displays the **Load** dialog box, which you can use to select a file with drawing content or download online content to **DesignCenter**.
Back	Select to show the content of the last selected file, or choose the flyout to access a list of previously viewed content.
Forward	Pick after using the **Back** button to show the content of the last selected file, or choose the flyout to access a list of previously viewed content.
Up	Moves up one level in the **Folder List** tree to a file, folder, drive, My Computer, or the desktop.
Search	Displays the **Search** dialog box, which you can use to locate drawing content on any drive that meets search criteria and load the content to **DesignCenter**.
Favorites	Navigates to the Autodesk folder in your Favorites folder. To add commonly used content to the Favorites folder, right-click on an item in the **Folder List** area and select **Add to Favorites**.
Home	Navigates to the **DesignCenter** folder. To change the "home" location, right-click on an item in the **Folder List** area and select **Set as Home**.
Tree View Toggle	Toggles the display of the **Tree View** pane.
Preview	Toggles the display of the **Preview** pane.
Description	Toggles the display of the **Description** pane.
Views	Allows you to show content in the **Content** pane using large icons, small icons, or a list or detail format.
Preview pane	Displays a saved image of the item selected in the **Content** pane, typically a block.
Description pane	Displays a saved description of the item selected in the **Content** pane.
Autodesk Seek **Autodesk Seek**	Launches the Autodesk Seek Web site, where you can download content from contributing manufacturers and community members.

Exercise 5-7

Access the Student Web site (www.g-wlearning.com/CAD) and complete Exercise 5-7.

Template Development
Chapter 5

For detailed instructions on adding layers to each of your drawing templates, go to the Student Web site (www.g-wlearning.com/CAD), select this chapter, and select **Template Development**.

Chapter Test

Answer the following questions. Write your answers on a separate sheet of paper or go to the Student Web site (www.g-wlearning.com/CAD) and complete the electronic chapter test.

1. Identify the following linetypes:

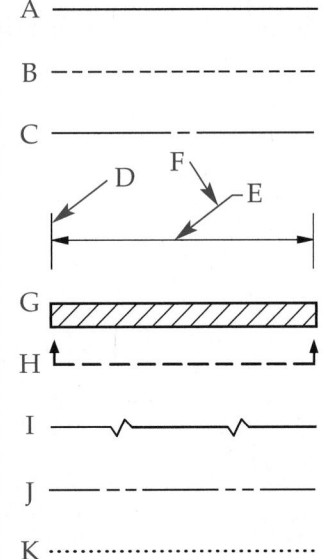

2. Identify two ways to access the **Layer Properties Manager**.
3. How can you tell if a layer is off, thawed, or unlocked by looking at the **Layer Properties Manager**?
4. Should you draw on layer 0? Explain.

5. How can you enter several new layer names consecutively without using the **New Layer** button in the **Layer Properties Manager**?
6. How do you make another layer current in the **Layer Properties Manager**?
7. How do you make another layer current using the ribbon?
8. How can you display the **Select Color** dialog box from the **Layer Properties Manager**?
9. List the seven standard color names and numbers.
10. How do you change the linetype assigned to a layer in the **Layer Properties Manager**?
11. What is the default linetype in AutoCAD?
12. What condition must exist before you can assign a linetype to a layer?
13. Describe the basic procedure to change layer linetype to HIDDEN.
14. What is the function of the linetype scale?
15. Explain the effects of using a global linetype scale.
16. Why do you have to be careful when changing linetype scales?
17. What is the state of a layer *not* displayed on-screen and *not* calculated by the computer when the drawing regenerates?
18. Explain the purpose of locking a layer.
19. Explain the difference between a locked layer state and layer transparency.
20. Identify the following layer status icons:

   A.   D.

   B.   E.

   C.   F.

21. Identify at least three layers that you cannot delete from a drawing.
22. Describe the purpose of layer filters.
23. Which button in the **Layer Properties Manager** allows you to save layer settings so they can be restored later?
24. In the **Tree View** pane of **DesignCenter**, how do you view the content categories of one of the listed open drawings?
25. How do you display all the available layers in a drawing in the **DesignCenter**?

Drawing Problems

Start AutoCAD if it is not already started. Start a new drawing from scratch or use an appropriate template of your choice. The template should include layers for drawing the given objects. Add layers as needed. Draw all objects using appropriate layers. Follow the specific instructions for each problem. Use only drawing tools and techniques you have already learned. Do not draw dimensions or text. Use your own judgment and approximate dimensions when necessary.

▼ Basic

1. Draw the hex head bolt pattern shown. Save the drawing as P5-1.

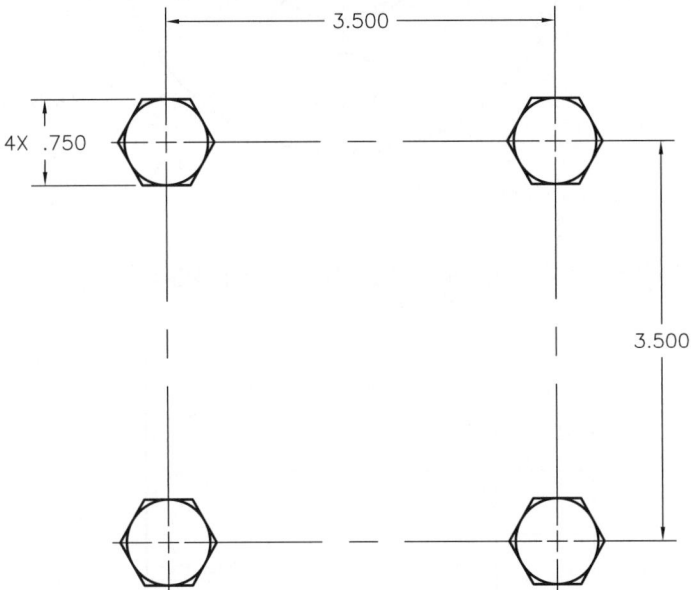

2. Draw the 1/2″ hex nut with 3/4″ across the flats and a .422″ minor diameter. Save the drawing as P5-2.

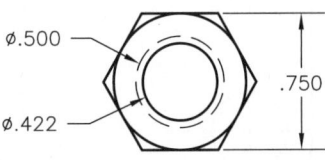

3. Draw the part view shown. Save the drawing as **P5-3**.

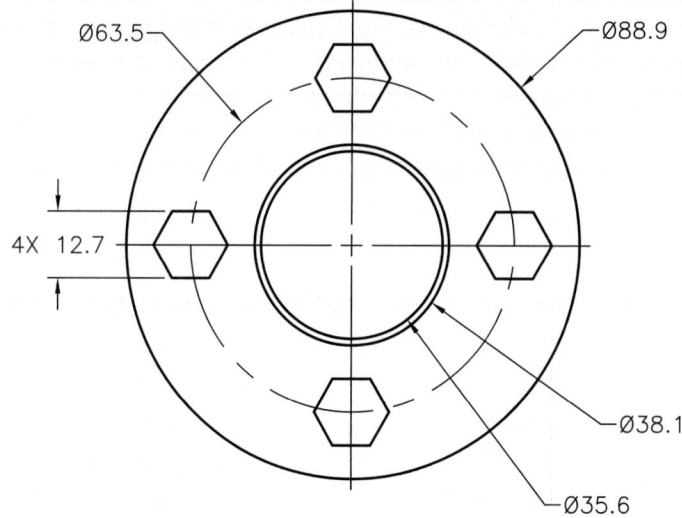

4. Draw the part view shown. Save the drawing as **P5-4**.

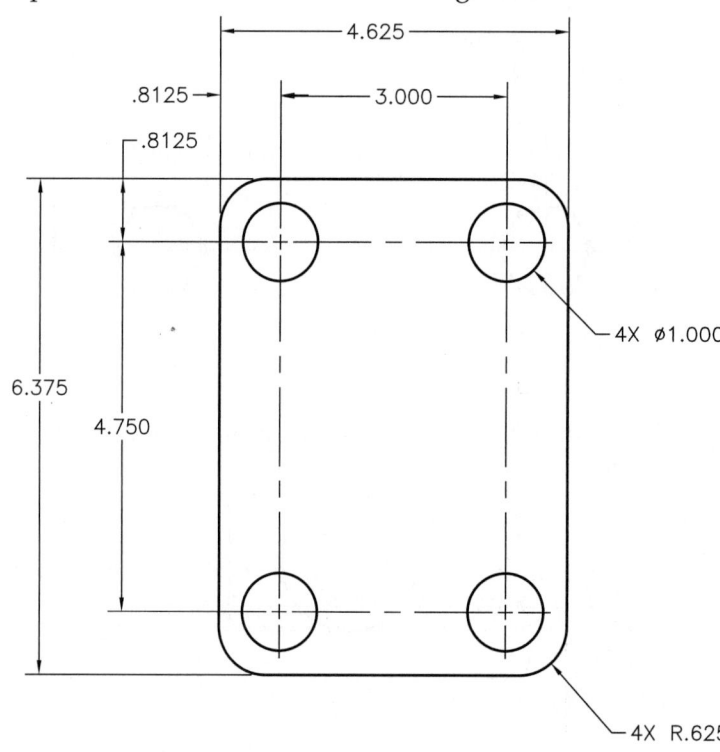

▼ Intermediate

5. Open P4-3, create or import a new layer for centerlines, and draw the centerlines. Save the drawing as P5-5.

6. Open P4-7, create or import a new layer for centerlines, and draw the centerlines. Save the drawing as P5-6.

▼ Advanced

7. Open P4-19, create or import a new layer for centerlines, and draw the centerlines. Change the global linetype scale to achieve an effect similar to the centerlines shown in Chapter 4. Save the drawing as P5-7.

8. Draw the plot plan shown. Use the linetypes shown, which include Continuous, HIDDEN, PHANTOM, CENTER, FENCELINE2, and GAS_LINE. Draw objects proportionate to the drawing shown. Use dimensions based on your experience, research, or measurements. Save the drawing as P5-8.

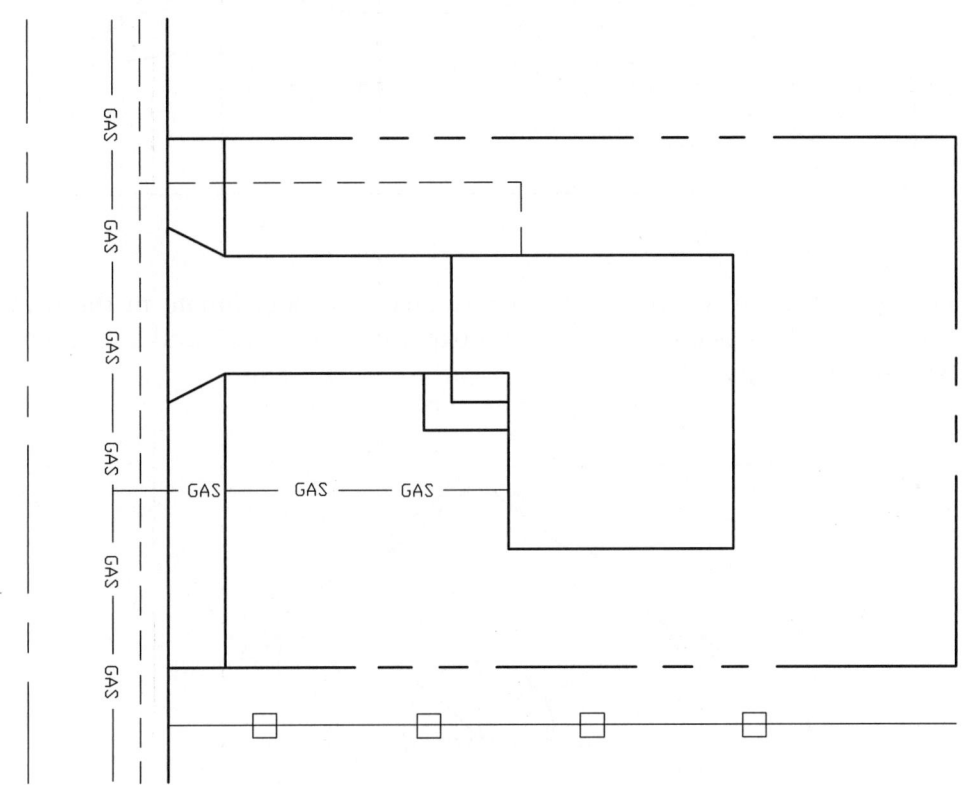

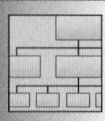

9. Draw the line chart shown. Use the linetypes shown, which include Continuous, HIDDEN, PHANTOM, CENTER, FENCELINE1, and FENCELINE2. Draw objects proportionate to the drawing. Save the drawing as P5-9.

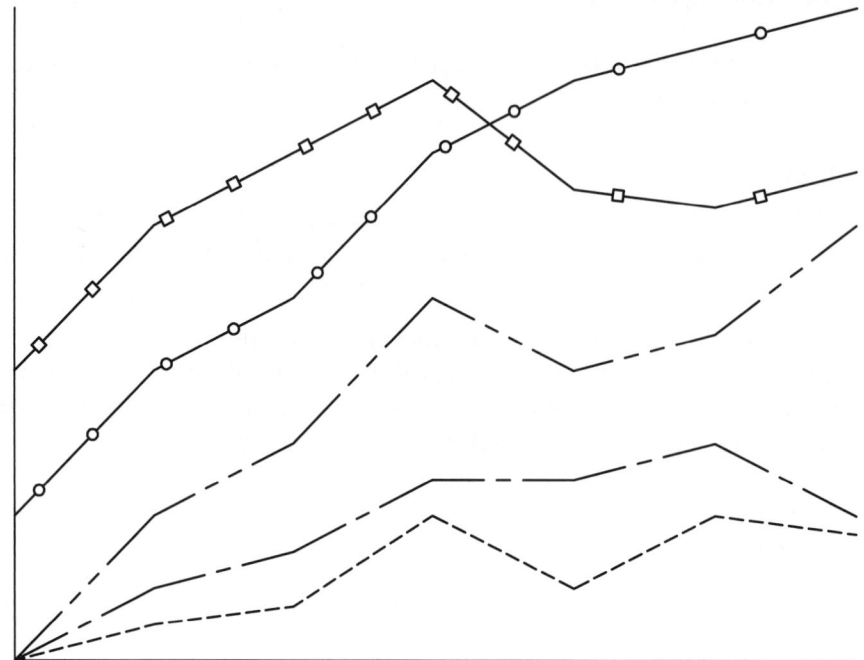

10. Draw the front elevation shown. Draw objects proportionate to the drawing shown. Use dimensions based on your experience, research, and measurements. Save the drawing as P5-10.

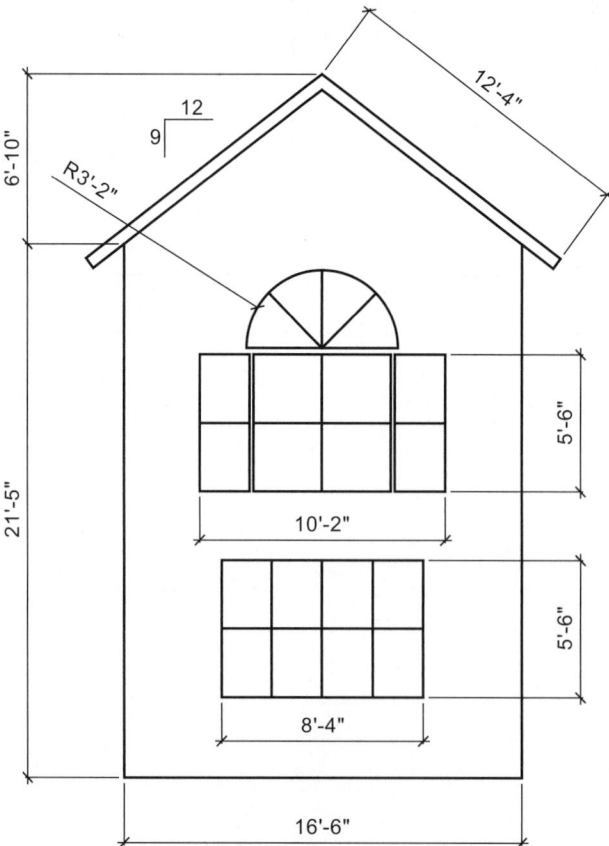

11. Create the controller integrated circuit diagram shown. Use a ruler or scale to keep the proportion as close as possible. Save the drawing as P5-11.

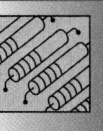

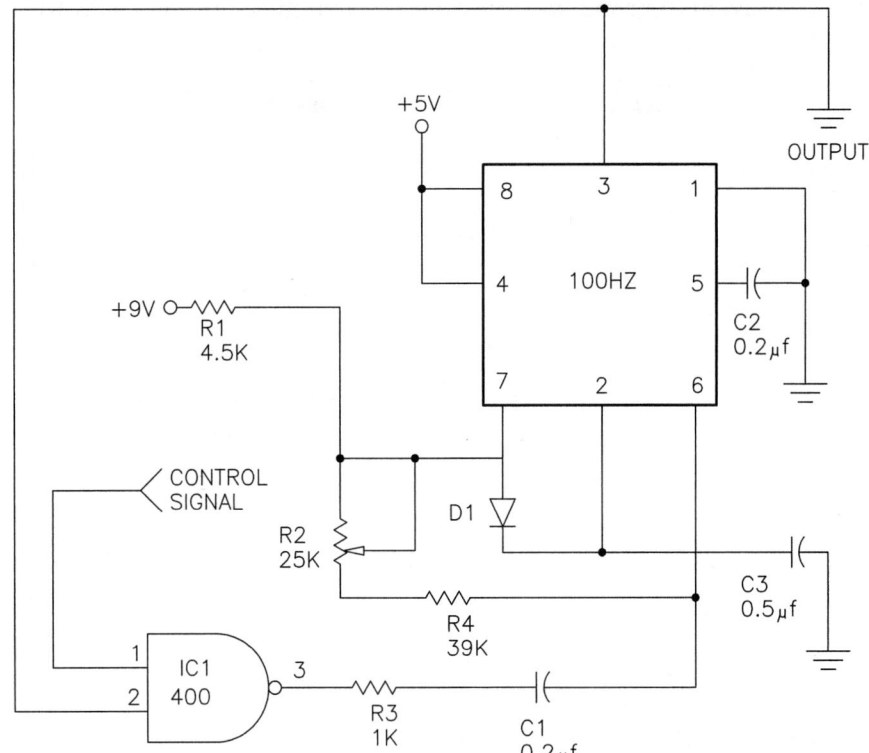

12. Draw a drift boat similar to the drift boat shown. Use dimensions based on your experience, research, or measurements. Use layers to group specific objects. Save the drawing as P5-12.

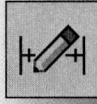

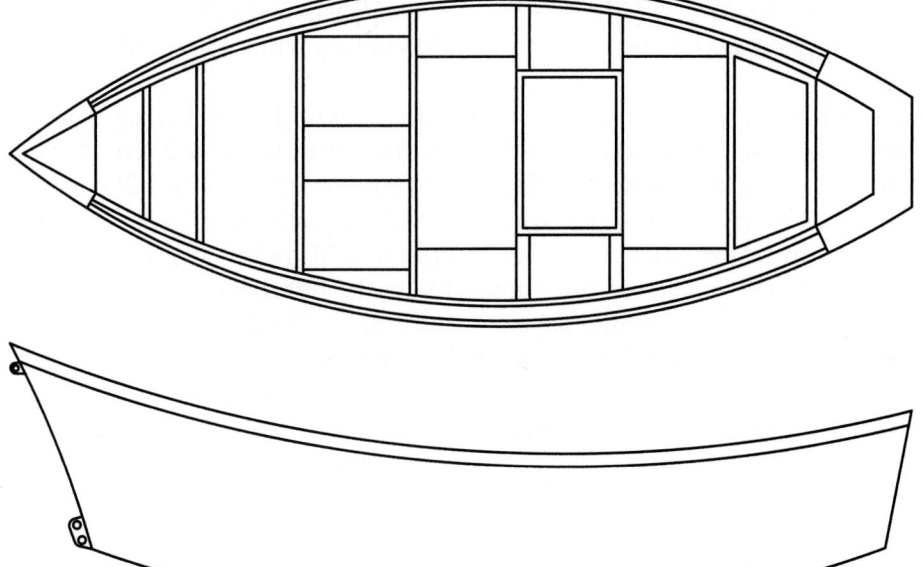

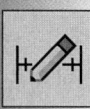

13. Draw a fishing boat similar to the fishing boat shown. Use the overall dimensions shown, and add dimensions based on your experience, research, or measurements. Use layers to group specific objects. Save the drawing as P5-13.

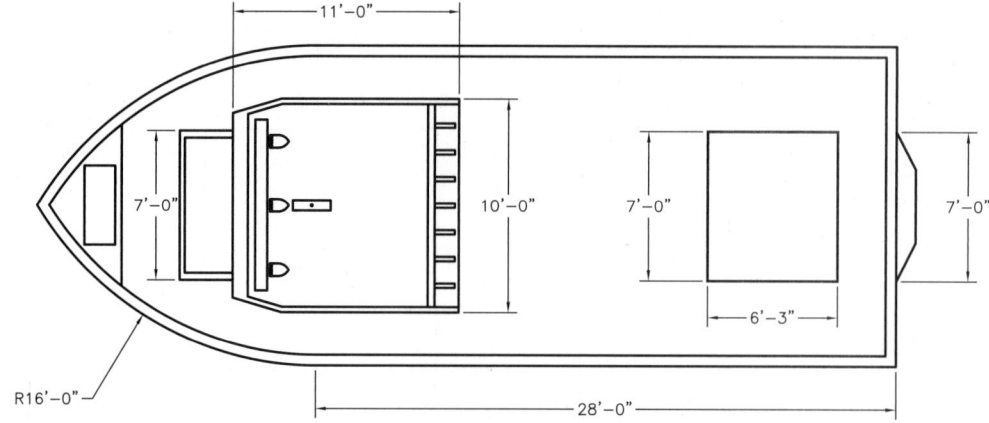

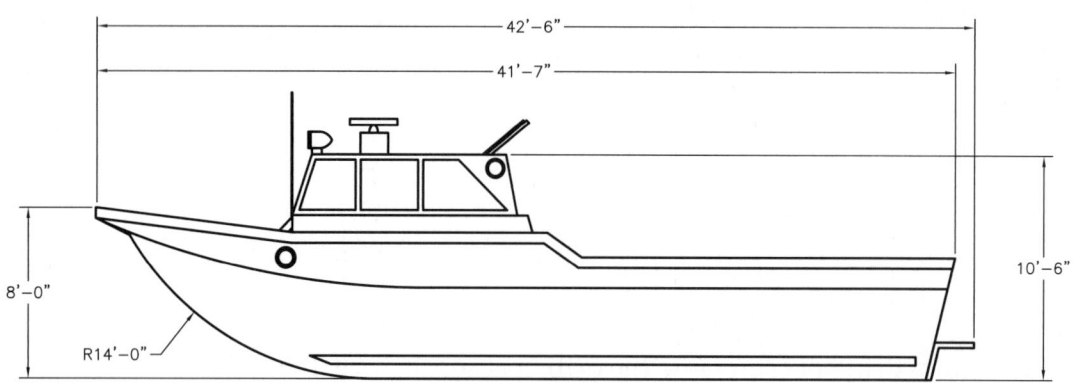

14. Research and write a report of approximately 500 words covering the American Institute of Architects (AIA) *CAD Layer Guidelines*. Include at least three lists of layers applied to specific disciplines, and explain what you would draw on each layer.

15. Research the design of an existing nut driver with the following specifications: fastens 1/2" hex head screws and bolts, minimum 6" overall length, solid zinc-plated steel shaft, plastic handle. Hand-draw a dimensioned 2D sketch of the existing design from the manufacturer's specifications, or from measurements taken from an actual nut driver. Start a new drawing from scratch or use a decimal-unit template of your choice. Draw the nut driver from your sketch. Do not dimension the drawing. Save the drawing as P5-15.

16. Create a dimensioned 2D sketch of the floor plan of a kitchen, complete with fixtures and appliances. Use a tape measure to dimension the size and location of kitchen features accurately. Start a new drawing from scratch or use an architectural unit template of your choice. Draw the kitchen from your sketch. Save the drawing as P5-16.

AutoCAD Certified Associate Exam Practice

Answer the following questions. Write your answers on a separate sheet of paper.

1. Which line widths are recommended by ASME Y14.2? *Select all that apply.*
   A. extra fine
   B. thin
   C. thick
   D. 3X
   E. 4X

2. Which of the following line characteristics would you typically assign to a layer for drawing object lines on a mechanical part view drawing? *Select the one item that best answers the question.*
   A. thick, HIDDEN linetype
   B. 4X, Continuous linetype
   C. extra fine, Continuous linetype
   D. 0.3 mm, Continuous linetype
   E. 0.6 mm, Continuous linetype

3. Which of the following operations are possible on a locked layer? *Select all that apply.*
   A. drawing new objects
   B. editing objects
   C. erasing objects
   D. selecting objects
   E. displaying objects on-screen

AutoCAD Certified Professional Exam Practice

Follow the instructions in each problem. Write your answers on a separate sheet of paper.

1. **Navigate to this chapter on the Student Web site and open CPE-05linetype.dwg.** Create a new layer called Centerline and assign it the color blue. Load the CENTER linetype and apply it to the Centerline layer. Then select the existing line and change it to the Centerline layer. Enter **LTSCALE** and specify a linetype scale of 2.0. The centerline linetype consists of long dashes alternating with short dashes. How many *short* dashes appear on the line at the current linetype scale?

2. **Navigate to this chapter on the Student Web site and open CPE-05layers.dwg.** Use the **Layer Control** drop-down list and the **Layer Properties Manager** to find the following information: On which layer was Line A drawn, and what line-weight is assigned to that layer?

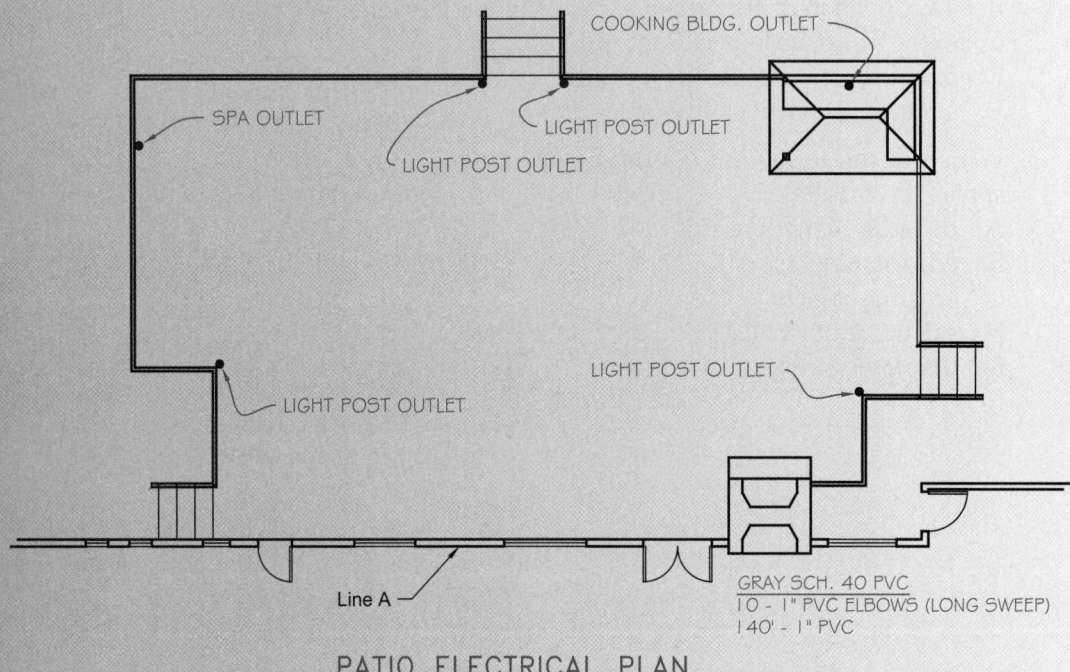

COOKING BLDG. OUTLET

SPA OUTLET

LIGHT POST OUTLET

LIGHT POST OUTLET

LIGHT POST OUTLET

LIGHT POST OUTLET

Line A

GRAY SCH. 40 PVC
10 - 1" PVC ELBOWS (LONG SWEEP)
140' - 1" PVC

PATIO ELECTRICAL PLAN
SCALE 1/8"=1'

6

View Tools and Basic Plotting

Learning Objectives

After completing this chapter, you will be able to do the following:

✓ Adjust the display window to view specific portions of a drawing.
✓ Use display tools transparently.
✓ Control object display order.
✓ Isolate or hide selected objects.
✓ Create named views for instant recall.
✓ Create multiple viewports in the drawing window.
✓ Perform general utility tasks such as regenerating and cleaning the screen.
✓ Print and plot drawings.

As you create drawings that are more complex and draw large and small objects, you will realize the importance of using view tools to adjust the drawing display. This chapter describes several view tools that you will use frequently during the drawing process. This chapter also introduces printing and plotting so that you can begin printing your drawings. Later chapters describe printing and plotting in more detail.

Navigation Bar

View tools are available from the ribbon, keyboard entry, shortcut menus, the navigation bar, SteeringWheels, and the ViewCube. This chapter introduces SteeringWheels and the ViewCube later. The navigation bar is a view toolbar positioned near the upper-right corner of the drawing window by default. See **Figure 6-1.** The navigation bar includes tool buttons for accessing common view tools associated with the current work environment. Right-click on a tool button or pick the **Settings** flyout to access options for changing the navigation bar.

A tool or option accessible from the navigation bar appears as a graphic in the margin of this textbook. The graphic indicates picking a navigation bar button. The example shown in this margin illustrates accessing the **Pan** tool from the navigation bar.

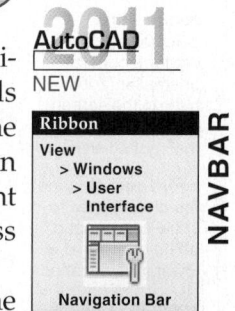

AutoCAD 2011
NEW

Ribbon
View
> Windows
> User Interface
Navigation Bar
Type
NAVBAR

NAVBAR

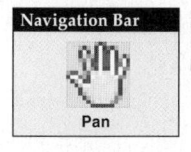

Navigation Bar
Pan

PAN

Figure 6-1.
The default
navigation bar in
model space. The
tools available from
the navigation bar
change when you
enter a different
work environment.

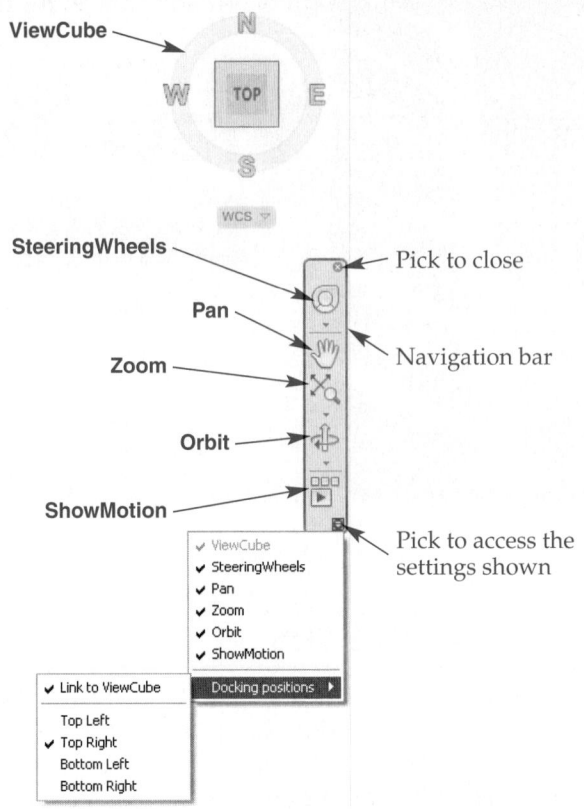

Some of the view tools available in the default **2D Drafting & Annotation** workspace are appropriate for 3D applications only. *AutoCAD and Its Applications—Advanced* explains 3D and animation view tools.

Zooming

zoom: Make objects appear bigger (zoom in) or smaller (zoom out) on the screen without affecting their actual size.

AutoCAD provides several methods for *zooming*. As described in Chapter 3, the easiest way to zoom is to use a mouse with a scroll wheel. To *zoom out*, roll the mouse wheel forward. To *zoom in*, roll the mouse wheel back. This technique also pans to the location of the crosshairs while zooming. Double-click the wheel to zoom to the furthest extents of objects in the drawing.

zoom out: Change the display area to show a larger part of the drawing at a lower magnification.

Additional zooming options are available from the **ZOOM** tool, depending on the portion of the drawing you want to display. The ribbon and navigation bar provide effective ways to access a **ZOOM** tool option, because they provide a direct link to the individual tool options. See **Figure 6-2**. In contrast, when you issue the **ZOOM** tool using dynamic input or the command line, you must choose a specific option to receive appropriate prompts.

zoom in: Change the display area to show a smaller part of the drawing at a higher magnification.

Figure 6-2. **ZOOM** tool options in the **Zoom** flyout on the **Navigate** panel of the **View** ribbon tab and on the navigation bar.

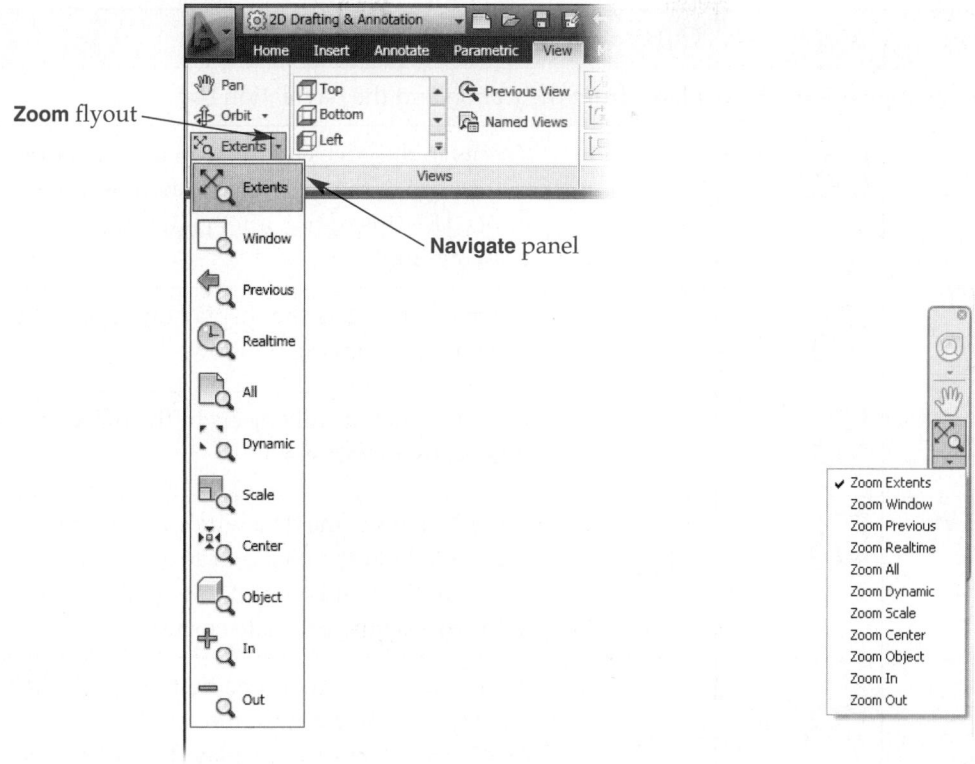

Ribbon   Navigation Bar

Realtime Zooming

Access the **Realtime** option to apply *realtime zooming*. The zoom cursor appears as a magnifying glass with plus and minus symbols. Press and hold the left mouse button and move the cursor up to zoom in or down to zoom out. Release the mouse button when you achieve the appropriate display. The **Realtime** option includes a shortcut menu that you can access while the zoom cursor is active. The menu provides a quick way to select an alternative view option, as described later in this chapter. When you are finished zooming, press [Esc], [Enter], or the space bar, or right-click and pick **Exit**.

realtime zoom: A zoom that you view as it occurs.

Additional Zoom Options

The mouse wheel and the **Realtime** option of the **ZOOM** tool are effective for most zooming requirements. Apply one of the other zoom options to achieve a specific display. **Figure 6-3** provides a brief description of the most useful options.

NOTE

The **Previous, In, Out, Center,** and **Dynamic** options of the **ZOOM** tool provide functions that you can achieve more easily using other view tools.

Figure 6-3. Zooming options available from the ribbon, the navigation bar, and the shortcut menu that appears when you right-click while using the **Realtime** option of the **ZOOM** tool.

Option	Button	Cursor	Function
The following options are available from the ribbon and the navigation bar.			
All			Zooms to the edges of the drawing limits, or to the edge of the geometry drawn past the limits. Use this option after changing the drawing limits.
Object			Zooms and centers the display on objects you select in the drawing window.
Extents*			Zooms to include all objects in the drawing (the "drawing extents").
Window*			Zoom to objects inside a window you create. Press and hold the pick button at the first corner of the window, and release the button at the diagonally opposite corner.
Scale			Zooms according to a specified magnification scale factor. The **nX** option scales the display relative to the current display. The **nXP** option scales a drawing in model space relative to paper space, as described later in this textbook.
The following options are available from the **Realtime** shortcut menu.			
Pan			Adjust the placement of the drawing on-screen using the **Realtime** option of the **PAN** tool.
Zoom			Return from the **Realtime** option of the **PAN** tool to the **Realtime** option of the **ZOOM** tool.
3D Orbit			View a 3D object as described in *AutoCAD and Its Applications—Advanced*.
Zoom Original		(No cursor)	Restores the previous display before any realtime zooming or panning occurred; useful if the modified display is not appropriate.

*Also available from the **Realtime shortcut menu.**

Exercise 6-1

Access the Student Web site (www.g-wlearning.com/CAD) and complete Exercise 6-1.

Panning

Ribbon

View
> Navigate

Navigation Bar

Type
PAN
P

PAN

The easiest way to *pan* is to use a mouse with a scroll wheel. Press and hold the mouse wheel and then move the mouse. An alternative is to access the **PAN** tool to apply *realtime panning*. The pan cursor appears as a hand. Press and hold the left mouse button and move the cursor in the direction to pan. Right-click to display the same shortcut menu available for realtime zooming. To exit realtime panning, press [Esc], [Enter], or the space bar, or right-click and pick **Exit**.

Another, but less effective, way to pan involves using drawing window scroll bars. To display the scroll bars, check **Display scroll bars in drawing window** in the **Window Elements** area of the **Display** tab in the **Options** dialog box.

pan: Change the drawing display so that different portions of the drawing are visible on-screen.

realtime panning: A panning operation in which you can see the drawing move on-screen as you pan.

> **NOTE**
>
> AutoCAD supports some high performance mice that include additional buttons and functions.

> **NOTE**
>
> By default, when you use the **U** tool after multiple zooming and panning operations, zooms and pans are grouped together, allowing you to return to the original view. To make each zoom and pan operation count individually, deselect the **Combine zoom and pan commands** check box in the **Undo/Redo** area of the **User Preferences** tab in the **Options** dialog box.

Exercise 6-2

Access the Student Web site (www.g-wlearning.com/CAD) and complete Exercise 6-2.

Introduction to SteeringWheels

Type
NAVSWHEEL

NAVSWHEEL

AutoCAD SteeringWheels provide an alternative way to access and use certain view tools. A *navigation wheel* is a specific SteeringWheel. Some navigation wheels and many of the tools available from navigation wheels are most appropriate for 3D modeling. This textbook focuses on the default navigation wheels and the **ZOOM**, **CENTER**, **PAN**, and **REWIND** tools for 2D applications. *AutoCAD and Its Applications—Advanced* explains the settings for navigation wheels.

The **Full Navigation Wheel** appears by default in model space, and the UCS icon changes to a 3D display. The **2D Navigation Wheel** is the only SteeringWheel available in layout space. See **Figure 6-4.** To access a different navigation wheel, select from the **SteeringWheels** flyout on the navigation bar, the shortcut menu that appears when you right-click while using a navigation wheel, or the flyout in the lower-right corner of a navigation wheel. The default format is big, but mini navigation wheels are available.

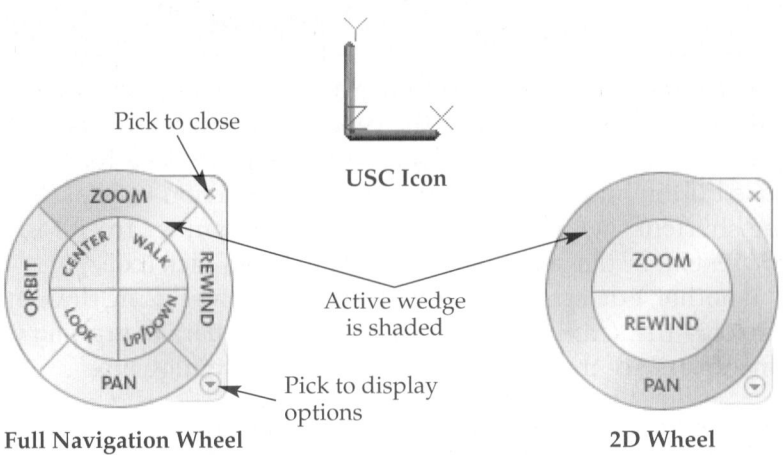

Figure 6-4.
The **Full Navigation Wheel** appears by default in model space. The **2D Wheel** is the only navigation wheel available in a layout. You can also display the **2D Wheel** in model space.

Pick to close

USC Icon

Active wedge is shaded

Pick to display options

Full Navigation Wheel

2D Wheel

wedges: The parts of a navigation wheel that contain navigation tools.

Navigation wheels display next to the cursor. *Wedges* contain the individual navigation tools and function similar to tool buttons. Hover over a wedge to highlight it. Some tools are activated when you pick a wedge, and other tools require that you hold down the left mouse button on the wedge.

A navigation wheel remains on-screen until you close it. This allows you to use multiple navigation tools. To close a navigation wheel, pick the **Close** button in the upper-right corner of the wheel, press [Esc], [Enter], or the space bar, or right-click and pick **Close Wheel**.

> **NOTE**
>
> The flyout in the lower-right corner of a navigation wheel provides access to other navigation wheels and SteeringWheel settings. The flyout also includes a **Fit to Window** option that zooms and pans to show all objects centered in the drawing window, and a **Close Wheel** option.

Zooming with the Navigation Wheel

The **ZOOM** navigation tool offers realtime zooming. Press and hold the left mouse button on the **ZOOM** wedge on the **Full Navigation Wheel** to display the pivot point icon and zoom navigation cursor. See **Figure 6-5.** The pivot point is the location where you press the **ZOOM** wedge. Move the zoom navigation cursor up or to the right to zoom in. Move the cursor down or to the left to zoom out. The pivot point icon also zooms in or out as a visual aid to zooming. Release the left mouse button when you achieve the appropriate display.

Using the Center Navigation Tool

The **CENTER** navigation tool centers the display screen at a picked point, without zooming. Press and hold the left mouse button on the **CENTER** wedge. The pivot point icon appears when you move the cursor over an object. Release the mouse button to pan so the object at the pivot point is displayed in the center of the drawing window when you release the mouse button. See **Figure 6-6.**

Figure 6-5.
To use the **ZOOM** navigation tool, hold down the left mouse button and move the cursor up or to the right to zoom in, or down or to the left to zoom out.

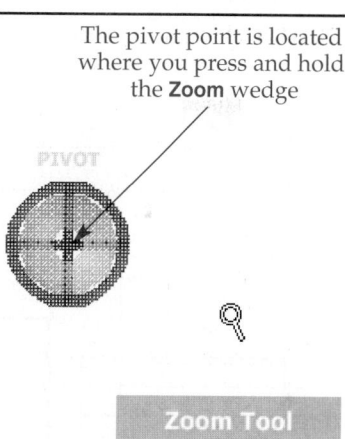

The pivot point is located where you press and hold the **Zoom** wedge

Zoom Tool

Figure 6-6.
To use the **CENTER** navigation tool, hold down the left mouse button and move the cursor over an object at the point you want to center in the drawing area and release the left mouse button.

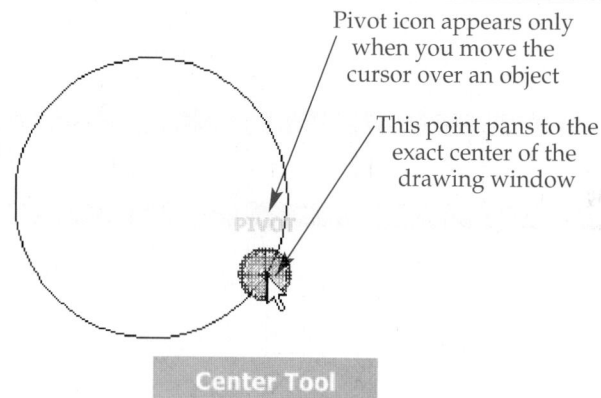

Pivot icon appears only when you move the cursor over an object

This point pans to the exact center of the drawing window

Center Tool

Panning with the Navigation Wheel

The **PAN** navigation tool offers realtime panning. Press and hold the left mouse button on the **PAN** wedge to display the pan navigation cursor. Move the pan navigation cursor in the direction to pan. Release the left mouse button when you achieve the desired display.

Rewinding

The **REWIND** navigation tool allows you to observe display changes and return to a previous display. For example, if you use the navigation wheel to zoom in, then pan, then zoom out, you can rewind through each action and return to the original zoomed-in display, the panned display, and then back to the current zoomed-out display. You can rewind through view actions created using most view tools, not just navigation wheel tools.

Pick the **REWIND** tool once to return to the previous display. Thumbnail images appear in frames as the previous view is restored. The thumbnail with an orange frame surrounded by brackets indicates the restored display and its location in the sequence of events. See **Figure 6-7**. Pick the **REWIND** button repeatedly to cycle back through prior views. Another option is to press and hold the left mouse button on the **REWIND** wedge to display the framed view thumbnails. Then, while still holding the left mouse button, move the brackets left over the thumbnails to cycle through earlier views, and right to return to later views. Release the left mouse button when you achieve the desired display.

Figure 6-7. Use the **REWIND** navigation tool to step back through and restore previous display configurations.

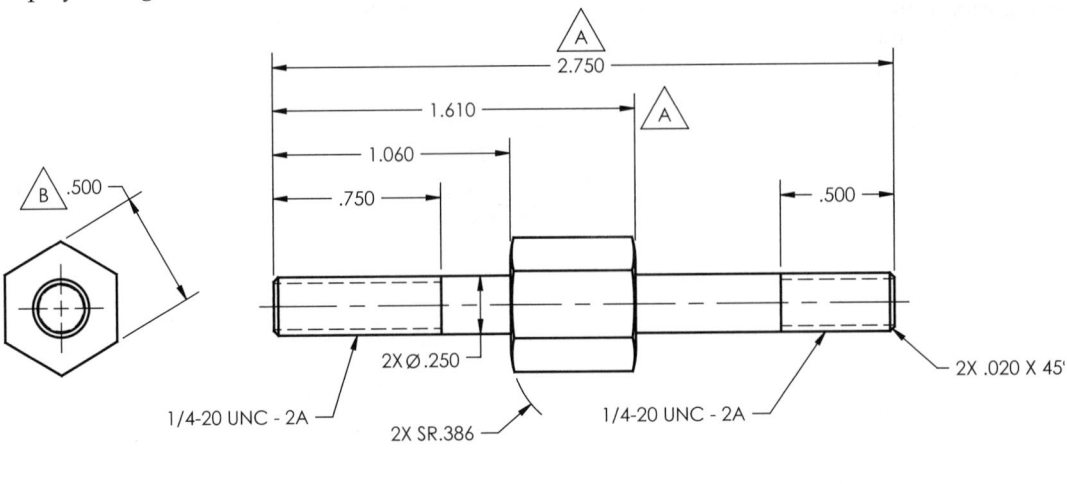

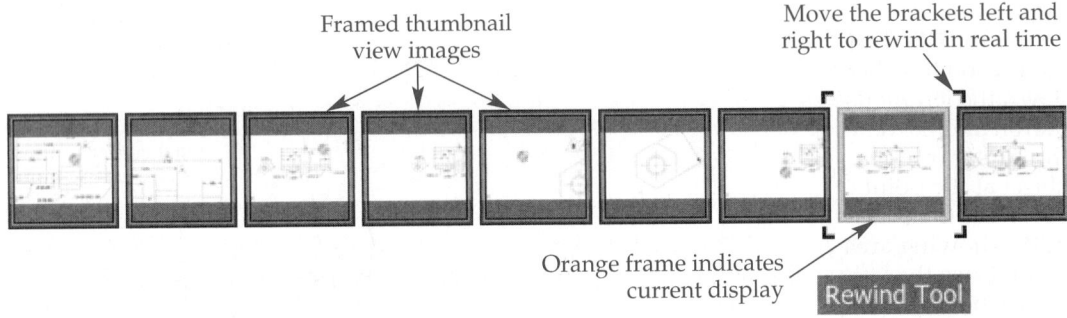

Framed thumbnail view images

Move the brackets left and right to rewind in real time

Orange frame indicates current display

Rewind Tool

NOTE

If you access and use a view tool from a source other than the navigation wheel, such as the ribbon, a rewind icon appears in place of the thumbnail. A thumbnail displays as you move the brackets over the rewind icon.

Exercise 6-3

Access the Student Web site (www.g-wlearning.com/CAD) and complete Exercise 6-3.

AutoCAD 2011
NEW

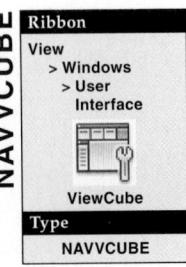

NAVVCUBE

Ribbon
View
> Windows
> User
Interface
[icon]
ViewCube
Type
NAVVCUBE

Introduction to the ViewCube

The ViewCube appears near the upper-right corner of the drawing window by default. See **Figure 6-8**. The ViewCube includes a **WCS** menu that is useful for some 2D drawing applications. However, the primary purpose of the ViewCube is to view a 3D model precisely using a labeled cube. Until you are ready to create 3D models, use the **NAVVCUBE** tool to turn off the ViewCube. If you change the view orientation, pick the **Home** button and then the **TOP** face to return to the default 2D view. *AutoCAD and Its Applications—Advanced* provides complete information on the ViewCube.

Figure 6-8.
This is how the
ViewCube should
look when you
create a 2D drawing.

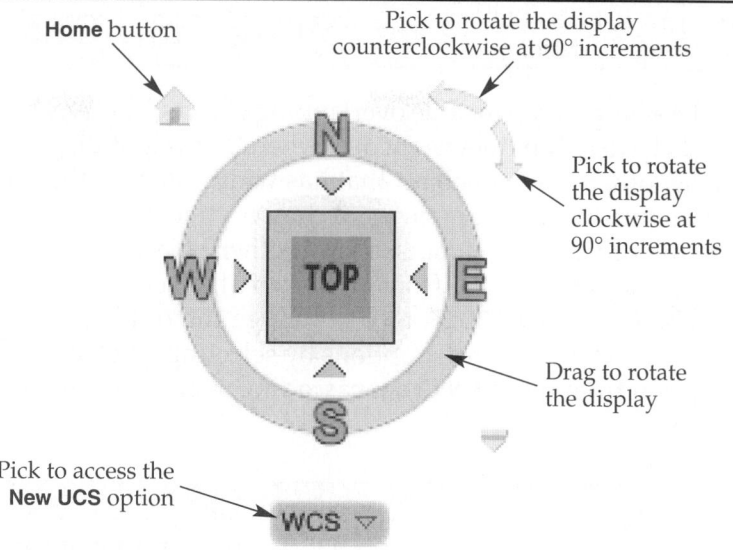

Home button

Pick to rotate the display
counterclockwise at 90° increments

Pick to rotate
the display
clockwise at
90° increments

Drag to rotate
the display

Pick to access the
New UCS option

WCS ▽

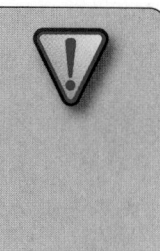
Rotating the display of the 2D drawing plane using a tool such as the **ViewCube** is inappropriate for most 2D applications. The coordinate system may not behave as expected. For example, text, which should always be horizontal, may appear at an unacceptable angle. Use the **ROTATE** tool to rotate *objects* as needed in 2D drawings, not just the display.

Using Tools Transparently

Activating a tool usually cancels the tool in progress and starts the new tool. However, you can use some tools *transparently*. After completing the transparent operation, the interrupted tool resumes. Therefore, it is not necessary to cancel the initial tool. You can use many display tools transparently, including **PAN**, **ZOOM**, SteeringWheels, and the ViewCube.

An example of when transparent tools are useful is drawing a line when one end of the line is somewhere off the screen. One option is to cancel the **LINE** tool, zoom out, and then reactivate the **LINE** tool. A more efficient method is to use **PAN** or **ZOOM** transparently with the **LINE** tool. To do so, begin the **LINE** tool and pick the first point. At the Specify next point: prompt, pan or zoom to display the next line endpoint. You can use any access method, but using the mouse wheel is often quickest. When the correct view appears, pick the second line endpoint. You can also activate tools transparently by typing an apostrophe (') before the tool name. For example, to enter the **ZOOM** tool transparently, type 'Z or 'ZOOM.

transparently:
When referring
to tool access,
describes
temporarily
interrupting the
active tool to use a
different tool.

PROFESSIONAL TIP

You can activate and adjust drawing aids such as **Grid**, **Snap**, and **Ortho** transparently. However, the quickest activation and adjustment methods are using the appropriate button on the status bar or pressing a function key.

Controlling Draw Order

Drawings often include overlapping objects. The overlap is difficult to see when all objects have a thin lineweight and when lineweight display is off. To help understand display order, view an object that has width, such as the donuts shown in **Figure 6-9**. The donuts in this example were drawn after the other objects. You can change the drawing order of the donuts, and all other objects, to place the items above or below selected objects or to the front or back of all objects.

Use the **DRAWORDER** tool to change the order of objects in a drawing. You can also set certain draw order options by selecting an object, right-clicking, and choosing an option from the **Draw Order** cascading submenu. **Figure 6-10** describes draw order options.

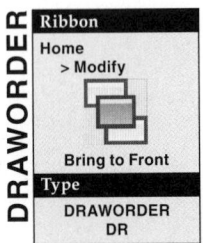

DRAWORDER

Ribbon
Home
> Modify
Bring to Front

Type
DRAWORDER
DR

NOTE

You may need to use the **DRAWORDER** tool on several objects until the objects display correctly. Objects move to the front of the drawing when you modify them.

Figure 6-9.
Change the order of objects to place selected objects under or above other objects.

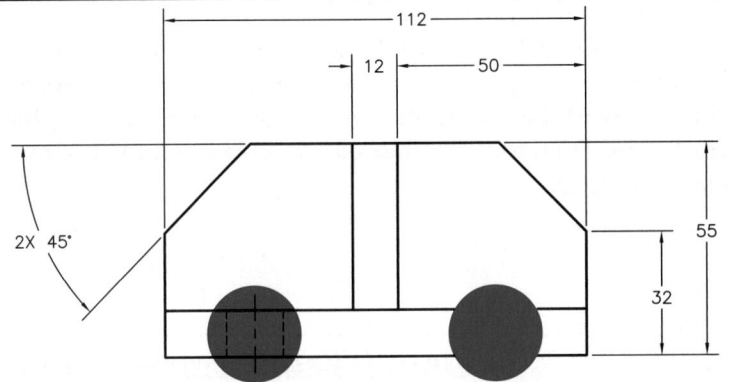

Figure 6-10.
The options available for rearranging the order of objects in a drawing. The text, dimension, and hatch options are available from the ribbon and apply to all text, dimension, or hatch objects in the drawing.

Option	Function
Bring to Front	Places the selected objects at the front of the drawing.
Send to Back	Places the selected objects at the back of the drawing.
Bring Above Objects	Moves the selected objects above the reference object.
Send Under Objects	Moves the selected objects below the reference object.
ABC Bring Text to Front	Places all text objects above other objects.
Bring Dimensions to Front	Places all dimension objects above other objects.
Send Hatches to Back	Moves all hatch objects below other objects.

Exercise 6-4

Access the Student Web site (www.g-wlearning.com/CAD) and complete Exercise 6-4.

Isolating or Hiding Objects

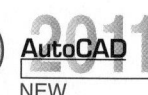
NEW

Layer states allow you to use layers to control the display of objects. AutoCAD includes other tools that allow you to display (isolate) or hide only selected objects. These functions are view tools for temporarily isolating or hiding objects to clarify the drawing and focus on specific items.

Access the **ISOLATEOBJECTS** tool to hide all objects except the objects you pick. An easy way to access the tool is to pick the **Isolate Objects** button on the right end of the status bar and pick the **Isolate Objects** option, or right-click and select **Isolate Objects** from the **Isolate** cascading submenu. See **Figure 6-11A.** Pick the objects to isolate as shown in **Figure 6-11B.**

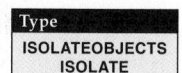

Access the **HIDEOBJECTS** tool to hide the objects you pick. An easy way to access the tool is to pick the **Isolate Objects** status bar button followed by the **Hide Objects** option, or right-click and select **Hide Objects** from the **Isolate** cascading submenu. Pick the objects to hide as shown in **Figure 6-11C.**

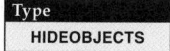

You can use the **ISOLATEOBJECTS** and **HIDEOBJECTS** tools at the same time to isolate and hide objects. You can also add objects to the set of isolated or hidden objects as needed.

Use the **UNISOLATEOBJECTS** tool to redisplay all hidden objects. An easy way to access the tool is to pick the **Isolate Objects** status bar button followed by the **End Object Isolation** option, or right-click and select **End Object Isolation** from the **Isolate** cascading submenu.

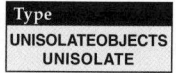

NOTE

The status bar tray icon indicates whether the drawing includes isolated or hidden objects. Use the **OBJECTISOLTATIONMODE** system variable to control whether isolation and hiding remains active when you close and reopen a drawing.

Exercise 6-5

Access the Student Web site (www.g-wlearning.com/CAD) and complete Exercise 6-5.

Figure 6-11. A—Use the status bar or shortcut menu to access object isolation and hiding tools. B—An example of using the **ISOLATEOBJECTS** tool and window selection to show only objects within a portion of a mechanical part view. C—An example of using the **HIDEOBJECTS** tool to hide several dimension and multileader objects on a structural detail.

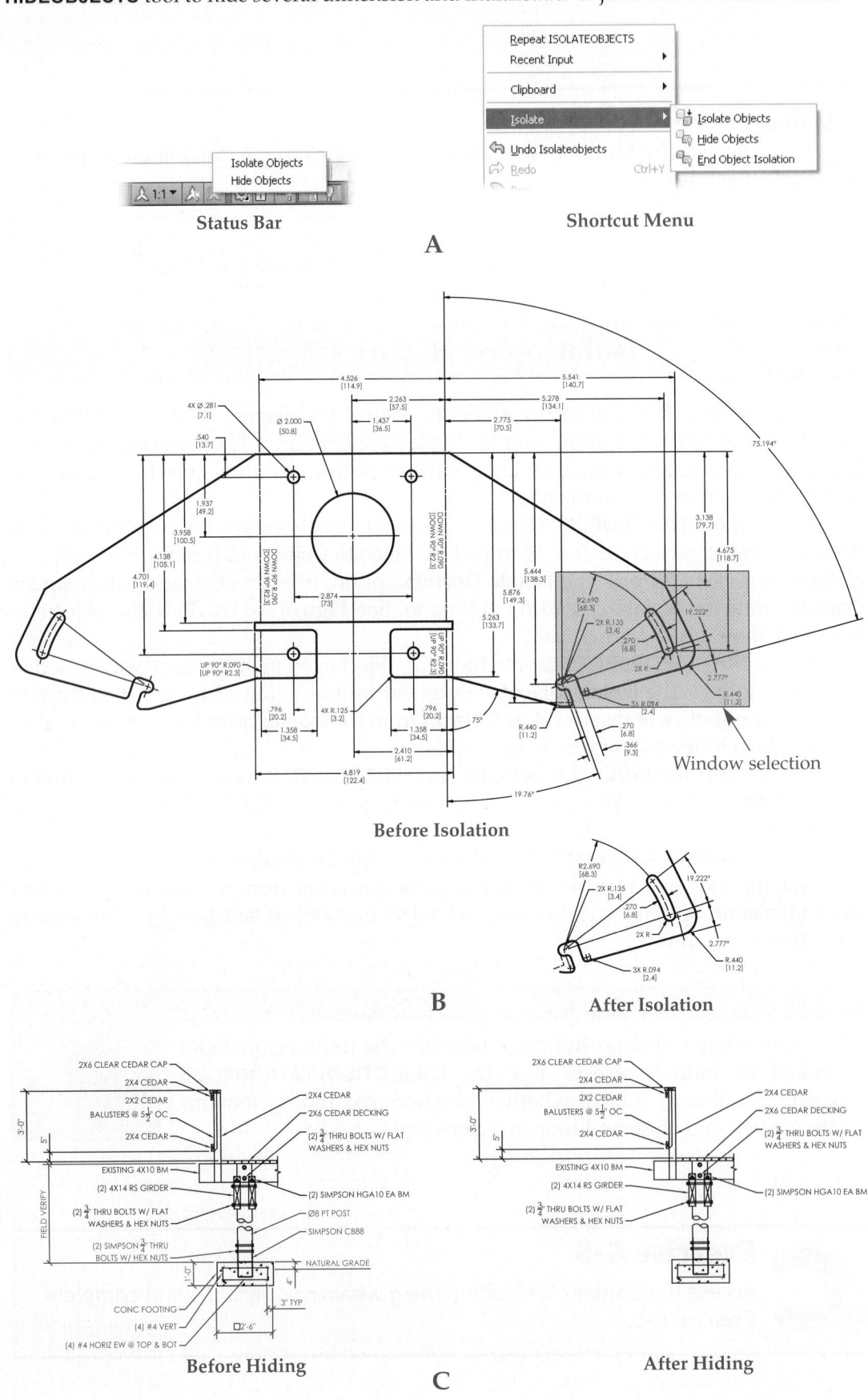

Status Bar

Shortcut Menu

A

Window selection

Before Isolation

After Isolation

B

Before Hiding

C

After Hiding

Named Views

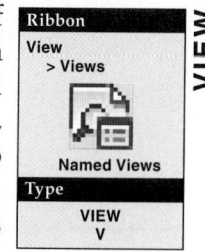

Use the **View Manager** to save a *named view*. A named view can be a portion of the drawing, such as a mechanical part drawing view or detail or a room or area on an architectural floor plan. A named view can also show an entire design or enlarged area. The advantage of naming views is that you can quickly recall a specific display, without searching for objects or using multiple view tools. Named views are also important to sheet sets, as explained in Chapter 32.

Figure 6-12 shows the **View Manager** and an architectural example that includes named views. The tree on the left side of the **View Manager** lists each type of view. Pick a view type to display information about the type. Pick the plus sign (+) to list related views, except for **Current**. The **Current** node lists the properties of the current display in the drawing window. The **Model Views** node lists named model views, and the **Layout Views** node lists named layout views. The **Preset Views** node lists all preset orthogonal and isometric views. This chapter focuses on the use of named model views. You will learn about layout views later in this textbook. *AutoCAD and Its Applications— Advanced* explains preset views.

named view: A specific drawing display saved for easy recall and future use, analogous to taking a picture.

Figure 6-12. Use the **View Manager** to assign new named views and to control existing named views. This example shows a named view of an overall floor plan titled FLOOR PLAN. The other named views display specific remodel areas for easy recall and future use.

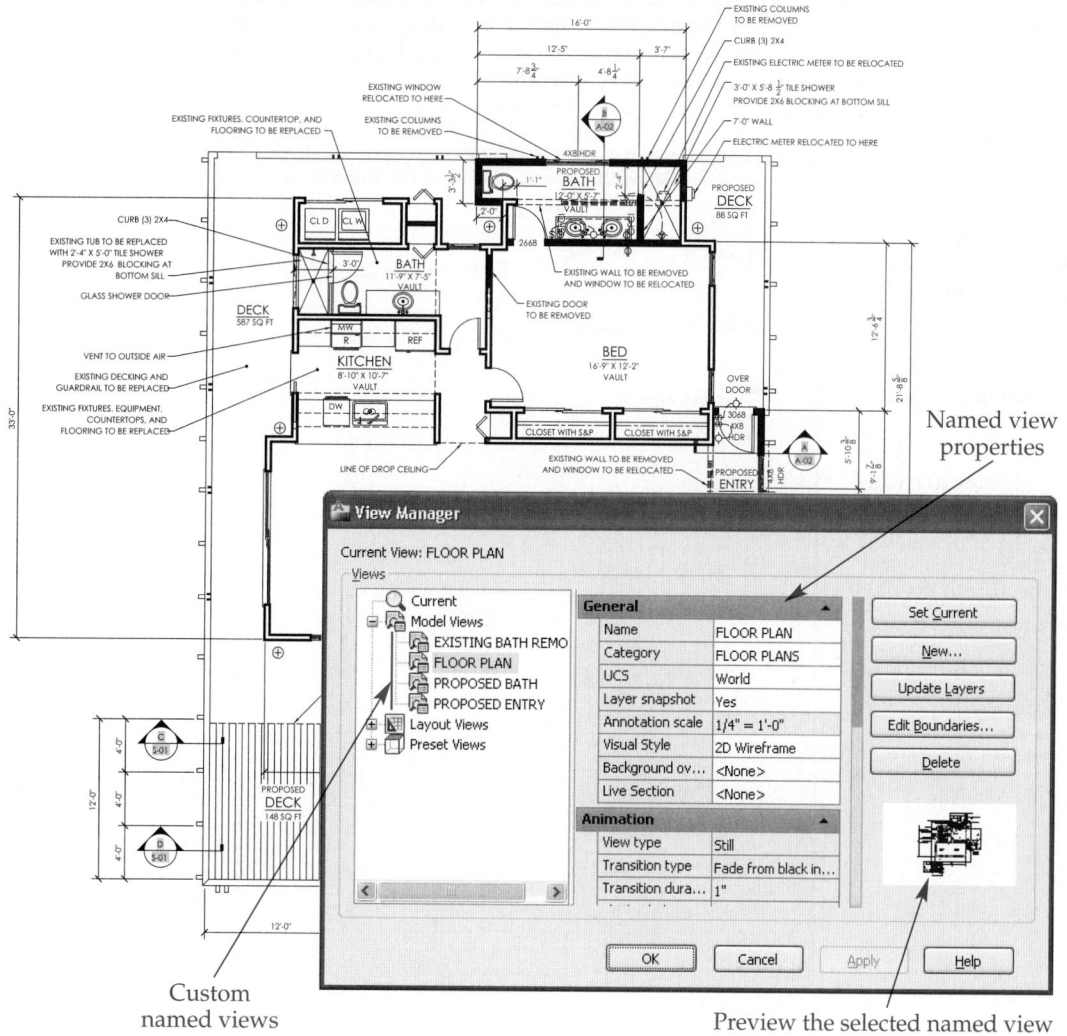

Named view properties

Custom named views

Preview the selected named view

Pick a model view to list its properties in the middle portion of the **View Manager**. You can modify some properties, such as **Name**. Other properties are read-only and are set during view configuration. The right side of the **View Manager** contains buttons to create and control views. The options are also available from the shortcut menu that appears when you right-click on a view.

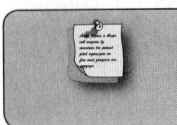

New Views

To save a display as a named view, pick the **New...** button or right-click on a view node or view and select **New...** to access the **New View/Shot Properties** dialog box. See **Figure 6-13A.** Type the view name in the **View name:** text box.

To create a basic 2D view, select **Still** from the **View type** drop-down list, and focus on the settings in the **View Properties** tab. The **Current display** radio button, which is the default, prepares the view boundary according to the current display in the drawing window. To construct a view boundary, pick the **Define window** radio button. The **New View/Shot Properties** dialog box disappears temporarily so you can pick two opposite

---

Figure 6-13. A—Use the **New View/Shot Properties** dialog box to save the current display as a view, or define a window to set as the view. B—Specifying a view boundary using the **Define window** option. This example shows creating a view boundary around the proposed bathroom that corresponds to the PROPOSED BATH named view.

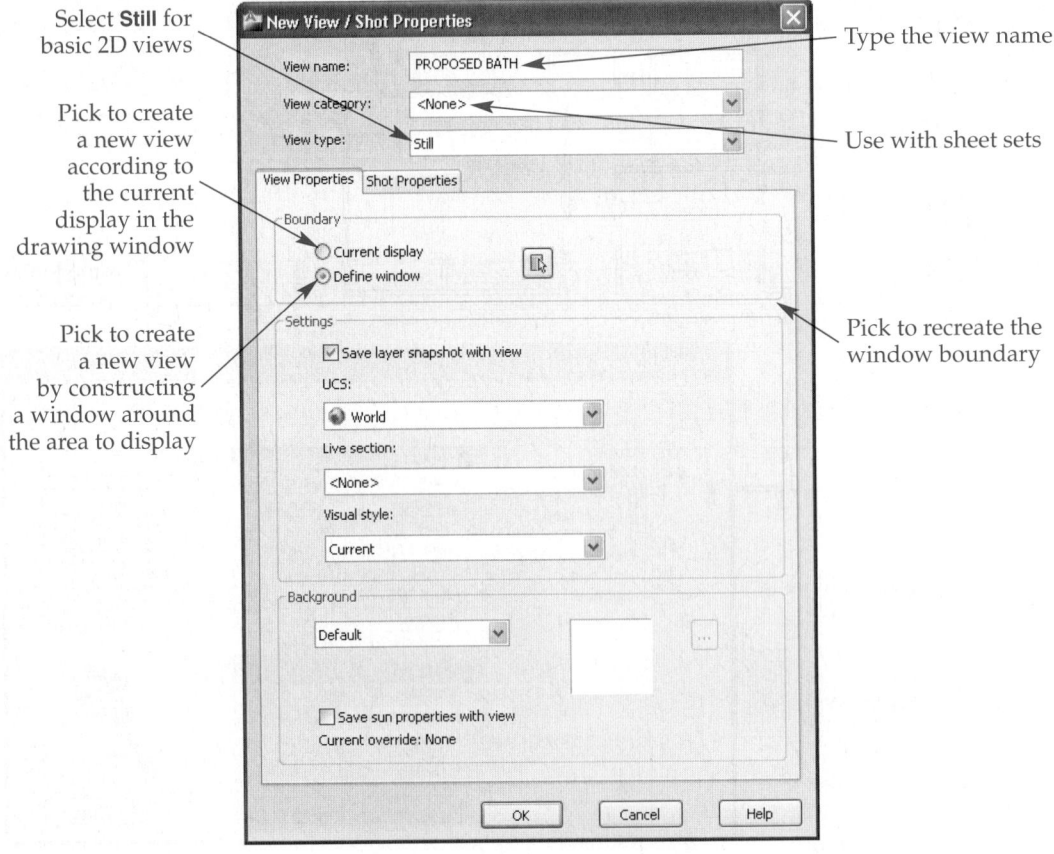

A

corners to define a window around the area to display. See **Figure 6-13B**. Press [Enter] or right-click to return to the **New View/Shot Properties** dialog box.

Select the **Save layer snapshot with view** check box to save the current layer settings when you save the new view. Saved layer settings are then recalled each time the view is set current. Pick the **OK** button to add the view name to the list in the **View Manager**. Pick the **OK** button in the **View Manager** to finish the new view and exit.

NOTE

AutoCAD and Its Applications—Advanced describes the other options in the **New View/Shot Properties** dialog box, which are applicable to 3D model animations and the UCS (user coordinate system).

Figure 6-13. Continued.

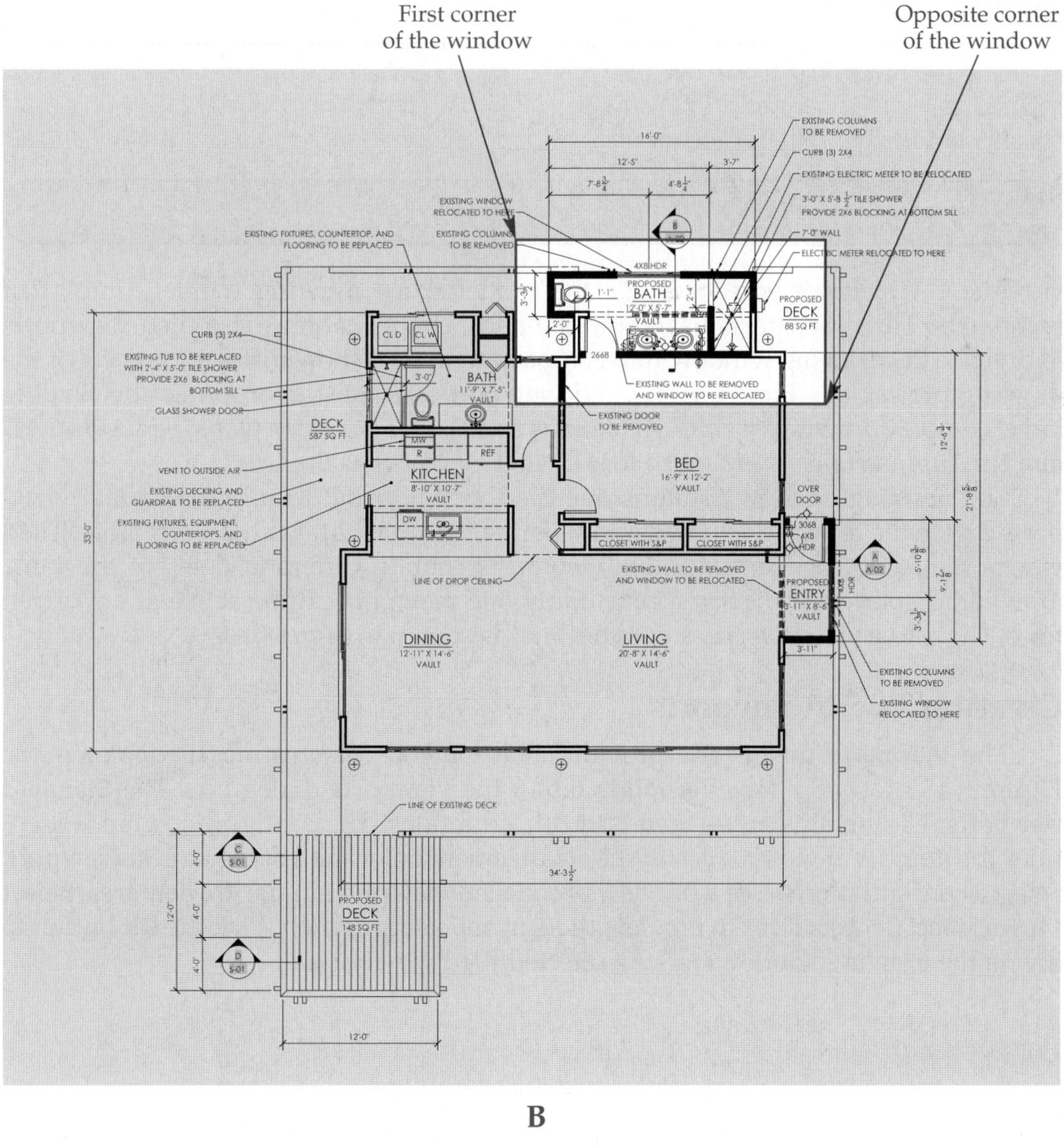

First corner of the window

Opposite corner of the window

B

Activating a View

To display a named view in the drawing window without accessing the **View Manager**, select the view from the list in the **Views** panel of the **View** ribbon tab. To make a named view current from inside the **View Manager**, select the view from the list and pick the **Set Current** button or right-click and choose **Set Current**. The name of the current view appears in the **Current View:** label above the **Views** area. Pick the **Apply** button to display the view, or pick the **OK** button to display the view and exit the dialog box.

Managing Views

Return to the **View Manager** to adjust named views using the appropriate button or shortcut menu option. Apply the **Update Layers** feature to update layers displayed in the view according to changes made to layer states. Use the **Edit Boundaries...** function to define or redefine the view boundary using a window. Use the **Delete** function to remove a named view from the drawing.

Exercise 6-6

Access the Student Web site (www.g-wlearning.com/CAD) and complete Exercise 6-6.

Tiled Viewports

tiled viewports: A window or frame within which a drawing is visible in model space.

AutoCAD allows you to divide the model space drawing window into *tiled viewports*. Tiled viewports have both 2D and 3D applications. Use tiled viewports to divide a 2D drawing window into compartments that show different aspects of the drawing project. See **Figure 6-14**. Tiled viewports are most appropriate for viewing large, complex drawings, such as site plans and profiles or floor plans. See *AutoCAD and Its Applications—Advanced* for 3D tiled viewport examples.

The drawing window contains one tiled viewport by default. Additional viewports divide the drawing window into separate tiles that butt against each other. Tiled viewports cannot overlap. Multiple viewports contain different views of the same drawing, displayed at the same time. Only one viewport can be active at any given time. The active viewport has a bold outline, as shown in **Figure 6-14**.

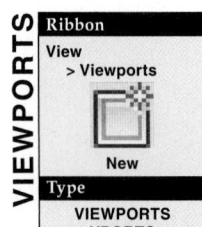

Creating Tiled Viewports

The **Viewports** dialog box provides one method for creating tiled viewports. **Figure 6-15** shows the **New Viewports** tab of the **Viewports** dialog box. The **Standard viewports:** list contains preset viewport configurations. The configuration name identifies the number of viewports and the arrangement or location of the largest viewport. Select a configuration to see a preview of the tiled viewports in the **Preview** area. Select *Active Model Configuration* to preview the current configuration. Pick the **OK** button to divide the drawing window into the selected tiled viewports.

Figure 6-14. A basic example of a mechanical part drawing viewed using three tiled viewports. Each viewport contains the same drawing, but can present a unique display. Titled viewports are most useful when you are viewing large, complex drawings.

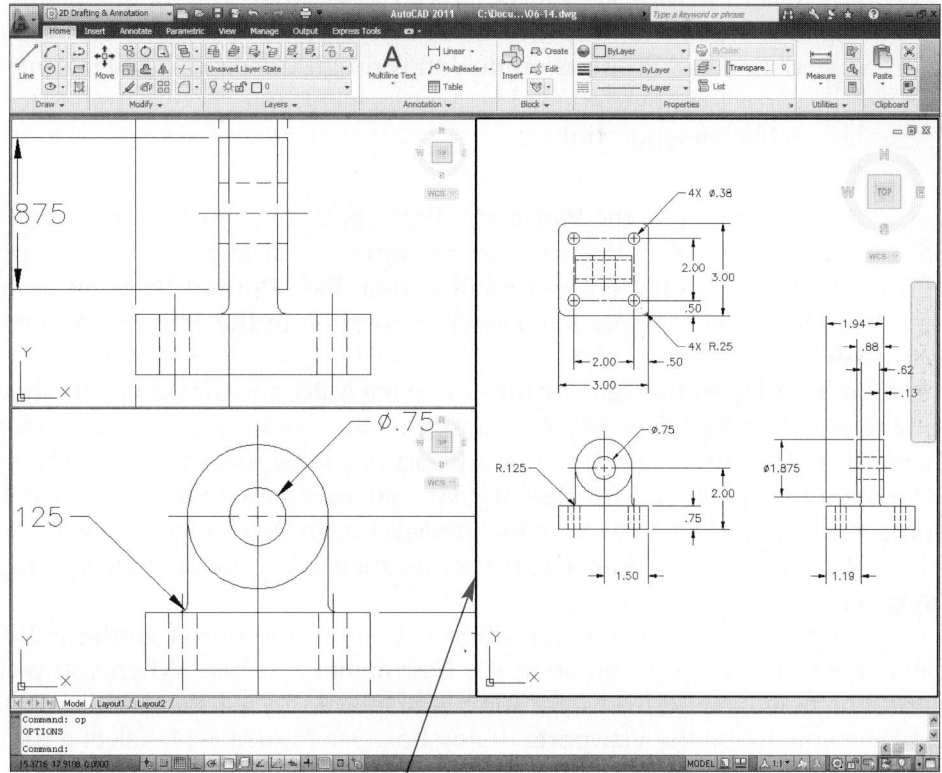

Thick outline around the active viewport

Figure 6-15. Specify the number and arrangement of tiled viewports in the **New Viewports** tab of the **Viewports** dialog box.

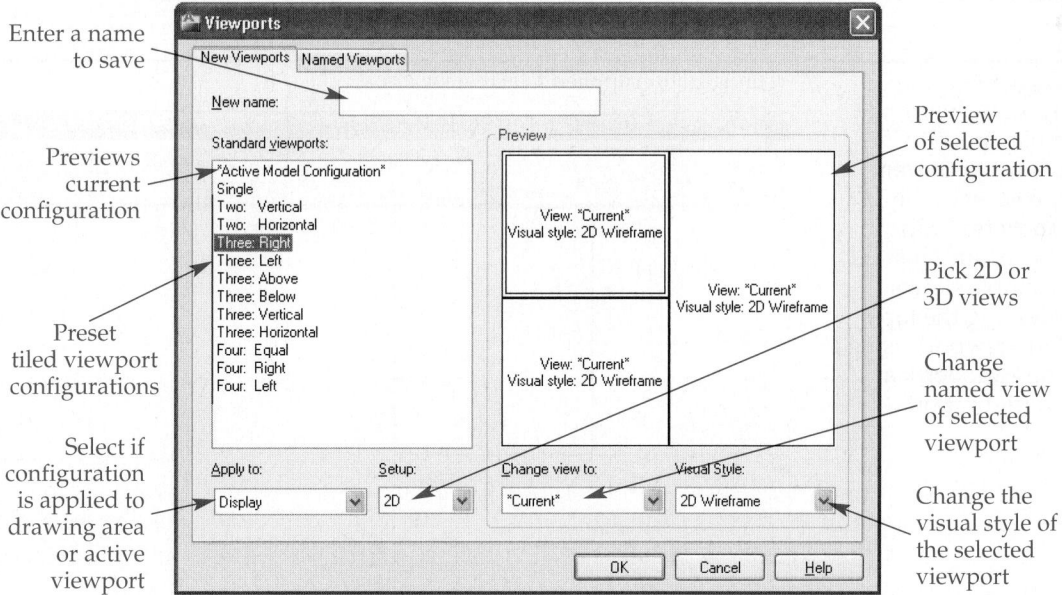

The additional options in the **Viewports** dialog box are useful when two or more viewports already exist. Select **Display** from the **Apply to:** drop-down list to apply the viewport configuration to the entire drawing area. Pick **Current Viewport** from the **Apply to:** drop-down list to apply the new configuration in the active viewport only. See **Figure 6-16.**

The default setting in the **Setup:** drop-down list is **2D**, and all viewports show the 2D drawing plane, or top view. If you choose the **3D** option, the different viewports display various 3D views of the drawing. At least one viewport shows a 3D isometric view. The other viewports show different views, such as a top view or side view. The viewport configuration is displayed in the **Preview** image. To change a view in a viewport, pick the viewport in the **Preview** image and then select the new viewpoint from the **Change view to:** drop-down list.

Create a unique viewport configuration if none of the preset configurations is acceptable. Enter a descriptive name in the **New name:** text box. When you pick the **OK** button, the new viewport configuration is displayed in the **Named Viewports** tab the next time you access the **Viewports** dialog box. See **Figure 6-17.** Select a different named viewport configuration and pick **OK** to apply changes to the drawing area. Named viewport configurations apply to the active viewport only.

Figure 6-16.
You can subdivide a viewport by choosing **Current Viewport** in the **Apply to:** drop-down list. This example shows dividing the top-left viewport using the **Two: Vertical** configuration.

Configuration applied to active viewport

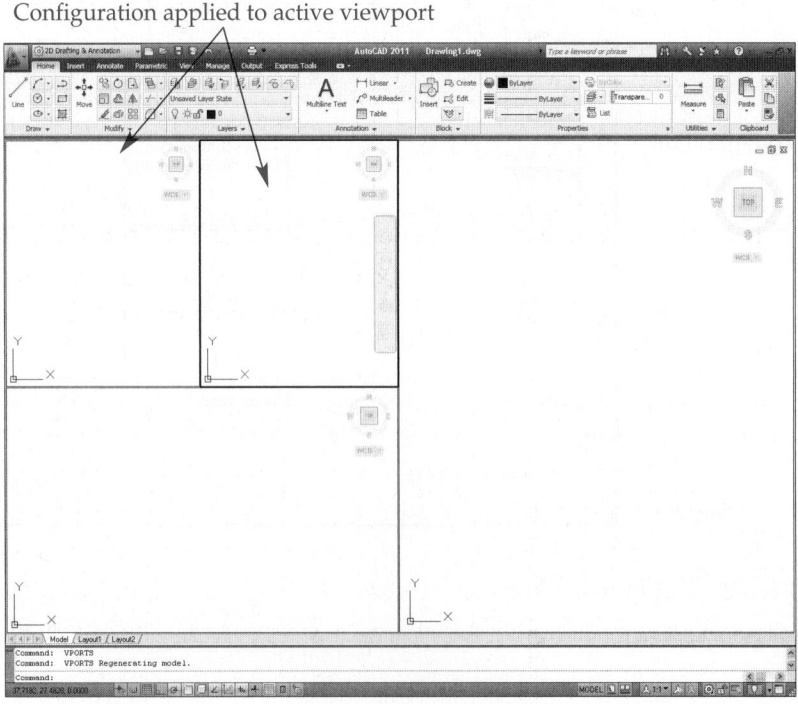

Figure 6-17. The **Named Viewports** tab displays custom viewports.

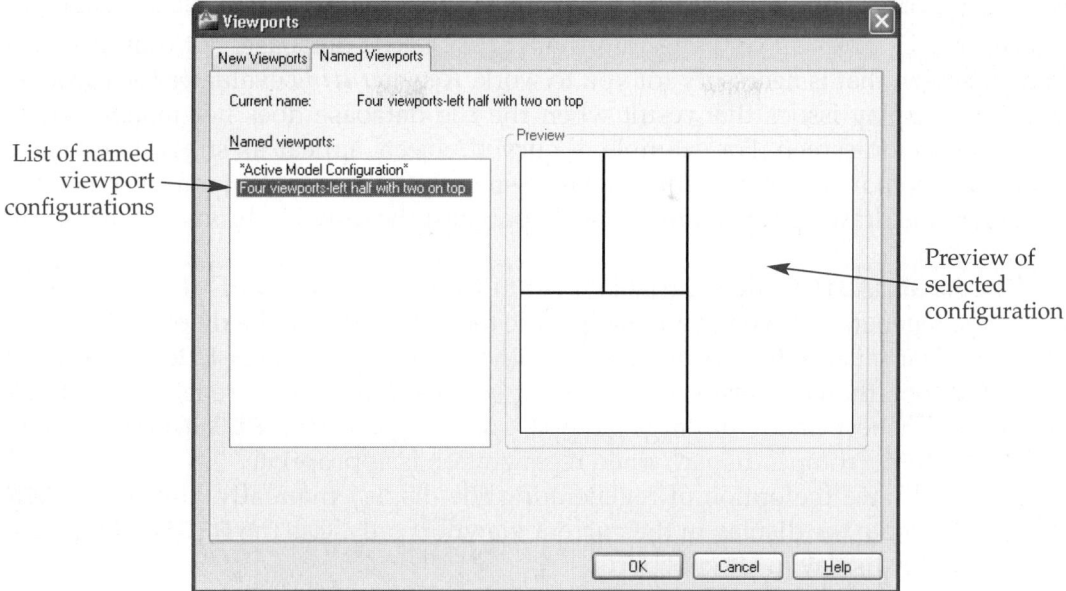

List of named viewport configurations

Preview of selected configuration

Working in Tiled Viewports

After you select the viewport configuration and return to the drawing area, move the mouse and notice that only the active viewport contains crosshairs. The cursor is an arrow in the other viewports. To make an inactive viewport active, move the cursor into the inactive viewport and pick.

Depending on the zoom level, as you draw in one viewport, objects appear in other viewports. Try drawing lines and other shapes and notice how drawing affects the viewports. Use a display tool, such as **ZOOM**, in the active viewport and notice the results. Only the active viewport reflects the use of the **ZOOM** tool.

Joining Tiled Viewports

Use the **Join Viewports** tool to join two viewports. Select the dominant viewport, which is the viewport that shows the view you want to display in the joined viewport, or press [Enter] to select the active viewport. Then select the viewport to join with the dominant viewport. AutoCAD joins the two viewports together and retains the dominant view.

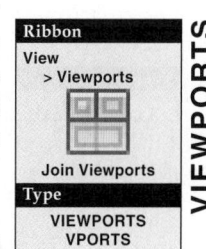

Ribbon

View
> Viewports

Join Viewports

Type

VIEWPORTS
VPORTS

VIEWPORTS

NOTE

The two viewports you join cannot create an L-shape viewport. The adjoining edges of the viewports must be the same size in order to join.

Exercise 6-7

Access the Student Web site (www.g-wlearning.com/CAD) and complete Exercise 6-7.

Regenerating the Screen

regenerating: Recalculating and redisplaying all objects on-screen to correspond to the information in the file database.

AutoCAD stores all drawing information in the file database, but only displays data on-screen that is necessary for you to work. *Regenerating* evaluates the drawing to correct display issues that result when the file database does not match exactly what you see on-screen. For example, if curved objects appear as straight segments when you zoom in, regenerate the display to smooth the curves. You may also need to regenerate the drawing if you are unable to pan past the drawing limits or the current display area.

The **REGENAUTO** system variable is set to **ON** by default. AutoCAD performs an automatic regeneration when you use specific tools that change the display. Examples of actions that cause automatic regeneration include using the **All** or **Extents** option of the **ZOOM** tool, thawing layers, or switching layouts. If automatic regeneration takes too much time, especially on large, complex drawings, set the **REGENAUTO** system variable to **OFF.** Prompts display when regeneration is appropriate.

You also have the option of regenerating the display manually. Use the **REGEN** tool to regenerate the display in the current viewport only. Use the **REGENALL** tool to regenerate the display in all viewports.

Type
REGEN

Type
REGENALL

redrawing: An process that was once useful for refreshing the screen display without regenerating the drawing.

NOTE

Redrawing is different from regenerating, and is an old function that was important when computers and graphics were slower and less advanced. The **REDRAW** tool redraws the display of the current viewport only. The **REDRAWALL** tool redraws the display in all viewports. *Regenerate* the display when necessary.

Cleaning the Screen

Type
[Ctrl]+[0]

The AutoCAD window can become crowded with multiple interface items, such as palettes, in the course of a drawing session. As the drawing area gets smaller, less of the drawing is visible, and drafting becomes more difficult. Use the **Clean Screen** tool to clear the AutoCAD window of all palettes, toolbars, and title bars. See **Figure 6-18.** An easy way to toggle the **Clean Screen** tool is to pick the **Clean Screen** button on the far right side of the status bar.

PROFESSIONAL TIP

The **Clean Screen** tool can be helpful when displaying multiple drawings. The active drawing appears when you use the **Clean Screen** tool. This allows you to work more efficiently within one of the drawings.

Supplemental Material

View Transitions and Resolution
For information about view transitions and view resolution, go to the Student Web site (www.g-wlearning.com/CAD), select this chapter, and select **View Transitions and Resolution.**

Figure 6-18.
Using the **Clean Screen** tool.
A—Initial display with the **Properties** palette and **Layer Properties Manager** displayed.
B—Display after using the **Clean Screen** tool.

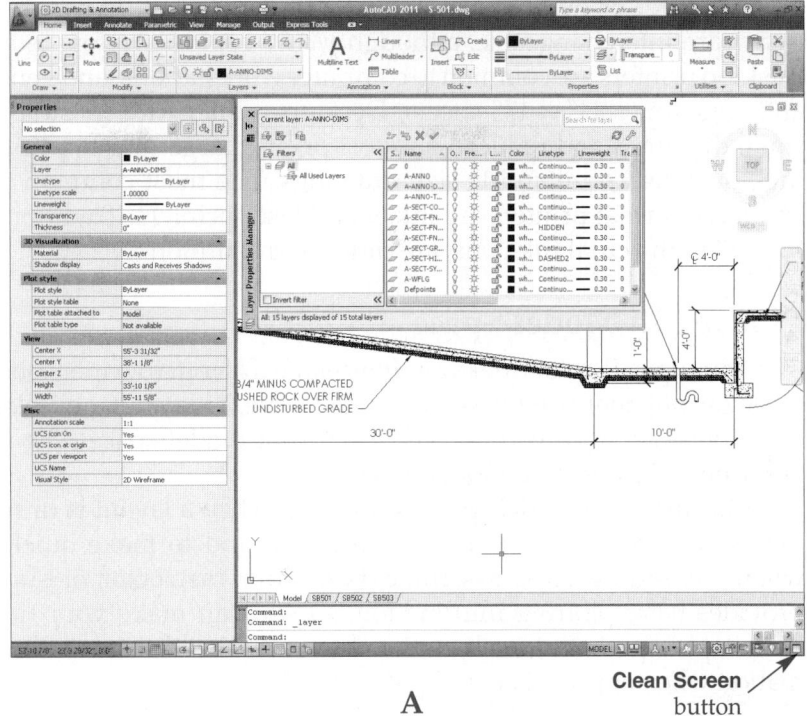

A

Clean Screen button

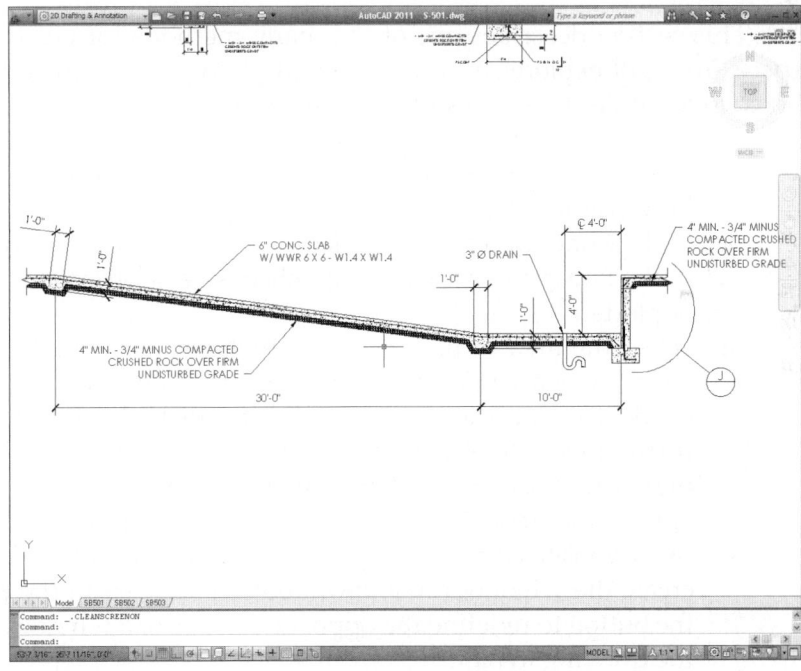

B

Introduction to Printing and Plotting

A *soft copy* appears on the computer monitor, making a drawing inconvenient to use for many manufacturing and construction purposes. A *hard copy* is useful on the shop floor or at a construction site. A design team can check and redline a hard copy without a computer or CADD software. CADD is the standard throughout the world for generating drawings, and electronic data exchange is becoming increasingly popular. However, hard-copy drawings are still a vital tool for communicating a design.

soft copy: The electronic data file of a drawing.

hard copy: A physical drawing produced by a printer or plotter.

A printer or plotter transfers soft copy images onto paper. The terms *printer* and *plotter* are interchangeable, although *plotter* typically refers to a large-format printer. Desktop printers are common to computer workstations, and generally print 8 1/2″ × 11″ and sometimes 11″ × 17″ sheets. Desktop printers are most appropriate for printing small drawings and reduced-size test prints. Large-format printers print larger drawings, such as C-size and D-size drawings. The most common types of both desktop and large-format printers are inkjet and laser printers. Traditional pen plotters, which "draw" with actual ink pens, are much less common.

Plotting in Model Space

You typically plot final drawings using a layout in paper space. A layout represents the sheet of paper used to organize and scale, or lay out, and plot or export a drawing or model. However, you can also plot from model space. The following information describes plotting from model space only.

Plotting from model space is common when a layout is unnecessary, to view how model space objects will appear on paper, and to make quick hard copies, such as when submitting basic assignments to your instructor or supervisor. This chapter provides basic plotting information, so you can make your first plot. This textbook fully explains creating and plotting layouts and additional printing and plotting information when appropriate.

Making a Plot

This section describes one of the many methods for creating a plot from model space. You will explore several additional plot options and settings later in the textbook. Refer to **Figure 6-19** as you read the following plotting procedure.

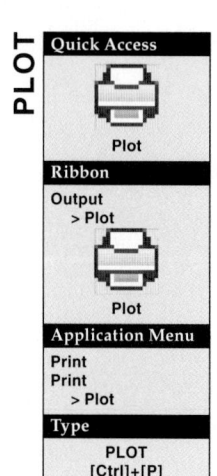

PLOT

Quick Access

Plot

Ribbon

Output
> Plot

Plot

Application Menu

Print
Print
> Plot

Type

PLOT
[Ctrl]+[P]

1. Access the **Plot** dialog box. If the column on the far right of the dialog box shown in **Figure 6-19** is not visible, pick the **More Options** button (>) in the lower-right corner.
2. In the **Printer/plotter** area, select a local or network printer or plotter.
3. In the **Paper size** area, choose a sheet size appropriate for the selected printer or plotter.
4. Select the area to plot from the **Plot area** section. The **Limits** option is the default when you plot from model space, and allows you to plot everything inside the specified drawing limits. Pick the **Extents** option to plot the furthest extents of objects in the drawing. Select the **Display** option to plot the current screen display, exactly as shown. When you select the **Window** option, the **Page Setup** dialog box disappears temporarily so you can pick two opposite corners to define a window around the area to plot. Once you create the window, a **Window...** button appears in the **Plot area** section. Pick the button to redefine the opposite corners of a window around the portion of the drawing to plot.
5. Select an option in the **Drawing orientation** area. Choose **Portrait** to orient the drawing vertically (*portrait*) or **Landscape** to orient the drawing horizontally (*landscape*). The **Plot upside-down** option rotates the drawing 180° on the paper.
6. Set the scale in the **Plot scale** area. The scale is a ratio of inches or millimeters to drawing units. Select a scale from the **Scale:** drop-down list or type values in the custom fields. Choose the **Fit to paper** check box to let AutoCAD increase or decrease the plot scale to fill the paper.

portrait: A vertical paper orientation.

landscape: A horizontal paper orientation.

Figure 6-19.
The **Plot** dialog box.

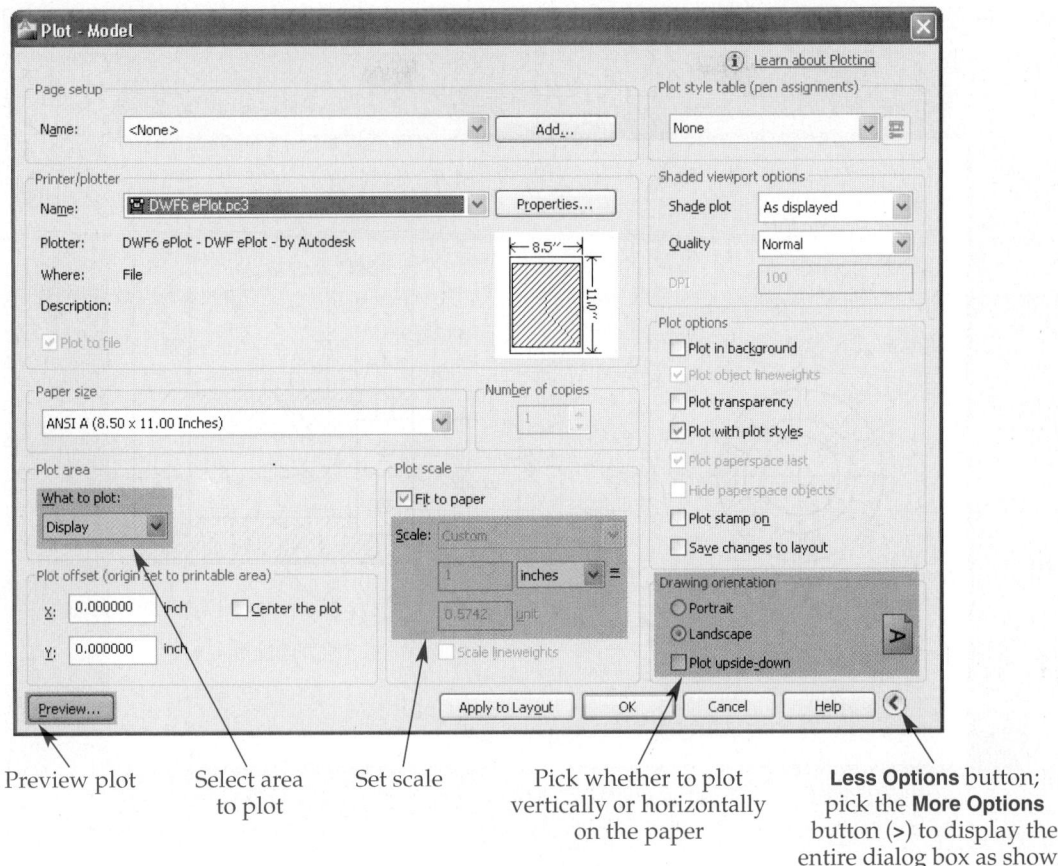

Preview plot — Select area to plot — Set scale — Pick whether to plot vertically or horizontally on the paper — **Less Options** button; pick the **More Options** button (>) to display the entire dialog box as shown

7. If necessary, use the **Plot offset (origin set to printable area)** area to set additional left and bottom margins around the plot, or to center the plot.
8. Pick the **Preview...** button to display the sheet as it will look when it plots. See **Figure 6-20.** The cursor appears as a magnifying glass with + and – symbols. Hold the left mouse button and move the cursor to increase or decrease the displayed image to view more or less detail. Press [Esc] to exit the preview.
9. Pick the **OK** button in the **Plot** dialog box to send the data to the plotting device.

Exercise 6-8

Access the Student Web site (www.g-wlearning.com/CAD) and complete Exercise 6-8.

Figure 6-20. A plot preview of mechanical part views drawn in model space. The preview shows exactly how the drawing will appear on paper.

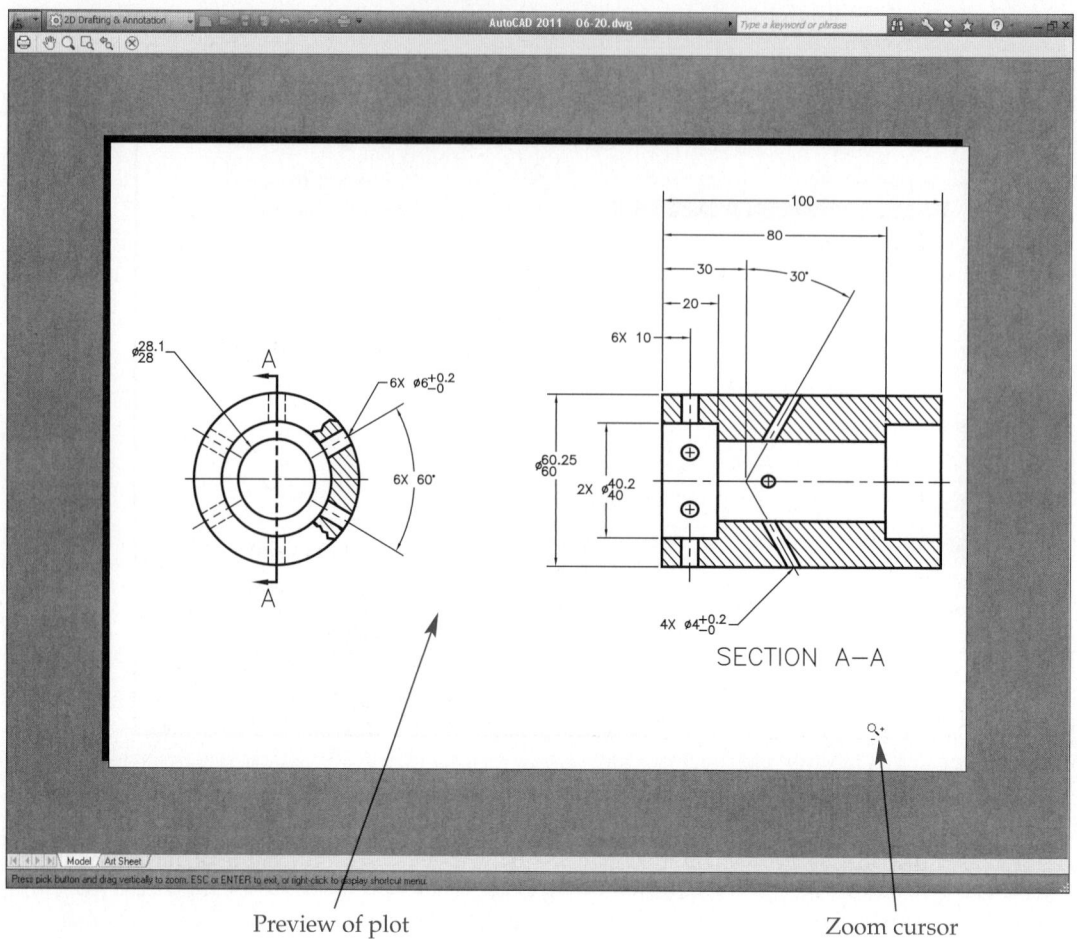

Preview of plot   Zoom cursor

Template Development
Chapter 6

For instructions on zooming to the drawing limits in each template, go to the Student Web site (www.g-wlearning.com/CAD), select this chapter, and select **Template Development**.

Chapter Test

Answer the following questions. Write your answers on a separate sheet of paper or go to the Student Web site (www.g-wlearning.com/CAD) and complete the electronic chapter test.

1. Briefly explain how to use the **Realtime** zoom option.
2. What is the difference between zooming and panning?
3. Which **SteeringWheels** navigation tools are most appropriate for 2D drafting applications?
4. Explain how to use the **CENTER** tool on the **Full Navigation Wheel**.
5. What feature of the **Full Navigation Wheel** allows you to return to previous display settings?

6. Why should you avoid using the ViewCube to rotate the display of a 2D drawing?
7. How do you enter a display tool transparently at the keyboard?
8. Which tool changes the order in which objects are displayed in a drawing?
9. Explain the difference between using layer states and object isolation or object hiding to hide objects.
10. How do you create a named view of the current screen display?
11. How do you display an existing named view?
12. What type of viewport occurs in model space?
13. How can you specify whether a new viewport configuration applies to the entire drawing window or the active viewport?
14. Explain the procedures and conditions that must exist for joining viewports.
15. Provide an example when regenerating the display is necessary.
16. Which tool regenerates all of the viewports?
17. Define *hard copy* and *soft copy*.
18. Identify four ways to access the **Plot** dialog box.
19. Describe the difference between the **Display** and **Window** options in the **Plot area** section of the **Plot** dialog box.
20. What is the major advantage of doing a plot preview?

Drawing Problems

Start AutoCAD if it is not already started. Start a new drawing from scratch or use an appropriate template of your choice. The template should include layers for drawing the given objects. Add layers as needed. Draw all objects using appropriate layers. Follow the specific instructions for each problem. Use only drawing tools and techniques you have already learned. Do not draw dimensions or text. Use your own judgment and approximate dimensions when necessary.

▼ Basic

1. Draw the surface-mounted fluorescent light fixture shown below. Zoom in and out on the drawing. Pan the screen display. Save the drawing as **P6-1**. Print an 8.5″ × 11″ copy of the drawing extents, fit to paper, using a portrait orientation.

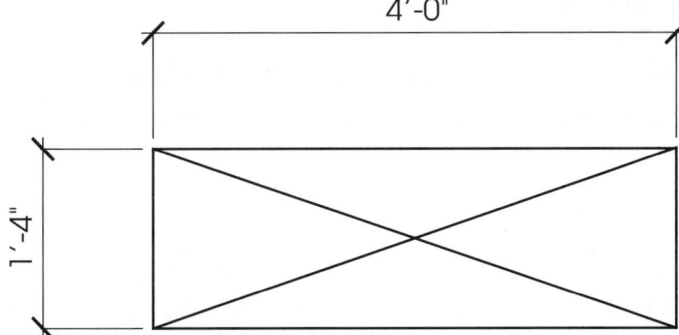

Surface-Mounted Fluorescent Fixture

2. Draw the surface-mounted light fixture shown below. Zoom in and out on the drawing. Pan the screen display. Save the drawing as P6-2. Print an 8.5″ × 11″ copy of the drawing extents, fit to paper, using a portrait orientation.

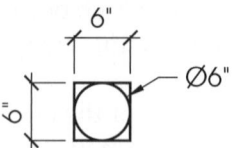

Surface-Mounted Fixture

3. Open the drawing named VW252-03-1200.dwg in the AutoCAD 2011\Sample\Sheet Sets\Manufacturing folder. Pick the Model tab below the drawing window to activate model space. Zoom to the extents of the drawing. Zoom in on each drawing view. Use a variety of view tools to view the gears in the full side view, the partial side views, and the isometric view. Close the drawing without saving.

4. Open the drawing named A-02.dwg in the AutoCAD 2011\Sample\Sheet Sets\ Architectural folder. Pick the Model tab below the drawing window to activate model space. Zoom to the extents of the drawing and print using the **Fit to paper** option. Use a variety of view tools to locate and view the following items:
   A. Front elevation.
   B. Doors on the right elevation
   C. Downspouts on the rear elevation.
   D. Column on the left elevation.
   E. Main entrance.

   Mark the location of each item on your hard copy. Close the drawing without saving.

5. Open the drawing named Erosion Control Plan.dwg in the AutoCAD 2011\Sample\ Sheet Sets\Civil folder. Pick the Model tab below the drawing window to activate model space. Zoom to the extents of the drawing and print using the **Fit to paper** option. Use a variety of view tools to locate and view the following items on the plan:
   A. Coburn Avenue.
   B. Proposed track and field.
   C. Proposed high school.
   D. Proposed tennis courts.
   E. Two proposed baseball fields.
   F. Two proposed softball fields.
   G. Accessible parking near the northeast corner of the high school.

   Mark the location of each item on your hard copy. Close the drawing without saving.

▼ Intermediate

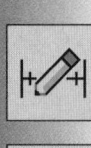

6. Create a freehand sketch of the default navigation bar that appears in model space. Label each tool button and briefly describe those tools that are most appropriate for 2D drafting applications.

7. Create a freehand sketch of the **Full Navigation Wheel**. Label each wedge and briefly describe those tools that are most appropriate for 2D drafting applications.

8. Draw the gasket shown. Save the drawing as P6-8. Print an 8.5″ × 11″ copy of the drawing extents, using a 1:1 scale and a landscape orientation.

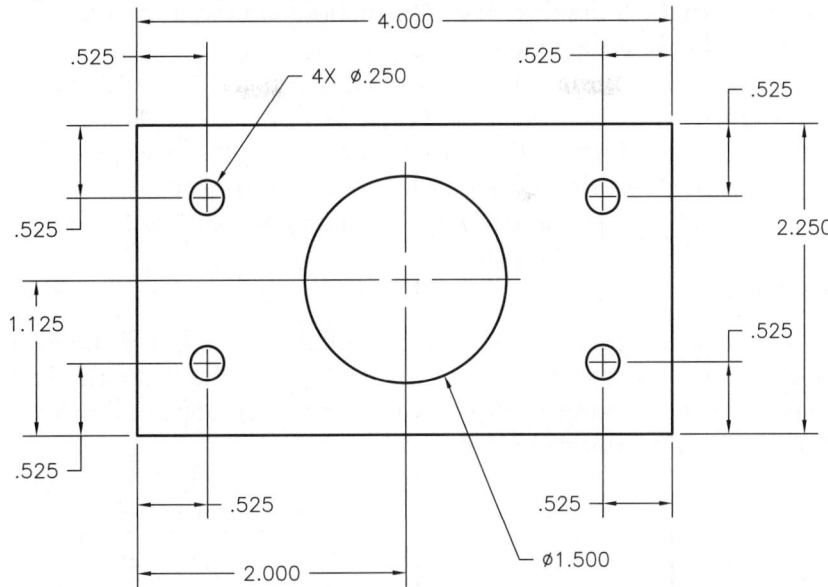

9. Open the drawing named blocks_and_tables_-_imperial.dwg at www.autodesk.com/autocad-samples. Save a copy of the drawing as P6-9. The P6-9 file should be active. Perform the following display functions on the drawing:

   A. Pick the Model tab to switch the drawing to model space.
   B. Zoom to the drawing extents.
   C. Zoom to create a display of the dining room and create a view of this display named Dining Room.
   D. Zoom to create a display of the kitchen and create a view of this display named Kitchen.
   E. Zoom to create a display of the master bedroom suite and create a view of this display named Master Suite.
   G. Display the view named Dining Room.
   H. Resave the drawing.

▼ Advanced

10. Open the drawing named Kitchens.dwg in the AutoCAD 2011\Sample\DesignCenter folder. Save a copy of Kitchen as P6-10. The P6-10 file should be active. Perform the following display functions on the drawing:

   A. Zoom to the drawing extents.
   B. Zoom in on each symbol and research if necessary to identify what the symbol represents.
   C. Create a named view of the extents of each symbol using the **Define Window** option in the **New View** dialog box. Use an appropriate name for each view.
   D. Systematically make each named view current. Edit the boundary if the view does not behave as anticipated.
   E. Resave the drawing.

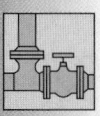

11. Open the drawing named Pipe Fittings.dwg in the AutoCAD 2011\Sample\ DesignCenter folder. Save a copy of Pipe Fittings as P6-11. The P6-11 file should be active. Perform the following display functions on the drawing:
   A. Zoom to the drawing extents.
   B. Zoom in on each symbol and research if necessary to identify what the symbol represents.
   C. Create a named view of the extents of each symbol using the **Define Window** option in the **New View** dialog box. Use an appropriate name for each view.
   D. Systematically make each named view current. Edit the boundary if the view does not behave as anticipated.
   E. Resave the drawing.

12. Draw the enclosed gazebo roof and floor plan shown. Use dimensions based on your experience or research. Zoom in and out on the drawing. Pan the screen display. Save the drawing as P6-12. Print an 8.5″ × 11″ copy of the drawing extents, fit to paper, using a portrait orientation.

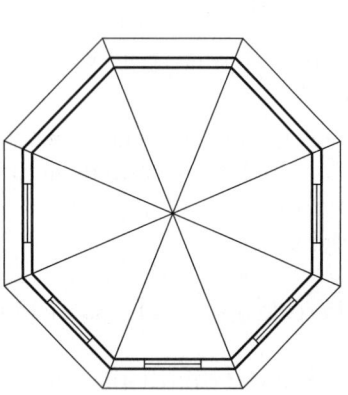

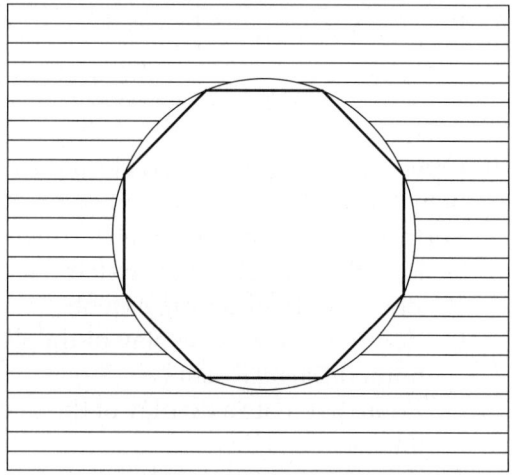

13. Research the design of an existing exercise dumbbell with the following specifications: steel, one-piece hexagon shape, five pounds. Create a dimensioned 2D sketch of the existing design from manufacturer's specifications or from measurements taken from an actual dumbbell. Research the mass properties of steel to design the dumbbell to weigh exactly five pounds. Start a new drawing from scratch or use a decimal-unit template of your choice. Draw the dumbbell from your sketch. Save the drawing as P6-13. Print an 8.5″ × 11″ copy of the drawing extents, using a 1:1 scale and a landscape orientation. Do not dimension the drawing.

AutoCAD Certified Associate Exam Practice

Answer the following questions. Write your answers on a separate sheet of paper.

1. Which of the following actions enters a view tool or drawing aid transparently? *Select all that apply.*
   A. picking a button on the status bar
   B. picking a button on the ribbon
   C. picking a button on the navigation bar
   D. typing a colon (:) before the tool name
   E. using the mouse wheel

2. How can you display a named view in a drawing? *Select all that apply.*
   A. select the view from the list in the **Views** panel of the **View** ribbon tab
   B. type the view name at the command line
   C. double-click the view name in the **View Manager**
   D. right-click and select the view name

3. When a drawing contains two or more tiled viewports, how can you activate a different viewport? *Select all that apply.*
   A. press the [F3] key
   B. press the space bar
   C. pick anywhere in the viewport to activate
   D. right-click and select the view to activate

AutoCAD Certified Professional Exam Practice

Follow the instructions in each problem. Write your answers on a separate sheet of paper.

1. **Navigate to this chapter on the Student Web site and open CPE-06zoom.dwg.**
   Use the view tool of your choice to zoom in on the notes in the lower-left corner of the drawing. Which ANSI standard should be used to interpret the graphic symbols for the electrical and electronic elements in this drawing?

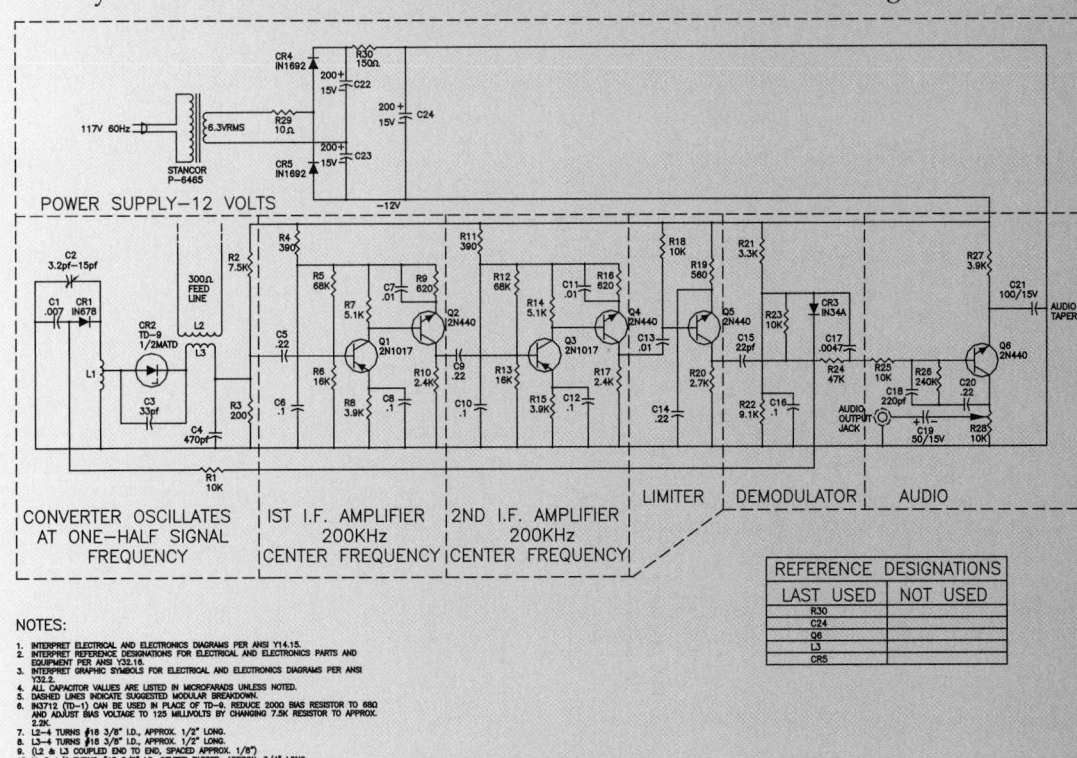

2. **Navigate to this chapter on the Student Web site and open CPE-06viewport.dwg.**
   Create tiled viewports using the **Three: Left** viewport configuration. In the left
   viewport, zoom to the drawing extents. In the top-right viewport, zoom to show
   the general drawing notes (not shown here). Answer the following questions.
   A. What is the scale of VIEW A?
   B. What is the current revision level for this drawing?

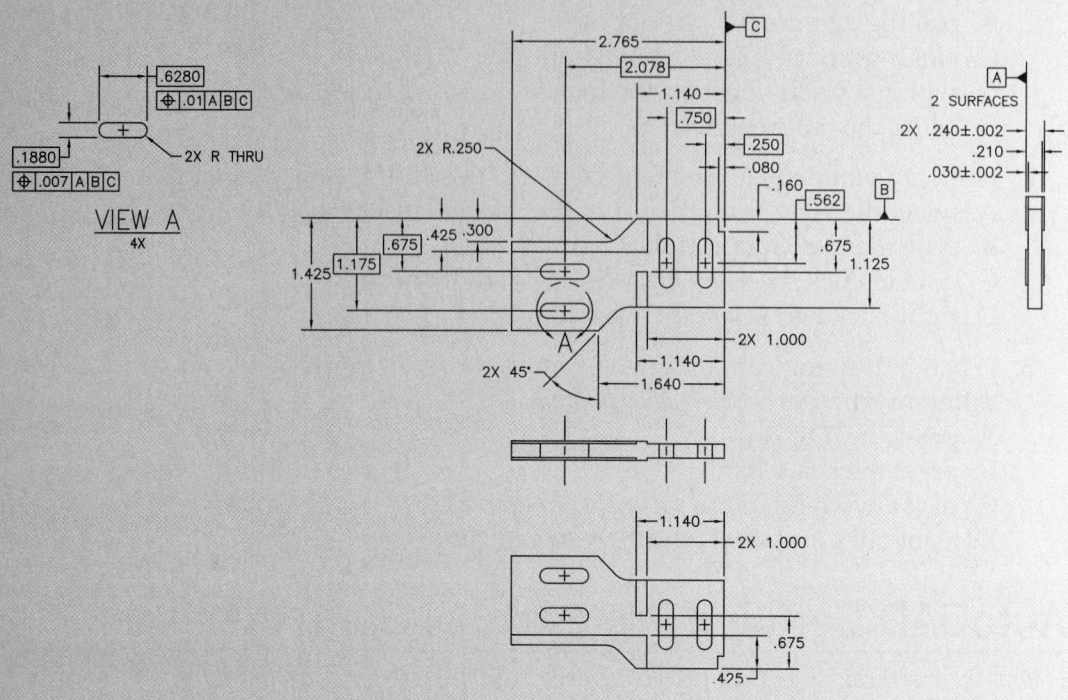

Object Snap and AutoTrack

Learning Objectives

After completing this chapter, you will be able to do the following:

✓ Set running object snap modes for continuous use.
✓ Use object snap overrides for single point selections.
✓ Select appropriate object snaps for various drawing tasks.
✓ Use AutoSnap™ features to speed up point specifications.
✓ Use AutoTrack™ to locate points relative to other points in a drawing.

This chapter explains how to use object snap and AutoTrack tools to draw accurately. Object snap and AutoTrack tools are very useful and efficient drawing aids. Object snaps and AutoTrack help you create accurate geometric constructions, but alone do not constrain, or apply relationships between, objects. Object snaps are also an important aid to parametric drafting. Chapter 22 explains how to use parametric drafting tools to constrain objects.

Object Snap

Object snap increases drafting performance and accuracy through the concept of *snapping*. See **Figure 7-1.** Use object snap with any tool that requires a point selection. Object snap *modes* identify the object snap point. The AutoSnap feature, which controls object snap, is on by default and displays *markers* while you draw. After a brief pause, a tooltip appears, indicating the object snap mode. See **Figure 7-2.** Refer to the list of standard object snap modes in **Figure 7-3** to identify the appropriate object snap for each drafting task. Object snap use becomes second nature with practice, and greatly increases productivity and accuracy.

object snap: A tool that locates an exact point, such as an endpoint, midpoint, or center point, on or in relation to an existing object.

snapping: Picking a point near the intended position to have the crosshairs "snap" exactly to the specific point.

markers: Visual cues that appear at the snap point to confirm object snap mode and location.

NOTE

If you cannot see an AutoSnap marker because of the size of the current screen display, you can still confirm the point before picking by reading the tooltip, which indicates if a point is acquired beyond the visible area.

Figure 7-1.
An example of object snaps used to aid construction of specific objects in a part drawing view. Object snaps aid geometric construction for any drawing application.

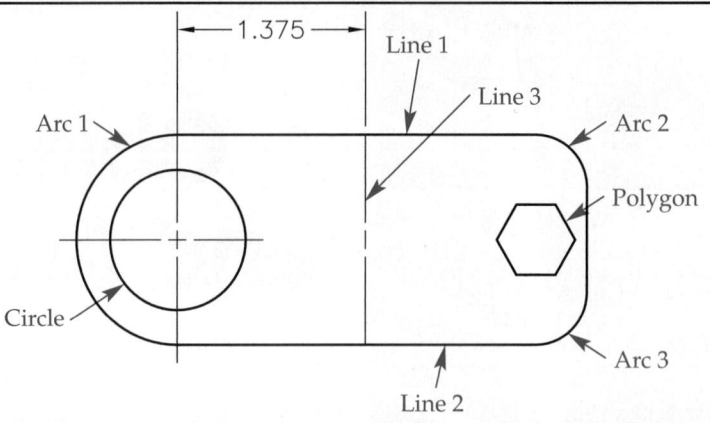

Object Snap	Construction Example
Parallel	Draw Line 2 parallel to Line 1
Endpoint	Begin and end Arc 1 at the endpoints of Line 1 and Line 2
Midpoint	Begin Line 3 at the midpoint of Line 1
Perpendicular	End Line 3 perpendicular to Line 2
Mid Between 2 Points	Locate the center of the Polygon at the midpoint between the center points of Arc 2 and Arc 3

Figure 7-2. The AutoSnap marker and related tooltip that appears when you snap to an endpoint and a point of tangency.

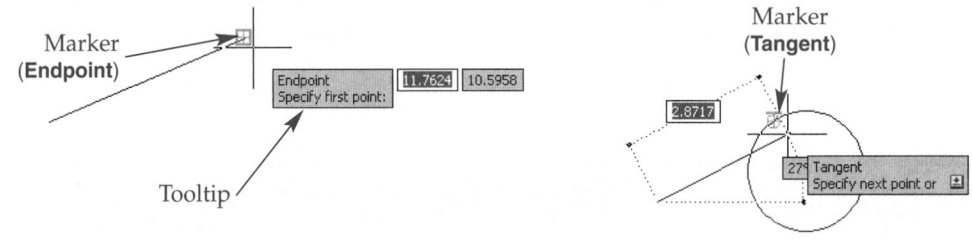

Snapping to an Endpoint   **Snapping to a Tangent**

Running Object Snaps

Type
DSETTINGS
DS
SE

running object snaps: Automatic object snap modes that run in the background while you work.

Running object snaps are on by default and are often the quickest and most effective way to use object snap. The **Endpoint, Center, Intersection,** and **Extension** running object snap modes are active by default. Right-click on the **Object Snap** or **Object Snap Tracking** button on the status bar and pick the modes to activate or deactivate. See **Figure 7-4A.** You can also set running object snaps using the **Object Snap** tab of the **Drafting Settings** dialog box. See **Figure 7-4B.** A quick way to access the **Object Snap** tab is to right-click on the **Object Snap** or **Object Snap Tracking** button on the status bar and select **Settings….**

To use most running object snaps, move the crosshairs near the location on an existing object where the object snap should occur. When you see the appropriate

Figure 7-3. Standard object snap modes.

Mode	Marker	Description
Endpoint	□	Locates the nearest endpoint of a line, arc, polyline, elliptical arc, spline, ellipse, ray, solid, or multiline.
Midpoint	△	Finds the point halfway between the endpoints of a line, polyline, circular arc, elliptical arc, polyline arc, spline, or multiline, or finds the start point of an xline.
Center	○	Finds the center point of radial objects, including circles, arcs, ellipses, elliptical arcs, and radial solids.
Node	⊗	Locates a point object drawn with the **POINT**, **DIVIDE**, or **MEASURE** tool, or a dimension definition point.
Quadrant	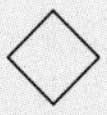 ◇	Locates the closest of the four quadrant points on circles, arcs, elliptical arcs, ellipses, and radial solids. (Some of these objects may not have all four quadrants.)
Intersection	×	Locates the closest intersection of two objects.
Extension	+	Finds a point along the imaginary extension of an existing line, polyline, arc, polyline arc, elliptical arc, spline, ray, xline, solid, or multiline.
Insertion	⌐⌐	Locates the insertion point of text objects and blocks.
Perpendicular	⊥	Finds a point that is perpendicular to an object from the previously picked point.
Tangent	○	Finds points of tangency between radial and linear objects.
Nearest	⊠	Locates the point on an object that is closest to the crosshairs.
Apparent Intersection	⊠	Locates the intersection between two objects that appear to intersect on-screen in the current view, but may not actually intersect in 3D space. Creating and editing 3D objects is described in *AutoCAD and Its Applications—Advanced*.
Parallel	//	Finds any point along an imaginary line parallel to an existing line or polyline.
None		Temporarily turns running object snap off during the current selection.

marker and tooltip, pick to locate the point at the exact position on the object. See **Figure 7-2.**

Toggle running object snaps off and on by picking the **Object Snap** button on the status bar, pressing [F3], right-clicking on the **Object Snap** button on the status bar and selecting the **Enabled** option, or using the **Object Snap On (F3)** check box on the **Object Snap** tab of the **Drafting Settings** dialog box. Turn off running object snaps to locate points without the aid, or to avoid possible confusion of object snap modes. The selected running object snap modes are restored when you reactivate running object snaps.

Figure 7-4. A—Right-click on the **Object Snap** or **Object Snap Tracking** button on the status bar to activate or deactivate running object snap modes. B—You can also set running object snap modes using the **Drafting Settings** dialog box.

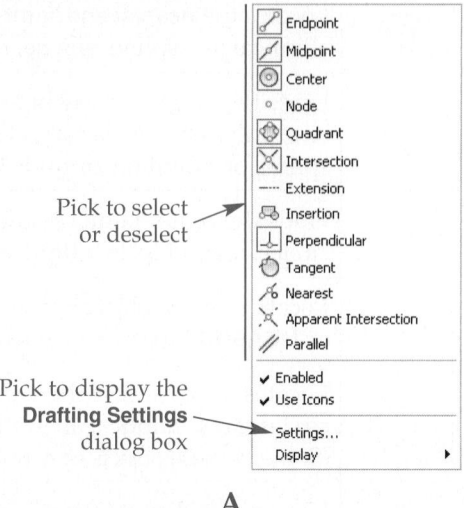

Pick to select or deselect

Pick to display the **Drafting Settings** dialog box

A

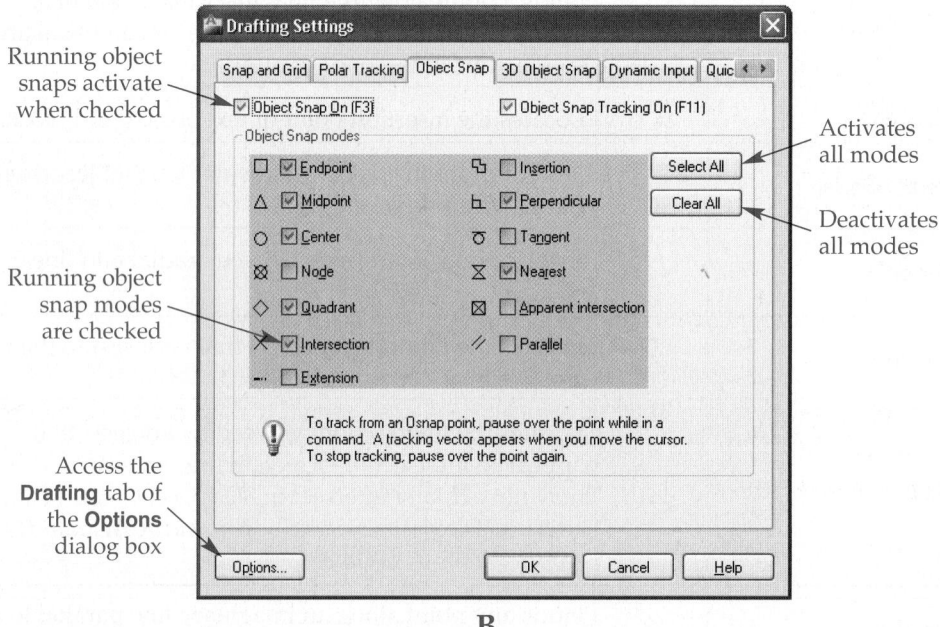

Running object snaps activate when checked

Running object snap modes are checked

Access the **Drafting** tab of the **Options** dialog box

Activates all modes

Deactivates all modes

B

PROFESSIONAL TIP

Activate only the running object snap modes that you use most often. Too many running object snaps can make it difficult to snap to the appropriate location, especially on detailed drawings with several objects near each other. Use object snap overrides to access object snap modes that you use less often.

NOTE

By default, a keyboard point entry overrides running object snaps. Use the **Priority for Coordinate Data Entry** area on the **User Preferences** tab of the **Options** dialog box to adjust the default setting.

Object Snap Overrides

Use an *object snap override* to select a specific point if you experience conflicting running object snaps, or to use an object snap that is not running. Running objects snaps return after you make the object snap override selection. All running object snap modes are available as object snap overrides, but some specific object snap options are only available as object snap overrides.

After you access a tool and are ready to apply an object snap, hold [Shift] or [Ctrl] and then right-click and choose an object snap override from the **Object Snap** shortcut menu. See **Figure 7-5**. An alternative, when you right-click and AutoCAD does not select the previous point, is to right-click without holding [Shift] or [Ctrl] and select from the **Snap Overrides** cascading submenu. Once you activate an object snap override, move the crosshairs near the location on an existing object where the object snap should occur. When you see the corresponding marker and tooltip, pick to locate the point at the exact position on the object.

object snap override: A method of isolating a specific object snap mode while using a tool. The selected object snap temporarily overrides the running object snap modes.

> **NOTE**
>
> You can activate an object snap override by entering the first three letters of the object snap name. For example, enter END to activate the **Endpoint** object snap or CEN to activate the **Center** object snap.

> **PROFESSIONAL TIP**
>
> Remember that object snap modes function with the active tool. An error message appears if you try to apply an object snap when no tool is active.

Endpoint Object Snap

To snap to an endpoint using the **Endpoint** object snap mode, move the crosshairs near the endpoint of a line, arc, polyline, spline, or ray. When the endpoint marker and tooltip appear, pick to locate the point at the exact endpoint. See **Figure 7-6**.

Figure 7-5.
The **Object Snap** shortcut menu provides quick access to object snap overrides.

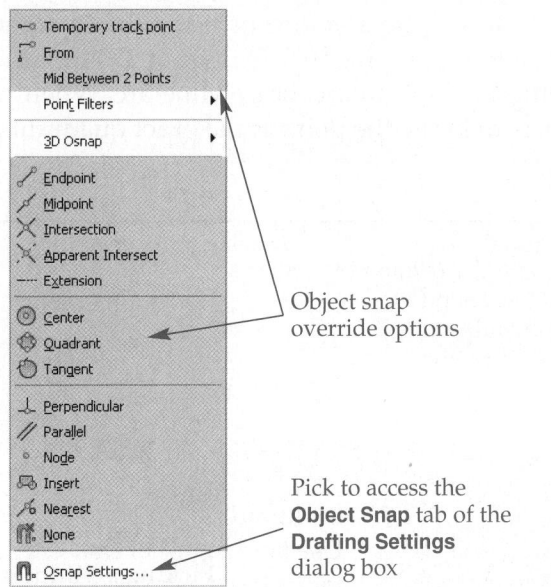

Object snap override options

Pick to access the **Object Snap** tab of the **Drafting Settings** dialog box

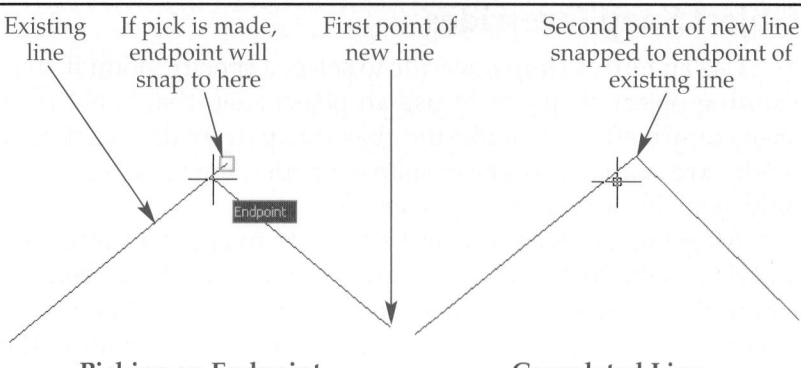

Figure 7-6.
Using the **Endpoint** object snap to locate the endpoint of an existing line. When using running object snaps, be sure the correct snap marker and tooltip appear before you pick.

Existing line

If pick is made, endpoint will snap to here

First point of new line

Second point of new line snapped to endpoint of existing line

Endpoint

Picking an Endpoint

Completed Line

Midpoint Object Snap

To snap to a midpoint using the **Midpoint** object snap mode, move the crosshairs near the midpoint of a line, arc, or polyline, or the start point of an xline. When the midpoint marker and tooltip appear, pick to locate the point at the exact midpoint. See **Figure 7-7.**

Exercise 7-1

Access the Student Web site (www.g-wlearning.com/CAD) and complete Exercise 7-1.

Center Object Snap

To snap to a center point using the **Center** object snap mode, move the crosshairs near the *perimeter*, not the center point, of a circle, arc, donut, ellipse, elliptical arc, or polyline arc. You must move the crosshairs near the perimeter of a circular object, especially if the object is large, to acquire the center point. When you see the center marker and tooltip, pick to locate the point at the exact center. See **Figure 7-8.**

Quadrant Object Snap

quadrant: A point on the circumference at the horizontal or vertical quarter of a circle, arc, donut, or ellipse.

To snap to a *quadrant* using the **Quadrant** object snap mode, move the crosshairs near the appropriate 0°, 90°, 180°, or 270° point on the circumference of a circle, arc, donut, ellipse, elliptical arc, or polyline arc. When you see the quadrant marker and tooltip, pick to locate the point at the exact quadrant position. See **Figure 7-9.**

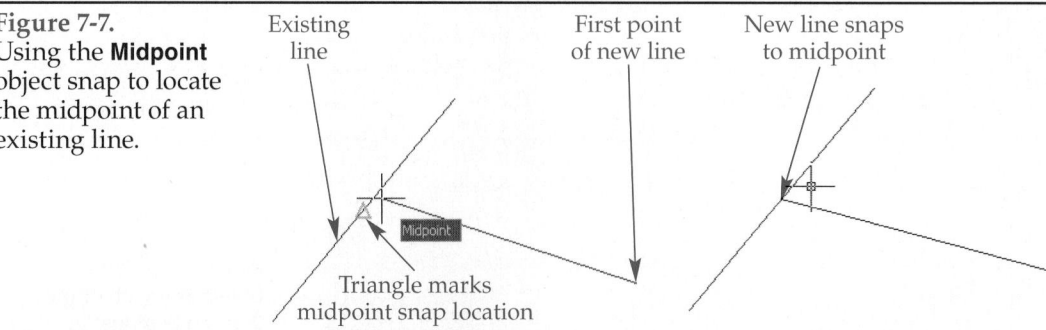

Figure 7-7.
Using the **Midpoint** object snap to locate the midpoint of an existing line.

Existing line

First point of new line

New line snaps to midpoint

Midpoint

Triangle marks midpoint snap location

Picking a Midpoint

Completed Line

Figure 7-8. Using the **Center** object snap to locate the center point of existing circles.

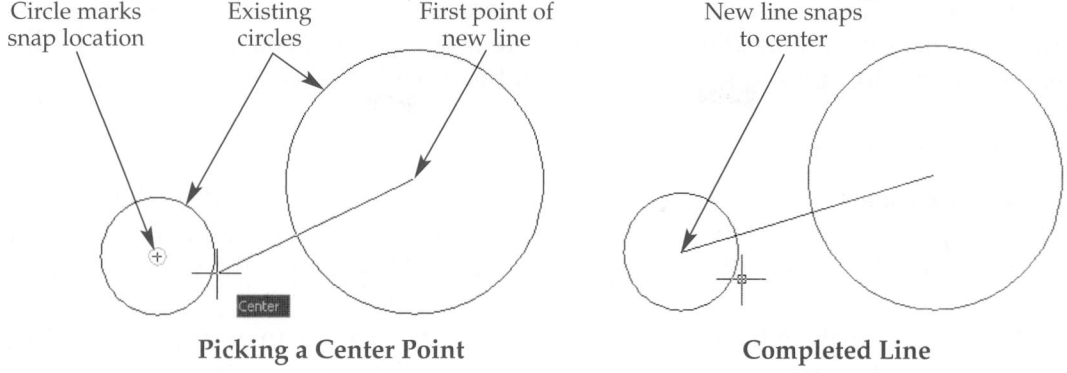

Circle marks snap location

Existing circles

First point of new line

New line snaps to center

Picking a Center Point

Completed Line

Figure 7-9. Using the **Quadrant** object snap to locate a quadrant point on the circumference of a circle.

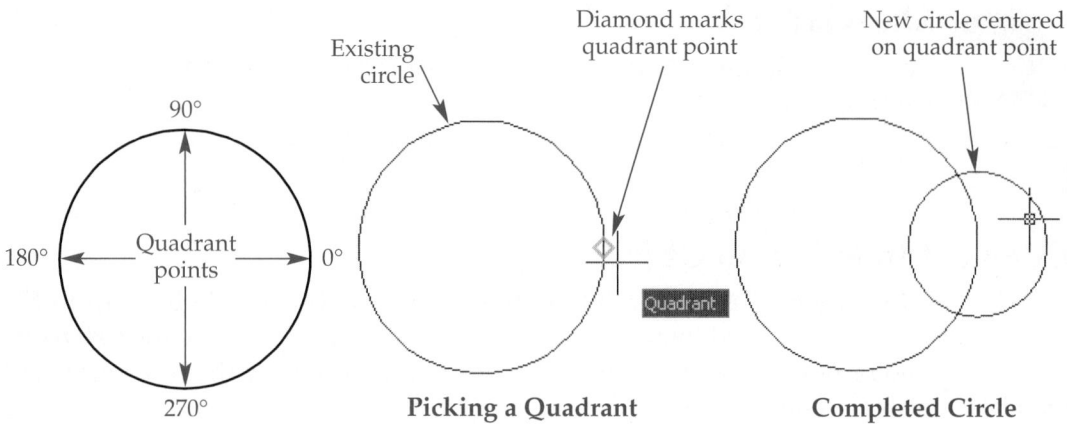

Diamond marks quadrant point

Existing circle

New circle centered on quadrant point

90°

180° Quadrant points 0°

270°

Picking a Quadrant

Completed Circle

> **NOTE**
>
> The current angle zero direction does not affect quadrant points, but quadrant points always coincide with the angle of the X and Y axes. The quadrant points of circles, arcs, and donuts are at the right (0°), top (90°), left (180°), and bottom (270°), regardless of the rotation of the object. However, the quadrant points of ellipses and elliptical arcs rotate with the object.

Exercise 7-2

Access the Student Web site (www.g-wlearning.com/CAD) and complete Exercise 7-2.

Intersection Object Snap

To snap to an intersection using the **Intersection** object snap mode, move the crosshairs near the intersection of two or more objects. When you see the intersection marker and tooltip, pick to locate the point at the exact intersection. See **Figure 7-10.**

Extension Object Snap

acquired point: A point found by moving the crosshairs over a point on an existing object to reference the point when picking a new point.

extension path: A dashed line or arc that extends from an acquired point to the current location of the crosshairs.

The **Extension** object snap mode uses *acquired points* instead of direct point selection. To snap to an extension, hover near the endpoint of a curve, but do not select. A point symbol (+) marks the location when AutoCAD acquires the point. Move the crosshairs away from the acquired point to display an *extension path*. Specify the location of a point along the extension path. **Figure 7-11** shows an example of using an **Extension** object snap twice to draw a line a specific distance away from two acquired points. In this example, type the .8 distance when you see the extension path. Dynamic input is not required to enter a value.

Exercise 7-3

Access the Student Web site (www.g-wlearning.com/CAD) and complete Exercise 7-3.

Extended Intersection Object Snap

Use the **Extension** or **Extended Intersection** object snap override to snap to the location where objects would intersect if they were long enough. To use the **Extension** object snap mode, hover near the endpoint of one curve to acquire the first point, and then hover near the endpoint of another curve to acquire the second point. Then move

---

Figure 7-10.
Using the **Intersection** object snap to locate the intersection of a line and an arc.

First point of new line

Second point snaps to this intersection

Intersection

Existing line and arc

Figure 7-11. Using the **Extension** object snap to create a line .8 units away from a rectangle.

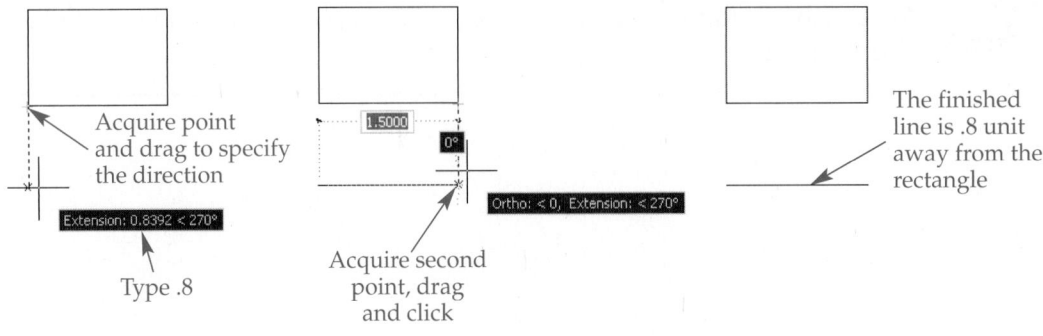

Acquire point and drag to specify the direction

Type .8

Extension: 0.8392 < 270°

1.5000

0°

Ortho: < 0, Extension: < 270°

Acquire second point, drag and click

The finished line is .8 unit away from the rectangle

---

the crosshairs away from the acquired point, near the location of where the objects would intersect. When you see two extension paths and an intersection icon, pick to locate the point. See **Figure 7-12A.**

To use the **Extended Intersection** object snap override, select objects one at a time using the **Intersection** object snap override. Once you activate the **Intersection** object snap override, move the cursor over one of the objects to display the intersection marker with an ellipsis (...), and pick the object. Then move the cursor over the other object to display the intersection marker at the extended intersection, and pick. See **Figure 7-12B.**

Exercise 7-4

Access the Student Web site (www.g-wlearning.com/CAD) and complete Exercise 7-4.

Figure 7-12. Locating the center of a circle at the extended intersection of a line and an arc. A—Using the **Extension** object snap. B—Using the **Extended Intersection** object snap.

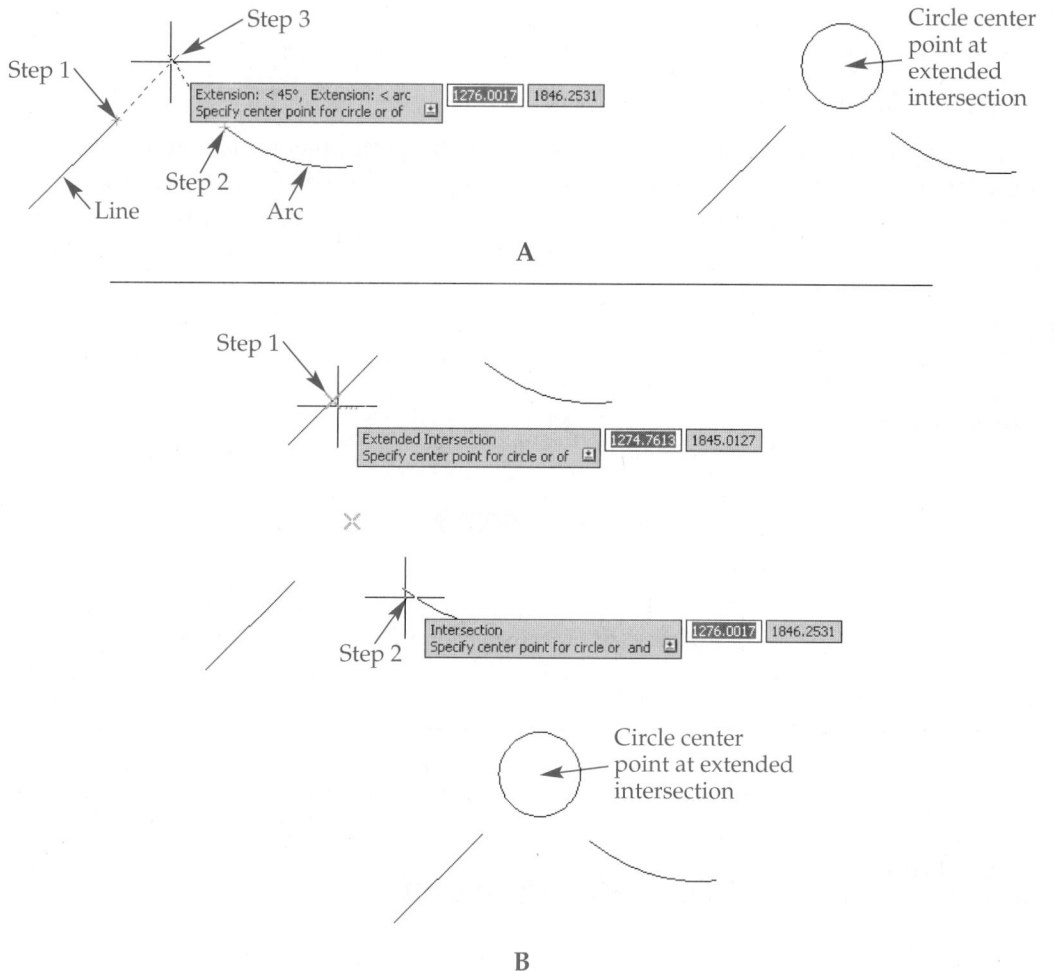

Perpendicular Object Snap

To snap to a perpendicular point using the **Perpendicular** object snap mode, move the crosshairs near the point of perpendicularity on a line, arc, elliptical arc, ellipse, spline, xline, multiline, polyline, or circle, or the endpoint of a line, arc, polyline, or spline. When you see the perpendicular marker and tooltip, pick to locate the point exactly perpendicular to the existing object. See **Figure 7-13**.

Figure 7-14 shows using the **Perpendicular** object snap mode to begin a line perpendicular to an existing object. The tooltip reads Deferred Perpendicular, and the perpendicular marker includes an ellipsis (...). The second endpoint determines the location of the line in a *deferred perpendicular* condition.

deferred perpendicular: A calculation of the perpendicular point that is delayed until you pick another point.

NOTE

Perpendicularity is determined from the point of intersection. Therefore, it is possible to draw a line perpendicular to a circle or arc.

Exercise 7-5

Access the Student Web site (www.g-wlearning.com/CAD) and complete Exercise 7-5.

Tangent Object Snap

To snap to the point of tangency using the **Tangent** object snap mode, move the crosshairs near an arc, circle, ellipse, elliptical arc, or spline. When you see the tangent marker, pick to locate the point at the exact point of tangency. See **Figure 7-15**.

Figure 7-13.
Drawing a line from a point perpendicular to an existing line.

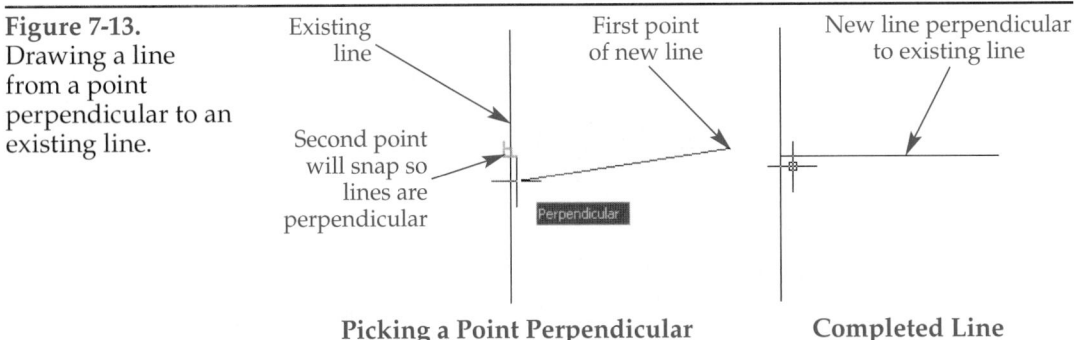

Picking a Point Perpendicular   Completed Line

Figure 7-14.
Deferring the second point of a line to establish a perpendicular construction.

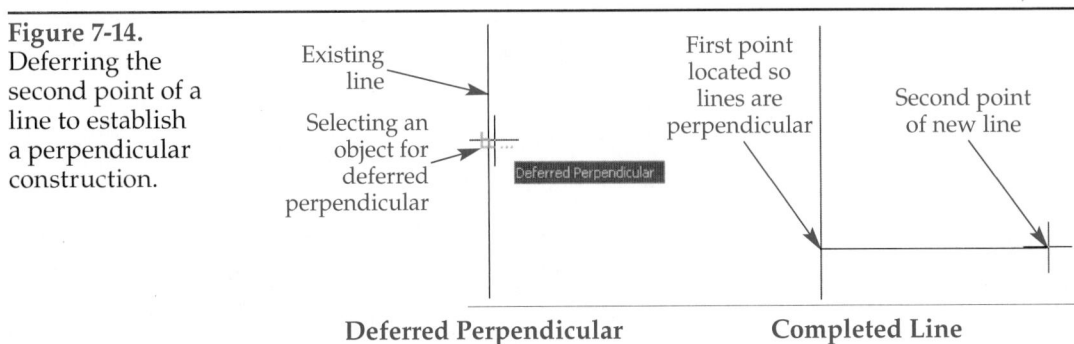

Deferred Perpendicular   Completed Line

Figure 7-15. Using the **Tangent** object snap to end a line tangent to a circle.

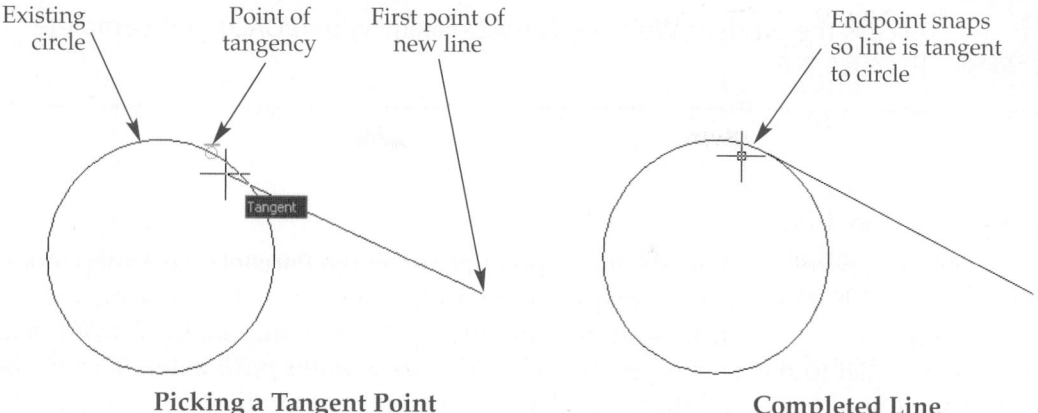

Existing circle

Point of tangency

First point of new line

Endpoint snaps so line is tangent to circle

Picking a Tangent Point

Completed Line

When drawing an object tangent to two objects, you may need to pick multiple points to fix the point of tangency. Until you identify both endpoints, the object snap specification is for *deferred tangency*. When AutoCAD recognizes both endpoints and calculates the tangency, you can draw the object in the correct location. See **Figure 7-16.**

deferred tangency: A calculation of the point of tangency that is delayed until you pick both points.

Figure 7-16. Drawing a line tangent to two circles.

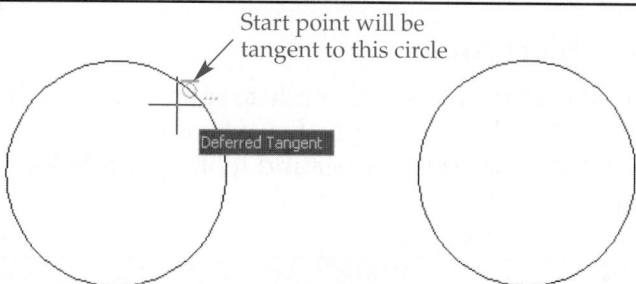

Start point will be tangent to this circle

First Tangent Point Deferred

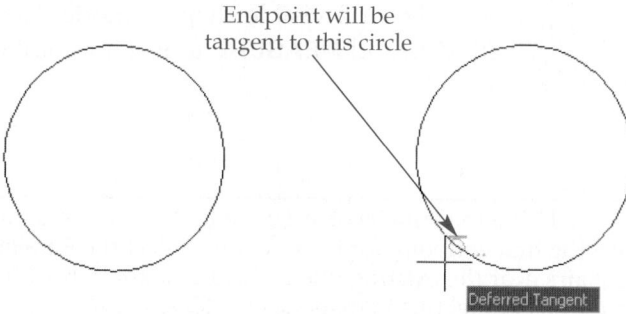

Endpoint will be tangent to this circle

Picking Second Tangent Point

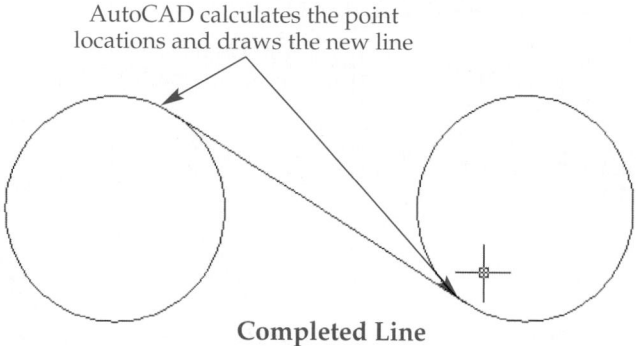

AutoCAD calculates the point locations and draws the new line

Completed Line

Exercise 7-6

Access the Student Web site (www.g-wlearning.com/CAD) and complete Exercise 7-6.

Parallel Object Snap

To snap to a point parallel to a line or polyline using the **Parallel** object snap mode, hover near the existing object to display the parallel marker, but do not pick. Then move the crosshairs away from and near parallel to the existing object. As you near a position parallel to the existing object, a *parallel alignment path* extends from the location of the crosshairs, and the parallel marker reappears to indicate acquired parallelism. Specify a point along the parallel alignment path. See **Figure 7-17**.

parallel alignment path: A dashed line parallel to an existing line that extends from the location of the crosshairs.

Exercise 7-7

Access the Student Web site (www.g-wlearning.com/CAD) and complete Exercise 7-7.

Node Object Snap

Use the **Node** object snap mode to snap to a point drawn using the **POINT**, **DIVIDE**, or **MEASURE** tool, or the origin of an extension line. Move the crosshairs near the node. When you see the node marker and tooltip, pick to locate the point at the exact node, or point.

> **NOTE**
>
> In order for the **Node** object snap to find a point object, the point must be in a visible display mode. Chapter 8 explains the **POINT**, **DIVIDE**, and **MEASURE** tools and point display mode controls.

Figure 7-17. Using the **Parallel** object snap to draw a line parallel to an existing line. A—Select the first endpoint for the new line, select the **Parallel** object snap, and then move the crosshairs near the existing line to acquire a point. B—Move the crosshairs near the location of the parallel line to display an extension path.

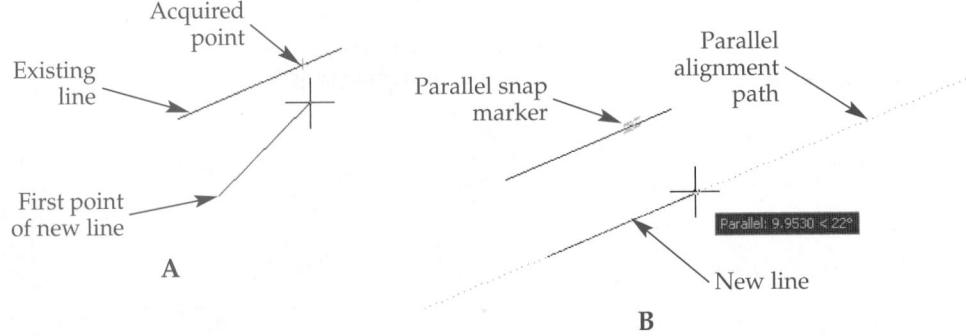

Nearest Object Snap

Use the **Nearest** object snap mode to specify a point that is directly on an object, but not at a critical location. Move the crosshairs near an existing object. When you see the nearest marker and tooltip, pick to locate the point at the location on the object that is closest to the crosshairs.

Exercise 7-8

Access the Student Web site (www.g-wlearning.com/CAD) and complete Exercise 7-8.

Temporary Track Point Snap

The **Temporary track point** snap mode is available only as an object snap override. It allows you to locate a point aligned with or relative to another point. For example, use the **Temporary track point** snap to place the center of a circle at the center of an existing rectangle. At the Specify center point for circle or [3P/2P/Ttr (tan tan radius)]: prompt, select the **Temporary tracking point** snap. Then use the **Midpoint** object snap to pick the midpoint of one of the vertical lines to establish the Y coordinate of the center of the rectangle. See **Figure 7-18A**. When the Specify center point for circle or [3P/2P/Ttr (tan tan radius)]: prompt reappears, reselect the **Temporary tracking point** snap mode. Then use the **Midpoint** object snap mode to pick the midpoint of one of the horizontal lines to establish the X coordinate of the center of the rectangle. See **Figure 7-18B**. Finally, pick to locate the center of the circle where the two tracking vectors intersect, and specify the circle radius. See **Figure 7-18C**.

> **NOTE**
>
> The direction in which you move the crosshairs from the temporary tracking point determines the X or Y alignment. Switch between horizontal or vertical tracking as needed.

Figure 7-18. Using temporary tracking to locate the center of a rectangle. A—Acquiring the midpoint of the left line. B—Acquiring the midpoint of the bottom line. C—Locating the center point of the circle at the intersection of the tracking vectors.

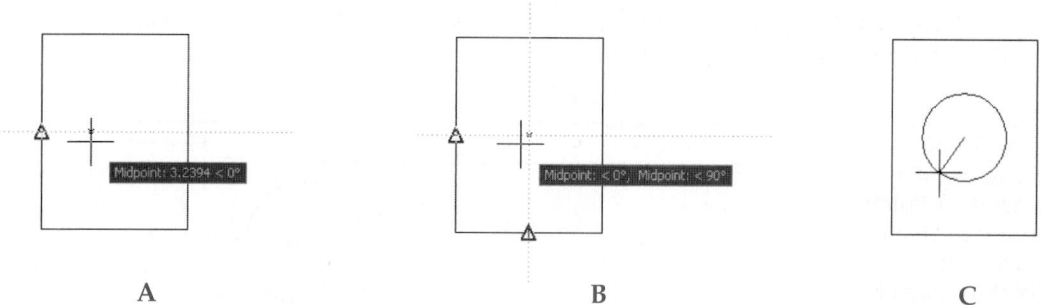

A   B   C

Snap From

The **From** snap mode is available only as an object snap override and allows you to locate a point using coordinate entry from a specified reference base point. For example, use the **From** snap to place the center of a circle using a polar coordinate entry from the midpoint of an existing line. At the Specify center point for circle or [3P/2P/Ttr (tan tan radius)]: prompt, select the **From** snap mode, and then use the **Midpoint** object snap to pick the midpoint of the line. At the <Offset>: prompt, enter the polar coordinate @2<45 to establish the center of the circle 2 units and at a 45° angle from the midpoint of the line. Specify the radius of the circle to complete the operation. See **Figure 7-19**.

Mid Between 2 Points Snap

The **Mid Between 2 Points** snap function is available only as an object snap override and is very effective for locating a point exactly halfway between two specified points. Use object snaps or coordinate point entry to pick reference points accurately. **Figure 7-20** shows locating the center of a circle between two line endpoints.

NOTE

Object snaps are also important when constructing a parametric drawing, especially when inferring geometric constraints. Chapter 22 explains parametric drafting. 3D object snaps are available for 3D applications, as described in *AutoCAD and Its Applications—Advanced*.

Figure 7-19.
An example of using the **From** point selection mode to locate the center of a circle using the **Midpoint** object snap and polar coordinate entry.

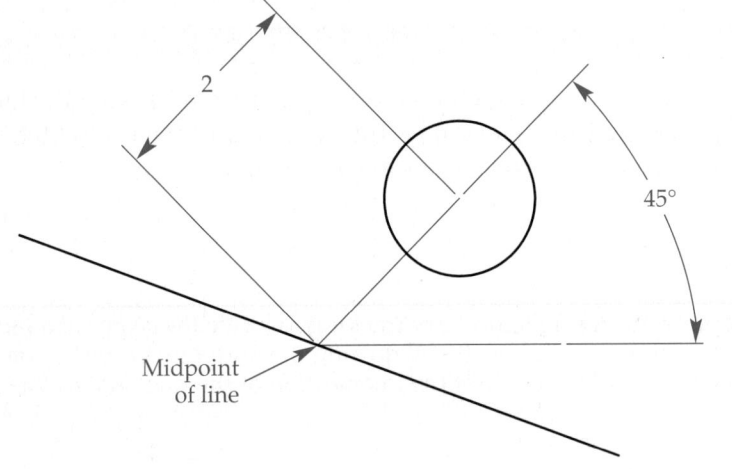

Figure 7-20.
Using the **Mid Between 2 Points** option to create a circle with center point located at an exactly equal distance between two line endpoints.

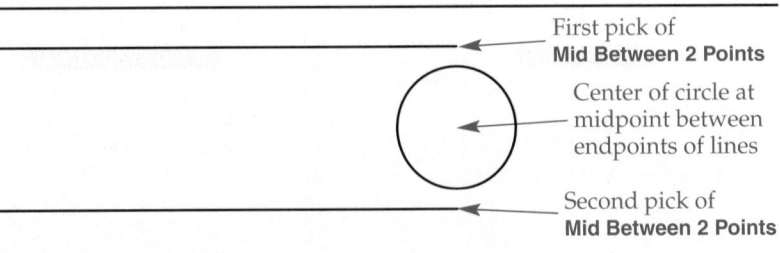

Exercise 7-9

Access the Student Web site (www.g-wlearning.com/CAD) and complete Exercise 7-9.

AutoTrack

AutoTrack offers an object snap tracking mode and a polar tracking mode. Snap and polar tracking are helpful for common drafting tasks, including basic geometric constructions. AutoTrack uses *alignment paths* and *tracking vectors* as drawing aids. Use AutoTrack with any tool that requires a point selection.

> **alignment paths:** Temporary lines and arcs that coincide with the position of existing objects.

Object Snap Tracking

Object snap tracking has two requirements: running object snaps must be active, and the crosshairs must hover over the intended selection long enough to acquire the point. Turn object snap on and off by picking the **Object Snap Tracking** button on the status bar, pressing [F11], or checking **Object Snap Tracking On (F11)** in the **Object Snap** tab of the **Drafting Settings** dialog box. Object snap tracking mode works with running object snaps. You must activate object snap tracking, running object snaps, and the appropriate running object snap modes in order for object snap tracking to function properly.

> **tracking vectors:** Temporary lines that display at specific angles, 0°, 90°, 180°, and 270° by default.

> **object snap tracking:** Mode that provides horizontal and vertical alignment paths for locating points after acquiring a point with object snap.

Figure 7-21 shows an example of using object snap tracking with the **Perpendicular** and **Midpoint** running object snaps to draw a line 2 units long, perpendicular to the existing slanted line. Running object snaps, the **Perpendicular** and **Midpoint** running object snap modes, and object snap tracking must be active before you use the **LINE** tool to draw the line.

Figure 7-22 shows an example of using object snap tracking with the **Midpoint** running object snap to locate the center point of a circle directly above the midpoint of a horizontal line and to the right of the midpoint of an angled line. Running object snaps, the **Midpoint** running object snap mode, and object snap tracking must be active before you use the **Circle, Radius** tool to draw the circle.

PROFESSIONAL TIP

Use object snap tracking whenever possible to complete tasks that require you to reference locations on existing objects. Often the combination of running object snaps and object snap tracking is the quickest way to construct geometry.

Exercise 7-10

Access the Student Web site (www.g-wlearning.com/CAD) and complete Exercise 7-10.

Figure 7-21.
Using object snap tracking to draw a line perpendicular to and at the midpoint of an existing line.

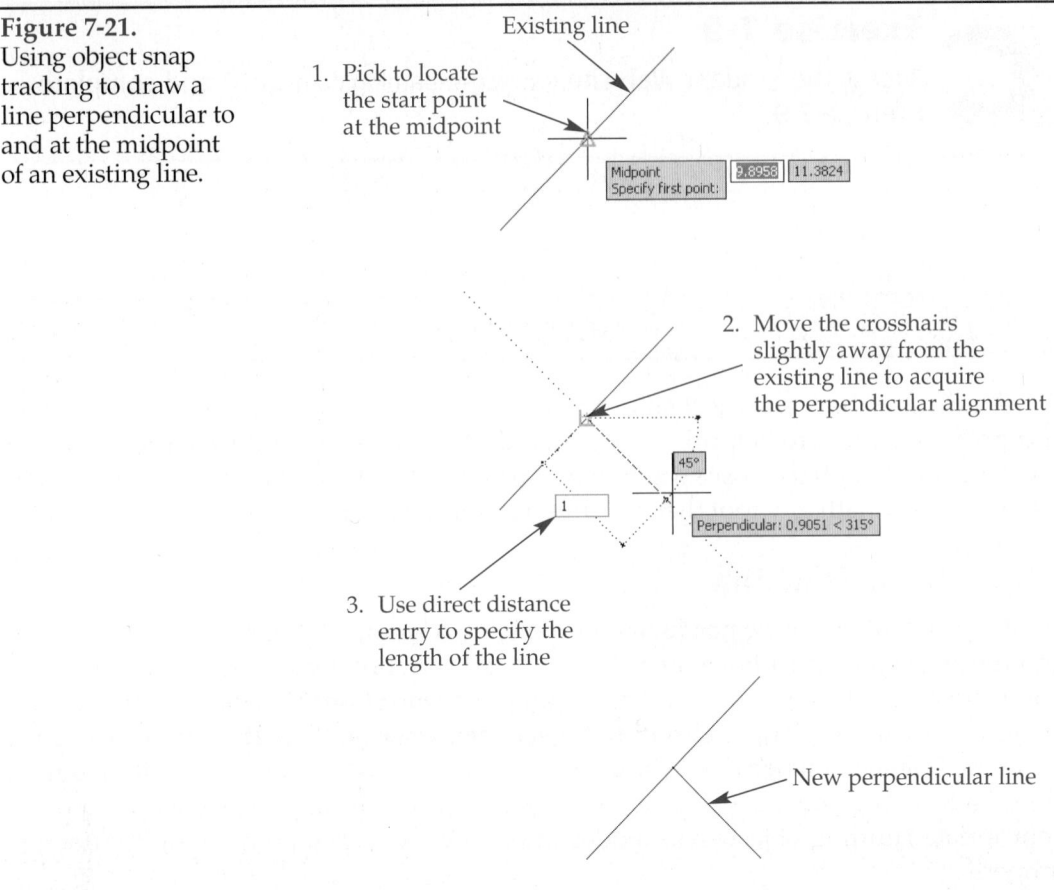

Existing line

1. Pick to locate the start point at the midpoint

Midpoint
Specify first point: | 9.8958 | 11.3824

2. Move the crosshairs slightly away from the existing line to acquire the perpendicular alignment

45°

Perpendicular: 0.9051 < 315°

3. Use direct distance entry to specify the length of the line

New perpendicular line

Figure 7-22. Using object snap tracking to locate the center point of a circle in line with the midpoints of two lines.

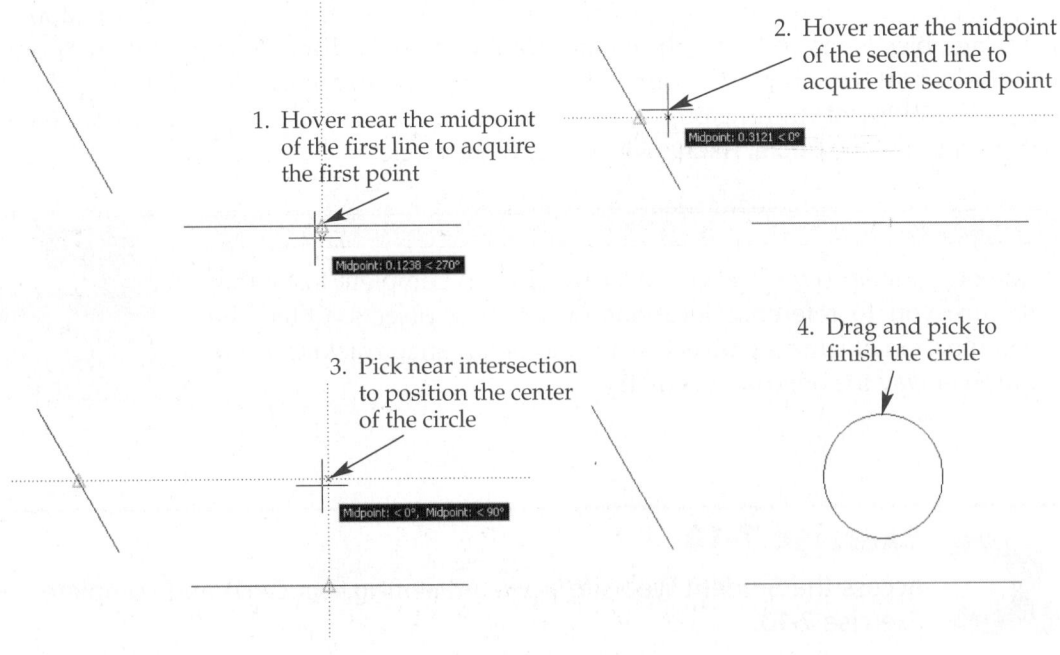

2. Hover near the midpoint of the second line to acquire the second point

Midpoint: 0.3121 < 0°

1. Hover near the midpoint of the first line to acquire the first point

Midpoint: 0.1238 < 270°

4. Drag and pick to finish the circle

3. Pick near intersection to position the center of the circle

Midpoint: < 0°, Midpoint: < 90°

Polar Tracking

Polar tracking causes the drawing crosshairs to "snap" to predefined angle increments and is an accurate method of using direct distance entry. Turn polar tracking on or off by picking the **Polar Tracking** button on the status bar, pressing [F10], or checking **Polar Tracking On (F10)** in the **Polar Tracking** tab of the **Drafting Settings** dialog box. As you move the crosshairs toward a polar tracking angle, AutoCAD displays an alignment path and tooltip. The default polar angle increments are 0°, 90°, 180°, and 270°.

Right-click on the **Polar Tracking** button on the status bar and pick an available polar tracking increment angle, or access the **Polar Tracking** tab in the **Drafting Settings** dialog box for total control. See **Figure 7-23**. A quick way to access the **Polar Tracking** tab is to right-click on the **Polar Tracking** button on the status bar and select **Settings…**. Use the **Increment angle** drop-down list to select the angle increments at which polar tracking vectors occur. These are the same angles available when you right-click on the **Polar Tracking** button on the status bar. The default increment is 90, which displays polar tracking vectors at 0°, 90°, 180°, or 270°. The 30° setting shown in **Figure 7-23** provides polar tracking at 30° increments. **Figure 7-24** shows an example of drawing a parallelogram using the **LINE** tool and polar tracking set to 30° angle increments.

To add specific polar tracking angles that are typically not associated with the increment angle, pick the **New** button in the **Polar Angle Settings** area and type an angle in the text box that appears in the **Additional angles** window. The angles you add work with the increment angle setting when you use polar tracking. AutoCAD only recognizes the specific additional angles you enter, not each increment of the angle. Use the **Delete** button to remove angles from the list. Uncheck **Additional angles** to make additional angles inactive.

The **Object Snap Tracking Settings** area sets the angles available with object snap tracking. If you select **Track orthogonally only**, only horizontal and vertical alignment paths are active. If you select **Track using all polar angle settings**, alignment paths are active for all polar snap angles.

The **Polar Angle measurement** setting determines whether the polar snap increments are constant or relative to the previous segment. If you choose **Absolute**, polar snap angles are measured from the base angle of 0° set for the drawing. If you pick **Relative to last segment**, each increment angle is measured from a base angle established by the previously drawn segment.

Figure 7-23. The **Polar Tracking** tab of the **Drafting Settings** dialog box.

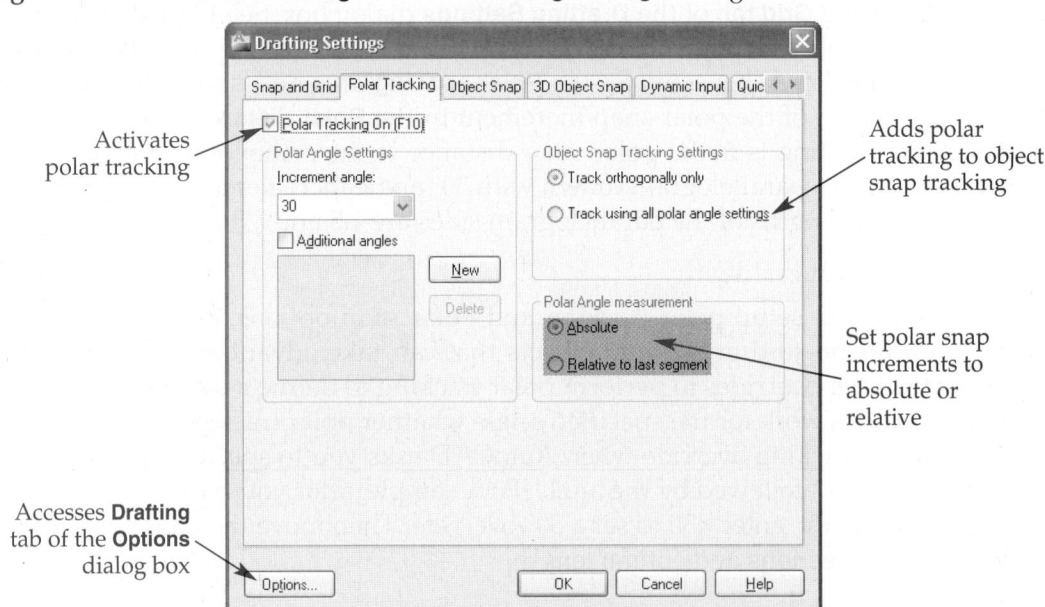

Figure 7-24. Using polar tracking with 30° angle increments to draw a parallelogram.

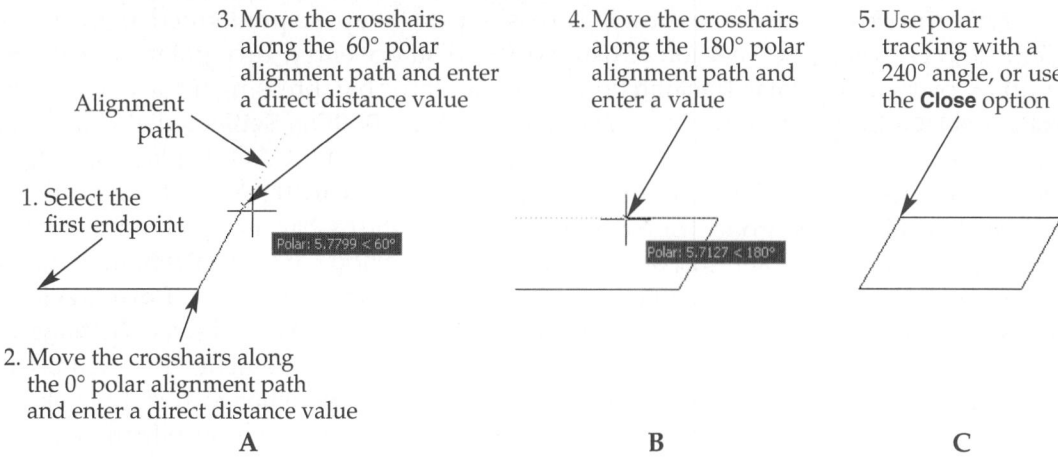

3. Move the crosshairs along the 60° polar alignment path and enter a direct distance value

4. Move the crosshairs along the 180° polar alignment path and enter a value

5. Use polar tracking with a 240° angle, or use the **Close** option

Alignment path

1. Select the first endpoint

Polar: 5.7799 < 60°

Polar: 5.7127 < 180°

2. Move the crosshairs along the 0° polar alignment path and enter a direct distance value

A   B   C

NOTE

AutoCAD automatically turns **Ortho** off when polar tracking is on, and it turns polar tracking off when **Ortho** is on.

Exercise 7-11

Access the Student Web site (www.g-wlearning.com/CAD) and complete Exercise 7-11.

Polar Tracking with Polar Snaps

You can also use polar tracking with polar snaps. For example, if you use polar tracking and polar snaps to draw the parallelogram in **Figure 7-24**, there is no need to type the length of the line, because you set the angle increment with polar tracking and a length increment with polar snaps. Establish the angle and length increments using the **Snap and Grid** tab of the **Drafting Settings** dialog box. See **Figure 7-25.**

To activate polar snap, pick the **PolarSnap** radio button in the **Snap type & style** area of the dialog box. This activates the **Polar spacing** area and deactivates the **Snap** area. Set the length of the polar snap increment in the **Polar distance:** text box. If the **Polar distance:** setting is 0, the polar snap distance is the orthogonal snap distance. **Figure 7-26** shows a parallelogram drawn with 30° angle increments and length increments of .75. The lengths of the parallelogram sides are 1.5 and .75.

Polar Tracking Overrides

It takes time to setup polar tracking and polar snap options, but it is worth the effort if you intend to draw several objects that can take advantage of this feature. Use polar tracking overrides to perform polar tracking to define a unique point. Polar tracking overrides work for the specified angle whether polar tracking is on or off. To activate a polar tracking override when AutoCAD asks you to specify a point, type a less than symbol (<) followed by the angle. For example, after you access the **LINE** tool and pick a first point, enter <30 to set a 30° override. Then move the crosshairs in one of the possible directions and enter a length.

Figure 7-25.
Use the **Snap and Grid** tab of the **Drafting Settings** dialog box to set polar snap distance.

Activates snap

Polar snap spacing

Select grid or polar snap

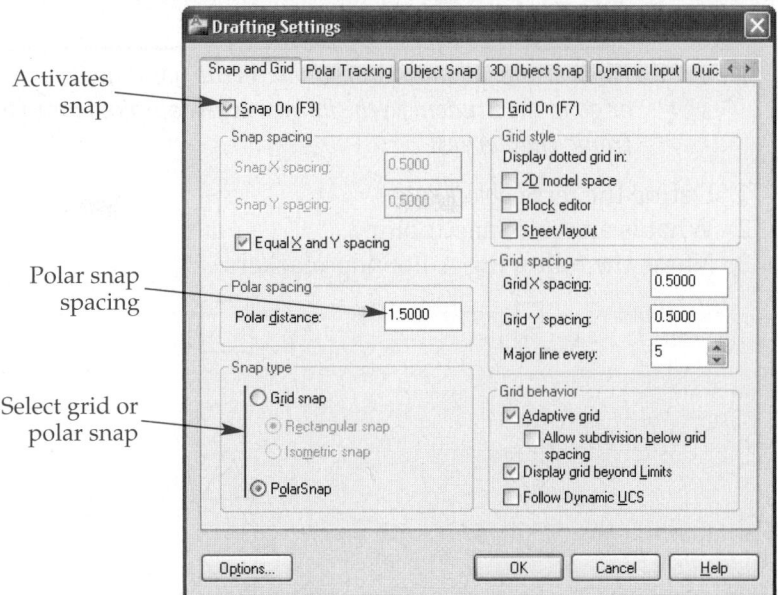

Figure 7-26. Drawing a parallelogram with polar snap. Notice the values that automatically appear in the input fields.

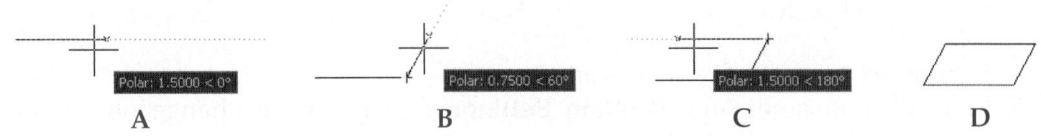

A   B   C   D

Exercise 7-12

Access the Student Web site (www.g-wlearning.com/CAD) and complete Exercise 7-12.

Supplemental Material

AutoSnap and AutoTrack Options
For information about options for controlling the appearance and function of AutoSnap and AutoTrack, go to the Student Web site (www.g-wlearning.com/CAD), select this chapter, and select **AutoSnap and AutoTrack Options**.

Template Development
Chapter 7

For detailed instructions on setting object snaps and polar tracking in your templates to save time and increase efficiency, go to the Student Web site (www.g-wlearning.com/CAD), select this chapter, and select **Template Development**.

Chapter Test

Answer the following questions. Write your answers on a separate sheet of paper or go to the Student Web site (www.g-wlearning.com/CAD) and complete the electronic chapter test.

1. Define the term *object snap*.
2. What is an AutoSnap tooltip?
3. Name the following AutoSnap markers:

A. E. I.

B. F. J.

C. G. K.

D. H. L.

4. Define the term *running object snap*.
5. How do you access the **Drafting Settings** dialog box to change object snap settings?
6. How do you set running object snaps?
7. What is the easiest way to turn off the running object snaps temporarily to make several point specifications without the aid of object snap?
8. Why should you activate only the running object snaps you use most often?
9. Describe object snap override.
10. How do you access the **Object Snap** shortcut menu?
11. Where are the four quadrant points on a circle?
12. What is the situation when the tooltip reads Extended Intersection?
13. What does it mean when the tooltip reads Deferred Perpendicular?
14. Give the tool and entries needed to draw a line tangent to an existing circle and perpendicular to an existing line:
    A. Tool: _____
    B. Specify first point: _____
    C. to _____
    D. Specify next point or [Undo]: _____
    E. to _____
15. What is a deferred tangency?
16. What conditions must exist for the tooltip to read Tangent?
17. Which object snaps depend on acquired points to function?
18. What two display features does AutoTrack use to help you align new objects with existing geometry?
19. What are the two requirements to use object snap tracking?
20. What would you enter to specify a 40° polar tracking override?

Drawing Problems

Start AutoCAD if it is not already started. Start a new drawing from scratch or use an appropriate template of your choice. The template should include layers for drawing the given objects. Add layers as needed. Draw all objects using appropriate layers. Follow the specific instructions for each problem. Use only drawing tools and techniques you have already learned. Use object snap and AutoTrack when possible. Do not draw dimensions or text. Use your own judgment and approximate dimensions when necessary.

▼ Basic

1. Draw the part view shown using object snap modes. Save the drawing as P7-1.

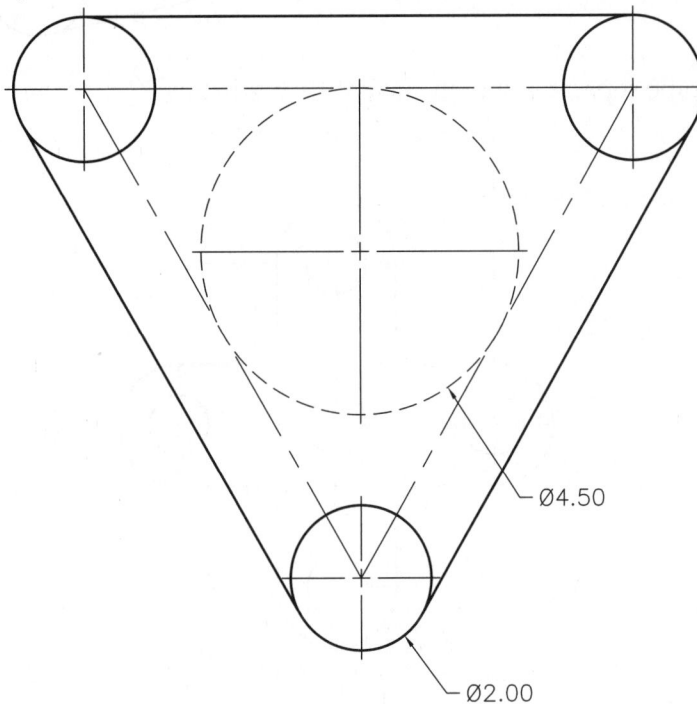

Ø4.50

Ø2.00

2. Draw the highlighted objects shown, and then use the object snap modes indicated to draw the remaining objects. Save the drawing as P7-2.

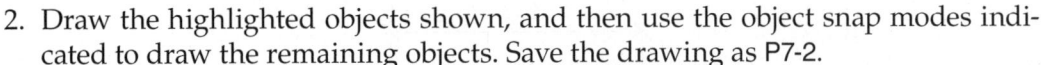

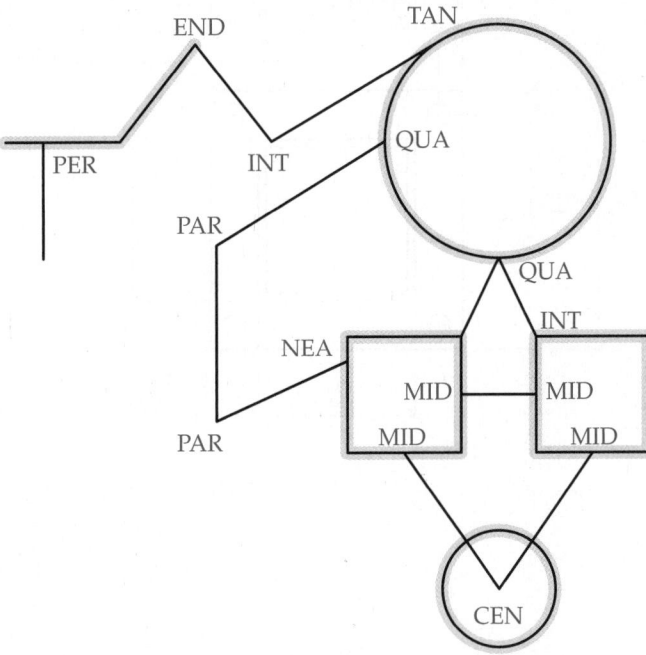

3. Draw the schematic shown using the **Endpoint**, **Tangent**, **Perpendicular**, and **Quadrant** object snap modes. Save the drawing as P7-3.

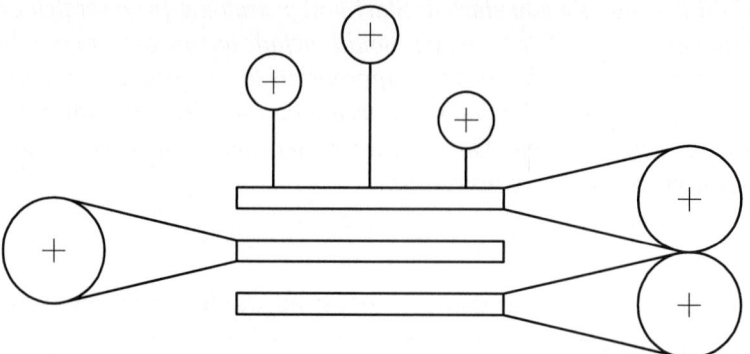

4. Draw the pipe separator shown. Save the drawing as P7-4.

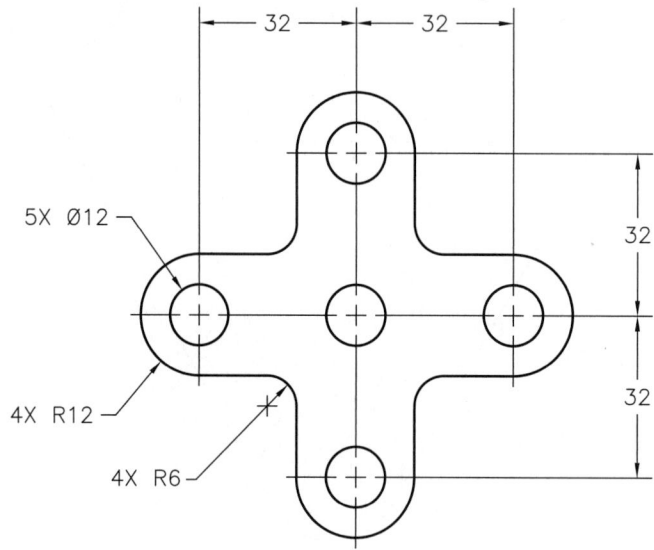

5. Draw the column base detail shown. Save the drawing as P7-5.

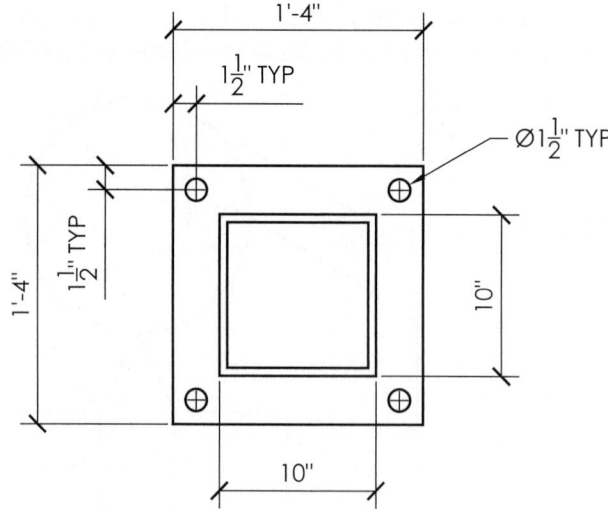

6. Draw the elbow shown. Save the drawing as P7-6.

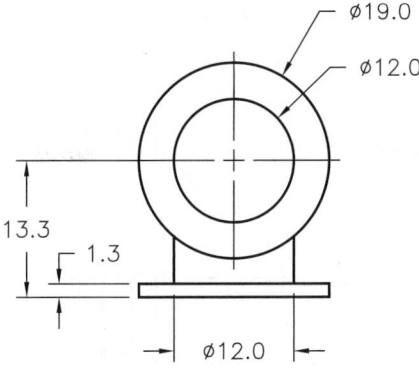

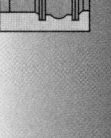

▼ Intermediate

7. Draw the electrical switch schematics shown. Use the **Midpoint**, **Endpoint**, **Tangent**, **Perpendicular**, and **Quadrant** object snap modes. Save the drawing as P7-7.

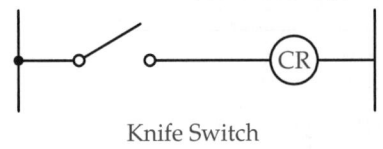

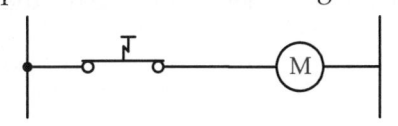

Knife Switch

Maintained Contact
Pushbutton

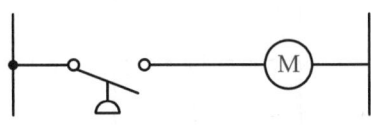

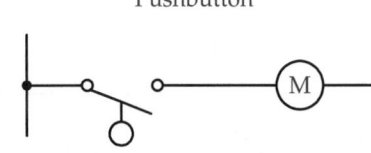

Pressure Switch
(Start on Rise in Pressure)

Level Switch
(Start on High Level)

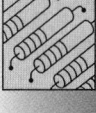

8. Draw the pressure cylinder shown. Use the **Arc** option of the **ELLIPSE** tool to draw the cylinder ends. Save the drawing as P7-8.

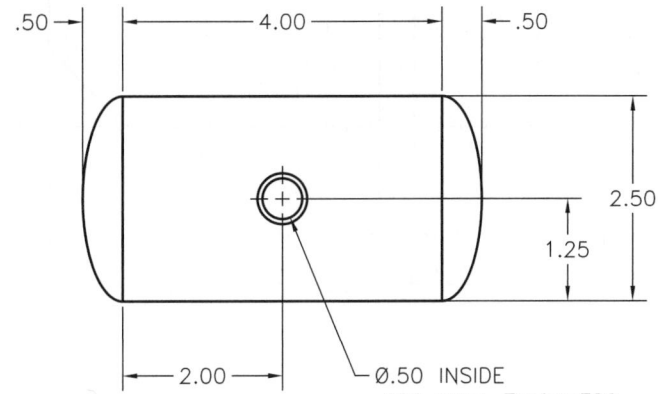

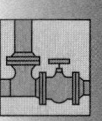

9. Draw the stud shown. Save the drawing as P7-9.

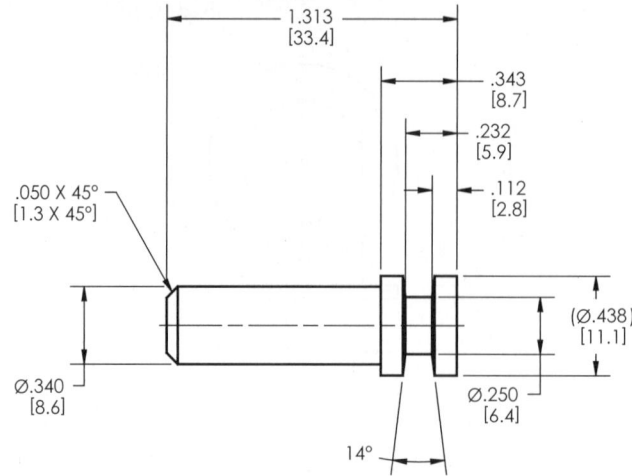

10. Draw the part view shown. Save the drawing as P7-10.

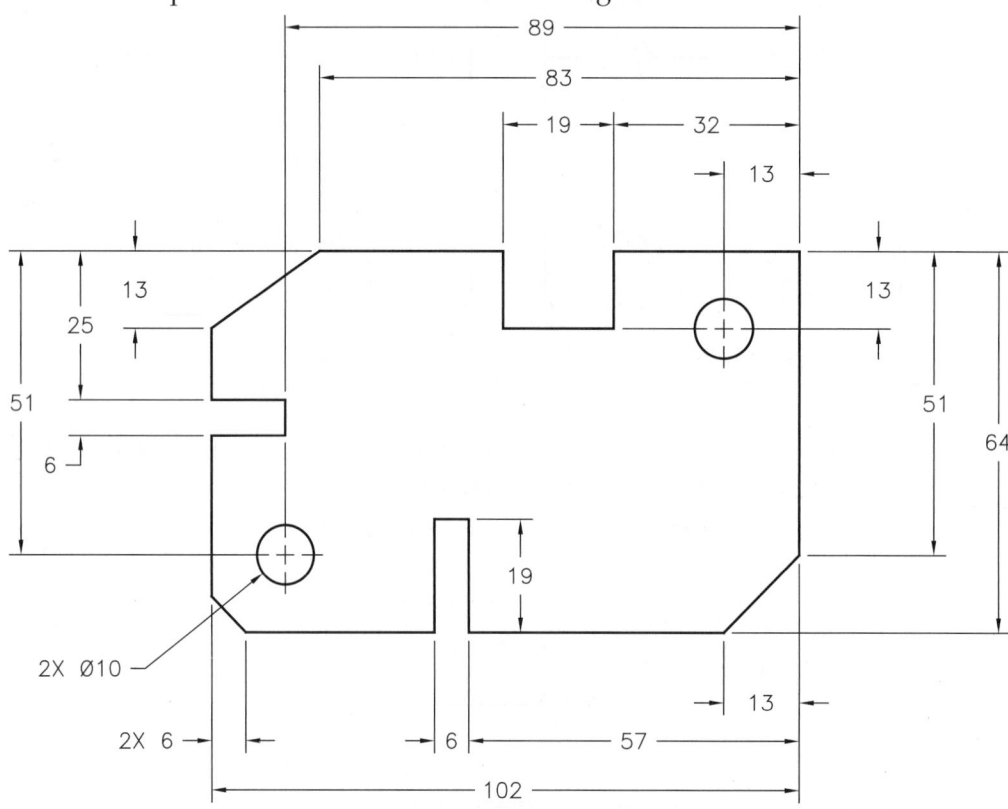

11. Draw the window elevation symbol shown. Save the drawing as P7-11.

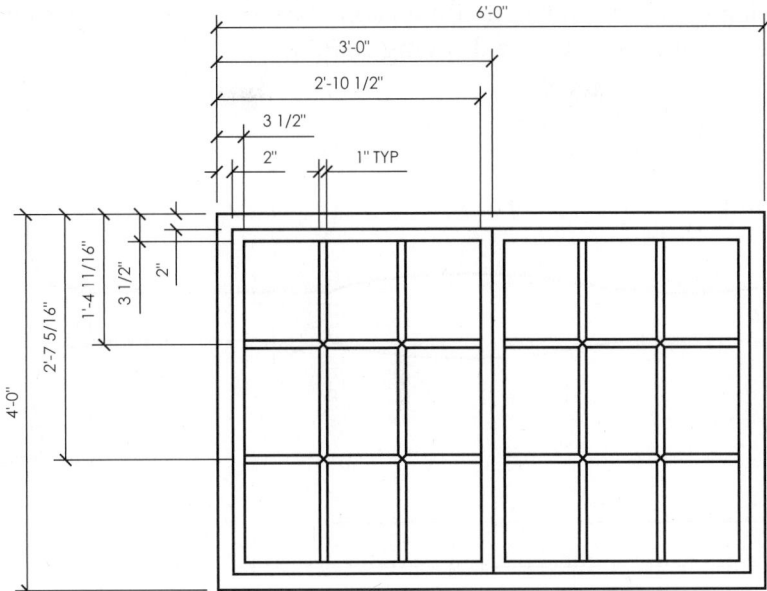

▼ **Advanced**

12. Use object snap modes to draw the elementary diagram shown. Save the drawing as P7-12.

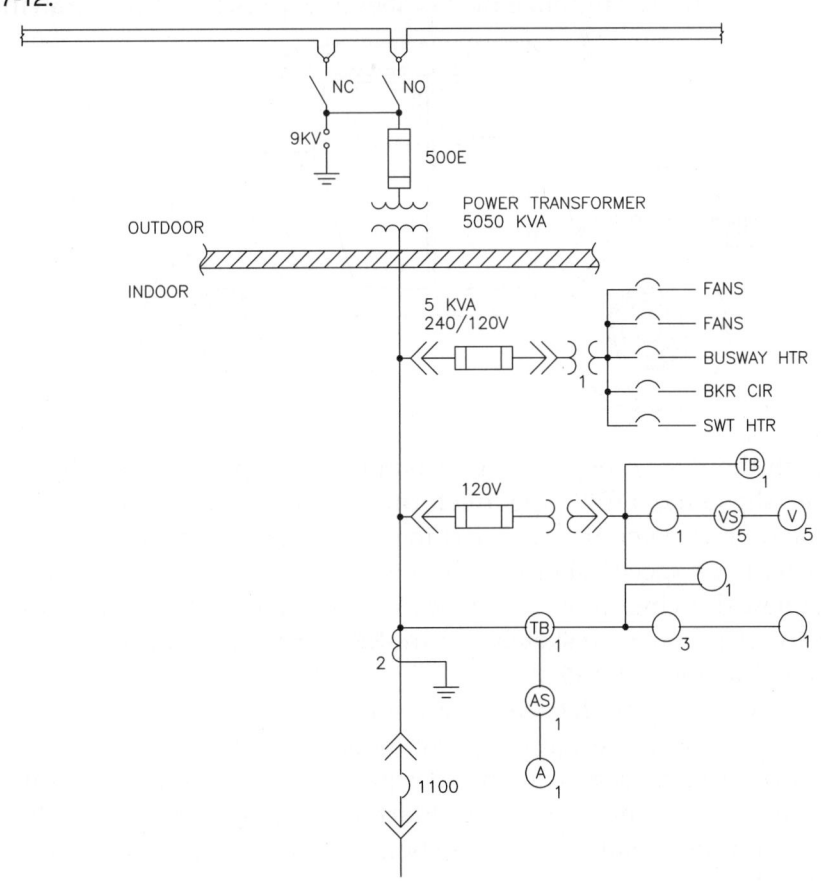

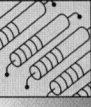

13. Design and draft a hammer similar to the hammer shown. Use the overall dimensions shown, and add dimensions based on your experience, research, and measurements. Save the drawing as P7-13.

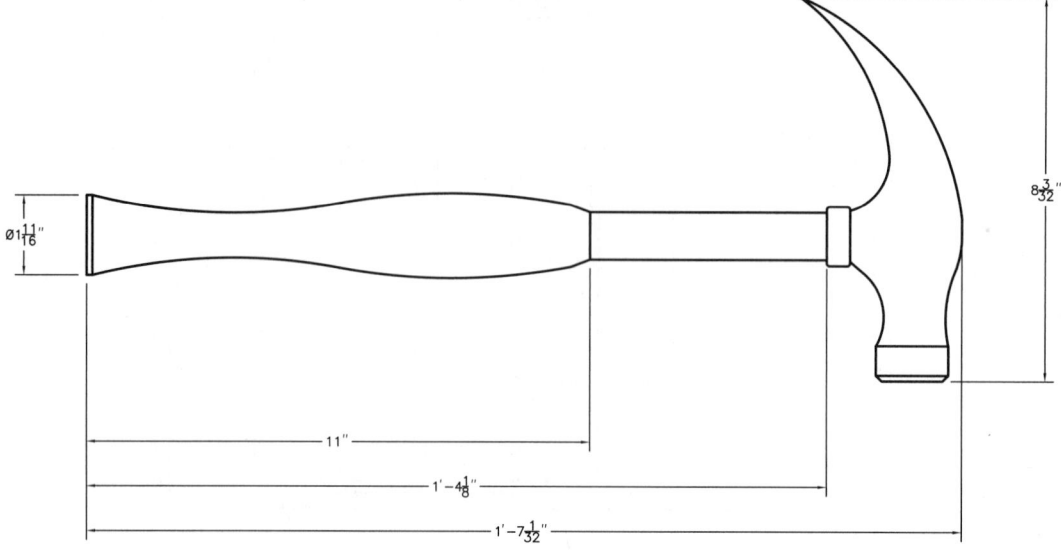

14. Create a drawing from the sketch of a truck design shown. Draw the truck using appropriate size and scale features. Use a tape measure to measure an actual truck for reference if instructed. Consider the tools and techniques used to draw the truck, and try to minimize the number of objects. Save your drawing as P7-14.

15. Research the design of an existing handlebar grip with the following specifications: slips onto a ∅1″ pipe, freeform ergonomic design with finger grooves, silicone rubber material. Create a dimensioned 2D sketch of the design from the manufacturer's specifications or from measurements taken from an actual grip. Start a new drawing from scratch or use a decimal-unit template of your choice. Draw the grip from your sketch. Use the **SPLINE** tool to draw the freeform curves. Save the drawing as P7-15.

16. Create a dimensioned 2D sketch of the front elevation of a residential groundwater pump house. Design the pump house to fit an 8′-0″ × 8′-0″ concrete slab foundation. Use a traditional style design. Use dimensions based on your experience, research, or measurements. Start a new drawing from scratch or use an architectural-unit template of your choice. Draw the elevation from your sketch. Save the drawing as P7-16.

AutoCAD Certified Associate Exam Practice

Answer the following questions. Write your answers on a separate sheet of paper.

1. Which of the labeled points shown can you select using the AutoSnap feature, without entering an object snap override, if the **Midpoint**, **Endpoint**, and **Center** object snaps are set as running object snaps? *Select the one item that best answers the question.*

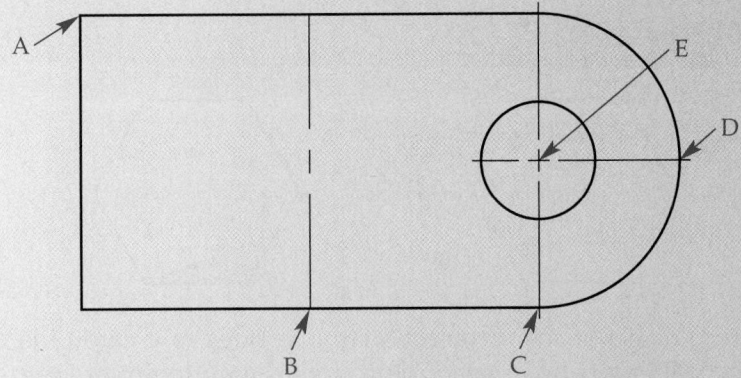

A. points A, B, and C
B. points A, C, and D
C. points A, B, D, and E
D. points A, B, C, and E
E. points A and E only

2. Which of the following positions describe quadrant points on a circle? *Select all that apply.*
A. 0°
B. 30°
C. 60°
D. 90°
E. 180°

3. Which of the following points can be selected using the **Endpoint** object snap? *Select all that apply.*
A. a corner of a rectangle
B. the center of a circle
C. the end of an arc
D. a vertex of a polygon
E. the midpoint of a line

AutoCAD Certified Professional Exam Practice

Follow the instructions in each problem. Write your answers on a separate sheet of paper.

1. **Navigate to this chapter on the Student Web site and open the CPE-07snaps. dwg file.**

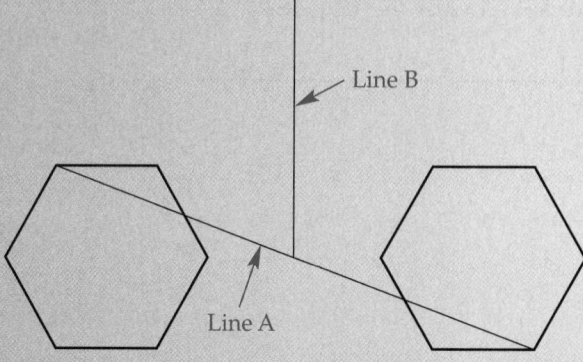

Use running object snaps or object snap overrides to create Line A as shown. Restart the **LINE** tool and create Line B from the midpoint of Line A, extending 1.5 units upward vertically. What are the coordinates of the upper endpoint of Line B?

2. **Navigate to this chapter on the Student Web site and open the CPE-07polar. dwg file.**

Use the **Drafting Settings** dialog box to create additional polar angles of 20, 40, and 80. Make sure **Polar Angle measurement** is set to **Absolute**. Then use polar tracking to create the following line segments:

A. A line starting at the right endpoint of the existing line and extending 3 units at 80°.

B. A line starting at the upper endpoint of the previous line and extending 4.5 units at 20°.

C. A line starting at the right endpoint of the previous line and extending 3 units upward vertically.

D. A line starting at the upper endpoint of the previous line and extending 6.3 units at 40°.

What are the coordinates of the upper endpoint of the last line you drew?

Construction Tools and Multiview Drawings

Learning Objectives

After completing this chapter, you will be able to do the following:

✓ Use the **OFFSET** tool to draw parallel and concentric objects.
✓ Place construction points.
✓ Mark points on objects at equal lengths using the **DIVIDE** tool.
✓ Mark points on objects at designated increments using the **MEASURE** tool.
✓ Create construction lines using the **XLINE** and **RAY** tools.
✓ Create multiview drawings.

This chapter explains how to create parallel offsets, divide objects, place point objects, and use construction lines. You can use these skills and your existing geometric construction skills to create multiview drawings. This chapter describes tools for producing accurate geometric constructions. These tools do not constrain, or apply relationships between, objects. Chapter 22 explains how to use parametric drafting tools to constrain objects.

Parallel Offsets

The **OFFSET** tool is a common geometric construction tool that is useful for many different drafting tasks. For example, you can offset lines, polylines, or xlines to construct multiviews or form the thickness of architectural floor plan walls. Offset circles, arcs, or other curves to form concentric objects. For example, you can offset a circle to create the wall thickness of a pipe.

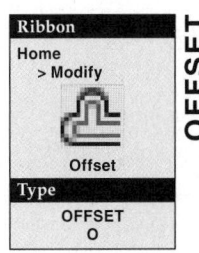

Ribbon
Home
> Modify
Offset
Type
OFFSET
O

OFFSET

Specifying the Offset Distance

Often the best way to use the **OFFSET** tool is to enter an offset value at the Specify offset distance or [Through/Erase/Layer] <*current*>: prompt. For example, to draw a circle concentric to and 1 unit from an existing circle, access the **OFFSET** tool, and specify an offset distance of 1. Pick the circle to offset, and then pick the side of the circle on which the offset occurs. See **Figure 8-1**. The **OFFSET** tool remains active, allowing you to pick another object to offset using the same offset distance. To exit, press [Enter], [Esc], or the space bar, or choose the **Exit** option.

Figure 8-1.
Drawing an offset circle using a designated distance.

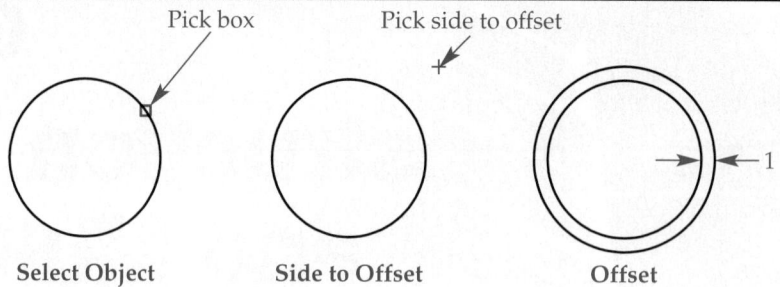

Select Object   Side to Offset   Offset

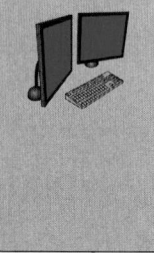

Through Option

Another option to specify the offset distance is to pick a point through which the offset occurs. Access the **OFFSET** tool and specify the **Through** option at the Specify offset distance or [Through/Erase/Layer] <current>: prompt, instead of picking an object to offset. Then pick the object to offset, and pick the point through which the offset occurs. See **Figure 8-2**. The **OFFSET** tool remains active, allowing you to pick another object to offset using the **Through** option. Exit the tool when you are finished offsetting.

Figure 8-2.
Drawing an offset through a given point.

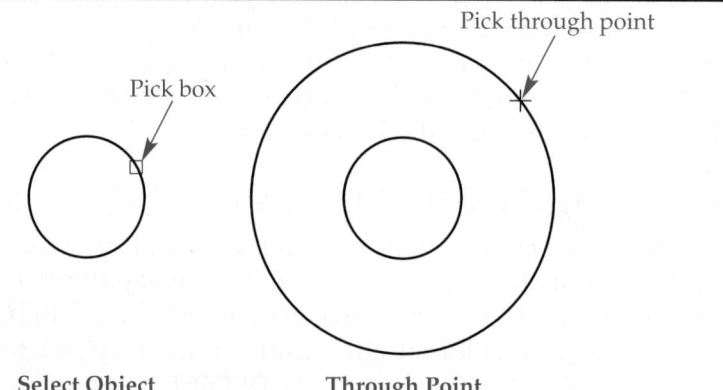

Select Object   Through Point

Erasing the Original Object

Use the **Erase** option of the **OFFSET** tool to erase the original, or source, object during the offset. Start the **OFFSET** tool, activate the **Erase** option, and choose **Yes** at the Erase source object after offsetting? prompt. The **Yes** option remains set as default until you change the setting to **No**. Be sure to change the **Erase** setting back to **No** if the source object should remain the next time you use the **OFFSET** tool. Exit the tool when you are finished offsetting.

Layer Option

By default, offsets use the same properties as the source object, including layer. Use the **Layer** option of the **OFFSET** tool to place the offset object on the current layer, regardless of the layer assigned to the source object. First, make the layer to apply to the offset current. Then start the **OFFSET** tool, activate the **Layer** option, and choose **Current** at the Enter layer option for offset objects: prompt. The **Current** option remains set as default until you change the setting to **Source**. Be sure to change the **Layer** setting back to **Source** if the layer assigned to the source object should apply to the offset the next time you use the **OFFSET** tool. Exit the tool when you are finished offsetting.

Multiple Option

The **Multiple** option is useful for offsetting more than once, using the same distance between objects, without having to reselect the object to offset. Access the **OFFSET** tool, specify the offset distance, and pick the source object. Then select the **Multiple** option and begin picking to specify the offset direction. See **Figure 8-3.** Exit when finished offsetting.

> **NOTE**
>
> You can use the **Undo** option, when available, to undo the last offset without exiting the **OFFSET** tool.

Exercise 8-1

Access the Student Web site (www.g-wlearning.com/CAD) and complete Exercise 8-1.

Figure 8-3.
Use the **Multiple** option to create multiple offsets of the same distance, without having to reselect the source object.

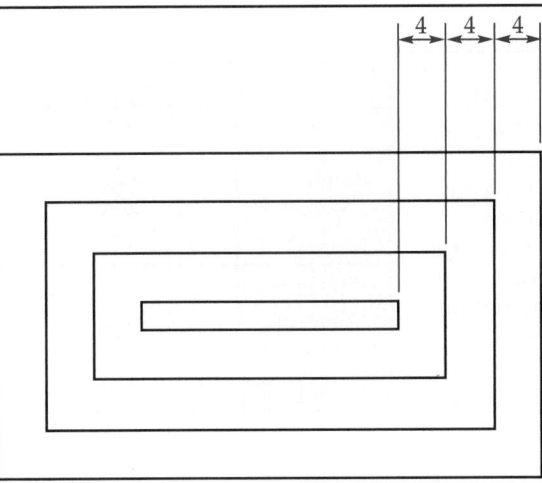

Ribbon
Home
> Draw

Multiple Points
Type
POINT
PO

Ribbon
Home
> Utilities

Point Style
Type
DDPTYPE

Drawing Points

Point objects are useful for identifying locations on a drawing and marking positions on objects. You can use the **POINT** tool to draw points anywhere in the drawing. Use any appropriate method to specify the location of a point object. To place a single point object and then exit the **POINT** tool, enter **POINT** or **PO** at the keyboard. To draw multiple points without exiting the **POINT** tool, access the **Multiple Points** function from the ribbon. Press [Esc] to exit the tool.

Setting Point Style

Points appear as one-pixel dots by default. The default appearance is functional and does not interfere with objects. However, the one-pixel style is difficult to see and can get lost. Change the point style and size using the **Point Style** dialog box, shown in **Figure 8-4.** Pick the image of the point style to make current.

Enter a value in the **Point Size:** text box to set the point size. Pick the **Set Size Relative to Screen** button to change the point size relative to the screen magnification, or zoom level. You may need to regenerate the display to view the relative sizes. Pick the **Set Size in Absolute Units** option button to make points appear the same size regardless of the screen magnification. See **Figure 8-5.** Pick the **OK** button to exit the **Point Style** dialog box. All existing and new points change to the current style and size.

Figure 8-4.
The **Point Style** dialog box provides a quick way to select the point style and change the point size.

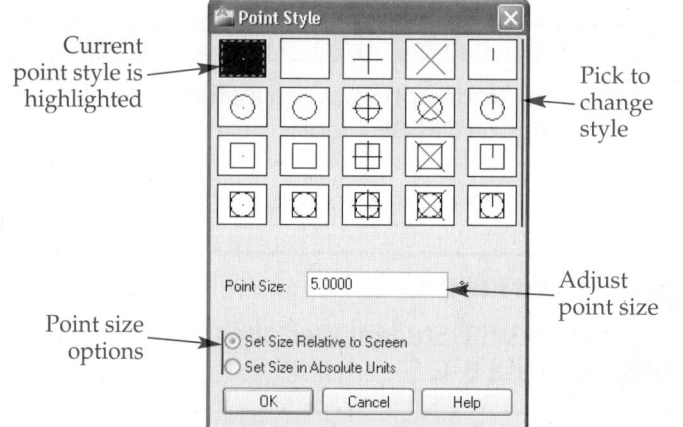

Current point style is highlighted

Pick to change style

Adjust point size

Point size options

Figure 8-5.
Points sized with the **Set Size Relative to Screen** setting change size as you zoom in and out. Points sized with the **Set Size in Absolute Units** setting remain a constant size.

Size Setting	Original Point Size	2X Zoom	.5 Zoom
Relative to Screen	⊠	⊠	⊠
Absolute Units	⊠	⊠	⊠

Exercise 8-2

Access the Student Web site (www.g-wlearning.com/CAD) and complete Exercise 8-2.

Marking an Object at Specified Increments

Use the **DIVIDE** tool to place point objects or blocks at equally spaced locations on a line, circle, arc, polyline, or spline. AutoCAD calculates the distance between marks based on the number of segments you specify. The **DIVIDE** tool does not break an object into an equal number of segments. Access the **DIVIDE** tool and select the object to mark. Enter the number of segments, and then exit the tool. The point style determines the appearance of the point objects. **Figure 8-6** shows marking 7 segments with points.

The **Block** option of the **DIVIDE** tool allows you to place a *block* at each increment, instead of a point object. Select the **Block** option at the Enter the number of segments or [Block]: prompt to insert a block. AutoCAD asks if the block should align with the object, such as rotate around a circle. You will learn about blocks later in this textbook.

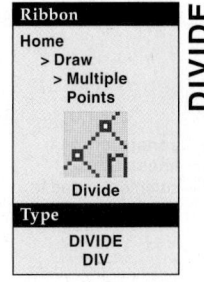

block: A symbol or shape saved for repeated use.

Marking an Object at Specified Distances

Use the **MEASURE** tool to place point objects or blocks a specified distance apart on a line, circle, arc, polyline, or spline. In contrast to the **DIVIDE** tool, the length of each segment and total length of the object determines the number of segments. The **MEASURE** tool does not break an object at specific lengths.

Access the **MEASURE** tool and select the object to mark. Measurement begins at the end closest to where you pick the object. Enter the distance between points, and then exit the tool. All increments are equal to the specified segment length except the last segment, which may be shorter. The point style determines the appearance of point objects. **Figure 8-7** shows marking .75 unit length segments with points. Use the **Block** option of the **MEASURE** tool to place a block at each interval.

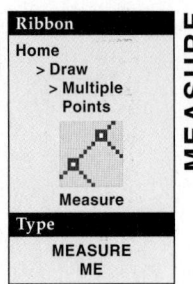

Figure 8-6.
Marking seven equal segments with points on a circle and a line using the **DIVIDE** tool. An × point style replaces the default point appearance in these examples. Notice that points do not appear at the endpoints of open objects, such as the line.

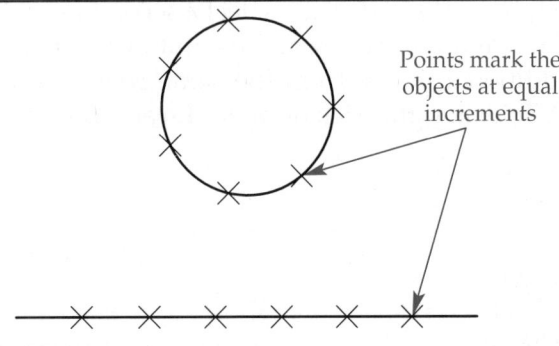

Points mark the objects at equal increments

Figure 8-7.
Using the **MEASURE** tool to place point objects on a line at .75 unit intervals. Notice that the last segment may be short, depending on the specified interval and total length of the object.

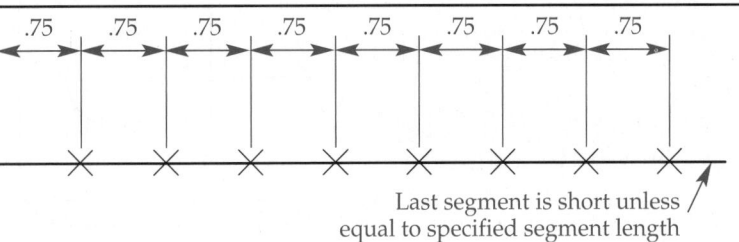

Last segment is short unless equal to specified segment length

Exercise 8-3

Access the Student Web site (www.g-wlearning.com/CAD) and complete Exercise 8-3.

Construction Lines and Rays

construction lines: Lines commonly used to lay out a drawing.

The tracking vectors and alignment paths available with object snap and AutoTrack tools are examples of *construction lines* generated by AutoCAD. Object snap and AutoTrack are very efficient for constructing geometry because vector and alignment lines appear as you draw. Often, however, drawings require construction lines that remain on-screen for reference and future use. You can draw construction geometry using any drawing tool, such as **LINE**, **ARC**, or **CIRCLE**. The **XLINE** and **RAY** tools are specifically designed for adding construction lines to help lay out a drawing. See **Figure 8-8**.

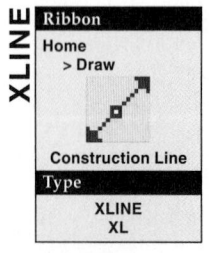

PROFESSIONAL TIP

Create construction geometry on a separate construction layer, named CONST, CONSTRUCTION, or A-ANNO-NPLT, for example. Turn off or freeze the construction layer when unneeded, or you can easily recognize and erase objects drawn on the construction layer if necessary.

Ribbon
Home
> Draw

Construction Line
Type
XLINE
XL

Using the XLINE Tool

Use the **XLINE** tool to draw an infinitely long AutoCAD construction line object, or *xline*. To draw a basic xline, specify the location of the first point through which the xline passes, or *root point*. Then select a second point through which the xline passes. The **XLINE** tool remains active, and the initial root point acts as an axis point. Continue locating additional points from the same root point to create additional xlines. See **Figure 8-9**. To exit, right-click or press [Enter], [Esc], or the space bar.

xline: A construction line in AutoCAD that is infinite in both directions; often helpful for creating accurate geometry and multiviews.

root point: The first point specified to create a construction line or ray.

Figure 8-8.
An example of a drawing laid out using construction lines.

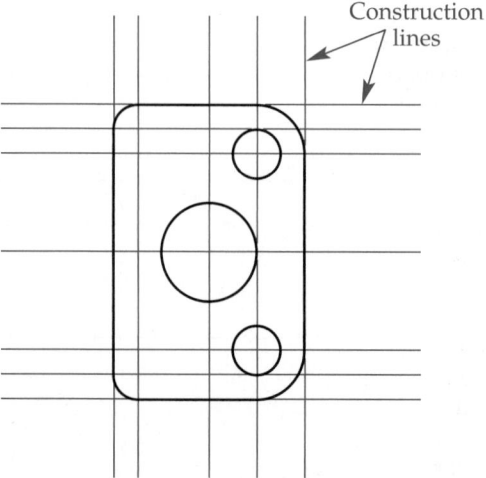

Construction lines

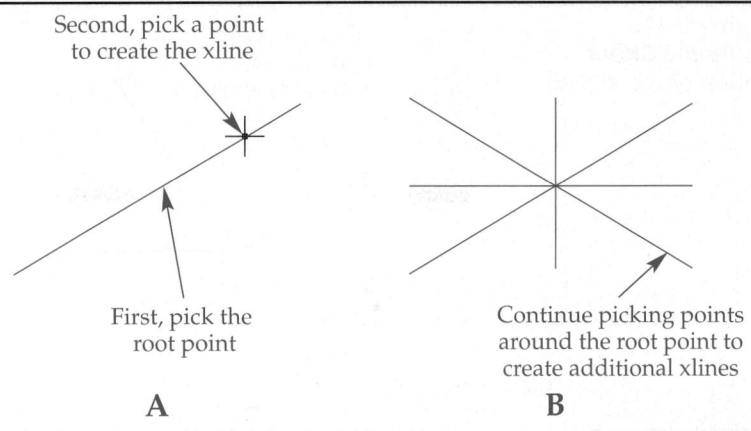

Figure 8-9.
A—Using the **XLINE** tool to draw an infinitely long construction line by picking two points through which the line passes. B—Constructing multiple xlines that intersect the root point before exiting the tool.

Second, pick a point to create the xline

First, pick the root point

Continue picking points around the root point to create additional xlines

A

B

Hor and Ver Options

Xline options are available as alternatives to selecting two points. The **Hor** option draws a horizontal xline through a single specified point. The **Ver** option draws a vertical xline through a single specified point. Use the **Hor** or **Ver** option when you know construction lines should be horizontal or vertical. The **XLINE** tool remains active with the **Hor** or **Ver** option, allowing you to draw additional horizontal or vertical xlines. Exit when you are finished placing xlines.

Ang Option

Use the **Ang** option to draw an xline at a precise angle through a selected point. Specify an angle by entering a value or picking two points, and then pick a point through which the xline passes. The **Reference** option of the **Ang** option allows you to reference the angle of an existing line object to use as the xline angle. The **Reference** option is useful when you do not know the angle of the xline, but you do know the angle between an existing object and the xline. See **Figure 8-10.**

Bisect Option

The **Bisect** option draws an xline that bisects a specified angle, using the root point as the vertex. See **Figure 8-11.** The **Bisect** option is useful for bisecting an angle and similar applications.

Offset Option

The **Offset** option draws an xline parallel to a selected linear object. The **Offset** option of the **XLINE** tool functions much like the **OFFSET** tool, except that the **Offset** option of the **XLINE** tool offsets an xline from the selected object, instead of the object itself. As with the **OFFSET** tool, specify an offset distance or use the **Through** option to pick a point through which to draw the xline.

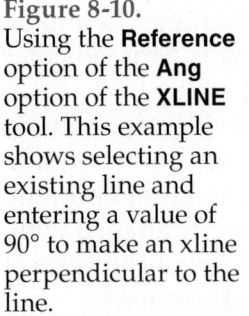
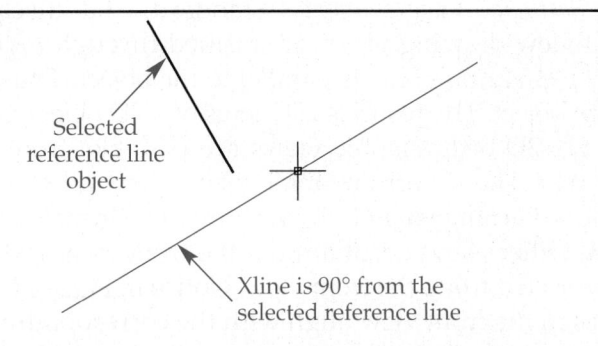

Figure 8-10.
Using the **Reference** option of the **Ang** option of the **XLINE** tool. This example shows selecting an existing line and entering a value of 90° to make an xline perpendicular to the line.

Selected reference line object

Xline is 90° from the selected reference line

Figure 8-11.
Using the **Bisect** option of the **XLINE** tool.

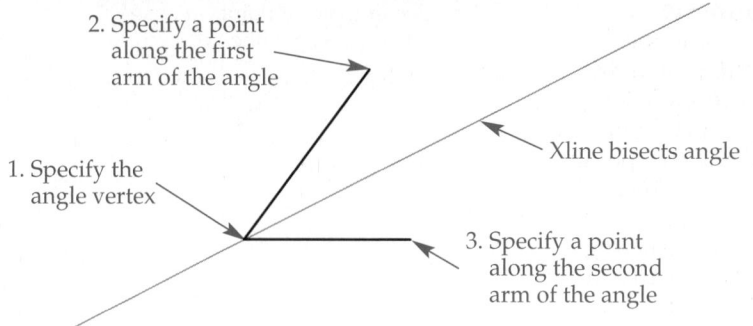

2. Specify a point along the first arm of the angle

Xline bisects angle

1. Specify the angle vertex

3. Specify a point along the second arm of the angle

NOTE

Although xlines are infinite, they do not change the drawing extents, and they have no effect on zooming operations.

Exercise 8-4

Access the Student Web site (www.g-wlearning.com/CAD) **and complete Exercise 8-4.**

Using the RAY Tool

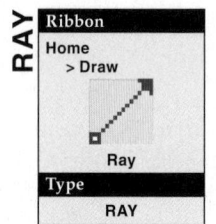

RAY

Ribbon
Home
> Draw

Ray

Type
RAY

ray: A linear AutoCAD object that is infinite in one direction only; considered semi-infinite.

Use the **RAY** tool to draw an AutoCAD *ray* object. A ray begins at an origin point and extends though another point, similar to the default option of the **XLINE** tool. However, a ray is infinite only in the direction of the second point. To draw a ray, specify the location of the root point, followed by a second point through which the ray passes. Continue locating points to create additional rays from the same root point. To exit, right-click or press [Enter], [Esc], or the space bar.

Multiview Drawings

multiview drawing: Presentation of drawing views created through orthographic projection.

A *multiview drawing* presents views of a product. The general multiview concept applies to most drafting fields. Mechanical drafting uses multiview drawings to represent part and assembly features. Architectural drafting uses plans, elevations, and sections to show building construction and layout. Electronics drafting uses schematic diagrams with electronic symbols to show circuit layout. Civil drafting uses plans and profiles show the topography of land.

This textbook explains multiview drawings based on the ASME Y14.3, *Multiview and Sectional View Drawings* standard, and discipline specific drafting practices. Multiview drawing views are formed through *orthographic projection*. The imaginary *projection plane* is parallel to the object. Thus, the line of sight is perpendicular to the object. The result is 2D views of a 3D object. See **Figure 8-12.**

orthographic projection: Projecting object features onto an imaginary plane.

projection plane: An imaginary projection plane parallel to the object.

Six 2D orthographic views are possible: front, right side, left side, top, bottom, and rear. The six orthographic views show all sides of an object and are drawn in a standard arrangement for readability. The front view is the central, or most important, view. Other views occur around the front view and usually are directly aligned with, or projected from, the front view. Notice in **Figure 8-13** that the horizontal and vertical edges in the front view align with the corresponding edges in the other views.

2011
TAX RATE SCHEDULES

ESTATES AND TRUSTS [§1 (e)]:

If taxable income is:	The tax is:
Not over $2,300	15% of taxable income.
Over $2,300 but not over $5,450	$345.00, plus 25% of the excess over $2,300.
Over $5,450 but not over $8,300	$1,132.50, plus 28% of the excess over $5,450.
Over $8,300 but not over $11,350	$1,930.50, plus 33% of the excess over $8,300.
Over $11,350	$2,937.00, plus 35% of the excess over $11,350.

CORPORATIONS

If Taxable Income Is: Over—	But Not Over—	The Tax Is:	Of the Amount Over—
$ 0	$ 50,000	15%	$ 0
50,000	75,000	$ 7,500 + 25%	50,000
75,000	100,000	13,750 + 34%	75,000
100,000	335,000	22,250 + 39%	100,000
335,000	10,000,000	113,900 + 34%	335,000
10,000,000	15,000,000	3,400,000 + 35%	10,000,000
15,000,000	18,333,333	5,150,000 + 38%	15,000,000
18,333,333		6,416,667 + 35%	18,333,333

UNIFIED CREDIT AMOUNT FOR ESTATE AND GIFT TAX

Year of Gift/Year of Death	Amount of Credit	Exemption Equivalent[a] (or Applicable Exclusion Amount)
January through June, 1977	$ 30,000 (6,000)[b]	$ 120,666 (30,000)[b]
July through December, 1977	30,000	120,666
1978	34,000	134,000
1979	38,000	147,333
1980	42,500	161,563
1981	47,000	175,625
1982	62,800	225,000
1983	79,300	275,000
1984	96,300	325,000
1985	121,800	400,000
1986	155,800	500,000
1987 through 1997	192,800	600,000
1998	202,050	625,000
1999	211,300	650,000
2000	220,550	675,000
2001	220,550	675,000
2002 and 2003	345,800	1,000,000
2004 and 2005	555,800 (345,800)[b]	1,500,000 (1,000,000)[b]
2006, 2007, and 2008	780,800 (345,800)[b]	2,000,000 (1,000,000)[b]
2009	1,455,800 (345,800)[b]	3,500,000 (1,000,000)[b]
2010	1,730,800[c] (330,800)[b]	5,000,000[c] (1,000,000)[b]
2011 and 2012	1,730,800[c,d]	5,000,000[c,d]

[a] For estate tax purposes in 2011 and 2012, this amount is called the basic exclusion amount.
[b] The numbers in parentheses represent the credit and exemption equivalent amounts for the gift tax.
[c] This amount applies if the executor opts to have the estate subject to the estate tax and FMV basis rule in 2010.
[d] This amount will be indexed for inflation in 2012.

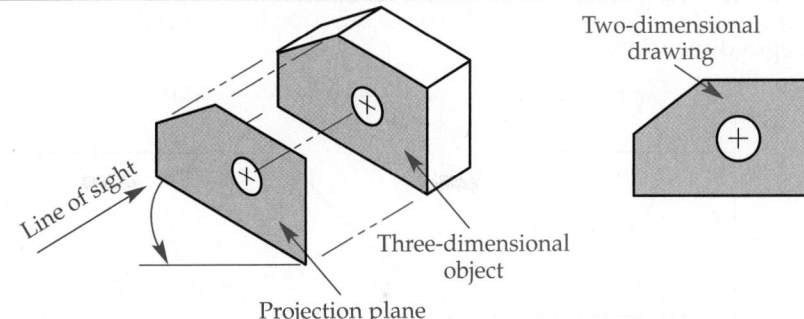

Figure 8-12.
Obtaining a
front view with
orthographic
projection.

Line of sight

Projection plane

Three-dimensional
object

Two-dimensional
drawing

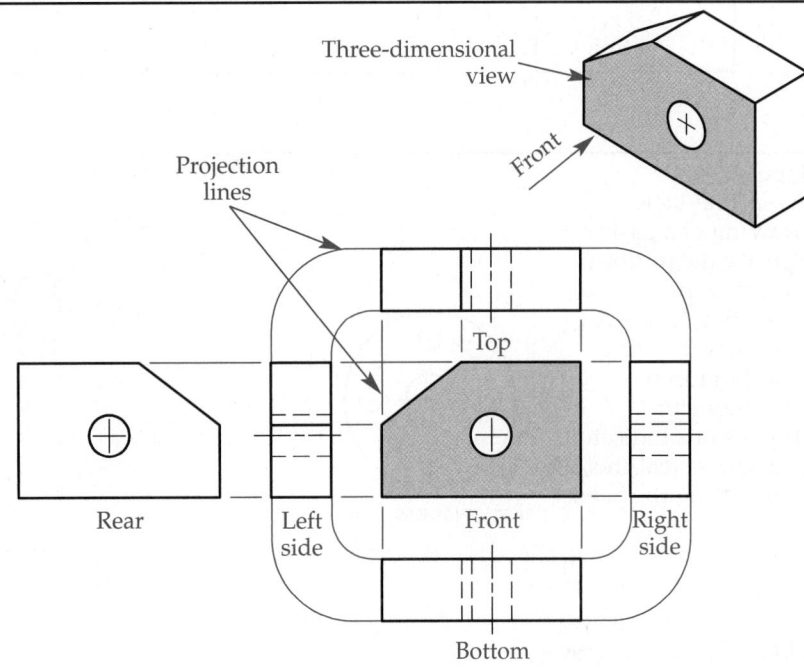

Figure 8-13.
Arrangement of the
six orthographic
views. The front
view is typically
central.

Three-dimensional
view

Front

Projection
lines

Top

Rear

Left
side

Front

Right
side

Bottom

Selecting the Front View

The front view is central to most multiview drawings. Consider the following
rules when selecting the front view:
- ✓ Most descriptive
- ✓ Most natural position
- ✓ Most stable position
- ✓ Provides the longest dimension
- ✓ Contains the least number of hidden features

Choosing Additional Views

Select additional views relative to the front view. Very few products require all
six views. The required number of views depends on the complexity of the object.
Use only enough views to describe the object completely. Drawing too many views
is time-consuming and can clutter the drawing. **Figure 8-14** shows an example of an
object that needs only two views. The two views completely describe the width, height,
depth, and features of the object. In some cases, a single view is enough to describe the
object. The example shown in **Figure 8-14** could be a one-view drawing with a note
specifying the uniform depth, or material. You can often draw a thin part that has a
uniform thickness, such as a gasket, with one view. If necessary, provide the thickness
or material specification as a general note or in the title block. See **Figure 8-15.**

Figure 8-14. The views you choose to describe the object should show all height, width, and depth dimensions.

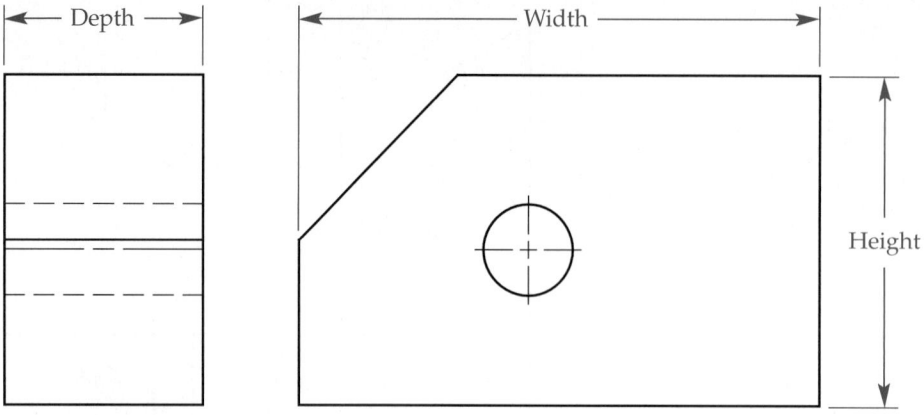

Figure 8-15. A—A one-view drawing of a gasket. Specify the uniform thickness in a general note. B—A one-view drawing of a thumbscrew. The diameter dimensions indicate cylindrical features, eliminating the need for a side view.

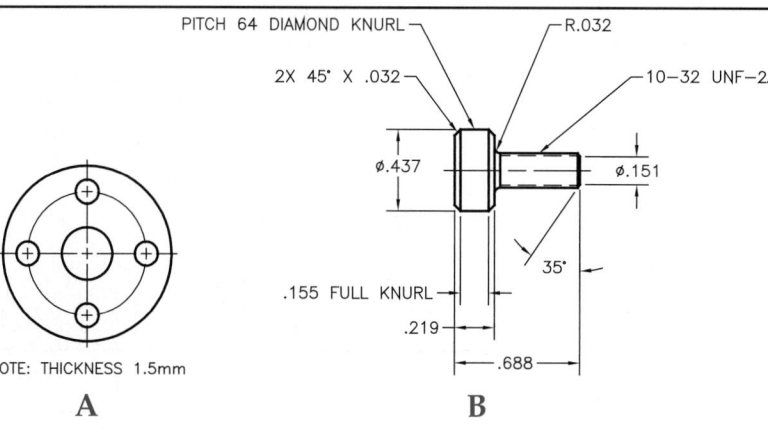

Auxiliary Views

You can sometimes completely describe an object using one or more of the six standard views. However, you must use an *auxiliary view* to describe a surface that appears *foreshortened* in standard orthographic views. Draw an auxiliary view using projection lines perpendicular to a slanted surface. One projection line is sometimes included on the drawing to connect the auxiliary view to the view where the slanted surface appears as a line. The resulting auxiliary view shows the surface at its true size and shape. A *partial auxiliary view* is enough for most applications. See **Figure 8-16.**

Removed Views

Sometime there is not enough room on a drawing to project directly from one view to another. This requires that you create a *removed view* to locate a view elsewhere on the drawing. An auxiliary view is a common example of a removed view in mechanical drafting, but you can relocate any view if necessary. See **Figure 8-17.** In other disciplines, such as architectural drafting, separate views, and even the same view, do not align and often occur on different sheets.

Draw a *viewing-plane line* parallel to the view in which the surface appears as a line. The standard viewing-plane line terminates with bold arrowheads that point toward the surface. A letter labels each end of the viewing-plane line. The letters correlate to the removed view title, such as **VIEW A-A**, below the removed view to key the viewing plane with the removed view. When you remove more than one view from direct projection, labels continue with **B-B** through **Z-Z**, if necessary. Do not use letters *I, O, Q, S, X,* and *Z,* because they can be confused with numbers.

Figure 8-16.
Auxiliary views
show the true size
and shape of an
inclined surface. Use
a partial auxiliary
view to show only
the inclined surface,
because the other
features appear
foreshortened and
reduce clarity.

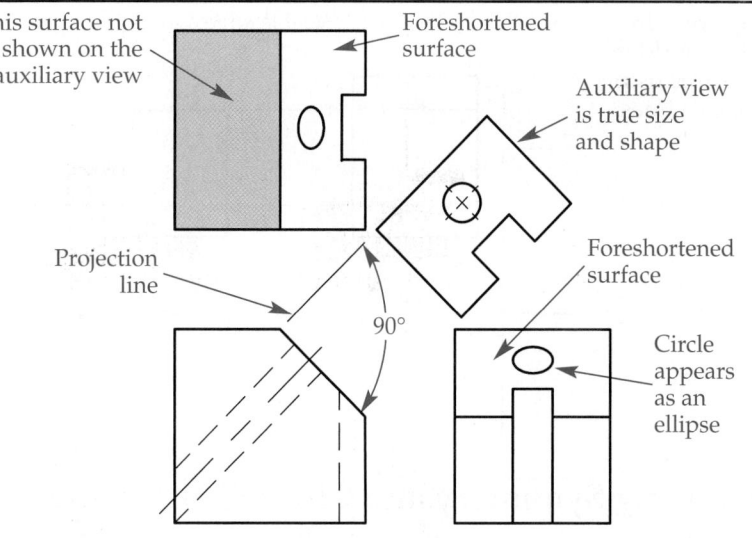

Figure 8-17.
A viewing-plane line
creates the flexibility
to move a view to a
location where there
is enough space
for the view. This
process creates a
removed view.

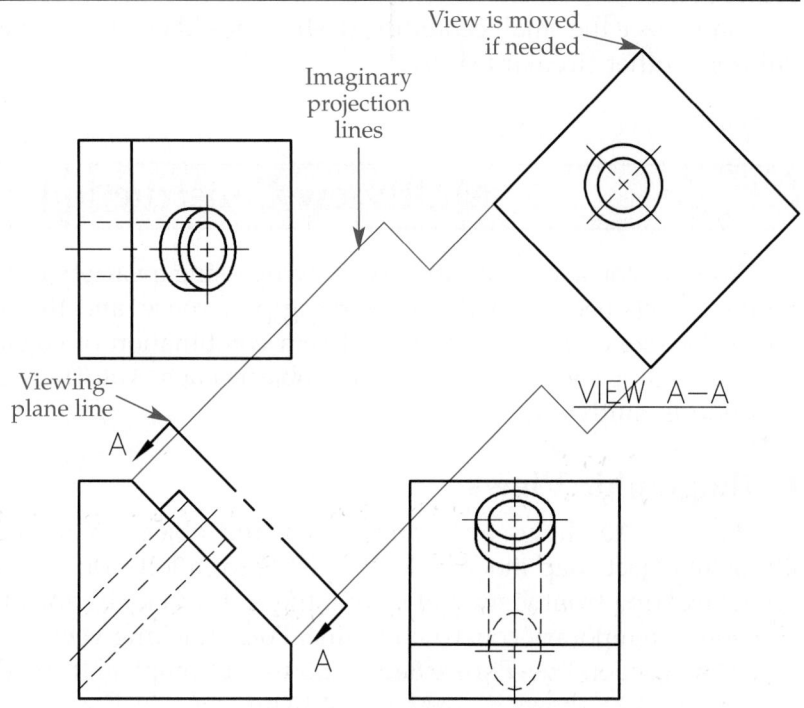

NOTE

A removed view retains the same angle as if it were projected
directly, which is especially important for an auxiliary view.

Showing Hidden Features

A multiview drawing typically shows hidden features of an object, even though
they are not visible in the view at which you are looking. Visible edges appear as object
lines. Hidden edges appear as hidden lines. Hidden lines are thin to provide contrast
with thick object lines. See **Figure 8-18.**

Figure 8-18.
Draw hidden features using hidden lines.

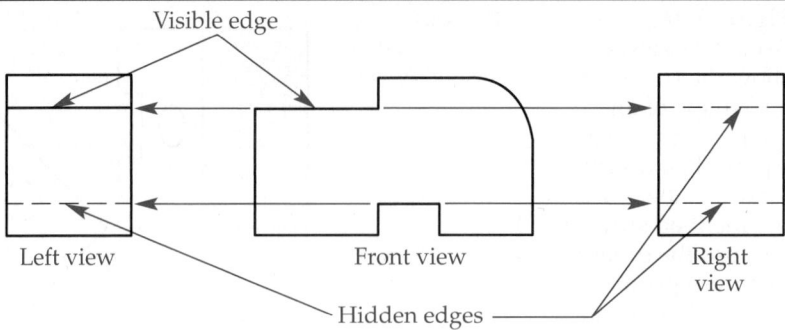

Visible edge

Left view   Front view   Right view

Hidden edges

Showing Symmetry and Circle Centers

Centerlines indicate the centerlines of symmetrical objects and the centers of circles. For example, in the circular view of a cylinder, centerlines cross to show the center of the cylinder. In the other view, a centerline identifies the axis. See **Figure 8-19.** The only place the small centerline dashes should cross is at the center of a circle, arc, ellipse, or other circular feature.

Multiview Construction

You can construct a multiview drawing using a variety of techniques, depending on the objects needed, personal working preference, and the information you know about the size and shape of items. Use a combination of construction methods and tools, including coordinate point entry, object snaps, AutoTrack, and construction lines to produce multiviews.

Orthographic Views

Figure 8-20 shows an example of using object snap tracking and a running **Endpoint** object snap mode to locate points for a left-side view by referencing points on the existing front view. Notice that the AutoTrack alignment path in **Figure 8-20A** provides a temporary construction line. Polar tracking vectors offer a similar temporary construction line. **Figure 8-20B** shows the complete front and left-side views.

Figure 8-21 shows an example of using construction lines to form three views. This example shows offsetting vertical and horizontal xlines to form an xline grid. Use the **Intersection** object snap mode to select the intersecting xlines when drawing line and arc endpoints and the center point of the arc. Notice that a single infinitely long xline can provide construction geometry for multiple views.

Figure 8-19.
Use of centerlines in multiview drawings.

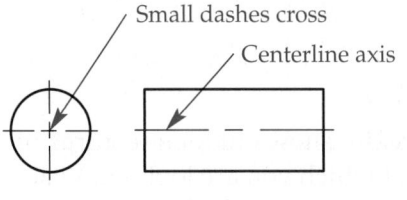

Small dashes cross

Centerline axis

Centerlines of a Cylinder

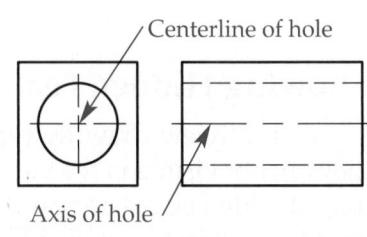

Centerline of hole

Axis of hole

Centerlines of a Hole

Figure 8-20.
An example of using object snap tracking to create an additional view. A—Referencing points from the front view to establish the first line of the left-side view. B—The completed front and left-side views.

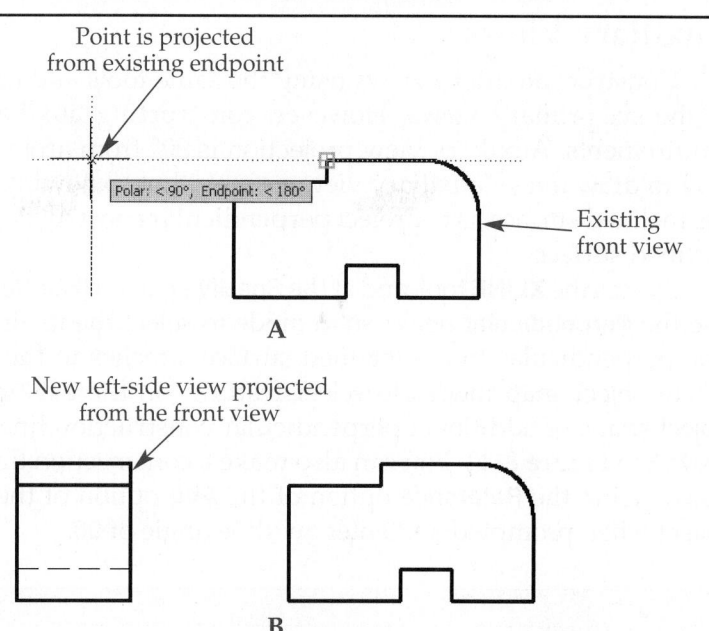

Point is projected from existing endpoint

Polar: < 90°, Endpoint: < 180°

Existing front view

A

New left-side view projected from the front view

B

Figure 8-21. Using a complete grid of construction lines to form a multiview drawing by "connecting the dots" at the intersections of the construction lines. You can quickly draw the rectangular outlines of the right side, left side, and top views using the **RECTANGLE** tool.

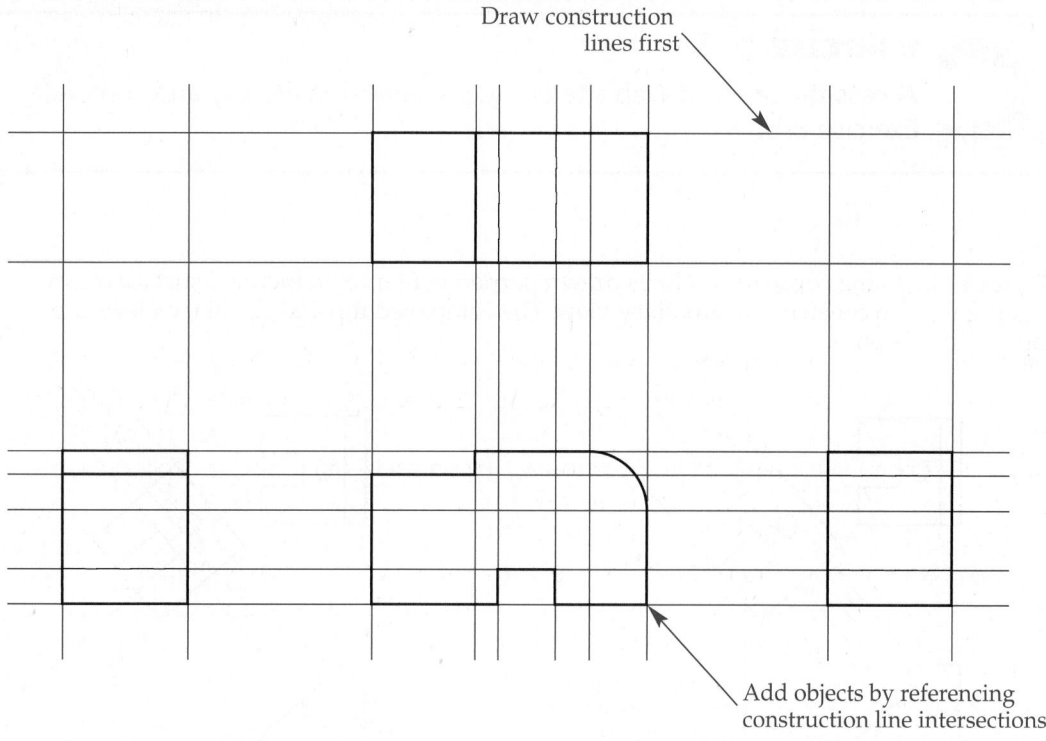

Draw construction lines first

Add objects by referencing construction line intersections

Exercise 8-5

Access the Student Web site (www.g-wlearning.com/CAD) and complete Exercise 8-5.

Auxiliary Views

Construct auxiliary views using the same tools and options you use to draw any of the six primary views. However, constructing auxiliary views presents unique requirements. Auxiliary view projection is 90° from an inclined surface. An effective way to draw a new auxiliary view, even without knowing or calculating the angle of the inclined surface, is to project perpendicular construction lines from features on the inclined surface.

Access the **XLINE** tool, and at the Specify a point or [Hor/Ver/Ang/Bisect/Offset]: prompt, use the **Perpendicular** object snap mode to select the inclined surface. A construction line perpendicular to the inclined surface attaches to the crosshairs. Use the appropriate object snap modes to select features on the existing view. You can then use object snaps or additional perpendicular construction lines to complete the auxiliary view. See **Figure 8-22.** You can also make a construction line perpendicular to a linear object using the **Reference** option of the **Ang** option of the **XLINE** tool. Select the line object when prompted and enter an xline angle of 90.

> **NOTE**
>
> You can also use parametric tools, explained in Chapter 22, in addition or as an alternative to other techniques for constructing multiview drawings.

 **Exercise 8-6**

Access the Student Web site (www.g-wlearning.com/CAD) and complete Exercise 8-6.

Figure 8-22. Using construction lines drawn perpendicular to an inclined surface on an existing view to construct an auxiliary view. The completed top and auxiliary views are shown for reference.

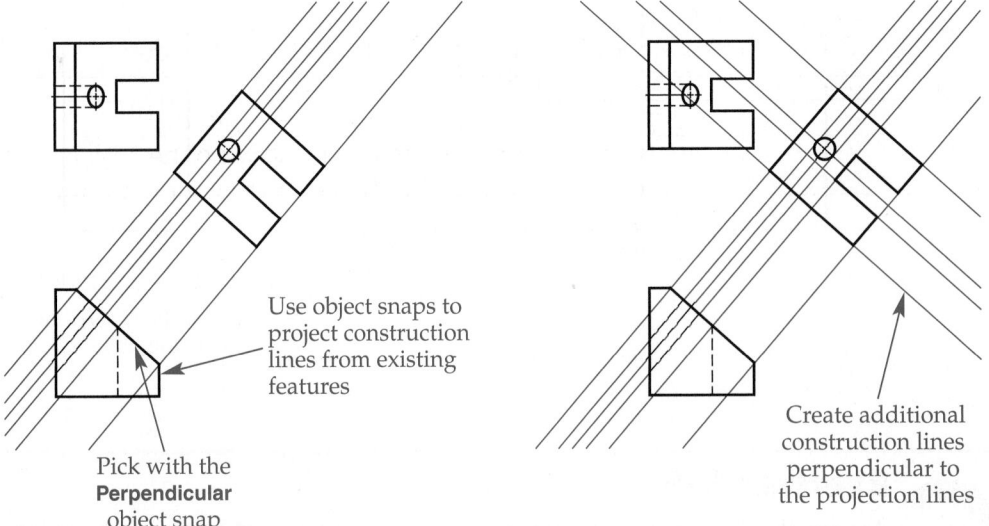

Use object snaps to project construction lines from existing features

Pick with the **Perpendicular** object snap

Create additional construction lines perpendicular to the projection lines

Template Development
Chapter 8

For detailed instructions on choosing a more appropriate point style to use for construction purposes, go to the Student Web site (www.g-wlearning.com/CAD), select this chapter, and select **Template Development**.

Chapter Test

Answer the following questions. Write your answers on a separate sheet of paper or go to the Student Web site (www.g-wlearning.com/CAD) and complete the electronic chapter test.

1. List two ways to establish an offset distance using the **OFFSET** tool.
2. Which option of the **OFFSET** tool allows you to remove the source offset object?
3. How do you draw a single point, and how do you draw multiple points?
4. How do you access the **Point Style** dialog box?
5. If you use the **DIVIDE** tool and nothing seems to happen, what should you do to make the points more visible?
6. How do you change the point size in the **Point Style** dialog box?
7. What tool can you use to place point objects that mark 24 equal segments on a line?
8. What is the difference between the **DIVIDE** and **MEASURE** tools?
9. Why is it a good idea to put construction lines on their own layer?
10. Name the tool that allows you to draw infinite construction lines.
11. Name the option that allows you to bisect an angle with a construction line.
12. What is the difference between the construction lines drawn with the tool identified in Question 10 and rays drawn with the **RAY** tool?
13. What ASME drafting standard applies to multiview drawings?
14. Provide at least four guidelines for selecting the front view of an orthographic multiview drawing.
15. How do you determine how many views of an object are necessary in a multiview drawing?
16. When can you describe a part with only one view?
17. When does a drawing require an auxiliary view, and what does an auxiliary view show?
18. List two methods of aligning the views in a multiview drawing.
19. What is the angle of projection from the slanted surface into the auxiliary view?
20. Describe an effective method of constructing an auxiliary view even if you do not know the angle of the inclined surface.

Drawing Problems

Start AutoCAD if it is not already started. Start a new drawing from scratch or use an appropriate template of your choice. The template should include layers for drawing the given objects. Add layers as needed. Draw all objects using appropriate layers. Follow the specific instructions for each problem. Use only drawing tools and techniques you have already learned. Use object snap and AutoTrack when possible. Do not draw dimensions or text. Use your own judgment and approximate dimensions when necessary.

▼ Basic

1. Draw the front and side views of the offset support shown. Save the drawing as **P8-1**.

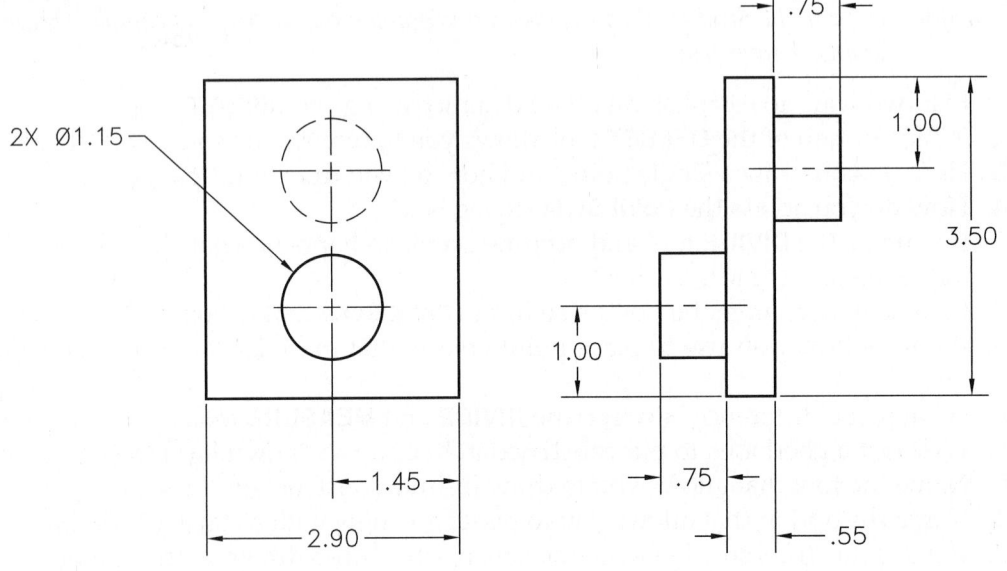

2. Draw the front and top views of the hitch bracket shown. Save the drawing as **P8-2**.

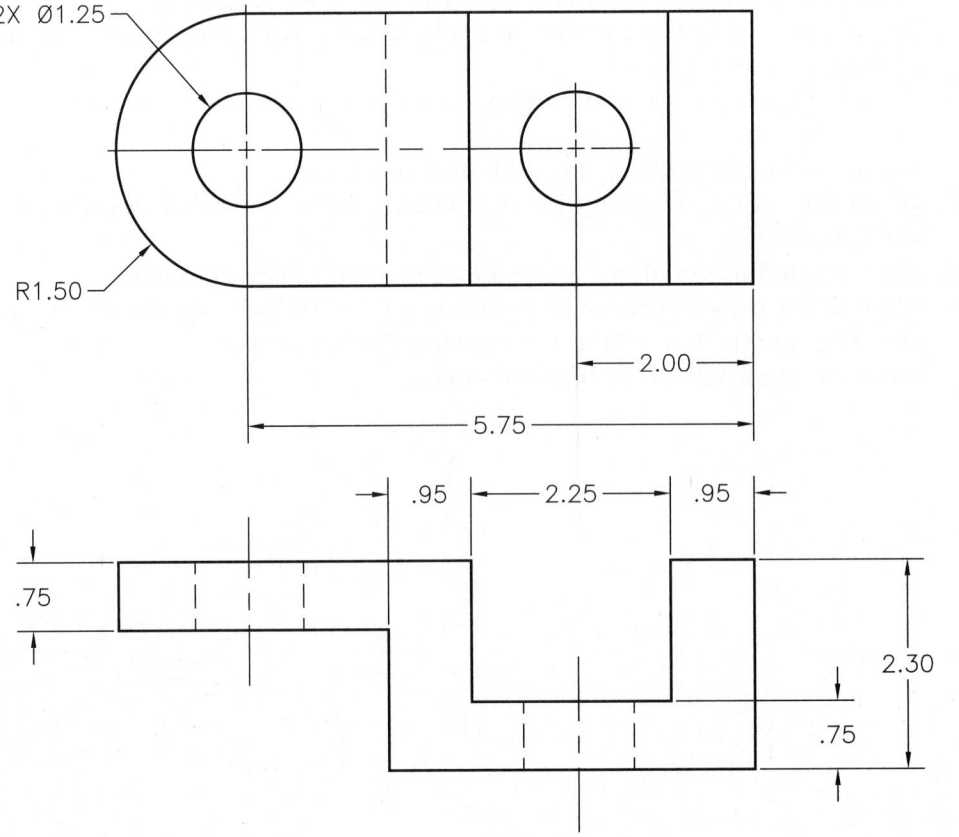

3. Draw the spring shown using the **PLINE** tool with a width of .024. Save the drawing as P8-3.

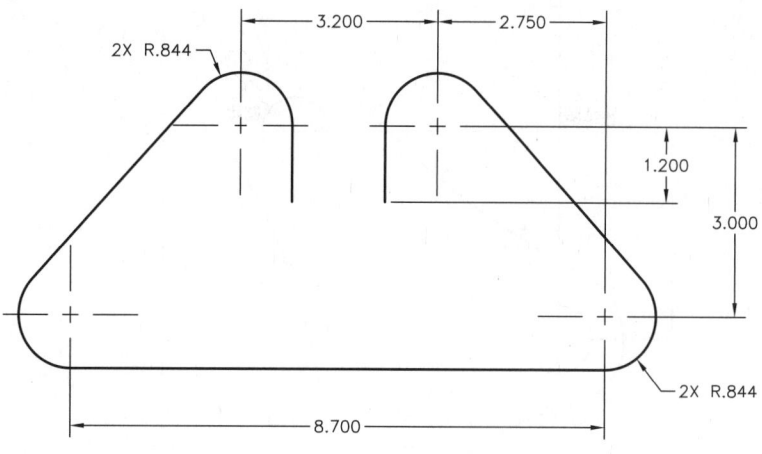

(Art courtesy of Bruce L. Wilcox)

4. Draw the sheet metal chassis shown. Save the drawing as P8-4.

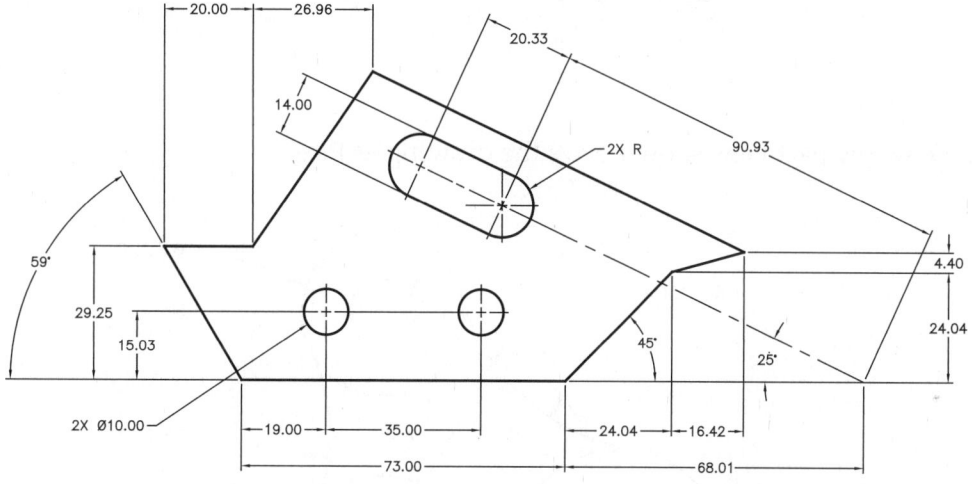

(Art courtesy of Bruce L. Wilcox)

▼ Intermediate

5. Draw the views of the elbow shown. Save the drawing as P8-5.

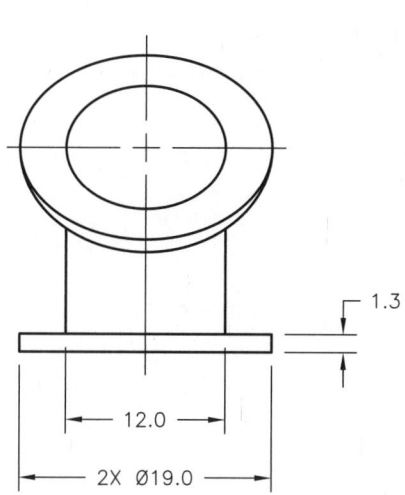

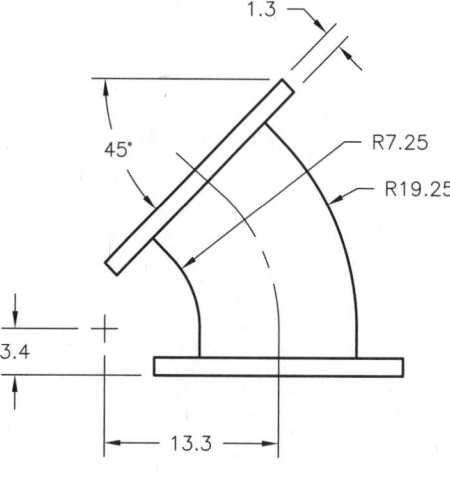

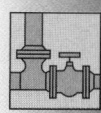

6. Draw the part view shown. Save the drawing as **P8-6**.

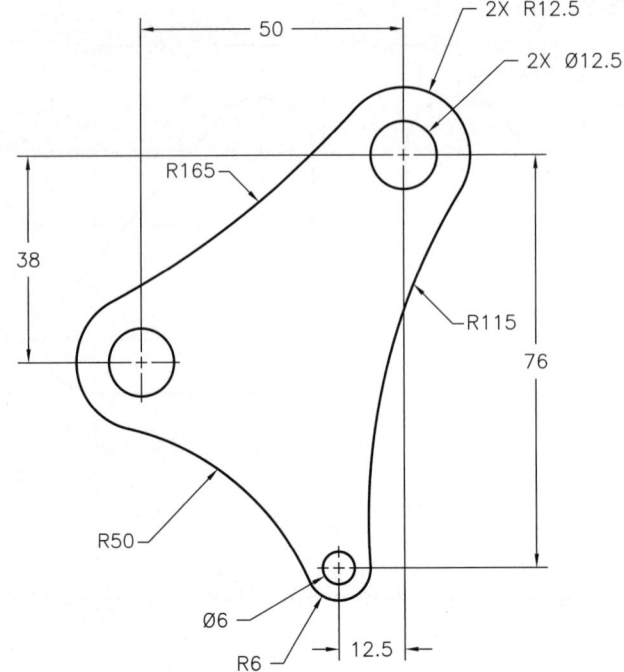

7. Draw the part view shown. Save the drawing as **P8-7**.

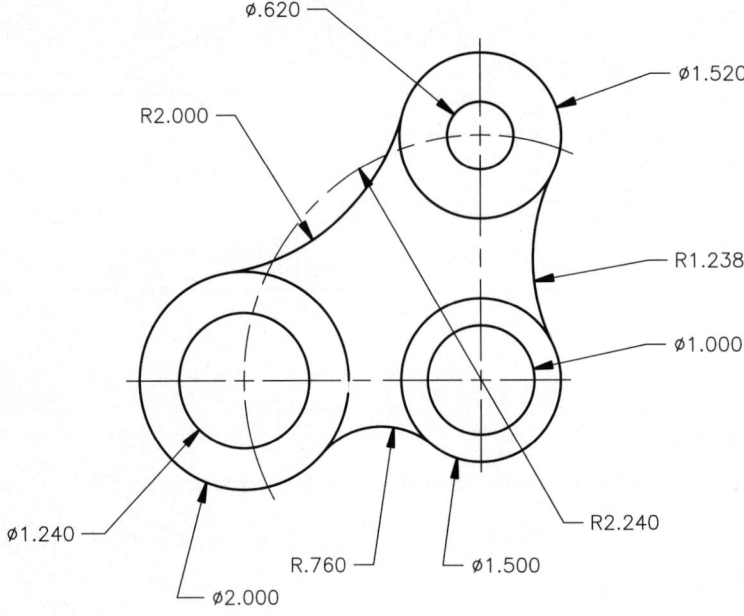

(Art courtesy of Bruce L. Wilcox)

8. Draw the views of the elbow shown. Save the drawing as **P8-8**.

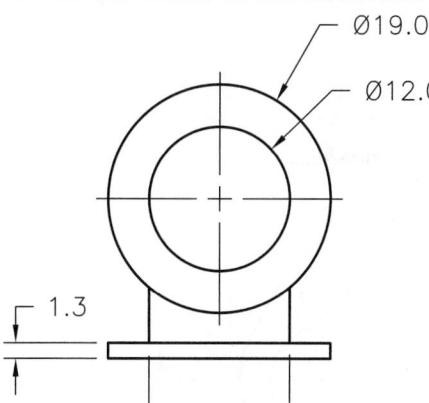
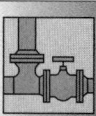
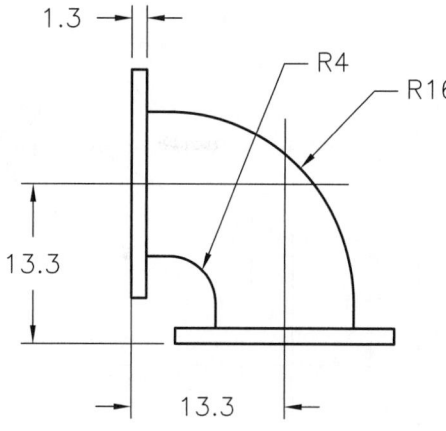

9. Use the **OFFSET** tool to draw the elevation of the desk shown. Center 1″ × 4″ rectangular drawer handles 2″ below the top of each drawer. The top of the legs begin 1″ from the edge of the bottom of the desk. Save the drawing as **P8-9**.

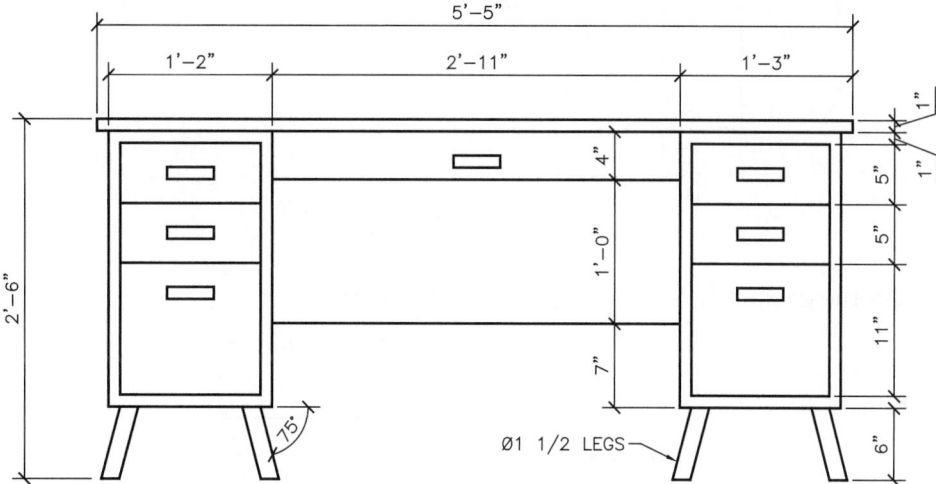

10. Draw the aluminum spacer shown. Save the drawing as **P8-10**.

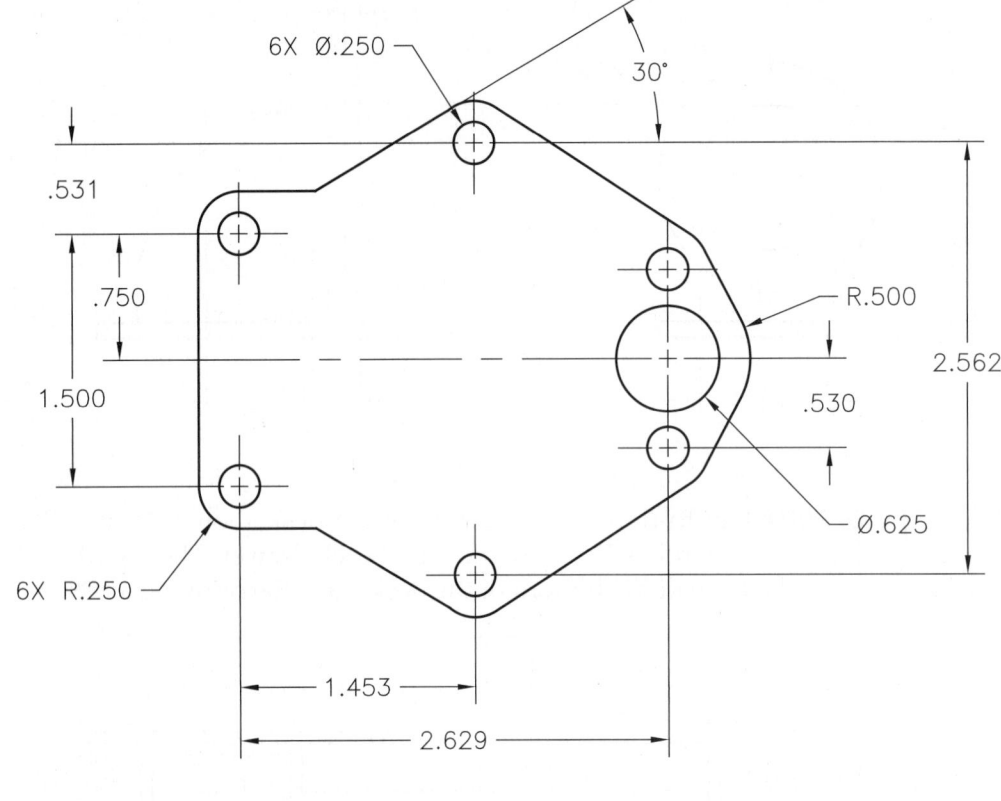

6X Ø.250

30°

.531

.750

1.500

R.500

2.562

.530

Ø.625

6X R.250

1.453

2.629

.250 THK

11. Draw the gasket shown. Save the drawing as **P8-11**.

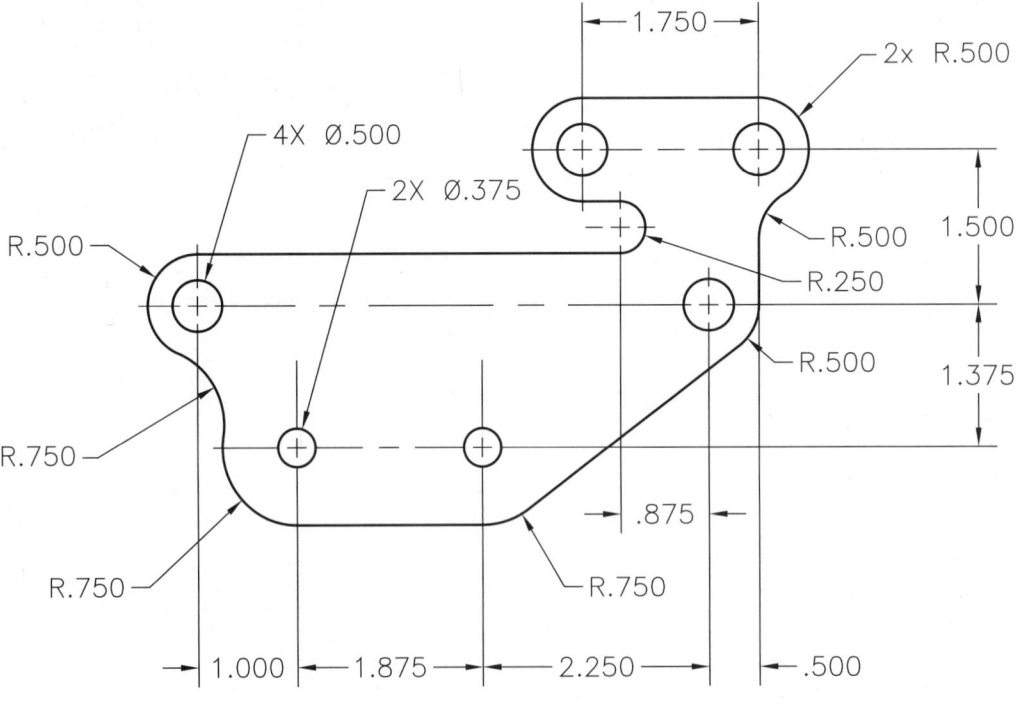

1.750

2x R.500

4X Ø.500

2X Ø.375

R.500

1.500

R.500

R.250

R.750

R.500

1.375

R.750

.875

R.750

1.000   1.875   2.250   .500

12. Draw the views of the cup shown. Save the drawing as **P8-12**.

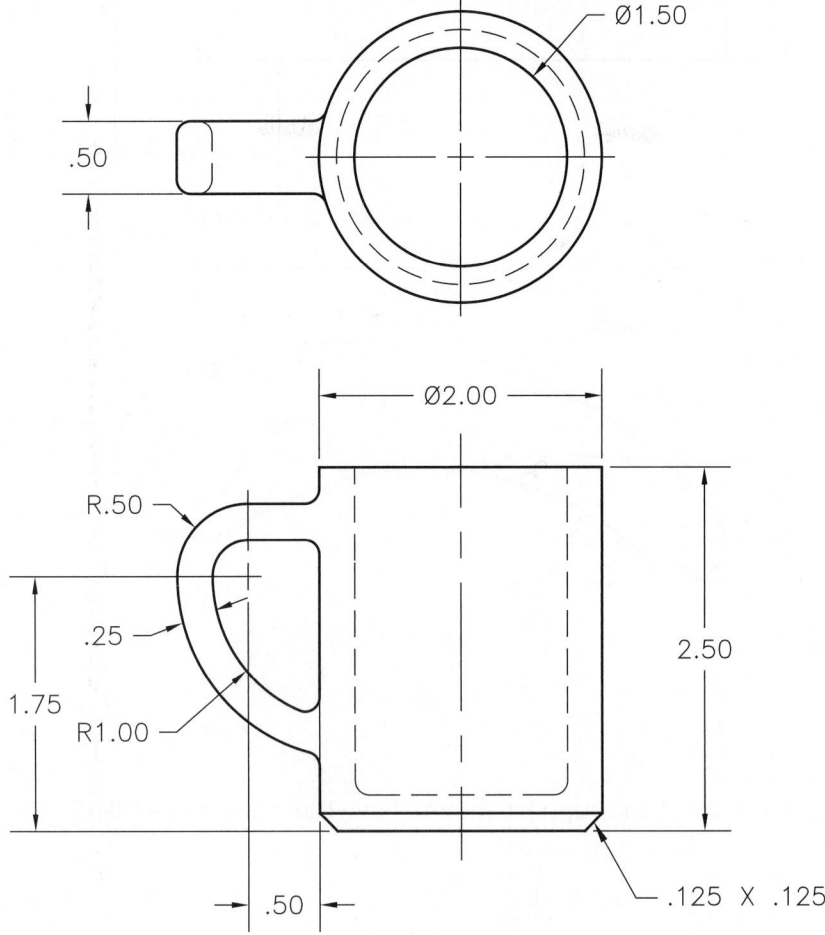

FILLETS AND ROUNDS R.10

13. Draw the views of the bushing shown. Save the drawing as **P8-13**.

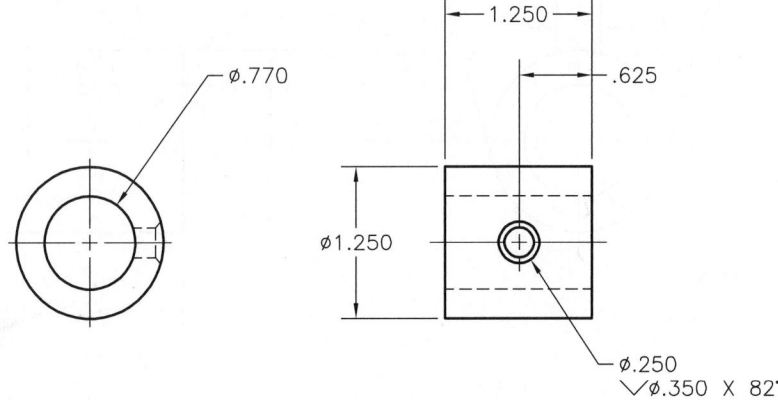

14. Draw the views of the wrench shown. Save the drawing as P8-14.

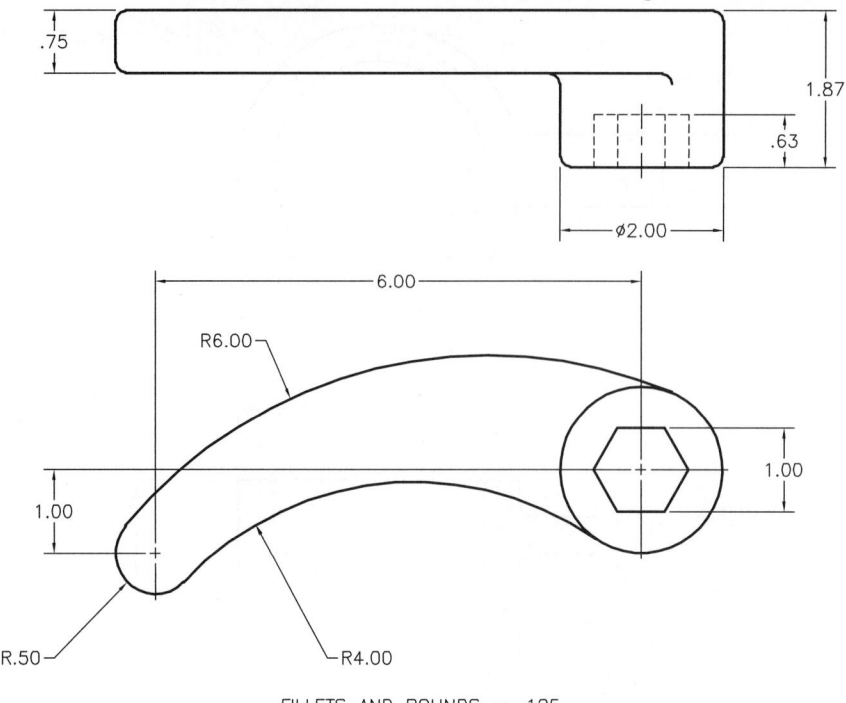

FILLETS AND ROUNDS = .125

15. Draw the views of the support shown. Save the drawing as P8-15.

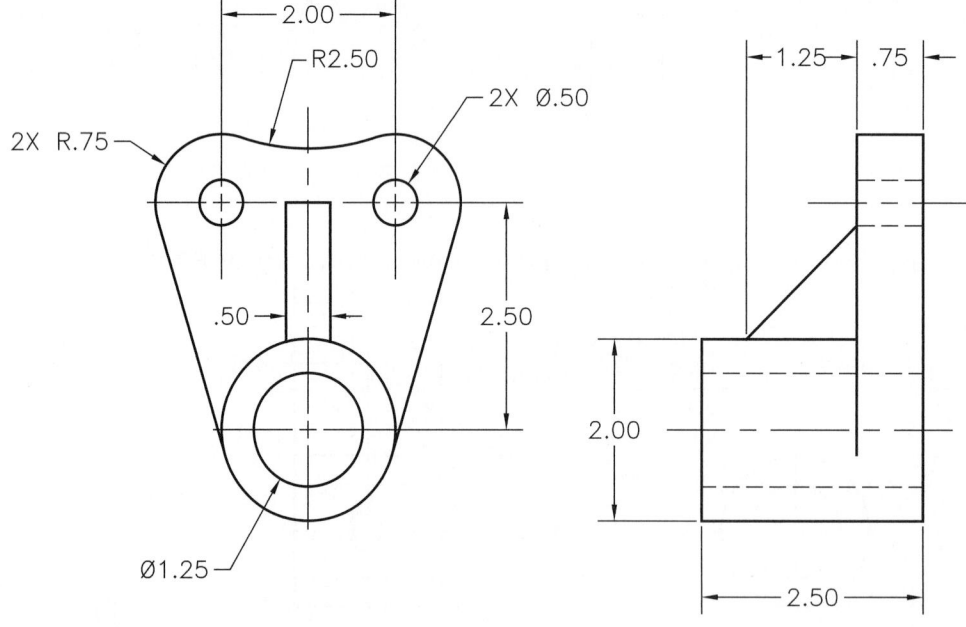

▼ Advanced

For Problems 16 through 18, draw the orthographic views needed to describe the part completely. Save the drawings as **P8-16**, **P8-17**, *and* **P8-18**.

16.

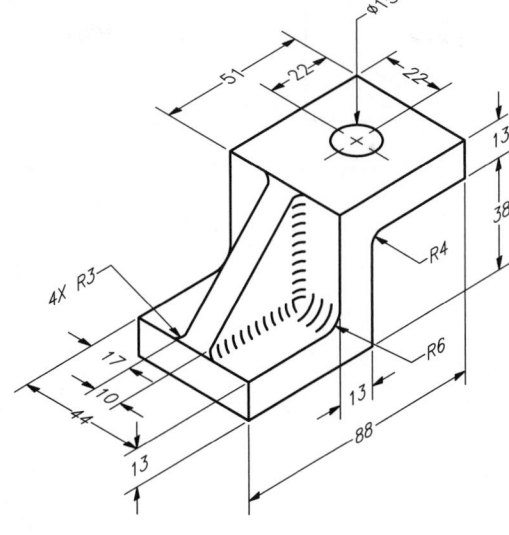

Brace

17.

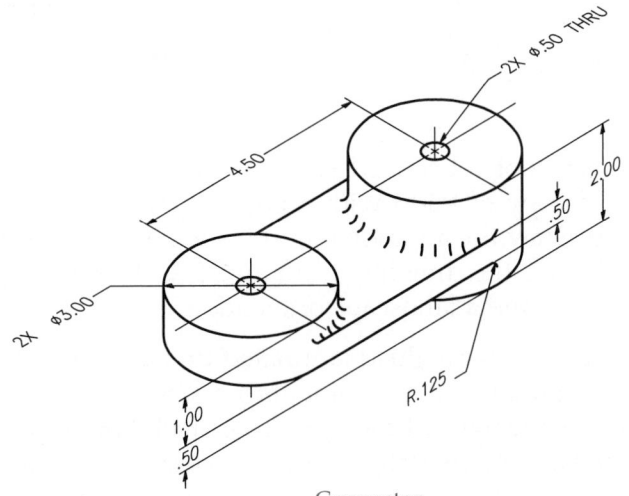

Connector

18.

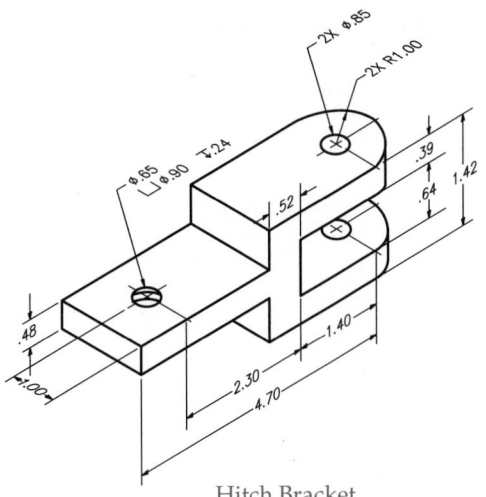

Hitch Bracket

19. Draw all views of the pillow block shown. Save the drawing as P8-19.

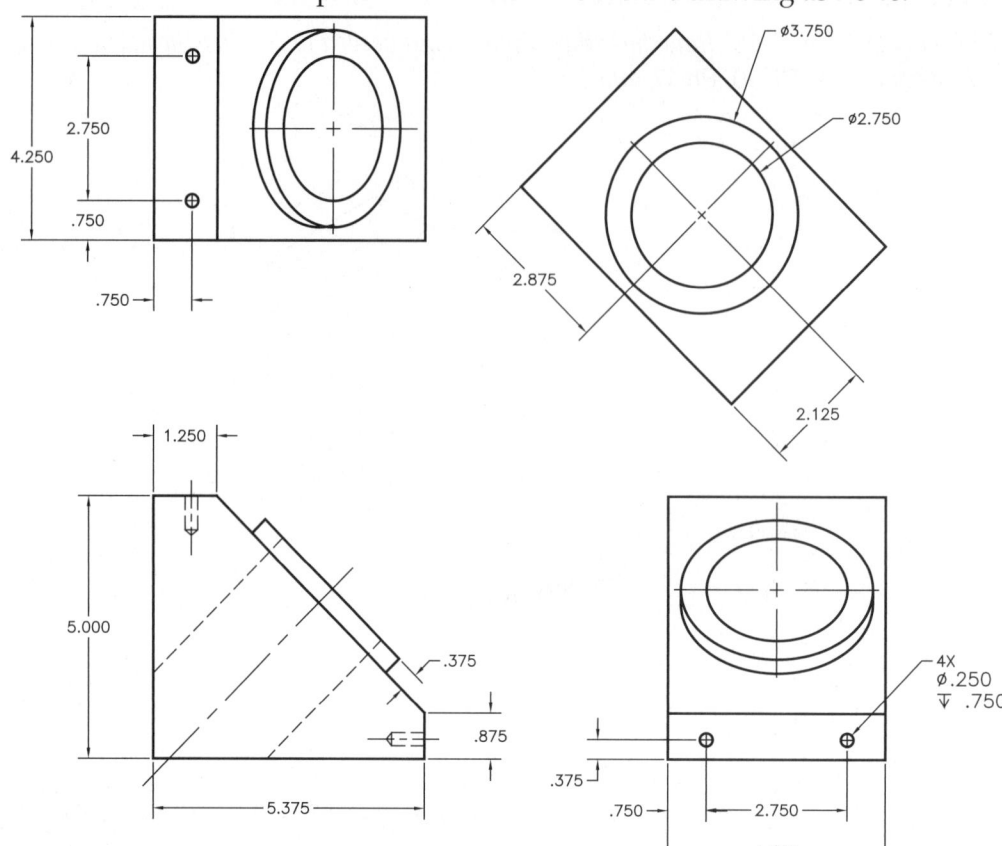

20. Open P5-15. If you have not yet created P5-15, go to Chapter 5 and complete the problem now. Save a copy of P5-15 with a new file name of P8-20. The P8-20 file should be active. Draw the additional multiview needed to describe the nut driver completely. Resave the drawing. Print an 8.5″ × 11″ copy of the drawing extents, using a 1:1 scale and a landscape orientation.

21. Research the specifications for a glued laminated timber (glulam) beam hanger with the following requirements: face-mounts a 5-1/8″ × 10″ glulam beam to a wood member, attaches using 16d nails, 12-gage steel, hot-dipped galvanized. Create a dimensioned 2D sketch of the design from the manufacturer's specifications, or from measurements taken from an actual hanger. Start a new drawing from scratch or use a decimal, fractional, or architectural unit template of your choice. Draw the front, top, right side, and left side views of the hanger from your sketch using the 0 layer. Save the drawing as P8-21.

AutoCAD Certified Associate Exam Practice

Answer the following questions. Write your answers on a separate sheet of paper.

1. Which of the following operations can you complete using the **OFFSET** tool? *Select all that apply.*
   A. create an exact copy of a line at a specified distance from the original
   B. create an exact copy of an arc at a specified distance from the original
   C. create a circle concentric with an existing circle
   D. create an arc concentric with an existing arc
   E. create an exact copy of a line through a specified point

2. Which of the following operations can you complete using the **MEASURE** tool? *Select all that apply.*
   A. place point objects anywhere in the drawing area
   B. convert point objects into blocks
   C. break a circle into a specified number of pieces
   D. place point objects at specified intervals along a line
   E. place point objects at a specified number of equally spaced locations on an arc

3. Which of the following are primary 2D orthographic views for a mechanical part drawing? *Select all that apply.*
   A. front
   B. rear
   C. auxiliary
   D. central
   E. top

AutoCAD Certified Professional Exam Practice

Follow the instructions in each problem. Write your answers on a separate sheet of paper.

1. **Navigate to this chapter on the Student Web site and open the CPE-08offset.dwg file.**

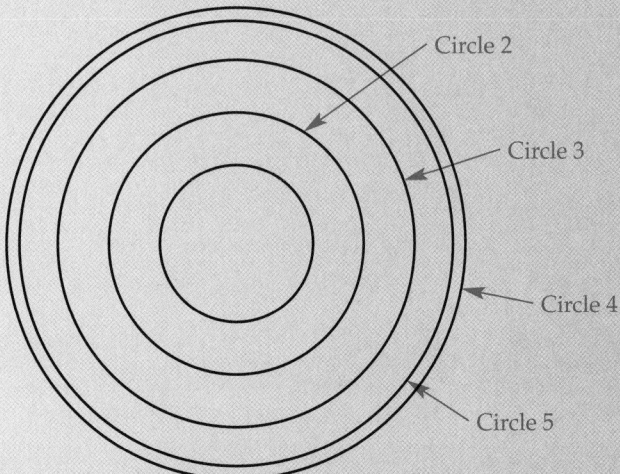

   Use the **Multiple** option of the **OFFSET** tool to offset the existing circle to the outside, using an offset distance of 2, to create Circle 2, Circle 3, and Circle 4. Then offset the outermost circle to the inside using an offset distance of .5 to create Circle 5. What are the coordinates of the top quadrant point of Circle 5?

2. **Navigate to this chapter on the Student Web site and open the CPE-07multiview.dwg file.**

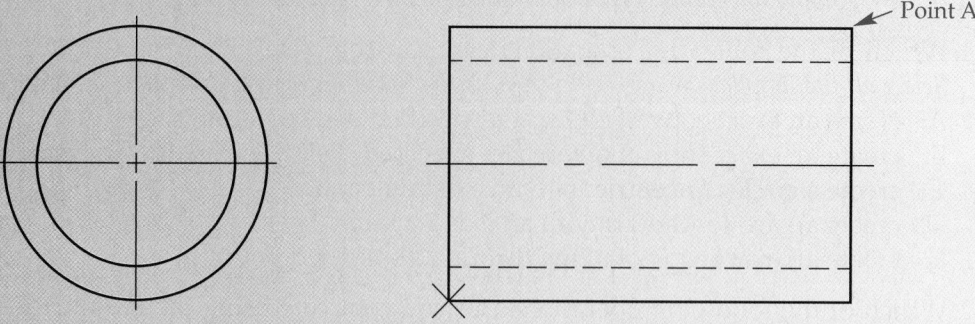

This file contains the front view of a cylindrical spacer, as well as the starting point for the lower-left corner of the right side view. Change the point display to an × to make it more visible. Then create the right side view, assuming that the spacer has a total length of 4 units. Use any method of construction described in this chapter to create the view accurately. Use hidden lines to show the inner diameter of the spacer, and include a center line to show the axis. Place the hidden lines and centerlines on the correct layers. What are the coordinates of Point A?

AutoCAD and Its Applications—Basics

Text Styles and Multiline Text

Learning Objectives

After completing this chapter, you will be able to do the following:

✓ Describe and use proper text standards.
✓ Calculate drawing scale and text height.
✓ Develop and use text styles.
✓ Use the **MTEXT** tool to create multiline text objects.

Annotation, dimensions, and symbols with *text* provide necessary information about features on a drawing. AutoCAD offers tools and settings to add uniform, easy-to-read text drawn according to drafting standards. This chapter introduces text standards and composition and explains how to use the **MTEXT** tool to prepare a text object that can include multiple lines of text, such as paragraphs or a list of general notes. Chapter 10 describes how to create single-line text objects using the **TEXT** tool, and additional text tools.

annotation: Textual information presented in notes, specifications, comments, and symbols.

text: Lettering on a CADD drawing.

Text Standards and Composition

Industry and company standards dictate how text should appear on a drawing. Consistent text type, format, height, and spacing are critical to legibility and drawing clarity. A drawing should use the same text *font* and format throughout, except for specific cases such as text in traditional architectural title blocks or on maps. Refer to **Figure 9-1** as you read the following information about text type and format.

font: The face design of a letter or number.

The ASME *Line Conventions and Lettering* standard applies to the process of hand lettering each character using one or more single straight or curved elements, in a Gothic font. For example, the letter A has three single-stroke lines. You can achieve the ASME standard with AutoCAD using a font such as Romans (roman simplex), Arial, or Century Gothic. The U.S. National CAD Standard (NCS) recommends a SansSerif font, though some companies prefer a slightly different font such as Arial or Century Gothic. Some architectural companies prefer the Stylus BT, ArchiText, or CountryBlueprint font, because these fonts provide a more traditional architectural hand lettering appearance.

Vertical text is most common. However, inclined text is an approved ASME standard and is used by some companies, most often in structural drafting, and for specific drawing requirements, such as water feature labels on maps. The recommended slant

Figure 9-1. Examples of common text typefaces and formats.

DIMENSIONS AND TOLERANCES PER ASME Y14.5–2009.

ASME Y14.2 standard: vertical UPPERCASE, Romans font

BEND DOWN 90° R.50

ASME Y14.2 standard: vertical UPPERCASE, Arial font

REMOVE ALL BURRS AND SHARP EDGES.

ASME Y14.2 standard: vertical UPPERCASE, Century Gothic font

SIMPSON LCC5.25-3.5 TYP

U.S. National CAD standard: vertical UPPERCASE, SansSerif font

HOOD W/FAN, VENT TO OUTSIDE AIR

Traditional architecture format: vertical UPPERCASE, Stylus BT font

ALL FRAMING LUMBER TO BE DFL #2 OR BETTER

Traditional architecture format: vertical UPPERCASE, CountryBlueprint font

TYP EACH END TWO FLANGES

ASME Y14.2 standard variation: inclined UPPERCASE, Arial font

Mississippi River

River identification on a map: inclined lowercase, SansSerif font

for inclined text is 68° from horizontal, though some drafters find 75° more appropriate. Uppercase text is standard. However, some companies use lowercase letters, most often on civil plans or maps.

A drawing displays specific text heights for different purposes. **Figure 9-2** lists minimum letter heights based on the ASME Y14.2, *Line Conventions and Lettering* standard. The NCS and many companies, especially those who produce architectural and civil drawings, depart slightly from the ASME standard. The NCS specifies a minimum text height of 3/32″ (2.4 mm). Most text is 1/8″ (3 mm) high, with titles and similar text 1/4″ (3 mm) high.

Numbers in dimensions and notes are the same height as standard text. AutoCAD provides several methods for stacking text in fractions. When dimensions contain fractions, the fraction bar should usually appear horizontally between the numerator and denominator. However, many notes have fractions displayed with a diagonal fraction bar (/). In this case, use a dash or space between the whole number and the fraction. **Figure 9-3** shows examples of text for numbers and fractions in different unit formats.

AutoCAD text tools provide great control over text *composition*. You can lay out text horizontally, as is typical when adding notes, or draw text at any angle according to specific requirements. AutoCAD automatically spaces letters and lines of text to help maintain the identity of individual notes. See **Figure 9-4**.

composition: The spacing, layout, and appearance of text.

Figure 9-2. Minimum letter heights based on the ASME Y14.2, *Line Conventions and Lettering* standard.

Application	Height INCH	Height METRIC (mm)
Most text (dimension values, notes)	.12	3
Drawing title, drawing size, CAGE code, drawing number, revision letter	.24* .12**	6* 3**
Section and view letters	.24	6
Zone letters and numerals in borders	.24	6
Drawing block headings	.10	2.5

*D, E, F, H, J, K, A0, and A1 size sheets

**A, B, C, G, A2, A3, and A4 size sheets

Figure 9-3. Examples of fractional text for different unit formats.

Decimal Inch	Fractional Inch			Millimeter		
2.750 .25	$2\frac{3}{4}$	2–3/4	2 3/4	2.5	3	0.7

PROFESSIONAL TIP

Text presentation is important. Refer to appropriate industry, company, or school standards, and consider the following tips when adding text:
- Plan your drawing using rough sketches to allow room for text and notes.
- Arrange text to avoid crowding.
- Place related notes in groups to make the drawing easy to read.
- Place all general notes in a common location. Locate notes in the lower-left corner or above the title block when using ASME standards, the upper-left corner when using military (MIL) standards, or the note block when using the NCS.
- Always use the spell checker.

Drawing Scale and Text Height

Ideally, you should determine drawing scale, scale factors, and text heights before you begin drawing. Incorporate these settings into drawing template files, and make changes when necessary. The drawing scale factor determines how text height appears on-screen and plots.

To understand the concept of drawing scale, look at the portion of a floor plan shown in **Figure 9-5.** You should draw everything in model space at full scale. This means that the bathtub, for example, is actually drawn 5' long. However, at this scale, text size becomes an issue, because full-scale text that is 1/8" high is too small compared

Figure 9-4. An example of general notes on a part drawing, typed according to the ASME Y14.2, *Line Conventions and Lettering* standard. The standard spacing is also appropriate for use on drawings for other disciplines.

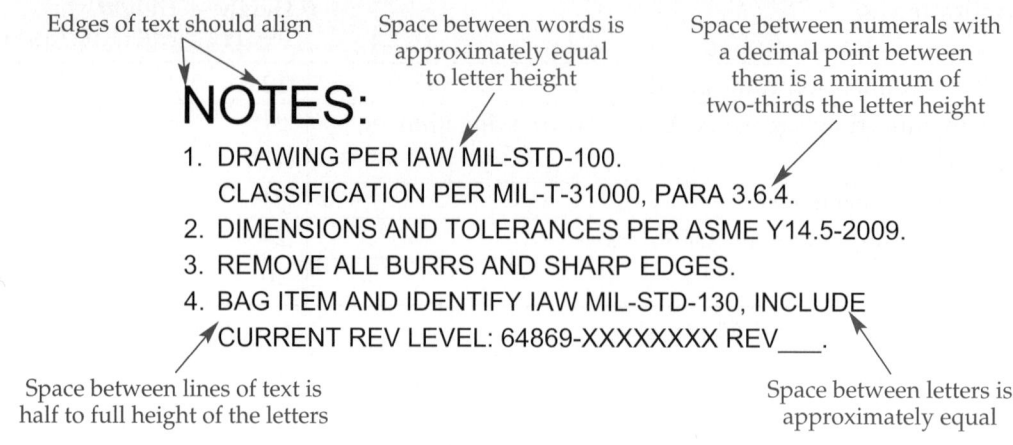

Edges of text should align

Space between words is approximately equal to letter height

Space between numerals with a decimal point between them is a minimum of two-thirds the letter height

NOTES:

1. DRAWING PER IAW MIL-STD-100.
   CLASSIFICATION PER MIL-T-31000, PARA 3.6.4.
2. DIMENSIONS AND TOLERANCES PER ASME Y14.5-2009.
3. REMOVE ALL BURRS AND SHARP EDGES.
4. BAG ITEM AND IDENTIFY IAW MIL-STD-130, INCLUDE
   CURRENT REV LEVEL: 64869-XXXXXXXX REV___.

Space between lines of text is half to full height of the letters

Space between letters is approximately equal

Figure 9-5. An example of a portion of a floor plan drawn at full scale in model space. A— Text drawn at full scale (1/8" high) is too small compared to the large objects. B—Text scaled to display and plot correctly.

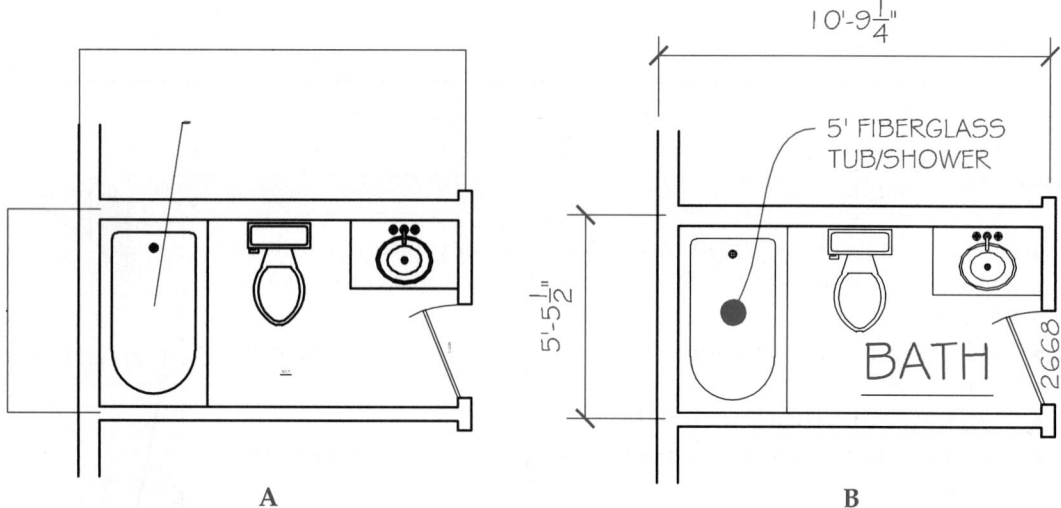

A

B

to the other full-scale objects. See **Figure 9-5A.** As a result, you must adjust the text height according to the drawing scale. See **Figure 9-5B.** You can calculate the scale factor manually and apply it to text height, or you can allow AutoCAD to calculate the scale factor using annotative text.

Scaling Text Manually

text height: The specified height of text, which may be different from the plotting size for text scaled manually.

scale factor: The reciprocal of the drawing scale.

paper text height: The plotted text height.

To adjust *text height* manually according to a specific drawing scale, you must calculate the drawing *scale factor.* **Figure 9-6** provides examples of calculating scale factor. You then multiply the scale factor by the *paper text height* to get the model space text height.

For example, a site plan plotted at a 1" = 60' scale has a scale factor of 720. Text drawn 1/8" high is almost invisible, because the drawing is 720 times larger than it is when plotted at the proper scale. Therefore, multiply the scale factor of 720 by the text height of 1/8" (.125") to find the 90" scaled text height for model space. The proper height of 1/8" text in model space at a 1" = 60' scale is 90".

Figure 9-6. Examples of calculating scale factor.

Example	Scale	Conversion	Calculation	Scale Factor
Mechanical	1:2	None	2 ÷ 2 = 1	2
Civil	1″ = 60′	1″ = 720″ (60′ contains 720″)	720 ÷ 1 = 720	720
Architectural	1/4″ = 1′-0″	1/4″ (.25″) = 12″ (1′ contains 12″)	12 ÷ .25 = 48	48
Metric to Inch	1:1	1″ = 25.4 mm	25.4 ÷ 1 = 25.4	25.4
Metric to Inch	1:2	1″ = 25.4 mm × 2 (50.8)	50.8 ÷ 1 = 50.8	50.8

Annotative Text

AutoCAD scales *annotative text* according to the *annotation scale* you select, which eliminates the need for you to calculate the scale factor. Once you choose an annotation scale, AutoCAD applies the corresponding scale factor to annotative text and all other annotative objects. For example, if you manually scale 1/8″ text for a drawing with a 1/4″ = 1′-0″ scale, or a scale factor of 48, you must draw the text using a text height of 6″ (1/8″ × 48 = 6″) in model space. When placing annotative text, using this example, you set an annotation scale of 1/4″ = 1′-0″. Then you draw the text using a paper text height of 1/8″ in model space. The 1/8″ high text is scaled to 6″ automatically according to the preset 1/4″ = 1′-0″ annotation scale.

Annotative text offers several advantages over manually scaled text, including the ability to control text appearance based on the drawing scale and paper text height, while reducing the need to focus on the scale factor. Annotative text is especially effective when the drawing scale changes or when a single sheet includes views at different scales.

annotative text: Text scaled by AutoCAD according to the specified annotation scale.

annotation scale: The drawing scale AutoCAD uses to calculate the height of annotative text.

PROFESSIONAL TIP

If you anticipate preparing scaled drawings, you should use annotative text and other annotative objects instead of manual scaling. However, scale factor does influence non-annotative items and is still an important value to identify and use throughout the drawing process.

Setting the Annotation Scale

You should usually set the annotation scale before you begin typing text so that the text height is scaled automatically. However, this is not always possible. It may be necessary to adjust the annotation scale throughout the drawing process, especially if you prepare views at different scales on one sheet. This textbook approaches annotation scaling in model space only, using the process of selecting the appropriate annotation scale before typing text. To draw text using another scale, pick the new annotation scale and then type the text.

The **Select Annotation Scale** dialog box appears when you access a text tool and an annotative text style is current. This dialog box provides a convenient way to set annotation scale before typing. You will learn about text styles later in this chapter. You can also select the annotation scale from the **Annotation Scale** flyout on the status bar. See **Figure 9-7**. The annotation scale is typically the same as the drawing scale.

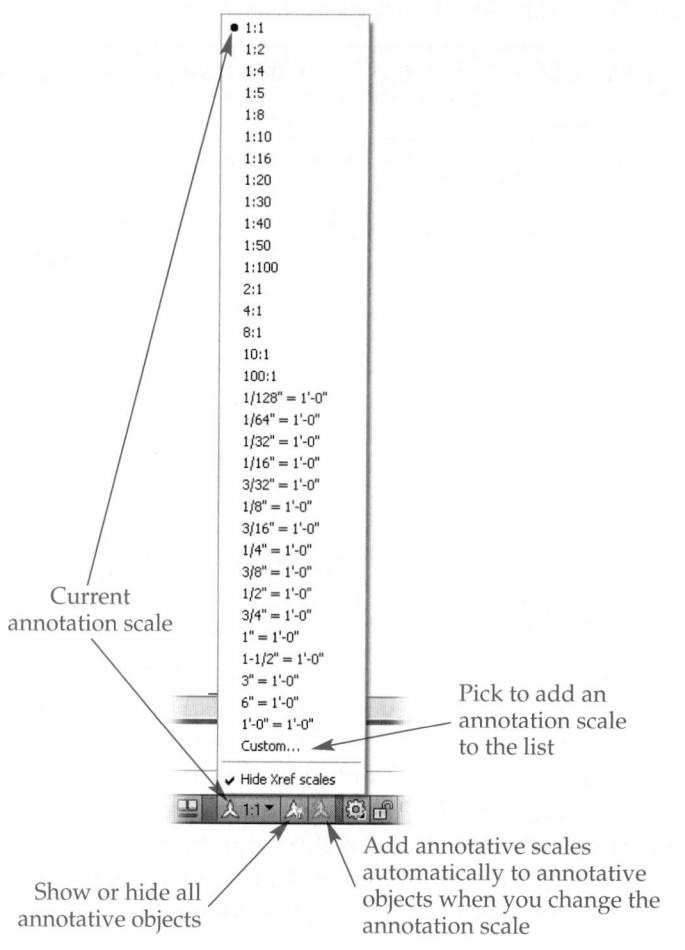

Current
annotation scale

Pick to add an
annotation scale
to the list

Add annotative scales
automatically to annotative
objects when you change the
annotation scale

Show or hide all
annotative objects

NOTE

This textbook describes many additional annotative object tools. Some of these tools are more appropriate for working with layouts, as explained later in this textbook.

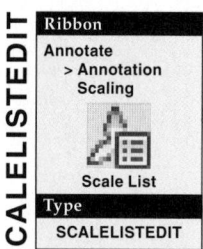

SCALELISTEDIT

Ribbon
Annotate
> Annotation
Scaling

Scale List

Type
SCALELISTEDIT

Editing Annotation Scales

If a scale is unavailable, or to change an existing scale, pick the **Annotation Scale** flyout on the status bar and choose **Custom…** to access the **Edit Scale List** dialog box. Move the highlighted scale up or down in the list using the **Move Up** or **Move Down** button. To remove the highlighted scale from the list, pick the **Delete** button.

Select the **Edit…** button to open the **Edit Scale** dialog box, where you can change the name of the scale and adjust the scale by entering the paper and drawing units. For example, a scale of 1/4″ = 1′-0″ has a paper units value of .25 or 1 and a drawing units value of 12 or 48.

To create a new annotation scale, pick the **Add…** button to display the **Add Scale** dialog box, which provides the same options as the **Edit Scale** dialog box. Pick the **Reset** button to restore the list to display the default annotation scales. Once you select an annotation scale, you are ready to type annotative text.

Changes you make in the **Edit Scale List** dialog box are stored with the drawing and are specific to the drawing. To make changes to the default scale list saved to the system registry, pick the **Default Scale List...** button in the **User Preferences** tab of the **Options** dialog box to access the **Default Scale List** dialog box. The options are the same as those in the **Edit Scale List** dialog box, but changes are saved as the default for new drawings and resetting the **Edit Scale List** dialog box.

Text Styles

A *text style* presets many text characteristics. Create a text style for each unique text appearance or function. For example, use an annotative text style to draw annotative text, and a non-annotative text style to draw non-annotative text. Another example is creating text styles that correspond to a specific text height or other characteristic. Add text styles to your drawing templates for repeated use. Avoid adjusting text format independently of the text style assigned to the text.

text style: A saved collection of settings for text height, width, oblique angle (slant), and other text effects.

Text Style Dialog Box

Create, modify, and delete text styles using the **Text Style** dialog box. See **Figure 9-8.** The **Styles** list box displays existing text styles. The Annotative text style allows you to create annotative text, as indicated by the icon to the left of the style name. The Standard text style does not use the annotative function.

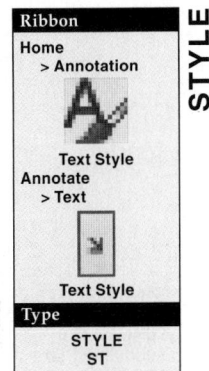

Figure 9-8. Use the **Text Style** dialog box to create, rename, delete, and set the characteristics of a text style. The **Big Font:** drop-down list replaces the **Font Style:** drop-down list when you select the **Use Big Font** check box. The **Height** text box replaces the **Paper Text Height** text box when you deselect the **Annotative** check box.

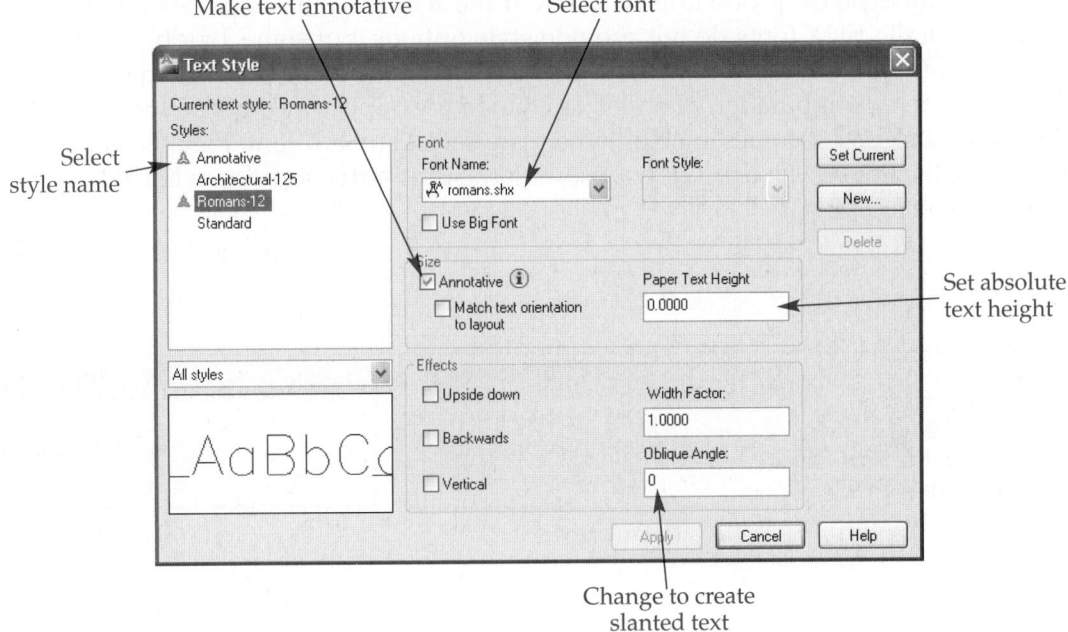

Make text annotative   Select font

Select style name

Set absolute text height

Change to create slanted text

To make a text style current, double-click the style name, right-click the name and select **Current**, or pick the name and select the **Current** button. Below the **Styles** list box is a drop-down list that you can use to filter the number of text styles displayed in the **Text Style** dialog box. Pick the **All Styles** option to show all text styles in the file, or pick the **Styles in use** option to show only the current style and styles used in the drawing.

Creating New Text Styles

To create a new text style, select an existing text style from the **Styles** list box to use as a base for formatting the new text style. Then pick the **New...** button to open the **New Text Style** dialog box. See **Figure 9-9**. Notice that style1 appears in the **Style Name** text box. Replace the default name with a more descriptive name. For example, the name ROMANS-12 describes a text style that uses a Romans font and characters .12" high. The name ARCHITECTURAL-125 describes a text style that uses the Stylus BT font and characters 1/8" high.

Text style names can have up to 255 characters, including uppercase and lowercase letters, numbers, dashes (–), underlines (_), and dollar signs ($). After typing the text style name, pick the **OK** button. The new text style appears in the **Styles** list box of the **Text Style** dialog box, and you are ready to adjust text style characteristics. Pick the **Apply** button to apply changes, and the **Close** button to exit the **Text Style** dialog box.

PROFESSIONAL TIP

Record the names and details about the text styles you create and keep the information in a log for future reference.

Font Options

Use the **Font Name** drop-down list in the **Font** area of the **Text Style** dialog box to select a font. The list includes TrueType fonts installed on your computer and fonts linked to AutoCAD shape files. TrueType fonts are *scalable fonts* and have an outline. By default, TrueType fonts appear and plot filled. You can recognize fonts from AutoCAD shape files (SHX fonts) by the .shx file extension and AutoCAD compass icon.

scalable fonts: Fonts that can be displayed or printed at any size while retaining proportional letter thickness.

The **Font Style** drop-down list is active if the selected font includes options, such as bold or italic. SHX fonts do not provide style options, but some TrueType fonts do. For example, the SansSerif font has Regular, Bold, BoldOblique, and Oblique options. Select a style or combination of styles to change the appearance of the font. The **Use Big Font** check box becomes enabled when you select an SHX font. Pick the check box to replace the **Font Style:** drop-down list with the **Big Font:** drop-down list, where you can choose a *big font*.

big font: A supplement that provides Asian and other large-format fonts that have characters and symbols not present in other font files.

Figure 9-9.
Enter a descriptive name for the new text style in the **New Text Style** dialog box.

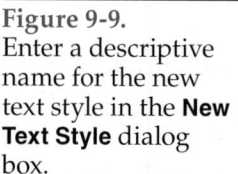

Default Style

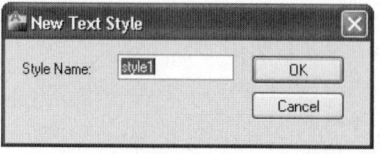

New Style

Reference Material

AutoCAD Fonts

For a sample of the many fonts available with AutoCAD, go to the **Reference Material** section on the Student Web site (www.g-wlearning.com/CAD) and select **AutoCAD Fonts**.

Size Options

The **Size** area of the **Text Style** dialog box contains options for defining text style height. Select the **Annotative** check box to set the text style as annotative and display the **Paper Text Height** text box. Deselect the **Annotative** check box to scale text manually and display the **Height** text box.

The default text height is 0. If you set a value other than 0, the text height is fixed for the text style and applies each time you use the text style. As a result, you can only use the specified text height to create single-line text, and you do not have the option of assigning a different text height to objects that reference the text style, such as dimensions.

PROFESSIONAL TIP

Use a text style height of 0 to provide the greatest flexibility when drawing. A prompt asks you to specify a text height when you create single-line text, and you can assign a text height to dimension, multileader, and table styles.

As an alternative, use a specific value to limit text height. In this case, the text style fully controls the height applied to single-line text and dimension, multileader, and table styles. This restricts text objects to a certain height, which can increase productivity and accuracy, but requires that you create a text style for each unique height. Dimension, multileader, and table styles are explained later in this textbook.

The **Match text orientation to layout** check box becomes enabled when you pick the **Annotative** check box. Check **Match text orientation to layout** to match the orientation of text in layout viewports with the layout orientation. Layouts are described later in this textbook.

Effects

The **Effects** area of the **Text Style** dialog box includes options to set the text format. It contains options for drawing text upside-down, backwards, and vertically. See **Figure 9-10**. The **Vertical** check box is available for SHX fonts. Text on drawings is normally horizontal. Vertical text is appropriate for special effects and graphic designs, and usually works best with a 270° rotation angle.

Use the **Width Factor** text box to specify the text character width relative to its height. You can set the width factor between 0.01 and 100. A width factor of 1 is default

Figure 9-10.
Special effects for text styles can be set in the **Effects** area of the **Text Style** dialog box.

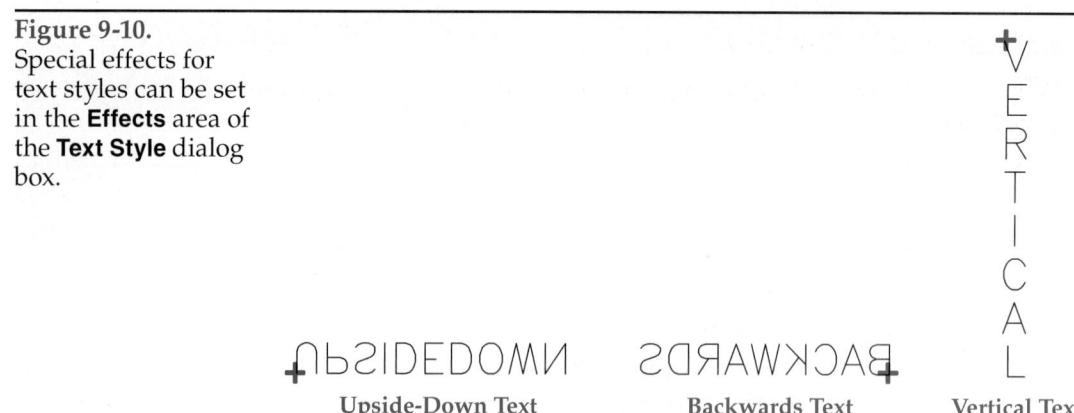

Upside-Down Text   Backwards Text   Vertical Text

and is recommended for most drawing applications. A width factor greater than 1 expands characters, and a factor less than 1 compresses characters. If necessary, reduce the width slightly, and only if you cannot reduce the height. See **Figure 9-11.**

The **Oblique Angle** text box allows you to set the angle at which text inclines. The 0 default draws vertical characters. A value greater than 0 slants characters to the right, and a negative value slants characters to the left. See **Figure 9-12.** Some fonts, such as the italic SHX font, are already slanted.

PROFESSIONAL TIP

AutoCAD text slant is measured from vertical. Use a 22° oblique angle to slant text according to the 68° horizontal incline standard.

NOTE

The **Preview** area of the **Text Style** dialog box displays an example of the selected font and font effects. This is a convenient way to see what the font looks like before using it in a new style.

Figure 9-11.
Examples of width factor settings for text.

Width Factor	Text
1	ABCDEFGHIJKLM
.5	ABCDEFGHIJKLMNOPQRSTUVWXY
1.5	ABCDEFGHI
2	ABCDEFG

Figure 9-12.
Examples of oblique angle settings for text.

Obliquing Angle	Text
0	ABCDEFGHIJKLM
15	*ABCDEFGHIJKLM*
–15	ABCDEFGHIJKLM

Exercise 9-1

Access the Student Web site (www.g-wlearning.com/CAD) and complete Exercise 9-1.

Changing, Renaming, and Deleting Text Styles

Select a text style from the **Styles** list box to edit. Make the necessary changes and pick the **Apply** button to apply changes. If you make changes to a text style, such as selecting a different font, all existing text objects assigned the modified text style update. Use a different text style with unique characteristics when appropriate.

To rename a text style using the **Text Style** dialog box, slowly double-click on the name or right-click on the name and select **Rename**. To delete a text style using the **Text Style** dialog box, right-click on the name and select **Delete**, or pick the style and select the **Delete** button. You cannot delete a text style that is assigned to text objects. To delete a style that is in use, assign a different style to the text objects that reference the style. You cannot delete or rename the Standard style.

> **NOTE**
>
> You can also rename styles using the **Rename** dialog box. Select **Text styles** in the **Named Objects** list to rename the style.

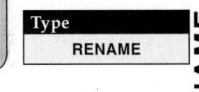

RENAME

Setting a Text Style Current

Set a text style current using the **Text Style** dialog box by double-clicking the style in the **Styles** list box, right-clicking on the style and selecting **Set current**, or picking the style and selecting the **Set current** button. To set a text style current without opening the **Text Style** dialog box, use the **Text Style** list on the expanded **Annotation** panel of the **Home** ribbon tab or on the **Text** panel of the **Annotate** ribbon tab. See **Figure 9-13.**

> **PROFESSIONAL TIP**
>
> You can import text styles from existing drawings using **DesignCenter**. See Chapter 5 for more information about using **DesignCenter** to reuse drawing content.

Figure 9-13. The fastest way to set a style current is to use the drop-down list on the ribbon.

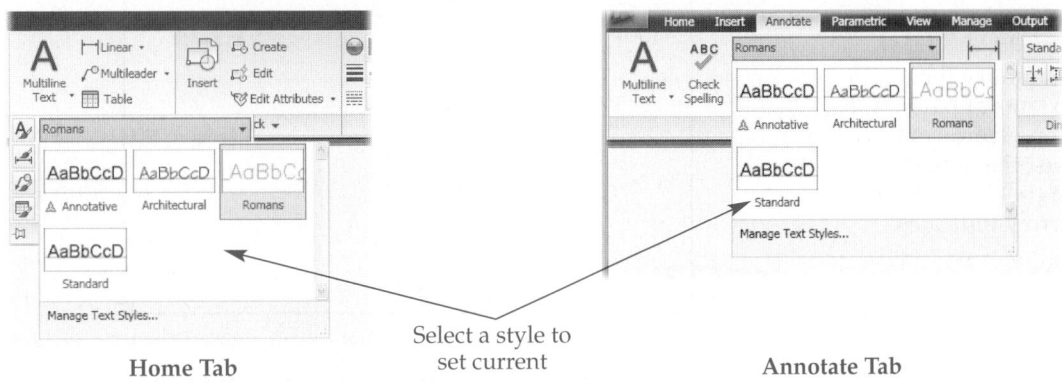

Select a style to set current

Home Tab   Annotate Tab

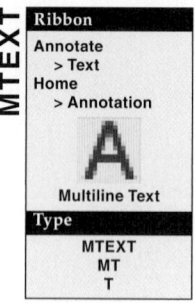

Ribbon

Annotate
> Text
Home
> Annotation

A

Multiline Text

Type

MTEXT
MT
T

text boundary: An imaginary box that sets the location and width for multiline text.

Multiline Text

The **MTEXT** tool draws a single multiline text, or mtext, object that can include extensive paragraph formatting, lists, symbols, and columns. It is good practice to set the appropriate text style current before you access the **MTEXT** tool. Activate the **MTEXT** tool to display letters near the crosshairs that indicate the current text style and height. Pick the first corner of the *text boundary*. A prompt then asks you to specify the opposite corner or choose an option. Use the options to preset text **Style** and **Height**, boundary **Justification**, **Rotation**, and **Width**, **Line spacing**, and use of **Columns**. However, it is typically easier to set mtext options while you are typing. **Rotation** is the only option you cannot adjust while typing. Use the **Rotation** option before selecting the opposite corner to rotate the text boundary, or rotate the mtext object after using an editing tool after you exit the tool.

Mtext uses dynamic columns by default to help you organize multiple text columns in an mtext object. Disable columns for typical text requirements without columns. Before selecting the second corner of the text boundary, choose the **Columns** option and then the **No columns** option. An arrow in the boundary shows the direction of text flow and where the boundary will expand as you type, if necessary. Pick the opposite corner of the text boundary to continue. See **Figure 9-14**. You will learn to format columns later in this chapter.

Using the Text Editor

text editor: The area of the multiline or single-line text system where you type text.

Once you select the opposite corner of the text boundary, the **Text Editor** contextual ribbon tab and the *text editor* appear. **Figure 9-15** shows the display with columns disabled. Typing mtext is similar to typing using word processing software such as Microsoft® Word. The **Text Editor** ribbon tab provides tools for adjusting and formatting text in the text editor. You can access many of the same options found in **Text Editor** ribbon tab, and Windows Clipboard functions, from the shortcut menu that appears when you right-click away from the ribbon. See **Figure 9-16**.

NOTE

If you close the ribbon, the **Text Formatting** toolbar appears instead of the **Text Editor** ribbon tab. This textbook focuses on using the **Text Editor** ribbon tab to add mtext. The **Text Formatting** toolbar provides the same functions.

Figure 9-14.
The text boundary is the box within which you type. Consider the text boundary the extents of paragraph. Long words extend past the boundary in the direction the arrow indicates.

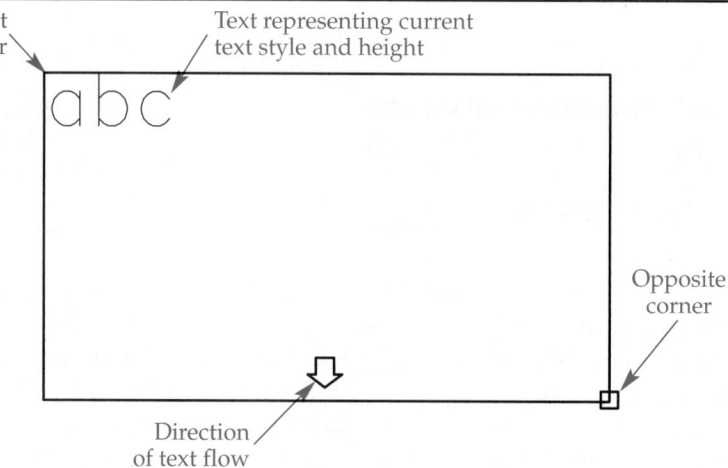

First corner

Text representing current text style and height

abc

Opposite corner

Direction of text flow

Figure 9-15. The **Text Editor** contextual ribbon tab provides options for working with mtext.

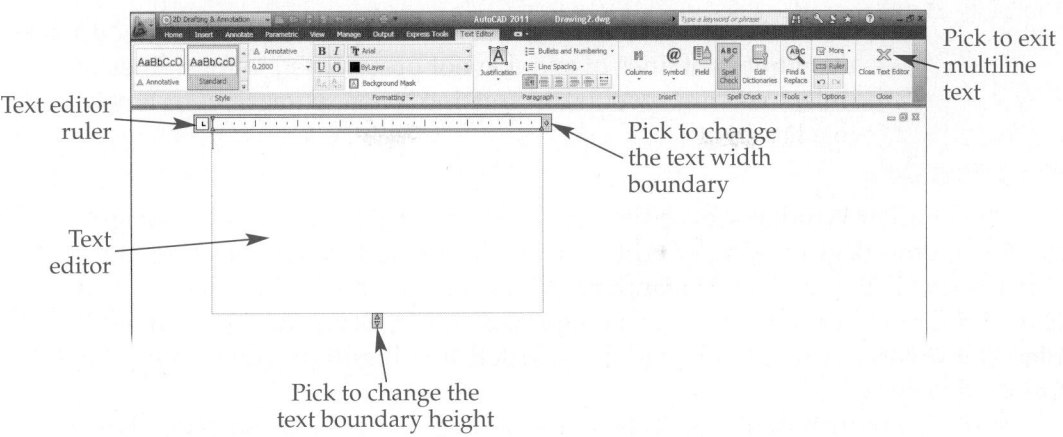

Text editor ruler

Text editor

Pick to change the text width boundary

Pick to exit multiline text

Pick to change the text boundary height

Figure 9-16.
Display the text editor shortcut menu by right-clicking away from the ribbon while the text editor is active. Use the shortcut menu as an alternative to the ribbon, or to select options that are not available from the ribbon.

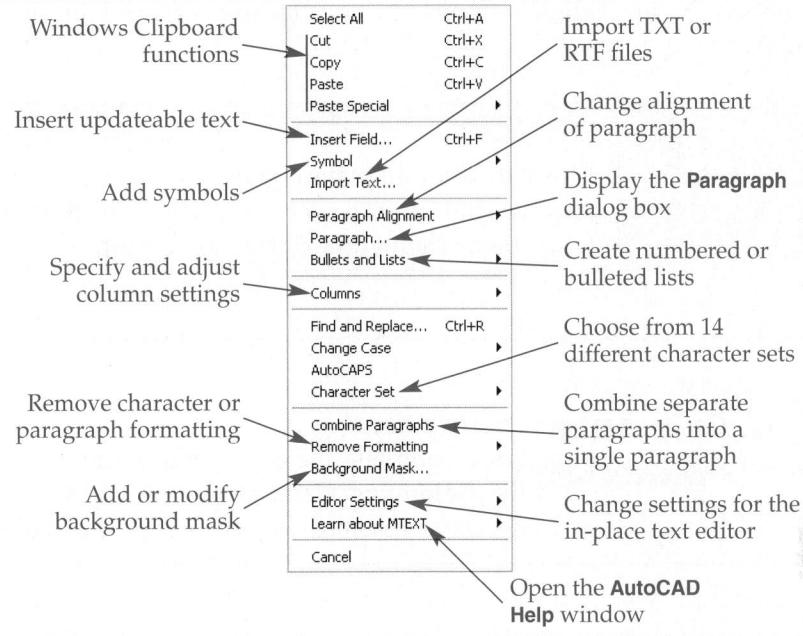

Windows Clipboard functions

Insert updateable text

Add symbols

Specify and adjust column settings

Remove character or paragraph formatting

Add or modify background mask

Import TXT or RTF files

Change alignment of paragraph

Display the **Paragraph** dialog box

Create numbered or bulleted lists

Choose from 14 different character sets

Combine separate paragraphs into a single paragraph

Change settings for the in-place text editor

Open the **AutoCAD Help** window

The text editor indicates the initial size of the area in which you type. When columns are not active, long words and paragraphs extend past the text editor limits. The text editor is transparent by default so that you can see how the text appears on-screen relative to other objects. Use the **Opaque Background** option to make the text editor opaque. The text editor includes a ruler that displays indent and tab stops and indent and tab markers. Use the **Ruler** option to turn the ruler on or off.

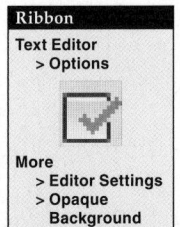

Ribbon
Text Editor
> Options

More
> Editor Settings
> Opaque Background

NOTE

Use the **Undo** and **Redo** tools to undo or redo text editor operations.

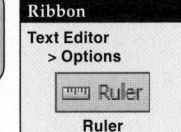

Ribbon
Text Editor
> Options

Ruler

To change the width of the text editor when you are not using columns, drag the arrows on the right end of the ruler. An alternative is to right-click on the ruler or the arrows at the bottom of the text editor and choose **Set Mtext Width...** to use the **Set Mtext Width** dialog box. To change the height of the text editor, drag the arrows at the bottom of the text editor, or right-click on the ruler or the arrows at the bottom of the text editor and select **Set Mtext Height...** to use the **Set Mtext Height** dialog box.

Change the width and height of the text editor to increase or decrease the number of lines of text. Do not press [Enter] to form lines of text, unless you are specifically creating a new paragraph or a new item in a list.

The familiar Windows text editor cursor displays at the current text height within the text editor. Begin typing or editing text. The procedure for selecting and editing existing text is the same as in standard Windows text editors. To select all text in the text editor, right-click inside the text editor and choose **Select All**. You can use the **Text Highlight Color...** option to change the selected text highlight color using the **Select Color** dialog box.

When you finish typing, exit the mtext system using the **Close Text Editor** option, or pick outside of the text editor. You can also press [Esc] or right-click and select **Cancel**, but AutoCAD prompts you to save changes to the mtext. The easiest way to reopen the text editor to make changes to text content is to double-click on an mtext object.

Ribbon
Text Editor
> Close

Close

NOTE

The text editor displays text horizontally, right-side up, and forward. Any special effects such as vertical, backwards, or upside-down take effect when you exit the text editor.

Reference Material
Shortcut Keys
For a complete list of keyboard shortcuts for text editing, go to the **Reference Material** section of the Student Web site (www.g-wlearning.com/CAD) and select **Shortcut Keys**.

Exercise 9-2

Access the Student Web site (www.g-wlearning.com/CAD) and complete Exercise 9-2.

Stacking Text

By default, the **AutoStack Properties** dialog box appears each time you type a fraction followed by pressing the space bar or [Enter]. See **Figure 9-17**. The **AutoStack Properties** dialog box allows you to activate and control AutoStacking, which causes the fraction to stack with a horizontal or diagonal fraction bar. You can also remove the leading space between a whole number and the fraction. If you do not want the dialog box to pop up each time you create a fraction, pick the **Don't show this dialog again; always use these settings** check box. Pick the **OK** button to apply the stack or the **Cancel** button to continue without stacking.

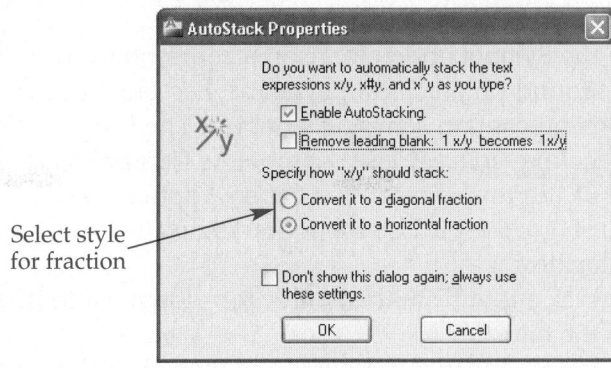

Figure 9-17.
The **AutoStack Properties** dialog box.

Manual Stacking

Use the **Stack** option to manually stack selected text vertically or diagonally. To draw a vertically stacked fraction, place a forward slash (/) between the top and bottom characters. Then select the text and pick the **Stack** option. To form a *tolerance stack*, use the caret (^) character between characters. To use a diagonal fraction bar, type a number sign (#) between characters. See **Figure 9-18**. To return stacked text to the original unstacked format, select the stacked text and the **Stack** ribbon option, or use the **Unstack** shortcut menu option.

Stack Settings

Adjust stack settings by selecting stacked text, right-clicking and choosing **Stack Properties** to display the **Stack Properties** dialog box. **Figure 9-19** briefly identifies the **Stack Properties** dialog box features. Select 100% from the **Text size** drop-down list to conform to ASME standards. This is an appropriate standard to follow for all disciplines.

Ribbon

Text Editor
> Formatting

Stack

tolerance stack: Text stacked vertically without a fraction bar.

Figure 9-18.
Examples of stacked characters. ASME standards recommend that the text height of stacked fraction numerals be the same as the height of other dimension numerals.

	Selected Text	Stacked Text
Vertical Fraction	1/2	$\frac{1}{2}$
Tolerance Stack	1^2	$\frac{1}{2}$
Diagonal Fraction	1#2	$\frac{1}{2}$

Figure 9-19.
The **Stack Properties** dialog box. Select 100% from the **Text size** drop-down list to conform to ASME standards.

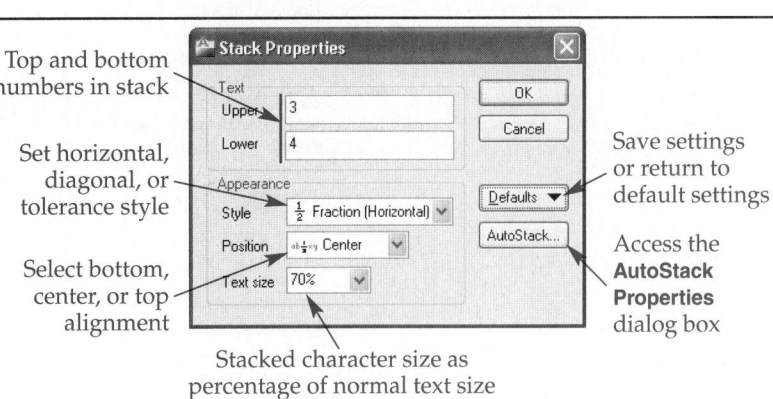

Top and bottom numbers in stack

Set horizontal, diagonal, or tolerance style

Select bottom, center, or top alignment

Save settings or return to default settings

Access the **AutoStack Properties** dialog box

Stacked character size as percentage of normal text size

Adding Symbols

non-breaking space: A symbol that you insert in place of a space to keep separate words together on one line, instead of wrapping the words that occur past the text boundary to the next line.

Use the **Symbol** option to insert a common drafting symbol or other unique character not found on a typical keyboard. See **Figure 9-20**. The first two sections in the **Symbol** menu contain common symbols. The third section contains the option to add a *non-breaking space*. Pick a symbol or **Non-breaking Space** to insert at the current location of the text cursor. The **Other...** option opens the **Character Map** dialog box, shown in **Figure 9-21**. Use the following steps to insert a symbol from the **Character Map** dialog box:

1. Pick a font from the **Font:** drop-down list to display symbols associated with the font.
2. Locate and pick a symbol, and then pick the **Select** button. The symbol appears in the **Characters to copy:** box. You can copy multiple symbols to the box.
3. Pick the **Copy** button to copy the symbols to the Clipboard.
4. Close the **Character Map** dialog box.
5. In the text editor, place the text cursor at the location where the symbols are to be inserted.
6. Right-click and select **Paste** to paste the symbols at the location of the cursor.

Exercise 9-3

Access the Student Web site (www.g-wlearning.com/CAD) and complete Exercise 9-3.

Style Settings

The **Style** panel of the **Text Editor** ribbon tab includes options for changing the text style and for overriding the annotative setting and text height. A single mtext object can use a combination of character formatting and text heights, but can only be

Figure 9-20.
Access the **Symbol** flyout to add symbols to the text editor.

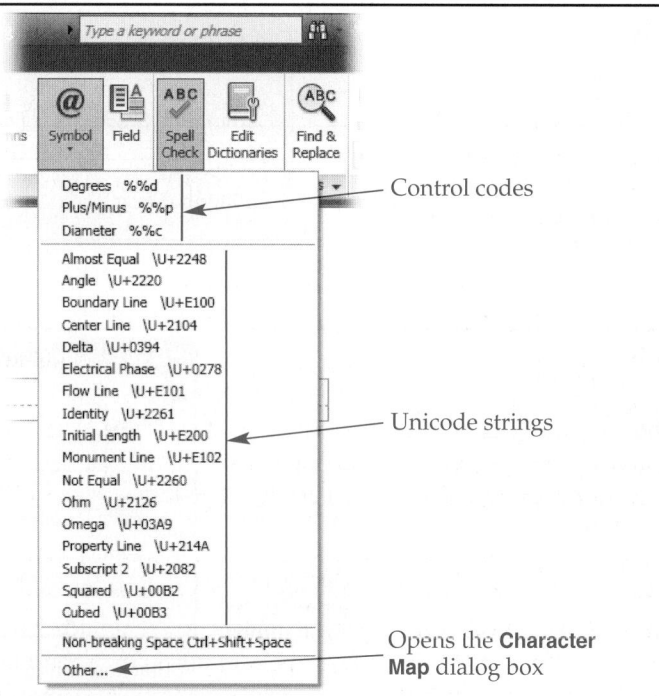

AutoCAD and Its Applications—Basics

Figure 9-21.
The **Character Map** dialog box.

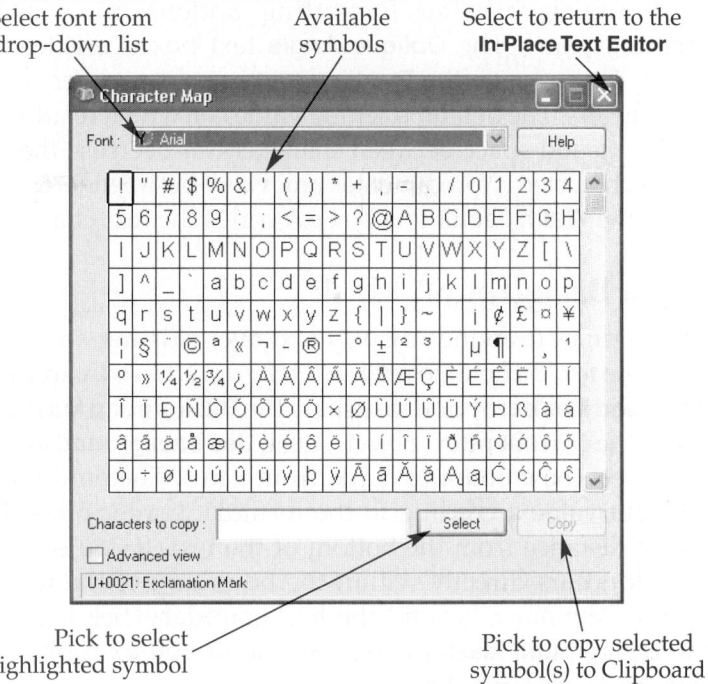

Select font from drop-down list | Available symbols | Select to return to the **In-Place Text Editor**

Pick to select highlighted symbol

Pick to copy selected symbol(s) to Clipboard

assigned one text style and can only be annotative or non-annotative. Use the scroll buttons to the right of the text styles to locate styles, or pick the expansion arrow to display styles in a temporary window. Pick a style different from the current style to apply to all text in the text editor.

Use the **Size** drop-down list to set the text height. The text height for annotative text is the paper text height. The text height for non-annotative text is the text height multiplied by the scale factor. You should usually only change the text height if the current text style uses a 0 height. Otherwise, you override the specified text style height. You can use the **Annotative** button to override the annotative setting of the current text style, but this is typically not appropriate.

Character Formatting

Use the **Formatting** panel of the **Text Editor** ribbon tab to adjust character format. Some of the same settings are also available from the shortcut menu. A single mtext object can use a combination of character formats. Remember, however, that making changes to character formatting overrides specified text style format and preset object properties, such as color. You should usually avoid this practice.

The **Bold** and **Italic** buttons are enabled for some TrueType fonts. Select the appropriate button(s) to make text bold and/or italic. Pick the **Underline** button to underline text. Select the **Overline** button to place a line over text. Use the **Make Uppercase** button to make all selected text uppercase, or use the **Make Lowercase** button to make all selected text lowercase. The **Font** drop-down list allows you to override the text font. The text color is set to ByLayer by default, but you can change the color by picking a color or option from the **Color** drop-down list. Although you should usually define color as ByLayer, a single mtext object can have a combination of text colors.

NOTE

The **AutoCAPS** option turns [Caps Lock] on for typing uppercase text in the mtext editor. [Caps Lock] turns off when you exit the text editor so that text in other programs is not all uppercase.

Ribbon
Text Editor
> **Tools**
  > **AutoCAPS**

Additional character formatting options are available from the expanded **Formatting** panel. The **Oblique Angle** text box overrides the angle at which text is inclined. The value in the **Tracking** text box determines the amount of space between text characters. The default tracking value is 1, which results in normal spacing. Increase the value to add space between characters, or decrease the value to tighten the spacing between characters. You can enter any value between 0.75 and 4.0. See **Figure 9-22**. The value in the **Width Factor** text box overrides the text character width.

Using a Background Mask

Sometimes drawings display text over existing objects, such as graphic patterns, making the text difficult to read. A *background mask* can solve this problem. Access the **Background Mask...** option to display the **Background Mask** dialog box. See **Figure 9-23**. To mask the current mtext object, check **Use background mask**. The **Border offset factor:** text box sets the amount of mask, from 1 to 5. The border offset factor works with the text height value according to the formula: border offset factor × text height = total masking distance from the bottom of the text. If you set the border offset factor to 1, the mask occurs directly within the boundary of the text. Use a value greater than 1 to offset the mask beyond the text boundary. See **Figure 9-24**. The **Fill Color** area of the **Background Mask** dialog box allows you to apply color to the mask using the background color or a different color.

background mask: A mask that hides a portion of objects behind and around text so that the text is unobstructed.

NOTE

The **Character Set** cascading submenu, available from the **More** flyout in the **Options** panel or the shortcut menu, displays a menu of code pages. A code page provides support for character sets used in different languages. Select a code page to apply it to selected text.

Exercise 9-4

Access the Student Web site (www.g-wlearning.com/CAD) and complete Exercise 9-4.

Figure 9-22.
The **Tracking** option for mtext determines the spacing between characters. Normal spacing is typically appropriate for all text on a drawing and adheres to most drafting standards.

AutoCAD tracking
Normal Spacing

AutoCAD tracking
Tracking = 0.75

A u t o C A D   t r a c k i n g
Tracking = 2.0

Figure 9-23.
The **Background Mask** dialog box controls text mask settings.

Determines how much of the background is masked

Sets mask color same as background color

Background Mask

☑ Use background mask

Border offset factor:
1.5000

Fill Color
☐ Use drawing background color   ■ Red

OK   Cancel

Figure 9-24. The border offset factor determines the size of the background mask. The text in the figure is 1/8″ with different border offset factors.

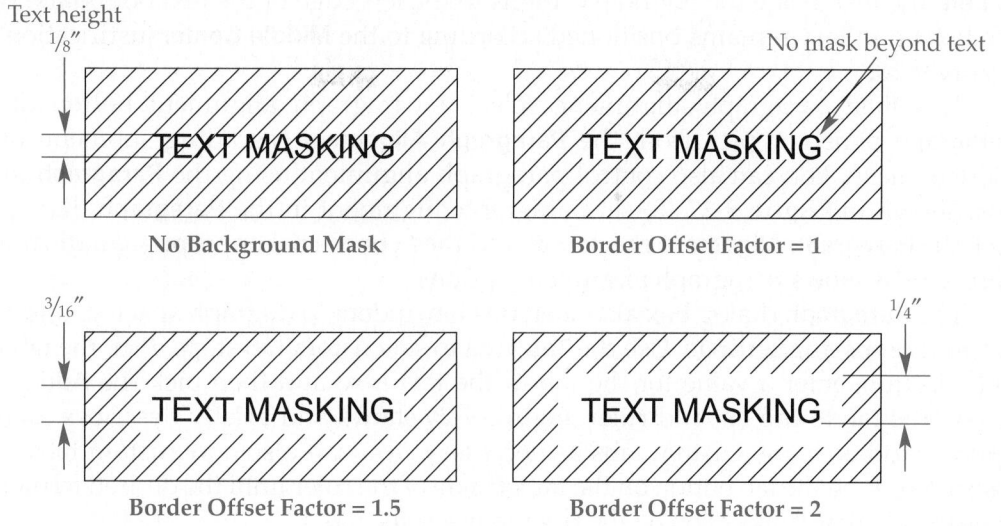

Paragraph Formatting

Use the **Paragraph** panel of the **Text Editor** ribbon tab to adjust paragraph formatting. Some of the same settings are also available from the shortcut menu. *Justify* the text boundary to control the arrangement and location of text within the text editor. You can also justify the text within the boundary independently of the text boundary justification. This provides flexibility for determining the location and arrangement of text. Justification also determines the direction of text flow. To justify the text boundary, select an option from the **Justification** flyout. See **Figure 9-25**.

justify: Align the margins or edges of text. For example, left-justified text aligns along an imaginary left border.

Figure 9-25. Options for justifying the mtext boundary.

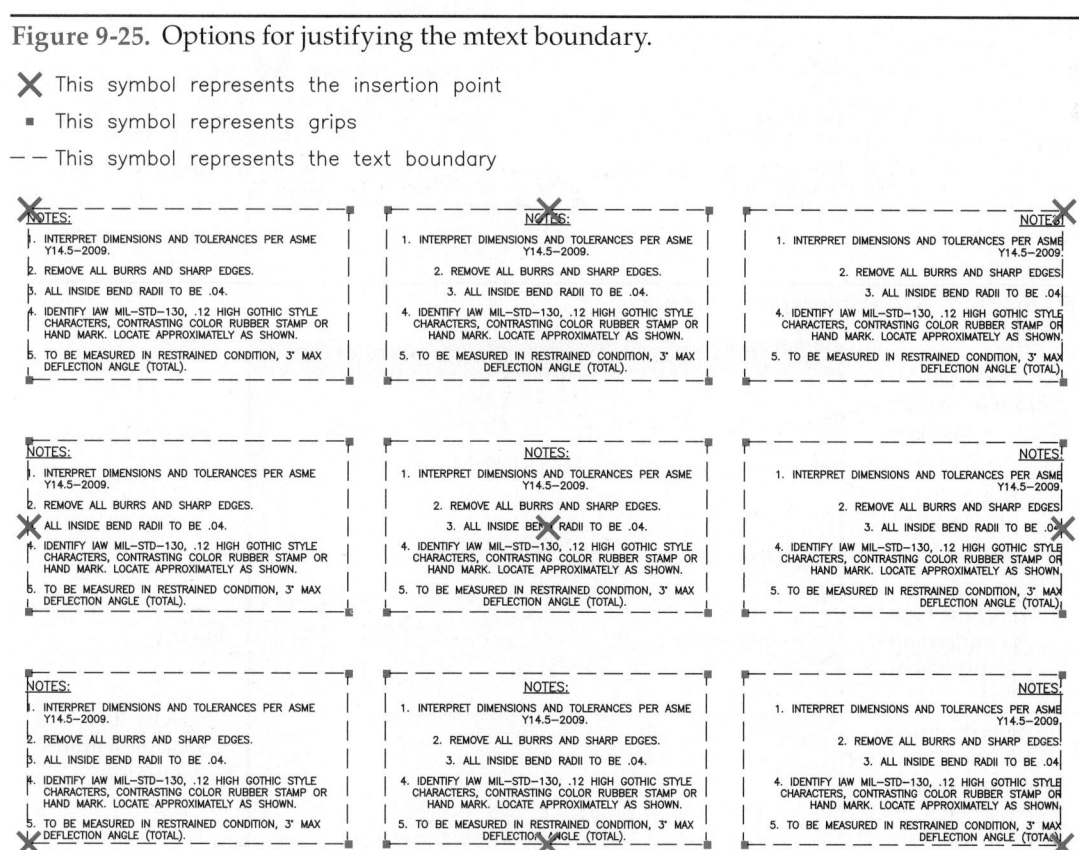

Ribbon

Text Editor
> Paragraph

Paragraph

Paragraph alignment occurs inside the text boundary. For example, when you apply a **Middle Center** text boundary justification, then set the paragraph alignment to **Left**, the text inside the boundary aligns to the left edge of the text boundary, while the text boundary remains positioned according to the **Middle Center** justification. See **Figure 9-26.**

To adjust paragraph alignment, select a paragraph alignment button on the **Paragraph** panel, or pick from the **Paragraph Alignment** cascading submenu of the shortcut menu. You can also control paragraph alignment using the **Paragraph** dialog box, shown in **Figure 9-27.** To set paragraph alignment in the **Paragraph** dialog box, pick the **Paragraph Alignment** check box, and then choose the appropriate radio button. **Figure 9-28** shows paragraph alignment options.

The **Paragraph** dialog box also includes tab, indent, paragraph spacing, and paragraph line spacing settings. Use the **Tab** area to set custom tab stops. Pick the tab type radio button, enter a value for the tab in the text box, and then pick the **Add** button to add the tab to the list and ruler. **Figure 9-29** shows and briefly describes each tab option. Add as many custom tabs as necessary. You can also add custom tabs to the ruler by picking the tab button on the far left side of the ruler until the desired tab symbol appears. Then pick a location on the ruler to insert the tab.

Figure 9-26. You can adjust paragraph alignment independently of text boundary justification.

X This symbol represents the insertion point

■ This symbol represents grips

— — This symbol represents the text boundary

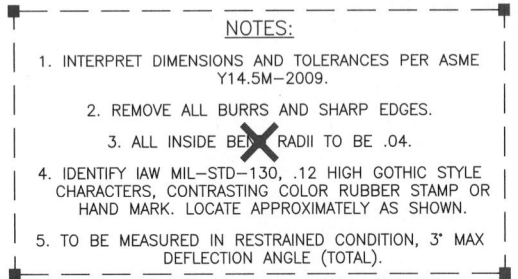
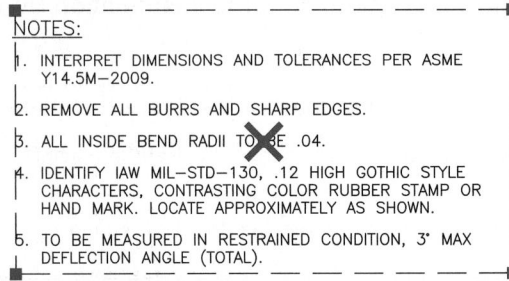

Figure 9-27. The **Paragraph** dialog box.

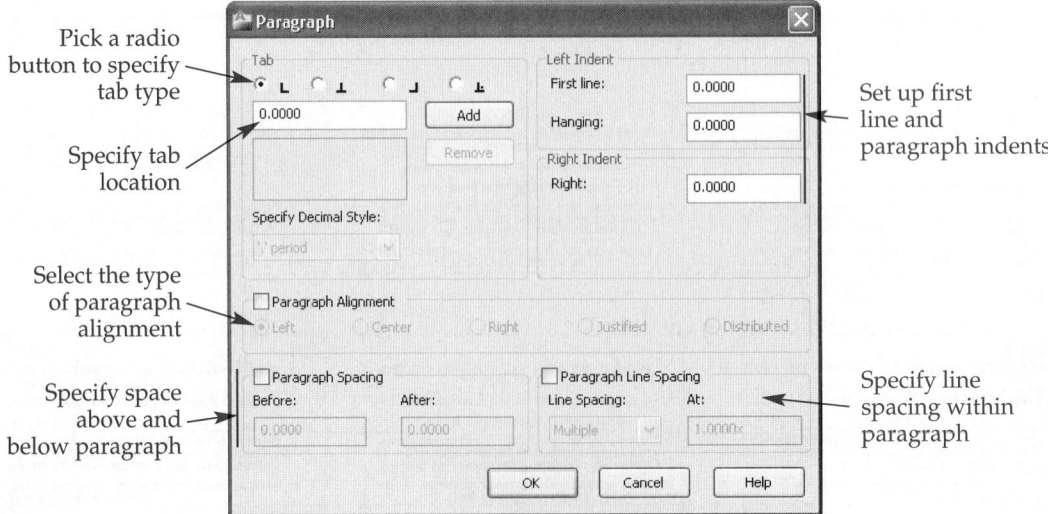

Pick a radio button to specify tab type

Specify tab location

Select the type of paragraph alignment

Specify space above and below paragraph

Set up first line and paragraph indents

Specify line spacing within paragraph

AutoCAD and Its Applications—Basics

Figure 9-28. Paragraph alignment options for mtext. In each of these examples, the text boundary justification is set to Top Left.

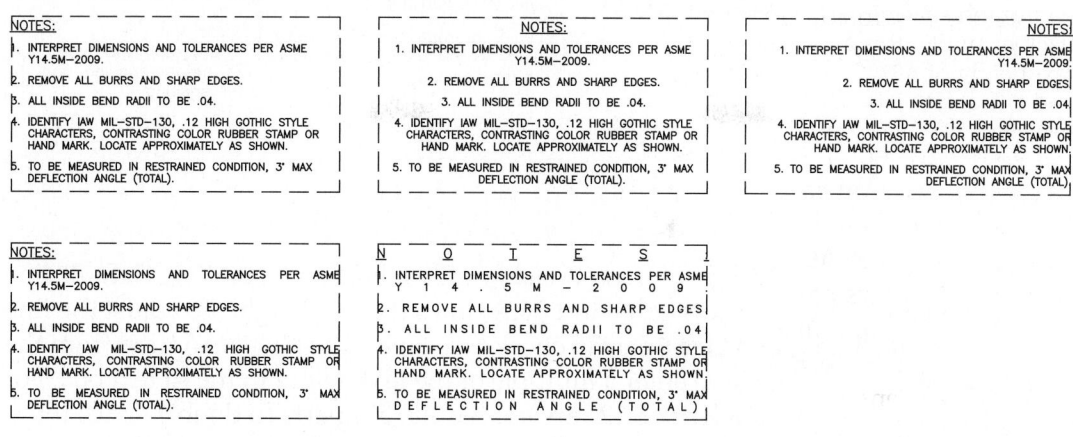

Figure 9-29. Using custom tabs to position text in the text editor. When you press [Tab], the cursor moves to the tab position. The type of tab determines text behavior.

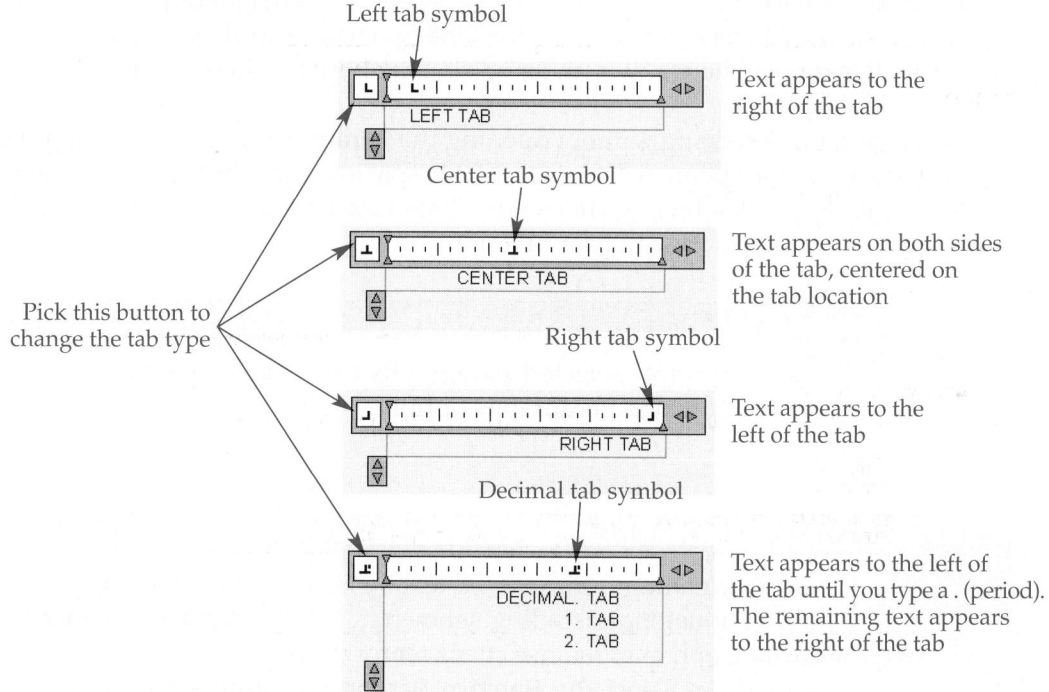

The options in the **Left Indent** area set the indentation for the first line of a paragraph of text and the remaining portion of a paragraph. The **First line** indent applies each time you start a new paragraph. As text wraps to the next line, the **Hanging** indent is used. The options in the **Right Indent** area set the indentation for the right side of a paragraph. As you type, the right indent value, not the right edge of the text boundary, determines when the text wraps to the next line.

The options in the **Paragraph Spacing** area define the amount of space before and after paragraphs. To set paragraph line spacing, pick the **Paragraph Spacing** check box. Then enter the spacing above a paragraph in the **Before** text box, and the spacing below a paragraph in the **After** text box. **Figure 9-30** shows examples of paragraph spacing settings.

Figure 9-30.
Examples of paragraph spacing. Each example uses a text height of .1875" and a first line left indent of .5".

Paragraph one typed with no paragpah spacing. Paragraph two typed with no paragraph spacing	Paragraph one typed with .25 before spacing and no after spacing.	Paragraph one typed with .125 before spacing and .5 after spacing.
	Paragraph two typed with .25 before spacing and no after spacing.	Paragraph two typed with .125 before spacing and .5 after spacing.
Before: 0" After: 0"	Before: .25" After: 0"	Before: .125" After: .5"

line spacing: The vertical distance from the bottom of one line of text to the bottom of the next line.

The options in the **Paragraph Line Spacing** area adjust *line spacing*. Default line spacing for single lines of text is equal to 1.5625 times the text height. To adjust the line spacing, pick the **Paragraph Line Spacing** check box. Select the **Multiple** option from the **Line Spacing** drop-down list to enter a multiple of the text height in the **At** text box. For example, lines with a text height of .12" are spaced .1875" apart. To double-space lines, you could enter a value of 3.125x, making the space between lines of text .375".

To force the line spacing to be the same for all lines of text, select the **Exactly** option from the **Line Spacing** drop-down list and enter a value in the **At** text box. If you enter an exact line spacing that is less than the text height, lines of text stack on top of each other. To add spaces between lines automatically based on the height of the characters in the line, choose the **At Least** option from the **Line Spacing** drop-down list and enter a value in the **At** text box. The result is an equal spacing between lines, even if the text has different heights.

You can also set line spacing without opening the **Paragraph** dialog box, using the **Line Spacing** flyout of the ribbon. Select an available spacing, pick the **More...** button to display the **Paragraph** dialog box, or choose the **Clear Line Spacing** option to apply an automatic spacing similar to the **At Least** function.

Ribbon
Text Editor
> Paragraph

Line Spacing

Ribbon
Text Editor
> Paragraph
> Combine
Paragraphs

NOTE

Combine multiple selected paragraphs to form a single paragraph using the **Combine Paragraphs** option.

PROFESSIONAL TIP

Remove formatting from selected text by right-clicking and using the **Remove Formatting** cascading submenu. Pick the **Remove Character Formatting** option to remove character formatting, such as bold, italic, or underline. Select the **Remove Paragraph Formatting** option to remove paragraph formatting, including lists. Pick the **Remove All Formatting** option to remove all character and paragraph formatting.

Exercise 9-5

Access the Student Web site (www.g-wlearning.com/CAD) and complete Exercise 9-5.

Lists

Drawings often include lists to organize information. Lists provide a way to arrange related items in a logical order and help make lines of text more readable. General notes are usually in list format. Mtext includes tools for automating the process of creating and editing numbered, bulleted, and alphabetical lists. You can create lists as you enter text or apply list formatting to existing text. Lists can contain sublevel items designated with double numbers, letters, or bullets. Default tab settings apply unless you adjust the paragraph options.

List tools are available from the **Numbering** flyout on the **Paragraph** panel of the **Text Editor** ribbon tab or the **Bullets and Lists** cascading submenu of the shortcut menu. The **Allow Bullets and Lists** option is active by default and is required to create a list. Unchecking **Allow Bullets and Lists** converts any list items in the text object to plain text characters and disables bullet and list options.

Choose an option from the **Lettered** cascading submenu to create an alphabetical list. Use the default **Uppercase** option to use uppercase lettering, or pick **Lowercase** to use lowercase lettering. Choose the **Numbered** option to form a numbered list. Select the **Bulleted** option to create a bulleted list using the default solid circle bullet symbol.

Another method of creating lists is to use the **Allow Auto-list** option. This option, which is active by default, detects characters that frequently start a list and automatically assigns the first list item. For example, if a line of text begins with a number or letter and a period, AutoCAD assumes that you are starting a list and formats additional lines of text to continue the list.

To create a numbered or lettered auto-list, you must include punctuation, such as a period, parenthesis, or colon, and press [Tab] after the number or letter that begins the first item. When you press [Enter] to start a new line of text, the new line has the same formatting as the previous line, and the next consecutive number or letter appears. To end the list, press [Enter] twice. **Figure 9-31** shows an example of a numbered list.

When creating a bulleted auto-list, you can use typical keyboard characters, such as a hyphen [-], tilde [~], bracket [>], or asterisk [*], at the beginning of a line. Another option is to insert a symbol at the beginning of a line. Then, to form the list, press [Tab] and type the line of text. When you press [Enter] to start a new line of text, the new line uses the same formatting bullet symbol as the previous line. To end the list, press [Enter] twice. See **Figure 9-32.**

Figure 9-31.
Framing notes arranged in a numbered list, using the traditional architectural Stylus BT font.

FRAMING NOTES:
1. ALL FRAMING NOTES TO BE DFL #2 OR BETTER.
2. ALL HEATED WALLS @ HEATED LIVING AREA TO BE 2 X 6 @ 16" OC. FRAME ALL EXTERIOR NON-BEARING WALLS W/2 X 6 STUDS @ 24" OC.
3. USE 2 X 6 NAILER AT THE BOTTOM OF ALL 2-2 X 12 OR 4 X HEADERS @ EXTERIOR WALLS, BACK HEADER W/2" RIGID INSULATION.
4. BLOCK ALL WALLS OVER 10'-0" HIGH AT MID HEIGHT.

Figure 9-32. In addition to the standard solid circle bullet symbol, you can use other keyboard characters or symbols to create a bulleted list.

- An elevation of the beam with end views or sections
- Complete locational dimensions for holes, plates, and angles
- Length dimensions

Bulleted List with Bullet Symbols

~ Connection specifications
~ Cutouts
~ Miscellaneous notes for the fabricator

Bulleted List with Tilde Characters

> **NOTE**
>
> Picking the **Use Tab Delimiter Only** option limits unwanted list formatting by instructing AutoCAD to recognize only tabs to start a list. If the **Use Tab Delimiter Only** option is unchecked, list formatting occurs when a space or tab follows the initial list item character.

You can convert multiple lines of text to a list by selecting the lines of text and picking a list format. AutoCAD detects where you press [Enter] to start a new line of text and lists the lines in sequence. When you create a list in this manner, a tab automatically occurs after the number, letter, or symbol preceding the text. Set tabs and indents to adjust spacing and appearance.

Additional options are available for controlling lists. Use the **Off** option to remove list characters or bulleting from selected text. Pick the **Start** option to renumber or re-letter selected items to create a new list. The numbering or lettering restarts from the beginning, using 1 or A, for example. Choose the **Continue** option to add selected items to a list that exists above the selected line of text. The number of the selected line of text continues from the previous list. Items below the selected line are also renumbered.

Exercise 9-6

Access the Student Web site (www.g-wlearning.com/CAD) and complete Exercise 9-6.

Columns

Sometimes it is necessary to group text into multiple sections, or columns. A common example is dividing lengthy general notes into columns. See **Figure 9-33**. Mtext with columns is still a single mtext object. This eliminates the need to create multiple text objects to form separate columns of text. You can create columns as you enter text or apply column formatting to existing text.

Earlier in this chapter, you were told to turn columns off before accessing the text editor. This approach is appropriate for typical text requirements without columns, especially as you learn to create mtext. However, mtext is set to form dynamic columns using the **Manual height** option by default. Column tools are also available while the text editor is active, from the **Columns** flyout on the **Insert** panel of the **Text Editor** ribbon tab or from the **Columns** cascading submenu of the shortcut menu.

Dynamic Columns

dynamic columns: Columns calculated automatically by AutoCAD according to the amount of text and the specified height and width of the columns.

To form *dynamic columns*, choose an option from the **Dynamic Columns** cascading submenu. Pick the **Auto height** option to produce columns of equal height. **Figure 9-34** shows methods for adjusting dynamic columns using **Auto height**. Increase column width or height to reduce the number of columns, or decrease column width or height to produce more columns. Pick the **Manual height** option to create columns you can adjust individually for height to produce distinct groups of information. Drag the arrows at the bottom of each column to adjust column height. See **Figure 9-35**.

Static Columns

static columns: Columns in which you divide the text into a specified number of columns.

To form *static columns*, choose the number of columns from the **Static Columns** cascading submenu. The display of text in static columns depends on how much text is in the text editor and the height and width of the columns. However, the selected number of columns does not change even if text is not completely filled or extends past a column. **Figure 9-36** shows methods for adjusting static columns. Increasing column width or height rearranges the text in the specified number of columns, but the number of static columns does not change based on column width or height.

Figure 9-33.
An example of general construction notes created as a single mtext object and divided into three columns.

1.01 RELATED WORK

A. REQUIREMENTS: PROVIDE METAL FABRICATION IN ACCORDANCE WITH CONTRACT DOCUMENTS.

1.02 SUBMITTALS

A. SHOP DRAWINGS: INCLUDE PLANS AND ELEVATIONS AT NOT LESS THAN 1" = 1'-0" SCALE, AND INCLUDE DETAILS OF SECTIONS AND CONNECTIONS AT NOT LESS THAN 3" = 1'-0" SCALE. SHOW ANCHORAGE AND ACCESSORY ITEMS. SHOP DRAWINGS FOR ITEMS SPECIFIED BY DESIGN LOAD SHALL INCLUDE ENGINEERING CALCULATIONS AND SHALL BEAR SEAL AND SIGNATURE OF PROFESSIONAL ENGINEER REGISTERED IN STATE IN WHICH PROJECT IS LOCATED.

1.03 DELIVERY, STORAGE AND HANDLING

A. DELIVERY: DELIVER ITEMS, WHICH ARE TO BE BUILT INTO WORK OF OTHER SECTIONS IN TIME TO NOT DELAY WORK.

B. STORAGE: STORE IN UNOPENED CONTAINERS. STORE OFF GROUND AND UNDER COVER, PROTECTED FROM DAMAGE.

C. HANDLING: HANDLE IN MANNER TO PROTECT SURFACES. PREVENT DISTORTION OF, AND OTHER DAMAGE TO, FABRICATED PIECES.

2.01 MATERIALS

A. STRUCTURAL STEEL SHAPES: ASTM A36.

B. STEEL PLATES: ASTM A283 GRADE C FOR BENDING OR FORMING COLD.

C. STEEL TUBING: ASTM A500, GALVANIZED WHERE INDICATED.

D. STEEL BARS AND BAR SHAPES: ASTM A675, GRADE 65; OR ASTM A36.

E. COLD FINISHED STEEL BARS: ASTM A108, GRADE AS SELECTED BY FABRICATOR.

F. STAINLESS STEEL: ASTM A167, TYPE 302 OR 304; NUMBER 4 FINISH.

G. BOLTS AND NUTS: ASTM A307, GRADE A BOLTS.

H. MACHINE SCREWS: F FF-S-92. TYPE COMPATIBLE WITH METALS BEING FASTENED AND FINISHED TO MATCH METAL FINISH.

2.02 FABRICATION, GENERAL

A. INCLUDE SUPPLEMENTARY BARS NECESSARY TO COMPLETE METAL FABRICATION WORK THOUGH NOT DEFINITELY INDICATED.

B. USE MATERIALS OF SIZE AND THICKNESS INDICATED, OR IF NOT INDICATED, OF REQUIRED SIZE AND THICKNESS TO PRODUCE ADEQUATE STRENGTH AND DURABILITY IN FINISHED PRODUCT FOR INTENDED USE.

C. FORM EXPOSED WORK TRUE TO LINE AND LEVEL WITH ACCURATE ANGLES AND SURFACES AND STRAIGHT SHARP EDGES. EASE EXPOSED EDGES TO RADIUS OF APPROXIMATELY 1/32 INCH UNLESS OTHERWISE INDICATED. FORM BENT-METAL CORNERS TO SMALLEST RADIUS WITHOUT CAUSING GRAIN SEPARATION OF OTHERWISE IMPAIRING WORK.

3.01 INSPECTION

A. EXAMINATION: EXAMINE SUBSTRATES, ADJOINING CONSTRUCTION AND CONDITIONS UNDER WHICH WORK IS TO BE INSTALLED. DO NOT PROCEED WITH WORK UNTIL UNSATISFACTORY CONDITIONS HAVE BEEN CORRECTED.

3.02 PREPARATION

A. FIELD MEASUREMENTS: VERIFY DIMENSIONS BEFORE PROCEEDING WITH WORK. OBTAIN FIELD MEASUREMENTS FOR WORK REQUIRED TO BE ACCURATELY FITTED TO OTHER CONSTRUCTION. BE RESPONSIBLE FOR ACCURACY OF SUCH MEASUREMENTS AND PRECISE FITTING AND ASSEMBLY OF FINISHED WORK.

3.03 INSTALLATION

A. INSTALL WORK IN LOCATIONS INDICATED, PLUMB, LEVEL, AND IN LINE WITH ADJACENT MATERIALS WHERE REQUIRED. PROVIDE FASTENINGS INDICATED.

B. FILL SPACE BETWEEN SLEEVES AND POSTS OF RAILINGS WITH SETTING COMPOUND. SLOPE TOP SURFACE TO DRAIN AWAY FROM POSTS.

3.04 ADJUSTING AND CLEANING

A. TOUCH-UP MARRED AND ABRADED SURFACES WITH SPECIFIED PAINT AFTER FIELD ERECTION.

3.05 PROTECTION

A. PROTECT FINISHED SURFACES AGAINST DAMAGE DURING SUBSEQUENT CONSTRUCTION OPERATIONS. REMOVE PROTECTION AT TIME OF SUBSTANTIAL COMPLETION.

Figure 9-34. Controlling columns using the dynamic column **Auto Height** option. Notice that column text flows automatically from one column to the next.

Drag here to increase or decrease column width

Drag here to increase or decrease the space between columns (gutter)

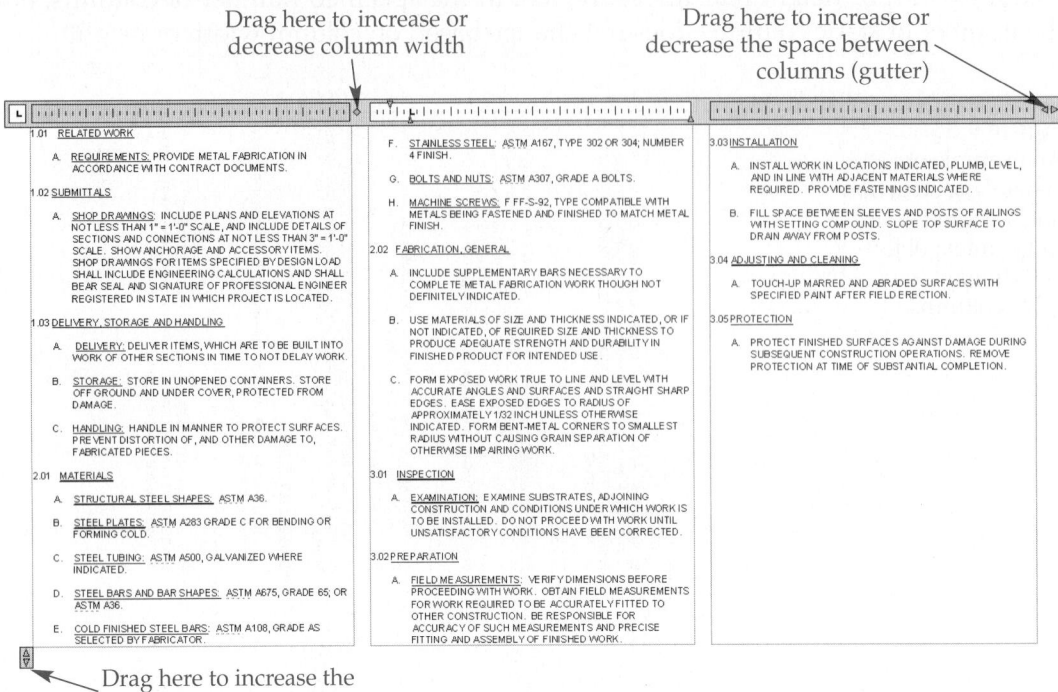

Drag here to increase the height of all columns

Figure 9-35. Controlling the length of dynamic columns individually, or manually.

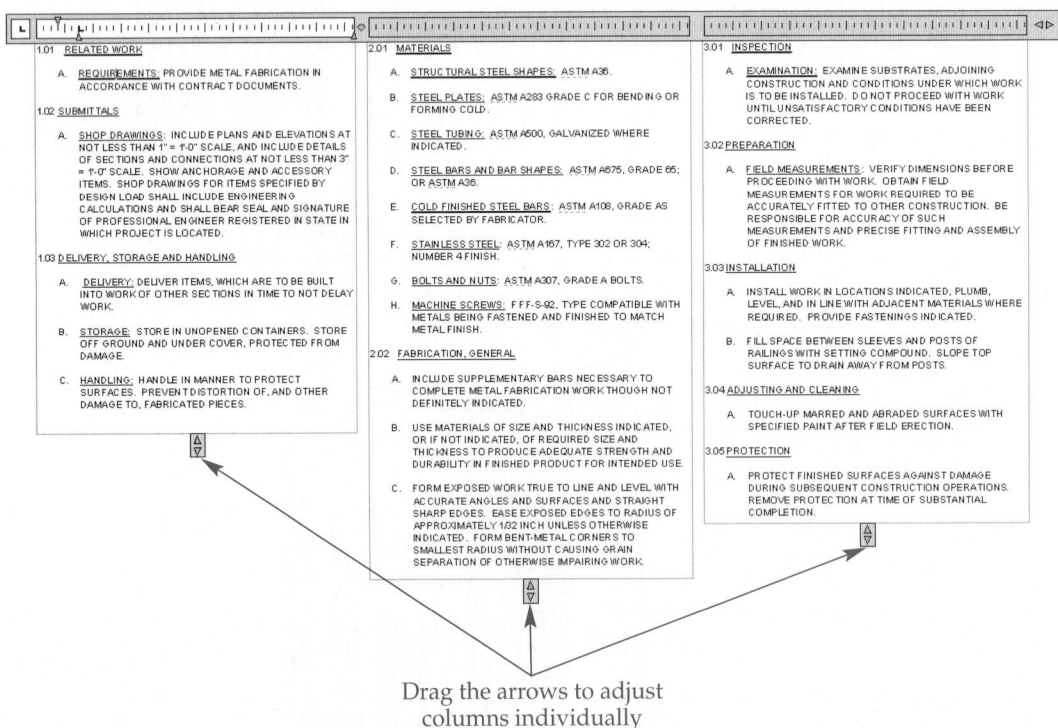

Drag the arrows to adjust columns individually

Figure 9-36. Controlling static columns.

Drag here to increase or decrease column width

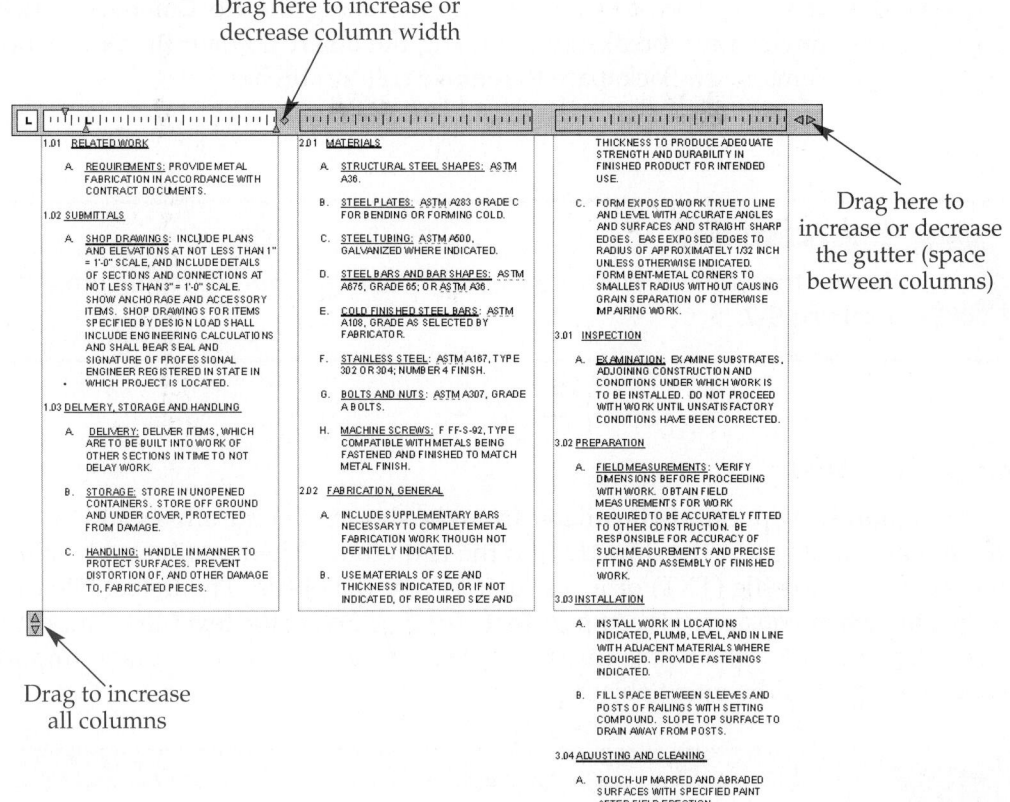

Drag here to increase or decrease the gutter (space between columns)

Drag to increase all columns

NOTE

To create more than six static columns, pick the **More...** option to access the **Column Settings** dialog box and enter the number of columns in the **Column Number** text box.

Using the Column Settings Dialog Box

You can use the **Column Settings...** dialog box as an alternative method to create columns. To create dynamic columns, select the **Dynamic Columns** radio button, and then pick the **Auto height** or **Manual height** radio button. To create static columns, choose the **Static Columns** radio button and enter the number of static columns in the **Column Number** text box.

Additional controls become available depending on the selected column type radio buttons. The **Height** text box allows you to enter the height for all static or dynamic columns. The **Width** area allows you to set column width and the *gutter*. Enter the column width in the **Column** text box and the gutter width in the **Gutter** text box. The **Total** text box is available only with static columns, and allows you to enter the total width of the text editor, which is the sum of the width of all columns and the gutter spacing between columns. To eliminate columns, pick the **No Columns** radio button.

gutter: The space between columns of text.

Controlling Column Breaks

Use the **Insert Column Break** option to specify the line of text at which a new column begins. To assign a column break, first form a dynamic or static column. Then place the cursor at a location in the text editor where a new column is to start, such as the start of a paragraph. Pick the **Insert Column Break** option to form the break. The text shifts to the next column at the location of the break. Continue applying column breaks as needed to separate sections of information.

Exercise 9-7

Access the Student Web site (www.g-wlearning.com/CAD) and complete Exercise 9-7.

Importing Text

The **Import Text** option, also available from the shortcut menu, allows you to import text from an existing text file directly into the text editor. The text file can be either a standard ASCII text file (TXT) or a rich text format (RTF) file. The **Select File** dialog box appears when you access the **Import Text...** option. Select the text file to import and pick the **Open** button. The text is inserted at the location of the text cursor. Imported text becomes part of the mtext object.

Template Development
Chapter 9

For detailed instructions on adding text styles to each drawing template, go to the Student Web site (www.g-wlearning.com/CAD), select this chapter, and select **Template Development**.

Chapter Test

Answer the following questions. Write your answers on a separate sheet of paper or go to the Student Web site (www.g-wlearning.com/CAD) and complete the electronic chapter test.

1. Define *font*.
2. Which ASME standard contains guidelines for lettering?
3. What is text composition?
4. Determine the AutoCAD text height for text to be plotted .188″ high using a half (1:2) scale. Show your calculations.
5. Determine the AutoCAD text height for text to be plotted .188″ high using a scale of 1/4″ = 1′-0″. Show your calculations.
6. Explain the function of annotative text and give an example.
7. What is the relationship between the drawing scale and the annotation scale for annotative text?

8. Define *text style*.
9. Describe how to create a text style that has the name ROMANS-12_15, uses the romans.shx font, has a fixed height of .12, a text width of 1.25, and an oblique angle of 15.
10. What are "big fonts"?
11. When setting text height in the **Text Style** dialog box, what value do you enter so that you can alter the text height when you create single-line text?
12. How would you specify text to display vertically on-screen?
13. What does a width factor of .5 do to text compared to the default width factor of 1?
14. Describe a fast way to make a text style current.
15. Name the tool that lets you create multiline text objects.
16. How does the width of the mtext boundary affect what you type?
17. What happens if the mtext you type exceeds or is not as long as the boundary length that you initially establish?
18. What happens by default when you type a fraction in the mtext editor, and what does this allow you to do?
19. How can you draw stacked fractions manually when using the **MTEXT** tool?
20. What is the purpose of tracking?
21. What text feature allows you to hide parts of objects behind and around text?
22. What is the difference between text boundary justification and paragraph alignment?
23. Explain how to convert multiple lines of text into a numbered list.
24. Briefly describe the difference between dynamic columns and static columns.
25. From what two file formats can you import text?

Drawing Problems

Start AutoCAD if it is not already started. Start a new drawing for each problem using an appropriate template of your choice. The template should include layers and text styles, when necessary, for drawing the given objects. Add layers and text styles as needed. Draw all objects using appropriate layers and text styles, justification, and format. Follow the specific instructions for each problem. Use only drawing tools and techniques you have already learned. Use your own judgment and approximate dimensions when necessary.

▼ Basic

1. Use the **MTEXT** tool to type your name using a text style of your choosing and a text height of 1". Save the drawing as P9-1. Print an 8.5" x 11" copy of the drawing extents, using a 1:1 scale and a landscape orientation. Construct the sheet into a name tag.

2. Use the **MTEXT** tool to type the definition of the following terms using a text style with the Arial font and a .12 text height. Save the drawing as P9-2.
   • annotation
   • text
   • composition
   • font
   • justify

3. Use the **MTEXT** tool to type the definition of the following terms using a text style with the Romand font and a .12 text height. Save the drawing as P9-3.
   • scale factor
   • annotative text
   • annotation scale
   • text height
   • paper text height

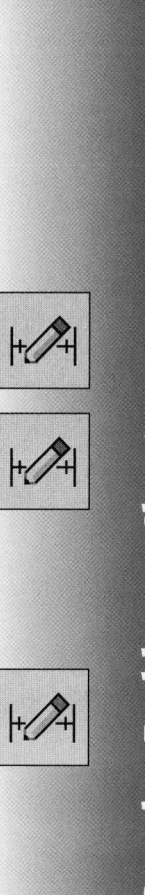

4. Use the **MTEXT** tool to type the key notes shown. Use a text style with the Stylus BT font. The heading text height is .25 and the note text height is .125. Save the drawing as P9-4.

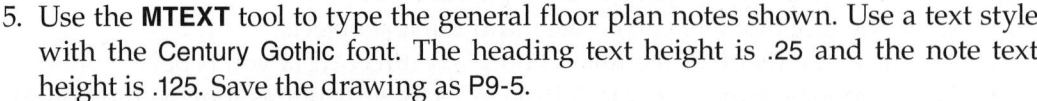

KEY NOTES
1.   SLOPING SURFACE
2.   DIAGONAL SUPPORT STRUT
3.   VENT- PROVIDE NEW CANT FLASHING
4.   BRICK CHIMNEY- REMOVE TO BELOW
      DECK SURFACE

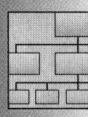

5. Use the **MTEXT** tool to type the general floor plan notes shown. Use a text style with the Century Gothic font. The heading text height is .25 and the note text height is .125. Save the drawing as P9-5.

GENERAL NOTES

1.   ALL PENETRATIONS IN TOP OR BOTTOM PLATES FOR PLUMBING OR ELECTRICAL RUNS TO BE SEALED. SEE ELECTRICAL PLANS FOR ADDITIONAL SPECIFICATIONS.
2.   PROVIDE 1/2" WATERPROOF GYPSUM BOARD AROUND ALL TUBS, SHOWERS, AND SPAS.
3.   VENT DRYER AND ALL FANS TO OUTSIDE AIR THRU VENT WITH DAMPER.

▼ **Intermediate**

6. Draw the basic organizational chart shown below. Save the drawing as P9-6.

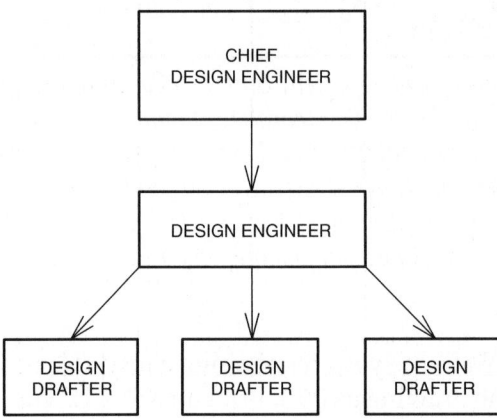

7. Use the **MTEXT** tool to type the general notes for a part drawing shown. Use a text style with the Romans font. The heading text height is 6 mm and the note text height is 3 mm. Save the drawing as P9-7.

NOTES:
1. DIMENSIONS AND TOLERANCES PER ANSI Y14.4—2009.
2. REMOVE ALL BURRS AND SHARP EDGES.

CASTING NOTES UNLESS OTHERWISE SPECIFIED:
1. .31 WALL THICKNESS
2. R.12 FILLETS
3. R.06 CORNERS
4. 1.5°—3.0° DRAFT
5. TOLERANCES
    ± 1° ANGULAR
    ± .03 TWO—PLACE DIMENSIONS
6. PROVIDE .12 THK MACHINING STOCK ON ALL MACHINED SURFACES.

8. Use the **MTEXT** tool to type the common framing notes shown. Use a text style with the Stylus BT font. The heading text height is .188 and the note text height is .125. After typing the text exactly as shown, edit the text with the following changes:
   A. Change the \ in item 7 to 1/2.
   B. Change the [in item 8 to 1.
   C. Change the 1/2 in item 8 to 3/4.
   D. Change the ^ in item 10 to a degree symbol.
   E. Check your spelling after making the changes.

Save the drawing as P9-8.

COMMON FRAMING NOTES:
1. ALL FRAMING LUMBER TO BE DFL #2 OR BETTER.
2. ALL HEATED WALLS @ HEATED LIVING AREAS TO BE 2 X 6 @ 24" OC.
3. ALL EXTERIOR HEADERS TO BE 2-2 X 12 UNLESS NOTED, W/ 2" RIGID INSULATION BACKING UNLESS NOTED.
4. ALL SHEAR PANELS TO BE 1/2" CDX PLY W/8d @ 4" OC @ EDGE, HDRS, & BLOCKING AND 8d @ 8" OC @ FIELD UNLESS NOTED.
5. ALL METAL CONNECTORS TO BE SIMPSON CO. OR EQUAL.
6. ALL TRUSSES TO BE 24" OC. SUBMIT TRUSS CALCS TO BUILDING DEPT. PRIOR TO ERECTION.
7. PLYWOOD ROOF SHEATHING TO BE \ STD GRADE 32/16 PLY LAID PERP TO RAFTERS. NAIL W/8d @ 6" OC @ EDGES AND 12" OC @ FIELD.
8. PROVIDE [1/2" STD GRADE T&G PLY FLOOR SHEATHING LAID PERP TO FLOOR JOISTS. NAIL W/10d @ 6" OC @ EDGES AND BLOCKING AND 12" OC @ FIELD.
9. BLOCK ALL WALLS OVER 10'-0" HIGH AT MID.
10. LET-IN BRACES TO BE 1 X 4 DIAG BRACES @ 45^ FOR ALL INTERIOR LOAD-BEARING WALLS.

9. Use the **MTEXT** tool to type the caulking notes shown. Use a text style with the San Serif font. The heading text height is .188 and the note text height is .125. Save the drawing as P9-9.

CAULKING NOTES:

CAULKING REQUIREMENTS BASED ON
OREGON RESIDENTIAL ENERGY CODE

1. SEAL THE EXTERIOR SHEATHING AT CORNERS, JOINTS, DOORS, WINDOWS, AND FOUNDATION SILL WITH SILICONE CAULK.
2. CAULK THE FOLLOWING OPENINGS W/ EXPANDED FOAM, BACKER RODS, OR SIMILAR:
   - ANY SPACE BETWEEN WINDOW AND DOOR FRAMES
   - BETWEEN ALL EXTERIOR WALL SOLE PLATES AND PLY SHEATHING
   - ON TOP OF RIM JOIST PRIOR TO PLYWOOD FLOOR APPLICATION
   - WALL SHEATHING TO TOP PLATE
   - JOINTS BETWEEN WALL AND FOUNDATION
   - JOINTS BETWEEN WALL AND ROOF
   - JOINTS BETWEEN WALL PANELS
   - AROUND OPENINGS

10. Using **MTEXT**, create the electrical notes shown below. Format the notes properly to make them easier to read.
    A. Use the Stylus BT font.
    B. Add the heading "ELECTRICAL NOTES:" on a separate line.
    C. Number each item separately.
    D. Use all capital letters and set the notes in two columns.
    Save the drawing as P9-10.

    All garage and exterior plugs and light fixtures to be on GFCI circuit. All kitchen plugs and light fixtures to be on GFCI circuit. Provide a separate circuit for microwave oven. Provide a separate circuit for personal computer. Verify all electrical locations with owner. Exterior spotlights to be on photoelectric cell with timer. All recessed lights in exterior ceilings to be insulation cover rated. Electrical outlet plate gaskets to be insulated on receptacle, switch, and any other boxes in exterior wall. Provide thermostatically controlled fan in attic with manual override; verify location with owner. All fans vent to outside air; all fan ducts to have automatic dampers. Hot water tanks to be insulated to R-11 minimum. Insulate all hot water lines to R-4 minimum; provide alternate bid to insulate all pipes for noise control. Provide 6 sq. ft. of vent for combustion air to outside air for fireplace connected directly to firebox; provide fully closable air inlet. Heating to be electric heat pump; provide bid for single unit near garage or for a unit each floor (in attic). Insulate all heating ducts in unheated areas to R-11; all HVAC ducts to be sealed at joints and corners.

11. Draw the general construction notes exactly as shown in Figure 9-33 using columns. Save the drawing as P9-11.

12. Draw the flowchart shown. Save the drawing as P9-12.

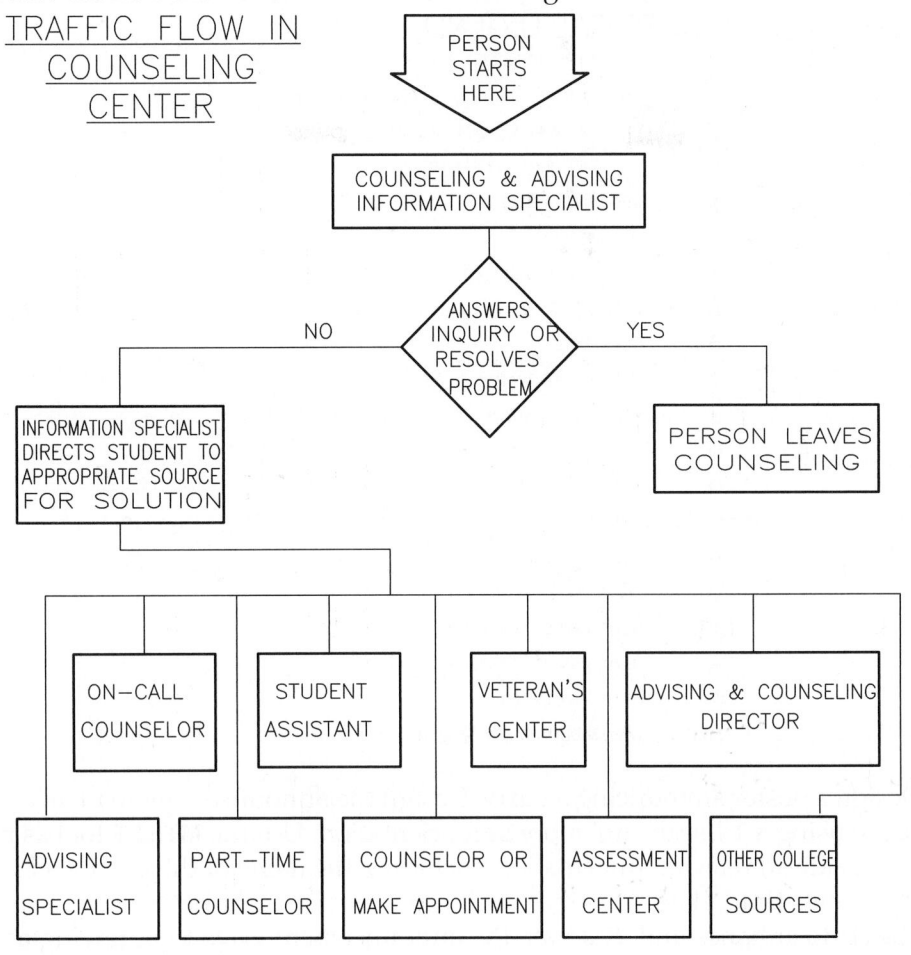

TRAFFIC FLOW IN COUNSELING CENTER

13. Draw the controller schematic shown. Save the drawing as P9-13.

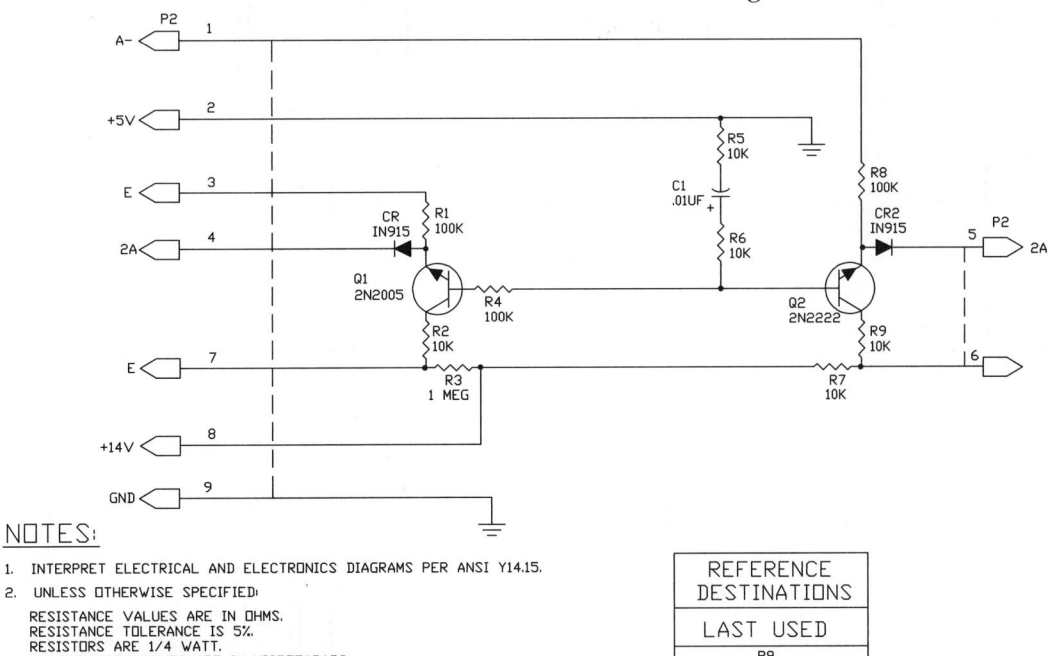

NOTES:

1. INTERPRET ELECTRICAL AND ELECTRONICS DIAGRAMS PER ANSI Y14.15.

2. UNLESS OTHERWISE SPECIFIED:

   RESISTANCE VALUES ARE IN OHMS.
   RESISTANCE TOLERANCE IS 5%.
   RESISTORS ARE 1/4 WATT.
   CAPACITANCE VALUES ARE IN MICROFARADS.
   CAPACITANCE TOLERANCE IS 10%.
   CAPACITOR VOLTAGE RATING IS 20V.
   INDUCTANCE VALUES ARE IN MICROHENRIES.

REFERENCE DESTINATIONS
LAST USED
R9
C1
CR2
Q2

14. Draw the electrical legend shown. Save the drawing as P9-14.

ELECTRICAL LEGEND:

⌽	110 VOLT DUPLEX CONVENIENCE OUTLET
⌽ GFCI	110 VOLT GROUND FAULT CIRCUIT INTERRUPT DUPLEX OUTLET
⌽WP GFCI	110 VOLT WATERPROOF GFCI DUPLEX OUTLET
⌽	110 VOLT SPLIT WIRED OUTLET
⌽	220 VOLT OUTLET
-⌽-	JUNCTION BOX
TV	CABLE TELEVISION OUTLET
-C-	CLOCK OUTLET
⌴	DOOR BELL
$	SINGLE POLE SWITCH
$³	THREE-WAY SWITCH
O	CEILING-MOUNTED LIGHT
-◇-	WALL-MOUNTED LIGHT
▭	FLUORESCENT LIGHT
⊙	CIRCULAR RECESSED LIGHT
▣	SQUARE RECESSED LIGHT
⊙F	LIGHT, FAN COMBINATION
⊙F H	LIGHT, FAN, HEAT COMBINATION
● SD	CEILING-MOUNTED SMOKE DETECTOR
⌴SD	WALL-MOUNTED SMOKE DETECTOR

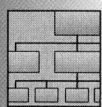

15. Design a poster announcing a party. Design the announcement to fit an 8.5″ × 11″ sheet, using a 1:1 scale and a portrait orientation. Use the **MTEXT** tool as needed to provide all relevant information, including the name of the party and a theme statement, time, date, location, and your contact information. Draw non-text objects to enhance and illustrate the announcement. Save the drawing as P9-15. Print 8.5″ × 11″ copies of the drawing extents, centered on the sheet, using a 1:1 scale and a portrait orientation. Distribute and post copies of the announcement. Throw the party.

16. Design a greeting card. Design the card to fit an 8.5″ × 11″ sheet, using a 1:1 scale and a portrait orientation, and using the format shown. Do not draw the dimensions, sheet edges, or fold lines. Use the **MTEXT** tool as needed to provide all relevant information, including the occasion, name of the card recipient, and a greeting. Draw non-text objects to enhance and illustrate the card. Save the drawing as **P9-16**. Print an 8.5″ × 11″ copy of the drawing extents, centered on the sheet, using a 1:1 scale and a portrait orientation. Fold the card and give it to the recipient.

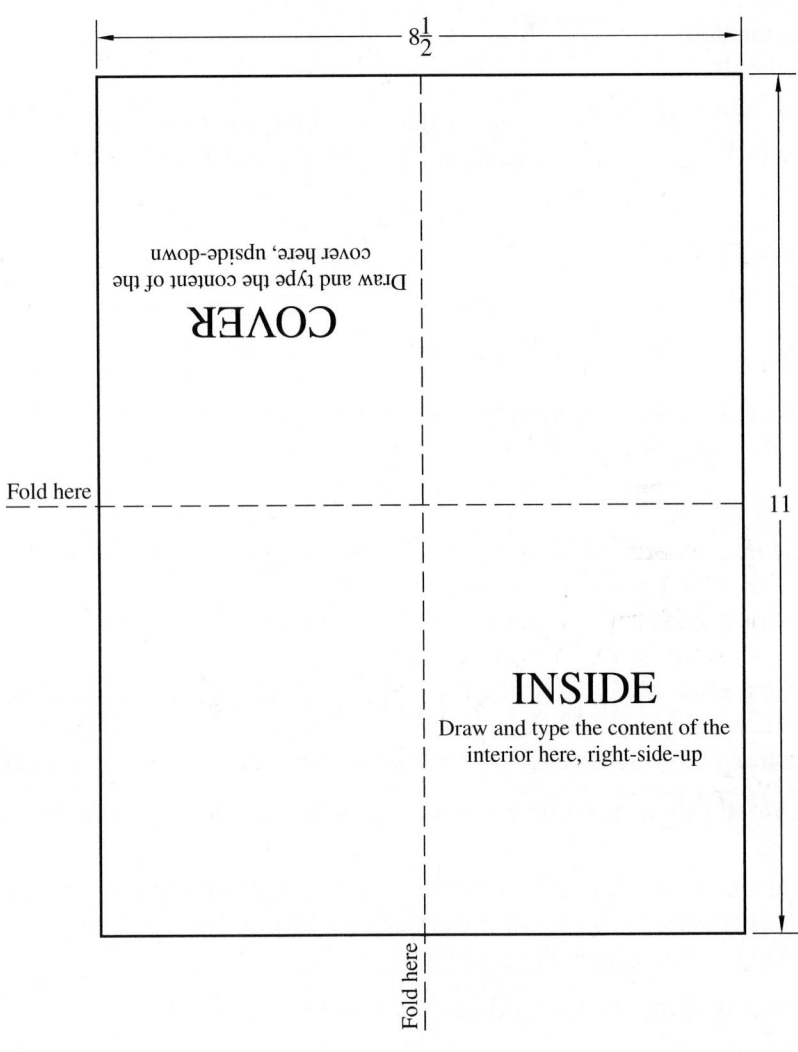

AutoCAD Certified Associate Exam Practice

Answer the following questions. Write your answers on a separate sheet of paper.

1. Which of the following options are available for AutoCAD SHX (shape) fonts? *Select all that apply.*
   A. backwards
   B. bold
   C. italic
   D. underscore
   E. vertical

2. Which of the following oblique angles should you specify in AutoCAD to slant text according to the 68° horizontal incline standard? *Select the one item that best answers the question.*
   A. 0°
   B. −22°
   C. 22°
   D. 68°
   E. −68°

3. Which of the following symbols can be used to stack selected mtext manually? *Select all that apply.*
   A. *
   B. ^
   C. /
   D. #
   E. ~

AutoCAD Certified Professional Exam Practice

Follow the instructions in each problem. Write your answers on a separate sheet of paper.

1. **Navigate to this chapter on the Student Web site and open the CPE-09columns. dwg file.**

   Edit the text to use dynamic columns with the **Auto height** option. Use the arrows on the text editor to create columns with a width of 5.44 units and a height of 2.41 units. How many columns result?

2. **Open a new drawing file and save it as CPE-09mtext.dwg.**

   Create a text style called SansSerif using the SansSerif font and a text height of .12. Enter the **MTEXT** tool and set a text boundary of 3 units. Use the SansSerif text style to insert the legal description shown below into the drawing using all uppercase text. Disable columns. Resave the file. How many lines of text does the legal description occupy with these settings?

   > Beginning at a point 20 feet north of center line of Unger Road, north for a length of 655.18', thence S89°33'10"E for a length of 447.75', thence south for a length of 475.53', thence N84°53'42"W for a length of 224.77', thence north for a length of 92.02', thence S81°12'15"W for a length of 196.19', thence south for a length of 256.56', thence S86°55'3"W for a length of 30.23' to the point of beginning.

Single-Line Text and Additional Text Tools

Learning Objectives

After completing this chapter, you will be able to do the following:

✓ Use the **TEXT** tool to create single-line text.
✓ Insert and use fields.
✓ Check spelling.
✓ Edit existing text.
✓ Search for and replace text automatically.

This chapter describes how to use the **TEXT** tool to place a single-line text object. The **TEXT** tool is most useful for adding a single character, word, or line of text. Use the **MTEXT** tool for all other text requirements. This chapter also presents methods for editing text and other valuable text tools, including fields, spell checking, and ways to find and replace text. You can apply most of the additional text tools described in this chapter to mtext or single-line text objects.

Single-Line Text

It is good practice to set the appropriate text style current before you access the **TEXT** tool. Then activate the **TEXT** tool to create a single-line text object. Left is the default justification. To use a different justification, choose the **Justify** option at the Specify start point of text [Justify/Style]: prompt before you pick the start point of the text. **Figure 10-1** shows all of the justification options except the **Align** and **Fit** options, which are described later in this chapter. Choose a justification option according to where and how you want text to form.

Pick a point to locate the text according to the specified justification, known as the *justification point*. Next, if the current text style uses a height of 0, enter the text height. If the current text style is annotative, enter the paper text height. If the current text style is not annotative, enter the text height multiplied by the scale factor. The next prompt asks for the text rotation angle. The default value is 0, which draws horizontal text. Specify a rotation angle to pivot the text around the start point in a counterclockwise direction. See **Figure 10-2**.

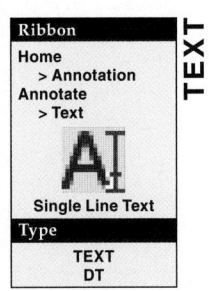

Ribbon
Home
> Annotation
Annotate
> Text

Single Line Text

Type
TEXT
DT

TEXT

justification point: The point from which text is justified according to the current justification option.

Figure 10-1. Standard justification options available for drawing single-line text. The difference between some options is only evident when you use values that extend below the baseline, such as the "y" in the word "Justify."

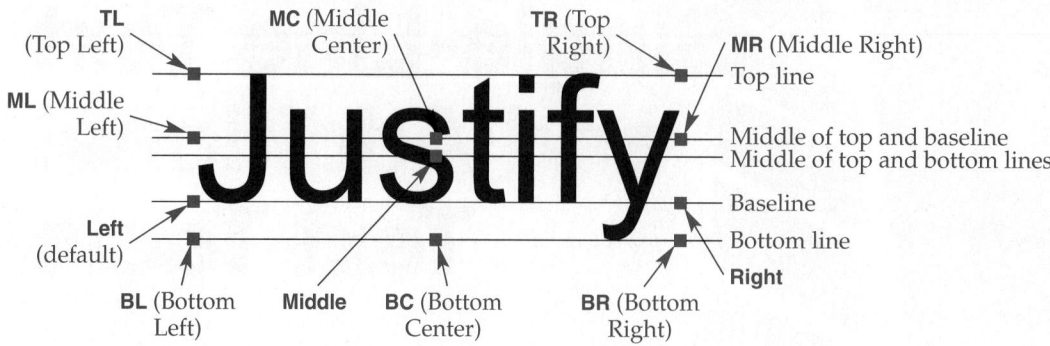

Figure 10-2. Examples of rotating single-line. The plus sign indicates the start point.

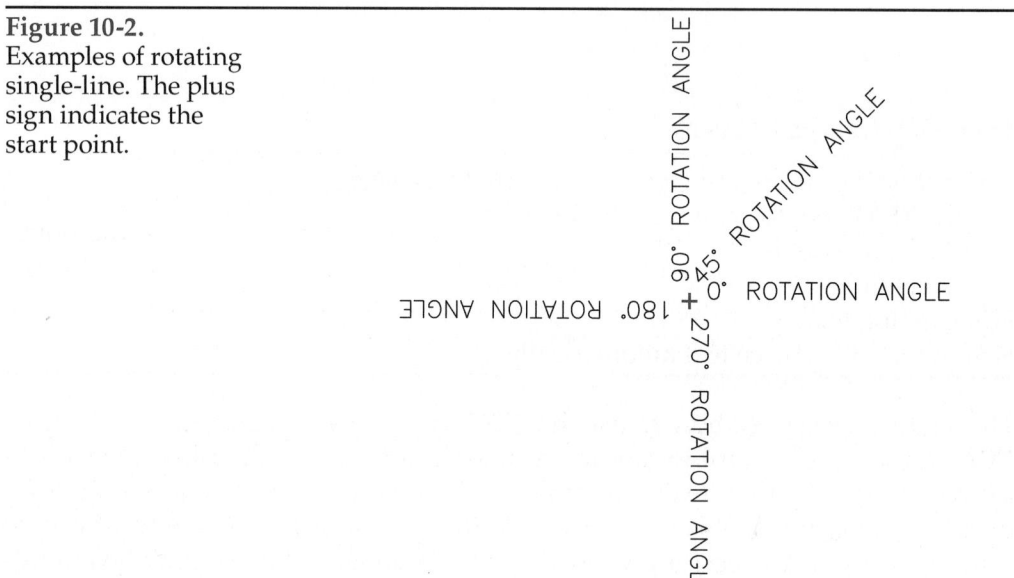

NOTE

Changes you make to the default text angle orientation or direction affect the text rotation.

Once you set the justification, height, and rotation angle, a text editor and cursor equal in height to the text height appears on-screen at the start point. As you type, the text editor increases in size to display the characters. See **Figure 10-3.** Right-click to display a shortcut menu of text options, similar to those available for the **MTEXT** tool.

Press [Enter] at the end of each line of text to move the cursor to a start point one line below the preceding line. Each new line of text is a new single-line text object, not a grouped paragraph. When you are finished typing, press [Enter] twice to exit the **TEXT** tool. Cancel the **TEXT** tool and remove incomplete lines of text by pressing [Esc].

NOTE

To change selected text to uppercase, right-click and select **UPPER-CASE** from the **Change Case** cascading submenu. Use the **lowercase** option to change all text to lowercase.

Figure 10-3.
Typing text using the **TEXT** tool and default left justification.

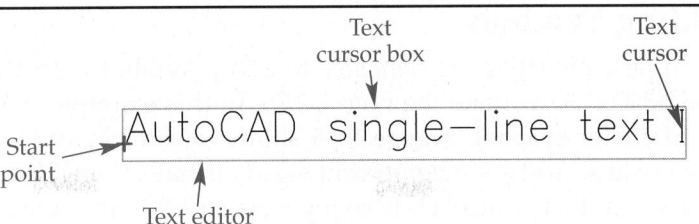

Text cursor box

Text cursor

Start point

Text editor

AutoCAD single—line text

Align or Fit Justification

Align and **Fit** justification options are available from the **Justify** option at the Specify start point of text [Justify/Style]: prompt, as an alternative to the previous method of creating single-line text. The **Align** option requires you to select the start point and endpoint of the line of text. AutoCAD adjusts the text height to form between the start point and endpoint. The height varies according to the distance between the points and the number of characters. The **Fit** option requires you to select the start point and endpoint of the line of text, *and* the text height. AutoCAD adjusts character width to fit between the specified points, while keeping text height constant. **Figure 10-4** shows the effects of the **Align** and **Fit** options.

Exercise 10-1

Access the Student Web site (www.g-wlearning.com/CAD) and complete Exercise 10-1.

Figure 10-4 Examples of using the **Align** and **Fit** justification options to create aligned and fit text. The plus signs indicate the start point and endpoint.

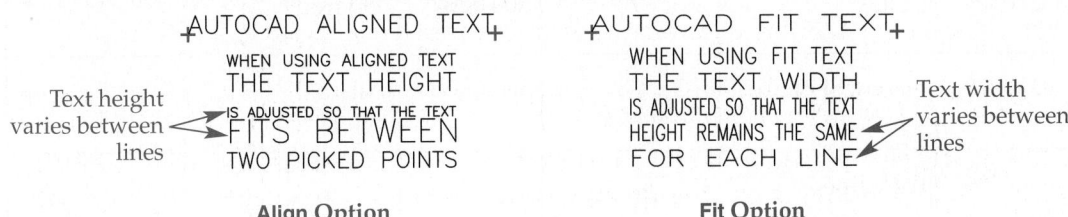

Text height varies between lines

AUTOCAD ALIGNED TEXT
WHEN USING ALIGNED TEXT
THE TEXT HEIGHT
IS ADJUSTED SO THAT THE TEXT
FITS BETWEEN
TWO PICKED POINTS

Align Option

AUTOCAD FIT TEXT
WHEN USING FIT TEXT
THE TEXT WIDTH
IS ADJUSTED SO THAT THE TEXT
HEIGHT REMAINS THE SAME
FOR EACH LINE

Text width varies between lines

Fit Option

Adding Symbols

Type a *control code sequence* to add a symbol with the **TEXT** tool. For example, type %%C2.75 to create the note Ø2.75. In this example, %%C is the code used to add the diameter symbol. **Figure 10-5** shows several symbol codes and the symbol the code creates. Add a single percent sign normally. However, when a percent sign must precede another control code sequence, use %%% to force a single percent sign.

Underscoring or Overscoring Text

Type %%U in front of text to underscore (underline) and %%O in front of text to overscore. For example, type %%UUNDERSCORING TEXT to create the note UNDERSCORING TEXT. Use both control code sequences to underscore and overscore text. For example, the control code sequence %%O%%ULINE OF TEXT produces LINE OF TEXT.

The %%U and %%O control codes are toggles that turn underscoring and overscoring on and off. Type %%U before a word or phrase to be underscored, and then type %%U after the word or phrase to turn underscoring off. Any text following the second %%U appears without underscoring. For example, enter %%UDETAIL A%%U HUB ASSEMBLY to create DETAIL A HUB ASSEMBLY.

Figure 10-5. Common control code sequences used to add symbols to single-line text.

Control Code or Unicode	Type of Symbol	Appearance	Control Code or Unicode	Type of Symbol	Appearance
%%d	Degrees	°	\U+2261	Identity	≡
%%p	Plus/Minus	±	\U+E200	Initial length	
%%c	Diameter	Ø	\U+E102	Monument line	
%%%	Percent	%	\U+2260	Not equal	≠
\U+2248	Almost equal	≈	\U+2126	Ohm	Ω
\U+2220	Angle	∠	\U+03A9	Omega	Ω
\U+E100	Boundary line		\U+214A	Property line	
\U+2104	Centerline		\U+2082	Subscript 2	2
\U+0394	Delta	△	\U+00B2	Squared	2
\U+0278	Electrical phase	φ	\U+00B3	Cubed	3
\U+E101	Flow line				

AutoCAD and Its Applications—Basics

Underline labels such as <u>SECTION A-A</u> or <u>DETAIL B</u> instead of drawing a line or polyline object under the text. In addition, use the **Middle** or **Center** justification mode. The view labels are automatically underlined and centered under the views or details they identify.

Exercise 10-2

Access the Student Web site (www.g-wlearning.com/CAD) and complete Exercise 10-2.

Fields

A *field* references drawing properties, AutoCAD functions, and information-related objects, and then displays the content in a text object. For example, insert the **Title** field below a drawing view to display the title of the drawing. You can update fields when changes occur to the reference data. For example, insert the **Date** field into a title block to update the field with the current date as necessary. Fields allow you to create "intelligent" text that uses existing drawing data and displays current information that changes throughout the course of a project.

field: A text object that can display a specific property value, setting, or characteristic.

Inserting Fields

Use the **FIELD** tool to add a field to an mtext or text object. To insert a field in an active mtext editor, access the **Field** option, also available by right-clicking and selecting **Insert Field**, or by pressing [Ctrl]+[F]. To insert a field in an active single-line text editor, right-click and select **Insert Field...** or press [Ctrl]+[F].

The **Field** dialog box appears, allowing you to select a field. See **Figure 10-6.** The **Field** dialog box includes many preset fields. You can filter the list of fields by selecting a category from the **Field category** drop-down list. Fields related to the category appear in the **Field names** list box. Pick a field from the list and then choose a format from the **Examples:** list box. If you cannot find an adequate example, create a custom format by typing in the **Data format:** text box.

Pick the **OK** button to insert the field. The field assumes the current text style. By default, field text displays a light gray background. See **Figure 10-7.** This keeps you aware that the text is actually a field, and the value may change. You can deactivate the background in the **Fields** area of the **User Preferences** tab of the **Options** dialog box. See **Figure 10-8.**

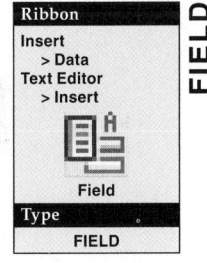

Ribbon
Insert
> Data
Text Editor
> Insert
Field
Type
FIELD

FIELD

Updating Fields

Update fields automatically or manually as changes occur to the referenced data. Examples include updating a **Date** field to correspond to the date today, a **Filename** field to match changes made to the filename, or an **Object** field to match changes made to the properties of an object. Set automatic field updates using the **Field Update Settings** dialog box. To access this dialog box, pick the **Field Update Settings...** button in the **Fields** area of the **User Preferences** tab of the **Options** dialog box. Whenever a selected event, such as saving or regenerating, occurs, all associated fields are automatically updated.

update: The AutoCAD procedure for changing text in a field based on the current value of field.

Figure 10-6. Select fields using the **Field** dialog box.

Selected field   Current value for field

Select category to limit field list

All available fields listed

Information related to the selected field type

Select text format for field

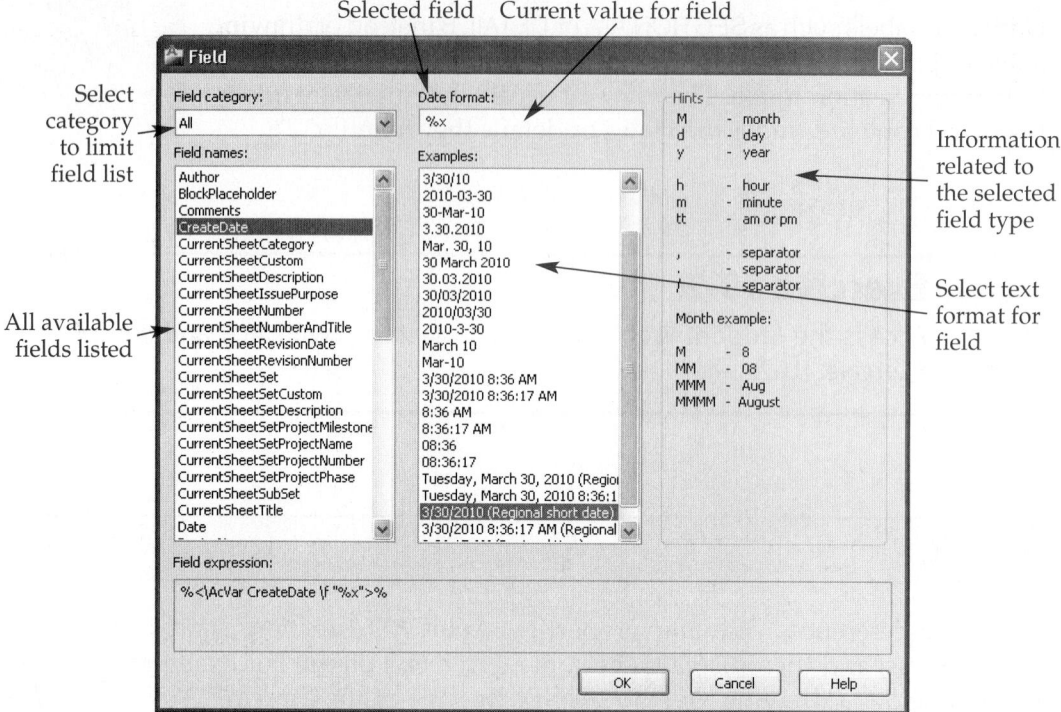

Figure 10-7.
A date and time field added to an mtext object. The gray background identifies the text as a field. The date and time field references the computer date and time you inserted the field.

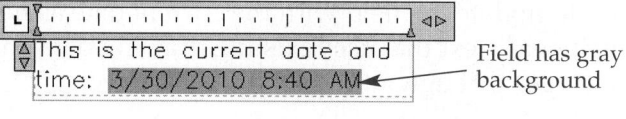

Field has gray background

Figure 10-8. Control the background display for fields in the **User Preferences** tab of the **Options** dialog box.

Controls display of field background

Pick to change automatic update settings

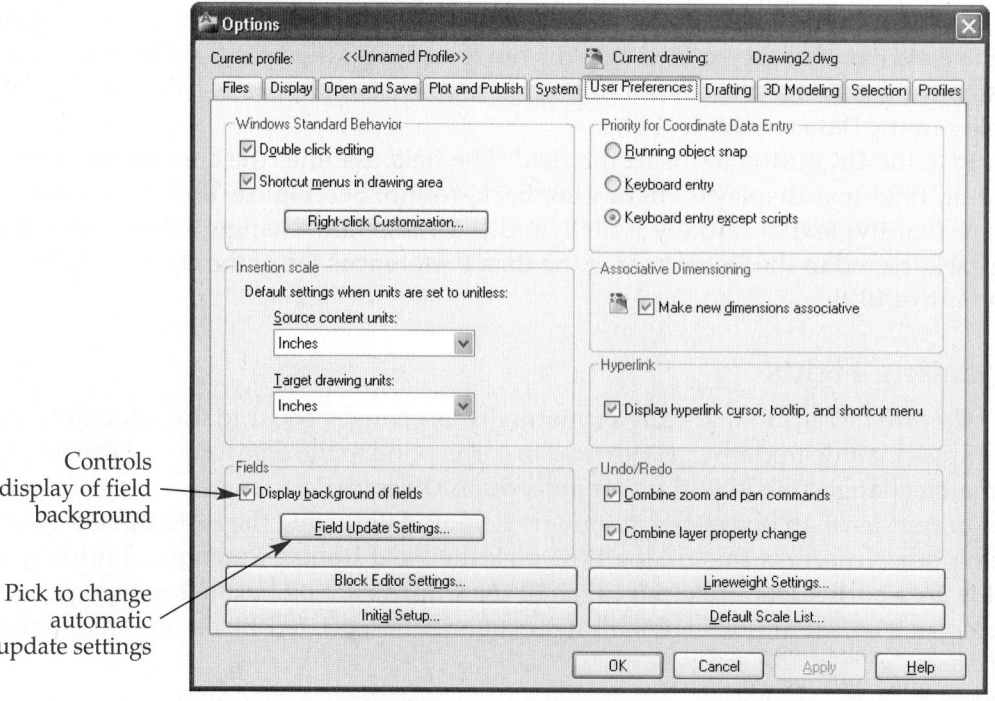

Update fields manually using the **Update Fields** tool. After selecting the tool, pick the fields to update. Use the **All** selection option to update all fields in a single operation. You can also update a field within the text editor by right-clicking on the field and selecting **Update Field**.

Ribbon
Insert
> Data

Update Fields
Type
UPDATEFIELD

UPDATEFIELD

Editing and Converting Fields

To edit a field, first activate the text object containing the field for editing. A quick way to edit text is to double-click on the text object. Then double-click on the field to display the **Field** dialog box. You can also right-click in the field and pick **Edit Field...**. Use the **Field** dialog box to modify the field settings and pick the **OK** button to apply changes.

To convert a field to standard text, activate the text object for editing, right-click on the field, and pick **Convert Field To Text**. When you convert a field to text, the current field value becomes text, the association to the field data is lost, and the value can no longer be updated.

> **NOTE**
>
> You can use fields with many AutoCAD tools, including inquiry tools, drawing properties, attributes, and sheet sets. You will learn specific field applications where appropriate throughout this textbook.

Exercise 10-3

Access the Student Web site (www.g-wlearning.com/CAD) and complete Exercise 10-3.

Checking Spelling

The quickest way to check for correct spelling in text objects is to use the **Spell Check** tool available in the current text editor. The **Spell Check** tool is active by default. To toggle the **Spell Check** tool on or off in the mtext or single-line text editor, select the **Check Spelling** option from the **Editor Settings** cascading submenu available from the shortcut menu or select **Spell Check** from the **Spell Check** panel on the **Text Editor** ribbon tab. You can also turn the **Spell Check** tool on and off in an active mtext editor by deselecting the **Spell Check** button on the **Options** panel of the **Text Editor** ribbon tab.

A red dashed line appears under a word that the AutoCAD dictionary does not recognize. Right-click on the underlined word to display options for adjusting the spelling. See **Figure 10-9.** The first section at the top of the shortcut menu provides suggested replacements for the word. Pick a word to change the spelling in the text editor. If you do not see the correct suggestion, you may be able to find the correct spelling from the **More Suggestions** cascading submenu.

If you still cannot find a correct spelling from the suggestions, the word is spelled correctly but not found in the dictionary, or is spelled so incorrectly that AutoCAD cannot suggest a replacement. If the word is spelled correctly, pick the **Add to Dictionary** option to add the current word to the custom dictionary. You can add words with up

Figure 10-9. Checking spelling using the **Spell Check** tool in the mtext editor. The tool functions the same in the single-line text editor.

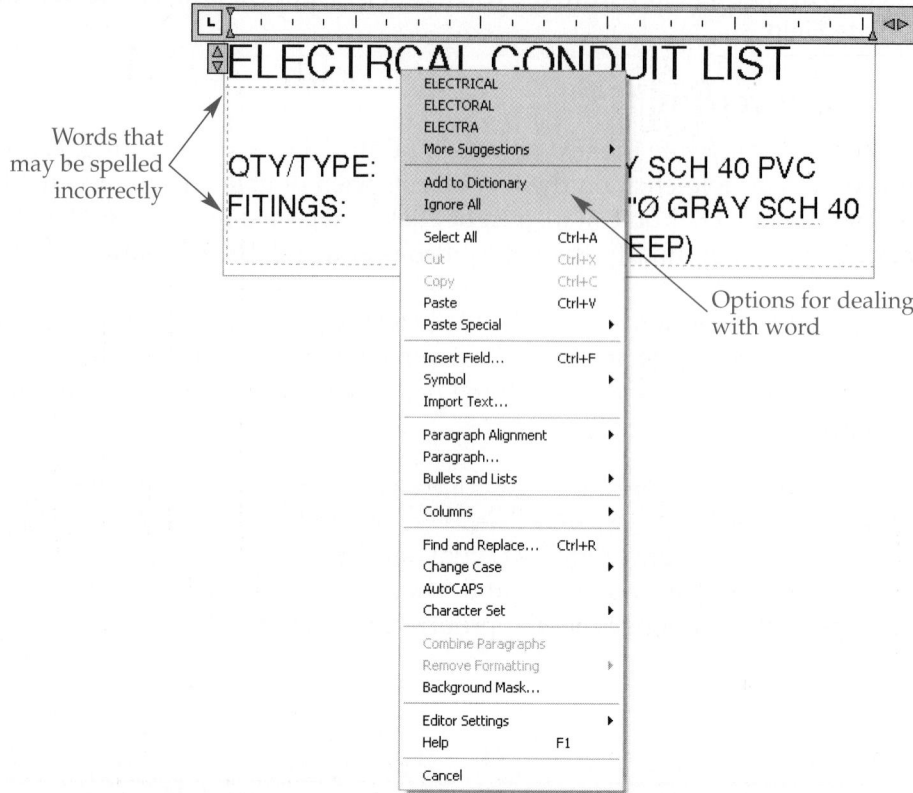

Words that may be spelled incorrectly

Options for dealing with word

to 63 characters. To use the current spelling without adding the word to the dictionary, pick the **Ignore All** option. Spell checking ignores all words that match the spelling in the active text editor, and hides underline. Add common drafting words and abbreviations to the dictionary, such as the abbreviation for the word SCHEDULE (SCH) in **Figure 10-9**, or ignore the words.

Using the SPELL Tool

The **SPELL** tool uses the **Check Spelling** dialog box, shown in **Figure 10-10**, to check the spelling of text objects without activating a text editor. To check spelling, first identify the portion of the drawing to check by selecting an option from the **Where to Check** drop-down list. Pick the **Entire drawing** option to check the spelling of all text objects in the drawing file, including model space and layouts, or choose the **Current space/layout** to check spelling only of text objects in the active layout or in model space, if model space is active. You can also check the spelling of certain text objects by picking the **Select text objects** button, next to the **Where to Check** drop-down list, to enter the drawing window and select the text objects to check. You do not need to choose the **Selected objects** option from the **Where to Check** drop-down list to check selected objects.

After you define what and where to check, pick the **Start** button to begin spell checking. The first word that may be misspelled becomes highlighted in the drawing window and is active in the **Check Spelling** dialog box. Pick the appropriate button to add, ignore, or change the spelling. Use the **Suggestions:** text box and a change option to type a different spelling that is not available from the list.

Figure 10-10. The **Check Spelling** dialog box.

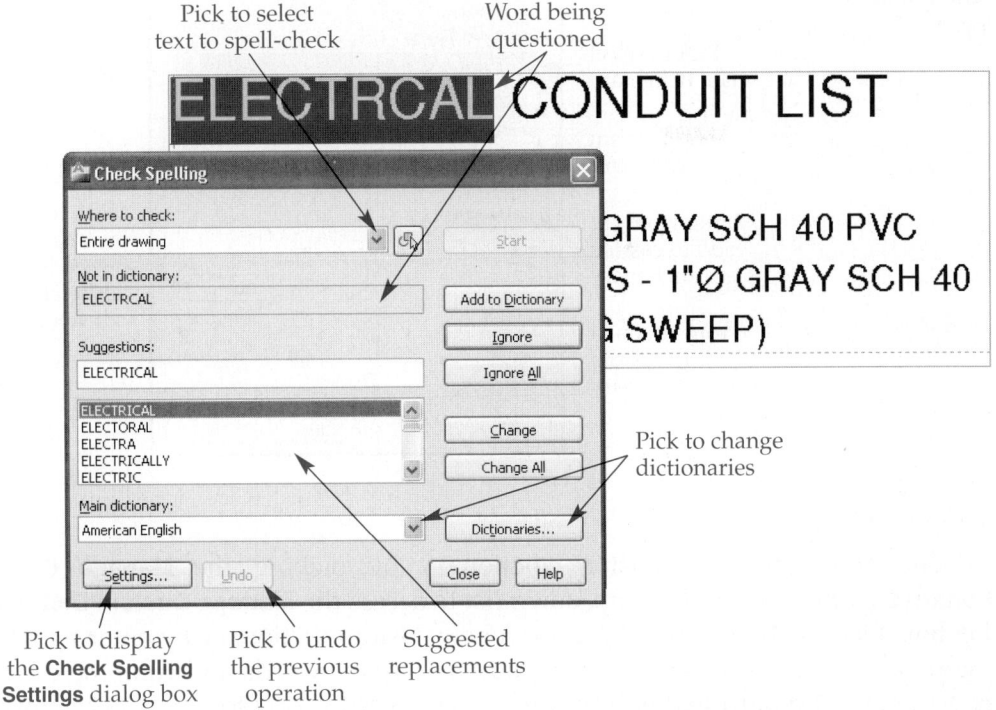

Pick to select
text to spell-check

Word being
questioned

Pick to change
dictionaries

Pick to display
the **Check Spelling**
Settings dialog box

Pick to undo
the previous
operation

Suggested
replacements

PROFESSIONAL TIP

Before you check spelling, you may want to adjust some of the spell-checking preferences provided in the **Check Spelling Settings** dialog box. Access this dialog box by picking the **Settings...** button in the **Check Spelling** dialog box, or select the **Check Spelling Settings...** option from the **Editor Settings** cascading submenu available from the text editor shortcut menu. If the mtext editor is already open, pick the small arrow in the lower-right corner of the **Spell Check** panel on the **Text Editor** ribbon tab. The settings apply to spelling checked using the **Spell Check** tool in the active text editor and using the **Check Spelling** dialog box.

Changing Dictionaries

To change the dictionary used when checking spelling, pick the **Dictionaries...** button of the **Check Spelling** dialog box. You can also select the **Dictionaries...** option from the **Editor Settings** cascading submenu available from the text editor shortcut menu to access the **Dictionaries** dialog box. See **Figure 10-11**.

Use the **Main dictionary** list to select a language dictionary to use as the current main dictionary. You cannot add definitions to the main dictionary. Use the **Custom dictionary** list to select the active custom dictionary. The default custom dictionary is sample.cus. Type a word in the **Content** text box to add or delete from the custom dictionary. For example, ASME Y14.5 is custom text used in engineering drafting. Pick the **Add** button to accept the custom words in the text box, or pick the **Delete** button to remove the words from the custom dictionary. Custom dictionary entries can use up to 63 characters.

Ribbon

Text Editor
> Spell Check

Edit Dictionaries

Figure 10-11.
The **Dictionaries**
dialog box.

Pick to select
main dictionary

Current
dictionary

Enter words to
add to custom
dictionary

Words defined
in custom
dictionary

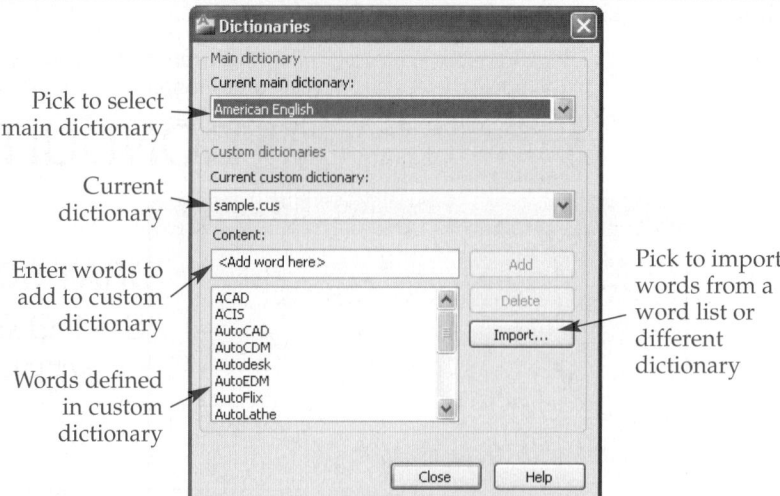

Pick to import
words from a
word list or
different
dictionary

Create and manage a custom dictionary by picking the **Manage Custom Dictionaries...** option from the drop-down list to access the **Manage Custom Dictionary** dialog box. Pick the **New** button to create a new custom dictionary by entering a new file name with a .cus extension. You can add and delete words and combine dictionaries using any standard text editor. If you use a word processor such as Microsoft® Word, be sure to save the file as *text only*, with no special text formatting or printer codes. Add a custom dictionary by picking the **Add** button, and choose the **Remove** button to delete a custom dictionary from the list. You can also add existing custom dictionaries by picking the **Import...** button from the **Custom dictionary** area.

PROFESSIONAL TIP

Create custom dictionaries for various disciplines. For example, add common abbreviations and brand names for mechanical drawings to a mech.cus file. A separate file named arch.cus might contain common architectural abbreviations and frequently used brand names.

Revising Text

The easiest way to reopen the text editor to make changes to text content is to double-click on an mtext or text object. Another technique to re-enter the text editor is to pick the text object to modify and then right-click and select **Mtext Edit...** to revise mtext, or **Edit...** to modify single-line text. A third option is to type **DDEDIT** to edit mtext or single-line text, or type **MTEDIT** to edit mtext.

Exercise 10-4

Access the Student Web site (www.g-wlearning.com/CAD) and complete Exercise 10-4.

Cutting, Copying, and Pasting Text

Clipboard functions allow you to copy, cut, and paste text from any text-based application, such as Microsoft® Word, into a text editor. You can also copy or cut and paste text from the text editor into other text-based applications. Access clipboard functions from the shortcut menu when an mtext or text editor is active. Text that you paste retains the original text properties.

AutoCAD provides additional paste options for pasting text into the active mtext text editor. Right-click and select an option from the **Paste Special** cascading submenu. Pick **Paste without Character Formatting** to paste text without applying preset character formatting such as bold, italic, or underline. Select the **Paste without Paragraph Formatting** option to paste text without applying current paragraph formatting, including lists. Pick the **Paste without Any Formatting** option to paste text without applying any current character and paragraph formatting.

> **PROFESSIONAL TIP**
>
> Cutting or copying and pasting text is useful if someone has already created specification notes in a program other than AutoCAD and you want to place the same notes in your drawings.

Finding and Replacing Text

AutoCAD provides tools for searching for and replacing text with a different word or phrase. You can search for and replace text in an active mtext or single-line text editor, or without opening a text editor.

Using the Find and Replace Tool

Use the **Find and Replace** tool to find and replace text in the active mtext or single-line text editor. Right-click and select **Find and Replace…**. The tool is also available in the mtext editor using the **Find & Replace** option. The **Find and Replace** dialog box displays. See **Figure 10-12**.

Type the text to search for in the **Find what:** text box. Type the text to substitute in the **Replace with:** text box. Then pick the **Find Next** button to highlight the next instance of the search text. You can then pick the **Replace** or **Replace All** button to replace just the highlighted text or all words that match the search criteria. Check boxes control the characters and words that are recognized.

Ribbon
Text Editor
> Tools

Find & Replace

Figure 10-12. Using the **Find and Replace** dialog box in the mtext editor. The tool functions the same in the single-line text editor.

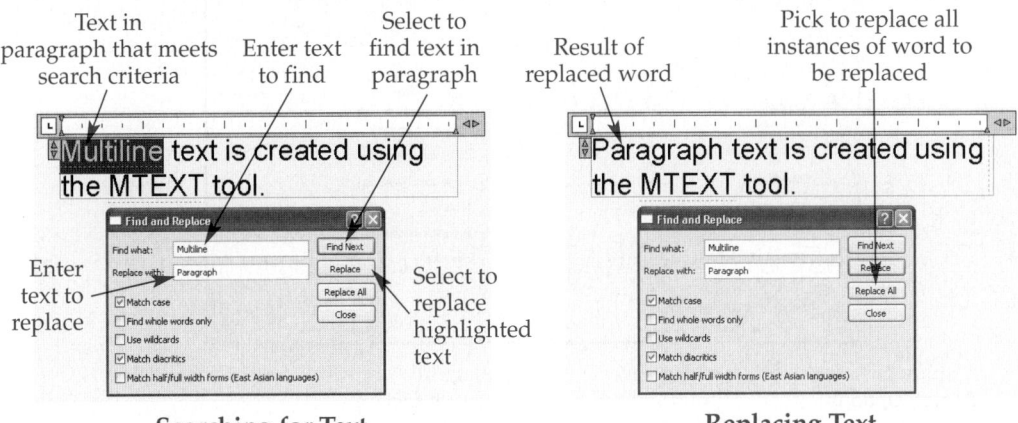

Searching for Text   Replacing Text

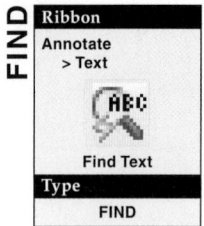

Using the FIND Tool

The **FIND** tool uses the **Find and Replace** dialog box, shown in **Figure 10-13**, to find and replace text objects without activating a text editor. Another method for accessing the **Find and Replace** dialog box is to enter the text string to find in the **Find Text** text box in the **Text** panel of the **Annotation** ribbon tab and press [Enter]. You can also activate the **FIND** tool by right-clicking when no tool is active and selecting **Find...**.

To find and replace text, first identify the portion of the drawing to search by selecting an option from the **Where to Check** drop-down list. The options are similar to those from the **Find Where** drop-down list in the **Check Spelling** dialog box. The **Find and Replace** dialog box is much like the dialog box of the same name that appears when you find and replace text within a text editor. However, the **FIND** tool version allows you to display the search results in a table within the dialog box, and provides more search options. Pick the **More Options** button to display check boxes used to control the characters and words recognized when you are finding and replacing text.

NOTE

The find and replace strings are saved with the drawing file for future use.

Scaling Text

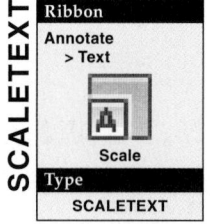

The **SCALETEXT** tool is one option for changing the height of mtext and/or text objects. Access the **SCALETEXT** tool and select the text objects to scale. At the prompt, specify the justification for the base point of the scale operation. The justification point determines the point from which the increase or decrease in size occurs. **Figure 10-1** shows the location of all justification points. The **Existing** option scales text objects using their existing justification setting as the base point. See **Figure 10-14**.

Figure 10-13. Using the version of the **Find and Replace** dialog box that appears when you use the **Find** tool.

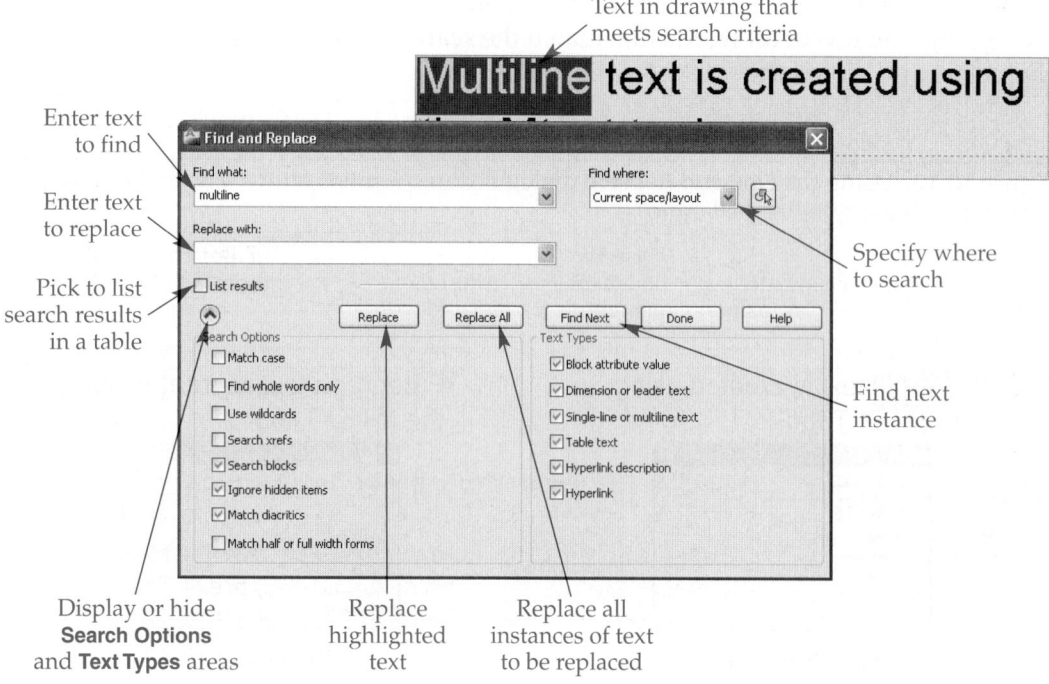

Figure 10-14.
The **Existing** option of the **SCALETEXT** tool scales text objects using their individual justification settings.

BL Justification
MC Justification
TR Justification
Original Text

BL Justification
MC Justification
TR Justification
**Text Scaled Using
Existing Base Point Option**

After you specify the justification point to use as the base point, AutoCAD prompts for the scaling type. The default **Specify new model height** option allows you to type a new value for the text height of non-annotative objects. If the selected text is annotative, AutoCAD ignores the value you enter. Use the **Paper height** option to type a new paper text height for the annotative objects. If the selected text is non-annotative, AutoCAD ignores the paper height value you enter.

Use **Match object** option to match the height of the text to the height of a different selected text object. Use the **Scale factor** option to scale text objects that have different heights relative to their current heights. For example, a scale factor of 2 scales all selected text objects to twice their current size.

> **CAUTION**
>
> Only use the **SCALETEXT** tool to scale non-annotative text.

Changing Justification

Use the **JUSTIFYTEXT** tool to change the justification point without moving the text. Pick the text for which you want to change the justification, and then select a new justification option.

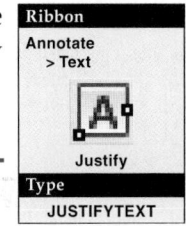

Ribbon
Annotate
> Text

Justify
Type
JUSTIFYTEXT

JUSTIFYTEXT

Exercise 10-5

Access the Student Web site (www.g-wlearning.com/CAD) and complete Exercise 10-5.

Supplemental Material

Isometric Text
For information about constructing text for isometric views, go to the Student Web site (www.g-wlearning.com/CAD), select this chapter, and select **Isometric Text**.

Express Tools
Chapter 10

The **Text** panel of the **Express Tools** ribbon tab includes additional text tools. For information about the most useful text express tools, go to the Student Web site (www.g-wlearning.com/CAD), select this chapter, and select **Text Express Tools**.

Chapter Test

Answer the following questions. Write your answers on a separate sheet of paper or go to the Student Web site (www.g-wlearning.com/CAD) and complete the electronic chapter test.

1. List two ways to access the **TEXT** tool.
2. Write the control code sequence required to draw the following symbols when using the **TEXT** tool:
   A. 30°
   B. 1.375 ± .005
   C. Ø24
   D. <u>NOT FOR CONSTRUCTION</u>
3. Briefly explain the function and purpose of fields.
4. What is different about the on-screen display of fields compared to that of text?
5. How can you access the **Field Update Settings** dialog box?
6. Explain how to convert a field to text.
7. What is the quickest way to check your spelling within a current text editor?
8. How do you change the **Current word** if you do not think the word displayed in the **Suggestions:** text box of the **Check Spelling** dialog box is the correct word, but one of the words in the list of suggestions is the correct word?
9. Identify three ways to access the AutoCAD spell checker.
10. How do you change the main dictionary for use in the **Check Spelling** dialog box?
11. Why might you want to create more than one custom dictionary?
12. What happens if you double-click on multiline text?
13. Briefly describe how to find and replace text when an mtext or single-line text editor is open.
14. Name the tool that allows you to find text and replace it with different text in a single instance or for every instance in the drawing.
15. When using the **SCALETEXT** tool, which base point option would you select to keep the current justification point of the text object?

Drawing Problems

Start AutoCAD if it is not already started. Start a new drawing using an appropriate template of your choice. The template should include layers and text styles, when necessary, for drawing the given objects. Add layers and text styles as needed. Draw all objects using appropriate layers and text styles, justification, and format. Follow the specific instructions for each problem. Use only drawing tools and techniques you have already learned. Use your own judgment and approximate dimensions when necessary.

▼ Basic

1. Create text styles according to the list shown Use the **TEXT** tool and the appropriate text style to type the text shown. Use a .25 unit text height and 0° rotation angle. Save the drawing as P10-1.

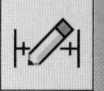

ARIAL - A VERY BASIC FONT USED FOR GENERAL-PURPOSE TEXT.

ROMANS — A FONT THAT CLOSELY DUPLICATES THE SINGLE—STROKE LETTERING THAT HAS BEEN THE STANDARD FOR DRAFTING.

ROMANC — A MULTISTROKE DECORATIVE FONT THAT IS GOOD FOR USE IN DRAWING TITLES.

ITALICC — AN ORNAMENTAL FONT THAT IS SLANTED TO THE RIGHT AND HAS THE SAME LETTER DESIGN AS THE COMPLEX FONT.

2. Create text styles according to the list shown. Use the **TEXT** tool and the appropriate text style to type the text shown. Use a .25 unit text height. Save the drawing as P10-2.

ARIAL-EXPAND THE WIDTH BY THREE.

MONOTXT-SLANT TO THE LEFT -30°.

ROMANS-SLANT TO THE RIGHT 30°.

ROMANC-BACKWARDS.

ITALICC-UNDERSCORED AND OVERSCORED.

ROMANS-USE 16d NAILS @ 10"OC.

ROMANT-ⵁ32 (812.8).

ROMANDC VERTICAL

3. Open P7-7 and save the file as P10-3. (If you have not yet completed P7-7, work the problem now.) The P10-3 file should be active. Use a text style with the Arial font to add text and titles to the electrical switch schematics as shown in Problem 7-7. Resave the drawing.

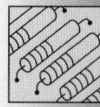

4. Open P5-11 and save the file as P10-4. (If you have not yet completed P5-11, work the problem now.) The P10-4 file should be active. Use a text style with the Romans font to add text to the circuit diagram as shown in Problem 5-11. Resave the drawing.

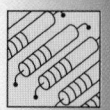

5. Open P7-12 and save the file as P10-5. (If you have not yet completed P7-12, work the problem now.) The P10-5 file should be active. Use a text style with the Romans font to add text to the elementary diagram as shown in Problem 7-12. Resave the drawing.

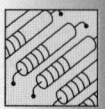

▼ Intermediate

6. Create text styles with a .375 height and the following fonts: Arial, BankGothic Lt BT, CityBlueprint, Stylus BT, Swis721 BdOul BT, Vineta BT, and Wingdings. Use each text style with the **TEXT** tool to type the complete alphabet and numbers 1–10. In addition, type all symbols available on the keyboard and the diameter, degree, and plus/minus symbols. Save the drawing as P10-6.

7. Draw the interior finish schedule shown. Use a text style with the Stylus BT font to add the text. Save the drawing as P10-7. You will learn to create tables using the **TABLE** tool in Chapter 11. The purpose of this problem is to practice using the **TEXT** tool to place text objects in specific areas, using appropriate justification and format. In general, the **TABLE** tool is more appropriate for drawing schedules.

INTERIOR FINISH SCHEDULE											
ROOM	FLOOR				WALLS				CEILING		
	VINYL	CARPET	TILE	HARDWOOD	CONCRETE	PAINT	PAPER	TEXTURE	SPRAY	SMOOTH	BROCADE	PAINT
ENTRY					●							
FOYER			●			●			●			●
KITCHEN			●				●			●		
DINING				●		●			●		●	●
FAMILY		●				●			●		●	●
LIVING		●				●		●				
MSTR. BATH			●							●		
BATH #2			●					●	●			
MSTR. BED		●				●					●	●
BED #2		●				●				●	●	●
BED #3		●				●				●	●	●
UTILITY	●					●				●	●	●

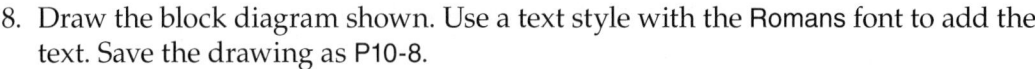
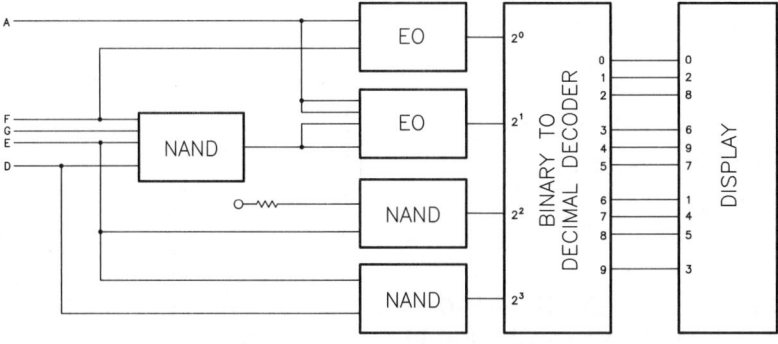

8. Draw the block diagram shown. Use a text style with the Romans font to add the text. Save the drawing as P10-8.

9. Draw the block diagram shown. Use a text style with the Romans font to add the text. Use polylines to create the arrowheads. Save the drawing as P10-9.

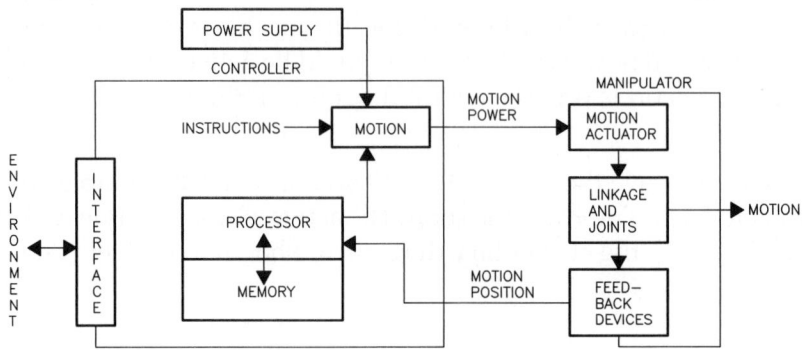

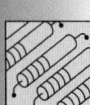

10. Draw the AND/OR schematic shown. Save the drawing as P10-10.

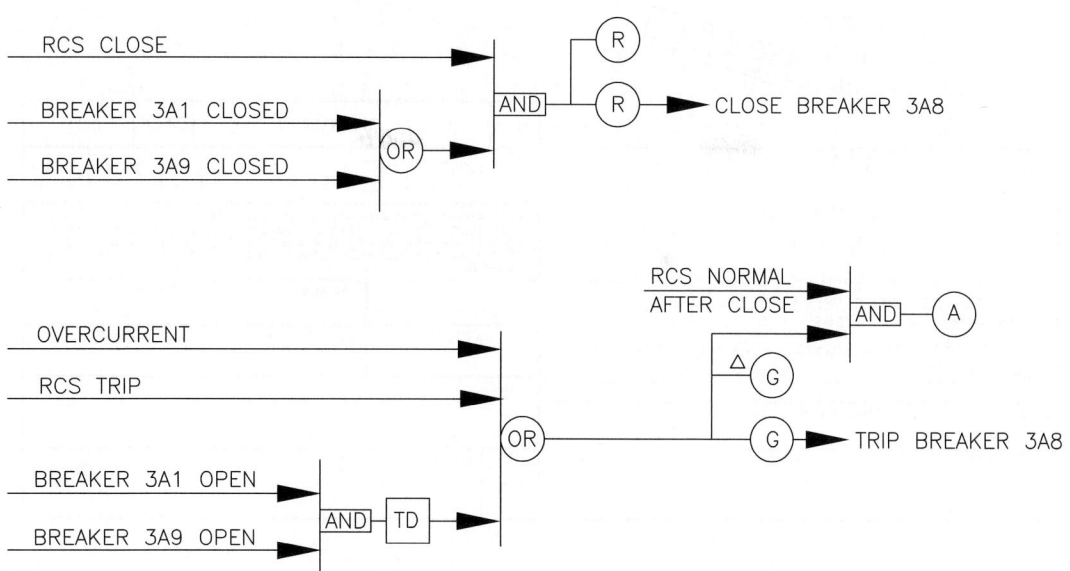

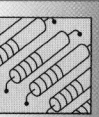

▼ **Advanced**

11. Open **EX2-5** and save the file as **P10-11**. (If you have not yet completed Exercise 2-5, complete it now.) The P10-11 file should be active. Use a text style with the Century Gothic font and the **MTEXT** tool to type the text shown. Use a .25 unit text height. Type text for the titles, and insert fields to add the values. Use appropriate field options to create the list exactly as shown, except that the Author, Approved by, and Checked By values will be specific to your drawing properties. Next, change the Title, Subject, Keywords, Comments, and Revision drawing file properties to values according to this problem. Use a revision value of A. Regenerate the display to apply an automatic update to all fields. Resave the drawing.

> Filename: P10-11.dwg
> Date: 03-30-2010
> Title: EXERCISE 2-5
> Subject: Exercise 2-5
> Author: ABC
> Keywords:Exercise 2-5
> Comments: This is Chapter 2, exercise number five.
> Approved by: ABC
> Checked by: ABC
> Revision level: 0
> Web site: www.g-w.com

12. Draw the mechanical drafting title block shown.

R -	CHANGE	DATE	ECN

HYSTER COMPANY

THIS PRINT CONTAINS CONFIDENTIAL INFORMATION WHICH IS THE PROPERTY OF HYSTER COMPANY. BY ACCEPTING THIS INFORMATION THE BORROWER AGREES THAT IT WILL NOT BE USED FOR ANY PURPOSE OTHER THAN THAT FOR WHICH IT IS LOANED.

SPECIFICATIONS

UNLESS OTHERWISE SPECIFIED DIMENSIONS ARE IN ~~INCHES~~ MILLIMETERS AND TOLERANCES FOR:
_____ PLACE DIMS± _____ :_____ PLACE DIMS± _____
ANGLES ± _____ : WHOLE DIMS± _____

DR.	SCALE	DATE
CK. MAT'L.	CK. DESIGN	REL. ON ECN
NAME		

MODEL	DWG. FIRST USED	SIMILAR TO
DEPT.	PROJECT	LIST DIVISION

H	PART NO.		R

13. Draw the mechanical drafting title block and parts list shown. Save the drawing as P10-13.

3	HOLDING PINS	12
2	SIDE COVERS	3
1	MAIN HOUSING	1
KEY	DESCRIPTION	QTY

PARTS LIST

JANE'S DESIGN

UNLESS OTHERWISE SPECIFIED
ALL DIMENSIONS IN
INCHES
AND TOLERANCES FOR:
1 PLACE DIMS: ±.1
2 PLACE DIMS: ±.01
3 PLACE DIMS: ±.005
ANGULAR: ±30'
FRACTIONAL: ±.1/32
FINISH: 125? in.

DR: JANE	SCALE: FULL	DATE: XX–XX–XX	APPD:

MATERIAL:
MILD STEEL

NAME:
XXX–XXXX

FIRST USED ON:	SIMILAR TO:	B	PART NO. 123–321	REV: 0

14. Create a dimensioned 2D sketch of a map providing driving or walking directions from your home to your school or office. Label all features, including roads and distances. Use available measuring devices, such as the odometer in your car, tape measure, or surveying equipment to measure features. Draw the map from your sketch using real-world units. Add text to label features and distances, but do not draw actual dimension objects. Save the drawing as P10-17.

15. Draw the architectural title block shown. Save the drawing as P10-14.

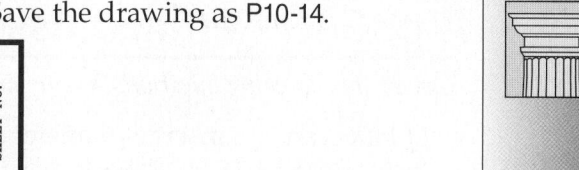

16. Draw title blocks with borders for electrical, piping, and general drawings. Research sample title blocks to come up with your designs. Save the drawings as P10-15A, P10-15B, and P10-15C.

17. Draw the engineering change notice shown. Save the drawing as P10-16.

Engineering Change Notice

ECN NO.

Disposition of production stock:
A =Alter or rework U=Use in production
T=Transfer to service stock S=Scrap

Qty.	Drawing Size Part No.	R/N	Description	Change	Other Usage in Production	D/S
01						
02						
03						
04						
05						
06						
07						
08						
09						
10						
11						
12						
13						
14						
15						
16						
17						
18						

Reason:

Castings & forgings affected? ☐ Yes ☐ No	Design engineer:	Supervisor approval:	Release date:	Page

AutoCAD Certified Associate Exam Practice

Answer the following questions. Write your answers on a separate sheet of paper.

1. How can you insert a diameter symbol into single-line text? *Select all that apply.*
   A. type %%D
   B. type %%C
   C. type (D)
   D. select it from the **Symbol** menu on the **Text Editor** ribbon tab
   E. right-click and select Diameter

2. What is the name of the file in which AutoCAD stores the default custom dictionary? *Select the one item that best answers the question.*
   A. dictionary.smp
   B. sample.cus
   C. sample.dct
   D. sample.dic
   E. sample.dwt

3. Which of the following tasks can you perform using a field? *Select all that apply.*
   A. display the date a drawing was created
   B. display drawing properties in the drawing
   C. change the name of a drawing
   D. change the names of layers
   E. update property displays to reflect their current status

AutoCAD Certified Professional Exam Practice

Follow the instructions in each problem. Write your answers on a separate sheet of paper.

1. **Navigate to this chapter on the Student Web site and open the CPE-10spell.dwg file.**
   Use the default spell checker or the **SPELL** tool to check the text in the drawing. What are the first three alternate spellings AutoCAD suggests for "ASME"?

2. **Navigate to this chapter on the Student Web site and open the CPE-10scale. dwg file.**
   Use the **SCALETEXT** tool to scale the text using the existing justification point and a scale factor of 2.67. What is the height of the text after the **SCALETEXT** operation?

Tables

Learning Objectives

After completing this chapter, you will be able to do the following:

✓ Create and modify table styles.
✓ Insert tables into a drawing.
✓ Edit tables.
✓ Create formulas in table cells to perform calculations.

This chapter describes how to create *tables*, which are common elements on technical drawings. Examples of table applications include bills of materials, parts lists, schedules, legends, tabular and chart dimensioning, revision history and status blocks, and other *associated lists*. **Figure 11-1** shows an example of a schedule and a parts list, and highlights the features of a table.

table: An arrangement of rows and columns that organize data to make it easier to read.

associated list: The ASME term describing tables added or related to engineering drawings.

Table Styles

A *table style* presets many table characteristics. Create a table style for each unique table appearance or function. For example, use a table style preset to the standard format of a parts list to draw a parts list. Use a different table style preset to the standard format of a wire list to draw a wire list. Add table styles to drawing templates for repeated use. Avoid adjusting table formats independently of the table style assigned to the table.

table style: A saved collection of table settings, including direction, text appearance, and margin spacing.

Table Style Dialog Box

Create, modify, and delete table styles using the **Table Style** dialog box. See **Figure 11-2.** The **Styles** list box displays existing table styles. The Standard table style is the default. To make a table style current, double-click the style name; right-click the name and select **Set current**; or pick the name and select the **Set current** button. Below the **Styles** list box is a drop-down list that you can use to filter the number of table styles displayed in the **Table Style** dialog box. Pick the **All Styles** option to show all table styles in the file, or pick the **Styles in use** option to show only the current style and styles used in the drawing.

Ribbon
Home
> Annotation

Table Style

Annotate
> Tables

Table Style

Type
TABLESTYLE
TS

TABLESTYLE

Figure 11-1. A—An example of a window schedule added to an architectural floor plan to identify windows and related information. This table uses a down direction. B—An example of a parts list added to a mechanical assembly drawing to identify assembly components. This table uses an up direction.

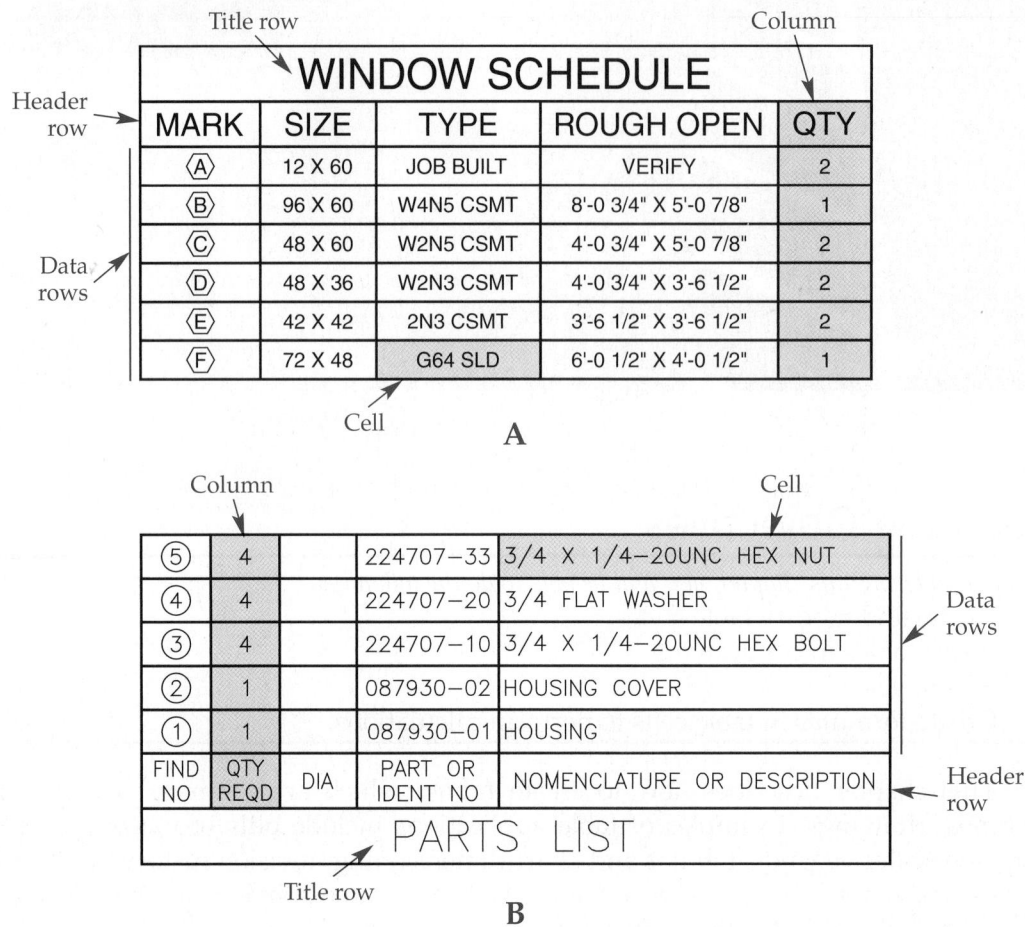

Figure 11-2. The **Table Style** dialog box.

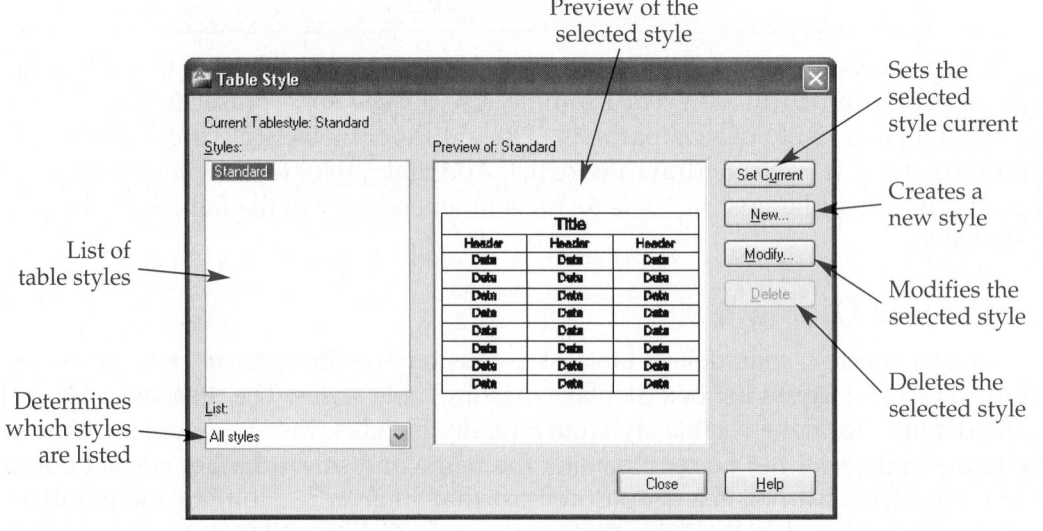

You can also open the **Table Style** dialog box from the **Insert Table** dialog box, described later in this chapter, by picking the **Launch the Table Style dialog** button.

Creating New Table Styles

To create a new table style, select an existing table style from the **Styles** list box to use as a base for formatting the new table style. Then pick the **New…** button to open the **Create New Table Style** dialog box. See **Figure 11-3**. You can base the new table style on the formatting of a different table style by selecting from the **Start With** drop-down list. Notice that Copy of followed by the name of the existing style appears in the **New Style Name** text box. Replace the default name with a more descriptive name, such as Parts List, Parts List No Heading, or Door Schedule.

Table style names can have up to 255 characters, including uppercase and lowercase letters, numbers, dashes (–), underlines (_), and dollar signs ($). After typing the table style name, pick the **Continue** button to open the **New Table Style** dialog box and adjust table style settings. See **Figure 11-4**. Pick the **OK** button to apply changes and close the **New Table Style** dialog box. Pick the **Close** button to exit the **Table Style** dialog box.

Figure 11-3.
In the **Create New Table Style** dialog box, specify the name of the new table style and the existing style to copy as a basis for the new style.

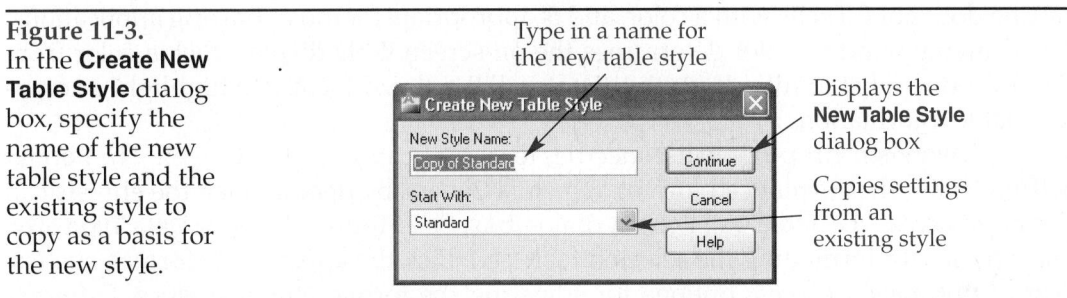

Type in a name for the new table style

Displays the **New Table Style** dialog box

Copies settings from an existing style

Figure 11-4. Use the **New Table Style** dialog box to specify the formatting properties of a new table style. This figure shows adjusting the **Data** cell style.

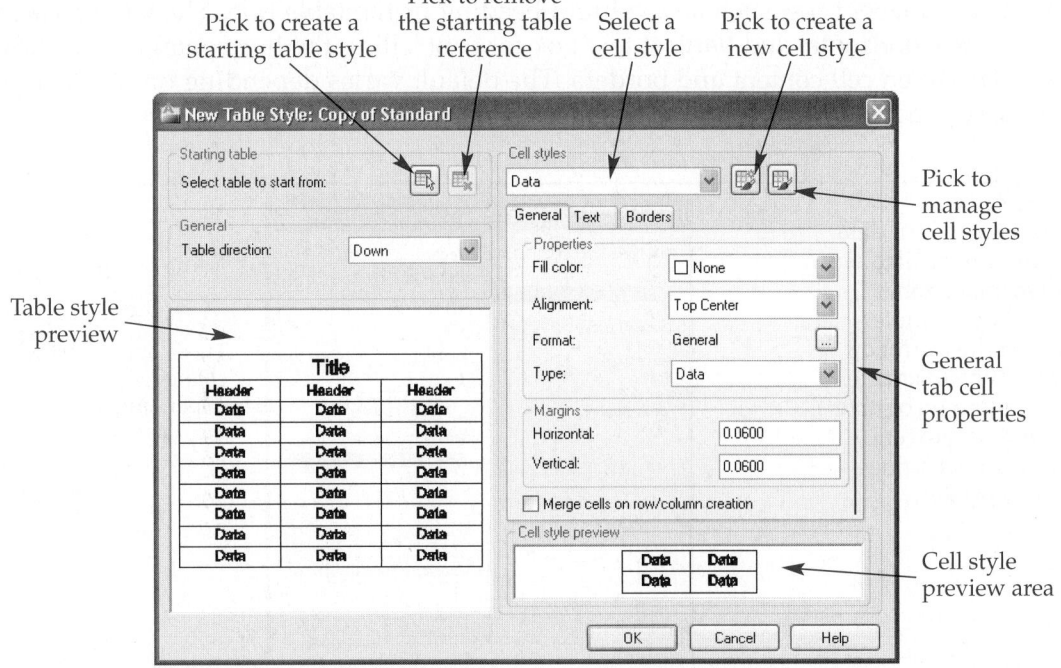

Pick to create a starting table style

Pick to remove the starting table reference

Select a cell style

Pick to create a new cell style

Pick to manage cell styles

Table style preview

General tab cell properties

Cell style preview area

Record the names and details about the table styles you create and keep this information in a log for future reference.

Table Direction

The **Table direction** setting in the **General** area of the **New Table Style** dialog box determines the placement of title and header rows and the order of data rows. Select **Down** from the drop-down list to place data rows below the title and header rows. Select **Up** to place data rows above the title and header rows. See **Figure 11-1**.

Cell Styles

cell styles: Styles that allow you to assign specific formatting to data, header, and title row cells.

Use the **Cell Styles** area of the **New Table Style** dialog box to control *cell styles*. Pick the **Data**, **Header**, or **Title** option from the **Cell Styles** drop-down list to display the properties corresponding to the selected row. **Figure 11-4** shows the **Data** cell style selected. Set cell formatting properties using the **General**, **Text**, and **Borders** tabs. The options in these tabs are the same for adjusting data, header, and title cell styles.

General Tab Settings

The **General** tab, shown in **Figure 11-4**, allows you to set general table characteristics. The **Fill color** drop-down provides options for filling cells. The default None setting does not fill cells with a color, and is appropriate for most drafting applications. The drawing window color determines the on-screen table display. Pick a color from the drop-down list to fill cells with the color. Fill cells with color to highlight or organize table information.

The **Alignment** drop-down list specifies text justification within the cell. The **Format** setting shows the current cell format, which is General by default. Pick the ellipsis (…) button to access the **Table Cell Format** dialog box. See **Figure 11-5**. The **Data Type** area lists options for formatting the selected table cell. Pick the appropriate format, such as **Text** or **Currency**, to access options for adjusting the format characteristics. Different options are available depending on the selected format.

Use the **Type** drop-down list of the **New Table Style** dialog box to specify the cell data type. Pick the **Data** option to define a data cell type. Choose the **Label** option if the cell is a label type, such as a column heading or the table title. The **Margins** area provides a **Horizontal** and **Vertical** text box for controlling the horizontal and vertical space between cell content and borders. The default varies depending on the current units, such as .06 (1.5 mm) when using decimal units.

Figure 11-5.
Many different data types are available to format a table cell. For example, select the **Currency** data type to enable the cell to recognize values as currency and format values appropriately.

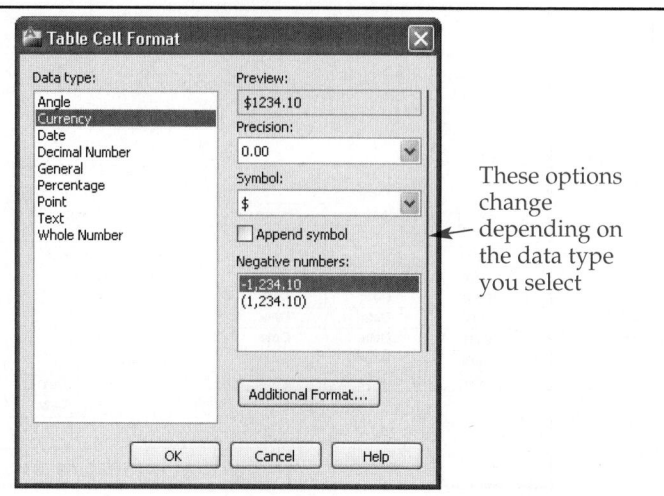

These options change depending on the data type you select

Pick the **Merge cells on row/column creation** check box to merge the row of cells together to form a single cell. This box is checked by default for the **Title** cell style. The title cell provides an example of when it is suitable to merge cells. The title applies to the entire table, or to each column.

Text Tab Settings

The **Text** tab, shown in **Figure 11-6,** allows you to set text characteristics for the selected cell style. The **Text style** drop-down list displays the text styles found in the current drawing. Select a style or pick the ellipsis (**...**) button to the right of the drop-down list to open the **Text Style** dialog box to create or modify a text style.

Use the **Text height** text box to specify the text height. The default varies depending on the current units and cell style, such as .18 (4.5 mm) for data and header and .25 (4.5 mm) for title when the drawing specifies decimal units. The **Text height** text box is inactive if you assign a text height other than 0 to the text style. Use the **Text color** drop-down list to set the text color. The **Text angle** text box controls the rotation angle of text within the table cell. **Figure 11-7** shows an example of a 90° text angle applied to the **Header** cell style.

Borders Tab Settings

The **Borders** tab, shown in **Figure 11-8,** allows you to control the border display and characteristics for the selected cell style. Use the **Lineweight** drop-down list to assign a unique lineweight to cell borders. Use the **Linetype** drop-down list to assign a unique linetype to cell borders. As when creating layers, you must load linetypes in order to apply linetypes to borders. Use the **Color** drop-down list to set the cell border color.

Pick the **Double line** check box to add another line around the default single line border style. The **Spacing** edit box is available when you check **Double line**, allowing you to enter the distance between the double lines. The default spacing varies depending on the current units, such as .045 (1.125 mm) when the drawing uses decimal units.

The **Border** buttons control how the **Lineweight**, **Linetype**, **Color**, and **Double line** properties apply to cell borders. From right to left, the options are **All Borders, Outside Borders, Inside Borders, Bottom Border, Left Border, Top Border, Right Border,** and **No Borders.** Once you set border properties, select or deselect the buttons as needed. See **Figure 11-9.**

Figure 11-6.
The **Text** tab in the **New Table Style** dialog box allows you to set text properties.

General	Text	Borders

Properties

Text style:	Standard	...
Text height:	0.1800	
Text color:	ByBlock	
Text angle:	0	

Figure 11-7.
In this table, a 90° text angle has been applied to the header cell style. This table is an example of a room schedule added to an architectural floor plan to list the characteristics of floor areas.

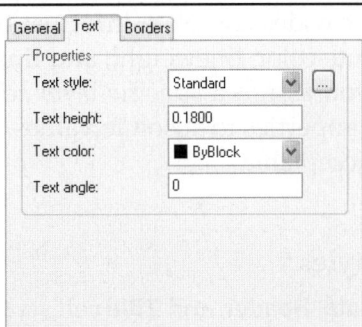

	ROOM SCHEDULE				
NUMBER	NAME	LENGTH	WIDTH	HEIGHT	AREA
1	BEDROOM 1	11'-0"	10'-0"	9'-0"	110 SQ. FT.
2	BEDROOM 2	10'-0"	11'-0"	9'-0"	110 SQ. FT.
3	MASTER BEDROOM	12'-0"	14'-0"	9'-0"	168 SQ. FT.
4	LIVING ROOM	12'-0"	16'-0"	9'-0"	192 SQ. FT.
5	DINING ROOM	11'-0"	12'-0"	9'-0"	132 SQ. FT.
6	KITCHEN	11'-0"	10'-0"	9'-0"	110 SQ. FT.

Figure 11-8.
The **Borders** tab in the **New Table Style** dialog box allows you to set cell border properties.

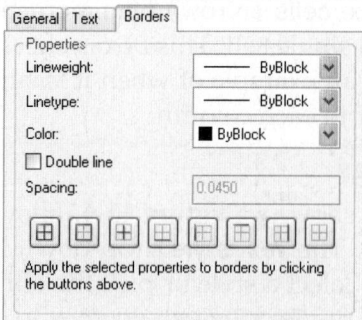

Figure 11-9. Border options available for table cells. This figure shows applying border options to data cell borders.

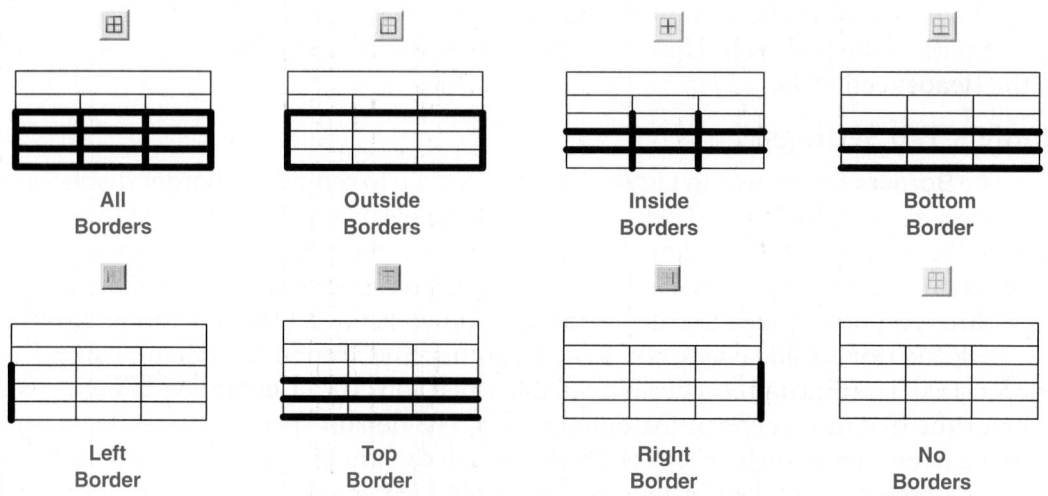

> **NOTE**
>
> AutoCAD treats a table like a block. Chapter 24 explains blocks and provides complete information on using ByBlock, ByLayer, or absolute color, lineweight, and linetype with blocks. For now, as long as you assign a specific layer to a table, and do not change the table properties to absolute values, the default ByBlock cell properties are acceptable.

Creating Cell Styles

The default **Data**, **Header**, and **Title** cell styles are adequate for typical table applications. However, you can develop additional cell styles to increase the flexibility and options for creating tables. For example, create a cell style called Data Yellow that is the same as the **Data** cell style but fills cells with a yellow color. Then when you draw a table, you can choose the **Data** or the **Data Yellow** cell style, depending on the application.

To create a new cell style, select an existing cell style from the **Cell Styles** area drop-down list to use as a base for formatting the new cell style. Then pick the **Create new cell style...** button from the **Cell Styles** area, or select **Create new cell style...** from the **Cell Styles** area drop-down list to display the **Create New Cell Style** dialog box. Type a name for the new cell style in the **New Style Name** text box. You can base the new cell style on the formatting of a different cell style by selecting from the **Start With** drop-down list.

Use the **Manage Cell Styles** dialog box, shown in **Figure 11-10**, to create, rename, and delete cell styles. To access this dialog box, pick the **Manage Cell Style dialog...** button from the **Cell Styles** area, or select **Manage cell styles...** from the **Cell Styles** area drop-down list.

NOTE

The **Preview** and **Cell style preview** areas of the **New Table Style** dialog box allow you to see how the selected table style characteristics appear in a table. This provides a convenient way to observe changes made to a table style, without creating a table.

Exercise 11-1

Access the Student Web site (www.g-wlearning.com/CAD) and complete Exercise 11-1.

Starting Table Styles

One technique for creating a table is to use a starting table style to base a new table on an existing table. You can consider a starting table style to be a table template that includes preset table properties and specific rows, columns, and data entries. Using a starting table style is much like copying a complete table and editing the table as needed. A starting table style can save time if you often prepare similar tables. For example, use a starting table style of a standard parts list to create a parts lists quickly. Another example is using a starting table style of a finished door schedule to add a similar door schedule to a plan that contains most of the same doors.

A starting table style references the characteristics of an existing table, including the number of columns and rows and the table direction. Other table style characteristics, such as text style, are set according to the selected base table style. As a result, it is usually most appropriate to create a new starting table style using a base table style that is the same as that used to draw the reference table. For example, if you create a door schedule using a table style named Door Schedule, you should base the new starting table style on the Door Schedule table style.

Figure 11-10.
Use the **Manage Cell Styles** dialog box to create new cell styles and to rename and delete existing cell styles.

Right-click to access **New**, **Rename**, and **Delete** options from the shortcut menu

Pick to display the **Create New Cell Style** dialog box

Pick to rename the selected cell style

Pick to delete the selected cell style

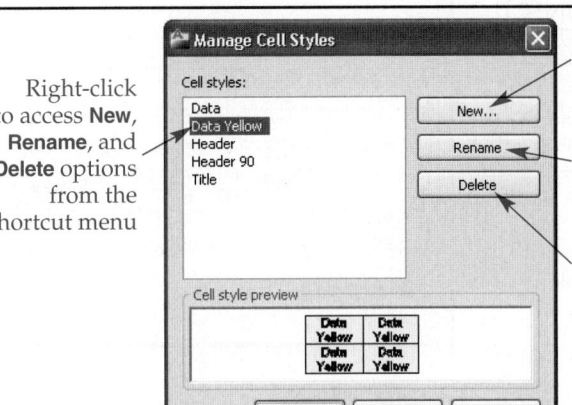

To create a starting table style, pick the **Select table to start from** button in the **Starting table** area. Then pick a border line of the existing table to reference. The preview displays the selected table and the table style settings of the base table style. See **Figure 11-11.** Modify the table direction and cell style options using the **General** and **Cell Styles** areas. Pick the **Remove Table** button to remove the table reference from the table style. Pick the **Start from Table style** insertion option, described later in this chapter, to add a table to a drawing using a starting table style.

Changing, Renaming, and Deleting Table Styles

Select a table style from the **Styles** list box to edit. Then pick the **Modify** button to access the **Modify Table Style** dialog box, which is the same as the **New Table Style** dialog box. If you make changes to a table style, such as merging cells, all existing table objects assigned the modified table style are updated. Use a different table style with unique characteristics when appropriate.

To rename a table style using the **Table Style** dialog box, slowly double-click the name or right-click on the name and select **Rename**. To delete a table style using the **Table Style** dialog box, right-click on the name and choose **Delete**, or pick the style and select the **Delete** button. You cannot delete a table style that is assigned to table objects. To delete a style that is in use, assign a different style to the tables that reference the style. You cannot delete or rename the Standard style.

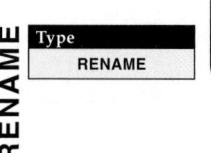

NOTE

You can also rename styles using the **Rename** dialog box. Select **Table styles** in the **Named Objects** list to rename the style.

Figure 11-11. Creating a starting table style that references an existing table. The table in this example is a list of reference designations, identifying last used components on an electrical schematic.

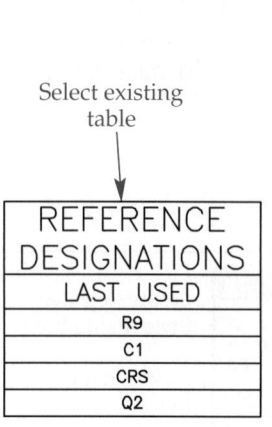

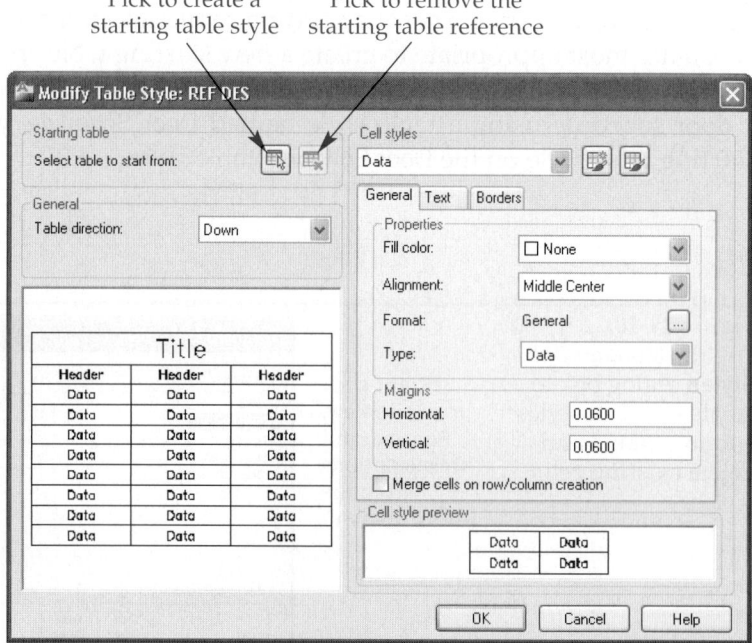

Setting a Table Style Current

Set a table style current using the **Table Style** dialog box by double-clicking the style in the **Styles** list box, right-clicking on the style and selecting **Set current**, or picking the style and selecting the **Set current** button. To set a table style current without opening the **Table Style** dialog box, use the **Table Style** flyout of the expanded **Annotation** panel of the **Home** ribbon tab, or the **Tables** panel of the **Annotate** ribbon tab. See **Figure 11-12.**

PROFESSIONAL TIP

You can import table styles from existing drawings using **DesignCenter**. See Chapter 5 for more information about using **DesignCenter** to reuse drawing content.

Inserting Tables

The **TABLE** tool allows you to insert an empty table with a specified number of rows and columns. After you insert the table, you can type text and insert content into the table cells. The **TABLE** tool also provides other methods for inserting tables, such as beginning a table using a starting table style, forming a table from data in an existing Microsoft® Excel spreadsheet or CSV (comma-separated) file, and creating a table by referencing AutoCAD data. Access the **TABLE** tool to display the **Insert Table** dialog box. See **Figure 11-13.**

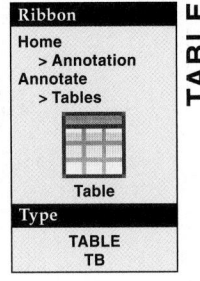

Ribbon
Home
> Annotation
Annotate
> Tables

Table

Type
TABLE
TB

Placing an Empty Table

To place an empty table, select a table style from the **Table Style** drop-down list, or pick the ellipsis (...) button to create or modify a table style. Next, pick the **Start from empty table** radio button in the **Insert options** area to create an empty table. The preview area shows a representation of a table using the current table style, but it does not adjust to column and row settings. Pick the **Specify insertion point** radio button in the **Insertion Behavior** area to create a table using the values in the **Column & row settings** area, and then select a single point to place the table in the drawing.

Figure 11-12.
The fastest way to set a style current is to use one of the drop-down lists on the ribbon.

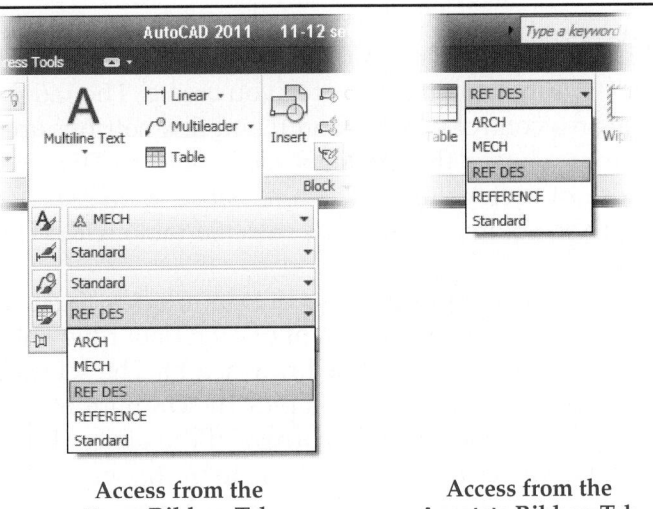

Access from the
Home Ribbon Tab

Access from the
Annotate Ribbon Tab

Figure 11-13. The **Insert Table** dialog box, shown with the **Start from empty table** insert option selected.

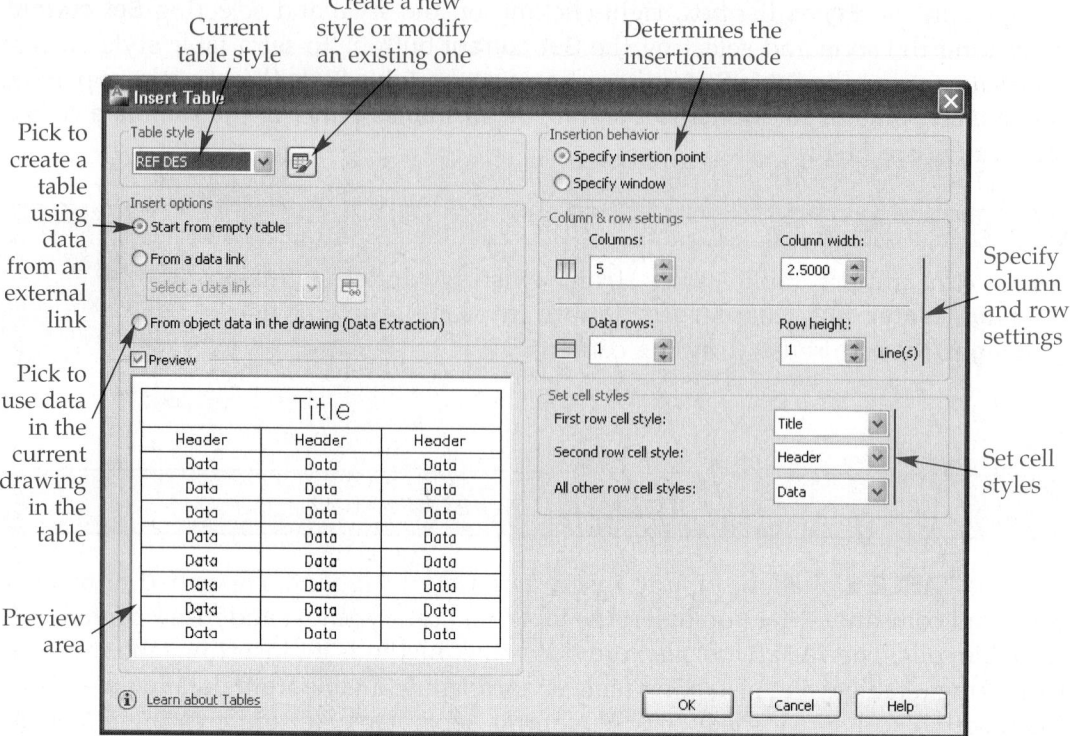

Use the **Columns** text box to specify the total number of table columns. Choose a **Column width** value to establish the initial width of each column. To help avoid initial crowding, enter a column width larger than necessary and then resize the columns later. Use the **Data rows** text box to specify the total number of data rows. Choose a **Row height** value to establish the initial height of each row based on the number of lines typed and the margin settings assigned to the table style. When you pick the **OK** button, AutoCAD prompts you to specify the table insertion point. See **Figure 11-14A.**

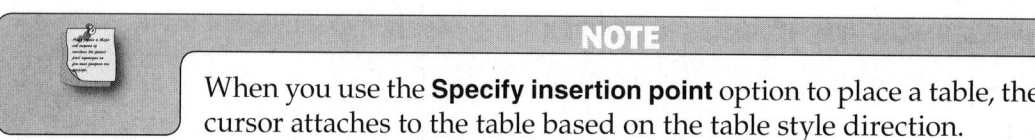

NOTE

When you use the **Specify insertion point** option to place a table, the cursor attaches to the table based on the table style direction.

Pick the **Specify window** radio button in the **Insertion Behavior** area to create a table that fits within a rectangular area you create. The radio buttons in the **Column & row settings** area control which column and row settings are active. To set a fixed number of columns, choose the **Columns** radio button. The selected table width determines the width of each column. The alternative is to pick the **Column width** radio button to set a fixed column width. The selected table width determines the total number of columns.

Choose the **Data rows** radio button to set a fixed number of rows. The selected table height determines the height of each data row. The alternative is to pick the **Row height** radio button to set a fixed row height. The selected table height determines the total number of rows. When you pick the **OK** button, AutoCAD prompts you to select the upper-left and lower-right corners of the table. AutoCAD uses the fixed **Column & row settings** values to adjust the table to fit the window. See **Figure 11-14B.**

Figure 11-14. Two ways to insert an empty table. A—Using the **Specify insertion point** radio button to select a single insertion point to create a table with three fixed columns and five fixed data rows. B—Using the **Specify window** radio button to specify an area using two pick points, creating a table with three columns and five data rows that adjust according to the window size.

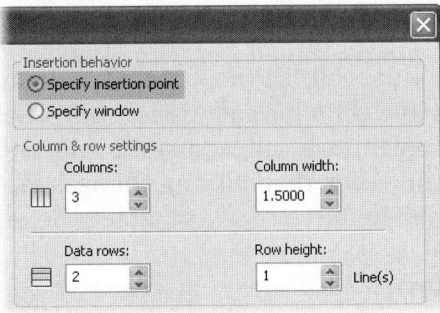
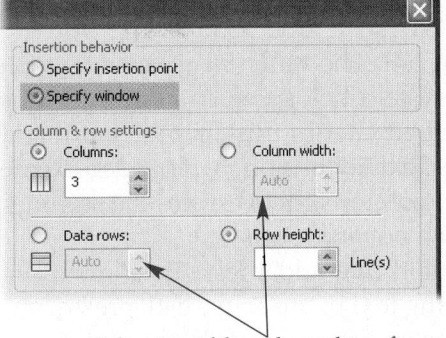

Column width and number of rows determined by size of window

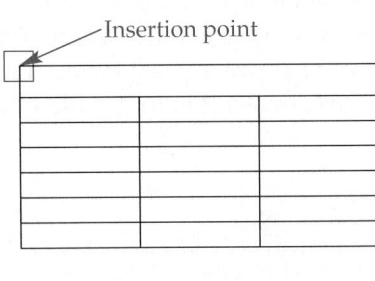

Insertion point

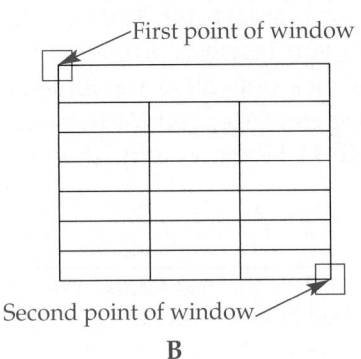

First point of window

Second point of window

A   B

NOTE

You specify the total number of *data* rows when constructing a table. By default, the table will also include a header row and title row, depending on cell style settings. The current table style text height and cell margin settings determine the default value for row height. For example, enter a row height of 1 if you plan to have a single line of text in each cell.

PROFESSIONAL TIP

You can add, delete, and fully adjust rows and columns as needed. Therefore, it is not critical that you enter the exact number and size of columns and rows before inserting a table.

Exercise 11-2

Access the Student Web site (www.g-wlearning.com/CAD) and complete Exercise 11-2.

Adding Cell Content

When you insert a table, the **Text Editor** contextual ribbon tab appears, with the text editor cursor in the title cell ready for typing. See **Figure 11-15.** Typing in a cell is like typing mtext. The options and settings available in the **Text Editor** ribbon tab and shortcut menu function the same in table cells as when editing mtext.

A dashed line around the border and a light gray background indicates the active cell. The *table indicator* identifies individual cells in the table. The identification system helps you to assign formulas to table cells for calculation purposes, as described later in this chapter. Before adding content to a cell, adjust the text settings in the **Text Editor** ribbon, if needed. Remember, however, that making changes to some text characteristics overrides the settings specified in the text style or table style, which is often not appropriate.

Hold [Alt] and press [Enter] to insert a return within the cell. When you finish entering text in the active cell, press [Tab] to move to the next cell. Hold [Shift] and press [Tab] to move the cursor backward (to the left or up) and make the previous cell active. Press [Enter] to make the cell directly below the current cell active, or exit the text editor if the cursor is at last cell. You can also use the arrow keys to navigate table cells.

When you finish typing, exit the text editor system using the **Close Text Editor** option, or pick outside of the table editor. You can also press [Esc] twice. The easiest way to reopen the text editor to make changes to text in a cell is to double-click in the cell. **Figure 11-16** shows a finished table.

table indicator: The grid of letters and numbers that identify individual cells in a table.

CLOSE

Ribbon
Text Editor
> Close

Close Text Editor

Figure 11-15. Use the **Text Editor** ribbon tab to add and modify table cell text. A blinking cursor, dashed border, and light gray background indicate the active cell.

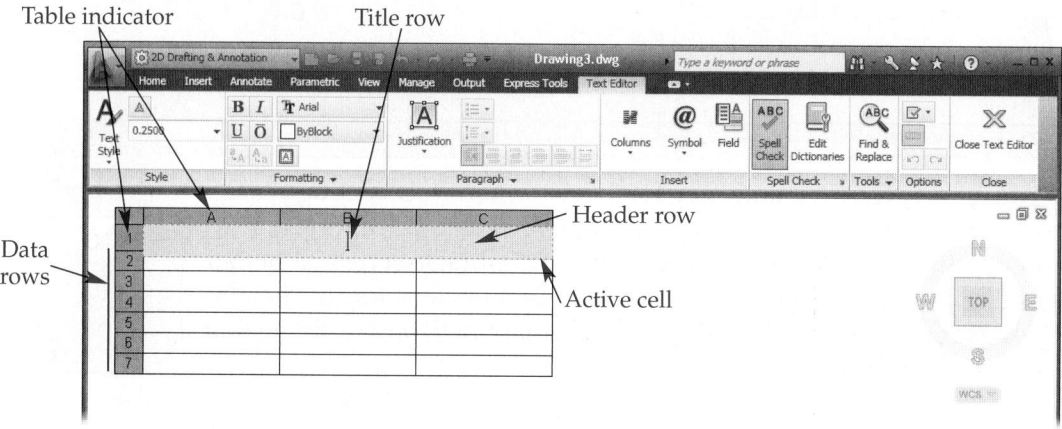

Figure 11-16. A completed parts list table added to a mechanical assembly drawing to identify assembly components.

PARTS LIST				
FIND NO	QTY REQD	DIA	PART OR IDENT NO	NOMENCLATURE OR DESCRIPTION
1	1		100-TBL-001	TABLE
2	2		100-CLJA-45	CLAMP JAWS
3	2		202-PIV-32	PIVOT ARM
4	1		340-HAND-06	LOCKING HANDLE
5	3		38009561	1/4-28UNF NYLOCK NUT
6	2		567-ADJR-98	ADJUSTING ROD HANDLE
7	2		786-SPG-64	1/8 SPRING PIN

Exercise 11-3

Access the Student Web site (www.g-wlearning.com/CAD) and complete Exercise 11-3.

Using a Starting Table Style

To place a table using a starting table style, select a starting table style from the **Table Style** drop-down list or select the ellipsis (**...**) button to create or modify a starting table style. The **Start from Table Style** radio button becomes activated in the **Insert options** area. See **Figure 11-17**. The preview area shows a preview of the parent table with the current table style settings and table options.

The **Specify insertion point** option is the only method for inserting a table using a starting table style. However, you can add columns and rows to the table using the **Additional columns** and **Additional rows** text boxes. You can also select the items from the parent table to include in the new table using the check boxes in the **Table options** area. For example, pick the **Data cell text** check box to create a new table that contains all the text added to the data cells of the parent table.

Pick the **OK** button and specify the insertion point of the table. The **Text Editor** ribbon tab appears with the text editor cursor in the title cell ready for adding new content or editing existing values. Exit the text editor when you are finished. **Figure 11-18** shows a table created by referencing an existing starting table style, with two additional rows.

Exercise 11-4

Access the Student Web site (www.g-wlearning.com/CAD) and complete Exercise 11-4.

Figure 11-17. You can use the **Insert Table** dialog box to create a new table using a starting table style.

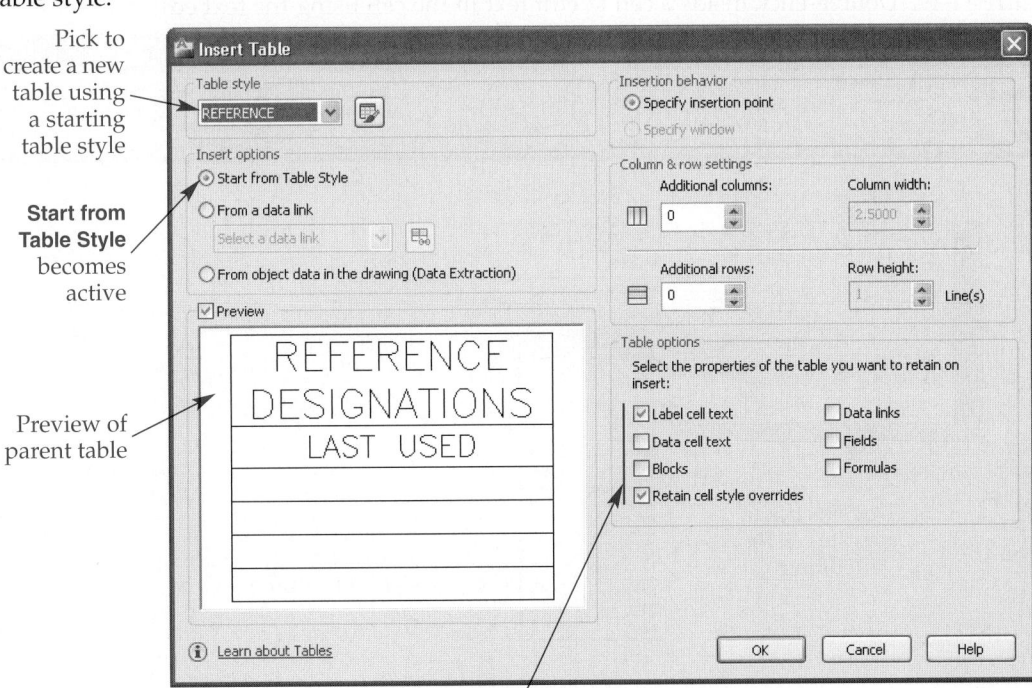

Figure 11-18.
Use a starting table style to create a new or modified table quickly. This example shows creating a new table of electronic reference designations using the starting table style created in Figure 11-11.

Existing table style used to form a starting table style

REFERENCE DESIGNATIONS	
LAST USED	
R9	
C1	
CRS	
Q2	

In the new table, all table options are retained and two rows are added

REFERENCE DESIGNATIONS	
LAST USED	
R9	
C1	
CRS	
Q2	
T4	
R6	

Editing Tables

AutoCAD provides several options to edit existing tables. One option is to re-enter the mtext editor to edit the text in a table cell. Use this method to modify cell content or change text format. Another option is to make changes to the table layout. Table layout changes include adding, removing, and resizing rows and columns, and wrapping table columns to break a large table into sections.

Text Editor

To edit the text in a table cell, double-click inside the cell or pick inside the cell, right-click, and select **Edit Text**. The cell becomes a text editor and the **Text Editor** ribbon tab appears. See **Figure 11-19**. This is the same format presented when you first insert a table. When you finish editing, use the **Close Text Editor** option, or pick outside of the table editor. You can also press [Esc] twice.

Figure 11-19. Double-click inside a cell to edit text in the cell using the text editor.

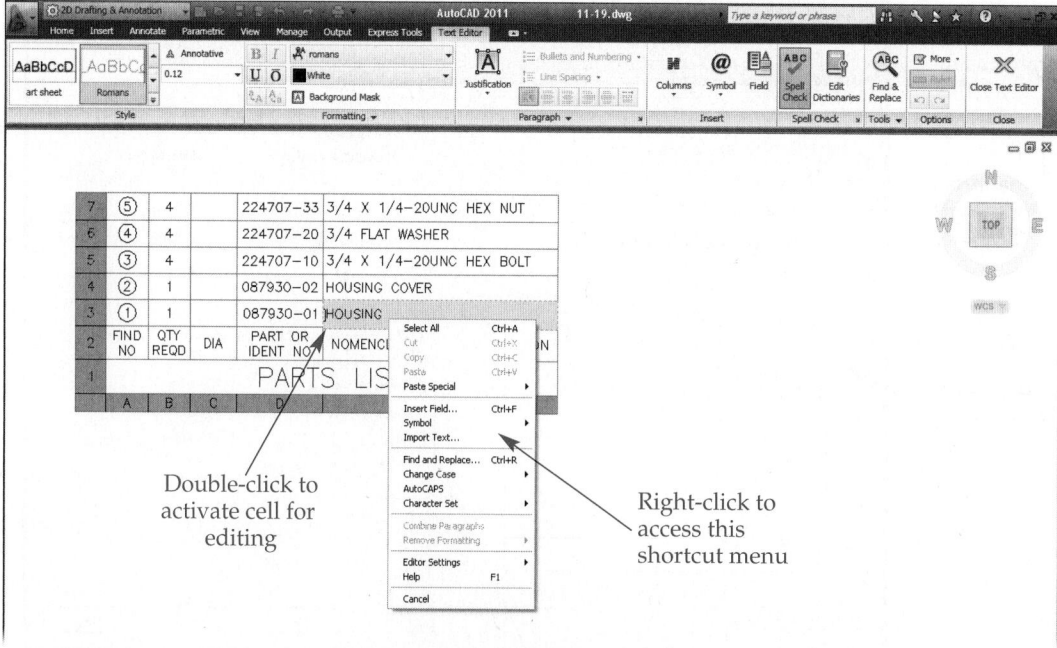

Exercise 11-5

Access the Student Web site (www.g-wlearning.com/CAD) and complete Exercise 11-5.

Table Cell Editor

You can access several table layout settings by picking (single-clicking) inside a cell to make the cell active and display the **Table Cell** contextual ribbon tab. The highlighted cell includes *grips*. The **Table Cell** ribbon tab contains options for adjusting table and individual cell layout. You can access many of the same options in **Table Cell** ribbon tab and Windows Clipboard functions from the shortcut menu that appears when you right-click away from the ribbon. See **Figure 11-20**. Use an option shown in **Figure 11-21** to select multiple cells and apply changes to all the cells at once.

grips: Small boxes that appear at strategic points on an object, allowing you to edit the object directly.

> **NOTE**
>
> Make sure you pick completely inside of the cell. If you accidentally select one of the cell borders, the entire table becomes the selected object. Editing table layout by selecting a cell border is described later in this chapter.

Auto-Fill

The most effective method for copying the content of one cell to multiple cells is to use the *auto-fill* function. **Figure 11-22A** shows the basic steps to use auto-fill. Pick inside the cell that contains the content to copy. Select the diamond-shaped auto-fill grip, and then right-click to choose an auto-fill option, if necessary. Finally, move the cursor to the last cell to fill and pick inside the cell.

auto-fill: A table function that fills selected cells based on the contents of another cell.

Figure 11-20. Pick inside a cell to access several options for modifying the table layout.

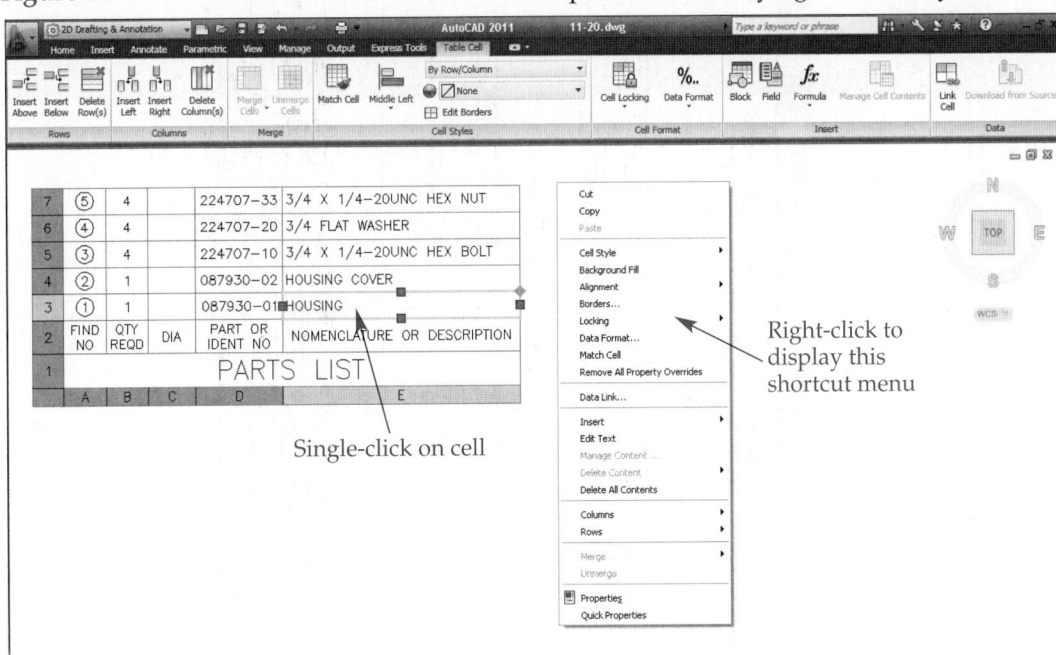

Figure 11-21. Selecting multiple cells in a table to edit. A—Using the pick-and-drag method. B—Picking a range of cells using [Shift]. C—Selecting a row, column, or the entire table.

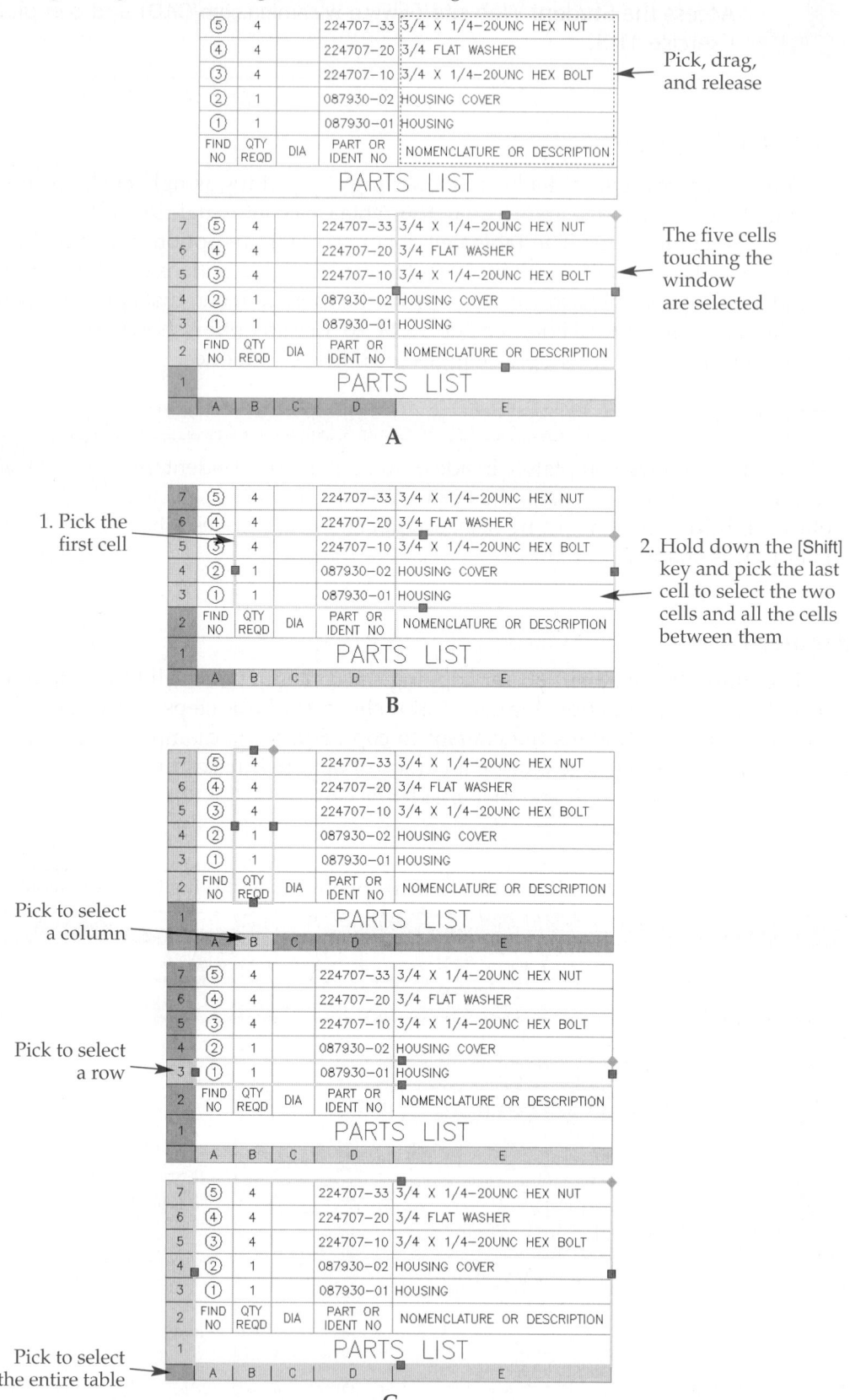

Figure 11-22. A—Using the auto-fill function to copy cell content to multiple cells. B—Using the **Fill Series** option to fill sequential whole number data. C—Using the **Copy Cells** option to copy data that would fill sequentially when using the **Fill Series** option. D—The completed door schedule uses auto-fill seven times to fill cells quickly. A door schedule typically appears on an architectural floor plan to identify doors and related information.

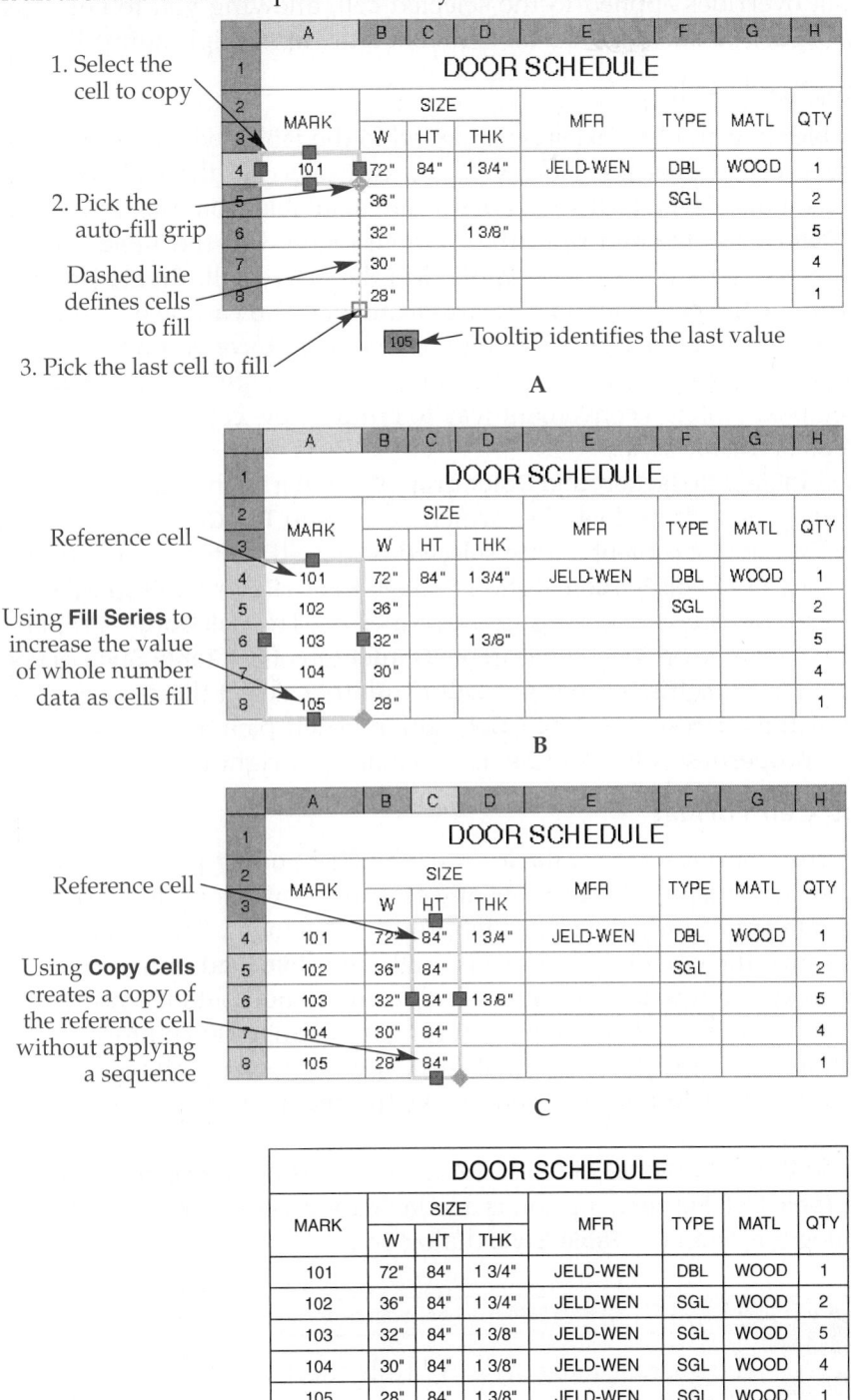

The **Fill Series** option fills cells with the content of the selected cell and applies format overrides. This option also automatically increases or decreases values of certain data types, such as dates and whole numbers, as the fill occurs. See **Figure 11-22B**. The **Fill Series Without Formatting** option fills cells with the content of the selected cell, but does not include format overrides.

The **Copy Cells** option copies the content of the selected cell and applies format overrides, but creates a static cell copy that does not adjust data values. See **Figure 11-22C**. The **Copy Cells Without Formatting** option copies the content of the selected cell, but does not include any format overrides. The **Fill Formatting Only** option fills the cells only with format overrides applied to the selected cell, allowing you to enter cell content manually. **Figure 11-22D** shows a table finished using multiple auto-fills.

Modifying Cell Style

Ribbon

Table Cell
> Cell Styles
> By Row/
Column

The table style and the text style assigned to the table style determine the appearance of most cell properties. However, you can override the cell style assigned to specific cells if necessary. Cell style options are available from the **Cell Styles** panel of the **Table Cell** ribbon tab and from the shortcut menu. Use the **Table Cell Style** drop-down list to override the cell style applied to the active cell. **Create New Cell Style...** and **Manage Cell Style...** functions are also available. You can save changes made to a cell as a new cell style by right-clicking and selecting **Save as New Cell Style...** from the **Cell Style** cascading submenu. Enter a name for the style in the **Save as New Cell Style** dialog box. This is a convenient way to build a new cell style that you can apply to other cells or a table style.

Ribbon

Table Cell
> Cell Styles

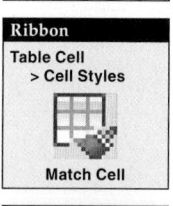

Background Color

Use the **Table Cell Background Color** drop-down list to change the cell background color. The alignment drop-down list, which defaults to **Top Center**, allows you to override the justification of content within selected cells. Cell content is placed in relation to cell borders. Use the **Cell Borders** option to open the **Cell Border Properties** dialog box, where you can override cell border display properties. The **Cell Border Properties** dialog box contains the same options found in the **Border** tab of the **Table Style** dialog box.

Ribbon

Table Cell
> Cell Styles

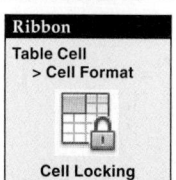

Top Center

To copy format settings from one cell to another, select the cell with the settings to copy, and then access the **Match Cell** option. Then pick a destination cell, which receives the properties. Select another cell to match, or right-click to exit.

Adjusting Cell Format

Ribbon

Table Cell
> Cell Styles

Edit Borders

Cell format options are available from the **Cell Format** panel of the ribbon and from the shortcut menu. The **Cell Locking** feature provides options for locking cells to protect data from unintended or inappropriate changes. The locked icon appears when you move the cursor over a locked cell. The **Unlocked** option unlocks the cell for you to make changes to cell content and format. The **Content Locked** option locks only the content of the cell, allowing you to make changes to cell format. The **Format Locked** option locks only the cell format, allowing you to make changes to cell content. The **Content and Format Locked** option locks the cell against changes in content and format.

Ribbon

Table Cell
> Cell Styles

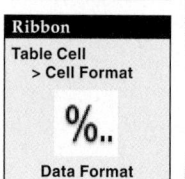

Match Cell

Override the data format of cells, if necessary, using the **Data Format...** function. A **Custom Table Cell Format...** option is available for access to the same **Table Cell Data Format** dialog box from the **Table Style** dialog box.

Ribbon

Table Cell
> Cell Format

Cell Locking

PROFESSIONAL TIP

The current table style controls most cell style and format properties. If you plan to make significant changes to cell properties, modify the table style or create a new style.

Ribbon

Table Cell
> Cell Format

%..

Data Format

NOTE

Right-click and select **Remove All Property Overrides** to restore selected cells to their original properties defined in the selected table style.

Inserting Fields and Blocks

In addition to text, table cells can contain fields, formulas, and blocks. To insert these items, use the tools available from the **Insert** panel of the **Table Cell** ribbon tab, or from the **Insert** cascading submenu of the shortcut menu. You will learn about formulas later in this chapter. Choose the **Field...** option to insert a field into a table cell using the same **Field** dialog box available for creating mtext and text objects. You can also insert fields into a cell using the text editor after double-clicking inside the cell to activate it.

Blocks are AutoCAD symbols that are useful in tables for applications such as creating a legend, displaying a view or flag note symbol in a parts list, and adding tags to a schedule. This chapter briefly describes options for inserting a block in a table. You will learn about blocks later in this textbook. Select the **Block...** option to insert a block into a table cell using the **Insert a Block in a Table Cell** dialog box. **Figure 11-23** briefly describes the options available in this dialog box. Double-click on a block to reopen the **Insert a Block in a Table Cell** dialog box to make changes. A cell can contain both text and blocks.

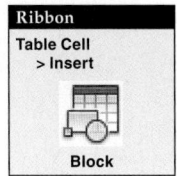

Adding and Resizing Columns and Rows

You can add, delete, and resize existing columns and rows as needed. Select a single cell or a group of cells to add, depending on the requirement. To delete and resize columns and rows, you do not need to select entire columns and rows. The following options are available from the **Columns** panel of the **Table Cell** ribbon tab or the **Columns** cascading submenu of the shortcut menu:

- **Insert Left.** Add a new column to the left of the selection.
- **Insert Right.** Add a new column to the right of the selection.
- **Delete.** Eliminate entire columns.
- **Size Equally.** Size multiple columns to the width of the widest column.

The following options are available from the **Rows** panel of the **Table Cell** ribbon tab or the **Rows** cascading submenu of the shortcut menu:

- **Insert Above.** Add a new row above the selection.
- **Insert Below.** Add a new row below the selection.
- **Delete.** Delete entire rows.
- **Size Equally.** Size multiple rows to the height of the tallest row.

Figure 11-23. Options in the **Insert a Block in a Table Cell** dialog box.

Feature	Description
Name	Used to choose the block from a drop-down list of the blocks stored in the current drawing.
Browse	Displays the **Select Drawing File** dialog box, where a drawing file can be selected and inserted into the table cell as a block.
AutoFit	Scales the block automatically to fit inside the cell.
Scale	Sets the block insertion scale. For example, a value of 2 inserts the block at twice its original size. A value of .5 inserts the block at half its created size. The **Scale** option is not available if the **AutoFit** check box is checked.
Rotation angle	Rotates the block to the specified angle.
Overall cell alignment	Determines the justification of the block in the cell and overrides the current cell alignment setting.

PROFESSIONAL TIP

You can also adjust column and row size using grips. Grip boxes appear in the middle of cell border lines. To resize a column or row, select a grip, move the crosshairs, and pick. Chapter 14 explains grips in detail.

Merging Cells

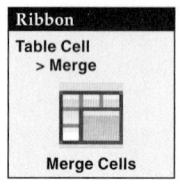

Ribbon
Table Cell
> Merge

Merge Cells

Merging allows you to combine adjacent cells. The default title cell style is an example of merged cells. Merge tools are available from the **Merge** panel of the ribbon and from the **Merge** cascading submenu in the shortcut menu. Select the cells to merge and then select the appropriate **Merge cells** option. Select the **All** option to merge all cells into one cell. The **By Row** and **By Column** options allow you to merge cells in multiple rows or columns without removing the horizontal or vertical borders. Use the **Unmerge Cells** option to separate merged cells back to individual cells.

NOTE

The **Delete All Contents** option deletes the contents in the selected cell. You can accomplish the same task by picking a cell and pressing [Delete].

Exercise 11-6

Access the Student Web site (www.g-wlearning.com/CAD) and complete Exercise 11-6.

Picking a Cell Edge to Edit Table Layout

Pick the edge, or border, of a cell to access additional methods for adjusting table layout. The display includes the table indicator grid, grips you can use to adjust row height and column width, and the table break function. Once you pick a cell border, right-click to display the shortcut menu shown in **Figure 11-24**.

Adjusting Table Style

Select a table style from the **Table Style** cascading submenu to apply a different table style to the selected table. Pick the **Set as Table in Current Table Style** option to create a starting table style based on the selected table and the current table style. This is a convenient technique for creating a starting table style without opening the **Table Style** dialog box. If the selected table was drawn using a starting table style, selecting the **Set as Table in Current Table Style** redefines the starting table. To save modifications made to the table as a new table style, pick the **Save as New Table Style...** option and enter a name for the style in the **Save as New Table Style** dialog box.

Figure 11-24. Pick a cell border to access several additional options for modifying table layout.

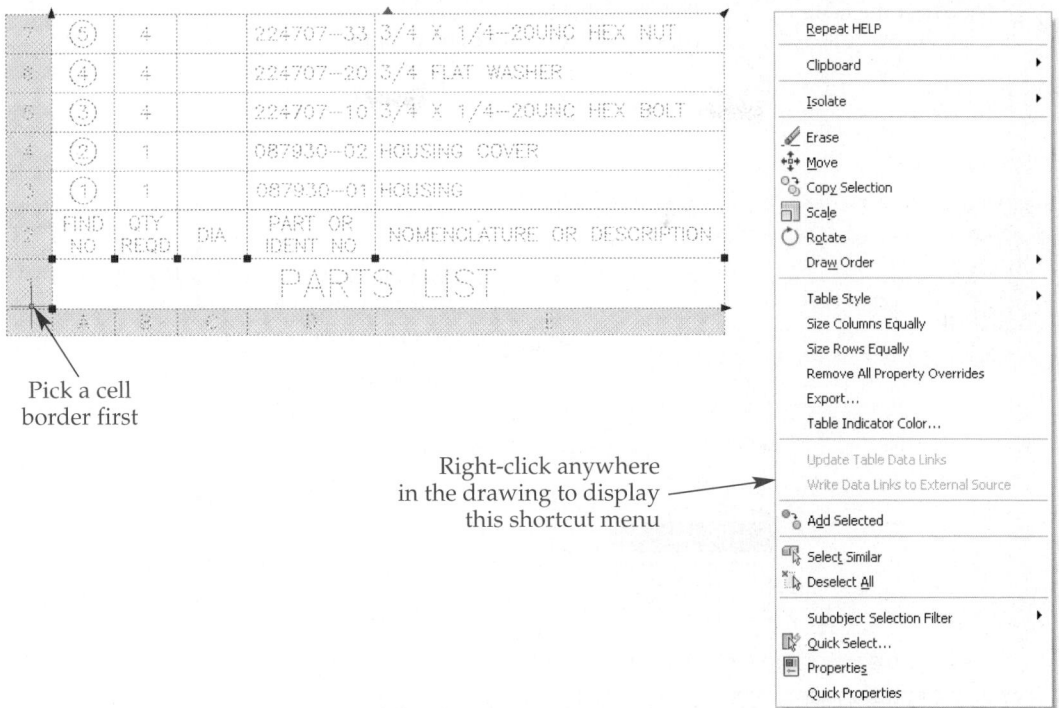

Pick a cell border first

Right-click anywhere in the drawing to display this shortcut menu

Resizing Columns and Rows

Use the grip boxes or arrowheads at the corners of columns and rows to adjust column and row size. To resize a column or row, select a grip box, move the crosshairs, and pick. Use the arrowhead grips to increase or decrease row height and/or column width uniformly. Chapter 14 explains grips in detail.

The **Size Columns Equally** option sizes all columns to the same width. AutoCAD divides the total width of the table evenly among the columns. The **Size Rows Equally** option sizes all rows to match the height of the tallest row in the table.

> **NOTE**
>
> The default grip box stretches the column or row without changing the size of the table. Hold [Ctrl] while stretching to increase or decrease the size of the table with the column or row resize.

Table Breaks

Use the table break function to break a table into separate sections while maintaining a single table object. Breaking a table is common when it is necessary to fit a long table in a specific area or on a certain size sheet. The table breaking grip is located midway between the sides of the table at the top or the bottom of the table, depending on the table direction. See **Figure 11-25.**

To break a table, select the table breaking grip and move the crosshairs into the table to display a preview of the table sections and a vector line. The crosshairs determines the location of the break. The closer to the table title and headers you move the crosshairs, the more sections you create, as shown in the table preview. When the preview of the table looks correct, pick the location to form the table breaks.

Figure 11-25. The procedure for breaking, or wrapping, a table into sections. This example shows wrapping a long parts list that was conflicting with the assembly drawing views.

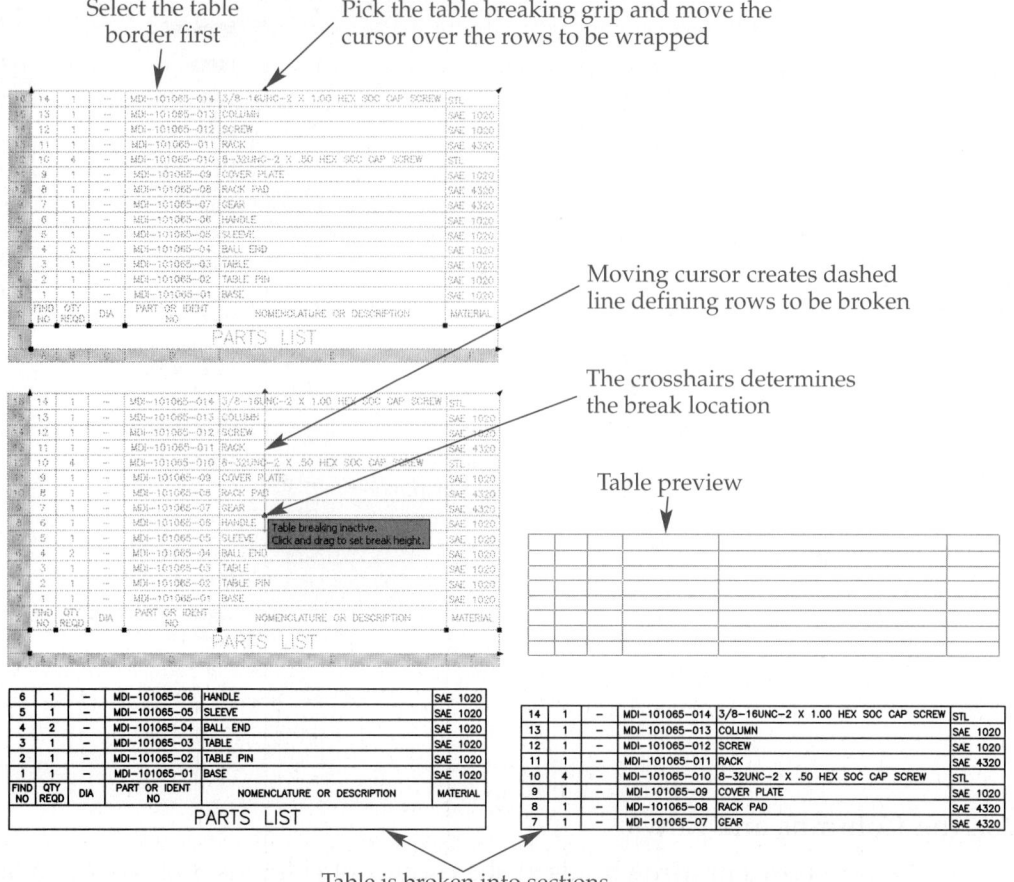

Select the table border first

Pick the table breaking grip and move the cursor over the rows to be wrapped

Moving cursor creates dashed line defining rows to be broken

The crosshairs determines the break location

Table preview

Table is broken into sections

After you add table breaks, several options become available from the **Properties** palette for adjusting the table sections. Chapter 14 covers using the **Properties** palette.

Additional Table Layout Options

The following additional table options are available from the shortcut menu:

- **Remove All Property Overrides.** Restores the original properties to the table, defined according to the selected table style.
- **Export.** Exports the table as a CSV file.
- **Table Indicator Color....** Allows you to change the color of the table indicator shown when you pick inside a cell.

Exercise 11-7

Access the Student Web site (www.g-wlearning.com/CAD) and complete Exercise 11-7.

Calculating Values in Tables

Performing calculations on table data using *formulas* is a common requirement. Examples include calculating and showing the total number of parts in a parts list, the total cost of items in a bill of materials, or the total glazing area in a window schedule. Formulas calculate operations based on numeric data in table cells. AutoCAD allows you to write formulas for sums, averages, counts, and other mathematical functions.

formulas: Mathematical expressions that allow you to perform calculations within table cells.

The table indicator grid that appears when you edit a table cell provides an identification system for cells. Letters identify columns, and numbers identify rows. Use the combination of column letter and row number to describe cells in formulas. For example, C6 identifies the cell located in Column C, Row 6. See **Figure 11-26.**

Creating Formulas

A formula evaluates data from other cells to display a result. The result updates when you edit data in the table linked to the formula. You often write a formula to calculate all cells in a row or column, or at least a range of continuous cells. For example, add the values of all cells in a column to display the total in a new cell at the bottom of the column. However, you can also write a formula that evaluates cells that do not share a common border. Formulas are field objects, as indicated by a light gray highlight.

You must enter the proper syntax in the table cell to create an accurate formula. An example of a complete expression using the standard syntax is =(C3+D4). The = sign tells AutoCAD to perform a calculation. The open parenthesis marks the beginning of the expression. Type C3+D4 to tell AutoCAD to add the value of cell C3 to the value of cell D4. The closing parenthesis marks the end of the expression.

When identifying a cell in an expression, you must enter the letter before the number. For example, you cannot enter 3C to designate the cell C3. Common operators used for mathematical functions include + for addition, – for subtraction, * for multiplication, / for division, and ^ for exponentiation. If you enter an incorrect expression or an expression evaluating cells without numeric data, AutoCAD displays the pound character (#) to indicate the error.

NOTE

Parentheses are unnecessary in some expressions, but other expressions cannot be calculated without them. It is good practice to use parentheses in all expressions.

Figure 11-26.
Column letters and row numbers identify table cells. The table indicator grid provides a reference for identifying each cell. This example shows a room schedule, which often includes square footage calculations for various areas.

Table indicator   Column

	A	B	C	D
1	SQUARE FOOTAGE			
2	**OFFICE**	**WIDTH (FT)**	**LENGTH (FT)**	
3	101	12	10	
4	102	20	15	
5	103	15	14	
6	201	24	20	
7	202	10	12	

Row

Cell C6

Input a formula using the text editor. **Figure 11-27** shows an example of typing the multiplication formula =(B3*C3) in cell D3. The result appears when you close the text editor of the cell, such as when you move to another cell.

You can use grouped expressions in formulas by enclosing expression sets in parentheses. For example, the expression =(E1+F1)*E2 multiplies the sum of E1 and F1 by E2. Another example: =(E1+F1)*(E2+F2)/G6 multiplies the sum of E1 and F1 by the sum of E2 and F2 and divides the product by G6.

Sum, Average, and Count Formulas

An alternative to entering formulas manually is to select a formula from AutoCAD to calculate the sum, average, or count of a range of cells. Pick inside a cell where the calculation is to occur, and then choose a formula using the **Formula** drop-down list, which is also available by right-clicking and selecting from the **Formula** cascading submenu of the **Insert** cascading submenu.

Select the **Sum** option and then use window selection to add the values of selected cells. See **Figure 11-28A**. The range, or window, can include cells from several columns and rows. Be sure to select all of the cells to be included in the calculation. When you select the second point, the expression appears in the cell. Notice in **Figure 11-28B** that the resulting expression is =Sum(D3:D7). This formula specifies that the selected cell is equal to the sum of cells D3 through D7. The colon (:) indicates the range of cells for the calculation. **Figure 11-28** shows an example of calculating the square footage for each office, and then calculating the total square footage.

The **Average** option creates a formula that calculates the average value of selected cells. The average is the sum of the selected cells divided by the number of cells selected. The **Count** option creates a formula that counts the number of selected cells. The count only includes cells that contain a value.

You can type sum, average, and count formulas directly into a cell without using the supplied formulas. If you calculate a value over a range of cells, use the colon symbol (:) to designate the range. You can also write an expression that evaluates individual cells instead of a range. The cells do not have to share a common border. To write an expression using nonadjacent cells, use a comma to separate the cell names. For example, to average cells D1, D3, and D6, type =Average(D1,D3,D6).

You can include a range of cells and individual cells in the same expression. For example, to count cells A1 through B10 in addition to cells C4 and C6, enter =Count(A1: B10,C4,C6). **Figure 11-29** shows examples of sum, average, and count formulas.

Figure 11-27.
Entering a multiplication formula to calculate the square footage of a room. A—Type the expression in the table cell using the correct syntax. B—The calculation occurs when you close the text editor of the cell.

	A	B	C	D
1	SQUARE FOOTAGE			
2	OFFICE	WIDTH (FT)	LENGTH (FT)	
3	101	12	10	=(B3*C3) ← Expression
4	102	20	15	
5	103	15	14	
6	201	24	20	
7	202	10	12	

A

SQUARE FOOTAGE			
OFFICE	WIDTH (FT)	LENGTH (FT)	
101	12	10	120 ← Result
102	20	15	
103	15	14	
201	24	20	
202	10	12	

B

Figure 11-28.
Creating a sum formula in a table cell. A—Pick a cell to hold the formula and select a range of cells for the formula by windowing around the cells. B—After you pick the second point of the window, the formula displays in the cell.

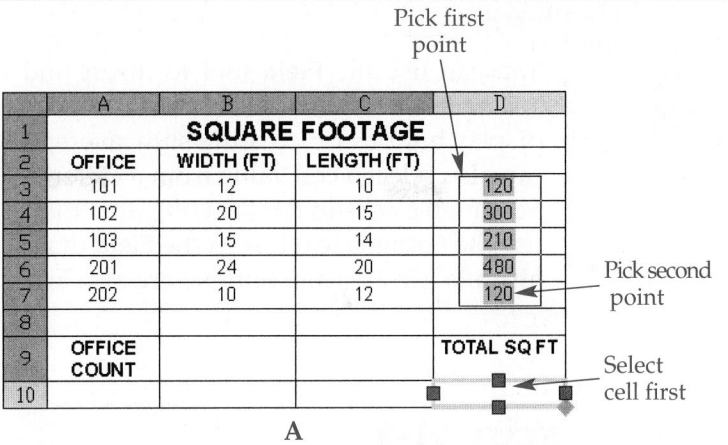

Figure 11-29.
Examples of sum, average, and count formulas and their resulting values.

	A	B	C	D
1	**SQUARE FOOTAGE**			
2	**OFFICE**	**WIDTH (FT)**	**LENGTH (FT)**	**SQ FT**
3	101	12	10	120
4	102	20	15	300
5	103	15	14	210
6	201	24	20	480
7	202	10	12	120
8				
9	**OFFICE COUNT**	**AVERAGE SQ FT PER ROOM**		**TOTAL SQ FT**
10	5	246		1230

=Count(A3:A7)   =Average(D3:D7)   =Sum(D3:D7)

NOTE

When using architectural units in a drawing, you can type the foot (′) and inch (″) symbols in table cells for use in values and formulas. When you use the foot symbol for a cell value, a formula in another cell automatically converts the resulting value to inches and feet.

Other Formula Options

The **Formula** drop-down list and **Insert** cascading submenu contain additional options for writing table formulas. The **Cell** option allows you to select a cell from a different table in the drawing to insert the contents in the current cell. You can then use the cell value in a formula. Select the **Equation** option to place an equal sign (=) in the current cell. You can then type the expression manually.

You can use the **Field** tool to insert and edit table cell formulas. Select **Formula** from the **Field names** list in the **Field** dialog box to display buttons for creating sum, average, and count formulas. You can also select a cell value from a different table as a starting point. Select table cells in the drawing area to define the formula. You can use the **Formula** text box in the **Field** dialog box to add to or edit the formula. Unit format options are also available.

Exercise 11-8

Access the Student Web site (www.g-wlearning.com/CAD) and complete Exercise 11-8.

Supplemental Material

Linking a Table to Excel Data

For information about using existing data entered in a Microsoft® Excel spreadsheet or a CSV file to create an AutoCAD table, go to the Student Web site (www.g-wlearning.com/CAD), select this chapter, and select **Linking a Table to Excel Data**.

Supplemental Material

Extracting Table Data

For information about using existing AutoCAD text to create a table, go to the Student Web site (www.g-wlearning.com/CAD), select this chapter, and select **Extracting Table Data**.

Template Development
Chapter 11

For detailed instructions on adding table styles to each drawing template, go to the Student Web site (www.g-wlearning.com/CAD), select this chapter, and select **Template Development**.

Chapter Test

Answer the following questions. Write your answers on a separate sheet of paper or go to the Student Web site (www.g-wlearning.com/CAD) and complete the electronic chapter test.

1. What is the purpose of creating a table style?
2. Briefly describe the procedure for creating a table style based on an existing table style.
3. What is the purpose of the **Alignment** setting in the **New Table Style** dialog box?
4. Which setting would you adjust in the **New Table Style** dialog box to increase the spacing between the text and the top of the cell?
5. How can creating a new table using a starting table style save time?
6. How can you make a table style current without opening the **Table Style** dialog box?
7. List two ways to open the **Insert Table** dialog box.
8. Describe the two ways to insert an empty table and explain how the methods differ.
9. By default, what two types of rows are at the top of a table?
10. What ribbon tab opens when you insert a table?
11. If you finish typing in a cell and want to move to the next cell in the same row, what two keyboard keys can you use?
12. List two ways to make a cell active for editing.
13. Explain how to insert a field into a table cell.
14. How can you insert a new row at the bottom of a table?
15. How are table cells identified in formulas?
16. Write the table cell formula that adds the value of C3 plus the value of D4.
17. What is the function of the colon (:) in the formula =Sum(D3:D7)?
18. What is the difference between a sum formula and a count formula?
19. Write the table cell formula that averages the values of cells D1, D3, and D6.
20. Explain how to write a formula that calculates a function for cells that do not share common borders.

Drawing Problems

Start AutoCAD if it is not already started. Start a new drawing using an appropriate template of your choice. The template should include layers, text styles, and table styles when necessary for drawing the given objects. Add layers, text styles, and table styles as needed. Draw all objects using appropriate layers, text styles, table styles, justification, and format. Follow the specific instructions for each problem. Use only drawing tools and techniques you have already learned. Use your own judgment and approximate dimensions when necessary.

▼ Basic

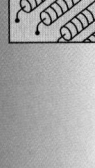

1. Create the electronic schematic reference designations list shown. Save the drawing as P11-1.

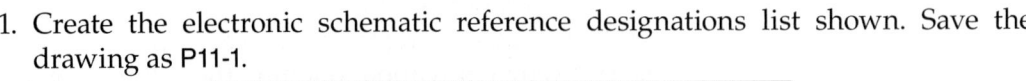

REFERENCE DESIGNATIONS	
LAST USED	DATE
R9	1/30/2010
C1	1/30/2010
CRS	1/30/2010
Q2	1/30/2010

2. Create the parts list shown in Figure 11-1B. Do not draw the circles around the find numbers. Save the drawing as P11-2.

3. Create the parts list shown. Save the drawing as P11-3.

5	1	–	210014–29	1/2–12UNC HEX NUT
4	1	–	320014–33	1/2 FLAT WASHER
3	2	–	632043–43	7/16 EXTERNAL SNAP RING
2	2	–	255010–41	1/4–20UNC WING NUT
1	2	–	803010–11	3/4 X 1/4–20UNC BOLT
FIND NO	QTY REQD	DIA	PART OR IDENT NO	NOMENCLATURE OR DESCRIPTION
PARTS LIST				

4. Create the window schedule shown in Figure 11-1A. Do not draw the polygons around the marks. Save the drawing as P11-4.

▼ Intermediate

5. Draw the finish schedule shown. Use the **Symbol** option of the text editor to locate and insert bullet symbols as shown. Save the drawing as P11-5.

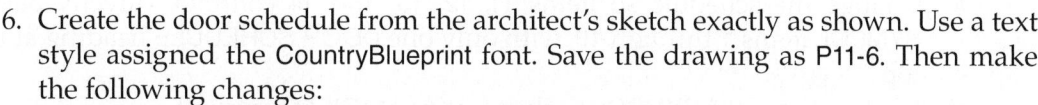

INTERIOR FINISH SCHEDULE										
ROOM	FLOOR				WALLS				CEIL	
	CARPET	VINYL	TILE	HARDWOOD	PAINT	PAPER	TEXTURE	SPRAY	SMOOTH	BROCADE	PAINT
FOYER			•		•		•			•	•
KITCHEN			•			•		•	•		•
DINING				•	•		•			•	•
FAMILY	•				•		•			•	•
LIVING	•				•		•			•	•
MASTER BED	•				•		•			•	•
MASTER BATH			•			•		•	•		•
BATH 2		•				•		•	•		•
BED 2	•				•		•			•	•
BED 3	•				•		•			•	•
UTILITY		•				•		•	•		•

6. Create the door schedule from the architect's sketch exactly as shown. Use a text style assigned the CountryBlueprint font. Save the drawing as P11-6. Then make the following changes:

- Edit the text style to use the SansSerif font.
- Replace the abbreviation SYM. with the word MARK (no period).
- Remove the period after the abbreviation QTY.
- Remove the periods from the abbreviation S.C.
- Replace the abbreviation RP. with the words RAISED PANEL.
- Remove the period after the abbreviation SLDG.

Resave the drawing.

DOOR SCHEDULE			
SYM.	SIZE	TYPE	QTY.
1	36x80	S.C. RP. METAL INSULATED	1
2	36x80	S.C. FLUSH METAL INSULATED	2
3	32x80	S.C. SELF CLOSING	2
4	32x80	HOLLOW CORE	5
5	30x80	HOLLOW CORE	5
6	30x80	POCKET SLDG.	2

7. Create the window schedule from the architect's sketch exactly as shown. Use a text style assigned the CityBlueprint font. Save the drawing as P11-7. Then make the following changes:
   - Edit the text style to use the SansSerif font.
   - Replace the abbreviation SYM. with the word MARK (no period).
   - Remove the period after the abbreviations QTY, SLDG, and AWN.
   - Replace the abbreviation CSM. with the abbreviation CSMT (no period).

   Resave the drawing.

		WINDOW SCHEDULE		
SYM.	SIZE	MODEL	ROUGH OPEN	QTY.
A	12x60	JOB BUILT	VERIFY	2
B	96x60	W4N5 CSM.	8'-0 3/4" x 5'-0 7/8"	1
C	48x60	W2N5 CSM.	4'-0 3/4" x 5'-0 7/8"	2
D	48x36	W2N3 CSM.	4'-0 3/4" x 3'-6 1/2"	2
E	42x42	2N3 CSM.	3'-6 1/2" x 3'-6 1/2"	2
F	72x48	G64 SLDG.	6'-0 1/2" x 4'-0 1/2"	1
G	60x42	G536 SLDG.	5'-0 1/2" x 3'-6 1/2"	4
H	48x42	G436 SLDG.	4'-0 1/2" x 3'-6 1/2"	1
J	48x24	A41 AWN.	4'-0 1/2" x 2'-0 7/8"	3

8. Create the door schedule shown using a table break. Save the drawing as P11-8. Make the following changes:
   - Change the schedule so items 11, 12, 13, and 14 continue directly below SYMBOL items 1 through 10, with only one DOOR SCHEDULE heading at the top.
   - Replace the word SYMBOL with the word MARK (no period).
   - Replace the word QUANTITY with the abbreviation QTY (no period).
   - Replace the abbreviations S.C. R.P. with the words SOLID CORE RAISED PANEL (no period).
   - Replace the abbreviation S.C.- with the words SOLID CORE (no hyphen, but include a space).
   - Replace the abbreviation H.C. with the words HOLLOW CORE (no period).
   - Replace WOOD FRAME-TEMP. SLDG GL. with the abbreviations TMPD SGD (no period).

   Resave the drawing.

	DOOR SCHEDULE				DOOR SCHEDULE		
SYMBOL	SIZE	MODEL	QUANTITY	SYMBOL	SIZE	MODEL	QUANTITY
1	3'-0" X 6'-8"	S.C. R.P. METAL INSULATED	1	11	4'-0" X 6'-8"	BI-FOLD	1
2	3'-0" X 6'-8"	S.C.-FLUSH-METAL INSULATED	2	12	2'-0" X 6'-0"	SHATTER PROOF	1
3	2'-8" X 6'-8"	S.C.-SELF CLOSING	2	13	6'-0" X 6'-8"	WOOD FRAME-TEMP. SLDG GL.	1
4	2'-8" X 6'-8"	H.C.	5	14	9'-0" X 7'-0"	OVERHEAD GARAGE	2
5	2'-6" X 6'-8"	H.C.	3				
6	2'-6" X 6'-8"	POCKET	2				
7	2'-4" X 6'-8"	POCKET	1				
9	5'-0" X 6'-0"	BI-PASS	2				
10	3'-0" X 6'-8"	BI-FOLD	1				

▼ Advanced

9. Open P11-3 and save the file as P11-9. The P11-9 file should be active. Make the following changes:

   - Change PARTS LIST to PURCHASE PARTS LIST.
   - Change Part Number 803010-11 as follows: Find No: 7, Name: HEX HD, Description: $\frac{1}{4}$-20UNC-2 X $\frac{3}{4}$ BOLT.
   - Change Part Number 255010-41 as follows: Find No: 11, Name: WING NUT, Description: $\frac{1}{4}$-20UNC.
   - Change Part Number 632043-43 as follows: Find No: 15, Name: SNAP RING, Description: Ø $\frac{7}{16}$ EXTERNAL.
   - Change Part Number 320014-33 as follows: Find No: 19, Name: WASHER, Description: Ø $\frac{1}{2}$ FLAT.
   - Change Part Number 210014-29 as follows: Find No: 21, Name: NUT, Description: $\frac{1}{2}$ -12UNC-2 HEX.

   Resave the drawing.

10. Create a table of your own design and use at least six of the applications of calculating values in tables described in this chapter. Save the drawing as P11-10.

11. Access the Student Web site content for this chapter and review Supplement 11A, "Linking a Table to Excel Data." Use this information to create a table by linking to Microsoft® Excel data. To do this, create your own Excel spreadsheet or find an existing Excel spreadsheet containing suitable data. Link a table to the Excel data. Save the drawing as P11-11.

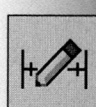

12. Access the Student Web site content for this chapter and review Supplement 11B, "Extracting Table Data." Use the description to create a table similar to the given examples and then extract the table data into an AutoCAD drawing. Save the drawing as P11-12.

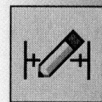

13. Research the requirements for a set of working drawings for a mechanical assembly. Identify a mechanical assembly consisting of several parts and possibly subassemblies. Use the **TABLE** tool to create a parts list identifying each component. Save the drawing as P11-13.

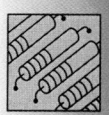

14. Research an example of a residential home design. Use the **TABLE** tool to create a door and window schedule identifying all of the doors and windows in the home. Save the drawing as P11-14.

15. Research an example of an electronic wiring harness schematic. Use the **TABLE** tool to create a wire list identifying all of the required wires. Save the drawing as P11-15.

16. Obtain a copy of leveling field notes prepared by a surveyor. Use the **TABLE** tool to reproduce the notes and calculate unspecified values. Save the drawing as P11-16.

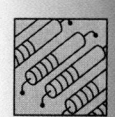

AutoCAD Certified Associate Exam Practice

Answer the following questions. Write your answers on a separate sheet of paper.

1. What is the meaning of the formula =((C3*D2)/4)? *Select the one item that best answers the question.*
   A. add the values of C3 and D2 and divide the result by 4
   B. multiply the values of both C3 and D2 by 4 and add the results
   C. multiply the value of C3 by the value of D2 and divide the result by 4
   D. divide the value of D2 by 4 and multiply the result by the value of C3

2. How can you remove existing breaks in a table? *Select all that apply.*
   A. select the table, right-click, and select **Remove All Property Overrides**
   B. move the table breaking grip down to the last row
   C. select the table breaking grip and press [Delete]
   D. use the **Properties** palette to set **Table Breaks Enabled** to No

3. In a table that uses the **Down** direction, what is the cell identification for a cell in the fourth row from the top, in the fifth column from the left? *Select the one item that best answers the question.*
   A. 4E
   B. 5D
   C. D4
   D. D5
   E. E4

AutoCAD Certified Professional Exam Practice

Follow the instructions for the following problem. Write your answer on a separate sheet of paper.

1. **Navigate to this chapter on the Student Web site and open CPE-11formula.dwg.** Perform the following tasks on the existing table:
   A. In the first data row of the AREA column, create a formula to calculate the area (length × width) of each room listed in the table.
   B. Use auto-fill to copy the formula to the remaining rows in the AREA column.
   C. Add a row at the bottom of the table.
   D. In the new bottom row, merge cells A11 through E11, set the alignment to **Top Right**, and enter the text TOTAL AREA.
   E. In the bottom-right cell, create a formula to calculate the total area of all the rooms. What is the total area of the house?

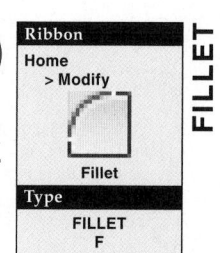

CHAPTER 12

Modifying Objects

Learning Objectives

After completing this chapter, you will be able to do the following:

✓ Use the **FILLET** tool to draw fillets, rounds, and other radius corners.
✓ Place chamfers and angled corners with the **CHAMFER** tool.
✓ Separate objects using the **BREAK** tool and combine objects using the **JOIN** tool.
✓ Use the **TRIM** and **EXTEND** tools to edit objects.
✓ Change objects using the **STRETCH** and **LENGTHEN** tools.
✓ Edit the size of objects using the **SCALE** tool.
✓ Use the **EXPLODE** tool.

This chapter explains methods for changing the geometry of existing objects using basic editing tools. Use editing tools to complete common drafting tasks, improve efficiency, and modify a drawing. Editing tools include many options. As you work through this chapter, experiment with each option to see which is most effective for different situations.

Using the FILLET Tool

Drafting terminology refers to a rounded interior corner as a *fillet*, and a rounded exterior corner as a *round*. AutoCAD refers to all rounded corners as *fillets*. The **FILLET** tool draws a rounded corner between intersecting or nonintersecting lines, circles, arcs, and polylines. See **Figure 12-1**.

Setting Fillet Radius

Access the **FILLET** tool and then use the **Radius** option to specify the fillet radius. The radius determines the size of a fillet and must be set before you select objects. Now select the objects to fillet. AutoCAD stores the radius as the new default radius, allowing you to place additional fillets of the same size.

FILLET

Ribbon
Home
> Modify

Fillet

Type
FILLET
F

fillet: A rounded interior corner used to relieve stress or ease the contour of inside corners.

round: A rounded exterior corner used to remove sharp edges or ease the contour of exterior corners.

Figure 12-1. Using the **FILLET** tool to add fillets and rounds.

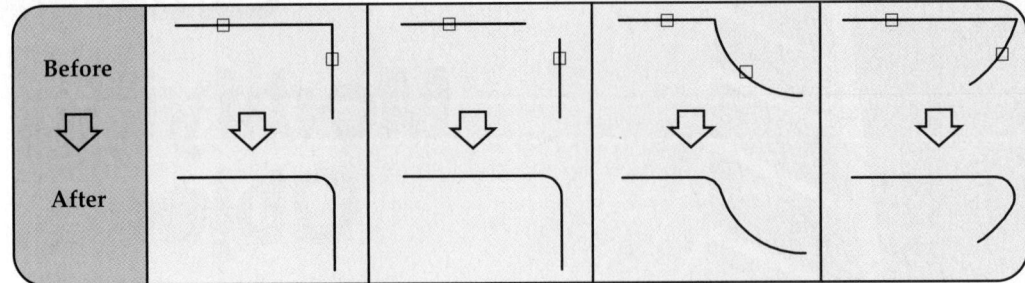

Use a fillet radius of 0 to connect two objects at a sharp corner. You can also create a zero-radius fillet without setting the radius to 0 by holding down the [Shift] key when you pick the second object. This is a convenient way to connect objects at a corner, or to form a square corner if edges are perpendicular.

Exercise 12-1

Access the Student Web site (www.g-wlearning.com/CAD) and complete Exercise 12-1.

Creating Full Rounds

You can use the **FILLET** tool to draw a full round between parallel lines. The radius of a fillet between parallel lines is always half the distance between the two lines, regardless of the radius setting. Use this method to create a full round, such as the end radii of a slot.

Polyline Option

Use the **Polyline** option to fillet all corners of a closed polyline. See **Figure 12-2**. Remember to set the appropriate radius before selecting the **Polyline** option. If you originally drew the polyline without using the **Close** option, the beginning corner does not fillet, as shown in **Figure 12-2**.

Trim Settings

The **Trim** option controls whether the **FILLET** tool trims object segments that extend beyond the fillet radius point of tangency. See **Figure 12-3**. Use the default **Trim** setting to trim objects. When you set the **Trim** option to **No trim**, the fillet occurs, but the filleted objects do not change.

Figure 12-2.
Using the **Polyline** option of the **FILLET** tool.

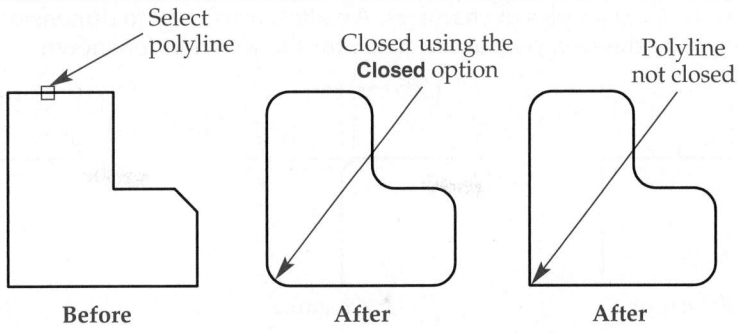

Before   After   After

Figure 12-3.
 Comparison of the **Trim** and **No trim** options of the **FILLET** tool.

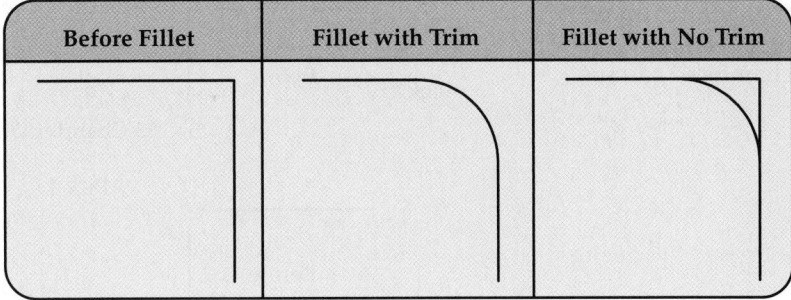

Before Fillet	Fillet with Trim	Fillet with No Trim

Multiple Option

Use the **Multiple** option to make several fillets without exiting the **FILLET** tool. The prompt for a first object repeats after each fillet is drawn. To exit, press [Enter], the space bar, [Esc], or right-click and select **Enter**. While using the **Multiple** option, you can select the **Undo** option to discard the previous fillet if necessary.

Exercise 12-2

Access the Student Web site (www.g-wlearning.com/CAD) and complete Exercise 12-2.

Using the CHAMFER Tool

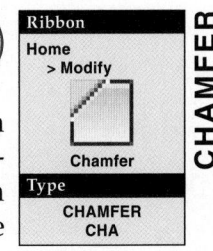

Ribbon
Home
> Modify

Chamfer

Type
CHAMFER
CHA

CHAMFER

In drafting terminology, a *chamfer* is a small, angled surface used to relieve a sharp corner. The **CHAMFER** tool allows you to draw an angled corner between intersecting and nonintersecting lines, polylines, xlines, and rays. Determine the size of a chamfer based on the distance from the corner. A 45° chamfer is the same distance from the corner in each direction. See **Figure 12-4.** Typically, two distances or one distance and one angle identify the size of a chamfer. For example, a value of .5 for both distances produces a 45° × .5 chamfer.

chamfer: A small, angled surface used to relieve a sharp corner.

Setting Chamfer Distances

Access the **CHAMFER** tool and then use the **Distance** option to specify the chamfer distances from a corner. You must set chamfer distances before you select objects. Then select the objects to chamfer. See **Figure 12-5.** AutoCAD stores the distances as the new default distances, allowing you to place additional chamfers of the same size.

Figure 12-4. Examples of chamfers. An alternative way to dimension a chamfer is to specify the angle by the size, such as 45° × .125 for the 45° chamfer shown.

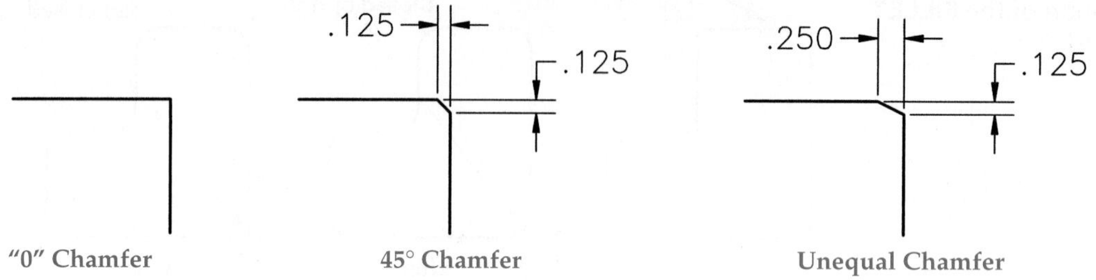

.125

.125

.250

.125

"0" Chamfer

45° Chamfer

Unequal Chamfer

Figure 12-5.
Using the **CHAMFER** tool to create chamfered corners.

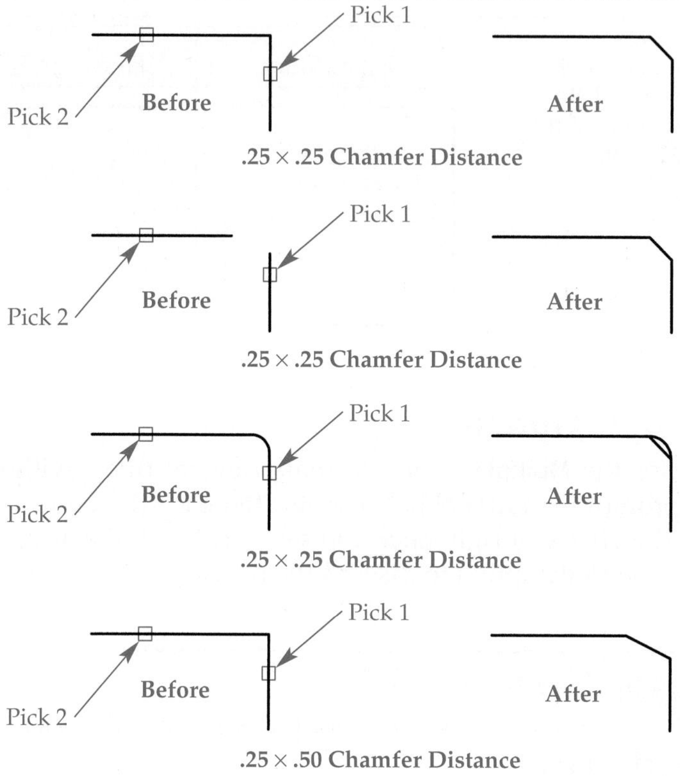

Pick 1

Pick 2   Before   After

.25 × .25 Chamfer Distance

Pick 1

Pick 2   Before   After

.25 × .25 Chamfer Distance

Pick 1

Pick 2   Before   After

.25 × .25 Chamfer Distance

Pick 1

Pick 2   Before   After

.25 × .50 Chamfer Distance

Setting Chamfer Angle

Use the **Angle** option as an alternative to setting two chamfer distances. Specify the chamfer distance along the first selected curve, followed by the chamfer angle. Now select the objects to chamfer. See **Figure 12-6.** AutoCAD stores the distance and angle, allowing you to place additional chamfers of the same size.

Method Option

AutoCAD maintains the specified chamfer distances or the distance and angle until you change the values. You can set the values for each method without affecting the other. Use the **Method** option to toggle between drawing chamfers using the **Distance** and **Angle** options.

PROFESSIONAL TIP

Use the **CHAMFER** tool to form sharp corners by specifying chamfer distances or an angle and distance of 0, or by holding [Shift] when you pick the second object.

Figure 12-6.
Using the **Angle** option of the **CHAMFER** tool with the chamfer length set at .5 and the angle set at 30°. Notice that the selection order determines where the distance and angle apply.

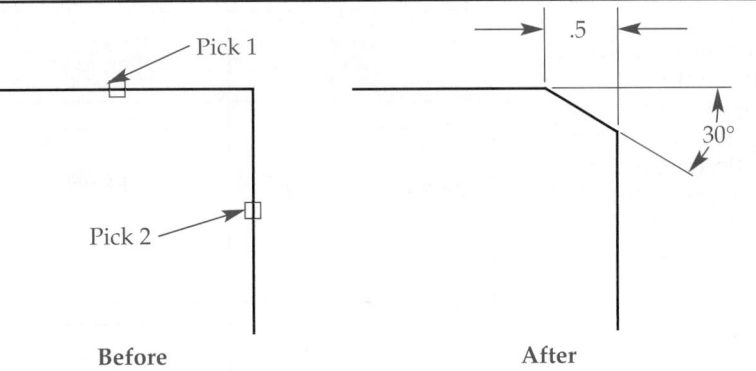

Before

After

NOTE

Only corners large enough to accept the specified chamfer size are eligible for chamfering. If the chamfer is too large, AutoCAD displays the message Distance is too large *Invalid*.

Exercise 12-3

Access the Student Web site (www.g-wlearning.com/CAD) and complete Exercise 12-3.

Additional Chamfer Options

The **CHAMFER** tool includes the same **Polyline**, **Trim**, and **Multiple** options as the **FILLET** tool. Similar rules apply when using these options with the **CHAMFER** tool. Use the **Polyline** option to chamfer all corners of a closed polyline, as shown in **Figure 12-7**. The **Trim** option controls whether the **CHAMFER** tool trims object segments that extend beyond the intersection, as shown in **Figure 12-8**. Use the **Multiple** option to make several chamfers without exiting the **CHAMFER** tool.

Exercise 12-4

Access the Student Web site (www.g-wlearning.com/CAD) and complete Exercise 12-4.

Figure 12-7.
Using the **Polyline** option of the **CHAMFER** tool. If you originally drew the polyline without using the **Close** option, the beginning corner does not chamfer.

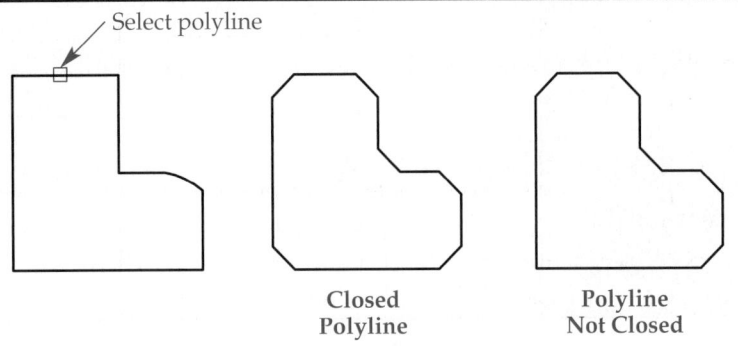

Closed Polyline

Polyline Not Closed

Figure 12-8.
Use the default **Trim** setting to trim objects. When you set the **Trim** option to **No trim**, the chamfer occurs, but chamfered objects do not change.

Before Chamfer	Chamfer with Trim	Chamfer with No Trim

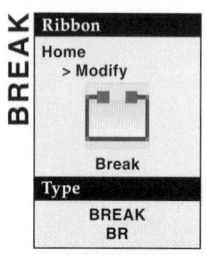

Ribbon
Home > Modify
Break
Type
BREAK BR

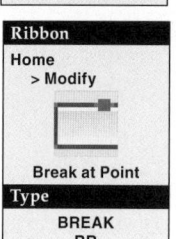

Ribbon
Home > Modify
Break at Point
Type
BREAK BR

Using the BREAK Tool

The **BREAK** tool can remove a portion of an object or split an object at a single point, depending on the points and option you select. By default, the point you pick when you select the object to break also locates the first break point. To select a different, possibly more accurate first break point, use the **First point** option at the Specify second break point or [First point]: prompt. See **Figure 12-9.**

If you select the same point for the first and second break points, the **BREAK** tool splits the object without removing a portion. At the Specify second break point or [First point]: prompt, use object snaps, coordinate entry, or enter @ to select the same coordinates as the first break point. See **Figure 12-10.** Another option is to use the **Break at Point** tool instead of the standard **BREAK** tool, which automates the process.

Select points in a counterclockwise direction when breaking circular objects to ensure that you remove the correct portion of the object. See **Figure 12-11.** Notice in **Figure 12-11** that you can break off the end of an open object by picking the first point on the object and the second point slightly beyond the end to cut off. AutoCAD selects the endpoint nearest the point you pick in space.

Figure 12-9. Using the **BREAK** tool to break an object. When you use the default method, the first pick selects the object and the first break point. Use the **First point** option to select the object to break and then specify accurate break points, such as the **Endpoint** object snaps shown.

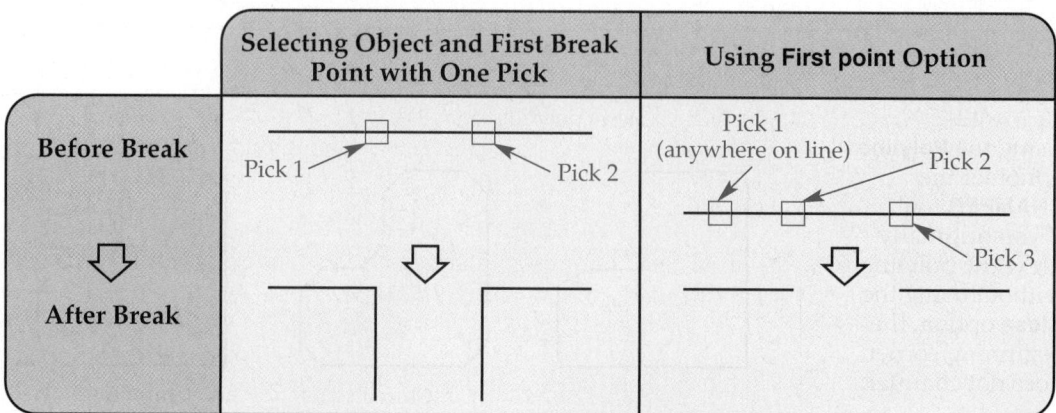

AutoCAD and Its Applications—Basics

Figure 12-10.
Using the **BREAK** tool to break an object at a single point without removing any of the object. Select the same point for the first and second break points. You can also use the **Break at Point** tool to automate the process.

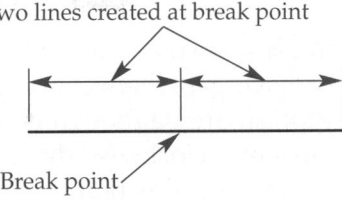

Pick Point 1, and then use object snaps, coordinate entry, or the @ option to pick the same point

Line to be broken

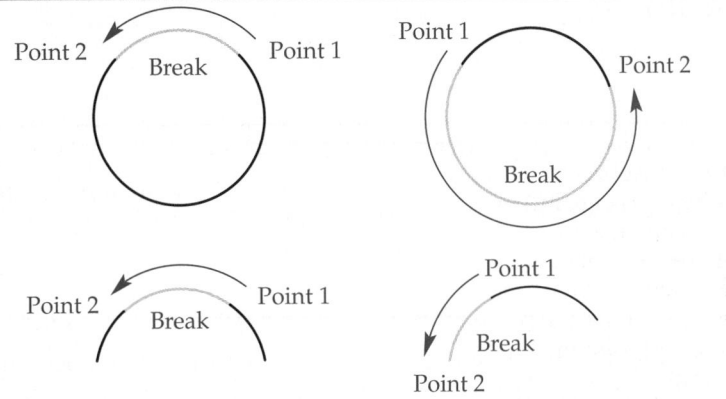

Two lines created at break point

Break point

Figure 12-11.
Select points in a counterclockwise direction when using the **BREAK** tool on circular objects, such as the circle shown here.

Point 2 — Break — Point 1

Point 1 — Point 2 — Break

Point 2 — Break — Point 1

Point 1 — Break — Point 2

PROFESSIONAL TIP

Use object snaps to pick a point accurately when using the **First point** option of the **BREAK** tool. However, it is necessary to turn running object snaps off if they conflict with points you try to pick.

Exercise 12-5

Access the Student Web site (www.g-wlearning.com/CAD) and complete Exercise 12-5.

Using the JOIN Tool

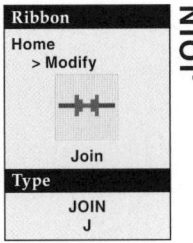

Ribbon
Home
> Modify

Join

Type

JOIN
J

JOIN

While drawing and editing, you sometimes create multiple objects that should be one object. These multiple objects are cumbersome to work with and increase the size of the drawing file. The **JOIN** tool is one option for combining lines, polylines, splines, arcs, and elliptical arcs. You can join objects of the same type, or specific combinations of objects.

Joining the Same Object Type

Access the **JOIN** tool and select, in any order, objects of the same type to join. Lines must be collinear, but can share the same endpoint, overlap, or have gaps between segments. See **Figure 12-12**. Polylines must share a common endpoint and cannot have gaps between segments or overlap. See **Figure 12-13**. The same rules apply for joining splines.

Arcs must share the same center point and radius, but can share the same endpoint, overlap, or have gaps between segments. See **Figure 12-14**. Similar rules apply for joining elliptical arcs, although elliptical arcs must share the same axes. Pick arcs or elliptical arcs in a clockwise direction to close the nearest clockwise gap, or pick in a counterclockwise direction to close the nearest counterclockwise gap. Depending on your selections, you may be prompted to convert arcs to a circle. To maintain the original object type, choose the **No** option and reselect the arcs in a counterclockwise direction.

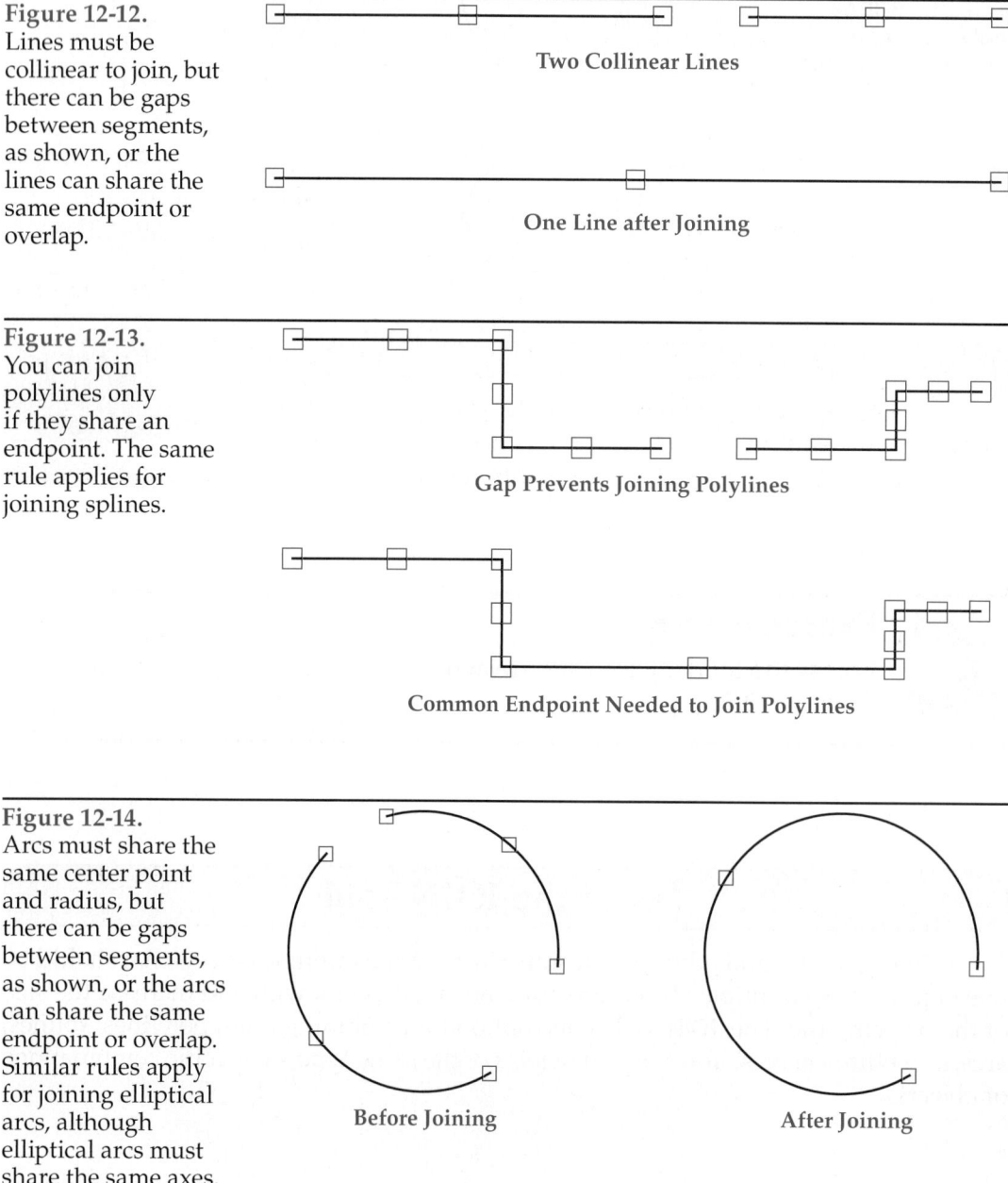

Figure 12-12.
Lines must be collinear to join, but there can be gaps between segments, as shown, or the lines can share the same endpoint or overlap.

Two Collinear Lines

One Line after Joining

Figure 12-13.
You can join polylines only if they share an endpoint. The same rule applies for joining splines.

Gap Prevents Joining Polylines

Common Endpoint Needed to Join Polylines

Figure 12-14.
Arcs must share the same center point and radius, but there can be gaps between segments, as shown, or the arcs can share the same endpoint or overlap. Similar rules apply for joining elliptical arcs, although elliptical arcs must share the same axes.

Before Joining

After Joining

AutoCAD and Its Applications—Basics

Joining Different Object Types

You can join lines, arcs, and polylines to polylines, or join lines, arcs, and polylines to splines. Access the **JOIN** tool and select the most complex object first, followed by the other objects. To join lines or arcs to a polyline, select the polyline first. To join lines, arcs, and polylines to a spline, select the spline first. Apply the same rules to join a combination of objects as to join objects of the same type. However, segments cannot have gaps or overlap. The final object becomes the most complex of the original objects.

Trimming

Use the **TRIM** tool to cut lines, polylines, circles, arcs, ellipses, splines, xlines, and rays that extend beyond an intersection. Access the **TRIM** tool, pick as many *cutting edges* as necessary, and then right-click or press [Enter] or the space bar. Then pick the objects to trim to the cutting edges. To exit, right-click or press [Enter] or the space bar. See **Figure 12-15**.

Automatic windowing with the crossing function is often the quickest and most effective method for trimming multiple objects. You can also use window or crossing polygons. The **TRIM** tool also offers **Crossing** and **Fence** options that provide standard crossing and fence selection. **Figure 12-16** shows using the **Crossing** option to trim multiple objects. **Figure 12-17** shows using the **Fence** option to trim multiple objects.

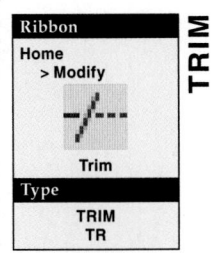

cutting edge: An object such as a line, arc, or text that defines the point (edge) at which the object you trim will be cut.

Figure 12-15.
Using the **TRIM** tool. Note the cutting edges.

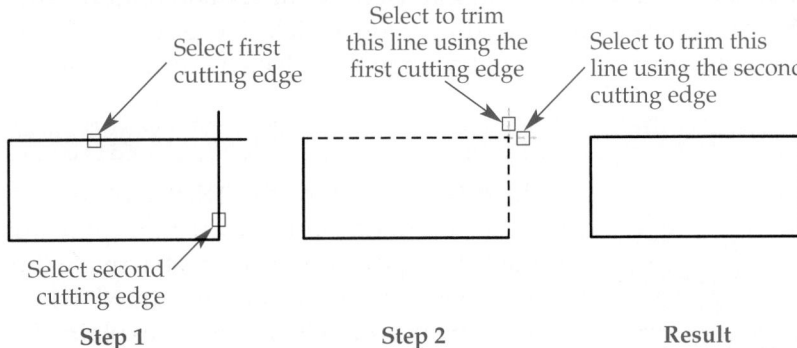

Figure 12-16.
The only objects trimmed with the **Crossing** option are those that cross the edges of the crossing window. Automatic windowing accomplishes the same task.

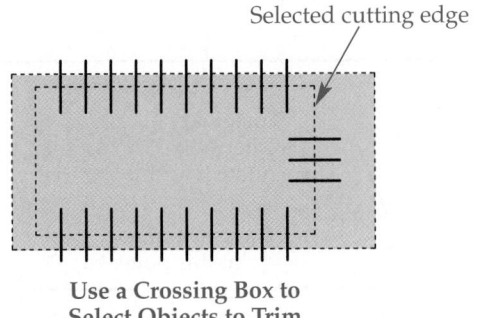

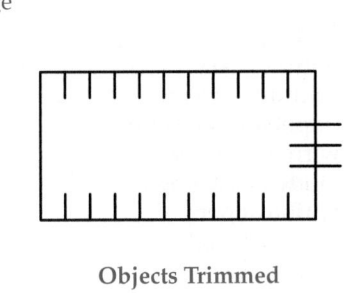

Figure 12-17. The **Fence** option allows you to select around objects. In this example, the cutting edge consists of the rectangle drawn using the **RECTANGLE** tool.

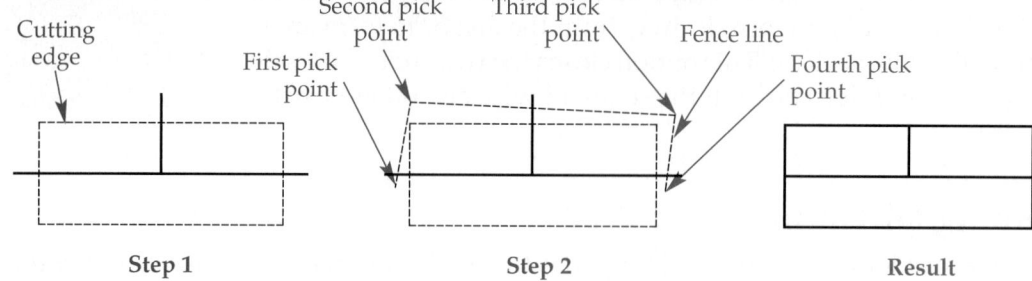

| Step 1 | Step 2 | Result |

NOTE

To access the **EXTEND** tool while using the **TRIM** tool, after selecting the cutting edge(s), hold [Shift] and pick objects to extend to the cutting edge. The **EXTEND** tool is described later in this chapter.

Trimming without Selecting a Cutting Edge

To trim objects to the nearest intersection without selecting a cutting edge, access the **TRIM** tool and, at the first Select objects or <select all>: prompt, right-click or press [Enter] or the space bar instead of picking a cutting edge. Then pick the objects to trim. You can continue selecting objects to trim without restarting the **TRIM** tool. To exit, right-click or press [Enter], the space bar, or [Esc].

Trimming to an Implied Intersection

implied intersection: The point at which objects would meet if they were extended.

Use the **Edge** option of the **TRIM** tool to trim to an *implied intersection*. The **No extend** mode is active by default, and does not allow you to trim objects that do not intersect. To trim nonintersecting objects, access the **TRIM** tool, pick the cutting edges, and select the **Edge** option followed by the **Extend** option. AutoCAD now recognizes implied intersections and allows you to pick objects to trim. See **Figure 12-18.** Adjusting the **Edge** function does not change the selected cutting edges.

NOTE

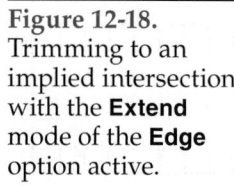

Use the **eRase** option of the **TRIM** tool to erase objects selected to trim. Use the **Undo** option to restore previously trimmed objects without leaving the tool. You must activate the **Undo** option immediately after performing an unwanted trim. The **Project** option applies to trimming 3D objects, as explained in *AutoCAD and Its Applications—Advanced*.

Figure 12-18. Trimming to an implied intersection with the **Extend** mode of the **Edge** option active.

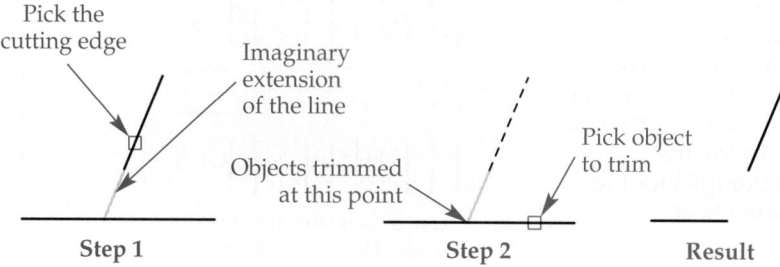

| Step 1 | Step 2 | Result |

AutoCAD and Its Applications—Basics

Extending

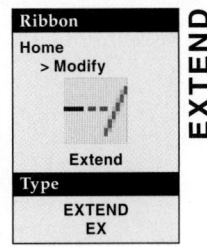

Use the **EXTEND** tool to extend lines, elliptical arcs, rays, open polylines, and arcs to meet other objects. You cannot extend a closed object because an unconnected endpoint does not exist. Access the **EXTEND** tool, pick as many *boundary edges* as necessary, and then right-click or press [Enter] or the space bar. Now pick the objects to extend to the boundary edges. To exit, right-click or press [Enter] or the space bar. See **Figure 12-19.**

Automatic windowing with the crossing function is often the quickest and most effective method for extending multiple objects. You can also use window or crossing polygons. The **EXTEND** tool also offers **Crossing** and **Fence** options that provide standard crossing and fence selection. **Figure 12-20** shows using the **Crossing** option to extend multiple objects. **Figure 12-21** shows an example of using the **Fence** option to extend multiple objects.

The **EXTEND** tool includes the same **Edge**, **Undo**, and **Project** options as the **TRIM** tool, and similar rules apply when using these options with the **EXTEND** tool. Use the **Extend** mode of the **Edge** option to extend to an implied intersection, as shown

> **boundary edge:** The edge to which objects such as lines, arcs, and polylines extend.

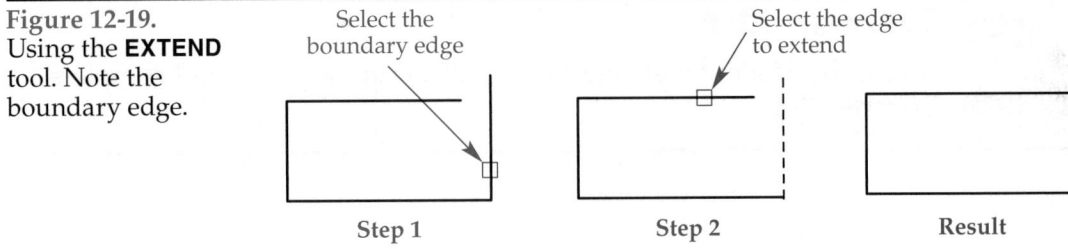

Figure 12-19. Using the **EXTEND** tool. Note the boundary edge.

Select the boundary edge — Step 1

Select the edge to extend — Step 2

Result

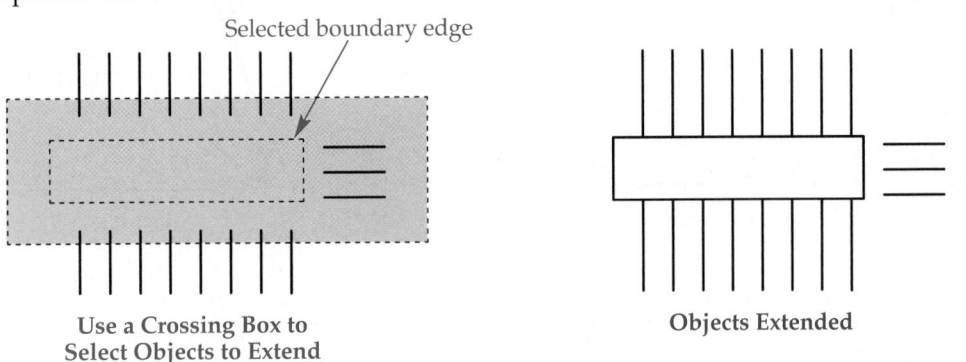

Figure 12-20. Selecting objects to extend using the **Crossing** option. Automatic windowing accomplishes the same task.

Selected boundary edge

Use a Crossing Box to Select Objects to Extend

Objects Extended

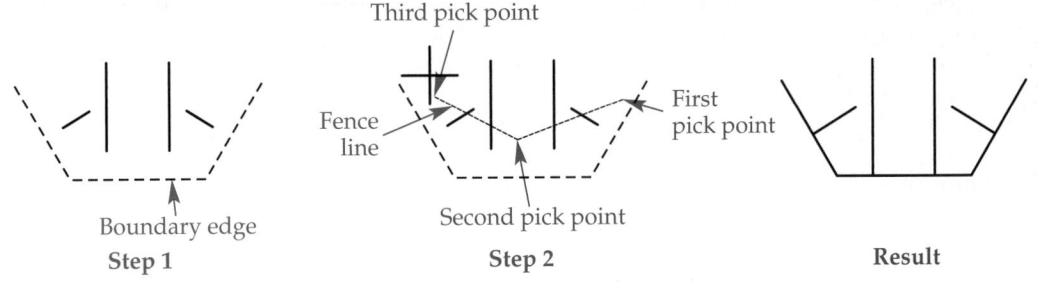

Figure 12-21. Extending multiple lines to a boundary edge using the **Fence** option.

Third pick point

Fence line

First pick point

Second pick point

Boundary edge

Step 1

Step 2

Result

in **Figure 12-22**. Select the **Undo** option immediately after performing an unwanted extend to restore previous objects without leaving the tool. The **Project** option applies to extending 3D objects, as explained in *AutoCAD and Its Applications—Advanced.*

PROFESSIONAL TIP

Figure 12-23 illustrates how to combine the **EXTEND** and **TRIM** tools, without selecting a boundary edge, to insert a wall in a floor plan. You can apply this process to a variety of applications.

NOTE

When you trim one infinite end of an xline, the object becomes a ray. When you trim both infinite ends of an xline, or the infinite end of a ray, the object becomes a line. Therefore, in many cases, you can modify xlines and rays to become a portion of the actual drawing.

Exercise 12-6

Access the Student Web site (www.g-wlearning.com/CAD) and complete Exercise 12-6.

Figure 12-22. Extending to an implied intersection with the **Extend** mode.

Pick the object to extend

Imaginary extension of the lines

Implied intersection

Select the boundary edge

Imaginary extension of the line

Command Sequence

Result

Figure 12-23.
To extend objects to the nearest intersection without selecting a boundary edge, right-click or press [Enter] or the space bar instead of picking a boundary edge. Then pick objects to extend. Hold down [Shift] to toggle between extending and trimming.

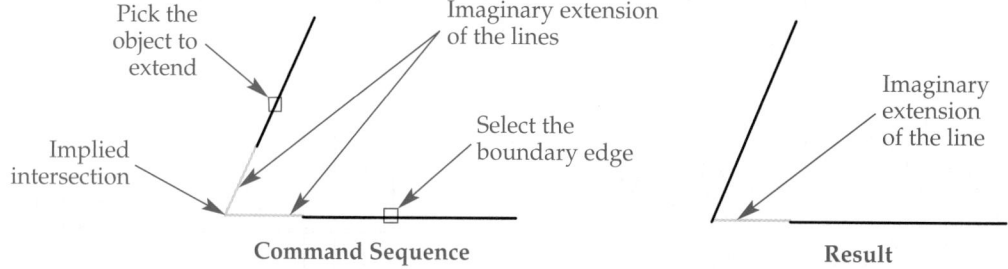

Pick Lines to Extend

Hold [Shift] and Pick Line to Trim

Finished Objects

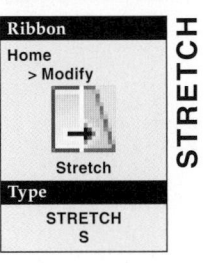

Ribbon

Home
> Modify

Stretch

Type

STRETCH
S

STRETCH

Stretching

The **STRETCH** tool allows you to modify certain dimensions of an object without changing other dimensions. In mechanical drafting, for example, you can stretch a screw body to create a longer or shorter screw. In architectural design, you can stretch room sizes to increase or decrease square footage.

Once you access the **STRETCH** tool, you must use a crossing box or crossing polygon to select only the objects to stretch. This is a very important requirement and is different from selection using other editing tools. See **Figure 12-24.** If you select using the pick box or a window, the **STRETCH** tool works like the **MOVE** tool, described in Chapter 13.

After selecting the objects to stretch, specify the *base point* from which the objects will stretch. Although the position of the base point is often not critical, you may want to select a point on an object, the corner of a view, or the center of a circle. The selection stretches or compresses as you move the crosshairs. Specify a second point to complete the stretch.

> **base point:** The initial reference point AutoCAD uses when stretching, moving, copying, and scaling objects.

PROFESSIONAL TIP

Use object snap modes while editing. For example, to stretch a rectangle to make it twice as long, use the **Endpoint** object snap to select the endpoint of the rectangle as the base point, and another **Endpoint** object snap to select the opposite endpoint of the rectangle as the second point.

Displacement Option

The **Displacement** option allows you to stretch objects relative to the origin, or 0,0,0 point. To stretch using a *displacement*, access the **STRETCH** tool and use a crossing box or crossing polygon to select only the objects to stretch. Then choose the **Displacement** option instead of defining the base point. At the Specify displacement <0,0,0>: prompt, enter an absolute coordinate to stretch the objects from the origin to the coordinate point. See **Figure 12-25.**

> **displacement:** The direction and distance in which an object moves.

Figure 12-24.
Using the **STRETCH** tool to edit specific dimensions.

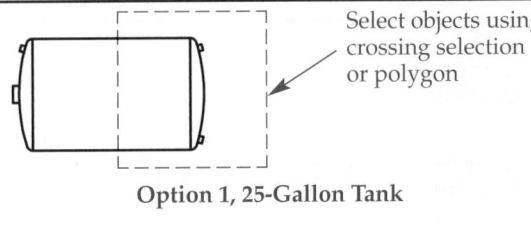

Select objects using crossing selection or polygon

Option 1, 25-Gallon Tank

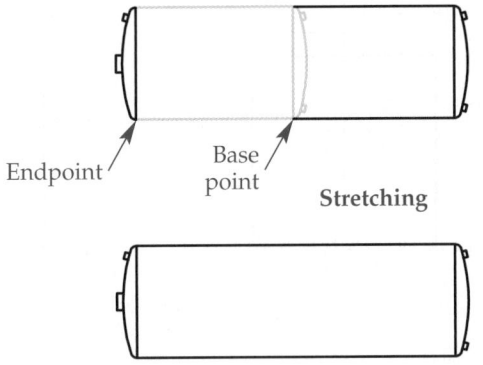

Endpoint   Base point   **Stretching**

Option 2, 50-Gallon Tank

Figure 12-25.
Using the **Displacement** option of the **STRETCH** tool. A—An example of a 1 × 1 rectangle to stretch. B—Stretching the rectangle using a 1,0 displacement.

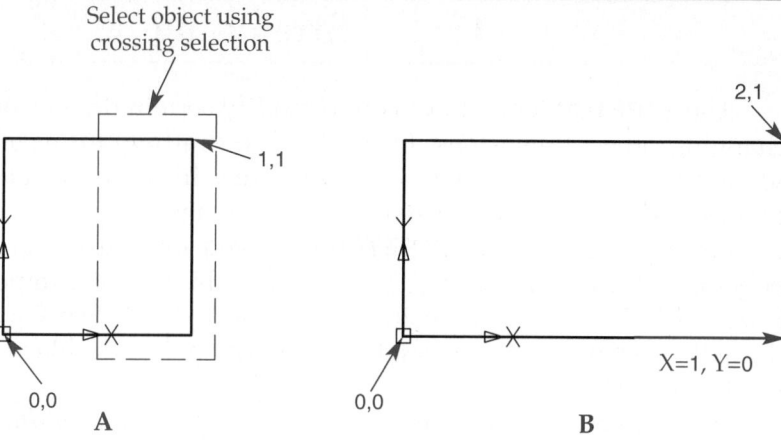

Using the First Point as Displacement

Another method for stretching an object is to use the first point as the displacement. The coordinates you use to select the base point automatically define the coordinates for the direction and distance for stretching the object. Access the **STRETCH** tool and use a crossing box or crossing polygon to select only the objects to stretch. Then specify the base point, and instead of locating the second point, right-click or press [Enter] or the space bar to accept the <use first point as displacement> default. See **Figure 12-26.**

PROFESSIONAL TIP

Objects often do not align conveniently for using crossing selection to pick objects to stretch. Consider using a crossing polygon to make selection easier. If the stretch is not as expected, press [Esc] to cancel. The **STRETCH** tool and other editing tools work well with polar tracking or **Ortho** mode.

Figure 12-26.
A—An example of a 1 × 1 rectangle to stretch. B—Stretching using the selected base point (1,1) as the displacement.

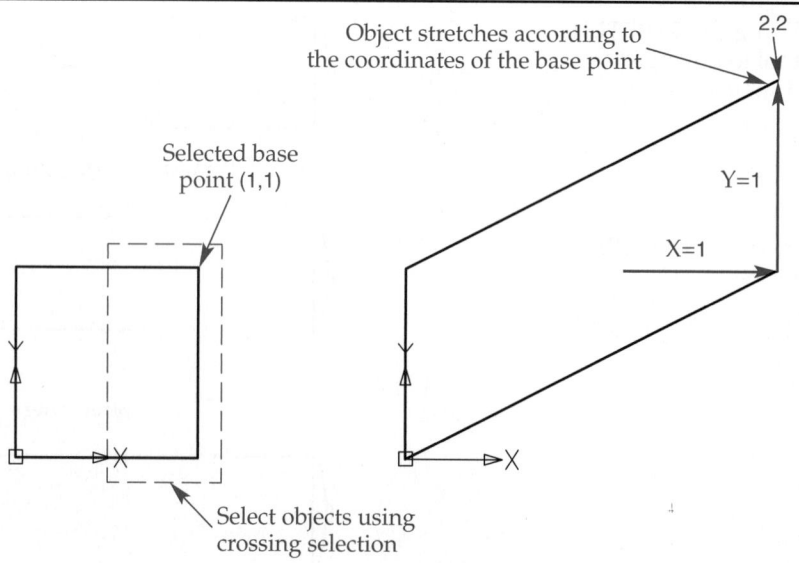

Using the LENGTHEN Tool

Use the **LENGTHEN** tool to change the length of a line, polyline, spline, or elliptical arc, or the included angle of an arc. You can only lengthen one object at a time. You cannot lengthen a closed object because an unconnected endpoint does not exist. Access the **LENGTHEN** tool and select the object to change. AutoCAD gives you the current length or included angle. The initial selection is for reference only. Choose an option and follow the prompts to complete the operation.

The **DElta** option allows you to specify a positive or negative change in length, measured from the endpoint of the selected object. The change in length occurs closest to the selection point. See **Figure 12-27**. Use the **Angle** function of the **DElta** option to change the included angle of an arc according to a specified angle. See **Figure 12-28**.

The **Percent** option allows you to change the length of an object or the angle of an arc by a specified percentage. The original length is 100 percent. Specify a percentage less than 100 to make the object shorter, or more than 100 to increase the length. See **Figure 12-29**.

Ribbon
Home
> Modify
Lengthen
Type
LENGTHEN
LEN

LENGTHEN

Figure 12-27.
Using the **DElta** option of the **LENGTHEN** tool with values of .75 and –.75.

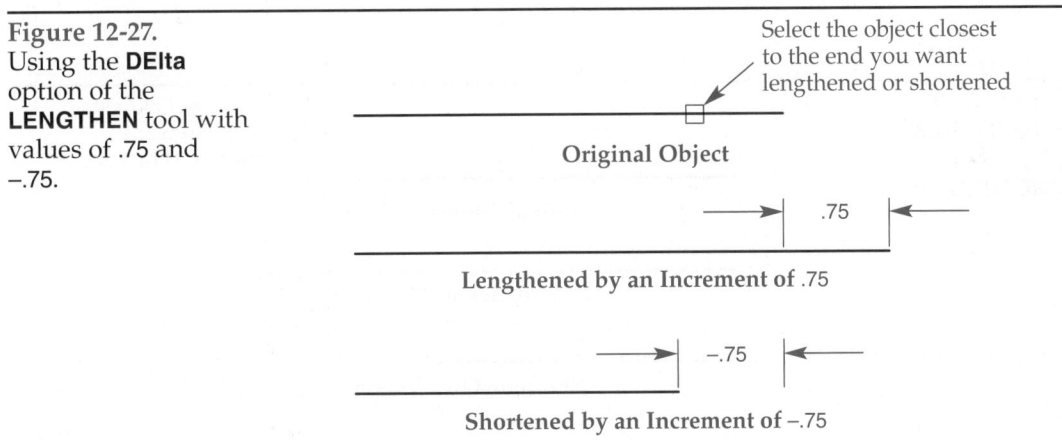

Select the object closest to the end you want lengthened or shortened

Original Object

.75

Lengthened by an Increment of .75

–.75

Shortened by an Increment of –.75

Figure 12-28.
Using the **Angle** function of the **DElta** option to increase or decrease the included angle of an arc by 45°.

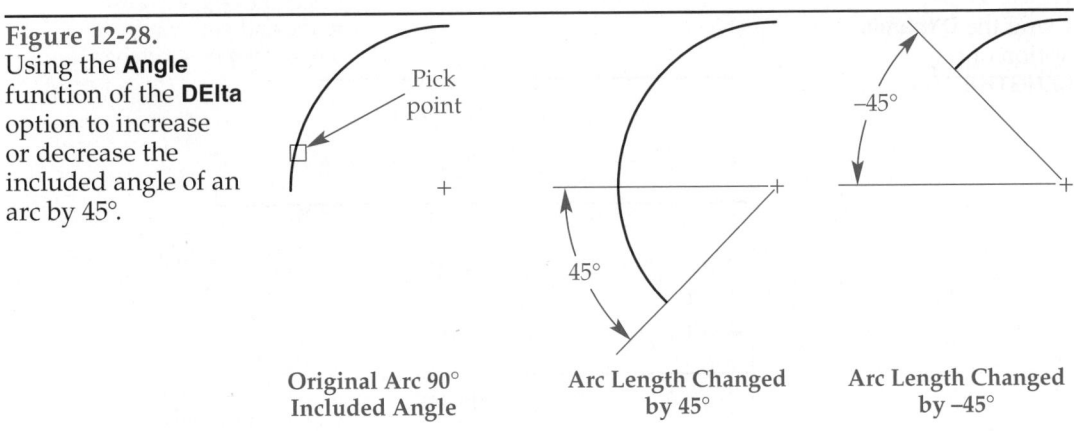

Pick point

–45°

45°

Original Arc 90°
Included Angle

Arc Length Changed by 45°

Arc Length Changed by –45°

Figure 12-29.
Examples of changing the length of a line using the **Percent** option of the **LENGTHEN** tool.

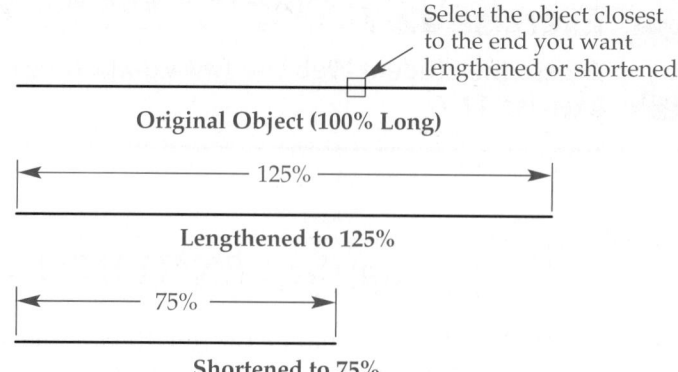

Select the object closest to the end you want lengthened or shortened

Original Object (100% Long)

────── 125% ──────

Lengthened to 125%

────── 75% ──────

Shortened to 75%

The **Total** option allows you to set the total length or angle of the object after the **LENGTHEN** operation. See **Figure 12-30.** The **DYnamic** option lets you drag the endpoint of the object to the desired length or angle using the crosshairs. See **Figure 12-31.** It is helpful to use dynamic input with polar tracking or **Ortho** mode or to have the grid and snap set to usable increments when using this option.

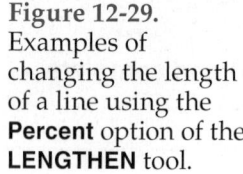

NOTE

You can only lengthen lines and arcs dynamically, and you can only decrease the length of a spline.

Figure 12-30.
Using the **Total** option of the **LENGTHEN** tool.

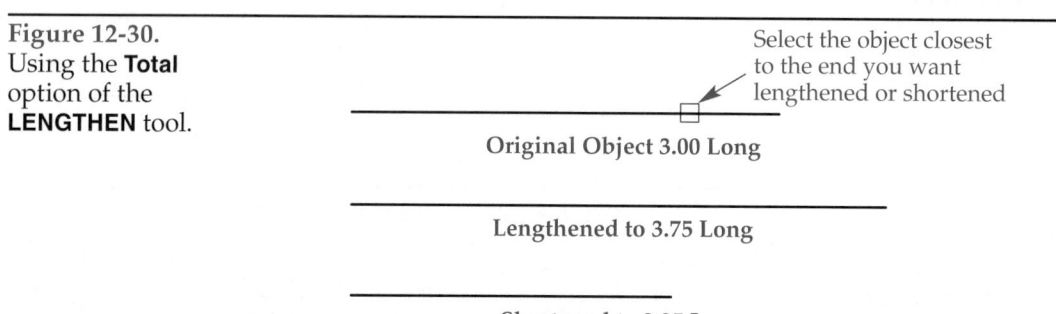

Select the object closest to the end you want lengthened or shortened

Original Object 3.00 Long

Lengthened to 3.75 Long

Shortened to 2.25 Long

Figure 12-31.
Using the **DYnamic** option of the **LENGTHEN** tool.

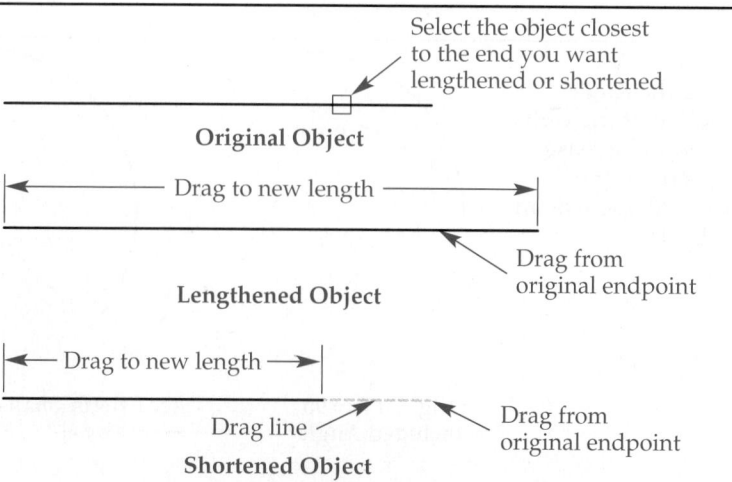

Select the object closest to the end you want lengthened or shortened

Original Object

────── Drag to new length ──────

Drag from original endpoint

Lengthened Object

── Drag to new length ──

Drag line   Drag from original endpoint

Shortened Object

You do not have to select the object before entering one of the **LENGTHEN** tool options, but doing so indicates the current length and, if the object is an arc, the angle. This is especially helpful when you are using the **Total** option.

Exercise 12-8

Access the Student Web site (www.g-wlearning.com/CAD) and complete Exercise 12-8.

Using the SCALE Tool

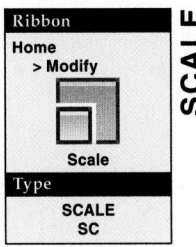

Ribbon
Home
> Modify
Scale
Type
SCALE
SC

SCALE

The **SCALE** tool allows you to proportionately enlarge or reduce the size of objects. After you access the **SCALE** tool, pick a base point to define where the increase or decrease in size occurs. The change in object size occurs away from or toward the base point during scaling. The next step is to specify the scale factor. Enter a number to indicate the amount of enlargement or reduction. For example, to make the objects twice the current size, type 2 at the Specify scale factor or [Copy/Reference] <*current*>: prompt. See Figure 12-32. You can also use coordinate entry or drawing aids to define the scale factor. Figure 12-33 provides examples of scale factors.

Figure 12-32.
Using the **SCALE** tool to make objects twice the previous size. The points associated with the selected objects adjust according to the location of the base point.

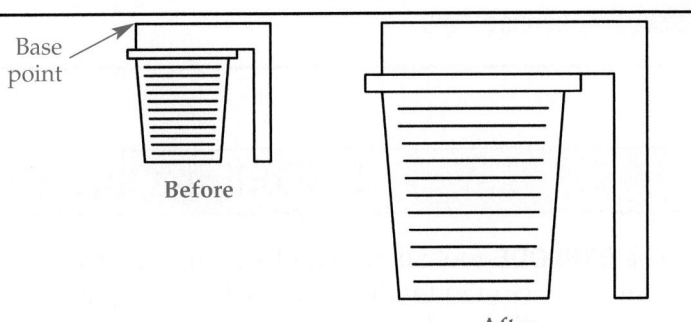

Base point

Before

After

Figure 12-33.
Scale factors and the resulting sizes.

Scale Factor	Resulting Size
10	10 times bigger
5	5 times bigger
2	2 times bigger
1	Equal to existing size
.75	3/4 of original size
.50	1/2 of original size
.25	1/4 of original size

Reference Option

The **Reference** option is an alternative to entering a scale factor, and allows you to specify a new size in relation to an existing dimension. For example, use the **Reference** option to change the size of a part with an overall dimension of 2.50″ to an overall dimension of 3.00″ proportionately. Choose the **Reference** option and specify the current length, 2.5 in the example, at the Specify reference length: prompt. Next, specify the length the dimension should be, 3 in the example. See **Figure 12-34.**

PROFESSIONAL TIP

Specify the reference length and new length using specific values; or choose points on existing objects. Picking points is especially effective when you do not know the exact reference and new lengths.

Copying While Scaling

The **Copy** option of the **SCALE** tool copies and scales the selected objects, leaving the original object unchanged. The copy moves to the specified location.

NOTE

The **SCALE** tool changes all dimensions of an object proportionately. Use the **STRETCH** or **LENGTHEN** tool to change only the length, width, or height.

Exercise 12-9

Access the Student Web site (www.g-wlearning.com/CAD) and complete Exercise 12-9.

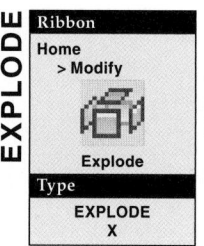

EXPLODE

Ribbon
Home
> Modify
Explode
Type
EXPLODE
X

Exploding Objects

The **EXPLODE** tool allows you to change a single object that consists of multiple items into a series of individual objects. For example, you can explode a polyline object into individual line and arc objects. See **Figure 12-35.** Another example is exploding an mtext object to create several text objects. You can explode a variety of other objects,

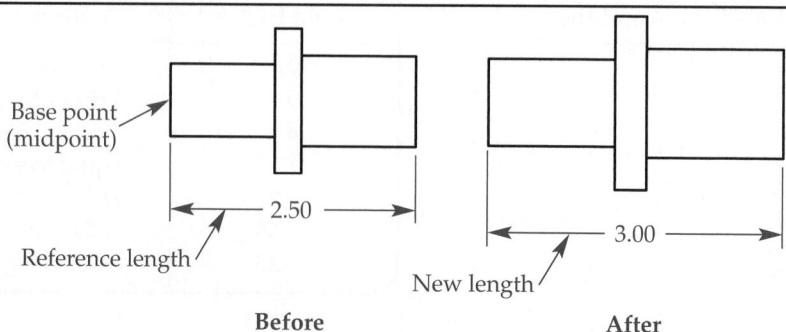

Figure 12-34.
Using the **Reference** option of the **SCALE** tool.

Base point (midpoint)

2.50

Reference length

3.00

New length

Before

After

Figure 12-35.
Using the **EXPLODE** tool to explode a polyline. In this example, the polyline becomes two collinear arcs with no polyline width or tangency information. Exploded polyline lines and arcs occur along the centerline of the original polyline.

Original Polyline   **Exploded Polyline**

including multilines, regions, dimensions, leaders, and blocks. This textbook explains these objects when appropriate. Access the **EXPLODE** tool, pick the object to explode, and right-click or press [Enter] or the space bar to cause the explosion.

CAUTION

Exploding eliminates the original object properties, characteristics, and associations. The need to explode objects is usually rare, and is only appropriate if no other tool or option can produce the desired effect.

Exercise 12-10

Access the Student Web site (www.g-wlearning.com/CAD) and complete Exercise 12-10.

Chapter Test

Answer the following questions. Write your answers on a separate sheet of paper or go to the Student Web site (www.g-wlearning.com/CAD) and complete the electronic chapter test.

1. How do you specify the size of a fillet?
2. Explain how to set the radius of a fillet to .50.
3. Which option of the **CHAMFER** tool would you use to specify a .125 × .125 chamfer?
4. What is the purpose of the **Method** option in the **CHAMFER** tool?
5. Describe the difference between the **Trim** and **No trim** options in the **CHAMFER** and **FILLET** tools.
6. How can you split an object in two without removing a portion?
7. In what direction should you pick points to break a portion out of a circle or arc?
8. What tool can you use to combine two collinear lines into a single line object?
9. What two requirements must be met before you can join two arcs?
10. Name the tool that trims an object to a cutting edge.
11. Which tool performs the opposite function of the **EXTEND** tool?
12. Name the tool associated with boundary edges.
13. Name the **TRIM** and **EXTEND** tool option that allows you to trim or extend to an implied intersection.
14. Which panel of the ribbon contains the **TRIM**, **EXTEND**, and **STRETCH** tools?
15. List two locations drafters normally choose as the base point when using the **STRETCH** tool.
16. Define the term *displacement*, as it relates to the **STRETCH** tool.
17. Identify the **LENGTHEN** tool option that corresponds to each of the following descriptions:
    A. Allows a positive or negative change in length from the endpoint.
    B. Changes a length or an arc angle by a percentage of the total.
    C. Sets the total length or angle to the value specified.
    D. Drags the endpoint of the object to the desired length or angle.
18. What tool would you use to reduce the size of an entire drawing by one-half?
19. Write the command aliases for the following tools:
    A. **CHAMFER**
    B. **FILLET**
    C. **BREAK**
    D. **TRIM**
    E. **EXTEND**
    F. **SCALE**
    G. **LENGTHEN**
20. Which tool removes all width characteristics and tangency information from a polyline?

Drawing Problems

Start AutoCAD if it is not already started. Start a new drawing for each problem using an appropriate template of your choice. The template should include layers, text styles, and table styles, when necessary, for drawing the given objects. Add layers, text styles, and table styles as needed. Draw all objects using appropriate layers, text styles, table styles, justification, and format. Follow the specific instructions for each problem. Use only drawing and editing tools and techniques you have already learned. Do not draw dimensions. Use your own judgment and approximate dimensions when necessary.

▼ Basic

1. Draw Object A using the **LINE** and **ARC** tools. Make sure the corners overrun and center the arc on the lines, but the arc should not touch the lines. Use the **TRIM**, **EXTEND**, and **STRETCH** tools to make Object B. Save the drawing as P12-1.

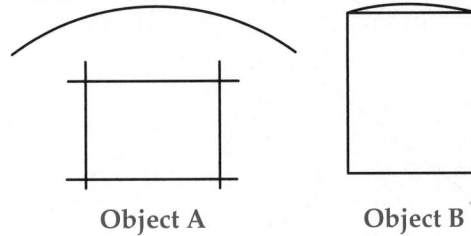

2. Open P12-1 and save the file as P12-2. The P12-2 file should be active. Use the **STRETCH** tool to convert Object A to Object B. Resave the drawing.

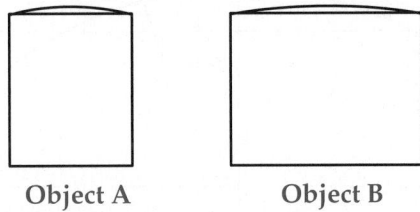

3. Refer to **Figure 12-24** in this chapter. Draw the object shown in Option 1. Stretch the object to twice its length, as shown in Option 2. Stretch the object again to one and a half times its length. *Hint:* Use endpoint and midpoint object snap modes to stretch accurately. Save the drawing as P12-3.

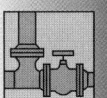

4. Draw the part view shown. Use the **CHAMFER** tool to create the inclined surface. Save the drawing as P12-4.

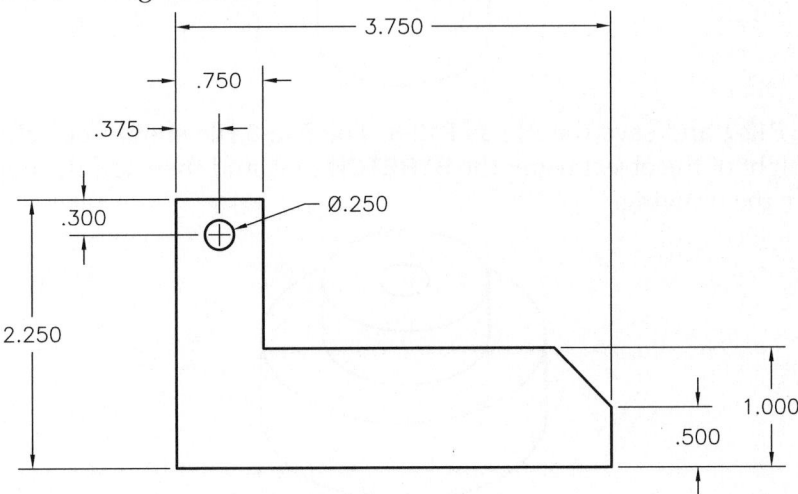

▼ Intermediate

5. Draw the wrench shown. Save the drawing as P12-5.

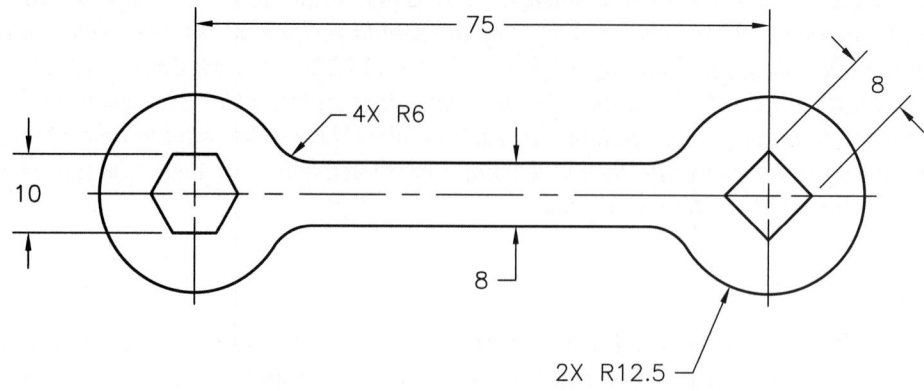

6. Draw the part view shown. Save the drawing as P12-6.

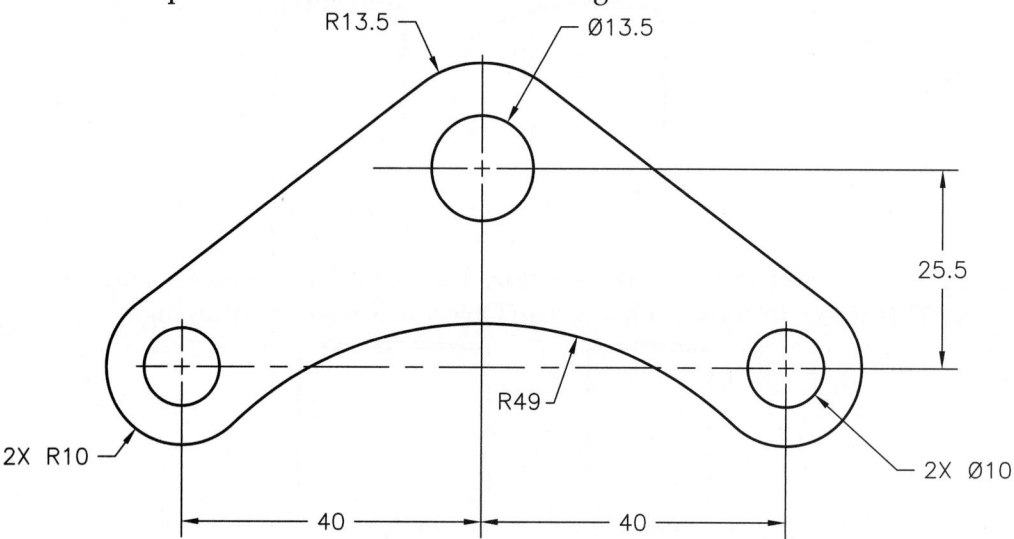

7. Draw the bushing shown using the **ELLIPSE** and **LINE** tools. Draw the ellipses using a 30° rotation angle. Use the **BREAK** or **TRIM** tool when drawing and editing the lower ellipse. Save the drawing as P12-7.

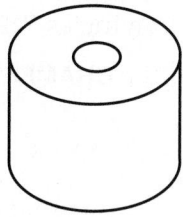

8. Open P12-7 and save the file as P12-8. The P12-8 file should be active. Shorten the height of the object using the **STRETCH** tool, and then add the object shown. Resave the drawing.

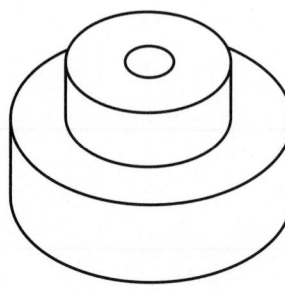

9. Use the **TRIM** and **OFFSET** tools to assist drawing the part view shown. Save the drawing as P12-9.

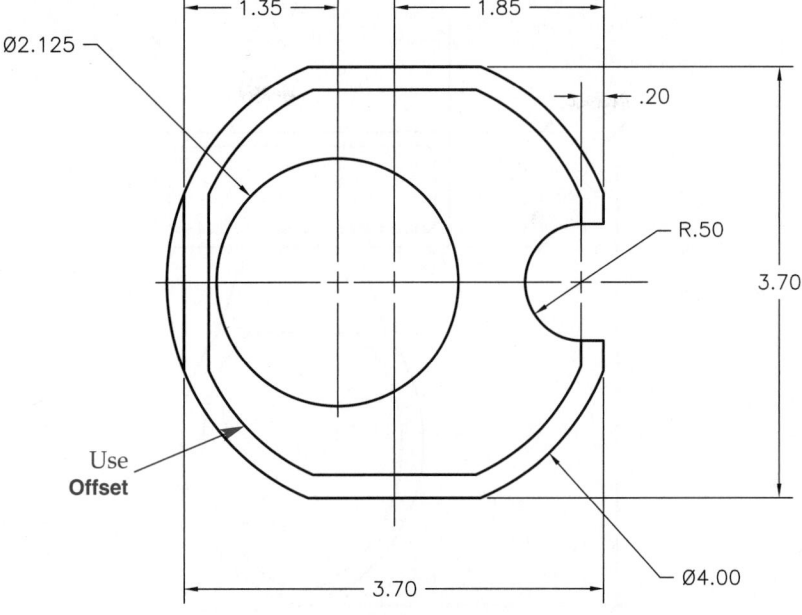

10. Draw the plate shown. Use the **FILLET** tool where appropriate. Save the drawing as P12-10.

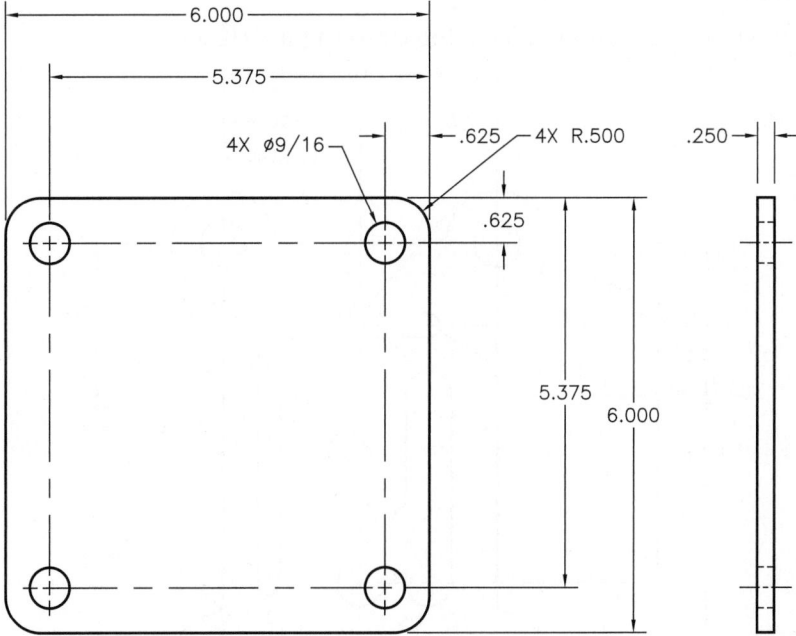

11. Draw the toilet shown. Use dimensions of your choice for undimensioned objects. Save the drawing as P12-11.

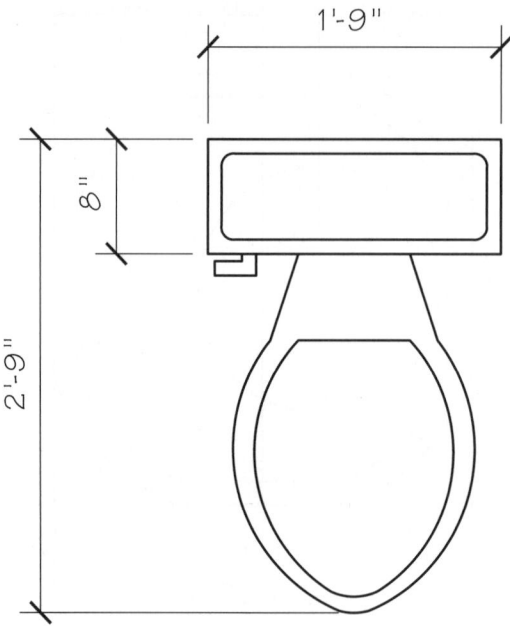

▼ Advanced

12. Draw the part view shown. Save the drawing as P12-12.

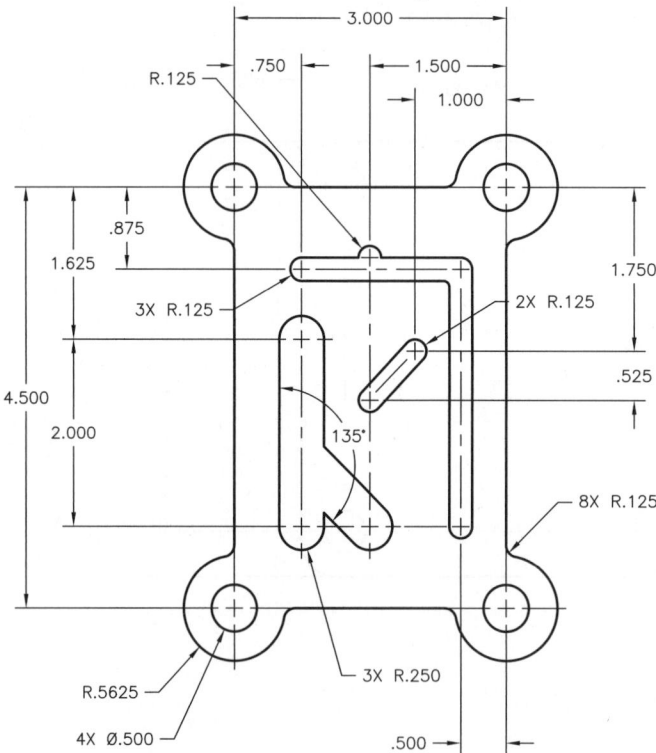

13. Draw the housing shown. Add rounds using the **FILLET** tool and chamfers using the **CHAMFER** tool. Use the trim mode setting to your advantage. Save the drawing as P12-13.

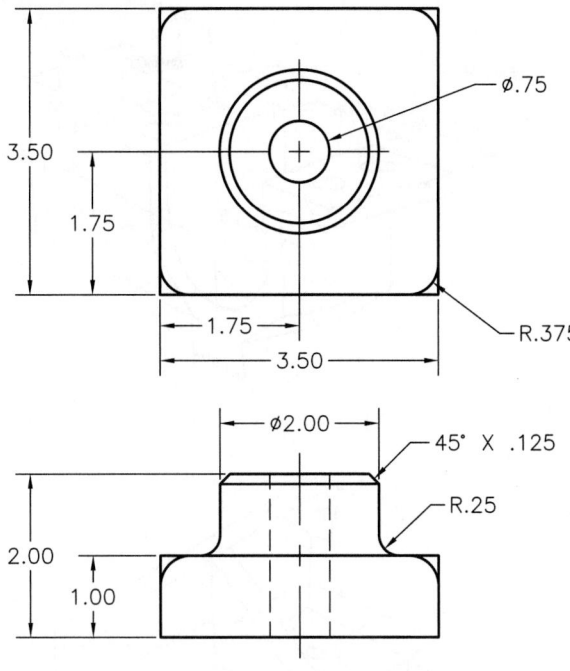

14. Draw the beam wrap detail shown. Save the drawing as P12-14.

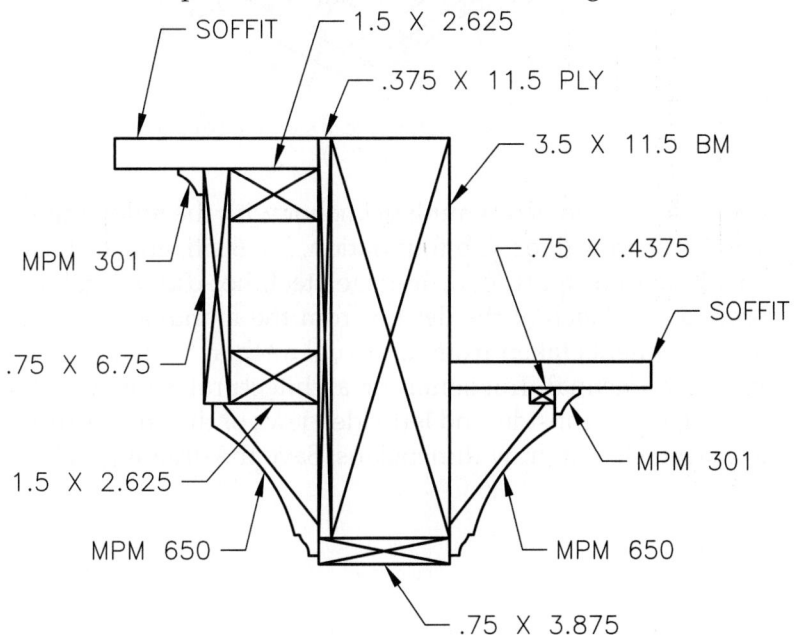

For Problems 15 and 16, draw the orthographic views needed to describe the part completely. Save the drawings as **P12-15** *and* **P12-16**.

15.

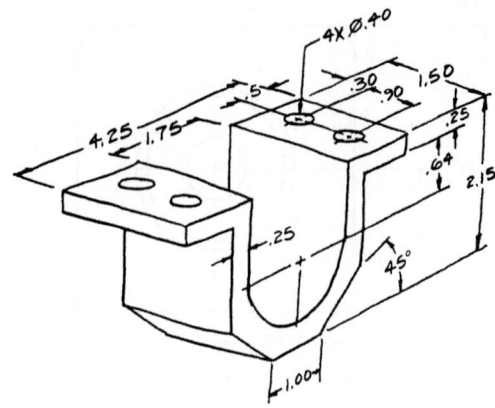

Journal Bracket (Engineer's Rough Sketch)

16.

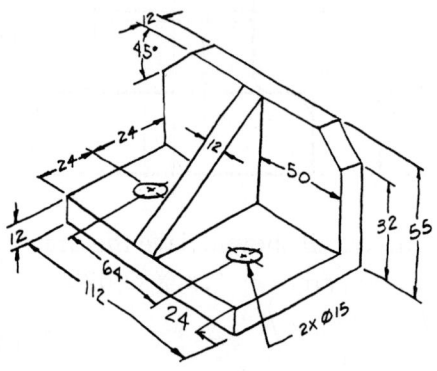

Angle Bracket (Engineer's Rough Sketch)
(Metric)

17. Research the specifications of a mudsill anchor with the following requirements: appropriate for stem wall or slab foundation, 2 × 6 sill, attaches using 10d nails, minimum 700-pound uplift load, 16-gage steel, hot-dipped galvanized. Create a dimensioned 2D sketch of the design from the manufacturer's specifications, or from measurements taken from an actual anchor. Start a new drawing from scratch or use a decimal, fractional, or architectural template of your choice. Draw the front, top, right-side, and left-side views of the anchor from your sketch using the 0 layer. Do not draw dimensions. Save the drawing as P12-17.

AutoCAD Certified Associate Exam Practice

Answer the following questions. Write your answers on a separate sheet of paper.

1. Which of the following can you use to extend two line segments to meet exactly at a sharp point? *Select all that apply.*
   A. **CHAMFER** tool with a distance of 0
   B. **Extend** mode of the **EXTEND** tool
   C. **Extend** mode of the **TRIM** tool
   D. **FILLET** tool with a radius of 0
   E. **LENGTHEN** tool with a delta of 0

2. Which of the following tools can resize a rectangle from 2″ × 4″ to 2″ × 8″ in a single operation? *Select all that apply.*
   A. **EXTEND**
   B. **JOIN**
   C. **LENGTHEN**
   D. **SCALE**
   E. **STRETCH**

3. Which keyboard key or keys can you press to trim an object while the **EXTEND** tool is active? *Select the one item that best answers the question.*
   A. [Alt]
   B. [Ctrl]
   C. [F2]
   D. [Shift]
   E. [Shift]+[Ctrl]

AutoCAD Certified Professional Exam Practice

Follow the instructions in each problem. Write your answers on a separate sheet of paper.

1. **Navigate to this chapter on the Student Web site and open CPE-12fillet.dwg.**

   Use an appropriate option of the **FILLET** tool to round all of the corners of the polyline using a fillet radius of 1.5 as shown in the figure. What are the coordinates of Point 1 (the center of the bottom-right radius)?

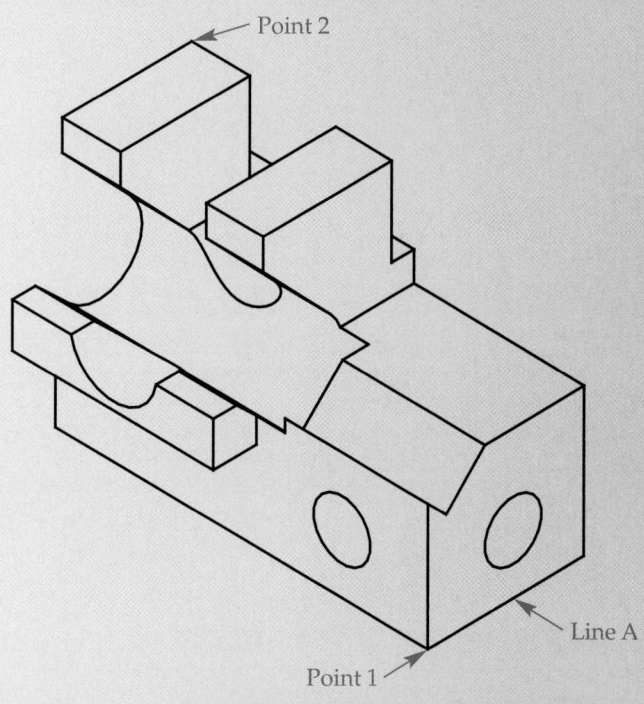

2. **Navigate to this chapter on the Student Web site and open CPE-12scale.dwg.**

Enlarge the entire object using the **Reference** option of the **SCALE** tool. Use Point 1 as the base point, and use Line A to set the reference length. Specify a new length of 1.35. Zoom out to see the result. What are the coordinates of Point 2?

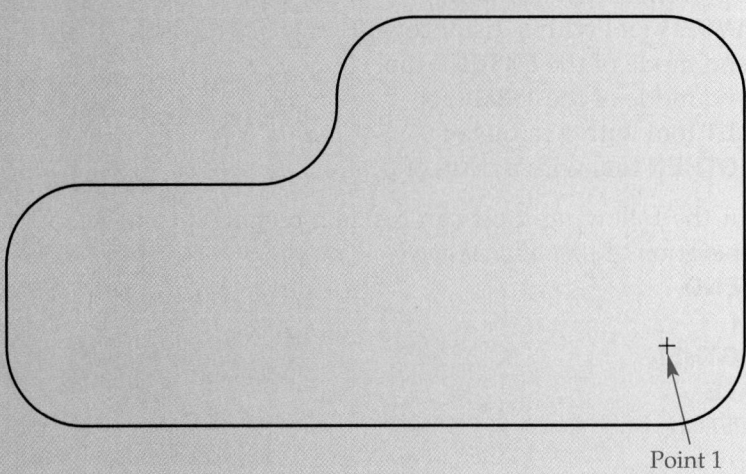

Point 1

Arranging and Patterning Objects

Learning Objectives

After completing this chapter, you will be able to do the following:

✓ Relocate objects using the **MOVE** tool.
✓ Change the angular positions of objects using the **ROTATE** tool.
✓ Use the **ALIGN** tool to move and rotate objects at the same time.
✓ Make copies of objects using the **COPY** tool.
✓ Draw mirror images of objects using the **MIRROR** tool.
✓ Use the **REVERSE** tool.
✓ Create patterns of objects using the **ARRAY** tool.

This chapter explains methods for arranging and patterning objects using basic editing tools. Use editing tools to complete common drafting tasks, improve efficiency, and modify drawings. Editing tools include many options. As you work through this chapter, experiment with each option to see which is most effective for different situations.

Moving Objects

Use the **MOVE** tool to move objects to a different location. Access the **MOVE** tool and select objects to move. At the next prompt, specify the base point from which the objects will move. Although the position of the base point is often not critical, you may want to select a point on an object, the corner of a view, or the center of a circle. The selection moves as you move the crosshairs. Specify a second point to complete the move. See **Figure 13-1**.

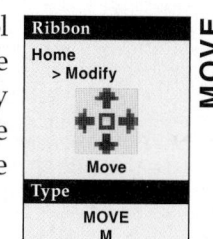

Ribbon	MOVE
Home	
> Modify	
Move	
Type	
MOVE	
M	

Displacement Option

The **Displacement** option allows you to move objects relative to the origin, or 0,0,0 point. To move using a displacement, access the **MOVE** tool and select objects to move. Then choose the **Displacement** option instead of defining the base point. At the Specify displacement <0,0,0>: prompt, enter an absolute coordinate to move the objects from the origin to the coordinate point. See **Figure 13-2**.

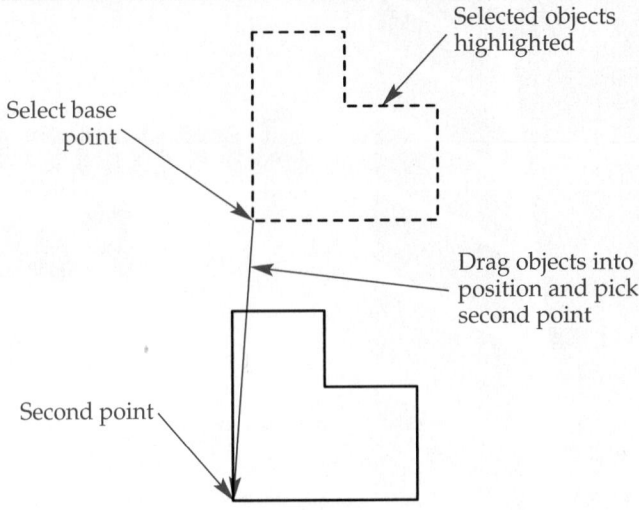

Figure 13-1.
Using the **MOVE** tool to relocate objects.

Selected objects highlighted

Select base point

Drag objects into position and pick second point

Second point

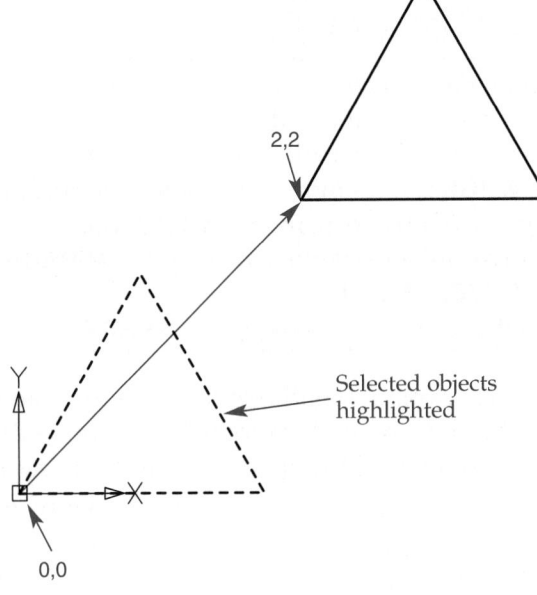

Figure 13-2.
Using the **Displacement** option of the **MOVE** tool to move objects. In this example, the origin is the base point and the absolute coordinate point 2,2 is the displacement.

2,2

Selected objects highlighted

0,0

Using the First Point As Displacement

Another method for moving an object is to use the first point as the displacement. The coordinates you use for the base point automatically define the coordinates for the direction and the distance for moving the object. Access the **MOVE** tool and select objects to move. Then specify the base point, and instead of locating the second point, right-click or press [Enter] or the space bar to accept the <use first point as displacement> default. See **Figure 13-3.**

PROFESSIONAL TIP

Use object snap modes while editing. For example, to move an object to the center of a circle, use the **Center** object snap mode to select the center of the circle.

Figure 13-3.
Moving a circle
using the selected
base point, 1,1 in
this example, as the
displacement.

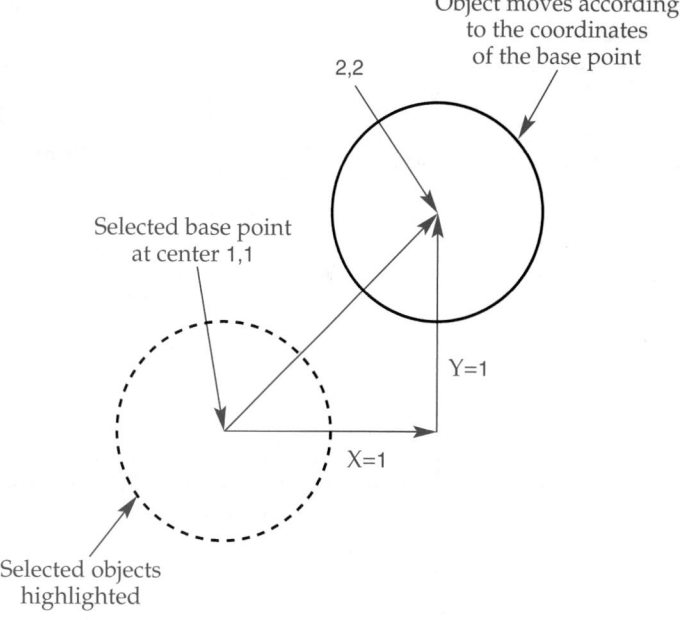

Object moves according
to the coordinates
of the base point

2,2

Selected base point
at center 1,1

Y=1

X=1

Selected objects
highlighted

Exercise 13-1

Access the Student Web site (www.g-wlearning.com/CAD) **and complete Exercise 13-1.**

Rotating Objects

Use the **ROTATE** tool to rotate objects. For example, rotate furniture to adjust an interior design plan, or rotate the north arrow on a site plan. Access the **ROTATE** tool and select objects to rotate. Proceed to the next prompt and specify the base point, or axis of rotation, around which the objects rotate. Next, enter a value or pick a point to specify a rotation angle at the Specify rotation angle or [Copy/Reference] <*current*>: prompt. See **Figure 13-4.**

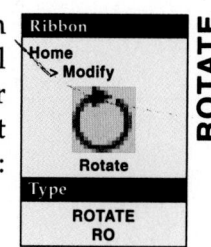

Reference Option

The **Reference** option is an alternative to entering a rotation angle, and allows you to specify a new angle in relation to an existing angle. For example, use the **Reference** option to rotate a north arrow from 150° to 90°. Choose the **Reference** option and specify the current angle, 150° in the example, at the Specify reference angle: prompt. Next, specify the angle the objects should be, 90° in the example. See **Figure 13-5A.**

PROFESSIONAL TIP

Specify the reference and new angles using specific values; or choose points, often on existing objects, as shown in **Figure 13-5B.** Picking points is especially effective when you do not know the exact reference and new angles.

Figure 13-4. Rotating a north arrow on a site plan –30° (330°) and 30°.

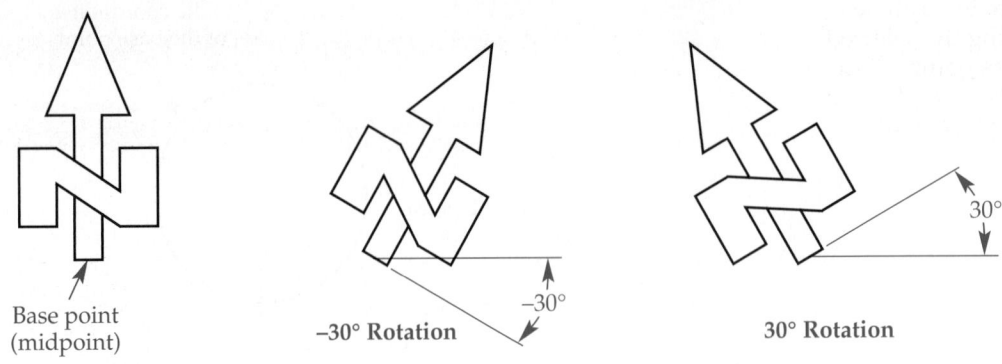

Base point
(midpoint)

–30° Rotation

30° Rotation

Figure 13-5. Using the **Reference** option of the **ROTATE** tool to rotate a north arrow on a site plan according to the current angle of the objects. A—Entering reference angles. B—Selecting points on a reference line.

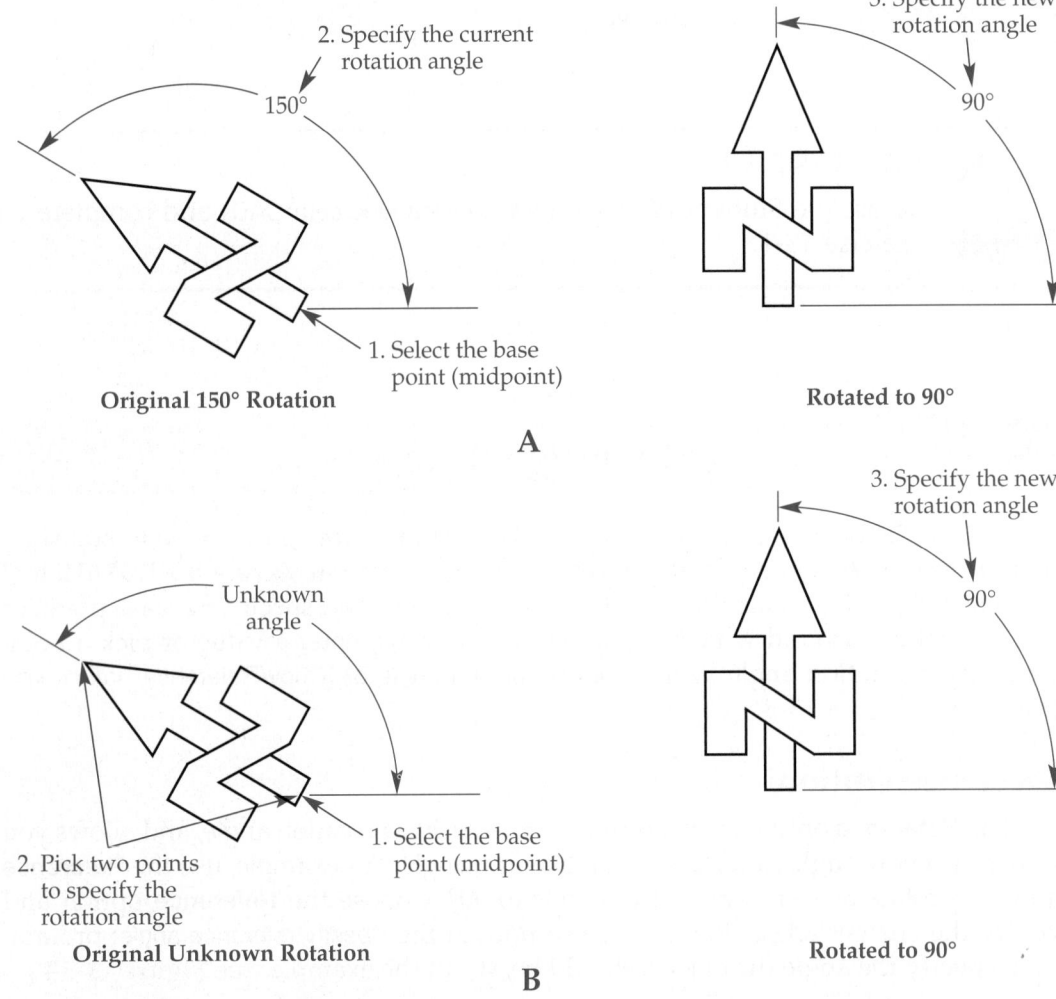

2. Specify the current
rotation angle

150°

1. Select the base
point (midpoint)

Original 150° Rotation

3. Specify the new
rotation angle

90°

Rotated to 90°

A

Unknown
angle

1. Select the base
point (midpoint)

2. Pick two points
to specify the
rotation angle

Original Unknown Rotation

3. Specify the new
rotation angle

90°

Rotated to 90°

B

Copying While Rotating

The **Copy** option of the **ROTATE** tool copies and rotates the selected objects, leaving the original object unchanged. The copy rotates to the specified angle.

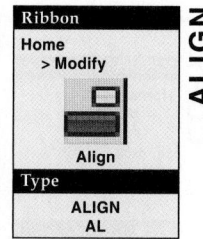

Exercise 13-2

Access the Student Web site (www.g-wlearning.com/CAD) and complete Exercise 13-2.

Aliging Objects

Use the **ALIGN** tool to move and rotate objects in one operation. The **ALIGN** tool is primarily meant for 3D applications, but it can be used for 2D drawings. Access the **ALIGN** tool and select objects to align. Then specify *source points* and *destination points*. Pick the first source point, followed by the first destination point. Then pick the second source point and the second destination point. Two source and destination points are adequate for aligning 2D objects. Right-click or press [Enter] or the space bar when the prompt requests the third source and destination points. See **Figure 13-6**. The last prompt allows you to change the size of the source objects. Choose **Yes** to scale the source objects if the distance between the source points is different from the distance between the destination points. See **Figure 13-7**.

source points: Points to define the original position of an object during an **ALIGN** operation.

destination points: Points to define the new location of objects during an **ALIGN** operation.

Figure 13-6. Using the **ALIGN** tool to move and rotate a kitchen cabinet layout against a wall. Select the **No** choice of the **Scale** option to apply this example.

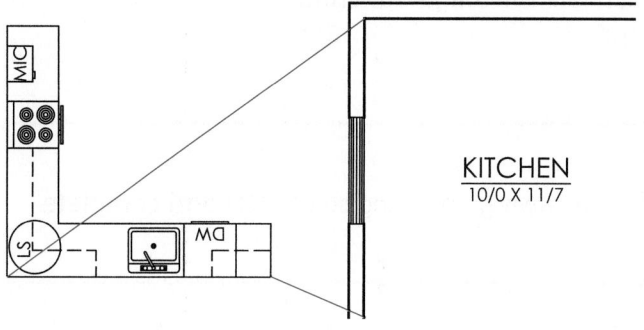
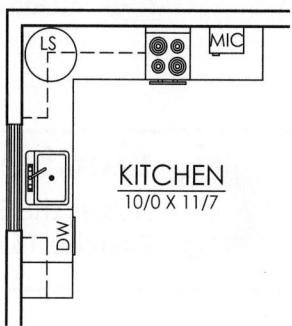

Figure 13-7. Select the **Yes** choice of the **Scale** option of the **ALIGN** tool to change the size of an object during the alignment.

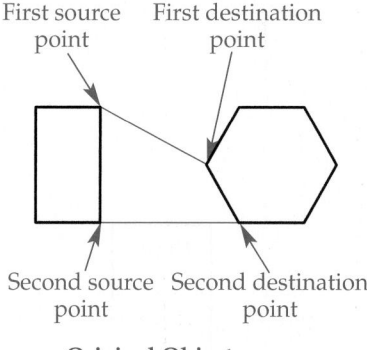
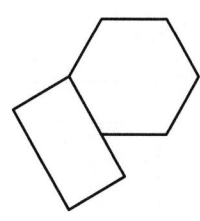
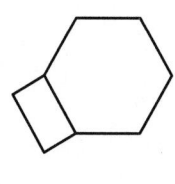

First source point   First destination point

Second source point   Second destination point

Original Objects   **Rectangle Not Scaled**   **Rectangle Scaled**

Exercise 13-3

Access the Student Web site (www.g-wlearning.com/CAD) and complete Exercise 13-3.

Access the Student Web site (www.g-wlearning.com/CAD) and complete Exercise 13-3.

COPY

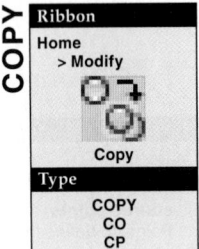

Ribbon
Home
> Modify

Copy

Type
COPY
CO
CP

Copying Objects

Use the **COPY** tool to copy objects. The **COPY** tool is similar to the **MOVE** tool, except that when you pick a second point, the original objects remain in place and a copy appears. See **Figure 13-8**. Access the **COPY** tool, select objects to copy, specify a base point, and pick a location to locate the copy. By default, you can continue creating copies of the selected objects by specifying additional points. Press [Enter] or the space bar or right-click and select **Enter** to exit.

The **COPY** tool provides the same options as the **MOVE** tool, allowing you to specify a base point and a second point, choose a displacement using the **Displacement** option, or define the first point as displacement.

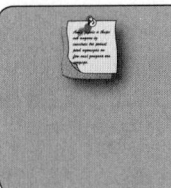

> **NOTE**
>
> The **Multiple** copy mode is active by default and allows you to create several copies of the same object using a single **COPY** operation. To make a single copy and exit the tool after placing the copy, use the **mOde** option and activate the **Single** function.

Exercise 13-4

Access the Student Web site (www.g-wlearning.com/CAD) and complete Exercise 13-4.

Access the Student Web site (www.g-wlearning.com/CAD) and complete Exercise 13-4.

Figure 13-8.
Using the **COPY** tool to duplicate objects.

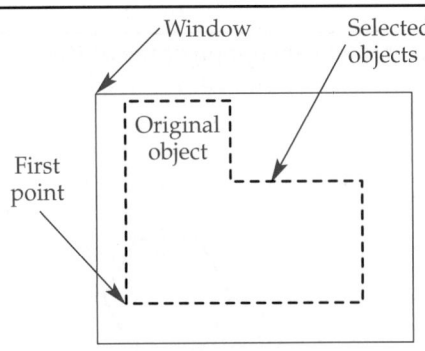
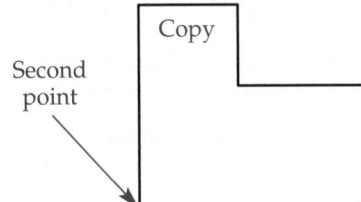

AutoCAD and Its Applications—Basics

Mirroring Objects

Ribbon

Home
> Modify

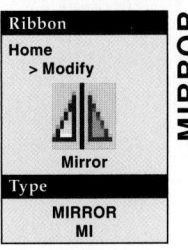

Mirror

Type

MIRROR
MI

MIRROR

The **MIRROR** tool allows you to reflect, or mirror, objects. For example, in mechanical drafting, mirror a part to form the opposite component of a symmetrical assembly. In architectural drafting, mirror a floor plan to create a duplex residence or to accommodate a different site orientation. Access the **MIRROR** tool and select the objects to mirror. Then create an imaginary *mirror line* at any angle by specifying two points. After you locate the second mirror line point, you have the option to delete the original objects. See **Figure 13-9**.

mirror line: The line of symmetry across which objects are mirrored.

NOTE

The **MIRRTEXT** system variable, which is set to 0 by default, prevents text from reversing during a mirror operation. Change the **MIRRTEXT** value to 1 to mirror text in relation to the original object. See **Figure 13-10**. Backward text is generally not acceptable, except for applications such as reverse imaging.

Figure 13-9. Using the **MIRROR** tool to reflect objects over an imaginary mirror line. You have the option of erasing the original objects.

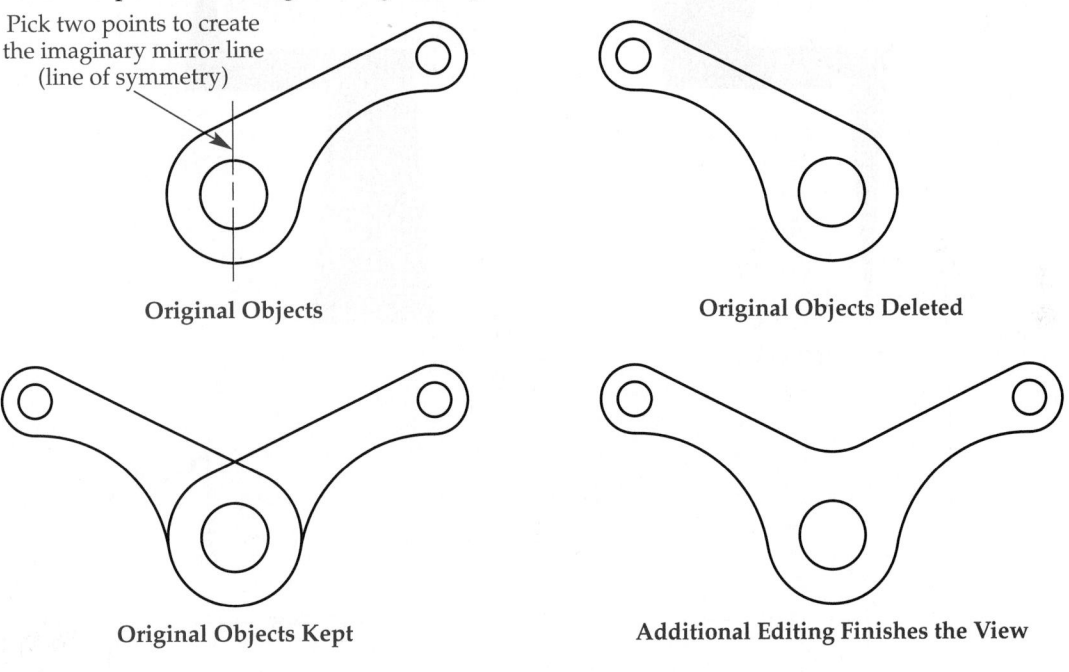

Figure 13-10. The **MIRRTEXT** system variable options.

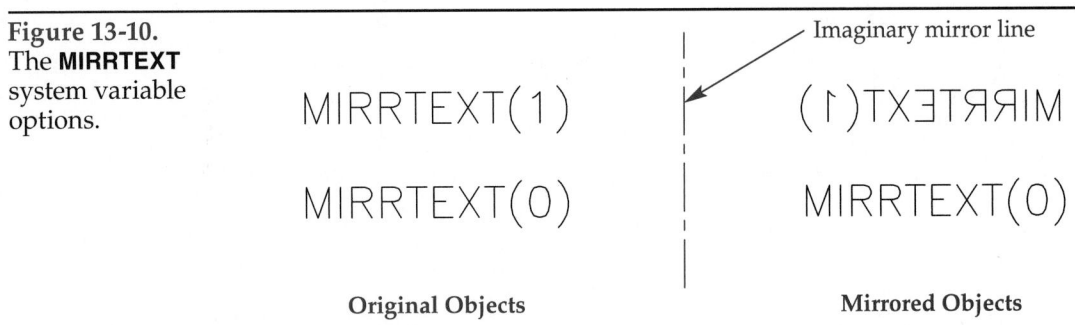

Exercise 13-5

Access the Student Web site (www.g-wlearning.com/CAD) and complete Exercise 13-5.

Reversing an Object's Point Calculation

REVERSE

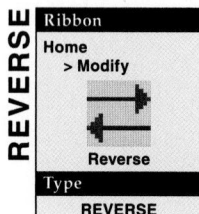

Ribbon
Home > Modify
Reverse
Type
REVERSE

The **REVERSE** tool reverses the calculation of points along lines, polylines, splines, and helixes. The previous start point becomes the new endpoint, and the previous endpoint becomes the new start point. As shown in Figure 13-11, reversing is apparent when applied to specific objects, such as polylines with varying width and lines or polylines assigned a linetype that includes text. AutoCAD attempts to orient text included with linetypes correctly by default for all objects. You should typically avoid reversing text included with linetypes.

Figure 13-11. A—Using the **REVERSE** tool to reverse a polyline with varying width. B—Reversing a polyline assigned a linetype that includes text.

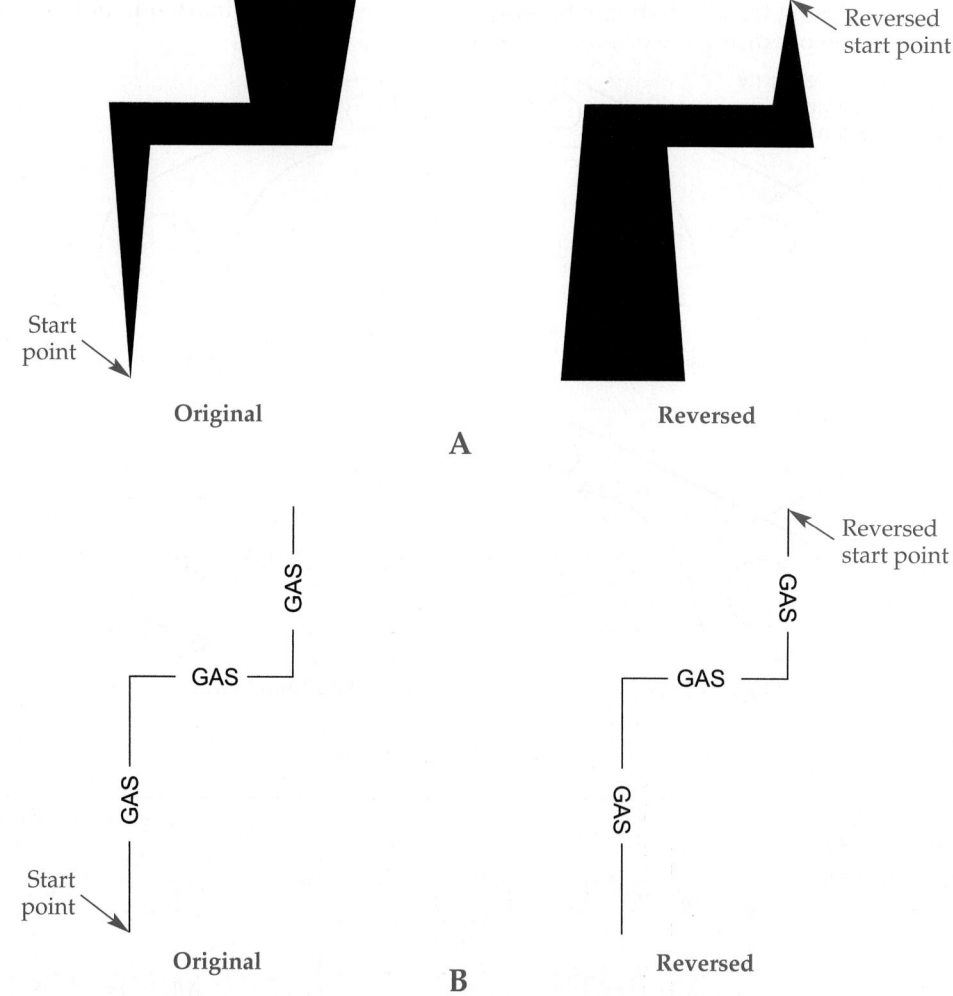

You can also use the **rEverse** option of the **PEDIT** tool to reverse polylines, and the **rEverse** option of the **SPLINEDIT** tool to reverse splines, as explained later in this textbook. Reversing affects the vertex options of the **PEDIT** tool and control point options of the **SPLINEDIT** tool.

Arraying Objects

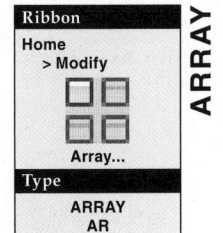

Use the **ARRAY** tool to form a rectangular or circular pattern, or *array*, of objects. For example, create a *rectangular array* of computer workstations on a classroom design plan, or create a *circular array* (also called a *polar array*) of screws on a mechanical assembly drawing. **Figure 13-12** shows examples of basic arrays. Access the **ARRAY** tool to display the **Array** dialog box, shown in **Figure 13-13**.

array: Multiple copies of an object arranged in a pattern.

rectangular array: A pattern made up of columns and rows of objects.

circular (polar) array: A circular pattern of objects.

Figure 13-12.
Examples of basic arrayed objects.

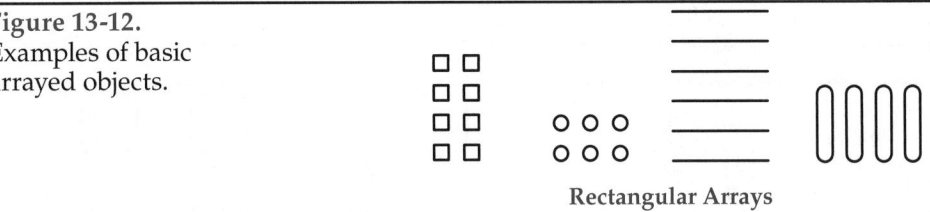

Rectangular Arrays

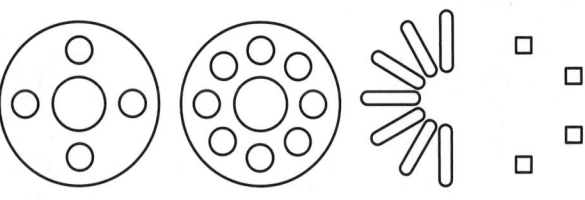

Polar Arrays

Figure 13-13.
The **Array** dialog box options for a rectangular array.

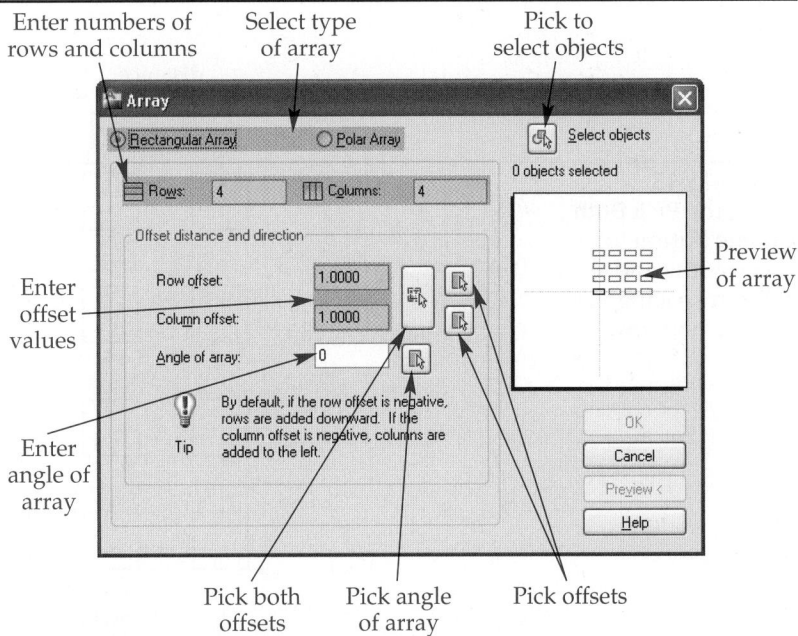

Rectangular Array

The **Rectangular Array** radio button is active by default, and displays options for building a rectangular pattern of rows and columns. See **Figure 13-13**. Pick the **Select objects** button to return to the drawing area and select the objects to array. Right-click or press [Enter] or the space bar to return to the **Array** dialog box.

Next, specify the array characteristics. For example, to create a rectangular pattern of a .5-unit square with four rows, four columns, and a .5 spacing between squares, type 4 in the **Rows:** and **Columns:** text boxes and 1.0000 in the **Row offset:** and **Column offset:** text boxes. As shown in **Figure 13-14**, the offset refers to the distance between a point on an object and the corresponding point in the next row or column.

You can also specify row and column offset by picking points. One option is to use the **Pick Row Offset** and **Pick Column Offset** buttons in the **Array** dialog box to select each distance separately. The second option is to select the **Pick Both Offsets** button to specify both distances in one pick. See **Figure 13-15**. An array can occur in the four directions shown in **Figure 13-16**. Adjust the direction using positive or negative values for row and column offset.

To rotate the array, type an angle in the **Angle of array:** text box or choose the **Pick Angle of Array** button to pick the angle on-screen. The column and row alignment rotate, not the objects. See **Figure 13-17**.

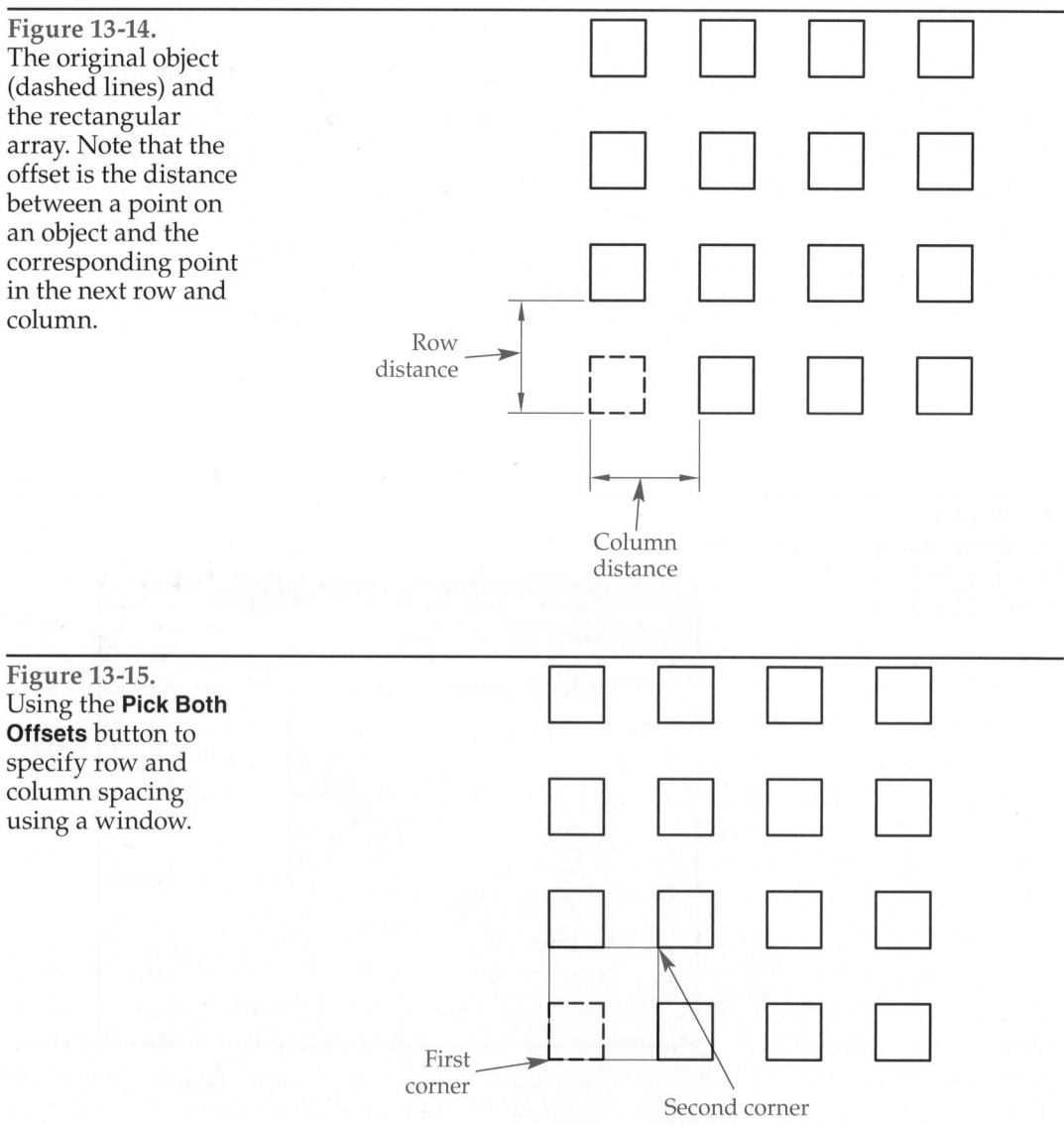

Figure 13-14.
The original object (dashed lines) and the rectangular array. Note that the offset is the distance between a point on an object and the corresponding point in the next row and column.

Row distance

Column distance

Figure 13-15.
Using the **Pick Both Offsets** button to specify row and column spacing using a window.

First corner

Second corner

Figure 13-16. Positive and negative offset distances determine the direction in which an array will grow.

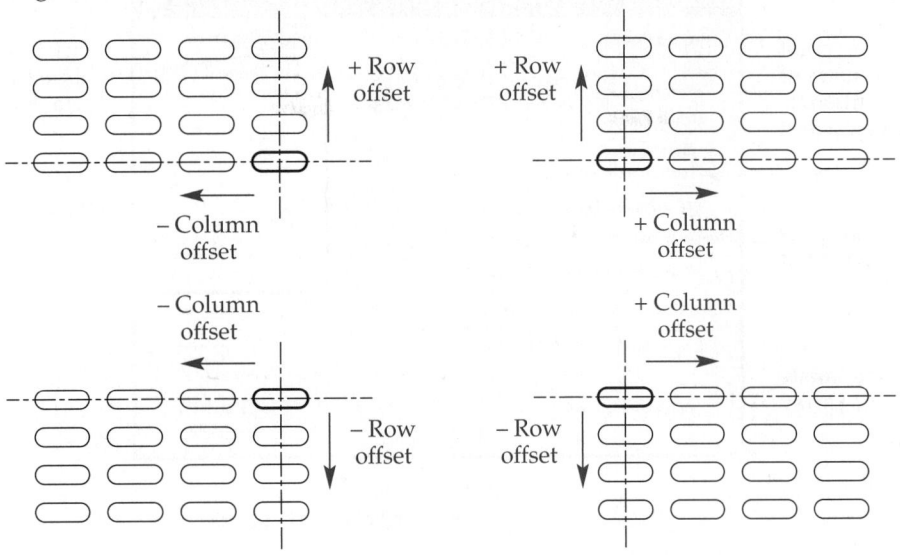

Figure 13-17. Rectangular arrays can be set at an angle using the **Angle of array:** setting.

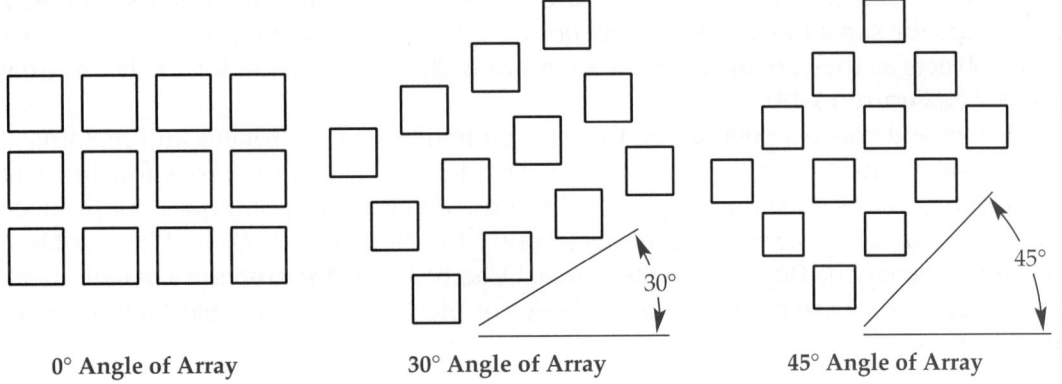

0° Angle of Array   30° Angle of Array   45° Angle of Array

Circular Array

Pick the **Polar Array** radio button to create a circular pattern of objects around a center point. See **Figure 13-18.** Pick the **Select objects** button to return to the drawing area and select the objects to array. Right-click or press [Enter] or the space bar to return to the **Array** dialog box.

Next, specify the center point around which the objects will be arrayed. Enter the coordinates for the center point in the **X:** and **Y:** text boxes or select the **Pick Center Point** button to pick the center point on-screen. Then specify the type of polar array using the **Method:** drop-down list. The method determines the settings available in the dialog box. Three methods are available:

- Total number of items & Angle to fill
- Total number of items & Angle between items
- Angle to fill & Angle between items

The **Total number of items:** setting is the total number of objects in the array, including the original object. Enter a positive angle in the **Angle to fill:** text box to array objects in a counterclockwise direction, or enter a negative angle to array objects in a clockwise direction. Enter 360 to create a complete circular array. The **Angle between items:** setting specifies the angular distance between adjacent objects in the array. For

Figure 13-18. The **Array** dialog box options for a polar array.

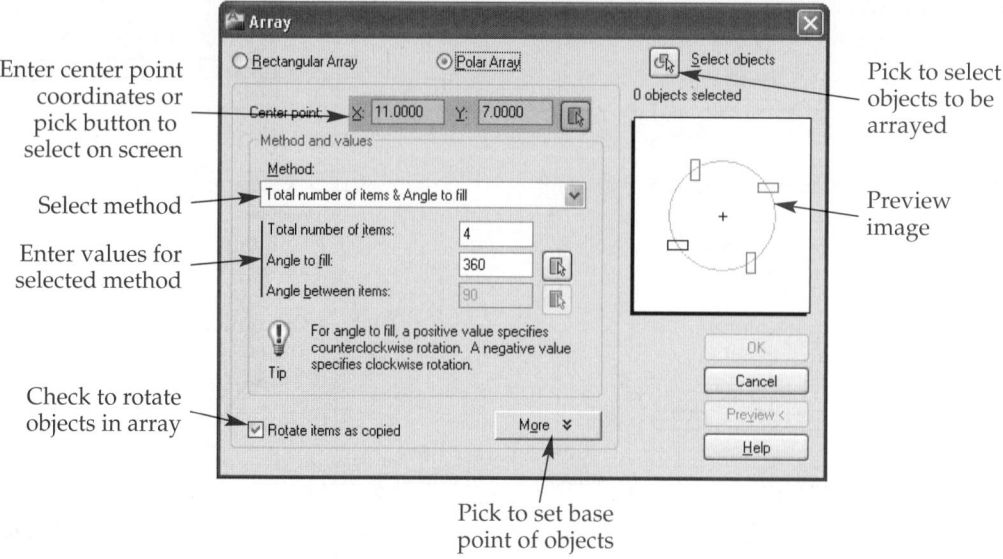

Enter center point coordinates or pick button to select on screen

Select method

Enter values for selected method

Check to rotate objects in array

Pick to select objects to be arrayed

Preview image

Pick to set base point of objects

example, to create a circular pattern of five items spaced 18° apart, enter 5 in the **Total number of items:** text box and 18 in the **Angle between items:** text box.

You can set objects to rotate as they are arrayed by checking **Rotate items as copied**. This keeps the same face of each object pointing toward the center point. If you do not rotate objects as they are arrayed, they remain in the same orientation as the original object. See **Figure 13-19.**

When you create a polar array, the base point of the object rotates and remains at a constant distance from the center point. The default base point varies for different types of objects, as shown in **Figure 13-20.** If the default base point does not produce the desired array, choose a different base point for the selected object. Pick the **More** button to display the **Object base point** area. Deactivate the **Set to object's default** check box. Enter a new base point in the text boxes or pick the button to select a base point on-screen.

Figure 13-19.
Rotating objects in a polar array. A—Check **Rotate items as copied** to rotate the square during the array. B—Uncheck **Rotate items as copied** to maintain the original orientation of objects during the array.

A   B

Figure 13-20.
Default base points for objects.

Object Type	Default Base Point
Arc, circle, ellipse	Center
Rectangle, polygon	First corner
Line, polyline, donut	Start point
Block, text	Insertion point

Exercise 13-6

Access the Student Web site (www.g-wlearning.com/CAD) and complete Exercise 13-6.

Chapter Test

Answer the following questions. Write your answers on a separate sheet of paper or go to the Student Web site (www.g-wlearning.com/CAD) and complete the electronic chapter test.

1. List two locations drafters normally choose as the base point when using the **MOVE** tool.
2. How would you rotate an object 45° clockwise?
3. Briefly describe the two methods of using the **Reference** option of the **ROTATE** tool.
4. Name the tool that you can use to move and rotate an object at the same time.
5. How many points must you select to align an object in a 2D drawing?
6. Which ribbon tab and panel contains the **MOVE** and **COPY** tools?
7. Explain the difference between the **MOVE** and **COPY** tools.
8. Briefly explain how to make several copies of the same object.
9. Which tool allows you to draw a reflected image of an existing object?
10. What is the purpose of the **REVERSE** tool?
11. What is the difference between polar and rectangular arrays?
12. What four values should you know before you create a rectangular array?
13. Suppose an object is 1.5″ (38 mm) wide and you want to create a rectangular array with .75″ (19 mm) spacing between objects. What should you specify for the distance between columns?
14. How do you specify a clockwise circular array rotation?
15. What values should you know before you create a circular array?

Drawing Problems

Start AutoCAD if it is not already started. Start a new drawing for each problem using an appropriate template of your choice. The template should include layers, text styles, and table styles, when necessary, for drawing the given objects. Add layers, text styles, and table styles as needed. Draw all objects using appropriate layers, text styles, table styles, justification, and format. Follow the specific instructions for each problem. Use only drawing and editing tools and techniques you have already learned. Do not draw dimensions. Use your own judgment and approximate dimensions when necessary.

▼ Basic

1. Open P12-1 and save the file as P13-1. (If you have not yet completed problem 12-1, complete it now.) The P13-1 file should be active. Rotate the object 90 degrees to the right and mirror the object to the left. Use the vertical base of the object as the mirror line. The final drawing should look like the example below. Resave the drawing.

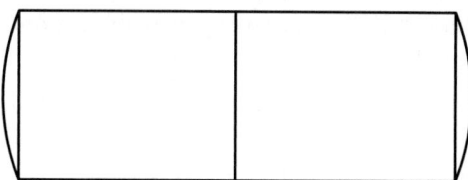

2. Open P12-2 and save the file as P13-2. (If you have not yet completed problem 12-2, complete it now.) The P13-2 file should be active. Make two copies of the object to the right of the original object. Scale the first copy 1.5 times the size of the original object. Scale the second copy 2 times the size of the original object. Move the objects so they are approximately centered in your drawing area. Move the objects as needed to align the bases of all objects and provide an equal amount of space between the objects. The final drawing should look like the example below. Resave the drawing.

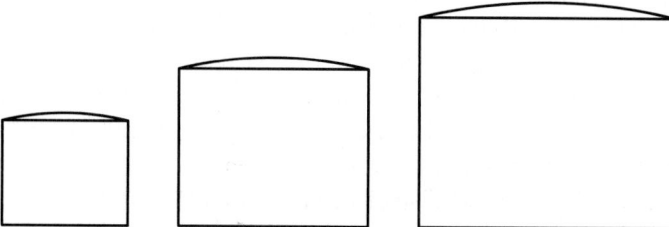

3. Draw Objects A, B, and C shown. Make a copy of Object A two units up. Make four copies of Object B three units up, center to center. Make three copies of Object C three units up, center to center. Save the drawing as P13-3.

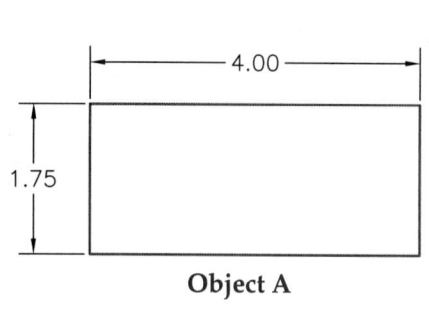

Object A

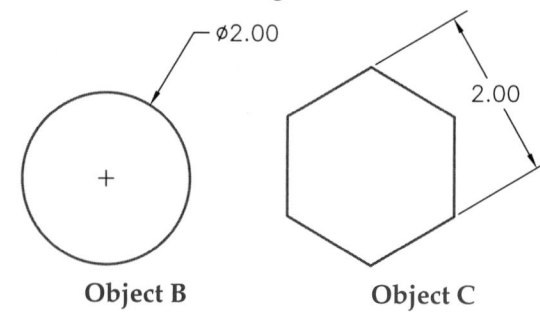

Object B   Object C

4. Open P12-4 and save the file as P13-4. (If you have not yet completed problem 12-4, complete it now.) The P13-4 file should be active. Draw a mirror image as Object B. Then remove the original view and move the new view so that Point 2 is at the original Point 1 location. Resave the drawing.

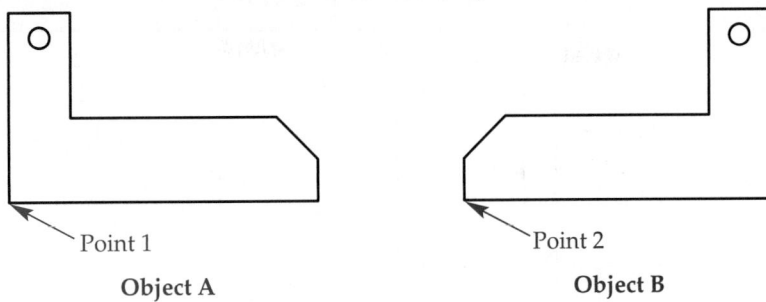

Object A

Object B

▼ Intermediate

5. Draw the part view shown. The object is symmetrical; therefore, draw only one half. Mirror the other half into place. Use the **CHAMFER** and **FILLET** tools to your best advantage. All fillets and rounds are .125. Use the **JOIN** tool where necessary. Save the drawing as P13-5.

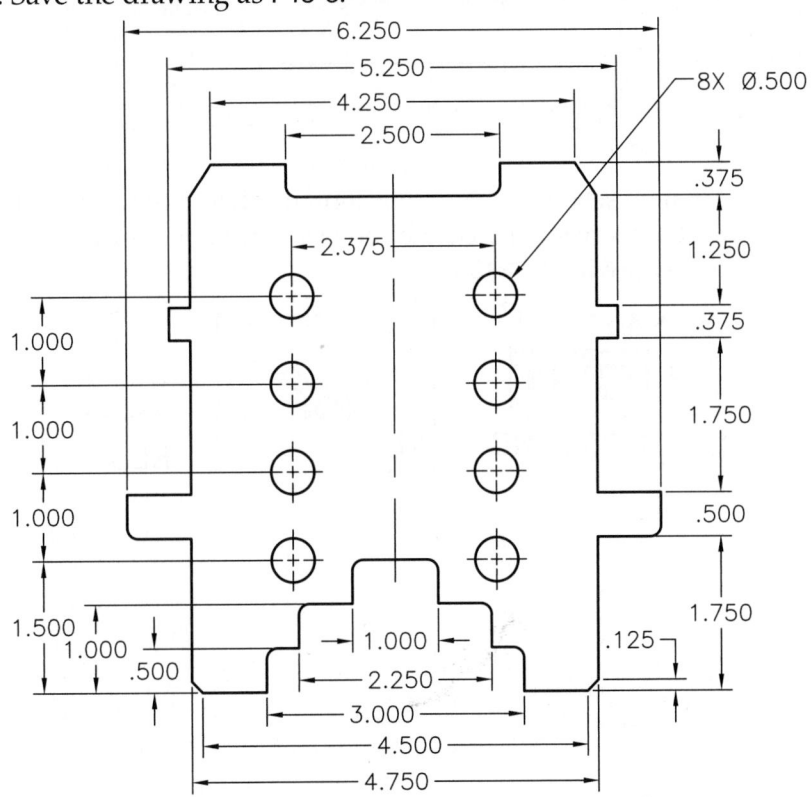

6. Draw the portion of the part view shown. Mirror the right half into place. Use the **CHAMFER** and **FILLET** tools to your best advantage. Save the drawing as P13-6.

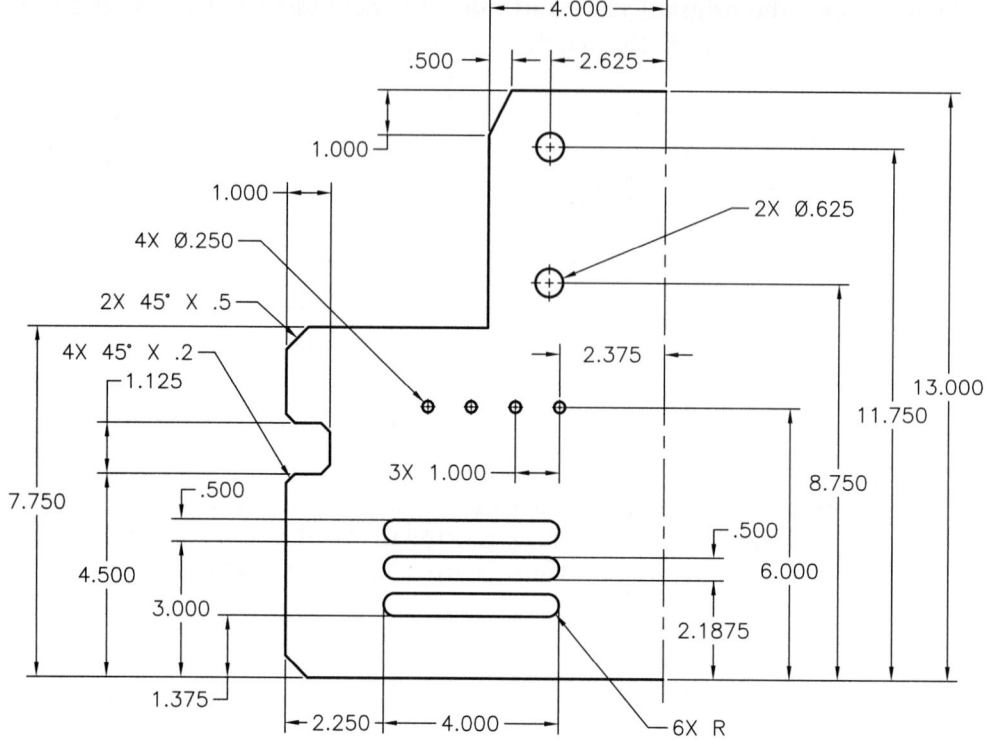

7. Draw the electronic schematic symbols shown. Mirror the drawing, but make sure the text remains readable. Delete the original image during the mirroring process. Save the drawing as P13-7.

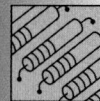

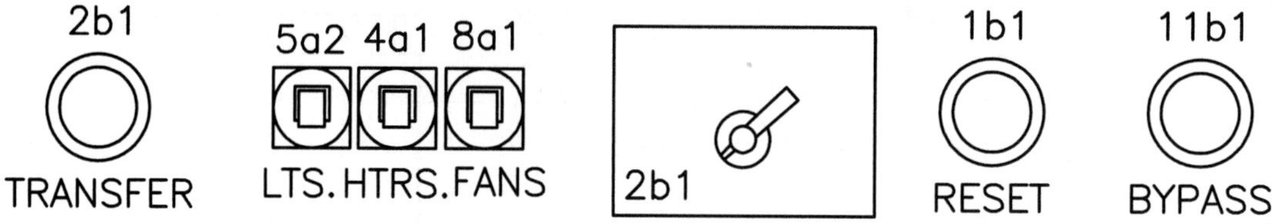

2b1

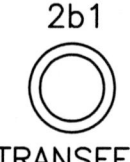

TRANSFER

5a2 4a1 8a1

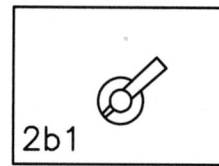

LTS. HTRS. FANS

2b1

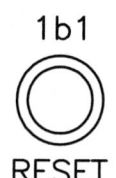

1b1

RESET

11b1

BYPASS

Drawing Problems - Chapter 13

8. Draw the timer schematic shown. Save the drawing as P13-8.

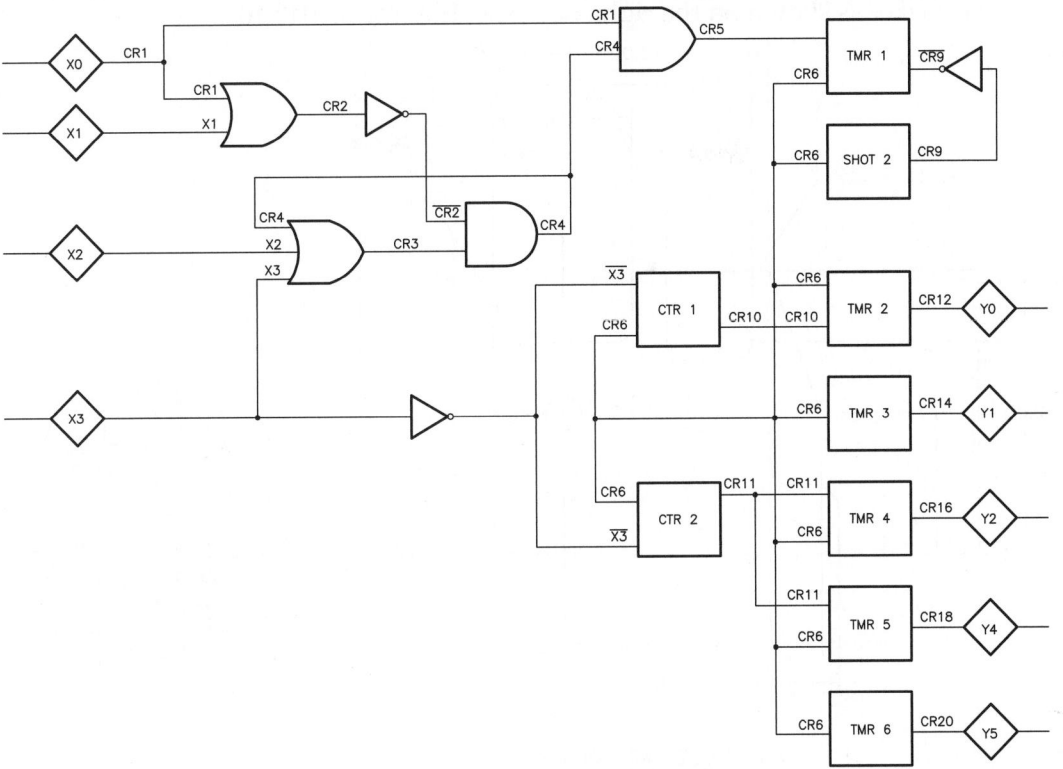

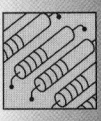

9. Use tracking and object snaps to draw the board shown, based on the following instructions:
   A. Draw the outline first, followed by the ten Ø.500 holes (A).
   B. The holes labeled B are located vertically halfway between the centers of the holes labeled A. They have a diameter one-quarter the size of the holes labeled A.
   C. The holes labeled C are located vertically halfway between the holes labeled A and B. Their diameter is three-quarters of the diameter of the holes labeled B.
   D. The holes labeled D are located horizontally halfway between the centers of the holes labeled A. These holes have the same diameter as the holes labeled B.
   E. Draw the rectangles around the circles as shown.
   F. Do not draw dimensions, notes, or labels.
   G. Save the drawing as P13-9.

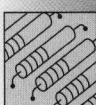

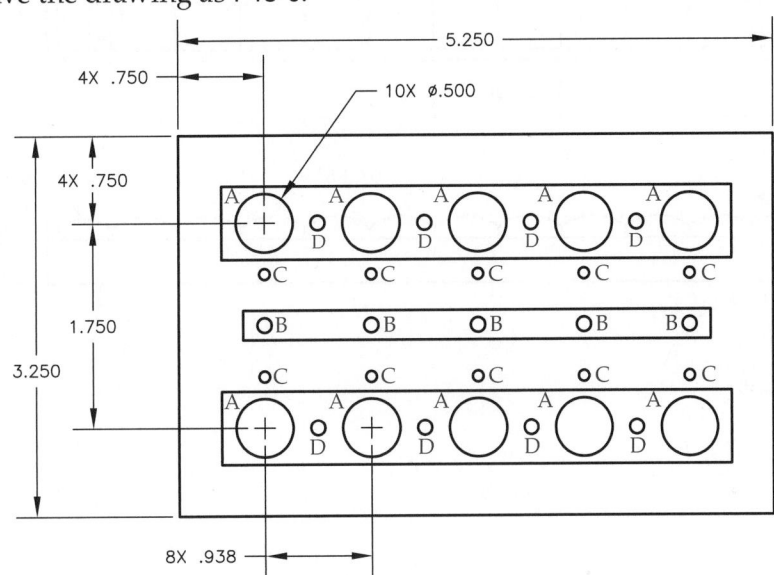

10. Draw the portion of the gasket shown on the left. Use the **MIRROR** tool to complete the gasket as shown on the right. Save the drawing as P13-10.

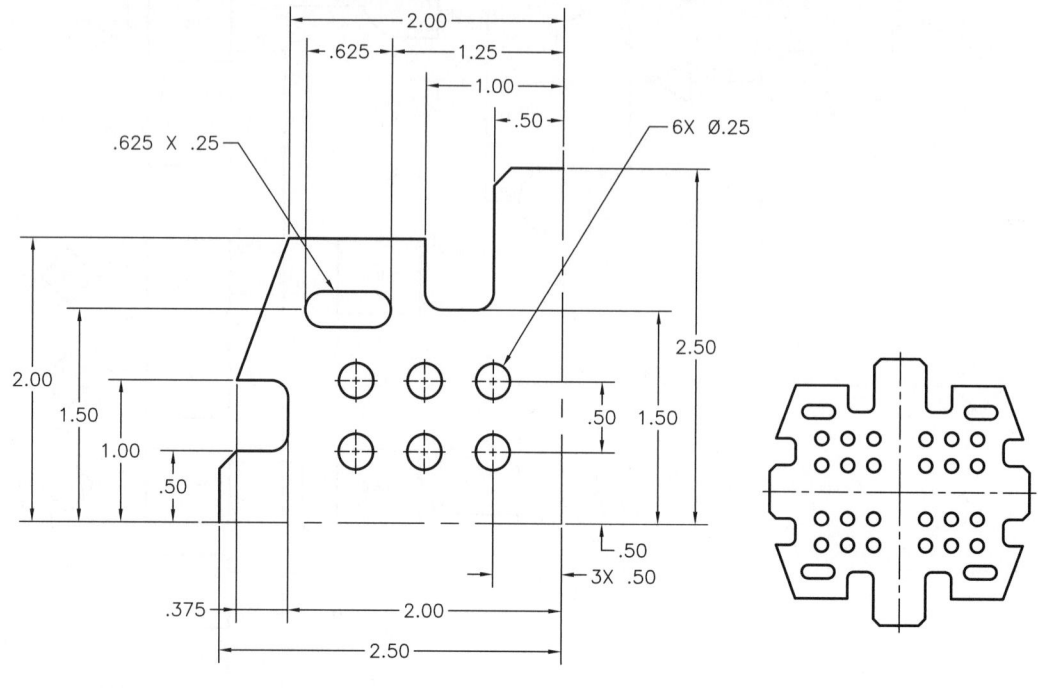

ALL FILLETS AND ROUNDS R.125.
CHAMFERS 45° X .125

11. Draw the padded bench shown. Use the **COPY** and **ARRAY** tools as needed. Save the drawing as P13-11.

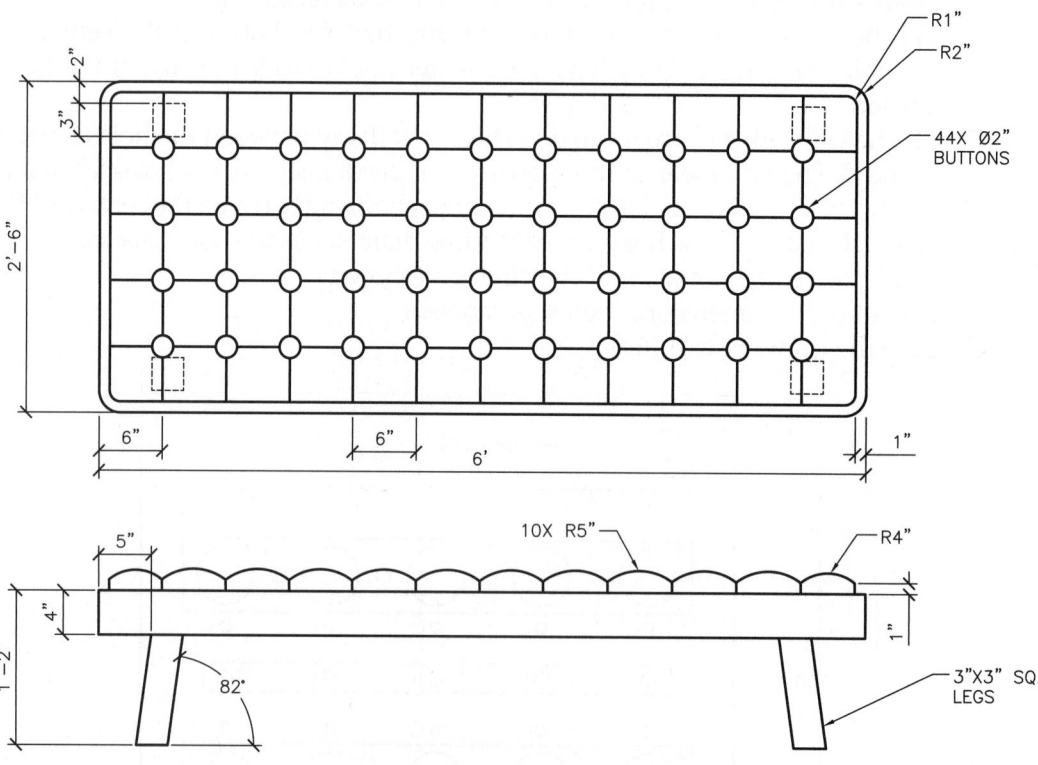

12. Draw the hand wheel shown. Use the **ARRAY** tool to draw the spokes. Save the drawing as P13-12.

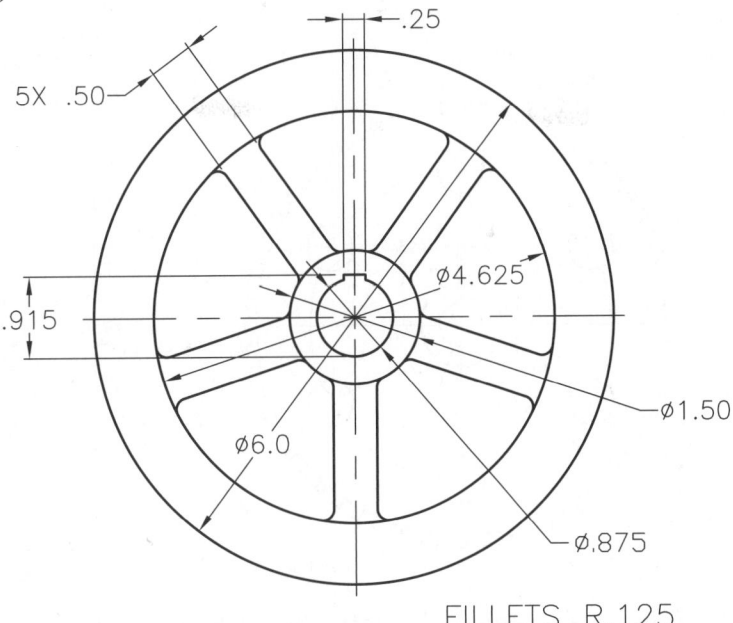

.25

5X .50

Ø4.625

.915

Ø6.0

Ø1.50

Ø.875

FILLETS R.125

▼ Advanced

13. Use the engineer's sketch and notes shown to draw the sprocket. Create a front and side view of the sprocket. Use the **ARRAY** tool as needed. Save the drawing as P13-13.

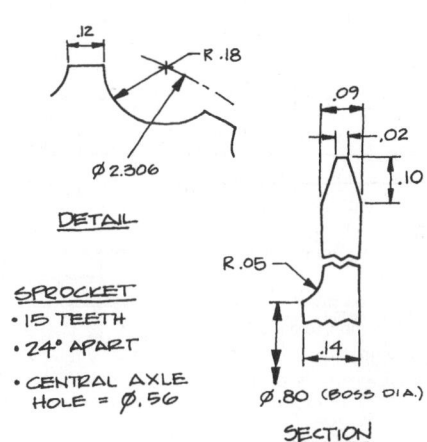

.12

R .18

Ø 2.306

DETAIL

SPROCKET
- 15 TEETH
- 24° APART
- CENTRAL AXLE HOLE = Ø.56

.09

.02

.10

R .05

.14

Ø.80 (BOSS DIA.)

SECTION

14. Draw the views of the sprocket shown. Use **ARRAY** to construct the hole and tooth arrangements. Save the drawing as P13-14.

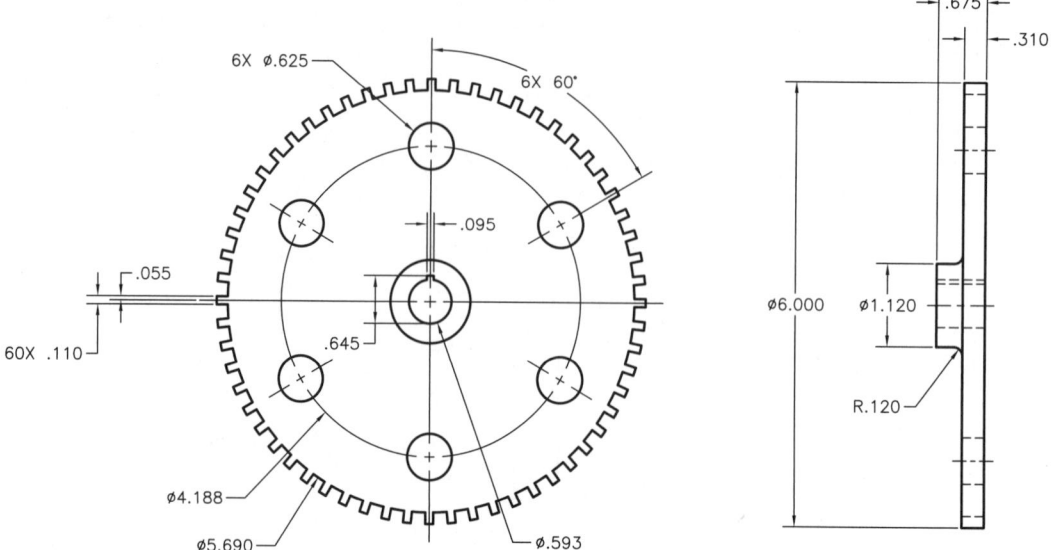

15. Draw the refrigeration system schematic shown. Save the drawing as P13-15.

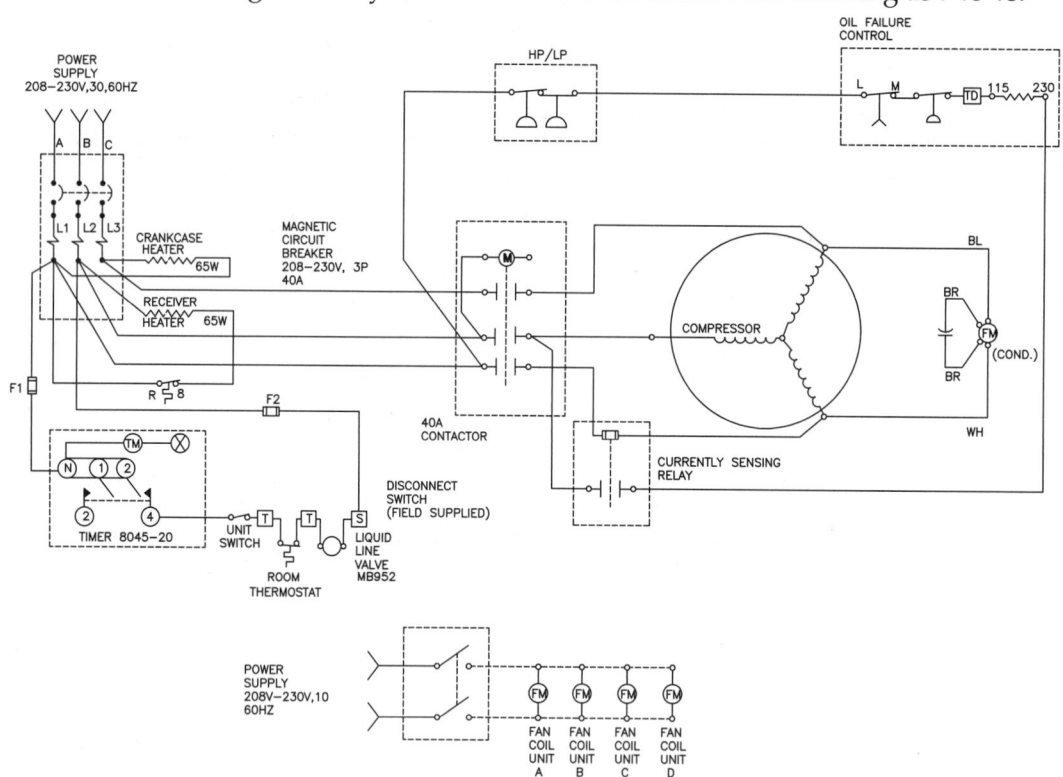

16. The structural sketch shown is a steel column arrangement on a concrete floor slab for a new building. The *I*-shaped symbols represent the steel columns. The columns are arranged in "bay lines" and "column lines." The column lines are numbered *1*, *2*, and *3*. The bay lines are labeled *A* through *G*. The width of a bay is 24'-0". Line balloons, or tags, identify the bay and column lines. Draw the arrangement, using **ARRAY** for the steel column symbols and the tags. The following guidelines will help:

A. Begin a new drawing using an architectural template.
B. Select architectural units and set up the drawing to print on a 36 × 24 sheet size. Determine the scale required for the floor plan to fit on this sheet size and specify the drawing limits accordingly.
C. Draw the steel column symbol to the dimensions given.
D. Set the grid spacing at 2'-0" (24").
E. Set the snap spacing at 12".
F. Draw all other objects.
G. Place text inside the balloon tags. Set the running object snap mode to **Center** and justify the text to **Middle**. Make the text height 6".
H. Save the drawing as P13-16.

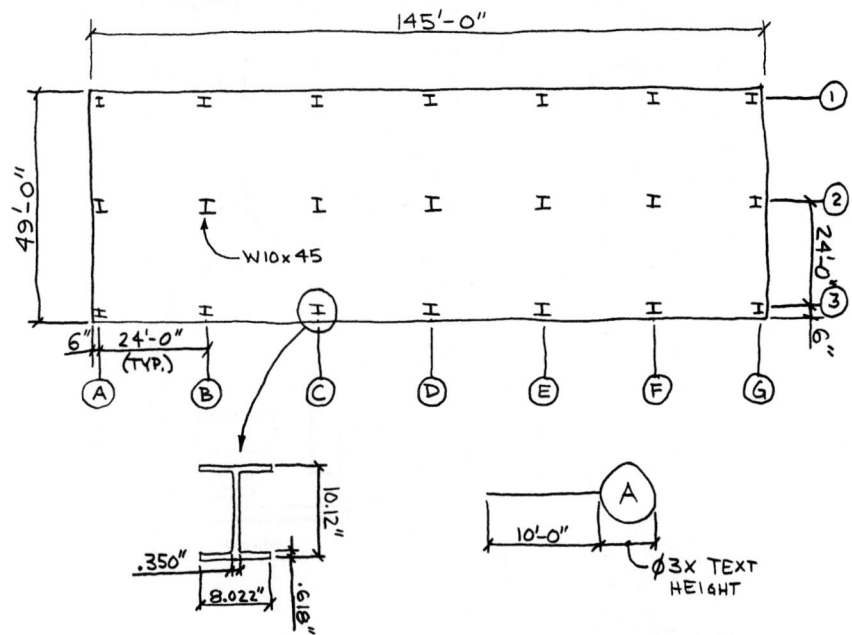

17. The sketch shown is a proposed classroom layout of desks and chairs. One desk is shown with the layout of a chair, keyboard, monitor, and tower-mounted computer (drawn with dotted lines). All of the desk workstations should have the same configuration. The exact sizes and locations of the doors and windows are not important for this problem. Use the following guidelines to complete this problem:
A. Begin a new drawing.
B. Choose architectural units.
C. Set up the drawing to print on a C-size sheet, and be sure to create the drawing in model space.
D. Use the appropriate drawing and editing tools to complete this problem quickly and efficiently.
E. Draw the desk and computer hardware to the dimensions given.
F. Do not dimension the drawing.
G. Save the drawing as P13-17.

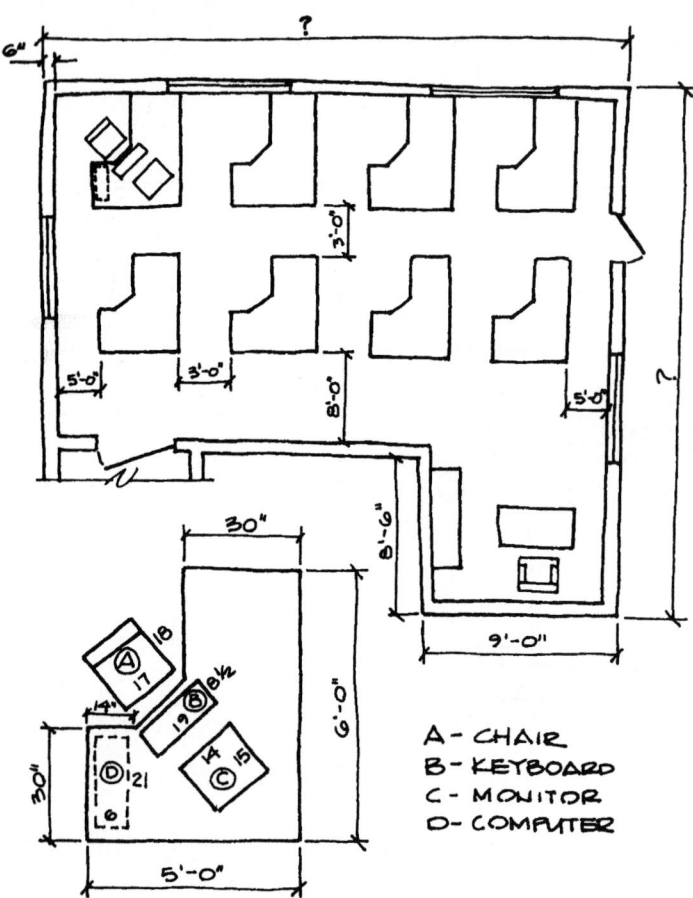

A - CHAIR
B - KEYBOARD
C - MONITOR
D - COMPUTER

18. Draw the front elevation of this house. Create the features proportional to the given drawing. Use the **ARRAY** and **TRIM** tools to place the siding and porch rails evenly. Save the drawing as P13-18.

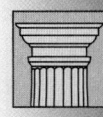

19. Create a dimensioned 2D sketch of a new design for an automobile wheel. Sketch a front view and a side view. Use dimensions based on your experience, research, and measurements. The design must include a circular repetition of features. Start a new drawing from scratch or use a decimal-unit template of your choice. Draw the views of the wheel from your sketch. Use the **ARRAY** tool to draw the circular pattern of features. Save the drawing as P13-19.

AutoCAD Certified Associate Exam Practice

Answer the following questions. Write your answers on a separate sheet of paper.

1. Which of the following can you do using the **MOVE** tool? *Select all that apply.*
   A. move objects relative to the origin (0,0,0)
   B. move objects from a base point to a second specified point
   C. rotate objects during the move operation
   D. use the first point you pick as the point of displacement
   E. use a scale factor

2. In which order do you pick the source and destination points when using the **ALIGN** tool? *Select the one item that best answers the question.*
   A. destination point 1, destination point 2, source point 1, source point 2
   B. destination point 1, source point 1, destination point 2, source point 2
   C. destination point 2, source point 2, destination point 1, source point 1
   D. source point 1, destination point 1, source point 2, destination point 2
   E. source point 1, source point 2, destination point 1, destination point 2

3. In the array shown below, what would you enter for the row and column offsets?
   Select the one item that best answers the question.
   A. row offset 1.00, column offset 2.00
   B. row offset 2.00, column offset 1.00
   C. row offset 2.00, column offset 4.00
   D. row offset 4.00, column offset 2.00
   E. row offset 5.00, column offset 6.00
   F. row offset 6.00, column offset 5.00

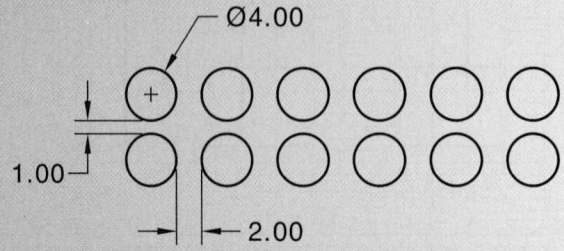

AutoCAD Certified Professional Exam Practice

Follow the instructions in each problem. Write your answers on a separate sheet of paper.

1. **Navigate to this chapter on the Student Web site and open CPE-13array.dwg.**
   Use the **ARRAY** tool to finish the view of a fan plate as shown. Analyze the drawing and use the most appropriate options for the polar array. What are the coordinates of Point 1?

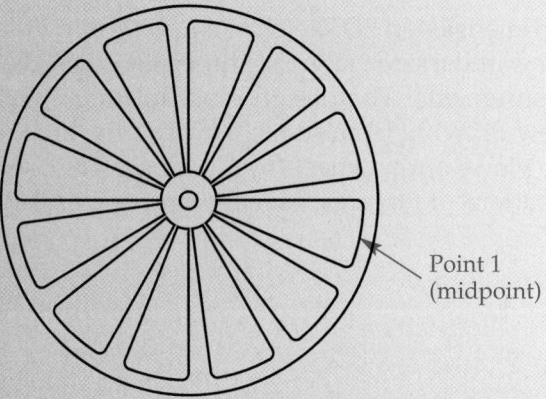

Point 1
(midpoint)

2. **Navigate to this chapter on the Student Web site and open CPE-13mirror.dwg.**
   Create a mirror line starting at absolute coordinates 13′,8′ and extending 5′ at 120°. Mirror the couch across this line. What are the coordinates of Point 1?

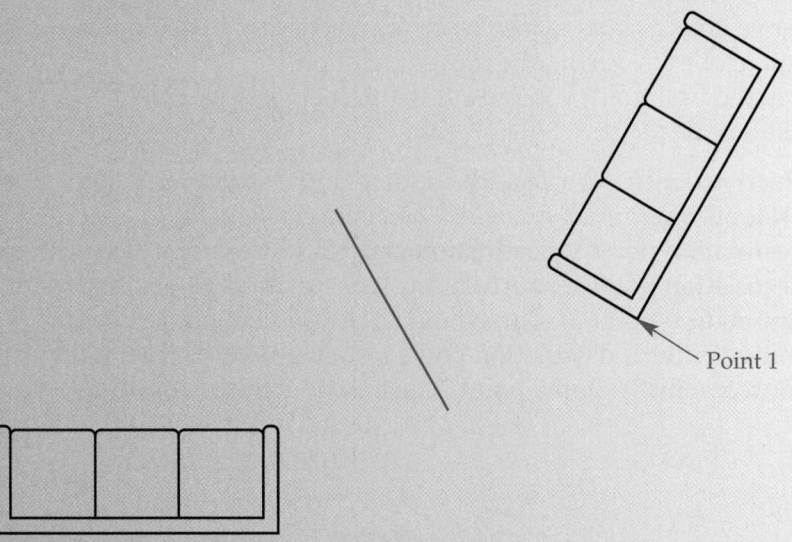

Point 1

Grips, Properties, and Additional Selection Techniques

Learning Objectives

After completing this chapter, you will be able to do the following:

✓ Use grips to stretch, move, rotate, scale, mirror, and copy objects.
✓ Adjust object properties using the **Quick Properties** panel and the **Properties** palette.
✓ Use the **MATCHPROP** tool to match object properties.
✓ Edit between drawings.
✓ Use the **ADDSELECTED** tool to draw an object based on an existing object.
✓ Create selection sets using the **SELECTSIMILAR** and **Quick Select** tools.

The traditional approach to editing is to access a tool, such as **ERASE**, **FILLET**, **MOVE**, or **COPY**, select the objects to modify, and follow prompts to complete the operation. This chapter explains the alternative approach of selecting objects first, and then using editing tools or object properties to make changes. This chapter also describes additional selection options, selection set filters, and related tools.

Grips

Use the crosshairs to select objects and display *grips*. See **Figure 14-1**. Selected objects become highlighted and grips initially appear in an *unselected grip* state. Unselected grips are blue (Color 140) by default. Grips are specific to object type. All objects include the standard filled-square grips at critical and editable points on the object. Arcs include filled-arrow grips for adjusting the shape of the arc. Several objects, including mtext, tables, polylines, splines, hatch, and blocks, have specialized grips. This textbook explains the grips specific to these objects when applicable.

Move the crosshairs over an unselected grip to snap to the grip. Then pause to change the color of the grip to pink (Color 11). Hovering over an unselected grip and allowing it to change color helps you select the correct grip, especially when multiple grips are close together. A tooltip or options may appear, depending on the object and grip.

Pick a grip to perform an editing operation at the location of the grip. A common *selected grip* appears red (Color 12) by default. If you select more than one object displaying unselected grips, what you do with the selected grips affects all selected objects. Objects having unselected and selected grips become part of the current selection set.

grips: Small boxes that appear at strategic points on a selected object, allowing you to edit the object directly.

unselected grips: Grips that you have not yet picked to perform an operation.

selected grip: A grip that you have picked to perform an operation.

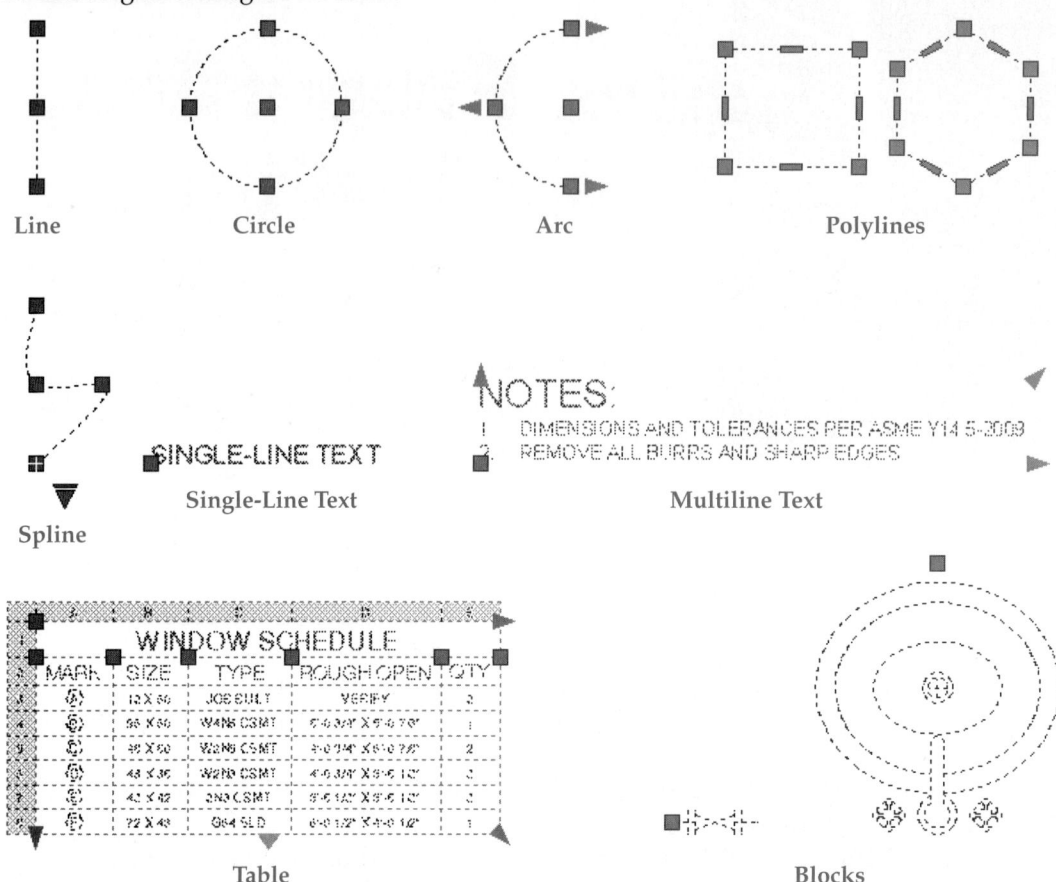

Figure 14-1. Grips appear at specific locations on objects when you select the objects while no drawing or editing tool is active.

Line

Circle

Arc

Polylines

Spline

SINGLE-LINE TEXT

Single-Line Text

NOTES:
1. DIMENSIONS AND TOLERANCES PER ASME Y14.5-2009
2. REMOVE ALL BURRS AND SHARP EDGES

Multiline Text

WINDOW SCHEDULE

Table

Blocks

To remove objects from a selection set, hold down [Shift] and pick the objects to deselect. Select additional objects, without pressing [Shift], to add to the grip selection set. [Shift] also allows you to select multiple grips. Hold down [Shift] and then select each grip. Remember not to release [Shift] until you pick all the grips to activate. While still holding down [Shift], pick a selected (red) grip to return the grip to the unselected (blue) state. **Figure 14-2** shows an example of modifying two circles at the same time using selected grips.

Press [Esc] to deselect all selected grips. Press [Esc] again to deselect all objects and hide grips. You can also right-click and pick **Deselect All** to hide all grips.

NOTE

Use the options in the **Grip Size** and **Grips** areas of the **Selection** tab in the **Options** dialog box to control grip size and color.

noun/verb selection: Performing tasks in AutoCAD by selecting the objects before activating a tool.

verb/noun selection: Performing tasks in AutoCAD by activating a tool before selecting objects.

PROFESSIONAL TIP

You can perform some conventional operations by selecting objects before you access a tool. For example, you can select objects to erase and then activate the **ERASE** tool or press [Delete]. This technique is available by default and is controlled by the **Noun/verb selection** check box in the **Selection Modes** area of the **Selection** tab in the **Options** dialog box.

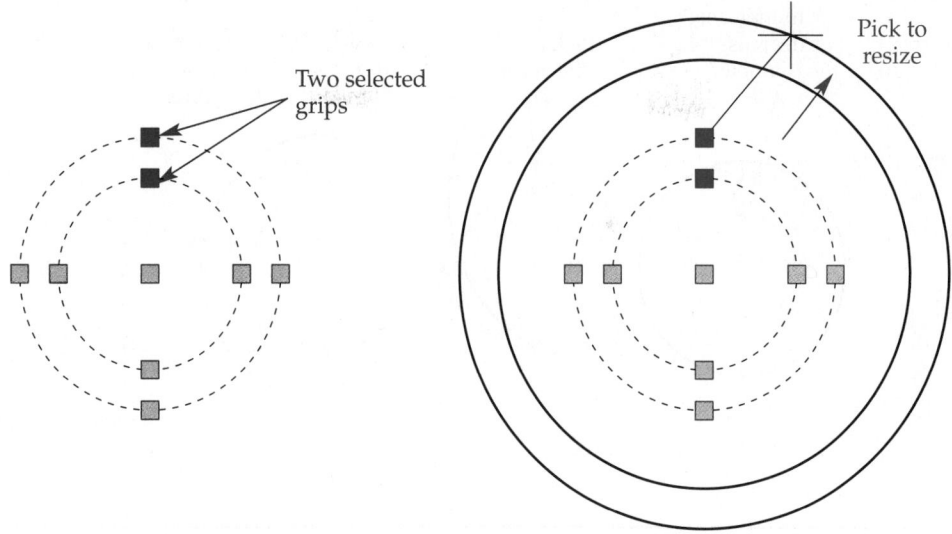

Figure 14-2. You can modify multiple objects at the same time by pressing [Shift] to select additional grips. In this example, if you only select one grip, you can only edit one circle.

Two selected grips

Pick to resize

Standard Grip Tools

Most grips provide access to the **STRETCH**, **MOVE**, **ROTATE**, **SCALE**, and **MIRROR** tools. In addition, the **Copy** option of the **MOVE** tool and sometimes, depending on the selected grip, the **STRETCH** tool imitate the **COPY** tool. Select grips to display options at the dynamic input cursor and the command line. Do not attempt to use conventional means of tool access, such as the ribbon. The first tool is **STRETCH**, as indicated by the ** STRETCH ** Specify stretch point or [Base point/Copy/Undo/eXit]: prompt. Use the **STRETCH** tool, or press [Enter] or the space bar or right-click and select **Enter** to cycle through other tools:

```
** STRETCH **
Specify stretch point or [Base point/Copy/Undo/eXit]: ↵
** MOVE **
Specify move point or [Base point/Copy/Undo/eXit]: ↵
** ROTATE **
Specify rotation angle or [Base point/Copy/Undo/Reference/eXit]: ↵
** SCALE **
Specify scale factor or [Base point/Copy/Undo/Reference/eXit]: ↵
** MIRROR **
Specify second point or [Base point/Copy/Undo/eXit]: ↵
** STRETCH **
Specify stretch point or [Base point/Copy/Undo/eXit]:
```

An alternative to cycling through tools is to select grips, right-click, and select an option from the shortcut menu. A third method to activate a tool is to enter the first two characters of the tool name. Type MO for **MOVE**, MI for **MIRROR**, RO for **ROTATE**, SC for **SCALE**, or ST for **STRETCH**.

Stretching

Stretching using grips is similar to stretching using the **STRETCH** tool, except that the selected grip acts as the stretch base point. In addition, depending on the selected grip and type of object, stretching using a grip can produce a move or scale operation, instead of stretching. See **Figure 14-3.** Stretch individual grips, or select multiple grips to combine operations. See **Figure 14-4.**

Figure 14-3. Using the **STRETCH** grip tool. Note the selected grip in each case. These examples apply only to unconstrained geometry.

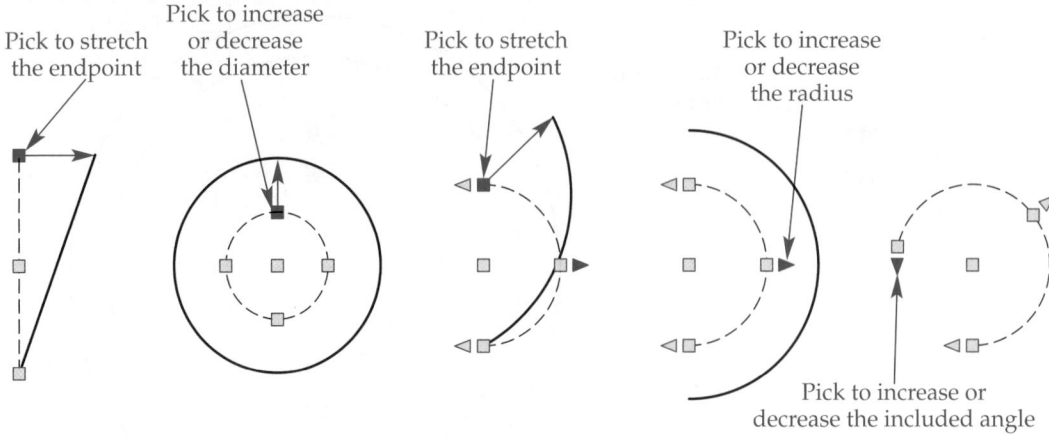

Pick to stretch the endpoint

Pick to increase or decrease the diameter

Pick to stretch the endpoint

Pick to increase or decrease the radius

Pick to increase or decrease the included angle

Figure 14-4. Stretching a polyline drawn using the **RECTANGLE** tool. A—Select corners to stretch individually. B—Hold down [Shift] to select multiple grips to stretch. These examples only apply to unconstrained geometry.

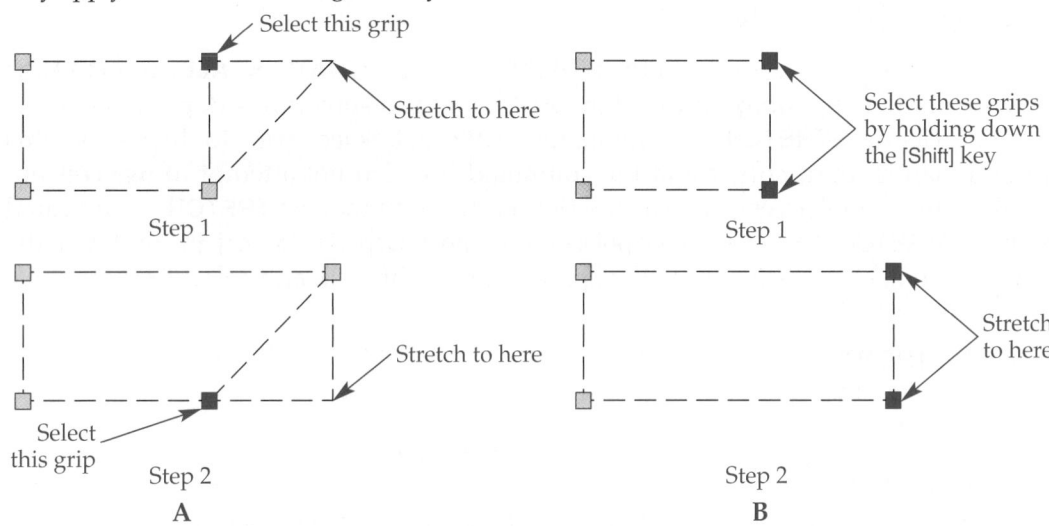

Select this grip

Stretch to here

Step 1

Select this grip

Stretch to here

Step 2

A

Select these grips by holding down the [Shift] key

Step 1

Stretch to here

Step 2

B

Use the **Base point** option to specify a base point instead of using the selected grip as the base point. Select the **Undo** option to undo the previous operation. Choose the **eXit** option or press [Esc] to exit without completing the stretch. When you finish stretching, the selected grips return to the unselected state. Press [Esc] to hide the grips.

Dynamic input is especially effective with the **STRETCH** grip tool. **Figure 14-5** shows an example of using dimensional input to modify the size of a circle or offset a circle by a specific distance. In this example, enter the new radius of the circle in the distance input field, or press [Tab] to enter an offset in the other distance input field. This is just one example of using dynamic input with grips. You can apply similar processes to edit most objects.

PROFESSIONAL TIP

Use grid snaps, coordinate entry, polar tracking, object snaps, and object snap tracking with any grip editing tool to improve accuracy.

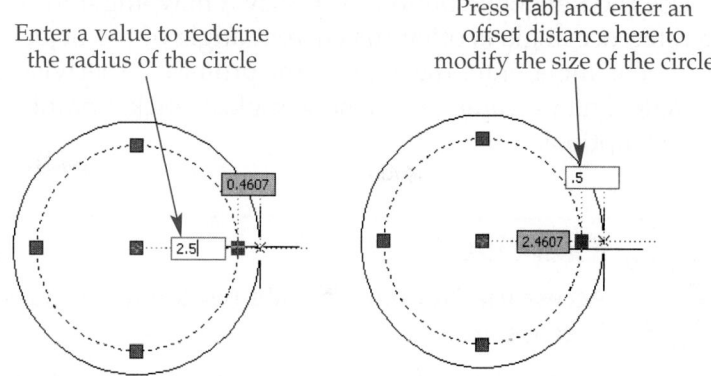

Figure 14-5.
Using the dimensional input feature of dynamic input with the **STRETCH** grip tool.

Enter a value to redefine the radius of the circle

0.4607

2.5

Press [Tab] and enter an offset distance here to modify the size of the circle

.5

2.4607

Exercise 14-1

Access the Student Web site (www.g-wlearning.com/CAD) and complete Exercise 14-1.

Moving

To move objects using grips, select the objects to move, pick grips to use as the base point, and activate the **MOVE** grip tool. Specify a new location for the base point to move the objects. See **Figure 14-6.** The **Base point**, **Undo**, and **eXit** options are similar to those for the **STRETCH** grip tool.

Exercise 14-2

Access the Student Web site (www.g-wlearning.com/CAD) and complete Exercise 14-2.

Rotating

To rotate objects using grips, select the objects to rotate, pick a grip to use as the base point, and activate the **ROTATE** grip tool. Specify a rotation angle to rotate the objects. The **Base point**, **Undo**, and **eXit** options are similar to those for the **STRETCH** grip tool.

Figure 14-6.
The selected grip is the default base point when you use the **MOVE** grip tool.

Pick a grip to be a base point

Step 1

Move the rectangle to this point

Step 2

Use the **Reference** option to specify a new angle in relation to an existing angle. The reference angle is often the current angle of the objects. If you know the value of the current angle, enter the value at the prompt. Otherwise, pick two points to identify the angle. Enter a value for the new angle or pick a point. Figure 14-7 shows **ROTATE** grip tool options.

Exercise 14-3

Access the Student Web site (www.g-wlearning.com/CAD) and complete Exercise 14-3.

Scaling

To scale objects using grips, select the objects to scale, pick a grip to use as the base point, and activate the **SCALE** grip tool. Enter a scale factor or pick a point to increase or decrease the size of the objects. The **Base point**, **Undo**, and **eXit** options are similar to those for the **STRETCH** grip tool.

Use the **Reference** option to specify a new size in relation to an existing size. The reference size is often the current length, width, or height of the objects. If you know the current size, enter the value at the prompt. Otherwise, pick two points to identify the size. Enter a value for the new size or pick a point. Figure 14-8 shows **SCALE** grip tool options.

Figure 14-7.
Using the **ROTATE** grip tool with the default rotation angle option, and with the alternative **Reference** option.

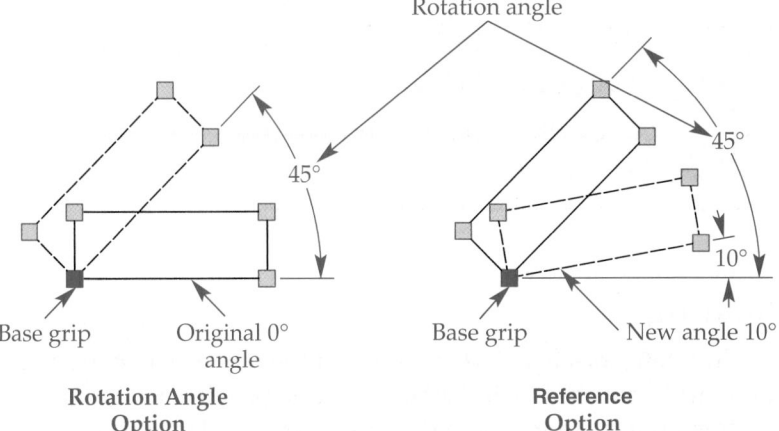

Figure 14-8.
When using the **SCALE** tool with grips, enter a scale factor or use the **Reference** option.

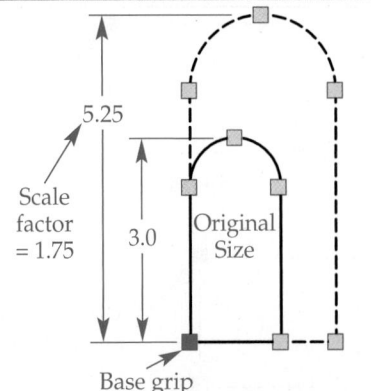

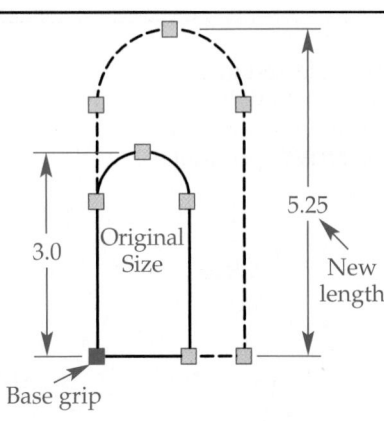

Exercise 14-4

Access the Student Web site (www.g-wlearning.com/CAD) and complete Exercise 14-4.

Mirroring

To mirror objects using grips, select the objects, pick a grip to use as the first point of the mirror line, and activate the **MIRROR** grip tool. Then pick another grip or any point on-screen to locate the second point of the mirror line. See **Figure 14-9**. Unlike the standard **MIRROR** tool, the grip version does not give you the immediate option to delete the old objects. Old objects are deleted automatically. To keep the original objects, use the **Copy** option of the **MIRROR** grip tool. The **Base point, Undo**, and **eXit** options are similar to those for the **STRETCH** tool.

Exercise 14-5

Access the Student Web site (www.g-wlearning.com/CAD) and complete Exercise 14-5.

Copying

Each standard grip editing tool includes the **Copy** option. The effect of using the **Copy** option depends on the selected objects, grip, and tool. The original selected objects remain unchanged, and the copy stretches when the **STRETCH** grip tool is active, rotates when the **ROTATE** grip tool is active, or scales when the **SCALE** grip tool is active. The **Copy** option of the **MOVE** grip tool is the true copy operation, allowing you to copy from any selected grip. The selected grip acts as the copy base point. Create as many copies of the selected object as needed, and then exit the tool.

Exercise 14-6

Access the Student Web site (www.g-wlearning.com/CAD) and complete Exercise 14-6.

Figure 14-9.
When you use grips to access the **MIRROR** tool, the selected grip becomes the first point of the mirror line, and the original object is automatically deleted.

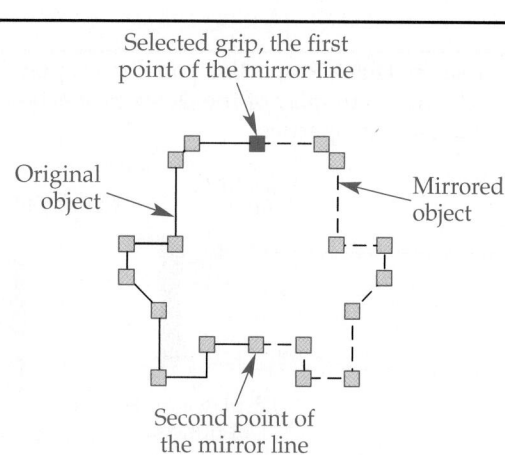

Selected grip, the first point of the mirror line

Original object

Mirrored object

Second point of the mirror line

Object Properties

Every object has specific properties. Properties include geometry characteristics, such as the location of the endpoints of a line in X,Y,Z space, the diameter of a circle, or the area of a rectangle. Layer is another property associated with all objects. The layer on which you draw an object defines other properties, including color, linetype, and lineweight. Most objects also include object-specific properties. For example, text objects have text properties, and tables have column, row, and cell properties.

AutoCAD provides many options for adjusting object properties, depending on the object and properties. One method is to use modification tools, such as **STRETCH**, **ROTATE**, or grip editing to make changes. Another method is to adjust layer characteristics using layer tools. You can also use the multiline text editor to adjust existing multiline text properties. A different technique to view and make changes to the properties of any object is to use the **Quick Properties** panel or the **Properties** palette. These tools are especially effective for modifying a particular property or set of properties for multiple objects at once.

PROFESSIONAL TIP

You can view object, color, layer, and linetypes properties by hovering over an object. This is a quick way to reference basic object information. See **Figure 14-10**.

Using the Quick Properties Panel

The **Quick Properties** panel, shown in **Figure 14-11**, appears by default when you pick an object. The **Quick Properties** panel floats by default above and to the right of the crosshairs. The drop-down list at the top of the **Quick Properties** panel identifies the selected object. Properties associated with the selected object are displayed below the drop-down list in rows. For example, if you pick a circle, the **Quick Properties** panel lists rows of circle properties.

Figure 14-10.
Hover over an object to view an object's color, layer, and linetype properties.

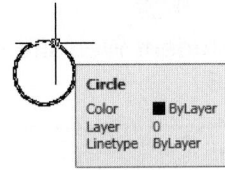

Figure 14-11. Use the **Quick Properties** panel to display and modify certain object properties. A—The initial display of the **Quick Properties** panel when you select a line object. B—The expanded list of properties.

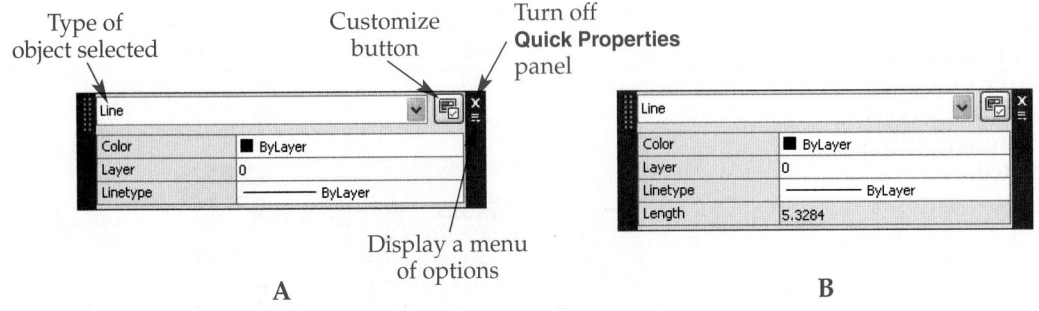

When you pick multiple objects, use the **Quick Properties** panel to modify all of the objects, or pick a specific object type from the drop-down list to modify. See **Figure 14-12.** Select All (*n*) to change the properties of all selected objects. Only properties shared by all selected objects appear when you choose All (*n*). Select the appropriate object type to modify a single type of object.

The **Quick Properties** panel lists the most common properties associated with the selected objects. You should recognize most of the properties. By default, three properties display, unless the selected objects contain fewer properties. If more properties are available, hover over a row or a **Quick Properties** panel side bar to expand the list.

To change a property, pick the property or current value. The way you change a value depends on the property. Some properties display a text box, such as the **Radius** property of an arc or circle or the **Text height** property of an mtext or text object. Enter a new value in the text box to change the property. Most text boxes display a calculator icon on the right side that opens the **QuickCalc** tool for calculating values. Chapter 16 covers using **QuickCalc**. Other properties, such as the **Layer** property, display a drop-down list of selections. A pick button is available for geometric properties, such as the **Center X** and **Center Y** properties of a circle. Select the pick button to specify a new coordinate. Choose an **...** (ellipsis) button to open a dialog box related to the property.

Press [Esc] or pick the **Close** button in the upper-right corner of the panel to hide the **Quick Properties** panel. Closing the **Quick Properties** panel does not disable the tool. If you choose not to use the **Quick Properties** panel, a quick way to disable or enable the panel is to pick the **Quick Properties** button on the status bar.

Exercise 14-7

Access the Student Web site (www.g-wlearning.com/CAD) and complete Exercise 14-7.

Quick Properties Panel Options

For information about adjusting **Quick Properties** panel options, go to the Student Web site (www.g-wlearning.com/CAD), select this chapter, and select **Quick Properties Panel Options**.

Using the Properties Palette

The **Properties** palette, shown in **Figure 14-13**, provides the same function as the **Quick Properties** panel, but allows you to view and adjust *all* properties related to the selected objects. You can dock, lock, and resize the **Properties** palette in the drawing area. You can access tools and continue to work while displaying the **Properties** palette. To close the palette, pick the **X** in the top-left corner, select **Close** from the shortcut menu, or press [Ctrl]+[1].

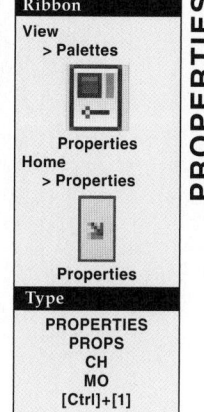

PROPERTIES

Ribbon
View
> Palettes

Properties

Home
> Properties

Properties

Type
PROPERTIES
PROPS
CH
MO
[Ctrl]+[1]

Figure 14-12.
The **Quick Properties** panel with three objects selected. You can edit the objects individually or select All (3) to edit all of the objects together.

Total number of objects selected

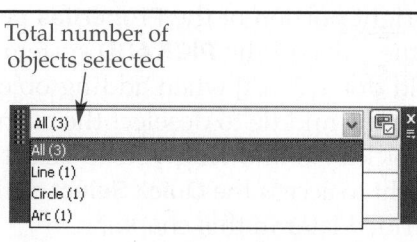

All (3)
All (3)
Line (1)
Circle (1)
Arc (1)

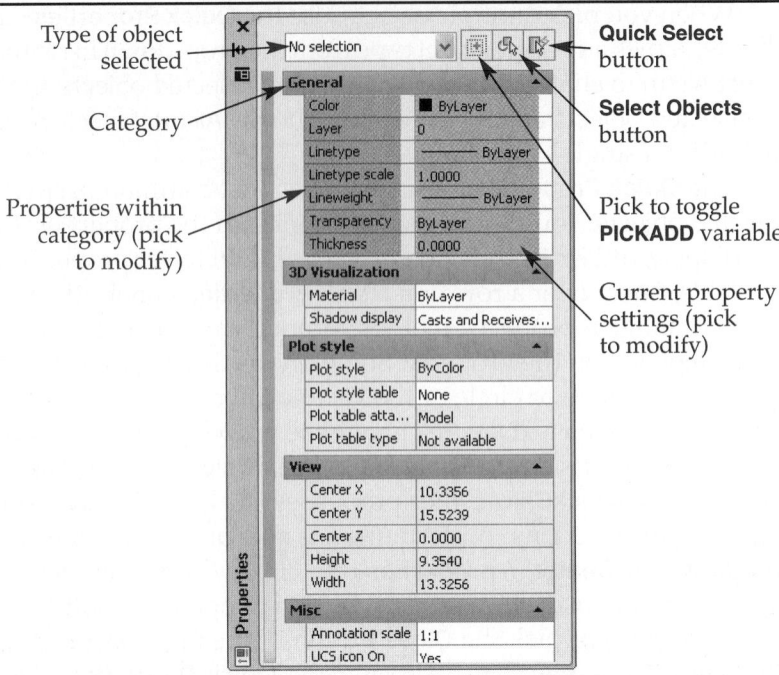

Figure 14-13.
Use the **Properties** palette to modify drawing settings and object properties.

Type of object selected

Category

Properties within category (pick to modify)

Quick Select button

Select Objects button

Pick to toggle **PICKADD** variable

Current property settings (pick to modify)

NOTE

If you already selected an object, you can access the **Properties** palette by right-clicking and selecting **Properties**. You can also double-click specific objects to select the object and open the **Properties** palette automatically.

Working with properties in the **Properties** palette is similar to working with properties in the **Quick Properties** panel. The drop-down list at the top of the **Properties** palette identifies the selected object. Properties associated with the selected object display below the drop-down list in categories and property rows. The categories and rows update to display properties associated with your selections. If you do not select an object, the **General**, **3D Visualization**, **Plot style**, **View**, and **Misc** categories list the current drawing settings.

When you pick multiple objects, use the **Properties** palette to modify all of the objects, or pick a specific object type from the drop-down list to modify. See **Figure 14-14**. Select All (*n*) to change the properties of all selected objects. Only properties shared by all selected objects appear when you choose All (*n*).

You should recognize most of the properties listed in the **Properties** palette. Do not adjust properties that you do not recognize. For example, the **3D Visualization** category and any properties related to the Z axis are for use in 3D applications.

To change a property, pick the property or current value. The way you change a value depends on the property, just as it does in the **Quick Properties** panel. Use the appropriate text box, drop-down list, or button to modify the value. After you make changes to the objects, press [Esc] to clear grips and remove the objects from the **Properties** palette. Close the **Properties** palette when you are finished.

The upper-right portion of the **Properties** palette contains three buttons. The left button toggles the value of the **PICKADD** system variable, which determines whether you need to hold down [Shift] when adding objects to a selection set. Pick the **Select Objects** button in the middle to deselect the currently selected objects and change the crosshairs to a pick box, allowing you to select other objects. Pick the **Quick Select** button on the right to access the **Quick Select** dialog box, where you can create a selection set, as described later in this chapter.

Figure 14-14.
The **Properties** palette with four objects selected. You can edit the objects individually or select All (4) to edit all of the objects together.

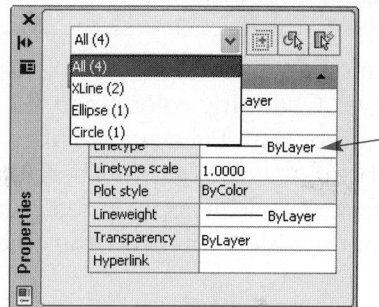

When All is selected, only properties common to all selected objects appear

General Properties

The **General** category of the **Properties** palette allows you to modify general object properties such as color, layer, linetype, linetype scale, plot style, lineweight, transparency, and thickness. See **Figure 14-15**. The **Quick Properties** panel also lists certain general properties.

NOTE

You can change the layer of a selected object by choosing a layer from the **Layer Control** drop-down list in the **Layers** panel on the **Home** ribbon tab. You can override color, linetype, lineweight, and plot style by choosing from the appropriate drop-down list in the **Properties** panel on the **Home** ribbon tab. Override transparency by selecting from the flyout and using the slider, also in the **Properties** panel on the **Home** ribbon tab.

AutoCAD 2011
NEW

Figure 14-15. A—The **Properties** palette with a Line object selected. Line objects have options in only three property categories. B—The **Properties** palette with a Circle object selected.

Type of object selected

General properties

Start point and endpoint coordinates

These values cannot be directly modified, but change if endpoints are modified

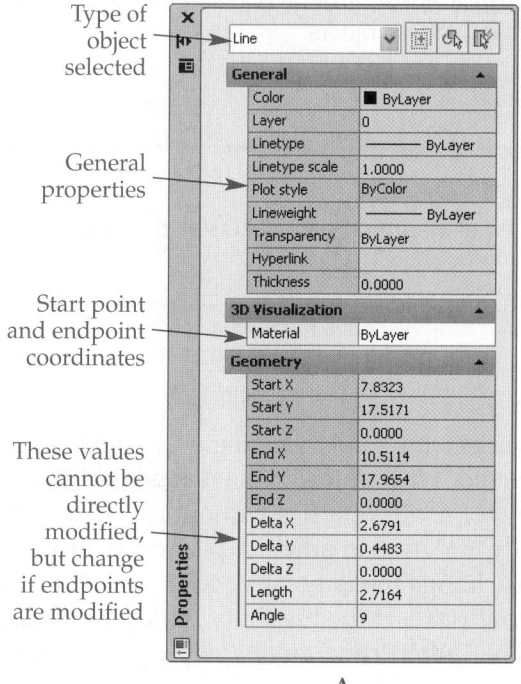

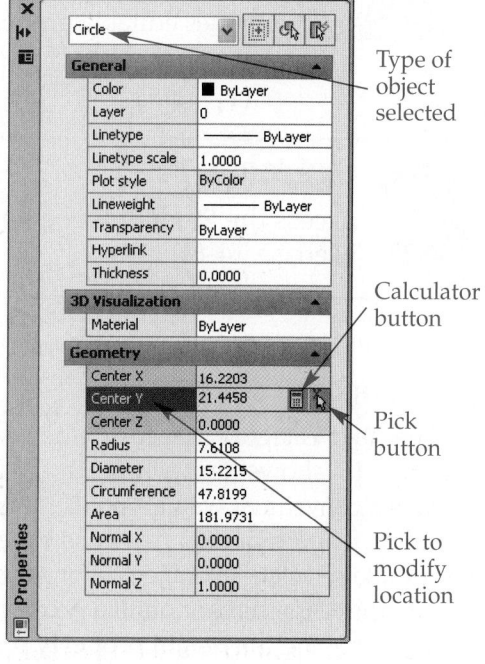

Type of object selected

Calculator button

Pick button

Pick to modify location

A

B

CAUTION

Color, linetype, lineweight, and transparency should typically be set as ByLayer. Changing color, linetype, lineweight, or transparency to a value other than ByLayer overrides logical properties, making the property an *absolute value*. Therefore, if the color of an object is set to red, for example, it appears red regardless of the color assigned to the layer on which you draw the object.

CAUTION

For most applications, linetype scale should be set globally so the linetype scale of all objects is constant. Adjusting the linetype scale of individual objects can create nonstandard drawings and make it difficult to adjust linetype scale globally. For most applications, you should not override color, linetype, linetype scale, plot style, lineweight, transparency, or thickness.

Geometry Properties

The **Geometry** category of the **Properties** palette allows you to modify object coordinates and dimensions. Refer again to **Figure 14-15**. The properties in the **Geometry** category vary depending on the selection. **Figure 14-15A** highlights the X, Y, and Z coordinates that you can use to relocate the start point and endpoint of a line. **Figure 14-15B** highlights the X, Y, and Z coordinates that you can use to relocate the center of a circle. Enter a value, select the calculator to calculate a value, or use the pick button to specify a point on-screen. The **Quick Properties** panel also lists certain geometry properties.

PROFESSIONAL TIP

The **Radius**, **Diameter**, **Circumference**, and **Area** properties are especially useful for modifying the dimension of a circle. Circle properties are an example of the useful information and instinctive adjustments often available using the **Properties** palette. The **Properties** palette provides editable properties for most objects.

Exercise 14-8

Access the Student Web site (www.g-wlearning.com/CAD) and complete Exercise 14-8.

Text Properties

The **Text** category appears when you select an mtext or single-line text object. **Figure 14-16** shows text properties associated with mtext. The **Properties** palette provides a convenient way to modify a variety of text properties without re-entering the text editor. The **Properties** palette is especially effective to adjust a particular property for multiple selected text objects. For example, change the annotative setting of all text in the drawing using the **Annotative** property row, or reset the height of multiple mtext or text objects using the **Height** property row. The **Quick Properties** panel also lists certain text-specific properties.

Figure 14–16.
The **Properties**
palette shows
the properties of
selected multiline
text. The properties
of single-line text
are slightly different
from those of mtext.

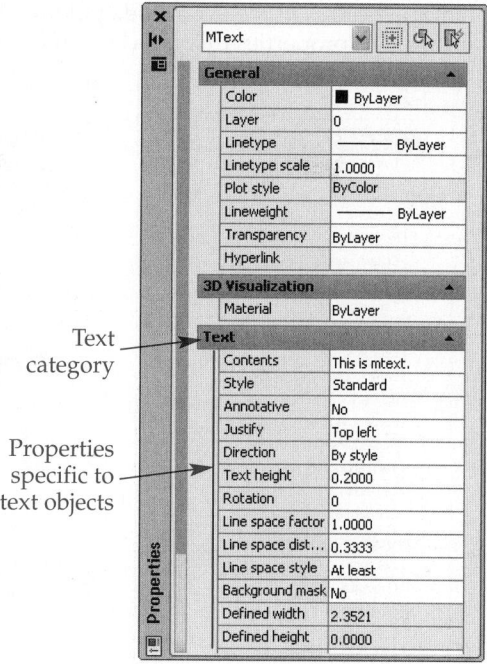

Text
category

Properties
specific to
text objects

Exercise 14-9

Access the Student Web site (www.g-wlearning.com/CAD) and complete
Exercise 14-9.

Table Properties

The **Properties** palette displays certain table properties depending on whether you
select inside a cell or pick a cell edge. See **Figure 14-17**. The **Cell** and **Content** categories
appear when you select inside a cell, and allow you to adjust the properties of the selected
cell. The **Table** and **Table Breaks** categories appear when you select a cell edge, and include
common table settings and table break properties. The **Quick Properties** panel also lists
certain table-specific properties.

PROFESSIONAL TIP

If the height of table rows is taller than desired, or if rows become
unequal in height, enter a very small value in the **Table height** row of
the **Table** category to return all rows to the smallest height possible
based on the margin spacing between cell content and cell borders.

Several useful options are available in the **Table Breaks** category of the **Properties**
palette for adjusting table breaks. The **Enabled** option toggles between the broken and
unbroken display. The **Yes** value appears when you create table breaks and enable
breaking. Pick **No** to return the table to an unbroken display. The **Direction** option
defines direction of broken table flow, or wrap. The default **Right** option wraps the
table to the right. Select **Left** to wrap the table to the left or pick **Up** to wrap the table
above.

Figure 14-17. Table properties in the **Properties** palette. A—The properties displayed when you select inside a cell. B—The properties displayed when you pick a cell edge.

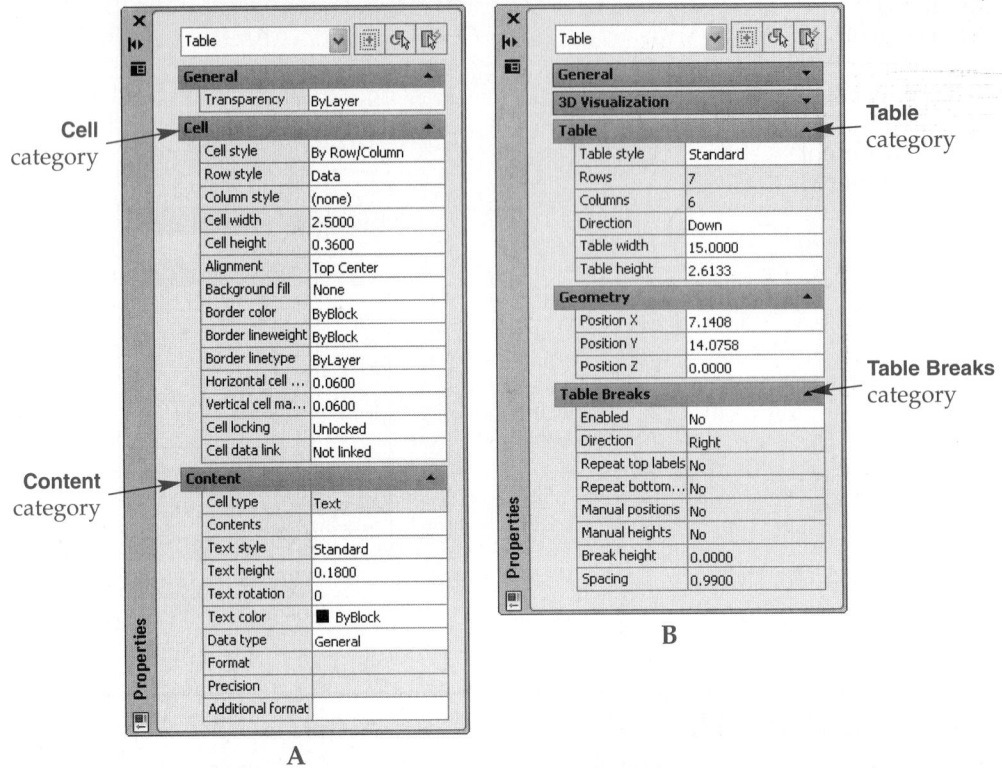

A

B

Cell category

Content category

Table category

Table Breaks category

The **Repeat top labels** option repeats cells that use a **Label** cell type at the beginning of each table section. Typically, the title cell and header cells use a **Label** cell type. Choose **Yes** to add the title and header cells to the wrapped table sections. The **Repeat bottom labels** option repeats cells that use a **Label** cell type at the end of each section. The **Manual positions** option allows you to move table sections independently while maintaining the table as a single object. When you select **No**, table sections move as a group.

The **Manual height** option adds a table-breaking grip to each section, which allows you to adjust the number of rows in each section independently and add additional breaks. When you select **No**, the table-breaking grip appears at the original section only and controls the number of breaks. The **Break height** text box allows you to define the height of each table section. The selected height determines the number of sections. The **Spacing** text box allows you to define the spacing between table sections. A value of 0 places the sections together.

PROFESSIONAL TIP

Fields provide an effective way to display drawing information within mtext and text objects. You can use fields with many AutoCAD tools, including inquiry tools, drawing properties, attributes, and sheet sets. You can update fields when changes occur to the reference data. Chapter 10 explains using fields. **Figure 14-18** shows acquiring object properties to display in fields.

Figure 14-18. Pick the Object field to add a property for a specific object to a field. Pick the **Select object** button to select the object. Properties specific to the object type appear. Select the property and format for the field.

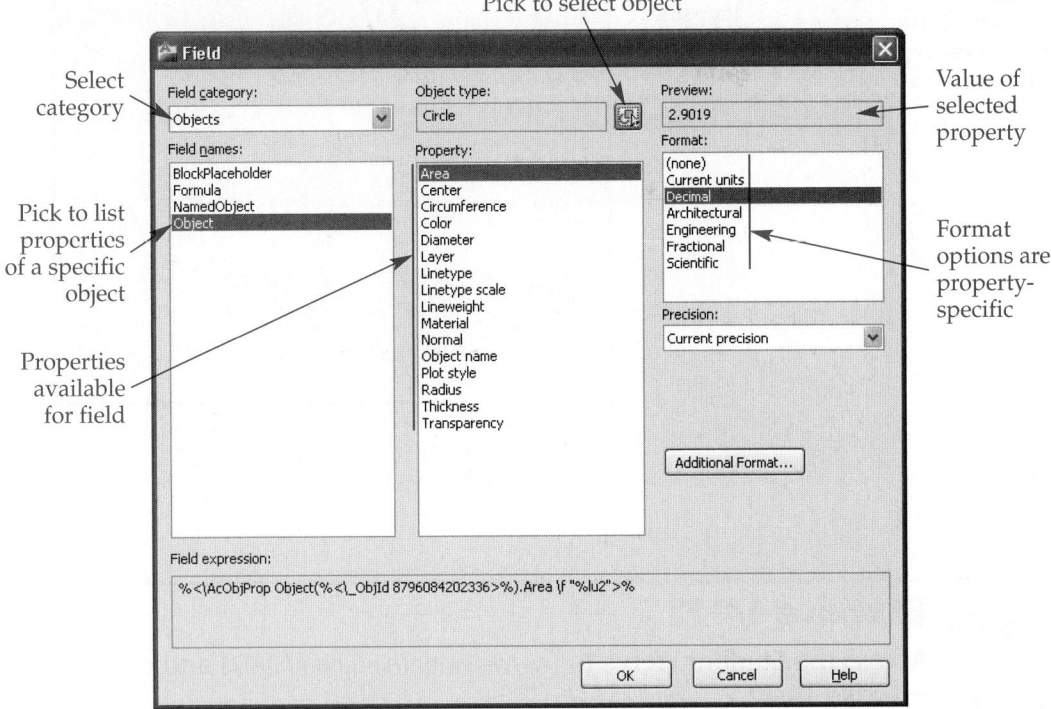

Pick to select object

Select category

Pick to list properties of a specific object

Properties available for field

Value of selected property

Format options are property-specific

Exercises 14-10 and 14-11

Access the Student Web site (www.g-wlearning.com/CAD) and complete Exercise 14-10 and Exercise 14-11.

Matching Properties

The **MATCHPROP** tool allows you to copy, or "paint," properties from one object to other objects. You can match properties in the same drawing or between drawings. When you first access the **MATCHPROP** tool, AutoCAD prompts you for the *source object*. After you select the source object, AutoCAD displays the properties it will paint. The next prompt allows you to pick the *destination objects*.

To change the paint properties, select the **Settings** option before picking the destination objects. The **Property Settings** dialog box appears, showing the properties to paint. See **Figure 14-19.** Properties are replaced in the destination objects if the corresponding **Property Settings** dialog box check boxes are active. For example, to paint only the layer property and text style of one text object to another text object, uncheck all boxes except the **Layer** and **Text** property check boxes. Pick the **OK** button to select destination objects.

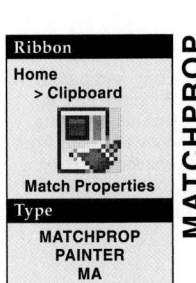

Ribbon
Home
> Clipboard

Match Properties
Type
MATCHPROP
PAINTER
MA

MATCHPROP

source object: When matching properties, the object with the properties you want to copy to other objects.

destination object: When matching properties, the object that receives the properties of the source object.

Figure 14-19.
The **Property Settings** dialog box for the **MATCHPROP** tool. Select the properties to paint to the destination objects.

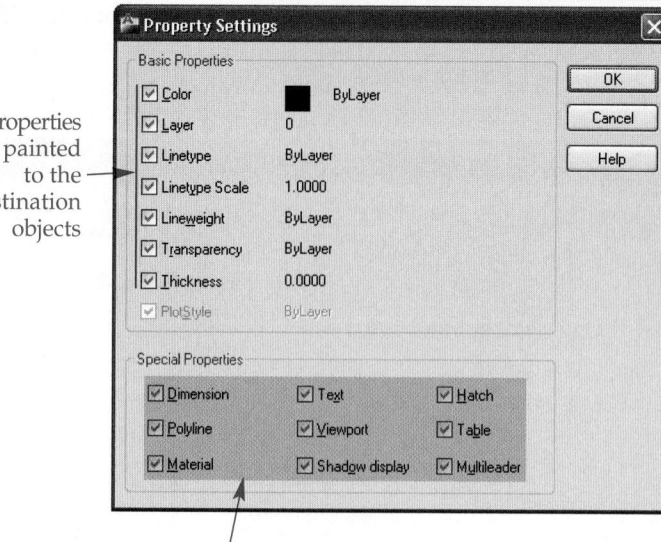

Properties painted to the destination objects

Properties particular to specific objects

Exercise 14-12

Access the Student Web site (www.g-wlearning.com/CAD) and complete Exercise 14-12.

Editing between Drawings

You can edit in more than one drawing at a time and edit between open drawings. For example, you can copy objects from one drawing to another. You can also refer to a drawing to obtain information, such as a distance, while working in a different drawing.

Figure 14-20 shows two drawings, each of a different section for the same home remodel project, tiled vertically. The Windows *copy and paste* function allows you to copy objects from one drawing to another. For example, copy the rafters and exterior studs from the Proposed Entry Section A drawing to paste and reuse in the Proposed Bath Section B. Select the objects to copy from the source drawing and choose a copy option. Then switch to the destination drawing and select a paste option.

copy and paste: A Windows function that allows you to copy an object from one location and paste it into another.

You can cut, copy, and paste between documents using options from the **Clipboard** panel on the **Home** ribbon tab, the **Clipboard** cascading shortcut menu, or the Windows-standard keyboard shortcuts. **Figure 14-21** briefly explains cut, copy, and paste options available when you right-click after selecting objects or after cutting or copying objects. Many of the same options are available from the **Clipboard** panel on the **Home** ribbon tab, and by typing, as shown.

PROFESSIONAL TIP

You may find it more convenient to use the **MATCHPROP** tool to match properties between drawings. To use the **MATCHPROP** tool between drawings, select the source object from one drawing and the destination object from another.

Figure 14-20. Tile multiple drawings to make editing between drawings easier.

Active drawing

Docked
Properties
palette

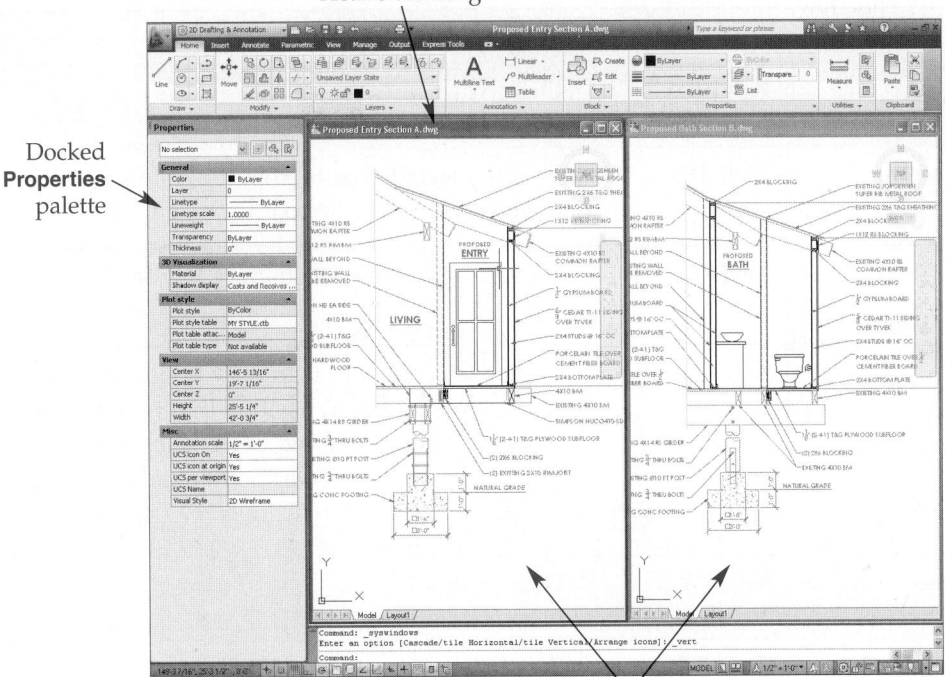

Cut or copy and paste, or use the
MATCHPROP tool to work between open drawings

Exercise 14-13

Access the Student Web site (www.g-wlearning.com/CAD) and complete
Exercise 14-13.

Add Selected

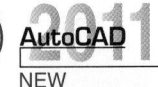
NEW

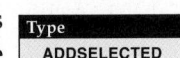

The **ADDSELECTED** tool allows you to draw a new object using the properties
of an existing object, without locating and selecting the object tool or presetting the
layer or other properties. An easy way to access the **ADDSELECTED** tool is to select
the object to replicate and then right-click and choose **Add Selected**. AutoCAD initiates the drawing tool and assigns properties corresponding to the selected object. For
example, pick a circle, right-click and choose **Add Selected**, and draw a circle as if you
had accessed the **CIRCLE** tool. AutoCAD applies the properties of the selected circle to
the new circle, regardless of the current settings.

Select Similar

NEW

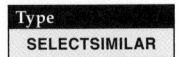

The **SELECTSIMILAR** tool provides another method of creating a selection set.
AutoCAD selects all objects in the drawing that match certain properties of objects
you select. An easy way to access the **SELECTSIMILAR** tool is to pick the object type
you want to select throughout the drawing and then right-click and choose **Select**

Figure 14-21. Options available for cutting, copying, and pasting objects in the active drawing or between drawings.

Cutting or Copying		
Option	**Keyboard Shortcut**	**Description**
Cut	[Ctrl]+[X]	Erases selected objects from the drawing and places the objects in the Clipboard.
Copy	[Ctrl]+[C]	Copies selected objects to the Clipboard.
Copy with Base Point	[Ctrl]+[Shift]+[C]	Copies selected objects to the Clipboard using a specific base point to position the copied objects for pasting. When prompted, select a logical base point, such as a corner or center point of an object.
Pasting		
Option	**Keyboard Shortcut**	**Description**
Paste	[Ctrl]+[V]	Pastes the objects on the Clipboard to the drawing. If you used the **Copy with Base Point** option, the objects attach to the crosshairs at the specified base point.
Paste as Block	[Ctrl]+[Shift]+[V]	Pastes and "joins" all objects on the Clipboard to the drawing as a block. The pasted objects act as a single object. Blocks are covered later in this textbook. Use the **EXPLODE** tool to break up the block.
Paste to Original Coordinates		Pastes the objects on the Clipboard to the same coordinates at which they were located in the original drawing.

Similar. By default, all objects of the same type and layer are selected. For example, pick a polyline object drawn on a HIDDEN layer, and then right-click and choose **Select Similar** to create a selection set of all polylines drawn on the HIDDEN layer.

To specify the properties for selecting similar objects, you must type SELECTSIMILAR before picking objects, and then choose the **SEttings** option to display the **Select Similar Settings** dialog box. Use the check boxes to filter the properties that must match the objects you pick in order for other objects to select. The more boxes you check, the more properties must match in order for AutoCAD to select objects.

NOTE

You can pick multiple objects with different properties to select all similar objects. For example, pick a line, arc, and spline, each assigned a unique layer, to select all lines, arcs, and splines with matching layers.

Quick Select

Ribbon
Home
> Utilities

Quick Select

Type
QSELECT

QSELECT

The **QSELECT**, or **Quick Select**, tool is similar to the **SELECTSIMILAR** tool, but provides additional filters. For example, use the **SELECTSIMILAR** tool to pick all circles in a drawing, but use the **Quick Select** tool to pick Ø2″ circles. Access the **Quick Select** tool to display the **Quick Select** dialog box shown in **Figure 14-22**. The **Quick Select** dialog box provides options for specifying the exact objects to include in or exclude from the selection set.

Begin the process by selecting the **Entire drawing** option from the **Apply to:** drop-down list to have access to all object types in the drawing for creating a selection set. An alternative is to pick specific objects to create an initial filter of just the selected objects. Pick objects before accessing the **Quick Select** tool, or choose the **Select Objects** button to return to the drawing window temporarily to pick objects. The **Apply to:** drop-down list then displays **Current selection**. Choose **Entire drawing** option or check **Append to current selection set** at the bottom of the dialog box to return to the entire drawing format.

Pick a specific object type from the **Object type:** drop-down list to create a selection set according to the object type. The **Multiple** option displays properties common to different objects in the entire drawing or the selected objects. Pick a property from the **Properties:** list to narrow the selection set. The items in the **Properties:** list vary depending on the specified object type or **Multiple** option.

The **Value:** text box or drop-down list allows you to specify a property value to narrow the selection set. Use the **Operator:** drop-down list to assign a *relative operator* to control which objects are selected according to the specified property value. For example, to select all Ø2″ circles in the drawing, select the **Entire drawing** option, a **Circle** object type, the **Diameter** property, and the **= Equals** operator, and type a value of 2.

> **relative operators:** In math, functions that determine the relationship between data items.

The **Include in new selection set** radio button creates a selection set according to the quick select settings, as previously described. The **Exclude from new selection set** radio button reverses the selection set to select all objects except those you specify. Using the previous example, all objects except Ø2″ circles would be selected. Pick the **OK** button to create the selection set.

Figure 14-22.
Use the **Quick Select** dialog box to create a specific selection set.

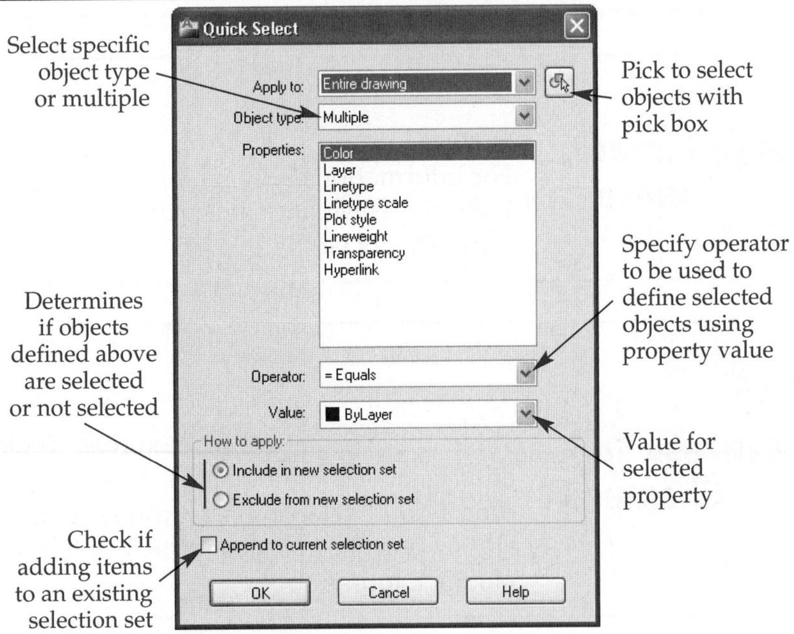

Select specific object type or multiple

Pick to select objects with pick box

Specify operator to be used to define selected objects using property value

Determines if objects defined above are selected or not selected

Value for selected property

Check if adding items to an existing selection set

PROFESSIONAL TIP

Creating a selection set according to specific properties can be very useful. For example, suppose you design a sheet metal part with many different size holes (circle objects) at different locations, and 20 of the holes accept 1/8″ screws. A design change occurs, and a request specifies to use 3/16″ screws instead. You could select and modify each circle individually, but it is more efficient to create a selection set of the 20 circles of the same size and modify them at the same time. Use the **Quick Properties** panel or the **Properties** palette to adjust properties of objects selected using the **SELECTSIMILAR** or **Quick Select** tools. You can also use parametric tools, explained in Chapter 22, to make all the circles equal in size. Then, when you change the diameter of one circle, all circles change to the new value.

Exercise 14-14

Access the Student Web site (www.g-wlearning.com/CAD) and complete Exercise 14-14.

Object Selection Filters

For detailed information about selecting multiple objects using the **Object Selection Filters** dialog box, go to the Student Web site (www.g-wlearning.com/CAD), select this chapter, and select **Object Selection Filters**.

Object Groups

For information about creating object groups, go to the Student Web site (www.g-wlearning.com/CAD), select this chapter, and select **Object Groups**.

Express Tools
Chapter 14

The **Modify** panel of the **Express Tools** ribbon tab includes additional editing tools. For information about the most useful modify and selection set express tools, go to the Student Web site (www.g-wlearning.com/CAD), select this chapter, and select **Modify Express Tools**.

Chapter Test

Answer the following questions. Write your answers on a separate sheet of paper or go to the Student Web site (www.g-wlearning.com/CAD) and complete the electronic chapter test.

1. Name the editing tools that are available using standard grips.
2. How can you select a grip tool other than the default **STRETCH**?
3. What is the purpose of the **Base Point** option in the grip tools?
4. Explain the function of the **Undo** option in the grip tools.
5. What happens when you choose the **eXit** option from the grips shortcut menu?
6. Which option of the **ROTATE** grip tool would you use to rotate an object from an existing 60° angle to a new 25° angle?
7. Describe the options for editing object properties.
8. Where does the **Quick Properties** panel appear by default when you select an object?
9. By default, how many properties appear in the **Quick Properties** panel?
10. Identify at least two ways to access the **Properties** palette.
11. Explain how to change the radius of a circle from 1.375 to 1.875 using the **Properties** palette.
12. How can you change the linetype of an object using the **Properties** palette?
13. For most applications, what value should you use for the color, linetype, and lineweight of objects?
14. What tool changes the properties of existing objects to match the properties of a different object?
15. Briefly explain how the Windows copy and paste function works to copy an object from one drawing to another.
16. Name the paste option that joins a group of objects as a block when pasted.
17. When you use the option described in Question 16, how do you separate the objects back into individual objects?
18. What is the purpose of the **ADDSELECTED** tool? Provide an example.
19. What is the purpose of the **SELECTSIMILAR** tool? Provide an example.
20. List the information you would specify in the **Quick Select** dialog box to select all ⌀6″ circles in a drawing.

Drawing Problems

Start AutoCAD if it is not already started. Start a new drawing for each problem using an appropriate template of your choice. The template should include layers, text styles, and table styles, when necessary, for drawing the given objects. Add layers, text styles, and table styles as needed. Draw all objects using appropriate layers, text styles, table styles, justification, and format. Follow the specific instructions for each problem. Use only drawing and editing tools and techniques you have already learned. Do not draw dimensions. Use your own judgment and approximate dimensions when necessary.

▼ Basic

1. Draw the objects labeled A. Then use **STRETCH** grip tool to make the objects look like the objects labeled B. Save the drawing as P14-1.

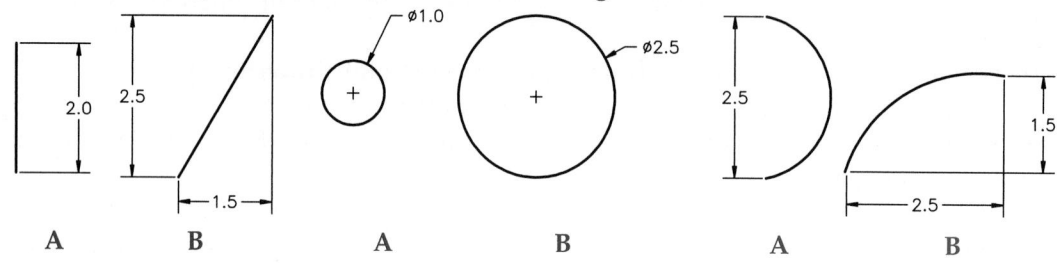

2. Draw the object labeled A. Use the **Copy** option of the **MOVE** grip tool to copy the object to the position labeled B. Edit Object A so it resembles Object C. Edit Object B so it looks like Object D. Save the drawing as P14-2.

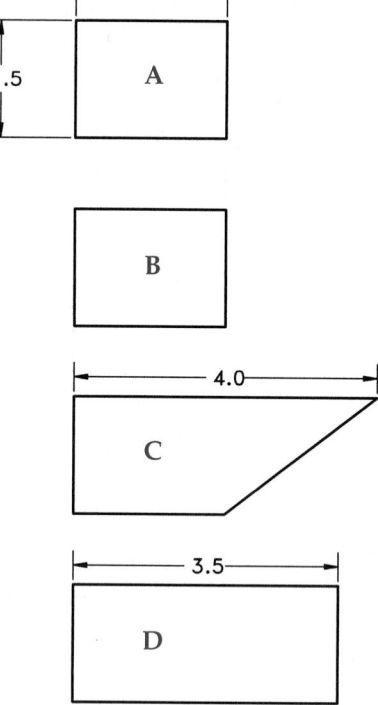

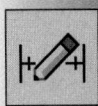

3. Draw the view labeled A. Copy the object, without rotating it, to a position below, as indicated by the dashed lines. Rotate the object 45°. Copy the rotated object labeled B to a position below, as indicated by the dashed lines. Use the **Reference** option to rotate the object labeled C to 25°, as shown. Save the drawing as P14-3.

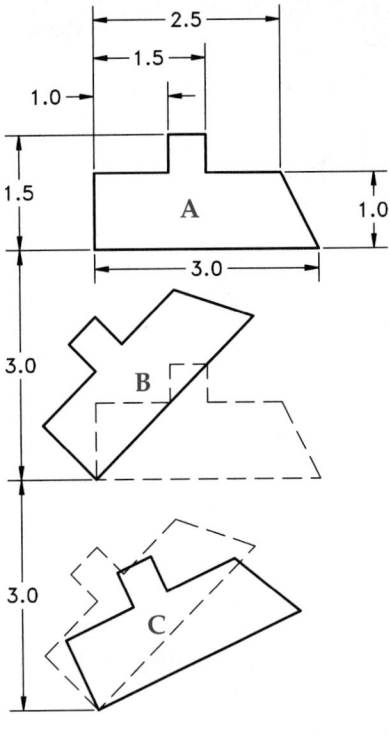

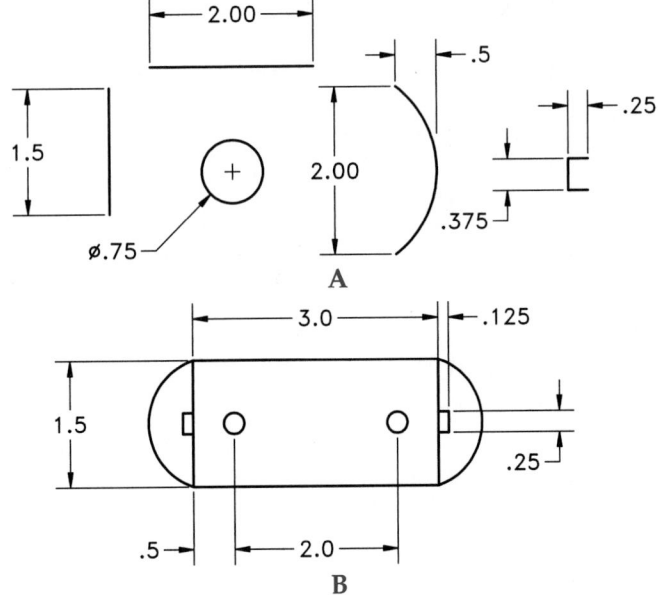

▼ Intermediate

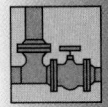

4. Draw the individual objects (vertical line, horizontal line, circle, arc, and polyline shape) in A using the dimensions given. Use these objects and grips to create the view shown in B. Save the drawing as P14-4.

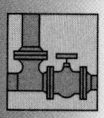

5. Open P14-4 and save the file as P14-5. The P14-5 file should be active. Copy the view two times to positions B and C. Use the **SCALE** grip tool to scale the view in position B to 50 percent of its original size. Use the **Reference** option of the **SCALE** grip tool to enlarge the view in position C from the existing 3.0 length to a 4.5 length, as shown in C. Resave the drawing.

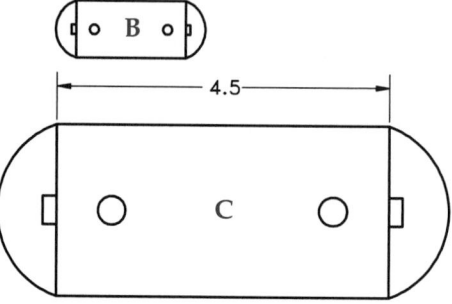

6. Draw the portion of the gasket shown in A. Use the **MIRROR** grip tool to complete the gasket as shown in B. Save the drawing as P14-6.

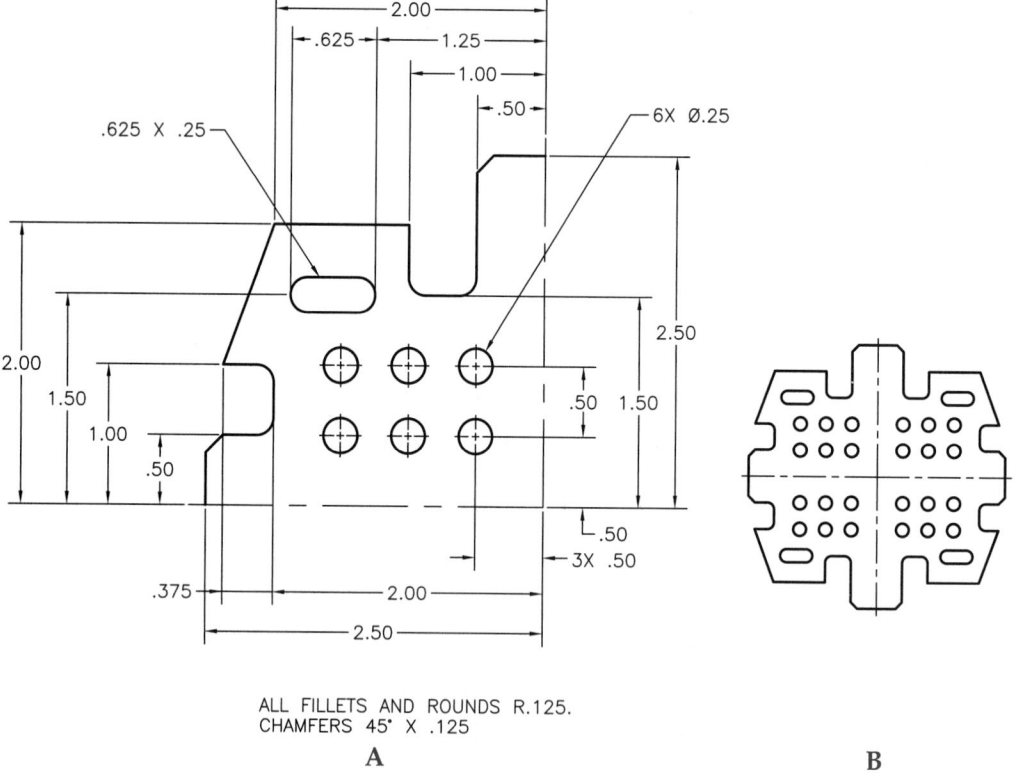

ALL FILLETS AND ROUNDS R.125.
CHAMFERS 45° X .125

A

B

7. Open P14-6 and save the file as P14-7. The P14-7 file should be active. Use the **Properties** palette to change the diameters of the circles from .25 to .125. Change the layer assigned to the slots to a layer that uses a PHANTOM linetype. Be sure the linetype scale allows the linetypes to display correctly. Resave the drawing.

8. Draw an assembly view similar to the one shown within the boundaries of the given dimensions. All other dimensions are flexible. Save the drawing as P14-8.

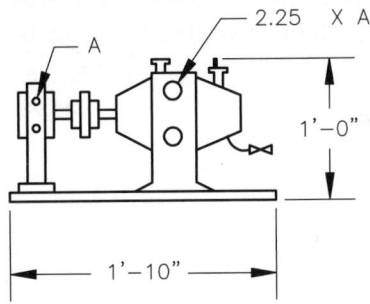

9. Draw the half of the gasket shown. Mirror the drawing to complete the other half of the gasket. Save the drawing as P14-9.

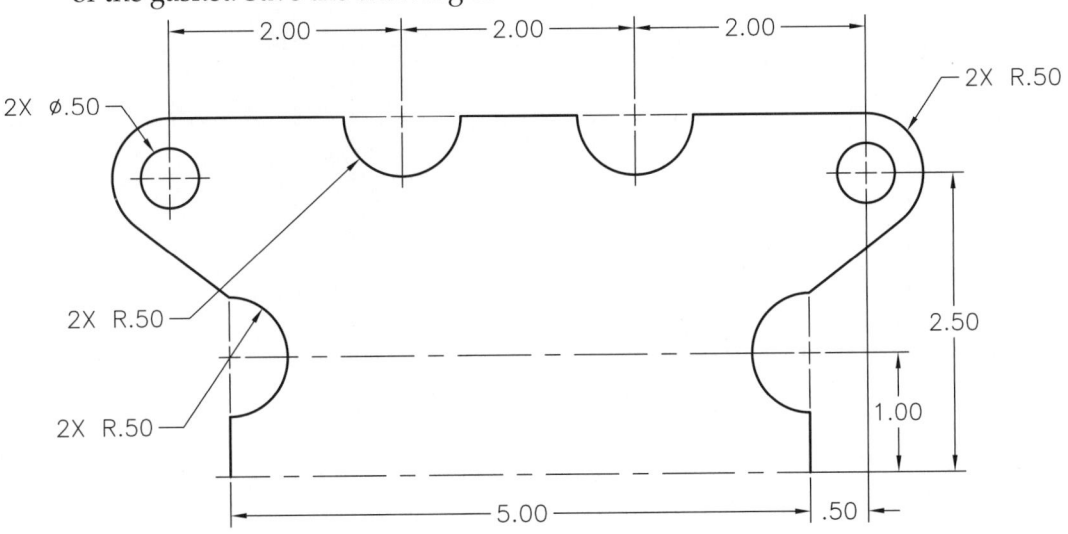

10. Draw the control diagram shown. Draw one branch (including text) and use the **COPY** grip tool to your advantage. Use text editing tools as needed. Save the drawing as P14-10.

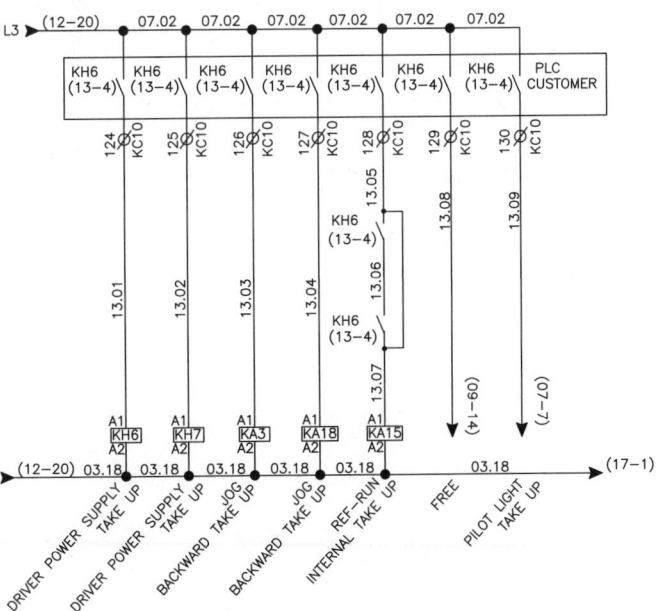

(Design and drawing by EC Company, Portland, Oregon)

▼ **Advanced**

11. Draw the folded and flat pattern views of the sheet metal bracket shown. The part material is 18-gauge steel. Save the drawing as P14-11.

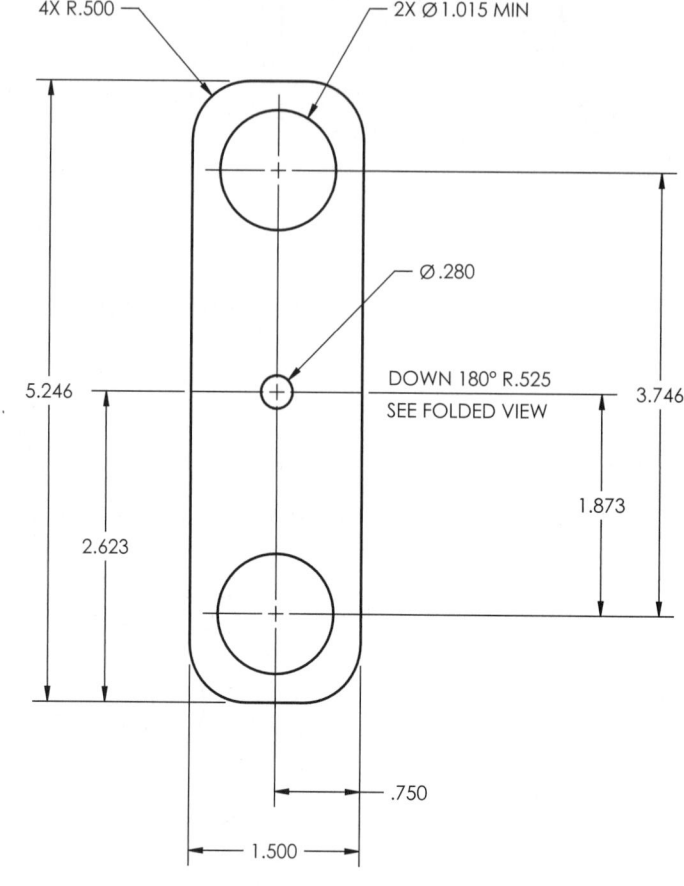

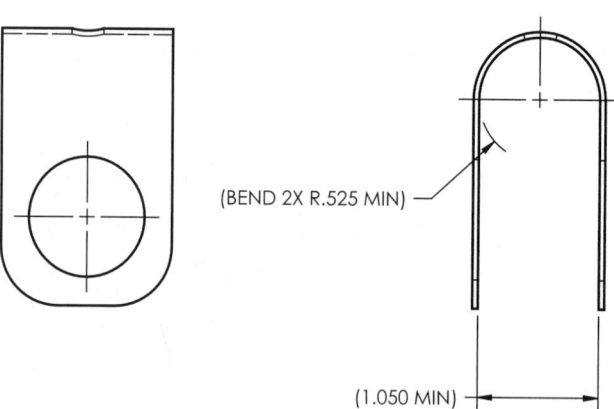

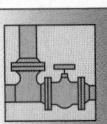

12. Draw a tank similar to the one shown within the boundaries of the given dimensions. All other dimensions are flexible. After drawing the tank, create a page for a vendor catalog, as follows:
   - All labels should be ROMAND text, centered directly below the view. Use a text height of .125".
   - Label the drawing ONE-GALLON TANK WITH HORIZONTAL VALVE.
   - Keep the valve at the same scale as the original drawing in each copy.
   - Copy the original tank to a new location and scale it so it is 2 times its original size. Rotate the valve 45°. Label this tank TWO-GALLON TANK WITH 45° VALVE.
   - Copy the original tank to another location and scale it to 2.5 times the size of the original. Rotate the valve 90°. Label this tank TWO-AND-ONE-HALF-GALLON TANK WITH 90° VALVE.
   - Copy the two-gallon tank to a new position and scale it so it is 2 times this size. Rotate the valve to 22°30′. Label this tank FOUR-GALLON TANK WITH 22°30′ VALVE.
   - Left-justify this note at the bottom of the page: Combinations of tank size and valve orientation are available upon request.
   - Use the **Properties** palette to change all tank labels to ROMANC, .25" high.
   - Change the note at the bottom of the sheet to ROMANS, centered on the sheet, using uppercase letters.
   - Save the drawing as P14-12.

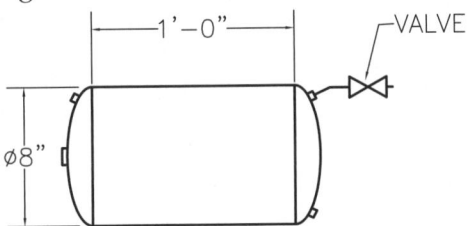

13. Create the interior finish schedule shown using the **TABLE** tool. Make the measurements for the rows and columns approximately the same as in the given table. Use the **Properties** palette as you construct the schedule. Save the drawing as P14-13.

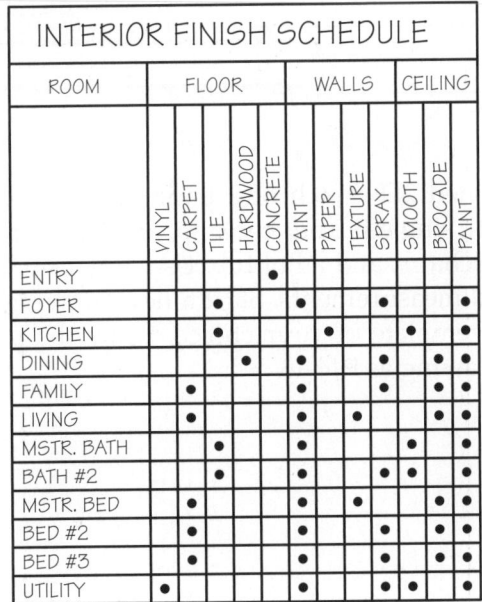

INTERIOR FINISH SCHEDULE											
ROOM	FLOOR					WALLS				CEILING	
	VINYL	CARPET	TILE	HARDWOOD	CONCRETE	PAINT	PAPER	TEXTURE	SPRAY	SMOOTH	BROCADE	PAINT
ENTRY					●							
FOYER			●			●			●			●
KITCHEN			●				●			●		●
DINING				●		●			●		●	●
FAMILY		●				●			●		●	●
LIVING		●				●		●			●	●
MSTR. BATH			●			●				●		●
BATH #2			●			●			●	●		●
MSTR. BED		●				●		●			●	●
BED #2		●				●			●		●	●
BED #3		●				●			●		●	●
UTILITY	●					●			●	●		●

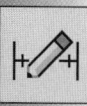

14. Draw the three views of a sports car. Save the drawing as P14-14.

15. Draw the sailboat shown. Save the drawing as P14-15.

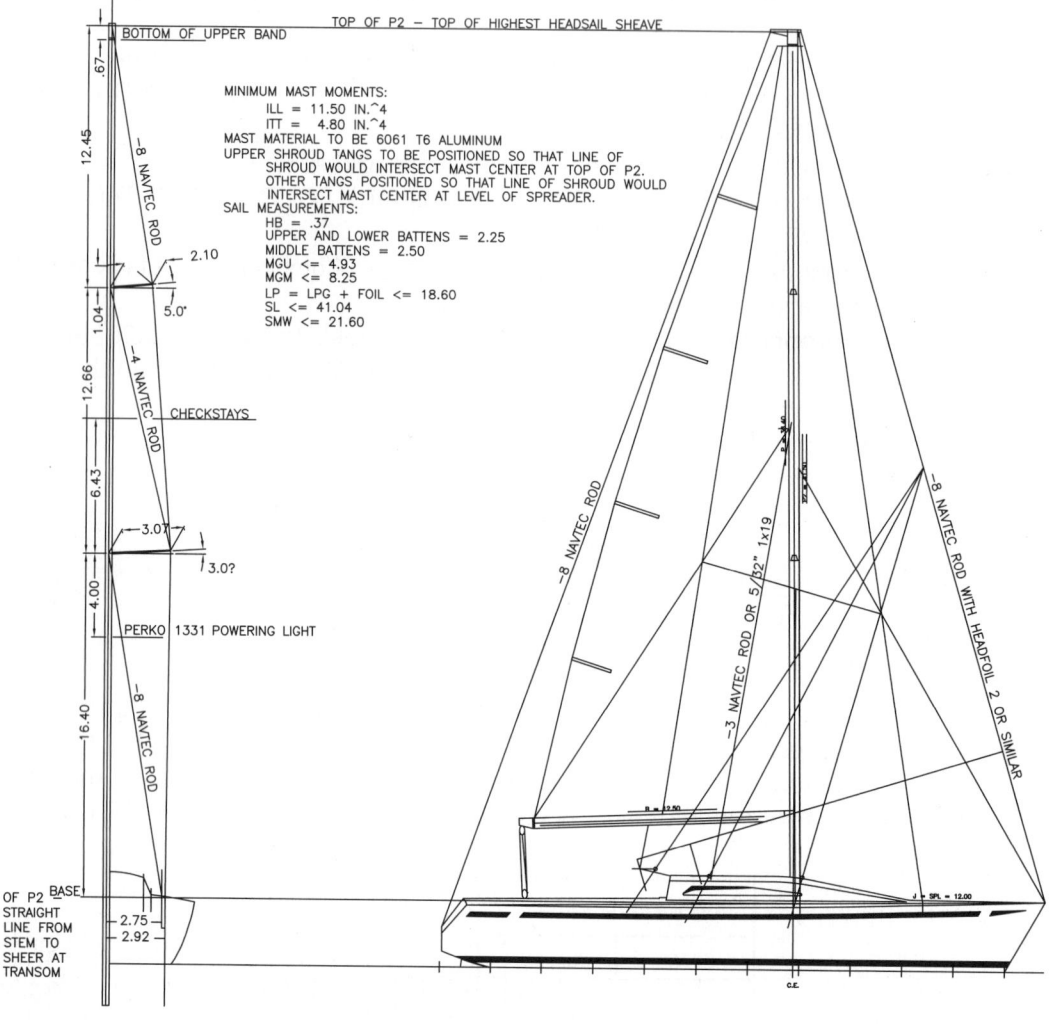

16. Create a dimensioned 2D sketch of a patio or deck plan. Include an outdoor kitchen with a grill, single-burner cooktop, and refrigerator. Add ample seating areas, a table with chairs, and a hot tub. Use dimensions based on your experience, research, and measurements. Start a new drawing from scratch or use an architectural-unit template of your choice. Draw the patio or deck from your sketch. Save the drawing as P14-16.

AutoCAD Certified Associate Exam Practice

Answer the following questions. Write your answers on a separate sheet of paper.

1. Which of the following operations can be performed using grips? *Select all that apply.*
   A. exploding a polygon into individual lines
   B. reflecting an object to create a mirror image
   C. reversing the order of point calculation for an object
   D. rotating an object by 17°
   E. scaling an object to half its current size

2. If you do not use the **Base point** option of a grip tool, which point does AutoCAD automatically select as the base point for the grip editing operation? *Select the one item that best answers the question.*
   A. the lower-left corner of the object
   B. the origin (0,0,0)
   C. a point you specify
   D. the selected grip

3. Which of the following relative operators are available for filtering data? *Select all that apply.*
   A. *
   B. /
   C. =
   D. <
   E. >
   F. >=

AutoCAD Certified Professional Exam Practice

Follow the instructions in each problem. Write your answers on a separate sheet of paper.

1. **Navigate to this chapter on the Student Web site and open CPE-14grips.dwg.**

   Use grips to rotate the metal plate 23.5°, as shown. Select the appropriate grip or use the **Base point** option to select the base point for the rotation. What are the coordinates of the center of the hole?

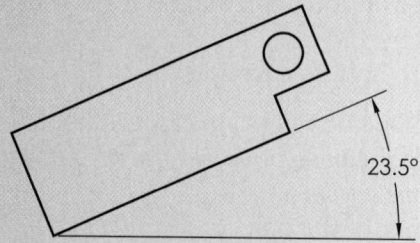

2. **Navigate to this chapter on the Student Web site and open CPE-14select.dwg.**

   Enter the **SELECTSIMILAR** tool using the command line or dynamic input and specify the **SEttings** option. Disable all of the **Similar Based On** check boxes except **Color, Layer,** and **Name**. Select the port in the lower-left corner of the connector system and press [Enter]. How many ports are selected based on your settings?

Polyline and Spline Editing Tools

Learning Objectives

After completing this chapter, you will be able to do the following:

✓ Edit polylines with the **PEDIT** tool.
✓ Use context-sensitive polyline grip tools.
✓ Create polyline boundaries.
✓ Edit splines with the **SPLINEDIT** tool.
✓ Use context-sensitive polyline grip tools.
✓ Convert polylines and splines.

You can modify polyline and spline objects using standard editing tools such as **ERASE**, **STRETCH**, and **SCALE**, but AutoCAD also provides specific tools to edit polylines and splines. Use the **PEDIT** tool or polyline grip tools to modify polylines. Use the **SPLINEDIT** tool or spline grip tools to modify splines. This chapter also describes how to create polyline boundaries and explores additional options for converting polylines and splines.

Using the PEDIT Tool

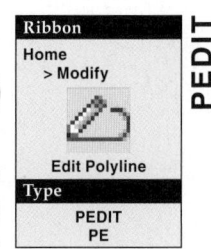

Ribbon
Home
> Modify

Edit Polyline

Type
PEDIT
PE

PEDIT

Access the **PEDIT** tool and select a polyline to edit, or choose the **Multiple** option to select multiple polylines to edit. To select a wide polyline, pick the edge of a polyline segment rather than the center. Choose an option to activate the appropriate editing function. To access polyline edit options without first issuing the **PEDIT** tool, pick a polyline to edit and then right-click and choose an option from the **Polyline** cascading submenu.

You can also use the **PEDIT** tool to convert a line, arc, or spline to a polyline. Access the **PEDIT** tool and select the object to convert. A prompt asks if you want to turn the object into a polyline. Select the **Yes** option to make the conversion, and continue using the **PEDIT** tool as normal.

AutoCAD
NEW

NOTE

You can also access **PEDIT** tool options by double-clicking on a polyline, or by right-clicking on a polyline and choosing **Edit Polyline** from the **Polyline** cascading submenu.

Opening and Closing a Polyline

Use the **Open** option to open a closed polyline and the **Close** option to close an open polyline. See **Figure 15-1.** The **Close** option is available if you close the polyline by drawing the final segment manually, or use the **Open** option of the **PEDIT** tool. The **Open** option is available if you use the **Close** option of the **PLINE** or **PEDIT** tools.

Join Option

The **Join** option provides the same function as the **JOIN** tool, allowing you to create a single polyline object from connected polylines or from a polyline connected to lines and arcs. As when you use the **JOIN** tool, the objects to join must share a common endpoint and cannot overlap or have gaps between segments. Choose the **Join** option and pick the objects to join. You can include the original polyline in the selection set, but it is not necessary. See **Figure 15-2.**

Figure 15-1.
Open and closed polylines.

Open Polyline   Closed Polyline

Figure 15-2.
Joining a polyline to other connected lines and an arc.

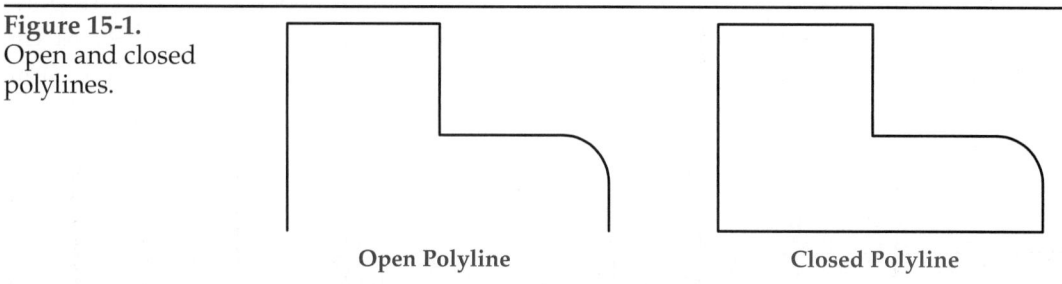

Window other lines

Select polyline

Changing Polyline Width

Choose the **Width** option and specify a new width to assign to the polyline. See **Figure 15-3**. The width of the original polyline can be constant, or it can vary, but *all* segments change to the new, constant width.

Exercise 15-1

Access the Student Web site (www.g-wlearning.com/CAD) and complete Exercise 15-1.

Edit Vertex Option

The **Edit vertex** option allows you to perform several operations at a *polyline vertex*. When you enter the **Edit vertex** option, an "X" marker appears on-screen at the first polyline vertex. The **Edit vertex** option is more difficult to use than other editing tools. It includes **Break**, **Insert**, **Move**, and **Straighten** functions that you can perform more easily using standard editing tools such as **BREAK** and **STRETCH**, or context-sensitive polyline grips. You will learn to grip-edit polylines later in this chapter. The **Tangent** and **Width** options are unique to the **Edit vertex** option and are sometimes useful. The **Tangent** option is most appropriate when used with the **Fit** option, as explained later in this chapter.

polyline vertex: The point at which two polyline segments meet.

> ### NOTE
> If an **Edit vertex** option does not appear to take effect, use the **Regen** option to regenerate the polyline. Use the **eXit** option to return to the **PEDIT** prompt.

Width Option

Use the **Width** function to change the starting and ending widths of a polyline segment. Enter the **Edit vertex** option and use the **Next** and **Previous** options to move the "X" marker to the first vertex where you want to change the polyline width. Activate the **Width** function and specify the starting and ending width of the polyline segment. See **Figure 15-4**.

Exercise 15-2

Access the Student Web site (www.g-wlearning.com/CAD) and complete Exercise 15-2.

Figure 15-3.
Changing the width of a polyline.

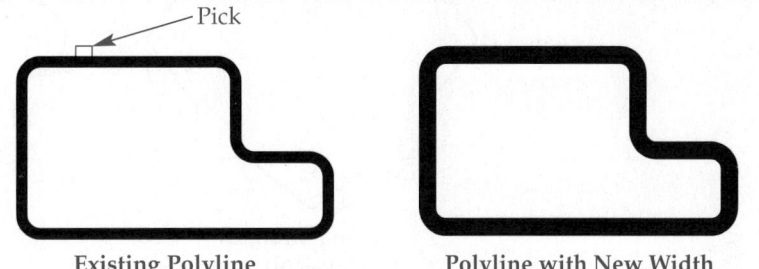

Existing Polyline   Polyline with New Width

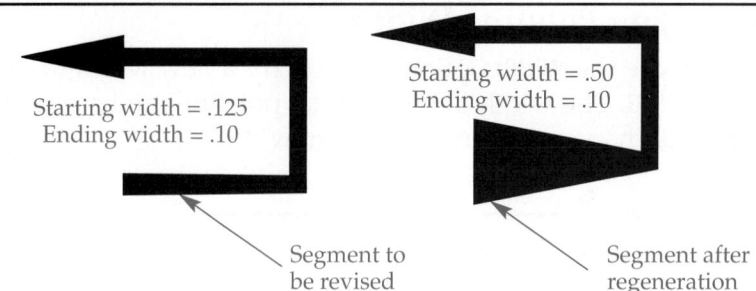

Figure 15-4.
Changing the width of a polyline segment with the **Width** vertex editing option. Use the **Regen** option to display the change if the width does not appear to change.

Starting width = .125
Ending width = .10

Starting width = .50
Ending width = .10

Segment to be revised

Segment after regeneration

Fit Option

curve fitting:
Converting a polyline into a series of smooth curves.

The **Fit** option of the **PEDIT** tool uses *curve fitting* to convert straight polyline segments to a series of smooth curves. For example, you could use curve fitting to draw lines on a graph, add an underlayment symbol to a structural section, or construct a freeform shape by picking accurate points and drawing straight polyline segments. Then use the **Fit** option to smooth the segments. The **Fit** option creates a *fit curve* by constructing pairs of arcs that pass through control points. You can specify the control points, or use the vertices of the polyline.

fit curve: A curve that passes through all of its fit points.

Prior to curve fitting, you can use the **Tangent** function of the **Edit vertex** option to assign each vertex a tangent direction. AutoCAD then fits the curve based on the preset tangent directions. Specifying tangent directions is optional, as a way to edit vertices when the **Fit** option of the **PEDIT** tool does not produce the best results. Enter the **PEDIT** tool, select the **Edit vertex** option, and use the **Next** and **Previous** options to move the "X" marker to the first vertex to change. Choose the **Tangent** option and specify a tangent direction in degrees or pick a point in the expected direction. An arrow at the vertex indicates the direction. Continue moving the marker to vertices and use the **Tangent** option as necessary.

Once all vertices you want to change include a specified tangent direction, enter the **Fit** option to create the curve. You can also enter the **PEDIT** tool, select a polyline, and enter the **Fit** option without adjusting tangencies. **Figure 15-5** shows a polyline formed into a smooth curve using the **Fit** option. If the resulting curve does not look correct, use the **Edit vertex** option to make changes as necessary.

Spline Option

When you edit a polyline with the **Fit** option, the resulting curve passes through each polyline vertex. The **Spline** option also smoothes the corners of a straight-segment polyline, but creates a *spline curve* that approximates a true B-spline. See **Figure 15-6**.

spline curve: A curve that passes through the first and last fit points and is influenced by the other fit points.

Figure 15-5.
Using the **Fit** option of the **PEDIT** tool to turn a polyline into a smooth curve.

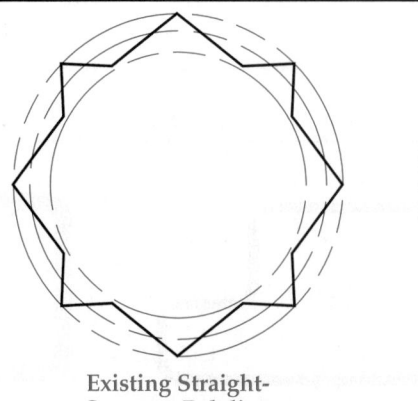
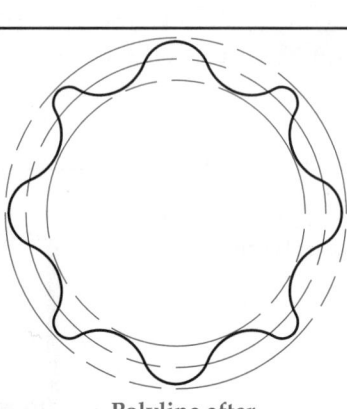

Existing Straight-Segment Polyline

Polyline after Curve Fitting

Figure 15-6.
A comparison of
polylines edited
with the **Fit** and
Spline options of
the **PEDIT** tool.
The **SPLINETYPE**
system variable
controls whether the
Spline option uses
a quadratic or cubic
curve.

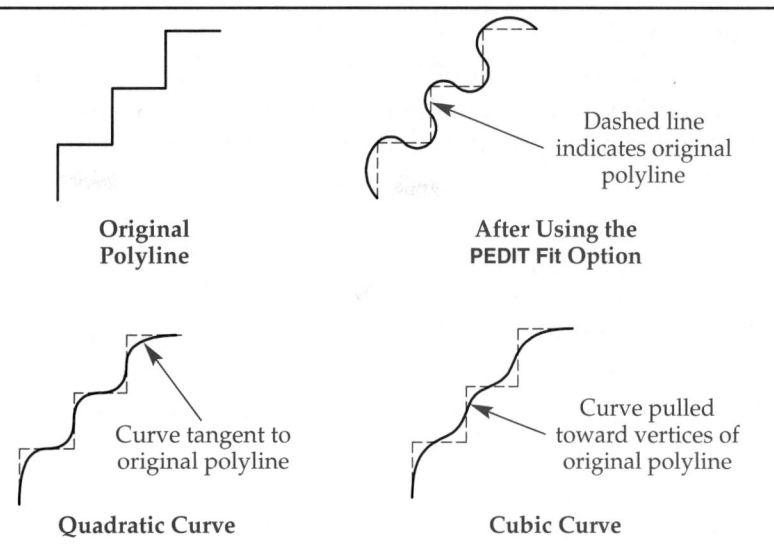

Original
Polyline

After Using the
PEDIT Fit Option

Dashed line
indicates original
polyline

Curve tangent to
original polyline

Curve pulled
toward vertices of
original polyline

Quadratic Curve

Cubic Curve

After Using the PEDIT Spline Option

You can choose to create a *cubic* or *quadratic* calculation before using the **Spline** option by adjusting the **SPLINETYPE** system variable. The default setting of 6 draws a cubic curve. Change the value to 5 to generate a quadratic curve.

Set the number of line segments used to construct spline curves by entering a value in the **Segments in a polyline curve** text box in the **Display resolution** area of the **Display** tab of the **Options** dialog box. After changing the value, you must reissue the **Spline** option of the **PEDIT** tool to apply the setting. The default value is 8, which creates a smooth spline curve with moderate regeneration time. Increasing the **Segments in a polyline curve** value creates a smoother spline curve, but increases regeneration time and drawing file size. See **Figure 15-7**.

cubic curve: A very smooth curve created by the **PEDIT** Spline option with **SPLINETYPE** set at 6.

quadratic curve: A curve created by the **PEDIT** Spline option with **SPLINETYPE** set at 5. The curve is tangent to the polyline segments between the intermediate control points.

NOTE

The **Fit** and **Spline** options of the **PEDIT** tool create approximations of a B-spline curve. Use the **SPLINE** tool to create a true B-spline curve.

Exercise 15-3

Access the Student Web site (www.g-wlearning.com/CAD) and complete Exercise 15-3.

Figure 15-7. A comparison of curves drawn with different display resolution settings.

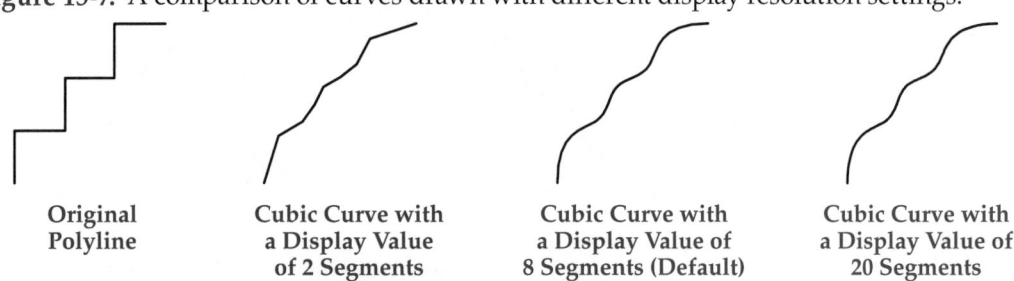

Original
Polyline

Cubic Curve with
a Display Value
of 2 Segments

Cubic Curve with
a Display Value of
8 Segments (Default)

Cubic Curve with
a Display Value of
20 Segments

Straightening All Polyline Segments

The **Decurve** option of the **PEDIT** tool returns a polyline edited with the **Fit** or **Spline** option to its original form. Specified tangent directions remain, however, for future reference. You can also use the **Decurve** option to straighten arc segments of a polyline. See **Figure 15-8.**

Exercise 15-4

Access the Student Web site (www.g-wlearning.com/CAD) and complete Exercise 15-4.

Linetype Generation

The **Ltype gen** option determines how linetypes other than Continuous generate in relation to polyline vertices. For example, if you use a Center linetype and disable the **Ltype gen** option, the polyline has a long dash at each vertex. When you activate the **Ltype gen** option, the polyline generates with a constant pattern in relation to the polyline as a whole. See **Figure 15-9.**

Figure 15-8.
The **Decurve** option straightens all curved segments of a polyline.

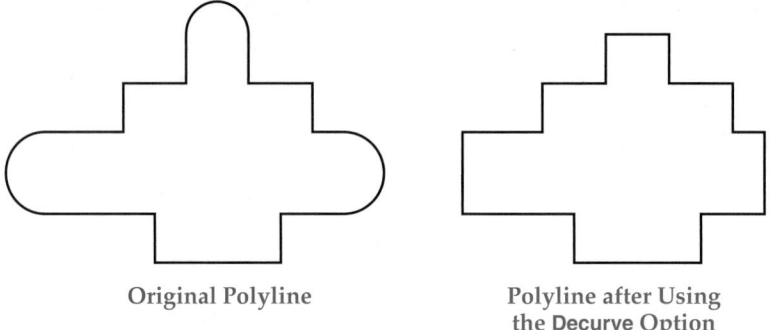

Original Polyline

Polyline after Using the **Decurve** Option

Figure 15-9.
A comparison of polylines and splined polylines with the **Ltype gen** option of the **PEDIT** tool on and off.

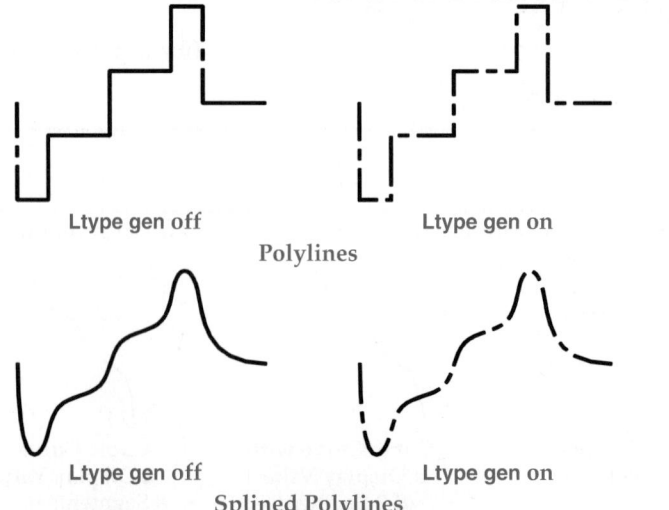

Ltype gen off

Ltype gen on

Polylines

Ltype gen off

Ltype gen on

Splined Polylines

Polyline Grip Tools

Pick a polyline object to display primary grips at each vertex and secondary grips at the midpoint of each segment. See **Figure 15-10.** Vertex grips have the standard filled-square grip appearance, and the midpoint grips display as filled rectangles. Use any of the grips to apply standard grip editing tools, including **STRETCH**, **MOVE**, **ROTATE**, **SCALE**, **MIRROR**, and **Copy**. Polyline grips also offer tools specific to working with polylines. These context-sensitive tools are often the best way to add or remove a vertex, convert a straight segment to an arc, or convert an arc to a straight segment.

Figure 15-10. Pick a polyline object to display grips at each vertex and at the midpoint of each segment. Apply one of the following methods to access context-sensitive polyline grip tools. A—Hover over an unselected grip to display a menu of options, and then pick an option from the list. B—Pick a grip and then right-click and select an option. C—Pick a grip and then press [Ctrl] to cycle though options.

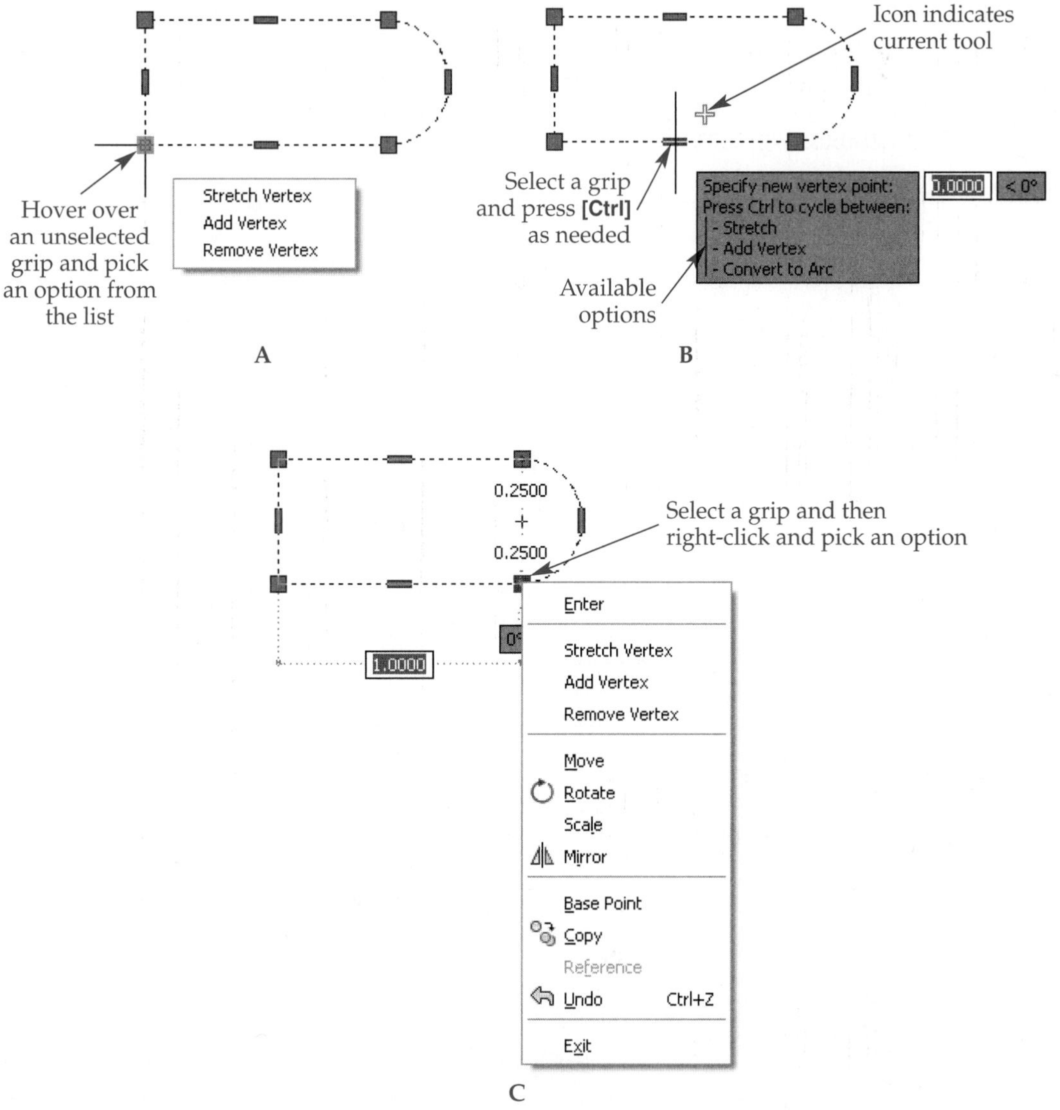

Hover over an unselected grip and pick an option from the list

| Stretch Vertex |
| Add Vertex |
| Remove Vertex |

A

Select a grip and press **[Ctrl]** as needed

Available options

Icon indicates current tool

Specify new vertex point:
Press Ctrl to cycle between:
- Stretch
- Add Vertex
- Convert to Arc

0.0000   < 0°

B

0.2500
+
0.2500

0°
1.0000

Select a grip and then right-click and pick an option

| Enter |
| Stretch Vertex |
| Add Vertex |
| Remove Vertex |
| Move |
| ↻ Rotate |
| Scale |
| ◢◣ Mirror |
| Base Point |
| ⊘ Copy |
| Reference |
| ↰ Undo   Ctrl+Z |
| Exit |

C

You can access and apply the same context-sensitive polyline grip tools in three different ways. **Figure 15-10** briefly explains and illustrates each technique. An icon identifies the current operation. Different options are available depending on whether you hover over or select a vertex or a midpoint grip, and whether the segment is straight or an arc. **Figure 15-11** illustrates and explains the process of using polyline grip tools to edit polylines. Specify a point if necessary to complete an operation. **Base point**, **Copy**, **Undo**, and **eXit** options are available for stretching a vertex. These options behave the same as when using the standard **STRETCH** grip edit tool.

Figure 15-11. Examples of options available for modifying polylines using grips.

Option	Process	Result
Stretch Vertex Stretches the polyline at the selected vertex	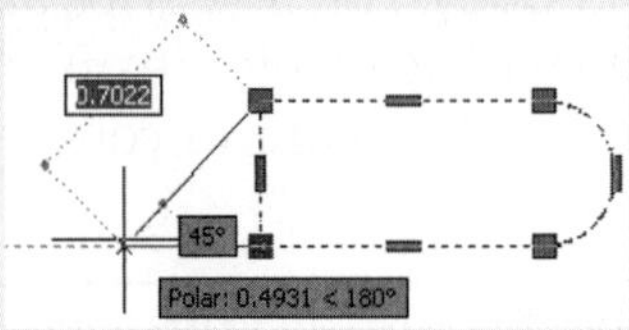	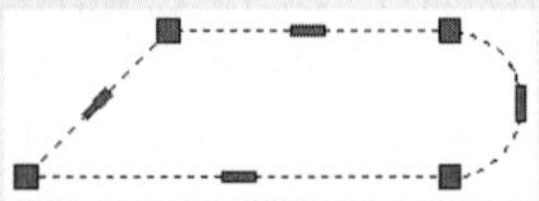
Stretch (straight segment) Stretches the polyline at the selected midpoint	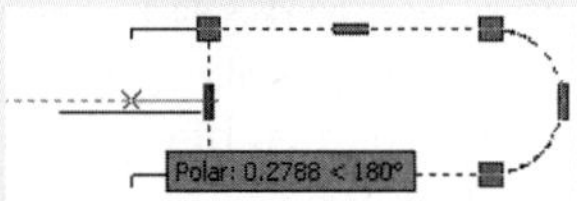	
Stretch (arc) Changes the radius of the arc at the selected midpoint	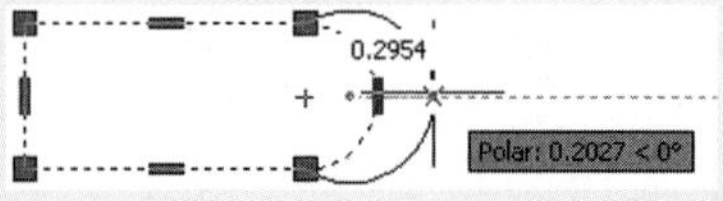	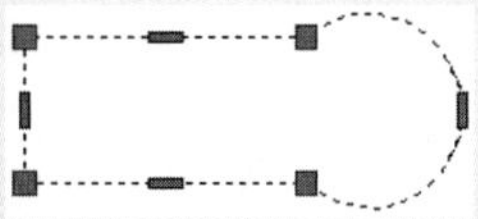
Add Vertex (straight segment) Adds a vertex using a selected vertex or midpoint	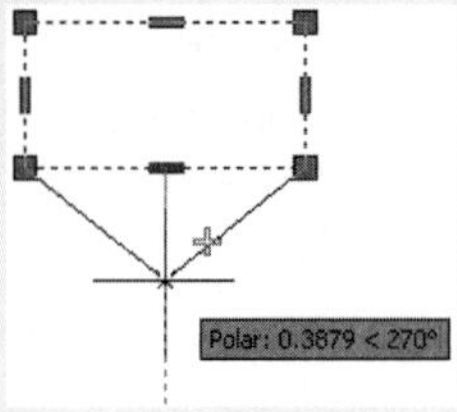	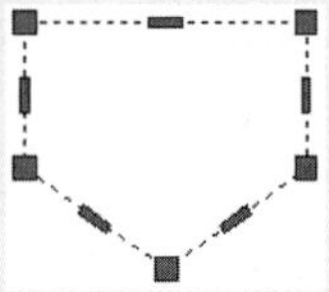
Add Vertex (arc) Adds a vertex using a selected vertex or midpoint	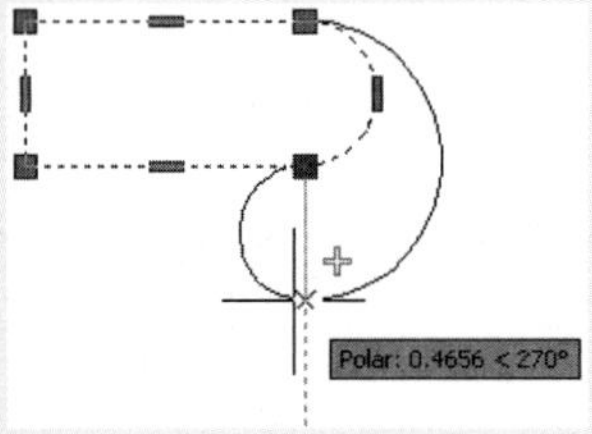	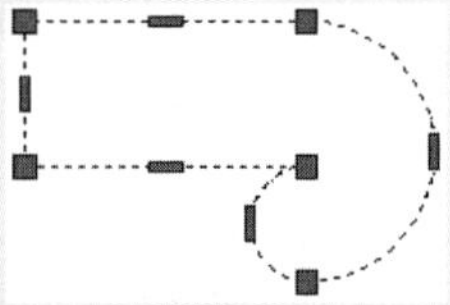
Remove Vertex Removes a selected vertex	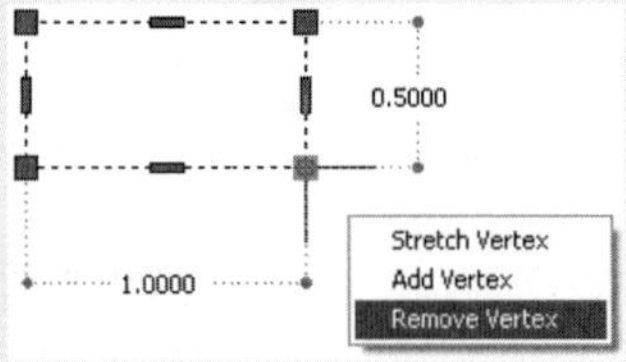	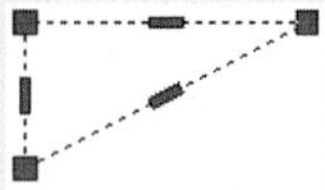
Convert to Line Converts an arc to a straight segment at the selected midpoint	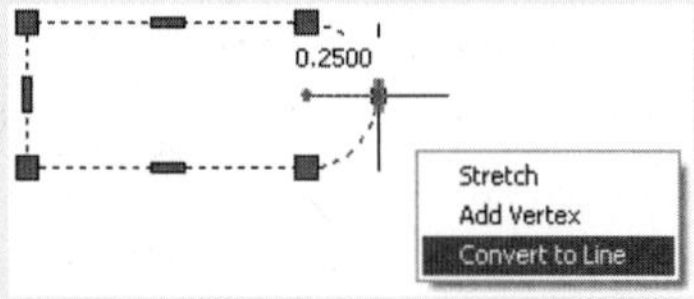	
Convert to Arc Converts a straight segment to an arc at the selected midpoint	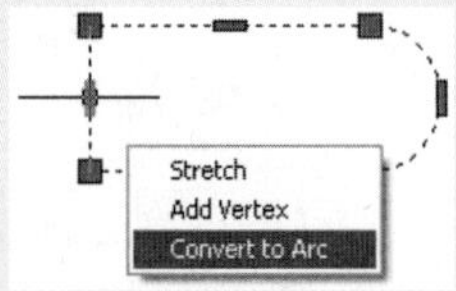	

NOTE

To select specific segments of a polyline object, instead of all segments, hold down [Ctrl] while picking. The polyline still is edited as one continuous object.

PROFESSIONAL TIP

Use grid snaps, coordinate entry, polar tracking, object snaps, and object snap tracking with any grip editing tool to improve accuracy.

Exercise 15-5

Access the Student Web site (www.g-wlearning.com/CAD) and complete Exercise 15-5.

Creating a Polyline Boundary

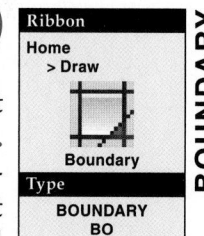

Ribbon
Home
> Draw

Boundary
Type
**BOUNDARY
BO**

BOUNDARY

region: A closed 2D area that can have physical properties such as centroids and products of inertia.

boundary set: The part of the drawing AutoCAD evaluates to define a boundary.

island: A closed area inside a boundary.

Access the **BOUNDARY** tool to create a polyline boundary from linear objects that form a closed area. The **Boundary Creation** dialog box appears as shown in **Figure 15-12.** Select the default **Polyline** option from the **Object type:** drop-down list to create a polyline around the specified area. Select **Region** from the **Object type:** drop-down list to create a *region* that you can use for area calculations, shading, extruding a solid model, and other purposes.

The **Current viewport** setting is active in the **Boundary set** drop-down list by default. This setting defines the *boundary set* from everything in the current viewport, even if it is not in the current display. An alternative is to pick the **New** button to return to the drawing window and select objects to use to create a boundary set. When you are finished selecting objects, right-click or press [Enter] or the space bar. The **Boundary Creation** dialog box returns with **Existing set** active in the **Boundary set** drop-down list to indicate that the boundary set references the selected objects.

The **Island detection** setting specifies whether *islands* within the boundary apply as boundary objects. See **Figure 15-13.** Check **Island detection** to form separate boundaries from islands within a boundary.

Figure 15-12.
The **Boundary Creation** dialog box.

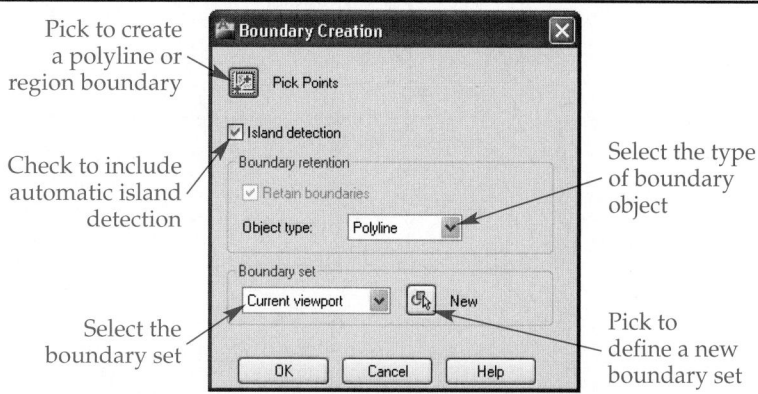

Pick to create a polyline or region boundary

Check to include automatic island detection

Select the type of boundary object

Select the boundary set

Pick to define a new boundary set

Figure 15-13.
You can include or exclude islands when defining a boundary set.

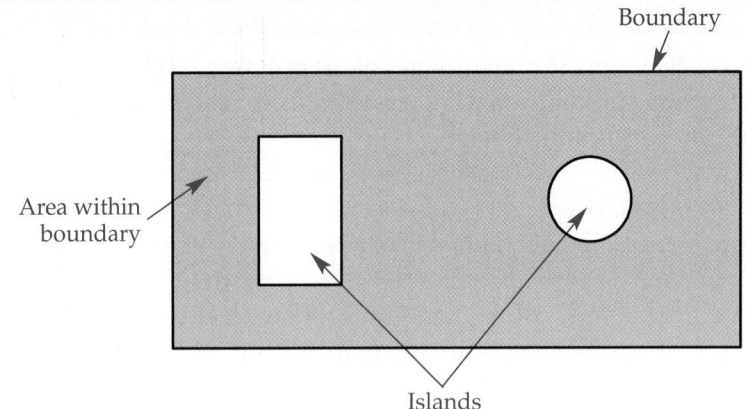

Finally, to create boundaries, select the **Pick Points** button, located in the upper-left corner of the **Boundary Creation** dialog box. Pick a point in each appropriate boundary area. If a point you pick is inside a closed area, the boundary becomes highlighted, as shown in **Figure 15-14.** The **Boundary Definition Error** alert box appears if the point you pick is not within a closed polygon. Pick **OK** and try again.

Unlike an object created with the **JOIN** tool or **Join** option of the **PEDIT** tool, a polyline boundary created with the **BOUNDARY** tool does not replace the original objects. The polyline traces over the defining objects with a polyline. The separate objects still exist underneath the newly created boundary. To avoid duplicate geometry, move the boundary to another location on-screen, erase the original objects, and then move the boundary back to its original position.

PROFESSIONAL TIP

You can simplify area calculations by using the **BOUNDARY** tool or by joining objects with the **JOIN** tool or **Join** option of the **PEDIT** tool before using the **AREA** tool. To retain the original objects, explode the polyline after the area calculation if you used the **JOIN** tool or **Join** option of the **PEDIT** tool. Erase the polyline boundary after the calculation if you used the **BOUNDARY** tool. Chapter 16 covers the **AREA** tool.

Figure 15-14.
Pick inside closed areas to highlight the boundary.

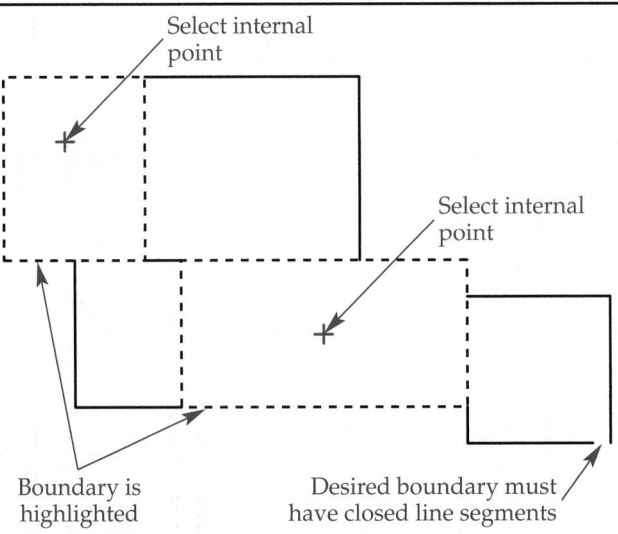

Using the SPLINEDIT Tool

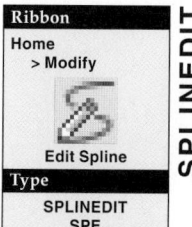

Ribbon
Home
> Modify

Edit Spline

Type

SPLINEDIT
SPE

SPLINEDIT

Splines are complex curves that you can adjust and calculate using a variety of methods. This chapter introduces specialized spline editing tools. Access the **SPLINEDIT** tool and select a spline to edit. Fit point grips locate *fit points* and identify a **Fit**-created spline. Control vertex grips locate control vertices and identify a **CV**-created spline. See **Figure 15-15**. Choose an option to activate the appropriate editing function. To access several spline editing options without first issuing the **SPLINEDIT** tool, pick a spline to edit and then right-click and choose an option from the **Spline** cascading submenu.

fit points: Points through which the spline passes that determine the shape of the spline.

NOTE

You can also access the **SPLINEDIT** tool by double-clicking on a spline.

PROFESSIONAL TIP

Select the **Undo** option immediately after performing an unwanted edit to restore the previous spline without leaving the tool. Use the **Undo** option more than once to step back through each operation. The **eXit** option is one way to cancel the **SPLINEDIT** tool.

Opening and Closing a Spline

Use the **Open** option to open a closed spline and the **Close** option to close an open spline. See **Figure 15-16**. The **Open** option is available if you close the spline by drawing the final segment manually or if you use the **Close** option of the **SPLINE** or **SPLINEDIT** tools. The effect of closing a spline varies depending on the spline creation method and associated options.

Figure 15-15. Access the **SPLINEDIT** tool to display fit point or vertex grips and a list of options for editing splines.

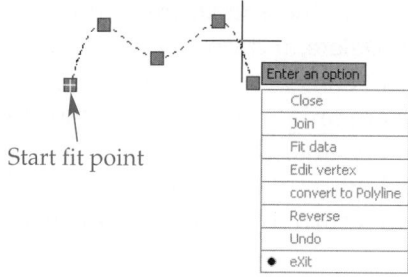

Start fit point

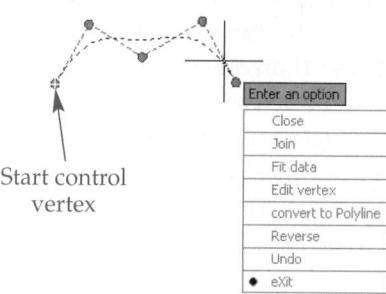

Start control vertex

Fit Creation Method Control

Control Vertices Creation Method

Figure 15-16. Closing an open spline. Note the significant difference between closing a spline created using the **Fit** method and a spline created using the **CV** method, even though the open spline is the same shape.

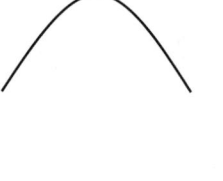

Original Open Spline

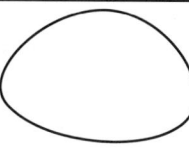

Closed Fit Points Spline

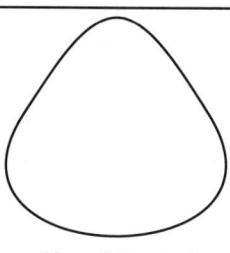

Closed Control Vertices Spline

Join Option

The **Join** option provides the same function as the **JOIN** tool, allowing you to create a single spline object from connected splines or from a spline connected to polylines, lines, or arcs. As when you use the **JOIN** tool, the objects to be joined must share a common endpoint and cannot overlap or have gaps between segments. Choose the **Join** option and pick the objects to join. You can include the original spline in the selection set, but it is not necessary. See **Figure 15-17**.

PROFESSIONAL TIP

Once you join objects into a continuous spline, use the **Close** option to close the spline if necessary.

Fit Data Option

The **Fit data** option allows you to perform several operations at a spline fit point. If you apply the **Fit** option to a spline showing control vertices, the spline converts to show fit points. The **Fit data** option is more difficult to use than other editing tools. It includes **Add**, **Close**, **Delete**, **Move**, **Purge**, and **Tangents** functions that you can perform more easily using standard editing tools or context-sensitive spline grips. You will learn to grip-edit splines later in this chapter.

The **toLerance** option is unique to the **Fit data** option and allows you to adjust fit tolerance values. The results are immediate, so you can adjust the fit tolerance as necessary to produce different results. Use the **eXit** function to return to the **SPLINEDIT** prompt.

Edit Vertex Option

The **Edit vertex** option allows you to perform several operations at a spline control vertex. If you apply a specific **Edit vertex** function to a spline showing fit points, the spline converts to show control vertices. Like the **Fit Data** option, the **Edit vertex** option is more difficult to use than other editing tools. It includes **Add**, **Delete**, and **Move** functions that you can perform more easily using standard editing tools or context-sensitive spline grips.

The **Elevate order**, add **Kink**, and **Weight** options are unique to the **Edit vertex** option and are sometimes useful. **Figure 15-18** briefly explains and illustrates these functions. When using the **Weight** option, apply the **Next**, **Previous**, and **Select point** functions to navigate to different vertices. Use the **eXit** function to return to the **SPLINEDIT** prompt.

Figure 15-17.
Joining a spline to other connected objects. The single object is now a complex spline that you can further edit to create a freeform shape.

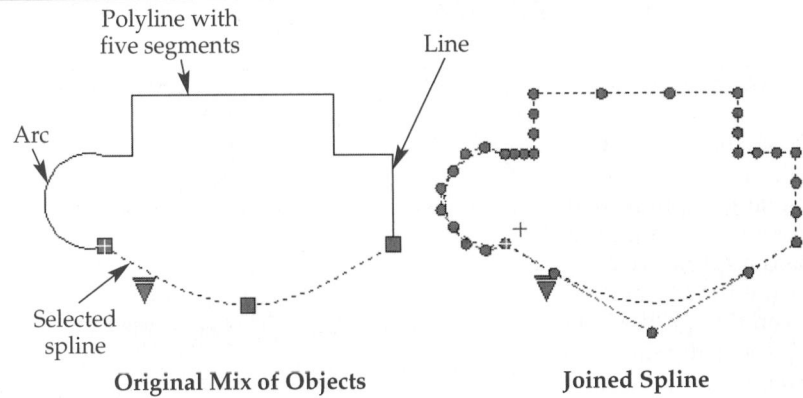

Polyline with five segments

Line

Arc

Selected spline

Original Mix of Objects

Joined Spline

Converting Splines and Polylines

The **Convert to Polyline** option of the **SPLINEDIT** tool allows you to convert a spline to a polyline. Select the spline to convert and enter a value at the Specify a precision <current>: prompt. The higher the specified precision, the more vertices are added to the polyline, making the polyline smoother. See **Figure 15-19.**

Use the **Object** option of the **SPLINE** tool to convert a spline-fitted polyline object, created using the **PEDIT** tool, to a spline object. When you access the **SPLINE** tool, activate the **Object** option instead of defining points. Then pick a spline-fitted polyline object to convert the polyline to a spline.

> **NOTE**
>
> The **rEverse** option of the **SPLINEDIT** tool applies the same operation as the **REVERSE** tool. Reversing affects the fit point and vertex options of the **SPLINEDIT** tool.

Figure 15-18. An introduction to spline editing functions that are unique to the **Edit vertex** option of the **SPLINEDIT** tool.

Option	Process	Result
Elevate order Adds control points for greater control of spline shape and spline *order* refinement. Specify a value between the current number of vertices and 26.	3 Original Control Vertices	Order Elevated to 10
add Kink Adds a sharp point known as a kink. Pick a location on the spline.	Specify a point on the spline <exit>: 7.8365 8.2070	Before Editing / After Editing
Weight Adjusts the spline weight at the selected vertex. The larger the weight, the closer the spline pulls toward the vertex. Specify a value greater than or equal to 1.	Original Weight of 1 Applied to the Second Vertex	Modified Weight of 5 Applied to the Second Vertex

order: In a spline, the degree of the spline polynomial + 1.

Figure 15-19. The effects of changing precision when converting a spline to a polyline.

Original Spline
Converted with Default Precision of 10
Converted with Precision of 1

Exercise 15-6

Access the Student Web site (www.g-wlearning.com/CAD) and complete Exercise 15-6.

Spline Grip Tools

Pick a spline object to display grips at each fit point or vertex, depending on the creation method. See **Figure 15-20**. A parameter grip appears near the start point of the spline. Pick the grip and then select the **Show Fit Points** option to change the spline to use fit points, or pick the **Show Control Vertices** option to change spline to use control vertices. These options are also available when you select a spline and right-click.

Fit point grips have the standard filled-square grip appearance, and vertex grips display as filled-circles. A "+" mark though the grip indicates the start point of the spline. Use any of the grips to apply standard grip editing tools, including **STRETCH**, **MOVE**, **ROTATE**, **SCALE**, **MIRROR**, and **Copy**. Spline grips also offer tools specific to working with splines. These context-sensitive tools are often the best way to move, add, or remove a fit point or vertex, adjust tangent direction, and refine vertices.

There are three different ways to access and apply the same context-sensitive spline grip tools. **Figure 15-20** briefly explains each technique. An icon identifies the current operation. Different options are available depending on whether you hover over or select a fit point or a vertex, and whether the point is at the end of the spline. **Figure 15-21** briefly explains examples of using spline grip tools to edit splines. **Base point**, **Copy**, **Undo**, and **eXit** options are available for stretching a fit point or vertex. They behave the same as in the standard **STRETCH** grip edit tool.

Exercise 15-7

Access the Student Web site (www.g-wlearning.com/CAD) and complete Exercise 15-7.

Figure 15-20. Pick a spline object to display grips at each fit point or vertex and a parameter grip near the start point. Apply one of the following methods to access context-sensitive spline grip tools. A—Hover over an unselected grip to display a menu of options, and then pick an option from the list. B—Pick a grip and then press [Ctrl] to cycle through options. C—Pick a grip, right-click, and select an option.

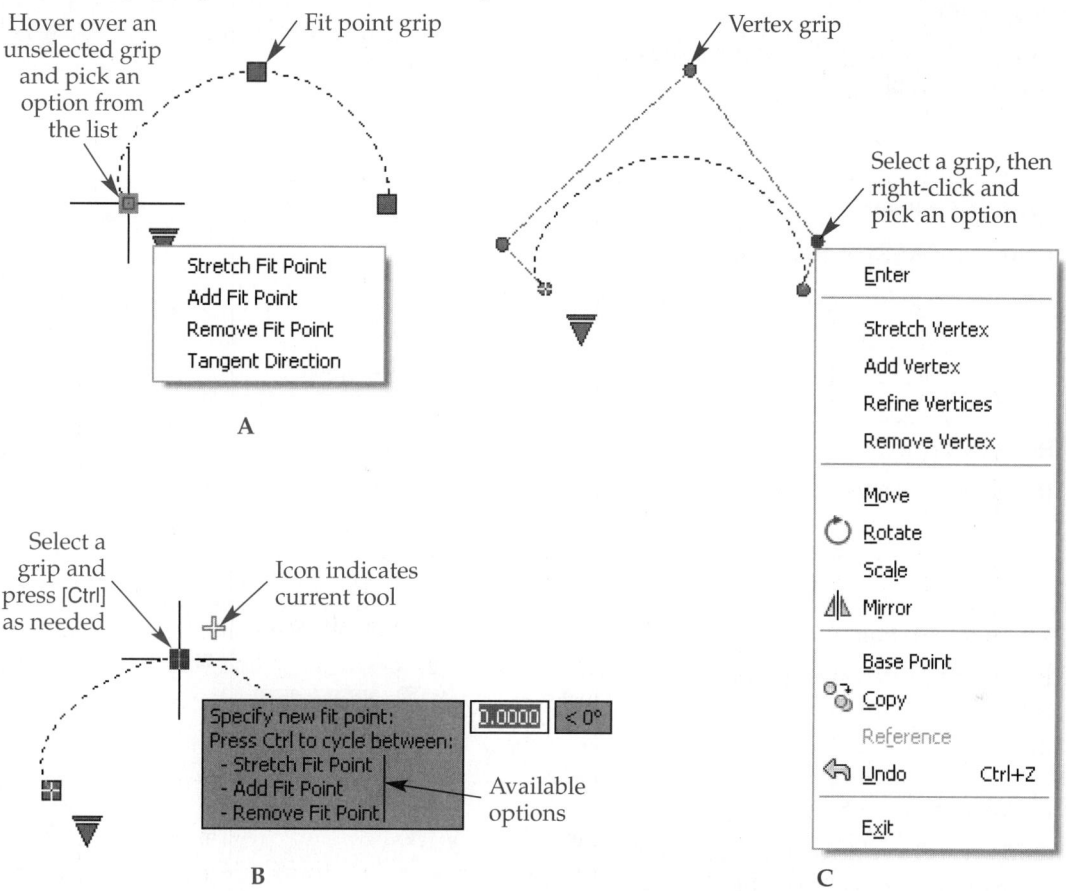

Figure 15-21. Examples of options available for modifying splines using grips.

Option	Process	Result
Stretch Fit Point Stretches the spline at the selected fit point	Polar: 0.7231 < 315°	
Stretch Vertex Stretches the spline at the selected vertex	Polar: 1.2145 < 225°	

(Continued)

Figure 15-21. *(Continued)*

Option	Process	Result
Add Fit Point Adds a fit point to the left of the selected fit point	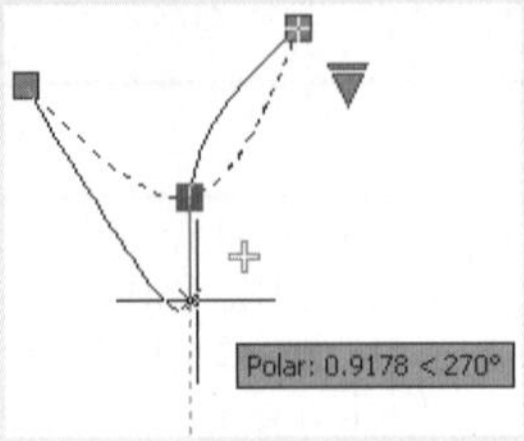	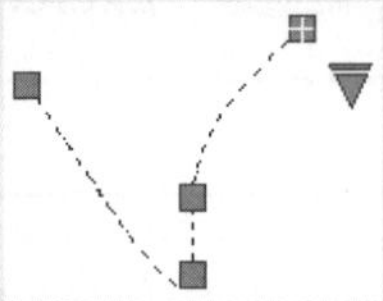
Add Vertex Adds a vertex to the left of the selected vertex	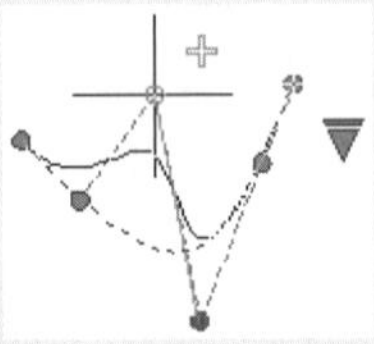	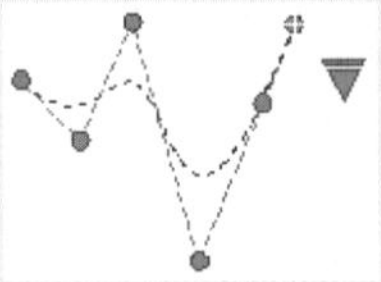
Remove Fit Point Removes a selected fit point	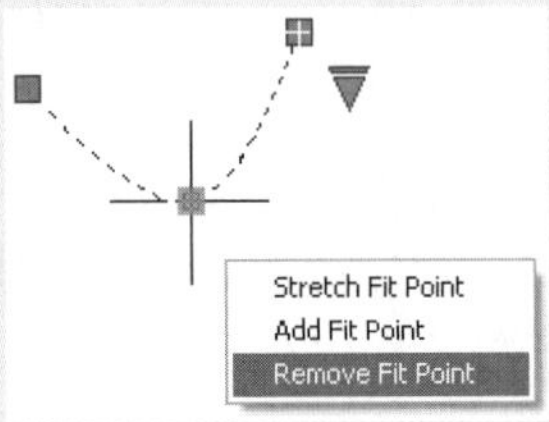	
Remove Vertex Removes a selected vertex	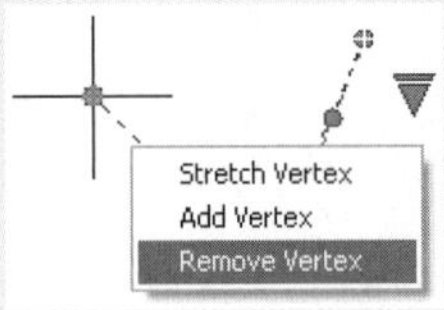	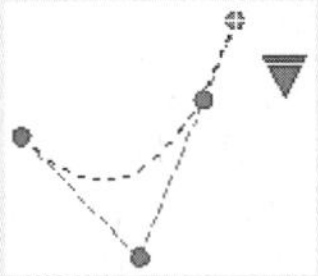
Tangent Direction Edits the selected start point or endpoint tangent direction for fit point splines	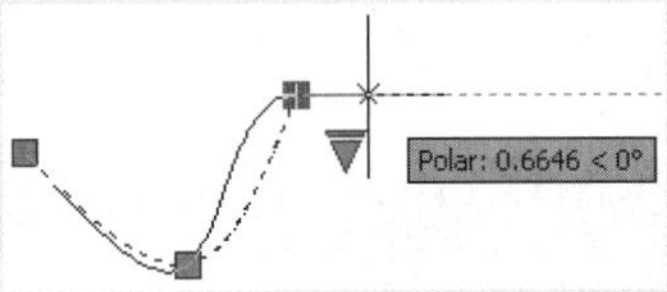	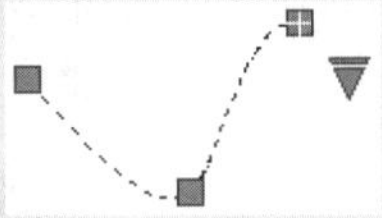
Refine Vertices Adds vertices relative to the selected vertex to fine-tune the spline for editing	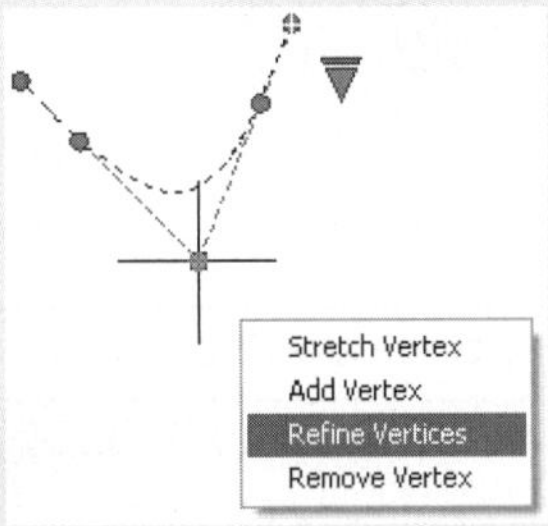	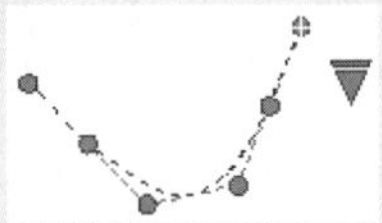

Chapter Test

Answer the following questions. Write your answers on a separate sheet of paper or go to the Student Web site (www.g-wlearning.com/CAD) and complete the electronic chapter test.

1. Name the tool and option required to turn three connected lines into a single polyline.
2. When you enter the **Edit vertex** option of the **PEDIT** tool, where does AutoCAD place the "X" marker?
3. Why might it appear that nothing happens when you change the starting and ending widths of a polyline?
4. Which **PEDIT** tool option and function allow you to change the starting and ending widths of a polyline?
5. How do you move the "X" marker to edit a different polyline vertex?
6. Name the **PEDIT** tool option and function used for curve fitting.
7. Explain the difference between a fit curve and a spline curve.
8. Compare a quadratic curve, cubic curve, and fit curve.
9. Which **SPLINETYPE** system variable setting allows you to draw a quadratic curve?
10. Explain how you can adjust the way polyline linetypes are generated using the **PEDIT** tool.
11. Describe how to use grips to stretch a straight polyline segment at the midpoint.
12. Describe how to use grips to straighten a polyline arc.
13. Name the tool used to create a polyline boundary.
14. Which **Fit data** function of the **SPLINEDIT** tool allows you to add a sharp point to a spline?
15. Identify the **Fit data** function of the **SPLINEDIT** tool that lets you increase, but not decrease, the number of control points appearing on a spline curve.
16. Name **Fit data** function of the **SPLINEDIT** tool that controls the pull exerted by a control point on a spline.
17. Name the **SPLINE** tool option that allows you to turn a spline-fitted polyline into a true spline.
18. Describe how to use grips to add a fit point to a control vertices spline.
19. Describe how to use grips to remove a vertex from a fit points spline.
20. Which spline grip option do you use to add vertices relative to a selected vertex to fine-tune the spline?

Drawing Problems

Start AutoCAD if it is not already started. Start a new drawing for each problem using an appropriate template of your choice. The template should include layers, text styles, and table styles, when necessary, for drawing the given objects. Add layers, text styles, and table styles as needed. Draw all objects using appropriate layers, text styles, table styles, justification, and format. Follow the specific instructions for each problem. Use only drawing and editing tools and techniques you have already learned. Do not draw dimensions. Use your own judgment and approximate dimensions when necessary.

▼ Basic

1. Use the **LINE** tool to draw two connected lines. Use the **PEDIT** tool to convert one of the lines to a polyline, and then use the **Join** option to convert the line and polyline into a single polyline object. Use the **LINE** tool to draw a rectangle. Use the **PEDIT** tool to convert one of the lines to a polyline, and then use the **Join** option to convert the three remaining lines and polyline into a single polyline object. Save the drawing as P15-1.

2. Use the **SPLINE** tool to draw a spline of your own design with at least four fit points. Use the **Convert to Polyline** option of the **SPLINEDIT** tool to convert the spline to a polyline. Save the drawing as P15-2.

3. Use the **RECTANGLE** tool to draw a 50 mm × 25 mm rectangle. Use grip editing to convert the straight 25 mm segments to R25 mm arcs, creating a full-round slot. Save the drawing as P15-3.

4. Use the **POLYGON** tool to draw the hexagon shown in A. Use the **Remove Vertex** and **Stretch** polyline grip edit tools to edit the hexagon as shown in B. Save the drawing as P15-4.

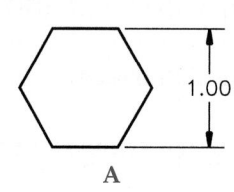

A

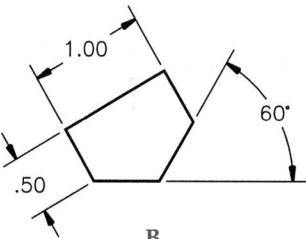

B

▼ Intermediate

5. Open P4-15 and save the file as P15-5. If you have not yet completed problem 4-15, do so now. The P15-5 file should be active. Use polyline editing to change the original objects to a rectangle as shown. Use the **Decurve** and **Width** options of the **PEDIT** tool and polyline grip editing. Resave the drawing.

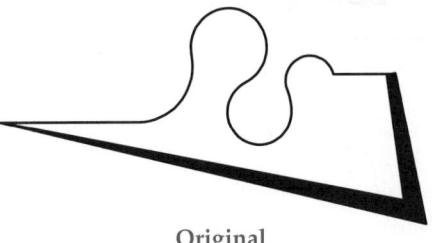

Original

After Editing

6. Open P4-16 and save the file as P15-6. If you have not yet completed problem 4-16, do so now. The P15-6 file should be active. Make the following changes.
   A. Combine the two polylines using the **Join** option of the **PEDIT** tool.
   B. Change the beginning width of the left arrow to 1.0 and the ending width to .2.
   C. Draw a polyline .062 wide, similar to Line A, as shown.
   Resave the drawing.

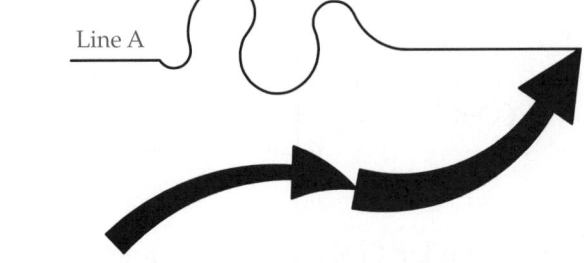

Line A

7. Draw four polylines .032 wide, using the following absolute coordinates for all four objects.

Point	Coordinates	Point	Coordinates	Point	Coordinates
1	1,1	5	3,3	9	5,5
2	2,1	6	4,3	10	6,5
3	2,2	7	4,4	11	6,6
4	3,2	8	5,4	12	7,6

Leave the first polyline as drawn. Use the **Fit** option of the **PEDIT** tool to smooth the second polyline. Use the **Spline** option of the **PEDIT** tool to turn the third polyline into a quadratic curve. Make the fourth polyline into a cubic curve. Use the **Decurve** option of the **PEDIT** tool to return one of the three edited polylines to its original form. Save the drawing as P15-7.

8. Use the **PLINE** tool to draw four copies of a patio plan similar to the plan shown in A. Draw the house walls 6″ wide. Leave the first plan as drawn. Use the **PEDIT** tool to create the designs shown. Use the **Fit** option for B, a quadratic spline for C, and a cubic spline for D. Change the **SPLINETYPE** system variable as required. Save the drawing as P15-8.

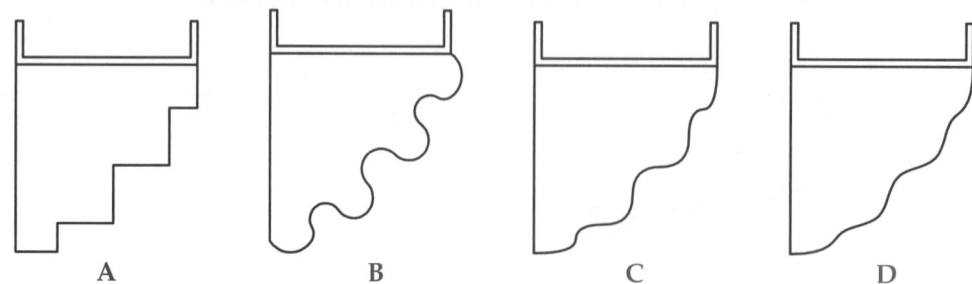

9. Open P15-8 and save the file as P15-9. The P15-9 file should be active. Use grip editing to create four new patio designs similar to A, B, C, and D below. Resave the drawing.

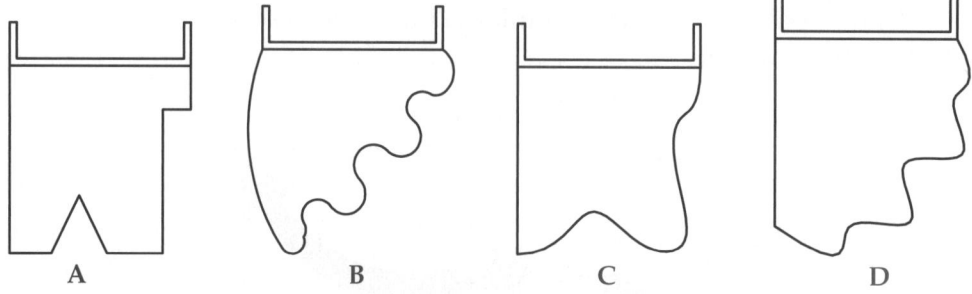

10. Draw a fit point spline similar to the original spline shown. Copy the spline seven times to create a layout similar to the layout shown. Use the **SPLINEDIT** tool or grip editing to perform the specified operations. Save the drawing as P15-10.

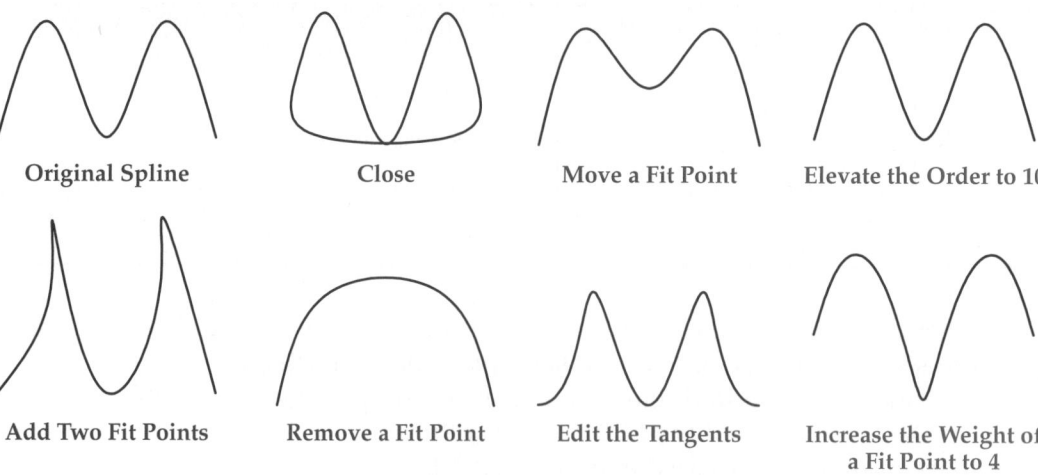

Original Spline   Close   Move a Fit Point   Elevate the Order to 10

Add Two Fit Points   Remove a Fit Point   Edit the Tangents   Increase the Weight of a Fit Point to 4

▼ Advanced

11. Draw the exterior door elevation shown. Use polylines and the **OFFSET** tool to draw the features. Save the drawing as P15-11.

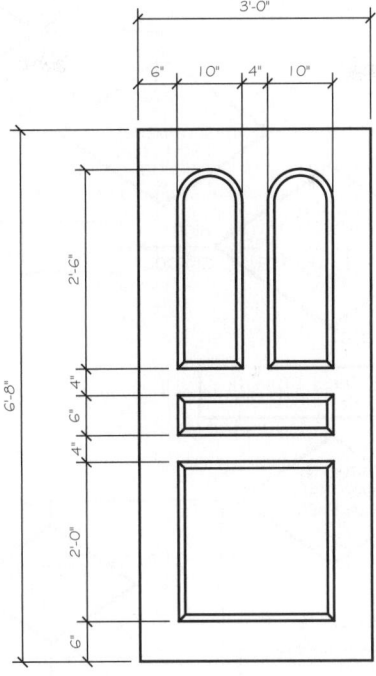

12. Draw the flow chart shown. Use polylines to draw the connecting lines, arrows, and diamonds. Save the drawing as P15-12.

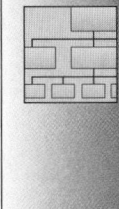

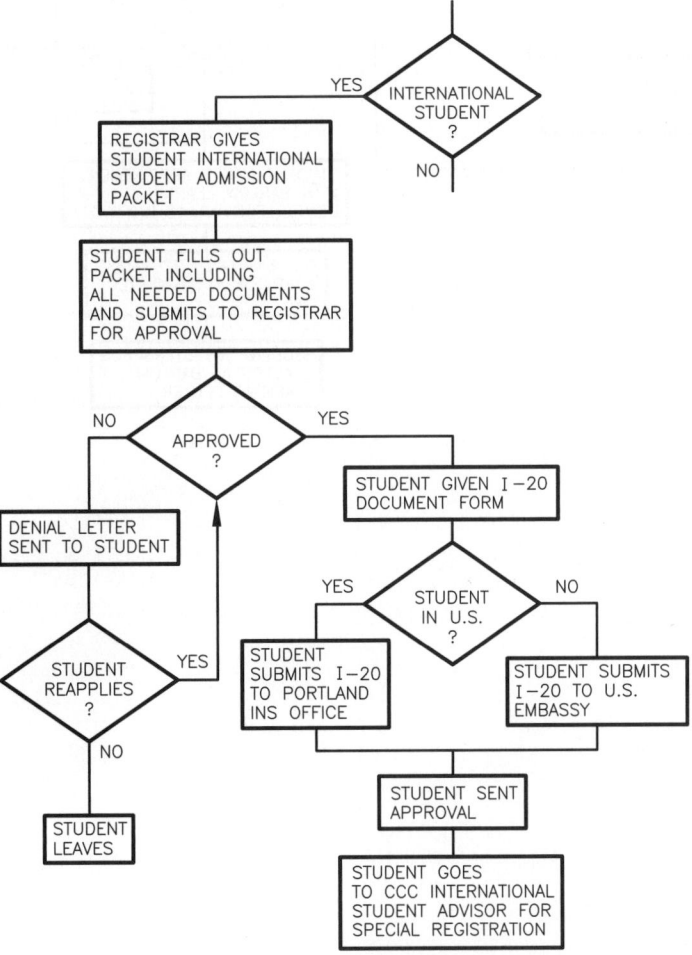

13. Draw the flow chart shown. Use polylines to draw the connecting lines, arrows, and diamonds. Save the drawing as P15-13.

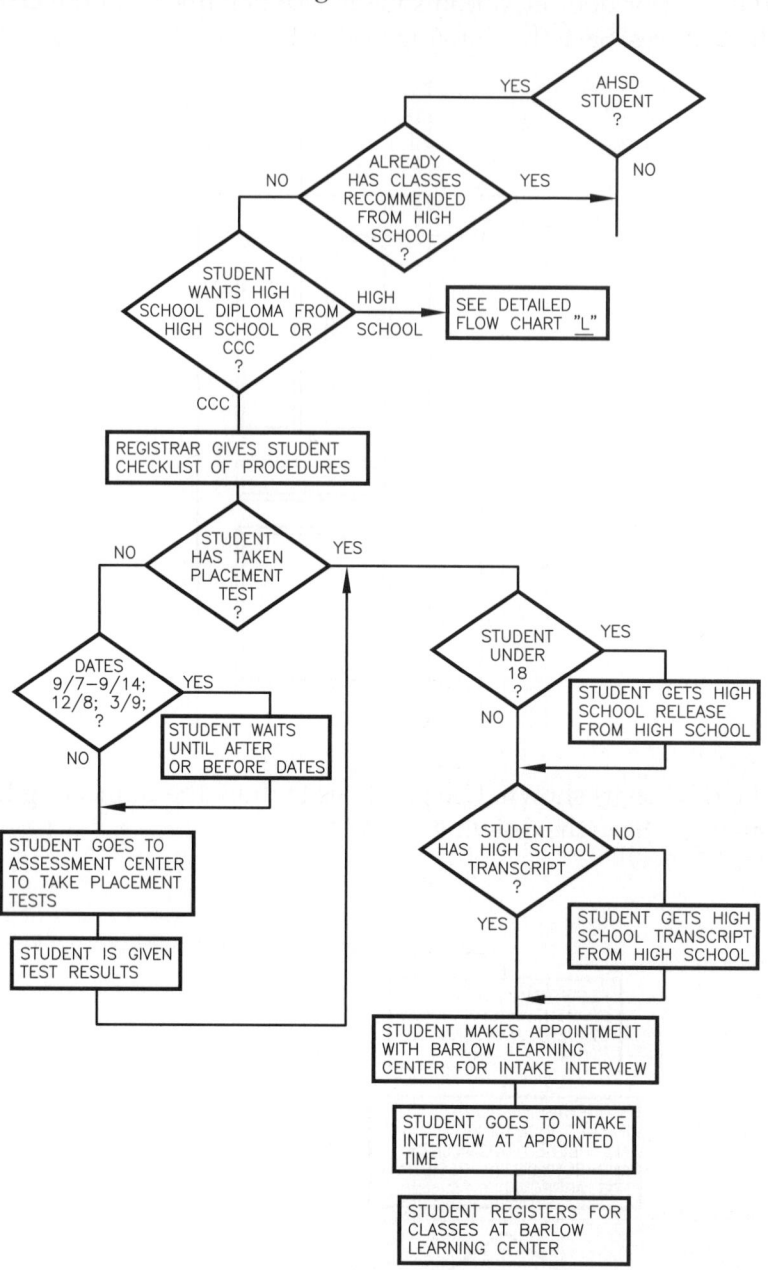

14. Draw the part views shown. Save the drawing as P15-14.

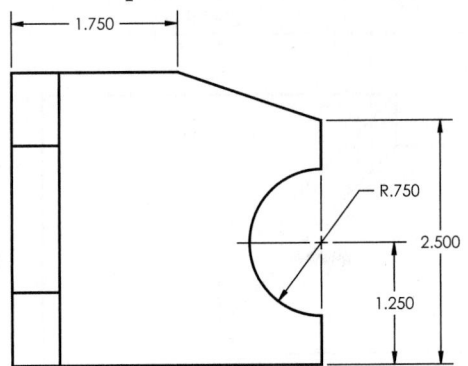

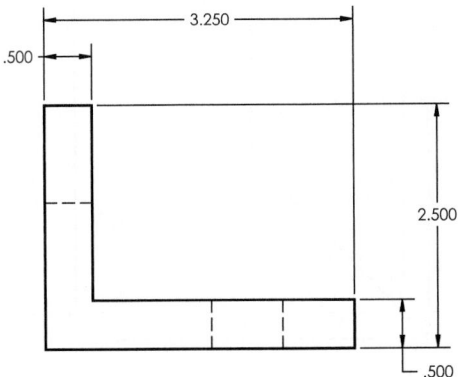

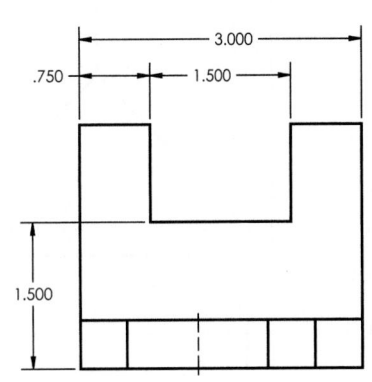

15. Use **SPLINE** and other tools, such as **ELLIPSE**, **MIRROR**, and **OFFSET**, to design an architectural door knocker similar to the knocker shown. Use an appropriate text tool and font to place your initials in the center. Save the drawing as P15-15.

16. Draw the roof plan shown. Save the drawing as P15-16.

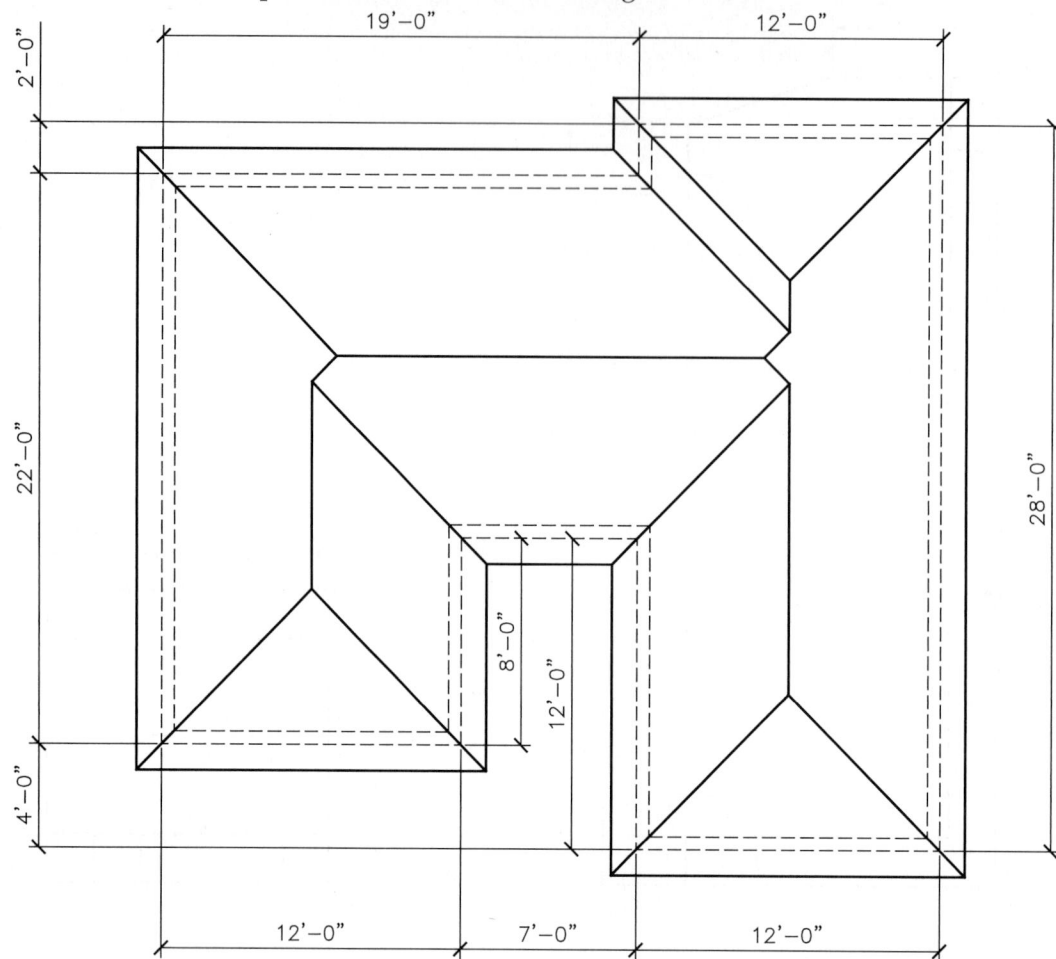

17. Find a tree appropriate for residential landscaping. Create a 2D sketch of the tree elevation. Use available measuring devices, such as a tape measure, to dimension the size and location of features accurately. Start a new drawing from scratch or use an architectural-unit template of your choice. Draw the tree elevation from your sketch. Save the drawing as P15-17.

18. Create a dimensioned 2D sketch of a view of a new design for a cordless phone. Include circles, ellipses, polylines, and freeform ergonomic edges in the design. Use available measuring devices, such as a tape measure and caliper, to measure an actual cordless phone for reference if necessary. Start a new drawing from scratch or use a decimal-unit template of your choice. Draw all of the views needed to describe the cordless phone completely from your sketch. Use the **SPLINE** tool to draw the freeform curves. Save the drawing as P15-18.

AutoCAD Certified Associate Exam Practice

Answer the following questions. Write your answers on a separate sheet of paper.

1. Which of the following operations can you use to convert all of the curves in a polyline to straight segments? *Select all that apply.*
   A. hover over the midpoint grip on each curve and choose **Convert to Line**
   B. select the polyline, right-click, and select **Polyline** and **Decurve**
   C. use the **PEDIT Decurve** option
   D. use the **PEDIT Fit** option
   E. use the **Straighten** function of the **PEDIT Edit Vertex** option

2. Which of the following statements are true about boundaries created using the default options? *Select all that apply.*
   A. The original objects are deleted when you create the boundary.
   B. They are created in exactly the same location as the original objects.
   C. They are polyline objects.
   D. They have physical properties such as centroids and products of inertia.

3. How can you show the control vertex grips on a spline that was created using the fit points method? *Select all that apply.*
   A. select the spline, right-click, and pick **Spline** and **Display Control Vertices**
   B. use the **SPLINEDIT Convert to Polyline** option
   C. select a fit point grip, right-click, and pick **Remove Fit Point**
   D. select the parameter grip and pick **Show Control Vertices**

AutoCAD Certified Professional Exam Practice

Follow the instructions in each problem. Write your answers on a separate sheet of paper.

1. **Navigate to this chapter on the Student Web site and open the CPE-15spline.dwg file.**
   Convert the spline into a polyline using a precision of 2. How many segments are present in the resulting polyline?

2. **Navigate to this chapter on the Student Web site and open the CPE-15pedit.dwg file.**
   Use the **PEDIT** tool to achieve the polyline shown below the centerline. Mirror the result using the centerline as the mirror line. What are the coordinates of Point 1?

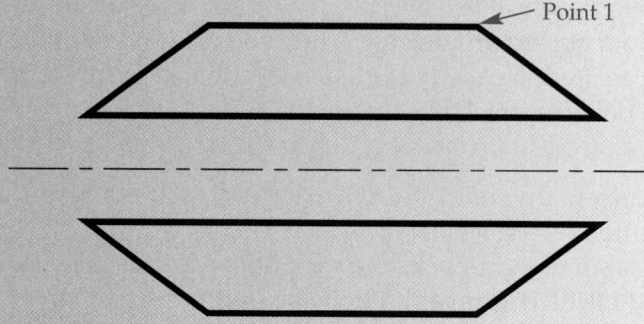

Point 1

Obtaining Drawing Information

Learning Objectives

After completing this chapter, you will be able to do the following:

✓ Identify a point location and basic object dimensions.
✓ Find the distance between points.
✓ Measure radii, diameters, and angles.
✓ Calculate area.
✓ List data related to a single point, an object, a group of objects, or an entire drawing.
✓ Determine the drawing status.
✓ Determine the amount of time spent in a drawing session.
✓ Perform calculations using the **QuickCalc** calculator.

This chapter describes tools that allow you to retrieve geometric values such as point coordinates, distance, angle, and area. It also explains additional tools for referencing object data, determining drawing status, and calculating time spent working on a drawing. This chapter also describes how to use the **QuickCalc** tool to calculate values while you work.

Taking Measurements

Taking measurements from a drawing is common during designing and drafting processes. Mechanical drafting examples include measuring a circle to confirm the size of a hole, measuring the angle between two surfaces, and calculating the volume of a part. Architectural drafting examples include checking the dimensions of a room, measuring the location of features within a room, and calculating square footage.

Using Grips

Grips provide one way to view basic object dimensions. To identify the location of a point that corresponds to a grip, confirm that the coordinate display field in the status bar is on. Then pick the object to activate grips and hover over a grip. The coordinates of the point appear in the coordinate display field. Use grips and dynamic input to view dimensions between grips. Pick the object to activate grips and hover over a grip to display dimensions. The information that appears varies depending on the object type and the selected grip. See **Figure 16-1**.

Figure 16-1.
Examples of hovering over grips to display dimensions at the dynamic input cursor. Dynamic input must be active to view dimensions, but it does not have to be active to list the coordinates of a grip in the status bar.

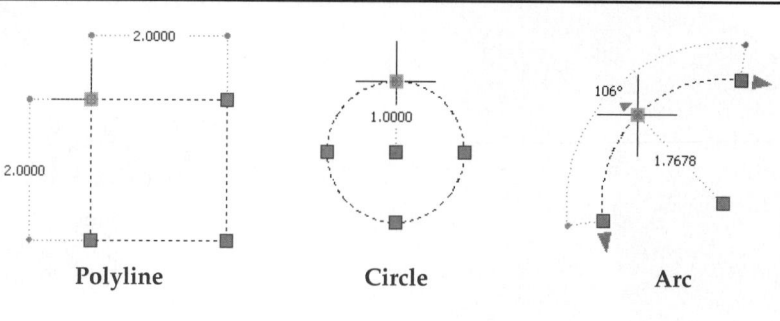

Polyline   Circle   Arc

Exercise 16-1

Access the Student Web site (www.g-wlearning.com/CAD) and complete Exercise 16-1.

Using the MEASUREGEOM Tool

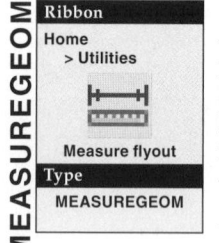

MEASUREGEOM

Ribbon

Home
> Utilities

Measure flyout

Type
MEASUREGEOM

The **MEASUREGEOM** tool allows you to measure distance, radius, angle, area, perimeter, and volume. The ribbon is an effective way to access **MEASUREGEOM** tool options. See **Figure 16-2.** When you access the **MEASUREGEOM** tool by typing, you must activate a measurement option before you begin. The **MEASUREGEOM** tool remains active after you take measurements, allowing you to continue measuring without reselecting the tool. Select the **eXit** option or press [Esc] to exit the tool.

Measuring Distance

Use the **Distance** option of the **MEASUREGEOM** tool to find the distance between points. Specify the first point, followed by the second point. The linear distance between the points, angle in the XY plane, and delta (change in) X and Y values appear on-screen, as shown in **Figure 16-3,** and at the command line. In a 2D drawing, the angle *from* the XY plane and delta Z values are always 0, as indicated at the command line. The first point you specify defines the vertex of the angular dimension, as shown in **Figure 16-3.**

Once you specify the first point, you can choose the **Multiple points** function to measure the distance between multiple points. AutoCAD calculates the distance between each point and displays the value at the command line during selection.

Figure 16-2.
Use the flyout in the **Utilities** panel of the **Home** ribbon tab to access specific **MEASUREGEOM** tool options.

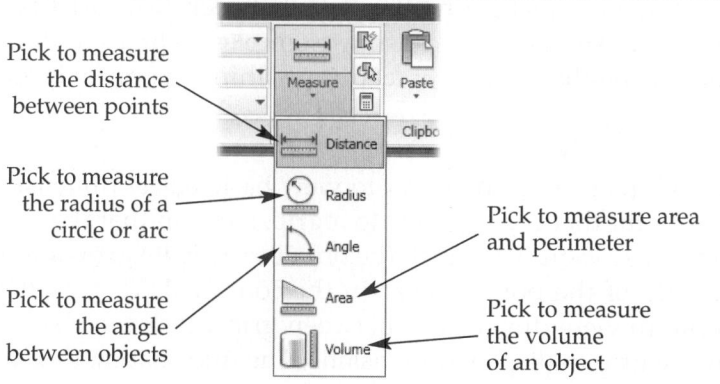

Pick to measure the distance between points

Pick to measure the radius of a circle or arc

Pick to measure the angle between objects

Pick to measure area and perimeter

Pick to measure the volume of an object

Figure 16-3.
The data provided by the **Distance** option. Notice that the first point defines the vertex of the angular value.

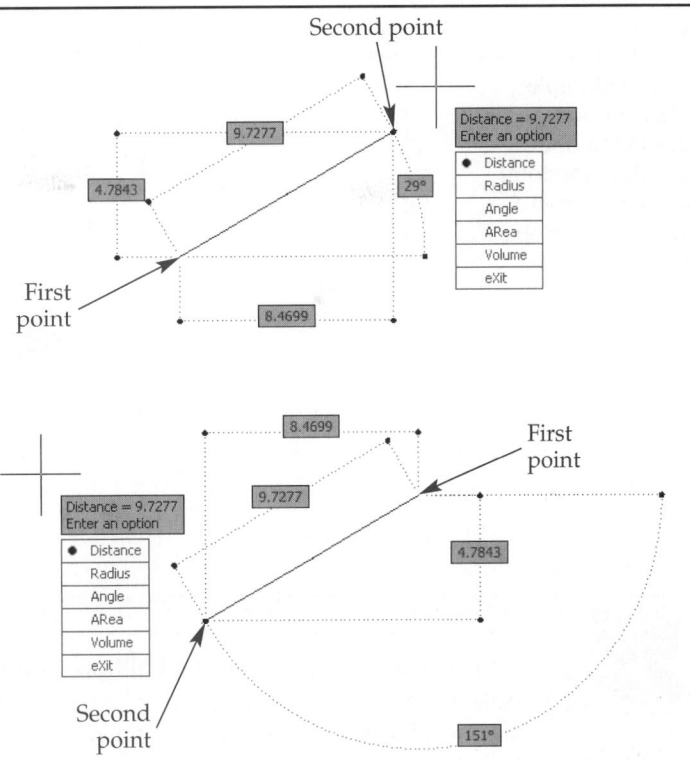

Several options are available for picking multiple points, as described in **Figure 16-4.** When you finish measuring, use the **Total** or **Close** option to display the total distance between all points. **Figure 16-5** shows an example of using the **Multiple points** function to calculate the perimeter of a shape.

> **NOTE**
>
> Use coordinate entry, object snap modes, and other drawing aids to pick points when using the **MEASUREGEOM** tool.

Figure 16-4.
Options available for the **Multiple points** function of the **Distance** option.

Option	Description
Arc	Measures the length of an arc; includes the same functions available for drawing arcs. Choose the **Line** function to return to measuring the distance between linear points.
Length	Measures the specified length of a line.
Undo	Cancels the effects of an unwanted selection, returning to the previous measurement point.
Total	Finishes multiple point selection and calculates the total distance between points.
Close	Connects the current point to the first point; finishes multiple point selection and calculates the total distance between points.

Figure 16-5.
An example of using the **Multiple points** function of the **Distance** option to calculate the total distance between several points along lines and an arc.

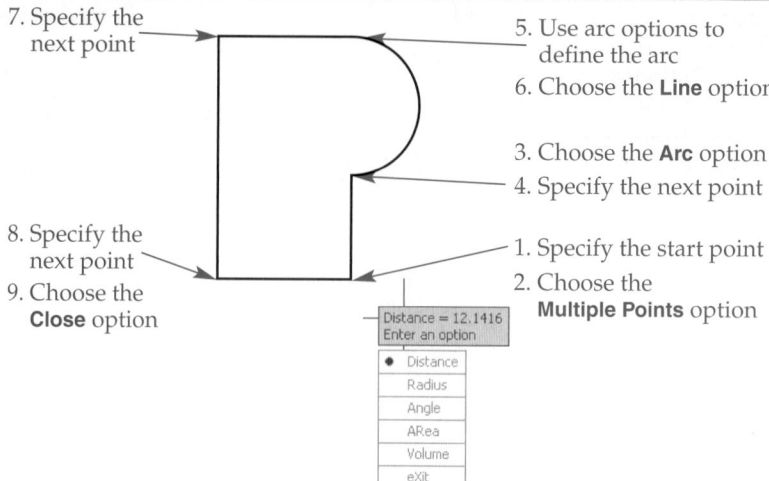

7. Specify the next point

8. Specify the next point

9. Choose the **Close** option

5. Use arc options to define the arc

6. Choose the **Line** option

3. Choose the **Arc** option

4. Specify the next point

1. Specify the start point

2. Choose the **Multiple Points** option

Distance = 12.1416
Enter an option

- Distance
- Radius
- Angle
- ARea
- Volume
- eXit

PROFESSIONAL TIP

You should typically use the **Multiple points** function of the **Distance** option to calculate the total distance between points of an open shape. The **Area** option of the **MEASUREGEOM** tool, described later in this chapter, is more suited to calculating the perimeter of a closed shape.

Measuring Radius and Diameter

Specify the **Radius** option of the **MEASUREGEOM** tool and pick an arc or circle to measure radius and diameter. The dimensions appear on-screen, as shown in **Figure 16-6,** and at the command line.

Measuring Angles

Use the **Angle** option of the **MEASUREGEOM** tool to find the angle between lines or points. To measure the angle between lines, select the first line followed by the second line. The dimension appears on-screen, as shown in **Figure 16-7A,** and at the command line. Select an arc to measure the angle between arc endpoints. See **Figure 16-7B.**

NOTE

Measuring an angle by selecting a circle and a point is typically most suitable for measuring 3D objects such as a cylinder.

Figure 16-6.
The data provided by the **Radius** option when you measure a circle or arc.

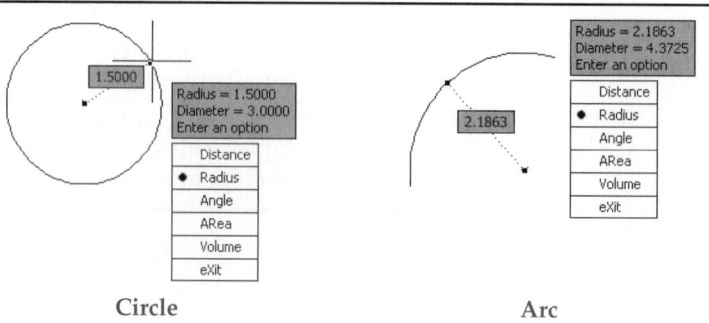

1.5000

Radius = 1.5000
Diameter = 3.0000
Enter an option

- Distance
- Radius
- Angle
- ARea
- Volume
- eXit

Circle

Radius = 2.1863
Diameter = 4.3725
Enter an option

- Distance
- Radius
- Angle
- ARea
- Volume
- eXit

2.1863

Arc

Figure 16-7. The data provided by the **Angle** option. A—Selecting two lines. B—Picking an arc.

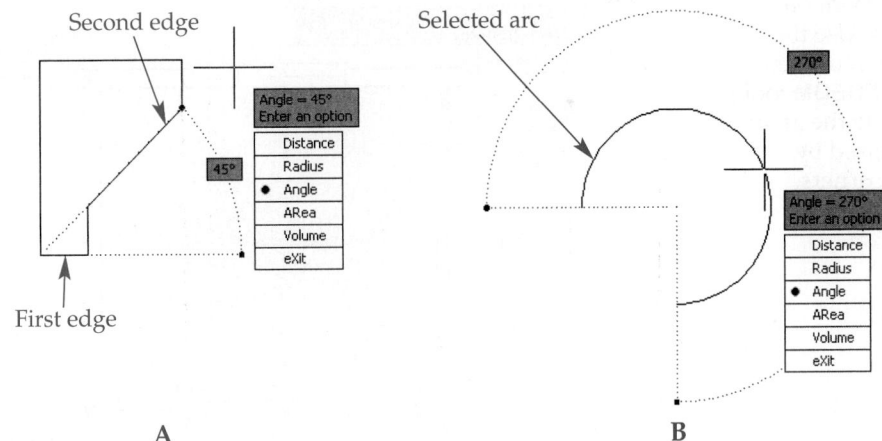

Choose the **Specify vertex** option when it is more appropriate to measure the angle between points, instead of selecting objects. Then select the angle vertex, followed by the first angle endpoint, and finally the second angle endpoint. See **Figure 16-8.**

Exercise 16-2

Access the Student Web site (www.g-wlearning.com/CAD) and complete Exercise 16-2.

Measuring Area

Use the **Area** option of the **MEASUREGEOM** tool to find the area between selected points or the area of an object. Specify the first point (corner) of the area to measure, followed by all other points (corners). The **Arc, Length,** and **Undo** options work the same as they do for measuring distance using the **Multiple points** function of the **Distance** option. A green (color 100) background fills the area to help you visualize the area. When you finish specifying perimeter corners, use the **Total** or **CLose** option to display the area between the points and the perimeter. The values appear on-screen, as shown in **Figure 16-9,** and at the command line.

Figure 16-8. Examples of when it is more appropriate to specify a vertex to measure an angle.

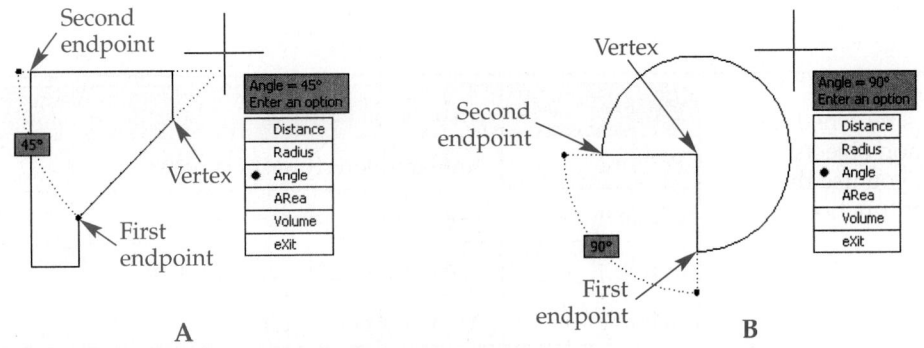

Figure 16-9.
Measuring the
area of a room on a
floor plan. Use the
Area option of the
MEASUREGEOM tool
to calculate the area
encompassed by
selected corners.

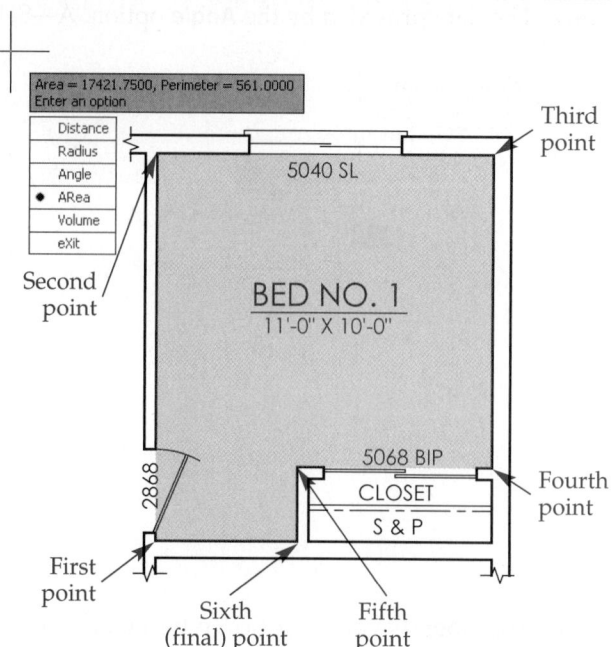

Use the **Object** function of the **Area** option to find the area of a polyline object, circle, or spline without picking corners. Access the **Area** option, activate the **Object** function instead of picking vertices, and then select the object to display values. AutoCAD displays the area of the object and a second value. The second value returned by the **Object** function varies, depending on the object type, as shown in **Figure 16-10**.

NOTE

You can calculate the area of an open polyline or spline object, but only if the endpoints show an apparent closure.

The **Area** option includes functions that allow you to calculate the sum of multiple different areas during a single operation. Before selecting corners or an object, activate the **Add area** option and define the first area by picking corners or using the **Object** function. Continue adding areas as needed, or use the **Subtract area** option to remove areas from the selection set. AutoCAD calculates a running total of the area as you add or remove areas. The **Area** option remains in effect until you exit.

Figure 16-11 shows an example of using the **Add area** and **Subtract area** functions of the **Area** tool in the same operation. In this example, select the **Add area** option, and then select the **Object** option and pick the rectangle (polyline). Right-click or press [Enter] or the space bar at the (ADD mode) select objects: prompt to continue. The area and perimeter of the rectangle and a total area appear.

Figure 16-10.
Values returned for
common objects
when you use the
Object function.

Object	Values Returned
Polyline	Area and length or perimeter
Circle	Area and circumference
Spline	Area and length or perimeter
Rectangle	Area and perimeter

Figure 16-11.
Measuring the area of a part view. To calculate the area of a rectangle drawn with the **RECTANGLE** tool, first select the outer boundary of the rectangle using the **Add area** function of the **Area** option. Select the inner circle boundaries using the **Subtract area** option. The total calculation appears.

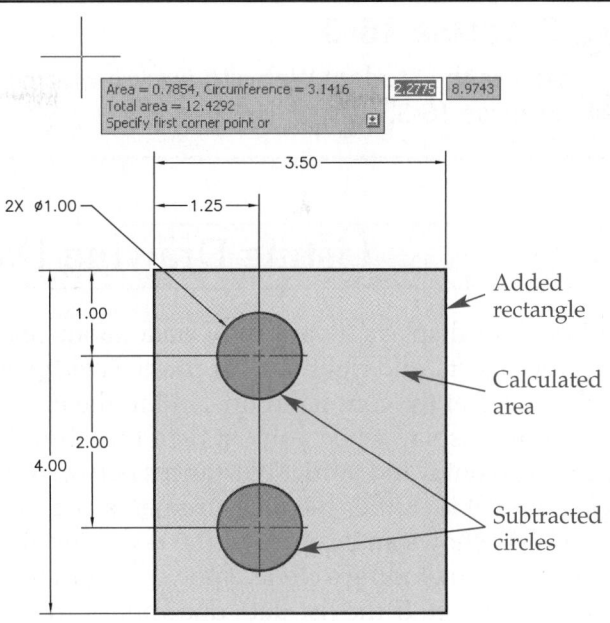

Then choose the **Subtract area** option to enter **SUBTRACT** mode. Select the **Object** option and pick the circles to subtract the area of the circles from the area of the rectangle. The area and circumference of each circle appear, along with the total area of the rectangle, minus the total area of the subtracted circles. Right-click or press [Enter] or the space bar at the (SUBTRACT mode) select objects: prompt to continue. Press [Enter] or the space bar, or right-click and choose **Enter** to display the total area and return to the **MEASUREGEOM** tool prompt.

PROFESSIONAL TIP

Calculating the area, circumference, and perimeter of shapes drawn with the **LINE** tool can be time-consuming, because you must specify each vertex. Use the **PLINE** tool when possible to construct a single object, or join existing objects. Use the **Object** function of the **Area** option to add or subtract objects.

NOTE

You can use the **Volume** option of the **MEASUREGEOM** tool to measure the volume of a basic drawing in 2D multiview format, but the option is most appropriate for measuring 3D objects. The **Region/Mass Properties** tool provides data related to the properties of a 2D region or 3D solid. *AutoCAD and Its Applications— Advanced* describes the **Volume** option of the **MEASUREGEOM** tool and the **Region/Mass Properties** tool.

NOTE

Traditional inquiry tools are available by typing command names. The **ID** tool displays the coordinates of a selected point. The **DIST** tool finds the distance between points, and the **AREA** tool calculates area. These tools function much like the options available with the **MEASUREGEOM** tool, but they are not as interactive.

Exercise 16-3

Access the Student Web site (www.g-wlearning.com/CAD) and complete Exercise 16-3.

Listing Drawing Data

LIST

Ribbon
Home
> Properties
List

Type
LIST
LI
LS

The **LIST** tool displays a variety of data about selected objects. Access the **LIST** tool, select the objects, and right-click or press [Enter] or the space bar. The data for each object is displayed at the command line and in the text window. **Figure 16-12A** shows the text window display when you list data for a line. The Delta X and Delta Y values indicate the horizontal and vertical distances between the *from point* and *to point* of the line. **Figure 16-12B** identifies the measurements of a line provided by the **LIST** tool.

Figure 16-13 shows an example of the text window listing data for a selection set of multiple objects, including a circle, a polyline drawn using the **RECTANGLE** tool, and a multiline text object. If the list data does not fit in the window, AutoCAD prompts you to press [Enter] to display additional data.

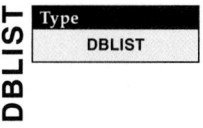

DBLIST

Type
DBLIST

NOTE

The **DBLIST** (database list) tool lists all data for every object in the current drawing. The information appears in the same format used by the **LIST** tool, although the text window does not appear automatically.

Figure 16-12.
A—The text window displayed when you use the **LIST** tool to list the properties of a line. B—The various data and measurements of a line provided by the **LIST** tool.

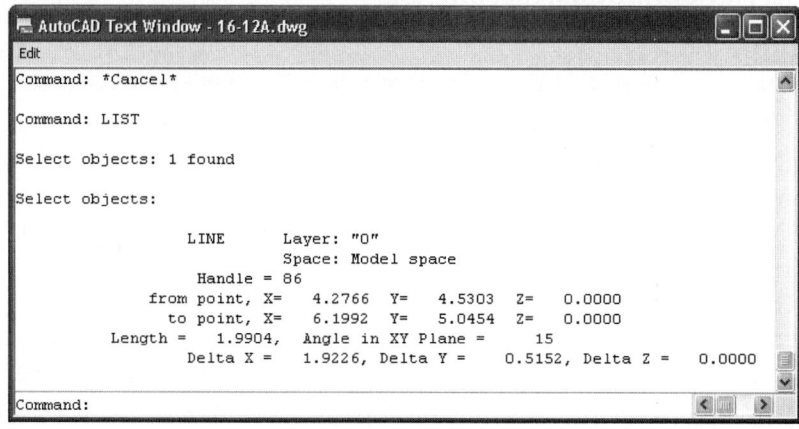

A

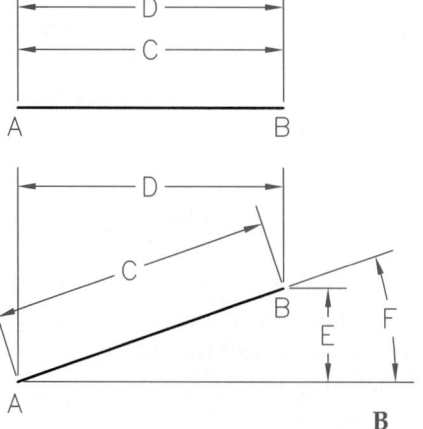

B

Figure 16-13.
Using the **LIST** tool to list the properties of multiline text, a circle, and a rectangle.

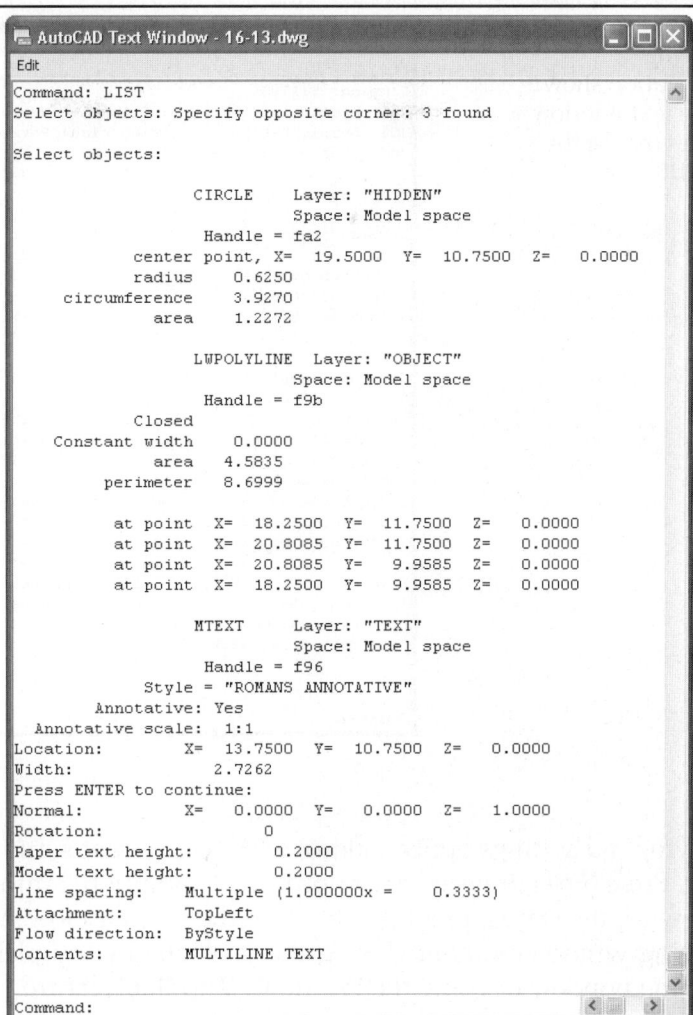

```
AutoCAD Text Window - 16-13.dwg
Edit
Command: LIST
Select objects: Specify opposite corner: 3 found

Select objects:

                    CIRCLE     Layer: "HIDDEN"
                                Space: Model space
                Handle = fa2
            center point, X=  19.5000  Y=  10.7500  Z=   0.0000
            radius    0.6250
        circumference    3.9270
                area    1.2272


                    LWPOLYLINE  Layer: "OBJECT"
                                Space: Model space
                Handle = f9b
            Closed
    Constant width    0.0000
                area    4.5835
        perimeter    8.6999

            at point  X=  18.2500  Y=  11.7500  Z=   0.0000
            at point  X=  20.8085  Y=  11.7500  Z=   0.0000
            at point  X=  20.8085  Y=   9.9585  Z=   0.0000
            at point  X=  18.2500  Y=   9.9585  Z=   0.0000


                    MTEXT     Layer: "TEXT"
                                Space: Model space
                Handle = f96
            Style = "ROMANS ANNOTATIVE"
        Annotative: Yes
    Annotative scale:  1:1
Location:       X=  13.7500  Y=  10.7500  Z=   0.0000
Width:             2.7262
Press ENTER to continue:
Normal:         X=   0.0000  Y=   0.0000  Z=   1.0000
Rotation:          0
Paper text height:        0.2000
Model text height:        0.2000
Line spacing:    Multiple (1.000000x =    0.3333)
Attachment:      TopLeft
Flow direction:  ByStyle
Contents:        MULTILINE TEXT

Command:
```

PROFESSIONAL TIP

The **LIST** tool provides most of the information about an object, including the area and perimeter of polylines. The **LIST** tool also reports object color and linetype, unless both are BYLAYER.

Exercise 16-4

Access the Student Web site (www.g-wlearning.com/CAD) and complete Exercise 16-4.

Reviewing the Drawing Status

The **STATUS** tool provides a method to display a variety of drawing information at the command line and in the text window, as shown in **Figure 16-14**. The number of objects in a drawing refers to the total number of objects—erased and existing. Free dwg disk (C:) space: represents the space left on the drive that contains the drawing file.

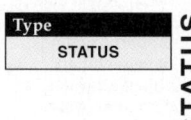

Type	
STATUS	

STATUS

Figure 16-14.
Drawing
information shown
in the text window
when you use the
STATUS tool.

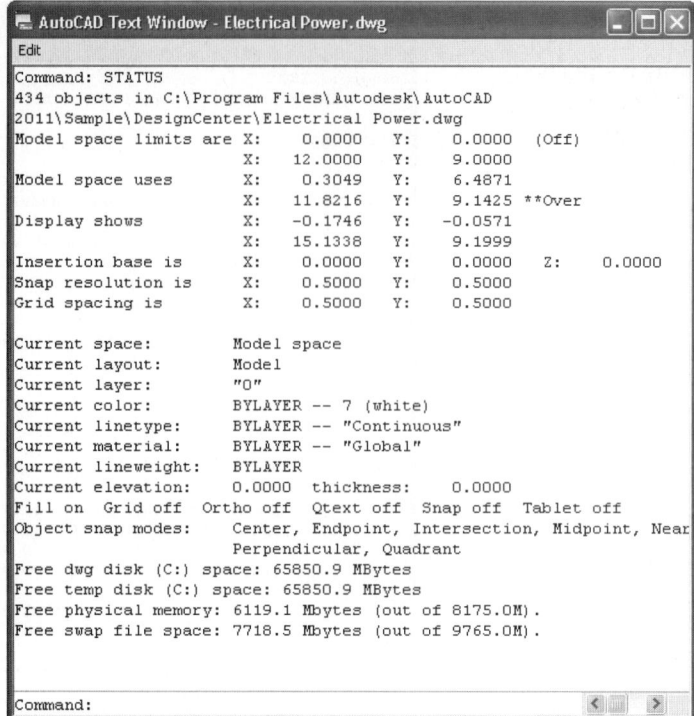

Drawing aid settings appear, along with the current settings for layer, linetype, and color. Press [Enter] if necessary to proceed to additional information. When you finish reviewing the status, press [F2] to close the text window. You can also switch to the drawing window without closing the text window by picking anywhere inside the drawing window or using the Windows [Alt]+[Tab] feature.

Checking the Time

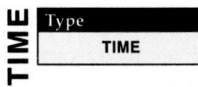

The **TIME** tool displays the current time and time related to the current drawing session. **Figure 16-15** shows an example of drawing time data displayed in the text window. The drawing creation time starts when you begin a new drawing, not when you first save a new drawing. The **SAVE** tool affects the Last updated: time. However, all drawing session time is lost when you exit AutoCAD without saving.

NOTE

The Windows operating system maintains the date and time settings for the computer. You can change these settings in the Windows Control Panel.

PROFESSIONAL TIP

field: A text object that displays a property, setting, or value for an object, drawing, or computer system.

Fields are an effective way to display drawing information within mtext and text objects. You can use fields with many AutoCAD tools, including inquiry tools, drawing properties, attributes, and sheet sets. You can update fields when changes occur to the reference data. Chapter 10 explains using fields.

Figure 16-15.
Information displayed in the text window when you use the **TIME** tool.

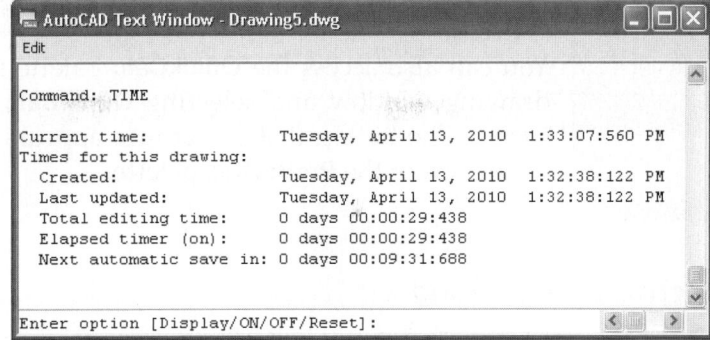

```
AutoCAD Text Window - Drawing5.dwg
Edit

Command: TIME

Current time:                Tuesday, April 13, 2010   1:33:07:560 PM
Times for this drawing:
  Created:                   Tuesday, April 13, 2010   1:32:38:122 PM
  Last updated:              Tuesday, April 13, 2010   1:32:38:122 PM
  Total editing time:        0 days 00:00:29:438
  Elapsed timer (on):        0 days 00:00:29:438
  Next automatic save in:    0 days 00:09:31:688

Enter option [Display/ON/OFF/Reset]:
```

Exercise 16-5

Access the Student Web site (www.g-wlearning.com/CAD) and complete Exercise 16-5.

Using QuickCalc

Most drafting projects require you to make calculations. For example, when working from a sketch with missing dimensions, you may need to calculate a distance or angle, or you may need to double-check dimensions. Often drafters make calculations using a handheld calculator. An alternative is to use **QuickCalc**, which is a palette containing a basic calculator, scientific calculator, units converter, and variables feature. See **Figure 16-16.** Use **QuickCalc** as you would a handheld calculator. You can also use **QuickCalc** while a tool is active to paste calculations when a prompt asks for a specific value.

Ribbon
View
> Palettes

Quick Calculator

Type
QUICKCALC
QC

QUICKCALC

Figure 16-16.
The **QuickCalc** palette allows you to perform a variety of calculations.

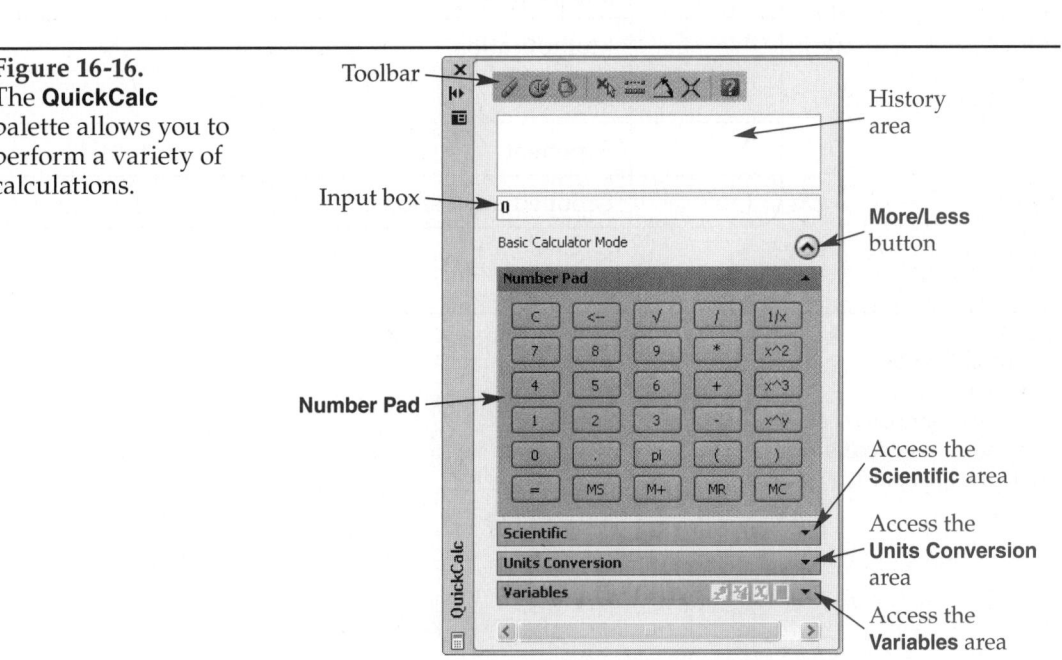

Toolbar

Input box

Number Pad

History area

More/Less button

Access the **Scientific** area

Access the **Units Conversion** area

Access the **Variables** area

Entering Expressions

The basic math functions used in numeric expressions include addition, subtraction, multiplication, division, and exponential notation. You can enter grouped expressions by using parentheses to break up the expressions to be calculated separately. For example, to calculate 6 + 2 and then multiply the sum by 4, enter (6+2)*4. The result will be wrong if you do not add the parentheses. **Figure 16-17** shows the symbols used for basic math operators.

Add expressions in the input box by picking buttons on the **Number Pad** or using keyboard keys. After creating the expression, pick the equal (=) button on the number pad or press [Enter] to evaluate the expression. **Figure 16-18** shows options found on the basic **Number Pad** that are not available from the keyboard.

The result of an evaluated expression appears in the input box, and the expression moves to the history area. **Figure 16-19** displays the **QuickCalc** palette after calculating 96.27 + 23.58. When you use only the input box of **QuickCalc**, pick the **More/Less** button below the input box to hide the additional sections, saving valuable drawing space. When all areas of the **QuickCalc** palette are displayed, the button is an up arrow and its tooltip reads **Less**. Pick the button again to display hidden areas.

Figure 16-17.
Common math operators.

Symbol	Function	Example
+	Addition	3+26
−	Subtraction	270–15.3
*	Multiplication	4*156
/	Division	265/16
^	Exponent	22.6^3
()	Grouped expressions	2*(16+2^3)

Figure 16-18.
The basic **Number Pad** area contains additional options that you cannot access using the keyboard.

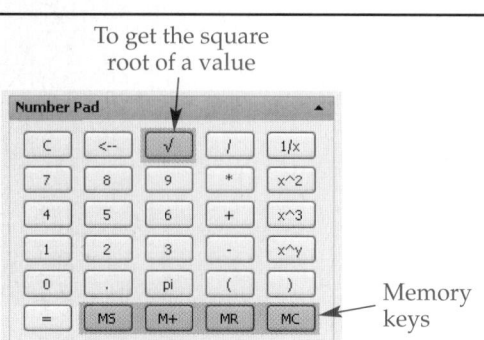

Figure 16-19.
A—Add an expression to the input box. B—After creating the expression, press [Enter] to evaluate the expression. The history area stores the expression and result.

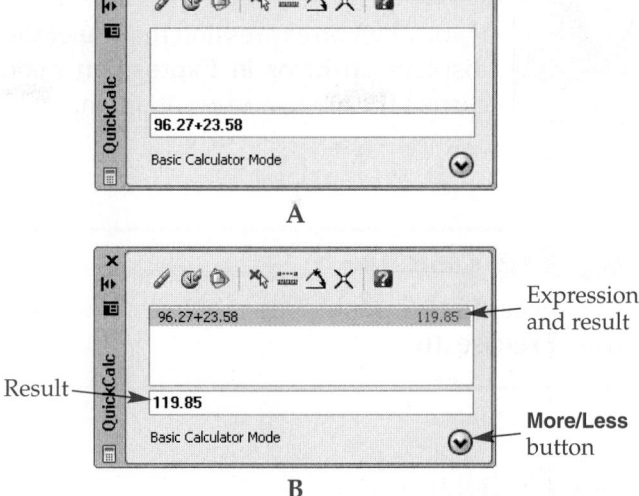

A

B

Result

Expression and result

More/Less button

Clearing the Input and History Areas

After picking the equal (=) button or pressing [Enter] to evaluate an expression, you can create a new expression without clearing the last result. AutoCAD automatically starts a new expression. You can clear the input box manually by placing the cursor in the input box and pressing [Backspace] or [Delete], or by picking the **Clear** button from the **QuickCalc** toolbar. To clear the history area, pick the **Clear History** button. See **Figure 16-20.**

Figure 16-20.
Use the buttons on the **QuickCalc** toolbar to clear the input box and history areas.

Pick to clear history area

Pick to clear the input box

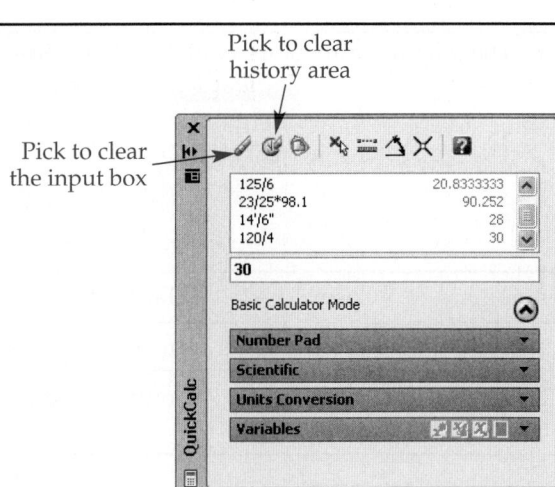

Exercise 16-6

Access the Student Web site (www.g-wlearning.com/CAD) and complete Exercise 16-6.

Scientific Calculations

The **Scientific** area of **QuickCalc** includes trigonometry, exponential, and some geometric functions. See **Figure 16-21**. To use one of the functions, add a value to the input box, pick the appropriate function button, and pick the equal (=) button or press [Enter]. When you pick a function button, the input box value appears in parentheses after the expression. For example, to get the sine of 14, clear the input box, type 14 in the input box, and pick the **sin** button. The input box now reads sin(14). Pick the equal (=) button or press [Enter] to view the result.

NOTE

You can pick a function button first, but doing so puts a default value of 0 in parentheses. Place the cursor in the input box to type a different number in the parentheses if needed.

Converting Units

The **Units Conversion** area allows you to convert one unit type to another. The unit types available are **Length**, **Area**, **Volume**, and **Angular**. For example, to use the unit converter to convert 23 centimeters to inches, pick in the **Units type** field to display the drop-down list. See **Figure 16-22**. Pick the drop-down list button to display the different unit types and select Length. Activate the **Convert from** field and select Centimeters from

Figure 16-21. The scientific functions available in **QuickCalc**.

	1	2	3	4	5
A	Sine	Cosine	Tangent	Base–10 Log	Base–10 Exponent
B	Arcsine	Arccosine	Arctangent	Natural Log	Natural Exponent
C	Convert Radians to Degrees	Convert Degrees to Radians	Absolute Value	Round	Truncate

Figure 16-22.
Picking the current unit type activates the field and displays the drop-down list button.

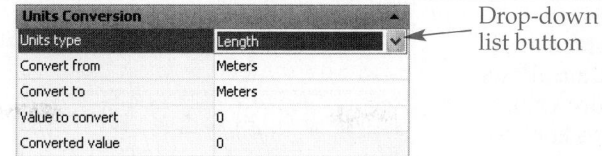

Drop-down list button

the drop-down list. Activate the **Convert to** field and select Inches from the drop-down list. Type 23 in the **Value to convert** field and pick the equal (=) button or press [Enter]. The **Converted value** field displays the converted units.

To pass the converted value to the input box for use in an expression, pick the **Return Conversion to Calculator Input Area** button. See **Figure 16-23.** If the button is not visible, pick once on the converted units in the **Converted value** field.

Exercise 16-7

Access the Student Web site (www.g-wlearning.com/CAD) and complete Exercise 16-7.

Using Variables

If you use an expression or value frequently, you can save it as a *variable.* Use the **Variables** area, shown in **Figure 16-24,** to create, edit, delete, and pass variables to the input box. The **Variables** area of **QuickCalc** includes two types of predefined variables: *constant* and *function.*

To create a new variable, select the **New Variable...** button to open the **Variable Definition** dialog box shown in **Figure 16-25.** Type a name for the variable in the **Name:** field. Select a group to contain the variable using the **Group with:** field. Type the value or the expression for the variable in the **Value or expression:** field. Give a description for the variable in the **Description** field. Pick the **OK** button to save the variable and display it in the **Variables** area.

To edit a variable, pick the variable to modify and select the **Edit Variable** button to reopen the **Variable Definition** dialog box. Pick the **Delete** button to delete the selected variable. Pick the **Return Variable to Input Area** button or double-click the variable name to pass the selected variable to the input box.

variable: A text item that represents another value and is available for future reference.

constant: An expression or value that stays the same.

function: An expression or value that asks for user input to get values to pass to the expression.

Figure 16-23.
After you convert a value, pass the value to the input box for use in an expression.

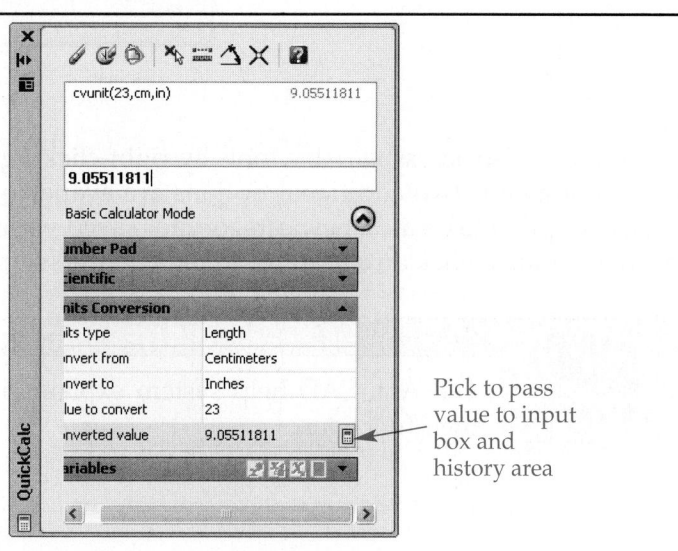

Pick to pass value to input box and history area

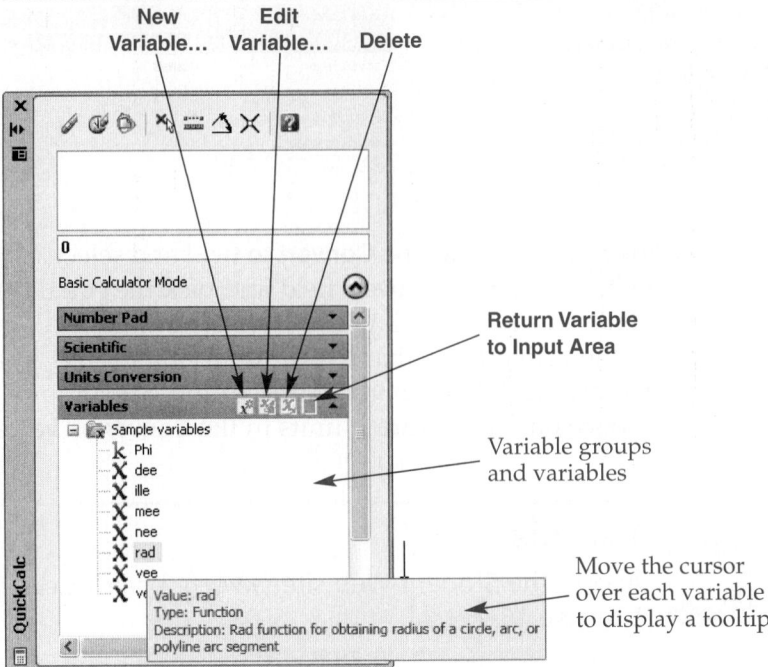

Figure 16-24.
The **Variables** area of **QuickCalc** allows you to store values and expressions for later use.

New Variable...   **Edit Variable...**   **Delete**

Return Variable to Input Area

Variable groups and variables

Move the cursor over each variable to display a tooltip

Value: rad
Type: Function
Description: Rad function for obtaining radius of a circle, arc, or polyline arc segment

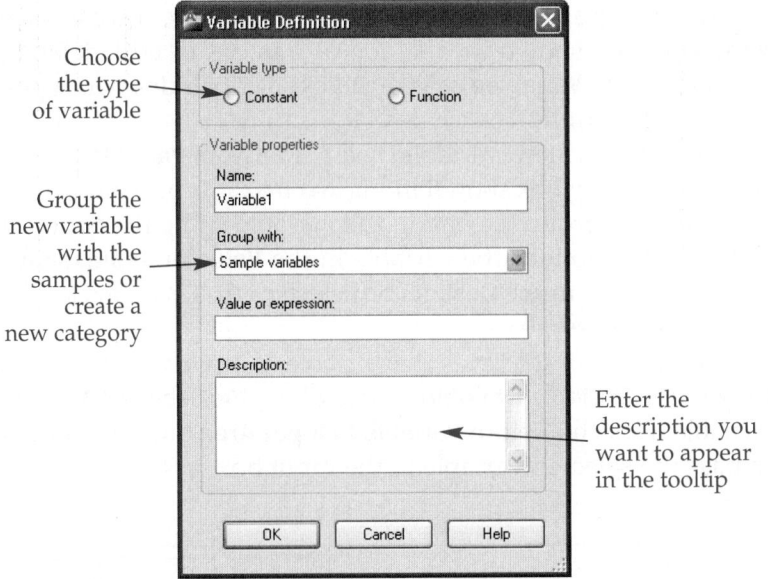

Figure 16-25.
Use the **Variable Definition** dialog box to define new variables.

Choose the type of variable

Group the new variable with the samples or create a new category

Enter the description you want to appear in the tooltip

You can also access variable tools by right-clicking in the **Variable** area to display a shortcut menu. Two additional options are available from the menu. Pick the **New Category** option to create a new category for saved variables. Select the **Rename** option or slowly double-click on a variable to rename the selected variable.

PROFESSIONAL TIP

The AutoCAD help system explains the predefined variables and their functions.

Using Drawing Values

Tools available from the **QuickCalc** toolbar allow you to pass values from the drawing to the **QuickCalc** input box, and from the input box to the drawing. When you select any of the buttons shown in **Figure 16-26**, the **QuickCalc** palette temporarily disappears so that you can select points from the drawing window.

Pick the **Get Coordinates** button to select a point from the drawing window and display the X,Y,Z coordinates in the input box. Pick the **Distance Between Two Points** button and select two points from the drawing area to display the distance between the points in the input box. Select the **Angle of Line Defined by Two Points** button and pick two points on a line to calculate the angle of the line and display the angle in the input box. Select the **Intersection of Two Lines Defined by Four Points** button to find the intersection of two lines by picking points on the two lines. The X,Y,Z coordinates of the intersection appear in the input box.

Using QuickCalc with Tools

The previous information focuses on using the **QuickCalc** palette to calculate unknown values while you are drafting, much like using a handheld calculator or the Windows Calculator. You can also use **QuickCalc** while a tool is active to pass a calculated value to the command line as a response to a prompt. AutoCAD provides a few alternatives for using **QuickCalc** while a tool is active.

If the **QuickCalc** palette is active when you access a tool, when the prompt requesting an unknown value appears, calculate the value using the **QuickCalc** palette and then press the **Paste value to command line** button to pass the value as a response to the prompt. For example, to draw a line a distance of 14′8″ + 26′3″ horizontally from a start point, activate the **QuickCalc** palette, access the **LINE** tool, and pick a start point. Then use polar tracking or **Ortho** mode to move the crosshairs to the right or left of the start point so the line is at a 0° or 180° angle. At the Specify next point or [Undo]: prompt, enter 14′8″ + 26′3″ in the **QuickCalc** palette input box and pick the equal (=) button or press [Enter]. The result in the input box is 40′11″. Pick the **Paste value to command line** button to respond to the prompt with a 40′11″ value. Press [Enter] or the space bar or right-click and select **Enter** to draw the 40′11″ line.

If the **QuickCalc** palette is not active while you are using a tool, you can still calculate and use a value. When the prompt requesting an unknown value appears, access **QuickCalc** by right-clicking and selecting **QuickCalc** or typing ′QC. A **QuickCalc** *window*, which is not the same as the **QuickCalc** palette, opens in command calculation mode. See **Figure 16-27**. Use the necessary tools to evaluate an expression. Then pick the **Apply** button to pass the value back to the command line, and close the **QuickCalc** window.

PROFESSIONAL TIP

The units you use in **QuickCalc** must match the drawing units. In the preceding example, which uses architectural units, the drawing units must also be architectural. If needed, use the **Drawing Units** dialog box to change the drawing units to Architectural.

Figure 16-26.
Use buttons on the **QuickCalc** toolbar to pass values from **QuickCalc** to AutoCAD and retrieve values from AutoCAD to pass to **QuickCalc**.

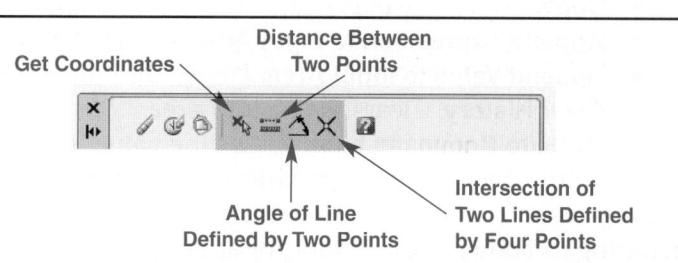

Get Coordinates

Distance Between Two Points

Angle of Line Defined by Two Points

Intersection of Two Lines Defined by Four Points

Figure 16-27.
The **QuickCalc**
window appears
when you access
QuickCalc while a
tool is active. The
Apply and **Close**
buttons are available
at the bottom of the
window.

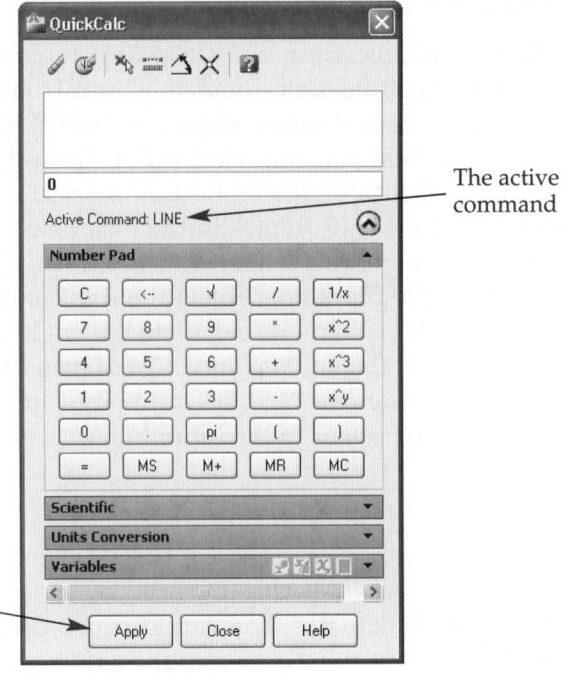

The active
command

Pick to pass
value back
to command

Exercise 16-8

Access the Student Web site (www.g-wlearning.com/CAD) **and complete**
Exercise 16-8.

Using QuickCalc with Object Properties

QuickCalc also allows you to calculate expressions for an object while using the
Properties palette. Pick a field that contains a numeric value to display the calculator
icon. **Figure 16-28** shows a selected circle and the active **Radius** field in the **Properties**
palette. Pick the calculator icon to open the **QuickCalc** window, again not the same item
as the **QuickCalc** palette, in property calculation mode. Use expressions and values in
the same manner as when using **QuickCalc** at any other time. Once you evaluate the
expression in the input box, pick the **Apply** button to pass the value to the property field
in the **Properties** palette. The object automatically updates based on the new value.

Additional QuickCalc Options

The history area contains settings and features that you can only access from a
shortcut menu, shown in **Figure 16-29.** Right-click anywhere in the history area to
access the menu with the following options:
- **Expression Font Color.** Changes the color of the expression font.
- **Value Font Color.** Changes the color of the value font.
- **Copy.** Copies the expression and value to the Windows clipboard.
- **Append Expression to Input Area.** Passes the expression to the input box.
- **Append Value to Input Area.** Passes the value to the input box.
- **Clear History.** Clears the history area.
- **Paste to Command Line.** Passes the value to the Command: prompt.

As with other palettes, picking the **Properties** button on the **QuickCalc** palette
displays a shortcut menu. The settings allow you to change the palette appearance,
including its ability to dock, hide, or appear transparent.

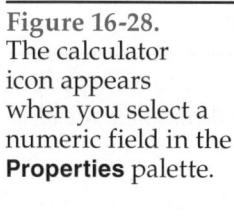

Figure 16-28.
The calculator icon appears when you select a numeric field in the **Properties** palette.

Selected object

Pick to access **QuickCalc**

Active field

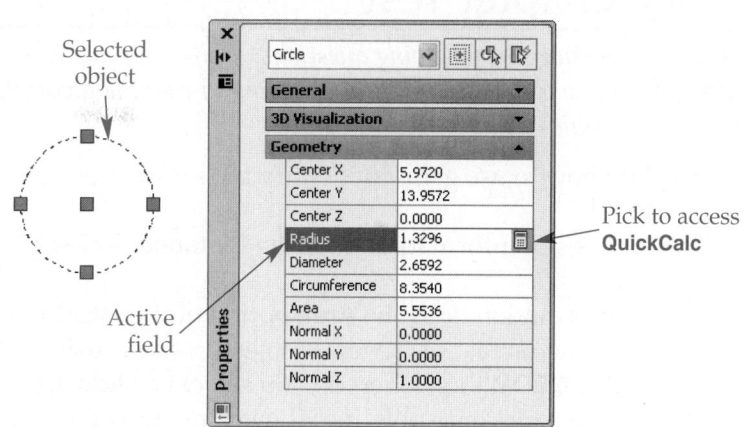

Figure 16-29.
The history area shortcut menu contains additional **QuickCalc** functions and settings.

Shortcut menu

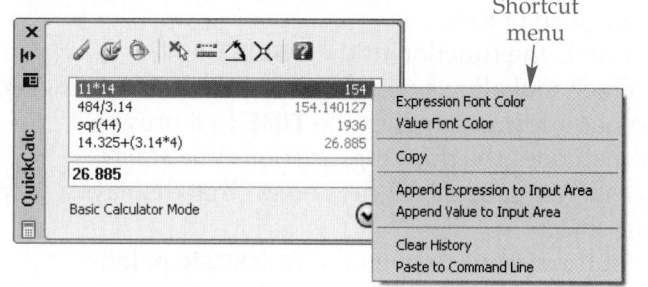

Chapter Test

Answer the following questions. Write your answers on a separate sheet of paper or go to the Student Web site (www.g-wlearning.com/CAD) and complete the electronic chapter test.

1. Explain how to use grips to identify the location of a point and the dimensions of an object.
2. What types of information does the **Distance** option of the **MEASUREGEOM** tool provide?
3. What information does the **Area** option of the **MEASUREGEOM** tool provide?
4. To add the areas of several objects when using the **Area** option of the **MEASUREGEOM** tool, when do you select the **Add area** function?
5. Explain how picking a polyline when using the **Area** option of the **MEASUREGEOM** tool is different from measuring the area of an object drawn with the **LINE** tool.
6. What is the purpose of the **LIST** tool?
7. Describe the meaning of *delta X* and *delta Y*.
8. What tool, other than **MEASUREGEOM** and **AREA**, provides the area and perimeter of an object?
9. What is the function of the **DBLIST** tool?
10. Which tool allows you to list drawing aid settings for the current drawing?
11. What information does the **TIME** tool provide?
12. When does the drawing creation time start?
13. What term describes a text object that displays a set property, setting, or value for an object?
14. List three ways to open the **QuickCalc** palette.
15. Name the four sections of the **QuickCalc** palette.
16. Give the proper symbol to use for the following math functions:
    A. Addition
    B. Subtraction
    C. Multiplication
    D. Division
    E. Exponent
    F. Grouped expressions
17. Under which section of the **QuickCalc** palette can you find the square root function?
18. Under which section of the **QuickCalc** palette can you find the arccosine function?
19. When using one of the scientific functions, which should you do first: pick the scientific function button or type in the value to use in the input box? Why?
20. Name the four types of units that you can convert using **QuickCalc**.
21. What term describes a text item that represents another value and can be accessed later as needed?
22. Which tool button passes the value in the **QuickCalc** input box to respond to a prompt?
23. How can you start **QuickCalc** while a command is active?
24. When using **QuickCalc** while a tool is active, how do you pass the value to respond to a prompt?
25. When the **Properties** palette is open, what do you need to do first to see the calculator icon to use **QuickCalc**?

Drawing Problems

Start AutoCAD if it is not already started. Start a new drawing for each problem using an appropriate template of your choice. The template should include layers, text styles, and table styles, when necessary, for drawing the given objects. Add layers, text styles, and table styles as needed. Draw all objects using appropriate layers, text styles, table styles, justification, and format. Follow the specific instructions for each problem. Use only drawing and editing tools and techniques you have already learned. Do not draw dimensions. Use your own judgment and approximate dimensions when necessary.

▼ Basic

1. Use **QuickCalc** to calculate the result of the following equations.
   A. 27.375 + 15.875
   B. 16.0625 – 7.1250
   C. 5 × 17'-8"
   D. 48'-0" ÷ 16
   E. (12.625 + 3.063) + (18.250 – 4.375) – (2.625 – 1.188)
   F. 7.25^2

2. Use **QuickCalc** to convert 4.625" to millimeters.

3. Use **QuickCalc** to convert 26 mm to inches.

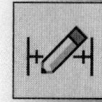

4. Use **QuickCalc** to convert 65 miles to kilometers.

5. Use **QuickCalc** to convert 5 gallons to liters.

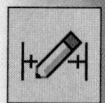

6. Use **QuickCalc** to find the square root of 360.

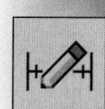

7. Use **QuickCalc** to calculate 3.25 squared.

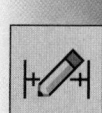

▼ Intermediate

8. Show the calculation and answer used with the **LINE** tool to make an 8" line .006 in./in. longer in a pattern to allow for shrinkage in the final casting. Show only the expression and answer.

9. Solve for the deflection of a structural member. The formula is written as $PL^3/48EI$, where P = pounds of force, L = length of beam, E = modulus of elasticity, and I = moment of inertia. The values to be used are P = 4000 lbs, L = 240", and E = 1,000,000 lbs/in^2. The value for I is the result of the beam (width × height^3)/12, where width = 6.75" and height = 13.5".

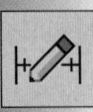

10. Calculate the coordinate located at 4,4,0 + 3<30.

11. Calculate the coordinate located at (3 + 5,1 + 1.25,0) + (2.375,1.625,0).

12. Draw the part view shown. Check the time when you start the drawing. Draw all the features using the **PLINE** and **CIRCLE** tools. Use the **Area** option of the **MEASUREGEOM** tool and the **Object, Add area**, and **Subtract area** functions to calculate the following:
    A. The area and perimeter of Object A.
    B. The area and perimeter of area B. The slot ends are full radius.
    C. The area and circumference of one of the circles.
    D. The area of Object A, minus the area of Object B.
    E. The area of Object A, minus the areas of the other three features.

    Enter the **TIME** tool and note the editing time spent on your drawing. Save the drawing as P16-12.

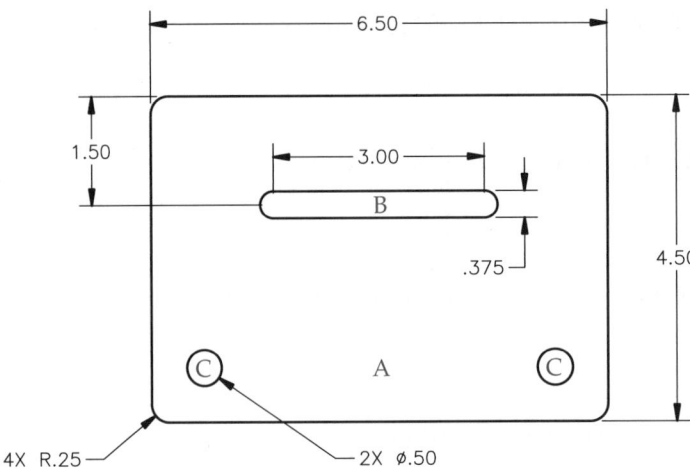

13. Draw the deck shown using the **PLINE** tool. Using the **POLYGON** tool, draw the hot tub. Use the following guidelines to complete this problem:
   A. Specify architectural units for your drawing. Use 1/2" fractions and decimal degrees. Leave the remaining settings for the drawing units at the default values.
   B. Set the limits to 100',80' and use the **All** option of the **ZOOM** tool.
   C. Set the grid spacing to 2' and the snap spacing to 1'.
   D. Calculate the measurements listed below.
      a. The area and perimeter of the deck.
      b. The area and perimeter of the hot tub.
      c. The area of the deck minus the area of the hot tub.
      d. The distance between Point C and Point D.
      e. The distance between Point E and Point C.
      f. The coordinates of Points C, D, and F.
   E. Enter the **DBLIST** tool and check the information listed for the drawing.
   F. Enter the **TIME** tool and note the total editing time spent on the drawing.
   G. Save the drawing as P16-13.

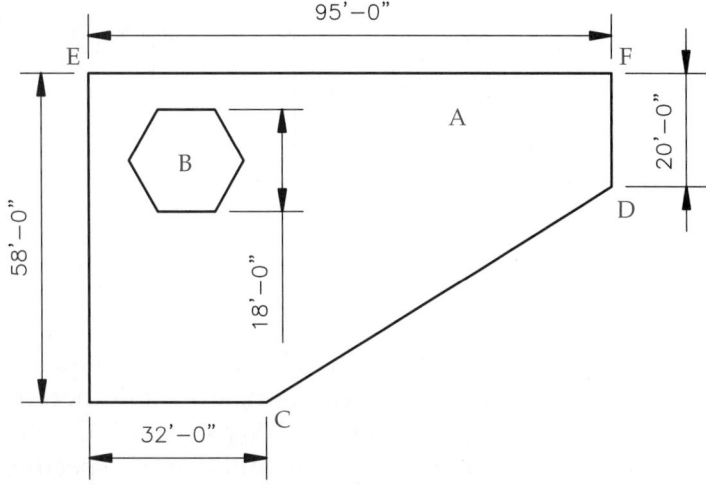

14. The drawing shown is a side view of a pyramid. The pyramid has four sides. Create an auxiliary view showing the true size of a pyramid face. Save the drawing as P16-14. Calculate the following:
   A. The area of one side.
   B. The perimeter of one side.
   C. The area of all four sides.
   D. The area of the base.
   E. The true length (distance) from the midpoint of the base on one side to the apex.

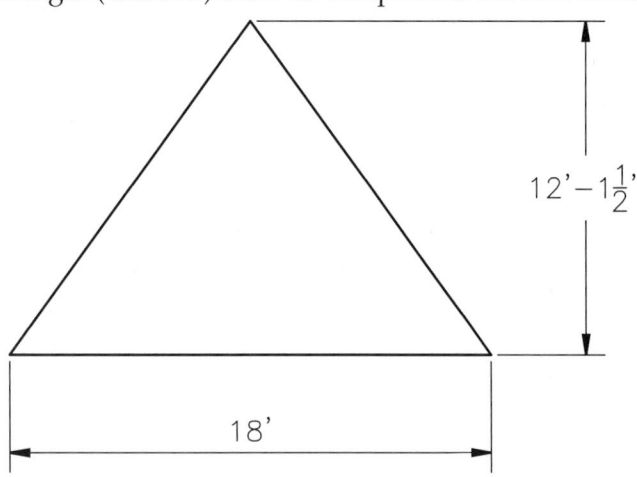

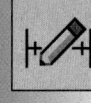

15. Make the following calculations given the right triangle shown.
    A. Length of side c (hypotenuse).
    B. Sine of angle *A*.
    C. Sine of angle *B*.
    D. Cosine of angle *A*.
    E. Tangent of angle *A*.
    F. Tangent of angle *B*.

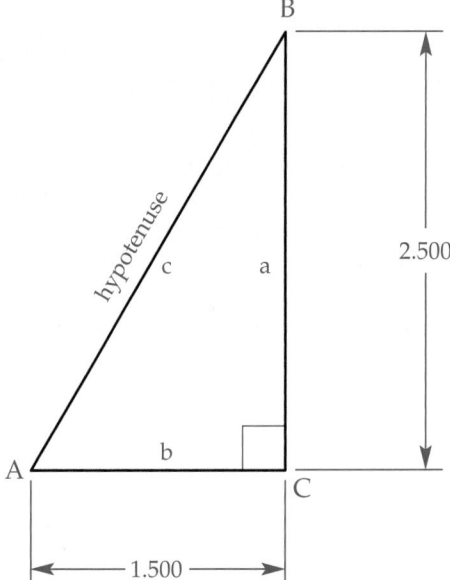

16. Research the design of an existing ball valve with the following specifications: brass body, chrome-plated brass ball, full port, lever style, non-threaded (solder) female ends to accept a ∅1″ pipe, rated for 500 psi at 100°. Create a dimensioned 2D sketch of the existing design from manufacturer's specifications, or from measurements taken from an actual valve. Start a new drawing from scratch or use a decimal-unit template of your choice. Draw the views needed to describe the valve completely from your sketch. Save the drawing as P16-19. Print an 8.5″ × 11″ copy of the drawing extents using a 1:1 scale and a landscape orientation.

17. Draw the house elevation shown. Draw the windows as single lines only (the location of the windows is not critical). The spacing between each of the second-floor windows is 3". The width of this end of the house is 16'-6". The length of the roof is 40'. Use the **PLINE** tool to assist in creating the specific shapes in this drawing, except as previously noted. Save the drawing as P16-16. Calculate the following:
   A. The total area of the roof.
   B. The diagonal distance from one corner of the roof to the other.
   C. The area of the first-floor window.
   D. The total area of all second-floor windows, including the 3" spaces between each of them.
   E. Siding will cover the house. What is the total area of siding for this end?

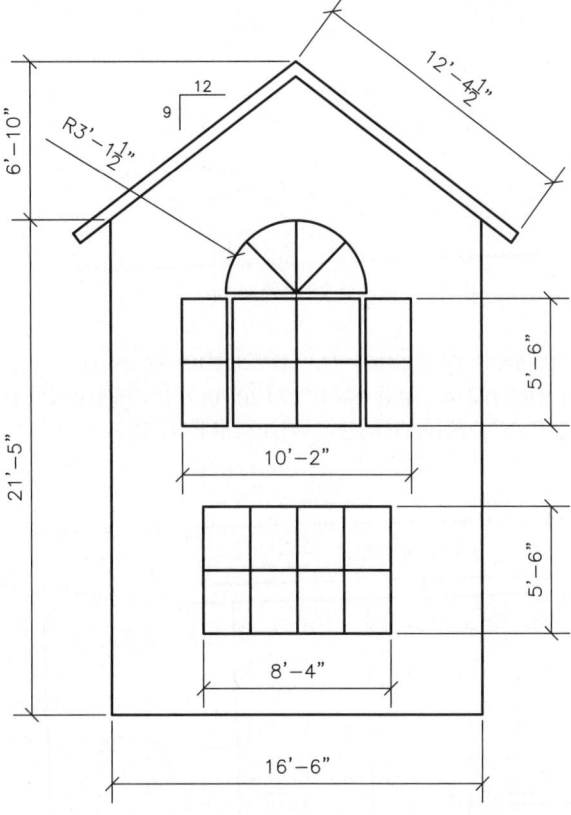

18. Draw the property plat shown. Label property line bearings and distances only if required by your instructor or supervisor. Calculate the area of the property plat in square feet and convert to acres. Save the drawing as P16-17.

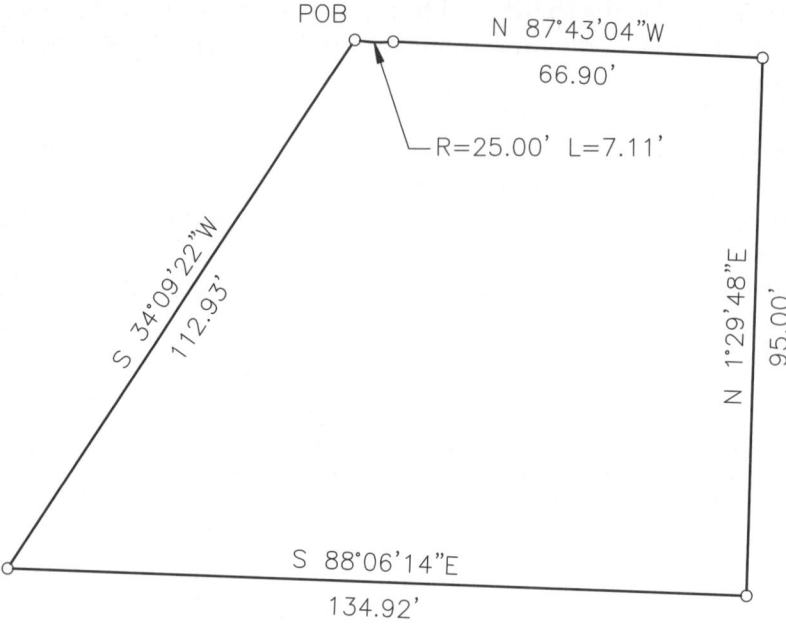

19. Draw the subdivision plat shown. Label the drawing as shown. Calculate the acreage of each lot and record each value as a label inside the corresponding lot (for example, .249 AC). Save the drawing as P16-18.

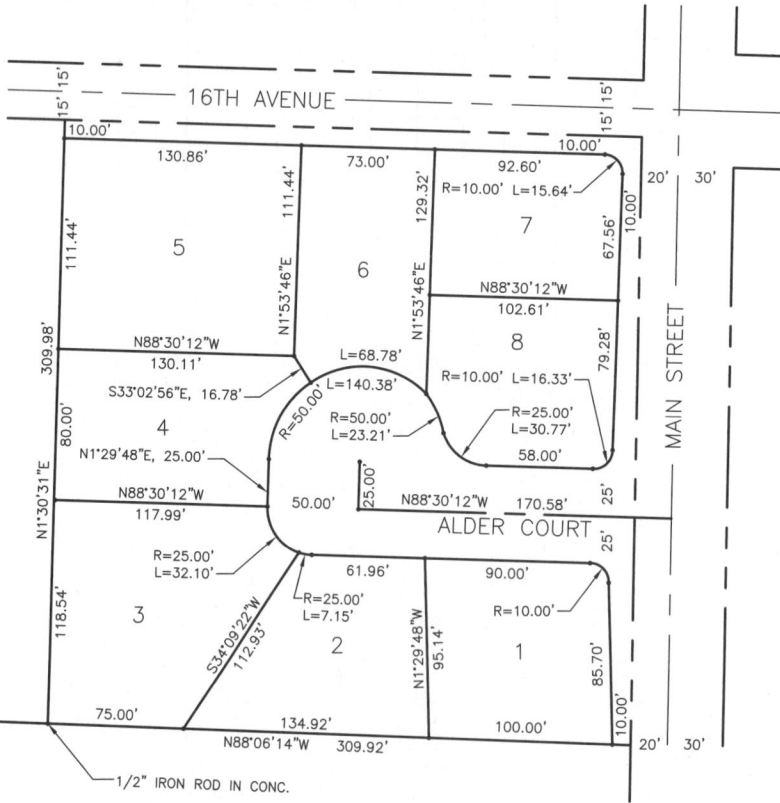

AutoCAD Certified Associate Exam Practice

Answer the following questions. Write your answers on a separate sheet of paper.

1. Which of the following tools can you use to find the length of a line? *Select all that apply.*
   A. **DBLIST**
   B. **DIST**
   C. **LIST**
   D. **MEASUREGEOM**
   E. **TIME**

2. Which of the following expressions in **QuickCalc** adds 3.7, 4.2, and 8.5, then divides the result by the sum of 9.8 and 17.4? *Select the one item that best answers the question.*
   A. 3.7+4.2+8.5÷9.8+17.4
   B. (3.7+4.2+8.5)÷(9.8+17.4)
   C. 3.7+4.2+8.5/9.8+17.4
   D. (3.7+4.2+8.5)/(9.8+17.4)
   E. =sum(3.7,4.2,8.5)/sum(9.8,17.4)

3. Which of the following conversions are possible in **QuickCalc**? *Select all that apply.*
   A. cubic feet to cubic meters
   B. degrees Fahrenheit to degrees Celsius
   C. degrees to radians
   D. miles to kilometers
   E. ounces to milligrams

AutoCAD Certified Professional Exam Practice

Follow the instructions in each problem. Write your answers on a separate sheet of paper.

1. **Navigate to this chapter on the Student Web site and open CPE-16circum.dwg.**

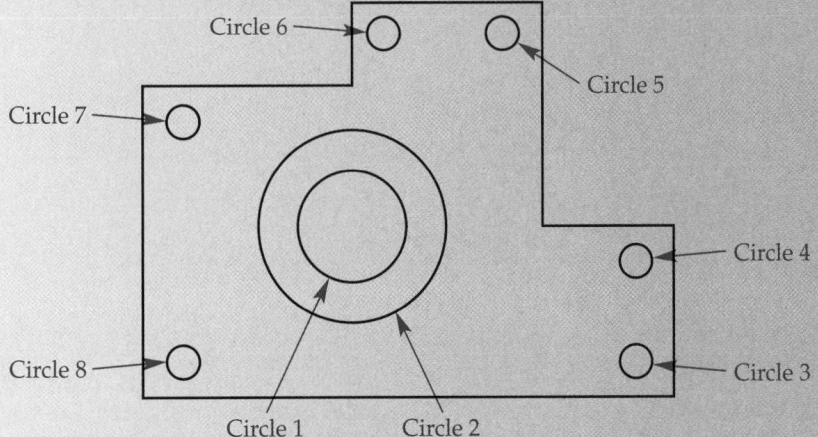

Use appropriate tools to find the answers to the following questions:
A. What is the circumference of Circle 1?
B. What is the total area of Circles 3, 4, 5, 6, 7, and 8?

2. **Navigate to this chapter on the Student Web site and open CPE-16perimeter.dwg.**

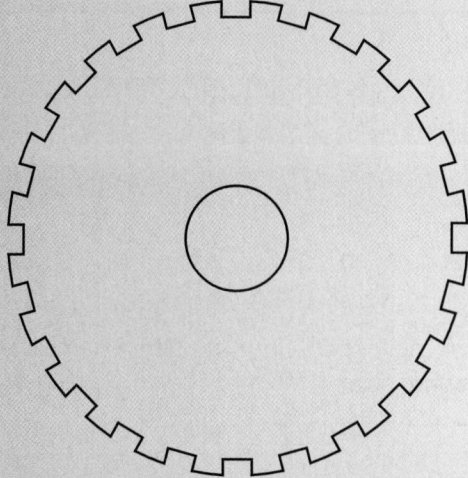

What is the perimeter of the gear?

CHAPTER 17

Dimension Standards and Styles

Learning Objectives

After completing this chapter, you will be able to do the following:

✓ Describe common dimension standards and practices.

✓ Create dimension styles.

✓ Manage dimension styles.

A *dimension* typically includes numerical values, lines, symbols, and notes. **Figure 17-1** shows typical dimension elements and dimensioning applications. Use dimension tools to dimension the size and location of features and objects. Dimension styles control the appearance of dimension elements. Dimensional constraint tools, explained in Chapter 22, allow you to use dimensions to control object size and location.

dimension: A description of the size, shape, or location of features on an object or structure.

Dimension Standards and Practices

Dimensions help communicate drawing information. Each drafting field uses different dimensioning practices. Dimensioning practices often depend on product requirements, manufacturing or construction accuracy, standards, and tradition. It is important for you to draw dimensions according to industry and company standards. Dimension standards help to ensure that product manufacturing or construction is accurate. In addition, consistent dimension formatting is critical to legibility and drawing clarity. A drawing should use the same general dimension format throughout when possible.

This textbook presents mechanical drafting dimensioning standards according to ASME Y14.5-2009, *Dimensioning and Tolerancing*, published by the American Society of Mechanical Engineers (ASME). When appropriate, this textbook also references International Standards Organization (ISO) standards and discipline-specific standards, including the United States National CAD Standard® (NCS) and American Welding Society (AWS) standards.

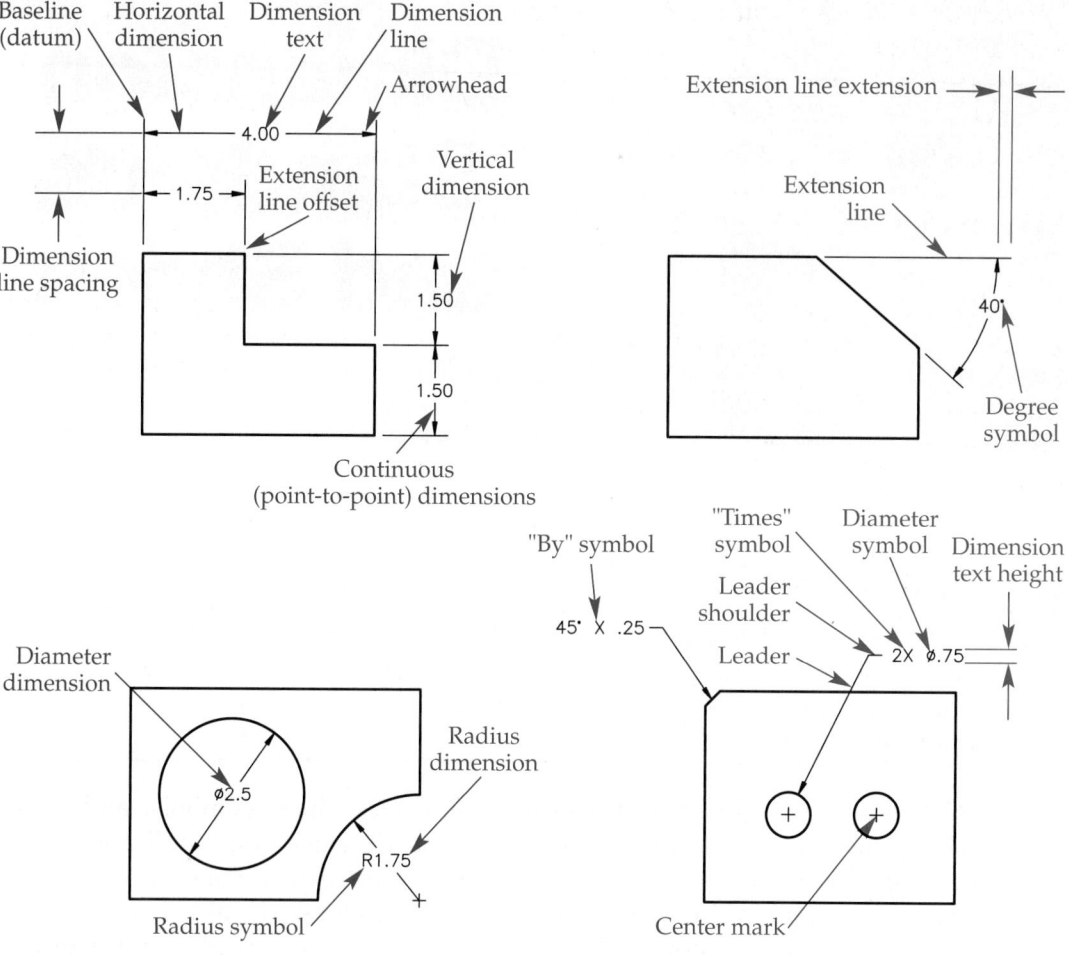

Figure 17-1. Dimensions describe the size and location of objects and features. Follow accepted conventions when dimensioning.

Unidirectional Dimensioning

unidirectional dimensioning: A dimensioning system in which all dimension values are displayed horizontally on the drawing.

Unidirectional dimensioning is common in mechanical drafting. The term *unidirectional* means "in one direction." Unidirectional dimensioning allows you to read all dimensions from the bottom of the sheet. Unidirectional dimensions normally have arrowheads at the ends of dimension lines. The dimension value usually appears in a break near the center of the dimension line. See **Figure 17-2.**

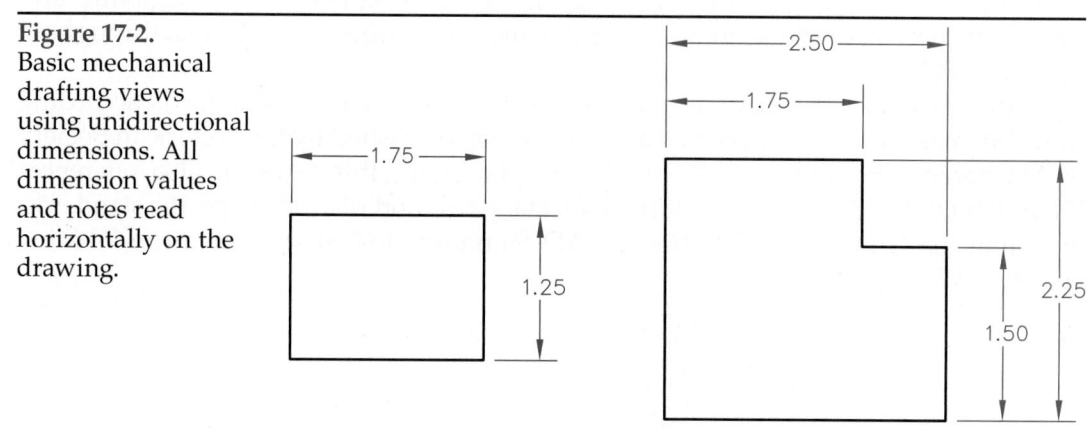

Figure 17-2. Basic mechanical drafting views using unidirectional dimensions. All dimension values and notes read horizontally on the drawing.

Aligned Dimensioning

Aligned dimensions are most common on architectural and structural drawings. Dimension values read at the same angle as the dimension line. Horizontal values read horizontally, and vertical values rotate 90° to read from the right side of the sheet. Notes usually read horizontally. Tick marks, dots, or arrowheads commonly terminate aligned dimension lines. In architectural drafting, you generally place the dimension number above the dimension line and use tick mark terminators. See **Figure 17-3.**

Size and Location Dimensions

Size dimensions provide the size of physical geometric *features*. See **Figure 17-4.** *Location dimensions* locate features. See **Figure 17-5.** Dimension to the center of circular features, such as holes and arcs, in the view in which they appear circular. Dimension to the edges of rectangular features. The *rectangular coordinate system* and the *polar coordinate system* are the two basic systems for creating location dimensions. See **Figure 17-6.** An example of location dimensions used in architectural drafting is dimensioning to the center of windows and doors on a floor plan.

aligned dimensioning: A dimensioning system in which dimension values align with dimension lines.

size dimensions: Dimensions that provide the size of physical features.

feature: Any physical portion of a part or object, such as a surface, hole, window, or door.

location dimensions: Dimensions that locate features on an object without specifying the size of the feature.

rectangular coordinate system: A system for locating dimensions from surfaces, centerlines, or center planes using linear dimensions.

polar coordinate system: A coordinate system in which angular dimensions locate features from surfaces, centerlines, or center planes.

Figure 17-3. An example of aligned dimensioning in architectural drafting. Notice the tick marks used instead of arrowheads and the placement of the dimensions above the dimension line.

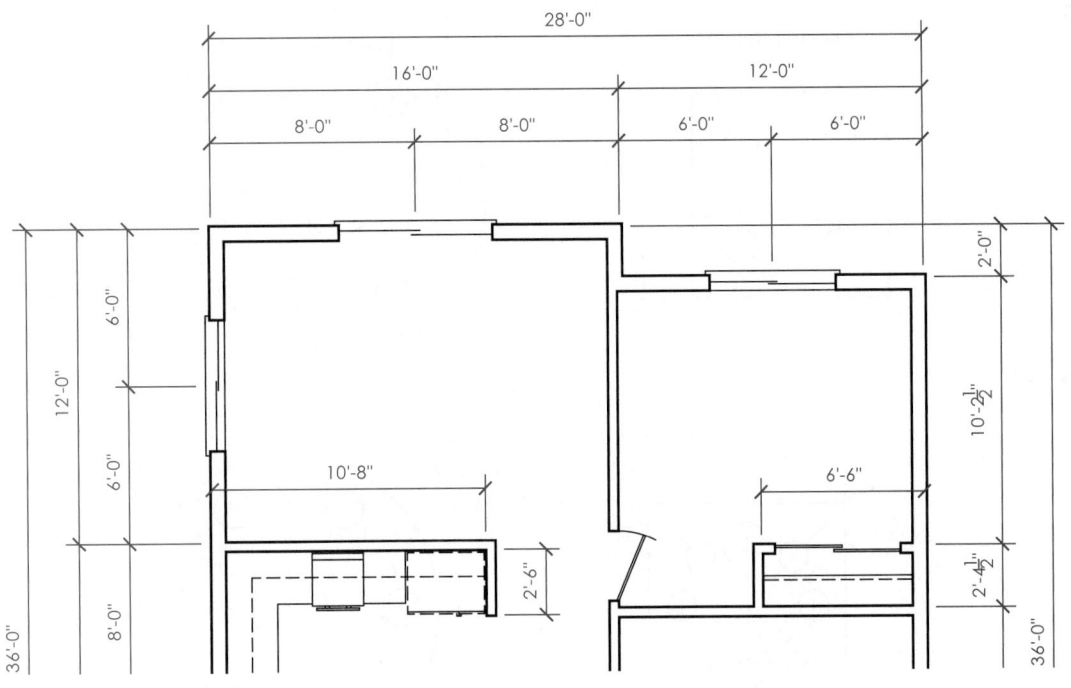

Figure 17-4. Size dimensions describe feature size, such as the features of this part view.

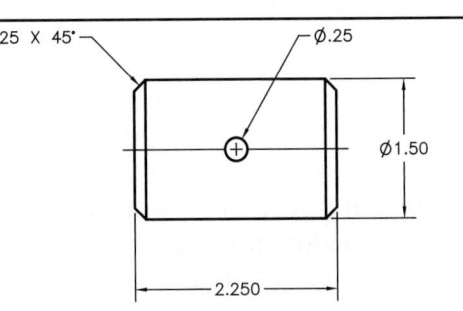

Figure 17-5. Using location dimensions to locate circular and rectangular features on part drawings.

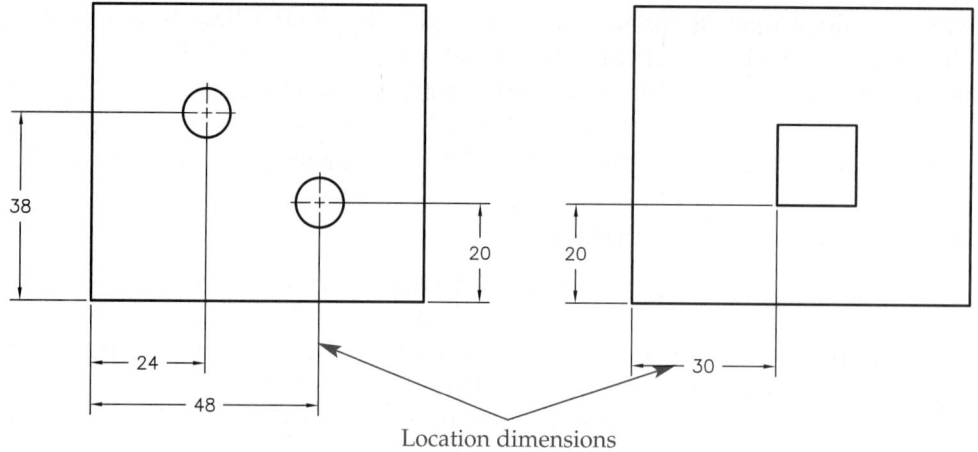

Location dimensions

Figure 17-6. A—Rectangular coordinate location dimensions. B—Polar coordinate location dimensions.

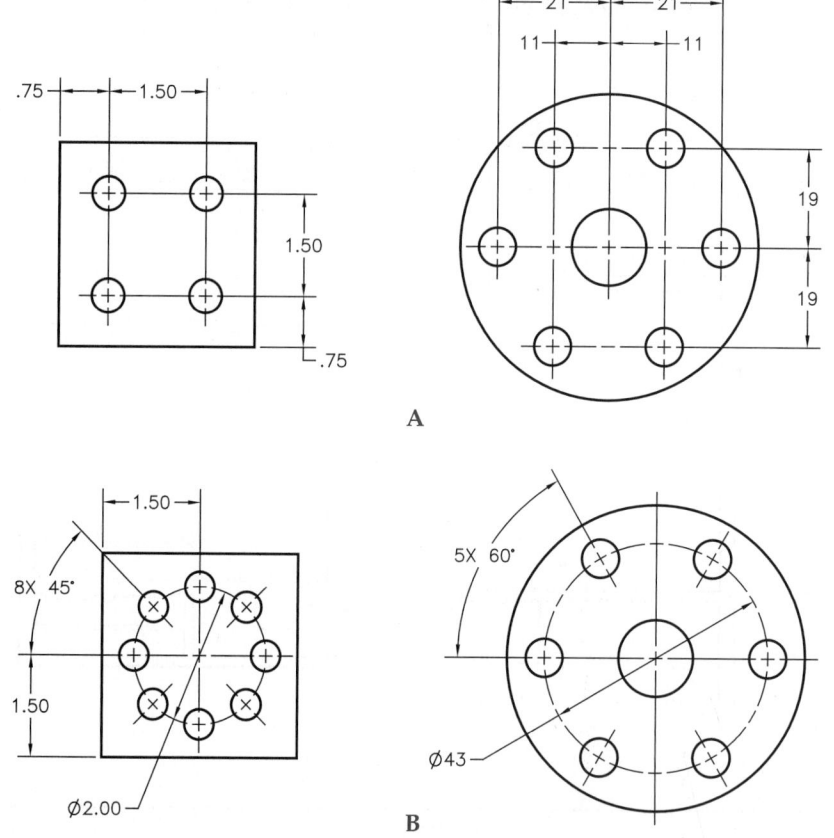

Notes

Specific notes and *general notes* are another way to describe feature size, location, or additional information. See **Figure 17-7.** Specific notes are attached to the dimensioned feature using a leader line. Place general notes in the lower-left corner, upper-left corner, or above or next to the title block, depending on sheet size and industry, company, or school practice.

Figure 17-7. A—A specific note added to a mechanical part drawing. B—A specific note added to an architectural roof plan. C—General notes on a mechanical part drawing. D—General notes on an architectural floor plan.

IDENTIFY IAW MIL-STD-130, .12 HIGH GOTHIC STYLE CHARACTERS, CONTRASTING COLOR RUBBER STAMP OR HAND MARK. LOCATE APPROX AS SHOWN FARSIDE

A

3 - 24" X 76" SOLAR PANELS
SUPPLIED BY OWNER
INSTALLED BY PLUMBING CONTRACTOR

B

NOTES:
1. DIMENSIONS AND TOLERANCES PER ASME Y14.5-2009.
2. REMOVE ALL BURRS AND SHARP EDGES R.020 MAX UNLESS OTHERWISE SPECIFIED.
3. HEAT TREAT H900 TO Rc 42-44.

C

GENERAL NOTES:
1. PROVIDE SCREENED VENTS @ EA. 3RD. JOIST SPACE @ ALL ATTIC EAVES.
2. PROVIDE SCREENED ROOF VENTS @ 10'-0" O.C. (1/300 VENT TO ATTIC SPACE).
3. USE 1/2" CCX PLY. @ ALL EXPOSED EAVES.
4. USE 300# COMPOSITION SHINGLES OVER 15# FELT.

D

Dimensioning Features and Objects

In mechanical drafting, you dimension flat surfaces using measurements for each feature. If you provide an overall dimension, you should omit one dimension, because the overall dimension controls the omitted value. See **Figure 17-8A**. In architectural drafting, it is common to place all dimensions without omitting any when possible to help make construction easier. See **Figure 17-8B**.

Figure 17-8.
A—Dimensioning flat surfaces.
B—Dimensioning architectural features.

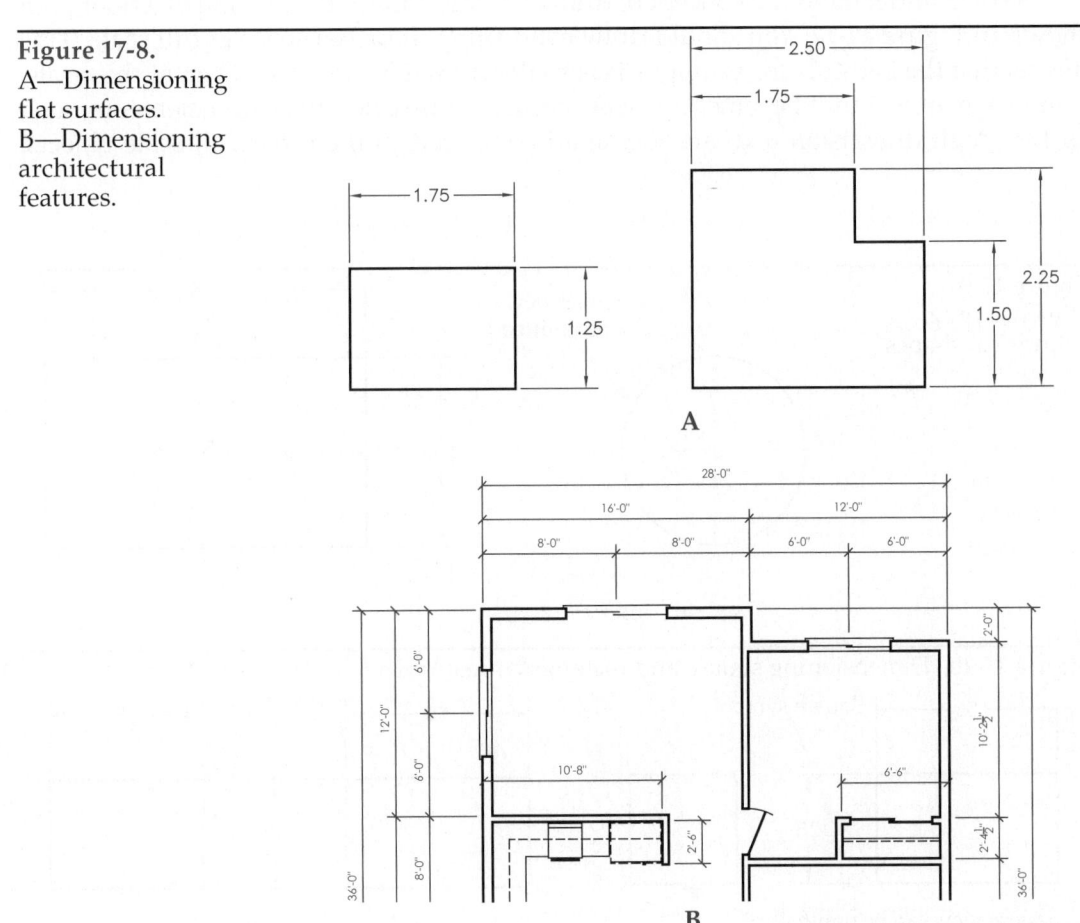

A

B

Dimensioning Cylindrical Shapes

You typically dimension the diameter and the length of a cylindrical shape in the view in which the cylinder appears rectangular. See **Figure 17-9.** The diameter symbol next to the dimension indicates that the part is a cylinder. This allows you to omit the view in which the cylinder appears as a circle.

Dimensioning Square and Rectangular Features

You usually dimension square and rectangular features in the views that show the length and height. If appropriate, add a square symbol preceding the dimension for a square feature to eliminate the need for an additional view. See **Figure 17-10.**

Dimensioning Cones and Regular Polygons

One method to dimension a conical shape is to dimension the length and the diameters at both ends. An alternative is to dimension the taper angle and the length. Regular polygons that have an even number of sides are usually dimensioned by giving the distance across the flats and the length. **Figure 17-11** shows examples of dimensioning cones and regular polygons.

Drawing Scale and Dimensions

Ideally, you should determine drawing scale, scale factors, and dimension size characteristics before you begin drawing. Incorporate these settings into your drawing template files, and make changes when necessary. The drawing scale factor determines how dimensions appear on-screen and plot.

To help understand the concept of drawing scale, look at the portion of a floor plan shown in **Figure 17-12.** You should draw everything in model space at full scale. This means that the bathtub, for example, is actually drawn 5′ long. However, at this scale, dimension appearance becomes an issue, because full-scale dimension elements, such as 1/8″ high dimension text, are too small compared to the other full-scale objects.

Figure 17-9.
Dimensioning cylindrical shapes.

Circular view can be omitted

56

ø32

Figure 17-10. Dimensioning square and rectangular features.

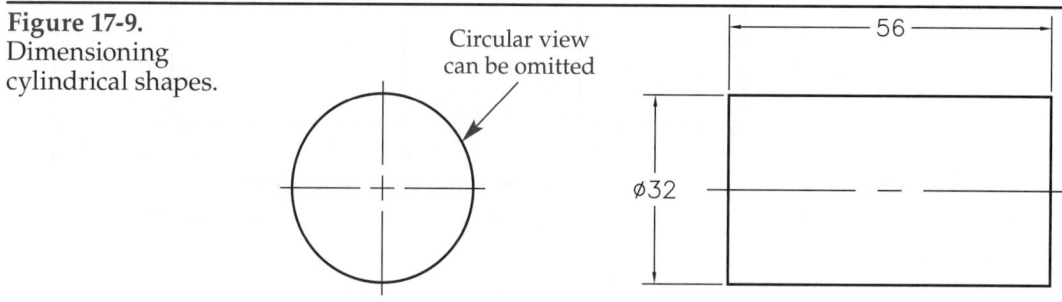

50   Square symbol

□28

Square view can be omitted

50

28

38

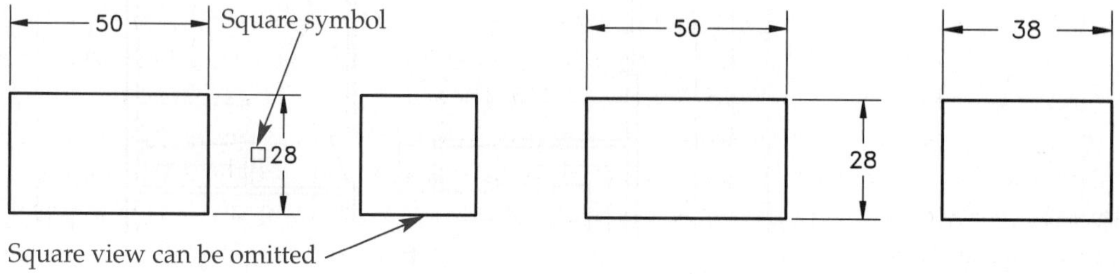

Figure 17-11. Dimensioning cones and hexagonal cylinders.

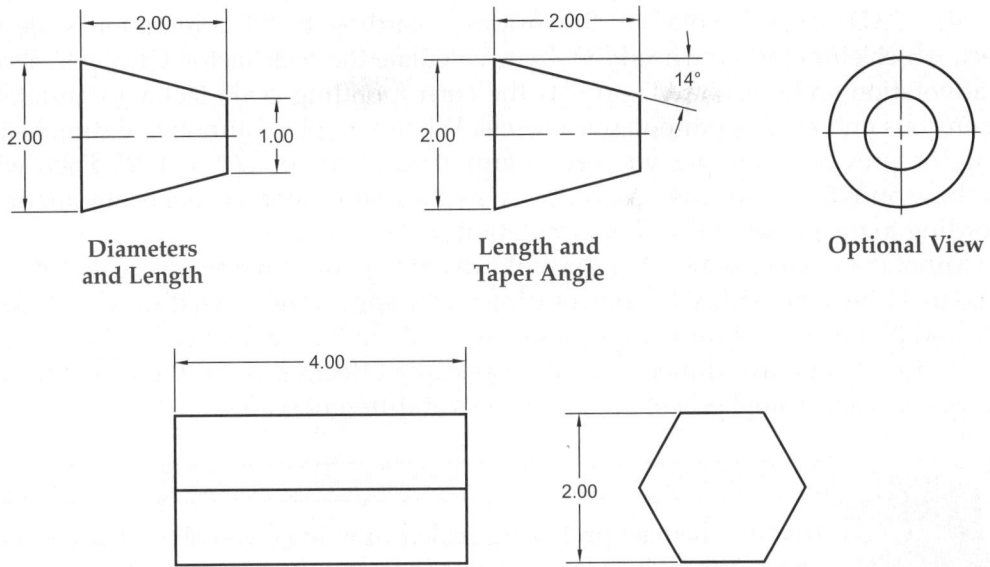

Diameters and Length

Length and Taper Angle

Optional View

Figure 17-12. A portion of a floor plan drawn at full scale in model space. If you draw dimensions at full scale, as shown in A, the dimensions are very small compared to the large objects. You must scale the dimensions, as shown in B, in order to see and plot them correctly.

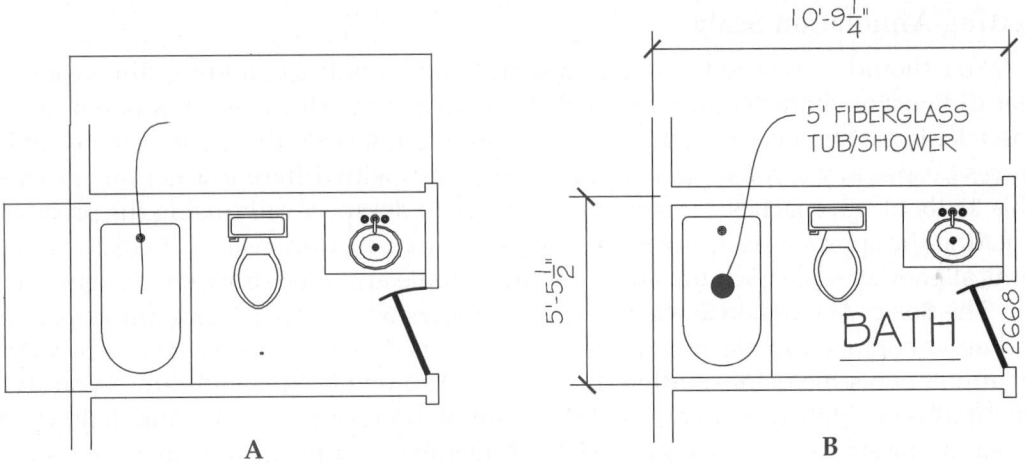

A

B

See **Figure 17-12A.** You must adjust the size of dimension characteristics according to the drawing scale. See **Figure 17-12B.** You can calculate the scale factor manually and apply it to dimensions, or you can allow AutoCAD to calculate the scale factor using annotative dimensions.

Scaling Dimensions Manually

To adjust the size of dimension elements manually according to a specific drawing scale, you must calculate the drawing scale factor. You then multiply the scale factor by the plotted size of dimension elements to get the model space size of dimension elements. Apply the scale factor to all dimension elements by entering the scale factor in the **Fit** tab of the **New** (or **Modify**) **Dimension Style** dialog box, described later in this chapter. For example, if you manually scale dimensions for a drawing with a 1/4″ = 1′-0″ scale, or a scale factor of 48, you must enter 48 in the **Fit** tab of the **New** (or **Modify**) **Dimension Style** dialog box. Refer to Chapter 9 for information on determining the drawing scale factor.

Annotative Dimensions

AutoCAD scales annotative dimensions according to the annotation scale you select, which eliminates the need for you to calculate the scale factor. Once you choose an annotation scale, AutoCAD applies the corresponding scale factor to annotative dimensions and all other annotative objects. When you place annotative dimensions, using the previous example, you set an annotation scale of 1/4″ = 1′-0″. Then when you draw annotative dimensions, AutoCAD scales dimension elements automatically according to the preset 1/4″ = 1′-0″ annotation scale.

Annotative dimensions offer several advantages over manually scaled dimensions, including the ability to control dimension appearance based on the drawing scale and plotted size of dimension elements, while reducing the need to focus on the scale factor. Annotative dimensions are especially effective when the drawing scale changes or when a single sheet includes views at different scales.

> **PROFESSIONAL TIP**
>
> If you anticipate preparing scaled drawings, you should use annotative dimensions and other annotative objects instead of manual scaling. However, scale factor does influence non-annotative items and is still an important value to identify and use throughout the drawing process.

Setting Annotation Scale

You should usually set annotation scale before you begin adding dimensions so that dimension characteristics are scaled automatically. However, this is not always possible. It may be necessary to adjust the annotation scale throughout the drawing process, especially if you prepare multiple drawings with different scales on one sheet. This textbook approaches annotation scaling in model space only, using the process of selecting the appropriate annotation scale before placing dimensions. To draw dimensions at another scale, pick the new annotation scale and then draw the dimensions.

The **Select Annotation Scale** dialog box appears when you access a dimension tool and an annotative dimension style is current. This dialog box is a convenient way to set annotation scale before adding dimensions. You will learn about dimension styles later in this chapter. You can also select the annotation scale from the **Annotation Scale** flyout on the status bar. See **Figure 17-13**. Remember that the annotation scale is typically the same as the drawing scale.

> **NOTE**
>
> This textbook describes many additional annotative object tools. Some of these tools are more appropriate for working with layouts, as explained later in this textbook.

Editing Annotation Scales

SCALELISTEDIT

Ribbon
Annotate
> Annotation
Scaling

Scale List

Type
SCALELISTEDIT

If a scale is unavailable, or to change an existing scale, pick the **Annotation Scale** flyout on the status bar and choose **Custom...** to access the **Edit Scale List** dialog box. Move the highlighted scale up or down in the list using the **Move Up** or **Move Down** button. To remove the highlighted scale from the list, pick the **Delete** button.

Select the **Edit...** button to open the **Edit Scale** dialog box where you can change the name of the scale and adjust the scale by entering the paper and drawing units. For example, a scale of 1/4″ = 1′-0″ uses a paper units value of .25 or 1 and a drawing units value of 12 or 48.

Figure 17-13.
Pick the **Annotation Scale** flyout on the status bar to activate an annotation scale.

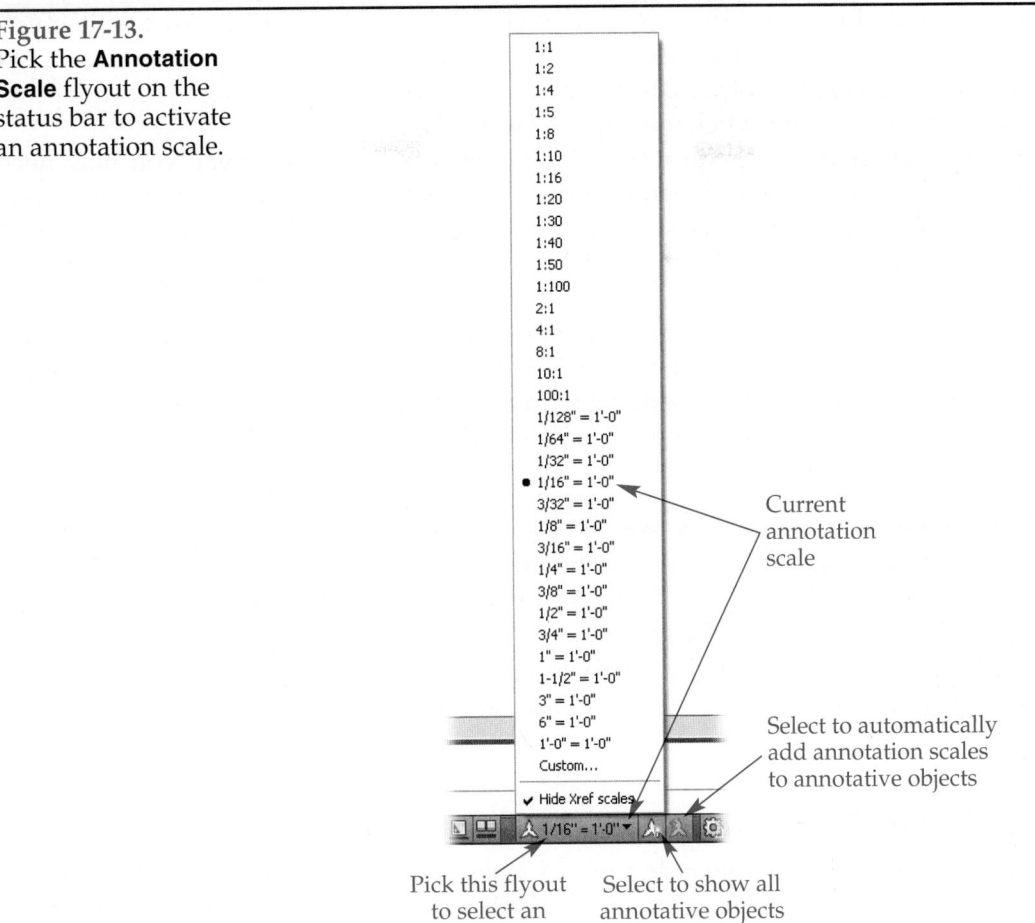

Current annotation scale

Select to automatically add annotation scales to annotative objects

Pick this flyout to select an annotation scale

Select to show all annotative objects

To create a new annotation scale, pick the **Add...** button to display the **Add Scale** dialog box, which provides the same options as the **Edit Scale** dialog box. Pick the **Reset** button to restore the list to display the default annotation scales. Once you select an annotation scale, you are ready to type annotative text.

> **NOTE**
>
> Changes you make in the **Edit Scale List** dialog box are stored with the drawing and are specific to the drawing. To make changes to the default scale list saved to the system registry, pick the **Default Scale List...** button in the **User Preferences** tab of the **Options** dialog box to access the **Default Scale List** dialog box. The options are the same as those in the **Edit Scale List** dialog box, but changes are saved as the default for new drawings and reset the **Edit Scale List** dialog box.

Dimension Styles

A *dimension style* presets many dimension characteristics. Dimension style settings usually apply to a specific drafting field or dimensioning application and correspond to appropriate drafting standards. For example, a mechanical drafting dimension style may use unidirectional placement, reference a text style assigned the Romans, Arial, or Century Gothic font, center text in a break in the dimension line,

dimension style: A saved configuration of dimension appearance settings.

and terminate dimension lines with arrowheads. See **Figure 17-2.** An architectural drafting dimension style may use an aligned dimension format, reference a text style assigned the SansSerif or Stylus BT font, place text above the dimension line, and terminate dimension lines with tick marks. See **Figure 17-3.**

Some drawings only require a single dimension style. However, you may need multiple dimension styles, depending on the variety of dimensions you apply and different dimension characteristics. You should generally create a dimension style for each dimensioning requirement. Add dimension styles to drawing templates for repeated use.

Create a dimension style for each frequently used dimension appearance or function. For example, create a dimension style for unspecified tolerances and a different dimension style for a common specified tolerance. Another example is developing a separate dimension style to add dimensions with a common prefix or suffix.

> **NOTE**
>
> AutoCAD provides the flexibility to control the appearance of dimensions for various dimensioning requirements without using a separate dimension style. For example, you can change the precision of or add a prefix to a limited number of special-case dimensions, instead of creating separate dimension styles.

Dimension Style Manager

Create, modify, and delete dimension styles using the **Dimension Style Manager** dialog box. See **Figure 17-14.** The **Styles:** list box displays existing dimension styles. The Annotative dimension style allows you to create annotative dimensions, as indicated by the icon to the left of the style name. The Standard dimension style does not use the annotative function.

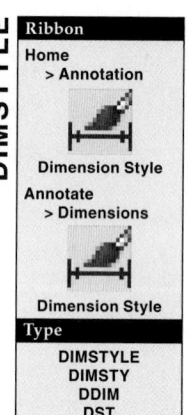

DIMSTYLE

Ribbon
Home
  > Annotation

Dimension Style

Annotate
  > Dimensions

Dimension Style

Type
DIMSTYLE
DIMSTY
DDIM
DST
D

Figure 17-14. The **Dimension Style Manager** dialog box.

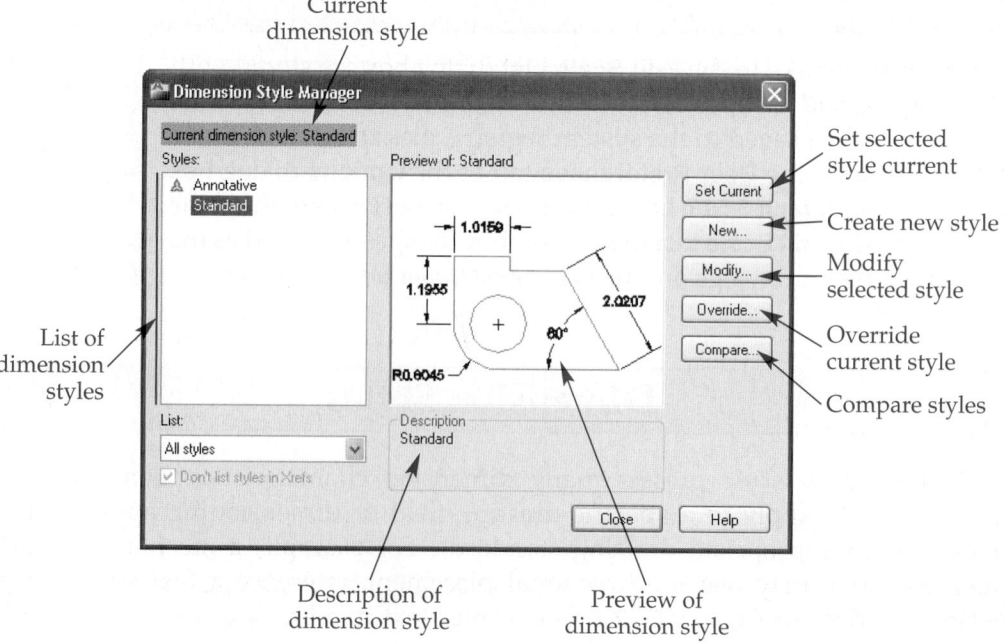

To make a dimension style current, double-click the style name, right-click on the name and select **Set current**, or pick the name and select the **Current** button. Use the **List:** drop-down list to filter the number of dimension styles displayed in the **Styles:** list box. Pick the **All Styles** option to show all dimension styles in the file or pick the **Styles in use** option to show only the current style and styles used in the drawing. If the current drawing contains external references (xrefs), use the **Don't list styles in Xrefs** box to eliminate xref-dependent dimension styles from the **Styles:** list box. This setting is valuable because you cannot set xref dimension styles current or use them to create new dimensions. You will learn about external references later in this textbook.

The **Description** area provides information about the selected dimension style. The **Preview of:** image displays a representation of the dimension style and changes according to the selections you make. If you change dimension settings without creating a new dimension style, the changes are automatically stored as a dimension style override.

Creating New Dimension Styles

To create a new dimension style, select an existing dimension style from the **Styles:** list box to use as a base for formatting the new dimension style. Then pick the **New...** button to open the **Create New Dimension Style** dialog box. See **Figure 17-15.** You can base the new dimension style on the formatting of a different dimension style by selecting from the **Start With** drop-down list. Notice that Copy of followed by the name of the existing style appears in the **New Style Name** text box. Replace the default name with a more descriptive name, such as Mechanical or Architectural. Dimension style names can have up to 255 characters, including uppercase or lowercase letters, numbers, dashes (–), underlines (_), and dollar signs ($).

Pick the **Annotative** check box to make the dimension style annotative. You can also make the dimension style annotative by selecting the **Annotative** check box in the **Fit** tab of the **New** (or **Modify**) **Dimension Style** dialog box, described later in this chapter. The Use for drop-down list specifies the type of dimensions to which the new style applies. Use the All dimensions option to create a new dimension style for all types of dimensions. If you select the Linear dimensions, Angular dimensions, Radius dimensions, Diameter dimensions, Ordinate dimensions, or Leaders and Tolerances option, you create a sub-style of the dimension style specified in the Start With: text box.

Pick the **Continue** button to open the **New Dimension Style** dialog box and adjust dimension style settings. See **Figure 17-16.** The **Lines**, **Symbols and Arrows**, **Text**, **Fit**, **Primary Units**, **Alternate Units**, and **Tolerances** tabs display groups of settings for specifying dimension appearance, as described in this chapter. After completing the style definition, pick the **OK** button to return to the **Dimension Style Manager** dialog box. Pick the **Close** button to exit the **Dimension Style Manager** dialog box.

Figure 17-15.
The **Create New Dimension Style** dialog box.

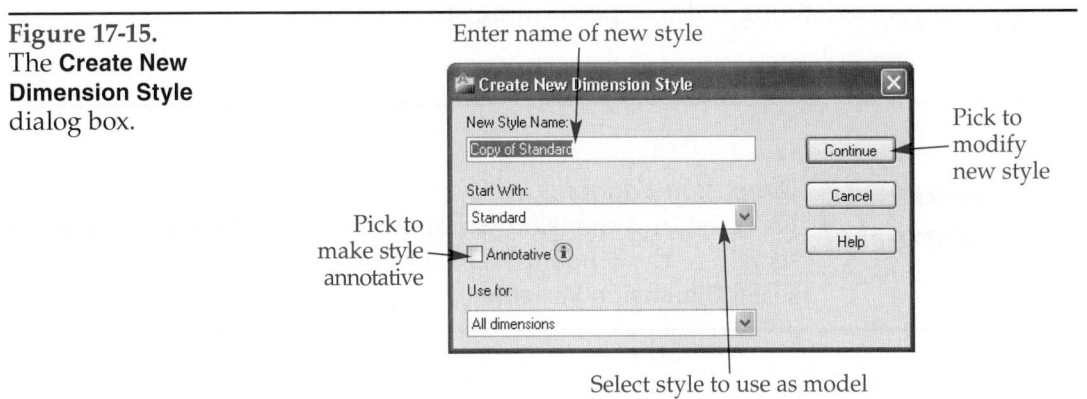

Enter name of new style

Pick to modify new style

Pick to make style annotative

Select style to use as model

Figure 17-16. The **Lines** tab of the **New** (or **Modify**) **Dimension Style** dialog box.

Select tab to change
dimension style settings

Dimension
line settings

Extension
line settings

Preview image
displayed in
all tabs

The preview image shown in the upper-right corner of each **New** (or **Modify**) **Dimension Style** dialog box tab displays a representation of the dimension style and changes according to the selections you make.

---

dimension variables: System variables that store the values of dimension style settings.

CAUTION

AutoCAD stores dimension style settings as *dimension variables*. Dimension variables have limited practical uses and are more likely to apply to advanced applications such as scripting and customizing. Changing dimension variables by typing the variable name is not a recommended method for changing dimension style settings. Changes made in this manner can introduce inconsistencies with other dimensions. You should make changes to dimensions by redefining styles or performing style overrides.

Reference Material

Dimension Variables

For a list of dimension variables, go to the **Reference Material** section of the Student Web site (www.g-wlearning.com/CAD) and select **Dimension Variables**.

AutoCAD and Its Applications—Basics

Lines Tab

Figure 17-16 shows the **Lines** tab of the **New** (or **Modify**) **Dimension Style** dialog box. The **Lines** tab controls the display of dimension and extension lines. A dimension style presets the appearance of dimension and extension lines for common applications. You can edit specific dimensions when necessary without using a separate dimension style.

Dimension Line Settings

The **Dimension lines** area of the **Lines** tab allows you to set dimension line format. **Color, Linetype,** and **Lineweight** drop-down lists are available for changing the dimension line color, linetype, and lineweight. *Associative dimensions* function as block objects. Chapter 24 explains blocks and provides complete information on using ByBlock, ByLayer, or absolute color, lineweight, and linetype with blocks. For now, as long as you assign a specific layer to a dimension object and do not change the dimension properties to absolute values, the default ByBlock properties are acceptable.

The **Extend beyond ticks** text box is inactive unless you select oblique or architectural tick terminators from the **Symbols and Arrows** tab of the **New** (or **Modify**) **Dimension Style** dialog box. Architectural tick marks or oblique arrowheads are common dimension line terminators on architectural drawings. An architectural dimensioning format sometimes extends dimension lines past extension lines, as shown in **Figure 17-17.** The 0.00 default draws dimension lines that do not extend past extension lines.

Use the **Baseline spacing** text box to change the spacing between the dimension lines of baseline dimensions created with the **DIMBASELINE** tool. The default spacing is too close for most drawings, as shown in **Figure 17-18.** ASME standards recommend a minimum spacing of .375″ (10 mm) from a drawing feature to the first dimension line and a minimum spacing of .25″ (6 mm) between dimension lines. A minimum spacing of 3/8″ is common for architectural drawings. These minimum recommendations are generally less than the spacing required by actual company or school standards. A value of .5″ (12 mm) or .75″ (19 mm) is usually more appropriate.

> **associative dimension:** A dimension in which all elements are linked to, or associated with, the dimensioned object; updates when the associated object changes.

Figure 17-17.
Using the **Extend beyond ticks** setting to allow the dimension line to extend past the extension line. With the default value of 0, the dimension line ends at the extension line.

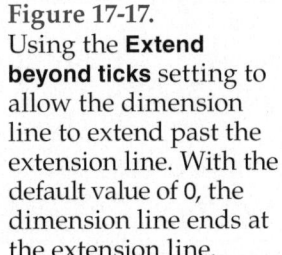

Figure 17-18.
The **Baseline spacing** setting controls the spacing between dimension lines when you use the **DIMBASELINE** tool.

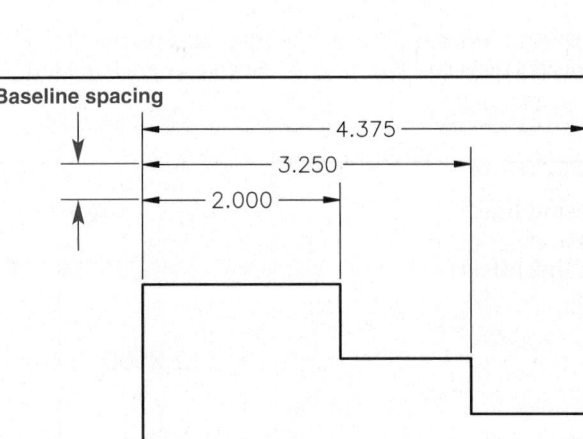

Check the **Suppress** boxes to hide the first, second, or both sides of dimension lines and dimension line terminators for dimension lines broken by a value. The **Dim line 1** and **Dim line 2** check boxes refer to the first and second points you pick when drawing a dimension. Both dimension lines appear by default. **Figure 17-19** shows the result of using dimension line suppression options.

Extension Line Settings

The **Extension lines** area of the **Lines** tab allows you to set extension line format. **Color, Linetype ext line 1, Linetype ext line 2**, and **Lineweight** drop-down lists are available for changing the extension line color, linetype, and lineweight from the default ByBlock setting, if necessary. You can use the **Linetype ext line 1** and **Linetype ext line 2** drop-down lists to override the linetype applied to each extension line. Extension lines 1 and 2 correspond to the first and second points you pick when drawing a dimension.

Use the **Extend beyond dim lines** option to set the distance the extension line runs past the dimension line. See **Figure 17-20**. ASME standards recommend a .125″ (3 mm) extension line extension. The **Offset from origin** option specifies the distance between the object and the beginning of the extension line. Most applications require this small offset. ASME standards recommend a .063″ (1.5 mm) extension line offset. When an extension line meets a centerline, however, use a setting of 0.0 to prevent a gap.

The **Fixed length extension lines** check box sets a given length for extension lines. Check this box to activate the **Length** text box. The value in the **Length** text box sets a restricted length for extension lines, measured from the dimension line toward the extension line origin.

Check the **Suppress** boxes to hide the first, second, or both extension lines. The **Ext line 1** and **Ext line 2** check boxes refer to the first and second points you pick when drawing a dimension. Both extension lines appear by default. **Figure 17-21** shows a common example of suppressing extension lines when they coincide with object lines.

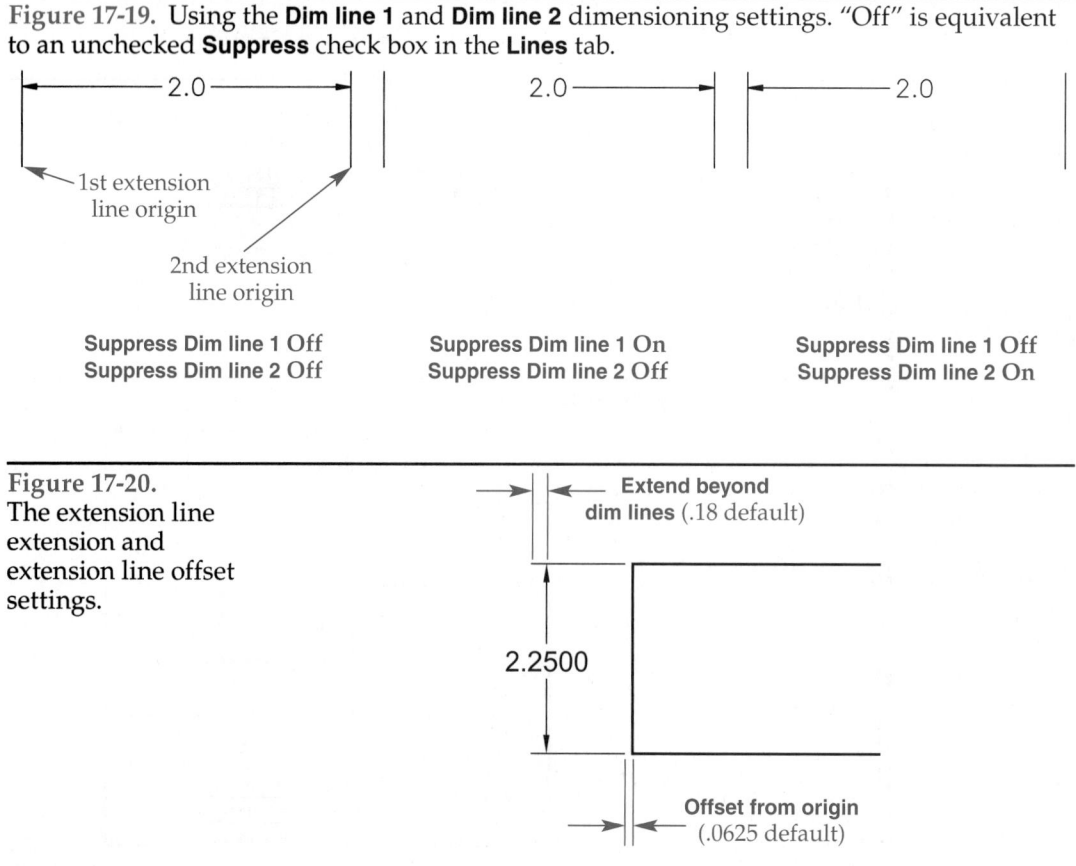

Figure 17-19. Using the **Dim line 1** and **Dim line 2** dimensioning settings. "Off" is equivalent to an unchecked **Suppress** check box in the **Lines** tab.

Figure 17-20.
The extension line extension and extension line offset settings.

Figure 17-21.
Examples of when it is appropriate to suppress extension lines. Place dimension lines away from objects, when possible, to display both extension lines.

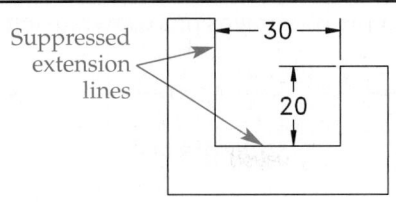

Symbols and Arrows Tab

Figure 17-22 shows the **Symbols and Arrows** tab of the **New** (or **Modify**) **Dimension Style** dialog box. The **Symbols and Arrows** tab controls the appearance of dimension line and leader terminators, center marks, and other symbol components of dimensions. A dimension style presets the appearance of symbols and arrows for common applications. You can edit specific dimensions when necessary without using a separate dimension style.

Arrowhead Settings

Use the appropriate drop-down list in the **Arrowheads** area to select the arrowhead to use for the first, second, and leader arrowheads. The default arrowhead is **Closed filled**, which is recommended by ASME standards, although **Closed blank**, **Closed**, or **Open** arrowheads are sometimes used. A leader pointing to a surface in a view where the surface appears as a plane uses a small dot. Figure 17-23 shows arrowhead styles. If you pick a new arrowhead in the **First:** drop-down list, AutoCAD automatically makes the same selection for the **Second:** drop-down list. When you select the **Oblique** or **Architectural tick** arrowhead, the **Extend beyond ticks:** text box in the **Lines** tab becomes activated.

Notice that Figure 17-23 does not contain an example of a user arrow. The **User Arrow...** option allows you to access a custom arrowhead. You must first design an arrowhead that fits inside a 1 unit square (unit block) with a dimension line "tail"

Figure 17-22. The **Symbols and Arrows** tab of the **New** (or **Modify**) **Dimension Style** dialog box.

Select tab to specify arrow style

Arrowhead properties

Center mark properties

Dimension break size

Arc length dimension settings

Jog symbol angle setting

Jog text height setting

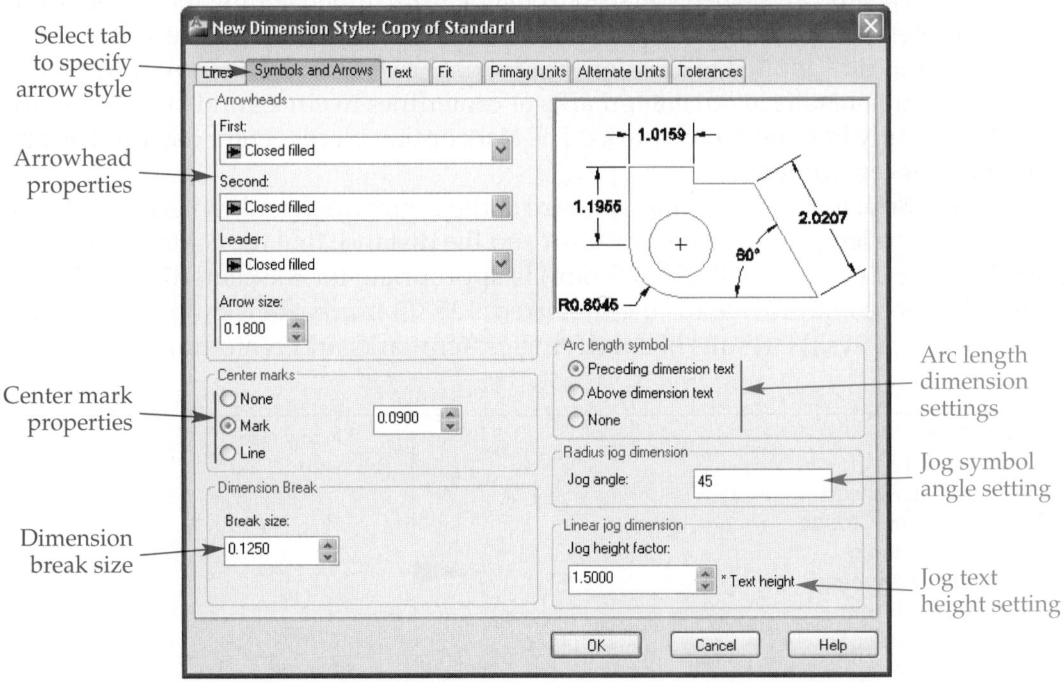

Figure 17-23. Examples of dimensions drawn using the options in the **Arrowheads** drop-down lists.

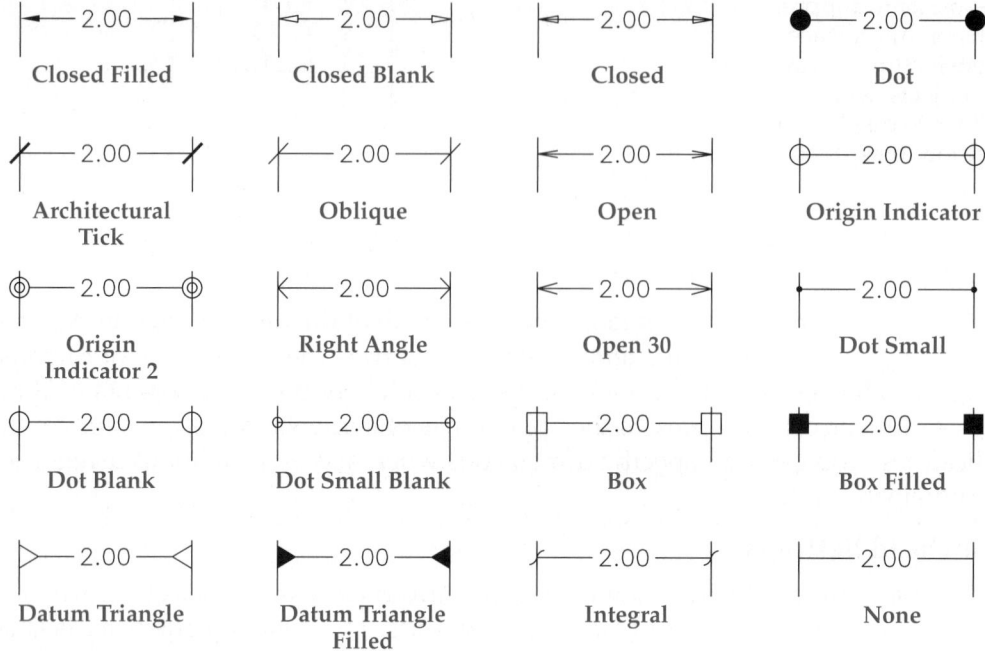

1 unit in length, and save the arrowhead as a block. Blocks are described later in this textbook. The **Select Custom Arrow Block** dialog box appears when you pick **User Arrow...** from an **Arrowheads** drop-down list. Type the name of the custom arrow block in the **Select from Drawing Blocks:** text box or pick a block from the drop-down list and then pick **OK** to apply the arrowhead to the style.

Use the **Arrow size:** text box to change arrowhead size. **Figure 17-24** shows the measurement you specify to set the arrowhead size. A .125″ (3 mm) arrowhead size is most common, especially on mechanical drawings.

Center Mark Settings

The **Center marks** area allows you to select the way center dashes and centerlines appear in circles and arcs when you use circular feature dimensioning tools. The ASME standard refers to AutoCAD center marks as the center dashes of centerlines. Center marks are typically applied to circular objects that are too small to receive centerlines. The **None** option results in no center marks or centerlines in circles and arcs. Fillets and rounds generally have no center marks. The **Mark** option places center dashes. The **Line** option places centerlines.

Use the **Size:** text box to change the size of the center mark and centerline. The size defines half the length of a centerline dash and the distance that the centerline extends past the object. A value of .0625″ (1.5 mm) is appropriate for the centerline dash half-length, but does not provide for the preferred .125″ (3 mm) extension past the object. **Figure 17-25** shows the results of specifying center marks and centerlines.

Figure 17-24.
ASME standards specify an arrowhead size of .125″. The **Closed filled**, **Closed blank**, and **Closed** arrowhead styles adhere to the standard 3:1 ratio of length to width.

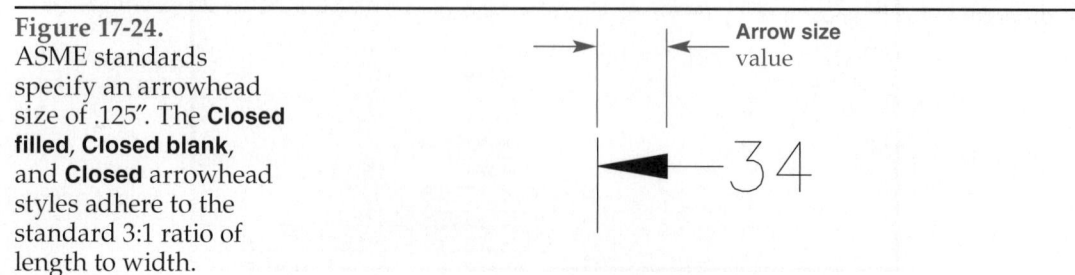

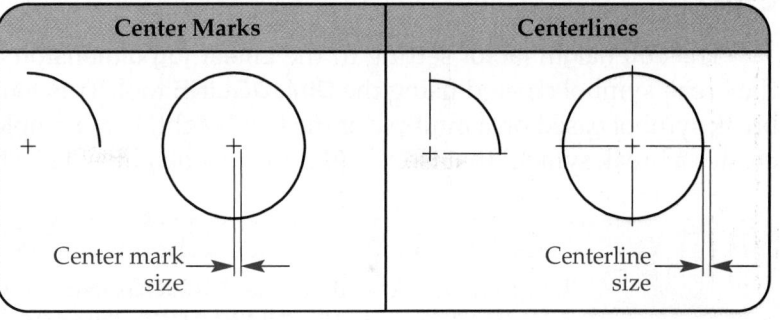

Figure 17-25.
Arcs and circles displayed with center marks and centerlines. Use a size of .0625" to achieve ASME standards for center marks, but not the extension past objects.

Adjusting Break Size

The **Dimension Break** area controls the amount of extension line that is hidden when you use the **DIMBREAK** tool. Specify a value in the **Break size:** text box to set the total length of the break. **Figure 17-26** shows an example of a 3 mm extension line break. The default size is .125" (3 mm). ASME standards do not recommend breaking extension lines.

Adding an Arc Length Symbol

The **Arc Length Symbol** area controls the placement of the arc length symbol when you use the **DIMARC** tool. The default **Preceding dimension text** option places the symbol in front of the dimension value. Select the **Above dimension text** radio button to place the arc length symbol over the length value. See **Figure 17-27**. Pick the **None** radio button to hide the symbol.

Adjusting Jog Angle

Use the **Jog angle** setting in the **Radius jog dimension** area to set the appearance of the break line applied to the jog symbol when you use the **DIMJOGGED** tool. This value sets the incline formed by the line connecting the extension line and dimension line. The default angle is 45°.

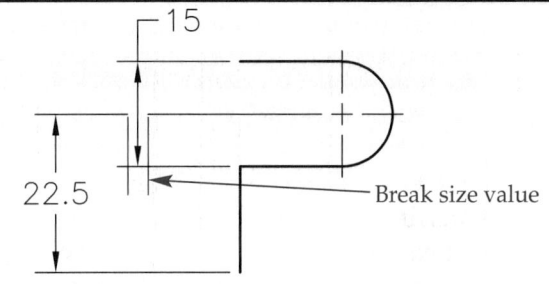

Figure 17-26.
Use the **Break size** setting to specify the length of the break created using the **DIMBREAK** tool.

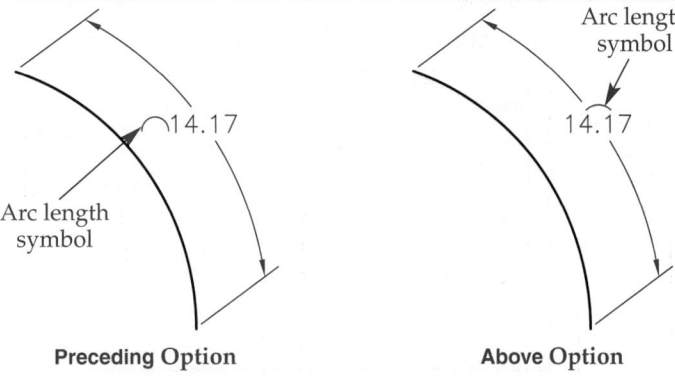

Figure 17-27.
You can place the arc length symbol in front of or above the arc dimension text.

Setting Jog Height

The **Jog height factor** setting in the **Linear jog dimension** area controls the size of the break symbol created using the **DIMJOGLINE** tool. This value sets the height of the break symbol based on a multiple of the text height. For example, the default value of 1.5 creates a break symbol that is .18″ tall if the text height is .12″. The default angle is 45°.

NOTE

Chapter 18 describes the **DIMJOGLINE** tool in more detail, and Chapter 19 covers the **DIMJOGGED**, **DIMARC**, and **DIMBREAK** tools.

Exercise 17-1

Access the Student Web site (www.g-wlearning.com/CAD) and complete Exercise 17-1.

Text Tab

Figure 17-28 shows the **Text** tab of the **New** (or **Modify**) **Dimension Style** dialog box. Use the **Text** tab to control the display of dimension text. A dimension style presets the appearance of dimension text for common applications. You can edit specific dimensions when necessary without using a separate dimension style.

Text Appearance Settings

Use the **Text appearance** area to set the dimension text style, color, height, and frame. A dimension style references a text style for the appearance of dimension values. Pick an existing text style from the **Text style** drop-down list. To create or modify a text style, pick the ellipsis (…) button next to the drop-down list to launch the **Text Style**

Figure 17-28. The **Text** tab of the **New** (or **Modify**) **Dimension Style** dialog box.

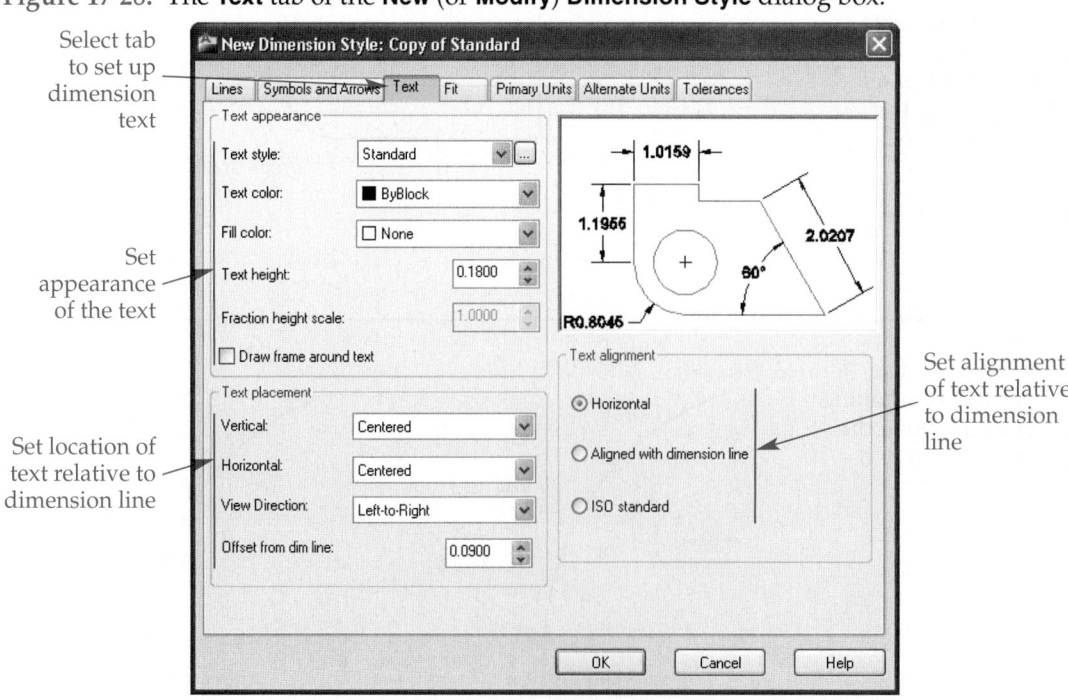

dialog box. Use the **Text color** drop-down list to specify the appropriate text color, which should be ByBlock for typical applications.

Use the **Text height** text box to specify the dimension text height. Dimension text height is commonly the same as the text height used for most other drawing text, except for titles, which are often larger. The default dimension text height of .18″ (2.5 mm) is an acceptable standard. Many companies use a text height of .125″ (3 mm). The ASME standard recommends a .12″ (3 mm) text height. The text height for titles and labels is usually .24″ (6 mm).

The **Fraction height scale** setting controls the height of fractions for architectural and fractional unit dimensions. The value in the **Fraction height scale** box is multiplied by the text height value to determine the height of the fraction. A value of 1.0 creates fractions that are the same text height as regular (nonfractional) text, which is the accepted standard. A value less than 1.0 makes the fraction smaller than the regular text height.

Select the **Draw frame around text** check box to create a box around the dimension text. A *basic dimension* is a common application for framed text, as described later in this textbook. The setting for the **Offset from dim line** value, explained later in this chapter, determines the distance between the text and the frame.

Text Placement Settings

The **Text placement** area controls text placement relative to the dimension line. See **Figure 17-29.** The **Vertical:** drop-down list provides vertical justification options. Use the default **Centered** option to place dimension text centered in a gap in the dimension line. This is the most common dimensioning practice in mechanical drafting and many other fields.

Select the **Above** option to place the dimension text horizontally above horizontal dimension lines. For vertical and angled dimension lines, the text appears in a gap in the dimension line. This option is common for architectural drafting and building construction. Architectural drafting typically uses aligned dimensioning, in which the dimension text aligns with the dimension lines and all text reads from either the bottom or the right side of the sheet.

Pick the **Outside** option to place the dimension text outside the dimension line and either above or below a horizontal dimension line or to the right or left of a vertical dimension line. The direction you move the cursor determines the above/below and left/right placement. Choose the **JIS** option to align the text according to the Japanese Industrial Standards (JIS).

Figure 17-29. Dimension text justification options. A—Vertical justification options, with the horizontal Centered justification. B—Horizontal justification options, with the vertical Centered justification.

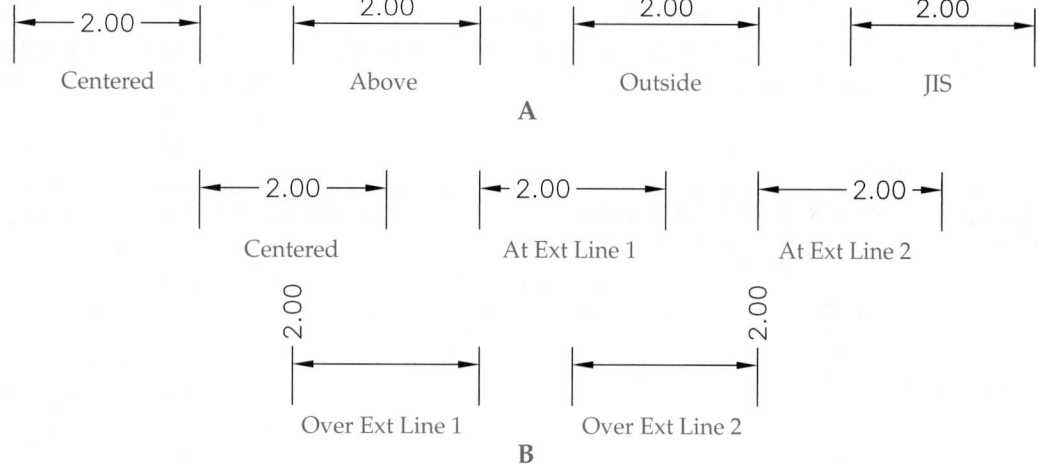

The **Horizontal:** drop-down list provides options for controlling the horizontal placement of dimension text. Pick the default **Centered** option to center dimension text between the extension lines. Select the **At Ext Line 1** option to locate the text next to the extension line you place first, or choose **At Ext Line 2** to locate the text next to the extension line you place second. Pick **Over Ext Line 1** to place the text aligned with and over the first extension line, or select **Over Ext Line 2** to place the text aligned with and over the second extension line. Placing text aligned with and over an extension line is not common practice.

The **View Direction:** drop-down list determines the reading direction of dimension text. Use the default **Left-to-Right** option to make text readable from left to right or from bottom to top, depending on the text placement and alignment. Choose the **Right-to-Left** option to flip dimension text. Text may appear inverted and reads from right to left or from top to bottom, depending on the text placement and alignment. Changing text view direction to right-to-left is not common practice.

The **Offset from dim line:** text box sets the gap between the dimension line and dimension text, the distance between the leader shoulder and text, and the space between text and a frame. The gap should be half the text height for most applications. **Figure 17-30** shows the gap in linear and leader dimensions.

Text Alignment Settings

Use the **Text alignment** area to specify unidirectional or aligned dimensions. The **Horizontal** option draws the unidirectional dimensions that are commonly used in mechanical drafting. The **Aligned with dimension line** option creates aligned dimensions, typical for architectural drafting. The **ISO Standard** option creates aligned dimensions when the text falls between the extension lines, and horizontal dimensions when the text falls outside the extension lines.

Fit Tab

Figure 17-31 shows the **Fit** tab of the **New** (or **Modify**) **Dimension Style** dialog box. The settings in the **Fit** tab establish dimension *fit format*. A dimension style presets fit format for common applications. You can edit specific dimensions when necessary without using a separate dimension style.

fit format: The arrangement of dimension text and arrowheads on a drawing.

Fit Options

The **Fit options** area controls how text, dimension lines, and arrows behave when there is not enough room between the extension lines to accommodate all of the items. The dimension style settings, such as the size of dimension text, offset, and arrowheads, influence fit performance. All fit options place text and dimension lines with arrowheads inside the extension lines if space is available. All fit options except the **Always keep text between ext lines** option place arrowheads, dimension lines, and text outside the extension lines when space is limited.

Choose the default **Either text or arrows (best fit)** radio button to move either the dimension value or the arrows outside extension lines first. Pick the **Arrows** radio

---

Figure 17-30. The **Offset from dim line** value controls the space between dimension text and the dimension line, leader shoulder, and frame.

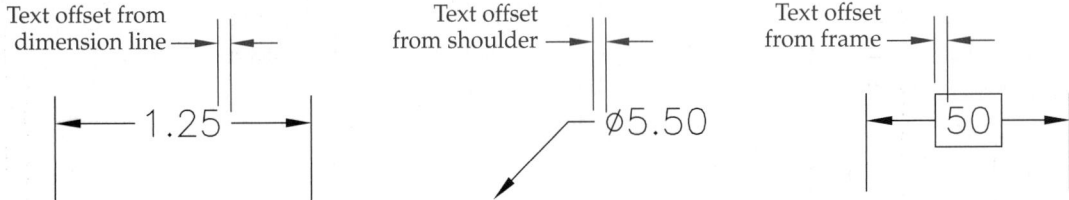

Figure 17-31. The **Fit** tab of the **New** (or **Modify**) **Dimension Style** dialog box.

Select tab to set up fit options

Description of selected option

Text and arrows fit options

Placement of grip-edited dimension text

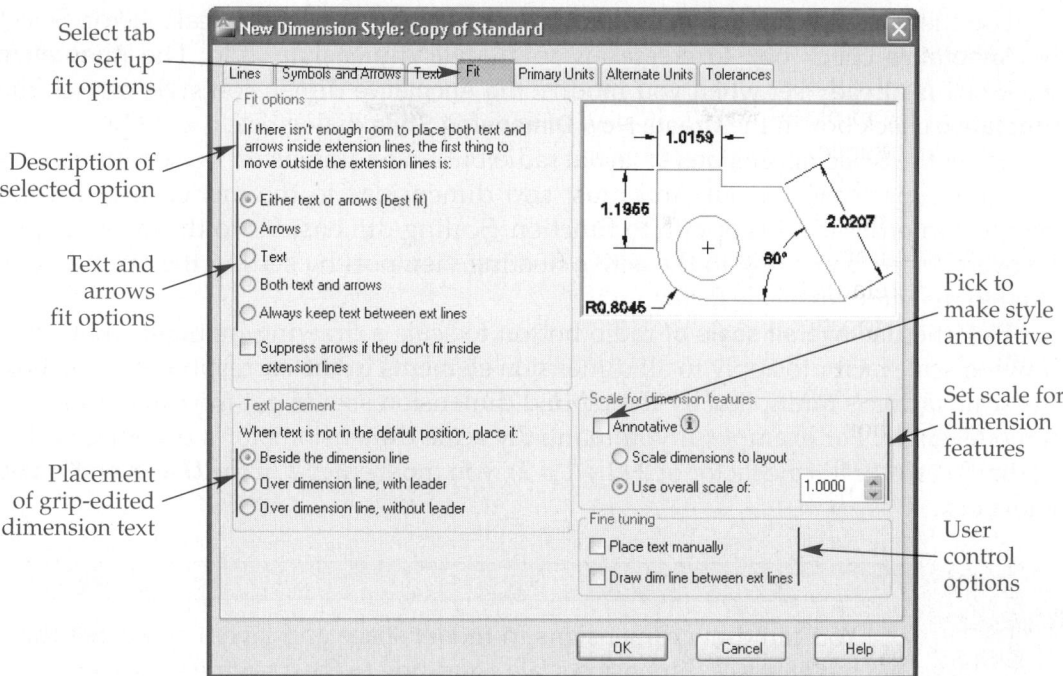

Pick to make style annotative

Set scale for dimension features

User control options

button to attempt to place arrowheads outside extension lines first, followed by text. Pick the **Text** radio button to attempt to place text outside extension lines first, followed by arrowheads. Choose the **Both text and arrows** radio button to move both text and arrowheads outside extension lines.

Select the **Always keep text between ext lines** radio button to place the dimension value between extension lines. This option typically causes interference between the dimension value and extension lines when there is limited space between extension lines. Pick the **Suppress arrows if they don't fit inside extension lines** radio button to remove the arrowheads if they do not fit between extension lines. Use this option with caution, because it can create dimensions that violate standards.

Text Placement Settings

Sometimes it becomes necessary to move the dimension text from its default position. You can stretch the dimension text independently of the dimension. The selected option in the **Text placement** area presets the effect of stretching a dimension text.

Select the **Beside the dimension line** radio button to restrict dimension text movement. You can stretch the text with the dimension line, but only within the same plane as the dimension line. Pick the **Over dimension line, with leader** radio button to stretch the text in any direction away from the dimension line. A leader line forms connecting the text to the dimension line. Choose the **Over dimension line, without leader** radio button to stretch the text in any direction away from the dimension line without including a leader.

PROFESSIONAL TIP

To return the dimension text to its default position, select the dimension, right-click, and select **Home text** from the **Dim Text position** cascading submenu.

Text Scale Options

Use the **Scale for dimension features** area to set the dimension scale factor. Select the **Annotative** check box to create an annotative dimension style. The **Annotative** check box is already set when you modify the Annotative dimension style or pick the **Annotative** check box in the **Create New Dimension Style** dialog box.

Select the **Scale dimensions to layout** radio button to dimension in a floating viewport in a paper space layout. You must add dimensions to the model in a floating viewport in order for this option to function. Scaling dimensions to the layout adjust the overall scale according to the active floating viewport by setting the overall scale equal to the viewport scale factor.

Pick the **Use overall scale of** radio button to scale a drawing manually. Enter the drawing scale factor to apply to all dimension elements in the corresponding text box. The scale factor is multiplied by the plotted dimension size to get the dimension size in model space. For example, if you manually scale dimensions for a drawing with a 1:2 (half) scale, or a scale factor of 2 (2 ÷ 1 = 2), you must enter 2 in the **Use overall scale of** text box.

PROFESSIONAL TIP

You can draw dimensions in model space and layout space. Set the model space dimension scale according to the drawing scale factor to achieve the correct dimension appearance. Associative paper space dimensions automatically adjust to model modifications and do not require scaling. In addition, if you dimension in paper space, you can dimension the model differently in two viewports. However, paper space dimensions are not visible when you work in model space, so you must be careful not to move a model space object into a paper space dimension. Avoid using non-associative paper space dimensions.

Fine Tuning Settings

The **Fine tuning** area provides additional options for controlling the placement of dimension text. Select the **Place text manually** check box to increase flexibility when placing dimensions, allowing you to locate text to the side within extension lines or outside of extension lines. However, the **Place text manually** feature can make it more cumbersome to offset dimension lines equally, and it is not necessary for standard dimensioning practices.

The **Draw dim line between ext lines** option forces AutoCAD to place the dimension line inside the extension lines, even when the text and arrowheads are outside. The default application is to place the dimension line and arrowheads outside the extension lines. See Figure 17-32. Although some companies prefer the appearance, forcing the dimension line inside the extension lines is not an ASME standard.

Exercise 17-2

Access the Student Web site (www.g-wlearning.com/CAD) and complete Exercise 17-2.

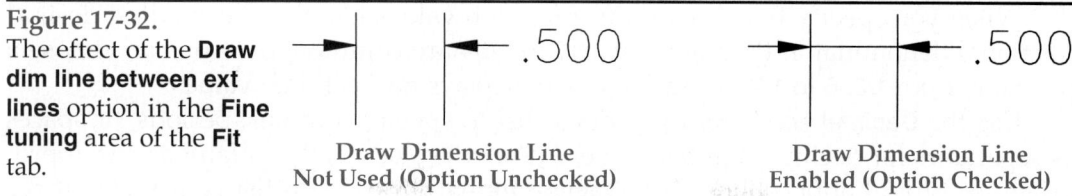

Figure 17-32.
The effect of the **Draw dim line between ext lines** option in the **Fine tuning** area of the **Fit** tab.

Draw Dimension Line
Not Used (Option Unchecked)

Draw Dimension Line
Enabled (Option Checked)

Primary Units Tab

Figure 17-33 shows the **Primary Units** tab of the **New** (or **Modify**) **Dimension Style** dialog box. The **Primary Units** tab controls linear and angular dimension units. A dimension style presets units for typical dimensioning requirements. You can edit specific dimensions when necessary without using a separate dimension style.

Linear Dimension Settings

The **Linear dimensions** area allows you to specify settings for primary linear dimensions. The options in the **Unit format** drop-down list are the same as those in the **Length** area of the **Drawing Units** dialog box. Typically, primary linear dimension unit format is the same as the corresponding drawing units.

The **Precision** drop-down list sets the precision applied to dimensions, which may be the same as the related drawing units precision. A drawing often includes different precisions applied to specific dimensions. With decimal units, precision determines the number of zeros that follow the decimal place.

Precision settings in mechanical drafting depend on the accuracy required to manufacture specific features. Some features require greater precision, generally due to fits between mating parts. For example, a precision setting of 0.00 represents less exactness than a setting of 0.0000. Chapter 20 further explains this concept. Common precisions in mechanical drafting include 0.0000, 0.000, and 0.00.

Figure 17-33. The **Primary Units** tab of the **New** (or **Modify**) **Dimension Style** dialog box.

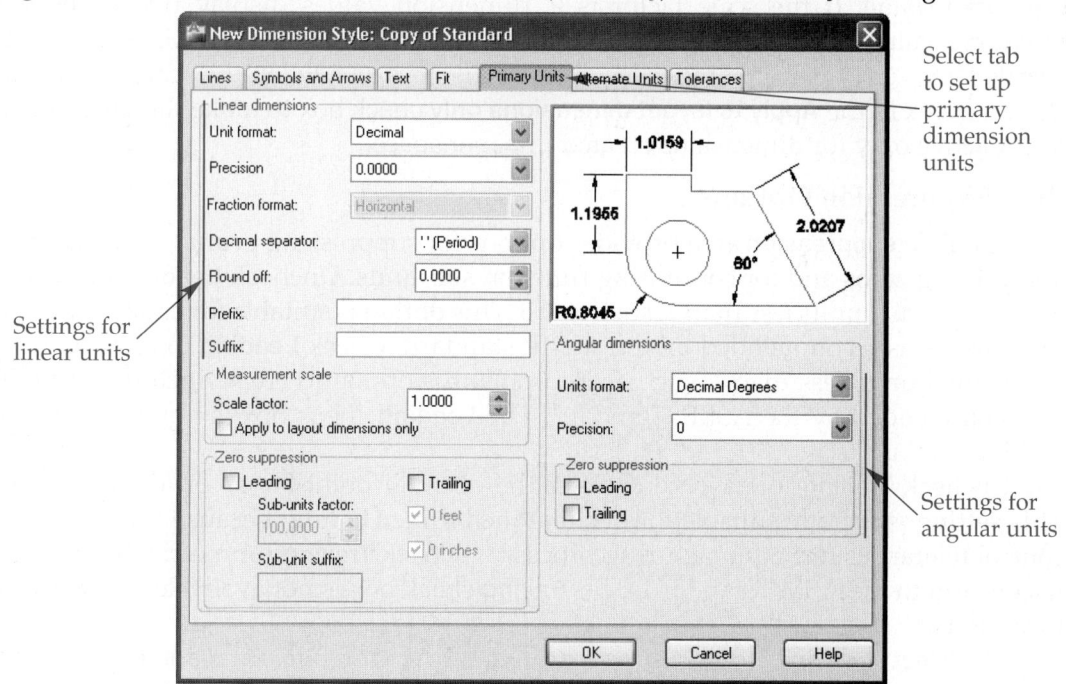

Select tab to set up primary dimension units

Settings for linear units

Settings for angular units

When you specify fractional units, precision values identify the smallest desired fractional denominator. Precisions of 1/16 to 1/64 are common, but you can choose a precision from 1/256 to 1/2. A precision of 0 displays no fractional values.

Use the **Decimal separator** drop-down list to specify commas, periods, or spaces as separators for decimal numbers. The '.' **(Period)** option is the default and is appropriate for typical applications. The **Fraction format** drop-down list is available if the unit format is **Architectural** or **Fractional**. The options for controlling the display of fractions are **Diagonal**, **Horizontal**, and **Not Stacked**.

The **Round off** text box specifies the accuracy of rounding for dimension numbers. The default is zero, which means that no rounding takes place and all associated dimensions specify the value exactly as measured. If you enter a value of .1, all dimensions round to the closest .1 unit. For example, an actual measurement of 1.188 rounds to 1.2. Rounding is inappropriate for most applications.

prefixes: Special notes or applications placed before the dimension value.

suffixes: Special notes or applications placed after the dimension value.

Enter a value in the **Prefix** text box to add a *prefix* to dimensions. A typical application for a prefix is SR3.5, where SR means "spherical radius." The prefix replaces the ∅ or R symbol when applied to a diameter or radius dimension. Enter a value in the **Suffix** text box to add a *suffix* to dimensions. A typical application for a suffix is 3.5 MAX, where MAX is the abbreviation for "maximum." Other examples include adding the suffix in (for inch) when you are placing a limited number of inch dimensions on a metric drawing, or using the suffix mm (for millimeter) when you are placing a limited number of millimeter dimensions on an inch drawing.

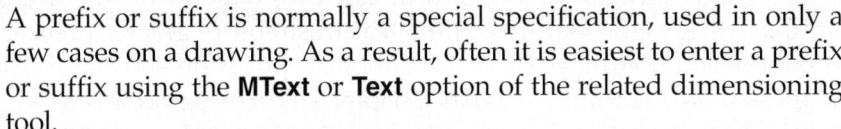

PROFESSIONAL TIP

A prefix or suffix is normally a special specification, used in only a few cases on a drawing. As a result, often it is easiest to enter a prefix or suffix using the **MText** or **Text** option of the related dimensioning tool.

Set the scale factor of linear dimensions in the **Scale factor:** text box of the **Measurement scale** area. If you set a scale factor of 1, dimension values display their measured value. If the scale factor is 2, dimension values display two times the measured value. For example, an actual measurement of 2 inches displays as 2 with a scale factor of 1, but the same measurement displays as 4 when the scale factor is 2. Place a check in the **Apply to layout dimensions only** check box to make the linear scale factor active only for dimensions created in paper space.

Zero Suppression Options

The **Zero suppression** area provides options for suppressing primary unit leading and trailing zeros and for controlling function sub-units. Uncheck **Leading** to leave a zero on decimal units less than 1, such as 0.5. This option is suitable for creating metric dimensions as recommended by the ASME standard. Check **Leading** to remove the 0 on decimal units less than 1, such as .5. Apply this option to create inch dimensions as recommended by the ASME standard. The **Leading** check box is not available for architectural units.

Uncheck **Trailing** to leave zeros after the decimal point based on the precision. This setting is usually suitable for decimal inch dimensioning because trailing zeros control tolerances for manufacturing processes. Check **Trailing** for metric dimensions to conform to the ASME standard. The **Trailing** check box is not available for architectural units.

The **0 feet** and **0 inches** check boxes are available for architectural and engineering units. Check **0 feet** to remove the zero in dimensions given in feet and inches when there are zero feet. For example, check **0 feet** to display a dimension as 11″, or uncheck **0 feet** to display the same dimension as 0′-11″.

Check **0 inches** to remove the zero when the inch portion of dimensions displayed in feet and inches is less than one inch, such as 12'-7/8". If **0 inches** is unchecked, the same dimension reads 12'-0 7/8". In addition, this option removes the zero from a dimension with no inch value; for example, 12' appears instead of 12'-0".

The **Sub-units factor** and **Sub-unit suffix** text boxes become available when you use decimal units and select the **Leading** check box. Most drawings use a single format for all dimension values. For example, all dimensions on a decimal inch drawing are measured in inches, or decimals of an inch. *Sub-units* allow you to apply a different unit format to dimensions that are smaller than the primary unit format, without using decimals. For example, if you use meters to dimension most objects on a metric civil engineering drawing, you can use a **Sub-units factor** value of 100 (100 cm/m) and a **Sub-unit suffix** of cm to dimension objects smaller than one meter using centimeters instead of decimals of a meter. Then, when you dimension an object that is 0.5 meters, the dimension reads 500 cm.

sub-units: Unit formats smaller than the primary unit format. For example, centimeters can be defined as a sub-unit of meters.

> **NOTE**
>
> For drawings that do not require sub-units but do suppress leading zeros, specify no sub-unit suffix. As long as you do not add a suffix, there is no need to change the sub-unit factor, although a factor of 0 also disables sub-units.

Angular Dimension Settings

The **Angular dimensions** area allows you to specify settings for primary angular dimensions. The options in the **Units format** drop-down list are the same as those in the **Angle** area of the **Drawing Units** dialog box. Typically, the primary angular dimension unit format is the same as the corresponding drawing units. Use the **Precision** drop-down list to set the appropriate angular dimension value precision. The **Zero suppression** area has check boxes for suppressing leading and trailing zeros on angular dimensions. Zero suppression for angular units is usually the same as applied to linear dimensions.

Alternate Units Tab

Figure 17-34 shows the **Alternate Units** tab of the **New** (or **Modify**) **Dimension Style** dialog box. Use the **Alternate Units** tab to set *alternate units*, or *dual dimensioning units*. Dual dimensioning practices are no longer a recommended ASME standard. ASME recommends that drawings be dimensioned using inch units or metric units only. However, other applications do use alternate units. Some companies who use manufacturers and vendors both in the U.S. and internationally require dual dimensioning.

alternate units (dual dimensioning units): Dimensions in which measurements in one system, such as inches, are followed by bracketed measurements in another system, such as millimeters.

Select the **Display alternate units** check box to enable alternate units. The **Alternate Units** tab includes most of the same settings found in the **Primary Units** tab. The value in the **Multiplier for alt units** text box is multiplied by the primary unit to establish the value for the alternate unit. A value of 25.4 allows you to use millimeters as alternate units on an inch-unit drawing. The **Placement** area controls the location of the alternate-unit dimension value. You can place alternate units either after or below the primary value.

> **NOTE**
>
>
> Chapter 20 describes the **Tolerances** tab found in the **New** (or **Modify**) **Dimension Style** dialog box.

Figure 17-34. The **Alternate Units** tab of the **New** (or **Modify**) **Dimension Style** dialog box.

Pick to activate
dual dimensioning units

Select tab to set
up alternate
units

Settings for
alternate units

Location of
alternate units

Exercise 17-3

Access the Student Web site (www.g-wlearning.com/CAD) and complete
Exercise 17-3.

Developing Dimension Styles

Creating and using dimension styles is an important element of drafting with
AutoCAD. Carefully evaluate the characteristics of dimensions, and check school,
company, and national standards to verify the accuracy of dimension settings.
Figure 17-35 provides possible settings for three common dimension styles. Use the
AutoCAD default values for settings not listed.

PROFESSIONAL TIP

To save valuable drafting time, add dimension styles to template
drawings.

Exercise 17-4

Access the Student Web site (www.g-wlearning.com/CAD) and complete
Exercise 17-4.

Figure 17-35. This chart shows dimension settings for typical mechanical and architectural drawings.

Setting	Mechanical—Inch	Mechanical—Metric (mm)	Architectural—U.S. Customary
Baseline spacing	.5	12	1/2″
Extend beyond dimension lines	.125	3	1/8″
Offset from origin	.063	1.5	1/16″ or 3/32″
Arrowhead options	Closed filled, Closed, or Open	Closed filled, Closed, or Open	Architectural tick, Dot, Closed filled, Oblique, or Right angle
Arrow size	.125	3	1/8″
Center marks	Line	Line	Mark
Center mark size	.0625	1.5	1/16″
Text style	Romans, Arial, or Century Gothic	Romans, Arial, or Century Gothic	SansSerif, Arial, Century Gothic, Stylus BT, or ArchiText
Text height	.12	3	1/8″
Vertical and horizontal text placement	Centered	Centered	Vertical: Above Horizontal: Centered
View direction	Left-to-right	Left-to-right	Left-to-right
Offset from dimension line	.063	1.5	1/16″
Text alignment	Horizontal	Horizontal	Aligned with dimension line
Linear unit format	Decimal	Decimal	Architectural
Linerar precision	0.0000	0.00	1/16″
Linear zero suppression	Suppress only the leading zero	Suppress only the trailing zero	Suppress only the 0 feet zero
Sub-units factor	0	Disabled	Disabled
Sub-units suffix	None	Disabled	Disabled
Angular unit format	Decimal degrees	Decimal degrees	Decimal degrees
Angular precision	0	0	0
Angular zero suppression	Suppress only the leading angular dimension zero	Suppress only the trailing angular dimension zero	Suppress only the leading angular dimension zero
Alternate units	Do not display	Do not display	Do not display
Tolerances	By application	By application	None

Changing Dimension Styles

Use the **Dimension Style Manager** to change the characteristics of an existing dimension style. Pick the **Modify** button to open the **Modify Dimension Style** dialog box. When you make changes to a dimension style, such as selecting a different text style or linear precision, all existing dimensions assigned the modified dimension style are updated. Use a different dimension style with unique characteristics when appropriate to prevent updating existing dimensions.

override: A temporary change to the current style settings; the process of changing a current style temporarily.

child: A style override.

parent: The dimension style from which a style override is formed.

To *override* a dimension style, pick the **Override** button in the **Dimension Style Manager** to open the **Override Current Style** dialog box. An example of an override is including a text prefix for a few of the dimensions in a drawing. The **Override** button is only available for the current style. Once you create an override, it is current and appears as a branch, called the *child*, of the *parent* style. Override settings are lost when any other style, including the parent, is set current.

Sometimes it is useful to view the details of two styles to determine their differences. Select the **Compare...** button in the **Dimension Style Manager** to display the **Compare Dimension Styles** dialog box. Compare two styles by selecting the name of one style from the **Compare:** drop-down list and the name of the other from the **With:** drop-down list. The differences between the selected styles display in the dialog box.

> **NOTE**
>
> The **New Dimension Style, Modify Dimension Style**, and **Override Current Style** dialog boxes have the same tabs.

Renaming and Deleting Dimension Styles

To rename a dimension style using the **Dimension Style Manager**, slowly double-click on the name or right-click on the name and select **Rename**. To delete a dimension style using the **Dimension Style Manager**, right-click on the name and select **Delete**. You cannot delete a dimension style assigned to dimension objects. To delete a style that is in use, first assign a different style to the dimension objects that reference the style to be deleted.

> **NOTE**
>
> You can also rename styles using the **Rename** dialog box. Select **Dimension styles** in the **Named Objects** list to rename a dimension style.

Type
RENAME

RENAME

Setting a Dimension Style Current

Set a dimension style current using the **Dimension Style Manager** by double-clicking the style in the **Styles** list box, right-clicking on the name and selecting **Set current**, or picking the style and selecting the **Set current** button. To set a text style current without opening the **Dimension Style Manager**, use the **Dimension Style** list in the expanded **Annotation** panel of the **Home** ribbon tab or on the **Dimensions** panel of the **Annotate** ribbon tab.

You can import dimension styles from existing drawings using **DesignCenter**. See Chapter 5 for more information about using **DesignCenter** to import file content.

Exercise 17-5

Access the Student Web site (www.g-wlearning.com/CAD) and complete Exercise 17-5.

The **Dimension** panel of the **Express Tools** ribbon tab includes a **DIMEX** tool that allows you to export a dimension style as a separate .dim file, and a **DIMIM** tool that allows you to import a .dim file as a dimension style into the current drawing. For most applications, use **DesignCenter** to reuse dimension styles from existing drawings or templates, without creating a separate file.

Template Development Chapter 17

For instructions on adding dimension styles to each drawing template, go to the Student Web site (www.g-wlearning.com/CAD), select this chapter, and select **Template Development**.

Chapter Test

Answer the following questions. Write your answers on a separate sheet of paper or go to the Student Web site (www.g-wlearning.com/CAD) and complete the electronic chapter test.

1. List at least three factors that influence a company's dimensioning practices.
2. Name the current ASME document that specifies mechanical drafting dimensioning practices.
3. Name two basic coordinate systems used to create location dimensions.
4. Define the term *general notes*.
5. Briefly explain the difference between placing specific and general notes on a drawing.
6. Explain how to dimension a cylinder using a single view.
7. Describe two ways to dimension a cone.
8. When is the best time to determine the drawing scale and scale factors for a drawing?
9. Explain how to add a scale to the **Annotation Scale** flyout in the status bar.
10. Define *dimension style*.
11. Name the dialog box used to create dimension styles.
12. Identify two ways to access the dialog box identified in Question 11.
13. Name the dialog box tab used to control the appearance of dimension lines and extension lines.
14. Name at least four arrowhead types that are available in the **Symbols and Arrows** tab for common use on architectural drawings.
15. Name the dialog box tab used to control the settings that display the dimension text.
16. What has to happen before you can assign a text style to a dimension style?
17. What is the ASME-recommended height for dimension numbers and notes on drawings?
18. Name the dialog box tab used to control settings that adjust the location of dimension lines, dimension text, arrowheads, and leader lines.
19. How can you delete a dimension style from a drawing?
20. How do you set a dimension style current?

Drawing Problems

Start AutoCAD if it is not already started. Follow the specific instructions for each problem.

▼ Basic

1. Start a new drawing from a template and create a RomanS text style using the romans font. Create the Mechanical (Inch) dimension style shown in **Figure 17-35**. Use the default AutoCAD settings for the dimension style settings not listed. Save the drawing as P17-1.

2. Start a new drawing from a template and create a RomanS text style using the romans font. Create the Mechanical (Metric) dimension style shown in **Figure 17-35**. Use the default AutoCAD settings for the dimension style settings not listed. Save the drawing as P17-2.

3. Start a new drawing from a template and create a Stylus BT text style using the Stylus BT font. Create the Architectural dimension style shown in **Figure 17-35**. Use the default AutoCAD settings for the dimension style settings not listed. Save the drawing as P17-3.

4. Write a short report explaining the difference between unidirectional and aligned dimensioning. Use a word processor and include sketches giving examples of each method.

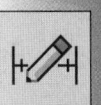

5. Write a short report explaining the difference between size and location dimensions. Use a word processor and include sketches giving examples of each method.

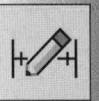

6. Write a short report describing the difference between dimensioning for mechanical drafting (drafting for manufacturing) and architectural drafting. Use a word processor and include sketches giving examples of each method.

7. Make sketches showing the standard practice for dimensioning a cylindrical object, a square object, and a conical object.

8. Make sketches showing the standard practice for dimensioning angles. Make one sketch showing coordinate dimensioning and another showing angular dimensioning.

▼ Intermediate

9. Find a copy of the ASME Y14.5-2009, *Dimensioning and Tolerancing* standard and write a report of approximately 350 words explaining the importance and basic content of this standard.

10. Interview your drafting instructor or supervisor and determine what dimension standards exist at your school or company. Write them down and keep them with you as you learn AutoCAD. Make notes as you progress through this textbook on how you use these standards. Also, note how you could change the standards to match the capabilities of AutoCAD.

▼ Advanced

11. Create a freehand sketch of **Figure 17-1**. Label each dimension item. To the side of the sketch, write a short description of each item.

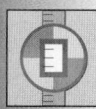

12. Research civil drafting and create a template establishing the dimension styles for a civil drawing.

13. Visit a local manufacturing company at which design drafting work is part of the business. Write a report with sketched examples identifying the standards used at the company.

14. Visit a local architect or architectural designer. Write a report with sketched examples identifying the standards used at the company.

15. Visit a local civil engineering company at which design drafting work is part of the business. Write a report with sketched examples identifying the standards used at the company.

AutoCAD Certified Associate Exam Practice

Answer the following questions. Write your answers on a separate sheet of paper.

1. Which of the following items are common components of a dimension? *Select all that apply.*
   A. boundaries
   B. lines
   C. numerical values
   D. symbols
   E. xlines

2. What is the term for a dimension style in which all text reads from the bottom of the sheet? *Select the one item that best answers the question.*
   A. aligned dimensioning
   B. polar dimensioning
   C. rectangular dimensioning
   D. unidirectional dimensioning

3. What is the smallest number of views that can be used to dimension a cylindrical shape? *Select the one item that best answers the question.*
   A. one
   B. two
   C. three
   D. four

AutoCAD Certified Professional Exam Practice

Follow the instructions in each problem. Write your answers on a separate sheet of paper.

1. **Navigate to this chapter on the Student Web site and open CPE-17annoscale.dwg.**
   What annotation scale is currently assigned to this drawing?

2. **Navigate to this chapter on the Student Web site and open CPE-17dimstyle.dwg.**
   What text style is assigned to the Mechanical dimension style? What font is assigned to the text style?

Linear and Angular Dimensioning

Learning Objectives

After completing this chapter, you will be able to do the following:
- ✓ Add linear dimensions to a drawing.
- ✓ Add angular dimensions to a drawing.
- ✓ Draw datum and chain dimensions.
- ✓ Dimension multiple objects using the **QDIM** tool.

A drawing often requires a variety of dimensions to describe the size and shape of features. Linear and angular dimensions are two of the most common dimensions. This chapter covers the process of adding linear and angular dimensions to a drawing using several dimensioning tools. You will also learn how to add a break symbol to a dimension line and use the **QDIM** tool.

Linear Dimensions

Linear dimensions usually measure straight distances, such as distances between horizontal, vertical, or slanted surfaces. Use the **DIMLINEAR** tool to draw a single linear dimension. Dimension tools reference the current dimension style and the points or objects you select to create a dimension object. When you use the **DIMLINEAR** tool, for example, you create a dimension object that includes all related dimension style characteristics, dimension and extension lines, arrowheads, and a dimension value associated with the distance between selected points.

Access the **DIMLINEAR** tool, pick a point to locate origin of the first extension line, and then pick a point to locate the origin of the second extension line. See **Figure 18-1**. Use object snap modes and other drawing aids to pick the exact origin of extension lines. Once you establish the extension line origins, use the options that appear at the Specify dimension line location or [Mtext/Text/Angle/Horizontal/Vertical/Rotated] prompt as needed. To apply the default settings and create a linear dimension, specify a point to locate the dimension line. See **Figure 18-2**.

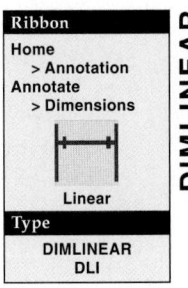

Ribbon
Home
> Annotation
Annotate
> Dimensions

Linear

Type
DIMLINEAR
DLI

DIMLINEAR

Figure 18-1.
Establishing
extension line origins.
The **Endpoint** and
Intersection object
snap modes are
useful for locating
origins accurately.

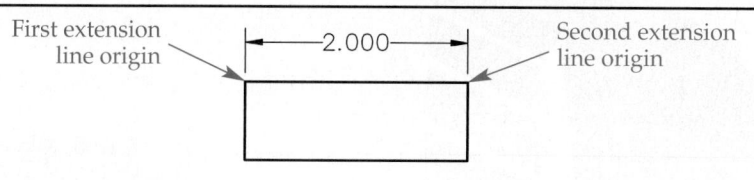

First extension line origin

Second extension line origin

2.000

Figure 18-2.
Establishing
the location of a
dimension line.
ASME standards
recommend a
minimum spacing of
.375″ (10 mm) from
a drawing feature to
the first dimension
line and a minimum
spacing of .25″ (6 mm)
between dimension
lines. A value of
.5″ (12 mm) or .75″
(19 mm) is usually
more appropriate.
Maintain consistent
spacing throughout a
drawing.

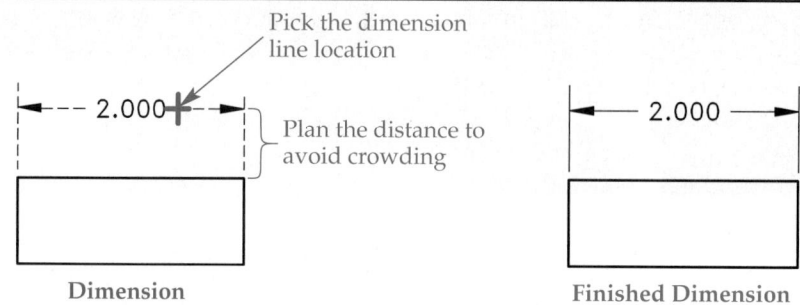

Pick the dimension line location

2.000

Plan the distance to avoid crowding

Dimension Being Positioned

2.000

Finished Dimension

NOTE

When you dimension objects with AutoCAD, the objects are measured exactly as drawn. This makes it important for you to draw objects and features accurately and to select the origins of extension lines accurately.

PROFESSIONAL TIP

Use preliminary plan sheets and sketches to help determine proper dimension line location and distances between dimension lines to avoid crowding. ASME standards recommend a minimum spacing of .375″ (10 mm) from a drawing feature to the first dimension line and a minimum spacing of .25″ (6 mm) between dimension lines. A minimum spacing of 3/8″ is common for architectural drawings. These minimum recommendations are generally less than the spacing required by actual company or school standards. A value of .5″ (12 mm) or .75″ (19 mm) is usually more appropriate. Create offset construction geometry to pick with object snap modes when placing dimension lines, or use drawing aids such as AutoSnap and Auto-Track or **Grid** and **Snap** modes.

Exercise 18-1

Access the Student Web site (www.g-wlearning.com/CAD) and complete Exercise 18-1.

Selecting an Object to Dimension

An alternative method to locate extension line origins is to pick a line, polyline segment, circle, or arc to dimension. You can use this option whenever you see the Specify first extension line origin or <select object>: prompt. Press [Enter] or the space bar or right-click and then pick the object to dimension. When you select a line, polyline segment, or arc, extension lines originate from the endpoints. When you pick a circle, extension lines originate from the quadrant closest to the selection and the opposite quadrant. See Figure 18-3.

Adjusting Dimension Text

The value attached to the dimension corresponds to the distance between the origins of extension lines. Use the **Mtext** option to adjust the dimension value using the mtext editor. See Figure 18-4. The highlighted value represents the current dimension value. Add to or modify the dimension text and then close the text editor. The **DIMLINEAR** tool continues, allowing you to pick the dimension line location.

The **Text** option uses the single-line text editor to change dimension text, even though the final dimension value is mtext. The current dimension value appears in brackets. Add to or modify the value as necessary, and then press [Enter] to exit the option. The **DIMLINEAR** tool continues, allowing you to pick the dimension line location.

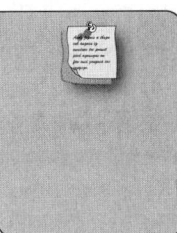

NOTE

Dimension values are horizontal or aligned with the dimension line, according to the current dimension style format. The **Angle** option has limited applications, but allows you to rotate the dimension text. Enter the desired angle at the Specify angle of dimension text: prompt to use this option.

Including Symbols with Dimension Text

Some AutoCAD dimension tools automatically place appropriate symbols with the dimension value. For example, when you dimension an arc using the **DIMRADIUS** tool, an R appears before the dimension value. When you dimension a circle using the **DIMDIAMETER** tool, a ∅ symbol appears before the dimension value. The ASME standard recommends these symbols. However, dimension tools such as **DIMLINEAR** do not automatically place certain symbols or add necessary characters.

Figure 18-3.
AutoCAD can determine extension line origins automatically when you use the **Select object** option to pick a line, polyline segment, arc, or circle.

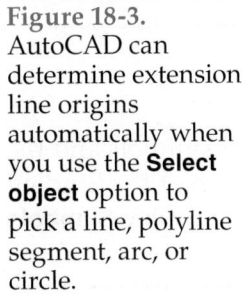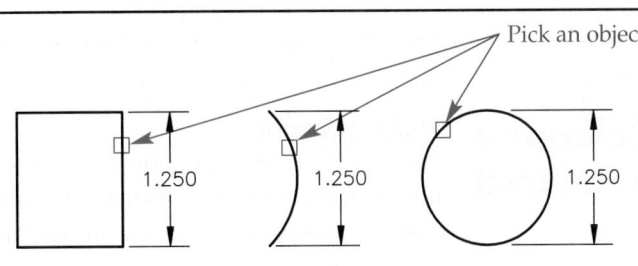

Figure 18-4. When you use the **Mtext** option, the **Text Editor** ribbon tab appears with the dimension value calculated by AutoCAD in a text box for editing.

Multiline
Text tab
of the
ribbon
appears

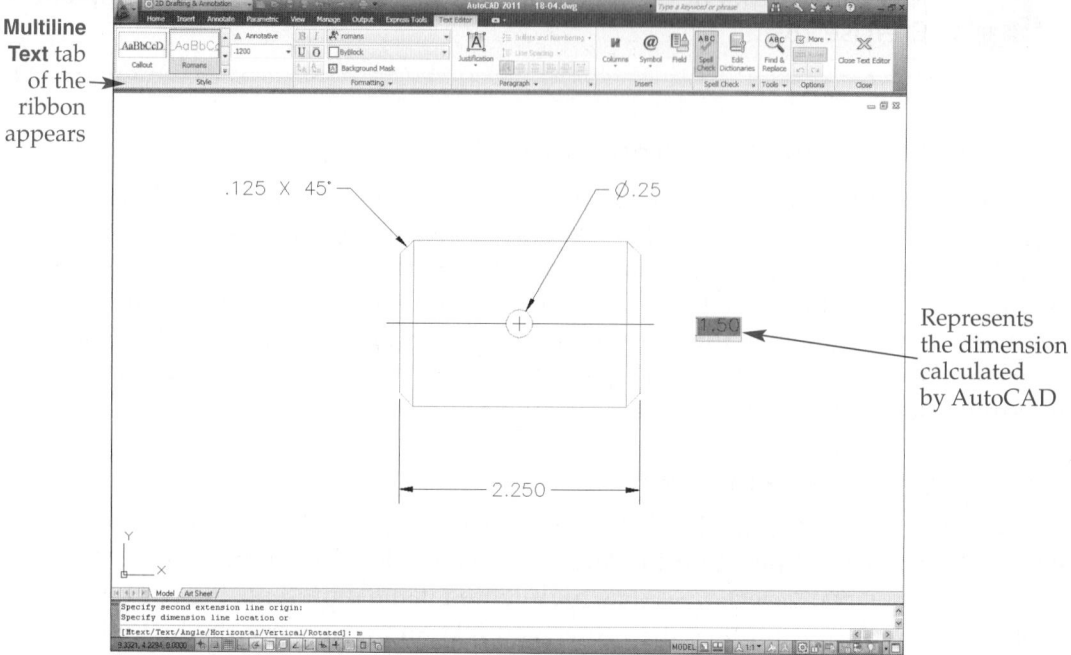

Represents
the dimension
calculated
by AutoCAD

One option is to use the **Mtext** option to activate the multiline text editor. Place the cursor at the location to add a symbol and then use options from the **Symbol** flyout or cascading submenu, or type characters. For example, pick the **Diameter** symbol from the **Symbol** flyout to add ∅ before the associated dimension value. Another example is enclosing a reference dimension in parentheses, as recommended by the ASME standard. To create a reference dimension, type open and close parentheses around the highlighted value.

You can also add content using the **Text** option and the single-line text editor. Place the cursor at the location to add a symbol and type control codes or characters. For example, type %%C to display ∅ or type parentheses around the value to create a reference dimension.

Another way to place symbols with dimension text is to create a dimension style that references a text style using the gdt.shx font. A text style with the gdt.shx font allows you to place common dimension symbols, including geometric dimensioning and tolerancing (GD&T) symbols, using the lowercase letter keys.

PROFESSIONAL TIP

Although you can add a prefix and suffix to a dimension style, usually it is more appropriate to adjust the limited number of dimensions that require a prefix or suffix.

Reference Material

Drafting Symbols
For more information about common drafting symbols and the gdt.shx font, go to the **Reference Material** section of the Student Web site (www.g-wlearning.com/CAD) and select **Drafting Symbols** in the list.

Exercise 18-2

Access the Student Web site (www.g-wlearning.com/CAD) and complete
Exercise 18-2.

Controlling the Dimension Line Angle

The **Horizontal** option restricts the **DIMLINEAR** tool to dimension only a horizontal distance. The **Vertical** option restricts the **DIMLINEAR** tool to dimension only a vertical distance. These options are helpful when it is difficult to produce the appropriate horizontal or vertical dimension line, such as when you are dimensioning the horizontal or vertical distance of a slanted surface. The **Mtext**, **Text**, and **Angle** options are available to change the dimension text value if necessary.

The **Rotated** option allows you to specify a dimension line angle. Practical applications include dimensioning angled surfaces and auxiliary views. This technique is different from other dimensioning tools because you provide a dimension line angle. See **Figure 18-5.** At the Specify angle of dimension line <0>: prompt, enter a value or specify two points on the line.

PROFESSIONAL TIP

AutoCAD dimensioning should be accurate and neat. You can achieve consistent, professional results by using the following guidelines:

- Never truncate, or round off, decimal values when entering locations, distances, or angles. For example, enter .4375 for 7/16, rather than .44.
- Set the precision to the most common precision level in the drawing before adding dimensions. Adjust the precision as needed for each dimension.
- Always use drawing aids, such as object snaps, to ensure the accuracy of dimensions.
- Never type a different dimension value from what appears highlighted or in <> brackets. To change a dimension, revise the drawing or dimension settings. Only adjust dimension text when it is necessary to add prefixes and suffixes, or to use a different text format.

Figure 18-5.
Rotating a
dimension for an
angled view.

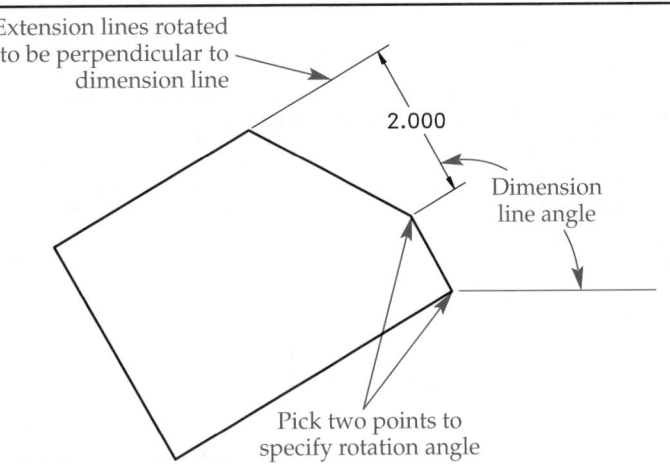

Extension lines rotated
to be perpendicular to
dimension line

2.000

Dimension
line angle

Pick two points to
specify rotation angle

Chapter 18 Linear and Angular Dimensioning

Exercise 18-3

Access the Student Web site (www.g-wlearning.com/CAD) and complete Exercise 18-3.

Dimensioning Angled Surfaces and Auxiliary Views

When you dimension a surface drawn at an angle, such as an auxiliary view, it is often necessary to align the dimension line with the surface, with extension lines perpendicular to the surface. In order to dimension these features properly, use the **DIMALIGNED** tool or the **Rotated** option of the **DIMLINEAR** tool.

Figure 18-6 shows the results of using the **DIMALIGNED** tool. Notice the difference between the aligned dimension in this figure and the rotated dimension in **Figure 18-5**. You can usually use the **DIMALIGNED** tool when the length of the extension lines is equal. The **Rotated** option of the **DIMLINEAR** tool is often necessary when extension lines are unequal.

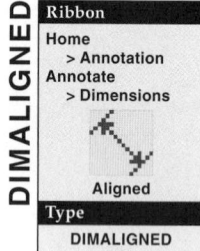

DIMALIGNED

Ribbon
Home > Annotation Annotate > Dimensions

Aligned

Type
DIMALIGNED DAL

Exercises 18-4 and 18-5

Access the Student Web site (www.g-wlearning.com/CAD) and complete Exercise 18-4 and Exercise 18-5.

Dimensioning Long Objects

When you create a drawing of a long part that has a constant shape, the view may not fit on the sheet, or it may look strange compared to the rest of the drawing. To overcome this problem, use a *conventional break* (or *break*) to shorten the view. **Figure 18-7** shows examples of standard break lines. For many long parts, a conventional break is required to display views or increase view scale without increasing sheet size. Dimensions added to conventional breaks describe the actual length of the product in its unbroken form. The dimension line includes a break symbol to indicate that the drawing view is broken and that the feature is longer than it appears. See **Figure 18-8**.

Use the **DIMJOGLINE** tool to add a break symbol to dimension lines created using the **DIMLINEAR** or **DIMALIGNED** tool. Access the **DIMJOGLINE** tool and pick a linear or aligned dimension line. Then pick a location on the dimension line to place the break symbol, as shown in **Figure 18-8**. An alternative to selecting the location of the break

conventional break (break): Removal of a portion of a long, constant-shaped object to make the object fit better on the sheet.

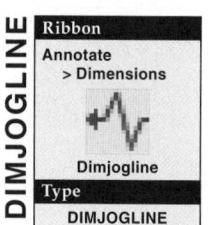

DIMJOGLINE

Ribbon
Annotate > Dimensions

Dimjogline

Type
DIMJOGLINE

Figure 18-6.
The **DIMALIGNED** tool allows you to place dimension lines parallel to angled features.

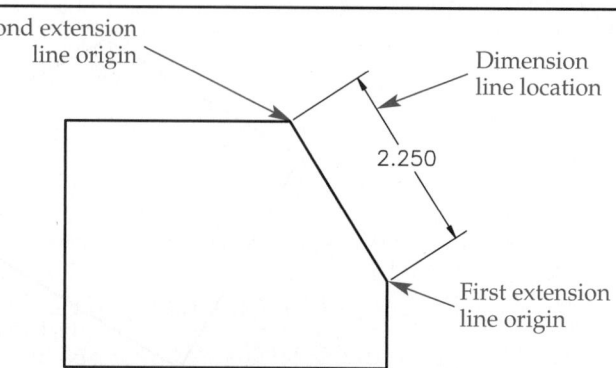

Second extension line origin

Dimension line location

2.250

First extension line origin

Figure 18-7. Standard break lines.

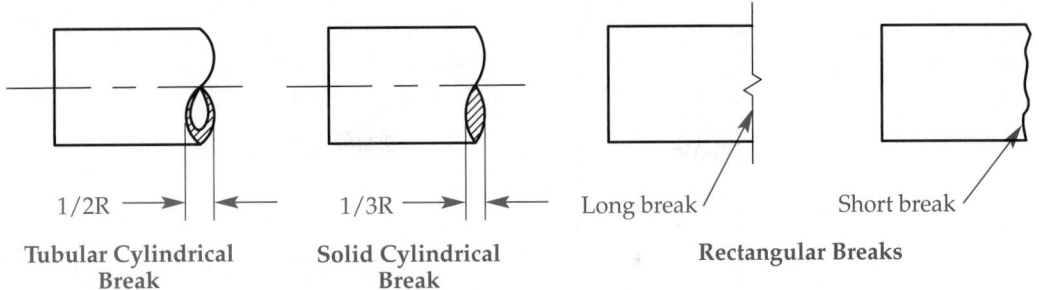

| 1/2R | 1/3R | Long break | Short break |
| Tubular Cylindrical Break | Solid Cylindrical Break | Rectangular Breaks | |

Figure 18-8. Using the **DIMJOGLINE** tool to place a break symbol on a dimension line.

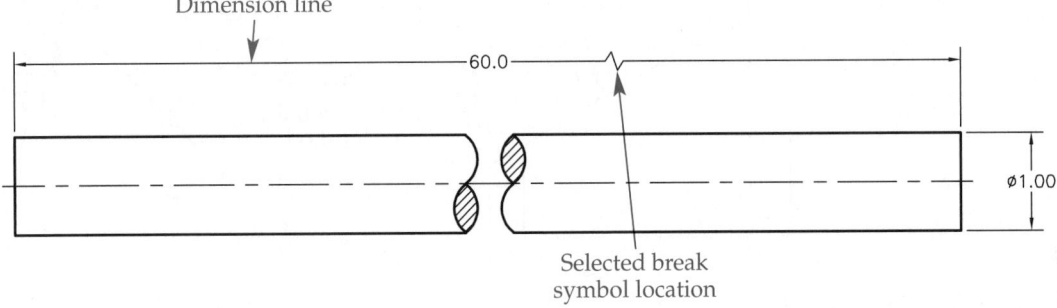

Dimension line

60.0

Ø1.00

Selected break symbol location

symbol is to press [Enter] to accept the default location. You can move the break later using grip editing or by reusing the **DIMJOGLINE** tool to select a different location. To remove the break symbol, access the **DIMJOGLINE** tool and select the **Remove** option.

> **NOTE**
>
> You can add only one break symbol to a dimension line.

Exercise 18-6

Access the Student Web site (www.g-wlearning.com/CAD) and complete Exercise 18-6.

Dimensioning Angles

Coordinate or angular dimensioning are accepted methods for dimensioning angles. **Figure 18-9** shows an example of *coordinate dimensioning* using the **DIMLINEAR** tool.

Figure 18-10 shows an example of *angular dimensioning* using the **DIMANGULAR** tool. You can dimension the angle between any two nonparallel lines from the *vertex* of the angle. AutoCAD automatically draws extension lines if needed.

coordinate dimensioning: A method of dimensioning angles in which dimensions locate the corner of the angle.

angular dimensioning: A method of dimensioning angles in which one corner of an angle is located with a dimension and the value of the angle is provided in degrees.

vertex: The point at which the two lines that form an angle meet.

Ribbon	
Home > Annotation Annotate > Dimensions	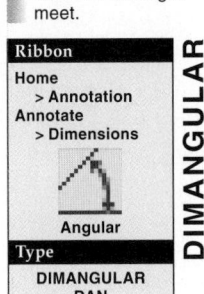
	Angular
Type	
DIMANGULAR DAN	

DIMANGULAR

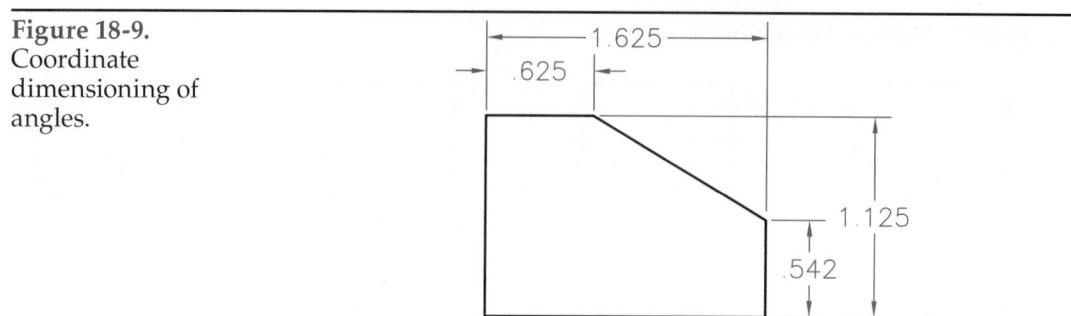

Figure 18-9.
Coordinate dimensioning of angles.

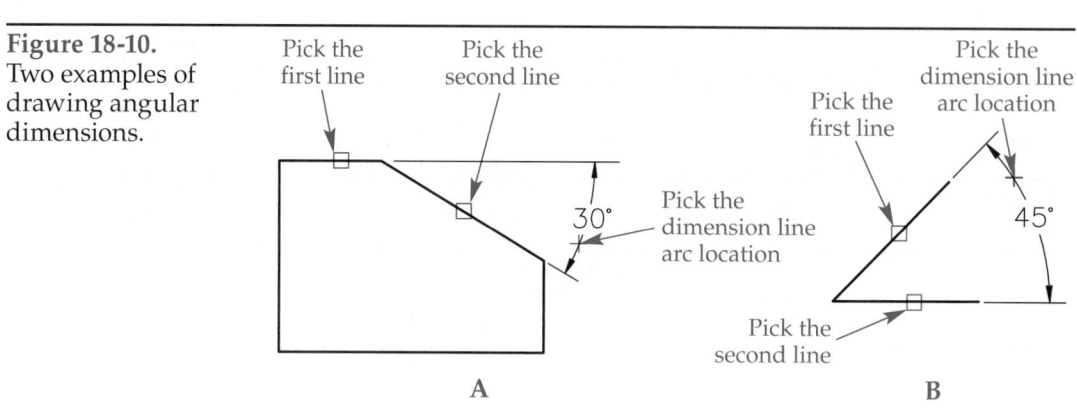

Figure 18-10.
Two examples of drawing angular dimensions.

Pick the first line

Pick the second line

Pick the dimension line arc location

Pick the first line

Pick the dimension line arc location

Pick the second line

30°

45°

A

B

Access the **DIMANGULAR** tool, pick the first leg of the angle to dimension, and then pick the second leg of the angle. The last prompt asks you to pick the location of the dimension line arc. **Figure 18-11** shows examples of angular dimensions and the effect that limited space may have on dimension fit and placement. Fit characteristics apply to most dimensions.

> **PROFESSIONAL TIP**
>
> You can create four different dimensions (two different angles) with an angular dimension. To preview these options before selecting the dimension line location, use the cursor to move the dimension around an imaginary circle. You can use the **Quadrant** option to isolate a specific quadrant of the imaginary circle and force the dimension to produce the value found in the selected quadrant.

Figure 18-11. The location of the dimension line determines the arrangement of the dimension line arc, text, and arrows.

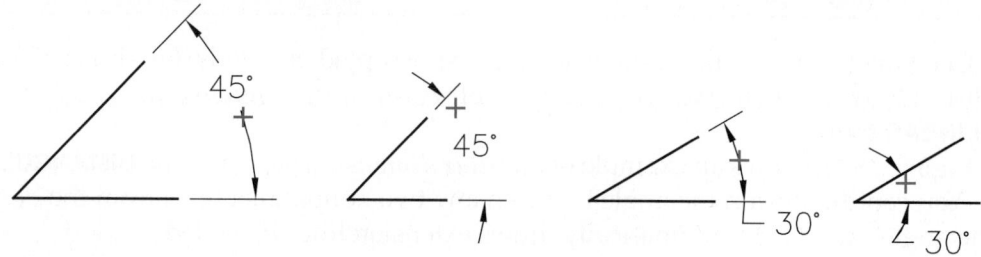

45°

45°

30°

30°

Dimensioning Angles on Arcs and Circles

Use the **DIMANGULAR** tool to dimension the included angle of an arc or a portion of a circle. When you dimension an arc, the center point becomes the angle vertex, and the two arc endpoints establish the extension line origins. See **Figure 18-12.**

When you dimension a circle using **DIMANGULAR**, the center point becomes the angle vertex, and two specified points locate the extension line origins. See **Figure 18-13.** The point you pick to select the circle locates the origin of the first extension line. You then select the second angle endpoint, which locates the origin of the second extension line.

> ### PROFESSIONAL TIP
>
> Using angular dimensioning for circles increases the number of possible solutions for a given dimensioning requirement, but the actual uses are limited. One application is dimensioning an angle from a quadrant point to a particular feature without first drawing a line to dimension. Another benefit of this option is the ability to specify angles that exceed 180°.

Angular Dimensioning through Three Points

You can also use the **DIMANGULAR** tool to establish an angular dimension according to the vertex and two angle line endpoints. See **Figure 18-14.** To apply this technique, press [Enter] or the space bar, or right-click after the first prompt. Then pick the vertex, followed by the two points. This method can also be used to dimension angles over 180°.

Exercise 18-7

Access the Student Web site (www.g-wlearning.com/CAD) and complete Exercise 18-7.

Figure 18-12.
Placing angular
dimensions on arcs.

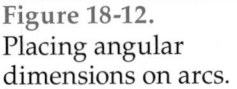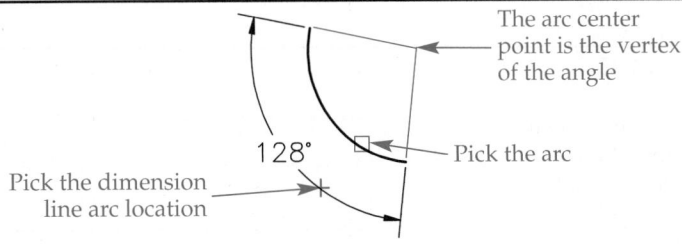

The arc center
point is the vertex
of the angle

128°

Pick the arc

Pick the dimension
line arc location

Figure 18-13.
Placing angular
dimensions on
circles.

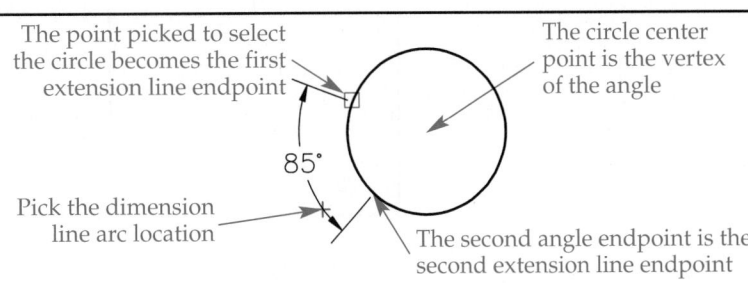

The point picked to select
the circle becomes the first
extension line endpoint

The circle center
point is the vertex
of the angle

85°

Pick the dimension
line arc location

The second angle endpoint is the
second extension line endpoint

Chapter 18   Linear and Angular Dimensioning

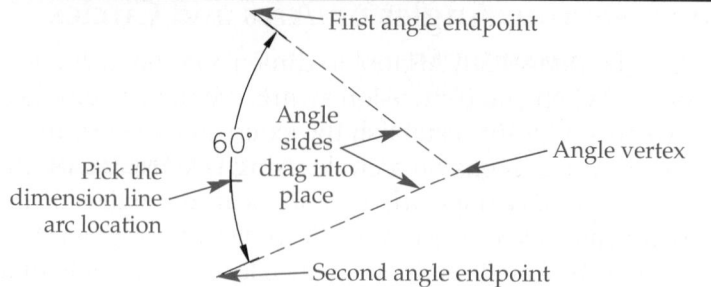

Figure 18-14.
Placing angular dimensions using three points.

First angle endpoint

Angle sides drag into place

60°

Angle vertex

Pick the dimension line arc location

Second angle endpoint

---

baseline dimensioning:
A method of dimensioning in which several dimensions originate from a common surface, centerline, or center plane.

datum:
Theoretically perfect surface, plane, point, or axis from which measurements can be taken.

chain dimensioning:
A method of dimensioning in which dimensions appear in a line from one feature to the next.

direct dimensioning: A type of dimensioning applied to control the specific size or location of one or more specific features.

Baseline, Chain, and Direct Dimensioning

Mechanical drafting often requires *baseline dimensioning*, in which each dimension is independent of the others and references a *datum*. This achieves more accuracy in manufacturing. **Figure 18-15** shows an object dimensioned with baseline dimensioning and surface datums.

Mechanical drafting sometimes uses *chain dimensioning*. However, this method provides less accuracy than baseline dimensioning because each dimension is dependent on other dimensions in the chain, resulting in tolerance buildup. In mechanical drafting, it is common to leave one dimension out and provide an overall dimension that controls the missing value. See **Figure 18-16**. Architectural drafting uses chain dimensioning in most applications to reduce the need to calculate or find dimension values during construction. Architectural drafting practices usually show dimensions for all features, plus an overall dimension.

Direct dimensioning controls the specific size or location of one or more specific features, often resulting in the least tolerance buildup. **Figure 18-17** shows an example of direct dimensioning on a part view. Baseline or chain dimensioning could be used to dimension the view, but would create more tolerance accumulation.

Baseline Dimensioning

The **DIMBASELINE** tool controls baseline dimensioning and allows you to select several points to define a series of baseline dimensions. You can create baseline dimensions with linear, angular, and ordinate dimensions. Chapter 19 describes ordinate dimensions.

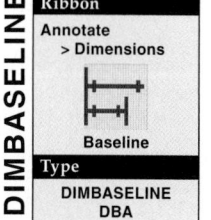

DIMBASELINE

Ribbon
Annotate > Dimensions
Baseline
Type
DIMBASELINE DBA

Figure 18-15.
Baseline dimensioning on a part view. Maintain consistent spacing throughout the drawing.

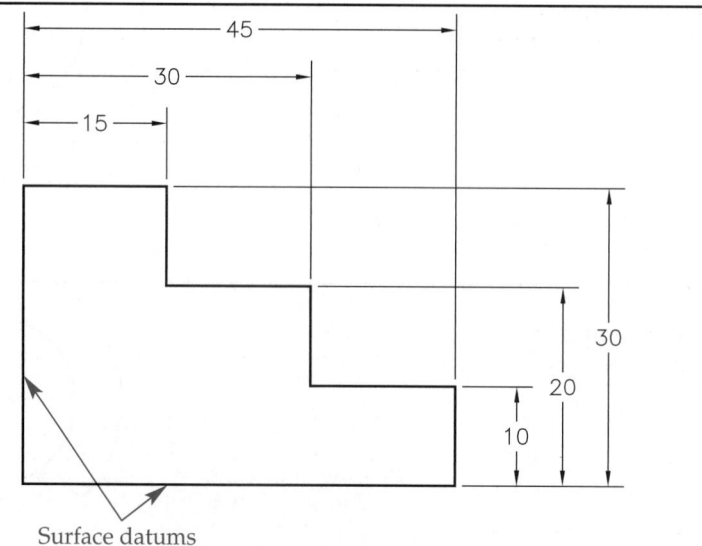

Surface datums

45
30
15
30
20
10

Figure 18-16. Chain dimensioning on a part view. The example on the left is more common, depending on the design and dimensioning requirements. The example on the right includes an optional reference dimension.

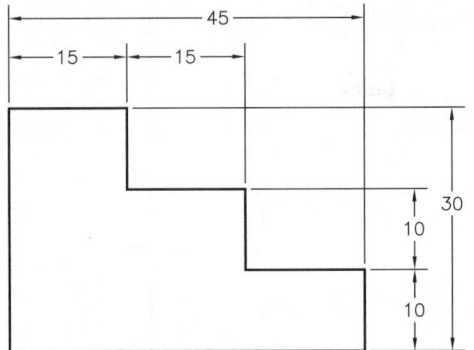

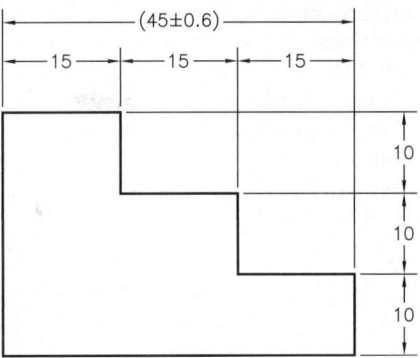

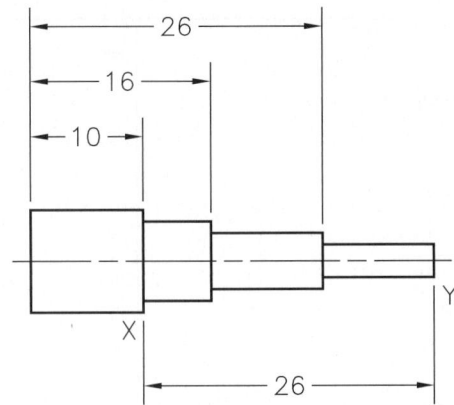

Figure 18-17. An example of direct dimensioning between surfaces X and Y. Baseline dimensioning locates the other surfaces.

The **DIMBASELINE** tool continues from an existing dimension. Therefore, you must create the first dimension using a suitable dimensioning tool. For example, for linear dimensions, use the **DIMLINEAR** tool. The first point you select when drawing the linear dimension defines the datum. Then access the **DIMBASELINE** tool and pick the next second extension line origin. Continue picking extension line origins until you have dimensioned all the features. Press [Enter] or the space bar or right-click twice, once at the Specify a second extension line origin or: prompt, and again at the Select base dimension: prompt, to create the dimensions and exit the tool. Notice that as you pick additional extension line origins, AutoCAD automatically places the dimension text; you do not specify a location. **Figure 18-18** shows an example of using the **DIMBASELINE** tool to pick two additional extension line origins to add to an existing linear dimension.

AutoCAD automatically selects the most recent dimension as the base dimension unless you specify a different dimension. To add baseline dimensions to an existing dimension other than the most recent dimension, use the **Select** option by pressing [Enter] or the space bar, or by right-clicking and selecting **Enter** at the first prompt. At the Select base dimension: prompt, pick the dimension to serve as the base. The extension line nearest the point where you select the dimension establishes the datum. Then select the new second extension line origins as described.

You can also draw baseline dimensions to angular features. First, draw an angular dimension. Then enter the **DIMBASELINE** tool. **Figure 18-19** shows angular baseline dimensions. As with linear dimensions, you can pick an existing angular dimension other than the most recent dimension.

Figure 18-18.
Using the
DIMBASELINE tool
to add baseline
dimensions.
AutoCAD
automatically places
the extension lines,
dimension lines,
arrowheads, and
text.

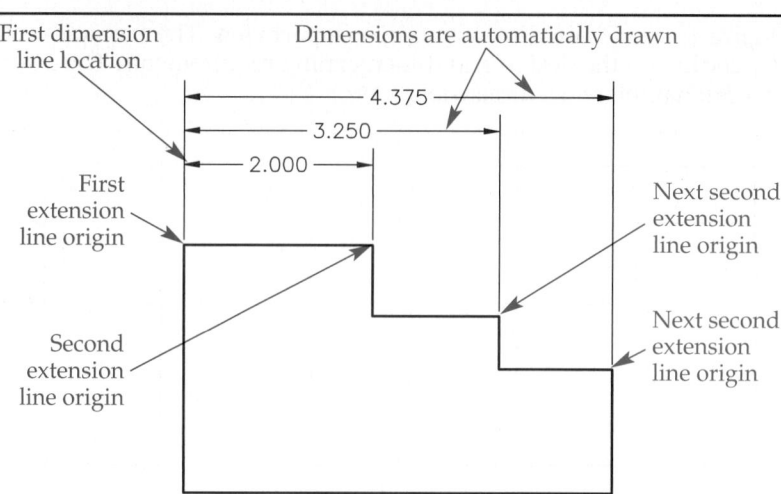

Figure 18-19.
Using the
DIMBASELINE tool
to add baseline
dimensions to
angular features.

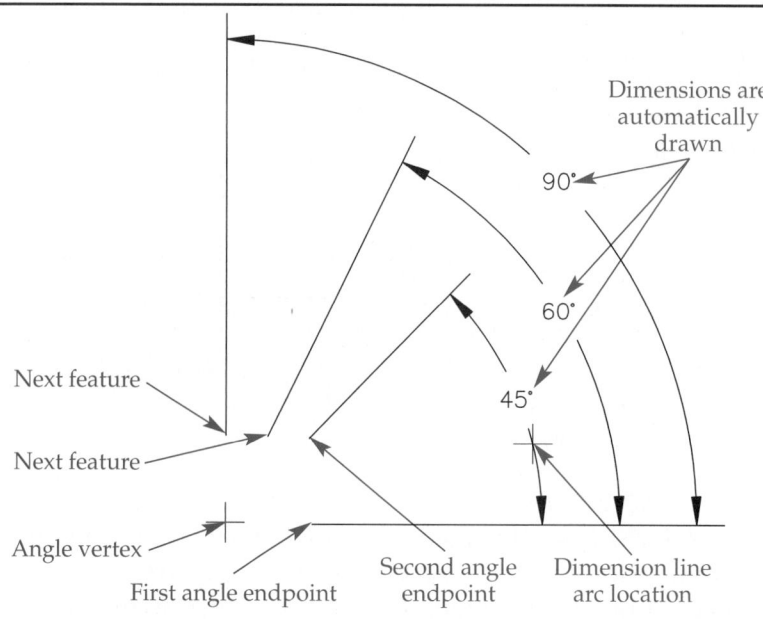

NOTE

Specify the distance between dimension lines in the **Lines** tab of the **New** (or **Modify**) **Dimension Style** dialog box. The ASME minimum distance between dimension lines is .375 (10 mm), but this is usually too close. A distance of .75 (19 mm) from the object to the first dimension line and .5 (12 mm) between other dimension lines is often ideal.

continued dimensioning: The AutoCAD term for chain dimensioning.

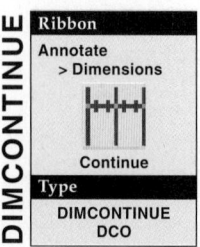

Chain Dimensioning

AutoCAD refers to chain dimensioning as *continued dimensioning*. The **DIMCONTINUE** tool controls chain dimensioning and allows you to select several points to define a series of chain dimensions. **Figure 18-20** shows chain dimensioning.

Use the **DIMBASELINE** and **DIMCONTINUE** tools in the same manner. When creating chain dimensions, you will see the same prompts and options you see when you create baseline dimensions. As with baseline dimensions, you can create continued dimensions with linear, angular, and ordinate dimensions.

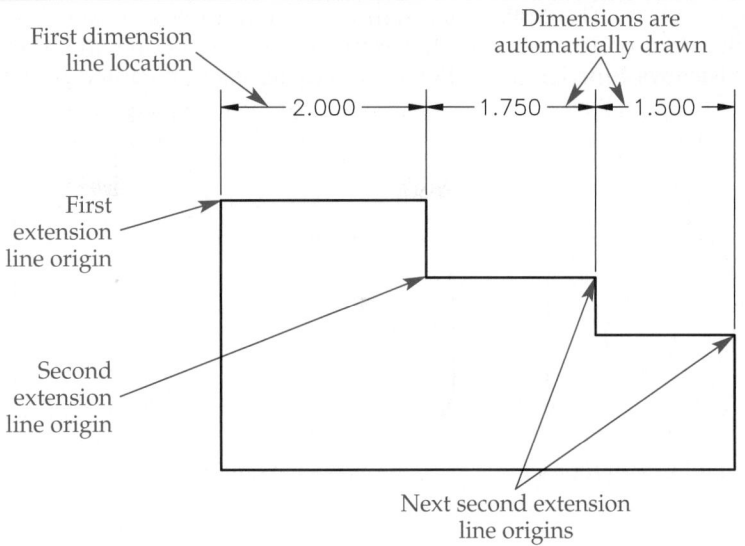

Figure 18-20.
Using the
DIMCONTINUE
tool to create chain
dimensions.

First dimension
line location

Dimensions are
automatically drawn

2.000 — 1.750 — 1.500

First
extension
line origin

Second
extension
line origin

Next second extension
line origins

NOTE

Use the **Undo** option in the **DIMBASELINE** and **DIMCONTINUE** tools
to undo previously drawn dimensions.

PROFESSIONAL TIP

You do not have to use **DIMBASELINE** or **DIMCONTINUE** immediately after you create the base or chain dimension. Use the **Select**
option later during the drawing session to pick the base or chain
dimension.

Exercise 18-8

Access the Student Web site (www.g-wlearning.com/CAD) and complete
Exercise 18-8.

Using QDIM to Dimension

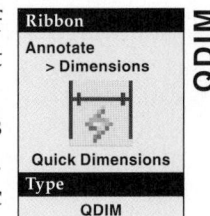

The **QDIM** tool automates the dimensioning processing by creating a group of
dimensions based on the objects you select. You can also use the **QDIM** tool to edit
dimensions, as explained in Chapter 21.

Access the **QDIM** tool and select the objects to dimension. Right-click or press
[Enter] or the space bar to display a preview of the dimensions attached to the cursor.
By default, AutoCAD establishes an extension line from every line, polyline, and arc
endpoint, and circle and arc center point.

To apply chain dimensioning, use the default **Continuous** option and specify the
location of the dimension lines. See **Figure 18-21A.** To apply baseline dimensioning,
choose the **Baseline** option and then specify the location of the first dimension line.

Figure 18-21. The **QDIM** tool can dimension multiple selected objects, without you having to pick extension line origins. This example shows selecting all objects initially, and then using the **Remove** function of the **Edit** option to deselect unwanted points.

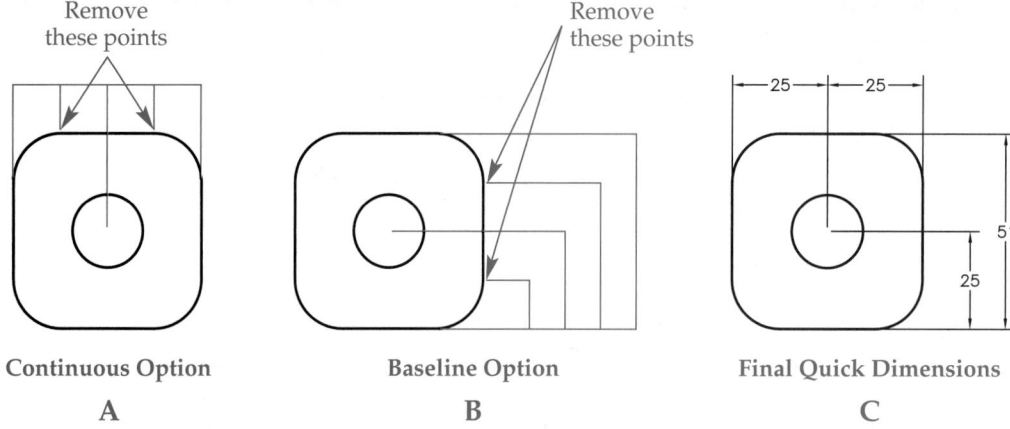

Continuous Option
A

Baseline Option
B

Final Quick Dimensions
C

See **Figure 18-21B.** If the **QDIM** tool does not reference the appropriate datum, use the **datum Point** option before locating the dimensions to specify a different datum point.

Use the **Edit** option before locating the dimensions to add dimensions to, or remove dimensions from, the current set. Marks indicate the points acquired by the **QDIM** tool. Use the **Add** function to specify a point to add a dimension, or use the **Remove** function to specify a point to remove the corresponding dimension. Right-click or press [Enter] or the space bar to return to the previous prompt and continue using the **QDIM** tool. **Figure 18-21C** shows a view dimensioned using the **QDIM** tool twice. The **Remove** function of the **Edit** option was used each time to remove unwanted dimensions.

The **Ordinate** option allows you to apply rectangular coordinate dimensioning without dimension lines, as explained in Chapter 19. The **Diameter** option dimensions all selected circles and arcs with diameter dimensions and no linear dimensions. The **Radius** option dimensions all selected circles and arcs with radius dimensions and no linear dimensions. Chapter 19 describes diameter and radius dimensions.

NOTE

The **Settings** option provides an **Endpoint** or **Intersection** toggle meant to set the object snap mode for locating extension line origins. The **Staggered** option creates a unique grouping of dimensions, similar to baseline dimensioning, but beginning from the center objects and expanding outward.

Exercise 18-9

Access the Student Web site (www.g-wlearning.com/CAD) and complete Exercise 18-9.

Chapter Test

Answer the following questions. Write your answers on a separate sheet of paper or go to the Student Web site (www.g-wlearning.com/CAD) and complete the electronic chapter test.

1. Name the two **DIMLINEAR** options that allow you to change dimension text.
2. Give two examples of symbols that automatically appear with some dimensions.
3. What is the purpose of the AutoCAD gdt.shx font?
4. Name the two dimensioning tools that provide linear dimensions for angled surfaces.
5. Which tool allows you to place a break symbol in a dimension line?
6. Name the tool used to dimension angles in degrees.
7. Describe a way to specify an angle in degrees if the angle is greater than 180°.
8. Which type of dimensioning is generally preferred for manufacturing because of its accuracy?
9. Define *direct dimensioning*.
10. How do you place a baseline dimension from the origin of the previously drawn dimension?
11. How do you place a baseline dimension from the origin of a dimension drawn during a previous drawing session?
12. What is the conventional term for the type of dimensioning AutoCAD refers to as continuous dimensioning?
13. Which tool other than **DIMBASELINE** creates baseline dimensions?
14. Explain how to remove dimensions from the current set when you use the **QDIM** tool.
15. Name at least three options for dimensioning that are available through the **QDIM** tool.

Drawing Problems

- *Start AutoCAD if it is not already started. Start a new drawing for each problem using an appropriate template of your choice.*

- *The template should include layers and text, dimension, multileader, and table styles, when necessary, for drawing the given objects. Add layers and text, dimension, multileader, and table styles as needed.*

- *Draw all objects using appropriate layers and text, dimension, multileader, and table styles, justification, and format.*

- *Follow the specific instructions for each problem. Use only drawing and editing tools and techniques you have already learned. Use your own judgment and approximate dimensions when necessary.*

- *Apply dimensions accurately using ASME or appropriate industry standards.*

Note: *Some of the problems in this chapter are built on problems from previous chapters. If you have not yet completed those problems, complete them now.*

▼ Basic

1. Start a new drawing from scratch or use a fractional unit template of your choice. Save the file as P18-1. Open P3-7 and copy one instance of Object A and Object B to the P18-1 drawing. The P18-1 file should be active. Dimension the views as shown.

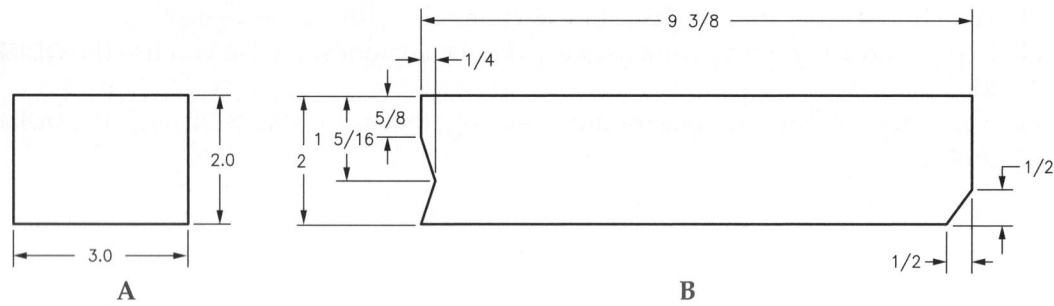

2. Open P3-5 and save the file as P18-2. The P18-2 file should be active. Dimension the drawing as shown.

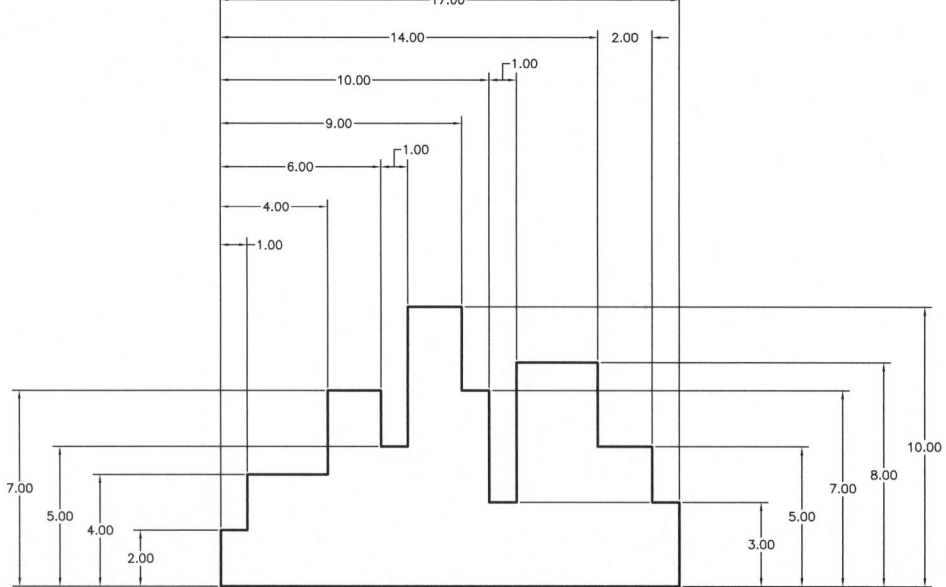

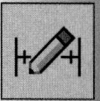

3. Open **P3-10** and save the file as **P18-3**. The P18-3 file should be active. Dimension the views as shown.

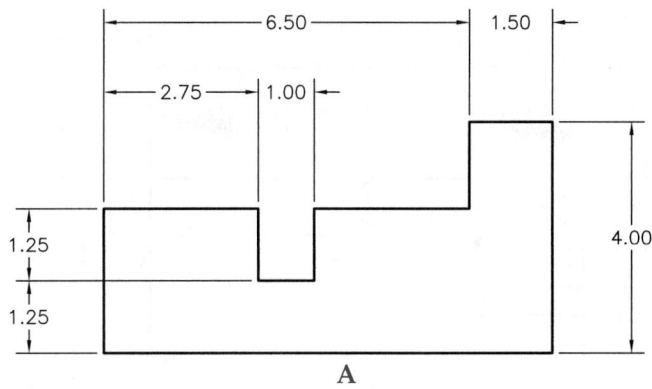

A

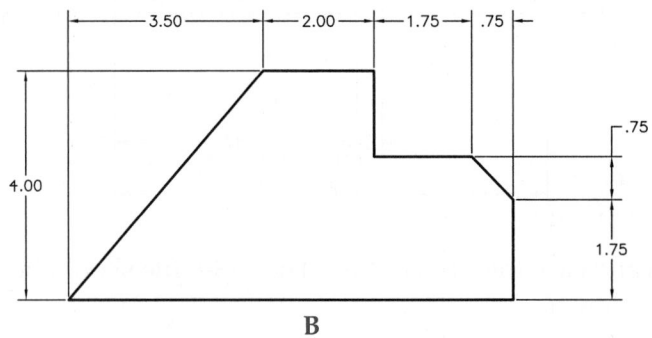

B

4. Open **P3-11** and save the file as **P18-4**. The P18-4 file should be active. Dimension the view as shown.

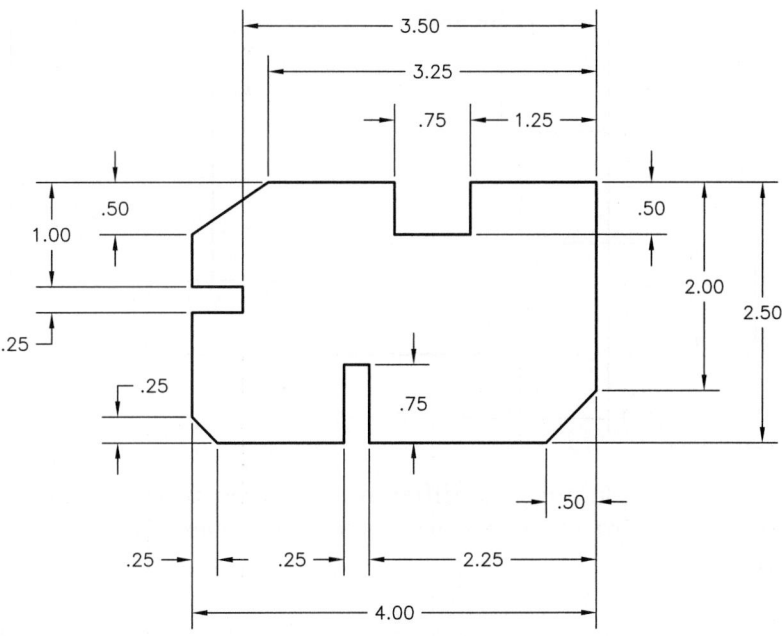

5. Open P3-12 and save the file as P18-5. The P18-5 file should be active. Dimension the views as shown. Note that this is a metric drawing.

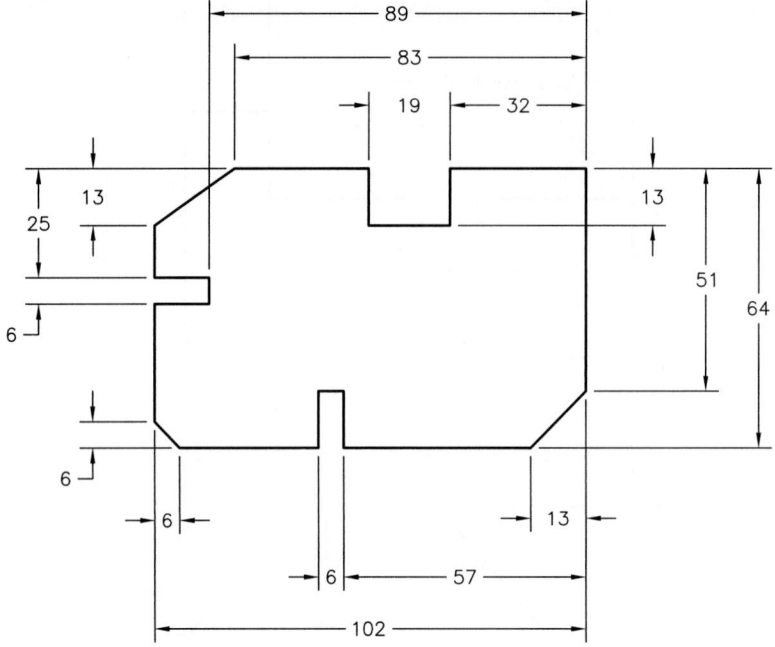

6. Open P3-8 and save the file as P18-6. The P18-6 file should be active. Dimension the view as shown.

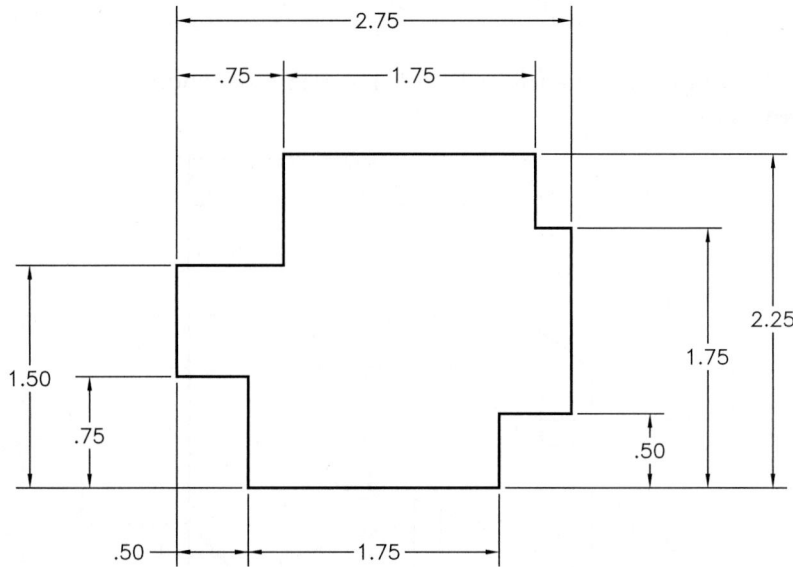

7. Write a report explaining the difference between baseline and chain dimensioning. Use a word processor and include sketches giving examples of each method.

8. Open P3-9 and save the file as P18-7. The P18-7 file should be active. Dimension the view as shown.

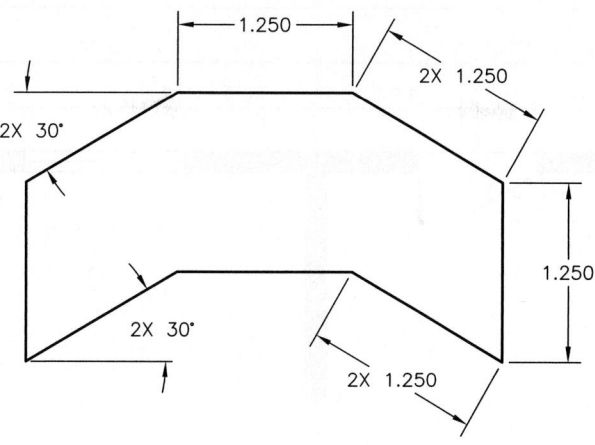

▼ Intermediate

9. Draw and dimension the views of a shaft shown. Save the drawing as P18-9.

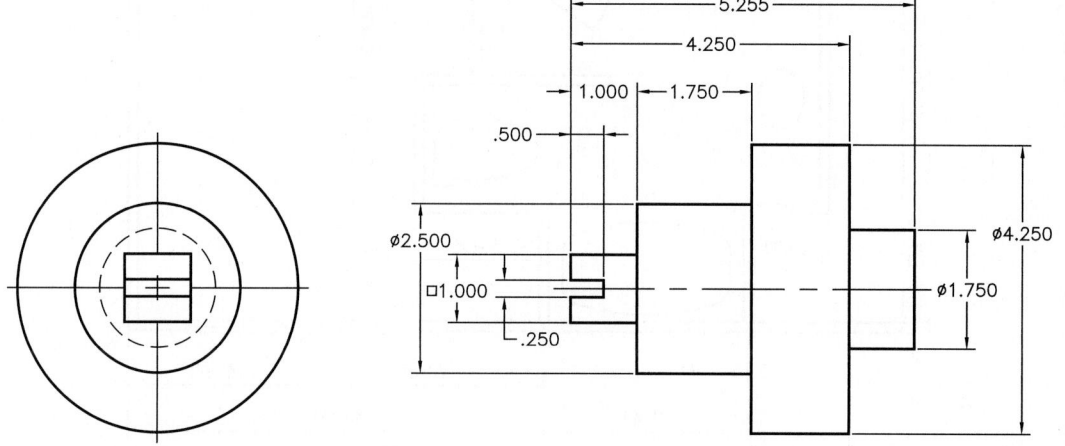

10. Open P3-13 and save the file as P18-10. The P18-10 file should be active. Dimension the view as shown.

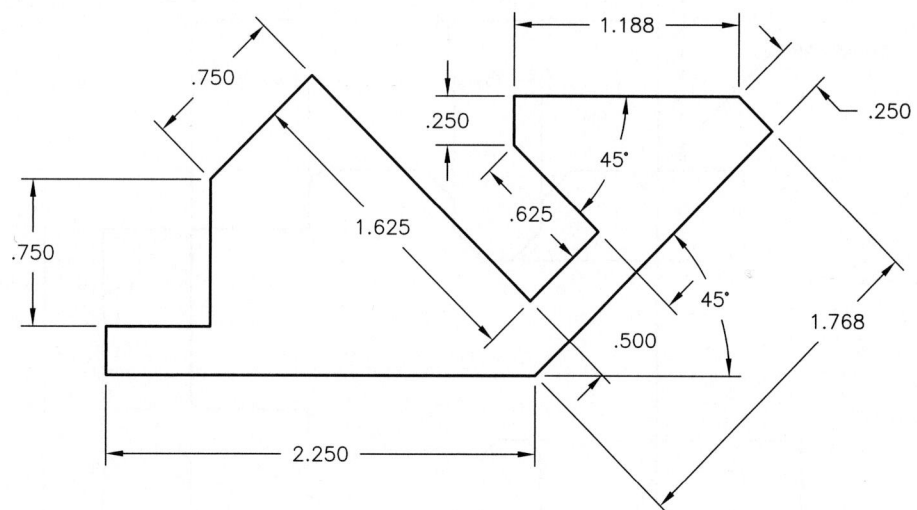

11. Draw and dimension the partial floor plan shown. Save the drawing as P18-11.

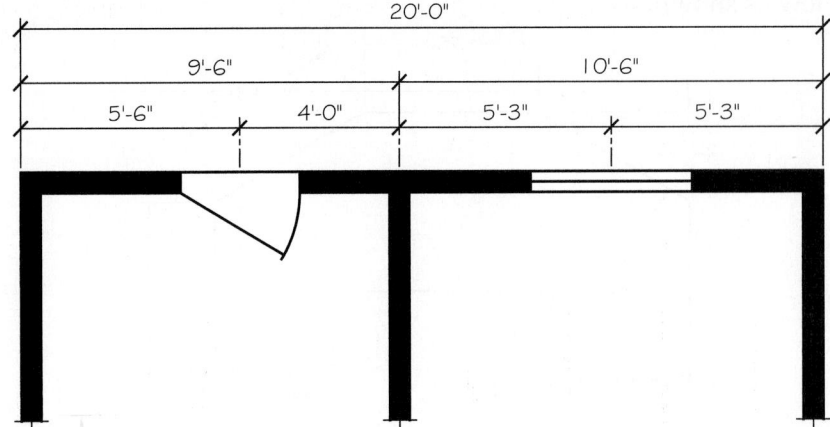

12. Draw and dimension the partial floor plan shown. Save the drawing as P18-12.

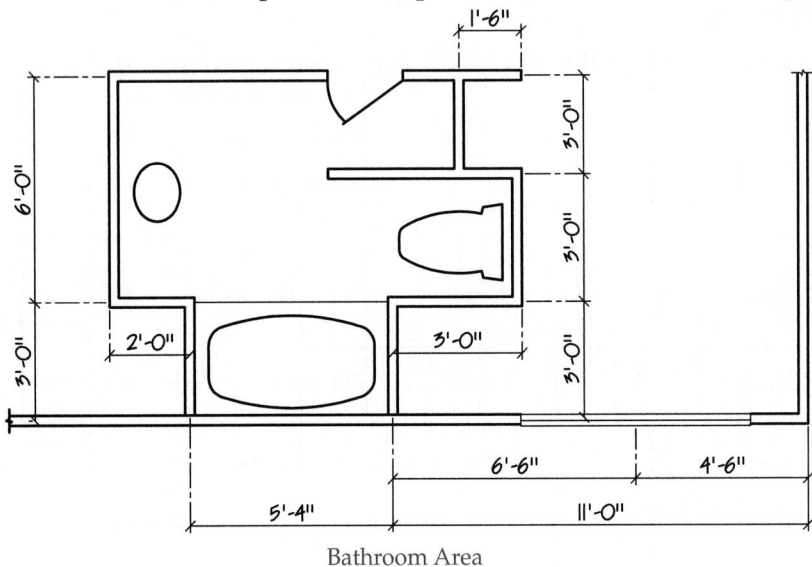

Bathroom Area

13. Draw and dimension the part view shown. Save the drawing as P18-13.

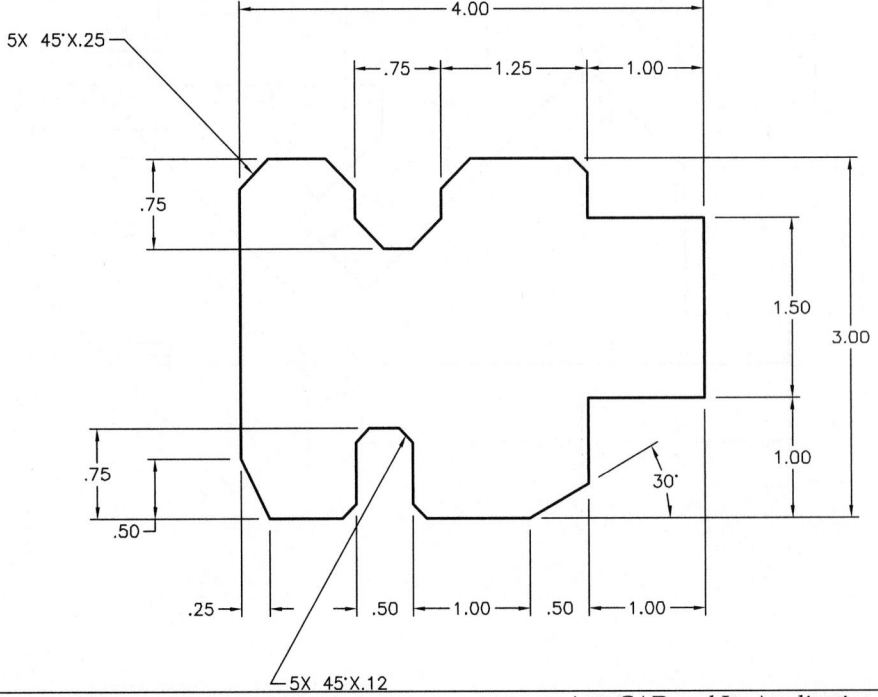

14. Draw and dimension the part view shown. Save the drawing as **P18-14**.

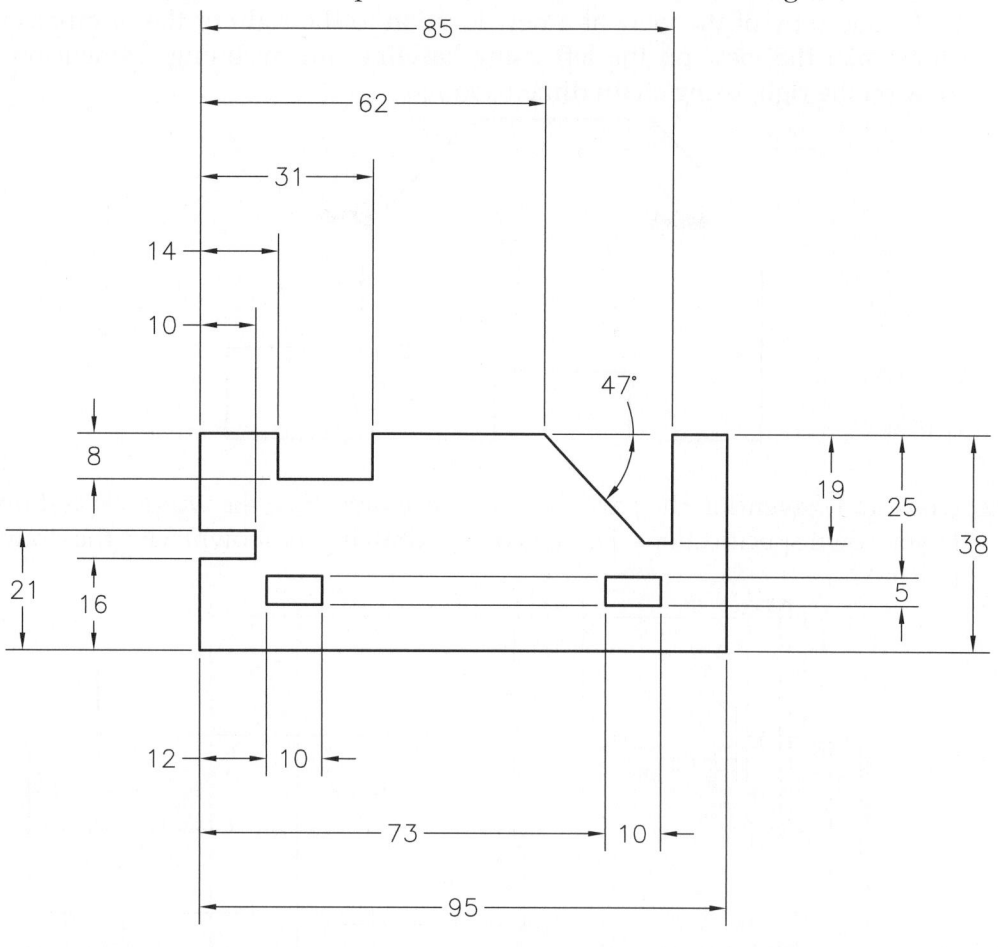

▼ Advanced

15. Open **P8-9** and save the file as **P18-16**. The P18-16 file should be active. Dimension the desk as shown.

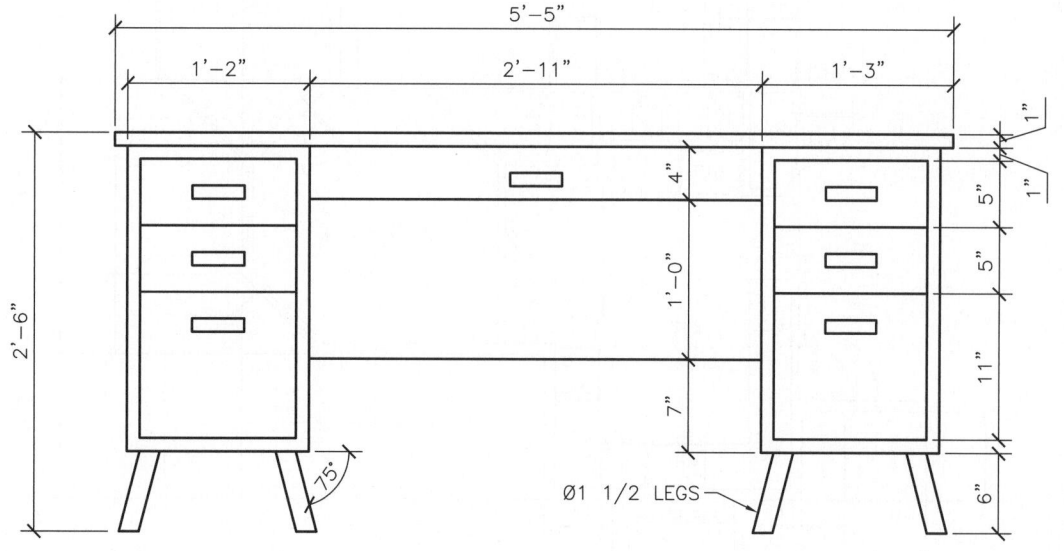

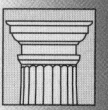

16. Open **P3-3** shown and save the file as **P18-15**. The **P18-15** file should be active. Make one copy of the view at a new location to the right of the original view. Dimension the view on the left using baseline dimensioning. Dimension the view on the right using chain dimensioning.

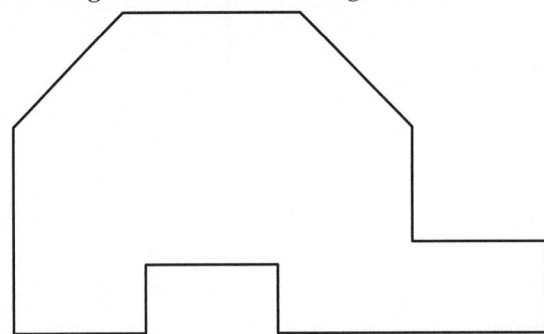

17. Draw and dimension the partial floor plan shown. Size the windows and doors to your own specifications. Dimension the drawing as shown. Save the drawing as **P18-17**.

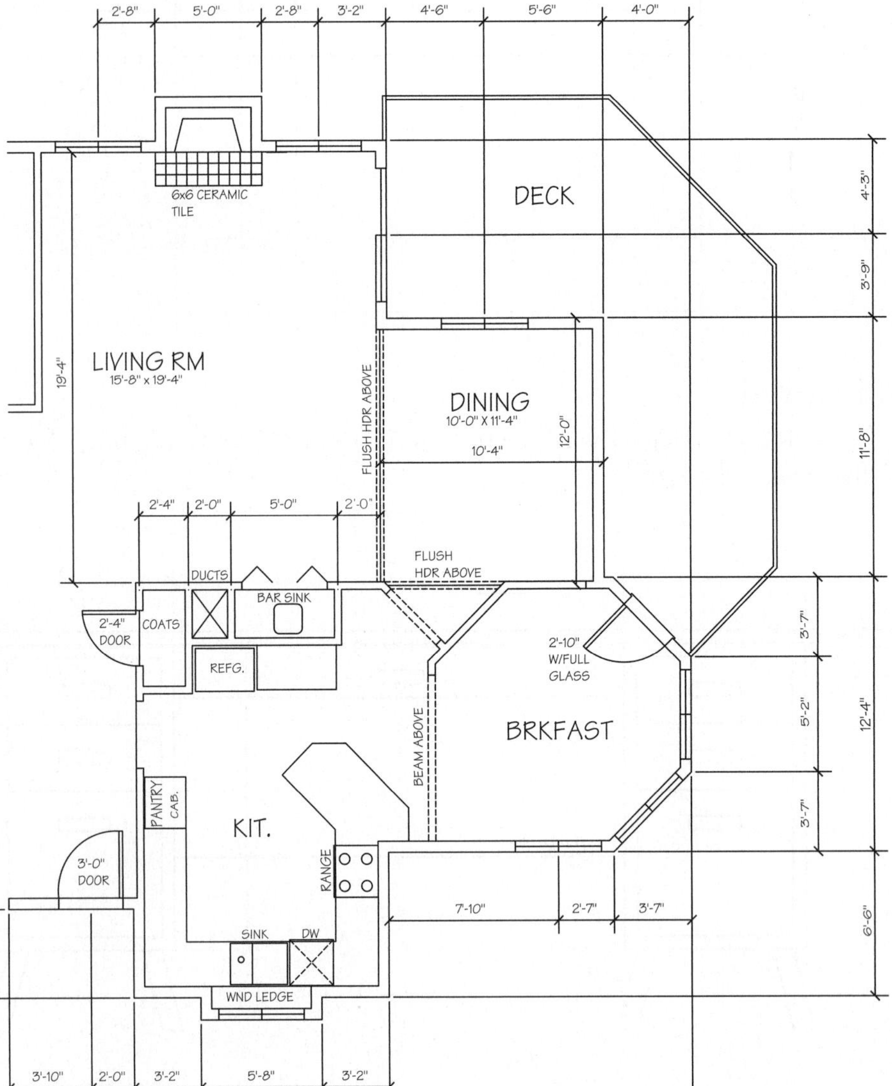

AutoCAD Certified Associate Exam Practice

Answer the following questions. Write your answers on a separate sheet of paper.

1. Which of the following is the *minimum* ASME-recommended spacing from the object to the first dimension line? *Select all that apply.*
   A. .375″
   B. .5″
   C. .75″
   D. 10 mm
   E. 19 mm
   F. 12 mm

2. How can you add a symbol to dimension text? *Select all that apply.*
   A. apply control codes or characters
   B. create a dimension style that references the gdt.shx font
   C. hold [Ctrl] and press an appropriate letter key
   D. press the appropriate function key
   E. use the **Mtext** option of the dimensioning tool
   F. use the **Text** option of the dimensioning tool

3. Which of the following tools continues dimensioning from a previously placed dimension? *Select all that apply.*
   A. **DIMANGULAR**
   B. **DIMBASELINE**
   C. **DIMCONTINUE**
   D. **DIMJOGLINE**
   E. **DIMLINEAR**

AutoCAD Certified Professional Exam Practice

Follow the instructions in each problem. Write your answers on a separate sheet of paper.

1. **Navigate to this chapter on the Student Web site and open CPE-18angles.dwg.**

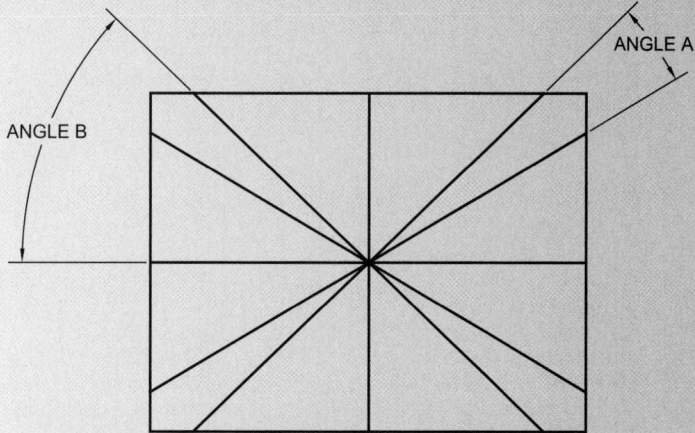

   What are the measured values of ANGLE A and ANGLE B? Use the appropriate dimensioning tool(s) to find the measurements.

2. **Navigate to this chapter on the Student Web site and open CPE-18baseline.dwg.**

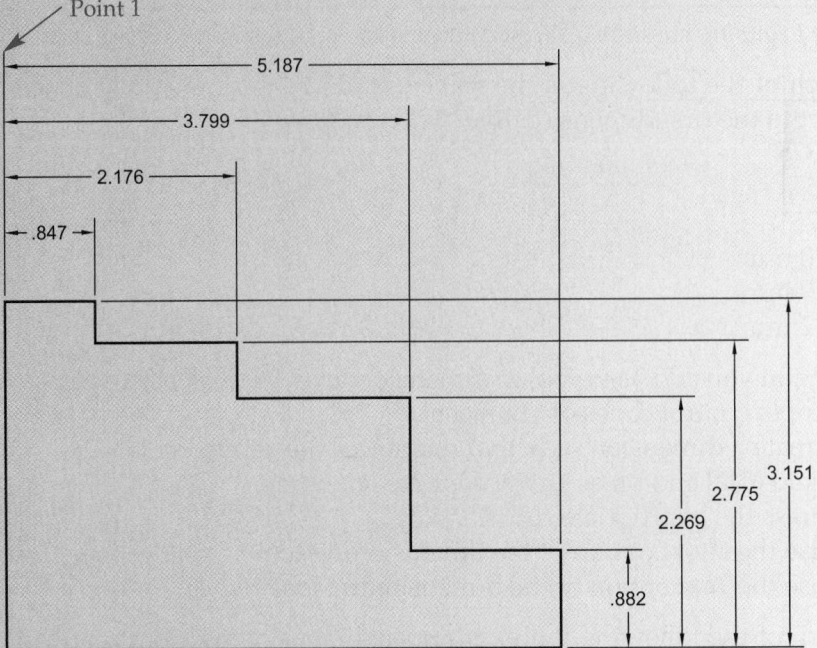

Use the **Dimension Style Manager** to change the baseline spacing in the Standard dimension style to .5, and leave all other settings as they are currently set. Use **DIMBASELINE** to finish the dimensions as shown. What are the coordinates of Point 1?

Dimensioning Features and Alternate Practices

Learning Objectives

After completing this chapter, you will be able to do the following:

✓ Dimension circles and arcs.
✓ Create and use multileader styles.
✓ Draw leaders using the **MLEADER** tool.
✓ Apply alternate dimensioning practices.
✓ Dimension using the **DIMORDINATE** tool.
✓ Mark up a drawing using the **REVCLOUD** and **WIPEOUT** tools.

A drawing must describe the size and location of all features for manufacturing or construction. This chapter explains options for dimensioning object features and introduces alternate mechanical drafting dimensioning practices. This chapter also introduces basic redlining techniques using the **Revision Cloud** and **Wipeout** tools.

Dimensioning Circles

The **DIMDIAMETER** tool allows you to dimension a circle or arc with a diameter. However, diameter is usually used to describe the size of circles. The ASME standard for dimensioning arcs is to identify the radius. Access the **DIMDIAMETER** tool and select a circle or arc to display a leader line and a diameter dimension value attached to the crosshairs. Specify a point to locate the dimension value. See **Figure 19-1**.

Like other dimension tools, the **DIMDIAMETER** tool references the current dimension style and the object you select to create a dimension object. The dimension includes all related dimension style characteristics, centerlines, leader, arrowheads, and a dimension value associated with the diameter. The leader points to the center of the circle or arc, as recommended by the ASME standard.

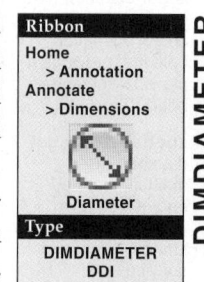

Ribbon
Home
> Annotation
Annotate
> Dimensions

Diameter

Type
DIMDIAMETER
DDI

DIMDIAMETER

NOTE

The **DIMDIAMETER** tool includes the **Mtext**, **Text**, and **Angle** options. Use the **Mtext** or **Text** option to add information to or change the dimension value. The **Angle** option changes the dimension text angle, although this practice is not common.

Figure 19-1. Using the **DIMDIAMETER** tool to dimension a circle.

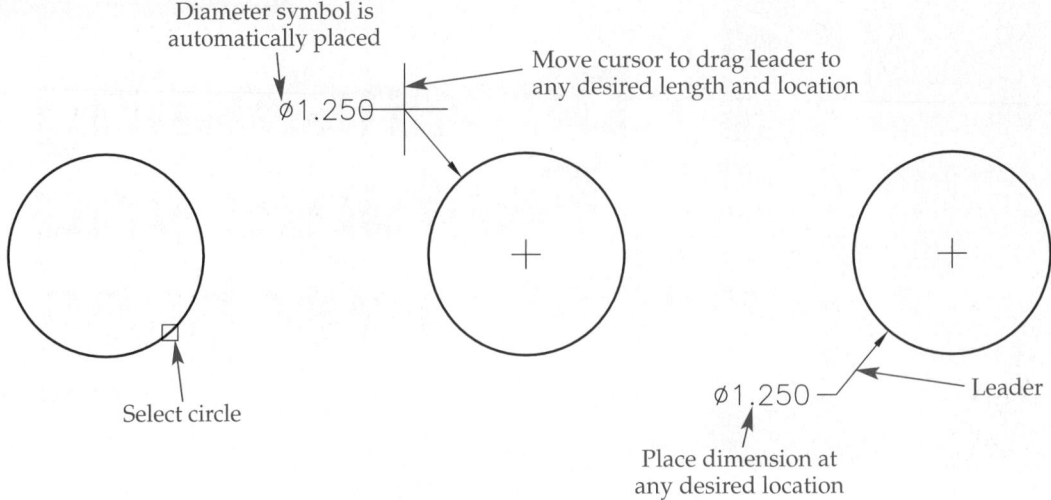

Diameter symbol is automatically placed

Move cursor to drag leader to any desired length and location

Ø1.250

Select circle

Ø1.250

Leader

Place dimension at any desired location

Exercise 19-1

Access the Student Web site (www.g-wlearning.com/CAD) and complete Exercise 19-1.

Dimensioning Holes

Dimension holes in the view in which they appear as circles. Give location dimensions to the center and a leader showing the diameter. The **DIMDIAMETER** tool is effective for dimensioning holes. To note multiple holes of the same size, dimension the size of one hole using the **DIMDIAMETER** tool and the **Mtext** or **Text** option. Precede the diameter with the number of holes followed by X and then a space. See the 2X Ø.50 dimension in **Figure 19-2.**

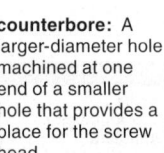

PROFESSIONAL TIP

The ASME standard recommends a small space between the object and the extension line. To specify the space, adjust the **Offset from origin** setting in the dimension style to an appropriate positive value, such as .063 (1.5 mm). This is very useful *except* when you dimension to centerlines to locate circular features. When you pick the endpoint of the centerline, a positive value leaves an unacceptable space between the centerline and the beginning of the extension line. Change the **Offset from origin** setting to 0 to remove the gap. Be sure to change back to the positive setting before dimensioning other objects.

counterbore: A larger-diameter hole machined at one end of a smaller hole that provides a place for the screw head.

spotface: A larger-diameter hole machined at one end of a smaller hole that provides a smooth, recessed surface for a washer; similar to a counterbore, but not as deep.

countersink: A cone-shaped recess at one end of a hole that provides a mating surface for a screw head of the same shape.

block: A symbol previously created and saved for reuse.

Dimensioning for Manufacturing Processes

Counterbore, spotface, and *countersink* manufacturing processes are examples of features dimensioned using symbols. Dimension manufacturing processes in the view in which they appear as circles, with a leader providing machining information in a note. See **Figure 19-3.** The **Mtext** option of the **DIMDIAMETER** tool provides a convenient method for dimensioning manufacturing processes. Many symbols are available in the gdt.shx font. You can also create custom symbols as *blocks*. Blocks are described later in this textbook.

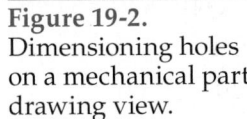

Figure 19-2.
Dimensioning holes on a mechanical part drawing view.

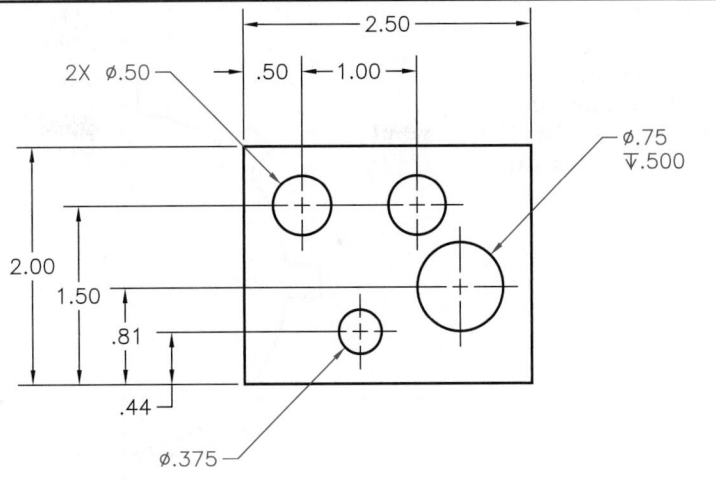

Figure 19-3.
Dimension notes for machining processes. You can insert symbols as blocks or use lowercase letters in the gdt.shx font.

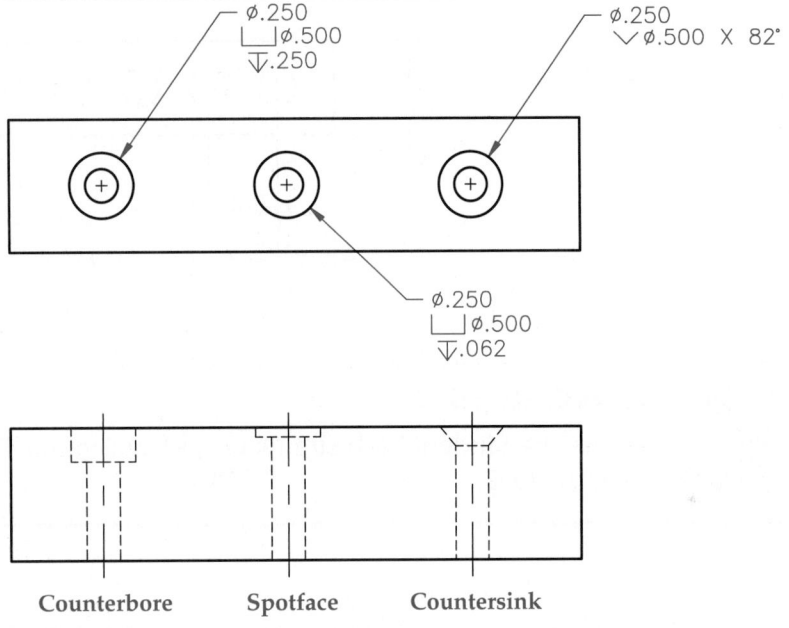

Counterbore   Spotface   Countersink

Drafting Symbols

For more information about common drafting symbols and the gdt.shx font, go to the **Reference Material** section of the Student Web site (www.g-wlearning.com/CAD) and select **Drafting Symbols** in the list.

Dimensioning Repetitive Features

Dimension *repetitive features* with the number of repetitions followed by an X, a space, and the dimension value. See **Figure 19-4.** Use a dimension tool appropriate for the application, and use the **Mtext** or **Text** option to add repetitive information to the dimension value. Use the **MLEADER** tool, described later in this chapter, to create the 8X note shown in **Figure 19-4.**

repetitive features: Many features having the same shape and size.

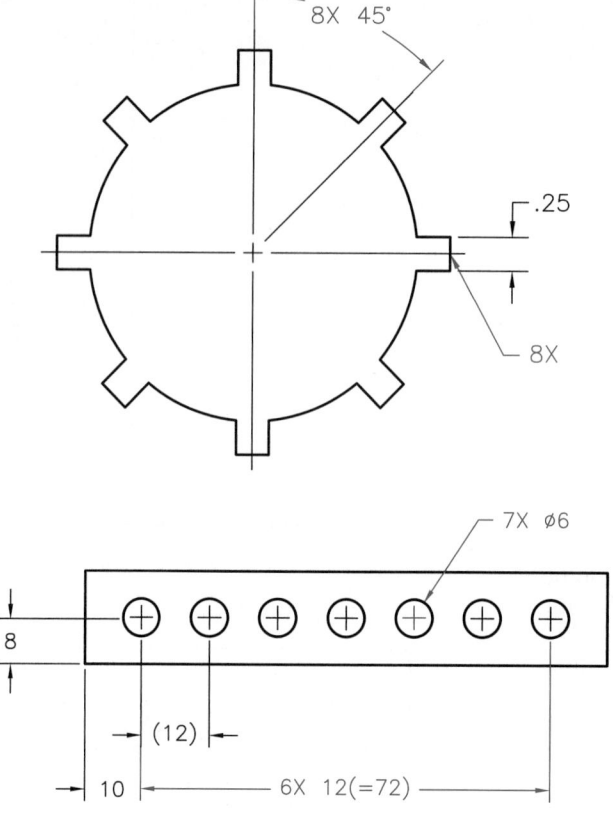

Figure 19-4.
Dimensioning
repetitive features
(shown in color) on
a drawing view of
different mechanical
parts.

Exercise 19-2

Access the Student Web site (www.g-wlearning.com/CAD) and complete
Exercise 19-2.

Dimensioning Arcs

The **DIMRADIUS** tool allows you to dimension an arc or circle with a radius.
However, the radius is usually used to describe the size of arcs. The ASME standard
for dimensioning circles is to identify the diameter. Access the **DIMRADIUS** tool and
select an arc or circle to display a leader line and a radius dimension value attached to
the crosshairs. Specify a point to locate the dimension value. See **Figure 19-5**.

Like other dimension tools, the **DIMRADIUS** tool references the current dimension
style and the object you select to create a dimension object. The dimension includes all
related dimension style characteristics, centerlines, leader, arrowheads, and a dimension value associated with the radius. The leader points to the center of the arc or circle,
as recommended by the ASME standard.

> **NOTE**
>
> The **DIMRADIUS** tool includes the **Mtext**, **Text**, and **Angle** options.
> Use the **Mtext** or **Text** option to add information to or change the
> dimension value. The **Angle** option changes the dimension text
> angle, although this practice is not common.

Figure 19-5. Using the **DIMRADIUS** tool to dimension arcs.

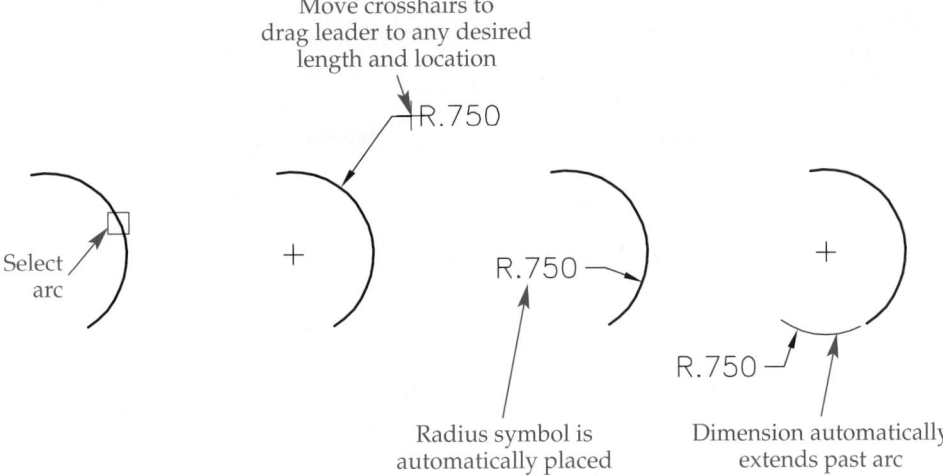

Move crosshairs to
drag leader to any desired
length and location

R.750

Select
arc

R.750

Radius symbol is
automatically placed

R.750

Dimension automatically
extends past arc

Dimensioning Arc Length

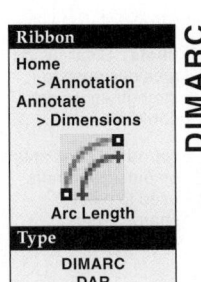

Access the **DIMARC** tool to dimension the length of an arc. Select an arc or polyline arc segment to display the arc length symbol and dimension value attached to the crosshairs. Specify a point to locate the dimension value. By default, the arc length symbol occurs before the text. The ASME standard recommends placing the symbol over the text, as shown in **Figure 19-6**. The dimension style controls the symbol placement.

Before placing the arc length dimension, add information to or change the dimension value using the **Mtext** or **Text** option. The **Angle** option is available to change the text angle. Use the **Partial** option to dimension a portion of the arc length. Select two points on the arc to dimension the length between the points. The **Leader** option, which is available when the arc is greater than 90°, allows you to add a leader pointing to the arc.

Dimensioning Large Arcs

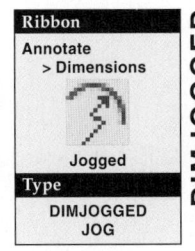

Use the **DIMJOGGED** tool to dimension an arc that is so large that the center point cannot appear on the layout. Jogging a dimension line is most appropriate for large arcs, but you can select a circle. Access the **DIMJOGGED** tool and pick an arc or circle. Then pick a location for the origin of the center. This point represents the center of the arc or circle. The associated radius value does not change. Select a location for the dimension line and then pick a location for the break symbol. See **Figure 19-7**. You can move the components of the dimension by grip editing after you place the dimension.

Figure 19-6.
Using the **DIMARC**
tool to dimension
the length of an arc.

Length
dimension

Arc length
symbol

Dimension
line

8.900

Arc

Figure 19-7.
Using the
DIMJOGGED tool
to place a radius
dimension for a
large arc.

Arc

Dimension
line

R28.14

Radius
dimension

Jog symbol

Center point
origin (override)

Dimensioning Fillets and Rounds

fillets: Small inside
arcs designed to
strengthen inside
corners.

rounds: Small arcs
on outside corners
used to relieve
sharp corners.

You can dimension *fillets* and *rounds* individually as arcs, using the **DIMRADIUS** tool, or collectively in a general note. See **Figure 19-8.** On mechanical drawings, it is common to include a general note such as ALL FILLETS AND ROUNDS R.125 UNLESS OTHERWISE SPECIFIED on the drawing.

Exercise 19-3

Access the Student Web site (www.g-wlearning.com/CAD) and complete Exercise 19-3.

Dimensioning Curves

Dimension curves as arcs when possible. When an arc does not have a constant radius, dimension to points along the curve using the **DIMLINEAR** tool. See **Figure 19-9.**

Adding Center Dashes and Centerlines

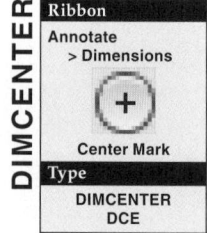

DIMCENTER

Ribbon
Annotate
> Dimensions
Center Mark
Type
DIMCENTER
DCE

Depending on the current dimension style setting, when you use the **DIMDIAMETER** and **DIMRADIUS** tools, small circles or arcs automatically receive center dashes, and large circles or arcs display center dashes or centerlines. Use the **DIMCENTER** tool to add center dashes or centerlines to objects that are not dimensioned using the **DIMDIAMETER** or **DIMRADIUS** tools. Access the **DIMCENTER** tool and pick a circle or an arc to display center marks.

The **DIMCENTER** tool references the current dimension style and the size of the circle or arc to place center dashes, centerlines, or no symbol. The ASME standard refers to AutoCAD center marks as the center dashes of centerlines. Center marks typically apply to circular objects that are too small to receive centerlines. Center marks are also common for rectangular coordinate dimensioning without dimension lines, regardless of circular object size, as described later in this chapter.

Figure 19-8.
Dimensioning fillets and rounds.

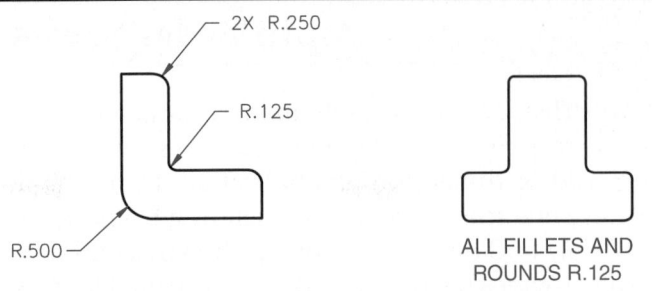

Figure 19-9.
Dimensioning curves that do not have a constant radius.

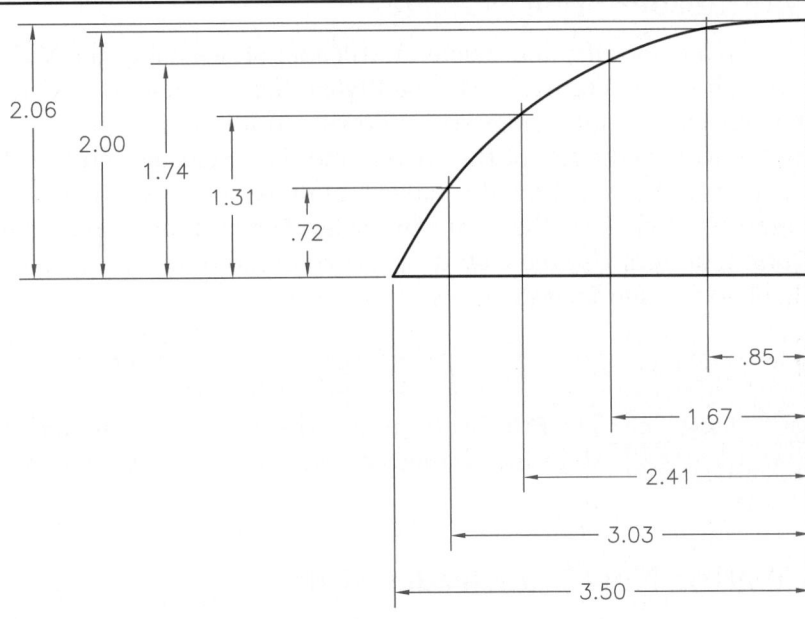

Drawing Leader Lines

The **DIMDIAMETER** and **DIMRADIUS** tools automatically place *leader lines* when you dimension circles and arcs. AutoCAD multileaders created using the **MLEADER** tool allow you to add leader lines for other applications, such as specific notes. Multileaders consist of single or multiple lines of *annotations*, including symbols, with the leader. Multileader styles control multileader characteristics, such as leader format, annotation style, and arrowhead size. You can create multi-segment leaders and align and group separate leaders. Chapter 21 describes adding and removing multiple leader lines and aligning leaders.

leader line: A line that connects a note or symbol to a specific feature or location on a drawing.

annotation: Textual information presented in notes, specifications, comments, and symbols.

NOTE

QLEADER and **LEADER** tools are available to create leader lines, but provide fewer options than the **MLEADER** tool.

multileader styles: Saved configurations for the appearance of leaders.

shoulder: A short horizontal line usually added to the end of straight leader lines.

A *multileader style* presets many multileader characteristics. Multileader style settings correspond to appropriate drafting standards and usually apply to a specific drafting field or dimensioning application. In mechanical drafting, properly drawn leaders have one straight segment extending from the feature to a horizontal *shoulder* that is 1/8"–1/4" (3 mm–6 mm) long. While most other fields also use straight leaders, AutoCAD provides the option of drawing curved leaders, which are common in architectural drafting. See **Figure 19-10.**

Multileader Style Manager

Ribbon
Home
> Annotation

Multileader Style
Annotate
> Leaders

Multileader Style

Type
MLEADERSTYLE
MLS

Create, modify, and delete multileader styles using the **Multileader Style Manager** dialog box. See **Figure 19-11.** The **Styles:** list box displays existing multileader styles. The Annotative multileader style allows you to create annotative leaders, as indicated by the icon to the left of the style name. The Standard multileader style does not use the annotative function. To make a multileader style current, double-click the style name, right-click on the name and select **Set current**, or pick the name and select the **Current** button. Use the **List:** drop-down list to filter the number of multileader styles displayed in the **Styles:** list box.

> **NOTE**
>
> The **Preview of:** image displays a representation of the multileader style and changes according to the selections you make.

Creating New Multileader Styles

To create a new multileader style, select an existing multileader style from the **Styles:** list box to use as a base for formatting the new multileader style. Then pick the **New...** button to open the **Create New Multileader Style** dialog box. See **Figure 19-12.**

Figure 19-10. Multileader styles control the display of leaders created using the **MLEADER** tool.

PITCH 64 RAISED
DIAMOND KNURL

Annotation using
a ROMANS font

Straight
leader line

Annotation using
a STYLUS BT font

Spline
leader line

30" SINGLE SINK

Architectural

Mechanical

Figure 19-11. The **Multileader Style Manager** dialog box.

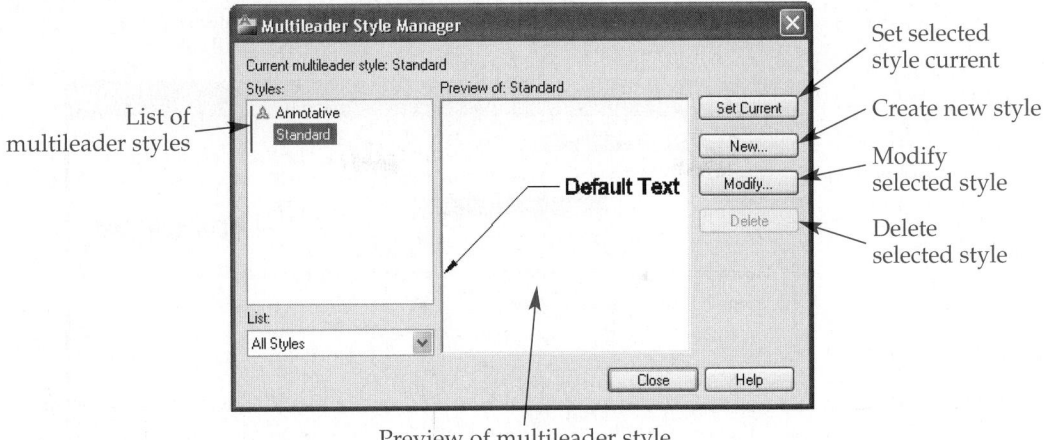

List of multileader styles

Set selected style current

Create new style

Modify selected style

Delete selected style

Preview of multileader style

Figure 19-12.
The **Create New Multileader Style** dialog box.

Name new style

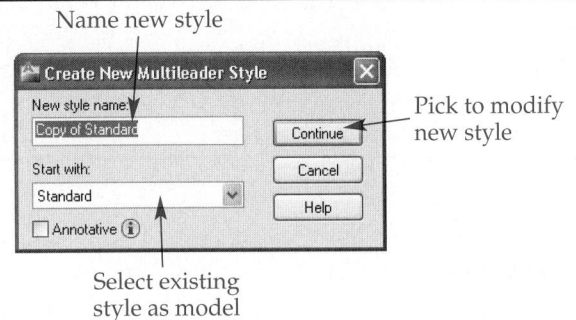

Pick to modify new style

Select existing style as model

You can base the new multileader style on the formatting of a different multileader style by selecting from the **Start With** drop-down list. Notice that Copy of followed by the name of the existing style appears in the **New Style Name** text box. Replace the default name with a more descriptive name, such as Mechanical, Architectural, Straight, or Spline. Multileader style names can have up to 255 characters, including uppercase or lowercase letters, numbers, dashes (–), underlines (_), and dollar signs ($).

Pick the **Annotative** check box to make the multileader style annotative. **Pick the Continue** button to access the **Modify Multileader Style** dialog box, shown in **Figure 19-13.** The **Leader Format**, **Leader Structure**, and **Content** tabs display groups of settings for specifying leader appearance, as described in this chapter. After completing the style definition, pick the **OK** button to return to the **Multileader Style Manager** dialog box.

NOTE

The preview image in the upper-right corner of each **Modify Multileader Style** dialog box tab displays a representation of the multileader style and changes according to the selections you make.

Leader Format Tab

Figure 19-13 shows the **Leader Format** tab of the **Modify Multileader Style** dialog box. The **Leader Format** tab presets the appearance of the leader line and arrowhead. You can edit specific leaders when necessary without using a separate multileader style.

Figure 19-13. The **Leader Format** tab of the **Modify Multileader Style** dialog box.

General multileader format settings

Multileader arrowhead settings

Multileader break size setting

Preview image is displayed in all tabs

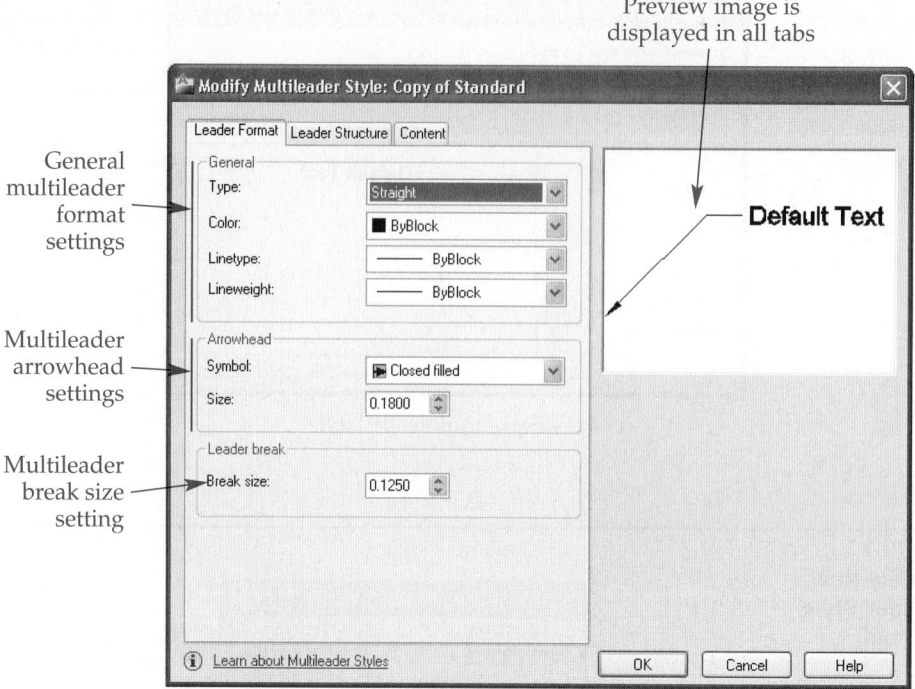

General Settings

The **General** area contains a **Type** drop-down list that you can use to specify the leader line shape. The **Straight** option produces leaders with straight-line segments. The **Spline** option produces curved leader lines, which are common in architectural drafting. Pick the **None** option to create a multileader style that does not use a leader line. Use the **None** option to create a leader that you can associate with other leaders using the **MLEADERALIGN** and **MLEADERCOLLECT** tools, described in Chapter 21.

Color, **Linetype**, and **Lineweight** drop-down lists are available for changing the dimension line color, linetype, and lineweight. Multileaders are block objects. Chapter 24 explains blocks and provides complete information on using ByBlock, ByLayer, or absolute color, lineweight, and linetype with blocks. For now, as long as you assign a specific layer to a multileader and do not change the *multileader* properties to absolute values, the default ByBlock properties are acceptable.

Arrowhead Settings

The **Arrowhead** area sets the leader arrowhead style and size. Select the arrowhead style from the **Symbol:** drop-down list. The arrowhead symbol options are the same as those for dimension style arrowheads. Set the arrowhead size using the **Size:** text box. A .125" (3 mm) arrowhead size is most common, especially on mechanical drawings. Leader arrowheads are typically the same size as dimension arrowheads.

Adjusting Break Size

The **Leader Break** area controls the amount of leader line hidden by the **DIMBREAK** tool. Specify a value in the **Break size:** text box to set the total length of the break. The default size is .125" (3 mm). ASME standards do not recommend breaking leader lines.

AutoCAD and Its Applications—Basics

Leader Structure Tab

Figure 19-14 shows the **Leader Structure** tab of the **Modify Multileader Style** dialog box. Use the **Leader Structure** tab to control leader construction and size. You can edit specific leaders when necessary without using a separate multileader style.

Setting Constraints

The **Constraints** area restricts the number of points you can select to create a leader, and the leader line angle. Pick the **Maximum leader points** check box to set a maximum number of vertices on the leader line. The multileader automatically forms once you pick the maximum number of points. To use fewer than the maximum number of points, press [Enter] at the Specify next point: prompt. Deselect the **Maximum leader points** check box to allow an unlimited number of vertices.

Use the **First segment angle** and **Second segment angle** check boxes to restrict the first two leader line segments to certain angles. Deselect the check boxes to draw leader lines at any angle. Select the appropriate check boxes and pick a value from the drop-down list to restrict the angle of the leader segment according to the selected value. **Ortho** mode overrides angle constraints, so it is advisable to turn **Ortho** mode off while you are placing leaders.

PROFESSIONAL TIP

The ASME standard for leaders recommends that leader lines have angles not less than 15° and not greater than 75° from horizontal. Use the **First segment angle** and **Second segment angle** settings to help maintain this standard.

Landing Settings

The **Landing settings** area controls the display and size of the *landing* and is only available with straight-line multileader styles. Select the **Automatically include landing** check box to display a shoulder automatically when you select the second leader line

> **landing:** The AutoCAD term for a leader shoulder.

Figure 19-14. The **Leader Structure** tab of the **Modify Multileader Style** dialog box.

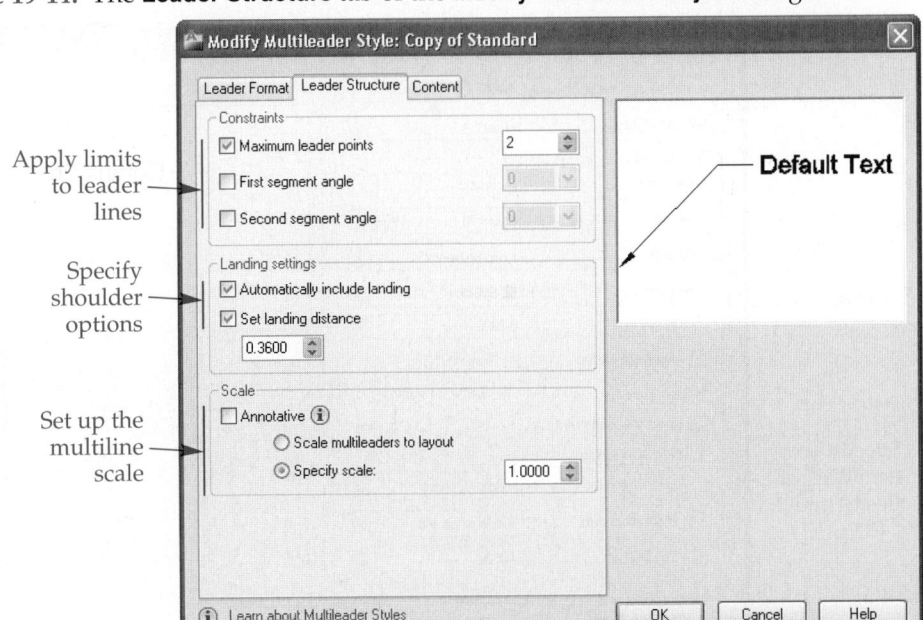

point. This is the preferred method for creating straight leader lines. Deselect the check box to create leaders without shoulders, or to pick a third point to draw the shoulder manually. When you check **Automatically include landing**, the **Set landing distance** check box becomes enabled. Check **Set landing distance** to define a specific shoulder length, typically 1/8″–1/4″ (3 mm–6 mm), in the text box. If you deselect the text box, a prompt asks for the shoulder length when you place a leader.

Scale Options

The **Scale** area sets the multileader scale factor. Select the **Annotative** check box to create an annotative multileader style. The **Annotative** check box is already set when you modify the Annotative multileader style or pick the **Annotative** check box in the **Create New Multileader Style** dialog box.

Select the **Scale dimensions to layout** radio button to add leaders in a floating viewport in a paper space layout. You must add leaders to the model in a floating viewport in order for this option to function. Scaling leaders to the layout allows the overall scale to adjust according to the active floating viewport by setting the overall scale equal to the viewport scale factor.

Pick the **Use overall scale of** radio button to scale a drawing manually. Enter the drawing scale factor to apply to all leader elements in the corresponding text box. The scale factor is multiplied by the plotted leader size to get the size of the leader in model space. For example, if you manually scale multileaders for a drawing with a 1:2 (half) scale, or a scale factor of 2 (2 ÷ 1 = 2), you must enter 2 in the **Use overall scale of** text box.

Content Tab

Figure 19-15 shows the **Content** tab of the **Modify Multileader Style** dialog box. The **Content** tab controls the display of text or a block with the leader line. Use the **Multileader type:** drop-down list to select the type of object to attach to the end of the leader line or shoulder. **Figure 19-16** shows an example of a leader drawn with each content option. You can edit specific leaders when necessary, without using a separate multileader style.

Figure 19-15. The **Content** tab of the **Modify Multileader Style** dialog box with the **Mtext** multileader type selected.

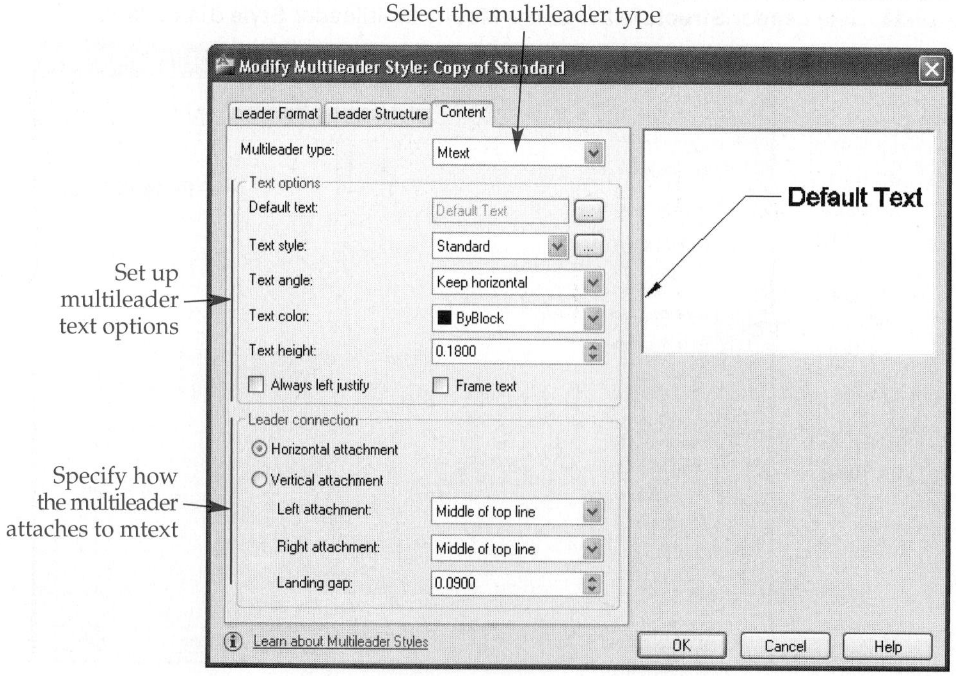

AutoCAD and Its Applications—Basics

Figure 19-16. Examples of each multileader content type.

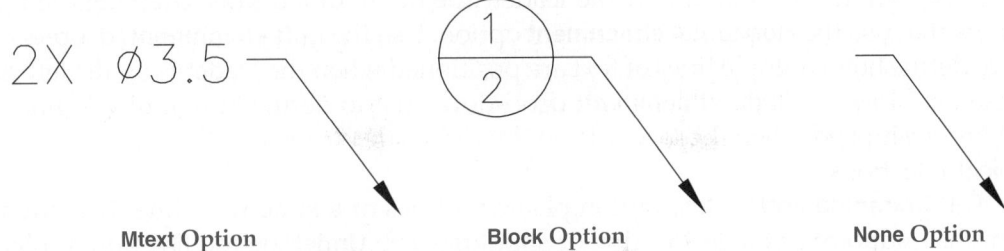

Mtext Option   Block Option   None Option

Attaching Mtext

Pick the **Mtext** option from the **Multileader type:** drop-down list, as shown in **Figure 19-15**, to attach multiline text to the leader. The **Text options** and **Leader connection** areas of the **Content** tab appear when you select the **Mtext** content type. The **Default text** option allows you to specify a value to attach leaders during leader placement. This is useful when the same note or symbol is required throughout a drawing. Pick the ellipsis (...) button to return to the drawing window and use the multiline text editor to enter the default text value. Close the text editor to return to the **Modify Multileader Style** dialog box.

A multileader style references a text style for the appearance of leader text. Pick an existing text style from the **Text style** drop-down list. To create or modify a text style, pick the ellipsis (…) button next to the drop-down list to launch the **Text Style** dialog box.

Select an option from the **Text angle** drop-down list to control the angle at which text appears in reference to the angle of the leader line or shoulder. See **Figure 19-17.** Use the **Text color** drop-down list to specify the text color, which should be ByBlock for typical applications. Use the **Text height** text box to specify the leader text height. Leader text height is usually the same as dimension text height.

The **Always left justify** option forces leader text to left-justify, regardless of the leader line direction. Pick the **Frame text** check box to create a box around the leader text. A basic dimension is a common application for framed text, as described later in this book.

Figure 19-17. Text angle options available for mtext.

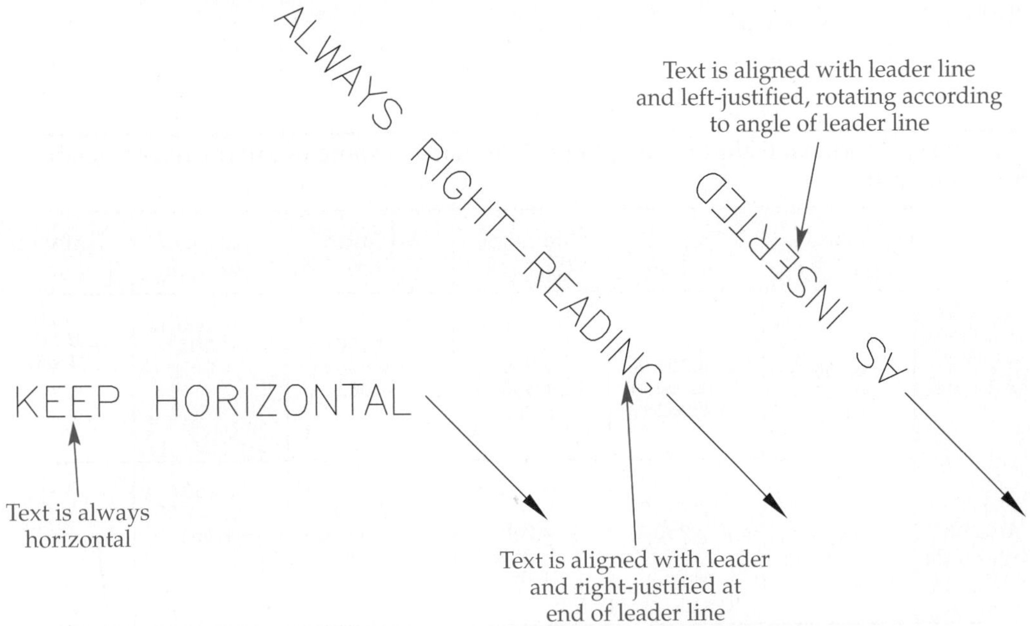

ALWAYS RIGHT–READING

AS INSERTED

Text is aligned with leader line and left-justified, rotating according to angle of leader line

KEEP HORIZONTAL

Text is always horizontal

Text is aligned with leader and right-justified at end of leader line

The **Leader connection** area contains options that determine how mtext is positioned relative to the endpoint of the leader line or shoulder. Most drawings require leaders that use the **Horizontal attachment** option. Use the **Left attachment:** drop-down list to define how multiple lines of text are positioned when the leader is on the left side of the text. Use the **Right attachment:** drop-down list to define how multiple lines of text are positioned when the leader is on the right side of the text. **Figure 19-18** shows typical selections.

The **Underline bottom line** option places all lines of text above a line that extends from the endpoint of the leader line or shoulder. The **Underline top line** option places the first line of text above a line that extends from the endpoint of the leader line or shoulder. The **Underline all text** option places the first line of text above a line that extends from the endpoint of the leader line or shoulder, and underlines the lines of text below. The **Leading gap** text box specifies the space between the leader line or shoulder and the text. The default is .09, but .063 (1.5 mm) is standard.

PROFESSIONAL TIP

Common drafting practice is to use the **Middle of bottom line** option for left attachment and the **Middle of top line** option for right attachment. The **Middle of text** option is sometimes necessary to display a single line of text that includes a horizontally stacked fraction.

Selecting the **Vertical attachment** radio button is uncommon. This option eliminates the possible use of a shoulder and connects the leader endpoint to the top center or bottom center of the text, depending on the leader line position. Use the **Top attachment:** drop-down list to define how text is positioned when the leader is above the text. Use the **Bottom attachment:** drop-down list to define how text is positioned when the leader is below the text. **Figure 19-19** shows each option.

Attaching a Symbol

Pick the **Block** option from the **Multileader type:** drop-down list, as shown in **Figure 19-20**, to attach a block to the leader. Blocks are described later in this textbook. Several blocks are available by default from the **Source block:** drop-down list. Pick the **User Block...** option to select a custom saved block. The **Select Custom Content Block** dialog box appears when you pick the **User Block...** option. Pick a block in the current drawing from the **Select from Drawing Blocks:** drop-down list and then pick the **OK** button.

Figure 19-18. Horizontal alignment options. The shaded examples are the recommended ASME standards.

	Top of Top Line	Middle of Top Line	Bottom of Top Line	Middle of Multiline Text	Middle of Bottom Line	Bottom of Bottom Line
Text on Left Side	⌀.250 ⌴⌀.500 ▽.062	⌀.250 ⌴⌀.500 ▽.062	⌀.250 ⌴⌀.500 ▽.062	⌀.250 ⌴⌀.500 ▽.062	⌀.250 ⌴⌀.500 ▽.062	⌀.250 ⌴⌀.500 ▽.062
Text on Right Side	⌀.250 ⌴⌀.500 ▽.062	⌀.250 ⌴⌀.500 ▽.062	⌀.250 ⌴⌀.500 ▽.062	⌀.250 ⌴⌀.500 ▽.062	⌀.250 ⌴⌀.500 ▽.062	⌀.250 ⌴⌀.500 ▽.062

Figure 19-19.
Vertical alignment
options.

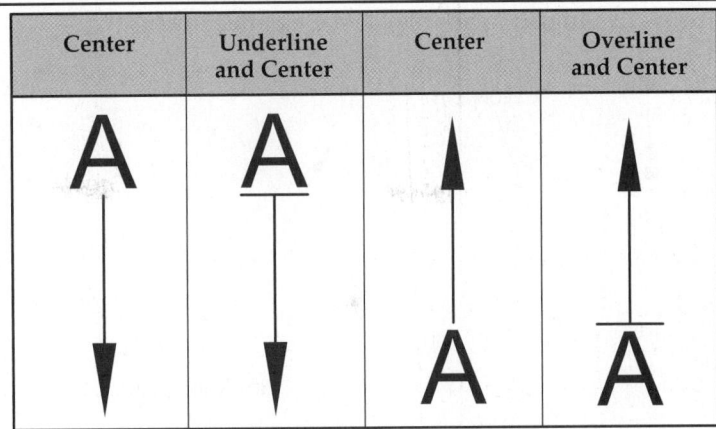

Center	Underline and Center	Center	Overline and Center

Figure 19-20. The **Content** tab of the **Modify Multileader Style** dialog box with the **Block** multileader type selected.

Select the
multileader type

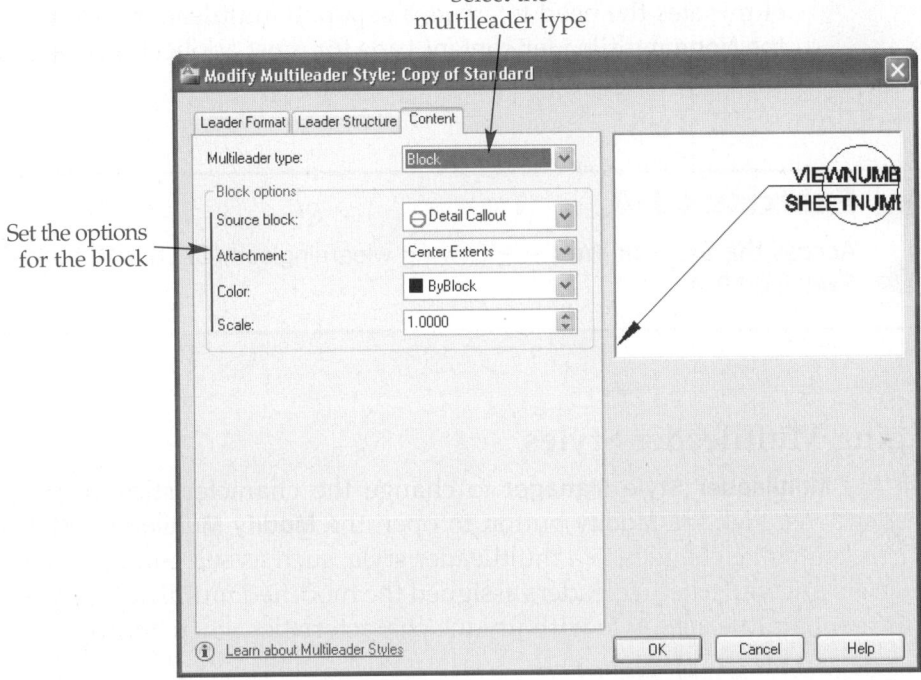

Set the options
for the block

Use the **Attachment:** drop-down list to specify how to attach the block to the leader. Pick the **Insertion point** option to attach the block to the leader according to the block insertion point, or base point. Choose the **Center extents** option to attach the block directly to the leader, aligned to the center of the block, even if the block insertion point is not on the block itself. See **Figure 19-21.**

Use the **Color** drop-down list to specify the block color, which should be ByBlock for typical applications. Use the **Scale** text box to proportionately increase or decrease the block size. Scale does not affect the appearance of the leader line, arrowhead, or shoulder, or the scale applied to the multileader object.

Using No Content

Select the **None** option from the **Multileader type:** drop-down list to end the leader without annotation. Use the **None** option when you need to create only a leader, without text or a symbol attached to the leader line or shoulder.

Figure 19-21. Adjusting multileader block attachment.

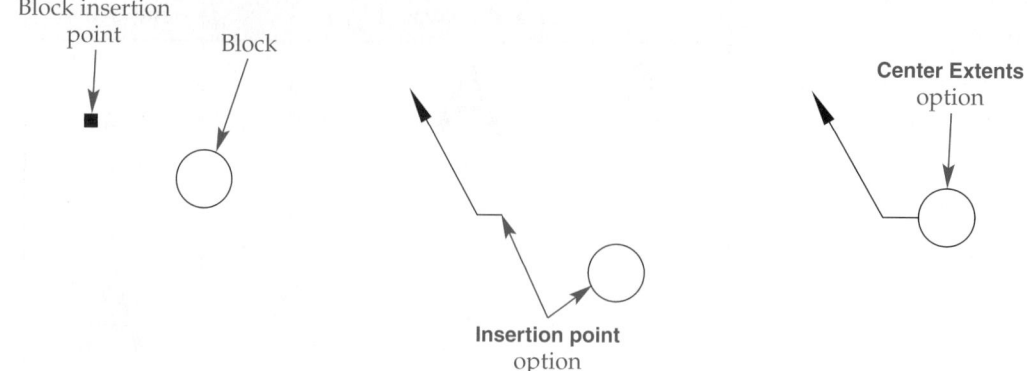

Block insertion
point

Block

Center Extents
option

Insertion point
option

> **NOTE**
>
> Add leaders to existing multileaders using the **Add Leader** tool. This eliminates the need to create a separate multileader style that uses the **None** multileader content type for most applications.

Exercise 19-4

Access the Student Web site (www.g-wlearning.com/CAD) and complete Exercise 19-4.

Changing Multileader Styles

Use the **Multileader Style Manager** to change the characteristics of an existing multileader style. Pick the **Modify** button to open the **Modify Multileader Style** dialog box. When you make changes to a multileader style, such as selecting a different text or arrowhead style, all existing leaders assigned the modified multileader style update. Use a different multileader style with unique characteristics when appropriate.

Renaming and Deleting Multileader Styles

To rename a multileader style using the **Multileader Style Manager**, slowly double-click on the name or right-click on the name and select **Rename**. To delete a multileader style using the **Multileader Style Manager**, right-click the name and select **Delete**. You cannot delete a multileader style assigned to leaders. To delete a style that is in use, assign a different style to the leaders that reference the style to be deleted.

> **NOTE**
>
> You can also rename styles using the **Rename** dialog box. Select **Multileader styles** in the **Named Objects** list to rename a multileader style.

Setting a Multileader Style Current

Set a multileader style current using the **Multileader Style Manager** by double-clicking the style in the **Styles** list box, right-clicking on the name and selecting **Set current**, or picking the style and selecting the **Set Current** button. To set a multileader style current without opening the **Multileader Style Manager**, use the **Multileader Style** drop-down list located in the expanded **Annotation** panel on the **Home** ribbon tab or the **Leaders** panel on the **Annotate** ribbon tab.

PROFESSIONAL TIP

You can import multileader styles from existing drawings using **DesignCenter**. See Chapter 5 for more information about using **DesignCenter** to import file content.

Inserting Multileaders

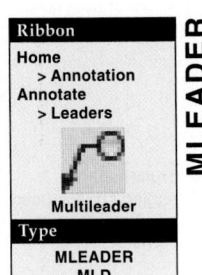

Use the **MLEADER** tool to insert a leader. How you insert a leader depends on the current multileader style settings and the option you choose to construct the leader. In general, there are three methods for inserting a multileader, depending on what portion of the leader you locate first. Review the components of a leader, shown in **Figure 19-22**, before reading the options for creating a multileader.

To use the default **Specify leader arrowhead location** option, specify the point at which the arrowhead touches first. Then specify a point to locate where the leader ends and the shoulder begins. If the **Mtext** option is active, enter leader text using the multiline text editor.

Choose the **leader Landing first** option to specify a point to locate where the leader ends and the shoulder begins first. Then specify the point at which the arrowhead touches. If the **Mtext** option is active, enter leader text using the multiline text editor.

Figure 19-22. Examples of leaders created using the **MLEADER** tool. A—An architectural leader created using a spline leader line, the **Specify leader arrowhead location** option, and three leader points. B—A mechanical leader created using a straight leader line, the **leader Landing first** option, and two leader points.

Use the **Content first** option to define the leader content first. The **Mtext** option allows you to type text using the multiline text editor. Then specify the point at which the arrowhead touches.

Select **Options** to access a list of options to override the current multileader style characteristics. The options are the same as those found in the **Modify Multileader Style** dialog box.

Exercise 19-5

Access the Student Web site (www.g-wlearning.com/CAD) and complete Exercise 19-5.

Dimensioning Chamfers

chamfer: An angled surface used to relieve sharp corners.

Dimension *chamfers* of 45° with a leader giving the angle and linear dimension, or with two linear dimension values. See **Figure 19-23**. Place the leader using the **MLEADER** tool. Chamfers other than 45° must include either the angle and a linear dimension or two linear dimensions. See **Figure 19-24**. Use the **DIMLINEAR** and **DIMANGULAR** tools for this purpose.

Exercise 19-6

Access the Student Web site (www.g-wlearning.com/CAD) and complete Exercise 19-6.

Figure 19-23.
Dimensioning 45° chamfers.

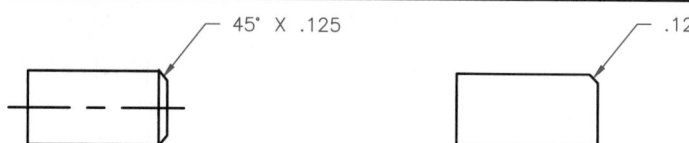

Figure 19-24.
Dimensioning chamfers that are not 45°.

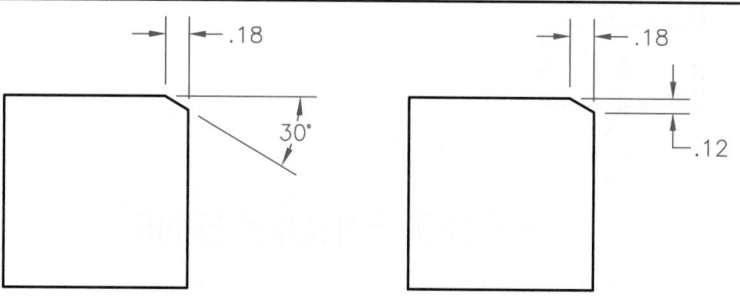

Thread Drawings and Notes

Figure 19-25 shows the elements of external and internal screw threads. However, threads commonly appear on a drawing as a simplified representation in which a hidden line indicates thread depth. See **Figure 19-26**. Threaded parts often include a chamfer to help engage the mating thread.

Thread representations show the reader that a thread exists, but the thread note gives the exact specifications. The thread note typically connects to the thread with a leader. See **Figure 19-27**. The most common thread forms are the Unified and metric screw threads, but a variety of other thread forms are required for specific applications.

Figure 19-25.
Features of external and internal screw threads.

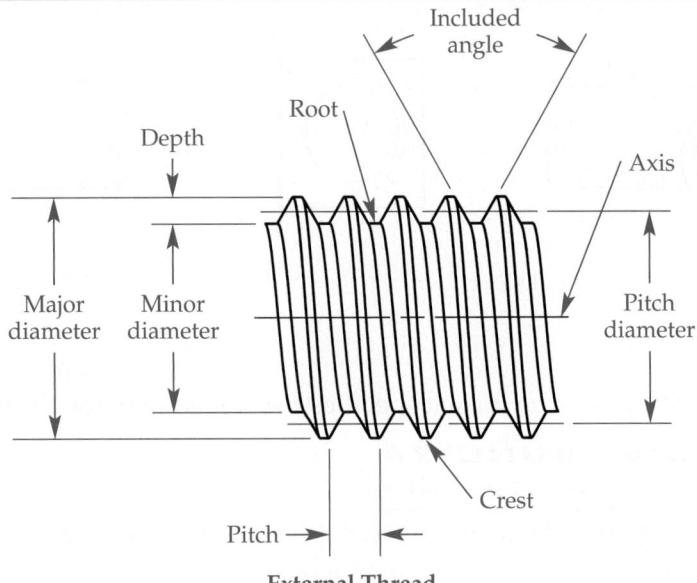

External Thread

Internal Thread

Figure 19-26.
Simplified thread
representations.

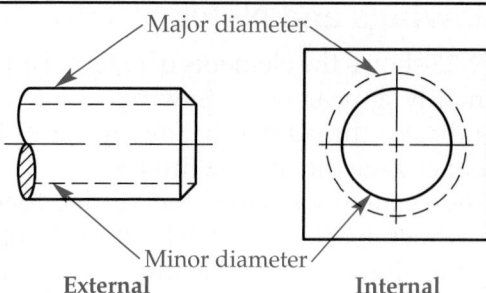

The following format specifies the thread note for Unified screw threads.

3/4-10UNC-2A
   (1)   (2)   (3)   (4)(5)

(1) Major diameter of thread, given as a fraction or number.
(2) Number of threads per inch.
(3) Thread series: UNC = Unified National Coarse, UNF = Unified National Fine.
(4) Class of fit: 1 = large tolerance, 2 = general-purpose tolerance, 3 = tight tolerance.
(5) Thread type: A = external thread. B = internal thread.

The following format specifies the thread note for metric threads.

M14X2
 (1) (2)   (3)

(1) M = metric thread.
(2) Major diameter in millimeters.
(3) Pitch in millimeters.

There are too many screw threads to describe in detail in this textbook. Refer to the *Machinery's Handbook*, published by Industrial Press Inc., or a comprehensive mechanical drafting text for more information.

Figure 19-27. Displaying the thread note with a leader.

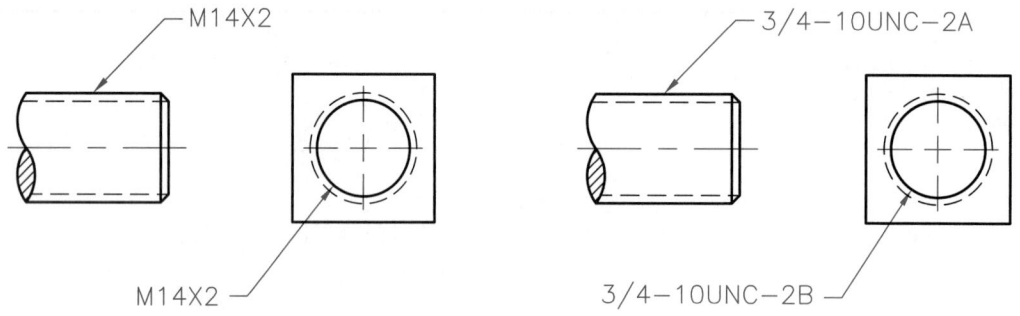

NOTE

The **Dimension** panel of the **Express Tools** ribbon tab includes **QLATTACH**, **QLATTACHSET**, and **QLDETACHSET** tools that allow you to attach and detach an annotation object to leaders created using the **QLEADER** and **LEADER** tools. Use multileaders instead of these leader and express tools.

Exercise 19-7

Access the Student Web site (www.g-wlearning.com/CAD) and complete Exercise 19-7.

Alternate Dimensioning Practices

Omitting dimension lines is common for drawings in industries that use computer-controlled machining processes, and when unconventional dimensioning practices are required because of product features. Rectangular coordinate dimensioning without dimension lines, tabular dimensioning, and chart dimensioning are examples of dimensioning methods that omit dimension lines.

Rectangular Coordinate Dimensioning without Dimension Lines

Rectangular coordinate dimensioning without dimension lines is popular in mechanical drafting for specific applications, such as precision sheet metal part drawings and electronics drafting, especially for chassis layout. Each dimension represents a measurement originating from a *datum*. See **Figure 19-28**. Identification letters label holes or similar features. Often a table, keyed to the identification letters, indicates feature size or specifications.

Tabular Dimensioning

In *tabular dimensioning*, each feature receives a label with a letter or number that correlates to a table. See **Figure 19-29**. Some companies take this practice one step further and display the location and size of features in the table from an X and a Y axis. The depth of features is also provided from the Z axis where appropriate. Each feature is labeled with a letter or number that correlates to the table, as shown in **Figure 19-30**.

Chart Dimensioning

Chart dimensioning may take the form of unidirectional, aligned, rectangular coordinate dimensioning without dimension lines, or tabular dimensioning. Chart dimensioning provides flexibility when dimensions change as the requirements of the product change. See **Figure 19-31**.

rectangular coordinate dimensioning without dimension lines: A type of dimensioning that includes only extension lines and text aligned with the extension lines.

datum: The 0 dimension, baseline, or common point from which all measurements are made while dimensioning.

tabular dimensioning: A form of rectangular coordinate dimensioning without dimension lines in which dimensions appear in a table.

chart dimensioning: A type of dimensioning in which the variable dimensions are shown with letters that correlate to a chart in which the possible dimensions are given.

Figure 19-28. Rectangular coordinate dimensioning without dimension lines, or arrowless dimensioning.

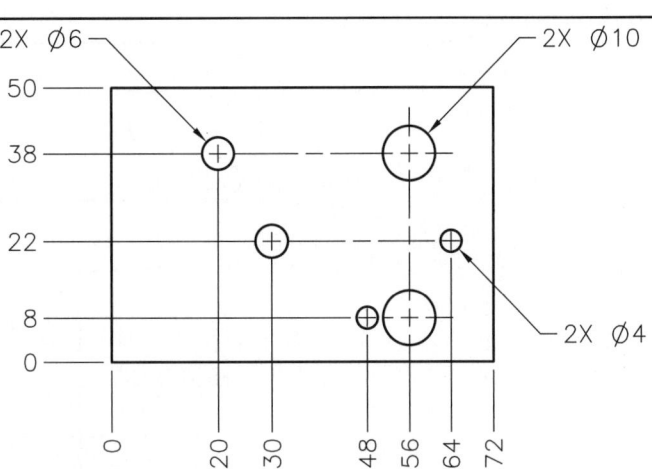

Figure 19-29.
Tabular dimensioning. Letters reference holes, and the table presents the related information.

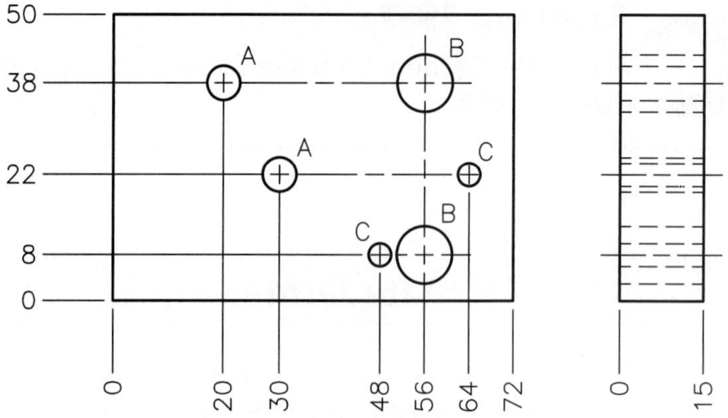

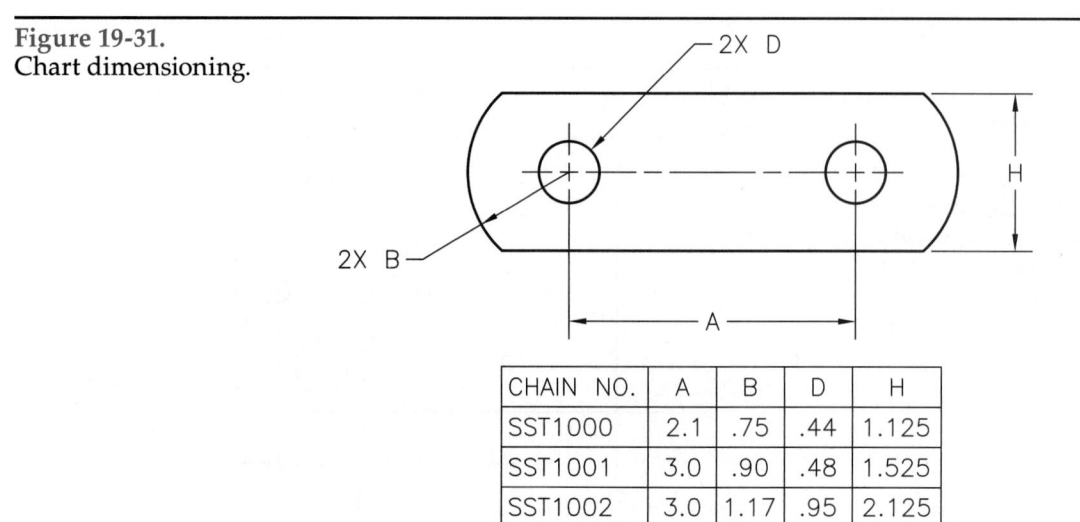

HOLE	A	B	C
DIA.	6	10	4

Figure 19-30.
Holes can be located with X, Y, and Z references given in a table with tabular dimensioning.

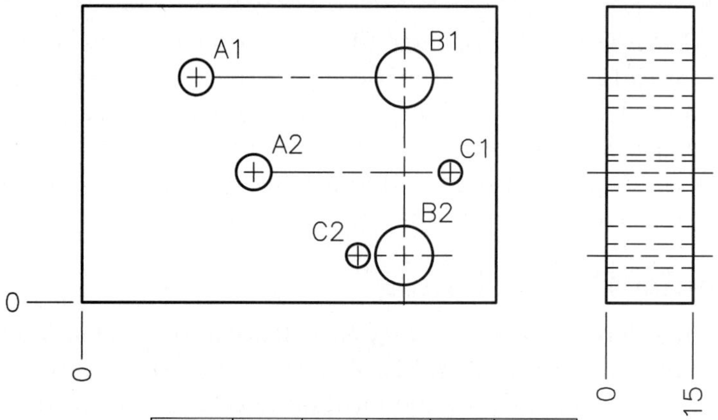

HOLE	QTY.	DIA.	X	Y	Z
A1	1	6	20	38	THRU
A2	1	6	30	22	THRU
B1	1	10	56	38	THRU
B2	1	10	56	8	THRU
C1	1	4	64	22	THRU
C2	1	4	48	8	THRU

Figure 19-31.
Chart dimensioning.

CHAIN NO.	A	B	D	H
SST1000	2.1	.75	.44	1.125
SST1001	3.0	.90	.48	1.525
SST1002	3.0	1.17	.95	2.125

Creating Ordinate Dimension Objects

AutoCAD refers to rectangular coordinate dimensioning without dimension lines as *ordinate dimensioning*. In order to create ordinate dimension objects accurately, you must move the default origin (0,0,0 coordinate) to the object datum. This involves understanding the AutoCAD world coordinate system and user coordinate systems. Once you establish the datum by temporarily moving the origin, use the **DIMORDINATE** tool to place ordinate dimension objects.

ordinate dimensioning: The AutoCAD term for rectangular coordinate dimensioning without dimension lines.

Introduction to WCS and UCS

The origin of the *world coordinate system (WCS)* has been at the 0,0,0 point for the drawings you have created throughout this textbook. In most cases, this is appropriate. However, when you apply rectangular coordinate dimensioning without dimension lines, it is best to originate dimensions from a primary datum, which is often a corner of the object. Depending on how you draw the object, this point may or may not align with the WCS origin.

world coordinate system (WCS): The AutoCAD rectangular coordinate system. In 2D drafting, the WCS contains four quadrants, separated by the X and Y axes.

The WCS is fixed, but the origin of a *user coordinate system (UCS)* can move to any point. The UCS is described in detail in *AutoCAD and Its Applications—Advanced*. In general, a UCS allows you to set your own coordinate system and origin. Measurements made with the **DIMORDINATE** tool originate from the current UCS origin. By default, this is the 2D 0,0 origin. A quick method for relocating the origin is to pick the **Origin** button from the **Coordinates** panel of the **View** ribbon tab. Then specify a new origin point, such as the corner of an object or another appropriate datum. See **Figure 19-32**.

user coordinate system (UCS): A temporary override of the WCS in which the origin (0,0,0) is moved to a location specified by the user.

When you finish drawing dimensions from a datum, you can leave the UCS origin at the datum or move it back to the WCS origin. To return to the WCS, pick the **World** button from the **Coordinates** panel of the **View** ribbon tab, or select the WCS option from the **WCS** menu of the **ViewCube**.

Using the DIMORDINATE Tool

The **DIMORDINATE** tool automatically places an extension line and a dimension at the point you specify. The dimension measures an X or Y coordinate distance from the UCS origin. Since you are working in the XY plane, you may want to set vertical and horizontal polar tracking or turn on **Ortho** mode before using the **DIMORDINATE** tool. In addition, if the drawing includes circular features, use the **DIMCENTER** tool to

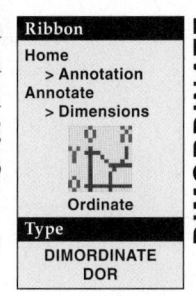

Ribbon

Home
> Annotation
Annotate
> Dimensions

Ordinate

Type

DIMORDINATE
DOR

DIMORDINATE

Figure 19-32.
Before you use the **DIMORDINATE** tool, move the UCS origin to the appropriate datum location and add center marks to circular features that you plan to dimension.

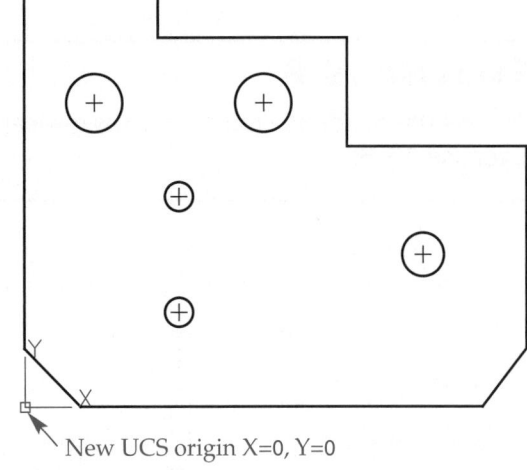

New UCS origin X=0, Y=0

place center dashes as shown in **Figure 19-32.** This conforms to ASME standards and provides something to pick when you dimension circular features.

Access the **DIMORDINATE** tool, and when the Specify feature location: prompt appears, pick a point to locate the origin of the extension line. If the feature is the corner of the object, pick an endpoint. If the feature is a circle, pick the end of the center dash, as shown in **Figure 19-33,** not the center of the object. This leaves the required space between the center mark and the extension line. Zoom in if needed and use object snap modes when necessary. The next prompt asks for the leader endpoint, which refers to the extension line endpoint. Specify the endpoint of the extension line.

If the X axis or Y axis distance between the feature and the extension line endpoint is large, the axis AutoCAD uses for the dimension by default may not be correct. When this happens, use the **Xdatum** or **Ydatum** option to specify the axis from which the dimension originates. The **Mtext, Text,** and **Angle** options are identical to the options available with other dimensioning tools. Pick the extension line endpoint to complete the process.

Figure 19-34A shows ordinate dimensions placed on the object. Notice that the dimension text aligns with the extension lines. Aligned dimensioning is standard with ordinate dimensioning. Add missing lines, such as centerlines or fold lines, to complete the drawing. Identify the holes with letters and create a correlated dimensioning table if appropriate. See **Figure 19-34B.**

PROFESSIONAL TIP

Most ordinate dimensioning tasks work best with polar tracking or **Ortho** mode on. However, when the extension line is too close to an adjacent dimension, it is best to stagger the extension line as shown in the following illustration. With **Ortho** mode off, the extension line is automatically staggered when you pick the second extension line point, as shown.

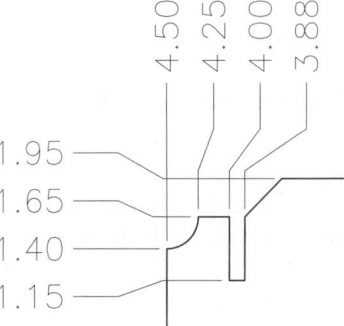

Exercise 19-8

Access the Student Web site (www.g-wlearning.com/CAD) **and complete Exercise 19-8.**

Figure 19-33.
Pick the endpoints of center marks to establish the correct offset, or develop a specific dimension style with an extension line origin offset of 0 for placing dimensions from center marks.

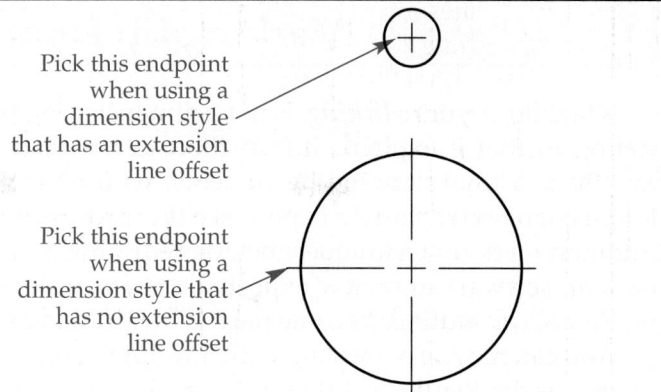

Pick this endpoint when using a dimension style that has an extension line offset

Pick this endpoint when using a dimension style that has no extension line offset

Figure 19-34.
A—Placing ordinate dimensions.
B—Completing the drawing.

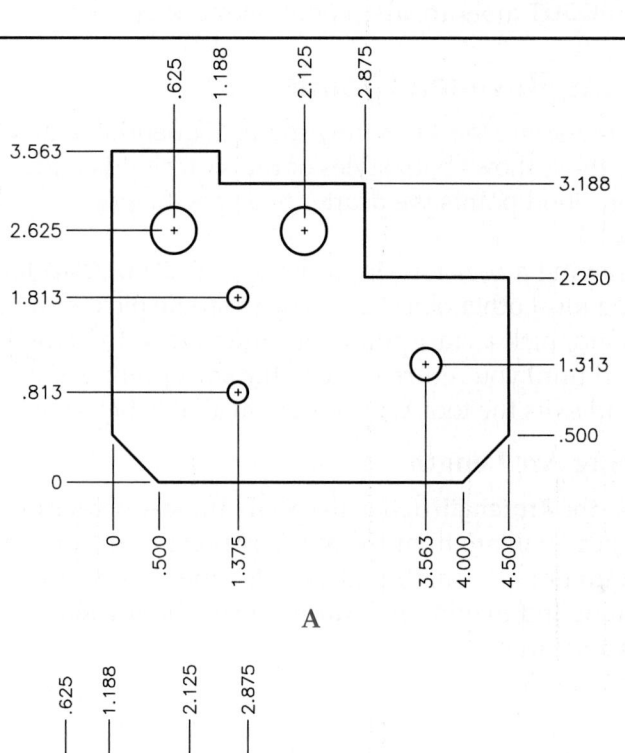

A

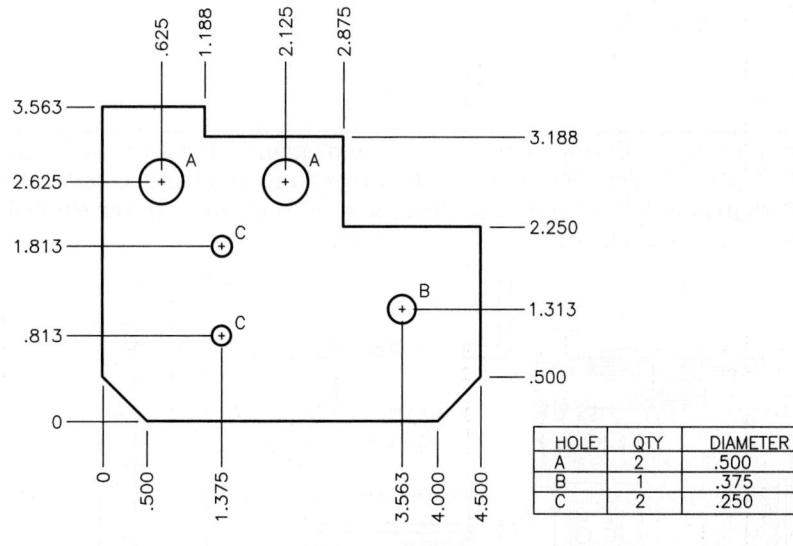

HOLE	QTY	DIAMETER
A	2	.500
B	1	.375
C	2	.250

B

marking up (redlining): The process of reviewing a drawing and marking required changes.

Marking up, or *redlining*, is not a dimensioning practice, but it is similar to dimensioning in that it explains information to the reader. Redlines are typically added directly to a final drawing by someone who reviews the drawing for accuracy and design changes. You might experience this process with your instructor or supervisor. Common mark-up techniques include redlining a plot with a red pen, using separate mark-up software to review exported drawings, or redlining directly in the drawing file. AutoCAD redlines become part of the drawing to document revision history.

You can redline a drawing with any appropriate AutoCAD tools, typically using a separate layer. Redlining often includes basic objects, text, and leaders. In some cases, you may add redline dimensions and even an entire drawing or detail. The **REVCLOUD** and **WIPEOUT** tools are also common mark-up tools.

Ribbon

Home
> Draw
Annotate
> Markup

Revision Cloud

Type

REVCLOUD

Creating Revision Clouds

revision cloud: A polyline of sequential arcs used to form a cloud shape around changes in a drawing.

A *revision cloud* is a polyline of sequential arcs forming a cloud-shaped object. **Figure 19-35** shows both styles of revision clouds with a leader and note attached. The revision cloud points the drafter to a specific portion of the drawing that may require an edit.

Drawing a revision cloud using the **REVCLOUD** tool is somewhat different than drawing most other objects, because a single pick is all that is required. To draw a revision cloud, pick a start point, and then move the crosshairs around the objects to be enclosed until you return close to the start point. AutoCAD closes the cloud automatically and exits the tool. Options are available before you pick the start point.

Defining Arc Length

Use the **Arc length** option to specify the size of revision cloud arcs. The value measures the length of an arc from the arc start point to the arc endpoint. AutoCAD prompts for the minimum arc length and then for the maximum arc length. Specifying different minimum and maximum values causes the revision cloud to have an uneven, hand-drawn appearance.

Figure 19-35. Examples of revision clouds identifying areas of a drawing to be modified. Notice the leaders describing the changes. You can create revision clouds using the **Calligraphy** style, as shown in the upper revision cloud, or the **Normal** style, as shown in the lower revision cloud.

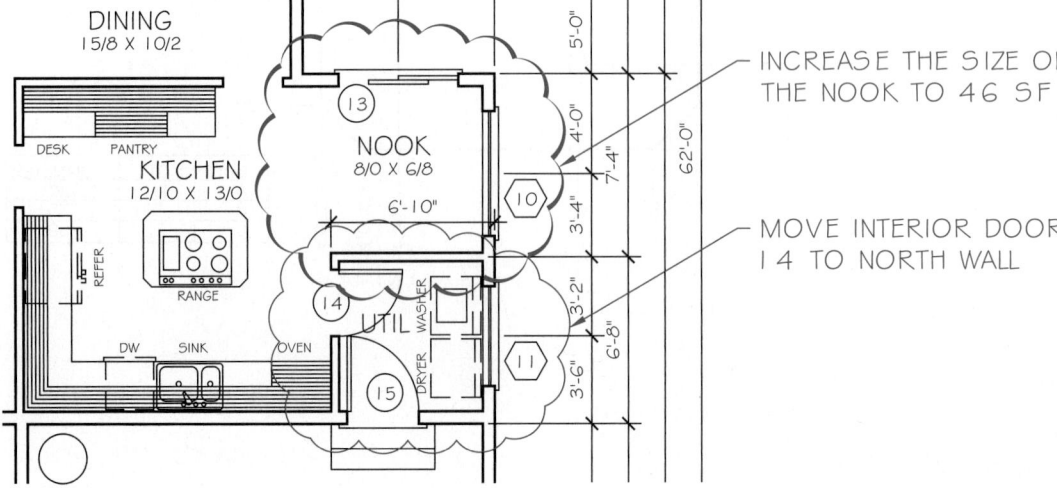

Converting Objects to Revision Clouds

Use the **Object** option to convert a circle, closed polyline, ellipse, polygon, or rectangle to a revision cloud. Pick the object to convert to a revision cloud. Use the **No** option at the Reverse direction: prompt, or use the **Yes** option to reverse the direction of the cloud arcs.

Changing Revision Cloud Style

Use the **Style** option to change the revision cloud style. The default style is **Normal**, which displays arcs with a consistent width. When you specify the **Calligraphy** style, the start and end widths of the individual arcs are different, creating a more stylized revision cloud. See **Figure 19-35**.

Exercise 19-9

Access the Student Web site (www.g-wlearning.com/CAD) and complete Exercise 19-9.

Using the WIPEOUT Tool

The **WIPEOUT** tool allows you to clear a portion of the drawing without erasing objects. The tool is sometimes appropriate for applications similar to those for **REVCLOUD**, most often redlining. **Figure 19-36** shows an example of a wipeout used to lay out the location of a proposed building site on a site plan.

Specify the first corner of the wipeout, followed by all other perimeter corners. Use the **Undo** option as needed to reverse the effects of an incorrect selection. Use the **Close** option, press [Enter] or the space bar, or right-click and choose **Enter** to create the wipeout.

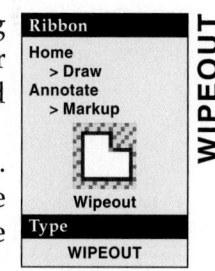

Figure 19-36. Using the **WIPEOUT** tool to clear a proposed building site on a site plan. Objects below the wipeout still exist. Further information has been added to the wipeout in this example.

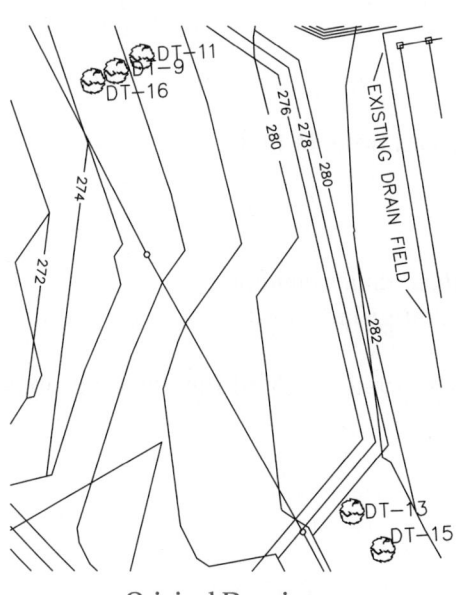

Pick points to create the wipeout

Original Drawing   Wipeout Added

An alternative to picking points is to use the **Polyline** option and select a closed polyline object to convert to a wipeout. Use the **Frames** option to turn the display of all wipeout boundaries on or off. You may need to regenerate the display to observe the effects of changing the frame setting. To reveal objects hidden by a wipeout, freeze or turn off the wipeout layer, use draw order tools, or erase the wipeout if it is no longer needed.

Template Development
Chapter 19

For detailed instructions on adding multileader styles to each drawing template, go to the Student Web site (www.g-wlearning.com/CAD), select this chapter, and select **Template Development**.

Chapter Test

Answer the following questions. Write your answers on a separate sheet of paper or go to the Student Web site (www.g-wlearning.com/CAD) and complete the electronic chapter test.

1. Which tool provides diameter dimensions for circles?
2. Which tool provides radius dimensions for arcs?
3. Explain how to add a center mark to a circle without using the **DIMDIAMETER** or **DIMRADIUS** tool.
4. What is the most common size for leader arrowheads?
5. What angle constraints should you use for leaders to maintain the ASME standard?
6. What is the usual length for the shoulder of a leader in mechanical drafting?
7. Describe two ways to dimension a 45° chamfer.
8. Identify the elements of this Unified screw thread note: 1/2-13UNC-2B.
   A. 1/2
   B. 13
   C. UNC
   D. 2
   E. B
9. Identify the elements of this metric screw thread note: M 14 X 2.
   A. M
   B. 14
   C. 2
10. Define *rectangular coordinate dimensioning without dimension lines*.
11. What term does AutoCAD use to refer to rectangular coordinate dimensioning without dimension lines?
12. Explain the importance of the user coordinate system (UCS) for drawing ordinate dimension objects.
13. What is the purpose of a revision cloud?
14. How do you close a revision cloud?
15. What is the purpose of the **WIPEOUT** tool?

Drawing Problems

- *Start AutoCAD if it is not already started. Start a new drawing for each problem using an appropriate template of your choice.*
- *The template should include layers and text, dimension, multileader, and table styles, when necessary, for drawing the given objects. Add layers and text, dimension, multileader, and table styles as needed.*
- *Draw all objects using appropriate layers and text, dimension, multileader, and table styles, justification, and format.*
- *Follow the specific instructions for each problem. Use only drawing and editing tools and techniques you have already learned. Use your own judgment and approximate dimensions when necessary.*
- *Apply dimensions accurately using ASME or appropriate industry standards.*

▼ Basic

1. Draw and dimension the part view shown. Save the drawing as P19-1.

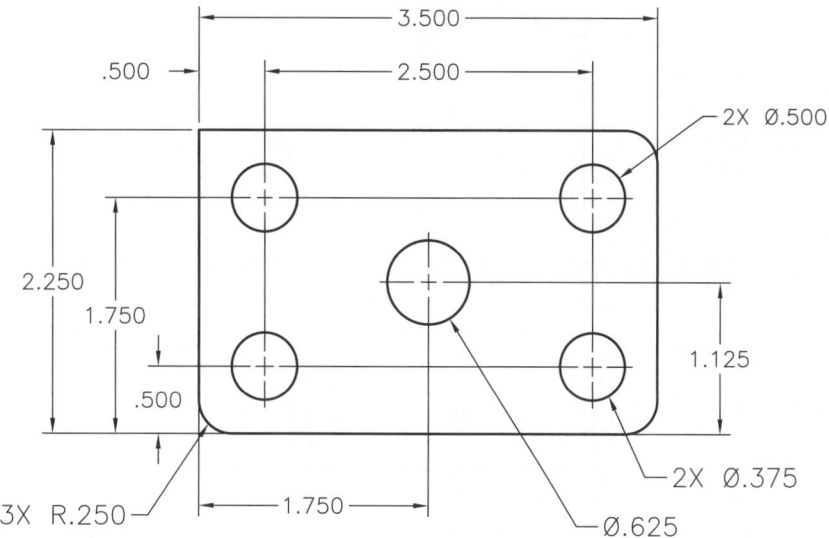

2. Draw and dimension the part views shown. Save the drawing as P19-2.

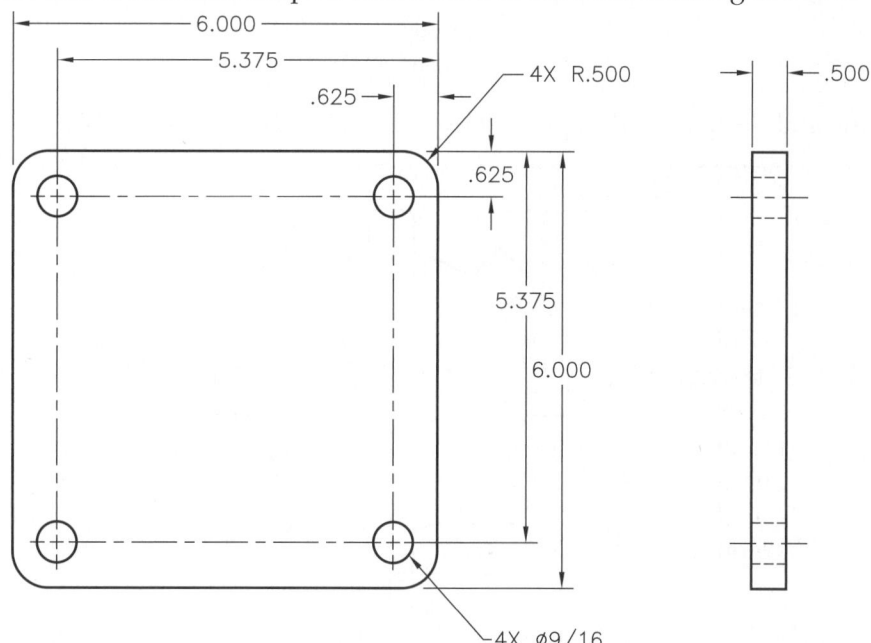

3. Draw and dimension the part view shown. Save the drawing as P19-3.

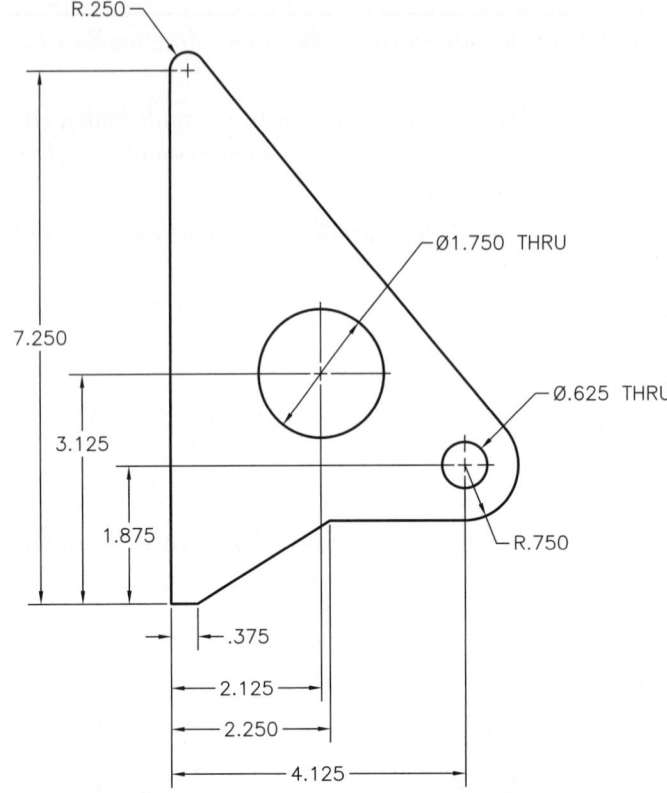

4. Draw and dimension the pin shown. Save the drawing as P19-4.

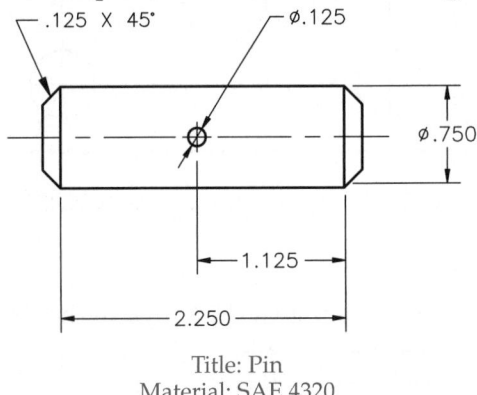

Title: Pin
Material: SAE 4320

5. Draw and dimension the spline shown. Save the drawing as P19-5.

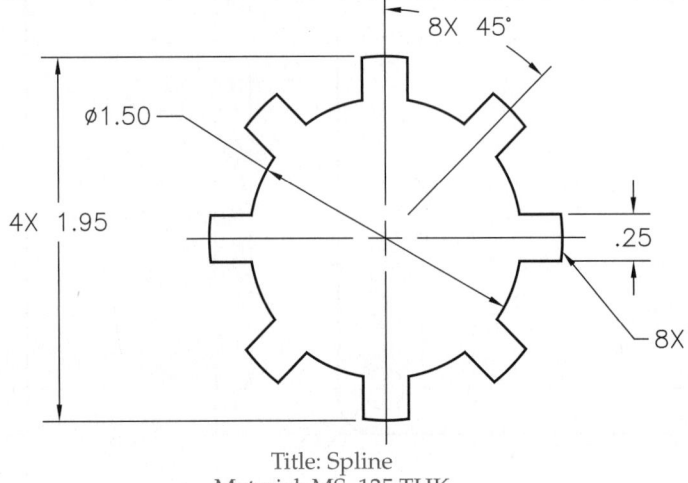

Title: Spline
Material: MS .125 THK

Drawing Problems - Chapter 19

6. Draw and dimension the gasket shown. Save the drawing as **P19-6**.

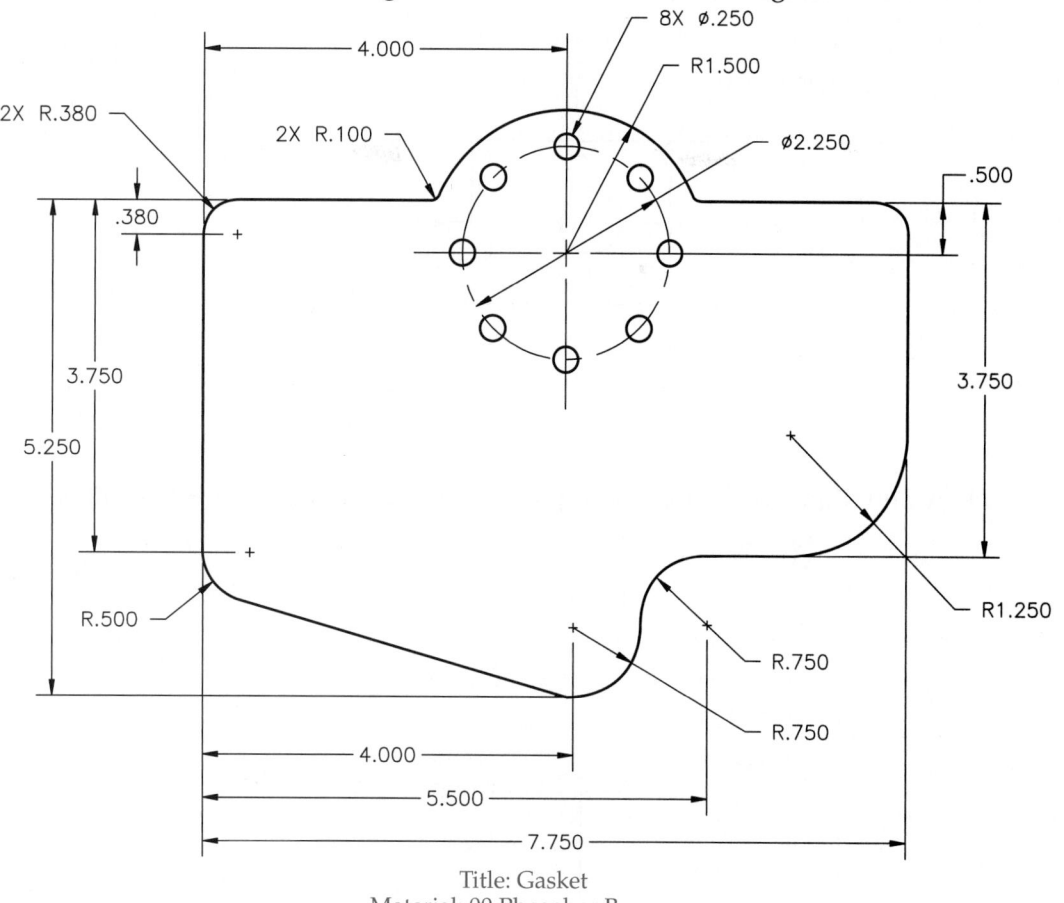

Title: Gasket
Material: 00 Phosphor Bronze

7. Draw and dimension the chain link shown. Save the drawing as **P19-7**.

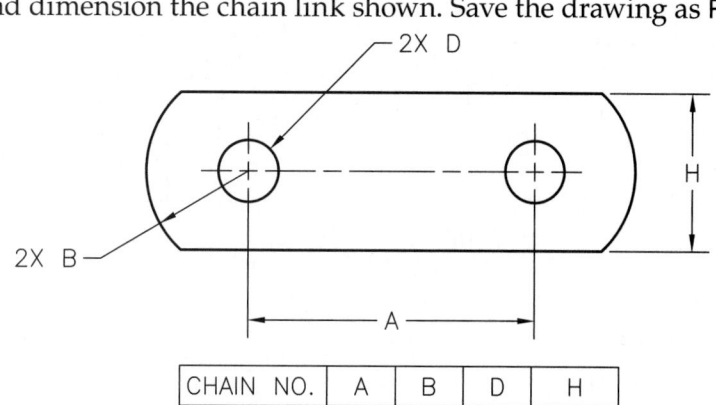

CHAIN NO.	A	B	D	H
SST1000	2.1	.75	.44	1.125
SST1001	3.0	.90	.48	1.525
SST1002	3.0	1.17	.95	2.125

8. Draw and dimension the part view shown. Save the drawing as P19-8.

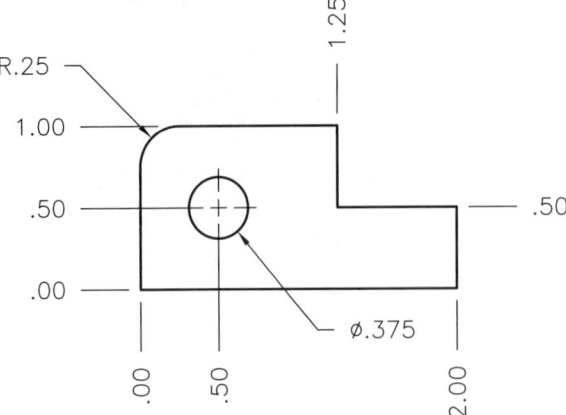

9. Draw and dimension the chassis spacer shown. Save the drawing as P19-9.

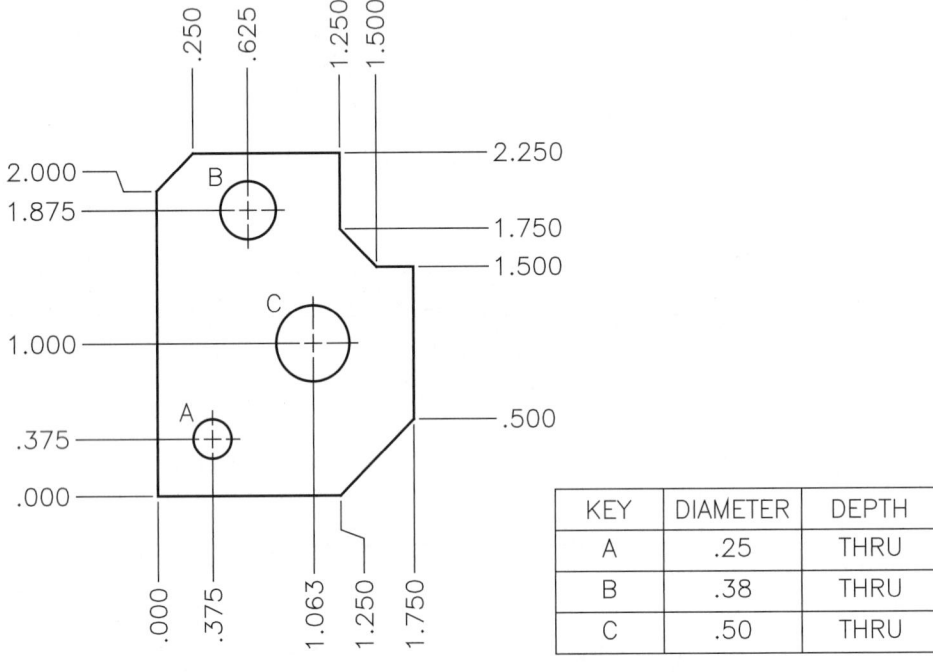

KEY	DIAMETER	DEPTH
A	.25	THRU
B	.38	THRU
C	.50	THRU

Title: Chassis Spacer
Material: .008 Aluminum

10. Draw and dimension the chassis shown. Save the drawing as P19-10.

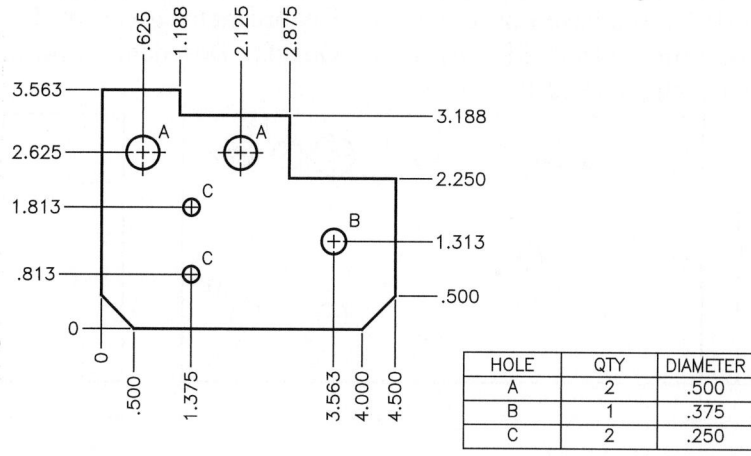

HOLE	QTY	DIAMETER
A	2	.500
B	1	.375
C	2	.250

Title: Chassis
Material: Aluminum .100 THK

11. Draw and dimension the part view shown. Save the drawing as P19-11.

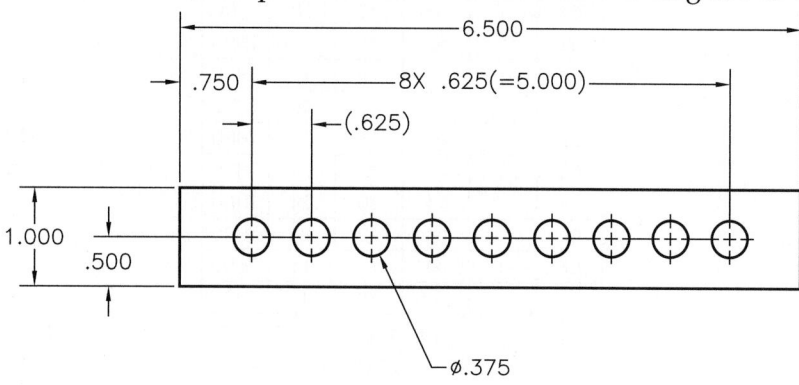

▼ Intermediate

12. Draw and dimension the thumb screw shown. Save the drawing as P6-8. Print an 8.5″ × 11″ copy of the drawing extents, using a 1:1 scale and landscape orientation.

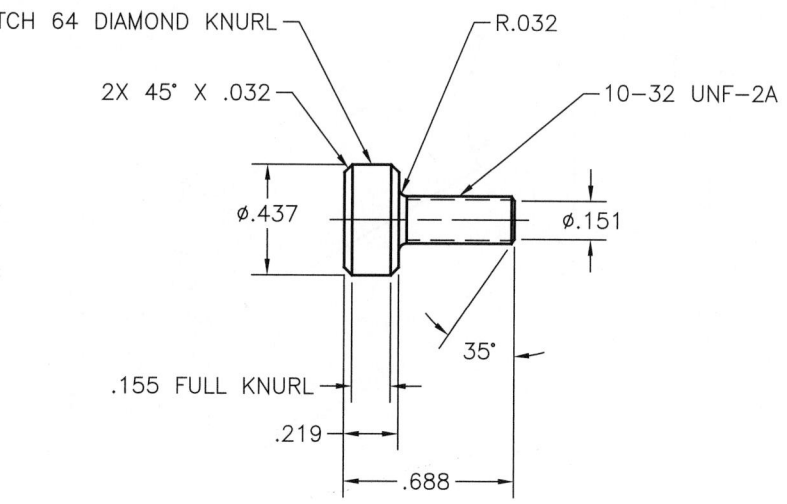

13. Convert the drawing shown to a drawing with the holes located using the **DIMORDINATE** tool based on the X and Y coordinates given in the table. Create a table columns for Hole (identification), Quantity, Description, and Depth (Z axis). Save the drawing as P19-13.

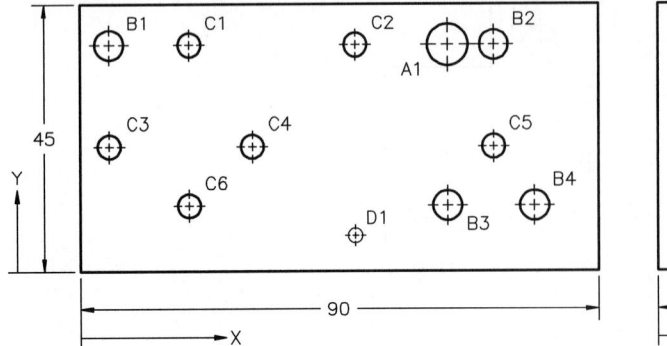

HOLE	QTY	DESC	X	Y	Z
A1	1	ø7	64	38	18
B1	1	ø5	5	38	THRU
B2	1	ø5	72	38	THRU
B3	1	ø5	64	11	THRU
B4	1	ø5	79	11	THRU
C1	1	ø4	19	38	THRU
C2	1	ø4	48	38	THRU
C3	1	ø4	5	21	THRU
C4	1	ø4	30	21	THRU
C5	1	ø4	72	21	THRU
C6	1	ø4	19	11	THRU
D1	1	ø2.5	48	6	THRU

Title: Base
Material: Bronze

For Problems 14 through 16, draw and dimension the orthographic views needed to describe the part completely. Save the drawings as P19-14, P19-15, *and* P19-16.

14.

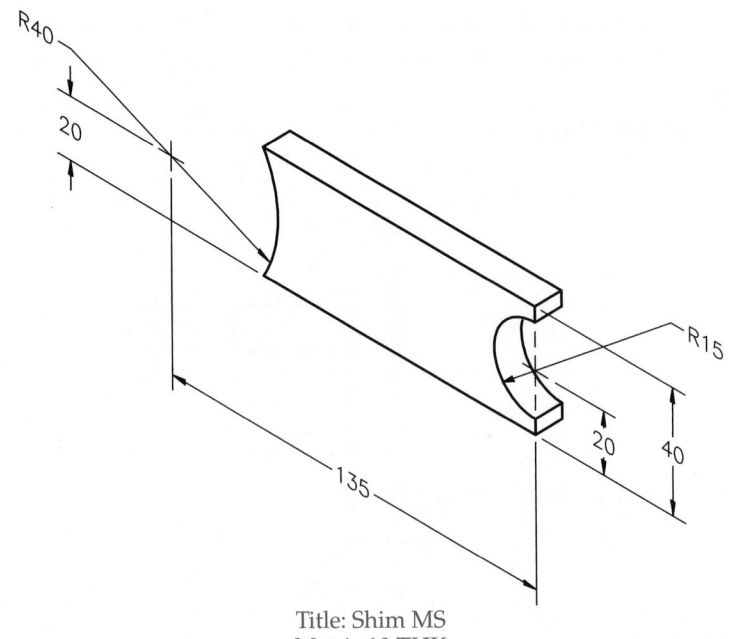

Title: Shim MS
Metric 10 THK

15. Half of the drawing is removed for clarity. Draw the entire part.

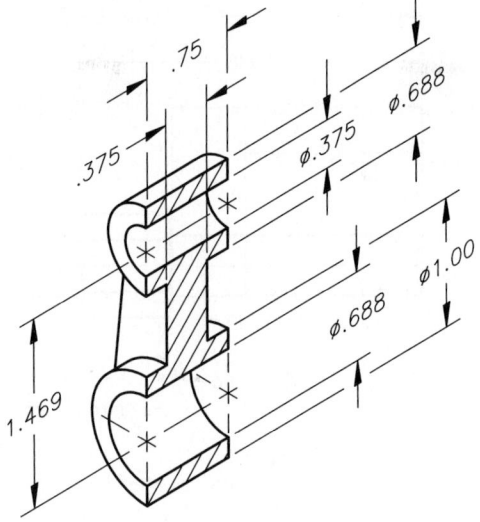

.75

.375

Ø.375

Ø.688

Ø.688

Ø1.00

1.469

FILLETS R.125

Title: Shaft Support
Material: Cast Iron (CI)

16. Half of the drawing is removed for clarity. Draw the entire part.

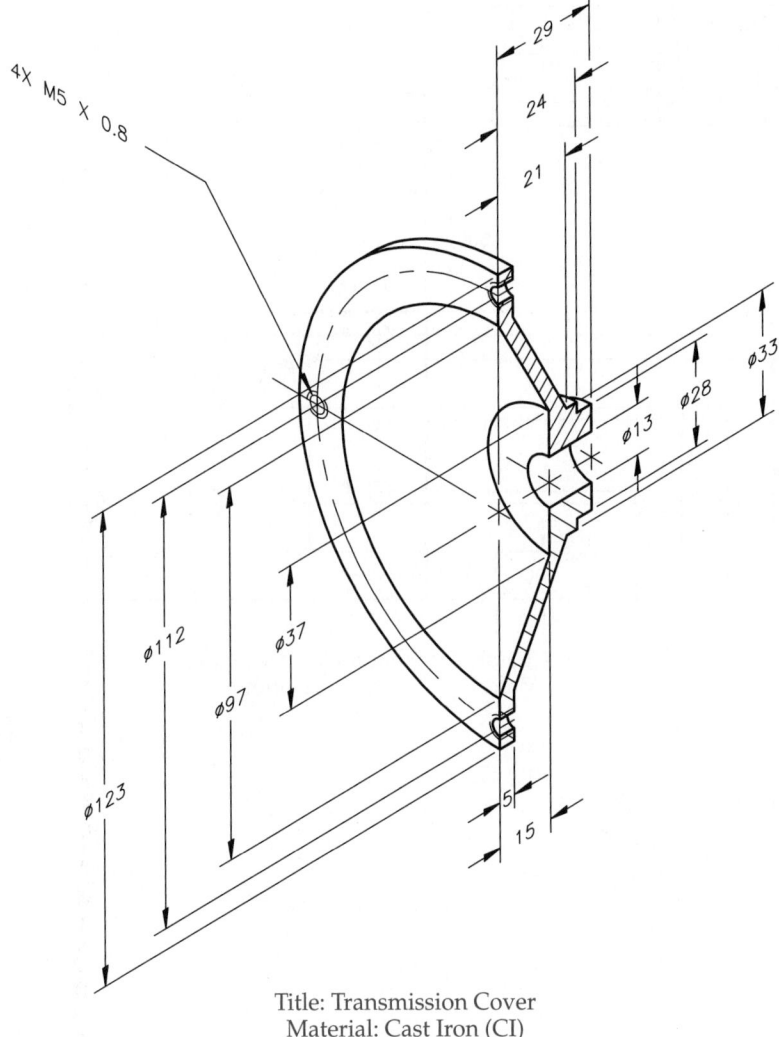

4X M5 X 0.8

29

24

21

Ø33

Ø28

Ø13

Ø112

Ø37

Ø97

Ø123

5

15

Title: Transmission Cover
Material: Cast Iron (CI)
Metric

17. Draw and dimension the part views shown. Save the drawing as P19-17.

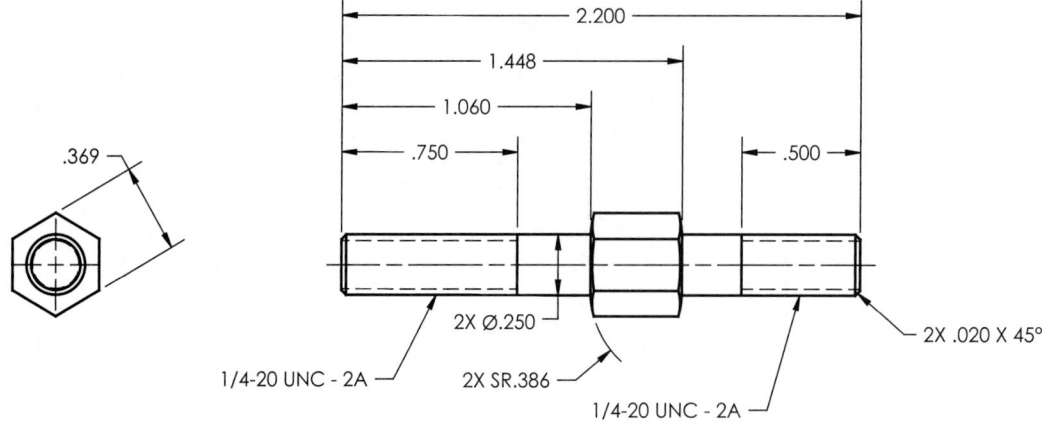

Title: Stud
Material: Stainless Steel

18. Draw and dimension the part view shown. Save the drawing as P19-18.

HOLE LAYOUT			
KEY	SIZE	DEPTH	NO. REQD
A	⌀.250	THRU	6
B	⌀.125	THRU	4
C	⌀.375	THRU	4
D	R.125	THRU	2

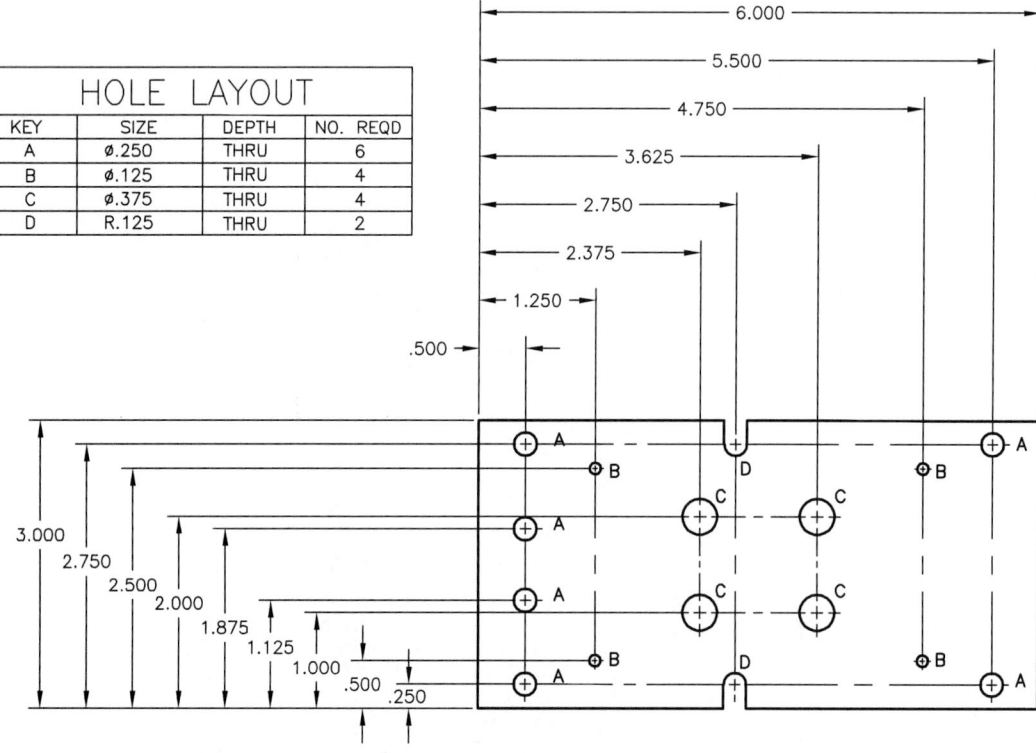

Title: Chassis Base (datum dimensioning)
Material: 12 gage Aluminum

19. Draw and dimension the part view shown. Save the drawing as P19-19.

HOLE LAYOUT			
KEY	SIZE	DEPTH	NO. REQD
A	⌀.250	THRU	6
B	⌀.125	THRU	4
C	⌀.375	THRU	4
D	R.125	THRU	2

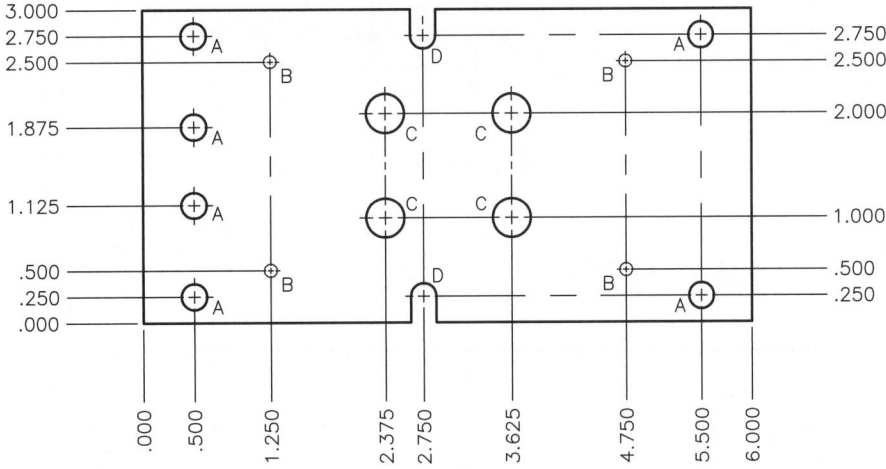

Title: Chassis Base (arrowless dimensioning)
Material: 12 gage Aluminum

20. Draw and dimension the part view shown. Save the drawing as P19-20.

HOLE LAYOUT				
KEY	X	Y	SIZE	TOL
A1	.500	2.750	⌀.250	±.002
A2	.500	1.875	⌀.250	±.002
A3	.500	1.125	⌀.250	±.002
A4	.500	.250	⌀.250	±.002
A5	5.500	2.750	⌀.250	±.002
A6	5.500	.250	⌀.250	±.002
B1	1.250	2.500	⌀.125	±.001
B2	1.250	.500	⌀.125	±.001
B3	4.750	2.500	⌀.125	±.001
B4	4.750	.500	⌀.125	±.001
C1	2.375	2.000	⌀.375	±.005
C2	2.375	1.000	⌀.375	±.005
C3	3.625	2.000	⌀.375	±.005
C4	3.625	1.000	⌀.375	±.005
D1	2.750	2.750	R.125	±.002
D2	2.750	.250	R.125	±.002

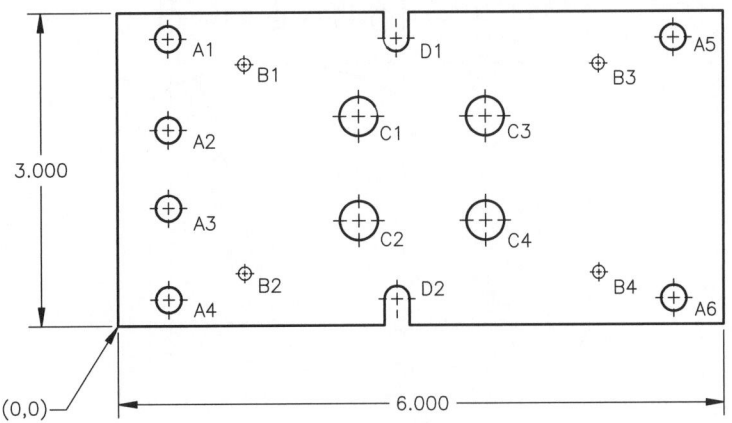

Title: Chassis Base (arrowless tabular dimensioning)
Material: 12 gage Aluminum

21. Draw and dimension the part views shown. Save the drawing as P19-21.

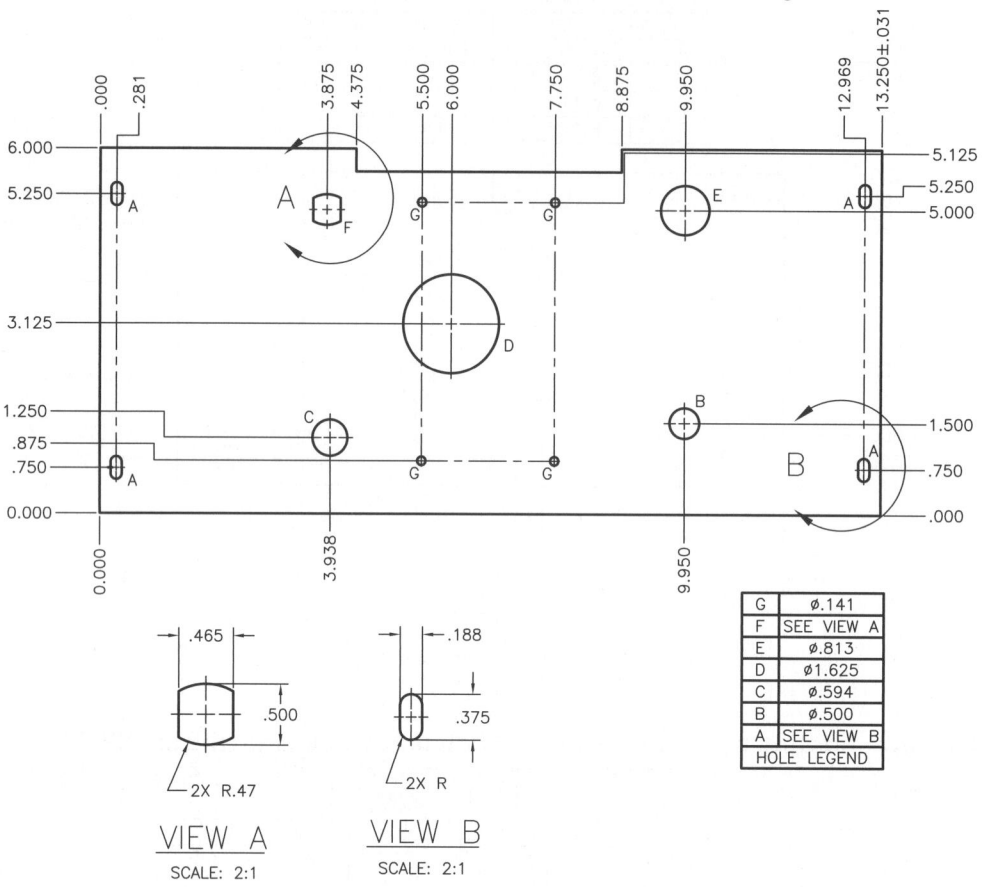

	HOLE LEGEND	
G	Ø.141	
F	SEE VIEW A	
E	Ø.813	
D	Ø1.625	
C	Ø.594	
B	Ø.500	
A	SEE VIEW B	

22. Draw and dimension the part views shown. Save the drawing as P19-22.

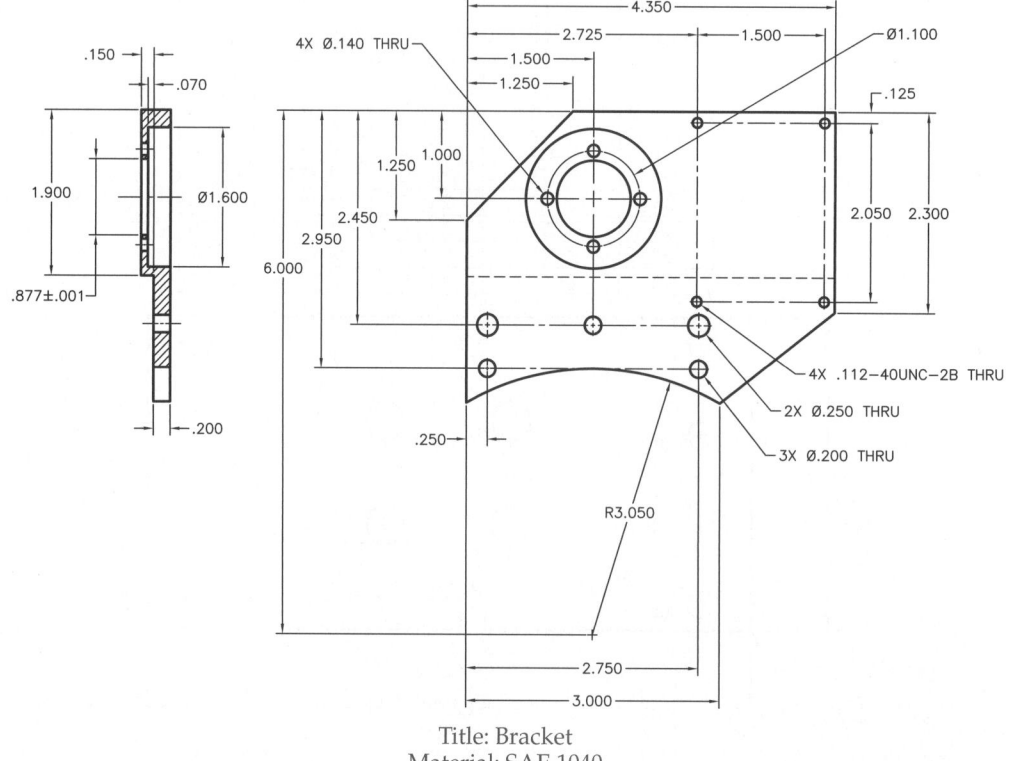

Title: Bracket
Material: SAE 1040

23. Draw and dimension the part views shown. Save the drawing as P19-23.

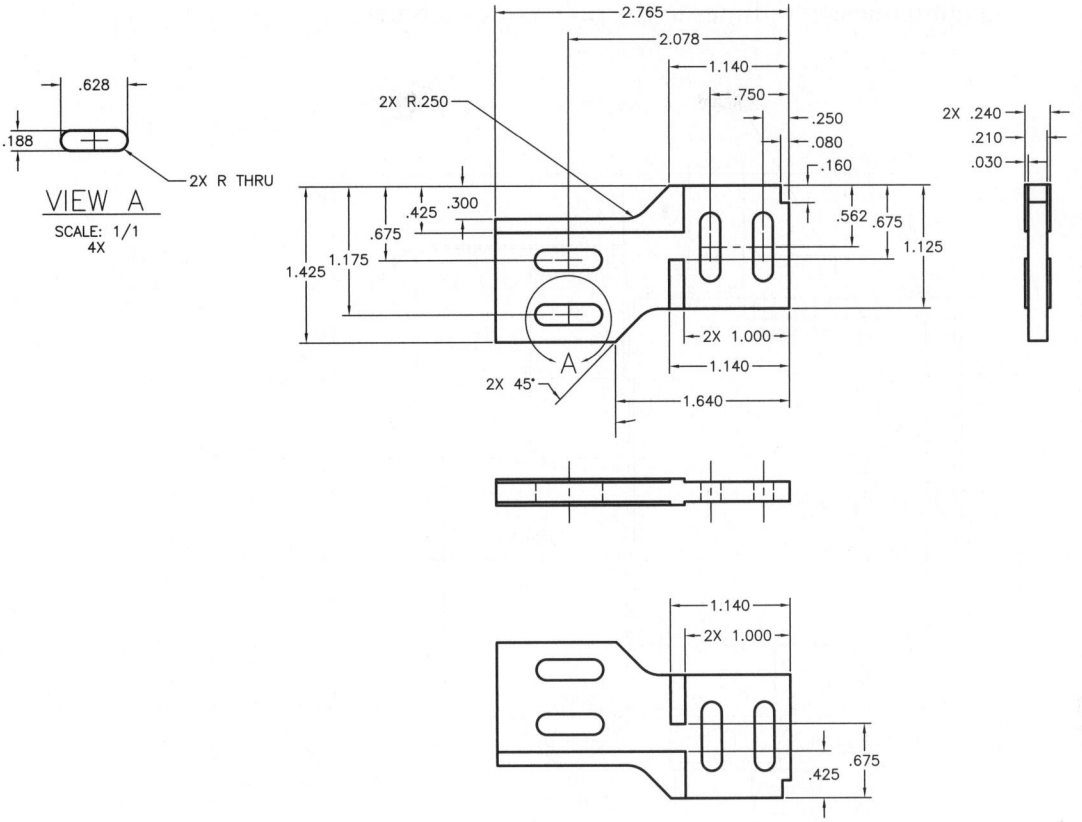

For Problems 24 and 25, draw and dimension the orthographic views needed to describe the part completely. Save the drawings as P19-24 and P19-25.

24.

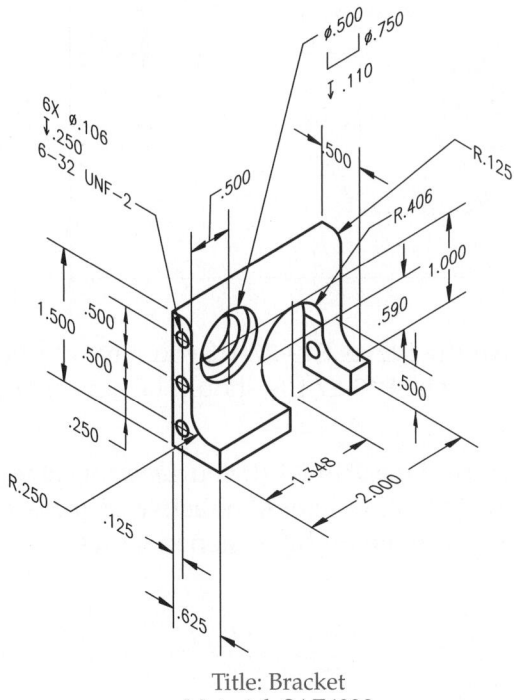

Title: Bracket
Material: SAE4320

25. Open P18-17 and save the file as P19-26. The P19-26 file should be active. Add the client-requested redlines to the floor plan as shown.

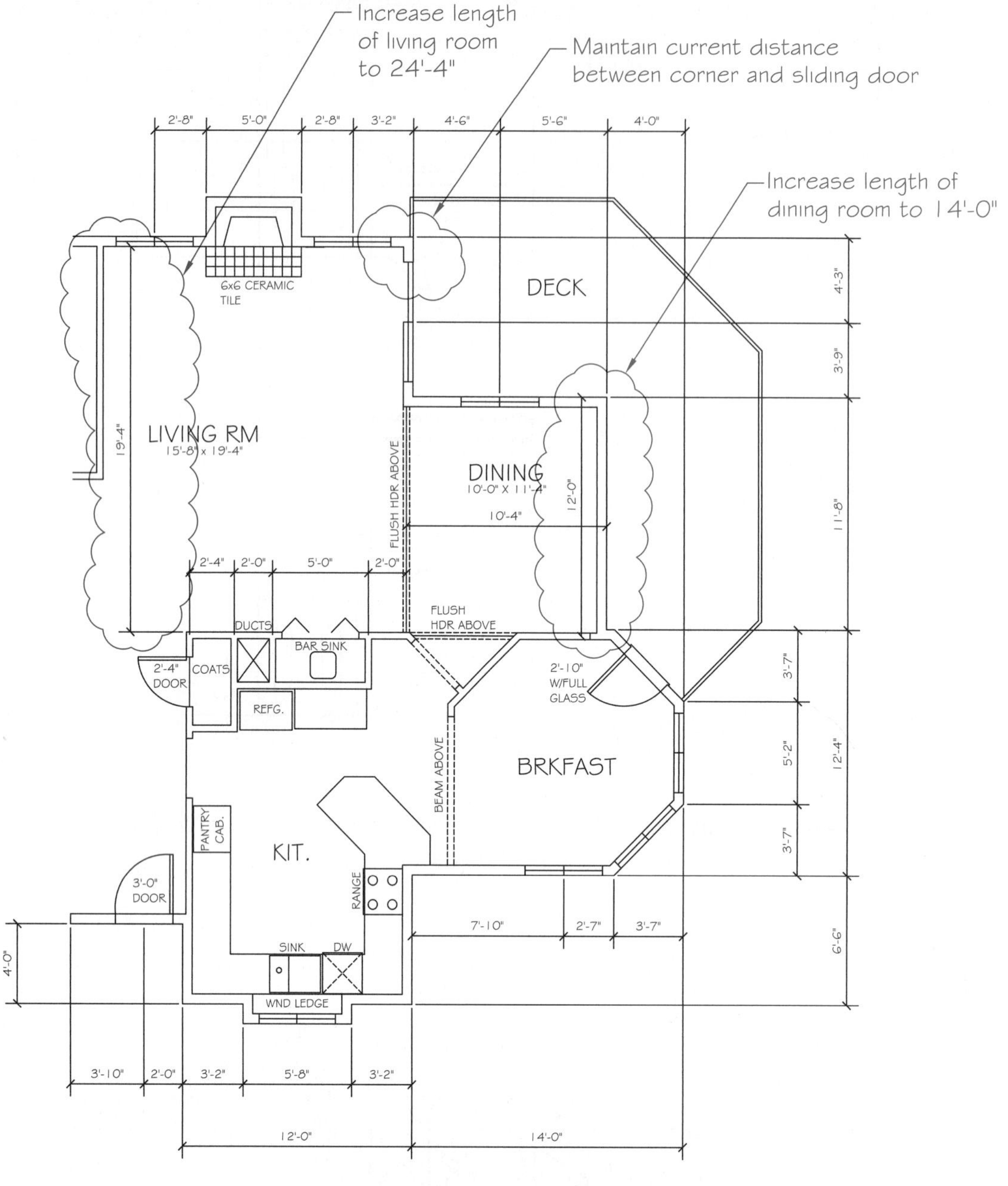

Increase length of living room to 24'-4"

Maintain current distance between corner and sliding door

Increase length of dining room to 14'-0"

DECK

LIVING RM
15'-8" x 19'-4"

6x6 CERAMIC TILE

DINING
10'-0" X 11'-4"

FLUSH HDR ABOVE

FLUSH HDR ABOVE

BRKFAST

2'-10" W/FULL GLASS

DUCTS

COATS

BAR SINK

REFG.

2'-4" DOOR

BEAM ABOVE

KIT.

PANTRY CAB.

RANGE

3'-0" DOOR

SINK

DW

WND LEDGE

26. Open P5-16 and save the file as P19-27. (If you have not yet completed problem 5-16, complete it now.) The P19-27 file should be active. Dimension the drawing of the kitchen.

27. Open P8-21 and save the file as P19-28. (If you have not yet completed problem 8-21, complete it now.) The P19-28 file should be active. Dimension the most important views of the hanger. Erase the undimensioned views.

Drawing Problems – Chapter 19

AutoCAD and Its Applications—Basics

28. Carefully evaluate the problem before beginning. Many of the given dimensions are provided to the inside surfaces of the bracket. This application is incorrect. Calculate the dimensions as needed to place baseline dimensioning from the surfaces labeled A and B. Do not place the A and B on your final drawing.

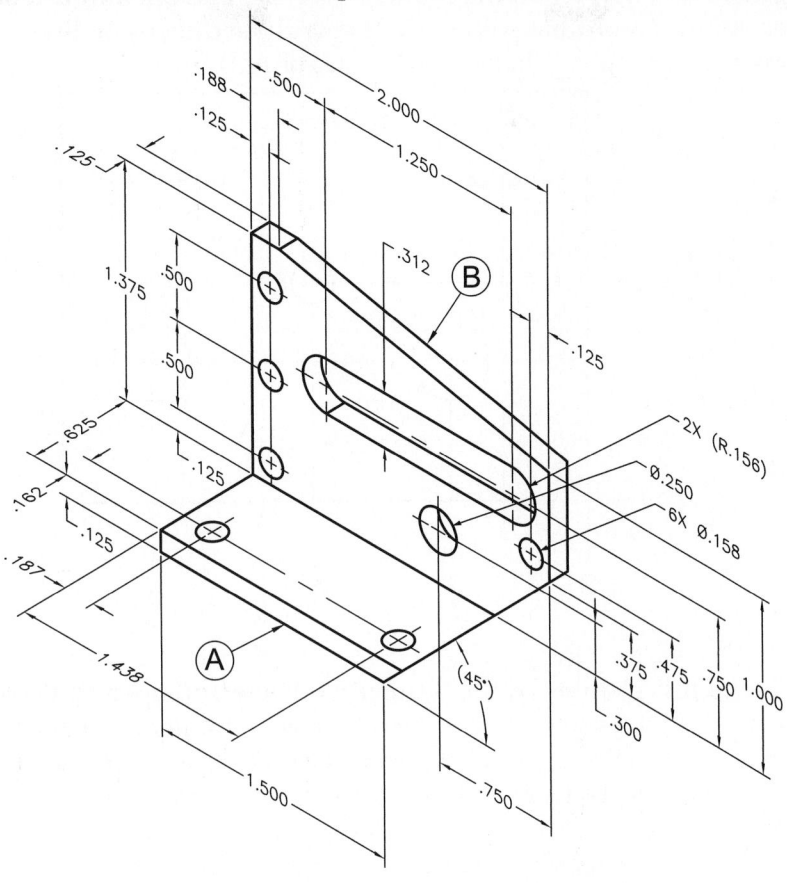

AutoCAD Certified Associate Exam Practice

Answer the following questions. Write your answers on a separate sheet of paper.

1. To comply with the ASME standard, what should the **Offset from origin** setting be when you dimension to a centerline? *Select all that apply.*
   A. 0
   B. .012
   C. .063
   D. .12 mm
   E. 1 mm
   F. 1.5 mm

2. What is the correct term for the shaded area in the hole shown below? *Select the one item that best answers the question.*
   A. counterbore
   B. countersink
   C. fillet
   D. landing
   E. round
   F. spotface

3. Which of the following tools can be used to dimension an arc? *Select all that apply.*
   A. **DIMARC**
   B. **DIMCENTER**
   C. **DIMJOGGED**
   D. **DIMJOGLINE**
   E. **DIMRADIUS**

AutoCAD Certified Professional Exam Practice

Follow the instructions in each problem. Write your answers on a separate sheet of paper.

1. **Navigate to this chapter on the Student Web site and open CPE-19ordinate.dwg.**
   Use rectangular coordinate dimensioning without dimension lines to dimension the drawing as shown. What are the values of A, B, and C?

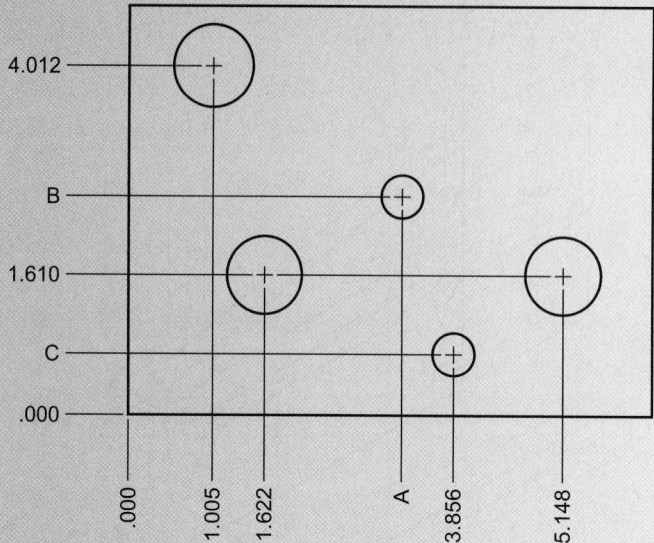

2. **Navigate to this chapter on the Student Web site and open CPE-19chart.dwg.**
   Create the drawing shown using the dimensions for item DRI203. Use the **Node** object snap to start the lower-right corner of the object at the point object provided in the drawing file. What are the coordinates of Point 1?

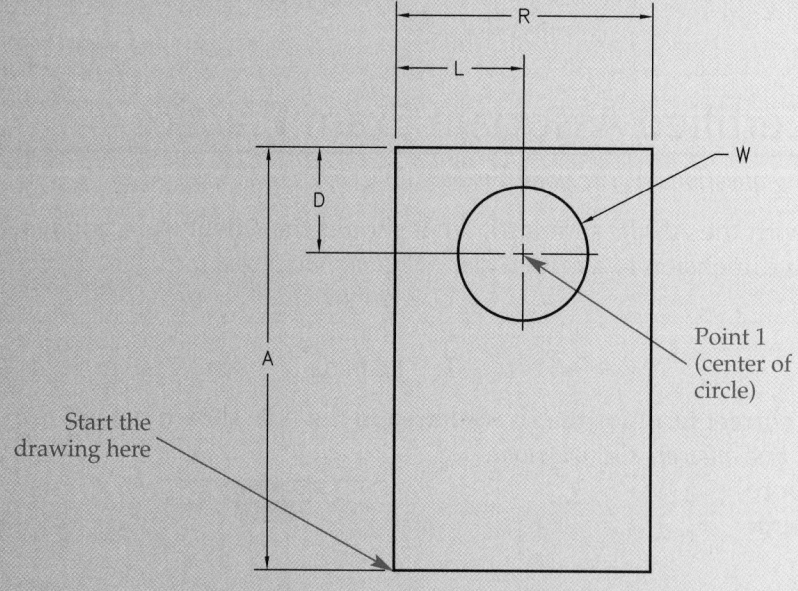

ITEM NO.	A	D	L	R	W
DRI201	4.000	1.000	1.250	2.500	1.261
DRI202	6.000	1.500	1.875	3.750	1.892
DRI203	9.500	2.375	2.969	5.938	2.995

Dimensioning with Tolerances

Learning Objectives

After completing this chapter, you will be able to do the following:

✓ Define and use dimensioning and tolerancing terminology.
✓ Set the precision for dimensions and tolerances.
✓ Set up the primary units for use with inch or metric dimensions.
✓ Create and use specified tolerance dimension styles.
✓ Explain the purpose of geometric dimensioning and tolerancing (GD&T).

This chapter introduces general tolerancing as applied to *conventional dimensioning* and explains how to create dimensions with specified tolerances for mechanical manufacturing drawings. This chapter also introduces geometric dimensioning and tolerancing (GD&T) symbols and offers information on how you can learn more about GD&T.

conventional dimensioning: Dimensioning without the use of geometric tolerancing.

Tolerancing Fundamentals

Each dimension has a *tolerance*, except for dimensions specifically identified as reference, maximum, minimum, or stock. The tolerancing practice depends on specific engineering and manufacturing applications, interrelated features, and industry and company preference. You can apply tolerance to dimensions indirectly using information in the title block or a general note. See **Figure 20-1**. Any dimension that requires a tolerance that is different from the general tolerances given in the title block or general note must have the specific tolerance applied directly to the dimension on the drawing. See **Figure 20-2**.

The dimension stated as 12.50±0.25 in **Figure 20-2A** is in a style known as *plus-minus dimensioning*. The tolerance of this dimension is the difference between the maximum and minimum *limits*. The plus-minus tolerance style applies when the variance is the same in the positive and negative directions. In this case, the upper limit is 12.75 (12.50 + 0.25 = 12.75), and the lower limit is 12.25 (12.50 – 0.25 = 12.25). To find the tolerance, subtract the lower limit from the upper limit. The tolerance in this example is 0.50 (12.75 – 12.25 = 0.50). The *specified dimension* of the feature shown in **Figure 20-2** is 12.50.

tolerance: The total amount by which a specific dimension is permitted to vary.

plus-minus dimensioning: A tolerance style in which the positive and negative variance is equal and is preceded by a ± symbol.

limits: The largest and smallest numerical values the feature can have.

specified dimension: The part of the dimension from which the limits are calculated.

Figure 20-1. The title block or a general note provides indirect tolerance specifications. A—An unspecified tolerance on an inch drawing. B—An unspecified tolerance on a metric drawing. Metric tolerancing is generally controlled by the ISO 2768—*General Tolerances* standard developed by the International Organization for Standardization (ISO).

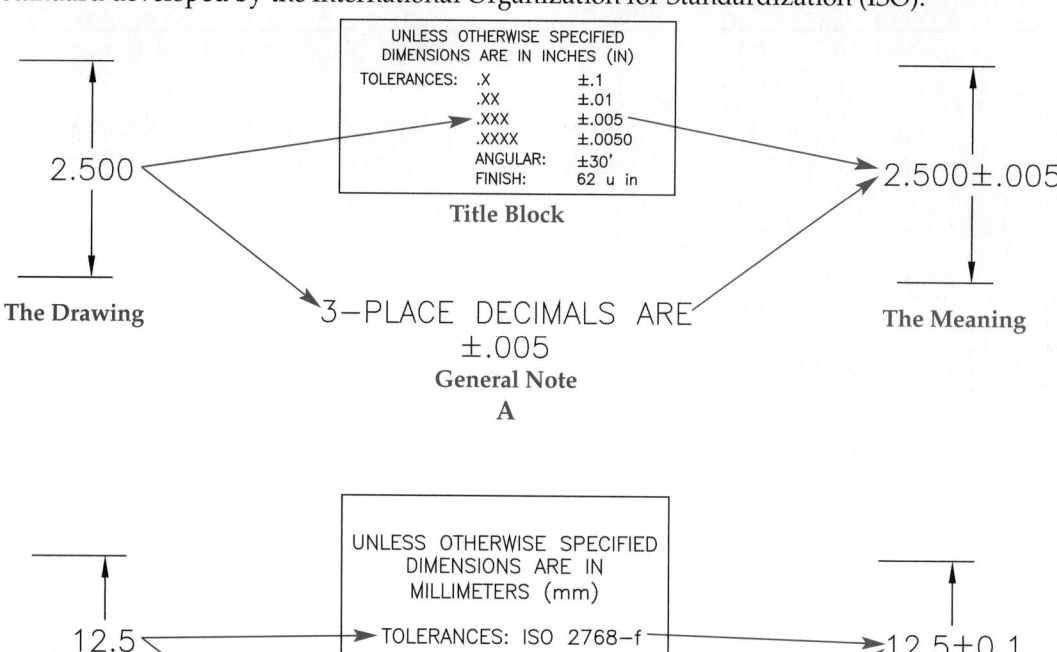

Figure 20-2. A—Plus-minus dimensioning. B—Limit dimensioning.

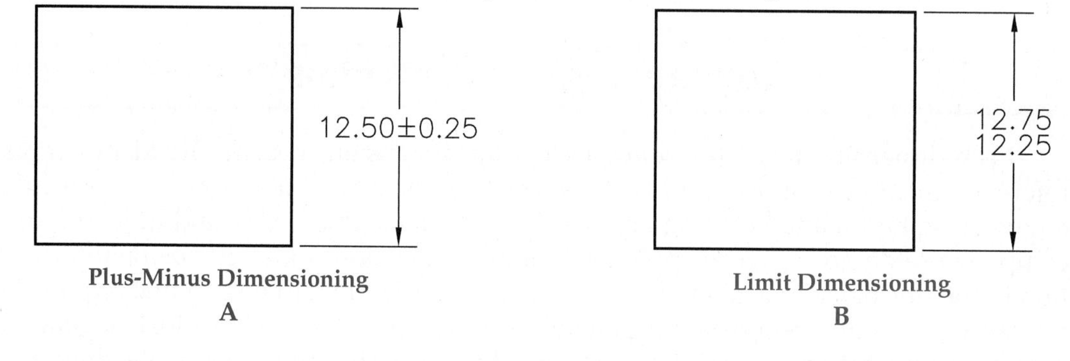

Plus-Minus Dimensioning
A

12.50±0.25

Limit Dimensioning
B

12.75
12.25

limit dimensioning:
Method in which the upper and lower limits are given, instead of the specified dimension and tolerance.

bilateral tolerance:
A tolerance style that permits variance in both the positive and negative directions from the specified dimension.

Limit dimensioning, shown in **Figure 20-2B**, is an alternative method of showing and calculating tolerance. Limit dimensioning is most common for defining fits between mating parts, such as a sliding fit between a hole and shaft or a press fit between a hole and bearing. Some companies, or departments within a company, such as an inspection department, prefer limits dimensioning because it does not require calculating limits. However, the actual dimension of the object in the drawing is unknown.

Plus-minus dimensioning uses a bilateral or unilateral tolerance format, depending on the application. **Figure 20-3** shows examples of equal and unequal *bilateral tolerances*. Bilateral tolerancing is the most common tolerancing method. Manufacturers typically

AutoCAD and Its Applications—Basics

Figure 20-3.
Examples of plus-minus dimensioning values using bilateral tolerances.

24 ± 0.1	$.750 \pm .005$	$45°30' \pm 0°5'$
Metric	Inch	Angular

Equal Bilateral Tolerance

$24^{+0.08}_{-0.20}$	$.750^{+.002}_{-.003}$	$45.5°^{+0.2°}_{-0.5°}$
Metric	Inch	Angular

Unequal Bilateral Tolerance

prefer equal bilateral tolerancing because they attempt to manufacture features as close to the specified dimension as possible. **Figure 20-4** shows examples of *unilateral tolerances*. Some companies use unilateral tolerances to define fits between mating parts. However, manufacturers who use the drawing to program computerized numerically controlled (CNC) machining equipment often avoid unilateral tolerancing.

Basic dimensions establish true position from datums and between interrelated features, and define true profile. A rectangle around the dimension value distinguishes a basic dimension from other types of dimensions. *Single limits* are sometimes applied to various features, such as chamfers, fillets, rounds, hole depths, and thread lengths. The abbreviation for minimum (MIN) or maximum (MAX) follows the dimension value to describe a single limit application. The design determines the unspecified limit.

unilateral tolerance: A tolerance style that permits a variation in only one direction from the specified dimension.

basic dimension: A theoretically exact dimension used in geometric dimensioning and tolerancing.

single limits: Limit dimensions used when the specified dimension cannot be any more than the maximum or less than the minimum given value.

Dimensioning Units

The ASME Y14.5-2009 *Dimensioning and Tolerancing* standard has separate recommendations for the display of inch, metric, and angular dimensions. **Figure 20-5**, **Figure 20-6**, and **Figure 20-7** briefly explain the rules for each type of dimension. The U.S. unit of measure commonly used on engineering drawings is the inch. The SI unit of measure commonly used on engineering drawings is the millimeter. Company or school policy and product requirements determine the actual units used on engineering drawings.

Place the general note UNLESS OTHERWISE SPECIFIED, ALL DIMENSIONS ARE IN INCHES (or MILLIMETERS) on the drawing when all dimensions are in inches or millimeters. Follow millimeter dimensions on an inch drawing with the abbreviation mm. Follow inch dimensions on a metric drawing with the abbreviation IN. **Figure 20-2**, **Figure 20-3**, and **Figure 20-4** show examples of displaying inch, metric, and angular dimensions with specified tolerances.

Figure 20-4.
A unilateral tolerance allows variation in only one direction from the specified dimension.

$24^{0}_{-0.2}$	$.625^{+.000}_{-.004}$	$25.5°^{0}_{-0.5°}$
$24^{+0.2}_{0}$	$.625^{+.004}_{-.000}$	$25.5°^{+0.5°}_{0}$
Metric	Inch	Angular

Figure 20-5. Dimensioning rules for inch dimensions.

Rules for Inch Dimensions	Examples
A zero does not precede a decimal inch that is less than one.	.5
Express a specified dimension to the same number of decimal places as its tolerance. Add zeros to the right of the decimal point if needed.	.250±.005 (additional zero added to .25)
Fractional inches generally indicate a larger tolerance, or give nominal sizes, such as in a thread callout.	Dimension value: 2 1/2±1/32 Thread: 1/2-13UNC-2B
Plus and minus values of an inch tolerance have the same number of decimal places.	$.250^{+.005}_{-.010}$ .255 .240
Unilateral tolerances use the + or – symbol, and the 0 value has the same number of decimal places as the value that is greater or less than 0.	$.250^{+.005}_{-.000}$ $.250^{+.000}_{-.005}$
Inch limit tolerance values have the same number of decimal points. When displaying limit tolerance values on one line, the lower value precedes the higher value, and a dash separates the values. When displaying stacked limit tolerance values, place the higher value above the lower value.	One line: 1.000–1.062 Stacked: $\frac{1.062}{1.000}$
Basic dimension values have the same number of decimal places as their associated tolerance.	2.000

Setting Primary Units

A dimension style controls the appearance of dimensions, including dimension values and tolerance. The initial phase of dimensioning with tolerances involves setting the appropriate values for the primary units of the dimension style. Use the **Primary Units** tab of the **New** (or **Modify**) **Dimension Style** dialog box, shown in **Figure 20-8,** to set the dimension units and precision.

Use the **Precision** drop-down list in the **Linear dimensions** area to set the number of zeros displayed after the decimal point of the specified dimension. The **Zero suppression** settings control the display of zeros before and after the decimal point. For inch dimensions, the **Leading** options should be on, and the **Trailing** options should be off. For typical metric dimensions, without using sub-units, the **Leading** options should be off, and the **Trailing** options should be on.

Figure 20-6. Dimensioning rules for metric dimensions.

Rules for Metric Dimensions	Examples
Omit the decimal point and zero when the dimension is a whole number.	12
A zero precedes a decimal millimeter that is less than one.	0.5
When the dimension is greater than a whole number by a fraction of a millimeter, follow the last digit to the right of the decimal point with a zero. This rule is true unless the dimension displays tolerance values.	12.5
Plus and minus values of a metric tolerance have the same number of decimal places. Add zeros to fill in where needed.	$24\begin{smallmatrix}+0.25\\-0.10\end{smallmatrix}$ 24.25 24.00
Metric limit tolerance values have the same number of decimal points. When displaying limit tolerance values on one line, the lower value precedes the higher value, and a dash separates the values. When displaying stacked limit tolerance values, place the higher value above the lower value. Examples in ASME Y14.5 show no zeros after the specified dimension to match the tolerance.	One line: 7.5–7.6 Stacked: $\begin{smallmatrix}7.6\\7.5\end{smallmatrix}$ 24±0.25 24.5±0.25
When applying unilateral tolerances, use a single 0 without a + or – sign for the 0 part of the value.	$24\begin{smallmatrix}0\\-0.2\end{smallmatrix}$ $24\begin{smallmatrix}+0.25\\0\end{smallmatrix}$
Basic dimension values follow the same display rules as stated for other metric numbers.	$\boxed{24}$ $\boxed{24.5}$

Figure 20-7. Dimensioning rules for angular dimensions.

Rules for Angular Dimensions	Examples
Establish angular dimensions in degrees (°) and decimal degrees (30.5°), or in degrees (°), minutes ('), and seconds (").	24°15'30"
The plus and minus tolerance values and the angle have the same number of decimal places.	30.0°±0.5° (not 30°±0.5°)
Where only specifying minutes or seconds, precede the number of minutes or seconds with 0° or 0°0', as applicable.	0°45'30" 0°0'45"

Figure 20-8. The **Primary Units** tab of the **New** (or **Modify**) **Dimension Style** dialog box sets the unit format and precision of linear dimensions.

Set the precision for specified dimensions

Set the zero suppression

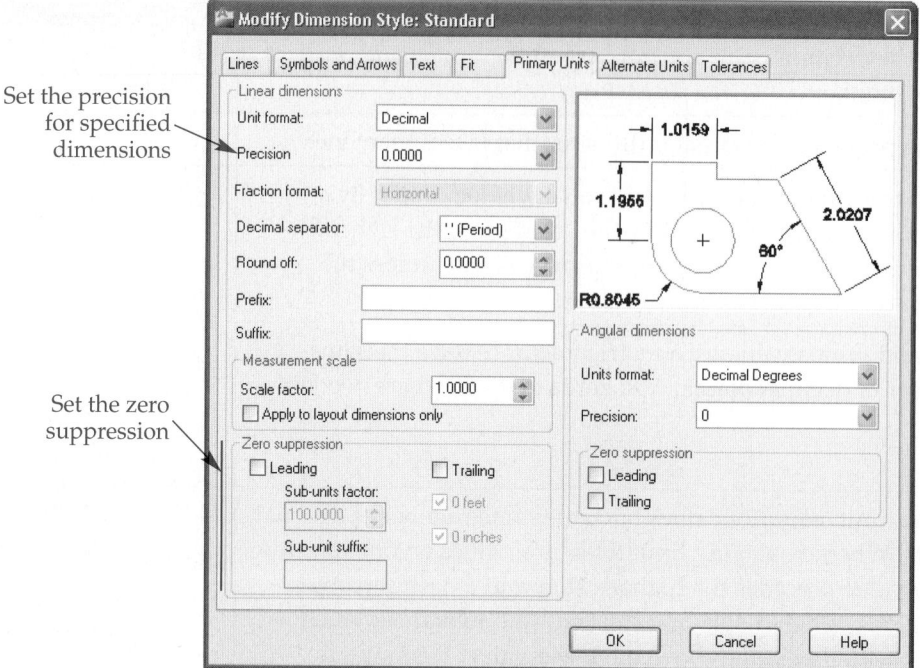

Setting Tolerance Methods

The **Tolerances** tab of the **New** (or **Modify**) **Dimension Style** dialog box, shown in **Figure 20-9**, allows you to create a specified tolerance dimension style. The default option in the **Method:** drop-down list is None. This means dimensions use an unspecified tolerance format. As a result, most of the options in the **Tolerances** tab are disabled. When you pick a different tolerance method from the drop-down list, appropriate options become enabled, and the preview image reflects the selected method. **Figure 20-10** shows the drop-down list options.

NOTE

The following information describes tolerance methods and the settings unique to each. You will learn about general settings, including tolerance precision, height, vertical position, alignment, and zero suppression, later in this chapter.

Symmetrical Tolerance Method

Select the **Symmetrical** option from the **Method:** drop-down list to create a *symmetrical tolerance*. Use the **Symmetrical** option to draw dimensions that display an equal bilateral tolerance in the plus-minus format. See **Figure 20-11**. Enter a tolerance value in the **Upper value:** text box. Although the **Lower value:** text box is disabled, you can see that the value in the **Lower value:** text box matches the value in the **Upper value:** text box.

symmetrical tolerance: The AutoCAD term for an equal bilateral tolerance.

Figure 20-9. The **Tolerances** tab of the **New** (or **Modify**) **Dimension Style** dialog box contains formatting settings for tolerance dimensions.

Select a tolerance method

Set the precision for tolerance dimensions

Settings should match the **Zero suppression** linear dimension settings in the **Primary Units** tab

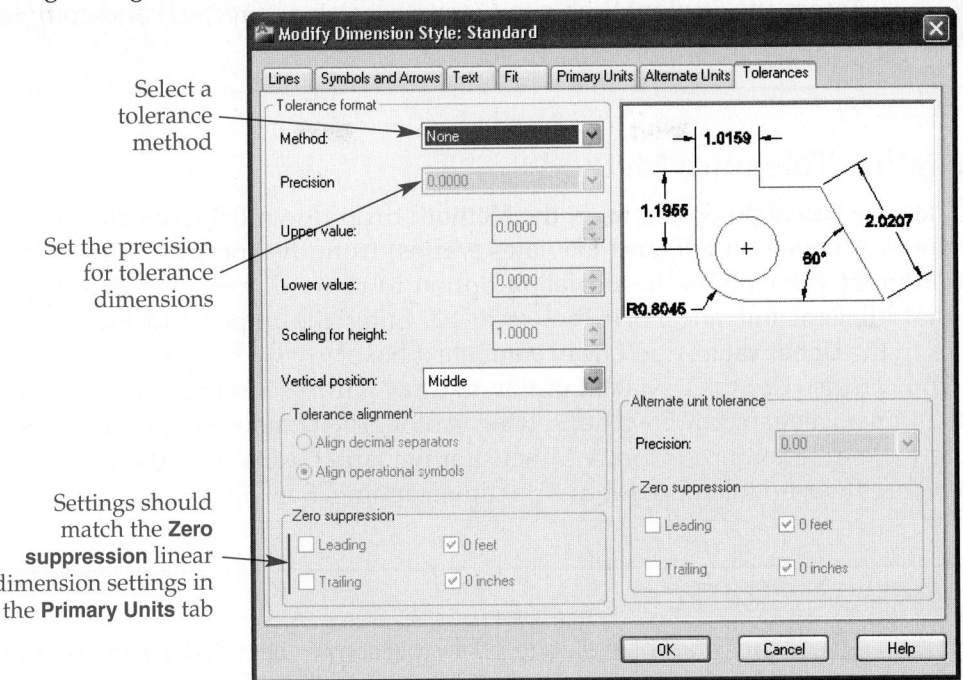

Figure 20-10. Select a tolerance method from the **Method:** drop-down list in the **Tolerance format** area.

Select a tolerance method

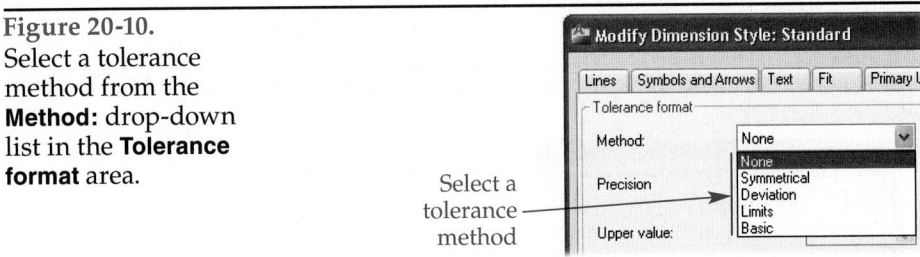

Figure 20-11. Setting the **Symmetrical** tolerance method option current, with an equal bilateral tolerance value of .005.

Specified tolerance method

Equal bilateral tolerance value

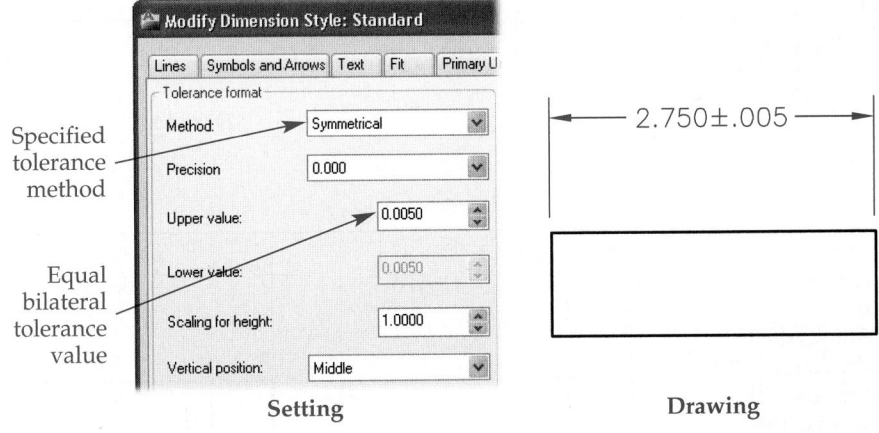

Setting   Drawing

Exercise 20-1

Access the Student Web site (www.g-wlearning.com/CAD) and complete Exercise 20-1.

Deviation Tolerance Method

deviation tolerance: The AutoCAD term for an unequal bilateral tolerance.

Pick the **Deviation** option from the **Method:** drop-down list to create a *deviation tolerance*. A deviation tolerance deviates (varies) from the specified dimension with two different values. Use the **Deviation** option to draw dimensions that display an unequal bilateral tolerance. See **Figure 20-12**. Enter the upper and lower tolerance values in the **Upper value:** and **Lower value:** text boxes.

You can also use the **Deviation** option to draw a unilateral tolerance by entering 0 for the **Upper value:** or **Lower value:** setting. AutoCAD includes the plus or minus sign before the zero tolerance for inch dimensioning. AutoCAD omits the plus or minus sign before the zero tolerance for metric dimensioning. See **Figure 20-13**.

Exercise 20-2

Access the Student Web site (www.g-wlearning.com/CAD) and complete Exercise 20-2.

Figure 20-12. Setting the **Deviation** tolerance method option current, with unequal bilateral tolerance values.

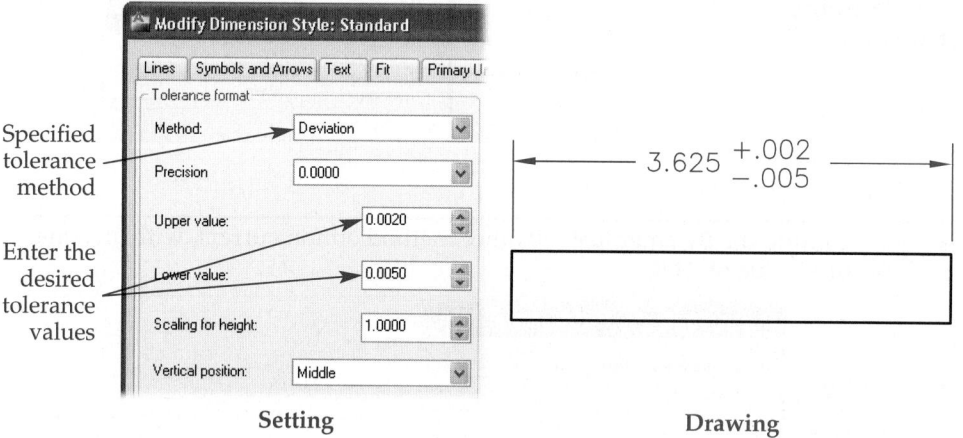

Figure 20-13. When you form a unilateral tolerance, AutoCAD automatically places the plus or minus symbol in front of the zero tolerance when using inch units. AutoCAD omits the plus symbol with metric units.

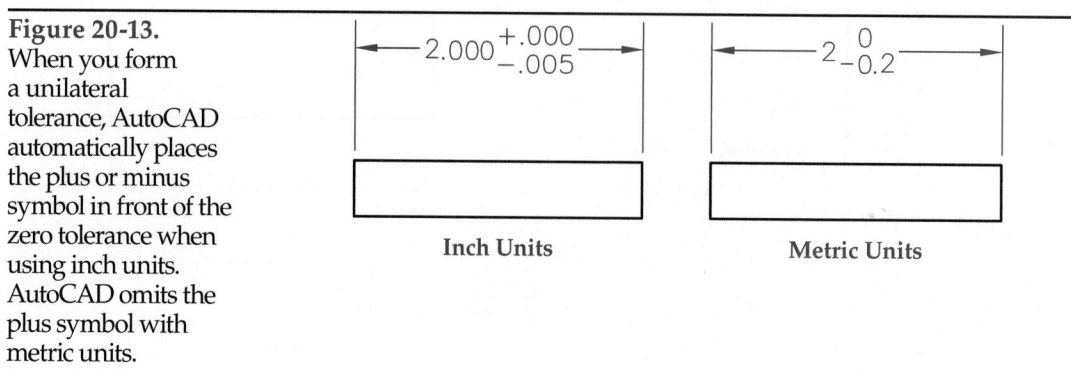

Limits Tolerance Method

Select the **Limits** option from the **Method:** drop-down list to apply limits dimensioning. See **Figure 20-14.** Use the **Upper value:** and **Lower value:** text boxes to enter the upper and lower tolerance values to add and subtract from the specified dimension. The upper and lower values can be equal or different.

Exercise 20-3

Access the Student Web site (www.g-wlearning.com/CAD) and complete Exercise 20-3.

Basic Tolerance Method

Pick the **Basic** option from the **Method:** drop-down list to draw basic dimensions. See **Figure 20-15.** Few options are enabled in the dialog box because a basic dimension has no tolerance. A rectangle around the dimension value distinguishes a basic dimension from other dimensions.

Figure 20-14. Selecting the **Limits** tolerance method and setting limit values.

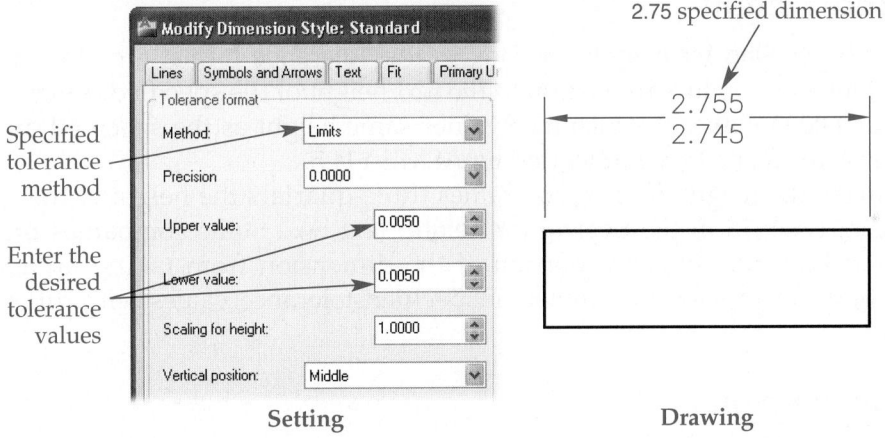

Setting   Drawing

Figure 20-15. Use the **Basic** tolerance method for basic dimensioning. The dimension text for a basic dimension appears inside a box.

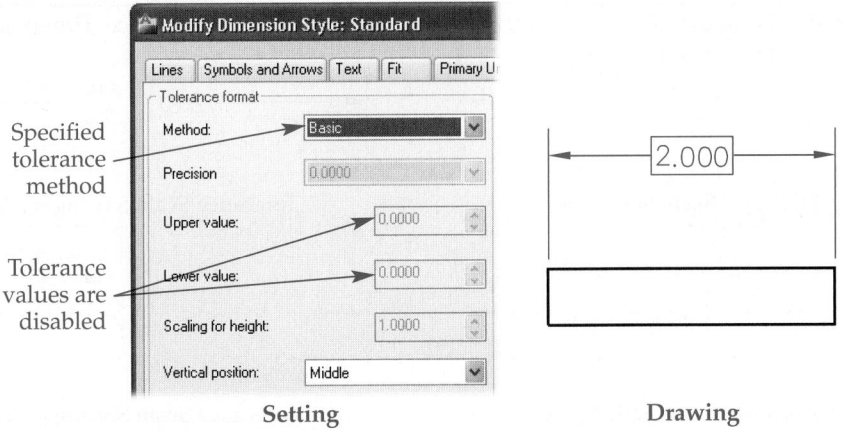

Setting   Drawing

Tolerance Precision

Adjust the tolerance precision after you choose the tolerance method. AutoCAD automatically makes the tolerance precision in the **Tolerances** tab the same precision you set in the **Primary Units** tab. If the tolerance precision does not reflect the correct level of precision, change the precision using the **Precision** drop-down list in the **Tolerance format** area.

Tolerance Height

Use the **Scaling for height:** text box in the **Tolerance format** area to set the text height of tolerance values in relation to the text height of the specified dimension. The default of 1.0000 makes the tolerance values same height as the specified dimension text. This is the format recommended by ASME Y14.5.

To make the height of tolerance values three-quarters the height of the specified dimension, type .75 in the **Scaling for height:** text box. Some companies prefer this practice to keep the tolerance portion of the dimension from taking up additional space. **Figure 20-16** shows examples of specified tolerance values with different text heights.

Vertical Position

Use the options in the **Vertical position:** drop-down list in the **Tolerance format** area to control the alignment, or justification, of deviation tolerance dimensions. The

Figure 20-16. Using different scale settings for the text height of tolerance dimensions. Use a scale of 1 to adhere to ASME standards.

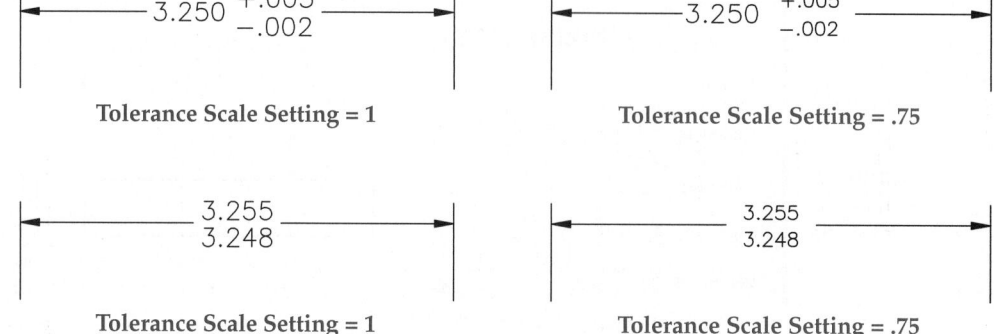

default **Middle** option centers the tolerance with the specified dimension. This is the format recommended by ASME Y14.5. The other justification options are **Top** and **Bottom**. **Figure 20-17** displays deviation tolerance dimensions with each justification option.

Tolerance Alignment

The options in the **Tolerance alignment** area become enabled when you use a deviation or limits tolerance method. Tolerance alignment controls the left and right tolerance justification. When using a deviation tolerance method, pick the **Align decimal separators** radio button to align the upper and lower tolerance value decimal points vertically. Select the **Align operational symbols** radio button to align the upper and lower tolerance plus and minus symbols vertically. See **Figure 20-18.** When using the limits tolerance method, pick the **Align decimal separators** radio button to align the upper and lower limit decimal points vertically. Select the **Align operational symbols** radio button to left-justify the upper and lower limits. See **Figure 20-19.**

Zero Suppression

You must select a tolerance method to enable the options in the **Zero suppression** area. The suppression settings for linear dimensions in the **Tolerances** tab should be the same as the **Zero suppression** tolerance format settings in the **Primary Units** tab. AutoCAD does not automatically match the tolerance setting to the primary units setting.

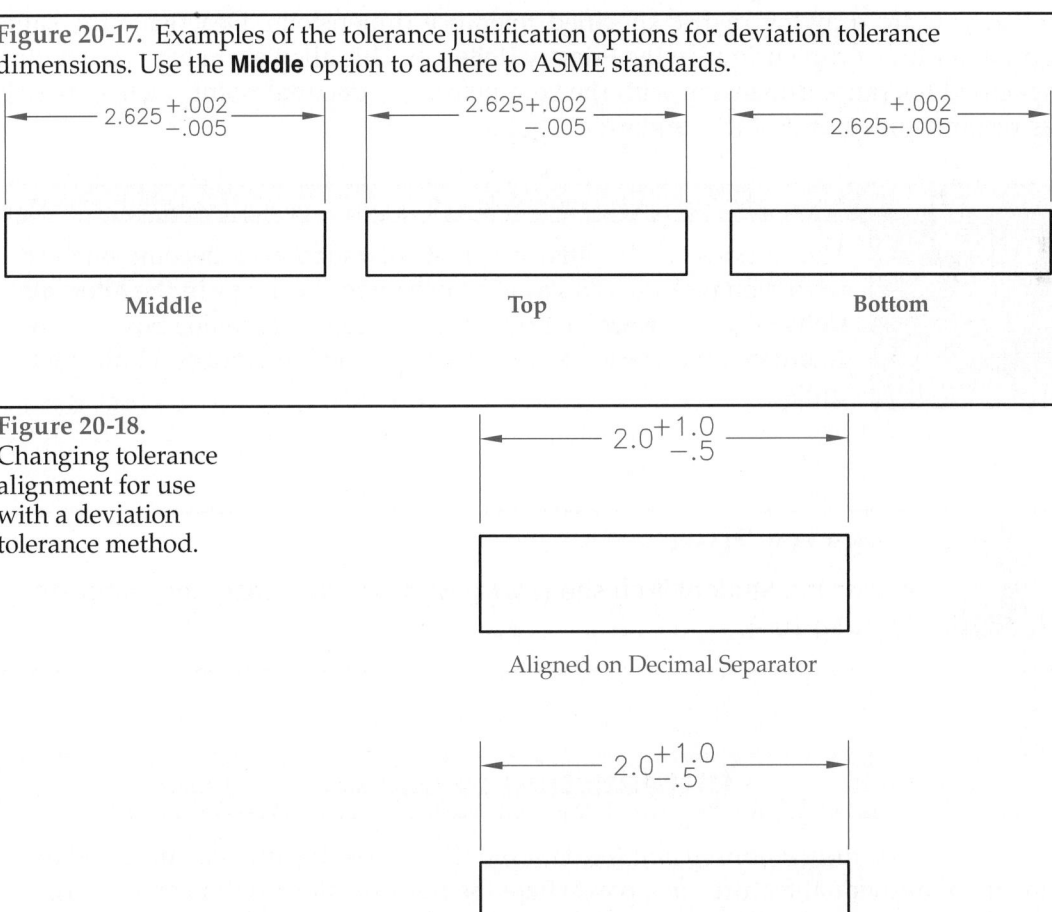

Figure 20-17. Examples of the tolerance justification options for deviation tolerance dimensions. Use the **Middle** option to adhere to ASME standards.

Middle   Top   Bottom

Figure 20-18.
Changing tolerance alignment for use with a deviation tolerance method.

Aligned on Decimal Separator

Aligned on Operational Symbols

Figure 20-19.
Changing tolerance
alignment for
use with a limits
tolerance method.

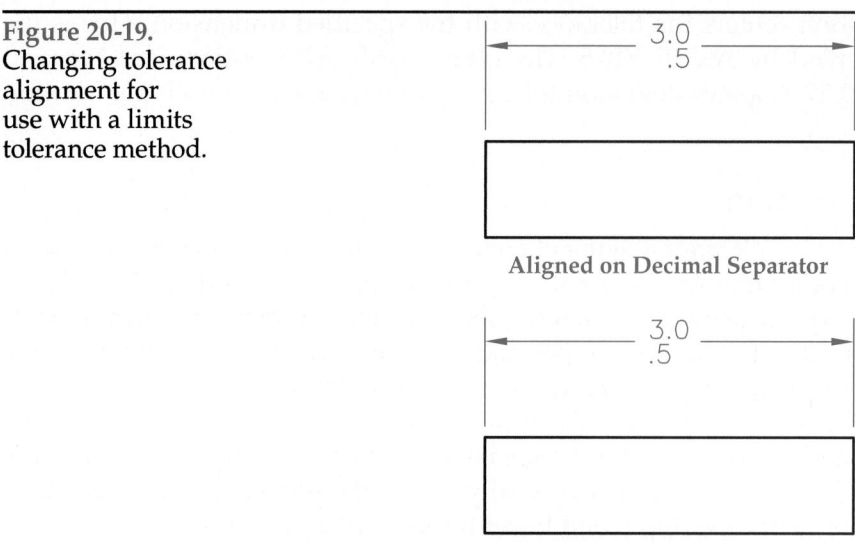

Aligned on Decimal Separator

Aligned on Operational Symbols

Select the **Leading** check box in the **Zero suppression** area of the **Tolerances** tab when you are drawing inch specified tolerance dimensions. Activate the same option for linear dimensions in the **Primary Units** tab. You can then draw inch specified tolerance dimensions without placing the zero before the decimal point, as recommended by ASME standards. These settings allow you to create a tolerance dimension such as .625±.005.

Deselect the **Leading** check box in the **Zero suppression** area of the **Tolerances** tab when you are drawing metric specified tolerance dimensions. Deactivate the same option for linear dimensions in the **Primary Units** tab. This allows you to place a metric specified tolerance dimension with the zero before the decimal point, such as 12±0.2, as recommended by ASME standards.

> **NOTE**
>
> The options in the **Alternate unit tolerance** area become enabled when you pick the **Display alternate units** check box in the **Alternate Units** tab of the **New** (or **Modify**) **Dimension Style** dialog box. Use the **Alternate unit tolerance** area to set specified tolerances for alternate units.

Exercise 20-4

Access the Student Web site (www.g-wlearning.com/CAD) and complete Exercise 20-4.

geometric dimensioning and tolerancing (GD&T): The dimensioning and tolerancing of individual features of a part where the permissible variations relate to characteristics of form, profile, orientation, runout, or the relationship between features.

Introduction to GD&T

Geometric dimensioning and tolerancing (GD&T) is the dimensioning and tolerancing of individual features of a part where the permissible variations relate to characteristics of form, profile, orientation, runout, or the relationship between features. For complete coverage of GD&T, refer to *Geometric Dimensioning and Tolerancing* by David A. Madsen, published by Goodheart-Willcox Company, Inc.

Reference Material

Drafting Symbols

For the names and examples of GD&T symbols and symbol applications, go to the **Reference Material** section of the Student Web site (www.g-wlearning.com/CAD) and select **Drafting Symbols** in the list.

Supplemental Material

GD&T with AutoCAD

For information about creating GD&T symbols using AutoCAD, go to the Student Web site (www.g-wlearning.com/CAD), select this chapter, and select **Using GD&T Tools in AutoCAD**.

Chapter Test

Answer the following questions. Write your answers on a separate sheet of paper or go to the Student Web site (www.g-wlearning.com/CAD) and complete the electronic chapter test.

1. Define the term *tolerance*.
2. What are the limits of the tolerance dimension 3.625±.005?
3. Give an example of an equal bilateral tolerance in inches and in metric units.
4. Give an example of an unequal bilateral tolerance in inches and in metric units.
5. Give an example of a unilateral tolerance in inches and in metric units.
6. What is the purpose of the **Symmetrical** tolerance method option?
7. What is the purpose of the **Deviation** tolerance method option?
8. What is the purpose of the **Limits** tolerance method option?
9. How do you set the number of zeros displayed after the decimal point for a tolerance dimension?
10. Explain the result of setting the **Scaling for height:** option to 1 in the **Tolerances** tab.
11. What setting should you use for the **Scaling for height:** option if you want the tolerance dimension height to be three-quarters of the specified dimension height?
12. Name the tolerance dimension justification option recommended by the ASME standards.
13. Which **Zero suppression** settings should you choose for linear and tolerance dimensions when using inch units?
14. Which **Zero suppression** settings should you choose for linear and tolerance dimensions when using metric units?
15. What is the purpose of geometric dimensioning and tolerancing?

Drawing Problems

- *Start AutoCAD if it is not already started. Start a new drawing for each problem using an appropriate template of your choice.*
- *The template should include layers and text, dimension, multileader, and table styles, when necessary, for drawing the given objects. Add layers and text, dimension, multileader, and table styles as needed.*
- *Draw all objects using appropriate layers and text, dimension, multileader, and table styles, justification, and format.*
- *Follow the specific instructions for each problem. Use only drawing and editing tools and techniques you have already learned. Use your own judgment and approximate dimensions when necessary.*
- *Apply dimensions accurately using ASME or appropriate industry standards.*

▼ Basic

1. Draw and dimension the part view shown. Save the drawing as P20-1.

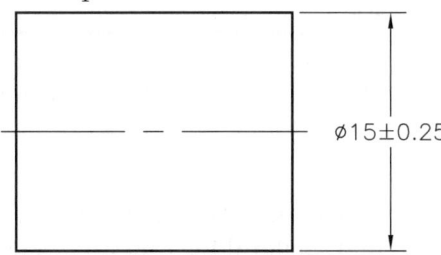

2. Draw and dimension the part view shown. Save the drawing as P20-2.

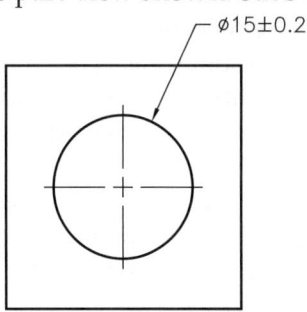

For Problems 3 through 6, draw and dimension the orthographic views needed to describe the part completely. Save the drawings as P20-3, P20-4, P20-5, and P20-6.

3.

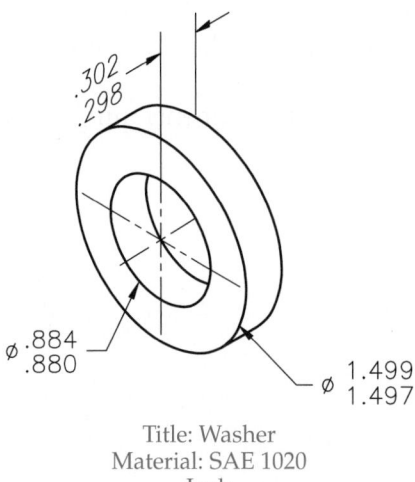

Title: Washer
Material: SAE 1020
Inch

4.

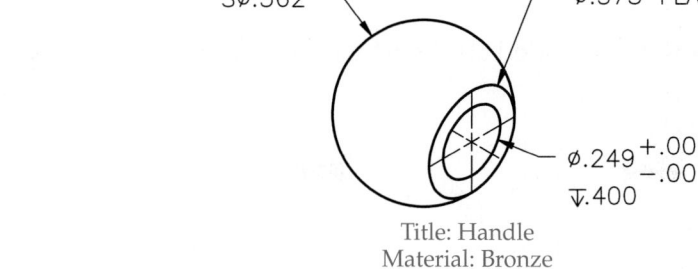

SØ.562   Ø.375 FLAT

Ø.249 $^{+.000}_{-.001}$

↧.400

Title: Handle
Material: Bronze
Inch

5.

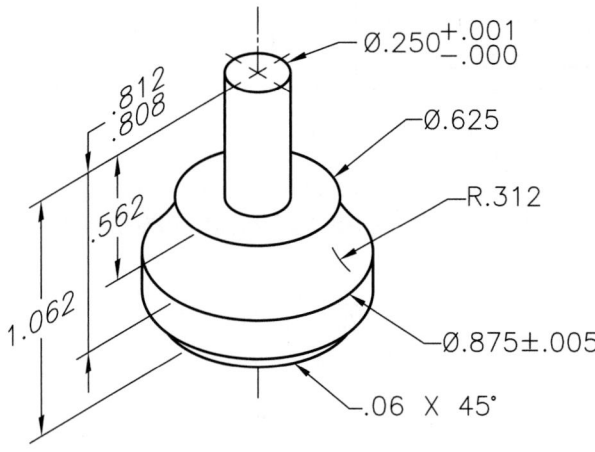

Ø.250 $^{+.001}_{-.000}$

Ø.625

R.312

.812
.808

.562

1.062

Ø.875±.005

.06 X 45°

ALL OTHER THREE PLACE DECIMALS ±.010

6.

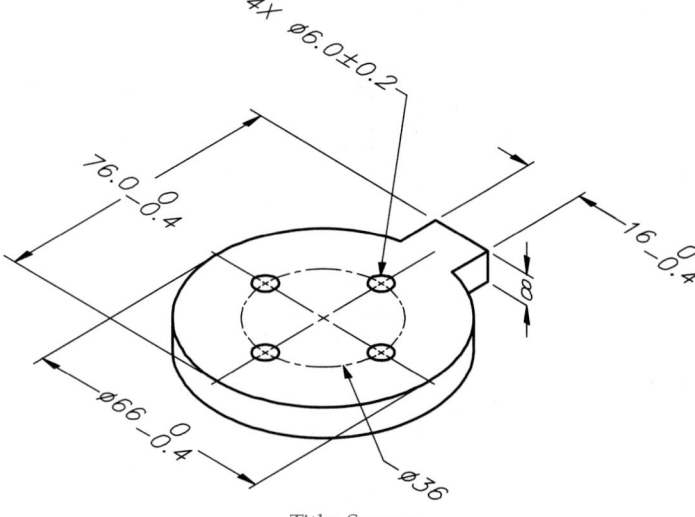

4X Ø6.0±0.2

76.0 $^{0}_{-0.4}$

16 $^{0}_{-0.4}$

8

Ø66 $^{0}_{-0.4}$

Ø36

Title: Spacer
Material: Cold Rolled Steel
Metric

▼ Intermediate

7. Draw and dimension the threaded stud part views shown. Save the drawing as P20-7.

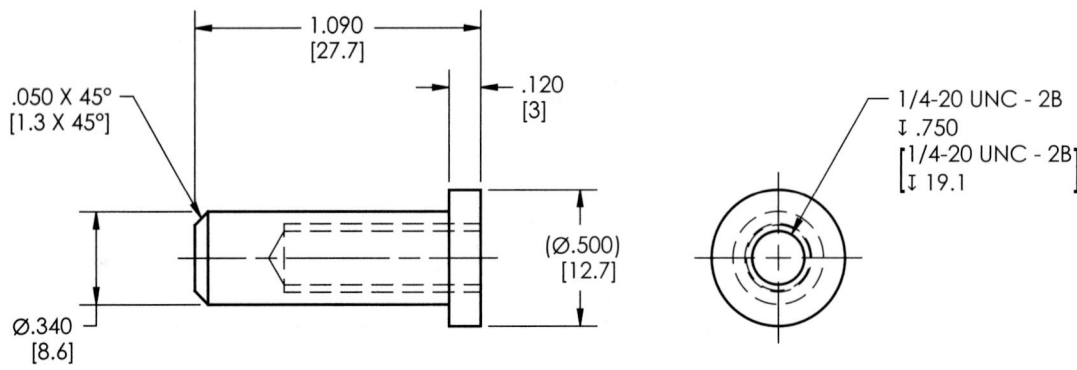

For Problems 8 through 10, draw and dimension the orthographic views needed to describe the part completely. Save the drawings as P20-8, P20-9, *and* P20-10.

8.

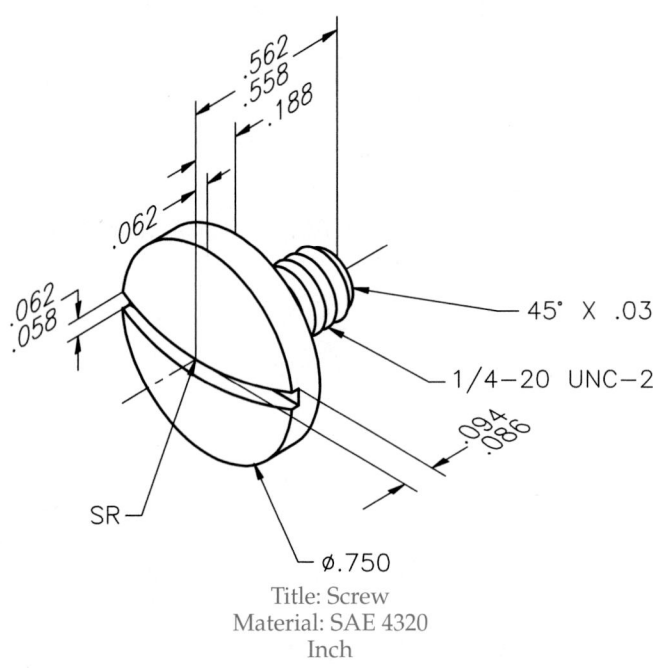

Title: Screw
Material: SAE 4320
Inch

Drawing Problems - Chapter 20

9. A portion of the drawing is removed for clarity. Draw the entire part.

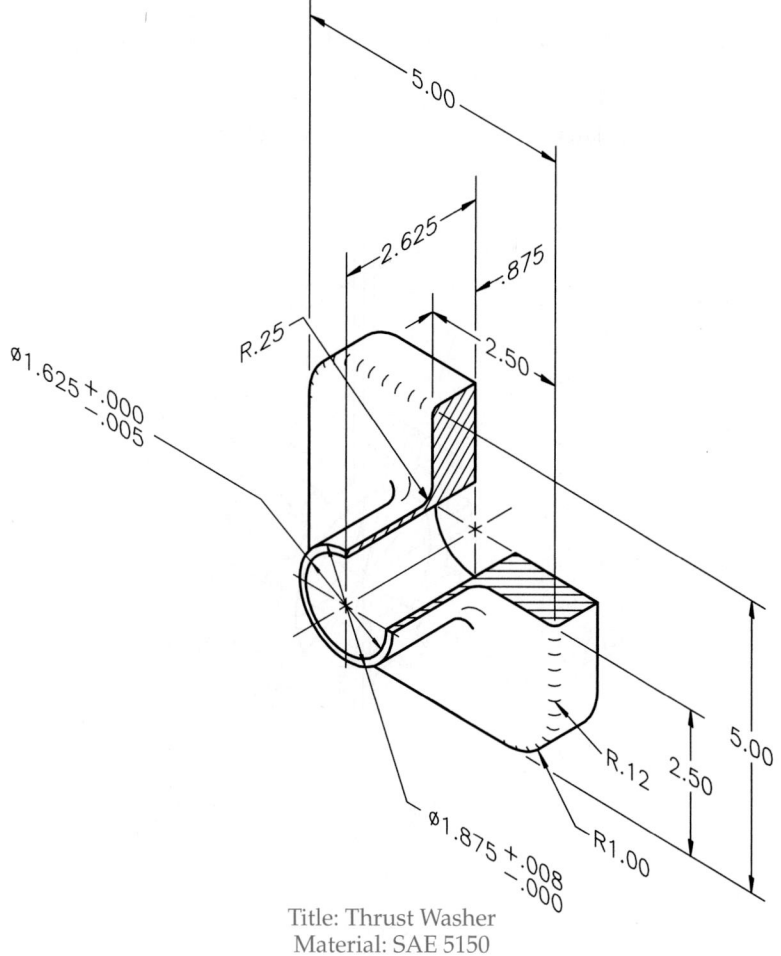

Title: Thrust Washer
Material: SAE 5150
Inch

▼ Advanced

10.

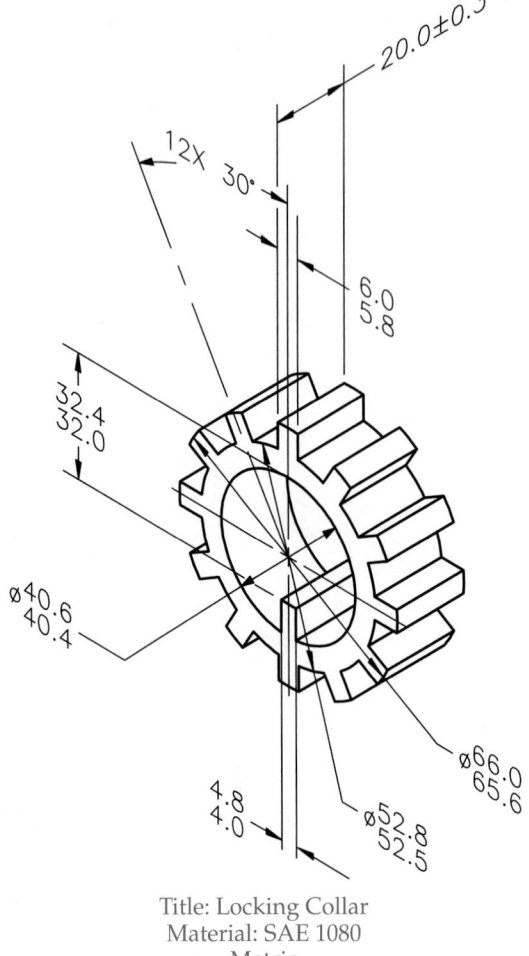

Title: Locking Collar
Material: SAE 1080
Metric

11. Draw and dimension the vise clamp part views shown. Save the drawing as P20-11.

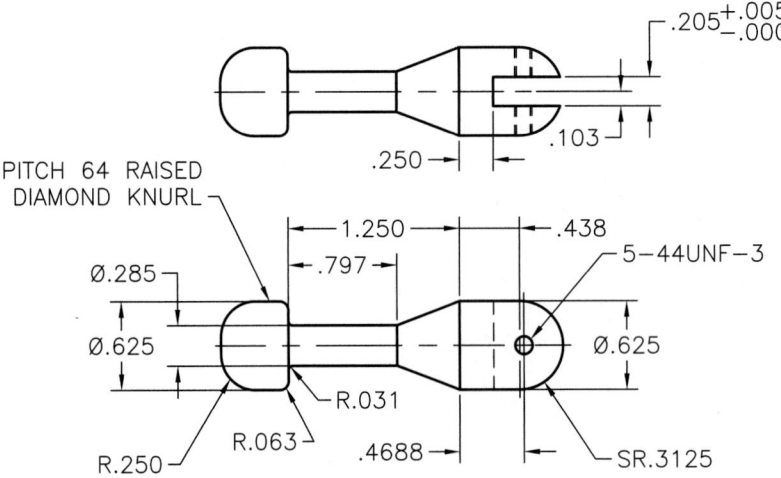

For Problems 12 through 16, draw and dimension the orthographic views needed to describe the part completely. Save the drawings as P20-12, P20-13, P20-14, P20-15, *and* P20-16. *Use the GD&T tools and practices described in the "Using GD&T Tools in AutoCAD" supplement available in the* Supplemental Material for this chapter on *the Student Web site.*

12. Untoleranced dimensions are ±0.3.

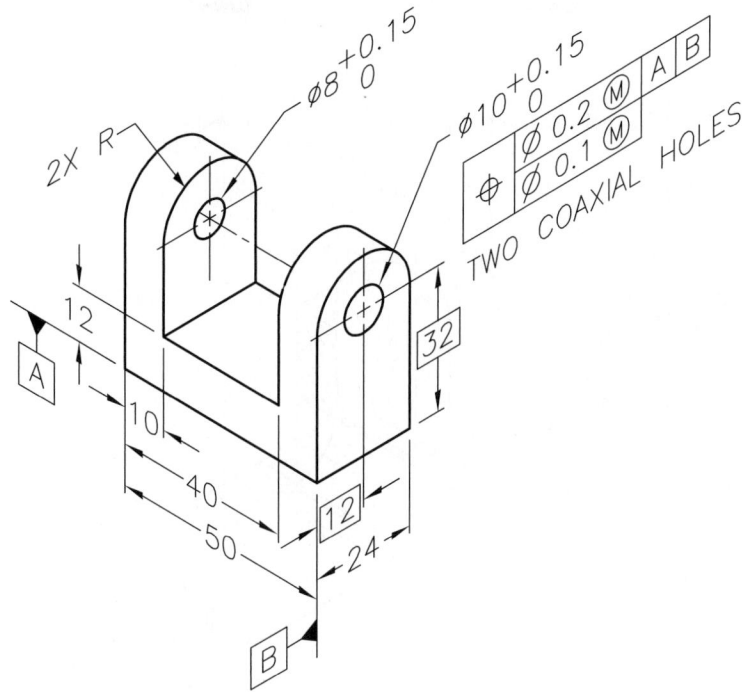

13. Open P20-9 and save the file as P20-13. The P20-13 file should be active. Add the geometric tolerancing applications shown. Untoleranced dimensions are ±.02 for two-place decimal precision and ±.005 for three-place decimal precision.

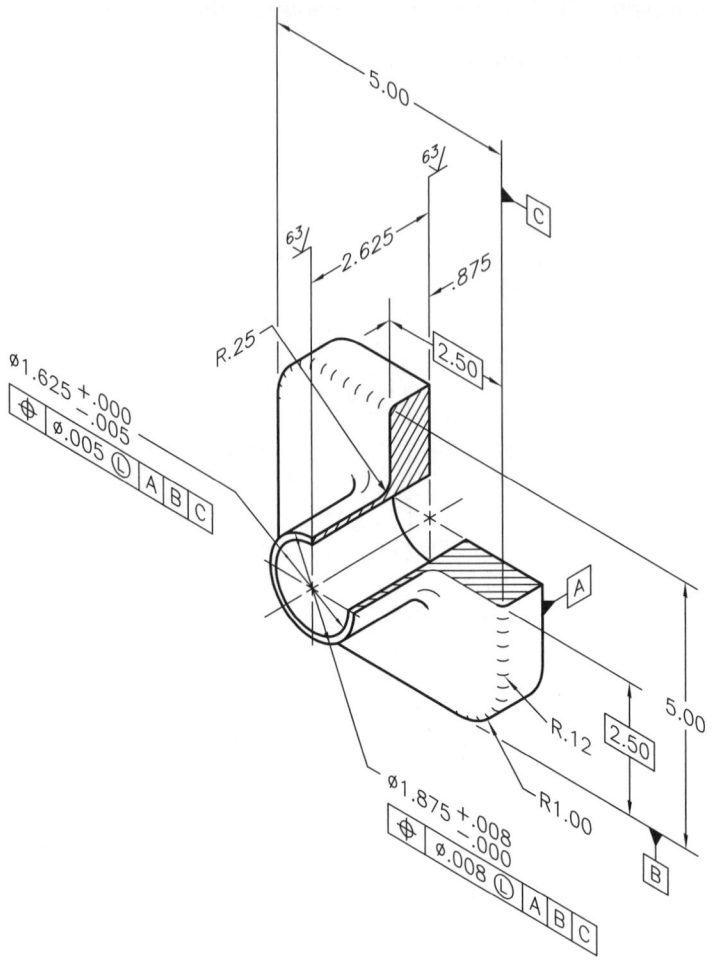

14. Open P20-6 and save the file as P20-14. The P20-14 file should be active. Add the geometric tolerancing applications shown. Untoleranced dimensions are ±0.5.

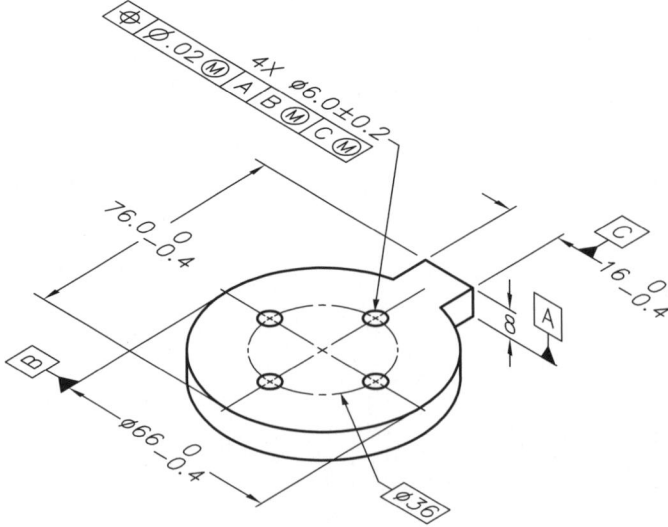

15. Open P20-10 and save the file as P20-15. The P20-15 file should be active. Add the geometric tolerancing applications shown.

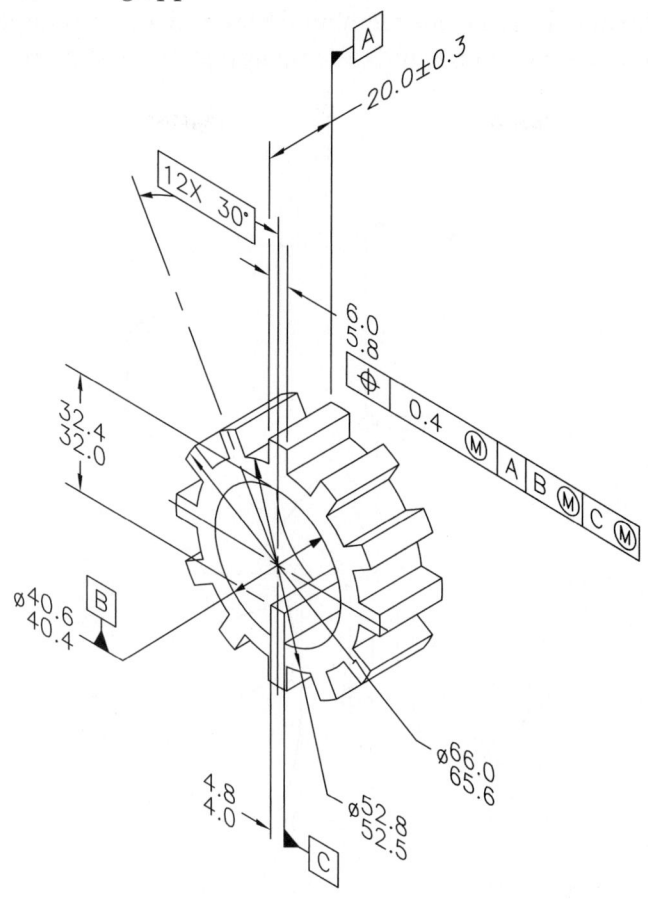

16. Half of the drawing is removed for clarity. Draw the entire part. Untoleranced dimensions are ±.010.

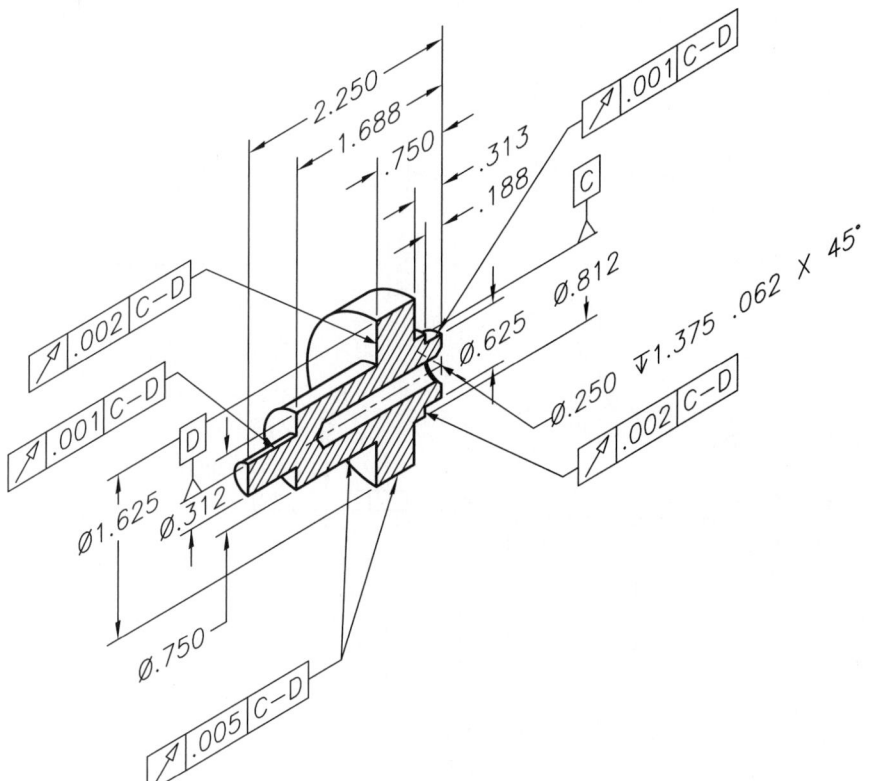

17. Open P19-22 and save the file as P20-17. The P20-17 file should be active. Use the GD&T tools and practices described in the "Using GD&T Tools in AutoCAD" supplement available in the Supplemental Material for this chapter on the Student Web site to add the geometric tolerancing applications shown.

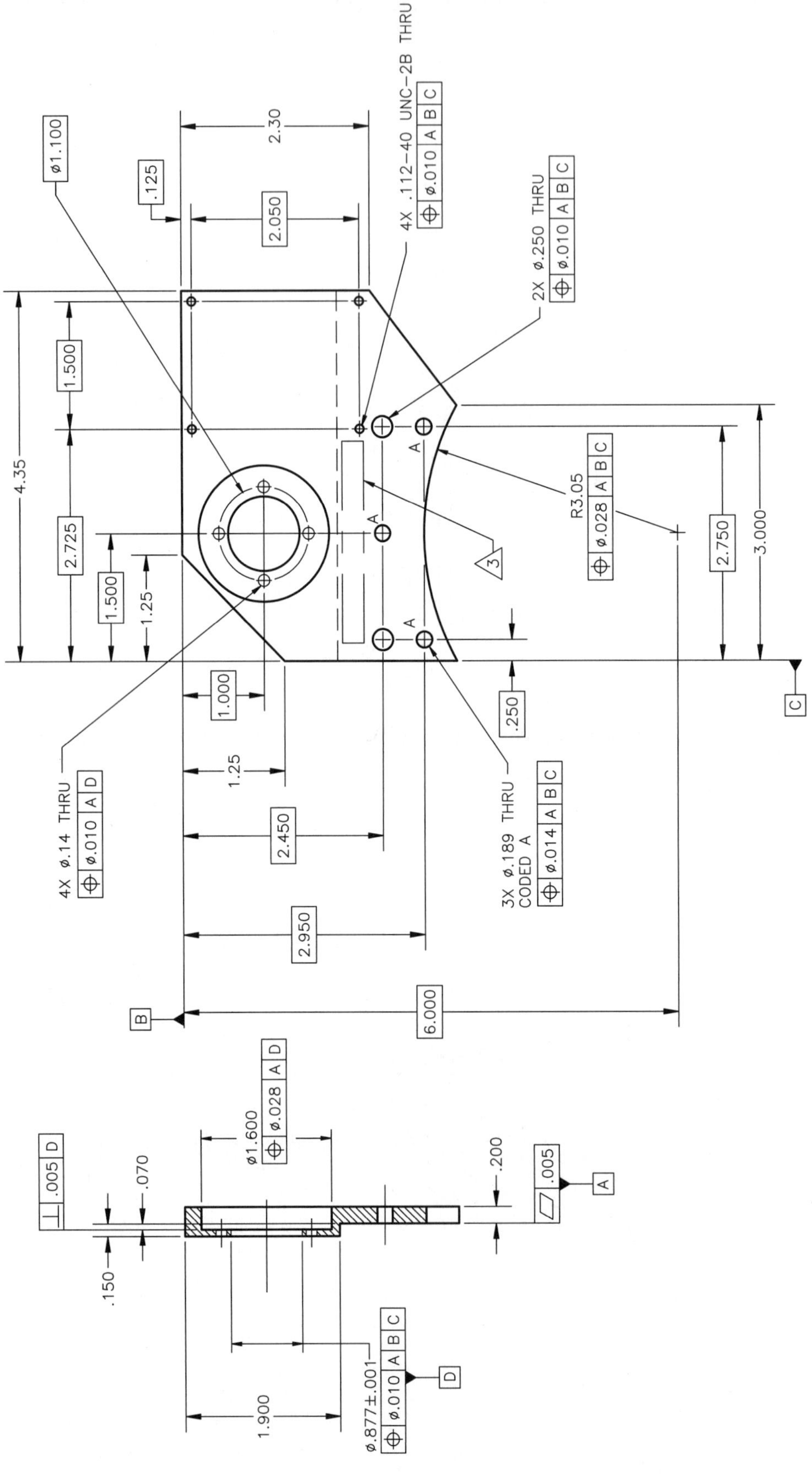

18. Draw and dimension the orthographic views needed to describe the part completely. Half of the drawing is removed for clarity. Draw the entire part. Untoleranced dimensions are ±.010. Use the GD&T tools and practices described in the "Using GD&T Tools in AutoCAD" supplement available in the Supplemental Material for this chapter on the Student Web site. Save the drawing as P20-18.

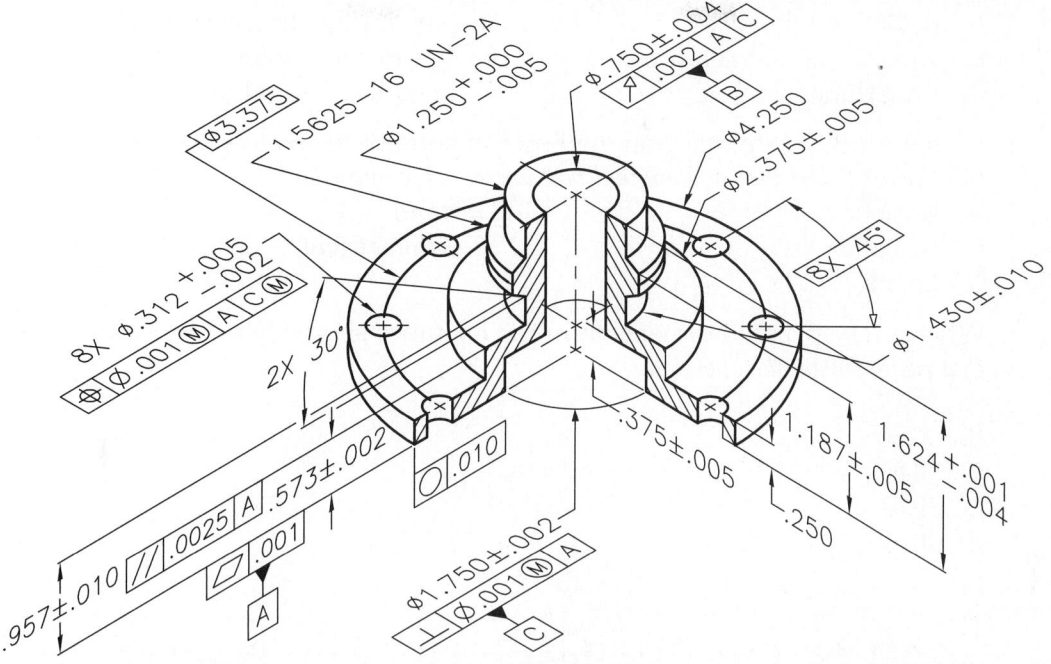

19. Research the design of an existing shaft collar with the following specifications: two-piece clamp-on, 1" bore, 1/4-28UNF screw threads. Create a dimensioned 2D sketch of the existing design from manufacturer's specifications, or from measurements taken from an actual shaft collar. Start a new drawing from scratch or use a decimal-unit template of your choice. Draw and dimension each part of the collar from your sketch. Save the drawing as P20-19.

AutoCAD Certified Associate Exam Practice

Answer the following questions. Write your answers on a separate sheet of paper.

1. Which of the following terms describes the dimension 18.75±.25? *Select all that apply.*
   A. deviation tolerance
   B. equal bilateral tolerance
   C. limit dimensioning
   D. plus-minus dimensioning
   E. symmetrical tolerance
   F. unequal bilateral tolerance

2. Which AutoCAD tolerancing method can you use to create an unequal bilateral tolerance? *Select the one item that best answers the question.*
   A. **Basic**
   B. **Deviation**
   C. **Limits**
   D. **None**
   E. **Symmetrical**

3. What is the specified dimension in the tolerance shown here? *Select the one item that best answers the question.*
   A. 10.17
   B. 10.50
   C. 10.60
   D. 10.62
   E. 10.67

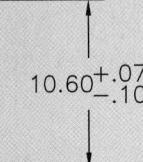

$10.60^{+.07}_{-.10}$

AutoCAD Certified Professional Exam Practice

Follow the instructions in each problem. Write your answers on a separate sheet of paper.

1. **Navigate to this chapter on the Student Web site and open CPE-20limits.dwg.** Create a new dimension style named Limits and select the **Limits** tolerancing method. Do not change any other settings. Use the Limits dimension style to create the two dimensions shown. What are the limits of dimensions A and B?

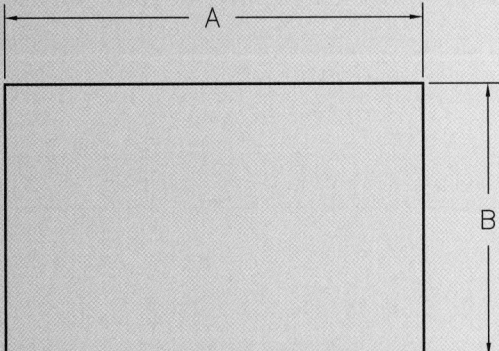

2. **Navigate to this chapter on the Student Web site and open CPE-20unilateral.dwg.** Create a new dimension style named Unilateral and select the appropriate tolerancing method to create a unilateral tolerance. Set an upper limit of 0 and a lower limit of −.021. Use the Unilateral dimension style to create the two dimensions shown. What are the limits of dimensions C and D?

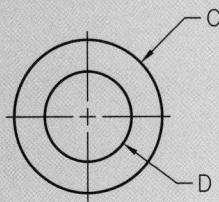

CHAPTER 21

Editing Dimensions

Learning Objectives

After completing this chapter, you will be able to do the following:

✓ Describe and control associative dimensions.
✓ Control the appearance of existing dimensions and dimension text.
✓ Update dimensions to reflect the current dimension style.
✓ Override dimension style settings and match dimension properties.
✓ Change dimension line spacing and alignment.
✓ Break dimension, extension, and leader lines.
✓ Create inspection dimensions.
✓ Edit existing multileaders.

You can modify dimensions using standard editing tools such as **ERASE** and **STRETCH**. AutoCAD also provides specific tools to adjust dimensions. This chapter describes techniques for editing dimension placement, value, and appearance.

Associative Dimensioning

A dimension is a group of elements treated as a single object. For example, you can access the **ERASE** tool and pick any portion of the dimension to erase the entire dimension. Additionally, dimensions reference objects or points. When you edit dimensioned objects with tools such as **STRETCH**, **MOVE**, **ROTATE**, and **SCALE**, dimensions change accordingly. See **Figure 21-1**.

An *associative dimension* forms by default when you select objects or pick points using object snaps. For example, if you dimension the ⌀1.0 circle in **Figure 21-1** using the **DIMDIAMETER** tool, and then change size of the circle to ⌀2.00, the diameter dimension adapts to show the correct size of the modified circle. Create associative dimensions when possible and practical by selecting objects or using object snaps. Associative dimensions relate best to object size and make revisions easier.

A *non-associative dimension* forms when you select points without using object snaps. A non-associative dimension is still a single object that updates when you make changes to the dimension, such as stretching the extension line origin. Non-associative dimensions are appropriate when associative dimensions would result

associative dimension: A dimension associated with an object. The dimension value updates automatically when the object changes.

non-associative dimension: A dimension linked to point locations, not an object; does not update when the object changes.

Figure 21-1. An example of a revised drawing. Dimensions adjust to the modified geometry, and the dimension values update to reflect the size and location of the modified geometry.

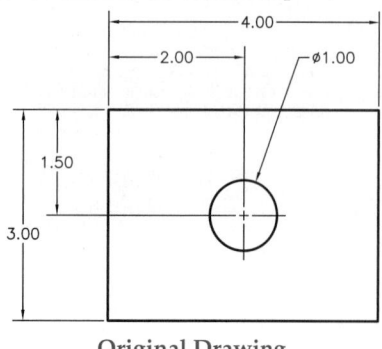

Original Drawing

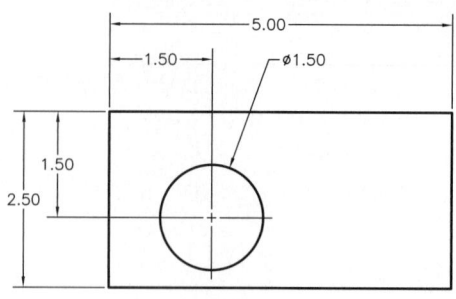

Revised Drawing

in dimensioning difficulty or unacceptable standards. When using non-associative dimensions, remember to edit the dimension with the object it dimensions, or adjust the dimension after the object changes.

NOTE

Refer to the **Associative** property in the **General** area of the **Properties** palette to determine whether a dimension is associative.

PROFESSIONAL TIP

Dimension tools allow you to dimension a drawing, but do not control object size and location. Chapter 22 explains how to use dimensional constraints to control object size and location. If you anticipate creating a drawing with features that will require significant or constant change, you may want to use dimensional constraints instead of, or in addition to, traditional dimensioning tools.

Associating Dimensions with Objects

Dimensions are associated with objects by default when you select objects or pick points using object snaps. To deactivate associative dimensioning for new objects, access the **Options** dialog box and deselect the **Make new dimensions associative** check box in the **Associative Dimensioning** area of the **User Preferences** tab.

Often the easiest way to convert a non-associative dimension to an associative dimension is to select the dimension to grip-edit, stretching the appropriate grip to the corresponding object snap point using the appropriate object snap mode. You can also convert dimensions using the **DIMREASSOCIATE** tool. Select the dimension to associate with an object. An X marker appears at a dimension origin, such as the origin of a linear dimension extension line or the center of a radial dimension. Select a point on an object to associate with the marker location. Repeat the process to locate the second object point for the first extension line, if required.

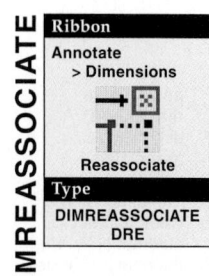

Ribbon

Annotate
> Dimensions

Reassociate

Type

DIMREASSOCIATE
DRE

Use the **Next** option to advance to the next definition point. Use the **Select object** option to select an object to associate with the dimension. The extension line endpoints automatically associate with the object endpoints.

Type

DIMDISASSOCIATE

> **NOTE**
>
> To disassociate a dimension from an object, grip-edit the dimension to stretch an appropriate grip point away from the associated object, or use the **DIMDISASSOCIATE** tool.

> **NOTE**
>
> The **Dimension** panel of the **Express Tools** ribbon tab includes a **DIMREASSOC** tool, not to be confused with the **DIMREASSOCIATE** tool, that allows you to change the overridden value of an associated dimension back to the actual associated dimension value. Access the **DIMREASSOC** tool and select associative dimensions to change. The **DIMREASSOCIATE** tool creates an associative dimension, but does not change an overridden dimension value.

Definition Points

Definition points, or *defpoints*, form automatically when you create a dimension. Use the **Node** object snap to snap to a definition point. If you select an object to edit and want to include dimensions in the edit, you must include the definition points in the selection set. AutoCAD automatically creates a Defpoints layer and places definition points on the layer. By default, the Defpoints layer does not plot. You can only plot definition points if you rename the Defpoints layer and then set the renamed layer to plot. Definition points are displayed even if you turn off or freeze the Defpoints layer.

definition points (defpoints): The points used to specify the dimension location and the center point of the dimension text.

Exercise 21-1

Access the Student Web site (www.g-wlearning.com/CAD) and complete Exercise 21-1.

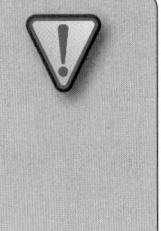

> **CAUTION**
>
> A dimension is a single object even though it consists of extension lines, a dimension line, arrowheads, and text. You may be tempted to explode the dimension using the **EXPLODE** tool to modify individual dimension elements. You should rarely, if ever, explode dimensions. Exploded dimensions lose layer assignment and association to related features and dimension styles.

> **PROFESSIONAL TIP**
>
> You can edit individual dimension properties without exploding a dimension using dimension shortcut menu options or the **Properties** palette to create a dimension style override.

Dimension Editing Tools

As the drawing process evolves and design changes occur, you will find it necessary to make changes to dimensioned objects and dimensions. AutoCAD includes dimension-specific editing tools and techniques to help you adjust dimensions as necessary.

Dimension Shortcut Menu Options

Select a dimension and then right-click to display the shortcut menu shown in Figure 21-2. The **Dim Text position** cascading submenu provides options to adjust the dimension value location. Pick **Above dim line** to move the dimension text above the dimension line. Select **Centered** to center the dimension text on the dimension line. Pick **Home text** to reposition the text at its original position. **Move text alone** allows you to move the text away from the dimension line. **Move with leader** allows you to move the text away from the dimension line and attach a leader from the text to the dimension line. **Move with dimension line** allows you to move the text, but maintain alignment between the text and the dimension line.

The **Precision** cascading submenu includes options to adjust the number of decimal places displayed with a dimension value. The **Precision** cascading submenu often provides the easiest way to specify an alternative tolerance. Use the **Dim Style** cascading submenu to assign a different dimension style to the dimension or to save a new dimension style based on the properties of the selected dimension.

Pick the **Flip Arrow** option to flip the direction of a dimension arrowhead to the opposite side of the extension line or object that the arrow touches. For example, if arrowheads and the dimension value are crowded inside extension lines, flip the arrowheads to the outside of extension lines to make the dimension easier to read. If the selected dimension includes two arrowheads, only the arrowhead closest to the point you pick when you select the dimension (not the right-click point) flips. This allows you to control the arrowheads independently.

Figure 21-2.
Select a dimension and then right-click to access this shortcut menu with options for adjusting individual dimensions.

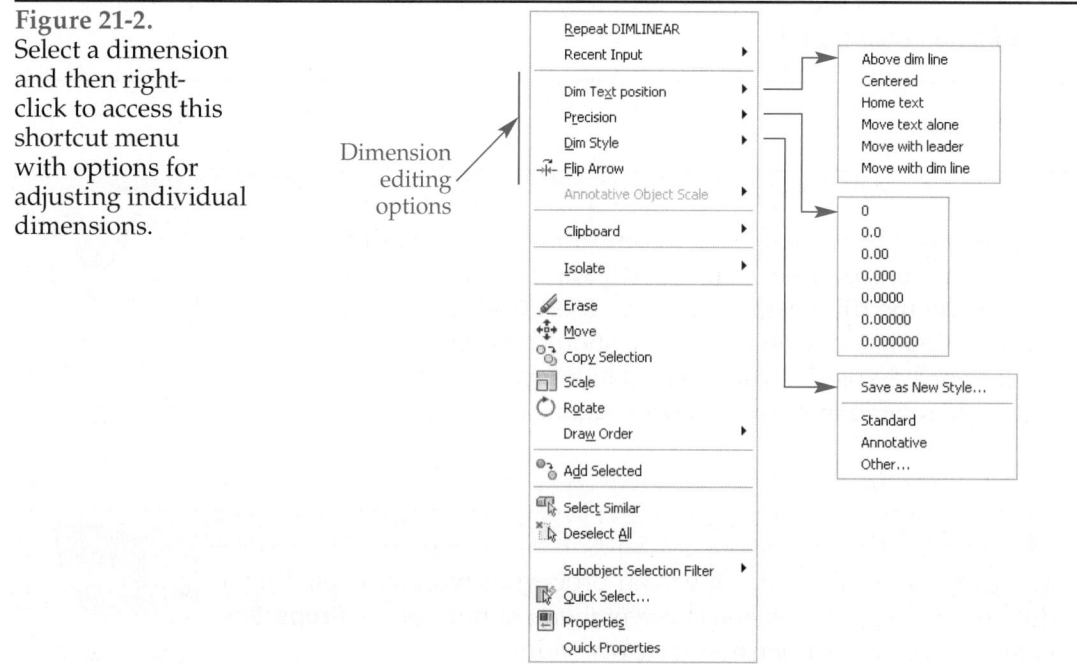

AutoCAD and Its Applications—Basics

Assigning a Different Dimension Style

To assign a different dimension style to existing dimensions, use the options on the **Dim Style** cascading submenu of the dimension shortcut menu. Another option is to pick the dimensions to change and select a different dimension style from the **Dimension Style** drop-down list on the **Home** or **Annotation** ribbon tab. A third option is to select the dimensions to change and choose a different dimension style from the **Quick Properties** panel or the **Properties** palette.

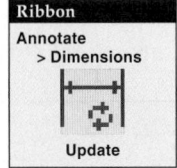

The **Update** dimension tool provides another technique to change the dimension style assigned to existing dimensions. Before you access the **Update** dimension tool, set the dimension style to be assigned to existing dimensions current. Then access the **Update** dimension tool and pick the dimensions to change them to the current style.

Editing the Dimension Value

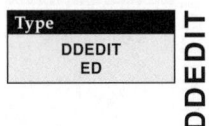

The **DDEDIT** tool allows you to add a prefix or suffix to the dimension value or edit the dimension text format. For example, use the **DDEDIT** tool to add a diameter symbol to a linear diameter dimension if you forget to use the **Mtext** or **Text** option of the **DIMLINEAR** tool. See **Figure 21-3.** Access the **DDEDIT** tool and select a dimension to enter the mtext editor. The highlighted value represents the current dimension value. Add to or modify the dimension text and then close the text editor. The **DDEDIT** tool continues, allowing you to edit other text if necessary.

CAUTION

You can replace the highlighted dimension value, but this action disassociates the dimension value with the object or points it dimensions. Therefore, leave the default value intact whenever possible.

Exercise 21-2

Access the Student Web site (www.g-wlearning.com/CAD) and complete Exercise 21-2.

Editing Dimension Text Placement

Proper dimensioning practice requires dimensions that are clear and easy to read. This sometimes involves moving the text of adjacent dimensions to separate the text elements. See **Figure 21-4.** You can use the dimension shortcut menu to adjust dimension text position, but the quickest method is to use grips. Select the dimension, pick the dimension text grip, and stretch the text to the new location. AutoCAD automatically reestablishes the break in the dimension line when you pick the new location.

Figure 21-3.
Using the **DDEDIT** tool to add a diameter symbol to an existing dimension.

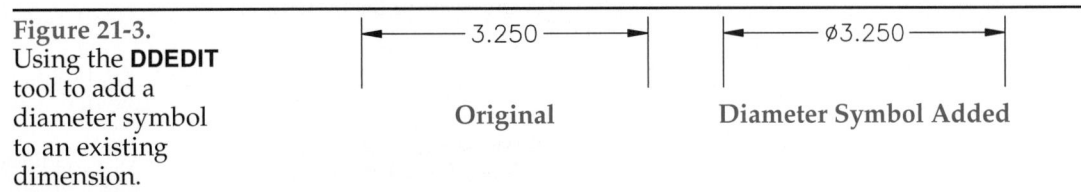

Original   Diameter Symbol Added

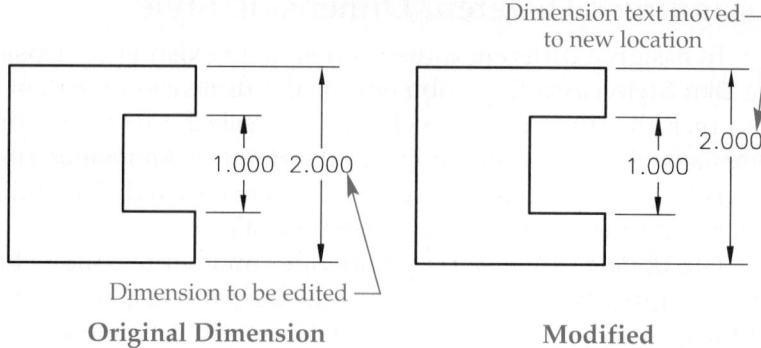

Figure 21-4.
Staggering dimension text for improved readability.

Dimension text moved to new location

1.000   2.000

1.000   2.000

Dimension to be edited

Original Dimension   **Modified**

DIMTEDIT

Ribbon

Annotate
> Dimensions

DIMTEDIT

Type
DIMTEDIT

Using the DIMTEDIT Tool

The **DIMTEDIT** tool allows you to change the placement and orientation of existing dimension text. Access the **DIMTEDIT** tool and select the dimension to alter. Specify a new point to stretch the text and automatically reestablish the break in the dimension line.

The **DIMTEDIT** tool also provides options to relocate dimension text to a specific position and rotate the text. However, it is usually quicker to select the appropriate button from the expanded **Dimensions** panel of the **Annotation** ribbon tab or select a similar option from the dimension shortcut menu. Use the **Text Angle (Angle)** option to rotate the dimension text. Select the **Left Justify (Left)** option to move horizontal text to the left and vertical text down. Use the **Center Justify (Center)** option to center the text on the dimension line. Choose the **Right Justify (Right)** option to move horizontal text to the right and vertical text up. Select the **Home** option to relocate text back to the original position. Figure 21-5 shows the result of using each **DIMTEDIT** tool option.

> **PROFESSIONAL TIP**
>
> Activate the **Place text manually** check box in the **Fit** tab of the **New** (or **Modify**) **Dimension Style** dialog box to provide greater flexibility for the initial placement of dimensions when necessary.

Figure 21-5.
A comparison of the **DIMTEDIT** tool options.

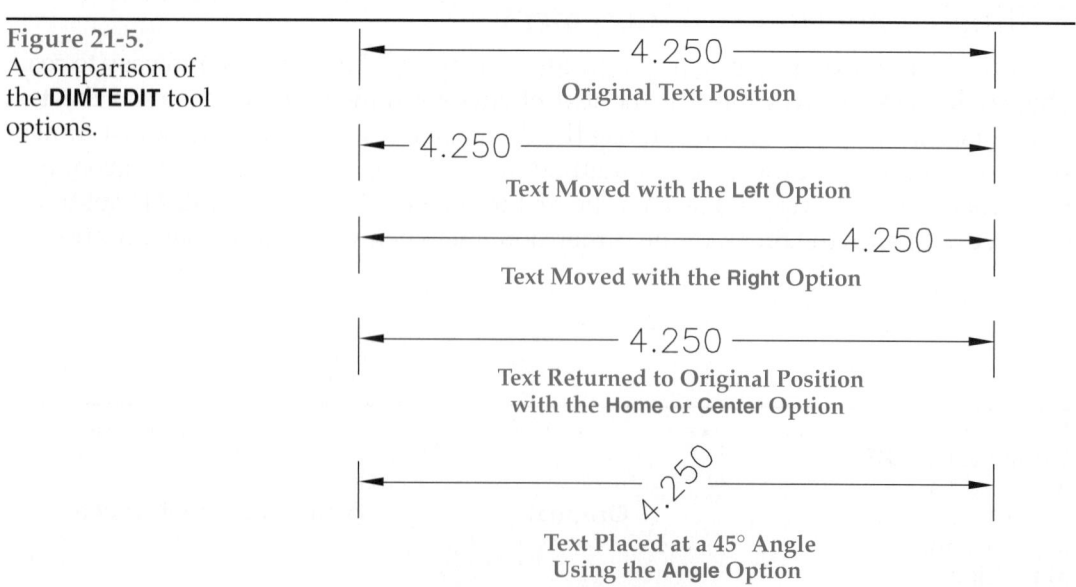

4.250
Original Text Position

4.250
Text Moved with the Left Option

4.250
Text Moved with the Right Option

4.250
Text Returned to Original Position with the **Home** or **Center** Option

4.250
Text Placed at a 45° Angle Using the **Angle** Option

Exercise 21-3

Access the Student Web site (www.g-wlearning.com/CAD) and complete Exercise 21-3.

Using the DIMEDIT Tool

The **DIMEDIT** tool, not to be confused with the **DIMTEDIT** tool, provides **Home** and **Rotate** options that function the same as the **Home** and **Angle** options of the **DIMTEDIT** tool. The **New** option is similar to using the **DDEDIT** tool to edit dimension values. When you activate the **New** option, the multiline text editor appears with the associated dimension value highlighted. Add to or modify the dimension text and then close the text editor.

Oblique Extension Lines

The **Oblique** option is unique to the **DIMEDIT** tool and allows you to change the extension line angle without affecting the associated dimension value. **Figure 21-6A** shows an example of adjusting the placement of dimensions when space is limited by changing existing linear dimensions to use oblique extension lines. **Figure 21-6B**

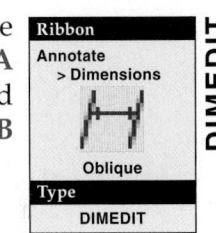

Ribbon
Annotate > Dimensions
Oblique
Type
DIMEDIT

Figure 21-6.
Drawing dimensions with oblique extension lines.

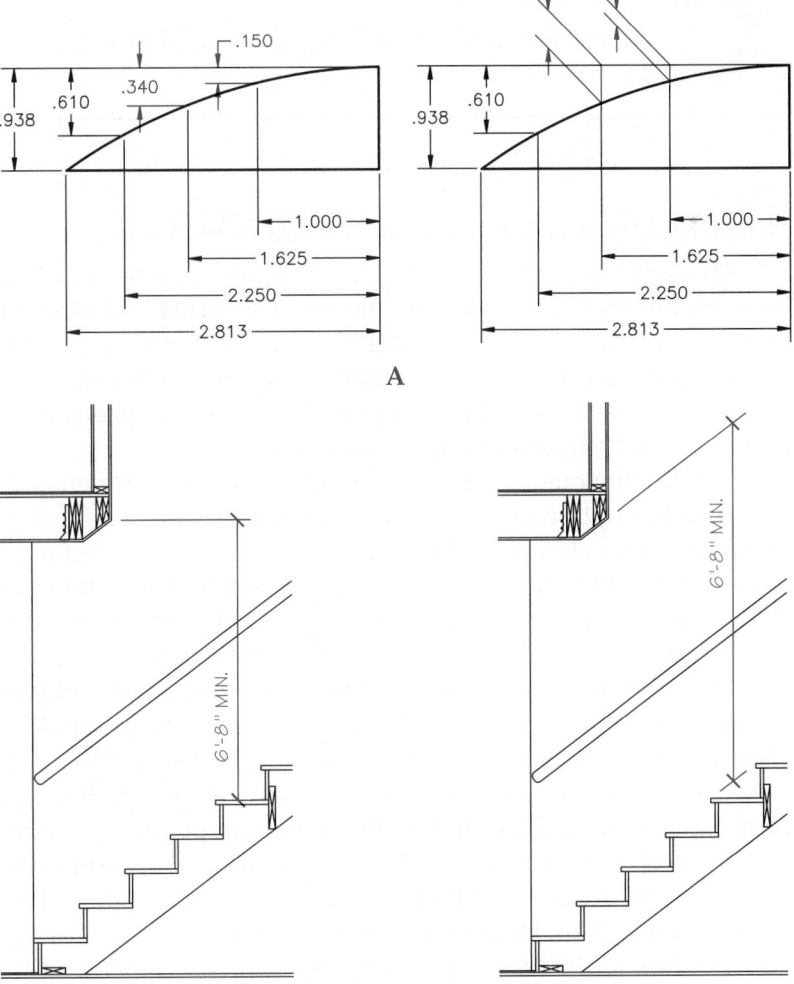

A

B

shows an example of using oblique extension lines to orient extension lines properly with the angle of the stairs in a stair section. Notice that the associated values and orientation of the dimension lines in these examples do not change.

To create oblique extension lines, dimension the object using the **DIMLINEAR** and **DIMALIGNED** tools as appropriate, even if the dimensions are crowded or overlap. Then access the **Oblique** option of the **DIMEDIT** tool. The quickest way to access the **Oblique** option is to pick the corresponding button from the expanded **Dimensions** panel of the **Annotation** ribbon tab. Then pick the linear and aligned dimensions to be redrawn at an oblique angle and specify the obliquing angle. Plan carefully to make sure you enter the correct obliquing angle. Obliquing angles originate from 0° East and revolve counterclockwise. Enter a specific value or pick two points to define the obliquing angle.

Supplemental Material

Isometric Dimensions

The **Oblique** option of the **DIMEDIT** tool is one option for dimensioning isometric drawings. For information about constructing dimensions for isometric views, go to the Student Web site (www.g-wlearning.com/CAD), select this chapter, and select **Isometric Dimensions**.

Exercise 21-4

Access the Student Web site (www.g-wlearning.com/CAD) and complete Exercise 21-4.

Editing Dimensions with the QDIM Tool

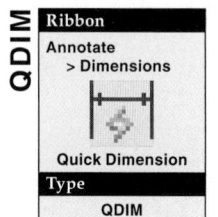

The **QDIM** tool provides options for replacing, adding, removing, and rearranging existing linear or ordinate dimensions. The **QDIM** tool does not change diameter or radius dimensions. Access the **QDIM** tool and select the dimensions to modify, and any other objects to dimension. The **QDIM** tool replaces the selected dimensions and adds dimensions to selected objects. Right-click or press [Enter] or the space bar to display a preview of the dimensions attached to the cursor.

The **Continuous** option changes selected linear dimensions to chain dimensions. The **Baseline** option changes selected linear dimensions to baseline dimensions. The **Ordinate** option changes selected linear dimensions to rectangular coordinate dimensions without dimension lines. You must reselect the location of the dimensions. If the **QDIM** tool does not reference the appropriate datum, use the **datum Point** option before locating the dimensions to specify a different datum point.

Use the **Edit** option before locating the dimensions to add dimensions to, or remove dimensions from, the current set. Marks indicate the points acquired by the **QDIM** tool. Use the **Add** function to specify a point to add a dimension, or use the **Remove** function to specify a point to remove the corresponding dimension. Right-click or press [Enter] or the space bar to return to the previous prompt and continue using the **QDIM** tool.

To create the dimensions shown in **Figure 21-7C** from the dimensions shown in **Figure 21-7A**, access the **QDIM** tool and select the existing dimensions. Then activate the **Baseline** option, followed by the **Edit** option. Choose the **Add** function and pick the point to add. Right-click or press [Enter] or the space bar, and then specify the location of the first dimension line.

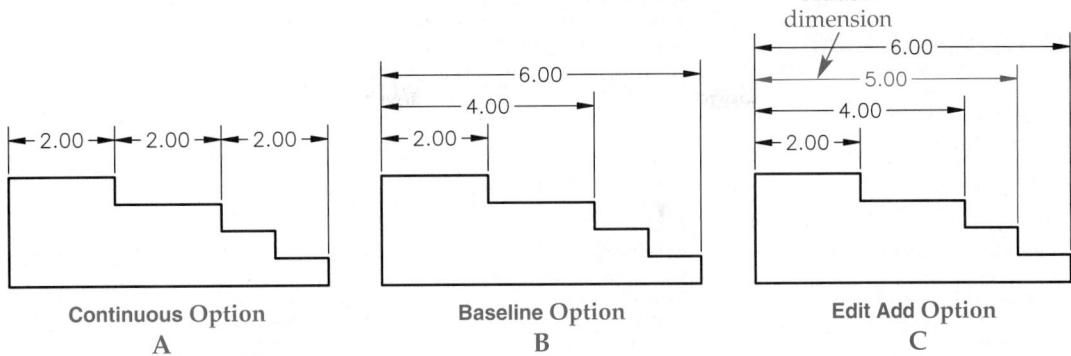

Continuous Option
A

Baseline Option
B

Edit Add Option
C

Exercise 21-5

Access the Student Web site (www.g-wlearning.com/CAD) and complete Exercise 21-5.

Overriding Dimension Style

A drawing often includes dimensions that require settings slightly different from the assigned dimension style. These dimensions may be too few to merit creating a new style. Perform a *dimension style override* for these situations. For example, use a dimension style with an **Offset from origin** value of .063 to conform to ASME standards for most dimensions. Apply a dimension style override with an **Offset from origin** value of 0 to three dimensions that should not display an extension line offset.

dimension style override: A temporary alteration of dimension style settings that does not actually modify the style.

Existing Dimensions

The **Properties** palette is an effective tool for overriding the dimension style assigned to existing dimensions. The **Properties** palette divides dimension properties into several categories. See **Figure 21-8**. To change a property, access the proper category, pick the property to highlight, and adjust the corresponding value. Most changes made using the **Properties** palette override the dimension style assigned to the selected dimension. The changes do not alter the original dimension style and do not apply to new dimensions.

NOTE

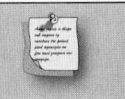

The **Quick Properties** panel provides a limited number of dimension properties and style overrides.

New Dimensions

Use the **Dimension Style Manager** to override the dimension style assigned to dimensions you are about to create. An example of an override is including a text prefix for a few dimensions. Select the dimension style to override from the **Styles** list and then pick the **Override** button to open the **Override Current Style** dialog box.

Figure 21-8. The **Properties** palette allows you to edit dimension properties and create dimension style overrides.

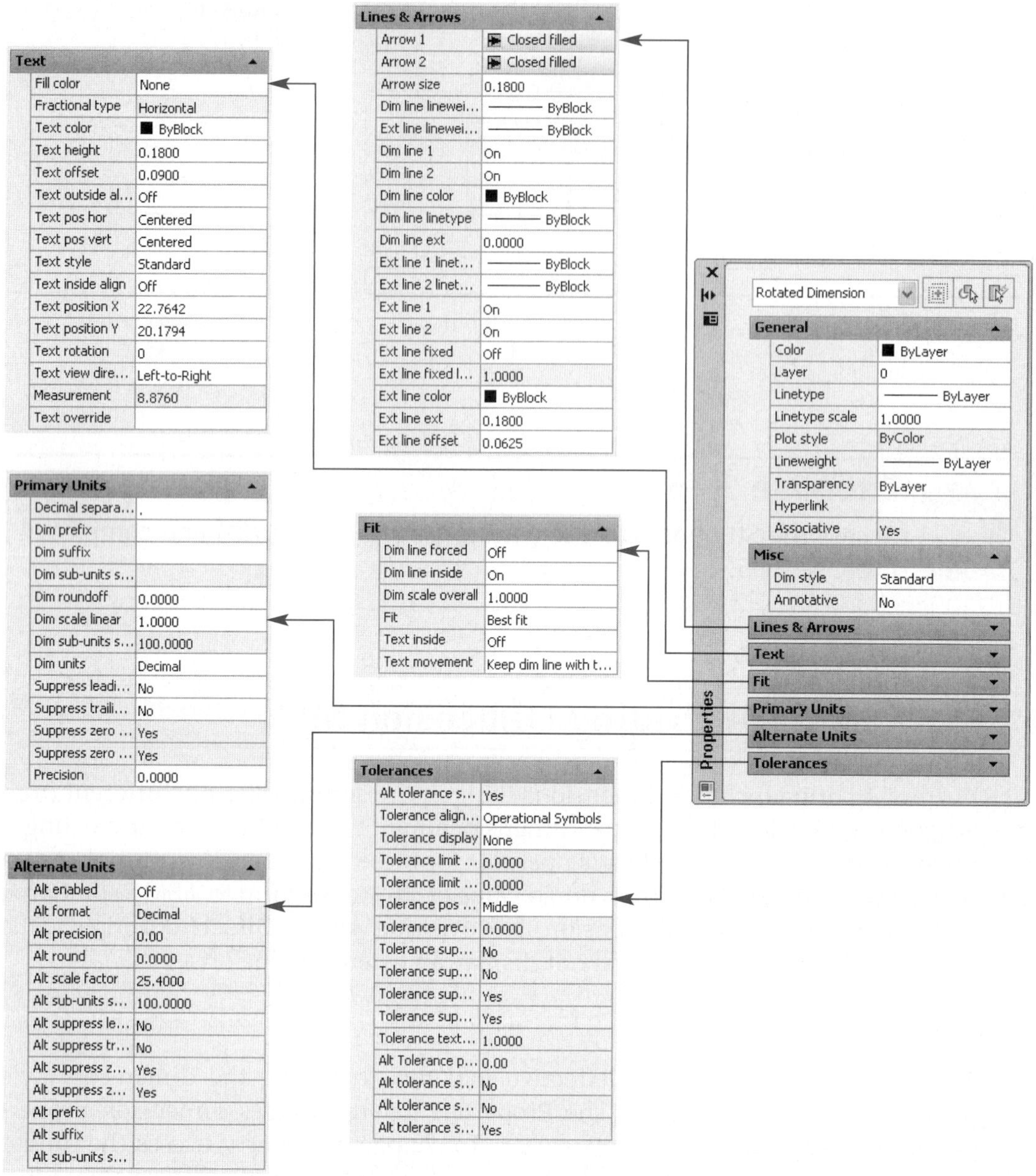

The **Override** button is only available for the current style. The **Override Current Style** dialog box includes the same tabs as the **New Dimension Style** and **Modify Dimension Style** dialog boxes. Make the necessary changes and pick the **OK** button. The override is current and appears as a branch under the original style labeled **<style overrides>**. Close the **Dimension Style Manager** and draw the unique dimensions.

To clear style overrides, return to the **Dimension Style Manager** and set a different style current. The override settings are lost when you set a different style, including the parent style, current. To incorporate the overrides into the overridden style, right-click on the **<style overrides>** name and select **Save to current style**. To save the changes to a new style, pick the **New...** button. Then select **<style overrides>** in the **Start With** drop-down list in the **Create New Dimension Style** dialog box. In the **New Dimension Style** dialog box, pick **OK** to save the overrides as a new style.

Exercise 21-6

Access the Student Web site (www.g-wlearning.com/CAD) and complete Exercise 21-6.

Using the MATCHPROP Tool

The **MATCHPROP** tool allows you to copy, or "paint," properties from one object to other objects, including dimensions. You can match properties in the same drawing or between drawings. Access the **MATCHPROP** tool, pick the source dimension with the desired properties, and then pick the destination dimensions to change. Press [Enter] or the space bar, or right-click and select **Enter** to exit. The style of the source dimension is applied to destination dimensions.

If you override the dimension style of the source dimension, the "base" style is applied along with the dimension style override. Reapplying the "base" style removes the overrides.

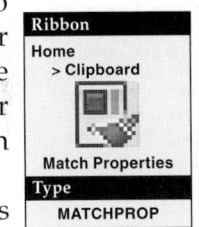

Ribbon
Home
> Clipboard

Match Properties
Type
MATCHPROP

MATCHPROP

NOTE

The **Property Settings** dialog box, available by selecting the **Settings** option before picking the destination objects, includes a **Dimension** check box. AutoCAD checks the box by default, allowing you to match dimensions.

Exercise 21-7

Access the Student Web site (www.g-wlearning.com/CAD) and complete Exercise 21-7.

Using the DIMSPACE Tool

The amount of space between a drawing view and the first dimension line and the space between dimension lines vary depending on the drawing and industry or company standard. ASME standards recommend a minimum spacing of .375″ (10 mm) from a drawing feature to the first dimension line and a minimum spacing of .25″ (6 mm) between dimension lines. A minimum spacing of 3/8″ is common for architectural drawings. These minimum recommendations are generally less than the spacing required by actual company or school standards. A value of .5 (12 mm) or .75 (19 mm) is usually more appropriate.

Typically, the spacing between dimension lines is equal, and chain dimensions align. See **Figure 21-9.** You generally determine the correct location and spacing of dimension lines before and while dimensioning. However, you can adjust dimension line spacing and alignment after you place dimensions. This is a common requirement when there is a need to increase or decrease the space between dimension lines, such as when the drawing scale changes, or when dimensions are unequally spaced or misaligned.

The **STRETCH, DIMTEDIT,** and **QDIM** tools or grips are common methods for adjusting the location and alignment of dimension lines. However, you must determine the exact location or amount of stretch applied to each dimension line before using these tools. An alternative is to use the **DIMSPACE** tool, which allows you to adjust the space equally between dimension lines or to align dimension lines.

Access the **DIMSPACE** tool and select the *base dimension,* followed by each dimension to space. Right-click or press [Enter] or the space bar to display the Enter value or [Auto]: prompt. Enter a value to space the dimension lines equally. For example, enter .5 to space the selected dimension lines .5" apart. Enter a value of 0 to align the dimensions. See **Figure 21-10.** Use the **Auto** option to space dimension lines using a value that is twice the height of the dimension text.

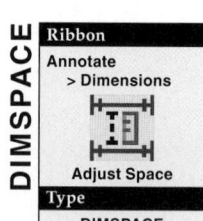

DIMSPACE

Ribbon
Annotate
> Dimensions

Adjust Space

Type
DIMSPACE

base dimension:
The dimension line that remains in the same location, with which other dimension lines align or spaced.

NOTE

Use the **DIMSPACE** tool to space and align linear and angular dimensions.

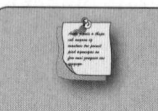

Exercise 21-8

Access the Student Web site (www.g-wlearning.com/CAD) and complete Exercise 21-8.

Figure 21-9. Correct drafting practice requires equal space and alignment between dimension lines for readability. The correct example uses a spacing of .75" (19 mm) from a drawing feature to the first dimension line and a spacing of .5" (12 mm) between dimension lines.

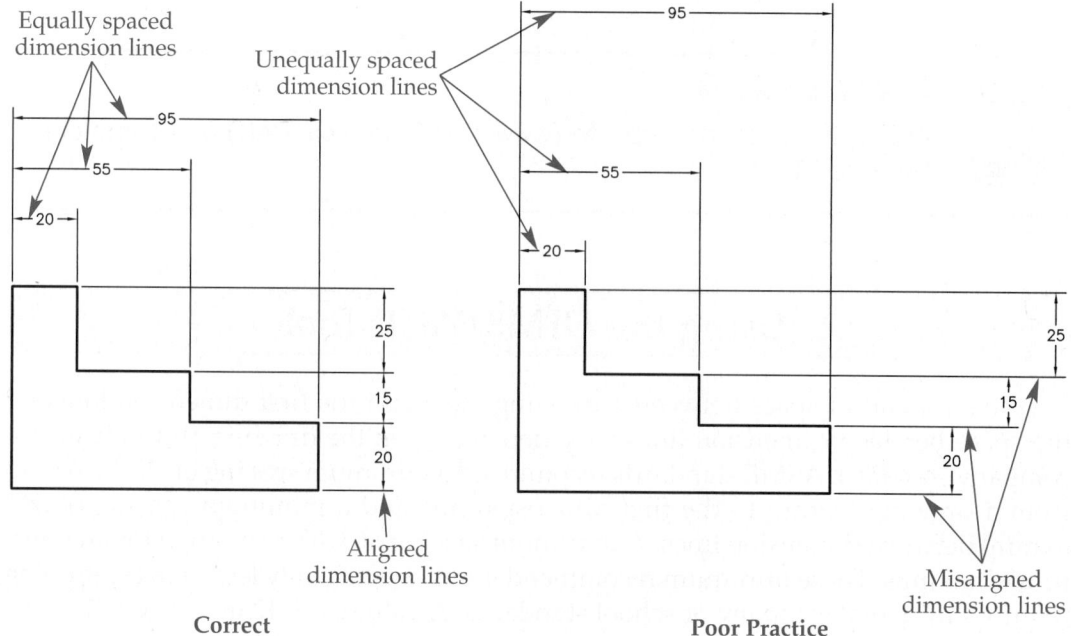

Figure 21-10.
Using the **DIMSPACE** tool to space and align dimension lines correctly.

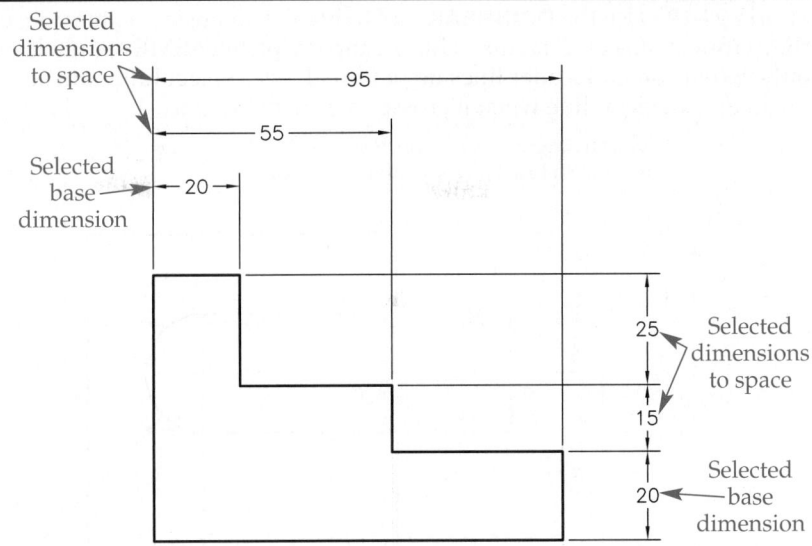

Using the DIMBREAK Tool

ASME and many other drafting discipline standards state that when dimension, extension, or leader lines cross a drawing feature or another dimension, neither line is broken at the intersection. See **Figure 21-11**. However, you can use the **DIMBREAK** tool to create breaks if desired.

Ribbon
Annotate **> Dimensions**
Break
Type
DIMBREAK

DIMBREAK

Access the **DIMBREAK** tool and select the dimension to break. This dimension contains the dimension, extension, or leader line to break across an object. If you pick a single dimension to break, the Select object to break dimension or [Auto/Restore/Manual]: prompt appears.

The **Auto** option is the default and breaks the dimension, extension, or leader line at the selected object. The **Dimension Break** setting of the current dimension style controls the break size. Pick additional objects if necessary to break the dimension at additional locations. See **Figure 21-12**. Use the **Manual** option to define the size of the break by selecting two points along the dimension, extension, or leader line, instead of using the break size set in the current dimension style. Activate the **Restore** option to remove a break created using the **DIMBREAK** tool.

Figure 21-11.
ASME and many other drafting discipline standards state that when dimension, extension, or leader lines cross a drawing feature or another dimension, the line is not broken at the intersection.

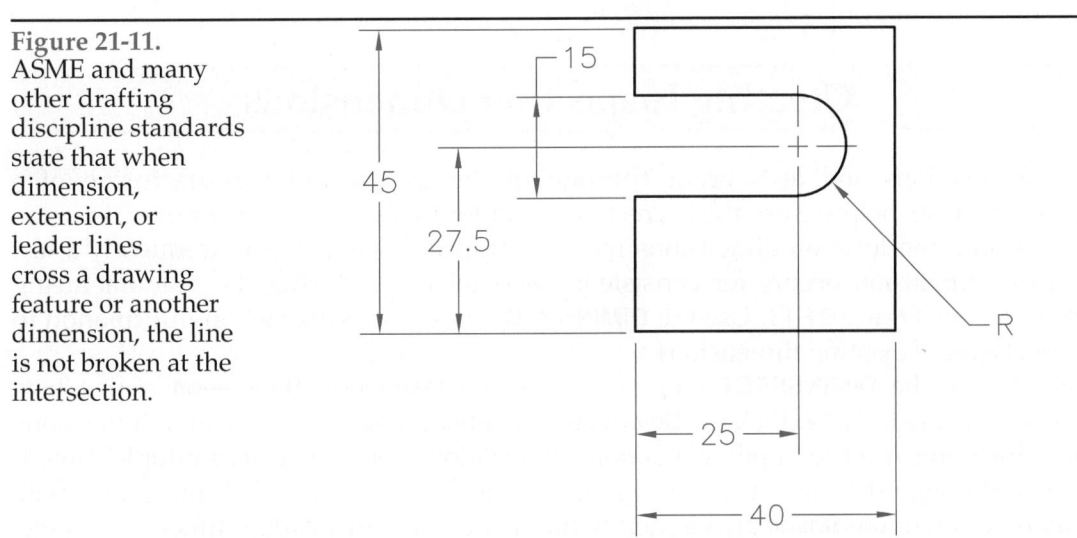

Figure 21-12. Use the **DIMBREAK** tool to break dimension, extension, or leader lines when they cross an object. *Caution:* This example violates ASME standards and is for reference only. Extension and leader lines do not break over object lines, but some drafters prefer to break an extension line when it crosses a dimension line.

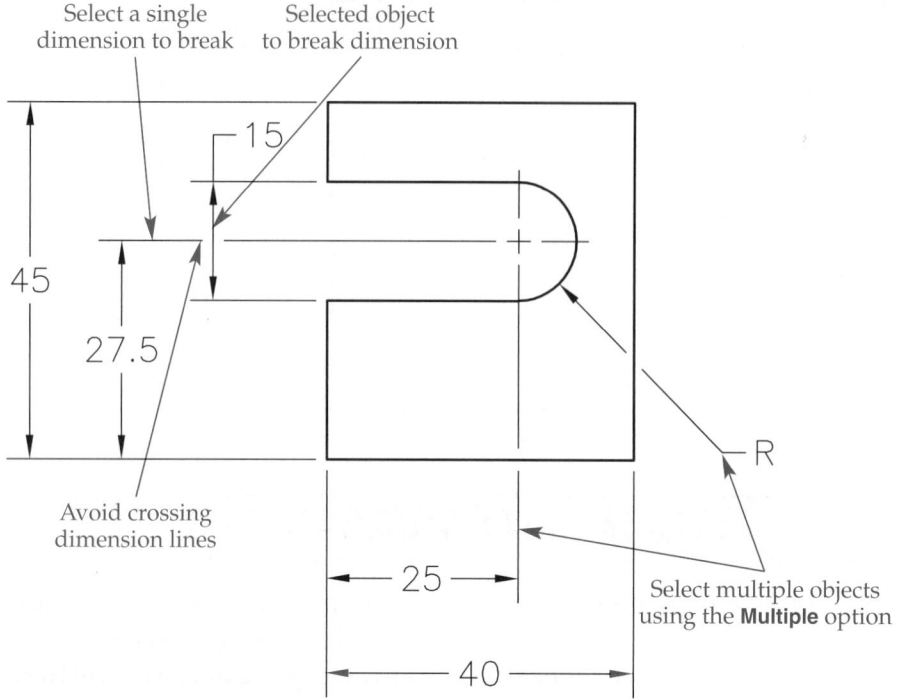

Another technique is to use the **Multiple** option to select more than one dimension. Right-click or press [Enter] or the space bar after you select dimensions to display the Enter an option [Break/Restore]: prompt. Select the **Break** option to break the selected dimension, extension, or leader lines everywhere they intersect another object. Use the **Restore** option to remove breaks created using the **DIMBREAK** tool.

Exercise 21-9

Access the Student Web site (www.g-wlearning.com/CAD) and complete Exercise 21-9.

Creating Inspection Dimensions

Inspections and tests occur throughout the design and manufacturing of a product. Tests help ensure the correct size and location of product features. In some cases, size and location dimensions include information about how frequently a test on the dimension occurs for consistency and tolerance during the manufacturing process. See **Figure 21-13.** Use the **DIMINSPECT** tool to add inspection information to most types of existing dimensions.

Access the **DIMINSPECT** tool to display the **Inspection Dimension** dialog box, shown in **Figure 21-14.** Pick the **Select dimensions** button and choose the dimensions to which you want to apply inspection information. You can select multiple dimensions, although the same inspection specifications apply to each. Pick the appropriate radio button in the **Shape** area to define the shape of the inspection dimension frame.

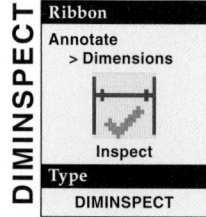

DIMINSPECT

Ribbon
Annotate
> Dimensions

Inspect

Type
DIMINSPECT

Figure 21-13. An inspection dimension added to a part drawing. This example shows an angular shape with a label, dimension, and inspection rate frame.

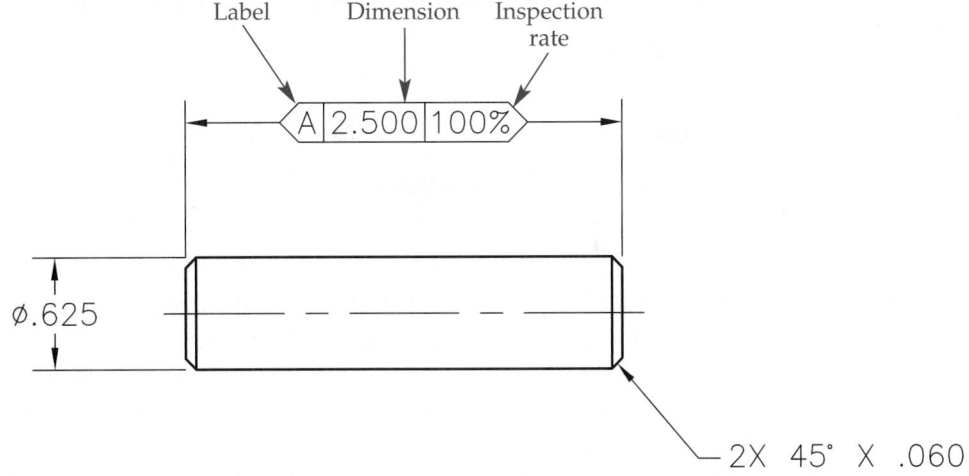

Figure 21-14.
The **Inspection Dimension** dialog box allows you to add inspection information to existing dimensions.

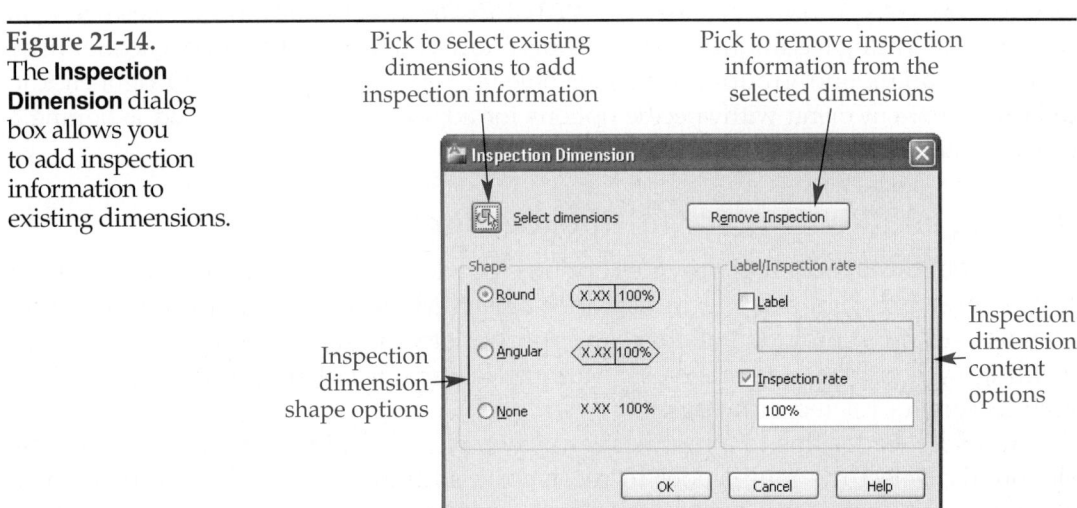

The inspection dimension contains the inspection label, the dimension value, and the inspection rate. Select the **None** option to omit frames around values.

Pick the **Label** check box to include a label, and type the label in the text box. The label appears on the left side of the inspection dimension and identifies the dimension. The inspection dimension shown in **Figure 21-13** is labeled A. The dimension frame houses the dimension value specified when you created the dimension. The length of the part shown in **Figure 21-13** is 2.500, as created when using the **DIMLINEAR** tool. The **Inspection rate** check box is active by default. Enter a value in the text box to indicate how often to test the dimension. The inspection rate for the dimension shown in **Figure 21-13** is 100%. This rate has different meanings depending on the application. In this example, the inspection rate of 100% means that the manufacturer must check the length of the part for tolerance every time the part is added to an assembly.

To remove an inspection dimension, access the **DIMINSPECT** tool, pick the **Select dimensions** button in the **Inspection Dimension** dialog box, and choose the dimensions from which you want to remove inspection information. Right-click or press [Enter] or the space bar to return to the **Inspection Dimension** dialog box, and pick the **Remove Inspection** button to return the dimension to its condition prior to adding the inspection content.

Exercise 21-10

Access the Student Web site (www.g-wlearning.com/CAD) and complete Exercise 21-10.

Editing Multileaders

Edit multileaders using methods similar to those you use to edit dimensions. Use editing tools such as **STRETCH, MOVE, ROTATE,** and **SCALE** as needed. Grips are particularly effective for adjusting the location of leader elements. Use the grip at the arrowhead to relocate the arrowhead. Use the grips at each end of a landing to stretch the landing, but be careful not to violate drafting standards. Use the grips at the middle of a landing or with leader content to relocate content.

To make changes to multileader text, double-click on the text to re-enter the mtext editor. Use the **Properties** palette or **Quick Properties** panel to override specific multileader properties. You can also use the **MATCHPROP** tool. In addition to these general multileader editing techniques, specific tools allow you to add and remove leader lines and space, align, and group multileader objects. Select a multileader and right-click to display a shortcut menu with specific options for adjusting multileaders and assigning a different multileader style.

Adding and Removing Multiple Leader Lines

The **MLEADEREDIT** tool provides options for adding leader lines to, and removing leader lines from, an existing multileader object. Multiple leaders are not a recommended ASME standard, but they are appropriate for some applications, such as welding symbols. See **Figure 21-15.** Multiple leaders are also appropriate for some architectural or related drawings.

To add a leader line to a multileader object, pick the **Add Leader** button from the ribbon and select the multileader to receive the additional leader line. You can also select the multileader, right-click, and choose **Add Leader.** Pick a location for the additional leader line arrowhead. You can place as many additional leader lines as needed without accessing the tool again. When you are finished, press [Enter], [Esc] or the space bar or right-click and select **Enter.** All leader lines are grouped to form a single multileader object.

To remove an unneeded leader line, pick the **Remove Leader** button from the ribbon and select the multileader object that includes the leader to remove. You can also select the multileader, right-click, and choose **Remove Leader.** Select the leader lines to remove and press [Enter], [Esc] or the space bar or right-click and select **Enter.**

MLEADEREDIT	
Ribbon	
Home	
> Annotation	
Annotate	
> Multileaders	
Add Leader	
Type	
MLEADEREDIT	

MLEADEREDIT	
Ribbon	
Home	
> Annotation	
Annotate	
> Multileaders	
Remove Leader	
Type	
MLEADEREDIT	

> **NOTE**
>
> If you type **MLEADEREDIT** to access the tool, you must activate the **Remove leaders** option to remove leader lines.

> **PROFESSIONAL TIP**
>
> To adjust the properties of a specific leader line in a group of leaders attached to the same content, hold down [Ctrl] and pick the leader to modify. Then access the **Properties** palette. Options specific to the selected leader appear, and all other properties are filtered out.

Figure 21-15.
Applications of
multiple leader
lines. A—*Caution:*
Do not use multiple
leader lines in
standard mechanical
applications.
B—Welding
applications often
require multiple
leader lines.

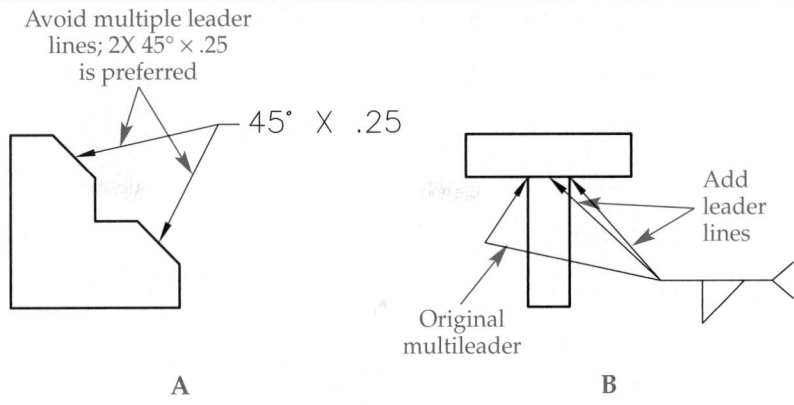

A   B

Exercise 21-11

Access the Student Web site (www.g-wlearning.com/CAD) and complete
Exercise 21-11.

Aligning Multileaders

An advantage of using multileaders is the ability to space and align leaders in an easy-to-read pattern. You typically determine the correct location and spacing of leaders before and while dimensioning. However, you can adjust leader spacing and alignment after you place multileaders. This is a common requirement when there is a need to increase or decrease the space between leaders, such as when the drawing scale changes, or when leaders are unequally spaced or misaligned. See **Figure 21-16.**

The **STRETCH** tool and grips are common methods for adjusting the location and alignment of leaders. However, you must determine the exact location of or amount of stretch applied to each leader before using these tools. An alternative is to use the **MLEADERALIGN** tool, which allows you to align and adjust the space between leaders.

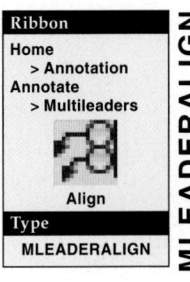

Ribbon
Home
> Annotation
Annotate
> Multileaders

Align

Type
MLEADERALIGN

Access the **MLEADERALIGN** tool and select the leaders to space and align. You can use the **MLEADERALIGN** tool to adjust the location of a single leader in reference to another leader, but for most applications, you should select several leaders. Select each leader to space or align and right-click or press [Enter] or the space bar. When a prompt asks you to select the multileader to align to, activate **Options** to change the multileader alignment.

Use Current Spacing Option

Apply the **Use current spacing** option to align and space the selected leaders equally according to the distance between one of the selected leaders and the next closest leader. Select the multileader with which all other leaders should align and space. Then specify the direction of the leader arrangement by entering or picking a point. The space between leaders is maintained if possible, depending on the selected direction. See **Figure 21-17.**

Distribute Option

Select the **Distribute** option to align and distribute the leaders, or place them at equally spaced locations between two points. The first point you specify identifies the location of one of the leaders and determines where distribution begins. The second point you specify identifies the location of the last leader. All other leaders are distributed equally between the two points. Leaders align with the first point. See **Figure 21-18.**

MLEADERALIGN

Figure 21-16. Leaders that are equally spaced and aligned improve drawing readability.

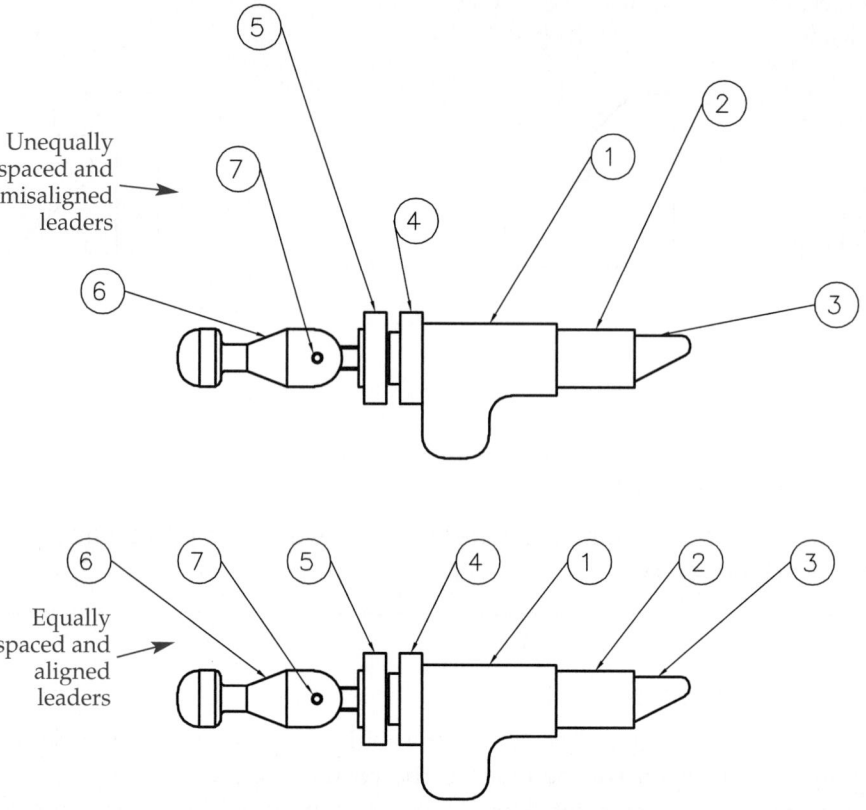

Unequally spaced and misaligned leaders

Equally spaced and aligned leaders

Figure 21-17. Using the **Use current spacing** option to align and equally space leaders.

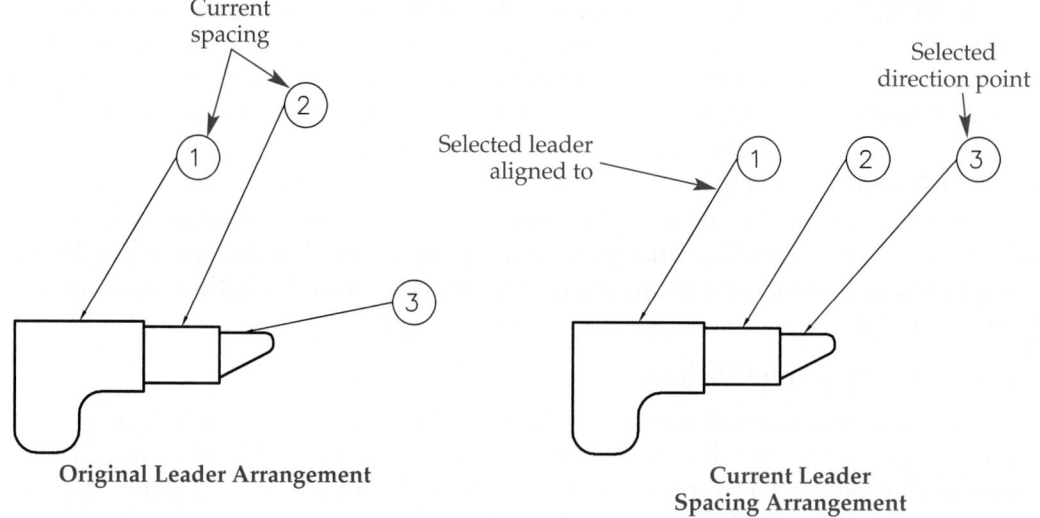

Current spacing

Selected direction point

Selected leader aligned to

Original Leader Arrangement

Current Leader Spacing Arrangement

Make Leader Segments Parallel Option

Use the **make leader segments Parallel** option to make all the selected leader lines parallel to one of the selected leader lines. Select an existing leader to keep in the same location and at the same angle. All other leaders form parallel to the selection. The length of each leader line, except for the leader aligned to, increases or decreases in order to become parallel with the first leader. See **Figure 21-19.**

Figure 21-18. Using the **Distribute** option to align and equally space leaders. This example uses horizontally aligned points.

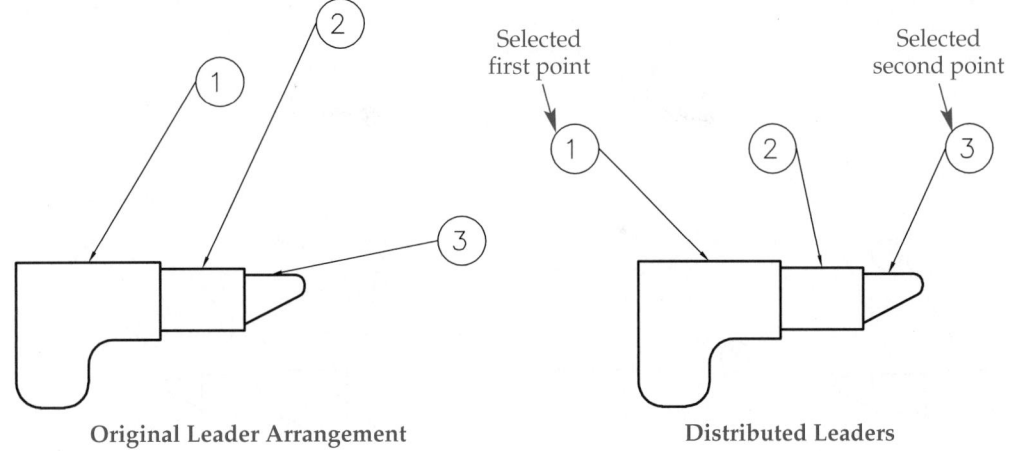

Original Leader Arrangement · Distributed Leaders

Selected first point · Selected second point

Figure 21-19. Using the **make leader segments Parallel** option to make leader lines parallel to each other.

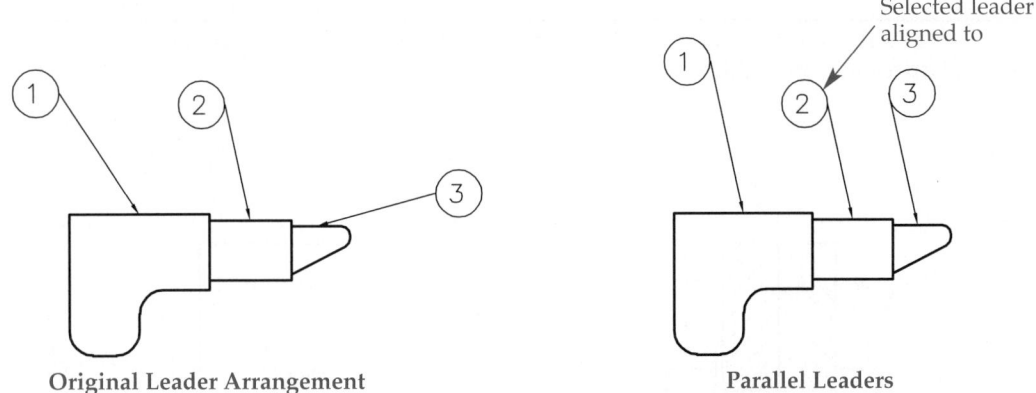

Original Leader Arrangement · Parallel Leaders

Selected leader aligned to

Specify Spacing Option

Choose the **Specify spacing** option to align and equally space the selected leaders according to the distance, or clear space, between the extents of the content of each leader. Select the multileader with which all other leaders should align and space. Specify the direction of the leader arrangement by entering or picking a point. See **Figure 21-20**.

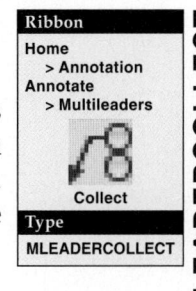

Ribbon

Home
> Annotation
Annotate
> Multileaders

Collect

Type
MLEADERCOLLECT

MLEADERCOLLECT

Exercise 21-12

Access the Student Web site (www.g-wlearning.com/CAD) and complete Exercise 21-12.

Grouping Multileaders

You can group separate multileaders created using a **Block** multileader content style to use a single leader line. This practice is common when adding *balloons* to assembly drawings. *Grouped balloons* allow you to identify closely related clusters of assembly components, such as a bolt, washer, and nut. See **Figure 21-21**. Use the **MLEADERCOLLECT** tool to group multiple existing leaders using a single leader line.

balloons: Circles that contain a number or letter to identify the assembly component and correlate the component to a parts list or bill of materials. Balloons connect to a component with a leader line.

grouped balloons: Balloons that share the same leader, which typically connects to the most obviously displayed component.

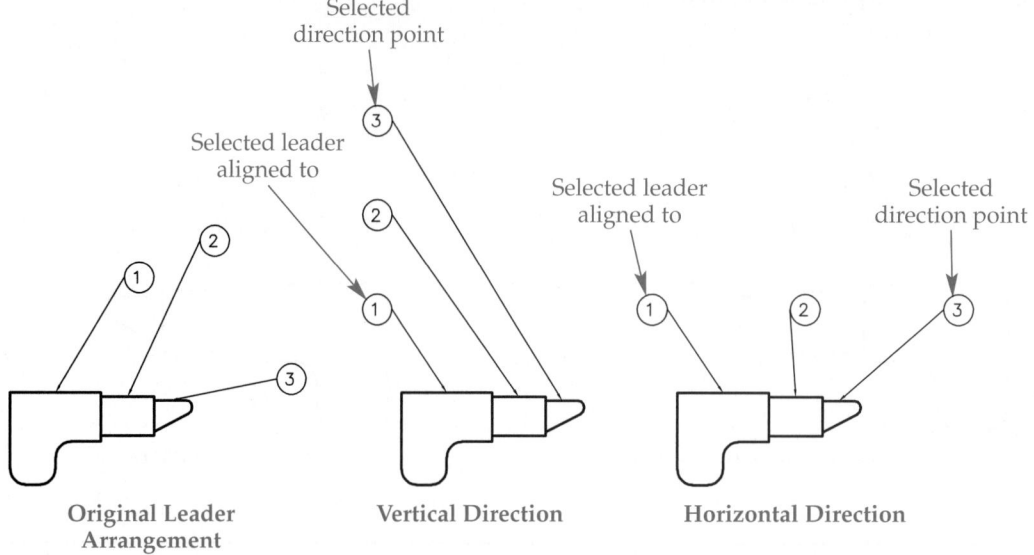

Figure 21-20. Using the **Specify spacing** option to align and equally space leaders.

Selected
direction point

Selected leader
aligned to

Selected leader
aligned to

Selected
direction point

Original Leader
Arrangement

Vertical Direction

Horizontal Direction

Figure 21-21. An example of grouped balloons identifying closely related parts. Some of the parts or features may be hidden.

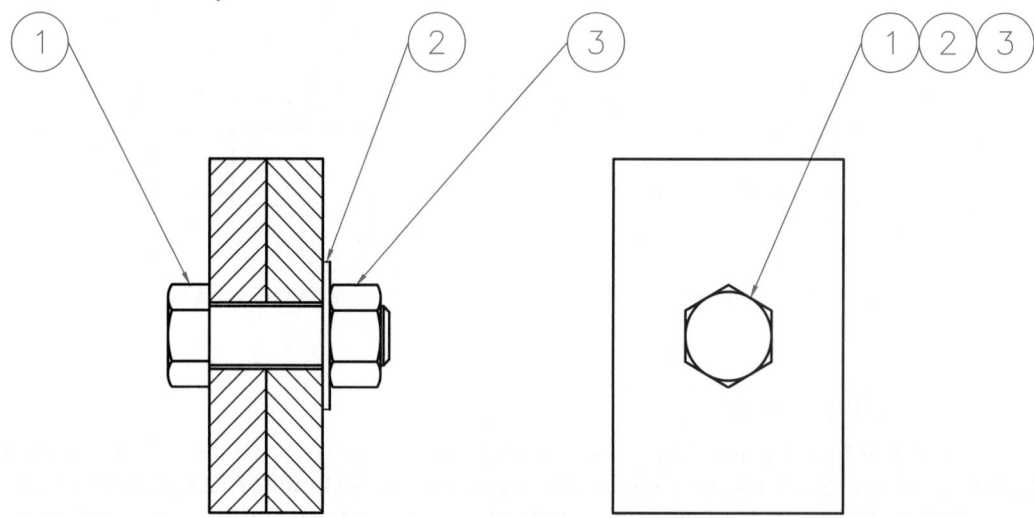

Access the **MLEADERCOLLECT** tool and select the leaders to group. The order in which you select leaders determines how the leaders are grouped. Select leaders in a sequential order, ending with the leader line to keep.

The options illustrated in **Figure 21-22** are available after you select the leaders. Select the **Horizontal** option to align grouped content horizontally, or the **Vertical** option to align grouped content vertically. Pick a point to locate the grouped leader. Select the **Wrap** option to wrap grouped content to additional lines as needed when the number of items exceeds a specified width or quantity. Enter the width at the Specify width prompt, or use the **Number** option to enter a quantity not to exceed before the grouped leaders wrap. Then pick a point to locate the grouped leader.

Figure 21-22. Options for grouping leaders using the **MLEADERCOLLECT** tool.

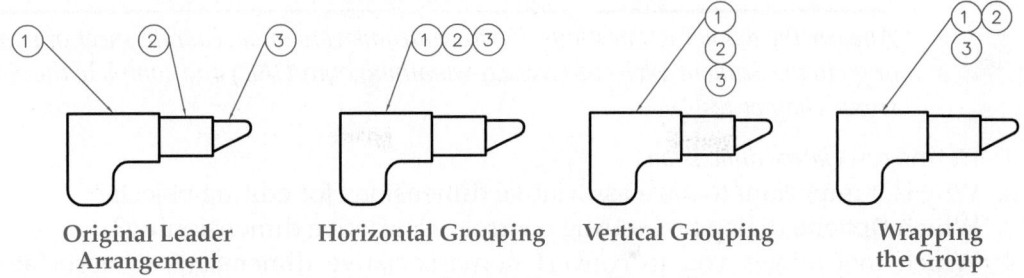

Original Leader
Arrangement
    Horizontal Grouping   Vertical Grouping   Wrapping
the Group

Exercise 21-13

Access the Student Web site (www.g-wlearning.com/CAD) and complete Exercise 21-13.

Chapter Test

Answer the following questions. Write your answers on a separate sheet of paper or go to the Student Web site (www.g-wlearning.com/CAD) and complete the electronic chapter test.

1. Define *associative dimension*.
2. Why is it important to have associative dimensions for editing objects?
3. Which **Options** dialog box setting controls associative dimensioning?
4. Which tool allows you to convert non-associative dimensions to associative dimensions?
5. Which tool allows you to convert associative dimensions to non-associative dimensions?
6. What are definition points?
7. Which four tool options related to dimension editing appear in the shortcut menu when you right-click on a dimension?
8. Name three methods of changing the dimension style of a dimension.
9. How does the **Dimension Update** tool affect selected dimensions?
10. Explain how to add a diameter symbol to a dimension text value using the **DDEDIT** tool.
11. Name the tool that allows you to control the placement and orientation of an existing associative dimension text value.
12. Name two applications in which you might need to create oblique extension lines.
13. Which tool and option can you use to add a new baseline dimension to an existing set of baseline dimensions?
14. When you use the **Properties** palette to edit a dimension, what is the effect on the dimension style?
15. How do you access the **Property Settings** dialog box?
16. Which tool can you use to adjust the space equally between dimension lines or align dimension lines without having to determine the exact location or amount of stretch needed?
17. What two options are available when you use the **Multiple** option of the **DIMBREAK** tool?
18. What tool allows you to add information about how frequently the manufacturer should test a dimension for consistency and tolerance during the manufacturing of a product?
19. Name an application in which leaders with multiple leader lines are common.
20. Identify the four options available to change multileader alignment.

Drawing Problems

- *Start AutoCAD if it is not already started. Start a new drawing for each problem using an appropriate template of your choice.*

- *The template should include layers and text, dimension, multileader, and table styles, when necessary, for drawing the given objects. Add layers and text, dimension, multileader, and table styles as needed.*

- *Draw all objects using appropriate layers and text, dimension, multileader, and table styles, justification, and format.*

- *Follow the specific instructions for each problem. Use only drawing and editing tools and techniques you have already learned. Use your own judgment and approximate dimensions when necessary.*

- *Apply dimensions accurately using ASME or appropriate industry standards.*

Note: Some of the problems in this chapter are built on problems from previous chapters. If you have not yet completed those problems, complete them now.

▼ Basic

1. Open P18-9 and save the file as P21-1. The P21-1 file should be active. Edit the drawing as follows:
   A. Erase the front (circular) view.
   B. Stretch the vertical dimensions to provide more space between dimension lines. Be sure the space you create is the same between all vertical dimensions.
   C. Stagger the existing vertical dimension text numbers if they are not staggered as shown in the original problem.
   D. Erase the 1.750 horizontal dimension and then stretch the 5.255 and 4.250 dimensions to make room for a new baseline dimension from the baseline to where the 1.750 dimension was located. This should result in a new baseline dimension that equals 2.750. Be sure all horizontal dimension lines are equally spaced.
   E. Resave the file.

2. Open P19-1 and save the file as P21-2. The P21-2 file should be active. Edit the drawing as follows:
   A. Stretch the total length from 3.500 to 4.000, leaving the holes the same distance from the edges.
   B. Fillet the upper-left corner. Modify the 3X R.250 dimension accordingly.
   C. Resave the drawing.

3. Open P18-12 and save the file as P21-3. The P21-3 file should be active. Edit the drawing as follows: Make the bathroom 8'-0" wide by stretching the walls and vanity that are currently 6'-0" wide to 8'-0". Do this without increasing the size of the water closet compartment. Provide two equally spaced oval sinks where there is currently one. Resave the drawing.

4. Open P19-19 and save the file as P21-4. The P21-4 file should be active. Edit the drawing as follows:
   A. Lengthen the part .250 on each side for a new overall dimension of 6.500.
   B. Change the width of the part from 3.000 to 3.500 by widening an equal amount on each side.
   C. Resave the drawing.

5. Open P19-17 and save the file as P21-5. The P21-5 file should be active. Edit the drawing as follows:
   A. Shorten the .75 thread on the left side to .50.
   B. Shorten the .388 hexagon length to .300.
   C. Resave the drawing.

6. Draw the shim shown at A. Then edit the .150 and .340 values using oblique dimensions as shown at B. Save the drawing as P21-6.

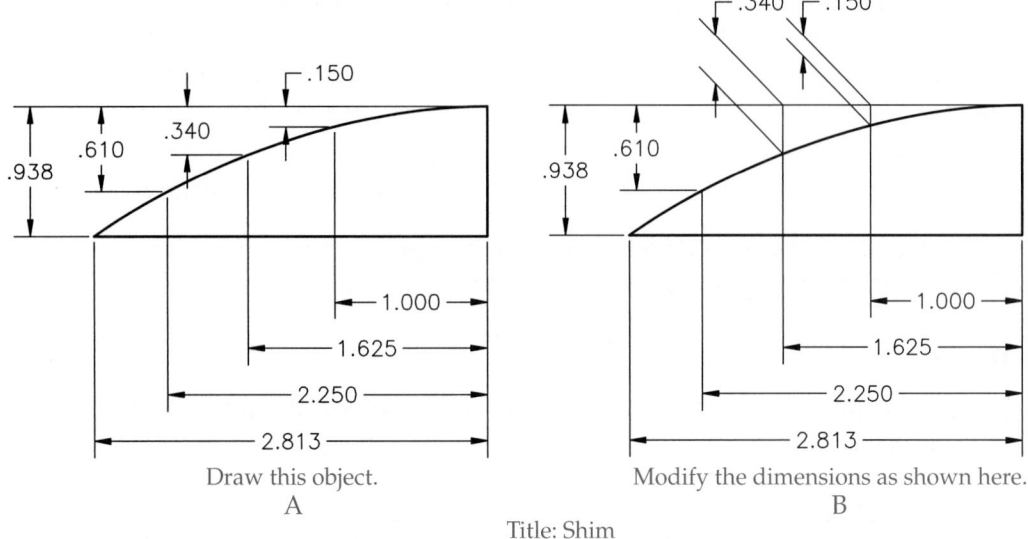

Draw this object.
A

Modify the dimensions as shown here.
B

Title: Shim

▼ Intermediate

7. Draw and dimension the swivel screw shown. Save the drawing as P21-7.

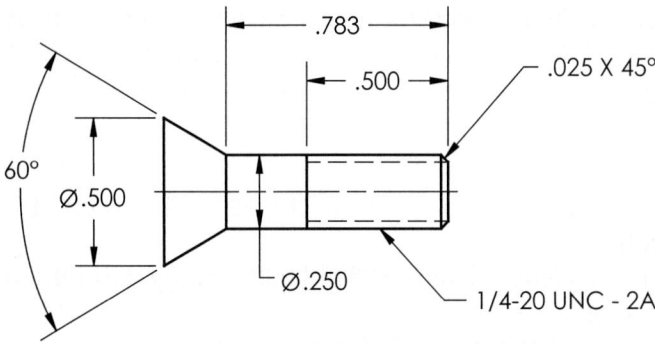

8. Open P19-4 and save the file as P21-8. The P21-8 file should be active. Edit the drawing as follows:
   A. Use the existing drawing as the model and make four copies.
   B. Leave the original drawing as it is and edit the other four pins in the following manner, keeping the Ø.125 hole exactly in the center of each pin.
   C. Give one pin a total length of 1.500.
   D. Create the next pin with a total length of 2.000.
   E. Edit the third pin to a length of 2.500.
   F. Change the last pin to a length of 3.000.
   G. Organize the pins on your drawing in a vertical row ranging in length from the smallest to the largest. You may need to change the drawing limits.
   H. Resave the drawing.

9. Open P19-5 and save the file as P21-9. The P21-9 file should be active. Edit the drawing as follows:
   A. Modify the spline to have twelve projections, rather than eight.
   B. Change the angular dimension, linear dimension, and 8X dimension to reflect the modification.
   C. Resave the drawing.

10. Open P19-11 and save the file as P21-10. The P21-10 file should be active. Edit the drawing as follows:
   A. Stretch the total length from 6.500 to 7.750.
   B. Add two more holes that continue the equally spaced pattern of .625 apart.
   C. Change the 8X .625(=5.00) dimension to read 10X .625(=6.250).
   D. Resave the drawing.

▼ Advanced

11. Draw and dimension the door elevation shown at A. Save the drawing as P21-7A. Open P21-7A and save the file as P21-7B. The P21-7B file should be active. Edit the drawing as shown at B.

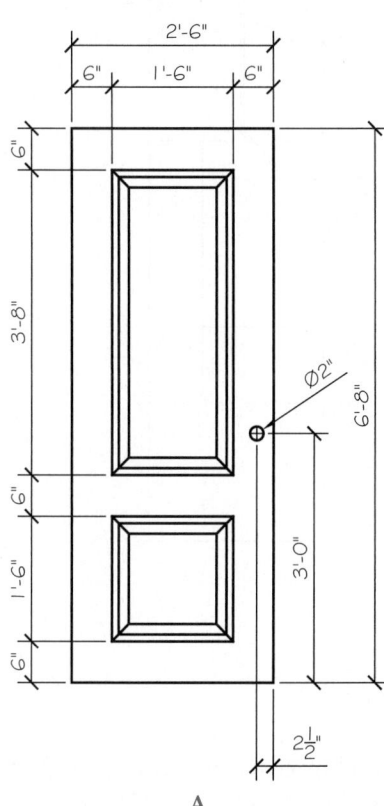

A

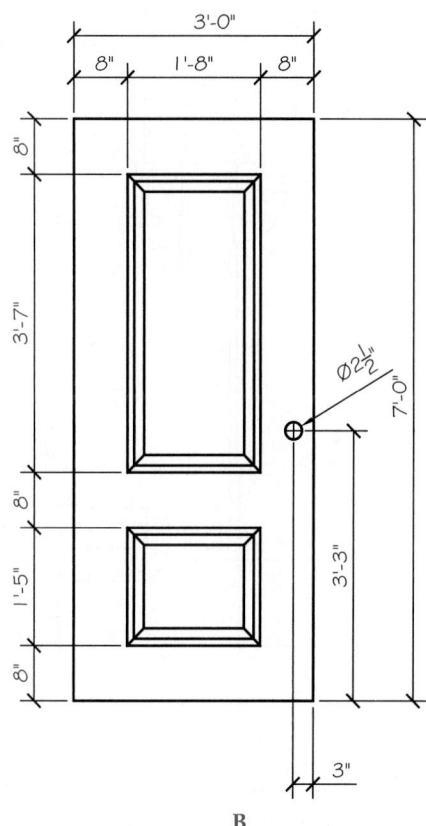

B

12. Open P18-17 and save the file as P21-12. The P21-12 file should be active. Make the client-requested revisions to the floor plan as shown. Make sure the dimensions reflect the changes.

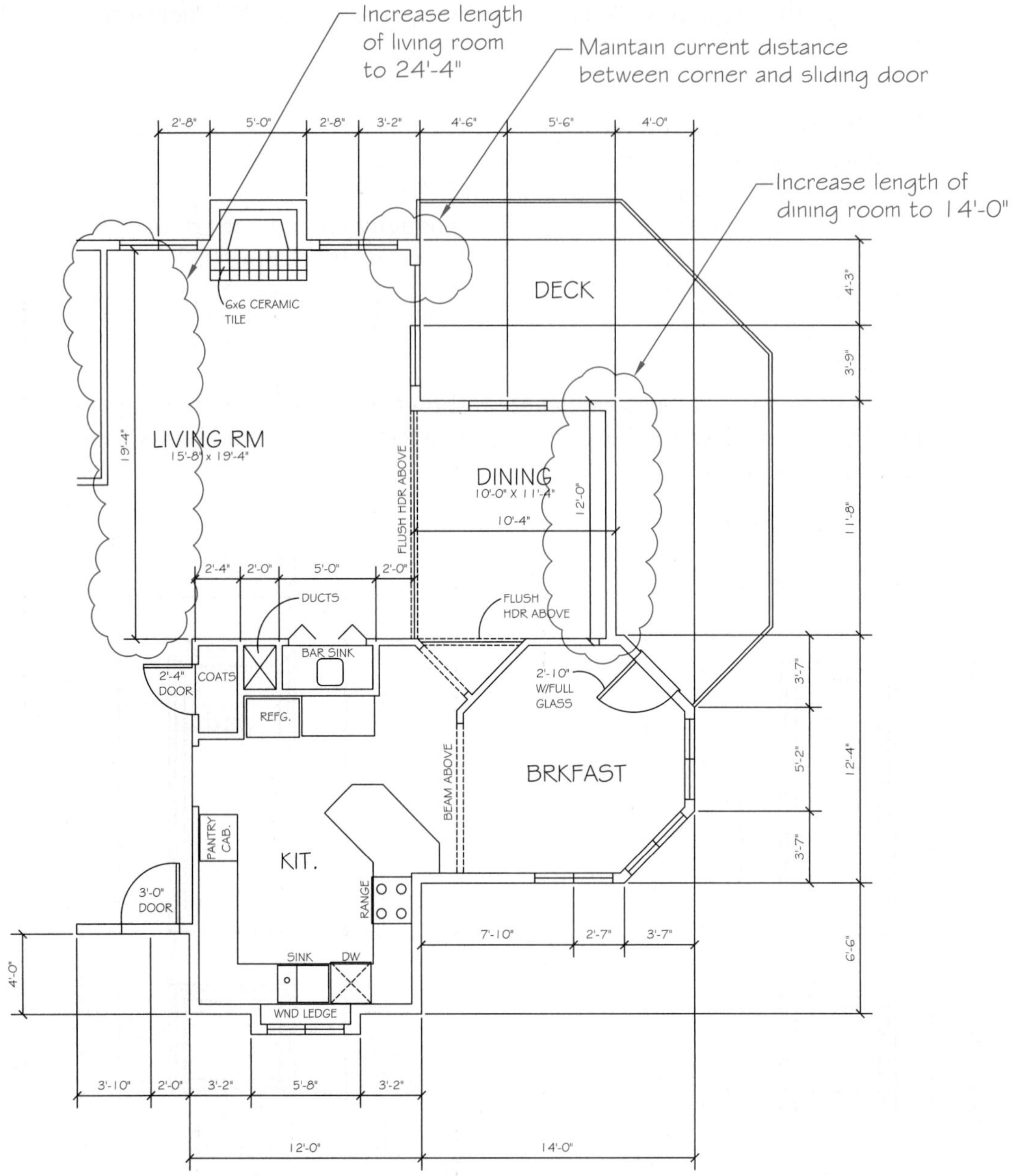

Increase length of living room to 24'-4"

Maintain current distance between corner and sliding door

Increase length of dining room to 14'-0"

DECK

6x6 CERAMIC TILE

LIVING RM
15'-8" x 19'-4"

FLUSH HDR ABOVE

DINING
10'-0" X 11'-4"

DUCTS

BAR SINK

FLUSH HDR ABOVE

COATS

REFG.

2'-4" DOOR

2'-10" W/FULL GLASS

BRKFAST

BEAM ABOVE

PANTRY CAB.

KIT.

RANGE

3'-0" DOOR

SINK   DW

WND LEDGE

13. Design and draw a vice clamp similar to the vice clamp shown in Figure 21-16. Add balloons and a parts list to the drawing. Save the drawing as P21-13.

14. Open P8-20 and save the file as P21-14. The P21-14 file should be active. Add balloons and a parts list to the drawing of the nut driver.

15. Open P12-17 and save the file as P21-15. The P21-15 file should be active. Dimension the most important views of the anchor. Erase the undimensioned views.

16. Draw and dimension the stairs cross section shown. Use oblique dimensions where necessary. Save the drawing as P21-16.

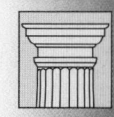

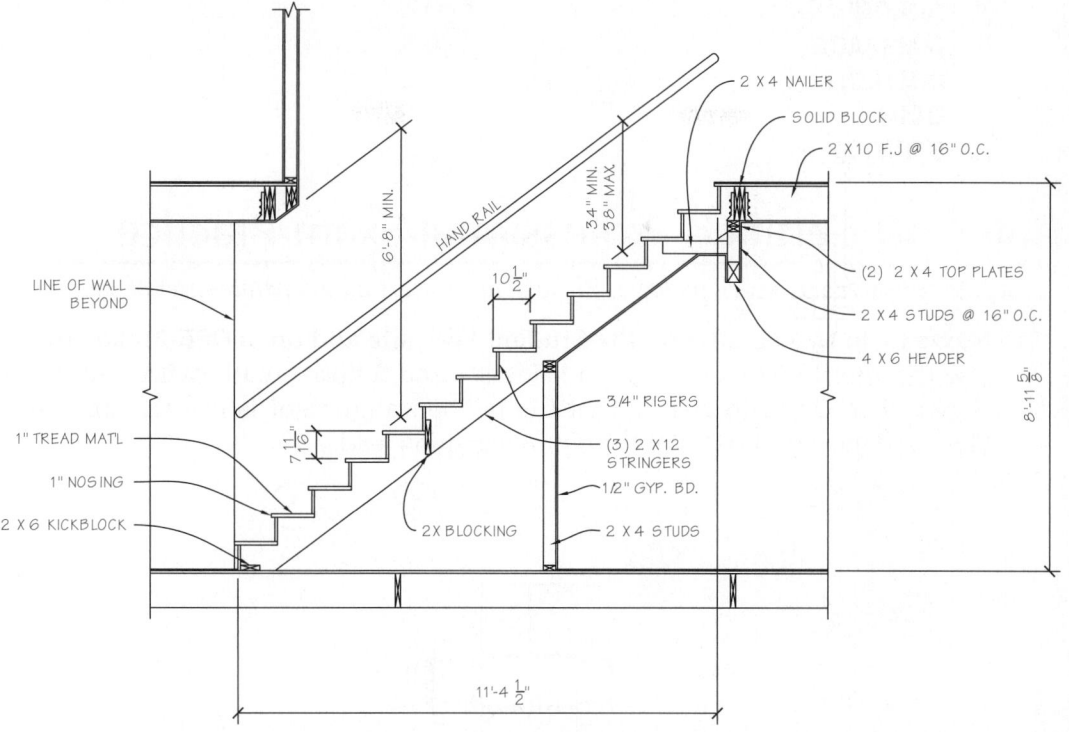

17. Use a word processor to write a report of at least 250 words explaining the importance of associative dimensioning. Site at least three examples from actual industry applications. Show at least four drawings illustrating your report.

AutoCAD Certified Associate Exam Practice

Answer the following questions. Write your answers on a separate sheet of paper.

1. Which of the following tools can you use to add a prefix to an existing linear dimension value? *Select all that apply.*
   A. **DDEDIT**
   B. **DIMEDIT New** option
   C. **DIMLINEAR Mtext** option
   D. **DIMTEDIT**
   E. **QDIM Edit** option

2. Which of the following tools allows you to space dimensions equally? *Select all that apply.*
   A. **DIMBASELINE**
   B. **DIMBREAK**
   C. **DIMORDINATE**
   D. **DIMSPACE**
   E. **MATCHPROP**

3. Which of the following tools allow you to adjust the location and alignment of dimension lines? *Select all that apply.*
   A. **DDEDIT**
   B. **DIMSPACE**
   C. **DIMTEDIT**
   D. **QDIM**
   E. **STRETCH**

AutoCAD Certified Professional Exam Practice

Follow the instructions in each problem. Write your answers on a separate sheet of paper.

1. **Navigate to this chapter on the Student Web site and open CPE-21align.dwg.** Use the appropriate tool to align leaders 1 and 3 horizontally with leader 2, as shown. Use **Ortho** to ensure that the balloon alignment is exactly horizontal. What are the coordinates of the balloon grip on leader 1?

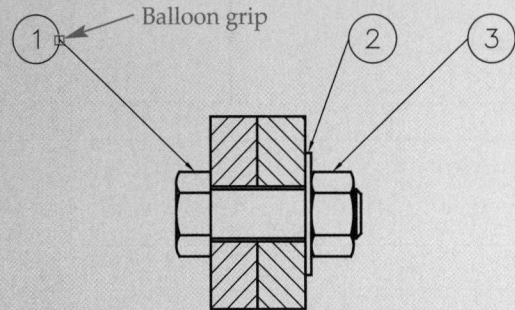

2. **Navigate to this chapter on the Student Web site and open CPE-21distribute.dwg.** Use the appropriate tool to distribute the four leaders equally between Point A and Point B. What are the coordinates of the balloon grip of leader 4?

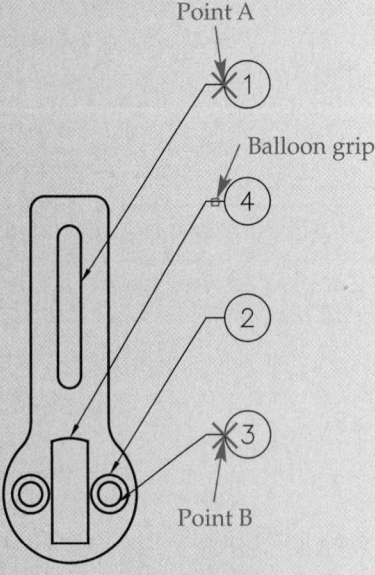

CHAPTER 22

Parametric Drafting

Learning Objectives

After completing this chapter, you will be able to do the following:

✓ Explain parametric drafting processes and applications.
✓ Create and edit parametric drawings.
✓ Add and manage geometric constraints.
✓ Add and manage dimensional constraints.
✓ Adjust the form of dimensional constraints.

Parametric drafting tools allow you to assign *parameters*, or *constraints*, to objects. The parametric concept, also known as *intelligence*, provides a way to associate objects and limit design changes. You cannot change a constraint so that it conflicts with other parametric geometry. A database stores and allows you to manage all parameters. You typically use parametric tools with standard drafting practices to create a more interactive drawing.

parametric drafting: A form of drafting in which parameters and constraints drive object size and location to produce drawings with features that adapt to changes made to other features.

parameters (constraints): Geometric characteristics and dimensions that control the size, shape, and position of drawing geometry.

Parametric Fundamentals

Parametric drafting can increase your ability to control every aspect of a drawing during and after the design and documentation process. Parametric tools can change the way you construct and edit geometry. However, in general, use parametric tools as a supplement to standard drafting practices and drawing aids. When used correctly, this technique allows you to produce accurate parametric drawings efficiently.

Understanding Constraints

Add parameters using *geometric constraints* and *dimensional constraints*. Well-defined constraints allow you to incorporate and preserve specific design intentions and increase revision efficiency. For example, if two holes through a part, drawn as circles, must always be the same size, use a geometric constraint to make the circles equal and add a dimensional constraint to size one of the circles. The size of both circles changes when you modify the dimensional constraint value. See **Figure 22-1**.

You must add constraints to make an object parametric. Dimensional constraints create parameters that direct object size and location. In contrast, a traditional

geometric constraints: Geometric characteristics applied to restrict the size or location of geometry.

dimensional constraints: Measurements that numerically control the size or location of geometry.

Figure 22-1. An example of a basic parametric relationship. The dimensional constraint controls the size of both circles with the aid of an equal geometric constraint.

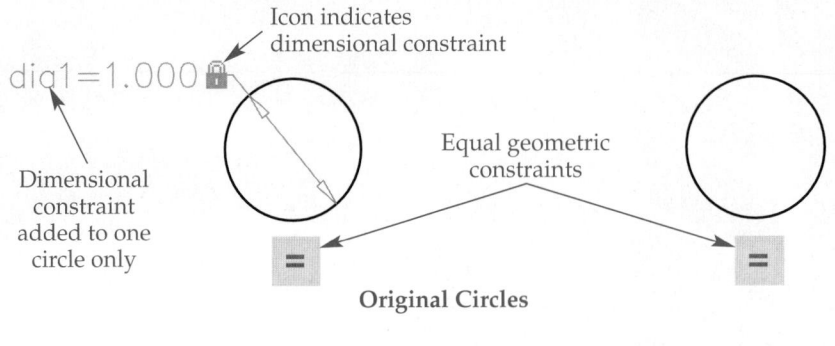

Icon indicates
dimensional constraint

dia1=1.000

Dimensional
constraint
added to one
circle only

Equal geometric
constraints

Original Circles

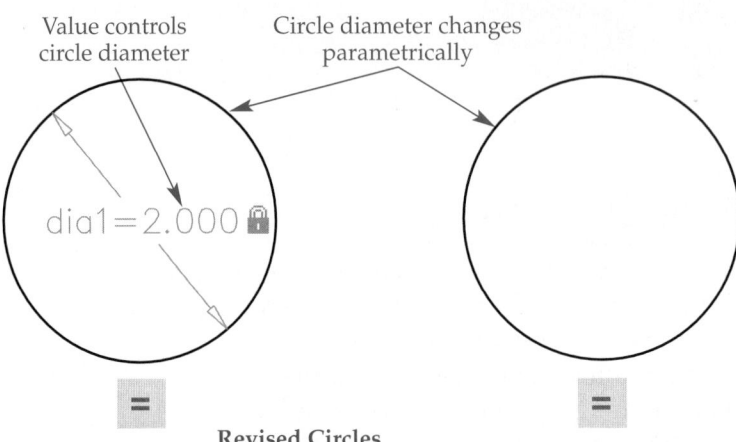

Value controls
circle diameter

Circle diameter changes
parametrically

dia1=2.000

Revised Circles

under-constrained:
Describes a drawing that includes constraints, but not enough to size and locate all geometry.

fully constrained:
Describes a drawing in which objects have no freedom of movement.

over-constrained:
Describes a drawing that contains too many constraints.

reference dimension: A dimension used for reference purposes only. Parentheses enclose reference dimensions to differentiate them from other dimensions.

associative dimension is associated with an object, but it does not control object size or location. **Figure 22-2** shows an example of a drawing that is *under-constrained*, *fully constrained*, and *over-constrained*. As you progress through the design process, you will often fully or almost fully constrain the drawing to ensure that the design is accurate. However, a message appears if you attempt to over-constrain the drawing. See **Figure 22-3**. AutoCAD does not allow you to over-constrain a drawing, as shown by the *reference dimension* in **Figure 22-2**.

Figure 22-4 shows an extreme example of constraining, for reference only. Study the figure to understand how constraints work, and how applying constraints differs from and compliments traditional drafting. Typically, you should prepare initial objects as accurately as possible using standard drawing tools and aids. Add geometric constraints while you are drawing, or add them later to existing objects. Apply dimensional constraints after creating the geometry.

Parametric Applications

Parametric tools aid the design and revision process, place limits on geometry to preserve design intent, and help form geometric constructions. Consider using constraints to help maintain relationships between objects in a drawing, especially during the design process, when changes are often frequent. However, you must decide if the additional steps required to make a drawing parametric are appropriate and necessary for the application.

Figure 22-2. Levels of parametric constraint.

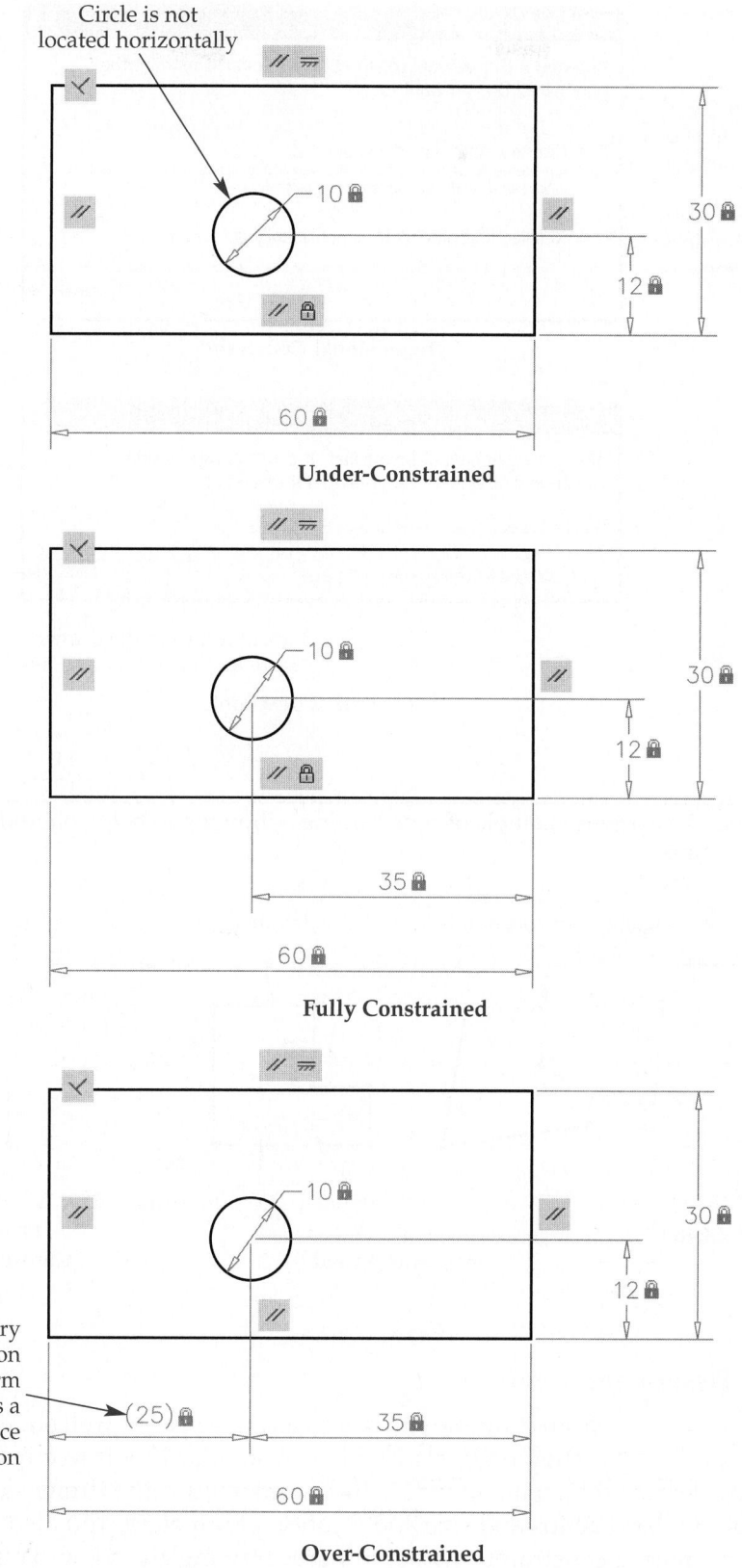

Circle is not located horizontally

Under-Constrained

Fully Constrained

Unnecessary dimension can form only as a reference dimension

Over-Constrained

Figure 22-3. Error messages appear when you attempt to over-constrain objects.

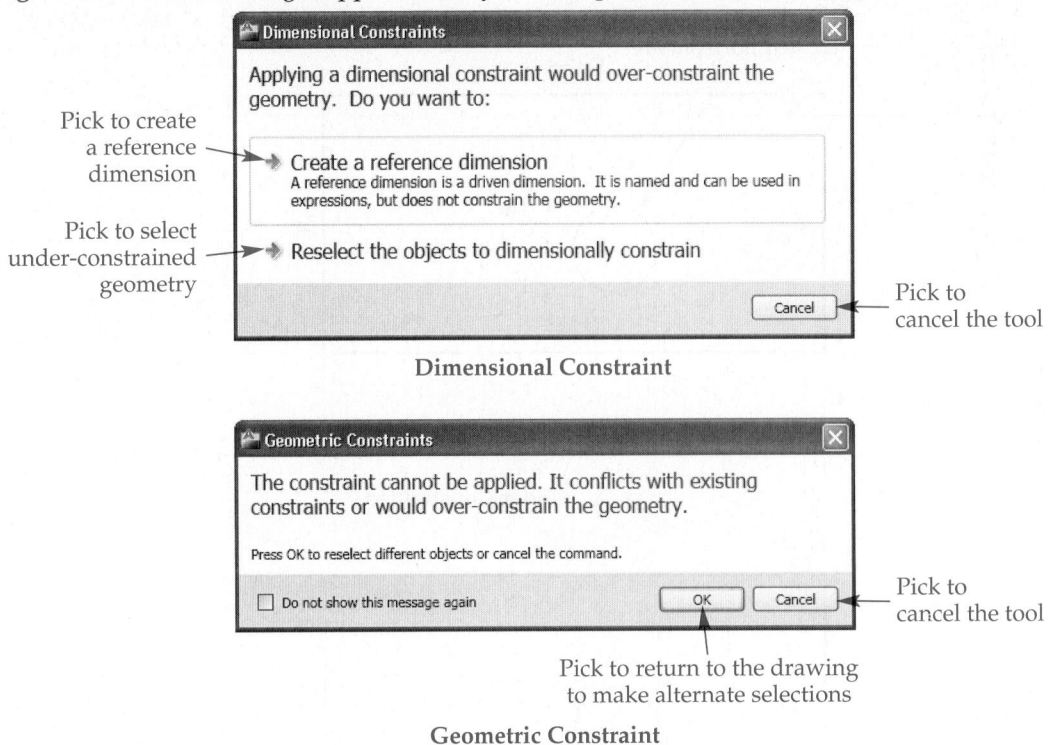

Pick to create a reference dimension

Pick to select under-constrained geometry

Pick to cancel the tool

Dimensional Constraint

Pick to cancel the tool

Pick to return to the drawing to make alternate selections

Geometric Constraint

Figure 22-4. An extreme example of constraining a drawing to help you understand how to apply constraints.

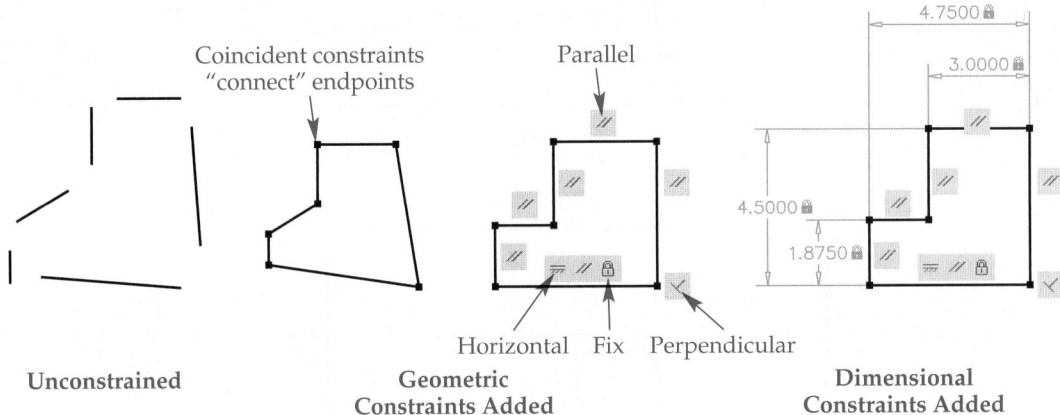

Coincident constraints "connect" endpoints

Parallel

Horizontal   Fix   Perpendicular

Unconstrained

Geometric Constraints Added

Dimensional Constraints Added

Product Design and Revision

Figure 22-5 shows an example of a front view of a spacer, well suited to parametric construction. First, as shown **Figure 22-5A,** use standard tools to create the geometry accurately. Next, as shown in **Figure 22-5B,** use geometric and dimensional constraints to add object relationships and size and location parameters. You also have the option to apply geometric constraints while you are drawing the view. This example uses centerlines, drawn on a separate construction layer, to apply the correct constraints. Then, as shown in **Figure 22-5C,** use the constraints to explore design alternatives and make changes to the drawing efficiently.

Figure 22-5. The front view of this spacer is a good candidate for parametric drafting. A—Accurate view geometry constructed using standard AutoCAD practices. B—Adding geometric and dimensional constraints to constrain the drawing. *(Continued.)*

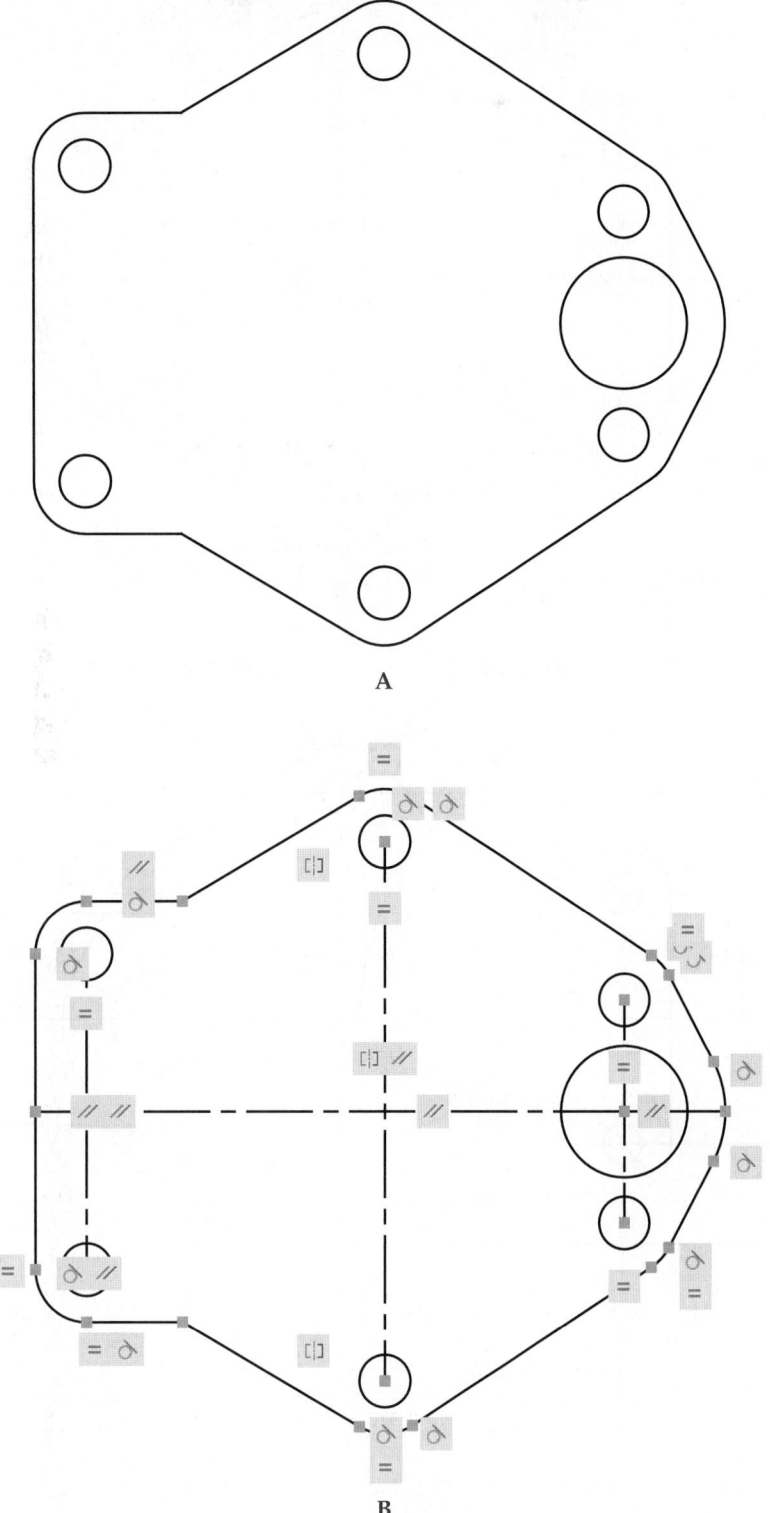

(Continued.)

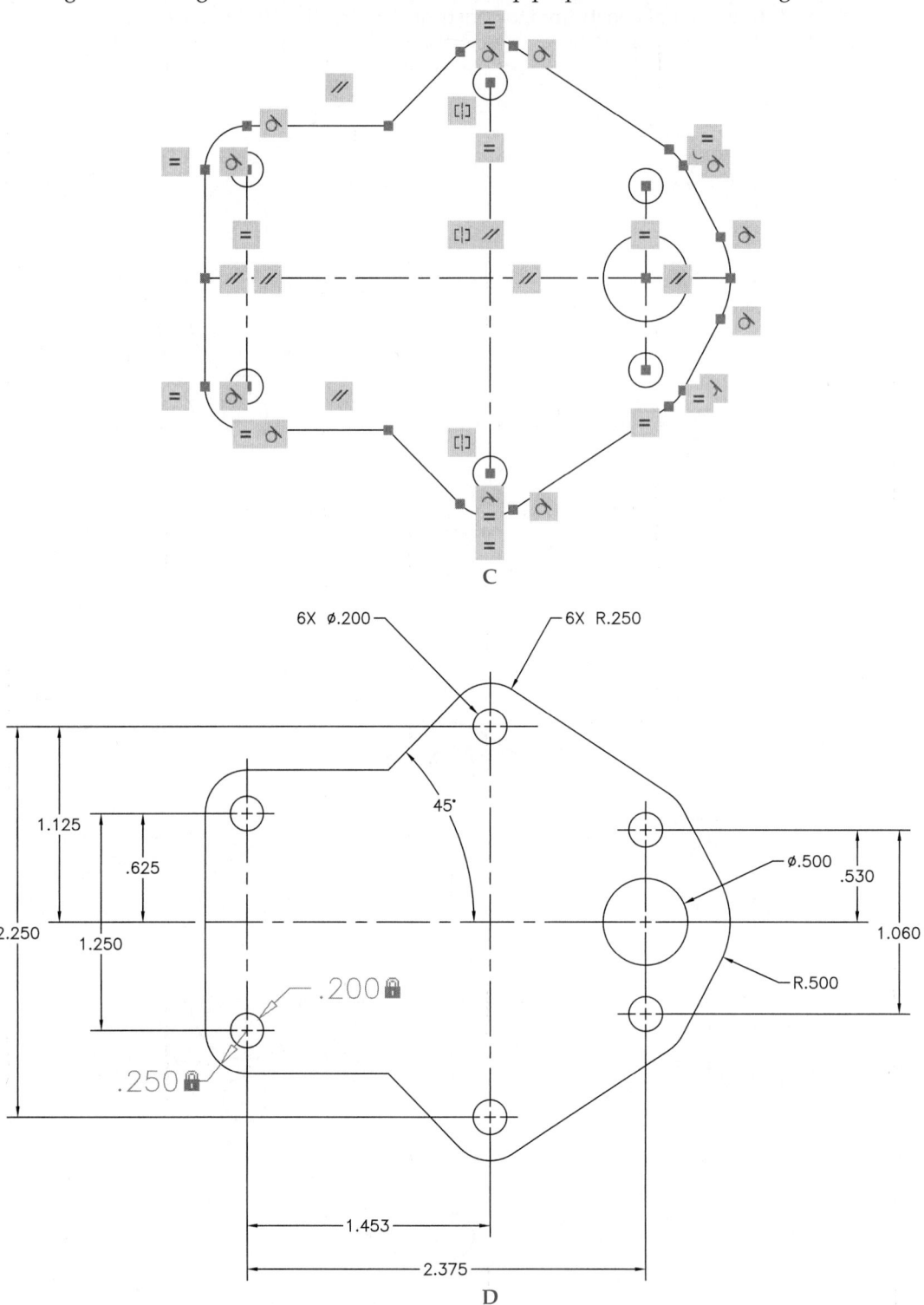

Figure 22-5D shows converting the dimensional constraint format to a formal appearance to which you can assign a dimension style. You can still use converted dimensions to adjust geometry parametrically. This example shows converting all dimensions except the .250 radius and diameter dimensions. Using standard associative .250 radial and diameter dimensions allows you to add the 6X prefix and relocate the dimensions. You can then hide the constraint information to view the finished drawing.

Geometric Construction

Use constraints to form geometric constructions when standard tools are inefficient or ineffective. For example, suppose you know that the angle of a line is 30°, and you know the line is tangent to a circle. However, you do not know the length of the line or the location of the line endpoints. One option is to position a 30° construction line, using the **Ang** option of the **XLINE** tool, anywhere in the drawing. See **Figure 22-6A.** Then use a **Tangent** geometric constraint to form a tangent relationship between the xline and circle. See **Figure 22-6B.** Then hide or delete the constraint if necessary.

Unsuitable Applications

You may find that parametric drafting is unsuitable or ineffective for some applications. For example, it may be unsuitable to add parameters to a drawing if the drawing is of a finalized product that will not require revision, or if you can easily modify drawing geometry without associating objects.

In addition, if your drawing includes a large number of objects, you may find it cumbersome to add the constraints required to form a fully intelligent drawing. For instance, you can use constraints to form all necessary relationships between objects in a floor plan. See **Figure 22-7.** In this example, constraints connect walls, specify walls as perpendicular or parallel, control wall thickness, position windows between walls, locate sinks on vanities, and form many other parametric relationships. You can then adjust dimensional constraints as needed to update the drawing.

If you effectively constrain *all* objects shown in **Figure 22-7,** you have the option, for example, to change the 11'-10 1/2" dimensional constraint to increase the width of the master bedroom. The entire floor plan adjusts to the modified room size. Consider, however, what this process requires. You must constrain all wall endpoints; the points where doors and windows meet walls; the distance between walls and objects, such as cabinets, sinks, and water closets; and form all other geometric and dimensional constraints.

NOTE

You can also use parametric tools when constructing blocks, as described later in this textbook.

Figure 22-6. A—A 30° xline placed near an associated circle. B—Using a **Tangent** geometric constraint to form a tangent construction. Notice the appropriate selection process. C—The final drawing.

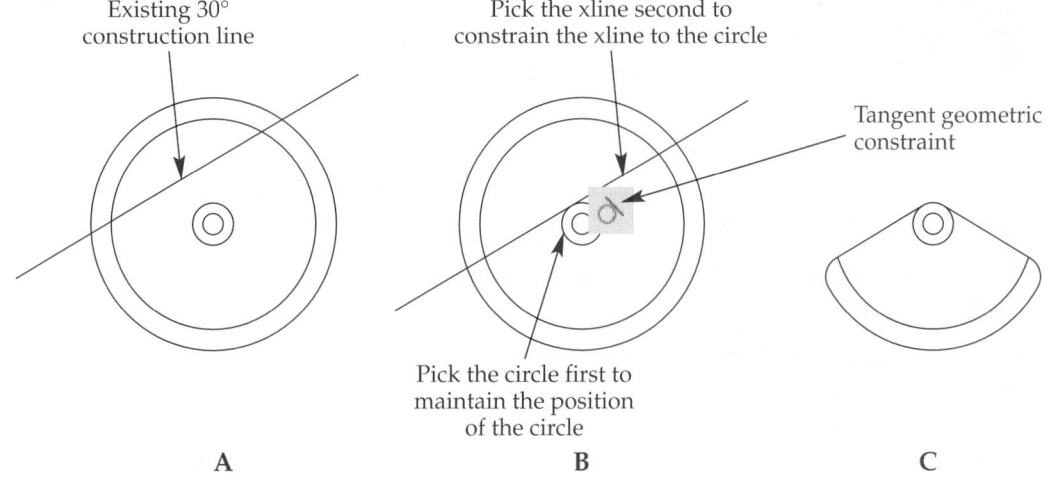

Existing 30° construction line

Pick the xline second to constrain the xline to the circle

Tangent geometric constraint

Pick the circle first to maintain the position of the circle

A   B   C

Figure 22-7. An architectural floor plan usually includes too many objects to constrain effectively and efficiently.

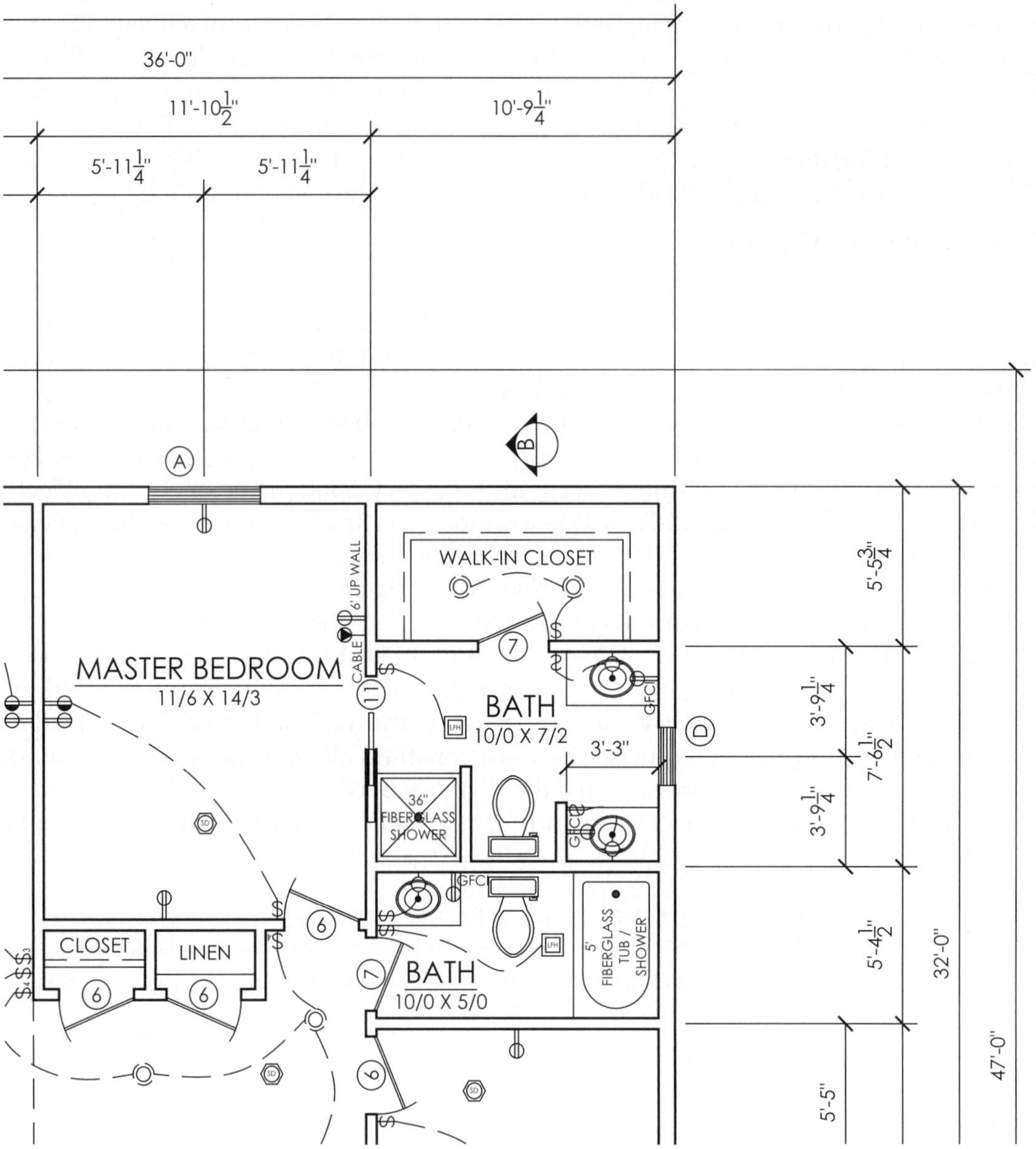

PROFESSIONAL TIP

Constraints can prove effective for multiview layout, to help maintain alignment between views.

Exercise 22-1

Access the Student Web site (www.g-wlearning.com/CAD) and complete Exercise 22-1.

Geometric Constraints

Geometric constraint tools allow you to add the geometric relationships required to build a parametric drawing. You typically add geometric constraints, or at least a portion of the necessary geometric constraints, before dimensional constraints to help preserve design intent. You can *infer* certain geometric constraints while drawing and editing, or manually apply geometric constraints to existing unconstrained geometry.

infer: Automatically detect and apply using logic.

Inferring constraints is the fastest way to add geometric relationships. However, often a combination of inferred and manually added geometric constraints is necessary. By default, a constraint-specific icon is visible when you infer constraints to indicate the presence of a geometric constraint. View, adjust, and remove geometric constraints as needed. **Figure 22-8** describes each geometric constraint.

PROFESSIONAL TIP

Placing too many geometric constraints can cause problems as you progress through the design process. Apply only the geometric constraints necessary to generate the required geometric constructions.

Figure 22-8. Geometric constraints form geometric relationships between points and/or objects. Only some of the geometric constraints can be inferred.

Constraint	Icon		Inferable	Description
Horizontal	⎯	Object	Yes	Horizontally aligns two points or a line, polyline, ellipse axis, mtext, or text object; positions geometry along the X axis on the default XY plane.
	⎯○⎯	Point-to-point		
Vertical		Object	Yes	Vertically aligns two points or a line, polyline, ellipse axis, mtext, or text object; positions geometry along the Y axis on the default XY plane.
		Point-to-point		
Parallel	//	Object-to-object	Yes	Creates a parallel constraint between a line, polyline, ellipse axis, mtext, or text object with another line, polyline, ellipse axis, mtext, or text object.
Perpendicular		Object-to-object	Yes	Forms a perpendicular constraint between a line, polyline, ellipse axis, mtext, or text object with another line, polyline, ellipse axis, mtext, or text object.
Tangent		Object-to-object	Yes	Forms a tangent constraint between a circle, arc, or ellipse and a line, polyline, circle, arc, or ellipse.
Collinear		Object-to-object	No	Aligns a line, polyline, ellipse axis, mtext, or text object with another line, polyline, ellipse axis, mtext, or text object.

(Continued.)

Figure 22-8. *(Continued.)*

Constraint	Icon		Inferable	Description
Concentric	◎	Object-to-object	No	Constrains the center of a circle, arc, or ellipse to the center of another circle, arc, or ellipse.
Equal	=	Object-to-object	No	Sizes and locates an object in reference to another object.
Symmetric	[⋮]	Object-to-object	No	Establishes symmetry between objects or points and a line, polyline, ellipse axis, mtext, or text object as the line of symmetry.
	⋮	Point-to-point		
	[⋮]	Line of symmetry		
Fix	🔒	Object	No	Secures an object to its current location in space.
	🔒	Point		
Smooth	⌐	Object-to-object	No	Connects and creates a curvature-continuous situation, or G2 curve, between a spline and a line, polyline, spline, or arc.

Inferring Geometric Constraints

The **CONSTRAINTINFER** system variable controls whether AutoCAD infers constraints as you create new geometry. The **Infer Constraints** button on the status bar provides a quick way to toggle **Infer Constraints** on and off. When **Infer Constraints** is on, constraints are inferred when you draw a new object. Appropriate object snaps and other drawing aids must be active in addition to the **Infer Constraints** tool in order for constraints to be inferred, except when you are using the **RECTANGLE** tool. For example, use the **LINE** tool and a horizontal (0° or 180°) or vertical (90° or 270°) polar tracking angle, or activate **Ortho** mode to constrain a horizontal or vertical line. See **Figure 22-9A**.

Constraints are also inferred when you edit an object. Some tools, such as **FILLET** and **CHAMFER**, infer constraints automatically. However, you must use grip editing and/or appropriate object snaps to infer constraints when stretching, moving, or copying. For example, use grip editing and the center point and midpoint grips or use the **MOVE** tool and **Center** and **Midpoint** object snap modes to move the center point of a circle coincident to the midpoint of a line. See **Figure 22-9B**.

NOTE

The **Quadrant**, **Intersection**, **Extension**, and **Apparent extension** object snaps do not infer constraints. The **OFFSET**, **BREAK**, **TRIM**, **EXTEND**, **SCALE**, **MIRROR**, **ARRAY**, and **MATCHPROP** tools do not infer constraints. Exploding a polyline removes all inferred constraints.

Figure 22-9. A—Inferring a horizontal and vertical constraint while drawing a line. B—Editing a drawing to infer a coincident constraint.

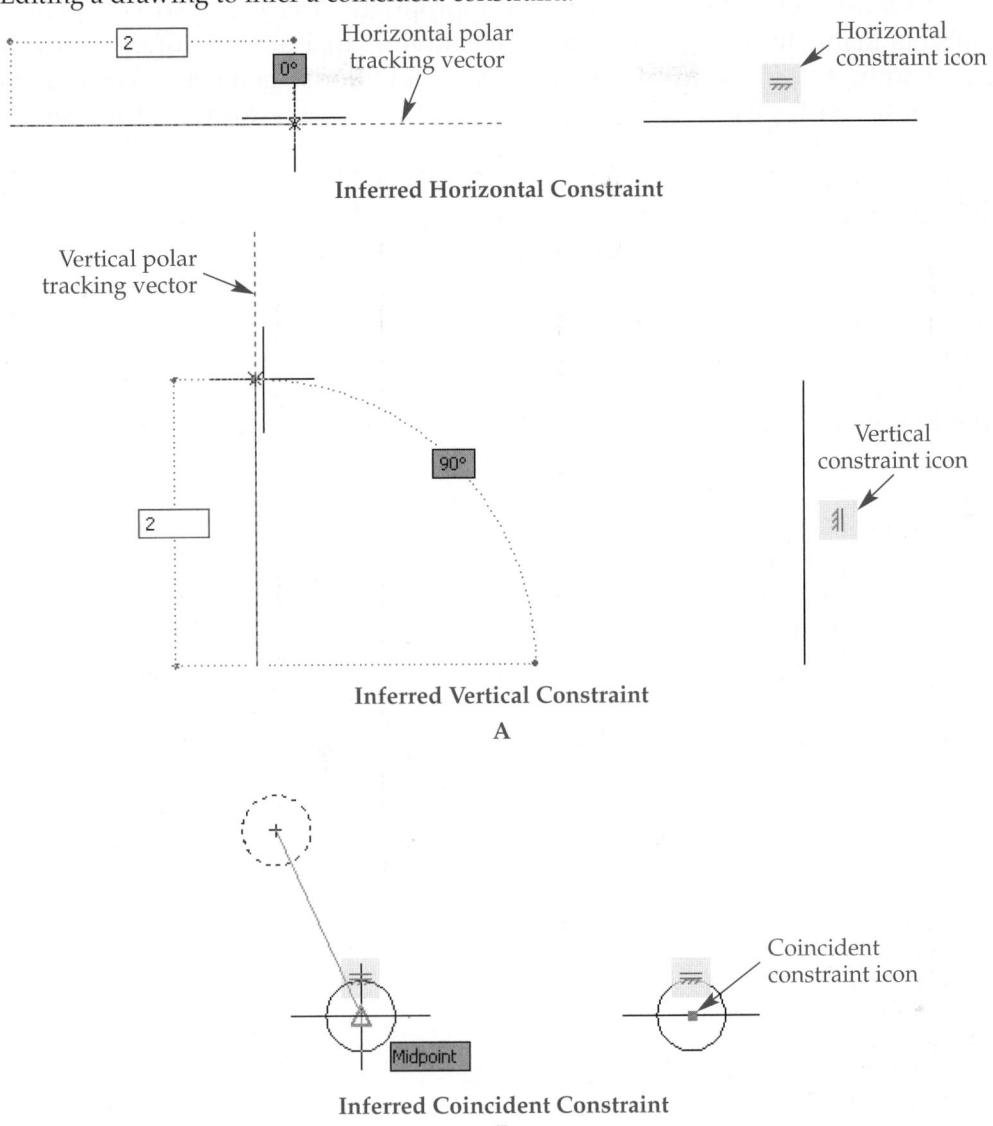

Inferred Horizontal Constraint

Inferred Vertical Constraint

A

Inferred Coincident Constraint

B

CAUTION

The **Infer Constraints** tool can save drafting time by placing geometric constraints while you draw or edit. However, use caution to ensure that appropriate geometric constructions occur. You may have to replace certain constraints manually.

Exercise 22-2

Access the Student Web site (www.g-wlearning.com/CAD) and complete Exercise 22-2.

Manual Geometric Constraints

Infer constraints when possible and appropriate. You can also add geometric constraints manually to apply geometric constraints that are not inferred automatically, as indicated in **Figure 22-8**, to include additional geometric constraints as needed, or to constrain a nonparametric drawing. The quickest way to place geometric constraints manually is to pick the appropriate button from the **Geometric** panel of the **Parametric** ribbon tab. You can also type **GC** followed by the name of the constraint, such as **GCTANGENT**, or select an option from the **GEOMCONSTRAINT** tool. Follow the prompts to make the required selection(s), form the constraint, and exit the tool.

Select objects, points, or an object and a point, depending on the objects and geometric constraint. **Figure 22-10** shows the point markers that appear as you move the crosshairs on an object to select a point. The object associated with a specific point highlights, allowing you to confirm that the point is on the appropriate object. Pick the marked location to apply the constraint to the object at that point. **Figure 22-10** also shows the ellipse axes and mtext and text constraint lines that appear for selection. Pick when you see the appropriate line to apply the constraint to the object using the line.

The **Fix** constraint requires a single object or point selection. All other geometric constraints require you to select two objects or points, or an object and a point. Generally, the first object or point you select remains the same. The second object or point you select changes in relation to the first selection, unless the first selection is fixed. For example, to create perpendicular lines using the **Perpendicular** constraint, first select the line that will remain in the same position at the same angle. Then select the line to make perpendicular to the first line, assuming the second line is not fixed.

Type
GEOMCONSTRAINT
GCON

Figure 22-10.
The points on objects you can select to create point-to-point or object-to-point constraints. This figure also shows selectable constraint lines at ellipse axes and through mtext and text objects. Use the lines to establish horizontal, vertical, parallel, perpendicular, or collinear constraints.

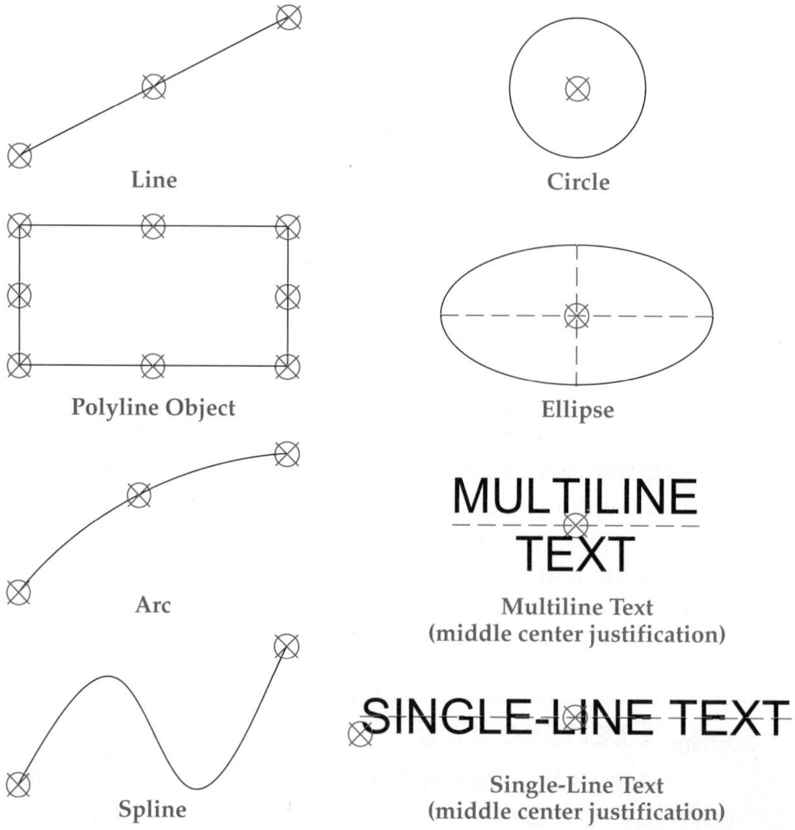

Line

Circle

Polyline Object

Ellipse

Arc

MULTILINE TEXT
Multiline Text
(middle center justification)

SINGLE-LINE TEXT
Single-Line Text
(middle center justification)

Spline

Coincident Constraints

Figure 22-11 shows *coincident* constraints applied to a basic multiview drawing. Reference this figure as you explore options for assigning coincident constraints.

Infer coincident constraints by turning on **Infer Constraints** and using specific drawing and editing tools and object snaps. When you use the **LINE** tool and draw a series of connected line segments, coincident constraints are inferred at adjoined endpoints. Use the **Close** option or an **Endpoint** object snap to infer a coincident constraint between the first and last points. When you use the **CHAMFER** tool, coincident constraints are inferred at each endpoint.

The **Endpoint**, **Midpoint**, **Center**, **Insertion**, and **Node** object snaps infer a point-to-point coincident constraint. For example, snap to the midpoint of a line to constrain the center of a donut to the midpoint of the line. The **Nearest** object snap infers an object-to-point coincident constraint. For example, snap to a nearest location on a line to constrain the center of a circle to the line. The center of the circle is free to move anywhere aligned with the line, and does not have to touch the line.

Use the **GCCOINCIDENT** or **GEOMCONSTRAINT** tool to create a coincident constraint manually. Move the pick box near a point on an existing object to display a point marker. Pick the marked location, and then pick a point on another object to make the two points coincide.

Use the **Object** function to select an object and a point, as required to constrain a point along a curve. The point does not have to contact the curve, and you can select the object first or second. The **Autoconstrain** function allows you to select multiple objects to form coincident constraints at every possible coincident intersection in a single operation. Right-click or press [Enter] or the space bar to use the **Autoconstrain** function.

coincident: A geometric construction that specifies two points sharing the same position.

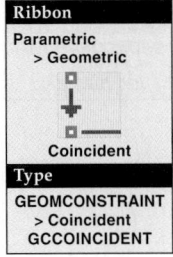

Ribbon

Parametric
> **Geometric**

Coincident

Type

GEOMCONSTRAINT
> **Coincident**
GCCOINCIDENT

NOTE

Connected polyline segments act as if they are constrained, but they do not use or accept coincident constraints at adjoined endpoints.

PROFESSIONAL TIP

When you select points, be sure to select the points corresponding to the surface to be constrained.

Figure 22-11. Coincident constraints required for a basic multiview drawing. For clarity, labels do not indicate all required coincident constraints. This drawing is used as an example throughout this chapter.

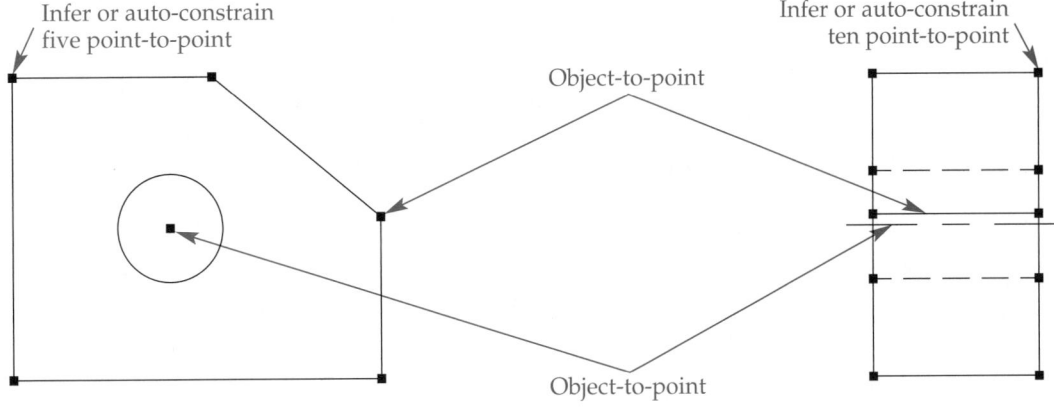

Exercise 22-3

Access the Student Web site (www.g-wlearning.com/CAD) and complete Exercise 22-3.

Horizontal and Vertical Constraints

Figure 22-12 shows basic examples of horizontally and vertically constrained objects and points. Horizontal and vertical constraints are commonly used to define a horizontal or vertical surface datum or to align points.

Infer a horizontal constraint while drawing a first line or polyline segment by turning on **Infer Constraints** and using a horizontal polar tracking angle (0° or 180°) or **Ortho** mode. See **Figure 22-9A.** A perpendicular constraint is inferred if the next line or polyline segment is vertical. Infer a vertical constraint while drawing a first line or polyline segment using a vertical polar tracking angle (90° or 270°) or **Ortho** mode. A perpendicular constraint is inferred if the next line or polyline segment is horizontal.

Use the **GCHORIZONTAL**, **GCVERTICAL**, or **GEOMCONSTRAINT** tool to create a horizontal or vertical constraint manually. Select a line, polyline, ellipse axis, mtext, or text object to constrain, or use the **2Points** function to pick two points to align horizontally or vertically.

Parallel and Perpendicular Constraints

parallel: A geometric construction that specifies that objects such as lines will never intersect, no matter how long they become.

perpendicular: A geometric construction that defines a 90° angle between objects such as lines.

Figure 22-13 shows *parallel* and *perpendicular* constraints applied to a basic multiview drawing. Parallelism and perpendicularity are common geometric characteristics that provide specific controls related to the orientation of features.

Infer parallel or perpendicular constraints by turning on **Infer Constraints** and using specific drawing and editing tools and object snaps. A perpendicular constraint is inferred if the next segment of a connected line or polyline is horizontal or vertical. When you use the **RECTANGLE** tool to draw a polyline object, parallel and perpendicular constraints are inferred to create a true rectangle. Additional parallel and perpendicular constraints are inferred when you use the **Chamfer** option of the **RECTANGLE** tool, depending on the specified distances. An additional perpendicular constraint is inferred when you use the **Fillet** option.

The **Parallel** object snap infers a parallel constraint between objects. The **Perpendicular** object snap infers a perpendicular and coincident constraint between objects.

Figure 22-12. Examples of vertically and horizontally constrained objects and points.

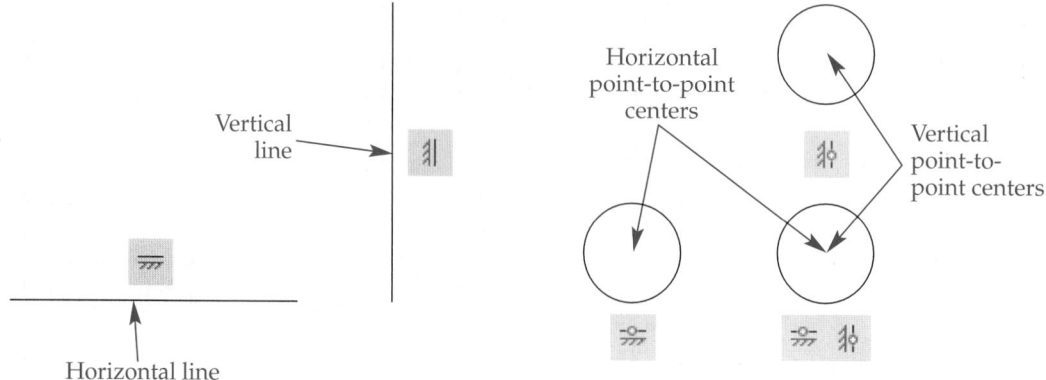

Figure 22-13. Parallel and perpendicular constraints required for the example multiview drawing.

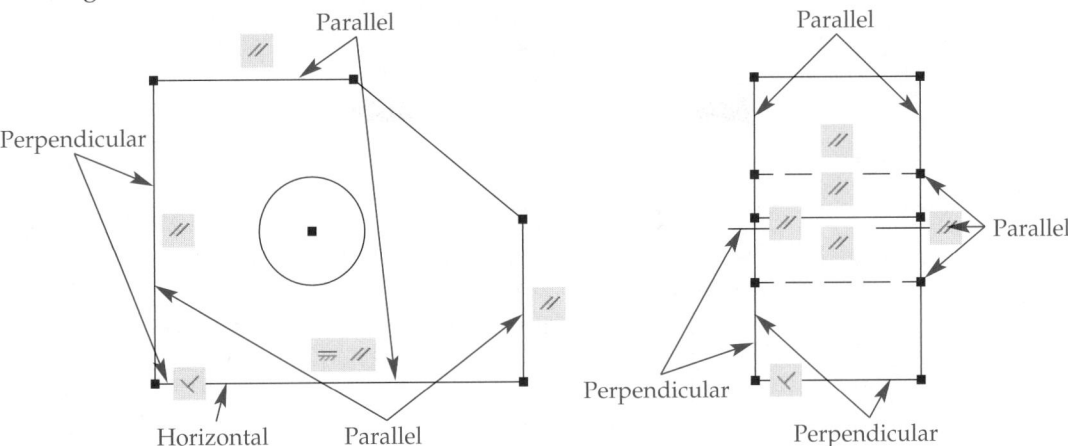

Use the **GCPARALLEL**, **GCPERPENDICULAR**, or **GEOMCONSTRAINT** tool to create a parallel or perpendicular constraint manually. Select a line, polyline, ellipse axis, mtext, or text object and a line, polyline, ellipse axis, mtext, or text object.

Exercise 22-4

Access the Student Web site (www.g-wlearning.com/CAD) and complete Exercise 22-4.

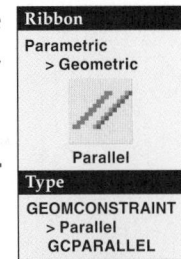

Tangent and Collinear Constraints

Figure 22-14 shows tangent and collinear constraints applied to a basic multiview drawing. Collinear constraints cannot be inferred.

Infer tangent constraints by turning on **Infer Constraints** and using the **FILLET** tool or the **Fillet** option of the rectangle tool with a radius greater than 0. You can also infer tangent constraints on arc segments of polylines, and using the **Tangent** object snap.

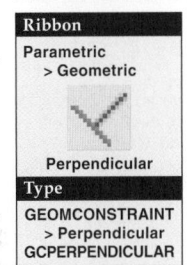

> **NOTE**
>
> The **Continue** option of the **ARC** tool does not infer a coincident or tangent constraint between the existing object and the new arc.

Use the **GCTANGENT** or **GEOMCONSTRAINT** tool to create a tangent constraint manually. Select a circle, arc, or ellipse and then a line, polyline, circle, arc, or ellipse. Use the **GCCOLLINEAR** or **GEOMCONSTRAINT** tool to create a collinear constraint manually. A collinear constraint is commonly used for applications such as aligning multiview surfaces. Select a line, polyline, ellipse axis, mtext, or text object and then another line, polyline, ellipse axis, mtext, or text object. Activate the **Multiple** function to select multiple objects to align in a single operation. Right-click or press [Enter] or the space bar to complete a multiple constrain operation.

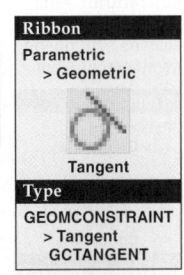

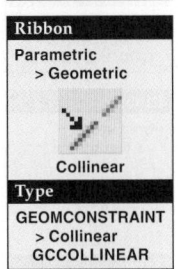

Figure 22-14. A—Collinear and tangent constraints required for the example multiview drawing. B—Common tangent constraint applications.

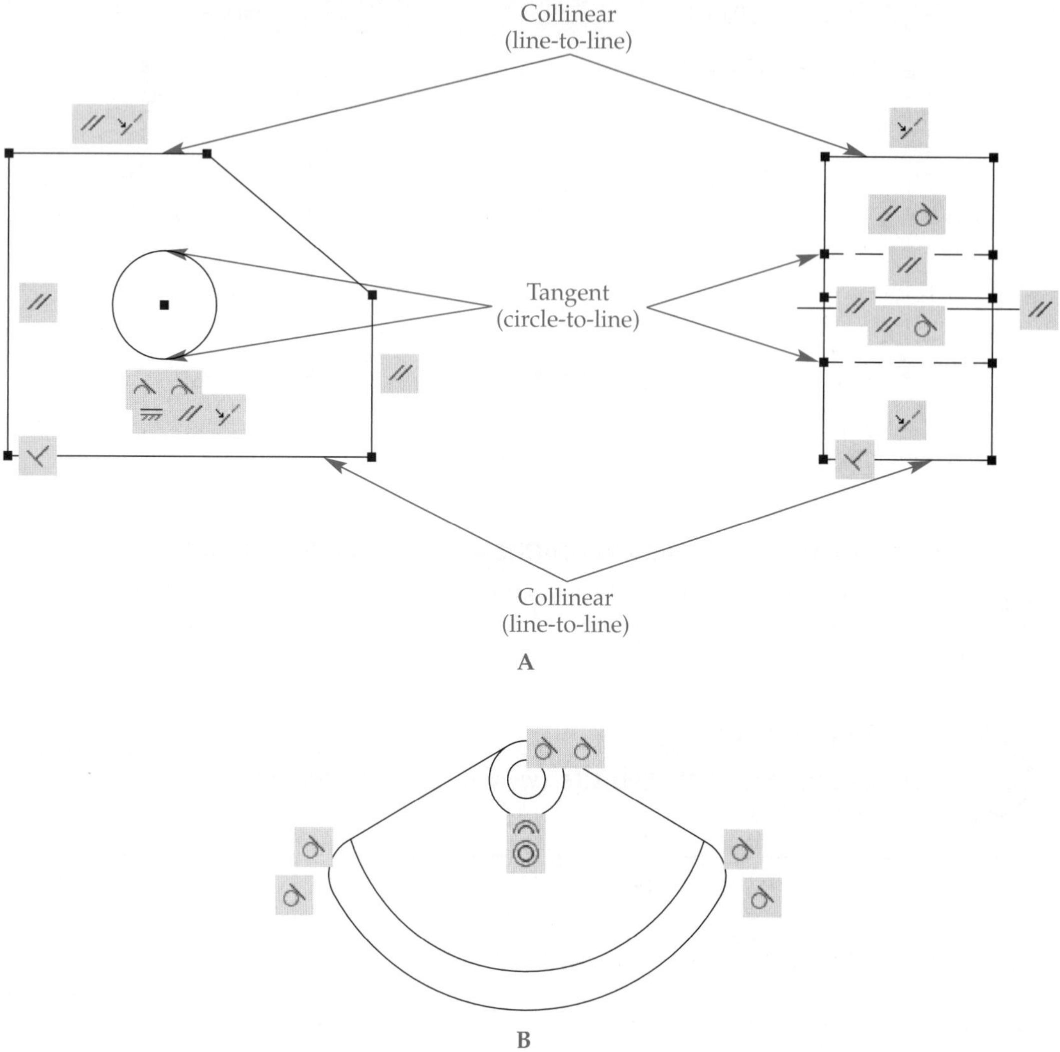

Collinear
(line-to-line)

Tangent
(circle-to-line)

Collinear
(line-to-line)

A

B

Access the Student Web site (www.g-wlearning.com/CAD) and complete Exercise 22-5 and Exercise 22-6.

Exercises 22-5 and 22-6

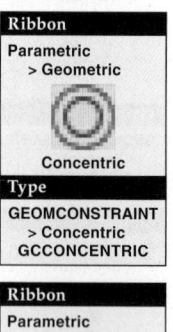

concentric: Arcs, circles, and/or ellipses sharing the same center point.

Ribbon
Parametric > Geometric
Concentric
Type
GEOMCONSTRAINT > Concentric GCCONCENTRIC

Ribbon
Parametric > Geometric
Equal
Type
GEOMCONSTRAINT > Equal GCEQUAL

Concentric and Equal Constraints

Use the **GCCONCENTRIC** or **GEOMCONSTRAINT** tool to assign a *concentric* constraint. Select a circle, arc, or ellipse and a second circle, arc, or ellipse. Use the **GCEQUAL** or **GEOMCONSTRAINT** tool to size objects equally and, in some cases, to locate objects. Select two objects, or activate the **Multiple** function to select multiple objects to equalize in a single operation. Right-click or press [Enter] or the space bar to complete a multiple constrain operation. **Figure 22-15** shows examples of concentric and equal constraints.

Figure 22-15.
Examples of concentric and equal constraints. All circles are concentric to an arc. All small arcs are equal, and all small circles are equal. Use the **Multiple** option to help make multiple objects equal in a single operation.

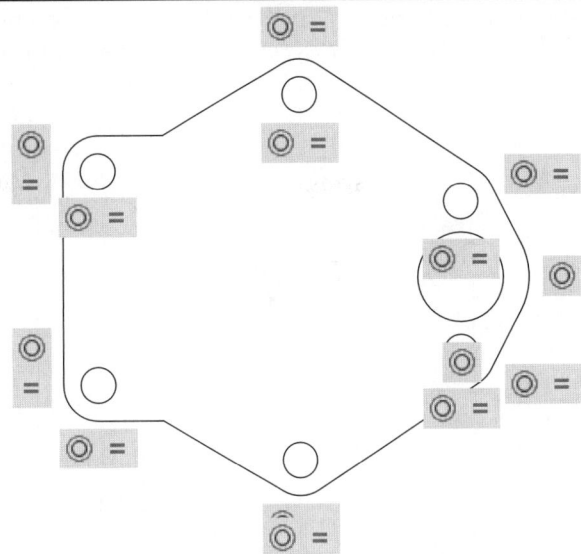

Symmetric, Fix, and Smooth Constraints

Use the **GCSYMMETRIC** or **GEOMCONSTRAINT** tool to establish symmetry between objects or points and a line, polyline, ellipse axis, mtext, or text object as the line of symmetry. Select one object, followed by another, and finally, a line of symmetry. Use the **2Points** option to pick points followed by the line of symmetry to constrain symmetrical points.

Use the **GCFIX** or **GEOMCONSTRAINT** tool to secure a point or object to its current location in space to help preserve design intent. A single fix constraint is often required to fully constrain a drawing. Use the default method to fix a point, or activate the **Object** function to select an object to fix. **Figure 22-16** shows examples of symmetric and fix constraints. Use the **GCSMOOTH** or **GEOMCONSTRAINT** tool to connect and create a curvature-continuous situation, or G2 curve, between a selected spline and a line, polyline, spline, or arc.

> **NOTE**
>
> When you apply a **Coincident** or **Smooth** constraint to a fit points spline, the spline converts to a control vertices spline.

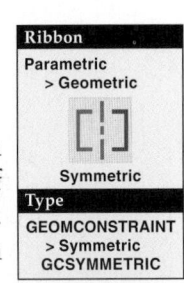

Exercise 22-7

Access the Student Web site (www.g-wlearning.com/CAD) and complete Exercise 22-7.

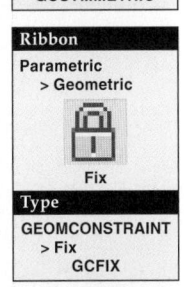

Using the AUTOCONSTRAIN Tool

Use the **AUTOCONSTRAIN** tool in an attempt to add all required geometric constraints in a single operation. Before using the **AUTOCONSTRAIN** tool, access the **AutoConstrain** tab of the **Constraint Settings** dialog box to specify the geometric constraints to apply. The constraint priority determines which constraints are applied first. The higher the priority, the more likely and often the constraint will form if

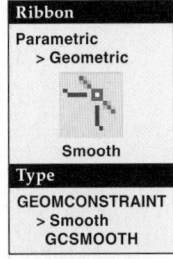

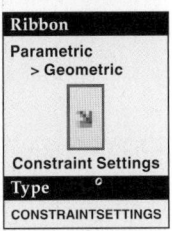

Figure 22-16. A symmetrical parametric drawing created by adding symmetric constraints to circles and arcs. A fix constraint secures the drawing in space.

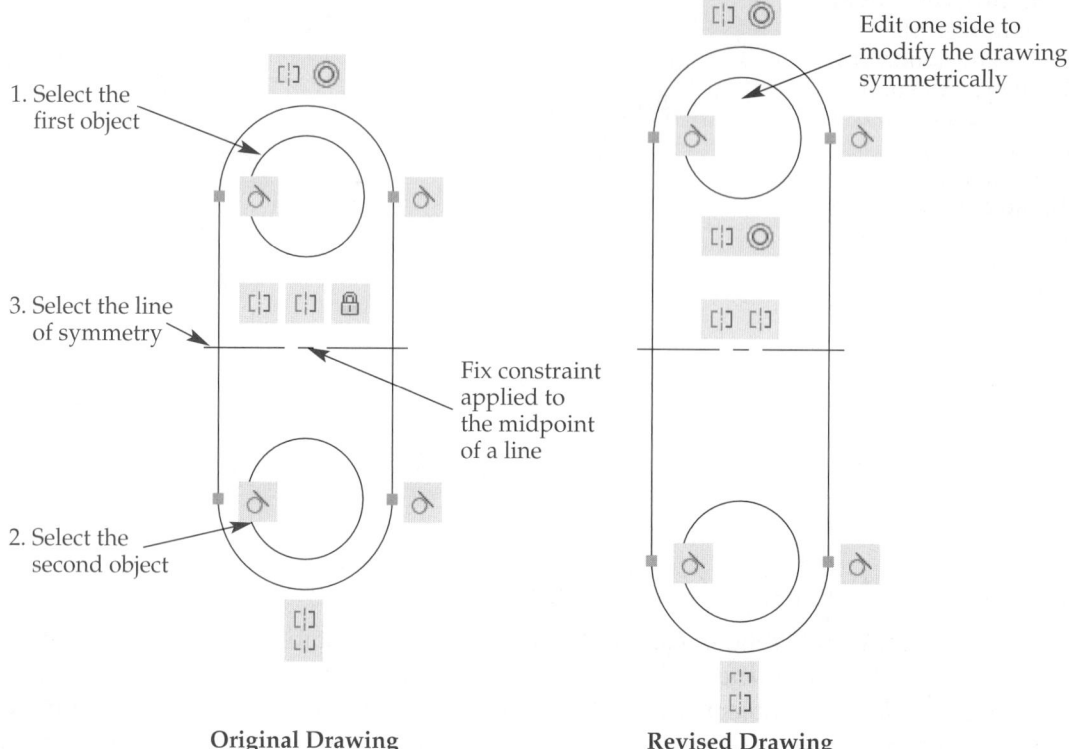

1. Select the first object

3. Select the line of symmetry

Fix constraint applied to the midpoint of a line

2. Select the second object

Edit one side to modify the drawing symmetrically

Original Drawing

Revised Drawing

appropriate geometry is available. Select a constraint and use the **Move Up** and **Move Down** buttons to change its priority. Use the corresponding **Apply** check marks and the **Select All** and **Clear All** buttons to omit specific constraints during the constraining procedure.

The check boxes determine whether tangent and perpendicular constraints can form if objects do not intersect. See **Figure 22-17**. The **Tolerances** area controls how specific constraints form based on the distance between and angle of objects. A distance less than or equal to the value specified in the **Distance** text box receives constraints. An angle less than or equal to the value specified in the **Angle** text box receives constraints. See **Figure 22-18**.

Once you specify the settings, access the **AUTOCONSTRAIN** tool and select the objects to constrain. The **Settings** option is available before selection to access the **AutoConstrain** tab of the **Constraint Settings** dialog box. A fix constraint does not occur.

NOTE

You can also access the **Constraint Settings** dialog box by right-clicking on the **Infer Constraints** button on the status bar and picking **Settings...**.

CAUTION

The **AUTOCONSTRAIN** tool can save drafting time by placing geometric constrains in a single operation. However, use caution to ensure that appropriate geometric constructions occur and geometry does not shift. You may have to replace certain constraints.

Figure 22-17. Examples of constraints that will form when you select the **Tangent objects must share an intersection** or the **Perpendicular objects must share an intersection** check box.

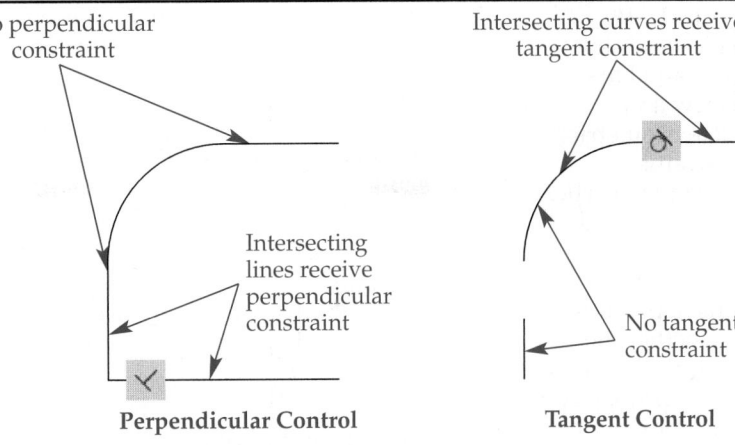

No perpendicular constraint

Intersecting lines receive perpendicular constraint

Perpendicular Control

Intersecting curves receive tangent constraint

No tangent constraint

Tangent Control

Figure 22-18. Examples of constraints that form based on **Distance** and **Angle** tolerance values.

	Distance between Objects > Distance Tolerance	Distance between Objects ≤ Distance Tolerance	Angle > Angle tolerance	Angle ≤ Angle tolerance
Before				
After				

Managing Geometric Constraints

Geometric *constraint bars* appear by default to indicate geometric constraints. See **Figure 22-19**. Refer to **Figure 22-8** if you need help recognizing constraint icons. The **CONSTRAINTBAR** tool includes options to show or hide constraint bars. The quickest way to access these options is to pick the appropriate button from the **Geometric** panel of the **Parametric** ribbon tab.

Pick the **Show/Hide** button, pick objects to manage, and then right-click or press [Enter] or the space bar to access options. Choose the **Show** option to display hidden constraint bars, the **Hide** option to hide visible constraint bars, or the **Reset** option to display hidden constraint bars and move constraint bars back to the default positions. Select the **Show All** button to display all constraint bars. Pick the **Hide All** button to hide all constraint bars. Hiding constraint bars does not remove geometric constraints.

Access the **Geometric** tab of the **Constraint Settings** dialog box to specify the geometric bars that appear and other geometric bar characteristics. Select the check boxes for individual constraints to display the constraints in constraint bars. Use the **Select All** and **Clear All** buttons to select or deselect all constraint type check boxes. By default, all constraint types are displayed. Limiting constraint bar visibility to specific constraint types often helps to locate and adjust constraints.

constraint bars: Toolbars that allow you to view and remove geometric constraints.

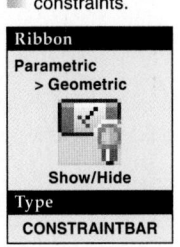

Ribbon
Parametric > Geometric

Show/Hide

Type
CONSTRAINTBAR

Figure 22-19.
Use geometric constraint bars to view and delete geometric constraints. Horizontal, vertical, symmetric, and fix constraints use different icons depending on whether the constraint is a point-to-point or object-to-point constraint.

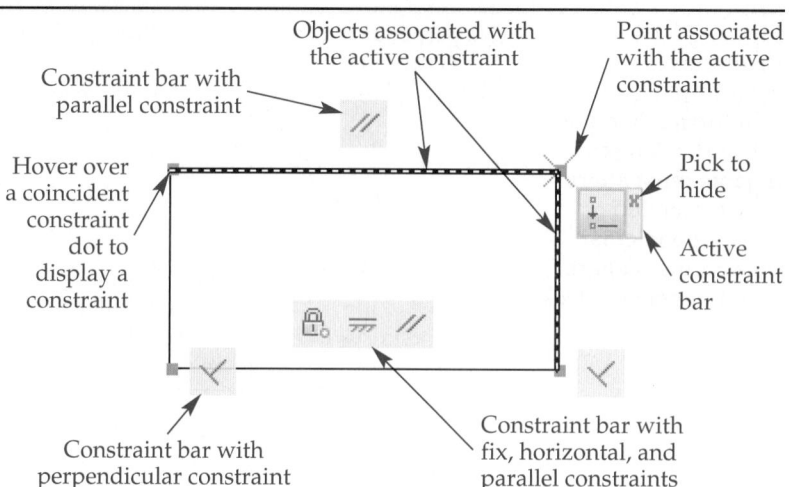

Constraint bar with parallel constraint

Objects associated with the active constraint

Point associated with the active constraint

Hover over a coincident constraint dot to display a constraint

Pick to hide

Active constraint bar

Constraint bar with perpendicular constraint

Constraint bar with fix, horizontal, and parallel constraints

Use the **Constraint bar transparency** slider or text box to adjust the constraint bar transparency. Check **Show constraint bars after applying constraints to selected objects** to display constraint bars after applying geometric constraints. Check **Show constraint bars when objects are selected** to display constraint bars when you select objects, even if constraint bars are hidden.

A coincident constraint initially appears as a dot. Hover over the dot to show the coincident constraint bar. All other constraints appear as constraint bars. Hover over an object to highlight constraint bars associated with constraints applied to the object. Hover over or select a constraint bar to highlight the corresponding constrained objects and display markers that identify constrained points. See **Figure 22-19.** The visual effects of hovering over an object or geometric bar helps you recognize the objects and points associated with the constraint.

If a constraint bar blocks your view, drag it to a new location. To hide a specific constraint bar, pick the **Hide Constraint Bar** button, or right-click and choose **Hide**. The right-click shortcut menu also includes options for hiding all constraint bars and for accessing the **Geometric** tab of the **Constraint Settings** dialog box.

Design changes sometimes require deleting existing constraints. To delete geometric constraints, hover over an icon in the constraint bar and press [Delete], or right-click and select **Delete**.

NOTE

You can also right-click with no objects selected to access a **Parametric** cascading submenu that provides options for displaying and hiding constraints and for accessing the **Constraint Settings** dialog box.

PROFESSIONAL TIP

To confirm that constraints, especially geometric constraints, are present and appropriate, select an object to display grips and attempt to stretch a grip. As an object becomes constrained, you should observe less freedom of movement. Stretching or attempting to stretch grips is one of the fastest ways to assess design options and to analyze where a constraint is still required. You know the drawing is constrained when you are no longer able to stretch the geometry.

Dimensional Constraints

Dimensional constraints establish size and location parameters. You must include dimensional constraints to create a truly parametric drawing. Dimensional constraints use a *dynamic format* by default, and their appearance is different from traditional associative dimensions. The easiest way to preset dimensional constraints to use the dynamic format is to pick the **Dynamic Constraint Mode** button from the expanded **Dimensional** panel of the **Parametric** ribbon tab.

You cannot modify how dynamic dimensional constraints appear, but you can change them to an *annotational format*. To preset new dimensional constraints to use an annotational format, pick the **Annotational Constraint Mode** button from the expanded **Dimensional** panel of the **Parametric** ribbon tab. The annotational format uses the current dimension style. This textbook focuses on using the **Dynamic Constraint Mode** function and then assigning annotational format later. View, adjust, and remove dimensional constraints as needed.

Adding Dimensional Constraints

The quickest way to create dimensional constraints is to pick the appropriate button from the **Dimensional** panel of the **Parametric** ribbon tab. You can also type **DC** followed by the name of the constraint, such as **DCLINEAR**, or select an option from the **DIMCONSTRAINT** tool. To create a dimensional constraint, follow the prompts to make the required selections, pick a location for the dimension line, enter a value to form the constraint, and exit the tool.

The process of selecting points or objects to locate dimensional constraint extension lines is the same as that for adding geometric constraints. When a dimensional constraint tool requires you to pick two points or objects, the first point or object you select generally remains the same. In some cases, you can consider the first point or object the datum. The second point or object you select changes in relation to the first selection, unless the first selection is fixed. When selecting points, be sure to select the points corresponding to the surface to constrain.

A text editor appears after you select the location for the dimension line, allowing you to specify the dimension value. See **Figure 22-20A**. Each dimensional constraint is a parameter with a specific name, expression, and value. By default, linear dimensions receive d names, angular dimensions receive ang names, diameter dimensions receive dia names, and radial dimensions receive rad names. Every parameter must have a unique name. The name of the first of each type of dimension includes a 1, such as d1. The next dimension includes a 2, such as d2, and so on. Use the text editor to enter a more descriptive name, such as Length, Width, or Diameter. Follow the name with the = symbol and then the dimension value. Changing the current dimension value modifies object size or location. Press [Enter] or pick outside of the text editor to form the constraint. See **Figure 22-20B**.

The most basic option to specify the value of a dimensional constraint is to type a value in the text editor. Dimensional constraint units reflect the current work environment and unit settings, including length, angle type, and precision. Accept the current value if the drawing is accurate. Enter a different value if the drawing is inaccurate, or to change object size.

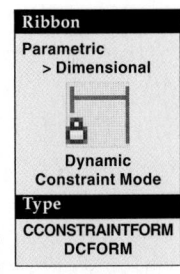

Ribbon

Parametric > Dimensional

Dynamic Constraint Mode

Type

CCONSTRAINTFORM
DCFORM

dynamic format: A dimensional constraint format specifically for controlling the size or location of geometry.

annotational format: A dimensional constraint format in which the constraints look like traditional dimensions, using a dimension style. Annotational dimensional constraints can still control the size or location of geometry.

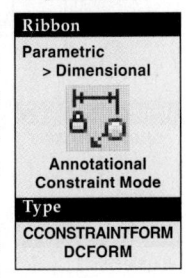

Ribbon

Parametric > Dimensional

Annotational Constraint Mode

Type

CCONSTRAINTFORM
DCFORM

Figure 22-20.
A—Use the text editor that appears after you establish the location of the dimension line to specify a parametric dimension. B—An example of modifying a parameter name and value. Notice that the dimension controls the object size.

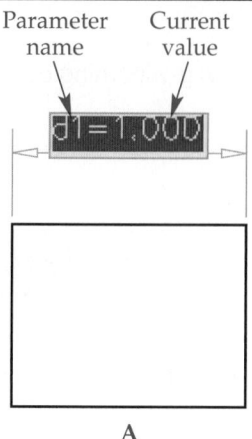

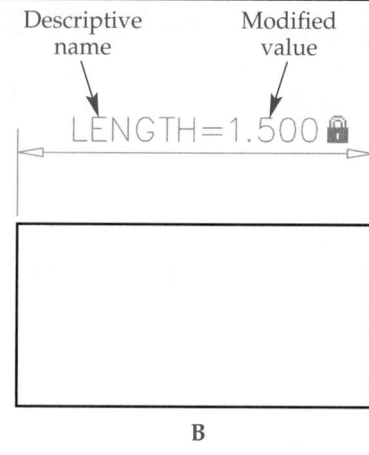

A

B

Another option is to enter an expression in the text editor. You can use an expression if you do not know an exact value, much like using a calculator. Usually, however, expressions include parameters to associate dimensional constraints. This enables the drawing to adapt according to parameter changes. In the active text editor, move the text cursor to the location to add the parameter, and then pick another existing dimensional constraint to copy its name to the expression. An alternative is to type the parameter name in the expression. An fx: in front of the dimension text indicates an expression. **Figure 22-21** shows an example of using an existing parameter in an expression to control the size of an object. In this example, the design requires that the height of the object always be half the value of the length.

NOTE

If you add an existing parameter to the text editor of a different dimensional constraint, without making a calculation, such as d1 = d2, the dimensional constraint uses the same value as the reference parameter. This is necessary for many applications, but use an equal geometric constraint when possible.

Ribbon
Parametric
> Dimensional

Linear

Type
DIMCONSTRAINT
> Linear
DCLINEAR

Ribbon
Parametric
> Dimensional

Horizontal

Type
DIMCONSTRAINT
> Horizontal
DCHORIZONTAL

Ribbon
Parametric
> Dimensional

Vertical

Type
DIMCONSTRAINT
> Vertical
DCVERTICAL

Linear Dimensional Constraints

Use the **DCLINEAR** or **DIMCONSTRAINT** tool to place a horizontal or vertical linear dimensional constraint. The **Horizontal** option sets the tool to constrain only a horizontal distance. The **Vertical** option sets the tool to constrain only a vertical distance. The **Horizontal** and **Vertical** options are helpful when it is difficult to produce the appropriate linear dimensional constraint, such as when you are dimensioning the horizontal or vertical distance of an angled surface.

Pick two points to specify the origin of the dimensional constraint, or use the **Object** function to select a line, polyline, or arc to constrain. Move the dimension line to an appropriate location and pick. Specify the dimension value and adjust the parameter name if desired. Press [Enter] or pick outside of the text editor to form the constraint. **Figure 22-20** and **Figure 22-21** show examples of linear dimensions.

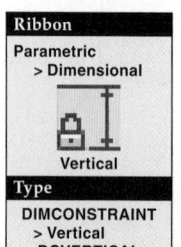

Exercise 22-9

Access the Student Web site (www.g-wlearning.com/CAD) and complete Exercise 22-9.

Figure 22-21. A—A modified parameter name and expression that references another parameter. B—The dimension that includes a parameter references the parameter when changes occur.

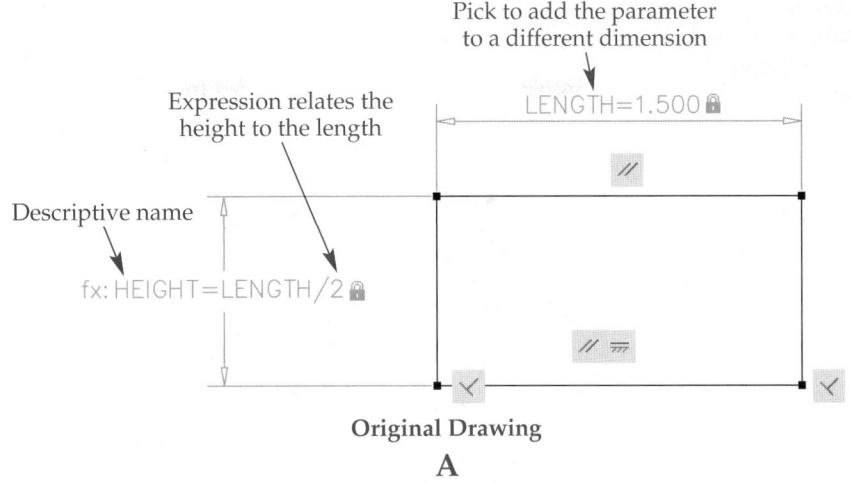

Original Drawing

A

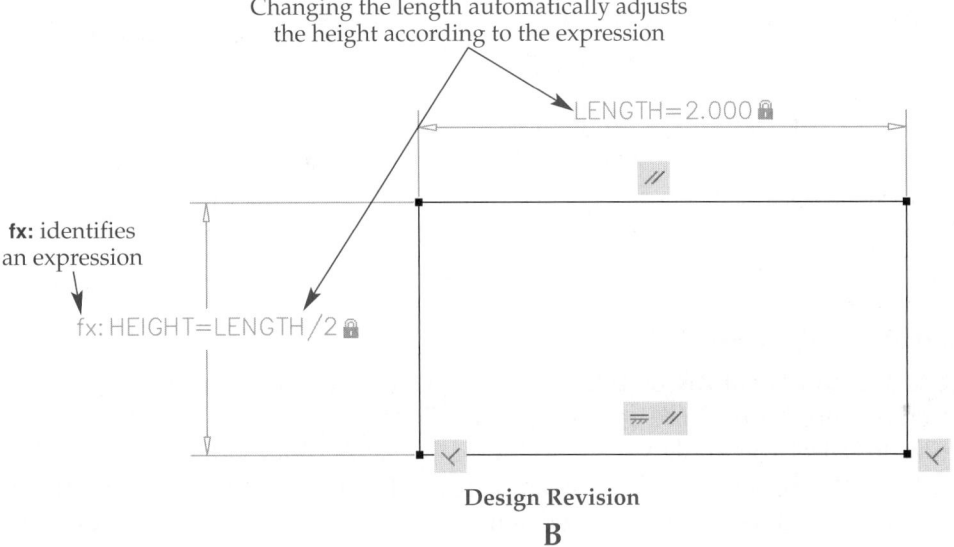

Design Revision

B

Aligned Dimensional Constraints

Use the **DCALIGNED** or **DIMCONSTRAINT** tool to place a linear dimensional constraint with a dimension line that is aligned with an angled surface, with extension lines perpendicular to the surface. Pick two points to specify the origin of the dimensional constraint, or use the **Object** function to select a line, polyline, or arc to constrain.

Often when you apply aligned dimensions, such as when you dimension an auxiliary view, it is necessary to pick a point and an aligned surface or two aligned surfaces. Use the **Point & Line** function to select a point and an alignment line. Use the **2Lines** function to select two alignment lines. Move the dimension line to an appropriate location and pick. Specify the dimension value, and adjust the parameter name if desired. Press [Enter] or pick outside of the text editor to form the constraint. **Figure 22-22** shows examples of aligned dimensional constraints created using each method.

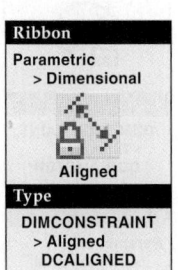

Ribbon

Parametric
> Dimensional

Aligned

Type

DIMCONSTRAINT
> Aligned
DCALIGNED

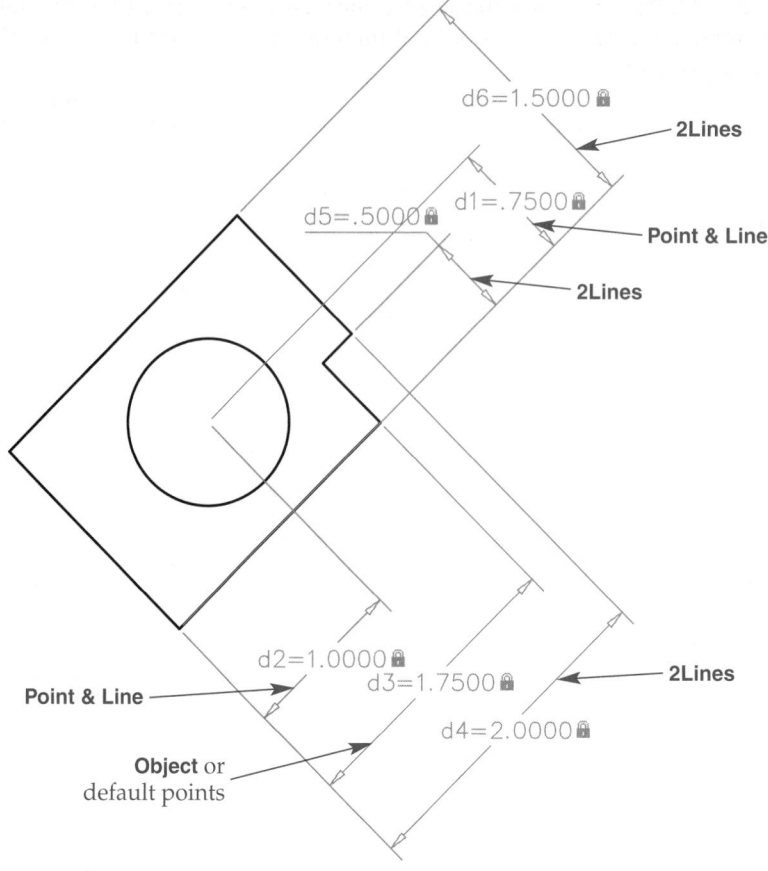

Figure 22-22.
An auxiliary view with full dimensional constraints created using the **Aligned** option.

d6=1.5000 🔒
2Lines
d5=.5000 🔒
d1=.7500 🔒
Point & Line
2Lines
Point & Line
d2=1.0000 🔒
d3=1.7500 🔒
2Lines
d4=2.0000 🔒
Object or default points

Angular Dimensional Constraints

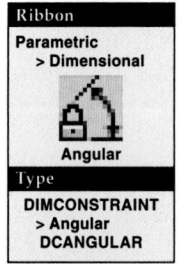

Use the **DCANGULAR** or **DIMCONSTRAINT** tool to place an angular dimension between two objects or three points. Pick two lines, polylines, or arcs, or use the **3Point** function to select the angle vertex, followed by two points to locate each side of the angle. Move the dimension line to an appropriate location and pick. Specify the dimension value, and adjust the parameter name if desired. Press [Enter] or pick outside of the text editor to form the constraint. Figure 22-23 shows examples of angular dimensional constraints created using each method.

Exercise 22-10

Access the Student Web site (www.g-wlearning.com/CAD) and complete Exercise 22-10.

Diameter and Radius Dimensional Constraints

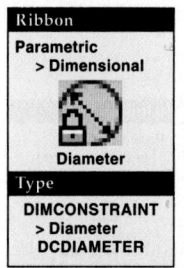

Access the **DCDIAMETER** or **DIMCONSTRAINT** tool to create a diameter dimensional constraint. Access the **DCRADIAL** or **DIMCONSTRAINT** tool to form a radius dimensional constraint. You can select a circle or arc when using either tool. In formal drafting, diameter constraints are applied to circles and radius constraints are applied to arcs. See Figure 22-24. In some parametric applications, however, it is appropriate to constrain arcs using a diameter and circles using a radius, most often when you are dimensioning construction geometry.

Figure 22-23. Forming angular dimensional constraints.

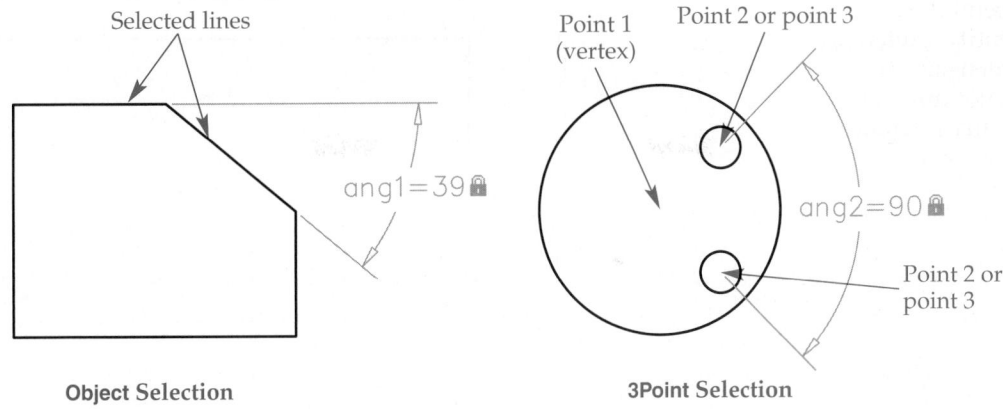

Selected lines

ang1=39🔒

Object Selection

Point 1 (vertex)

Point 2 or point 3

ang2=90🔒

Point 2 or point 3

3Point Selection

Figure 22-24.
Forming diameter and radius dimensional constraints. In this example, equal geometric constraints control the size of the undimensioned arcs.

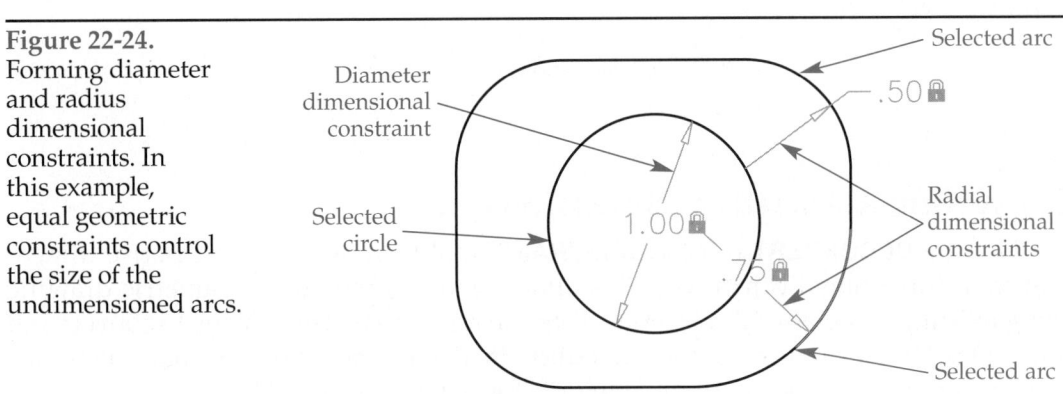

Diameter dimensional constraint

Selected circle

Selected arc

.50🔒

1.00🔒

.75🔒

Radial dimensional constraints

Selected arc

Reference Dimensional Constraints

When you try to constrain a fully constrained object, the drawing should become over-constrained. However, AutoCAD does not allow over-constraining to occur. You can either cancel the tool without accepting the dimension, or accept the dimension and allow it to become a reference dimension. See **Figure 22-25.** Reference dimensions are sometimes required to form specific parameters or expressions. You cannot edit a reference dimension to change the size of an object, but a reference dimension changes when you modify related dimensions.

NOTE

Dimensional constraints define and constrain drawing geometry. They use a unique AutoCAD style and do not comply with ASME standards. Do not be overly concerned about the placement or display characteristics of dimensional constraints, but if possible, apply dimensional constraints just as you would add dimensions to a drawing, using correct drafting practices. In addition, move and manipulate dimensional constraints so the drawing is as unclut-tered as possible. Use grips to make basic adjustments to dimensional constraint position.

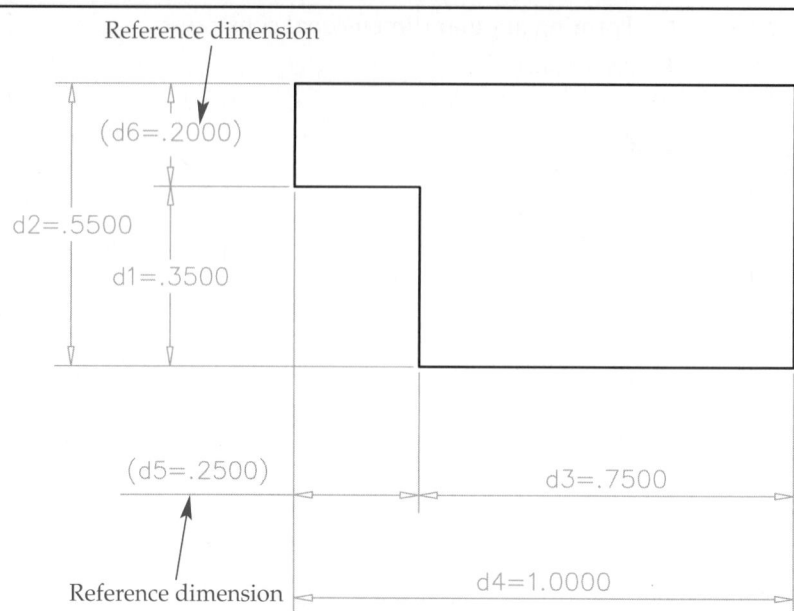

Figure 22-25.
Parentheses identify a reference dimension. You cannot directly modify reference dimensions.

Reference dimension

(d6=.2000)

d2=.5500

d1=.3500

(d5=.2500)

d3=.7500

d4=1.0000

Reference dimension

Converting Associative Dimensions

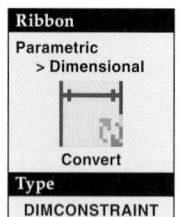

Ribbon

Parametric
> Dimensional

Convert

Type
DIMCONSTRAINT

Use the **DCCONVERT** or **DIMCONSTRAINT** tool to convert an associative dimension to a dimensional constraint. This allows you to prepare a parametric drawing using existing associative dimensions. Pick the associative dimensions to convert and press [Enter] or pick outside of the text editor. By default, new dimensional constraints and converted dimensions use the dynamic format. See **Figure 22-26.**

Managing Dimensional Constraints

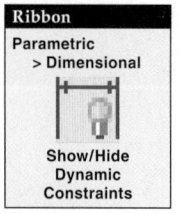

Ribbon

Parametric
> Dimensional

Show/Hide
Dynamic
Constraints

By default, all dimensional constraints are displayed in the dynamic format, include a lock icon, and include the parameter name and dimension value. The **DCDISPLAY** tool provides methods to show or hide dimensional constraints. The quickest way to access these options is to pick the appropriate button from the **Dimensional** panel of the **Parametric** ribbon tab. Pick the **Show/Hide** button, pick dimensional constraints to manage, and then right-click or press [Enter] or the space bar to access options. Choose the **Show** option to display hidden dimensional constraints, or the **Hide** option to hide visible dimensional constraints.

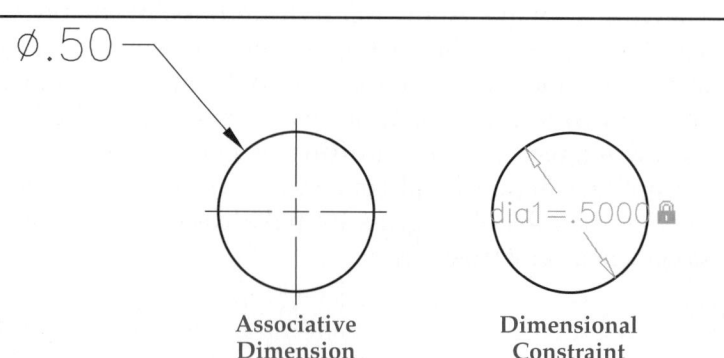

Figure 22-26.
Converting a dimension drawn using the **DIMDIAMETER** tool to a dimensional constraint. The default dimensional constraint format is dynamic.

Ø.50

Associative
Dimension

dia1=.5000

Dimensional
Constraint

Select the **Show All** button to display all dimensional constraints. Pick the **Hide All** button to hide all dimensional constraints. Hiding dimensional constraints does not remove them. You typically hide dimensional constraints to prepare a formal drawing, or when you no longer need to see dimensional constraints for the current design phase.

Use the **Dimensional** tab of the **Constraint Settings** dialog box to adjust additional dimensional constraint settings. The **Dimension name format** drop-down list allows you to display dimensional constraints with the parameter name and value, parameter name, or value. Use the **Show lock icon for annotational constraints** check box to toggle the lock icon on or off for new dimensional constraints. If you hide dimensional constraints and select the **Show hidden dynamic constraints of selected objects** check box, you can pick an object to show associated dimensional constraints temporarily.

Design changes sometimes require deleting existing constraints. Use the **ERASE** tool to eliminate specific dimensional constraints.

Ribbon
Parametric
> Dimensional

Constraint Settings

Type
CONSTRAINTSETTINGS

> **NOTE**
>
> You can also right-click with no objects selected to access a **Parametric** cascading submenu that provides options for displaying and hiding constraints, changing the dimension name format, and accessing the **Constraint Settings** dialog box. The options are also available when you pick a dimensional constraint and then right-click.

Working with Parameters

A *dimensional constraint parameter* automatically forms every time you add a dimensional constraint. You can adjust parameters by changing the dimensional constraint value or by using the options in the **Constraint** category of the **Properties** palette. The **Parameters Manager** allows you to manage all parameters in the drawing. See **Figure 22-27**.

dimensional constraint parameters: Parameters that form when you insert a dimensional constraint.

The list view pane on the right side of the **Parameters Manager** lists parameters in a table and provides parameter controls. Pick a parameter in the **Parameters Manager** to highlight the corresponding dimensional constraint in the drawing. To change the name of a parameter, pick inside a text box in the **Name** column to activate it, type the new name, and press [Enter] or pick outside of the text box. Enter a new value or expression for the parameter in an **Expression** column text box. The value appears in the **Value** column display box for reference. Use the **Delete** button or right-click on a parameter and select **Delete** to remove the parameter and the corresponding dimensional constraint.

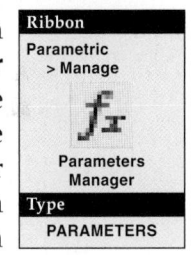

Ribbon
Parametric
> Manage

Parameters Manager

Type
PARAMETERS

To specify *user parameters*, pick the **User Parameters** button to display a **User Variables** node. User parameters function like dimensional constraints in the **Parameters Manager**. Create user parameters in order to access specific parameters throughout the design process. For example, if you know the thickness of a part will always be twice a certain dimensional constraint, create a user parameter similar to the parameter shown in **Figure 22-27** to define the thickness. You can then use the custom parameter for reference and in expressions when you place additional dimensional constraints.

user parameters: Additional parameters you define.

Pick the **Expand Parameters filter tree** button or right-click in the list pane and select **Show Filter Tree** to display the tree view pane on the left side of the **Parameters Manager**. *Parameter filters* are typically appropriate when it becomes difficult to manage a very large number of parameters. Filter a large list of parameters to make it easier to work with the parameters needed for a specific drawing task.

NEW

parameter filters: Settings that screen out, or filter, parameters you do not want to display in the list view pane of the **Parameters Manager**.

Parameter filters are listed in alphabetical order inside the **All** node. Select the **All** node to display all parameters in the drawing. Pick the **All Used in Expressions** filter to display only parameters used in or referenced by expressions. Pick the **Invert filter**

Figure 22-27.
The **Parameters Manager** is a good resource for reviewing and editing parameters and for creating user parameters. This figure shows the expanded parameters filter tree.

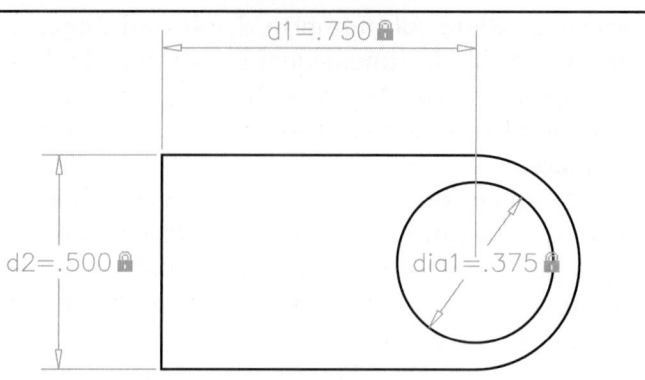

Pick to create a new group filter

Pick to delete a user parameter

Pick to delete the selected parameter

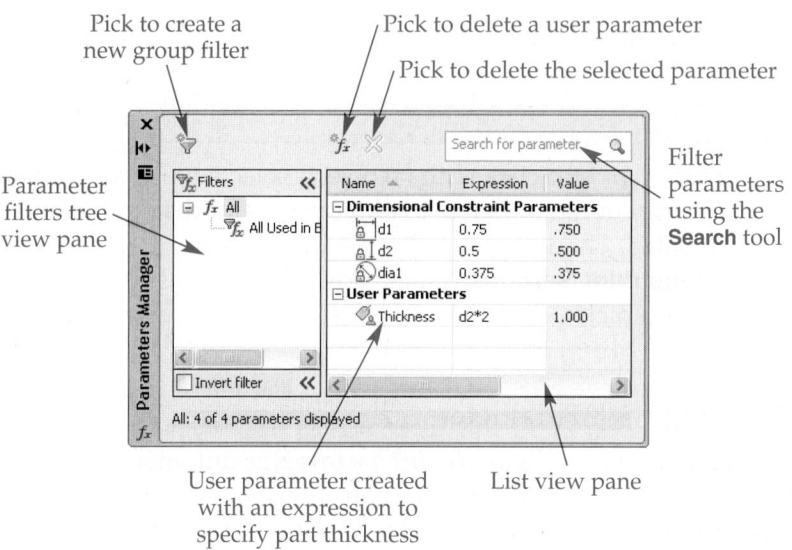

Parameter filters tree view pane

Filter parameters using the **Search** tool

User parameter created with an expression to specify part thickness

List view pane

check box to invert, or reverse, a parameter filter. Select the **Filter** button or right-click on a filter name and select **New Group Filter** to create a custom parameter group filter. A new group filter appears in the filter tree view ready to accept a custom name, if desired. Select the **All** node at the top of the filter tree area to display all the parameters in the drawing. Then, to add a parameter to the group filter, drag a parameter from the list and drop it onto the group filter name. Right-click on a filter name in the tree view or a parameter name in the list view to access options for managing group filters.

NOTE

Use the **Search** text box to search for specific parameters according to parameter name.

Exercise 22-11

Access the Student Web site (www.g-wlearning.com/CAD) and complete Exercise 22-11.

Dynamic and Annotational Form

This textbook focuses on using the default dynamic format for placing dimensional constraints. **Figure 22-28A** shows the dimensional constraints required to fully constrain the example multiview drawing in their dynamic format. The annotational format is more appropriate than the dynamic format for formal dimensioning practices. Annotational constraints still control object size and location.

The **CCONSTRAINTFORM** system variable sets the dimensional constraint form applied when you add new dimensional constraints. The easiest way to adjust the **CCONSTRAINTFORM** system variable is to pick the appropriate **Dynamic Constraint Mode** or **Annotational Constraint Mode** button from the expanded **Dimensional** panel of the **Parametric** ribbon tab. You can also preset the dimensional constraint format using the **DIMCONSTRAINT** tool by selecting the **Form** option, or by using the **DCFORM** tool before creating a dimensional constraint.

> **NOTE**
>
> The specified Annotational or Dynamic form is a system variable and applies to new dimensional constraints until you change it to the alternate setting.

Use the **Constraint Form** drop-down list in the **Constraint** category of the **Properties** palette to change the dimensional constraint form assigned to existing dimensions. **Figure 22-28B** shows the dimensional constraints in dynamic format that require changing to the annotational format for the example multiview drawing. Annotational dimensions, especially those converted from dynamic dimensions, often require that you make format and organizational changes to prepare the final drawing. You may also have to add non-parametric dimensions. Make the following changes to create the final drawing shown in **Figure 22-28C.**

- Hide all geometric constraints and dynamic dimensions.
- Disable the lock icon display.
- Change the dimension name format to **Value**.
- Make basic dimension style overrides and dimension location adjustments if necessary.

Exercise 22-12

Access the Student Web site (www.g-wlearning.com/CAD) and complete Exercise 22-12.

Parametric Editing

You can adjust existing parametric drawings in a variety of ways. Drawing additional unconstrained objects adds geometry that requires constraining to make the drawing fully parametric once again. You may need to delete or replace existing constraints to constrain new objects. Erasing objects and exploding polylines removes constraints. If you erase geometry associated with an expression, an alert appears asking if you want to convert the dimensional constraint to a user parameter, maintain the information, or remove the parameter with the dimensional constraint.

Figure 22-28.
The typical process
for changing a
parametric drawing
to a final, formal
appearance. A—A
fully constrained
drawing with
dynamic
dimensional
constraints. Notice
that dimensions
apply to all items,
including centerline
extensions and the
distance between
views. B—Changing
dynamic dimensions
to annotational
dimensions.
Change only
those dimensions
required for formal
dimensioning.
C—The appearance
of the final drawing.

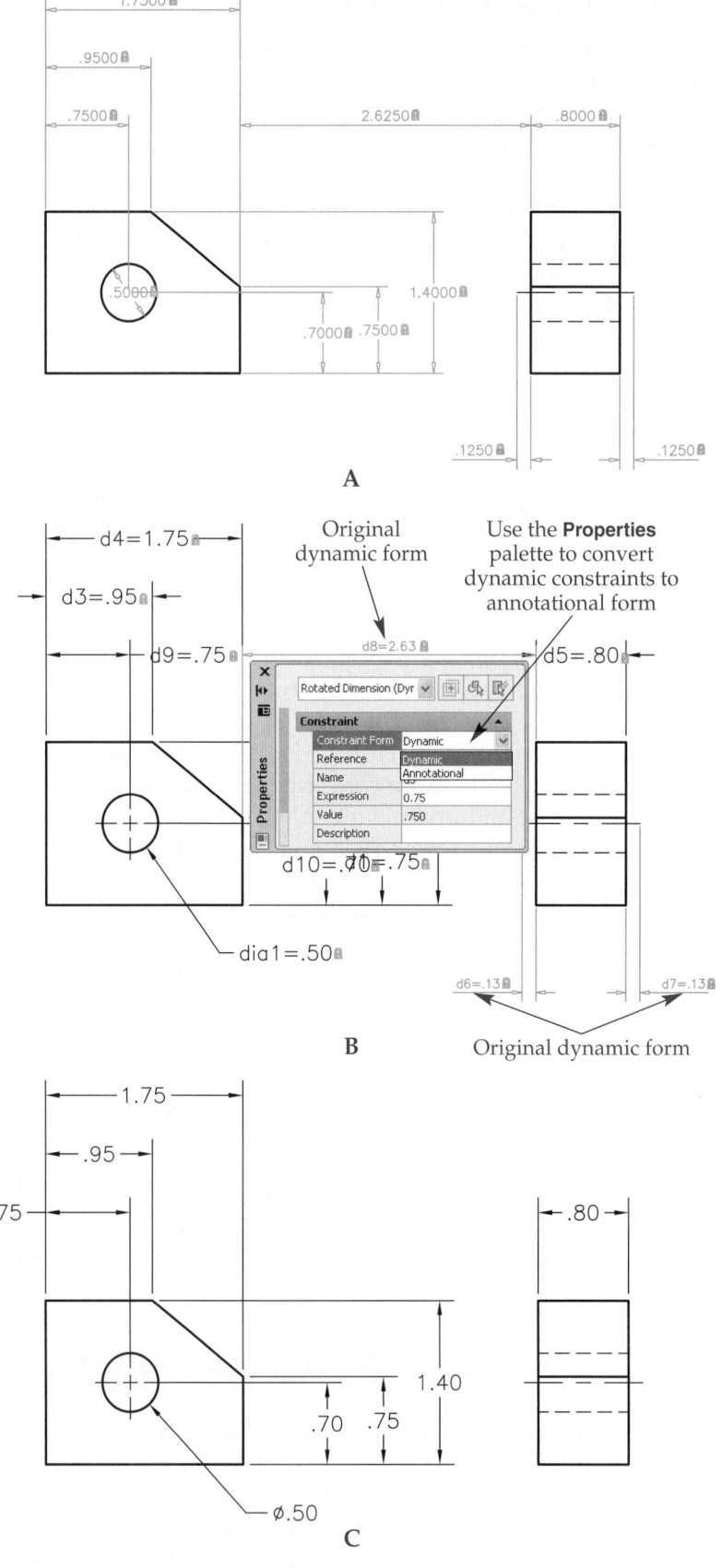

Modifying Dimensional Constraints

Adjust dimensional constraints to make design changes to a constrained drawing. To edit a dimensional constraint value, double-click on the value, or select the dimensional constraint, right-click, and pick **Edit Constraint**. The text editor appears, allowing you to make changes. Press [Enter] or pick outside of the text editor to complete the operation.

Another method is to pick a dimensional constraint and use parameter grips to change the value. See **Figure 22-29.** Parameter grip-editing is most appropriate for analyzing design options, when you do not know a specific value, or when using drawing aids such as object snaps to adjust the value. You can also modify a dimensional constraint value by entering a different expression in the **Expression** text box in the **Constraint** category of the **Properties** palette, or in the **Expression** text box of the **Parameters Manager**.

NOTE

If a drawing includes enough geometric constraints, and the geometric constraints are accurate, changing dimensions should maintain all geometric relationships.

Removing Constraints

Constraints limit your ability to make changes to a drawing. For example, you cannot rotate a horizontally or vertically constrained line. You may have to relax or delete constraints to make significant changes to a drawing. Relax constraints using standard editing practices. When you use a basic editing tool such as **ROTATE**, a message

---

Figure 22-29.
Using a parameter grip to change the dimensional constraint value.

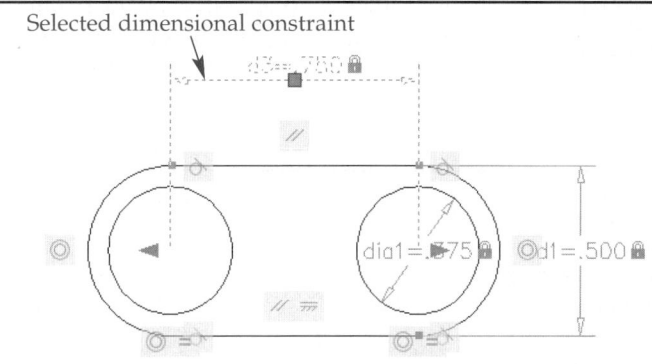

Selected dimensional constraint

Original Drawing

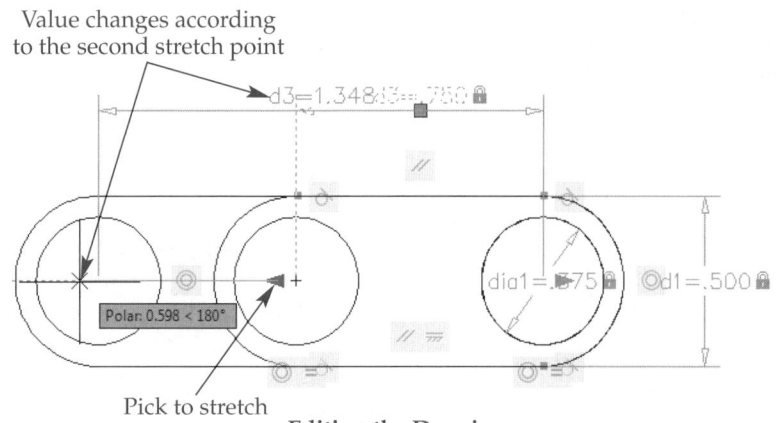

Value changes according to the second stretch point

Pick to stretch

Editing the Drawing

---

appears asking if you want to relax constraints. To relax constraints while stretching, moving, or scaling with grips, you may need to press [Ctrl] to toggle relaxing on and off. See **Figure 22-30A**. Other edits automatically remove constraints. See **Figure 22-30B**. The only constraints, if any, that you remove are those required to achieve the edit.

In addition to the methods described previously for deleting individual constraints, a **DELCONSTRAINT** tool is available. Access the tool and select the geometric and dimensional constraints to remove. The **DELCONSTRAINT** tool is especially effective for removing a significant number of constraints. Use the **All** selection option to remove all constraints from the drawing.

Ribbon
Parametric
> Manage

Delete Constraints
Type
DELCONSTRAINT

NOTE

Some editing techniques, such as mirroring or moving, may only require removal of fix constraints, especially when you are editing an entire drawing. Exploding a polyline removes all constraints.

PROFESSIONAL TIP

Occasionally, constraining geometry causes objects to twist out of shape, making it difficult to control the size and position of the drawing. Use the **UNDO** tool to return to the previous design. Consider the following suggestions to help avoid this situation:
- Use standard and accurate drafting practices to construct objects at or close to their finished size.
- Add as many geometric constraints as appropriate before dimensioning.
- Dimension the largest objects first.
- Move objects to a more appropriate location, if necessary, and change object size before constraining.

Figure 22-30. Examples of relaxing constraints. A—Access the **MOVE** tool and then press [Ctrl] to remove the concentric constraint. The process is similar for stretching and scaling. B—Rotating removes a vertical constraint in this example.

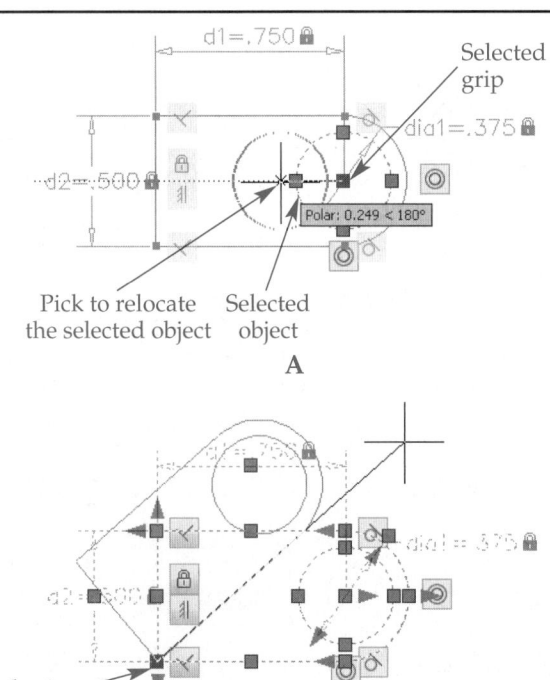

Exercise 22-13

Access the Student Web site (www.g-wlearning.com/CAD) and complete Exercise 22-13.

Chapter Test

Answer the following questions. Write your answers on a separate sheet of paper or go to the Student Web site (www.g-wlearning.com/CAD) and complete the electronic chapter test.

1. Give an example demonstrating how to use constraints to form a geometric construction when standard AutoCAD tools are inefficient or ineffective.
2. Describe two applications in which parametric drafting may be unsuitable or ineffective.
3. Briefly describe the purpose of geometric constraint tools, and identify what you see on-screen that indicates the presence of a geometric constraint.
4. Name the function that forms geometric constraints while you draw or edit.
5. Name the tools that allow you to assign geometric constraints manually.
6. When you use geometric constraint tools that allow you to pick two objects or points, describe what generally happens to the first and second objects you select.
7. List the object snaps that infer coincident constraints.
8. Identify common uses for horizontal and vertical constraints.
9. Describe how to infer horizontal and vertical constraints.
10. List the object types that can form parallel or perpendicular constraints.
11. Name the types of objects you can constrain with the **Tangent** constraint.
12. What does the **Collinear** constraint allow you to do?
13. Explain the basic function of the **Equal** constraint.
14. Describe the default function of the **Symmetric** constraint.
15. Name the tool you can use to attempt to add all required geometric constraints in a single operation.
16. Briefly describe how to specify the appearance and characteristics of geometric bars.
17. Compare the appearance of a coincident constraint with the display of other constraints.
18. Explain how to determine which objects and points are associated with a constraint.
19. What should you do if constraint bars block your view or if you want to hide constraint bars?
20. Name the tool that allows you to assign linear, diameter, radius, and angular dimensional constraints.
21. What is the most basic method to specify dimension values when you create a dimensional constraint?
22. Name the tools that allow you to place a linear dimensional constraint with a dimension line aligned with an angled surface with extension lines perpendicular to the surface.
23. Which tools allow you to place an angular dimension between two objects or three points?
24. Explain the options AutoCAD provides when you try to over-constrain a drawing.
25. Briefly explain how to convert an associative dimension to a dimensional constraint, and give the advantage of using this option.
26. What happens every time you add a dimensional constraint?
27. How do you adjust parameters?
28. Explain how to edit a dimensional constraint value.
29. Briefly describe how to relax constraints.
30. Which tool provides an efficient method of removing a significant number of constraints in a single operation?

Drawing Problems

- *Start AutoCAD if it is not already started. Start a new drawing for each problem using an appropriate template of your choice.*

- *The template should include layers and text, dimension, multileader, and table styles, when necessary, for drawing the given objects. Add layers and text, dimension, multileader, and table styles as needed.*

- *Draw all objects using appropriate layers and text, dimension, multileader, and table styles, justification, and format.*

- *Follow the specific instructions for each problem. Use only drawing and editing tools and techniques you have already learned. Use your own judgment and approximate dimensions when necessary.*

- *Apply formal dimensions accurately using ASME or appropriate industry standards.*

Note: *Dimensional constraints shown for reference are created using AutoCAD and may not comply with ASME standards.*

▼ Basic

1. Use the **POLYGON** tool to draw the hexagon as shown. Fully constrain the hexagon as shown. All sides are equal. Fix the midpoint of the construction line. Edit the d1 parameter to change the distance across the flats to 4.000. Save the drawing as P22-1.

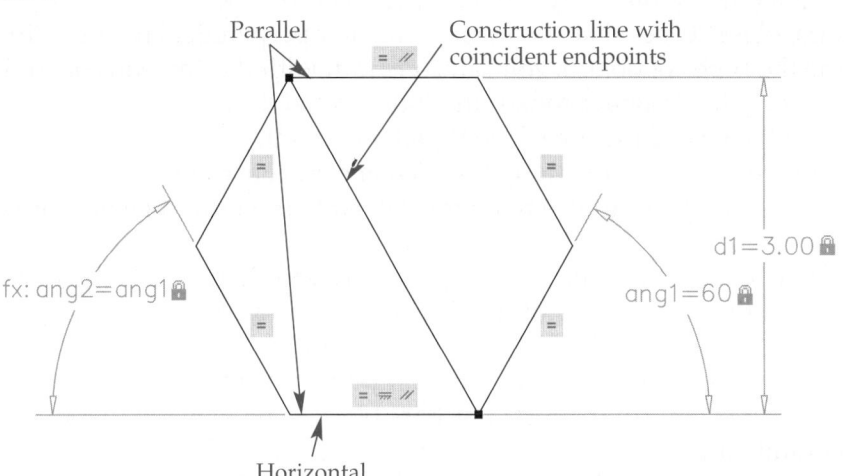

2. Use the **RECTANGLE** and **CIRCLE** tools to draw the view shown. Fully constrain the view as shown. The circle is tangent to the rectangle in two locations. Edit the d2 parameter to change the distance to 4.500. Edit the d3 parameter to change the distance to 2.000. Save the drawing as P22-2.

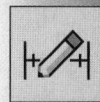

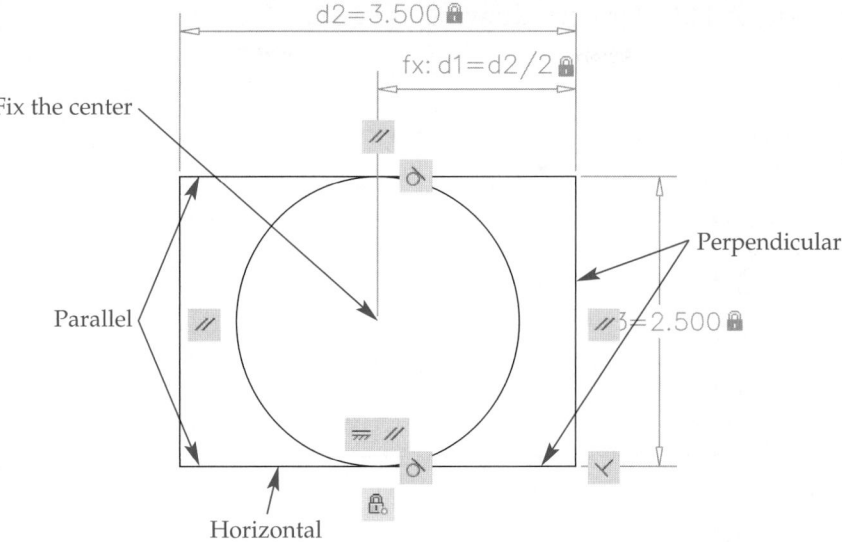

3. Draw and fully constrain the circles shown. Both of the smaller circles are tangent to the larger circle. Edit the dia1 parameter to change the diameter to 2.000. Save the drawing as P22-3.

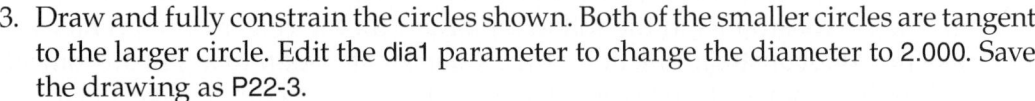

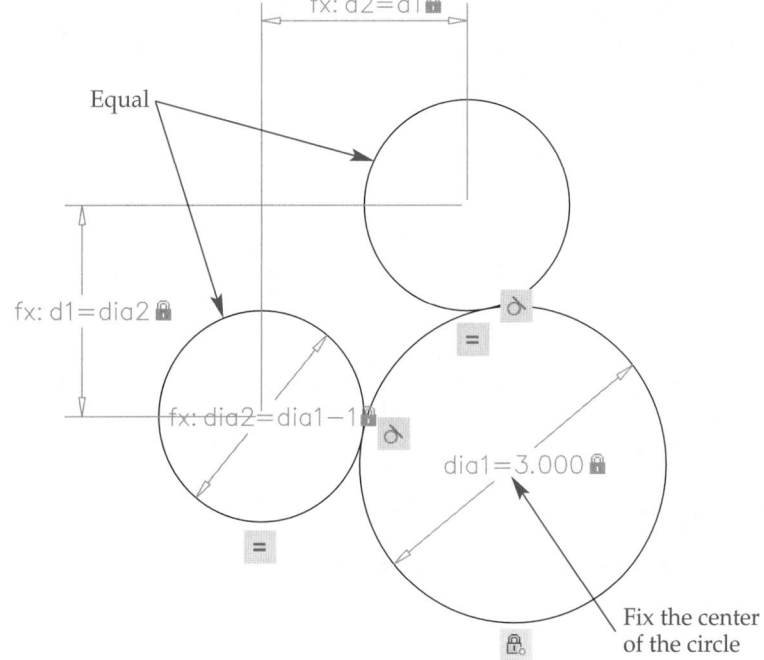

4. Draw and fully constrain the pipe spacer shown. Infer as many constraints as possible and appropriate. Use the **AUTOCONSTRAIN** tool, with default settings, to apply additional geometric constraints. Make all circles equal in size. Edit the d1 parameter to change the distance to 2.000. Edit the rad1 parameter to change the radius to 1.250. Save the drawing as P22-4.

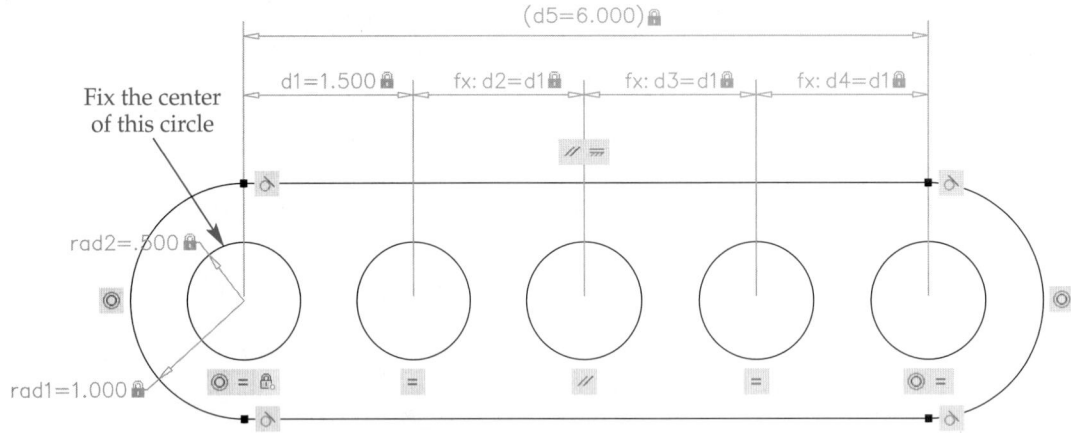

▼ Intermediate

5. Draw and fully constrain the view shown. Do not infer constraints. Apply geometric constraints in the following order: fix the center of the center circle; use the **Autoconstrain** function of the **Coincident** option to apply all coincident constraints; make all circles equal; make all small arcs equal; make all large arcs concentric to the appropriate circles; use the **AUTOCONSTRAIN** tool with default settings to apply the remaining geometric constraints. Edit the d1 parameter to change the distance to 1.750. Save the drawing as P22-5.

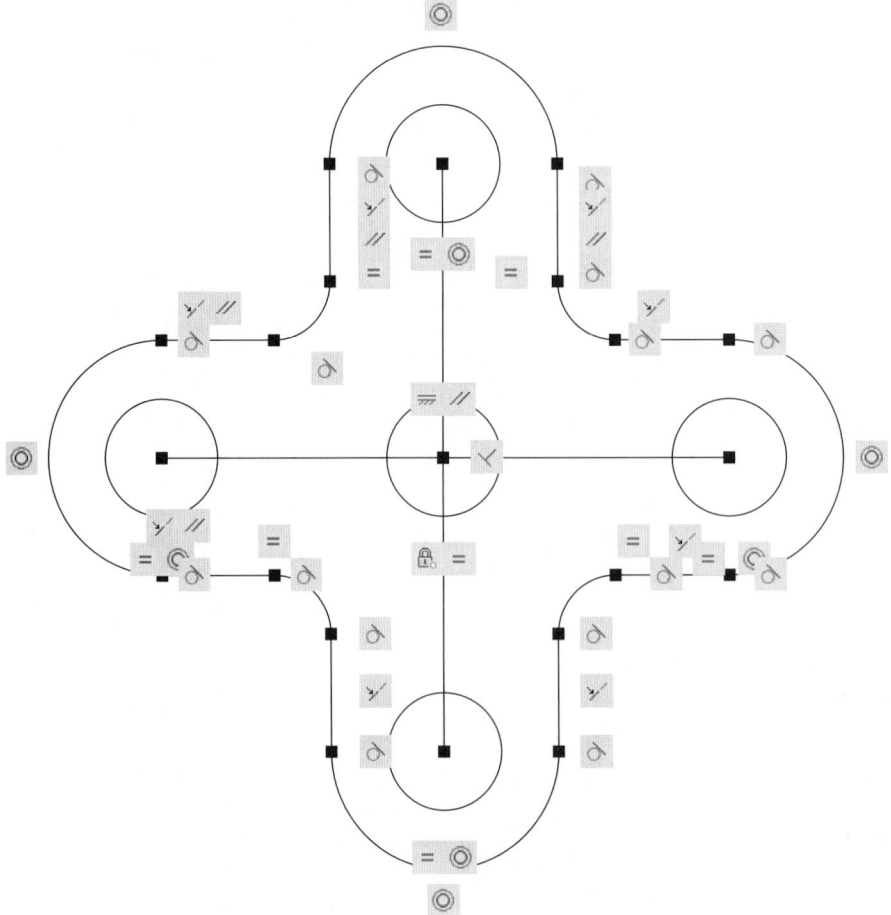

6. Draw and fully constrain the view shown. Follow the guidelines below.
   - Infer constraints when possible and appropriate.
   - Use the **Fillet** option of the **RECTANGLE** tool to create the 4.6250 by 6.3750 rectangle with .6250 rounded corners.
   - Use the **RECTANGLE** tool to create the construction rectangle and then add the circles. Notice that the circles are not concentric to the arcs.
   - Apply geometric constraints in the following order: fix the center of the lower-left circle; make all circles equal; make all arcs equal.
   - Use the **AUTOCONSTRAIN** tool with default settings to apply the remaining geometric constraints.
   - Edit the d1 parameter to change the distance to 1.0000.
   - Edit the d5 parameter to change the distance to 5.1250.
   - Save the drawing as P22-6.

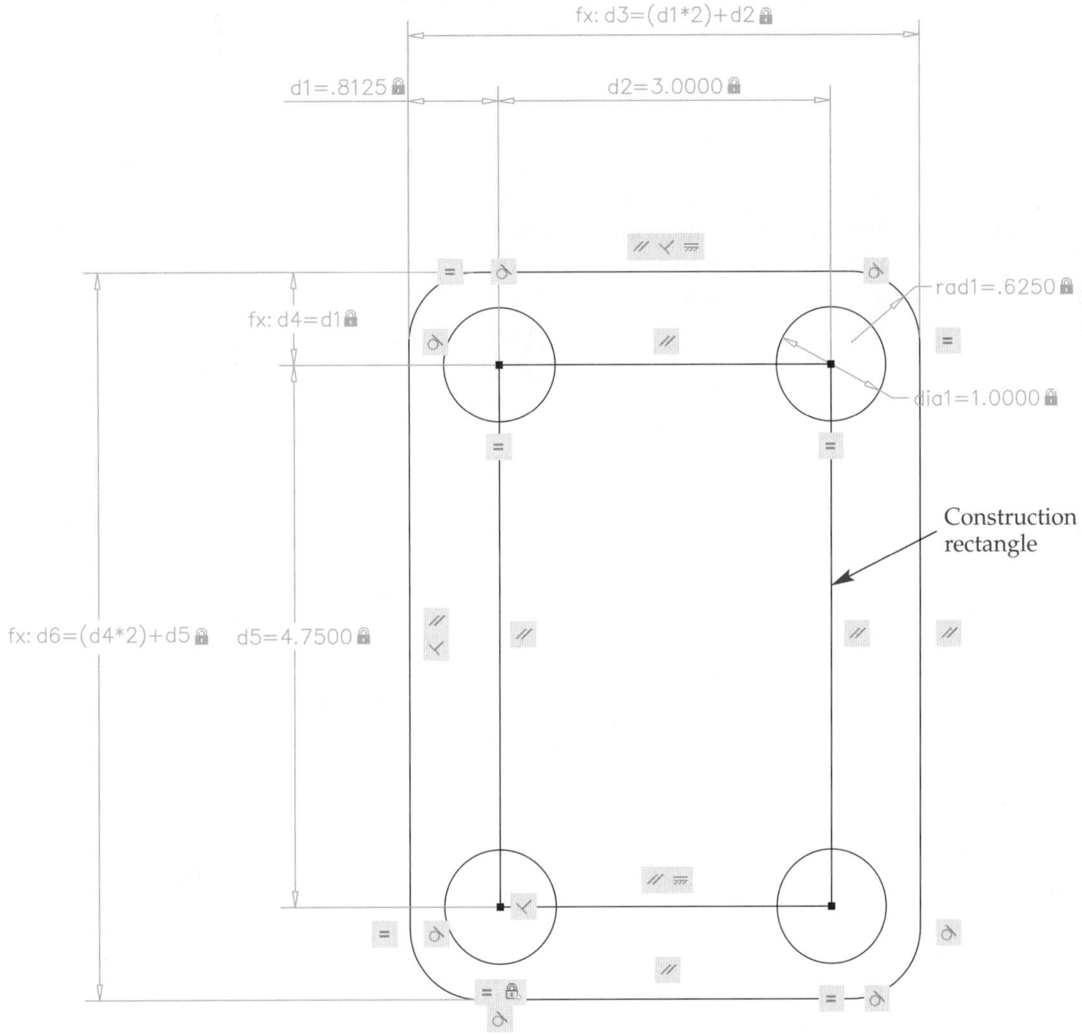

fx: d3=(d1*2)+d2

d1=.8125

d2=3.0000

fx: d4=d1

rad1=.6250

dia1=1.0000

Construction rectangle

fx: d6=(d4*2)+d5   d5=4.7500

▼ Advanced

7. Draw and fully constrain the view shown. Save the drawing as **P22-7**.

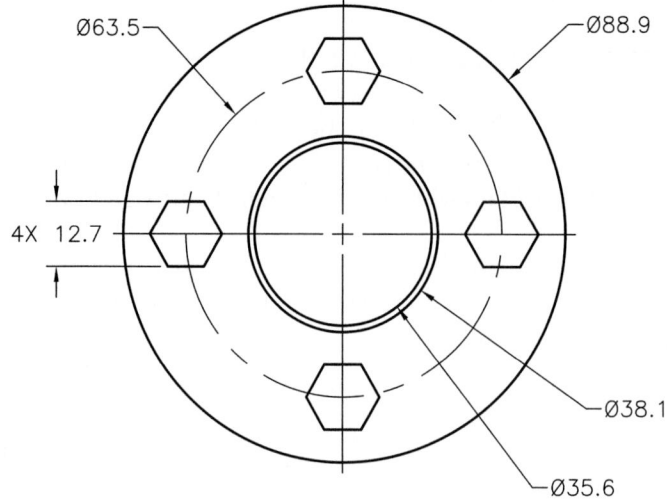

Ø63.5
Ø88.9
4X 12.7
Ø38.1
Ø35.6

8. Use the information below to draw the non-parametric view shown in A. Then fully constrain the view as shown in B. Edit the view as shown in C. Finish by converting dimensional constraints to create the formal drawing shown in D. Save the drawing as **P22-8**.

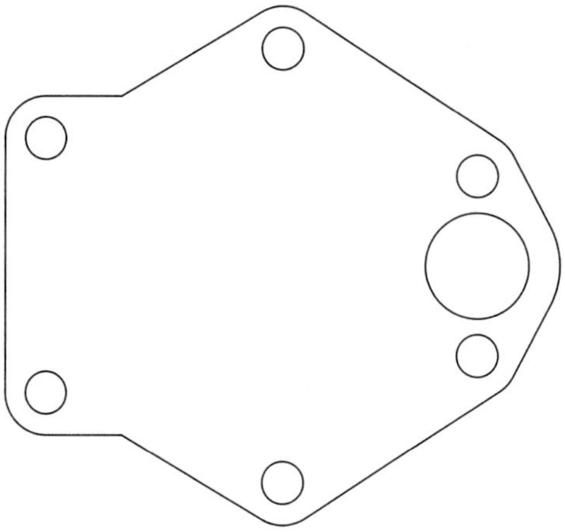

A

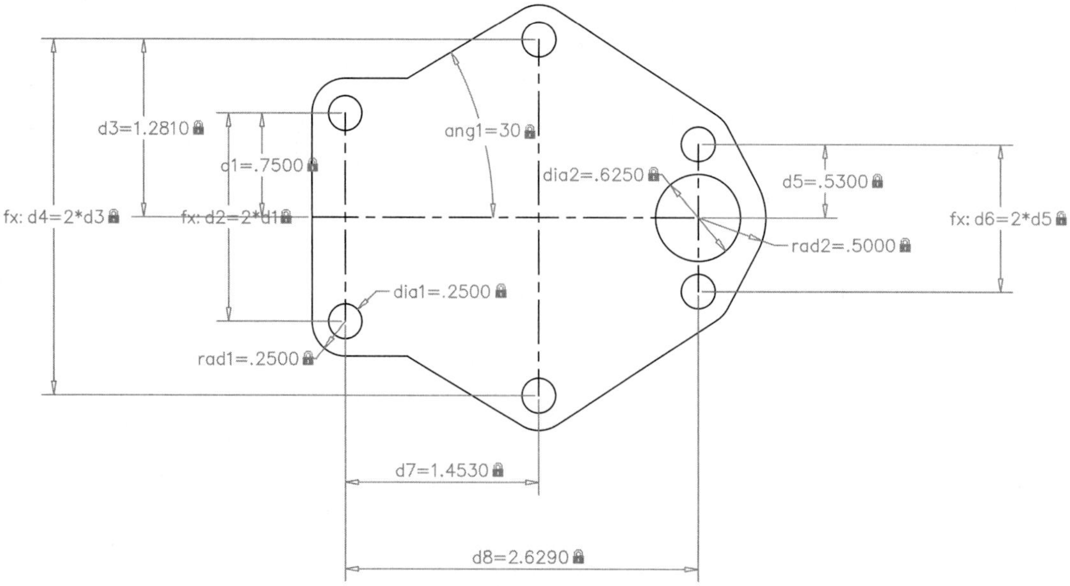

B

d3=1.2810
d1=.7500
fx: d4=2*d3
fx: d2=2*d1
ang1=30
dia2=.6250
d5=.5300
fx: d6=2*d5
rad2=.5000
dia1=.2500
rad1=.2500
d7=1.4530
d8=2.6290

(Continued.)

AutoCAD and Its Applications—Basics

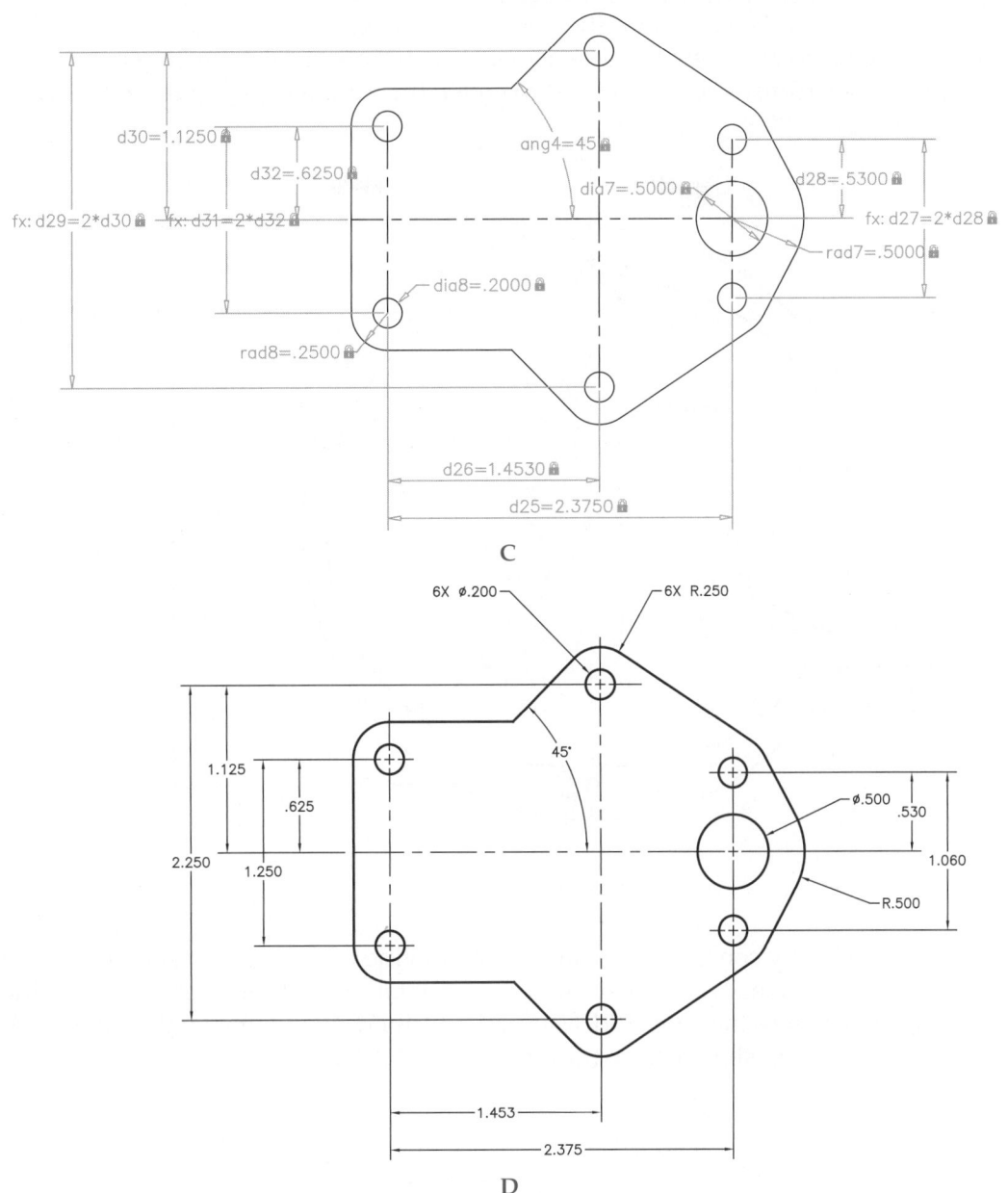

C

D

9. Draw and fully constrain the view shown. Convert dynamic dimensional constraints to annotational dimensional constraints. Adjust the drawing and add associative dimensions as needed to create the formal drawing shown. Save the drawing as P22-9.

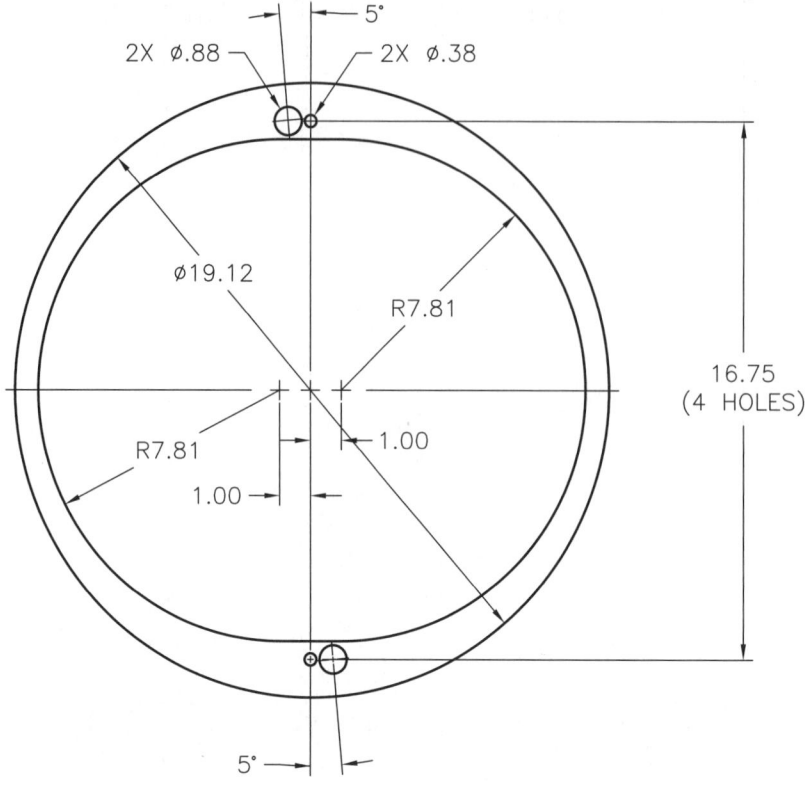

10. Draw and fully constrain the multiview drawing of the support shown. Convert dynamic dimensional constraints to annotational dimensional constraints. Adjust the drawing and add associative dimensions as needed to create the formal drawing shown. Save the drawing as P22-10.

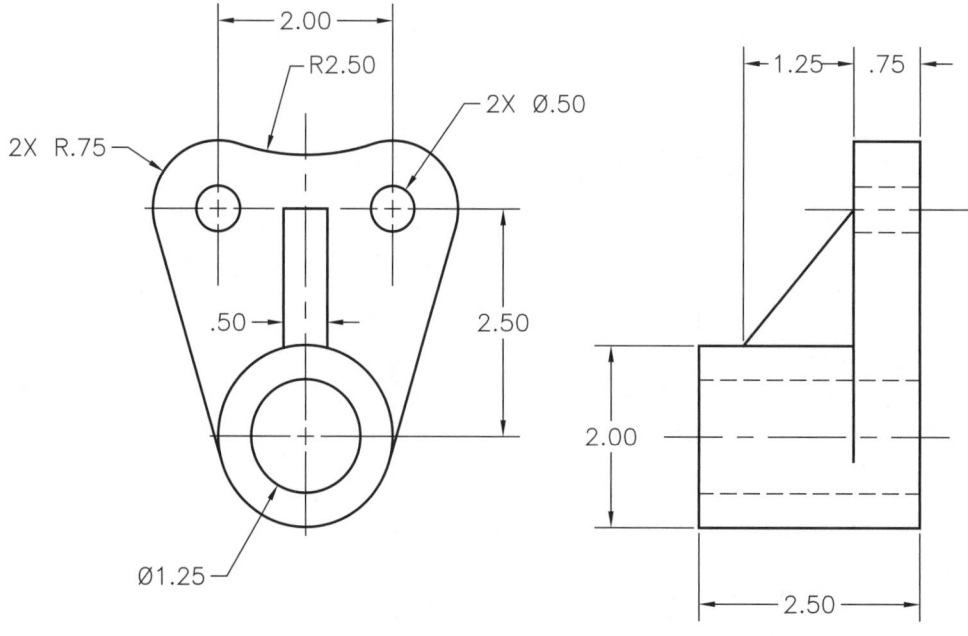

11. Use the isometric drawing provided to create a multiview orthographic drawing for the part. Include only the views necessary to fully describe the object. Draw and fully constrain the drawing. Convert dynamic dimensional constraints to annotational dimensional constraints. Adjust the drawing and add associative dimensions as needed to create a formal drawing. Save the drawing as P22-11.

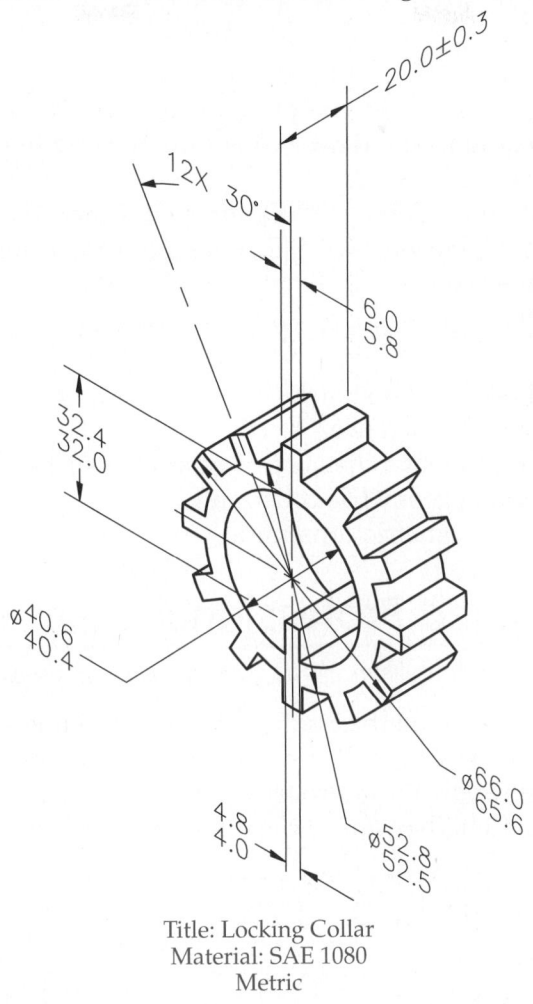

Title: Locking Collar
Material: SAE 1080
Metric

12. Research the design of an existing manifold with the following specifications: one-piece; nickel-plated 6061 aluminum, NPT female connections; two 1/2" inlets; eight 3/8" outlets on one side, 1" center-to-center; four mounting holes; for use with air, water, or hydraulic oil. Create a dimensioned 2D sketch of the existing design from manufacturer's specifications, or from measurements taken from an actual manifold. Start a new drawing from scratch or use a decimal-unit template of your choice. Draw and fully constrain a multiview orthographic drawing of the manifold. Include only the views necessary to fully describe the part. Convert dynamic dimensional constraints to annotational dimensional constraints. Adjust the drawing and add associative dimensions as needed to create a formal drawing. Save the drawing as P22-12.

AutoCAD Certified Associate Exam Practice

Answer the following questions. Write your answers on a separate sheet of paper.

1. Which of the following are forms of dimensional constraints? *Select all that apply.*
   A. annotational
   B. construction
   C. dynamic
   D. geometric
   E. static

2. What type of dimension can you place instead of a dimensional constraint if a dimensional constraint would over-constrain the drawing? *Select the one item that best answers the question.*
   A. annotational dimension
   B. construction dimension
   C. dynamic dimension
   D. inferred dimension
   E. reference dimension

3. Which of the following actions can you perform using the **DCLINEAR** tool? *Select all that apply.*
   A. constrain a horizontal distance
   B. constrain a vertical distance
   C. constrain the horizontal distance of an angled surface
   D. place a horizontal geometric constraint
   E. place a vertical geometric constraint

AutoCAD Certified Professional Exam Practice

Follow the instructions in each problem. Write your answers on a separate sheet of paper.

1. **Navigate to this chapter on the Student Web site and open CPE-22parameter.dwg.**
   Constrain the lines as shown. Begin by applying a fix constraint to the lower-left intersection. Then apply the appropriate constraints to achieve the figure shown. Do not change the length of any of the lines. What are the coordinates of Point A?

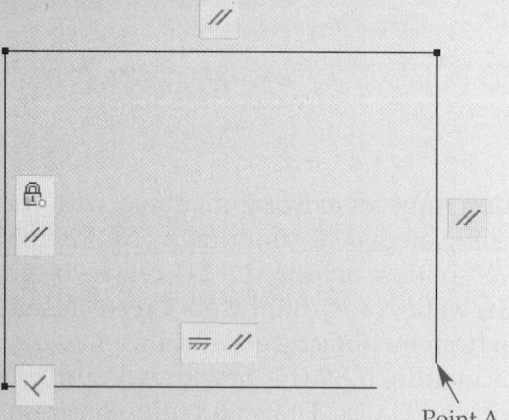

Point A

2. **Navigate to this chapter on the Student Web site and open CPE-22edit.dwg.**
   Show the dimensional constraints and edit the LENGTH dimension to 7.500. Do not change any other settings. What are the coordinates of Point A (the center of the right arc)?

Point A .

AutoCAD and Its Applications—Basics

Section Views and Graphic Patterns

Learning Objectives

After completing this chapter, you will be able to do the following:

✓ Identify sectioning techniques.
✓ Add graphic patterns using the **HATCH** tool.
✓ Insert hatch patterns using **DesignCenter** and tool palettes.
✓ Edit existing hatch patterns.

Drawings often require *graphic patterns* to describe specific information. For example, the front elevation of the house shown in **Figure 23-1** contains patterns and fills that graphically represent building materials and shading. One of the most common graphic patterns is a group of section lines added to a section view. This chapter focuses on using the **HATCH** tool to draw graphic patterns. You will also learn other methods of adding and edit hatches.

graphic pattern:
A patterned arrangement of objects or symbols.

Figure 23-1. Graphic patterns describe repetitive drawing information, such as the siding, brick, roofing, concrete, and shading added to the front elevation of a house. In this illustration, all of the items shown in color are graphic patterns.

Section Views

It is poor practice, and often not possible, to dimension internal, hidden features. *Section views*, also called *sectional views* or *sections*, clarify hidden features. Typically, you add section views to a multiview drawing to describe the exterior and interior features of a product. Often, as shown in **Figure 23-2,** a primary view is a section or includes a section.

When a drawing includes a section, one of the other views contains a *cutting-plane line* to show the location of the cut. The cutting-plane line is a thick dashed or phantom line in accordance with ASME Y14.2, *Line Conventions and Lettering*. The standard cutting-plane line terminates with bold arrowheads that point toward the cutting plane, indicating the line of sight when you are looking at the section view.

Each end of the cutting-plane line is labeled with a letter. The letters correlate to the section view title, such as SECTION A-A, below the section view to key the cutting plane with the section view. When you section more than one view, labels continue with B-B through Z-Z, if necessary. Do not use letters *I, O, Q, S, X,* and *Z*, because they can be confused with numbers. Labeling section views is necessary for drawings with multiple sections. You can often omit the label when only one section view is present and its location is obvious. *Section lines* are the graphic pattern used in a section view. They distinguish hidden features from exterior objects.

Other drafting fields, including architectural, structural, and civil drafting, also use sectioning. Cross sections through buildings show construction methods and materials. See **Figure 23-3.** Profiles and cross sections on a civil engineering drawing show the contour and construction of land for utility, transportation, and other civil engineering projects. Cutting-plane lines used in non-mechanical fields are often composed of letter and number symbols. This helps coordinate the large number of sections found in a set of drawings.

Figure 23-2. A two-view mechanical part drawing with a full section view and a broken-out section.

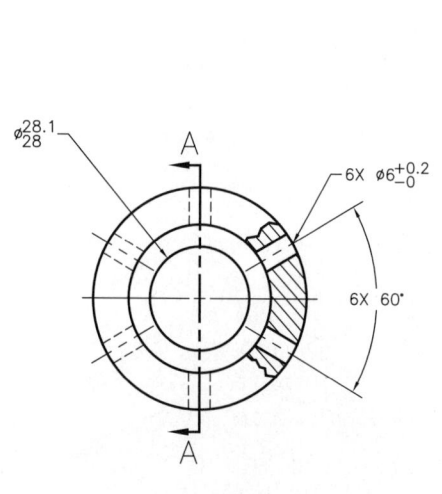

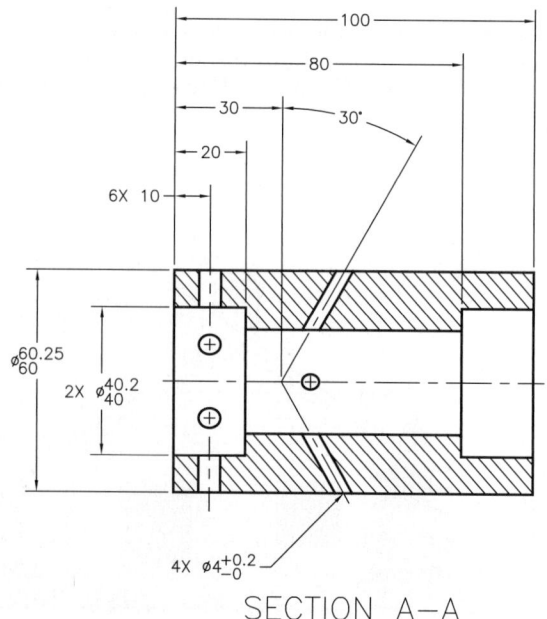

SECTION A—A

Figure 23-3. An architectural section view showing the construction of a proposed bathroom for a residential renovation project.

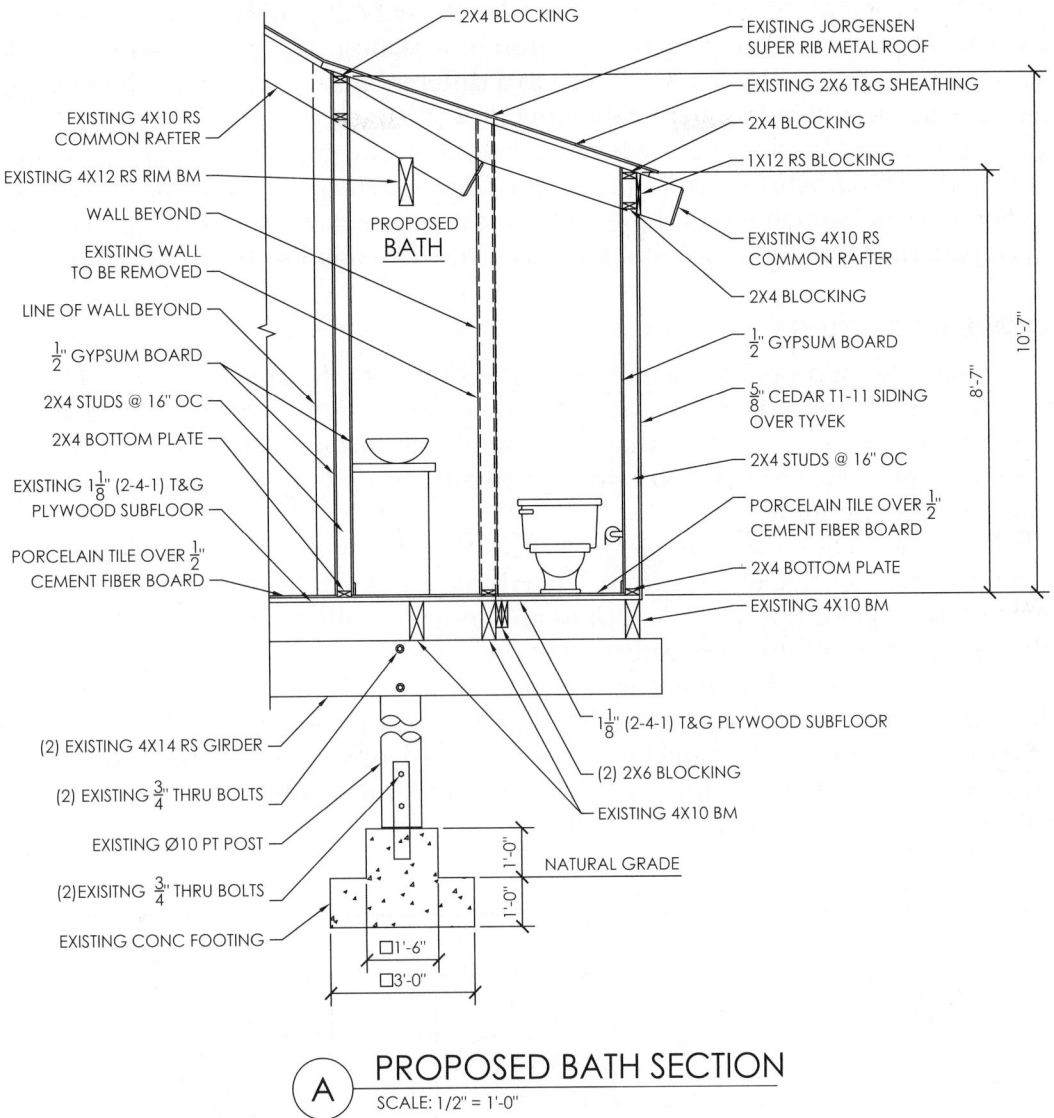

Section Lines

Section views include section line symbols to show where material is cut to reveal hidden features. The standard on basic mechanical drawings is 45° section lines, unless another angle is required to satisfy other section line rules. Avoid drawing section lines at angles greater than 75° or less than 15° from horizontal. Section lines should never be parallel or perpendicular to adjacent lines on the drawing. In addition, section lines should not cross object lines.

Equally spaced section lines, with a minimum .063″ (1.5 mm) spacing, are standard on mechanical drawings, and are adequate for basic applications like the drawing in **Figure 23-2.** Depending on the drawing and discipline, you may use different patterns to clarify the drawing or to represent specific material cut by the section. A specific material pattern is not necessary on a part drawing if the title block or a note clearly indicates the material. However, use different or coded section lines on an assembly drawing to represent each component or different material. Section line symbols on a non-mechanical drawing can be lines or can consist of graphic patterns that represent specific materials, such as insulation, earth, and concrete on an architectural or structural section. They may also be omitted for clarity, as is common on civil engineering profiles.

AutoCAD provides standard graphic patterns and section line symbols known as *hatches,* or *hatch patterns.* The acad.pat file stores standard hatch patterns. The ANSI31 pattern is a general section line symbol and is the default pattern in some templates. The ANSI31 pattern also represents cast iron in a section. The ANSI32 symbol identifies steel in a section. When you change to a different hatch pattern, the new pattern becomes the default in the current drawing until changed.

Use the Solid hatch pattern whenever it is necessary to create a solid filled area. The ASME Y14.3 *Multiview and Sectional View Drawings* standard recommends omitting section lines on section views showing thin features, such as ribs and lugs. The Solid hatch pattern is appropriate for thin sections if you do not follow the ASME standard.

hatches (hatch patterns): AutoCAD section line symbols and graphic patterns.

Types of Sections

Choose the appropriate type of section according to the application and features to be sectioned. For example, an object that includes a significant amount of hidden features may require a section that cuts completely through the object. In contrast, a drawing may require that you remove a small portion to expose and dimension a single, minor interior feature.

full sections: Sections that show half the object removed.

Figure 23-2 shows an example of a *full section.* The cutting plane applied to a full section passes completely through the view, typically along the center plane, as shown by the cutting-plane line. *Offset sections* are similar to full sections, except the cutting plane staggers to cut through features that are not in a straight line. See **Figure 23-4.**

offset sections: Sections that have a staggered cutting plane.

Figure 23-5 provides an example of an *aligned section.* The cutting plane cuts through the feature and then rotates to align with the center plane before projecting onto the section view. An aligned section shows the true size and shape of the aligned features. If you use direct projection, such as with a full or offset section, the section will appear foreshortened.

aligned sections: Sections used when a feature is out of alignment with the center plane.

Figure 23-4.
A two-view mechanical part drawing with an offset section view.

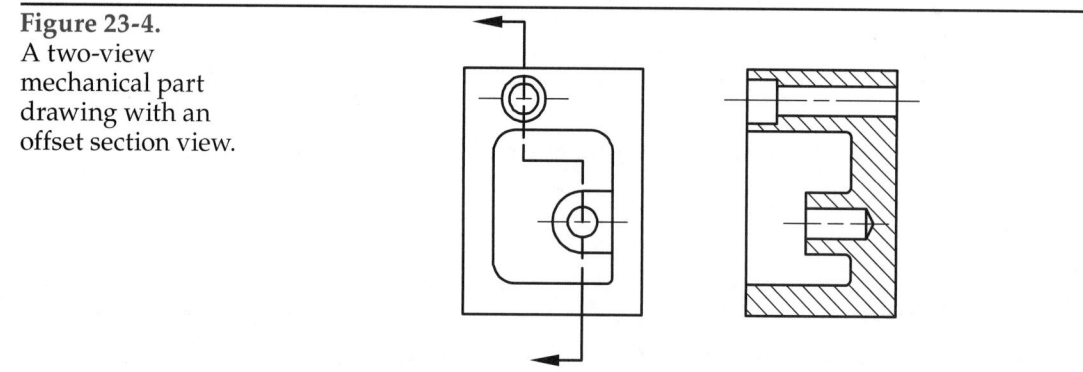

Figure 23-5.
A two-view mechanical part drawing with an aligned section view.

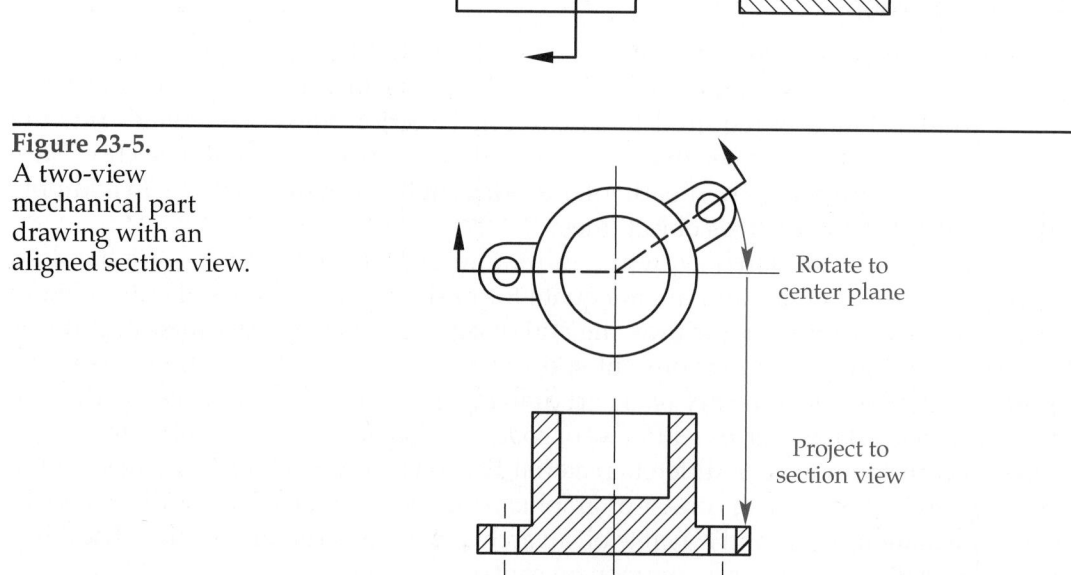

Figure 23-6 shows an example of a *revolved section*. A revolved section may appear in place within the object, or a portion of the view may be broken away to make dimensioning easier. Omit cutting-plane lines with revolved sections. Use a *removed section* when it is not possible to show a standard section in direct projection from the cutting plane, or when a revolved section is inappropriate. See **Figure 23-7.** A cutting-plane line identifies the location of the section. Multiple removed sections require labeled cutting-plane lines and related views. Drawing only the ends of the cutting-plane lines simplifies the views.

Figure 23-8 shows an example of a *half section*. The term *half* describes how half of the view appears in section, while the other half remains as an exterior view. Half sections are commonly used to draw symmetrical objects. A centerline separates the sectioned portion of the view from the unsectioned portion. You normally omit hidden lines from the unsectioned half. *Broken-out sections* clarify specific hidden features. See **Figure 23-9. Figure 23-2** also shows a broken-out section.

revolved sections: Sections that clarify the contour of objects that have the same shape throughout their length.

removed sections: Standard section views, but removed from direct projection from the cutting plane.

half sections: Sections that show one-quarter of the object removed.

broken-out sections: Sections that show a small portion of the object removed.

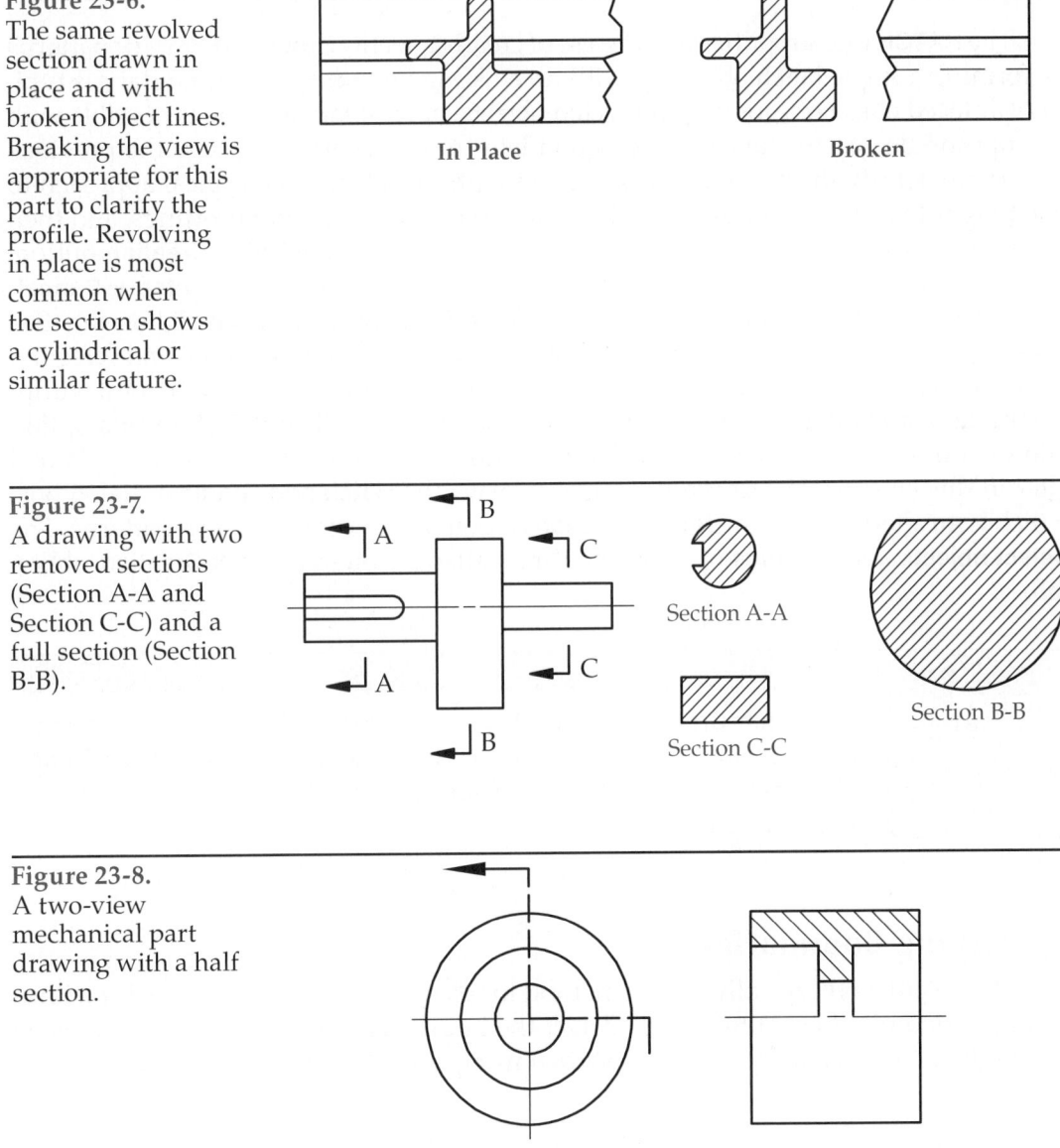

Figure 23-6.
The same revolved section drawn in place and with broken object lines. Breaking the view is appropriate for this part to clarify the profile. Revolving in place is most common when the section shows a cylindrical or similar feature.

In Place   Broken

Figure 23-7.
A drawing with two removed sections (Section A-A and Section C-C) and a full section (Section B-B).

Section A-A
Section C-C
Section B-B

Figure 23-8.
A two-view mechanical part drawing with a half section.

Figure 23-9.
Use a broken-out section to display a small portion of a hidden feature.

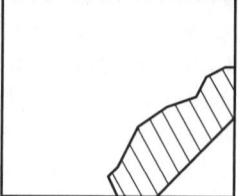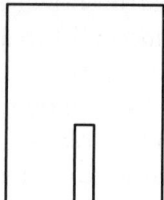

Using the HATCH Tool

The **HATCH** tool simplifies the process of creating section lines and graphic patterns by forming a single hatch object that fills an existing *boundary*. The boundary is typically a closed object or group of connected objects, but a small opening is possible with an appropriate gap tolerance, as explained later in this chapter. Review the previous figures to identify the boundaries associated with each view. The typical approach to hatching is to specify boundaries, adjust hatch properties and other settings, and then create the hatch and exit the **HATCH** tool by picking the **Close Hatch Creation** button, pressing [Esc], [Enter], or the space bar, or right-clicking and selecting **Enter** or **Cancel**.

Access the **HATCH** tool to display the **Hatch Creation** contextual ribbon tab. See **Figure 23-10.** Some options are also available by typing, or right-clicking and selecting from the shortcut menu. The default method for placing a hatch is to pick a point within a boundary, and allow AutoCAD to identify the boundary. The **Select objects** option allows you to select objects in addition to or instead of internal points, as explained later in this chapter. The **SeTtings** option displays the **Hatch and Gradient** dialog box, which is an alternative to the **Hatch Creation** ribbon tab for creating hatch patterns. The **Select objects** and **SeTtings** options are also available from the **Hatch Creation** ribbon tab.

boundary: The area filled by a hatch.

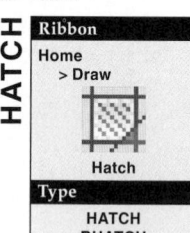

Ribbon
Home
> Draw

Hatch

Type
HATCH
BHATCH
BH
H

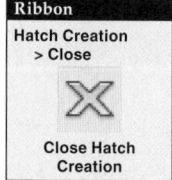

Ribbon
Hatch Creation
> Close

Close Hatch Creation

Specifying Boundaries

The default and typically easiest method for placing hatch is to pick a point within a boundary and allow AutoCAD to detect the boundary. Move the crosshairs inside a boundary to preview the hatch, as shown in **Figure 23-10.** Use the preview to help

Figure 23-10. The **Hatch Creation** contextual ribbon tab. Use the default **Pick Points** option and the crosshairs to preview the boundary to hatch.

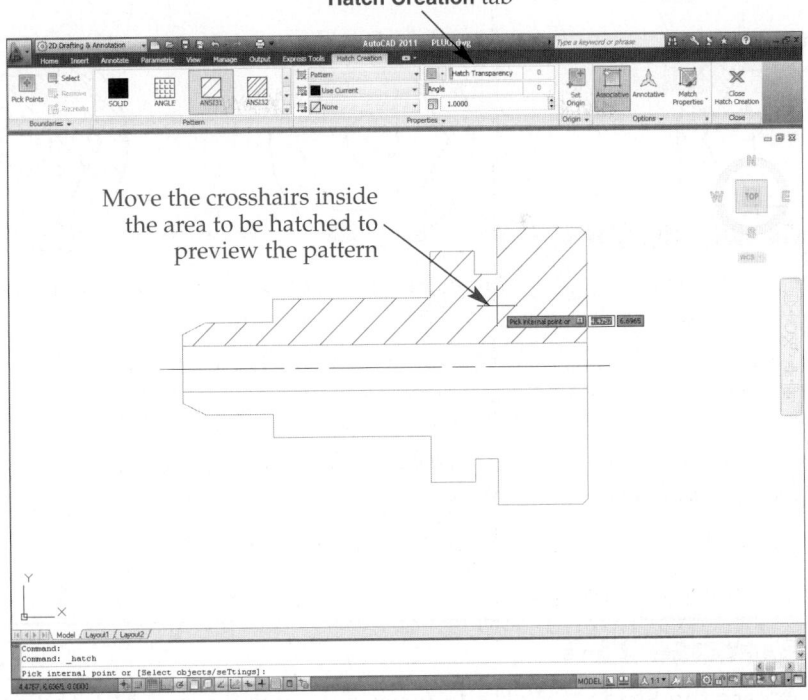

identify the boundary. The initial preview may not use the correct hatch pattern or boundary properties, but should allow you to determine if selecting the point will fill the acceptable boundary. Adjust the pattern and boundary properties interactively once you specify boundaries.

If the boundary looks correct, pick the point to apply the hatch and highlight the boundary. Continue picking points to specify additional boundaries to include with the hatch object. If a preview does not appear, AutoCAD cannot detect the boundary or the current hatch scale is too large for the size of the boundary. The most common reason AutoCAD cannot detect a boundary is because the boundary contains gaps. Exit the **HATCH** tool and edit the drawing to create a closed boundary. Use the **Hatch Pattern Scale** option to adjust the hatch scale, as described later in this chapter.

Island Detection

When picking points to specify hatch boundaries, you may need to adjust how AutoCAD treats *islands*, as shown in **Figure 23-11.** Use the flyout in the expanded **Options** panel to specify island detection. Pick the **Normal Island Detection** option to hatch every other boundary, stepping inward from the outer boundary. Select the **Outer Island Detection** option to hatch only the outermost boundary. Choose the **Ignore Island Detection** option to ignore all islands and hatch everything within the outer boundary.

islands:
Boundaries inside another boundary.

Ribbon
Hatch Creation
> Options

Normal Island Detection

Outer Island Detection

Ignore Island Detection

> **NOTE**

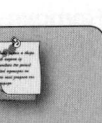

The **No Island Detection** option applies to hatches applied with previous versions of AutoCAD.

Figure 23-11. Adjusting island detection when picking a single internal point. The **Outer Island Detection** option is appropriate for this example and for most applications.

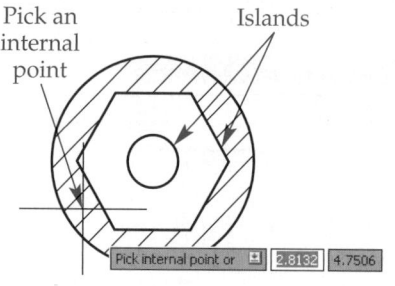

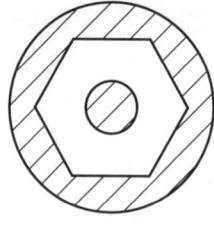
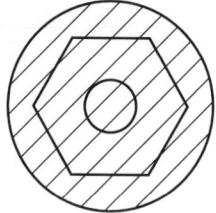

Outer Island Detection   Normal Island Detection   Ignore Island Detection

PROFESSIONAL TIP

Pick the **Outer** island display style to ensure that inner islands are not hatched unintentionally.

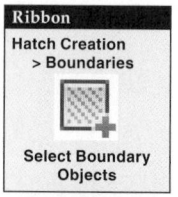

Exercise 23-1

Access the Student Web site (www.g-wlearning.com/CAD) and complete Exercise 23-1.

Selecting Objects

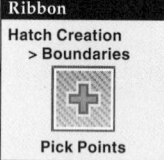

Ribbon
Hatch Creation
> Boundaries

Select Boundary Objects

An alternative method to specify a boundary is to use the **Select Boundary Objects** option to select objects that form a boundary. A common example is selecting a closed object such as a polyline, circle, or group of connected objects to hatch an area that would be difficult or time-consuming to hatch by picking points because of numerous internal boundaries. See **Figure 23-12.** When necessary, select objects within the hatch boundary to exclude from the hatch pattern. See **Figure 23-13.** The preview automatically updates according to the selections. Use the **Pick Points** option to return to internal point selection mode.

Ribbon
Hatch Creation
> Boundaries

Pick Points

NOTE

If you specify the wrong boundary, use the **U** tool as needed to undo the selection without exiting the **HATCH** tool.

Removing Boundaries

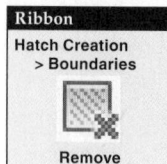

Ribbon
Hatch Creation
> Boundaries

Remove

The **Remove boundaries** option is available after you specify a boundary. Use the **Remove boundaries** option to select unwanted boundaries or objects to remove from the selection set.

Figure 23-12.
An example of an architectural elevation on which it is easier to use the **Select Boundary Objects** option to specify a hatch boundary. The closed polyline around the area to be hatched is for construction purposes only.

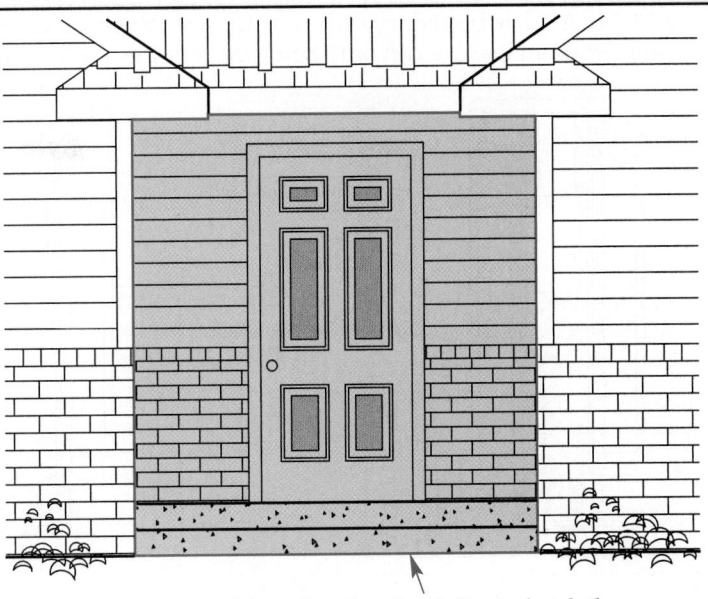

Select this closed polyline to hatch the area instead of picking multiple points

Figure 23-13. Using the **Select Boundary Objects** option to exclude a polyline hexagon and text object from the hatch pattern.

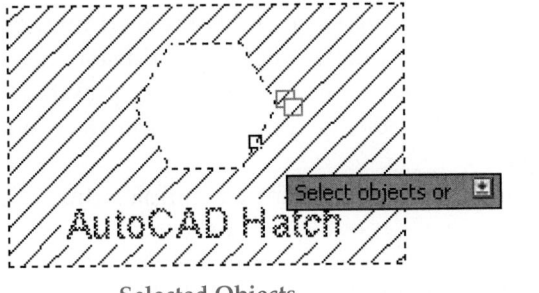

Selected Objects

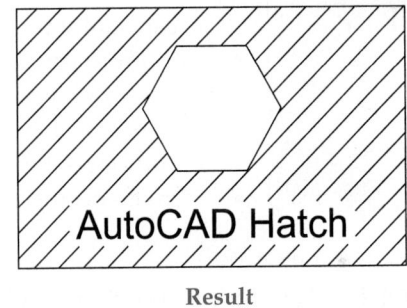

Result

Exercise 23-2

Access the Student Web site (www.g-wlearning.com/CAD) and complete Exercise 23-2.

Boundary Set

By default, the **HATCH** tool evaluates the entire current viewport to detect boundaries. To limit the evaluation area, possibly increasing hatch performance, pick the **Select new boundary set** option and use a window to define the area to evaluate. See **Figure 23-14A**. Right-click, or press [Enter] or the space bar to create the boundary set. Toggle between the **Use Boundary Set** and **Use Current Viewport** option from the **Specify Boundary Set** drop-down list in the expanded **Boundaries** panel. Creating a new boundary set overrides the previous boundary set. **Figure 23-14B** shows a new hatch pattern applied to boundaries within the boundary set.

Ribbon
Hatch Creation > Boundaries

Select new boundary set

Figure 23-14. A—The boundary set limits the area that AutoCAD evaluates during a hatching operation. B—You can only hatch boundaries within the boundary set.

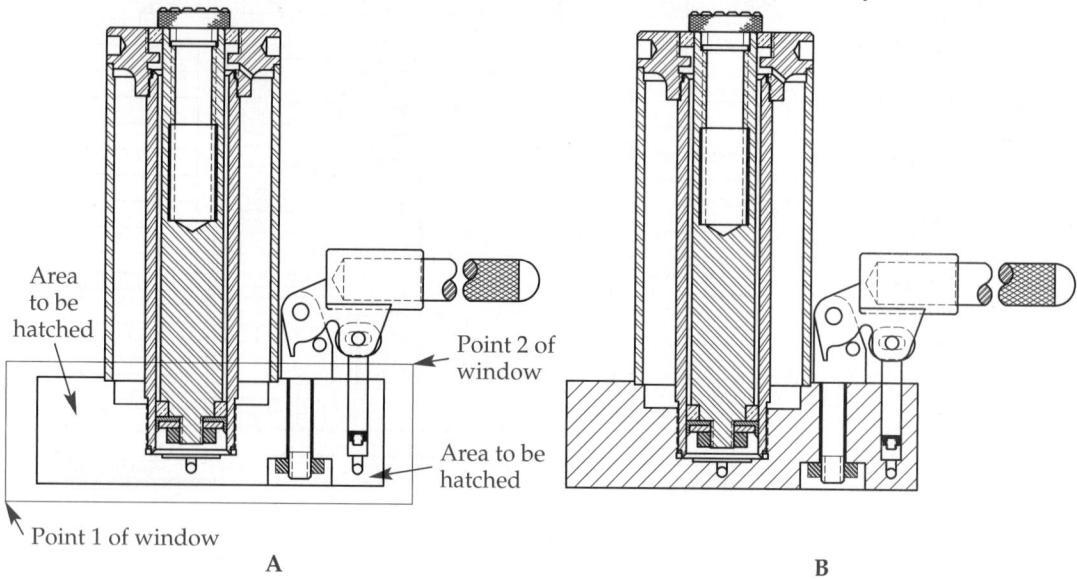

Area to be hatched

Point 2 of window

Area to be hatched

Point 1 of window

A

B

PROFESSIONAL TIP

Apply the following techniques to specify a boundary area and save time, especially when you are hatching large and complex drawings:
- Zoom in on the boundary area to be hatched to aid selection.
- Use previews to confirm correct boundaries before picking.
- Turn off layers assigned to objects that might interfere with boundary definition.
- Create boundary sets of small areas within a complex drawing.

Hatching Unclosed Areas and Correcting Boundary Errors

The **HATCH** tool works well unless there is a gap in a boundary, or you pick a point or select objects outside a likely boundary. When you select a point or objects where no boundary can form, an error message states that a valid boundary cannot be determined. Close the message and try again to specify the boundary. When you try to hatch an area that does not close because of a small gap, you will see the error message and circles shown in **Figure 23-15.** Close the message and eliminate the gap to create the hatch.

For most applications, it is best to identify and close a gap. However, you can hatch an unclosed boundary by setting a *gap tolerance* using the **Gap Tolerance** option. Use the slider or enter a value in the text box up to 5000. AutoCAD ignores any gaps in the boundary less than or equal to the tolerance value.

Retaining Boundaries

By default, a hatch pattern boundary forms according to objects in the drawing. The boundary is essentially temporary, which is appropriate for most applications. Select the **Retain Boundary - Polyline** option to form a separate polyline object overlapping the boundary. Choose the **Retain Boundary - Region** option to form a separate *region* object overlapping the boundary. Retaining a boundary forms additional boundary objects that you can use even if you remove or edit the original objects.

Ribbon

Hatch Creation > Options > Gap Tolerance

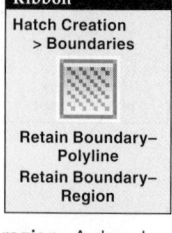

gap tolerance: The amount of gap allowed between segments of a boundary to be hatched.

Ribbon

Hatch Creation > Boundaries

Retain Boundary–Polyline

Retain Boundary–Region

---

region: A closed two-dimensional area.

Figure 23-15. Close a boundary to create a hatch pattern.

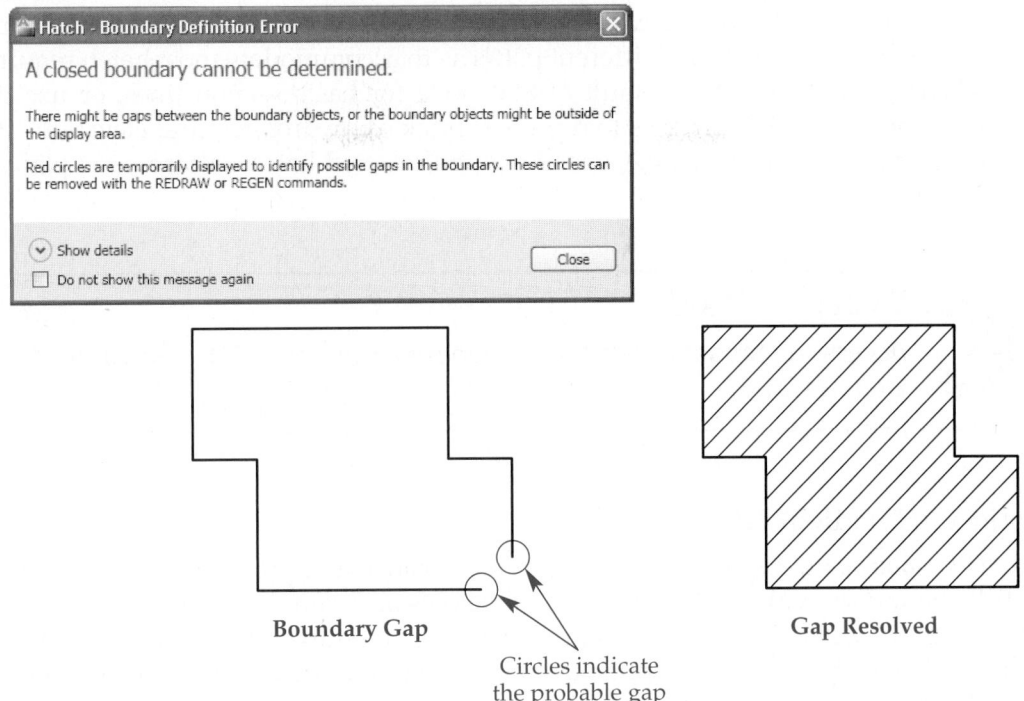

Boundary Gap

Gap Resolved

Circles indicate
the probable gap

Selecting a Hatch Pattern

The **Pattern** panel includes all of the hatch patterns and fills supplied with AutoCAD. Use the scroll buttons to the right of the patterns to locate a pattern, or pick the expansion arrow to display patterns in a temporary window. See **Figure 23-16.** The **Hatch Type** drop-down list in the **Properties** panel includes **Solid**, **Gradient**, **Pattern**, and **User defined** categories to help you locate specific hatches in the **Pattern** panel, essentially filtering the list. Select a category to display related hatches in the **Pattern** panel. Select a hatch pattern from the **Pattern** panel to apply to the specified boundaries.

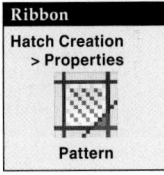

Ribbon

Hatch Creation
> Properties

Pattern

Figure 23-16. Select a hatch pattern from the **Pattern** panel of the **Hatch Creation** ribbon tab.

Choose a category to view related
hatches in the Pattern panel

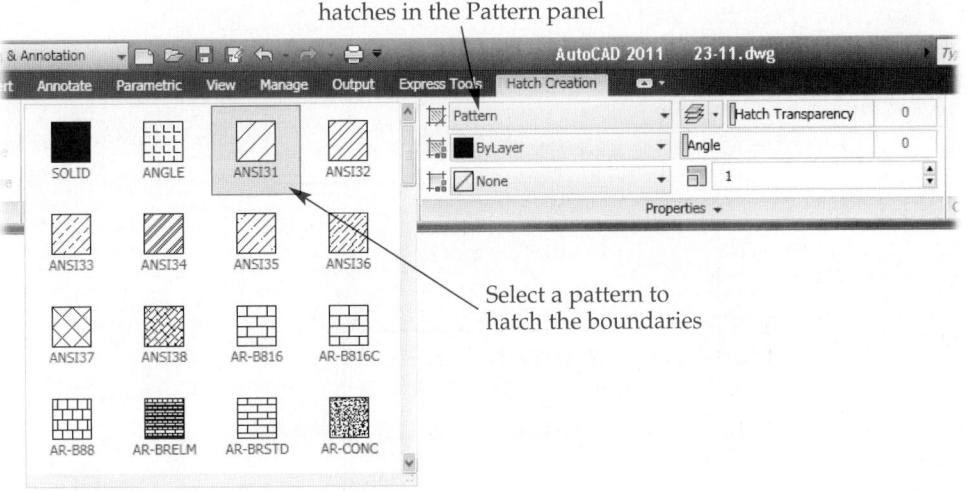

Select a pattern to
hatch the boundaries

Patterns

The **Pattern** hatch type provides patterns stored in the acad.pat and acadiso.pat files. AutoCAD includes many different patterns to accommodate most hatch requirements. For example, use the default ANSI31 style for basic section lines, or use the BRICK or one of the AR-B patterns to represent brick on an architectural elevation. The **Properties** panel provides settings specific to the selected hatch pattern, as explained later in this chapter.

Exercise 23-3

Access the Student Web site (www.g-wlearning.com/CAD) and complete Exercise 23-3.

Solid and Gradient Fills

The **Solid** hatch type and corresponding SOLID hatch provide an effective way to fill a boundary with a solid. **Figure 23-17** shows an example of several boundaries filled with the SOLID hatch. This example uses specific transparent layers assigned to different hatch objects. Use an option associated with the **Gradient** hatch type to create a gradient fill, as explained later in this chapter.

Exercise 23-4

Access the Student Web site (www.g-wlearning.com/CAD) and complete Exercise 23-4.

Figure 23-17. A portion of a storm water pollution control plan with a transparent SOLID hatch. The solid fills represent different impervious and non-impervious surfaces.

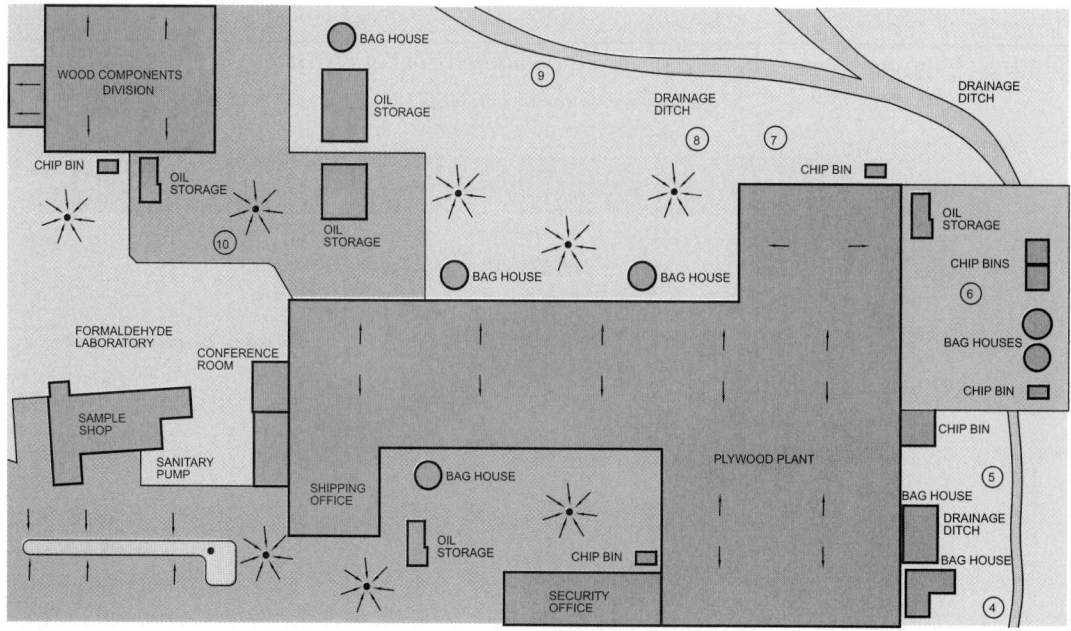

The **SOLID** tool allows you to draw basic solid shapes without creating a boundary. Access the **SOLID** tool and pick points in a specific sequence to form different shapes. The SOLID hatch applied using the **HATCH** tool is typically a better method of creating solid fills.

User Defined Hatch

The **User defined** hatch type and corresponding USER hatch creates a pattern of equally spaced lines for basic hatching applications. The lines use the linetype assigned to the current layer. Use options in the **Properties** panel of the **Hatch Creation** ribbon tab to adjust the USER hatch appearance, as explained later in this chapter.

Create and save custom hatch patterns in PAT files. Add the files to the AutoCAD search path to have access to custom hatch from the **Pattern** panel. *AutoCAD and Its Applications—Advanced* provides more information about customizing hatch-related dialog boxes.

Pattern Size

The **Properties** panel provides hatch pattern appearance control. Scale, or spacing, is a primary hatch property. Use the **Hatch Pattern Scale** option to adjust hatches of the **Pattern** type. The default scale is 1. If the pattern appears too small or large, specify a different scale. See **Figure 23-18.** For example, by default, the ANSI31 hatch is a pattern of lines spaced .125″ (3 mm) apart. If you change the scale to 2, the pattern of lines is spaced .25″ (6 mm) apart.

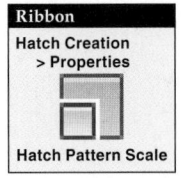
The **Hatch Spacing** option replaces the **Hatch Pattern Scale** option when you select the USER hatch. Specify the exact distance between lines. Changes to scale or spacing update automatically in the preview of the specified boundaries.

Use a smaller hatch size for small objects and a larger hatch size for larger objects. This makes section lines look appropriate for the drawing scale. Often you must use your best judgment when selecting a hatch size.

Use an appropriate hatch scale or spacing to display the hatch pattern on-screen and plot correctly according to the drawing scale. To understand the concept of hatch size, look at the section view shown in **Figure 23-19.** In this example, which uses

Figure 23-18.
Hatch pattern scale applies to hatches of the **Pattern** type and to custom hatch patterns.

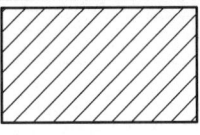

Scale = 1

Scale = 2

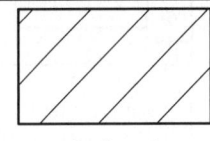

Scale = 3

Figure 23-19. The hatch pattern may appear incorrect if the drawing scale changes.

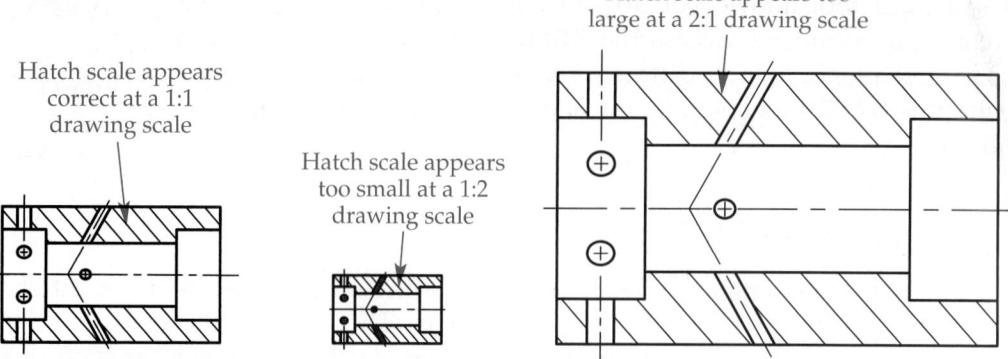

Hatch scale appears correct at a 1:1 drawing scale

Hatch scale appears too small at a 1:2 drawing scale

Hatch scale appears too large at a 2:1 drawing scale

the ANSI31 hatch pattern, the section line spacing should be the same distance apart regardless of drawing scale. The section lines on the full-scale (1:1) drawing display correctly. However, the section lines are too close on the half-scale (1:2) drawing, and they are too far apart on the double-scale (2:1) drawing. To obtain the correct results, you must adjust the hatch size according to the drawing scale. You can calculate scale factor manually and apply it to hatch scale or spacing, or you can allow AutoCAD to calculate the scale factor using annotative hatch patterns.

Scaling Hatch Patterns Manually

To adjust hatch size manually according to a specific drawing scale, you must first calculate the drawing scale factor. Then multiply the scale factor by the plotted hatch scale or spacing to get the model space hatch scale or spacing. Specify the scale of predefined or custom hatch patterns using the **Hatch Pattern Scale** option. Specify the spacing of the USER hatch using **Hatch Spacing** option. Figure 23-20 shows examples of adjusting hatch scale according to drawing scale. Refer to Chapter 9 for information on determining the drawing scale factor.

Annotative Hatch Patterns

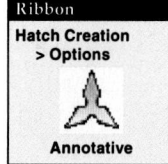

Ribbon

Hatch Creation > Options

Annotative

Pick the **Annotative** button in the **Options** panel to make the hatch pattern annotative. AutoCAD scales annotative hatches according to the annotation scale you select, which eliminates the need for you to calculate the scale factor. Once you choose an annotation scale, AutoCAD applies the corresponding scale factor to annotative hatches and all other annotative objects.

Figure 23-20. The hatch pattern scale may require adjusting, depending on the drawing scale.

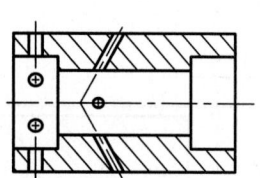

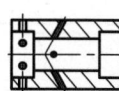

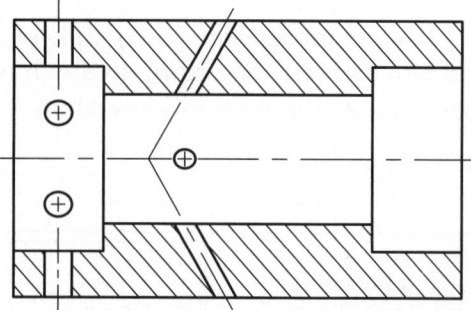

Drawing scale: 1:1
Drawing scale factor: 1
Hatch scale: 1

Drawing scale: 1:2
Drawing scale factor: 2
Hatch scale: 2

Drawing scale: 2:1
Drawing scale factor: .5
Hatch scale: .5

The hatch pattern is displayed at the proper size regardless of the drawing scale, much like the example shown in **Figure 23-20**, but without requiring you to change the hatch scale or spacing. For example, if you specify a value using the **Hatch Pattern Scale** or **Hatch Spacing** option appropriate for an annotation scale of 1/4″ = 1′-0″, and then change the annotation scale to 1″ = 1′-0″, the appearance of the hatch pattern relative to the drawing scale does not change. It looks the same on the 1/4″ = 1′-0″ scale drawing as it does on the 1″ = 1′-0″ scale drawing. Refer to Chapter 9 for information on setting annotation scale.

Relative to Paper Space Option

The **Relative to Paper Space** option in the expanded **Properties** panel allows you to scale the hatch pattern relative to the scale of the active layout viewport. You must enter a floating layout viewport in order to select the **Relative to Paper Space** option. The hatch scale automatically adjusts according to the viewport scale. For example, a floating viewport scale set to 4:1 uses a scale factor of .25 (1 ÷ 4 = .25). If you enter a hatch scale of 1, the hatch automatically appears at a scale of .25 (1 × .25 = .25).

Ribbon
Hatch Creation
> Properties

Relative to Paper Space

NOTE

You can control the ISO pen width for predefined ISO patterns using the **ISO Pen Width:** drop-down list in the expanded **Properties** panel.

Ribbon
Hatch Creation
> Properties
> ISO Pen Width

Additional Pattern Properties

The **Properties** panel provides other settings that you can preview interactively as you make changes. The **Hatch Angle** option controls pattern rotation. Use the slider or enter a value up to 359 in the text box to rotate the pattern relative to the X axis. For example, the ANSI31 hatch is a pattern of 45° lines. Change the angle to 15° to form a pattern of 60° (45+15=60) lines. The **Double** option is available with the USER hatch and allows you to create a pattern of double lines. **Figure 23-21** shows examples of user-defined hatch patterns.

The **Background Color** option allows you to fill the specified boundaries with the hatch pattern and a background color similar to a solid fill. See **Figure 23-22**. Hatching with a solid fill and pattern is not a common drafting practice, but is appropriate in

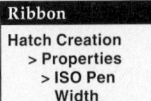

Ribbon
Hatch Creation
> Properties
> Hatch Angle

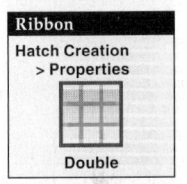

Ribbon
Hatch Creation
> Properties

Double

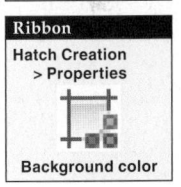

Ribbon
Hatch Creation
> Properties

Background color

Figure 23-21. Examples of user-defined hatch patterns with different hatch angles and spacing.

Angle	0°	45°	0°	45°
Spacing	.125	.125	.250	.250
Single Hatch				
Double Hatch				

Figure 23-22.
Use the **Background Color** option of the **Properties** panel to fill boundaries with a color and a hatch pattern. This example shows an architectural window elevation with background Color 9 and the ANSI34 pattern.

some applications. Choose a color from the drop-down list or pick the **Select Colors...** option to pick a color from the **Select Color** dialog box. The color must be different from the color assigned to the pattern layer.

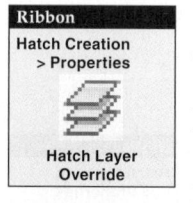

Use the **Hatch Layer Override** option to apply a different layer to the hatch without exiting the **HATCH** tool and making the different layer current. The **Hatch Color** and **Hatch Transparency** options override the color and transparency assigned to the current layer. For most applications, you should not override color or transparency.

Setting the Hatch Origin Point

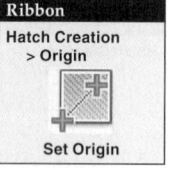

The **Origin** panel includes options that control the position of hatch patterns. Select an option from the expanded **Origin** panel, or pick the **Set Origin** button. The default setting is **Use Current Origin**, which refers to the current UCS origin to define the point from which the hatch pattern forms and how the pattern repeats. In some cases, it is important that a hatch pattern align with, or originate from, a specific point. A common example is hatching a representation of bricks. To specify a different origin point, pick the **Set Origin** button and select an origin point. See **Figure 23-23.**

The expanded **Origin** panel includes **Bottom Left, Bottom Right, Top Right, Top Left,** and **Center** options. Select an option to align the hatch origin point with the corresponding point on the hatch boundary. For example, use the **Bottom right** option to create the pattern shown in **Figure 23-23B.** Select the **Store as Default Origin** option to save the custom origin point.

Figure 23-23.
A—The default **Use current origin** setting. B—Pick the **Set Origin** button and select the lower-left corner (endpoint) of the rectangle. Notice that the pattern, or in this example the first brick, starts exactly at the corner of the hatched area.

A

B

To start hatch here, pick endpoint as the origin point

Gradient Fill

Select the **Gradient** hatch type and choose a gradient style from the **Pattern** panel to create a *gradient fill*. See Figure 23-24. Gradient fills are commonly used to simulate color-shaded objects and to create the appearance of a lit surface with a gradual transition from an area of highlight to a darker area. Use two colors to simulate a transition from light to dark between the colors. Several different gradient fill patterns are available to create linear sweep, spherical, radial, or curved shading.

The **Gradient Colors** button is active by default to specify a fill using a smooth transition between two colors. Use the **Gradient Color 1** and **Gradient Color 2** drop-down lists to specify gradient colors. Deselect the **Gradient Colors** button to create a fill that has a smooth transition between the darker shades and lighter tints of one color. The **Gradient Tint and Shade** option becomes enabled when you use the single-color option. Use the slider or enter a value up to 100 in the text box to specify the *tint* or *shade* of a color used for a one-color gradient fill.

The **Centered** origin button is active by default and applies a symmetrical configuration. If you deselect the **Centered** origin button, the gradient fill shifts to simulate the projection of a light source from the left of the object. Use the **Angle** option to specify the gradient fill angle relative to the current UCS. The default angle is 0°.

gradient fill: A shading transition between the tones of one color or two separate colors.

Ribbon
Hatch Creation
> Properties

Gradient Colors

Ribbon
Hatch Creation
> Properties

Gradient Tint and Shade

tint: A specific color mixed with white.

shade: A specific color mixed with black.

Exercise 23-5

Access the Student Web site (www.g-wlearning.com/CAD) and complete Exercise 23-5.

Hatch Composition Options

The **HATCH** tool creates an *associative hatch pattern* by default. To create a *non-associative hatch pattern*, deselect the **Associative** button in the **Options** panel. An associative hatch is appropriate for most applications. If you stretch, scale, or otherwise

associative hatch pattern: A hatch pattern that updates automatically when you edit associated objects.

non-associative hatch pattern: A hatch that is independent of objects and updates when the boundary changes, but not when you make changes to objects.

Figure 23-24. Select a gradient style from the **Pattern** panel to access options for creating gradient fills, such as this two-color lagoon representation.

Select a gradient from the Pattern panel

Deselect to create a single-color gradient

Select the color for a single-color gradient, or color 1 for a two-color gradient

Select color 2 for a two-color gradient

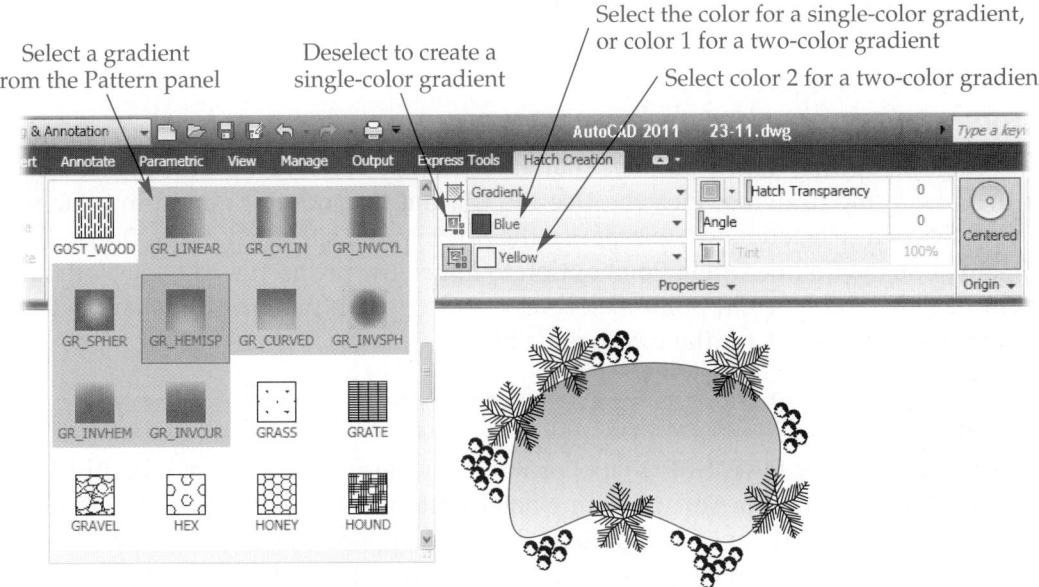

edit the objects that define the boundary of an associative hatch, the pattern automatically adjusts to fill the modified boundary. A non-associative hatch pattern does not respond to changes made to the original boundary. Instead, non-associative hatch boundary grips are available for changing the extents of the hatch, separate from the original boundary objects.

You can select multiple points and objects during a single hatch operation. By default, multiple boundaries form a single hatch object. Selecting and editing one of the hatch patterns selects and edits all patterns created during the same operation. If this is not the preferred result, select the **Create Separate Hatches** option before applying the hatch. Individual hatch patterns form for each boundary.

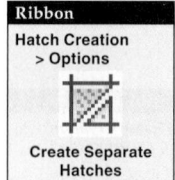
Ribbon
Hatch Creation
> Options

Create Separate
Hatches

PROFESSIONAL TIP

When you create an associative hatch, it is often best to specify a single internal point per hatch. If you specify more than one internal point in the same operation, AutoCAD creates one hatch object from all points you pick. This can cause unexpected results when you try to edit what appears to be a separate hatch object.

Controlling the Draw Order

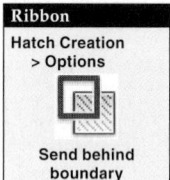
Ribbon
Hatch Creation
> Options

Send behind
boundary

The draw order drop-down list in the **Options** panel provides options for controlling the order of display when a hatch pattern overlaps other objects. The **Send behind boundary** option is the default and makes the hatch pattern appear behind the boundary. Select the **Bring in front of boundary** option to make the hatch pattern appear on top of the boundary. Select the **Do not assign** option to have no automatic drawing order setting assigned to the hatch.

Use the **Send to back** option to send the hatch pattern behind all other objects in the drawing. Any objects that are in the hatched area appear as if they are on top of the hatch pattern. Use the **Bring to front** option to bring the hatch pattern in front of, or on top of, all other objects in the drawing. Any objects that are in the hatched area appear as if they are behind the hatch pattern.

NOTE

Use the **DRAWORDER** tool to change the draw order setting after creating a hatch pattern.

Reusing Existing Hatch Properties

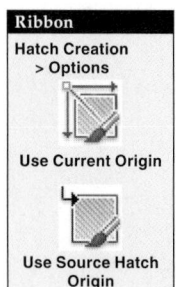
Ribbon
Hatch Creation
> Options

Use Current Origin

Use Source Hatch
Origin

You can specify hatch pattern characteristics by referencing an identical hatch pattern from the drawing. Pick the **Use the Current Origin Point** option to match the properties of a selected hatch, except use the origin point specified in the **Origin** panel. Pick the **Use the Source Origin Point** option to match the properties of a selected hatch, including the hatch origin point. Select an existing hatch pattern to match, and then specify the boundaries for the new hatch object.

PROFESSIONAL TIP

The **MATCHPROP** tool provides an alternate method of inheriting the properties of an existing hatch pattern and applying the properties to a different hatch pattern. This tool applies existing hatch patterns to objects in the current drawing or to objects in other open drawing files.

Exercise 23-6

Access the Student Web site (www.g-wlearning.com/CAD) and complete Exercise 23-6.

Hatching Using DesignCenter

To pattern a boundary using **DesignCenter**, use the **Tree View** pane to locate and select a PAT file to display the patterns in the **Content** pane. See **Figure 23-25A**. The most effective technique to transfer a hatch pattern from **DesignCenter** to the active drawing is to use a drag-and-drop operation. Press and hold down the pick button on the pattern to import, and then drag the cursor to the drawing window. A hatch pattern symbol appears with the cursor. See **Figure 23-25B**. Release the pick button in a boundary to apply the hatch pattern. See **Figure 23-25C**.

An alternative to drag and drop is copy and paste. Right-click on a hatch pattern in **DesignCenter** and pick **Copy**. Move the cursor into the active drawing, right-click, and select **Paste** from the **Clipboard** cascading submenu. A hatch pattern symbol appears with the crosshairs. Pick in a boundary to apply the hatch pattern. You can also use **DesignCenter** with the **HATCH** tool. Right-click on a hatch pattern in **DesignCenter** and select **BHATCH...** to access the **Hatch Creation** ribbon tab with the selected hatch pattern active.

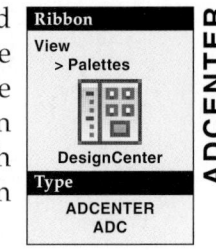

Figure 23-25. A—Pick a PAT file in DesignCenter to display the available hatch patterns in the Content pane. B—The hatch pattern symbol appears under the cursor during the drag-and-drop and paste operations. C—Pick a point to apply the hatch pattern.

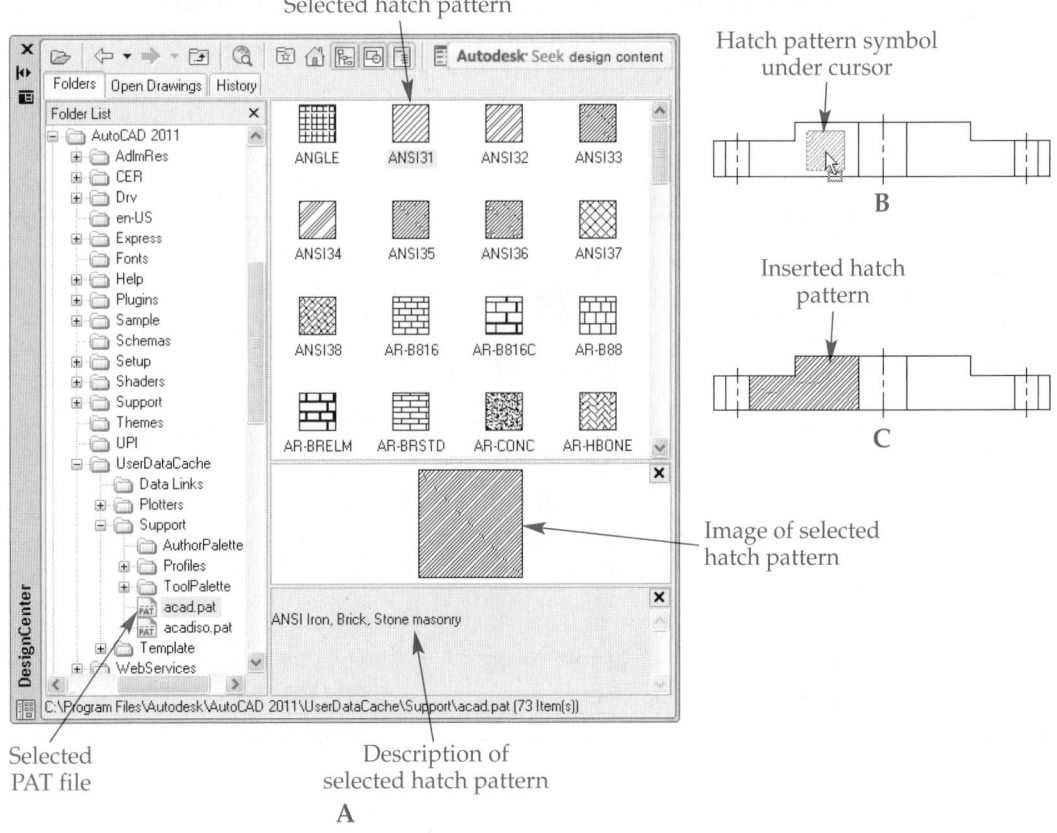

The same rules that apply to the **HATCH** tool also apply to dragging and dropping or copying and pasting hatches. When you insert hatch patterns using **DesignCenter**, the angle, scale, and island detection settings match the settings of the previous hatch pattern. Edit the hatch pattern, as described later in this chapter, to change the settings after you insert the hatch pattern.

NOTE

AutoCAD includes two PAT files: acad.pat and acadiso.pat. To verify the location of AutoCAD support files, access the **Files** tab in the **Options** dialog box and check the path listed under the Support File Search Path.

Exercise 23-7

Access the Student Web site (www.g-wlearning.com/CAD) **and complete Exercise 23-7.**

Hatching Using Tool Palettes

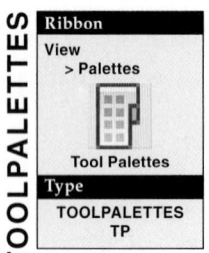

TOOLPALETTES	
Ribbon	
View	
> Palettes	
Tool Palettes	
Type	
TOOLPALETTES **TP**	

tool palette: A palette that contains tabs to help organize tools and other features.

The **Tool Palettes** palette, shown in **Figure 23-26,** provides an alternative means of storing and inserting hatch patterns. *Tool palettes* can also store and activate other drawing content and tools, such as blocks, images, tables, external reference files, drawing and editing tools, user-defined macros, script files, and Visual Lisp expressions. The **Command Tools Samples** tool palette contains examples of custom tools. For more information on AutoCAD customization and using tool palettes, refer to *AutoCAD and Its Applications—Advanced.*

Figure 23-26.
You can use the **Tool Palettes** palette to access and insert hatch patterns.

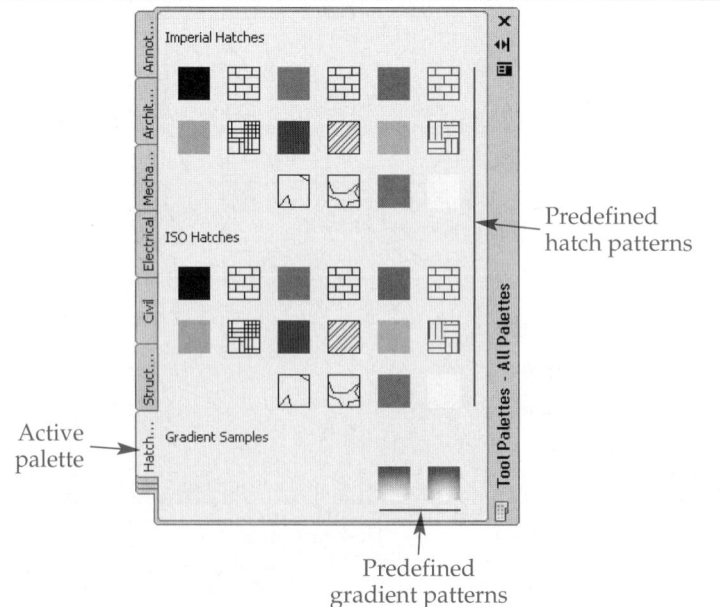

Predefined hatch patterns

Active palette

Predefined gradient patterns

AutoCAD and Its Applications—Basics

Locating and Viewing Content

Tabs along the side of the **Tool Palettes** palette divide each tool palette. Pick a tab to view related content in a tool palette. If the **Tool Palettes** palette contains more palettes than can be displayed on-screen, pick on the edge of the lowest tab to display a menu listing the palette tabs. Select the name of the tab to access the related tool palette. Use the scroll bar or scroll hand to view large lists of tool palette content. The scroll hand appears when you place the cursor in an empty area in the tool palette. Picking and dragging scrolls the tool palette up and down.

> **NOTE**
>
> By default, icons represent the tools in each tool palette. Several tool palette view options are available, including the ability to display a tool as an image of your choice. For more information on adjusting tool palette display, refer to *AutoCAD and Its Applications—Advanced*.

Inserting Hatch Patterns

To insert a hatch pattern from the **Tool Palettes** palette, access a tool palette containing hatches and fills. To drag and drop a pattern, press and hold down the pick button on the hatch to be inserted, and then drag the cursor into the drawing. A hatch pattern symbol appears with the cursor. Release the pick button in a boundary to apply the hatch pattern. An alternative to the drag-and-drop method is to pick once on the hatch image to attach the hatch to the crosshairs, and then pick a boundary in the drawing to apply the hatch pattern. Edit the hatch pattern, as described later in this chapter, to change the settings after you insert the hatch pattern.

> **NOTE**
>
> You can add tool palettes to the **Tool Palettes** palette and add tools to tool palettes. For more information on creating and modifying tool palettes, refer to *AutoCAD and Its Applications—Advanced*.

Exercise 23-8

Access the Student Web site (www.g-wlearning.com/CAD) and complete Exercise 23-8.

Editing Hatch Patterns

A hatch pattern is a single object that you can edit using standard editing tools such as **ERASE, COPY, MOVE**, or the **Properties** palette. AutoCAD also provides specific tools to edit hatches. Edit a hatch object to apply a different pattern or pattern properties, or when the drawing changes, such as when you add or remove objects that change existing hatch boundaries.

Click on a hatch object to display the Hatch Editor contextual ribbon tab, or double-click to display both the **Properties** palette and the **Hatch Editor** ribbon tab. The **Hatch**

Editor ribbon tab is similar to the **Hatch Creation** ribbon tab, but focuses on options for adjusting the existing hatch.

The **Recreate Boundary** and **Display Boundary Objects** options are specific to the **Hatch Editor** ribbon tab. The most practical application for the **Recreate Boundary** option is to recreate erased boundary geometry. See **Figure 23-27**. Pick the **Recreate Boundary** button and follow the prompts to recreate the boundary as a region or polyline. You can also specify whether to associate the hatch with the objects. The **Display Boundary Objects** option, available for associative hatches, selects the associative boundary. Use grips to make changes to the size and shape of the boundary.

Ribbon
Hatch Editor
> Boundaries

Recreate

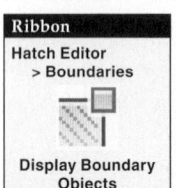

Ribbon
Hatch Editor
> Boundaries

Display Boundary
Objects

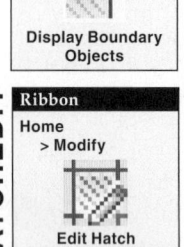

HATCHEDIT

Ribbon
Home
> Modify

Edit Hatch

Type
HATCHEDIT
HE

> **NOTE**
>
> The **HATCHEDIT** tool also allows you to change hatch characteristics, but uses the **Hatch Edit** dialog box instead of the **Hatch Editor** ribbon tab.

Exercise 23-9

Access the Student Web site (www.g-wlearning.com/CAD) and complete Exercise 23-9.

Adding and Removing Boundaries

Use the **Pick Points**, **Select Objects**, and **Remove Boundaries** options of the **Hatch Editor** ribbon tab to add boundaries to and remove boundaries from existing hatch objects. For example, **Figure 23-28** shows drawing a rectangle to create a window on a portion of an architectural elevation. To add the window as an island in the boundary, double-click the hatch pattern to display the **Hatch Editor** ribbon tab, and then use the **Select Objects** option to pick the rectangle. Close the **Hatch Editor** to complete the operation.

Editing Associative Hatch Patterns

When you edit an object associated with a hatch pattern, the hatch pattern changes to adapt to the edit. **Figure 23-29** shows examples of stretching an associated object and removing an island from an associative boundary. As long as you edit the objects associated with the boundary, the hatch pattern updates.

Figure 23-27.
Using the **Recreate Boundary** button to recreate a lost object associated with the hatch boundary.

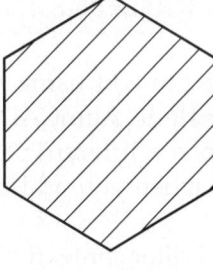

Original Hatched
Polygon

Polygon Erased

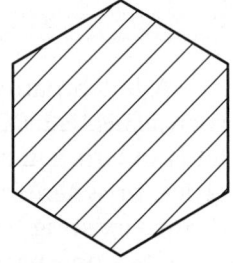

Recreated Polygon
Boundary

Figure 23-28. Adding an object to an existing hatch pattern boundary.

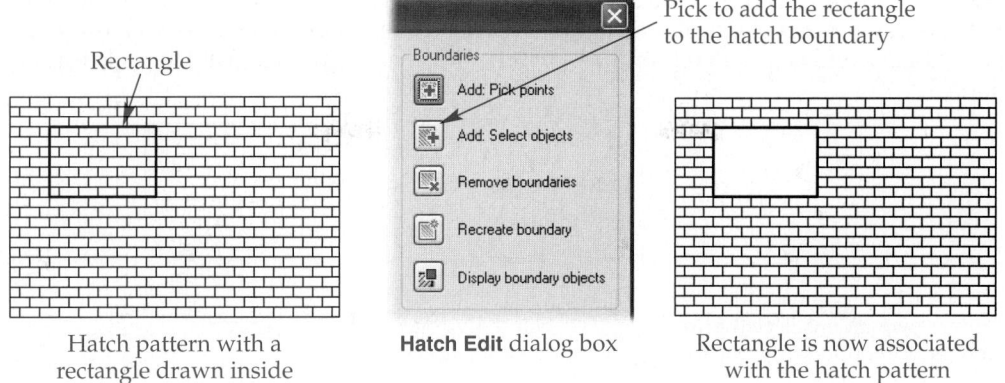

Rectangle

Pick to add the rectangle to the hatch boundary

Boundaries
- Add: Pick points
- Add: Select objects
- Remove boundaries
- Recreate boundary
- Display boundary objects

Hatch pattern with a rectangle drawn inside

Hatch Edit dialog box

Rectangle is now associated with the hatch pattern

Figure 23-29. Editing objects with associative hatch patterns. A—The hatch pattern stretches with the object. B—The hatch pattern revises to fill the area of an erased island.

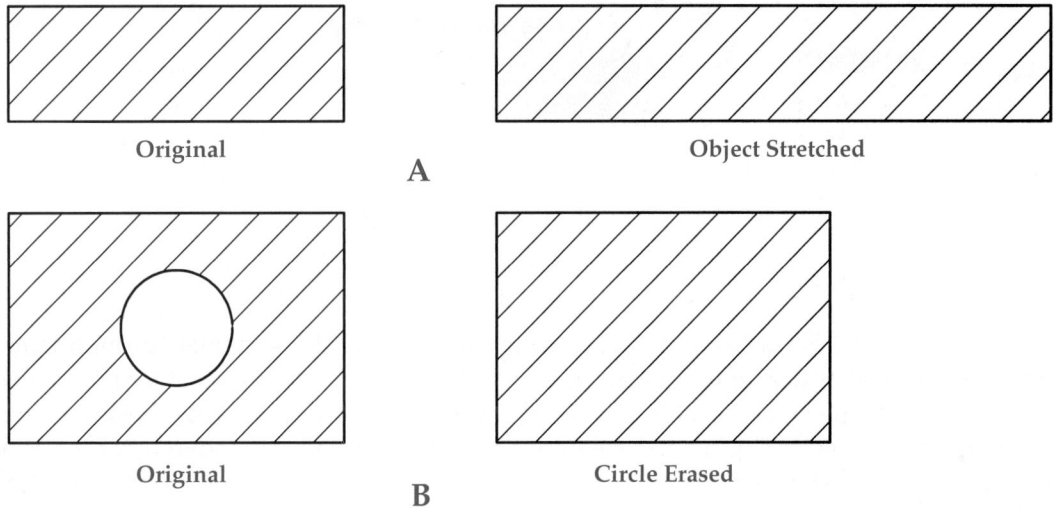

Original

Object Stretched

A

Original

Circle Erased

B

Exercise 23-10

Access the Student Web site (www.g-wlearning.com/CAD) and complete Exercise 23-10.

Center Grip Editing

The circle center grip that appears when you select a hatch object with the cross-hairs provides convenient access to hatch editing options. There are three different ways to access and apply the same context-sensitive hatch grip tools. **Figure 23-30** briefly explains and illustrates each technique. The **Stretch** option functions as a primary grip, providing access to the standard **STRETCH, MOVE, ROTATE, SCALE,** and **MIRROR** tools. Use the **Origin Point** option to specify a new origin point for the hatch. Use the **Hatch Angle** option to rotate the hatch, and use the **Hatch Scale** option to edit the pattern size.

Figure 23-30. Use the center hatch object grip to edit a hatch pattern. Apply one of the following methods to access context-sensitive hatch grip tools. A—Hover over the unselected grip to display a menu of options, and then pick an option from the list. B—Pick the grip and then right-click and select an option. C—Pick the grip and then press [Ctrl] to cycle through options.

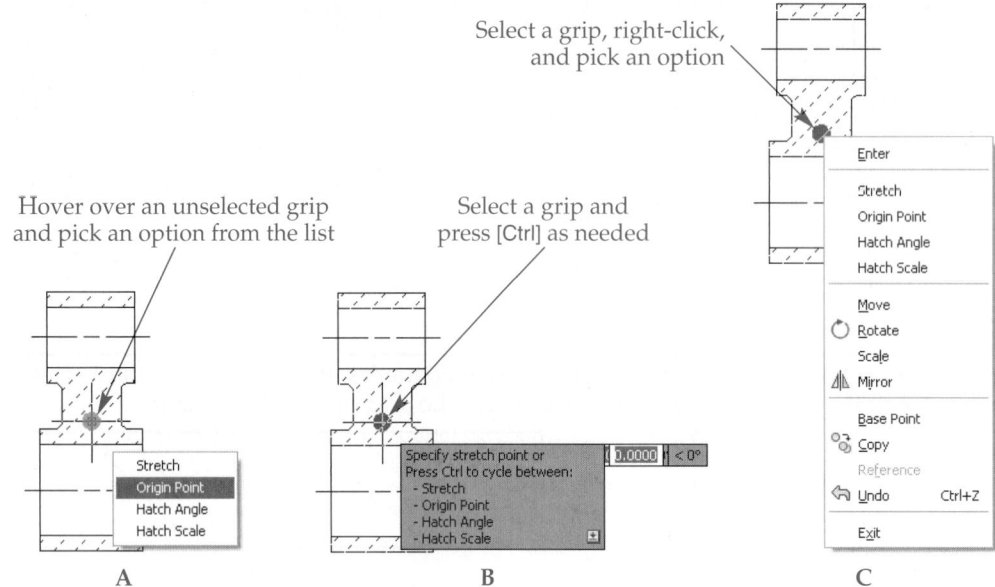

Hover over an unselected grip
and pick an option from the list

Select a grip and
press [Ctrl] as needed

Select a grip, right-click,
and pick an option

A   B   C

Editing Non-Associative Hatch Patterns

Create a non-associative hatch pattern by deselecting the **Associative Boundaries** option in the **Hatch Creation** or **Hatch Editor** ribbon tab. A non-associative hatch also forms when you move an associative hatch pattern away from or erase the associated boundary objects. The objects you reference to create a non-associative hatch pattern do not control the size and shape of the hatch. However, you can edit non-associative hatch patterns using standard and grip editing tools.

Pick a non-associative hatch object to display the center grip previously described, primary grips at each vertex, and secondary grips at the midpoint of each boundary segment. See **Figure 23-31.** Non-associative hatch grips provide the same function as the polyline context-sensitive grip tools described in Chapter 15. Use one of the options shown in **Figure 23-30** to access and apply the same context-sensitive hatch grip tools. You may be able to add a vertex to create a new line or arc, remove a vertex to eliminate a line or arc, or convert a line to an arc or an arc to a line. **Figure 23-31** shows the process of making several changes to a boundary using grip editing techniques.

PROFESSIONAL TIP

When working with associative and non-associative hatch patterns, remember that associative hatch patterns are associated with objects. The objects define the hatch boundary. Non-associative hatch patterns are not associated with objects, but they do show association with the hatch boundary.

Figure 23-31. Using the grips that appear when you select a non-associative hatch pattern. A—The original non-associative hatch. B—Moving an island out of the boundary and adjusting edge grips. C—Adjusting edge and point grips. D—Moving an island back into the boundary and adjusting edge and point grips.

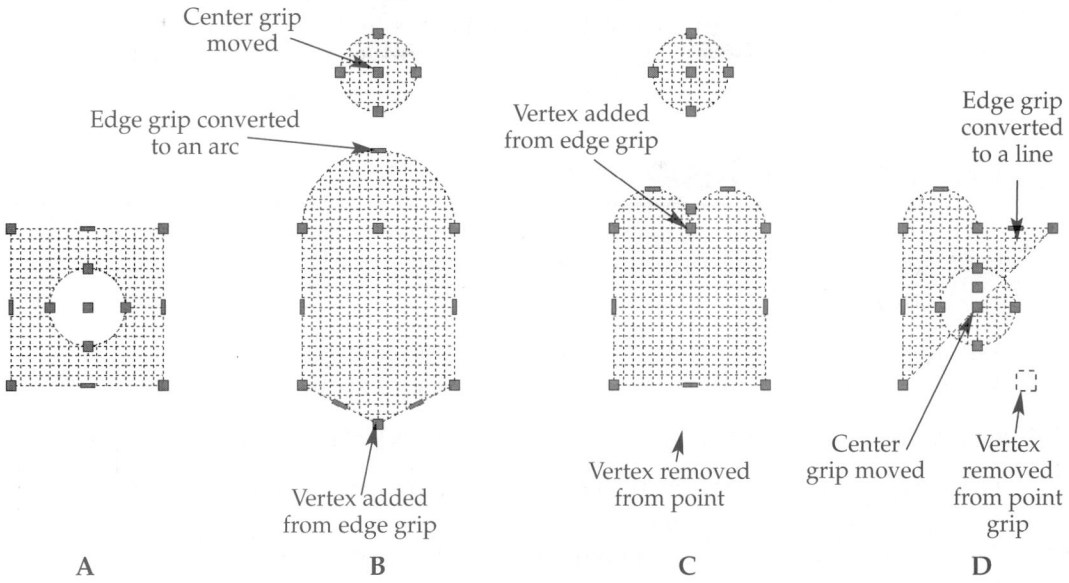

A   B   C   D

NOTE

The **MIRRHATCH** system variable is set to 0 by default. This setting prevents a hatch from reversing during a mirror operation. Change the **MIRRHATCH** value to 1 to mirror a hatch in relation to the original object. See **Figure 23-32**.

Exercise 23-11

Access the Student Web site (www.g-wlearning.com/CAD) and complete Exercise 23-11.

Figure 23-32. The **MIRRHATCH** system variable options.

Mirror line

Original Objects   MIRRHATCH=0   MIRRHATCH=1

Express Tools
Chapter 23

The **Draw** panel of the **Express Tools** ribbon tab includes a **SUPERHATCH** tool. For information about the **SUPERHATCH** tool, go to the Student Web site (www.g-wlearning.com/CAD), select this chapter, and select **The SUPERHATCH Tool**.

Chapter Test

Answer the following questions. Write your answers on a separate sheet of paper or go to the Student Web site (www.g-wlearning.com/CAD) and complete the electronic chapter test.

1. What is the AutoCAD term for standard section line symbols?
2. Which AutoCAD hatch pattern provides a general section line symbol?

For Questions 3–8, name the type of section identified in each of the following statements:

3. Half of the object is removed; the cutting-plane line generally cuts completely through along the center plane.
4. The cutting-plane line is staggered through features that do not lie in a straight line.
5. The section is turned in place to clarify the contour of the object.
6. The section is rotated and is located away from the object. A cutting-plane line normally identifies the location of the section.
7. The cutting-plane line cuts through one-quarter of the object; used primarily on symmetrical objects.
8. A small portion of the view is removed to clarify an internal feature.
9. Explain the three island detection style options.
10. Describe the basic difference between using the **Pick Points** and **Select Objects** options in the **Hatch Creation** ribbon tab.
11. How do you limit AutoCAD hatch evaluation to a specific area of the drawing?
12. What is the purpose of the **Gap Tolerance** setting in the **Hatch Creation** ribbon tab?
13. Explain how to select a hatch pattern or fill using the **Hatch Creation** ribbon tab.
14. Name the two files supplied with AutoCAD that contain hatch patterns.
15. What considerations should you take into account when choosing a hatch scale?
16. How do you change the hatch angle in the **Hatch Creation** ribbon tab?
17. What is a gradient fill? How do you create a gradient fill with the **HATCH** tool?
18. Define *associative hatch pattern*.
19. What is the result of stretching an object associated with an associative hatch pattern?
20. Explain how to use an existing hatch pattern on a drawing as the pattern for another hatch.
21. Explain how to use drag and drop to insert a hatch pattern from **DesignCenter** into an active drawing.
22. Explain two ways to use drag and drop to insert a hatch pattern from a tool palette into a drawing.
23. What is typically the easiest way to access the **Hatch Editor** ribbon tab?
24. How does the **Hatch Editor** ribbon tab compare to the **Hatch Creation** ribbon tab?
25. What happens if you erase an island inside an associative hatch pattern?

Drawing Problems

- *Start AutoCAD if it is not already started. Start a new drawing for each problem using an appropriate template of your choice.*
- *The template should include layers and text, dimension, multileader, and table styles, when necessary, for drawing the given objects. Add layers and text, dimension, multileader, and table styles as needed.*
- *Draw all objects using appropriate layers and text, dimension, multileader, and table styles, justification, and format.*
- *Follow the specific instructions for each problem. Use only drawing and editing tools and techniques you have already learned. Use your own judgment and approximate dimensions when necessary.*
- *Apply formal dimensions accurately using ASME or appropriate industry standards.*

▼ Basic

1. Draw the game board shown. Save the drawing as P23-1.

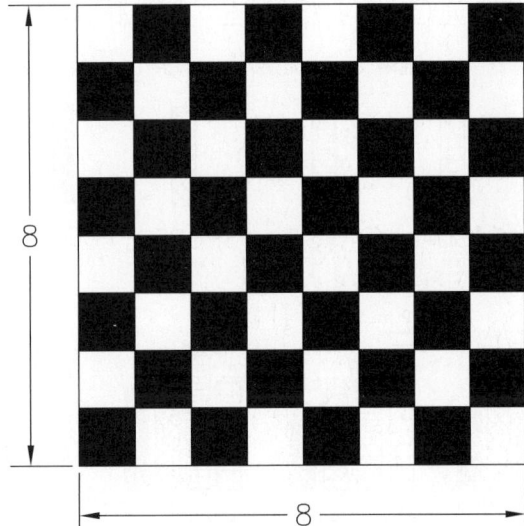

2. Draw the bar graph shown. Save the drawing as P23-2.

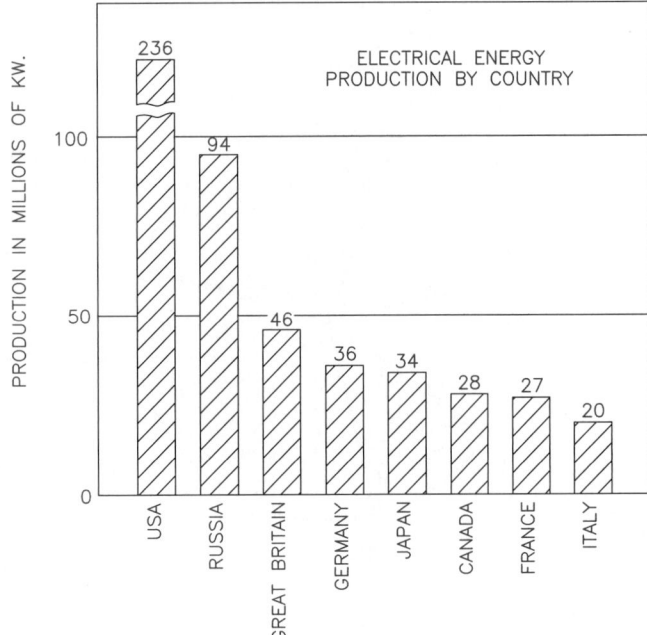

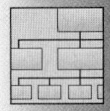

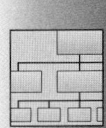

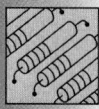

3. Draw the component layout shown. Save the drawing as P23-3.

COMPONENT LAYOUT

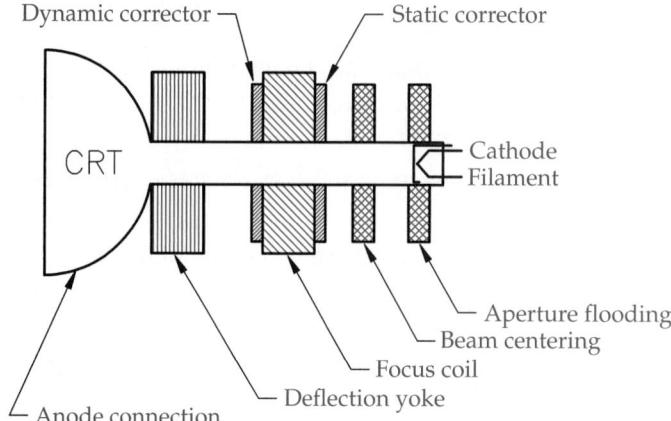

Dynamic corrector — Static corrector

CRT

Cathode
Filament

Aperture flooding
Beam centering
Focus coil
Deflection yoke
Anode connection

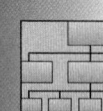

4. Draw the bar graphs shown. Save the drawing as P23-4.

SOLOMAN SHOE COMPANY

PERCENT OF TOTAL SALES EACH DIVISION

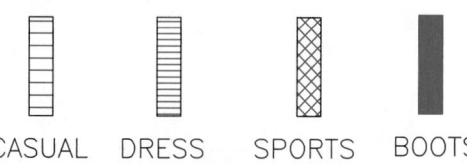

CASUAL   DRESS   SPORTS   BOOTS

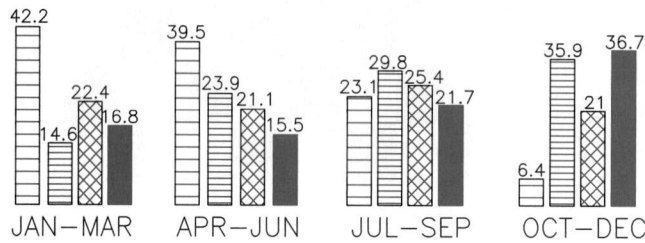

42.2
14.6   22.4   16.8
JAN—MAR

39.5
23.9   21.1   15.5
APR—JUN

23.1   29.8   25.4   21.7
JUL—SEP

35.9   36.7
6.4   21
OCT—DEC

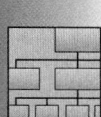

5. Draw the pie chart shown. Save the drawing as P23-5.

DIAL TECHNOLOGIES
EXPENSE BUDGET
FISCAL YEAR

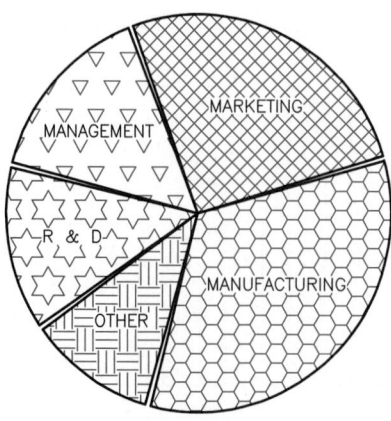

MANAGEMENT
MARKETING
R & D
MANUFACTURING
OTHER

6. Draw the bar graph shown. Save the drawing as P23-6.

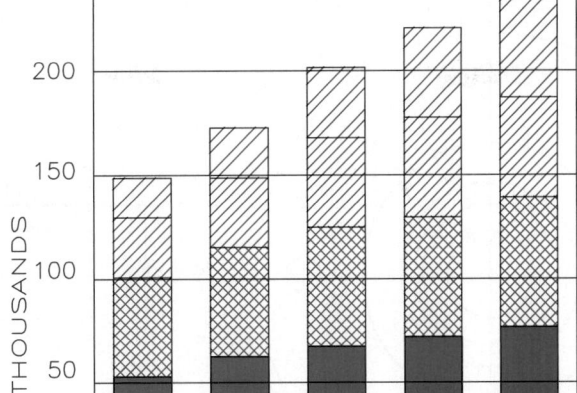

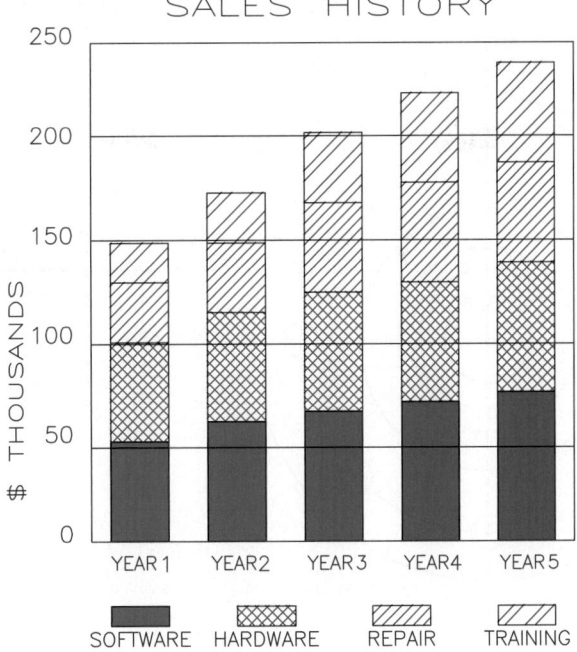

▼ Intermediate

7. Draw and dimension the views shown, which include aligned and broken-out sections. Save the drawing as P23-7.

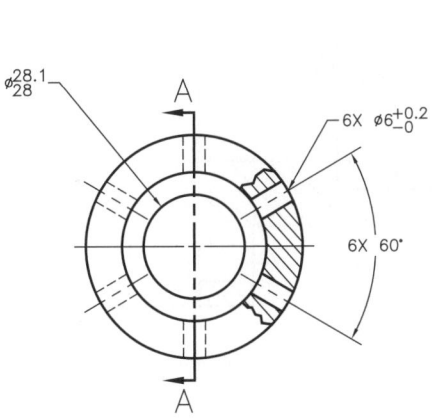

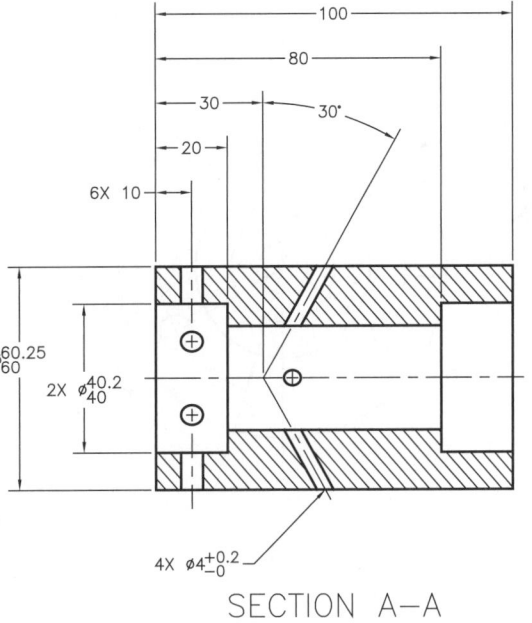

SECTION A—A

8. Draw and dimension the views shown. Save the drawing as **P23-8**.

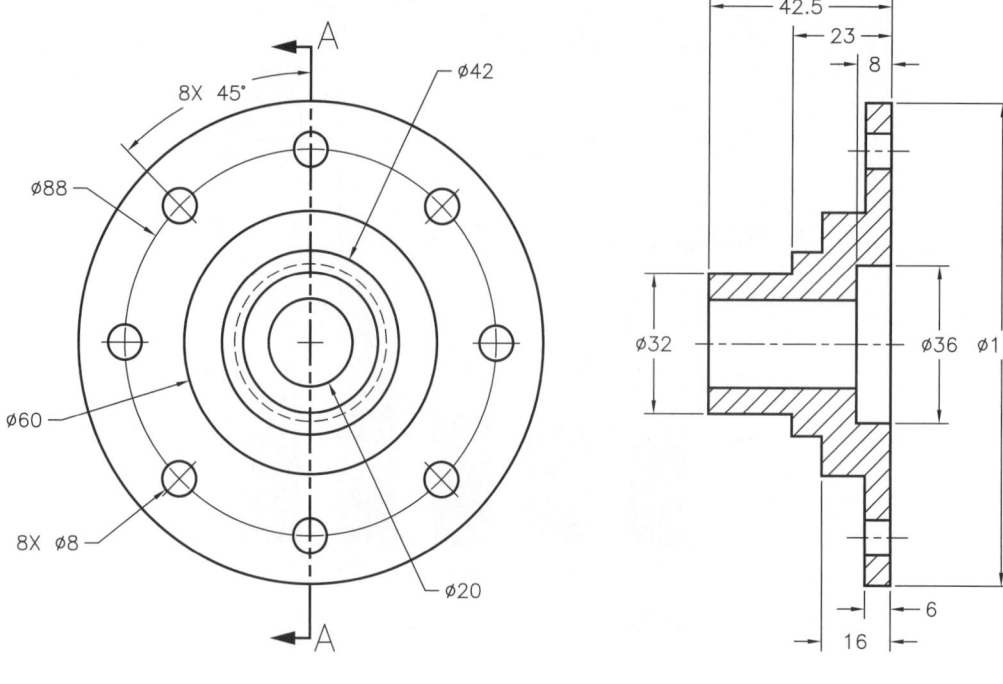

SECTION A–A

9. Draw and dimension the views shown. Save the drawing as **P23-9**.

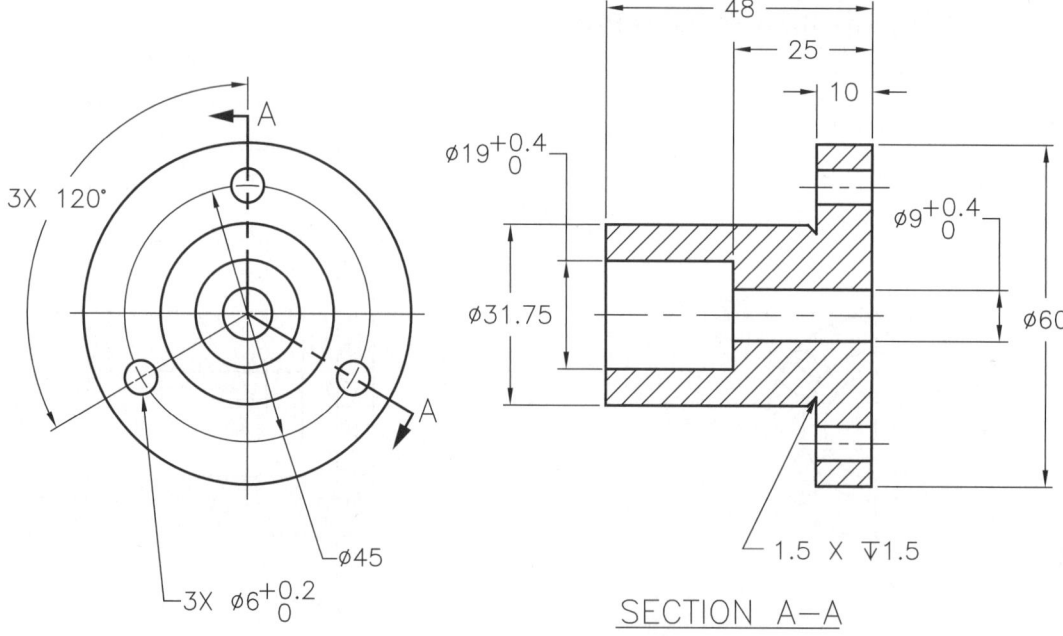

SECTION A–A

10. Draw and dimension the views of the chain guide as shown. Save the drawing as P23-10.

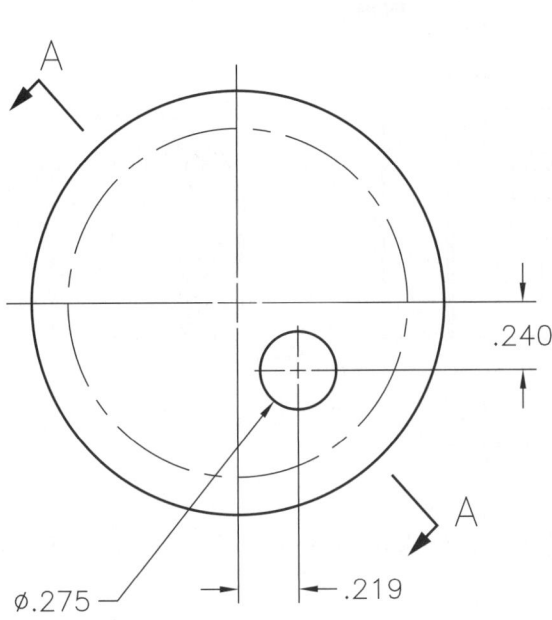

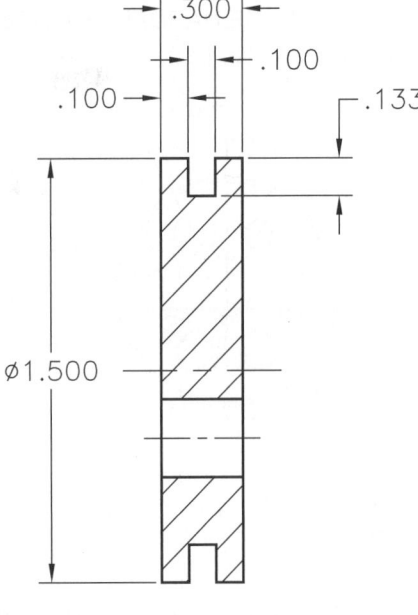

SECTION A–A

11. Draw and dimension the views of the sleeve and add the notes as shown. Save the drawing as P23-11.

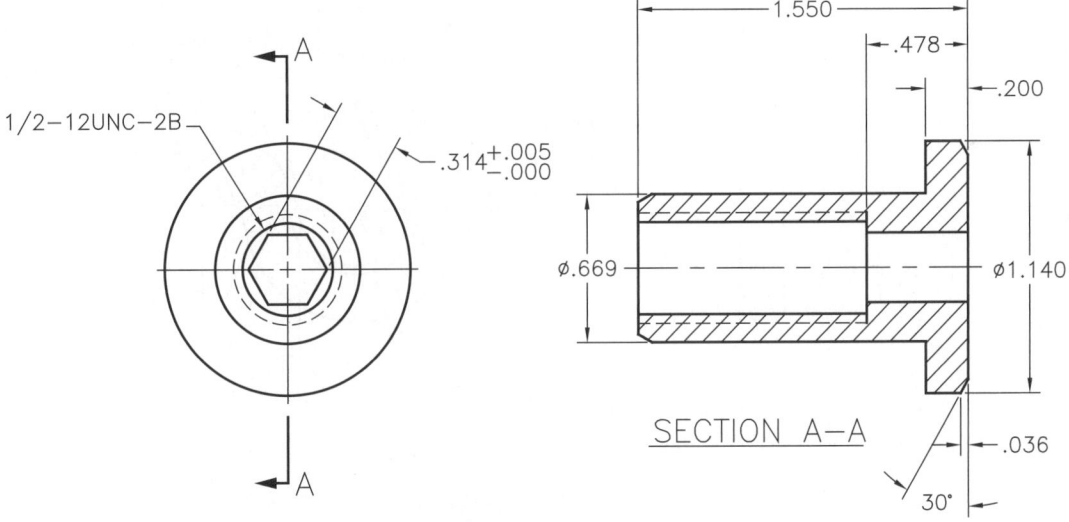

SECTION A–A

1. INTERPRET ALL DIMENSIONS AND
   TOLERANCES PER ASME Y14.5M–1994.
2. REMOVE ALL BURRS AND SHARP EDGES.
3. CASE HARDEN 45–50 ROCKWELL.
4. PAINT ACE GLOSS BLACK ALL OVER.

▼ Advanced

12. Draw and dimension the views shown. Add the following notes: OIL QUENCH 40-45C, CASE HARDEN .020 DEEP, and 59-60 ROCKWELL C SCALE. Save the drawing as P23-12.

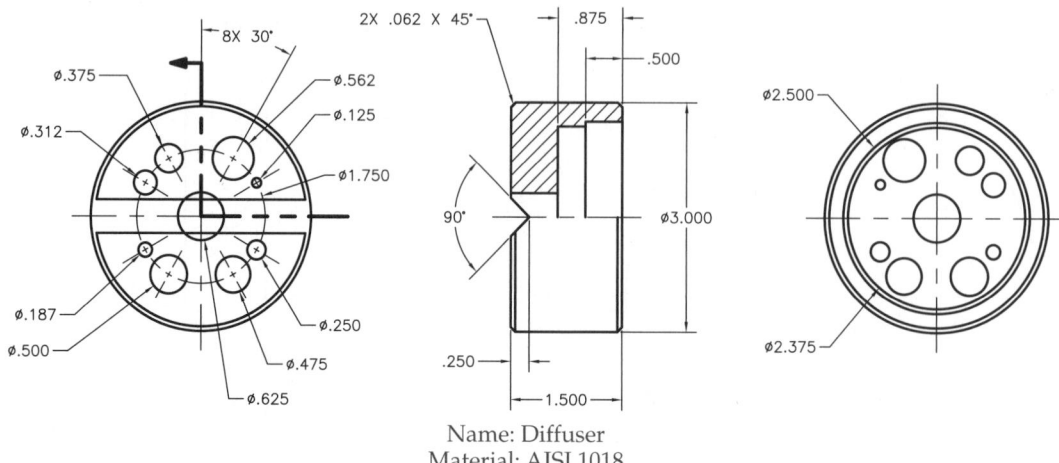

Name: Diffuser
Material: AISI 1018

13. Draw and dimension the views of the tow hook as shown. Save the drawing as P23-13.

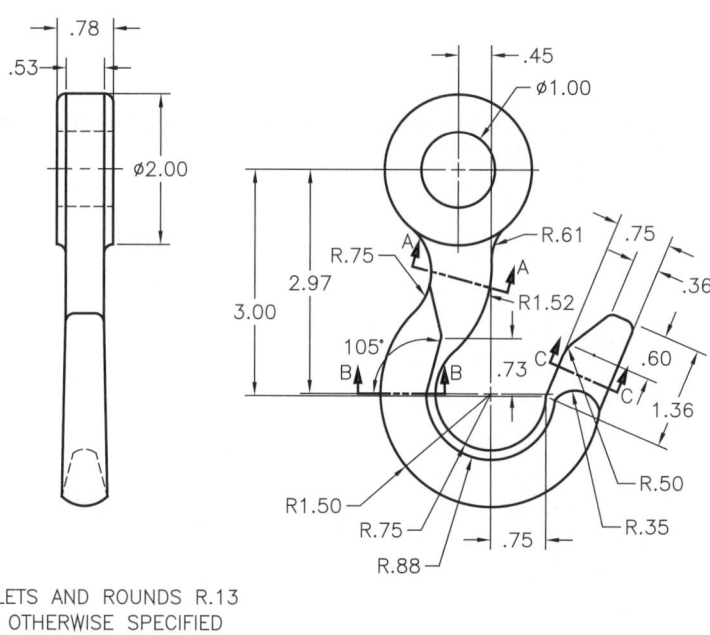

ALL FILLETS AND ROUNDS R.13
UNLESS OTHERWISE SPECIFIED

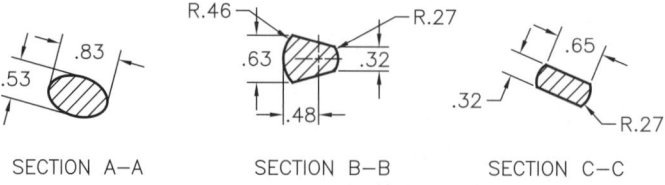

SECTION A–A   SECTION B–B   SECTION C–C

14. Draw the stair detail as shown. Save the drawing as P23-14.

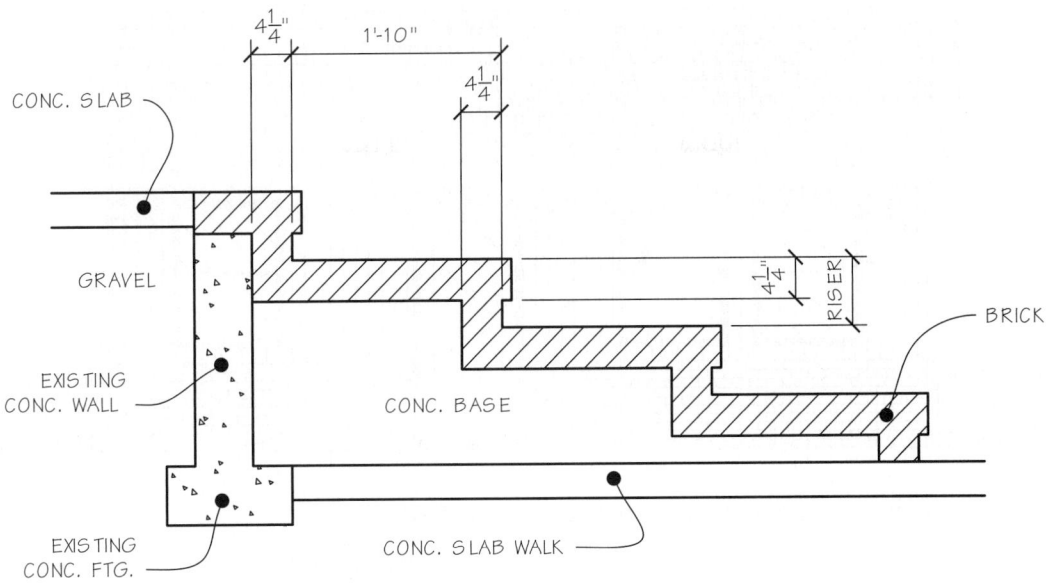

15. Draw the foundation detail shown, but make the following changes:
    A. Use the SansSerif font
    B. Use .125" leader shoulders
    C. When text is on the left side of a leader, position text at the middle of the bottom line
    D. When text is on the right side of a leader, position text at the middle of the top line
    Save the drawing as P23-15.

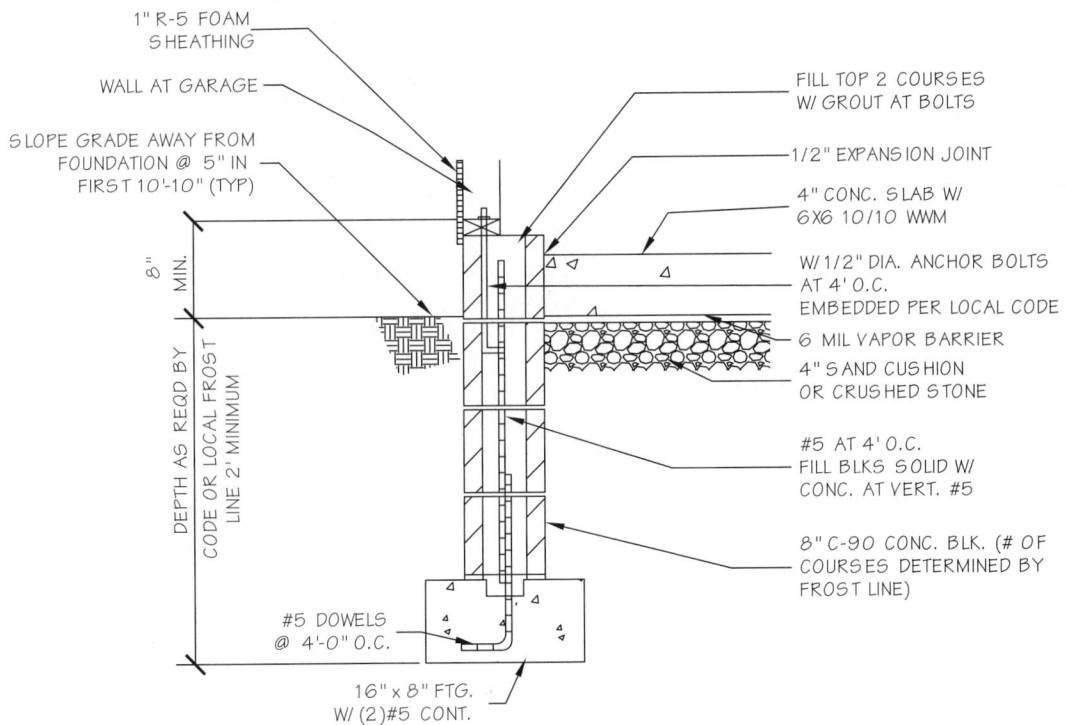

16. Draw the front elevation shown. Save the drawing as P23-16.

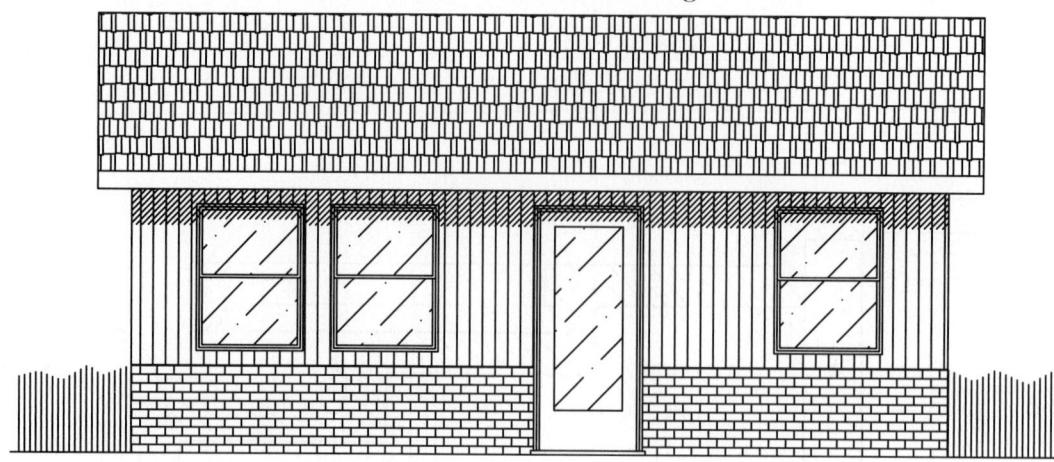

17. Draw the plan shown. Save the drawing as P23-17.

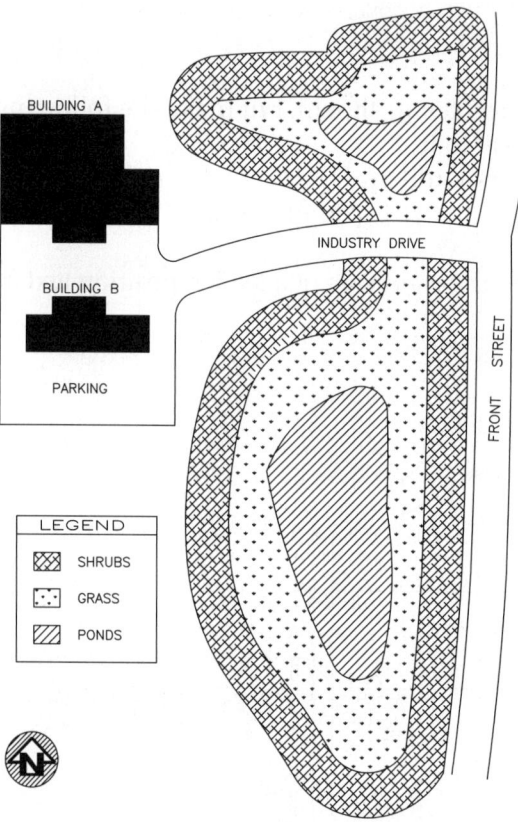

AutoCAD and Its Applications—Basics

18. Draw the plan shown. Save the drawing as P23-18.

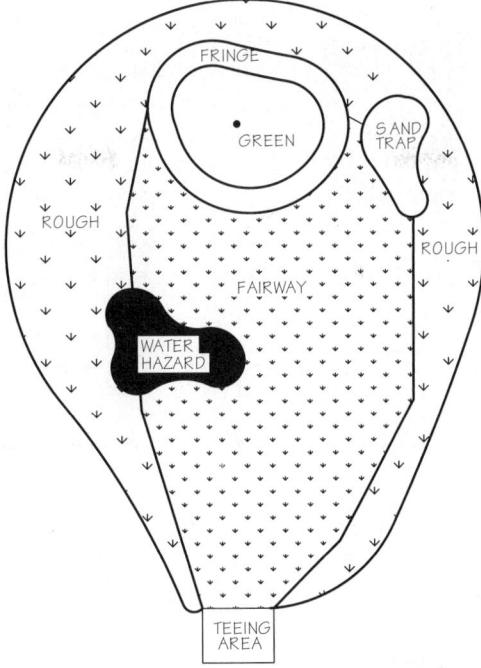

19. Draw the plan shown. Save the drawing as P23-19.

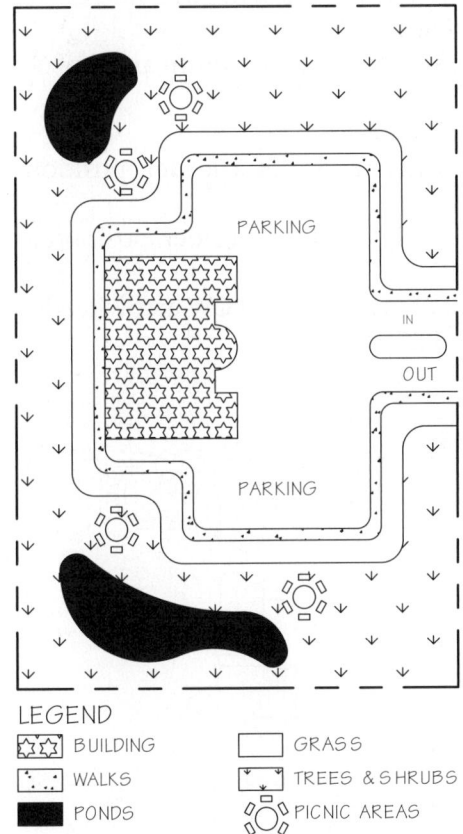

20. Draw the profile shown. Save the drawing as P23-20.

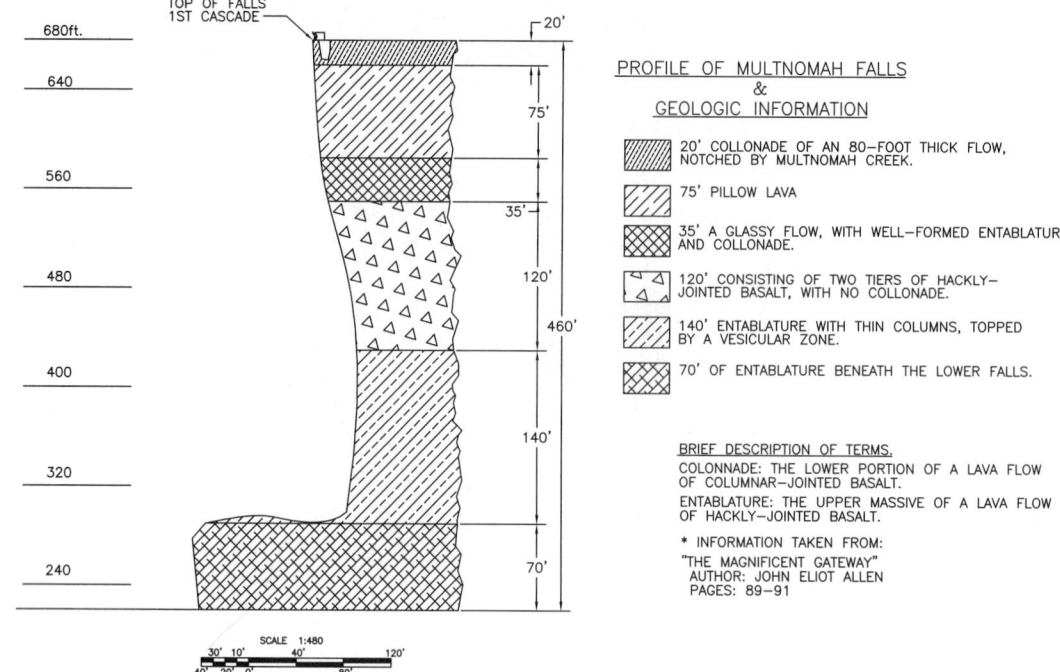

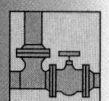

21. Draw the drop cleanout detail shown, but make the following changes:
    A. Use the SansSerif font
    B. Use diagonal leader lines at a maximum angle of 60° and a minimum angle of 30°
    C. Use .125" leader shoulders
    D. When text is on the left side of a leader, position text at the middle of the bottom line
    E. When text is on the right side of a leader, position text at the middle of the top line
    F. Use the **PLINE** tool to create the FLOW arrowheads.
    Save the drawing as P23-21.

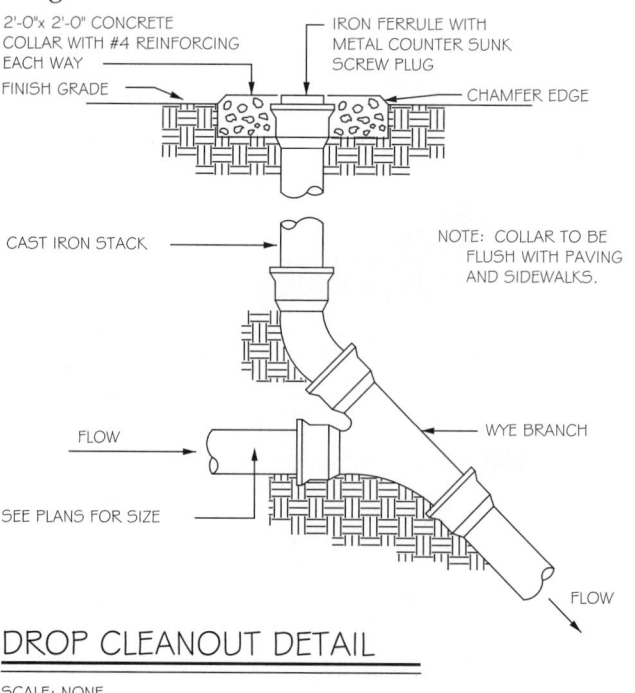

DROP CLEANOUT DETAIL

SCALE: NONE

22. Draw the map shown, using the **SPLINE** tool to create the curved shapes. Draw the map at full scale as close as possible to the map shown. Save the drawing as P23-22.

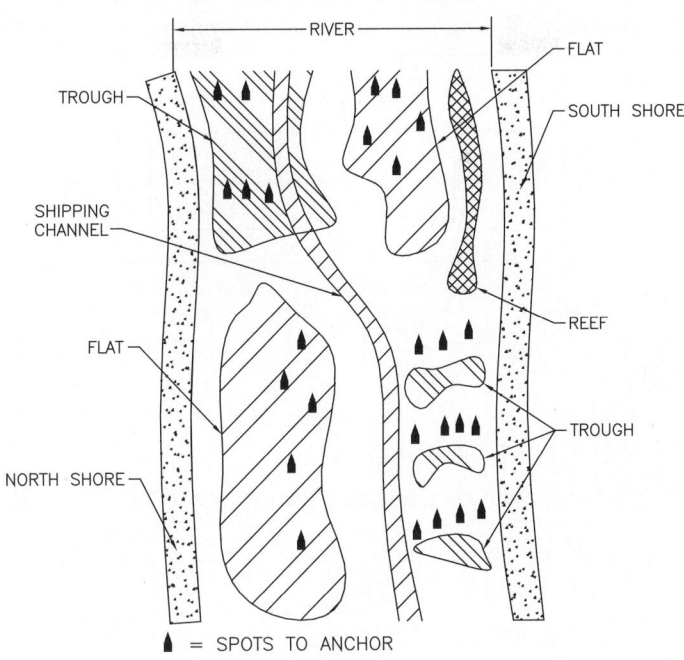

AutoCAD Certified Associate Exam Practice

Answer the following questions. Write your answers on a separate sheet of paper.

1. Which of the following sections would show all of the internal features of the part most efficiently? *Select the one item that best answers the question.*

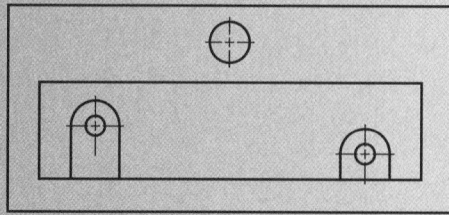

   A. broken-out section
   B. full section
   C. offset section
   D. removed section
   E. revolved section

2. Which of the following can be used as a boundary for a hatch? *Select all that apply.*

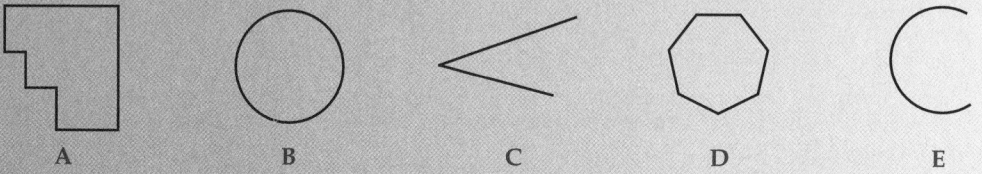

3. Which of the following options would you choose to create the hatch shown? *Select the one item that best answers the question.*
   A. **Ignore Island Detection**
   B. **No Island Detection**
   C. **Normal Island Detection**
   D. **Outer Island Detection**

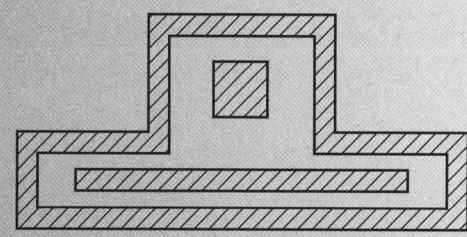

AutoCAD Certified Professional Exam Practice

Follow the instructions in each problem. Write your answers on a separate sheet of paper.

1. **Navigate to this chapter on the Student Web site and open CPE-23scale.dwg.** What is the scale of the hatch in this drawing?

2. **Navigate to this chapter on the Student Web site and open CPE-23boundary.dwg.** Recreate the boundary for the hatch. Use the boundary and the appropriate measurement tool to answer the following question: What is the total area of the hatched object?

Standard Blocks

24

Learning Objectives

After completing this chapter, you will be able to do the following:
- ✓ Create and save blocks.
- ✓ Insert blocks into a drawing.
- ✓ Edit a block and update the block in a drawing.
- ✓ Create blocks as drawing files.
- ✓ Construct and use a symbol library.
- ✓ Purge unused content from a drawing.

The ability to create and use *blocks* is a major benefit of drawing with AutoCAD. The **BLOCK** tool stores a block within a drawing as a *block definition*. The **WBLOCK** tool saves a *wblock* as a separate drawing file. You can insert blocks as often as needed and share blocks between drawings. You also have the option to scale, rotate, and adjust blocks to meet specific drawing requirements.

block: A symbol saved and stored in a drawing for future use.

block definition: Information about a block stored within the drawing file.

wblock: A block definition saved as a separate drawing file.

Constructing Blocks

A block can consist of any object or group of objects, including annotation, or can be an entire drawing. Review each drawing and project to identify items you can use more than once. Screws, punches, subassemblies, plumbing fixtures, and appliances are examples of items to consider converting to blocks. Draw the objects once and then save them as a block for multiple use.

Selecting a Layer

Identify the appropriate layer on which to create block elements before drawing the objects. To do this, you must understand how layers and object properties apply when using blocks. The 0 layer is the preferred layer on which to draw block objects. If you originally create block objects on the 0 layer, the block inherits the properties of the layer you assign to the block. Draw the objects for all blocks on the 0 layer and then assign the appropriate layer to each block when you insert the block. If you draw block objects on a layer other than layer 0, place all the objects on layer 0 before creating the block.

A second method is to create block objects using one or more layers other than layer 0. If you originally create block objects on a layer other than layer 0, the block belongs to the layer you assign to the block, but the objects retain the properties of the layers you use to create the objects. The difference is only noticeable if you place the block on a layer other than the layer you use to draw the block objects.

A third technique is to create block objects using the ByBlock color, linetype, lineweight, and transparency. If you originally create block objects using ByBlock properties, the block belongs to the layer you assign to the block, but the objects take on the color, linetype, lineweight, and transparency you assign to the block, regardless of the layer on which you place the block. Using the ByBlock setting is only noticeable if you assign absolute values to the block using the properties in the **Properties** panel of the **Home** ribbon tab or the **Properties** palette.

Another option is to create block objects using an absolute color, linetype, lineweight, and transparency. If you originally create block objects using absolute values, such as a Blue color, a Continuous linetype, a 0.05mm lineweight, and a 50 transparency value, the block belongs to the layer you assign to the block, but the objects display the specified absolute values regardless of the properties assigned to the drawing or the layer on which you place the block.

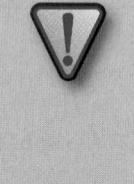

CAUTION

Drawing block objects on a layer other than layer 0, or using ByBlock or absolute properties, can cause significant confusion. The result is often a situation in which a block belongs to a layer, but the block objects display properties of a different layer, or absolute values. In most cases, you should draw block objects on layer 0, and then assign a specific layer to each block.

Drawing Block Elements

Draw the elements of a block as you would any other geometry. If you plan to define a block as annotative, to scale the block according to the drawing scale, you can include annotative or non-annotative objects, such as text, with the block. As long as you specify the block as annotative, all objects act annotative, even if some objects are non-annotative. However, you must use non-annotative objects when preparing a non-annotative block.

insertion base point: The point on a block that defines where the block is positioned during insertion.

When you finish drawing the objects, determine the best location for the *insertion base point*. When you insert the block into a drawing, the insertion base point positions the block. **Figure 24-1** shows examples of common blocks and a possible insertion base point for each.

PROFESSIONAL TIP

A single block allows you to create multiple features that are identical except for scale. In these cases, draw the base block to fit inside a one-unit square. This makes it easy to scale the block when you insert it into a drawing to create variations of the block.

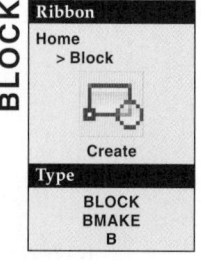

BLOCK

Ribbon
Home
> Block

Create

Type
BLOCK
BMAKE
B

Creating Blocks

Once you draw objects and identify an appropriate insertion base point, you are ready to save the objects as a block. Use the **BLOCK** tool and the corresponding **Block Definition** dialog box to create a block. See **Figure 24-2.**

Figure 24-1. Common drafting symbols and their insertion points for placement on drawings. Colored grips indicate the insertion points.

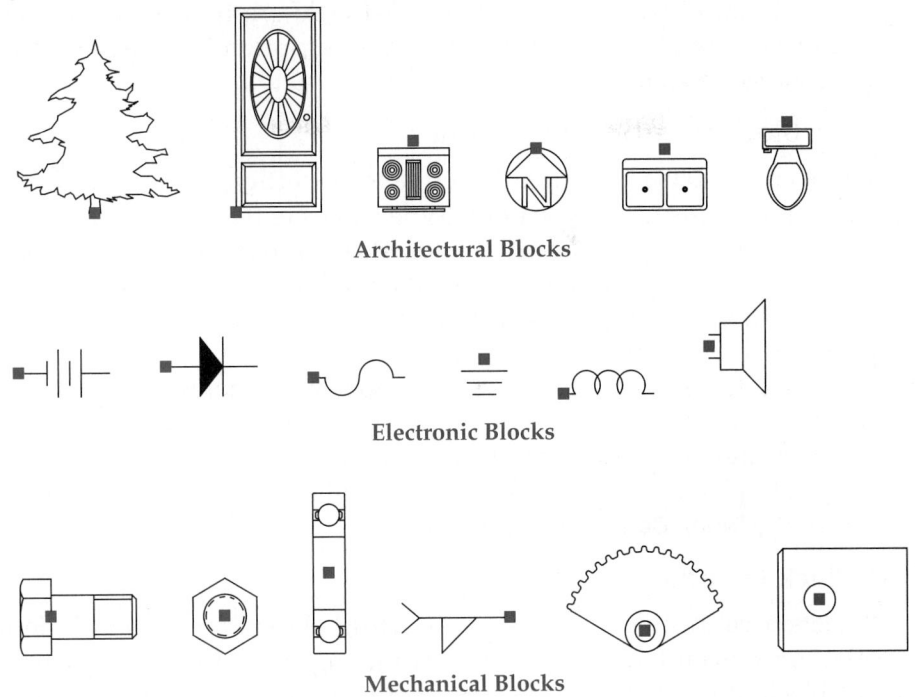

Architectural Blocks

Electronic Blocks

Mechanical Blocks

Figure 24-2. Use the **Block Definition** dialog box to create a block.

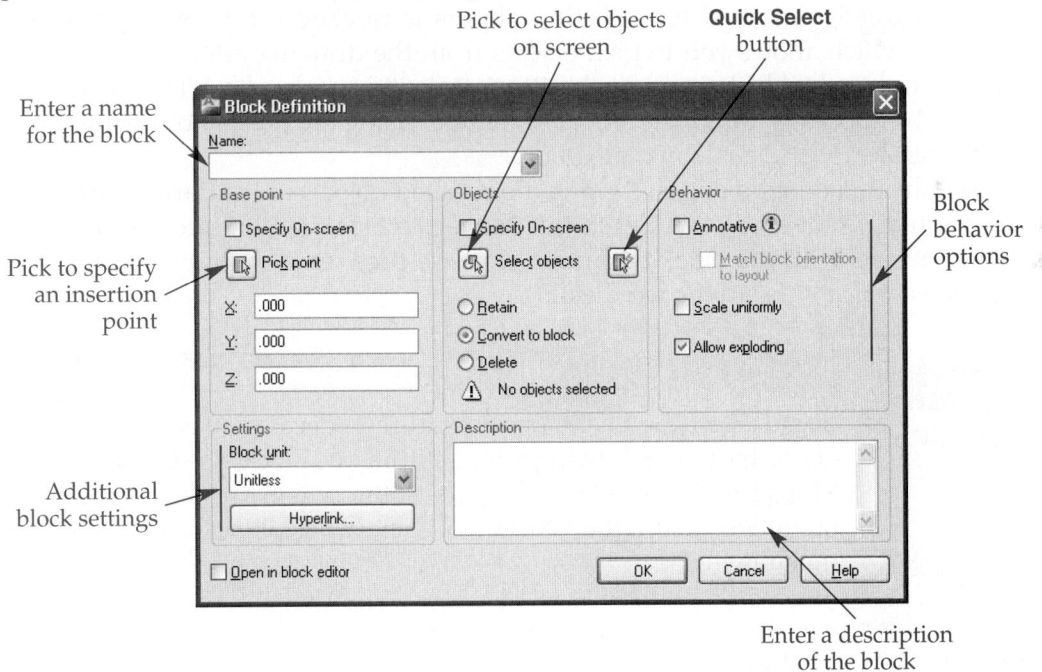

Pick to select objects on screen

Quick Select button

Enter a name for the block

Pick to specify an insertion point

Additional block settings

Block behavior options

Enter a description of the block

Naming and Describing the Block

Enter a descriptive name for the block in the **Name:** text box. For example, name a vacuum pump PUMP or a 3′ × 6′-8″ door DOOR_3068. The block name cannot exceed 255 characters. It can include numbers, letters, spaces, the dollar sign ($), hyphen (-), and underscore (_). Use the drop-down list to access an existing name to recreate a block or to use a block name as reference when naming a new block with a similar name.

A block name is often descriptive enough to identify the block. However, you can enter a description of the block in the **Description:** text box to help identify the block. For example, the PUMP block might include the description This is a vacuum pump symbol, or the DOOR_3068 block might include the description This is a plan view, 3′ wide by 6′-8″ tall, interior, single-swing door.

Defining the Block Insertion Base Point

Use options in the **Base point** area to define the insertion base point. If you know the coordinates for the insertion base point, type values in the **X:**, **Y:**, and **Z:** text boxes. However, often the best way to specify the insertion base point is to use object snap to select a point on an object. Choose the **Pick point** button to return to the drawing and select an insertion base point. The **Block Definition** dialog box reappears after you select the insertion base point.

An alternative technique is to choose the **Specify On-screen** check box, which allows you to pick an insertion base point in the drawing after you pick the **OK** button to create the block and exit the **Block Definition** dialog box. This method can save time by allowing you to pick the insertion base point without using the **Pick point** button and re-entering the **Block Definition** dialog box.

Selecting Block Objects

The **Objects** area includes options for selecting objects for the block definition. Pick the **Select objects** button to return to the drawing and select the objects that will compose the block. Press [Enter] or the space bar or right-click to redisplay the **Block Definition** dialog box. The number of selected objects appears in the **Objects** area, and an image of the selection appears next to the **Name:** drop-down list. To create a selection set, use the **QuickSelect** button and **Quick Select** dialog box to define a filter.

An alternative method for selecting objects is to choose the **Specify On-screen** check box, which allows you to pick objects from the drawing after you pick the **OK** button to create the block and exit the **Block Definition** dialog box. This method can save time by allowing you to select objects without using the **Select objects** button and re-entering the **Block Definition** dialog box.

Pick the **Retain** radio button to keep the selected objects in the current drawing in their original, unblocked state. Select the **Convert to block** radio button to replace the selected objects with the block definition. Choose the **Delete** radio button to remove the selected objects after defining the block.

PROFESSIONAL TIP

If you select the **Delete** option and then decide to keep the original geometry in the drawing after defining the block, use the **OOPS** tool. This returns the original objects to the screen and keeps the block definition. Using the **UNDO** tool removes the block definition from the drawing.

Block Scale Settings

Pick the **Annotative** check box in the **Behavior** area to make the block annotative. AutoCAD scales annotative blocks according to the annotation scale you select, which eliminates the need for you to calculate the scale factor. The **Match block orientation to layout** check box becomes enabled when you select the **Annotative** check box. Pick this check box to keep annotative blocks planar to the layout in a floating viewport, even if the drawing view rotates, such as if you rotate the UCS. Selecting the **Match block orientation to layout** option also prohibits you from using the **ROTATE** tool to rotate a block.

If you check **Scale uniformly** in the **Behavior** area, you do not have the option of specifying different X and Y scale factors when you insert the block. You will learn options for scaling blocks later in this chapter.

Additional Block Definition Settings

If you check **Allow exploding** in the **Behavior** area, you have the option of exploding the block. If you do not check **Allow exploding**, you cannot explode the block after inserting it. Select a unit type from the **Block unit** drop-down list in the **Settings** area to specify the insertion units of the block. Pick the **Hyperlink...** button to access the **Insert Hyperlink** dialog box to insert a hyperlink in the block. If you check **Open in block editor**, the new block immediately opens in the **Block Definition Editor** when you create the block and exit the **Block Definition** dialog box. The **Block Definition Editor** is described later in this chapter.

NOTE

To verify that a block has been saved properly, reopen the **Block Definition** dialog box. Pick the **Name:** drop-down list to display a list of blocks in the current drawing.

PROFESSIONAL TIP

You can use blocks to create other blocks. Insert existing blocks into a view and then save all of the objects as a block. This is a process known as *nesting*. You must give the top-level block a name that is different from any nested block. Proper planning and knowledge of all existing blocks can speed up the drawing process and the creation of complex views.

nesting: Creating a block that includes other blocks.

Exercise 24-1

Access the Student Web site (www.g-wlearning.com/CAD) and complete Exercise 24-1.

Inserting Blocks

block reference: A specific instance of a block inserted into a drawing.

AutoCAD provides several options for inserting a block into a drawing. Remember to make the layer you want to assign to the block current before inserting the block. You should also determine the proper size and rotation angle for the block before insertion. The term *block reference* describes an inserted block. *Dependent symbols* are any named objects, such as blocks and layers. AutoCAD automatically updates dependent symbols in a drawing the next time you open the drawing.

dependent symbols: Named objects in a drawing that have been inserted or referenced into another drawing.

Using the INSERT Tool

The **INSERT** tool provides a common method for inserting a block into a drawing. Access the **INSERT** tool to display the **Insert** dialog box. See **Figure 24-3**.

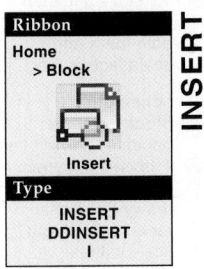

Ribbon
Home
> Block

Insert

Type

INSERT
DDINSERT
I

INSERT

Figure 24-3. The **Insert** dialog box allows you to select and prepare a block for insertion. Select a block from the drop-down list or enter the block name in the **Name:** text box.

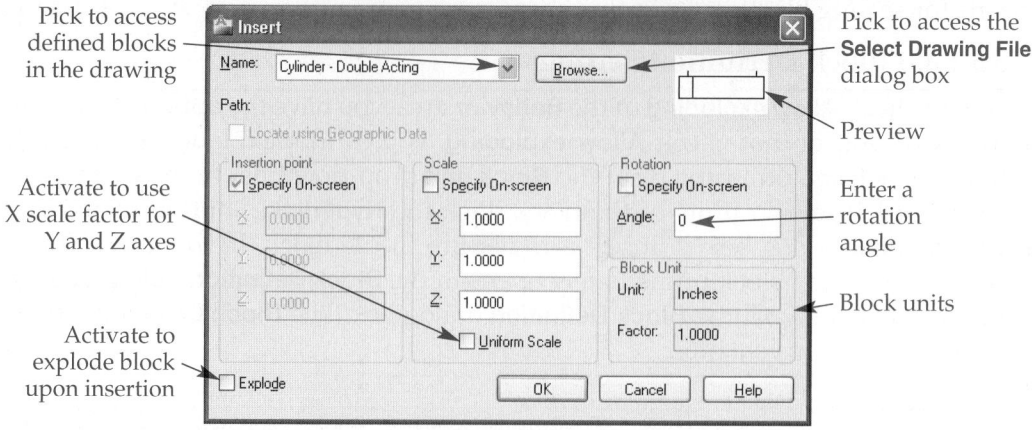

Pick to access defined blocks in the drawing

Activate to use X scale factor for Y and Z axes

Activate to explode block upon insertion

Pick to access the **Select Drawing File** dialog box

Preview

Enter a rotation angle

Block units

Selecting the Block to Insert

Use the **Name:** drop-down list to show the blocks defined in the current drawing and select the name of the block you want to insert. You can also type the name of the block in the **Name:** text box. Another option is to pick the **Browse...** button to display the **Select Drawing File** dialog box. This allows you to locate and select a drawing or DXF file (wblock) to insert as a block. Inserting a file as a block is described later in this chapter.

Specifying the Block Insertion Point

The **Insertion point** area contains options for specifying where to insert the block. Select the **Specify On-screen** check box to specify a location in the drawing when you pick the **OK** button. To insert the block using absolute coordinates, deselect the **Specify On-screen** check box and enter coordinates in the **X:**, **Y:**, and **Z:** text boxes.

Scaling Blocks

The **Scale** area allows you to specify scale values for the block in relation to the X, Y, and Z axes. Deselect the **Specify On-screen** check box to enter scale values in the **X:**, **Y:**, and **Z:** text boxes. Activate the **Uniform Scale** check box to specify a scale value for the X axis that also applies to the scale of the Y and Z axes. The **X** value is the only active axis value if you created the block with **Scale uniformly** checked in the **Block Definition** dialog box. Select the **Specify On-screen** check box to receive prompts for scaling the block during insertion.

It is possible to create a mirror image of a block by entering negative scale factor values. For example, enter –1 for the X and Y scale factor to mirror the block to the opposite quadrant of the original orientation, but retain the original size. **Figure 24-4** shows different scale and mirroring techniques.

Blocks are classified as real blocks, schematic blocks, or unit blocks, depending on how you scale the block during insertion. Examples of *real blocks* include a bolt, a bathtub, a pipe fitting, and the car shown in **Figure 24-5A.** Examples of *schematic blocks* include notes, detail bubbles, tags, and section symbols. See **Figure 24-5B.** Schematic blocks typically include annotative blocks. When you insert an annotative schematic block, AutoCAD automatically determines the block scale based on the annotation scale. When you insert a non-annotative schematic block, you must specify the scale factor.

real block: A block originally drawn at a 1:1 scale and then inserted using 1 for both the X and Y scale factors.

schematic block: A block originally drawn at a 1:1 scale and then inserted using the drawing scale factor for both the X and Y scale values.

AutoCAD and Its Applications—Basics

Figure 24-4. Negative and positive scale factors have different effects when used to insert a block. Colored grips indicate the insertion points.

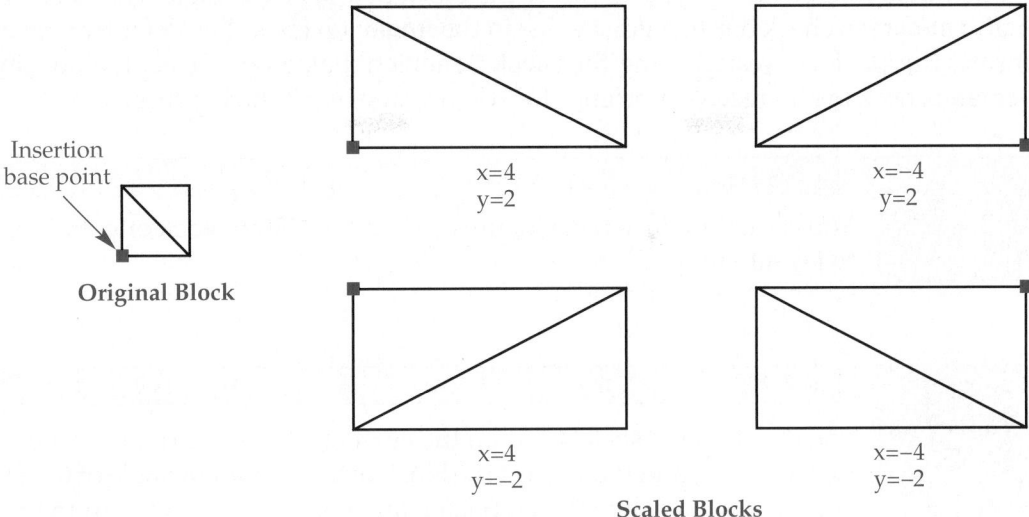

Insertion base point

Original Block

x=4
y=2

x=−4
y=2

x=4
y=−2

x=−4
y=−2

Scaled Blocks

Figure 24-5. A—Real blocks, such as this car, are drawn at full scale and inserted using a scale factor of 1 for both the X and Y axes. B—A schematic block is inserted using the scale factor of the drawing for the X and Y axes. C—A 2D unit block is often inserted at different scales for the X and Y axes.

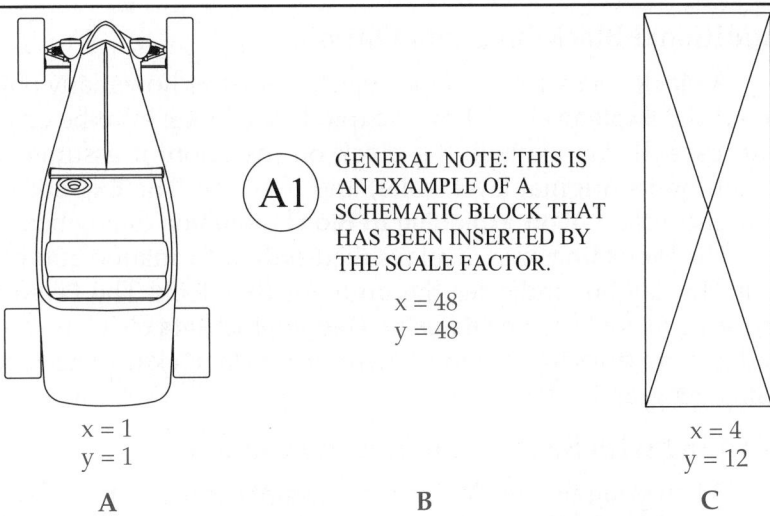

A1

GENERAL NOTE: THIS IS AN EXAMPLE OF A SCHEMATIC BLOCK THAT HAS BEEN INSERTED BY THE SCALE FACTOR.

x = 48
y = 48

x = 1
y = 1

x = 4
y = 12

A

B

C

NOTE

For most applications, insert annotative blocks at a scale of 1 to apply the annotation scale correctly. Entering a scale other than 1 adjusts the scale of the block by multiplying the scale value by the annotative scale factor.

unit block: A 1D, 2D, or 3D block drawn to fit in a 1-unit, 1-unit-square, or 1-unit-cubed area so that it can be scaled easily.

1D unit block: A 1-unit, one-dimensional object, such as a straight line segment, saved as a block.

2D unit block: A 2D object that fits into a 1-unit × 1-unit square, saved as a block.

3D unit block: A 3D object that fits into a 1-unit × 1-unit × 1-unit cube, saved as a block.

There are three general types of *unit blocks*. An example of a *1D unit block* is a 1″ blocked line object. An example of a *2D unit block* is a 1″ × 1″ square. A *3D unit block* is any blocked object that can fit inside a 1-unit × 1-unit × 1-unit (1″ × 1″ × 1″ for example) cube. To use a unit block, insert the block and determine the individual scale factors for each axis. For example, insert a 1″ 1D unit block line at a scale of 4 to create a 4″ line. When inserting a 2D unit block, assign different scale factors for the X and Y axes to change the block dimensions. For example, specify 4 for the X axis and 12 for the Y axis to create the 4″ × 12″ beam shown in **Figure 24-5C**. A 3D unit block allows you to adjust the scale of the X, Y, and Z axes.

Rotating Blocks

The **Rotation** area allows you to insert the block at a specific angle. Deselect the **Specify On-screen** check box to enter a value in the **Angle:** text box. The default angle of 0° inserts the block as created using the **Block Definition** dialog box. Select the **Specify On-screen** check box to receive a prompt for rotating the block during insertion.

NOTE

You cannot rotate a block defined using the **Match block orientation to layout** option.

PROFESSIONAL TIP

You can rotate a block based on the current UCS. Be sure the proper UCS is active, and then insert the block using a rotation angle of 0°. If you decide to change the UCS later, any inserted blocks retain their original angle.

Additional Block Insertion Options

A block is saved as a single object, no matter how many objects the block includes. Select the **Explode** check box to explode the block into the original objects for editing purposes. If you explode the block on insertion, it assumes its original properties, including its original layer, color, and linetype. The **Explode** check box is disabled if you unchecked **Allow exploding** in **Block Definition** dialog box.

The **Block Unit** area displays read-only information about the selected block. The **Unit:** display box indicates the units for the block. The **Factor:** display box indicates the scale factor. The **Locate using Geographic Data** check box is active when the block and current drawing include *geographic data*. Pick the check box to position the block using geographic data.

> **geographic data:** Information added to a drawing to describe specific locations and directions on Earth.

Working with Specify On-Screen Prompts

When you pick the **OK** button, prompts appear for any values defined as **Specify On-screen** in the **Insert** dialog box. If you specify the insertion point on-screen, the Specify insertion point or [Basepoint/Scale/X/Y/Z/Rotate/PScale/PX/PY/PZ/PRotate]: prompt appears. Enter or select a point to insert the block. The options allow you to specify a different base point; enter a value for the overall scale; enter independent scale factors for the X, Y, and Z axes; enter a rotation angle; and preview the scale of the X, Y, and Z axes or the rotation angle before entering actual values. If you use one of these options, the new value overrides the related setting in the **Insert** dialog box.

If you specify the X scale factor on-screen, the Enter X scale factor, specify opposite corner, or [Corner/XYZ] <1>: prompt appears. Pick a point or enter a value for the scale. You can also use the **Corner** option to scale the block. The Enter Y scale factor <use X scale factor>: prompt appears if you enter an X scale factor. Specify a value different from the X scale factor, or press [Enter] or the space bar, or right-click to accept the same scale specified for the X axis.

The X and Y scale factors allow you to stretch or compress the block to create modified versions of the block. See **Figure 24-6**. This is why it is a good idea to draw blocks to fit inside a one-unit square when appropriate. It makes the block easy to scale because you can enter the exact number of units for the X and Y dimensions. For example, if you want the block to be three units long and two units high, enter 3 when prompted to enter the X scale factor, and enter 2 when prompted to enter the Y scale factor.

Figure 24-6. A comparison of different X and Y scale factors used for inserting a 2D unit block. This example shows a block of a plan view window symbol inserted into a 6″ wall.

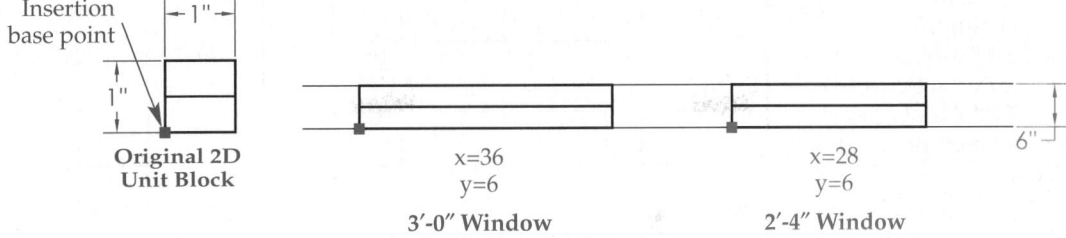

The insertion base point specified when the block was created may not always be the best point when you actually insert the block. Instead of inserting and then moving the block, use the **Basepoint** option to specify a different base point before locating the block. Select the **Basepoint** option when prompted to specify the insertion point. The block temporarily appears on-screen, allowing you to choose an alternate insertion base point. The block reattaches to the crosshairs at the new point and a message appears indicating that the tool is resuming, allowing you to pick the insertion point in the drawing.

Exercise 24-2

Access the Student Web site (www.g-wlearning.com/CAD) and complete Exercise 24-2.

Inserting Multiple Arranged Copies of a Block

The **MINSERT** tool combines the functions of the **INSERT** and **ARRAY** tools. **Figure 24-7** shows an example of an **MINSERT** tool application. To follow this example, set architectural units, draw a 4′ × 3′ rectangle, and save the rectangle as a block named DESK. Then access the **MINSERT** tool and enter DESK. Pick a point as the insertion point and then accept the X scale factor of 1, the Y scale factor of use X scale factor, and the rotation angle of 0. The arrangement is to be three rows and four columns. In order to make the horizontal spacing between desks 2′ and the vertical spacing 4′, you must consider the size of the desk when entering the distance between rows and columns. Enter 7′ (3′ desk depth + 4′ space between desks) at the Enter distance between rows of specify unit cell: prompt. Enter 6′ (4′ desk width + 2′ space between desks) at the Specify distance between columns: prompt.

The complete pattern takes on the characteristics of a block, except that you cannot explode the pattern. Therefore, you must use the **Properties** palette to modify the number of rows and columns, change the spacing between objects, or change other properties. If you rotate the initial block, all objects in the pattern rotate about their insertion points. If you rotate the patterned objects about the insertion point while using the **MINSERT** tool, all objects align on that point.

Type
MINSERT

Exercise 24-3

Access the Student Web site (www.g-wlearning.com/CAD) and complete Exercise 24-3.

Figure 24-7.
Creating an arrangement of desks using the **MINSERT** tool. An alternative is to use the **ARRAY** tool after you position one block.

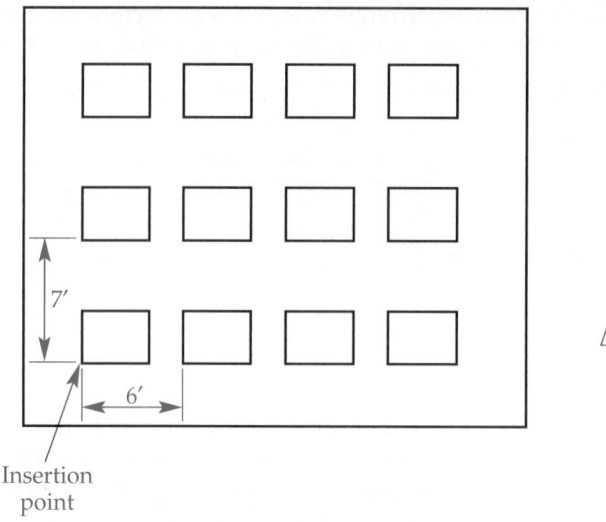

Insertion point

Insertion base point

Inserting Entire Drawings

The **INSERT** tool also allows you to insert an entire drawing into the current drawing as a block. Access the **INSERT** tool and pick the **Browse...** button in the **Insert** dialog box. Use the **Select Drawing File** dialog box to select a drawing or DXF file to insert.

When you insert a drawing into another drawing, the inserted drawing becomes a block reference and functions as a single object. The drawing is inserted on the current layer, but only objects drawn on the 0 layer inherit the color, linetype, lineweight, and transparency properties of the current layer. Explode the inserted drawing if necessary. Once exploded, the objects revert to their original layers. Inserting a drawing brings any existing block definitions and other drawing content, such as layers and dimension styles, into the current drawing.

By default, every drawing has an insertion base point of 0,0,0 when you insert it into another drawing. To change the insertion base point of the drawing, access the **BASE** tool and select a new insertion base point. Save the drawing before inserting it into another drawing.

When inserting a drawing as a block, you have the option of using the existing drawing to create a block with a different name. For example, to define a block named BOLT from an existing drawing named Fastener.dwg, access the **INSERT** tool and use the **Browse...** button to select the Fastener.dwg file. Use the **Name:** text box to change the name from Fastener to BOLT, and pick the **OK** button. You can then insert the file into the drawing or press [Esc] to exit the tool. A BOLT block definition is now available for use.

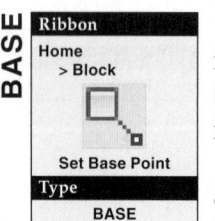

BASE

Ribbon
Home
> Block

Set Base Point
Type
BASE

Exercise 24-4

Access the Student Web site (www.g-wlearning.com/CAD) and complete Exercise 24-4.

Insert Blocks Using DesignCenter

DesignCenter provides an effective way to insert blocks or entire drawings as blocks in the current drawing. To insert a block using **DesignCenter**, use the folder list to locate and select a file containing the block to be inserted. Select the **Blocks** branch in the folder list or double-click on the **Blocks** icon in the content pane to display blocks defined in the file. See **Figure 24-8**. The most effective technique to transfer a block from **DesignCenter** to the active drawing is to use a drag-and-drop operation. Press and hold down the pick button on the block and drag the cursor to the drawing window. The block attaches to the cursor at the insertion base point. Release the pick button to insert the block at the location of the cursor.

An alternative to the drag-and-drop method is copy and paste. Right-click on a block in **DesignCenter** and pick **Copy**. Move the cursor into the active drawing, right-click, and select **Paste** from the **Clipboard** cascading submenu. The block attaches to the cursor at the insertion base point. Specify a point to insert the block. You can also use **DesignCenter** with the **Insert** dialog box. Right-click on a block in **DesignCenter** and select **Insert Block…** to access the **Insert** dialog box with the selected block active. This technique allows you to scale, rotate, or explode the block during insertion.

To insert a drawing or DXF file using **DesignCenter**, use the folder list to locate and select a folder to display the contents of the folder in the content pane. Drag and drop or copy and paste the file from the content pane into the current drawing. You can also right-click a file icon in the **Content** pane and select **Insert as Block…**.

> **NOTE**
>
> Blocks are inserted from **DesignCenter** based on the type of block units you specify when you created the block. For example, if the original block was a 1 × 1 square and you specified the block units as feet when you created the block, then the block inserts as a 12″ × 12″ square.

Figure 24-8. Use **DesignCenter** to insert blocks from files or drawings from folders. Several example blocks are available in the AutoCAD **Sample** folder shown.

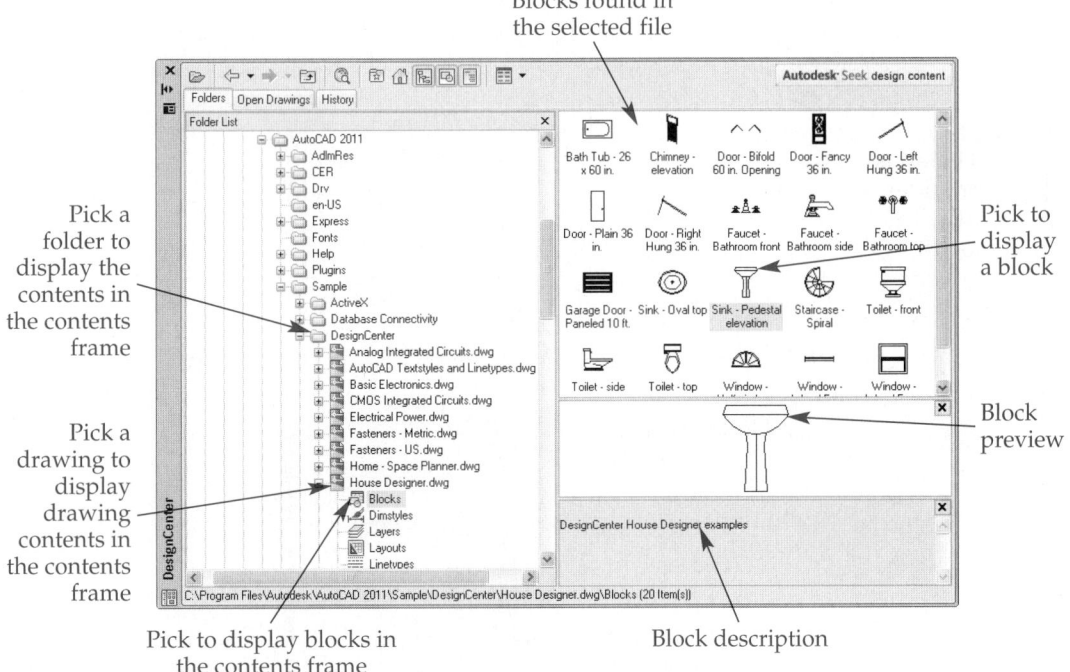

Insert Blocks Using Tool Palettes

block insertion tools: Blocks located on a tool palette.

The **Tool Palettes** palette, shown in **Figure 24-9**, provides another means of storing and inserting blocks. AutoCAD refers to blocks in a tool palette as *block insertion tools.* Tool palettes can also store and activate other drawing content and tools. For more information on AutoCAD customization and using tool palettes, refer to *AutoCAD and Its Applications—Advanced.*

To insert a block from the **Tool Palettes** palette, access the tool palette containing the block. Hover over the block icon to display the name and description. To drag and drop the block, press and hold down the pick button on the block and drag the cursor into the drawing. The block attaches to the cursor at the insertion base point. Release the pick button to insert the block at the location of the cursor. An alternative to the drag-and-drop method is to pick once on the block image to attach the block to the crosshairs, and then specify a point in the drawing to insert the block. This method offers an advantage over the drag-and-drop method by presenting options for adjusting the insertion base point, scale, and rotation.

Exercise 24-5

Access the Student Web site (www.g-wlearning.com/CAD) and complete Exercise 24-5.

Editing Blocks

A block reference, or inserted block, is a single object that you can edit using standard editing tools such as **ERASE**, **COPY**, **ROTATE**, grip editing, or the **Properties** palette. The grip box for a block appears at the insertion base point of the block.

A different form of block editing involves redefining the block by modifying the block definition or changing the objects that compose the block. You can redefine a block using the **Block Editor** or by exploding and then recreating the block.

Figure 24-9.
The **Tool Palettes** palette provides another way to insert blocks.

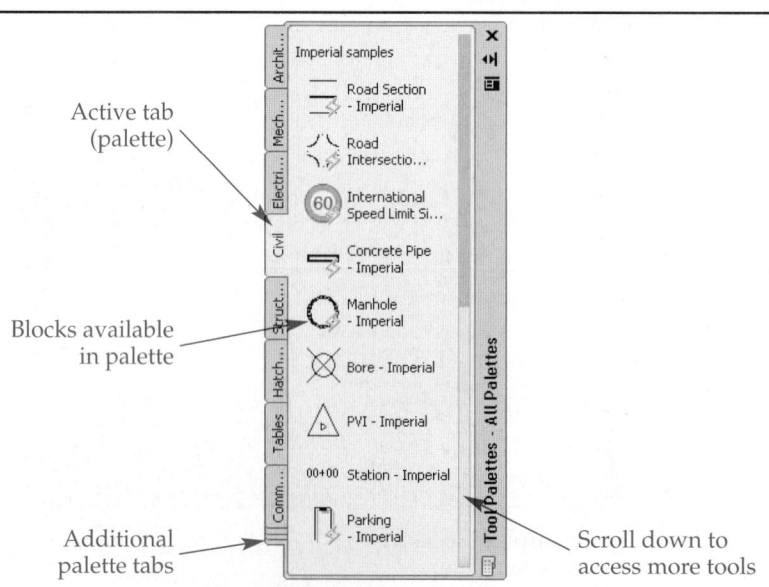

Active tab (palette)

Blocks available in palette

Additional palette tabs

Scroll down to access more tools

Changing Block Properties to ByLayer

If you originally set block element properties such as color, linetype, lineweight, and transparency to absolute values, and you want to change the properties to ByLayer, you can either edit the block definition or use the **SETBYLAYER** tool to accomplish the same task without editing the block definition. Access the **SETBYLAYER** tool and use the **Settings** option to display the **SetByLayer Settings** dialog box. Select the check boxes that correspond to the object properties you want to convert to ByLayer. Pick the **OK** button to exit the **SetByLayer Settings** dialog box.

Next, select the blocks with the properties you want to set to ByLayer and press [Enter] or the space bar, or right-click to display the Change ByBlock to ByLayer? prompt. Select the **Yes** option to change all object properties currently set to ByBlock to ByLayer. Pick the **No** option to change all object properties set to values other than ByBlock to ByLayer. The next prompt asks if you want to include blocks in the conversion. If the selection is a block, choose **Yes** to convert the properties of all references of the same block in the drawing to ByLayer. If you pick **No**, only the properties of the selected block are converted. All other references of the same block remain unchanged.

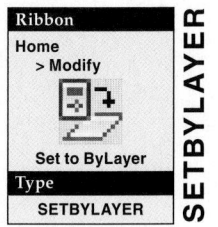

PROFESSIONAL TIP

To change the properties of several blocks, use the **Select Similar** or **Quick Select** tool to create a selection set of block references.

Using the Block Editor

Use the **BEDIT** tool to make changes to a block definition using the **Block Editor**. Access the **BEDIT** tool to display the **Edit Block Definition** dialog box. See **Figure 24-10**. Select the name of an existing block to edit from the list box. Pick the <Current Drawing> option to edit a block saved as the current drawing, such as a wblock. A preview and description of the selected block appear. You can create a new block by typing a unique name in the **Block to create or edit** field. Pick the **OK** button to open the selected block in the **Block Editor**. See **Figure 24-11**. If you typed a new block name, the drawing area is empty, allowing you to create a new block.

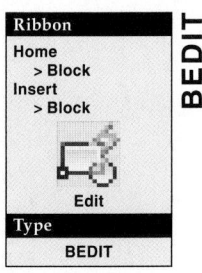

Modifying a Block

Use drawing and editing tools to modify or create the block definition. Specify the UCS origin, or 0,0,0 point, as the block insertion base point. The tools in the panels of the **Block Editor** ribbon tab are specifically for modifying and creating block geometry. **Figure 24-12** describes some of the basic tools available in the **Block Editor** ribbon.

Figure 24-10.
The **Edit Block Definition** dialog box.

Blocks available in current drawing

Block selected for editing

Preview of selected block

Block definition description

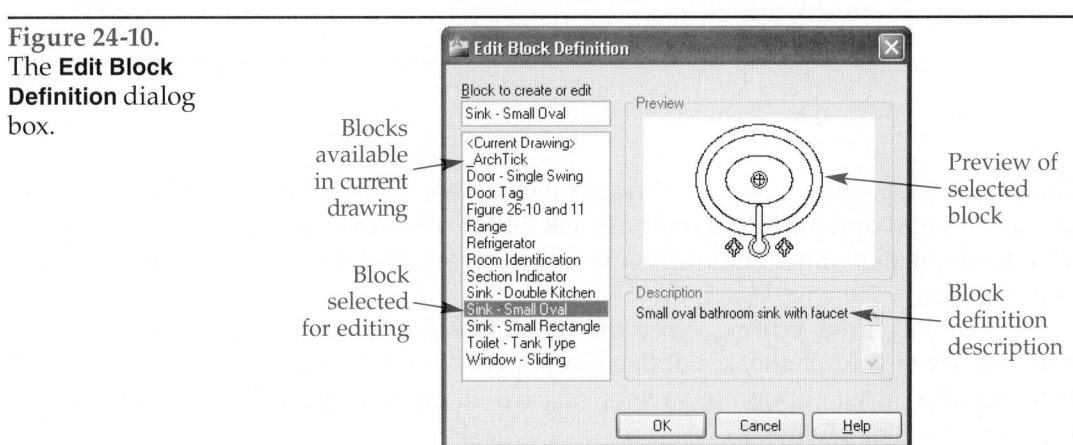

Figure 24-11. The context-sensitive **Block Editor** ribbon tab and the **Block Authoring Palettes** palette are available in block editing mode. Only the block geometry appears in the **Block Editor**.

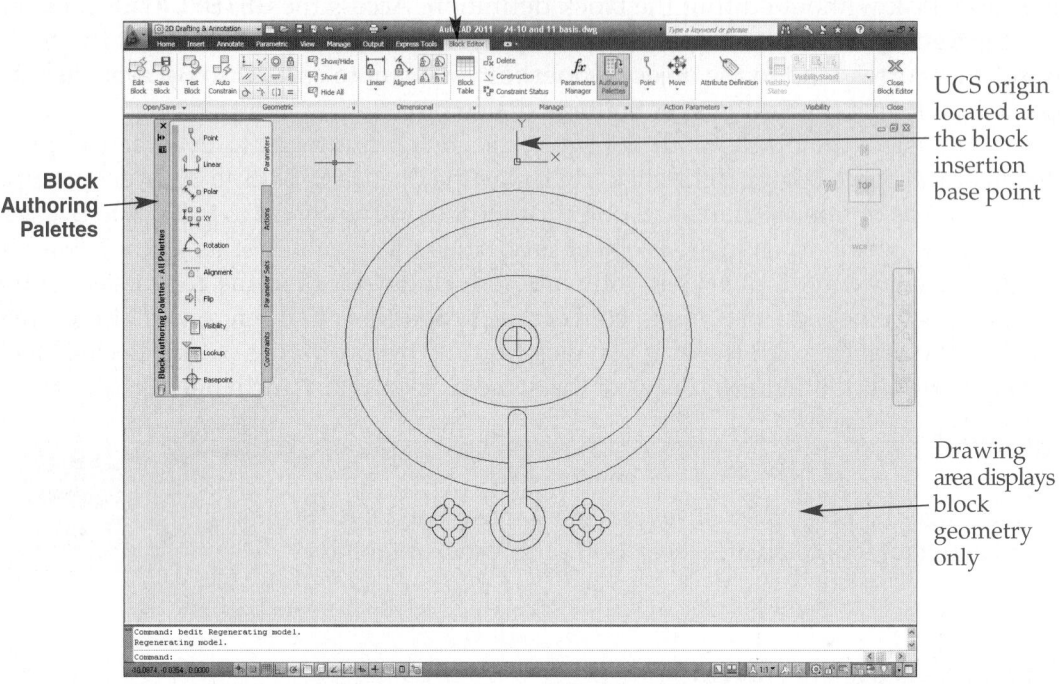

Block editing and construction tools available in the **Block Editor** ribbon tab

Block Authoring Palettes

UCS origin located at the block insertion base point

Drawing area displays block geometry only

Figure 24-12. The **Block Editor** ribbon tab contains several tools and options specifically for editing and constructing blocks. This table describes the most basic functions.

Button	Description
	Saves changes to the block and updates the block definition.
	Opens the **Save Block As** dialog box, allowing you to save the block as a new block, using a different name.
	Opens the **Edit Block Definition** dialog box, which is the same dialog box displayed when you enter block editing mode. You can select a different block to edit or specify the name of a new block to create from scratch.
	Toggles the **Block Authoring Palettes** palette off and on.
	Closes the **Block Editor**.

Parametric tools allow you to constrain block geometry and form block tables. Many of the tools and options found on the **Block Editor** ribbon tab relate to dynamic blocks. This textbook explains dynamic blocks, block tables, and other block editing tools in later chapters.

When you finish editing, close the **Block Editor** to return to the drawing. If you have not saved your changes, a dialog box appears asking if you want to save changes. Pick the appropriate option to save or discard changes, or pick the **Cancel** button to return to the **Block Editor**.

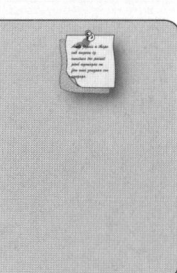

Double-click on a block to display the **Edit Block Definition** dialog box with the block selected. Open a block directly in the **Block Editor** by selecting the block and then right-clicking and choosing **Block Editor**. Another option is to open a block directly in the **Block Editor** when you create the block by selecting the **Open in block editor** check box in the **Block Definition** dialog box.

Adding a Block Description

To change the description assigned to the original block definition, open the block in the **Block Editor** and display the **Properties** palette with no objects selected. Make changes to the description using the **Description** property in the **Block** category. Pick the **Save Block Definition** button and the **Close Block Editor** button to return to the drawing.

You can also edit blocks in place using the **REFEDIT** tool. Chapter 31 describes in-place editing using the **REFEDIT** tool as it applies to external references. Use the same techniques to edit blocks.

Exercise 24-6

Access the Student Web site (www.g-wlearning.com/CAD) and complete Exercise 24-6.

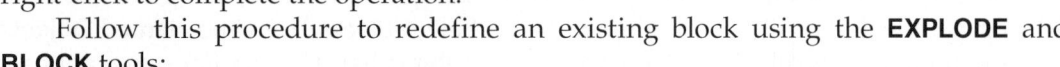

Exploding and Redefining a Block

You can explode a block during insertion by checking **Explode** in the **Insert** dialog box. This is useful when you want to edit the individual objects of the block. You can also use the **EXPLODE** tool after inserting the block to break it into the original objects, but only if you check **Allow exploding** in the **Block Definition** dialog box. Access the **EXPLODE** tool, select the objects to be exploded and press [Enter] or the space bar or right-click to complete the operation.

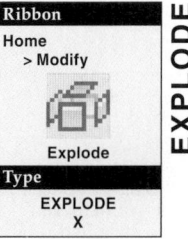

Follow this procedure to redefine an existing block using the **EXPLODE** and **BLOCK** tools:

1. Insert the block to redefine.
2. Make sure you know the exact location of the insertion base point, which is lost during the explosion.
3. Use the **EXPLODE** tool to explode the block.
4. Edit the elements of the block as needed.
5. Recreate the block definition using the **BLOCK** tool.
6. Assign the block the same original name and, if appropriate, the same insertion point.
7. Select the objects to include in the block.
8. Pick the **OK** button in the **Block Definition** dialog box to save the block. When a message appears asking if you want to redefine the block, pick **Yes**.

Exercise 24-7

Access the Student Web site (www.g-wlearning.com/CAD) and complete Exercise 24-7.

Understanding the Circular Reference Error

circular reference error: An error that occurs when a block definition references itself.

A *circular reference error* occurs when you try to redefine a block that already exists using the same name. AutoCAD informs you that the block references itself or has not been modified. A block can be composed of many objects, including other blocks. When you use the **BLOCK** tool to incorporate an existing block into a new block, AutoCAD detects all objects that compose the new block, including existing block definitions. A problem occurs if you select an instance of the redefined block as an element of the new definition. The new block refers to a block of the same name, or references itself. **Figure 24-13A** illustrates the process of correctly redefining a block named BOX to avoid a circular reference error. **Figure 24-13B** shows an incorrect redefinition resulting in a circular reference error.

Renaming Blocks

Type
RENAME
REN

Access the **RENAME** tool to rename a block using the **Rename** dialog box, without editing the block definition. See **Figure 24-14**. Select Blocks from the **Named Objects** list, and then pick the block to be renamed in the **Items** list. The current name appears in the **Old Name:** text box. Type the new block name in the **Rename To:** text box. Pick the **Rename To:** button to display the new name in the **Items** list. Pick the **OK** button to exit the **Rename** dialog box.

Updating Block Icons

Type
BLOCKICON

A block icon forms when you define a block. The icon appears when you insert and edit blocks to help you recognize the block. Block icons require updating when an icon does not appear, as is often the case when you store a block in a drawing created with an older version of AutoCAD, or if the icon does not reflect changes made to the block. To create or update a block icon, open the drawing that contains the block, access the **BLOCKICON** tool, enter the name of the block, and right-click or press [Enter] or the space bar.

Figure 24-13. A—The correct procedure for redefining a block. B—Redefining a block without first exploding the block creates an invalid circular reference.

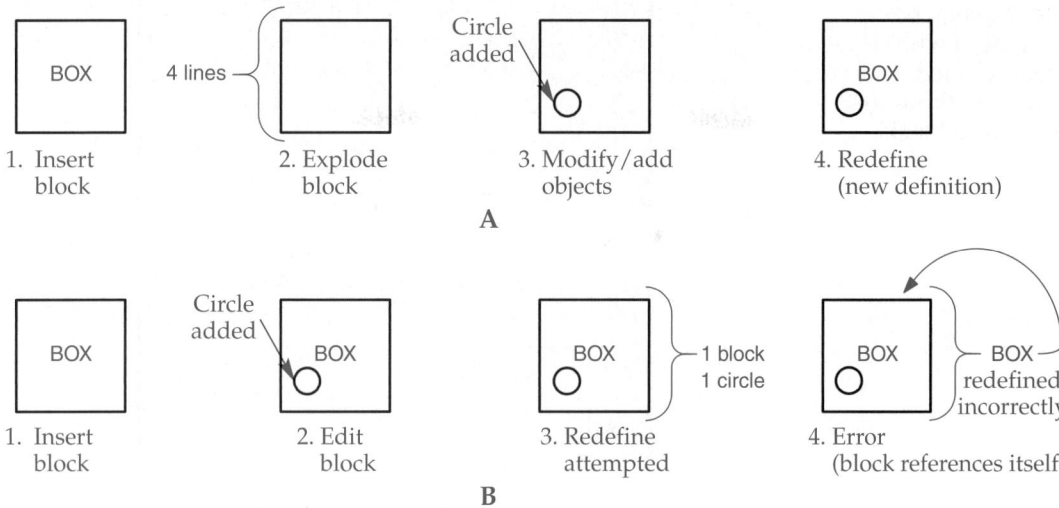

A

B

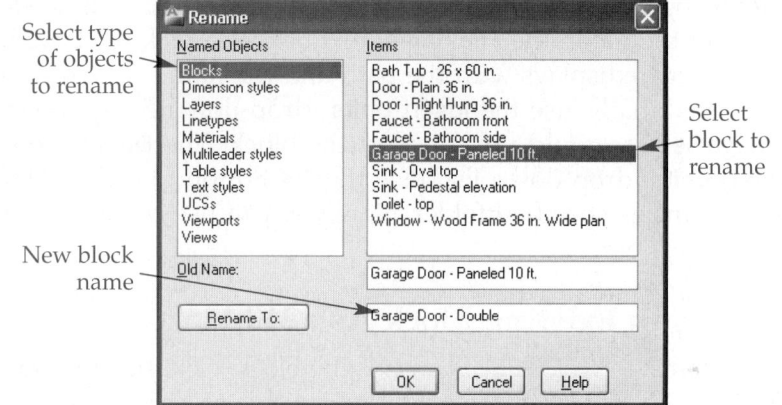

Figure 24-14.
The **Rename** dialog box allows you to change the name of blocks and other named objects.

Creating Blocks as Drawing Files

Blocks that you create with the **BLOCK** tool are stored with the drawing. A wblock created using the **WBLOCK** tool is saved as a separate drawing (DWG) file. You can also use the **WBLOCK** tool to create a block from any object. The object does not have to be a block definition. Insert the wblock as a block into any drawing. Access the **WBLOCK** tool to display the **Write Block** dialog box shown in **Figure 24-15.**

Type
WBLOCK

Creating a New Wblock

One purpose for creating a wblock is to create a new drawing file from existing objects that you have not converted to a block. To apply this technique, pick the **Objects** radio button in the **Source** area. The process of creating a wblock from existing non-block objects is similar to the process of creating a block using the **BLOCK** tool. Specify an insertion base point using options in the **Base point** area, and select the objects and the disposition of the objects using options in the **Objects** area. The **Base point** and **Objects** areas function the same as those found in the **Block Definition** dialog box.

In contrast to a block, a wblock is saved as a drawing file, not as a block in the current drawing. Enter a path and file name for the block in the **File name and path:** text

---

Figure 24-15.
Using the **Write Block** dialog box to create a wblock from selected objects without first defining a block.

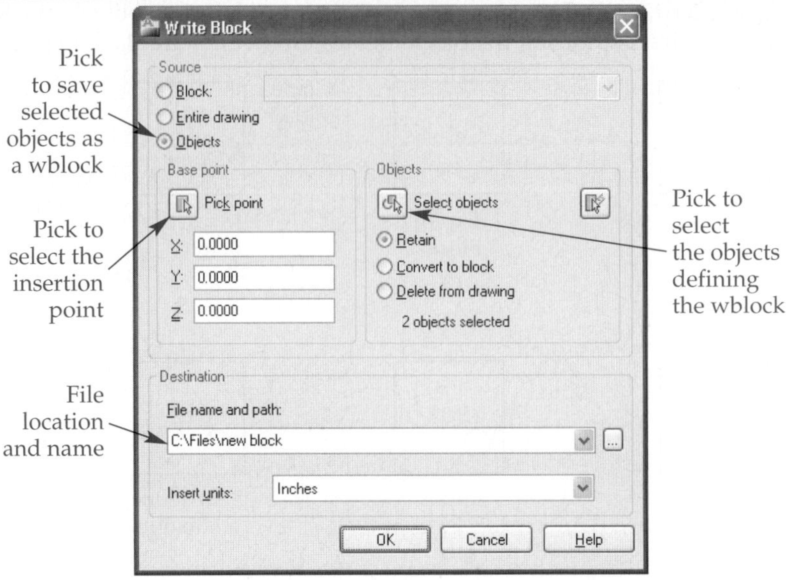

Pick to save selected objects as a wblock

Pick to select the insertion point

Pick to select the objects defining the wblock

File location and name

box or pick the ellipsis (**...**) button next to the text box to display the **Browse for Drawing File** dialog box. Navigate to the folder in which you want to save the file, confirm the name of the file in the **File name:** text box, and pick the **Save** button. The **Write Block** dialog box redisplays with the path and file name shown in the **File name and path:** text box. Finally, use the **Insert units:** drop-down list to select the type of units that **DesignCenter** should use to insert the block. The **Destination** area also includes the **Insert units:** drop-down list. Pick the **OK** button to finish. The objects are saved as a wblock in the specified folder. Now you can use the **INSERT** tool in any drawing to insert the block.

Saving an Existing Block As a Wblock

To create a wblock from an existing block, pick the **Block** radio button in the **Source** area. See **Figure 24-16.** Select the block to save as a wblock from the drop-down list. Use the options in the **Destination** area to locate the wblock, and pick the **OK** button to finish.

Figure 24-16. Using the **Write Block** dialog box to create a wblock from an existing block definition.

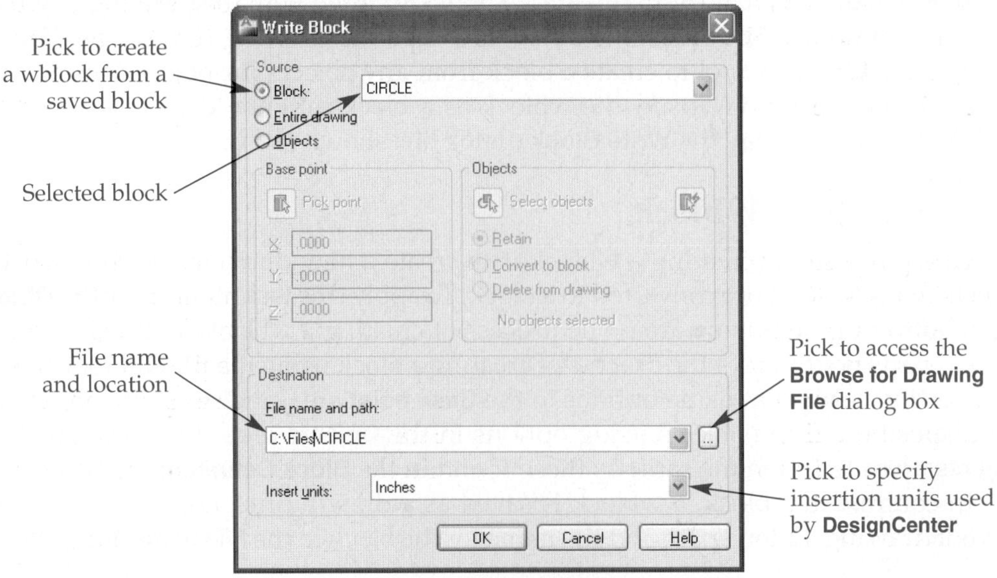

Pick to create a wblock from a saved block

Selected block

File name and location

Pick to access the **Browse for Drawing File** dialog box

Pick to specify insertion units used by **DesignCenter**

Storing a Drawing As a Wblock

To store an entire drawing as a wblock, pick the **Entire drawing** radio button in the **Source** area. Use the options in the **Destination** area to locate the wblock. In this case, the whole drawing is saved as if you are using the **SAVE** tool. However, all uninserted, or unused, blocks in the drawing are deleted. If the drawing contains any unused blocks, the **Entire drawing** method may reduce the size of a drawing considerably. Pick the **OK** button to finish.

Exercise 24-8

Access the Student Web site (www.g-wlearning.com/CAD) and complete Exercise 24-8.

Revising an Inserted Drawing

If you insert a wblock into multiple drawings and then need to make changes to the wblock, use the **INSERT** tool to access the original drawing file with the **Select Drawing File** dialog box. Then activate the **Specify On-screen** check box in the **Insertion point** area and pick the **OK** button. When a message asks to redefine the block, pick the **Yes** option. All of the wblock references update. Press [Esc] to cancel the tool so that you do not insert a new block.

> **PROFESSIONAL TIP**
>
> If you work on projects that use inserted drawings that require revision, use reference drawings, or xrefs, instead of inserting drawing files. Chapter 31 explains reference drawings placed using the **XREF** tool. All xrefs automatically update when you open a drawing file that contains the xref content.

Symbol Libraries

Store frequently used symbols in *symbol libraries* to increase productivity. Continue to add new symbols to libraries to increase the number of symbols available for reuse. Establish whether you will store symbols as blocks or drawing files, and identify a storage location and system.

symbol library: A collection of related blocks, shapes, views, symbols, or other content.

Creating Symbol Libraries

There are two general methods to create a symbol library. One option is to save multiple blocks in a single drawing. The other option is to save each block to a separate wblock file. Use the following guidelines when developing a symbol library:
- Follow industry and company or school standards for blocks and symbols.
- Identify each block with a descriptive name and insertion point location.
- When saving multiple blocks in a drawing file, save one group of symbols per drawing file and use folders to organize files.
- When using wblocks, give each file a meaningful name and use folders to organize files.

- Provide all users with a hard copy of the symbol library showing each symbol, insertion points, storage locations, and any other necessary information. See **Figure 24-17.**
- If a network is not in use, place symbol library files on each workstation in the classroom or office.
- Keep backup copies of all files in a secure location.
- When you revise symbols, update all files containing the edited symbols as appropriate.
- Inform all users of any changes to saved symbols.

Storing Symbol Libraries

Store symbol libraries on the local or network hard drive. This location is easy to access, quick, and more convenient to use than portable media. Removable media, such as a removable hard drive, USB flash drive, or CD, are appropriate for backup purposes if a network drive with an automatic backup function is not available. In the absence of a network, use removable media to transport files from one workstation to another.

Use a system of folders and files to store and organize symbol libraries. Store content outside of the AutoCAD system folders to keep the system folders uncluttered, and to differentiate your folders and files from AutoCAD system folders and files. A good method is to create a \Blocks folder for storing blocks, as shown in **Figure 24-18.**

If you save multiple symbols within a single drawing, use **DesignCenter** or the **Tool Palettes** palette to insert the symbols as needed. This system often works best when you use several drawing files to group similar symbols. For example, create different symbol libraries based on fastener, electronic, electrical, piping, mechanical, structural, architectural, landscaping, and mapping symbols. Limit the symbols in a drawing to a reasonable number so you can easily find and load the symbols.

Figure 24-17. A printed copy of a typical symbol library distributed to architectural drafters. The "X" symbols indicate insertion points and are not part of the blocks. (Courtesy of Ron Palma, 3D-DZYN)

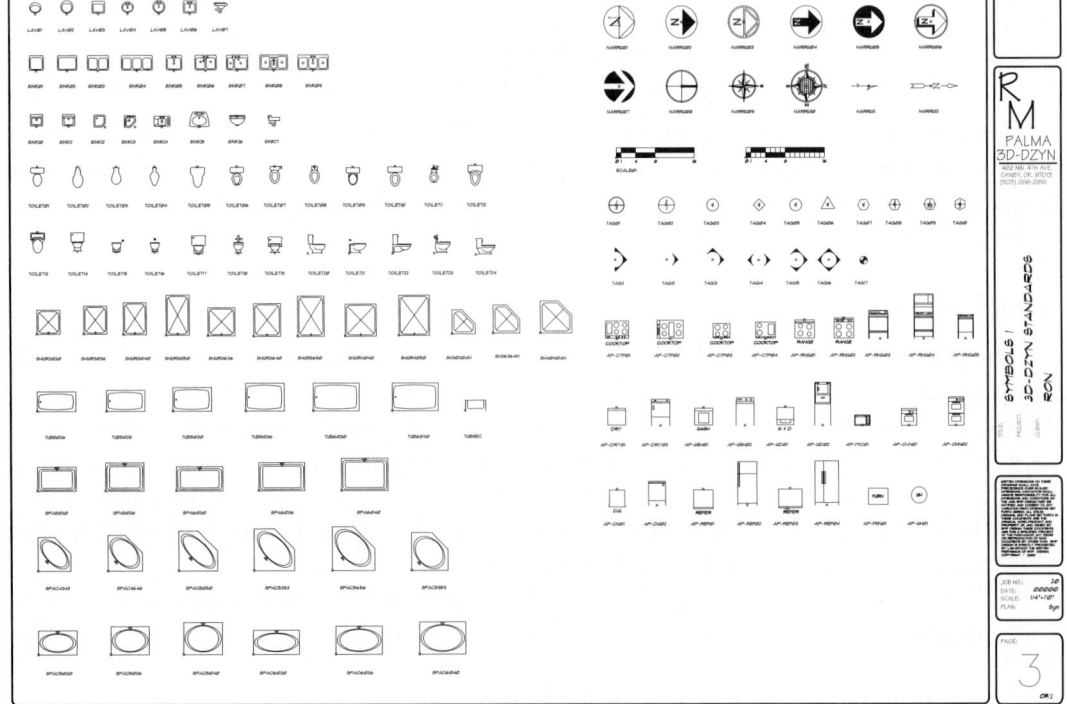

Figure 24-18. An efficient way to store blocks saved as drawing files is to set up a Blocks folder containing folders for each type of block on the hard drive.

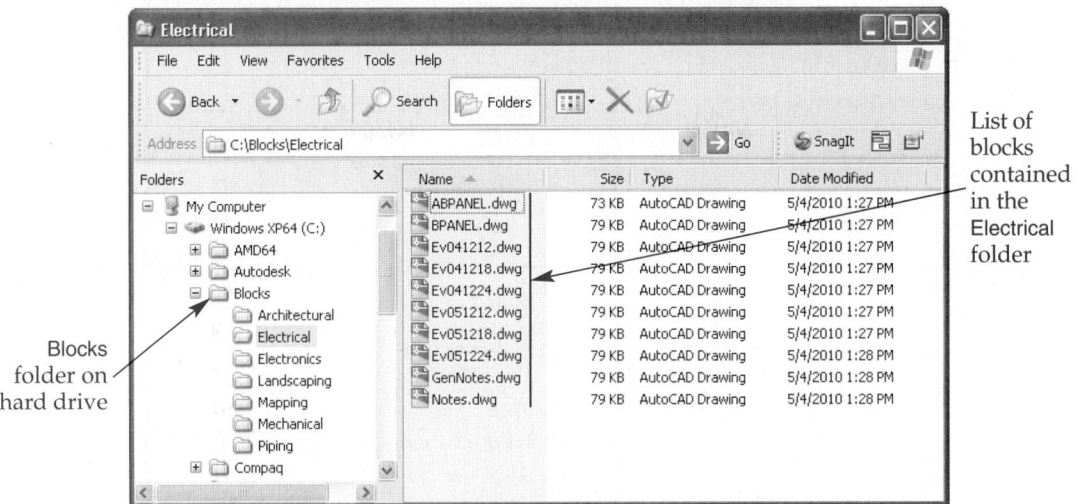

Blocks folder on hard drive

List of blocks contained in the Electrical folder

Arrange drawing files saved on the hard drive in a logical manner. All workstations in a non-networked classroom or office should have folders with the same names. Assign one person to update and copy symbol libraries to all workstations. Copy drawing files to each workstation from a master CD. Keep the master and backup versions of the symbol libraries in separate locations.

Purging Named Objects

A drawing typically accumulates unused *named objects* that may be unnecessary. Unused named objects increase drawing file size and may make it more difficult to locate and use content that is common and necessary. Use the **PURGE** tool to *purge* unused objects from the drawing if necessary. Access the **PURGE** tool to display the **Purge** dialog box. See **Figure 24-19**.

Select the appropriate radio button at the top of the dialog box to view content that can or cannot be purged. Before purging, select the **Confirm each item to be purged** check box to have an opportunity to review each item before deleting. Check **Purge nested items** to purge nested items. Selecting the **Purge zero-length geometry and empty text objects** check box is an effective way to erase all zero-length objects, such as a line or arc drawn as a dot and text that only includes spaces. These objects are often mistakes or unintended results of the drawing and editing processes.

To purge specific unused items, use the tree view to locate and highlight the items to purge, and then pick the **Purge** button. To purge all unused items, pick the **Purge All** button. Purging may cause other named objects to become unreferenced. As a result, you may need to purge more than once to purge the drawing of all unused named objects. Messages appear to guide you through the purge operation.

named objects: Blocks, dimension styles, layers, linetypes, materials, multileader styles, plot styles, shapes, table styles, text styles, and visual styles that have specific names.

purge: Delete unused named objects from a drawing file.

Type
PURGE
PU

Figure 24-19.
The **Purge** dialog box.

Select which items are listed below

Check to verify each item before purging

Pick to purge nested items

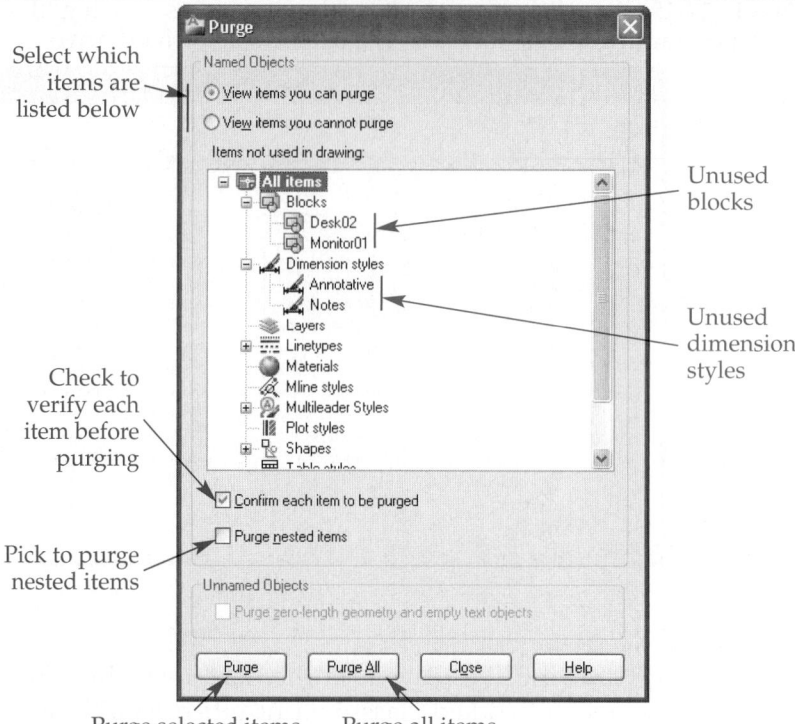

Unused blocks

Unused dimension styles

Purge selected items   Purge all items

Chapter Test

Answer the following questions. Write your answers on a separate sheet of paper or go to the Student Web site (www.g-wlearning.com/CAD) and complete the electronic chapter test.

1. Why would you draw blocks on the 0 layer?
2. What properties do blocks drawn on a layer other than layer 0 assume when they are inserted?
3. What characters can be used in a block name?
4. Define the term *nesting* in relation to blocks.
5. What is a block reference?
6. How can you access a listing of all blocks in the current drawing?
7. Describe the effect of entering negative scale factors when inserting a block.
8. What type of block is a one-unit line object?
9. How do you preset block insertion variables using the **Insert** dialog box?
10. Name a limitation of an array pattern created with the **MINSERT** tool.
11. What is the purpose of the **BASE** tool?
12. Briefly explain how to insert a block into a drawing from **DesignCenter**.
13. What tool allows you to change a block's layer without editing the block definition?
14. Identify the tool that allows you to break an inserted block into its individual objects for editing purposes.
15. Suppose you have found that a block was incorrectly drawn. Unfortunately, you have already inserted the block 30 times. How can you edit all of the blocks quickly?
16. What is the primary difference between blocks created with the **BLOCK** and **WBLOCK** tools?
17. Explain the advantage of storing a drawing as a wblock if you anticipate the need to insert the drawing into other drawings.
18. Define *symbol library*.
19. What is the purpose of the **PURGE** tool?
20. Explain how to remove all unused blocks from a drawing.

Drawing Problems

- *Start AutoCAD if it is not already started. Start a new drawing for each problem using an appropriate template of your choice.*
- *The template should include layers and text, dimension, multileader, and table styles, when necessary, for drawing the given objects. Add layers and text, dimension, multileader, and table styles as needed.*
- *Draw all objects using appropriate layers and text, dimension, multileader, and table styles, justification, and format.*
- *Follow the specific instructions for each problem. Use only drawing and editing tools and techniques you have already learned. Use your own judgment and approximate dimensions when necessary.*
- *Apply formal dimensions accurately using ASME or appropriate industry standards.*

Note: *Some of the problems in this chapter are built on problems from previous chapters. If you have not yet completed those problems, complete them now.*

▼ Basic

1. Open P13-16 and save as P24-1. The P24-1 file should be active. The sketch for this drawing is shown. Erase all copies of the symbols, leaving the original objects intact. These include the steel column symbols and the bay and column line tags. Then do the following:
   A. Make blocks of the steel column symbol and the tag symbols.
   B. Use the **MINSERT** tool or the **ARRAY** tool to place the symbols in the drawing.
   C. Dimension the drawing as shown.
   D. Resave the drawing.

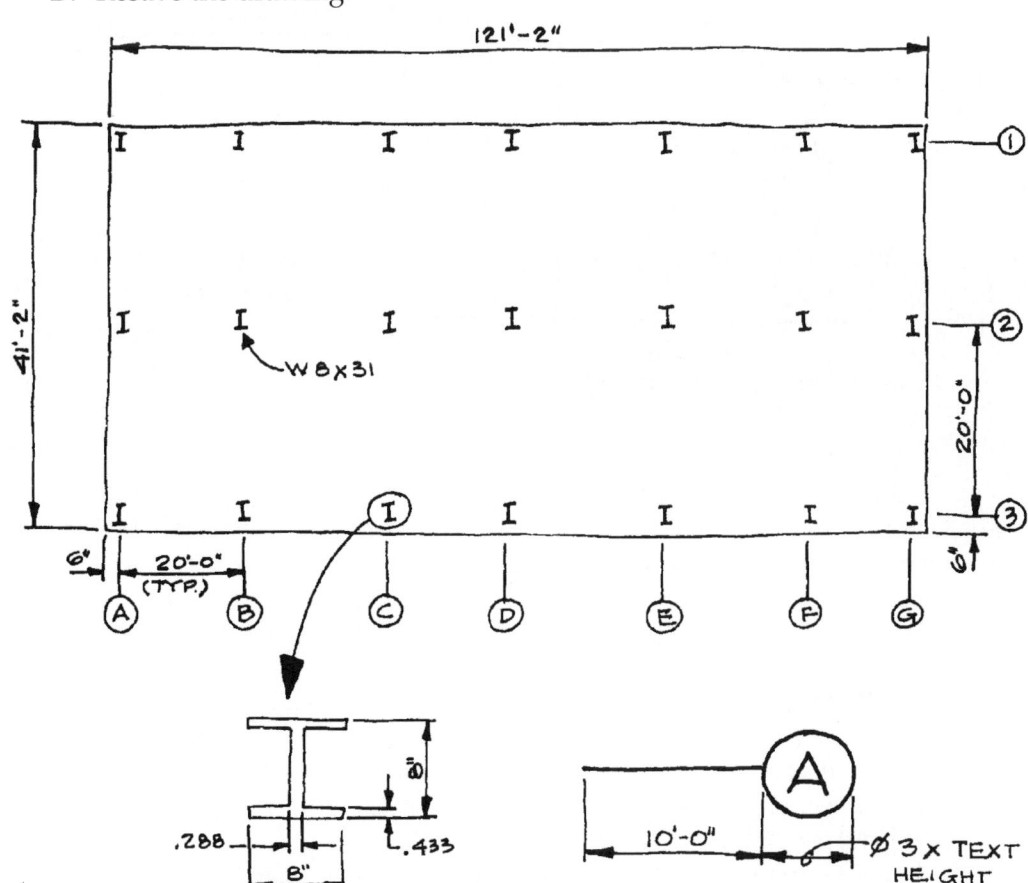

2. Open P13-17 and save as P24-2. The P24-2 file should be active. The sketch for this drawing is shown. Erase all of the desk workstations except one. Then do the following:

A. Create a block of the workstation.
B. Insert the block into the drawing using the **MINSERT** tool.
C. Dimension one of the workstations as shown.
D. Resave the drawing.

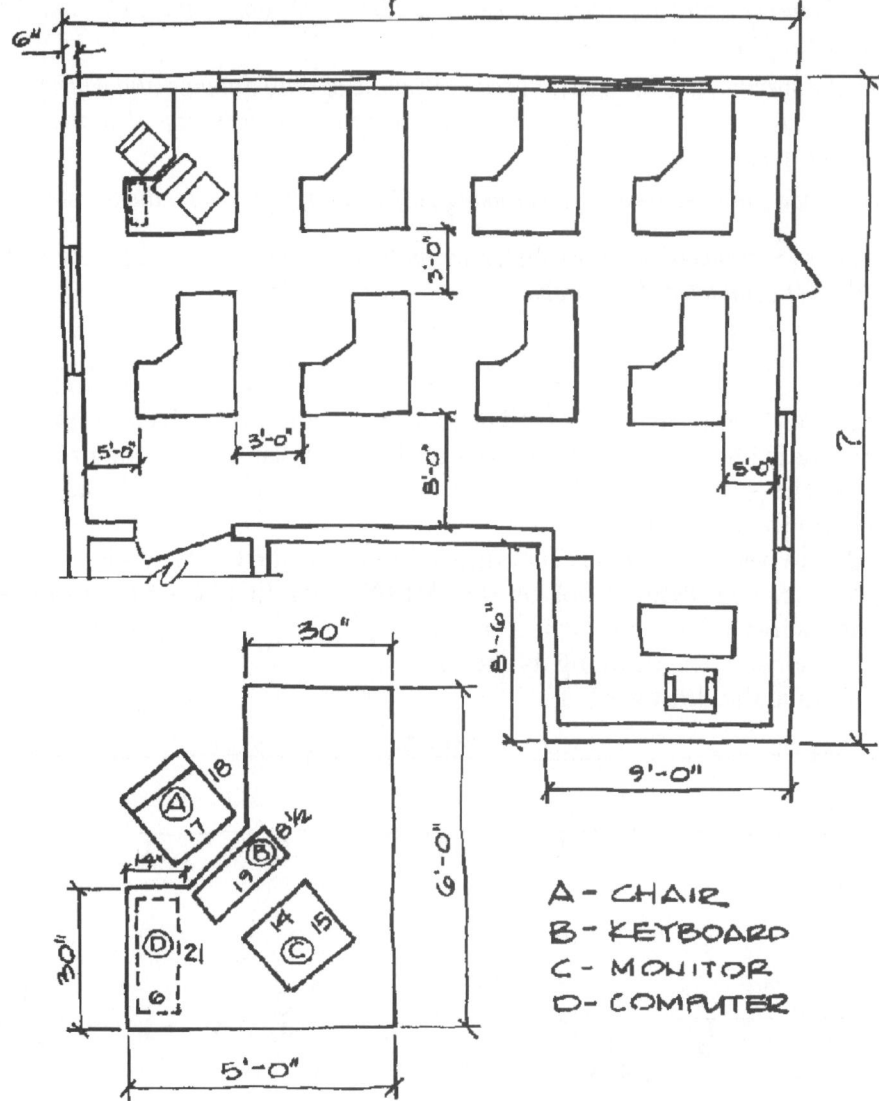

A – CHAIR
B – KEYBOARD
C – MONITOR
D – COMPUTER

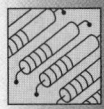

3. Complete this problem after completing Problem 24-7. Open **P24-7** and save as **P24-3**. The P24-3 file should be active. Modify the NAND gates to become XNOR gates, as shown, by modifying the block definition. Save the drawing as **P24-3**.

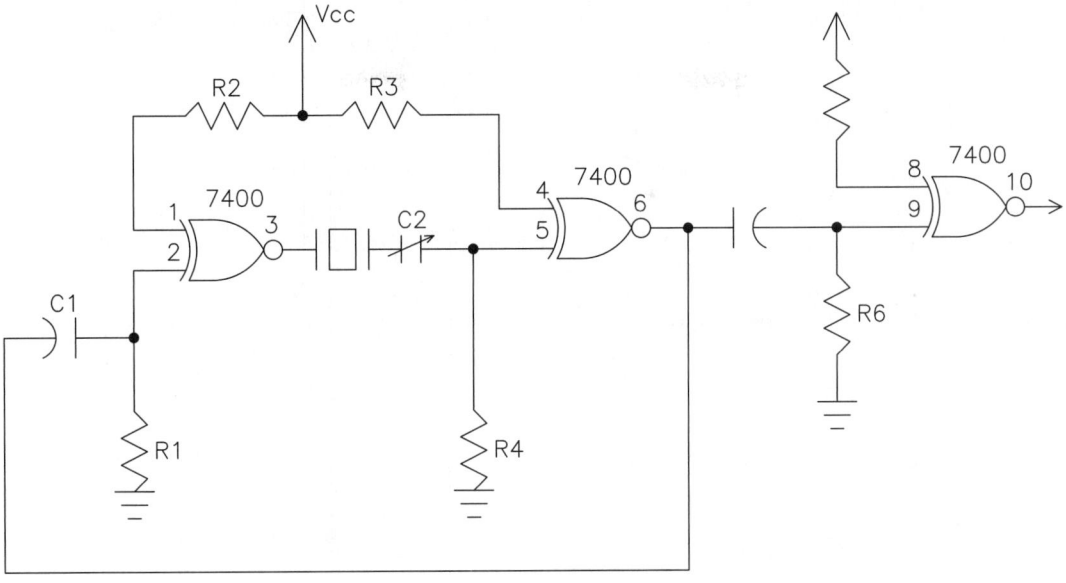

▼ Intermediate

Problems 4–7 represent a variety of diagrams created using symbols as blocks. Create each drawing as shown. The drawings are not to scale. Create the symbols first as blocks or wblocks and then save the symbols in a symbol library using one of the methods described in this chapter.

4. Draw the integrated circuit schematic for a clock. Save the drawing as **P24-4**.

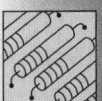

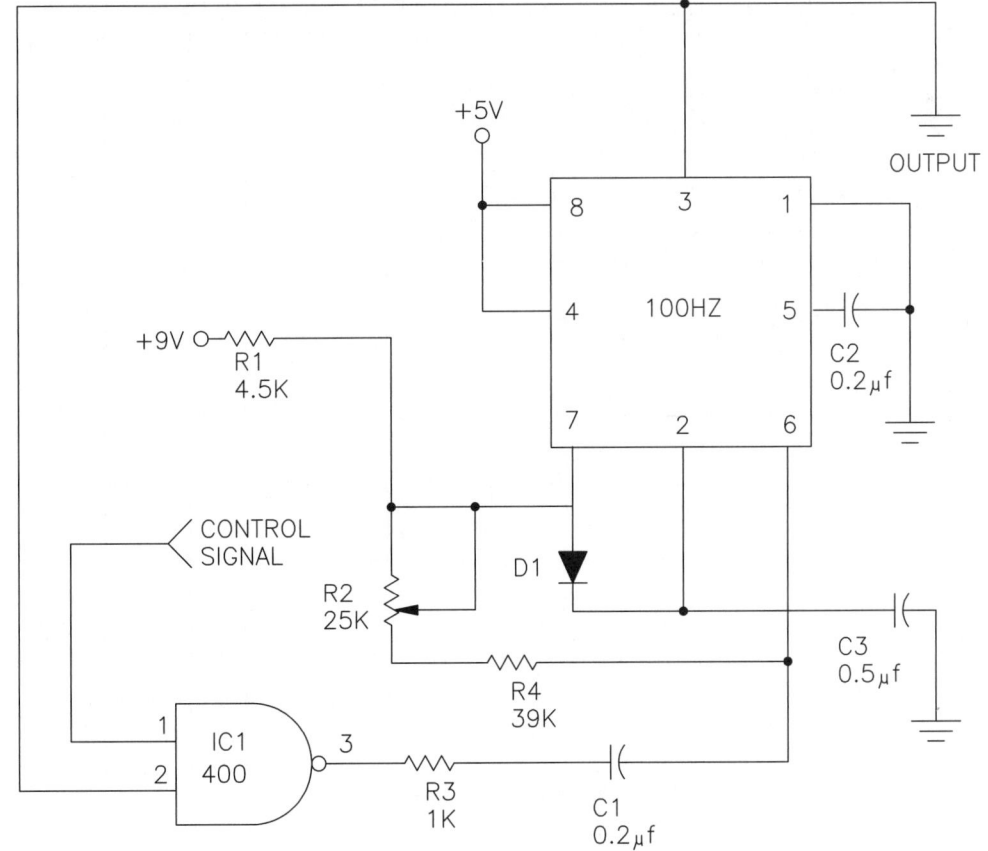

Integrated Circuit for Clock

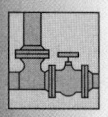

5. Draw the piping flow diagram. Save the drawing as P24-5.

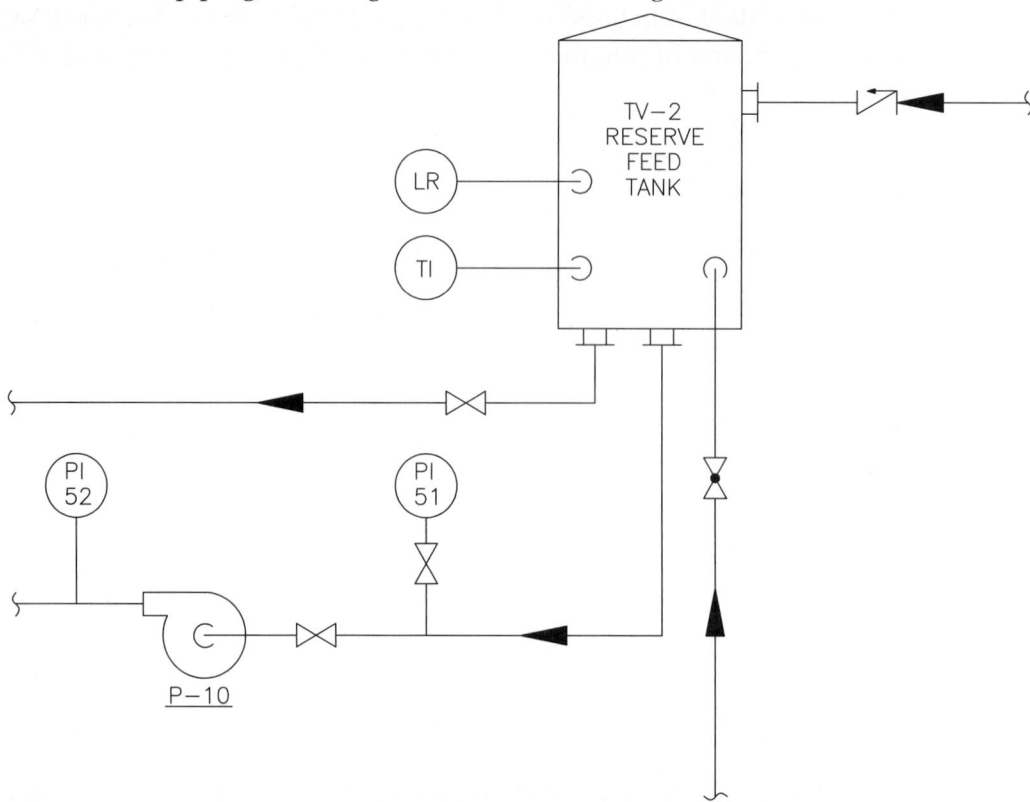

Piping Flow Diagram

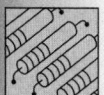

6. Draw the logic diagram of a marking system. Save the drawing as P24-6.

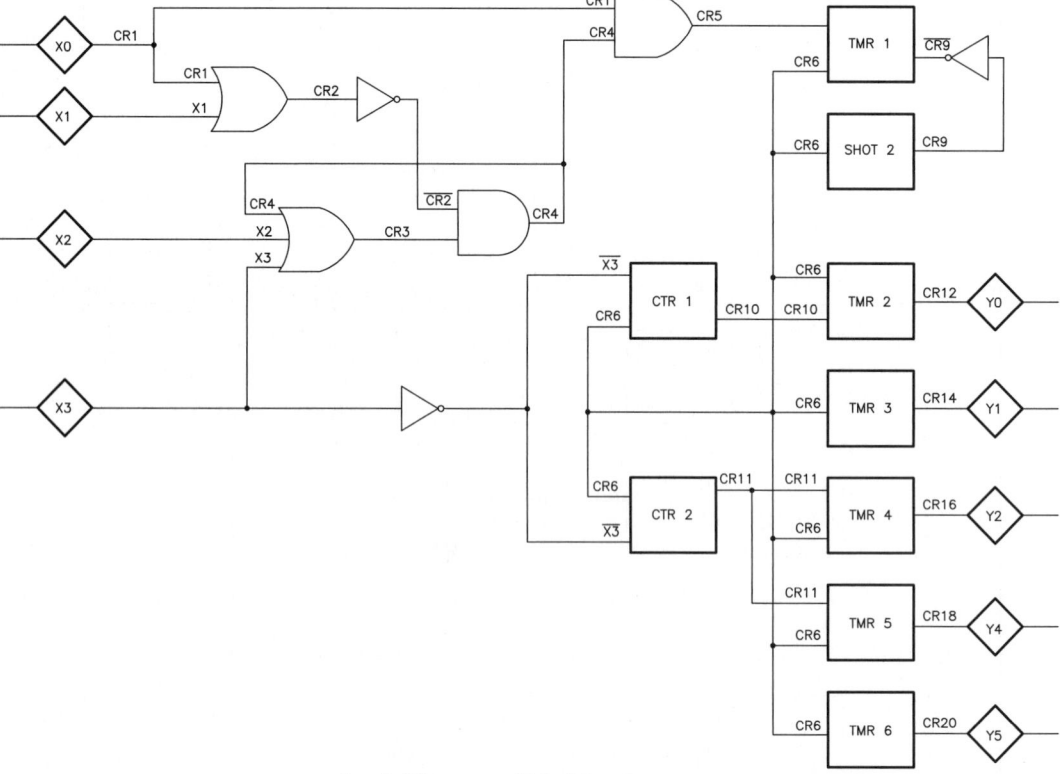

Logic Diagram of Marking System

7. Draw the digital logic circuit. Create each type of component in the circuit as a block. Save the drawing as P24-7.

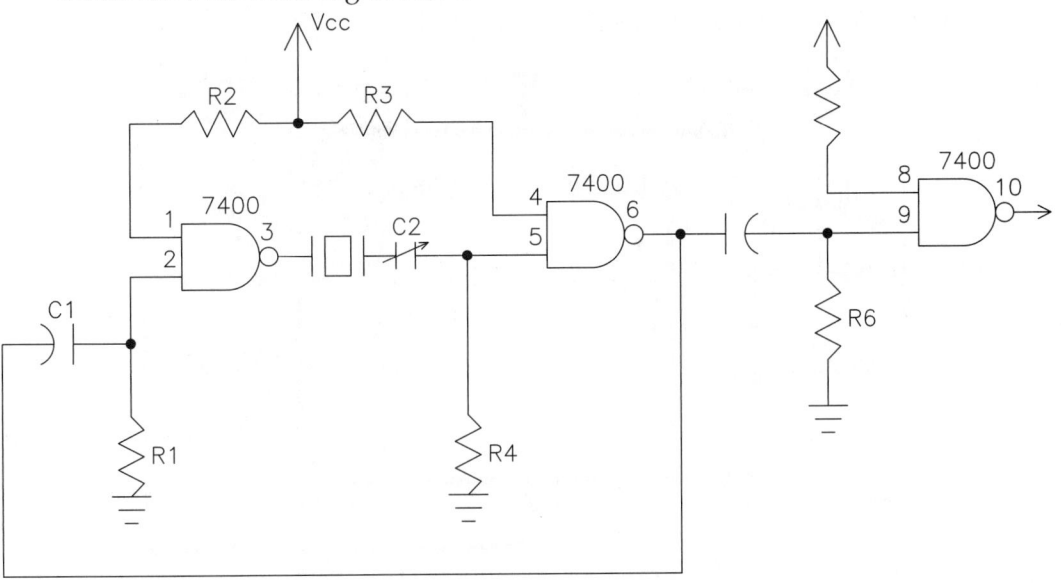

▼ Advanced

Problems 8–12 present engineering sketches of schematic drawings. The drawings are not to scale. Prepare a formal drawing from each sketch using symbols. Create the symbols first as blocks or wblocks and then save the symbols in a symbol library using one of the methods described in this chapter.

8. Draw the logic diagram of a portion of the internal components of a computer from the sketch shown. Save the drawing as P24-8.

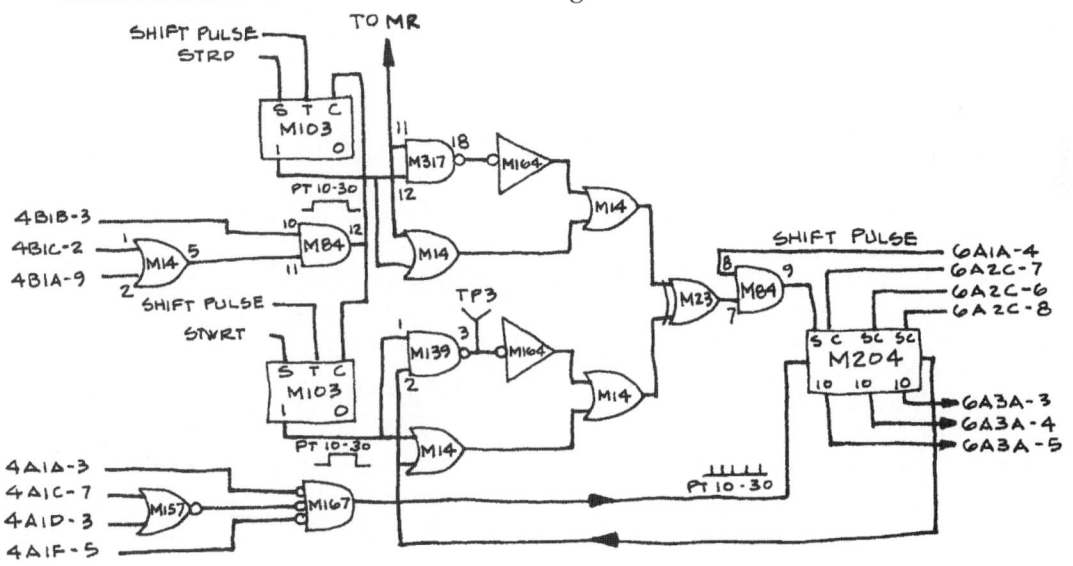

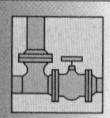

9. Draw the piping flow diagram of a cooling water system from the sketch shown. Look closely at this drawing before you begin. Draw the thick flow lines with polylines. Save the drawing as P24-9.

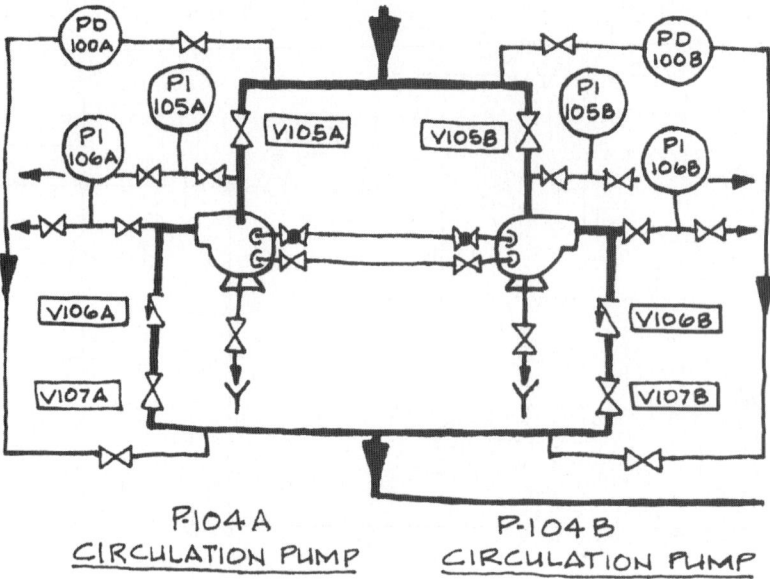

10. Draw the general arrangement of a basement floor plan for a new building from the sketch shown. The engineer has shown one example of each type of equipment. Use the following instructions to complete the drawing.
   A. All text should be 1/8" high, except the text for the bay and column line tags, which should be 3/16" high. The diameter of the line balloons for the bay and column lines should be twice the diameter of the text height.
   B. The column and bay steel symbols represent wide-flange structural shapes and should be 8" wide × 12" high.
   C. The PUMP and CHILLER installations (except PUMP #4 and PUMP #5) should be drawn per the dimensions given for PUMP #1 and CHILLER #1. Use the dimensions shown for the other PUMP units.
   D. TANK #2 and PUMP #5 (P-5) should be drawn per the dimensions given for TANK #1 and PUMP #4.
   E. Tanks T-3, T-4, T-5, and T-6 are all the same size and are aligned 12' from column line A.
   F. Plan this drawing carefully and create as many blocks as necessary to increase your productivity. Dimension the drawing as shown, and provide location dimensions for all equipment not shown in the engineer's sketch.
   G. Save the drawing as P24-10.

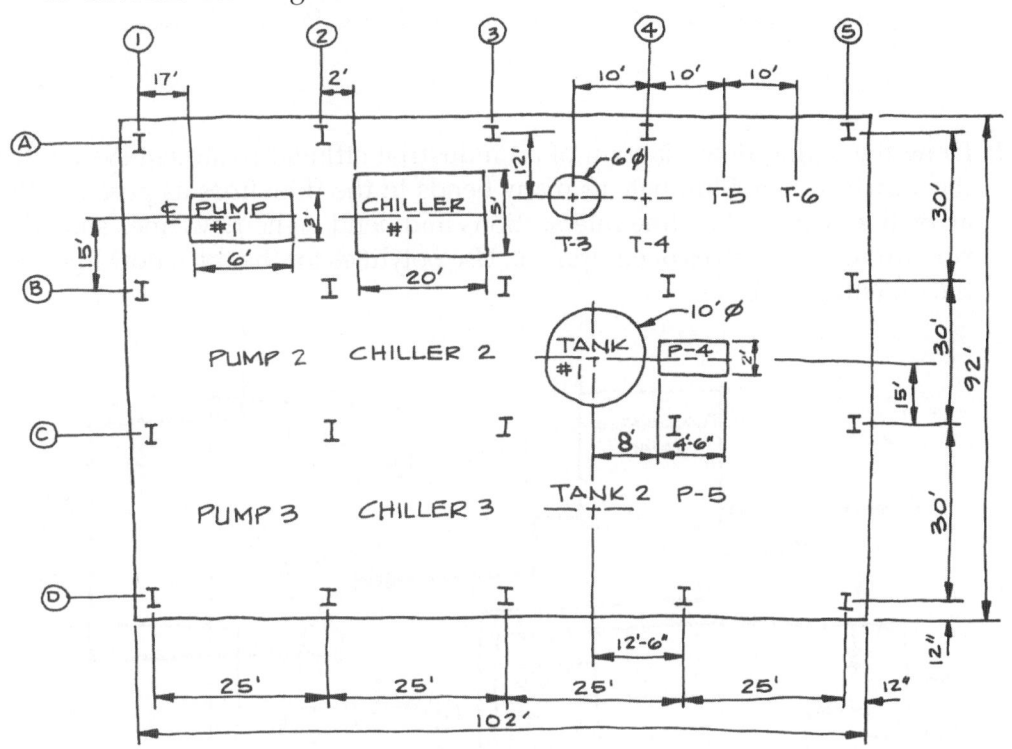

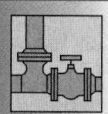

11. Open P24-10 and save as P24-11. The P24-11 file should be active. The engineer has provided you with a sketch of the necessary revisions to the drawing. It is up to you to alter the drawing as quickly and efficiently as possible. Do not add the dimensions shown on the sketch; the dimensions are provided for construction purposes only. Revise the drawing so all chillers and the four tanks reflect the changes. Save the drawing as P24-11.

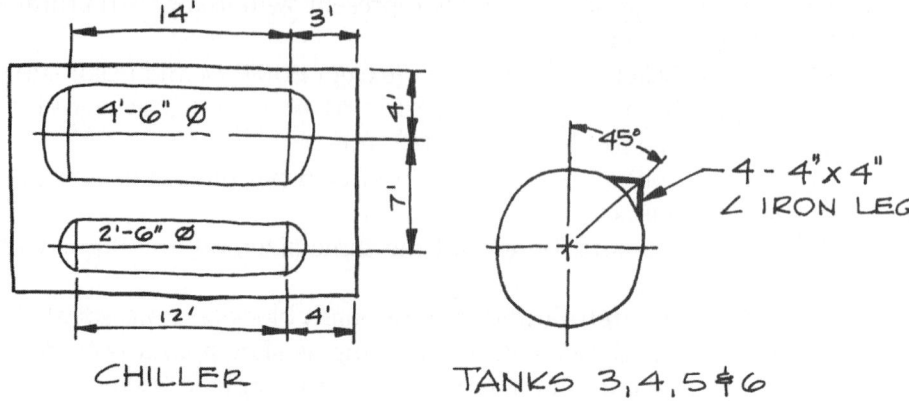

12. Draw the piping flow diagram of an industrial effluent treatment system from the sketch shown. Eliminate as many bends in the flow lines as possible. Place arrowheads at all flow line intersections and bends. The flow lines should not run through any valves or equipment. Use polylines for the thick flow lines. Save the drawing as P24-12.

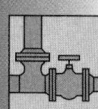

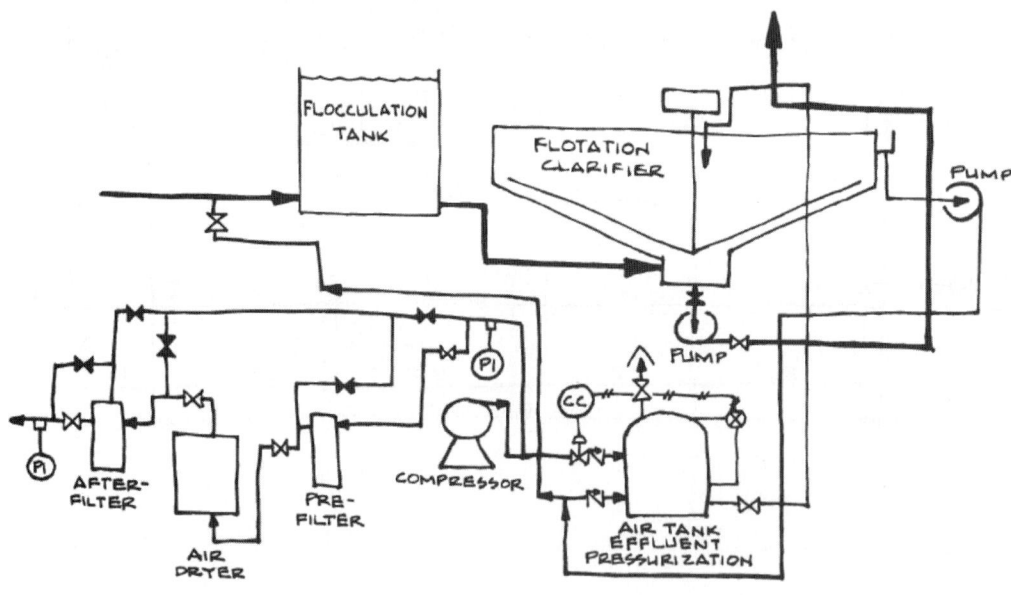

13. Create computer, plotter, and printer/copier blocks and then draw the network diagram shown. Save the drawing as P24-13.

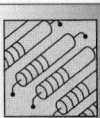

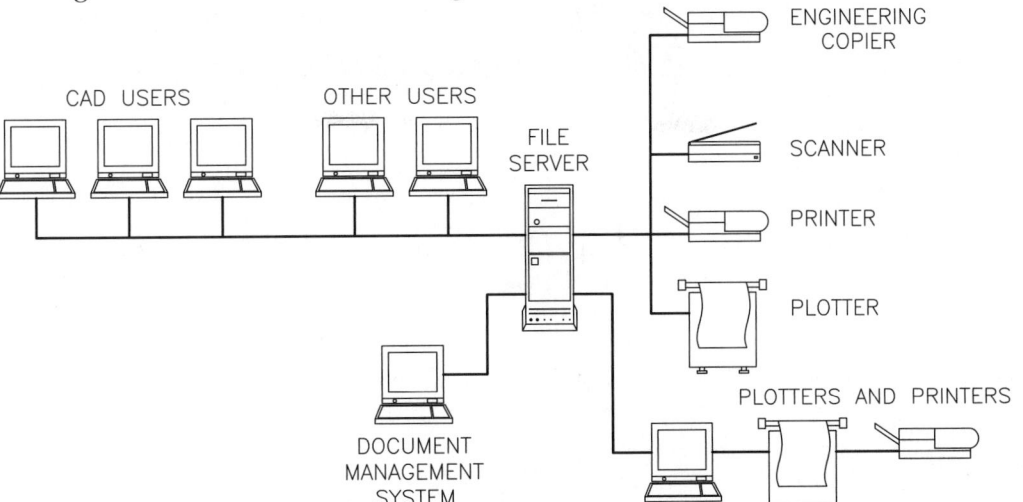

14. Draw the piping diagram, creating blocks for each type of fitting. Save the drawing as P24-14.

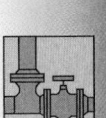

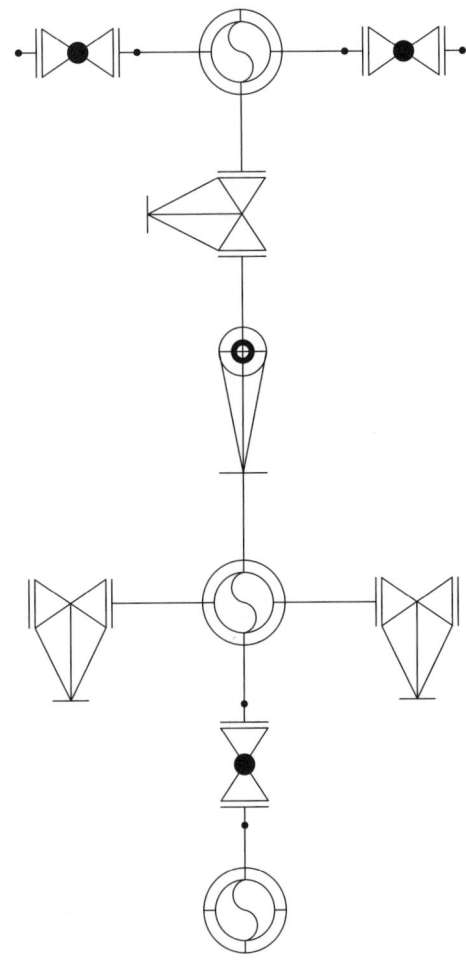

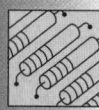
15. Create component blocks based on the dimensions shown. Then use the blocks to draw the schematic below. Save the drawing as P24-15.

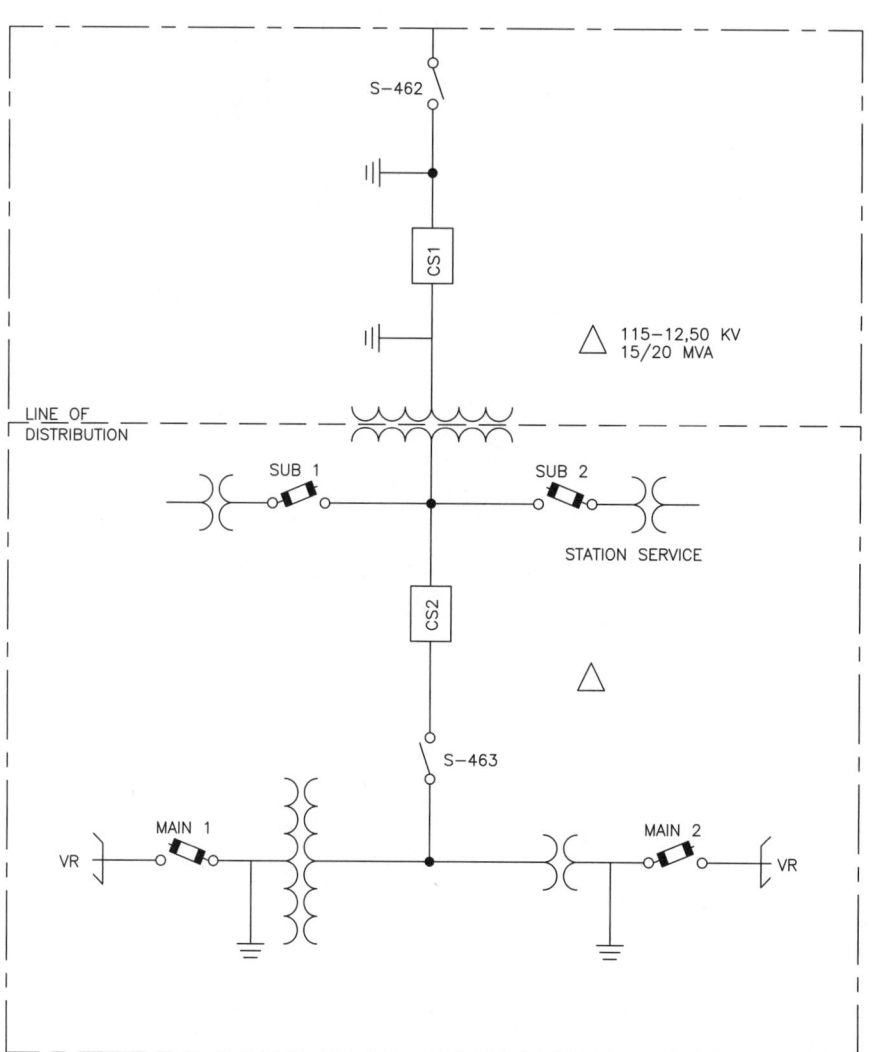

16. Create a symbol library for one of the drafting disciplines listed and save the symbol library as a template or drawing file. Then, after checking with your supervisor or instructor, draw a problem using the library. If you save the symbol library as a template, start the problem with the template. If you save the symbol library as a drawing file, start a new drawing and insert the symbol library into the new file. Specialty areas you might create symbols for include:

- Mechanical (machine features, fasteners, tolerance symbols)
- Architectural (doors, windows, fixtures)
- Structural (steel shapes, bolts, standard footings)
- Civil (mapping symbols, survey markers, utilities)
- Industrial piping (fittings, valves)
- Piping flow diagrams (tanks, valves, pumps)
- Electrical schematics (resistors, capacitors, switches)
- Electrical one-line (transformers, switches)
- Electronics (IC chips, test points, components)
- Logic diagrams (AND gates, NAND gates, buffers)
- GD&T (GD&T symbols)

Save the drawing as P24-16 or choose an appropriate file name, such as ARCH-PRO or ELEC-PRO. Display the symbol library created in this problem and print a hard copy. Put the printed copy in your notebook for reference.

AutoCAD Certified Associate Exam Practice

Answer the following questions. Write your answers on a separate sheet of paper.

1. A drawing has five layers: 0 (white), Objects (blue), Dimensions (red), Center (yellow), and Hidden (green). If you create objects on the 0 layer, assign the objects an absolute color of green, create a block of the objects, and then insert the block on the Objects layer, what color will the block be? *Select the one item that best answers the question.*
   A. blue
   B. green
   C. red
   D. white
   E. yellow

2. You have a 1″ × 1″ unit block of a window. To use the block to represent a 3′ window in a 4″ wall, which of the following scale factors would you use? *Select the one item that best answers the question.*
   A. x = 1, y = 1
   B. x = 3, y = 4
   C. x = 4, y = 30
   D. x = 30, y = 4
   E. x = 36, y = 4

3. Which of the following can you use to insert a block into a drawing? *Select all that apply.*
   A. **BLOCK** tool
   B. **DesignCenter**
   C. **INSERT** tool
   D. **Tool Palettes** palette
   E. **WBLOCK** tool

AutoCAD Certified Professional Exam Practice

Follow the instructions in each problem. Write your answers on a separate sheet of paper.

1. **Navigate to this chapter on the Student Web site and open CPE-24block.dwg.** This drawing contains a block named Hole. Insert the block using the default settings. Select the lower-left corner of the existing object as the insertion point. What are the coordinates of the center of the hole?

2. **Navigate to this chapter on the Student Web site and open CPE-23insert.dwg.** This drawing contains a 2D unit block named Door. Use the appropriate scale factors and rotation to place a 2′-4″ door 6″ above the intersection of the two walls. Edit the wall lines to finish the doorway as shown. What are the coordinates of Point A?

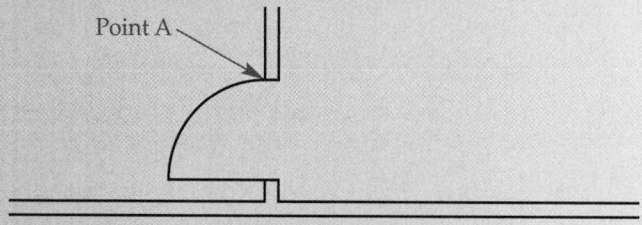

CHAPTER 25

Block Attributes

Learning Objectives

After completing this chapter, you will be able to do the following:

✓ Define attributes.
✓ Create and insert blocks that contain attributes.
✓ Edit attribute values and definitions in existing blocks.
✓ Create title blocks, revision blocks, and parts lists with attributes.
✓ Display attribute values in fields.

Attributes enhance blocks that require text or numerical information. For example, a door tag block contains a letter or number that links the door to a door schedule. Adding an attribute to the door tag block allows you to include a unique letter or number with the symbol, without adding block definitions for each door tag. You can also *extract* attribute data to automate drawing requirements, such as preparing schedules, parts lists, and bills of materials.

attributes: Text-based data assigned to a specific object. Attributes turn a drawing into a graphical database.

extract: Gather content from the drawing file database to display in the drawing or in an external document.

Defining Attributes

Attributes and geometry are often used together to create a block. See **Figure 25-1.** However, you can prepare blocks that only include attributes. Create attributes with other objects during the initial phase of block development. Add as many attributes as needed to describe the symbol or product, such as the name, number, manufacturer, type, size, price, and weight of an item.

Attribute Modes

Access the **ATTDEF** tool to assign attributes using the **Attribute Definition** dialog box. See **Figure 25-2.** Use the **Mode** area to set attribute modes. Symbols often require attributes to appear with the block. An alternative is to check **Invisible** to hide attributes, but still include attribute data in the drawing that you can reference and extract. The geranium symbol in **Figure 25-1** is an example of a block with attributes that might be invisible, depending on the application. The other symbols in **Figure 25-1** are examples of blocks with visible attributes. Blocks often include both visible and invisible attributes.

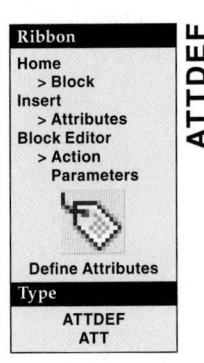

Ribbon

Home
> Block
Insert
> Attributes
Block Editor
> Action
  Parameters

Define Attributes

Type
ATTDEF
ATT

ATTDEF

Figure 25-1. Examples of blocks with defined attributes.

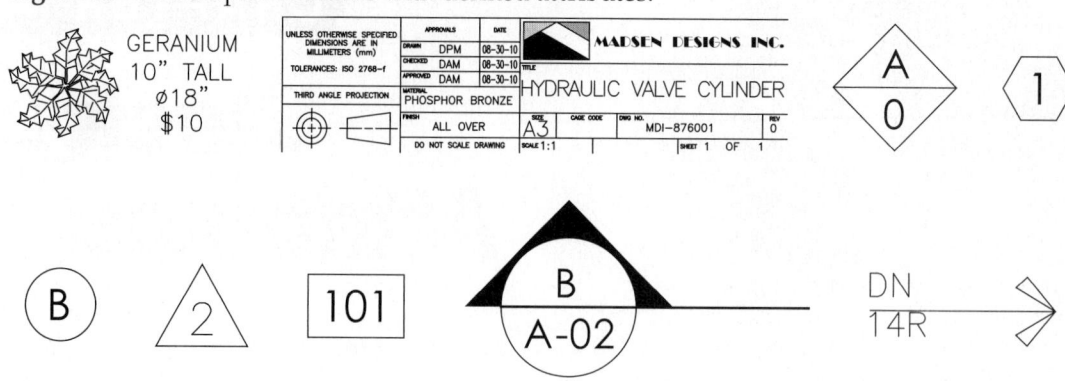

Figure 25-2.
Use the **Attribute Definition** dialog box to assign attributes to blocks.

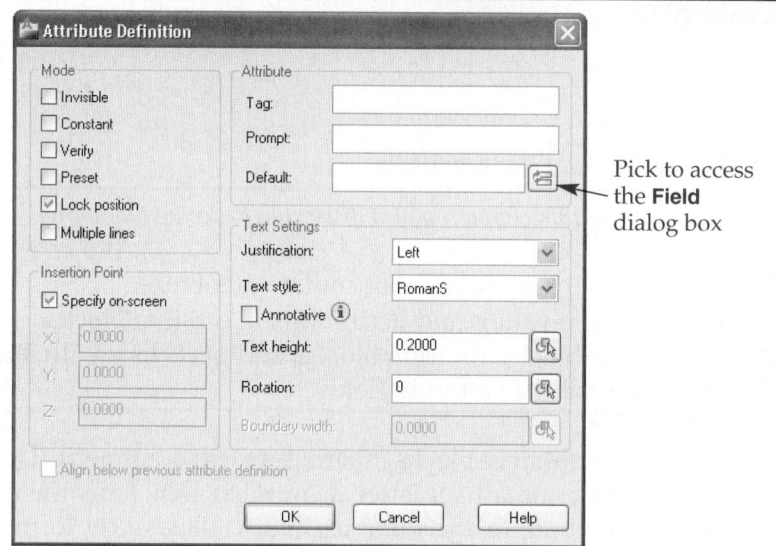

Pick the **Constant** check box if the value of the attribute should always be the same. All insertions of the block display the same value for the attribute, without prompting for a new value when you insert the block. Deselect the **Constant** check box to use different attribute values for multiple insertions of the block. Pick the **Verify** check box to display a prompt that asks if the attribute value is correct when you insert the block. Choose the **Preset** check box to have the attribute assume preset values during block insertion. The **Preset** option disables the attribute prompt. Uncheck **Preset** to display the normal prompt.

Deselect the **Lock position** check box to have the ability to move the attribute independently of the block after insertion. In addition, you must deselect the **Lock position** check box to include the attribute with the action selection set when you assign an action to a dynamic block. If **Lock position** is checked, the attribute is filtered out when you assign the action to the dynamic block. You will learn about dynamic blocks later in this textbook.

You can create single-line or multiple-line attributes. Pick the **Multiple lines** check box to activate options for creating a multiple-line attribute. Deselect the **Multiple lines** check box to create a single-line attribute.

Tag, Prompt, and Value

The **Attribute** area provides text boxes for assigning a tag, prompt, and default value to the attribute. Use the **Tag** text box to enter the attribute name, or tag. For example, the tag for a size attribute for a valve block could be SIZE. You must enter a tag in order to create an attribute. The tag cannot include spaces. The attribute definition applies uppercase characters to the tag, even if you type lowercase characters in the text box.

Type a statement in the **Prompt** text box that will display when you insert or edit the block. For example, if you specify SIZE as the attribute tag, you might specify What is the valve size? or Enter valve size: as the prompt. You have the option to leave the prompt blank. The **Prompt** text box is disabled when you select the **Constant** attribute mode.

Use the **Default** text box to specify a default attribute value or a description of an acceptable value for reference. For example, you might type the most common size for the SIZE attribute, or a message regarding the type of information needed, such as 10 SPACES MAX or NUMBERS ONLY. If you deselect the **Multiple lines** attribute mode, enter the default value directly in the text box.

Attribute values can include up to 255 characters. If the first character in an entry is a space, start the string with a backslash (\). If the first character is a backslash, begin the entry with two backslashes (\\). If you select the **Multiple lines** attribute mode, pick the ellipsis (...) button to enter the drawing area and place multiline text using the **Text Formatting** toolbar and text editor. See **Figure 25-3**. Enter the default text, and then pick the **OK** button on the toolbar to return to the **Attribute Definition** dialog box. Use the **Insert field** button to include a field in the default value. You have the option to leave the default value blank.

> **NOTE**
>
> The abbreviated **Text Formatting** toolbar shown in **Figure 25-3** appears by default. Set the **ATTIPE** system variable to 1 to display the complete **Text Formatting** toolbar. The **ATTIPE** system variable is set to 0 by default.

Text Settings

Use options in the **Text Settings** area to specify attribute text format. Use the **Justification** drop-down list to select a justification for the attribute text. The default justification is Left. In single-line attributes, the text itself is justified. In the **Multiple lines** attribute mode, the text boundary is justified.

Figure 25-3.
Define multiple-line attributes directly on-screen. The abbreviated **Text Formatting** toolbar appears instead of the **Text Editor** ribbon tab.

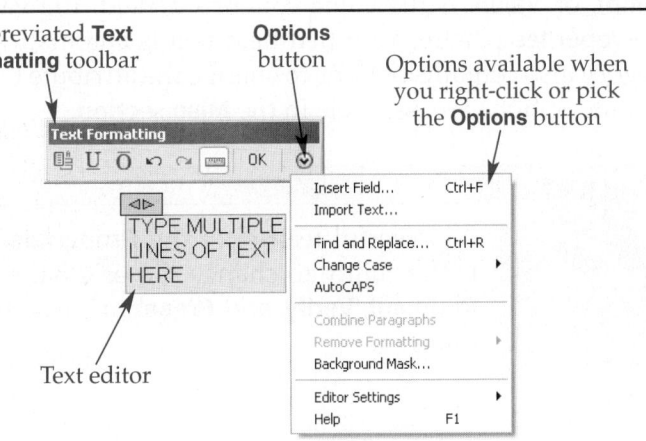

Use the **Text Style** drop-down list to select a text style available in the current drawing to assign to the attribute. Pick the **Annotative** check box to make the attribute text height annotative. AutoCAD scales annotative attributes according to the specified annotation scale, which eliminates the need to calculate the scale factor. If you plan to define a block as annotative, you can include annotative or non-annotative objects, such as attributes, with the block. However, you must use non-annotative objects when preparing a non-annotative block.

Specify the height of the attribute text in the **Height** text box, or pick the **Text Height** button next to the text box to pick two points in the drawing to set the text height. Identify the rotation angle for the attribute text in the **Rotation** text box, or pick the **Rotation** button next to the text box to pick two points in the drawing to set the text rotation. The **Boundary width** option is available in the **Multiple lines** attribute mode. Type a width in the **Boundary width** text box, or pick the **Boundary width** button next to the text box to pick two points in the drawing to set a text boundary width.

Defining the Attribute Insertion Point

Use options in the **Insertion Point** area to define how and where to position the attribute during insertion. Choose the **Specify On-screen** check box to pick an insertion point in the drawing after you pick the **OK** button to create the attribute and exit the **Attribute Definition** dialog box. An alternative is to type values in the **X:**, **Y:**, and **Z:** text boxes if you know the coordinates for the insertion point.

The **Align below previous attribute definition** check box is enabled if the drawing already contains at least one attribute. Check the box to place the new attribute directly below the most recently created attribute using the justification of that attribute. This is an effective technique for placing a group of different attributes in the same block. The **Text Options** and **Insertion Point** areas are deactivated.

Placing the Attribute

After defining all elements of the attribute, pick the **OK** button to close the **Attribute Definition** dialog box. The attribute tag appears on-screen if you specified coordinates for the insertion point, or if you used the **Align below previous attribute definition** option. Otherwise, AutoCAD prompts you to specify an insertion point. If the attribute mode is set to **Invisible**, do not be concerned that the tag is visible. The tag disappears when you include the attribute with a block definition.

Editing Attribute Properties

The **Properties** palette provides options for editing attributes before you include them in a block. See **Figure 25-4.** Change the color, linetype, or layer of the selected attribute in the **General** category. Use options in the **Text** category to adjust the **Tag**, **Prompt**, or **Value**. If the value contains a field, the value appears as normal text in the **Properties** palette. Modified field text is automatically converted to text. The **Text** category also contains options to change the attribute text settings. Additional text and attribute options are available in the **Misc** section.

PROFESSIONAL TIP

A powerful feature of the **Properties** palette for editing attributes is the ability to change the original attribute modes. The **Invisible**, **Constant**, **Verify**, and **Preset** mode settings are available in the **Misc** category.

Figure 25-4.
The **Properties** palette allows you to modify attributes.

Selected object to edit →

Pick to change the attribute tag →

Pick to change an attribute mode setting →

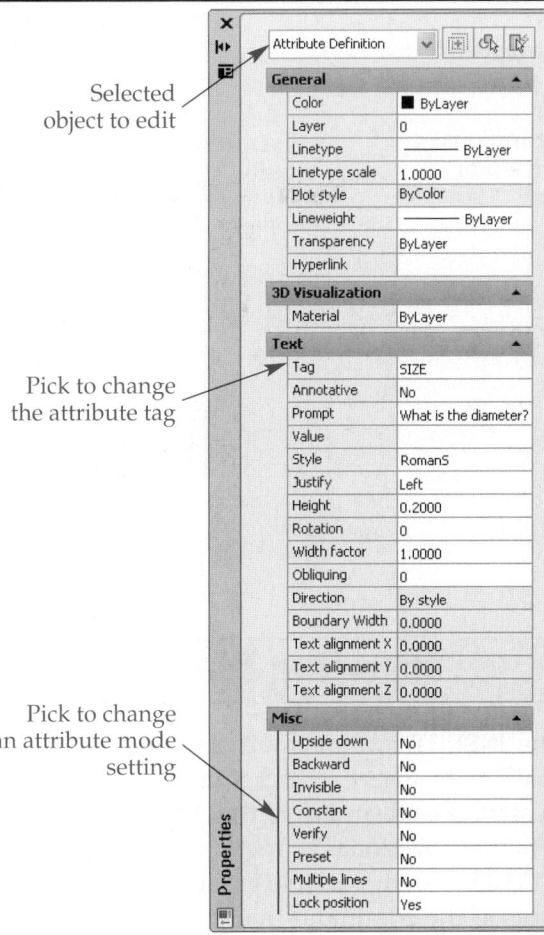

Creating Blocks with Attributes

Attributes are useful only when they are included with a block definition. Use the **BLOCK** or **WBLOCK** tool to define a block with attributes. Select all objects and attributes to be included with the block. The order in which you select attribute definitions is the order of prompts, or the order in which the attributes appear in the **Edit Attributes** dialog box. If you select the **Convert to Block** radio button in the **Block Definition** dialog box, the **Edit Attributes** dialog box appears when you create the block. See **Figure 25-5.** The **Edit Attributes** dialog box allows you to adjust attribute values when you insert or edit the block.

PROFESSIONAL TIP

If you create attributes in the order in which you want to receive prompts and then use window or crossing selection to select the attributes, the attribute prompts display in the *reverse* order of the desired prompting. To change the order, insert, explode, and then redefine the block using window or crossing selection again to pick the attributes. The attribute prompt order reverses again, placing the prompts in the desired order.

Figure 25-5.
The **Edit Attributes** dialog box allows you to enter attribute definitions when you insert or edit a block.

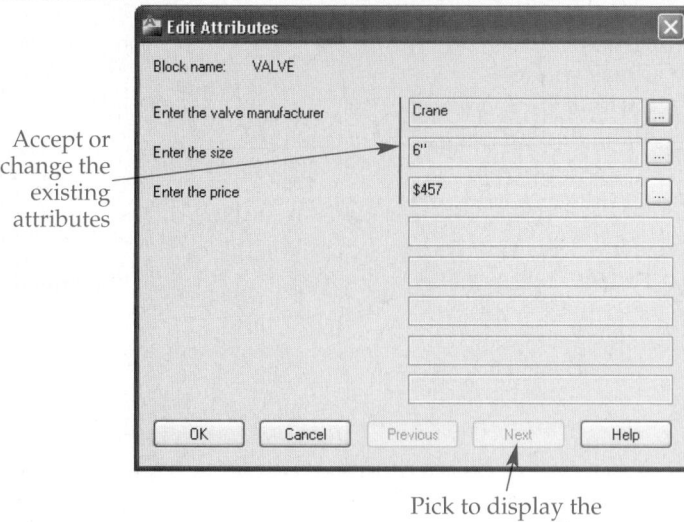

Accept or change the existing attributes

Pick to display the next page of attributes

Inserting Blocks with Attributes

Use the **INSERT** tool or another block insertion method, such as **DesignCenter** or a tool palette, to insert a block that contains attributes. The process of inserting a block with attributes is similar to that for inserting a block without attributes. The only difference is that additional prompts request values for each attribute.

The **ATTDIA** system variable is set to 0 by default, which displays single-line attribute prompts at the command line or dynamic input and displays multiple-line attribute prompts using the AutoCAD text window. A better method of entering attribute values is to set the **ATTDIA** system variable to 1 before inserting blocks. This enables the **Edit Attributes** dialog box. The dialog box appears after you specify the insertion point, scale, and rotation angle, allowing you to answer each attribute prompt. Type single-line attribute values in the text boxes. To define multiple-line attributes, select the ellipsis (...) button next to the text boxes to enter values on-screen as multiline text. If a value includes a field, you can right-click on the field to edit it or convert it to text.

Press [Tab] to move quickly through the attributes and buttons in the **Edit Attributes** dialog box. Press [Shift]+[Tab] to cycle through attributes and buttons in reverse order. If the block includes more than eight attributes, pick the **Next** button at the bottom of the **Edit Attributes** dialog box to display the next page of attributes. When you finish entering values, pick the **OK** button to close the dialog box and create the block.

Exercise 25-1

Access the Student Web site (www.g-wlearning.com/CAD) and complete Exercise 25-1.

Attribute Prompt Suppression

Some blocks may include attributes that always retain default values. In this case, there is no need to receive prompts for attribute values when you insert the block. Assign the **Constant** mode to a specific attribute during attribute definition, if you are confident the attribute value will not change, or turn off prompts for all attributes by setting the **ATTREQ** system variable to 0. To display attribute prompts again, change the setting back to 1. The **ATTREQ** system variable setting is saved with the drawing.

Controlling Attribute Display

Some attributes only provide content to generate parts lists or bills of materials and to speed accounting. These types of attributes usually do not display on-screen or plot. Use the **ATTDISP** tool to control the display of attributes on-screen. The easiest way to activate an **ATTDISP** tool option is to pick the corresponding button from the ribbon.

Use the default **Retain display** (**Normal**) option to display attributes exactly as created. Use the **Display all** (**ON**) option to display all attributes, both visible and invisible. Apply the **Hide all** (**OFF**) option to suppress the display of all attributes, including visible attributes.

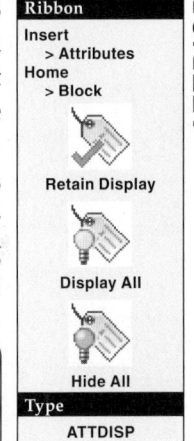
Ribbon
Insert
> Attributes
Home
> Block

Retain Display

Display All

Hide All

Type
ATTDISP

ATTDISP

Editing Attribute References

Once you insert a block with attributes, tools are available for editing attribute values and settings. One option is modify the attributes of a single block using the **EATTEDIT** tool. Access the **EATTEDIT** tool and pick the block to display the **Enhanced Attribute Editor**. See **Figure 25-6**. If you want to edit attributes in other blocks, pick the **Select block** button to return to the drawing to select a different block to modify.

The **Attribute** tab, shown in **Figure 25-6**, displays all of the attributes assigned to the selected block. Pick the attribute you want to modify and enter a new value in the **Value:** text box. If the attribute is a multiple-line attribute, pick the ellipsis (**...**) button to modify the text on-screen. Pick the **Apply** button after adjusting the value.

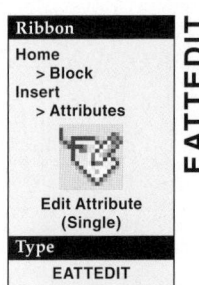
Ribbon
Home
> Block
Insert
> Attributes

Edit Attribute
(Single)
Type
EATTEDIT

EATTEDIT

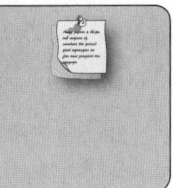

Type
ATTIPEDIT

Figure 25-6. Select the attribute to modify and change the value in the **Attribute** tab of the **Enhanced Attribute Editor**.

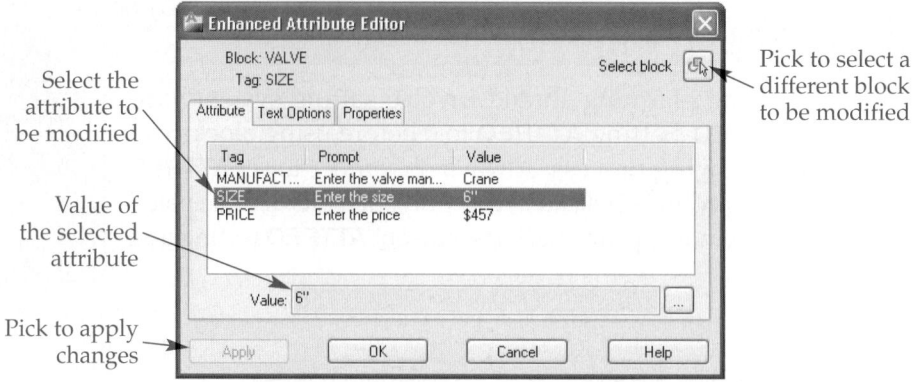

Select the attribute to be modified

Value of the selected attribute

Pick to apply changes

Pick to select a different block to be modified

Use the **Text Options** tab, shown in **Figure 25-7A,** to modify the text properties of an attribute. The **Properties** tab, shown in **Figure 25-7B,** provides object property adjustments for an attribute. Each attribute in a block is a separate item. The settings you apply in the **Text Options** and **Properties** tabs affect the active attribute in the **Attribute** tab. Pick the **Apply** button to view changes made to attributes. Pick the **OK** button to close the dialog box.

Figure 25-7. A—The **Text Options** tab provides options in addition to those set in the **Attribute Definition** dialog box. B—The **Properties** tab allows you to modify the properties of an attribute.

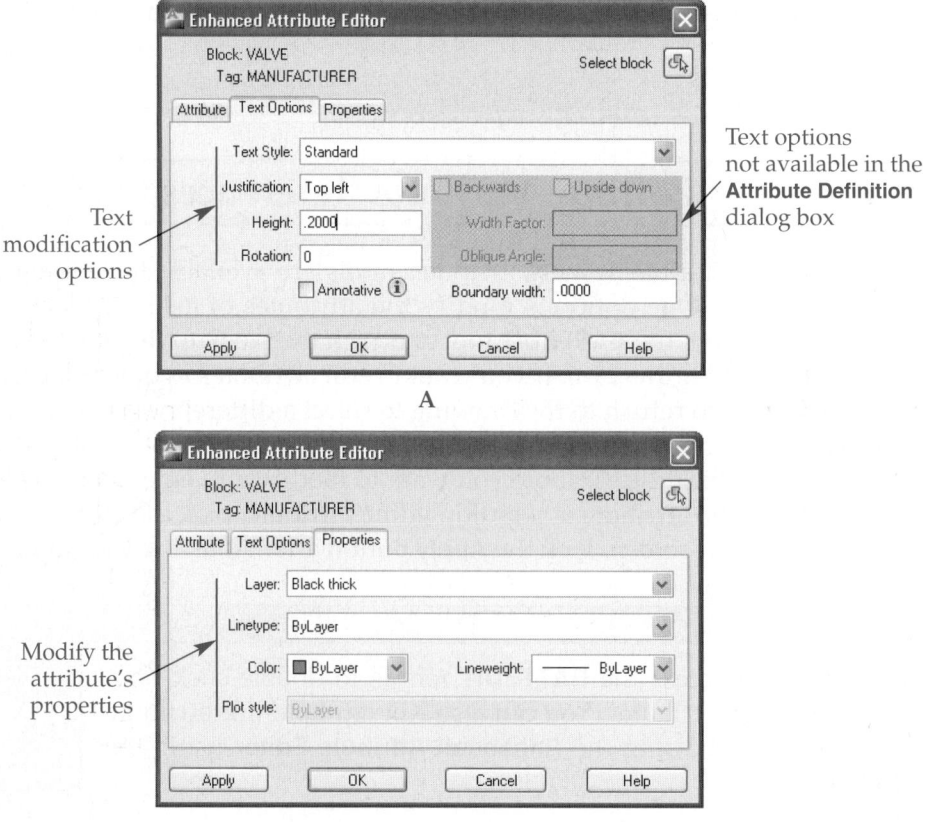

Text modification options

Text options not available in the **Attribute Definition** dialog box

A

Modify the attribute's properties

B

Exercise 25-2

Access the Student Web site (www.g-wlearning.com/CAD) and complete Exercise 25-2.

Using the FIND Tool to Edit Attributes

The **FIND** tool, which uses the **Find and Replace** dialog box described in Chapter 10, provides one of the quickest ways to edit attributes. You can also access the **FIND** tool when no tool is active by right-clicking in the drawing area and selecting **Find...**, or enter the text in the **Find text** text box in the **Text** panel of the **Annotation** ribbon tab and press [Enter]. Specify the portion of the drawing to search, the attribute value to find, and the replacement value.

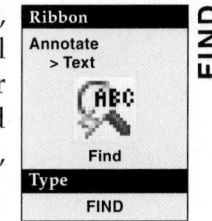

Ribbon
Annotate
> Text

FIND

Find

Type
FIND

Editing Multiple Attribute References

The **Enhanced Attribute Editor** allows you to edit attribute values and settings by selecting blocks one at a time. The **-ATTEDIT** tool edits the attributes of several blocks. When you access the **-ATTEDIT** tool, a prompt asks if you want to edit attributes individually. Use the default Yes option to select specific blocks with attributes to edit. Use the No option to apply *global attribute editing*.

If you choose the Yes option, prompts appear to specify the block name, attribute tag, and attribute value. To edit attribute values selectively, respond to each prompt with the correct name or value, and then select one or more attributes. If you see the message 0 found after selecting attributes, you picked an incorrectly specified attribute. It is often quicker to press [Enter] at each of the three specification prompts and then pick the attribute to edit. Select an option and follow the prompts to edit the attribute(s).

If you choose the No option, the Edit only attributes visible on screen? prompt appears. Select the Yes option to edit all visible attributes, or choose the No option to edit all attributes, including invisible attributes. The same three prompts previously described for individual block editing appear.

Figure 25-8A shows a VALVE block inserted three times with the manufacturer specified as CRANE. In this example, the manufacturer was supposed to be POWELL. To change the attribute for each insertion, access the **-ATTEDIT** tool and specify global

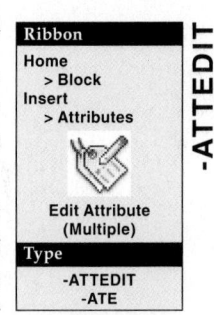

Ribbon
Home
> Block
Insert
> Attributes

-ATTEDIT

Edit Attribute
(Multiple)

Type
-ATTEDIT
-ATE

global attribute editing: Editing or changing all insertions, or instances, of the same block in a single operation.

Figure 25-8.
Using the global editing technique with the **-ATTEDIT** tool allows you to change the same attribute on several block insertions.

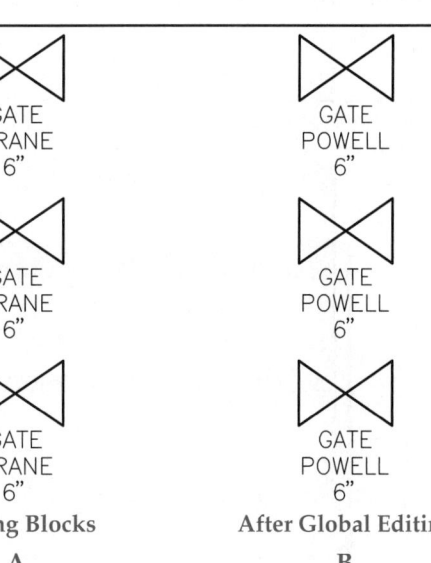

GATE
CRANE
6"

GATE
POWELL
6"

GATE
CRANE
6"

GATE
POWELL
6"

GATE
CRANE
6"

GATE
POWELL
6"

Existing Blocks

After Global Editing

A

B

---

editing. Press [Enter] at each of the three specification prompts. When the Select attributes: prompt appears, pick CRANE on each of the VALVE blocks and press [Enter]. At
the Enter string to change: prompt, enter CRANE, and at the Enter new string: prompt, enter
POWELL. See the result in **Figure 25-8B.**

PROFESSIONAL TIP

Use care when assigning the **Constant** mode to attribute definitions.
The **-ATTEDIT** tool displays 0 found if you attempt to edit a block attribute that has a **Constant** mode setting. Assign the **Constant** mode
only to attributes you know will not change.

NOTE

You can also use the **-ATTEDIT** tool to edit individual attribute values
and properties. However, it is more efficient to use the **Enhanced
Attribute Editor** to change individual attributes.

Exercise 25-3

Access the Student Web site (www.g-wlearning.com/CAD) and complete
Exercise 25-3.

Editing Attribute Definitions

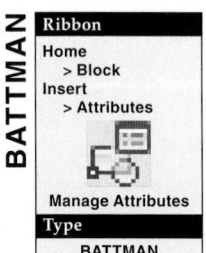

Ribbon
Home
> Block
Insert
> Attributes

Manage Attributes
Type
BATTMAN

Once you create a block with attributes, tools are available for modifying attribute
definitions. One option is to edit attribute definitions using the **BATTMAN** tool, which
displays the **Block Attribute Manager**. See **Figure 25-9.** To manage the attributes in a
block, choose the block name from the **Block:** drop-down list or pick the **Select block**
button to return to the drawing and pick a block.

The tag, prompt, default value, and modes for each attribute are listed by default. To
select the attribute properties listed in the **Block Attribute Manager**, pick the **Settings...**

Figure 25-9. Use the **Block Attribute Manager** to change attribute definitions, delete
attributes, and change the order of attribute prompts.

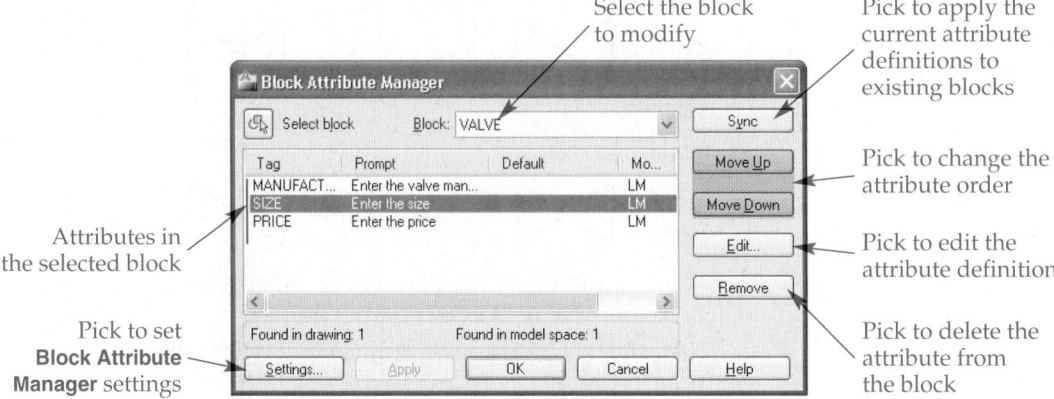

button to open the **Block Attribute Settings** dialog box. See **Figure 25-10.** Check the properties to list in the **Display in list** area. Select the **Emphasize duplicate tags** check box to highlight attributes with identical tags in red. Check **Apply changes to existing references** to apply changes made in the **Block Attribute Manager** to existing blocks. Pick the **OK** button to return to the **Block Attribute Manager.**

The attribute list in the **Block Attribute Manager** reflects the order in which prompts appear when you insert a block. Use the **Move Up** and **Move Down** buttons to change the order of the selected attribute within the list, modifying the prompt order. To delete an attribute, pick the **Remove** button. To modify an attribute, select the attribute and pick the **Edit...** button to display the **Edit Attribute** dialog box. See **Figure 25-11.** Use the **Attribute** tab to modify the modes, tag, prompt, and default value. The **Text Options** and **Properties** tabs of the **Edit Attribute** dialog box are identical to the tabs found in the **Enhanced Attribute Editor.** Check **Auto preview changes** at the bottom of the dialog box to display changes to attributes immediately in the drawing area.

After modifying the attribute definition in the **Edit Attribute** dialog box, pick the **OK** button to return to the **Block Attribute Manager.** Then pick the **OK** button to return to the drawing. When you modify attributes within a block, future insertions of the block reflect the changes. Existing blocks update only if you select the **Apply changes to existing references** check box in the **Settings** dialog box.

NOTE

The **Block Attribute Manager** modifies attribute definitions, not attribute reference values. Modify attribute values using the **Enhanced Attribute Editor.**

Figure 25-10.
The **Block Attribute Settings** dialog box controls the types of attributes displayed in the **Block Attribute Manager.**

Select the attribute properties to list in the **Block Attribute Manager**

Identifies duplicate tags

Updates existing blocks

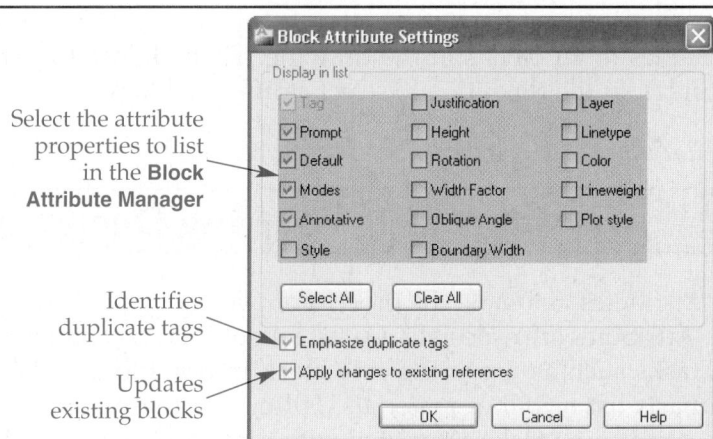

Figure 25-11. Use the **Edit Attribute** dialog box to modify attribute definitions and properties.

Use these tabs to modify attribute properties

Select modes

Modify attribute definition

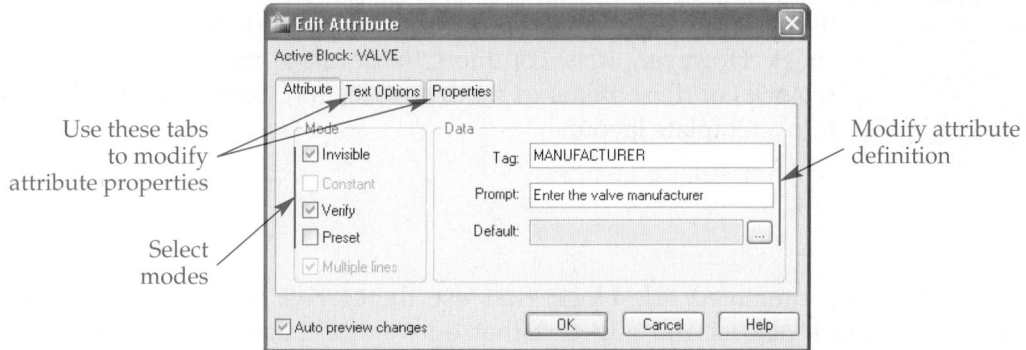

Redefining a Block with Attributes

To add attributes to or revise the geometry of a block, edit the block definition using the **BEDIT** or **REFEDIT** tools. Chapter 31 explains the **REFEDIT** tool. The **BEDIT** and **REFEDIT** tools allow you to make changes to a block definition, including attributes assigned to the block, without exploding the block.

> **NOTE**
>
> You can also explode and then redefine the block using the same name. Another option is to use the **ATTREDEF** tool. However, the **ATTREDEF** tool is text-based, and you must first explode the block. Use **BEDIT** or **REFEDIT** to edit the block.

Synchronizing Attributes

Redefining a block automatically updates the properties of all of the same blocks in the drawing, but does not apply changes made to attributes. For example, if you add an object to a block, all existing blocks of the same name update to display the new object. However, if you add an attribute to a block, all existing blocks of the same name continue to display the original attributes, without the new attribute. Synchronize the blocks to update the attribute redefinition.

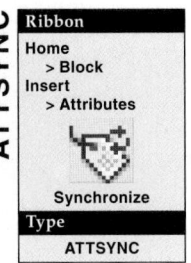

ATTSYNC

Ribbon
Home
> Block
Insert
> Attributes

Synchronize

Type
ATTSYNC

Synchronize blocks in the **Block Attribute Manager** by picking the **Sync** button. This method is convenient because it allows you to make changes to and remove attributes using the **Block Attribute Manager**. Use the **ATTSYNC** tool to synchronize attributes from outside the **Block Attribute Manager**. Access the **ATTSYNC** tool and use the default **Select** option to pick a block that contains the attributes you want to synchronize. An alternative is to use the **Name** option to type the block name, or use the **?** option to list the names of all blocks in the drawing. Then choose the **Yes** option to synchronize attributes, or the **No** option to select a different block.

Automating Drafting Documentation

Attributes automate the process of placing symbols that require textual information. Attributes are especially useful for automating common detailing or documentation tasks such as preparing title block information, revision block data, schedules, or a parts list or bill of materials. Filling out these items is usually one of the more time-consuming tasks associated with drafting documentation.

>
>
> **NOTE**
>
> You typically draw or place title blocks, revision blocks, and parts lists in a layout, as they are content usually added to the drawing sheet. However, it is common to develop the initial blocks or wblocks of these items in model space, and then insert the blocks into a template layout.

Title Blocks

To create an automated title block, first use the correct layer, typically layer 0, to draw title block objects and add text that does not change, such as the titles of compartments. Format the title block in accordance with industry and company or school standards. Include your company or school logo if appropriate. If you work in an industry that produces items for the federal government, also include the applicable *Commercial and Government Entity Code (CAGE Code)*. **Figure 25-12** shows a title block drawn in accordance with the ASME Y14.1 *Decimal Inch Drawing Sheet Size and Format* standard.

Next, define attributes for each area of the title block. As you create attributes, determine the appropriate text height and justification for each definition. Common title block attributes include drawing title, drawing number, drafter, checker, dates, drawing scale, sheet size, material, finish, revision letter, and tolerance information. See **Figure 25-13**. Create approval attributes with a prompt such as ENTER INITIALS OR SEEK SIGNATURE, providing the flexibility to type initials or leave the cell blank for written initials. Apply the same practice to date attributes. Include any other information that may be specific to the organization or drawing application. Assign default values to the attributes wherever possible. For example, if you consistently specify the same tolerances for dimensions, assign default values to the tolerance attributes.

PROFESSIONAL TIP

The size of each area within the title block limits the number of characters displayed in a line of text. Include a reminder about the maximum number of characters in the attribute prompt, such as Enter drawing name (15 characters max). Each time you insert a block or drawing containing the attribute, the prompt displays the reminder.

After you define each attribute in the title block, you are ready to create the block. One option is to use the **BLOCK** tool to create a block of the title block within the current file. When specifying the insertion base point, pick a corner of the title block

Figure 25-12. A title block must comply with applicable standards. This title block complies with the ASME Y14.1 standard, *Decimal Inch Drawing Sheet Size and Format.*

Figure 25-13. Define attributes for each area of the title block. Attributes should define all information that might possibly change, including general tolerances. This figure shows the attributes in color for illustrative purposes only.

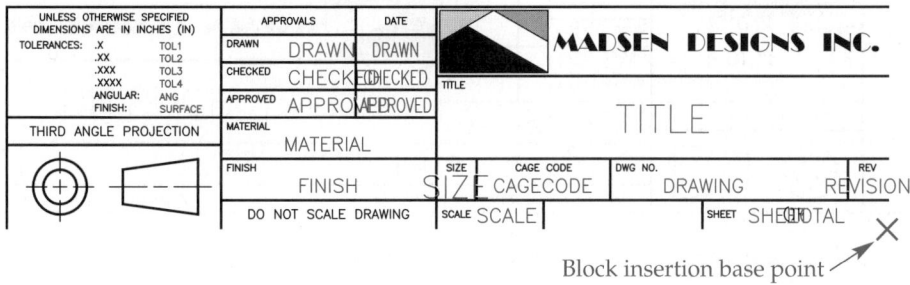

Block insertion base point

that is convenient to use each time you insert the block. **Figure 25-13** shows the insertion base point that is appropriate for that particular title block. Use the **Delete** option in the **Block Definition** dialog box to remove the selected objects from the drawing.

Another option is to use the **WBLOCK** tool to save the drawing as a file. Give the file a descriptive name, such as TITLE_B or FORMAT_B for a B-size title block. **Figure 25-14** shows the attribute block created in **Figure 25-13**, inserted and completely filled out using attributes.

> **NOTE**
>
> If you are creating a template, insert the block at the appropriate location and save the file as a drawing template. Edit the values in an existing title block using the **Enhanced Attribute Editor**.

Revision Blocks

It is almost certain that a detail drawing will require revision. Typical changes include design improvements and the correction of drafting errors. The first revision is usually assigned the revision letter *A*. If necessary, revision letters continue with *B* through *Y*, but the letters *I*, *O*, *Q*, *S*, *X*, and *Z* are not used because they might be confused with numbers.

revision block: A block that provides space for the revision letter, a description of the change, the date, and approvals.

zones: A system of letters and numbers used on large drawings to help direct the attention of the person reading the print to a location on the drawing.

Drawing layout formats include an area with columns specifically designated to record drawing changes. This area, commonly called the *revision block*, is normally located at the upper-right corner of the drawing sheet. A column for *zones* is included only if applicable.

The **TABLE** tool is an excellent tool for preparing a revision block. An alternative is to use blocks and attributes to document revisions. The process is similar to creating a title block, but a revision block requires two separate blocks. The first block consists of only lines and text and forms the title and heading rows. See **Figure 25-15A**. Insert the second block, which includes attributes, whenever a revision is required. See **Figure 25-15B**.

Format the revision block according to industry and company or school standards, and use the correct layer, typically layer 0. As you create attributes, determine the appropriate text height and justification for each definition. Define attributes for the zone (if necessary), revision letter, description, date, and approval. Assign the APPROVED attribute a prompt such as ENTER INITIALS OR SEEK SIGNATURE, providing the flexibility to type initials or leave the cell blank for written initials. Apply the same practice to the date attribute.

Figure 25-14. The title block after insertion of the attributes. Add dates and approvals when the drawing is complete.

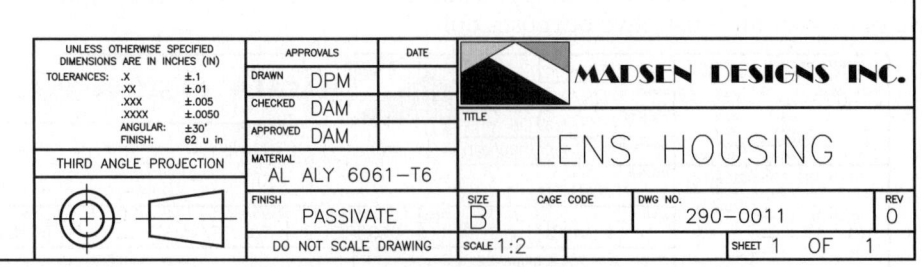

Figure 25-15. Creating a revision block using two separate blocks. A—The first block forms the title and heading rows. B—The second block includes attributes and is added each time an engineering change is employed. The revision block shown complies with the ASME Y14.1 standard, *Decimal Inch Drawing Sheet Size and Format*. This figure shows the attributes in color for illustrative purposes only.

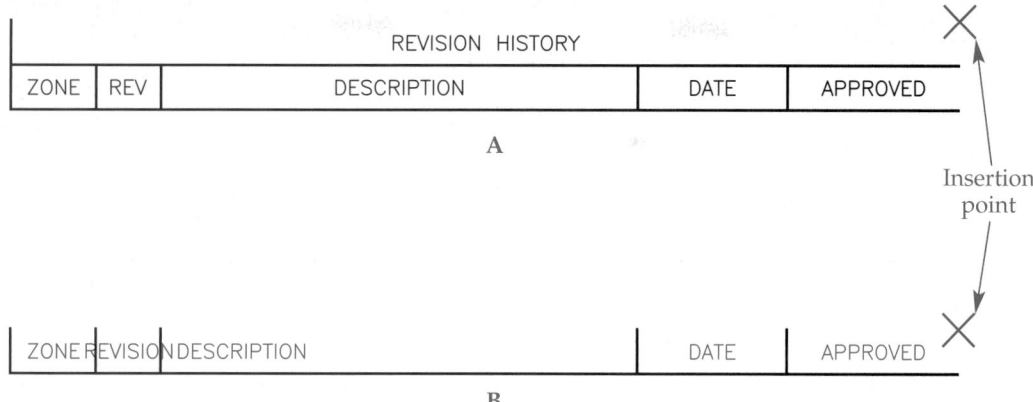

Use the **BLOCK** or **WBLOCK** tool to create the blocks. If you create wblocks, use descriptive file names such as REVBLK or REV. **Figure 25-16** shows an example of revision information added by inserting the two blocks created in **Figure 25-15** in the upper-left inside corner of the border.

Parts Lists

Assembly drawings require a parts list, or bill of materials, that provides information about each component of the assembly or subassembly. Columns can identify a variety of information depending on the organization and application. Common elements include the list type (parts list, index list, application list, data list, wire list), design activity, contract number, find or item number, quantity required, CAGE Code (when necessary), part or identification number, and nomenclature or description. Companies often include the parts list on the face of the assembly drawing. A parts list on an assembly drawing usually appears directly above the title block, depending on industry and company standards. Other organizations create the parts list as a separate document, often in an 8-1/2″ × 11″ format.

The **TABLE** tool is an excellent tool for preparing a parts list. An alternative is to use blocks and attributes. The process is very similar to creating a revision block. The first block consists of only lines and text and forms the title (if used) and heading rows. See **Figure 25-17A**. The second block includes attributes and is inserted as many times as necessary to document each assembly component. See **Figure 25-17B**.

Format the parts list according to industry and company or school standards, and use the correct layer, typically layer 0. As you create attributes, select the appropriate text height and justification for each definition. Define attributes for the column or cell in the parts list.

Figure 25-16. The completed revision block after inserting two blocks.

REVISION HISTORY				
ZONE	REV	DESCRIPTION	DATE	APPROVED
C3	A	ADDED .125 CHAMFER	08−30−10	

Figure 25-17. Creating a parts list using two separate blocks. A—The first block forms the title (if used) and heading rows. B—The second block includes attributes and is inserted as many times as necessary to define each assembly component. The revision block shown complies with the ASME Y14.1 standard, *Decimal Inch Drawing Sheet Size and Format*.

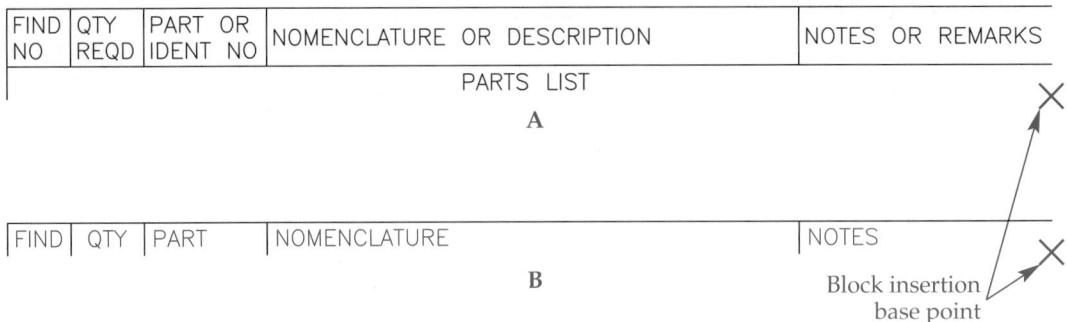

Use the **BLOCK** or **WBLOCK** tool to create the blocks. If you save wblocks, use descriptive file names, such as PL for parts list or BOM for bill of materials. **Figure 25-18** shows an example of the beginning of a parts list developed by inserting the blocks created in **Figure 25-17**.

Using Fields to Reference Attributes

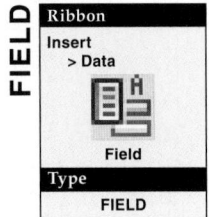

Use fields to link text to attribute values. To display a field as an attribute value, access the **Field** dialog box from within the **MTEXT** or **TEXT** tool, or use the **FIELD** tool. In the **Field** dialog box, pick **Objects** from the **Field category:** drop-down list, and pick **Object** in the **Field names:** list box. Then pick the **Select object** button to return to the drawing window and select the block containing the attribute.

When you select the block, the **Field** dialog box reappears with the available properties (attributes) listed. Pick an attribute tag to display the corresponding value in the **Preview:** box. Select the format and pick the **OK** button to insert the attribute value as a field in the text object.

Figure 25-18. The beginning of a parts list after inserting blocks and editing attribute values.

FIND NO	QTY REQD	PART OR IDENT NO	NOMENCLATURE OR DESCRIPTION	NOTES OR REMARKS
4	4	74–0080	SLEEVE	SAE1020
3	12	85741	8–32UNC–2 X .50 HEX SOC CAP SCREW	SAE 4320
2	2	2569–01	RACK PAD	UHMW BLACK
1	1	52451	MOUNTING PLATE	AL ALY 6061–T6

PARTS LIST

UNLESS OTHERWISE SPECIFIED DIMENSIONS ARE IN INCHES (IN)
TOLERANCES: .X ±.1 .XX ±.01 .XXX ±.005 .XXXX ±.0050 ANGULAR: ±30' FINISH: 62 u in

APPROVALS	DATE
DRAWN DPM	
CHECKED DAM	
APPROVED DAM	

MADSEN DESIGNS INC.

THIRD ANGLE PROJECTION

MATERIAL VARIES

FINISH ALL OVER

TITLE

VOR MULTIPLIER

SIZE B

CAGE CODE

DWG NO. 290–0011

REV 0

SCALE 1:2

DO NOT SCALE DRAWING

SHEET 1 OF 1

Supplemental Material

Extracting Attribute Data
For information about using attributes to create a table and exporting attribute data to an external file, go to the Student Web site (www.g-wlearning.com/CAD), select this chapter, and select **Extracting Attribute Data**.

Chapter Test

*Answer the following questions. Write your answers on a separate sheet of paper or go to the Student Web site (**www.g-wlearning.com/CAD**) and complete the electronic chapter test.*

1. What is an attribute?
2. Explain the purpose of the **ATTDEF** tool.
3. Describe the function of the following attribute modes:
   A. **Invisible**
   B. **Constant**
   C. **Verify**
   D. **Preset**
4. What is the purpose of the **Default** text box in the **Attribute Definition** dialog box?
5. How can you edit attributes before including the attributes with a block?
6. How can you change an existing attribute from visible to invisible?
7. If you select attributes using the **Window** or **Crossing** selection method to define a block, in what order will attribute prompts appear?
8. What purpose does the **ATTREQ** system variable serve?
9. List the three options for attribute display.
10. Explain how to change the value of an inserted attribute.
11. What does *global attribute editing* mean?
12. After you save a block with attributes, what method can you use to change the order of prompts when you insert the block?
13. List examples of detailing or documentation tasks that attributes can help automate.
14. What element of an assembly drawing provides information about each component of the assembly or subassembly?
15. How can you link text to an attribute value?

Drawing Problems

- *Start AutoCAD if it is not already started. Start a new drawing for each problem using an appropriate template of your choice.*
- *The template should include layers and text, dimension, multileader, and table styles, when necessary, for drawing the given objects. Add layers and text, dimension, multileader, and table styles as needed.*
- *Draw all objects using appropriate layers and text, dimension, multileader, and table styles, justification, and format.*
- *Follow the specific instructions for each problem. Use only drawing and editing tools and techniques you have already learned. Use your own judgment and approximate dimensions when necessary.*
- *Apply dimensions accurately using ASME or appropriate industry standards.*

Note: *Some of the problems in this chapter are built on problems from previous chapters. If you have not yet completed those problems, complete them now.*

▼ Basic

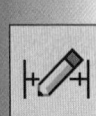

1. Use a word processor to list each attribute mode. Provide a brief description of each.

2. Draw the structural steel wide flange shape shown. Do not dimension the drawing. Create attributes for the drawing using the information given. Make a block of the drawing and name it W12 X 40. Insert the block once to test the attributes. Save the drawing as P25-2.

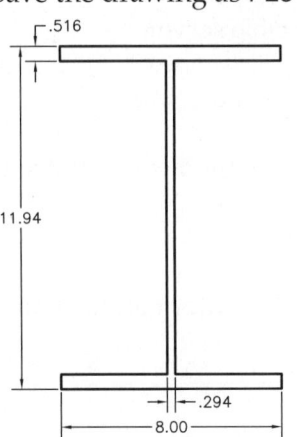

Attributes			
Steel	W12 × 40	Visible
Mfr.	Ryerson	Invisible
Price	$.30/lb	Invisible
Weight	40 lbs/ft	Invisible
Length	10′	Invisible
Code	03116WF	Invisible

▼ Intermediate

3. Open P25-2 and save it as P25-3. The P25-3 file should be active. Construct the floor plan shown. Dimension the drawing. Insert the block W12 X 40 six times as shown. The chart below the drawing provides the required attribute data. Enter the appropriate information for the attributes as prompted. Note that the steel columns labeled 3 and 6 require slightly different attribute data. You can speed the drawing process by using **ARRAY** or **COPY**. Resave the drawing.

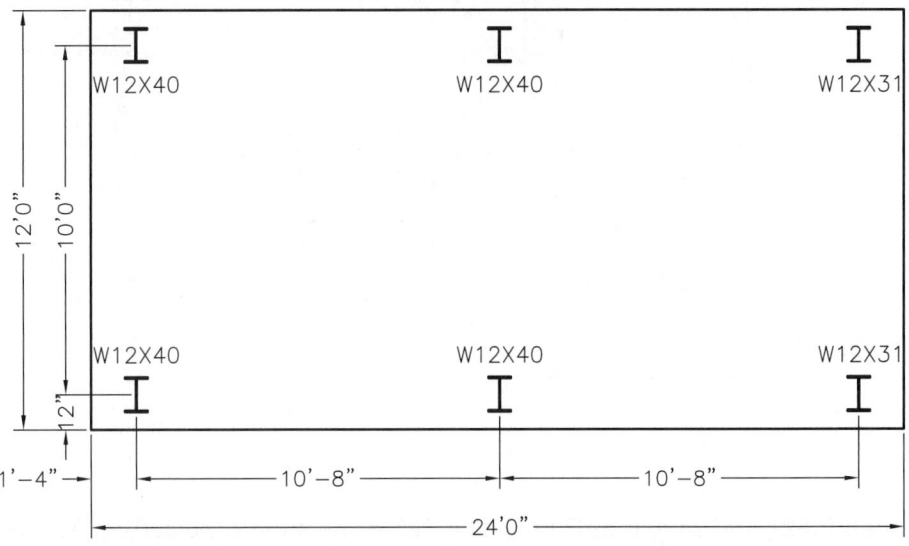

	Steel	Mfr.	Price	Weight	Length	Code
Blocks ①, ②, ④, & ⑤	W12 × 40	Ryerson	$.30/lb	40 lbs/ft	10′	03116WF
Blocks ③ & ⑥	W12 × 31	Ryerson	$.30/lb	31 lbs/ft	8.5′	03125WF

4. Open P25-2 and save it as P25-4. The P25-4 file should be active. Edit the W12 X 40 block in the newly saved drawing according to the following information. Resave the drawing.

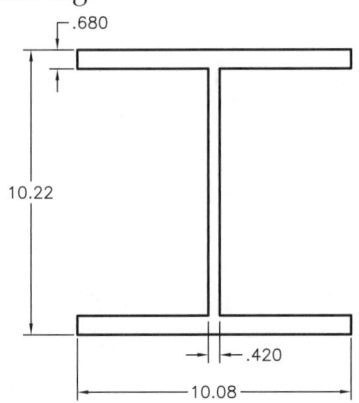

	Steel	W10 × 60	Visible
Attributes	Mfr.	Ryerson	Invisible
	Price	$.25/lb	Invisible
	Weight	60 lbs/ft	Invisible
	Length	10′	Invisible
	Code	02457WF	Invisible

▼ Advanced

5. Draw the structural detail shown. Save the drawing as P25-5.

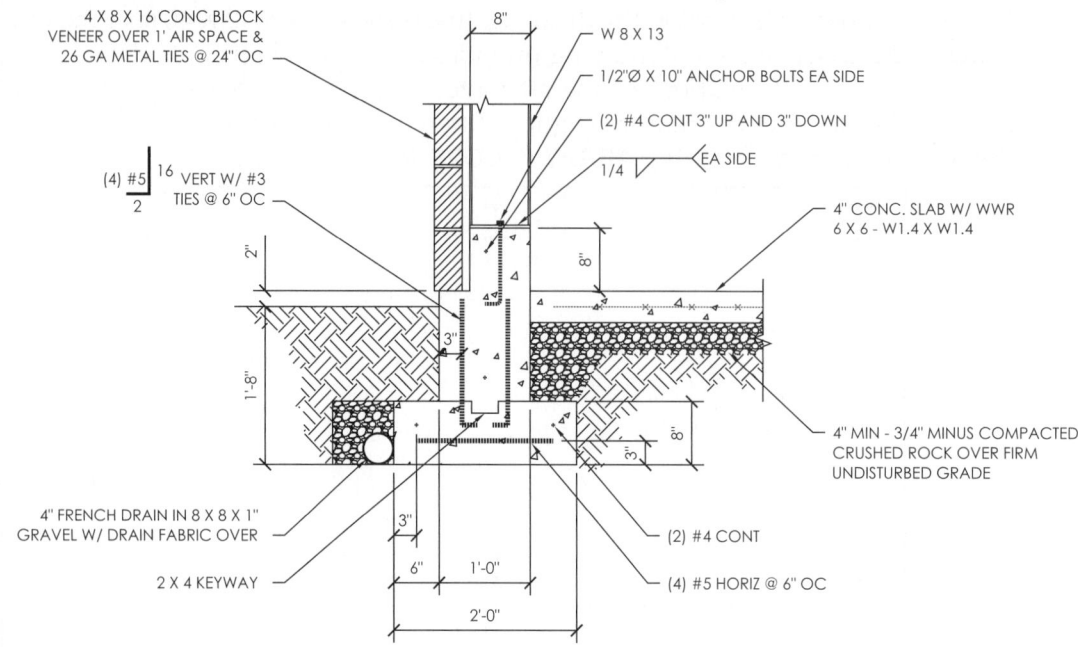

6. Open P8-21 and save it as P25-6. The P25-6 file should be active. Add constant, invisible attributes to each view of the glulam (glued laminated) beam hanger to identify all necessary specifications. Create a block of each view with the attributes. Insert the block of each view. Resave the drawing.

7. Open P12-17 and save it as P25-7. The P25-7 file should be active. Add constant, invisible attributes to each view of the mudsill anchor to identify all necessary specifications. Create a block of each view with the attributes. Insert the block of each view. Resave the drawing.

8. Open P25-2 and save it as P25-8. The P25-8 file should be active. Create a tab-separated extraction file for the blocks in the drawing. Extract the following information for each block:
   - Block name
   - Steel
   - Manufacturer
   - Price
   - Weight
   - Length
   - Code

   Resave the drawing. Save the tab-separated extraction file as P25-8.

9. Open P25-2 and save it as P25-9. The P25-9 file should be active. Create a table from the block attribute data and insert the table into the drawing. Resave the drawing.

10. Select a drawing from Chapter 24 and create a bill of materials for the drawing using the **Data Extraction** wizard. Use the comma-separated format to display the file. Display the file in Windows Notepad. Save the drawing and the comma-separated extraction file as P25-10.

11. Create a drawing of the computer workstation layout in the classroom or office in which you are working. Provide attribute definitions for all of the items listed here.
    - Workstation ID number
    - Computer brand name
    - Model number
    - Processor chip
    - Amount of RAM
    - Hard disk capacity
    - Video graphics card brand and model
    - CD-ROM/DVD-ROM speed
    - Date purchased
    - Price
    - Vendor phone number
    - Other data as you see fit

    Generate and extract a file for all of the computers in the drawing. Save the drawing and extracted file as P25-11.

AutoCAD Certified Associate Exam Practice

Answer the following questions. Write your answers on a separate sheet of paper.

1. Which group of **ATTDEF** settings is *most* efficient for an attribute that is not expected to change and that will be used only to tabulate data? *Select the one item that best answers the question.*
   A. **Invisible, Constant, Lock position**
   B. **Invisible, Verify, Preset**
   C. **Visible, Constant, Preset**
   D. **Visible, Constant, Verify**
   E. **Visible, Verify, Lock position**

2. Which of the following tools can you use to change attribute modes after an attribute has been created? *Select all that apply.*
   A. **-ATTEDIT**
   B. **ATTREDEF**
   C. **BATTMAN**
   D. **EATTEDIT**
   E. **Properties** palette

3. Which of the following tools allow you to add attributes to a block without exploding the block? *Select all that apply.*
   A. **ATTREDEF**
   B. **BEDIT**
   C. **EATTEDIT**
   D. **FIELD**
   E. **REFEDIT**

AutoCAD Certified Professional Exam Practice

Follow the instructions in each problem. Write your answers on a separate sheet of paper.

1. **Navigate to this chapter on the Student Web site and open CPE-25attribute.dwg.** Insert the existing BUSH block into the drawing. Without exploding the block, change the attribute mode from **Invisible** to **Visible**, and change the text height to 12. What type of plant is this, and how much does it cost?

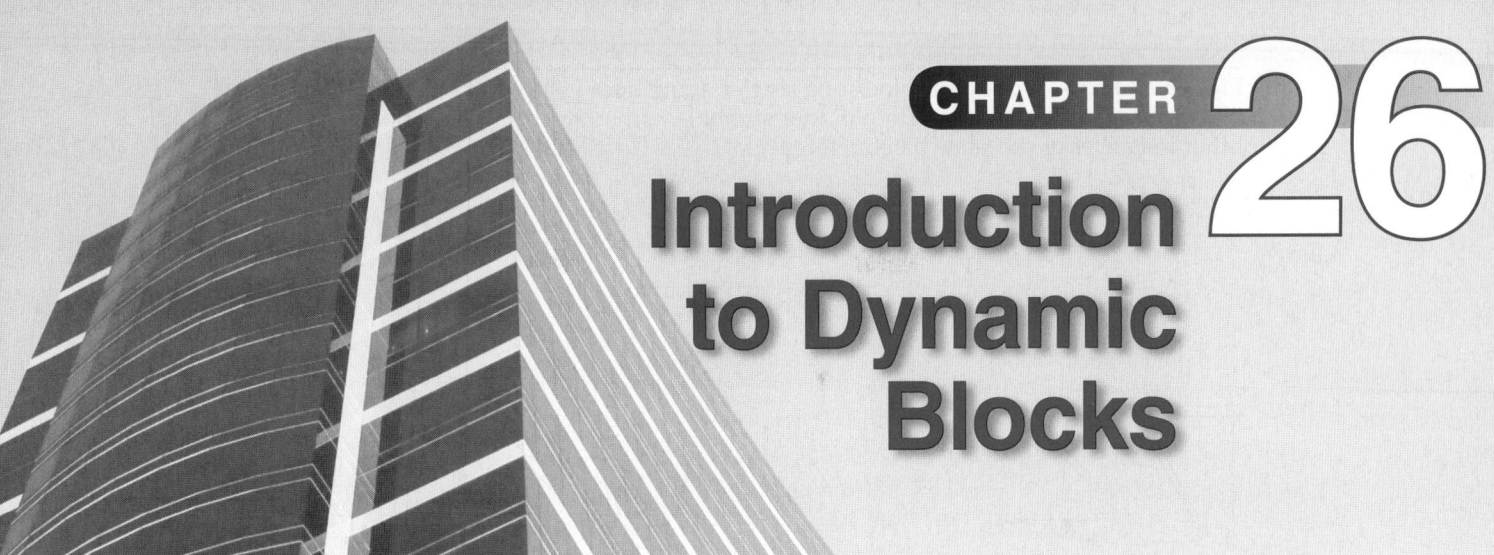

CHAPTER 26

Introduction to Dynamic Blocks

Learning Objectives

After completing this chapter, you will be able to do the following:
- ✓ Explain the function of dynamic blocks.
- ✓ Assign action parameters and actions to blocks.
- ✓ Modify parameters and actions.

A standard block typically represents a very specific item, such as a specific style of a bolt that is 1″ long. In this example, if the same style of bolt is available in three other lengths, you must create three additional standard blocks. An alternative is to create a single *dynamic block* that can be adjusted to show each different bolt length. Dynamic blocks can increase productivity and reduce the size of symbol libraries, making symbol libraries more manageable.

dynamic block: An adjustable block that you can assign parameters, actions, and/or geometric constraints and constraint parameters.

Dynamic Block Fundamentals

A dynamic block is a parametric symbol that you can adjust to change size, shape, and geometry without drawing additional blocks, and without affecting other instances of the block reference. **Figure 26-1** shows an example of a dynamic block of a plan view single-swing door symbol. In this example, the dynamic properties of the block allow you to create many different single-swing door symbols according to specific parameters, such as door size, wall thickness, swing location, swing angle representation, wall angle, and exterior or interior usage.

The process of constructing and using dynamic blocks is identical to the process for creating standard blocks, except for the addition of *action parameters* and (usually) *actions* that control block geometry. AutoCAD refers to action parameters as *parameters* in the context of dynamic blocks. A dynamic block can contain multiple parameters, and a single parameter can include multiple actions. You can use geometric constraints and *constraint parameters* as an alternative or in addition to parameters and actions. Many different tools and options exist for constructing dynamic blocks, depending on the purpose of the block.

action parameter (parameter): A specification for block construction that controls block characteristics such as positions, distances, and angles of dynamic block geometry.

action: A definition that controls how dynamic block parameters behave.

constraint parameters: Dimensional constraints that control the size or location of block geometry numerically.

Figure 26-1. A—A dynamic block of a single-swing door symbol. B—The dynamic block allows you to create many different door symbols without creating new blocks or affecting other instances of the same block reference.

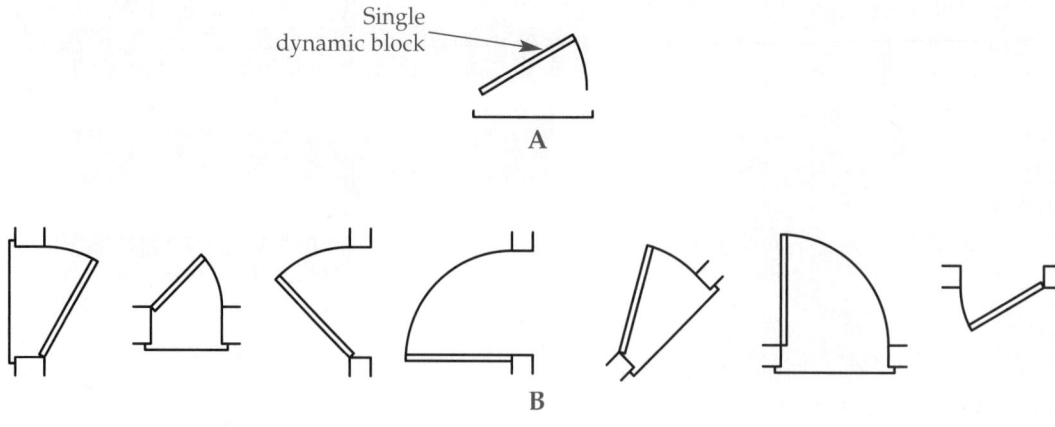

Single dynamic block

A

B

Figure 26-2A shows an example of a bolt symbol created as a dynamic block and selected for grip editing. The bolt shaft objects include a linear parameter with a stretch action, as indicated by the *parameter grips*. The length of the bolt increases when you stretch the right-hand linear parameter grip to the right. See **Figure 26-2B**.

parameter grips: Special grips that allow you to change the parameters of a dynamic block.

NOTE

As you learn to create and use dynamic blocks, you will notice that many actions function like editing tools with which you are already familiar, allowing operations such as stretch, move, scale, array, and rotate.

Figure 26-2. A linear parameter with a stretch action assigned to the shaft objects in the block of a bolt. A—Selecting the block displays the linear grips. B—Selecting and moving a linear grip stretches the bolt shaft.

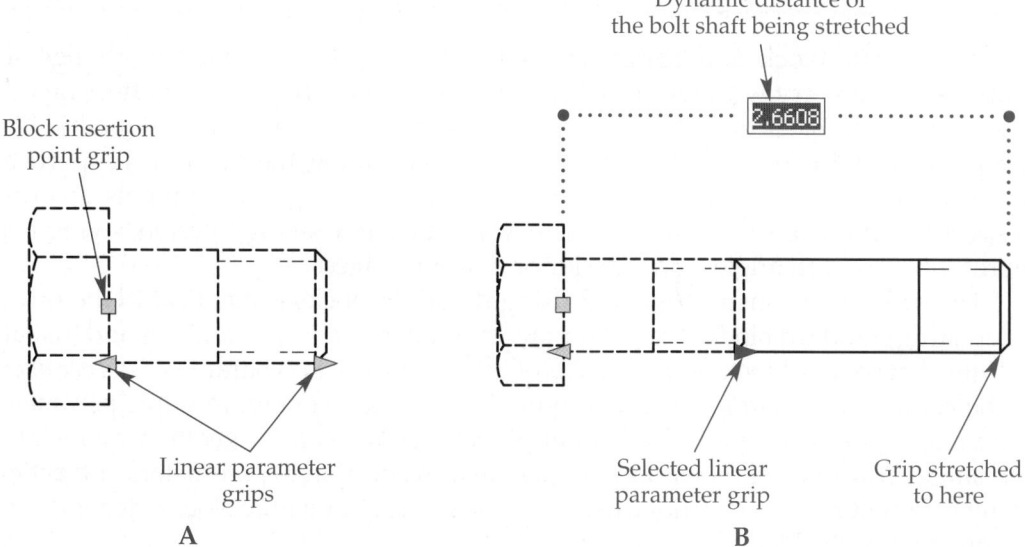

Dynamic distance of the bolt shaft being stretched

2.6608

Block insertion point grip

Linear parameter grips

Selected linear parameter grip

Grip stretched to here

A

B

Assigning Dynamic Properties

Edit an existing block in the **Block Editor** to assign dynamic properties. Access the **BEDIT** tool to display the **Edit Block Definition** dialog box shown in **Figure 26-3** and select the block from the list box. A preview and the description of the selected block appear. Pick the **OK** button to open the selection in the **Block Editor**. See **Figure 26-4**.

To create a dynamic block from scratch within the **Block Editor**, type a name for the new block in the **Block to create or edit** text box. To edit a block saved as the current drawing, such as a wblock, pick the <Current Drawing> option.

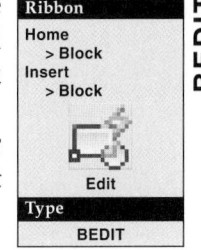

Ribbon
Home
> Block
Insert
> Block
Edit
Type
BEDIT

BEDIT

NOTE

Double-click a block to display the **Edit Block Definition** dialog box with the block selected. You can open a block directly in the **Block Editor** by selecting the block, right-clicking, and choosing **Block Editor**. Another option is to open a block directly in the **Block Editor** during block creation by selecting the **Open in block editor** check box in the **Block Definition** dialog box.

The **Block Editor** ribbon tab and **Block Authoring Palettes** palette provide easy access to tools and options for assigning dynamic block properties and creating attributes. The **Block Authoring Palettes** palette contains parameter, action, and constraint tools. Although you can type BPARAMETER or BACTION to activate the **BPARAMETER** or **BACTION** tool and then select a parameter or action as an option, it is easier to use the **Block Editor** ribbon tab or **Block Authoring Palettes**.

You can also assign actions to certain parameters, such as point parameters, by double-clicking on the parameter and selecting an action option. You can assign only specific actions to a given parameter. The process of assigning an action is slightly different, depending on the method used to access the action. If you type BACTION, you

Figure 26-3.
The **Edit Block Definition** dialog box.

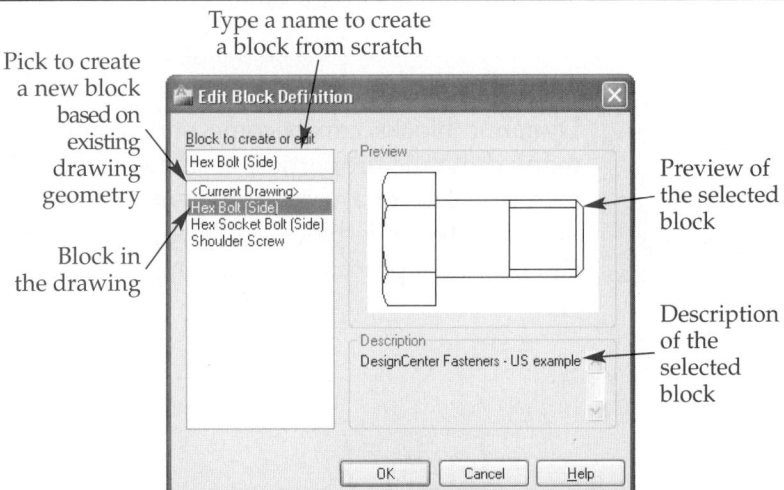

Pick to create a new block based on existing drawing geometry

Type a name to create a block from scratch

Block in the drawing

Preview of the selected block

Description of the selected block

Figure 26-4. The **Block Editor** ribbon tab and the **Block Authoring Palettes** are available in block editing mode. Notice the drawing window background, which has changed color to indicate block editing mode, and the location of the block relative to the origin.

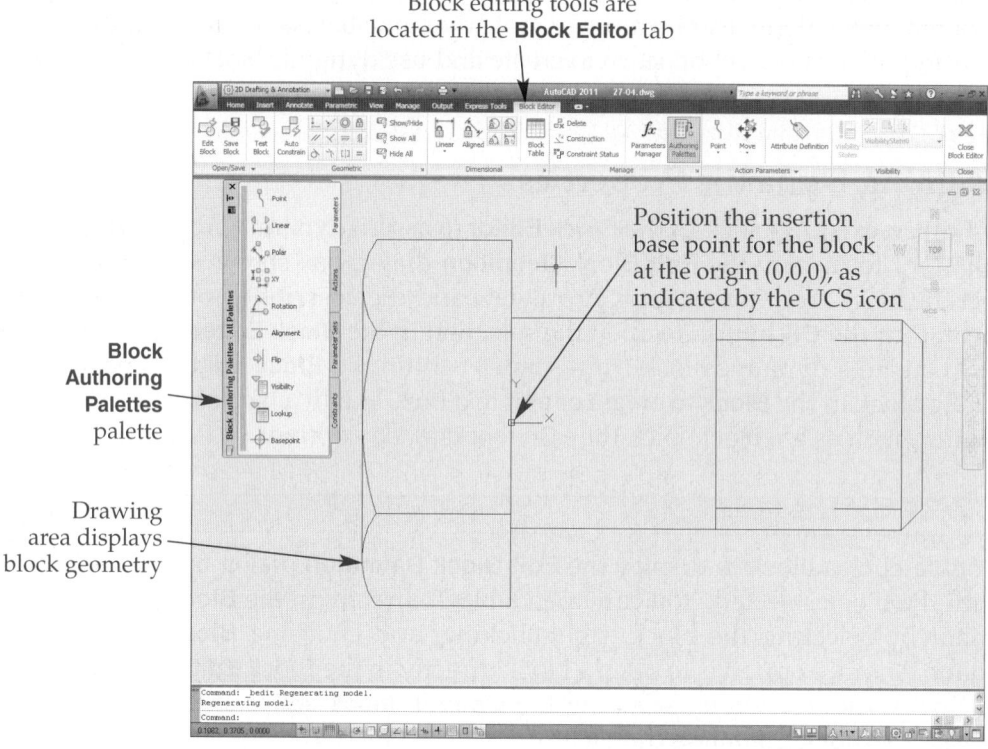

Block editing tools are located in the **Block Editor** tab

Position the insertion base point for the block at the origin (0,0,0), as indicated by the UCS icon

Block Authoring Palettes palette

Drawing area displays block geometry

must first select the parameter and then specify the action type. If you pick the action from the **Action Parameters** panel in the **Block Editor** ribbon tab or the **Block Authoring Palettes**, the specific action is active and a prompt asks you to pick the parameter. If you double-click on the parameter, the parameter becomes selected, but you must choose the action type.

Saving a Block with Dynamic Properties

Once you add one or more parameters to a block and assign actions to the parameters, you are ready to save and use the dynamic block. Use the **BSAVE** tool to save the block, or use the **BSAVEAS** tool to save the block using a different name. Remember that saving changes to a block updates all blocks of the same name in the drawing. Use the **BCLOSE** tool to exit the **Block Editor** when you are finished.

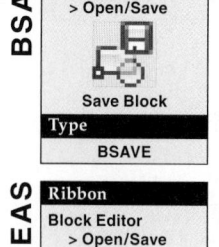

> **NOTE**
>
> Dynamic blocks can become very complex with the addition of many dynamic properties. A single dynamic block can potentially take the place of a very large symbol library. This chapter focuses on basic dynamic block applications, fundamental use of parameters, and the process of assigning a single action to a parameter.

Point Parameters

A *point parameter* creates a position property to which you can assign move and stretch actions. For example, assign a point parameter with a move action to a door tag that is part of a door block so you can move the tag independently of the door. Point parameters also provide multiple insertion point options. For example, add point parameters to the ends of a weld symbol reference line to create two insertion point options.

Figure 26-5 provides an example of adding a point parameter. Access the **Point** parameter option and specify a location for the parameter. The parameter location determines the base point from which dynamic actions occur. **Figure 26-5** shows picking the center of the door tag circle to identify the base point of a move action. Adjust the parameter location after initial placement if necessary. The yellow alert icon indicates that no action is assigned to the parameter.

Once you specify the parameter location, pick a location for the *parameter label*. All parameters include a parameter label. The label appears only in block editing mode. By default, the label for the first point parameter is Position. Move the label as needed after initial placement.

Next, enter the number of grips to associate with the parameter. The default **1** option creates a single grip at the parameter location that allows you to use grip editing to carry out the assigned action. If you choose the **0** option, you can only use the **Properties** palette to adjust the block.

Parameter options are available before you specify the parameter location. Most of the options are also available from the **Properties** palette if you have already created the parameter. Use the **Label** option to enter a more descriptive label name. The **Name** option allows you to specify a name for the parameter that displays as the **Parameter type** in the **Properties** palette. The **Chain** option specifies whether a chain action can affect the parameter. Chain actions are described later in this chapter. The **Description** option allows you to type a description, such as the purpose of or application for the parameter. The description displays in the drawing area as a tooltip. The **Palette** option determines whether the label appears in the **Properties** palette when you select the block.

point parameter: A parameter that defines an XY coordinate location in the drawing.

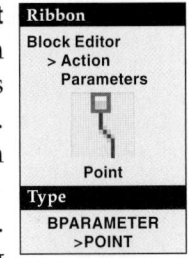

Ribbon

Block Editor
> Action
> Parameters

Point

Type

**BPARAMETER
>POINT**

parameter label: A label that indicates the purpose of a parameter.

Figure 26-5.
A point parameter consists of the grip location and a label. This example shows adding a point parameter to the tag of a plan view door symbol to allow the tag to be positioned independently of the door.

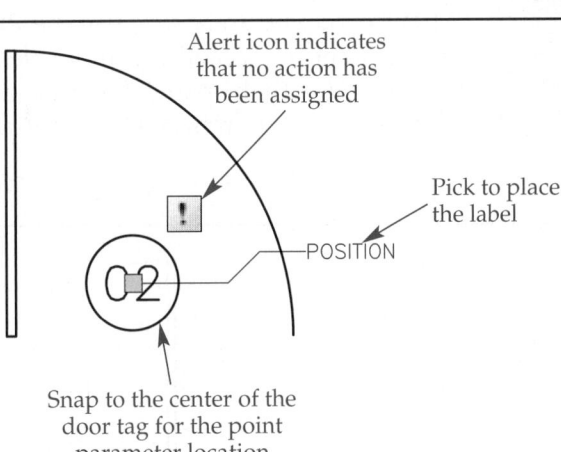

Alert icon indicates that no action has been assigned

Pick to place the label

POSITION

Snap to the center of the door tag for the point parameter location

Change the parameter label name to something more descriptive, and add a description. Naming labels and describing parameters helps organize parameters and helps you identify each parameter when you are controlling a block dynamically. This is especially important when you add multiple parameters to a block. Consider keeping the default parameter type as part of the name. For example, change the name of the door symbol point parameter from Point to Point – Tag Center.

Exercise 26-1

Access the Student Web site (www.g-wlearning.com/CAD) and complete Exercise 26-1.

Assigning a Move Action

move action: An action used to move a block object independently of other objects in the same block.

Figure 26-6 illustrates the process of adding a *move action* to the door block example. First, access the **Move** action option and pick the point parameter. Then select the objects that make up the door tag and the associated parameter. Press [Enter] or the space bar or right-click to assign the action. Test the block, as explained later in this chapter. Save the block and exit the **Block Editor**. The dynamic block is now ready to use.

Ribbon
Block Editor
> Action
Parameters

Move
Type
BACTIONTOOL
>MOVE

NOTE

Typically, when you select objects to include with an action, you should also select the associated parameter. Otherwise, the parameter grip will be left behind when you apply the action.

After you create an action, use the **Properties** palette to change the action name to something more descriptive, but keep the default action type with the name. For example, change the name of the door symbol move action from Move to Move – Tag.

Figure 26-6.
Assigning a move action to a point parameter.

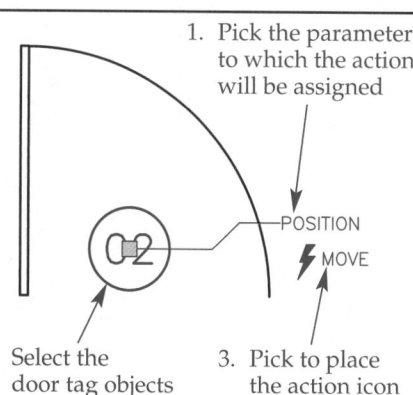

1. Pick the parameter to which the action will be assigned
POSITION
MOVE
2. Select the door tag objects
3. Pick to place the action icon

Using a Move Action Dynamically

Figure 26-7A shows the door block reference, selected for editing. The point parameter grip appears as a light blue square in the center of the door tag. The insertion base point specified when the block was created appears as a standard unselected grip. Select the point parameter grip and move the door tag as shown in **Figure 26-7B**. Pick a point to specify a new location for the door tag. See **Figure 26-7C**.

NOTE

During block insertion, press [Ctrl] to cycle through the positions of any parameters added to the dynamic block. This is one method of selecting a different insertion base point, corresponding to the position of a parameter, to use when inserting the block.

PROFESSIONAL TIP

During block insertion, use the **Properties** palette to adjust dynamic properties. If you do not include grips with a parameter, the options in the **Custom** category are the only way to adjust the block.

Testing and Adjusting Dynamic Properties

After you exit the **Block Editor**, you can insert a block and use grip editing or the **Properties** palette to confirm appropriate dynamic function. If the block does not respond as desired, however, you must re-enter the **Block Editor** to make changes. A more convenient option is to access the **BTESTBLOCK** tool from inside the **Block Editor** to enter the **Test Block Window**. The **Test Block Window** provides standard AutoCAD tools and options, allowing you to test dynamic function without exiting block editing mode. Pick the **Close Test Block Window** button to re-enter the **Block Editor**. AutoCAD

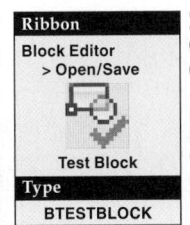

Ribbon
Block Editor
> Open/Save

Test Block
Type
BTESTBLOCK

BTESTBLOCK

Figure 26-7. Dynamically moving an action assigned to a point parameter. A—Select the block to display grips. The point parameter grip is shown as a light blue square. B—Select and move the point parameter grip. C—The door tag is at a new location, but it is still part of the block.

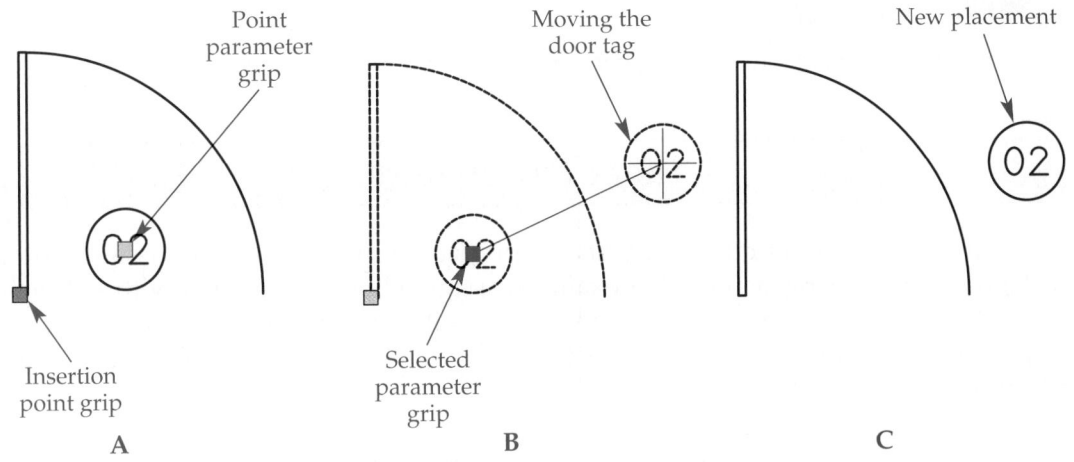

discards changes made while testing so that you can adjust the original block as needed. Block testing is especially important when a block includes multiple dynamic properties.

Adjusting Parameters

Use standard editing tools such as **MOVE** to make changes to existing parameter labels or grips. You can move parameter grips independently of the parameter label, which is often required if multiple grips are stacked or are near the same location. Use the **ERASE** tool to remove a parameter or parameter grips.

Grip editing is especially effective for adjusting parameters. When you select a parameter, grips appear at the parameter location and label. Use the **Properties** palette to adjust the properties of the selected parameter. The settings in the **Properties** palette change depending on the type of parameter. Limited property options are also available by selecting a parameter and right-clicking. Use the **Grip Display** cascading submenu to redefine the number of grips or to relocate grips with the parameter location. Use the **Rename** option to change the name of the label.

Adjusting Actions

action bars:
Toolbars that allow you to view, remove, and adjust actions.

Action bars appear by default when you assign actions. See **Figure 26-8A.** Each action displays an icon to identify and control the action. When you hover over or select an icon, the objects and parameter corresponding to the action become highlighted and markers identify action points. This display allows you to recognize the objects, parameter, and points associated with the action. If action bars block your view, drag them to a new location. To hide an action bar, pick the **Close** button located to the right of the icons. Hiding action bars does not remove actions. **Figure 26-8B** briefly describes the options available when you right-click on an action icon.

> **NOTE**
>
> To hide or show all actions, pick the **Hide All Actions** or **Show All Actions** button from the **Manage Parameters** panel of the **Block Editor** ribbon tab. You can also right-click with no objects selected to access an **Action Bars** cascading submenu that provides options for displaying and hiding action bars.

Exercise 26-2

Access the Student Web site (www.g-wlearning.com/CAD) and complete Exercise 26-2.

Linear Parameters

linear parameter:
A parameter that creates a measurement reference between two points.

A *linear parameter* creates a distance property to which you can assign move, scale, stretch, and array actions. For example, assign a linear parameter with a stretch action to a block of a bolt symbol to make the bolt shaft longer or shorter. Assign a second linear parameter and stretch action to the bolt head to control the bolt head diameter.

Figure 26-8. A—Action bars appear by default when you add actions. B—Options for adjusting actions when you right-click on an action icon.

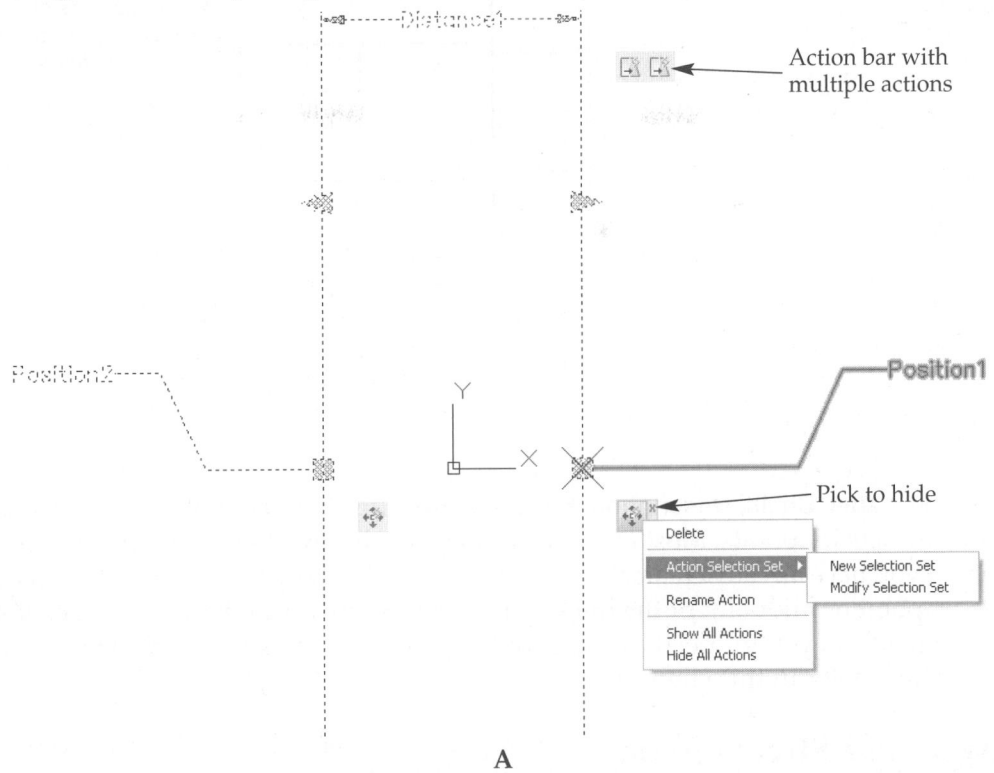

Action bar with multiple actions

Position1

Pick to hide

Option	Description
Delete	Deletes the action.
New Selection Set	Allows you to select objects to associate with the action; eliminates the original selection set.
Modify Selection Set	Adds objects to associate with the action.
Rename Action	Provides a text box for renaming the action.
Show All Actions	Displays all actions.
Hide All Actions	Hides all actions.

B

Figure 26-9 provides an example of adding a linear parameter. For this example, activate the **Linear** parameter option and use the **Label** function to name the linear parameter Shaft Length. Next, pick the start and endpoints of the linear parameter to determine the locations from which dynamic actions occur. If you plan to assign a single action to the parameter, select the point associated with the action second. **Figure 26-9** shows picking the endpoint of the lower edge of the shaft and then using polar tracking or the extension object snap to pick the point where the edge of the shaft would meet the end if extended. You must select points that are horizontal or vertical to each other to create a horizontal or vertical linear parameter.

Once you select the start and endpoints, pick a location for the parameter label. Next, enter the number of grips to associate with the parameter. The default **2** option creates grips at the start and endpoints, allowing you to use grip editing to carry out the action assigned to either point. Select the **1** option to assign a grip at the endpoint only, as shown in **Figure 26-9.** You will be able to grip-edit the block only if an action is associated with the endpoint. If you choose the **0** option, you can only use the **Properties** palette to adjust the block.

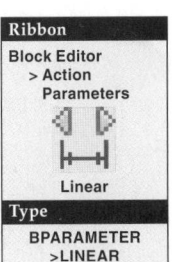

Ribbon

Block Editor > Action Parameters

Linear

Type

BPARAMETER >LINEAR

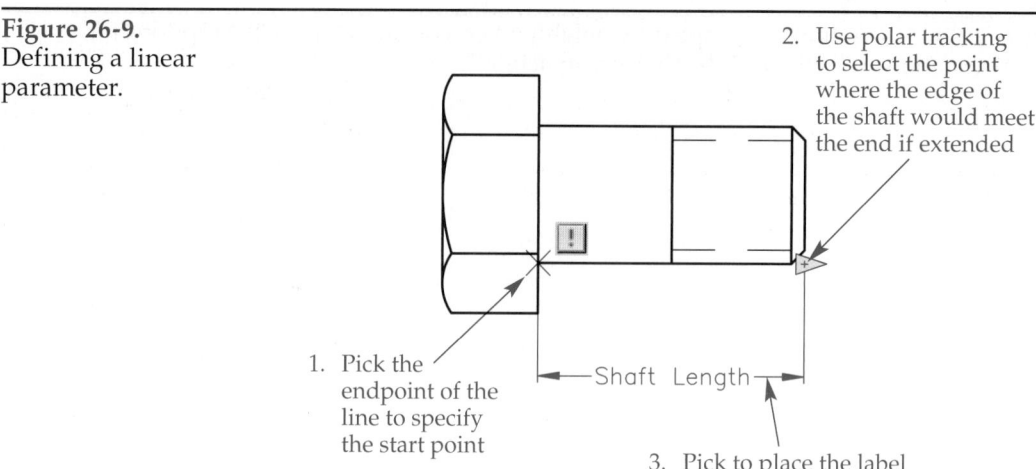

Figure 26-9.
Defining a linear parameter.

2. Use polar tracking to select the point where the edge of the shaft would meet the end if extended

1. Pick the endpoint of the line to specify the start point

Shaft Length

3. Pick to place the label

Name, **Label**, **Chain**, **Description**, **Base**, **Palette**, and **Value set** options are available before you specify points. Most of these options are also available from the **Properties** palette if you have already created the parameter. The **Base** option allows you to assign the start point or midpoint of the linear parameter as the action base point. The **Value set** option allows you to specify values for the action. The **Base** and **Value set** options are described later in this chapter.

Assigning a Stretch Action

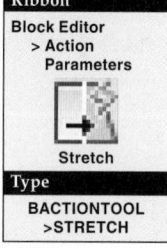

stretch action: An action used to change the size and shape of block objects with a stretch operation.

Ribbon

**Block Editor
> Action
Parameters**

Stretch

Type

**BACTIONTOOL
>STRETCH**

Figure 26-10 illustrates the process of adding a *stretch action* to the bolt symbol example. Access the **Stretch** action option and pick the Shaft Length parameter. Then specify a parameter point to associate with the action. Move the crosshairs near the appropriate parameter point to display the red snap marker, and pick to select. Alternatives include choosing the **sTart point** option to pick the start point of the linear parameter or the **Second point** option to select the endpoint. If you plan to use grip editing to control the block, and added a single grip, specify the point with the grip.

Next, create a window to define the stretch frame. This is the same technique you apply when using the **STRETCH** tool. See **Figure 26-10A.** Then pick the objects to

Figure 26-10.
Assigning a stretch action to a linear parameter. A—Specify the parameter and parameter grip, and create a window for the stretch frame. B—Select the objects to be included in the stretch action.

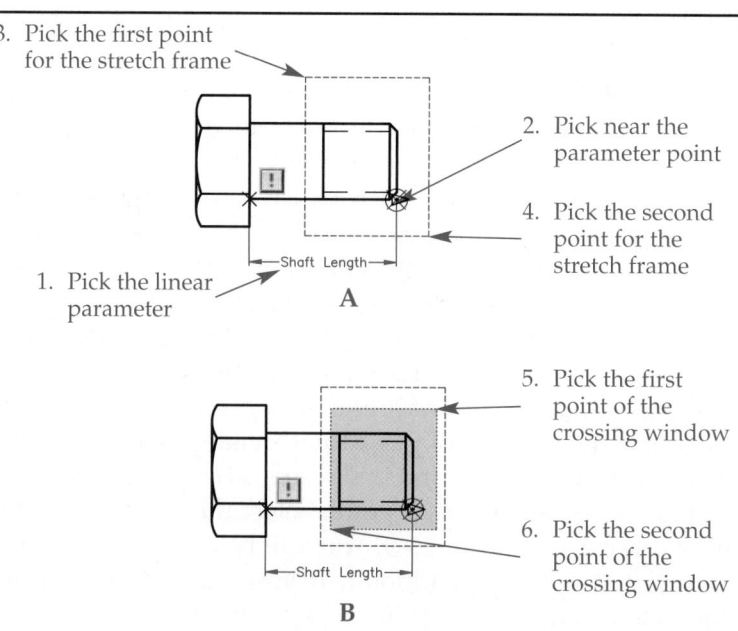

3. Pick the first point for the stretch frame

2. Pick near the parameter point

4. Pick the second point for the stretch frame

Shaft Length

1. Pick the linear parameter

A

5. Pick the first point of the crossing window

6. Pick the second point of the crossing window

Shaft Length

B

stretch, including the associated parameter. You do not need to use a crossing window, because the previous operation defines the stretch. However, crossing selection is often quicker. See **Figure 26-10B.** Press [Enter] or the space bar or right-click to place the action icon. Test and save the block, and exit the **Block Editor.** The dynamic block is now ready to use.

Using a Stretch Action Dynamically

Figure 26-11 shows the bolt block reference selected for editing. The linear parameter grip is a light blue arrow at the far end of the bolt shaft. The insertion base point specified when the block was created appears as a standard unselected grip. Select the parameter grip and stretch the shaft to the new length. Use dynamic input to view the stretch dimension, and enter an exact length value in the distance field. You can also use the **Properties** palette to define the distance.

PROFESSIONAL TIP

The dynamic input distance field is a property of the linear parameter, allowing you to enter an exact distance. To get the best results when using a linear parameter, it is important that you locate the first and second points correctly.

Exercise 26-3

Access the Student Web site (www.g-wlearning.com/CAD) and complete Exercise 26-3.

Stretching Objects Symmetrically

The **Linear** parameter option includes a **Base** function that allows you to assign the start point or midpoint of the linear parameter as the action base point. Use the **Midpoint** setting to specify the midpoint as the action base point. The midpoint base point maintains symmetry when you adjust the block. You can set the **Base** preference before picking the first point or later using the **Properties** palette.

Figure 26-12 shows an example of a linear parameter with a stretch action assigned to the objects composing the bolt head. For this example, activate the **Linear** parameter option and use the **Base** option to choose the **Midpoint** setting. Next, use the **Label** option to change the label name to Head Diameter. Select the start and endpoints of the linear parameter to define the parameter and automatically calculate the midpoint.

Figure 26-11.
Selecting the inserted block in the drawing displays parameter grips.

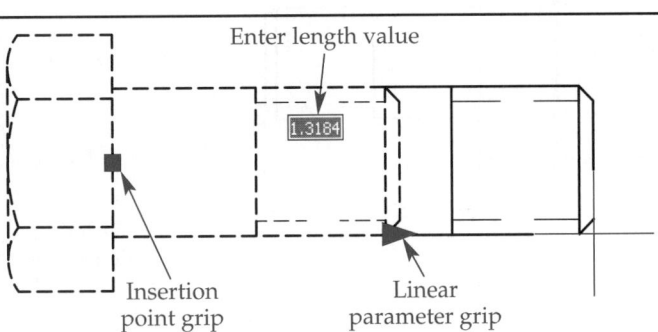

Figure 26-12.
The base point of
a linear parameter
appears as an X.
Use the **Midpoint**
option to locate the
base point halfway
between the start
and endpoints.

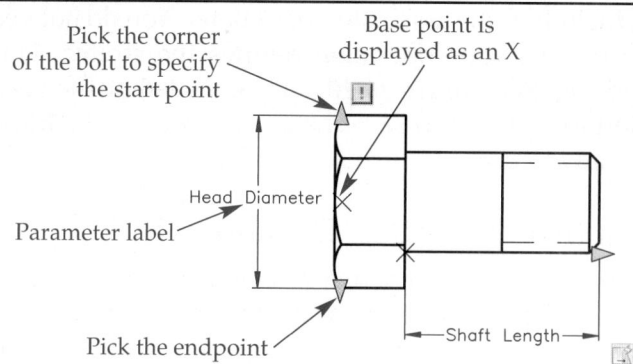

This example uses the upper-right and lower-left corners of the bolt head. After you
select the start and endpoints, pick a location for the parameter label. Next, enter the
number of grips to associate with the parameter. The **Figure 26-12** example uses the
default **2** option to create grips at the start and endpoints.

Figure 26-13 demonstrates the process of assigning a stretch action to one side of
the bolt head. First, access the **Stretch** action option and pick the Head Diameter parameter. Then pick the upper linear parameter point to associate with the action. Create a
crossing window to define the stretch frame, as shown in **Figure 26-13A**. Then select
the objects to stretch, including the associated parameter, as shown in **Figure 26-13B**.
Press [Enter] or the space bar or right-click to place the action icon.

Repeat the previous sequence to assign a second stretch action to the opposite side
of the bolt head. Test and save the block, and exit the **Block Editor**. The dynamic block is
now ready to use. **Figure 26-14** illustrates using the lower grip point or dynamic input
to stretch the bolt block reference. Use either grip to stretch the bolt head. You can also
use the **Properties** palette to define the distance.

Assigning a Scale Action

Figure 26-15 shows a block of a vanity symbol that includes a sink. In this example,
a *scale action* is assigned to a linear parameter to adjust the size of the sink while
maintaining the dimensions of the vanity. Activate the **Linear** parameter option and
use the **Base** option to choose the **Midpoint** setting. Next, use the **Label** option to change

scale action: An
action often used
to scale some of
the objects within a
block independently
of the other objects.

Figure 26-13. Assigning a stretch action to one side of the bolt head. A—Create a crossing
window around the top of the bolt head. B—Select the objects to be included in the stretch
action.

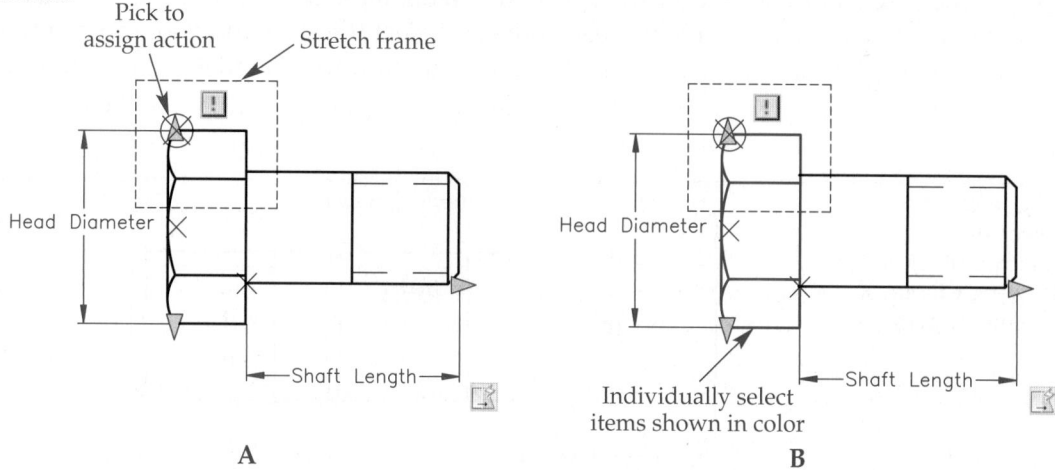

Figure 26-14.
Dynamically stretching the bolt head. Notice that the head stretches symmetrically.

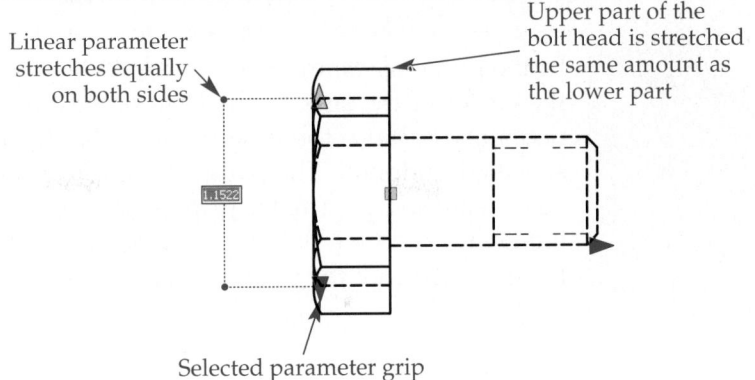

Linear parameter stretches equally on both sides

Upper part of the bolt head is stretched the same amount as the lower part

Selected parameter grip

Figure 26-15.
A linear parameter assigned to the sink objects in a block of a vanity with a sink. Locate the parameter base point and independent base type at the center of the sink to scale the sink symmetrically.

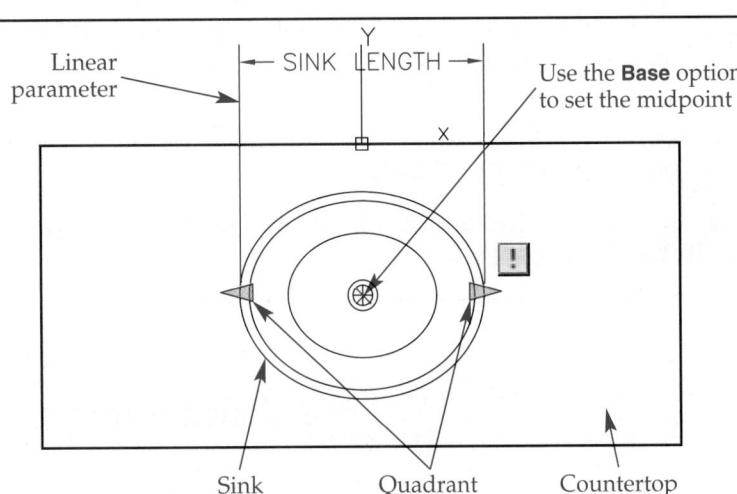

Linear parameter

SINK LENGTH

Use the **Base** option to set the midpoint

Sink   Quadrant   Countertop

the label name to SINK LENGTH. Select the start and endpoints of the linear parameter to define the parameter and automatically calculate the midpoint. This example uses two quadrants of the sink. After you select the start and endpoints, pick a location for the parameter label. Next, choose the number of grips to associate with the parameter. The **Figure 26-15** example uses the default **2** option to create grips at the start and endpoints.

Now assign a scale action to the parameter. First, access the **Scale** action option and pick the SINK LENGTH linear parameter. Then select the objects to include in the scale action, including the associated parameter. Press [Enter] or the space bar or right-click to assign the action.

When using a scale action, it is critical to scale objects relative to the correct base point. Access the **Properties** palette and display the properties of the scale action. The **Overrides** category includes options for adjusting the base point. The default **Base type** option is **Dependent**, which scales the objects relative to the base point of the associated parameter. Choose the **Independent** option to specify a different location. The **Base X** and **Base Y** values default to the parameter start point. Enter the coordinates relative to the block insertion base point, or use the pick button that appears when you select the **Base X** and **Base Y** values to choose points on-screen. For the sink example, it is important that the objects be scaled relative to the exact center of the sink so that the sink will be centered within the vanity as the scale changes. Test and save the block, and exit the **Block Editor**. The dynamic block is now ready to use.

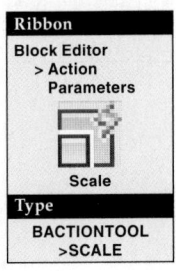

Ribbon
Block Editor
> Action
Parameters

Scale

Type
BACTIONTOOL
>SCALE

Using a Scale Action Dynamically

Figure 26-16 shows using the right grip or dynamic input to scale the sink in the vanity block reference. You can use either grip to scale the sink. You can also use the **Properties** palette to define the distance.

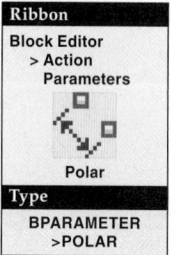

Exercise 26-4

Access the Student Web site (www.g-wlearning.com/CAD) and complete Exercise 26-4.

Polar Parameters

polar parameter:
A parameter that includes a distance property and an angle property.

Ribbon
Block Editor
> Action
Parameters
Polar
Type
BPARAMETER
>POLAR

A *polar parameter* provides the same function as a linear parameter, but creates an angle, or rotation, property in addition to a distance property. You can assign move, scale, stretch, polar stretch, and array actions to a polar parameter. For example, assign a polar parameter with a polar stretch action to the steel channel shape shown in **Figure 26-17** to adjust the depth to create different size channels, and rotate the block at the same time if necessary. See **Figure 26-18**.

To insert the polar parameter, access the **Polar** parameter option. Use the **Label** option to change the label name to Depth, but keep the default angle name. Then specify the base point, such as the left endpoint shown. Pick an endpoint aligned with the base point, such as the opposite endpoint shown. After you select the start and endpoints, pick a location for the parameter label. Next, enter the number of grips to associate

Figure 26-16.
Scaling the sink dynamically. Notice that the vanity portion of the block remains the same.

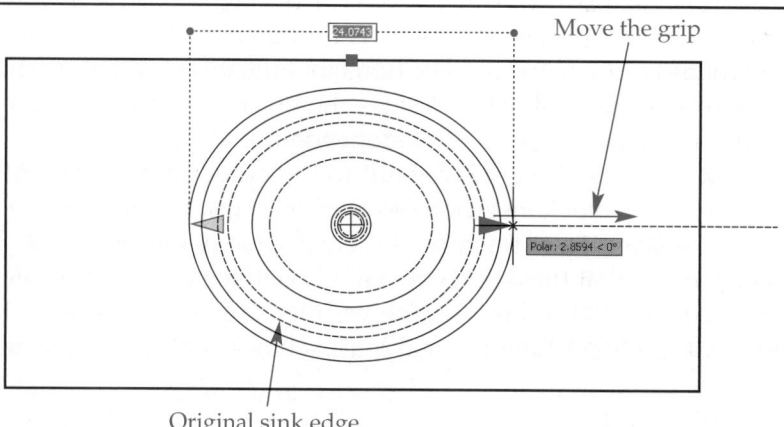

Move the grip

Original sink edge

Figure 26-17.
Adding a polar
parameter.

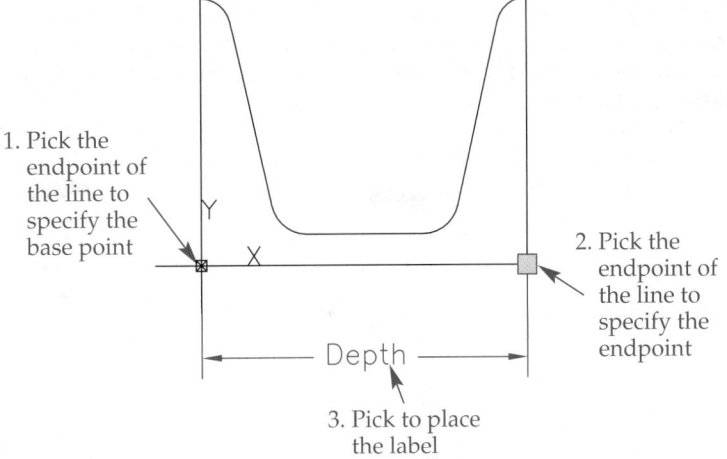

1. Pick the endpoint of the line to specify the base point

2. Pick the endpoint of the line to specify the endpoint

Depth

3. Pick to place the label

Figure 26-18.
An example of a portion of a motor mount with side views of different steel channel shapes created and rotated using a single block with a polar parameter, assigned a polar stretch action.

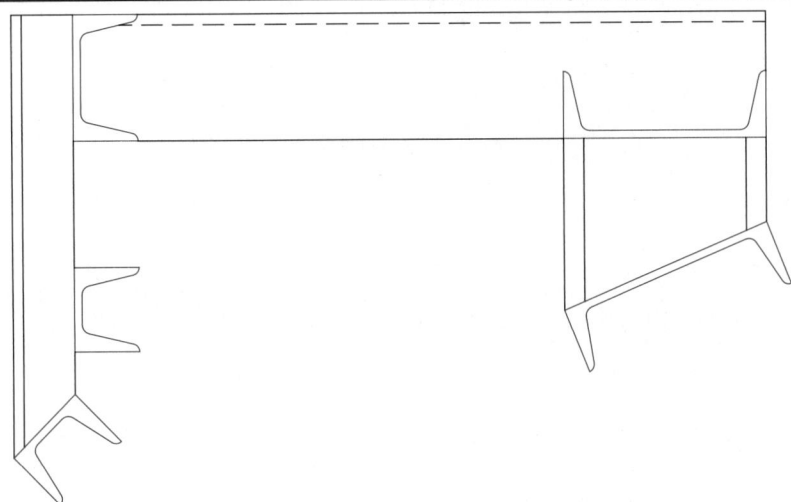

with the parameter. Select the **1** option to assign a grip at the endpoint only, as shown in **Figure 26-17**. You will be able to grip-edit the block only if an action is associated with the endpoint.

> **NOTE**
>
> **Name**, **Label**, **Chain**, **Description**, **Palette**, and **Value set** options are available before you specify the parameter. Most of these options are also available from the **Properties** palette if you have already created the parameter.

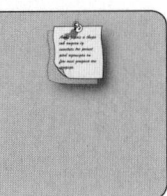

polar stretch action: An action used to change the size, shape, and rotation of block objects with a stretch operation.

Ribbon

Block Editor
> Action
Parameters

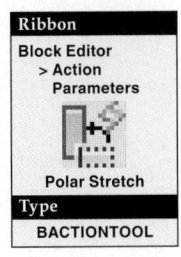

Polar Stretch

Type
BACTIONTOOL

Assigning a Polar Stretch Action

Figure 26-19 illustrates the process of adding a *polar stretch action* to the steel channel shape example. Access the **Polar Stretch** action option and pick the Depth parameter. Then specify a parameter point to associate with the action. Move the crosshairs near the appropriate parameter point to display the red snap marker, and pick to select. Alternatives include choosing the **sTart point** option to pick the start point of the polar parameter, or the **Second point** option to select the endpoint. If you plan to use grip editing to control the block, and added a single grip, specify the point with the grip.

Figure 26-19. Assigning a polar stretch action to a polar parameter. A—Specify the parameter and parameter grip, and create a window for the stretch frame. B—Select the objects to be included in the stretch action. C—Select the objects to be included in the rotation action.

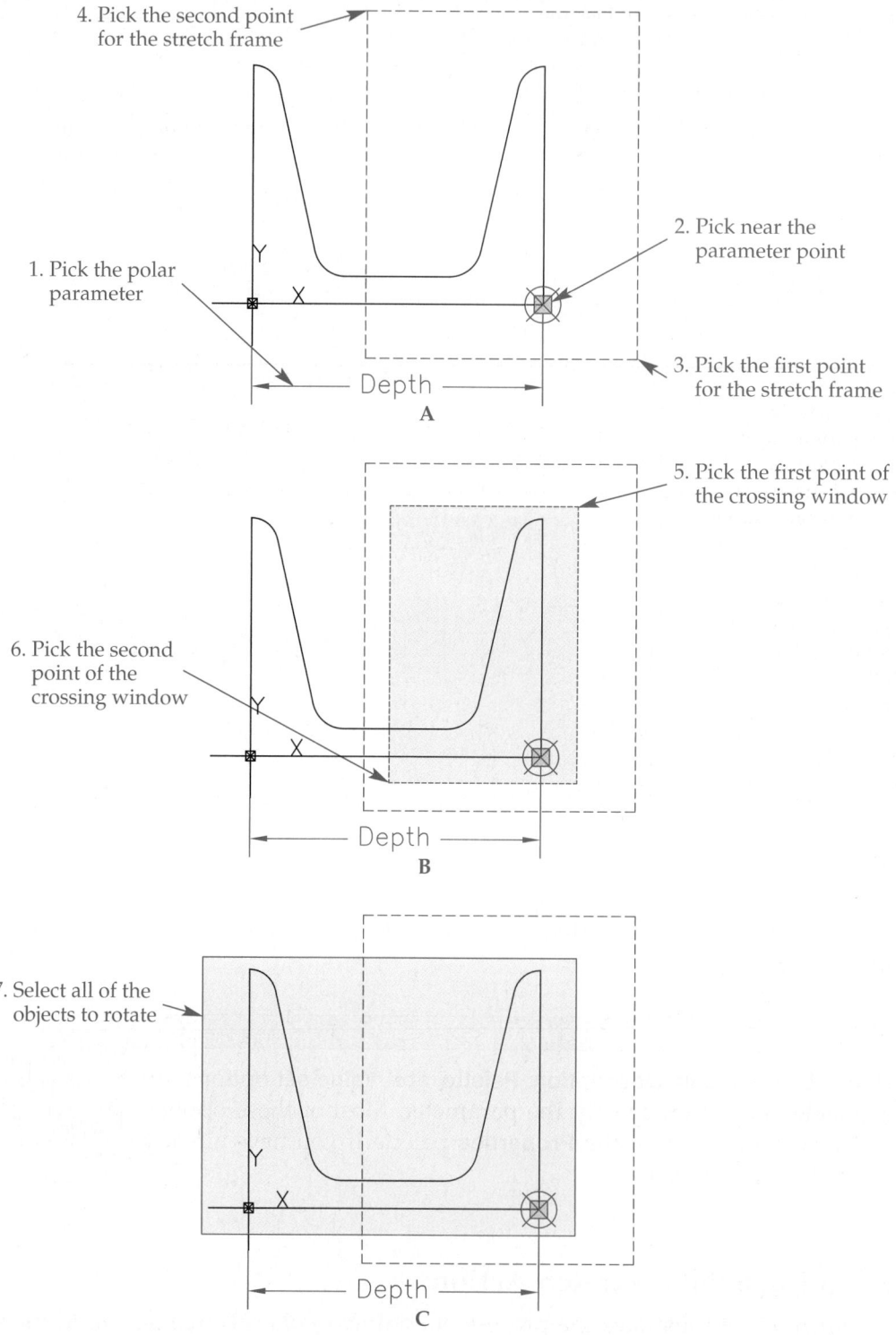

Next, create a window to define the stretch frame. This is the same technique you apply when using the **STRETCH** tool. See **Figure 26-19A.** Pick the objects to stretch, including the associated parameter. You do not need to use a crossing window, because the previous operation defines the stretch. However, crossing selection is often quicker. See **Figure 26-19B.** Then select the objects to rotate, which are often the objects of a block.

See **Figure 26-19C**. Press [Enter] or the space bar or right-click to place the action icon. Test and save the block, and exit the **Block Editor**. The dynamic block is now ready to use.

Using a Polar Stretch Action Dynamically

Figure 26-20 shows the steel channel shape block reference selected for editing. The polar parameter grip appears as a light blue arrow at the far end of the channel depth. The insertion base point specified when the block was created appears as a standard unselected grip. Select the parameter grip and stretch the channel depth to the new length and angle. Use dynamic input to view the stretch dimension and rotation angle, and enter an exact length value in the distance field and rotation angle in the angle field. You can also use the **Properties** palette to define the distance.

> **NOTE**
>
> The **Properties** palette includes **Multiplier** and **Angle Offset** options for move, stretch, and polar stretch actions. Enter a value in the **Multiplier** text box to multiply by the parameter value when adjusting the block. For example, if you assign a distance multiplier of 2 to a move action and move an object 4 units, the object actually moves 8 units. Enter an angle in the **Angle Offset** text box to change the parameter grip angle. For example, if you assign an offset angle of 45 to a move action and move an object 10°, the object actually moves 55°.

Exercise 26-5

Access the Student Web site (www.g-wlearning.com/CAD) and complete Exercise 26-5.

Figure 26-20. An example of applying the polar stretching action. Selecting the inserted block in the drawing displays parameter grips.

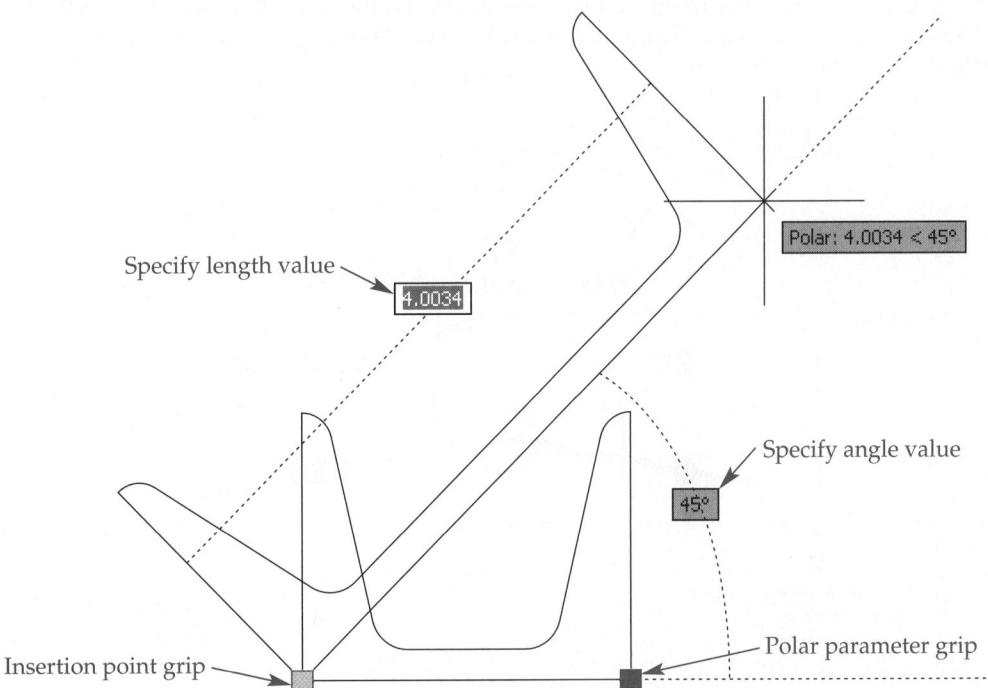

Rotation Parameters

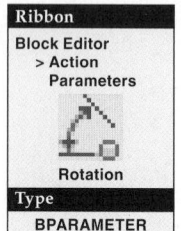

rotation parameter: A parameter that allows objects in a block to rotate independently of the block.

Ribbon

Block Editor
  > Action
    Parameters

Rotation

Type

BPARAMETER
>ROTATION

A *rotation parameter* creates a rotation property to which you can assign a rotate action. For example, assign a rotation parameter with a rotate action to the needle in the speedometer block shown in **Figure 26-21** to rotate the needle around the circumference of the dial. To insert the rotation parameter, access the **Rotation** parameter option and pick the center of the circular base of the needle as the rotation base point. Then pick a point, such as the needle endpoint shown, to specify the parameter radius. Set the default rotation angle from 0° east, or if rotation should originate from an angle other than 0°, use the **Base angle** option. **Figure 26-21** shows using the **Base angle** option to base the rotation at 0° and specifying a default rotation angle of 200° to align the rotation with the 120 and 0 marks.

After you define the rotation parameter, pick a location for the parameter label. Next, enter the number of grips to associate with the parameter. The default **1** option creates a single grip at the parameter radius that allows you to use grip editing to carry out the rotate action.

> **NOTE**
>
> **Name**, **Label**, **Chain**, **Description**, **Palette**, and **Value set** options are available before you specify the parameter. Most of these options and the **Base angle** setting are also available from the **Properties** palette if you have already created the parameter.

Assigning a Rotate Action

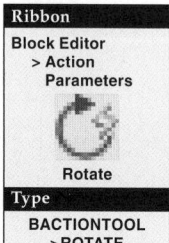

rotate action: An action used to rotate objects within a block without affecting the other objects in the block.

Ribbon

Block Editor
  > Action
    Parameters

Rotate

Type

BACTIONTOOL
>ROTATE

To assign a *rotate action* to the speedometer example, access the **Rotate Action** option and pick the rotation parameter. Then select the objects that make up the needle and the rotation parameter. Press [Enter] or the space bar, or right-click to place the

Figure 26-21. A rotation parameter with a rotate action allows you to rotate the needle in a speedometer block to indicate different speeds. Use the **Base angle** option to set a base angle other than 0°.

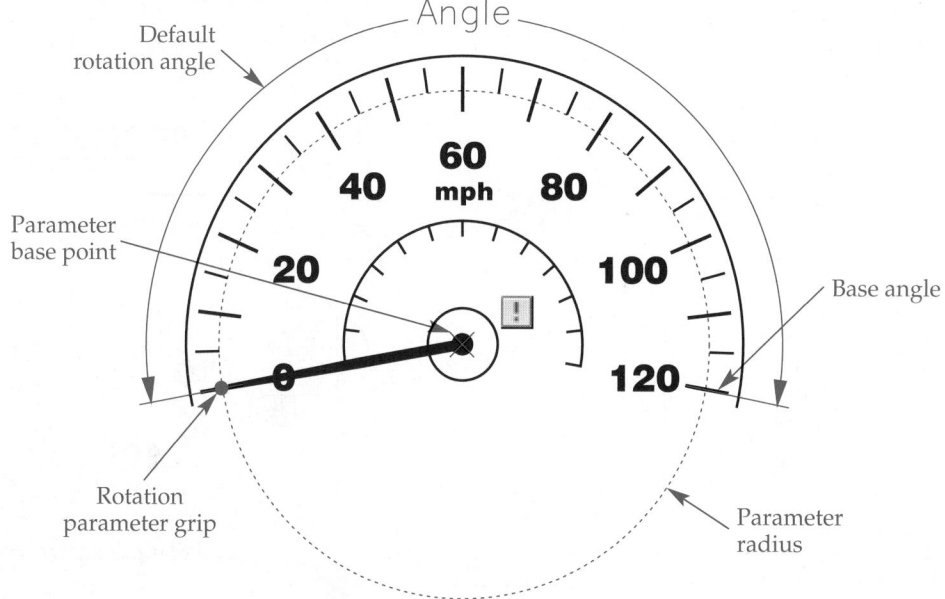

action. If necessary, access the **Properties** palette and adjust the **Base type** option. The default **Dependent** option sets the rotation point as the base point of the rotation parameter, which is appropriate for the speedometer example. Test and save the block, and exit the **Block Editor**. The dynamic block is now ready to use.

Using a Rotate Action Dynamically

Figure 26-22 shows using the rotation parameter grip or dynamic input to rotate the needle inside a reference of the speedometer block. An endpoint object snap is most appropriate to select a specific speed for this example. You can also use the **Properties** palette to define the angle.

Exercise 26-6

Access the Student Web site (www.g-wlearning.com/CAD) and complete Exercise 26-6.

Alignment Parameters

An *alignment parameter* creates an alignment property. When you move a block with an alignment parameter near another object, the block rotates to align with the object based on the angle and alignment line defined in the block. An alignment parameter saves time by eliminating the need to rotate a block or assign a rotation parameter. An alignment parameter affects the entire block, and therefore requires no action.

alignment parameter: A parameter that aligns a block with another object in the drawing.

Creating an Alignment Parameter

Figure 26-23 provides an example of adding an alignment parameter to the block of a gate valve symbol to align the gate valve with pipes. Access the **Alignment** parameter option and pick the point in the center of the valve to locate the parameter grip and define the first point of the alignment line. Next, specify the alignment direction, or use the **Type** option to specify the alignment type. Alignment type does not affect how the block aligns; it determines the direction of the alignment grip. Select the **Perpendicular** option to point the grip perpendicular to the alignment line, or choose the **Tangent** option to point the grip tangent to the alignment line. Set the **Tangent** option for the gate valve example.

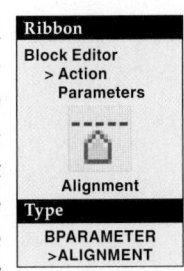

Ribbon
Block Editor > Action Parameters
Alignment

Type
BPARAMETER >ALIGNMENT

Figure 26-22.
Dynamically rotating the needle in a speedometer block using a rotate action assigned to a rotation parameter.

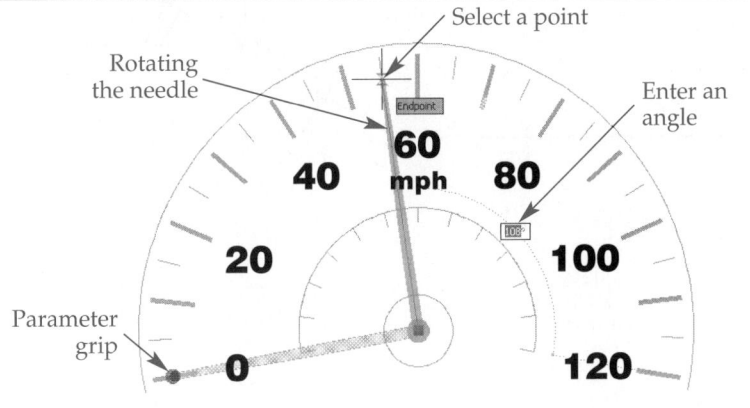

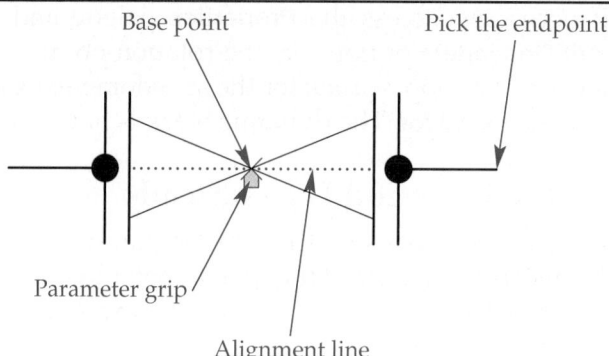

Figure 26-23.
Adding an alignment parameter to a gate valve block.

Base point

Pick the endpoint

Parameter grip

Alignment line

After specifying the base point and alignment type, pick a second point to set the alignment direction. The angle between the first point and the second point defines the alignment line. The alignment line determines the default rotation angle. **Figure 26-23** shows selecting the endpoint of the valve symbol. The alignment parameter grip is an arrow that points in the direction of alignment, perpendicular or tangent to the object with which the block will align. Test the block by drawing a line in the **Test Block Window** and attempting to align the block with the line. When you are finished, save the block and exit the **Block Editor**. The dynamic block is now ready to use.

> **NOTE**
>
> Use the **Name** option before you specify the parameter to rename the parameter. Alignment parameters do not include labels. You can also adjust the alignment type from the **Properties** palette if you have already created the parameter.

Using an Alignment Parameter Dynamically

Figure 26-24 shows using the alignment parameter grip to align the gate valve block with a pipeline. Select the block to display grips and then pick the parameter grip. Move the block near another object to align the block with the object. The rotation depends on the alignment path and type and the angle of the other object.

Figure 26-24. Move the gate valve block near a line to align the block with the line.

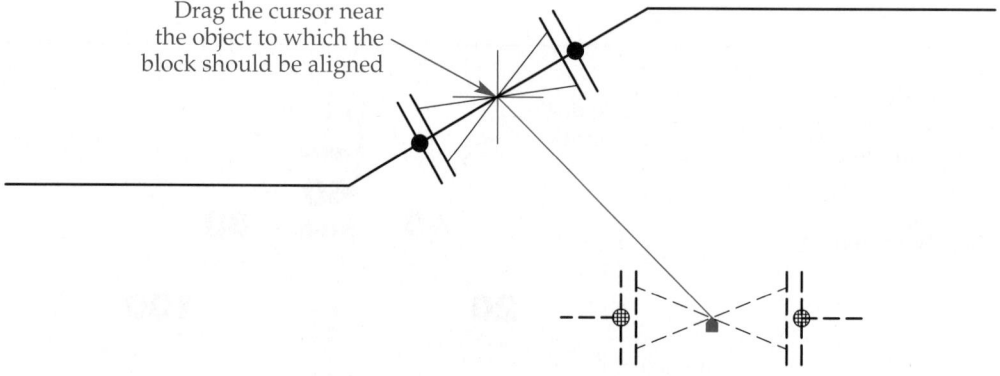

Drag the cursor near the object to which the block should be aligned

Exercise 26-7

Access the Student Web site (www.g-wlearning.com/CAD) and complete Exercise 26-7.

Flip Parameters

A *flip parameter* creates a flip property to which you can assign a flip action. For example, assign a flip parameter with a flip action to a door symbol to provide the option to place the door on either side of a wall. A flip parameter can also be used to control the side of a reference line on which a weld symbol appears for arrow side or other side applications.

Figure 26-25 shows an example of adding a flip parameter. Access the **Flip Parameter** option and pick the base point, followed by the endpoint of the reflection line. See **Figure 26-25A**. Pick a location for the parameter label, and then enter the number of grips to associate with the parameter. The default **1** option creates a single flip grip that allows you to use grip editing to carry out the flip action.

Flipping a block mirrors the block over the reflection line. However, for the door symbol, with the line in the position shown in **Figure 26-25A**, an incorrect flip will result when you flip the block to the other side of a wall. To mirror the block properly, you must locate the reflection line to account for wall thickness. To place the door on a 4" wall, for example, use the **MOVE** tool to move the reflection line 2" lower than the door. The label and parameter grip also move. In addition, move the parameter grip horizontally to the middle of the door opening to help place and flip the block properly. See **Figure 26-25B**.

flip parameter:
A parameter that mirrors selected objects within a block.

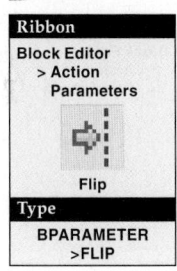

Ribbon
Block Editor
> Action
Parameters

Flip

Type
BPARAMETER
>FLIP

Figure 26-25. A—Inserting a flip parameter. B—Moving the parameter so the block will flip correctly about the centerline of a wall.

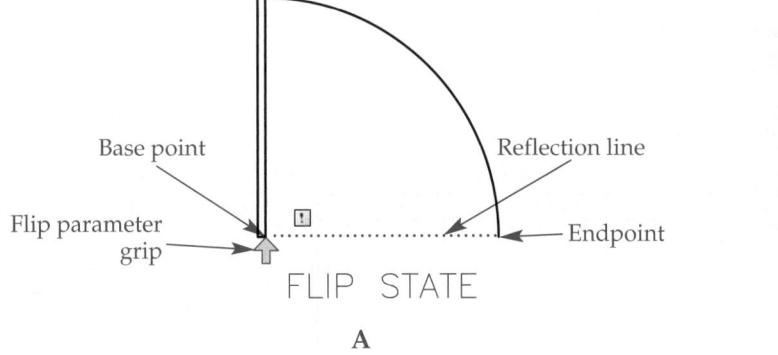

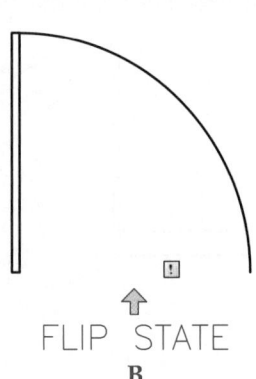

A   B

Name, **Label**, **Description**, and **Palette** options are available before you specify the parameter. Most of these options are also available from the **Properties** palette if you have already created the parameter.

PROFESSIONAL TIP

A block reference with a flip parameter mirrors about the reflection line. You must place the reflection line in the correct location so the flip creates a symmetrical, or mirrored, copy. This typically requires the reflection line to be coincident with the block insertion point.

Assigning a Flip Action

flip action: An action used to flip the entire block.

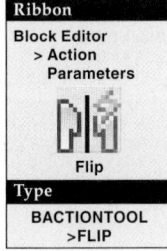

Ribbon
Block Editor **> Action** **Parameters**
Flip
Type
BACTIONTOOL >FLIP

To assign a *flip action* to the door example, access the **Flip** action option and pick the flip parameter. Then select the objects that make up the door and the flip parameter. Press [Enter] or the space bar or right-click to place the action. Test and save the block, and exit the **Block Editor**. The dynamic block is now ready to use.

Using a Flip Action Dynamically

Figure 26-26A shows a reference of the door block, selected for editing. Pick the flip parameter grip to flip the block to the other side of the reflection line, as shown in **Figure 26-26B.** Unlike other parameters and actions that require stretching, moving, or rotating, a single pick initiates a flip action.

PROFESSIONAL TIP

Add another flip parameter with a flip action to a door symbol to flip the door from side to side. This allows one block takes the place of four blocks to accommodate different door positions.

Figure 26-26. A—Select the block to display the flip parameter grip. B—Pick the flip parameter grip to flip the block about the reflection line. The entire block flips because all of the objects within the block are included in the selection set for the action.

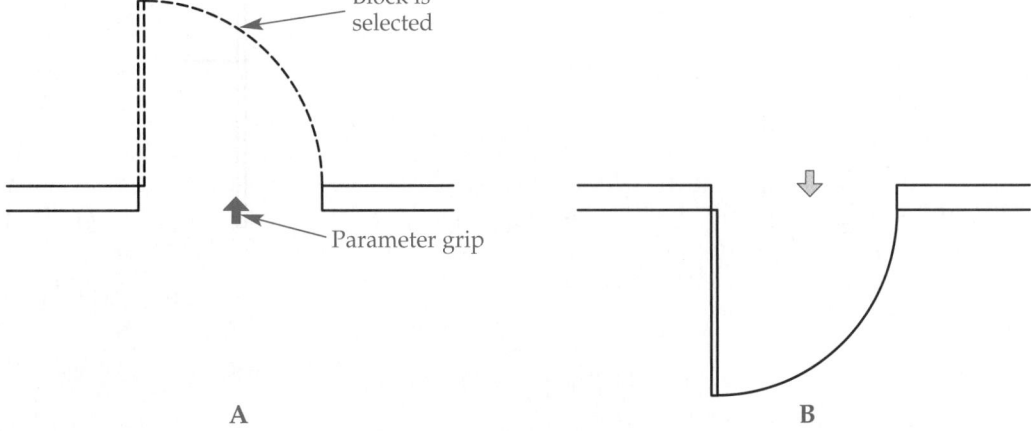

Exercise 26-8

Access the Student Web site (www.g-wlearning.com/CAD) and complete Exercise 26-8.

XY Parameters

An *XY parameter* creates horizontal and vertical distance properties. You can assign move, scale, stretch, and array actions to XY parameters. The XY parameter can include up to four parameter grips—one at each corner of a rectangle defined by the parameter. You can use the XY parameter for a variety of applications, depending on the assigned actions.

Figure 26-27 provides an example of inserting an XY parameter. Access the **XY** parameter option and pick the base point, which is the origin of the X and Y distances. Next, pick a point to specify the XY point, which is the *corner* opposite the base point. Finally, enter the number of grips to associate with the parameter. The default **2** option creates grips at the start and endpoints, allowing you to use grip editing to carry out the action assigned to either point. Select the 4 option, as shown in **Figure 26-27**, to assign a grip at each XY corner to maximize flexibility, or choose a smaller number to limit dynamic options. If you choose the **0** option, you can only use the **Properties** palette to adjust the block.

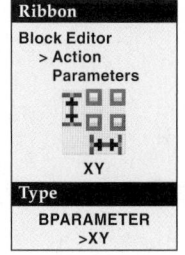

XY parameter: A parameter that specifies distance properties in the X and Y directions.

Ribbon
Block Editor
> Action
Parameters
XY
Type
BPARAMETER
>XY

> **NOTE**
>
> **Name**, **Label**, **Chain**, **Description**, **Palette**, and **Value set** options are available before you specify the parameter. Most of these options and the **Base angle** setting are also available from the **Properties** palette if you have already created the parameter.

Assigning an Array Action

Figure 26-28 illustrates using an *array action* assigned to an XY parameter. This example shows dynamically arraying the block of an architectural glass block to create an architectural feature of glass blocks, such as a wall, without using a separate array operation. Access the **Array** action option and pick the XY parameter. Then select the objects to be included in the array, and press [Enter] or the space bar or right-click to accept the selection.

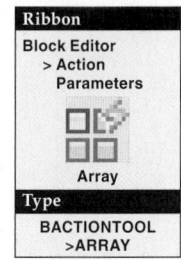

array action: An action used to array objects within the block based on preset specifications.

Ribbon
Block Editor
> Action
Parameters
Array
Type
BACTIONTOOL
>ARRAY

Figure 26-27.
Adding an XY parameter to a block of an architectural glass block. The XY parameter consists of X and Y distance properties and four grips.

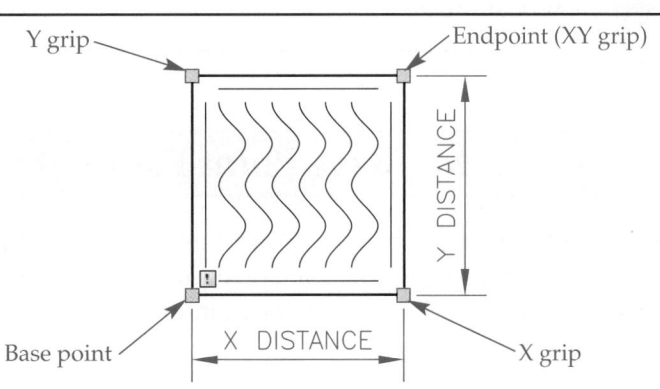

Figure 26-28.
Dynamically creating an array of architectural glass blocks using a block with an XY parameter and an array action. The pattern of rows and columns forms as you move the XY parameter. Notice the grout joints that form between the glass blocks because of proper action definition.

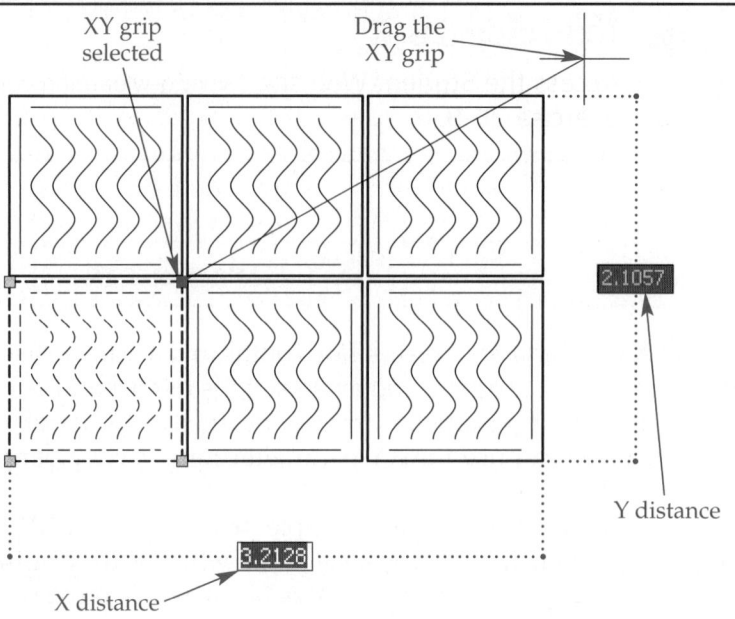

At the Enter the distance between rows or specify unit cell: prompt, enter a value for the distance between rows or pick two points to set the row and column values. At the Enter the distance between columns: prompt, specify a value for the distance between columns. The second prompt does not appear if you select two points to define the row and column values. In the glass block example, be sure to allow for a grout joint when setting the row and column distance. Before assigning the action, you may want to draw a construction point offset from the block by the width of the grout joint. Then you can pick two points to define the row and column values. Be sure to erase the construction point before saving the block. Test and save the block, and exit the **Block Editor**. The dynamic block is now ready to use.

Using an Array Action Dynamically

Figure 26-28 illustrates using the upper-right grip or dynamic input to array a reference of the architectural glass block. You can use any available grip to apply an array, depending on where you want the array to occur. You can also use the **Properties** palette to define the array. Notice that proper action definition produces grout joints. The resulting array remains a single block.

Exercise 26-9

Access the Student Web site (www.g-wlearning.com/CAD) and complete Exercise 26-9.

Base Point Parameters

The **Block Editor** origin (0,0,0 point) determines the default location of the block insertion base point. Typically, you construct blocks in the **Block Editor** in reference to the origin, using the origin as the location of the insertion base point. The base point you choose when creating a block using the **BLOCK** tool attaches to the origin when you open the block in the **Block Editor**. Add a *base point parameter* to override the default origin base point.

Access the **Basepoint** parameter option and pick a point to place the base point parameter. The parameter appears as a circle with crosshairs. After you save the block, the location of the base point parameter becomes the new base point for the block. You cannot assign actions to a base point parameter, but you can include a base point parameter in the selection set for actions.

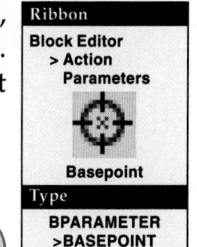

base point parameter: A parameter that defines an alternate base point for a block.

Ribbon
Block Editor
> Action
Parameters

Basepoint
Type
BPARAMETER
>BASEPOINT

Parameter Value Sets

A *value set* helps to ensure that you select an appropriate value when dynamically controlling a block. This can often increase the usefulness of a dynamic block. For example, if a window style is only available in widths of 36″, 42″, 48″, 54″, and 60″, add a value set to a linear parameter with a stretch action to limit selection to these sizes. See **Figure 26-29**. You can use a value set with linear, polar, XY, and rotation parameters.

value set: A set of allowed values for a parameter.

Creating a Value Set

To create a value set, select the **Value set** option available at the first prompt after you access a parameter option, and then pick a value set type. Choose the **List** option to create a list of possible sizes. Type all of the valid values for the parameter separated by commas. For the window block example, enter 36,42,48,54,60. Then press [Enter] or the space bar or right-click to return to the initial parameter prompt, and add the parameter. After you insert the parameter, the valid values appear as tick marks.

Select the **Increment** option to specify an incremental value. Minimum and maximum values are also set to provide a limit for the increments. For the window block example, use the **Value set** option again to set 6″ width increments. This time choose the **Increment** option and type 6 for the distance increment, 36 for the minimum distance, and 60 for the maximum distance. The initial parameter prompt returns after you enter the maximum distance.

After you add a parameter with a value set, assign an action to the parameter. For the window block in **Figure 26-29**, assign a stretch action to the linear parameter. This allows the window to stretch to the valid widths specified in the value set. Test and save the block, and exit the **Block Editor**. The dynamic block is now ready to use.

Figure 26-29.
When you adjust a block that includes a value set, tick marks appear at locations corresponding to the values in the value set. You can only adjust the block to one of the tick marks.

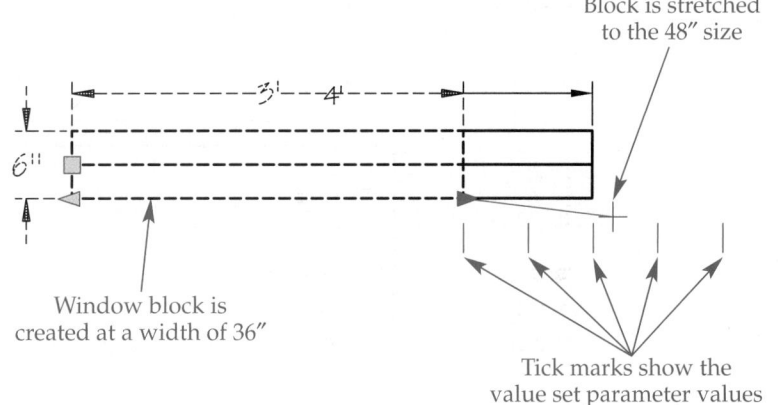

Block is stretched to the 48″ size

Window block is created at a width of 36″

Tick marks show the value set parameter values

Using a Value Set with a Parameter

Figure 26-29 shows using a linear parameter grip with a stretch action to specify the width of a window block reference. Tick marks appear at the positions of valid values. As you stretch the grip, the modified block snaps to the nearest tick mark. When using dynamic input, you can also enter a value in the input field. If you type a value that is not included in the value set, the nearest valid value applies. You can also use the **Value Set** category of the **Properties** palette to select a value.

Exercise 26-10

Access the Student Web site (www.g-wlearning.com/CAD) and complete Exercise 26-10.

Chain Actions

chain action: An action that triggers another action when you modify a parameter.

A *chain action* limits the number of edits that you have to perform by allowing one action to trigger other actions. For example, **Figure 26-30** shows using a chain action to stretch the block of a table and chairs, and array the chairs along the table at the same time. You can use a chain action with point, linear, polar, XY, and rotation parameters.

Figure 26-30.
A—A block of a table with six chairs. B—Use a chain action with a linear parameter to array the chairs automatically when you stretch the table.

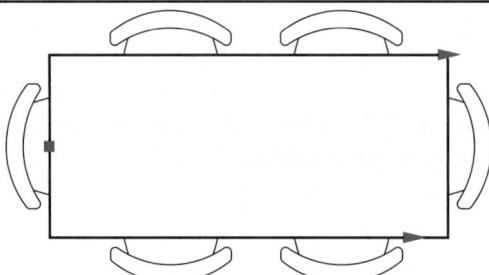

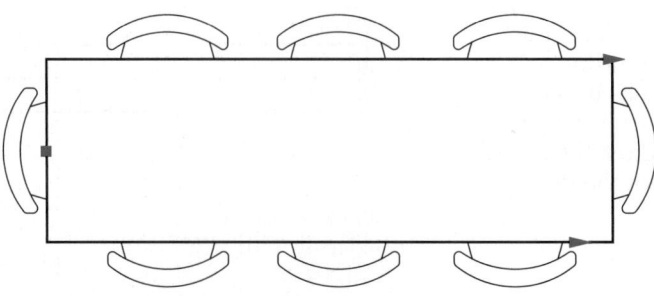

Creating a Chain Action

To create a chain action, select the **Chain** option available at the first prompt after you access a parameter option to display the Evaluate associated actions when parameter is edited by another action? [Yes/No]: prompt. The default **No** setting does not create a chain action. Select the **Yes** option to create a chain action.

Figure 26-31 shows the default arrangement of the table and chairs block example. For this example, access the **Linear** parameter option and use the **Label** option to change the label name to CHAIR ARRAY. Next, choose the **Chain** option and select **Yes**. To complete the parameter, select the start and endpoints shown in **Figure 26-31A**, and assign a single grip to the endpoint. Then assign an array action to the parameter, selecting the chairs on the top and bottom of the table as the objects to array. At the Enter the distance between rows or specify unit cell: prompt, use object snaps to snap to the endpoint of one of the chairs and then snap to the equivalent endpoint on the chair next to the first chair.

Add another single-grip linear parameter, labeled TABLE STRETCH, as shown in **Figure 26-31B**. Assign a stretch action to the parameter associated with the TABLE STRETCH parameter grip. Use a crossing window around the right end of the table and the CHAIR ARRAY parameter grip. See **Figure 26-31C**. Select the table, the chair at the right end of the table, and the CHAIR ARRAY parameter as the objects to stretch. Test and save the block, and exit the **Block Editor**. The dynamic block is now ready to use.

PROFESSIONAL TIP

The keys to successfully creating a chain action are to set the **Chain** option to **Yes** for the parameter affected automatically and to include the parameter in the object selection set when creating the action that drives the chain action.

Applying a Chain Action

Figure 26-32 shows using a linear parameter grip or dynamic input to stretch the table and chairs block reference. Stretching the table triggers the array action. You can also use the **Properties** palette to define the table length.

Exercise 26-11

Access the Student Web site (www.g-wlearning.com/CAD) and complete Exercise 26-11.

Figure 26-31.
A—Inserting a linear parameter to use with an array action for the chairs. B—Inserting a linear parameter to stretch the table. C—Assigning a stretch action to the linear parameter. When you specify the crossing window, be sure to include the **CHAIR ARRAY** parameter grip in the frame.

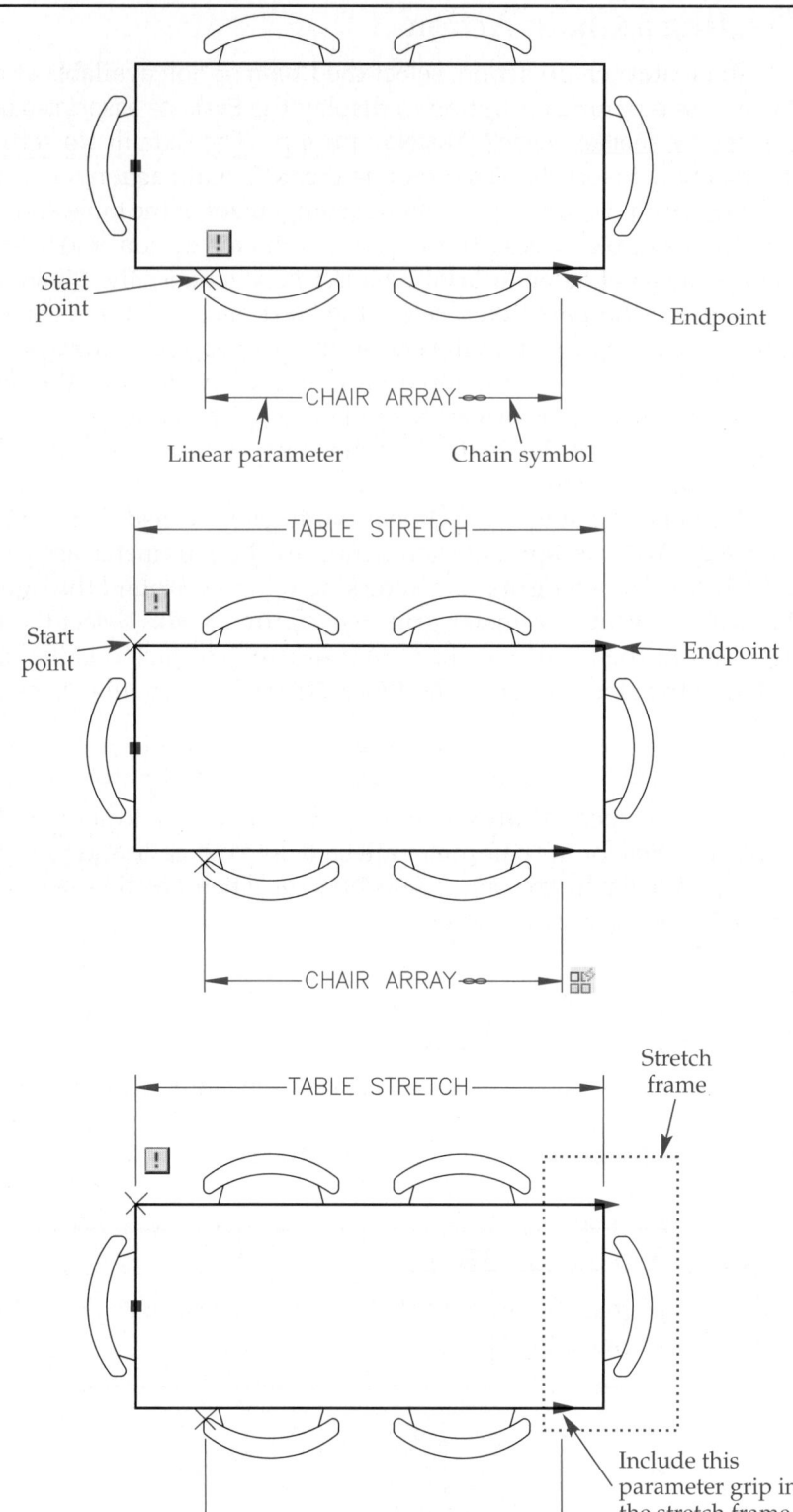

Figure 26-32.
As you stretch the parameter grip, the table stretches and the chairs are arrayed at the same time.

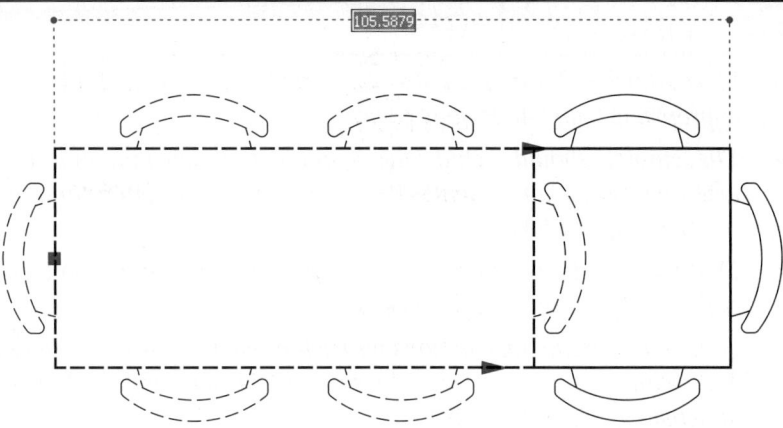

Chapter Test

Answer the following questions. Write your answers on a separate sheet of paper or go to the Student Web site (www.g-wlearning.com/CAD) and complete the electronic chapter test.

1. Define *dynamic block*.
2. What is the function of a dynamic block?
3. How are standard blocks and dynamic blocks the same? How are they different?
4. Identify the property that forms when you create a point parameter and list the actions you can assign.
5. What is the purpose of a move action?
6. When do action bars appear?
7. What information can you get by hovering over or selecting an action bar?
8. What is the basic function of a linear parameter?
9. Explain the function of a stretch action.
10. Briefly describe how to use a stretch action symmetrically.
11. What is the basic function of a scale action?
12. Describe the polar parameter type and list the actions that you can assign to the parameter.
13. Identify the property that forms when you create a rotation parameter and list the actions you can assign.
14. Describe what happens when you move a block with an alignment parameter near another object in the drawing. How does this save drawing time?
15. Give at least one practical example of using a flip parameter.
16. Briefly describe the properties an XY parameter creates and list the actions that you can assign to the parameter.
17. Give an example of using an array action assigned to an XY parameter.
18. When would you add a base point parameter?
19. Describe the basic use of a value set.
20. Explain the function of a chain action.

Drawing Problems

- *Start AutoCAD if it is not already started. Start a new drawing for each problem using an appropriate template of your choice.*

- *The template should include layers and text, dimension, multileader, and table styles, when necessary, for drawing the given objects. Add layers and text, dimension, multileader, and table styles as needed.*

- *Draw all objects using appropriate layers and text, dimension, multileader, and table styles, justification, and format.*

- *Follow the specific instructions for each problem. Use only drawing and editing tools and techniques you have already learned. Use your own judgment and approximate dimensions when necessary.*

- *Apply dimensions accurately using ASME or appropriate industry standards.*

Note: *Some of the problems in this chapter are built on problems from previous chapters. If you have not yet completed those problems, complete them now.*

▼ Basic

1. Open P24-1 and save it as P26-1. The P26-1 file should be active. Erase all copies of the steel column symbols except for the one in the lower-left corner. Insert an XY parameter into the steel column block and associate an array action with the parameter. Use the proper values for the array action to array the block dynamically to match the drawing. Use the dynamic block to create the rest of the steel columns in the drawing. Resave the drawing.

2. Create a block named WIRE ROLL as shown. Do not include the dimensions. Insert a linear parameter on the entire length of the roll. Use a value set with the following values: 36″, 42″, 48″, and 54″. Assign a stretch action to the parameter and associate the action with either parameter grip. Create a crossing window that will allow the length of the roll to stretch. Select all of the objects on one end and the length lines as the objects to stretch. Insert the WIRE ROLL block four times into a drawing and stretch each block to use a different value set length. Save the drawing as P26-2.

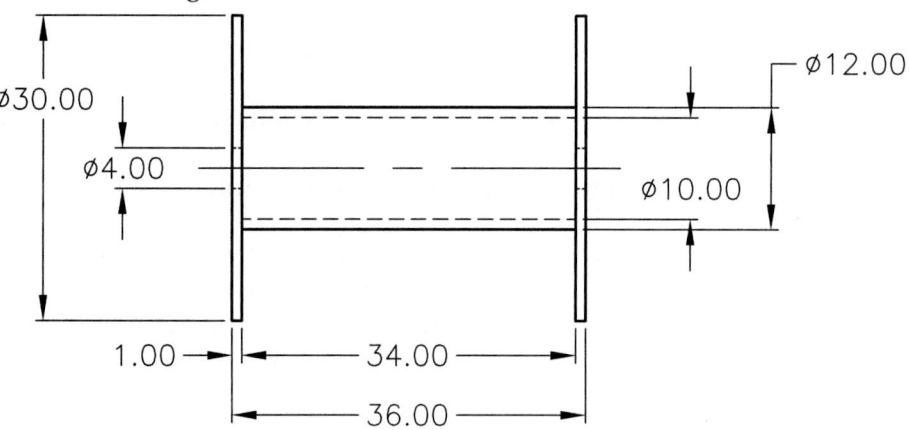

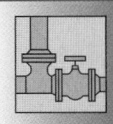

3. Create a block named **90D ELBOW** as shown on the left. Do not include the dimensions. Insert two flip parameters and two flip actions. The purpose of one of the flip parameter/action combinations is to flip the elbow horizontally. The second flip parameter/action combination flips the elbow vertically. Use the dynamic block to create the drawing shown on the right. Save the drawing as P26-3.

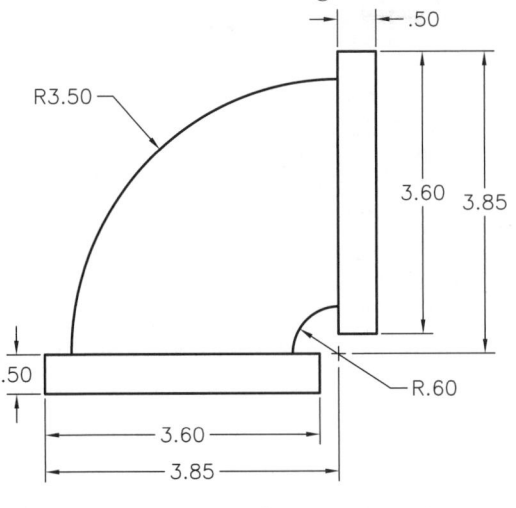

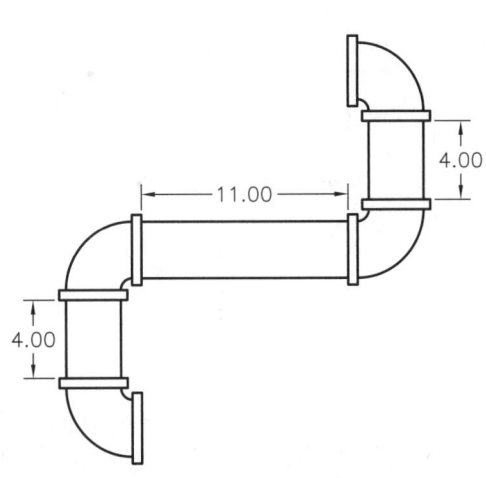

4. Create a block of the 48″ window shown on the left. Do not include the dimensions. Insert an alignment parameter so the length of the window can align with a wall. Then draw the walls shown on the right. Insert the window block as needed. Use the alignment parameter to align the window to the walls. Center the windows on wall segments unless dimensioned. Save the drawing as P26-4.

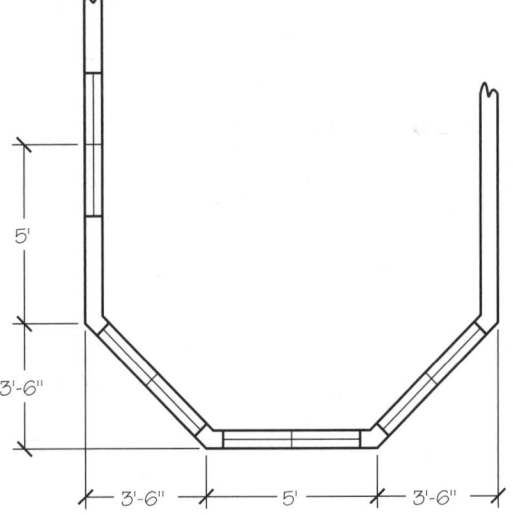

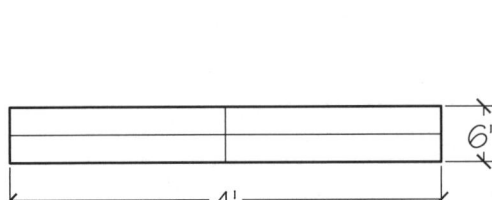

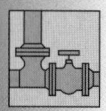

5. Create a block named **CONTROL VALVE** as shown on the left. Include the label in the block. Insert a point parameter and assign a move action to the parameter. Select the two lines of text as the objects to which the action applies. Insert the **CONTROL VALVE** block into the drawing three times. Use the point parameter to move the text to match the three positions shown. Save the drawing as **P26-5**.

CONTROL VALVE
PART #336HR

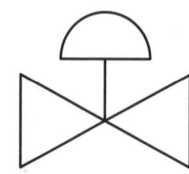

CONTROL VALVE
PART #336HR

CONTROL VALVE
PART #336HR

▼ Intermediate

6. Create a block named **FLANGE** as shown. Do not include dimensions. Insert a rotation parameter specifying the center of the flange as the base point. Assign a rotate action to the parameter, selecting the six ⌀.2 circles as the objects to which the action applies. Insert the **FLANGE** block into the drawing twice. Use the rotation parameter to create the two configurations shown. Save the drawing as **P26-6**.

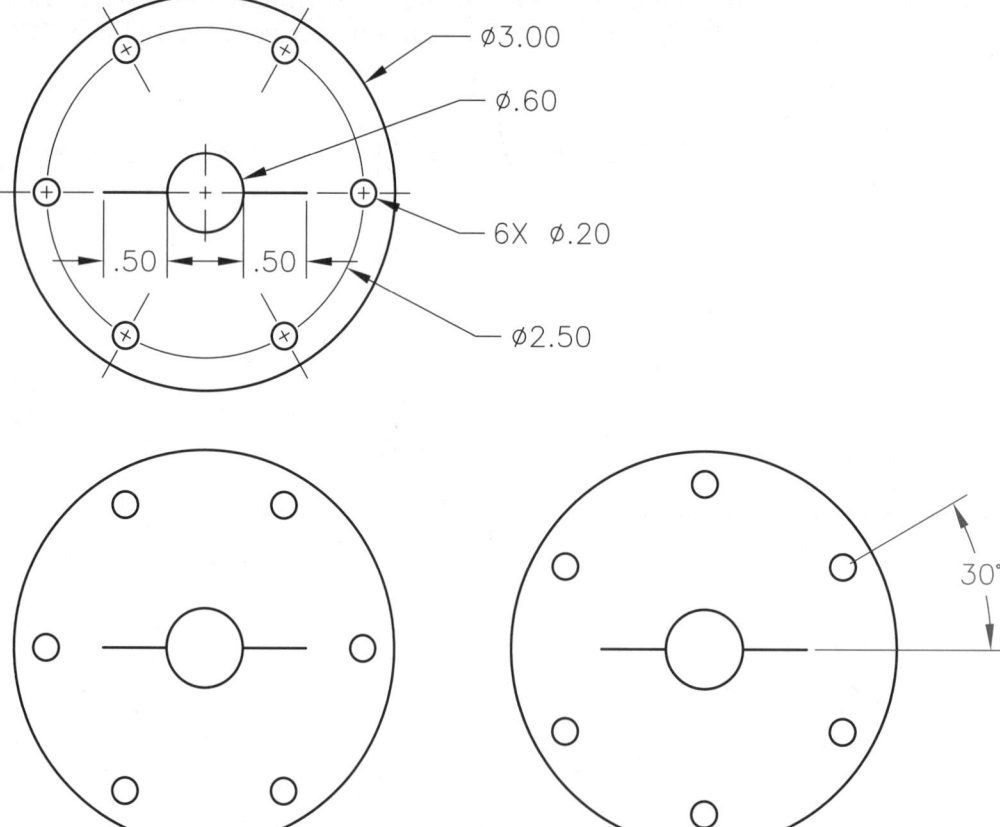

Drawing Problems - Chapter 26

7. Open P26-6 and save it as P26-7. The P26-7 file should be active. Open the FLANGE block in the **Block Editor** and use the **Properties** palette to apply the following settings to the rotation parameter:

A. **Angle label**—BOLT HOLES
B. **Angle description**—ROTATION OF BOLT HOLE PATTERN
C. **Ang type**—INCREMENT
D. **Ang increment**—30
E. Save the changes and exit the **Block Editor**. Save the drawing.

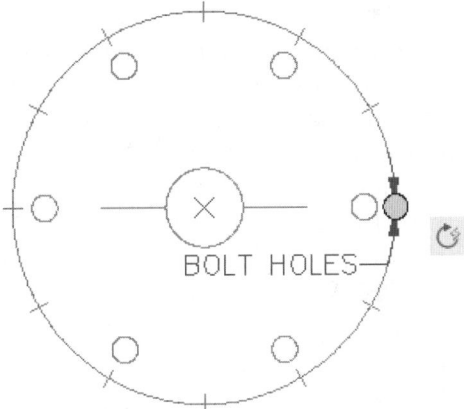

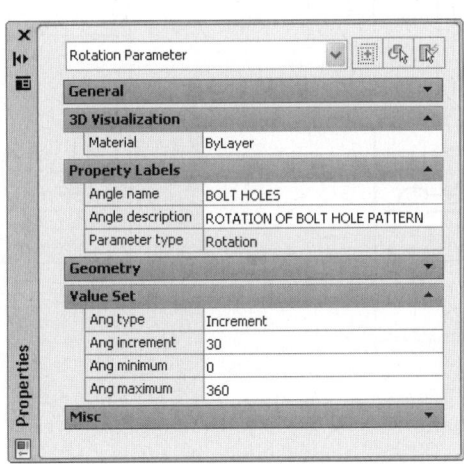

8. The drawing shown is a fan with an enlarged view of the motor. This fan can have one of three motors of different sizes. Create the fan as a dynamic block.

   A. Draw all the objects. Do not dimension the drawing or draw the enlarged view.

   B. Create a block named FAN consisting of the objects shown in the enlarged view.

   C. Open the block in the **Block Editor** and insert a linear parameter along the top of the motor (the 1.50″ dimension). Use a value set with the following values: 1.5, 1.75, and 2.

   D. Assign a scale action to the linear parameter. Select all of the objects that make up the motor as the objects to which the action applies. Use an independent base point type and specify the base point as the lower-left corner of the motor (the implied intersection).

   E. Save the block and exit the **Block Editor**.

   F. Insert the block three times into the drawing. Use the linear parameter grip to scale the motor to the three different sizes, as shown below on the right.

   G. Save the drawing as P26-8.

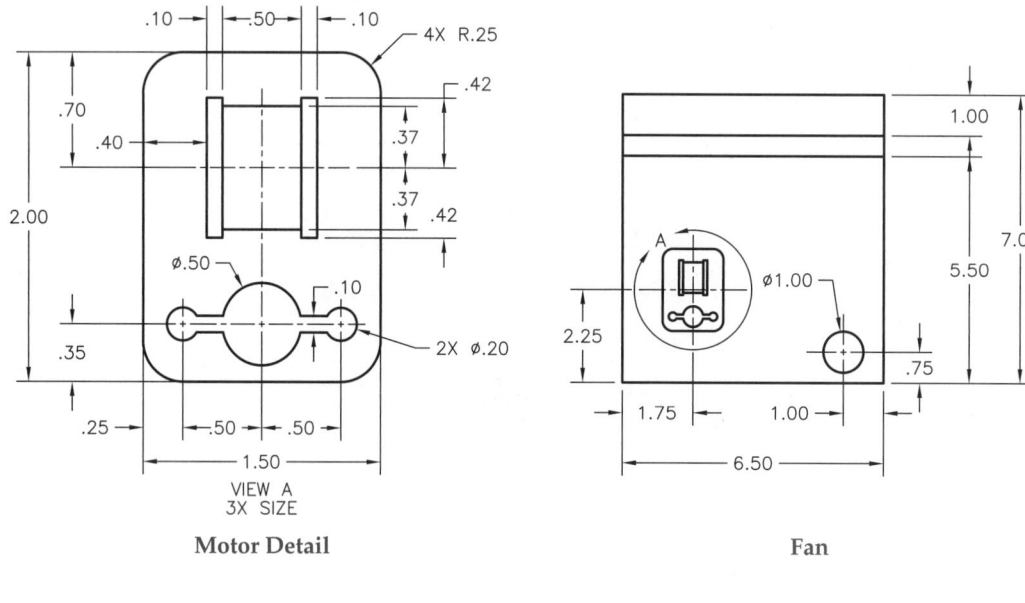

Motor Detail   **Fan**

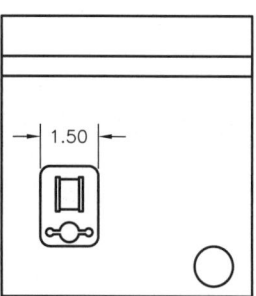   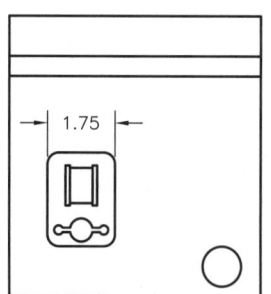   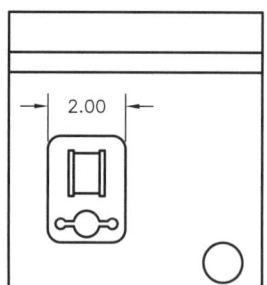

9. Construct a block of an architectural glass block similar to the block shown. Use an XY parameter with an array action to create a glass block wall of 10 rows and 15 columns. Construct the block to include an appropriate grout joint. Save the drawing as P26-9.

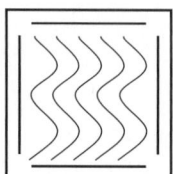

10. Construct a block of a steel C4×5.4 shape. Reference the American Institute of Steel Construction (AISC) manual for dimensions. Add a polar parameter with a polar stretch action to adjust the depth and angle of block references. Insert and adjust the block as needed to create a portion of a motor mount similar to the drawing shown. Save the drawing as P26-10.

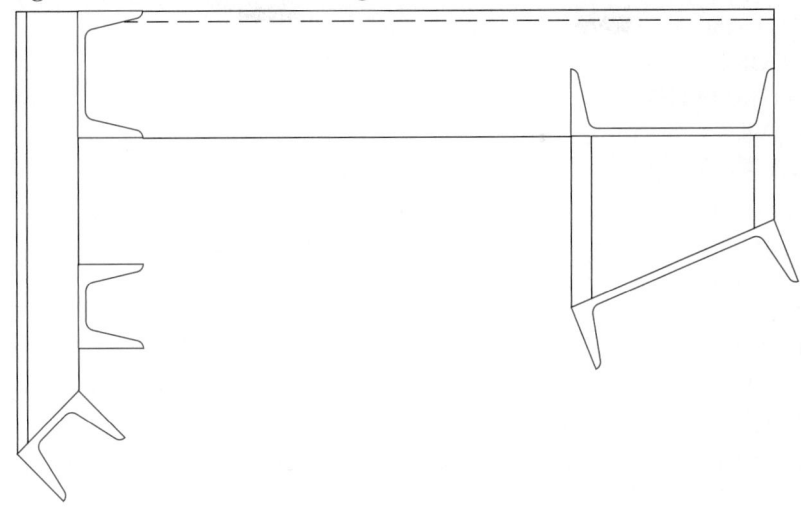

11. Construct a block of a speedometer similar to the speedometer shown. Add a rotation parameter with a rotate action to adjust the needle reading for block references. Insert the block four times and use the dynamic needle to create a speedometer that reads 5 mph, 25 mph, 55 mph, and 110 mph. Save the drawing as P26-11.

12. Construct a block of a table with six chairs similar to the block shown. Use linear parameters with array, stretch, and chain actions as needed to stretch and add chairs to block references. Insert the block twice and use the dynamic stretch and array to create a table with eight chairs and a table with ten chairs. Save the drawing as P26-12.

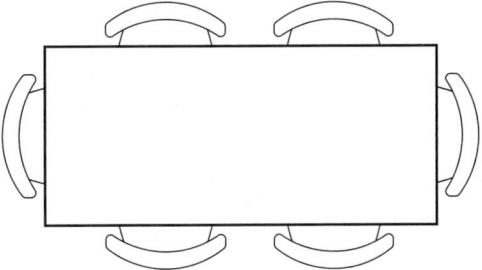

Drawing Problems – Chapter 26

AutoCAD Certified Associate Exam Practice

Answer the following questions. Write your answers on a separate sheet of paper.

1. Which of the following tools can be used to save a dynamic block? *Select all that apply.*
   A. **BACTION**
   B. **BLOCK**
   C. **BPARAMETER**
   D. **BSAVE**
   E. **BSAVEAS**

2. Which of the following actions can be assigned to a point parameter? *Select all that apply.*
   A. **FLIP**
   B. **MOVE**
   C. **ROTATE**
   D. **SCALE**
   E. **STRETCH**

3. Which of the following block properties can be changed using a polar stretch action? *Select all that apply.*
   A. color
   B. layer
   C. shape
   D. size
   E. rotation

AutoCAD Certified Professional Exam Practice

Follow the instructions in each problem. Write your answers on a separate sheet of paper.

1. **Navigate to this chapter on the Student Web site and open CPE-26align.dwg.** Edit the existing SOFA block to include an alignment parameter that will align the middle of the back of the sofa with a wall. Insert the block into the drawing. Use the alignment parameter and other appropriate tools to center the sofa on the window as shown, exactly 4″ from the wall. What are the coordinates of the middle of the sofa back? (Use the coordinates of the quadrant point on the sofa back.)

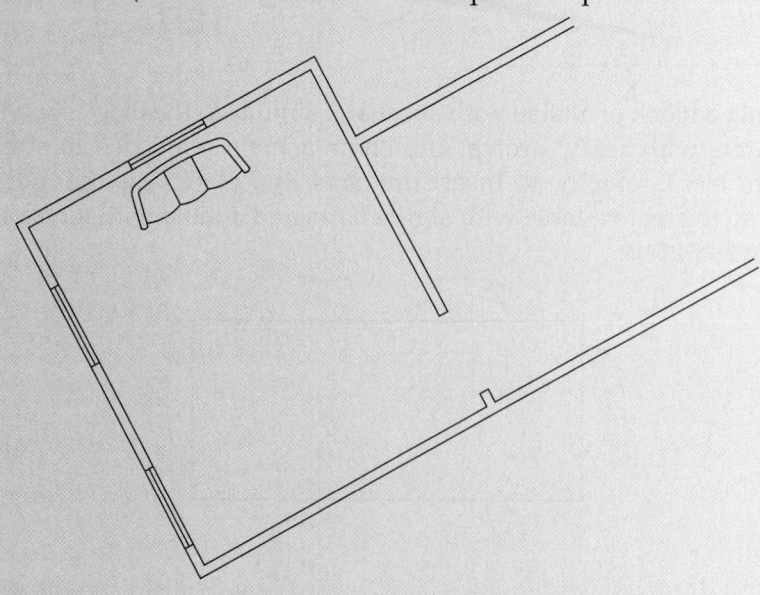

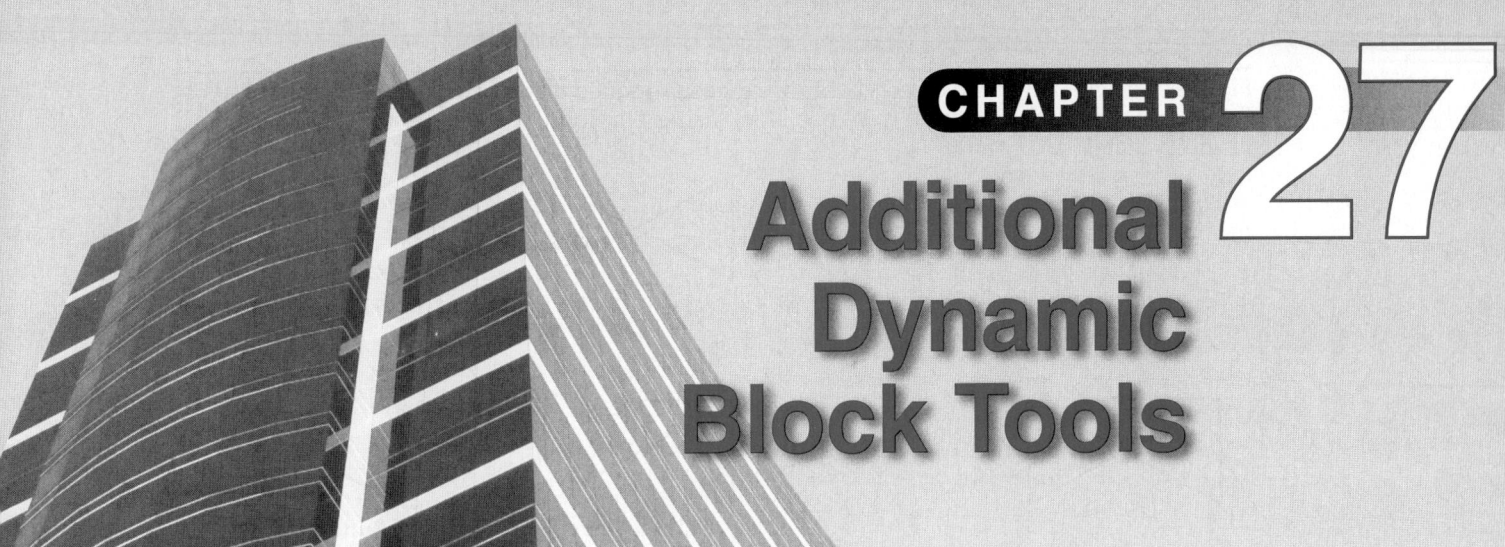

Additional Dynamic Block Tools

Learning Objectives

After completing this chapter, you will be able to do the following:

✓ Apply visibility and lookup parameters.
✓ Use parameter sets.
✓ Constrain block geometry.
✓ Use a block properties table.

This chapter describes adding visibility and lookup parameters to enhance the usefulness of blocks. You will also learn to apply geometric constraints and constraint parameters to blocks as an alternative or in addition to parameters and actions. Finally, this chapter explores the process of using a block properties table.

Visibility Parameters

A *visibility parameter* allows you to assign *visibility states* to objects within a block. Selecting a visibility state displays the only objects in the block associated with the visibility state. Visibility states expand the capacity of blocks in a symbol library by allowing you to hide or make visible specific objects and even completely different symbols. A block can include one visibility parameter. Visibility parameters do not require an action.

Figure 27-1 provides an example of using a visibility parameter to create four different symbols from a single block. To create the block, draw all of the objects representing the different variations, as shown in **Figure 27-1A**. Then assign a visibility parameter and add visibility states that identify the objects that are visible in each variation. Insert the block and select a visibility state to display the corresponding objects. See **Figure 27-1B**.

To add a visibility parameter, access the **Visibility Parameter** option and pick a location for the parameter label. The parameter automatically includes a single grip. When you insert the block and select the grip, a shortcut menu appears listing visibility states. There is no prompt to select objects because the visibility parameter is associated with the entire block.

visibility parameter: A parameter that allows you to assign multiple views to objects within a block.

visibility states: Views created by selecting block objects to display or hide.

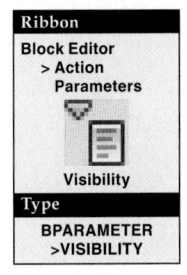

Ribbon

Block Editor > Action Parameters

Visibility

Type

BPARAMETER >VISIBILITY

Figure 27-1. A—All of the objects composing each unique valve symbol shown together. B—Create each different valve from one block using a visibility parameter with different visibility states.

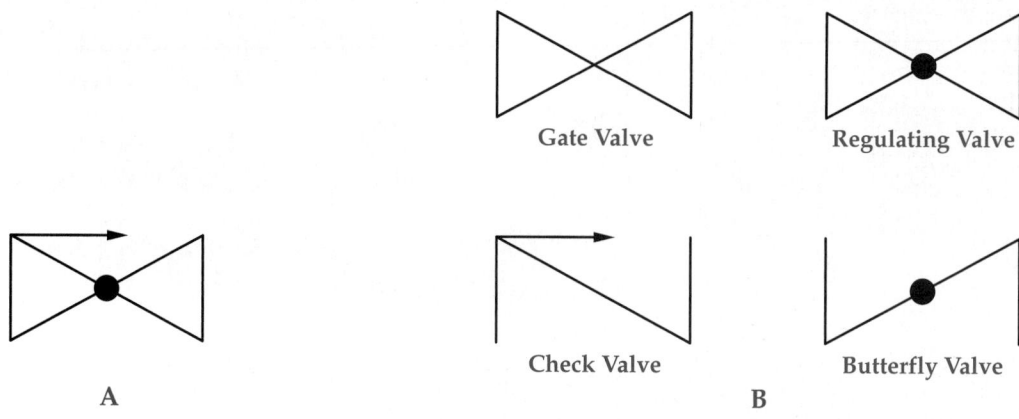

Gate Valve

Regulating Valve

Check Valve

Butterfly Valve

A

B

> **NOTE**
>
>  **Name**, **Label**, **Description**, and **Palette** options are available before you specify the parameter. Most of the options are also available from the **Properties** palette if you have already created the parameter.

Creating Visibility States

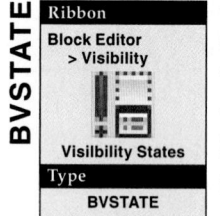

BVSTATE

Ribbon

Block Editor > Visibility

Visibility States

Type

BVSTATE

The tools in the **Visibility** panel of the **Block Editor** ribbon tab become enabled when you add a visibility parameter. See **Figure 27-2**. To create a visibility state, access the **BVSTATE** tool to display the **Visibility States** dialog box. See **Figure 27-3A**. Pick the **New...** button to open the **New Visibility State** dialog box shown in **Figure 27-3B**. Type the name of the new visibility state in the **Visibility state name:** text box. For the valve block example shown in **Figure 27-1**, an appropriate name could be GATE VALVE, REGULATING VALVE, CHECK VALVE, or BUTTERFLY VALVE, depending on which valve the visibility state represents.

Pick the **Hide all existing objects in new state** radio button to make all of the objects in the block invisible when you create the new visibility state. This allows you to choose only the objects that should be visible for the visibility state. Pick the **Show all existing objects in new state** radio button to make all of the objects in the block visible when you create the new visibility state. This allows you to hide objects that should be invisible for the visibility state. Select the **Leave visibility of existing objects unchanged in new state** radio button to display the objects that are currently visible when you create the new visibility state.

Figure 27-2.
The visibility tools in the **Visibility** panel of the **Block Editor** ribbon tab.

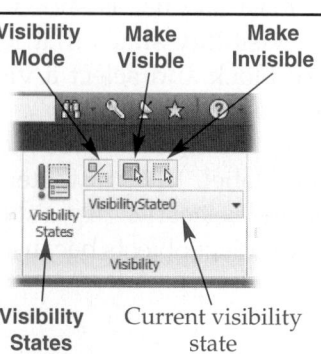

Visibility Mode

Make Visible

Make Invisible

Visibility States

Current visibility state

Figure 27-3.
A—Manage
visibility states
using the **Visibility
States** dialog box.
B—Create new
visibility states
using the **New
Visibility State**
dialog box.

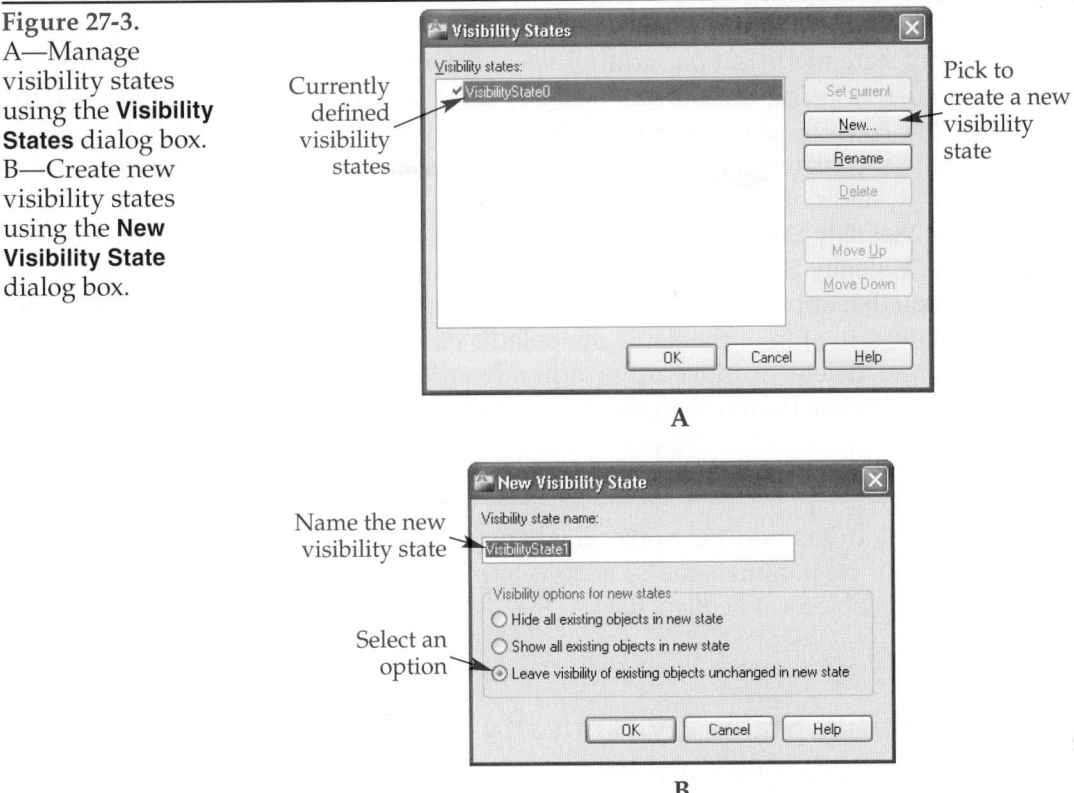

Currently
defined
visibility
states

Pick to
create a new
visibility
state

A

Name the new
visibility state

Select an
option

B

Pick the **OK** button to create the new visibility state. The new state is added to the
list in the **Visibility States** dialog box and becomes the current state, as indicated by the
check mark next to the name. Pick the **OK** button to return to block editing mode.

Next, use the **BVSHOW** and **BVHIDE** tools to display only the objects that should
be visible in the current state. Pick the **Make Visible** button to select objects to make
visible. Invisible objects are temporarily displayed semitransparently for selection.
Pick the **Make Invisible** button to select objects to make invisible. For example, to make
a visibility state to depict the gate valve shown in **Figure 27-4B** from the valve block
shown in **Figure 27-4A**, use the **Make Invisible** tool to turn off the filled circle and the
arrow. The changes are saved to the visibility state automatically. Use the **BVMODE** tool
to toggle the visibility mode on and off. Turn on visibility mode to display invisible
objects as semitransparent. Turn off visibility mode to display only visible objects.

Repeat the process to create additional visibility states for the block. The valve
block example requires four visibility states. The **Current visibility state** drop-down list
displays the current visibility state. Select a state from the drop-down list to make the
state current. After you create all visibility states, test and save the block and exit the
Block Editor. The dynamic block is now ready to use.

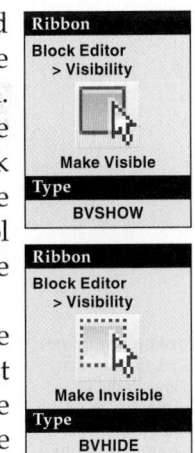

Ribbon
Block Editor > Visibility
Make Visible
Type
BVSHOW

Ribbon
Block Editor > Visibility
Make Invisible
Type
BVHIDE

Figure 27-4.
A—The VALVE block
with all objects
visible. B—The
VALVE block after
making the arrow
and filled circle
invisible to create
the GATE VALVE
visibility state.

VISIBILITY

A

VISIBILITY

B

Modifying Visibility States

Visibility state modification requires special consideration. Set the state you want to modify current using the **Current visibility state** drop-down list, and then use the **BVSHOW** and **BVHIDE** tools to change the visibility of objects as needed. When you add objects to the current visibility state, the objects are automatically set as invisible in all visibility states other than the current state.

Use the **Visibility States** dialog box to rename and delete visibility states. You can also use the **Visibility States** dialog box to arrange the order of visibility states in the shortcut menu that appears when you insert the block and pick the visibility parameter grip. The state at the top of the list is the default view for the block. Pick the visibility state to rename, delete, or move up or down from the **Visibility states:** list box. Then select the appropriate button to make the desired change.

> **PROFESSIONAL TIP**
>
> If you add new objects when modifying a state, be sure to update the parameters and actions applied to the block to include the new objects, if needed.

Using Visibility States Dynamically

Figure 27-5A shows the valve block reference selected for editing. Select the visibility grip to display a shortcut menu containing each visibility state. A check mark indicates the current visibility state. To switch to a different view of the block, select the name of the visibility state from the list. See **Figure 27-5B**. You can also use the **Properties** palette to select a visibility state.

Exercise 27-1

Access the Student Web site (www.g-wlearning.com/CAD) **and complete** Exercise 27-1.

Lookup Parameters

lookup parameter: A parameter that allows tabular properties to be used with existing parameter values.

lookup action: An action used to select a preset group of parameter values to carry out actions with stored values.

A *lookup parameter* creates a lookup property to which you can assign a *lookup action*. For example, **Figure 27-6** shows three valve symbols created from a single

---

Figure 27-5.
A—Pick the visibility parameter grip to display a shortcut menu with the available visibility states. The current state is checked. B—Select a different visibility state from the shortcut menu to change the appearance of the block.

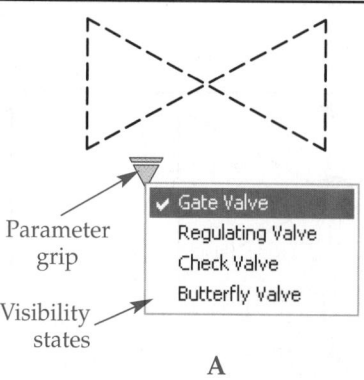

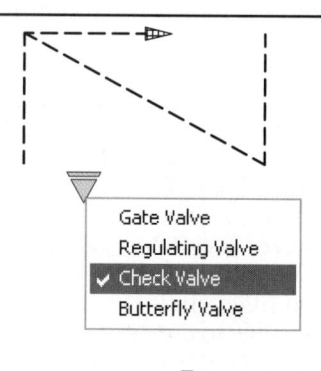

A   B

Figure 27-6.
A lookup parameter allows you to create these three valve symbols using the same block. Notice how the geometry changes.

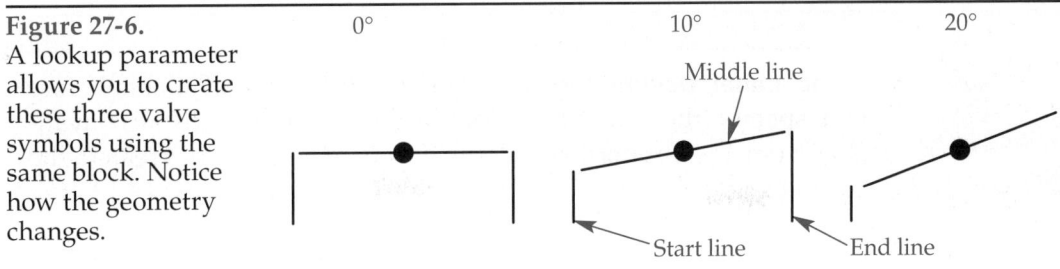

block by adjusting the rotation parameter of the middle line. The lookup action allows the middle line rotation to control the length of the start and end lines.

To create the valve block shown in **Figure 27-7**, first draw the geometry of the 0° symbol. Then add a linear parameter and label it Start Line. Select the start point as the bottom of the start line, and the endpoint as the top of the start line. Assign a stretch action to the parameter, associated with the top parameter grip. Draw the crossing window around the top of the start line and select the start line as the object to stretch.

Add another linear parameter, labeled End Line. Select the bottom of the end line as the start point and the top of the end line as the endpoint. Assign a stretch action to the parameter, associated with the top parameter grip. Draw the crossing window around the top of the end line and select the end line as the object to stretch.

Next, add a rotation parameter labeled Middle Line. Specify the center of the circle as the base point. Select the right endpoint of the middle line to set the radius, and specify the default rotation angle as 0. Assign a rotation action to the parameter. Pick the center of the circle as the rotation base point, and select the middle line as the object to rotate.

To add a lookup parameter, access the **Lookup Parameter** option and pick a location for the parameter label. Then enter the number of grips to associate with the parameter. The default **1** option creates a single lookup grip that allows you to use grip editing to carry out the lookup action. When you insert the block and select the grip, a shortcut menu appears listing rotation options. There is no prompt to select objects because a lookup parameter is associated with the entire block.

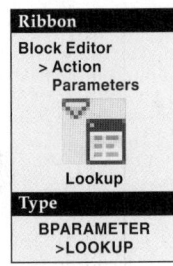

Figure 27-7. The block of the valve symbol example with linear parameters and stretch actions assigned to the start and end lines and a rotation parameter and rotate action assigned to the middle line.

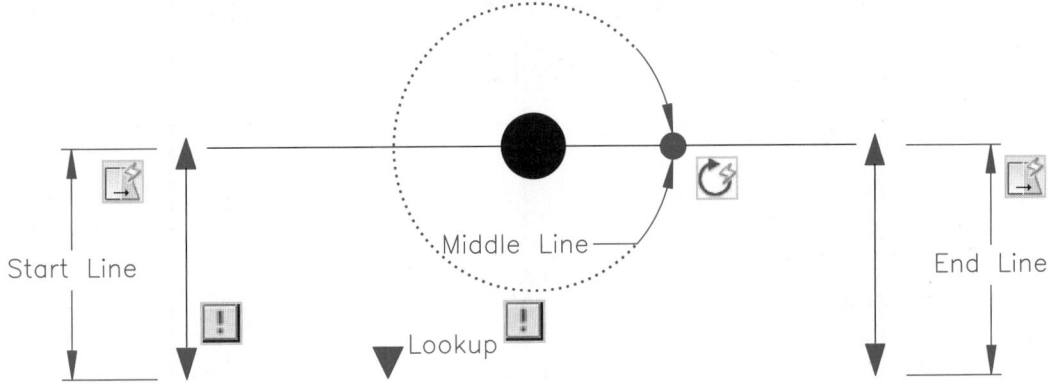

Assigning a Lookup Action

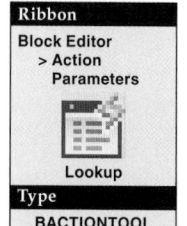

Ribbon

**Block Editor
> Action
Parameters**

Lookup

Type

**BACTIONTOOL
>LOOKUP**

lookup table: A table that groups the properties of parameters into custom-named lookup records.

To assign a lookup action, access the **Lookup Action** option and select a lookup parameter. The **Property Lookup Table** dialog box appears, allowing you to create a lookup table. See **Figure 27-8.**

Creating a Lookup Table

A *lookup table* groups parameter properties into custom-named lookup records. The **Action name:** display box indicates the name of the lookup action associated with the table. The table is initially blank. To add a parameter property, pick the **Add Properties...** button to open the **Add Parameter Properties** dialog box. See **Figure 27-9.**

All parameters in the block containing property values appear in the **Parameter properties:** list. Lookup, alignment, and base point parameters do not contain property values. Notice that the property name is the parameter label. The **Property type** area determines the type of property parameters shown in the list. By default, the **Add input properties** radio button is active, which displays available input property parameters. To display available lookup property parameters, select the **Add lookup properties** radio button.

To add parameter properties to the lookup table, select the properties in the **Parameter properties:** list and pick the **OK** button. A new column, named as the parameter property, forms for each parameter in the **Input Properties** area of the **Property Lookup Table** dialog box. See **Figure 27-10.** Use the **Input Properties** area to specify a value for parameters added to the table. Type a value in each cell in the column. Add a custom name for each row, or record, in the **Lookup** column in the **Lookup Properties**

Figure 27-8. The **Property Lookup Table** dialog box.

Pick to add
a property

Action
name

Input
properties

Lookup
properties

Property Lookup Table

Action name:

Lookup1

Add Properties ...

Audit

Input Properties

Lookup Properties

Lookup

Custom

Read only

OK   Cancel   Help

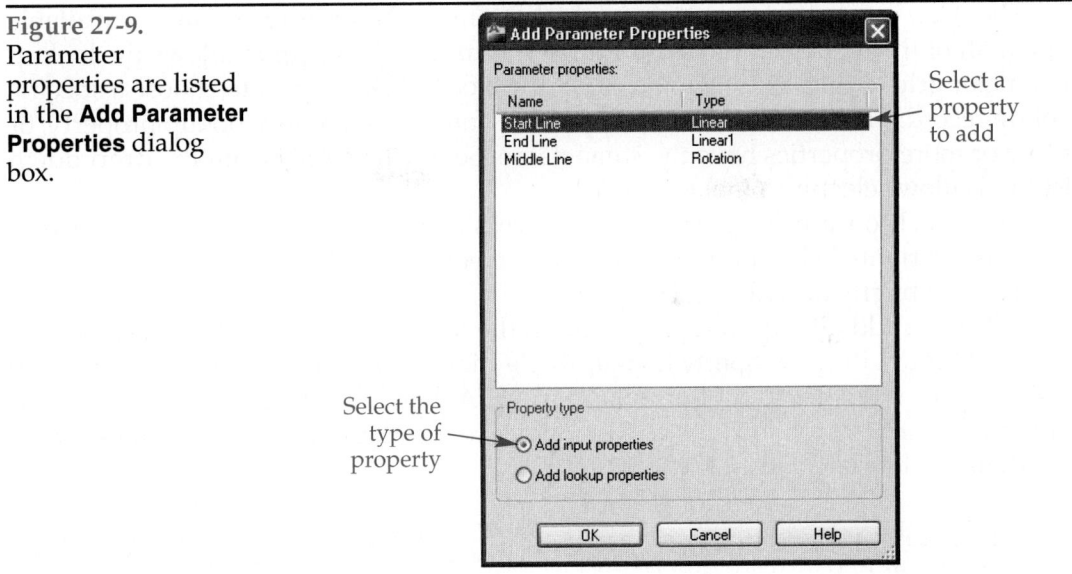

Figure 27-9.
Parameter properties are listed in the **Add Parameter Properties** dialog box.

Select a property to add

Select the type of property

Figure 27-10. A lookup table with multiple parameters and values added.

Parameter properties

Parameter values for the property

Custom names for each row (record)

Custom property record

Select to display the lookup parameter grip in the drawing

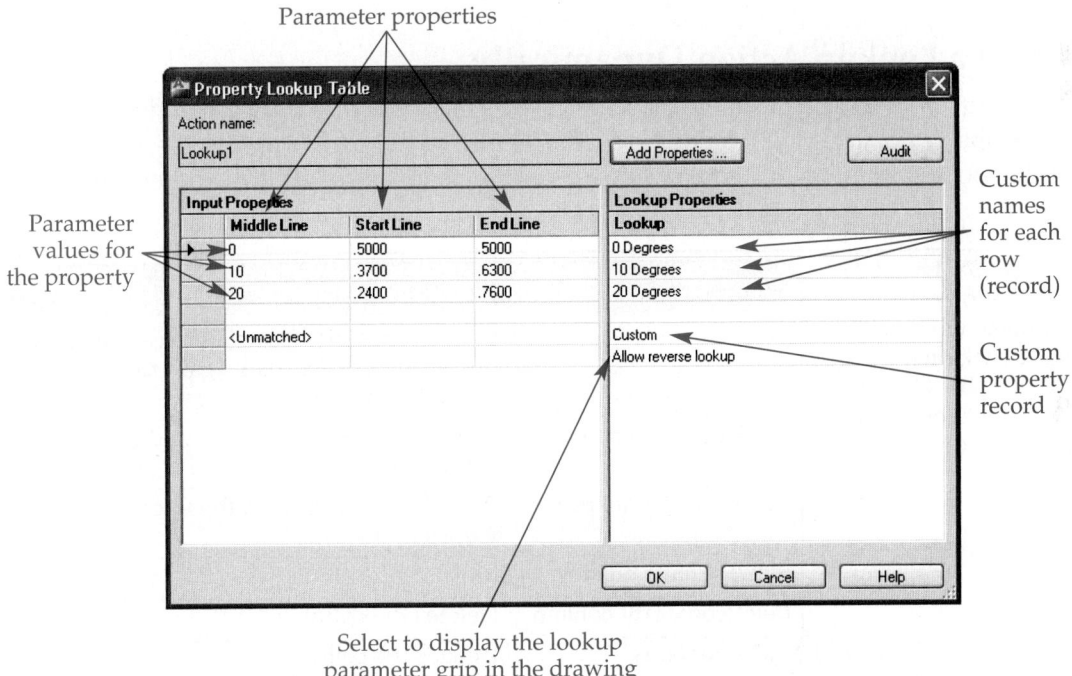

area. This area displays the name that appears in the shortcut menu when you insert the block and select the lookup parameter grip.

For the valve symbol example, add the Middle Line, Start Line, and End Line parameter properties to the table. Then complete the lookup table as shown in **Figure 27-10.** Start with the Middle Line values. Press [Enter] after typing the value to add a new blank row and then type the remaining values in each cell. Use the [Enter], [Tab], arrow keys, or pick in a different cell to navigate through the table.

The row, or record, that contains the <Unmatched> value, named Custom in the **Lookup** column, applies when the current parameter values of the block do not match a record in the table. This allows you to adjust the block using parameter values other than those specified in the lookup table. You cannot add any values to the row, but you can change the name of **Custom**.

The Allow reverse lookup setting at the bottom of the **Lookup** column is available only if all of the names in the lookup table are unique. This option allows the lookup parameter grip to display when you select the block. Pick the grip to choose a specific lookup record. The Read only setting appears if you do not name a lookup property, or if two or more properties have the same name. Select **Read only** from the drop-down list to disallow selecting a lookup record.

Right-click on a column heading to access a menu with options for adjusting columns, or right-click on a row to access a menu with options for adjusting rows. **Figure 27-11** briefly describes each option.

After you add all required properties to the table and assign values to each, pick the **Audit** button in the **Property Lookup Table** dialog box to check each record in the table to make sure they are all unique. If AutoCAD does not find errors, pick the **OK** button to return to the **Block Editor**. Test and save the block, and exit the **Block Editor**. The dynamic block is now ready to use.

NOTE

To redisplay the **Property Lookup Table** dialog box, right-click on a lookup action and pick **Display lookup table**.

Using a Lookup Action Dynamically

Figure 27-12 shows a valve block reference selected for editing. The figure shows the **Property Lookup Table** dialog box for reference only. Since Allow reverse lookup is set in the lookup table, the lookup parameter grip appears along with the other parameter

Figure 27-11.
A—Options available when you right-click on a column. B—Options available when you right-click on a row.

Menu Option	Function
Sort	Sorts the records (rows) in ascending or descending order. Pick again to reverse the sort order.
Maximize all headings	Adjusts all columns to the width of the column headings.
Maximize all data cells	Adjusts all columns to the width of the values in the cells.
Size columns equally	Makes all columns equal in width.
Delete property column	Deletes the column.
Clear contents	Deletes the cell values.

A

Menu Option	Function
Insert row	Inserts a new row above the selected row.
Delete row	Deletes the record (row).
Clear contents	Deletes the cell values.
Move up	Moves the row up by one row.
Move down	Moves the row down by one row.
Range syntax examples	Displays the online documentation examples of how to enter values into a lookup table.

B

Figure 27-12. The lookup parameter grip appears when you select the block. The list of available lookup records is displayed when you pick the lookup parameter grip. Notice the correlation between the available options and the lookup property names in the **Property Lookup Table** dialog box.

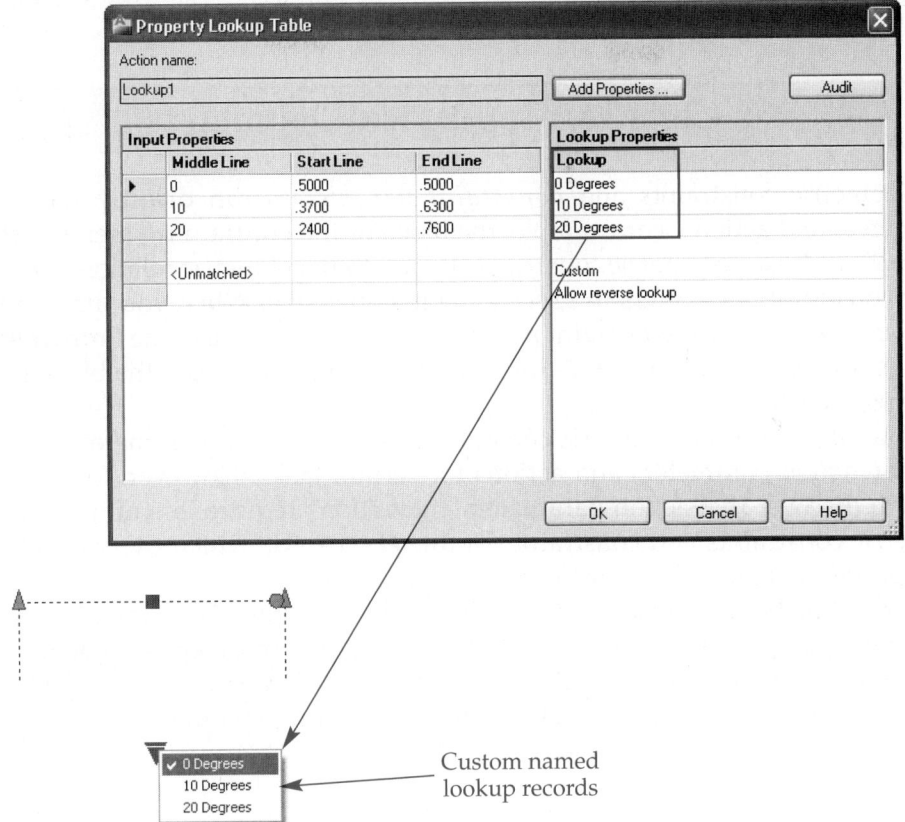

Custom named lookup records

grips. Pick the lookup parameter grip to display a shortcut menu containing each lookup record. The entries in the menu match the entries in the **Lookup** column of the **Property Lookup Table** dialog box. A check mark indicates the current record. To switch to a different view of the block, select the name of the record from the list.

You can change other parameters assigned to the block, such as the linear and rotation parameters of the example block, independently of the named records. When you change any of the parameters, the lookup parameter becomes Custom, because the current parameter values do not match one of the records in the lookup table.

Exercise 27-2

Access the Student Web site (www.g-wlearning.com/CAD) and complete Exercise 27-2.

Parameter Sets

The **Parameter Sets** tab of the **Block Authoring Palettes** window contains common parameters and actions grouped to enhance productivity. Follow the prompts to create a parameter and automatically associate an action with the parameter. The action forms without any selected objects, as is indicated by the yellow alert icon. If the parameter set contains an action that must include associated objects, as most do, double-click on the action icon and select objects. The prompts may differ depending on the type of action.

Constraining Block Geometry

constraint parameters: Dimensional constraints available for block construction to control the size or location of block geometry numerically.

Geometric constraints and *constraint parameters* can directly replace action parameters and actions. For example, the block of the cut framing member shown in **Figure 27-13A** uses geometric constraints to maintain geometric relationships and two linear constraint parameters to specify the member size. When you insert and select the block to edit, use the constraint parameter grips or options in the **Properties** palette to adjust the block. See **Figure 27-13B**. An alternative is to create the block using two linear parameters.

You may find that geometric constraints and constraint parameters are easier to use than action parameters and actions for certain tasks. However, for some blocks, you will discover that action parameters and actions require less effort than adding geometric constraints and constraint parameters. Decide which dynamic block tools and options are appropriate for the blocks you create.

A combination of dynamic properties is also effective. For example, parameters and actions such as alignment, array, and flip offer dynamic controls that are often not possible using geometric constraints and constraint parameters. **Figure 27-14** shows how adding an alignment parameter to the cut framing member block allows you to size and align instances of the block.

Figure 27-13.
A—A cut framing member block made dynamic using geometric constraints and constraint parameters. B—Using the default 2x4 block to create a 4x4 symbol.

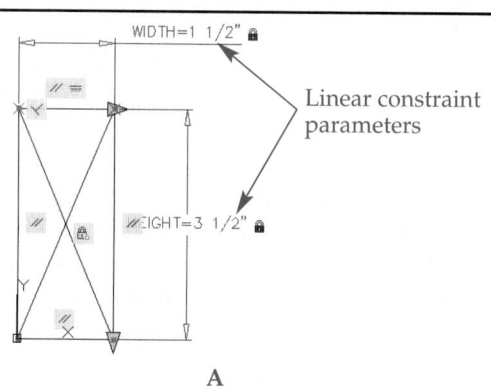

Linear constraint parameters

A

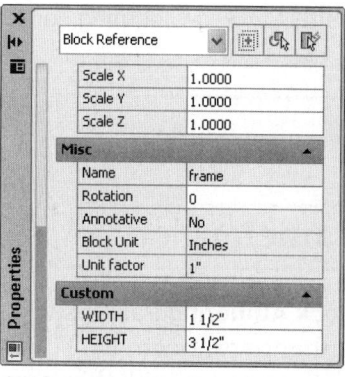

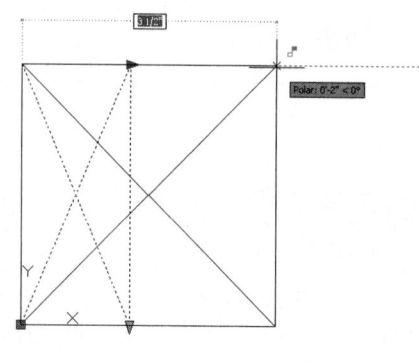

B

AutoCAD and Its Applications—Basics

Figure 27-14. Using geometric constraints and constraint parameters to adjust the size of a cut framing member symbol. An alignment parameter aligns each member for specific applications.

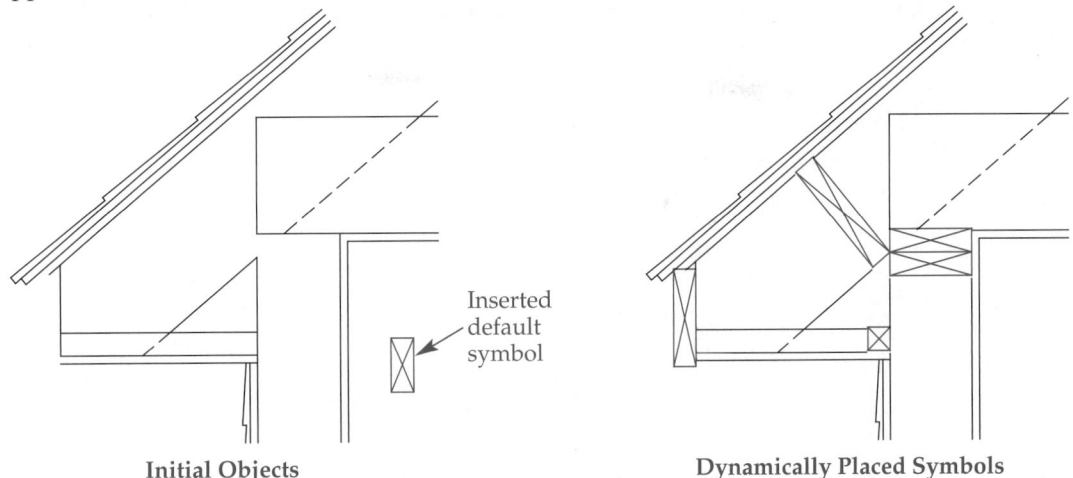

Inserted default symbol

Initial Objects   Dynamically Placed Symbols

Using Geometric Constraints

The geometric constraint tools and options available in the **Block Editor** are identical to those you use to constrain a parametric drawing geometrically. The tools in the **Geometric** panel of the **Parametric** ribbon tab are duplicates of the tools in the **Geometric** panel of the **Block Editor** ribbon tab. Use the geometric constraints in the **Block Editor** as you would in the drawing environment, including the options for relaxing and deleting constraints. The same shortcut menu, **Constraint Settings** dialog box, and **Properties** palette functions apply. Review Chapter 22 for information on adding geometric constraints.

Assign constraints to block objects before you define the block or during block editing to create a dynamic block. See **Figure 27-15A**. Once you define and insert the block, only constraint parameters, action parameters, or actions influence geometric constraints. This allows you to use blocks as objects in parametric drawings. For example, you can insert and rotate the block, as shown in **Figure 27-15B**, even though the block definition includes a horizontal constraint. Use constraints in the drawing to locate blocks and establish geometric relationships between blocks and other objects. See **Figure 27-15C**.

> **NOTE**
>
> Use geometric constraints in the block environment to form geometric constructions in specific situations when standard AutoCAD tools are inefficient or ineffective.

Exercise 27-3

Access the Student Web site (www.g-wlearning.com/CAD) and complete Exercise 27-3.

Figure 27-15. A—A wide flange block made dynamic using geometric constraints and constraint parameters. B—You can rotate the block reference in the drawing, because the constraints define the size and shape of block geometry during definition and when the block is adjusted dynamically. C—Constrain blocks in a drawing as you would any other geometry.

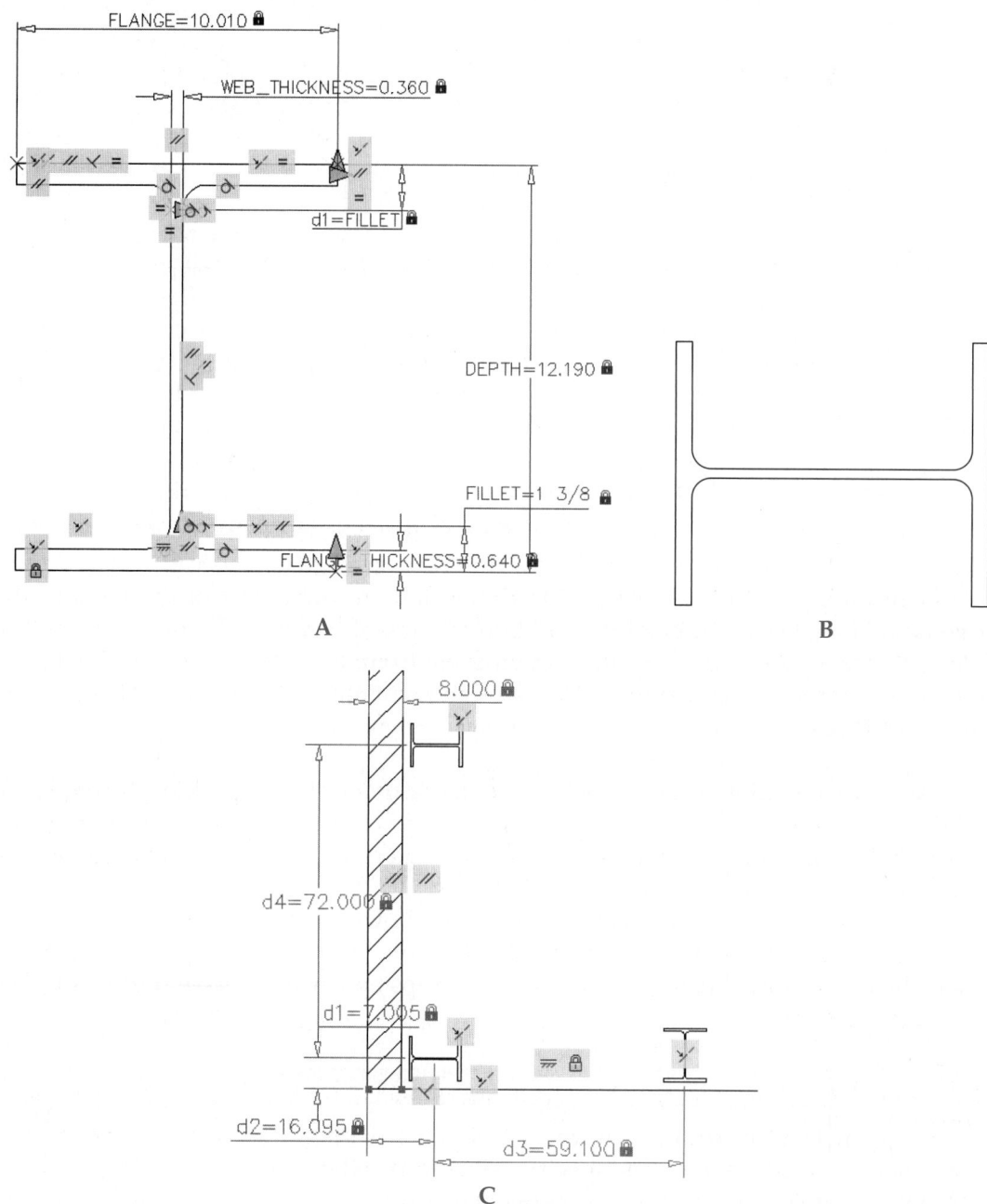

Using Constraint Parameters

Constraint parameters replace dimensional constraints in the **Block Editor**. To help avoid confusion, remember that dimensional constraints constrain a parametric drawing, including block references, as shown in **Figure 27-15C**. Constraint parameters constrain the size and location of block components. By default, dimensional constraints are gray and constraint parameters are blue. You also have the option of converting dimensional constraints to constraint parameters.

You can often use constraint parameters instead of action parameters and actions. If you do not use action parameters, you must include constraint parameters to create a dynamic block. The constraint parameter tools and options available in the **Block Editor** function much like those you use to constrain a parametric drawing dimensionally. Review Chapter 22 for information on adding dimensional constraints.

Using the BCPARAMETER Tool

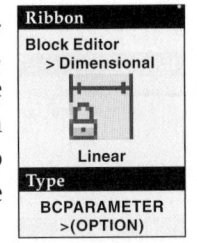

Ribbon
Block Editor
> Dimensional

Linear

Type
BCPARAMETER
>(OPTION)

The **BCPARAMETER** tool replaces the **DIMCONSTRAINT** tool in the **Block Editor**, and provides **Linear**, **Horizontal**, **Vertical**, **Aligned**, **Diameter**, and **Radius** options. The **Linear** option is the default in the **Block Editor** ribbon tab. You can also use the **BCPARAMETER** tool to convert dimensional constraints to constraint parameters. Each constraint parameter is a separate **DIMCONSTRAINT** tool option. The quickest way to add or convert constraint parameters using the **DIMCONSTRAINT** tool is to pick the appropriate button from the **Dimensional** panel of the **Block Editor** ribbon tab.

The process of adding constraint parameters is identical to that for adding dimensional constraints, except that constraint parameters can include grips. Constraint parameters are essentially a combination of dimensional constraints and action parameters. The constraint parameters given custom names in **Figure 27-16** are those that can be adjusted for specific block references. As when creating a parametric drawing, the other constraint parameters are required to define the block and define specific geometric relationships. Notice the expressions applied to these values.

To create a constraint parameter, follow the prompts to make the required selections, pick a location for the dimension line, and enter a value to form the constraint. When prompted, specify the number of grips. The radius constraint parameter allows you to add 0 or 1 grip. All other constraint parameters can include 0, 1, or 2 grips. If you plan to assign a single grip to a constraint parameter, select the point associated with the grip second. If you choose the 0 option, you can only use the **Properties** palette to adjust the block.

> **NOTE**
>
> If you attempt to over-constrain a block, a message appears indicating that adding the geometric constraint or constraint parameter is not allowed. You cannot create reference constraint parameters.

Figure 27-16.
Using constraint parameters to form a dynamic block of a spacer. A single grip is all that is required for these constraint parameters. Do not assign or rename constraint parameters that do not control geometry.

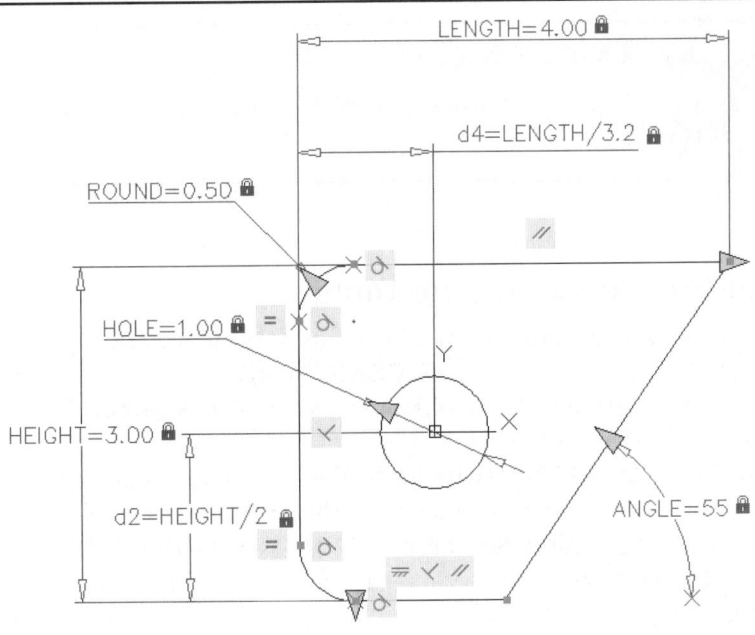

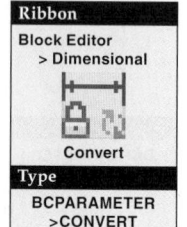

As when adding dimensional constaints or action parameters, change the constraint parameter name to a custom, more descriptive name. Naming labels helps organize parameters and identify each parameter when you control the block dynamically. Custom parameters also appear in the **Custom** category of the **Properties** palette.

Ribbon
Block Editor
> Dimensional

Convert

Type
BCPARAMETER
>CONVERT

Use the **Convert** option of the **BCPARAMETER** tool to convert a dimensional constraint to a constraint parameter. This allows you to prepare a dynamic block using existing dimensional constraints. Access the **Convert** option and pick the dimensional constraint to convert. The dimensional constraint becomes the corresponding constraint parameter and includes the default number of grips.

Controlling Constraint Parameters

Control and adjust constraint parameters using a combination of the same techniques you use to manage dimensional constraints and action parameters. Many of the options from shortcut menus, the **Constraint Settings** dialog box, and the **Properties** palette apply. Right-click with no objects selected to access options for displaying and hiding parametric constraints and for accessing the **Constraint Settings** dialog box. Select a constraint parameter and then right-click to display a shortcut menu with options for editing the constraint, changing the name format, and redefining the grips.

As with dimensional constraints and the action parameters, the **Properties** palette provides an effective way to control and enhance constraint parameters. You can also use the **Parameters Manager**. **Figure 27-17** shows a foundation detail block with linear constraint parameters. Notice the multiple options available in the **Properties** palette for adjusting the selected constraint parameter.

Use the options in the **Value set** category of the **Properties** palette to assign value sets to a constraint parameter. Each constraint parameter in the **Figure 27-17** example uses an incremental value to help ensure that you select an appropriate value when adjusting a block reference. You can also create a list of possible sizes. The processes of creating a value set in the **Properties** palette and using value sets are identical for constraint parameters and action parameters.

Exercise 27-4

Access the Student Web site (www.g-wlearning.com/CAD) and complete Exercise 27-4.

Additional Parametric Tools

The **Block Editor** offers additional options for adding constraints to blocks. Many of the tools, such as the **DELCONSTRAINT** tool, function the same in block editing mode as in drawing mode. However, the **Block Editor** does offer some unique parametric construction tools.

The **BCONSTRUCTION** tool allows you to create construction geometry to aid geometric construction and constraining. Construction geometry appears only in the block definition. See **Figure 27-18**. Access the **BCONSTRUCTION** tool and select the objects to convert to or revert from construction geometry. Press [Enter] or the space bar, or right-click and pick **Enter**. Next, choose the **Convert** option to convert

Ribbon
Block Editor
> Manage

Construction
Geometry

Type
BCONSTRUCTION

BCONSTRUCTION

Figure 27-17. Adjust constraint parameters as you would dimensional constraints and action parameters. Use the **Properties** palette to add value sets.

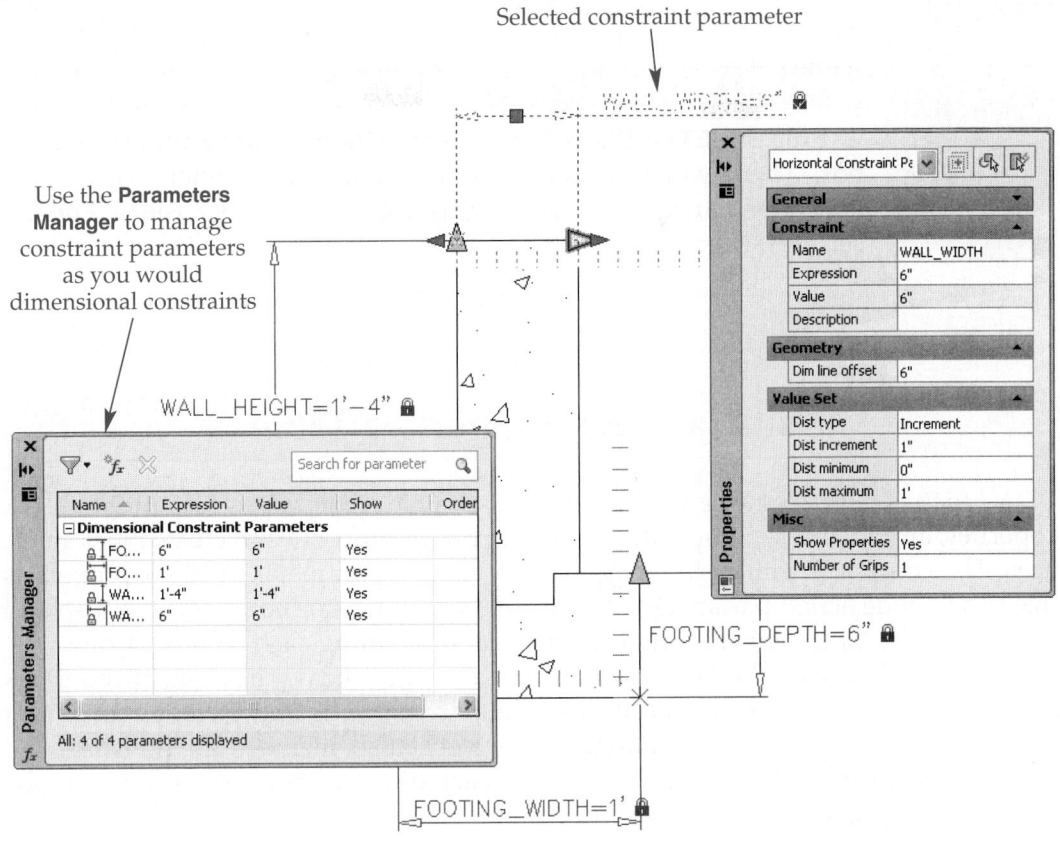

Selected constraint parameter

Use the **Parameters Manager** to manage constraint parameters as you would dimensional constraints

Figure 27-18. A weld nut block in which construction geometry aids geometric construction and constraining.

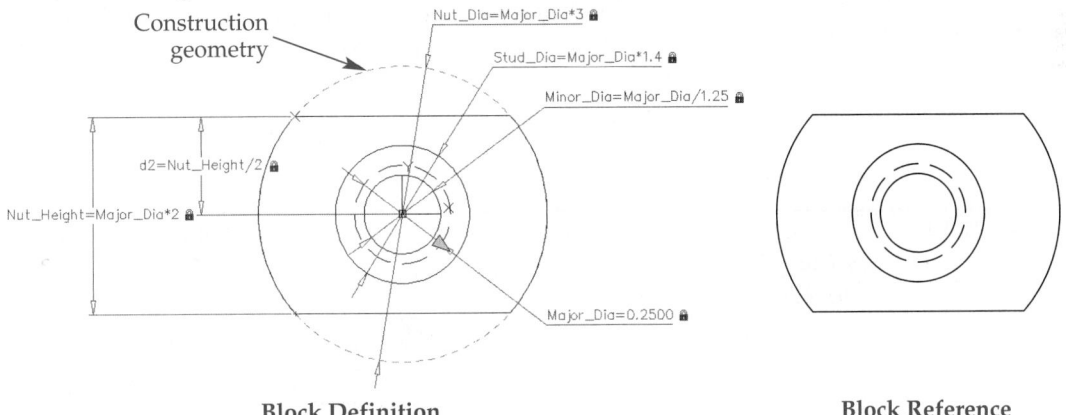

Construction geometry

Block Definition

Block Reference

non-construction objects to the construction format, or choose **Revert** to return construction geometry to the standard format. You can also use the **Hide all** option to hide all existing construction geometry before selecting objects, or use the **Show all** option to display all construction geometry.

Use the **BCONSTATUSMODE** tool to toggle constraint status identification on and off. When you turn constraint status mode on, objects with no constraints appear white (black) by default, objects assigned some form of constraints are blue, and fully constrained geometry is magenta. If the block contains a constraint error, objects associated with the error are red. Using constraint status is helpful, especially if you want to constrain objects in a certain order or confirm that geometry has been fully constrained.

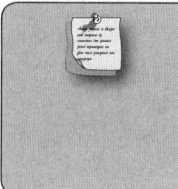

NOTE

Use the **BESETTINGS** tool to access the **Block Editor Settings** dialog box. There you can adjust parameter and parameter grip color and appearance, constraint status colors, and other **Block Editor** settings.

Using a Block Properties Table

block properties table: A table of action parameters and/or constraint parameters that allows you to create multiple block properties and then select them to create block references.

A *block properties table* allows you to assign specific values to multiple block properties, and then select a specific group, or row, of properties to create block references. The concept is similar to using a lookup action parameter. A block properties table can include action parameters, constraint parameters, or both. You can also add attributes to the table, which is often appropriate for naming each record, or row.

Figure 27-19 shows the block of the front view of a heavy hex nut in the **Block Editor**. The block includes an appropriate level of constraints and includes constraint parameters to direct dynamic changes. The block also includes an invisible and preset attribute for defining the designation of each different nut and, as shown in the **Parameters Manager**, a user-defined parameter for the nut thickness.

PROFESSIONAL TIP

It is critical that you assign the **Preset** mode to attributes that you include in a block properties table. This allows the attribute value to adjust to the selected block record. The **Preset** mode requires no default value, and you will not receive a prompt to adjust the value.

Figure 27-19. A heavy hex nut block definition ready to use to create a block properties table.

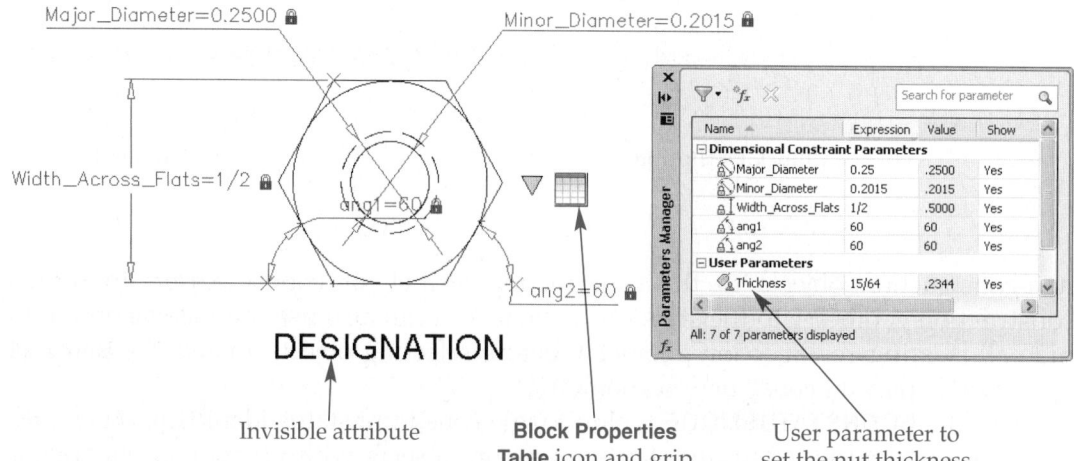

After you create parameters and attributes, access the **BTABLE** tool and select the parameter location. Next, enter the number of grips to associate with the parameter. The default **1** option creates a single grip that allows you to select a table record from the grip shortcut menu. If you choose the **0** option, you can only use the **Properties** palette to select a record. The **Palette** option, available before you specify the parameter location or from the **Properties** palette, determines whether the label appears in the **Properties** palette when you select the block reference. The **Block Properties Table** dialog box appears, allowing you to create a block properties table. See **Figure 27-20**.

Ribbon
Block Editor
> Dimensional
Block Table
Type
BTABLE
BTABLE

Creating a Block Properties Table

A block properties table groups the properties of parameters into custom records, or rows. To add parameter properties, pick the **Add Properties...** button to open the **Add Parameter Properties** dialog box. See **Figure 27-21**. All parameters in the block that contain property values appear in the **Parameter properties:** list. Lookup, alignment, and base point parameters do not contain property values. Notice that the property name is the parameter label.

To add parameter properties to the table, select the properties in the **Parameter properties:** list and pick the **OK** button. A column appears in the table for each parameter property. Type a value in each cell in the column. A new row forms automatically when you enter a value in a cell. See **Figure 27-22**. Press [Enter], [Tab], [Shift]+[Enter], the arrow keys, or pick in a different cell to navigate through the table.

For the nut block example, complete the table as shown in **Figure 27-22**. The DESIGNATION column references the attribute property. The value you enter in the DESIGNATION text box in each row specifies the record name. This value appears in the shortcut menu when you insert the block and select the block properties table parameter grip.

> **NOTE**
>
> Right-click on a column heading to access a menu with options for adjusting columns. Right-click on a row to access a menu with options for adjusting rows. The options are the same as those for adjusting lookup table columns and rows.

Figure 27-20. The **Block Properties Table** dialog box.

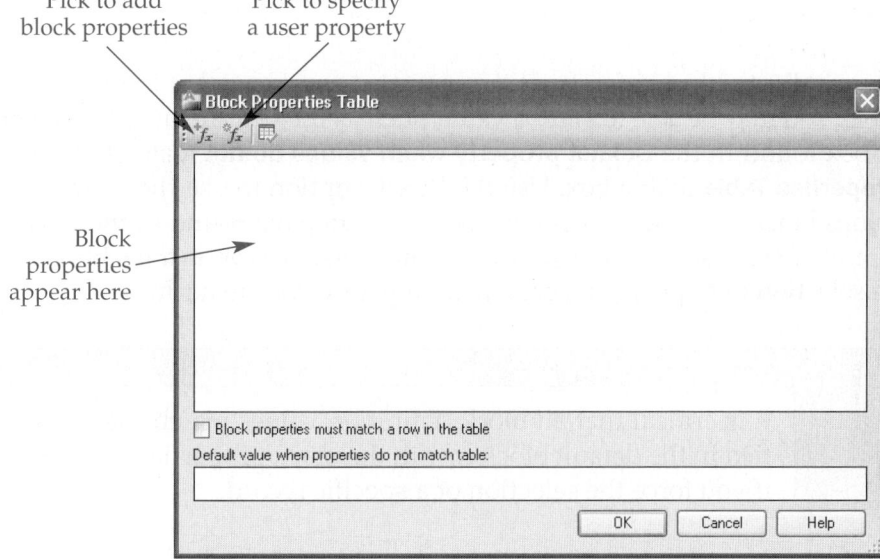

Pick to add block properties

Pick to specify a user property

Block properties appear here

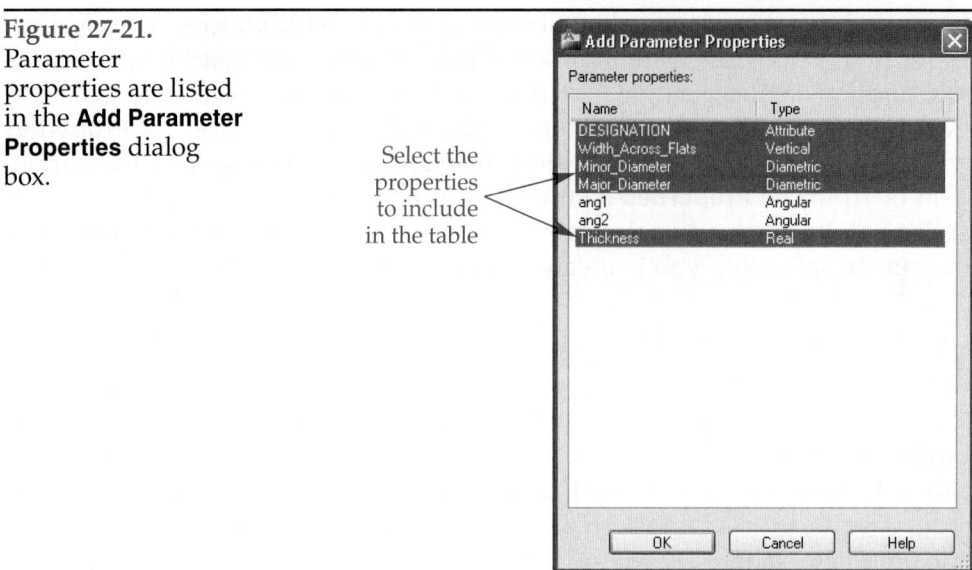

Figure 27-21.
Parameter
properties are listed
in the **Add Parameter
Properties** dialog
box.

Select the
properties
to include
in the table

Figure 27-22. A block properties table with multiple parameters and values added.

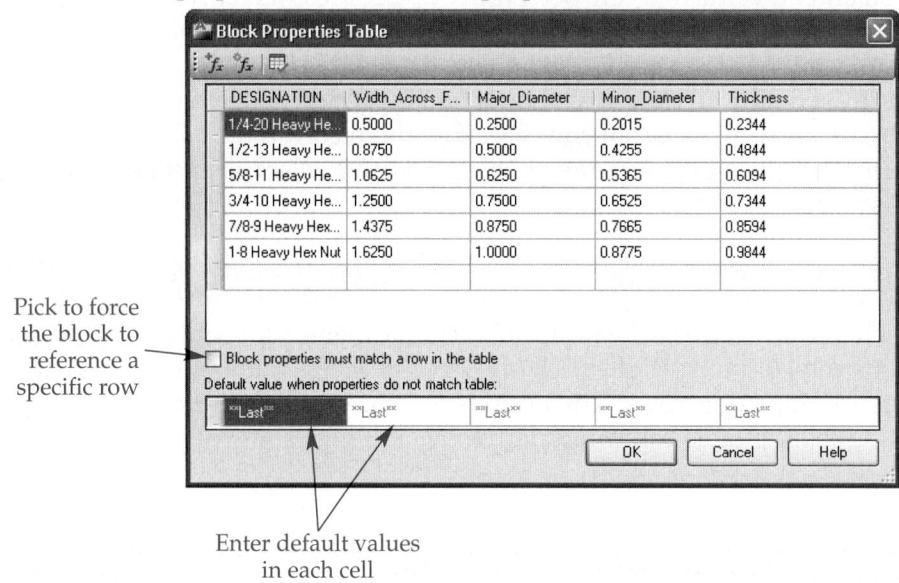

Pick to force
the block to
reference a
specific row

Enter default values
in each cell

You can adjust a block reference using parameter values other than those specified in the table. You may be able to enter a value, such as the value of an attribute property, in a text box found in the **Default property when values do not match table** area of the **Block Properties Table** dialog box. Use the **Last** option to use the value assigned to the previous block reference when you specify a value not found in the table. Often it is appropriate to choose the **Block properties must match a row in the table** check box to force the selection of a specific record, matching all values in a row.

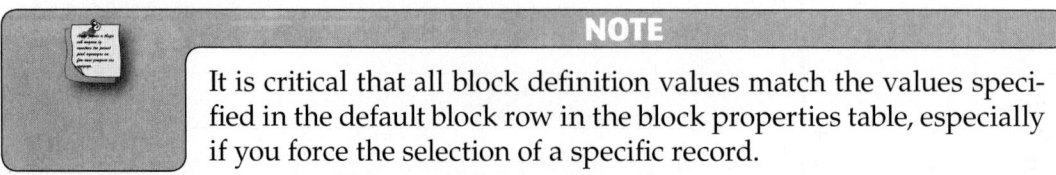

NOTE

It is critical that all block definition values match the values specified in the default block row in the block properties table, especially if you force the selection of a specific record.

After you add all required properties to the table and assign values to each, pick the **Audit** button in the **Block Properties Table** dialog box to check each record in the table. Make sure the records are unique and that there are no discrepancies between the block definition and the table values. If AutoCAD does not find errors, pick the **OK** button to return to the **Block Editor**. Test and save the block, and exit the **Block Editor**. The dynamic block is now ready to use.

> **NOTE**
>
> To redisplay the **Block Properties Table** dialog box, double-click on the parameter, or access the **BTABLE** tool.

Using a Block Properties Table Dynamically

Figure 27-23 shows the inserted nut block selected for editing. Since the block table parameter includes a grip, a grip appears that you can select to choose a specific block style. The entries in the grip menu match the rows in the **Block Properties Table** dialog box. A check mark indicates the current record. To switch to a different view of the block, select the name of the record from the list. You can also pick the **Properties Table...** option to display the **Block Properties Table** in drawing mode. Double-click a row to activate it. In this example, no other grips were assigned to blocks. This makes the table and the **Properties** palette the only two methods to select a block reference format.

> **PROFESSIONAL TIP**
>
> The options for developing dynamic blocks and creating parametric drawings can become confusing. Keep the following concepts in mind as you proceed:
> - Use constraints as an alternative or in addition to action parameters and actions.
> - Constraints allow you to create a parametric drawing *or* a dynamic block.
> - Assign constraints to create a dynamic block during block definition or while editing the block.
> - Treat inserted blocks like any other object when preparing a parametric drawing.

Figure 27-23.
The block table parameter grip displays when you select the block. The list of available records appears when you pick the parameter grip. Notice the correlation between the available options and the names in the **Block Properties Table** dialog box.

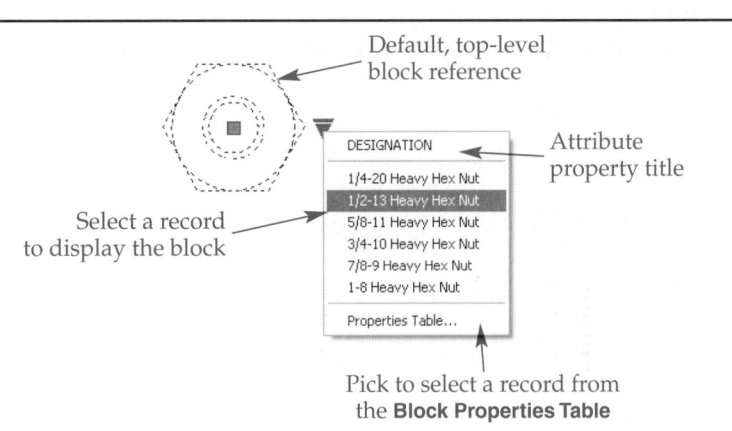

Exercise 27-5

Access the Student Web site (www.g-wlearning.com/CAD) and complete Exercise 27-5.

Express Tools

Chapter 27

The **Block** and **Draw** panels of the **Express Tools** ribbon tab include additional tools related to blocks. For information about the most useful block express tools, go to the Student Web site (www.g-wlearning.com/CAD), select this chapter, and select **Block Express Tools**.

Chapter Test

Answer the following questions. Write your answers on a separate sheet of paper or go to the Student Web site (www.g-wlearning.com/CAD) and complete the electronic chapter test.

1. Define *visibility parameter*.
2. What are visibility states?
3. How do you display the shortcut menu that allows you to select from the existing visibility states of a block?
4. When you select a block and display the visibility parameter shortcut menu, what indicates the current visibility state?
5. Briefly describe a lookup parameter.
6. Explain the basic function of a lookup action.
7. Identify the basic function of a lookup table.
8. What is a parameter set?
9. What ribbon tab, in addition to the **Parametric** ribbon tab, contains geometric constraint tools?
10. When can you assign constraints to block objects to create a dynamic block?
11. What takes the place of dimensional constraints in the **Block Editor**?
12. What tool and option allow you to convert a dimensional constraint to a constraint parameter?
13. How can you create construction geometry to aid geometric construction in the **Block Editor**?
14. Explain how to toggle constraint status identification on and off in the **Block Editor**.
15. What does a block properties table allow you to do?

Drawing Problems

- *Start AutoCAD if it is not already started. Start a new drawing for each problem using an appropriate template of your choice.*
- *The template should include layers and text, dimension, multileader, and table styles, when necessary, for drawing the given objects. Add layers and text, dimension, multileader, and table styles as needed.*
- *Draw all objects using appropriate layers and text, dimension, multileader, and table styles, justification, and format.*
- *Follow the specific instructions for each problem. Use only drawing and editing tools and techniques you have already learned. Use your own judgment and approximate dimensions when necessary.*
- *Apply dimensions accurately using ASME or appropriate industry standards.*

Note: *Constraint parameters shown for reference are created using AutoCAD and may not comply with ASME standards.*

Note: *Some of the problems in this chapter are built on problems from previous chapters. If you have not yet completed those problems, complete them now.*

▼ Basic

1. Use **DesignCenter** to insert the HEAVY HEX NUT block you created in Exercise 27-5. Insert or copy the block to create six total symbols. Use the block table parameter to display each size nut as shown. Save the drawing as P27-1.

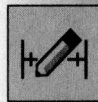

   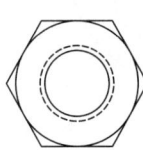 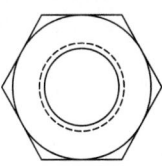 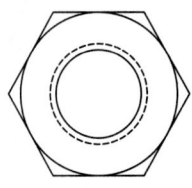

2. Open P22-2 and save as P27-2. The P27-2 file should be active. Create a block named FIXTURE, select all objects, and pick the center of the circle as the insertion base point. Open the block in the **Block Editor** and convert the dimensional constraints to constraint parameters. Insert the FIXTURE block into the drawing three times to create the 4x4, 6x6, and 4x5 symbols as shown. Resave the drawing.

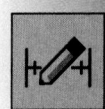

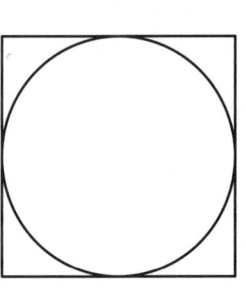 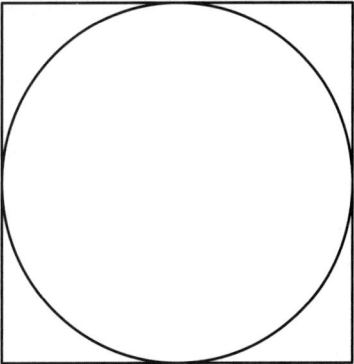 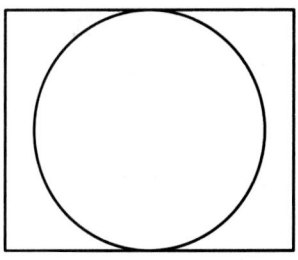

3. Open P22-5 and save as P27-3. The P27-3 file should be active. Create a block named PLATE, select all objects and pick the center of the plate as the insertion base point. Open the block in the **Block Editor** and convert the construction rectangle to construction geometry. Convert the dimensional constraints to constraint parameters. Insert the PLATE block into the drawing and create the drawing shown. Do not add dimensions. Resave the drawing.

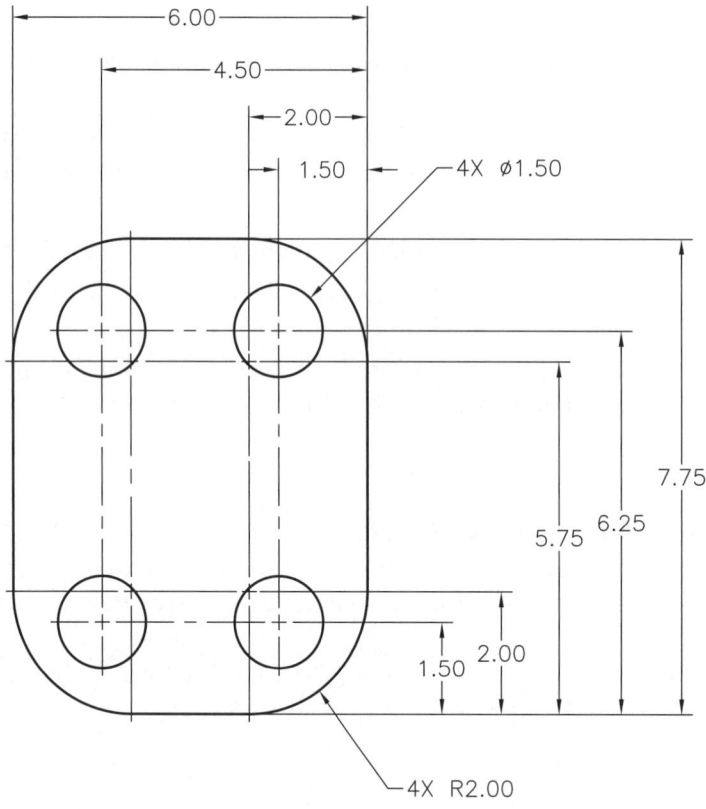

▼ Intermediate

4. Open P22-6 and save as P27-4. The P27-4 file should be active. Create a block named SELECTOR, select all objects, and pick the center of the center circle as the insertion base point. Open the block in the **Block Editor** and convert the construction lines to construction geometry. Convert the dimensional constraints to constraint parameters. Insert the SELECTOR block into the drawing three times and create three different symbols of your own design. Resave the drawing.

5. Create a single block that can be used to represent each of the three door blocks shown below. Name the block 30 INCH DOOR. Do not include labels. Create an appropriately named visibility state for each view: 90 OPEN, 60 OPEN, and 30 OPEN. Insert the 30 INCH DOOR block into the drawing three times. Set each block to a different visibility state. Save the drawing as P27-5.

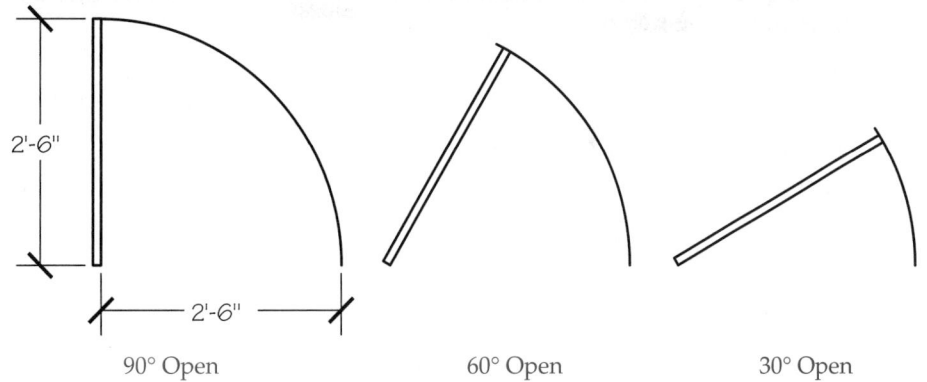

2'-6"

2'-6"

90° Open   60° Open   30° Open

6. Create a cut framing member block that can be used to represent each of the symbols shown below. Name the block FRAME. Add geometric constraints and constraint parameters as needed, and assign an alignment parameter. Use the block to create the portion of the detail shown. Save the drawing as P27-6.

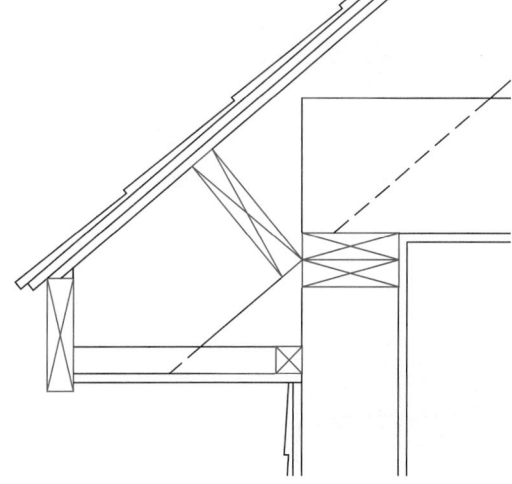

7. Open P25-6 and save it as P27-7. The P27-7 file should be active. Explode the glulam beam hanger blocks. Use the geometry and attributes as needed to create a single block using a visibility parameter. Stack the views on top of each other using an appropriate insertion base point location in the block definition so that each view occurs at the correct location when you select a visibility state. Insert the block multiple times and adjust the visibility to display each view. Resave the drawing.

8. Open P25-7 and save it as P27-8. The P27-8 file should be active. Explode the mudsill anchor blocks. Use the geometry and attributes as needed to create a single block using a visibility parameter. Stack the views on top of each other using an appropriate insertion base point location in the block definition so that each view occurs at the correct location when you select a visibility state. Insert the block multiple times and adjust the visibility to display each view. Resave the drawing.

▼ Advanced

9. Create a foundation footing and wall block that can be used to represent various construction requirements. Name the block Foundation. Add the geometric constraints and constraint parameters shown. Include 1″ increment value sets for each constraint parameter. The block should stretch symmetrically as shown. Save the drawing as P27-9.

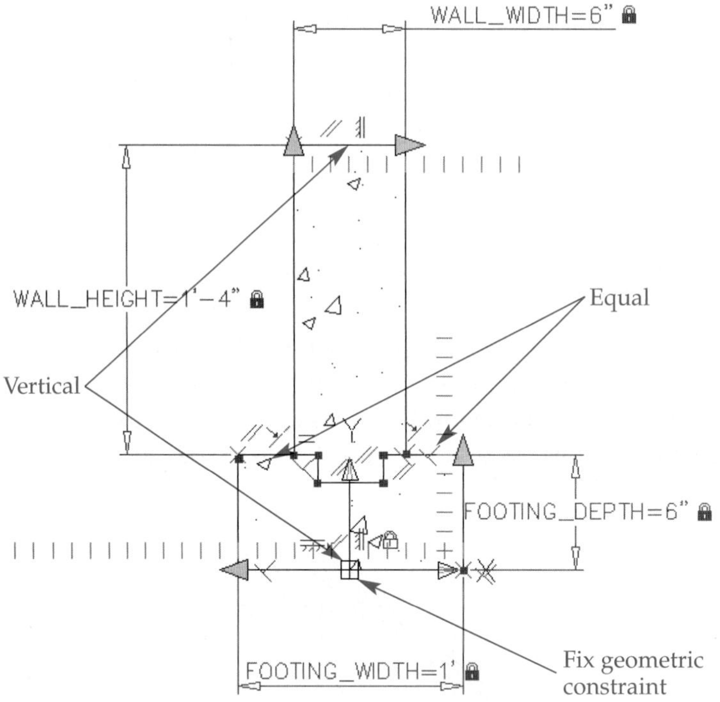

WALL_WIDTH=6″ 🔒

WALL_HEIGHT=1′−4″ 🔒

Equal

Vertical

FOOTING_DEPTH=6″ 🔒

Fix geometric constraint

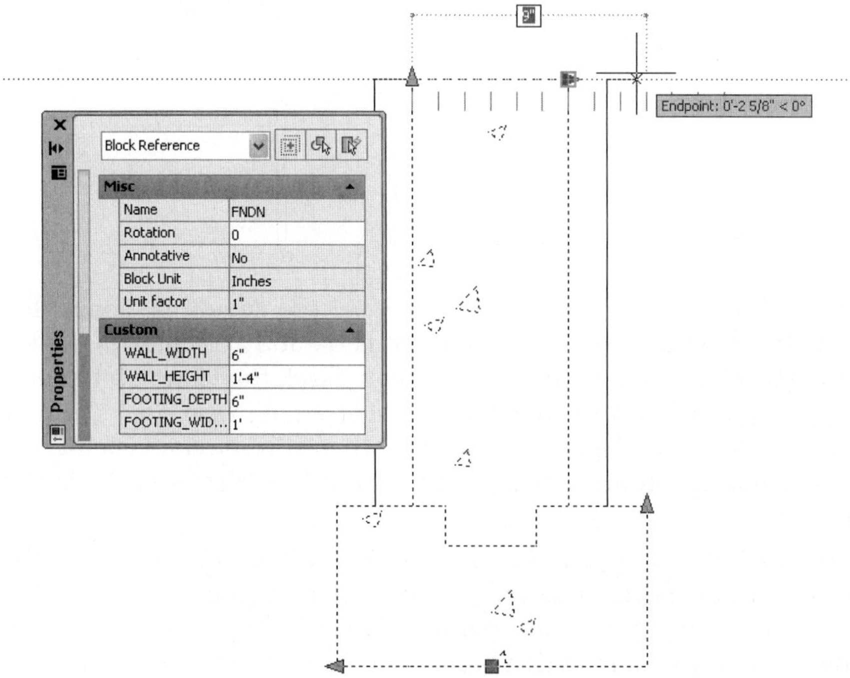

FOOTING_WIDTH=1′ 🔒

Endpoint: 0′-2 5/8″ < 0°

Block Reference		
Misc		▲
Name	FNDN	
Rotation	0	
Annotative	No	
Block Unit	Inches	
Unit factor	1″	
Custom		▲
WALL_WIDTH	6″	
WALL_HEIGHT	1′-4″	
FOOTING_DEPTH	6″	
FOOTING_WID...	1′	

10. The bolt shown in the drawing below is available in four different lengths. As the length increases, the size of the bolt head increases for added strength. Create a dynamic block that will allow the length of the shaft and the size of the bolt head to be changed in a single operation.
    A. Draw the objects that make up the bolt and create a block named BOLT. Do not include dimensions.
    B. Insert a linear parameter along the length of the shaft from the bottom of the bolt head to the end of the shaft. Label it SHAFT LENGTH.
    C. Assign a stretch action to the SHAFT LENGTH parameter. Associate the action with the parameter grip at the end of the shaft. Create a crossing window around the end of the shaft that includes the threads. Select the end of the shaft, threads, and edges of the shaft.
    D. Insert a linear parameter along the depth of the bolt head (the .3″ dimension). Label it HEAD THICKNESS.
    E. Assign a scale action to the HEAD THICKNESS parameter and select the objects that compose the bolt head. Use an independent base point type and specify the midpoint of the vertical line where the shaft meets the bolt head.
    F. Insert a lookup parameter and assign a lookup action to it.
    G. Add the SHAFT LENGTH and the HEAD THICKNESS parameters to the lookup table. Complete the table with the following properties:

Shaft Length	Head Thickness	Lookup
1	0.3	1″ Length
1.5	0.333	1.5″ Length
2	0.366	2″ Length
2.5	0.4	2.5″ Length

    H. Set the table to allow reverse lookup, save the block, and exit the **Block Editor**.
    I. Insert the block four times into the drawing. Specify a different lookup property for each block.
    J. Save the drawing as P27-10.

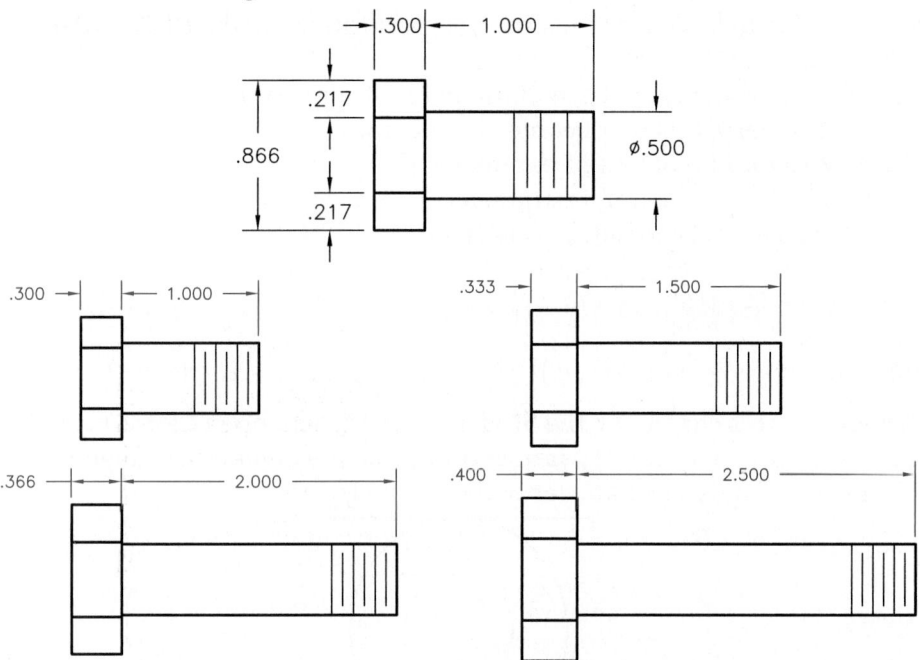

11. Repeat Problem 27-10, but this time use geometric constraints, constraint parameters, and a block properties table instead of action parameters. Save the drawing as P27-11.

AutoCAD Certified Associate Exam Practice

Answer the following questions. Write your answers on a separate sheet of paper.

1. How many visibility parameters can you assign to a block? *Select the one item that best answers the question.*
   A. 1
   B. 2
   C. 4
   D. 16
   E. unlimited number

2. Study the property lookup table for a pipeline valve. Which option would you choose from the lookup parameter grip to display the valve in the 45° position? *Select the one item that best answers the question.*
   A. Full Flow
   B. No Flow
   C. Normal Flow
   D. Reduced Flow

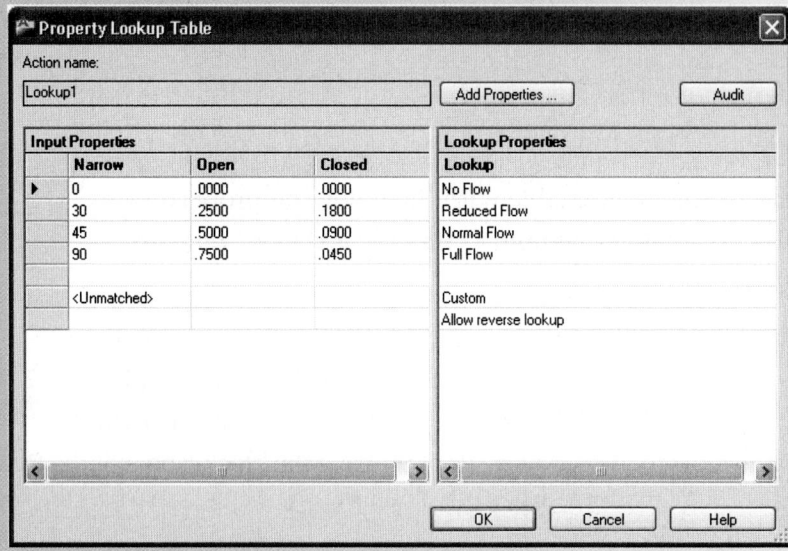

3. Which of the following actions can you perform using the **BCPARAMETER** tool? *Select all that apply.*
   A. convert a dimensional constraint to constraint parameter
   B. create a perpendicular geometric constraint
   C. create a radius constraint parameter
   D. place a linear constraint parameter
   E. place a parallel geometric constraint

AutoCAD Certified Professional Exam Practice

Follow the instructions in the problem. Write your answers on a separate sheet of paper.

1. **Navigate to this chapter on the Student Web site and open CPE-27constraint.dwg.** Use the existing constraint parameter to make the outer circle tangent to the line, as shown. What is the diameter of the inner circle?

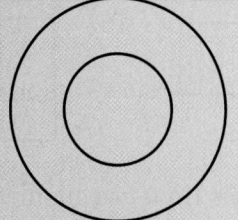

Learning Objectives

After completing this chapter, you will be able to do the following:
- ✓ Describe the purpose for and proper use of layouts.
- ✓ Begin to prepare layouts for plotting.
- ✓ Manage layouts.
- ✓ Use the **Page Setup Manager** to define plot settings.
- ✓ Use plot styles and plot style tables.

You may often print or plot a drawing in model space to make a quick hard copy for check or reference purposes. Ordinarily, however, you create a drawing in model space and then lay out the drawing for plotting in paper space. Hard-copy plots are required for a variety of reasons. For example, it is typically easier for workers in a machine shop or a construction crew in the field to refer to a print than to use a computer to view the drawing file. Most of the same steps you follow to prepare a drawing for plotting apply to exporting a drawing to an electronic format.

Introduction to Layouts

The first step to make an AutoCAD drawing is to create a *model* in *model space*. See **Figure 28-1A.** Model space is usually active by default. You have been using model space throughout this textbook to create objects and dimensioned drawing views. Once you complete a model, use a *layout* in *paper space* to prepare the final drawing for plotting. See **Figure 28-1B.** A layout represents the sheet of paper used to lay out and plot a drawing. A layout often includes the following items, depending on the drawing:

- Floating viewports to display content from model space
- Border and title block
- Revision history block
- General notes
- Bill of materials, parts list, schedules, legend, and other associated lists
- Sheet annotation and symbols such as titles, north arrow, and graphic scale
- Page setup information

model: A 2D or 3D drawing composed of various objects, such as lines, circles, and text, usually created at full size.

model space: The environment in AutoCAD in which you create drawings and designs.

layout: A specific arrangement of views or drawings for plotting or printing on paper.

paper space: The environment in AutoCAD in which you create layouts.

Figure 28-1. A—Design and draft objects in model space. B—Use paper space to finalize and lay out drawings and designs on paper for plotting or export.

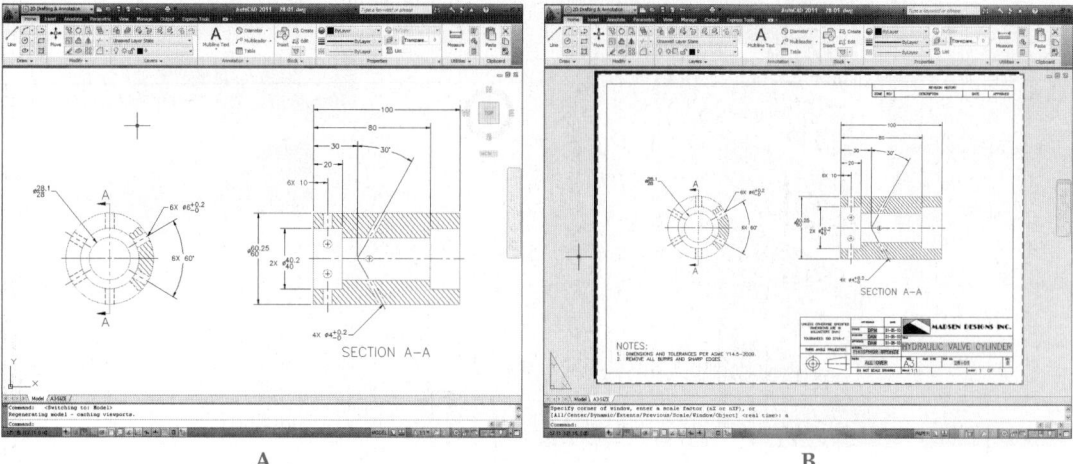

A   B

floating viewport: A viewport added to a layout in paper space to display objects drawn in model space.

A major element of the layout system is the *floating viewport*. Consider a layout to be a virtual sheet of paper and a floating viewport as a window cut into the paper to show objects drawn in model space. In **Figure 28-1B**, a single viewport exposes objects drawn in model space. Draw the floating viewport on a layer that you can turn off or freeze so the viewport does not plot and is not displayed on-screen. Chapter 29 explains using floating viewports.

Layouts with floating viewports offer the ability to construct properly scaled drawings. A single drawing can have multiple layouts, each representing a different paper space, or plot, definition. Each layout can include multiple floating viewports to provide additional or alternate drawing views, prepared at different scales if necessary. You can use a single drawing file to prepare several different final drawings and drawing views. For example, an architectural drawing file might include several details that are too large to place on a single sheet of paper. You can use multiple layouts, and if necessary differently scaled floating viewports, to prepare as many sheets as needed to plot all of the details found in the drawing.

Working with Layouts

Learn to use tools and options for displaying and managing layouts before you prepare a layout for plotting. The layout and model tabs and model space and paper space tools in the status bar are available by default. These are the most effective tools for navigating between model space and layouts, and for managing layouts. You can also type MODEL to return to model space from a layout.

Layout and Model Tabs

The model and layout tabs appear directly below the drawing window. See **Figure 28-2A**. The model space tab is furthest to the left, followed by layout tabs arranged in the order they were created, from left to right. If the drawing includes so many layouts that the tabs spread past the screen, use the forward and reverse buttons to the left of the tabs to access model space or the appropriate layout. Hover over an inactive tab to display a preview of the contents. Pick a layout tab to enter paper space with the selected layout current, or pick the **Model** tab to re-enter model space.

Figure 28-2. A—Using the layout and model tabs to activate model space and paper space. B—Options available when you right-click on a tab.

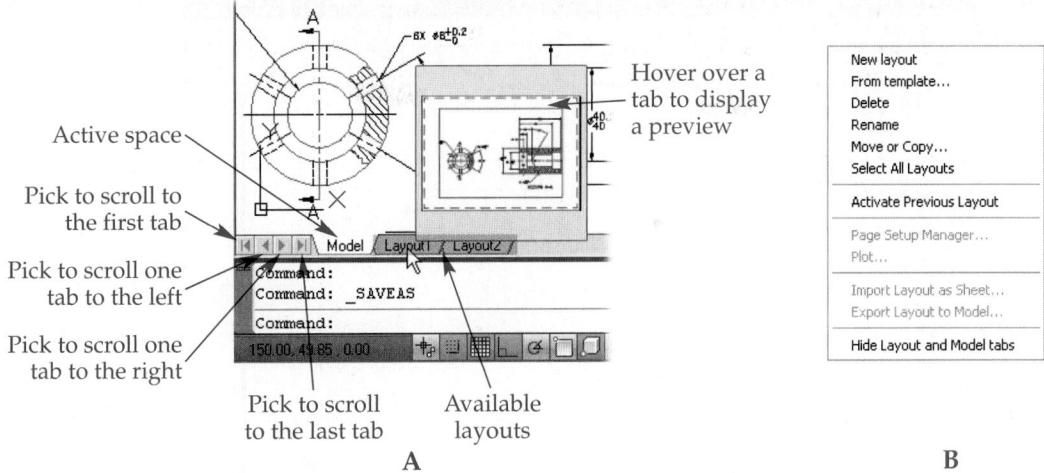

A

B

Right-click on a tab to access a shortcut menu with options for controlling layouts and the layout and model tabs. See **Figure 28-2B.** Pick **Activate Model Tab** to enter model space. Select **Activate Previous Layout** to make the previously current layout current. Pick **Select All Layouts** to select all layouts in the drawing. The **Select All Layouts** option is valuable for selecting all layouts for purposes such as publishing or deleting. The shortcut menu is also the primary resource for adding layouts and moving, renaming, and deleting existing layouts.

Figure 28-3 shows an example of using the supplied acad.dwt drawing template and picking the **Layout1** tab to display the default **Layout1** layout. The layout uses default settings based on an 8.5″ × 11″ sheet of paper in a landscape (horizontal) orientation. The white rectangle you see on the gray background is a representation of the sheet. Dashed lines mark the sheet *margin*. A large, rectangular floating viewport reveals model space objects, in this example a dimensioned multiview drawing. The acad.dwt file includes an additional layout named **Layout2**.

margin: The extent of the printable area; objects drawn past the margin (dashed lines) do not print.

NOTE

The **Layout elements** area of the **Display** tab in the **Options** dialog box includes several settings that affect the display and function of layouts. Use the default settings until you are comfortable working with layouts.

PROFESSIONAL TIP

Look at the user coordinate system (UCS) icon to confirm whether you are in model space or paper space. When you enter a layout, the UCS icon changes from two lines to a triangle that indicates the X and Y coordinate directions.

Model and Paper Buttons

The status bar provides other convenient tools for managing layouts. See **Figure 28-4.** The **Quick View Layouts** and **Quick View Drawings** tools are described later in this chapter. Pick the **MODEL** button to exit model space and enter paper space. If the file

Figure 28-3. Pick the **Layout1** tab to display **Layout1** provided in the default acad.dwt template.

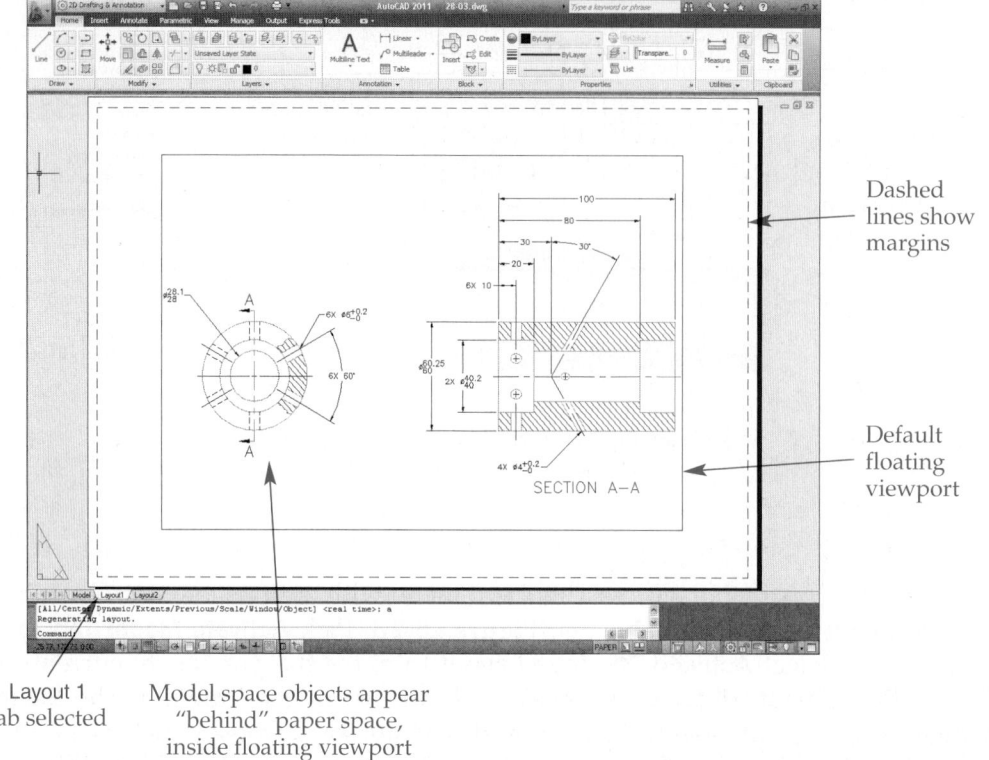

Dashed lines show margins

Default floating viewport

Layout 1 tab selected

Model space objects appear "behind" paper space, inside floating viewport

Figure 28-4. The status bar provides additional tools for activating model and paper space and managing layouts.

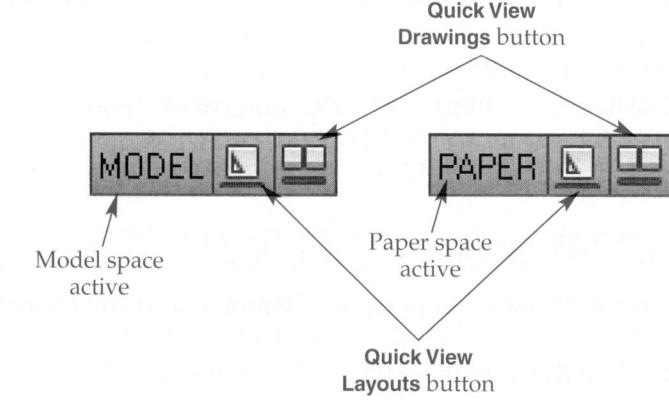

Quick View **Drawings** button

Model space active

Paper space active

Quick View **Layouts** button

contains multiple layouts, the top-level layout is displayed unless you previously accessed a different layout. While a layout is active, pick the **PAPER** button to use the **MSPACE** tool, which activates a floating viewport. The **MSPACE** tool does not return you to model space. Select the **PAPER** button to deactivate a floating viewport.

Type
MSPACE

Exercise 28-1

Access the Student Web site (www.g-wlearning.com/CAD) and complete Exercise 28-1.

The Quick View Layouts Tool

The **Quick View Layouts** tool is similar to the layout and model tabs, but provides additional options and a visual format for displaying and adjusting layouts in the current file. The quickest way to access the **Quick View Layouts** tool is to pick the **Quick View Layouts** button on the status bar. The active **Quick View Layouts** tool appears in the lower center of the AutoCAD window. See **Figure 28-5.**

Type
QVLAYOUT

The **Model** thumbnail image is on the left, followed by layout thumbnails in the order they were created, from left to right. If the drawing includes so many layouts that thumbnails spread past the screen, hover the cursor over the furthest right and left thumbnails to scroll though the options. Hover over a thumbnail to highlight the image and show additional options. See **Figure 28-6.** Pick a layout thumbnail to enter paper space with the selected layout current, or pick the **Model** thumbnail to re-enter model space.

> **NOTE**
>
> Icons represent model and layout thumbnails until you enter a layout for the first time (initialize the layout). The icon then changes to a thumbnail image of the layout.

A small toolbar appears below the thumbnail images in the **Quick View Layouts** tool, as shown in **Figure 28-6.** By default, the **Quick View Layouts** tool disappears when you pick a thumbnail to switch layouts or enter model space. To keep the tool on-screen, pick the **Pin Quick View Layouts** button. Pick the **New Layout** button to create a

Figure 28-5.
The **Quick View Layouts** tool offers an effective visual method for changing between model space and paper space and provides options for managing layouts.

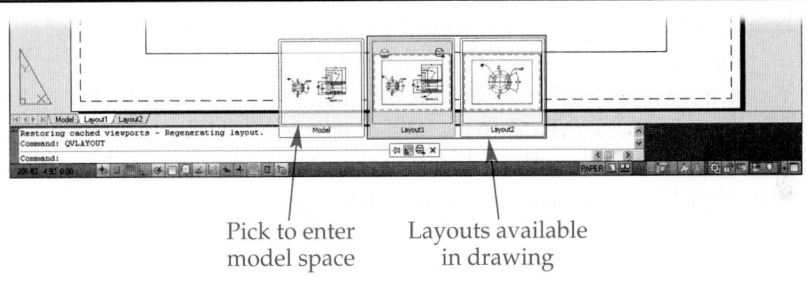

Pick to enter model space

Layouts available in drawing

Figure 28-6.
Hover over a thumbnail to display **Plot...** and **Publish...** buttons.

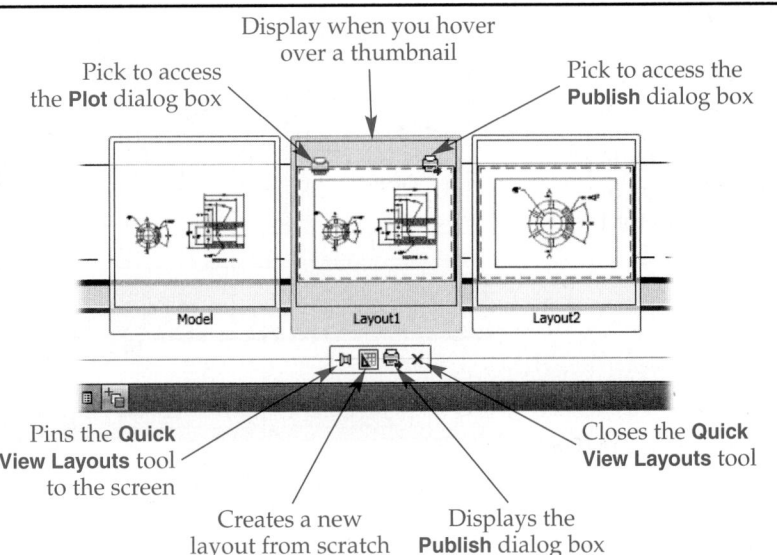

Display when you hover over a thumbnail

Pick to access the **Plot** dialog box

Pick to access the **Publish** dialog box

Pins the **Quick View Layouts** tool to the screen

Closes the **Quick View Layouts** tool

Creates a new layout from scratch

Displays the **Publish** dialog box

new layout from scratch, as described later in this chapter. Pick the **Publish...** button to access the **Publish** dialog box, explained later in this textbook. Select the **Close** button to exit the **Quick View Layouts** tool.

> **NOTE**
>
>
>
> If you pin the **Quick View Layouts** tool to the screen, close the tool and then access the tool again, the **Quick View Layouts** tool appears in the pinned state.

Right-click on a tab to access the same shortcut menu available when you right-click on the model or a layout tab, excluding the **Hide Layout and Model tabs** option. See **Figure 28-2B.** You can also access some menu options from a shortcut menu that displays when you right-click directly on the **Quick View Layouts** button on the status bar. An option selected from this menu applies to the current file and the current layout.

The Quick View Drawings Tool

Type

QVDRAWING

The **Quick View Drawings** tool provides the same features for working with layouts as the **Quick View Layouts** tool, but allows you to manage the layouts in all open drawings. Use **Quick View Drawings** tool to increase productivity when you are working between existing drawings. The quickest way to access the **Quick View Drawings** tool is to pick the **Quick View Drawings** button on the status bar. Refer to Chapter 2 for information on basic **Quick View Drawings** tool features, such as using the tool to work with multiple open documents.

Access the **Quick View Drawings** tool and hover over a drawing file. The model and layout thumbnail images appear above the highlighted drawing. Move the cursor over the model or a layout thumbnail to enlarge the display. See **Figure 28-7.** Pick a layout thumbnail to switch to the highlighted file and enter paper space with the selected layout active, or pick the **Model** thumbnail to switch to the highlighted file in model space. Right-click on a thumbnail to access the same shortcut menu that displays when you right-click on a thumbnail using the **Quick View Layouts** tool. Right-click on a thumbnail to make the associated file current.

Figure 28-7.
Use the **Quick View Drawings** tool to manage layouts located in other open files. Hover over a file thumbnail to display model and layout thumbnails for the file.

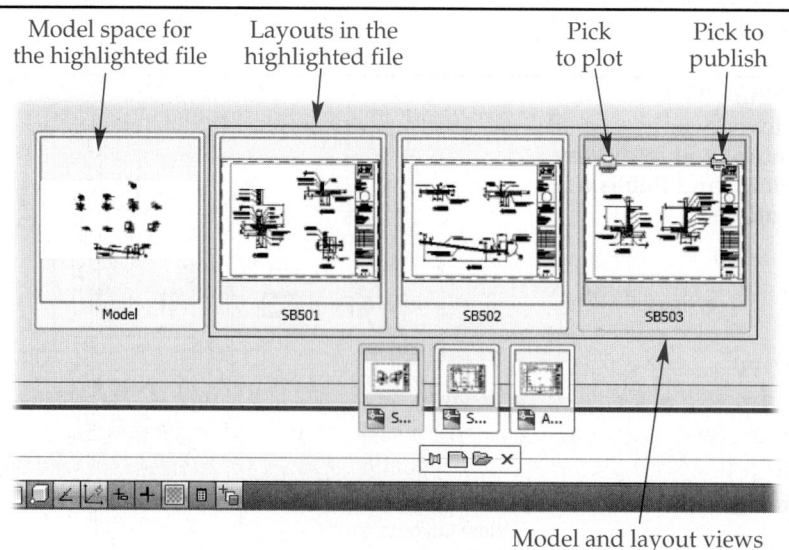

Model space for the highlighted file

Layouts in the highlighted file

Pick to plot

Pick to publish

Model and layout views enlarge when hovered over

Adding Layouts

To add a new layout to a drawing, you can create a new layout from scratch, use the **Create Layout** wizard, or reference an existing layout. Referencing an existing, preset layout is often the most effective approach. You can also insert a layout from a different DWG, DWT, or DXF file into the current file or create a copy of a layout in the current file.

Starting from Scratch

To create a new layout from scratch, right-click on the model or a layout tab, a **Quick View Layouts** or **Quick View Drawings** thumbnail image, or the **Quick View Layouts** button on the status bar, and pick **New Layout**. A new layout appears on the far right of the layout list. The settings applied to the new layout depend on the template used to create the original file. The name of the layout is set according to the names of other existing layouts. For example, when you add a new layout to a default drawing started from the acad.dwt template, a new layout named **Layout3** appears and includes an 8.5″ × 11″ sheet of paper, a landscape (horizontal) orientation, and a large floating viewport.

Using the Create Layout Wizard

Use the **Create Layout** wizard to build a layout from scratch using values and options you enter in the wizard. The wizard provides options for naming the new layout and selecting a printer, paper size, drawing units, paper orientation, title block, and viewport configuration. The pages of the wizard guide you through the process of developing the layout.

Type
LAYOUTWIZARD

Using a Template

To create a new layout from a layout stored in an existing DWG, DWT, or DXF file, right-click on the model or a layout tab, a **Quick View Layouts** or **Quick View Drawings** thumbnail image, or on the **Quick View Layouts** button on the status bar, and pick **From Template…**. The **Select Template From File** dialog box appears. See **Figure 28-8A**. The Template folder in the path set by the AutoCAD Drawing Template File Location appears by default. Select the file containing the layout you want to add to the current drawing and pick the **Open** button. The **Insert Layout(s)** dialog box appears, listing all layouts in the selected file. See **Figure 28-8B**. Highlight the layout(s) to copy and pick the **OK** button.

Using DesignCenter

DesignCenter provides an effective way to add existing layouts to the current drawing. Use the folder list to locate and select a drawing or template file. Pick the **Layouts** branch in the folder list, or double-click on the **Layouts** icon in the content pane. See **Figure 28-9**. Select the layout(s) to copy from the content pane and then drag and drop, or use the **Add Layout(s)** or **Copy** and **Paste** options from the shortcut menu to insert the layouts into the current drawing.

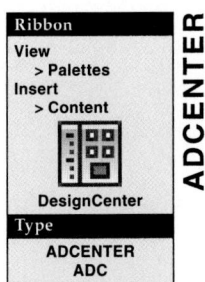

Ribbon
View
> Palettes
Insert
> Content

DesignCenter

Type
ADCENTER
ADC

ADCENTER

Figure 28-8.
Adding a layout using an existing layout stored in a different drawing, drawing template, or DXF file. A—Select the file containing the layout. B—Highlight the layout to add to the current drawing.

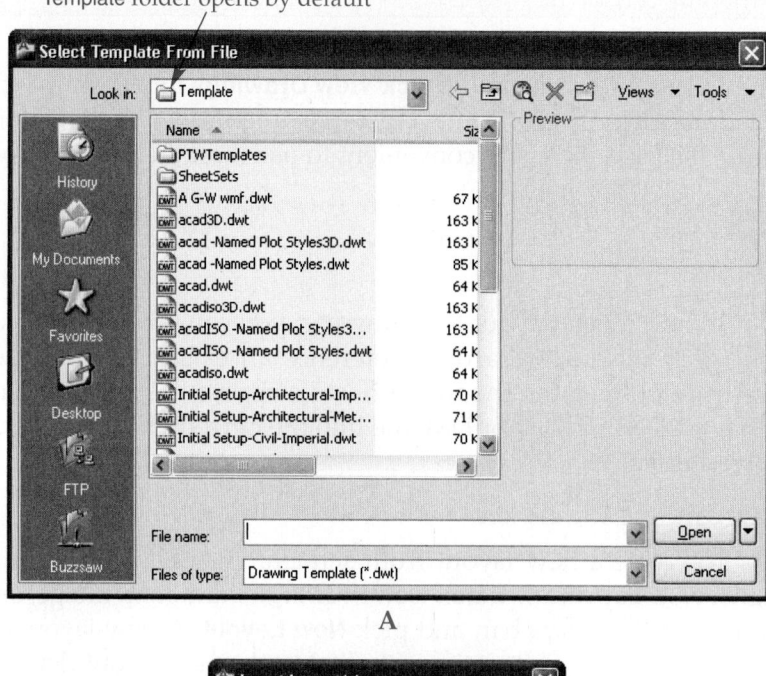

Template folder opens by default

A

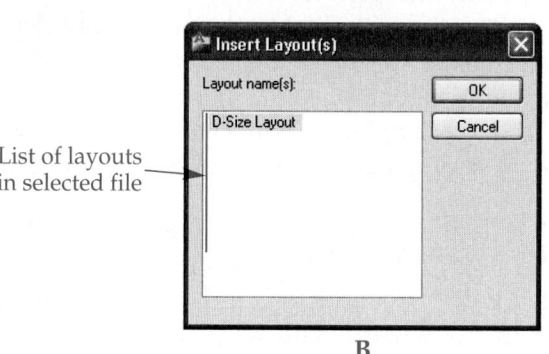

List of layouts in selected file

B

Figure 28-9.
Using **DesignCenter** to share layouts between drawings.

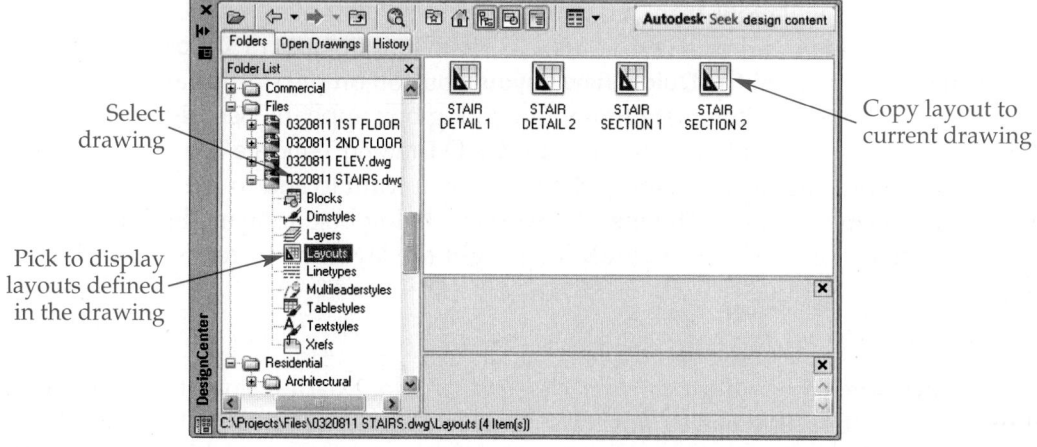

Select drawing

Pick to display layouts defined in the drawing

Copy layout to current drawing

Copying and Moving Layouts

To create a copy of a layout, right-click on a layout tab, a **Quick View Layouts** or **Quick View Drawings** thumbnail image, or make the layout to copy current and right-click on the **Quick View Layouts** button on the status bar. Then pick **Move or Copy...**

to display the **Move or Copy** dialog box. See **Figure 28-10.** To create a copy, select the **Create a copy** check box and pick the layout that will appear to the right of the new layout, or pick (move to end) to place the copy to the right of all other layouts. The default name of the new layout is the name of the current or selected layout plus a number in parentheses.

Move a layout using the **Move or Copy...** dialog box without selecting the **Create a copy** check box. When you add and rename layouts, the layouts do not automatically rearrange into a predetermined order. Organize layouts in an appropriate order to reduce confusion and aid in the publishing process, described in Chapter 32.

Renaming Layouts

Layouts are easier to recognize and use when they have descriptive names. To rename a layout, right-click on a layout tab or a **Quick View Layouts** or **Quick View Drawings** thumbnail image and pick **Rename**. You can also slowly double-click on the current name to activate it for editing. When the layout name highlights, type a new name and press [Enter].

Deleting Layouts

To delete an unused layout from the drawing, right-click on the layout tab or the **Quick View Layouts** or **Quick View Drawings** thumbnail image and pick **Delete**. An alert message warns that the layout will be deleted permanently. Pick the **OK** button to remove the layout.

Exporting a Layout to Model Space

The **EXPORTLAYOUT** tool allows you to save the current layout display as a separate DWG file. The **EXPORTLAYOUT** tool produces a "snapshot" of the layout display that you can use for applications in which it is necessary to combine model space and paper space objects, such as when exporting a file as an image. (Model space and paper space are not exported together as an image.)

The quickest way to access the **EXPORTLAYOUT** tool is to right-click on a layout tab or a **Quick View Layouts** or **Quick View Drawings** thumbnail image and pick **Export Layout to Model....** The **Export Layout to Model Space** dialog box appears and functions much like the **Save As** dialog box. Pick a location for the file, use the default file name or enter a different name, and pick the **SAVE** button. Everything shown in the layout, including objects drawn in model space, are converted to model space and are saved as a new file.

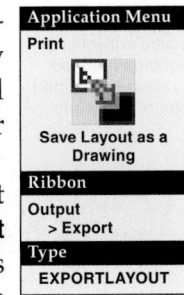

| Application Menu |
| Print |
| Save Layout as a Drawing |
| Ribbon |
| Output > Export |
| Type |
| EXPORTLAYOUT |

Figure 28-10.
The **Move or Copy** dialog box allows you to reorganize layouts and copy layouts within a drawing.

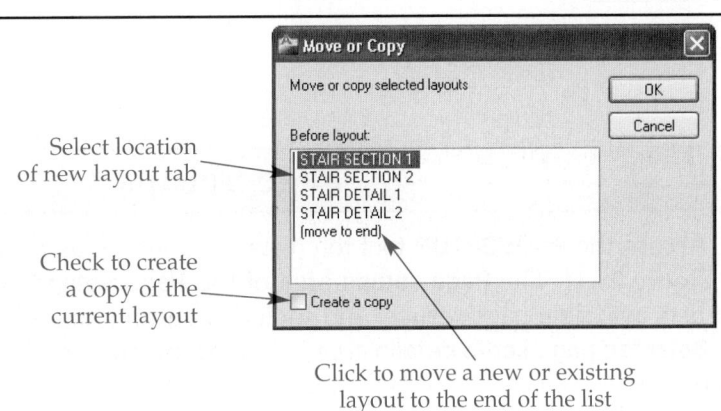

Select location of new layout tab

Check to create a copy of the current layout

Click to move a new or existing layout to the end of the list

The **EXPORTLAYOUT** tool eliminates the relationship between model space and paper space. Export a layout only when it is necessary to export model space and paper space together as a single unit. Use a descriptive name to differentiate between the exported layout file and the original file.

Exercise 28-2

Access the Student Web site (www.g-wlearning.com/CAD) and complete Exercise 28-2.

Initial Layout Setup

Preparing a layout for plotting involves creating and modifying floating viewports, adjusting plot settings, and adding layout content such as annotation, symbols, a border, and a title block. This chapter focuses on the process of preparing layouts for plotting using the **Page Setup Manager**. When you complete this initial phase, you will be better prepared to add content to layouts and create and manage floating viewports, as described in Chapter 29.

page setup: A saved collection of settings required to create a finished plot of a drawing.

A *page setup* establishes most of the settings that determine how a drawing plots. Plot settings include printer selection, paper size and orientation, plot area and offset, plot scale, and plot style. The **Page Setup Manager** and related **Page Setup** dialog box allow you to create and modify saved page setups that control how layouts appear on-screen and plot. This is where initial layout setup occurs. You then use the **Plot** dialog box to create the actual plot using the saved page setup. The **Page Setup** and **Plot** dialog boxes include most of the same settings.

PROFESSIONAL TIP

Layout setup usually involves several steps. A well-defined page setup decreases the amount of time required to prepare a drawing for plotting. Once a layout is set up, only a few steps are required to produce a plot. Add fully defined layouts to drawing templates for convenient future use.

Page Setups

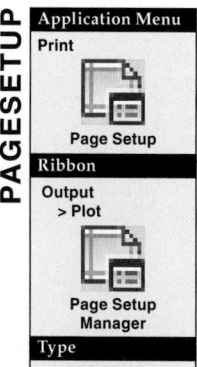

Access the **PAGESETUP** tool to create page setups using the **Page Setup Manager**. See **Figure 28-11**. The **Page setups** area of the **Page Setup Manager** contains a list box that lists available page setups, and includes buttons to add and modify page setups. The **Selected page setup details** area provides information about the highlighted page setup.

Figure 28-11.
Use the **Page Setup Manager** to modify existing page setups and to create and import page setups.

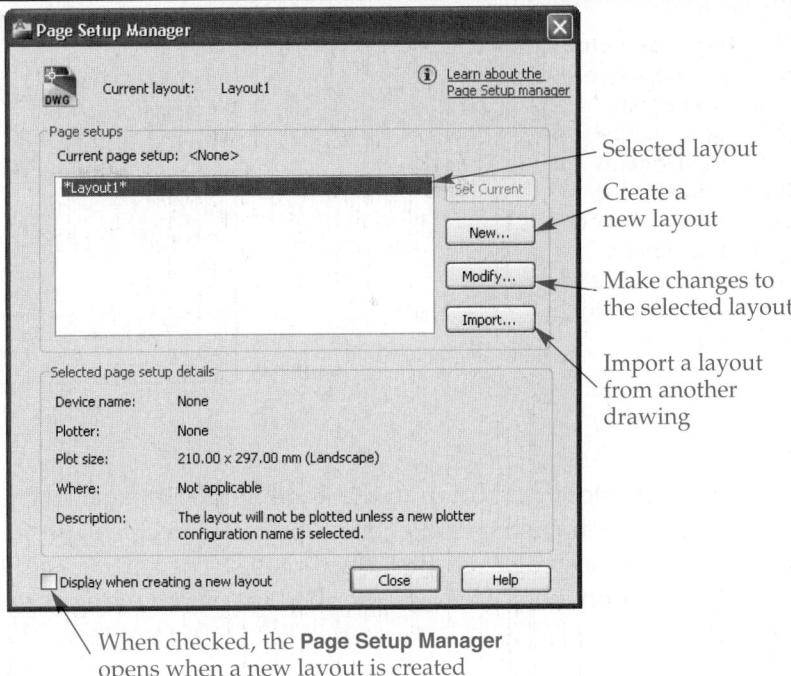

Selected layout

Create a new layout

Make changes to the selected layout

Import a layout from another drawing

When checked, the **Page Setup Manager** opens when a new layout is created

NOTE

You can also access the **Page Setup Manager** by right-clicking on the model or a layout tab, a **Quick View Layouts** or **Quick View Drawings** thumbnail image, or on the **Quick View Layouts** button on the status bar, and selecting **Page Setup Manager...**.

When you access the **Page Setup Manager** in model space, *Model* appears in the **Page Setups** list box. When you access the **Page Setup Manager** in paper space, the name of the current layout appears in the **Page Setups** list box. When preparing a layout for plotting, check to be sure that you are in paper space and that the appropriate layout is current. Each layout can have a unique page setup. Asterisks (*) before and after the layout name indicate the page setup assigned to the current layout. You have the option to create or use other page setups instead of the page setup associated with the layout.

Create a new page setup to use different plot characteristics without overriding plot settings or spending time making page setup changes. For example, create two page setups to plot to two different printers or plotters. Pick the **New...** button to create a new page setup using the **New Page Setup** dialog box. See **Figure 28-12.** Type a name for the new page setup and choose an option from the **Start with:** list box. Pick the **OK** button to create the page setup and display the **Page Setup** dialog box. Pick the **Import...** button to use existing page setups from a DWG, DWT, or DXF file.

To attach a different page setup to the current layout, select a page setup from the list in the **Page Setup Manager** and pick the **Set Current** button, or right-click on a page setup and choose **Set Current**. The layout will now plot according to the selected page setup. When you make a different page setup current, the selected page setup overrides the layout page setup. The page setup name appears in parentheses next to the layout name. To rename or delete an existing page setup, right-click on the page setup and pick **Rename** or **Delete**.

Figure 28-12.
The **New Page Setup** dialog box appears when you create a new page setup. Selecting **None** in the **Start with:** list box does not select a printer. **Default** selects the default printer assigned to the computer.

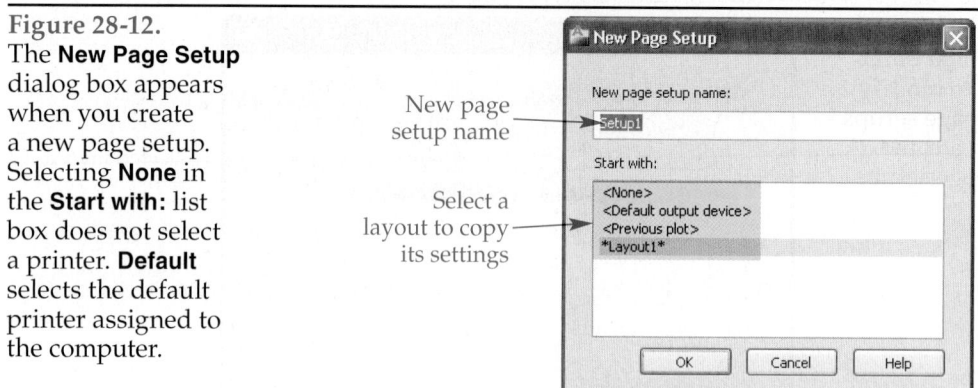

New page setup name

Select a layout to copy its settings

Select the **Modify...** button in the **Page Setup Manager** to change the settings of an existing page setup using the **Page Setup** dialog box. See **Figure 28-13.** The **Page Setup** dialog box defines page setup characteristics. The settings control layout appearance and plot function. Each area, as described in the following sections, controls a specific plot setting.

Plot Device

plot device: The printer, plotter, or alternative plotting system to which the drawing is sent.

configured: Installed and ready to use.

Use the **Printer/plotter** area of the **Page Setup** dialog box, shown in **Figure 28-14,** to select the appropriate *plot device* and adjust the plot device configuration if necessary. The default None setting indicates that no plot device is specified. Select a *configured* plot device to print or plot to from the **Name:** drop-down list.

Figure 28-13. The **Page Setup** dialog box allows you to adjust the plot settings for the selected page setup. This is where the initial phase of layout setup begins.

Current layout

Page setup name

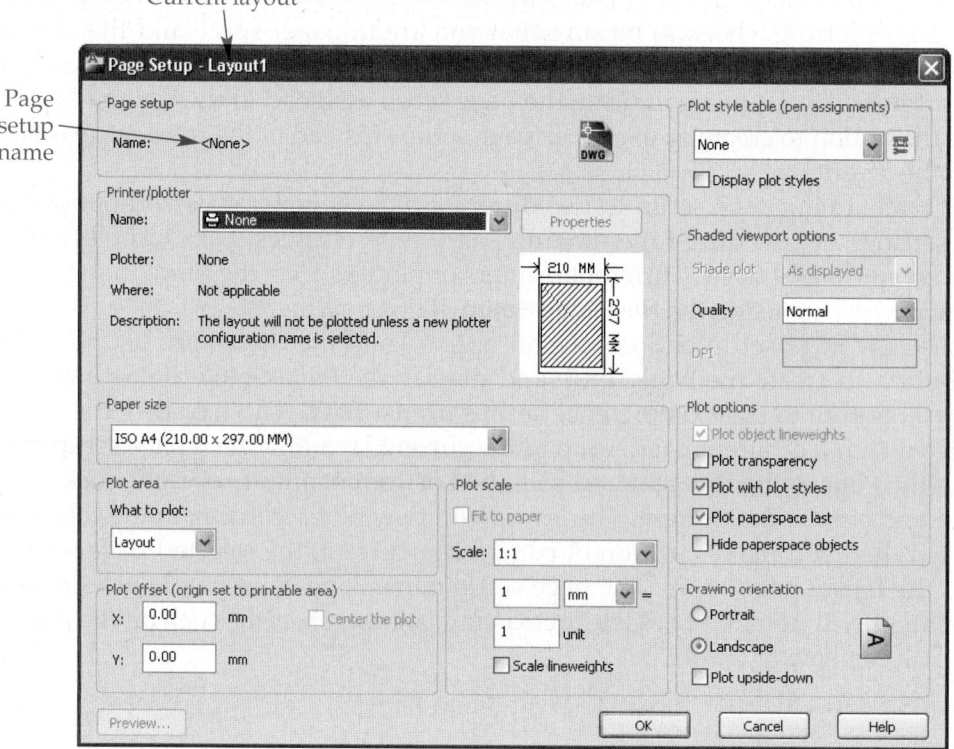

AutoCAD and Its Applications—Basics

Figure 28-14.
The **Printer/plotter**
area of the **Page
Setup** dialog box.

Select a printer

After a printer is selected, additional changes can be made

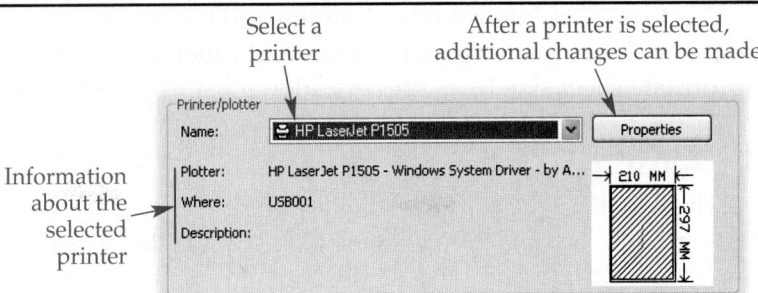

Information about the selected printer

Electronic Plots

Exporting a drawing is an effective way to display and share a drawing for some applications. One way to export a drawing is to plot a layout to a different file type. Electronic plotting uses the same general process as hard-copy plotting, but the plot exists electronically instead of on an actual sheet of paper.

A common electronic plotting method is to select the DWG To PDF.pc3 option to plot to a portable document format (PDF) file. For example, send a PDF file of a layout to a manufacturer, vendor, contractor, agency, or plotting service. The recipient uses common Adobe® software to view the plot electronically, and to plot the drawing to scale without having the AutoCAD software. This method also helps avoid inconsistencies that sometimes occur when sharing AutoCAD files. Select the DWF6 ePlot.pc3 or DWFX ePlot (XPS compatible).pc4 option to plot to the appropriate design web format (DWF) file. The recipient of a DWF file uses a viewer such as the Autodesk Design Review software to view and mark up the plot.

exporting:
Transferring electronic data from a database, such as a drawing file, to a different format used by another program.

NOTE

You will explore additional information on creating electronic plots later in this textbook and in *AutoCAD and Its Applications—Advanced.*

PROFESSIONAL TIP

If you use a plotting service or blueprint shop to plot large sheets, ask if the printer accepts PDF files. Plotting a layout to a PDF file and then using the PDF file to create a hard copy is often the most convenient way to share a drawing and ensure that the hard copy is exactly as expected.

Supplemental Material

Plotter Configuration
For more information about managing and configuring plot devices, go to the Student Web site (www.g-wlearning.com/CAD), select this chapter, and select **Plotter Configuration**.

Sheet Size

The **Paper size** area, shown in **Figure 28-15**, controls the *sheet size*. The sheet size determines the size of the virtual sheet of paper displayed in a layout and corresponds to the actual sheet size you plan to use when plotting. To determine sheet size, take into account the size of the drawing and additional space for dimensions, notes,

sheet size: The size of the paper used to lay out and plot drawings.

border, clear space between the drawing and border, title block, revision history block, zoning, and an area for general notes and other annotations and symbols. Select the appropriate sheet size from the drop-down list in the **Paper size** area.

Standard Sheet Sizes

The ASME Y14.1, *Decimal Inch Drawing Sheet Size and Format*, and ASME Y14.1M, *Metric Drawing Sheet Size and Format* standards specify the American Society of Mechanical Engineers (ASME) standard sheet sizes and formats. **Figure 28-16** shows the ASME Y14.1 sheet size specifications in inches. **Figure 28-17** shows the ASME Y14.1M sheet size specifications in metric units.

Figure 28-18 shows standard ASME sheet sizes. To describe sheet size values verbally, generally state the vertical measurement and then the horizontal measurement. For example, describe a C-size sheet as 22 (horizontal) × 17 (vertical). Longer lengths are known as elongated and extra-elongated drawing sizes. These are available in multiples of the short side of the sheet size.

Figure 28-15.
The **Paper size** area allows you to define the sheet size applied to the layout, which corresponds to the sheet size on which you plan to plot.

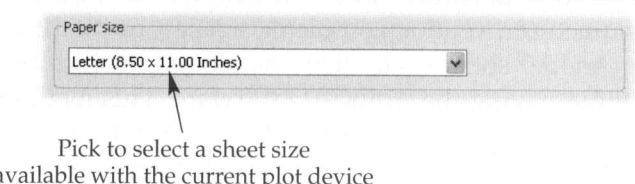

Pick to select a sheet size
available with the current plot device

Figure 28-16.
ASME Y14.1 standard sheet sizes for U.S. customary (inch) drawings.

Size Designation	Size (in inches)	
	Vertical	Horizontal
A	8 1/2 11	11 (horizontal format) 8 1/2 (vertical format)
B	11	17
C	17	22
D	22	34
E	34	44
F	28	40
Sizes G, H, J, and K are roll sizes.		

Figure 28-17.
ASME Y14.1M standard sheet for metric drawings.

Size Designation	Size (in millimeters)	
	Vertical	Horizontal
A0	841	1189
A1	594	841
A2	420	594
A3	297	420
A4	210	297

Figure 28-18. A—Standard drawing sheet sizes (ASME Y14.1). B—Standard metric drawing sheet sizes (ASME Y14.1M).

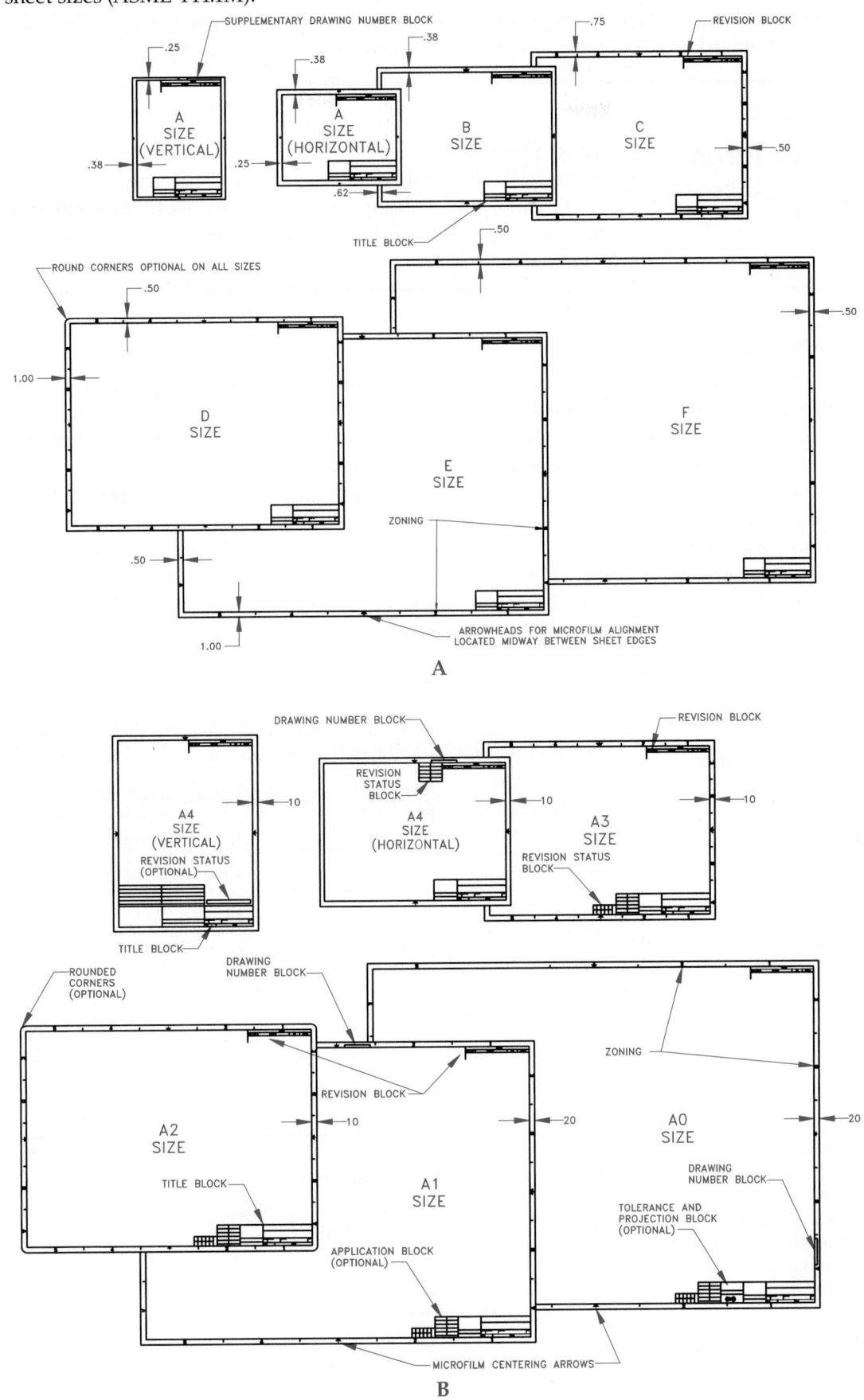

Some companies that prepare architectural or related drawings prefer inch-unit architectural sheet sizes, which vary slightly from the ASME standard. AutoCAD includes architectural and modified architectural sheet sizes depending on the specified plot device. Standard architectural sheet sizes in inches are shown in **Figure 28-19**.

Reference Material

Drawing Sheets
For tables describing sheet characteristics, including sheet size, drawing scale, and drawing limits, go to the **Reference Material** section of the Student Web site (www.g-wlearning.com/CAD) and select **Drawing Sheets**.

Drawing Orientation

The **Drawing orientation** area, shown in **Figure 28-20**, controls the plot rotation. Landscape orientation is the most common engineering drawing orientation and is the default in most AutoCAD-supplied templates. Portrait orientation is the standard for most text-based documents printed on 8.5″ × 11″ paper.

Pick the **Plot upside-down** check box to produce variations of the standard landscape and portrait orientations. When you select an upside-down orientation, it may help to consider the landscape format to be a rotation angle of 0° and portrait format to be a rotation angle of 90°. Therefore, an upside-down landscape format rotates the drawing 180°, and an upside-down portrait orientation rotates the drawing 270°. Use the preview image to help select the appropriate orientation.

Figure 28-19.
Architectural sheet sizes.

Size Designation	Size (in inches)	
	Vertical	**Horizontal**
A	9	12 (horizontal format)
	12	9 (vertical format)
B	12	18
C	18	24
D	24	36
E	36	48

Figure 28-20.
The **Drawing orientation** area contains options for adjusting the drawing angle of rotation.

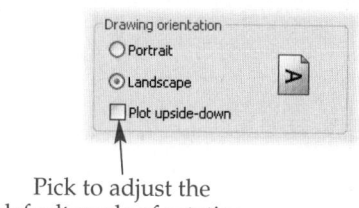

Pick to adjust the default angle of rotation

AutoCAD and Its Applications—Basics

The way in which a sheet feeds into a printer or plotter can affect the sheet size and drawing orientation you select. Sheets of paper, especially large sheets, often feed into a plotter with the short side of the sheet entering first. This may require you to use a sheet size that orients the sheet in a portrait format, for example D-Size 22x34 instead of D-Size 34x22, while still using a landscape drawing orientation.

Exercise 28-3

Access the Student Web site (www.g-wlearning.com/CAD) and complete Exercise 28-3.

Plot Area

The **Plot area** section, shown in Figure 28-21, allows you to choose the portion of the drawing to plot. Select an option from the **What to plot:** drop-down list. The **Layout** option is available when you plot a layout. When you select this option, everything inside the margins of the layout plots. The **Layout** option is the default and is the most common setting for plotting a layout. Use other plot area options primarily for plotting in model space, or to adjust the area to plot in paper space.

The **View** option is available when named views exist in the drawing, and if the model space or paper space environment associated with the current page setup includes a named view. When you pick the **View** option, an additional drop-down list appears in the **Plot area** section, allowing you to select a specific view to define as the plot area. Refer to Chapter 6 for information about other **Plot area** options.

Plot Offset

The **Plot offset** area, shown in Figure 28-22, controls distance the drawing is offset from the plot origin. You can specify the plot origin as the lower-left corner of the printable area or the lower-left corner of the sheet by selecting the appropriate radio button in the **Specify plot offset relative to** area in the **Plot and Publish** tab of the **Options** dialog box.

The **Plot offset (origin set to printable area)** title appears when you use the default **Printable area** option of the **Options** dialog box. The values you enter in the **X:** and **Y:** text boxes define the offset from the printable area. Use the default values of 0 to locate the plot origin at the lower-left corner of the printable area, which corresponds to the lower-left corner of the layout margin (dashed rectangle). To move the drawing away from the default printable area origin, enter positive or negative values in the text boxes. For example, to move the drawing one unit to the right and two units above the lower-left corner of the margin, enter 1 in the **X:** text box and 2 in the **Y:** text box.

Figure 28-21.
Use the **Plot area** section to define the portion of the drawing to plot.

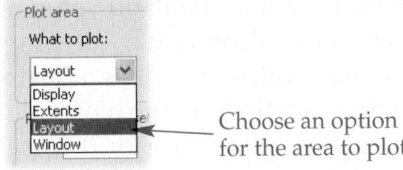

Choose an option for the area to plot

Figure 28-22.
The **Plot offset** area controls how far the drawing is offset from the lower-left corner of the printable area or layout border.

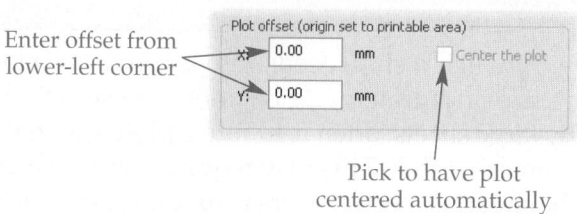

Enter offset from lower-left corner

Pick to have plot centered automatically

Select the **Edge of paper** radio button in the **Options** dialog box to display the **Plot offset (origin set to layout border)** title. The values you enter in the **X:** and **Y:** text boxes define the offset from the edge of the sheet. Use the default values of 0 to locate the plot origin at the lower-left corner of the sheet. Change the values in the text boxes to move the drawing away from the sheet origin.

When you select any option other than the **Layout** option from the **What to plot:** drop-down list in the **Plot area** section, the **Center the plot** check box becomes active. Check **Center the plot** to shift the plot origin automatically as needed to center the selected plot area in the printable area.

PROFESSIONAL TIP

If a drawing does not center on the sheet when you plot using the **Layout** option, open the **Options** dialog box and select the **Plot and Publish** tab. Pick the **Edge of paper** radio button in the **Specify plot offset relative to** area. Then use values of 0 in the X and Y offset text boxes in the **Page Setup** dialog box to locate the plot origin at the lower-left corner of the sheet. Depending on the specific plot configuration, you may also need to pick the **Plot upside-down** check box in the **Drawing orientation** area of the **Page Setup** dialog box to locate the origin exactly at the lower-left corner of the sheet. Alternatively, resolve the issue by changing the plot offset to the X and Y values of the lower-left corner of the printable area.

Plot Scale

Always draw objects at their actual size, or full scale, in model space, regardless of the size of the objects. For example, if you draw a small machine part and the length of a line in the drawing is 2 mm, draw the line 2 mm long in model space. If you draw a building and the length of a line in the drawing is 80′, draw the line 80′ long in model space. For layout and printing purposes, you must then scale most drawings to fit properly on a sheet, according to a specific *drawing scale*.

drawing scale: The ratio between the actual size of objects in the drawing and the size at which the objects plot on a sheet of paper.

When you scale a drawing, you increase or decrease the displayed size of model space objects. A properly scaled floating viewport in a layout allows for this process, as described in Chapter 29. When setting up a layout for plotting, remember that the layout is also at full scale. One difference between model space and paper space is that objects in model space can be very large or very small, while objects in paper space always correspond to sheet size. In order for objects on the layout and in model space to appear correct when plotted, you must plot a layout at full scale, or 1:1.

Use the **Plot scale** area of the **Page Setup** dialog box to specify the plot scale. See **Figure 28-23.** The **Scale:** drop-down list provides several predefined decimal and architectural or related scales, as well as a **Custom** option. For most applications, when setting up a layout for plotting, set the plot scale to 1:1. This ensures that the layout and scaled floating viewports plot correctly. If you choose a scale other than 1:1, the layout does not plot to scale.

Figure 28-23.
Use the **Plot scale** area to adjust the scale at which the drawing plots. The plot scale is typically set to 1:1 to plot a layout even though the drawing scale may not be 1:1.

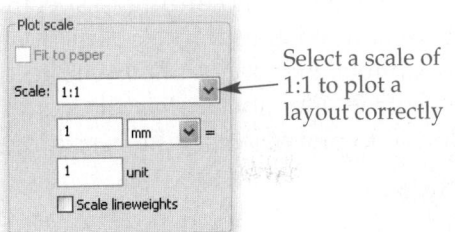

Select a scale of 1:1 to plot a layout correctly

When preparing to plot in model space, you may choose to select a scale other than 1:1. For example, to plot an architectural floor plan, you might set the plot scale to 1/4″ = 1′-0″. If the desired scale is not available, enter values in the text boxes below the drop-down list of predefined scales and select the correct unit of measure from the drop-down list. The **Custom** option automatically displays when you enter values. For example, 1 inch = 600 units is a custom scale entry used to plot at a scale of 1″ = 50′ (50′ x 12″ = 600). Refer to Chapter 9 for more information about drawing scale and scale factors.

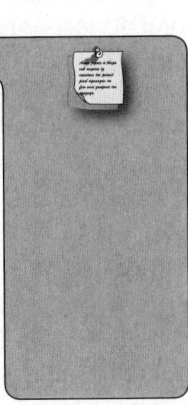

Pick the **Fit to paper** check box to adjust the plot scale automatically to fit on the selected sheet. Fitting to paper is useful if you are not concerned about plotting to scale, such as when you are creating a check copy on a sheet that is too small to plot at the appropriate scale. Select the **Scale lineweights** check box to scale (increase or decrease the weight of) lines when the plot scale changes.

In the event that you need to plot an inch drawing on a metric sheet, use a custom scale of 1 inch = 25.4 units. Conversely, use a custom scale of 25.4 mm = 1 unit to plot a metric drawing on an inch sheet.

Exercise 28-4

Access the Student Web site (www.g-wlearning.com/CAD) and complete Exercise 28-4.

Plot Styles

Object properties control the appearance of objects on-screen. By default, what you see on-screen is what plots. For example, if you draw objects on a layer that uses a Red color, Continuous linetype, and 0.60 mm lineweight, the objects display and plot red, continuous, and thick, assuming you show lineweights on-screen and use a color plotter. If this is the result you want, you are ready to continue with the page setup and plotting process.

However, to define exactly how objects plot regardless of what displays on-screen, you must assign *plot styles* to objects. Use plot styles to maintain object properties in

plot styles:
Properties, including color, linetype, lineweight, line end treatment, and fill style, that are applied to objects for plotting purposes only.

the drawing, but plot objects according to specific plotting properties. For example, to plot all objects in a drawing as dark as possible, you should plot them using the color black. In this example, plot styles allow you to plot all objects black without making them black on-screen. Plot styles also allow you to plot objects using shades of gray instead of color, or to plot objects lighter or darker than they display on-screen.

Plot Style Tables

plot style table: A configuration, saved as a separate file, that groups plot styles and provides complete control over plot style settings.

color-dependent plot style table: A file that contains plot style settings used to assign plot values to object colors.

named plot style table: A file that contains plot style settings used to assign plot values to objects or layers.

Plot style tables contain plot styles. Choose to use either a *color-dependent plot style table* or a *named plot style table*. A color-dependent plot style table forces objects to plot according to object color. Color-dependent plot style tables contain 255 preset plot styles—one for each AutoCAD Color Index (ACI) color. Each color-dependent plot style is linked to an index color. Plot style properties control how to treat objects of a certain color when the objects plot. For example, the plot style Color 1, which is Red, defines how all objects that are red on-screen plot. If you assign the Black plot color to plot style Color 1, all red objects are plotted in black, even though the objects are red on-screen.

A named plot style table forces objects to plot according to named plot style values, which you can assign to a layer or object. Any layer or object assigned a named plot style plots using the settings specified for that plot style. For example, create a layer named OBJECT that uses the Red color and a plot style named BLACK that uses a Black color. Then assign the BLACK plot style to the OBJECT layer. Objects drawn on the OBJECT layer plot using the BLACK plot style and plot black in color, even though the objects are red on-screen.

Ideally, decide which plot style table is appropriate before you begin drawing. The templates created in the Template Development feature of this textbook, for example, assume that drawings plot so that all objects appear dark, or black, with different object linetypes and lineweights. You can use a color-dependent plot style table or a named plot style table to create this effect. Default AutoCAD plot style behavior uses color-dependent plot style tables. For most applications, it is usually best to use color-dependent plot style tables, because they are the default and do not require you to assign named plot styles to layers or objects.

Configuring Plot Style Table Type

To configure the plot style type used by default when you create new drawings, pick the **Plot Style Table Settings...** button in the **Plot and Publish** tab of the **Options** dialog box. This opens the **Plot Style Table Settings** dialog box shown in **Figure 28-24.**

To use a named plot style table, pick the **Use named plot styles** radio button from the **Default plot style behavior for new drawings** area *before* you start a new drawing file. Select a specific plot style table to use as the default for new drawings from the **Default plot style table:** drop-down list in the **Current plot style table settings** area. When you select the **Use named plot styles** radio button, the **Default plot style for layer 0:** and **Default plot style for objects:** options become active.

> **NOTE**
>
> When you use a template to create a new drawing, the plot style settings defined in the template override the settings you specify in the **Plot Style Table Settings** dialog box. For example, if you configure the template to use named plot style tables, you can only select a named plot style table to apply to the plot, even if you select the **Use color dependent plot styles** radio button in the **Plot Style Table Settings** dialog box.

Figure 28-24.
Use the **Plot and Publish** tab of the **Options** dialog box to set up the default plot style types and tables for new drawings.

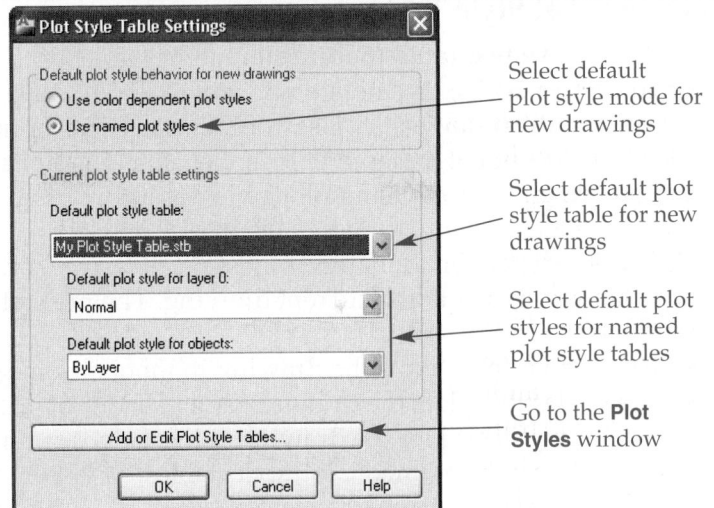

Select default plot style mode for new drawings

Select default plot style table for new drawings

Select default plot styles for named plot style tables

Go to the **Plot Styles** window

Pick the **Add or Edit Plot Style Tables...** button in the **Plot Style Table Settings** dialog box to open the **Plot Styles** window. See **Figure 28-25**. The **Plot Styles** window lists available color-dependent and named plot style tables saved in the Plot Style Table Search Path, as defined in the expanded **Printer Support File Path** option in the **Files** tab of the **Options** dialog box. Color-dependent plot style table files (CTB) use the .ctb extension. Named plot style table files (STB) include an .stb extension. Double-click on **Add-A-Plot Style Table Wizard** to create a new plot style table, or double-click on an existing plot style table file to edit the file.

Creating and Editing Plot Style Tables

For detailed information about creating and editing plot style tables, go to the Student Web site (www.g-wlearning.com/CAD), select this chapter, and select **Creating and Editing Plot Style Tables**.

Figure 28-25.
The **Plot Styles** window lists available plot style files and allows you to create and edit plot style tables.

Named plot style icon

Double-click to create a new plot style table

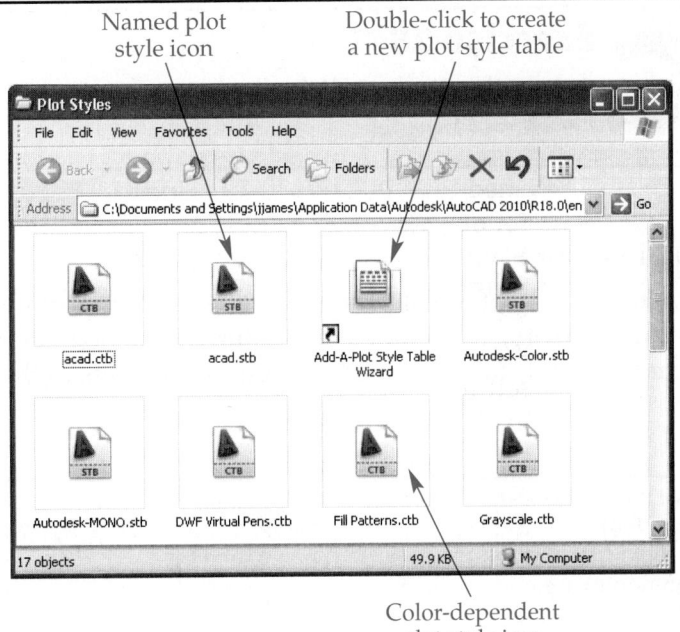

Color-dependent plot style icon

Selecting a Plot Style Table

Use the **Plot style table (pen assignments)** area of the **Page Setup** dialog box, shown in **Figure 28-26**, to activate and manage plot style tables. Select a plot style table from the drop-down list. Use the default **None** option instead of selecting a specific color-dependent or named plot style table. The **None** option plots exactly what appears on-screen without using plot styles, assuming you use a color plotter to plot objects with color.

Only color-dependent or named plot style tables appear, depending on the type of plot style table assigned to the current drawing. The most often used color-dependent plot style tables are:

- Monochrome.ctb—plots the drawing in monochrome (black and white).
- Grayscale.ctb—plots the drawing using shades of gray.
- Screening files—plot the drawing using faded, or screened, colors.

When a drawing uses named plot style tables, it is common to select one of the following:

- Autodesk-Color.stb—provides access to named plot styles for plotting the drawing using solid and faded colors.
- Monochrome.stb—references a named plot style for plotting the drawing in monochrome.
- Autodesk-MONO.stb—provides access to named plot styles for plotting objects monochrome, in color, and in faded monochrome.

PROFESSIONAL TIP

You cannot select named plot style tables if you start the drawing with color-dependent plot style tables. Conversely, you cannot select color-dependent plot style tables if you start the drawing with named plot style tables. You can type CONVERTPSTYLES to access the **CONVERTPSTYLES** tool, which allows you to switch between table modes in a drawing. However, you should avoid converting plot style tables when possible. Instead, use the appropriate plot style type when beginning a new drawing.

Exercise 28-5

Access the Student Web site (www.g-wlearning.com/CAD) and complete Exercise 28-5.

Applying Plot Styles

After you select a plot style table from the drop-down list in the **Plot style table (pen assignments)** area of the **Page Setup** dialog box, the plot styles contained in the selected plot style table are ready to assign to objects in the drawing. When you select

Figure 28-26.
Use the **Plot style table (pen assignments)** area to select, create, and edit plot style tables.

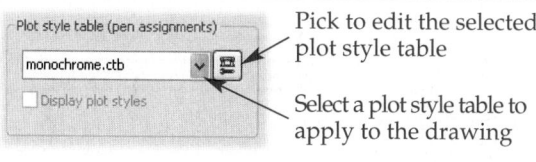

Pick to edit the selected plot style table

Select a plot style table to apply to the drawing

AutoCAD and Its Applications—Basics

a color-dependent plot style table, plot styles are automatically applied to objects according to object color. No additional steps are required to apply color-dependent plot styles to objects.

When you select a named plot style table, the named plot styles contained in the table are ready to assign to layers or individual objects. Any layer or object assigned a named plot style plots using the settings specified for that style. Named plot style tables contain as many plot styles as have been created. For example, the monochrome.stb plot style table contains the default Normal plot style and a style named Style 1. When you apply the Normal plot style to layers or objects, objects plot exactly as they appear on-screen. Style 1 assigns the color Black to all layers or objects that use Style 1 for plotting. In order to plot all objects in the drawing black, even if the objects have different colors on-screen, you must apply Style 1 to all layers.

Assign named plot styles to layers in the **Layer Properties Manager** palette. See **Figure 28-27.** Select a layer and then pick the current plot style, such as **Normal**, from the **Plot Style** column. The **Select Plot Style** dialog box appears. See **Figure 28-28.** Select a named style to assign to the highlighted layer. Any object drawn on a layer assigned to a named plot style plots using the settings in the named plot style.

You can also assign named plot styles to individual objects. If you assign a plot style to an object drawn on a layer that has already been assigned a named plot style, the plot style assigned to the object overrides the plot style settings for the layer. Assign plot styles to objects using the **Properties** palette or the **Plot Style Control** drop-down list in the **Properties** panel on the **Home** ribbon tab. See **Figure 28-29.**

NOTE

If the current drawing is set to use a named plot style table, the default plot style for all layers is Normal. The default plot style for all objects is ByLayer. Objects plotted with these settings keep their original properties.

Figure 28-27. Assign named plot styles to layers using the **Layer Properties Manager**. This example uses the monochrome.stb plot style table and the Style 1 plot style assigned to all layers to plot all objects black.

Pick plot style name for layer
to select a different plot style

Figure 28-28.
Use the **Select Plot Style** dialog box to assign a plot style to a layer.

Pick plot style for layer from list of plot styles in plot style table

Current plot style table

Identifies current layout tab

Access **Plot Style Table Editor** dialog box

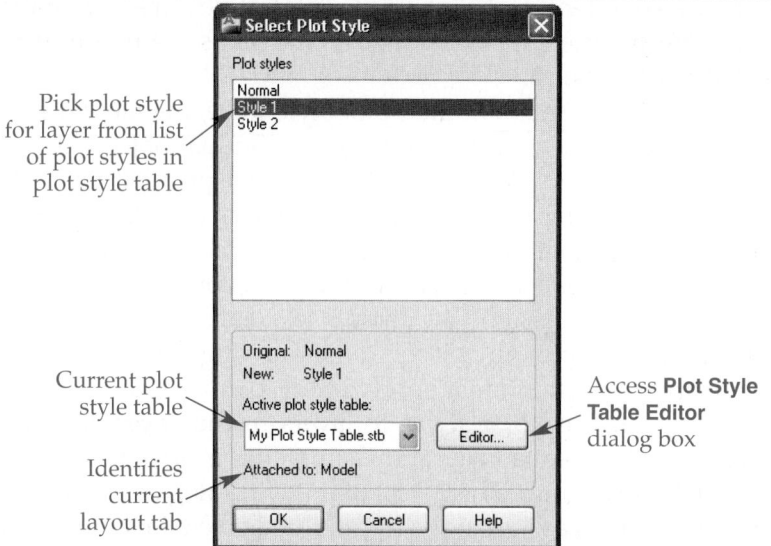

Figure 28-29.
You can assign a plot style to individual objects using A— the **Properties** palette or B—the **Plot Style Control** drop-down list in the ribbon.

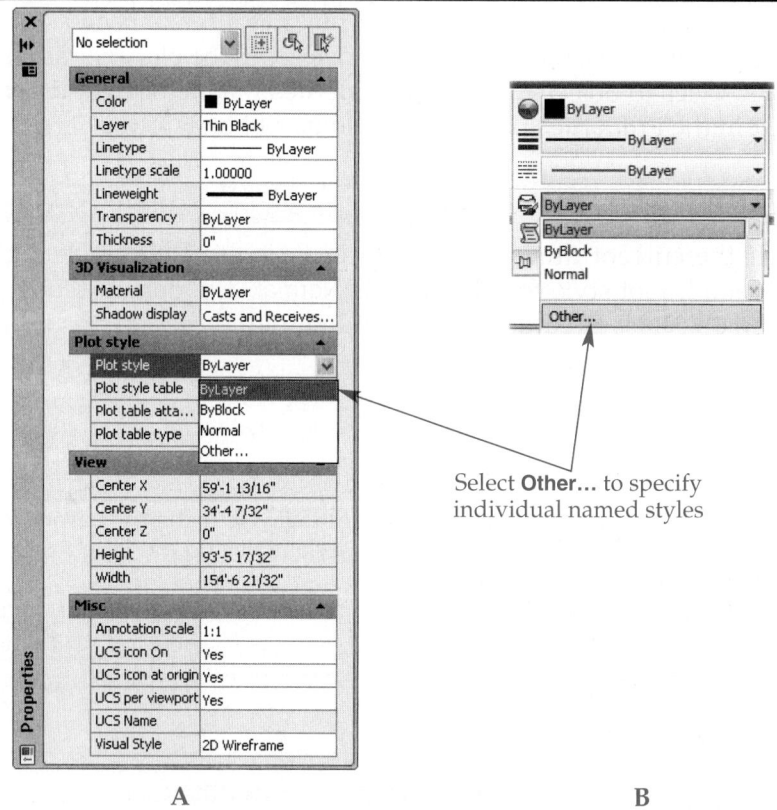

Select **Other...** to specify individual named styles

A

B

Exercise 28-6

Access the Student Web site (www.g-wlearning.com/CAD) and complete Exercise 28-6.

Viewing Plot Style Effects On-Screen

To display plot style effects on-screen, pick the **Display plot styles** check box in the **Plot style table** area in the **Page Setup** dialog box. Objects appear on-screen as they will plot. Typically, it is not appropriate to work with objects displayed as they will

AutoCAD and Its Applications—Basics

plot, especially if you print in monochrome. In this example, the color assigned to a layer appears black, which defeats the purpose of assigning colors to layers. A better practice is to use the preview feature of the **Page Setup** or **Plot** dialog box, as described later in this chapter, to preview the effects of plot styles before plotting.

Other Plotting Options

The **Plot options** area of the **Page Setup** dialog box contains additional options that affect how specific items plot. If you plan to plot objects using a plot style table, be sure to select the **Plot with plot styles** check box. The main purpose of this check box is to toggle the use of plot styles on and off. This allows you to create a plot quickly with or without using plot styles.

When you deselect the **Plot with plot styles** check box, the **Plot object lineweights** check box becomes enabled and selected. When this box is checked, all objects with a lineweight greater than 0 plot using the assigned lineweight. Deselect the check box to plot all objects using a 0, or thin, lineweight.

The **Plot transparency** check box provides the flexibility to plot transparent objects transparent or opaque. Check **Plot transparency** for objects that are assigned to a transparent layer and objects in which the style has been overridden to appear transparent. For many drawings, transparency should be reproduced on the plot, as shown in **Figure 28-30**, especially if you are using transparent fills. However, sometimes transparency is only for on-screen display proposes. For this application, deselect the **Plot transparency** check box.

Pick the **Plot paperspace last** check box to plot paper space objects after model space objects. This option ensures that objects in paper space that overlap objects in model space plot over the model space objects. The **Plot paperspace last** check box is disabled when you plot in model space, because model space does not include paper space objects. Select the **Hide paperspace objects** check box to remove hidden lines from 3D objects created in paper space. This option is only available when you plot from a layout tab and affects only objects drawn in paper space. It does not affect any 3D objects in a viewport.

NOTE

The **Shaded viewport options** area of the **Page Setup** dialog box provides settings that control viewport shading. These options set the type and quality of shading for plotting 3D models from a shaded or rendered viewport. *AutoCAD and Its Applications— Advanced* explains 3D models.

Completing Page Setup

After you select all appropriate page setup options, pick the **Preview** button in the lower-left corner of the **Page Setup** dialog box to preview the effects of the page setup. What you see on-screen is the exact plot appearance, assuming you use a color plotter to make color prints. The **Realtime Zoom** tool is automatically activated in the preview window. Additional view tools are available from the toolbar near the top of the window or from a shortcut menu. Use view tools to help confirm that the plot settings are correct. When you finish previewing the plot, pick the **Close** button on the toolbar, press [Esc] or [Enter], or right-click and select **Exit** to return to the **Page Setup** dialog box. Pick the **OK** button to exit the **Page Setup** dialog box, and pick **Close** button to exit the **Page Setup Manager**.

Exercise 28-7

Access the Student Web site (www.g-wlearning.com/CAD) and complete Exercise 28-7.

Figure 28-30. An example of an architectural elevation with transparent layers plotted to show the existing structure. Opaque layers identify the proposed structure.

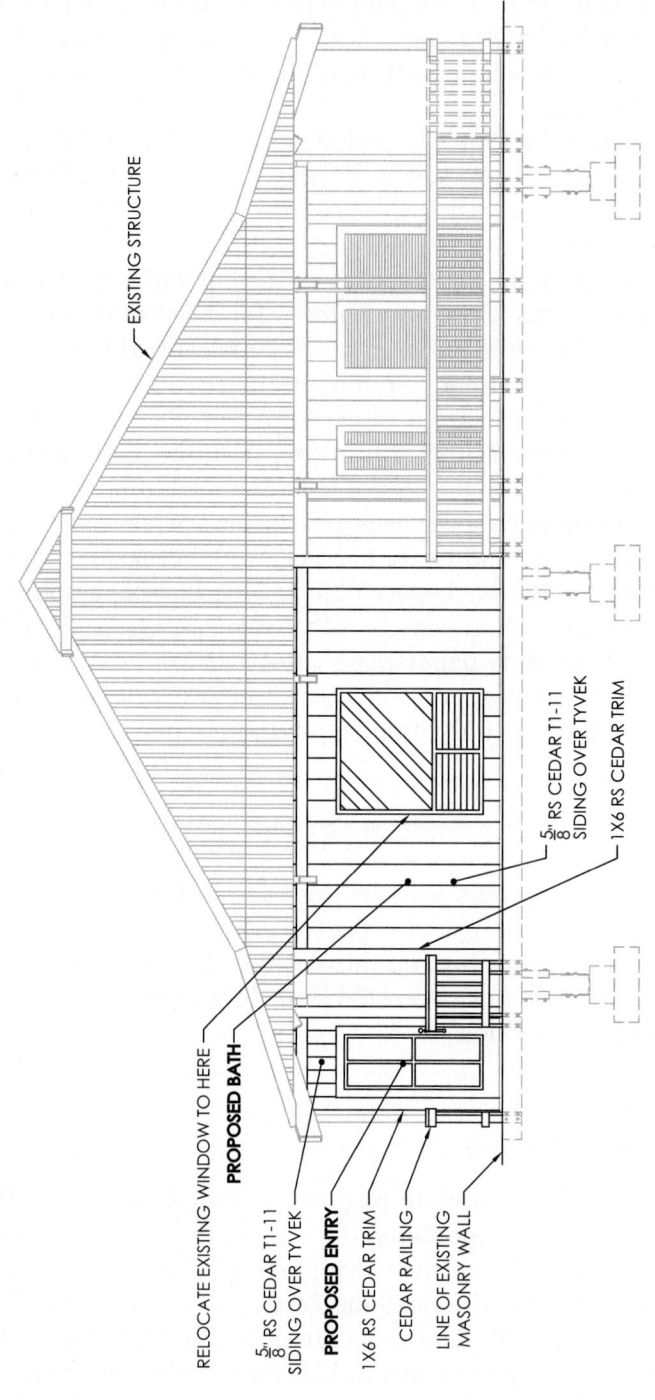

Chapter Test

Answer the following questions. Write your answers on a separate sheet of paper or go to the Student Web site (www.g-wlearning.com/CAD) and complete the electronic chapter test.

1. What is a model?
2. Define *model space*.
3. What is the purpose of a layout?
4. What is paper space?
5. What is the purpose of a floating viewport?
6. What is the purpose of the dashed rectangle that appears on the default layout?
7. If you pick the **MODEL** button to enter paper space and the file contains multiple layouts, none of which you previously accessed, which layout is displayed by default?
8. Briefly describe the function of the **Quick View Layouts** tool.
9. What does the **Quick View Drawings** tool allow you to do?
10. What is a page setup?
11. Briefly describe the basic function of the **Page Setup Manager** and the related **Page Setup** dialog box.
12. Briefly describe the function of the **Plot** dialog box and explain when it is used in relation to the **Page Setup Manager** and **Page Setup** dialog box.
13. Explain the importance of a well-defined page setup.
14. How can you identify which page setup is tied to the current layout?
15. What is a plot device?
16. Define *sheet size*.
17. What factors should you consider when you select a sheet size for a drawing?
18. Which ASME standards specify sheet sizes?
19. What is the plot offset of a layout?
20. Define *drawing scale*.
21. What are plot styles?
22. Briefly explain the purpose of a plot style table.
23. How do you assign plot styles in a color-dependent plot style?
24. Briefly explain the function of a named plot style table.
25. How can you be certain that your page setup options will produce the desired plot?

Drawing Problems

Start AutoCAD if it is not already started. Follow the specific instructions for each problem.

Note: *Some of the problems in this chapter are built on problems from previous chapters. If you have not yet completed those problems, complete them now.*

▼ Basic

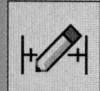

1. Use a word processor to list five items commonly found in a layout. Provide a brief description of each item.

2. Start a new drawing using the acad.dwt template. Create a plot style table named Black35mm.cbt that will plot all colors in the AutoCAD drawing in black ink on the paper, with a lineweight of 0.35 mm. (*Hint:* To make the same change to a property of all the plot styles, select the first plot style in the list, in this case Color 1, then scroll to the end of the list, hold down the [Shift] key, and select the last plot style in the list, in this case Color 255.) Save the drawing as P28-2.

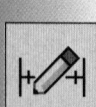

3. Start a new drawing using the acad -Named Plot Styles.dwt template. Create a plot style table named BlackShades.stb. Create the following plot styles:
   - Black100% with color set to black, all other properties set to their default values.
   - Black50% with color set to black, screening set to 50, all other properties set to their default values.
   - Black25% with color set to black, screening set to 25, all other properties set to their default values.

   Save the drawing as P28-3.

▼ Intermediate

4. Open P12-15 and save as P28-4. The P28-4 file should be active. Delete the default **Layout2**. Create a new B-size sheet layout by following these steps:
   A. Rename the default **Layout1** to **B-SIZE**.
   B. Select the **B-SIZE** layout and access the **Page Setup Manager**.
   C. Modify the **B-SIZE** page setup according to the following settings:
   - **Printer/Plotter:** Select a printer or plotter that can plot a B-size sheet
   - **Paper size:** Select the appropriate B-size sheet (varies with printer or plotter)
   - **Plot area:** Layout
   - **Plot offset:** 0,0
   - **Plot scale:** 1:1 (1 inch = 1 unit)
   - **Plot style table:** monochrome.ctb
   - **Plot with plot styles**
   - **Plot paperspace last**
   - Do not check **Hide paperspace objects**
   - **Drawing orientation:** Select the appropriate orientation (varies with printer or plotter)

   Resave P28-4.

5. Open P12-16 and save as P28-5. The P28-5 file should be active. Delete the default **Layout2**. Create a new A2-size sheet layout according to the following steps:

A. Rename the default **Layout1** to **A2-SIZE**.

B. Select the **A2-SIZE** layout and access the **Page Setup Manager**.

C. Modify the **A2-SIZE** page setup according to the following settings:
   - **Printer/Plotter:** Select a printer or plotter that can plot an A2-size sheet
   - **Paper size:** Select the appropriate A2-size sheet (varies with printer or plotter)
   - **Plot area:** Layout
   - **Plot offset:** 0,0
   - **Plot scale:** 1:1 (1 mm = 1 unit)
   - **Plot style table:** monochrome.ctb
   - **Plot with plot styles**
   - **Plot paperspace last**
   - Do not check **Hide paperspace objects**
   - **Drawing orientation:** Select the appropriate orientation (varies with printer or plotter)

Resave P28-5.

6. Open P8-18 and save as P28-6. The P28-6 file should be active. Delete the default **Layout2**. Create a new B-size sheet layout according to the following steps:

A. Rename the default **Layout1** to **B-SIZE**.

B. Select the **B-SIZE** layout and access the **Page Setup Manager**.

C. Modify the **B-SIZE** page setup according to the following settings:
   - **Printer/Plotter:** Select a printer or plotter that can plot a B-size sheet
   - **Paper size:** Select the appropriate B-size sheet (varies with printer or plotter)
   - **Plot area:** Layout
   - **Plot offset:** 0,0
   - **Plot scale:** 1:1 (1 inch = 1 unit)
   - **Plot style table:** monochrome.ctb
   - **Plot with plot styles**
   - **Plot paperspace last**
   - Do not check **Hide paperspace objects**
   - **Drawing orientation:** Select the appropriate orientation (varies with printer or plotter)

Resave P28-6.

▼ Advanced

7. Use a word processor to write a report of approximately 250 words explaining the difference between model space and paper space and describing the importance of using layouts. Cite at least three examples from actual industry applications of using layouts to prepare a multi-sheet drawing. Use at least four drawings to illustrate your report.

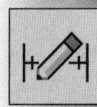

For Problems 8 through 11:

- *Start a new drawing for each problem using an appropriate template of your choice. The template should include layers and text, dimension, multileader, and table styles, when necessary, for drawing the given objects. Add layers and text, dimension, multileader, and table styles as needed.*

- *Draw all objects using appropriate layers and text, dimension, multileader, and table styles, justification, and format.*

- *Follow the specific instructions for each problem. Use only drawing and editing tools and techniques you have already learned. Use your own judgment and approximate dimensions when necessary.*

- *Apply dimensions accurately using ASME or appropriate industry standards.*

8. Draw and dimension the wood beam details shown. Establish the missing information using your own specifications, or determine the correct size of items not dimensioned. Prepare a single layout for plotting on a C-size sheet using the monochrome.ctb plot style. Delete all other layouts. Save the drawing as P28-8.

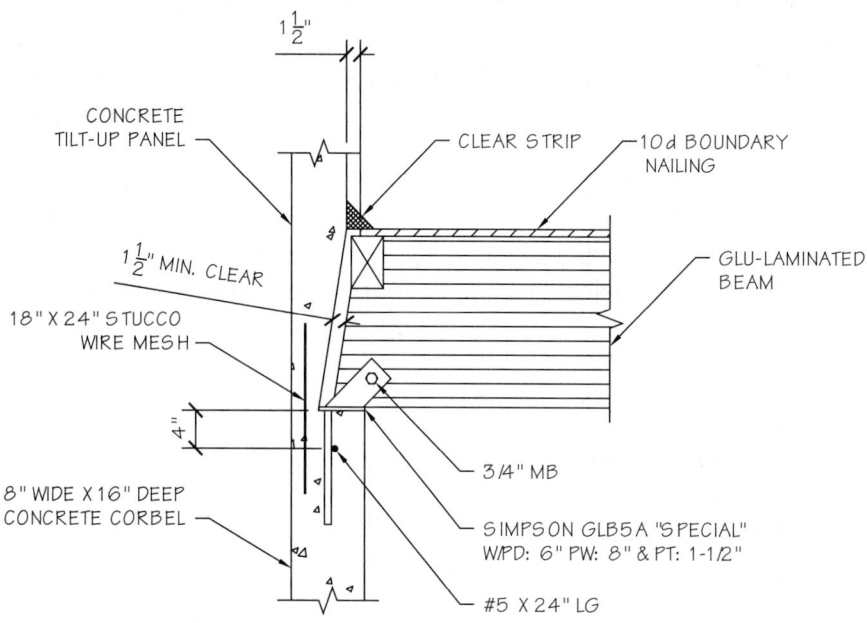

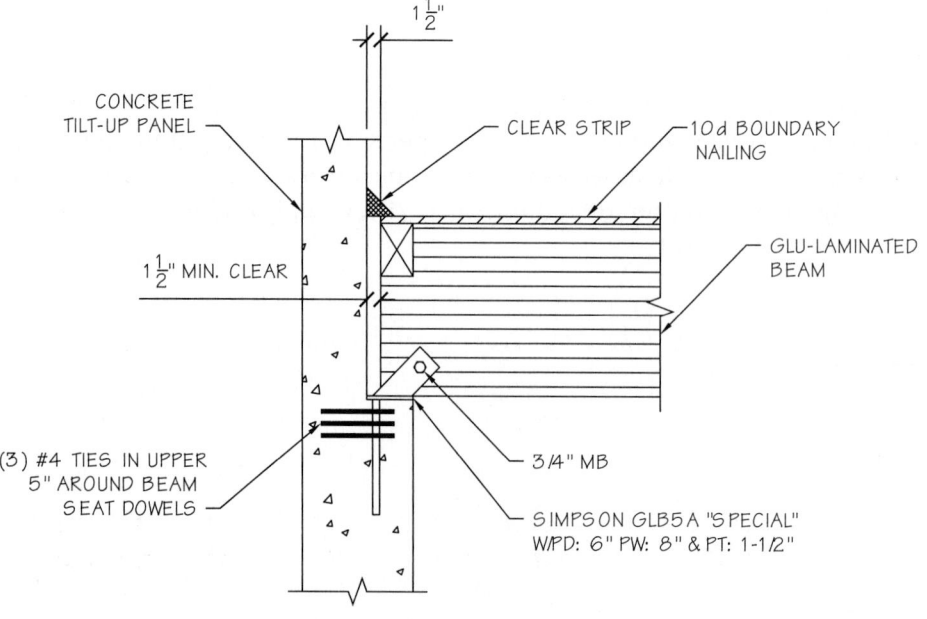

9. Draw and dimension the views of the support shown. Prepare a single layout for plotting on an A3-size sheet using the monochrome.ctb plot style. Delete all other layouts. Save the drawing as P28-9.

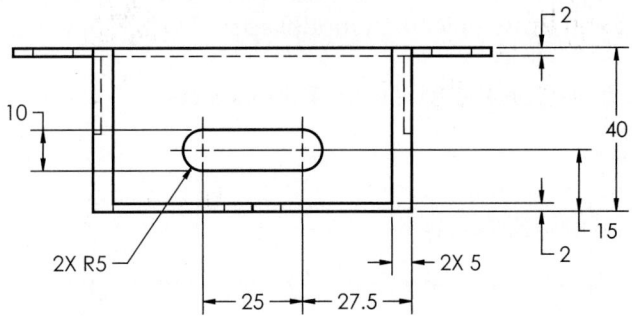

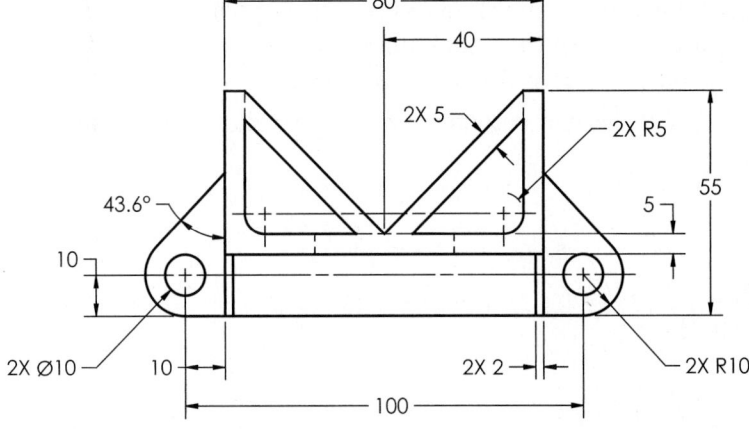

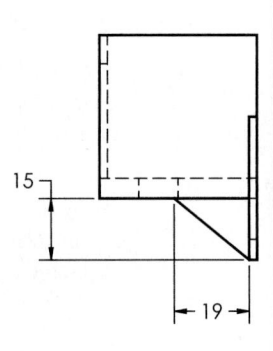

10. Research the design of an existing drive sprocket with the following specifications: single strand with hub, accepts ANSI 50 chain, 28 teeth, 5/8" pitch, finished 1" bore with 1/4"× 1/8" ANSI keyway and two set screws, steel material. Create a dimensioned 2D sketch of the existing design from manufacturer's specifications or from measurements taken from an actual sprocket. Start a new drawing from scratch or use a decimal-unit template of your choice. Draw and dimension the views required to document the design. Prepare a single layout for plotting on an appropriate sheet using the monochrome.ctb plot style. Delete all other layouts. Save the drawing as P28-10.

11. Create a dimensioned 2D sketch of the floor plan of a precast concrete restroom for a public park. Design the restroom to fit a 16'-0" × 16'-0" concrete slab foundation. Divide the restroom to provide separate stalls for men and women. Use dimensions based on your experience, research, and measurements. Start a new drawing from scratch or use an architectural template of your choice. Draw and dimension the floor plan from your sketch. Prepare a single layout for plotting on an appropriate sheet using the monochrome.ctb plot style. Delete all other layouts. Save the drawing as P28-11.

AutoCAD Certified Associate Exam Practice

Answer the following questions. Write your answers on a separate sheet of paper.

1. At what scale should you draw objects in model space? *Select the one item that best answers the question.*
   - A. choose a scale based on the true size of the objects
   - B. full scale (1:1)
   - C. half scale (1:2)
   - D. quarter scale (1:4)
   - E. no particular scale is necessary

2. Which of the following methods can you use to create a new layout? *Select all that apply.*
   - A. pick **New** and **Layout** from the **Application Menu**
   - B. pick the **New...** button in the **Page Setup Manager**
   - C. pick the **New Layout** button in the **Quick View Drawings** tool
   - D. pick the **New Layout** button in the **Quick View Layouts** tool
   - E. right-click on a current layout and select **New layout**

3. Which of the following plot styles can you use in a drawing that uses named plot styles? *Select all that apply.*
   - A. acad.stb
   - B. Fill Patterns.ctb
   - C. grayscale.ctb
   - D. monochrome.stb
   - E. My Plot Style Table.stb

AutoCAD Certified Professional Exam Practice

Follow the instructions in the problem. Write your answers on a separate sheet of paper.

1. **Navigate to this chapter on the Student Web site and open CPE-28pagesetup.dwg.** Assuming that you print this drawing using a color printer, in what color will objects drawn on the **Objects** layer plot?

2. **Navigate to this chapter on the Student Web site and open CPE-28sheetsize.dwg.** Use appropriate inquiry tools to determine the answer to this question. What sheet size is Layout 1 most likely designed to plot?

Learning Objectives

After completing this chapter, you will be able to do the following:

✓ Add layout content.
✓ Use floating viewports.
✓ Create properly scaled final drawings.
✓ Preview and plot layouts.

This chapter explores the additional steps to complete layout setup. You will learn to add content to a layout and to place and use floating viewports. You will also use the **PLOT** tool to preview the plot and send the layout to a printer, plotter, or alternate electronic format.

Layout Content

Model space provides an environment to create drawing views and add dimensions and annotations directly to views. Layouts provide an effective method to display model space content using floating viewports and to add items such as:

• Border and title block
• Revision history block
• General notes
• Bill of materials, parts list, schedules, legend, and other associated lists
• Sheet annotation and symbols such as titles, north arrow, and graphic scale

Layouts provide flexibility to lay out, scale, and prepare a final drawing. Consider the objects placed in model space to be drawing content and the objects you add to a layout to be sheet content. A complete drawing forms when you bring drawing and sheet content together. See Figure 29-1.

Drawing in Paper Space

A layout is a representation of a flat piece of paper. As a result, paper space is a 2D drawing environment. Most 2D drawing and editing tools and options described throughout this textbook function the same in paper space as in model space. However, some tools are specific to or most commonly used in either model space or paper

Figure 29-1. Dimensioned drawing views created in model space, combined with a border, title block, revision history block, and general notes created in paper space, form the final drawing.

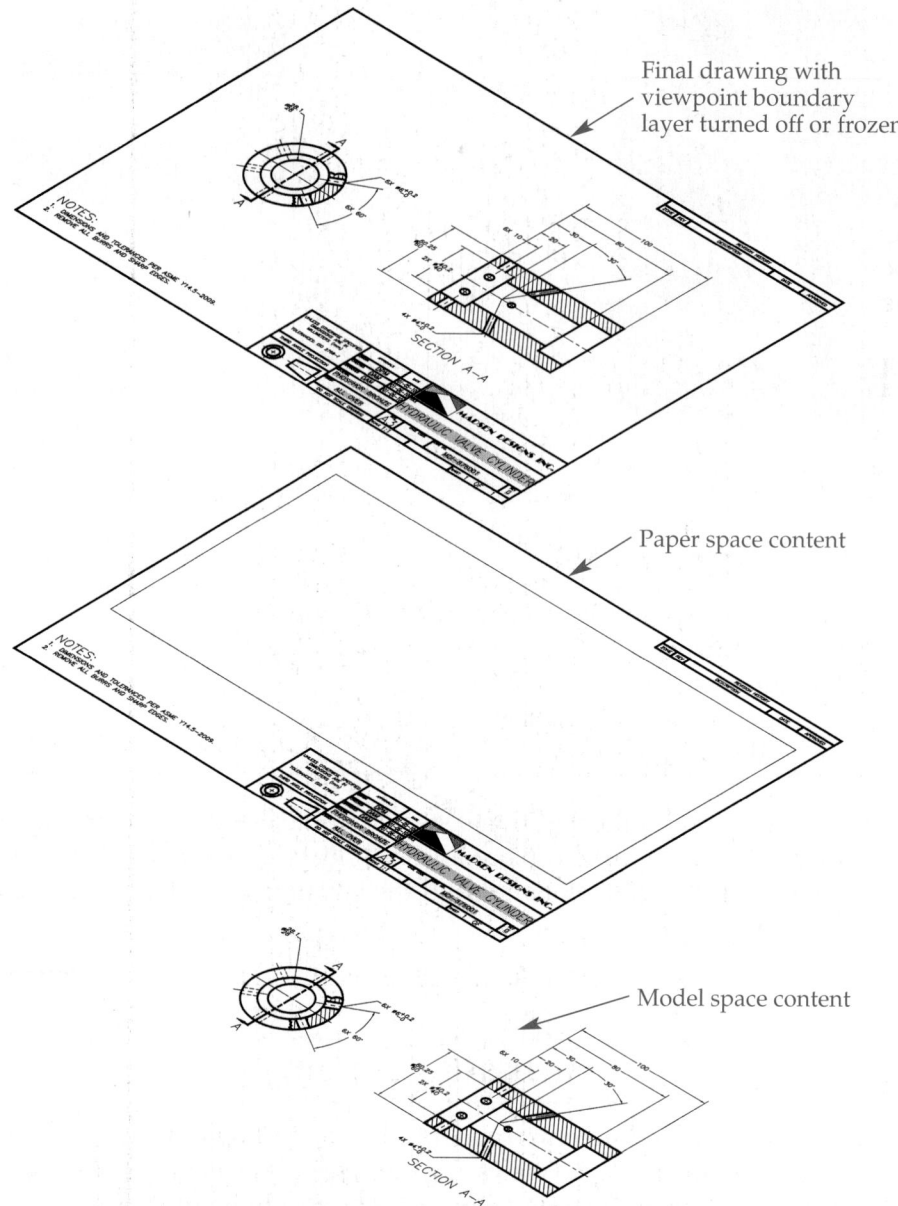

Final drawing with viewpoint boundary layer turned off or frozen

Paper space content

Model space content

space. For example, the **Full Navigation Wheel** appears by default when you access the **SteeringWheel** view tool in model space. The **2D Navigation Wheel** appears in paper space and is specific to 2D drafting.

> **NOTE**
>
> Although paper space is a 2D environment, you can display 3D models created in model space in paper space floating viewports.

As in model space, you typically draw geometry on a layout at full scale. One difference between model space and paper space is that objects in model space may be very large or very small, while paper space objects always correspond to the sheet size. Draw all layout content using the actual size you want the objects to appear on the plotted sheet. Use multiline or single-line text or blocks with attributes to add layout content such as general notes, view titles, and similar annotations to a layout. Place a bill of materials, parts list, schedules, or similar tabular information using the **TABLE** tool or blocks with attributes. Typically, you will create items such as a border, title block, and revision history block as blocks, often with attributes, and then insert these items into the layout.

Use layers appropriate for the layout and the objects added to the layout. Consider using a single layer named SHEET, for example, on which you draw all layout content. Another option is to use layers specific to layout items, such as a BORDER layer for the border and a TITLE or A-ANNO-TTBL layer for the title block. Assign a layer named Viewport, VPORT, or A-ANNO-NPLT, for example, to floating viewports so you can turn off, freeze, or set the viewport boundary to "no plot" before plotting.

NOTE

The default floating viewport boundary assumes the layer that is current when you first access a layout. If you use the default viewport, it may be necessary to change the layer on which it is drawn.

The Layout Origin

Most drawing and editing in paper space occurs on the sheet, which is the white rectangle you see on the gray background. However, it is possible, and necessary in some applications, to create objects off the sheet. When drawing and editing on a layout, remember that the origin (0,0) is controlled by the X and Y values you enter in the **Plot offset** area of the **Page Setup** dialog box. For example, if you draw a line with a start point of (1,1), the line begins 1 unit to the left and 1 unit up from the plot origin. The default origin position is at the lower-left corner of the printable area. See Figure 29-2. Refer to Chapter 28 for more information about plot origin and the **Plot offset** area of the **Page Setup** dialog box.

Layout content often references the edge of the sheet. For example, you might position a border 1/2" inside of the sheet edge. In this situation, it is usually best to define the layout origin as the lower-left corner of the sheet. The best option is to select the **Edge of paper** radio button in the **Specify plot offset relative to** area in the **Publish and Plot** tab of the **Options** dialog box. In the **Plot offset** area of the **Page Setup** dialog box, use values of 0.000 in the X and Y offset text boxes to locate the plot origin at the lower-left corner of the sheet. This is an excellent way to center the drawing on the sheet.

Figure 29-2.
The default location of the plot origin is often not appropriate, because all point entry is in reference to the lower-left corner of the printable area. Change the location of the plot origin to define the lower-left corner of the sheet as the (0,0) point.

The default origin is located at the lower-left corner of the printable area

Set the plot origin at the lower-left corner of the sheet

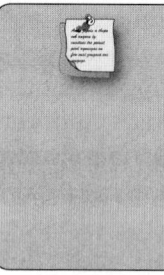
A second option to relate content to the lower-left corner of the sheet is to select the **Printable area** radio button in the **Specify plot offset relative to** area in the **Publish and Plot** tab of the **Options** dialog box. Then identify the values of the lower-right corner of the printable area. Information about the printable area is available in the **Device and Document Settings** tab of the plotter **Configuration Editor**. Next, in the **Plot offset** area of the **Page Setup** dialog box, change the X and Y plot offset values to the values of the lower-left corner of the printable area. The values you enter must be negative. The origin offsets from the printable area, so if you use a different plotter or plot configuration, the printable area may change, causing the offset to shift.

Exercise 29-1

Access the Student Web site (www.g-wlearning.com/CAD) and complete Exercise 29-1.

Floating Viewports

The primary advantage of using floating viewports in a paper space layout is the ability to prepare scaled drawings without increasing or decreasing the actual size of drawing views or sheet content. You can also create multiple viewports on a single layout to show differently scaled or alternate drawing views. For example, a single sheet might contain a floor plan drawn at a 1/4″ = 1′-0″ scale, an eave detail drawn at a 3/4″ = 1′-0″ scale, and a foundation detail drawn at a 3/4″ = 1′-0″ scale. See **Figure 29-3**.

A floating viewport boundary is the portion of the viewport that you see. Everything inside the viewport shows through from model space. Use tools such as **MOVE, ERASE, STRETCH,** and **COPY** to modify the viewport boundary in paper space. Use display tools such as **VIEW, PAN,** and **ZOOM** to modify the display of model space objects in the floating viewport. Additional options are available for adjusting how objects appear, according to the layers you assign to objects. Layer control allows you to define how the drawing appears within the viewport. Be sure a layout tab is current as you work through the following sections describing floating viewports.

Figure 29-3. An example of an architectural layout, ready to plot, that includes three floating viewports used to display drawing views at different scales. The layer on which the viewports are drawn is off or frozen for plotting.

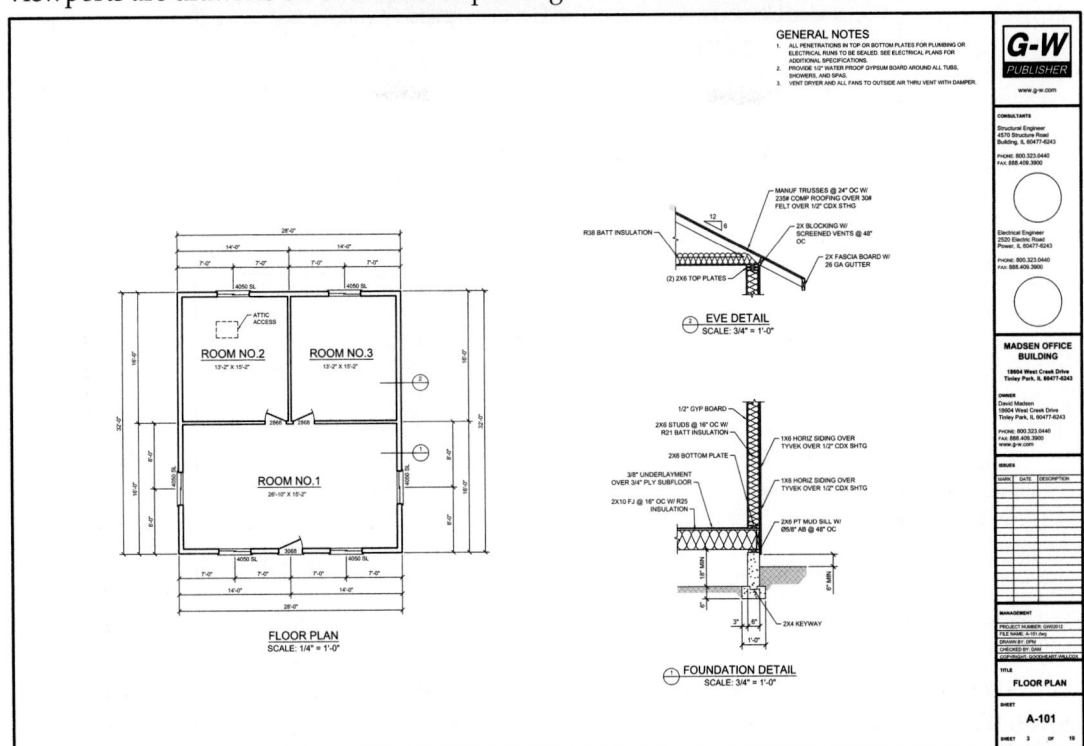

PROFESSIONAL TIP

When you first select a layout and enter paper space, a rectangular floating viewport appears, showing the objects in model space. As part of layout setup, consider using the **ERASE** tool to erase the default viewport and draw a new viewport (or several viewports). Erasing the default viewport, or erasing everything in the layout, does not erase objects in model space.

Creating Floating Viewports

AutoCAD provides a variety of ways to create new floating viewports in paper space. The **Viewports** dialog box provides options for creating one to four new viewports according to a specific viewport configuration. The **MVIEW** tool is a text-based method for creating new viewports. The **MVIEW** tool provides the same options found in the **Viewports** dialog box, plus additional viewport definition options. You can also access many of the methods for creating new viewports directly from the **Viewports** panel on the **View** ribbon tab.

Using the Viewports Dialog Box

The **Viewports** dialog box, shown in **Figure 29-4**, looks and functions the same in paper space as in model space, except for a few differences. One difference is that the **Viewport spacing:** text box replaces the **Apply to:** drop-down list in the **New Viewports** tab in paper space. The **Viewport spacing:** text box is available only when you select a standard viewport configuration that places two or more viewports, as shown in **Figure 29-4**. Enter a value to define the space between multiple viewports.

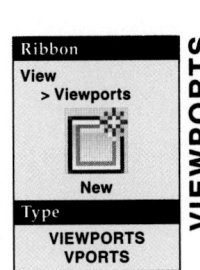

Ribbon

View
> Viewports

New

Type
VIEWPORTS
VPORTS

VIEWPORTS

Figure 29-4. The **Viewports** dialog box with the **New Viewports** tab selected. The **Viewport Spacing:** setting is available when paper space is active.

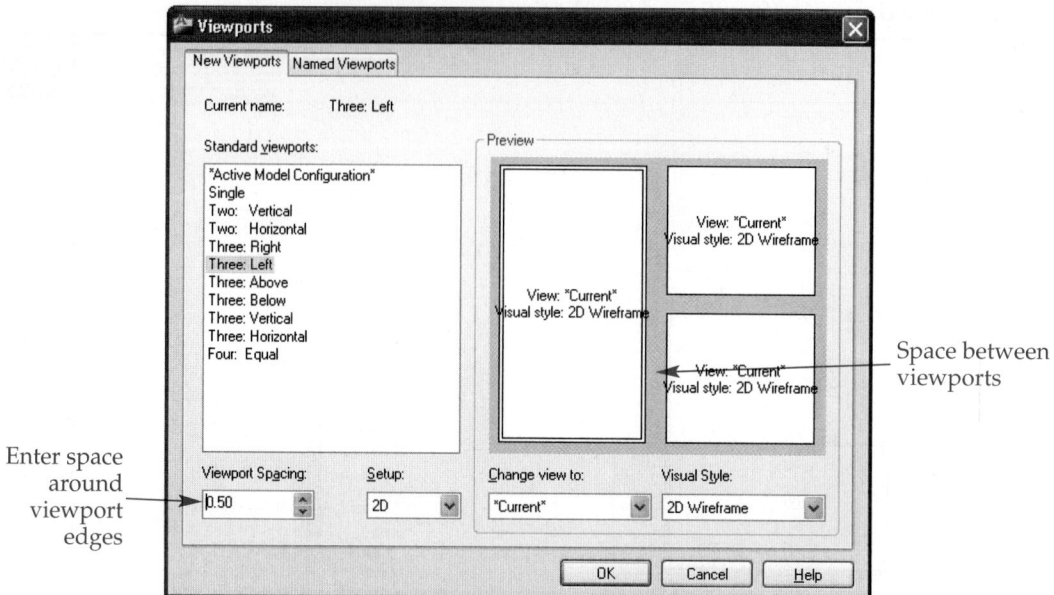

Enter space around viewport edges

Space between viewports

Another difference is that when you pick the **OK** button to create floating viewports, the viewports do not automatically appear, as in model space. Instead, you must specify a first and second corner to define the area occupied by the viewport configuration. See **Figure 29-5**. If you use the **Fit** option, AutoCAD fits the viewport(s) into the printable area without requiring you to pick points. Refer to Chapter 6 for more information about the **Viewports** dialog box.

Exercise 29-2

Access the Student Web site (www.g-wlearning.com/CAD) and complete Exercise 29-2.

Using the MVIEW Tool

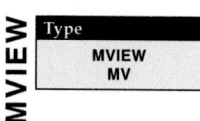

Type
MVIEW
MV

Access the **MVIEW** tool and create a single viewport by selecting opposite corners of the viewport, pressing [Enter] or the space bar, or right-clicking and choosing **Enter** to activate the **Fit** option. The **Fit** option creates a viewport that fills the printable area. The **2**, **3**, and **4** options provide preset viewport configurations similar to those available from the **Viewports** dialog box. The **Shadeplot** option includes the same options available from the **Visual Style** drop-down list in the **Viewports** dialog box, which is explained in *AutoCAD and Its Applications—Advanced.*

Figure 29-5. Select two points on the layout to specify the area to be filled by the viewport configuration. Notice that the viewport spacing forms as specified in the **Viewports** dialog box. This example shows the initial placement of three structural details using a three-viewport configuration. Each viewport will eventually display a single detail.

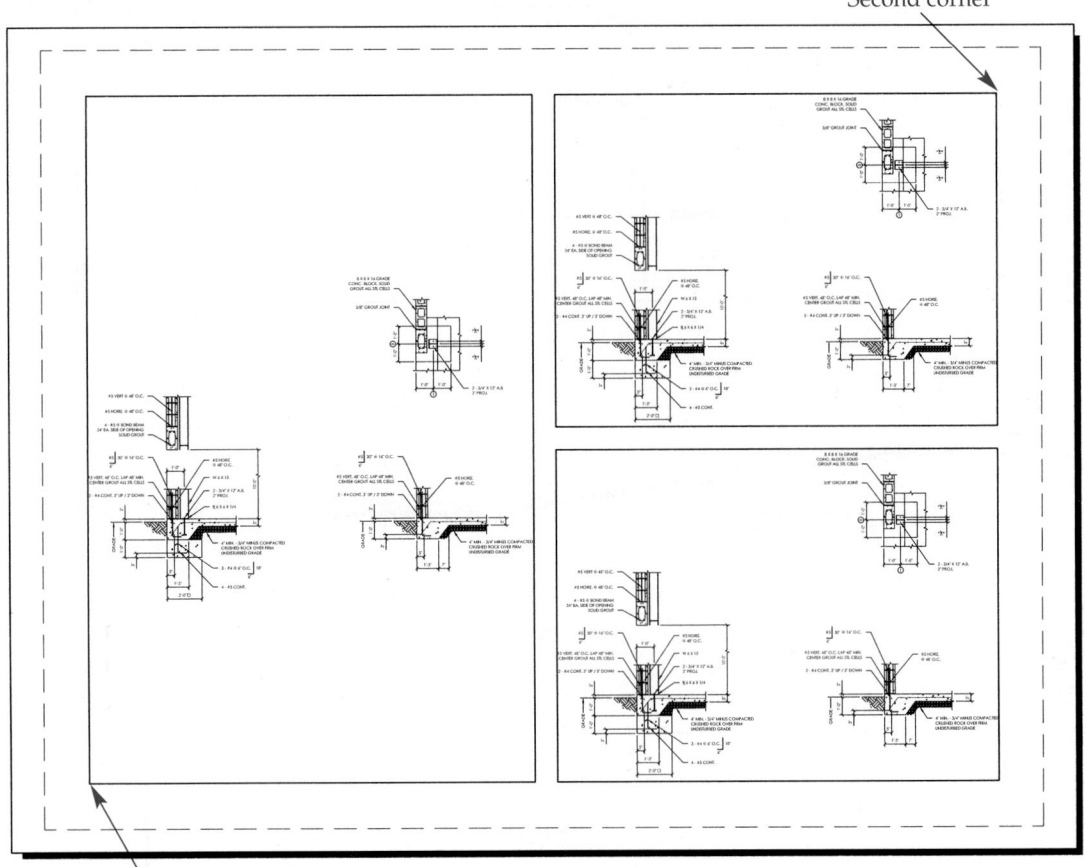

Second corner

First corner

Choose the **Restore** option to convert a saved viewport configuration into individual floating viewports. Typically, drafters use the **Restore** option to convert tiled viewports into floating viewports. For example, if model space displays two tiled viewports, use the **Restore** option to create two floating viewports. See **Figure 29-6.** After you access the **Restore** option, enter the viewport configuration name. In the previous example, select the **Active** option to use the two tiled viewports of the active viewport configuration in model space. Next, select opposite corners of the viewport, press [Enter] or the space bar, or right-click and choose **Enter** to activate the **Fit** option. The model space tiled viewport configuration now appears in paper space as floating viewports.

Figure 29-6. A—A **Two: Horizontal** tiled viewport configuration in model space. B—The model space tiled viewports converted to floating viewports using the **Restore** option of the **MVIEW** tool. This example shows the initial placement of two structural details using a two-viewport configuration. Each viewport will eventually display a single detail.

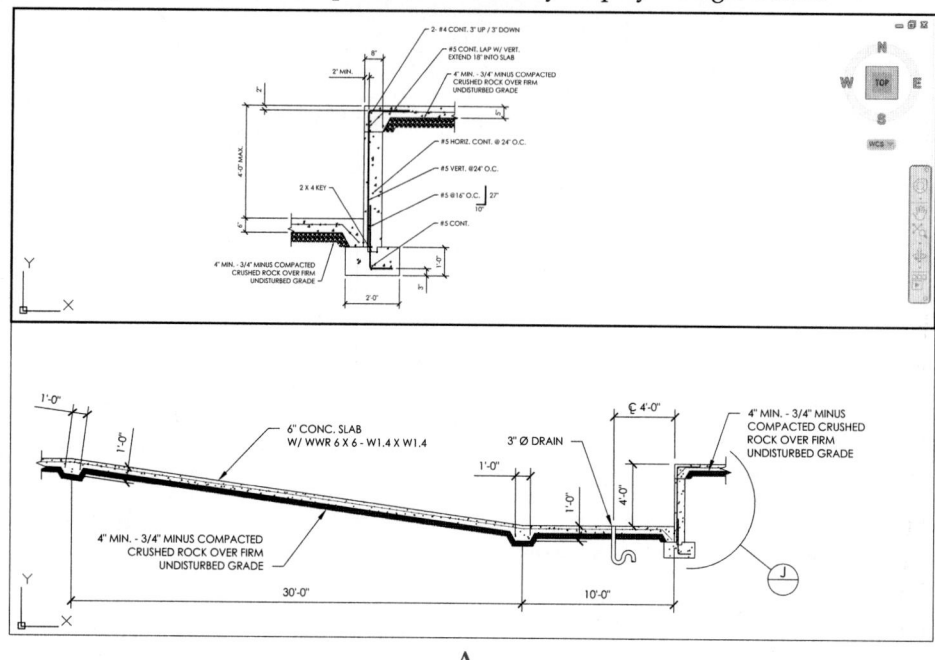

A

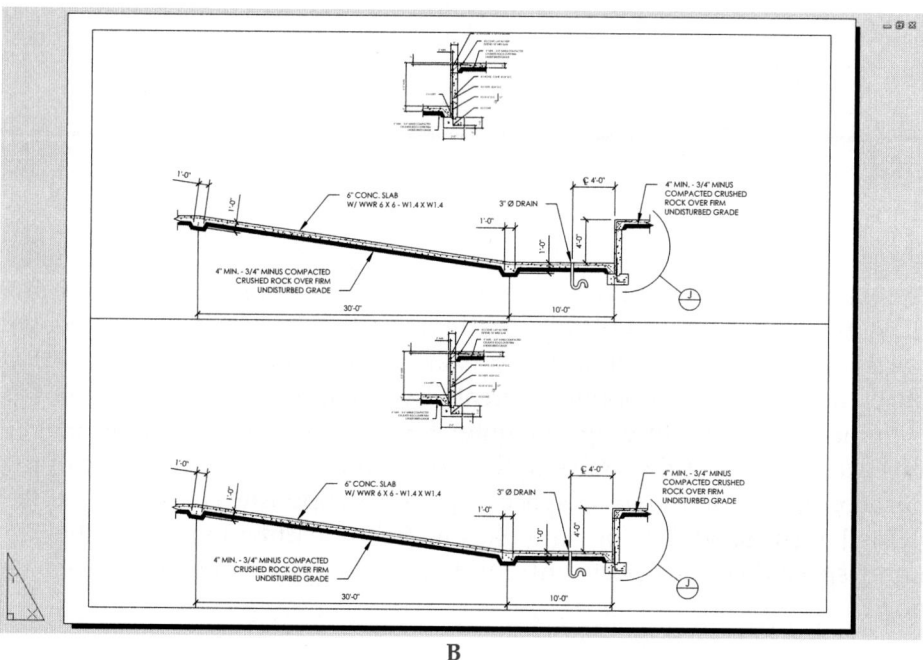

B

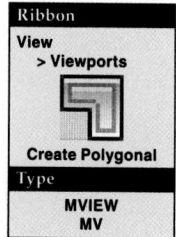

Ribbon

View
> **Viewports**

Create Polygonal

Type

MVIEW
MV

Forming Polygonal Floating Viewports

The most common shape for a floating viewport is rectangular, which is suitable for many applications. As an alternative, use the **Polygonal** option of the **MVIEW** tool to form a polygonal floating viewport boundary. Use the ribbon to access the **Polygonal** option easily. Construct a polygonal viewport using the same techniques you use to draw a closed polyline object. The viewport can be any closed shape composed of lines and arcs. **Figure 29-7** shows a polygonal floating viewport used to define the maximum drawing view area 1/2″ in from the border and title block.

Converting Objects to Floating Viewports

Use the **Object** option of the **MVIEW** tool to convert a closed object drawn in paper space to a floating viewport. Activate the **Object** option and select a closed shape, such as a circle, ellipse, or closed polyline shape, to convert the object to a viewport. **Figure 29-8** shows an example of a circle and rectangle converted to floating viewports.

Exercise 29-3

Access the Student Web site (www.g-wlearning.com/CAD) and complete Exercise 29-3.

Adjusting the Floating Viewport Boundary

For purposes of adjusting a floating viewport boundary, you should consider the boundary a closed object. For example, treat rectangular viewports like rectangles, polygonal viewports like closed polyline objects, circular viewports like circles, and elliptical viewports like ellipses. Use editing tools such as **MOVE**, **ERASE**, **STRETCH**, **COPY**, and grips as needed to modify the size, shape, and location of floating viewports. When you adjust a floating viewport, the "hole" cut through the sheet changes.

Figure 29-7. An example of a structural detail displayed in a polygonal floating viewport. The layer on which the viewport is drawn is turned off or frozen for plotting.

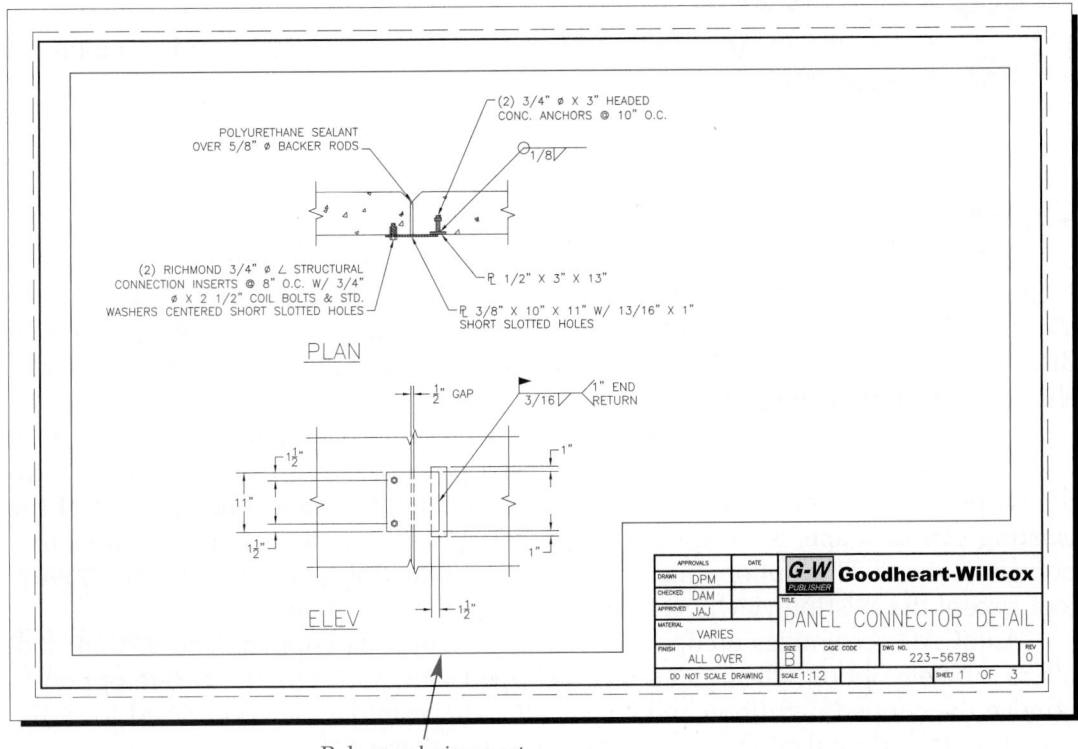

Polygonal viewport

Figure 29-8. You can convert any closed object to a floating viewport. This example shows a cover sheet with a plot plan viewport converted from a rectangle and a vicinity map converted from a circle. The layer on which these viewports are drawn remains on and thawed for plotting.

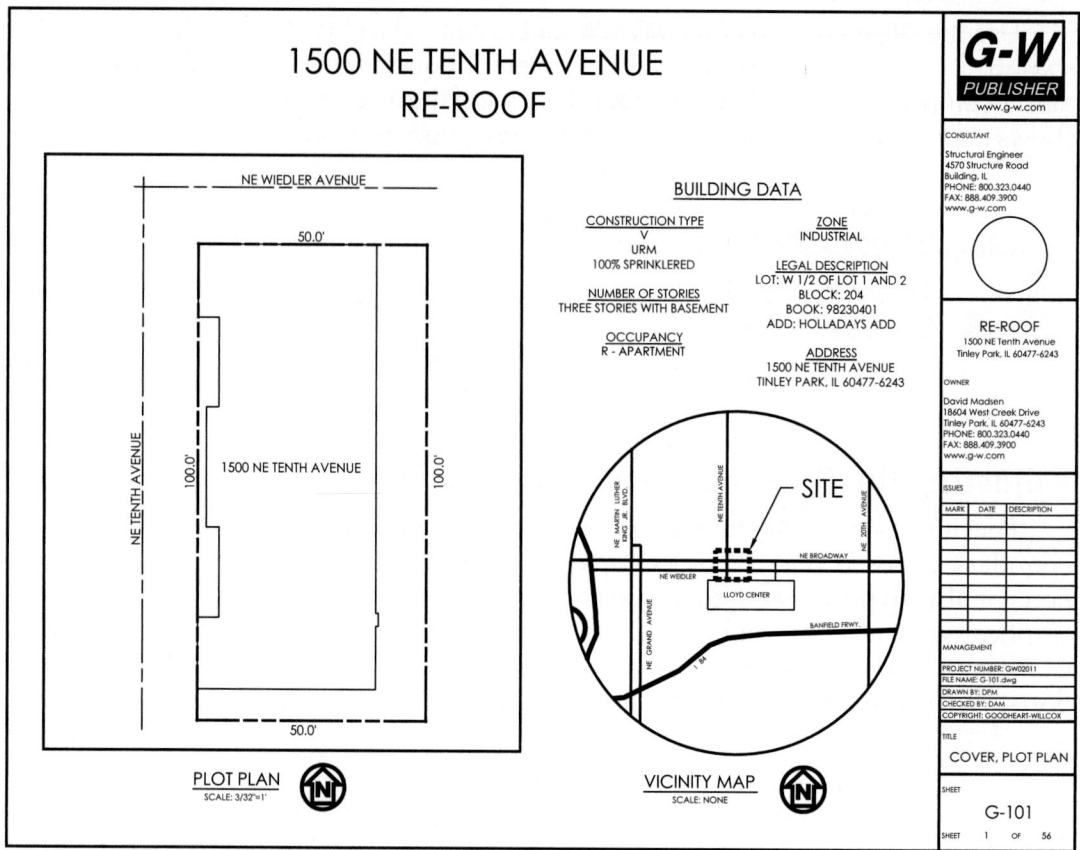

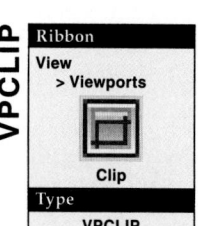

Exercise 29-4

Access the Student Web site (www.g-wlearning.com/CAD) and complete Exercise 29-4.

VPCLIP

Ribbon

View
> Viewports

Clip

Type

VPCLIP

Clipping Viewports

The **VPCLIP** tool allows you to redefine the boundary of an existing viewport. To access the tool from a shortcut menu, select a viewport and then right-click and pick **Viewport Clip**. You can clip a floating viewport to an existing closed object that you draw before accessing the **VPCLIP** tool, or you can clip the viewport to a polygonal shape that you create while using the tool.

After you access the **VPCLIP** tool, select the viewport to clip. Then select an existing closed shape, such as a circle, ellipse, or closed polyline, to recreate the viewport in the shape of the selected object. See **Figure 29-9**. An alternative, once you select the existing closed shape, is to use the **Polygonal** option to redefine the viewport to a polygonal shape. This option functions the same as the **Polygonal** option of the **MVIEW** tool, except the existing viewport transforms into the new shape.

AutoCAD recognizes a clipped floating viewport as clipped. The **VPCLIP** tool offers a **Delete** option when you select a clipped viewport. Use the **Delete** option to remove the clipped definition and convert the shape into a viewport sized to fit the extents of the original clipping object or polygonal shape.

Figure 29-9. An example of clipping a viewport showing a wall section to a closed polyline to create an eave detail. AutoCAD removes the original viewport and converts the rectangle to a viewport.

Polyline created using the **RECTANGLE** tool

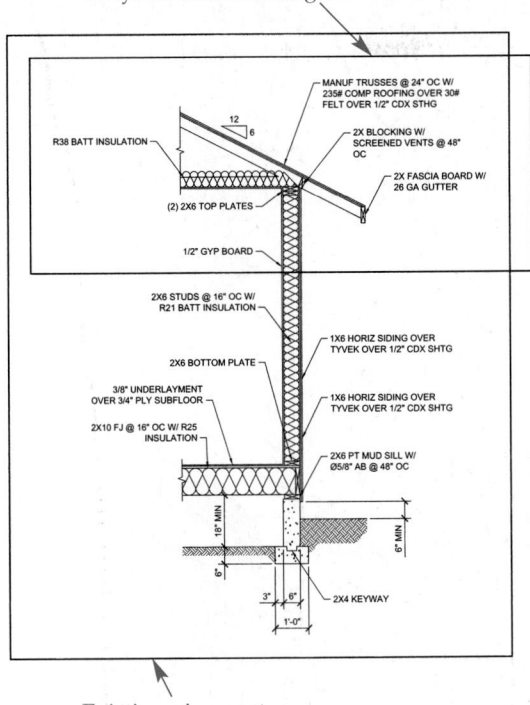

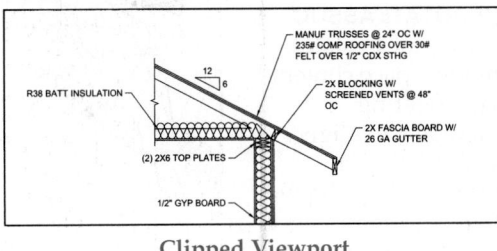

Clipped Viewport

Existing viewport

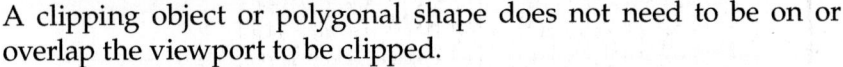

NOTE

A clipping object or polygonal shape does not need to be on or overlap the viewport to be clipped.

PROFESSIONAL TIP

Create floating viewports and adjust the size and shape of viewport boundaries after you insert the border, title block, and other layout content. This will allow you to position viewports so they do not interfere with layout information.

Rotating Model Space Content

The **VPROTATEASSOC** system variable setting determines what happens to model space content when you rotate a floating viewport. The variable uses a value of 1 by default. As a result, when you rotate a viewport, the display of objects in model space rotates to align with the viewport. See **Figure 29-10A**. The orientation of objects in model space does not change. In order to maintain the original alignment of model space content in a floating viewport, as shown in **Figure 29-10B**, access the **VPROTATEASSOC** system variable before rotating the viewport and enter a value of 0.

Figure 29-10.
An example of a highway cut and fill plan shown through a viewport. A—The default **VPROTATEASSOC** setting of 1 rotates model space content on a floating viewport to align with viewport rotation. B—Change the value to 0 to maintain the original model space orientation when you rotate a viewport.

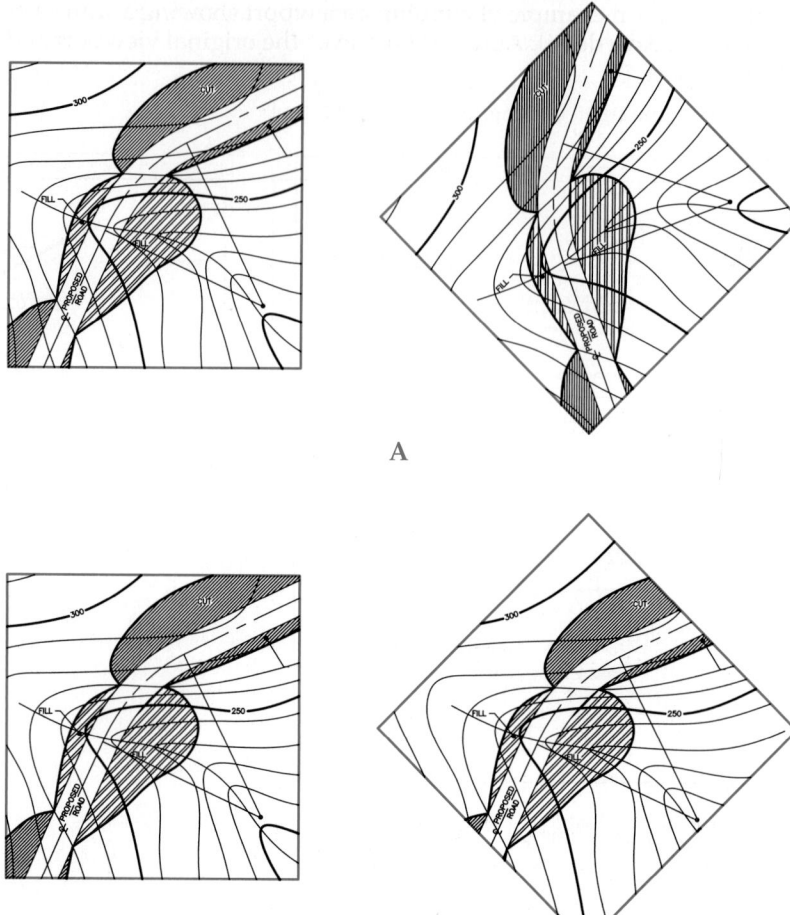

A

B

Activating and Deactivating Floating Viewports

Activate a floating viewport to work with model space objects while in paper space. This allows you to adjust the display of the model space drawing shown in the viewport. Repeat the process of activating and adjusting a viewport for every floating viewport in the layout to achieve the final drawing.

To activate a floating viewport, double-click inside the viewport area, press the **PAPER** button on the status bar, or type MSPACE or MS. If the layout contains a single viewport, the viewport appears highlighted, indicating that it is current. On the layout, the UCS icon disappears, and the model space UCS icon displays in the corner of each layout viewport. You are now working directly in model space, through the paper space viewport. The active and highlighted viewport is the viewport you double-click on or the newest viewport, depending on how you access the **MSPACE** tool. See Figure 29-11. To make a different viewport active, pick once inside the viewport.

Highlighted viewport is active

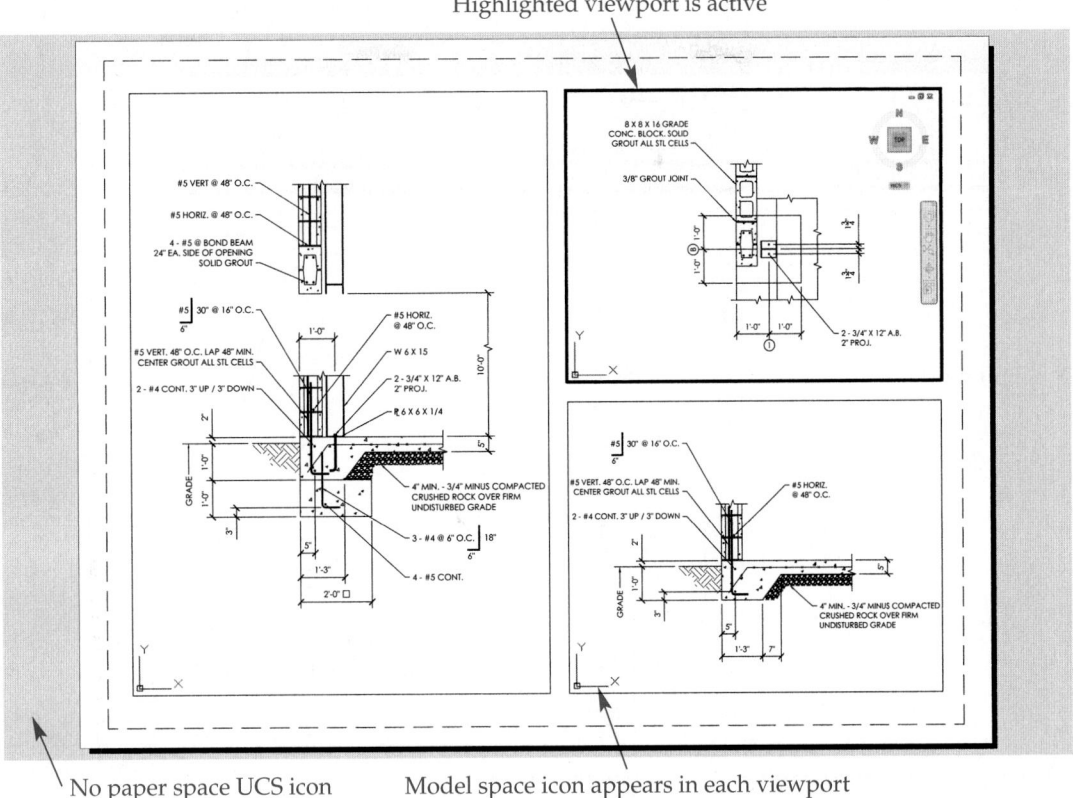

No paper space UCS icon   Model space icon appears in each viewport

After you adjust the display of all floating viewports, you must re-enter paper space to plot and continue working with the layout. To activate paper space, double-click outside a viewport, press the **MODEL** button on the status bar, or type PSPACE or PS. The layout space UCS icon reappears, and the model space UCS icon disappears from the corners of the viewports.

Scaling a Floating Viewport

The scale you assign to a floating viewport is the same as the drawing scale. The quickest way to set viewport scale is to activate a viewport, or pick a viewport boundary in paper space without activating the viewport. Then select the appropriate scale from the **Viewport Scale** flyout on the status bar. See Figure 29-12. An alternative is to pick the viewport to be scaled in paper space and access the **Properties** palette. Then choose a viewport scale from the **Standard scale** drop-down list.

If a scale is unavailable, or to change an existing scale, pick the **Annotation Scale** flyout on the status bar and choose **Custom...** to access the **Edit Scale List** dialog box. Move the highlighted scale up or down in the list using the **Move Up** or **Move Down** button. To remove the highlighted scale from the list, pick the **Delete** button.

Select the **Edit...** button to open the **Edit Scale** dialog box, where you can change the name of the scale and adjust the scale by entering the paper and drawing units. For example, a scale of 1/4″ = 1′-0″ uses a paper units value of .25 or 1 and a drawing units value of 12 or 48. To create a new annotation scale, pick the **Add...** button to display the **Add Scale** dialog box, which provides the same options as the **Edit Scale** dialog box. Pick the **Reset** button to restore the list to display the default scales.

Figure 29-12. Using the **Viewport Scale** flyout button on the status bar to set the drawing scale. This example shows scaling a multiview part drawing in a single viewport.

Active or selected viewport   Select a drawing scale from the list

Viewport scale flyout

NOTE

Changes you make in the **Edit Scale List** dialog box are stored with the drawing and are specific to the drawing. To make changes to the default scale list saved to the system registry, pick the **Default Scale List...** button in the **User Preferences** tab of the **Options** dialog box to access the **Default Scale List** dialog box. The options are the same as those in the **Edit Scale List** dialog box, but changes are saved as the default for new drawings, resetting the **Edit Scale List** dialog box.

CAUTION

Setting viewport scale is a zoom function that increases or decreases the *displayed* size of the drawing in the viewport. You can also use the **XP** option of the **ZOOM** tool to specify the scale of the active viewport. If you use an option of the **ZOOM** tool other than a specific **XP** value to adjust the drawing inside an active floating viewport, the drawing loses the correct scale. Once the viewport scale is set, do not zoom in or out. Lock the viewport, as described later in this chapter, to help ensure that the drawing remains properly scaled.

Scaling Annotations

You should always draw objects at their actual size, or full scale, in model space, regardless of the size of the objects. However, this method requires special consideration for annotations, hatches, and similar items added to objects in model space. You can adjust the appearance of annotations manually, but it is often best to use annotative objects to automate the process. Scaled viewports and annotative objects function together to scale drawings properly and increase multiview drawing flexibility. Chapter 30 explains annotative objects.

Controlling Linetype Scale

Adjust the **LTSCALE** system variable to make a global change to the linetype scale to increase or decrease the lengths of the dashes and spaces found in some linetypes. Modify the **LTSCALE** value as needed to make linetypes match standard drafting practices. However, depending on the size of objects in model space and the specified floating viewport scale, an **LTSCALE** value in model space may not be appropriate for paper space.

For example, an **LTSCALE** value of .5 is appropriate for an inch unit mechanical part drawing plotted at full scale. In this example, apply an **LTSCALE** value of .5 to model space and paper space because both environments function at full scale. If you scale the drawing to 2:1, a linetype scale of .25 (scale factor of 1/2 × **LTSCALE** value of .5 = .25) is needed in model space and paper space in order for lines to appear correct in both environments. By default, AutoCAD calculates the appropriate linetype scale display in model space and paper space according to the **LTSCALE** setting.

The **CELTSCALE**, **PSLTSCALE**, and **MSLTSCALE** system variables control how the **LTSCALE** system variable applies, or does not apply, to linetypes in model space and paper space. The **CELTSCALE**, **PSLTSCALE**, and **MSLTSCALE** system variables are set to 1 by default, and should be set to 1 in order for the **LTSCALE** value to apply correctly in model space and paper space. All linetypes will then appear with the same lengths of dashes and dots regardless of the floating viewport scale, and no matter whether you are in paper space or model space.

Using the previous example, lines will appear correctly in model space and at a scale of 1:1 and 2:1 in paper space. However, when you scale a floating viewport or change the annotation scale in model space, remember to use the **REGEN** tool to regenerate the display. Otherwise, the linetype scale will not update according to the new scale. The **MSLTSCALE** system variable is associated with the selected annotation scale, as described in Chapter 30.

Adjusting a View

When you first create a floating viewport, AutoCAD performs a **ZOOM Extents** to display everything in model space through the viewport. The **Scale to fit viewport scale** option accomplishes the same task. When you scale a viewport, AutoCAD adjusts the view from the center of the viewport, which often results in the appropriate display. However, you must adjust the view when you change the size or shape of the viewport, when a centered view is not appropriate, or to display a specific portion of the drawing. Use the **PAN** tool in an active viewport to redefine the displayed location of the view.

Boundary Adjustment

The viewport boundary can "cut off" a scaled model space drawing. This may be acceptable to display a portion of a view. However, to display the entire view, you can either increase the size of the viewport boundary or select a different scale to reduce the displayed size of the view to fit the viewport. If it is not appropriate to increase the size of the viewport or decrease the scale, use a larger sheet size. **Figure 29-13** shows

Figure 29-13. An example of a multiview part drawing in which it is appropriate to show all model space objects, but also necessary to display only a portion of model space to create a view enlargement. Use the **PAN** tool to adjust the position of model space objects in floating viewports.

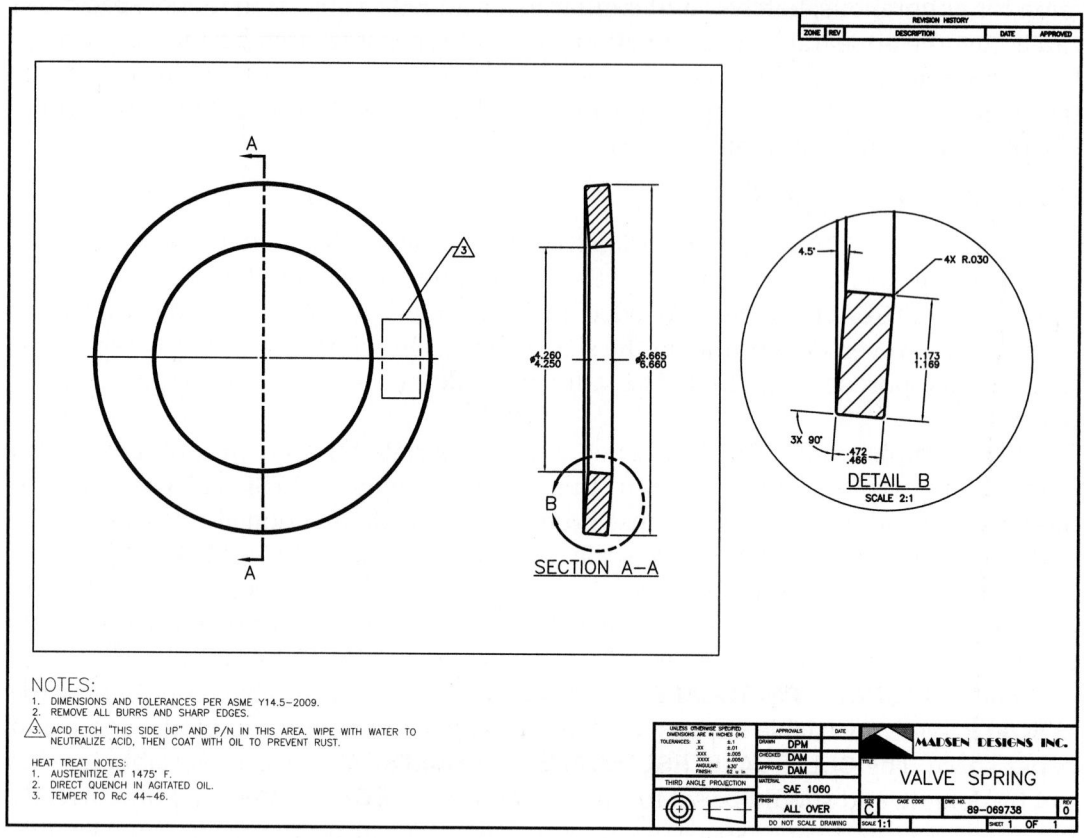

a drawing with two viewports. The rectangular viewport shows everything in model space at full scale. The circular viewport cuts off model space objects and displays objects at a 2:1 scale to create a detail.

Precision Adjustment and Alignment

The **PAN** tool is effective for adjusting model space content in a floating viewport, but it offers limited precision, especially when you are attempting to align views in different viewports. One way to adjust and align views precisely is to use the **MOVE** tool to move viewports, because objects shown in a viewport move with the viewport. Draw construction geometry, such as a line, on the layout or use object snaps and AutoTrack to reference specific points between views. Access the **MOVE** tool and select the viewport as the object to move, but specify the base point and second point on objects in model space or on construction geometry on the layout. Use object snaps to aid point selection. See **Figure 29-14.**

Type
MVSETUP

The **MVSETUP** tool provides another way to adjust and align views precisely. Choose the **Align** option and then select the **Horizontal** option to align views horizontally or the **Vertical alignment** option to align views vertically. A viewport becomes activated when you select an alignment option. Pick inside the viewport with the model space view to pan. Then specify a base point in model space from which model space pans. Use object snaps, AutoTrack, or construction geometry to aid point selection. Activate the viewport that contains the model space view with which to align, and specify a stationary point in model space to which the base point will pan horizontally or vertically. See **Figure 29-15.** Continue using the **MVSETUP** tool or cancel to exit.

Figure 29-14. Moving a floating viewport to position the center of the front elevation of this home in the center of a sheet. A—Select the viewport to be moved and a base point associated with model space objects. The X identifies the specified point for illustrative purposes only. B—Move the viewport to a point on the layout. This example uses construction lines to aid selection. Object snap and AutoTrack are also effective.

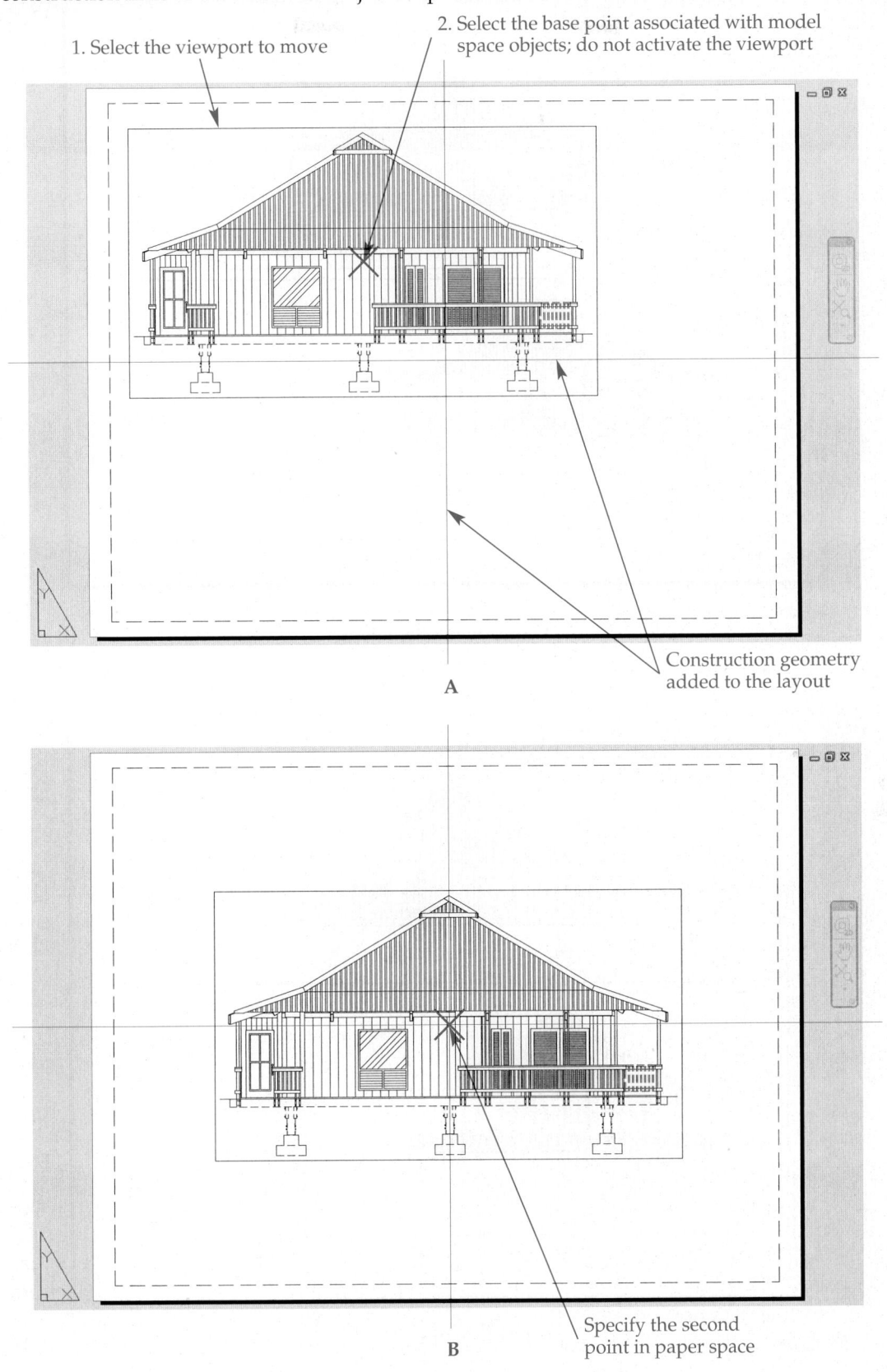

1. Select the viewport to move

2. Select the base point associated with model space objects; do not activate the viewport

Construction geometry added to the layout

A

Specify the second point in paper space

B

Figure 29-15. Using the **MVSETUP** tool, **Align** option, and **Vertical alignment** function to align views vertically in different floating viewports. The same process applies to using the **Horizontal** function of the **Align** option to align views horizontally.

Selected base point

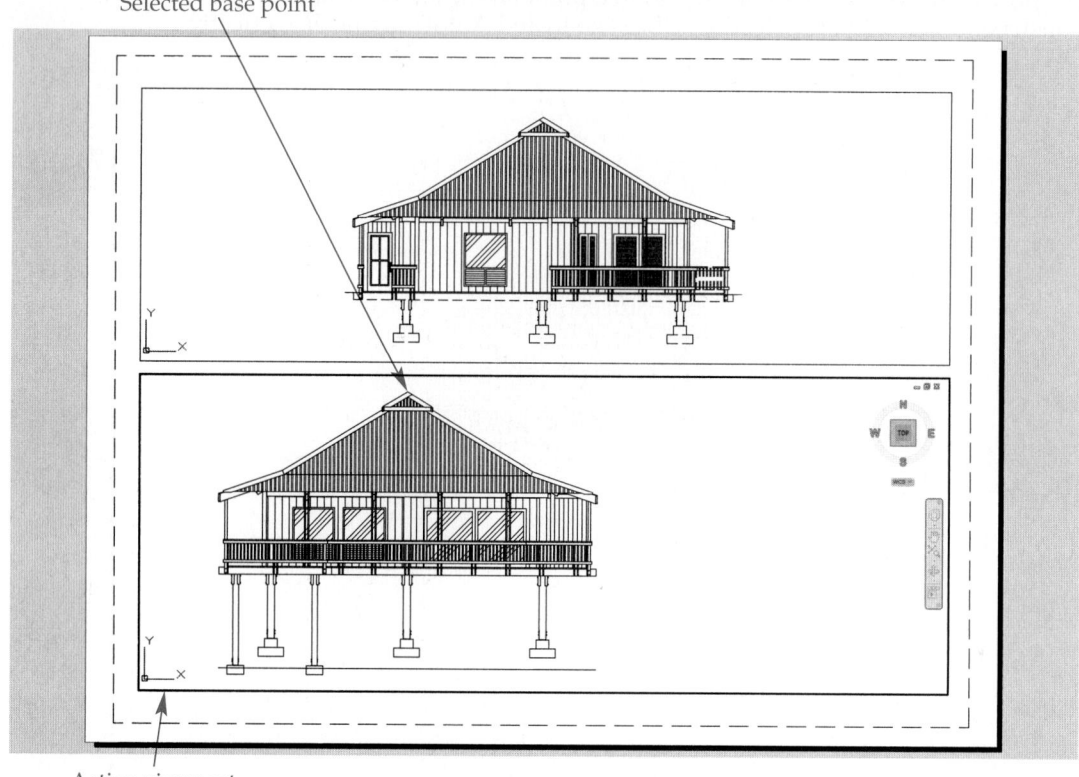

Active viewport

1. Specify the Base Point

Selected alignment point   Active viewpoint

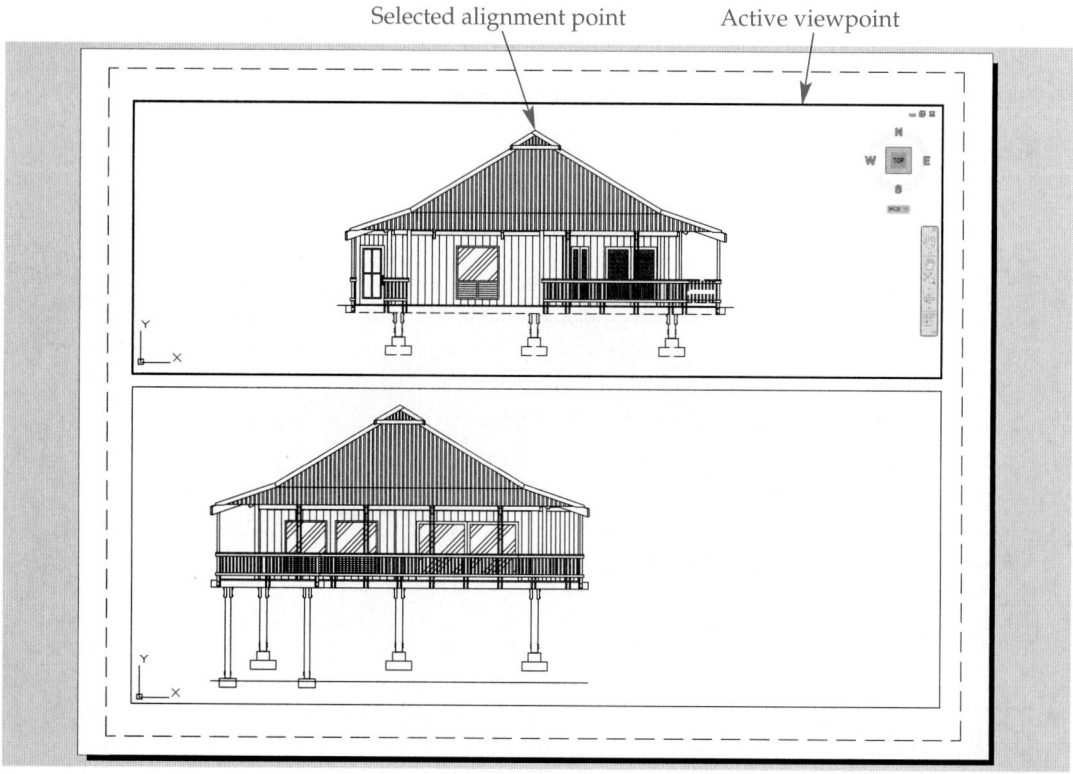

2. Specify the Alignment Point

Figure 29-15. *(Continued.)*

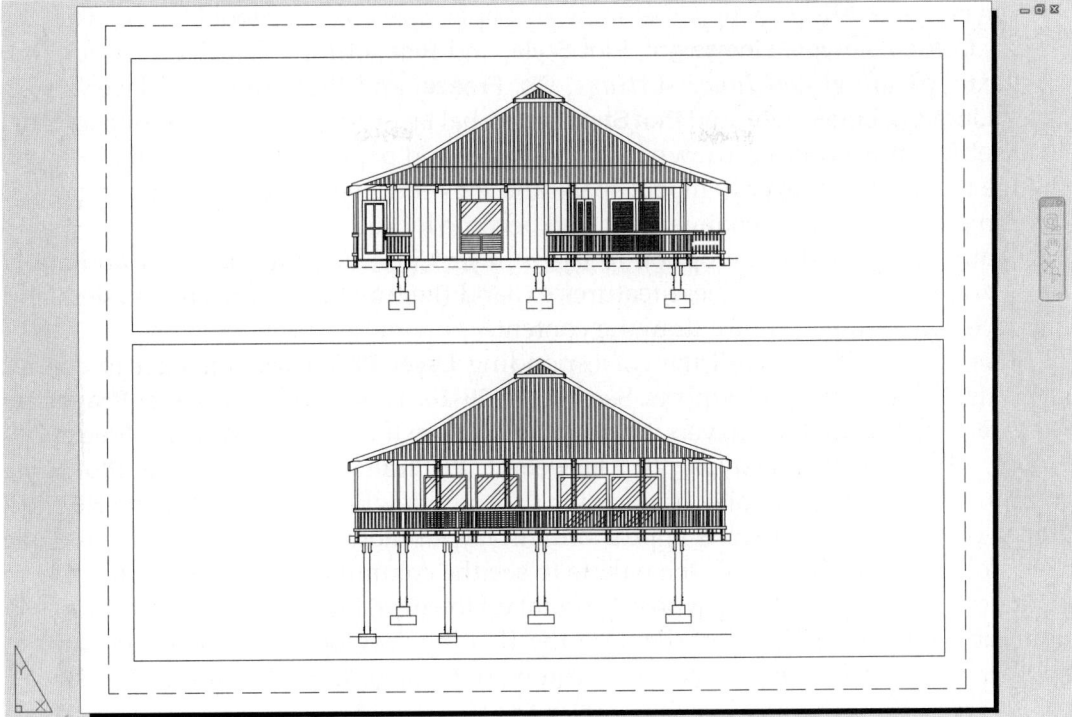

Aligned View

NOTE

The **MVSETUP** tool includes several additional options that are outdated, perform operations that you can accomplish more easily using other tools, or have limited application.

Locking and Unlocking Floating Viewports

After you adjust the drawing in the viewport to reflect the proper scale and view, lock the viewport so the scale and view orientation do not accidentally change. Locking the viewport allows you to use display tools such as **ZOOM** and **PAN** to aid in working with objects in model space without changing the scale or position of the view in the floating viewport.

The quickest way to lock or unlock a viewport is to select a viewport in paper space and right-click. From the **Display Locked** cascading submenu, select **Yes** to lock the viewport or select **No** to unlock the viewport. A second option is to select a viewport in paper space and access the **Properties** palette. From the **Display Locked** drop-down list of the **Misc** category, select **Yes** to lock the viewport or select **No** to unlock the viewport. You can also use the **Lock** option of the **MVIEW** tool. Follow the prompts to select the viewport(s) to lock or unlock.

Exercise 29-5

Access the Student Web site (www.g-wlearning.com/CAD) and complete Exercise 29-5.

Controlling Layer Display

Layers generally function the same in paper space as in model space. The **On**, **Freeze**, **Color**, **Linetype**, **Lineweight**, **Plot Style**, and **Plot** settings described throughout this textbook are *global layer settings*. **On**, **Freeze**, and **Plot** are global layer states. **Color**, **Linetype**, **Lineweight**, and **Plot Style** are global layer properties. Changing a global layer setting affects objects drawn in model space and paper space. For example, if you change the color of a layer in model space and lock the layer, all objects drawn on that layer in paper space also change color and become locked.

AutoCAD provides the option to freeze layers in a floating viewport and apply *layer property overrides*. These features expand the function of the layer system and improve your ability to reuse drawing content.

Use the **LAYER** tool and the corresponding **Layer Properties Manager** to control layer display in floating viewports. See **Figure 29-16**. This is the same **Layer Properties Manager** used to manage layers throughout this textbook. The **NEW VP Freeze**, **VP Freeze**, **VP Color**, **VP Linetype**, **VP Lineweight**, **VP Transparency**, and **VP Plot Style** columns control layer display options for floating viewports. Except for the **NEW VP Freeze** column, these columns appear only in layout mode. You probably need to use the scroll bar at the bottom of the palette to see the columns. The options can apply to layout content, such as the viewport boundary. However, layer settings typically apply to an active floating viewport. Be sure the floating viewport to which you want to apply layer control settings is active as you work through the following sections.

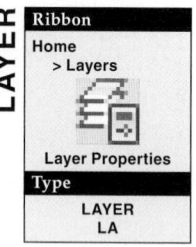

Ribbon
Home
> Layers

Layer Properties

Type
LAYER
LA

> **NOTE**
>
> The **VPLAYER** tool is a text-based tool that also controls layer display in floating viewports. The **Layer Properties Manager** is faster and easier to use than the **VPLAYER** tool.

Figure 29-16. Use the **Layer Properties Manager** to control the display of layers in floating viewports.

Controls freezing in new viewports Controls freezing in the active viewports Layer property overrides

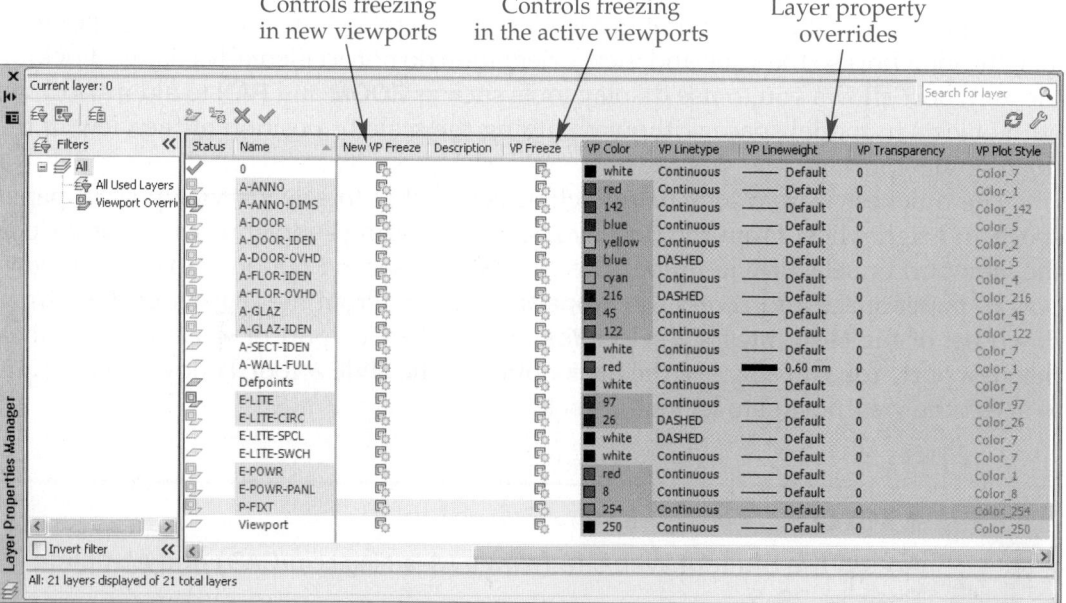

Freezing and Thawing

Freeze layers in the active viewport to create different views using a single drawing. For example, **Figure 29-17A** shows the model space display of a floor plan with electrical plan content added directly to the floor plan using electrical plan layers. **Figure 29-17B** shows two layouts from the same drawing file. One layout displays a floor plan with no electrical information, and the other layout displays an electrical plan without specific floor plan content.

In the **Figure 29-17** example, you draw many objects, such as doors, walls, and windows, on layers that maintain the global **Thaw** setting. As a result, these objects appear in model space and in both floating viewports. Freeze layers in specific viewports (**VP Freeze**) to create two different drawings. This example shows viewport layer

Figure 29-17. Creating a floor plan and separate electrical plan using the same drawing file. A—An example of "overlapping" layers in model space. B—Layers frozen in separate layouts to create two different drawing views.

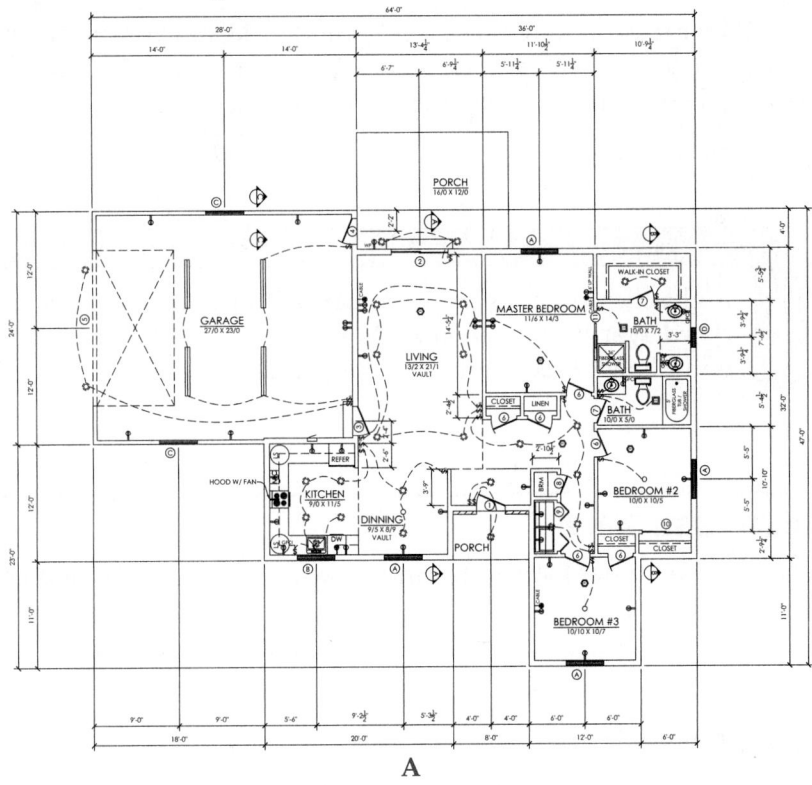

A

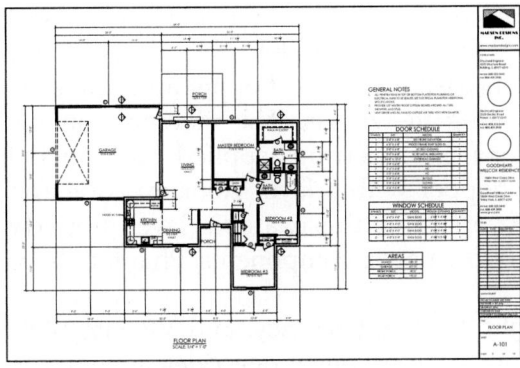

Floor Plan Layout
Created by freezing electrical layers
in the floating viewport

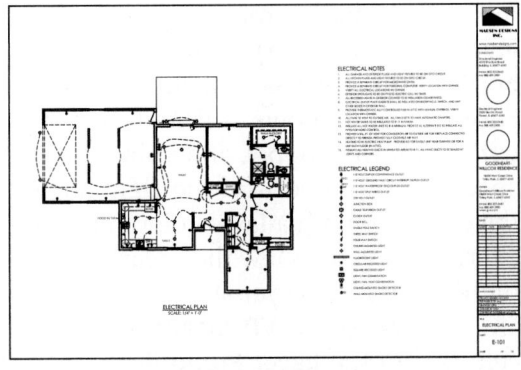

Electrical Plan Layout
Created by freezing floor plan
layers in the floating viewport

B

freezing in two different viewports, each viewport in a different layout, but you can apply the same concept to multiple viewports in the same layout.

VP Freeze

VP Thaw

The **VP Freeze** column of the **Layer Properties Manager** palette controls freezing and thawing layers in the current viewport. Pick the **VP Thaw** icon or the **VP Freeze** icon to toggle freezing and thawing in the current viewport. The **VP Freeze** icon freezes layers only in the selected floating viewport, while the **Freeze** icon freezes layers globally in all floating viewports. To freeze or thaw a layer in all layout viewports, including those created before picking the **VP Freeze** icon or **VP Thaw** icon, right-click and pick **VP Freeze Layer in All Viewports** or **VP Thaw Layer in All Viewports**.

PROFESSIONAL TIP

The **VP Freeze** function is also available in the **Layer Control** drop-down list in the **Layers** panel on the **Home** ribbon tab. This provides a quick way to freeze and thaw layers in a viewport without accessing the **Layer Properties Manager**.

New VP Freeze

New VP Thaw

The **New VP Freeze** column of the **Layer Properties Manager** controls freezing and thawing of layers in newly created floating viewports. Pick the **VP Thaw** icon or the **VP Freeze** icon to toggle freezing and thawing in any new floating viewport. This feature has no effect on the active viewport. Use the **New VP Freeze** option to freeze specific layers in any new floating viewports.

NOTE

Right-click on a layer in the **Layer Properties Manager** and select **New Layer VP Frozen in All Viewports** to create a new layer preset with the **VP Freeze** and **New VP Freeze** icons selected.

Exercise 29-6

Access the Student Web site (www.g-wlearning.com/CAD) and complete Exercise 29-6.

Layer Property Overrides

You can use layer property overrides to create different views without changing individual object properties, creating separate drawing files, or readjusting global layer properties. For example, **Figure 29-18A** shows the model space display of a hopper and conveyer system with unique layers assigned to the hopper and conveyer. **Figure 29-18B** shows a layout with two floating viewports. The viewport on the left shows the hopper and conveyer with global layer settings applied, as in model space. The viewport on the right shows the hopper with a layer color override and the conveyer with a layer color and linetype override. In this example, layer property overrides create a view that clearly shows the two separate components. Phantom lines highlight the conveyer as the mechanism.

The **VP Color**, **VP Linetype**, **VP Lineweight**, **VP Transparency**, and **VP Plot Style** columns in the **Layer Properties Manager** control the property overrides assigned to layers. The **VP Plot Style** column appears only when a named plot style is in use. Layer property overrides apply only to floating viewports in paper space. AutoCAD does not identify layers that contain layer property overrides in model space.

Figure 29-18. A—A hopper and conveyer drawn in model space. B—Using property overrides to create different layout views.

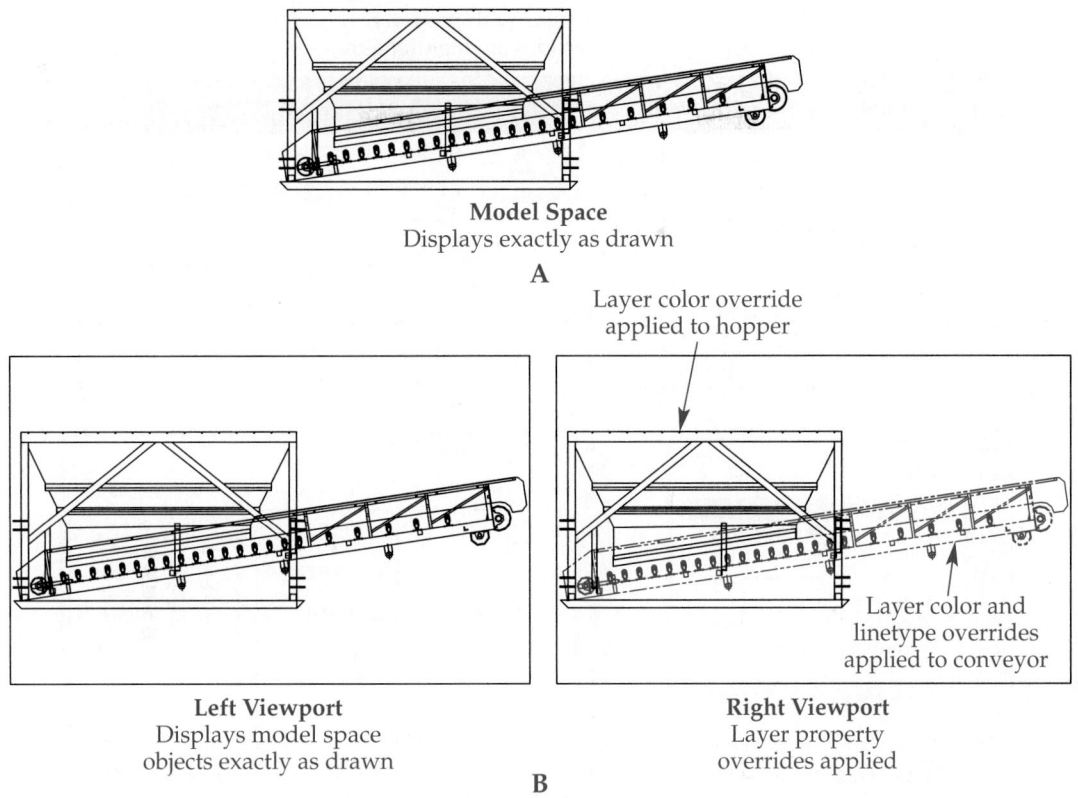

Model Space
Displays exactly as drawn

A

Layer color override
applied to hopper

Layer color and
linetype overrides
applied to conveyor

Left Viewport
Displays model space
objects exactly as drawn

Right Viewport
Layer property
overrides applied

B

The general process of overriding a layer property is just like that for changing a global value. For example, to override the color assigned to a layer, pick the color swatch and choose a color from the **Select Color** dialog box. The difference is that layer property overrides apply only to specific layers in an active floating viewport. Object properties do not change from **Bylayer**, and the model space display does not change.

When viewed in paper space, the **Properties** palette, **Layer Properties Manager**, and **Layer Control** drop-down list of the **Layers** ribbon tab indicate which layers include layer property overrides. See **Figure 29-19**. The **Layer Properties Manager** identifies layers that contain layer property overrides with a sheet and viewport icon in the status column. The layer names, global properties affected by the overrides, and the property overrides are highlighted. Use the **Viewport Overrides** filter to quickly display and manage only those layers that include layer property overrides. You can also save layer property overrides in a layer state.

The **Properties** palette highlights layer names that contain layer property overrides. Properties affected by the override are also highlighted and are identified as **Bylayer (VP)**. The **Layer Control** drop-down list in the **Layers** ribbon tab also highlights layers that include layer property overrides.

NOTE

The **Viewport Overrides** icon appears in the status bar when you activate a floating viewport or assign layer property overrides to the active viewport.

If layer property overrides are no longer necessary, you should remove the overrides from the layer. Changing a property back to the original, or global, value does

Figure 29-19. Layers with property overrides are highlighted in the **Properties Manager** palette, the **Layer Properties Manager**, and the **Layer Control** drop-down list on the ribbon.

Layers with property
overrides are highlighted

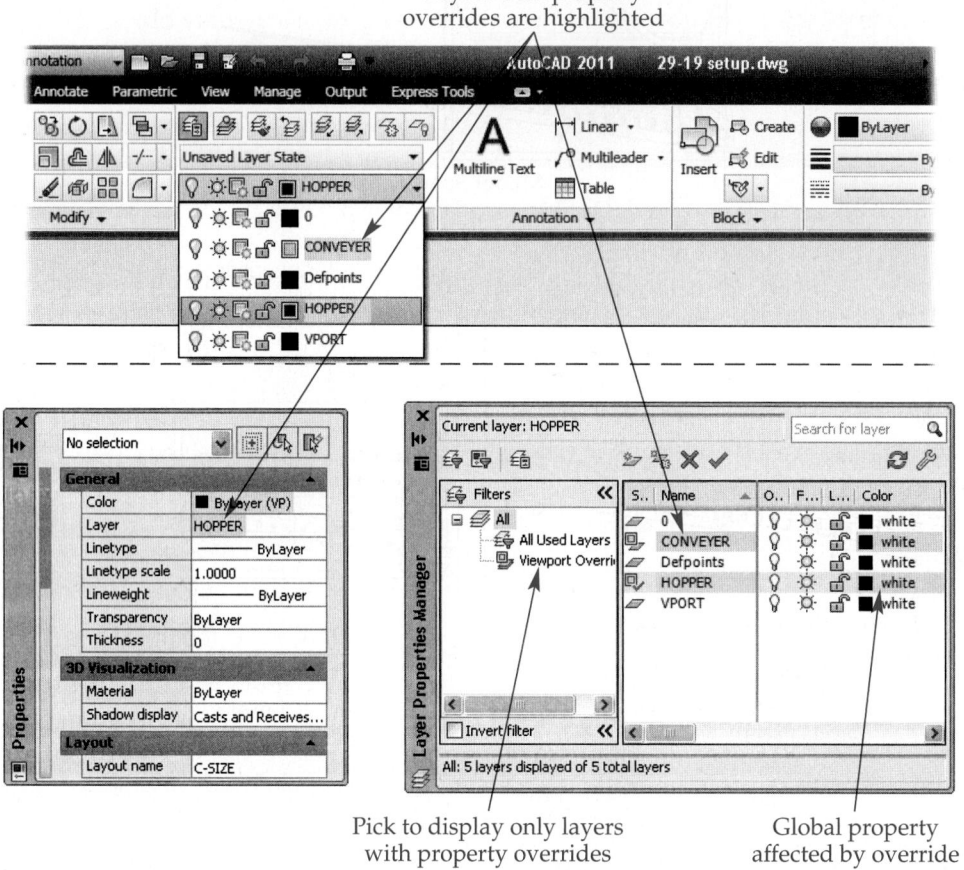

Pick to display only layers
with property overrides

Global property
affected by override

not remove the override. Right-click on a layer that contains layer property overrides in the **Layer Properties Manager** and pick **Remove Viewport Layer Overrides for** to access a cascading submenu of options for removing layer property overrides. Pick **Selected Layers** and then **In Current Viewport Only** or **In All Viewports** to remove layer property overrides from the current viewport or from all viewports that include overrides.

NOTE

You can also use the **Layer** option of the **MVIEW** tool and the **Reset** option of the **VPLAYER** tool to remove layer property overrides.

Exercise 29-7

Access the Student Web site (www.g-wlearning.com/CAD) and complete Exercise 29-7.

Turning Off Floating Viewport Objects

By default, objects appear in floating viewports, allowing you to view model space through the viewports. You can hide objects in the floating viewport without removing

AutoCAD and Its Applications—Basics

the viewport, which is convenient, for example, to plot a certain view, but still have access to the viewport. One option to toggle the display of objects in the viewport on and off is to select a viewport in paper space and right-click. From the **Display Viewport Objects** cascading menu, select **No** to hide objects or **Yes** to display objects.

Another option is to select a viewport in paper space and access the **Properties** palette. From the **On** drop-down list, select **No** to hide objects or **Yes** to show objects. You can also use the **ON** and **OFF** options of the **MVIEW** tool. Follow the prompts to select the viewport(s).

Maximizing Floating Viewports

When you activate a floating viewport, you are working in model space from within the paper space display. The primary function of activating a floating viewport is to adjust the display of model space to prepare a final drawing. Avoid working inside an active viewport to make changes to model space objects.

One alternative to activating a floating viewport is to maximize the viewport by picking the **Maximize Viewport** button on the status bar or by selecting a viewport, right-clicking, and choosing **Maximize Viewport**. When you maximize a viewport, you fill the entire drawing window with the selected floating viewport. See **Figure 29-20**. This allows you to work more effectively than when the layout content covers much of the window. In addition, a maximized viewport displays objects exactly as they appear in the floating viewport, including frozen layers and layer overrides. Typically, you should maximize a floating viewport to use view tools such as **ZOOM** and **PAN** and make changes to objects in model space while remaining in paper space.

Figure 29-20. Maximize a floating viewport to work in a model-space-like environment, but with layout characteristics, such as layers frozen in the viewport and layer property overrides.

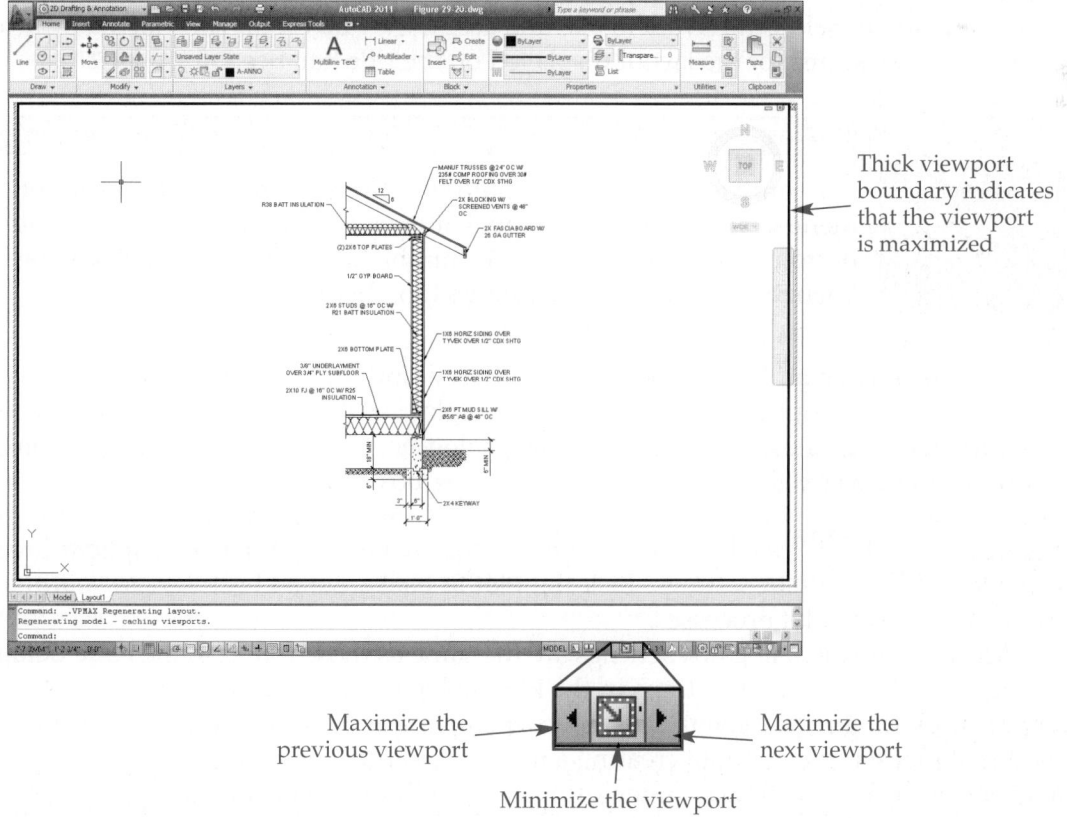

If the drawing includes multiple viewports, use the **Maximize Previous Viewport** and **Maximize Next Viewport** buttons on the status bar to change to other floating viewports in a maximized display. To redisplay the entire layout, pick the **Minimize Viewport** button on the status bar, right-click and choose **Minimize Viewport**, or type **VPMIN**.

NOTE

You can maximize a floating viewport even if the viewport is not active.

PROFESSIONAL TIP

If you do not want to see floating viewport boundaries on the plot, remember to freeze or turn off the layer assigned to the viewport before plotting.

Exercise 29-8

Access the Student Web site (www.g-wlearning.com/CAD) and complete Exercise 29-8.

Plotting

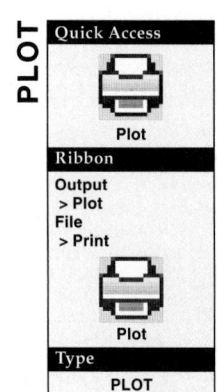

PLOT

Quick Access

Plot

Ribbon

Output
> Plot
File
> Print

Plot

Type

PLOT
[Ctrl]+[P]

After you prepare a layout for plotting, you are ready to plot. If you develop an appropriate page setup and layout, the process of creating the actual print should be almost automatic. Select the layout to plot and access the **PLOT** tool. The **Plot** dialog box appears with the name of the layout displayed on the title bar. See **Figure 29-21**.

NOTE

You can also access the **Plot** dialog box by selecting from the shortcut menu available from the model or layout tab, or by picking the **Plot** button in a **Model** or a layout thumbnail image in the **Quick View Layouts** or **Quick View Drawings** tool display.

The **Page Setup** and **Plot** dialog boxes are very similar, except the **Plot** dialog box provides additional options specific to creating a plot. All the settings in the **Plot** dialog box correspond to those in the **Page Setup** dialog box. Pick the **>**, or **More Options**, button in the lower-right corner of the **Plot** dialog box to toggle the display of additional dialog box areas, as shown in **Figure 29-21**. Specify a number in **Number of copies** text box to indicate how many copies of the layout to plot. The **Plot options** area provides additional plot settings. Pick the **Plot in background** check box to continue working while the plot processes.

Most of the **Plot** dialog box settings are the same as those found in the **Page Setup** dialog box. Changing plot settings in the **Plot** dialog box overrides the page setup for a specific plotting requirement. This is a convenient way to make a plot using slightly modified plot settings without creating a new page setup. For example, you can make a "check print" by selecting a printer, using an A- or B-size sheet and scaling the plot to

Figure 29-21. Use the **Plot** dialog box to finalize the layout and send the drawing to a printer, plotter, or file.

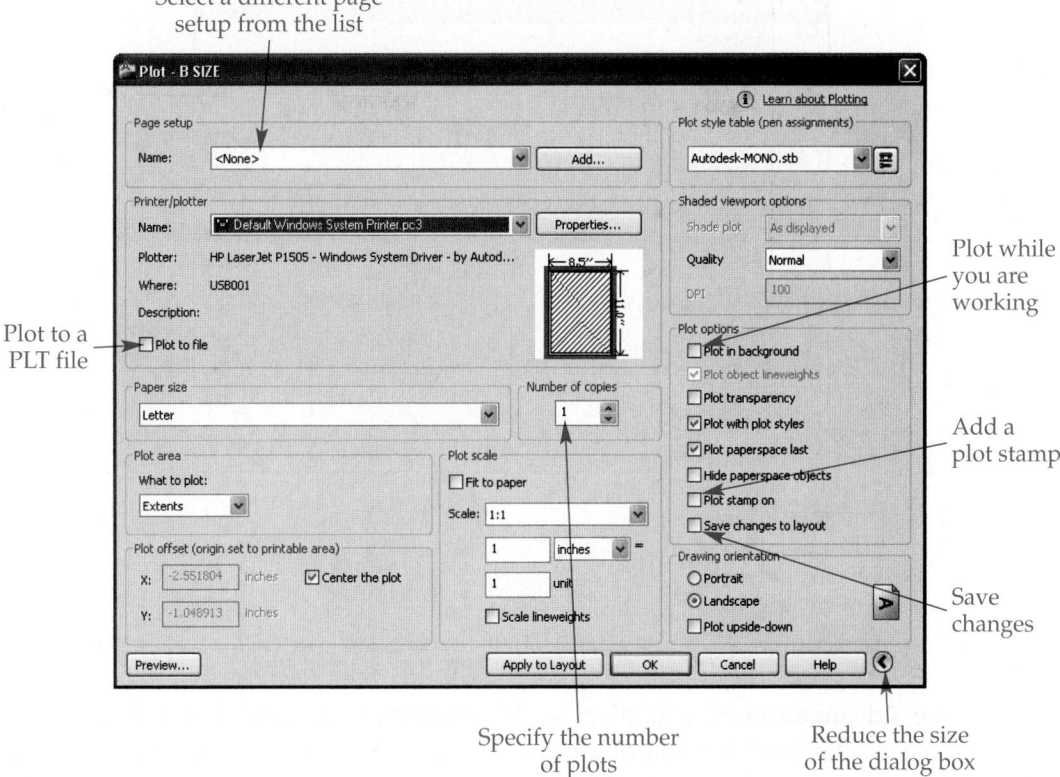

Select a different page setup from the list

Plot to a PLT file

Plot while you are working

Add a plot stamp

Save changes

Specify the number of plots

Reduce the size of the dialog box

fit the paper. After the drawing prints, the settings return to those originally assigned in the page setup, allowing you to plot the final drawing using the appropriate printer, sheet size, and 1:1 scale.

Adding a Plot Stamp

Pick the **Plot stamp on** check box in the **Plot options** area of the **Plot** dialog box to add a *plot stamp* to the plot. When you select the check box, the **Plot Stamp Settings…** button appears. Pick the button to display the **Plot Stamp** dialog box. See Figure 29-22.

Pick the check boxes in the **Plot stamp fields** area to identify the information to include in the plot stamp. To create additional plot stamp fields, pick the **Add/Edit** button in the **User defined fields** area, and use the **User Defined Fields** dialog box to add, edit, and delete custom fields. For example, add a field for the client name, project name, or contractor who uses the drawing. Select the fields from the drop-down lists in the **User defined fields** area.

The **Preview** area provides a preview of the location and orientation of the plot stamp. The preview does not show the actual plot stamp text. Plot stamp settings are saved in a plot stamp parameter (PSS) file. Pick the **Save As** button to save the current settings as a new PSS file, or pick the **Load** button to access and use an existing PSS file.

plot stamp: Text added only to the hard copy that includes information such as the drawing name or the date and time the drawing was printed.

NOTE

The log file settings are independent of the plot stamp settings. You can produce a log file without creating a plot stamp or have a plot stamp without producing a log file.

Figure 29-22. Use the **Plot Stamp** dialog box to specify the information included in the plot stamp.

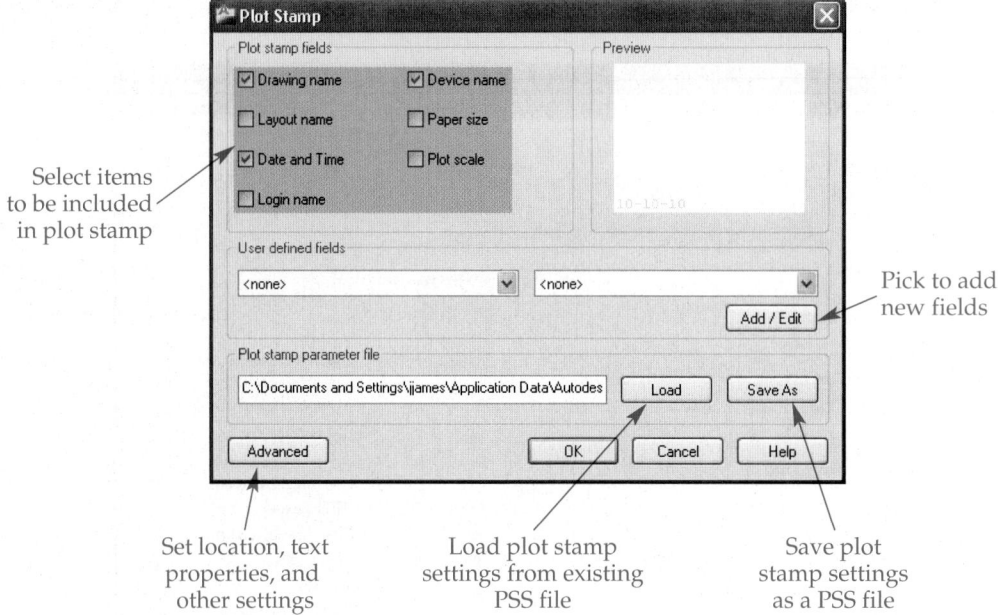

Select items to be included in plot stamp

Pick to add new fields

Set location, text properties, and other settings

Load plot stamp settings from existing PSS file

Save plot stamp settings as a PSS file

Pick the **Advanced** button to display the **Advanced Options** dialog box shown in **Figure 29-23**. The **Location and offset** area includes options to define the position of the plot stamp. Use the **Location** drop-down list to select the corner in which the plot stamp begins. To print the plot stamp upside-down, pick the **Stamp upside-down** check box. Pick **Horizontal** or **Vertical** from the **Orientation** drop-down list to specify the orientation of the plot stamp. Use the **X Offset** and **Y Offset** text boxes to set the offset distances for the plot stamp and pick whether the distances are measured from the edge of the printable area or the paper border.

The **Text properties** area provides options for controlling plot stamp text characteristics. Use the **Font** drop-down list to select a font and the **Height** text box to specify

Figure 29-23. The **Advanced Options** dialog box allows you to define the plot stamp location, orientation, text font and size, and units.

Pick corner where stamp is located

Set plot stamp orientation

Offset distances

Pick where offsets are measured from

Log file name

Select font

Enter text height

Units for text height and offsets

Pick log file location

the text height. Pick the **Single line plot stamp** check box to contain the plot stamp to a single line. If this box is left unchecked, the plot stamp prints on two lines.

Use the **Units** drop-down list to select the units for the plot stamp offset and text height. The plot stamp units can be different from the drawing units. Select the **Log file location** check box to create a log file of plotted items. Specify the name of the log file in the text box. Pick the **Browse...** button to locate the log file.

> **NOTE**
>
> You can also configure plot stamp settings by picking the **Plot Stamp Settings...** button on the **Plot and Publish** tab of the **Options** dialog box.

Saving Changes to the Layout

If you make changes in the **Plot** dialog box and want to save changes to the layout page setup for future plots, pick the **Save changes to layout** check box in the **Plot options** area. You can also save changes by picking the **Apply to Layout** button. If you do not select the **Save changes to layout** check box or pick the **Apply to Layout** button, changes made in the **Plot** dialog box are discarded, and the original page setup appears the next time you open the **Plot** dialog box.

Page Setup Options

The **Plot** dialog box provides an alternate means of creating a page setup. To apply this technique, access the **Plot** dialog box and make changes to plot settings, just as you would in the **Page Setup** dialog box. Then select the **Add...** button in the **Page setup** area to display the **Add Page Setup** dialog box. Enter a name for the page setup in the **New page setup name:** text box. All current settings in the **Plot** dialog box are saved with the new page setup. Select a page setup from the **Name:** drop-down list to restore the settings in the **Plot** dialog box. Pick the **<Previous plot>** option to reference the setting used to create the last plot, or pick the **Import...** button to import a page setup from a DWG, DWT, or DXF file.

> **NOTE**
>
> When using the **Plot** dialog box to define settings for a page setup, name the page setup *after* you make changes to settings. If you name the page setup and want to make changes later, such as changes to a plot style, use the **Page Setup Manager** dialog box instead.

Previewing the Plot

The final step before plotting is to preview the plot. The plot preview shows exactly what the plot should look like based on plot and layout settings. Always preview the plot to check the drawing for errors and view the effects of plot settings before sending the information to the plot device. This will help you eliminate unnecessary plots. To preview the plot, pick the **Preview** button in the lower-left corner of the **Plot** dialog box to enter preview mode. See **Figure 29-24**. What you see on-screen is exactly what will plot, assuming you use a color plotter to make color prints and load the correct sheet size in the plot device.

The **Realtime Zoom** tool is automatically active in the preview window. Additional view tools are available from the toolbar near the top of the window or from a shortcut

Figure 29-24. Previewing a plot is an excellent way to help confirm that the plot will be correct before sending the information to the plot device.

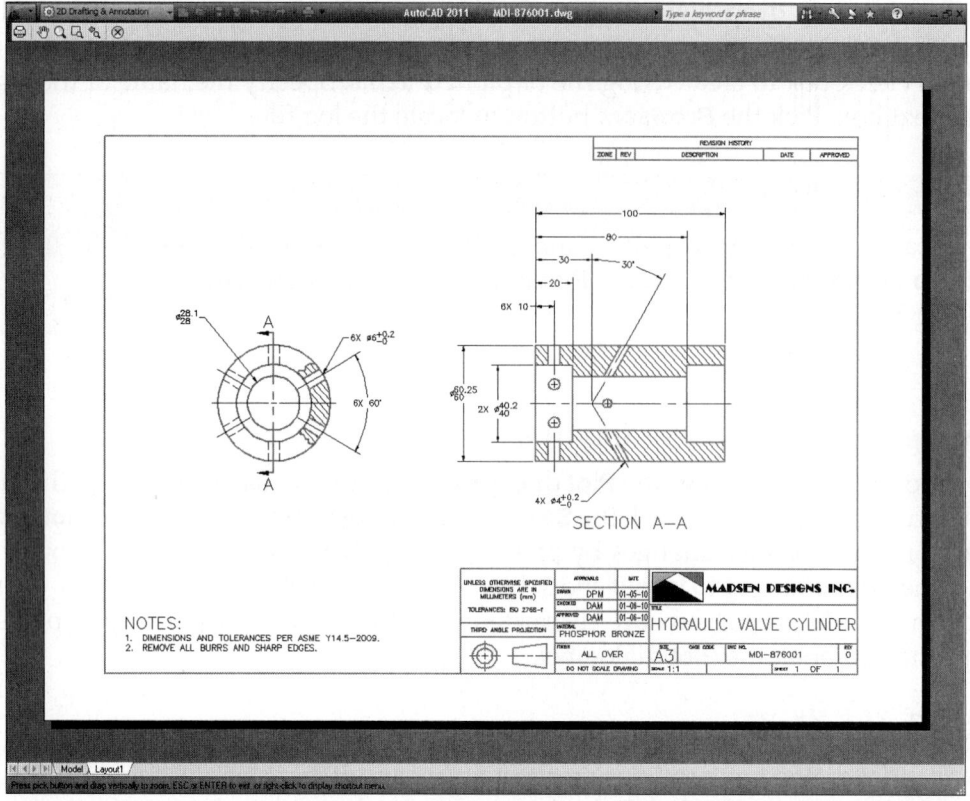

menu. Use view tools to help confirm that the plot settings are correct. When you finish previewing the plot and are ready to plot, pick the **Plot** button on the toolbar, or right-click and select **Plot**. When you finish previewing the plot, pick the **Close** button on the toolbar, press [Esc] or [Enter], or right-click and select **Exit** to return to the **Plot** dialog box.

> **NOTE**
>
> You must select a plot device other than **None** in order to activate the **Preview...** button.

Output

When plotting to a plotter or printer, pick the **OK** button to send the plot to the plot device and close the **Plot** dialog box. When plotting to a PDF file, pick the **OK** button to display the **Browse for Plot File** dialog box. Specify a location and name for the file and then pick the **Save** button to close the **Plot** dialog box and open the PDF file automatically using installed Adobe® software. When plotting to a DWF or DWFX file, pick the **OK** button to display the **Browse for Plot File** dialog box. Specify a location and name for the file and then pick the **Save** button to close the **Plot** dialog box. View the DWF or DWFX file using Autodesk Design Review software.

By default, AutoCAD notifies you of the success or failure of a hard copy or electronic plot with a message from the status bar tray. To view additional details about

AutoCAD and Its Applications—Basics

the plot, pick **Click to view plot and publish details...** to display the **Plot and Publish Details** dialog box. You can also access the **Plot and Publish Details** dialog box using the **VIEWPLOTDETAILS** tool.

> **NOTE**
>
> AutoCAD provides additional tools for exporting drawings, automating the process of transmitting drawings electronically (**eTransmit**), and *publishing*. Publishing a set of sheets is described later in this textbook.

publishing: Preparing a sequential set of multiple drawings for hard copy or electronic plotting of the set.

Exercise 29-9

Access the Student Web site (www.g-wlearning.com/CAD) and complete Exercise 29-9.

Plotting to a PLT File

If a plot device is not available, but you are ready to plot, an alternative is to plot to a file. A plot file saves with a PLT extension. The file stores all the drawing geometry, plot styles, and plot settings assigned to the drawing. Some offices or schools with only one printer or plotter attach a *plot spooler* to the printer or plotter to plot a PLT file. The plot spooler device usually allows you to take a PLT file from a storage disk and copy it to the plot spooler, which in turn plots the drawing.

plot spooler: A disk drive with memory that allows you to plot files.

To plot to a file, open the **Plot** dialog box, select the plot device from the **Name:** drop-down list, and check the **Plot to file** check box. The setting in the **Plot and Publish** tab of the **Options** dialog box determines the location in which the plot file is saved. To specify the path, pick the ellipsis (...) button for the **Select default location for all plot-to-file operations** dialog box.

Supplemental Material

Additional Plotting Options

For information about several additional plot settings in the **Plot and Publish** tab of the **Options** dialog box, go to the Student Web site (www.g-wlearning.com/CAD), select this chapter, and select **Additional Plotting Options**.

Express Tools
Chapter 29

The **Layout** panel of the **Express Tools** ribbon tab includes additional layout tools. For information about the most useful layout express tools, go to the Student Web site (www.g-wlearning.com/CAD), select this chapter, and select **Layout Express Tools**.

Template Development
Chapter 29

For detailed instructions on adding layouts to each drawing template, go to the Student Web site (www.g-wlearning.com/CAD), select this chapter, and select **Template Development**.

Chapter Test

Answer the following questions. Write your answers on a separate sheet of paper or go to the Student Web site (www.g-wlearning.com/CAD) and complete the electronic chapter test.

1. Name the two types of content that are brought together to create a complete drawing.
2. What tools can you use to modify the boundary of a floating viewport?
3. What **MVIEW** option can form a floating viewport outline using a polyline?
4. What **MVIEW** option converts a closed object drawn in paper space into a floating viewport?
5. How do you activate a floating viewport?
6. How can you tell that a viewport is active in paper space?
7. How do you reactivate paper space after activating a floating viewport for editing?
8. How does the scale you assign to a floating viewport compare with the drawing scale?
9. To what value should the **CELTSCALE**, **PSLTSCALE**, and **MSLTSCALE** system variables be set so that the **LTSCALE** value will be applied correctly in model space and paper space?
10. Viewport edges may cut off the drawing when the viewport is correctly scaled. List three options to display the entire view.
11. Why should you lock a viewport after you adjust the drawing in the viewport to reflect the proper scale and view?
12. Give an example of why you would hide objects in a floating viewport without removing the viewport.
13. What is a plot stamp?
14. If you make changes to the page setup using the **Plot** dialog box, how can you save these changes to the page setup so that the changes apply to future plots?
15. Give at least two reasons why you should always preview a plot before sending the information to the plot device.

Drawing Problems

- *Start AutoCAD if it is not already started.*
- *Start a new drawing for each problem using an appropriate template of your choice. The template should include layers and text, dimension, multileader, and table styles, when necessary, for drawing the given objects. Add layers and text, dimension, multileader, and table styles as needed.*
- *Draw all objects using appropriate layers and text, dimension, multileader, and table styles, justification, and format.*
- *Follow the specific instructions for each problem. Use only drawing and editing tools and techniques you have already learned. Use your own judgment and approximate dimensions when necessary.*
- *Apply dimensions accurately using ASME or appropriate industry standards.*

Note: *Some of the problems in this chapter are built on problems from previous chapters. If you have not yet completed those problems, complete them now.*

▼ Basic

1. Follow the instructions in the Template Development portion of the Student Web site to add and set up layouts for the Mechanical-Inch template file.

2. Follow the instructions in the Template Development portion of the Student Web site to add and set up layouts for the Mechanical-Metric template file.

3. Follow the instructions in the Template Development portion of the Student Web site to add and set up layouts for the Architectural-US template file.

4. Follow the instructions in the Template Development portion of the Student Web site to add and set up layouts for the Architectural-METRIC template file.

5. Follow the instructions in the Template Development portion of the Student Web site to add and set up layouts for the Civil-US template file.

6. Follow the instructions in the Template Development portion of the Student Web site to add and set up layouts for the Civil-METRIC template file.

7. Open P28-4 and save as P29-7. The P29-7 file should be active. Make the **B-SIZE** layout current. Create a new layer named **VPORT**. Delete the default floating viewport and create a single floating viewport .5" in from the edges of the sheet on the **VPORT** layer. Scale model space in the viewport to 1:1. Plot the layout, leaving the **VPORT** layer on and thawed. Resave the file.

8. Open P28-5 and save as P29-8. The P29-8 file should be active. Activate the **A2-SIZE** layout. Create a new layer named **VPORT**. Delete the default floating viewport and create a single floating viewport 10 mm from the edges of the sheet on the **VPORT** layer. Scale model space in the viewport to 1:1. Plot the layout, leaving the **VPORT** layer on and thawed. Resave the file.

9. Open P28-6 and save as P29-9. The P29-9 file should be active. Activate the **B-SIZE** layout. Create a new layer named **VPORT**. Delete the default floating viewport and create a single floating viewport .5″ from the edges of the sheet on the **VPORT** layer. Scale model space in the viewport to 1:1. Plot the layout, leaving the **VPORT** layer on and thawed. Resave the file.

▼ Intermediate

10. Open P28-8 and save as P29-10. The P29-10 file should be active. Create a floating viewport and scale model space in the viewport using an appropriate scale. Plot the layout, leaving the **VPORT** layer on and thawed. Resave the file.

11. Open P8-1 and save as P29-11. The P29-11 file should be active. Delete the default **Layout2**. Create a new A-size sheet layout according to the following steps:
    A. Rename the default **Layout1** to **A-SIZE**.
    B. Select the **A-SIZE** layout and access the **Page Setup Manager**.
    C. Modify the **A-SIZE** page setup according to the following settings:
       - **Printer/Plotter:** Select a printer or plotter that can plot an A-size sheet
       - **Paper size:** Select the appropriate A-size sheet (varies with printer or plotter)
       - **Plot area:** Layout
       - **Plot offset:** 0,0
       - **Plot scale:** 1:1 (1 in. = 1 unit)
       - **Plot style table:** monochrome.ctb
       - **Plot with plot styles**
       - **Plot paper space last**
       - Do not check **Hide paper space objects**
       - **Drawing orientation:** Select the appropriate orientation (varies with printer or plotter)
    D. Create a new layer named **VPORT**.
    E. Delete the default floating viewport and create a single floating viewport .5″ from the edges of the sheet on the **VPORT** layer.
    F. Scale model space in the viewport to 1:2. Plot the layout, leaving the **VPORT** layer on and thawed.
    G. Resave the file.

12. Open P8-11 and save as P29-12. The P29-12 file should be active. Create layouts and floating viewports as needed to plot the drawing at an appropriate scale.

Drawing Problems - Chapter 29

▼ Advanced

13. Open P29-13 from the Student Web site. Create a layout, plot style, and page setup so the layout can be plotted as follows: Using color-dependent plot styles, have the equipment (shown in color in the diagram) plot with a lineweight of 0.8 mm and 80% screening on an A-size sheet oriented horizontally. Plotted text height should be 1/8". Plot in paper space at 1:1. Save the drawing as P29-13.

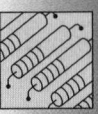

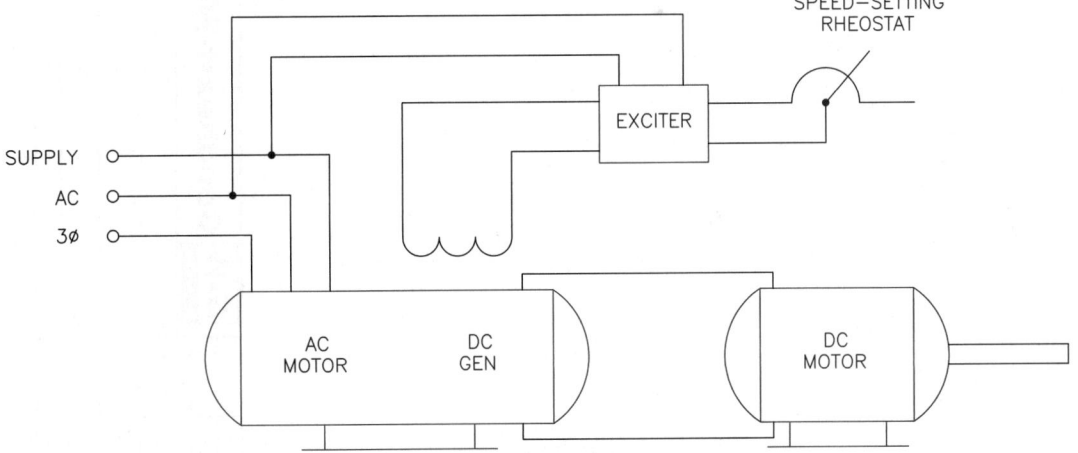

14. Open P29-14 from the Student Web site. Create four layouts with names and displays as follows:
    - The **Entire Schematic** layout plots the entire schematic on a B-size sheet.
    - The **3 Wire Control** layout plots only the 3 Wire Control diagram on an A-size sheet, horizontally oriented.
    - The **Motor** layout plots the motor symbol and connections in the lower center of the schematic on an A-size sheet, oriented vertically.
    - The **Schematic** layout plots schematic without the 3 Wire Control and motor components on an A-size sheet, oriented horizontally.

    Set up the layouts so they will plot with a text height of 1/8". Plot in paper space at a scale of 1:1. Save the drawing as P29-14.

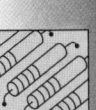

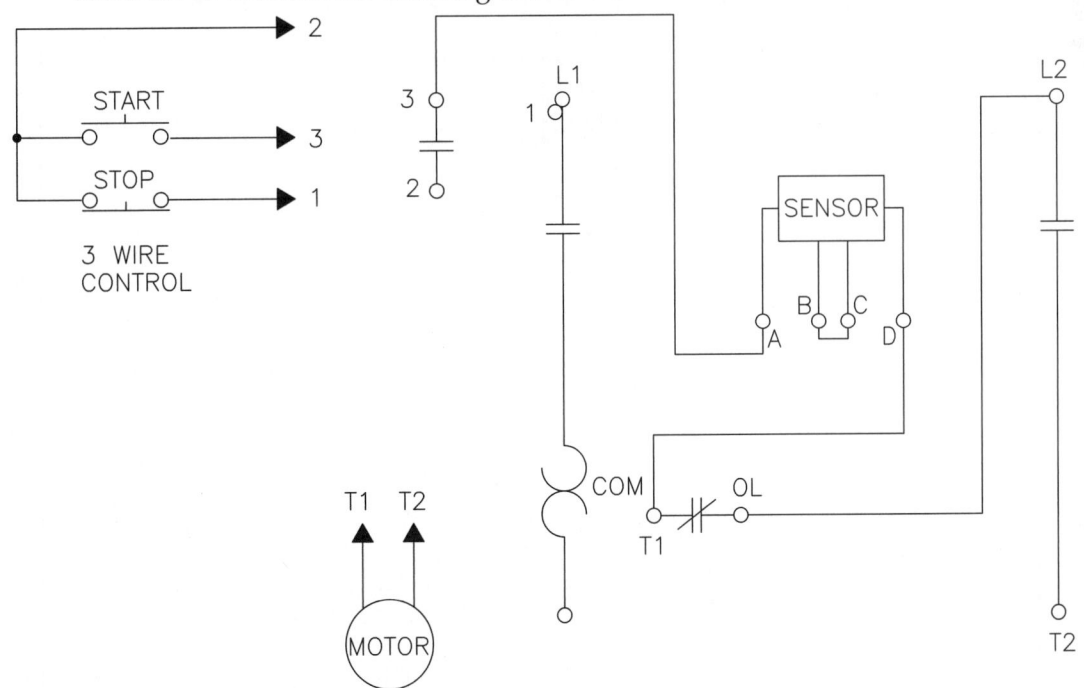

15. Draw and dimension the female insert shown. Use a layout to plot the drawing. Save the drawing as P29-15.

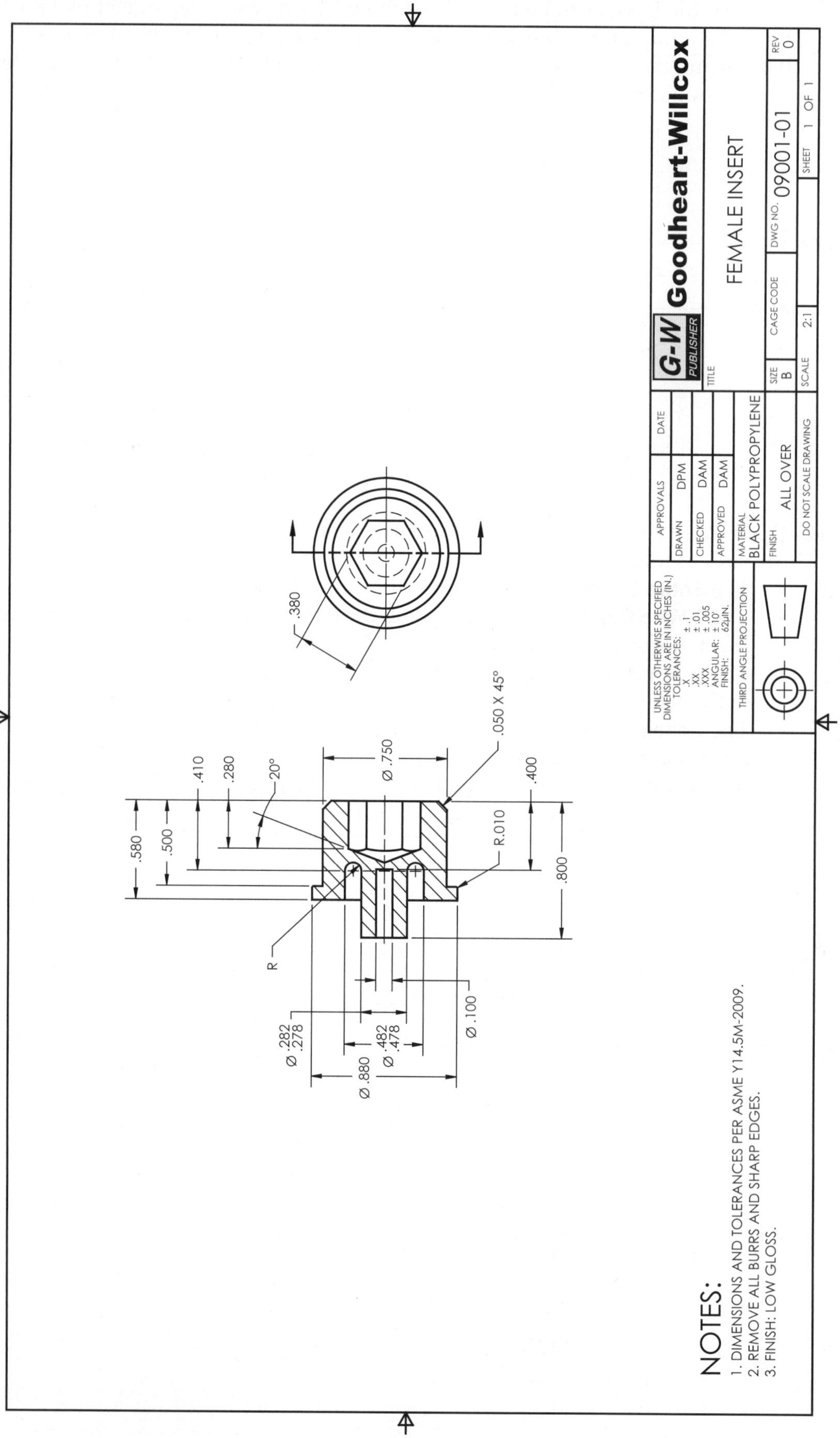

.380

Ø .750

.050 X 45°

.400

R.010

.800

.410

.280

20°

.580

.500

R

Ø .282
Ø .278

Ø .880

.482
.478

Ø .100

NOTES:
1. DIMENSIONS AND TOLERANCES PER ASME Y14.5M-2009.
2. REMOVE ALL BURRS AND SHARP EDGES.
3. FINISH: LOW GLOSS.

APPROVALS		DATE
DRAWN	DPM	
CHECKED	DAM	
APPROVED	DAM	

UNLESS OTHERWISE SPECIFIED
DIMENSIONS ARE IN INCHES (IN.)
TOLERANCES:
.X   ± .1
.XX   ± .01
.XXX   ± .005
ANGULAR: ± .10
FINISH: 62µIN.

THIRD ANGLE PROJECTION

MATERIAL
BLACK POLYPROPYLENE

FINISH   ALL OVER

DO NOT SCALE DRAWING

G-W *PUBLISHER* **Goodheart-Willcox**

TITLE
FEMALE INSERT

SIZE B | CAGE CODE | DWG NO. 09001-01 | REV 0

SCALE 2:1 | SHEET 1 OF 1

AutoCAD Certified Associate Exam Practice

Answer the following questions. Write your answers on a separate sheet of paper.

1. Which of the following drawing elements should you typically create in paper space? *Select all that apply.*
   A. border
   B. size and location dimensions
   C. general drawing notes
   D. thread notes
   E. title block

2. Which of the following methods can you use to create a floating viewport? *Select all that apply.*
   A. **EXPORTLAYOUT** tool
   B. **MIVEW** tool
   C. **Viewports** dialog box
   D. **Viewports** panel on the **View** ribbon tab
   E. **VPCLIP** tool

3. Which of the following features of the **Layer Properties Manager** apply layer property overrides? *Select all that apply.*
   A. **Freeze**
   B. **New VP Freeze**
   C. **New VP Thaw**
   D. **Thaw**
   E. **VP Plot Style**

AutoCAD Certified Professional Exam Practice

Follow the instructions in the problem. Write your answers on a separate sheet of paper.

1. **Navigate to this chapter on the Student Web site and open CPE-29adjust.dwg.** Move the polygonal viewport up so its top edge aligns with the top edge of the rectangular viewport and the left edge of the upper portion of the polygonal viewport is .25" from the rectangular viewport, as shown. What are the 2D coordinates of point A?

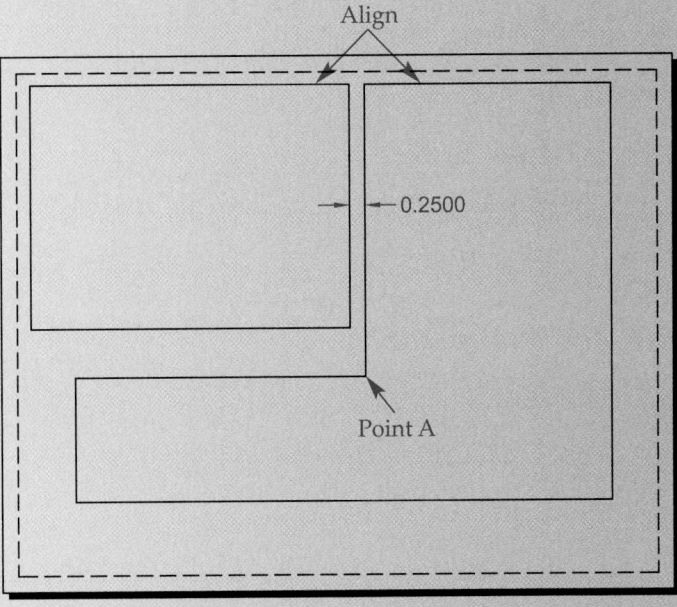

2. **Navigate to this chapter on the Student Web site and open CPE-29rotate.dwg.**
Make the Stair Detail layout current. Set the contents of the existing viewport to
display at a scale of 1/4″ = 1′-0″. Do not make any other changes. What are the 2D
coordinates of point B in the layout?

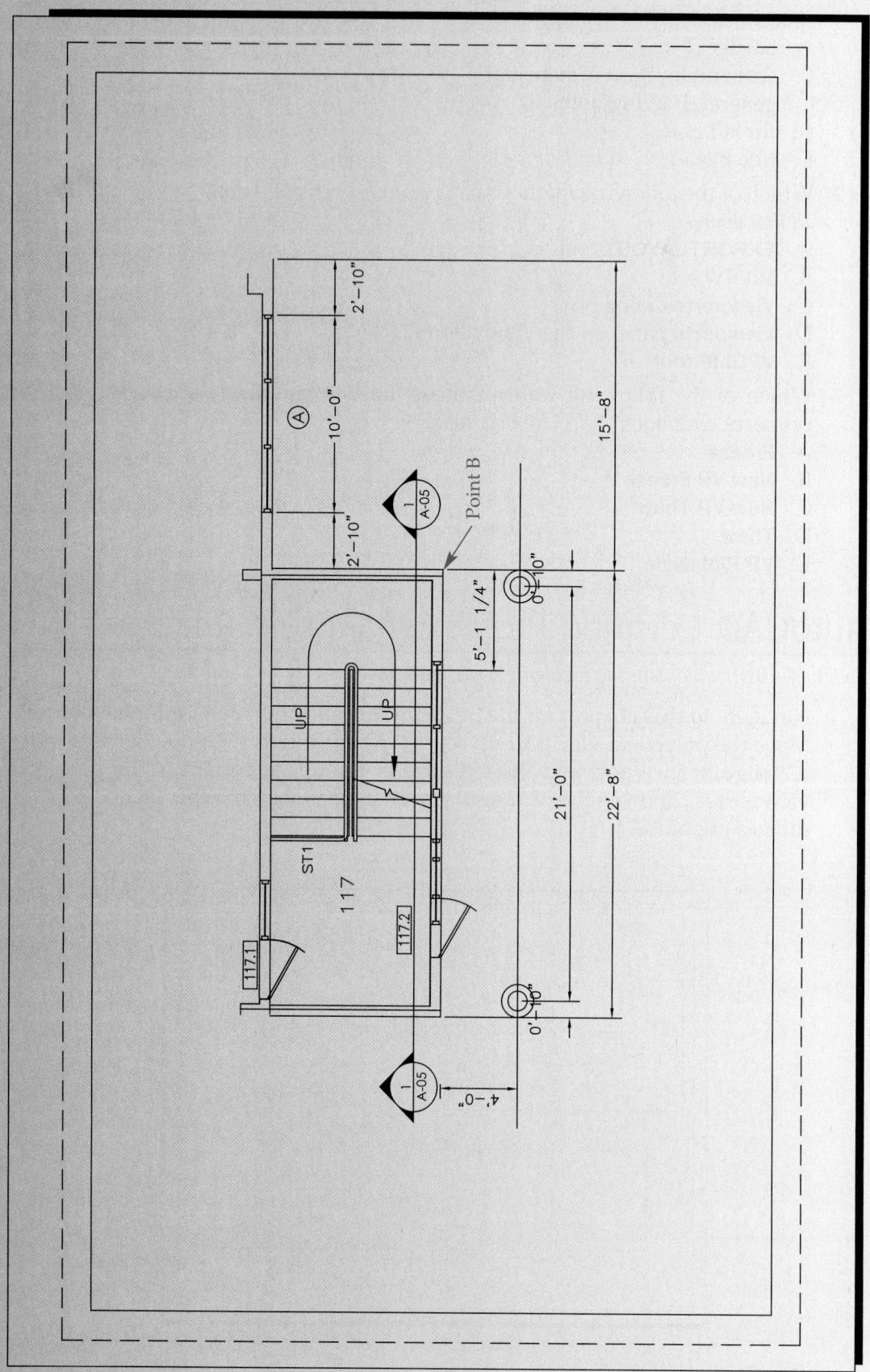

Annotative Objects

Learning Objectives

After completing this chapter, you will be able to do the following:

✓ Explain the differences between manual and annotative object scaling.
✓ Specify objects as annotative.
✓ Create and use annotative objects in model space.
✓ Display annotative objects in scaled layout viewports.
✓ Adjust the scale of annotations according to a new drawing scale.
✓ Use annotative objects to help prepare multiview drawings.

You must scale *annotations* and related items, such as dimension objects and hatch patterns, so that information appears on-screen and plots correctly relative to scaled objects. AutoCAD provides annotative tools to automate the process of scaling *annotative objects*. Annotative tools also provide flexibility for working with layouts to create multiview drawings.

annotations: Letters, numbers, words, and notes used to describe information on a drawing.

annotative objects: AutoCAD objects that can adapt automatically to the current drawing scale.

Introduction to Annotative Objects

As explained in previous chapters, always draw objects at their actual size, or full scale, in model space, regardless of the size of the objects. For example, if you draw a small machine part and the length of a line in the drawing is 2 mm, draw the line 2 mm long in model space. If you draw a building and the length of a line in the drawing is 80', draw the line 80' long in model space. These examples describe drawing objects that are too small or too large for layout and printing purposes. To fit these objects properly on a sheet, you *scale* them to a specific drawing scale.

When you scale a drawing, you increase or decrease the displayed size of model space objects. A properly scaled floating viewport in a layout allows for this process. Scaling a drawing greatly affects the display of items added to objects in model space, such as annotations, because these items should be the same size on a plotted sheet, regardless of the displayed size, or scale, of the rest of the drawing. See **Figure 30-1.**

Traditional manual scaling of annotations, hatches, and other objects requires determining the scale factor of the drawing scale and then multiplying the scale factor by the plotted size of the objects. In contrast, annotative objects are scaled automatically

scale: (verb) The process of enlarging or reducing objects to fit properly on a sheet of paper. (noun) The ratio between the actual size of drawing objects and the size at which objects plot on a sheet of paper.

Figure 30-1. The large drawing features in this example of a residential site plan require scaling in order to fit on a standard size sheet. Annotations are scaled according to the plotted size of the drawing; otherwise, they would be too small to see.

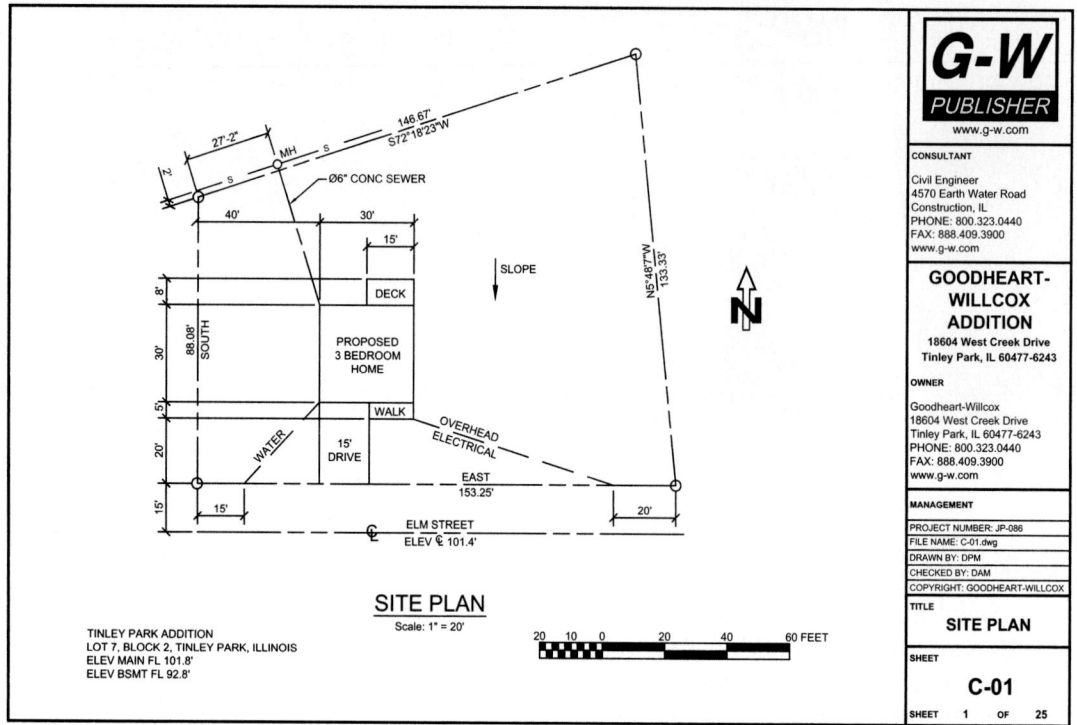

according to the selected annotation scale, which is the same as the drawing scale. This eliminates the need for you to calculate the scale factor and manually adjust the size of objects according to the drawing scale.

PROFESSIONAL TIP

Use annotative objects instead of traditional manual scaling even if you do not anticipate using a drawing scale other than 1:1.

Defining Annotative Objects

Annotative objects include single-line and multiline text, dimensions, leaders and multileaders, GD&T symbols created using the **TOLERANCE** tool, hatch patterns, blocks, and attributes. The method you use to define objects as annotative varies depending on the object type. You can make objects annotative when you first draw them or convert non-annotative objects to annotative status as needed.

Creating New Annotative Objects

Single-line and multiline text is annotative when it is drawn using an annotative text style. To make a text style annotative, pick the **Annotative** check box in the **Size** area of the **Text Style** dialog box. See **Figure 30-2.** A drawing may include a combination of annotative and non-annotative text, dimension, and multileader styles. An example of text that is typically *not* annotative is text added directly to a layout, which is printed at a scale of 1:1.

Figure 30-2.
Single-line and multiline text objects are annotative when you draw them using an annotative text style.

Pick to make the text style annotative

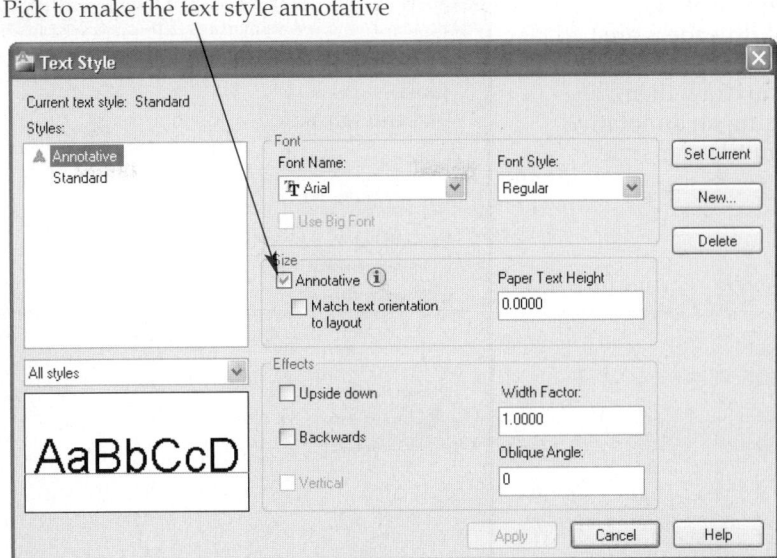

Dimensions, standard leaders, and GD&T symbols created using the **TOLERANCE** tool are annotative when they are drawn using an annotative dimension style. To make a dimension style annotative, pick the **Annotative** check box in the **Fit** tab of the **New** (or **Modify**) **Dimension Style** dialog box. See **Figure 30-3.**

Multileaders are annotative when they are drawn using an annotative multileader style. To make a multileader style annotative, pick the **Annotative** check box in the **Leader Structure** tab of the **Modify Multileader Style** dialog box. See **Figure 30-4.**

NOTE

When you create an annotative multileader using the block multileader type, the block automatically becomes annotative, even if the block is not set as annotative.

Figure 30-3.
Dimensions, leaders, and GD&T symbols created using the **TOLERANCE** tool are annotative when you draw them using an annotative dimension style.

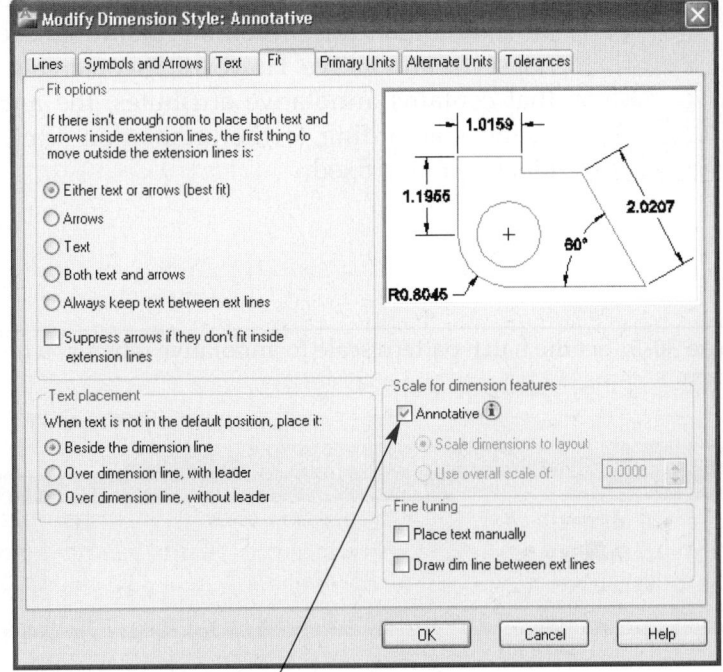

Pick to make the dimension style annotative

Figure 30-4.
Multileaders are annotative when you draw them using an annotative multileader style.

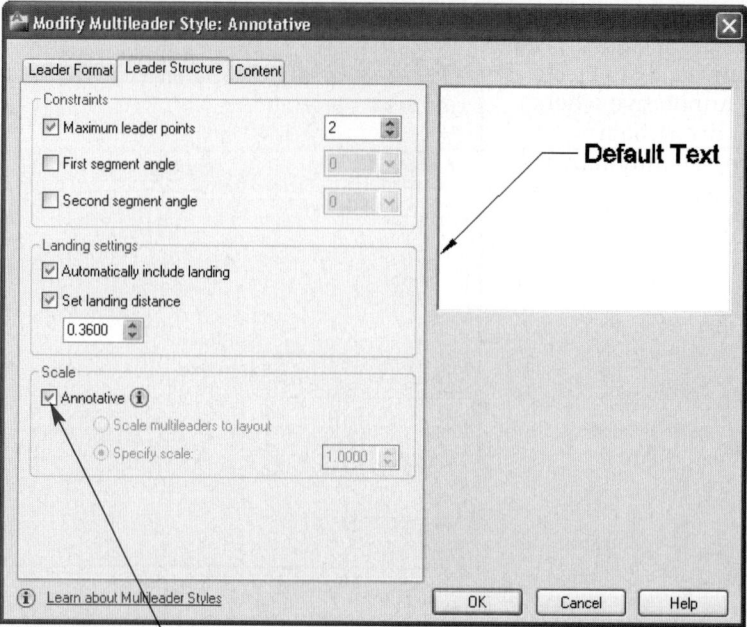

Pick to make the multileader style annotative

Hatch patterns are annotative when you set the hatch scale as annotative during hatch creation or edit. Pick the **Annotative** button in the **Options** panel of the **Hatch Creation** or **Hatch Editor** ribbon tab. See **Figure 30-5.**

To make attribute text height and spacing annotative, pick the **Annotative** check box in the **Attribute Definition** dialog box. See **Figure 30-6A.** To make a block annotative, pick the **Annotative** check box in the **Behavior** area of the **Block Definition** dialog box. See **Figure 30-6B.**

NOTE

When you make a block annotative, any attributes included in the block automatically become annotative, even if the attributes are not set as annotative. However, if you create a non-annotative block that contains annotative attributes, the annotative attribute scale changes according to the annotation scale, while the size of the block remains fixed.

Figure 30-5. Set the hatch pattern scale to annotative when you create or edit the hatch pattern.

Pick to make the hatch scale annotative

Figure 30-6. Set attributes (A) and blocks (B) as annotative during definition.

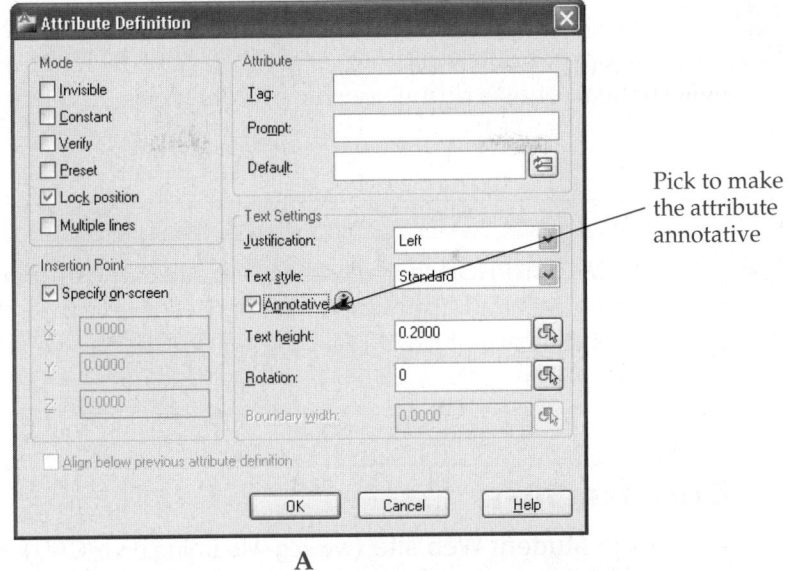

Pick to make the attribute annotative

A

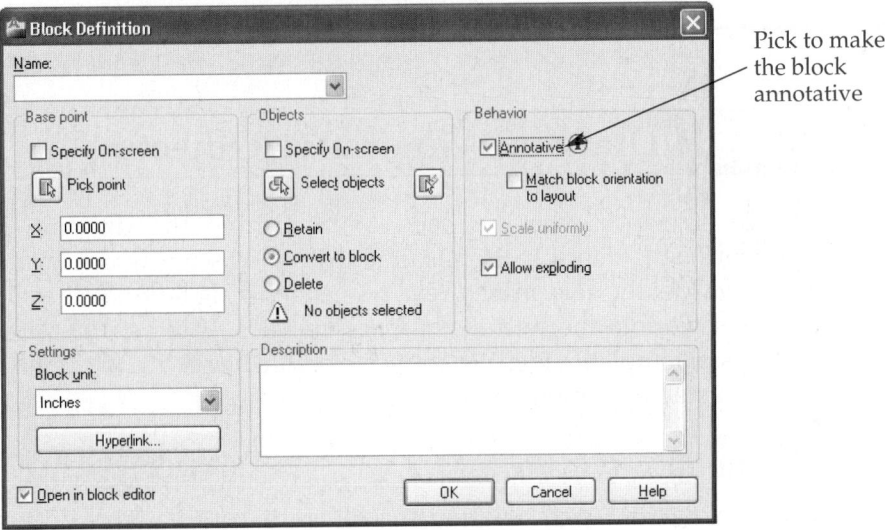

Pick to make the block annotative

B

Making Existing Objects Annotative

Specify objects as annotative when you first create them in model space when possible. However, you can assign annotative status to objects originally drawn as non-annotative. The appropriate style controls the annotative status of single-line and multiline text, dimensions, standard leaders and multileaders, and GD&T symbols created using the **TOLERANCE** tool. Change the style assigned to the object to an annotative style to make the object annotative. You must edit or recreate existing hatch patterns, blocks, and attributes in order to make the objects annotative.

One way to make existing objects annotative is to override the non-annotative status using the **Properties** palette. This technique is most effective to make a limited number of objects annotative. The location of the annotative properties in the **Properties** palette varies depending on the selected object. The **Annotative** and **Annotative scale** properties are common to all annotative objects. Select **Yes** from the **Annotative** drop-down list to make non-annotative objects annotative, or choose **No** to make annotative objects non-annotative.

Exercise 30-1

Access the Student Web site (www.g-wlearning.com/CAD) and complete Exercise 30-1.

Drawing Annotative Objects

Annotative objects reduce the need to determine the drawing scale factor. However, you must still identify the appropriate drawing scale, which is the same as the *annotation scale*. Ideally, determine drawing scale during template development and incorporate the scale into the settings in template files. If you do not apply drawing scales to settings in templates, identify the scale before beginning a drawing, or at least before you begin placing annotations.

annotation scale: The scale AutoCAD uses to calculate the scale factor applied to annotative objects.

Setting Annotation Scale

In general, you set the annotation scale before you begin adding annotations so that annotations are scaled automatically. However, it may be necessary to adjust the annotation scale throughout the drawing process, especially if the drawing scale changes or when you are preparing multiple drawings with different scales on one sheet. Approach the process of scaling annotations in model space by first selecting an annotation scale and then placing annotative objects. To draw annotations at a different scale, select the new annotation scale before placing annotative objects.

The **Select Annotation Scale** dialog box may appear when you add an annotative object. This dialog box provides a convenient way to set annotation scale before creating the object. The other primary means of specifying the annotation scale is to choose a scale from the **Annotation Scale** flyout on the status bar. See **Figure 30-7**. The annotation scale is typically the same as the drawing scale. You can also set the annotation scale in the **Properties** palette when no objects are selected by choosing the annotation scale from the **Annotation Scale** option in the **Misc** category.

If a scale is unavailable, or to change an existing scale, pick the **Annotation Scale** flyout on the status bar and choose **Custom...** to access the **Edit Scale List** dialog box. The **Edit Scale List** dialog box is also available by picking the **Edit Scale List...** button in the **User Preferences** tab of the **Options** dialog box. The **Edit Scale List** dialog box is the same dialog box used to edit floating viewport scales, as explained in Chapter 29.

Figure 30-7.
The status bar includes several annotation scale options. If you display the drawing status bar, the **Annotation Scale** button moves from the application status bar to the drawing status bar.

- 1:1
- 1:2
- 1:4
- 1:5
- 1:8
- 1:10
- 1:16
- 1:20
- 1:30
- 1:40
- 1:50
- 1:100
- 2:1
- 4:1
- 8:1
- 10:1
- 100:1
- 1/128" = 1'-0"
- 1/64" = 1'-0"
- 1/32" = 1'-0"
- 1/16" = 1'-0"
- 3/32" = 1'-0"
- 1/8" = 1'-0"
- 3/16" = 1'-0"
- 1/4" = 1'-0"
- 3/8" = 1'-0"
- 1/2" = 1'-0"
- 3/4" = 1'-0"
- 1" = 1'-0"
- 1-1/2" = 1'-0"
- 3" = 1'-0"
- 6" = 1'-0"
- 1'-0" = 1'-0"
- Custom...

Current annotation scale

Pick the **Custom...** option to add an annotation scale to the list

Hide Xref scales

Pick this flyout to select an annotation scale

> **NOTE**
>
> Annotation scale sets the drawing scale in model space for controlling annotative objects. Viewport scale sets the drawing scale in a layout floating viewport to define the drawing scale. Both scales should be the same and should match the drawing scale.

Controlling Model Space Linetype Scale

The **CELTSCALE**, **PSLTSCALE**, and **MSLTSCALE** system variables control how the **LTSCALE** system variable applies to linetypes in model space and paper space. Leave the **CELTSCALE**, **PSLTSCALE**, and **MSLTSCALE** system variables at their default setting of 1 to apply the **LTSCALE** value correctly according to the current annotation scale. However, when you change the annotation scale, remember to use the **REGEN** tool to regenerate the display. Otherwise, the linetype scale will not update according to the new scale.

> **PROFESSIONAL TIP**
>
> When you open a drawing in AutoCAD 2011 that was created in an AutoCAD version earlier than AutoCAD 2008, the **MSLTSCALE** system variable is set to 0. Change the value to 1 to take advantage of annotative linetype scaling.

Annotative Text

Draw annotative text using the same tools you use to draw non-annotative text. The difference is the value you enter for text height. To create annotative multiline text, use an annotative text style or pick the **Annotative** button. Then enter the paper text height, such as 1/4", in the **Size** text box. See **Figure 30-8**. The text scale, which includes spacing, width, and paragraph settings, automatically adjusts according to the current annotation scale.

To create annotative single-line text, use an annotative text style. After you pick the start point, specify the paper text height. The text scale automatically adjusts according to the current annotation scale.

> **NOTE**
>
> The **Properties** palette contains specific annotative text properties in addition to those displayed for all annotative objects. For example, use the **Paper text height** property to specify a paper text height. The **Model text height** property is a reference value that identifies the height of the text after the scale factor is applied.

Annotative Dimensions and Multileaders

Draw annotative dimensions, leaders, GD&T symbols created using the **TOLERANCE** tool, and multileaders using the same tools you use to draw non-annotative dimensions and multileaders. Once you activate an annotative dimension or multileader style and select the appropriate annotation scale, the process of placing correctly scaled dimensions and multileaders is automatic.

However, you must still determine the correct dimension and text location and spacing from objects when you add dimensions and text to scaled drawings. This involves multiplying the scale factor by the plotted spacing. For example, if the first dimension line should be 3/4" from an object when plotted at a 1/4" = 1'-0" scale, the correct spacing in model space is 36" from the object. The scale factor is $48 \times 3/4" = 36"$.

Figure 30-8. Create annotative multiline text using an annotative text style, or pick the **Annotative** option.

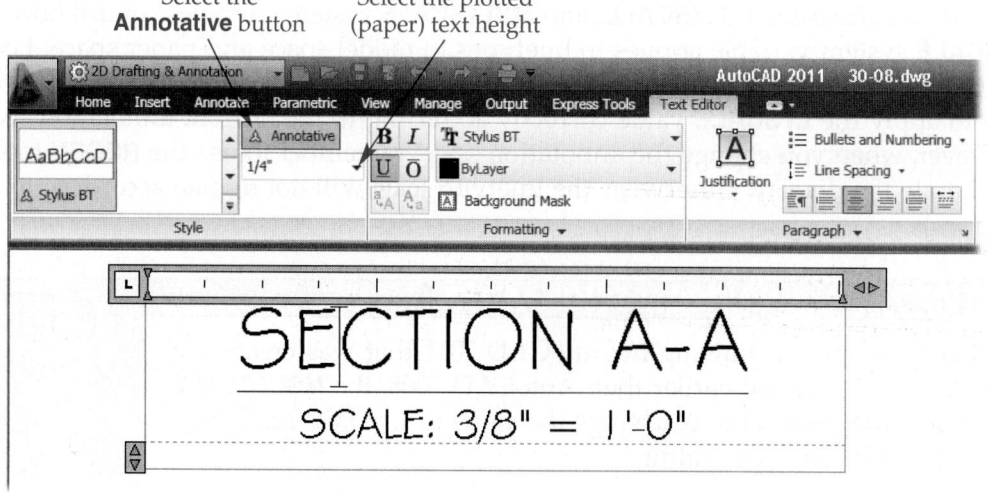

Annotative Hatch Patterns

The difference between annotative and non-annotative hatch patterns is the way in which the drawing scale affects the hatch scale. When you create annotative hatch patterns, the scale you enter in the **Scale:** text box produces the same results regardless of the specified annotation scale. For example, if you enter a value in the **Scale:** text box that is appropriate for an annotation scale of 1:1, and then change the annotation scale to 4:1, the hatch pattern scale does not change relative to the drawing display. It looks the same on the 1:1 scaled drawing as on the 4:1 scaled drawing.

In contrast, when you create non-annotative hatch patterns, if you enter a value in the **Scale:** text box that is appropriate for a drawing scaled to 1:1 and then change the drawing scale to 4:1, the displayed scale of the hatch pattern increases. The hatch looks four times as large on the 4:1 drawing as on the 1:1 drawing.

Annotative Blocks and Attributes

Annotative blocks, often classified as *schematic blocks*, are commonly used for annotation purposes. When you insert an annotative schematic block, AutoCAD determines the block scale based on the current annotation scale, eliminating the need for you to enter a scale factor. For most applications, insert annotative blocks at a scale of 1 to apply the annotation scale correctly. Entering a scale other than 1 adjusts the scale of the block by multiplying the block scale by the annotation scale.

schematic block:
A block originally drawn at a 1:1 scale.

PROFESSIONAL TIP

When you create unit and schematic blocks that contain text and attributes, you should usually not make the text and attributes annotative. The text height you specify is set according to the full-scale size of the block, not necessarily the paper height. Any non-annotative text and attributes you select when you make a block annotative also automatically become annotative.

Exercise 30-2

Access the Student Web site (www.g-wlearning.com/CAD) and complete Exercise 30-2.

Displaying Annotative Objects in Layouts

Once you create drawing features and symbols and add annotative objects according to the appropriate annotation scale, you are ready to display and plot the drawing using a paper space layout. Refer to Chapter 29 to review the process of using and scaling floating viewports. **Figure 30-9** shows a drawing scaled to 3/8″ = 1′-0″. In this example, drawing features are drawn at full scale in model space. The annotation scale in model space was set to 3/8″ = 1′-0″, and annotative text, dimensions, multileaders, hatch patterns, and blocks were added. The annotative objects in paper space are automatically scaled according to the 3/8″ = 1′-0″ annotation scale.

In the **Figure 30-9** example, the viewport scale and the annotation scale are the same, which is typical when scaling annotative objects. If you select a different viewport scale from the **Viewport Scale** flyout, the annotation scale automatically

Figure 30-9. Scaling a drawing in a floating paper space viewport. The **Viewport Scale** flyout provides one of the easiest ways to set the viewport scale. A button is also available to synchronize the viewport and annotation scale if they do not match.

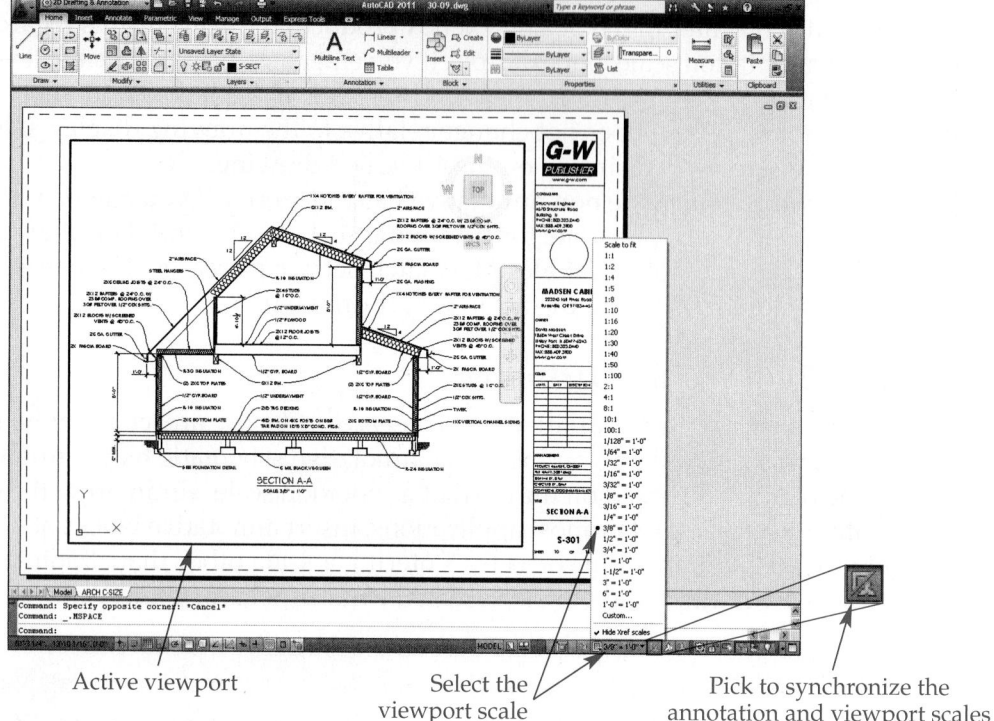

Active viewport   Select the viewport scale   Pick to synchronize the annotation and viewport scales

adjusts according to the viewport scale. However, if you adjust the viewport scale by zooming, for example, the annotation scale does not change. The viewport scale and the annotation scale must match in order for the drawing and annotative objects to be scaled correctly. Pick the button to the right of the **Viewport Scale** flyout, identified in Figure 30-9, to synchronize the viewport and annotation scales.

The **Properties** palette also provides viewport and annotation scale controls. You must be in paper space and pick a floating viewport to access viewport properties. Choose a viewport scale from the **Standard scale** drop-down list. Adjust the annotation scale using the **Annotation scale** option. See Figure 30-10.

PROFESSIONAL TIP

Lock the viewport display to avoid zooming and disassociating the viewport scale from the annotation scale. Refer to Chapter 29 for more information on locking and unlocking floating viewports.

Exercise 30-3

Access the Student Web site (www.g-wlearning.com/CAD) and complete Exercise 30-3.

Figure 30-10. The **Properties** palette also allows you to set the viewport and annotation scale.

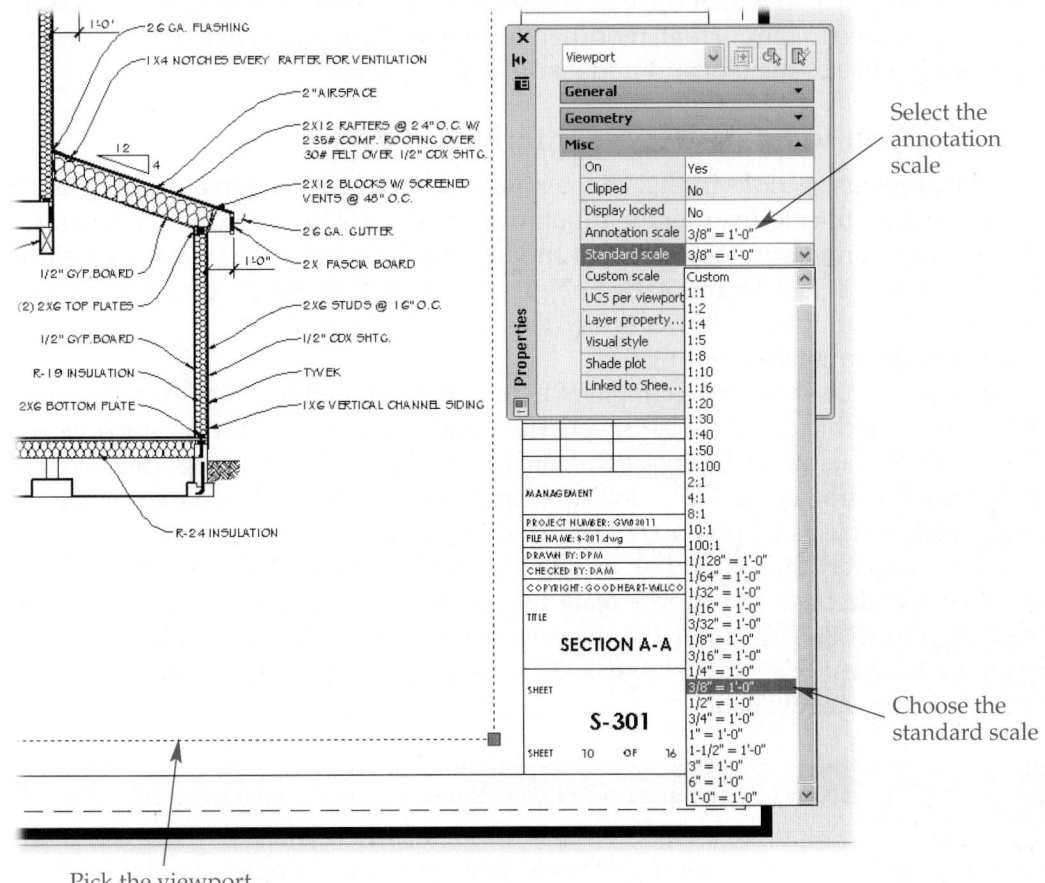

Pick the viewport

Select the annotation scale

Choose the standard scale

Changing Drawing Scale

No matter how much you plan a drawing, drawing scale can change throughout the drawing process. Reduce the drawing scale if it is necessary to use a smaller sheet. Increase the drawing scale if drawing features are redesigned and become larger, or if additional drawing detail is required.

Changing the drawing scale affects the size and position of annotations. If you change the drawing scale, remember that the annotation scale is the same as the drawing scale.

To change the annotation scale in model space, select a new annotation scale from the **Annotation Scale** flyout. To change the annotation scale in an active viewport in a layout, adjust the viewport scale by selecting the drawing scale from the **Viewport Scale** flyout. Again, the viewport and annotation scales should be the same for most applications.

Using the ANNOUPDATE Tool

When you create single-line text using a non-annotative text style and then change the style to annotative, text drawn using the style becomes annotative. However, the properties of the annotative text remain set according to the non-annotative text style. When you create annotative text using an annotative text style and then change the style to non-annotative, text drawn in the style becomes non-annotative. However, the properties of the non-annotative text remain set according to the annotative style.

Chapter 30   Annotative Objects

Use the **ANNOUPDATE** tool to update text properties to reflect the current properties of the text style in which the text is drawn. When prompted to select objects, pick the text to update to the current, modified text style. Then right-click or press [Enter] or the space bar to exit the tool and update the text.

Introduction to Scale Representations

The previous sections in this chapter assume that you develop a drawing using a single annotation scale. In order for annotative object scale to change when the drawing scale changes, annotative objects must support the new scale. This involves assigning new annotation scales to annotative objects. If annotative objects do not support the new scale, the annotative object scale does not change, and objects may disappear, depending on annotative settings.

Figure 30-11A shows an example of a drawing prepared at a 3/8″ = 1′-0″ scale and placed on an architectural C-size sheet. The annotation scale in this example is set to 3/8″ = 1′-0″, to scale annotative objects according to a 3/8″ = 1′-0″ drawing scale. To change the scale of the drawing to 1/2″ = 1′-0″ to display additional detail, you must ensure that the annotative objects support a 1/2″ = 1′-0″ scale.

After you add the 1/2″ = 1′-0″ annotation scale to annotative objects, change the annotation scale or the viewport scale to 1/2″ = 1′-0″ to scale the objects correctly. See Figure 30-11B. The annotative objects in the Figure 30-11 example support two annotation scales: 3/8″ = 1′-0″ and 1/2″ = 1′-0″. As a result, two *annotative object representations* are available.

annotative object representation: Display of an annotative object at an annotation scale that the object supports.

NOTE

Annotative objects display an icon when you hover the crosshairs over the objects. Objects that support a single annotation scale display the annotative icon shown in Figure 30-12A. Annotative objects that support more than one annotation scale display the annotative icon shown in Figure 30-12B. The icons appear by default according to selection preview settings in the **Selection** tab of the **Options** dialog box.

Understanding Annotation Visibility

Before changing the current annotation scale, you should understand how the annotation scale affects annotative object visibility. The annotative object scale does not change if annotative objects do not support the selected annotation scale. In addition, annotative objects disappear when an annotation scale that the objects do not support is current. For example, if annotative objects only support an annotation scale of 3/8″ = 1′-0″, and you set an annotation scale of 1/2″ = 1′-0″, the annotative object scale remains set at 3/8″ = 1′-0″, and the objects disappear.

The easiest way to turn annotative object visibility on and off according to the current annotation scale is to pick the **Annotation Visibility** button on the status bar. See Figure 30-13. Turning on annotation visibility is most effective when you are adding annotation scales to or deleting them from annotative objects. If you add multiple annotation scales to annotative objects, the annotative object representation is based on the current scale.

Figure 30-11. A—A drawing created using an annotation scale of 3/8″ = 1′-0″ on an architectural C-size sheet. Annotative objects automatically appear at the correct scale. B—The same drawing shown in A, modified to an annotation scale of 1/2″ = 1′-0″ and placed on an architectural D-size sheet. An annotation scale of 1/2″ = 1′-0″ is added to all of the annotative objects, allowing the objects to adapt to the new scale automatically.

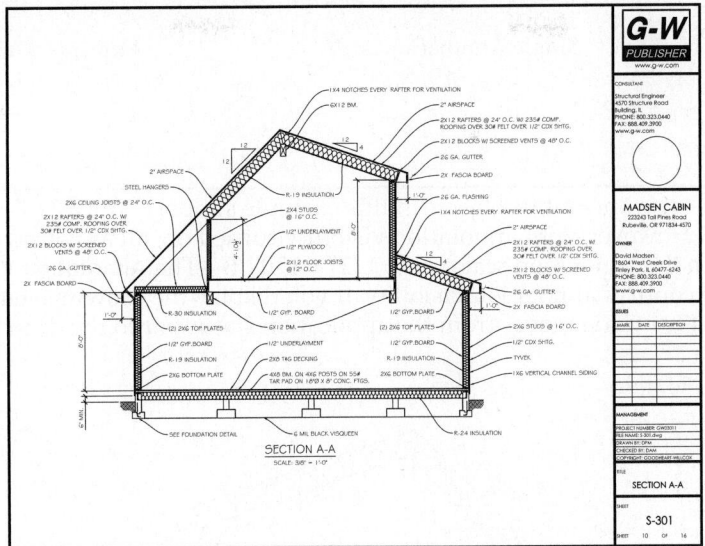

A

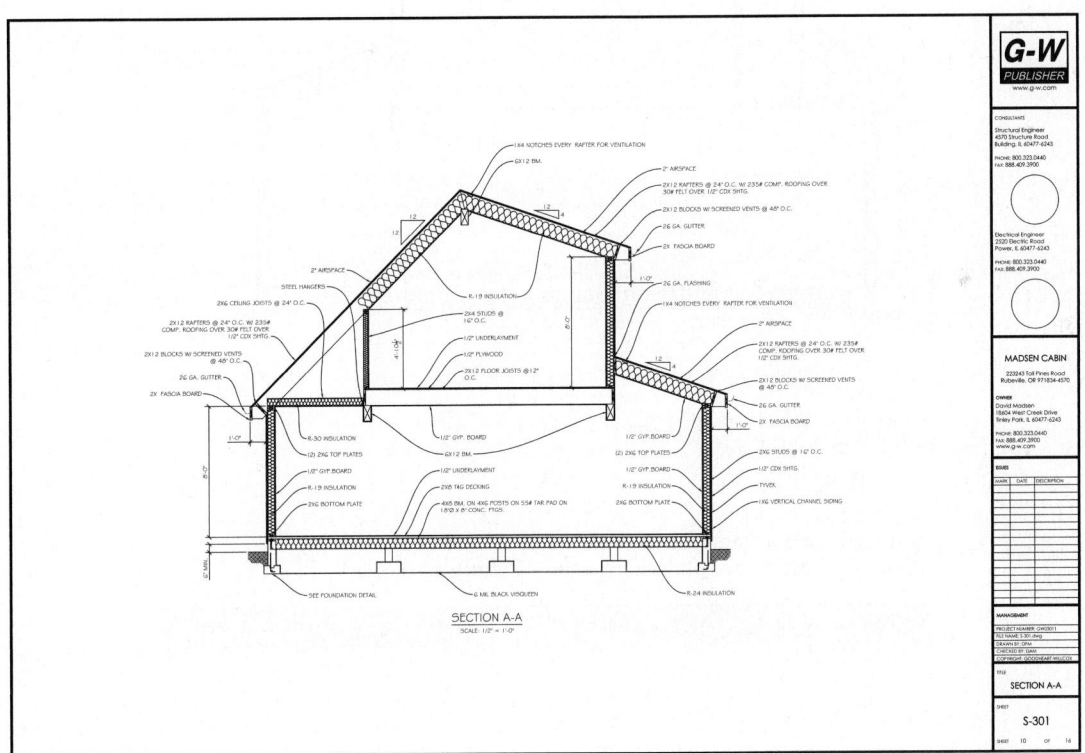

B

Figure 30-12.
The icons displayed
when annotative
objects support
single or multiple
annotation scales.

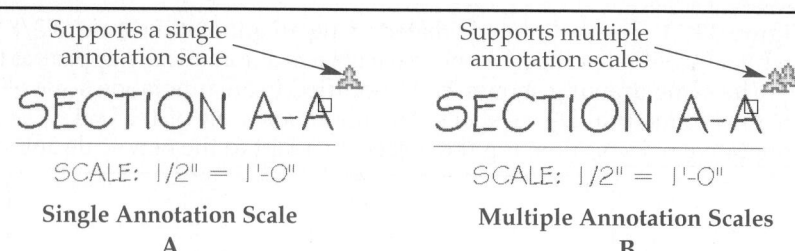

Supports a single
annotation scale

Supports multiple
annotation scales

Single Annotation Scale
A

Multiple Annotation Scales
B

Figure 30-13. A—The annotative objects in this example support only a 3/8″ = 1′-0″ annotation scale. However, with annotation visibility turned on, all annotative objects appear, even with the annotation scale set to 1/2″ = 1′-0″. B—The **Annotation Visibility** button on the status bar controls annotation visibility. If you display the drawing status bar, the **Annotation Visibility** button moves from the application status bar to the drawing status bar.

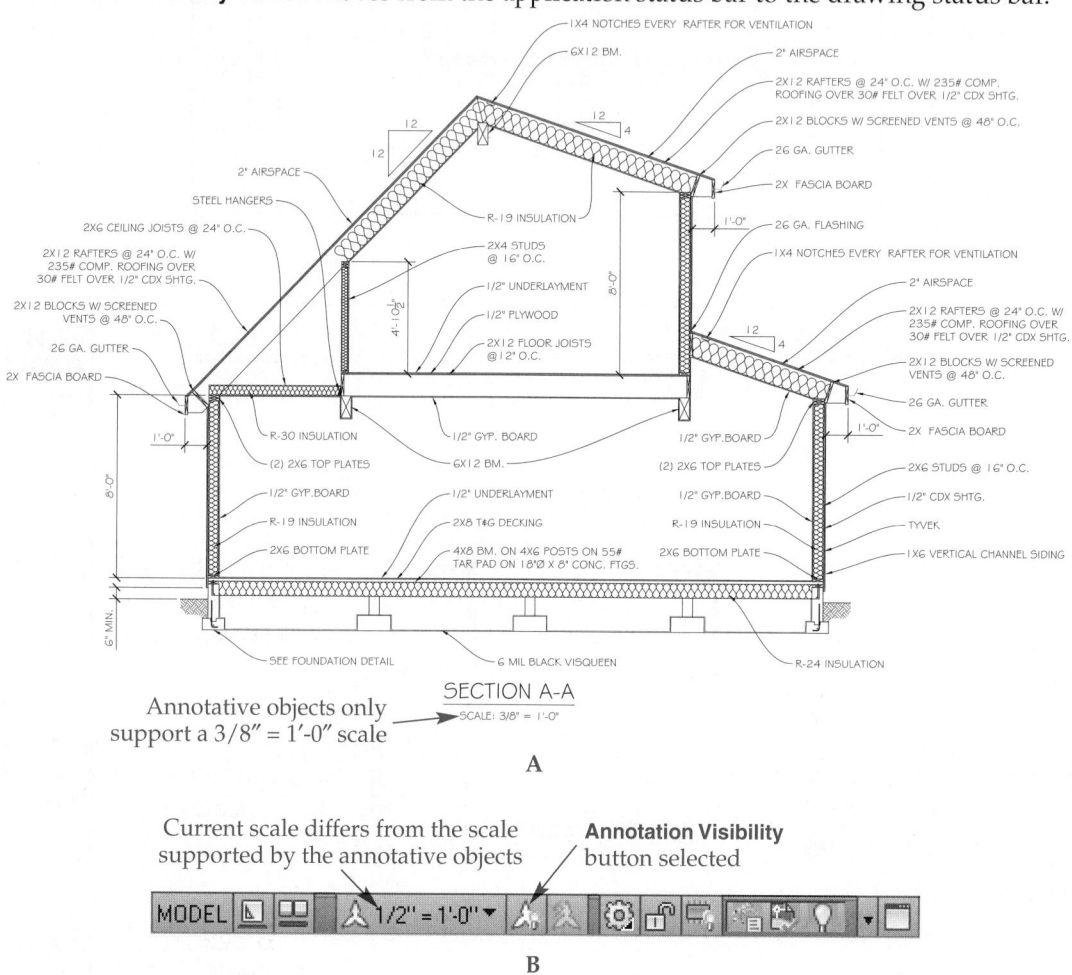

Annotative objects only
support a 3/8″ = 1′-0″ scale

A

Current scale differs from the scale
supported by the annotative objects

Annotation Visibility
button selected

B

Deselect the **Annotation Visibility** button to display only the annotative objects that support the current annotation scale. Any annotative objects unsupported by the current annotation scale disappear. See **Figure 30-14.** Turning annotation visibility off is most effective when you are annotating a drawing, or a portion of a drawing, using a different annotation scale without showing annotative object representations specific to a different annotation scale. Turning off visibility of annotative objects that do not support the current annotation scale is also effective for preparing multiview drawings because it eliminates the need to create separate layers for objects displayed at different scales. This practice is described later in this chapter.

AutoCAD and Its Applications—Basics

Figure 30-14. Deselect the **Annotation Visibility** button to display only the annotative objects that support the current annotation scale. The annotative objects in this example do not appear because they support only a 3/8″ = 1′-0″ annotation scale, and the current annotation scale is 1/2″ = 1′-0″.

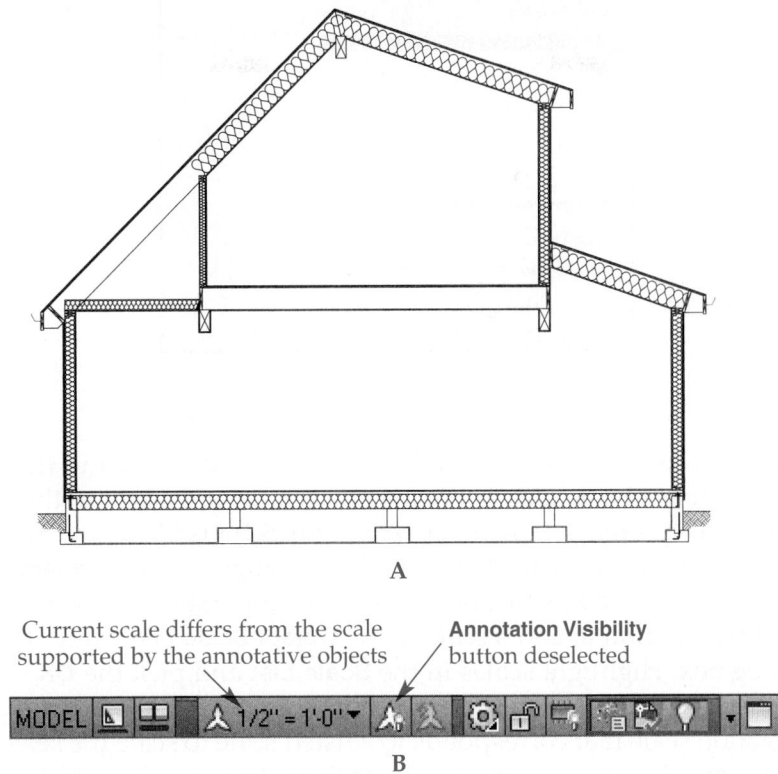

Current scale differs from the scale supported by the annotative objects

Annotation Visibility button deselected

Adding and Deleting Annotation Scales

One method for assigning additional annotation scales to annotative objects is to add the scales to selected objects. This method is appropriate whenever the drawing scale changes, but it is especially effective for adding annotation scales only to specific objects, such as when you are creating multiview drawings.

Delete an annotation scale from annotative objects if the annotation scale is no longer in use, should not display in a specific view, or makes it difficult to work with annotative objects. When you delete an annotation scale from annotative objects, the scale can no longer be applied to them. Add or delete annotation scales from selected objects using annotation scaling tools or the **Properties** palette.

Using the OBJECTSCALE Tool

The **OBJECTSCALE** tool provides one method of adding and deleting annotation scales supported by annotative objects. A quick way to access the **OBJECTSCALE** tool is to select an annotative object and then right-click and pick **Add/Delete Scale...** from the **Annotative Objects Scales** cascading submenu. If you activate the **OBJECTSCALE** tool by right-clicking on objects, the **Annotation Object Scale** dialog box appears, allowing you to add or remove annotation scales from the selected objects. See **Figure 30-15**. If you access the **OBJECTSCALE** tool before selecting objects, all annotative objects are displayed, even those objects that do not support the current annotation scale. Select the annotative objects to modify and right-click or press [Enter] or the space bar to display the **Annotation Object Scale** dialog box.

The **Object Scale List** shows the annotation scales associated with the selected annotative objects. A scale must appear in the list in order for the scale to apply to

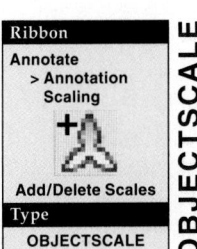

Ribbon
Annotate
> Annotation
   Scaling
Add/Delete Scales
Type
OBJECTSCALE

OBJECTSCALE

Figure 30-15. Use the **Annotation Object Scale** dialog box to add annotation scales to and delete them from annotative objects.

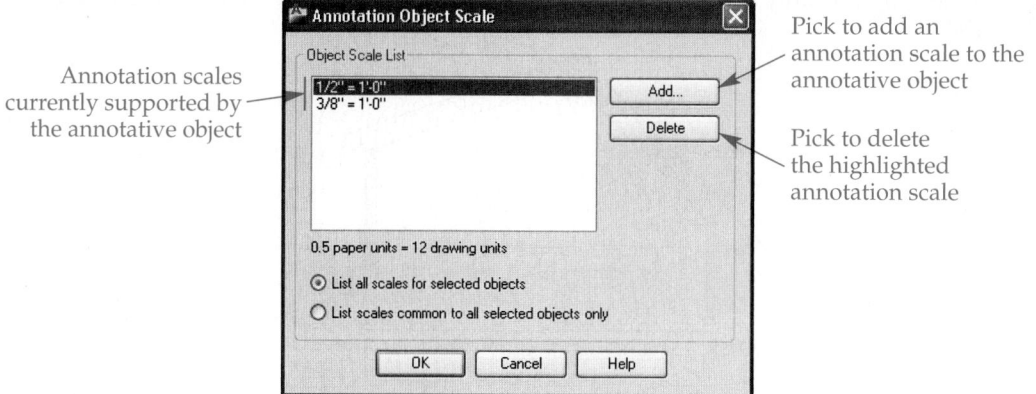

Annotation scales currently supported by the annotative object

Pick to add an annotation scale to the annotative object

Pick to delete the highlighted annotation scale

the annotative objects. If you select a different annotation scale, and that scale is not displayed in the **Object Scale List**, annotative objects do not adapt to the new annotation scale, and you have the option to make the objects invisible. In the example shown in Figure 30-13 and Figure 30-14, 1/2″ = 1′-0″ must appear in the **Object Scale List** in order for the annotative objects to adapt to the new annotation scale of 1/2″ = 1′-0″.

Pick the **Add...** button to add a scale to the **Object Scale List** using the **Add Scales to Object** dialog box. Highlight scales in the **Scale List** and pick the **OK** button to add the scales to the **Object Scale List**. Once you add a scale to the **Object Scale List**, you can pick an annotation scale that corresponds to a listed scale to scale the selected annotative objects. To remove a scale from the **Object Scale List**, highlight the scale and pick the **Delete** button.

If you select multiple annotative objects, pick the **List scales common to all selected objects only** radio button to display only the annotative scales common to the selected objects. Pick the **List all scales for selected objects** radio button to show all annotation scales associated with any of the selected objects, even if some of the objects do not support the listed scales. Listing all scales for selected objects is helpful when you want to delete a scale that applies only to certain objects.

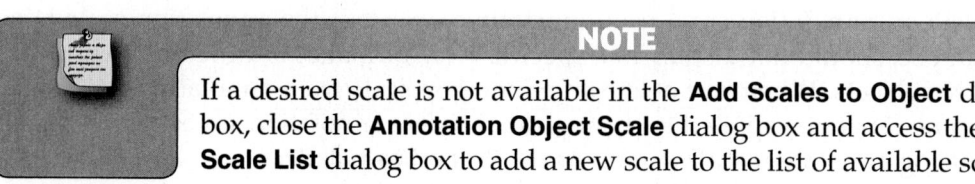

NOTE

If a desired scale is not available in the **Add Scales to Object** dialog box, close the **Annotation Object Scale** dialog box and access the **Edit Scale List** dialog box to add a new scale to the list of available scales.

Using the Properties Palette

The **Properties** palette also allows you to add annotation scales to selected annotative objects. See Figure 30-16. The location of the annotative properties in the **Properties** palette varies depending on the selected object. The **Annotative scale** property displays the annotation scale currently applied to the selected annotative objects and contains an ellipsis button (...) that you can pick to open the **Annotation Object Scale** dialog box.

Automatically Adding Annotation Scales

Another technique for assigning additional annotation scales to annotative objects is to add a selected annotation scale automatically to all annotative objects in the drawing. This eliminates the need to add annotation scales to individual annotative objects and quickly produces newly scaled drawings.

Figure 30-16.
The **Annotation scale** property in the **Properties** palette provides another way to access the **Annotation Object Scale** dialog box.

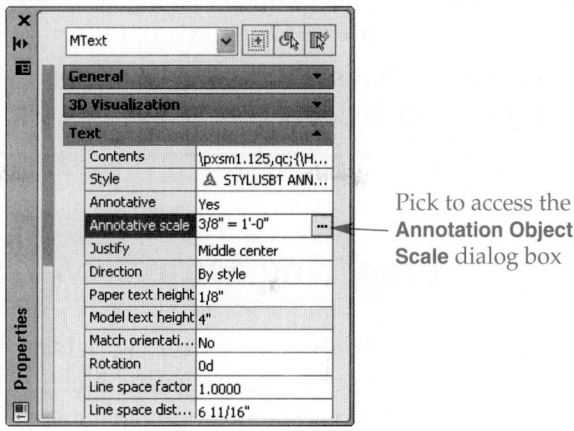

Pick to access the **Annotation Object Scale** dialog box

The **ANNOAUTOSCALE** system variable controls the ability to add an annotation scale to all existing annotative objects. Enter 1, –1, 2, –2, 3, –3, 4, or –4, depending on the desired effect. **Figure 30-17A** describes each option. After you enter the initial value, the easiest way to toggle the **ANNOAUTOSCALE** system variable on and off is to pick the button on the status bar shown in **Figure 30-17B**.

CAUTION

Use caution when adding annotation scales automatically. Due to the effectiveness and transparency of the tool, annotation scales are often added to annotative objects unintentionally. Although you can later delete scales, this causes additional work and confusion.

Figure 30-17. A—**ANNOAUTOSCALE** system variable options. B—After you enter the initial **ANNOAUTOSCALE** system variable setting, use the button on the status bar to toggle **ANNOAUTOSCALE** on and off. If you display the drawing status bar, the **ANNOAUTOSCALE** button moves from the application status bar to the drawing status bar.

Value	Mode	Description
1	On	Adds the selected annotation scale to annotative objects, not including those drawn on a layer that is turned off, frozen, locked, or frozen in a viewport.
–1	Off	1 behavior is used when **ANNOAUTOSCALE** is turned back on.
2	On	Adds the selected annotation scale to annotative objects, not including those drawn on a layer that is turned off, frozen, or frozen in a viewport.
–2	Off	2 behavior is used when **ANNOAUTOSCALE** is turned back on.
3	On	Adds the selected annotation scale to annotative objects, not including those drawn on a layer that is locked.
–3	Off	3 behavior is used when **ANNOAUTOSCALE** is turned back on.
4	On	Adds the selected annotation scale to all annotative objects regardless of the status of the layer on which the annotative object is drawn. 4 is the AutoCAD default setting when toggled on.
–4	Off	4 behavior is used when **ANNOAUTOSCALE** is turned back on. –4 is the AutoCAD default setting when toggled off.

A

Pick to toggle the **ANNOAUTOSCALE** system variable on or off

B

Exercise 30-4

Access the Student Web site (www.g-wlearning.com/CAD) and complete Exercise 30-4.

Preparing Multiview Drawings

Drawings for many different engineering fields often contain views, sections, and details drawn at different scales. Annotative objects offer several advantages for these drawings, especially when views in model space appear at different scales in layouts. Use scaled viewports to display multiple views using a single file. You can assign a different annotation scale to each drawing view that contains annotative objects, reducing the need to calculate multiple drawing scale factors, while maintaining the appropriate scale of previously drawn annotative objects. Additionally, by adjusting annotative scale representation visibility and position, you can prepare differently scaled multiview drawings, while eliminating the need to use separate, scale-specific layers and annotations.

Creating Differently Scaled Drawings

Figure 30-18A shows an example of two different drawing views, both drawn at full scale in model space. The full section in **Figure 30-18A** uses a 3/8″ = 1′-0″ scale. To prepare the full section, set the annotation scale in model space to 3/8″ = 1′-0″, and then add annotative objects. The annotative objects are automatically scaled according to the 3/8″ = 1′-0″ annotation scale. The stair section in **Figure 30-18A** uses a 1/2″ = 1′-0″ scale. To prepare the stair section, change the annotation scale in model space from 3/8″ = 1′-0″ to 1/2″ = 1′-0″, and then add annotative objects. These annotative objects are automatically scaled according to the 1/2″ = 1′-0″ annotation scale. If you look closely, you can see the different scales applied to the drawing views.

Figure 30-18A shows annotation visibility on, allowing you to see all annotative objects and observe the effects of using different scales. **Figure 30-18B** shows annotation visibility off to show only annotative objects that support the current annotation scale, which is 1/2″ = 1′-0″ in this example.

The next step is to display and plot the drawing using multiple paper space viewports. **Figure 30-19** shows an architectural D-size sheet layout with two floating viewports. One viewport displays the full section at a viewport scale of 3/8″ = 1′-0″. The other viewport displays the stair section at a viewport scale of 1/2″ = 1′-0″. Notice that the annotative objects are the same size in both views.

Exercise 30-5

Access the Student Web site (www.g-wlearning.com/CAD) and complete Exercise 30-5.

Reusing Annotative Objects

Often the same drawing features appear in different views at different scales. For example, you may plot a drawing on a large sheet using a large scale, and plot the same drawing on a smaller sheet using a smaller scale. Another example is preparing a view enlargement or detail.

Figure 30-18. Two different drawing views drawn at full scale in model space. The full section uses an annotation scale of 3/8″ = 1′-0″, and the stair section uses an annotation scale of 1/2″ = 1′-0″. A—Annotation visibility is on. B—Annotation visibility is off with the current annotation scale set to 1/2″ = 1′-0″ (stair section view scale).

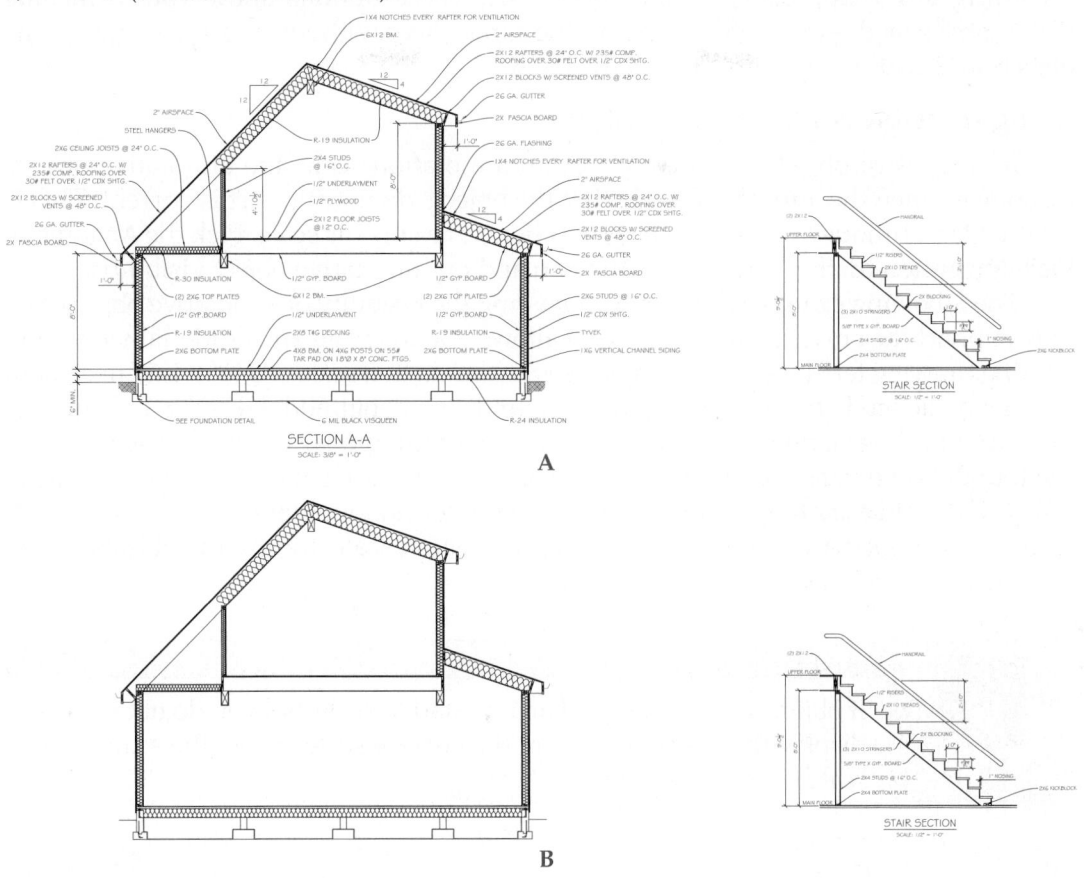

Figure 30-19. Using viewports with different scales to create a multiview drawing. Notice that the annotative objects are the same size in both views.

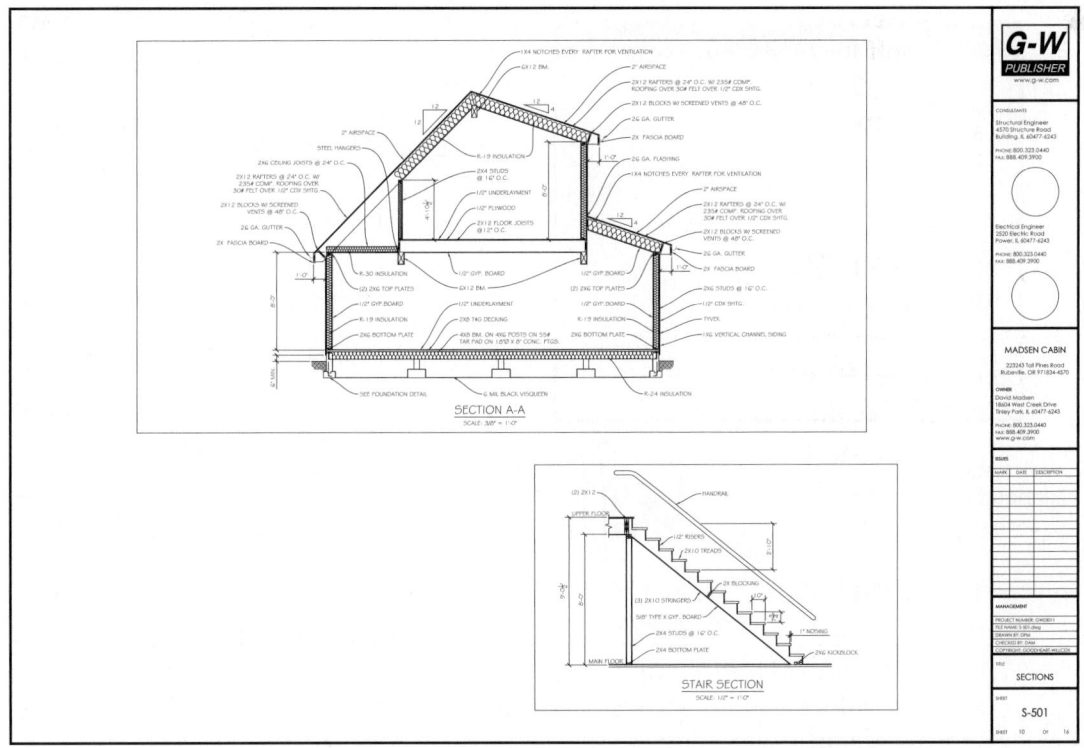

Annotative objects significantly improve the ability to reuse existing drawing features. Use annotation visibility to hide annotative objects not supported by the current annotation scale. You can also adjust the position of scale representations according to the appropriate annotation scale. These options allow you to include differently scaled annotative objects on the same sheet without creating copies of the objects and without using scale-specific layers.

Using Invisible Scale Representations

If annotative objects do not support an annotation scale, the annotative objects disappear when the annotation scale that the objects do not support is current. This is a valuable technique for displaying certain items at a specific scale. Pick the **Annotation Visibility** button on the status bar to turn on and off annotative object visibility.

The following example shows how adjusting the visibility of annotative objects that only support the current annotation scale allows you to create an additional view from existing drawing features. This example uses an annotation scale of 3/4″ = 1′-0″ to create a foundation detail. To begin constructing the foundation detail, add the 3/4″ = 1′-0″ annotation scale to the existing earth hatch pattern so it will appear on the full section and the foundation detail. See **Figure 30-20.** Next, with the current annotation scale set to 3/4″ = 1′-0″, add annotative objects specific to the foundation detail. See **Figure 30-21.** These objects support only the 3/4″ = 1′-0″ annotation scale, hiding the objects on the full section, which uses a 3/8″ = 1′-0″ scale.

PROFESSIONAL TIP

If objects already support an annotation scale, but you do not want to display those annotations at the current scale, delete the annotation scale from the objects.

Figure 30-20. Reuse the earth hatch pattern by adding the 3/4″ = 1′-0″ foundation detail scale to the annotative hatch pattern.

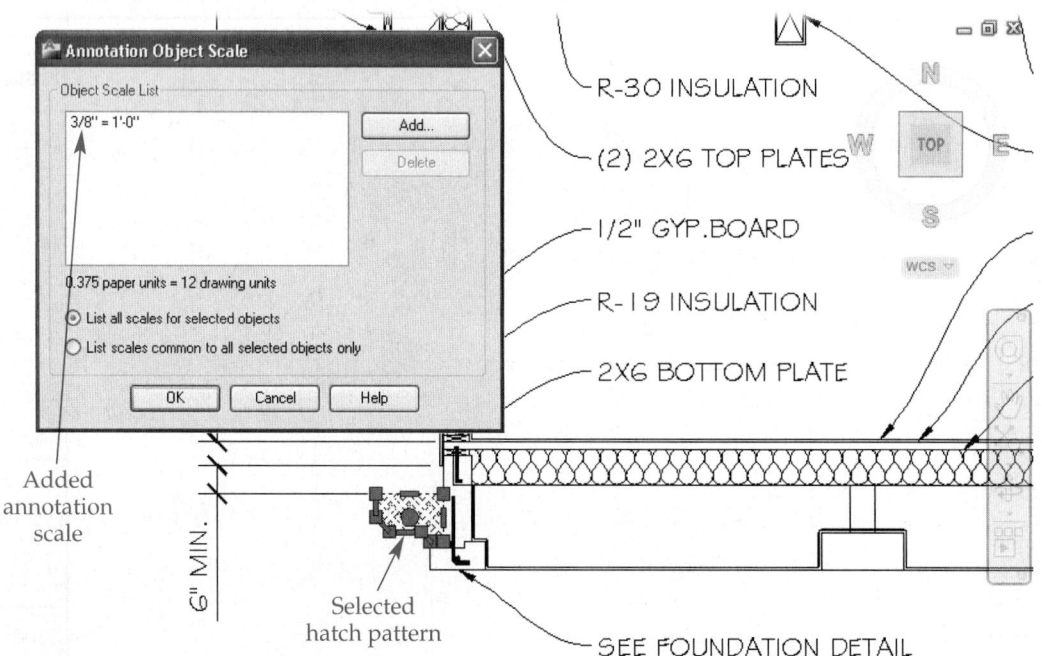

AutoCAD and Its Applications—Basics

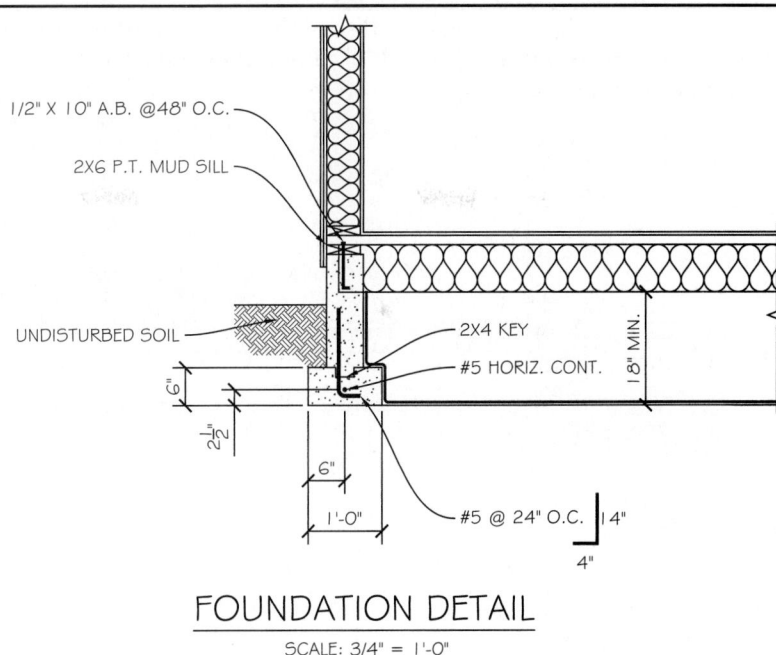

Figure 30-21.
Adding annotative text, dimensions, multileaders, and hatch patterns specific to the foundation detail using a 3/4″ = 1′-0″ annotation scale.

1/2″ X 10″ A.B. @48″ O.C.

2X6 P.T. MUD SILL

UNDISTURBED SOIL

2X4 KEY

#5 HORIZ. CONT.

18″ MIN.

6″

2 1/2″

6″

1′-0″

#5 @ 24″ O.C.

4″

4″

FOUNDATION DETAIL

SCALE: 3/4″ = 1′-0″

Adjusting Scale Representation Position

When you reuse annotative objects, the location and spacing of annotative objects on one scale are often not appropriate for another scale. Reposition each scale representation to overcome this issue.

In the foundation detail example in **Figure 30-21,** some of the existing 3/8″ = 1′-0″ scaled dimensions and multileaders from the full section are reused in the foundation detail. See **Figure 30-22A.** The first step is to add a 3/4″ = 1′-0″ annotation scale to the objects. Next, with **Annotation Visibility** turned off, as shown in **Figure 30-22B,** you can see the resulting position of the selected objects, which is initially the same as the position of the 3/8″ = 1′-0″ objects. The only difference is that now the 3/8″ = 1′-0″ objects also support a 3/4″ = 1′-0″ scale.

Use grip editing to adjust the position of annotation scale representations. When you select annotative objects that support more than one annotation scale, all scale representations appear by default. See **Figure 30-23.** An annotative object is a single object, but it can contain several scale representations. Grips are displayed on the scale representation that corresponds to the current annotation scale. Using grips to edit scale representations is similar to editing the object used to create the scale representation. The difference when editing a scale representation is that you adjust a scaled copy of the object. **Figure 30-24** shows the effects of editing the position of dimension and multileader scale representations on the foundation detail. The figure shows selecting the representations to help demonstrate the effects of editing scale representation position. Notice that you can edit all elements of the scale representation to produce the desired annotations at the appropriate locations.

PROFESSIONAL TIP

Use the **DIMSPACE** and **MLEADERALIGN** tools to adjust dimension spacing and multileader alignment after changing the drawing scale.

Chapter 30 Annotative Objects

Figure 30-22. A—Reusing some of the existing 3/8″ = 1′-0″ scaled objects to create another drawing view. B—Adding a 3/4″ = 1′-0″ annotation scale to existing objects and setting the annotation scale to 3/4″ = 1′-0″.

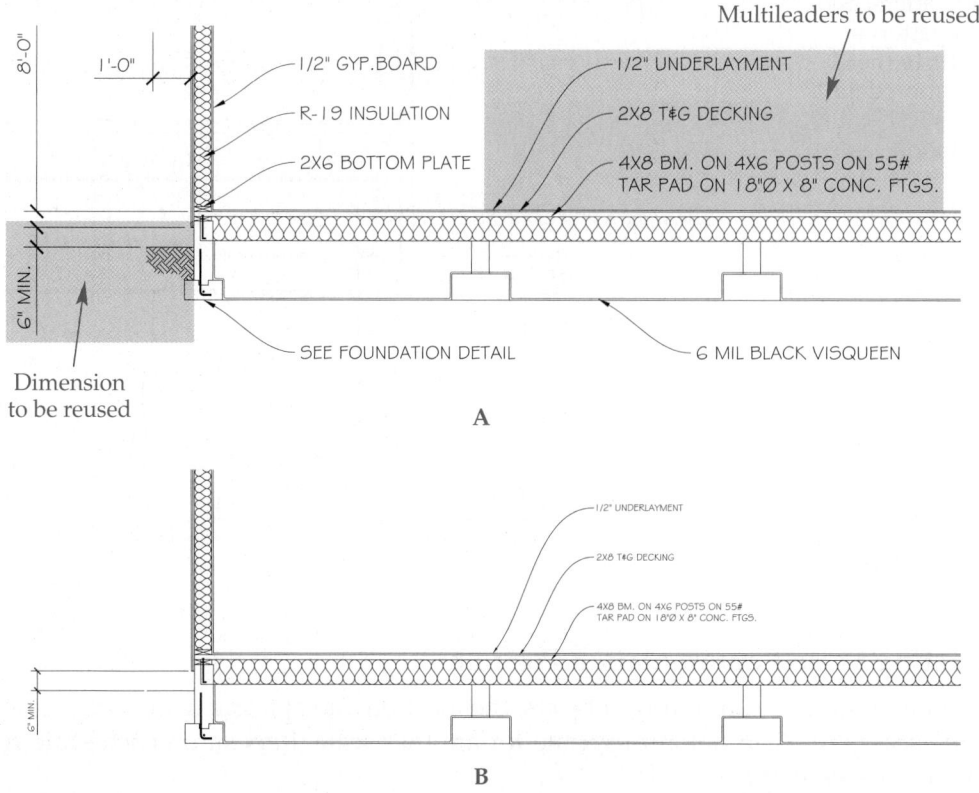

A

B

Figure 30-23. Adjust the position of annotation scale representations using grip editing. When you select annotative objects that support more than one annotation scale, all scale representations appear by default.

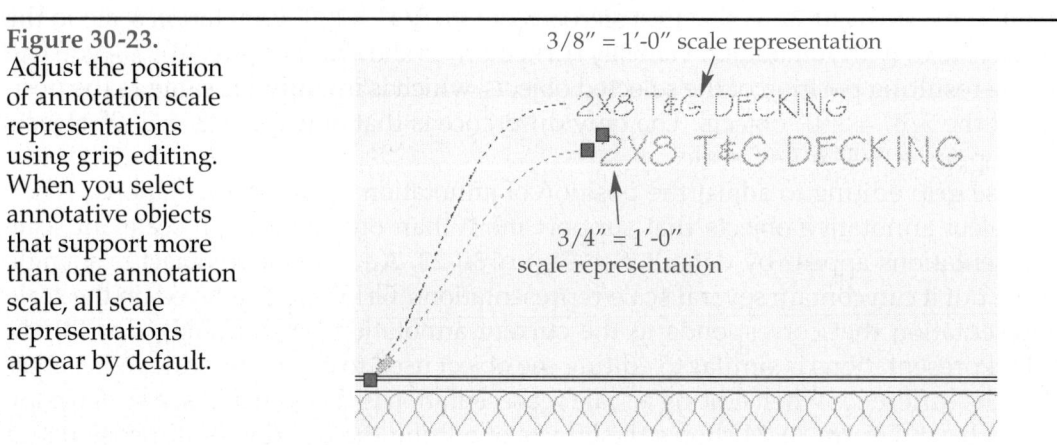

The **SELECTIONANNODISPLAY** system variable controls the display of selected scale representations and is set to 1 by default. As a result, all scale representations display and appear dimmed when you pick an annotative object that supports multiple annotation scales. See **Figure 30-24.** The display can be confusing if the selected object supports several annotation scales. Set the **SELECTIONANNODISPLAY** system variable to 0 to display only the scale representation that corresponds to the current annotation scale.

Figure 30-24. Editing the position of scale representations is much like creating scaled copies of existing annotations.

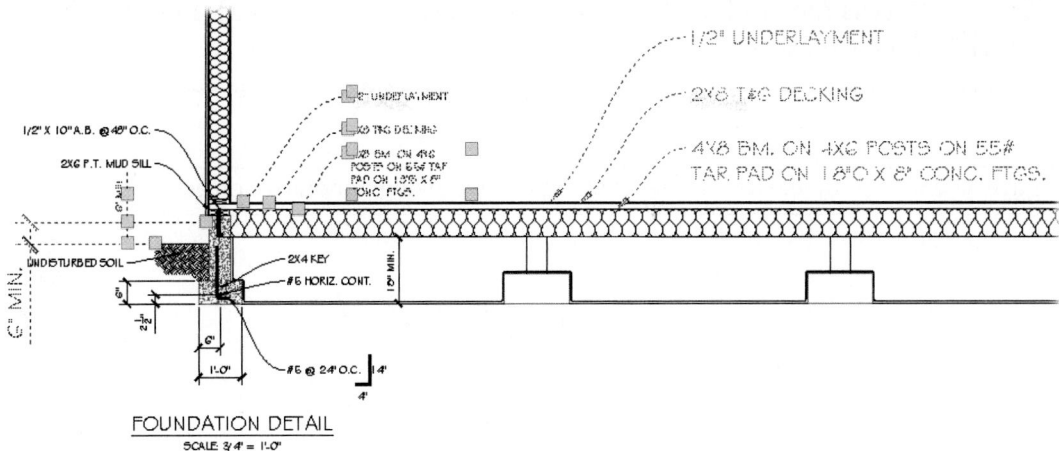

FOUNDATION DETAIL
SCALE 3/4" = 1'-0"

Resetting Scale Representation Position

The **ANNORESET** tool removes multiple scale representation positions, allowing you to change the position of all selected scale representations to the position of the scale representation that is set for the current annotation scale. A quick way to access the **ANNORESET** tool is to select annotative objects, right-click and pick the option from the **Annotative Object Scale** cascading submenu. If you activate the **ANNORESET** tool by right-clicking on objects, the position of the selected objects resets. If you access the tool before selecting objects, pick the annotative objects. Then right-click or press [Enter] or the space bar to exit the tool and reset the scale representation positions.

Ribbon

Annotate
> Annotation
Scaling

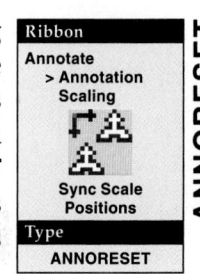

Sync Scale
Positions

Type

ANNORESET

ANNORESET

Completing a Multiview Drawing

The last step in creating a multiview drawing is to display and plot the drawing using multiple paper space viewports. **Figure 30-25** shows an architectural D-size sheet layout with three floating viewports. One viewport displays the full section at a 3/8" = 1'-0" viewport scale. A second viewport displays the stair section at a 1/2" = 1'-0" viewport scale. A third viewport displays the foundation detail at a 3/4" = 1'-0" viewport scale.

Exercise 30-6

Access the Student Web site (www.g-wlearning.com/CAD) and complete Exercise 30-6.

Figure 30-25. A complete multiview drawing created using annotative objects.

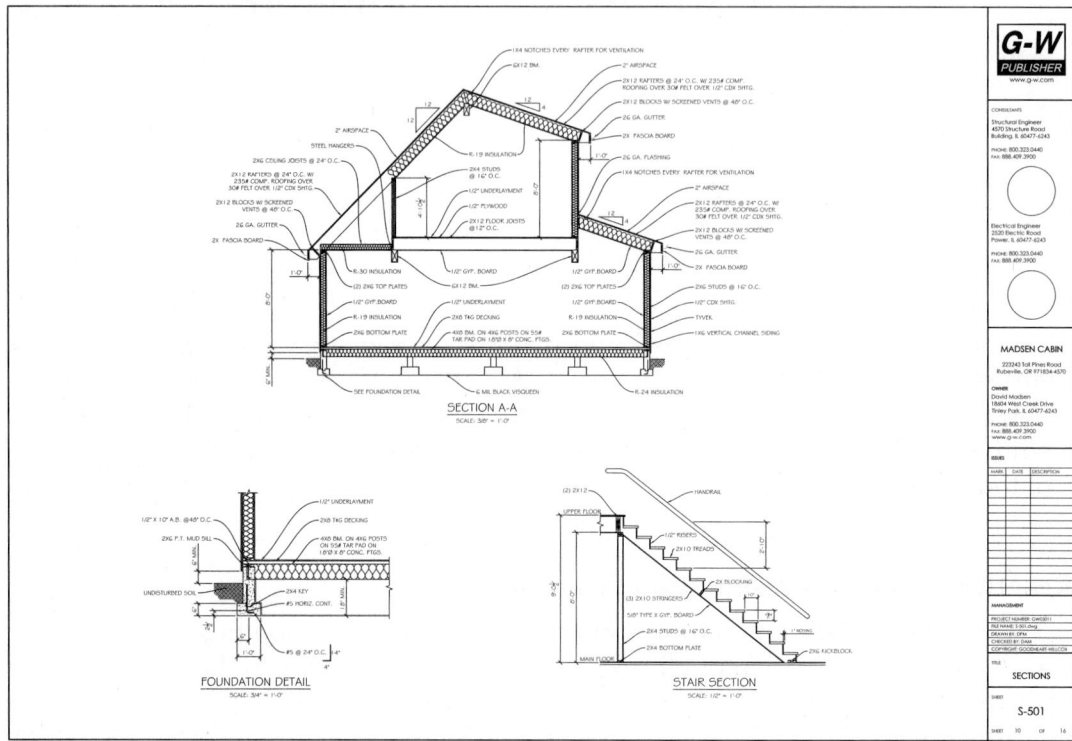

Chapter Test

Answer the following questions. Write your answers on a separate sheet of paper or go to the Student Web site (www.g-wlearning.com/CAD) and complete the electronic chapter test.

1. What are annotative objects?
2. Explain the practical differences between manual and annotative object scaling.
3. Identify at least four types of objects that you can make annotative.
4. How do you set text scale, including spacing, width, and paragraph settings, to adjust automatically according to the current annotation scale?
5. Identify an important relationship between the viewport scale and the annotation scale.
6. Which **MSLTSCALE** system variable setting should you use so you do not have to calculate the drawing scale factor when entering an **LTSCALE** value?
7. Name the tool used to update text properties according to the current properties of the text style on which the text is drawn.
8. What is an annotative object representation?
9. Briefly describe the result of setting the **ANNOAUTOSCALE** system variable to a value of 4.
10. Briefly explain the effect of turning annotation visibility on and off.

Drawing Problems

- *Start AutoCAD if it is not already started.*

- *Start a new drawing for each problem using an appropriate template of your choice. The template should include layers and text, dimension, multileader, and table styles, when necessary, for drawing the given objects. Add layers and text, dimension, multileader, and table styles as needed.*

- *Draw all objects using appropriate layers and text, dimension, multileader, and table styles, justification, and format.*

- *Follow the specific instructions for each problem. Use only drawing and editing tools and techniques you have already learned. Use your own judgment and approximate dimensions when necessary.*

- *Apply dimensions accurately using ASME or appropriate industry standards.*

Note: *Some of the problems in this chapter are built on problems from previous chapters. If you have not yet completed those problems, complete them now.*

▼ Basic

1. Open P23-9 and save as P30-1. The P30-1 file should be active. Convert all the non-annotative objects to annotative objects. Resave the drawing.

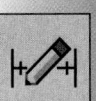

2. Open P24-10 and save as P30-2. The P30-2 file should be active. Convert all of the non-annotative objects to annotative objects. Resave the drawing.

▼ Intermediate

3. Draw the section view and side view shown. Use annotative objects to prepare a full-scale drawing of the part. Change the annotation scale to 2:1 and adjust the scale representations as needed according to the new scale. Save the drawing as P30-3.

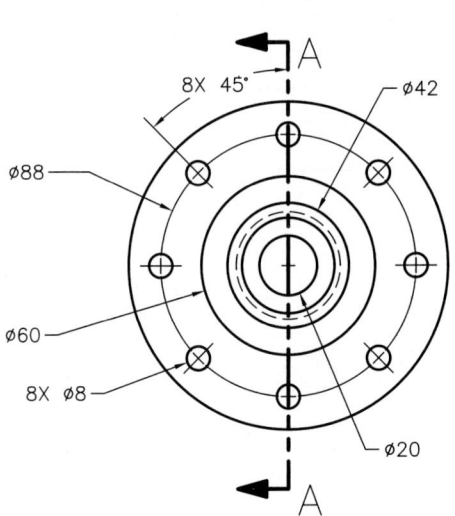

Name: Hub
Material: Cast Iron

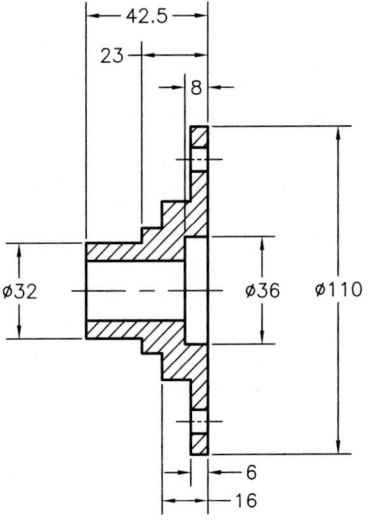

SECTION A—A

4. Draw the section view and side views shown. Use annotative objects to prepare a full-scale drawing of the part. Change the annotation scale to 2:1 and adjust the scale representations as needed according to the new scale. Save the drawing as P30-4.

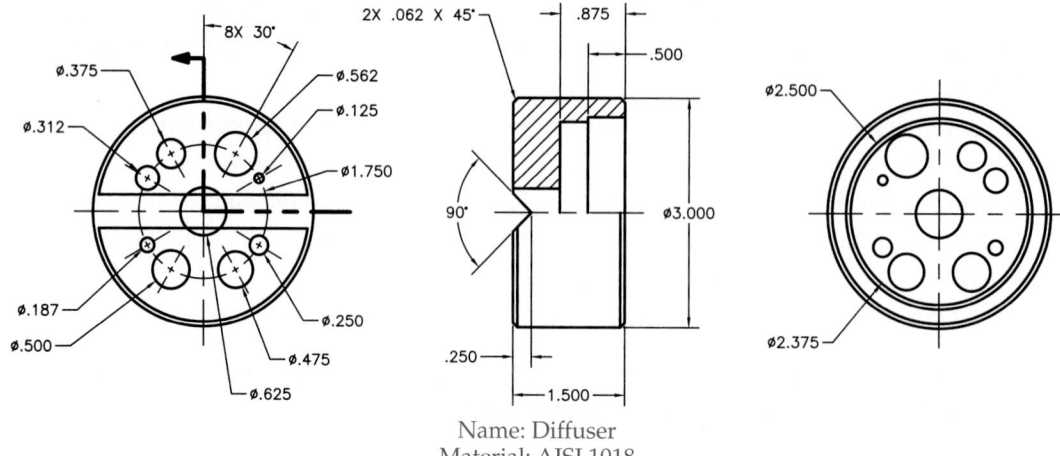

Name: Diffuser
Material: AISI 1018

5. Draw the fan shown at full scale in model space. Use annotative objects to prepare a full-scale view of the fan as shown and a view enlargement of the motor. You should not have to create a copy of the motor or develop scale-specific layers. Save the drawing as P30-5.

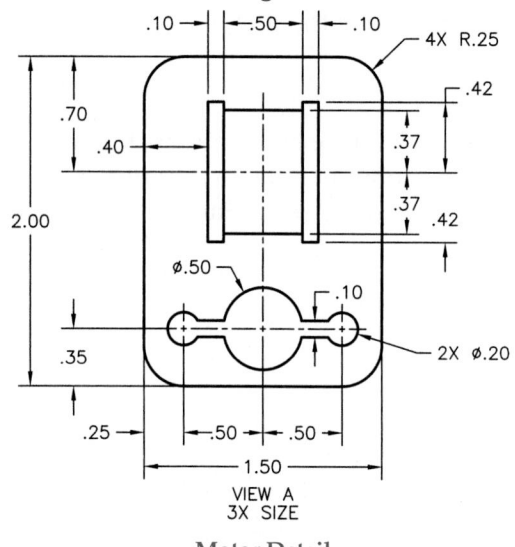

VIEW A
3X SIZE

Motor Detail

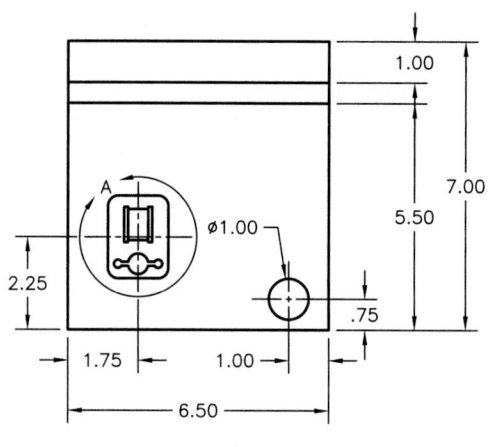

Fan

▼ Advanced

6. Draw the floor plan shown at full scale in model space. Use annotative objects to prepare a 1/4″ = 1′-0″ view. Change the annotation scale to 1/8″ = 1′-0″ and adjust the scale representations as needed according to the new scale. Save the drawing as P30-6.

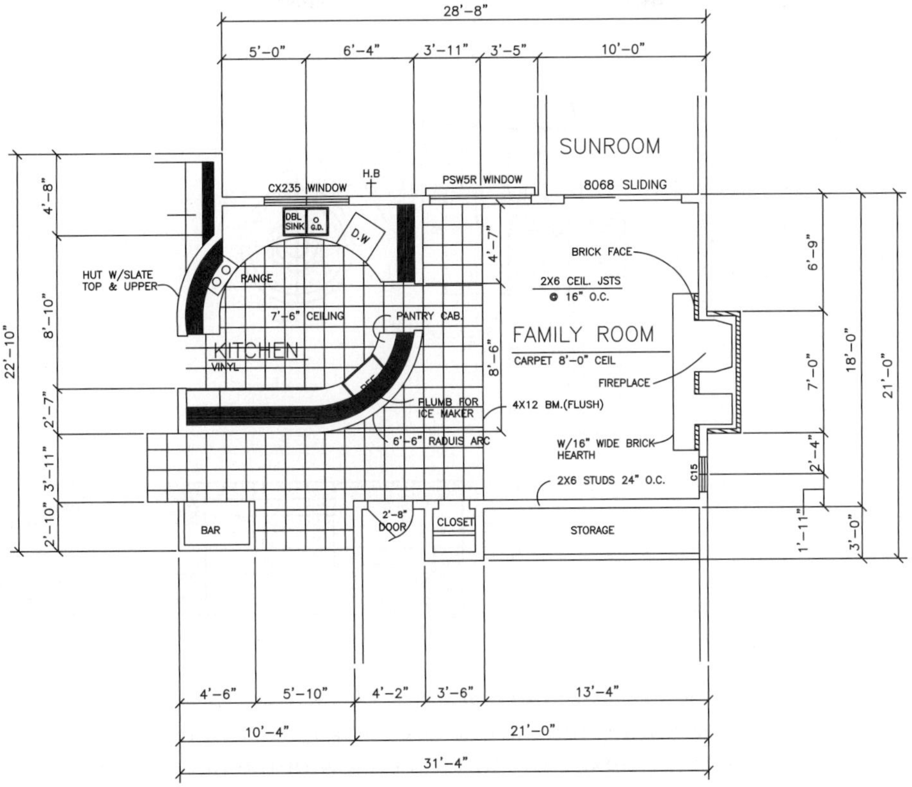

7. Draw the part shown at full scale in model space. Use annotative objects to prepare the full-scale view and the view enlargement shown. You should not have to create a copy of the part or develop scale-specific layers. Plot the layout. Save the drawing as P30-7.

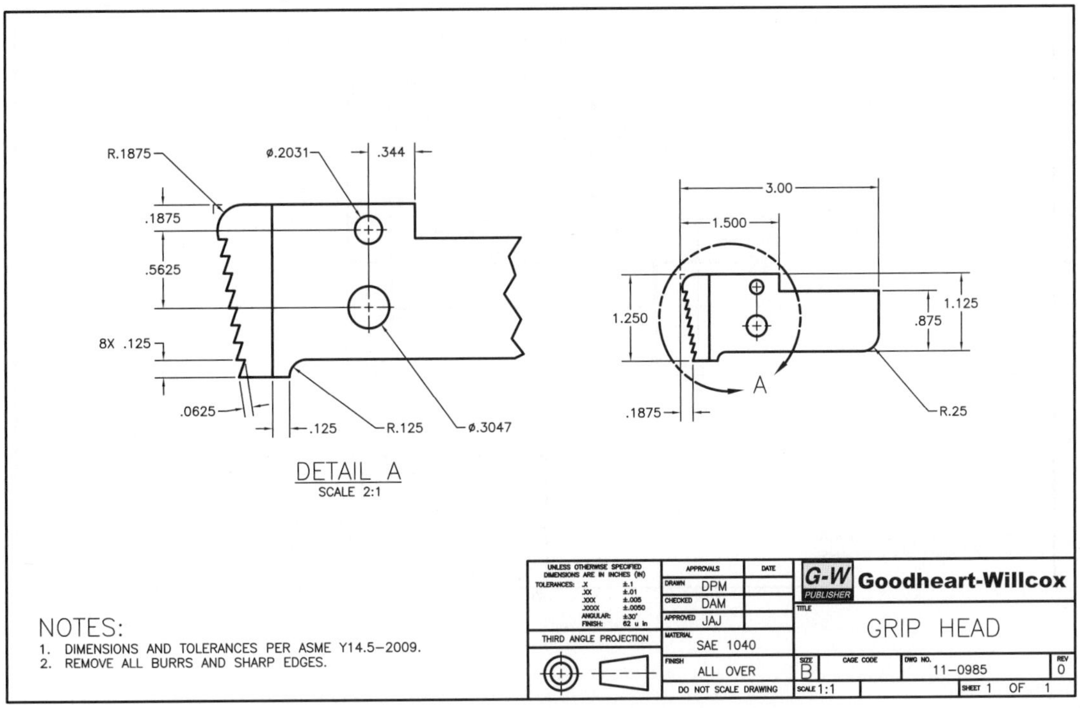

8. Draw, dimension, and plot using a layout the male insert shown. Use annotative objects. Use a larger sheet and annotative object scaling to plot a 4:1 scale drawing of the insert. You should not have to create a copy of the part or develop scale-specific layers. Save the drawing as P30-8.

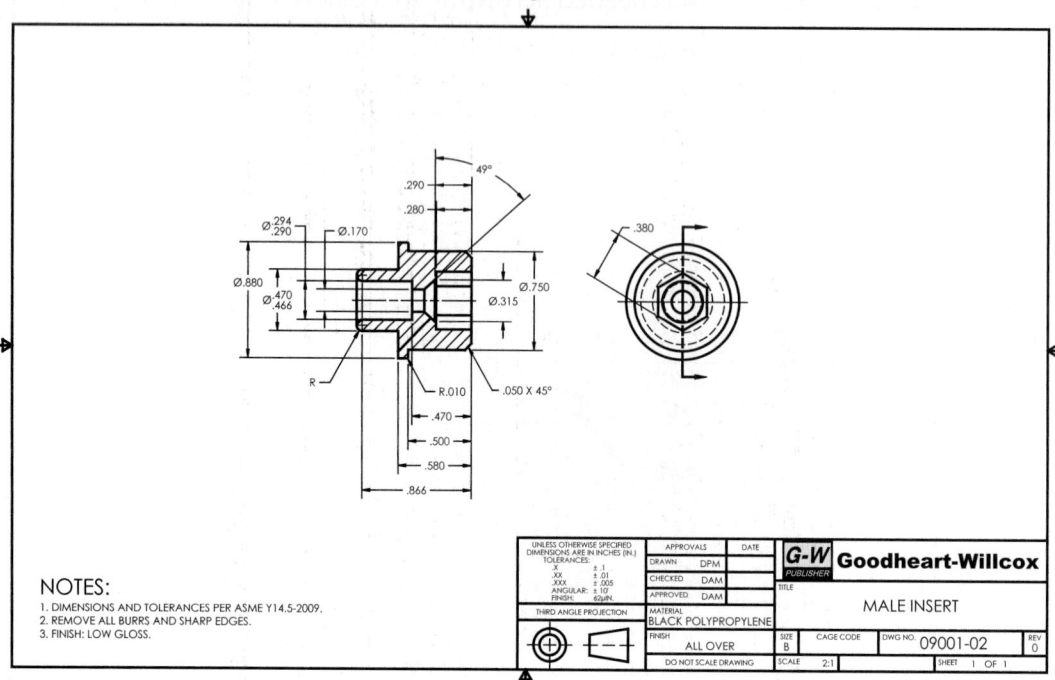

9. Draw the sheet metal flat pattern shown. Design the shape of punch A using your own judgment and dimensions proportionate to other part features. Use annotative objects to prepare the full-scale view of the flat pattern and the view enlargement of the punch. Dimension the punch. You should not have to create a copy of the part or develop scale-specific layers. Plot the layout. Save the drawing as P30-9.

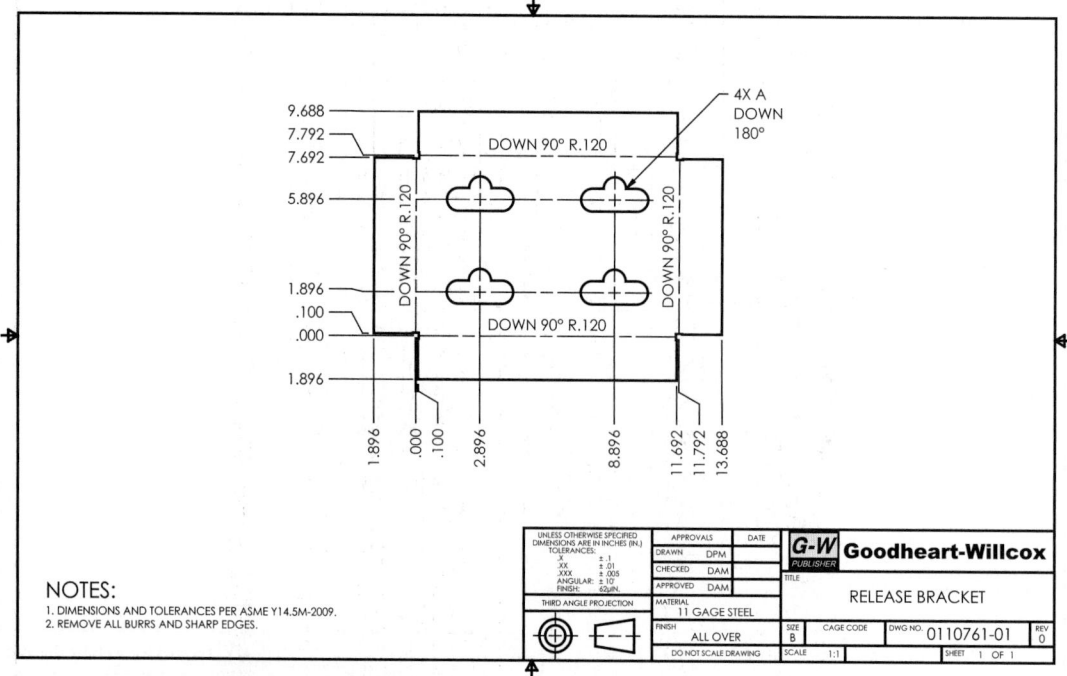

10. Research the design of an existing paper-cutting scissors consisting of at least three separate parts. Create dimensioned 2D sketches of the existing design from manufacturer's specifications, or from measurements taken from actual scissors. Start a new drawing from scratch or use a decimal template of your choice. Prepare detail drawings of each part and an assembly drawing with balloons and a parts list. Use annotative objects and separate layouts for each drawing to prepare a set of drawings in one file. Plot each drawing. Save the drawing as P30-10.

11. Create a dimensioned 2D sketch of a complete floor plan for a home with three bedrooms and two bathrooms. Start a new drawing from scratch or use an architectural template of your choice. Draw, dimension, and plot the floor plan from your sketch using a layout. Use annotative objects. Save the drawing as P30-11.

12. Obtain a hard copy of a plot plan of a small residential subdivision, or a portion of a subdivision. Draw, dimension, and plot the subdivision using a layout. Use annotative objects. Save the drawing as P30-12.

AutoCAD Certified Associate Exam Practice

Answer the following questions. Write your answers on a separate sheet of paper.

1. A drawing of a mechanical part is set up to be printed at a scale of 2:1 in a layout in paper space. The length of one feature on the part is 35.125″. How long should that feature be drawn in model space? *Select the one item that best answers the question.*
   A. 3.513″
   B. 17.563″
   C. 35.125″
   D. 70.250″

2. Which of the following statements are true about blocks? *Select all that apply.*
   A. Attributes included in an annotative block automatically become annotative even if they are not set to be annotative.
   B. Attributes included in an annotative block change according to the annotation scale, but the block remains fixed.
   C. You can make a block annotative when you originally create the block.
   D. You can make a block annotative after its creation by using the **Properties** palette.

3. How can you change the overall annotation scale of a layout? *Select all that apply.*
   A. right-click and select an annotation scale from the cascading list
   B. select **Scale List** in the **Annotation Scaling** panel of the **Annotate** ribbon tab
   C. use the **Annotation Scale** flyout
   D. use the **Properties** palette
   E. use the **Viewport Scale** flyout

AutoCAD Certified Professional Exam Practice

Follow the instructions in the problem. Write your answers on a separate sheet of paper.

1. **Navigate to this chapter on the Student Web site and open CPE-30annoscale.dwg.** Change the annotation scale to 1/2″=1′-0″ to display annotative hatch patterns created at that scale. What hatch pattern is used for the undisturbed soil in this drawing?

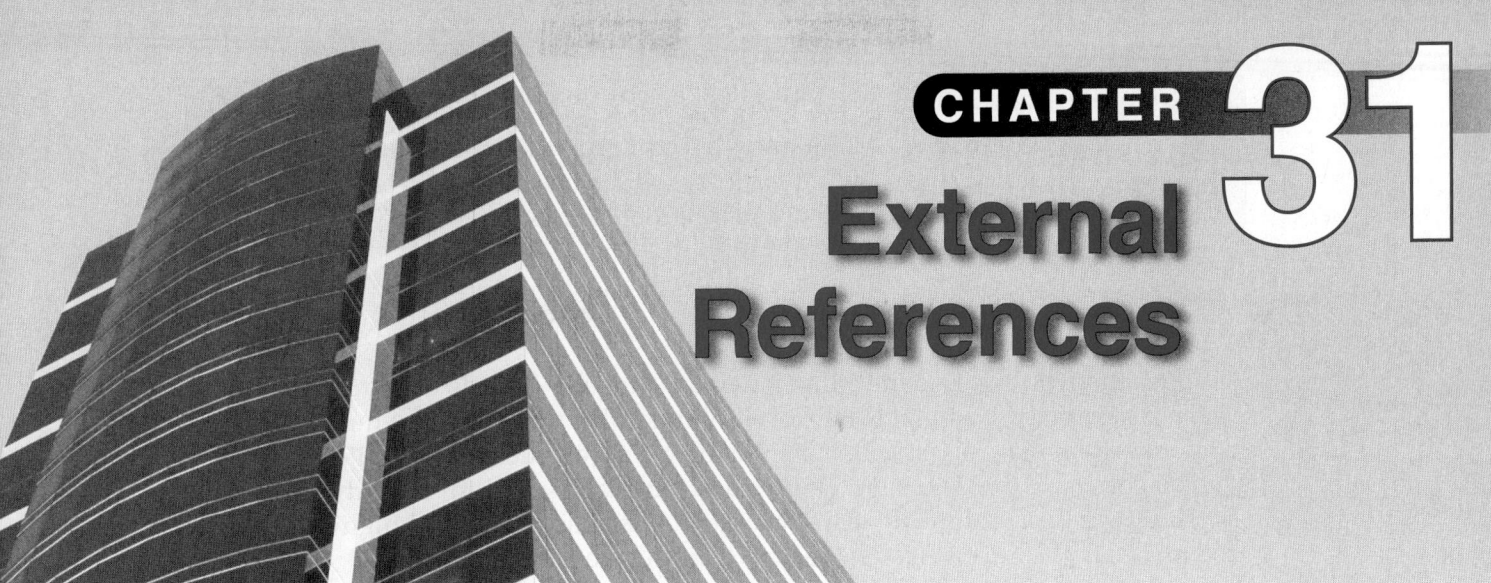

External References

Learning Objectives

After completing this chapter, you will be able to do the following:

✓ Explain the function of external references.
✓ Attach existing drawings to the current drawing.
✓ Use **DesignCenter** and tool palettes to attach external references.
✓ Bind external references and selected dependent objects to a drawing.
✓ Edit external references in the current drawing.

External references (xrefs) expand on the concept of reusing existing content in AutoCAD. Xrefs provide an effective way to relate existing base drawings, complex symbols, images, and details to other drawings. Xrefs also help multiple users share content. This chapter focuses on using xref drawings and provides common xref applications.

external reference (xref): A DWG, DWF, DWFx, raster image, DNG, or PDF file incorporated into a drawing for reference only.

Introduction to Xrefs

An xref is a drawing (DWG), design web format (DWF and DWFx), raster image, digital negative (DNG), or portable document format (PDF) file that you reference into a *host drawing*. Inserting an xref is similar to inserting an entire drawing as a block. However, unlike a block, which is actually stored in the file in which you insert the block, the file geometry in a *reference file* is not added to the host drawing. File data appears on-screen for reference only. The result is usable information, but the host file remains much smaller host than if you insert a block or copy and paste objects. Xrefs are also easier to manage in a host drawing than blocks or pasted objects.

host drawing: The drawing into which xrefs are incorporated.

reference file: An xref; a file referenced by the host.

Another major benefit of using xrefs is the link between reference and host files. Any changes you make to reference files are reflected in host drawings, so the host drawings display the most recent reference content. AutoCAD reloads each xref whenever the host drawing loads. This allows you or a design drafting team to work on a multi-file project, with the assurance that any revisions to reference files are displayed in host drawings.

Xref Files

Files that you can reference into a current drawing include existing DWG, DWF, DWFx, raster image, DNG, and PDF files. DWF and DWFx files are drawings compressed for publication, viewing, and mark-up using a viewer, such as the Autodesk Design Review software. DWF and DWFx files are commonly used to share drawings with members of a design drafting team who do not use AutoCAD. The high compression also makes DWF and DWFx files easy to transmit electrically.

Raster image and DNG file reference is appropriate for adding an image to a drawing, such as for a company logo in a title block. PDF file reference allows you to reuse PDF file content. Externally referencing an image or PDF file into a drawing is an excellent technique, because the large file sizes often associated with images and PDF files do not affect the host drawing.

Xref Applications

DWG files are the most common xref files and are the focus of this chapter. The term *xref* often applies specifically to referenced DWG files. In general, use xrefs to reuse existing drawing information and help develop other drawings. There are countless applications for xref drawings in every drafting field. The following sections provide typical xref drawing applications. As you work with AutoCAD, you will discover a variety of uses for xref drawings.

Reference Existing Geometry

One of the most common applications for xref drawings is to reference existing geometry to use as a pattern or source of needed information in the host drawing. For example, a floor plan includes size and shape information required to prepare additional plans, elevations, sections, and details. **Figure 31-1** shows an example of referencing a floor plan file into a new drawing to use as an outline for creating a roof plan file.

Figure 31-2 shows an example of the roof plan file created in **Figure 31-1** attached to a new drawing as an xref and then used to project an elevation. The roof plan xref includes a *nested* floor plan xref. In this example, the elevation file references the roof plan. The roof plan in turn references the floor plan.

nested xrefs: Xrefs contained within other xrefs.

Create a Multiview Drawing

Another xref application is to create commonly used drawings, such as sections and details, as separate drawing files and then attach each drawing as an xref to a host drawing, known as the *master drawing*. Use floating viewports and layer viewport freezing to create a multiview layout. You can prepare a multiview drawing entirely from existing xref drawings or from a combination of objects created "in place" in the master drawing and attached xrefs.

master drawing: A host drawing created by attaching several frequently used xrefs.

Figure 31-1. Using a floor plan xref drawing as a pattern, or outline, to draw a roof plan.

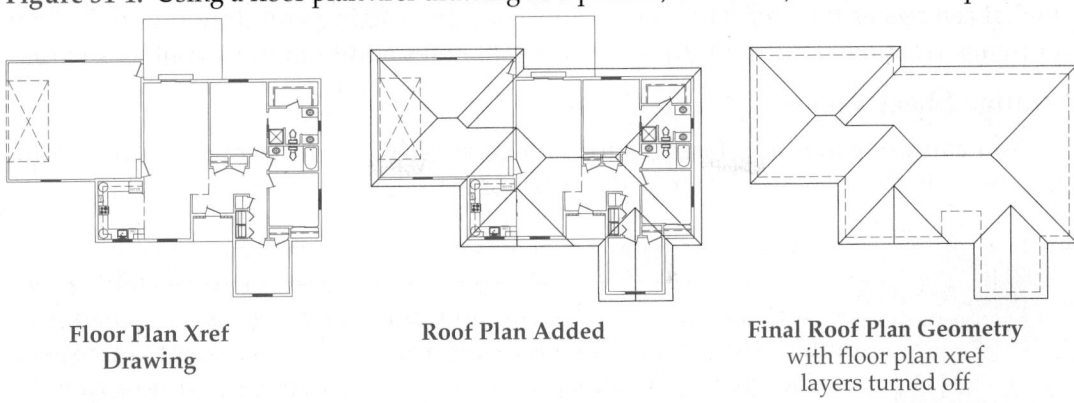

Floor Plan Xref
Drawing

Roof Plan Added

Final Roof Plan Geometry
with floor plan xref
layers turned off

Figure 31-2.
Using a roof plan
xref drawing that
contains a nested
floor plan xref
drawing as a pattern
for projecting
geometry needed to
create an elevation.
The projection lines,
drawn using the
XLINE tool, are for
reference.

Roof plan xref includes
the nested floor plan xref

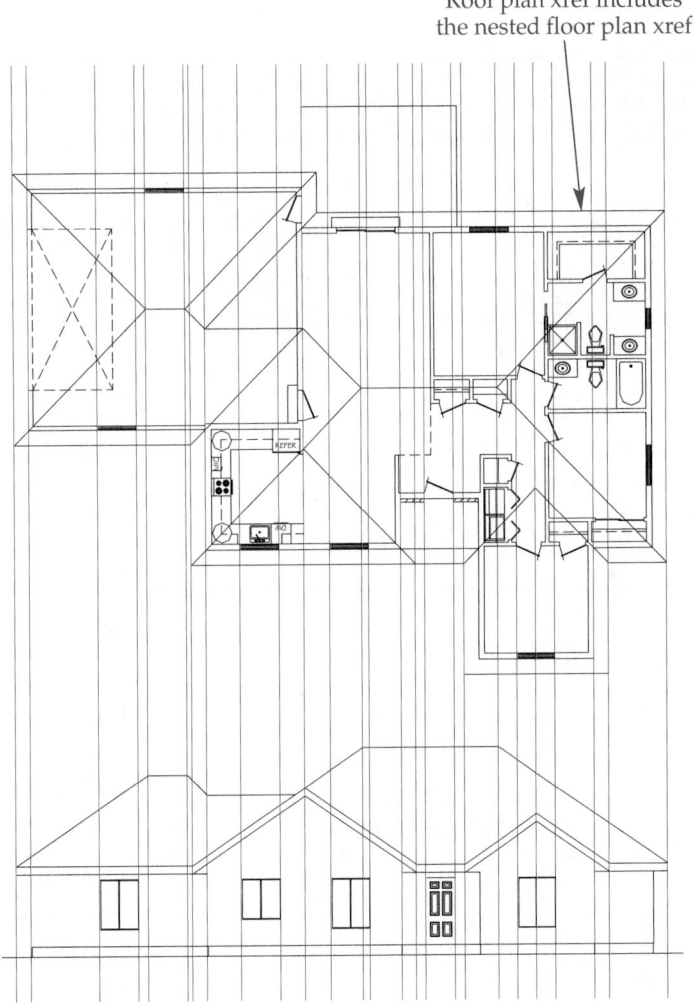

Figure 31-3A shows an example of five stock details referenced into the model space environment of a new drawing. Floating viewports arrange the details in a layout, as shown in **Figure 31-3B**. When you make changes to details in the referenced detail files, the files are updated in the host file.

Add Layout Content

Layout content, such as a title block or general notes, typically has a standard format. If the format requires modification, such as adding a new note to a list of general notes, you can make changes to the xref drawing and easily update each host file that references the xref. This is the same concept as using xref drawings to build a multiview drawing. **Figure 31-3B** shows general notes added to the layout as an xref.

Arrange Sheet Views

You can use external references to arrange sheet views in layouts when you are working with sheet sets. Chapter 32 describes sheet sets.

PROFESSIONAL TIP

You can use blocks, wblocks, and non-block objects in a manner similar to xref drawings. However, xrefs are much easier to manage, provide greater flexibility, and update automatically in host drawings. Always use xref drawings if you plan to use the drawing in multiple host drawings, and if the design might change.

Figure 31-3. A—Xref frequently used drawing views into model space, reducing the size of the file and providing the ability to change instances of the view used in multiple host drawings. B—Arrange referenced views in floating viewports like other model space objects.

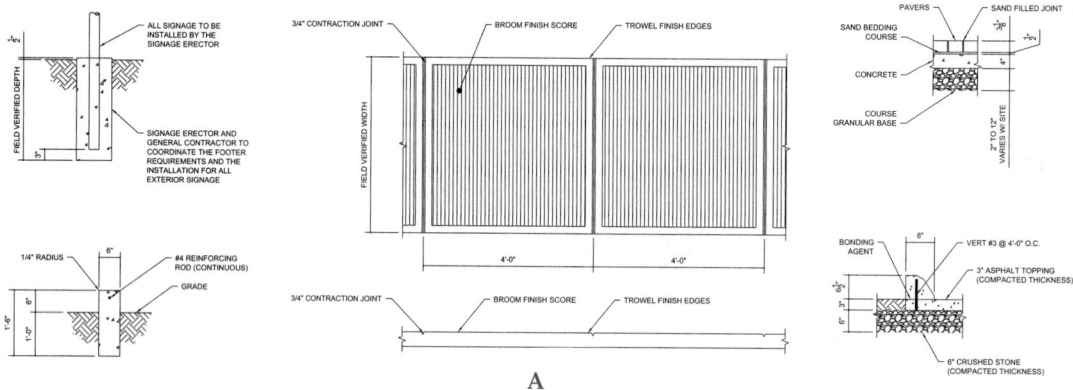

A

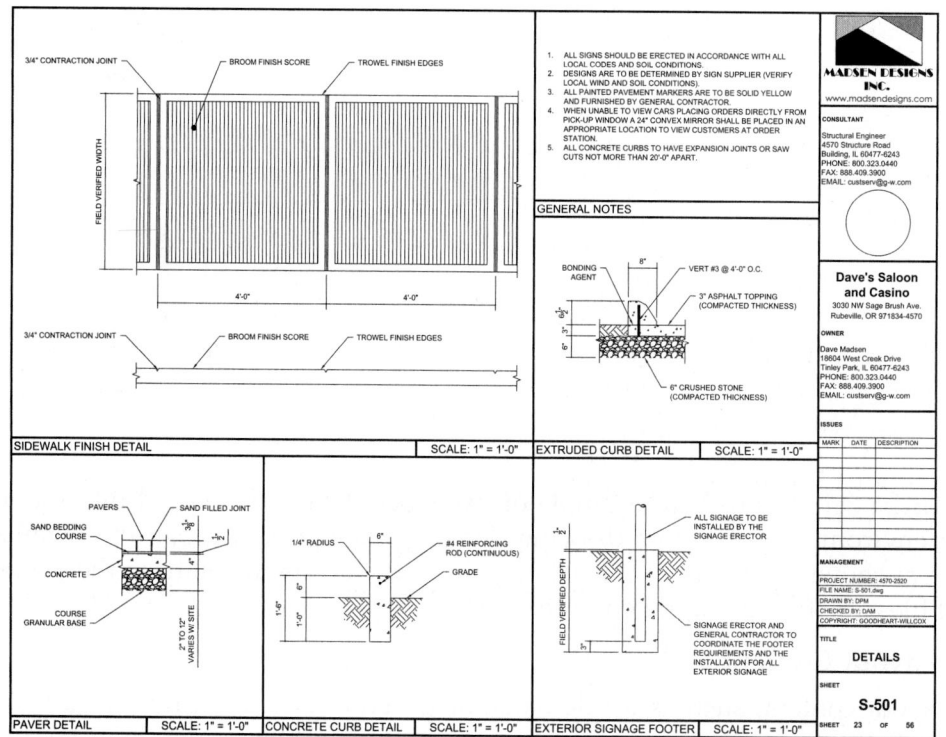

B

AutoCAD and Its Applications—Basics

Preparing Xref and Host Drawings

Before you begin placing xref drawings, you should prepare the xref and host drawing files for xref insertion. When you place an xref drawing, everything you see in model space is inserted into the host file as a single item. Layout content is not included. The default insertion base point for an xref file is the model space origin, or 0,0,0. The insertion base point attaches to the crosshairs or appears at the specified insertion point when you insert the xref into the host drawing. If it is critical that xref objects coincide with the 0,0,0 point for insertion, move all objects in model space as needed in the xref file.

An alternative to moving objects to the origin is to use the **BASE** tool to change the insertion base point of the drawing. Access the **BASE** tool, and then select a new insertion base point. Save the drawing before using it as an xref.

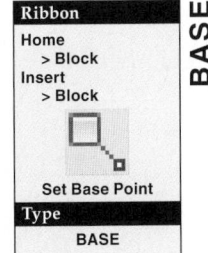

If you use an appropriate template, little effort is necessary to prepare the host file to accept an xref. The host file should include a unique layer (named XREF or A-ANNO-REFR, for example) assigned to xrefs. As you will learn, layers in a referenced drawing file remain intact when you add the xref to a host drawing. Therefore, properties and states that you assign to the XREF layer have no effect on xref objects. The main purpose of the XREF layer is to contain the xref on a specific layer. Set the XREF layer current and proceed to place the xref drawing.

Placing Xref Drawings

To place an xref, access the **ATTACH** tool to display the **Select Reference File** dialog box. The dialog box is set to display image files by default. Pick **Drawing (*.dwg)** from the **Files of type:** drop-down list to show and reference only drawings. Use the **Select Reference File** dialog box to locate the drawing file to add to the host file as an xref. Then pick the **Open** button to display the **Attach External Reference** dialog box. See **Figure 31-4.**

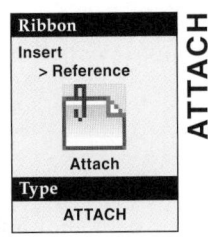

The **Attach External Reference** dialog box includes options for specifying how and where to place the selected file in the host drawing as an xref. If an external reference already exists in the current drawing, place another copy by choosing the file from the **Name:** drop-down. To place a different xref drawing, pick the **Browse...** button and select the new file in the **Select Reference File** dialog box.

You can also place an xref using the **External References** palette shown in **Figure 31-5.** The **External References** palette is a complete external reference management tool. To place an xref drawing using the **External References** palette, pick the **Attach DWG** button from the **Attach** flyout, or right-click on the **File References** pane and select **Attach DWG...**. The **Select Reference File** dialog box appears, displaying only drawing files. Locate and select a file to add as an xref and pick the **Open** button to display the **Attach External Reference** dialog box.

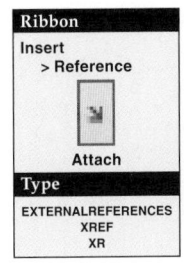

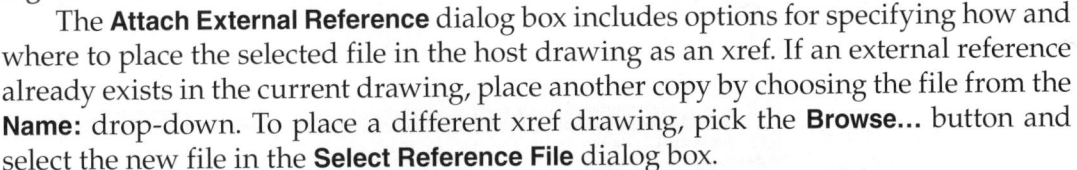
NOTE

The **XATTACH** tool is identical to the **ATTACH** tool, but it initially displays only drawing files in the **Select Reference File** dialog box.

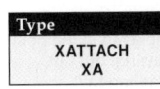

Figure 31-4. Use the **Attach External Reference** dialog box to specify how to place an xref in the host drawing. Pick the **Show Details** button to display additional file details, as shown.

Pick to access existing xrefs   Pick to select a new file to attach

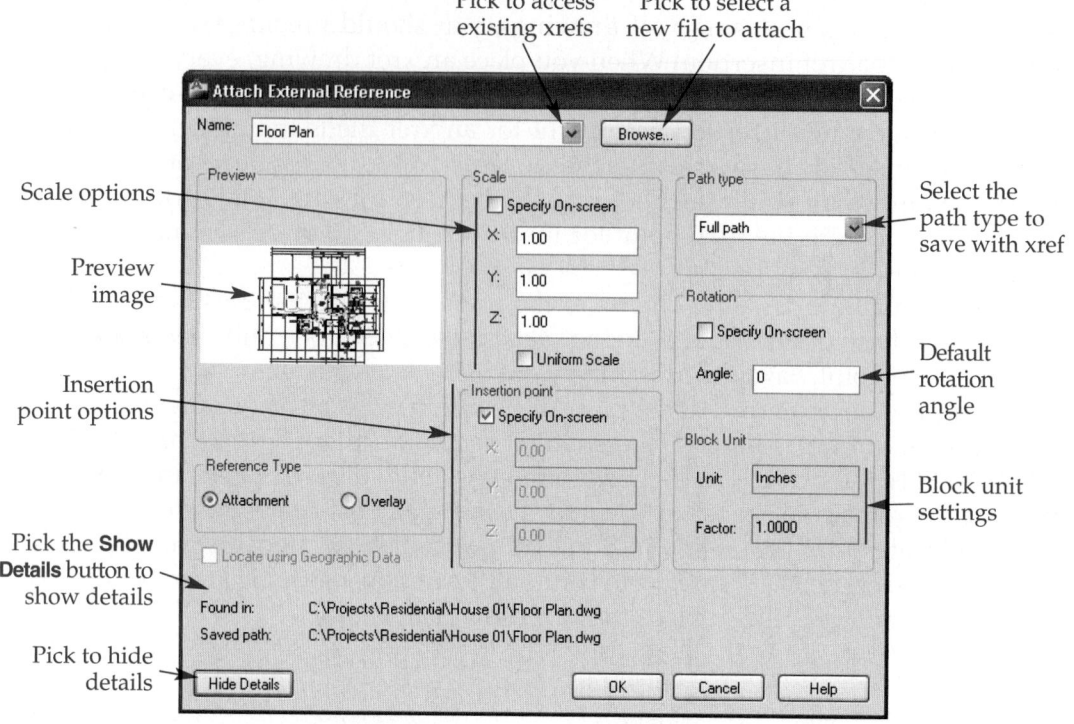

Scale options

Preview image

Insertion point options

Pick the **Show Details** button to show details

Pick to hide details

Select the path type to save with xref

Default rotation angle

Block unit settings

Figure 31-5. The **External References** palette provides access to all options for externally referenced files.

Pick to add an xref drawing to the host file

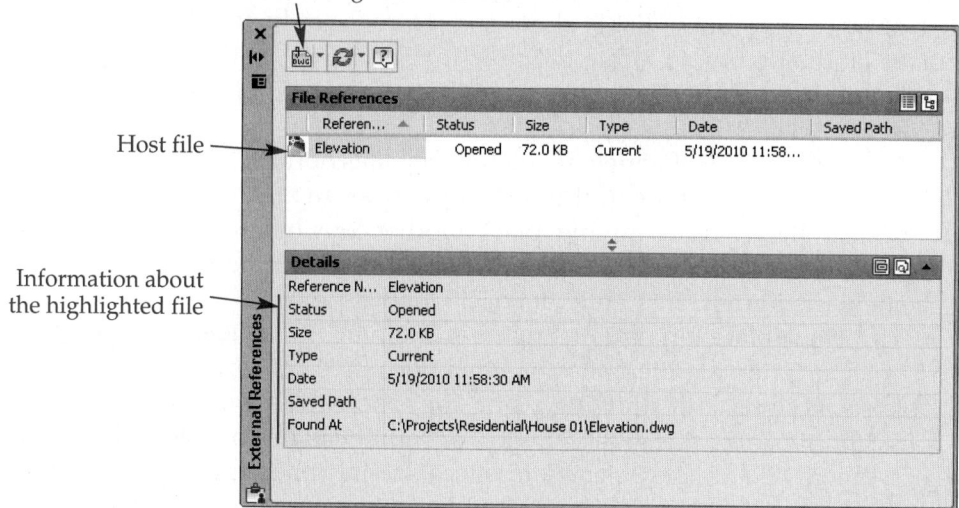

Host file

Information about the highlighted file

Attachment vs. Overlay

attachment: An xref linked with or referenced into the current drawing.

overlay: An xref displayed in the host drawing, but not attached to it.

parent xref: An xref that contains one or more other xrefs.

You can choose to insert an xref drawing as an *attachment* or an *overlay* by selecting the **Attachment** or **Overlay** radio button in the **Reference Type** area. Attach xrefs for most applications. An xref overlay allows you to share content with others in a design drafting team, typically while working in a networked environment. You can overlay drawings without referencing nested xrefs.

Nesting occurs when an xref file references another xref file. An attached xref that has nested xrefs is the *parent xref.* When you attach an xref, the host drawing receives any nested xrefs that the xref contains. This does not happen when you overlay an xref.

AutoCAD and Its Applications—Basics

Furthermore, if you overlay an xref in a host drawing and then attach the host drawing to the current drawing, the overlaid xref does not appear in the current drawing.

For example, suppose you attach a floor plan xref to a host file to create a foundation plan, and then attach the foundation plan xref to a host file to draw a section. Attaching the foundation plan brings the foundation and floor plan geometry into the section file for reference. If a member of your design drafting team uses your section, or is working on a drawing that already has the floor and/or foundation plan attached, she or he can overlay the section xref into a drawing without bringing in the floor plan and foundation plan.

> **NOTE**
>
> You can change an overlay to an attachment or an attachment to an overlay after insertion. Managing xrefs is described later in this chapter.

Selecting the Path Type

Use the **Path type** drop-down list in the **Path Type** area to set how AutoCAD stores the path to the xref file. The path locates the xref file when you open the host file. The path appears in the **Attach External Reference** dialog box when you pick the **Show Details** button, and later appears in the **External References** palette. See **Figure 31-6.**

The default **Full path** option saves an *absolute path*. When using the **Full path** option, you must locate xref drawings in the drive and folder specified in the saved path. You can move the host drawing to any location, but the xref drawings must remain in the saved path. This option is acceptable if it is unlikely that you will move or copy the host and xref drawings to another computer, drive, or folder.

absolute path: A path to a file defined by the location of the file on the computer system.

The **Relative path** option is often more appropriate if you share drawings with a client or eventually archive drawings. The **Relative path** option saves a *relative path*. If the host drawing and xref files are located in a single folder and subfolders, you can copy the folder to any location without losing the connection between files. For example, copy the folder from the C: drive of one computer to the D: drive of another computer, to a folder on a CD, or to an archive server. If you perform these types of transfers with the **Full path** option, you need to open the host drawing after copying

relative path: A path to a file defined according to the location of the file relative to the host drawing.

Figure 31-6. You can reference a file using a full path, a relative path, or no path. The path type is displayed in the **Save Path** column in the **External References** palette.

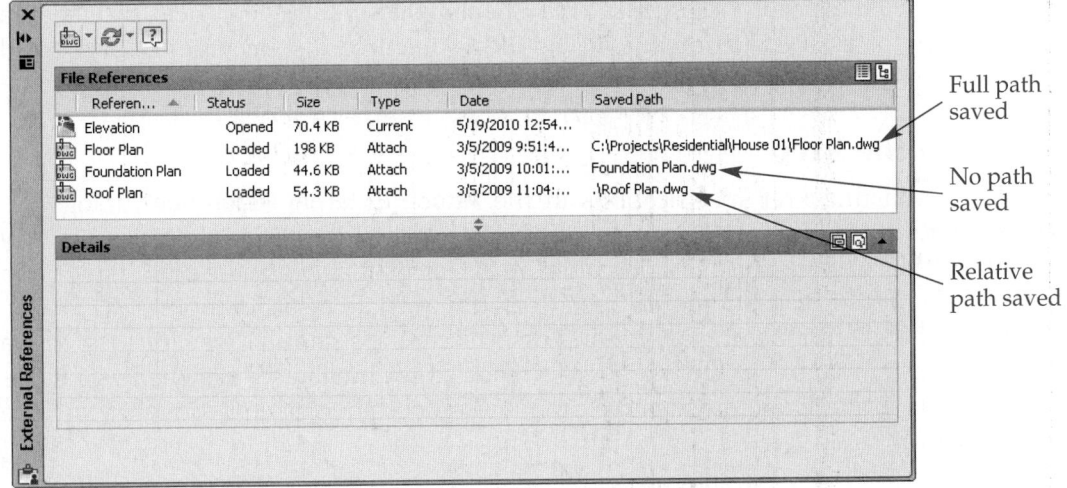

and redefine the saved paths for all xref files. You cannot use a relative path if the xref file is on a drive other than the drive on which the host file is stored.

Select the **No Path** option if you do not want to save the path to the xref file. If you choose the **No Path** option, the xref file loads only if you include the path to the file in one of the Support File Search Path locations or if the xref file is in the same folder as the host file. Specify the Support File Search Path locations in the **Files** tab of the **Options** dialog box.

NOTE

AutoCAD searches for xref files in all paths of the current project name. Project search paths are listed under Project Files Search Path in the **Files** tab of the **Options** dialog box. Create a new project as follows:
1. Pick Project Files Search Path to highlight it, and then pick the **Add...** button.
2. Enter a project name.
3. Pick the plus sign icon (+), and then pick the word Empty.
4. Pick the **Browse...** button and locate the folder that is to become part of the project search path. Then pick **OK**.
5. Complete the project search path definition by entering the **PROJECTNAME** system variable and specifying the same name you specified in the **Options** dialog box.

Additional Xref Placement Options

The remaining items in the **Attach External Reference** dialog box allow you to control or identify xref insertion location, scaling, rotation angle, and block unit settings. Deselect the **Specify On-screen** check box in the **Insertion point** area to enter 2D or 3D coordinates in the text boxes for insertion of the xref. Activate the **Specify On-screen** check box to specify the insertion location on-screen. The **Locate using Geographic Data** check box is active if the xref and host drawings include *geographic data*. Pick the check box to position the xref using geographic data.

geographic data: Information added to a drawing to describe specific locations and directions on Earth.

Use the **Scale** area to set xref scale factor. AutoCAD sets the X, Y, and Z scale factors to 1 by default. Enter different values in the corresponding text boxes or activate the **Specify On-screen** check box to display scaling prompts when you insert the xref. Select the **Uniform Scale** check box to apply the X scale factor to the Y and Z scale factors.

The rotation angle for the inserted xref is 0 by default. Specify a different rotation angle in the **Angle:** text box, or select the **Specify On-screen** check box to display a rotation prompt for the rotation angle. The **Block Unit** area displays the unit type and scale factor stored with the selected drawing file.

Inserting the Xref

After adjusting xref specifications in the **Attach External Reference** dialog box, pick the **OK** button to insert the xref into the host drawing. If you chose the **Specify On-screen** check box in the **Insertion point** area, the xref attaches to the crosshairs and a prompt asks for the insertion point. Specify an appropriate insertion point for the xref.

The options for attaching an xref are essentially the same as those for inserting a block. However, remember that xrefs are not added to the database of the host file, as are inserted blocks. Therefore, using external references helps keep your drawing file size to a minimum.

Placing Xrefs with DesignCenter and Tool Palettes

To place an xref into the current drawing using **DesignCenter**, first use the **Tree View** pane to locate the folder containing the drawing you want to attach. Then display the drawing files located in the selected folder in the **Content** pane. Right-click on the drawing file in the **Content** pane and select **Attach as Xref...** Another method is to drag and drop the drawing into the current drawing area using the right mouse button. When you release the button, select the **Attach as Xref...** option. The **Attach External Reference** dialog box appears. Enter the appropriate values and pick the **OK** button to place the xref.

You must add an xref or drawing file to a tool palette in order to use the **Tool Palettes** palette to place the file as an xref. To add an xref to a tool palette, drag an existing xref from the current drawing or an xref from the **Content** pane of **DesignCenter** into the **Tool Palettes** palette. Use drag and drop to attach the xref to the current drawing from the palette.

Xref files in tool palettes display an external reference icon. A drawing file (not an xref) added to a tool palette from the current drawing or using **DesignCenter**, is a block tool. To convert the block tool to an xref tool, right-click on the image in the **Tool Palettes** palette and select **Properties...** to display the **Tool Properties** dialog box. Then change the **Insert as** field status from Block to Xref using the **Insert as** drop-down list. The **Reference type** row controls whether the xref is inserted as an attachment or an overlay.

Working with Xref Objects

An xref is inserted as a single object. Xref drawings appear faded by default to help differentiate the xref from the host drawing. Xref fading is an on-screen display function only and does not apply to plots. The **XDWGFADECTL** system variable controls fading of xref drawings on-screen. The easiest way to adjust fading is to use the options in the expanded **Reference** panel of the **Insert** ribbon tab. See **Figure 31-7A**. Pick the **Xref Fading** button to activate or deactivate xref fading, and use the slider or text box to increase or decrease fading. The default value of 70% creates significant fading. See **Figure 31-7B**.

Select an xref in the **External References** palette to highlight all visible instances of the xref in the drawing. Select an xref in the drawing to highlight the name in the **External References** palette. Use editing tools such as **MOVE** and **COPY** to modify the xref as needed. However, there are some significant differences between xrefs and other objects. For example, if you erase an xref, the xref definition remains in the file, similar to an erased block. You must detach an xref to remove it from the file completely.

NOTE

In order to select an xref, pick an object displayed on-screen that is part of the xref.

Figure 31-7.
A—Use options in the expanded **Reference** panel of the **Insert** ribbon tab to control xref fading. B—Default fading applied to xref objects.

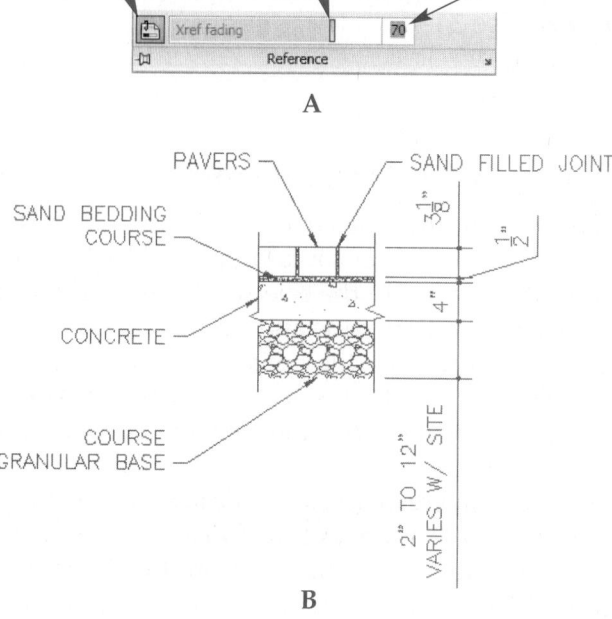

Deselect to remove fading

Slide right to increase fading

Type a fade percentage

A

B

Dependent Objects

When you place an xref in a drawing, the host file receives all named objects in the xref file, such as layers and blocks, as *dependent objects*, even if the xref file does not use the objects. Dependent objects are displayed in the host drawing for reference only. The xref drawing stores the actual object definitions.

When you attach an xref, dependent objects are assigned unique names that consist of the xref file name followed by the actual object name, separated by a vertical bar symbol (|). For example, a layer named A-DOOR in a reference drawing named Floor Plan comes into the host drawing as Floor plan|A-DOOR. See **Figure 31-8.** This name

Figure 31-8. The xref drawing name and a vertical bar symbol (|) precede xref-dependent layer names in the host drawing.

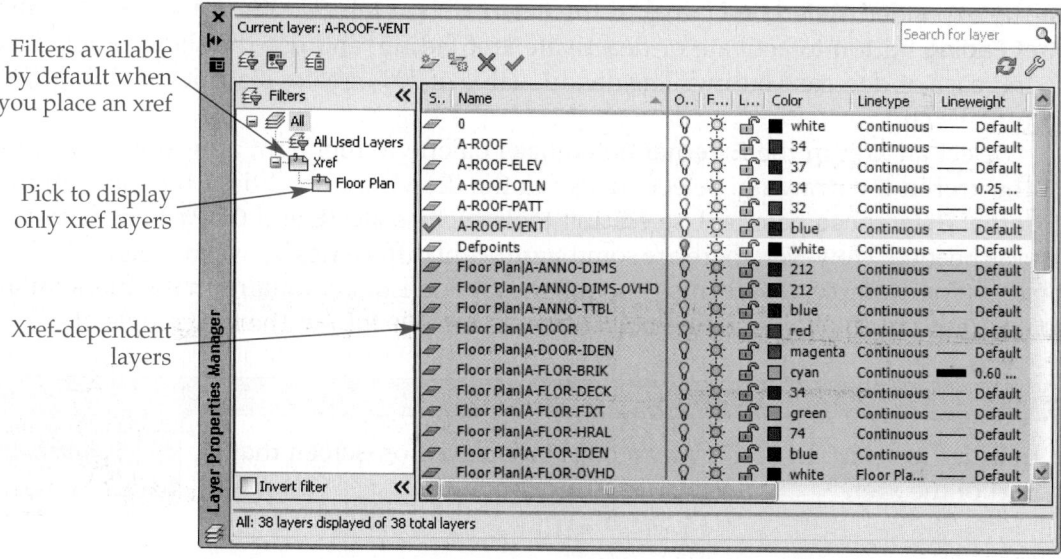

Filters available by default when you place an xref

Pick to display only xref layers

Xref-dependent layers

distinguishes xref-dependent layers from layers that may have the same name in the host drawing. The names also make it easier to manage layers when several xrefs are attached to the host drawing, because the layers from each reference file are preceded by their file names. You cannot rename xref-dependent objects.

When you attach an xref, dependent objects such as layers are added to the host drawing only in order to support the display of the objects in the reference file. You cannot set xref layers current, and as a result, you cannot draw on xref layers. However, you can turn xref layers on and off, thaw and freeze them, and lock or unlock them as needed. You can also change the colors and linetypes of xref layers.

NOTE

Use the Xref filter in the **Layer Properties Manager** palette to display and manage dependent layers. You can also save dependent layers in a layer state.

PROFESSIONAL TIP

When you attach a drawing as an xref, the reference file comes into the host drawing with the same layer colors and linetypes used in the original file. If you reference a drawing to check the relationship of objects between two drawings, consider changing the xref layer colors to make it easier to differentiate between the content of the host drawing and the xref drawing. Changing xref layer colors affects only the display in the current drawing and does not alter the original reference file.

Exercise 31-2

Access the Student Web site (www.g-wlearning.com/CAD) and complete Exercise 31-2.

Managing Xrefs

The **External References** palette is the primary tool for managing and accessing current information about xrefs found in a host drawing. The **External References** palette displays an upper **File References** pane and a lower **Details** pane. See Figure 31-9. Display the **File References** pane in list view or tree view and with details or a preview.

List View Display

The list view display shown in Figure 31-9 is active by default. Pick the **List View** button or press the [F3] key to activate list view mode while in tree view mode. The labeled columns displayed in list view provide information about and management options for xrefs.

The **Reference Name** column displays the current drawing file name followed by the names of all existing xrefs in alphabetical or chronological order. The standard AutoCAD drawing file icon identifies the host drawing, and a sheet of paper with a

Figure 31-9. The **External References** palette allows you to view and manage referenced files. The **File References** pane appears in **List View** mode and the **Details** pane displays in **Details** mode.

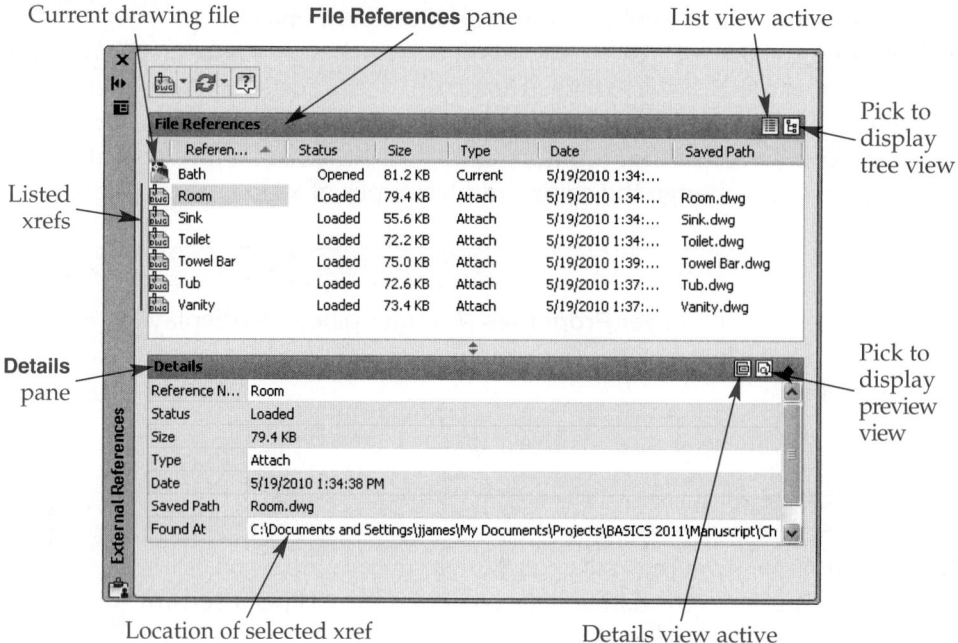

Current drawing file   **File References** pane   List view active

Listed xrefs

Details pane

Pick to display tree view

Pick to display preview view

Location of selected xref   Details view active

paper clip icon identifies xref drawings. Each xref type displays a different icon. The **Status** column describes the status of each xref, which can be:

- **Loaded.** The xref is attached to the drawing.
- **Unloaded.** The xref is attached but cannot be displayed or regenerated.
- **Unreferenced.** The xref has nested xrefs that are not found or are unresolved. An unreferenced xref is not displayed.
- **Not Found.** The xref file is not found in the specified search paths.
- **Unresolved.** The xref file is missing or cannot be found.
- **Orphaned.** The parent of the nested xref cannot be found.

The **Size** column lists the file size for each xref. The **Type** column indicates whether the xref is attached or referenced as an overlay. The **Date** column indicates the date the xref was last modified.

The **Saved Path** column lists the path name saved with the xref. If only a file name appears, the path was not saved. Prefixes describe the relative paths to xref files. In **Figure 31-6,** the characters .\ precede the Roof Plan reference file. The period (.) represents the folder containing the host drawing. From that folder, AutoCAD looks in the House 01 folder that contains the Roof Plan drawing. The Elevation reference file in **Figure 31-10** uses a similar specification. In this example, the same folder contains the Elevation xref and the host drawing. The characters ..\ precede the specification for the Wall xref. The double period instructs AutoCAD to move up one folder level from the current location. The double period repeats to move up multiple folder levels. For example, AutoCAD locates the Panel xref in **Figure 31-10** by moving up two folder levels from the folder of the host drawing and opening the Symbols folder.

Figure 31-10. Relationship between the symbols in the **Saved Path** list and file locations within the folder structure.

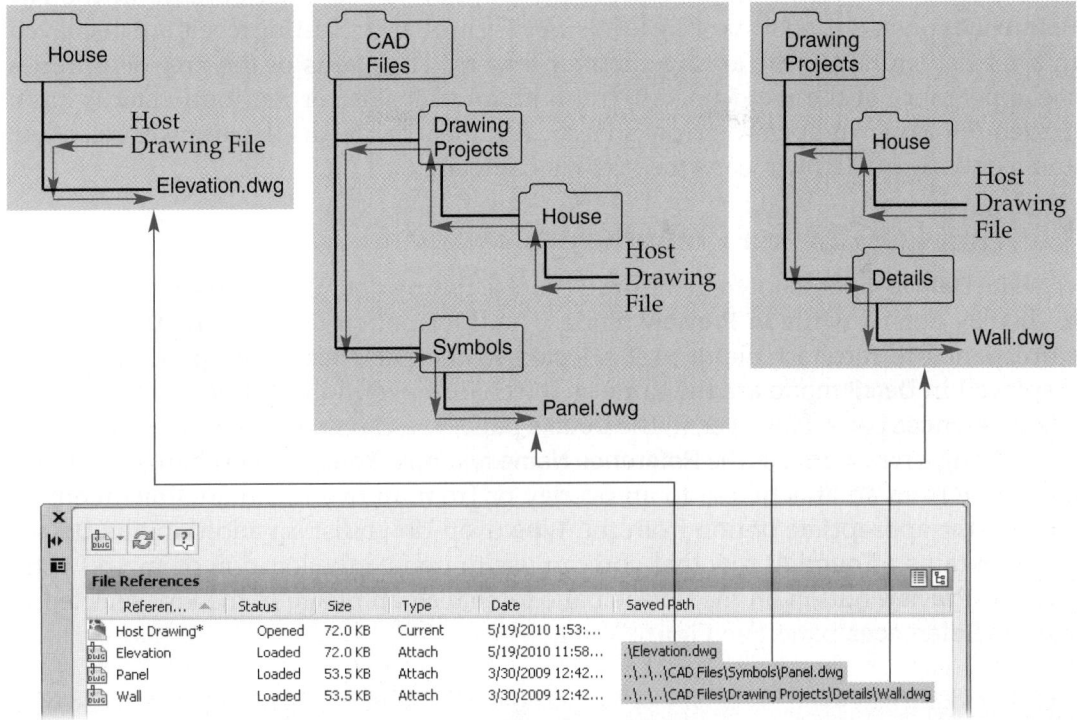

The path saved to the xref is one of several locations AutoCAD searches when you open a host drawing and an xref requires loading. AutoCAD searches path locations to load xref files in the following order:

1. The full or relative path associated with the xref
2. The current folder of the host drawing
3. The project paths specified in the Project Files Search Path
4. The support paths specified in the Support File Search Path
5. The Start in: folder path specified for the AutoCAD application shortcut associated using the **Properties** option in the desktop icon shortcut menu

Adjust the column widths in list view mode as necessary to view complete information. To adjust the width of a column, move the cursor to the edge of the button at the top of the column until the cursor changes to a horizontal resizing cursor. Press and hold the left mouse button and drag the column to the desired width. If columns extend beyond the width of the dialog box, a horizontal scroll bar appears at the bottom of the list.

Tree View Display

Pick the **Tree View** button or press the [F4] key to see a list of xrefs in the **File References** pane, and show nesting levels. See **Figure 31-11**. Nesting levels are displayed in a format similar to the arrangement of folders. The status of the xref determines the appearance of the xref icon. An xref with an unloaded or not found status has a grayed-out icon. An upward arrow shown with the icon means the xref was reloaded, and a downward arrow means the xref was unloaded.

Viewing Details or a Preview

The **Details** mode, shown in **Figure 31-9**, is active by default. Pick the **Details** button to display details while in **Preview** mode. The information listed in the **Details** pane corresponds to the host file or xref selected in the **File References** pane. The rows displayed in **Detail** mode are the same as the columns found in **List View** mode of the **File References** pane. However, in the **Details** pane, you can modify the reference name by entering a new name in the **Reference Name** text box. You can also change the reference type from an attachment to an overlay or from an overlay to an attachment by picking the appropriate option from the **Type** drop-down list. In addition, the **Details** pane contains a **Found At** row that you can use to update the location of an xref path. Pick the **Preview** button on the **Details** pane to display an image of the xref selected in the **File References** pane. See **Figure 31-11**.

> **NOTE**
>
> You can also use the **External References** palette to manage data extractions.

Detaching, Reloading, and Unloading Xrefs

Each time you open a host drawing containing an attached xref, the xref loads and appears on-screen. This association remains permanent until you *detach* the xref. Erasing an xref does not remove the xref from the host drawing. To detach an xref, right-click on the reference name in the **File References** pane of the **External References**

detach: Remove an xref from a host drawing.

Figure 31-11.
The **File References** pane in **Tree View** mode shows nested xref levels. The **Details** pane in **Preview** mode shows a thumbnail preview of the selected xref.

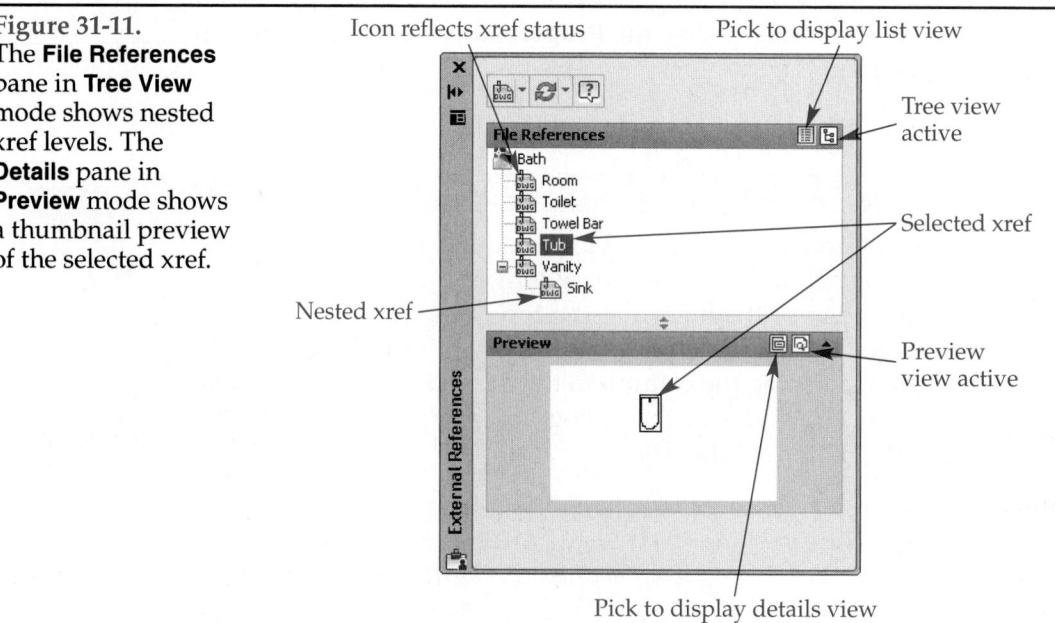

Icon reflects xref status

Pick to display list view

Tree view active

Selected xref

Nested xref

Preview view active

Pick to display details view

palette and pick **Detach**. All instances of the xref and all of its nested xrefs are detached from the current drawing, along with all referenced data.

In some situations, you may need to update, or *reload*, an xref file in the host drawing. For example, if you edit an xref while the host drawing is open, the updated version may be different from the version you see. To update the xref, right-click the reference name in the **File References** pane of the **External References** palette and pick **Reload**, or pick the **Reload All References** button from the flyout to reload all unloaded xrefs. Reloading xrefs forces AutoCAD to read and display the most recently saved version of each xref.

To *unload* an xref, right-click on the reference name in the **File References** pane of the **External References** palette and pick **Unload**. An unloaded xref is not displayed or regenerated, so performance increases. Reload the xref to redisplay it.

reload: Update an xref in the host drawing.

unload: Suppress the display of an xref without removing the xref from the host drawing.

> **NOTE**
>
> If AutoCAD cannot find an xref, an alert appears when you open the host drawing. Choose the appropriate option to ignore the problem or fix the problem using the **External References** palette.

Updating the Xref Path

A file path saved with an xref is displayed in the **Saved Path** column of the **File References** pane and the **Saved Path** row of the **Details** pane in the **External References** palette. If the **Saved Path** location does not include an xref file, when you open the host drawing, AutoCAD searches the *library path*. A link to the xref forms if AutoCAD finds a file with a matching name. In such a case, the **Saved Path** location differs from where AutoCAD actually found the file.

library path: The path AutoCAD searches by default to find an xref file, including the current folder and locations set in the **Options** dialog box.

Check for matching paths in the **External References** palette by comparing the path listed in the **Saved Path** column of the **File References** pane and **Saved Path** row of the **Details** pane with the listing in the **Found At** row of the **Details** pane. When you move an xref and the new location is not in the library path, the xref status is Not Found. To update or find the **Saved Path** location, select the path in the **Found At** edit box and pick the **Browse...** button to the right of the edit box to access the **Select new path** dialog box. Use the **Select new path** dialog box to locate the new folder and select the desired file. Then pick the **Open** button to update the path.

The Manage Xrefs Icon

By default, when you edit, save, and close an xref, and then open the host drawing, changes made to the xref automatically appear without any notification. If you make changes to an xref while the host drawing is open, a notification appears in the status bar tray. Changes are indicated by the appearance of the **Manage Xrefs** icon, a balloon message, or both.

The **Tray Settings** dialog box controls notifications in the status bar tray for xref changes and other system updates. Select **Tray Settings...** from the status bar shortcut menu to access the **Tray Settings** dialog box. Select the **Display icons from services** check box to display the **Manage Xrefs** icon in the status bar tray when you attach an xref to the current drawing. If you modified an xref in the current file since opening the file, the **Manage Xrefs** icon appears with an exclamation sign. Pick the **Manage Xrefs** icon or right-click on the **Manage Xrefs** icon and select **External References...** to open the **External References** palette to reload the xref.

Select the **Display notifications from services** check box in the **Tray Settings** dialog box to display a balloon message notification with the name of the modified xref file. See **Figure 31-12A.** You can then pick the xref name in the balloon message to reload

---

the file. The example in **Figure 31-12** shows adding a Towel Bar xref to the Room parent xref drawing. The xref reloads in the host drawing named Bath. See **Figure 31-12B**. You can also reload xrefs by right-clicking on the **Manage Xrefs** icon and selecting **Reload DWG Xrefs**.

Figure 31-12. The **Manage Xrefs** icon in the status bar tray provides a notification when you modify and save an xref file. A—A balloon message and an exclamation point appear at the icon. B—Reloading the xref file updates the current drawing and changes the appearance of the icon.

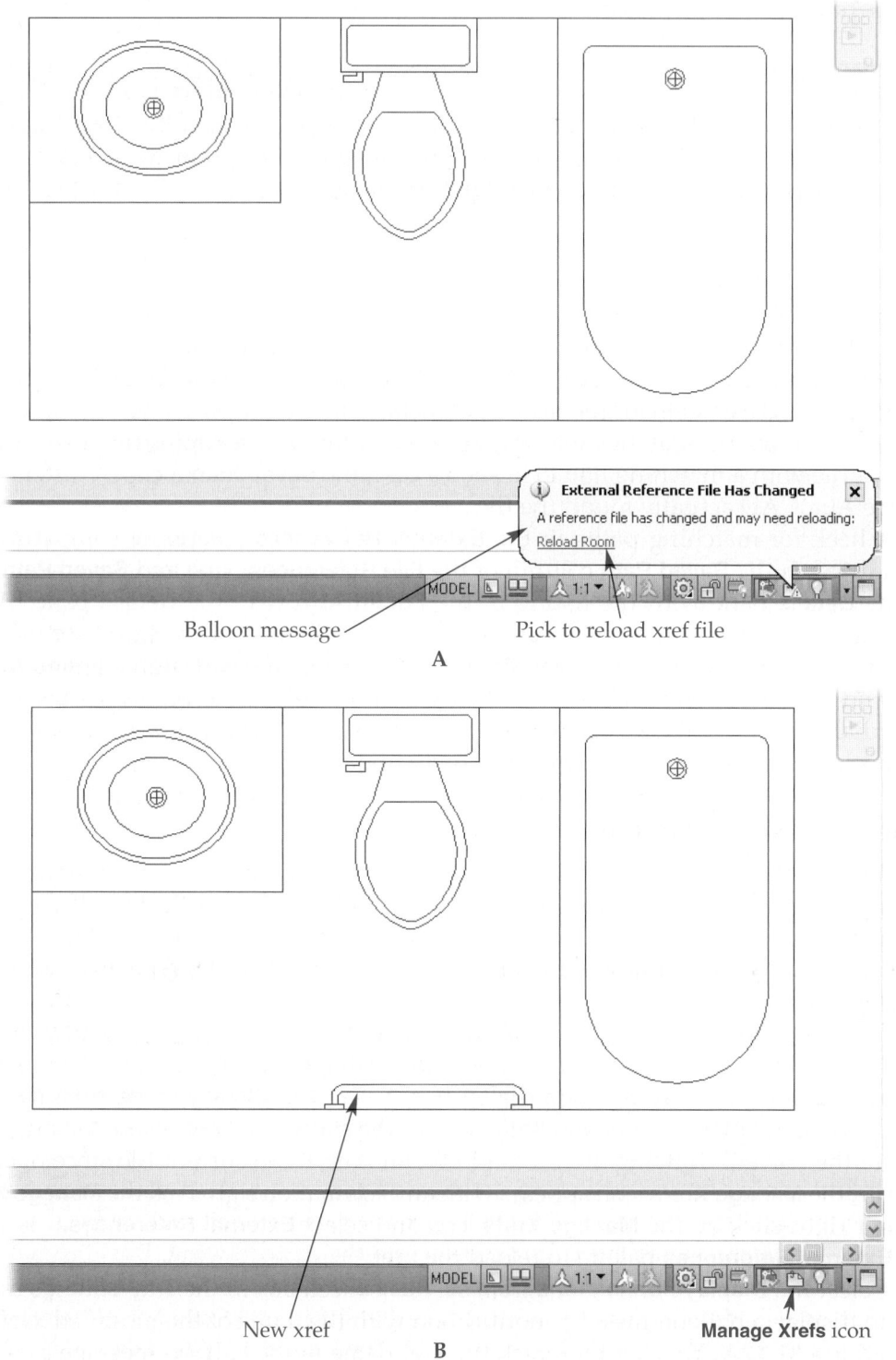

Exercise 31-3

Access the Student Web site (www.g-wlearning.com/CAD) and complete Exercise 31-3.

Clipping Xrefs

Clip, or crop, an xref to display only a specific portion, or an xref *subregion*. All geometry that falls outside the clipping boundary is invisible, and objects that are partially within the subregion appear trimmed at the boundary. Although clipped objects appear trimmed, the xref file does not change. Clipping applies to a selected instance of an xref, not to the actual xref definition.

subregion: The displayed portion of a clipped xref.

Use the **XCLIP** tool to create and modify clipping boundaries. A quick way to access the **XCLIP** tool is to select an object that is part of the xref file, then right-click and select **Clip Xref**. If you access the **XCLIP** tool before selecting an xref, pick an object associated with the xref to clip. Then press [Enter] to accept the default **New boundary** option and select the clipping boundary.

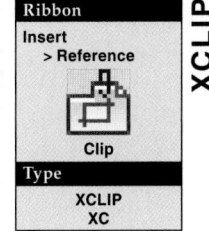

When you select the **New boundary** option, a prompt asks you to specify the clipping boundary. Use the default **Rectangular** option to create a rectangular boundary. Then pick the corners of the rectangular boundary. See **Figure 31-13.** Note that the geometry outside the clipping boundary no longer appears after clipping. The **New boundary** option includes additional options for specifying the clip boundary and area to clip, as briefly described in **Figure 31-14.**

Edit a clipped xref as you would an unclipped xref. The clipping boundary moves with the xref. Note that nested xrefs are clipped according to the clipping boundary for the parent xref.

The clipping boundary, or frame, is invisible by default. Use the **XCLIPFRAME** system variable to toggle the display of the clipping boundary frame. Set the value of **XCLIPFRAME** to 1 to turn on the frame.

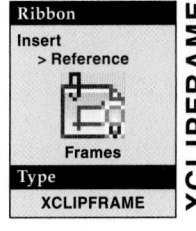

The other options of the **XCLIP** tool apply after you define a clip boundary. The **ON** and **OFF** options turn the clipping feature on or off. The **Clipdepth** option allows you to define front and back clipping planes to control the portion of a 3D drawing that displays. Clipping 3D models is described in *AutoCAD and Its Applications—Advanced.* Use the **Delete** option to remove an existing clipping boundary, returning the xref to its unclipped display. Use the **generate Polyline** option to create and display a polyline object at the clip boundary to frame the clipped portion.

Exercise 31-4

Access the Student Web site (www.g-wlearning.com/CAD) and complete Exercise 31-4.

Demand Loading and Xref Editing Controls

Demand loading controls how much of an xref loads when you attach the xref to the host drawing. Demand loading improves performance and saves disk space because only a portion of the xref file loads into the host drawing. For example, data on frozen layers and data outside of clipping regions does not load.

demand loading: Loading only the portion of an xref file necessary to regenerate the host drawing.

Demand loading occurs by default. Use the **Open and Save** tab of the **Options** dialog box to check or change the setting. The **Demand load Xrefs:** drop-down list in the **External References (Xrefs)** area contains each demand loading option. Select the **Enabled with copy** option to turn on demand loading. Other users can edit the original drawing because AutoCAD uses a copy of the referenced drawing. Alternatively, pick the **Enabled** option to turn on demand loading. If you use this option, the xref file is considered "in use" while you are referencing the drawing, preventing other users from editing the file. Select the **Disabled** option to turn off demand loading.

Figure 31-13. Clipping a large site plan xref to display a specific area. A—Using the **Rectangular** boundary selection option. B—The clipped xref.

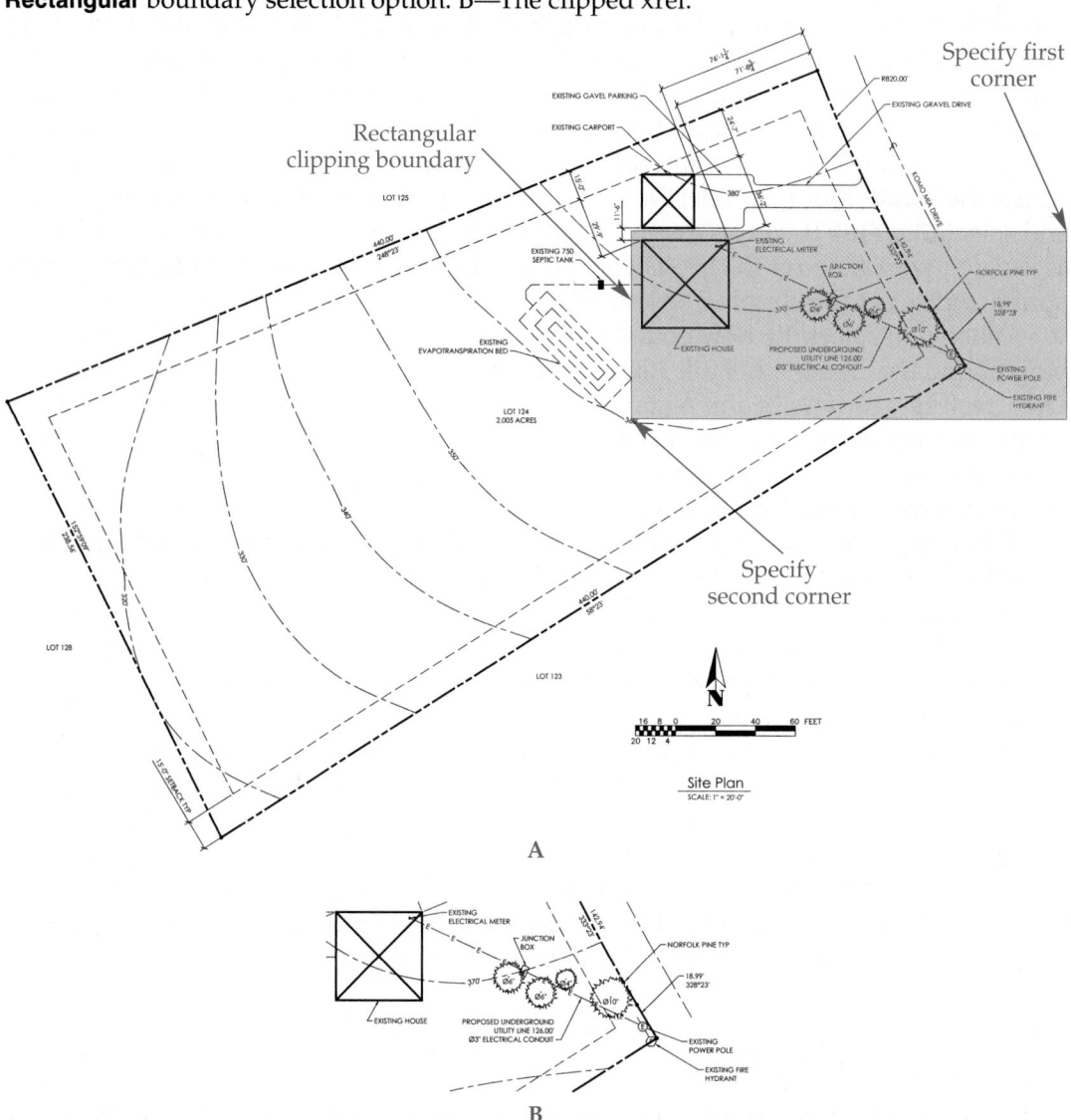

Figure 31-14. Additional options available for the **New boundary** function of the **XCLIP** tool.

Option	Description
Select Polyline	Select an existing polyline object as the clip boundary. If the polyline does not close, the start and endpoints of the boundary connect.
Polygonal	Draw an irregular polygon as a boundary.
Invert clip	Inverts the selection so that the portion of the xref that lies outside of the clipping boundary is clipped. Only the portion of the xref outside of the boundary is displayed.

AutoCAD and Its Applications—Basics

Two additional settings in the **Open and Save** tab of the **Options** dialog box control the effects of changes made to xref-dependent layers and in-place reference editing. The **Retain changes to Xref layers** check box allows you to keep all changes made to the properties and states of xref-dependent layers. Any changes to layers take precedence over layer settings in the xref file. Edited properties remain even after you reload the xref. The **Allow other users to Refedit current drawing** check box controls whether the current drawing can be edited in place by others while it is open and when it is referenced by another file. Both check boxes are selected by default.

PROFESSIONAL TIP

If you plan to use a drawing as an external reference, save the file with *spatial indexes* and *layer indexes*. These lists help improve performance when you reference drawings with frozen layers and clipping boundaries. Use the following procedure to create spatial and layer indexes:

1. Access the **Save Drawing As** dialog box.
2. Pick **Options...** from the **Tools** flyout button and select the **DWG Options** tab of the **Saveas Options** dialog box.
3. Select the type of index required from the **Index type:** drop-down list.
4. Pick the **OK** button and save the drawing.

spatial index: A list of objects ordered according to their location in 3D space.

layer index: A list of objects ordered according to the layers to which they are assigned.

Binding an Xref

Bind an xref to make the xref a permanent part of the host drawing, as if you were inserting the file using the **INSERT** tool. Binding is useful when you need to send the full drawing file to another location or user, such as a plotting service or client. To bind an xref using the **External References** palette, right-click on the reference name and pick **Bind....** The **Bind Xrefs** dialog box that appears contains **Bind** and **Insert** radio buttons.

bind: Convert an xref to a permanently inserted block in the host drawing.

Using the Insert and Bind Options

The **Insert** option converts the xref into a normal block, as if you had used the **INSERT** tool to place the file. In addition, the drawing is added to the block definition table, and all named objects, such as layers, blocks, and styles, are incorporated into the host drawing as named in the xref. For example, if you bind an xref file named PLATE that contains a layer named OBJECT, the xref-dependent layer PLATE|OBJECT becomes the locally defined layer OBJECT. All other xref-dependent objects lose the xref name and assume the properties of the locally defined objects with the same name. The **Insert** binding option provides the best results for most purposes.

The **Bind** option also converts the xref into a normal block. However, the xref name remains with all dependent objects. Two dollar signs with a number between them replace the vertical line in each name. For example, an xref layer named Title|Notes becomes Title0Notes. The number inside the dollar signs is automatically incremented if a local object definition with the same name exists. For example, if Title0Notes already exists in the drawing, the newly bound layer becomes Title1Notes. In this manner, all xref-dependent object definitions that are bound receive unique names. Use the **RENAME** tool or other appropriate method to rename bound objects.

Binding Specific Dependent Objects

Binding an xref allows you to make all dependent objects in the xref file a permanent part of the host drawing. Dependent objects include named items such as blocks, dimension styles, layers, linetypes, and text styles. Before binding, you cannot directly use any dependent objects from a referenced drawing in the host drawing. For example, you cannot make an xref layer or text style current in the host drawing.

In some cases, you may only need to incorporate one or more specific named objects, such as a layer or block, from an xref into the host drawing, instead of binding the entire xref. If you only need selected items, it can be counterproductive to bind an entire drawing. Instead, use the **XBIND** tool and corresponding **Xbind** dialog box, shown in **Figure 31-15,** to select specific named objects to bind.

Xrefs have AutoCAD drawing file icons. Expand a group to select an individually named object. To select an object for binding, highlight the object and pick the **Add** button. The names of all objects selected and added are displayed in the **Definitions to Bind** list. Pick the **OK** button to complete the operation. A message displayed on the command line indicates how many objects of each type are bound.

Individual objects bound using the **XBIND** tool rename in the same manner as objects bound using the **Bind** option in the **Bind Xrefs** dialog box. An automatic linetype bind performs so that a layer that includes a linetype not loaded in the host drawing can reference the required linetype definition. The linetype includes a new linetype name, such as xref1$0$hidden. In a similar manner, a previously undefined block may automatically bind to the host drawing because of binding nested blocks. Use the **RENAME** tool or other appropriate method to rename objects.

Exercise 31-5

Access the Student Web site (www.g-wlearning.com/CAD) and complete Exercise 31-5.

Editing Xref Drawings

reference editing:
Editing reference drawings from within the host file.

One option for editing an xref drawing is to use in-place editing, or *reference editing,* within the host drawing. You can save any changes made to the xref to the original xref drawing from within the host drawing. Alternatively, you can edit the xref in a separate drawing window as you would any other drawing file.

Figure 31-15.
Use the **Xbind** dialog box to bind xref-dependent objects individually to the host drawing.

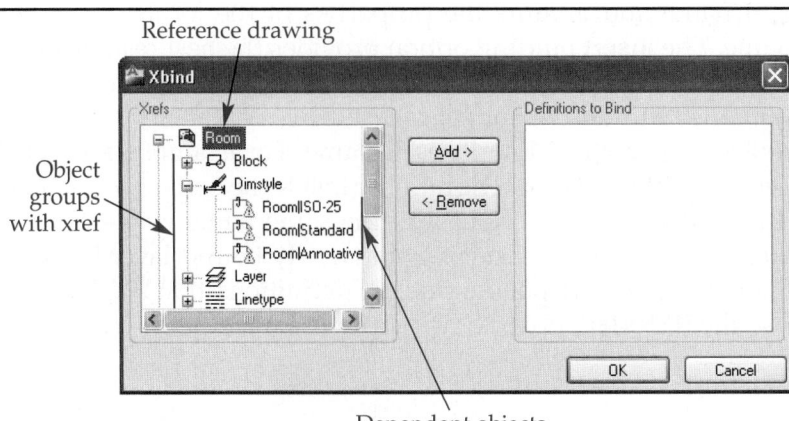

Reference Editing

The **REFEDIT** tool allows you to edit xref drawings in place. Quick ways to initiate reference editing include double-clicking on an xref, or selecting an xref and then right-clicking and selecting **Edit Xref In-place**. If you access the **REFEDIT** tool without first selecting an xref, you must then pick the xref to edit. The **Reference Edit** dialog box opens with the **Identify Reference** tab active. See **Figure 31-16**. The example shows the Room reference drawing selected for editing. Notice that nested blocks, like the Bath Tub 26 x 60 in. block found in the Tub reference, are listed under their parent xref.

The **Automatically select all nested objects** radio button in the **Path:** area is active by default. Use this option to make all xref objects available for editing. To edit specific xref objects, pick the **Prompt to select nested objects** radio button. The Select nested objects: prompt displays after you pick the **OK** button, allowing you to pick objects that belong to the selected xref. Pick all the geometry you want to edit and press [Enter]. The nested objects you select make up the *working set*. If multiple instances of the same xref appear, be sure to pick objects from the original xref you select.

Additional options for reference editing are available in the **Settings** tab of the **Reference Edit** dialog box. The **Create unique layer, style, and block names** option controls the naming of selected layers and *extracted* objects. Check the box to assign the prefix n, with *n* representing an incremental number, to object names. This is similar to the renaming method used when you bind an xref.

The **Display attribute definitions for editing** option is available if you select a block object in the **Identify Reference** tab of the **Reference Edit** dialog box. Check the box to edit any attribute definitions included in the reference. To prevent accidental changes to objects that do not belong to the working set, check the **Lock objects not in working set** option. This makes all objects outside of the working set unavailable for selection in reference editing mode.

If the selected xref file contains other references, the **Reference name:** area lists all nested xrefs and blocks in tree view. In the example given, Toilet, Tub, Vanity, and Towel Bar are nested xrefs in the Room xref. If you pick the drawing file icon next to Vanity in the tree view, for example, an image preview appears and the selected xref is highlighted in the drawing window.

When you finish adjusting settings, pick the **OK** button to begin editing the xref. The primary difference between the drawing and reference editing environments is the **Edit Reference** panel that appears in each ribbon tab. See **Figure 31-17**. Use the tools in the **Edit Reference** panel to add objects to the working set, remove objects from the working set, and save or discard changes to the original xref file.

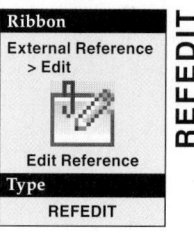

working set:
Nested objects selected for editing during a **REFEDIT** operation.

extracted:
Temporarily removed from the drawing for editing purposes.

Figure 31-16. The **Reference Edit** dialog box lists the name of the selected reference drawing and displays an image preview.

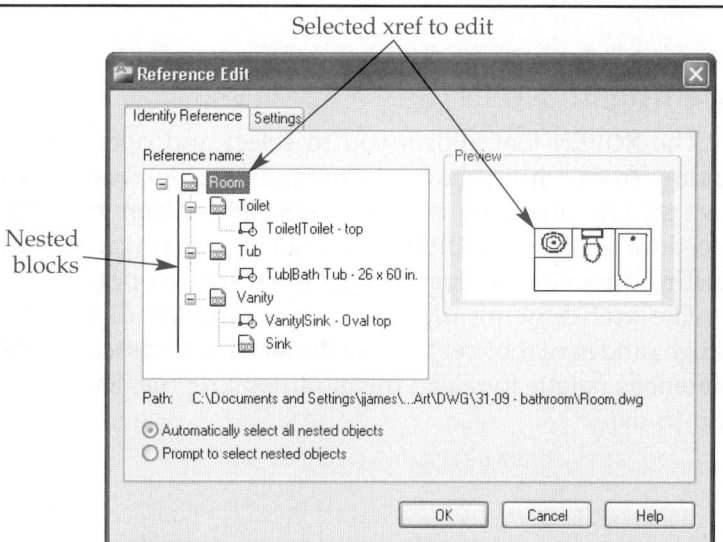

Figure 31-17.
The **Edit Reference** panel appears in each ribbon tab during reference editing. Most other drawing tools and options function the same in the drawing and reference editing environments.

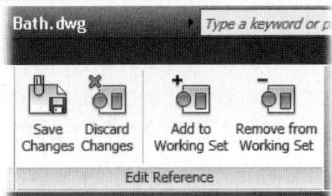

Any object you draw during the in-place edit is automatically added to the working set. Use the **Add to Working Set** button to add existing objects to the working set. When you add an object to the working set, the object is extracted, or removed, from the host drawing. The **Remove from Working Set** button allows you to remove selected objects from the working set. Removing a previously extracted object adds the object back to the host drawing.

Figure 31-18A shows reference-editing the Vanity xref nested in the Room xref. Notice that all objects not in the working set become faded. The objects in the working set appear in normal display mode. Once you define the working set, use drawing and editing tools to alter the xref. Pick the **Save Changes** button to save the changes. Pick the **OK** button when AutoCAD asks if you want to continue with the save and redefine the xref. All instances of the xref are updated. **Figure 31-18B** shows the xref after editing to redesign the sink and add a faucet. Pick the **Discard Changes** button to exit reference editing without saving changes.

NOTE

In-place reference editing is best suited for minor revisions. Conduct major xref revisions in the reference drawing file.

CAUTION

All edits made using reference editing are saved back to the reference drawing file and affect any host drawing that references the file. For this reason, it is critically important that you edit external references only with the permission of your supervisor or instructor.

Opening an Xref File

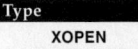

Type
XOPEN

The **XOPEN** tool allows you to select and open an xref in a separate drawing window from within the host drawing. A quick way to access the **XOPEN** tool is to select an xref and then right-click and pick **Open Xref**. This is essentially the same procedure as using the **OPEN** tool, but faster. If you access the **XOPEN** tool without first selecting an xref, you must then pick the xref to open.

The xref drawing file opens in a separate drawing window. After you make changes and save the xref file, use the **Manage Xrefs** icon in the status bar or the **External References** palette to reload the modified xref file. Reloading ensures that the host file is up-to-date.

Figure 31-18.
Reference editing.
A—Objects in the
drawing that are not
a part of the working
set appear faded
during the reference-
editing session.
B—All instances of
the xref immediately
update after reference
editing.

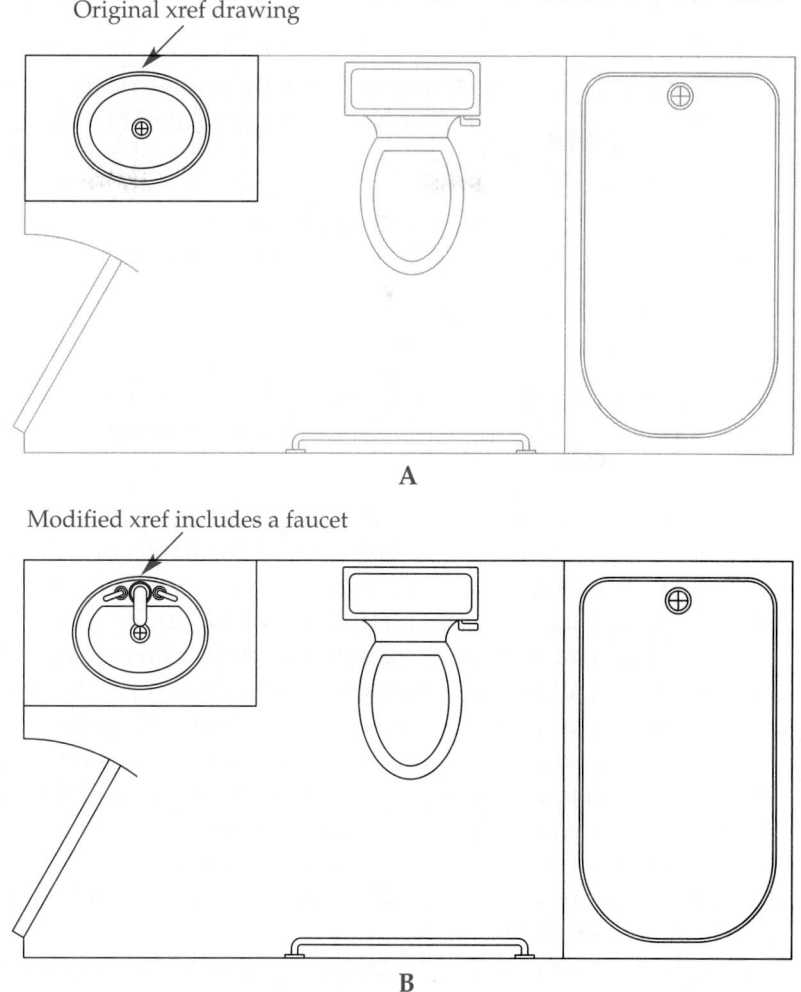

Original xref drawing

A

Modified xref includes a faucet

B

NOTE

You can also open an xref in the **External References** palette by right-clicking the xref name and selecting **Open**.

PROFESSIONAL TIP

Select an xref to display the **External References** ribbon tab. This provides a convenient location to access tools for reference editing, opening, and clipping an xref. An option is also available for accessing the **External References** palette.

Exercise 31-6

Access the Student Web site (www.g-wlearning.com/CAD) and complete Exercise 31-6.

Express Tools

Chapter 31

The **Block** and **Modify** panels of the **Express Tools** ribbon tab include additional tools related to xrefs and blocks. For information about the most useful xref express tools, go to the Student Web site (www.g-wlearning.com/CAD), select this chapter, and select **Xref Express Tools**.

Chapter Test

Answer the following questions. Write your answers on a separate sheet of paper or go to the Student Web site (www.g-wlearning.com/CAD) and complete the electronic chapter test.

1. What types of files can you reference into an AutoCAD drawing?
2. What effect does the use of referenced drawings have on drawing file size?
3. What is a nested xref?
4. List at least three common applications for xrefs.
5. On what layer should you insert xrefs into a host drawing?
6. Which tool allows you to attach an xref drawing to the current file?
7. What is the difference between an overlaid xref and an attached xref?
8. What is the difference between an absolute path and a relative path?
9. Describe the process of placing an xref using **DesignCenter.**
10. What must you do before you can use a tool palette to place an xref?
11. If you attach an xref file named FPLAN to the current drawing, and FPLAN contains a layer called ELECTRICAL, what name will appear for this layer in the **Layer Properties Manager**?
12. What is the purpose of the **Detach** option in the **External References** palette?
13. When are xrefs updated in the host drawing?
14. What could you do to suppress an xref temporarily without detaching it from the master drawing?
15. Which tool allows you to display only a specific portion of an externally referenced drawing?
16. What are spatial and layer indexes, and what function do they perform?
17. Why would you want to bind a dependent object to a master drawing?
18. What does the layer name WALL0NOTES mean?
19. What tool allows you to edit external references in place?
20. What tool allows you to open a parent xref drawing into a new AutoCAD drawing window by selecting the xref in the host drawing?

Drawing Problems

- *Start AutoCAD if it is not already started.*
- *Start a new drawing for each problem using an appropriate template of your choice. The template should include layers and text, dimension, multileader, and table styles, when necessary, for drawing the given objects. Add layers and text, dimension, multileader, and table styles as needed.*
- *Draw all objects using appropriate layers and text, dimension, multileader, and table styles, justification, and format.*
- *Follow the specific instructions for each problem. Use only drawing and editing tools and techniques you have already learned. Use your own judgment and approximate dimensions when necessary.*
- *Apply dimensions accurately using ASME or appropriate industry standards.*

Note: *Some of the problems in this chapter are built on problems from previous chapters. If you have not yet completed those problems, complete them now.*

▼ Basic

1. Attach a dimensioned problem from Chapter 18 into a new drawing as an xref. Save the drawing as P31-1.

2. Attach a dimensioned problem from Chapter 19 into a new drawing as an xref. Save the drawing as P31-2.

3. Attach a dimensioned problem from Chapter 20 into a new drawing as an xref. Save the drawing as P31-3.

▼ Intermediate

4. Attach the EX29-9.dwg file used in Exercise 29-9 into a new drawing as an xref. Copy the xref three times. Use the **XCLIP** tool to create a clipping boundary on each view. Apply an inverted rectangular clip to the original xref, a polyline boundary on the first copy, and a polygonal boundary on the second copy. Save the drawing as P31-4.

5. Attach the EX29-9.dwg file used in Exercise 29-9 into a new drawing as an xref. Bind the xref to the new drawing. Rename the layers to the names assigned to the original EX29-9 (xref) file. Explode the block created by binding the xref. Save the drawing as P31-5.

6. Create the multi-detail drawing shown according to the following information:
   - Use the Mechanical-Inch.dwt drawing template file available on the Student Web site.
   - Set drawing units to fractional.
   - Xref the following files into model space: Detail-Item 1.dwg, Detail-Item 2.dwg, Detail-Item 3.dwg, Detail-Item 4.dwg, Detail-Item 5.dwg, and Detail-Item 6.dwg. These files are available on the Student Web site.
   - Use six floating viewports on the **C-SIZE** layout to arrange and scale the details. Use a 1:2 scale.
   - Adjust the title block information using the drawing property fields and attributes.
   - Plot the drawing.

   Save the drawing as P31-6.

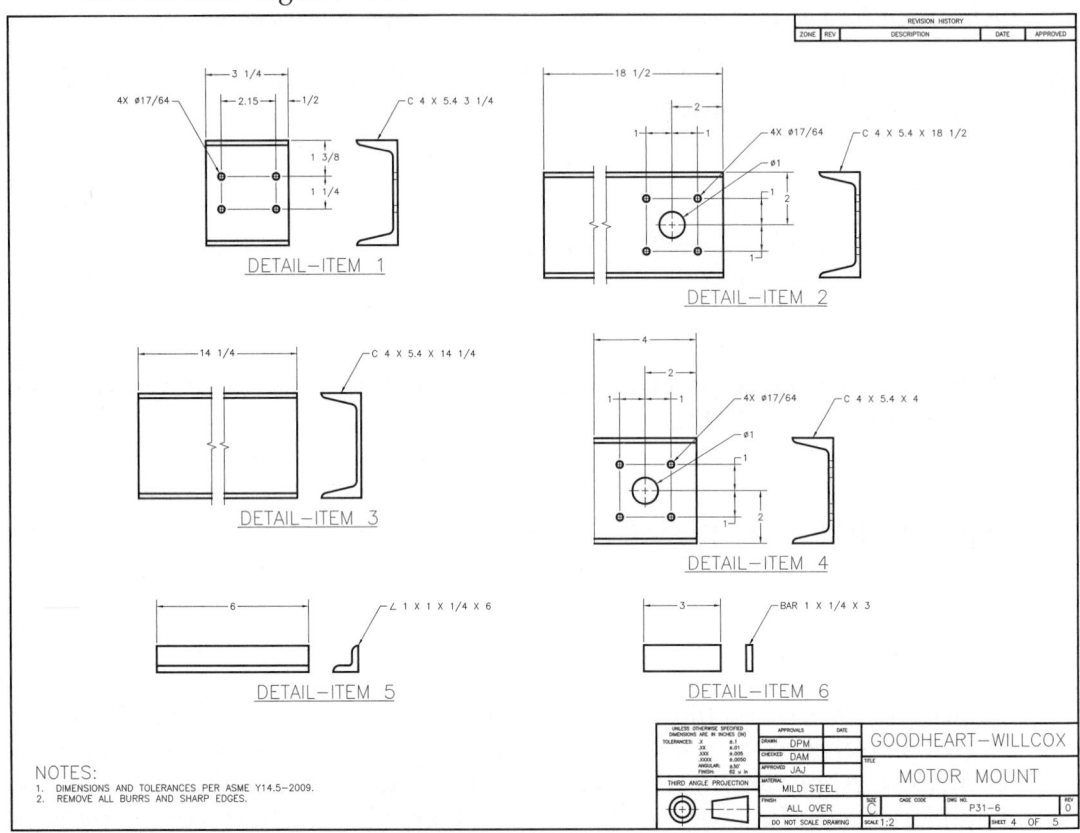

▼ Advanced

7. Design and draw a basic residential floor plan using an appropriate template. Save the file as P31-7FLOOR. Xref the P31-7FLOOR file into a new file as an attachment. Use the xref to help draw a roof plan. Save the roof plan file as P31-7ROOF.

8. Xref the P31-7ROOF file into a new file as an attachment. Use the xref to help draw front and rear elevations. Save the elevation file as P31-8.

9. Use a word processor to write a report of approximately 250 words explaining the purpose of external references. Include a brief description of the types of files that you can reference. Cite at least three examples from actual industry applications of using external references to help prepare drawings. Use at least four sketches to illustrate your report.

10. Xref the P28-11 file into a new file as an attachment. Use the xref to help draw a roof plan. Save the file as P31-10ROOF. Xref the P28-11 file into a new file as an attachment. Use the xref to help draw a slab foundation plan. Save the file. Xref the P31-10ROOF file and the P31-10FDTN files into a new file as attachments. Use corresponding insertion base points to overlap the plans exactly. Use the xrefs to help draw front, rear, right-side, and rear exterior elevations and an interior elevation for each wall. Save the elevation file as P31-10.

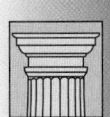

11. Draw the details shown in Figure 31-3A using a separate file for each detail and name the files according to the detail names shown in Figure 31-3B. Xref the files to create the layout shown in Figure 31-3B. Plot the layout. Save the complete drawing as P31-11.

AutoCAD Certified Associate Exam Practice

Answer the following questions. Write your answers on a separate sheet of paper.

1. Which of the following file types can be referenced into a host drawing? *Select all that apply.*
   A. DNG
   B. DOC
   C. DWFx
   D. PDF
   E. XLS
2. What is the default insertion base point for an xref file? *Select the one item that best answers the question.*
   A. lower-left corner of the geometry
   B. lower-left corner of the layout
   C. model space origin
   D. upper-right drawing limit
3. Which of the following terms describes an xref that is displayed in the host drawing but is not linked to it? *Select the one item that best answers the question.*
   A. attached xref
   B. clipped xref
   C. nested xref
   D. overlaid xref
   E. parent xref

AutoCAD Certified Professional Exam Practice

Follow the instructions in the problem. Write your answers on a separate sheet of paper.

1. **Navigate to this chapter on the Student Web site and open CPE-31backyard.dwg.** What layers in this drawing are former xrefs that have been bound to the drawing?

CHAPTER 32

Sheet Sets

Learning Objectives

After completing this chapter, you will be able to do the following:

✓ Describe the functions of an AutoCAD sheet set.
✓ Create and manage sheet sets.
✓ Add subsets and sheets to a sheet set.
✓ Use sheet views.
✓ Insert callout and view label blocks.
✓ Create sheet list tables
✓ Manage sheet set fields.
✓ Publish and archive a sheet set.

A design project typically requires a set of drawings and documents that completely specify the design. Preparing accurate drawings and making revisions in a timely manner involves significant organization, especially when a project includes multiple related *sheets* and *views*. *Sheet sets* help organize a set of drawings and simplify project management. This chapter focuses on creating sheet sets from given sheet set elements such as drawing templates, blocks, and fields, and assumes that you have an understanding of these items, as explained throughout this textbook. This chapter also describes how to prepare objects specifically related to sheet set applications.

sheet: A printed drawing or electronic layout that displays project design requirements.

view: 2D representations of an object.

sheet set: A collection of drawing sheets for a project; the AutoCAD tool that aids project organization.

Introduction to Sheet Sets

A sheet set is an electronic database of information about a project and the set of drawings required to document the design. A sheet set provides a way to organize files related to a set of drawings, similar to using Windows Explorer and a folder with subfolders to contain files. The most basic application of a sheet set is to group drawings in the proper order for easy access and quick opening. A sheet set also provides functions that automate managing and creating a set of drawings, which improves speed and accuracy. **Figure 32-1** shows an example of using a sheet set to manage the drawings for a small architectural project of a Cappuccino Express drive-through coffee stand. The sheet set organizes the four required layouts in the appropriate order for viewing, editing, *publishing*, and *archiving*.

publishing: Preparing a sequential set of multiple drawings for hard copy or electronic plotting of the set.

archiving: Gathering and storing all drawings and associated files related to a project.

Figure 32-1. Using a sheet set to manage a set of architectural drawings. The **Sheet Set Manager** is a palette for creating and working with sheet sets.

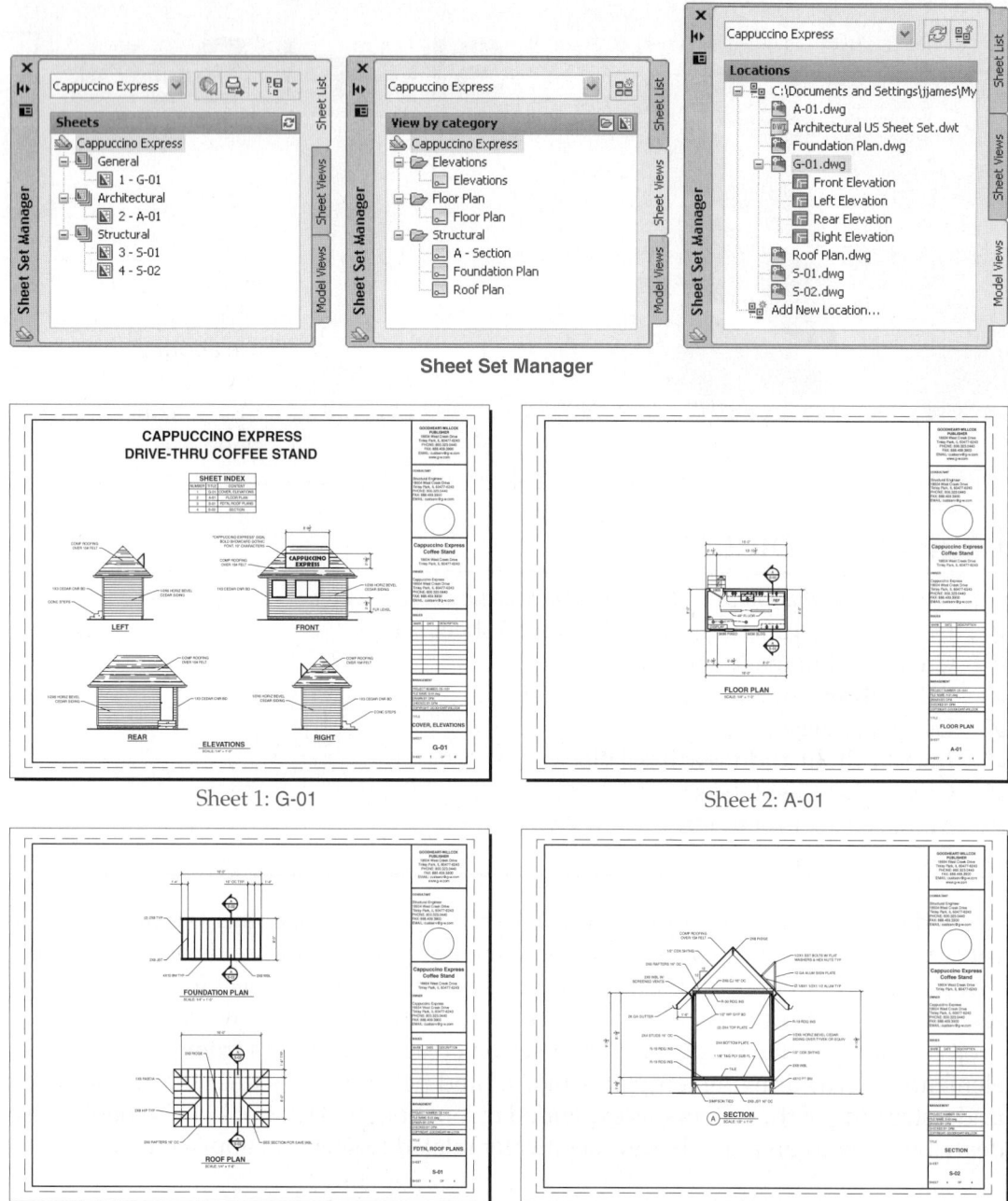

Sheet Set Manager

Sheet 1: G-01

Sheet 2: A-01

Sheet 3: S-01

Sheet 4: S-02

Sheet Set

Every sheet set has a sheet set data (DST) file specific to the project. A DST file is essentially an electronic version of a design project. It is similar to a folder containing subfolders and each sheet in a set of drawings. The purpose of a DST file is to manage the paths to files related to a set of drawings and the procedures required for the sheet set to function properly. A sheet set stores and displays all information about the project, including:

- Paths to required drawing layouts, or sheets
- The structure and organization of sheets in the sheet set
- Project properties common to all sheets and usually found in title blocks, such as the name and number of the project

- A path to a template file and storage location for creating new sheets
- Paths to drawing and model space views
- Paths to blocks with attributes containing fields that link information from one drawing or view to another drawing or view on different sheets of the sheet set
- A path to a page setup used to plot all sheets using the same settings, if appropriate

Introduction to Sheet Set Fields

One way to enhance the usefulness of a sheet set is to use text and blocks with attributes that include *fields* linked to elements of the sheet set. **Figure 32-2** highlights some of the fields used in the Cappuccino Express sheet set shown in **Figure 32-1**. The most common applications for sheet set fields include titles, title blocks, *callout blocks*, *view label blocks*, and *sheet list tables*. You will learn more about these items later in this chapter.

Fields display properties and allow values to change during the course of the project. For example, the SHEET NUMBER attribute in the title block on each sheet uses a **CurrentSheetNumber** field that increments the sheet number when you add a sheet to

field: A text object that can display a specific property value, setting, or characteristic.

callout block: A block that uses attributes containing fields that link the view number and sheet title between the sheet set and drawing (sheet) views.

view label block: A block that uses attributes containing fields that link the view name, number, and scale to drawing (sheet) views.

sheet list table: An AutoCAD table that references a table style and selected items in a sheet set to create a list of sheets in the sheet set and related information.

Figure 32-2. Examples of fields added to text and attributes linked to sheet set properties. Use the same tools and options to add fields that reference sheet set data as you would for fields associated with other items.

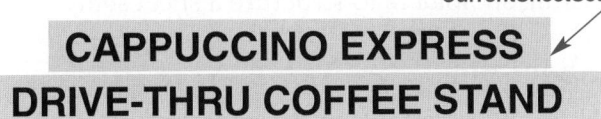

Mtext

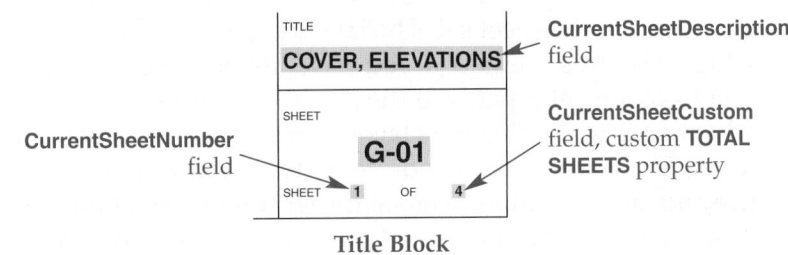

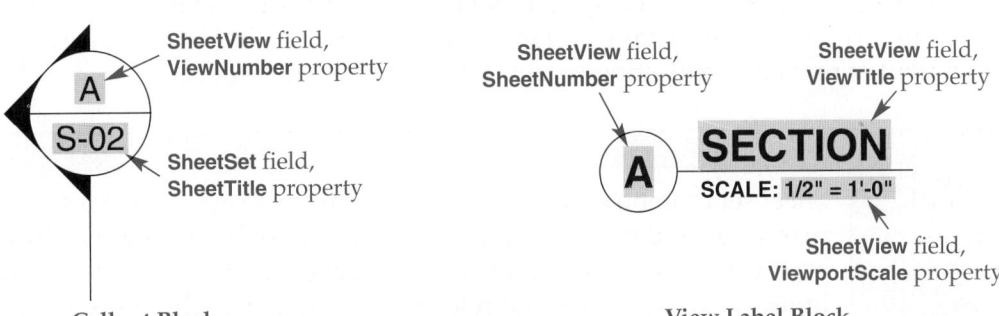

Sheet List Table

the set. Fields are also associated with sheets and views. For example, the title under each view is a block that includes a VIEW attribute with a **SheetView** field that displays the name of the view. The title updates when you change the name of the view.

Preparing for a Sheet Set

Preparing to create a sheet set involves several processes. You can adjust every aspect of a sheet set whenever necessary, but for best efficiency, prepare for a sheet set in advance by identifying and creating all of the required elements. Preparing for a sheet set includes considering basic properties, such as the project name and number, and identifying where you will store the DST file. Preparation also includes developing a drawing template (DWT) file for creating new sheets, drawing blocks with attributes containing sheet set fields, and defining a page setup to plot all sheets using the same settings.

A sheet in a sheet set is a layout in paper space. Although you can add multiple layouts to a drawing file, you can only open and use one layout in a drawing assigned to a sheet set. Therefore, prepare a single layout per drawing if you plan to use a sheet set. Delete all other layouts found in existing drawings and in the template you intend to assign to the sheet set. Use an external reference to reuse model space content in other layouts, and in different drawing files when necessary.

If you plan to organize existing drawings in a sheet set, store all files related to the project in a designated folder when possible. Use a limited number of subfolders to group files, such as an Architectural folder to group architectural drawings and a Structural folder to group structural drawings for a building project. AutoCAD allows you to reference existing subfolders to structure a sheet set.

Developing a Sheet Set

AutoCAD includes multiple tools and techniques for developing and managing a sheet set. However, there are two primary options for building a set of drawings in a sheet set during or after you create a new sheet set file. One option is to link, or import, existing layouts to the sheet set. The layouts typically represent final or nearly complete drawings. Use this method if you have already prepared layouts for each sheet in a set, but have not yet organized the sheets in a sheet set.

The second option is to develop new layouts in which you display existing or new model space geometry. Sheet sets include tools for creating new drawings using a specific template and layout, similar to using the **NEW** tool, and at the same time incorporate the new layouts into the sheet set. Use this technique to add a new drawing to the set. Externally reference existing model space content to the new sheet, or use the drawing as a blank sheet for developing new geometry. Projects often require a combination of referencing existing layouts and creating new sheets.

NOTE

Sheet sets combine many AutoCAD features to automate and organize a set of drawings. To understand and effectively apply sheet sets, you must understand templates, layouts, fields, blocks, attributes, views, and external references. If you have difficulty understanding an aspect of sheet sets, review the associated underlying concept.

The Sheet Set Manager

The **Sheet Set Manager**, shown in **Figure 32-1** and **Figure 32-3**, is a palette that allows you to create, organize, and access sheet sets. Like other palettes, **Sheet Set Manager** can be resized, docked, and set to auto-hide. The **Sheet Set Manager** also makes use of detailed tooltips and shortcut menus for accessing tools and options.

Use the **Sheet Set Control** drop-down list at the top of the **Sheet Set Manager** to open and create sheet sets. The buttons next to the drop-down list control the items listed in the **Sheet Set Manager** and vary depending on the current tab. Right-click on the **Sheets** list area and select **Preview/Details Pane** to display the **Preview** or **Details** pane. Pick the **Details** or **Preview** button to toggle the corresponding display. The **Details** pane, shown in **Figure 32-3**, lists properties associated with the item selected in the **Sheet Set Manager**. The **Preview** pane displays an image of a selected sheet or view.

The **Sheet List** tab is the primary resource for managing sheets within a sheet set. Some projects require using only the **Sheet List** tab. The **Sheet Views** tab allows you to organize and place named views on layouts. Sheet views also provide a method to insert blocks that relate information on one sheet to a view on another sheet, such as the section bubbles shown in **Figure 32-1**, and sheet blocks associated with views, such as the view titles shown in **Figure 32-1**. The **Model Views** tab allows you to open files related to the current sheet set, and includes an option to create new layout views using existing model space content.

SHEETSET
Quick Access

Sheet Set Manager
Ribbon
View
> Palettess
Sheet Set Manager
Type
SHEETSET
SSM

> **NOTE**
>
> When no drawing is open, the **Sheet Set Manager** button appears in the **Quick Access** toolbar. Pick the button to access the **Sheet Set Manager** without opening a drawing.

Creating Sheet Sets

To create a new sheet set, first begin a new file or open an existing file, even if the file does not relate to the sheet set. Then access the **NEWSHEETSET** tool to display the **Create Sheet Set** wizard. See **Figure 32-4**. The **NEWSHEETSET** tool is also available

Type
NEWSHEETSET

Figure 32-3.
The **Sheet Set Manager** contains **Sheet List, Sheet Views,** and **Model Views** tabs. Pick the **Sheet Set Control** drop-down list to access options to create or open a sheet set.

Figure 32-4.
Select the **An example sheet set** radio button on the **Begin** page to use an existing sheet set as a template for building a new sheet set, or to create a sheet set from scratch. Pick the **Existing drawings** radio button to create a new sheet set without referencing an existing sheet set, but with the option to add existing drawing layouts as sheets in the set.

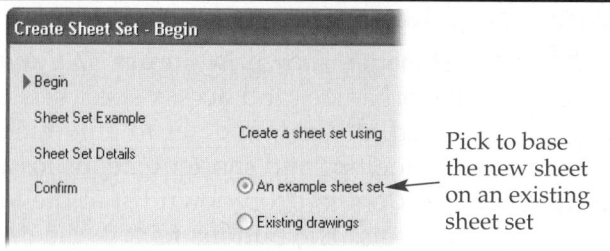

Pick to base the new sheet on an existing sheet set

from the **Sheet Set Manager** by picking the **New Sheet Set...** option from the **Sheet Set Control** drop-down list. Use the **Create Sheet Set** wizard to create a sheet set from an *example sheet set*, from scratch without selecting existing layouts to include as sheets, or from scratch but with the option to select existing layouts to include as sheets.

example sheet set: An existing sheet set used as a template for developing a new sheet set.

An Example Sheet Set Option

Pick the **An example sheet set** radio button on the **Begin** page of the **Create Sheet Set** wizard to generate a new sheet set from an existing sheet set that has properties and settings similar to those you want to apply to the new sheet set. This is much like using a drawing template to begin a new drawing. Later, you can modify the characteristics from the example sheet set in the new sheet set as needed. Beginning with an example sheet set is useful if a sheet set is available that closely matches the sheet set you intend to create. For example, use the Cappuccino Express sheet set shown in **Figure 32-1** as an example sheet set for projects with similar characteristics. All properties and many settings that you assign to the example sheet set, such as the General, Architectural, and Structural *subsets* shown in **Figure 32-1,** are reproduced in the new sheet set.

subsets: Groups of similar layouts, such as those in the same discipline, sometimes based on folder hierarchy.

PROFESSIONAL TIP

Avoid using an example sheet set if the new sheet set is significantly different from an available example sheet set. It may take more time to modify the sheet set than to create a new sheet set that is specific to the new project.

Sheet Set Example Page

Pick the **Next** button to display the **Sheet Set Example** page. See **Figure 32-5.** When you create a sheet set from an example sheet set, you start from an existing DST file. The **Select a sheet set to use as an example** radio button is active by default, and a list box displays all DST files in the default Template folder. Select an example sheet set from the list, or pick the **New Sheet Set** option in the **Select a sheet set to use as an example** list box to begin a new sheet set from scratch.

You can use any existing sheet set as an example sheet set. To use an example sheet set not saved in the Template folder, pick the **Browse to another sheet set to use as an example** radio button and then select the ellipsis (...) button. Use the **Browse for sheet set** dialog box to locate and select a DST file in another folder.

Figure 32-5.
Use the **Sheet Set Example** page to select an example sheet set.

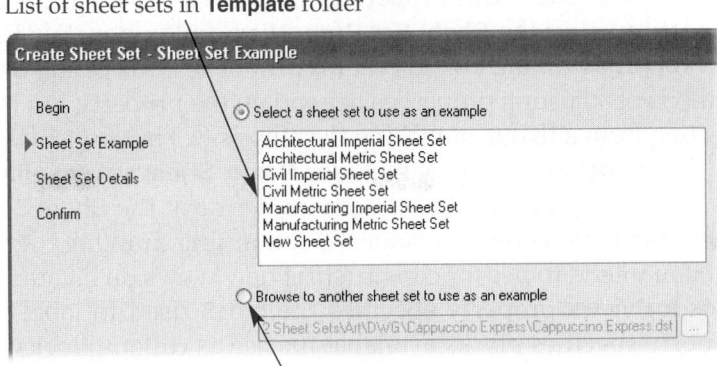

List of sheet sets in **Template** folder

Select a template from the **Browse for Sheet Set** dialog box

Sheet Set Details Page

Select the **Next** button to display the **Sheet Set Details** page. See **Figure 32-6.** Use the **Sheet Set Details** page to modify the existing sheet set data and create settings for the new project. Most sheet set details are specific to a project. Enter the name, or title, of the sheet set in the **Name of new sheet set** text box. The name is typically the project number or a short description of the project. Type a description for the sheet set in the **Description (optional)** area. The **Store sheet set data file (.dst) here** text box determines where the sheet set file is saved. Pick the ellipsis (**...**) button and select a folder in the **Browse for sheet set folder** dialog box to change the default DST file location. Pick the **Create a folder hierarchy based on subsets** check box to allow AutoCAD to create subfolders that match the subsets in the example sheet set. Layouts in each folder are listed under each subset.

Figure 32-6. On the **Sheet Set Details** page, type a name and description for the sheet set and specify the location of the DST file. You can also access additional sheet set properties.

Type a name   Type a description

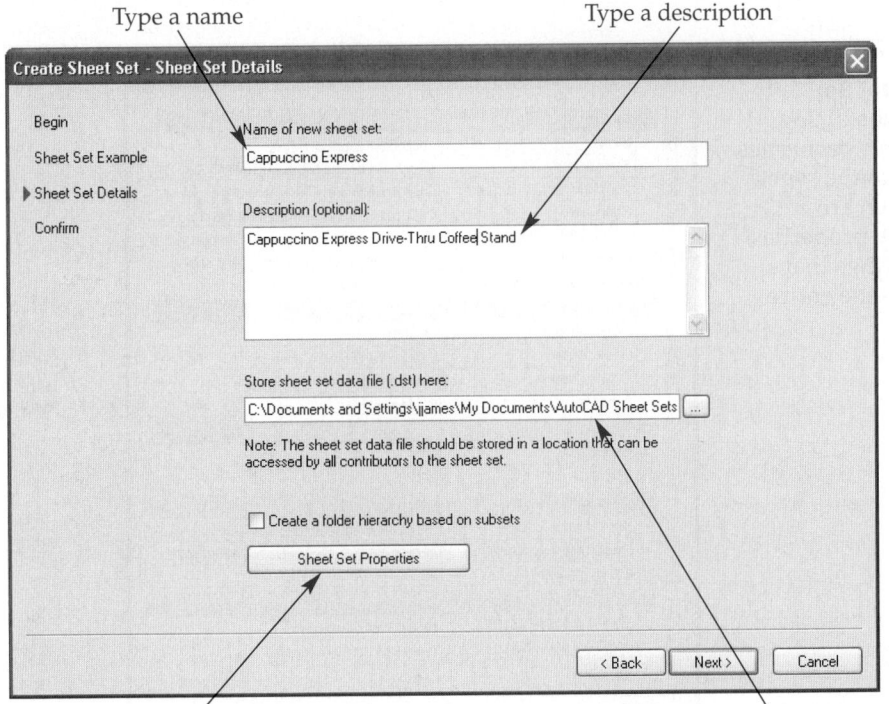

Pick to open the **Sheet Set Properties** dialog box   Specify a location for the DST file

Pick the **Sheet Set Properties** button to adjust and create additional sheet set properties using the **Sheet Set Properties** dialog box. See **Figure 32-7.** Use the **Sheet Set Properties** dialog box to edit all properties except the **Sheet set data file** property. Methods of adjusting properties depend on the property, but include typing in a text box, selecting from a flyout, or picking the ellipsis (**...**) button to navigate to a specific location.

The **Sheet Set** category includes **Name, Sheet set data file,** and **Description** properties that correspond to the values you define at the **Sheet Set Details** page. The **Model view** property specifies the folder(s) containing drawing files with model space content that you intend to use for constructing new views on layouts in the sheet set. The **Label block for views** property specifies the block used to label views. The **Callout blocks** property specifies blocks available for use as callout blocks. The **Page setup overrides file** property determines the location of a DWT file containing a page setup that applies to all sheets in the sheet set. The **Project Control** category lists properties common to most projects, including **Project number, Project name, Project phase,** and **Project milestone.**

The **Sheet Set Manager** includes an option to create a new sheet and drawing file without referencing an existing layout. Use the **Sheet storage location** property in the **Sheet Creation** category to specify where to store new sheets. Remember the specified location so that you can locate the new drawings. Use the **Sheet creation template** property to define the drawing template and layout for creating new sheets. The **Select Layout as Sheet Template** dialog box appears when you select the ellipsis (**...**) button. See **Figure 32-8.** All layouts in the selected template appear in the list box. Select the appropriate layout and pick the **OK** button. Set the **Prompt for template** property to **No** to use the specified **Sheet creation template** property to create all new sheets. Select **Yes** to have the option to choose a different template to create a new sheet.

The **Sheet Set Custom Properties** category lists custom properties that you create by picking the **Edit Custom Properties** button to access the **Custom Properties** dialog box. Custom properties are necessary to specify additional information on sheets, such as the properties shown in **Figure 32-7,** which are linked to fields in attributes of the title block. Use the **Add** and **Delete** buttons in the **Custom Properties** dialog box to add and delete custom properties. After you set all values in the **Sheet Set Properties** dialog box, pick the **OK** button to return to the **Sheet Set Details** page.

Figure 32-7.
The **Sheet Set Properties** dialog box stores properties related to the sheet set, which are typically properties and settings that apply to the entire project.

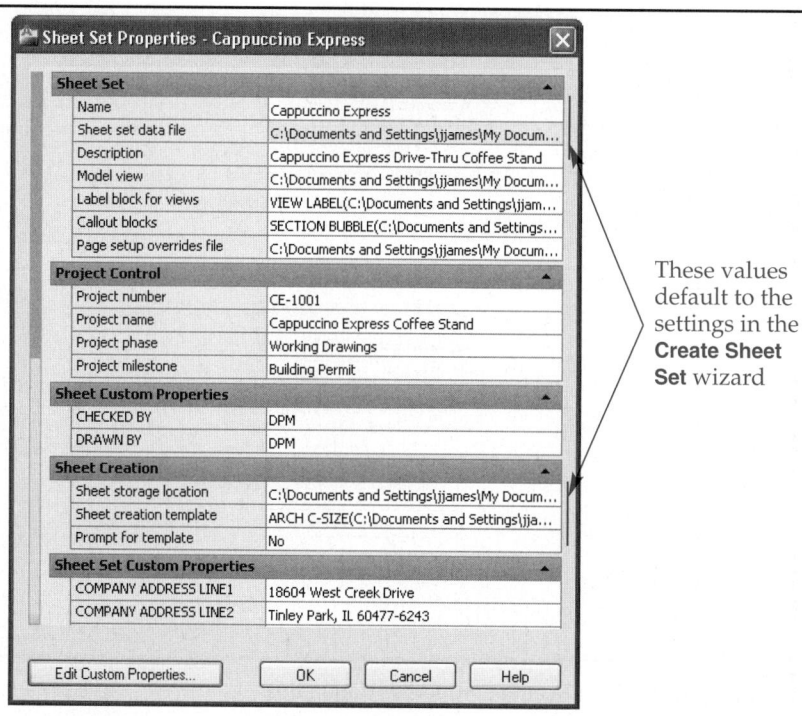

These values default to the settings in the **Create Sheet Set** wizard

AutoCAD and Its Applications—Basics

Figure 32-8.
Selecting an existing
layout as a template
for new sheets in a
sheet set.

Pick to select a different template file

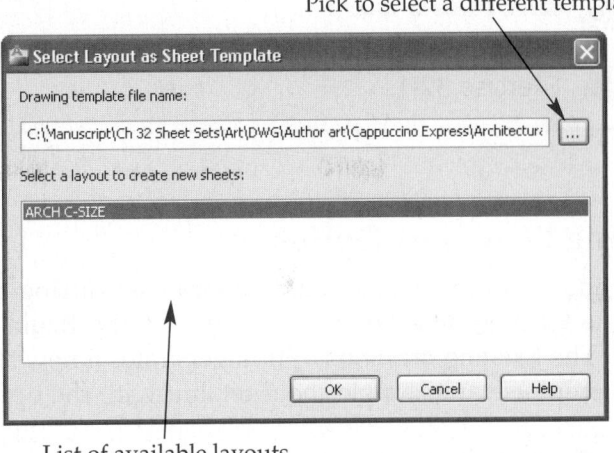

List of available layouts

NOTE

You are required to specify all relevant sheet set details if you choose the **New Sheet Set** option of the **Sheet Set Example** page.

Confirm Page

Pick the **Next** button to display the **Confirm** page. See **Figure 32-9**. The **Sheet Set Preview** area displays all information associated with the sheet set. Use the **Back** button to return to previous pages to make changes. Pick the **Finish** button to create the sheet set.

PROFESSIONAL TIP

Copy and paste the information in the **Sheet Set Preview** area of the **Confirm** page into a word processing program to save and print for reference.

Figure 32-9. Use the **Confirm** page to preview settings before creating the sheet set.

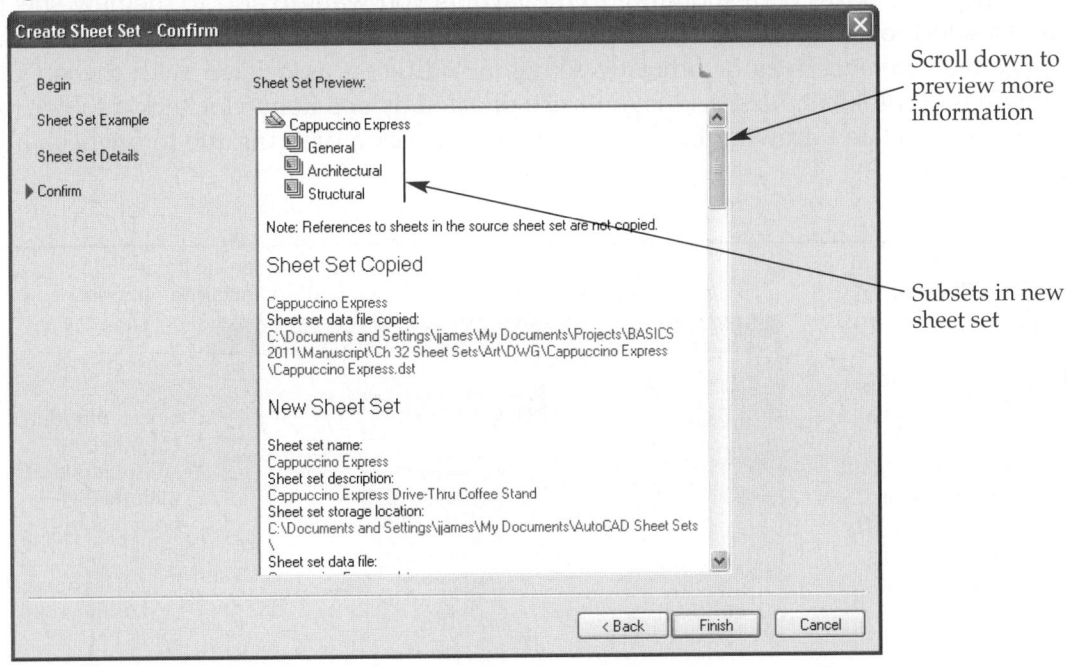

Scroll down to preview more information

Subsets in new sheet set

Exercise 32-1

Access the Student Web site (www.g-wlearning.com/CAD) and complete Exercise 32-1.

Existing Drawings Option

To add existing layouts to a new sheet set during the sheet set creation process, select the **Existing drawings** radio button on the **Begin** page of the **Create Sheet Set** wizard. The **Existing drawings** option generates a new sheet set from scratch, without the option to use an example sheet set, but with the option to add existing layouts as sheets.

The **Existing drawings** option is useful if an example sheet set is unavailable or inappropriate, and if you have already developed multiple final or nearly final layouts. If you choose to apply the **Existing drawings** option, it is especially important that all drawings only include a single layout. In addition, organize files in a structured hierarchy of folders before creating the sheet set. This saves time because you can reproduce the subfolders as subsets in the new sheet set.

Sheet Set Details Page

Select the **Next** button to display the **Sheet Set Details** page. This is nearly the same page that appears when you create a new sheet set from an example sheet set, as shown in **Figure 32-6**. Use the **Sheet Set Details** page to define sheet set data and create properties for the new project. Because the **Existing drawings** option does not use an example sheet set, you must specify all relevant details, including custom properties.

Choose Layouts Page

Pick the **Next** button to display the **Choose Layouts** page. See **Figure 32-10**. The **Choose Layouts** page allows you to specify layouts in existing drawings to add to the sheet set as sheets. Pick the **Browse...** button to display the **Browse for Folder** dialog box, and select the folder containing the drawing files with the desired layouts. The list box displays the selected folder, subfolders, drawing files, and all layouts within the drawings. Repeat the process to add other folders to the list box as needed.

Check the boxes corresponding to the layouts you want to add to the new sheet set. Deselect layouts that you do not want to add to the sheet set, such as layouts in unneeded reference files or other drawings not directly associated with the set of drawings. Subfolders, files, and layouts are selected as one item. Uncheck a folder to uncheck all related drawing files and layouts. Uncheck a drawing file to uncheck all related layouts.

Figure 32-10.
Use the **Choose Layouts** page to link existing layouts to a new sheet set. AutoCAD refers to the process as *importing layouts,* but the operation does not technically import layouts; it references layouts.

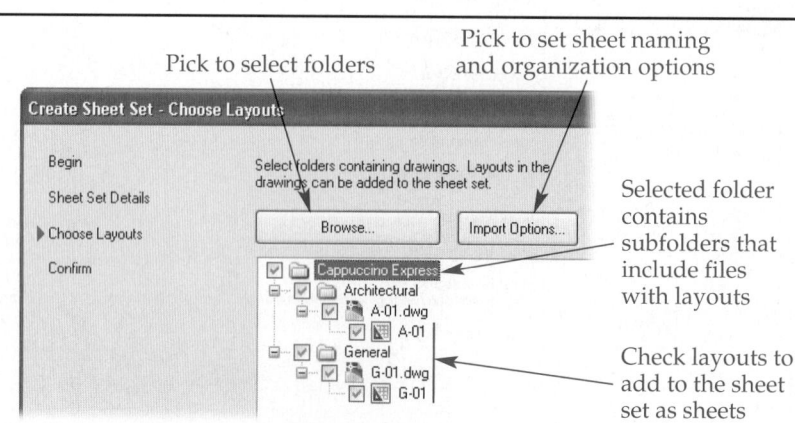

AutoCAD and Its Applications—Basics

To adjust sheet naming and subset options, pick the **Import Options...** button to display the **Import Options** dialog box. See **Figure 32-11**. The name of a drawing with one layout, the name of the layout, and the name of the sheet in the sheet set are often the same. However, when you create a sheet set using existing layouts, especially when you select multiple layouts in a single file, you may need to adjust sheet naming. Select the **Prefix sheet titles with file name** check box to include the drawing file name with the name of the layouts that become sheets. For example, the sheet name Electrical Plan – First Floor Electrical forms from a layout named First Floor Electrical imported from the drawing file Electrical Plan.dwg.

Select the **Create subsets based on folder structure** check box to organize a sheet set so that subfolders are grouped into subsets. Layouts in each folder are listed in each subset. The **Ignore top level folder** option determines whether the top level folder creates a subset. **Figure 32-12A** shows the **Choose Layouts** page with layouts imported from the Cappuccino Express folder for the Cappuccino Express sheet set. This sheet set uses the **Create subsets based on folder structure** and **Ignore top level folder** options, but not the **Prefix sheet titles with file name** option. **Figure 32-12B** shows the result of the configuration in the **Sheet Set Manager**. As shown in **Figure 32-12B**, each sheet can include a number preceding the sheet name, separated by a dash.

Confirm Page

Pick the **Next** button to display the **Confirm** page. This is the same page that appears when you create a new sheet set from an example sheet set. The **Sheet Set Preview** area displays all information associated with the sheet set. Use the **Back** button to return to previous pages to make changes. Pick the **Finish** button to create the sheet set.

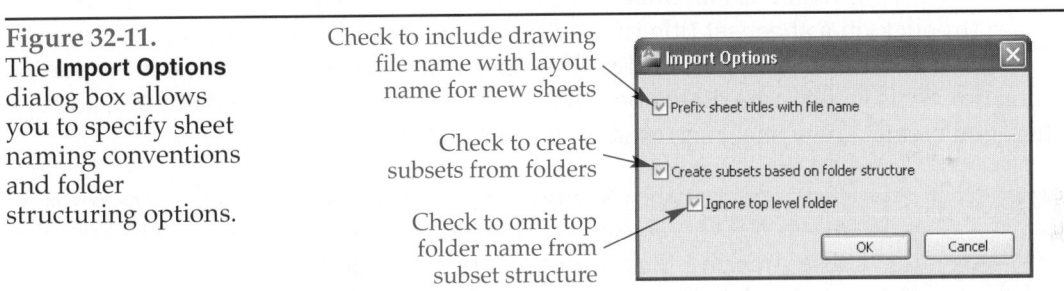

Figure 32-11.
The **Import Options** dialog box allows you to specify sheet naming conventions and folder structuring options.

Check to include drawing file name with layout name for new sheets

Check to create subsets from folders

Check to omit top folder name from subset structure

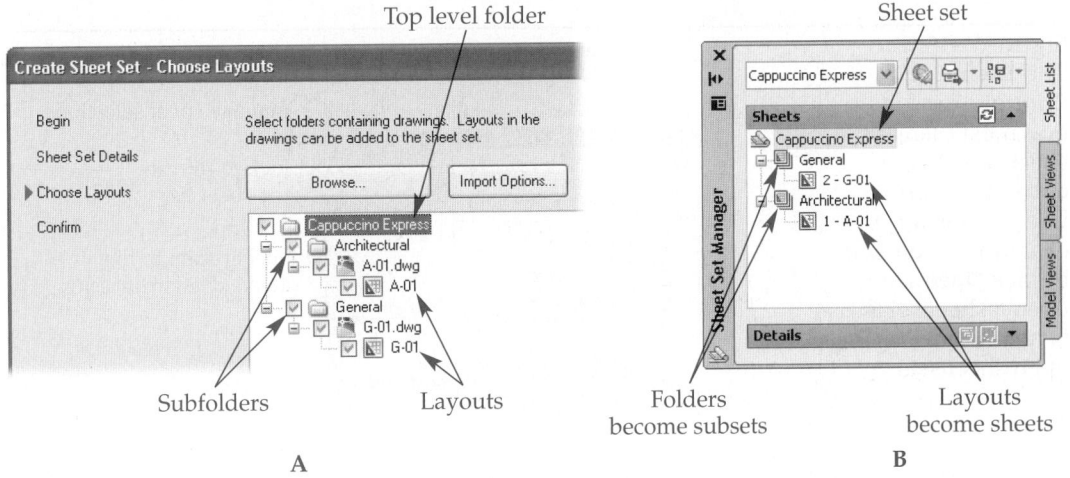

Figure 32-12. Creating a sheet set named Cappuccino Express with subsets. A—Layouts imported from the Architectural and General subfolders in the Cappuccino Express folder. Subfolders are designated as subsets for the new sheet set. B—Subsets shown in the **Sheet Set Manager**.

Top level folder

Subfolders

Layouts

A

Sheet set

Folders become subsets

Layouts become sheets

B

Exercise 32-2

Access the Student Web site (www.g-wlearning.com/CAD) and complete Exercise 32-2.

Managing Sheet Sets

Options for opening, closing, and controlling sheet sets are available from the **Sheet Set Control** drop-down list, buttons, flyouts, and shortcut menus. Opening a sheet set is similar to accessing a folder in Windows Explorer. You can open any sheet set, regardless of the active drawing file. A sheet set remains open until you close it or exit AutoCAD. Make an open sheet set current to use the sheet set and display the sheet set content in the **Sheet Set Manager** tabs.

The top portion of the **Sheet Set Control** drop-down list displays sheet sets that are open in the current AutoCAD session. See **Figure 32-13**. Pick a sheet set from the list to make it current. The list clears when you exit AutoCAD. Use the **Recent** cascading submenu to open a recently opened sheet set. Select **Open...** to display the **Open Sheet Set** dialog box. Then navigate to a DST file and open the file in the **Sheet Set Manager**.

To close a sheet, right-click on an open sheet set in the **Sheet Set Control** drop-down list or on the sheet set title in the **Sheet List** tab, and select **Close Sheet Set**. Sheet sets automatically close when you exit AutoCAD. Closing a sheet set removes the sheet set from the **Sheet Set Manager** and allows you to delete the DST file if necessary. To save all of the drawing files with layouts associated with the current sheet set at the same time, right-click on a sheet set title in the **Sheet List** tab and select **Resave All Sheets**.

Right-click on the sheet set and pick **Properties...** to display the **Sheet Properties** dialog box. This is the same dialog box that is available from the **Sheet Set Details** page when you create a new sheet set, as shown in **Figure 32-7**.

NOTE

Close drawing files with layouts associated with the current sheet set to update the sheet set according to changes made to the drawings. To update changes to the sheet list manually, pick the **Refresh Sheet Status** button. See **Figure 32-13**.

Figure 32-13.
The **Sheet Set Control** drop-down list displays sheet sets that are currently open. Use the **Recent** cascading submenu or pick **Open...** to open a sheet set that is not in the list of open sheet sets.

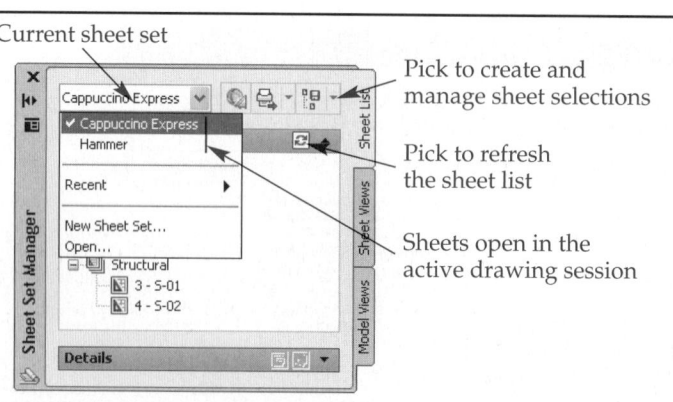

Current sheet set

Pick to create and manage sheet selections

Pick to refresh the sheet list

Sheets open in the active drawing session

Subsets

Subsets provide a way to organize sheets in a sheet set, similar to using subfolders to organize files with Windows Explorer. The example in **Figure 32-10** uses a General subset to group all general sheets for a building project, an Architectural subset to group all architectural sheets, and a Structural subset to group all structural sheets. Another example is using subsets to organize assemblies, subassemblies, and parts for a mechanical design project. Although subsets are not required, they can provide significant help in managing a sheet set, especially when the sheet set includes multiple sheets. For example, you can set a subset not to publish instead of taking the time to set each individual sheet not to publish.

Creating Subsets

The **Existing drawings** option for creating a new sheet set includes the **Create subsets based on folder structure** function that allows you to form subsets based on an existing folder hierarchy during the process of creating a sheet set. For existing sheet sets, use the **Sheet List** tab of the **Sheet Set Manager** to create new subsets. Add a subset to a sheet set or to an existing subset to create the desired subset hierarchy. Right-click on the sheet set or subset name in the **Sheet List** tab and select **New Subset...** to open the **Subset Properties** dialog box. See **Figure 32-14**. Type the name of the subset in the **Subset name** text box. For example, name a subset Structural to contain all structural sheets in a sheet set for a building project. Select **Yes** from the **Create Folder Hierarchy** drop-down list to create a new folder that corresponds to the subset.

The **Publish Sheets in Subset** property determines whether sheets in the subset are published. The **Do Not Publish Sheets** setting prevents sheets in the subset from being published. An icon identifies subsets set not to publish. The **New Sheet Location** property determines the path to which new sheets are saved when you add a new sheet from the subset. The default location is the folder associated with the sheet set or subset in which you create the new subset, or the folder you specified when you created the sheet set.

Use the **Sheet Creation Template** property to specify a drawing template and layout to use when creating new sheets in the subset. For example, assign a specific drawing template and layout to an Architectural subset to create new architectural discipline sheets, and assign a different drawing template and layout to a Structural subset to create new structural discipline sheets. The process for specifying a sheet creation template and layout for a subset is identical to the process for selecting the sheet creation template and layout for a sheet set. Use the **Prompt for Template** drop-down list to indicate whether a prompt should ask for a sheet template instead of using the specified sheet creation template.

Managing Subsets

Drag and drop subsets as needed to restructure the sheet set. Right-click on a subset in the **Sheet List** tab and pick **Collapse** to collapse the nodes of a subset. To make changes to an existing subset, right-click on the subset and select **Properties...**

Figure 32-14.
The **Subset Properties** dialog box allows you to define a new subset.

Enter a name for the new subset

Path to which new sheets are saved

Template layout for new sheets

to redisplay the **Subset Properties** dialog box. The **Rename Subset...** shortcut menu option also opens the **Subset Properties** dialog box. To delete a subset, right-click on the subset and select **Remove Subset**. The **Remove Subset** option is not available if the subset contains sheets.

 **Exercise 32-3**

Access the Student Web site (www.g-wlearning.com/CAD) and complete Exercise 32-3.

Sheets

A sheet set or subset contains sheets, just as a folder or subfolder contains drawing files in Windows Explorer. A sheet is a path to a single layout in a drawing file. See **Figure 32-15**. To open a sheet, double-click on the sheet or right-click on the sheet and select **Open**. The drawing file that contains the referenced layout tab opens and displays the layout corresponding to the sheet. You can also open a sheet as *read-only*.

read-only:
Describes a drawing file opened for viewing only. You can make changes to the drawing, but you cannot save changes without using the SAVEAS tool.

NOTE

When you use any technique to open a file, including opening files from the **Sheet Set Manager**, the files are added to the open files list. Use the **Quick View Drawings** tool or window control tools on the ribbon to view open files. Save and close any files that you do not need open.

Figure 32-15.
Sheets in the set of drawings for the example Cappuccino Express building project. Hover over a sheet to display a detailed tooltip.

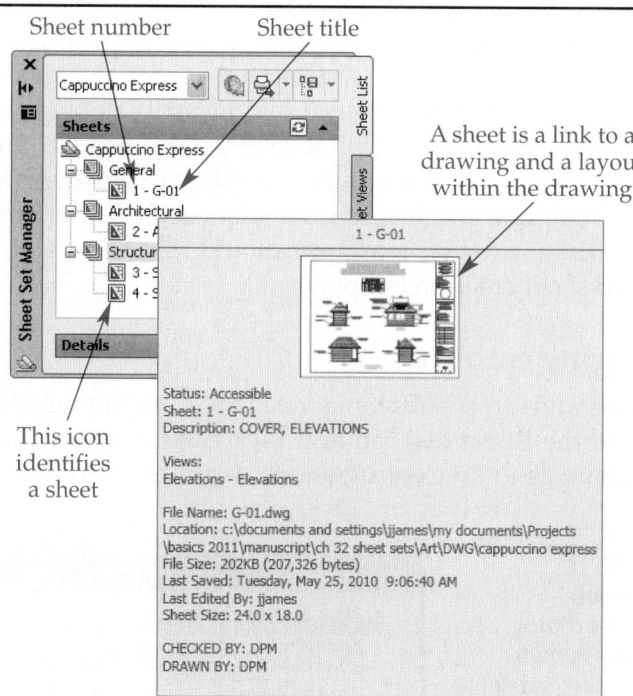

Adding a Layout As a Sheet

The **Existing drawings** option for creating a new sheet set includes the **Choose Layouts** page that allows you to add existing layouts to a sheet set as sheets. You can also add a layout to an existing sheet set using the **Sheet Set Manager** or directly from an open drawing. To add an existing layout to a sheet set using the **Sheet Set Manager**, right-click on the sheet set or the subset that will contain the sheet, and select **Import Layout as Sheet...**. The **Import Layouts as Sheets** dialog box appears. See **Figure 32-16**.

Pick the **Browse for Drawings** button to select a drawing file. All layouts in the drawing file appear in the list box and are checked for import by default. The **Status** column indicates whether the layout can be imported into the sheet set. You can only use a layout in one sheet set. In other words, you cannot import a layout that has already been consumed by a sheet set. Each checked layout is imported as a separate sheet. Importing layouts only links layouts to the sheet set. The original file remains unchanged, and no new drawing files or layouts form. Uncheck a box to exclude a layout from importing. Select the **Prefix sheet titles with file name** check box to include the name of the file in the sheet title. Pick the **Import Checked** button to import the selected layouts as sheets.

A layout tab, the **Quick View Layouts** tool, and the **Quick View Drawings** tool provide a way to add existing layouts to a sheet set directly from an open drawing. Right-click on the layout tab or thumbnail image you want to import and select **Import Layout as Sheet...**. The **Import Layouts as Sheets** dialog box appears with the selected layout listed. You must save the drawing and set up the layout to make the **Import Layout as Sheet...** menu option available.

> **NOTE**
>
> Right-click on a subset in the **Sheet Set Manager** and select **Import Layout as Sheet...** to import layouts into the subset. Importing a layout from a layout tab, the **Quick View Layouts** tool, or the **Quick View Drawings** tool does not provide an initial option to add layouts as sheets in a subset. You must drag and drop the sheets into the appropriate subset after importing.

Figure 32-16.
Use the **Import Layouts as Sheets** dialog box to link existing layouts to a sheet set as sheets. AutoCAD refers to the process as importing layouts, but the operation does not technically import layouts; it references layouts.

Pick to locate and select a drawing file

Uncheck to exclude a layout from importing

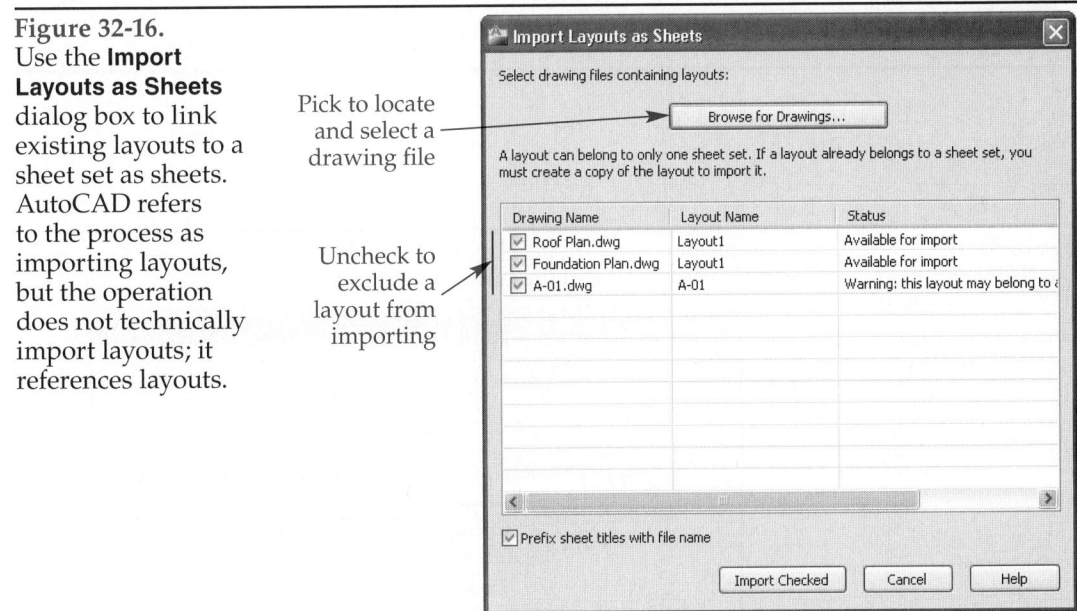

Adding a Sheet Using a Template

Another option for adding a sheet to a sheet set is to create a new drawing using a specific template and layout, and at the same time incorporate the new layout into the sheet set as a sheet. Externally reference existing model space content to the new sheet, or use the drawing as a blank sheet for developing new geometry.

Before adding a sheet from a template, consider assigning a specific drawing template to use for new sheet creation in the **Sheet creation template** setting in the **Sheet Set Properties** and **Subset Properties** dialog boxes. Then set the **Prompt for template** property to **No** to force AutoCAD to use only the specified template, or choose **Yes** to have the option to select a different template when you create a new sheet.

Right-click on the sheet set or subset that will contain the new sheet, and select **New Sheet….** If you do not assign a drawing template to use for new sheet creation, or if you selected the **Prompt for template** option, AutoCAD displays the **Select Layout as Sheet Template** dialog box. The **New Sheet** dialog box appears if a specified template layout exists, or after you select the template layout. See **Figure 32-17.**

Type the sheet number in the **Number** text box and the sheet name in the **Sheet title** text box. A new sheet creates a new drawing file, and the sheet title becomes the name of the layout in the drawing file. Enter the file name in the **File name** text box. The file name is the sheet number and title by default. Edit the drawing file name, if necessary. For example, you might remove the sheet number from the name. The **Folder path** display box shows where the drawing file will be saved, as specified in the **Sheet Set Properties** or **Subset Properties** dialog box. Check the **Open in drawing editor** to open the file and display the layout.

Exercise 32-4

Access the Student Web site (www.g-wlearning.com/CAD) and complete Exercise 32-4.

Figure 32-17.
Use the **New Sheet** dialog box to create a new sheet, and a corresponding drawing file and layout, from a drawing template.

Type the sheet number

Type a name for the sheet and the corresponding layout

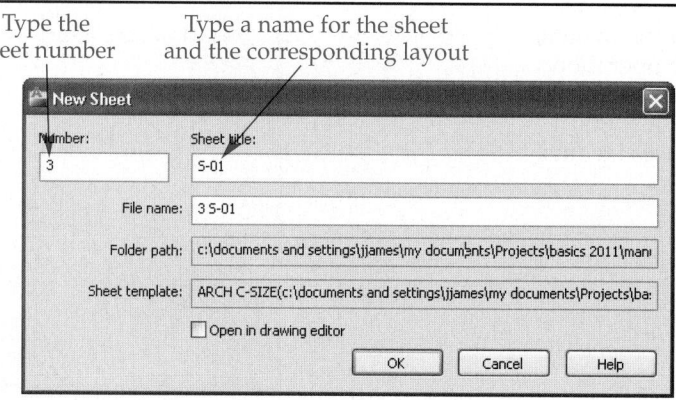

Managing Sheets

Drag and drop sheets as needed to restructure the sheet set and move sheets from the sheet set to subsets or between subsets. Right-click on a sheet in the **Sheet Set Manager** and pick **Rename & Renumber...** to access the **Rename & Renumber Sheet** dialog box. Use the **Number:** text box to renumber the sheet and the **Sheet title:** text box to rename the sheet. Check **Rename layout to match: Sheet title** to name the layout to match the modified sheet name. The **Layout name:** text box is available if you deselect the **Rename layout to match: Sheet title** check box, and allows you to change the layout name independently of the sheet name. The **Prefix with sheet number** check box is also available.

Options for renaming the file are available only if the drawing file is closed. Check **Rename drawing file to match: Sheet title** to name the file to match the modified sheet name. The **File name:** text box is available if you deselect the **Rename drawing file to match: Sheet title** check box, and allows you to change the file name independently of the sheet name. The **Prefix with sheet number** check box is also available. If the sheet is one of several in a subset, pick the **Next** and **Previous** buttons to access different sheets in the subset.

Right-click on a sheet and pick **Properties...** to display the **Sheet Properties** dialog box. See **Figure 32-18.** The **Sheet Properties** dialog box offers another way to change the sheet name and number, and provides additional properties. Use the text boxes to type the appropriate information. It is important that you specify all relevant information to completely define the project, so that text and blocks containing attributes with fields display the correct content. The **Include for publish** option determines whether the sheet is published or plotted with the sheet set. The default value is **Yes**.

The **Expected layout** and **Found layout** text boxes display the path to the file where you initially saved the sheet and the path to the file where AutoCAD found the sheet. If the paths are different, pick the ellipsis (**...**) button to update the **Expected layout** setting using the **Import layout as sheet** dialog box. The **Sheet Properties** dialog box includes the same **Rename options** area found in the **Rename & Renumber Sheet** dialog box.

Right-click on a sheet and select **Remove Sheet** to remove the sheet from the sheet set. Removing a sheet does not delete the drawing file.

Figure 32-18.
The **Sheet Properties** dialog box allows you to modify sheet properties. Add all relevant sheet details that will appear in title blocks and similar content.

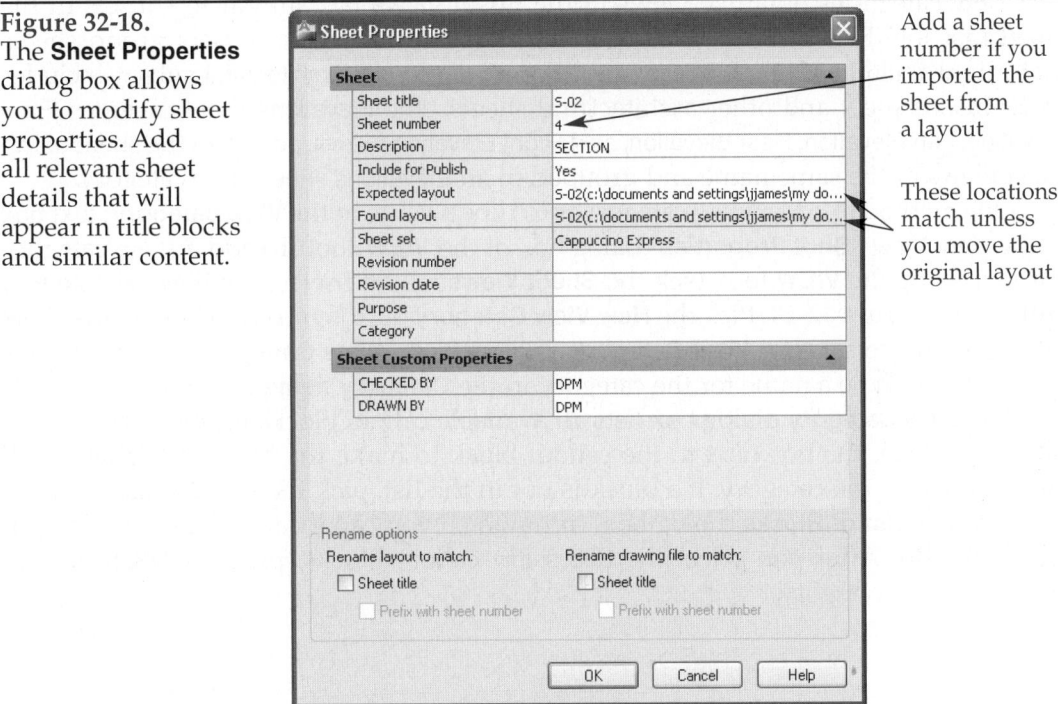

Add a sheet number if you imported the sheet from a layout

These locations match unless you move the original layout

NOTE

When you change the location of a drawing file that has layouts associated with a sheet set, the association with the sheet set is broken. Update the specified path to the drawing file in the **Sheet Properties** dialog box or re-import the layouts into the sheet set.

Exercise 32-5

Access the Student Web site (www.g-wlearning.com/CAD) and complete Exercise 32-5.

Sheet Views

sheet view:
A layout or model view saved for use in a sheet set; allows you to add views to layouts and insert callout and view label blocks.

Use the **Sheet Views** tab of the **Sheet Set Manager** to group views by category, open views for viewing and editing, and add callout and view label blocks. *Sheet views* provide a way to access specific views and to link drawing views to sheets in the sheet set. You must create sheet views to add callout and view label blocks from the **Sheet Set Manager**. Callout and view label blocks use attributes containing fields that link data between the sheet set and drawing views. The fields update automatically to reflect changes in sheet numbering and organization. See **Figure 32-19**.

One option to create a sheet view is to use the **VIEW** tool in paper space to prepare a named view of a layout. This technique essentially forms a copy of a sheet as a sheet view that you can reference to add callout and view label blocks. The second option to create a sheet view is to add a *model view* to a layout. You will learn about model views later in this chapter.

model view:
A drawing file or named model space view added to a layout to create a sheet view.

View Categories

View categories organize views in the **Sheet Views** tab, similar to subsets in the **Sheet List** tab. However, view categories group views, while subsets group sheets that might include several sheet views. For example, an Architectural subset includes an Elevations sheet and other architectural sheets. The Elevations sheet includes Front Elevation, Left Elevation, Rear Elevation, and Right Elevation views, added to the sheet using sheet views of the same name and grouped in an Elevations sheet view category.

One method to add a view category is to type a value in the **View category:** text box in the **New View / Shot Properties** dialog box of the **VIEW** tool. To add a view category without using the **VIEW** tool, pick the **Sheet Views** tab and select the **View by category** button. See **Figure 32-20**. Pick the **New View Category** button or right-click on the sheet set name and select **New View Category...** to open the **View Category** dialog box. See **Figure 32-21**. Type a name for the category in the **Category name** text box.

The **View Category** dialog box lists all available callout blocks for the current view category. Check the box next to the callout block to make the block available for all views added to the category. If a block is not in the list, pick the **Add Blocks...** button to access the **List of Blocks** dialog box, from which you can locate a drawing file with blocks to add. After you select the necessary callout blocks, pick the **OK** button to create the new category.

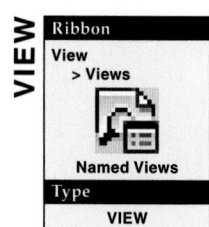

VIEW	
Ribbon	
View	
> Views	
	Named Views
Type	
VIEW	
V	

AutoCAD and Its Applications—Basics

Figure 32-19. Sheet views allow you to access specific views and add callout and view label blocks that link drawing views to sheets throughout the sheet set.

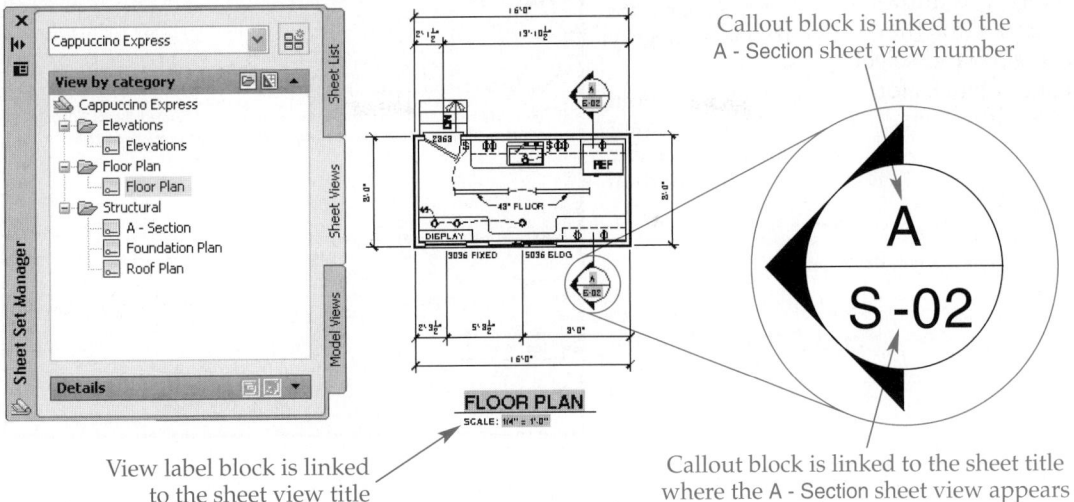

Callout block is linked to the A - Section sheet view number

View label block is linked to the sheet view title

Callout block is linked to the sheet title where the A - Section sheet view appears

Floor Plan Sheet View

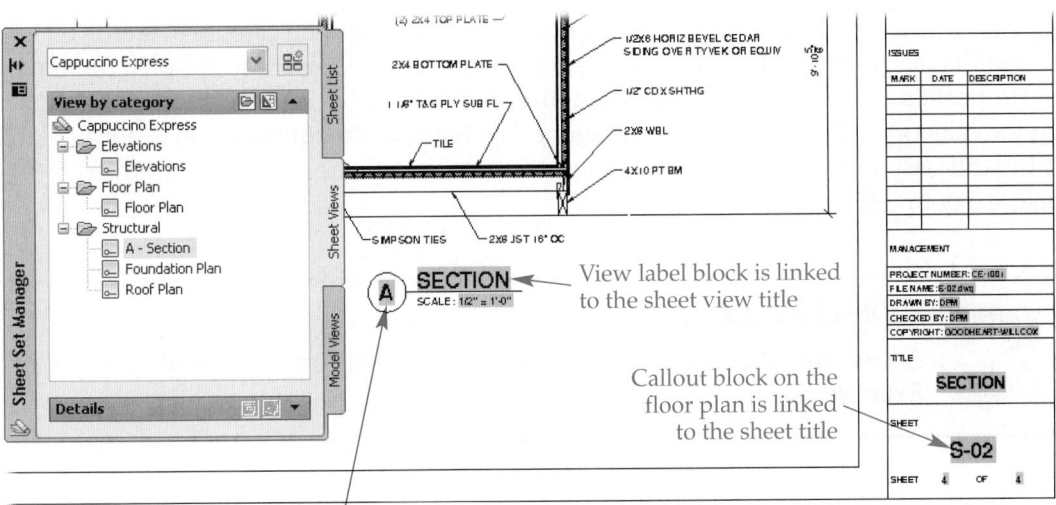

View label block is linked to the sheet view title

Callout block on the floor plan is linked to the sheet title

View label block is linked to the sheet view number, which is linked to the callout block on the floor plan

A - Section Sheet View

Figure 32-20. Create view categories in the **Sheet Views** tab of the **Sheet Set Manager**.

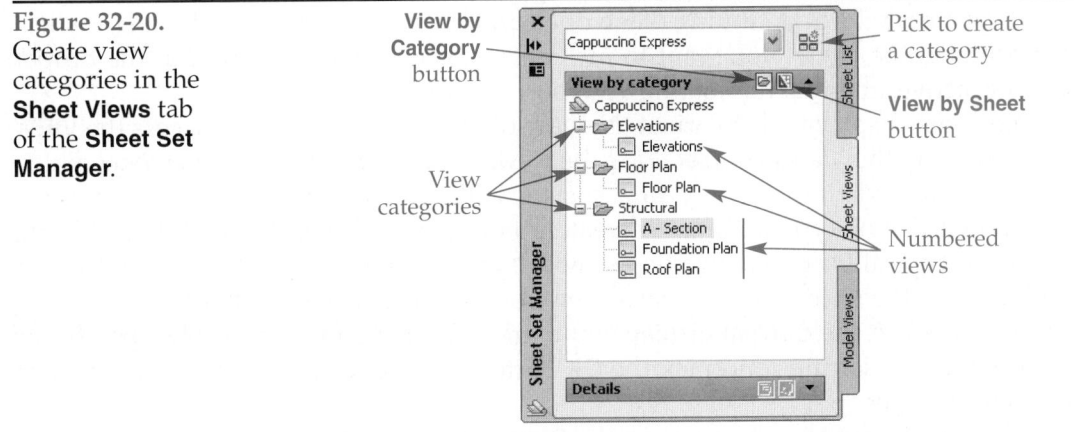

View by Category button

View categories

Pick to create a category

View by Sheet button

Numbered views

Figure 32-21.
The **View Category** dialog box allows you to name the category and select callout blocks for use with views.

Type a name for the view category

Check the callout blocks you want to make available for insertion

Pick to locate additional callout blocks in existing files

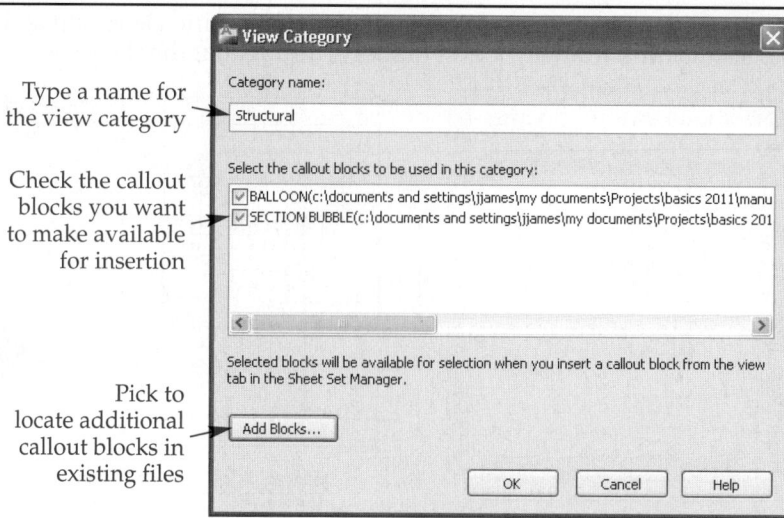

Managing View Categories

View categories are listed alphanumerically. To change the category name and add callout blocks, right-click on a view category in the **Sheet Views** tab and pick **Rename...** or **Properties...** to reopen the **View Category** dialog box. To delete a category, right-click on the category and select **Remove Category**. The **Remove Category** option is not available if the category includes sheet views. You must remove all sheet views from the category before deleting the category.

Exercise 32-6

Access the Student Web site (www.g-wlearning.com/CAD) and complete Exercise 32-6.

Creating Sheet Views from Layouts

Using the **VIEW** tool in paper space creates a layout view that is added to the sheet set as a sheet view. You can then reference the sheet view to place callout and view label blocks. A sheet must be a part of the sheet set to include a sheet view. If the sheet set does not reference the layout you intend to capture as a named view, add the layout to the sheet set before continuing. Then open and activate the sheet set. Open the sheet that contains the layout you want to include as a sheet view. Ensure that the proper layout is active, and that no floating viewport is active.

Next, use display tools to orient the view of the layout as needed. Access the **VIEW** tool to display the **View Manager**. Pick the **New...** button to open the **New View** dialog box. Select an existing category to associate with the view from the **View category** drop-down list, or type a name to create a new category. See **Figure 32-22.** Layout views are typically not as specific as model views. The main purpose is to assign the layout to the sheet set as a sheet view for callout and view label block requirements. Therefore, the **Current display** boundary option is often acceptable. Specify the remaining view settings and pick the **OK** button as needed to save the view and exit the **View Manager.**

The new layout view appears in the **Sheet Set Manager** in the specified view. To display the view from the **Sheet Set Manager,** double-click on the view or right-click

Figure 32-22.
Use the **VIEW** tool and the associated **View Manager** and **New View / Shot Properties** dialog boxes to create a sheet view.

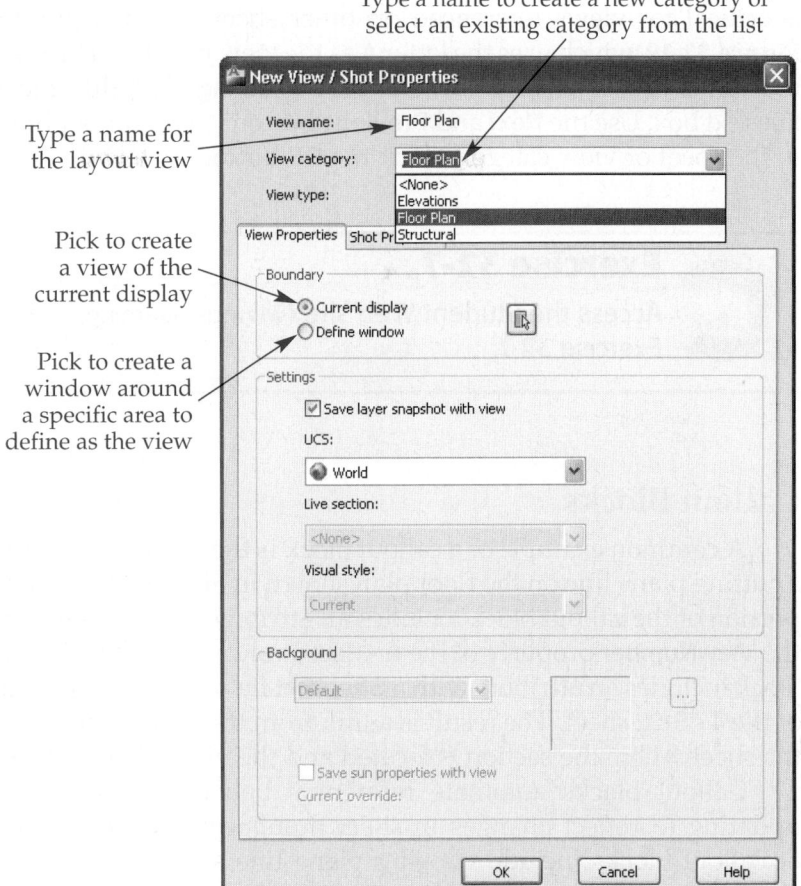

Type a name for the layout view

Type a name to create a new category or select an existing category from the list

Pick to create a view of the current display

Pick to create a window around a specific area to define as the view

on the view and select **Display**. If the drawing file is open, the view is set current. If the drawing file is not open, the file opens and displays the view.

Managing Sheet Views

Display sheet views by category or sheet using the appropriate button shown in **Figure 32-20.** Sheet views are listed alphanumerically in both formats. Pick the **View by category** button to display sheet views within view categories. Pick the **View by sheet** button to display sheet views in the sheets where they are located. The **View by sheet** display also provides an option to change the category assigned to a sheet view. Right-click on a sheet view and select a different category from the **Set category** cascading submenu.

To change the name or number of a sheet view, right-click on the sheet view in the **Sheet Views** tab and select **Rename & Renumber...** to display the **Rename & Renumber View** dialog box. See **Figure 32-23.** Enter a number or letter for the view in the **Number** text box. A view number is typically not required for views that are not linked to other

Figure 32-23.
Use the **Rename & Renumber View** dialog box to renumber or rename a sheet view.

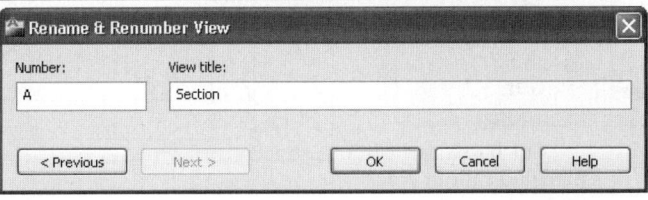

sheets, such as the Floor Plan view shown in **Figure 32-19.** However, the view number is critical for views referenced on other sheets, such as the Section view shown in **Figure 32-19,** which uses the letter A as the view number. The view number is displayed in front of the view name in the **Sheet Set Manager.** Modify the view name in the **View title** text box. Use the **Next** and **Previous** buttons to renumber or rename different views in the sheet or view category. Pick the **OK** button when you are finished.

Exercise 32-7

Access the Student Web site (www.g-wlearning.com/CAD) and complete Exercise 32-7.

Callout Blocks

A common example of a callout block is the section view information at the end of a cutting plane line on the floor plan shown in **Figure 32-24.** In this example, the upper portion of the callout block includes an attribute with a **SheetView** field that references the **ViewNumber** property of the A - Section sheet view. The lower portion of the callout block includes an attribute with a **SheetSet** field that references the **SheetTitle** property of the 4 - S-02 sheet. The result is a link from the cutting-plane line on the floor plan to the sheet where the section is located and the view identification.

Callout blocks automate references between drawing content and views by updating to reflect changes in sheet numbering and organization. Other examples of callout blocks include viewing plane line symbols, such as exterior and interior elevation bubbles, and detail identification. You can also use callout blocks as balloons on an assembly drawing to associate components with a parts list, as found in a set of drawings. A callout block typically appears on a different sheet from the sheet view it references. Callout blocks can also include hyperlink fields, or *hyperlinks,* that provide convenient access to the reference sheet view.

hyperlinks: Links in a document that connect it to related information in other documents or on the Internet.

Figure 32-24. Using a callout block assigned to a sheet view to link a cutting plane on a floor plan to a section view on a separate sheet.

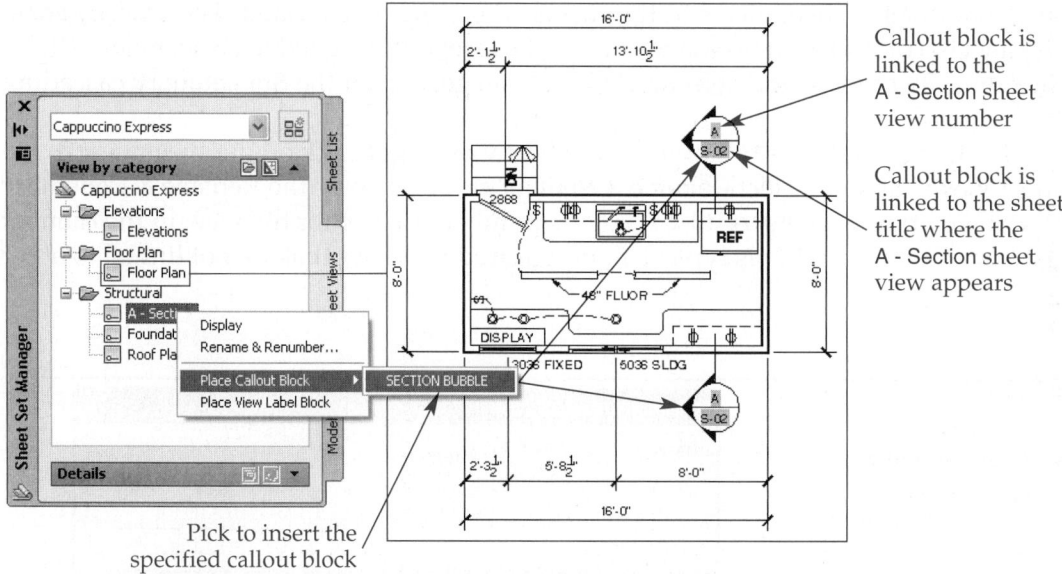

Callout block is linked to the A - Section sheet view number

Callout block is linked to the sheet title where the A - Section sheet view appears

Pick to insert the specified callout block

Use dynamic blocks with suitable parameters, such as rotational, flip, and visibility parameters, to reduce the number of blocks needed for a sheet set.

Before you can insert a callout block from the **Sheet Set Manager**, the block must be available to the sheet set and assigned to the view category. A sheet set or view category can reference multiple callout blocks. Callout blocks are often added to a sheet set during sheet set creation. To assign callout blocks to an existing sheet set, right-click on the sheet set in the **Sheet Set Manager** and pick **Properties...** to display the **Sheet Properties** dialog box. Specify the available blocks in the **Callout blocks** text box. Pick the ellipsis (...) button to access the **List of Blocks** dialog box. See **Figure 32-25**. Pick the **Add...** button to access the **Select Block** dialog box, and then pick the ellipsis button to navigate to and select the drawing or template file that contains callout blocks.

If the file consists of only the objects that make up the block, choose the **Select the drawing file as a block** radio button to use the file as a callout block. If the file includes blocks saved as blocks, pick the **Choose blocks in the drawing file:** radio button and select the blocks to use as callout blocks. Use the **Delete** button to remove a block from the **List of Blocks** dialog box.

After you add callout blocks to a sheet set, you must assign the appropriate callout blocks to each view category. To specify the callout blocks available for a view category, right-click on the category and select **Properties...** to open the **View Category** dialog box. See **Figure 32-21**. Use the check boxes to select the callout blocks to assign to the view category. Only check those callouts that apply to the specific category. Pick the **Add Blocks...** button to add new blocks to the view category using the **Select Block** dialog box.

Figure 32-25. All of the callout blocks available to a sheet set appear in the **List of Blocks** dialog box.

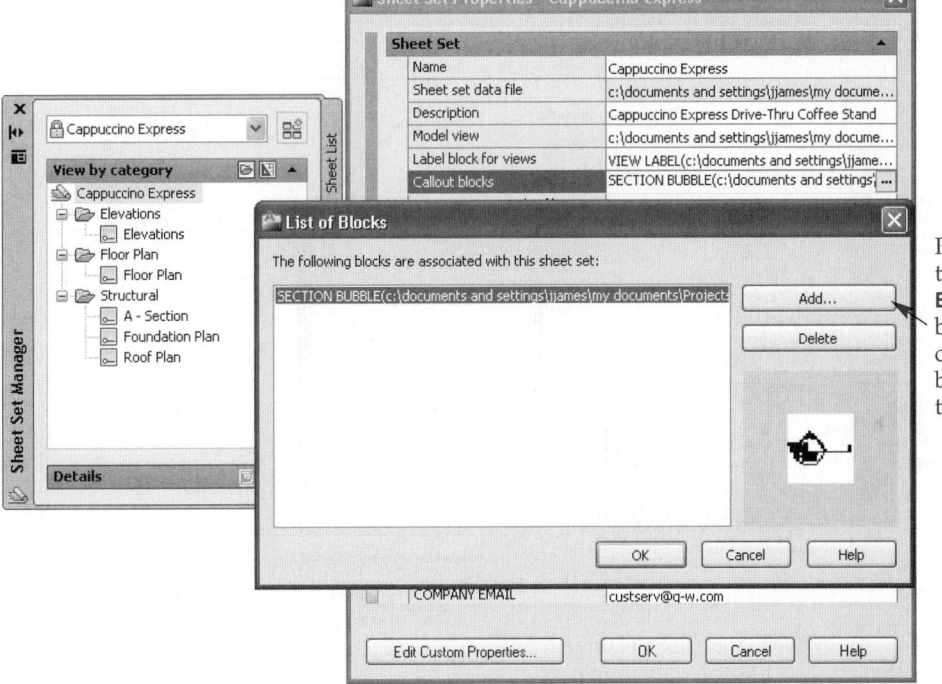

To insert a callout block, open the sheet on which the reference is to appear and activate model space to add the symbol to model space. For example, open the floor plan shown in **Figure 32-24** to add the cutting-plane line callouts referencing the section view. Then pick the **Sheet Views** tab of the **Sheet Set Manager**, right-click on the sheet view to reference, and select the block from the **Place Callout Block** cascading submenu. For example, right-click on the A - Section sheet view to create the cutting-plane line reference shown in **Figure 32-24**. Specify an insertion point for the block and follow the prompts to modify the block as needed.

Exercise 32-8

Access the Student Web site (www.g-wlearning.com/CAD) and complete Exercise 32-8.

View Label Blocks

View label blocks automate reference between drawing views and view identification by updating to reflect changes in view number, title, and scale. A common example of a view label block is the view title and scale information displayed under the section view shown in **Figure 32-26**. In this example, the bubble portion of the view label block includes an attribute with a **SheetView** field that references the **ViewNumber** property of the A - Section sheet view. The title includes an attribute with a **SheetView** field that references the **ViewTitle** property of the A - Section sheet view. The scale includes an attribute with a **SheetView** field that references the **ViewportScale** property of the A - Section sheet view.

NOTE

View label blocks can also include hyperlinks, but hyperlinks are usually not useful in view label blocks because a view label block typically appears on the same sheet as the sheet view it references.

Figure 32-26. Using a view label block assigned to a sheet view to title a section view on the sheet where the sheet view is located.

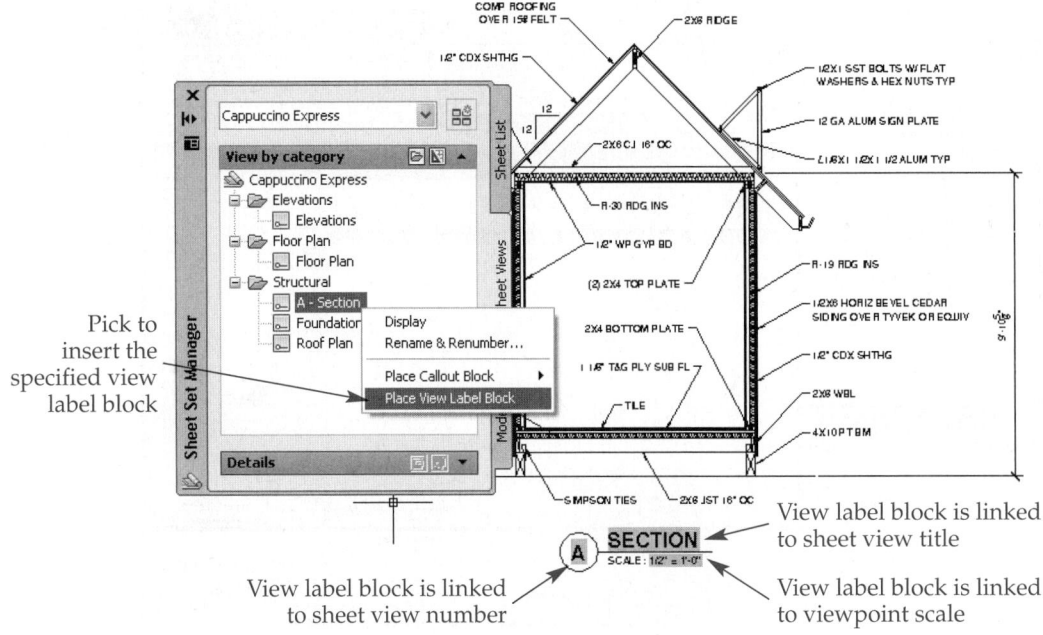

Before you can insert a view label block from the **Sheet Set Manager**, the block must be available to the sheet set. A sheet set can only reference a single view label block, and you cannot assign different view label blocks to each view category. View label blocks are often added to a sheet set during sheet set creation. To assign a view label block to an existing sheet set, right-click on the sheet set in the **Sheet Set Manager** and pick **Properties...** to display the **Sheet Properties** dialog box.

Specify the view label block in the **Label block for views** text box. Pick the ellipsis (**...**) button to access the **Select Block** dialog box, and then pick the ellipses button to navigate to and select the drawing or template file that contains the view label block. If the file consists of only the objects that make up the block, choose the **Select the drawing file as a block** radio button to use the file as a view label block. If the file includes blocks saved as blocks, pick the **Choose blocks in the drawing file:** radio button and select the block to use as the view label block.

To insert a view label block, open the sheet containing the view to be labeled. For example, open the section view layout shown in **Figure 32-26** to add the view label referencing the section view. Items such as labels are often created in paper space, but you can insert a view label into model space if necessary. Pick the **Sheet Views** tab of the **Sheet Set Manager**, right-click on the sheet view to reference, and select **Place View Label Block**. For example, right-click on the A - Section sheet view to create the view label shown in **Figure 32-26**. Specify an insertion point for the block and follow the prompts to modify the block as needed.

If the view label block includes a **SheetView** field that references the **ViewportScale** property, AutoCAD only recognizes the viewport scale of sheet views created from model views. You will learn about model views later in this chapter. If you add a sheet view from a layout view, the scale appears as a series of pound (#) symbols to indicate an inability to reference the required information. To work around this problem, link the SCALE attribute value directly to the floating viewport object using the **EATTEDIT** tool. See **Figure 25-27**.

Figure 32-27. Using a field to display the correct viewport scale when referencing a layout view to place a view label.

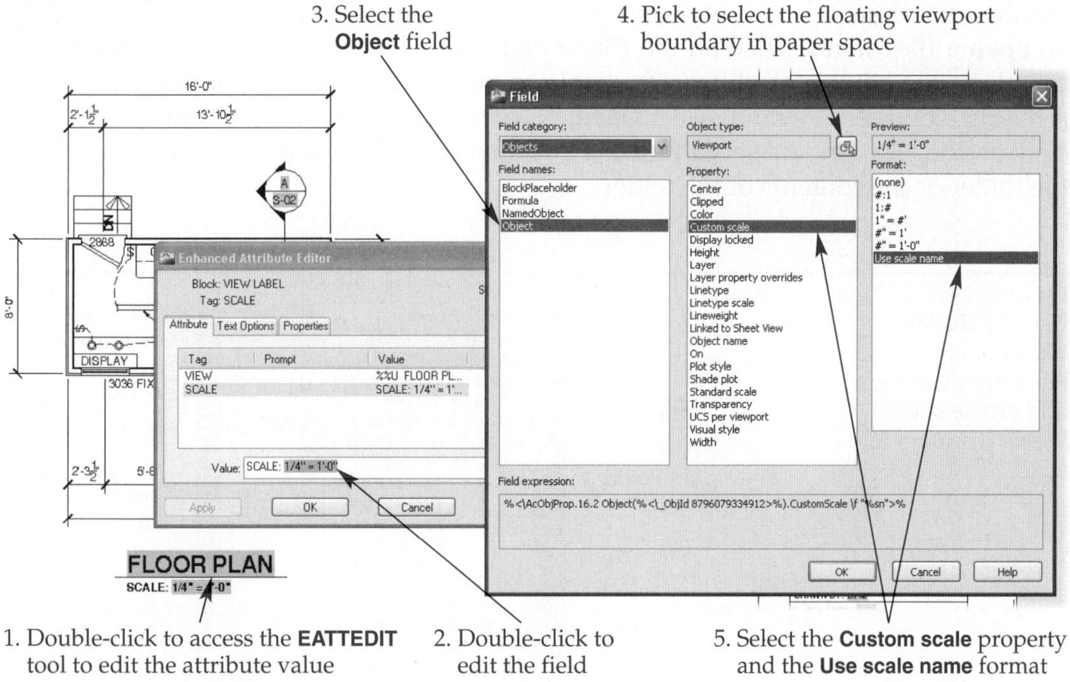

3. Select the **Object** field

4. Pick to select the floating viewport boundary in paper space

1. Double-click to access the **EATTEDIT** tool to edit the attribute value

2. Double-click to edit the field

5. Select the **Custom scale** property and the **Use scale name** format

A quick way to access the **EATTEDIT** tool is to double-click on a block containing attributes. Edit the field in the SCALE attribute to use an **Object** field. Pick the **Select object** button and pick the appropriate floating viewport boundary in paper space. When the **Field** dialog box returns, select the **Custom scale** property and **Use scale name** format. Pick the **OK** button to display the correct scale.

Exercise 32-9

Access the Student Web site (www.g-wlearning.com/CAD) and complete Exercise 32-9.

Model Views

resource drawings: Drawing files that include named model space views referenced for use as sheet views.

The **Model Views** tab of the **Sheet Set Manager** allows you to access *resource drawings*. See **Figure 32-28**. Add folders to the **Model Views** tab to list drawing files, drawing template files, and named model views found in the files. One purpose of resource drawings is to access files associated with the project, but not included as sheets. This function is similar to locating files in a different folder using Windows Explorer. The other purpose of resource drawings is to create sheet views from model space content or named model views. You can use this function in addition or as an alternative to creating sheet views from layout views.

Folders are often added to the **Model Views** tab during sheet set creation. To add a folder to an existing sheet set, double-click on the Add New Location entry, pick the **Add New Location** button, or right-click on the Add New Location entry or a folder and select **Add New Location....** Then use the **Browse for Folder** dialog box to locate and select the folder containing the desired files. The folder and all of drawing and drawing template files found in the folder appear in the **Locations** list box. Named model space views are listed under the drawing files that contain them.

Right-click on a folder and pick **Collapse** to collapse the nodes of the folder. Right-click on a drawing and select **See Model Space Views** to expand the list of model space views in the drawing. This is the same as picking the + sign next to the drawing file. To open a file, double-click on the file or right-click on the file and select **Open**. You can also open a file as read-only. To display a model view, double-click on the view or right-click on the view and select **Open**. To remove a location from a sheet set, right-click on the location and select **Remove Location**. Removing a location does not delete the folder or the contents of the folder.

Figure 32-28.
Use the **Model Views** tab to access resource drawings and create sheet views from model space.

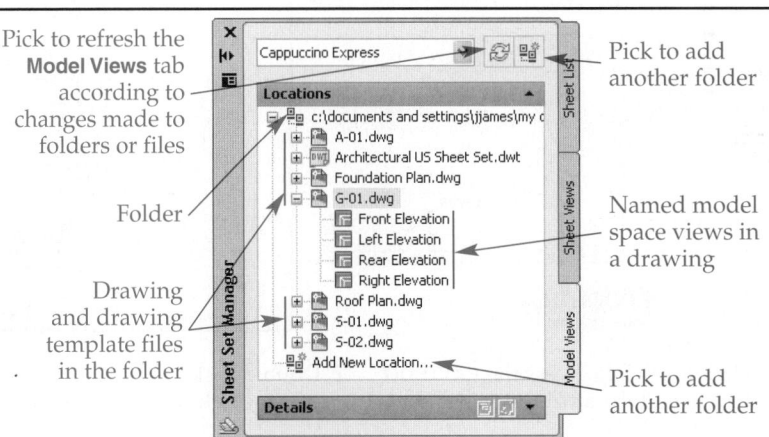

Pick to refresh the **Model Views** tab according to changes made to folders or files

Folder

Drawing and drawing template files in the folder

Pick to add another folder

Named model space views in a drawing

Pick to add another folder

Creating Sheet Views from Model Views

Create a sheet view from an entire model space drawing or from a named model space view listed in the **Model Views** tab. When you create a sheet view from a drawing or model view, AutoCAD combines and automates the traditional process of adding an xref to a new drawing, creating a floating viewport, scaling the viewport, and adding a view label block.

To create a sheet view from the entire drawing in model space, ensure that the resource folder includes the drawing file. To create a sheet view from a named model view, open the file containing the model space content to reference. Then use the **VIEW** tool in model space to create a named model view. Type the name of an existing view category, or type a name to create a new category.

To create a sheet view from model space content, activate the sheet in the sheet set that will receive the sheet view, and erase any existing floating viewports. Create a new sheet if necessary, and assign the sheet to the sheet set. Set an appropriate viewport layer current. Drag and drop the drawing or view from the **Model Views** folder or right-click on the drawing or view and select **Place on Sheet**. An alert appears if the sheet set does not include the current layout.

The model view attaches to the cursor. Right-click before specifying the insertion point and select the appropriate viewport scale. The scale is stored as the **ViewportScale** property of the **SheetView** field. See Figure 32-29A. Then specify a location to place the view. The result is a floating viewport on the layout with the view label assigned to the sheet set at the lower-right corner of the viewport. The model space content you see is attached as an xref in model space and shows through the viewport. A new sheet view appears in the **Sheet Views** tab corresponding to the inserted model view. See Figure 32-29B.

Exercise 32-10

Access the Student Web site (www.g-wlearning.com/CAD) and complete Exercise 32-10.

Figure 32-29 Referencing a drawing as a model view to create a sheet view. The same basic process applies to forming sheet views from named model views. A—Drag and drop the drawing and select the viewport scale. B—Specify the location for the view.

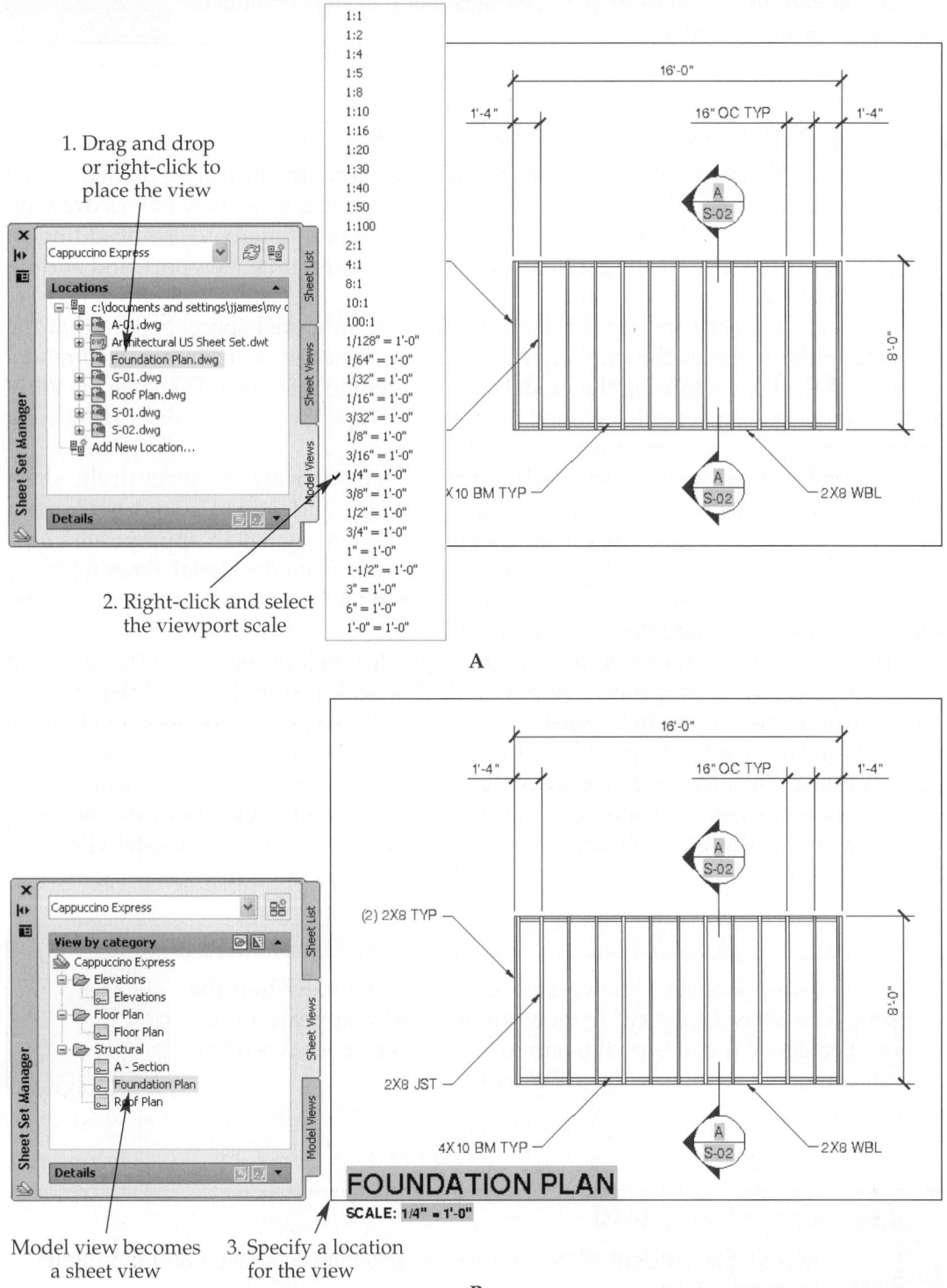

A

B

Sheet List Tables

A sheet list table automates the processes of collecting information about the sheet set and organizing the data in a table. A common example of a sheet list table is the sheet index typically found on the cover of a set of drawings for a construction project. See **Figure 32-30.** You can also use a sheet list table to prepare a parts list, bill of materials, or similar table. A sheet list table acquires properties from each sheet in the sheet set. Therefore, you typically add a sheet list table as the last step in developing a sheet set. However, the table data is linked to the sheet set and updates as you make changes to sheet properties.

Inserting a Sheet List Table

To insert a sheet list table, access the **Sheet Set Manager** and open the sheet on which you want to place the table. Right-click on the sheet set, a subset, or a sheet in the **Sheet Set Manager** and select **Insert Sheet List Table...** to open the **Sheet List Table** dialog box. See **Figure 32-31.** For most applications, right-click on the sheet set to access the **Sheet List Table** dialog box to create a sheet list table that is initially set to include all subsets and sheets. Right-clicking on a subset or sheet to access the **Sheet List Table** dialog box initially limits the sheets in the table, although you can add and remove sheets from the table as needed.

Select a table style to apply to the sheet list table from the **Table Style name** drop-down list, or pick the ellipsis (**...**) button to access the **Table Style** dialog box. The preview area displays a representation of the table. Select the **Show Subheader** check

---

Figure 32-30. A sheet list table used to create a sheet index on the cover of a set of architectural drawings. This figure shows the **Sheet Set Manager** for reference. Notice the information linked between the sheet set and the sheet list table.

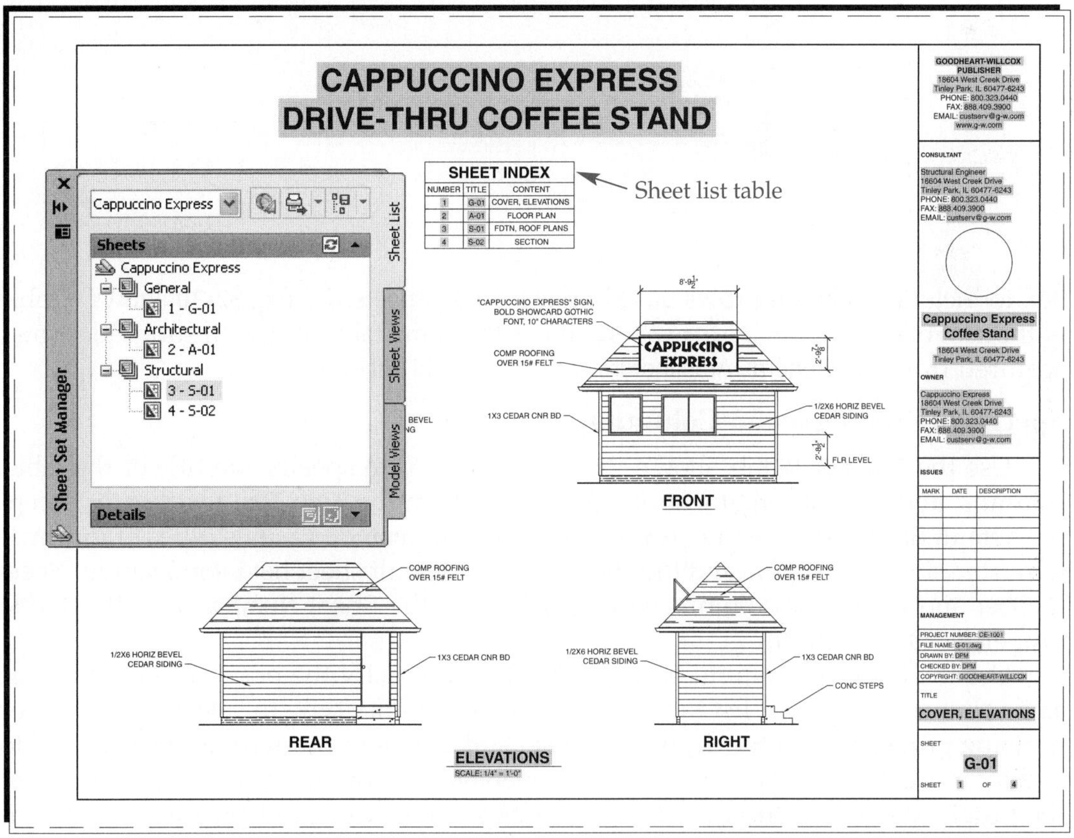

Figure 32-31. Use the **Sheet List Table** dialog box to set up the display characteristics and sheet properties assigned to a sheet list table.

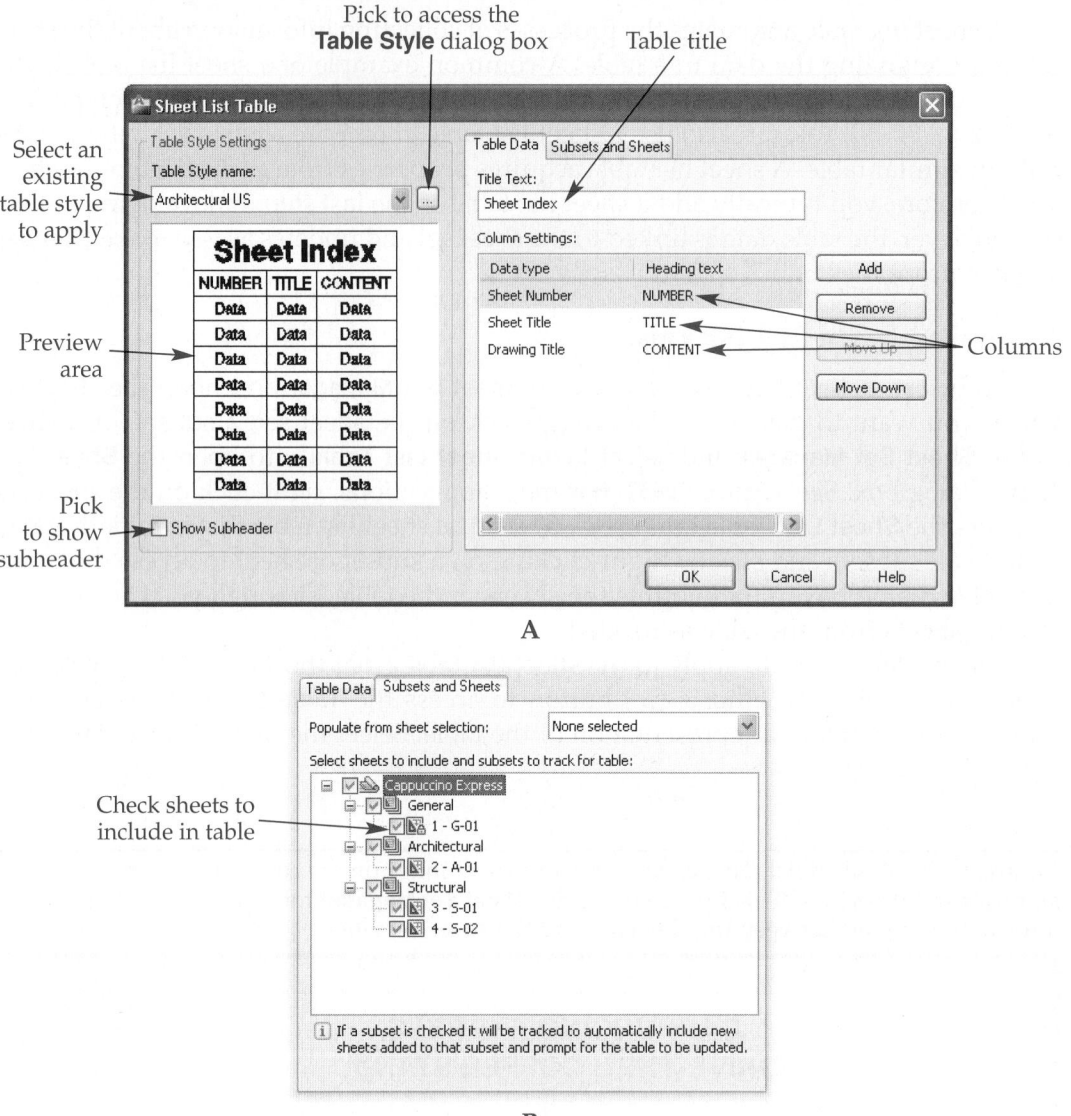

A

B

box to include subheader rows based on selected subsets. **Figure 32-30** shows a table without subheader rows. **Figure 32-32** shows the same table, but with subheader rows acquired from the General, Architectural, and Structural subsets.

Specifying the Title and Columns

Use the **Table Data** tab, shown in **Figure 32-31A,** to specify the title of the table, columns, and column organization. Type the title in the **Title Text** text box or accept the default Sheet List Table title. A sheet list table can include various types of information from the drawing file and the sheet set. The default sheet list table includes Sheet Number and Sheet Title columns corresponding to the **Sheet Number** and **Sheet Title** properties of each sheet.

Use the **Data type** column of the dialog box to specify the properties to reference as a column in the sheet list table. Pick the existing data type to select a sheet set or drawing property from the drop-down list. Add a custom property to the sheet set to add a different data type to the list. The **Heading text** column in the dialog box uses the property name as the default heading. Select the name and type a new value if

Figure 32-32. A sheet list table with subheaders added by referencing subsets.

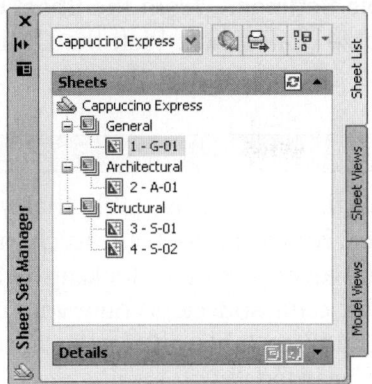

SHEET INDEX		
NUMBER	TITLE	CONTENT
General		
1	G-01	COVER, ELEVATIONS
Architectural		
2	A-01	FLOOR PLAN
Structural		
3	S-01	FDTN, ROOF PLANS
4	S-02	SECTION

appropriate. The table shown in previous figures has headings that are different from the property names, which is common.

Use the **Add**, **Remove**, **Move Up**, and **Move Down** buttons as necessary to add, remove, and organize columns. A new column is initially displayed under the last column in the list. The column at the top of the list appears on the far right side of the table as the first column in the table.

Specifying Rows

The **Subsets and Sheets** tab, shown in **Figure 32-31B,** allows you to specify table rows by selecting check boxes to include sheets in the table. Each row is a sheet reference. When you right-click on a sheet set to access the **Sheet List Table** dialog box, all subsets and sheets in the sheet set are initially selected for addition to the table. Use the appropriate check boxes to add and remove sheets from the table.

Checked sheets are the only items that appear in the table. You do not need to check subsets to display subheaders. However, you must check sheet sets and subsets to include sheet sets and subsets during updates. If you make changes to the sheet set, a prompt appears to update only the subsets you check in the **Subsets and Sheets** tab. The **Populate from sheet selection** drop-down list provides access to *sheet selections*. Choose a sheet selection to check only the sheets associated with the saved selection. You will learn more about sheet selections later in this chapter. Pick the **OK** button and specify an insertion point to insert the table.

sheet selections: Groups of subsets and/or sheets that are often used to publish the same group of sheets.

> **NOTE**
>
>
> You can only insert a sheet list table into a layout of a drawing file that is a part of the sheet set. The **Insert Sheet List Table...** option is not available if the drawing file is not part of the sheet set or if model space is current.

Editing a Sheet List Table

The information in a sheet list table is linked directly to the data source, or property, field. Update a sheet list table to display changes made to the sheet set. For example, update a sheet list table after changing the sheet numbers in the **Sheet Set Manager** or after adding a sheet to the sheet set. Use the **DATALINKUPDATE** tool to update a sheet list table. A quick way to access the tool is to select the table to update, right-click, and select **Update Table Data Links**. You can also select inside a table header or data cell and then right-click and pick **Update Sheet List Table** from the **Sheet List Table** cascading submenu.

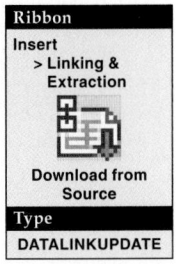

Ribbon

Insert
> Linking &
Extraction

Download from
Source

Type

DATALINKUPDATE

To modify the properties for the table, select inside a table header or data cell and then right-click. Choose **Edit Sheet List Table Settings...** from the **Sheet List Table** cascading submenu to reopen the **Sheet List Table** dialog box. Pick the **OK** button to update the sheet list table.

NOTE

Use the same techniques to modify a sheet list table that you use to modify any other table object. For example, you can change text or add columns and rows. However, avoid unlocking cells and overriding values linked to the data source. When you use the **DATALINKUPDATE** tool on the modified table, an alert indicates that manual modifications will be discarded.

Sheet List Table Hyperlinks

The **Sheet Number** and **Sheet Title** properties contain hyperlinks that you can use to access sheets. To open a sheet using a hyperlink, hover the crosshairs over a sheet number or sheet title until the hyperlink icon and tooltip appear. Hold down the [Ctrl] key and pick the hyperlink to open the selected sheet.

Exercise 32-11

Access the Student Web site (www.g-wlearning.com/CAD) and complete Exercise 32-11.

Sheet Set Fields

Throughout this chapter, you have experienced how text and blocks with attributes containing fields link text information to elements of the sheet set. Text and multiline text objects, title blocks, callout blocks, view label blocks, and sheet list tables use sheet set fields to automate documentation and the process of changing values during the course of the project. The following sections provide additional information on applying and using sheet set fields.

AutoCAD provides specific field types for use with sheet sets. In the **Field** dialog box, pick **SheetSet** from the **Field category:** drop-down list to filter fields specific to sheet sets in the **Field names:** list box. See **Figure 32-33.** Use fields in the **SheetSet** category to display values defined in the sheet set, subset, sheet, or sheet view. Some fields have several property and format options.

PROFESSIONAL TIP

When you prepare attributes with fields, avoid using the **Multiple lines** option, because multiple-line attributes with fields often display an inappropriate format. Use several single-line attributes and custom properties as needed. In addition, choose the **Preset** option in the **Attribute Definition** dialog box or **Properties** palette to have the attribute assume preset sheet set property values during block insertion.

Figure 32-33. An example of a link between a current sheet set field and the corresponding sheet set property.

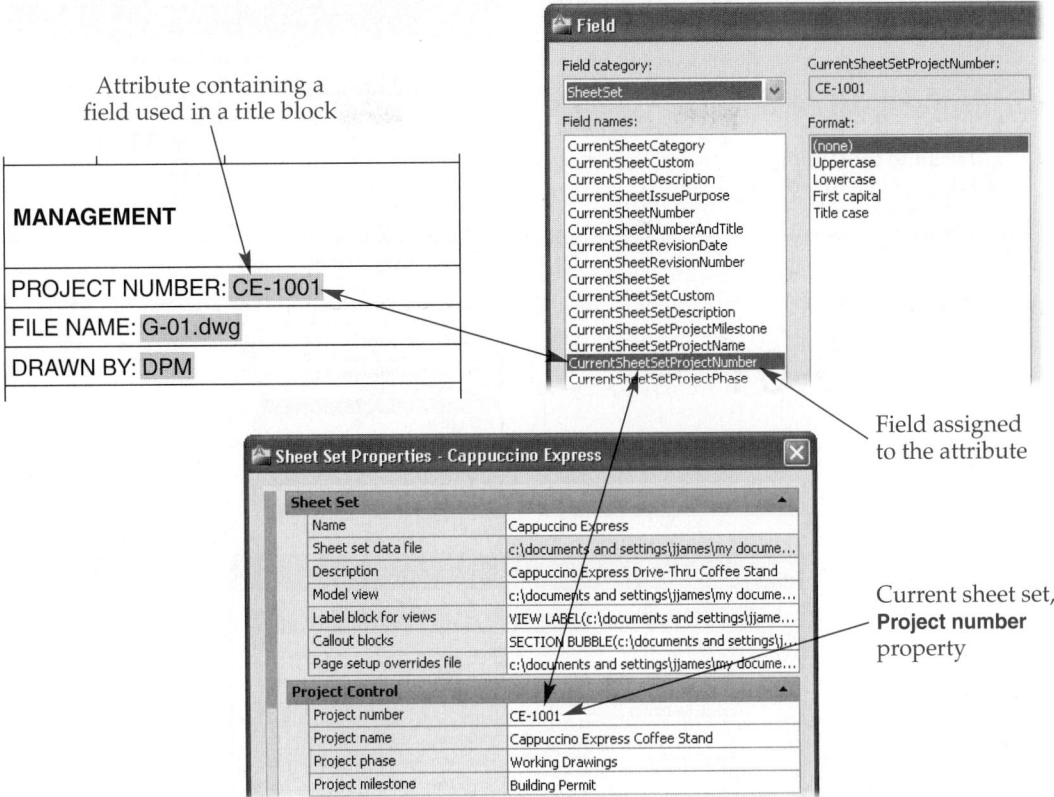

Attribute containing a field used in a title block

Field assigned to the attribute

Current sheet set, **Project number** property

Current Sheet Set Fields

Current sheet set fields, such as the **CurrentSheetSetProjectNumber** field shown in **Figure 32-33**, are linked to properties assigned in the **Sheet Set Properties** dialog box. The field value is specific to the current sheet set, which is where the field is located. For example, if you insert a title block onto a new sheet in a sheet set named Big House, the **SheetSetProjectName** field will display Big House. If you insert the same title block onto a new sheet in a sheet set named Little House, the **SheetSetProjectName** field displays Little House.

Current Sheet Fields

Current sheet fields, such as the **CurrentSheetTitle** field shown in **Figure 32-34**, is linked to properties assigned in the **Subset Properties** or **Sheet Set Properties** dialog boxes. The field value is specific to the current sheet, which is where the field is located. For example, a title block with an attribute containing the **CurrentSheetNumber** field displays 1 on sheet 1 and 2 on sheet 2 in a sheet set.

Sheet Set Fields

The various **CurrentSheetSet** and **CurrentSheet** fields are appropriate for most applications, but they link values only to the current project. Pick the **SheetSet** field to display options for linking values to any existing sheet set. See **Figure 32-35**. Use the **Sheet set:** drop-down list to display the contents of an open sheet set in the **Sheet navigation tree**, or pick the ellipsis (**...**) button to open another sheet set. Select the sheet set, a subset, or a sheet to specify the field value.

Figure 32-34. An example of a link between a current sheet field and the corresponding sheet property.

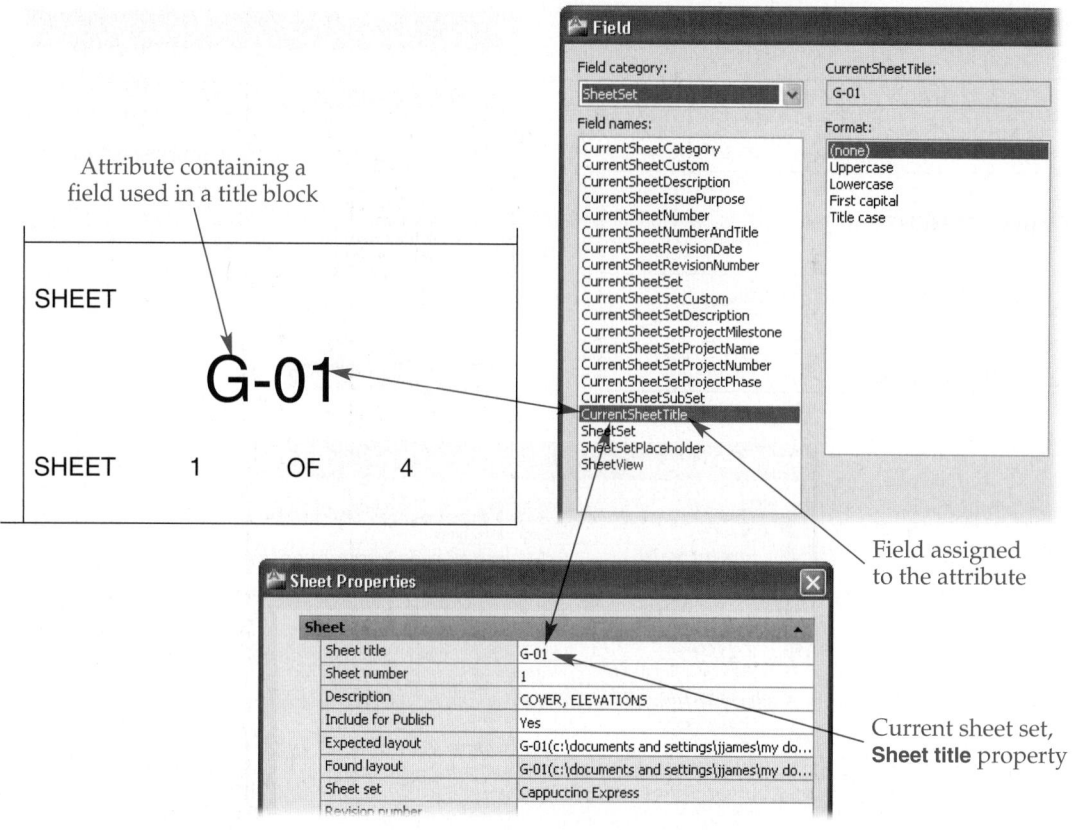

Attribute containing a field used in a title block

Field assigned to the attribute

Current sheet set, **Sheet title** property

Figure 32-35. The **SheetSet** field allows you to associate a value to a specific sheet set, typically related to a different project from the current sheet set.

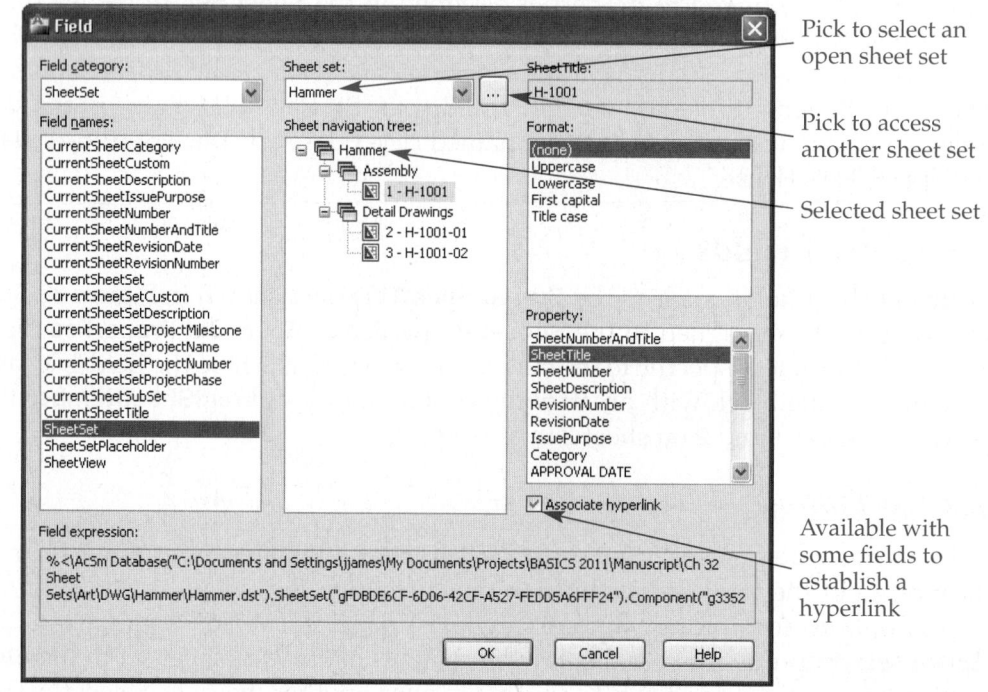

Pick to select an open sheet set

Pick to access another sheet set

Selected sheet set

Available with some fields to establish a hyperlink

The **Property** list box, which appears when you pick the sheet set or a sheet, allows you to select a property to associate with the sheet set or sheet. Use the **Format** list box to override the format used in the **Sheet Set Properties**, **Subset Properties**, or **Sheet Properties** dialog box, depending on the selection. For example, if you type Assembly in the **Subset Properties** dialog box, pick the **Uppercase** format to force AutoCAD to display ASSEMBLY. Pick the **Associate hyperlink** check box to include a hyperlink to the property with the field.

NOTE

Custom sheet set and sheet fields are available from the **Property** list box.

Sheet Set Placeholder Fields

The **SheetSetPlaceholder** field inserts a *sheet set placeholder* that allows you to prepare text or a block without knowing the specific location of the property that the field will reference. Callout and view label blocks use **SheetSetPlaceholder** fields. See **Figure 32-36**. When you add a callout or view label block to a drawing in a sheet set, AutoCAD locates the information corresponding to the placeholders. The placeholders automatically become **CurrentSheet**, **CurrentSheetSet**, or **SheetView** fields, depending on the type of placeholder, and display the correct values.

sheet set placeholder: A temporary value for a field that later references specific properties for values.

Sheet View Fields

SheetView fields typically form when you use callout and view label blocks with attributes containing sheet set placeholder fields. Select the **SheetView** field to display options for linking values to any existing sheet view, or to place values without using callout or view label blocks. The process for assigning a **SheetView** field is similar to that for assigning a **SheetSet** field, except that you select a sheet, view category, or sheet view from the **Sheet navigation tree**.

Figure 32-36. A view label block in the **Block Editor**. Callout and view label blocks use **SheetSetPlaceholder** fields to assign a field with the necessary characteristics.

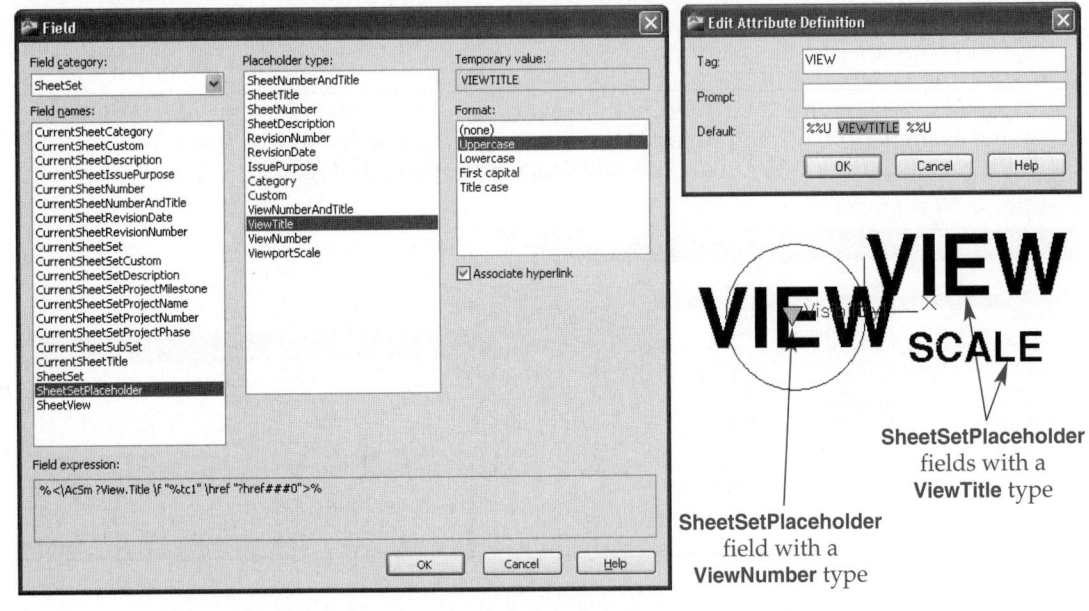

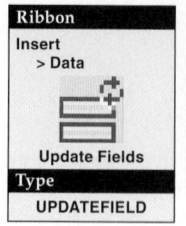

PROFESSIONAL TIP

If a field does not display the expected value, update the field manually using the **UPDATEFIELD** tool, or use the **REGEN** tool to apply an automatic update. In some cases, you may need to delete and then reinsert a block to display the correct field values.

Custom Properties

Custom properties are necessary to include additional information about a sheet set and sheets. For example, many of the properties referenced by fields in a title block are custom properties. To add or modify custom properties, access the **Sheet Set Properties** dialog box and pick the **Edit Custom Properties** button to display the **Custom Properties** dialog box. See **Figure 32-37.**

Use the **Add** button to add custom properties using the **Add Custom Property** dialog box. See **Figure 32-37B.** Specify the name, default value, and owner of the property. The **Sheet Set** owner creates a custom sheet set property that applies to all sheets in the set. The **Sheet** owner creates a custom sheet property that might vary from sheet to sheet. Use the **Delete** button to delete custom properties. Custom sheet set and sheet properties appear in the **Sheet Set Properties** dialog box. Custom sheet properties also appear in the **Sheet Properties** dialog box.

Custom Property Fields

Choose the **CurrentSheetCustom** field to reference a custom sheet set property associated with the current sheet set. Use the **CurrentSheetSetCustom** field to reference a custom sheet property associated with the current sheet. When you are developing a block or template, and no sheet set is current, type the name of intended custom property in the **Custom property name** text box of the **Field** dialog box. AutoCAD correlates the name you enter with the property of the same name when you use the block or template in the current sheet set. Custom properties appear in the **Custom property name** drop-down list of the **Field** dialog box when a sheet set is current.

NOTE

If you create a sheet set from an example sheet set, any custom properties in the example sheet set are added to the new sheet set.

Figure 32-37. A—Use the **Custom Properties** dialog box to add and delete custom properties. Study the examples of custom properties and default values added to this sheet set. B—Define a custom property using the **Add Custom Property** dialog box.

Existing custom properties

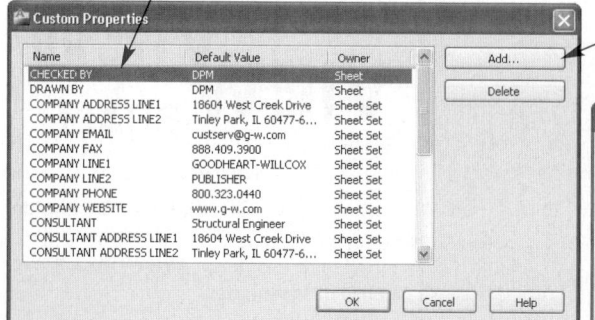

Pick to create a custom sheet set or sheet property

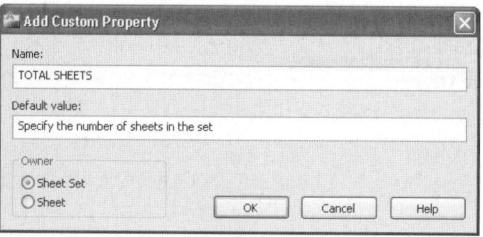

A   B

AutoCAD does not calculate the total number of sheets in a sheet set. To display the total number of sheets, such as in a title block, create a custom **TOTAL SHEETS** property owned by the sheet set. At the end of the project, view the number assigned to last sheet and type the value in the **TOTAL SHEETS** property in the **Sheet Set Properties** dialog box.

Exercise 32-12

Access the Student Web site (www.g-wlearning.com/CAD) and complete Exercise 32-12.

Publishing a Sheet Set

A sheet set provides options to publish the sheet set, subsets, or individual sheets in the sheet set. Publishing a sheet set is a convenient way to create a hard copy or electronic version of a set of drawings, without plotting each layout separately. As when plotting a single layout, you have the option to publish hard copies to a printer or plotter or to create a portable document format (PDF) file or design web format (DWF or DWFx) file.

AutoCAD also provides tools for exporting drawings and publishing without referencing a sheet set using the **PUBLISH** tool. *AutoCAD and Its Applications—Advanced* provides additional information on exporting and publishing drawings.

Publish Options

Pick the sheet set to publish, or press [Shift] or [Ctrl] to select specific items to publish, such as individual subsets or sheets. Access publish options from the **Publish** flyout, shown in **Figure 32-38**, or right-click on the sheet set, subsets, or sheets and select the **Publish** to display a cascading submenu. Pick the appropriate **Publish to DWF, Publish to DWFx**, or **Publish to PDF** option to create a DWF, DWFx, or PDF file from the selected items. A dialog box appears, allowing you to specify a name and location for the file. The resulting file contains multiple pages with each sheet on a separate page. Use the **Publish to Plotter** option to plot the selected items to the default printer or plotter using the plot settings from each layout.

The **Publish using Page Setup Override** option is available if you assigned a named page setup from a file to the **Page setup overrides file** property of the **Sheet Set Properties** dialog box. Pick the option to publish all sheets using the settings specified in the saved page setup. Use the **Include for Publish** option to identify whether the selected items will be published. Pick the **Edit Subset and Sheet Publish Settings...** option to display the **Publish Sheets** dialog box. Check specific sheets to include for publishing.

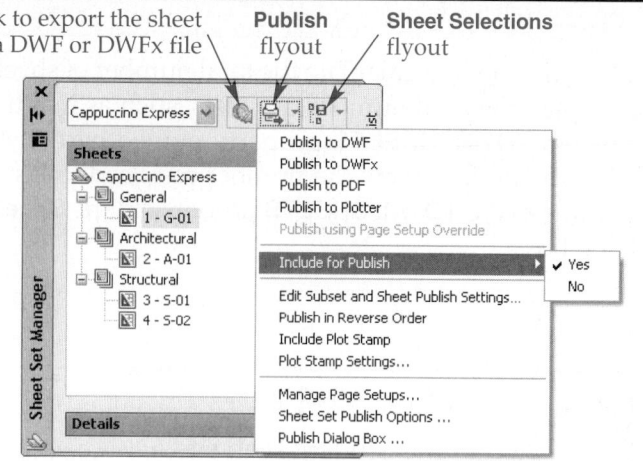

Figure 32-38.
The **Publish** flyout provides options for preparing a selected sheet set, or subsets or sheets within the sheet set, for publishing.

Pick to export the sheet set as a DWF or DWFx file

Publish flyout

Sheet Selections flyout

The **Publish in Reverse Order** option publishes sheets in the opposite order from the order displayed in the **Sheet Set Manager**. With certain printers, publishing a sheet set in reverse order is helpful so that the last sheet is on the bottom of the stack, at the end of the set. Select the **Include Plot Stamp** option to plot the plot stamp assigned to the layout or page setup override with the selected sheets. Select the **Plot Stamp Settings...** option to open the **Plot Stamp** dialog box to specify the plot stamp settings. The **Manage Page Setups...** option opens the **Page Setup Manager**, allowing you to create or modify a page setup. The **Sheet Set Publish Options...** selection displays the **Sheet Set Publish Options** dialog box, which includes settings for creating a DWF, DWFx, or PDF file. The **Publish Dialog Box...** option opens the **Publish** dialog box, which lists the sheets in the current sheet set or the sheet selection.

Sheet Selections

Sheet selections provide a way to group specific subsets or sheets for publishing or for populating rows in a sheet list table. The most common application for a sheet selection is to create a selection set of specific subsets or sheets to publish. For example, create a sheet selection named Plans and Elevations from the Plans and Elevations subsets to publish only the plan and elevation sheets in the sheet set.

To save a sheet selection, pick the subsets or sheets to be included in the selection set. Then pick the **Sheet Selections** flyout on the **Sheet Set Manager** and select **Create...** to access the **New Sheet Selection** dialog box. Enter a name for the selection set and pick the **OK** button. The new selection set appears when you pick the **Sheet Selections** button. Pick a sheet selection from the **Sheet Selections** flyout to highlight the associated sheets in the **Sheet Set Manager**. To rename or delete a sheet selection, pick **Manage...** from the **Sheet Selections** flyout to display the **Sheet Selections** dialog box. Select the sheet selection and pick the **Rename** or **Delete** button.

Archiving a Sheet Set

Archive sets of drawings as necessary throughout a project. For example, when you present a set of drawings to the client for the first time, the client may want to make design changes. Archive the files at this phase for future reference before making modifications. Archive copies of all drawings and related files to a single location. Related files include external references, font files, plot style table files, template files, and other documents associated with the project.

Access the **ARCHIVE** tool to archive a sheet set using the **Archive a Sheet Set** dialog box. See **Figure 32-39.** A quick way to activate the **ARCHIVE** tool is to right-click on the sheet set in the **Sheet Set Manager** and select **Archive...**. The **Sheets** tab, shown in **Figure 32-39A,** displays all subsets and sheets in the sheet set. Check the sheets you want to archive. The **Files Tree** tab shown in **Figure 32-39B** and the alternative **Files Table** tab shown in **Figure 32-39C** list drawing files and related files. Pick the **Add a File...** button in the **Files Tree** or **Files Table** tab to access the **Add File to Archive** dialog box. Use the dialog box to include files that are not part of the sheet set in the archive. You can include any type of file with the archive—the archive is not limited to AutoCAD files.

Use the **Enter notes to include with this archive** text box to type descriptive information about the archive, such as the design phase or items added to the archive. Pick the **View Report** button to list all files included in the archive in the **View Archive Report** dialog box. The **View Archive Report** dialog box includes a **Save As...** button that allows you to save the report to a text file.

Select the **Modify Archive Setup...** button in the **Archive a Sheet Set** dialog box to display the **Modify Archive Setup** dialog box for adjusting archive settings. See **Figure 32-40.** Use the **Archive package type** drop-down list to specify the archive format. Choose the **Folder (set of files)** option to copy all archived files into a single folder. Select the **Self-extracting executable (*.exe)** option to compress all files into a self-extracting *zip file.* Choose the **Zip (*.zip)** option to compress all files into a normal zip file. Use a program that works with zip files to extract the files.

Select an earlier version of AutoCAD in the **File Format** drop-down list to convert the archived files to the selected version. The **Archive file folder** drop-down list defines where the archive is saved. Select a location from the list or pick the **Browse...** button to choose a different location.

The **Archive file name** drop-down list provides options for naming the archive. Choose the **Prompt for a filename** option to display the **Specify Zip File** dialog box so that you can specify a name for the archive package. Pick the **Overwrite if necessary** option to overwrite the file name if a file with the same name already exists. Select the **Increment file name if necessary** option to create a new file with an incremental number added to the file name if a file with the same name already exists. This option allows you to save multiple versions of the archive.

zip file: A file that contains one or more folders and/or files compressed using the Windows ZIP file format.

Figure 32-39. A—The **Archive a Sheet Set** dialog box allows you to specify archive settings and files to archive. Use the **Sheets** tab to select sheets in the set to archive. B—Use the **Files Tree** tab to include other documents that relate to a project in the archive. C—The **Files Table** tab provides an alternative display for selecting documents to archive.

Type descriptive information about the archive

Checked items are included in the archive

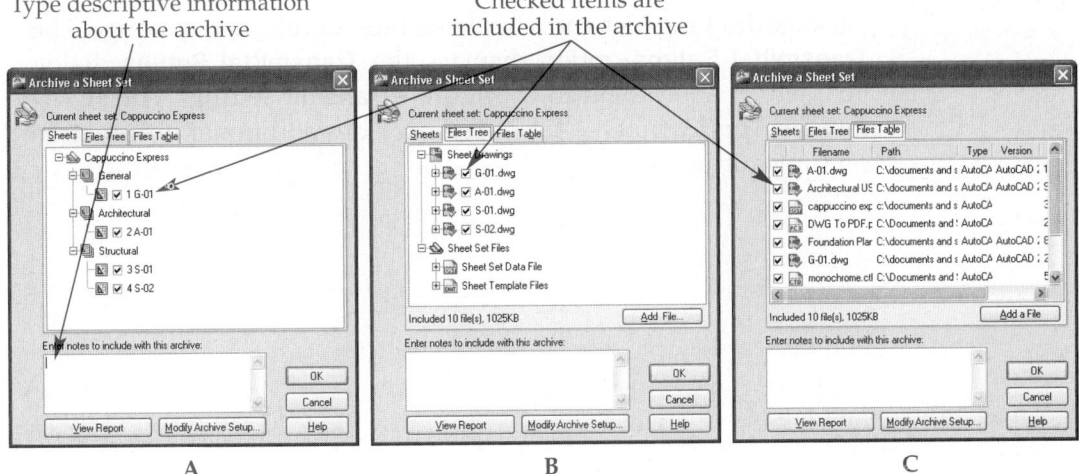

A   B   C

Figure 32-40. Specify archive file settings using the **Modify Archive Setup** dialog box.

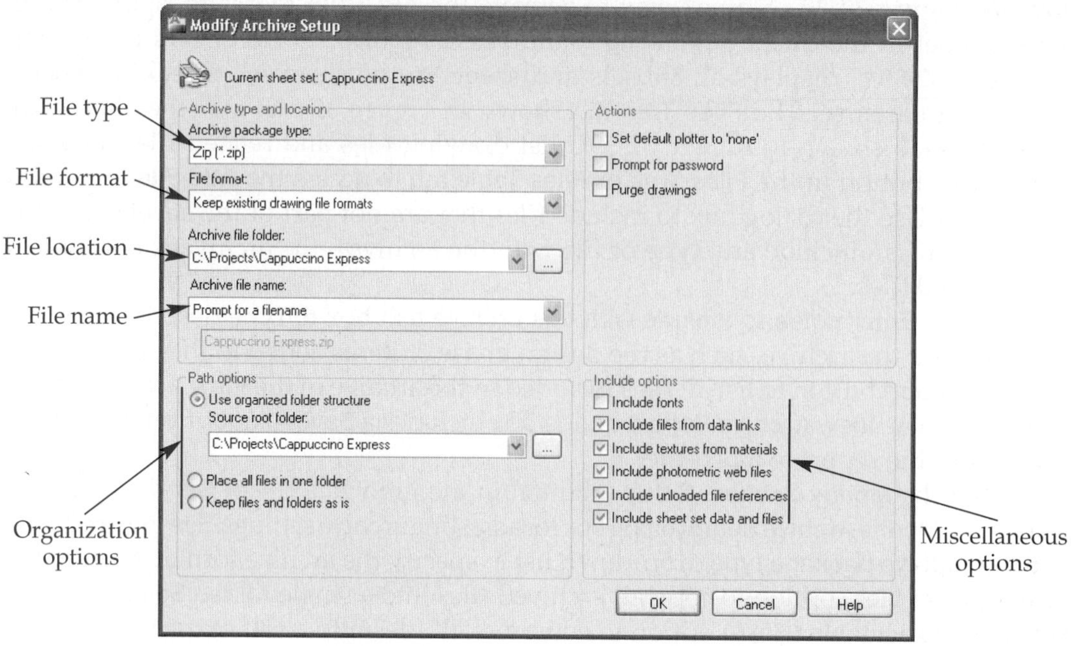

Select the **Use organized folder structure** radio button to allow the archive file to duplicate the folder structure for the files. The **Source root folder** setting determines the root folder for files that use relative paths, such as xrefs. Pick the **Place all files in one folder** radio button to archive all files into a single folder. Select the **Keep files and folders as is** radio button to use the same folder structure for all the files in the sheet set.

The **Set default plotter to 'none'** check box disassociates the plotter name from the drawing files, which is useful if you send files to someone using a different plotter. Select the **Prompt for password** check box to set a password for the archive. If you select this option, the password you choose is required to open the archive package. The **Purge drawings** action purges all drawings in the archive to eliminate unused content and reduce file size. Use the check boxes in the **Include options** area to specify items to include with the archive.

> **NOTE**
>
> Right-click on a sheet set name and select **eTransmit** to display the **Create Transmittal** dialog box for use with the **eTransmit** feature. This option, which is similar to the **Archive** option, allows you to package drawing files and associated files for Internet exchange. The **Transmittal Setups** option displays the **Transmittal Setups** dialog box, which allows you to configure **eTransmit** settings. *AutoCAD and Its Applications—Advanced* provides additional information on transmitting drawings.

Chapter Test

Answer the following questions. Write your answers on a separate sheet of paper or go to the Student Web site (www.g-wlearning.com/CAD) and complete the electronic chapter test.

1. What is a sheet set?
2. What is the purpose of a sheet set data file, and what extension does the file have?
3. What does the term *sheet* refer to in relation to a sheet set and a drawing file?
4. What is a sheet list table?
5. What is the purpose of fields in a sheet set?
6. Explain when you would add existing layouts to a sheet set and when you should add a new layout.
7. Briefly describe the general options for creating a new sheet set.
8. What are subsets in relation to a sheet set?
9. How do you add a custom property to a sheet set?
10. Explain how to create a subset in an existing sheet set.
11. What is the purpose of the **Import Layouts as Sheets** dialog box?
12. How do you modify a sheet name or number?
13. What is a sheet view?
14. Explain why AutoCAD callout blocks and view labels update automatically when you make changes to the related sheet set.
15. Briefly explain how to create a view category from the **Sheet Set Manager** and associate callout blocks to the category.
16. What information do the upper and lower values in a callout block typically provide?
17. Explain how to insert a callout block into a drawing.
18. What are resource drawings?
19. Explain how to add a column heading to a sheet list table.
20. How can you update a sheet list table to reflect changes made in the **Sheet Set Manager**?
21. Briefly explain how to publish a sheet set to a DWF, DWFx ,or PDF file.
22. How do you create a sheet selection set?
23. What is the purpose of archiving a sheet set?
24. What is a zip file?
25. List the three packaging types available for archiving a sheet set.

Drawing Problems

Start AutoCAD if it is not already started. Follow the specific instructions for each problem.

Note: *Some of the problems in this chapter are built on problems from previous chapters. If you have not yet completed those problems, complete them now.*

▼ Basic

1. Create a new sheet set using the **Create Sheet Set** wizard and the New Sheet Set example sheet set. Name the new sheet set My Sheet Set.

2. Create a new sheet set using the **Create Sheet Set** wizard and the Civil Imperial Sheet Set example sheet set. Name the new sheet set Civil Sheet Set.

▼ Intermediate

3. Complete the Hammer sheet set you started in Exercise 32-1. Save a copy of the drawing files H-1001.dwg, H-1001-01.dwg, and H-1001-02.dwg from the Student Web site to the Hammer folder you created during Exercise 32-1. Open the Hammer sheet set created in Exercise 32-1. Continue creating the sheet set as follows:

A. Access the **Sheet Set Properties** dialog box and adjust the properties as shown in A, but use APPROVED BY, CHECKED BY, DRAWN BY, and COMPANY values appropriate to your drawings.

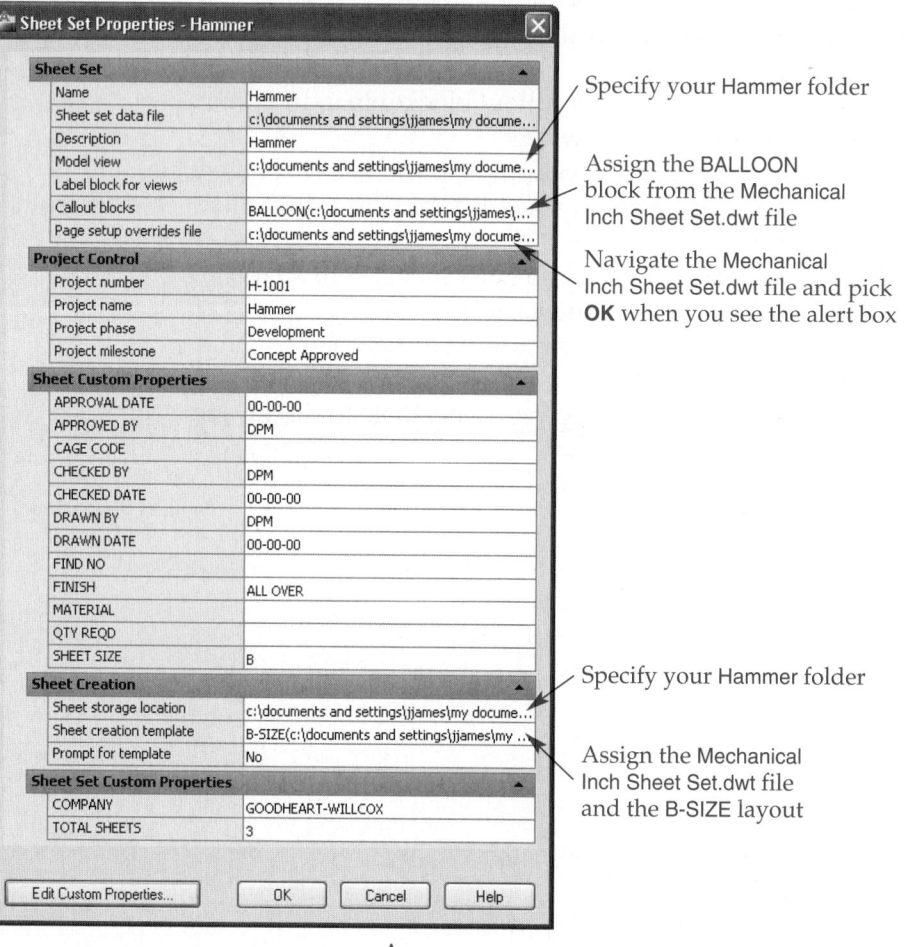

A

B. Import the H-1001 layout into the Assembly subset and the H-1001-01 and H-1001-02 layouts into the Detail Drawings subset. Access the **Sheet Properties** dialog box for each sheet and adjust the properties as shown in B.

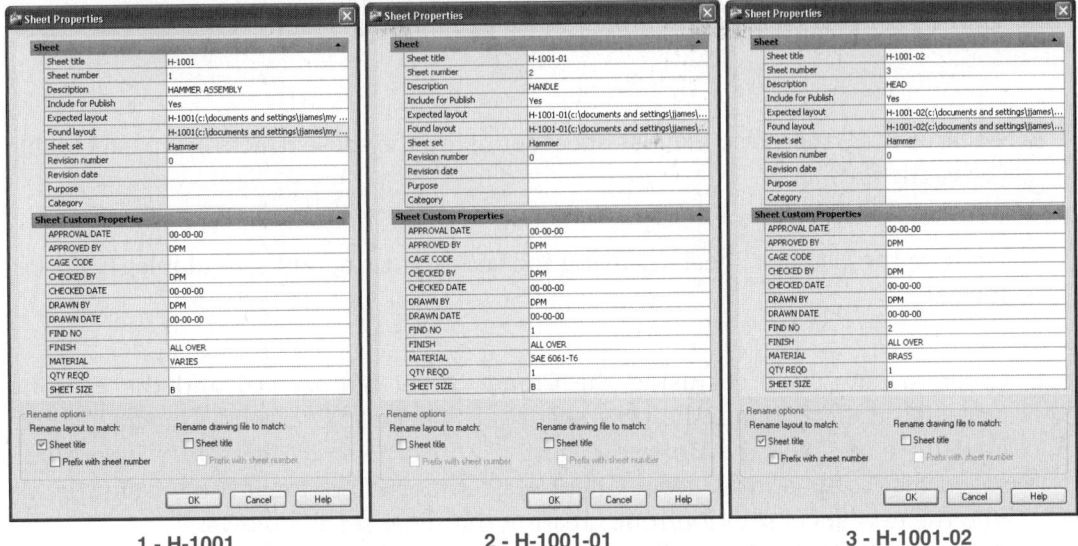

1 - H-1001   2 - H-1001-01   3 - H-1001-02

B

C. Create a sheet view of the 2 - H-1001-01 layout. Number the view 1 and name it HANDLE. Create a sheet view of the 3 - H-1001-02 layout. Number the view 2 and name it HEAD. Assign the BALLOON callout block to both views.

D. Complete the H-1001 layout as shown in C. Use multileaders and callout blocks from the 1 - HANDLE and 2 - HEAD sheet views in model space to create the identification balloons. Create the parts list using a sheet list table.

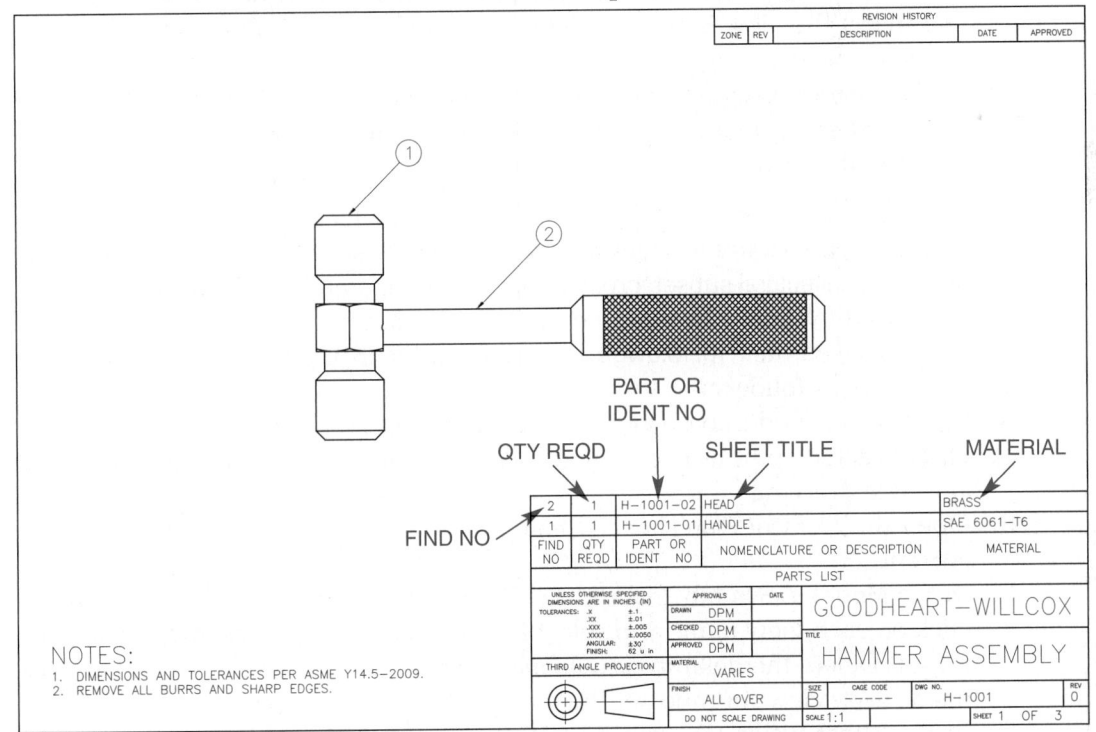

C

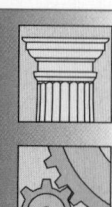

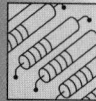

4. Publish the Cappuccino Express sheet set to a plotter or PDF file.

5. Publish the Hammer sheet set to a plotter or PDF file.

6. Archive the Cappuccino Express sheet set using the self-extracting zip executable (EXE) file format.

7. Archive the Hammer sheet set using the self-extracting zip executable (EXE) file format.

8. Create a new sheet set using the **Create Sheet Set** wizard and the **Existing drawings** option. Name the new sheet set Schematic Drawings. On the **Choose Layouts** page, pick the **Browse...** button and browse to the folder where you saved the P29-14.dwg file from Chapter 29. Import all of the layouts from the file into the new sheet set. Continue creating the sheet set as follows:
   A. In the **Sheet Set Properties** dialog box, assign the layout named ISO A1 Layout from the Tutorial-mMfg.dwt template file in the AutoCAD 2011 Template folder as the sheet creation template.
   B. Open a new drawing file using a template of your choice and create a block for a view label. Save the drawing file and then assign the block to the sheet set using the **Label block for views** setting in the **Sheet Set Properties** dialog box.
   C. Create a new view category and name it Schematics.
   D. Open the 3 Wire Control layout, create a new view, and add it to the Schematics view category. Double-click on the new view name in the **Sheet Views** tab and insert the view label block you previously created. Renumber the view and save the drawing.
   E. Add a custom property to the sheet set named Checked by and set the owner type to **Sheet**. Add another custom property named Client and set the owner type to **Sheet Set**.

9. Create a new sheet set using the **Create Sheet Set** wizard and the Architectural Imperial Sheet Set example sheet set. Name the new sheet set Floor Plan Drawings. Under the Architectural subset, create a new sheet named Floor Plan. Number the sheet A1. In the **Model Views** tab, add a new location by browsing to the folder where you saved the P18-16.dwg file from Chapter 18. Open the P18-16.dwg file and continue as follows:
   A. Create three model space views named Kitchen, Living Room, and Dining Room. Orient each display as needed to describe the area of the floor plan. Save and close the drawing.
   B. Open the A1-Floor Plan sheet. Create a new layer named Viewport and set it current.
   C. In the **Model Views** tab, expand the listing under the P18-16.dwg file. Right-click on each view name and select **Place on Sheet**. Insert each view into the layout. Delete the default view labels inserted with the views. Double-click inside each viewport and set the viewport scale as desired.
   D. In the **Sheet Views** tab, renumber the views. Insert a new view label block under each view.
   E. Save and close the drawing.

10. Use a word processor to write a report of approximately 250 words explaining the purpose of sheet sets. Cite at least three examples from actual industry applications of using sheet sets to help manage a set of drawings. Use at least two sketches to illustrate your report.

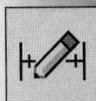

▼ Advanced

11. Design and draw an arbor press. Prepare layouts for the assembly and each component. Then create a new sheet set to organize the drawings and layouts. Publish and archive the final sheet set.

12. Plan a new shopping center for your area. Determine how many stores to include. If possible, obtain a copy of a survey for vacant land in your area suitable for building the shopping center. Determine the components of a complete set of plans for the shopping center, including a site plan, floor plans, foundation plans, roof plans, elevations, and any needed sections. Establish the components for a new sheet set to organize the drawings and layouts.

13. Plan a new residence with approximately 3500–4000 square feet, four bedrooms, three baths, a den/office, kitchen, dining room, nook, family room, and three-car garage. Create a complete set of plans for the residence, including a site plan, floor plans, foundation plans, roof plans, elevations, and any needed sections. Prepare layouts for each drawing. Then create a new sheet set to organize the drawings and layouts. Archive the final sheet set.

AutoCAD Certified Associate Exam Practice

Answer the following questions. Write your answers on a separate sheet of paper.

1. Which of the following actions can you perform using the **Sheet Set Manager**? *Select all that apply.*
   A. add sheets to a sheet set
   B. change the name of a sheet set data file
   C. organize files related to a project
   D. open drawing files that contain layouts referenced in a sheet set
   E. purge unused blocks from a sheet set

2. Which of the following methods can you use to create a sheet view? *Select all that apply.*
   A. add a model view
   B. double-click an existing sheet
   C. right-click on an existing sheet
   D. use the **VIEW** tool

3. To which of the following file types can you publish a sheet set? *Select all that apply.*
   A. DST
   B. DWF
   C. EXE
   D. PDF
   E. ZIP

Index

AutoCAD and Its Applications—Basics

Index–Basics

spline grip tools, 446–448
Spline Options, 130
SPLINE tool, 129–130, 437
    options, 130
SPLINETYPE system variable, 437
spotface, 544
stacked objects, 102
    cycling through, 102
standards, 24
static columns, 286–287
status bars, 38–39
status toggle buttons, 38
STATUS tool, 467–468
SteeringWheels, 183–186
sticky panel, 36
stretch action, 782
    assigning, 782–783
    using dynamically, 783
stretching objects, 363–364
STRETCH tool, 363–364, 405–407, 409–410, 433,
       435, 439–440, 446, 609, 620, 624–625, 782,
       788, 870, 875
    Displacement option, 363–364
STYLE tool, 269
STYLESMANAGER tool, 855
subregion, 951
Subset Properties dialog box, 975–976, 978, 995, 997
subsets, 968
    creating, 975
    managing, 975–976
sub-units, 511
suffices, 510
SUPERHATCH tool, 704
surface model, 22
symbol libraries, 735–737
    creating, 735–736
    storing, 736–737
symmetrical tolerance, 590
system options, 41
system variables, 156
    ANNOAUTOSCALE, 921
    ATTDIA, 756
    ATTIPE, 753
    ATTREQ, 757
    CCONSTRAINTFORM, 665
    CELTSCALE, 881, 911
    CONSTRAINTINFER, 646
    LTSCALE, 156, 881, 911
    MIRRHATCH, 703
    MIRRTEXT, 385
    MSLTSCALE, 881, 911
    OJBECTISOLATIONMODE, 189
    PSLTSCALE, 881, 911
    REGENAUTO, 198
    SELECTIONANNODISPLAY, 926
    SPLINETYPE, 437
    VPROTATEASSOC, 877–878
    XDWGFADECTL, 943

T

tab, 36
Table Cell ribbon tab, 333, 335–338
    auto-fill, 333, 335–336
    Cell Format panel, 336
    Cell Styles panel, 336
    Column panel, 337
    Field option, 337
    Insert panel, 337
    Merge panel, 338

    Rows panel, 337
table indicator, 330
tables, 319–344
    adding cell content, 330
    breaks, 339–340
    calculating values in, 341–344
    editing, 332–340
    extracting data, 344
    inserting, 327–331
    linking to Excel data, 344
    picking cell edge to edit table layout, 338–340
    placing empty table, 327–329
    starting table style, 331
    styles, 319–327
Table Style dialog box, 991–992
table styles, 319–327
    cell styles, 322–325
    changing, renaming, and deleting, 326
    creating new, 321
    setting current, 327
    starting table styles, 325–326
    table direction, 322
    Table Styles dialog box, 319–321
TABLESTYLE tool, 319
TABLE tool, 328, 764, 869
tabular dimensioning, 563
tangent, 113
Tangent object snap, 218–219
template development, 74–76, 202, 227, 251, 290,
       344, 515, 570
Template Options dialog box, 75
templates, 51
    starting from, 52–53
Temporary Track Point snap, 221
text, 263
    cutting, copying, and pasting, 309
    finding and replacing, 309
    justification, 311
    revising, 308–311
    scaling, 266, 310–311
text boundary, 274
text box, 30
Text Editor ribbon tab, 274–275, 330, 332
    Close option, 276, 330, 332
    Mtext option, 522
    Paragraph panel, 281–282, 285
text height, 265–269
TEXTSCR tool, 80
text standards, 263–265
Text Style dialog box, 269–273
text styles, 269–273
    changing, renaming, and deleting, 273
    creating new, 270
    effects, 271–272
    font options, 270–271
    size options, 271
TEXT tool, 299–301, 766
thread drawings and notes, 561–562
tiled viewports, 194, 196–197
    creating, 194, 196
    joining, 197
    working in, 197
time, checking, 468–469
TIME tool, 468–469
tint, 695
title blocks, 762–764
tolerance, 585
    alignment, 595
    height, 594
    precision, 594

Index–Basics